REFERENCE
ONLY

Hoover's Handbook of

World Business 2014

HOOVERS™
A D&B COMPANY

Austin, Texas

Hoover's Handbook of World Business 2014 is intended to provide readers with accurate and authoritative information about the enterprises covered in it. Hoover's researched all companies and organizations profiled, and in many cases contacted them directly so that companies represented could provide information. The information contained herein is as accurate as we could reasonably make it. In many cases we have relied on third-party material that we believe to be trustworthy, but were unable to independently verify. We do not warrant that the book is absolutely accurate or without error. Readers should not rely on any information contained herein in instances where such reliance might cause financial loss. The publisher, the editors, and their data suppliers specifically disclaim all warranties, including the implied warranties of merchantability and fitness for a specific purpose. This book is sold with the understanding that neither the publisher, the editors, nor any content contributors are engaged in providing investment, financial, accounting, legal, or other professional advice.

The financial data (Historical Financials sections) in this book are from a variety of sources. Morningstar, Inc., provided selected data for the Historical Financials sections of publicly traded companies. For private companies and for historical information on public companies prior to their becoming public, we obtained information directly from the companies or from trade sources deemed to be reliable. Hoover's, Inc., is solely responsible for the presentation of all data.

Many of the names of products and services mentioned in this book are the trademarks or service marks of the companies manufacturing or selling them and are subject to protection under US law. Space has not permitted us to indicate which names are subject to such protection, and readers are advised to consult with the owners of such marks regarding their use. Hoover's is a trademark of Hoover's, Inc.

HOOVERS™
A D&B COMPANY

10 9 8 7 6 5 4 3 2 1

Publishers Cataloging-in-Publication Data

Hoover's Handbook of World Business 2014

Includes indexes.

ISBN 978-1-63053-001-3

ISSN 1055-7199

1. Business enterprises — Directories. 2. Corporations — Directories.

HF3010 338.7

Hoover's Company Information is also available on the Internet at Hoover's Online (www.mergent/hoovers.com). A catalog of Hoover's products is available on the Internet at www.mergent/hooversbooks.com.

U.S. AND WORLD BOOK SALES

Mergent Inc.

580 Kingsley Park Drive
Fort Mill, SC
29715
Phone: 800-342-5647
e-mail: orders@mergent.com
Web: www.mergents.com

Mergent Inc.

CEO: Jonathan Worrall

Executive Managing Director: John Pedernales

Executive Vice President of Sales: Fred Jenkins

Managing Director of Relationship Management: Chris Henry

Managing Director of Print Products: Thomas Wecera

Production Research Assistant: Erin Keane

MERGENT CUSTOMER SERVICE

Support and Fulfillment Manager: Melanie Horvat

ABOUT MERGENT, INC.

Mergent, Inc. is a leading provider of business and financial data on global publicly listed companies. Based in the U.S, the company maintains a strong global presence, with offices in New York, Charlotte, San Diego, London, Tokyo and Melbourne.

Founded in 1900, Mergent operates one of the longest continuously collected databases of: descriptive and fundamental information on domestic and international companies; pricing and terms and conditions data on fixed income and equity securities; and corporate action data. In addition, Mergent's Indxis subsidiary develops and licenses equity and fixed income investment products based on its proprietary investment methodologies. Our licensed products have over $9 billion in assets under management and are offered by major investment management firms. The Indxis calculation platform is the chosen technology for some of the world's largest index companies. Its index calculation and pricing distribution protocols are used to administer index rules and distribute real-time pricing data.

Abbreviations

AB – Aktiebolag (Swedish)*
ADR – American Depositary Receipts
AG – Aktiengesellschaft (German)*
AFL-CIO – American Federation of Labor and Congress of Industrial Organizations
AMEX – American Stock Exchange
A/S – Aktieselskab (Danish)*
ASA – Allmenne Aksjeselskaper (Norwegian)*
ATM – asynchronous transfer mode; automated teller machine
CAD/CAM – computer-aided design/computer-aided manufacturing
CASE – computer-aided software engineering
CD-ROM – compact disc – read-only memory
CEO – chief executive officer
CFO – chief financial officer
CMOS – complementary metal-oxide semiconductor
COMECON – Council for Mutual Economic Assistance
COO – chief operating officer
DAT – digital audio tape
DOD – Department of Defense
DOE – Department of Energy
DOT – Department of Transportation
DRAM – dynamic random-access memory
DVD – digital versatile disc/digital video disc
EC – European Community
EPA – Environmental Protection Agency
EPS – earnings per share
EU – European Union
EVP – executive vice president
FCC – Federal Communications Commission
FDA – Food and Drug Administration
FDIC – Federal Deposit Insurance Corporation
FTC – Federal Trade Commission
GATT – General Agreement on Tariffs and Trade
GmbH – Gesellschaft mit beschränkter Haftung (German)*
GNP – gross national product
HDTV – high-definition television
HMO – health maintenance organization
HR – human resources
HTML – hypertext markup language
ICC – Interstate Commerce Commission
IMF – International Monetary Fund
IPO – initial public offering
IRS – Internal Revenue Service
KGaA – Kommanditgesellschaft auf Aktien (German)*
LAN – local-area network
LBO – leveraged buyout
LNG – liquefied natural gas
LP – limited partnership
Ltd. – Limited
MFN – Most Favored Nation
MITI – Ministry of International Trade and Industry (Japan)
NAFTA – North American Free Trade Agreement
Nasdaq – National Association of Securities Dealers Automated Quotations
NATO – North Atlantic Treaty Organization
NV – Naamlose Vennootschap (Dutch)*
NYSE – New York Stock Exchange
OAO – open joint stock company (Russian)
OAS – Organization of American States
OECD – Organization for Economic Cooperation and Development
OEM – original equipment manufacturer
OOO – limited liability company (Russian)
OPEC – Organization of Petroleum Exporting Countries
OS – operating system
OTC – over-the-counter
P/E – price-to-earnings ratio
PLC – public limited company (UK)*
RAM – random-access memory
R&D – research and development
RISC – reduced instruction set computer
ROA – return on assets
ROI – return on investment
SA – Société Anonyme (French)*; Sociedad(e) Anónima (Spanish and Portuguese)*
SA de CV – Sociedad Anónima de Capital Variable (Spanish)*
SEC – Securities and Exchange Commission
SEVP – senior executive vice president
SIC – Standard Industrial Classification
SpA – Società per Azioni (Italian)*
SPARC – scalable processor architecture
SVP – senior vice president
VAR – value-added reseller
VAT – value-added tax
VC – venture capitalist
VP – vice president
WAN – wide-area network
WWW – World Wide Web
ZAO – closed joint stock company (Russian)
z o.o. – z ograniczona odpowiedzialnoscia (Polish)*

* These abbreviations are used in companies' names to convey that the companies are limited liability enterprises; the meanings are usually the equivalent of *corporation* or *incorporated.*

Contents

List of Lists vi
Companies Profiled vii
About *Hoover's Handbook of World Business 2014* ix
Using Hoover's Handbooks x
A List-Lover's Compendium 1a
The Companies 1
Index of Company Executives 495

List of Lists

HOOVER'S RANKINGS

The 100 Largest Companies by Sales in *Hoover's Handbook of World Business 2014*....2a
The 100 Most Profitable Companies in *Hoover's Handbook of World Business 2014*....3a
The 100 Largest Employers in *Hoover's Handbook of World Business 2014*....4a

Companies Profiled

77 Bank, Ltd. (The) (Japan) 1
A.P. Moller - Maersk A/S 1
AB Electrolux (Sweden) 2
ABB Asea Brown Boveri Ltd. (Switzerland) 4
ABB Ltd 4
Abbey National Treasury Services PLC (United Kingdom) 6
Accenture plc 6
ACE, Ltd. 8
ACS Actividades de Construccion y Servicios, S.A. 9
Adecco S.A. (Switzerland) 11
Adidas AG 12
AEGON N.V. 13
Aeon Co. Ltd. (Japan) 15
Ageas NV 16
Agricultural Bank of China 17
Agrium, Inc. 17
Air France-KLM 18
Airbus Group NV 19
Aisin Seiki Co., Ltd. 21
Akzo Nobel N.V. (Netherlands) 22
Alcatel-Lucent 24
Alecta pensionsforsakring, omsesidigt (Sweden) 26
Alimentation-Couche Tard, Inc. 26
Allianz SE 27
Allied Irish Banks Plc 28
Alstom 30
America Movil, S.A.B. de C.V. 31
AMP Ltd. 32
ANA Holdings Inc. 33
Anglo American Plc (United Kingdom) 34
Anheuser-Busch Inbev SA 36
AP Moller AS 37
ArcelorMittal SA 38
Assicurazioni Generali S.p.A. 40
Associated British Foods Plc 41
AstraZeneca Plc 43
AUDI AG Vormals Audi-NSU Auto Union AG 45
Australia and New Zealand Banking Group Ltd 45
Aviva Plc (United Kingdom) 46
AXA S.A. 48
BAE Systems Plc 50
Balfour Beatty Plc 52
Baloise Holding AG 53
Banca Popolare dell'Emilia 54
Banco Bilbao Vizcaya Argentaria SA (BBVA) 55
Banco Bradesco S.A. 56
Banco De Sabadell SA 57
Banco Espirito Santo S.A. 58
Banco Popular Espanol, S.A. 58
Banco Santander Brasil SA 59
Banco Santander SA 59
Bangkok Bank Public Co., Ltd. (Thailand) 61
Bank Hapoalim B.M. (Israel) 62
Bank Leumi Le-Israel B.M. 62
Bank of China Ltd., Beijing 63
Bank of Communications Co., Ltd. 64
Bank of East Asia Ltd. 65
Bank of Ireland (Ireland) 66
Bank of Kyoto, Ltd. (Japan) 67
Bank of Montreal 67
Bank of Nova Scotia Halifax 68
Bank of Yokohama, Ltd. 69
Bankinter, S.A. 70
Banque Nationale de Belgique (National Bank of Belgium) 71
Baoshan Iron & Steel Co Ltd 71
Barclays Africa Group Ltd 71
Barclays Bank Plc 72
Barclays PLC 73
BASF SE 74
Bayer AG 76
Bayerische Landesbank (Germany) 78
Bayerische Motoren Werke AG 79
BCE Inc. 81
Bertelsmann AG (Germany, Fed. Rep.) 83
BG Group Plc 84
Bharat Petroleum Corp., Ltd. (India) 85
BHP Billiton Ltd. 86
BHP Billiton Plc 88
BNP Paribas (France) 89
Boc Hong Kong Holdings Ltd 90
Bombardier Inc. 90
Bouygues S.A. 92
BP p.l.c. 94
Bridgestone Corp. (Japan) 95
British American Tobacco Plc (United Kingdom) 97
BT Group Plc 98
Bunge Ltd. 101
Byucksan Enginering & Construction Co Ltd. 103
Caixa Geral de Depositos, S.A. 103
Canadian Imperial Bank of Commerce 103
Canon, Inc. 105
Carnival Corp. 106
Carrefour S.A. 108
Casino Guichard Perrachon S.A. 110
Cathay Financial Holding Co 111
Celesio AG 112
Cemex S.A.B. de C.V. 113
Central Bank of Ireland (Ireland) 115
Centrica Plc 115
Chiba Bank, Ltd 117
China Communications Construction Company Ltd. 117
China Construction Bank Corp 118
China International United Petroleum & Chemicals Co Ltd 118
China Life Insurance Co Ltd 118
China Merchants Bank Co Ltd 118
China Minsheng Banking Corp Ltd 119
China Mobile Limited 119
China Petroleum & Chemical Corp. Inc 120
China Railway Construction Corp Ltd 121
China Railway Group Ltd 121
China Shenhua Energy Co., Ltd. 121
China Telecom Corp Ltd 121
China Unicom (Hong Kong) Ltd 122
China United Network Communications Ltd 123
Christian Dior SA 123
Chugoku Bank, Ltd. (The) 124
Chuo Mitsui Trust & Banking Co., Ltd. 124
CNH Industrial N.V. 124
Cnooc Ltd. 125
CNP Assurances S.A. 125
Co-operative Bank p.l.c. (The) (United Kingdom) 126
Colas SA Boulogne 126
Commerzbank AG (Germany, Fed. Rep.) 128
Commonwealth Bank of Australia 129
Compagnie de Saint-Gobain 130
Compagnie Generale des Etablissements Michelin (France) 132
Compass Group PLC (United Kingdom) 133
Continental AG (Germany, Fed. Rep.) 134
Cosmo Oil Co., Ltd. 136
CPC Corporation, Taiwan 137
Credit Suisse Group 138
CTBC Financial Holdings Ltd 139
Dai Nippon Printing Co., Ltd. 140
Dai-Ichi Life Insurance Co., Ltd. 141
Daimler AG 142
Danone 144
Danske Bank AS (Denmark) 146
DBS Group Holdings Ltd. 147
Dekabank Deutsche Girozentrale 148
Denso Corp. (Japan) 148
Deutsche Bank AG 149
Deutsche Bundesbank (Germany, Fed. Rep.) 149
Deutsche Lufthansa AG (Germany, Fed. Rep.) 150
Deutsche Post AG 151
Deutsche Post RG 152
Deutsche Postbank AG 153
Deutsche Telekom AG 153
Diageo Plc 154
DNB ASA 156
DZ Bank AG Deutsche Zentral-Genossenschaftsbank 157
E.ON SE 158
Ecopetrol SA 159
EDF Trading Ltd 160
EDP Energias de Portugal S.A. 160
Endesa S.A. 162
ENI S.p.A. 162
Ergo Versicherungsgruppe AG 164
Ericsson 165
Erste Group Bank AG 166
Espirito Santo Financial Group S.A. (Luxembourg) 167
Etablissements Delhaize Freres et Cie Le Lion S.A. (Belgium) 168
European Investment Bank 170
Fiat SPA 171
Finmeccanica S.p.A. 172
First Commercial Bank 174
Flextronics International Ltd. 174
Fomento de Construcciones y Contratas, S.A. 176
Fomento Economico Mexicano, S.A.B. de C.V. 177
Formosa Petrochemical Corp 178
Fresenius SE & Co KGaA 178
Fuji Heavy Industries, Ltd. 179
FUJIFILM Holdings Corp 181
Fujitsu Ltd. 183
Fukoku Mutual Life Insurance Co (Japan) 184
Gas Natural SDG, S.A. 185
Gazprom Neft 186
Gazprom OAO 186
GDF SUEZ 188
GlaxoSmithKline Plc 190
Glencore Xstrata PLC 192
Great-West Lifeco Inc. 193
Gunma Bank, Ltd. (The) (Japan) 193
Hachijuni Bank, Ltd. (Japan) 194
Hang Seng Bank Ltd. 194
Hannover Rueckversicherung SE 195
HDFC Bank Ltd. 196
HeidelbergCement AG 196
Heineken N.V. (Netherlands) 197
Henkel AG & Co KGAA 201
Hennes & Mauritz AB 202
Heraeus Holding GmbH (Germany Fed. Rep.) 204
Hindustan Petroleum Corp., Ltd. (India) 205
Hino Motors, Ltd. 205
Hiroshima Bank, Ltd. (The) (Japan) 206
Hitachi, Ltd. 207
Hochtief AG 209
Hokuhoku Financial Group Inc. 210
Holcim Ltd 211
Hon Hai Precision Industry Co., Ltd. 212
Honda Motor Co., Ltd.(Honda Giken Kogyo Kabushiki Kaisha) (Japan) 213
HSBC Bank Canada 215
HSBC Bank Plc (United Kingdom) 216
HSBC Holdings Plc 216
Hutchison Whampoa Ltd. 218
Hyundai Heavy Industries Co., Ltd. 220
Hyundai Motor Co., Ltd. 221
Iberdrola SA 222
ICICI Bank Ltd (India) 223
Idemitsu Kosan Co Ltd 224
Imperial Oil Ltd. 225
Imperial Tobacco Group Plc 226
Indian Oil Corp., Ltd. (India) 227
Industria De Diseno Textil (Inditex) SA 227
Industrial and Commercial Bank of China Ltd 229
Industrial Bank Co., Ltd. 229
ING Bank N.V. (Netherlands) 230
ING Groep N.V. 230
International Consolidated Airlines Group SA 232
Internetq Plc, London 233
Intesa Sanpaolo S.P.A. 233
Investec plc 235
Isuzu Motors, Ltd. (Japan) 235
Itau Unibanco Holding S.A. 237
ITOCHU Corp. (Japan) 237
J. Sainsbury PLC 239
Japan Tobacco Inc. 240
Jardine Matheson Holdings Ltd. 242
Jardine Strategic Holdings Ltd (Bermuda) 242

Companies Profiled (continued)

JBS S.A. 242
JFE Holdings Inc 243
Johnson Matthey Plc (United Kingdom) 244
Joyo Bank, Ltd. 245
JX Holdings, Inc. 246
Kansai Electric Power Co., Inc. (Kansai Denryoku K. K.) (Japan) 246
KB Financial Group, Inc. 247
KBC Group NV 247
KDDI Corp 248
Kia Motors Corp. (South Korea) 248
Kingfisher PLC 249
Kirin Holdings Co Ltd 251
Komatsu, Ltd. 252
Koninklijke Ahold NV 253
Koninklijke KPN NV 255
Koninklijke Philips N.V. 256
Korea Electric Power Corp 258
Korea Gas Corp. (South Korea) 259
Kuehne & Nagel International AG 259
L'Air Liquide S.A. (France) 260
Landesbank Baden-Wurttemberg 262
Landesbank Berlin - Gironzentrale (Germany, Fed. Rep.) 262
Landesbank Berlin Holding AG (Berlin) 263
Landesbank Hessen-Thueringen Girozentrale (Helaba) (Germany, Fed. Rep.) 264
Landwirtschaftliche Rentenbank (Germany, Fed. Rep.) 264
Legal & General Group PLC (United Kingdom) 264
Lenovo Group Ltd 265
LG Electronics Inc 267
Linde AG (Germany, Fed. Rep.) 268
Lloyds Banking Group Plc 269
Loblaw Cos. Ltd. 270
LVMH Moet Hennessy Louis Vuitton 270
LyondellBasell Industries NV 272
Macquarie Group Ltd 272
Magna International Inc. 273
Malayan Banking Berhad 275
Man SE 276
Manulife Financial Corp. 277
Mapfre SA 278
Marks & Spencer Group PLC 279
Marubeni Corp. 281
Mazda Motor Corp. (Japan) 282
Mediobanca Banca Di Credito Finanziario SpA 284
Mega International Commercial Bank Co Ltd 285
Metallurgical Corp China Ltd 285
Metro AG 285
Migros-Genossenschafts-Bund (Switzerland) 287
Mitsubishi Chemical Holdings Corp 288
Mitsubishi Corp 288
Mitsubishi Electric Corp. 290
Mitsubishi Motors Corp. (Japan) 292
Mitsubishi UFJ Financial Group Inc 293
Mitsui & Co., Ltd. 294
Mitsui Life Insurance Co., Ltd 296
MOL Hungarian Oil and Gas Plc 296
Morrison (Wm.) Supermarkets Plc 297
MS&AD Insurance Group Holdings 298
Muenchener Rueckversicherungs-Gesellschaft AG (Germany) 299
National Australia Bank Ltd 300
National Bank of Abu Dhabi 302
National Bank of Canada 302
National Bank Of Greece S A 303
National Grid plc 304
National Westminster Bank Plc 305
NEC Corp 305
Nedbank Group Ltd 307
Nestle S.A. 307
Nippon Life Insurance Co. (Japan) 310
Nippon Steel & Sumitomo Metal Corp 311
Nippon Telegraph & Telephone Corp. (Japan) 313
Nishi-Nippon City Bank Ltd 314
Nissan Motor Co., Ltd. 315
NKSJ Holdings, Inc. 316
Noble Group Ltd 317
Nokia Corp 317
Nomura Holdings Inc 319
Nordea Bank AB 320
Nordea Bank Denmark A/S 321
North Pacific Bank, Ltd. 321
Novartis AG Basel 322
Novo-Nordisk A/S 324
NTT DOCOMO, Inc. 325
Obayashi Corp. (Japan) 327
Oil and Natural Gas Corp. Ltd. 328
Oil Co Lukoil 328
Old Mutual Plc 329
OMV AG (Austria) 331
Orange 332
Orix Corp. (Japan) 334
Otto Versand (GmbH & Co.) (Germany, Fed. Rep.) 334
Oversea-Chinese Banking Corp. Ltd. (Singapore) 336
Panasonic Corp 336
Pegatron Corp 338
PetroChina Co Ltd 339
Petroleo Brasileiro S.A. 339
Petroliam Nasional Berhad (Malaysia) 341
Peugeot S.A. (France) 341
PICC Property and Casualty Co Ltd 342
Ping An Insurance (Group) Co of China Ltd. 343
Piraeus Bank SA 343
POSCO (South Korea) 344
Power Corp. of Canada 345
Power Financial Corp 346
Prudential Plc 347
PT Resource Alam Indonesia TBK 348
PTT Public Co Ltd. 348
QBE Insurance Group Ltd. 349
Quanta Computer Inc 350
Rallye S.A. 351
Randstad Holding N.V. 352
Reliance Industries Ltd 353
Renault S.A. (France) 354
Repsol S.A. 355
Resona Holdings Inc Osaka 356
Ricoh Co., Ltd. 357
Rio Tinto Ltd 358
Rio Tinto Plc 360
Roche Holding Ltd. 361
Rolls Royce Holdings Plc 363
Rosneft Oil Co OJSC (Moscow) 365
Royal Bank of Canada 365
Royal Bank of Scotland Group Plc 367
Royal Bank of Scotland plc 369
Royal Dutch Shell Plc 369
RWE AG 370
S-Oil Corp 372
SABMiller Plc (United Kingdom) 372
Safran S.A. 374
SAIC Motor Corp Ltd 376
Saipem S.p.A. 376
Samsung Electronics Co., Ltd. 377
San Miguel Corp 378
Sandvik AB (Sweden) 380
Sanofi 381
SAP AG 383
Saudi Basic Industries Corp - SABIC (Saudi Arabia) 385
Sberbank Russia 386
Schlumberger Ltd. 386
Schneider Electric S.A. 386
Seven & i Holdings Co. Ltd. 388
Sharp Corp. (Japan) 389
Shenzhen Development Bank Co., Ltd. 391
Shinhan Financial Group Co. Ltd. 391
Shinsei Bank Ltd. (Japan) 392
Shizuoka Bank, Ltd. (Japan) 393
Showa Shell Sekiyu K.K. 393
Siam Commercial Bank Public Co., Ltd. (The) 394
Siemens AG (Germany) 394
Sistema JSFC 397
SK Holdings Co Ltd 397
SK Innovation Co Ltd 397
SK Telecom Co Ltd (South Korea) 398
Skandinaviska Enskilda Banken 398
Skanska AB 400
Societe Generale 401
Sodexo 402
Softbank Corp. (Japan) 404
Sojitz Corp 405
Solvay S.A. 406
Sony Corp 407
SSE PLC 409
Standard Chartered Plc 410
Standard Life Assurance Co. (United Kingdom) 412
Standard Life Plc 412
Statoil ASA 413
Storebrand ASA 415
Sumitomo Chemical Co., Ltd. 415
Sumitomo Corp. (Japan) 416
Sumitomo Electric Industries, Ltd. (Japan) 418
Sumitomo Life Insurance Co. (Japan) 419
Sumitomo Mitsui Financial Group Inc Tokyo 420
Sumitomo Mitsui Trust Holdings Inc 421
Sun Life Financial Inc 421
Suncor Energy Inc 422
Suncorp Group Ltd. 423
Suzuki Motor Corp. (Japan) 424
Svenska Handelsbanken 425
Swedbank A B 426
Swiss Re Ltd. 426
T&D Holdings Inc 427
Taiwan Cooperative Bank 427
Taiwan Semiconductor Manufacturing Co., Ltd. 428
Talanx AG 429
Tata Motors Ltd 430
Telecom Italia SPA 431
Telefonaktiebolaget LM Ericsson (Sweden) 433
Telefonica, S.A. 433
Telenor ASA 434
TeliaSonera A B 435
Telstra Corp., Ltd. 437
Tesco PLC (United Kingdom) 438
Teva Pharmaceutical Industries Ltd 440
THALES 442
ThyssenKrupp AG 444
Tokio Marine Holdings Inc 445
Tokyo Electric Power Co. Inc. (The) (Japan) 446
TonenGeneral Sekiyu K.K. 447
Toppan Printing Co., Ltd. 448
Toronto Dominion Bank 449
Toshiba Corp 450
Total S.A. 452
Toyota Motor Corp 454
Toyota Tsusho Corp 456
TUI AG 456
TUI Travel Plc 458
Turkiye Garanti Bankasi A.S. 459
UBS AG (Switzerland) 460
Umicore S.A. 462
Unicredito S.p.A. Roma 463
Unilever N.V. 464
Unilever Plc (United Kingdom) 465
Unione Di Banche Italiane S.c.p.a. 466
United Overseas Bank Ltd. (Singapore) 466
Vale S. A. 467
Valeo S.A. (France) 468
Veolia Environnement 470
Vinci SA 471
Vivendi 473
Vodafone Group Plc 474
Volkswagen A.G. (Germany, Fed. Rep.) 476
Volvo AB 478
Wesfarmers Ltd. 480
Westdeutsche Genossenschafts- Zentralbank EG (Germany, Fed. Rep.) 481
WestLB AG 481
Weston (George) Limited 482
Westpac Banking Corp 483
Wilmar International Ltd 485
Wolseley Plc Jersey 485
Woolworths Ltd 487
Woori Finance Holdings Co., Ltd 488
ZF Friedrichshafen AG (Germany) 489
Zurich Insurance Group Ltd 490

About Hoover's Handbook of World Business 2014

This edition of *Hoover's Handbook of World Business* is focused on its mission of providing you with premier coverage of the global business scene. Featuring 450 of the world's most influential companies based outside of the United States, this book is one of the most complete sources of in-depth information on large, non-US-based business enterprises available anywhere.

Hoover's Handbook of World Business is one of our four-title series of handbooks that covers, literally, the world of business. The series is available as an indexed set, and also includes *Hoover's Handbook of American Business*, *Hoover's Handbook of Private Companies*, and *Hoover's Handbook of Emerging Companies*. This series brings you information on the biggest, fastest-growing, and most influential enterprises in the world.

HOOVER'S ONLINE FOR BUSINESS NEEDS

In addition to Hoover's widely used MasterList and Handbooks series, comprehensive coverage of more than 40,000 business enterprises is available in electronic format on our Web site at www.hoovers.com. Our goal is to provide our customers the fastest path to business with insight and actionable information about companies, industries, and key decision makers, along with the powerful tools to find and connect to the right people to get business done. Hoover's has partnered with other prestigious business information and service providers to bring you all the right business information, services, and links in one place.

We welcome the recognition we have received as the premier provider of high-quality company information — online, electronically, and in print — and continue to look for ways to make our products more available and more useful to you.

We believe that anyone who buys from, sells to, invests in, lends to, competes with, interviews with, or works for a company should know all there is to know about that enterprise. Taken together, this book and the other Hoover's products and resources represent the most complete source of basic corporate information readily available to the general public.

HOW TO USE THIS BOOK

This book has four sections:

1. "Using Hoover's Handbooks" describes the contents of our profiles and explains the ways in which we gather and compile our data.

2. "A List-Lover's Compendium" contains lists of the largest, fastest-growing, and most valuable companies of global importance.

3. The company profiles section makes up the largest and most important part of the book — 450 profiles of major business enterprises, arranged alphabetically.

4. Three indexes complete the book. The first sorts companies by industry groups, the second by headquarters location. The third index is a list of all the executives found in the Executives section of each company profile.

Using Hoover's Handbooks

SELECTION OF THE COMPANIES PROFILED

The 300 profiles in this book include a variety of international enterprises, ranging from some of the largest publicly traded companies in the world — Daimler AG, for example — to Malaysia's largest and oldest conglomerate, Sime Darby Berhad. It also includes many private businesses, such as Bertelsmann AG and LEGO, as well as a selection of government-owned entities, such as Mexico's Petróleos Mexicanos. The companies selected represent a cross-section of the largest, most influential, and most interesting companies based outside the United States.

In selecting these companies, we followed several basic criteria. We started with the global giants, including Toyota and Royal Dutch Shell, and then looked at companies with substantial activity in the US, such as Vivendi and Diageo. We also included companies that dominate their industries (e.g., AB Electrolux, the world's #1 producer of household appliances), as well as representative companies from around the world (an Indian conglomerate, Tata; two firms from Finland, Nokia and Stora Enso Oyj; and two companies from Russia, OAO Gazprom and OAO LUKOIL). Companies that weren't necessarily global powerhouses but that had a high profile with consumers (e.g., IKEA) or had interesting stories (Virgin Group) were included. Finally, because of their truly global reach, we added the Big Four accounting firms (even though they are headquartered or co-headquartered in the US).

ORGANIZATION

The profiles are presented in alphabetical order. You will find the commonly used name of the enterprise at the beginning of the profile; the full, legal name is found in the Locations section. For some companies, primarily Japanese, the commonly translated English name differs from the actual legal name of the company, so both are provided. (The legal name of Nippon Steel Corporation is Shin Nippon Seitetsu Kabushiki Kaisha.) If a company name starts with a person's first name (e.g., George Weston Limited), it is alphabetized under the first name. We've also tried to alphabetize companies where you would expect to find them — for example, Deutsche Lufthansa is in the L's and Grupo Televisa can be found under T.

The annual financial information contained in the profiles is current through fiscal year-ends occurring as late as June 2013. We have included certain nonfinancial developments, such as officer changes, through September 2013.

OVERVIEW

In the first section of the profile, we have tried to give a thumbnail description of the company and what it does. The description will usually include information on the company's strategy, reputation, and ownership. We recommend that you read this section first.

HISTORY

This extended section, which is present for most companies, reflects our belief that every enterprise is the sum of its history and that you have to know where you came from in order to know where you are going. While some companies have limited historical awareness, we think the vast majority of the enterprises in this book have colorful backgrounds. We have tried to focus on the people who made the enterprises what they are today. We have found these histories to be full of twists and ironies; they make fascinating reading.

EXECUTIVES

Here we list the names of the people who run the company, insofar as space allows. We have shown age and pay information where available, although most non-US companies are not required to report the level of detail revealed in the US.

Although companies are free to structure their management titles any way they please, most modern corporations follow standard practices. The ultimate power in any corporation lies with the shareholders, who elect a board of directors, usually including officers or "insiders," as well as individuals from outside the company. The chief officer, the person on whose desk the buck stops, is usually called the chief executive officer (CEO) in the US. In other countries, practices vary widely. In the UK, traditionally, the Managing Director performs the functions of the CEO without the title, although the use of the term CEO is on the rise there. In Germany it is customary to have two boards of directors: a managing board populated by the top executives of the company and a higher-level supervisory board consisting of outsiders.

As corporate management has become more complex, it is common for the CEO to have a "right-hand person" who oversees the day-to-day operations of the company, allowing the CEO plenty of time to focus on strategy and long-term issues. This right-hand person is usually designated the chief operating officer (COO) and is often the president of the company. In other cases one person is both chairman and president.

We have tried to list each company's most important officers, including the chief financial officer (CFO) and the chief legal officer. For companies with US operations, we have included the names of the US CEO, CFO, and top human resources executive, where available.

The people named in the Executives section are indexed at the back of the book.

The Executives section also includes the name of the company's auditing (accounting) firm, where available.

LOCATIONS

Here we include the company's full legal name and its headquarters, street address, telephone and fax numbers, and Web site, as available. We also list the same information for the US office for each company, if one exists. Telephone numbers of foreign offices are shown using the standardized conventions of international dialing. The back of the book includes an index of companies by headquarters location.

In some cases we have also included information on the geographic distribution of the company's business, including sales and profit data. Note that these profit numbers, like those in the Products/Operations section below, are usually operating or pretax profits rather than net profits. Operating profits are generally those before financing costs (interest income and payments) and before taxes, which are considered costs attributable to the whole company rather than to one division or part of the world. For this reason the net income figures (in the Historical Financials section) are usually much lower, since they are after interest and taxes. Pretax profits are after interest but before taxes.

PRODUCTS/OPERATIONS

This section lists as many of the company's products, services, brand names, divisions, subsidiaries, and joint ventures as we could fit. We have tried to include all its major lines and all familiar brand names. The nature of this section varies by company and the amount of information available. If the company publishes sales and profit information by type of business, we have included it (in US dollars).

COMPETITORS

In this section we have listed enterprises that compete with the profiled company. This feature is included as a quick way to locate similar companies and compare them. Because of the difficulty in identifying companies that only compete in foreign markets, the list of competitors is still weighted to large international companies with a strong US presence.

HISTORICAL FINANCIALS

Here we have tried to present as much data about each enterprise's financial performance as we could compile in the allocated space. Financial data for all companies is presented in US dollars, using the appropriate exchange rate at fiscal year-end.

While the information presented varies somewhat from industry to industry, it is less complete in the case of private companies that do not release data (although we have always tried to provide annual sales and employment). The following information is generally present.

A five-year table, with relevant annualized compound growth rates, covers:

- Sales — fiscal year sales (year-end assets for most financial companies)
- Net income — fiscal year net income (before accounting changes)
- Net profit margin — fiscal year net income as a percent of sales (as a percent of assets for most financial firms)
- Employees — fiscal year-end or average number of employees
- Stock price — the fiscal year close
- P/E — high and low price/earnings ratio
- Earnings per share — fiscal year earnings per share (EPS)
- Dividends per share — fiscal year dividends per share

The information on the number of employees is intended to aid the reader interested in knowing whether a company has a long-term trend of increasing or decreasing employment. As far as we know, we are the only company that publishes this information in print format.

The numbers on the left in each row of the Historical Financials section give the month and the year in which the company's fiscal year actually ends. Thus, a company with a September 30, 2010, year-end is shown as 9/10.

In addition, we have provided in graph form a stock price history for companies that trade on the major US exchanges. The graphs, covering up to five years, show the range of trading between the high and the low price, as well as the closing price for each fiscal year. For public companies that trade on the OTC or Pink Sheets or that do not trade on US exchanges, we graph net income. Generally, for private companies, we have graphed net income, or, if that is unavailable, sales.

Key year-end statistics in this section generally show the financial strength of the enterprise, including:

- Debt ratio (long-term debt as a percent of shareholders' equity)
- Return on equity (net income divided by the average of beginning and ending common shareholders' equity)
- Cash and cash equivalents
- Current ratio (ratio of current assets to current liabilities)
- Total long-term debt (including capital lease

obligations)

- Number of shares of common stock outstanding
- Dividend yield (fiscal year dividends per share divided by the fiscal year-end closing stock price)
- Dividend payout (fiscal year dividends divided by fiscal year EPS)
- Market value at fiscal year-end (fiscal year-end closing stock price multiplied by fiscal year-end number of shares outstanding)
- Fiscal year sales for financial institutions.

Per share data has been adjusted for stock splits. The data for public companies with sponsored American Depositary Receipts has been provided to us by Morningstar, Inc. Other public company information was compiled by Hoover's, which takes full responsibility for the content of this section.

In the case of private companies that do not publicly disclose financial information, we usually did not have access to such standardized data. We have gathered estimates of sales and other statistics from numerous sources.

Hoover's Handbook of

World Business

A List-Lover's Compendium

The 100 Largest Companies by Sales in Hoover's Handbook of World Business 2014

Rank	Company	Sales ($ thous)
1	Copperbelt Energy Corp Plc	$1,358,747,000,000
2	Zambeef Products Plc	$1,306,212,000,000
3	Exxon Mobil Corp.	$482,295,000,000
4	Royal Dutch Shell Plc	$481,700,000,000
5	Wal-Mart Stores, Inc.	$469,162,000,000
6	China Petroleum & Chemical	$446,893,625,854
7	Byucksan Enginering & Constru	$393,378,326,847
8	BP plc	$381,589,000,000
9	PetroChina Co Ltd	$352,134,940,126
10	Oil and Natural Gas Corp. Lt	$298,969,328,082
11	Volkswagen A.G. (Germany)	$253,956,503,535
12	Chevron Corporation	$241,909,000,000
13	Total S.A.	$240,279,103,978
14	Toyota Motor Corp	$234,495,805,515
15	PT Resource Alam Indonesia	$214,901,931,000
16	Glencore Xstrata PLC	$214,436,000,000
17	EDF Trading Ltd	$212,057,410,532
18	China International United P	$204,650,577,741
19	Samsung Electronics Co., Ltd	$188,351,632,900
20	Phillips 66	$182,922,000,000
21	E.ON SE	$174,687,689,157
22	Apple Inc	$170,910,000,000
23	ENI S.p.A.	$169,719,960,629
24	Berkshire Hathaway Inc.	$162,463,000,000
25	AXA S.A.	$158,689,204,448
26	Gazprom OAO	$156,607,432,658
27	General Motors Co.	$152,256,000,000
28	Daimler AG	$150,649,102,559
29	General Electric Co	$147,359,000,000
30	Petroleo Brasileiro S.A.	$144,103,000,000
31	Valero Energy Corp.	$139,250,000,000
32	Oil Co Lukoil	$139,171,000,000
33	Industrial and Commercial Ba	$135,669,965,398
34	Hon Hai Precision Industry Co	$134,567,503,639
35	Ford Motor Co. (DE)	$134,252,000,000
36	Allianz SE	$132,970,104,749
37	Statoil ASA	$129,328,113,710
38	BNP Paribas (France)	$128,541,458,463
39	GDF SUEZ	$127,900,886,411
40	AT&T Inc	$127,434,000,000
41	Fannie Mae	$127,230,000,000
42	CVS Caremark Corporation	$123,133,000,000
43	McKesson Corp.	$122,455,000,000
44	Hewlett-Packard Co	$120,357,000,000
45	JX Holdings, Inc.	$119,239,335,530
46	ING Groep N.V.	$118,467,606,211
47	Verizon Communications Inc	$115,846,000,000
48	China Construction Bank Corp	$114,738,967,390
49	Nippon Telegraph & Telephone	$113,726,287,639
50	SK Holdings Co Ltd	$112,088,941,726
51	Fiat S.P.A Torino	$110,659,481,032
52	UnitedHealth Group Inc	$110,618,000,000
53	Assicurazioni Generali S.p.A	$109,109,454,832
54	Banco Santander SA	$108,980,285,982
55	HSBC Holdings Plc	$108,851,000,000
56	JPMorgan Chase & Co.	$108,184,000,000
57	Societe Generale	$107,290,546,535
58	Costco Wholesale Corp	$105,156,000,000
59	Honda Motor Co., Ltd.	$104,981,734,142
60	Agricultural Bank of China	$104,724,284,700
61	International Business Machi	$104,507,000,000
62	BASF SE	$103,768,718,298
63	Carrefour S.A.	$103,414,162,985
64	Siemens AG (Germany)	$102,419,883,291
65	Nissan Motor Co., Ltd.	$102,342,053,219
66	Bayerische Motoren Werke	$101,289,467,208
67	Rosneft Oil Co OJSC	$101,114,793,180
68	Cardinal Health, Inc.	$101,093,000,000
69	Nestle S.A.	$100,713,817,016
70	Federal Reserve System	$100,526,000,000
71	Bank of America Corp.	$100,078,000,000
72	Bank of China Ltd., Beijing	$99,711,810,417
73	Tesco PLC	$98,950,732,475
74	Kroger Co.	$96,751,000,000
75	Hitachi, Ltd.	$96,087,508,070
76	Noble Group Ltd	$94,045,115,000
77	Express Scripts Holding Co	$93,858,100,000
78	PTT Public Co Ltd.	$91,301,486,703
79	Wells Fargo & Co.	$91,247,000,000
80	Citigroup Inc	$90,708,000,000
81	China Mobile Limited	$89,892,660,580
82	Prudential Plc	$89,419,912,611
83	Lloyds Banking Group Plc	$88,336,738,242
84	Metro AG	$87,965,304,913
85	AmerisourceBergen Corp.	$87,959,167,000
86	Munich Re Group	$87,956,078,567
87	Prudential Financial, Inc.	$84,815,000,000
88	ArcelorMittal SA	$84,213,000,000
89	Procter & Gamble Co	$84,167,000,000
90	Marathon Petroleum Corp.	$82,492,000,000
91	Telefonica, S.A.	$82,188,293,998
92	Boeing Co.	$81,698,000,000
93	Freddie Mac	$80,635,000,000
94	Indian Oil Corp., Ltd. (India	$80,378,189,122
95	Hyundai Motor Co., Ltd.	$79,113,495,991
96	Microsoft Corporation	$77,849,000,000
97	China Railway Construction C	$77,685,881,040
98	Panasonic Corp	$77,615,958,925
99	Philip Morris International	$77,393,000,000
100	Nippon Life Insurance Co.	$77,167,430,083

SOURCE: HOOVER'S, INC., DATABASE, OCTOBER 2013

The 100 Most Profitable Companies in Hoover's Handbook of World Business 2014

Rank Company	Net Income ($ thous)
1 Copperbelt Energy Corp Plc	$109,322,000,000
2 Oil and Natural Gas Corp. Lt	$55,319,147,897
3 Exxon Mobil Corp.	$44,880,000,000
4 Gazprom OAO	$38,850,189,176
5 Industrial and Commercial Ba	$38,261,560,873
6 Apple Inc	$37,037,000,000
7 China Construction Bank Corp	$30,986,744,201
8 Volkswagen A.G. (Germany, Fe	$28,624,080,774
9 Royal Dutch Shell Plc	$26,592,000,000
10 Chevron Corporation	$26,179,000,000
11 PT Resource Alam Indonesia T	$23,591,717,000
12 Agricultural Bank of China	$23,273,702,955
13 Bank of China Ltd., Beijing	$22,365,493,752
14 Microsoft Corporation	$21,863,000,000
15 Samsung Electronics Co., Ltd	$21,715,190,371
16 JPMorgan Chase & Co.	$21,284,000,000
17 China Mobile Limited	$20,736,106,771
18 Wells Fargo & Co.	$18,897,000,000
19 PetroChina Co Ltd	$18,498,787,455
20 Fannie Mae	$17,224,000,000
21 Wal-Mart Stores, Inc.	$16,999,000,000
22 International Business Machi	$16,604,000,000
23 Berkshire Hathaway Inc.	$14,824,000,000
24 Zambeef Products Plc	$14,583,000,000
25 Pfizer Inc	$14,570,000,000
26 Total S.A.	$14,095,221,246
27 HSBC Holdings Plc	$14,027,000,000
28 General Electric Co	$13,641,000,000
29 Statoil ASA	$12,317,814,535
30 BP plc	$11,582,000,000
31 Nestle S.A.	$11,575,260,088
32 Sberbank Russia	$11,458,362,528
33 Mitsubishi UFJ Financial Gro	$11,362,532,268
34 Procter & Gamble Co	$11,312,000,000

Rank Company	Net Income ($ thoud)
35 Rosneft Oil Co OJSC (Moscow)	$11,202,126,210
36 Petroleo Brasileiro S.A.	$11,034,000,000
37 Intel Corp	$11,005,000,000
38 Oil Co Lukoil	$11,004,000,000
39 Freddie Mac	$10,982,000,000
40 Oracle Corp.	$10,925,000,000
41 BHP Billiton Plc	$10,876,000,000
42 BHP Billiton Ltd.	$10,876,000,000
43 Johnson & Johnson	$10,853,000,000
44 Google Inc	$10,737,000,000
45 Alecta pensionsforsakring, om	$10,446,343,742
46 Roche Holding Ltd.	$10,405,843,557
47 ENI S.p.A.	$10,264,969,428
48 China Petroleum & Chemical C	$10,246,466,918
49 Toyota Motor Corp	$10,225,762,526
50 Cnooc Ltd.	$10,216,310,908
51 Cisco Systems, Inc.	$9,983,000,000
52 Novartis AG Basel	$9,505,000,000
53 Bank of Communications Co.,	$9,363,280,788
54 Coca-Cola Co (The)	$9,019,000,000
55 Philip Morris International	$8,800,000,000
56 BNP Paribas (France)	$8,637,178,308
57 Sumitomo Mitsui Financial Gr	$8,439,171,706
58 ConocoPhillips	$8,428,000,000
59 Ecopetrol SA	$8,328,675,582
60 Daimler AG	$8,033,511,642
61 Hyundai Motor Co., Ltd.	$8,018,919,677
62 China Shenhua Energy Co., Lt	$7,837,033,778
63 Central Bank of China	$7,762,363,496
64 Citigroup Inc	$7,541,000,000
65 Goldman Sachs Group, Inc.	$7,475,000,000
66 Royal Bank of Canada	$7,462,274,017
67 GlaxoSmithKline Plc	$7,358,171,120
68 AT&T Inc	$7,264,000,000

Rank Company	Net Income ($ thous)
69 China Merchants Bank Co Ltd	$7,261,984,327
70 Anheuser-Busch Inbev SA	$7,243,000,000
71 Twenty-First Century Fox Inc	$7,097,000,000
72 Commonwealth Bank of Austral	$7,081,065,198
73 America Movil, S.A.B. de C.V	$7,037,237,089
74 Qualcomm, Inc.	$6,853,000,000
75 Allianz SE	$6,812,997,814
76 Bayerische Motoren Werke AG	$6,716,780,201
77 Saudi Basic Industries Corp -	$6,607,188,763
78 Sanofi $6,546,751,817	
79 BASF SE	$6,430,763,462
80 AstraZeneca Plc	$6,297,000,000
81 Westpac Banking Corp	$6,230,388,953
82 Comcast Corp	$6,203,000,000
83 British American Tobacco Plc	$6,191,179,687
84 General Motors Co.	$6,188,000,000
85 Toronto Dominion Bank	$6,187,811,470
86 Itau Unibanco Holding S.A.	$6,179,413,592
87 Pepsico Inc.	$6,178,000,000
88 Merck & Co., Inc	$6,168,000,000
89 Disney (Walt) Co. (The)	$6,136,000,000
90 Wharf (Holdings) Ltd. (The)	$6,097,089,112
91 Bank of Nova Scotia Halifax	$6,039,408,278
92 China Minsheng Banking Corp	$6,025,267,097
93 Abbott Laboratories	$5,962,920,000
94 Australia and New Zealand Ba	$5,907,911,535
95 Unilever N.V.	$5,904,861,715
96 Unilever Plc (United Kingdom)	$5,904,861,715
97 Gazprom Neft	$5,791,466,400
98 Siemens AG (Germany)	$5,782,224,770
99 Taiwan Semiconductor Manufac	$5,725,303,863
100 Caterpillar Inc.	$5,681,000,000

SOURCE: HOOVER'S, INC., DATABASE, OCTOBER 2013

The 100 Largest Employers in Hoover's Handbook of World Business 2014

Rank	Company	Employees
1	Wal-Mart Stores, Inc.	2200000
2	Hon Hai Precision Industry Co	1290000
3	Tesco PLC	954225
4	G4S Plc 648254	
5	Randstad Holding N.V.	611020
6	Kelly Services, Inc.	568100
7	Volkswagen A.G. (Germany, Fe	549763
8	PetroChina Co Ltd	548355
9	Metro AG	536744
10	Yum! Brands, Inc.	523000
11	Compass Group PLC (United Ki	508714
12	Agricultural Bank of China	501762
13	Deutsche Post RG	473626
14	Deutsche Post AG	472321
15	McDonald's Corp	440000
16	International Business Machi	434246
17	Pou Chen Corp	427965
18	Sodexo	427921
19	Industrial and Commercial Ba	427356
20	Yue Yuen Industrial (Holding	423000
21	Gazprom OAO	417000
22	United Parcel Service Inc	399000
23	China Petroleum & Chemical C	376201
24	Hitachi, Ltd.	374775
25	Carrefour S.A.	364969
26	Siemens AG (Germany)	362400
27	Target Corp	361000
28	China Construction Bank Corp	355290
29	Kroger Co.	343000
30	Home Depot Inc	340000
31	Nestle S.A.	339000
32	Toyota Motor Corp	333498
33	Hewlett-Packard Co	331800
34	Nippon Telegraph & Telephone	324713
35	Rallye S.A.	321385
36	Veolia Environnement	318376
37	Casino Guichard Perrachon S.	316711
38	China Telecom Corp Ltd	305676
39	General Electric Co	305000
40	Bank of China Ltd., Beijing	302016
41	Panasonic Corp	293742
42	China Railway Group Ltd	289343
43	Berkshire Hathaway Inc.	288500
44	Sberbank Russia	286019
45	CVS Caremark Corporation	280000
46	Securitas AB	279641
47	Pepsico Inc.	278000
48	Daimler AG	275087
49	Accenture plc	275000
50	ArcelorMittal SA	273811
51	Aramark Holdings Corp	272000
52	HSBC Holdings Plc	270000
53	Wells Fargo & Co.	269200
54	Bank of America Corp.	267000
55	Citigroup Inc	259000
56	JPMorgan Chase & Co.	258965
57	Onex Corp.	250000
58	Hutchison Whampoa Ltd.	250000
59	Walgreen Co.	248000
60	Sears Holdings Corp	246000
61	Lowe's Companies Inc	245000
62	China Railway Construction C	244523
63	AT&T Inc	242000
64	GDF SUEZ	236156
65	Deutsche Telekom AG	229686
66	Koninklijke Ahold NV (Nether	225000
67	China Unicom (Hong Kong) Ltd	218598
68	United Technologies Corp.	218000
69	Fiat S.P.A Torino	214836
70	General Motors Co.	213000
71	China Resources Enterprise, L	211000
72	Sumitomo Electric Industries,	206323
73	Toshiba Corp	206087
74	Darden Restaurants, Inc. (Un	206000
75	Peugeot S.A. (France)	204287
76	HCA Holdings Inc	204000
77	Robert Half International In	203000
78	Wesfarmers Ltd.	200000
79	Woolworths Ltd.	197637
80	Canon, Inc.	196968
81	Compagnie de Saint-Gobain	192781
82	Vinci SA	192701
83	Honda Motor Co., Ltd.	190338
84	Ping An Insurance (Group) Co	190284
85	Banco Santander SA	188779
86	BNP Paribas (France)	188551
87	Costco Wholesale Corp	184000
88	Verizon Communications Inc	183400
89	China Mobile Limited	182487
90	Fomento Economico Mexicano,	182260
91	Starbucks Corp.	182000
92	TJX Companies, Inc.	179000
93	Pegatron Corp	177948
94	Yamato Holdings Co., Ltd.	177108
95	Jabil Circuit, Inc.	177000
96	Macy's, Inc.	175700
97	Disney (Walt) Co. (The)	175000
98	Boeing Co.	174400
99	Unilever N.V.	172000
100	Unilever Plc (United Kingdom	172000

SOURCE: HOOVER'S, INC., DATABASE, OCTOBER 2013

Hoover's Handbook of

World Business

The Companies

77 Bank, Ltd. (The) (Japan)

Unlike 77 Sunset Strip 77 Bank's name doesn't denote its address but its order in the history of Japanese banking. 77 Bank was founded in 1878 as the 77th national bank in Japan. Operating more than 140 branches in the northern area of Japan's largest island Honshu 77 Bank provides the usual banking services of savings and lending as well some other operations such as temporary employment property appraisal and credit-document custody. 77 Bank also provides financial-related services that include leasing credit investigation computer-based contract services and a credit card.

EXECUTIVES

President and Director, Hiroshi Kamata
Deputy President and Director, Teruhiko Ujiie
Senior Managing Director and Board Member, Yoshiaki Nagayama
Managing Director and Board Member, Reiichi Sato
Managing Director and Board Member, Kimitsugu Nagao
Managing Director and Board Member, Masayuki Yamada
Managing Director and Board Member, Mitsutaka Kambe
President and Director, Hiroshi Kamata
Senior Managing Director and Board Member, Yoshiaki Nagayama
Managing Director and Board Member, Reiichi Sato
Managing Director and Board Member, Kimitsugu Nagao
Managing Director and Board Member, Mitsutaka Kambe
Auditors: DeloitteToucheTohmatsu

LOCATIONS

HQ: 77 Bank, Ltd. (The) (Japan)
3-3-20 Chuo, Aoba-ku, Sendai, Miyagi 980-8777
Phone: (81) 22 267 1111
Web: www.77bank.co.jp

COMPETITORS

Fukuoka Financial Group
Gunma Bank
Ito-Yokado
Japan Post
Sumitomo Mitsui

HISTORICAL FINANCIALS

Company Type: Public

Income Statement FYE: March 31

	ASSETS ($ mil.)	NET INCOME ($ mil.)	INCOME AS % OF ASSETS	EMPLOYEES
03/13	87,798	132	0.2%	3,038
03/12	92,853	130	0.1%	3,128
03/11	75,086	(367)	—	3,149
03/10	63,237	124	0.2%	3,062
03/09	57,316	78	0.1%	3,003
Annual Growth	11.3%	14.0%	—	0.3%

2013 Year-End Financials

Return on assets: 0.1%
Return on equity: 3.7%
Long-term debt ($ mil.): —
No. of shares (mil.): 373
Sales ($ mil): 1,191
Dividends
Yield: —
Payout: —
Market value ($ mil.): —

	STOCK PRICE ($) FY Close	P/E High/Low	PER SHARE ($) Earnings	Dividends	Book Value
03/13	0.00	— —	0.35	0.00	10.45
03/12	5.15	— —	0.35	0.00	10.37
03/11	5.15	— —	(0.97)	0.00	9.87
03/10	5.35	— —	0.33	0.00	10.06
Annual Growth	—	— —	1.8%	—	1.0%

A.P. Moller - Maersk A/S

Oceangoing containers mean big money for A.P. Moller - Morsk. Operating in about 130 countries the conglomerate specializes in global container shipping and related services led by Maersk Line which transports cargo via a fleet of more than 500 containerships Damco which provides freight forwarding and supply chain management services and APM Terminals a major container terminal operator. Other activities include marine transportation of crude oil and natural gas (Maersk Tankers) oil and gas exploration and production (Maersk Oil and Gas) and marine towing and salvage (Svitzer). It also owns one of Denmark's largest retail chain store operators Dansk Supermarked.

In line with a recovering global economy and as a result of cost-saving measures that it began undertaking in 2008 the company achieved its best profit so far in 2010 after a loss in 2009. It made a DKK 28.2 billion ($5 billion) profit in 2010 compared to a loss of DKK 5.5 billion ($1 billion) in the prior year. Most of its business units contributed to the overall profit including its container shipping oil and gas terminal drilling and retail operations. The main factors were increased container rates and volumes reduced costs per unit and increased oil prices. Only those in its tanker and offshore business segment including Maersk Tankers Maersk FPSO and Maersk LNG recorded losses for the year.

Moving forward the company's main goal is to expand business and maintain high profitability within two primary industries —shipping and oil and gas. Within the shipping industry container shipping and terminal activities are its key priorities for investment. Investments in Maersk Tankers Damco and Svitzer will be driven by market opportunities. It is pushing Maersk Line to gain market share by sharpening its customer focus and improving its fleet. It has committed at least $3.8 billion to buy 20 of the world's largest most energy-efficient container vessels known as Triple-E. They are expected to be delivered between 2013 and 2015. Meanwhile APM Terminals aims to be the leading global port operator and a significant contributor to the group's cash flows and earnings. It is divesting certain non-core port terminals and entering into agreements to establish port terminals in such emerging markets as Brazil and Liberia.

In the oil and gas industry Maersk Oil and Maersk Drilling (including Maersk Supply Service) are marked as the group's main priorities for investment. Maersk Oil is trying to stabilize production by 2014 and thereafter gradually grow to reach a stable production rate of 400000 barrels of oil equivalent per day. As fields in the North Sea mature Maersk Oil is investing in promising oil fields in Brazil and the Gulf of Mexico. It also obtained several licenses in Greenland Norway and the UK. Maersk Drilling aims to be one of the leading drilling contractors within deep water and ultra harsh environments having already committed about $3.8 billion to the construction of four deep-water drillships and two ultra harsh jack-up rigs.

Founded by Peter Maersk Moller and his son Arnold Peter Moller A.P. Moller - Maersk styles the company and family name as "Maersk" but uses "Maersk" for the names of most of its subsidiaries. A.P. Moller - Maersk's main shareholder is The A.P. Moller and Chastine Mc-Kinney Moller Foundation which was established by company founder A.P. Moller in 1953.

HISTORY

Arnold Peter Moller and his father sea captain Peter Maersk Moller founded Aktieselskabet Dampskibsselskabet Svendborg (Steamship Company Svendborg) in 1904 in Svendborg Denmark. Their first ship a second-hand steamer bore on its funnel a white seven-pointed star on a blue background which had been on Peter's first ship. Later known as the Maersk star the logo adorned all subsequent ships of the company as well as ships of a second company formed eight years later — Dampskibsselskabet af 1912 Aktieselskab (Steamship Company of 1912). At that point six ships were in the Maersk fleet.

In 1917 the company began building its own ships after establishing the Odense Steel Shipyard. It launched regular liner service between the US and the Far East in 1928 calling the operation the Maersk Line. With the addition of its first tankers that year Maersk owned 35 ships.

Maersk Mc-Kinney Moller A.P.'s son became a partner in the company in 1940. That year with Germany occupying Denmark he fled to the US with his bride on one of the last ships out. Refusing to take orders from the Nazis A.P. transferred control of the company to the US where the 26-year-old Maersk had established operations. Most of the Maersk fleet flew under British or US flags during the war which took the life of 148 Maersk seamen and claimed 25 ships. Maersk Mc-Kinney Moller returned to Denmark in 1947.

A.P. Moller formed the Maersk Company in 1951 in London as a shipbroker; it became one of the world's largest shipowners. The early 1960s saw A.P. Moller diversifying as it moved into oil and gas exploration and production in Denmark in 1962 and established supermarket chain Dansk Supermarked in 1964. A.P. died the next year having run the company for more than 60 years. Prior to his death he had created three foundations to hold most of the company's shares. His son Maersk took command of A.P. Moller and the Maersk fleet which contained 88 ships. Under his leadership the company expanded even further and became more international; his business savvy became apparent when he sold some of the company's tanker fleet in the 1970s just prior to prices going down.

In 1970 A.P. Moller established domestic carrier Maersk Air. A.P. Moller began seeing its first oil production in the North Sea in 1972. The next year the company acquired its first container vessel the "Svendborg Maersk".

Maersk Container Industri was formed in 1991 to produce intermodal containers. That year Maersk and rival Sea-Land entered into a transpacific vessel-sharing agreement which was expanded into a global alliance in 1995. In 1999 just months after buying South Africa's Safmarine Container Lines Maersk bought Sea-Land's international liner services and 18 terminals. The Maersk Line and Sea-Land operations were merged to form Maersk Sealand.

In 2000 A.P. Moller planned to extend its Bilka grocery chain into southern Sweden. That year Maersk Sealand decided to shift its transshipment hub in Singapore to a Malaysian port. In 2001 Maersk Air and Scandinavian Airlines System

(SAS) were together fined $45 million by the European Commission for infringing on the EC's competition rules by entering into a secret deal to monopolize certain air routes in Scandinavia. As a result Maersk Air's chairman and managing director stepped down and were replaced.

A.P. Moller which through the years had continued to operate through two separately listed companies — Aktieselskabet Dampskibsselskabet Svendborg and Dampskibsselskabet af 1912 Aktieselskab —reorganized in 2003 and wound up with a single publicly traded company —A.P. Moller - Maersk A/S —at its head.

A.P. Moller - Maersk purchased the majority of Kerr-McGee's North Sea oil assets in late 2005. Also that year the passenger transportation business of Maersk Air was sold to an Icelandic investment group.

Maersk Line was launched as a brand in 2006 as a result of the combined operations of Maersk Sealand and Royal P&O Nedlloyd which was acquired by A.P. Moller - Maersk in 2005. Consolidating the businesses proved to be more difficult than expected however. The container shipping operations lost money in 2006 before posting a small profit in 2007. That year CEO Jess Soderberg stepped down two years ahead of schedule and Nils Smedegaard Andersen CEO of brewer Carlsberg and a director of A.P. Moller - Maersk replaced him. In addition Maersk Line's management structure was simplified.

Throughout 2008 the company worked on cutting costs and in September 2009 the company combined its Maersk Logistics and Damco divisions keeping the Damco name.

EXECUTIVES

Chairman, Michael P. Rasmussen, age 59
Founder, Arnold Moller
Senior Vice President, Carsten Plougmann
Director, Sir John R. H. Bond, age 71
Vice Chairman, Poul J. Svanholm, age 79
Director, Jan Leschly, age 72
Director, Jan Topholm, age 66
Director, Lars E. Kann-Rasmussen, age 73
Vice Chairman, Ane Maersk Mc-Kinney Uggla, age 64
Director, Leise Maersk Mc-Kinney Moller, age 71
Director, Cecilie M. Hansen, age 38
Director, Lars Pallesen, age 65
Director, John Axel Poulsen, age 66
Auditors: GrantThornton

LOCATIONS

HQ: A.P. Moller - Maersk A/S
Esplanaden 50, Copenhagen K DK-1098
Phone: (45) 33 63 33 63
Web: www.maersk.com

2010 Sales

	% of total
Denmark	20
US	12
UK	9
Qatar	9
Other	50
Total	**100**

PRODUCTS/OPERATIONS

2010 Sales

	% of total
Shipping	
Container	45
Tankers offshore & other	10
Retail	18
Oil &	18
Terminal	7
Other	2
Total	**100**

Selected Business Areas

Container shipping & related
- Damco (freight forwarding and supply chain management services)
- Maersk Container Industry (manufacturing of dry and reefer containers)
- Maersk Line (global container shipping)
- MCC Transport (intra-Asia container shipping)
- Safmarine (Africa Middle East and Indian subcontinent container shipping)

Oil and gas activities
- Maersk Oil (oil and gas exploration and production)

Retail & other
- Dansk Supermarked (owner of several chains of supermarkets department stores and discount markets)
- Svitzer (specialized marine services including towing salvage and emergency response)

Tankers offshore & related
- Maersk Drilling (offshore drilling activities and operation of land rigs through 50% ownership in Egyptian Drilling Company)
- Maersk FPSOs (floating oil and gas production units)
- Maersk LNG (liquefied natural gas transportation)
- Maersk Supply Service (anchor handling and platform supply vessels)
- Maersk Tankers (tanker shipping of crude oil oil products and gas)

Technology
- Maersk Fluid Technology
- Maersk Maritime Technology

Terminal activities
- APM Terminals (port operations inland transportation and container repair)

COMPETITORS

BP
CMA CGM
COSCO Group
China Shipping
Coop Danmark
DP World
Evergreen Marine
Frontline
Hanjin Shipping
Hapag-Lloyd
Hess Corporation
Hutchison Port Holdings
Hyundai Merchant Marine
ICA AB
John Swire & Sons
Kawasaki Kisen
Mediterranean Shipping Company
Mitsui O.S.K. Lines
NYK Line
Neptune Orient
Orient Overseas
PSA International
SSA Marine
Singamas
Statoil

HISTORICAL FINANCIALS

Company Type: Public

Income Statement FYE: December 31

	REVENUE ($ mil.)	NET INCOME ($ mil.)	NET PROFIT MARGIN	EMPLOYEES
12/12	60,432	3,829	6.3%	121,105
12/11	56,114	2,642	4.7%	117,080
12/10	56,630	4,750	8.4%	108,110
12/09	50,333	(1,360)	—	115,386
12/08	58,508	3,182	5.4%	120,000
Annual Growth	0.8%	4.7%	—	0.2%

2012 Year-End Financials

Debt ratio: 4.6%
Return on equity: 10.7%
Cash ($ mil.): 2,298
Current ratio: 1.15
Long-term debt ($ mil.): 17,333
No. of shares (mil.): 4
Dividends
Yield: 0.0%
Payout: 0.0%
Market value ($ mil.): 67

	STOCK PRICE ($) FY Close	P/E High	P/E Low	PER SHARE ($) Earnings	Dividends	Book Value
12/12	15.45	0	0	876.65	0.01	8,447.54
Annual Growth	—	—	—	—	—	—

AB Electrolux (Sweden)

AB Electrolux has a hunting license for dust bunnies. The firm a top maker of household appliances worldwide operates through two segments: consumer durables (residential kitchen fabric care and cleaning) and professional products (industrial kitchens restaurants and laundries). It cranks out washing machines stoves refrigerators and freezers under the AEG Electrolux Eureka Frigidaire and Zanussi names. It's also the #1 maker globally of vacuum cleaners (Electrolux Eureka brands). Electrolux's presence in the commercial market has it making foodservice and laundry equipment under the Electrolux and Zanussi labels. CEO Hans Straberg left the company at the end of 2010.

Straberg joined Electrolux in 1983 and became the company's top executive in 2002. Since then he worked to make the Electrolux name a global brand (particularly in the US with its campaign that features TV personality Kelly Ripa) restructured the company and spun off the firm's outdoor unit. COO Keith McLoughlin succeeded Straberg at the start of 2011. Previously head of Electrolux Major Appliances North America McLoughlin brought with him expertise in R&D manufacturing and purchasing as well as 20 years of experience at DuPont.

While the company's executive suite changed hands Electrolux has been streamlining its manufacturing. It shuttered a Canadian factory and cut 800 jobs in Europe. The company in 2011 shut down its consumer washing machine and dryer manufacturing center in Webster City Iowa. The closings wrap up a restructuring program Electrolux began in 2004. Since then the company has largely shifted North American and Western European consumer durables production to plants in Asia Mexico and Eastern Europe. Electrolux also laid off some 3000 employees worldwide in 2009. The streamlining strategy seems to be paying off. Electrolux in 2009 cited an uptick in business in Europe and North America thanks to a combination of lowering its production costs and raising its prices.

Meanwhile the company has been refocusing its professional products division to cater to the key food service and laundry markets. As such Electrolux has been disposing of operations that don't complement its strategy. In 2011 Electrolux Professional sold its heating element business to NIBE Industrier. The heating element business which has been part of Electrolux since 1978 manufactured an assortment of products for heating control and measurement at facilities in Switzerland.

Electrolux boasts a global reach as its products are sold in more than 150 markets. Its consumer durables business spans four regions (Europe North America Latin America and Asia/Pacific) while its professional products unit with a hefty 10% profit margin and 7% of sales focuses on a single global business area. Its largest markets are Europe and North America. Looking beyond established markets to emerging markets in Central and Eastern Europe the company acquired a washing machine factory in the Ukraine. The early 2011 purchase will broaden Electrolux's manufacturing base in emerging markets and enable the firm to better supply CIS markets from within the area. Turning to another lucrative emerging market Electrolux acquired the Egyptian company Olympic Group in later in the year after seeing the deal almost collapse due to the political turmoil. Olympic is the largest manufacturer of washing machines refrigerators and cookers (stoves) in the Middle East and North Africa; it boasts a roughly

30% market share in Egypt. To further expand its reaches into emerging markets Electrolux has decided to purchase Chilean appliance manufacturer Compania Tecno Industrial (CTI) maker of Fensa Mademsa and Somela appliances. Electolux plans to introduce higher-end appliances into the Chilean and Argentine marketplaces.

Its breadth has made Electrolux a behemoth in the household appliances industry. Electrolux sells some 40 million products worldwide; nearly half of them were sold under its namesake brand. Its consumer durables segment generated 93% of its 2009 revenue.

With declining housing starts in the US and retailers struggling to lure shoppers to buy products Electrolux has seen the US market stagnate. Tax incentives to entice US consumers to purchase energy-efficient large appliances have helped to offset sales declines however. Some 60% of Electrolux's appliances in the US are sold by four big-box retailers: Lowe's Sears Home Depot and Best Buy.

Through Investor AB –which also has stakes in Saab and other multinational companies –the Wallenberg family controls about 26% of Electrolux's voting power.

HISTORY

Swedish salesman Axel Wenner-Gren saw an American-made vacuum cleaner in a Vienna Austria store window in 1910 and envisioned selling the cleaners door-to-door a technique he had learned in the US. Two years later he worked with fledgling Swedish vacuum cleaner makers AB Lux and Elektromekaniska to improve their existing designs. The two companies merged to form AB Electrolux in 1919. When the board of the new company balked at Wenner-Gren's suggestion to mass-produce vacuum cleaners he guaranteed Electrolux's sales through his own sales company.

In the 1920s the company used the "Every home —an Electrolux home" slogan as Wenner-Gren drove his sales force on and launched new sales companies in Europe and North and South America. He scored a publicity coup by securing the blessing of Pope Pius XI to vacuum the Vatican gratis for a year. By the end of the 1920s Electrolux had purchased most of Wenner-Gren's sales companies (excluding Electrolux US) and had gambled on refrigerator technology and won. By buying vacuum cleaner maker Volta (Sweden 1934) it gained retail distribution.

Despite the loss of Eastern European subsidiaries during WWII the company did well until the 1960s when it backed an unpopular refrigeration technology. Swedish electrical equipment giant ASEA controlled by Marcus Wallenberg bought a large stake in Electrolux in 1964 and in 1967 he installed Hans Werthen as chairman. Werthen slashed overhead and sold the company's minority stake in Electrolux US to Consolidated Foods. (The US Electrolux business was taken private in 1987.)

Since 1970 Electrolux has bought more than 300 companies (many of them troubled appliance makers) updated their plants and gained global component manufacturing efficiencies. Acquisitions included National Union Electric (Eureka vacuum cleaners US 1974) Tappan (appliances US 1979) Zanussi (appliances industrial products; Italy; 1984) White Consolidated Industries (appliances industrial products; US; 1986) and Lehel (refrigerators Hungary 1991). By 1996 the company had acquired a 41% interest in Refrigerac?o Parana Brazil's #2 manufacturer of appliances. (Electrolux owned it all by 1998.)

To better focus on its "white goods" (washers refrigerators etc.) in 1996 Electrolux began selling noncore businesses. In 1997 under new CEO Michael "Mike the Knife" Treschow the company launched a restructuring plan involving the closing of about 25 plants and the elimination of more than 12000 jobs mostly in Europe. The plan worked: Electrolux's profits more than quadrupled in 1998. Also that year the company launched a joint venture in India with Voltas Limited forming that country's largest refrigerator manufacturer.

Electrolux acquired the European operations of chainsaw maker McCulloch in 1999. To strengthen its Asian presence Electrolux teamed up with Toshiba for future collaboration on household appliances. Also that year the company said it would sell its vending machine unit and professional refrigeration business. That year AB Electrolux agreed to buy the major appliance business of Email Ltd. Australia's top household appliance maker.

In January 2002 it finalized the sale of its leisure appliance operations —mostly refrigerators for recreational vehicles –to private equity firm EQT Northern Europe. In April 2002 Electrolux CEO Michael Treschow resigned (but remained as a director) and was replaced by board member Hans Straberg. The firm acquired Diamant Boart International a world-leading manufacturer and distributor of diamond tools and related equipment in June 2002.

As part of a restructuring effort to combat the effects of diminishing consumer demand and higher material costs Electrolux cut nearly 5000 jobs (about 6% of its workforce) during 2003.

Electrolux relaunched its flagship brand of vacuum cleaners in North America during 2004 having bought the rights from long-unaffiliated vacuum maker Electrolux LLC (now Aerus). Also that year former CEO Michael Treschow reappeared in a leadership position assuming the role of chairman. Treschow left the company again in 2007. Hans Straberg who had joined Electrolux in 1983 was appointed CEO of the business in 2002.

The firm exited its outdoor segment which consisted of chainsaws and lawn and garden equipment (Husqvarna Jonsered brands) and diamond tools (Dimas Diamant Boart names) through a spinoff in 2006.

EXECUTIVES

SVP General Counsel and Secretary, Cecilia Vieweg, age 57
President and Chief Executive Officer; Director, Keith R. McLoughlin, age 57
Deputy Chairman, Peggy B. Bruzelius, age 63
VP Investor Relations and Financial Information, Peter Nyquist
Chief Financial Officer Senior Vice President, Tomas Eliasson, age 51
Head of Major Appliances North America Executive Vice President, Jack G. Truong, age 52
Chairman, Marcus Wallenberg, age 58
Deputy Chairman, Ronnie Leten, age 57
Manager Financial Information, Maria Norin
Head of Major Appliances Asia/Pacific Executive Vice President, Gunilla Nordstrom, age 55
SVP Group Staff Human Resources and Organizational Development Electrolux Group, Carina Malmgren Heander
Head of Major Appliances Latin America Executive Vice President, Ruy Hirschheimer, age 65
EVP and Head of Electrolux Major Appliances Europe, Enderson Guimaraes, age 53
Head of Major Appliances Europe Middle East and Africa Executive Vice President, Jonas Samuelson, age 45
Head of Professional Products Executive Vice President, Alberto Zanata, age 53
Talent Management Specialist, Irwin Sjafril
VP Commuications Europe, Christina Lindberg
SVP and Chief Design Officer, Stefano Marzano, age 63
Chief Technology Officer Senior Vice President, Jan Brockmann, age 48
Head of Small Appliances Executive Vice-President, Henrik Bergstrom, age 42
Chief Marketing Officer Senior Vice President, MaryKay Kopf
President and Chief Executive Officer; Director, Keith R. McLoughlin, age 57
Director, Hasse Johansson, age 64
Deputy Chairman, Peggy B. Bruzelius, age 63
Director, John S. Lupo, age 66
Deputy Chairman, Ronnie Leten, age 57
Director, Barbara M. Thoralfsson, age 54
Director, Torben B. Sorensen, age 61
Director, Ulrika Saxon
Auditors: PricewaterhouseCoopersAB

LOCATIONS

HQ: AB Electrolux (Sweden)
S:t Gloransgatan 143, Stockholm S-105 45
Phone: (46) 8 738 60 00 **Fax:** (46) 8 738 74 61
Web: www.electrolux.com

PRODUCTS/OPERATIONS

2009 Sales

	% of total
Consumer	93
Professional	7
Total	**100**

Selected Products and Brands

Consumer durables
Core A
Floorcare products
Professional products
Foodservice equipment
Laundry equipment

COMPETITORS

Ali SpA
BISSELL
BSH Bosch und Siemens Hausgerate
Fisher & Paykel Appliances Holdings
Franke Group
GE Appliances & Lighting
Gree Electrical Appliances
Haier Group
Hobart Corp.
Indesit
LG Electronics
Miele
Philips Electronics
Royal Appliance
SEB
Samsung Group
Whirlpool
WinWholesale

HISTORICAL FINANCIALS

Company Type: Public

Income Statement

FYE: December 31

	REVENUE ($ mil.)	NET INCOME ($ mil.)	NET PROFIT MARGIN	EMPLOYEES
12/12	16,884	398	2.4%	59,478
12/11	14,730	299	2.0%	52,916
12/10	15,856	596	3.8%	51,544
12/09	15,323	366	2.4%	51,750
12/08	13,418	46	0.3%	52,034
Annual Growth	5.9%	70.8%	—	3.4%

2012 Year-End Financials

Debt ratio: 2.5%
Return on equity: 12.8%
Cash ($ mil.): 1,049
Current ratio: 1.10
Long-term debt ($ mil.): 1,535
No. of shares (mil.): 286
Dividends
Yield: 3.5%
Payout: 3.1%
Market value ($ mil.): 15,234

STOCK PRICE ($) FY Close		P/E High/Low		PER SHARE ($) Earnings	Dividends	Book Value
12/12	53.24	0	0	1.39	1.91	10.61
12/11	31.49	0	0	1.05	0.05	10.46
12/10	56.75	0	0	2.08	1.11	10.80
12/09	46.75	0	0	1.29	0.00	9.30
12/08	17.40	1	0	0.17	1.43	7.40
Annual Growth	32.3%	—	—	70.3%	7.6%	9.4%

ABB Asea Brown Boveri Ltd. (Switzerland)

LOCATIONS

HQ: ABB Asea Brown Boveri Ltd. (Switzerland)
P.O. Box 8131, Zurich CH-8050
Phone: (41) 317 7111 **Fax:** (41) 311 7958
Web: www.abb.com

HISTORICAL FINANCIALS

Company Type: Public

Income Statement FYE: December 31

	REVENUE ($ mil.)	NET INCOME ($ mil.)	NET PROFIT MARGIN	EMPLOYEES
12/12	39,336	2,704	6.9%	146,100
12/11	37,990	3,168	8.3%	0
12/10	31,589	2,561	8.1%	0
12/98	123	640	518.4%	199,232
12/97	124	643	519.1%	213,057
Annual Growth	46.8%	10.0%	—	(2.5%)

2012 Year-End Financials

Debt ratio: 20.5%
Return on equity: 16.5%
Cash ($ mil.): 6,875
Current ratio: 1.48
Long-term debt ($ mil.): 7,534
No. of shares (mil.): —
Dividends
Yield: —
Payout: —
Market value ($ mil.): —

STOCK PRICE ($) FY Close		P/E High/Low		PER SHARE ($) Earnings	Dividends	Book Value
12/12	0.00	—	—	1.18	0.00	7.36
12/11	0.00	—	—	1.38	0.00	6.89
Annual Growth	—	—	—	(1.0%)	—	0.4%

ABB Ltd

You could be forgiven for thinking that ABB is short for "A Bunch of Businesses" –though that bunch has evolved over some 130 years. ABB engineers power and automation technologies for a broad base of utility industrial and commercial customers. Its lines run from robots to light switches. Power products include transmission and distribution components as well as turnkey substation systems. Automation technologies are used to monitor and control equipment and processes in industrial plants and utilities. The company has established a presence in about 100 countries with its core businesses concentrated in power and automation markets.

Geographic Reach

ABB's operations extend to around 100 countries. A large portion of the company's production and development facilities reside in Canada China Finland Germany India Italy Norway Sweden Switzerland and the US.

Europe accounted for 36% of its total sales in 2012; the Americas and Asia each generated 27% while Africa and the Middle East brought in 10%.

Operations

ABB operates through five segments: Power Products Power Systems Discrete Automation and Motion Low Voltage Products and Process Automation. The Power Products and Power Systems segments are driven primarily by the capital expenditures of electrical utilities.

The Automation Products Process Automation and Low Voltage Products segments are impacted by the health of several industries including automotive consumer products metals and minerals paper and pulp and pharmaceuticals. A global presence and competitive cost base however have helped to buffer ABB's exposure to regional recessions and slow economies.

Major subsidiaries owned by ABB include ABB Inc. ABB Limited Baldor Electric Company Thomas & Betts Ventyx Tropos Networks ABB AG ABB Ltda. Power-One and ABB Contracting.

Sales and Marketing

ABB sells its products through direct sales and external channel partners like wholesalers distributors system integrators EPCs and OEMs.

Financial Performance

ABB generated $39.3 billion in revenues for 2012 a historic milestone for the company; this represented a 3% increase from the $37.8 billion it earned in 2011. The spike in revenues was mainly due to a solid order level as well as the favorable impact of its 2012 Thomas & Betts acquisition.

While ABB has enjoyed three straight years of revenue growth its profits slipped by 15% from $3.2 billion in 2011 to $2.7 billion in 2012 due to an increase in the cost of sales. This was the result of an unfavorable business mix coupled with higher prices involved with restructuring its segments.

Strategy

As the global economy moves away from the recession ABB has been making some milestone acquisitions to boost its product offerings operations and geographic reach. In mid-2013 it purchased Power-One a major provider of solar inverters technology used to convert the sun's energy into electricity. ABB made the $1 billion deal to boost its renewable energy business and expand its solar product portfolio.

In 2012 ABB bought Thomas & Betts (T&B) for about $3.9 billion. T&B sells electrical connectors HVAC equipment and transmission towers. The acquisition significantly added to ABB's North American presence giving it access to T&B's network of more than 6000 distributor locations and wholesalers throughout the continent. Shortly after that transaction was made ABB snapped up Tropos Networks a California firm that makes wireless technologies and products for distribution area communication networks. The acquisition broadened ABB's communications systems portfolio and enabled it to better cater to North American clients in the power transportation and mining sectors.

In 2011 ABB acquired the Trasfor Group which advanced its portfolio of specialty dry-type transformers used in drives railway rolling stock offshore wind power and other renewable energy applications. Months earlier ABB swallowed up Baldor Electric for $3.1 billion. Baldor Electric a US industrial motors business strengthened ABB's energy efficient offerings most notably in North America.

Other completed acquisitions that year include ABB's takeover of Mincom an Australia-based software and services company with clients ranging from mining companies (Rio Tinto and Anglo American) to big manufacturing companies (Boeing and Caterpillar). Not only did the deal bring an estimated $200 million in revenues but it also expanded ABB's software capabilities.

HISTORY

Asea Brown Boveri (ABB) was formed in 1988 when two giants ASEA AB of Sweden and BBC Brown Boveri of Switzerland combined their electrical engineering and equipment businesses. Percy Barnevik head of ASEA became CEO.

ASEA was born in Stockholm in 1883 when Ludwig Fredholm founded Electriska Aktiebolaget to manufacture an electric dynamo created by engineer Jonas Wenstrom. In 1890 the company merged with Wenstrom's brother's firm to form Allmanna Svenska Electriska Aktiebolaget (ASEA) a pioneer in industrial electrification. Early in the 1900s ASEA began its first railway electrification project. By the 1920s it was providing locomotives and other equipment to Sweden's national railway and by the next decade ASEA was one of Sweden's largest electric equipment manufacturers. In 1962 it bought 20% of appliance maker Electrolux. ASEA created the nuclear power venture ASEA-ATOM with the Swedish government in 1968 and bought full control in 1982.

BBC Brown Boveri was formed in 1891 as the Brown Boveri and Company partnership between Charles Brown and Walter Boveri in Baden Switzerland. It made power generation equipment and produced the first steam turbines in Europe in 1900. BBC entered Germany (1893) France (1894) and Italy (1903) and diversified into nuclear power equipment after WWII.

By 1988 BBC the bigger company had a West German network that ASEA the more profitable company coveted. Both had US joint ventures. In an unusual merger ASEA (which became ABB AB) and BBC (later ABB AG) continued as separate entities sharing equal ownership of ABB. Barnevik crafted a unique decentralized management structure under which national subsidiaries were closely linked to their local customers and labor forces. In six years ABB took over more than 150 companies worldwide.

An ABB-led consortium built one of the world's largest hydroelectric plants in Iran in 1992 and in 1995 ABB merged its transportation segment into Adtranz (a joint venture with Daimler-Benz) to form the world's #1 maker of trains.

Tragedy struck in 1996. Robert Donovan CEO of ABB's US subsidiary died in a plane crash along with Commerce Secretary Ron Brown and other executives on a trade mission. Donovan's death hastened the US unit's restructuring.

In 1997 Barnevik gave up the title of CEO remaining as chairman and was succeeded by Goran Lindahl an engineer who worked his way up the ranks at ASEA. (Barnevik remained chairman until 2001.) After 1997 profits dipped drastically Lindahl scrapped Barnevik's vaunted regional matrix structure in favor of one organized by product areas under a strong central management. Though the Asian financial crisis slowed orders ABB still pulled in large contracts including one to build the world's largest cracker plant in Texas in 1998.

In 1999 ABB acquired Elsag Bailey a Dutch maker of industrial control systems for about $1.5 billion and sold its 50% stake in Adtranz to DaimlerChrysler for about $472 million. ABB and France's ALSTOM combined their power generation businesses to form the world's largest power plant equipment maker. That year ABB AB and ABB AG were at last united under a single stock through holding company ABB Ltd.

ABB scaled back its power plant-related activities in 2000. The company sold its nuclear power business to BNFL for $485 million and its 50% stake in ABB Alstom Power to ALSTOM for $1.2 billion. (Areva acquired ALSTOM's transmission and distribution business in 2004.) In 2001 Lindahl resigned and Jorgen Centerman head of the company's automation business replaced him. Centerman promptly reorganized ABB's industrial operations into four segments based on customer type and two based on product type.

Also in 2001 ABB acquired French company Entrelec a supplier of industrial automation and control products. With economic slowdowns occurring in the company's key markets ABB announced plans in 2001 to cut 12000 jobs over 18 months. Later that year amid rising numbers of asbestos claims against US subsidiary Combustion Engineering ABB took a $470 million fourth-quarter charge to cover asbestos liabilities. The claims charged asbestos exposures stemming from products supplied before the mid-1970s by Combustion Engineering which ABB acquired in 1990.

In 2002 ABB found itself embroiled in controversy after revealing not only a record loss but also payments of large pensions to former chairman Barnevik and former chief executive Lindahl. The former executives agreed that year to return a part (about $82 million) of their pension payouts to ABB. That year the company which faced $4.4 billion in debts after industry slumps affected its sales of power systems and equipment industrial automation and controls sold part of its financial services unit to GE Commercial Finance for $2.3 billion.

The day after the company sold its structured finances unit ABB's chief executive Jorgen Centerman resigned and was replaced by the chairman Jurgen Dormann. That year ABB sold its metering business to Germany-based Ruhrgas for $244 million.

In 2003 as part of its settlement with asbestos plaintiffs ABB placed Combustion Engineering into bankruptcy. Later that same year the company announced that it would sell its Sirius International reinsurance business to the Bermuda-based White Mountains; the deal was completed in 2004 for about $425 million. ABB also sold its upstream oil gas and petrochemicals unit to Candover Partners 3i and J.P. Morgan Partners for $925 million in 2004. (To clear the way for the sale ABB also agreed to pay US regulators $16 million in fines to settle bribery cases at US-based ABB Vetco Gray and Scotland-based ABB Vetco UK. The subsidiaries –part of the petroleum business that was sold –allegedly paid off government officials in Angola Kazakhstan and Nigeria in order to win oil contracts between 1998 and 2003.)

Sulzer CEO Fred Kindle succeeded Dormann as ABB's CEO in 2005. (Dormann remained chairman until his retirement in 2007.) The company made a number of small dispositions in 2005 including its Japanese control valves business its foundry business and several cable and power line businesses.

ABB ended years of litigation –and a major corporate headache –when it reached a settlement on an asbestos liability case related to US subsidiary Combustion Engineering in 2006. As part of the settlement ABB committed more than $1.4 billion to pay settled claims.

After consolidating its remaining businesses into the two areas power technologies and automation technologies ABB restructured its operations into five divisions in 2006: Power Products Power Systems Automation Products Process Automation and Robotics. It took further steps to streamline operations and position itself for growth for example by moving its main robotics operation from Detroit to Shanghai.

In 2006 ABB voluntarily disclosed to the US Department of Justice and the SEC that the company made payments in the Middle East that might have violated anti-bribery laws. The following year ABB disclosed similar suspect payments at subsidiaries in Asia Europe and South America.

Kindle left ABB in 2008 due to what the company called "irreconcilable differences" concerning the leadership of the company; former GE Healthcare CEO Joe Hogan became CEO of ABB later that year.

In 2008 the company dug deeper into its investment purse spending $653 million to complete 12 deals. Most notably ABB purchased Kuhlman Electric a US-based transformer manufacturer from The Carlyle Group for $513 million including assumed debt. Kuhlman Electric was integrated into ABB's Power Products division in North America and deepens ABB's geographic footprint and product offerings in the industrial and electric utility sectors.

ABB's bunch of businesses has been peeled back too. Several divestitures were completed in 2008 and 2007; ABB exited its 50% interest in South Africa's ABB Powertech Transformers to Powertech owned by the Altron Group for $11 million. In 2007 ABB sold subsidiary ABB Lummus Global to Chicago Bridge & Iron Co. for some $870 million in cash as well as its Building Systems business in Germany and power plant interests in India and Morocco to Abu Dhabi National Oil. Power Lines businesses in Brazil and Mexico were also put on the sale block for $20 million.

ABB plowed in $209 million in 2009 adding eight new operations. Among them the company acquired the assets of Sinai Engineering a designer and provider of services for electrical generation and transmission systems planning as well as construction management. The transaction completed through its US ABB Inc. expanded ABB's presence in western Canada. On the other side of the world ABB picked up South Africa's Westingcorp (Pty) Ltd. The move ramped up ABB's line of power capacitors (machines that add to a system's power quality and energy efficiency) and opened the door to local and global electric utilities and mining markets.

ABB in mid-2010 acquired K-TEK a maker of level detection technology used in the oil and gas industry as well as water and other industries. Its instrumentation and sensing technologies which number more than 350000 installations enhanced ABB's slate of measurement products part of its Process Automation division. The deal garnered K-TEK's facilities in the US the Netherlands China India and South Africa.

ABB picked up US software provider Insert Key Solutions in late 2010. Its combination with the earlier acquisition of Ventyx (valued at approximately $1 billion) from Vista Equity Partners created a comprehensive portfolio of software for managing asset-intensive businesses engaged in the utility energy and communications industries. Ventyx and Insert Key Solutions joined ABB's network management business.

EXECUTIVES

Chief Executive Officer; Member of the Executive Committee, Joseph M. (Joe) Hogan, age 56, $1,798,924 total compensation
Region Manager Central Europe, Peter Smits, age 61, $788,357 total compensation
Head of Marketing and Customer Solutions, Greg Scheu, age 52
Head of Global Markets, Frank Duggan, age 54
Head of Power Products Division, Bernhard Jucker, age 59, $754,215 total compensation
Head of Power Systems Division, Brice Koch, age 49
Head of Human Resources, Gary Steel, age 60, $619,854 total compensation
EVP and CFO, Eric Elzvik, age 53
Corporate Communications, Thomas Schmidt
Group SVP and Head Investor Relations, Michel Gerber, age 45
Region Manager North America, Enrique Santacana
CEO, Ulrich Spiesshofer, age 49, $775,921 total compensation
Head of Process Automation Division, Veli-Matti Reinikkala, age 56, $532,046 total compensation
General Counsel, Diane de Saint Victor, age 58, $647,952 total compensation
Executive Committee Member Power Systems Division, Peter Leupp, age 62, $770,005 total compensation
Chairman, Hubertus von Grunberg, age 71
Corporate Communications, Wolfram Eberhardt
Region Manager Northern Europe, Sten Jakobsson, age 64
Region Manager South America, Sergio Gomes
Region Manager North Asia, Claudio Facchin
Region Manager South Asia, BoonKiat Sim
CFO, Michel Demare
Head of Low Voltage Products Division, Tarak Mehta, age 47
Group SVP and Chief Counsel Corporate and Finance, Richard A. Brown
CTO, Prith Banerjee
Head of Discrete Automation and Motion Division, Pekka Tiitinen, age 47
Director, Michael Treschow, age 70
Director, Michel de Rosen, age 62
Director, Jacob Wallenberg, age 58
Director, Roger Agnelli, age 54
Director, Ying Yeh, age 65
Director, Hans Ulrich Marki, age 66
Director, Louis R. Hughes, age 64
Director, Bernd W. Voss, age 73
Non-Executive Member of the Board of Directors, Hans Maerki
Auditors: Ernst&YoungLtd.

LOCATIONS

HQ: ABB Ltd
P.O. Box 1831, Affolternstrasse 44, Zurich CH-8050
Phone: (41) 43 317 7111 **Fax:** (41) 43 317 7992
Web: www.abb.com

2012 Sales

	$ mil.	% of total
Europe	14,073	36
Americas	10,699	27
Total	**39,336**	**100**

PRODUCTS/OPERATIONS

2012 Sales

	$ mil.	% of total
Power Products	10,717	25
Process Automation	8,156	19
Low Voltage Products	6,638	16
Total	**39,336**	**100**

Selected Mergers and Acquisitions

FY2013
Power-One Inc. ($1 billion; Camarillo California; maker of solar inverters)
FY2012
Thomas & Betts Corporation ($3.9 billion; Memphis Tennessee; electrical connectors HVAC equipment and transmission towers)
Tropos Networks Inc. (Silicon Valley California; wireless technologies and products for distribution area communication networks)
FY2011

Trasfor Group (Switzerland; specialty dry-type transformers)
Baldor Electric ($3.1 billion; Fort Smith Arkansas; industrial motors)

Selected Products

Automation Products
- Breakers
- Control products
- DIN-rail components
- Drives
- Enclosures
- Generators
- Instrumentation
- Low-voltage switchgear
- Motors
- Power electronics systems
- Switches
- Wiring accessories

Electrical Products
- Boxes and covers (Bowers Commander Steel City)
- Cable ties (Catamount Ty-Fast Ty-Rap)
- Connectors (Blackburn Color-Keyed)
- Lighting (Carlon Red Dot Lumacell)
- Wire management systems (Carlon T&B)

HVAC
- Evaporative cooling and energy recovery equipment (International Energy Saver)
- Heaters (EK Campbell Reznor)
- Heating mechanical and refrigeration supplies (T&B)

Power Products
- Circuit breakers for all current and voltage levels
- High- and medium-voltage switchgear and apparatus
- Power and distribution transformers
- Sensors

Power Systems
- Power plant automation and electrification solutions
- Transmission and distribution systems

Process Automation
- Automation products and solutions
- Controls
- Industry-specific application knowledge and services
- Plant optimization

Robotics
- Industrial robots
- Industrial software products
- Robot contollers and software

Steel Structures
- Power connectors and accessories (Elastimold)
- Steel poles (Meyer)
- Transmission towers (Lehigh)

COMPETITORS

ALSTOM
AREVA
Baldor Electric
Bharat Heavy Electricals
Cisco Systems
Cooper Industries
Crompton Greaves
Danaher
Durr
Eaton
Emerson Electric
Endress + Hauser
Ericsson
FANUC
GE
Hitachi
Honeywell International
Hyosung
Hyundai Corporation
Invensys
KUKA
Kawasaki Heavy Industries
Larsen & Toubro
Legrand
Metso
Mitsubishi Heavy Industries
Nokia
Rittal Corp.
Rockwell Automation
SPX
Schneider Electric
Siemens AG
Toshiba
Voith
WEG Industrias
Yaskawa Electric
Yokogawa Electric

HISTORICAL FINANCIALS

Company Type: Public

Income Statement FYE: December 31

	REVENUE ($ mil.)	NET INCOME ($ mil.)	NET PROFIT MARGIN	EMPLOYEES
12/12	39,336	2,704	6.9%	146,100
12/11	37,990	3,168	8.3%	133,600
12/10	31,589	2,561	8.1%	116,500
12/09	31,795	2,901	9.1%	116,100
12/08	34,912	3,118	8.9%	119,600
Annual Growth	3.0%	(3.5%)	—	5.1%

2012 Year-End Financials

Debt ratio: 20.5%
Return on equity: 16.5%
Cash ($ mil.): 8,481
Current ratio: 1.48
Long-term debt ($ mil.): 7,534
No. of shares (mil.): —
Dividends
Yield: 3.3%
Payout: 53.7%
Market value ($ mil.): —

	STOCK PRICE ($) FY Close	P/E High	P/E Low	PER SHARE ($) Earnings	Dividends	Book Value
12/12	20.79	19	13	1.18	0.69	7.36
12/11	18.83	20	12	1.38	0.67	6.89
12/10	22.45	20	14	1.12	0.47	6.52
12/09	19.10	17	9	1.27	0.43	6.02
12/08	15.01	24	7	1.36	0.45	4.89
Annual Growth	8.5%	—	—	(3.5%)	11.2%	10.8%

Abbey National Treasury Services PLC (United Kingdom)

LOCATIONS

HQ: Abbey National Treasury Services PLC (United Kingdom)
2 Triton Square, Regent' s Place, London NW1 3AN
Phone: (44) 870 607 6000 **Fax:** (44) 20 7224 5306
Web: www.ants.co.uk

HISTORICAL FINANCIALS

Company Type: Public

Income Statement FYE: December 31

	ASSETS ($ mil.)	NET INCOME ($ mil.)	INCOME AS % OF ASSETS	EMPLOYEES
12/12	351,245	425	0.1%	717
12/11	340,444	531	0.2%	817
12/10	393,221	714	0.2%	679
12/09	458,091	612	0.1%	560
12/01	164,161	0	—	947
Annual Growth	7.2%	—	—	(2.5%)

2012 Year-End Financials

Return on assets: 0.1%
Return on equity: 7.0%
Long-term debt ($ mil.): —
No. of shares (mil.): —
Sales ($ mil): 6,919
Dividends
Yield: —
Payout: —
Market value ($ mil.): —

Accenture plc

For Accenture the accent is on helping businesses improve their performance. The world's largest consulting firm Accenture offers a well-balanced portfolio of management consulting technology and business process outsourcing (BPO) services to some of the top companies and government organizations in the world. Corporate clients span a broad spectrum of industries —from retail to communications —and include more than three-quarters of the FORTUNE 500. Clients use Accenture's services to enter new markets increase revenue in existing markets improve operational performance and deliver new products to market. Accenture is domiciled in Dublin but headquartered in New York.

Geographic Reach

Accenture serves clients in more than 200 cities spanning 120 countries. The majority of its revenue is balanced between the Americas and Europe Middle East and Africa (EMEA). The US is its largest individual market generating about one-third of total revenue. The remainder is made in the Asia/Pacific region.

Operations

Accenture's business is divided into five operating groups: Communications Media & Technology; Financial Services; Health & Public Service; Products; and Resources. Although revenue generated by these operating groups is well dispersed Products is the company's largest segment serving mainly consumer-oriented industries including automotive consumer goods life sciences retail transportation and travel services.

Accenture has a global network of innovation centers in the US Australia China Japan Singapore India France and South Africa.

Financial Performance

As the global economy has improved and the demand for its consulting and outsourcing services has increased Accenture recognized a 9% spike in revenue ($27.4 billion to $29.7 billion) and a 12 % rise in profits ($2.3 billion to $2.6 billion) from 2011 to 2012.

The recent growth was attributed to double digit growth across all its five operating groups. Accenture has also benefited from its growth strategy that is focused on further differentiating its products and services in the marketplace and improving its competitiveness. It has also been helped from a positive increase in the local currency.

Strategy

Accenture's strategy is focused on deepening and differentiating its industry and technology capabilities from competitors. It is doing so in part by investing in analytics cloud computing insight-driven health interactive and digital marketing mobility and smart grid. Acquisitions joint ventures and alliances are key means through which Accenture enhances and adds to its offerings. One such partnership is a five-year research collaboration with MIT announced in early 2013 to develop advanced analytics specifically how to harness the challenges of big data and develop new approaches to improve the science of decision-making. In late 2012 Accenture and GE Aviation formed a joint venture company called Taleris to provide global airlines and cargo carriers with intelligent operations services to improve efficiency.

From a geographic standpoint the company is focusing expansion efforts on certain emerging markets in particular such as Brazil China India Mexico Russia South Africa South Korea Turkey and certain countries in Southeast Asia and the Middle East.

Mergers and Acquisitions

To help its clients more effectively measure and monitor the progress of their change programs Accenture in 2013 acquired ChangeTrack Research an Australia-based provider of analytics-based tools and services for change management usage. The acquisition complemented Accenture's suite of tools and capabilities to help its clients achieve the goals of their most significant organizational transformations.

Adding to its footprint in Asia/Pacific Accenture acquired in 2012 Singapore-based Newspage Pte Ltd a provider of distributor management and mobility software that helps consumer goods companies improve their operations sales performance and data visibility.

Earlier in 2012 the company expanded its operations through the purchase of Octagon Research Solutions a provider of clinical and regulatory information management solutions and software for the pharmaceutical industry. The deal gives Accenture a means to provide clinical and regulatory services to pharmaceutical companies.

HISTORY

Accenture traces its history back to the storied accounting firm of Arthur Andersen & Co. Founded by Northwestern University professor and accounting legend Arthur Andersen in 1913 the firm's expanding scope of operations led it into forensic accounting and advising clients on financial reporting processes forming the basis for a management consulting arm. Arthur Andersen led the firm until his death in 1947. His successor Leonard Spacek split off the consulting operations as a separate unit in 1954.

The consulting business grew quickly during the 1970s and 1980s thanks in part to an orgy of US corporate re-engineering. By 1988 consulting accounted for 40% of Andersen's sales. Chafing at sharing profits with the auditors (who faced growing price pressures and a rising tide of legal action due to the accounting irregularities of their clients) the consultants sought more power within the firm. The result was a 1989 restructuring that established Andersen Worldwide (later Andersen) as the parent of two independent units Arthur Andersen and Andersen Consulting (AC). The growing revenue imbalance between the operations remained unresolved however and a year later Arthur Andersen poured gas on the flames by establishing its own business consultancy.

Meanwhile AC continued to expand during the 1990s by forming practices focused on manufacturing finance and government. It addressed the shift from mainframes to PCs by forming alliances with technology heavyweights Hewlett-Packard Sun Microsystems and Microsoft. In 1996 AC teamed up with Internet service provider BBN (acquired by GTE in 1997) to form ServiceNet a joint venture to develop Internet commerce and other systems.

The Andersen family feud took a turn for the worse in 1997 with the retirement of CEO Lawrence Weinbach. A deadlocked vote for a new leader led the board to appoint accounting partner Robert Grafton as CEO angering the consulting partners. Later that year AC asked the International Chamber of Commerce to negotiate a breakup of Andersen Worldwide. George Shaheen to whom many attributed the heightened tensions between the units resigned as CEO of AC in 1999 and was replaced by Joe Forehand.

While the separation dispute dragged on the consulting business grew and diversified amid increasing consolidation in the industry. In 1999 the company moved into e-commerce venture funding with the formation of Andersen Consulting Ventures and in 2000 it inked partnership deals with Microsoft (Microsoft system implementation services) Sun Microsystems (for B2B Internet office supply sales) and BT (Internet-based human resources services).

That year an international arbitrator finally approved AC's separation from its parent ruling that the consultancy must change its name and pay Andersen Worldwide $1 billion (far less than the $15 billion demanded by the accounting partners). Renamed Accenture the company went public in 2001. While the new name (a made-up word) might have struck some as a marketing challenge having an identity distinct from that of its former parent proved to be a stroke of luck for Accenture. Andersen broke apart in 2002 after becoming embroiled in the accounting scandals of energy giant Enron.

In 2004 Accenture successfully bid on a $10 billion 10-year contract to create a system to identify visitors and immigrants coming into the country. Dubbed US-VISIT (United States Visitor and Immigrant Status Indicator Technology) the system was to be employed by the Department of Homeland Security to prevent terrorists from entering the US. However Accenture's bid nearly ran afoul of congressional critics who tried to pass spending amendments barring firms headquartered outside the US from winning security-related business.

Forehand stepped down as CEO of Accenture in 2004 and was replaced by company veteran William Green. Forehand remained chairman until he retired in 2006 when Green was named to that post as well.

Accenture acquired Capgemini's North American health practice in 2005 for $175 million in order to strengthen its offerings to hospitals and health care systems. In 2006 the firm expanded its outsourcing operations by buying NaviSys a leading provider of software for the life insurance industry along with key assets of Kansas-based accountant Savista.

In mid-2008 Accenture swallowed up ATAN an industrial and automation services provider based in Brazil that caters to the mining energy and utilities sectors. It also obtained SOPIA a Tokyo-based consulting firm specializing in Oracle systems integration. During that year Accenture added to its transportation and travel services operations (located within its Products Division) when it bought AddVal Technology. AddVal provided software and technology used for freight order management and the deal enhanced Accenture's ability to integrate and simplify its clients' freight management services capabilities.

In late 2009 Accenture looked to solidify its position in a vital market when it obtained the Symbian professional services unit of Nokia. The unit offers engineering and support services for the Symbian operating system one of the world's most widely used operating systems for smart phones. The acquired operations provided a broad range of embedded software services for mobile devices and were rebranded Accenture Embedded Mobility Services.

Accenture obtained RiskControl a consulting firm based in Brazil in early 2010. Also that year Accenture bought Beijing Genesis Interactive Technology Company an embedded software firm providing mobile software outsourcing services to companies in China. The acquisitions furthered Accenture's penetration into the cutting-edge smart phone support services market.

Focusing on beefing up its Financial Services segment in 2011 Accenture acquired Duck Creek Technologies a provider of software and tools catering to the insurance and health care sectors. At the time of the transaction Duck Creek served about 60 clients throughout North America and the UK.

At the beginning of 2011 Pierre Nanterme the former head of the company's financial services operations was promoted to become the company's newest CEO. Green remains with Accenture as chairman.

EXECUTIVES

Senior Managing Director Strategic Initiatives; CEO Accenture Interactive, R. Timothy S. (Tim) Breene, age 63, $1,583,681 total compensation

Group Chief Executive - Financial Services, Richard A. Lumb, age 52

International Chairman, Karl-Heinz Floether, age 61, $1,237,338 total compensation

Chairman, William D. (Bill) Green, age 59, $1,237,500 total compensation

Group Chief Executive-Technology, Kevin M. Campbell, age 52, $1,122,529 total compensation

International Chairman Strategic Countries, Diego Visconti, $1,995,154 total compensation

Chief Financial Officer, Pamela J. (Pam) Craig, age 56, $1,175,265 total compensation

Director Public Relations, Fred J. Hawrysh

Principal Accounting Officer and Controller, Anthony G. (Tony) Coughlan, age 56

Chief Marketing and Communications Officer, Roxanne Taylor

Group Chief Executive - Health & Public Service, Stephen J. (Steve) Rohleder, age 56, $1,175,265 total compensation

Chief Geographic Strategy & Operations Officer, David C. Thomlinson

Managing Director North America, Jorge L. Benitez, age 53

Senior Director Investor Relations, David Straube

Group Chief Executive-Technology, Martin I. (Marty) Cole, age 57

Group Chief Executive-North America, Robert N. (Bob) Frerichs, age 61, $1,102,577 total compensation

Chief Human Resources Officer, Jill B. Smart

Chief Leadership Officer, Adrian J. Lajtha, age 56

CTO and Managing Director Technology, Donald J. (Don) Rippert

Executive Director Office of the CEO, Lori L. Lovelace

Chairman and Chief Executive Officer, Pierre Nanterme, age 54

Chief Financial Officer, David P. Rowland, age 52

Group Chief Executive Products, Gianfranco Casati, age 54

Managing Director US Federal Business, Lisa M. Mascolo, age 53

Group Chief Executive Management Consulting, Alexander (Sander) van 't Noordende, age 50

Managing Director Security Services, Alastair MacWillson

Managing Director Management Consulting North America, Walt Shill

Chief Accounting Officer; Corporate Controller, Richard P. Clark

Global Managing Director Retail Practice, Janet L. Hoffman

Country Managing Director Singapore; Managing Director Customer Relationship Management, Lay Lim Teo

Global Managing Director Electronics and High-Tech Group, Jean-Laurent Poitou

Managing Director Strategy Management Consulting Group, Mark Spelman

Chief Operating Officer, Johan G. (Jo) Deblaere, age 51

Group Chief Executive - Business Process Outsourcing, Michael J. (Mike) Salvino

Chief Strategy Officer, Shawn Collinson, age 52

Country Managing Director Brazil, Roger Ingold

Chairman Greater China, Gong Li

Chairman and Georgraphy Managing Director India, Harsh Manglik

Country Managing Director Spain, Vicente Moreno
General Counsel Secretary and Chief Compliance Officer, Julie S. Sweet, age 47
Chief Performance Officer, Jeffrey (Jeff) Osborne
Global Managing Director Research and Development and Alliances, Gavin Michael
Head Legal UK and Ireland, Patrick B. F. Rowe
Senior Manager Corporate Communications, Ben J. Geschwind
Group COO Management Consulting, Sylvie Ouziel
Executive Director Business Applications, Kenneth (Ken) Corless
Executive Director Global Infrastructure, Vidya S. (Vid) Byanna
CIO, Frank B. Modruson
Senior Director IT Business Operations, Robert E. (Bob) Kress
Group Chief Executive Resources, Jean-Marc Ollagnier, age 52
Managing Director United Kingdom, Oliver (Olly) Benzecry, age 51
Group Chief Executive-Management Consulting, Alexander M. (Sander) van't Noordende
Group Chief Executive - Management Consulting Growth Platform, Alexander Noordende
Lead Independent Director, Mark Stuart
Group Chief Executive - Communications Media & Technology, Robert E. (Bob) Sell
President ASM Research, Jim Traficant
Director, Charles H. Giancarlo, age 55
Director, Dina Dublon, age 60
Director, Nobuyuki Idei, age 76
Lead Director, Sir Mark Moody-Stuart, age 72
Director, Robert I. (Bob) Lipp, age 75
Director, Dennis F. Hightower, age 70
Director, Wulf von Schimmelmann, age 67
Director, Blythe J. McGarvie, age 57
Director, Marjorie (Marge) Magner, age 63
Director, William L. (Bill) Kimsey, age 71
Chairman & CEO, Pierre Nanterme, age 53
Independent Director, Gilles Pelisson
Auditors: KPMGLLP

LOCATIONS

HQ: Accenture plc
1 Grand Canal Square, Grand Canal Harbour, Dublin 2
Phone: (353) 1 646 2000
Web: www.accenture.com

2012 Sales

	$ mil.	% of total
Americas	45	
Asia/Pacific	15	

PRODUCTS/OPERATIONS

2012 Sales

	$ mil.	% of total
Products	23	
Financial services	22	
Health & public service	15	

2012 Sales

Consulting	56	
Total	**0**	**100**

Selected Mergers and Acquisitions

FY2013
ChangeTrack Research Pty Ltd (Sydney Australia; analytics-based tools and services)
FY2012
Octagon Research Solutions Inc. (clinical and regulatory information management services and software)
FY2011
Duck Creek Technologies (software and tools for insurance and health care)
CAS Computer Anwendungs- und Systemberatung (CRM and mobility software)
FY2010
Beijing Genesis Interactive Technology Co. (embedded software services)
Knowledge Rules (provider of business solutions utilizing BPM software)
Acceria (technology and consulting business services)
CadenceQuest (customer data and analytics)
Risk Control (risk management)

Selected Practice Areas

Communications and high technology
- Communications
- Electronics and high technology
- Media and entertainment

Products
- Automotive
- Consumer goods and services
- Health and life sciences
- Industrial equipment
- Retail
- Transportation and travel services

Financial services
- Banking
- Capital markets
- Insurance

Resources
- Chemicals
- Energy
- Natural resources
- Utilities

Government

Selected Services

Business consulting
- Customer relationship management
- Finance and performance management
- Human performance
- Strategy
- Supply chain management

Outsourcing
- Application outsourcing
- Business process outsourcing (BPO)
  - Customer contact
  - Finance and accounting
  - Human resources
  - Learning
  - Procurement
- Infrastructure outsourcing

Systems integration and technology
- Enterprise architecture
- Information management
- Infrastructure consulting
- Intellectual property
- Research and development

COMPETITORS

Bain & Company
Booz Allen
Boston Consulting
Capgemini
Capgemini North America
Charteris
Computer Sciences Corp.
Deloitte Consulting
HP Enterprise Services
IBM
McKinsey & Company
Unisys

HISTORICAL FINANCIALS

Company Type: Public

Income Statement

FYE: August 31

	REVENUE ($ mil.)	NET INCOME ($ mil.)	NET PROFIT MARGIN	EMPLOYEES
08/13	30,394	3,281	10.8%	275,000
08/12	29,777	2,553	8.6%	257,000
08/11	27,352	2,277	8.3%	236,000
08/10	23,094	1,780	7.7%	204,000
08/09	23,170	1,589	6.9%	177,000
Annual Growth	7.0%	19.9%	—	11.6%

2013 Year-End Financials

Debt ratio: 0.1%
Return on equity: 72.0%
Cash ($ mil.): 5,631
Current ratio: 1.45
Long-term debt ($ mil.): 25
No. of shares (mil.): 666
Dividends
Yield: 0.0%
Payout: 32.8%
Market value ($ mil.): 48,144

	STOCK PRICE ($) FY Close	P/E High/Low		PER SHARE ($) Earnings	Dividends	Book Value
08/13	72.25	16	12	4.93	1.62	7.44
08/12	61.60	17	13	3.84	1.35	6.13
08/11	53.59	18	10	3.40	0.90	5.62
08/10	36.60	16	12	2.66	1.13	4.11
Annual Growth	25.4%	—	—	16.7%	9.5%	16.0%

ACE, Ltd.

This ACE aims to provide a full house of insurance services. Through subsidiaries ACE Limited sells property/casualty insurance life insurance and reinsurance through subsidiaries around the globe. It primarily provides property/casualty insurance to commercial and personal customers. Policies offered include general liability homeowners auto accident workers' compensation and specialty crop and marine coverage. The company's ACE Tempest Re businesses provide reinsurance to property/casualty insurers in North America and Europe. ACE's life insurance and life reinsurance operations are focused in the US and other select markets. Products are primarily marketed through independent brokers.

Geographic Reach

The North American insurance segment which includes property/casualty subsidiaries ACE USA ACE Bermuda and ACE Canada is ACE's largest business segment accounting for about 40% of revenue. The company's ACE International and ACE Global Markets property/casualty insurance units reach into the rest of the world while its smaller ACE Life insurance division primarily operates in emerging markets in Asia Europe and the Americas.

With its operating subsidiaries located in more than 50 countries ACE serves customers in more than 170 nations.

ACE moved its place of incorporation home from the Caymans to Switzerland in 2008. It kept executive offices in Bermuda and New York.

Strategy

ACE regularly looks to expand its product offerings and geographical presence through acquisitions and organic measures. For instance the firm launched a new property/casualty division catering to high-net-worth individuals in 2008.

To expand in high-growth geographic markets it established new offices in Turkey and Panama in 2009 and 2008. Then in early 2012 the company opened a representative office in Kiev that will allow it to directly engage in the Ukraine insurance market.

Mergers and Acquisitions

In recent years ACE has focused its geographic expansion on smaller acquisitions in emerging global marketplaces. In 2011 ACE entered two new markets for life insurance in North Asia after acquiring New York Life's life insurance operations in Hong Kong and Korea for about $425 million.

In 2012 ACE acquired Indonesian general insurance firm Asuransi Jaya Proteksi for some $130 million. It closed its purchase of Mexican surety insurer Fianzas Monterrey from New York Life for $285 million in 2013 as well as its purchase of another Mexican insurance firm ABA Seguros from Ally Financial for $865 million.

ACE broadened its specialty holdings through the 2010 acquisition of the 80% of Rain and Hail Insurance Service which it did not already own for

$1.1 billion in cash. Through the deal ACE secured one of the largest crop insurers in North America. Continuing this trend in 2011 ACE acquired another agribusiness insurer Penn Miller Holding for $107 million.

Past purchases include the $2.6 billion acquisition of Combined Insurance Company of America in 2008 from insurance broker Aon Corporation. The purchase expanded the company's worldwide accident supplemental health and life underwriting business specifically for small businesses and middle-income individuals. A lull in acquisitions carried ACE through 2009 due to economic conditions.

EXECUTIVES

Division President ACE Westchester, Bruce L. Kessler
Chief Investment Officer ACE Group, Timothy A. Boroughs
Chairman and Chief Executive Officer, Evan G. Greenberg, age 58, $1,200,000 total compensation
Chief Financial Officer, Philip V. Bancroft, age 53, $670,000 total compensation
Chief Accounting Officer ACE Group, Paul B. Medini, age 55
Chairman Insurance - North America, John Lupica
Chief Risk Officer and Chief Actuary ACE Limited, Sean Ringsted
President ACE Life, Russell G. Bundschuh
Chief Communications Officer ACE Group, Patrick F. McGovern
Division President ACE Bermuda, Rees Fletcher
General Counsel, Robert F. (Bob) Cusumano, age 56, $515,000 total compensation
Division President ACE Tempest Re USA, James E. Wixtead
Vice Chairman and Chief Operating Officer ACE Limited Chairman ACE Overseas General, John W. Keogh, age 48, $675,000 total compensation
Division President Global Personal Lines and Small Commercial Insurance and COO Overseas General Insurance, Juan C. Andrade, age 44
Regional President ACE Latin America, Jorge Luis Cazar
Division President Accident, Edward Levin
Treasurer ACE Group, Ken Koreyva
Division President ACE Tempest Re Canada, Constantin (Tino) Petalas
President Combined Insurance, Brad Bennett
Chief Administration Officer, Samantha Froud
CEO ACE Private Risk Services, Robert Courtemanche
Regional President ACE Asia Pacific, Damien Sullivan
Chief Auditor ACE Group, Julie Schaekel
CIO ACE Group, Kevin Shearan
Managing Director ACE Tempest Re International, Steve Roberts
Regional President, David Robinson
COO Continental Europe, Jeff Moghrabi
Country President France, Nadia Cote
Chief Actuary, Stephen Wilson
President - Australia & New Zealand, Giles Ward
President ACE Argentina, Fernando Mendez
President ACE Chile, Juan Merchan
President ACE Puerto Rico, Judith Hernandez
Vice President General Manager, Carl Nagle
Director, Leo F. Mullin, age 70
Director, Robert M. Hernandez, age 68
Director, Michael G. (Mike) Atieh, age 60
Director, Robert Ripp, age 71
Director, Michael P. Connors, age 56
Director, Peter Menikoff, age 72
Director, Thomas J. (Tom) Neff, age 75
Director, John A. (Jack) Krol, age 75
Director, Bruce L. Crockett, age 68
Director, Eugene B. Shanks Jr.
Director, Olivier Steimer, age 57
Vice Chairman ACE Limited and ACE Group Holdings; CEO Insurance North America; Chairman and CEO USA; Chairman Westchester; Chairman and President ACE INA Holdings, Brian E. Dowd, age 49
Vice Chairman ACE Limited and ACE Group Holdings; Chairman Insurance Overseas General, John W. Keogh, age 47
Director, Mary A. Cirillo-Goldberg, age 64
Director, Theodore E. (Ted) Shasta, age 61
Auditors: PricewaterhouseCoopersLLP

LOCATIONS

HQ: ACE, Ltd.
Baerengasse 32, Zurich CH-8001
Phone: (41) 43 456 76 00
Web: www.acegroup.com

PRODUCTS/OPERATIONS

2010 Premiums

	% of total
Insurance - North	42
Insurance - overseas	39
Life	11
Global	8
Total	**100**

COMPETITORS

AEGON
AIG
AXA
Aetna
Allianz
Allstate
American Financial Group
Berkshire Hathaway
CNA Surety
Chubb Corp
Fairfax Financial Holdings
General Re
Hannover Re
Humana
ING
Liberty Mutual
Loews
MetLife
Munich Re America
Munich Re Group
Old Republic
Swiss Re
The Hartford
Travelers Companies
W. R. Berkley
White Mountains Insurance Group
XL Group plc

HISTORICAL FINANCIALS

Company Type: Public

Income Statement FYE: December 31

	ASSETS ($ mil.)	NET INCOME ($ mil.)	INCOME AS % OF ASSETS	EMPLOYEES
12/12	92,545	2,706	2.9%	17,000
12/11	87,505	1,585	1.8%	16,500
12/10	83,355	3,108	3.7%	16,000
12/09	77,980	2,549	3.3%	15,000
12/08	72,057	1,197	1.7%	15,000
Annual Growth	6.5%	22.6%	—	3.2%

2012 Year-End Financials

Return on assets: 3.0%
Return on equity: 10.3%
Long-term debt ($ mil.): —
No. of shares (mil.): 340
Sales ($ mil): 17,936
Dividends
Yield: 3.0%
Payout: 30.6%
Market value ($ mil.): 27,158

	STOCK PRICE ($) FY Close	P/E High/Low		PER SHARE ($) Earnings	Dividends	Book Value
12/12	79.80	10	9	7.89	2.41	80.90
12/11	70.12	16	13	4.65	1.38	72.76
12/10	62.25	7	5	9.11	1.30	68.59
12/09	50.40	7	4	7.55	1.46	58.44
12/08	52.92	18	11	3.53	0.26	43.30
Annual Growth	10.8%	—	—	22.3%	74.5%	16.9%

ACS Actividades de Construccion y Servicios, S.A.

Turning the rains (and the wind) on the plains of Spain into electricity provides the current for growth at ACS Actividades de Construccion y Servicios one of Spain's largest construction and infrastructure groups. ACS Group operates in five primary business areas: construction concessions environment industrial services and energy. The company's activities include civil engineering installation and maintenance for energy facilities transport services and highway management. ACS has grown by investing in such firms as former construction rival Dragados and Germany-based infrastructure giant HOCHTIEF. The group is active in more than 50 countries mainly in Europe and Latin America.

The group's largest and fastest-growing arm is its industrial services and energy segment which provides applied engineering construction and maintenance for the energy and communications sectors. ACS has invested in the segment's growth including making investments in renewable energies. The group develops such projects as wind farms and solar energy plants as well as traditional power stations and toll systems.

Another key arm for ACS is its construction segment which is engaged in civil commercial and residential building. Typical construction projects include roads railways parking garages sports facilities and hospitals. ACS focuses on public-private partnership arrangements for jobs such as public protection housing developments. The segment expanded with its 2009 acquisition of US builder Pulice Construction for $114 million. The deal added a Phoenix-based civil work specialist and a prime contractor for the Arizona Department of Transportation.

Through units including Urbaser and Dragados ACS' environmental segment provides facility management waste management and port and logistics chain services. It offers services for facilities including health care centers hotels office buildings schools and courthouses. In 2011 ACS sold its stake in interior cleaning services unit Clece to private equity firms for E608 million (some $865 million); the capital should help ACS develop its core businesses.

ACS's concessions unit develops designs builds and maintains infrastructure projects primarily in Europe and North America. Holdings include a minority stake in Abertis one of the largest infrastructure companies in Europe and a stake in energy company IBERDROLA. Through Dragados ACS took an approximately two-thirds stake in Polish building firm Pol-Aqua in 2009.

Also that year ACS sold its controlling stake in electric utility Union Fenosa to pay down debts incurred through its investments in HOCHTIEF and IBERDROLA (which it had originally planned to merge with Union Fenosa). In 2010 the company made a successful hostile takeover bid to increase its stake in HOCHTIEF from about 30% to more than 50% –it ultimately wants to buy the firm outright —to better take advantage of the German company's geographic reach and to cut costs. ACS is focusing its energy business on IBERDROLA.

The global recession hurt construction firms as projects dried up or customers struggled to keep up with payments. ACS was no exception and it began looking for other noncore assets to sell. In one such deal it sold port operator Dragados Servicios Portuarios y Logisticos to a group of investors for some E720 million (approximately $952 million) in 2010.

HISTORY

In war-torn Europe in 1942 the Spanish construction company Obras y Construcciones Industriales (Ocisa) was born. The company soon began a 50-year association with Spain's hydroelectric industry marked by the completion of the dam and reservoir project Presa de Bachimana in 1950. The company built nine more dam and reservoir projects in Spain (including Presa de la Llosa completed in 1997).

As the demand for public works projects decreased and competition increased Spanish constructors began working abroad especially in Latin America where Ocisa was contracted in 1975 to create an irrigation tunnel in Venezuela's Andes.

A six-year economic expansion measured by the success of Spain's "Big Seven" construction companies including #5 Ocisa reached its end in 1992 when the Spanish government the country's biggest builder was forced to cut spending on infrastructure. This triggered consolidation in Spain's construction industry including Ocisa's 1993 acquisition of Construcciones Padros in which Ocisa held a 25% stake. Adopting the new name OCP Construcciones it also absorbed the assets of its installation and assembly subsidiary Compania de la Distribucion de Electricidad (Grupo Cobra).

The slowdown in public works projects continued and companies sought additional pooling of resources and diversification of activities at home and abroad. In 1996 OCP bought a 40% stake in the state-owned construction firm Auxini increased to 100% a year later. Also in 1997 the OCP group led by its president Florentino Perez acquired Gines Navarro Construcciones controlled (79%) by the powerful investment group led by brothers Carlos and Juan March. The two companies combined to create Spain's third-largest construction group Actividades de Construcciones y Servicios or Grupo ACS.

Perez became chairman of the new group and promised to make it Spain's most profitable public construction company through further diversification international contracts and selective investment in real estate. Grupo March which now controlled about 37% of ACS joined with OCP shareholders including former VP Juan Torres and the Roa family to offer a portion of their shares on the market yet retained 50% of the new company among themselves. A public offering of shares in ACS was completed that year following a 4-for-1 share split.

ACS began restructuring placing its construction activities including Auxini under its subsidiary Puertos y Obras. In 1998 ACS was first listed on the IBEX-35 index of top Spanish companies.

With the construction industry continuing to consolidate Grupo ACS benefited from a boom in construction work in Spain led by liberalization of the energy markets and continued international growth especially in Latin America.

ACS further diversified into transportation in 1999 with the purchase of Continental Auto a Spanish passenger coach company and an increased stake in its subsidiary Transportes Alsina. It also placed a bid for Enatcar Spain's state-owned transportation company. The next year the group joined Finnish telecommunications firm Sonera and France's Vivendi to form a consortium to operate under one of Spain's third-generation wireless phone licenses. ACS and Sonera agreed in 2001 to form a new venture to explore additional markets in Europe and the US for 3G wireless operations.

In 2002 ACS took a major step toward expanding further by acquiring the 24% controlling stake in rival Dragados from Banco Santander Central Hispano. The next year Dragados accepted a bid by ACS for another 10% of its shares and the two companies merged operations. By combining the operations of Dragados with its own ACS built itself into one of Spain's largest construction companies.

The company acquired a 50% stake in Brazilian port authority Terminal de Santa Catarina for E25.5 million in 2006. ACS has invested further in international port terminals particularly in Brazil and India.

EXECUTIVES

Vice Chairman, Pablo Vallbona Vadell
Chairman and CEO ACS Actividades de Construccion y Servicios, Florentino Perez Rodriguez, age 64
General Manager Iridium, Francisco Fernandez Lafuente
Chairman and CEO Services Communications and Energy; Chairman and CEO of Cobra and Chairman of Etra and Imesapi, Eugenio Llorente Gomez
Finance Manager, Jose Zornoza Soto
Executive Vice Chairman, Antonio Garcia Ferrer, age 66
Subsidiary Companies Manager Dragados, Octavio del Real Sanchez
Secretary, Jose Luis del Valle Perez
Corporate General Manager ACS Actividades de Construccion y Servicios, Angel Manuel Garcia Altozano
General Manager, Jose Luis Lopez Molinillo
Director Investments and Management Control, Christina Aldamiz-Echevarria Gonzalez de Durana
CEO Vias y Contrucciones SA, Gonzalo Gomez-Zamalloa Baraibar
Chairman and CEO Construction Environment & Logistics and Concesisons; Chairman and CEO Dragados, Marcelino Fernandez Verdes
Secretary General of Construction Environment & Logistics and Concesisons, Luis Nogueira Miguelsanz
Executive Assistant Environment and Logistics, Antonio Alfonzo Sanchez
General Manager Dragados, Ignacio Segura Surinach
Civil Works Manager Dragados, Ricardo Martin de Bustamante
Building Manager Dragados, Juan Perez Luis Garcia-Gelabert Perez
Contracting Manager Dragados, Maximiliano Navascues Redondo
Technical Services Manager Dragados, Alfonso Costa Cuadrench
Chairman Vias y Construcciones, Manuel Perez Beato
Civil Works Manager Vias y Construcciones, Manuel Alvarez Mu?oz
Building Manager Vias y Construcciones, Ignacio Legorburu Escobar
General Manager Tecsa, Jose Maria Aguirre Fernandez
CEO Seis, Botteghelz Canga Botteghelz
General Manager Seis, Pablo Quiros Gracian
General Manager Drace Medio Ambiente, Fernando Garcia Arribas
General Manager FPS, Juan Mata Arbide
CEO Geocisa, Alejandro Canga Botteghelz
Chairman and CEO Urbaser, Javier Polanco Gomez-Lavin
General Manager Urbaser, Jose Maria Lopez-Pi?ol
Chairman and CEO Clece, Cristobal Valderas Alvarado
Chairman and CEO Iridium, Manuel Garcia Buey
General Manager Iridium, Victor Revuelta Garcia
General Manager Services Communications and Energy, Jose Alfonso Nebrera Garcia
Secretary General ACS Services Communications and Energy, Jose Romero de Avila Gonzalez-Albo
CEO Semi and Maessa, Daniel Vega Baladron
General Manager Cymi and Masa, Vicente Prados Tejada
General Manager Large Contract Dragados Industrial, Pablo Garcia Arenal
CEO Initec Intecsa and Makiber, Raul Llamazares de la Puente
General Manager Dragados Offshore Dragados Industrial, Pedro Ascorbe Trian
Chairman Sice Technology and Systems Dragados Industrial, Juan Enrique Ruiz Gonzalez
Vice Chairman, Pablo Vallbona Vadell
Chairman and CEO ACS Actividades de Construccion y Servicios, Florentino Perez Rodriguez, age 64
Executive Vice Chairman, Antonio Garcia Ferrer, age 66
Director, Juan March de la Lastra
Director, Jose Maria Aguirre Gonzalez
Director, Agustin Bateucas Torrego
Director, Jose Alvaro Cuervo Garcia
Director, Manuel Delgado Solis
Director, Javier Echenique Landiribar
Director, Sabina Flaxa Thienemann
Director, Jaon-David Grima i Terre
Director, Jose Maria Loizaga Viguri
Director, Pedro Lopez Jimenez
Director, Santos Marinze-Conde Gutierrez-Barquin
Director, Javier Nonzon de Caceres
Director, Miquel Roca i Junyent
Director, Julio Sacristan Fidalgo
Director, Francisco Servando Verdu Pons
Auditors: DeloitteSL

LOCATIONS

HQ: ACS Actividades de Construccion y Servicios, S.A.
Avda. Pio XII, 102, Madrid 28036
Phone: (34) 91 343 9200 **Fax:** (34) 91 343 9456
Web: www.grupoacs.com

PRODUCTS/OPERATIONS

2009 Sales

	% of total
Industrial	43
Construction	39
Environment	17
Concessions	1
Total	**100**

Selected Subsidiaries

Concessions
- Concesiones Viarias Chile S.A. (infrastructures)
- Iridium Concesiones de Infraestructuras S.A.

Construction
- Acainsa S.A. (real estate development)
- Ave Lalin
- Consorcio Tecdra S.A.
- Constructora Norte Sur S.A. (48% Chile)
- Desaladora Barcelona (28%)
- Guadarrama Iv (33%)
- Inmobiliaria Alabega S.A. (real estate development)
- Isla Verde Ute (35%)
- Soterram. Basurto Ute Tecsa-Necso (50%)
- Terminal Aeropuerto (70%)

Environment
- Consenur S.A. (management and treatment of hospital waste)
- Empordanesa de Neteja S.A. (urban solid waste management and street cleaning)
- Mapide S.A. (interior cleaning)
- Publimedia Sistemas Publicitarios S.L. (advertising services)
- RetraOil S.L. (treatment of oils and marpoles)
- Servicios Generales de Jaen S.A. (75% water)
- Somasur S.A. (intermediary company Morocco)
- Urbaser de Mejico S.A. (collection of urban solid waste and street cleaning)

Urbaser Valencia C.A. (collection of urban solid waste and street cleaning)
Ute Ecoparc V (20% USW treatment)
Vertederos de Residuos S.A. (84% VERTRESA collection of urban solid waste and street cleaning)
Industrial Services
ACS industrial Services LLC (energy production US)
Actividades de Servicios e Instalaciones Cobra S.A. (auxiliary energy and communications distribution Guatemala)
Andasol 1 S.A. (energy production)
API Movilidad S.A. (road maintenance)
BTOB Construccion Ventures S.L. (administrative management)
Central Termica de Mejillones S.A. (engineering supply and construction Chile)
Cobra Ingenieria de Montajes S.A. (installations and assembly)
Cobra Peru S.A. (auxiliary energy and communications distribution)
Coinsal Instalaciones y Servicios S.A. de C.V. (installations and assembly El Salvador)
Cymi Holding S.A. (securities holding company Brazil)
Dragados Gulf Construction Ltd. (Saudi Arabia)
Emurtel S.A. (50% electrical installations)
Enq S.L. (electrical installations)
Etra Catalu?a S.A. (electrical installations)
Extresol-1 S.L. (energy production)
Gerovitae La Guancha S.A. (senior social and health center operations)
Humiclima Est S.A. (air conditioning)
Incro S.A. (50% engineering)
Infraest. Energeticas Medioambi. Extreme?as S.L. (services)
Instalaciones y Servicios Codeven C.A. (air conditioning)
Mantenimiento y Montajes Industriales S.A. (industrial maintenance and assemblies)
Mexsemi S.A. de C.V. (99.7% assemblies Mexico)
Opade Organizac. y Promoc de Actividades Deportivas S.A. (athletic activities organization and promotion)
Parque Eolico Marmellar S.L. (70% energy production)
Portumasa S.A. (manufacture and sale of electical equipment Portugal)
Semi Maroc S.A. (99.7% assemblies)
Serveis Catalans Serveica S.A. (electrical installations)
SICE LLC. (design construction installation and maintenance of traffic and trade)
Sistemas Radiantes F. Moyano S.A. (telecommunications)
Tecnotel de Canarias S.A. (air conditioning)
Ute C.T. Andasol 1 (80% fossil fuel plant)
Venezolana de Limpiezas Indust. C.A. (83% VENELIN Venezuela)
Services
Valdemingomez 2000 S.A. (34% Valdemingomez degasification)

COMPETITORS

Abengoa
Acciona
Aker Solutions
Andrade Gutierrez
Balfour Beatty
Bechtel
Bilfinger Berger
Black & Veatch
Brisa
Cintra
DP World
FCC Barcelona
Ferrovial
Grupo San Jose
Hyundai Engineering and Construction
Impregilo
Kellogg Brown & Root UK
OHL
Odebrecht
Skanska
TECNOCOM
VINCI

HISTORICAL FINANCIALS

Company Type: Public

Income Statement FYE: December 31

	REVENUE ($ mil.)	NET INCOME ($ mil.)	NET PROFIT MARGIN	EMPLOYEES
12/12	51,173	(2,539)	—	164,342
12/11	37,520	1,244	3.3%	164,923
12/10	21,110	1,756	8.3%	138,542
12/09	23,248	2,811	12.1%	142,085
12/08	23,519	2,523	10.7%	138,936
Annual Growth	21.5%	—	—	4.3%

2012 Year-End Financials

Debt ratio: 34.2%
Return on equity: (-64.3%)
Cash ($ mil.): 5,967
Current ratio: 1.06
Long-term debt ($ mil.): 9,027
No. of shares (mil.): 314
Dividends
Yield: —
Payout: —
Market value ($ mil.): —

Adecco S.A. (Switzerland)

Any way you stack it Adecco is the world's largest employment agency serving some 100000 clients from more than 5500 offices worldwide. The company primarily provides temporary staffing services (more than 90% of sales) but also offers permanent employee placement project assistance outsourcing and other human resources-related services. Besides its core industrial and office staffing services Adecco maintains six professional lines: Engineering & Technical; Finance & Legal; Human Capital Solutions; Information Technology; Medical & Scientific; and Sales Marketing & Events. Adecco traces its roots to 1957 and has a history of growing through mergers and acquisitions.

Adecco's list of secondary and specialty brands includes DIS Deutscher Industrie Service DNC De Nederlanden Lee Hecht Harrison Career Services Altedia and Office Angels.

In early 2011 the company improved its position in an important emerging market when it established FESCO Adecco a human resource services joint venture catering to China. Months later Adecco obtained Drake Beam Morin (DBM) a human resources consulting firm specializing in employee selection development retention and transition. Adecco bought DBM for $216 million and merged it with Lee Hecht Harrison.

Adecco made big waves throughout the staffing industry when it acquired rival MPS Group for $1.3 billion in January 2010. The purchase of MPS Group an IT staffing leader with a network of more than 220 offices globally added girth to Adecco's operations worldwide. MPS Group particularly strengthened Adecco's engineering legal staffing IT and finance/accounting offerings. Adecco rolled MPS Group in with its Adecco Group North America division. MPS Group subsidiaries (which include Modis Idea Integration and Accounting Principals) now function as subsidiaries of Adecco.

HISTORY

Swiss accountant Henri-Ferdinand Lavanchy founded Adia in 1957 when a client asked him to find someone to fill a job. The company expanded internationally in the 1960s with offices in Belgium and elsewhere in Europe and entered the US in 1972. When Adia went public in Switzerland in 1979 Lavanchy retired from active management. Martin Pestalozzi succeeded him. The US operation Adia Services went public in 1984.

Pestalozzi's management group was ousted when retailer Asko Deutsche Kaufhaus and Swiss investor Klaus Jacobs bought about 50% of Adia in 1991 after a scandal involving the sale of part of the company to Swiss financier (later fugitive) Werner Ray. Jacobs bought out Asko in 1993 as well as Adia's US investors bringing US operations under company ownership again.

Adia and Ecco SA one of the top French employment services companies merged in 1996 to form Adecco. (Adia chairman Jacobs and Ecco chairman Philippe Foriel-Destezet began a revolving chairmanship and former Adia executive John Bowmer became CEO.) After the merger Adecco bought ICON Recruitment (IT recruiting Australia; 1996) Seagate Associates (outplacement consulting New Jersey; 1997) and Massachusetts-based TAD Resources International the largest private staffing services company in the US in 1997. The company bought rival Olsten's staffing and IT business in 2000 to further solidify Adecco as the world's largest temporary staffing firm.

Adecco restructured around four divisions (Adecco Staffing Ajilon Staffing and Managed Services Career Services and e-Recruiting and Executive Search) in 2001. In 2002 Klaus retired from the company; Bowmer became chairman and 10-year company veteran Jerome Caille took over as CEO. Adecco sold jobpilot an online job board to Monster Worldwide in 2004. In 2005 the company acquired French human resources firm Altedia. Caille left the company in 2005 and Jacobs came back on board as chairman and interim CEO. In 2006 Dieter Scheiff was named as the new CEO.

Adecco augmented its German operations in mid-2007 when it acquired German staffing company Tuja Holding GmbH for about $1 billion. Tuja's estimated revenue for 2007 was around $870 million.

After years of acquisitions (and a failed attempt to buy rival Michael Page International in 2008) the company appointed Patrick De Maeseneire as the new CEO effective June 2009. A former Adecco executive De Maeseneire had served as the CEO of chocolate maker Barry Callebaut since 2002. Adecco made a megadeal in January 2010 with the acquisition of rival MPS Group for $1.3 billion.

EXECUTIVES

Regional Head North America, Robert P. Crouch, age 44
CEO, Baron Patrick G. De Maeseneire, age 55, $1,011,570 total compensation
CFO and Head of Global Solutions, Dominik de Daniel, age 39, $951,030 total compensation
Chairman, Rolf Dorig, age 55
Global Head Human Capital Solutions; President and COO Lee Hecht Harrison, Peter Alcide
Regional Head Japan and Asia, Mark Du Ree, $163,402 total compensation
Chief Sales Officer, Sergio Picarelli, age 47, $187,500 total compensation
Vice Chairman, Andreas Jacobs, age 50
Regional Head France Switzerland and India, Alain Dehaze, age 51, $166,784 total compensation
Chief Human Resources Officer, Christian Vasino, age 42, $579,159 total compensation
Regional Head France Switzerland and India, Francois Davy, age 56, $830,048 total compensation
Regional Head North America, Theron I. (Tig) Gilliam Jr., age 48, $708,734 total compensation
Head of Investor Relations, Karin Selfors-Thomann, age 38
Director Group Communications, Lilian Furrer
Country Manager Australia/New Zealand, Jeff Doyle
Country Manager Benelux, Erwin Iersel
Regional Head Germany and Austria, Andreas Dinges, age 55, $175,123 total compensation
Regional Head Italy and Eastern Europe, Federico Vione, age 42, $125,088 total compensation
Country Manager Nordics, Per-Arne Gulbrandsen
Manager China and North East Asia, Cynthia Chew
Group Internal Audit, Pierlaurent Barbieri
Regional Head UK and Ireland, Peter Searle, $118,344 total compensation

Regional Head Iberia and South America, Enrique Sanchez, age 47, $161,296 total compensation
Head Group Communications, Stephan Howeg
Group Communications Manager, Jacqueline Maag-Spieler
CIO, Frank Meyer
Country Manager Switzerland and Austria, Michael Agoras
Manager India and Middle East, Sudhakar Balakrishnan
General Counsel and Corporate Secretary, Urs Waelchli
Manager Eastern Europe, Christos Misailidis
Manager South East Asia, Lynne Ng
Regional Head Northern Europe, Martin Alonso, age 53
Chief Operating Officer, Michael Schwartz
Chairman of the Board, Ofer Kotler
Controller, Orit Hillel
Chief Executive Officer, Shlomo Zohar
Chief Financial Officer, Yaron Zaltsman
Chief Scientific Officer, Nobuyoshi Maeji
Director, David N. Prince, age 63
Director, Wanda Rapaczynski, age 67
Director, Jakob Baer, age 68
Director, Thomas O'Neill, age 69
Vice Chairman, Andreas Jacobs, age 50
Director, Didier Lamouche
Director, Alexander Gut
External Director, Eyal Gibor
Auditors: Ernst&YoungLtd.

LOCATIONS

HQ: Adecco S.A. (Switzerland)
Saegereistrasse 10, P.O. Box, Glattbrugg 8152
Phone: (41) 44 878 88 88 **Fax:** (41) 44 829 88 88
Web: www.adecco.com

COMPETITORS

Insperity
Kelly Services
ManpowerGroup
Randstad Holding
Robert Half
Synergie
Technical Aid Corporation
Volt Information

HISTORICAL FINANCIALS

Company Type: Public

Income Statement FYE: December 31

	REVENUE ($ mil.)	NET INCOME ($ mil.)	NET PROFIT MARGIN	EMPLOYEES
12/12	27,067	496	1.8%	32,987
12/11	26,573	671	2.5%	32,826
12/10	24,968	566	2.3%	31,279
12/09	21,316	11	0.1%	28,508
12/08	27,912	692	2.5%	37,055
Annual Growth	(0.8%)	(7.9%)	—	(2.9%)

2012 Year-End Financials

Debt ratio: 28.4%
Return on equity: 10.0%
Cash ($ mil.): 1,453
Current ratio: 1.27
Long-term debt ($ mil.): 2,024
No. of shares (mil.): 184
Dividends
Yield: 3.6%
Payout: 62.6%
Market value ($ mil.): 4,883

	STOCK PRICE ($) FY Close	P/E High/Low	PER SHARE ($) Earnings	Dividends	Book Value
12/12	26.45	24 15	2.64	0.95	26.39
12/11	20.86	25 12	3.52	1.18	28.90
12/10	32.62	27 16	2.90	0.19	27.31
12/09	27.65	1519593	0.06	0.43	25.75
12/08	16.75	12 12	3.79	0.00	22.42
Annual Growth	12.1%	— —	(8.7%)	—	4.2%

Adidas AG

From famous athletes to school kids adidas wants to help everyone get in the game. The company sells sports shoes apparel and equipment sporting its iconic three-stripe logo in 170 countries. The #2 sporting goods manufacturer (behind NIKE) focuses on football soccer basketball running and training gear and apparel as well as lifestyle goods including SLVR and Y-3 fashion brands. adidas' wholesale division gets adidas and Reebok products to retailers while the retail group runs its own 2445 Reebok and adidas shops. Other businesses include TaylorMade-adidas Golf Rockport and Reebok-CCM Hockey. Founder Adi Dassler brother of PUMA creator Rudi began making shoes in the early 1920s.

Geographic Reach

Germany's adidas rings up half of its sales in Europe. Greater China and North America contribute 16% and 13% of sales respectively. It also sells and distributes its shoes and apparel in Latin America and other markets in Asia. Key growth markets for the company include North America China Russia Latin America Japan and the UK.

Operations

Adidas brand shoes are the company's cash cow accounting for three-quarters of total sales. The Reebok brand and TaylorMade-adidas Golf each represent about 10%. While the company operates its own retail stores and sells shoes online wholesaling is the bigger business representing nearly two-thirds of total sales. The company supplies adidas and Reebok brand shoes to retailers.

Financial Performance

Adidas delivered strong sales growth in 2012 despite macroeconomic challenges in many regions but especially in Europe its largest market. Sales increased 14% in 2012 versus 2011 to nearly $19.7 billion. However net income was down 20% over the same period. With the exception of the Reebok brand whose sales fell 14% in 2012 versus 2011 adidas's other brands all posted healthy sales gains. Indeed the core adidas brand posted a 15% uptick in annual sales while TaylorMade-adidas Golf's sales rose 29%.

The company's Retail business segment posted a 21% gain in annual sales while the wholesale unit posted a 7% gain. The hottest growth markets for the German firm were Greater China and European Emerging Markets each with sales up 15%. Latin America and other Asian markets reported 8% and 7% gains respectively. Overall sales in North America rose a modest 2%. 2012 marked the third consecutive year of rising sales for the company following a decline during the global financial crisis.

Strategy

In 2010 adidas unveiled its strategic business plan –called "Route 2015" –outlining its strategies and objectives for the next five years. The plan set ambitious total group sales growth targets of 45% to 50% (on a currency-neutral basis). Aiming to grow its bottom line faster than its top line adidas hopes to grow annual earnings at a compound annual growth rate of 15% and reach an operating margin of 11% sustainably by 2015. (In 2012 its operating margin was 8%.) Three markets singled out for their growth potential are North America Greater China and Russia which are expected to contribute about 50% of the total group growth under the Route 2015 plan. In the US the company believes its brands have enormous opportunity to gain market share by focusing on improved distribution and launching more innovative products.

To fulfill its goal of growth in China adidas says it will add 2500 stores there by 2015 putting up-scale outlets in the large cities and teen-targeted casual NEO shops in smaller markets. Other moves include expanding e-commerce through a venture with China's biggest online retailer Taobao.com; sponsoring running competitions; and partnering with workout center chains.

Going forward one of the company's strategies for success is to continue offering products with both mass and niche appeal allowing each of its brands to maintain a unique identity. Part of the innovation is a fashion and sport line of apparel from a deal with Giorgio Armani to go with adidas' SLVR and Y-3 lines. Another example is the mi line that combines technology and gear in customizable shoes digital coaches online support heart rate sensing apparel and mobile hardwear to connect it all.

Mergers and Acquisitions

In November 2011 the company acquired Five Ten a leading brand in the technical outdoor markets and outdoor action sports community for $25 million. As part of its Route 2015 strategy adidas expects sales in the outdoor segment to exceed ?500 million ($662.7 million) by 2015.

HISTORY

adidas grew out of an infamous rift between German brothers Adi and Rudi Dassler who created athletic shoe giants adidas and Puma. As WWI was winding down Adi scavenged for tires rucksacks and other refuse to create slippers gymnastics shoes and soccer cleats at home. His sister cut patterns out of canvas. By 1926 the shoes' success allowed the Dasslers to build a factory. At the 1928 Amsterdam Olympics German athletes first showcased Dassler shoes to the world. In 1936 American Jesse Owens sprinted to Olympic gold in Dassler's double-striped shoes.

Business boomed until the Nazis commandeered the Dassler factory to make boots for soldiers. Although both Rudi and Adi were reportedly members of the Nazi party only Rudi was called to service. Adi remained at home to run the factory. When Allied troops occupied the area Adi made friends with American soldiers –even creating shoes for a soldier who wore them at the 1946 Olympics. Rudi came home from an American prison camp and joined his brother; together they scavenged the war-torn landscape for tank materials and tents to make shoes.

Soon a dispute between the brothers split the business. Rumors circulated that Rudi resented that Adi had failed to use his American connections to help spring him from prison camp. Rudi set up his own factory facing Adi across the River Aurach. The brothers never spoke to each other again except in court. Rudi's company was named Puma and Adi's became adidas. Adi added a third stripe to the Dassler's trademark shoe while Rudi chose a cat's paw in motion. Thus began one of the most intense rivalries in Europe. The children of Puma and adidas employees attended separate elementary schools and the employees even distinguished themselves by drinking different beers.

With Adi's innovations throughout the late 1940s and 1950s (such as the replaceable-cleat soccer shoe) adidas came to dominate the world's athletic shoe market. In the late 1950s it capitalized on the booming US market overtaking the canvas sneakers made by P.F. Flyers and Stride Rite (Keds). The company also initiated the practice of putting logos on sports bags and clothing.

adidas continued to expand globally in the 1960s and 1970s to maintain its dominant position. However a flood of new competitors following the 1972 Munich Olympics and the death of Adi in 1978 signaled the end of an era. As NIKE and Reebok captured the North American market during the 1980s adidas made one of its biggest missteps —it turned down a sneaker endorsement offer from a young Michael Jordan in 1984.

French politician and entrepreneur Bernard Tapie bought the struggling company in 1989 but he stepped down in 1992 amid personal political and business scandals. The next year Robert Louis-Dreyfus became CEO. He shifted production to Asia pumped up the advertising budget and brought in former NIKE marketing geniuses to re-establish the company's identity.

adidas became adidas-Salomon in 1997 with its $1.4 billion purchase of Salomon a French maker of skis and other sporting goods. The company also opened its first high-profile store in Portland Oregon that year. In a 1998 reorganization Louis-Dreyfus sacked Jean-Francois Gautier as Salomon's president in the wake of disappointing sales particularly from TaylorMade Golf Salomon's golf subsidiary.

Amid a 10% slide in revenue several key executives decided to leave the company in 2000 including adidas America CEO Steve Wynne. Citing poor health Louis-Dreyfus soon followed (but remained as chairman); he was replaced by the new CEO of adidas America Ross McMullin who soon after was diagnosed with cancer. Later that year the company announced it would consolidate its apparel under the Heritage label to reinforce its position in the burgeoning casual wear market.

In 2001 Louis-Dreyfus retired as chairman and in March COO Herbert Hainer became chief executive. That year adidas-Salomon opened adidas Originals retail stores in Tokyo and Berlin; that was followed with a New York City store in 2002. Despite slumping sales in the US amid deep discounting by competitors adidas announced in 2003 that it would not offer discounts and still intended to capture 20% of the country's shoe market.

Britain's Barclays Bank PLC became adidas' largest shareholder in 2004 raising its stake to 5.4%. The company changed its name in 2006 to adidas AG.

In May 2008 adidas AG won a $305 million award from a federal jury in Oregon for trademark violation of its three-stripe design by Collective Brands the operator of the Payless and Stride Rite shoe-store chains.

In November 2011 adidas acquired outdoor specialist Five Ten adding to its outdoor portfolio.

EXECUTIVES

Chairman, Igor Landau, age 69
Member Executive Board Global Brands, Erich Stamminger, age 57
CEO, Herbert Hainer, age 60
Member Executive Board Finance, Robin Stalker, age 56
Member Executive Board Global Operations, Glenn Bennett, age 51
Deputy Chairwoman; Chairwoman Central Works Council, Sabine Bauer, age 50
Chief Marketing Officer adidas Sport Style, Hermann Deininger
Sales Director Customer Service Market Central and Director, Hans Ruprecht, age 59
Chief Corporate Communication Officer, Jan Runau, age 48
Corporate Public Relations Manager, Kirsten Keck, age 40
Senior Corporate Public Relations Manager, Katja Schreiber, age 35
Deputy Chairman, Willi Schwerdtle, age 60
VP Investor Relations, John-Paul O'Meara
Junior Investor Relations Manager, Johannes Fink
Founder, Adi Dassler
Director, Christian Tourres, age 75
Director, Herbert Kauffmann, age 62
Deputy Chairwoman; Chairwoman Central Works Council, Sabine Bauer, age 50
Director, Heidi Thaler-Veh, age 51
Director, Stefan Jentzsch, age 53
Sales Director Customer Service Market Central and Director, Hans Ruprecht, age 59
Director, Roland Nosko, age 55
Deputy Chairman, Willi Schwerdtle, age 60
Director, Alexander Popov, age 42
Director, Dieter Hauenstein, age 56
Director, Wolfgang Jager, age 58
Auditors: KPMGDeutscheTreuhand-GesellschaftAG

LOCATIONS

HQ: Adidas AG
Adi-Dassler-Strasse 1, Herzogenaurach D-91074
Phone: (49) 91 32 84 0 **Fax:** (49) 91 32 84 2241
Web: www.adidas-group.com

2012 Sales

% of total	
Western	27
European Emerging	23
Greater	16
North	13
Latin	11
Other Asian	10
Total	**100**

PRODUCTS/OPERATIONS

2012 Sales by Segment

	% of total
Wholesale	64
Retail	23
Other	13
Total	**100**

2012 Sales by Product

	% of total
Footwear	47
Apparel	42
Hardware	11
Total	**100**

2012 Sales by Brand

	% of total
adidas	76
Reebok	11
TaylorMade-adidas	9
Rockport	2
Reebok-CCM	2
Total	**100**

COMPETITORS

ASICS
Amer Sports
Beam
Benetton
Callaway Golf
Columbia Sportswear
Converse
Cutter & Buck
Deckers Outdoor
FUBU
Fila Korea
Fila USA
Head N.V.
Huffy Corporation
K-Swiss
Mizuno
NIKE
New Balance
PUMA SE
PVH
Quiksilver
Ralph Lauren
Rawlings Sporting Goods
Rollerblade
Rossignol
Saucony
Skechers U.S.A.
Trek Bicycle
Under Armour
VF Corporation
Victoria' s Secret Stores

HISTORICAL FINANCIALS

Company Type: Public

Income Statement FYE: December 31

	REVENUE ($ mil.)	NET INCOME ($ mil.)	NET PROFIT MARGIN	EMPLOYEES
12/12	19,616	693	3.5%	46,306
12/11	17,259	867	5.0%	46,824
12/10	16,047	758	4.7%	42,541
12/09	14,954	352	2.4%	39,596
12/08	15,097	897	5.9%	39,982
Annual Growth	6.8%	(6.3%)	—	3.7%

2012 Year-End Financials

Debt ratio: 16.8%
Return on equity: 9.8%
Cash ($ mil.): 2,201
Current ratio: 1.57
Long-term debt ($ mil.): 1,590
No. of shares (mil.): 209
Dividends
Yield: 1.0%
Payout: 23.5%
Market value ($ mil.): 9,373

	STOCK PRICE ($)	P/E		PER SHARE ($)		
	FY Close	High/Low		Earnings	Dividends	Book Value
12/12	44.80	31	22	3.32	0.46	33.41
12/11	32.61	24	16	4.14	0.74	32.93
12/10	32.70	24	14	3.63	0.15	29.53
12/09	27.15	50	20	1.76	0.23	25.97
12/08	19.35	25	7	4.29	0.28	24.46
Annual Growth	23.4%	—	—	(6.2%)	12.6%	8.1%

AEGON N.V.

Not only has AEGON expanded across Europe it has also spread Transamerica. The Dutch life insurance giant is using its expertise in acquisition (US rival Transamerica was its largest catch) and consolidation to build a transnational collection of financial service businesses serving 40 million customers worldwide. Its subsidiaries operate primarily in the US the Netherlands and the UK offering personal and commercial life insurance pensions and annuities and accident and supplemental health insurance as well as retirement and savings advice and management services. AEGON also has insurance operations in 15 other countries in the Americas Europe and Asia as well as banking operations in the Netherlands.

The company has established a strong growth pattern for existing and new international markets largely through strategic acquisitions though its pace has slowed some due to economic downturns in 2008 and 2009. AEGON which derives about 60% of its revenues from life insurance premiums is focused on organic expansion in the high-growth regions of Asia central and eastern Europe and Latin America. To consolidate its market position in Spain AEGON in mid-2013 inked an exclusive 25-year strategic partnership with Banco Santander SA. As part of the agreement AEGON acquired a 51% stake in the joint venture which consists of a life insurance company and a non-life insurance company. The venture distributes life and general insurance products through Banco Santander's SA branch network while AEGON Spain provides back-office services.

In the Asia/Pacific region AEGON is broadening its operations partially through its Beijing-based insurance joint venture with the Chinese National Offshore Oil Corporation (CNOOC). It also formed a mutual fund joint venture with China-based Industrial Securities Co. in 2008 and it has an annuities partnership with Sony Life in Japan that began operations in 2009.

European expansion efforts include AEGON's 2009 buyout of former partner Banca Transilvania's shares in BT AEGON the Romanian pension business set up by the two companies the previous year. Acquisitions in other regions include the 2009 purchase of a 50% stake in Brazilian life insurance firm Mongeral SA. AEGON has also been focusing on broadening its global distribution channels which include independent agents brokers direct response workplace marketing banks and other financial institutions.

The company began scaling back on growth efforts in 2008 due to global economic conditions announcing plans to focus on high-growth and high-return investments in the emerging geographic markets. Later in 2008 as global financial conditions worsened AEGON secured a ?3 billion ($3.8 billion) capital infusion from the Dutch government to help it ward off economic woes. (This was fully repaid in 2011.) The funding was part of the Dutch government's bailout package designed to keep a group of banks and insurers from falling victim to the downturn in the global credit and equity markets.

To further ward off the impact of a slowing economy (and pay off its loan from the Dutch government) the company has initiated cost-containment and risk-reduction measures. It has been working to cut costs in its established market operations by reorganizing its Dutch US and UK divisions; it also restructured some global management responsibilities. In 2009 the company sold its Taiwanese life business for $84 million to Zhongwie Company. Also in 2009 it sold its Dutch real estate brokerage business and in early 2010 AEGON sold its funeral insurance business in the Netherlands.

The company announced additional restructuring measures to further streamline its operations in 2010. To reduce costs and risk exposures AEGON made plans to sharpen its focus on life pension and asset management operations and as such began seeking a buyer for Transamerica Reinsurance its US-based global life reinsurance business. The company sold Transamerica Re to French reinsurance firm SCOR for some $900 million in 2011. The sale included all of the life reinsurance operations although AEGON retained the annuity guarantee business. Further reorganization that year included cutting 300 positions in the Netherlands with associated costs of about $80 million which are expected to be accounted for before year-end. The company expects to achieve most of its cost savings in 2012.

In 2011 AEGON repurchased ?750 million in securities held by the Dutch state and completed the final repayment of the government bailout funds. Overall the company spent ?4.1 billion to repay the original ?3 billion loan including premium and interest payments. AEGON was the first company to repay the Dutch government funds issued through the 2008 bailout program. Although repayment frees AEGON to resume its acquisition activities the firm plans to continue its focus on organic growth efforts especially in Asia.

For several years AEGON has been restructuring its UK division around its core retirement and workplace savings units. In 2011 the company sold off its closed UK-based Guardian life and pensions business to private equity group Cinven for GBP275 million in cash. The sale provided proceeds for the company to recapitalize its Scottish Equitable business.

Independent trust Association AEGON (or Vereniging AEGON) controls about 33% of the company. Association AEGON is charged with safeguarding the interests of AEGON's shareholders and helped facilitate its bailout by issuing shares to the Dutch government.

HISTORY

AEGON traces its roots to 1844 when former civil servant and funeral society agent J. Oosterhoff founded Algemeene Friesche a burial society for low-income workers. The next year a similar organization Groot-Noordhollandsche was founded. These companies later became insurers and expanded nationwide. Meanwhile Olveh a civil servants' aid group was founded in 1877. The three companies merged in 1968 to form mutual insurer AGO.

AEGON's other operations came from different traditions. Vennootschap Nederland was founded in 1858 as a tontine (essentially a death pool with the survivors taking the pot) by Count A. Langrand-Dumonceau an ex-French Foreign Legionnaire from Belgium. In 1913 the company merged with Eerste Nederlandsche whose accident and health division had been previously spun off as Nieuwe Eerste Nederlandsche.

A year after Vennootschap was founded C. F. W. Wiggers van Kerchem founded a similar scheme Nillmij in the Dutch East Indies. The government promoted Nillmij to colonial civil servants and military people and for a while the company enjoyed a monopoly in the colony. Nillmij's Indonesian operations were nationalized after independence in 1957 but its Dutch subsidiaries continued to operate. All insurers were hit by fast-growing postwar government social programs. As a result industry consolidation came early to the Netherlands. In 1969 Eerste Nederlandsche Nieuwe Eerste Nederlandsche and Nillmij merged to form Ennia.

AGO demutualized in 1978 and became AGO Holding N.V. which was owned by Vereniging AGO. Meanwhile the shrinking Dutch insurance market forced companies to look overseas. AGO moved into the US in 1979 by buying Life Investors; by 1982 half of its sales came from outside the Netherlands. Ennia meanwhile expanded in Europe (it entered Spain in 1980) and the US (buying Arkansas-based National Old Line Insurance in 1981).

AGO and Ennia merged in 1983 to form AEGON. Vereniging AGO became Vereniging AEGON and received a 49% stake in the combined entity. (This stake was later reduced.) The company made more purchases at home and abroad and spent much of the rest of the decade assimilating operations.

AEGON's US units accounted for about 40% of sales in the mid-1980s and the firm increased that figure with acquisitions. In 1986 it bought Baltimore-based Monumental Corp. (life and health insurance) and expanded the company's US penetration.

This left AEGON underrepresented in Europe as deregulation paved the way for economic union and social service cutbacks spurred opportunities in private financial planning in the region. So in the 1990s AEGON began buying European companies including Regency Life (UK 1991) and Allami Biztosito (Hungary 1992). It formed an alliance with Mexico's Grupo Financiero Banamex in 1994. This reduced its reliance on US sales. It continued buying specialty operations in the US particularly asset management lines.

In 1997 AEGON began to concentrate on life insurance and financial services and shed its other operations. It bought the insurance business of Providian (now part of Washington Mutual) and sold noncore lines such as auto coverage. The next year it sold FGH Bank (mortgages) to Germany's Bayerische Vereinsbank (now Bayerische Hypotheken und Vereinsbank) and in 1999 sold auto insurer Worldwide Insurance.

That year AEGON expanded further in the US with the $9.7 billion purchase of Transamerica and bought the life and pensions businesses of the UK's Guardian Royal Exchange. In 2000 the company sold Labouchere N.V. a Dutch banking subsidiary to Dexia. Also in 2000 AEGON acquired UK-based third-party administrator HS Administrative Services.

Following the Transamerica acquisition the company divested several assets to focus on life insurance and pensions. In 2003 and 2004 diverse parts of Transamerica Finance (including its real estate tax unit and trailer leasing business) were sold to various companies including First American GE Commercial Finance and a joint venture held by Goldman Sachs and Cerberus Capital Management.

In 2005 the company sold off its German subsidiary AEGON Lebensversicherngs-AG operating as MoneyMaxx to Deutscher Ring. In 2006 it acquired a 49% stake in Mexican insurer Seguros Argos.

To expand in central and eastern Europe the company acquired pension fund management company PTE Ergo Hestia in Poland in 2007 as well as Dutch employee benefit and life insurance company OPTAS. To expand in Asia AEGON formed an annuities partnership with Sony Life in Japan in 2007. Also in 2007 AEGON USA purchased two Merrill Lynch insurance units and insurance services firm Clark Consulting.

In 2008 the company expanded in Europe by purchasing Turkish life and retirement services provider Ankara Emeklilik Hungarian pension fund UNIQA and Polish pension fund PTE Skarbiec-Emerytura as well as stakes in two similar Spanish firms.

AEGON slowed its acquisition efforts that year due to economic difficulties and began to control costs by restructuring and shedding some assets. In 2008 AEGON decided to discontinue an Indian life insurance and asset management joint venture with Ranbaxy.

EXECUTIVES

CEO AEGON The Netherlands and Member Management Board, Marco Keim, age 52

Chairman of the Executive Board and CEO, Alexander R. (Alex) Wynaendts, age 52, $1,251,311 total compensation

Global Head Sustainability, Marc A. van Weede

Member Management Board; CEO Americas, Mark W. Mullin, age 51

Senior Vice President, Greg Tucker

Member of the Executive Board and Management Board; Chief Financial Officer, Jan Nooitgedagt, age 60

CFO AEGON UK, Clare Bousfield

Member of the Management Board; Chief Executive Officer - Aegon UK, Adrian Grace

Member Supervisory Board, Irving W. Bailey II, age 71

Member of the Supervisory Board, Leo M. van Wijk, age 67

Member of the Supervisory Board, Antony Burgmans, age 66

Member of the Supervisory Board, Kornelis J. (Kees) Storm, age 71

Member of the Supervisory Board, Ben van der Veer, age 61

Member of the Supervisory Board, Dirk P. M. Verbeek, age 61

Member of the Supervisory Board, Shemaya Levy, age 67

Member of the Supervisory Board, Karla M.H. Peijs, age 69

Auditors: Ernst&YoungAccountants

LOCATIONS

HQ: AEGON N.V.
AEGONplein 50, P.O. Box 85, The Hague 2501 CB
Phone: (31) 70 344 3210
Web: www.aegon.com

2010 Sales

	% of total
The	43
UK	31
The	19
Other	7
Total	**100**

PRODUCTS/OPERATIONS

2010 Premiums

Life insurance	87
General insurance	3

Selected Subsidiaries and Affiliates

The Americas
- AEGON USA LLC Cedar Rapids Iowa (US)
- Transamerica Advisors Life Insurance Company Little Rock Arkansas (US)
- Transamerica Advisors Life Insurance Company of New York New York New York (US)
- Monumental Life Insurance Company Cedar Rapids Iowa (US)
- Stonebridge Casualty Insurance Company Columbus Ohio (US)
- Stonebridge Life Insurance Company Rutland Vermont (US)
- Transamerica Financial Life Insurance Company Inc. Purchase New York (US)
- Transamerica Life Insurance Company Cedar Rapids Iowa (US)
- Western Reserve Life Assurance Co. of Ohio Columbus Ohio (US)
- Transamerica Life Canada Toronto Ontario (Canada)

The Netherlands
- AEGON Bank NV Utrecht
- AEGON Levensverzekering NV The Hague
- AEGON Schadeverzekering NV The Hague
- OPTAS Pensioenen NV Rotterdam

The UK
- Scottish Equitable plc Edinburgh
- Origen Financial Services Ltd. London
- Positive Solutions (Financial Services) Ltd. Newcastle

Other regions
- AEGON Espa?a S.A. Madrid Spain (99.98%)
- AEGON Magyarorszag Altalanos Biztosito Zrt. Budapest Hungary
- AEGON Towarzystwo Ubezpiecze na ycie Spoka Akcyjna. Warsaw Poland
- AEGON Asset Management Company Mumbai India (75%)

Selected Joint Ventures

AEGON Sony Life Insurance Cy (50%) life insurance Tokyo
AEGON-CNOOC Life Insurance Company Ltd (50%) life insurance Shanghai
AMVEST Vastgoed BV (50%) property management and development; Utrecht Netherlands
CAN Vida y Pensiones Sociedad Anonima de Seguros (50%) life insurance and pension; Pamplona Spain
Caixa Terrassa Vida y Pensiones Sociedad Anonima de Seguros (50%) life and accident insurance and pension; Terrassa Spain

COMPETITORS

AIG
AXA
Allianz
Allstate
American General
Ameriprise
Aviva
Aviva Life Insurance India
BMO Financial Group
Canada Life
Delta Lloyd
Desjardins Financial Security
E-L Financial
Eureko
FMR
Fidelity & Guaranty Life
Franklin Templeton
Generali Deutschland
ING
Industrial Alliance Insurance and Financial Servic
Jackson National Life
John Hancock Financial Services
Legal & General Group
Lincoln Financial Group
Lloyds Banking Group
Manulife Financial
MassMutual
MetLife
Munich Re Group
Mutual of Omaha
Nationwide
New York Life
Old Mutual
OppenheimerFunds
Power Corporation of Canada
Primerica
Principal Financial
Prudential
Prudential plc
Putnam
RBC Insurance
Rabobank
SNS REAAL
Standard Life
Sun Life
Swiss Life
Symetra
T. Rowe Price
The Hartford
The Vanguard Group
Western & Southern Financial
Zurich Insurance Group

HISTORICAL FINANCIALS

Company Type: Public

Income Statement

FYE: December 31

	ASSETS ($ mil.)	NET INCOME ($ mil.)	INCOME AS % OF ASSETS	EMPLOYEES
12/12	482,493	2,017	0.4%	24,407
12/11	446,987	1,124	0.3%	25,288
12/10	444,745	2,354	0.5%	27,474
12/09	430,203	293	0.1%	28,382
12/08	401,614	(1,512)	—	31,425
Annual Growth	4.7%	—	—	(6.1%)

2012 Year-End Financials

Return on assets: 0.4%
Return on equity: 5.5%
Long-term debt ($ mil.): —
No. of shares (mil.): 1,943
Sales ($ mil): 57,339

Dividends
Yield: 3.5%
Payout: 51.2%
Market value ($ mil.): 12,515

	STOCK PRICE ($) FY Close	P/E High/Low		PER SHARE ($) Earnings	Dividends	Book Value
12/12	6.44	17	10	0.88	0.23	20.11
12/11	4.02	—	—	(0.08)	0.00	17.69
12/10	6.13	17	10	1.11	0.00	18.36
12/09	6.41	—	—	(0.23)	0.00	15.93
12/08	6.05	—	—	(1.29)	0.96	12.18
Annual Growth	1.6%	—	—	—	(29.9%)	13.3%

Aeon Co. Ltd. (Japan)

Japanese giant AEON CO. has enough retail ventures to last for eons. The holding company has about 180 subsidiaries and 25 affiliated companies. It runs the Aeon and Jusco chains of general merchandise stores and Japan's #1 supermarket chain with 1300 stores under the MaxValu and other banners as well as 3500-plus MINISTOP convenience stores. AEON also operates specialty chains including The Body Shop and Laura Ashley stores in Japan. It has a joint venture in Japan with Sports Authority and also operates HapYcom a leading drugstore chain in Japan. Other operations include shopping center development and financial services. Facing slow growth at home AEON is expanding in China and other Asian economies.

To that end AEON's China-based subsidiary and its MaxValu supermarket chain in 2012 formed a joint venture to operate supermarkets in China.

Sales across the vast AEON group inched up less than 1% in fiscal 2011 (ends February) vs. the previous year. Sales in Japan rose 4% while sales in the rest of Asia fell.

AEON has adopted a holding company structure in a bid to increase its responsiveness to changing (mostly negative) retail trends in Japan where it rings up about 95% of its total sales. A prolonged economic slump aging and shrinking population and weakness in the supermarket and department store sectors have the Japanese retailer looking abroad for future growth. Important Asian markets for AEON include China Hong Kong Malaysia South Korea and Thailand. The company beat a hasty retreat from North America with the sale of its majority stake in ladies apparel chain The Talbots in 2010 to better focus on its retail and financial service operations in Asia.

To grow in China AEON established a subsidiary in Shenzhen and greatly increased its investment there. At the end of fiscal 2011 (ends February) AEON had about 80 stores in China including specialty and general merchandise stores and supermarkets. Also AEON operates two mall-style shopping centers located in Beijing and in Huizhou northeast of Shenzhen. The malls are populated by specialty shops including AEON-owned banners such as Jusco and The Body Shop.

To adapt to changing demographics in its home country AEON is focusing on the "senior market" by developing products especially for seniors and developing senior-friendly floor plans and stores as well as services. The company's My Basket chain of more than 220 small-size urban supermarkets was developed specifically to serve Japan's aging and increasingly urban population. In early 2012 the retailer spun off its My Basket division into a wholly-owned subsidiary with the aim of tripling its store count in the Tokyo metro area by the end of fiscal 2013.

Among Japanese retailers AEON is one of the most proactive in preparing to defend its business from foreign competitors including the world's #1 retailer Wal-Mart and Britain's Tesco. To compete it has cut prices and distribution costs adopted western sales techniques and has acquired smaller retailers. The company is upgrading its computer systems to rival those of US giant Wal-Mart. Also AEON beat out Wal-Mart to buy eight hypermarkets in Japan operated by France's Carrefour which abandoned the Japanese market. In mid-2012 AEON agreed to acquired a 50% stake in Tesco Japan a subsidiary of UK's largest retailer Tesco plc for just 1 yen. Tesco Japan operates about 120 small Tesco and Tsurukame supermarkets in and around Tokyo. AEON is expected to acquire the remainder of Tesco Japan in the future.

EXECUTIVES

President, Motoya Okada, age 62
Chairman, Naoki Hayashi
EVP, Noriyuki Murakami
VP, Atsunobu Agata
SEVP, Yoshiki Mori

VP; President AEON Mall, Soichi Okazaki
EVP, Hiroshi Yokoo
EVP, Jerry Black
EVP, Shouhei Murai
EVP, Masaaki Toyoshima
VP; CEO ASEAN, Nagahisa Oyama
VP; CEO China, Haruyoshi Tsuji
President and Director, Motoya Okada, age 60
VP and Director, Naoki Hayashi
Director, Masaharu Ikuta
Director, Hideki Kurashige
VP and Director, Yoshiki Mori
Director, Masami Ishizaka
Director, Takejiro Sueyoshi
Director, Keiichi Tadaki
President, Motoya Okada, age 62
Chairman, Naoki Hayashi
EVP, Noriyuki Murakami
VP, Atsunobu Agata
SEVP, Yoshiki Mori
VP; President AEON Mall, Soichi Okazaki
EVP, Hiroshi Yokoo
EVP, Jerry Black
EVP, Shouhei Murai
VP; CEO ASEAN, Nagahisa Oyama
VP; CEO China, Haruyoshi Tsuji
President and Director, Motoya Okada, age 60
VP and Director, Naoki Hayashi
Director, Masaharu Ikuta
Director, Hideki Kurashige
VP and Director, Yoshiki Mori
Director, Masami Ishizaka
Director, Takejiro Sueyoshi
Director, Keiichi Tadaki
Auditors: DeloitteToucheTohmatsu

LOCATIONS

HQ: Aeon Co. Ltd. (Japan)
1-5-1 Nakase, Mihama-ku, Chiba 261-8515
Phone: (81) 43 212 6042 **Fax:** (81) 43 212 6849
Web: www.aeon.info

2011 Sales

	% of total
Japan	95
Asia & other	5
Total	**100**

PRODUCTS/OPERATIONS

2011 Sales

	% of total
General merchandise & other	69
Service & other	19
Specialty store	9
Shopping center	3
Total	**100**

Selected Store Names

Abilities Jusco (CDs DVDs and books)
Asbee (shoe stores)
Blue Grass (apparel for teenage girls)
Claire's Nippon (women's clothing)
Cox (family casual clothing)
HapYcom (drugstores)
Home Wide Corp. (home centers)
JUSCO (apparel food and household item superstores)
JUS-Photo (film developing)
Laura Ashley Japan (clothing and home furnishings)
Maxvalu (supermarkets)
Mega Sports (Sports Authority stores)
MINISTOP (convenience stores)
MYCAL Corporation (supermarkets)
My Basket (small-scale supermarkets)
Nustep (family footwear stores)
Petcity (pets & pet supplies)
Sports Authority (sporting goods)

COMPETITORS

A.S. Watson
A.S. Watson
Ito-Yokado
METRO AG
Carrefour
Carrefour
Costco Wholesale
Costco Wholesale
Dairy Farm International
Dairy Farm International
Fast Retailing
Fast Retailing
Heiwado
Heiwado
Isetan Mitsukoshi
Isetan Mitsukoshi
Ito-Yokado
METRO AG
Rakuten
Rakuten
Seiyu
Seiyu
Seven & i
Seven & i
Takashimaya
Takashimaya
Tesco
Tesco
The Gap
The Gap
Uny
Uny

HISTORICAL FINANCIALS

Company Type: Public

Income Statement

FYE: February 28

	REVENUE ($ mil.)	NET INCOME ($ mil.)	NET PROFIT MARGIN	EMPLOYEES
02/13	61,696	810	1.3%	91,646
02/12	64,736	830	1.3%	81,483
02/11	62,252	729	1.2%	74,465
02/10	56,874	350	0.6%	76,520
02/09	53,588	(28)	—	76,432
Annual Growth	3.6%	—	—	4.6%

2013 Year-End Financials

Debt ratio: 0.3%
Return on equity: 7.5%
Cash ($ mil.): 4,961
Current ratio: 0.99
Long-term debt ($ mil.): 10,822
No. of shares (mil.): 791
Dividends
Yield: 3.8%
Payout: —
Market value ($ mil.): 8,878

	STOCK PRICE ($) FY Close	P/E High/Low	PER SHARE ($) Earnings	Dividends	Book Value
02/13	11.22	— —	0.95	0.43	19.86
02/12	12.07	— —	0.95	0.26	20.72
02/11	12.07	— —	0.83	0.21	19.47
02/10	9.60	— —	0.44	0.00	16.83
02/09	9.65	— —	(0.04)	0.00	14.81
Annual Growth	3.8%	— —	—	—	7.6%

Ageas NV

ageas N.V. (known as Ageas) is hoping to offer insurance throughout the ages. The company formerly named Fortis N.V. provides life health and property/casualty insurance in Belgium and other European and Asian countries. Ageas was laid low by high debt and the contraction of credit markets in 2008. After receiving a hefty bailout from the Benelux governments it sold its Dutch operating units to the Netherlands government and its remaining bank operations to BNP Paribas. ageas N.V. and its sister company Belgian-traded ageas SA/NV have identical operations and are known simply as Ageas. In 2012 the companies announced plans to combine into one legal entity.

The Ageas companies have been undergoing a number of restructuring measures as part of a strategic review (launched following the BNP Paribas transaction) to determine the best path towards resolving legacy debt issues and prospering as an insurance business. Initiatives resulting from the review included the pruning of less-appealing insurance operations. As a stipulation of the BNP Paribas deal (which gave BNP Paribas rights to the Fortis brand) in 2010 the two sister companies also underwent a rebranding effort and changed their operating name to Ageas.

In addition the organization has working to simplify the complex legal structure of the Ageas group. To begin the simplification process in 2010 it announced plans to liquidate its Fortis Brussels subsidiary which had previously held the banking assets. The efforts culminated in 2012 when it announced plans to combine the two legal parent Ageas entities into one. Through the transaction all assets of ageas N.V. will be merged into ageas SA/NV and shareholders of ageas N.V. will receive an equal number of shares in ageas SA/NV (following which a reverse split will occur to reduce the total number of shares). The Belgium-based ageas SA/NV entity will continue as the surviving parent entity aligning the Ageas legal structure more closely with its remaining operational territories.

Through its operational reshuffling and rebranding efforts the Ageas organization has focused on its core insurance operations which are held by the Ageas Insurance (formerly Fortis Insurance) subsidiary. The insurance division includes the 75%-owned AG Insurance (formerly Fortis Insurance Belgium) subsidiary and the international insurances businesses including subsidiaries in the UK France and Hong Kong (Ageas Asia) as well as joint ventures elsewhere in Europe (including Luxembourg) and Asia.

Ageas continues to review and divest certain underperforming insurance operations. At the same time the organization has begun to see a turnaround in its finances and it is pursuing a cautious expansion strategy in high-growth insurance markets including continental Europe.

Ageas (then known as Fortis) began experiencing troubles after financial woes brought on by its part in the 2007 takeover of ABN AMRO were worsened by global economic conditions the following year. The Benelux governments (Belgium Luxembourg and the Netherlands) teamed together in September 2008 to bail Fortis out jointly paying about E11.2 billion ($16 billion) in return for significant stakes in the operations of each respective country.

Shortly after when the rescue plan failed to stabilize the organization the government of the Netherlands paid an additional E16.8 billion ($23 billion) to acquire all of the former Fortis' Dutch banking and insurance operations including the former ABN AMRO operations.

Fortis sold a 75% stake in its remaining banking operations in Luxembourg and Belgium (held by Fortis Banque now operating as BNP Paribas Fortis) and a 25% stake in the Belgian insurance business for some E4.4 billion ($5.5 billion) to BNP Paribas in 2009; the Belgium government gained the remaining 25% of Fortis Banque through the deal. The agreement was first reached in late 2008 but was delayed and revised twice after Belgian courts ruled that the government had overstepped its bounds by not considering the interests of Fortis' shareholders. The last version of the deal was reached in March 2009 and closed in May.

As part of the deal Fortis also split off its portfolio of risky structured investments (the collateralized debt obligations and US mortgage-backed securities at the center of the 2008 global banking crisis) into a separate entity (Royal Park Investments) with stakes in the entity going to Fortis (45%) the Belgian government (43%) and BNP Paribas (12%).

Ageas has gone through a number of leadership changes during the past few years of turmoil. Following the final transformation into a pure-play insurance company in mid-2009 it named Bart De Smet as CEO; De Smet was already leading the company's insurance division and is refocusing the company around those operations. In December 2008 restructuring expert Karel De Boeck was appointed CEO replacing interim CEO Filip Dierckx who took control shortly before the bailout was announced. Dierckx replaced Herman Verwilst who took a mere three-month stint at the helm and Verwilst had replaced ousted Jean-Paul Votron the leader who had overseen the company's participation in the ABN AMRO deal.

LOCATIONS

HQ: Ageas NV
Archimedeslaan 6, Utrecht 3584 BA
Phone: (31) 30 25 25 304 **Fax:** (31) 30 25 25 310
Web: www.ageas.com

HISTORICAL FINANCIALS

Company Type: Public

Income Statement FYE: December 31

	ASSETS ($ mil.)	NET INCOME ($ mil.)	INCOME AS % OF ASSETS	EMPLOYEES
12/12	127,999	979	0.8%	13,335
12/11	117,189	(747)	—	12,557
12/10	132,721	298	0.2%	11,707
12/09	134,323	1,717	1.3%	10,374
12/08	129,840	(39,177)	—	0
Annual Growth	(0.4%)	—	—	—

2012 Year-End Financials

Return on assets: 0.7%
Return on equity: 8.3%
Long-term debt ($ mil.): —
No. of shares (mil.): 231
Sales ($ mil): 20,614
Dividends
Yield: —
Payout: —
Market value ($ mil.): 7,013

	STOCK PRICE ($) FY Close	P/E High	P/E Low	PER SHARE ($) Earnings	Dividends	Book Value
12/12	30.25	17	1	4.13	0.00	56.35
12/11	1.52	—	—	(2.97)	0.00	41.71
12/10	2.25	9	4	1.20	0.00	42.73
12/09	3.89	2	0	6.91	0.00	48.60
12/08	1.16	—	—	(170.71)	0.00	37.75
Annual Growth	126.0%	—	—	—	—	10.5%

Agricultural Bank of China

LOCATIONS

HQ: Agricultural Bank of China
No. 69, Jianguomen Nei Avenue, Dongcheng District, Beijing 100005
Phone: (86) 10 85109619 **Fax:** (86) 10 85108557
Web: www.abchina.com

HISTORICAL FINANCIALS

Company Type: Public

Income Statement FYE: December 31

	ASSETS ($ mil.)	NET INCOME ($ mil.)	INCOME AS % OF ASSETS	EMPLOYEES
12/12	2,124,449	23,273	1.1%	501,762
12/11	1,855,232	19,370	1.0%	490,121
12/10	1,568,269	14,393	0.9%	485,800
12/09	1,300,906	9,518	0.7%	480,098
12/08	1,027,969	7,543	0.7%	475,640
Annual Growth	19.9%	32.5%	—	1.3%

2012 Year-End Financials

Return on assets: 1.1%
Return on equity: 20.6%
Long-term debt ($ mil.): —
No. of shares (mil.): —
Sales ($ mil): 104,724
Dividends
Yield: 3.3%
Payout: —
Market value ($ mil.): —

	STOCK PRICE ($) FY Close	P/E High	P/E Low	PER SHARE ($) Earnings	Dividends	Book Value
12/12	12.60	1	1	0.07	0.42	0.37
12/11	10.63	1	0	0.06	0.00	0.32
Annual Growth	18.5%	—	—	4.6%	217.9%	3.9%

Agrium, Inc.

It's no bull that Agrium is a top producer and marketer of fertilizers in the Americas. A leader in the production of nitrogen the company operates plants in 14 countries on six continents producing about 10 million tons of nitrogen potash and phosphate products per year. In addition to supplying wholesalers Agrium operates more than 800 fertilizer retail outlets in the US and South America. The company also owns 50% of Profertil a joint venture with Spain's Repsol YPF that runs Argentina's largest nitrogen plant and 25% of a nitrogen fertilizers plant in Egypt. After a 2009 bid for CF Industries fell short Agrium acquired Australian wheat exporter AWB Ltd. for $1.2 billion in 2010.

Agrium's revenues increased 18% in 2010 due to higher sales volumes and stronger product prices. Its Retail segment saw a 13% increase in sales based on higher crop nutrient margins and volumes; the Wholesale group was up 24% on stronger demand for potash while the Advanced Technologies unit sales grew 29% on increased sales of its Smart Nitrogen product. Global sales saw major gains in the Asia/Pacific and South America regions. Agrium's net income jumped 95% in 2010 due primarily to the rebound in crop nutrient demand and increased margins across all three business units.

The company's strategy is to expand across all three of its business segments with both strategic acquisitions and organic growth through a combination of capacity expansions improvements to its operating model and maintaining strong industry fundamentals. The company has primarily used acquisitions to expand its Retail and Advanced Technologies segments but finds growing its Wholesale business to be more capital-intensive.

Agrium sees the AWB deal as a way to enhance its market presence and improve its product and service offerings in Australia and New Zealand. However soon after the deal closed Agrium sold AWB's commodity management businesses to Cargill Incorporated in a deal valued at $917 million. Agrium absorbed the rest of AWB's assets.

In 2012 Agrium expanded its presence in retail operations by agreeing to acquire the agri-products business of Viterra from Glencore International (since renamed Glencore Xstrata) after the latter closes on its acquisition of Viterra. The buy for about $1.8 billion will give Agrium about 90% of Viterra's Canadian retail facilities all of its Australian retail facilities and a minority stake in its nitrogen plant in Alberta.

In 2011 Agrium acquired CerealToscana S.A. a fertilizer distribution company in Italy and Agroport its subsidiary in Romania for $27 million. The combined companies have a stable financial record with gross sales of some $200 million. The deal enhances Agrium Europe's existing fertilizer distribution business.

Agrium made its $5.2 billion hostile offer for CF Industries amidst a four-company year-long bidding war that also included Yara Industries and Terra Industries. Agrium withdrew its offer to buy CF Industries after that company successfully acquired Terra.

The company also purchased 24 retail farm centers in Argentina in 2010 from DuPont Crop Protection. The deal will expand Agrium's Loveland crop-protection products into additional South American countries.

In 2008 it bought agricultural products retailer UAP for $2.5 billion including assumed debt. In the latter half of the decade Agrium has implemented an aggressive expansion strategy by acquiring a number of businesses throughout the Americas. The deal for UAP was the largest by far. It greatly added to Agrium's North American retail operations and also expanded the company's international reach.

Other acquisitions have included agricultural products distributor Royster-Clark and two divisions of Spectrum Brands' Nu-Gro subsidiary. The Nu-Gro deal formed the base of Agrium's Advanced Technologies unit which supplies agricultural products and services in North and South America and sells branded micronutrients and other industrial products worldwide (such as controlled-released fertilizers for the turf grass horticulture and consumer agriculture markets).

HISTORY

Agrium was formed in 1992 to facilitate the reorganization of Cominco's fertilizer division and to acquire the fertilizer business of the Alberta Energy Company (1993). Cominco was founded in 1896 as the Smelting and Refining Company when Fritz Heinze fired up his first smelter at Trail Creek Landing British Columbia. Using the ores of the nearby Rossland mines the company soon diversified into other products (such as fertilizers) and new metallurgical technologies. In 1906 the Smelting and Refining Company the Rossland mines and the nearby St. Eugene Mine merged to form the Consolidated Mining and Smelting Company of Canada Limited.

During WWI the Canadian government conscripted all the company's lead zinc and chemical production and instructed the company to make explosive-grade ammonium nitrate at its fertilizer plants. Cominco became the company's official name in 1966.

Alberta Energy was formed in 1973 to lessen Alberta's dependence on foreign oil in response to the OPEC oil embargo. In 1989 its petrochemical division established fertilizer (ammonium nitrate) subsidiaries in the US.

Agrium was established to compete in the rapidly consolidating fertilizer market (the number of North American ammonia producers fell from 55 in 1980 to 26 at the end of 1996). The phosphate and potash industries also consolidated albeit on a smaller scale.

Between 1993 and 1996 the company expanded its US operations by acquiring Crop Protection Services and Western Farm Service (both retail operations) AG-BIO (the phosphate-based fertilizer business of Imperial Oil) and Nu-West Industries. Agrium expanded into South America in 1995 by opening retail sales units for selling fertilizer agricultural chemicals and other services in the farming regions of Argentina.

In 1996 Agrium acquired Viridian a Canadian fertilizer producer with nitrogen- and phosphate-based fertilizer plants in Alberta. Expanding its supply base the company bought a phosphate mine in Alberta in 1997. The company also bought back 10% of its shares in 1998.

Agrium opened a phosphate rock mine in Ontario in 1999 to reduce its reliance on phosphate rock imported from West Africa. In 2000 Agrium bought Unocal's nitrogen-based fertilizer operations for around $325 million thereby increasing its nitrogen production capacity some 60%. Also that year Agrium's Profertil nitrogen plant a joint venture with Spain's industrial giant Repsol-YPF began production in Argentina but the plant was shut down by a government agency following an accidental discharge of ammonia (the plant was reopened later in 2000).

The company continued to expand its retail business in North and South America through acquisitions in 2006 of other agricultural products and services such as Nu-Gro and Pursell Technologies.

EXECUTIVES

Chair, Frank W. Proto, age 70
Senior Vice President; President - Retail Business Unit, Richard L. Gearheard, age 63, $401,099 total compensation
VP and Treasurer, Patrick J. (Pat) Freeman
SVP Business Development and Chief Legal Officer, Leslie A. O'Donoghue, $340,398 total compensation
SVP Human Resources, James M. (Jim) Grossett
President; Chief Executive Officer; Director, Michael M. (Mike) Wilson, age 61, $1,009,274 total compensation
VP Marketing and Distribution, Kevin R. Helash
Senior Vice President; President - Wholesale Business Unit, Ronald A. (Ron) Wilkinson, $415,526 total compensation
Senior Director Investor Relations, Richard Downey
SVP; President Agrium Advanced Technologies, Andrew K. Mittag, age 53
Chief Financial Officer VP, Stephen G. (Steve) Dyer
VP Retail East Region, Thomas E. (Tom) Warner, age 61
Vice President Treasurer, Angela S. Lekatsas
Senior Director Corporate and Government Relations, Doug Beever
Corporate Secretary and Senior Legal Counsel, Gary J. Daniel
Executive Vice President - Corporate Development; Chief Risk Officer, Charles V. (Chuck) Magro
Manager Investor Relations, Todd Coakwell
Senior Vice President; Chief Legal Officer, Eric Miller
Vice President; Corporate Controller, Fredrick Thun
Executive Vice President Corporate Development & Strategy & Chief Risk Officer, Leslie ODonoghue
Director, Victor J. Zaleschuk, age 69
Director, Russell K. (Russ) Girling, age 50
Director, Derek G. Pannell, age 66
Director, Ralph S. Cunningham, age 72
President CEO and Director, Michael M. (Mike) Wilson, age 61
Director, Germaine Gibara, age 68
Director, Susan A. Henry, age 67
Director, Russell J. Horner, age 63
Director, A. Anne McLellan, age 62
Independent Director, David Lesar
Independent Director, John Lowe
Auditors: KPMGLLP

LOCATIONS

HQ: Agrium, Inc.
13131 Lake Fraser Drive S.E., Calgary, Alberta T2J 7E8
Phone: 403 225-7236 **Fax:** 403 225-7610
Web: www.agrium.com

2010 Sales

	$ mil.	% of total
US	7,899	75
Europe	583	5
South America	497	4
Australia & Asia	144	2
Total	**10,520**	**100**

PRODUCTS/OPERATIONS

2010 Sales

	$ mil.	% of total
Retail		
Crop nutrients	3,001	27
Crop protection products	2,703	24
Seeds services & other	1,265	11
Wholesale		
Nitrogen	1,343	12
Potash	646	6
Phosphate	548	5
Other	1,194	11
Advanced technologies	390	4
Adjustments	(570)	-
Total	**10,520**	**100**

COMPETITORS

BASF SE
CF Industries
K+S
Koch Industries Inc.
Potash Corp
SQM
Yara

HISTORICAL FINANCIALS

Company Type: Public

Income Statement

FYE: December 31

	REVENUE ($ mil.)	NET INCOME ($ mil.)	NET PROFIT MARGIN	EMPLOYEES
12/12	16,686	1,494	9.0%	14,500
12/11	15,470	1,371	8.9%	14,800
12/10*	10,743	713	6.6%	14,150
01/10	0	0	—	0
12/09	9,129	366	4.0%	11,153
Annual Growth	22.3%	59.8%	—	9.1%

*Fiscal year change

2012 Year-End Financials

Debt ratio: 24.7%
Return on equity: 22.3%
Cash ($ mil.): 726
Current ratio: 1.54
Long-term debt ($ mil.): 2,115
No. of shares (mil.): 149
Dividends
Yield: 1.0%
Payout: 10.4%
Market value ($ mil.): 14,916

	STOCK PRICE ($) FY Close	P/E High	P/E Low	PER SHARE ($) Earnings	Dividends	Book Value
12/12	99.87	11	7	9.55	1.00	46.31
12/11	67.11	11	7	8.68	0.28	40.70
12/10*	91.75	20	11	4.51	0.11	32.82
01/10	61.50	—	—	(0.00)	0.11	(0.00)
12/09	61.50	28	13	2.33	0.11	29.25
Annual Growth	12.9%	—	—	60.0%	108.7%	16.6%

*Fiscal year change

Air France-KLM

Air France and KLM represent years of French and Dutch airline tradition but Air France-KLM represents a first: a holding company made up of two national airlines. Together Air France-KLM is the second-largest airline in Europe after Deutsche Lufthansa and one of the largest in the world. Through its operating units the company serves more than 250 destinations in about 125 countries with a fleet of some 590 aircraft. Air France and KLM operate independently from hubs in Paris and Amsterdam but have coordinated their operations both as sister companies and as members of the SkyTeam alliance which also includes Alitalia Delta Air Lines and Korean Air Lines.

Anticipating further uncertainty in the world economy Air France-KLM announced a three-year plan in January 2012 to strengthen profitability that comprises decreased capacity growth debt reduction to E4.5 billion ($5.9 billion) and cost cutting measures that include a freeze on pay increases at Air France and wage moderation at KLM as well as the continuation of a hiring freeze begun in September 2011. To boost demand for seats the company will decrease its fleet by cutting more than E1 billion ($1.3 billion) from its budget for expansion.

With the goal of increasing productivity by 20% Air France is consolidating its European operations into three units. One of them tasked with serving smaller cities will include Brit Air Regional and Airlinair. The second will be focused on leisure operations and will include discount line Transavia which annually carries more than 5 million passengers on low-cost medium-haul flights to several vacation spots. As a third division Air France's short-haul brand will add no-frills service.

Though the company is prepared for a challenging economic climate year-over-year revenue grew 13% in fiscal 2011. The company's cargo segment 12% of revenue was profitable that year while the more significant passenger segment 77% of revenue broke even. Maintenance representing 5% of revenue was reported to have contributed to operating income.

The company's fuel bill increased 21% between 2010 and 2011 a setback that was further exacerbated by the appreciation of the dollar relative to the euro. However the company has been hopeful that its hedging strategy will have a positive effect on its fuel expenses. Fuel hedging is when airlines lock in a pre-determined price for future jet fuel purchases.

In addition to rising fuel prices the company has been challenged by competition from low-cost carriers particularly from airlines based in the Middle East. To meet those challenges Air France-KLM has been working to expand its SkyTeam alliance to Brazil and Asia especially India. It has also been working to create joint ventures similar to one already in place with Delta Air Lines and Alitalia with Chinese airlines.

In addition to its SkyTeam alliance Air France-KLM operates a trans-Atlantic joint venture with Delta and Alitalia that offers more than 260 flights on about 145 aircraft. The company plans to use this partnership to develop more service for Asia Latin America and Africa. Another area of focus for the joint venture is Florida which since 2011 has been served by more than a dozen new flights.

And supplementing its low-cost Transavia operations Air France-KLM formed a partnership with British economy carrier Flybe to provide about 45 flights between France and the UK.

The company's Paris and Amsterdam hubs are connected by what Air France-KLM calls the Paris-Amsterdam Hubway which is served by more than 10 daily flights between the two nodes. Each of the two hubs has its own geographical emphasis and they complement each other to create a broader service area. For instance KLM is focused more on East Africa while Air France provides more service for West Africa. A third hub Lyon-Saint Exupery connects regional centers in France with the rest of Europe.

The French government owns about 16% of the combined company; employees own about 10%. Air France-KLM's board includes six directors representing employees.

EXECUTIVES

President and Chief Executive Offi cer of KLM, Peter F. Hartman, age 64
Chief Operating Officer, Alain Bassil, age 57
EVP Marketing Revenue Management and Network; Chief Commercial Officer Air France, Bruno Matheu, age 50
Executive Vice President French Sales Air France-KLM, Christian Boireau, age 63
Chairman and CEO, Jean-Cyril Spinetta, age 70, $990,375 total compensation
CFO Air France-KLM Group and Director Air France, Philippe Calavia, age 65
EVP International & the Netherlands; Managing Director KLM, Erik Varwijk, age 51
Executive Vice-President Engineering and Maintenance, Franck Terner
Executive Vice-President Corporate Secretary, Jacques Pape
Executive Vice-President Commercial Sales and Marketing, Patrick Alexandre
Executive Vice-President Commercial Marketing, Pieter Bootsma
Director, Pierre Richard, age 72
Auditors: KPMGS.A.

LOCATIONS

HQ: Air France-KLM
2, rue Robert Esnault-Pelterie, Paris 75007
Phone: (33) 1 41 56 78 00 **Fax:** (33) 1 41 56 56 00
Web: www.airfranceklm-finance.com

2011 Sales

	% of total
Europe	30
Americas	27
Asia	20
Africa/Middle	16
Caribbean/Indian	7
Total	**100**

PRODUCTS/OPERATIONS

2011 Sales

	% of total
Passenger	77
Cargo	12
Maintenance	5
Other	6
Total	**100**

COMPETITORS

Aer Lingus
Air Berlin
American Airlines Group
Austrian Airlines
Brussels Airlines
IAG
Lufthansa
Ryanair
SAS
SNCF
United Continental
Virgin Atlantic Airways
easyJet

HISTORICAL FINANCIALS

Company Type: Public

Income Statement FYE: December 31

	REVENUE ($ mil.)	NET INCOME ($ mil.)	NET PROFIT MARGIN	EMPLOYEES
12/12	33,806	(1,571)	—	100,744
12/11*	24,672	(571)	—	102,277
03/11	33,607	872	2.6%	102,012
03/10	28,316	(2,102)	—	104,721
03/09	31,893	(1,082)	—	106,933
Annual Growth	1.5%	—	—	(1.5%)

*Fiscal year change

2012 Year-End Financials

Debt ratio: 54.0%
Return on equity: (-21.6%)
Cash ($ mil.): 4,507
Current ratio: 0.77
Long-term debt ($ mil.): 12,607
No. of shares (mil.): 296
Dividends
Yield: —
Payout: —
Market value ($ mil.): 2,863

	STOCK PRICE ($) FY Close	P/E High	P/E Low	PER SHARE ($) Earnings	Dividends	Book Value
12/12	9.67	—	—	(5.31)	0.00	21.92
12/11*	5.16	—	—	(1.94)	0.00	26.52
03/11	16.80	19	9	2.42	0.00	32.97
03/10	15.65	—	—	(7.15)	0.00	24.56
03/09	8.85	—	—	(3.67)	0.86	25.41
Annual Growth	2.2%	—	—	—	—	(3.6%)

*Fiscal year change

Airbus Group NV

European Aeronautic Defence and Space Company (EADS) succeeds in commercial and military aerospace and related services. Considered Europe's largest supplier it rivals Boeing in the competitive skies. EADS' largest segment is Airbus: its commercial division ranks among the top two makers of large commercial aircraft (seats 100-plus passengers) while its military division manufactures transport tankers and mission aircraft. Other segments include Eurocopter civil/military helicopters (holds a 33% world market share); Astrium's satellites and launcher systems; and Cassidian's defense and security business that makes combat aircraft missile systems radar defense electronics and unmanned aerial systems (UAS).

In September 2012 EADS announced it was considering a merger with UK-based BAE Systems a global provider of sensors flight controls and aircraft. However the proposed $45 billion merger —which would have created the largest global aerospace and defense player on the planet both in total sales and market value —was called off weeks later after it failed to pass European governmental and regulatory hurdles.

As a giant European industrial exporter EADS operates between a euro/dollar exchange rate rock (pounded by fluctuating market demand) and a global economic hard place. Among its solutions EADS adeptly hedges currency pitting the dollar against the euro as well as offsets the cost of US-built content (structures engines and avionics) — typically 35% to 45% of its jets —by paying in euros. Concurrently EADS aims for more aggressive Airbus sales by ramping up production and tapping promising emerging markets such as Brazil China and India. EADS also manages to correct the revenue ups and downs experienced in its Airbus commercial ventures with those of its other businesses thereby mitigating cyclical market downturns.

The company's strategy has reported some success; sales (in euros) increased almost 7% in 2010 over 2009 and its net income gained an altitude of E553 million (about $733 million) from a tailspin loss of E763 million (more than $1 billion) — with all segments posting a rise. Additionally EADS' orders increased more than 80% during 2010. After suffering a stall-out due to the global economic recession industry passenger travel revved up in 2010 more than 8% while freight increased in excess of 20%; the world aircraft fleet is expected to double in 20 years.

Preparing to capitalize on demand EADS hammered out its Vision 2020 goals under which it pursues the world's #1 position in air and space platforms systems and services. Services are targeted to achieve a 25% share of the business in less than 10 years. To this end EADS has been scouting deals in the services sector. In August 2011 it agreed to purchase Vizada a global satellite-based mobile communication services provider from French private-equity Apax France. The whopping E673 million ($969 million) deal bolsters EADS's subsidiary Astrium a top contractor of space-technology wares in Europe and furthers opportunities beyond Europe with maritime aerospace as well as land media and other commercial customers. Hard on its heels EADS took over more than 98% of Canada-based Vector Aerospace for C$625 million (about $341 million). Vector joins Eurocopter as a standalone business adding a multi-platform aviation repair and overhaul business.

Meanwhile EADS is moving toward a better balance between its commercial and defense segments intending to source as much as 40% of its content outside Europe. The company continues to create global industrial partnerships beyond Europe's perimeters especially in Asia (including Korea and Vietnam) the Middle East (especially Saudi Arabia) and the Americas. EADS formed a joint venture with India-based Larsen & Toubro (L&T; considered India's largest engineering/construction company by revenue) in early 2011. EADS will hold a minority share of 26% while L&T holds the rest. The India-based JV will manufacture electronics equipment for the defense and security industry.

In the same vein EADS Eurocopter created a subsidiary in India in 2010 and has broken ground to build a new rotary-wing facility at its Helicopteros do Brasil-Helibras (Helibras) subsidiary. Helibras will produce and assemble EC725 helicopters for the Brazilian armed forces. Also in 2010 EADS' Cassidian segment partnered with Brazil-based Odebrecht servicing regional defense and security needs. Previously the company strengthened its position in the Japanese marketplace by establishing EADS Japan K.K. subsidiary to drive regional marketing and industrial and aerospace alliances. The company's Tianjin manufacturing facility rolled out China's first Airbus A320 and Eurocopter's EC-175 civil helicopter took its maiden flight after being developed with Chinese partners.

US contracts are on its wish list and EADS North America —EADS prime contractor for defense products in the US —help to fill those orders especially helicopters to the US Army and Coast Guard. EADS is hunting for deals in the US where it can spend some of its almost E12 billion (almost $16 billion) in net cash. EADS has a preference for penetrating the North American market where the US military is the world's largest aerospace and defense customer (spending approximately $1.4 trillion per year); EADS North America teams up with US defense companies to jockey into position as a prime contractor to the Pentagon. Even with defense budget cuts the US still represents about half of global defense spending. The company's goal is to increase North American annual revenues to $10 billion (eight-fold) in a decade primarily by addressing defense cyber security and space related projects. EADS North America operates a number of business concerns involved in the development and manufacture of rotorcraft defense systems avionics and security and public safety products and equipment.

In addition to growing its geographic markets EADS is also boosting its technology offerings. It began test flights in 2010 for its hybrid X3 helicopter. In partnership with Northrop Grumman EADS'

Cassidian segment conducted maiden flights for its Euro Hawk UAS. As the demand for cyber security and cyber warfare (the protection of computer systems and data from interference) grows Cassidian seized the opportunity to acquire UK-based Regency IT in 2010 to boost its capabilities in this sector. Additionally the company developed an all-electric Cri-Cri aerobatic plane in partnership with Aero Composites Saintonge. It also backs the development of biofuels to power aircraft achieving the world's first flight of an aircraft running on pure biofuel made from algae.

EADS comprises four business segments. Airbus the largest represents almost two-thirds of sales. Its A320 family includes single-aisle aircraft; staggering sales worldwide make this the top selling commercial jetliner. Airbus A330/A340 twin-aisle jets include tankers that cater to markets wanting a plane that can lift more passengers and cargo and go farther. The twin-deck A380 XWB seats ore than 500 passengers and is expected to rival Boeing's Dreamliner.

Cassidian defense & security division which leads EADS' armed forces and civil security operations is the company's second largest unit after Airbus. Its activities range broadly from producing the Eurofighter (combat aircraft) to missile systems defense communication systems and electronics. Its MBDA subsidiary (owned along with BAE Systems and Finmeccanica) is recognized as the world's largest missile company. In 2012 Cassidian acquired 75% of Carl Zeiss Optronics from Carl Zeiss AG. Carl Zeiss Optronics makes optronic optic and precision-engineered products with a focus that includes border-surveillance systems vehicle sensors and submarine periscopes. In late 2011 Cassidian acquired the French company SurveyCopter maker of unmanned aerial vehicles (UAV). Partnered with Cassidian since 2003 SurveyCopter expertise is in robotic and autopilot vehicles for hostile environment utilization. The acquisition will boost Cassidian's plans to launch a new industrial line of tactical UAVs and VTOL UAVs for military and private export markets.

EADS Eurocopter commands more than one-third of the civil and public/private helicopter fleet. Eurocopter operations experienced a market downturn in 2009 for smaller commercial helicopters; the company responded by implementing its SHAPE restructuring program which included cutting costs reducing inventories and boosting technology to help the civil helicopter business weather the crisis. Eurocopter and its Helibras affiliate began construction on a new Brazil-based rotary-wing center scheduled for a production launch in 2012. Helibras will manufacture assemble and service EC725 helicopters for use by the Brazilian armed forces.

The Astrium space group supplies satellites launchers and space services to Europe's institutional and military space programs. Astrium has driven the design and development of high-profile projects such as Galileo the European satellite navigation system and the International Space Station's Columbus space laboratory and unmanned Automated Transfer Vehicle (ATV).

Daimler AG owns about 22.5% of EADS. SOGEPA (a French state holding company) and France-based Lagardere SCA together own approximately 22.5%. Spain owns 5%.

HISTORY

The growth of the European Aeronautic Defence and Space Company –EADS –is overshadowed by the long history of its components and by the obstacles overcome to cement the deal: The French and the Germans historically aren't overly fond of each other so how did it come to pass that Germany's DaimlerChrysler Aerospace AG (DASA) and France's Aerospatiale Matra put aside their differences to band together with Spain's Construcciones Aeronauticas SA (CASA)?

The US aerospace sector in the 1990s saw many companies consolidate scrambling to make their way in the post-Cold War era. Boeing the largest aerospace company in the world got that way by acquiring a number of operations including Rockwell International's aerospace and defense operations (1995) and most importantly McDonnell Douglas in a $16 billion deal (1997). In the same era defense giant Lockheed merged with Martin Marietta (1995) and acquired Loral (1997). These US companies had it relatively easy –they all paid taxes to Uncle Sam but acquisition deals in Europe were stymied by concerns over national security and privatization because much of Europe's defense industry was government-owned.

Spurred into action by their US rivals DASA and British Aerospace (now BAE SYSTEMS) – partners in Airbus –began merger talks in 1997. Fearful of being left out in the cold France's government-owned Aerospatiale – another Airbus partner –began talks to merge with Matra a French defense company controlled by Lagardere. Weeks after the Aerospatiale-Matra deal was announced in 1998 the chairman of DASA's parent company Jurgen Schrempp met with Lagardere's CEO Jean-Luc Lagardere and proposed a three-way deal. It never occurred and in 1999 the BAE SYSTEMS and DASA deal fell through as well.

Later that year Schrempp and Lagardere met again and laid the groundwork for a merger between DASA and Aerospatiale Matra. Less than three weeks after the Aerospatiale-Matra merger was completed Lagardere found itself pitching the DASA/Aerospatiale Matra merger idea to a stunned French government (which still held a 48% stake in Aerospatiale Matra). Marathon negotiations ensued. Late in the year Spain's Construcciones Aeronauticas SA (CASA) agreed to become part of EADS.

In 2000 EADS went public and Airbus announced that it would abandon its consortium structure in favor of incorporation. The next year EADS began pushing for a consolidation of army and naval equipment manufacturing among EU countries similar to the aerospace consolidation that created EADS. For Airbus the long-sought switch from consortium to corporation finally occurred in July 2001 when Airbus S.A.S. was incorporated.

EADS bought out BAE SYSTEMS' 25% share in their Astrium joint venture in 2003. In October 2004 EADS agreed to acquire US defense electronics maker Racal Instruments as part of its plan to increase defense sales in the US. Rumors surfaced the next month that EADS was discussing a merger deal with French defense company Thales.

In December 2004 EADS and BAE SYSTEMS gave Airbus the green-light to build the super-jumbo twin-deck A380 a plane that competes directly with Boeing's upcoming 787 Dreamliner. A few months later in early 2005 EADS was given preferred bidder status for the UK's Royal Air Force aerial refueling tanker contract. The program was valued at approximately $25 billion.

Claiming victory at last in 2006 Airbus beat Boeing on deliveries (434 vs. 398) but Boeing racked up a record 1004 plane orders while Airbus notched only 790. Moreover EADS' shares took a pounding in 2006 on Airbus' announcement that deliveries of the A380 would be delayed by six or seven months due to manufacturing glitches. A group of EADS shareholders cried foul and filed suit when it was revealed that co-CEO Noel Forgeard and five other EADS directors exercised stock options weeks before an internal investigation into the delays was launched. Two weeks later Forgeard fell on his sword and resigned. Louis Gallois former chairman of Societe Nationale des Chemins de Fer Francais (SNCF) France's state railway company was named to replace him. The same fate befell Airbus boss Gustav Humbert who was replaced by Christian Streiff a former executive at French building materials concern Compagnie de Saint-Gobain.

The production logjams at Airbus also prompted some of the company's airline customers to seek compensation in lieu of taking their business elsewhere (Boeing). EADS forecast that the production delays at Airbus would be a $2.5 billion drain on profits over four years. In the wake of the additional delivery delays Airbus CEO Christian Streiff was sent packing after only three months on the job. EADS Co-CEO Louis Gallois was named as his replacement.

In 2006 Daimler announced plans to gradually reduce its stake in EADS from about 30% to half that amount. Later that year EADS acquired Sofrelog of France (a maker of maritime monitoring systems). Russian bank Vneshtorgbank (100% controlled by the Russian government) also purchased a 5% stake in EADS for about $1.17 billion. The stake did not entitle Vneshtorgbank to a board seat but the move was expected to strengthen cooperation between EADS and the re-emerging Russian aerospace industry.

After long negotiations EADS shifted in 2007 to a new management structure aimed at cutting down on the damaging political bickering between its German and French management and shareholder factions. Politicians like German Chancellor Angela Merkel and French President Nicolas Sarkozy touted the compromise as a success. Others namely labor forces were more skeptical –calling the latest management shake-up just another round of musical chairs that leaves the power struggles between Paris and Munich largely unresolved.

EADS continued to expand into emerging markets especially regions including Asia the Middle East and North and South America. Deliveries included the company's (long-delayed) A380 model launched with Singapore Airlines in late 2008. Adding to Airbus's standing the all-new A350-XWB (made for the most part of lighter-weight composite materials) sliced into about two-thirds of jet demand in the Middle East. It also forged alliances and won contracts in Brazil China Japan and North America.

Airbus launched a cost-cutting initiative in 2008 that slashed some 10000 jobs. Dubbed Power8 the plan marched out cost-saving measures that aimed to reduce development cycles by two years and boost overall productivity by 20%. Central to Power8 was the spinoff of some of Airbus's manufacturing facilities to new partners. Partner funding of planes like the A350-XWB (spurred by assurances of subcontract work) plus plant sales risked an ongoing row between Airbus and unions as well as factory owners –stakeholders who feared plant divestitures and more job cuts. That year EADS captured its first big US military contract when Airbus North America was given the opportunity to make US Army light utility helicopters.

The company was awarded a contract to replace outdated KC-135 refueling tankers in conjunction with Northrop Grumman for the US Air Force –an upset protested by rival bidder Boeing. Soon after the Government Accountability Office (GAO) announced its findings of flaws in the bidding process. EADS and Northrop Grumman dropped out of the bidding in early 2010 with EADS vowing not to submit a proposal unless it was assured that it had a fair chance to win. By late summer – after US president Obama assured French president Nicolas Sarkozy that the Pentagon tanker bidding process would be fair –EADS announced that it would consider once again to enter into the bidding war. The contract to build the US tanker valued at approximately $35 billion went to Boeing in early 2011.

EXECUTIVES

Chief Strategy and Marketing Officer, Marwan Lahoud, age 47
Chairman North America, Ralph D. Crosby Jr., age 65
CEO and Director, Louis Gallois, age 69
CEO EADS Astrium, Francois Auque, age 57
President and CEO Airbus, Thomas (Tom) Enders, age 54
CEO North America, Sean C. O'Keefe, age 57
CTO, Jean J. Botti, age 56
President and CEO Eurocopter, Lutz Bertling, age 51
Chief Compliance Officer, Pedro Montoya, age 49
Head Corporate Communications, Pierre Bayle
Head Corporate Media Relations, Alexander Reinhardt
International Media Relations, Rod Stone
Head Airbus Military, Domingo Ure?a-Raso, age 55
Corporate Communications Spain, Jaime Perez-Guerra
SVP Latin America Strategy and Marketing, Anne Tauby
Head Investor Relations, Nathalie Errard
CFO, Harald Wilhelm
Chairman of EADS, Arnaud Lagard+?re
Chief Executive Officer - Cassidian; Member of the Executive Committee, Bernhard Bernhard Gerwert Gerwert
Head of Airbus Military; Chairman of EADS CASA; Member of the Executive Committee, Domingo Domingo Urena-Raso Urena-Raso
Chief Executive Officer - Airbus; Member of the Executive Committee, Fabrice Fabrice Bregier Bregier
Chief Operating Officer - Airbus; Member of the Executive Committee, Gunter Gunter Butschek Butschek
Chief Executive Officer - EADS North America ; Member of the Executive Committee, Sean Sean OKeefe OKeefe
Chief Human Resources Officer of EADS and Airbus; Member of the Executive Committee, Thierry Thierry Baril Baril
Non-Executive Chairman of the Board, Arnaud Arnaud Lagardere Lagardere
Director, Arnaud Lagardere, age 52
Director, Dominique D'Hinnin, age 52
Director, Lakshmi N. Mittal, age 62
Director, Michel Pebereau, age 70
CEO and Director, Louis Gallois, age 69
Director, Sir John Parker, age 69
Director, Juan Manuel Eguiagaray Ucelay, age 66
Director, Hermann-Josef Lamberti, age 56
Director, Rolf Bartke, age 66
Director, Wilfried Porth, age 54
Independent Director, Michel Michel Pebereau Pebereau
Auditors: KPMGAccountantsN.V.

LOCATIONS

HQ: Airbus Group NV
Mendelweg 30, Leiden 2333 CS
Phone:
Web: www.airbus-group.com

2010 Sales

	% of total
Europe	47
Asia/Pacific	25
Middle	13
North	8
Other	7
Total	**100**

PRODUCTS/OPERATIONS

2010 Sales

	% of total
Airbus	64
Cassidian	13
Astrium	11
Eurocopter	10
Other	2
Total	**100**

Selected Operations and Interests

Business aircraft (JV with Dassault Aviation 46%)
Commercial airplanes (Airbus)
- A320 (single-aisle aircraft)
- A330/A340
- A350 XWB (extra wide body)

Helicopters (Eurocopter SAS)
- EC135 (light twin engine)
- EC175 (multi-role)
- EC225 (Super Puma)
- EC725
- E225/ED725 (twin engine)
- NH90 (medium-weight multi-role)
- Tiger (medium-weight

Satellites (Astrium)
- Ariane 5 (heavy-lift satellite)
- Automated Transfer Vehicle (ATV)
- Eurostar 3000 (telecommunications satellite)

Security combat and missile systems (Cassidian)
- Cassidian Professional Mobile Radio (PMR)
- Eurofighter (aka " Typhoon")combat aircraft (JV with Dassault Aviation 46%)
- MBDA missile systems (JV with BAE systems and Finmeccanica)
- Radars
- Unmanned Aerial Systems (UAS; partnered with Northrop Grumman

Other businesses
- ATR (50- to 74-seat turboprop aircraft; JV with Alenia Aeronautica)
- EADS North America
- EADS UK

COMPETITORS

AgustaWestland
BAE SYSTEMS
BAE Systems Inc.
Boeing
Bombardier
E' Prime Aerospace
Embraer
GenCorp
Lockheed Martin
Northrop Grumman
Orbital Sciences
RUAG Holding
Raytheon
Textron

HISTORICAL FINANCIALS

Company Type: Public

Income Statement

FYE: December 31

	REVENUE ($ mil.)	NET INCOME ($ mil.)	NET PROFIT MARGIN	EMPLOYEES
12/12	74,443	1,618	2.2%	140,405
12/11	63,544	1,336	2.1%	133,115
12/10	61,233	740	1.2%	121,691
12/09	61,688	(1,099)	—	119,506
12/08	60,488	2,197	3.6%	118,349
Annual Growth	5.3%	(7.4%)	—	4.4%

2012 Year-End Financials

Debt ratio: 6.8%
Return on equity: 12.7%
Cash ($ mil.): 11,540
Current ratio: 0.93
Long-term debt ($ mil.): 4,621
No. of shares (mil.): 822
Dividends
Yield: 0.0%
Payout: 8.9%
Market value ($ mil.): 32,647

	STOCK PRICE ($) FY Close	P/E High/Low	PER SHARE ($) Earnings	Dividends	Book Value
12/12	39.71	48 34	1.98	0.18	16.69
12/11	31.40	53 32	1.64	0.12	14.05
12/10	23.45	74 43	0.91	0.00	14.59
12/09	19.90	— —	(1.35)	0.11	18.72
12/08	16.75	34 12	2.73	0.08	19.04
Annual Growth	24.1%	— —	(7.7%)	22.7%	(3.2%)

Aisin Seiki Co., Ltd.

Nothing stops Aisin Seiki from making its line of brake systems and powertrain components for cars. Aisin's main automotive business offers automotive-related products such as transmissions brakes and engine and car navigation systems. Its Life and Energy business offers items for more comfortable living with products that range from heating and cooling systems to toilets with jet sprays; well-care items include electric wheelchairs and reclining beds. The company has around 160 consolidated subsidiaries and companies worldwide. Separate business segments include Aisin AW Group Aisin Seiki Group Advics Group and Aisin Takaoka Group.

Operations

Aisin Seiki operates through nearly 160 subsidiaries that are spread throughout four main segments. Aisin AW Group is its largest segment (39 % of total sales in 2012) and makes automatic transmissions and car navigation systems. Aisin Seiki Group (36%) sells its automotive parts as well as its life and energy products. Advics Group is responsible for making brake components (15%) while Aisin Takaoka Group (5%) manufacturers the cart-iron parts for engines and brakes.

Financial Performance

Aisin Seiki saw its revenues increase by almost 3% from 2011 to 2012 but its net income decreased by roughly 20%. The slight jump in net sales was attributed to a 6% spike in sales from its Aisin AW Group segment. All other segments recorded a decrease in sales. The company's net income declined mainly due to a decrease in gross profits and an increase in selling general and administrative expenses.

Strategy

Aisin Seiki is looking to diversify its customer mix by expanding production overseas to achieve a 50% ratio by 2015. Its Advics segment in 2012 established production and sales companies in Haryana State North India and Karnataka State South India to produce brake parts that meet market demand and promote local procurement. To penetrate the most populous market in the word Advics also established a production company in Guangdong China that year.

Aisin Seiki continues to make automotive components and systems but it also focuses on increasing sales of main products such as transmissions car navigation systems and power sliding doors. The company's business segments have worked autonomously in the past; however Aisin Seiki is working to combine and link its individual businesses thus strengthening and maximizing the potential of the products and technologies that are cultivated by each company.

HISTORY

Aisin Seiki traces its roots to 1943 when Tokai Hikoki was founded to produce airplane engines for the Japanese war effort. After the war the company switched to manufacturing sewing machines and auto parts. Aisin Seiki took its present name in 1965 after Tokai Hikoki merged with Shinkawa Kogyo.

The company's operations were limited to Japan until 1969 when it signed a technical agreement with a German company regarding steering gears. International expansion continued as Aisin Seiki formed Aisin USA (to import aftermarket parts for imported cars) in 1970 Aisin Europe in 1971 and Aisin (UK) and Aisin (Australia) Pty. in 1972. Other operations sprung up in Mexico (1973) Brazil (1974) Singapore (1977) and Germany

(1978). In the late 1980s the company worked at expanding the sale of body components such as sunroofs and seats.

Although Aisin Seiki USA had been formed to import parts for imported cars by 1990 the unit imported more parts for domestic cars than it did for imports. In 1996 Aisin Seiki set up Tangshan Aisin Gear a joint venture with Tangshan Gear Works to produce manual transmissions in China. The next year the company's Kariya plant which produced brake and clutch parts used in many Toyotas burned down. The disruption forced Toyota — which accounted for about 80% of the Kariya plant's sales —to temporarily shut down its 20 Japanese auto plants. Also in 1997 Aisin Seiki formed Aisin GM Allison Co. a joint venture with General Motors to produce automatic transmissions in Japan and the Pacific Rim region. Aisin GM Allison was dissolved in 2007 as GM geared up to sell Allison Transmission.

In 1998 the company formed Aisin Europe Manufacturing in the UK its first manufacturing facility in Europe. Also that year it began work on subsidiary Aisin A W Co. to supply engine parts for the Toyota facility in West Virginia. Despite increasing sales Aisin Seiki announced in 2000 that it would post a loss due to a charge for retirement benefits.

EXECUTIVES

Auditor, Minoru Hayashi, age 70
Chairman, Kanshiro Toyoda, age 71
Vice Chairman, Yasuhito Yamauchi, age 69
Senior Managing Director and Director, Toshikazu Nagura
Managing Officer, Kenji Tsujimura
President and Director, Fumio Fujimori
EVP and Director, Shunichi Nakamura
Senior Managing Director and Director, Takashi Morita
Senior Managing Director and Director, Naofumi Fujie
Managing Officer, Takashi Enomoto
Managing Officer, Masayasu Saito
Managing Officer, Kazumi Usami
Senior Managing Director and Director, Makoto Mitsuya
Senior Managing Director and Director, Toshiyuki Mizushima
Managing Officer, Yoshiaki Kato
Managing Officer, Hitoshi Okabe
Senior Managing Director and Director, Yutaka Miyamoto
Auditor, Toshihiro Gonda
Auditor, Shoichiro Toyoda
Auditor, Ryo Kobayashi
Managing Officer, Yoshihiko Kanada
Managing Officer, Seiichi Takahashi
Managing Officer, Shinsuke Yagi
Managing Officer, Masayasu Sugiura
Managing Officer, Susumu Takase
Managing Officer, Ryuji Nakamura
Managing Officer, Naoki Katsurayama
Managing Officer, Masanobu Ishikawa
Managing Officer, Naoshi Ichino
Managing Officer, Takahisa Hirose
Vice Chairman, Yasuhito Yamauchi, age 69
Director, Toshiyuki Ishikawa
EVP and Director, Norio Oku, age 66
Senior Managing Director and Director, Toshikazu Nagura
President and Director, Fumio Fujimori
Director, Takeshi Kawata
EVP and Director, Shunichi Nakamura
Director, Tsuneo Uchimoto
Senior Managing Director and Director, Shinichiro Yamamura
Senior Managing Director and Director, Takashi Morita
Senior Managing Director and Director, Naofumi Fujie
Senior Managing Director and Director, Shizuo Shimanuki
Senior Managing Director and Director, Makoto Mitsuya
Senior Managing Director and Director, Toshiyuki Mizushima
Director, Masahiro Suo
Director, Tsutomu Ishikawa
Senior Managing Director and Director, Yutaka Miyamoto
Auditors: ChuoAoyamaAuditCorporation

LOCATIONS

HQ: Aisin Seiki Co., Ltd.
2-1 Asahi-machi, Kariya, Aichi 448-8650
Phone: (81) 566 24 8265
Web: www.aisin.co.jp

PRODUCTS/OPERATIONS

2012 Sales

	% of total
Aisin AW	39
Aisin Seiki	36
Advics	15
Aisin Takaoka	5
Other	5
Total	**100**

2012 Sales by Products

	% of total
Drivetrain	45
Brake &	20
Body-related	16
Engine-related	10
Information-related	5
Life energy &	4
Total	**100**

Selected Products

Automotive
- Drivetrain products (transmission and clutch systems)
- Brake and chassis products (drum brakes master cylinders air suspension systems)
- Body products (door frames and locks sunroofs power seats)
- Engine products (water pumps pistons exhaust manifolds)
- Information and other products (navigation systems Intelligent Parking Assist)
- Aftermarket products

Energy System
- GHP
- Cogeneration system
- Cryopump
- Cryocooler
- Peltier modules

Life and Amenity
- Bed furniture and fabric (ASLEEP)
- Housing equipment
- House remodeling service (Livelan)
- Home-use sewing machine
- Embroidery machine
- Facility consulting service (CONTRACT)
- Business consulting service (TSS)
- Audio equipment

COMPETITORS

APM Automotive
BorgWarner
Calsonic Kansei
DENSO
DURA Automotive
Dana Holding
Delphi Automotive Systems
Eaton
Faurecia
Haldex
Hitachi America
Lear Corp
Magna International
Meritor
Mitsubishi Electric
Modine Manufacturing
Panasonic Corp
Robert Bosch
Sumitomo Electric
TRW Automotive
Tenneco
Torotrak
Valeo
Visteon
ZF Friedrichshafen

HISTORICAL FINANCIALS

Company Type: Public

Income Statement

FYE: March 31

	REVENUE ($ mil.)	NET INCOME ($ mil.)	NET PROFIT MARGIN	EMPLOYEES
03/13	26,888	823	3.1%	83,378
03/12	28,089	676	2.4%	78,212
03/11	27,261	841	3.1%	74,671
03/10	21,994	177	0.8%	73,213
03/09	22,487	(255)	—	73,201
Annual Growth	4.6%	—	—	3.3%

2013 Year-End Financials

Debt ratio: 0.1%
Return on equity: 9.8%
Cash ($ mil.): 2,268
Current ratio: 1.47
Long-term debt ($ mil.): 2,853
No. of shares (mil.): 281
Dividends
Yield: —
Payout: —
Market value ($ mil.): 8,625

	STOCK PRICE ($) FY Close	P/E High/Low	PER SHARE ($) Earnings	Dividends	Book Value
03/13	30.60	— —	2.92	0.00	42.85
03/12	36.71	— —	2.40	0.00	41.94
03/11	24.25	— —	2.99	0.00	39.39
03/10	24.25	— —	0.63	0.00	33.19
Annual Growth	8.1%	— —	46.7%	—	6.6%

Akzo Nobel N.V. (Netherlands)

Akzo Nobel may be the world's largest paint manufacturer but it does more than just paint a pretty picture. The company is also among the world's largest chemical manufacturers and salt producers. Akzo Nobel divides its business into three main lines: Decorative Paints which produces consumer and commercial paints and primarily serves Europe and North America; Performance Coatings which manufactures marine and protective coatings packaging coatings automotive finishes and industrial coatings; and Specialty Chemicals which makes pulp and paper chemicals functional chemicals (flame retardants crop nutrients) industrial chemicals (salt and chlor-alkalis) surfactants and specialty starches.

Akzo Nobel's products include such brands as Dulux Eka International and Sikkens. Since its merger with ICI Akzo Nobel has established a global leadership position in Decorative Paints enjoying economies of scale while expanding its global footprint. In the US it has introduced its products in Wal-mart and relaunched the Glidden brand for its Home Depot sales. In Canada it markets through major retailer RONA. It has strengthened its presence in the high-growth markets of Asia Latin America and Eastern Europe. In China it has penetrated mass markets and in India it is gaining momentum with an investment in its flagship Dulux brand.

The company's Performance Coatings segment is represented in most markets of the industry including general industrial coatings for metals and plastic; and protective coatings for oil and gas airports and stadia power generation mining and minerals and water and wastewater markets. The segment holds market leadership positions in marine coatings protective coatings and yacht coatings and it also supplies coatings for commercial vehicles and aircraft. Its powder coatings unit provides electrostatically applied coatings that are sprayed and then cured by applying heat. And its wood finishes and adhesives are used for furniture flooring cabinets windows and doors.

Akzo Nobel's Specialty Chemicals segment holds a number of leading positions for various chemicals such as ethyline amines salt specialties and organic peroxides produced by its functional chemicals unit. Its industrial chemicals unit also is a leading producer of caustic lye and chlorine in Europe as well as salt. The pulp and paper chemicals unit produces bleaching chemicals and silica additives. The segment's products are used to make a number of everyday items including cosmetics detergents disinfectants ice cream paper plastics and soaps.

Akzo Nobel operates in more than 80 countries but most of its holdings are in Western Europe North America and the Asia/Pacific. It is expanding in emerging markets within Latin America and Eastern Europe.

Despite a globally challenging environment Akzo Nobel's revenues grew 7% in fiscal 2011 driven by higher pricing to offset increases in the cost of raw materials. However weak end markets and higher costs adversely affected the company's results and net income dropped to E477 ($585.4 million) compared to net income of E754 ($925 million) in fiscal 2010. The company's Specialty Chemicals and Performance Coatings segments both reported 8% growth in 2011 while its Decorative Paints unit grew 7%.

The company's strategy is to invest in its brands distribution system and people with a focus on expansion in mid-tier markets. Akzo Nobel is concentrating on growth in regions such as Asia Eastern Europe and Latin America as demand begins to decline in mature markets such as Western Europe and North America (though those two regions still account for about half of Akzo Nobel's business). In addition to growing in strong emerging markets the company seeks strategic bolt-on acquisitions and continues to make significant investments.

As part of its three-year performance improvement program launched in late 2011 Azko Nobel has been restructuring business lines such as its European and North American decorative paints and its performance coatings' wood finishes and adhesives. The company has managed to raise prices enough in 2012 to offset most of the raw material price increases. Although the costs of titanium dioxide continue to rise Akzo Nobel has been successful in passing on most of its raw material cost increases.

In early 2012 the company completed its acquisition of Boxing Oleochemicals a leading Chinese surfactants producer. Boxing makes nitrile amines and derivatives used for industrial and consumer applications ranging from asphalt additives to fabric softeners. The buy enhances Azko Nobel's position in specialty surfactants and broadens its reach in Asia. Boxing's operations will be integrated into the company's Surface Chemistry unit.

It is investing in a Ningbo China facility to convert a chlorine plant in Frankfurt to its membrane electrolysis technology. It is investing in Brazil also to supply two of the world's largest pulp mills.

In early 2012 the company also moved to strengthen its packaging coatings operations by trying to acquire the part of Italy's Packaging Coatings Metlac Group it doesn't own (it holds a 49% stake). However the UK's office of Fair Trading put the brakes on the deal because of competition concerns and referred the case to the UK's Competition Commission. Both Metlac and Akzo Nobel supply metal packaging coatings used in food and beverage cans.

In 2012 Akzon Nobel split its ICI Pakistan subsidiary into two new companies: AkzoNobel Pakistan Limited (comprising the paints and specialty chemicals business) and ICI Pakistan Limited (comprising all other businesses of ICI Pakistan). In the process AkzoNobel maintains 76% control of the paints business while seeking a buyer for ICI Pakistan.

To expand its industrial coatings business Akzo Nobel acquired Germany-based Schramm Holding in 2011. Akzo Nobel believes the acquisition makes it the global leader for specialty plastic coatings for the lucrative market serving mobile devices laptops TVs and auto interiors. Also in 2011 Akzo Nobel opened a new coatings plant in India.

That year the company's Decorative Paints unit expanded with the company's entry into a partnership in China with Quangxi CAVA Titanium Industry Co. to ensure a supply of titanium dioxide. It also invested E110 million ($135 million) in 2011 in a replacement manufacturing plant in the North East of England.

To raise cash to pay down debt in 2012 AkzoNobel agreed to divest its North American Decorative Paints business to PPG Industries for $1.05 billion.

HISTORY

The Akzo side of Akzo Nobel traces its roots to two companies —German rayon and coatings maker Vereinigte Glanzstoff-Fabriken (founded 1899) and Dutch rayon maker Nederlandsche Kunstzijdebariek (founded 1911 and known as NK or Enka). In 1928 NK built a plant near Asheville North Carolina in what later became the town of Enka. The two companies merged in 1929 to create Algemene Kunstzijde-Unie (AKU).

In 1967 two Dutch companies merged to form Koninklijke Zout-Organon (KZO). Two years later KZO bought US-based International Salt and merged with AKU to form Akzo. In the 1980s Akzo focused on building its chemicals coatings and pharmaceuticals businesses. Akzo sold its paper and pulp business to Nobel in 1993. A few months later the company reclaimed that business when it bought Nobel.

Best remembered for the prizes that bear his name (which were first awarded in 1901 through a bequest in his will) Alfred Nobel invented the blasting cap in 1863 making it possible to control the detonation of nitroglycerin. He then persuaded Stockholm merchant J. W. Smitt to help him finance Nitroglycerin Ltd. to make and sell the volatile fluid (1864). Nobel's quest to improve nitroglycerin led to his invention of dynamite in 1867.

After Nobel's death in 1896 Nitroglycerin Ltd. remained an explosives maker and in 1965 it changed its name to Nitro Nobel. In 1978 Swedish industrialist Marcus Wallenberg bought Nitro Nobel for his KemaNord chemical group known afterward as KemaNobel. Within six years industrialist Erik Penser controlled both KemaNobel and armaments maker Bofors and he merged them in 1984 as Nobel Industries.

Risky investments led Penser to ruin in 1991. His holdings including Nobel were taken over by a government-owned bank and conveyed into Securum a state-owned holding company (which still owns 18% of Akzo Nobel). In 1992 Nobel spun off its consumer-goods segment.

Akzo bought Nobel in 1994. Although the company had good financial results in 1995 it faced pressure from rising costs for raw materials and a difficult foreign-exchange environment. Akzo announced major closings and layoffs —it sold its polyethylene packaging resin business and moved some clothing-grade rayon operations to Poland.

The merger between Akzo and Nobel was legally completed in 1996. That year the company introduced Puregon a fertility drug and Remeron touted as a replacement for Prozac in the US and other countries. In 1997 Akzo Nobel put most of its worst-performing segment fibers into a joint venture with Turkish conglomerate Sabanci. It also sold its North American salt unit to Cargill.

Akzo Nobel acquired Courtaulds (coatings sealants and fibers) in 1998 and changed the firm's name to Akzo Nobel UK. AkzoNobel also bought BASF deco the European decorative-coatings business of BASF Coatings. Akzo Nobel combined its fiber business with AkzoNobel UK to form a new division Acordis. AkzoNobel then sold Acordis to investment firm CVC Capital Partners in 1999 for $859 million (AkzoNobel retains a minority share). That year AkzoNobel bought Hoechst's animal-health unit Hoechst Roussel Vet for $712 million. In 2000 the company bought Dexter Corporation's aircraft coatings business.

In 2001 Akzo Nobel sold its medical diagnostics division to French drugmaker bioMerieux-Pierre Fabre. Later that year the company picked up the vehicle refinishes business of MAC Specialty Coatings of the US. It also agreed to sell its printing inks business to a private equity firm.

CEO Cees van Lede retired in mid-2003 succeeded by Hans Wijers who immediately set about restructuring cutting costs and erasing debt. By year's end more than 3300 jobs were cut and AkzoNobel had sold off three big chemical units: catalysts (to Albemarle for about $750 million) coating resins and phosphorous chemicals (to Ripplewood Holdings for another $270 million).

The fruits of those sell-offs came with 2005 acquisitions in Germany France and Switzerland. The last purchase of Swiss Lack made Akzo Nobel the largest paint company in Switzerland as well. The following year the company made a bigger buy that of Canadian coatings maker Sico for $285 million.

Also in 2006 Akzo Nobel decided to pare down its operations further with the sale of its inks and adhesive resins business to Hexion Specialty Chemicals. The business was concentrated in Europe but had strong international operations as well. The deal brought the company about $100 million.

Early in 2006 Akzo announced plans to split off its pharmaceuticals segment Organon. It originally planned to float a minority share early in 2007 and then fully separate the new company by 2009. In a surprise move however Schering-Plough came in and bought the unit for $14.4 billion.

In what turned out to be a major turning point for the company Akzo Nobel approached UK coatings and chemicals maker ICI with a $14 billion takeover offer in late 2007. ICI's board rejected the price tag as insufficient. Akzo Nobel countered twice and ended up agreeing to a deal worth $16 billion. As part of the deal Henkel bought the adhesives and electronic materials businesses of ICI subsidiary National Starch and Chemical. The buy of ICI built up Akzo's coatings business even further. The acquired businesses have great strength in retail decorative paints and in North America both areas in which Akzo Nobel's coatings business had been lacking.

Another business acquired in the deal was Akzo Nobel's new Chemicals Pakistan division which was composed of the company's majority holdings in two publicly traded companies. Those subsidiaries made soda ash polyester fibers and pure terephthalic acid (PTA). In 2009 though the company sold its 75% stake in the subsidiary that makes PTA to Korean manufacturer KP Chemical.

Akzo Nobel subsidiary National Starch acquired Penford Australia's specialty grain wet milling and manufacturing facility in 2009 expanding National

Starch's reach into the Asia/Pacific region. However in 2010 Corn Products International (renamed Ingredion) acquired National Starch for $2.7 billion.

In 2010 Akzo Nobel acquired the powder coatings business of Dow Chemical Company. The deal brought technological know-how and significant synergy potential to Akzo Nobel's Powder Coatings line and enhanced the company's position in the US.

EXECUTIVES

Chairman, Karel Vuursteen, age 72
Deputy Chairman, Uwe-Ernst Bufe, age 69
Managing Director Canada AkzoNobel Decorative Paints, Pierre Dufresne
Managing Director AkzoNobel Marine and Protective Coatings, Bill McPherson
Member Board of Management Performance Coatings, Leif Darner, age 61, $803,415 total compensation
Corporate Director Communications, John McLaren
Member Management Committee Research Development & Innovation, Graeme D. Armstrong, age 49
Managing Director AkzoNobel Functional Chemicals, Robert (Bob) Margevich
Managing Director AkzoNobel Surface Chemistry, Frank Sherman
Managing Director AkzoNobel Powder Coatings, Rob Molenaar
Managing Director Continental Europe AkzoNobel Decorative Paints, Antoine Fady
Member Board of Management Integrated Supply Chain, Werner Fuhrmann
CFO, Keith Nichols, age 53, $771,324 total compensation
Managing Director AkzoNobel Polymer Chemicals, Alan Kwek, age 55
Corporate Director Purchasing, Ton Geurts
Managing Director Latin America AkzoNobel Decorative Paints, Jaap Kuiper
Media Officer, Tineke Dikken
Head of External Relations, Tim van der Zanden
General Counsel, Sven Dumoulin
Media Officer Specialty Chemicals and Performance Coatings, Oskar Bosson
Managing Director Northern and Eastern Europe AkzoNobel Decorative Paints, Ruud Joosten
Managing Director U.S. AkzoNobel Decorative Paints, Erik Bouts
Corporate Director Control, Hans de Vriese, age 48
Managing Director AkzoNobel Industrial Finishes, Bob Taylor
Member Board of Management Decorative Paints, Louis W. (Tex) Gunning, age 64, $544,616 total compensation
Managing Director UK Ireland and South Africa Building Adhesives AkzoNobel Decorative Paints, Richard Stuckes
Manager Investor Relations, Ivar Smits
Corporate Director Strategy and Mergers and Acquisitions, Jennifer Midura
Member of the Executive Committee; Responsible for Performance Coatings, Conrad Keijzer
Secretary Investor Relations, Els van der Hulst
Media Officer Decorative Paints, Christian Tardif
Managing Director South East Asia and Pacific AkzoNobel Decorative Paints, Jeremy Rowe
Managing Director India and South Asia AkzoNobel Decorative Paints, Amit Jain
Member Board of Management HR and Organizational Development, Marjan Oudeman, age 55
Corporate Director Investor Relations, Jonathan Atack
Vice President Corporate HR & Life Sciences, Asif Malik
Director, Antony Burgmans, age 66
Director, Peter Ellwood, age 69
Deputy Chairman, Uwe-Ernst Bufe, age 69
Director, Peggy B. Bruzelius, age 64
Director, Baroness Virginia Bottomley, age 65
Director, Dolf van den Brink, age 65
Director, Louis R. Hughes, age 65
Member of the Supervisory Board, Ben Verwaayen
Member of the Supervisory Board, Dolf Brink
Member of the Supervisory Board, Sari Baldauf
Auditors: KPMGAccountantsN.V.

LOCATIONS

HQ: Akzo Nobel N.V. (Netherlands)
Strawinskylaan 2555, P.O. Box 75730, Amsterdam 1070 AS
Phone: (31) 20 502 7555 **Fax:** (31) 20 502 7666
Web: www.akzonobel.com

2011 Sales

	% of total
Europe	
Western	38
Eastern	7
Asia/Pacific	22
North	20
Latin	10
Other	3
Total	**100**

PRODUCTS/OPERATIONS

2011 Sales

	$ mil.	% of total
Specialty Chemicals	34	
Performance Coatings	33	

Selected Products

Specialty chemicals
- Base chemicals
- Functional chemicals
- Polymer chemicals
- Pulp and paper chemicals
- Surfactants

Decorative paints
Performance coatings
- Car refinishes
- Industrial finishes
- Marine and protective coatings
- Powder coatings

COMPETITORS

Alfa SA
Asahi Kasei
BASF SE
Compass Minerals
DuPont
Eastman Chemical
Evonik Degussa
Ferro
Formosa Plastics
H.B. Fuller
Orica
PPG Industries
Sherwin-Williams
Valspar

HISTORICAL FINANCIALS

Company Type: Public

Income Statement

FYE: December 31

	REVENUE ($ mil.)	NET INCOME ($ mil.)	NET PROFIT MARGIN	EMPLOYEES
12/12	20,284	(2,858)	—	50,610
12/11	20,303	616	3.0%	57,240
12/10	19,593	1,009	5.2%	55,590
12/09	20,013	410	2.1%	57,060
12/08	21,551	(1,518)	—	60,040
Annual Growth	(1.5%)	—	—	(4.2%)

2012 Year-End Financials

Debt ratio: 29.7%
Return on equity: (-26.8%)
Cash ($ mil.): 2,309
Current ratio: 1.39
Long-term debt ($ mil.): 4,465
No. of shares (mil.): 239
Dividends
Yield: 2.2%
Payout: —
Market value ($ mil.): 5,379

	STOCK PRICE ($) FY Close	P/E High/Low		PER SHARE ($) Earnings	Dividends	Book Value
12/12	22.50	—	—	(12.05)	0.50	38.00
12/11	48.30	74	35	2.61	1.06	50.77
12/10	62.13	40	25	4.30	1.49	51.49
12/09	66.30	121	48	1.74	2.31	48.22
12/08	41.72	—	—	(6.10)	2.66	45.04
Annual Growth	(14.3%)	—	—	—	(34.2%)	(4.2%)

Alcatel-Lucent

Alcatel-Lucent found its calling: supplying high-tech equipment for telecommunications networks. The company's core network products unit sells network switching and transmission systems for wireline and wireless networks terrestrial and submarine optical systems microwave radio products and fixed-access gear. Its software and services division develops applications for IP television digital payment messaging and mobile communications while services range from application and systems integration to managed services and maintenance. Alcatel-Lucent's enterprise division provides corporate and government clients with unified communications systems data networking gear and contact center systems.

Alcatel-Lucent has undergone extensive integration and restructuring efforts since its formation in 2006 when Alcatel and Lucent Technologies merged. The company has struggled with organizational changes in a market that has been particularly hard-hit by a weak economy. Cost-cutting initiatives have included inking a 10-year alliance with Hewlett-Packard for HP to take over Alcatel-Lucent's IT infrastructure. The deal signed in 2009 also included a plan for joint product marketing.

Higher sales volumes and cuts in fixed operation expenses in general brought good results for Alcatel-Lucent in 2010. Revenue at the company was up more than 5% in 2010 over 2009. Gross profit went up to more than 34% in 2010 compared to more than 33% in 2009. More specifically Alcatel-Lucent enjoyed strong percentage growth in its IP division (24%) wireless business (14.6%) and networks segment (6.2%) but it weathered declines in its wireline and optic businesses down 4.4.% and 7% respectively.

Strong demand in the mobile market and other beneficial economic factors led to a 21% increase in 2010 US sales especially in the IP and wireless categories. Mainly because of poor demand in its wireless business European sales were weak that year. The European segment represented more than 31% of revenue in 2010 compared with more than 34% in 2009. Sales in Asia/Pacific were down 2% in 2010 compared with 2009 primarily because China decreased spending after a big 2009 push for 3G networks.

As consumers demand more from their smartphones and other devices Alcatel-Lucent is shifting the focus of its research and development efforts. In 2008 the company spent about 75% of its 2.5 billion-euro R&D budget on improving existing technologies. In 2010 the company spent 75% of that same R&D budget on new technologies.

The company's acquisition and divestiture strategy has aimed at building its service provider product portfolio and jettisoning non-core businesses. The company bought France-based mobile software and application development tool maker

OpenPlug in 2010. Late that year it sold its Adixen vacuum pump business to Germany-based Pfeiffer Vacuum Technology for E200 million (about $279 million). The business —which makes vacuum pumps leak detectors gauges plasma sensors valves flanges and fittings under the ADIXEN brand —was not considered core to Alcatel-Lucent's long-term strategy. The vacuum pump unit fits better as part of Pfeiffer Vacuum which also gained an expanded international sales network and access to Asian markets.

In 2011 Alcatel-Lucent announced receipt of a binding offer for its call center services unit Genesys. The UK-based private equity firm Permira proposed $1.5 billion for the business. Alcatel-Lucent had been considering its options with its entire Enterprise Applications unit ultimately deciding Genesys wasn't necessary to that business' contributions to a unified communications and data networking strategy.

HISTORY

In 1898 Pierre Azaria combined his electric generating company with three others to form Compagnie Generale d'Electricite (CGE). As one of Europe's pioneering electric power and manufacturing companies CGE expanded operations in France and abroad through acquisitions. After the French government nationalized electric utilities in 1946 CGE diversified into the production of telecommunications equipment consumer appliances and electronics.

In 1970 CGE bought Alcatel a French communications firm founded in 1879 that had introduced digital switching exchanges. CGE combined its telecom division with Alcatel to form CIT Alcatel.

The Mitterrand government nationalized CGE in 1982. The next year the company traded its electronics units for Thomson's communications businesses making CGE the world's fifth-largest telephone equipment maker. Later CGE combined Alcatel with ITT's phone equipment operations to form Alcatel NV a Brussels-based company that started off as the world's second-largest telecom enterprise after AT&T.

In 1987 the government sold CGE to the public. Two years later CGE and UK-based The General Electric Company plc (GEC now Marconi plc) combined their power systems and engineering businesses to create GEC Alsthom NV. The company adopted the Alcatel Alsthom name in 1991 (shortened to Alcatel in 1998) and purchased the transmission equipment unit of US-based Rockwell International (now Rockwell Automation).

Turnaround specialist Serge Tchuruk the former head of French oil giant TOTAL was chosen to lead the company in 1995. Deregulation and intense competition in the European telecom market along with massive write-offs of bad investments dating back to the 1980s led to a $5 billion loss in 1995 Alcatel's first loss and one of the largest to date by a French company. As a result Alcatel divested nonstrategic assets and cut its workforce by more than 12500 employees. The company bounced back with a profit in 1996.

Following the recommendation of the French government in 1998 Alcatel Dassault Industries and Aerospatiale joined forces to buy part of the state's stake in defense electronics group Thomson-CSF (now Thales). Intensifying its telecommunications focus Alcatel sold its main engineering unit (Cegelec) to GEC Alsthom in 1998 and then spun off the venture as ALSTOM. That year Alcatel bought networking specialists Packet Engines and DSC Communications to further push into the US market.

In 1999 Alcatel acquired several more US-based data network equipment makers including Xylan and Assured Access. The next year it swapped all but 10% of its stake in nuclear power company Framatome for an additional 10% of Thomson-CSF. The company pressed further into the US that year with the purchases of Genesys Telecommunications (computer-telephony software) and Canadian equipment maker Newbridge Networks.

Alcatel changed the name of its power and communication cables business one of the world's largest cable manufacturing operations to Nexans in 2000. The company also sold 20% of its optical components unit to create the first European tracking stock. Alcatel acquired Genesys Telecommunications Laboratories in 2000.

Genesys acquired IBM's CallPath computer-telephony software unit in 2001. Alcatel also took control of its satellite communications joint venture with Thales. A market slowdown that year led Alcatel to announce staff cuts of about 10%.

In mid-2001 Alcatel spun off Nexans to the public (it sold its remaining minority stake in the company in 2004) unloaded the rest of ALSTOM and bought a controlling stake in its joint venture in China with Shanghai Bell. The company beefed up its line of fiber-optic products when it bought passive component maker Kymata that year.

Alcatel sold its enterprise distribution and services operations in Europe in 2002 to Platinum Equity. The company also sold several of its European manufacturing facilities to contractor Sanmina-SCI; items produced at these locations included point-to-point microwave systems and wireline network access systems.

The company added to its optical transport products for metro networks with the acquisition of startup Astral Point that year and it announced that it would acquire privately held Telera a US-based provider of software for making Web content accessible by phone in order to strengthen Genesys' contact center software business. That year it sold its semiconductor business Alcatel Microelectronics to STMicroelectronics for about $345 million; the two companies will jointly develop chipsets for DSL networking equipment.

Alcatel bought iMagic and PacketVideo in 2003 as part of an effort to gain ground in the video networking market. The company that year also sold its power systems unit which comprised AEG SVS Power Supply Systems Alcatel Converters Harmer & Simmons and the Saft Power Systems business lines. It boosted its wireless equipment portfolio with the acquisition of mobile network switching products maker Spatial Wireless for $250 million in 2004. Alcatel also turned its attention to its IP routing products with the acquisitions of eDial and TiMetra that year. It acquired UK-based Native Networks a provider of carrier-class Ethernet network transport technology for $55 million in cash in 2005.

In 2006 Alcatel purchased a stake in home networking specialist 2Wire. (2Wire was sold to Pace in 2010.) It also acquired voice recognition software developer VoiceGenie Technologies through its contact center software unit Genesys.

Alcatel acquired US rival Lucent Technologies for $11.6 billion in late 2006 forming a new organization called Alcatel-Lucent. Tchuruk became chairman of the combined company; Lucent chief Patricia Russo was named CEO.

After the merger Alcatel-Lucent acquired the UMTS access network assets of Nortel Networks for $320 million.

In 2007 the company divested its stakes in two satellite-related joint ventures it formed with Finmeccanica: Alcatel Alenia Space and Telespazio Holding. It sold the satellite businesses along with transportation and security holdings to Thales increasing its stake in the defense giant to about 21%.

With Alcaltel-Lucent's losses widening both Tchuruk and Russo stepped down in 2008. The company named Philippe Camus and Ben Verwaayen to take over as chairman and CEO respectively.

Also in 2008 the company acquired Motive a developer of remote network management software used by service providers to deploy and support residential gateways for $68 million. It also sold its remaining 21% share of defense contractor Thales to airplane maker Dassault Aviation for $2.3 billion.

In 2009 Alcatel-Lucent bought UK-based content delivery network infrastructure and services provider Velocix. The deal was intended to expand the company's portfolio of services for ISPs and media companies. Velocix specialized in products that digitally delivered media content.

EXECUTIVES

SEVP and CFO, Paul J. Tufano, age 59
EVP; President Quality Assurance and Customer Care, Janet G. Davidson
Chairman, Philippe Camus, age 65
Chief Marketing and Communications Officer; President Europe Middle East and Africa, Stephen A. Carter, age 48
SEVP Sales, Robert Vrij, age 49
SEVP Operations, Philippe Guillemot, age 54
Corporate Media Relations, Mary Ward
CEO, Michel Combes, age 51
EVP; President Applications; CEO Genesys, Paul Segre
President IP Routing and Transport, Basil Alwan
President Wireless, Dave Geary
Executive Vice President of Alcatel-Lucent and President of a recently formed, Kenneth Frank
EVP; President Bell Laboratories, Jeong H. Kim, age 52
Chairman Management Board Deutschland, Alf H. Wulf, age 50
EVP Business and Information Technology Transformation, Robin Dargue
Executive Vice President of Alcatel-Lucent and President, Adolfo Hernandez
SVP Public Affairs, Gabrielle Gauthey
President Asia/Pacific, Rajeev Singh-Molares
President Enterprise succeeding, Tom Burns
General Counsel, Steve Reynolds
President 4G/LTE Wireless Networks, Ken Wirth
Vice President Alcatel-Lucent Ventures and Bell, Wim Sweldens
CEO Alcatel-Lucent Bell and VP Benelux, Luc Defieuw
Country Head India, Munish Seth
SEVP Strategy and Innovation, Philippe Keryer
VP Human Resources and Transformation, Christel Heydemann
EVP and Head of Operations, Rod Powell
President IP Platform, Andrew McDonald
President Fixed Networks, Federico Guillen
Director, Jean C. Monty, age 66
Director, Jean-Cyril Spinetta, age 70
CEO and Director, Bernardus J. (Ben) Verwaayen, age 60
Director, Stuart E. Eizenstat, age 71
Director, Olivier Piou, age 55
Director, Lady Sylvia Jay, age 66
Director, Carla Cico, age 52
Director, Daniel Bernard, age 66
Director, W. Frank Blount, age 74
Director, Louis R. Hughes, age 65
Auditors: Deloitte&Associes

LOCATIONS

HQ: Alcatel-Lucent
3 avenue Octave Greard, Paris 75007
Phone: (33) 1 40 76 10 10 **Fax:** (33) 1 40 76 14 00
Web: www.alcatel-lucent.com

2011 Sales

	$ mil.	% of total
Americas		
US	36	
Other countries	10	
Europe		
France	8	
Other countries	21	
Asia Pacific		
China	8	
Other countries	9	
Other regions	8	
Total	**0**	**100**

PRODUCTS/OPERATIONS

2011 Sales

	% of total
Networks	62
Software services &	28
Enterprise	8
Other	2
Total	**100**

COMPETITORS

Avaya
Brocade Communications
Cisco Systems
Corning
ECI Telecom
Ericsson
Fujitsu
Harris Corp.
Hitachi
Huawei Technologies
Juniper Networks
Motorola Solutions
NEC
Nokia Siemens Networks
Nortel Networks
Panasonic Mobile Communications
Tellabs
Toshiba
UTStarcom
ZTE
telent

HISTORICAL FINANCIALS

Company Type: Public

Income Statement FYE: December 31

	REVENUE ($ mil.)	NET INCOME ($ mil.)	NET PROFIT MARGIN	EMPLOYEES
12/12	19,040	(1,811)	—	72,344
12/11	19,824	1,416	7.1%	76,002
12/10	21,408	(447)	—	79,796
12/09	21,834	(754)	—	78,373
12/08	23,745	(7,291)	—	77,717
Annual Growth	(5.4%)	—	—	(1.8%)

2012 Year-End Financials

Debt ratio: 29.6%
Return on equity: (-47.2%)
Cash ($ mil.): 4,482
Current ratio: 1.28
Long-term debt ($ mil.): 5,211
No. of shares (mil.): —
Dividends
Yield: —
Payout: —
Market value ($ mil.): —

	STOCK PRICE ($) FY Close	P/E High/Low	PER SHARE ($) Earnings	Dividends	Book Value
12/12	1.39	— —	(0.80)	0.00	1.13
12/11	1.56	26 5	0.54	0.00	2.20
12/10	2.96	— —	(0.20)	0.00	2.10
12/09	3.32	— —	(0.33)	0.00	2.38
12/08	2.15	— —	(3.23)	0.00	2.87
Annual Growth	(10.3%)	— —	—	—	(20.7%)

Alecta pensionsforsakring, omsesidigt (Sweden)

LOCATIONS

HQ: Alecta pensionsforsakring, omsesidigt (Sweden)
Regeringsgatan 107, Stockholm SE-103 73
Phone: (46) 8 441 60 00 **Fax:** (46) 8 441 62 90
Web: www.alecta.com

HISTORICAL FINANCIALS

Company Type: Public

Income Statement FYE: December 31

	ASSETS ($ mil.)	NET INCOME ($ mil.)	INCOME AS % OF ASSETS	EMPLOYEES
12/12	85,837	10,446	12.2%	426
12/11	72,503	(13,343)	—	445
12/10	75,552	4,876	6.5%	459
12/09	66,096	12,758	19.3%	560
12/08	55,139	(12,255)	—	572
Annual Growth	11.7%	—	—	(7.1%)

2012 Year-End Financials

Return on assets: 12.8%
Return on equity: 50.7%
Long-term debt ($ mil.): —
No. of shares (mil.): —
Sales ($ mil): 12,445
Dividends
Yield: —
Payout: —
Market value ($ mil.): —

Alimentation-Couche Tard, Inc.

Alimentation Couche-Tard can gas up you and your car on both sides of the US-Canada border. It's the second-largest convenience store operator in North America and the leader in Canada with some 5875 outlets: Couche-Tard in Quebec; Mac's in central and western Canada; and more than 3500-plus Circle K shops in more than 40 US states. (It bought the Circle K chain in the US from ConocoPhillips in 2003.) Nearly 80% of its sales are rung up in the US. Alimentation Couche-Tard French for "food for those who go to bed late" sells gas at more than two-thirds of its stores. With an eye on Europe fast-growing Couche-Tard has acquired Statoil Fuel & Retail the largest acquisition in its history.

The $2.6-billion purchase of Statoil Fuel & Retail ASA with about 2300 locations in northern Europe mainly in Scandinavia closed in June 2012. Statoil is a Norway-based road transport fuel retailer and operates a network of retail stores across Scandinavia Poland the Baltic States and Russia. Statoil owns and operates a dozen key terminals as well as 38 depots in eight countries and a fleet of about 400 road tankers. Through its Circle K subsidiary Couche-Tard has license agreements for the operation of stores in Asia (including Japan and China) Mexico and the Middle East.

Couche-Tard operates more than 2000 convenience stores from Atlantic to Western Canada. Central Canada and the western half of Quebec Province are home to about 70% of the stores. The company divides the US market into eight geographic business units with the largest retail presence in the Great Lakes region and Arizona.

Sales at Couche-Tard's convenience stores in fiscal 2012 (ends April) climbed to $23 billion an increase of 21% vs. the prior year. Net income grew more than 23% over the same period. Indeed sales net income and cash flow from operations have all been on a steep upward trajectory over the past two years after relatively-flat annual comparisons during the recession. The recent rise is mainly attributable to an increase in fuel sales due to higher average prices at the pump as well as acquisitions and an increase in same-store merchandise sales at its stores in the US and Canada. Fuel sales (measure by volume) also increased in the US. Fuel accounted for 76 % of total US sales vs. 55% in Canada.

Acquisitions are a big part of Couche-Tard's growth strategy. Its purchase of Statoil is the latest and largest in a long chain of acquisitions that includes the purchase of Circle K nearly a decade ago. The Circle K acquisition established the Canadian firm as a major player in the US market and the company hopes to repeat that success in Europe. The fragmented US convenience store market and trend by major oil companies to cast off their retail operations has afforded Couche-Tard (and rival 7-Eleven) ample opportunity to acquire small independently-operated chains and occasionally a big fish. After a five-month struggle Couche-Tard in 2010 reluctantly abandoned its hostile $2-billion bid for Casey's General Stores. The purchase of Casey's which operates more than 1500 stores in the Midwestern US would have strengthened Couche-Tard's Circle K's retail business. Overall in fiscal 2012 the company acquired about 440 stores including 33 On the Run stores in Southern Louisiana from ExxonMobil and built only 28. With about 70% of its sales (even more in the US) coming from gas Couche-Tard is vulnerable to fluctuations in motor fuel prices. To protect itself from such volatility the retailer is focused on developing its in-store merchandise sales (especially fresh foods) which return higher margins and are less volatile.

FMR LLC is the company's largest shareholder with about 10% of the stock.

EXECUTIVES

VP Operations Western Canada, Kim J. Trowbridge
President CEO and Director, Alain Bouchard, $915,855 total compensation
Chairman, Richard Fortin, age 63, $413,033 total compensation
EVP and Director, Real Plourde, $454,900 total compensation
VP Administration and Director, Jacques D'Amours
COO, Brian P. Hannasch, $286,000 total compensation
VP Development, Butch Seber
VP Operations Eastern Canada, Michel Bernard
VP Operations Central Canada, Jean-Luc Meunier
VP Administration U.S., Robert G. Campau
VP Operations Arizona Region, Geoffrey C. (Geoff) Haxel
Senior Director Franchise Operations USA Mexico and Asia, Rick Hamlin
VP Operations U.S. Midwest Region, Darrell Davis
VP Operations U.S. Great Lakes Region, Paul Rodriguez
VP Operations Florida and Gulf Coast Region, Mike Struble
VP Operations U.S. West Coast Region, Tim Tourek
VP Operations Gulf, Jason Broussard

VP Operations U.S. Southeast Region, Matt McCure
VP and CFO, Raymond Pare
VP Operations U.S. Southwest Region, Lou Valdes
VP Purchasing and Supply Chain, Alain Brisebois
Vice-President Administration, Jacques DAmours
Vice-President and Chief financial Officer, Raymond Pare
Vice-President Operations Quebec East and Atlantic Canada, Pierre Peters
Vice-President Operations quebec West Canada, Michel Doucet
Vice President, Dennis Tewell
Vice-President Operations u.s, Bruce Landini
Vice-President oPERATIONS u.s, Bill Bartolomeo
President European Operations, Jacob Schram
President Fuel Americas & Operations, Jean Bernier
Director, Jean Turmel
President CEO and Director, Alain Bouchard
EVP and Director, Real Plourde
VP Administration and Director, Jacques D'Amours
Director, Roger Desrosiers
Director, Jean A. Elie
Director, Roger Longpre
Director, Jean-Pierre Sauriol
Director, Melanie Kau
Auditors: RaymondChabotGrantThornton

LOCATIONS

HQ: Alimentation-Couche Tard, Inc.
4204 Boulevard Industriel, Laval, Quebec H7L 0E3
Phone: 450 662-3272 **Fax:** 450 662-6633
Web: www.couche-tard.com

2012 Sales

	$ mil.	% of total
US	18,081	79
Canada	4,915	21
Total	**22,997**	**100**

2012 US Sales

	$ mil.	% of total
Gasoline	13,673	76
Merchandise & services	4,408	24
Total	**18,081**	**100**

2012 Canada Sales

	$ mil.	% of total
Gasoline	2,724	55
Merchandise & services	2,190	45
Total	**4,915**	**100**

2012 Stores

	No.
US	
Great Lakes	693
Arizona	639
West	543
Midwest	501
Florida	399
Southwest	385
Gulf	354
Southeast	331
Canada	
Quebec	551
Quebec East &	352
Central	747
West	308
Total	**5,803**

PRODUCTS/OPERATIONS

2012 Sales

	$ mil.	% of total
Gasoline	16,398	71
Merchandise & services	6,598	29
Total	**22,997**	**100**

Selected Proprietary Brands

Beverages
- Froster (frozen)
- Sloche (flavored)
- Sunshine Joe (coffee)

Sandwiches
- Handfull
- La Maisonnee

COMPETITORS

7-Eleven
Casey' s General Stores
Chevron
Cumberland Farms
Exxon Mobil
Gate Petroleum
Kroger
Kum & Go
Loblaw
Marathon Oil
Pilot Flying J
Publix
QuikTrip
Racetrac Petroleum
Royal Dutch Shell
Sheetz
Shell Oil
Sobeys
The Pantry
TravelCenters of America

HISTORICAL FINANCIALS

Company Type: Public

Income Statement FYE: April 28

	REVENUE ($ mil.)	NET INCOME ($ mil.)	NET PROFIT MARGIN	EMPLOYEES
04/13	35,543	572	1.6%	78,500
04/12	22,997	457	2.0%	60,000
04/11	18,550	369	2.0%	53,000
04/10	16,439	302	1.8%	53,000
04/09	15,781	253	1.6%	48,000
Annual Growth	22.5%	22.6%	—	13.1%

2013 Year-End Financials

Debt ratio: 34.1%
Return on equity: 21.3%
Cash ($ mil.): 658
Current ratio: 1.05
Long-term debt ($ mil.): 2,984
No. of shares (mil.): 187
Dividends
Yield: 0.0%
Payout: 9.7%
Market value ($ mil.): 10,986

	STOCK PRICE ($) FY Close	P/E High	P/E Low	PER SHARE ($) Earnings	Dividends	Book Value
04/13	58.57	19	12	3.07	0.30	17.15
04/12	42.55	17	10	2.49	0.28	12.15
04/11	26.60	14	9	1.96	0.18	10.78
04/10	18.33	12	7	1.60	0.14	8.79
04/09	10.10	12	8	1.29	0.12	7.07
Annual Growth	55.2%	—	—	24.2%	24.6%	24.8%

Allianz SE

One of the world's biggest insurers Allianz SE offers a range of insurance products and services –including life health and property/casualty coverage for individuals and businesses –through more than 1000 subsidiaries ventures and affiliates operating all over the globe (though its key markets are France Germany Italy and the US). The company serves some 78 million customers. In addition to selling insurance Allianz provides retail and institutional asset management services through Allianz Global Investors private equity investment through Allianz Capital Partners and banking services through Allianz Bank.

Geographic Reach

Allianz operates in more than 70 countries with most of its operations in Europe. It also operates in the Asia/Pacific region and the Americas.

Operations

On the insurance front Allianz gets about half of its revenues from its life and health division which operates under the Allianz brand and serves individual and group accounts. The property/casualty operations account for 45% of revenues. Allianz offers specialty property/casualty and marine insurance under the Allianz Global Corporate and Specialty brand. The unit has offices in more than a dozen locations and is one of the world's largest providers of marine insurance.

Though it has restructured to focus on core insurance and asset management offerings Allianz still has banking operations in Germany and other global regions.

Sales and Marketing

Allianz markets its products through independent agents and brokers dedicated agents bank representatives and direct marketing channels. It has about 150000 sales force associates 1200 distribution partners and about 2000 agencies in its worldwide network.

Financials

Allianz reported a 3% increase in revenues to some E106 billion in 2012 due to higher earnings in the property/casualty and asset management segments slightly offset by a decline in the life and health segment. Net income nearly doubled to E5.5 billion due to growth in operational performance and improved investment returns.

Strategy

Allianz is focused on achieving sustainable growth in its property/casualty life and health and asset management operations. It also seeks to achieve operational synergies among its businesses through shared technology investments capital allocations and best practice sharing. The company's investment strategy is conservative with the goal of providing stable returns.

While the US and Europe are Allianz's largest markets the company is pursuing growth in emerging markets as well. It has established significant operations in select Asian countries and it is expanding its presence in Central and Eastern Europe and the Asia/Pacific region. Targeted markets include China India and Russia.

Ownership

Allianz is part of a web of interlocking German corporate ownership. It holds a stake in reinsurance giant Munich Re which in turn has a small stake in Allianz. Munich Re is also the company's principal external reinsurer though Allianz itself reinsures a significant amount of its insurance companies' risk. Allianz also serves as a reinsurer for third parties.

HISTORY

Carl Thieme founded Allianz in Germany in 1890. That year the company took part in the creation of the Calamity Association of Accident Insurance Companies a consortium of German Austrian Swiss and Russian firms to insure international commerce.

By 1898 Thieme had established offices in the UK Switzerland and the Netherlands. His successor Paul von der Nahmer expanded Allianz into the Balkans France Italy Scandinavia and the US. After a hiatus during WWI Allianz returned to foreign markets.

In WWII Allianz insured Auschwitz Dachau and other death camps. Company documents show Allianz wasn't worried about risk at the SS troop-guarded camps. After the German defeat the victors seized Allianz's foreign holdings except for a stake in Spain's Plus Ultra. In the 1950s Allianz repurchased confiscated holdings in Italian and Austrian companies.

Allianz saturated the German market and began a full-scale international drive in the late 1950s and 1960s. It became Europe's largest insurer through a series of acquisitions beginning in 1973. Allianz formed Los Angeles-based Allianz Insurance in 1977.

In 1981 Allianz launched a takeover (which turned hostile) of the UK's Eagle Star insurance company. After a 1983 bidding joust with Britain's B.A.T Industries (now part of Zurich Financial Services) Allianz withdrew.

The firm consoled itself by shopping. In 1984 it won control of Riunione Adriatica di Sicurta (Ras) Italy's second-largest insurance company. Two years later the firm bought Cornhill (now Allianz Insurance plc) on its third try. As the Iron Curtain crumbled Allianz in 1989 acquired 49% of Hungaria Biztosito. Its "drang nach Osten" continued the next year after national reunification when it gained control of Deutsche Versicherungs AG East Germany's insurance monopoly. Allianz that year became the first German insurer licensed in Japan; it also bought the US's Fireman's Fund Insurance.

Natural disasters led to large claims and set the company back in 1992 the first time in 20 years it lost money from its German operations. Allianz restructured operations that year; profits surged in 1993 mostly from international business.

Allianz expanded in Mexico in 1995 forming a life and health insurance joint venture with Grupo Financiero BanCrecer (now owned by Grupo Financiero Banorte). The company set up an asset management arm in Hong Kong in 1996 with an eye to further Asian expansion getting a license in China the next year. In 1997 after Holocaust survivors sued Allianz and other insurers for failing to pay on life policies after WWII Allianz agreed to participate in a repayment fund.

In 1998 Allianz bought control of Assurances Generales de France; it was the white knight that prevented Assicurazioni Generali from taking the company. In 1999 Allianz said it would restructure some of its insurance operations including spinning off its marine and aviation lines to better compete in the multinational market. That year US subsidiary Allianz Life bought Life USA Holding. In 2000 Allianz bought 70% of PIMCO Advisors Holdings to strengthen its asset management operations. That year the company continued its push into Asia buying a 12% stake in Hana Bank of South Korea and planning to boost its ownership of Malaysia British Assurance Life. Also in 2000 Allianz acquired Dutch insurer Zwolsche Algemeene.

Allianz remained acquisitive in 2001 buying US investment manager Nicholas-Applegate and taking a majority stake in ROSNO one of Russia's largest insurers. Also that year it bought a nearly 96% stake in German banking giant Dresdner and acquired the remainder the following year.

Allianz paid out claims of some $1.3 billion relating to the terrorist attacks on the World Trade Center. The company set up a terrorism insurance unit offering coverage primarily for companies within the European Union.

After a year of record losses (primarily due to investment losses and Dresdner's struggles) former CEO Henning Schulte-Noelle stepped down and assumed the chair post in 2003. Allianz's stock lost more than 75% of its value in 2002.

Getting out of the red Allianz rebounded some in 2003 thanks to the upturn in the stock markets and the streamlining of its operations (the company reduced its employee total by some 8000 people). Allianz also raised some $5 billion to improve its capital base.

The company sold most of its Canadian property/casualty operations to ING Canada in 2004.

The company transitioned to a Societas Europaea a joint stock company that is ruled by European Union standards in 2006 and changed its name from Allianz AG to Allianz SE.

Also in 2006 Allianz consolidated its worldwide specialty property/casualty and marine insurance operations (including the Allianz Global Risks and Allianz Marine & Aviation units) under the Allianz Global Corporate & Specialty brand.

In 2008 Allianz invested $2.5 billion in ailing US insurer Hartford Financial Services giving Allianz an option to own about 20% of Hartford. (Hartford repurchased the debt in 2012.)

To focus on its insurance operations the company sold its Dresdner Bank subsidiary one of Germany's largest banks offering both retail and investment banking to Commerzbank in a $14.4 billion cash and stock transaction in early 2009.

EXECUTIVES

Chairman of the Management Board; Chief Executive Officer, Michael Diekmann, age 59, $1,623,840 total compensation
Member Management Board Insurance German Speaking Countries and Allianz Banking and Director Labor Relations, Gerhard Rupprecht, age 65, $1,030,330 total compensation
Vice Chairman, Gerhard Cromme, age 70
Member Management Board Global Insurance Lines & Anglo Markets, Clement B. Booth, age 59, $927,640 total compensation
Chairman, Henning Schulte-Noelle, age 71
Member Management Board Asset Management Worldwide, Jay Ralph, age 53
Member Management Board Insurance USA, Gary C. Bhojwani
Member Management Board Insurance German-Speaking Countries, Werner Zedelius, age 56, $1,030,330 total compensation
Member Management Board Insurance Europe I + II Africa South America P/C Sustainability Program, Enrico T. Cucchiani, age 63, $927,640 total compensation
Chairman Australia, John S. Curtis, age 63
Vice Chairman, Rolf Zimmermann, age 61
Chief Risk Officer, Thomas C. Wilson, age 52
Member of the Management Board; Chief Operating Officer, Christof Mascher, age 53, $279,698 total compensation
CIO Allianz SE and Allianz Managed Operations and Services (AMOS), Ralf Schneider, age 50
Member of the Management Board; Insurance Western & Southern Europe, Dieter Wemmer
Member of the Management Board; Insurance Iberia & Latin America ; Legal & Compliance; M&A, Helga Jung
Member of the Management Board with responsibility for Insurance Growth Markets, Manuel Bauer
Member of the Management Board; Chief Financial Officer, Maximilian Zimmerer
Member of the Management Board; Controlling; Reporting; Risk; IR, Oliver Baete
Board Member, Igor Landau, age 69
Board Member, Peter D. Sutherland, age 67
Vice Chairman, Gerhard Cromme, age 70
Board Member, Prof Renate Kocher, age 60
Board Member, Wulf H. Bernotat, age 65
Board Member, Jean-Jacques Cette, age 57
Board Member, Jorg Reinbrecht, age 56
Board Member, Godfrey R. (Geoff) Hayward, age 54
Vice Chairman, Rolf Zimmermann, age 61
Board Member, Peter Kossubek, age 60
Member of the Supervisory Board; Employee Representative, Franz Heiss
Member of the Supervisory Board, Renate Koecher
Auditors: KPMGDeutscheTreuhand-GesellschaftAG

LOCATIONS

HQ: Allianz SE
Koeniginstrasse 28, Munich D-80802
Phone: (49) 89 38 00 0 **Fax:** (49) 89 38 00 3425
Web: www.allianz.com

PRODUCTS/OPERATIONS

2012 Sales

Life & health insurance	49	
Asset management	6	
Corporate & other	1	
Total	**0**	**100**

Selected Operations and Brands

Allianz
Allianz Global Corporate and Specialty
Allianz Global Investors
Allianz Worldwide Care
Euler Hermes
PIMCO

COMPETITORS

AEGON
AXA
Allstate
Aviva
Berkshire Hathaway
CNP Assurances
Citigroup
ERGO
Generali
Generali Deutschland
Groupama
ING
Legal & General Group
MetLife
Munich Re Group
New York Life
Nippon Life Insurance
Old Mutual
Prudential
Prudential plc
RSA Insurance
State Farm
Swiss Re
Talanx
The Hartford
Victoria Versicherung
Zurich Insurance Group
ageas SA/NV

HISTORICAL FINANCIALS

Company Type: Public

Income Statement FYE: December 31

	ASSETS ($ mil.)	NET INCOME ($ mil.)	INCOME AS % OF ASSETS	EMPLOYEES
12/12	915,544	6,813	0.7%	144,094
12/11	829,713	3,291	0.4%	141,938
12/10	836,409	6,762	0.8%	151,338
12/09	841,357	6,190	0.7%	153,203
12/08	1,335,982	(3,416)	—	182,865
Annual Growth	(9.0%)	—	—	(5.8%)

2012 Year-End Financials

Return on assets: 0.7%
Return on equity: 10.4%
Long-term debt ($ mil.): —
No. of shares (mil.): 453
Sales ($ mil): 132,970
Dividends
Yield: 3.1%
Payout: —
Market value ($ mil.): 6,263

	STOCK PRICE ($) FY Close	P/E High	P/E Low	PER SHARE ($) Earnings	Dividends	Book Value
12/12	13.82	2	1	14.95	0.43	155.76
12/11	9.47	5	2	7.09	0.00	128.40
12/10	11.87	2	1	14.88	0.38	131.87
12/09	12.45	3	1	13.69	1.02	128.24
12/08	10.83	—	—	(7.65)	0.68	104.31
Annual Growth	6.3%	—	—	—	(10.9%)	10.5%

Allied Irish Banks Plc

Allied Irish Banks (AIB) one of Ireland's largest banks and private employers is looking beyond the Emerald Isle for its proverbial pot o' gold. The company offers retail and commercial accounts and loans life insurance financing leasing pension and trust services through some 275 branches in Ireland and another 50 in Northern Ireland where it operates First Trust Bank. In the UK AIB focuses on commercial clients through about 35 locations. The company's capital markets division offers commercial treasury services corporate finance and investment banking services. In the US AIB specializes in financial services for the not-for-profit sector. The Irish government took control of AIB in late 2010.

The seizure was the fourth such bank takeover since Ireland's financial system began teetering on the verge of collapse in 2008. The nation has been among the hardest-hit victims of the global financial crisis and the government has struggled to prevent the banks' complete failure. It provided cash injections to AIB Bank of Ireland and Irish Bank Resolution Corporation (formerly Anglo Irish Bank) in 2008.

The year 2010 proved even more difficult for AIB and its peers. The company reported a loss before taxation of more than E10 billion (more than $14 billion) largely due to bad real estate and construction loans. That year the government took over the bank leaving its shareholders with essentially nothing. The bank transferred some E20 billion ($27 billion) in loans to Ireland's National Asset Management Agency (NAMA) a "bad bank" agency created in late 2009 in response to the economic crisis.

The European Union also announced in 2010 that it would invest some tens of billions of euros in the still-weak Irish economy. Ireland's restructuring plan includes the closure of Irish Bank Resolution Corporation; AIB and Bank of Ireland are the two "banking pillars" to remain. AIB acquired deposits and assets of Anglo Irish Bank in early 2011. For its part AIB lost more than E13 billion in deposits in 2010 as skittish corporate and financial clients pulled their funds from the bank. The government now owns 92% of AIB.

The bank began selling assets primarily overseas assets to boost its own capital levels. In 2010 it sold its 70% stake in Poland's Bank Zachodni (which has some 500 branches) to Spain's Grupo Santander for some E3.1 billion ($3.7 billion). It also sold its more than 20% stake of New York-based M&T Bank as well as its stake in Goodbody Holding (parent of entities including Goodbody Stockbrokers). Plans were announced to sell its UK operations but they have been placed on the backburner while the economy recovers.

In 2011 AIB sold its Canadian operations to Raymond James Financial's Raymond James Bank. Also that year it struck a deal to sell some $600 million in US commercial property loans at a discount to Blackstone and Wells Fargo. At home the bank is selling AIB Asset Management Holdings Ireland to Prescient Holdings for an undisclosed sum.

Also in 2011 the company announced a simplified structure in which its divisions were integrated and its AIB and First Trust operations were more closely aligned. And on a more hopeful note the bank introduced mobile banking services to its offerings.

Prior to the financial downturn the small Irish market and its inevitable ties to the UK's economy made AIB look overseas to remain competitive. Indeed about a third of AIB's sales assets and pretax profits were coming from outside of Ireland. Meanwhile its home turf also faced intruders — namely European banks free to do business in the EU-opened Irish market. In response the firm positioned itself as an international bank establishing a presence in Eastern Europe the Baltic and southeastern Europe.

HISTORY

Allied Irish Banks was formed in 1966 by the "trinity" of Provincial Bank (founded 1825) The Royal Bank (founded 1836) and Munster and Leinster (founded 1885 but with origins back to the late 1600s). Both AIB and its then-larger rival Bank of Ireland had to consolidate in order to compete with North American banks entering Ireland. From its start AIB sought to expand overseas and by 1968 it had an alliance with Canada's Toronto-Dominion Bank.

In the 1970s AIB expanded its branch network to England and Scotland. The 1980s saw AIB boost its presence in the US market (it had already debuted AIB branches) with the acquisition of First Maryland Bancorp.

The Irish Parliament's Finance Act of 1986 instituted a withholding tax known as the Deposit Interest Retention Tax (DIRT) for Irish residents. Consequently (with a wink and a nod) AIB and other banks let customers create bogus non-resident accounts to avoid paying DIRT. An investigation indicated that at one point AIB's branch in Tralee had 14700 non-resident accounts on its rolls –more than half the local population. After tax authorities began probing many of the accounts in question were reclassified as "resident" and customers had to pay the taxes on them. In 1991 AIB was reprimanded but neither the bank nor its customers have paid the remaining $100 million tax bill.

Tom Mulcahy who integrated AIB's treasury investment and international banking activities became chief executive in 1994. Mulcahy a respected leader envisioned AIB as an international Ireland-based bank.

In 1995 AIB bought UK-based investment fund manager John Govett from London Pacific Group (now Berkeley Technology Limited). Mulcahy moved AIB the same year into Eastern Europe with a stake in Poland-based Wielkopolski Bank Kredytowy (or WBK).

AIB was busy in 1999. It gained a toehold in Asia by entering a cross-marketing agreement with Singapore's Keppet TatLee bank a survivor of the region's financial crisis. Liberalized Singapore banking laws allowed AIB the right to buy one-quarter of the bank by 2001. AIB also bought an 80% stake of Bank Zachodni in Poland in 1999.

That year AIB merged First Maryland Bancorp and its other US holdings into the renamed Allfirst Financial a sizable mid-Atlantic states bank.

To consolidate its power in Eastern Europe in 2001 AIB merged its Polish banks (Wielkopolski Bank Kredytowy and Bank Zachodni) into Bank Zachodni WBK. That year Mulcahy retired but was appointed by the Irish government to take over as chairman of troubled airline Aer Lingus.

AIB lost nearly $700 million from 1996 to 2002 apparently from bogus foreign exchange transactions made by rogue trader John Rusnak who pleaded guilty to bank fraud.

In 2003 AIB sold troubled Maryland-based bank Allfirst Financial to M&T Bank Corporation. As part of the deal AIB assumed ownership of more than 20% of M&T becoming the company's largest shareholder. Under AIB's direction Allfirst had grown into a major regional player with about 250 branches in Maryland Pennsylvania Virginia and Washington DC.

In the midst of the global financial crisis the Irish government injected E2 billion ($2.8 billion) into AIB in exchange for a 25% share in voting rights in 2008. Ireland also provided capital for Bank of Ireland and Irish Bank Resolution Corporation to help stabilize the plunging Irish financial system. AIB also sought capital from the private sector.

EXECUTIVES

CFO AIB Group, Bernard Byrne
Head Corporate Relations and Communications, Catherine Burke
Managing Director AIB Poland, Gerry Byrne, age 57
Managing Director AIB Bank, Robbie Henneberry, age 49
Manager Group Investor Relations, Rose O'Donovan
Managing Director Great Britan adn Northern Ireland, Nick Treble, age 53
Group Press Officer Corporate Relations and Communications, Ronan Sheridan
Deputy Chairman, Michael Somers, age 71
Chief Executive Officer, David Duffy
Senior Vice President with AIB Corporate Banking North America, Denise Magyer
Director, Robert G. (Bob) Wilmers, age 77
Director, Kieran Crowley, age 61
Director, Jennifer Winter, age 52
Director, Sean O' Driscoll, age 55
Director, Declan Collier, age 58
Director, Dick Spring, age 63
Director, Jim O'Hara, age 62
Director, Catherine Woods, age 51
Deputy Chairman, Michael Somers, age 70
Auditors: KPMG

LOCATIONS

HQ: Allied Irish Banks Plc
Bankcentre, Ballsbridge, Dublin 4
Phone: (353) 1 6600311 **Fax:** 212 339-8006
Web: www.aibgroup.com

COMPETITORS

Bank Millennium
Bank of America
Bank of Ireland
Barclays
Citigroup
HSBC
Irish Bank Resolution
Lloyds Banking Group
Royal Bank of Scotland
Ulster Bank

HISTORICAL FINANCIALS

Company Type: Public

Income Statement

FYE: December 31

	ASSETS ($ mil.)	NET INCOME ($ mil.)	INCOME AS % OF ASSETS	EMPLOYEES
12/12	161,482	(4,806)	—	14,708
12/11	176,751	(2,990)	—	16,716
12/10	194,361	(13,694)	—	23,208
12/09	251,111	(3,476)	—	23,275
12/08	254,652	1,072	0.4%	25,815
Annual Growth	(10.8%)	—	—	(13.1%)

2012 Year-End Financials

Return on assets: (-2.8%)
Return on equity: (-28.3%)
Long-term debt ($ mil.): —
No. of shares (mil.): —
Sales ($ mil): 4,370
Dividends
Yield: —
Payout: —
Market value ($ mil.): —

	STOCK PRICE ($) FY Close	P/E High/Low	PER SHARE ($) Earnings	Dividends	Book Value
12/12	0.60	— —	(0.01)	0.00	0.03
12/11	0.68	— —	(0.01)	0.00	0.04
12/10	0.88	— —	(7.55)	0.00	0.40
12/09	3.51	— —	(3.10)	0.00	17.48
12/08	4.69	120 10	1.16	0.00	14.16
Annual Growth	(40.2%)	— —	—	—	(78.8%)

Alstom

Alstom is all about speed and power. Alstom's Power segment is a world leader providing boilers turbines air quality systems generators and controls for coal gas hydroelectric and nuclear power generation. Turnkey power plant and wind farm setups are available as well as emission reduction systems. Alstom claims it has equipped 25% of the world's operating power plants. Its Transport business is a world-leading manufacturer of all things railroad-related from commuter trains and locomotives to signaling equipment to rail infrastructure. It also makes high-speed trains and provides complete turnkey railroad setup. Alstom's Grid segment mainly addresses the growing smart-grid market in the utility sector.

After seeing its revenue decrease in 2009 and 2010 Alstom enjoyed a 6% increase in its fiscal 2011 sales. Orders were also up in 2011 by 28%. Net income however was down 62% in 2011 over 2010.

Alstom operates in about 100 countries but the company has been reshifting its focus from the developed world to newly developing markets. Orders from clients in emerging countries grew from 35% of the global total in fiscal 2010 to 60% in fiscal 2011. Orders in the Brazil-Russia-India-China sector increased from 10% of the global total in fiscal 2010 to 25% in 2011. Alstom is building its BRIC operations by striking partnerships and joint-venture deals with several companies in those areas. Among them is a 50-50 venture with Shanghai Electric to make boilers. Meanwhile Alstom is correspondingly downsizing operations in Europe and North America where the company did experience some growth in 2011 but not as strong as that in emerging markets.

Alstom is also concentrating its R&D efforts on such promising technologies as turbine upgrades carbon capture and storage programs and tidal thermal and solar power in its Power segment; train control systems and VHS (very-high speed) in the Transport segment; and super grids as well as smart grids in its Grid operations. Alstom is anticipating strong growth in its new equipment service railway and transmission businesses.

Alstom had shed some business to focus on its Power and Transport segments but it has now added another major category to its operations Grid a business it has developed with the acquisition of Utility Integration Solutions and a partnership with Microsoft in the US and the acquisition of Psymetrix a smart grid services company in the UK.

Buoyed by strong orders in renewable energy technology Alstom has entered into an agreement with EDF Energies Nouvelles to develop offshore wind power. It also made an investment in BrightSource Energy a solar company.

HISTORY

GEC Alsthom was incorporated in the Netherlands in 1989 as a 50/50 joint venture between France's Compagnie Generale d'Electricite (or GCE later Alcatel and now Alcatel-Lucent) and The General Electric Company plc (GEC later Marconi and now telent) of the UK. Merging the power and transportation subsidiary of one to the other's power-systems unit suited a consolidating energy sector.

GEC Alsthom already had railway plants in Belgium France Spain and the UK and in 1994 the company expanded into Germany by purchasing 51% of Preussag AG's Linke-Hofmann-Busch GmbH. The following year GEC Alsthom expanded into Brazil when it bought 60% of CMW Equipamentos SA (railway signaling systems) from Odebrecht Group a Brazil-based holding company.

The formation of joint ventures and acquisitions continued throughout the 1990s. GEC Alsthom forged a joint venture with Romania-based turbogenerator maker General Turbo (1995); bought Elmac South America's largest maker of industrial electric motors from Siemens (1996); and purchased Wessex Traincare a UK rolling-stock repair firm (1998). Also in 1998 GEC Alsthom bought Cegelec (electrical contracting and industrial process control) from Alcatel. Later that year GEC Alsthom was taken public and it name changed to Alstom.

Alstom joined with ASEA Brown Boveri to form ABB Alstom Power (power generation) and sold its heavy-duty gas turbine business to General Electric (GE) in 1999. The company continued divesting non-core industrial units in 2000 by selling its diesel-engines unit to MAN. Later that year ALSTOM announced that its subsidiary Les Chantiers de l'Atlantique signed a letter of intent to build the largest cruise liner ever the Queen Mary 2 for Cunard Line.

The company bought ABB's share in ABB Alstom Power for around $1.2 billion in 2000 renaming it Alstom Power. Alstom also announced plans to open a new marine manufacturing facility in the Philadelphia Naval Yard to support US Navy and commercial vessel requirements for electrical equipment. The same year Alstom bought a 51% stake in rail equipment company Fiat Ferroviaria.

In 2001 Alcatel and Marconi sold their stakes in the company. To close out the year Alstom sold its contracting operations (electrical installation) to a management buyout group (financed by CDC Equity Capital and Charterhouse Development Capital) for about $660 million. The company launched "Restore Value" a debt reduction plan in early 2002 to be facilitated by the sale of additional shares in the company. Alstom announced the following year a plan to raise E3 billion by the end of 2004 through the sale of non-core businesses.

Alstom Power Conversion was sold in late 2005 to Barclays Private Equity in a management buyout. The business changed its name to Converteam.

In early 2006 Alstom reached an agreement with the Aker Yards unit (now STX Europe a subsidiary of South Korea-based STX Business Group) of Norwegian conglomerate Aker under which Aker Yards acquired 75% of a new company taking in the Alstom Marine business including the Chantiers de l'Atlantique shipbuilding subsidiary while Alstom retained a 25% stake in the business. Depending on financial performance Alstom agreed to sell the 25% stake to Aker Yards in 2010 for up to E125 million. Until that time Alstom had committed to investing an estimated E350 million in the marine business while four large banks extended E550 million in construction financing to the new entity. In March 2010 Alstom sold its remaining 25% stake in the Marine business.

By 2006 Alstom was largely out of crisis mode and on more secure financial footing. It was profitable and growing sales and had whittled its debt down to E1.2 billion (around $1.5 billion). Alstom was ready to resume acquisitions and to expand operations. The company signed a framework agreement with the Bouygues group that saw the construction firm acquire around one-quarter of Alstom's equity (most of it shares bought from the French government). Bouygues group became Alstom's reference shareholder and agreed to purchase a 50% stake in Alstom's hydro power business Alstom Hydro Holding. That 50/50 joint venture was formally established in late 2006.

In late 2006 Alstom sold its train renovation business in the UK to Railcare Ltd. The unit of Alstom Transport had annual sales of E60 million (about #40 million or $79 million) and employed 430 people at two facilities. While the business was similar in nature to railroad rolling stock manufacturing Alstom no longer made rolling stock in the UK and the business wasn't as profitable as the parent company would have liked.

By early 2007 Alstom had reduced its net debt to E64 million (nearly $89 million) through positive cash flow and the release of E700 million in cash collateral related to the company's bonds. In closing out the 2007 fiscal year the company announced that it was debt-free.

As part of its goal to increase its manufacturing capabilities the company made a number of acquisitions in 2007. Alstom picked up Ecotecnia a Spanish manufacturer of wind power generation equipment and solar panels for E350 million ($471 million). It also acquired the assets of Power Systems Mfg. (PSM) a subsidiary of Calpine for $242 million in cash. PSM provides parts and upgrades for gas turbines. Alstom made PSM part of its Power Service Sector. Qingdao Sizhou Electric Power Equipment a Chinese manufacturer of boiler auxiliaries also joined the pack. Sizhou specializes in coal-fired power generation. The firm has been renamed Alstom Sizhou.

Prior to the final disposal of the last of its Marine activities in November 2008 the company divested itself of its former Transmission & Distribution sector to shift its main focus on two sectors Transport and Power.

Alstom entered into a strategic partnership with Russian rail supplier Transmashholding (TMH) in 2008 creating a joint venture to make passenger rail cars in the Tver region of Russia in response to a bid from Russian Railways.

In 2009 Alstom purchased 51% of China-based manufacturer Wuhan Boiler to gain entry into the Chinese boiler sector. China is considered the largest market for coal-fired power plant boilers and Alstom has built a new energy-efficient boiler production facility in Hubei province. The facility which will serve as an exporting base and research and development center for Asia/Pacific began production in late 2009.

Also in 2009 French state-controlled nuclear reactor manufacturer AREVA selected Alstom and Schneider Electric as top bidders for its power transmission and distribution business. Bidding losers included non-French companies Toshiba and General Electric. The French consortium Alstom-Schneider has agreed not to lay off workers and will hire AREVA employees wherever possible. French president Nicolas Sarkozy who represents the government's 93% stake in AREVA supported the decision. The deal was completed in June 2010.

In 2009 Bouygues exchanged its 50% stake in Alstom Hydro for 4.4 million Alstom shares giving Bouygues a 32% stake in Alstom.

It also teamed up with India-based Bharat Forge a metal forming company to manufacture steam turbine islands in India in 2010.

Alstom further expanded in Russia in late 2010 when it signed strategic agreements with major Russian energy companies FSK Inter RAO Mosenergo (a subsidiary of Gazprom) Rosatom Rostechnologii and RusHydro to jointly provide hydropower generation thermal power generation nuclear power generation and electricity transmission.

The company made job cuts in Switzerland from its power transmission division in 2011 amid increased competition from Asia.

EXECUTIVES

Chairman and CEO, Patrick Kron, age 59, $408,288 total compensation
Deputy CEO Power Sector, Philippe Joubert, age 59
SVP Corporate Communications, Patrick Bessy
President Power Service Sector, Walter Graenicher
Chief Financial Officer, Nicolas Tissot, age 47
EVP; President Transport, Henri Poupart-Lafarge, age 44
Director Corporate Information, Philippe Kasse
EVP; President Grid Sector, Gregoire Poux-Guillaume
Managing Director North America Alstom Transport, Guillaume Mehlman
General Counsel, Keith Carr
President of Alstom Thermal Power and Executive Vice-President of Alstom, Philippe Cochet
EVP; President Renewable Power, Jerome Pecresse
SVP Human Resources, Bruno Guillemet, age 56
Senior Vice President for Alstom ?s steam business, Andreas Lusch
Director, Klaus J. Mangold, age 68
Director, Candace K. Beinecke
Director, Jean-Martin Folz, age 66
Director, Olivier Bouygues, age 61
Director, James W. (Jim) Leng, age 66
Director, Georges Chodron de Courcel, age 63
Director, Jean-Paul Bechat, age 68
Director, Pascal Colombani, age 66
Director, Gerard Hauser, age 71
Director, Alan M. Thomson, age 66
Director, Philippe Marien, age 57
Auditors: Ernst&Young

LOCATIONS

HQ: Alstom
3, avenue Andre Malraux, Levallois-Perret 92300
Phone: (33) 1 41 49 20 00
Web: www.alstom.com

2009 Sales by Origin

	% of total
Europe	70
North	15
Asia/Pacific	9
South & Central	4
Middle East &	2
Total	**100**

2009 Sales by Destination

	% of total
Europe	52
North	16
Middle East &	13
Asia/Pacific	13
South & Central	6
Total	**100**

PRODUCTS/OPERATIONS

2009 Sales

	% of total
Power	70
Transport	30
Total	**100**

Selected Products and Services

Power
- Air quality control systems
- Boilers
- Coal-fired (steam) power plants
- Control systems
- Energy recovery
- Environmental systems
- Gas-fired power plants
- Generators and turbogenerators
- Heat exchange
- Hydroelectric power plants
- Maintenance and service
- Nuclear power plants
- Product retrofitting
- Turbines
- Turnkey power plants
- Wind farms

Transport
- Communication systems
- Freight trains
- Information solutions
- Infrastructure maintenance
- Passenger trains
- Power supply
- Rolling stock services
- Station utilities
- Subsystems
- Track laying
- Trains (high speed very high speed regional commuter locomotives metros trams tram-trains)
- Turnkey systems
- Workshops and depots

COMPETITORS

ABB
Amsted Industries
Babcock & Wilcox
Bharat Heavy Electricals
Cummins
GE Energy
Global Power Equipment
Greenbrier Rail Services
Hitachi
Hyundai Heavy Industries
McDermott
Mitsui Engineering & Shipbuilding
Nippon Sharyo
Nordex
RailWorks
Siemens AG
Siemens Energy
Siemens Mobility
Toshiba
Trinity Industries
Vestas Wind Systems
Vossloh
Westinghouse Air Brake

HISTORICAL FINANCIALS

Company Type: Public

Income Statement FYE: March 31

	REVENUE ($ mil.)	NET INCOME ($ mil.)	NET PROFIT MARGIN	EMPLOYEES
03/13	25,994	1,028	4.0%	86,252
03/12	26,602	976	3.7%	93,998
03/11	29,767	657	2.2%	94,648
03/10	26,497	1,641	6.2%	77,740
03/09	24,928	1,475	5.9%	81,693
Annual Growth	1.1%	(8.6%)	—	1.4%

2013 Year-End Financials

Debt ratio: 20.1%
Return on equity: 17.1%
Cash ($ mil.): 2,814
Current ratio: 0.94
Long-term debt ($ mil.): 5,937
No. of shares (mil.): 308
Dividends
Yield: 0.0%
Payout: 4.7%
Market value ($ mil.): 1,242

	STOCK PRICE ($) FY Close	P/E High	P/E Low	PER SHARE ($) Earnings	PER SHARE ($) Dividends	PER SHARE ($) Book Value
03/13	4.03	3	2	3.39	0.16	20.85
03/12	3.84	5	2	3.28	0.17	19.61
03/11	5.90	8	5	2.22	0.15	19.62
03/10	6.50	4	3	5.64	0.29	18.77
Annual Growth	(14.7%)	—	—	(12.0%)	(13.9%)	2.7%

America Movil, S.A.B. de C.V.

offers wireless phone service from the Rio Grande to Tierra del Fuego. The company is Latin America's top mobile carrier with more than 225 million subscribers in 18 countries. In Mexico the company enjoys a 70% market share with nearly 65 million subscribers to its Telcel brand which has 260+ retail stores. Its second largest market is Brazil which serves more than 50 million subscribers through Claro. America Movil also provides fixed-line service in Central America and the Caribbean with more than 5 million lines. TracFone Wireless is America Movil's US presence. Majority owner Carlos Slim Helu combined America Movil with his fixed-line businesses Telmex in 2010 as part of a broader restructuring effort.

The $21 billion dollar deal was structured so that America Movil acquired the minority stakes in Telmex that Helu did not already own through a stock transaction with their controlling holding company Carso Global Telecom. The plan combined Helu's wired and wireless telecom interests in hopes of holding ground against increasing competition from smaller telephone companies and cable television operators like Televisa which offer bundled phone TV and Internet services. The combined wired operations of Telmex and the wireless business of America Movil provides phone TV and Internet services. As one company the merger was slated to save about $700 million in administrative costs following the delisting of Telint and Carso Global.

In the US the company operates through subsidiary TracFone which is a leading provider of prepaid wireless services. TracFone products feature a pay-as-you-go prepaid mobile phone with no annual contracts or activation fees. Its services account for more than 5% of America Movil's total revenue. The company also owns more than 71% of Telvista a call center company with locations in the US and Mexico.

America Movil's operating revenues rose more than 8% in 2010 over 2009.

In 2012 Tracfone acquired Simple Mobile which is one of the largest mobile virtual network operators for T-Mobile. The previous year America Movil paid $75 million for a license to provide Costa Rica with satellite television wireless phone and Internet service under its Claro brand. Currently the only telecom provider in the country is the government-controlled Instituto Costarricsense de Electricidad (Grupo ICE). Telefonica also plans to provide telecom services in Costa Rica.

America Movil is acquiring 100% control of Telmex by buying the 40+% of the company it doesn't already own. Telmex will be delisted from the exchanges it trades on when the acquisition is complete and it now operates as a brand that provides fixed-line service in Mexico and Columbia.

The family of Mexican billionaire Carlos Slim Helu (also the world's wealthiest person) controls more than 46% of America Movil; AT&T owns nearly one quarter of the company and operates as a competitor in some of its smaller markets.

HISTORY

The company was formed in 2000 as a result of a spinoff from Telmex which was at the time Mexico's largest local and long-distance phone service provider. In late 2006 America Movil acquired majority owner America Telecom in a move to streamline the structure of the company and to free up assets for share buybacks or dividends.

The company expanded its presence in the Caribbean region in 2007 with the acquisition of Puerto Rico Telephone from Verizon Communications and a handful of other shareholders for nearly $2 billion. The next year it bought Jamaican wireless service provider Oceanic Digital Jamaica and became licenced to provide wireless services in Panama.

Also in 2008 the company rebranded its operations in Argentina Paraguay and Uruguay to its Claro brand which America Movil now uses for all of its operations in Central America and the Caribbean. That year it bought Estesa Holding a cable TV and data services provider in Nicaragua for $48 million. The acquisition of Estesa boosted America Movil's cable television and broadband offerings and gave the company greater access to the Nicaraguan market.

EXECUTIVES

CEO and Director, Daniel Hajj Aboumrad, age 45
Director, Jaime Chico Pardo, age 62
Director, Rayford (Ray) Wilkins Jr., age 60
Director, Alejandro Soberon Kuri, age 51
Director, David Ibarra Mu?oz, age 82
Director, Carlos Bremer Gutierrez, age 51
Director, Pablo Roberto Gonzalez Guajardo, age 44
Director, Ernesto Vega Velasco, age 75
Director, Mike Viola, age 58
Auditors: ManceraS.C.

LOCATIONS

HQ: America Movil, S.A.B. de C.V.
Lago Zurich 245, Plaza Carso/Edificio Telcel, Piso 16, Colonia Granada Ampliacion, Mexico, D.F. 11529
Phone: (52) 55 2581 4449 **Fax:** (52) 55 2581 4422
Web: www.americamovil.com

2010 Sales

	% of total
Mexico	25
Mexico	18
Brazil	25
Columbia &	8
Southern	7
US	5
Andean	4
Caribbean	4
Central	2
Eliminations (3.3.)	
Total	**100**

PRODUCTS/OPERATIONS

2010 Sales

	% of total
Mobile voice	44
Fixed voice	23
Mobile data voice	13
Fixed data	11
Paid	2
Other	7
Total	**100**

Selected Operations

America Movil Peru (8.3 million subscribers)
AM Wireless Uruguay (800000 subscribers)
AMX Argentina (17 million subscribers)
AMX Paraguay (500000 subscribers)
Claro Chile (3.6 million subscribers)
Claro Panama (100000 subscribers)
Codetel (Dominican Republic 4.8 million subscribers)
Comcel (Colombia 27.7 million subscribers)
Conecel (Ecuador 9.4 million subscribers)
CTE (El Salvador 800000 subscribers)
ENITEL (Nicaragua 2.2 million subscribers)
Oceanic (Jamaica 400000 subscribers)
Sercom Honduras (1.4 million subscribers)
TELPRI (Puerto Rico 1.6 million subscribers)
TracFone (US 14.4 million subscribers)
Telgua (Guatemala 1.2 million subscribers)

COMPETITORS

AT&T
Alfa SA
Axtel
Brasil Telecom
Cable & Wireless Communications
Iusacell
Millicom
NII Holdings
Portugal Telecom
Sprint Nextel
TIM Participac?es
Tele Norte Leste
Telecom Argentina
Telefonica
Telefonica Brasil
Telefonica de Argentina
Telemig Celular
Vivo Participac?es

HISTORICAL FINANCIALS

Company Type: Public

Income Statement

FYE: December 31

	REVENUE ($ mil.)	NET INCOME ($ mil.)	NET PROFIT MARGIN	EMPLOYEES
12/12	59,648	7,037	11.8%	158,719
12/11	47,627	5,931	12.5%	158,694
12/10	49,032	7,350	15.0%	150,079
12/09	42,871	7,080	16.5%	53,661
12/08	24,946	4,293	17.2%	52,879
Annual Growth	24.4%	13.2%	—	31.6%

2012 Year-End Financials

Debt ratio: 3.2%
Return on equity: 31.0%
Cash ($ mil.): 3,500
Current ratio: 0.83
Long-term debt ($ mil.): 31,095
No. of shares (mil.): —
Dividends
Yield: 1.3%
Payout: 1.9%
Market value ($ mil.): —

	STOCK PRICE ($) FY Close	P/E High/Low		PER SHARE ($) Earnings	Dividends	Book Value
12/12	23.14	0	0	0.09	0.30	0.31
12/11	22.60	0	0	0.08	0.00	0.27
12/10	57.34	0	0	0.09	0.25	0.31
12/09	46.98	0	0	0.09	0.61	(0.00)
12/08	30.99	—	—	0.06	1.19	0.16
Annual Growth	(7.0%)	—	—	10.1%	(29.1%)	18.3%

AMP Ltd.

AMP is on top —down under. The company is one of Australia's largest insurance and investment management groups. Through its AMP Financial Services (AFS) division more than 2000 representatives sell the company's financial offerings which include life home vehicle travel and business insurance as well as retirement products financial planning and advice superannuation products (professionally managed retirement investment funds) and banking. AMP Capital Investors provides investment management to AFS and to other individual and institutional investors. AMP Limited also provides retail financial services under the Hillcross and Arrive Wealth Management brands.

AMP Limited is active mainly in Australia and New Zealand but is pursuing expansion in selected parts of Asia. It is also banking on its banking business which includes savings accounts home loans and American Express credit cards to be an area of growth.

AMP Limited which has more than A$100 billion of assets under management claims that approximately one in seven Australians and New Zealanders are AMP customers. And the company aims to increase its presence even more. In 2009 it offered to acquire the operations of AXA Asia Pacific in those two nations. However rival National Australia Bank entered the fray and outbid AMP but regulators nixed the deal citing antitrust concerns. AMP eventually signed an agreement with AXA to acquire AXA Asia Pacific in 2010 and sell the unit's operations in Asia back to AXA. The company hopes the deal which was completed the following year will boost its life insurance and wealth management business in Australia and New Zealand.

HISTORY

AMP was conceived in Sydney in 1848 by W. S. Walsh (a clergyman) Thomas Mort (a businessman) and Thomas Holt (a wool trader) who convened with two others to discuss forming a mutual life insurance company in Australia. (Many of the UK's and US's largest mutuals were also founded about this time.) The next year Australian Mutual Provident Society was born; it opened for business with a staff of two: secretary William Perry and a small boy. In its first year the company sold only 42 policies. Luckily no one died in the first three years of operations and the company was able to build up some reserves. The company grew slowly over the next decade appointing just two agents — in Auckland New Zealand and Hobart Australia.

Sales took off with the 1860 appointment of the company's first full-time agent Benjamin Short who had the novel idea of actively recruiting customers and actually "selling" policies. The company opened an office in New Zealand in 1871; it opened a branch in the UK in 1908.

In the next few decades the company helped build the Australian economy through investment of its reserves. It funded industry and infrastructure including farming communities as part of the South Australian Land Development Scheme. The company grew free of foreign competition protected by regulations severely restricting the activities of foreign companies in the banking and financial industries in Australia. In 1958 the company formed AMP Fire and General Insurance (changed to AMP General in 1990).

In 1988 AMP moved abroad with the acquisition of London Life Assurance. The following year it made history with its acquisition of funds management group Pearl Assurance then the largest takeover of a British financial firm by a foreign company.

The company founded AMP Asset Management in 1991 to manage its overseas assets. In 1995 the company expanded its international presence through a joint venture with the financial services arm of UK-based Virgin Group. The company also began offering mortgage and banking products in Australia through a new unit Priority One.

After a careful inquiry in 1996 AMP's board recommended demutualization; policyholders approved in 1997 and the conversion was completed the next year with the company taking the name AMP Limited. Trading got off to a rocky start however as the company imposed an unusual pricing mechanism by which the official initial stock price was linked to pricing activity over the first five days of trading. This was done to protect individual policyholders from typical opening-day stock gyrations but institutional investors were unable to value their investments for several days (a technical breach of accounting rules).

AMP bought Citibank's New Zealand retail banking business and UK fund manager Henderson in 1998. The next year AMP battled to buy general insurer GIO Australia Holdings picking up 57% after resistance to its original low-ball offer; it also bought UK mutual insurer National Provident Institution (NPI).

The company streamlined all of its investment-management operations into a single unit in 1999 and expanded Asian operations with offices in Beijing and Tokyo. In 2000 the problems arising from the GIO takeover resulted in a board shakeup; chairman Ian Burgess resigned.

Local rival Suncorp-Metway bought AMP's domestic general insurance unit in 2001 and Churchill Insurance (a subsidiary of Credit Suisse) acquired its similar operations in the UK that year.

AMP split off its UK-based operations as HHG at the end of 2003 (retaining a 10% share). HHG eventually changed its name to Henderson Group plc in 2005. AMP sold its shares in Henderson later that year.

EXECUTIVES

General Manager Public Affairs, Matthew Percival, $303,597 total compensation
Managing Director and CEO, Craig Dunn, age 49, $725,000 total compensation
Managing Director AMP Financial Services, Craig Meller, age 50
Managing Director AMP Capital Investors, Stephen Dunne, $427,221 total compensation
General Manager Human Resources, Fiona Wardlaw
Chairman, Peter Mason, age 66
Chief Information Officer, Lee Barnett
Chief Financial Officer, Colin Storrie, age 45
General Manager Group Strategy, Jonathan Deane
General Counsel, Brian Salter
Director, Richard H. (Rick) Allert, age 68
Managing Director and CEO, Craig Dunn, age 49
Director, John Palmer, age 65
Director, Paul A. Fegan, age 52
Director, Nora L. Scheinkestel, age 52
Director, Catherine Brenner, age 41
Director, Brian Clark, age 64
Director, Peter Shergold, age 66
Auditors: Ernst&Young

LOCATIONS

HQ: AMP Ltd.
Level 24, 33 Alfred Street, Sydney, New South Wales 2000
Phone: (61) 2 9257 5000 **Fax:** (61) 2 9257 7178
Web: www.amp.com.au

PRODUCTS/OPERATIONS

2009 Sales

	% of total
Investment	75
Fee	12
Life insurance premiums & related	10
Other	3
Total	**100**

COMPETITORS

AXA Asia Pacific
Australia and New Zealand Banking
Aviva
Commonwealth Bank of Australia
Macquarie Group
National Australia Bank
QBE
RSA Insurance
St. Andrew' s Australia
Suncorp-Metway
ageas SA/NV

HISTORICAL FINANCIALS

Company Type: Public

Income Statement FYE: December 31

	ASSETS ($ mil.)	NET INCOME ($ mil.)	INCOME AS % OF ASSETS	EMPLOYEES
12/12	123,395	731	0.6%	5,829
12/11	112,176	699	0.6%	6,000
12/10	90,783	788	0.9%	3,700
12/09	80,789	664	0.8%	3,500
12/08	59,796	399	0.7%	3,800
Annual Growth	19.9%	16.3%	—	11.3%

2012 Year-End Financials

Return on assets: 0.6%
Return on equity: 9.8%
Long-term debt ($ mil.): —
No. of shares (mil.): —
Sales ($ mil): 17,547
Dividends
Yield: —
Payout: —
Market value ($ mil.): —

	STOCK PRICE ($) FY Close	P/E High/Low		PER SHARE ($) Earnings	Dividends	Book Value
12/12	4.97	23	15	0.26	0.00	0.00
12/11	4.25	26	15	0.27	0.00	2.47
12/10	5.34	15	10	0.38	0.00	1.44
12/09	5.45	12	7	0.33	0.00	1.14
12/08	2.70	16	4	0.21	0.28	0.71
Annual Growth	16.5%	—	—	4.6%	—	(75.2%)

ANA Holdings Inc

ANA Holdings is the parent of All Nippon Airways one of Japan's leading carriers along with Japan Airlines. With a fleet of more than 210 aircraft ANA flies to some 130 domestic destinations and 40 international ones. It extends its network through code-sharing with members of the Star Alliance an airline marketing partnership that includes such carriers as United Continental's United Airlines and Continental and Lufthansa. (Code-sharing enables airlines to sell tickets on one another's flights.) Besides passenger service ANA's air transportation operations include cargo and mail hauling and aircraft maintenance and ground support. The company also sells travel packages and operates hotels.

Domestic passenger flights account for most of the company's air transportation business but ANA sees international passenger service and cargo operations as its main growth areas. ANA will be adding some flight schedules between the Americas and Asia in spring 2011 when its trans-Pacific joint venture with United Continental kicks off. The US Department of Transportation and the Japanese government have both approved the agreement. ANA and Lufthansa are in talks to form a joint venture. If the deal receives antitrust approval the two airlines will work together for flights between Europe and Japan.

The company is also working to add routes between Japan and China where it serves additional destinations via its code-sharing partnership with Air China and to other markets in East Asia. Another key to international growth for ANA is the expansion of Tokyo's Haneda Airport where a fourth runway is under construction. Along with its benefits for ANA the new runway is expected to bring more competitors to Haneda and ANA has indicated that it is considering starting a low-cost carrier in response.

In addition ANA plans to gradually add freighters to its cargo fleet which consists of four Boeing 767-300s. Its cargo routes are focused on Asia but also include US destinations. Up until late 2010 much of the company's cargo service was provided through subsidiaries Air Japan (AJX) and ANA & JP Express (AJV) when it rolled of its cargo operations into Air Nippon Network (AKX); once the merger was complete AKX was renamed ANA Wings. ANA acquired control of AJV –formerly a joint air cargo venture between ANA and Japan Post Nippon Express and Mitsui O.S.K. Lines –in April 2010. ANA merged AJX and AJV in mid-2010 in order to streamline the operations.

In June 2009 ANA agreed to spin off its helicopter maintenance operations from subsidiary ANA Aircraft Maintenance and sell that division to helicopter manufacturer Eurocopter. Besides All Nippon Airways' primary air transportation travel and hotel businesses the company has interests in information services logistics and trading companies.

HISTORY

Two domestic Japanese air carriers that started in 1952 –Nippon Helicopter and Aeroplane Transport and Far East Airlines –consolidated operations in 1957 as All Nippon Airways (ANA).

Throughout the 1960s ANA developed a domestic route network linking Japan's largest cities —Tokyo Osaka Fukuoka and Sapporo —and its leading provincial centers including Nagoya Nagasaki Matsuyama and Hakodate. During this period domestic traffic grew at an annual rate of 30% to 60%.

In 1970 the Japanese cabinet formulated routes for its major airlines giving ANA scheduled domestic service and unscheduled international flights. That year Tokuji Wakasa became ANA's chairman and the company began a program of diversification that led to the establishment of ANA Trading international charter service (starting with Hong Kong) and a hotel subsidiary. Air Nippon a regional domestic airline was started in 1974.

The company established Nippon Cargo Airlines a charter service set up jointly with four steamship lines in 1978. ANA carried 19.5 million passengers that year but its growth slowed between 1978 and 1980. High jet fuel prices caused a $45.6 million loss in 1979 but ANA rebounded a year later. In 1982 ANA opened international charter service to Guam. The company founded ANA Sports in 1984 to manage the company soccer team.

Japan deregulated air routes in 1985 allowing ANA to offer scheduled international flights. The airline offered its first regular flight from Tokyo to Guam in 1986 and soon added service to Los Angeles and Washington DC. Flights to China Hong Kong and Sydney began a year later.

Between 1988 and 1990 ANA added flights to Bangkok London Moscow Saipan Seoul Stockholm and Vienna. In 1988 ANA bought a minority stake in Austrian Airlines and set up the domestic computer reservation system (CRS). The company's international CRS INFINI (a joint venture with CRS co-op ABACUS) went online in 1990.

ANA started World Air Network Charter (WAC) in 1991 to serve travelers from Japan's smaller cities. That year ANA opened its first European hotel (in Vienna) was listed on the London Stock Exchange and opened a flight school in the US for its pilots.

In 1992 ANA premiered a hotel in Beijing. In 1995 the airline announced that it would increase its international traffic by more than 30%. As part of this strategy ANA and Air Canada began a code-sharing service in 1996 between Osaka and Vancouver and a year later ANA became the first Japanese airline to operate a Boeing 777 on an international route (between Tokyo and Beijing).

As the Asian financial crisis sent Japanese airlines to the brink a pilot strike in 1998 dashed ANA's hopes for a 15% pay cut. To cope ANA formed alliances with United Airlines (owned by United Continental formerly UAL Corporation) Lufthansa and Brazil's VARIG. ANA extended those partnerships in 1999 by joining the global Star Alliance. To shore up its financial strength ANA reorganized domestic routes dropping some unprofitable ones and shifting others to its Air Nippon unit; it also announced plans to launch low-cost air service for international routes in Asia. Competition intensified when Japan fully deregulated domestic fares in 2000 sparking a fare war.

The following year ANA avoided a potentially costly strike and began working toward expanding through partnerships. However terrorist attacks on the US caused a slump in worldwide air travel and ANA was forced to cut back on its flights. Then ANA had to trim more routes in response to a worldwide slump in air travel in 2003 due to the SARS outbreak.

In order to develop its own cargo business ANA sold its 27%-plus stake in Nippon Cargo Airlines to Nippon Yusen Kabushiki Kaisha in 2005.

In 2006 ANA formed a hotel management joint venture with hospitality industry leader InterContinental Hotels Group (IHG). The new company IHG ANA Hotels Group Japan took over management of ANA's 30 hotel properties.

EXECUTIVES

Corporate Auditor, Koichiro Ono
Chairman, Yoji Ohashi
President and CEO, Shinichiro Ito
Corporate Auditor, Koji Ohno
SEVP Public Relations General Administration Legal and Insurance, Shin Nagase
EVP Engineering and Maintenance and Director, Hiroyuki Ito
SVP Personnel; President ANA JINZAI Univeristy, Takashi Shiki
SVP and General Manager Tokyo Sales Office, Katsuyori Kikuchi
SVP Engineering and Maintenance, Shinsuke Maki
EVP Alliance and International Affairs Information Technology Services and Director, Keisuke Okada
SEVP Operations and Airport Services and Director, Mitsuo Morimoto
President All Nippon Airways, Osamu Shinobe
EVP Operations Airport Services and Director, Katsumi Nakamura
SVP Flight Operations, Shinichi Inoue
SVP and General Manager China, Kunio Yamazaki
SVP The Americas, Satoru Fujiki
SVP Flight Operations, Yusuke Jikumaru
EVP Government and Industrial Affairs Strategic Planning-Asia Pacific and Airport and Facilities Planning, Shigeyuki Takemura
SVP Marketing and Sales, Akihiko Nakamura
SVP and General Manager Nagoya Sales Office, Tsukasa Shibata
SVP and General Manager Osaka Airport, Kenji Maruyama
SVP and General Manager Tokyo International Airport, Mitsuhiko Ota
SVP Information Technology Services, Toru Sato
EVP Legal and Insurance General Administration and CSR Promotion, Yoshinori Maruyama
EVP Finance Accounting and Investor Relations, Kiyoshi Tonomoto
SVP Finance and Accounting, Eiji Kanazawa
SVP and General Manager Osaka Sales Office, Ken Nishimura
SVP and General Manager Nanita Airport, Katsumi Kobayashi
SEVP Human Resources Strategy Corporate Planning and Group Business Development, Shinya Katanozaka
SVP Corporate Planning, Akira Okada
SEVP International and Regulatory Affairs and Director, Hayao Hora
Director, Shosuke Mori, age 73
President CEO and Director, Shinichiro Ito
Director, Misao Kimura, age 76
SEVP Public Relations General Administration Legal and Insurance, Shin Nagase
EVP Engineering and Maintenance and Director, Hiroyuki Ito
EVP Investor Relations Associated Business Development Financial and Accounting and Purchasing and Director, Tomohiro Hidema
EVP Alliance and International Affairs Information Technology Services and Director, Keisuke Okada
SEVP Operations and Airport Services and Director, Mitsuo Morimoto
EVP Corporate Planning and B787 Launch Project and Director, Osamu Shinobe
SEVP International and Regulatory Affairs and Director, Hayao Hora
Auditors: Ernst&YoungShinNihon

LOCATIONS

HQ: ANA Holdings Inc
1-5-2 Higashi-Shinbashi, Minato-ku, Tokyo 105-7133
Phone: (81) 3 6735 1001 **Fax:** (81) 3 6735 1005
Web: www.anahd.co.jp

PRODUCTS/OPERATIONS

2010 Sales

	% of total
Air	81
Travel	12
Other	7
Total	**100**

2010 Sales

	% of total
Passenger	69
Cargo	7
Other	24
Total	**100**

COMPETITORS

Accor
Air France-KLM
American Airlines Group
American Express
British Airways
Carlson Wagonlit
Cathay Pacific
Central Japan Railway
China Airlines
China Eastern Airlines
China Southern Airlines
Delta Air Lines
EVA Air
East Japan Railway
Hyatt
Japan Airlines
Kintetsu
Korean Air
Qantas
Singapore Airlines
Virgin Atlantic Airways
West Japan Railway

HISTORICAL FINANCIALS

Company Type: Public

Income Statement FYE: March 31

	REVENUE ($ mil.)	NET INCOME ($ mil.)	NET PROFIT MARGIN	EMPLOYEES
03/13	15,767	458	2.9%	32,634
03/12	17,207	343	2.0%	32,884
03/11	16,395	281	1.7%	32,731
03/10	13,150	(614)	—	32,578
03/09	14,141	(43)	—	33,045
Annual Growth	2.8%	—	—	(0.3%)

2013 Year-End Financials

Debt ratio: 0.4%
Return on equity: 6.5%
Cash ($ mil.): 918
Current ratio: 1.57
Long-term debt ($ mil.): 8,019
No. of shares (mil.): —
Dividends
Yield: —
Payout: —
Market value ($ mil.): —

	STOCK PRICE ($) FY Close	P/E High/Low	PER SHARE ($) Earnings	Dividends	Book Value
03/13	4.20	— —	0.14	0.00	2.34
03/12	5.95	— —	0.14	0.00	2.68
03/11	6.05	— —	0.11	0.00	2.52
03/10	5.70	— —	(0.26)	0.00	2.04
03/09	7.72	— —	(0.02)	0.00	1.70
Annual Growth	(14.1%)	— —	—	—	8.3%

Anglo American Plc (United Kingdom)

Anglo American's name might be a little misleading —it has never been American. The UK-based company owns significant stakes in global producers of platinum (75% of Anglo Platinum) and diamonds (85% of De Beers S.A.). In addition Anglo American has interests in ferrous and base metals and industrial minerals. It ranks among the world's largest iron ore producers and is also a leading copper producer. Anglo is one of the world's largest coal miners and exporters of metallurgical coal a key raw material in steel production. It also produces thermal coal used to generate electricity. The founding Oppenheimer family no longer controls Anglo American.

Anglo American has been growing by strategic investments in long-life low-cost assets. It also has been increasing its organic growth by delivering projects ahead of or on schedule. For the past five years the company has been slimming down its operations setting strict targets and investing in strategic growth opportunities. It does not look to investments on the basis of short-term drivers but makes its decisions based on long-term investments that will be sound for the next decade or beyond. The company tries to look beyond current market volatility while making its investments.

It 2009 Anglo decided to continue investing in four major projects: Kolomela iron ore mine in South Africa Barro Alto (nickel) and Minas-Rio (iron ore) mines in Brazil and Los Bronces copper mine in Chile. By 2011 all but the Minas-Rio iron ore project had started production on or ahead of schedule. A discovery of caves at the Minas-Rio iron ore project caused a delay in the work schedule because of a need for specialized assessment.

In 2011 Anglo delivered a strong performance which was boosted by higher prices. The company achieved a record group operating profit that year of $11.1 billion up 14% from the prior year and driven in part by solid performances by its Kumba Iron Ore Metallurgical Coal and Thermal Coal divisions. However the company's net income dipped slightly from that in 2010 when the company posted larger gains on divestments.

Anglo also made acquisitions in 2011 that significantly increased its growth. Perhaps its most historic purchase in recent years was its agreement in late 2011 to acquire the Oppenheimer family's 40% stake in giant diamond company De Beers for $5.1 billion. The interest of the Oppenheimers —who had been in the diamond industry for more than a century —increased Anglo American's 45% stake to 85%. The government of Botswana holds the remaining 15%.

In addition to giving it majority control of the mining company Anglo American believes the acquisition will provide it with De Beers' expertise in administrative functions such as financial management supply chain and technical operations. The acquisition comes after a new 10-year sales agreement with the mining company's partner the government of Botswana. De Beers and Russia's ALROSA account for about half of the world's diamond production.

The company also stirred up controversy in 2011 by selling nearly 25% of its stake in Anglo American Sur copper mining subsidiary in Chile to Japan's Mitsubishi Corporation for $5.4 billion. The deal angered Chilean mining and government officials because Codelco Chile's state-owned resources company and the world's largest copper company wanted to exercise its option to buy a

49% stake in the company. Chile acted quickly to obtain a court injunction to block Anglo from selling any more of its shares of Anglo American Sur.

Although in 2012 a Chilean court rejected a bid by Codelco to have 49% of the dividends from Anglo American Sur frozen and held in escrow the dispute may drag on for years.

Anglo American and Lafarge SA agreed in 2011 to form a joint venture valued at $2.8 billion to combine their cement aggregates ready-mixed concrete asphalt and contracting businesses in the UK (Tarmac UK and Lafarge UK). The joint operations are expected to save a total of about $96 million a year through increased efficiency and improved logistics. The venture is designed to take advantage of an anticipated economic recovery. The UK's Competition Commission however ruled in 2012 that both Anglo and Lafarge would have to divest several operations including Lafarge's Hope cement plant in northern England –one of the largest in the UK.

The company also significantly expanded its metallurgical coal interests in 2011 with the acquisition of Peace River Coal Limited Partnership which holds exploration leases in British Columbia. Peace River Coal holds approximately 1 billion metric tons of high-quality coking coal.

In 2012 the company completed the final step of its $1.4 billion divestment of the Scaw Metals Group by selling Scaw South Africa an integrated steel maker to an investment consortium led by the Industrial Development Corporation of South Africa. The sale follows Anglo's disposal of Scaw's Moly-Cop and AltaSteel businesses to OneSteel in 2010.

HISTORY

In 1905 the Oppenheimers a German family with a major interest in the Premier Diamond Mining Company of South Africa began buying some of the region's richest gold-bearing land. The family formed Anglo American Corporation of South Africa in 1917 to raise money from J. P. Morgan and other US investors. The name was chosen to disguise the company's German background during WWI.

Under Ernest Oppenheimer the company bought diamond fields in German Southwest Africa (now Namibia) in 1920 breaking the De Beers hegemony in diamond production. Oppenheimer's 1928 negotiations with Hans Merensky the person credited with the discovery of South Africa's "platinum arc" led to Anglo American's interest in platinum.

The diamond monopoly resurfaced in 1929 when Anglo American won control of De Beers formed by Cecil Rhodes in 1888 with the help of England's powerful Rothschild family.

Anglo American and De Beers had become the largest gold producers in South Africa by the 1950s. They were also major world producers of coal uranium and copper. In the 1960s and 1970s Anglo American expanded through mergers and cross holdings in industrial and financial companies. It set up Luxembourg-based Minorco to own holdings outside South Africa and help the company avoid sanctions placed on firms doing business in the apartheid country.

Minorco sold its interest in Consolidated Gold Fields in 1989 and in 1990 it bought Freeport-McMoRan Gold Company (US). In 1993 Minorco bought Anglo American's and De Beers' South American European and Australian operations as part of a swap that put all of Anglo American's non-African assets except diamonds in Minorco's hands. Some analysts claimed the company had moved the assets to protect them from possible nationalization by the new black-controlled South African government. The company spun off insurer African Life to a group of black investors in 1994.

Anglo American bought a stake in UK-based conglomerate Lonrho (now Lonmin) in 1996. In 1997 Anglo American made mining acquisitions in Zambia Colombia and Tanzania and began reorganizing its gold and diamond operations. In 1998 the company's First National and Southern Life financial units merged with Rand Merchant Bank's Momentum Life Assurers to form FirstRand. (Anglo American has divested most of its interest in FirstRand.)

The company moved to the UK in 1999 and began trading on the London Stock Exchange in an effort to reach international investors. When it was based in South Africa Anglo American was unable to send its money overseas (the result of boycotts connected to that country's apartheid policies) so it bulked up on South African interests. Anglo American has evolved such that it can depend on product and geographic diversity to weather global economic turmoil. South African operations now make up less than half of the company's total sales and its base metals and platinum units each account for about a quarter of sales.

In 2000 the company bought UK building materials company Tarmac plc and later sold Tarmac America to Greece-based Titan Cement for $636 million. That year De Beers paid $590 million for Anglovaal Mining's stake in De Beers' flagship Venetia diamond mine and $900 million for Royal Dutch Shell's Australian coal mining business. On the disposal side Anglo American sold its 68% stake in LTA and its 14% stake in Li & Fung a Hong Kong trading company. Harry Oppenheimer died that year at the age of 92.

In a surprising move in early 2001 Anglo American announced that it had formed a consortium with Central Holding (the Oppenheimer family) and Debswana Diamond to acquire De Beers. In February De Beers agreed to be acquired in a deal worth about $17.6 billion. The deal –giving Anglo American and Central Holding 45% each and Debswana a 10% stake –was completed in June 2001.

In 2002 Anglo American and Japan-based conglomerate Mitsui pooled their Australian coal resources; Anglo American owns 51% of the joint venture. The company also completed a $1.3 billion deal that year for Chilean copper assets (two mines and a smelter) formerly owned by Exxon Mobil. In 2003 the company eyed the red hot iron ore market when it acquired a controlling stake in South Africa-based iron producer Kumba Resources.

Anglo American sold its 20% stake in Gold Fields to Norilsk Nickel in 2004 and reduced its stake in AngloGold Ashanti to 42% from its former 51% in 2006 then to below 20% the following year and finally entirely in 2009. In divesting its gold interests Anglo American seemed to capitulate to demands from the investor community and the idea that the gold industry is sufficiently different from the rest of the mining industry as to necessitate separate management.

The company set up new units in 2009 along product and geographical lines. The new divisions consisted of platinum (South Africa) copper (Chile) nickel (Brazil) metallurgical coal (Australia) thermal coal (South Africa) Kumba Iron Ore (of which Anglo American owned 65% South Africa) and Iron Ore Brazil. The change capped off several years of reorganization and divestment.

In 2009 the board of Anglo American rejected an offer to merge with rival Xstrata (renamed Glencore Xstrata in 2013). Although Xstrata called the bid a "merger of equals" based on similar capitalization sizes Anglo American's board was not convinced of the benefits of the $68 billion all stock deal. Although Anglo American used to have a majority stake in AngloGold Ashanti it divested its remaining shares in 2009.

In 2010 Anglo American through its subsidiary Anglo Zinc completed the divestment of its zinc assets to Vedanta Resources subsidiary Sterlite Industries in a $1.3 billion deal. That year the company also sold Tarmac's aggregates businesses in France Germany Poland and the Czech Republic as well as its French and Belgian concrete products operations for $483 million.

Nicky Oppenheimer grandson of the founder retired from the board in 2011.

EXECUTIVES

Group Director Human Resources and Communications, Mervyn Walker, age 53
Chairman, Sir John Parker, age 70
CEO Anglo Platinum, Neville F. Nicolau, age 53
Managing Director Tarmac, Karim Hajjar
Group Head Safety and Sustainable Development, Dorian Emmett, age 60
Executive Director Anglo American South Africa, Godfrey G. Gomwe, age 56
CEO Copper, John MacKenzie, age 44
Group Director Non-Core Assets, Duncan Wanblad, age 46
CEO Thermal Coal, Norman B. Mbazima, age 55
Group Head Corporate Communications and Branding, Anik Michaud
CEO Kumba Iron Ore, Chris Griffith, age 48
Group Director Mining and Technology, Brian Beamish, age 56
Group Director Business Performance and Projects, David Weston, age 54
Media Relations, James Wyatt-Tilby
Media Relations South Africa, Pranill Ramchander
Head Investor Relations South Africa, Anna Mulholland
CEO Anglo Nickel, Walter De Simoni, age 57
CEO Metallurgical Coal, Seamus French, age 50
CEO Iron Ore Brazil, Stephan Weber, age 51
Group Director Strategy and Business Development, Peter Whitcutt, age 47
Manager Internal and External Reporting, Hermien Botes
Chief Medical Officer, Brian Brink
Manager International Social and Community Development, Jonathan Samuel
Chief Financial Officer, Mark Gelmon
Chief Executive Officer; Director, Robin Forshaw
CEO and Board Member, Cynthia B. Carroll, age 55
Board Member, Jack E. Thompson, age 64
Board Member, Nicholas F. (Nicky) Oppenheimer, age 68
Board Member, Sir Chung-Kong (C.K.) Chow, age 61
Director Finance and Board Member, Rene Medori, age 55
Board Member, Sir Philip Hampton, age 60
Board Member, David Challen, age 70
Board Member, Tshmano Mohau Frederick (Fred) Phaswana, age 68
Board Member, Peter Woicke, age 70
Board Member, Ray O'Rourke, age 66
Director, Phuthuma F. Nhleko, age 53
Board Member, Mamphela Ramphele, age 66
Independent Director, Alaudin Sachedina
Independent Director, Richard Simpson
Auditors: DeloitteLLP

LOCATIONS

HQ: Anglo American Plc (United Kingdom)
20 Carlton House Terrace, London SW1Y 5AN
Phone: (44) 20 7968 8888 **Fax:** (44) 20 7968 8500
Web: www.angloamerican.com

PRODUCTS/OPERATIONS

2011 Sales

	% of total
Iron ore &	22
Platinum	20
Copper	14
Metallurgical	12
Thermal	10
Diamonds	9
Nickel	1
Other mining &	12
Total	**100**

Selected Subsidiaries

Platinum
- Anglo Platinum Corporation Limited (75% South Africa)

Base Metals
- Anglo American Sur (75% copper mines Chile)
  - Empresa Minera de Mantos Blancos SA (copper Chile)
  - Minera Loma de Niquel CA (91% nickel Venezuela)
  - Minera Quellaveco SA (80% copper Peru)
  - Minera Sur Andes Limitada (copper Chile)

Coal
- Anglo Coal (South Africa)
  - Anglo Coal (Callide) Pty Limited (Australia)

Ferrous Metals and Industries
- Kumba Resources Limited (65%; coal iron ore heavy minerals; South Africa)

Industrial Minerals
- Copebras Limitada (phosphate products Brazil)

Diamonds
- De Beers S.A. (45%)

COMPETITORS

BHP Billiton
Freeport-McMoRan
Glencore Xstrata
Impala Platinum
Norilsk Nickel
Pe?oles
Rio Tinto Limited
Teck
Vale
Vedanta Resources
Xstrata

HISTORICAL FINANCIALS

Company Type: Public

Income Statement FYE: December 31

	REVENUE ($ mil.)	NET INCOME ($ mil.)	NET PROFIT MARGIN	EMPLOYEES
12/12	28,761	(1,493)	—	106,000
12/11	30,580	6,169	20.2%	100,000
12/10	27,960	6,544	23.4%	100,000
12/09	20,858	2,425	11.6%	107,000
12/08	26,311	5,215	19.8%	105,000
Annual Growth	2.3%	—	—	0.2%

2012 Year-End Financials

Debt ratio: 22.3%
Return on equity: (-3.8%)
Cash ($ mil.): 9,094
Current ratio: 2.05
Long-term debt ($ mil.): 15,150
No. of shares (mil.): 1,390
Dividends
Yield: 2.2%
Payout: —
Market value ($ mil.): 21,713

	STOCK PRICE ($) FY Close	P/E High/Low		PER SHARE ($) Earnings	Dividends	Book Value
12/12	15.61	—	—	(1.19)	0.35	27.07
12/11	18.15	5	3	4.89	0.30	29.54
12/10	26.11	5	3	5.18	0.11	25.94
12/09	21.68	11	3	1.98	0.20	19.84
12/08	11.62	8	2	4.29	0.61	15.36
Annual Growth	7.7%	—	—	—	(13.0%)	15.2%

Anheuser-Busch Inbev SA

Anheuser-Busch InBev (AB InBev) knows how to say "beer" in a lot of languages. The company operates more than 140 breweries across six geographic regions worldwide. It boasts a product list of 200-plus brands including global best-sellers Budweiser (brewed by Anheuser Busch) Stella Artois and Beck's. The Belgian brewer holds a slew of regional beers including Leffe and Hoegaarden as well as local favorites Michelob Skol and Brahma. AB InBev controls Mexico's largest brewer Grupo Modelo which produces Corona Extra Modelo Especial and Pacifico. AB InBev isn't just for grown ups - it also makes and distributes soft drinks mostly in Latin America. All told it operates in some 20 countries worldwide.

Operations

In addition to its beverage production AB InBev has nearly 40 global facilities making everything from malt syrup to hop pellets to labels bottles and cans. It also has hop farms in Germany and the US.

Non-beer operations include an exclusive license to bottle and distribute PepsiCo products (Pepsi 7UP and Gatorade) in Brazil through its Ambev subsidiary. The unit also handles PepsiCo products in other parts of Latin America and has a exclusive deal to distribute Monster Energy drinks in Brazil. Soft drinks account for about 10% of AB InBev revenue.

Geographic Reach

The company brews beer and soda at plants spread across its six geographic zones. Latin America North and Asia Pacific have the highest number of factories with about 35 each. Latin America South and North America come in next with around 20 each. Western Europe the original home of the InBev part of AB InBev has about 15 and the Central and Eastern Europe region has around 10. Most of the facilities produce beer but nearly 20 produce both beer and soda and about a dozen (mostly in Latin America) make only soda.

North America original home of the AB part of AB InBev accounts for the majority of sales for the company.

Sales and Marketing

The company distributes it products globally according to local regulations and agreements. Generally it pursues direct distribution where possible and indirect distribution elsewhere. When using indirect distribution it strives to secure exclusive agreements. In regions where AB InBev has no direct affiliates it often licenses local brewers to produce its key brands.

Though the company has a long list of brands its employs a "focus brands" marketing strategy wherein its concentrates money people and attention on the brands that account for about 70% of its beer sales by volume. Those include its three global brands Budweiser Beck's and Stella Artois; what it calls multi-country brands (Leffe and Hoegaarden); and its "local champions" including Bud Light Jupiler Sibirskaya Korona Skol Harbin and Quilmes.

Financial Performance

AB InBev saw a modest 7% increase in revenue (adjusted to account for acquisitions and disposals) mainly due to price increases in North and South America as well as increased sales volume in Asia. Acquisitions and disposals also positively impacted nearly all the company's expenses resulting in a modest $9 million profit for 2012.

Strategy

In both developed and developing markets which each account for about half the company's sales AB InBev focuses its efforts on it core brands while developing regional favorites as well. It uses large events and social media to stay connected with its customers and introduce new products to bring in new customers.

The company also keeps costs in check through strict financial discipline and improving manufacturing efficiencies.

In 2013 the company expects to invest in new capacity projects in China Brazil and Argentina to meet future demand expectations in these growing markets.

Mergers and Acquisitions

In 2013 AB InBev acquired almost all of Mexico's largest beer company Grupo Modelo (it had already owned 50%) for some $20 billion. Owner of the ubiquitous south of the US border brands Corona Extra Modelo Especial and Pacifico Modelo will help expand AB InBev's annual revenues to around $47 billion with operations in 24 countries. The deal allows AB InBev further exposure in emerging markets like Mexico an economy that grew by 4.6% in the first quarter of 2012. Part of the arrangement include selling Grupo Modelo's US business to rival brewer Constellation Brands for about $5 billion.

HISTORY

Monks at the Leffe Abbey in Belgium were brewing beer as early as 1240 and surviving records from 1366 mention Belgium's Den Horen brewery. Belgian master brewer Sebastien Artois (best known for his Stella Artois lager) took over Den Horen in 1717. In 1853 the Piedboeuf family founded a brewery at Liege and established the Jupiler lager. Albert Van Damme assumed management of that brewery in 1920.

Over the years the Artois and Piedboeuf families took over or established operations both in and outside Belgium. Direct descendants (the clans de Spoelberch Van Damme and de Mevius) of the two families were still managing the companies in 1987 when they decided the key to survival in the fragmented European beer market was to merge.

Artois-Piedboeuf-Interbrew acquired the Hoegaarden brewery in Belgium in 1989. The company changed its name to Interbrew three years later acquired another Belgian brewery (Belle-Vue) and bought stakes in breweries in Bulgaria Croatia and Hungary. In 1995 Dommelsche Bierbrouwerij bought Allied Breweries Nederland an Allied Domecq subsidiary and Interbrew acquired the Oranjeboom breweries in the Netherlands.

The company purchased John Labatt Ltd. for $2 billion in 1995. As a result of the deal Interbrew gained control of Latrobe Brewing (Rolling Rock beer US) 22% of Mexico's FEMSA Cerveza (increased to 30% in 1998) the Toronto Argonauts football team 90% of the Toronto Blue Jays (it sold an 80% stake in the baseball team to cable firm Rogers Communications in 2000) and various broadcast properties.

Interbrew sold many noncore assets including Lehigh Valley Dairies (US) and John Labatt Retail (pubs UK) in 1996. Also that year the company established joint ventures in the Dominican Republic and the US (to import Mexican beers through FEMSA).

In 1998 Interbrew paid $250 million for 50% of the Doosan Group's Oriental Brewery South Korea's second-largest brewer and bought a majority stake in Russian brewer Rosar. The next year Interbrew combined its Russian operations with Sun Brewing forming Russian brewer Sun-Interbrew. It then bought Korea's Jinro-Coors Brewery for about $378 million. Hugo Powell was later named CEO of Interbrew.

Interbrew bought Britain's third-largest brewer Whitbread Beer Company in 2000 for $590 million. Having gained a foothold in the UK market the company then bought Bass Brewers from Bass PLC in 2000 for more than $3 billion. Interbrew went public on the Euronext (Brussels) exchange in 2000.

In 2001 Baron Paul De Keersmaeker retired as chairman and was replaced by Pierre Jean Everaert. That year the company took an 80% stake in Germany's tenth-largest brewer Diebels. Interbrew also sold Carling which controls about 18% of the UK beer market to Coors for $1.7 billion after being ordered to remedy unfair competition advantages related to the Bass Brewers purchase.

John Brock former COO of Cadbury Schweppes became CEO of Interbrew in 2003. That year it sold a minority stake of its Namibian Breweries in southern Africa to Diageo and Heineken.

In 2004 Interbrew purchased a 70% stake in Chinese brewer Zhejiang Shiliang which gave Interbrew nearly a 50% market share in China's Zhejiang province.

InBev was created through a 2005 merger of Interbrew and AmBev. The merger resulted in a series of transactions between Interbrew subsidiary Labatt and Mexico's FEMSA. By creating InBev Interbrew gave up interest in distributing FEMSA beer brands in the US. In return Interbrew retained full control of the US division of Labatt. InBev merged Labatt U.S.A. with what was Beck's North America to create its US operations.

Exiting the Slovenian market InBev sold its stake in Pivovarna Union to Pivovarna Lasko in 2005. That year it also acquired Russian premium brewer Tinkoff and sold its stake in soft-drink company Bremer Erfrischungsgetranke to Coca-Cola. It sold its minority stake in Spanish brewer Damm as well. At year-end Carlos Brito formerly zone president for the company's North American operations succeeded John Brock as CEO of InBev.

Saying it intended to concentrate on import brands in the US market in 2006 the company sold subsidiary InBev USA's domestic beer brand Rolling Rock to Anheuser-Busch for $82 million. Later in the year InBev and A-B struck an additional deal for A-B to serve as the exclusive distributor for some of its European brands such as Beck's Bass and Stella Artois. In addition it paid some $1 billion to increase its stake in Quinsa an Argentine brewer to 90% from 57% that year.

EXECUTIVES

Chairman, Kornelis J. (Kees) Storm, age 71
Chief People and Technology Officer, Claudio Garcia, age 45
Chief Executive Officer, Carlos Brito, age 53, $1,279,044 total compensation
CFO, Felipe Dutra, age 48
Chief Supply Officer, Sabine Chalmers, age 49
Chief Sales Officer, Bernardo Pinto Paiva, age 44
Chief Supply Officer, Claudio Braz Ferro, age 45
Zone President Asia Pacific, Michel Dimitrios Doukeris, age 37
Zone President Central and Eastern Europe, Stuart MacFarlane
President Asia Pacific, Ricardo Tadeu
Chief Supply Officer, Claudio Ferro
Director, Stefan Descheemaeker, age 53
Director, Kornelis J. (Kees) Storm, age 70
Director, August A. Busch IV, age 48
Director, Jorge Paulo Lemann, age 74
Director, Jean-Luc Dehaene, age 70
Director, Gregoire de Spoelberch, age 46
Director, Marcel H. Telles, age 63
Director, Roberto Moses Thompson Motta, age 55
Director, Carlos A. Sicupira, age 66
Director, Alexandre Van Damme, age 49
Director, Mark Winkelman, age 68
Director, Comte Arnoud de Pret, age 68
Auditors: PricewaterhouseCoopersBedrijfsrevisorenBCVBA

LOCATIONS

HQ: Anheuser-Busch Inbev SA
Brouwerijplein 1, Leuven 3000
Phone: (32) 16 27 6111 **Fax:** (32) 16 50 6111
Web: www.ab-inbev.com

2012 Sales

	$ mil.	% of total
North America	16,028	40
Latin America		
North	11,455	29
South	3,023	8
Europe		
Western	3,625	9
Central & Eastern	1,668	4
Asia/Pacific	2,690	7
Global Export & Holding Companies	1,270	3
Total	**39,758**	**100**

PRODUCTS/OPERATIONS

Selected Brands

Global brands
- Becks
- Budweiser
- Stella Artois

Multi-country brands
- Hoegaarden
- Leffe

Local brands
- Asia Pacific
  - Harbin
  - Sedrin
- Central & Eastern Europe
  - Chernigivske
  - Klinskoye
  - Sibirskaya Korona
- Latin America
  - Antarctica
  - Bohemia
  - Brahma
  - Quilmes
  - Skol
- North America
  - Bud Light
  - Bud Light Lime
  - Bud Light Lime Lime-A-Rita
  - Bud Light Platinum
  - Corona
  - Labatt
  - Michelob ULTRA
  - Modelo Especial
  - Natural Light
  - Pacifico
- Western Europe
  - Jupiler
  - Hasseroder
  - Lowenbrau
  - Spaten

Selected Subsidiaries and Affiliates

Anheuser-Busch Companies Inc. (US)
Bass Beers Worldwide Limited (UK)
Brasserie de L' Abbaye De Leffe S.A. (98% Belgium)
Brasserie de Luxembourg Mousel - Diekirch (96% Luxemburg)
Brauerei Beck GmbH & Co. KG (Germany)
Brauerei Diebels GmbH & Co. KG (Germany)
Brouwerij Van Hoegaarden N.V. (Belgium)
Cerveceria y Malteria Quilmes Saica y G (62% Argentina)
Cobrew N.V. (Belgium)
Companhia de Bebidas Das Americas - AmBev (62% Brazil)
Grupo Modelo S.A.B. de C.V. (95% Mexico)
Haake-Beck Brauerei GmbH & Co. KG (Germany)
Harbin Brewing Company Limited (China)
InBev Baisha (Hunan) Brewery Co. Ltd. (China)
InBev Double Deer Group Co. Ltd. (55% China)
Interbrew International B.V. (The Netherlands)
Labatt Brewing Company Limited (62% Canada)
Nanjing InBev Jinling Brewery Co. Ltd. (China)
PJSC Sun InBev Ukraine (99% Ukraine)
Spaten - Franziskaner - Brau GmbH (Germany)

COMPETITORS

Anchor Brewers
Asahi Breweries
Asia Pacific Breweries
Bavaria S.A.
Beijing Enterprises
Big Rock Brewery
Boston Beer
Carlsberg
Central European Distribution
Coca-Cola
Coca-Cola FEMSA
Constellation Brands
Craft Brew Alliance
Cuauhtemoc Moctezuma
Diageo
FEMSA
Fraser & Neave
Grolsch
Heineken
Holsten-Brauerei
Kirin Holdings Company
Lion
Molson Coors
Pyramid Breweries
Radeberger Gruppe
SABMiller
San Miguel Corporation
Sapporo
Suntory Holdings
Thai Beverage
Tsingtao
UB Group
Yuengling & Son

HISTORICAL FINANCIALS

Company Type: Public

Income Statement FYE: December 31

	REVENUE ($ mil.)	NET INCOME ($ mil.)	NET PROFIT MARGIN	EMPLOYEES
12/12	39,758	7,243	18.2%	117,632
12/11	39,046	5,855	15.0%	116,278
12/10	36,297	4,026	11.1%	114,313
12/09	36,758	4,613	12.5%	116,489
12/08	22,512	1,800	8.0%	119,874
Annual Growth	15.3%	41.6%	—	(0.5%)

2012 Year-End Financials

Debt ratio: 36.1%
Return on equity: 18.3%
Cash ($ mil.): 7,051
Current ratio: 1.01
Long-term debt ($ mil.): 38,951
No. of shares (mil.): 1,602
Dividends
Yield: 1.7%
Payout: 35.0%
Market value ($ mil.): 140,038

	STOCK PRICE ($) FY Close	P/E High/Low	PER SHARE ($) Earnings	Dividends	Book Value
12/12	87.41	20 13	4.45	1.56	25.68
12/11	60.99	17 14	3.63	1.18	23.46
12/10	57.09	25 18	2.50	0.49	22.13
12/09	52.03	18 13	2.90	0.00	19.06
Annual Growth	18.9%	— —	11.3%	—	7.7%

AP Moller AS

LOCATIONS

HQ: AP Moller AS
Esplanaden 50, Copenhagen K 1098
Phone: (45) 33 63 33 63
Web: www.maersk.com

HISTORICAL FINANCIALS

Company Type: Public

Income Statement FYE: December 31

	REVENUE ($ mil.)	NET INCOME ($ mil.)	NET PROFIT MARGIN	EMPLOYEES
12/12	60,432	3,829	6.3%	121,105
12/11	56,114	2,642	4.7%	117,080
12/10	56,630	4,750	8.4%	108,110
12/09	50,333	(1,360)	—	115,386
12/08	58,508	3,182	5.4%	119,599
Annual Growth	0.8%	4.7%	—	0.3%

2012 Year-End Financials

Debt ratio: 4.6%	No. of shares (mil.): 4
Return on equity: 10.7%	Dividends
Cash ($ mil.): 2,298	Yield: —
Current ratio: 1.15	Payout: —
Long-term debt ($ mil.): 17,333	Market value ($ mil.): —

ArcelorMittal SA

Few metal makers have the mettle of ArcelorMittal. The company is easily the largest steel-making entity in the world producing more than 90 million metric tons of crude steel annually about 6% of the world steel output. Operating in more than 60 countries ArcelorMittal manufactures the full range of steel products: slabs and coil coated steel and tinplate wire rod and rebar and billets and blooms as well as all manner of electrical steel products. It also has 20 mining operations and is one of the world's largest iron ore producers. In 2011 it produced 54 million metric tons of iron ore and 8 million metric tons of metallurgical coal. CEO and founder Lakshmi Mittal controls about 41% of ArcelorMittal.

ArcelorMittal operates through subsidiaries in Europe Africa Asia and the Americas. The company is the largest producer of steel in North and South America and Africa the second-largest steel producer in the Commonwealth of Independent States region and has a growing presence in Asia including investments in China. It is also the largest steel producer in the European Union. In addition many of ArcelorMittal's units have access to developing markets that are expected to experience significant future growth in steel consumption such as Central and Eastern Europe South America India Africa and Russia. Overall about 48% of its steel is produced in Europe 36% in the Americas and 16% in other countries such as Kazakhstan South Africa and Ukraine.

ArcelorMittal produces a wide variety of products across all steel-consuming industries including the automotive appliance engineering construction energy and machinery markets. The company sells its products in local markets and through a centralized marketing organization in more than 170 countries. It's strategy depends on maintaining its size and scale in the global steel market vertical integration of its operations producing a diverse portfolio of products and continuously improving its quality.

Following a dismal slide in 2009 ArcelorMittal rebounded to post a 20% increase in overall revenues for 2010. Still a far cry from the record numbers of 2008 the company's net income took a steep climb up almost 2500% in 2010 though it fell more than three times that amount the previous year due to the global recession. Its Flat Carbon Americas and Flat Carbon Europe segments showed significant sales gains in 2010 as did its Long Carbon Americas and Europe segment.

In 2011 the company spun off its stainless and specialty steels steel operations into Aperam which immediately became the world's sixth-largest stainless steel producer. ArcelorMittal made the decision in 2010 to spin off its stainless steel units in Europe and Brazil after determining that they were underperforming and would better thrive as a separate business.

Strategy

In 2013 ArcelorMittal formed a joint venture with Nippon Steel & Sumitomo Metal to buy ThyssenKrupp Steel USA from ThyssenKrupp for $1.5 billion. The deal is expected to deliver $60 million in annual savings.

To focus on its core businesses and pay down debt in 2013 the company sold 15% of its ArcelorMittal Mines Canada subsidiary to Chinese and Korean steelmakers for $1.1 billion.

In 2012 ArcelorMittal agreed to sell New Jersey-based Skyline Steel a North American steel foundation and piling products distributor and specialty steel plate and bar producer Astralloy to US-based Nucor for $605 million. Arcelor-Mittal will continue to use Skyline as a distributor of its piling and foundation products including sheet piling in North America and the Caribbean. Skyline serves the construction and infrastructure industries.

In 2012 ArcelorMittal decided to expand its presence in China. It agreed to increase its stake in a joint venture with Valin Group known as Valin ArcelorMittal Automotive (VAMA) from 33% to 49%. VAMA is trying to enhance its position in China as a supplier of high-strength steels and products for the automotive market. The joint venture scheduled to become operational in 2014 will increase its planned capacity from 1.2 million tons to 1.5 million tons.

After spinning its wheels in an escalating bidding war in 2011 ArcelorMittal joined rival Nunavut Iron Ore in making a joint acquisition of Canada-based Baffinland Iron Mines for $594 million. Both companies sought access to Baffinland's Mary River Project an undeveloped deposit of iron ore on sparsely populated North Baffin Island located inside the Arctic Circle as a source of raw materials. The venture faces stiff challenges including building an infrastructure around the mine's formidable location and shipping the ore out to Europe and other production sites.

Also that year the company agreed to buy a 40% stake in G Steel Public Company greatly expanding its presence in Asia. G Steel produces about 2.5 million ton of steel annually at its two slab-rolling plants in Thailand. The deal is part of ArcelorMittal's strategy of establishing a presence in emerging markets with with the potential for future growth.

In 2011 ArcelorMittal joined with Peabody Energy to make an offer to jointly acquire Macarthur Coal Ltd. and its extensive holdings (23 billion tons of reserves and the largest producer of pulverized coking coal) in Australia's Bowen Basin. ArcelorMittal would hold a 40% stake in Macarthur. However shortly after the companies gained a controlling stake (more than 59%) in Macarthur ArcelorMittal backed out of the deal. Peabody the world's largest private-sector coal company will take 100% of PEAMCoal its joint venture with ArcelorMittal that was acquiring Macarthur.

In 2010 ArcelorMittal sought to buy Zimbabwe Iron and Steel Works but the deal was rejected by the Zimbabwean government which owns a controlling stake in the operation. Government officials said they were looking for a smaller company to partner with the state-owned operation.

In 2009 ArcelorMittal completed its acquisition of the laser-welding steel activities of Noble International a leader in the niche industry. It also acquired Mexican steel producer Sicarsta for nearly $1.5 billion an acquisition that combined with its Lazaro Cardenas created Mexico's largest steel company.

Since its consolidation of Arcelor and Mittal Steel the company has been working to gather its Brazilian steel operations into one cohesive unit. ArcelorMittal Brasil is among that country's largest steel producers now. In 2008 ArcelorMittal agreed to pay London Mining $810 million to buy its Brazilian iron ore mining unit. The idea behind the deal is to vertically integrate more fully ArcelorMittal's steel operations by providing its own raw materials.

HISTORY

ArcelorMittal is the product of decades of steelmaking by India's Mittal family. In 1967 patriarch Mohan Mittal unsuccessfully tried to open a steel mill in Egypt. He and his four younger brothers then set up a steel company in India but squabbles pushed Mohan to chart his own course eventually giving rise to an empire that flourished under the Ispat name. Mohan's son Lakshmi began working part-time at the family steel mill while in school; he started full-time at 21 after graduating in 1971.

Mohan set up an operation in Indonesia in 1975 (Ispat Indo) and put Lakshmi in charge. The next year fueled by ambitions and held back by government regulations in India Lakshmi formed Ispat International in Jakarta Indonesia to focus on expansion through acquisitions. He spent the next decade strengthening the Indonesian operations and perfecting the minimill process using direct-reduced iron (DRI).

Ispat took advantage of the recessionary late 1980s and early 1990s by making a string of acquisitions. In 1988 it took over the management of Trinidad and Tobago's state steel companies (bought in 1994; renamed Caribbean Ispat).

In 1992 Ispat bought Mexico's third-largest (albeit bankrupt) steel and DRI producer. Two years later it acquired Canada's Sidbec-Dosco steelmaker. Also that year Lakshmi took exclusive control of international operations leaving his brothers Pramod and Vinod to control the Indian divisions.

The mid-1990s brought more acquisitions: In 1995 Ispat bought Germany's Hamburger Stahlwerks and a mill in Kazakhstan. The next year it purchased Ireland's only steelmaker Irish Steel. Lakshmi moved to London in 1996 and purchased a home on Bishops Avenue known as "millionaire's row." (Saudi Arabia's King Fahd was a neighbor.)

In 1997 the company bought the long-product (wire rod) division of Germany's Thyssen AG (renamed Ispat Stahlwerk Ruhrort and Ispat Walzdraht Hochfeld). It also completed a $776 million IPO.

Ispat acquired Chicago-based Inland Steel in 1998 (and renamed it Ispat Inland) including the steel-finishing operations of I/N Tek (60% Inland-owned joint venture with Nippon Steel) and I/N Kote (50% Inland-owned joint venture with NSC).

In 1999 Ispat formed a joint venture with Mexican steelmaker Grupo Imsa to make flat-rolled steel to sell throughout most of the Americas. It also paid $96 million for France-based Usinor's Unimetal Trefileurope and Societe Metallurgique de Revigny subsidiaries which specialize in carbon long products. That year Ispat Inland became the target of a US federal criminal grand jury investigation and a related civil lawsuit for allegedly defrauding the Louisiana Highway Department. (The case was settled for $30 million with the cost split between Ispat Inland and Contech Construction Products Inc. of Ohio.)

In 2000 the company responded to a downturn in the steel industry by starting a Web-based joint venture with Commerce One to connect buyers and sellers in the worldwide metals market. It also offered to buy VSZ Slovakia's #1 steelworks but was outbid by U.S. Steel.

After struggling with heavy debt high labor and energy costs new environmental regulations and EU steel quotas in 2001 Ispat closed down its subsidiary Irish Ispat which accounted for about 2% of the parent company's steel production.

In 2002 the company's 51%-owned pipe making subsidiary Productura Mexicana de Tuberia sold almost all of its production assets.

The present ArcelorMittal was forged in 2004 when Ispat International (of which the Mittal family owned 70%) purchased LNM Holdings (wholly owned by the Mittals) for $13 billion. In 2006 the former Mittal Steel agreed to buy rival Arcelor for about $34 billion to create ArcelorMittal.

Mittal Steel had established its hold on the world steel market through its 2005 purchase of the US-based International Steel Group (ISG) for $4.5 billion. The purchase made the company the largest steel producer (ahead of U.S. Steel and Nucor) in the US a market that had long been a targeted area for expansion for CEO Mittal. Once the deal closed the company combined ISG's operations with those of subsidiary Ispat Inland to form a single North American entity Mittal Steel USA (now ArcelorMittal USA.

Also in 2005 Mittal Steel acquired a 93% stake in Ukrainian state-run steel company KryvorizhStal with the winning $4.84 billion bid in an auction held by the Ukrainian government. The price was high but Mittal was anxious to gain a stronger foothold in the region –and to keep its rivals away from KryvorizhStal. (This fact incidentally went a long way to convincing Mittal it needed to combine with Arcelor; the competition for acquisitions was driving prices dramatically upward.)

The company also began to broaden its portfolio outside the steel industry dipping its toe into the energy business. In mid-2005 Mittal formed two joint ventures with India's government-controlled Oil & Natural Gas Corporation: one to buy stakes in foreign oil and gas projects the other involved in oil and gas trading and shipping. The ventures began to look for business in places like Indonesia Kazakhstan Angola and Trinidad and Tobago.

After consolidating his family's various steel interests in the early part of this decade Mittal began work on the steel industry as a whole and was soon the world's largest steel producer.

By 2006 Mittal Steel no longer was content to be merely the world's largest steel producer; it wanted to dominate the market. The company announced an offer to the shareholders of Arcelor then the industry's #2 player to buy that company and in the process create the world's first 100-million-ton steel producer. Arcelor and seemingly half the governments of Western Europe initially fought the attempt.

Mittal improved its proposed price however and Arcelor's board finally approved the offer when Mittal also made ownership/corporate governance concessions. The combined company is 43% owned by the Mittal family. After a few months of a transitional management team arrangement Lakshmi Mittal took over as CEO of the combined company toward the end of 2006.

EXECUTIVES

executive Vice-President of ArcelorMittal visited ArcelorMittal Ostrava, Gerhard Renz, age 65
EVP Finance, Bhikam C. Agarwal, age 61
Chairman and CEO, Lakshmi N. Mittal, age 62
SEVP Asia Africa Commonwealth of Independent States (excluding China and India); Distribution Solutions; Tubular Products and Corporate Responsibility, Gonzalo Urquijo, age 50
SEVP Long Carbon Worldwide, Michel Wurth, age 59
EVP; Chief Executive Stainless, Bernard Fontana, age 51
CFO, Aditya Mittal, age 37
President and CEO ArcelorMittal Mines Canada, Serge Miller
SEVP; Head Mining, Peter G. J. Kukielski, age 56
VP; CEO Long Carbon Europe, Augustine Kochuparampil
EVP and Head Marketing and Commercial Coordination, Michael B. Pfitzner, age 63
EVP; CEO India and China, Vijay K. Bhatnagar, age 67
EVP; CEO ArcelorMittal USA, Michael G. (Mike) Rippey, age 56
EVP; CEO ArcelorMittal Mining, Bill Scotting, age 55
EVP; CEO Flat Americas; CTO, Louis (Lou) Schorsch, age 64
Member Group Management Board Shared Services, Davinder K. Chugh, age 56
Member Group Management Board Corporate Finance Mergers and Acquisitions and Business Development including India (chapter 1) and Risk Management, Sudhir Maheshwari, age 49
Secretary, Henk Scheffer
Corporate Communications, Nicola Davidson
Media Contact North America, Bill Steers
VP ArcelorMittal North American Investor Relations, Thomas A. (Tom) McCue
CFO Stainless Steel, Julien Onillon, age 42
Member Group Management Board Technology and Projects Asia and Africa, Christophe Cornier, age 60
EVP; CEO Distribution Solutions, Philippe Darmayan, age 60
EVP and CTO, Pierre Gugliermina, age 61
EVP; CEO Flat Carbon Europe, Robrecht Himpe, age 55
EVP; CEO Africa and Commonwealth of Independent States (CIS), Arnaud Poupart-Lafarge, age 47
Secretary Group Management Board, Sujogya Dash
Head Media Relations, Giles Read
Corporate Media Contact, Arne Langner
Corporate Media Contact, Jean Lasar
Corporate Media Contact, Lynn Robbroeckx
Media Contact Spain, Ignacio Agreda
Director Investor Relations, Daniel Fairclough
CEO ArcelorMittal Kryviy Rih, Rinat Starkov
EVP and Head Human Resources, Willie Smit
VP; CEO Long Carbon Central and South America, Augusto Augusto Espeschit de Almeida Almeida
VP; CEO Flat Carbon South America, Benjamin Baptista
VP; CEO ArcelorMittal Mexico, Bill Bill Chisholm Chisholm
Vice President Chief Marketing Officer, Brian Aranha
Independent Member of Board of Directors, Bruno Bruno Lafont Lafont
VP; CEO - Flat Carbon Europe Business Division North, Geert Van Poelvoorde
Vice President Global research and development, Gregory Ludkovsky
Independent Member of Board of Directors, Guillaume Guillaume de Luxembourg Luxembourg
VP; CEO Flat Carbon Europe Business Division Southwest, Jean-Luc Maurange
Executive Vice President Long Carbon Americas, Jefferson Paula
Member of Management Committee and Vice President; CEO; ArcelorMittal Dofasco; Hamilton, Juergen Juergen Schachler Schachler
Member of Management Committee and Vice President; Mining Operations, Kleber Kleber Silva Silva
Member of Management Committee; Vice President; Chief Technology Officer, Marc Marc Vereecke Vereecke
VP; CEO ArcelorMittal South Africa, Nku Nymebezi-Heita
VP; CEO Long Carbon North America, PS (Venkat) Venkataramanan
Executive Vice President; Head of Mining Projects and Exploration; Member of the Management Committee, Philippus Philippus du Toit Toit
VP; CEO Flat Carbon Europe Business Division East; CEO ArcelorMittal Poland, Sanjay Sanjay Samaddar Samaddar
Vice President Chief Commercial Officer, Simon Wandke
Vice President and Head of Americas Iron Ore Operations, Steven Steven Wood Wood
VP and Director of Security; Health; Assets Safety; Environment and Mining Sustainability, Suresh Suresh Rajapakse Rajapakse
VP; CEO Distribution Solutions, Alain Le Grix
Executive Vice President, Henri Blaffart
Board Member, Lewis B. (Lew) Kaden, age 70
Board Member, Narayanan Vaghul, age 76
Board Member, Wilbur L. Ross Jr., age 75
Board Member, Vanisha Mittal Bhatia, age 32
Board Member, Antoine Spillmann, age 49
Board Member, Prince Guillaume de Luxembourg, age 49
Board Member, Suzanne P. Nimocks
Board Member, Jeannot Krecke, age 61
Non Independent Member of Board of Directors, Jeannot Jeannot Krecke Krecke
Independent Director, Tye Tye Burt Burt
Non Independent Member of Board of Directors, Vanisha Vanisha Mittal Bhatia Bhatia
Auditors: DeloitteS.A.

LOCATIONS

HQ: ArcelorMittal SA
19, Avenue de la Liberte, Luxembourg L-2930
Phone: (352) 4792 2484 **Fax:** (352) 4792 89 3937
Web: www.arcelormittal.com

2010 Sales

	$ mil.	% of total
Europe	37,446	48
Asia & Africa	12,564	16

PRODUCTS/OPERATIONS

2010 Sales

	$ mil.	% of total
Flat Carbon Products		
Americas	19,301	21
Steel Solutions & Services	15,744	17
Total	**78,025**	**100**

Segments and Selected Products
Flat Carbon Europe
Coated products
Coil
Cold-rolled
Hot-rolled
Plate
Slab
Tin plate
Flat Carbon Americas
Coated products
Steel
Plate
Coil
Cold-rolled
Hot-rolled
Slabs
Long Carbon Americas & Europe
Billets
Blooms
Rebar
Sections
Wire rod
Asia Africa & Comonwealth of Independent States
Flat products
Long products
Pipes
Tubes
ArcelorMittal Steel Solutions & Services (in-house trading and distribution arm)

COMPETITORS

AK Steel Holding Corporation
BHP Billiton
Baosteel
BlueScope Steel
China Steel

Essar Group
Evraz
Gerdau
JFE Holdings
Mechel OAO
Nippon Steel & Sumitomo Metal Corporation
Nucor
POSCO
Severstal
Shougang Corp.
Tata Steel
Tenaris
Ternium
ThyssenKrupp Steel
United States Steel

HISTORICAL FINANCIALS

Company Type: Public

Income Statement FYE: December 31

	REVENUE ($ mil.)	NET INCOME ($ mil.)	NET PROFIT MARGIN	EMPLOYEES
12/12	84,213	(3,726)	—	273,811
12/11	93,973	2,263	2.4%	260,523
12/10	78,025	2,916	3.7%	273,811
12/09	65,110	118	0.2%	281,703
12/08	124,936	9,399	7.5%	315,867
Annual Growth	(9.4%)	—	—	(3.5%)

2012 Year-End Financials

Debt ratio: 22.9%
Return on equity: (-6.8%)
Cash ($ mil.): 4,398
Current ratio: 1.33
Long-term debt ($ mil.): 21,965
No. of shares (mil.): 1,549
Dividends
Yield: 3.6%
Payout: 455.3%
Market value ($ mil.): 27,063

	STOCK PRICE ($) FY Close	P/E High/Low	PER SHARE ($) Earnings	Dividends	Book Value
12/12	17.47	— —	(2.41)	0.64	33.39
12/11	18.19	26 10	1.19	0.64	36.60
12/10	38.13	25 14	1.72	0.64	40.31
12/09	45.75	585214	0.08	0.64	40.44
12/08	24.59	15 2	6.78	1.28	40.41
Annual Growth	(8.2%)	— —	—	(15.9%)	(4.7%)

Assicurazioni Generali S.p.A.

Italy's largest insurance company (and one of the largest in Europe) Assicurazioni Generali writes insurance for risks as varied as pensions and car insurance. Present in more than 60 countries Generali's core businesses are involved in both personal and commercial insurance (including life accident health motor fire marine/aviation and reinsurance); the rest concentrate on other financial services and real estate. Generali is noted for being a leading insurer of satellite and space missions which it has been covering since 1964. In more earthbound realms the company targets individuals and small to midsized businesses and has been in business since 1831.

Generali operates through more than 500 companies throughout the world. Life insurance makes up the lion's share of its business with products that include savings and protection policies health business and supplementary pension policies. More than two-thirds of its written premiums are generated through its life insurance segment. Its non-life segment centers on retail markets.

Although Generali promotes its financial services operations including Banca Generali and BSI such services as wealth management and bank insurance products only account for about 10% of its revenues.

Italy Germany and France are Generali's largest markets with Austria and Spain significantly adding to sales. Its Italian property/casualty subsidiary Alleanza Toro holds a good chunk of Generali's domestic operations serving more than 3 million customers; it offers products under the Alleanza and Toro brands.

Generali's results in 2011 were affected by broadspread economic instabilities in the eurozone. Its life insurance results suffered impairment losses on Greek government bonds and its non-life markets were impacted by adverse trading conditions. Revenues for the year fell almost 13% to $104.9 billion down from the $120.3 billion achieved in 2010. Net income sank 44% to $1.5 billion down from $2.7 billion. Written premiums also dropped by 6%. At year end the company had more than $600 billion worth of assets and a $36.5 billion property portfolio. The company is looking to grow its operating results by 10% in 2012.

Generali's strategy for growth is based entering new market segments and countries. With its place firmly cemented in Western Europe it is looking to expand its presence in Eastern Europe Latin America and Asia through joint ventures and acquisitions. To that end Generali has targeted the fast-growing life insurance market of Vietnam and launched its Generali Vietnam Life Insurance Company subsidiary in 2011. Its BSI private banking division also received license to provide banking and investment services in Hong Kong that year.

Other strategic initiatives include improving its overall operating efficiencies including centralizing its IT operations into a single data center; optimizing its distribution networks and the developing proprietary networks; delivering innovative products; and diversifying its distribution methods. To reach younger customers it is particularly vested in providing direct channels via mobile applications and the web. The company leads in direct-to-consumers telephone and online channels in Italy Germany and France where it offers both life and property/casualty products.

The company's largest shareholder is Mediobanca with 13% of the its shares. Other institutional shareholders collectively own 55% of the company and retail shareholders own almost 32%.

HISTORY

Assicurazioni Generali was founded as Assicurazioni Generali Austro-Italiche in 1831 by a group of merchants led by Giuseppe Morpurgo in the Austro-Hungarian port of Trieste. Formed to provide insurance to the city's bustling trade industry the company offered life marine fire flood and shipping coverage. That year Morpurgo established what he intended to be Generali's headquarters in Venice. (While the company maintained offices in both cities Trieste ultimately won out.)

By 1835 Generali had opened 25 offices in Central and Western Europe; it had also expelled Morpurgo. The firm moved into Africa and Asia in the 1880s. In 1900 Generali began selling injury and theft insurance. In 1907 Generali's Prague office provided the young experimental writer Franz Kafka his first job. (He found it disagreeable and quit after a few months.)

During WWI the firm's Venice office pledged allegiance to Italy while the office in Trieste (still part of Austria-Hungary) stayed loyal to the Hapsburgs. After the war Trieste was absorbed by the new Italian republic. Under Edgardo Morpurgo Generali expanded further in the 1920s managing 30 subsidiaries and operating in 17 countries. As fascist Italy aligned itself with Germany in the 1930s adoption of anti-Semitic laws caused Morpurgo and a number of other high-ranking Jewish employees to flee the country. In 1938 Generali moved its headquarters to Rome (but moved them back to Trieste after war's end).

The firm maintained steady business both before and during Nazi occupation in WWII; in 1945 however the Soviets seized all Italian properties in Eastern Europe including 14 Generali subsidiaries. In 1950 Generali invaded the US market offering shipping and fire insurance and reinsurance. Generali established a cooperative agreement with Aetna Life and Casualty (now Aetna Inc.) in 1966 further cementing its US connections.

In 1988 Generali tried to acquire French insurer Compagnie du Midi. Foreshadowing Generali's later dealings with Istituto Nazionale delle Assicurazioni (INA) Midi escaped Generali's grasp through a merger with AXA. As the Iron Curtain frayed in 1989 Generali formed AB Generali Budapest through a joint venture with a Hungarian insurer. In 1990 the firm opened an office in Tokyo through an agreement with Taisho Marine and Fire Insurance (which became Mitsui Marine & Fire Insurance and is now Mitsui Sumitomo Insurance). By 1993 Generali had become Italy's largest insurer.

In 1997 the firm was accused along with other major European insurers of not paying on policies of Holocaust victims. (It moved to settle claims in 1999.)

The company focused on the German and Swiss markets in 1998 acquiring controlling interests in insurer AMB Aachener und Munchener (now AMB Generali) and in Banca della Svizzera Italiana. Also that year Generali and Commerzbank established an alliance that gave the companies more access to each other's markets.

In 1999 Generali succeeded in a hostile takeover of INA its largest domestic competitor. The move pre-empted INA's proposed merger with San Paolo IMI which would have knocked Generali to second place among the country's insurers.

Avoiding violation of the EU's antitrust laws in connection with the INA acquisition the company sold four subsidiaries (including Italian insurers Aurora and Navale) in 2000.

In 2002 Generali rolled together three Italian securities investments firms —Altinia Ina Sim and Prime Consult Sim —into Banca Generali.

The insurer entrenched itself in Germany by acquiring a controlling interest in one of the country's largest insurers AMB Generali (formerly Aachener und Munchener) and establishing an alliance with Commerzbank in 2006. In Spain the company boosted its presence with its 2009 acquisition of local insurers Estrella Seguros and Vitalicio Seguros. Generali also acquired the remaining shares of its majority-owned Italian life insurance firm Alleanza Assicurazioni in 2009 and then merged Alleanza with its Italian property/casualty subsidiary Toro Assicurazioni into a new company named Alleanza Toro.

Some of the company's acquisitions in Eastern Europe have drawn questions from its own board members. More specifically a joint venture struck in 2008 with Czech insurer PPF Group drew in Italy's market regulators. Citing differences with the company's strategy Cesare Geronzi resigned as chairman in 2011.

EXECUTIVES

Managing Director, Sergio Balbinot, age 53
Financial Reporting, Massimo Romano, age 54
Vice Chairman, Vincent Bollore, age 61
Vice Chairman, Francesco G. Caltagirone, age 70

Vice Chairman, Alberto N. Nagel, age 48
Assistant General Manager Mergers & Acquisitions, Amerigo Borrini
Assistant General Manager Group Communication, Mauro Giusto, age 53
Deputy General Manager Human Resources & Organization, Lodovico Floriani
Real Estate, Giancarlo Scotti
Assistant General Manager Group Control Strategic Planning and Tax, Stefano Meroi, age 48
General Manager and CFO, Raffaele Agrusti, age 56
Deputy General Manager Insurance Operations, Valter Trevisani, age 51
Head Research and Development, Lorenzo Savorelli, age 54
Assistant General Manager Technical Insurance Area and International and European Union Relations, Franco Urlini, age 53
Group Compliance, Antonio Cangeri
Head Group Internal Audit, Alessandro Busetti
Assistant General Manager Group Legal and Corporate Affairs, Oliviero E. Pessi
Chief Risk Officer, Stefano Ferri
Chief Information Technology Officer, Massimo Paltrinieri
Head Investor Relations, Salvatore Colotti
Chief Investment Officer, Philippe Setbon
Chairman, Eugenio Colucci
Chairman, Gabriele Galateri
Controller, Generali S.p.A
CEO, Mario Greco
Managing Director, Sergio Balbinot, age 53
Board Member, Paolo Scaroni, age 67
Vice Chairman, Vincent Bollore, age 61
Group CEO and Managing Director, Giovanni Perissinotto, age 58
Vice Chairman, Francesco G. Caltagirone, age 70
Board Member, Lorenzo Pellicioli, age 62
Board Member, Diego Della Valle, age 60
Board Member, Alessandro (Att) Pedersoli, age 84
Vice Chairman, Alberto N. Nagel, age 48
Board Member, Reinfried Pohl, age 85
Board Member, Petr Kellner, age 49
Chairman, Gabriele Galateri
Auditors: PricewaterhouseCoopersSpA

LOCATIONS

HQ: Assicurazioni Generali S.p.A.
Piazza Duca degli Abruzzi 2, P.O. Box 538, Trieste 34132
Phone: (39) 40 6711 **Fax:** (39) 40 671 600
Web: www.generali.com

2011 Written Premiums by Location

	% of total
Europe	
Italy	29
Germany	24
France	19
Austria	4
Spain	4
Switzerland	2
Other	10
Other	8
Total	**100**

PRODUCTS/OPERATIONS

2011 Revenues

	% of total
Life	59
Property/casualty	31
Financial	10
Total	**100**

2011 Written Premiums

	% of total
Life	67
Non-life	33
Total	**100**

Mergers Acquisitions Divestitur

2011
Sale of stake in Afore Banorte Generali (Mexican pension business operations
Sale of 51% stake in B-Source S.A. (Swiss banking services)

2010
Participation in Intesa Vita sold

2009
Merger of Alleanza Assicurazioni in Assicurazioni Generali and creation of Alleanza Toro
Agreement for the purchase of 30% stake in Guotai AMC (asset manager China)

2008
Generali PPF Holding acquires majority stakes in Ardaf e Rai (insurance companies Romania)
Joint venture with Czech Group PPF and incorporation of Generali PPF Holding (Generali owns a 51 stake)

2007
BSI acquires Banca del Gottardo (bank Switzerlan
Nuova Tirrena sold to Groupama

2006
Purchase of Toro Assicurazioni (65.5% insurance Italy)
Purchase of majority stake in Orel-G (insurance Bulgaria)
Purchase of majority stake in Garant Auto e Garant Life (insurance companies Ukraine)
Purchase of majority stake in Delta Osiguranje (insurance Serbia)
Purchase of Libertas Osiguranje (insurance Croatia)
BSI acquires Banca Unione di Credito (credit union bank Switzerlan
Squeeze out of minorities shareholders of Generali Schweiz Holding (Switzerla
Squeeze out of minorities shareholders of Generali Holding Vienna (Austria)
Partial squeeze out of minorities shareholders of AMB Generali Holding (Germany)

COMPETITORS

AIG
AXA
Allianz
Assurances Generales de France
Camfin
ERGO
Eureko
FonSai
ING
Milano Assicurazioni
Swiss Re
Unipol
Zurich Insurance Group
ageas SA/NV

HISTORICAL FINANCIALS

Company Type: Public

Income Statement FYE: December 31

	ASSETS ($ mil.)	NET INCOME ($ mil.)	INCOME AS % OF ASSETS	EMPLOYEES
12/12	582,241	118	0.0%	0
12/11	547,204	1,107	0.2%	81,997
12/10	565,381	2,277	0.4%	85,368
12/09	610,537	1,885	0.3%	85,322
12/08	536,780	1,203	0.2%	84,063
Annual Growth	2.1%	(44.0%)	—	—

2012 Year-End Financials

Return on assets: 0.0%
Return on equity: 0.5%
Long-term debt ($ mil.): —
No. of shares (mil.): 1,556
Sales ($ mil): 109,109
Dividends
Yield: 0.0%
Payout: 189.5%
Market value ($ mil.): 11,116

	STOCK PRICE ($) FY Close	P/E High/Low	PER SHARE ($) Earnings	Dividends	Book Value
12/12	7.14	238151	0.08	0.15	16.79
12/11	11.23	38 28	0.72	0.39	12.87
12/10	10.40	23 14	1.47	0.23	15.04
12/09	11.63	25 25	1.34	0.13	15.41
Annual Growth	(15.0%)	— —	(50.7%)	4.2%	2.2%

Associated British Foods Plc

Think you're the best thing since sliced bread? Associated British Foods (ABF) "is" sliced bread. ABF which introduced sliced bread in the UK during the 1930s makes and markets baked goods under the Allinson and Tip Top brands. Its grocery products which account for some one-third of sales include household staples Karo syrup Argo corn starch Kingsmill bread Silver Spoon sugar and Twinings tea. In the US it owns Fleischmanns Yeast and ingredient and spice maker ACH. Other divisions churn out sugar pharmaceutical ingredients specialty oils and animal feed. Beyond food ABF owns Primark a retail clothing chain in the UK and parts of Europe. ABF's activities span nearly 45 countries worldwide.

ABF benefits from a diversified basketful of international name brands. More than 50% of the company's sales and about 45% of its operating profits are generated outside of the UK. Grocery operations provide a slow-growth platform from which to pursue higher-growth yet more volatile commodity markets such as agriculture and sugar.

Despite a difficult global economy ABF has managed to shore up its performance. Following a two-year decline in 2010 year-over-year earnings (US currency) climbed more than 50% slipping slightly in 2011 on a modest acceleration in sales. Results were driven by more than a two-fold increase in demand from the Asia/Pacific region which helped offset a sharp decline in the Americas.

ABF's cash position which bounced up in 2010 and down the next year reflects a handful of capital investments. Among them the company has funded a new meat factory in Australia and launched Vivergo Fuels Ltd. The UK wheat bioethanol plant operational in 2012 is a joint venture among ABF BP and DuPont which produces bio-fuel and animal feed.

Sugar prices which marked a 30-year high during most of 2011 have also buoyed recent earnings. ABF's sugar business (representing about 20% of sales) took off in 2009 with the acquisition of Azucarera Ebro a beet sugar producer owned by Ebro Puleva. The takeover has strengthened ABF's business infrastructure; previously ABF orchestrated a long-term agreement for its African sugar processor Illovo to supply Azucarera Ebro with raw cane sugar. In addition Azucarera produces ethanol and animal feed. ABF bolsters operations further with a handful of cane sugar mills and beet sugar factories in China.

Elsewhere ABF is continuing to invest in Primark as it faces off lower consumer spending coupled with higher unemployment. Over the last 10 years the clothing retailer has doubled its store count expanding to generate more than one-quarter of the company's sales. Some 220 stores primarily in the UK but with a growing presence in Western Europe cater the latest fashion trends to the under 35-year-old woman. During 2011 retail operating profits slumped some 9% on more than a 10% uptick in sales over the prior year. ABF cited its decision to absorb the costs associated with increased cotton prices and higher UK taxes in order to preserve its customer base.

ABF's future in large part looks to its past. It is one of the UK's biggest family owned businesses. Founded in 1935 by W. Garfield Weston his great-grandson CEO George Weston and the Weston family own approximately 55% of ABF.

HISTORY

When Garfield Weston took over his father's company upon the elder Weston's death in 1924 George Weston Limited was one of Canada's largest bakeries. Ten years later taking advantage of the cheap prices afforded by a worldwide depression Garfield purchased a biscuit-making division from Scottish baker Mitchell & Muir and opened a factory in Edinburgh. He promptly purchased other UK bakeries and grouped them in 1935 as Allied Bakeries.

Allied went public that year with the Weston family controlling most of its shares. The company's early accomplishments included the introduction of sliced bread to the UK. By 1940 Allied had acquired more than 30 bakeries and had become Britain's largest baker by introducing inexpensive biscuits to the masses.

Garfield's son Garry joined Allied's board of directors in 1948. The following year the company acquired two Australian firms: Gold Crust Bakeries and Gartelle White. It also bought the Ryvita Company a maker of crispbread. Placed under Garry's control Ryvita eventually became a household name in the UK. Garry also helped the Burton's biscuit division launch the popular Wagon Wheels chocolate biscuits in 1951. Three years later he was sent to Australia to oversee the company's operations there.

To control the entire food-selling process Allied moved into retailing during the 1950s acquiring famous London department store Fortnum & Mason (later acquired by the Weston family). The company was renamed Associated British Foods (ABF) in 1960. During the 1960s ABF opened Primark clothing stores and bought the Fine Fare chain of supermarkets. By the time Garry returned to the UK to become CEO in 1966 his father had thrown together a number of businesses that made everything from flour to parrot food. To achieve a stronger focus Garry sold many of these.

Growth continued internally. In 1970 ABF opened the largest bakery in Western Europe in Glasgow Scotland. Frozen foods were added in 1978 the year Garfield died. The company's Twinings Tea subsidiary opened its first North American factory in 1980. Two years later ABF formed AB Ingredients to make new ingredients and additives for baked goods. The company sold the Fine Fare chain to Dee Corp. (now Somerfield) in 1986 and the following year it formed AB Technology to develop high-tech improvements for food processing.

After nearly 25 years without a major acquisition in 1991 the company purchased British Sugar one of the UK's two sugar processors from Berisford a diversified holdings firm. In 1995 the company acquired AC Humko a manufacturer of specialty oils in the US from Kraft. The next year ABF sold its supermarkets in the Irish Republic and Northern Ireland to the UK's biggest supermarket chain Tesco. Peter Jackson was appointed CEO in 1999. That year the company acquired German baking ingredients producer Rohr Enzymes and bought several mills from Dalgety Feed.

In 2000 ABF sold its UK ice-cream business to Richmond Foods (now R&R Ice Cream). Deputy chairman Harry Bailey took over as chairman when Garry became ill. ABF sold Burtons Biscuits (Wagon Wheels) that year to investment firm HM Capital Partners (then called Hicks Muse Tate & Furst) for about $187 million and it bought several Procter & Gamble commercial shortening and oil brands. In 2001 ABF sold AB Coatings its food coatings business and Nelsons its jam and preserves business. Also that year the company agreed to buy the UK bakery ingredients business of the Kerry Group.

In 2002 ABF's subsidiary ACH Food Companies purchased 19 of Unilever's North American brands including Mazola corn oil Argo and Kingsford's corn starches Karo corn syrup and Henri's salad dressings. Also in 2002 ABF acquired the food and beverages business of Novartis with the exception of Puerto Rican and US assets. (Brands included Caotina Ovomaltine and Ovaltine.) Later in the year the company sold off its Allied Glass Containers business to management.

In 2003 ABF sold six UK flour mills to Archer Daniels Midland. In 2004 the company acquired Unilever's Mexican oils and fats brands including Inca Mazola and Capullo in a $110 million cash transaction. Later that year it acquired Irish feed ingredients companies Vistavet and Nutrition Services Ltd. ABF's subsidiary ACH Food Companies also acquired the global yeast herbs and spice business of Australian company Burns Philp. The acquisition included Burns Philp's Fleischmann's Yeast brand and herb and spice company Tone Brothers.

In 2004 chief executive Peter Jackson unexpectedly announced he was stepping down. A member of ABF's founding and controlling family George Weston was chosen to succeed Jackson. (The Weston family also controls Canadian food processor and supermarket operator George Weston Limited).

ABF's Allied Grain unit formed a joint venture with Banks Cargill Agriculture Frontier in 2005. Frontier's products include grains and oilseeds. The 2005 purchase of retailer Littlewoods' stores added to ABF's Primark retail department-store operations.

In 2006 AFB bought the ethnic foods business of Heinz subsidiary HP Foods; it also acquired a 51% stake in South Africa's largest sugar producer Illovo for $599 million in cash. The next year it acquired Indian food maker Patak's. Its meal-accompaniment products Blue Dragon and Westmill Foods add to ABF's other ethnic cuisine offerings. The acquisition included Patak's assets and brands in all countries with the exception of India.

Already a player in the breakfast-food sector both in the US and internationally in 2007 the company added to its branded food product offerings with the acquisition of Jordans a UK maker of breakfast cereals cereal bars muesli and oat porridge.

EXECUTIVES

Finance Director and Director, John G. Bason, age 55, $1,009,023 total compensation
Chairman, Charles J. F. Sinclair, age 64
Chief Executive and Director, George G. Weston, age 49, $1,463,391 total compensation
Company Secretary, Paul Lister
Head External Affairs, Geoff Lancaster
IR Contact Officer, Chris Chris Barrie Barrie
Director, W. Galen Weston, age 71
Finance Director and Director, John G. Bason, age 55
Chief Executive and Director, George G. Weston, age 49
Director, Javier Ferran, age 55
Director, Peter Smith, age 67
Director, Timothy Clarke, age 56
Director, Lord Michael Jay, age 66
Non-Executive Director, Emma Emma Adamo Adamo
Independent Non-Executive Director, Javier Javier Ferran Ferran
Independent Non-Executive Director, Michael Michael Jay of Ewelme Ewelme
Auditors: KPMGAuditPlc

LOCATIONS

HQ: Associated British Foods Plc
Weston Centre, 10 Grosvenor Street, London W1K 4QY
Phone: (44) 20 7399 6500 **Fax:** (44) 20 7399 6580
Web: www.abf.co.uk

2011 Sales

	% of total
UK	43
Europe &	25
Asia/Pacific	21
The	11
Total	**100**

PRODUCTS/OPERATIONS

2011 Sales

Grocery	33	
Retail	28	
Sugar	19	
Agriculture	10	
Ingredients	10	
Total	**0**	**100**

Selected Products and Brands

Agriculture
- Animal feeds (AB Agri)

Grocery
- Bread baked goods and cereal
  - Allinson breads
  - Burgen breads
  - Jordans cereals
  - Kingsmill breads
  - Ryvita rye crispbread
  - Speedibake bakery products
  - Sunblest bread snacks and rolls
  - Tip Top bread and baked goods (Australia)
- Herbs and spices
  - Durkee (US)GraviesSaucesSeasoningsSoup basesSpices
  - Spice Islands (US)SeasoningsSpices
  - Tone's spices (US)
- Hot beverages sugar and sweeteners
  - Billington's cane sugars
  - Jacksons of Picadilly teas
  - Karo corn syrup
  - Ovaltine
  - Silver Spoon sugar (UK)
  - La Tisaniere teas and infusions (France)
  - Twinings teas
- Meat
  - Don Deligoods (Australia)
  - KRC (Australia)
- Vegetable oils
  - Capullo canola oil (Mexico)
  - Mazola corn oil (US)
- World foods
  - Blue Dragon (Asian)
  - Patak's (Indian)
- Other
  - Askeys ice cream and dessert accompaniments
  - Baking MadBaking adviceRecipesTips
  - Crusha milkshake mix

Ingredients
- Specialty ingredients
  - Enzymes
  - Specialty proteins and lipids
  - Yeast extracts
- Yeast and bakery ingredients
  - Argo corn starch

Retail clothing
- Primark
  - Accessories
  - Childrenswear
  - Footwear
  - Homeware
  - Hosiery
  - Lingerie
  - Menswear
  - Womenswear

Sugar
- Beet sugar

COMPETITORS

ADM	Morrisons
ALDI	Nestle
ASDA	Nine West

Armani
Bahlsen
Bakkavor
Bill Blass
Burberry
Carrefour
Celestial Seasonings
Chr. Hansen A/S
Cosun
Cumberland Packing
Danisco A/S
Donna Karan
Gap UK
General Mills
Greencore
Gucci
Harrods
Heinz
Hwa Hong
Iconix Brand Group
Imperial Sugar
Ingredion
J Sainsbury
Jones Group
Kenneth Cole
Kerry Group
Marks & Spencer
McCormick & Company
Merisant
Mondelez International
Nordzucker
Northern Foods
NutraSweet
Oscar Mayer Limited
PVH
Perry Ellis International
Premier Foods
Pura Foods
R.C. Bigelow
Ralph Lauren
Renshawnapier
Republic of Tea
Sara Lee North American Retail
St. John Knits
Stash Tea
Sucriere de Pithiviers
Sudzucker
T.K. Maxx
Tata Global Beverages
Tate & Lyle
Tereos
Tesco
Unilever
Unilever UK Foods
United Biscuits
Waitrose
Wal-Mart
Warburtons
kate spade

HISTORICAL FINANCIALS

Company Type: Public

Income Statement FYE: September 14

	REVENUE ($ mil.)	NET INCOME ($ mil.)	NET PROFIT MARGIN	EMPLOYEES
09/13	21,057	934	4.4%	112,652
09/12	19,870	900	4.5%	106,243
09/11	17,481	854	4.9%	102,253
09/10	15,893	853	5.4%	0
09/09	15,465	599	3.9%	96,251
Annual Growth	8.0%	11.7%	—	4.0%

2013 Year-End Financials

Debt ratio: 17.8%
Return on equity: 9.9%
Cash ($ mil.): 572
Current ratio: 1.36
Long-term debt ($ mil.): 1,220

No. of shares (mil.): 791
Dividends
Yield: 0.0%
Payout: 86.8%
Market value ($ mil.): 22,982

	STOCK PRICE ($) FY Close	P/E High/Low	PER SHARE ($) Earnings	Dividends	Book Value
09/13	29.03	101 71	1.18	1.03	12.25
09/12	20.67	79 58	1.14	0.85	11.95
09/11	17.74	68 55	1.09	0.86	11.47
09/10	16.29	60 42	1.08	0.77	10.45
09/09	14.03	97 43	0.76	0.69	10.02
Annual Growth	19.9%	— —	11.7%	10.5%	5.2%

AstraZeneca Plc

AstraZeneca's products run the gamut from A (blood pressure drug Atacand) to Z (prostate and breast cancer drug Zoladex). One of the world's major pharmaceutical firms AstraZeneca specializes in drugs for cardiovascular neurological gastrointestinal respiratory oncology and infection therapy areas. The firm's biggest sellers include cholesterol reducer Crestor cardiovascular drug Brilinta acid reflux remedy Nexium and Symbicort for asthma. AstraZeneca also markets drugs that aim to treat high cholesterol diabetes pain viral diseases and various cancers. The company's products are sold in more than 100 countries.

Geographic Reach

Sales in emerging markets were up about 10% in 2011 and 4% in 2012 thanks to sales growth in China and Russia. China was really the bright spot with a 17% increase in sales on the strength of the company's cardio and respiratory drugs. As a result the firm is increasing investments in emerging markets; for instance in 2011 it announced plans to build a new $200 million manufacturing plant to meet market needs in China. Later that year it acquired generic injectable drug manufacturer Guangdong BeiKang Pharmaceutical.

Growth in China and other emerging markets is key for AstraZeneca's as it sees sales dip in established markets due to patent expiration in its older medications.

Operations

In 2013 AstraZeneca sold its only non-pharma business Aptium Oncology which operates cancer treatment centers in the US. This came on the heels of selling its other non-core units Astra Tech (medical devices) and DENTSPLY (dental implant systems). The moves are part of the company's focus on streamlining its operations around core drug development and commercialization efforts in targeted therapeutic areas for the past few years as part of strategic restructuring efforts in the face of looming patent expirations and increasing generic competition.

The company estimates that by 2015 more than half of its current revenue will be subject to losses through patent expirations. Since 2010 the number of AstraZeneca's drugs with sales of more than $1 billion each dropped from 10 to seven: Crestor Atacand Nexium Seroquel IR Seroquel XR Zoladex and Symbicort. The firm has especially been feeling the effects of generic competition for some of its top sellers in the US (the company's largest market) where revenues were down 21% due to patent losses and increased generic competition. Established markets Western Europe and Canada also saw double digit drops as Crestor lost patent protection in Canada and sales of Seroquel IR Nexium Arimidex and Meronem decreased. Bestseller Seroquel IR lost European patent protection in 2012.

AstraZeneca has had several successes in its R&D organization as it works to keep the bestsellers coming and sales of newer drugs such as Crestor Symbicort and Seroquel XR have helped sustain overall revenues for the company. With a pipeline of about 85 drugs in various development stages as it also looks for acquisitions to boost its product development.

Financial Performance

In 2012 the patent loss of Seroquel IR caused revenues to drop 17% to about $28 billion. Net income also fell 37% to $6.3 billion. Despite struggling with patent losses in previous years AstraZeneca had managed to stay one step ahead of the game through its balanced growth and cost-control efforts. The firm reported increased revenues (though margins are dwindling) and profits in recent years including a 24% net income rise (to about $10 billion) in 2011 largely due to the sale of Astra Tech. Reported revenues showed a slight 1% increase (to some $33.6 billion) in 2011 though the company reported that with constant exchange rates sales were actually down by about 2%.

Strategy

The divestiture of Astra Tech in 2011 followed a strategic review seeking to maximize the subsidiary's value; the sale also fit nicely into AstraZeneca's broader strategy to focus on core drug development and commercialization efforts in targeted therapeutic areas.

As part of its cost-control efforts to reduce the impact of patent expirations AstraZeneca launched a program in early 2010 aiming to reduce its worldwide workforce by about 15% by the end of 2014. When that appeared to not be enough in early 2012 the company announced restructuring efforts to reduce its workforce by another 10%.

These efforts were led by CEO David Brennan until April 2012 when Brennan abruptly retired as shareholders exerted pressure on the firm to enact more aggressive growth strategies. The announcement followed the expiration of top seller Seroquel IR's patent in March 2012 which took a swift toll on AstraZeneca's earnings. Later that year the company named Roche executive Pascal Soriot as its new CEO with hopes that Soriot's experience in pharma strategy and innovation would help it turn around its finances.

The firm is making a concerted effort to strengthen its industry position ahead of patent expirations by overhauling its R&D organization including by building up its late-stage drug development pipeline through internal research and development acquisitions and collaborations. Through its MedImmune unit it is also building up its R&D programs for new biologic medicines which enjoy longer terms of patent protection. At the same time AstraZeneca is streamlining the pipeline to concentrate on the most promising research areas by reducing the number of disease targets within its six core therapy areas (cardiovascular gastrointestinal infection neuroscience oncology and respiratory/inflammation). These efforts have resulted in the consolidation of some R&D facilities. AstraZeneca also outsourced some early stage research functions to Charles River Laboratories in 2012.

While trials for a depression candidate under development with biotech firm Targacept were halted in 2012 AstraZeneca and Targacept continue to work on other neurological drugs together. Also in 2012 AstraZeneca formed a partnership with biotech firm Amgen to develop a portfolio of anti-inflammatory drugs.

Mergers and Acquisitions

Along with discovering its own new drugs and collaborating with its pharmaceutical cohorts AstraZeneca also expands its R&D pipeline through occasional acquisitions. In 2012 the company acquired US development firm Ardea Biosciences for some $1.3 billion to gain a promising gout treatment candidate. In mid-2012 AstraZeneca paid some $3.2 billion to expand its R&D partnership with BMS (following BMS' acquisition of diabetes firm Amylin).

In 2013 AstraZeneca focused expansion efforts on the cardiovascular market. It purchased AlphaCore a US-based private biotech firm and agreed to purchase Omthera which is working to develop heart medicines based on omega-3 fatty acids for some $443 million.

HISTORY

AstraZeneca forerunner Imperial Chemical Industries (ICI) was created from the 1926 merger of four British chemical companies —Nobel Industries; Brunner Mond and Company; United Alkali; and British Dyestuffs —in reaction to the German amalgamation that created I. G. Farben. ICI plunged into research recruiting chemists engineers and managers and forming alliances with universities. Between 1933 and 1935 at least 87 new products were created including polyethylene.

Fortunes declined as competition increased after WWII. In 1980 ICI posted losses and cut its dividend for the first time. In 1982 turnaround artist John Harvey-Jones shifted ICI from bulk chemicals to high-margin specialty chemicals such as pharmaceuticals and pesticides. That business became Zeneca which ICI spun off in 1993.

The takeover specter loomed large over the company during its first year. Zeneca had several drugs in its pipeline but it also had expiring patents on others making them fair game for competitors. Bankrolled by its agrochemical business Zeneca forged alliances with other pharmaceutical firms. In 1994 it entered a marketing alliance with Amersham International (now Amersham) to sell Metastron a nuclear-medicine cancer agent. The next year Zeneca formed a joint venture with Chinese companies Advanced Chemicals and Tianli to make textile-coating chemicals.

In 1995 Glaxo was forced to sell a migraine drug candidate to complete its merger with Wellcome. Zeneca's gamble in buying the then-unproven drug (Zomig) paid off when the product gained US FDA approval two years later.

By 1997 Zeneca completed its gradual acquisition of Salick Health Care formed to create more humane cancer treatment programs. The purchase followed a trend of large drug firms moving into managed care which raised concerns that centers might be pressured to use their parent companies' drugs but Zeneca maintained that Salick would remain independent except to the extent that it offered an opportunity to evaluate treatments.

In 1998 Zeneca got the FDA's OK to sell its brand of tamoxifen (Nolvadex) to women at high risk of contracting breast cancer. In 1999 it sued Eli Lilly to protect Nolvadex against Lilly's marketing claim that its osteoporosis treatment Evista reduced breast cancer risk a use for which it was not approved.

In 1999 Zeneca completed its purchase of Sweden's Astra to form AstraZeneca. That year the firm sold its specialty chemicals unit Zeneca Specialties to Cinven Group and Investcorp. With its agricultural business stagnated due to crippled markets in Asia and Europe AstraZeneca announced plans to merge the unit with the agrochemicals business of Novartis and spun it off as Syngenta. In 2000 Sweden approved ulcer drug Nexium as well as Symbicort Turbuhaler an asthma inhaler.

In 2001 AstraZeneca sold its genetic diversity testing services subsidiary Cellmark Diagnostics to Orchid Cellmark (with whom the company also announced a multi-year collaborative research agreement).

Chief executive Sir Tom McKillop retired at the close of 2005 and was succeeded by marketing expert David Brennan.

In 2006 the company acquired UK biotech firm KuDOS Pharmaceuticals which develops oncology products based on a proprietary DNA repair technology for $206 million.

The company in 2007 made a major push to bolster its biologics business by purchasing US biotech firm MedImmune for more than $15 billion cash. The acquisition expanded AstraZeneca's capability for vaccination research as well as its research in oncology infection and respiratory disorders; it also added manufacturing facilities.

The MedImmune purchase dovetailed with AstraZeneca's $1.3 billion acquisition of Cambridge Antibody Technology in 2006. The two were merged under the MedImmune name in late 2007. AstraZeneca also acquired UK biotech firm Arrow Therapeutics which has products for respiratory ailments and hepatitis under development for $147 million in 2007.

To absorb its many acquisitions and streamline its organization and to enhance its long term competitive position the company launched a multiphase restructuring program in 2007. As a result of the first phase the firm reduced its workforce by about 10% between 2007 and 2010 and reduced annual expenses by some $2.4 billion.

AstraZeneca also slowed its acquisition pace a bit focusing instead on its research and development and restructuring efforts. The company experienced a boost in demand for its H1N1 vaccines in 2009 due to a global pandemic.

Seroquel's profit margin received a hit in 2010 after AstraZeneca agreed to pay about $520 million to settle US Department of Justice claims it marketed the drug for unapproved uses such as a treatment for anxiety attention deficit hyperactivity disorder (ADHD) and bipolar maintenance.

EXECUTIVES

Non-Executive Chairman of the Board, Leif Johansson, age 62
Chief Financial Officer; Executive Director, Simon Lowth, age 52, $852,000 total compensation
Executive Vice President - Global Commercial Operations, Tony P. Zook
President North America, Rich Fante
IR Contact Officer, Ed Seage
Chief Medical Officer, Howard Hutchinson
Executive Vice President - Human Resources and Corporate Affairs, Lynn Tetrault
EVP Operations, David Smith
Media Relations UK, Neil McCrae
Investor Relations UK, Jonathan Hunt
Investor Relations UK, Karl Hard
Media Relations U.S., Tony Jewell
President and CEO AstraZeneca UK, Mark Jones
EVP Development, Anders Ekblom
General Counsel, Jeff Pott
Media Contact UK, Chris Sampson
Media Contact UK, Sarah Lindgreen
Media Contact Sweden, Anne-Charlotte Knutsson
Investor Relations U.S., Jorgen Winroth
VP and Head Oncology and Infection, Alan Barge
Investor Relations UK, Clive Morris
President Research and Development, Martin Mackay
Chief Executive Officer; Executive Director, Pascal Soriot, age 54
Company Secretary, Adrian Kemp
IR Contact Officer, James Ward-Lilley
Chief Compliance Officer, Katarina Ageborg
Executive Vice President; MedImmune, Bahija Jallal
Executive Vice President - Global Medicines Development, Briggs Morrison
Executive Vice President; Global Portfolio & Product Strategy, Marc Dunoyer
Executive Vice President; International, Mark Mallon
Executive Vice President - Innovative Medicines, Menelas Pangalos
Executive Vice President; North America, Paul Hudson
Director, Michele J. Hooper, age 61
Non-Executive Director Chairman of the Audit Committee, Rudy H. P. Markham, age 67
Director, John S. Varley, age 56
Director, Jean-Philippe Courtois, age 54
CEO and Director, David R. Brennan, age 58
Director, Jane E. Henney, age 66
CFO and Director, Simon Lowth, age 51
Director, Marcus Wallenberg, age 58
Director, Dame Nancy Rothwell, age 58
Director, Jean-Philippe Courtois, age 52
Director, Bruce Burlington, age 64
Non-Executive Independent Director, Shriti Vadera
Non-Executive Director, Genevieve Berger
Non-Executive Director, Graham Chipchase
Auditors: KPMGAuditPlc

LOCATIONS

HQ: AstraZeneca Plc
2 Kingdom Street, London W2 6BD
Phone: (44) 20 7604 8000 **Fax:** (44) 20 7604 8151
Web: www.astrazeneca.com

2011 Sales

	$ mil.	% of total
Americas		
US	13,745	41
Canada & other Americas	3,041	9
Europe		
Continental Europe	8,229	24
Total	**33,591**	**100**

PRODUCTS/OPERATIONS

2012 Sales

	$ mil.	% of total
Cardiovascular	9,531	34
Gastrointestinal	4,852	17
Respiratory & Inflammation	4,415	16
Neuroscience	3,923	14
Oncology	3,489	12
Infection & other	1,715	6
Other businesses	48	1
Total	**27,973**	**100**

Selected Products

Cardiovascular
- Atacand (angiotensin II antagonist for hypertension and heart failure)
- Crestor (statin for cholesterol-lowering drug)
- Onglyza (type 2 diabetes)
- Plendil (calcium antagonist for hypertension and angina)
- Seloken/Toprol-XL (beta-blocker for blood pressure heart failure angina)
- Zestril (ACE inhibitor for hypertension other)

Gastrointestinal
- Losec/Prilosec (acid reflux disease)
- Nexium (acid reflux disease)

Infection and Other Products
- FluMist (intranasal flu vaccine)
- Merrem/Meronem (intraveneous antibiotic for serious hospital infections)
- Synagis (for respiratory syncytial virus or RSV in infants)

Neuroscience
- Diprivan (general anesthetic)
- Local anesthetics (Carbocaine Citanest Naropin Xylocaine)
- Seroquel (anti-psychotic for schizophrenia and bipolar)
- Zomig (migraines)

Oncology
- Arimidex (aromatase inhibitor for breast cancer)
- Casodex (anti-androgen for prostate cancer)
- Faslodex (oestrogen receptor antagonist for breast cancer)
- Iressa (kinase inhibitor for non-small cell lung cancer)
- Nolvadex (breast cancer)
- Zoladex (LHRH agonist for prostate and breast cancer)

Respiratory & Inflammation
- Oxis (beta-agonist for asthma and chronic obstructive pulmonary disease)
- Pulmicort (anti-inflammatory for asthma)
- Rhinocort (topical nasal anti-inflammatory)
- Symbicort (anti-inflammatory and bronchodilator in one inhaler for asthma and chronic obstructive pulmonary disease)

Selected Subsidiaries

AstraZeneca AB (Sweden)
AstraZeneca BV (The Netherlands)
AstraZeneca Canada Inc.
AstraZeneca do Brasil Limitada
AstraZeneca Farmaceutica Spain SA
AstraZeneca GmbH (Germany)
AstraZeneca KK (Japan)
AstraZeneca LP (US)
AstraZeneca Pharmaceuticals Co. Limited (China)
AstraZeneca Pharmaceuticals LP (US)
AstraZeneca Pty Limited (Australia)
AstraZeneca SAS (France)
AstraZeneca SpA (Italy)
AstraZeneca UK Limited
IPR Pharmaceuticals Inc. (Puerto Rico)

MedImmune L.L.C. (US)
Novexel SA (France)
NV AstraZeneca SA (Belgium)
Zeneca Holdings Inc. (US)

COMPETITORS

Abbott Labs
Amgen
Aptium Oncology
Bard
Bayer AG
Bristol-Myers Squibb
Elan
Eli Lilly
Genentech
Gilead Sciences
GlaxoSmithKline
Johnson & Johnson
Memorial Sloan-Kettering
Merck
Novartis
Pfizer
Ranbaxy Laboratories
Roche Holding
Sanofi
Teva
US Oncology
Zimmer Holdings

HISTORICAL FINANCIALS

Company Type: Public

Income Statement FYE: December 31

	REVENUE ($ mil.)	NET INCOME ($ mil.)	NET PROFIT MARGIN	EMPLOYEES
12/12	27,973	6,297	22.5%	51,700
12/11	33,591	9,983	29.7%	57,200
12/10	33,269	8,053	24.2%	61,100
12/09	32,804	7,521	22.9%	62,700
12/08	31,601	6,101	19.3%	65,000
Annual Growth	(3.0%)	0.8%	—	(5.6%)

2012 Year-End Financials

Debt ratio: 19.2%
Return on equity: 26.7%
Cash ($ mil.): 7,701
Current ratio: 1.37
Long-term debt ($ mil.): 9,409
No. of shares (mil.): 1,246
Dividends
Yield: 6.0%
Payout: 57.2%
Market value ($ mil.): 58,935

	STOCK PRICE ($) FY Close	P/E High	P/E Low	PER SHARE ($) Earnings	Dividends	Book Value
12/12	47.27	10	8	4.98	2.85	19.04
12/11	46.29	7	6	7.30	2.70	17.99
12/10	46.19	10	7	5.57	2.41	16.47
12/09	46.94	9	6	5.19	2.09	14.24
12/08	41.03	12	8	4.20	1.90	10.99
Annual Growth	3.6%	—	—	4.4%	10.7%	14.7%

AUDI AG Vormals Audi-NSU Auto Union AG

LOCATIONS

HQ: AUDI AG Vormals Audi-NSU Auto Union AG
I/FF-12, P.O. Box 10 04 57, Ingolstadt D-85045
Phone: (49) 841 89 0 **Fax:** (49) 841 89 325 24
Web: www.audi.com

HISTORICAL FINANCIALS

Company Type: Public

Income Statement FYE: December 31

	REVENUE ($ mil.)	NET INCOME ($ mil.)	NET PROFIT MARGIN	EMPLOYEES
12/12	64,282	5,646	8.8%	67,231
12/11	57,036	5,676	10.0%	62,806
12/10	47,433	3,461	7.3%	59,513
12/09	42,986	1,872	4.4%	58,011
12/08	47,809	3,045	6.4%	57,533
Annual Growth	7.7%	16.7%	—	4.0%

2012 Year-End Financials

Debt ratio: 19.7%
Return on equity: 31.1%
Cash ($ mil.): 14,722
Current ratio: 1.45
Long-term debt ($ mil.): 512
No. of shares (mil.): 43
Dividends
Yield: —
Payout: —
Market value ($ mil.): 30,203

	STOCK PRICE ($) FY Close	P/E High	P/E Low	PER SHARE ($) Earnings	Dividends	Book Value
12/12	702.39	14	10	131.30	0.00	452.77
12/11	741.00	18	11	132.01	0.00	382.14
12/10	899.00	28	26	80.48	0.00	347.73
12/09	705.00	51	26	43.55	0.00	342.42
12/08	615.00	22	22	70.83	0.00	323.84
Annual Growth	3.4%	—	—	16.7%	—	8.7%

Australia and New Zealand Banking Group Ltd

Australia and New Zealand Banking Group (ANZ) one of Australia's Big Four banks and one of New Zealand's top banks offers commercial and retail banking and financial services from about 1400 branches and offices primarily in Australia and New Zealand but also across the Asia/Pacific region. Offerings include standard deposit and lending services credit cards wealth management agribusiness finance and insurance and foreign exchange services for other financial institutions. Altogether the group serves 8 million customers in more than 30 countries including China Germany India the UK and the US. ANZ traces its roots to the 1835 founding of Bank of Australasia.

ANZ which generates about 95% of its revenues in Australia and New Zealand is focused on expansion in the Asia/Pacific region where it has opened new branches and acquired existing operations. In 2009 it bought the businesses of Royal Bank of Scotland (which had been selling noncore operations) in six Asian countries (Hong Kong Indonesia Philippines Singapore Taiwan and Vietnam) for $550 million. ANZ typically teams with other firms to enter new markets or accelerate growth; the bank has taken minority stakes or formed partnerships with among others Metrobank (Philippines) Bank of Tianjin (China) Sacombank (Vietnam) Panin Bank (Indonesia) and AmBank Group (Malaysia).

To further its strategy of becoming a superregional bank ANZ entered an agreement with wheat marketer AWB Limited allowing the bank to exclusively market its offerings to AWB's 100000 customers. In 2010 the company acquired the loan and deposit books of Landmark Financial Services a division of AWB's Landmark rural arm. Landmark Financial Services provides services to some 10000 agribusiness customers.

In a bid to catch up with its rivals in domestic fund management the company formed OnePath (formerly ING Australia) a wealth management joint venture with Dutch financial services giant ING Groep. The division offers investment retirement insurance and superannuation products. In late 2009 ANZ bought out ING's 51% stake in the venture and rebranded it OnePath. OnePath has about A$54 billion in funds under management.

HISTORY

Captain Cook claimed Australia for the crown in 1770. By 1800 convicts and free immigrants had built a thriving wool trade with the mother country but the land needed financial infrastructure. In 1835 the Bank of Australasia was founded and two years later Union Bank of Australia both backed by London investors. In 1838 the Union Bank moved into New Zealand.

Economic depression during the 1840s helped both the Bank of Australasia and the Union Bank pick off some of their competitors. In 1852 English Scottish and Australia Bank was founded. A gold rush revived the economy and led to several decades of growth during which much of the banks' profits were returned to London.

In 1951 Australasia and Union banks merged to form ANZ. For the next 20-some years Australia's banks developed a large branch network. ANZ formed a savings bank subsidiary Australia and New Zealand Savings Bank in 1955. For the next 15 years the combined bank made sporadic overtures to English Scottish and Australia Bank and in 1970 the marriage finally took place. ANZ became the third-largest bank in Australia.

The company moved its headquarters from London to Australia in 1976. Merger mania hit Australia in the early 1980s as the industry geared up for foreign competition after an open-door policy was instituted. ANZ began building operations inside and outside the country. It bought UK-based Grindlays Bank Group and its offices in 40 countries.

During the 1980s and 1990s ANZ built up its holdings overseas and broadened its offerings into insurance leasing asset management and securities often through acquisitions while trimming a variety of operating companies it had accumulated. In 1995 alone it sold about 75 companies.

Although ANZ still derived about 75% of sales from its home markets its foreign exposure brought pain when the Asian currency crisis spread to Russia and South America in 1998. ANZ realigned its business and liquidated noncore Asian operations. As part of this effort in 1999 the company sold its retail brokerage operations to Citigroup's Salomon Smith Barney and bought a stake in E*Trade's Australian operations.

Also in 1999 ANZ reaffirmed its commitment to Asia. The company's Indonesian subsidiary PT ANZ Panin Bank bought the credit card operations of PT Bank Papan Sejahtera from the Indonesian Bank Restructuring Agency.

ANZ sold its Grindlays subsidiaries in 2000 to Standard Chartered in order to simplify operations.

In 2003 ANZ bought the National Bank of New Zealand from Lloyds Banking Group. Although the Reserve Bank of New Zealand initially required that the two banks remain separate legal entities it eventually permitted them to merge with caveats. The new subsidiary known as ANZ National Bank must see itself as a New Zealand company first and foremost and it must establish facilities that will allow it to operate as a stand alone in the event any of its foreign service providers including its Australian owner fails to deliver.

A year later ANZ sold the majority of its London-headquartered project finance business to Standard Chartered for about $1.5 billion. The business operated in four regions: the UK the US the Middle East and South Asia (especially India).

ANZ then expanded in the Pacific region buying Bank of Hawaii's operations in Papua New Guinea Vanuatu and Fiji. ANZ started selling mutual funds in India but abandoned those plans for a pan-Asian Internet bank it developed with Oversea-Chinese Banking Corporation of Singapore.

EXECUTIVES

CEO and Director, Michael R. P. Smith, age 57
Chairman, John P. Morschel, age 71
Deputy CEO, Graham K. Hodges, $872,700 total compensation
Chief Executive Officer, Philip (Phil) Chronican, age 57
CEO Global Wealth and Private, Joyce A. Phillips
Group Managing Director Human Resources, Susie Babani
CEO ANZ New Zealand, David Hisco
Chief Risk Officer, Nigel Williams
CIO, Anne Weatherston
General Manager Regional Commercial Banking, Tania Motton
CFO, Shayne Elliott
General Manager America and Head of Relationship Banking America, Doug Stolberg
Executive Director Head of Transaction Banking, William Evans
COO, Alistair Currie
Director, Ian J. Macfarlane, age 66
Director, Gregory J. Clark, age 69
CEO and Director, Michael R. P. Smith, age 57
Director, Alison M. Watkins, age 49
Director, David E. Meiklejohn, age 71
Auditors: KPMG

LOCATIONS

HQ: Australia and New Zealand Banking Group Ltd
Level 9, 833 Collins Street, Docklands, Melbourne, Victoria 3008
Phone: (61) 3 9273 5555 **Fax:** (61) 3 8542 5252
Web: www.anz.com

2010 Sales

	% of total
Australia	75
New	19
Asia/Pacific Europe and	6
Total	**100**

PRODUCTS/OPERATIONS

2010 Sales

	% of total
Retail	41
Institutional	35
Commercial	19
Wealth	3
Partnerships	2
Total	**100**

COMPETITORS

AMP Limited
Bank Central Asia
Bank Danamon Indonesia
Bank Mandiri
Bank Rakyat
Bank of East Asia
Commonwealth Bank of Australia
HBOS Australia
HSBC
Macquarie Group
National Australia Bank
Sumitomo Trust and Banking
Suncorp-Metway
Westpac Banking

HISTORICAL FINANCIALS

Company Type: Public

Income Statement FYE: September 30

	ASSETS ($ mil.)	NET INCOME ($ mil.)	INCOME AS % OF ASSETS	EMPLOYEES
09/12	670,134	5,907	0.9%	45,900
09/11	577,526	5,202	0.9%	50,439
09/10	514,775	4,357	0.8%	46,917
09/09	420,546	2,594	0.6%	37,687
09/08	378,909	2,669	0.7%	36,925
Annual Growth	15.3%	22.0%	—	5.6%

2012 Year-End Financials

Return on assets: 0.9%
Return on equity: 14.2%
Long-term debt ($ mil.): —
No. of shares (mil.): —
Sales ($ mil): 38,097
Dividends
Yield: 0.0%
Payout: 69.2%
Market value ($ mil.): —

	STOCK PRICE ($) FY Close	P/E High	P/E Low	PER SHARE ($) Earnings	Dividends	Book Value
09/12	25.69	13	8	2.15	1.49	15.90
09/11	18.58	14	8	1.93	1.39	14.08
09/10	22.94	12	7	1.69	0.91	12.95
09/09	21.43	13	3	1.14	0.85	11.43
09/08	15.50	62	4	1.30	1.23	10.46
Annual Growth	13.5%	—	—	13.2%	4.8%	11.0%

Aviva Plc (United Kingdom)

In the consolidating European insurance industry Aviva is a lively player. As the top insurance provider in the UK and a leading insurance firm worldwide Aviva offers both life and general insurance. Its long-term savings segment focuses on life insurance pensions unit trusts and other products while its general insurance segment includes the stuff which is called "non-life" or "property/casualty" elsewhere: home auto accident and fire coverage. Its Aviva Investors arm provides asset management globally. In the UK it also offers private medical insurance through employers. All of the company's businesses operate under the Aviva banner.

Geographic Reach

Aviva operates in about 20 countries. In addition to the UK which accounts for about a third of sales primary markets include Canada France Ireland Italy and Spain. The company also has operations in emerging markets such as China India Poland Turkey and Singapore.

Operations

Aviva's long-term insurance segment includes life insurance pensions annuities bonds savings and other investment and protection products and accounts for about three-fourths of annual revenues. General insurance offerings include personal and commercial property/casualty coverage as well as health plans and account for nearly a quarter of sales.

Sales and Marketing

Aviva distributes its products through many channels –including direct sales forces independent brokers partners and bank representatives –tailored to each market where it operates. The firm spent about #22 million ($36 million) on marketing efforts during 2012.

Financial Performance

Revenue has fluctuated for Aviva in recent years due to economic conditions and restructuring measures. In 2012 the company achieved 21% revenue growth (to some #47 billion or $75 billion) due to higher investment income levels. Increased revenue was especially seen in core markets including France Italy and Spain as well as certain emerging markets.

The company reported a net loss of #3 billion ($5 billion) in 2012 however due to changes in investment contract provisions and unallocated investment surplus charges.

Strategy

Through restructuring measures in recent years Aviva has refocused on producing attractive financial returns in its narrowed business markets reducing capital volatility to build financial strength and improving revenue growth and profits.

After taking a big hit in 2008 due to investment losses tied to the global recession Aviva has downsized its operations in subsequent years to try to repair the damage including the sale of noncore international operations. To further focus on priority markets where it has a strong presence in 2012 Aviva sold its Czech Hungarian and Romanian life insurance and pension operations to MetLife for an undisclosed price. It has also steadily reduced its stake in Netherlands-based Delta Lloyd lowering its interest to some 20% in 2012.

The company agreed to sell its Aviva USA division which includes life insurance and annuity operations to Athene Holding for some $1.8 billion in 2012. The sale includes related asset management operations; Aviva will retain certain third-party asset management operations in the US held by its Aviva Investors unit. In addition Aviva agreed to sell operations in Russia Malaysia and Sri Lanka that year.

To further simplify its business the company has combined the operations of a number of businesses especially in Europe to simplify its product range and shorten the time to launch new products. The company has also simplified its branding messages across its operations. Its global operations now operate as Aviva.

HISTORY

When insurers hiked premiums after the 1861 Great Tooley Street Fire of London merchants formed Commercial Union Fire Insurance (CU). It opened offices throughout the UK and in foreign ports and soon added life (1862) and marine (1863) coverage.

Over the next 20 years CU's foreign business thrived. The firm had offices across the US by the 1880s. In the 1890s CU entered Australia India and Southeast Asia. Foreign business eventually accounted for some 75% of CU's sales.

CU went shopping in the 20th century adding accident insurer Palatine Insurance Co. of Manchester in 1900 and rescuing two companies ruined by San Francisco's 1906 earthquake and fire. CU recovered from the Depression with the help of a booming auto insurance market and spent most of the 1930s and WWII consolidating operations to cut costs.

Profits suffered in the 1950s as CU faced increased competition in the US. To boost sales it merged with both multiline rival North British and Mercantile and life insurer Northern and Employers Assurance in the early 1960s. While US business continued to lag in the 1970s the company's European business grew.

From 1982 to 1996 CU cut its operations in the US entered new markets (Poland 1992; South Africa and Vietnam 1996) and sold its New

Zealand subsidiaries (1995). As competition in the UK increased the company in 1997 reorganized and merged with General Accident in 1998.

General Accident & Employers Liability Assurance Association (GA) was formed in 1885 in Perth Scotland to sell workers' compensation insurance. Within a few years GA had branches in London and Scotland. It diversified into insurance for train accidents (1887) autos (1896) and fire (1899); in 1906 its name changed to General Accident Fire and Life Assurance.

GA expanded into Australia Europe and Africa at the turn of the century. After WWI the company's auto insurance grew along with car ownership. During the 1930s the company entered the US auto insurance market. WWII put a stop to GA's growth.

The company expanded after the war forming Pennsylvania General Fire Insurance Association (1963) and acquiring the UK's Yorkshire Insurance Co. (1967). By the 1980s about one-third of its sales came from the US.

After 1986 GA acquired some 500 real estate brokerage agencies to cross-sell its home and life insurance. To increase presence in Asia and the Pacific the company in 1988 acquired NZI Corp. a New Zealand banking and insurance company whose failing operations cost GA millions. At the same time new US government regulations and a series of damaging storms hammered the company.

In response GA cut costs posting a profit by 1993. As the industry consolidated the company bought nonstandard auto insurer Sabre (1995) life insurer Provident Mutual (1996) and General Insurance Group Ltd. in Canada (1997). Unable to compete on its own GA merged with Commercial Union to form CGU in 1998.

After the merger CGU added personal pension plans and entered alliances to sell insurance in Italy and India. Merger costs and exceptional losses for 1998 hit operating profits hard. In 1999 CGU upped its stake in French bank Societe Generale to about 7% to help it fend off a hostile takeover attempt by Banque Nationale de Paris (now BNP Paribas).

In 2000 CGU merged with rival Norwich Union to form CGNU and made plans to exit the Canadian life and the US general insurance businesses. In 2001 CGNU sold its US property/casualty operations to White Mountains Insurance.

In an attempt to strengthen its brand name the company changed its name to Aviva in 2002. Following the name change the company merged and rebranded many of its subsidiaries. Aviva also made changes to its Asian operations in 2004 selling its general insurance business in Asia to Mitsui Sumitomo Insurance.

Back home Aviva acquired UK-based automotive service company RAC in 2005 (sold to The Carlyle Group in 2011) to gain access to its auto insurance and loan businesses. To get to the meaty middle Aviva stripped off RAC's non-core businesses including its fleet services which it sold to VT Group in 2006. At around the same time the company also divested its 50% ownership in Lex Vehicle Leasing to HBOS (which later merged with Lloyds TSB to become Lloyds Banking Group).

Looking to Asia for operational strategies Aviva moved more of its back-office operations to India and Sri Lanka but then reversed the trend in 2008 when it sold the business process outsourcing units to WNS.

Having entered Russia in March 2006 Aviva gained an 8% share of the Russian market by 2011 through a major push including the purchase of the Russian pension fund operations of ING in 2009. In 2010 the company re-entered the Singaporean insurance market after a five-year absence by offering direct online car insurance.

As part of an effort to focus on the Aviva brand the company changed the long-time UK brand name of Norwich Union to Aviva UK in 2009. It also changed brand names in Ireland and Poland in 2010.

The company expand its US investment management operations through the #83 million ($128 million) purchase of River Road Asset Management in 2010.

The company sold its Aviva Australia insurance and wealth management operations business to National Australia Bank in 2009 for $825 million. To loosen up a bit more cash Aviva then spun off about 40% of its Netherlands-based Delta Lloyd subsidiary in an initial public offering. It hoped to raise around $1.2 billion Euros but actually got $995 million. In 2011 the company reduced its stake in its Netherlands-based Delta Lloyd subsidiary to 43%. Aviva also exited its partnership in the United Arab Emirates that year.

Aviva also sold its UK roadside assistance and insurance unit RAC to The Carlyle Group for #1 billion (about $1.6 billion) in 2011 to focus on its insurance and savings businesses.

EXECUTIVES

Interim Executive Deputy Chairman, John McFarlane, age 66
Executive Director Developed Markets, Trevor J. Matthews, age 61
Chairman, Lord Colin M. Sharman, age 70, $969,309 total compensation
Director Corporate Affairs Aviva Investors, Paul Lockstone
Head Group Media Relations, Andrew Reid
CEO Aviva USA, Christopher J. (Chris) Littlefield, age 46
CEO of Aviva, Andrew Moss, age 55, $1,846,577 total compensation
Global Business Development Director Aviva Investors, Erich Gerth, age 50
CEO Aviva France, Jean-Pierre Menanteau, age 49
Director Corporate Affairs United Kingdom, Hayley Stimpson
Head Group Media Relations, Sue Winston
CEO Higher Growth Markets, Simon Machell, age 50
Marketing Director UK Business, Gary Price
Group Director Human Resources, John Ainley, age 56
COO, Cathryn Riley
Director Investor Relations, Charles Barrows, age 49
CEO UK General Insurance, David McMillan
Head Investor Relations, Jessie Burrows
Chief Executive; Aviva Europe; Executive Director, Igal Mayer, age 52
Regional Development and Strategy Director Aviva Asia, Anupam Sahay
Chief Risk Officer, Robin Spencer, age 43
Chief Executive - Aviva Investors, Alain Dromer, age 58
EVP and COO Operations and Technology Aviva Canada, Robert Merizzi
CEO Investors North America, Greg Boal
Director Global Investment Solutions, Richard Field
Chief Marketing and Communications Officer, Amanda Mackenzie, age 49
Chief Executive; Aviva North America, Richard Hoskins
Director Human Resources Aviva Investors, Nigel Clemson
EVP Claims and Procurement Aviva Canada, Jim Haskins
Head Consultant Relationship Management Aviva Investors, Jonathan May
Manager Investor Relations, Susie Yeoh
Company Secretary, Graham Jones
Chief Risk Officer North America, Dan Guilbert
Head Advertising and Media UK Life, Sue Helmont
CEO Aviva UK & Ireland General Insurance, Maurice Tulloch
Chief Actuary Aviva USA, John D. Currier Jr.
Director Group Communications, Nigel Prideaux
Deputy Director Strategy France, Pierre-Emmanuel Lefebvre, age 34
Secretary Executive Committee, Stanislas Belot, age 38
Deputy CFO and Chief Capital Officer, Tim Harris
Managing Director of Aviva NDB Insurance, Shah Rouf
Head Investor Relations, Jonathan Price
Director Corporate Risk Solutions, Dipak Warren
Director Corporate Affairs Europe, Jon Bunn
Chief Executive Officer; Aviva UK & Ireland Life, David Barral
CEO France, Philippe Maso
Head of Investor Relations, David Elliot
Director of Investor Relations, Sophie Garrett
Senior Manager, Anna Cardell
General Manager marketing and bancassurance, Amal Perera
Chief Accounting Officer, David Rogers
finance Director, John Lister
Vice President of corporate affairs, Sally Turney
Head of Investor Relations, Shaheen Iqbal
Business Development Director, Simon Warsop
Vice President of Claims, Wayne Ross
Group General Counsel; Company Secretary, Kirstine Cooper
Director, Michael J. (Mike) Hawker, age 53
Interim Executive Deputy Chairman, John McFarlane, age 66
Executive Director Developed Markets, Trevor J. Matthews, age 61
Director, Russell F. Walls, age 69
CEO of Aviva, Andrew Moss, age 55
Director, Richard K. Goeltz, age 70
Director, Scott Wheway, age 46
Director, Euleen Y. K. Goh, age 57
CFO and Director, Patrick C. (Pat) Regan, age 46
Non-Executive Independent Director, Gay Evans
Non-Executive Independent Director, Glyn Barker
Auditors: Ernst&YoungLLP

LOCATIONS

HQ: Aviva Plc (United Kingdom)
St. Helen' s, 1 Undershaft, London EC3P 3DQ
Phone: (44) 20 7662 8934
Web: www.aviva.com

2012 Revenues

UK & Ireland	46	
France	30	
High growth markets	5	
Total	**0**	**100**

PRODUCTS/OPERATIONS

2012 Revenues

	% of total
Long-term (life)	76
General insurance &	23
Fund	1
Total	**100**

COMPETITORS

AEGON
AXA
Ageas Insurance International
Allianz
Bank of Ireland
Canada Life
Friends Provident
Generali
ING
Legal & General Group
Lloyds Banking Group
Prudential plc
QBE
RSA Insurance
Royal Bank of Scotland
Standard Life
Zurich Insurance Group

HISTORICAL FINANCIALS

Company Type: Public

Income Statement FYE: December 31

	ASSETS ($ mil.)	NET INCOME ($ mil.)	INCOME AS % OF ASSETS	EMPLOYEES
12/12	508,848	(5,186)	—	33,122
12/11	482,575	347	0.1%	36,562
12/10	574,642	2,271	0.4%	45,142
12/09	573,964	1,757	0.3%	46,327
12/08	516,703	(1,333)	—	54,758
Annual Growth	(0.4%)	—	—	(11.8%)

2012 Year-End Financials

Return on assets: (-1.0%)
Return on equity: (-27.1%)
Long-term debt ($ mil.): —
No. of shares (mil.): —
Sales ($ mil): 69,463

Dividends
Yield: 6.6%
Payout: —
Market value ($ mil.): —

	STOCK PRICE ($) FY Close	P/E High/Low	PER SHARE ($) Earnings	Dividends	Book Value
12/12	12.41	— —	(1.82)	0.82	5.35
12/11	9.25	682353	0.09	2.06	7.35
12/10	12.41	70 39	0.77	0.73	7.70
12/09	13.07	105 83	0.61	0.00	6.76
Annual Growth	(1.7%)	— —	—	—	(5.7%)

AXA S.A.

The insurance world revolves around this AXA. The company which started as a sleepy collection of mutual insurance companies is today one of the world's largest insurers and a financial management powerhouse. In addition to its strong presence in France AXA owns US-based AXA Financial which controls life insurance firm AXA Equitable and investment manager AllianceBernstein. The company also has major subsidiaries in the UK (AXA UK) Germany (AXA Konzern) Japan (AXA Life) and Belgium (AXA Belgium). The AXA companies offer life insurance personal and commercial property and casualty insurance financial services and asset management services. AXA has about ?1 trillion (or $1.45 trillion) in assets under management.

Geographic Reach

Rather than trying to run a cross-border organization AXA instead buys and builds up businesses in each country rebranding them under the AXA name. The company serves more than 100 million customers in 60 countries primarily in Europe North America and Asia as well as in Africa Latin America and the Middle East. The central and eastern European market is the largest geographic segment accounting for about 30% of annual sales.

Operations

AXA's operations are divided into five segments with the largest business division –life and savings –accounting for about 60% of annual revenues. Life and savings products include savings retirement life insurance and health insurance offerings for groups and individuals; the division serves some 40 million customers in 30 countries around the globe. AXA's property/casualty segment accounting for about 30% of sales offers commercial and personal auto homeowners property and liability insurance primarily in Europe the Middle East and Latin America.

Meanwhile the asset management (investment fund management) international insurance (corporate solutions assurance offerings) and banking (retail banking savings and mortgage loans in Europe) segments together account for the remainder of revenues. The asset management business while small compared to AXA's two larger segments has a sizable presence in the investment market with assets under management of more than ?1000 billion.

Sales and Marketing

AXA markets its products through independent agents and brokers as well as through direct and salaried sales forces. It also has distribution partnerships with entities including banks car dealerships and other retail locations.

AXA sells its products both to individuals and to corporate groups. Its commercial property/casualty unit primarily targets small to midsized companies. The asset management business targets institutional investors (including AXA's insurance subsidiaries) and individuals.

Financial Performance

AXA reported revenues of some ?86 billion ($132 billion) in 2011 a decrease of about 19% from 2010 sales. A majority of the decline is due to the divestiture of operations in certain regions. However gains on asset sales caused AXA's net income to rise 46% to $4.5 billion.

Other factors impacting revenues included decreased insurance sales in regions including Latin America the Mediterranean Belgium France Japan and Central and Eastern Europe which was offset by growth in the US Switzerland Hong Kong and other Asian markets.

Strategy

AXA invests in a diverse spread of business to reduce risk and volatility across its operations and it focuses on building a solid business foundation and distribution network in each respective market where it operates.

To focus on core operations (life and savings property/casualty and asset management) as well as to free up capital and allow for expansion in emerging markets AXA is conducting some divestitures. For instance in 2013 the company sold the older books of life insurance policies issued by its MONY Life subsidiaries to Protective Life for some $1.1 billion to reduce its exposure to the underperforming North America market. AXA plans to focus on growth in the US in select markets where it has experienced momentum.

In addition in late 2011 the company sold its Canadian arm to Intact Financial for about $2.6 billion. Also in 2011 AXA exited its Australian and New Zealand joint venture operations through a complex transaction with Australian insurer AMP. (However AXA also expanded its Asian operations through the AMP deal.)

Mergers and Acquisitions

The transaction with AMP was one of the company's largest deals conducted in recent years. Through the transaction AXA took full control of the Asian operations of former majority-owned subsidiary AXA Asia Pacific (AXA APH) in 2011 for some A$9.8 billion ($9.4 billion) gaining full control of subsidiaries joint ventures and partnerships in China Hong Kong India Indonesia Malaysia the Philippines Singapore and Thailand. Former joint-venture partner AMP took full control of AXA APH's operations in Australia and New Zealand for some A$3.5 billion ($3.4 billion).

AXA further expanded its insurance operations in emerging markets in 2012 when it acquired the Asian (mainly Hong Kong and Singapore) and Latin American (Mexico) property/casualty operations of HSBC. The purchase also expanded AXA's bancassurance operations (where insurance is sold at partnering retail banks) in the regions.

Ownership

Mutuelles AXA (two mutuals) controls AXA through a more than 20% stake. In 2010 AXA voluntarily delisted its stock from the NYSE to focus on its larger-volume listing on the Euronext Paris exchange.

HISTORY

AXA dates to the 1817 formation of regional fire insurer Compagnie d'Assurances Mutuelles contre l'incendie in Rouen France (northwest of Paris). In 1881 France's first mutual life insurer was founded: Mutuelle Vie.

In 1946 these two operations and the younger Anciennes Mutuelles Accidents (founded 1922) were brought together by Sahut d'Izarn (general manager of Compagnie d'Assurances) as the Groupe Ancienne Mutuelle. Later members included Ancienne Mutuelle of Calvados (1946) Ancienne Mutuelle of Orleans (1950) Mutualite Generale (1953) and Participation (1954).

A long-term thinker d'Izarn named not only his successor Lucien Aubert but also Aubert's successor: Claude Bebear a 23-year-old friend of d'Izarn's son. Never having held a job Bebear found the whole thing amusing and decided to try it.

Groupe Ancienne Mutuelle prospered during the 1960s thanks to d'Izarn's disciplined management but his technophobia kept the company from entering the computer age.

D'Izarn died in 1972. Aubert capitulated to worker demands during a series of strikes in the early 1970s; Bebear ended a 1974 strike by threatening to use force against an employee sit-in then ousted Aubert. Bebear spent the rest of the 1970s upgrading the firm's technology. During this period the company became known as Mutuelles Unies.

Bebear then began building the firm through a series of spectacular acquisitions. In 1982 Mutuelles Unies gained control of crisis-ridden stock insurer Drouot. Two years later the company's name became AXA (which has no meaning and was chosen because it is pronounced the same in most Western languages). When another old-line insurer Providence went on the market AXA went after it. Providence's management was entertaining another offer when AXA bought tiny inactive Bayas Tudjus which held the right to a seat on the Providence board. Bebear capitalized on small stockholders' dissatisfaction to spark a bidding war and used a new issue of Drouot stock in 1986 to buy Providence –France's first hostile takeover.

AXA bought lackluster US firm Equitable (later named AXA Financial) in 1991 infusing $1 billion into the firm in return for the right to own up to 50% of its stock upon demutualization in 1992. AXA moved into Asia with the purchase of Australia's National Mutual in 1995.

Bebear consolidated the operations into a global organization. In 1996 AXA bought the ailing Union des Assurances de Paris which had done poorly since its 1994 privatization. It bought the 52% of Belgian insurer Royale Belge SA it didn't already own as well as Belgian savings bank Anhyp in 1998.

Bebear raised hackles when he supported the Societe Generale-Paribas bank merger then supported BNP's hostile takeover attempt of both (which garnered only Paribas). In 1999 AXA bought Guardian Royal Exchange then sold the life and pensions business to Dutch insurer AEGON; Bebear announced his retirement in 1999. In 2000 he stepped down from the management board but took over as chairman of the supervisory board. Henri de Castries was placed in the top executive position as chairman of the management board.

That year AXA took control of Japan's Nippon Dantai Life Insurance. It also bought the remaining shares of AXA Financial and the 44% of AXA UK (formerly Sun Life and Provincial Holdings) it didn't already own. The next year AXA unloaded its debt-heavy subsidiary Banque Worms to Deutsche Bank.

In an attempt to strengthen its US retail insurance and annuity business AXA through subsidiary AXA Financial bought MONY Group for some $1.5 billion in 2004. The deal was opposed by some of MONY's shareholders but it ultimately gained approval. On the down side AXA discontinued its slumping US-based reinsurance operations (AXA Corporate Solutions Reinsurance and AXA Corporate Solutions Life Reinsurance).

Also in 2004 the company exited its operations in Uruguay thus exiting the South American market and sold its Dutch brokerage and health insurance subsidiaries and its German mortgage lending business.

AXA made a major coup in the insurance industry when it acquired the Winterthur Group from Credit Suisse Group for ?7.9 billion ($11 billion) in 2006. Winterthur added subsidiaries in 17 countries with 13 million customers and especially strengthened AXA's European operations. The primary Swiss Winterthur division was renamed AXA Versicherungen. AXA also sold the assets of AXA Re that year.

In 2007 AXA sold noncore Dutch subsidiaries AXA Netherlands Winterthur Netherlands and DBV Netherlands. To expand its insurance operations in emerging markets AXA acquired South Korean car insurance provider Kyobo Auto (now Kyobo AXA General Insurance). In addition it formed a partnership with BNP Paribas to provide property/casualty insurance in the Ukraine.

That year the company's property fund division AXA Investment Managers announced plans to invest more than $15 billion in Asian real estate by 2013. In addition AXA established the AXA Research Fund in 2008 to invest $500 million in social science research institutions over five years.

After a long career at the center of AXA's operations Bebear retired as chairman of the supervisory board in 2008 but retained the title of honorary chairman of the company.

AXA bought out its Turkish joint venture partner pension fund Oyak for $525 million in 2008 to take full control of AXA Holding A.S. (formerly AXA Oyak) a provider of life and other insurance products in the fast-growing Turkish market. Later that year the company purchased #3 Mexican life insurance company ING Seguros (now AXA Seguros) for $1.5 billion from ING Groep. AXA also made an investment in the Russian property/casualty market.

To further expand in emerging markets by targeting the high-growth regions of Central and Eastern Europe in 2010 AXA entered the Romanian life insurance market with the buy of Omniasig Life. The deal followed AXA's buy of minority interests in Omniasig's Hungarian Czech and Polish subsidiaries from the European Bank for Reconstruction and Development in late 2009.

To focus on core operations in 2010 the company sold parts of its UK life insurance business (including traditional life and pension corporate pension and annuity operations) to acquisition vehicle Resolution Ltd. for ?3.3 billion ($4.1 million). Resolution added the acquired operations to another insurance firm Friends Provident picked up in 2009; the former AXA operations are now known as Friends Life. The asset sale allowed AXA UK to focus its life operations on high-growth wealth management services including its specialist pension and direct protection businesses. AXA UK also retained its property/casualty health insurance and investment management operations.

AXA also simplified its management organization to reduce complexities and create a nimble leadership team to face future customer needs and economic challenges. In 2010 the company streamlined its governance structure by combining its supervisory board and its management board into a single board of directors led by Henri de Castries as chairman and CEO; Castries had previously been chairman of the management board.

AXA took full control of the Asian operations of former majority-owned subsidiary AXA Asia Pacific (AXA APH in which it previously owned a 54% stake) in 2011 to strengthen its operations in the fast-paced region. The firm completed a deal with Australian insurer AMP through which AMP acquired all of AXA APH for some A$13.3 billion ($12.8 billion); AMP then sold the Asian operations to AXA for some A$9.8 billion ($9.4 billion) while retaining AXA APH's operations in Australia and New Zealand. The deal was agreed upon in late 2010 after a year-long bidding war for control of AXA APH between AMP and rival National Australia Bank (NAB).

Also in 2011 it sold its roughly 16% stake in Taikang Life (China's fourth-largest life insurer) to a group of shareholders for $1.2 billion to meet regulatory conditions for the AXA APH asset acquisition. (AXA gained a stronger position in another joint venture in China with Industrial and Commercial Bank of China through the AXA APH deal.)

EXECUTIVES

Chairman and CEO, Henri de Castries, age 59, $662,600 total compensation
Deputy CEO and Board Member, Denis Duverne, age 60, $569,836 total compensation
Vice Chairman, Norbert Dentressangle, age 59
CEO AXA UK, Paul J. Evans, age 48
CEO AXA Asia Pacific Holdings Australia, Andrew (Andy) Penn, age 50
CEO Northern Central and Eastern Europe, Jacques de Vaucleroy, age 53
CEO France, Nicolas Moreau, age 48, $580,835 total compensation
President and CEO AXA Financial and AXA Equitable, Mark Pearson, age 55
Vice Chairman Asia Pacific, John R. Dacey, $365,532 total compensation
General Counsel and Head of Human Resources, George Stansfield
CEO AXA Japan, Jean-Louis Laurent Josi, age 44
Member of the Executive Committee; Group Chief Operating Officer, Veronique Weill
CEO Mediterranean-Latin America Region (MedLA), Jean-Laurent Granier
Investor Marketing and Events, Laurence Letty
CEO Northern Central and Eastern Europe, Alfred Bouckaert
Chairman and CEO AllianceBernstein, Peter S. Kraus
SVP and Head Investor Relations, Mattieu Rouot
Financial Analyst France, Thomas Hude
Vice President, Yadl Gabel
Member of the Executive Committee; Chief Executive Officer of AXA Konzern AG, Thomas Buberl
Board Member, Jean-Martin Folz, age 66
Board Member, Michel Pebereau, age 70
Deputy CEO and Board Member, Denis Duverne, age 60
Vice Chairman, Norbert Dentressangle, age 59
Board Member, Jacques de Chateauvieux, age 63
Board Member, Anthony J. Hamilton, age 72
Board Member, Dominique Reiniche, age 57
Board Member, Giuseppe Mussari, age 51
Board Member, Wendy Cooper, age 63
Board Member, Francois Martineau, age 63
Board Member, Ramon de Oliveira, age 59
Board Member, Isabelle Kocher, age 47
Board Member, Suet-Fern Lee, age 55
Auditors: PricewaterhouseCoopersAudit

LOCATIONS

HQ: AXA S.A.
25, avenue Matignon, Paris 75008
Phone: (33) 1 40 75 57 00 **Fax:** 212 707-1805
Web: www.axa.com

2011 Sales

	% of total
Central & Eastern	31
France	24
Mediterranean & Latin	15
US	12
Asia/Pacific	10
UK &	5
Direct	3
Total	**100**

PRODUCTS/OPERATIONS

2011 Sales

	% of total
Life &	60
Property/casualty	31
Asset	4
International	4
Banking &	1
Total	**100**

Selected Brands and Divisions

Africa
- AXA Holding Maroc

Asia-Pacific
- AXA China
- AXA Japan
- AXA Financial Services (Singapore)
- Kyobo AXA General Insurance

Asset Management
- AXA Investment Managers (US)
- AllianceBernstein (US)

Europe
- AXA Bank (Germany)
- AXA Bank Europe (Belgium)
- AXA Banque (France)
- AXA Czech Republic Insurance
- AXA Czech Republic Pension Funds
- AXA France Assurance
- AXA Holdings Belgium
- AXA Holdings Ireland
- AXA Hungary
- AXA Insurance
- AXA Italia
- AXA Konzern (Germany)
- AXA Lebensversicherung (Germany)
- AXA Life
- AXA Life Europe
- AXA Luxembourg
- AXA Mediterranean
- AXA MPS Vita
- AXA MPS Danni
- AXA Poland Pension Funds
- AXA Poland
- AXA Portugal Companhia de Seguros
- AXA Portugal Companhia de Seguros de Vida
- AXA Turkey
- AXA UK
- AXA Versicherung (Germany)
- Seguro Directo

International Insurance
- AXA Assistance
- AXA Corporate Solutions Assurance
- AXA Corporate Solutions Life Reinsurance Company
- Colisee

North America
- AXA Financial (US)
- AXA Seguros (Mexico)

COMPETITORS

ACE Limited
AEGON
AIG
Ageas Insurance
JPMorgan Chase
Legal & General Group
Merrill Lynch

International
Allianz
Allstate
Aviva
BNP Paribas
Bank of America
Berkshire Hathaway
CIGNA
CNP Assurances
Citigroup
Dai-ichi Life
Eureko
Generali
ING
MetLife
Munich Re Group
Nationwide
New York Life
Nippon Life Insurance
Prudential
Prudential plc
State Farm
Sumitomo Life
Talanx
The Hartford
Travelers Companies
Zurich Insurance Group

HISTORICAL FINANCIALS

Company Type: Public

Income Statement FYE: December 31

	ASSETS ($ mil.)	NET INCOME ($ mil.)	INCOME AS % OF ASSETS	EMPLOYEES
12/12	1,004,154	5,472	0.5%	94,364
12/11	944,329	5,592	0.6%	96,999
12/10	979,224	3,679	0.4%	102,957
12/09	1,020,286	5,194	0.5%	103,432
12/08	941,636	1,290	0.1%	109,304
Annual Growth	1.6%	43.5%	—	(3.6%)

2012 Year-End Financials

Return on assets: 0.5%
Return on equity: 8.1%
Long-term debt ($ mil.): —
No. of shares (mil.): —
Sales ($ mil): 158,689
Dividends
Yield: 4.8%
Payout: 42.0%
Market value ($ mil.): —

	STOCK PRICE ($) FY Close	P/E High	P/E Low	PER SHARE ($) Earnings	Dividends	Book Value
12/12	18.22	19	10	2.16	0.89	29.61
12/11	12.86	25	11	2.26	0.89	26.85
12/10	16.65	45	21	1.45	1.25	28.98
12/09	23.68	42	9	2.18	1.10	29.42
12/08	22.47	198	55	0.62	1.86	25.33
Annual Growth	(5.1%)	—	—	36.9%	(16.9%)	4.0%

BAE Systems Plc

BAE Systems helped win the Battle of Britain in 1940 with its Spitfire and Mosquito fighters; today it is a leading military contractor and major foreign player in the US defense market. BAE's main operating groups –electronic systems cyber & intelligence and platforms & services –provide products and services that include electro-optical sensors flight controls commercial and financial security ship repair and modernization and aircraft. BAE's fighter aircraft include the Hawk Tornado and the next-generation Eurofighter Typhoon. North America is BAE's biggest market with the US Department of Defense (DoD) its largest single customer.

Financial Analysis

Struggling with declining budgets in customer markets the company weathered a year-over-year 2011 sales decline of 14%.

By segment platforms & services (UK) fell 4%. Operations in this segment which accounts for about 32% of revenue include UK-based air and maritime activities as well as such shared services as the Advanced Technology Center. Platforms & services (US) plummeted about 31%. This segment which represents about 27% of revenue is made up of the US-headquartered land & armaments business and operates additionally in the UK Sweden and South Africa.

Platforms & services (international) which operates in Australia India Oman and Saudi Arabia was down 12%. The segment accounting for 20% of revenue was busy with the first Saudi Typhoon squadron becoming operational and the launch of the first Royal Australian Navy Landing Helicopter Dock hull. Electronics systems –representing 14% of revenue –decreased about 11%. This segment's operations include electronic warfare systems military and commercial digital engine and flight controls and hybrid electric drive systems. Cyber & intelligence's 2011 year-over-year revenue rose 16%. The segment accounting for 7% of revenue handles cyber government and commercial security operations.

Strategy

Amid sharp reductions in defense spending in both of the company's biggest markets the US and UK BAE Systems has launched a strategy that besides focusing on electronics and cyber & intelligence includes developing more export business to support its platforms segments and expanding its operations internationally.

Also to further its focus on core businesses BAE Systems has disposed of several units in 2011 including Swiss-Photonics and BAE Systems' remaining share in Saab AB as well as its business in regional aircraft asset management and its US-based composites structures and California-based advanced ceramics units. In 2012 the company sold its safety products business.

Also in 2011 BAE Systems settled a tough legal situation agreeing to pay a fine of up to $79 million after reaching a civil settlement with the US Department of State for alleged violations of US defense export control regulations. The company's US subsidiary BAE Systems Inc. was not involved in the matter.

Mergers & Acquisitions

As a segment targeted for additional growth cyber & intelligence has expanded recently with some major acquisitions. In 2011 BAE Systems acquired the intelligence service businesses of L-1 Identity Solutions as well as ETI A/S a Danish cyber and intelligence company and Norkom Group which provides anti-money laundering services. In other business the segment enjoyed a boost in commercial sales for its Detica unit and invested in the UK Security Operations Center.

Company Background

In September 2012 BAE Systems agreed to merge with European Aeronautic Defence and Space Company (EADS). However the proposed $45 billion merger –which would have created the largest global aerospace and defense player on the planet both in total sales and market value –was called off weeks later after it failed to pass European governmental and regulatory hurdles.

HISTORY

Post-Wright brothers and pre-WWII a host of aviation companies sprang up to serve the British Empire –too many to survive after the war when the empire contracted. Parliament took steps in 1960 to save the industry by merging companies to form larger stronger entities –Hawker-Siddeley Aviation and British Aircraft Corporation (BAC).

Hawker-Siddeley made up of aircraft and missiles divisions was created by combining A.V. Roe Gloster Aircraft Hawker Aircraft Armstrong Whitworth and Folland Aircraft. It attained fame in the 1960s for developing the Harrier "jump jet."

BAC was formed from the merger of Bristol Aeroplane English Electric and Vicker-Armstrong. In 1962 it joined France's Aerospatiale to build the supersonic Concorde and became a partner in ventures to develop the Tornado and Jaguar fighters. The cost of these ventures plus the commercial failure of the Concorde was more than the company could bear. Realizing British aviation was again in trouble the British government nationalized BAC and Hawker-Siddeley in 1976 and merged them in 1977 with Scottish Aviation to form British Aerospace (BAe).

BAe joined the Airbus consortium in 1979. A partial privatization of the company began in 1981 when the government sold 52% to the public (the remaining stake sold in 1985). Also in 1981 BAe announced a joint venture with Comsat General and announced that it would be the prime contractor for L-SAT-1 the European Space Agency's telecommunications satellite. Later in the decade BAe bought Steinheil Optronik (optical equipment) and Ballast Nedam Groep (civil and marine engineering).

BAe formed Ballast Nedam Construction in 1990. It also began to restructure its troubled regional aircraft division in 1992 by laying off thousands of workers and closing a major plant. It divested its corporate jet business to Raytheon and won a $7.5 billion contract from Saudi Arabia for Tornado jets in 1993. BAe sold its satellite business in 1994. Matra BAe Dynamics the world's third largest maker of tactical missiles was formed in a 1996 merger between BAe and Lagardere subsidiary Matra Hachette. BAe joined Lockheed Martin in a competition to build fighter jets for the UK and the US.

BAe's emphasis on large jetliners led to the 1998 breakup of Aero International its two-year-old regional aircraft joint venture with Aerospatiale (France) and Alenia (Italy). Shortly thereafter BAe spent $454 million for a 35% stake in Swedish military jet maker Saab. Also in 1998 BAe bought Siemens' UK- and Australia-based defense electronics operations. In 1999 BAe acquired the electronic systems defense unit of Marconi Electronic Systems (MES) for $12.7 billion (including US-based Tracor). The company changed its corporate identity to BAE SYSTEMS to remove the British influence from its name.

The UK government agreed to loan BAE about $836 million in 2000 to support the Airbus A3XX superjumbo airliner project. The same year BAE acquired Lockheed Martin's control systems unit for about $510 million. The prime contractor for the UK's new Type 45 destroyer BAE was named to build two of the first three Type 45s. Late in the year BAE spent about $1.7 billion for a group of Lockheed Martin's defense electronics businesses including its Sanders airborne electronics unit. BAE sold its power and controls business (actuation equipment and starter motors) to Cobham.

Early in 2001 the company sold its 54% stake in BAE SYSTEMS CANADA (now known as CMC Electronics) to Oncap a Toronto-based investment fund as part of a $398 million management buyout of the affiliate. The same year the Airbus Industrie consortium finally became Airbus S.A.S. a corporation. In late 2001 BAE announced that it would phase out its regional aircraft business.

The following year (2002) BAE sold its defensive-countermeasures business to Esterline Technologies. Just a year later it took a 29% stake in Alvis maker of the Challenger main battle tank. In 2004 General Dynamics made a 280 pence a share bid for Alvis; BAE topped that offer in early June with a bid of 320 pence a share (about $650 million) and a deal was struck. BAE then combined Alvis with its RO Defence group to form a new business unit Land Systems. Prior to the Alvis deal BAE was reportedly in merger talks with US contractors (including General Dynamics).

BAE was selected as the prime contractor for the UK's next two aircraft carriers in 2003. In 2004 however the Ministry of Defence took away that designation and brought in Thales to work on the carrier project. The controversy was ratcheted up another notch in 2005 when Halliburton subsidiary Kellogg Brown & Root (now KBR an independent company) was brought in as the physical integrator of the project. A spending review by the UK's Ministry of Defence in 2006 however put any final decisions about Britain's future carrier plans on hold until mid-2007 when yet another deal was worked out. The new carrier plan combined the shipbuilding operations of BAE with those of VT Group –Britain's only remaining shipbuilding concerns.

The joint venture known as BVT Surface Fleet provided the Royal Navy with two new aircraft carriers in a contract valued at #3.8 billion (about $7.6 billion). The deal aimed not only to secure the jobs at the UK's last remaining shipbuilders during the life of the carrier contract but also to create a single UK-based shipbuilding concern that safeguarded jobs in the long term as VT and BAE's shipbuilding operations would no longer compete with each other for bringing big contracts to the UK. VT owned 45% of BVT and BAE owned the majority. VT had the option of selling its stake in BVT for a guaranteed minimum of #380 million (about $535 million) and it took that option in 2009 in order to focus on its growing support services business.

It was revealed in early 2005 that BAE was seeking buyers for its aerostructures business which made airframe components for such customers as Airbus Boeing Cessna and Raytheon. Around this time BAE reduced its stake in Saab from 35% to 22%. Also in 2005 BAE acquired – through its North American subsidiary –US-based United Defense Industries (UDI) in a deal worth about $4.2 billion as part of its push to get more US defense contracts. As part of the company's BAE Systems Land & Armaments business UDI made armored vehicles (including the Bradley Fighting Vehicle) landing craft and weapons systems. Upon closing the UDI deal BAE SYSTEMS North America changed its name to BAE Systems Inc.

The sale of the company's stake in Airbus to EADS for E2.75 billion (about $3.3 billion) in 2006 was effected in order to focus on its defense businesses –primarily in the US. Selling its Airbus stake to EADS helped fund expansion in the US defense sector. That same year BAE sold its aerostructures business which made Avro jet aircraft to Spirit AeroSystems. With the closure of its commercial aerospace unit and the sale of its stake in Airbus BAE essentially became a military contractor.

In 2007 BAE made its first move toward a major US defense acquisition since the completion of the EADS deal when it bought Armor Holdings for about $4.5 billion. The deal positioned it as a more powerful competitor in the tactical military vehicle sector; a fact that gained significance as the US military fleet of HUMVEEs aged driving demand for a next-generation replacement which turned out to be the Mine Resistant Ambush Protect (MRAP) vehicle. Prior to the acquisition Armor won a Marine Corps contract to build over 1000 MRAPs which was in addition to the more than 440 MRAPs that BAE already had contracts to build. The combined contracts were worth about $730 million.

The company had a good year in 2008. It acquired three companies. US-based MTC Technologies was purchased for $375 million; it brought technical and professional services used especially in equipment integration and modernization for the US military and intelligence agency sectors. It was incorporated into the company's EI&S group. To target the national security market Detica was acquired for #543 million (almost $960 million plus the assumption of net debt) in the fall. Supporting the company's Program & Support business Detica provides business and technology consultancy with expertise in security and threat intelligence. Investing down under BAE SYSTEMS paid about $650 million for Tenix Defence a leading Australian defense contractor. That same year Ian King (former COO) was appointed CEO after Mike Turner (CEO since 2002) retired after serving 42 years at BAE.

BAE SYSTEMS met with some turbulence in early 2010 when it lost out on a follow-up contract with the DoD; the deal had previously generated a whopping $2 billion in annual sales for the company. Instead the DoD awarded the contract to make medium tactical vehicles to Oshkosh Corporation.

EXECUTIVES

Board Member; President and CEO BAE Systems Inc., Linda P. Hudson, age 63
Group General Counsel, Philip Bramwell
Group Managing Director Programmes and Support, Nigel Whitehead
Director Group HR, Alastair Imrie
EVP Product Sectors, Tom Arseneault
SVP Strategy and Planning BAE Systems Inc., Douglas E. (Doug) Belair
Director Group Strategy, Andrew Davies
Director Group Communications, Charlotte Lambkin
EVP Service Sectors, Lawrence B. (Larry) Prior III, age 57
Director Group Strategy, Kevin Taylor
EVP Service Sectors, David A. (Dave) Herr
SVP Information Management and CIO BAE Systems Inc., D. Michael Bennett
SVP Corporate Communications BAE Systems Inc., John Suttle
CEO and Board Member, Ian King, age 57, $1,230,205 total compensation
Director Group Business Development, Alan Garwood, age 58
Group Managing Director International, Guy Griffiths
Secretary, David Parkes
SVP Human Resources BAE Systems Inc., Curt Grey
Director Group Media Relations, John Neilson
Head Financial Public Relations, Lindsay Walls
Manager Media Relations Land Systems, Mike Sweeney
Head of Communications BAE Systems Australia, Simon Latimer
Manager Media Relations Global Tectical Systems Land Systems South Africa, Natasha Pheiffer
VP Internal Audit BAE Systems Inc., Michelle Lamberton
SVP Finance BAE Systems Inc., Brad Jacobs
Group Finance Director, Peter Lynas
Non-Executive Independent Chairman of the Board, Keith Edelman
Senior Independent Non-Executive Director, William Tuffy
Chairman, Dick Oliver
Board Member; President and CEO BAE Systems Inc., Linda P. Hudson, age 63
Board Member, Nicholas C. (Nick) Rose, age 54
Board Member, Michael Hartnall, age 71
Board Member, Sir Peter J. Mason, age 67
Board Member, Carl G. Symon, age 66
CEO and Board Member, Ian King, age 57
Board Member, Paul Anderson
Group Finance Director, Peter Lynas
Non-Independent Non-Executive Director, John Chillcott
Non-Independent Non-Executive Director, Simon Peters
Auditors: KPMGAuditPlc

LOCATIONS

HQ: BAE Systems Plc
6 Carlton Gardens, London SW1Y 5 AD
Phone: (44) 1252 373232
Web: www.baesystems.com

2011 Sales

	% of total
US	41
Europe	
UK	21
Rest of	15
Middle East	
Saudi	13
Rest of Middle	-
Asia/Pacific	
Australia	6
Rest of	2
Africa & Central & South	2
Canada	-
Total	**100**

PRODUCTS/OPERATIONS

2011 Sales

	% of total
Platforms services	
Platforms & services	32
Platforms & services	27
Platforms & services	20
Electronic	14
Cyber &	7
Total	**100**

2011 Sales

	% of total
Long-term	53
Sale of	26
Provision of	21
Royalty	-
Total	**100**

Selected Products and Services

Air
- Avionics
- Combat aircraft
- Commercial aircraft
- Controls (flight and engine)
- Jet trainers
- Maintenance repair and upgrades
- Missiles and counter measures
- Reconnaissance aircraft
- Unmanned aerial vehicle (UAV)

Homeland Security
- Border and coastal surveillance

Information Technology
Intelligence Security & Resilience
Land
- Artillery
- Combat and tactical vehicles
- Munitions
- Radar
- Unmanned systems

Sea
- Amphibious and auxiliary ships
- Naval guns
- Submarines
- Underwater systems
- Warships

Systems Integration & Electronics
- C4ISR (Command Control Communications Computers Intelligence Surveillance Reconnaissance)
- Communications
- Electronic warfare & countermeasures
- Imaging systems
- Intelligence systems
- Navigation systems
- Sensor systems

Technology and Innovation
Through-Life Support

COMPETITORS

Astronautics
Boeing
Bombardier
Horstman Defence Systems
ITT Corp.

- DRS Technologies
- EADS
- Fabbrica D' Armi Pietro Beretta
- Finmeccanica
- GenCorp
- General Dynamics
- Goodrich Corp.
- High Performance Technologies
- Honeywell International
- L-3 Communications
- Lockheed Martin
- Meggitt-USA
- Navistar International
- Northrop Grumman
- RUAG Holding
- Rockwell Collins
- Sotera Defense
- Thales
- Ultra Electronics
- United Technologies

HISTORICAL FINANCIALS

Company Type: Public

Income Statement FYE: December 31

	REVENUE ($ mil.)	NET INCOME ($ mil.)	NET PROFIT MARGIN	EMPLOYEES
12/12	26,789	1,721	6.4%	81,000
12/11	27,452	1,915	7.0%	87,000
12/10	32,756	1,633	5.0%	92,000
12/09	32,997	(108)	—	98,000
12/08	24,294	2,542	10.5%	94,000
Annual Growth	2.5%	(9.3%)	—	(3.7%)

2012 Year-End Financials

Debt ratio: 21.6%
Return on equity: 26.7%
Cash ($ mil.): 5,407
Current ratio: 0.78
Long-term debt ($ mil.): 4,782
No. of shares (mil.): —
Dividends
Yield: 5.1%
Payout: 563.4%
Market value ($ mil.): —

	STOCK PRICE ($) FY Close	P/E High/Low	PER SHARE ($) Earnings	Dividends	Book Value
12/12	22.28	186126	0.53	1.15	1.84
12/11	17.66	155102	0.57	2.81	2.02
12/10	20.85	201132	0.47	0.95	2.43
12/09	23.18	— —	(0.03)	0.95	2.13
12/08	22.31	237 77	0.72	0.94	2.99
Annual Growth	(0.0%)	— —	(7.5%)	5.3%	(11.4%)

Balfour Beatty Plc

Talented? Check. In demand? Check. Handsome? You decide. Check out this Beatty –Balfour Beatty. The company provides infrastructure and commercial services including engineering design construction and maintenance. It operates primarily in the UK and North America but has been expanding and today operates in more than 80 countries around the world. Balfour Beatty works on a range of project types including roads and railways schools military housing hospitals and airports. It also provides financing and is an active participant in public-private partnerships. US units include Balfour Beatty Infrastructure and Balfour Beatty Construction.

Geographic Reach

The UK accounts for half of London-based Balfour Beatty's annual revenue. The US is the firm's second-largest market accounting for more than a third of it $15.3 billion in 2012 sales. Other strategic markets for the global infrastructure group include Australia Brazil Canada India and South Africa.

Operations

Construction Services is Balfour Beatty's largest business contributing nearly two-thirds of its annual revenue. The firm's construction activities include building refurbishment and fit-out mechanical and electrical services civil and ground engineering and rail engineering. Professional Services such as program management and project design accounts for more than 15% of sales while the firm's Support Services business including highways network management and the upgrading and maintenance of water gas and electric networks is about equal in size. Balfour Beatty's infrastructure investments include a sizable portfolio of long term public-private partnerships in the UK primarily in the fields of education health and roads and street lighting as well as airports. The company also has partnerships with French firms AREVA and VINCI to bid on contracts to build new nuclear power plants there. Balfour Beatty has aggressively moved in on the airport business bidding with a variety of partners on airport projects in the UK Ireland and the US.

Sales and Marketing

The firm's two largest customers are the US government and the UK government which contributed 24% and 23% of Balfour Beatty's revenue in 2012 respectively.

Financial Performance

Balfour Beatty's revenue was flat in 2012 compared with 2011 while its pre-tax profit from continuing operations fell 7%. The firm's Support Services business was the revenue driver in 2012 as the outsourcing trend among central and local governments utilities and commercial enterprises gained momentum. Also the firm's share of the UK highways maintenance market increased. Construction Services posted a 1% decline in revenue in 2012 versus 2011 as a result of government imposed austerity measures in the UK. Also the construction climate in the US remained depressed from historical highs.

Strategy

Balfour Beatty has grown rapidly thanks largely to an active schedule of acquisitions around the globe. Chief among these was the 2009 purchase of New York-based transportation engineering firm Parsons Brinckerhoff for some $625 million. The combination of Balfour Beatty and Parsons Brinckerhoff fell in line with both companies' strategies for global growth. Parsons Brinckerhoff retained its name and became a subsidiary of Balfour Beatty. The acquisition also underscored Balfour Beatty's increasing focus on infrastructure an area that offers added stability when the construction markets decline.

To those ends key strategic markets for the group include emerging markets in Asia Africa and South America. The UK and North American infrastructure landscapes are still recovering but look to provide plenty of opportunity for growth in the future.

Mergers and Acquisitions

In January 2013 the firm acquired Subsurface Group a US energy storage business. The purchase builds on Parsons Brinckerhoff's experience in the design and construction of underground sale caverns for the hydrocarbon storage. Other recent purchases in the US include Howard S. Wright a contracting firm on the West Coast which extends Beatty's reach in Northern California and the Pacific Northwest and Fru-Con Construction a water and wastewater contractor acquired in 2011.

Extending its reach in the UK fit-out market the company purchased Office Projects Group for #8 million in 2011.

HISTORY

BICC (now known as Balfour Beatty) was created by the 1945 merger of two leading UK electrical cable firms: Callender's Cable and Construction Company and British Insulated Cables. Both companies date to the beginning of the electrical cable industry.

William Callender moved out of the road-surfacing business and into electric wiring after he saw an 1882 demonstration of Edison's incandescent lighting in London. Son William invented a way to insulate copper wire with vulcanized bitumen and the Callender firm devised methods to lay cable beneath city streets.

James Atherton a fur trader who got the British rights to US paper-insulation patents established British Insulated Wire in 1890. With Italian inventor Sebastian de Ferranti on its board the company developed paper-insulated high-voltage cable. By 1903 it had merged with two other wiring firms to form British Insulated and Helsby Cables (BI).

BI and Callender's competed for or collaborated on nearly every major UK cable project. During WWII Callender's designed magnetic cable used extensively in ocean minesweeping and BI and Callender's helped build a gas pipeline across the Channel to support the D-day landing. At war's end the two companies merged to become British Insulated Callender's Cables (BICC).

In the next quarter-century BICC expanded internationally and branched into large-scale construction and civil engineering. In 1969 BICC bought Balfour Beatty a power construction-engineering company that became the group's most-profitable unit in the 1970s. The firm shortened its name to BICC in 1975. In 1979 BICC went into the expanding electronics field buying manufacturers Vero Boschert and Sealectro. In 1981 it teamed with Corning to manufacture fiber-optic cable in Wales.

A worldwide recession in the mid-1980s forced BICC to scale back its electronics division to refocus on cable. Cable purchases included Phillips Cablec and Brintec (bringing the Brand-Rex name); the buys made BICC the leading high-power cable maker in North America. BICC also moved into continental Europe acquiring Ceat Cavi and a 20% stake in GEGC Spain's top cable firm. In 1989 BICC acquired Andover Controls a leading maker of building-automation systems.

In the early 1990s the construction industry slid dragging Balfour Beatty into losses. BICC Cable and Balfour Beatty had both worked on the Channel Tunnel. In 1993 BICC bought KWO Kabel the former #1 cable manufacturer of East Germany. With the privatization of British Rail in 1996 Balfour Beatty bought three track-maintenance units from the former state monopoly.

As the European power industry deregulated utilities cut spending and the cable business declined. In 1997 BICC laid off Italian workers and entered a German joint venture Kabel Kwo Kabel with Dutch group NFK closing two factories. BICC froze new Asian investments during the region's financial crisis in 1998. It swapped its UK building-wire business for the heavy power cable business of UK firm Delta; 870 UK workers were subsequently laid off. The firm continued cutting jobs at European cable plants (2000 between 1997 and 1998).

In 1999 BICC sold its energy-cable businesses to General Cable for $440 million. BICC's energy-cable operations were combined with those of General Cable to form BICC General. BICC also sold its telecommunications-cabling businesses to Corning. After completing the sale in 2000 of its only remaining cable business data- and specialty-cabler Brand-Rex BICC changed its name to Balfour Beatty to reflect its new direction.

Balfour boosted its rail services in 2001 with the acquisition of the Rail Systems Division of US industrial group ABC-NACO and the rail electrication project business of Swiss engineering group ABB. The group's US civil and engineering company Balfour Beatty Construction Inc. acquired

National Engineering and Contracting an Ohio-based road and bridge contractor. The next year Balfour Beatty Construction along with Fluor and T. J. Lambrecht Construction was selected to build a $1 billion toll road one of the largest design/build transportation projects in the US.

In 2002 Balfour Beatty abandoned talks to buy J.A. Jones the US business of Philipp Holzmann the bankrupt German construction group. Instead it acquired another US-based company Security International an electronic access control provider that it integrated into a new security systems division within subsidiary Andover Controls. In 2003 the group acquired Mansell one of the UK's top construction and property services companies.

The company continued its acquisition strategy the next year with a Californian project management company JCM Group for $10 million which allowed it to augment its other operations there. Also in 2005 the company acquired Pennine Group a UK ground engineering specialist and SBB a German rail signalling specialist that has been renamed Balfour Beatty Rail Signal. The group's acquisition of rail rival Birse Group for #32 million in 2006 boosted Balfour Beatty's rail operations.

Balfour Beatty was a 20% shareholder in Metronet the London Underground building and maintenance company that in 2007 was placed in administration. The group wrote down some #27 million in equity investments and revenue losses related to the partnership.

In better 2007 news Balfour Beatty acquired Centex's construction unit that year. Renamed Balfour Beatty Construction the unit brought a strong presence in the Southeast US and a large piece of the military housing construction market to Balfour Beatty.

Balfour Beatty bought the military housing division of US real estate investment trust (REIT) GMH Communities for $350 million in 2008. That deal added established long-term contracts with federal agencies and strengthened its position in the US military housing market.

Also that year the company expanded its European business with the acquisition of German rail engineering company Schreck-Mieves for ?36 million. Its acquisitions of UK contracting firm Dean and Dyball and US management company Barnhart further helped it expand in those countries.

EXECUTIVES

Chairman, Steven (Steve) Marshall, age 56
Director Planning and Development, Peter J. L. Zinkin, age 60, $649,143 total compensation
CEO, Ian P. Tyler, age 53, $1,012,389 total compensation
Chairman and CEO Balfour Beatty Construction, Robert C. Van Cleave, age 48
Deputy CEO and Director, Anthony L. P. Rabin, age 58, $513,791 total compensation
Group Managing Director, James J. (Jim) Moynihan
Chairman Parsons Brinckerhoff, Keith J. Hawksworth
Director Human Resources, Paul Raby
Group Managing Director Engineering and Safety, Andy Rose
Group Managing Director Rail, Manfred Leger
Group Managing Director, Michael J. (Mike) Peasland, age 62
Manager Group Media Relations, Marjorie Hooper
Group Managing Director, Brian Osborne, age 57
COO, Andrew McNaughton, age 50
Chief Financial Officer, Duncan Magrath
Chief Executive Officer, George J. Pierson
General Counsel and Company Secretary, Chris Vaughan
Director Corporate Communications, Duncan Murray
Director, Robert J. W. (Rob) Walvis, age 66
Director, Hubertus Krossa, age 66
Director, Gordon H. Sage, age 67
Director, M. J. (Mike) Donovan, age 60
Deputy CEO and Director, Anthony L. P. Rabin, age 58
Director, Iain Ferguson, age 58
Director, Graham Roberts, age 54
Auditors: DeloitteLLP

LOCATIONS

HQ: Balfour Beatty Plc
130 Wilton Road, London SW1V 1LQ
Phone: (44) 20 7216 6800 **Fax:** (44) 20 7216 6950
Web: www.balfourbeatty.com

2012 Sales

	% of total
UK	50
US	36
Rest of	5
Rest of	9
Total	**100**

PRODUCTS/OPERATIONS

2012 Sales by Segment

	% of total
Construction	65
Professional	17
Support	16
Infrastructure	2
Corporate	-
Total	**100**

Selected Subsidiaries and Affiliates

Balfour Beatty Capital Ltd.
Balfour Beatty Capital Group Inc.
Balfour Beatty Civil Engineering Ltd.
Balfour Beatty Construction Group Inc. (US)
Balfour Beatty Construction Scottish & Southern Ltd.
Balfour Beatty Group Inc. (US)
Balfour Beatty Group Ltd.
Balfour Beatty LLC (US)
Balfour Beatty Rail Ltd.
BK Gulf LLC (Dubai 49%)
Delphian Insurance Company Ltd. (Isle of Man)
Dutco Balfour Beatty LLC (Dubai 49%)
Heery International Inc. (US)
Monteray Ltd. (25%)
Parsons Brinckerhoff Inc. (US)
PB Americas Inc.

COMPETITORS

ABB
ACS
AMEC
Amey
Bechtel
Bouygues
Bovis Lend Lease
Carillion
Clark Builders Group
Dragados
FCC Barcelona
Fluor
Hunt Companies
John Laing
Kier Group
Parsons Infrastructure & Technology
Peter Kiewit Sons'
Serco
Skanska
WS Atkins

HISTORICAL FINANCIALS

Company Type: Public

Income Statement FYE: December 31

	REVENUE ($ mil.)	NET INCOME ($ mil.)	NET PROFIT MARGIN	EMPLOYEES
12/12	15,285	70	0.5%	50,304
12/11	14,666	287	2.0%	50,301
12/10	14,340	222	1.5%	50,042
12/09	14,501	344	2.4%	51,543
12/08	12,038	285	2.4%	43,030
Annual Growth	6.2%	(29.4%)	—	4.0%

2012 Year-End Financials

Debt ratio: 24.3%
Return on equity: 3.4%
Cash ($ mil.): 873
Current ratio: 0.79
Long-term debt ($ mil.): 622
No. of shares (mil.): 688
Dividends
Yield: 1.7%
Payout: 392.4%
Market value ($ mil.): 6,261

	STOCK PRICE ($) FY Close	P/E High/Low	PER SHARE ($) Earnings	Dividends	Book Value
12/12	9.10	418 39	0.10	0.16	3.06
Annual Growth	—	— —	—	—	—

Baloise Holding AG

Founded in 1863 as a fire insurance company Baloise-Holding today is a general insurer that sells such standardized products as group and individual life policies and accident property and auto insurance to small firms and individuals. The company is one of the leading insurers in Switzerland operating primarily there and in Germany; together the countries account for about 80% of its sales. Through subsidiaries it also operates in six other nearby countries including Croatia and Serbia. Baloise also provides banking pension plans and other financial services through its Baloise Bank SoBa. The company uses its own sales force as well as partner distributors and independent brokers to sell its wares.

Baloise has been growing adding Croatia Liechtenstein and Serbia to the fold in 2007. Company strategy includes strengthening its brand to gain new customers and expanding regionally with "culturally compatibility" in mind. Its brands include Baloise Basler Deutcher Ring and Osiguranje Zagreb.

At the end of 2008 a challenging year for businesses worldwide Baloise declared a 50% drop in profits and that its stock lost about 30% of its value (beating the 35% lost by the Swiss Market Index on average). Believing its fundamentals are strong the company has been buying back shares and it paid shareholders their usual dividend.

In 2009 the company agreed to acquire the Luxembourg non-life insurance operations of Fortis Insurance for E23 million ($34 million). The purchase strenthens its property/casualty operations in the Luxembourg market.

HISTORY

In 1863 15 business leaders in Basel Switzerland formed the Baloise Fire Insurance Company. This was followed in 1864 by the formation of the Baloise transportation and life insurance companies.

Baloise-Holding was created in 1962 as a holding company for the previously independent insurance entities. In 1971 it merged all of its non-life companies into the Baloise Insurance Group.

Under its then-new chairman and president Rolf Schauble Baloise-Holding began in 1993 to reorganize its operations as it implemented a new corporate strategy. Key components of the strategy included a focus on the company's core European markets and a pattern of discarding less-profitable businesses. In 1998 Baloise-Holding sold off its US operations.

Strengthening its position as a full-fledged financial services company in 2000 Baloise acquired Swiss bank Solothurner (now Baloise Bank SoBa).

The same year it purchased Belgian bank HBK-Spaarbank Belgian insurer Amazon Insurance N.V. and Swiss regional bank Solothurner Bank SoBa. However in 2004 the company's Belgian unit Mercator sold its banking unit to ING.

The company acquired life insurer MONEY-MAXX Lebensversicherung AG from the Dutch Aegon Group in 2005.

EXECUTIVES

Head of Deutscher Ring Germany, Wolfgang Fauter, age 62
Head of Baloise Assurances Luxembourg, Andre Bredimus
Head of Baloise Bank SoBa, Alois Muller
Vice Chairman, Georg F. Krayer, age 70
Head Asset Management, Martin Wenk, age 56
Head of Corporate Development, Thomas Wodrich
Group CEO, Martin Strobel, age 47
Head of Information Systems and Logistics, Rene Guttinger
Head Finance, German Egloff, age 55
Head of Accounting/Controlling, Urs Bienz
Head of Basler Securitas Germany, Frank Grund
Head of Baloise Asset Management, Reto Diezi
Head of Real Estate/Mortgages, Urs Degen
Head of Baloise Fund Invest, Robert Antonietti
Head Corporate Center, Thomas Sieber
Head of Compliance, Peter Kalberer
Head of Runoff, Bruno Rappo
Chairman, Andreas Burckhardt, age 62
Head of Financial Management, Stefan Nolker
Corporate Human Resources, Markus Jordi, age 52
Head of Investment Strategy and Investment Controlling, Bernhard Casar
Member of the Corporate Executive Committee; Head of Division International, Jan Meulder
Member of Corporate Executive Committee; Head of Corporate Division Switzerland, Michael Mueller
Director, Werner Kummer, age 66
Director, Hansjorg Frei, age 71
Vice Chairman, Georg F. Krayer, age 70
Director, Gertrud Hohler, age 71
Director, Arend Oetker, age 72
Director, Christoph Albrecht, age 73
Director, Klaus Jenny, age 69
Director, Eveline Saupper, age 55
Non-Executive Independent Director, Michael Becker
Non-Executive Independent Director, Thomas Pleines
Non-Executive Independent Director, Andreas Beerli
Non-Executive Independent Director, Georges-Antoine Boccard
Non-Executive Independent Director, Hans Frei
Auditors: PricewaterhouseCoopersAG

LOCATIONS

HQ: Baloise Holding AG
Aeschengraben 21, Basel CH-4002
Phone: (41) 61 285 85 85 **Fax:** (41) 61 285 70 70
Web: www.baloise.com

PRODUCTS/OPERATIONS

2008 Sales

	% of total
Life	59
Other	41
Total	**100**

Selected Subsidiaries

Austria
Basler Versicherungen (insurance and pension products for private and business clients)
Belgium
Mercator Verzekeringen (personal and property insurance for individuals and small to mid-sized businesses)
Croatia
Osiguranje Zagreb (personal and property insurance for individuals and small to mid-sized businesses)
Germany
Basler Versicherungen (personal and property insurance for individuals small and mid-sized enterprises and selected industrial clients)
Deutscher Ring (insurance and pension products for individuals)
Luxembourg
Baloise Assurances (life personal and property insurance for private and business clients)
Serbia
Basler Osiguranja (personal and property insurance for individuals and small to mid-sized businesses)
Switzerland
Baloise Bank SoBa (banking products and services)
Basler Versicherungen (insurance and pension products for individuals and small to mid-sized enterprises)

COMPETITORS

AEGON
AIG
AXA
AXA Versicherungen
Allianz
Eureko
Hannover Re
Helvetia Group
ING
Itausa
Munich Re Group
Prudential plc
Swiss Life
Zurich Insurance Group

HISTORICAL FINANCIALS

Company Type: Public

Income Statement

FYE: December 31

	ASSETS ($ mil.)	NET INCOME ($ mil.)	INCOME AS % OF ASSETS	EMPLOYEES
12/12	80,208	958	1.2%	8,795
12/11	73,412	129	0.2%	9,141
12/10	69,878	929	1.3%	8,797
12/09	65,332	810	1.2%	9,400
12/08	57,573	700	1.2%	9,233
Annual Growth	8.6%	8.2%	—	(1.2%)

2012 Year-End Financials

Return on assets: 1.2%
Return on equity: 20.1%
Long-term debt ($ mil.): —
No. of shares (mil.): 46
Sales ($ mil): 10,199

Dividends
Yield: 0.0%
Payout: 3.4%
Market value ($ mil.): 370

	STOCK PRICE ($) FY Close	P/E High	P/E Low	PER SHARE ($) Earnings	Dividends	Book Value
12/12	7.89	1	1	9.91	0.34	112.25
12/11	9.71	11	9	1.37	0.37	87.76
12/10	9.15	1	1	9.50	0.25	92.83
12/09	10.25	1	1	8.32	0.20	87.80
Annual Growth	(8.4%)	—	—	4.5%	13.9%	6.3%

Banca Popolare dell'Emilia

Banca Popolare dell'Emilia Romagna is popular not just in its home region of Emilia Romagna but thanks to its local banking subsidiaries throughout 17 Italian regions. Renamed in 1992 and known as BPER the institution owns or has stakes in more than a dozen banks. Founded in 1867 on the initiative of Societa Operaia di Mutuo Soccorso it provides individuals and businesses with a variety of services including deposit banking lending and bancassurance (life insurance). Altogether BPER's network of banks boasts more than 1300 branches. Other BPER subsidiaries and affiliates offer such products and services as asset management factoring leasing and private banking.

EXECUTIVES

Deputy Chairman, Piero Ferrari
Deputy Chairman, Vittorio Fini, age 60
Chairman, Ettore Caselli, age 71
Managing Director and General Manager, Luigi Odorici, age 66
Manager Financial Reporting, Emilio Annovi
Deputy General Manager, Eugenio Garavini
Deputy General Manager, Fabrizio Togni
Director of Investor Relations, Gilberto Borghi
Director, Luigi Cremonini, age 74
Deputy Chairman, Piero Ferrari
Director, Mario Zucchelli, age 68
Director, Angelo Tantazzi, age 74
Deputy Chairman, Vittorio Fini, age 60
Director, Giulio Cicognani, age 66
Director, Alessandro Fagioli, age 75
Director, Giuseppe Lusignani, age 55
Director, Fioravante Montanari, age 72
Director, Erminio Spallanzani, age 67
Managing Director and General Manager, Luigi Odorici, age 66
Deputy Chairman, Alberto Marri, age 59
Non-Executive Independent Director, Deanna Rossi
Non-Executive Independent Director, Flavio Amadori
Non-Executive Independent Director, Giosue Boldrini
Independent Director, Giuseppina Amarelli
Independent Director, Manfredi Luongo
Independent Director, Valeriana Masperi

LOCATIONS

HQ: Banca Popolare dell' Emilia
Via San Carlo 8/20, Modena 41100
Phone: (39) 059 2021111 **Fax:** (39) 059 2022033
Web: www.bper.it

Selected Regions

Italy
ABRUZZO
BASILICATA
CALABRIA
CAMPANIA
EMILIA ROMAGNA
LAZIO
LIGURIA
LOMBARDIA
MARCHE
MOLISE
PUGLIA
SARDEGNA
SICILIA
TOSCANA
TRENTINO ALTO ADIGE
UMBRIA
VENETO
Abroad
China
Ireland
Luxembourg

COMPETITORS

Antonveneta
BNL bc
Banca Carige
Banca Popolare Di Spoleto
Banca Popolare dell' Etruria
Banca Popolare di Milano
Banca di Legnano
Banco Popolare
Banco di Desio
CREDEM
Intesa Sanpaolo
Monte dei Paschi di Siena
UniCredit

HISTORICAL FINANCIALS

Company Type: Public

Income Statement FYE: December 31

	ASSETS ($ mil.)	NET INCOME ($ mil.)	INCOME AS % OF ASSETS	EMPLOYEES
12/12	81,241	(14)	—	11,834
12/11	78,238	277	0.4%	11,965
12/10	78,292	392	0.5%	12,159
12/09	85,842	166	0.2%	12,278
12/08	73,780	186	0.3%	11,878
Annual Growth	2.4%	—	—	(0.1%)

2012 Year-End Financials

Return on assets: (-0.0%)
Return on equity: (-0.2%)
Long-term debt ($ mil.): —
No. of shares (mil.): 332
Sales ($ mil): 4,360

Dividends
Yield: —
Payout: —
Market value ($ mil.): —

Banco Bilbao Vizcaya Argentaria SA (BBVA)

It's not Cortez revisited but Banco Bilbao Vizcaya Argentaria (BBVA) –one of Spain's top banks –is conquering the New World. Although much of its business activity is in Spain (more than half of its loans) the company also operates in about 10 Latin American countries through subsidiaries including BBVA Bancomer in Mexico; Banco Bilbao Vizcaya Argentaria Chile; and BBVA Banco Frances in Argentina. With some 7400 offices in 30 countries the bank offers retail corporate and institutional banking; investment banking; asset management; insurance; and securities brokerage. BBVA also operates in other European countries and is expanding in China as well as in the US where it owns Compass Bank.

The company is focused on five geographic areas: Spain Mexico South America the US and Eurasia (which includes BBVA's Portugese and Turkish operations).

As one of Spain's largest banks (along with Santander) BBVA has been struggling with the worldwide financial downturn and the sovereign debt crisis. Unemployment in the country remains above 20% and the gross domestic product has been shrinking. More than a quarter of the bank's real estate loans are non-performing loans which has led to lower revenues. Another key market Mexico has seen some bright spots (mortgage activities have begun to rebound there) but is also still vulnerable to the troubled economic climate. Goodwill impairment in the US contributed to a loss in the market in 2011. That year BBVA's revenues grew 11% to $47.2 billion but net income fell 41% to $3.9 billion. A decrease in net interest income (due to an upturn in interest rates in the Eurozone) a decline in asset values slower customer activities and a reduction of earnings from portfolio sales all served to drag down the company's earnings.

As part of a larger restructuring of banks in Spain the company acquired Unnim Banc which had been taken over by the Bank of Spain for a symbolic ?1 in 2012. BBVA also assumed 20% of Unnim's real estate losses amounting to some ?300 million. The acquisition gives the bank more than 600 branches in Catalonia which has been a target market for BBVA. The deal also made BBVA Spain's largest bank by assets.

The company has worked to expand internationally to help diversify operations beyond its home market. BBVA has targeted Asia as a growth market forming an alliance with China's CITIC Group. In accordance the company owns a 30% stake in CITIC International Financial Holdings and a 15% stake in China Citic Bank.

BBVA is expanding in other markets too. In 2011 it acquired Credit Uruguay Banco from Credit Agricole to become one of Uruguay's largest financial institutions. The company also bought a 25% stake in Turkish bank Garanti which it jointly manages with Turkish conglomerate Dogus Group.

To better focus on its expansion in the US BBVA is selling its Puerto Rican operations to OFG Bancorp for $500 million. The sale represents less than 1% of BBVA's total assets. BBVA plans to sell other operations in Latin America including the Provida Bancomer and Horizonte Peru pension management companies.

HISTORY

Banco Bilbao Vizcaya Argentaria (BBVA) is the progeny of the 2000 merger of Banco Bilbao Vizcaya (BBV) and Argentaria Caja Postal y Banco Hipotecario. BBV formed when Banco de Bilbao and Banco de Vizcaya merged in 1988 while Argentaria Caja Postal y Banco Hipotecario coalesced from the 1991 merger of six government-owned banks.

In 1857 a group of Basque businessmen banded together to offer loans and other banking services to businesses. The bank –eventually Banco de Bilbao –helped fund the region's industrialization. Its first foray beyond the Basque region was Paris not Madrid in 1902. It later entered London Madrid and other major European cities.

Franco's rise to power and the isolation of WWII deterred industrial growth. In protectionist Spain Bilbao bought 16 banks between 1941 and 1943 and formed a unit to focus on US and Latin American partnerships.

In the 1960s Bilbao reorganized and formed a unit focused on industrial growth. It rolled with the punches as banking rules continued to change in the 1970s and 1980s. The bank expanded consumer services began issuing credit cards (1971) and bought banks that couldn't cope with changing regulations.

To compete in financially deregulated Europe Spain's overpopulated banking industry began to consolidate in the early 1990s. After #3 Bilbao failed to take over #2 Banco Espa?ol de Credito it merged with regional rival Banco de Vizcaya.

Formed in 1901 by Basque merchants Banco de Vizcaya expanded through purchases and had some 200 branches by 1935 including offices in Europe's leading cities. During the post-WWII bust it bought weaker banks and invested in Spain's industrial complex.

In the 1960s and 1970s Vizcaya added industrial banking insurance personal investment management and leasing. The bank refocused on international growth opening branches in London Mexico City New York and other cities. It entered consumer banking and became another participant in the branch race; by 1980 Vizcaya had some 900 offices. Looking to be a strong player in deregulated Europe the bank merged with Bilbao in 1988; together the two banks had nearly 3400 branches.

The merger almost unraveled after Vizcaya chair Pedro Toledo (set to lead the new bank with Bilbao chair Jose Angel Sanchez Asiain) died in 1989. The two banks fought over Toledo's replacement until the Bank of Spain suggested in 1990 Bilbao executive Emilio Ybarra y Churruca become the only chair.

Until 1992 government regulations and strong unions prevented BBV from cutting some 5000 jobs and 600 branches. After Europe's 1992 deregulation the company targeted Latin America buying banks in Mexico and Peru (1995); Argentina Colombia and Venezuela (1996); and Brazil and Chile (1997). The merger of rivals Banco Santander and Banco Central Hispanoamericano in 1999 prompted BBV to merge with Argentaria in 2000.

After the merger BBVA teamed with top Spanish telecom Telefonica to develop online banking services. The duo announced plans to merge BBVA's Uno-e online bank with First-e one of Europe's first Internet-only banks. The merger which would have created the largest Internet bank in the world collapsed as the dotcom crisis began and online banks experienced losses.

Also in 2000 BBVA bought 30% of Grupo Financiero Bancomer Mexico's #2 bank and merged it into its existing Mexican bank Grupo Financiero BBV-Probursa; the resulting Grupo Financiero BBVA-Bancomer is the country's largest bank. The bank completed the renaming of its subsidiaries to reflect their position as BBVA subsidiaries in 2002.

In 2004 BBVA bought the 40% of Mexico's BBVA Bancomer that it did not already own. To finance about half of the approximately $4 billion bid the company issued 195 million new shares.

The next year BBVA tried to buy the rest of Italian bank Banca Nazionale del Lavoro (BNL) (it already owned 15%). However Italian regulatory bodies nixed the deal and BNP Paribas bought BNL. BBVA later sold its stake in the Italian bank.

To break into the US market BBVA purchased Texas banks Laredo National Bancshares for $850 million in 2005 Texas Regional Bancshares for more than $2 billion in 2006 and State National Bancshares for $480 million in 2007. BBVA's strategy in the US was centered around capturing more of the lucrative business transacted between the US and Mexico and to access the exploding Spanish-speaking market in the states. BBVA expanded its US operations again when it bought Compass Bank in 2007.

Adding on to its US operations BBVA acquired the failed Guaranty Financial Group in 2009. The deal which was facilitated by the FDIC fit in with BBVA's strategy of expanding in the Sunbelt especially Texas. BBVA merged its previously acquired State National Bancshares Laredo National Bancshares and Texas Regional Bancshares into Compass.

EXECUTIVES

Head Legal Tax Audit and Compliance, Eduardo Arbizu Lostao
Head Risk, Manuel Castro
Head Brand and Communication, Gregorio Panadero Illera, age 44
Head South America, Vicente Rodero Rodero
Head Strategy and Development, Carlos Torres Vila
Secretary, Domingo Armengol Calvo
Director Investor Relations, Pedro Barahona
Head Human Resources and Services, Juan Ignacio Apoita Gordo
Chief Executive Officer; Executive Director, Angel Fernandez
General Secretary, Domingo Armengol
Head of Chairmans Office, Fernando Gutierrez
Director of Human Resources and Services, Juan Gordo
Chief Risk Officer, Manuel Aladro
Chief Financial Officer, Manuel Cid
Director of Innovation and Technology, Ramon Valls
Director, Jose Maldonado Ramos, age 60
Director, Ramon Bustamante y de la Mora, age 64

Director, Juan Carlos Alvarez Mezquiriz, age 54
Director, Ignacio Ferrero Jordi, age 68
Director, Enrique Medina Fernandez, age 70
Director, Jose Antonio Fernandez Rivero, age 63
Director, Carlos Loring Martinez de Irujo, age 66
Director, Susana Rodriguez Vidarte, age 57
Director, Tomas Alfaro Drake, age 61
Director, Rafael Bermejo Blanco, age 73
Director, Juan Pi Llorens, age 63
Independent Director, Belen Lopez
Independent Director, Carlos Irujo
Independent Director, Enrique Fernandez
aIndependent Director, Jose Rivero
Independent Director, Jose Garcia-Suelto
Independent Director, Juan Llorens
Independent Director, Ramon Mora
Independent Director, Susana Vidarte
Independent Director, Tomas Drake
Auditors: DeloitteSL

LOCATIONS

HQ: Banco Bilbao Vizcaya Argentaria SA (BBVA)
Plaza de San Nicolas, 4, Bilbao, Viscaya 48005
Phone: (34) 91 537 7000 **Fax:** (34) 91 537 6766
Web: www.bbva.com

2011 Sales

	% of total
Mexico	34
Spain	26
Eurasia	20
South	20
Total	**100**

PRODUCTS/OPERATIONS

2011 Sales

	% of total
Interest	61
Fees &	14
Net gains on financial assets &	3
Dividends	1
Other	21
Total	**100**

Selected Subsidiaries and Affiliates

BBVA Banco Frances (Argentina)
BBVA Bancomer S.A. DE C.V. (Mexico 99.9%)
BBVA Chile
BBVA Colombia (95%)
BBVA Compass (US)
BBVA Dinero Express S.A.U. (financial services)
BBVA Luxinvest S.A. (Luxembourg)
BBVA Patrimonios Gestora SGIIC S.A. (private bank)
BBVA Portugal
BBVA Puerto Rico
BBVA Seguros S.A. DE Seguros Y Reaseguros (insurance 99.9%)
CITIC International Financial Holdings Limited (Hong Kong 30%)
Seguros Bancomer S.A. DE C.V. (Mexico)
Uno-e Bank S.A. (online services)

Selected Acquisitions

2012
Unnim Banc S.A. (E1; Spain; savings bank)
2011
Turkiye Garanti Bankasi A.S. (E4.4 billion; Turkey; bank; 25%)
Credit Uruguay Banco (E78 million; Uruguay; bank)

COMPETITORS

ABN AMRO Group
BNP Paribas
Banamex
Banco Comercial Portugues
Banco Galicia
Banco Popular Espa?ol
Banco de la Nacion Argentina
Banco do Brasil
Bankinter
Banorte
Barclays
Credit Suisse
DEPFA BANK
Deutsche Bank
Espirito Santo
Grupo Santander
HSBC
JPMorgan Chase
Santander Rio
Societe Generale

HISTORICAL FINANCIALS

Company Type: Public

Income Statement

FYE: December 31

	ASSETS ($ mil.)	NET INCOME ($ mil.)	INCOME AS % OF ASSETS	EMPLOYEES
12/12	840,632	2,209	0.3%	113,924
12/11	773,080	3,885	0.5%	109,694
12/10	739,769	6,164	0.8%	104,755
12/09	770,798	6,064	0.8%	104,416
12/08	758,674	7,018	0.9%	111,936
Annual Growth	2.6%	(25.1%)	—	0.4%

2012 Year-End Financials

Return on assets: 0.2%
Return on equity: 4.2%
Long-term debt ($ mil.): —
No. of shares (mil.): —
Sales ($ mil): 51,786
Dividends
Yield: 5.6%
Payout: 213.2%
Market value ($ mil.): —

	STOCK PRICE ($) FY Close	P/E High/Low	PER SHARE ($) Earnings	Dividends	Book Value
12/12	9.42	53 27	0.42	0.53	10.05
12/11	8.57	39 20	0.83	1.10	10.16
12/10	10.17	32 12	1.53	0.94	10.84
12/09	18.04	40 10	1.54	0.39	11.26
12/08	12.49	40 11	1.83	1.13	9.57
Annual Growth	(6.8%)	— —	(30.7%)	(17.2%)	1.2%

Banco Bradesco S.A.

Big banking in Brazil is provided in part by Banco Bradesco which holds more than R$761 billion ($376 billion) in assets and has more than 65 million clients. As one of Brazil's largest private sector banks (Banco do Brasil is at the top) Banco Bradesco offers retail banking services through more than 4500 branches and offices. It also offers private middle-market and corporate banking savings plans leasing auto financing and credit cards. Brokerage subsidiary Bradesco Securities operates in the US and the UK while Banco Bradesco Europe provides asset management private banking and trade finance services across the European Union. Bradesco was founded as Banco Brasileiro de Descontos in 1943.

Banco Bradesco is present in all Brazilian cities and is continuing to expand its network in order to serve more customers in the growing country. The company has benefited from Brazil's economic growth and has seen its consumer lending operations increase with consumer confidence. Its two primary segments –banking and insurance – each account for about half of the company's profits.

The bank has grown through numerous acquisitions over the years including buying the Brazilian operations of other large multinational banks. In 2010 it entered an agreement with Banco do Brasil and Banco Santander (Brasil) to consolidate the operations of each company's external ATM networks; that deal increased Banco Bradesco's ATM network.

However Banco Bradesco's geographic diversity took a hit in 2011 when it lost its bid to offer financial services through 6000 Brazilian post offices. Banco do Brasil took over the duties the following year. Banco Bradesco had offered the service for 10 years prior.

The company's performance has been improving since the worst of the global financial crisis has passed. Banco Bradesco's revenues in 2011 grew 7% while profits grew by 13% that year. (Percentages in US dollars will be different due to conversion rates.) Both the banking and insurance segments saw growth in interest and noninterest earnings; banking noninterest income grew by more than 35% alone. The improvements were largely due to a simple increase in business volume a factor which also contributed to the 17% growth of the bank's loan portfolio.

Banco Bradesco is dedicated to both organic growth and expansion by acquisition. In 2011 the company opened more than 1000 new branches. Also that year the company acquired the state-controlled Banco do Estado do Rio de Janeiro (now Banco BERJ) in an auction. The deal also included the exclusive right to manage some 440000 bank accounts of public servants in Rio de Janeiro through 2014.

The company is also focused on improving its technological offerings. It recently adopted a biometric system in which customers can use a scan of their palm as a password for ATM usage.

EXECUTIVES

EVP, Arnaldo Alves Vieira, age 65
Vice Chairman, Antonio Bornia, age 78
Managing Officer, Milton Matsumoto, age 68
Managing Officer Bradesco Dia e Noite Equity and Customer Service, Armando Trivelato Filho, age 67
Managing Officer, Jose Alcides Munhoz, age 65
Managing Officer, Luiz Pasteur Vasconcellos Machado, age 65
Managing Officer, Odair Afonso Rebelato, age 68
Managing Officer IT, Aurelio Conrado Boni, age 62
VP, Julio de Siqueira Carvalho de Araujo, age 59
VP, Norberto Pinto Barbedo, age 61
Managing Officer, Paulo Eduardo D'Avila Isola, age 58
Managing Officer Bradesco Capitalizac?o Retail Bradesco Bradesco Empresas and Branch Network, Ademir Cossiello, age 58
Department Officer Bradesco Varejo (Retail) Department and Credit Collection Department, Adineu Santesso, age 61
Department Officer Systems Development, Airton Celso Exel Andreolli, age 65
Department Officer Treasury, Alfredo A. Lima de Menezes, age 51
Department Officer Products and Services, Altair A. de Souza, age 52
Department Officer Organization and Methods, Antonio C. Del Cielo
Managing Officer Customer Relations, Candido Leonelli, age 66
Department Officer Research and Technological Innovation, Douglas T. Francisco, age 51
Department Officer Cards, Jair D. Scalco, age 63
Department Officer Market Relations, Jean Philippe Leroy, age 49
Department Officer Human Resources, Jose Luiz Rodrigues Bueno, age 60
Department Officer Loan and Financing, Josue A. Pancini
Department Officer Systems Development, Luiz A. dos Santos, age 62
Department Officer Fiscal Audit, Luiz C. Angelotti, age 49
Department Officer Marketing, Luiz C.B. Cavalcanti Jr., age 51
Department Officer Loan, Luiz F. Peres, age 63
Department Officer Cards, Marcelo de Araujo Noronha, age 48
Department Officer Bradesco Dia&Noite, Marcos Bader, age 56

Department Officer General Controllership, Moacir Nachbar Jr., age 48
Department Officer General Inspectorship, Nilton P. Nogueira, age 59
Department Officer Assets, Ricardo Dias, age 63
Department Officer, Robert J. van Dijk, age 55
Department Officer Credit Collection, Roberto S. Hollander, age 62
Department Officer Purchasing, Paulo A. dos Santos, age 49
Member of the Executive Board; Managing Director, Alexandre Gluher
Member of the Executive Board; Managing Director, Alfredo Menezes
Member of the Executive Board; Managing Director, Andre Cano
Executive Vice President; Member of the Executive Board, Domingos Abreu
Member of the Executive Board, Joao Sabino
Executive Vice President; Member of the Executive Board, Julio Araujo
Executive Vice President; Member of the Executive Board, Laercio Cezar
Chairman of the Board, Lazaro Brandao
Chief Executive Officer; Member of the Executive Board; Director, Luiz Cappi
Executive Vice President; Member of the Executive Board, Marco Rossi
Chief Accounting Officer, Marcos Galende
Member of the Executive Board; Managing Director, Mauricio Minas
Member of the Executive Board, Paulo Ferreira
Executive Vice President; Member of the Executive Board, Sergio Clemente
CEO and Board Member, Luiz Carlos Trabuco Cappi, age 61
Vice Chairman, Antonio Bornia, age 78
Board Member, Marcio Artur Laurelli Cypriano, age 69
Board Member, Carlos Alberto Rodrigues Guilherme, age 70
Board Member, Mario da Silveira Teixiera Jr., age 67
Board Member, Joao Aguiar Alvarez, age 53
Board Member, Denise Aguiar Alvarez, age 56
Board Member, Ricardo Espirito Santo Silva Salgado, age 69
Auditors: PricewaterhouseCoopers

LOCATIONS

HQ: Banco Bradesco S.A.
Cidade de Deus S/N, Vila Yara, Osasco, SP 06029-900
Phone: (55) 11 3684 3702 **Fax:** (55) 11 3684 3213
Web: www.bradesco.com.br

PRODUCTS/OPERATIONS

2011 Sales

	% of total
Interest &	83
Fees &	11
Insurance & pension	3
Net gains of foreign currency transactions &	3
Total	**100**

Selected Subsidiaries

Alvorada Cart?es Credito Financiamento e Investimento S.A.
Banco Bankpar S.A.
Banco BERJ S.A.
Banco Boavista Interatlantico S.A.
Banco Bradesco Argentina S.A. (99.99%)
Banco Bradesco Cart?es S.A.
Bradesco Leasing S.A. Arrendamento Mercantil
Bradesco Seguros S.A.
Bradesco Auto/RE Companhia de Seguros S.A.
Bradesco Capitalizac?o S.A.
Bradesco Saude S.A.
Bradesco Vida e Previdencia S.A.

COMPETITORS

Banco Santander
Banco do Brasil
Caixa Economica Federal
Itau Unibanco

HISTORICAL FINANCIALS

Company Type: Public

Income Statement

FYE: December 31

	ASSETS ($ mil.)	NET INCOME ($ mil.)	INCOME AS % OF ASSETS	EMPLOYEES
12/12	391,868	5,522	1.4%	103,385
12/11	387,177	5,875	1.5%	104,684
12/10	363,225	5,987	1.6%	95,248
12/09	290,182	4,592	1.6%	85,072
12/08	194,901	3,268	1.7%	0
Annual Growth	19.1%	14.0%	—	—

2012 Year-End Financials

Return on assets: 1.4%
Return on equity: 17.2%
Long-term debt ($ mil.): —
No. of shares (mil.): —
Sales ($ mil): 49,553

Dividends
Yield: 2.7%
Payout: 7.6%
Market value ($ mil.): —

	STOCK PRICE ($) FY Close	P/E High	P/E Low	PER SHARE ($) Earnings	Dividends	Book Value
12/12	17.37	2	1	1.26	0.43	8.29
12/11	16.68	3	2	1.34	0.17	7.55
12/10	20.29	4	2	1.38	0.43	7.43
12/09	21.87	—	—	1.22	0.33	6.36
12/08	9.87	—	—	0.88	0.63	3.96
Annual Growth	15.2%	—	—	9.4%	(9.2%)	20.3%

Banco De Sabadell SA

Banco de Sabadell (also known as BancoSabadell) is one of the top banking groups in Spain offering corporate commercial and private banking through more than 2000 branches. The company operates under five banking brands: SabadellAtlantico and Banco Herrero for business banking; Solbank which specializes in providing banking services for tourists and the tourism industry; ActivoBank for online banking; and BancoUrquijo for private banking. BancoSabadell also offers bancassurance products asset management and securities brokerage. The company has a presence in about 20 countries. It is looking across the Atlantic for growth especially in Florida as well as in Mexico.

BancoSabadell acquired Miami-based Mellon United National Bank (which it rebranded Sabadell United Bank) and its 15 branches from The Bank of New York Mellon in 2010. The following year it acquired the assets and branches of the failed Lydian Private Bank further adding to its operations in the region. In 2007 the company acquired TransAtlantic Bank and BBVA's private banking business also both based in Miami.

Closer to home BancoSabadell acquired smaller rival Banco Guipuzcoano in 2010. The following year it acquired savings bank Caja de Ahorros del Mediterraneo (CAM) which had been seized by the government for a symbolic E1. That deal brought some 5 million additional customers to the bank increased its assets by around 75% and upped its branch numbers by more than 900. CAM (now SabadellCAM) will be integrated into BancoSabadell's operations over time.

In 2008 company sold a 50% stake in its insurance operations to Zurich Financial Services which is managing the business.

EXECUTIVES

Deputy General Manager, Blanca Corominas
Deputy General Director, Carlos Santamans
Deputy General Manager, Cirus Cabot
Deputy General Manager, Enric Masachs
Deputy General Manager, Federico Castillo
Deputy General Director, Fernando Munoz
Deputy General Manager, Ignacio Casellas
Chief Executive Officer; Executive Director, Jaime Romojaro
Deputy General Manager, Jaime Vallverdu
Deputy General Director, Jaume Balsells
Third Vice Chairman of the Board; Independent Director, Javier Landiribar
Deputy General Manager, Javier Hernandez
Deputy General Manager, Joan Sierra
Deputy General Manager, Jose Puig
General Controller; Director, Jose Rodriguez
Second Vice Chairman of the Board, Jose Bosch
Executive Chairman of the Board, Jose Creus
Deputy General Manager, Juan Alonso
Deputy General Manager, Luis Vall
Non-Member Secretary of the Board, Miguel Junyent
General Director, Miquel Guell
Deputy General Manager, Pablo Moreno
Deputy General Manager, Pedro Sologaistua
Deputy General Manager, Rafael Nauffal
Deputy General Director, Ramon Reina
Deputy General Manager, Salvador Terradas
Chief Financial Officer; General Director, Tomas Muina
Deputy General Manager, Ramon Pol
Independent Director, Francesc Selvas
Independent Director, Hector Moreno
Independent Director, Joan Andreu
Independent Director, Joaquin Corachan
Second Vice Chairman of the Board, Jose Bosch
Independent Director, Jose Sufrategui
Independent Director, Maria Lloveras
Independent Director, Sol Comadran
Auditors: PricewaterhouseCoopersAuditoresS.L.

LOCATIONS

HQ: Banco De Sabadell SA
Plaza de Sant Roc, 20, Barcelona, Sabadell 08201
Phone: (34) 93 902 323 555 **Fax:** (34) 93 935 916 062
Web: www.bancsabadell.com

COMPETITORS

BBVA
Banco Pastor
Banco Popular Espa?ol
Banco de Valencia
Grupo Santander

HISTORICAL FINANCIALS

Company Type: Public

Income Statement

FYE: December 31

	ASSETS ($ mil.)	NET INCOME ($ mil.)	INCOME AS % OF ASSETS	EMPLOYEES
12/12	212,927	18	0.0%	14,291
12/11	129,910	5	0.0%	10,675
12/10	129,954	3	0.0%	10,777
12/09	119,312	5	0.0%	9,466
12/08	112,375	2	0.0%	9,929
Annual Growth	17.3%	60.3%	—	9.5%

2012 Year-End Financials

Return on assets: 0.0%
Return on equity: 0.1%
Long-term debt ($ mil.): —
No. of shares (mil.): —
Sales ($ mil): 9,535

Dividends
Yield: —
Payout: —
Market value ($ mil.): —

	STOCK PRICE ($) FY Close	P/E High/Low	PER SHARE ($) Earnings	Dividends	Book Value
12/12	0.00	120 88	0.04	0.00	3.92
12/11	4.35	45 45	0.19	0.00	5.47
12/10	4.15	36 23	0.37	0.00	5.78
12/09	7.34	36 33	0.57	0.00	6.11
Annual Growth	—	— —	(48.7%)	—	(10.5%)

Banco Espirito Santo S.A.

Banco Espirito Santo (BES) is one the largest banks in Portugal with about 665 branches throughout the country and more than ?82 billion ($110 billion) in assets. It is the flagship of Espirito Santo Financial Group which holds a controlling stake in the bank. BES has subsidiaries that provide asset management investment banking private equity factoring and leasing and insurance services. It also has more than 100 branches outside its home country including Angola Spain and Libya. The bank's origins date back to 1869 when its namesake Jose Maria do Espirito Santo e Silva founded Caza de Cambio a streetside exchange in S?o Paulo.

The merger of Banco Internacional de Credito into Banco Espirito Santo was finalized in 2006. Banco Espirito Santo expanded even further into the Spanish market in 2005. The company first purchased Spanish asset management firms Lusogest and Lusopensiones then acquired Banco de Inversion from the Bank of Spain positioning itself for increased competition in Spain.

In 2007 the company suffered massive losses when it invested in a Florida company E.S. Bankest that went bankrupt. BDO Seidman was ordered to pay $170 million in fines and some $350 million in damages to Banco Espirito Santo; the accounting firm had audited E.S. Bankest and not uncovered the fraud.

EXECUTIVES

Vice-Chairman and CEO, Ricardo Espirito Santo Salgado, age 69
Chairman, Alberto Alves de Oliveira Pinto, age 81
Vice-Chairman, Bruno Bernard Marie Joseph de Laage de Meux
Vice-Chairman and CEO, Ricardo Espirito Santo Salgado, age 69
Vice-Chairman, Bruno Bernard Marie Joseph de Laage de Meux
Auditors: KPMG

LOCATIONS

HQ: Banco Espirito Santo S.A.
Avenida da Liberdade, no. 195, Lisbon 1250-142
Phone: (351) 21 359 7390 **Fax:** (351) 21 359 7309
Web: www.bes.pt

2012 Branches

	No.
Portugal	666
Angola	41
Libya	33
Spain	26
Cape	2
Other	7
Total	**775**

COMPETITORS

BNP Paribas
Banco BPI
Banco Comercial Portugues
Caixa Geral de Depositos
Citigroup
Grupo Santander

HISTORICAL FINANCIALS

Company Type: Public

Income Statement FYE: December 31

	ASSETS ($ mil.)	NET INCOME ($ mil.)	INCOME AS % OF ASSETS	EMPLOYEES
12/12	110,308	126	0.1%	9,944
12/11	103,783	(140)	—	9,863
12/10	111,962	683	0.6%	9,858
12/09	118,554	752	0.6%	9,359
12/08	105,117	562	0.5%	9,431
Annual Growth	1.2%	(31.1%)	—	1.3%

2012 Year-End Financials

Return on assets: 0.1%
Return on equity: 1.5%
Long-term debt ($ mil.): —
No. of shares (mil.): —
Sales ($ mil): 7,285

Dividends
Yield: 31.3%
Payout: 1,643.2%
Market value ($ mil.): —

	STOCK PRICE ($) FY Close	P/E High/Low	PER SHARE ($) Earnings	Dividends	Book Value
12/12	1.24	575 22	0.04	0.39	2.32
12/11	1.71	— —	(0.05)	0.21	4.96
12/10	3.73	34 14	0.55	0.25	7.96
12/09	6.65	39 13	0.71	1.79	8.23
12/08	8.90	23 17	1.13	0.00	12.64
Annual Growth	(38.9%)	— —	(56.8%)	—	(34.6%)

Banco Popular Espanol, S.A.

Banco Popular Espa?ol certainly lives up to its middle name. One of Spain's top banks (after giants Banco Santander and BBVA) Banco Popular offers commercial and retail banking services through more than 2200 branches. It operates mainly at home where it specializes in commercial loans to small and midsized businesses. Non-banking offerings include mutual funds asset management life insurance factoring and securities brokerage. Banco Popular also owns Banco Popular Portugal and mortgage bank Banco Popular Hipotecario and it owns a 60% stake in private bank Popular Banca Privada. (Dexia owns the rest.) The bank also sells property/casualty coverage by German insurer Allianz.

Banco Popular absorbed four of its smaller regional subsidiaries in 2008 to simplify its structure and reduce costs. The entities included Banco de Castilla Banco de Credito Balear Banco de Galicia and Banco de Vasconia. The bank merged with larger subsidiary Banco de Andalucia in 2009.

The company is working to extend its services to profitable business niches in strong economies. Banco Popular's 2007 deal to buy Miami's TotalBank marked the Spanish bank's first move into the US. TotalBank which operates some 15 branches in Miami-Dade County gives Banco Popular a foothold to grow in Florida and across the US. South Florida's proximity to Latin America and its wealth of Spanish-speaking professionals make it desirable for Spanish banks. Also in 2007 Banco Popular opened some 40 domestic MundoCredit branches to provide services for immigrants with little banking history.

The collapse of the Spanish real estate market in 2008 sent ripple effects across the country's financial sector. Banco Popular was one of several creditors that collectively took a controlling interest in troubled property developer Metrovacesa and a smaller 25% combined stake in Inmobiliaria Colonial in exchange for assuming the firms' debts.

HISTORY

Things got rolling in 1926 for Banco Popular Espa?ol then known as Banco Popular de los Previsores del Porvenir. Formed to provide "all the types of operations ... proper to credit companies" the bank endured the Spanish Civil War and WWII before adopting its present name in 1947.

Banco Popular grew rapidly in the 1960s as Spain's economy stabilized and banks grappled with a decree that they separate their commercial and investment operations. In 1962 Banco Popular implemented merchant banking services through Banco Europeo de Negocios or Eurobanco (Banco Popular acquired the rest of it in 1974.) Like most of its peers Banco Popular sidestepped the restrictive banking laws by launching specialized companies. In 1964 it joined forces with Heller Overseas (now a Fuji Bank subsidiary) to form Heller Factoring Espa?ola in 1964; it created investment fund manager Sogeval in 1965 and leasing company Iberleasing in 1966.

Banking restrictions also led to Banco Popular's 1967 creation of five ""Popularinsa"" regional banking companies: Banco de Andalucia Banco de Castilla Banco de Credito Balear Banco de Galicia and Banco de Vasconia. By the late 1970s legal changes allowed Banco Popular and the regional banks to act as one. In 1987 the "Popularinsa" banks were made subsidiaries. Two years later Javier Valls was tapped to join his elder brother Luis in the bank's chairmanship.

In 1991 the bank stuck a tentative toe in the international water forming Banco Popular Comercial in France. But while its peers scrambled furiously to become cross-border players the company's growth plan remained focused on domestic retail and commercial banking. Such dedication did not go unrewarded: Banco Popular has consistently been ranked as one of the world's most profitable banks.

To build on its products and services the bank allied with US-based Bankers Trust (now part of Deutsche Bank) in 1994 to offer investment services to its top-end customers in Spain. In 1996 it joined French credit company Cofinoga to issue private-label credit cards and on-the-spot credit in Spain; through agreements with foreign banks Banco Popular also moved into Canada Southeast Asia and Latin America that year.

German-based insurer Allianz bought into the bank in 1998 (its stake is now less than 10%). In 1999 the bank moved to cut costs by consolidating its fund management and private banking services. Banco Popular started Internet-based Bancopopular-e.com in 2000. Luis Valls resigned in 2004. Angel Ron then became co-chairman with

Javier Valls who resigned in 2006 and left Ron as the sole chair. Luis Valls died in 2006.

The company sold Banco Popular France to Credit Mutuel in 2008.

EXECUTIVES

Regional Manager Murcia, Antonio Perez
Director, Jose M. Lucia Aguire
Vice Chairman and CEO, Roberto Higuera
Director, Helena Irene Revoredo Delvecchio
Secretary and Director, Francisco Aparicio
Director, Jose M. Mas Millet, age 58
Director, Americo Ferreira de Amorim
Director, Luis Montuenga
Director, Eric Gancedo
Vice Chairman, Luis Herrando
Director, Manuel Morillo
Director, Miguel Nigorra
Director, Nicolas Osuna
Director, Jose R. Rodriguez
Director, Vincente Santana
Director, Miguel A. de Solis
Director, Vicente Tardio
Director, Casimiro Molins
Auditors: PricewaterhouseCoopersAuditoresS.L.

LOCATIONS

HQ: Banco Popular Espanol, S.A.
Velazquez 34, Madrid 28001
Phone: (34) 91 520 70 00 **Fax:** (34) 91 577 92 08
Web: www.bancopopular.es

2008 Sales

	% of total
Spain	94
Portugal	6
Total	**100**

PRODUCTS/OPERATIONS

2008 Sales

	% of total
Interest	82
Fees &	13
Net exchange	1
Investments	1
Other	3
Total	**100**

COMPETITORS

BBVA
Banco Espa?ol de Credito
Banco Pastor
Banco de Sabadell
Bankinter
Barclays
Espirito Santo
Grupo Santander
La Caixa

HISTORICAL FINANCIALS

Company Type: Public

Income Statement FYE: December 31

	ASSETS ($ mil.)	NET INCOME ($ mil.)	INCOME AS % OF ASSETS	EMPLOYEES
12/12	207,748	(3,243)	—	16,501
12/11	169,346	620	0.4%	14,062
12/10	174,175	789	0.5%	14,252
12/09	186,251	1,103	0.6%	14,431
12/08	154,315	1,470	1.0%	15,069
Annual Growth	7.7%	—	—	2.3%

2012 Year-End Financials

Return on assets: (-1.7%)
Return on equity: (-26.9%)
Long-term debt ($ mil.): —
No. of shares (mil.): —
Sales ($ mil): 8,300
Dividends
Yield: —
Payout: —
Market value ($ mil.): —

Banco Santander Brasil SA

If you're looking for a place to park a "brazillion" dollars Banco Santander (Brasil) is there. The bank which is part of Spain's Banco Santander provides a range of consumer and commercial financial services through some 3700 branches primarily in Brazil's southern and southeastern regions with a major presence in the states of S?o Paulo and Rio Grande do Sul. Santander Brasil also offers wholesale banking to large corporations. Additional services include asset management private banking and insurance. The company accounts for about a quarter of its parent's revenues making it the group's largest international unit. Banco Santander and its affiliates own more than 80% of Santander Brasil.

The parent company listed approximately 15% of its shares of its Brazilian unit on the New York Stock Exchange in a 2009 IPO. It turned out to be the world's largest IPO that year raising some R$13 billion ($8 billion). The proceeds from the offering have been used to drive growth by funding new branches and lending. It is also growing its insurance and credit card businesses; the company recently began offering its Santander-Ferrari credit card.

In late 2010 Santander rebranded its Brazilian brands –Banco Real and Santander Brasil –under the same name and platform. (It completed similar restructuring efforts in the UK and Mexico.) The parent company has high hopes for its Latin American operations especially in the high-growth markets of Brazil and Mexico. As such Santander is committed to investing in those units as it solidifies its position as a leading global bank. It expects to open an additional 600 Santander Brasil branches by 2014 as part of its efforts to make it Brazil's leading bank. Altogether Latin America account for about half of the group's sales.

Santander Brasil is the result of the 2006 merger of Banco Santander banks Banco Santander Brasil Banco Santander Meridional and Banco do Estado de S?o Paulo. The company added to its Brazilian bank empire when it acquired Banco Real in 2008. At the time Banco Real was the fourth largest non government-owned Brazilian bank. The acquisition boosted Santander Brasil into the top three of banks in Brazil (along with Banco Bradesco and Itau Unibanco)

Brazil is a promising region of the world for banking. The country was a resilient market during the economic downturn. Employment levels rose and a new middle class emerged. As the Brazilian economy expands Santander Brasil expects lending and overall demand for banking services to grow.

LOCATIONS

HQ: Banco Santander Brasil SA
Avenida Presidente Juscelino Kubitschek, 2235 and 2041 ? Bloco A, Sao Paulo 04543-011
Phone: (55) 11 3174 8589 **Fax:** (55) 11 3174 6751
Web: www.santander.com.br

HISTORICAL FINANCIALS

Company Type: Public

Income Statement FYE: December 31

	REVENUE ($ mil.)	NET INCOME ($ mil.)	NET PROFIT MARGIN	EMPLOYEES
12/12	30,184	2,664	8.8%	53,992
12/11	32,163	4,154	12.9%	54,602
12/10	30,314	4,447	14.7%	54,406
12/09	28,128	3,157	11.2%	51,241
12/08	12,328	1,020	8.3%	0
Annual Growth	25.1%	27.1%	—	—

2012 Year-End Financials

Debt ratio: —
Return on equity: 6.8%
Cash ($ mil.): 27,162
Current ratio: —
Long-term debt ($ mil.): —
No. of shares (mil.): —
Dividends
Yield: 4.1%
Payout: 3.8%
Market value ($ mil.): —

	STOCK PRICE ($)	P/E		PER SHARE ($)		
	FY Close	High/Low		Earnings	Dividends	Book Value
12/12	7.28	0	0	6.39	0.30	0.10
12/11	8.14	0	0	9.95	0.14	0.11
12/10	13.60	0	0	10.64	0.46	0.21
12/09	13.94	0	0	8.78	0.11	0.19
Annual Growth	(19.5%)	—	—	(7.6%)	27.6%	(14.4%)

Banco Santander SA

What started a contender in the running of the banks in Spain Banco Santander has expanded over the years to become one of the largest banks in the world. Beyond Spain it offers retail banking and consumer finance in Portugal the UK and other parts of Europe as well as the US. Subsidiaries such as Banco Santander Chile Banco Santander (Brasil) Santander Rio in Argentina and Grupo Financiero Santander make it a top banking group in Latin America which accounts for about 40% of the group's revenues. Other units offer asset management private banking corporate and investment banking and insurance. All told the company has some 100 million customers and 14800 locations in more than 40 countries.

Over the years Santander has expanded to become more geographically diverse –a key strategy for the company as it looks to reduce risk. The bank's strategy revolves around making acquisitions and boosting deposits in growth nations; it generates more than half of its profits in emerging markets. Santander has taken advantage of the economic downturn to snap up businesses and asset portfolios at bargain prices.

One target market for growth is Latin America where profits have been growing; the company hopes to further strengthen its presence in the region. In 2010 Santander took full control of its Mexico unit by acquiring Bank of America's 25% stake in Grupo Financiero Santander for ?2 billion ($2.5 billion) as well as the rest of Puerto Rican unit Santander BanCorp it didn't already own. It then acquired GE Capital's $2 billion consumer mortgage business in Mexico for $162 million plus the assumption of debt. The company has also been opening new branches in the region. While the financial downturn and the European sovereign debt crisis has been rough for Spain and Portugal Mexico holds promise for growth. Hoping to cash in on some of that growth Banco Santander spun off nearly 25% of Grupo Financiero Santander in a public offering worth more than $4 billion.

Banco Santander also made a big move into Eastern Europe. In 2011 it paid ?4 billion (nearly $6 billion) for Poland's Bank Zachodni. The acquisition may signal more acquisitions for Santander in neighboring East European countries.

In addition to Latin America and Europe Banco Santander is making its move in the US. The company's American holdings include Northeast regional bank Santander Holdings USA (formerly Sovereign Bancorp). In 2010 Santander bought a ?2.5 billion ($3 billion) auto loan portfolio from Citigroup.

Banco Santander also operates Santander UK the result of the 2010 merger of Abbey National Bradford & Bingley and the former Alliance & Leicester (all of which were acquired by Santander). Santander's acquisitions in the UK helped bump up profits from the region in 2009 and 2010 but in 2011 profits slipped as a result of remediation charges related to mis-sold payment protection insurance. In 2010 Santander announced plans to buy some 315 Royal Bank of Scotland branches in the UK for about ?2 billion ($3 billion) further expanding its presence there. That deal which has been delayed includes a wealth management business with some 84000 clients.

Santander also has started making inroads in China. The bank is seeking to acquire a 20% stake in Bank of Beijing Consumer Finance Company for CNY 306 million ($49.8 million). Previously in 2011 it established a rural bank joint venture with China Construction Bank. It is among several other foreign banks that are extending their presence to rural China where few people have access to financial services.

On the other hand Santander has been selling some assets in order to shore up its balance sheet and meet new capital reserve requirements. In 2011 the company announced plans to sell a 35% stake in its American automotive financing unit for more than $1 billion. It then sold a minority stake in Banco Santander Chile to further increase its core capital ratio. Santander also sold its Columbian unit to CorpBanca of Chile for $1.2 billion.

Despite the group's diverse operations the troubled debt market in Europe and the slowly recovering global economy have taken their toll on Santander. Although acquisitions helped Santander's revenues grow 25% in 2011 profits fell some 36% that year largely as a result of the slowdown in Spain and Portugal. The bank has never needed a bailout though and achieved its minimum capital requirements months early in 2011. Santander believes that as the economy continues to improve it is well-positioned around the world to grow even further.

The Botin family has led Grupo Santander since its founding in 1857. Emilio Botin Sanz de Sautuola y Garcia de los Rios Spain's richest man (depending on whom you ask) has been chairman since 1986.

HISTORY

In 1857 a group of Basque businessmen had formed Banco Santander to finance Latin American trade. The emergence of Cantabria as a leading province after WWI helped the bank expand first regionally and then nationally.

The Botin family has been closely identified with the bank for decades. Emilio Botin served first as a board member and then for a few years as chairman before his death in 1923. The post was held by his son Emilio Botin-Sanz de Sautuola from 1950 to 1986 when "his" son Emilio Botin Sanz de Sautuola y Garcia de los Rios (known as Don Emilio) took over.

Spanish banks were spared the worst of the Great Depression (thanks to their isolation and the country's shunning the gold standard) but Spain's civil war was draining. In the early 1940s Santander expanded into Madrid and other major Spanish cities and merged with a few rivals. In the 1950s and 1960s as interest rates were controlled and mergers halted banks competed by building branch networks and investing overseas particularly in Latin America. In 1965 Santander joined with Bank of America to form Bankinter (it divested most of its stake by the mid-1990s).

Tight economic controls were relaxed in the 1970s after Franco's death. Despite global recession Santander continued to invest in Latin America through the mid-1980s.

In the late 1980s Santander prepared to compete in a deregulated Spain and Europe forming alliances with Royal Bank of Scotland Kemper (now part of Zurich Financial Services) and Metropolitan Life Insurance. In 1989 the bank jump-started competition by introducing Spain's first high-interest account.

Santander focused on home in the 1990s. Spurned by Banco Hispano Americano (BHA) Santander acquired a 60% stake in the ailing Banco Espa?ol de Credito (Banesto) which became wholly owned in 1998. The bank took a hit when Latin America plunged into an economic crisis that year. With profit margins falling the bank merged with BCH in 1999.

BCH was formed by the 1991 merger of Banco Central and BHA. BHA had been established in 1900 by investors in Latin America; Central had been founded in 1919. The mixed banks offered both commercial and investment banking; they funded industrialization and investment in Latin America and became two of Spain's largest banks before the civil war.

After the war BHA sold its Latin American assets when the currency dried up while Central used mergers and acquisitions to expand across Spain. Isolated from WWII by Franco the two banks used their dual strategies to fund overseas investment and domestic-branch growth.

After Franco's death the banks faced increased competition at home and abroad. Central bought BHA in 1991 to remain competitive as Spain entered the European Economic Community (now the EU) in 1992.

Following the merger BCH trimmed 20% of its branches fired some 10000 employees and sold unprofitable holdings. Focused on Latin America the bank took small stakes in small banks. Losing its edge BCH merged with Santander in 1999.

In 2000 the newly merged BSCH focused on expanding in Europe and Latin America. Among its European moves was its alliance with Societe Generale to buy investment-fund management firms particularly in the US. In Latin America the bank bought Brazil's Banco Meridional Banco do Estado de S?o Paulo (Banespa) and Grupo Financiero Serfin Mexico's #3 bank. Critics questioned the $5 billion price tag BSCH paid for Banespa charging that the formerly state-run bank was overvalued in 2001. Executive in-fighting saw ex-Santander chairman Emilio Botin triumph over ex-BCH chairman Jose Maria Amusategui for control of BSCH's helm. Soon after the bank started doing business as simply Santander Central Hispano. The following year the bank sold off its shares of Germany's Commerzbank and France's Societe Generale.

In one of Europe's largest cross-border bank mergers ever Santander paid more than ?12 billion ($15 billion) for British bank Abbey National in 2004. It solidified its UK operations through the approximately ?1.25 billion ($2.6 billion) purchase of Alliance & Leicester. Abbey then acquired the retail deposit business of Bradford & Bingley after it was nationalized in 2008.

Another acquisition helped Santander grow in South America. In 2007 the company along with Royal Bank of Scotland and Fortis acquired the Netherlands-based ABN AMRO (the international retail banking giant with more than 4350 branches) for around ?71 billion ($87 billion). As part of the bid Banco Santander took ABN AMRO's Brazilian operations doubling its market share in Brazil. Also a part of the ABN AMRO deal Santander became the largest non-government-owned bank in Uruguay.

In 2009 the Venezuelan government took over Banco Santander subsidiary Banco de Venezuela the third-largest bank in the country. The government paid some ?755 million ($1 billion) to nationalize the bank.

Also that year Santander acquired the approximately three-quarters of Sovereign it didn't already own. Santander then purchased a more than ?3 billion ($4 billion) US car loan portfolio and a loan servicing platform from HSBC.

EXECUTIVES

Chairman, Emilio Botin Sanz de Sautuola y Garcia de los Rios, age 79
Second Vice Chairman, Matias Rodriguez Inciarte, age 65
EVP Strategy and Asia, Juan Rodriguez Inciarte, age 60
EVP Global Wholesale Banking, Jose Garcia Cantera, age 47
EVP Risk, Javier Peralta de las Heras, age 63
Third Vice Chairman, Guillermo de la Dehesa Romero, age 72
First Vice Chairman, Fernando de Asua Alvarez, age 81
Executive Vice President Finance and Investor Relations, Jose Antonio Alvarez Alvarez, age 53
EVP Global Private Banking and Asset Management, Javier Marin, age 47
EVP Human Resources, Jose Luis Gomez Alciturri, age 64
EVP Santander Totta, Nuno Amado, age 54
Chief Executive Officer, Javier Marin Romano, age 47
Second Vice Chairman, Matias Rodriguez Inciarte, age 65
Director, Luis Alberto Salazar-Simpson, age 72
EVP Strategy and Asia, Juan Rodriguez Inciarte, age 60
Director, Antonio Escamez Torres, age 61
EVP America and Director, Francisco Luzon Lopez, age 64
Second Vice Chairman and CEO, Alfredo Saenz Abad, age 69
Director, Lord Terence (Terry) Burns, age 69
CEO Santander UK; Director, Ana P. Botin, age 52
Fourth Vice Chairman, Manuel Soto Serrano, age 72
Third Vice Chairman, Guillermo de la Dehesa Romero, age 72
First Vice Chairman, Fernando de Asua Alvarez, age 81
Director, Antonio Basagoiti Garcia-Tu?on, age 70
Director, Javier Botin, age 38
Director, Rodrigo Echenique Gordillo, age 66
Director, Abel Matutes Juan, age 71
Director, Angel Jado Becerro de Bengoa, age 67
Director, Isabel Tocino Biscarolasaga, age 62
Director, Vittorio Corbo Lioi, age 69

LOCATIONS

HQ: Banco Santander SA
28660 Boadilla del Monte, Madrid
Phone: (34) 91 259 6514 **Fax:** (34) 91 254 1038
Web: www.gruposantander.com

PRODUCTS/OPERATIONS

2011 Sales

	% of total
Interest	67
Fees &	14
Income from insurance & reinsurance contracts	7
Net gains on financial assets &	3
Other	9
Total	**100**

COMPETITORS

BBVA
Banco Comercial Portugues
Banco Popular Espa?ol
Banco do Brasil
Bank of America
Citigroup
Deutsche Bank
Espirito Santo
HSBC
JPMorgan Chase

HISTORICAL FINANCIALS

Company Type: Public

Income Statement FYE: December 31

	ASSETS ($ mil.)	NET INCOME ($ mil.)	INCOME AS % OF ASSETS	EMPLOYEES
12/12	1,673,432	2,906	0.2%	188,779
12/11	1,618,788	6,921	0.4%	187,233
12/10	1,629,469	10,949	0.7%	172,909
12/09	1,599,794	12,882	0.8%	169,460
12/08	1,467,480	12,410	0.8%	170,961
Annual Growth	3.3%	(30.4%)	—	2.5%

2012 Year-End Financials

Return on assets: 0.1%
Return on equity: 2.9%
Long-term debt ($ mil.): —
No. of shares (mil.): —
Sales ($ mil): 108,980
Dividends
Yield: 7.8%
Payout: 290.0%
Market value ($ mil.): —

	STOCK PRICE ($) FY Close	P/E High	P/E Low	PER SHARE ($) Earnings	PER SHARE ($) Dividends	PER SHARE ($) Book Value
12/12	8.17	67	34	0.29	0.64	9.53
12/11	7.52	40	19	0.78	0.79	11.09
12/10	10.65	36	15	1.25	0.64	12.05
12/09	16.44	37	8	1.50	1.07	12.02
12/08	9.49	40	9	1.70	1.00	10.07
Annual Growth	(3.7%)	—	—	(35.7%)	(10.5%)	(1.4%)

Bangkok Bank Public Co., Ltd. (Thailand)

Bangkok Bank wants to protect the baht you've got. One of the largest commercial banks in Thailand Bangkok Bank provides a variety of banking services to individual and commercial clients including checking and savings accounts loans Internet banking and treasury and investment banking services. It operates about 850 branches serving 16 million customers throughout Thailand about a dozen other Southeast Asian countries the UK and the US. The bank was founded in 1944 in response to the difficulty Thai businessmen encountered in receiving credit facilities from foreign banks; it has since had a hand in developing its homeland's industry and agriculture.

Subsidiary Bualuang Securities offers brokerage investment banking and fund management services. Its BBL Asset Management provides mutual funds while Sinsuptawee Asset Management manages property and distributes assets transferred from Bangkok Bank.

Bangkok Bank plans to establish a banking subsidiary in China where it already has established customers through a handful of representative branches. The company believes that China's economy carries significant growth potential.

EXECUTIVES

President and Director, Chartsiri Sophonpanich, age 53
EVP Conglomerate 2, Yaowadee Nakhata
EVP Human Resources, Ruchanee Nopmuang
EVP Technology, Kajornvut Tayanukorn
EVP and Manager Japan Desk, Hitoshi Ozawa
Vice President, Ian Guy Gillard
EVP and Manager Multinational II, Bussakorn Pao-In
Vice President, Amphorn Purinthawarakun
Vice President; Company Secretary, Aphichat Romyarup
Vice President, Ayut Kritsanamara
Vice President of Finance Management, Bunsong Bunyasaranan
Vice President, Chaiyong Rattanacharoensiri
VP of Large Business Enterprises; Mgng.Dir. of Large Business Enterprises of Siam City Bank; Dir., Charnsak Fueangfu
Chairman of the Board, Chatri Sophonphanit, age 79
Vice President, Chirana O-sotsin
Vice President, Chitwatthana Charuwatthanachai
Vice President, Chok Ranong
Vice President, Khanit Si
Vice President, Kirati Laisathit
Vice President of International Banking Group, Korbsak Phutrakun
Chairman of the Executive Board; Director, Kosit Panpiemrat
Vice President, Krisorn Bharami-uaychai
Vice President, Kunthida Siwayathorn
Vice President of Regional Business Expansion; International Banking Group, Lin Kung
Vice President, Mali Sintraphannathorn
Vice President, Manusiri Karnchana
Vice President, Narin Ophamurathawong
Vice President, Natthaphorn Luengsuwan
Vice President, Niraman Laisathit
Vice President, Panit Tunwatthanachit
Vice President, Parnsak Pruksakit
Vice President, Phakorn Wanaptikun
Vice President, Phornnit Tunwatthanachit
Vice President of Audit and Control, Phornthep Kitsanayothin
Vice President, Piyada Sucharitkun
Vice President, Piyaphan Thananithi
Vice President, Pratsani Ui-yamaphan
Vice President, Ratchada Thiratharathorn
Vice President of Foreign Exchange Trading Department, Sa-ard Thirarotchanawong
Vice President of Human Resources, Saowani Siriphat
Vice President, Shairit Anuchitworawong
Vice President, Shuphorn Chantharawichai
Vice President, Siridet Ueang-udomsin
Vice President of Loan Recovery and Legal, Songkhram Sakunphram
Vice President of Credit Management, Suraphong Winyawong
Vice President of Special Credit; Executive Director; Director, Suwan Thaensathit
Vice President, Than Siriphokhi
Vice President, Thanit Sirichot
Vice President, Tharisa Thanyasiri
Vice President, Thawat Triwannakun
Assistant President ; Director, Thawilap Ritthaphirom
Vice President of Credit Management and Credit Acceptance, Thawisak Thanatsrang
Vice President, Thongchai A-nanthothai
Vice President of Correspondence Banking, Wanlapha Klinpathum
Vice President, Wirasak Sutanthawibun
Vice Chairman of the Executive Board; Director, Decha Tulanan
Senior Vice President of Technology, Suthira Sriphaibun
Vice President, Sutthirat Phashirat
President and Director, Chartsiri Sophonpanich, age 53
Vice Chairman, Staporn Kavitanon, age 70
Director, Piti Sithi-Amnuai, age 77
Member Board of Executive Directors, Amorn Chandarasomboon, age 80
Director, Charn Sophonpanich, age 69
Vice Chairman Board of Executive Directors, Deja Tulananda, age 75
SEVP and Director, Prasong Uthaisangchai, age 64
SEVP and Director, Suvarn Thansathit, age 66
Director, Phornthep Phornprapha, age 64
Director, Gasinee Witoonchart, age 63
Director, Adm. Prachet Siridej, age 75
Director, Kovit Poshyananda, age 75
Member Board of Executive Directors, Singh Tangtatswas, age 68
Director, Kanung Luchai, age 87
Director, Prince Mongkolchaleam Yugala, age 74
Chairman Board of Executive Directors, Kosit Panpiemras, age 68
Independent Director, Kesini Withunchat
Independent Director, Khanueng Ruechai
Chairman of the Executive Board; Director, Kosit Panpiemrat
Independent Director, Kowit Posayanon
Independent Director, Mongkhonchaloem Yukhon
Independent Director, Prachet Siridet
Auditors: DeloitteToucheTohmatsuJaiyos

LOCATIONS

HQ: Bangkok Bank Public Co., Ltd. (Thailand)
333 Silom Road, Bangkok 10500
Phone: (66) 0 2231 4333 **Fax:** 212 422-0728
Web: www.bangkokbank.com

PRODUCTS/OPERATIONS

2008 Sales

	% of total
Interest	
Loans	61
Investments	11
Interbank & money market	5
Noninterest	
Fees & service	17
Gain on	4
Gain on disposal of	1
Other	1
Total	**100**

COMPETITORS

Bank of Ayudhya
CIMB Group
DBS Group Holdings
KASIKORNBANK
Krung Thai
Siam Commercial
Standard Chartered
TMB Bank
Thanachart Capital
United Overseas Bank

HISTORICAL FINANCIALS

Company Type: Public

Income Statement FYE: December 31

	ASSETS ($ mil.)	NET INCOME ($ mil.)	INCOME AS % OF ASSETS	EMPLOYEES
12/12	79,046	1,079	1.4%	22,934
12/11	66,949	868	1.3%	21,503
12/10	64,913	818	1.3%	21,229
12/09	53,187	617	1.2%	20,735
12/08	48,208	584	1.2%	21,192
Annual Growth	13.2%	16.6%	—	2.0%

2012 Year-End Financials

Return on assets: 1.4%
Return on equity: 12.7%
Long-term debt ($ mil.): —
No. of shares (mil.): 1,908
Sales ($ mil): 4,320
Dividends
Yield: —
Payout: —
Market value ($ mil.): 10,289

	STOCK PRICE ($) FY Close	P/E High/Low		PER SHARE ($) Earnings	Dividends	Book Value
12/12	5.39	0	0	0.57	0.00	4.68
12/11	4.42	0	0	0.46	0.00	4.06
12/10	4.31	0	0	0.43	0.00	4.02
12/09	3.75	0	0	0.32	0.00	3.03
12/08	1.68	—	—	0.30	0.00	2.63
Annual Growth	33.8%	—	—	16.7%	—	15.5%

Bank Hapoalim B.M. (Israel)

The largest bank in Israel Bank Hapoalim caters to individual commercial and corporate clients at home and abroad. Within Israel the Bank Hapoalim Group has more than 270 full-service branches and business centers. Another 30 express branches are in the works. Overseas it has about 45 branches correspondent offices and financial subsidiaries in Asia Australia Europe Latin America and North America; its international focus is on private banking and the corporate sector. Bank Hapoalim provides investment banking services including the underwriting of and investment in companies; it also provides trust services to individuals and businesses.

Bank Hapoalim was founded in 1921. Shari Arison Israel's wealthiest person is the controlling shareholder.

The bank has undergone major shakeups in its leadership since Arison took control of the bank in 2007. Dan Dankner also came on board as chairman that year. In March 2009 Zvi Ziv resigned as CEO after clashing with Dankner; deputy CEO Zion Keinan was picked to replace him. Bank of Israel (the nation's central bank) then wrangled with Arison over Hapoalim's performance and leadership threatening to remove Dankner if significant changes weren't made. Dankner seemed to get the message and resigned in 2009. Yair Seroussi replaced him.

The company planned to acquire control of Ukraine bank OJSC Ukraininan Innovation Bank (Ukrinbank) but was blocked by Bank of Israel. As a result Bank Hapoalim has suspended its planned growth in Eastern Europe. However it is examining opportunities in other regions to add to such investments as Bank Pozitif in Turkey and DKB in Kazakhstan. Other international businesses include Hapoalim Switzerland The PAM Group and Bank Hapoalim (Cayman). Hapoalim Securities U.S.A. offers securities trading for customers in Israel and abroad.

EXECUTIVES

Member of the Management Board; Chief Financial Officer, Ran Oz, age 46
Chairman, Yair Seroussi, age 58
Head Information Technology, Zvi Naggan
Chief Legal Advisor, Ilan Mazur
Head Client Asset Management, Hanna Pri-Zan
Head International Banking, Orit Lerer
Head Global Treasury, Anat (Moti) Levin
Chief Accountant, Ofer Levy
Head Human Resources Logistics and Procurement, Efrat Yavetz
Chief Risk Officer, Dan Koller
Head Retail Banking, Lilach Asher-Topilsky
Head Corporate Banking, Shimon Gal
Vice President, Micha Shimoni
Chief Risk Officer, Tzahi Cohen
Deputy Chief Executive Officer; Head of Strategy; Member of the Management Board, Ari Pinto
Secretary, Yoram Weisberg
Director, Dan (Danny) Dankner, age 48
External Director, Yosef Yarom
Director, Irit Izakson
Director, Nira Dror
Director, Pnina Dvorin
Director, Moshe Koren
Director, Prof Yair E. Orgler, age 73
Director, Efrat Peled
Director, Nir Zichlinskey
Director, Oded Sarig
Director, Leslie Littner
Director, Mali Baron, age 66
Director, Iris Dror
Director, Ronen Israel
Director, Imri Tov
External Director, Amnon Deek
External Director, Dafna Schwartz
Auditors: SomekhChaikin

LOCATIONS

HQ: Bank Hapoalim B.M. (Israel)
50 Rothschild Blvd., Tel-Aviv 66883
Phone: (972) 3 567 3333 **Fax:** (972) 3 560 7028
Web: www.bankhapoalim.co.il

2009 Sales

	% of total
Israel	87
Europe	8
North	5
Total	**100**

COMPETITORS

Bank Leumi le-Israel
First International Bank of Israel
Israel Discount Bank
Mizrahi Tefahot
UBS

HISTORICAL FINANCIALS

Company Type: Public

Income Statement FYE: December 31

	ASSETS ($ mil.)	NET INCOME ($ mil.)	INCOME AS % OF ASSETS	EMPLOYEES
12/12	100,980	682	0.7%	13,484
12/11	93,300	718	0.8%	13,408
12/10	90,552	628	0.7%	13,605
12/09	81,934	348	0.4%	13,821
12/08	80,585	(235)	—	13,581
Annual Growth	5.8%	—	—	(0.2%)

2012 Year-End Financials

Return on assets: 0.6%
Return on equity: 10.0%
Long-term debt ($ mil.): —
No. of shares (mil.): 1,319
Sales ($ mil): 5,319
Dividends
Yield: —
Payout: —
Market value ($ mil.): 28,796

	STOCK PRICE ($) FY Close	P/E High/Low		PER SHARE ($) Earnings	Dividends	Book Value
12/12	21.82	0	0	1.03	0.00	5.44
12/11	16.05	1	1	0.54	0.02	4.71
12/10	26.50	1	1	0.47	0.00	4.92
12/09	19.60	1	0	0.26	0.00	4.13
12/08	10.78	—	—	(0.18)	0.00	3.75
Annual Growth	19.3%	—	—	—	—	9.8%

Bank Leumi Le-Israel B.M.

Bank Leumi le-Israel looms large as one of Israel's largest financial institutions. The company whose name translates as National Bank of Israel offers retail banking (for consumers and small businesses) commercial banking (middle-market businesses) corporate banking (large companies) and private banking (wealthy clients) through deposits mortgages and other loans credit cards trust services and investments. It has about 235 branches in Israel and more than 80 locations (including branches agencies and representative offices) in some 20 countries including the US. Subsidiary Leumi Partners provides corporate investment banking services and makes direct investments in nonbanking businesses.

Other subsidiaries include The Arab Israel Bank Leumi Mortgage Bank and retail and private banking units in the UK Switzerland Luxembourg and Romania. In 2011 Bank Leumi bought Geneva-based private bank Banque Safdie from the Safdie family. It plans to merge the firm with Bank Leumi Switzerland. In a restructuring move that will cut costs Bank Leumi plans to absorb Leumi Mortgage Bank in 2012. The company will then provide mortgage services through a newly created mortgage division.

After the Israeli parliament passed a number of capital market reform laws in 2005 Bank Leumi was compelled to sell its mutual fund and investment portfolio management operations. It has since focused on providing investment and pension counseling to its clients.

The Israeli government owns more than 10% of Bank Leumi but has been selling off its stake in the company and intends to eventually divest its entire holding.

HISTORY

At the beginning of the 20th century a group of prominent Jewish men led by Austrian Zionist Theodor Herzl founded the Jewish Colonial Trust (which would later become known as Otzar Hityashvut Hayehudim or OHH). An advocate of the Jewish settlement of Palestine the trust recognized the need for a financial institution to promote colonization in the region which was then part of the Ottoman Empire. In 1902 it established the Anglo-Palestine Company the forerunner of Bank Leumi le-Israel. A year later the London-based company opened its first Palestinian office in Jaffa (now Tel Aviv).

As WWI began the company had half a dozen branches. The outbreak of hostilities between Great Britain and the Ottoman Empire forced the London-based bank to close its offices but it continued to operate from the Spanish Consulate in Jerusalem. By the mid-1920s the company was known as the Anglo-Palestine Bank and was playing a significant role in the development of local agriculture.

During the following decade Palestine saw an influx of refugees from Nazism in Europe. The bank assisted in transferring assets to Palestine and anchored the area's economy through WWII. When Israel gained independence in 1948 the Anglo-Palestine Bank became the nation's fiscal agency and printed monetary notes for the new government. It began to focus its efforts on international operations and in 1950 opened its first US office in New York City. But even though it was the national bank of the newly formed Israeli state the bank was still based in London. In 1951 a company named leumi Le'Israel was founded in Tel Aviv and assumed control of the bank which took the name Bank Leumi le-Israel (National Bank of Israel) in 1954. Also that year the government formed the Bank of Israel and Bank Leumi resumed its commercial banking activities.

Bank Leumi maintained its status as Israel's leading bank until the 1980s when triple-digit inflation hit the country. The bottom fell out in 1983 when investors pulled out of the stock market fearing devaluation of the shekel. As they had done for several years Bank Leumi and Israel's other major banking groups reacted by taking out massive loans to buy their own stock and shield against losses in share price. The artificially inflated bank stocks crashed and thousands of individual investors lost their savings. The Israeli government intervened paying some $7 billion to bail out the banks. Though the state now held most of Bank Leumi's stock the OHH maintained voting rights.

In 1986 following a government inquiry into the stock scandal chairman Ernst Japhet and the company's board were forced to resign prompting more contention. On their way out Japhet and his officers received millions of dollars in severance pay and monthly pensions. The ramifications of what became known as "Leumigate" resulted in the company's next two chairmen also being ousted over the next two years. Rival Bank Hapoalim wrested the mantle of Israel's #1 bank from Bank Leumi in 1987.

The government sold off 10% of its interest in the firm to a unit of Deutsche Bank in 1993 and in 1995 mandated that banks sell their nonfinancial holdings. That year Galia Maor became CEO as the first woman head of an Israeli bank and Eitan Raff became chairman (he announced his retirement in 2010).

Controvery continued however. In 1997 Bank Leumi sold a majority stake in Migdal Insurance to Assicurazioni Generali which amplified questions regarding the buyer's handling of life insurance policies of Jewish Holocaust victims. The inquiry spread to Bank Leumi which released information about dormant accounts the next year but nonetheless faced government scrutiny and lawsuits from descendants of Holocaust victims.

In 2006 an Israeli law established a company to collect restitution for property deemed abandoned by Holocaust victims who had made bank deposits and bought real estate and bank shares in Israel in anticipation of the establishment of a Jewish homeland in Palestine. After years of wrangling The Company for Restitution of Holocaust Victims Assets in mid-2009 filed suit against Bank Leumi considered to be the holder of the most Jewish Holocaust assets; the lawsuit asked for NIS 300 million ($75 million) in restitution for more than 3500 victims. Denying any financial culpability the bank later that year offered NIS 20 million ($5 million). In 2010 it agreed to arbitration.

EXECUTIVES

Chairman, David Brodet, age 69
Deputy CEO and Head of Banking, Baruch Lederman
Deputy CEO and Head Operations and Information Systems, Itzhak Malach
President and CEO, Rakefet Russak-Aminoach, $876,253 total compensation
EVP and Head Economics and Finance, Ron M. Fainaro, age 46
Deputy CEO and Head Capital Markets, Prof Daniel Tsiddon
First EVP Chief Accounting Officer and Head of Accounting, Menachem Schwartz
EVP and Head Banking, Tamar Yassur
EVP and Head Structured Finance and Real Estate, Yoel Mintz
First EVP and Head Commercial Banking, Gideon Altman
First EVP and Head Corporate, Yaacov (Kobi) Haber
First EVP, Dan Cohen
Head of the Office of the Chief Executive Officer and the Strategy Department, Avner Mendelson
Vice President and Chief Executive Officer of Bank Leumi USA, Itzhak Aboulafia
Co-Chief Executive Officer, Ron Ron Fainaro Fainaro
EVP and Head Internal Audit, Sasson Mordechay
Head of Credit Dept., Shahar Malkiel
Vice President and Deputy Head of Operations; Administration & Systems Abroad, Shlomo Pergament
Bank and Group Secretary, Yael Rudnicki
EVP and Head Risk Management, Hedva Ber
EVP and Head Capital Markets, Itai Ben-Zeev
EVP and Head Accounting, Shlomo Goldfarb
EVP, Nomi Sandhaus
EVP and Head Operations and Information Systems, Dan Yerushalmi
Director, Doron Cohen
Director, Zvi Koren, age 71
Director, Yaacov Goldman, age 56
Director, Moshe Vidman
Director, Prof Israel Gilead
Director, Rami Avraham Guzman
Director, Jacob Mashaal
Director, Nurit Segal
Director, Moshe Dovrat
Director, Zipora Gal Yam
Director, Prof Arieh Gans
Director, Prof Efraim Sadka
Director, Reuven Adler
Director, Amos Sapir
Director, David Avner
Director, Prof Gabriela Shalev
External Director, Gabriella Shilo
External Director, Haim Samet
Director, Miryam (Miri) Katz
Director, Avraham (Rami) Guzman
Director, Prof Yedidia (Zvi) Stern
Director, Yehuda Drori
Director, Yoav Nardi
External Director, Zipora Samet
Auditors: SomekhChaikin

LOCATIONS

HQ: Bank Leumi Le-Israel B.M.
34 Yehuda Halevi Street, Tel-Aviv 65546
Phone: (972) 3 514 8111 **Fax:** (972) 3 566 1872
Web: www.bankleumi.com

COMPETITORS

Bank Hapoalim
Bank of America
Citigroup
First International Bank of Israel
HSBC
Israel Discount Bank
Mizrahi Tefahot
Standard Chartered
UniCredit

HISTORICAL FINANCIALS

Company Type: Public

Income Statement FYE: December 31

	ASSETS ($ mil.)	NET INCOME ($ mil.)	INCOME AS % OF ASSETS	EMPLOYEES
12/12	100,919	249	0.2%	13,407
12/11	95,697	494	0.5%	13,633
12/10	92,610	671	0.7%	13,490
12/09	85,168	533	0.6%	13,342
12/08	81,621	24	0.0%	13,424
Annual Growth	5.4%	79.3%	—	(0.0%)

2012 Year-End Financials

Return on assets: 0.2%
Return on equity: 3.8%
Long-term debt ($ mil.): —
No. of shares (mil.): 1,473
Sales ($ mil): 4,904
Dividends
Yield: —
Payout: —
Market value ($ mil.): 5,084

	STOCK PRICE ($) FY Close	P/E High	P/E Low	PER SHARE ($) Earnings	Dividends	Book Value
12/12	3.45	0	0	0.17	0.00	4.54
12/11	3.05	0	0	0.33	0.00	4.15
12/10	5.10	0	0	0.45	0.00	4.53
12/09	3.35	0	0	0.36	0.00	3.93
12/08	1.85	7	2	0.02	0.00	3.33
Annual Growth	16.9%	—	—	81.0%	—	8.1%

Bank of China Ltd., Beijing

The Bank of China (BOC) has its sights set on global conquest –of the financial kind. One of the largest banks in the world's most populous country BOC is a financial giant. It has more than 10000 domestic branches as well as foreign offices in about 30 countries. Commercial banking (including corporate and retail banking and treasury operations) accounts for about 90% of its revenues. BOC International provides investment banking services in China the UK the US and Singapore. BOC Group Insurance sells general and life insurance products in China. The group provides aircraft leasing through BOC Aviation. China's government owns about 70% of BOC one of the nation's four state-owned commercial banks.

Despite the sluggish economic climate around the world BOC's operating income and profits both grew by 19% in 2011. Additionally its assets grew by 13% to RMB 11.8 trillion ($1.9 trillion). The solid performance was credited to an increase in both interest and noninterest earnings and the bank's relatively low portfolio of bad loans decreased even further that year. Loan demand remains healthy and the bank expects to grow its domestic lending by more than 10% in 2012.

It could be argued that BOC's goal of becoming a premier multinational banking group was achieved in late 2011 when the company was named to the list of Global Systematically Important Financial Institutions (firms that are considered too big to fail). It was China's only company to be named to the list. BOC's strategic development plan for further growth includes efforts to streamline its structure expand internationally (it was the first major Chinese bank to offer RMB products in the US) and invest in its technology and branch network. In 2011 BOC divested some of its riskier holdings in bonds issued by Ireland Italy Greece Portugal and Spain.

HISTORY

The Bank of China (BOC) has always had strong ties to the government of China. Established as a central bank in 1912 right after the establishment of the Provisional Government of the Republic of China BOC became a government-chartered international exchange bank in 1928. Their first overseas branch was opened in London in 1929 leading to a global network of 34 overseas branches over the next two decades.

After WWII the bank specialized in foreign exchange supporting foreign trade and the development of China's national economy. Between 1984 and 2001 BOC issued bonds in the international capital market 27 times. In 1993 when China initiated reform in its foreign exchange system BOC played a key role in the unification of exchange rates foreign exchange purchases and sales and the incorporation of foreign-funded enterprises into the foreign exchange sales system.

In 1994 BOC began to transform from a specialized bank to a wider-based state-owned commercial bank by issuing its first BOC Hong Kong dollar notes and then Macao pataca notes. The issue of both notes helped stabilize their respective markets.

BOC International Holdings a wholly owned subsidiary of BOC specializing in investment banking was incorporated in Hong Kong in 1998. Three years later the group restructured its Hong Kong operations by merging 10 of its member banks into Bank of China (Hong Kong) Limited a locally registered bank that successfully listed on the Hong Kong Stock Exchange in July 2003.

The bank was not free of scandal. A 2002 probe into BOC's New York branch by the US Office of the Comptroller of the Currency revealed that preferential treatment was given to certain customers who had personal relationships with some members of the bank's previous management. Regulators from the US and China fined BOC $20 million for "unsafe and unsound" business practices.

In 2005 the Royal Bank of Scotland (RBS) formed a consortium that bought a 10% stake in BOC. In exchange BOC agreed to distribute the Scottish bank's credit cards and other products. RBS sold its stake in 2009 and the banks ended their partnership agreement.

BOC went public in 2006. Its IPO was estimated to be the world's largest in six years. Foreign banks and investors scrambled for a piece of the action; Saudi investor Prince Alwaleed bin Talal invested $2 billion in the bank. The successful IPO was fraught with symbolism for the banking industry in China which had been struggling. China had had to bail out two of the country's top banks BOC and China Construction Bank three times within six years. And for decades money in China's state banks had been used to support failing state companies leaving the banks with a mountain of bad loans.

To increase its non-interest income BOC acquired Singapore Aircraft Leasing (since renamed BOC Aviation) for $965 million in late 2006. The BOC Aviation portfolio includes more than 75 aircraft in about 20 countries.

BOC announced plans in 2008 to acquire 20% of French private bank La Compagnie Financiere Edmond de Rothschild but dropped those plans in 2009 after failing to get approval from Chinese regulators.

In early 2009 BOC faced selloffs by major investors as several subprime-battered financial institutions lined up to divest their stakes in the bank. UBS sold its entire 1% stake and Bank of America dumped its 3% share. Royal Bank of Scotland also sold its 4% stake in BOC. The two banks then cut their strategic partnership ties.

EXECUTIVES

EVP and Executive Director, Li Zaohang, age 57
EVP, Wang Yongli, age 48
Vice Chairman and President, Li Lihui, age 60
Secretary to the Board of Directors, Zhang Bingxun, age 63
Chairman of the Board, Gang Xiao
Vice Chairman of the Board; Head of Bank, Lihui Li
Chief Credit Risk Officer, Weijian Zhan
Chief Auditor, Yanfen Liu
Secretary of the Board, Yaosheng Fan
Director, Alberto Togni, age 75
EVP and Executive Director, Li Zaohang, age 57
Director, Anthony F. Neoh, age 66
EVP and Executive Director, Zhou Zaiqun, age 59
Vice Chairman and President, Li Lihui, age 60
Director, Hong Zhihua, age 58
Director, Huang Haibo, age 58
Director, Cai Haoyi, age 58
Director, Huang Shizhong, age 50
Director, Huang Danhan, age 63
Independent Non-Executive Director, Danhan Huang
Independent Non-Executive Director, Guoliang Dai
Non-Executive Director, Haoyi Cai
Non-Executive Director, Lina Liu
Independent Non-Executive Director, Nout Wellink
Non-Executive Director, Qi Zhang
Independent Non-Executive Director, Shizhong Huang
Independent Non-Executive Director, Wenyao Zhou
Non-Executive Director, Xiangdong Zhang
Non-Executive Director, Yansong Jiang
Auditors: PricewaterhouseCoopers

LOCATIONS

HQ: Bank of China Ltd., Beijing
No. 1 Fuxingmen Nei Dajie, Beijing 100818
Phone: (86) 10 6659 6688 **Fax:** (86) 10 6601 6871
Web: www.boc.cn

PRODUCTS/OPERATIONS

2011 Sales

	% of total
Interest	
Loans &	57
Securities & financial	11
Other	11
Noninterest	
Fees &	14
Net trading	2
Other	5
Total	**100**

Selected Subsidiaries

Bank of China Group Insurance Company Limited
BOC Aviation Private Limited
BOC Hong Kong (Group) Limited
Bank of China Group Investment Limited
Chiyu Banking Corporation Limited (commercial banking 47%)
Nanyang Commercial Bank Limited (commercial banking 66%)
Tai Fung Bank Limited (commercial banking 50.3%)

COMPETITORS

Agricultural Bank of China
Bank of East Asia
CITIC International Financial
Cathay Financial Holding
China Construction Bank
China Development Bank
China Merchants Bank
China Minsheng Banking
Chuo Mitsui Trust
HSBC
Hang Seng Bank
Industrial and Commercial Bank of China
Shanghai Pudong Development Bank

HISTORICAL FINANCIALS

Company Type: Public

Income Statement

FYE: December 31

	ASSETS ($ mil.)	NET INCOME ($ mil.)	INCOME AS % OF ASSETS	EMPLOYEES
12/12	2,034,025	22,365	1.1%	302,016
12/11	1,879,458	19,728	1.0%	289,951
12/10	1,586,847	15,841	1.0%	279,301
12/09	1,281,772	11,836	0.9%	262,566
12/08	1,019,373	9,311	0.9%	249,278
Annual Growth	18.9%	24.5%	—	4.9%

2012 Year-End Financials

Return on assets: 1.1%
Return on equity: 17.9%
Long-term debt ($ mil.): —
No. of shares (mil.): —
Sales ($ mil): 99,711
Dividends
Yield: 42.2%
Payout: 16.4%
Market value ($ mil.): —

	STOCK PRICE ($)	P/E		PER SHARE ($)		
	FY Close	High	Low	Earnings	Dividends	Book Value
12/12	11.36	1	0	0.08	0.02	0.47
12/11	9.15	1	0	0.07	0.01	0.41
12/10	13.08	1	1	0.06	0.02	0.35
12/09	13.46	1	1	0.05	0.01	0.30
Annual Growth	(5.5%)	—	—	13.2%	29.4%	12.4%

Bank of Communications Co., Ltd.

Bank of Communications (BoCom) is one of the largest commercial banks in China based on total assets. The company offers services in corporate banking personal banking and treasury operations. Its offerings include personal savings accounts personal loans corporate loans trade financing wealth management e-banking and credit card services. BoCom boasts 30 provincial branches and a network of more than 2600 outlets in some 180 cities –including overseas branches in New York Tokyo and Singapore and representative offices in London and Frankfurt. The bank is also one of China's oldest. HSBC Holdings holds close to a 20% interest in BoCom.

Geographic Reach

BoCom has a dozen overseas institutions that consist of branches located in Hong Kong New York Tokyo Singapore Seoul Frankfurt Macau Ho Chi Minh City Sydney and San Francisco. It also operates a representative office in Taipei and Bank of Communications (UK) Co. Ltd.

Operations

The bank organizes its operations into four segments. Its personal banking unit focuses on personal savings bank cards personal lending payment and settlement investment services insurance services and wealth management. BoComm's corporate banking segment comprises cash management supply chain financing investment banking financial institution banking and asset custody services. The company's international banking unit consists of foreign exchange wealth management document settlement remittance and bill services trade finance and offshore banking. BoComm's fourth segment e-banking provides personal online banking enterprise online banking telephone banking and self-help banking.

Strategy

The company has continued to expand its offerings by venturing into new lines of business. With its purchase of an 85% stake in Hubei International Trust and Investment Corporation BoComm entered the trust industry. Soon after it began to also cater to the insurance industry with the launch of BoCommLife Insurance a joint venture with the Commonwealth Bank of Australia. BoCom is among the nation's first commercial banks allowed to tap into the insurance industry.

EXECUTIVES

Vice Chairman and President, Ximing Niu, age 57
EVP and CFO, Yu Yali, age 56
EVP and CIO, Hou Weidong, age 54
EVP, Dicky Peter Yip, age 66
Chief Risk Officer, Yang Dongping, age 56
General Manager and Chief Accountant, Teng Tieqi
Director, Hu Huating
Director, Wong (Peter) Tung Shun
Director, Gu Mingchao
Director, Lei Jun
Director, Li (Eric) Ka-cheung

LOCATIONS

HQ: Bank of Communications Co., Ltd.
No. 188 Yincheng Zhong Road, Pudong New District, Shanghai 200120
Phone: (86) 21 58766688 **Fax:** (86) 21 58798398
Web: www.bankcomm.com

PRODUCTS/OPERATIONS

Selected Services

Personal Banking
- Personal Savings in Local and Foreign Currencies
- Bank Card
- Personal Lending
- Wealth Management

Corporate Banking
- Deposit Services
- Financing Services
- Settlement Services
- Wealth Management
- Financial Institutional Banking Services

International Banking
- ForexWealth Management
- Document Settlement
- Remittance and bill services
- Trade finance
- Offshore Banking

E-Banking
- Telephone Bank
- Personal Online Banking
- Corporate Online Banking

COMPETITORS

Bank of China
Bank of China (Hong Kong)
Bank of East Asia
China Construction Bank
China Development Bank
China Merchants Bank
China Minsheng Banking
Chong Hing Bank
Hang Seng Bank
Industrial and Commercial Bank of China
Public Financial Holdings
Shanghai Pudong Development Bank

HISTORICAL FINANCIALS

Company Type: Public

Income Statement FYE: December 31

	ASSETS ($ mil.)	NET INCOME ($ mil.)	INCOME AS % OF ASSETS	EMPLOYEES
12/12	845,872	9,363	1.1%	96,259
12/11	732,584	8,060	1.1%	90,149
12/10	599,489	5,922	1.0%	85,290
12/09	484,642	4,410	0.9%	79,122
12/08	393,192	4,161	1.1%	77,734
Annual Growth	21.1%	22.5%	—	5.5%

2012 Year-End Financials

Return on assets: 1.1%
Return on equity: 17.8%
Long-term debt ($ mil.): —
No. of shares (mil.): —
Sales ($ mil): 43,614

Dividends
Yield: —
Payout: —
Market value ($ mil.): —

	STOCK PRICE ($) FY Close	P/E High	P/E Low	PER SHARE ($) Earnings	Dividends	Book Value
12/12	0.74	0	0	0.14	0.00	0.82
12/11	0.67	0	0	0.13	0.00	0.70
12/10	0.97	0	0	0.10	0.00	0.55
12/09	1.19	0	0	0.08	0.00	0.45
12/08	0.70	0	0	0.08	0.00	0.41
Annual Growth	1.6%	—	—	16.3%	—	19.2%

Bank of East Asia Ltd.

Bank of East Asia provides retail and commercial banking services in Hong Kong and mainland China. Its offerings include deposit accounts consumer loans mortgages business loans credit cards private banking and investment management. Bank of East Asia has some 130 locations in Hong Kong and more than 60 in mainland China; internationally it has about 30 offices in the British Virgin Islands Malaysia Singapore the UK and Vietnam. The bank's subsidiaries include online securities and futures brokerage provider East Asia Securities Blue Cross (Asia-Pacific) Insurance and Tricor which performs outsourced business services.

Like many of its peers Bank of East Asia is seeking new revenue lines by branching into related industries. In 2009 it arranged to buy a minority stake in fund house Golden Eagle Asset Management allowing it to enter China's growing fund market. Bank of East Asia also launched a trust business in that country.

With an increased focus on Hong Kong and China the bank is also streamlining elsewhere. It sold a majority stake of its Canadian network (a half-dozen branches) to Industrial and Commercial Bank of China (ICBC) in 2010 and arranged to sell its US operations to that company the following year.

EXECUTIVES

Chairman and CEO, David K. P. Li, age 75
General Manager Personal Banking Division, Hon shing Tong
General Manager China Division, Raymond H. K. Yu
Director, Richard T. K. Li, age 45
Director, Isidro Faine Casas, age 71
Director, Allan C. Y. Wong, age 62
Director, Shau-Kee Lee, age 83
Director, Thomas P. K. Kwok, age 59
Deputy Chief Executive and Executive Director, Joseph Y. W. Pang, age 62
Director, Winston Yau-lai Lo, age 72
Director, William W. H. Doo, age 69
Director, Aubrey K. S. Li, age 62
Director, Fook-wo Li, age 97
Director, Chung-hin Wong, age 80
Director, Prof Arthur K. C. Li, age 68
Director, William M. W. Mong, age 84
Director, Kay peng Khoo, age 75
Director, Man-kou Tan, age 76
Director, Kenneth C. M. Lo, age 71
Director, Eric F. C. Li, age 84
Director, Stephen Charles K. S. Li, age 54
Director, Khoon ean Kuok, age 58
Independent Non-Executive Director, Kin Cheung
Auditors: KPMG

LOCATIONS

HQ: Bank of East Asia Ltd.
10 Des Voeux Road Central,
Phone: (852) 3608 3608 **Fax:** (852) 3608 6000
Web: www.hkbea.com

COMPETITORS

Bank of China (Hong Kong)
Bank of Communications
CITIC International Financial
China Development Bank
China Minsheng Banking
Chong Hing Bank
Dah Sing Banking
Dah Sing Financial Holdings Limited
Hang Seng Bank
Public Financial Holdings
Shanghai Pudong Development Bank

HISTORICAL FINANCIALS

Company Type: Public

Income Statement FYE: December 31

	ASSETS ($ mil.)	NET INCOME ($ mil.)	INCOME AS % OF ASSETS	EMPLOYEES
12/12	89,285	781	0.9%	12,441
12/11	78,707	561	0.7%	12,238
12/10	68,728	543	0.8%	11,412
12/09	55,978	330	0.6%	10,540
12/08	53,582	5	0.0%	10,863
Annual Growth	13.6%	253.0%	—	3.4%

2012 Year-End Financials

Return on assets: 0.9%
Return on equity: 11.5%
Long-term debt ($ mil.): —
No. of shares (mil.): —
Sales ($ mil): 3,901

Dividends
Yield: 0.0%
Payout: 0.5%
Market value ($ mil.): —

	STOCK PRICE ($) FY Close	P/E High	P/E Low	PER SHARE ($) Earnings	Dividends	Book Value
12/12	3.86	0	0	0.35	0.00	3.31
12/11	3.70	0	0	0.25	0.00	2.95
12/10	4.15	0	0	0.25	0.00	2.79
12/09	3.92	0	0	0.18	0.00	2.45
12/08	2.01	6	1	0.00	0.00	2.48
Annual Growth	17.7%	—	—	241.5%	(7.5%)	7.5%

Bank of Ireland (Ireland)

The one-time unofficial bank of the Irish state that traces its history to 1783 Bank of Ireland is now a full-blown financial services provider for consumers and businesses operating about 250 retail branches in Ireland and approximately 50 more in Northern Ireland. The bank offers traditional services such as deposits loans mortgages and life insurance. It provides similar services in the UK through some 11500 post office locations. Bank of Ireland also offers corporate finance and capital markets services in the US and Europe. The group's segments include Retail Ireland Bank of Ireland Life Retail UK and Corporate and Treasury.

Financial Performance

Still feeling the effects of the 2008 global financial crisis's blow to Ireland's economy Bank of Ireland reported a fifth straight year of reductions in revenue in 2012 (a 22% decline) which was attributed to lower interest income and fees. With the exception of 2011 the bank's net income has also been on a downward trajectory since 2008; in 2012 it reported a $2.4 billion dip into the red a decline driven by lower revenue and exacerbated by a minimal decline in expenses. The bank has been cutting back expenses including its operations and personnel costs but high regulatory costs and unfavorable current exchange rates offset its expense reductions. Strong capital and reductions in its leveraged debts were bright spots in the bank's finances in 2012.

Strategy

After its 2008 government bailout the Bank of Ireland was forced to sell off assets in order to strengthen its balance sheet. Among the divisions it sold was Bank of Ireland Asset Management which went to State Street Corporation. Other divestitures included Bank of Ireland Securities (formerly the largest Irish-owned asset administration provider) to Northern Trust the US business of its Foreign Currency Exchange subsidiary to Wells Fargo and asset-based lender Burdale Financial also to Wells Fargo.

Other divisions may be put up for sale further giving the bank a boost in capital. The bank is focused on reducing its operating expenses and debt levels.

Company Background

The Irish banking system was hit particularly hard by the global financial crisis in 2008 and a number of companies (including Bank of Ireland) required government bailouts. In mid-2011 Ireland's Central Bank Governor Patrick Honohan stated that his nation's banks had returned to financial soundness.

In late 2009 the government established the National Asset Management Agency or NAMA in response to the nation's fiscal troubles. NAMA is a "bad bank" charged with buying toxic property loans from Irish banks in exchange for government bonds; it was designed to help get bad loans off the banks' books while providing liquidity and credit to the nation. In 2011 Bank of Ireland completed its final asset transfers to NAMA. By then Ireland's banks and the global outlook looked healthier but the sovereign debt crisis threw Europe into turbulence that shook up both consumer and business confidence. This time though all eyes were turned toward other weakened nations such as Greece Spain and Portugal.

HISTORY

Bank of Ireland opened for business in Dublin in 1783 at Mary's Abbey. The bank had #600000 19 employees and a desire to offer more consistent service than the unstable private banks traders and merchants active at the time.

In 1784 Bank of Ireland began to print notes. As the government's unofficial banker it received all funds owed to the Irish treasury and administered all loans to and from the state.

By 1790 the bank's original building at Mary's Abbey had expanded into four. The bank's growth continued to outpace its premises. In 1803 the bank acquired Parliament House in College Green; after five years of remodeling the building was opened to the public. (It remained the bank's headquarters until the 1960s.)

Over time the bank ventured out of Dublin to open branch offices. Expansion began in 1825 with the establishment of seven branches; by 1883 the number had risen to 58 and by 1920 there were 75.

In 1926 the bank bought National Land Bank and renamed it National City Bank. More acquisitions followed —Hibernian Bank in 1958 and National Bank in 1965.

Much like its counterparts in the US the company was impacted by declining real estate values and higher unemployment rates in its home country. In 2008 the Irish government injected ?2 billion ($2.8 billion) into the bank in exchange for a 25% voting stake. Ireland also provided capital for Allied Irish Banks and Irish Bank Resolution to help stabilize the nation's financial system which plunged amid the global financial crisis and its own financial slump.

As part of the bailout the bank was compelled to sell off parts of itself. Bank of Ireland divested two units Iridian Asset Management and Guggenheim Alternative Investment Management in 2009. Other sales followed.

EXECUTIVES

Chief Executive Corporate and Treasury Division, Michael Torpey, age 55
CEO UK Division, Des Crowley, age 53, $409,895 total compensation
Group Communications, Dan Loughrey
Deputy Governor, Patrick H. O'Sullivan, age 64
Director, Kent Atkinson, age 68
Head of Non Core Division, Denis Donovan, age 59, $410,660 total compensation
Group CEO and Director, Richie Boucher, age 54, $346,834 total compensation
Group Treasury, Sean Crowe
Branch Network Ireland, Tim O'Neill
Group Payments, Vincent Brennan
Group Customer Operations, Joe Larkin
Business Banking Ireland and UK, Mark Cunningham
Global Markets, Austin Jennings
Group CFO, Andrew Keating
Consumer Banking Ireland and UK, Stephen Mason
Bank of Ireland UK, David McGowan
Corporate Banking, Tom Hayes
Post Office Financial and Travel Services, Patrick Waldron
Wealth Management, Mick Sweeney
Governor, Patrick J. Molloy, age 74
Divisional HR Capital Markets and Group Functions, Amy Burke
Group Investor Relations, Tony Joyce
Divisional HR Group Manufacturing, Marlene Shanley
HR Retail Ireland and UK, Neville Bourke
Chief Credit and Market Risk Officer, Vincent Mulvey, age 52
Chief Governance Risk Officer, Peter Morris
CEO Retail Ireland, Liam McLoughlin, age 50
Group Services, Orla Cunningham
Secretary, Helen Nolan
Group Regulatory and Operational Risk, John Murphy
Chief Customer and Operating Officer, Nick Fahy
Group Growth and Development, Donal Collins
Group IT, Larry Kiernan
Risk Strategy Analysis and Reporting, Declan Murray
Divisional Finance Retail Ireland and UK, Niall O?Shea
Head Group Manufacturing, Senan Murphy
Head of Group HR, Julie Sharp
COO, Kay Hanneffy
Credit and Market Risk Capital Markets, Tom McGivney
Retail Credit Ireland and UK, Tom Fee
Head of Acquisition Finance Germany, Ralph Betz
Governor, Archie Kane
Executive Vice President, Joe Connolly
Director, Patrick T. Kennedy, age 44
Deputy Governor, Patrick H. O'Sullivan, age 64
Director, Kent Atkinson, age 68
Director, Jerome J. Kennedy, age 64
Director, Paul M. Haran, age 55
Group CEO and Director, Richie Boucher, age 54
Director, Joe Walsh
Director, Tom Considine
Director, Pat Butler
Director, Patrick Mulvihill
Auditors: PricewaterhouseCoopers

LOCATIONS

HQ: Bank of Ireland (Ireland)
40 Mespil Road, Dublin 4
Phone: (353) 1 637 8000 **Fax:** (353) 76 623 4786
Web: www.bankofireland.com

COMPETITORS

AIB
Barclays
HSBC
Irish Bank Resolution
Lloyds Banking Group
NatWest
National Irish Bank
Nationwide Building Society
Northern Bank
Ulster Bank
permanent tsb

HISTORICAL FINANCIALS

Company Type: Public

Income Statement FYE: December 31

	ASSETS ($ mil.)	NET INCOME ($ mil.)	INCOME AS % OF ASSETS	EMPLOYEES
12/12	195,263	(2,404)	—	12,016
12/11	200,329	58	0.0%	13,234
12/10	224,141	(821)	—	14,235
12/09*	260,895	(2,103)	—	14,647
03/09	258,232	91	0.0%	15,868
Annual Growth	(6.7%)	—	—	(6.7%)

*Fiscal year change

2012 Year-End Financials

Return on assets: (-1.2%)
Return on equity: (-19.3%)
Long-term debt ($ mil.): —
No. of shares (mil.): —
Sales ($ mil): 8,207
Dividends
Yield: —
Payout: —
Market value ($ mil.): —

	STOCK PRICE ($) FY Close	P/E High/Low	PER SHARE ($) Earnings	Dividends	Book Value
12/12	6.50	— —	(0.09)	0.00	0.38
12/11	4.24	— —	(0.01)	0.00	0.44
12/10	2.65	— —	(0.29)	0.00	1.87
12/09*	7.66	— —	(2.43)	0.00	9.59
03/09	2.65	2235 20	0.08	0.00	9.48
Annual Growth	25.1%	— —	—	—	(55.4%)

*Fiscal year change

Bank of Kyoto, Ltd. (Japan)

For financial services in Kyoto proper protocol might involve a visit to The Bank of Kyoto. The regional bank serves Kyoto and neighboring prefectures through some 165 branch offices. The bank serves businesses particularly small and medium-sized local companies as well as individual consumers. In addition to traditional deposit banking and lending The Bank of Kyoto and its subsidiaries offer credit cards leasing stock brokerage and business consulting services. The bank has worked to expand its operations beyond its home base and has opened branches to the north in the Kinki Region. Founded in 1941 the bank has about $81 billion in assets and ranks as Kyoto Prefecture's largest retail bank.

Geographic Reach

The Bank of Kyoto operates 110 branches in Kyoto Prefecture 28 in Osaka Prefecture a dozen in Shiga eight in Hyogo and seven branches in Nara.

Strategy

The Bank of Kyoto is aggressively opening branches to expand its reach beyond Kyoto Prefecture. Since opening its first branch at Kusatsu in Shiga Prefecture in 2000 the bank has opened branches in five neighboring prefectures (Kyoto Osaka Shiga Nara and Hyogo).

EXECUTIVES

Chairman, Yasuo Kashihara
President and Director, Hideo Takasaki
Senior Managing Director, Issei Daido
Managing Director, Hisayoshi Nakamura
Managing Director, Yoshio Nishi
Managing Director, Katsuyuki Toyobe
Managing Director, Masayuki Kobayashi
Managing Director, Junji Inoguchi
Managing Director, Nobuhiro Doi
Managing Executive Officer, Hiroshi Okuno
Managing Executive Officer, Yojiro Nagayasu
Managing Executive Officer, Yuji Kitayama
President and Director, Hideo Takasaki
Senior Managing Director, Issei Daido
Managing Director, Hisayoshi Nakamura
Managing Director, Yoshio Nishi
Managing Director, Katsuyuki Toyobe
Managing Director, Masayuki Kobayashi
Managing Director, Junji Inoguchi
Managing Director, Nobuhiro Doi
Auditors: DeloitteToucheTohmatsu

LOCATIONS

HQ: Bank of Kyoto, Ltd. (Japan)
700 Yakushimae-cho, Karasuma-dori Matsubara-Agaru, Shimogyo-ku, Kyoto 600-8652
Phone: (81) 75 361 2211 **Fax:** (81) 75 343 1276
Web: www.kyotobank.co.jp

COMPETITORS

Mitsubishi UFJ Financial Group
Mizuho Financial
Resona
Sumitomo Mitsui
Sumitomo Trust and Banking

HISTORICAL FINANCIALS

Company Type: Public

Income Statement FYE: March 31

	ASSETS ($ mil.)	NET INCOME ($ mil.)	INCOME AS % OF ASSETS	EMPLOYEES
03/13	81,057	186	0.2%	3,570
03/12	89,714	189	0.2%	3,545
03/11	87,986	221	0.3%	3,485
03/10	76,174	167	0.2%	3,393
03/09	67,880	103	0.2%	3,263
Annual Growth	4.5%	16.0%	—	2.3%

2013 Year-End Financials

Return on assets: 0.2%
Return on equity: 4.0%
Long-term debt ($ mil.): —
No. of shares (mil.): 377
Sales ($ mil): 1,225
Dividends
Yield: —
Payout: —
Market value ($ mil.): —

	STOCK PRICE ($) FY Close	P/E High/Low	PER SHARE ($) Earnings	Dividends	Book Value
03/13	0.00	— —	0.46	0.00	13.02
03/12	8.56	— —	0.47	0.00	13.84
03/11	7.90	— —	0.55	0.00	14.31
03/10	8.30	— —	0.42	0.00	13.76
Annual Growth	—	— —	2.7%	—	(1.4%)

Bank of Montreal

Bank of Montreal is bilingual –it speaks Canadian and American business. Also known as BMO Financial Group (or BMO) the company offers retail banking wealth management and investment banking services in North America. Its BMO Bank of Montreal is one of Canada's oldest and biggest banks. Serving individuals government agencies and businesses it has about 900 branches that provide deposits mortgages and loans life insurance credit cards investments and wealth management services. In the US it owns BMO Harris Bank which offers personal and commercial banking through some 700 branches. Another subsidiary BMO Capital Markets performs institutional brokerage and investment banking services.

BMO is focused on building its business in North America and select global markets through acquisitions as well as organic growth. One of the company's goals is to have up to 1000 branches in the US. As part of that initiative it bought Milwaukee-based Marshall & Ilsley (M&I) which doubled its branch network in the Midwest and deepened its presence in Florida and Arizona where BMO had previously made modest forays. The deal which was completed in 2011 was the Canadian bank's largest in the US to date. M&I is combining with BMO Harris Bank.

Though competition is fierce since there are few major players in the Canadian banking industry BMO continues to grow its business there. It claims to serve approximately one-fifth of all households in the country.

Beyond North America BMO incorporated its first subsidiary in China in 2010. It offers banking and investment banking there and owns a stake in joint venture Fullgoal Fund Management. The company is adding to its infrastructure expanding its footprint and exploring new opportunities in China. One example is BMO's referral agreement with Agricultural Bank of China. BMO also is developing its corporate and investment banking capabilities in India.

BMO is pursuing growth in its private client segment which includes money manager BMO Nesbitt Burns online brokerage BMO InvestorLine BMO Insurance and BMO Harris Private Bank by emphasizing investor education and personalized advice and by adding new products and services such as exchange-traded funds. In 2012 BMO acquired US investment firm CTC Consulting which merged with Harris myCFO which is BMO's wealth management business in the US. The deal expanded BMO's focus on high net-worth clients and strengthened its geographic footprint along the West Coast and East Coast of the US.

The company also wants to expand the private client group's geographic penetration beyond North America. To that end in 2011 it bought Hong-Kong based wealth manager Lloyd George Management which has some $6 billion under management. The following year it took a 19.99% stake (the maximum allowed for foreign investors) in Chinese wealth manager COFCO Trust.

BMO's growth strategy has helped improve results despite slow economic growth. In 2011 net income rose by about 16% and revenue climbed by about 12%.

HISTORY

Montreal was a key port for fur and agriculture trade by the early 1800s. To finance these activities the Montreal Bank (Canada's first) opened in 1817. Chartered in 1822 the bank officially became Bank of Montreal. Its ties with the US were strong and nearly 50% of its original capital came from Yanks.

When the fur trade shifted northward to Hudson Bay in the 1820s the bank diversified. In 1832 Bank of Montreal financed Canada's first railroad the Champlain & St. Lawrence. The bank also grew through acquisitions including the Bank of Canada (1831) and the Bank of the People (1840). It opened a branch in New York in 1859.

Canada united as a confederation in 1867 and Bank of Montreal expanded west. During the 1860s it became Canada's de facto central bank until the 1935 creation of the Bank of Canada. By 1914 Bank of Montreal was the nation's largest. It bought the British Bank of North America (1918) Merchants Bank of Canada (1922) and Molsons Bank (1925). During the Depression however its growth ground to a halt.

WWII pumped up Canada's economy and the company's finances. Bank of Montreal enjoyed even greater growth during the postwar boom. It began expanding internationally particularly in Latin America. But the bank failed to capitalize on the growth of consumer and small-business lending during the 1960s and was the last major Canadian bank to issue a credit card (in 1972). In 1975 it hired William Mullholland a Morgan Stanley veteran to run the company. Mullholland closed unprofitable branches and modernized operations.

The bank bought Chicago-based Harris Bankcorp in 1984. As Canada's banking industry deregulated Bank of Montreal moved into investment banking acquiring one of Canada's largest brokerage firms Nesbitt Thomson in 1987.

The Latin American debt crisis and the recession of the late 1980s and early 1990s hit Bank of Montreal hard. It tumbled into the red in 1989 partly because of loan defaults. The next year Matthew Barrett replaced Mullholland as chairman and began overhauling operations focusing on consumer and middle-market business banking and on cutting costs.

By 1994 nonperforming assets were down and Bank of Montreal began growing again. It bought brokerage Burns Fry and merged it with Nesbitt Thomson to form Nesbitt Burns thus increasing its presence in merchant and investment banking and securities. It added to its Harris Bank network with the purchase of Suburban Bancorp. The next year Bank of Montreal expanded its private banking business for wealthy individuals; it also began targeting aboriginal Canadians.

Eyeing international growth Bank of Montreal bought an interest in Mexico's Grupo Financiero Bancomer in 1996 (now called BBVA Bancomer; it has since sold its interest) and opened branches in Beijing (1996) and Dublin Ireland (1997). It agreed in 1998 to merge with Royal Bank of Canada but Canada's finance minister rejected the merger.

Barrett stepped down as CEO and chairman in 1999; the firm named Anthony Comper its new CEO. The bank realigned its operations to focus on retail and commercial banking investment banking and wealth management and cut some 2450 jobs. Eyeing growth in the US Bank of Montreal in 2000 agreed to buy Florida's Village Banc of Naples as well as Seattle brokerage Freeman Welwood.

Continuing its southward push it bought Chicago-area community banks Lakeland Community Bank and New Lenox State Bank as well as Indiana-based Mercantile Bancorp in 2004.

Bank of Montreal sold US-based online brokerage Harrisdirect to E*TRADE in 2005. Comper retired in 2007 and was succeeded as CEO by former COO William Downe.

In 2009 BMO Financial bought the North American operations of Diners Club from Citigroup doubling its corporate credit card business.That year the company also bought American International Group's Canadian life insurance business adding about 400000 clients and expanding BMO's distribution channel.

BMO has been building its US banking operations. In 2010 Harris Bank acquired the failed Indiana-based institution AMCORE Bank in an FDIC-facilitated transaction. The company also bought First National Bank & Trust in Indiana in 2007 and Wisconsin's Merchants and Manufacturers Bancorporation and Ozaukee Bank the following year.

LOCATIONS

HQ: Bank of Montreal
129 Saint-Jacques Street, Montreal, Quebec H2Y 1L6
Phone: 416 867-6785 **Fax:** 416 867-6793
Web: www.bmo.com

PRODUCTS/OPERATIONS

2011 Sales

	% of total
Interest	
Loans	48
Securities	14
Deposits with	1
Noninterest	
Securities commissions &	7
Deposit & payment service	5
Securitization	5
Lending	3
Mutual fund	4
Trading	3
Underwriting & advisory	3
Other	7
Total	**100**

HISTORICAL FINANCIALS

Company Type: Public

Income Statement FYE: October 31

	ASSETS ($ mil.)	NET INCOME ($ mil.)	INCOME AS % OF ASSETS	EMPLOYEES
10/13	513,702	3,999	0.8%	45,500
10/12	526,880	4,126	0.8%	46,000
10/11	502,570	3,053	0.6%	47,000
10/10	404,083	2,758	0.7%	37,947
10/09	358,157	1,647	0.5%	36,173
Annual Growth	9.4%	24.8%	—	5.9%

2013 Year-End Financials

Return on assets: 0.7%
Return on equity: 14.1%
Long-term debt ($ mil.): —
No. of shares (mil.): 644
Sales ($ mil): 19,935
Dividends
Yield: 4.2%
Payout: 48.6%
Market value ($ mil.): 44,896

	STOCK PRICE ($) FY Close	P/E High/Low		PER SHARE ($) Earnings	Dividends	Book Value
10/13	69.70	10	8	5.99	2.88	45.14
10/12	59.12	10	8	6.17	2.83	44.16
10/11	59.17	14	10	4.86	2.88	41.41
10/10	59.25	13	9	4.66	3.44	37.92
10/09	46.37	15	5	2.84	1.94	33.75
Annual Growth	10.7%	—	—	20.5%	10.4%	7.5%

Bank of Nova Scotia Halifax

The last place to look for The Bank of Nova Scotia's headquarters is in Nova Scotia. Although the company (aka Scotiabank) was founded in that province in 1832 it moved to Toronto in 1900. One of Canada's Big Five banks (along with Royal Bank of Canada TD Bank Bank of Montreal and CIBC) Scotiabank provides retail corporate and investment banking services around the world. In addition to about 1000 domestic branches Scotiabank has approximately 1700 offices in more than 50 other countries mainly in the Caribbean and Central and South America. Services include deposit accounts loans insurance brokerage asset management mutual funds and trust services.

While its domestic competitors have been expanding in the US Scotiabank has been focused mainly on making inroads in the Caribbean Latin America and Asia. The bank plans growth in Mexico the Caribbean and South America in addition to its home market. As it looks outward for growth Scotiabank has benefitted from a strong Canadian dollar bolstered by the nation's natural resources sector. The company reported record net income for fiscal 2010.

In 2012 the company rebranded its Scotia Capital Scotia Waterous and ScotiaMocotta investment banking units as Scotiabank in an effort to solidify its brand. The firms became part of Scotiabank's Global Banking and Markets division which offers such services as securities underwriting and mergers and acquisitions advice to corporate clients.

Later that year Scotiabank acquired US-based Howard Weil a boutique investment bank focused on the energy sector. The company built its investment banking practice in South America through the 2010 acquisitions of Dresdner Bank Brazil from Germany's Commerzbank and Royal Bank of Scotland's wholesale banking operations in Colombia.

Domestically Scotiabank wants to be the dominant money manager. As part of its strategy it announced a consolidated wealth management arm in 2009: Scotia Asset Management which includes ScotiaFunds ScotiaMcLeod and Scotia Cassels Investment Counsel. The year before Scotiabank acquired a large minority stake of fund manager CI Financial from Sun Life Financial. In a similar move the company acquired Dundee Corporation's stake in DundeeWealth for some $2.3 billion in 2011. The acquisition gave Scotiabank control of another one of Canada's largest wealth managers.

In 2012 Scotiabank agreed to buy ING Bank of Canada from Dutch group ING for C$3.1 billion. ING Bank of Canada operating as ING Direct primarily serves its clients via the Internet and has marketed itself as an alternative to big banks. Scotiabank plans to continue to run ING Direct as a standalone bank. (ING Groep has been selling off parts of its business as it tries to gain capital strength.)

The company also expanded its wealth management segment with the 2010 acquisition of the money management operations of BNP Paribas in the Bahamas the Cayman Islands and Panama and an agreement to purchase The WaterStreet Group which caters to ultra-high-net-worth clients. Scotiabank is also growing its wealth management business by offering new investment products.

Increasing its focus on insurance as well Scotiabank in 2009 rebranded its ScotiaLife Financial business which offers credit travel life and health coverage. It has also built up its online brokerage capabilities acquiring TradeFreedom Securities in 2007 and E*TRADE Canada from E*TRADE in 2008. Other areas of focus for Scotiabank include mobile banking and global foreign exchange.

Beyond Canada the company owns interests in banks in Chile (Scotiabank Chile formerly Banco del Desarrollo) Mexico (Scotiabank Inverlat) and Central America (Scotiabank El Salvador and Groupo BNS de Costa Rica). In 2010 Scotiabank bought Royal Bank of Scotland's Chilean business and its wholesale banking operations in Colombia making it the only Canadian-owned institution with a presence in the latter country. More expansion in the Caribbean was achieved when Scotiabank acquired R&G Financial's troubled R-G Premier Bank of Puerto Rico. The transaction which was assisted by the FDIC added nearly 30 branches to Scotiabank's network on the island.

Scotiabank expanded in Peru one of South America's fastest-growing economies with its 2006 acquisition of some 80% of Banco Wiese Sudameris (now Scotiabank Peru) from Italian banking group Banca Intesa (now Intesa Sanpaolo) which held on to the rest. It also holds an interest in Peru-based pension-fund manager AFP ProFuturo. Scotiabank entered Uruguay for the first time in 2010 by buying controlling stakes in private bank Nuevo Banco Comercial and consumer lender Pronto. Further expanding in Latin America during 2011 the company acquired wholesale bank Dresdner Bank Brasil (now Scotiabank Brasil) and a majority stake in Colombia-based retail bank Banco Colpatria. In 2012 it announced plans to buy a majority of Colfondos a Colombian pension fund firm with more than $9 billion in assets under management.

Building its position in the Asia-Pacific region Scotiabank in 2009 increased its stake in Thailand's Thanachart Bank to 49% the Thai limit for foreign ownership. The next year Thanachart acquired Siam City Bank making it Thailand's fifth-largest bank. Scotiabank also upped its stake in China's Xi'an City Commercial Bank to almost 15% and arranged to acquire nearly 20% of the state-run Chinese institution Bank of Guangzhou.

EXECUTIVES

Chairman, John T. Mayberry, age 69
Group Head Global Corporate and Investment Banking and Co-Chief Executive Officer Scotia Capital, Stephen D. (Steve) McDonald
Group Head and Chief Risk Officer, Robert H. (Rob) Pitfield
President CEO and Director, Richard E. (Rick) Waugh, $1,000,000 total compensation
Group Head Global Human Resources and Communications, Sylvia D. Chrominska
Vice Chairman Chief Operating Officer, Sarabjit S. (Sabi) Marwah
Executive Vice President General Counsel Secretary, Deborah M. Alexander
Executive Vice President, Alberta G. Cefis
Group Head Global Wealth Management, Christopher J. (Chris) Hodgson
President, Brian J. Porter, $450,000 total compensation
Group Head International Banking, Dieter W. Jentsch
EVP Enterprise Effectiveness, Luc A. Vanneste, $400,000 total compensation
Executive Vice President and Chief Administration Officer Global Banking and Markets, Anne Marie O'Donovan
Group Head Global Capital Markets and Co-Chief Executive Officer Scotia Capital, Michael (Mike) Durland
EVP Latin America, Wendy G. Hannam
Executive Vice President Information Technology and Solutions, Kimberlee B. (Kim) McKenzie
Executive Vice President Chief Financial Officer, Sean McGuckin
Executive Vice President Global Wealth Management, Barbara F. (Barb) Mason
EVP Retail Products and Services Canadian Banking, Robin S. Hibberd
Group Head Canadian Banking, Anatol von Hahn
EVP and Chief Credit Officer, Stephen P. Hart
Executive Vice President Treasurer, Jeffrey C. (Jeff) Heath
EVP and President and CEO Grupo Financiero Scotiabank Mexico, Troy Wright
Executive Vice President Chief Administrative Officer, Marianne Hasold-Schilter
Executive Vice President; Chief Administration Officer - Scotia Capital, Anne ODonovan
Executive Vice President - Mexico; President & Chief Executive Officer - BNS Mexico, Nicole Polignac
EVP Global Human Resources, Sue Graham Parker
EVP Retail Distribution Canadian Banking, James McPhedran
Executive Vice President Global Human Resources, Sue Parker
Director, Barbara S. Thomas, age 62
Director, Ronald A. (Ron) Brenneman, age 66
Director, Paul D. Sobey, age 54
President CEO and Director, Richard E. (Rick) Waugh
Vice Chairman and COO, Sarabjit S. (Sabi) Marwah
Director, Thomas C. (Tom) O'Neill, age 66
Director, John C. Kerr, age 67
Director, C. J. Chen, age 65
Director, N. Ashleigh Everett, age 55
Director, Allan C. Shaw, age 68
Director, Michael J. L. Kirby, age 70
Director, Alexis E. Rovzar de la Torre, age 61
Director, Indira V. Samarasekera, age 59
Director, David A. Dodge
Auditors: KPMGLLP

LOCATIONS

HQ: Bank of Nova Scotia Halifax
Scotia Plaza, 44 King Street West, Toronto, Ontario M5H 1H1
Phone: 416 775-0798 **Fax:** 416 866-7867
Web: www.scotiabank.com

PRODUCTS/OPERATIONS

2010 Sales

	% of total
Interest	
Loans	51
Securities	18
Other	2
Noninterest	
Trading	4
Deposit & payment	4
Credit	4
Investment management brokerage & trust	3
Mutual	2
Underwriting fees & other	2
Card	2
Other	8
Total	**100**

Selected Canadian Subsidiaries

BNS Capital Trust
BNS Investment Inc.
Montreal Trust Company of Canada
Scotia Merchant Capital Corporation
Dundee Bank of Canada
Maple Trust Company
National Trustco Inc.
The Bank of Nova Scotia Trust Company
National Trust Company
RoyNat Inc.
Scotia Capital Inc.
1548489 Ontario Limited
Scotia iTrade Corp.
Scotia Asset Management L.P.
Scotia Capital Inc.
Scotia Dealer Advantage Inc.
Scotia Insurance Agency Inc.
Scotia Life Insurance Company
Scotia Mortgage Corporation
Scotia Securities Inc.
Scotiabank Capital Trust
Scotiabank Subordinated Notes Trust.
Scotiabank Tier 1 Trust

Selected International Subsidiaries

The Bank of Nova Scotia Berhad (Malaysia)
The Bank of Nova Scotia International Limited (Bahamas)
The Bank of Nova Scotia Asia Limited (Singapore)
The Bank of Nova Scotia Trust Company (Bahamas) Ltd.
Scotiabank & Trust (Cayman) Ltd. (Cayman Islands)
BNS (Colombia) Holdings Limited
Grupo BNS de Costa Rica S.A.
Scotia Insurance (Barbados) Limited
Scotiabank (Bahamas) Limited
Scotiabank (British Virgin Islands) Limited
Scotiabank Caribbean Treasury Limited (Bahamas)
Scotiabank (Hong Kong) Limited
Scotiabank (Ireland) Limited
Scotia Group Jamaica Limited (72%)
The Bank of Nova Scotia Jamaica Limited
Scotia DBG Investments Limited (77% Jamaica)
Grupo Financiero Scotiabank Inverlat S.A. de C.V. (97% Mexico)
Nova Scotia Inversiones Limitada (Chile)
Scotiabank Chile S.A.
Scotia Capital (USA) Inc.
Scotia Holdings (US) Inc.
The Bank of Nova Scotia Trust Company of New York
Scotiabanc Inc. (US)
Scotia International Limited (Bahamas)
Scotiabank Anguilla Limited
Scotiabank de Puerto Rico
Scotiabank El Salvador S.A.
Scotiabank Europe plc (UK)
Scotiabank Peru S.A.A.
Scotiabank Trinidad and Tobago Limited

COMPETITORS

BMO Financial Group
Banamex
Banco Santander Chile
Bank of America
Bicsa Panama
CIBC
Citigroup
HSBC Bank Canada
JPMorgan Chase
National Bank of Canada
RBC Financial Group
TD Bank

HISTORICAL FINANCIALS

Company Type: Public

Income Statement FYE: October 31

	ASSETS ($ mil.)	NET INCOME ($ mil.)	INCOME AS % OF ASSETS	EMPLOYEES
10/13	711,122	5,932	0.8%	0
10/12	669,863	6,039	0.9%	81,497
10/11	577,548	4,978	0.9%	75,362
10/10	516,989	3,963	0.8%	70,772
10/09	0	3,098***************%		
67,802				
Annual Growth	—	17.6%	—	—

2013 Year-End Financials

Return on assets: 0.8%
Return on equity: 14.7%
Long-term debt ($ mil.): —
No. of shares (mil.): 1,208
Sales ($ mil): 27,819
Dividends
Yield: 3.9%
Payout: 48.9%
Market value ($ mil.): 73,446

	STOCK PRICE ($) FY Close	P/E High/Low		PER SHARE ($) Earnings	Dividends	Book Value
10/13	60.77	11	9	4.92	2.34	35.32
10/12	54.38	11	8	5.23	2.18	33.56
10/11	52.61	14	10	4.64	2.06	30.20
10/10	53.51	14	10	3.84	1.92	26.01
10/09	41.78	12	4	3.05	1.81	(0.00)
Annual Growth	9.8%	—	—	12.7%	6.6%	—

Bank of Yokohama, Ltd.

The Bank of Yokohama concentrates its operations in its native Kanagawa prefecture and southern portions of neighboring Tokyo. The bank offers standard retail services such as deposits housing loans credit cards securities brokerage and investment products and advice. On the commercial side it provides small and medium-sized commercial financing including venture capital investment. The bank also has units that offer leasing and factoring. The Bank of Yokohama which was formed in 1920 operates more than 600 Japanese branches plus representative offices in Bangkok Hong Kong London New York and Shanghai. It also shares branches though a joint venture with Hamagin Tokai Tokyo Securities.

EXECUTIVES

Deputy President and Representative Director, Chiyuki Okubo
Chairman, Tadashi Ogawa, age 70
Managing Executive Officer and Director, Seiichi Yoneda

Managing Executive Officer and Director, Atsushi Mochizuki
Managing Executive Officer, Shunji Komatsu
President and Representative Director, Tatsumaro Terazawa
Managing Executive Officer and Representative Director, Kengo Takano
Managing Executive Officer and Director, Susumu Koshida
Managing Executive Officer, Shizumi Maesako
Managing Executive Officer, Yoshiyuki Hiranuma
Deputy President and Representative Director, Chiyuki Okubo
Representative Director, Masaki Itoh
Managing Executive Officer and Director, Seiichi Yoneda
Managing Executive Officer and Director, Atsushi Mochizuki
Managing Executive Officer and Director, Takashi Noguchi
President and Representative Director, Tatsumaro Terazawa
Managing Executive Officer and Representative Director, Kengo Takano
Auditors: DeloitteToucheTohmatsu

LOCATIONS

HQ: Bank of Yokohama, Ltd.
3-1-1 Minatomirai, Nishi-ku, Yokohama, Kanagawa 220-8611
Phone: (81) 45 225 1111 **Fax:** (81) 45 225 1160
Web: www.boy.co.jp

COMPETITORS

Mitsubishi UFJ Financial Group
Mizuho Financial
Norinchukin Bank
Sumitomo Mitsui
Suruga Bank
Tokyo Star Bank

HISTORICAL FINANCIALS

Company Type: Public

Income Statement FYE: March 31

	ASSETS ($ mil.)	NET INCOME ($ mil.)	INCOME AS % OF ASSETS	EMPLOYEES
03/13	143,144	588	0.4%	4,751
03/12	156,066	624	0.4%	4,752
03/11	151,202	568	0.4%	4,768
03/10	128,301	331	0.3%	4,784
03/09	122,209	74	0.1%	4,743
Annual Growth	4.0%	67.6%	—	0.0%

2013 Year-End Financials

Return on assets: 0.4%
Return on equity: 6.8%
Long-term debt ($ mil.): —
No. of shares (mil.): 1,308
Sales ($ mil): 3,124
Dividends
Yield: —
Payout: —
Market value ($ mil.): 30,330

	STOCK PRICE ($) FY Close	P/E High/Low	PER SHARE ($) Earnings	Dividends	Book Value
03/13	23.18	— —	0.44	0.00	7.27
03/12	19.90	— —	0.46	0.00	7.54
03/11	47.80	— —	0.42	0.46	6.99
03/10	48.75	— —	0.24	0.43	6.00
03/09	42.97	— —	0.05	0.46	5.33
Annual Growth	(14.3%)	— —	68.7%	—	8.1%

Bankinter, S.A.

Founded in 1965 as a joint venture between what is now Grupo Santander and Bank of America Bankinter is among the top six banks in Spain. The company offers a variety of consumer and business banking services through about 360 branch locations agents telephone services mobile banking and the Internet. A pioneer in Internet stock trading Bankinter conducts more than half of its transactions online. It serves corporations individuals and small enterprises. Bankinter provides mutual and pension funds mortgages leasing and securities brokerage focusing on convenient low-cost delivery and customer service. Investment firm Cartival S.A. owns about 23% of Bankinter.

Although Bankinter has about 360 branches in Spain more than half of its transactions are conducted on the Internet. The bank has pioneered technologies to make its online services more accessible including making Web pages compatible with software used by the visually impaired.

The bank is making a strong push to court the small and medium enterprise (SME) segment of the market. In recent years Bankinter launched dozens of new service centers catering to SMEs. The bank also continues to open other private banking and business management branches in fast-growing towns throughout the country.

Bankinter announced in 2009 it will buy the 50% of auto insurer Linea Directa Aseguradora it already does not own from Royal Bank of Scotland. The proposed shift follows a change in control at Royal Bank which was taken over by the government in 2008.

France's Credit Agricole owns about 20% of Bankinter. Through investment firm Cartival former Bankinter chairman Jaime Botin controls more than 15% of the bank's stock. The Botin family leads Grupo Santander which includes Spain's largest bank.

HISTORY

In 1962 Franco tried to end mixed banks in Spain with a decree that prevented banks from taking part in both commercial and investment operations. The banks circumvented this through cosmetic compliance spending the next decade nominally spinning off operations. In 1965 Banco Santander (now Grupo Santander) and Bank of America created Banco Intercontinental Espanol (Bankinter) in Madrid to specialize in industrial banking.

From 1970 to 1985 Bankinter evolved into a retail bank; it introduced credit cards personal loans and other services and offered financing to larger corporations. Bankinter was not consumed by the great branch race that defined banking-industry competition in Franco-era Spain; the bank had only 150 branches by 1985.

The bank became independent as both Bank of America (in 1987) and Santander (1994) reduced their stock holdings. Bankinter began diversifying its operations opening branches and gaining more clients. Bankinter's successful 1987 introduction of a high-interest special deposit account was dulled when other banks followed suit slowing growth. The bank took its current name in 1990 and in 1991 introduced some of Spain's first mutual funds. Within a recession-hammered economy Bankinter worked to cut costs through the introduction of telephone banking (1992) and other innovative conveniences.

Attracted by the low-cost liquidity of private banking Bankinter entered that segment in 1995. It took a step in the "allfinanz" direction that year creating an auto and home insurance alliance with Royal Bank of Scotland subsidiary Direct Line; the UK bank already had insurance ventures with Bankinter sibling Santander. Two years later Bankinter began BKNet Spain's first online stock-trading service.

In 1998 the bank opened a Mexican office to explore the possibility of transferring its high-tech operations into that country. As the financial industry's global consolidation continued the bank in 1999 said it was seeking a foreign ally possibly one that could help expand Bankinter's online technology.

The bank found willing partners later that year inking deals to form an Internet bank in Spain with a joint venture of US Web portal Lycos (now part of Terra Networks) and German media giant Bertelsmann as well as another Internet bank with Portugal's Banco Espirito Santo.

Although Bankinter recorded 2004 as a particularly profitable year with income up nearly 25% it also suffered the death of a deputy manager Jose Garcia in the March 11 terrorist attacks against Madrid.

In 2007 the bank sold 50% of its life insurance division to Spanish insurer Mapfre. The sale boosted Bankinter's capital.

In 2008 Credit Agricole increased its ownership in the bank to about 20%. It became the bank's largest shareholder edging out former chairman Jaime Botin.

EXECUTIVES

Chairman, Pedro Guerrero Guerrero
CEO, Maria Dolores Dancausa
Director, Jose Ramon Arce Gomez
Director, John de Zuleta Greenebaum
Director, Fabiola Arredondo de Vara
Director, Marcelino Botin-Sanz de Sautola y Naveda
Director, Fernando Masaveu Herrero
Auditors: PricewaterhouseCoopersAuditoresS.L.

LOCATIONS

HQ: Bankinter, S.A.
Paseo de la Castellana, 29, Madrid 28046
Phone: (34) 91 339 75 00 **Fax:** (34) 91 339 83 23
Web: www.bankinter.es

PRODUCTS/OPERATIONS

Selected Subsidiaries

Aircraft S.A.
Bankinter Consultoria Asesoramiento y Atencion Telefonica S.A.
Bankinter Gestion de Seguros S.A.
Bankinter International B.V. (Netherlands)
Bankinter Seguros de Vida S.A.
Gesbankinter S.A.
Hispamarket S.A.
Intergestora S.A.
Intergestora Nuevas Tecnologias S.C.R. S.A.
Intermobiliaria S.A.

COMPETITORS

AEGON
BBVA
Banco Espa?ol de Credito
Banco Guipuzcoano
Banco Popular Espa?ol
Banco de Sabadell
Deutsche Bank
Espirito Santo
Grupo Santander
La Caixa

HISTORICAL FINANCIALS

Company Type: Public

Income Statement FYE: December 31

	ASSETS ($ mil.)	NET INCOME ($ mil.)	INCOME AS % OF ASSETS	EMPLOYEES
12/12	76,665	164	0.2%	3,853
12/11	76,949	234	0.3%	3,904
12/10	72,475	201	0.3%	4,740
12/09	78,464	366	0.5%	4,694
12/08	74,755	352	0.5%	4,483
Annual Growth	0.6%	(17.4%)	—	(3.7%)

2012 Year-End Financials

Return on assets: 0.2%
Return on equity: 3.9%
Long-term debt ($ mil.): —
No. of shares (mil.): 563
Sales ($ mil): 3,814
Dividends
Yield: 5.1%
Payout: 51.9%
Market value ($ mil.): 2,453

	STOCK PRICE ($) FY Close	P/E High/Low		PER SHARE ($) Earnings	Dividends	Book Value
12/12	4.35	52	18	0.30	0.14	7.55
12/11	6.01	39	21	0.45	0.24	8.37
12/10	5.30	65	27	0.43	0.26	7.29
12/09	11.10	48	26	0.82	1.42	7.86
12/08	8.75	59	24	0.88	0.54	6.77
Annual Growth	(16.0%)	—	—	(23.4%)	(28.2%)	2.8%

Banque Nationale de Belgique (National Bank of Belgium)

No prizes for guessing the role of the Nationale Bank van Belgie. NBB is indeed the national central bank for Belgium and a member of the European System of Central Banks (ESCB). Founded in 1850 the institution performs a variety of functions aimed at maintaining stability and liquidity for Belgium's banks and financial markets including arranging fund transfers between banks overseeing settlement activities for securities markets and issuing banknotes and coins. The bank's chief executive known as its governor is appointed by the Belgian monarch. NBB is also known by its names in French (Banque nationale de Belgique) English (National Bank of Belgium) and German (Belgische Nationalbank).

The bank carries out various other functions within Belgium's financial system. As the nation's lender of last resort NBB is also able to provide emergency funds when times of exceptional financial crisis. It did as much in 2008 with the cross-national bailout of Fortis. NBB has also printed currency notes (and distributed coins struck by Belgium's Royal Mint) since 1851.

Auditors: Ernst&YoungReviseursd'EntreprisesSCC

LOCATIONS

HQ: Banque Nationale de Belgique (National Bank of Belgium)
Boulevard de Berlaimont 14, Brussels BE-1000
Phone: (32) 2 221 21 11 **Fax:** (32) 2 221 31 00
Web: www.nbb.be

COMPETITORS

Bank of England
Deutsche Bundesbank
Federal Reserve
Swiss National Bank

HISTORICAL FINANCIALS

Company Type: Public

Income Statement FYE: December 31

	ASSETS ($ mil.)	NET INCOME ($ mil.)	INCOME AS % OF ASSETS	EMPLOYEES
12/12	144,660	1,762	1.2%	2,103
12/11	165,193	1,162	0.7%	2,101
12/10	99,973	1,113	1.1%	2,065
12/09	146,160	2,754	1.9%	2,095
12/08	214,193	621	0.3%	2,143
Annual Growth	(9.3%)	29.8%	—	(0.5%)

	STOCK PRICE ($) FY Close	P/E High/Low		PER SHARE ($) Earnings	Dividends	Book Value
12/12	2,975.00	—	—	(0.00)	0.00	18,613
12/11	2,600.00	—	—	(0.00)	0.00	16,122
12/10	4,900.00	—	—	(0.00)	0.00	15,756
12/09	4,800.00	—	—	(0.00)	0.00	16,507
Annual Growth	(14.7%)	—	—	—	—	3.0%

Baoshan Iron & Steel Co Ltd

Blast furnaces and steel mills nsk

EXECUTIVES

Chairman, Wenbo He

LOCATIONS

HQ: Baoshan Iron & Steel Co Ltd
Baosteel Command Center, No. 885, Fujin Road, Baoshan District, Shanghai 201900
Phone: (86) 21 26647000 **Fax:** (86) 21 26646999
Web: www.baosteel.com/plc/

PRODUCTS/OPERATIONS

HISTORICAL FINANCIALS

Company Type: Public

Income Statement FYE: December 31

	REVENUE ($ mil.)	NET INCOME ($ mil.)	NET PROFIT MARGIN	EMPLOYEES
12/12	30,719	1,666	5.4%	32,598
12/11	35,405	1,169	3.3%	41,919
12/10	30,707	1,955	6.4%	42,308
12/09	21,752	851	3.9%	42,318
12/08	29,435	1,003	3.4%	43,789
Annual Growth	1.1%	13.5%	—	(7.1%)

2012 Year-End Financials

Debt ratio: 3.5%
Return on equity: 9.5%
Cash ($ mil.): 1,418
Current ratio: 0.84
Long-term debt ($ mil.): 2,015
No. of shares (mil.): —
Dividends
Yield: —
Payout: —
Market value ($ mil.): —

Barclays Africa Group Ltd

Can Absa help with your banking needs in Africa? Absa-lutely! Serving nearly 12 million consumers small businesses and commercial clients the company's Absa Bank is one of the largest retail banks and mortgage lenders in South Africa with about 700 branches and 9000 ATMs most of them in that country. The bank and other subsidiaries offer deposits loans credit cards insurance investments financial planning brokerage wealth management and investment banking services. British bank Barclays owns about 55% of Absa Group making it one of South Africa's largest foreign investors since apartheid ended in 1994.

Beyond South Africa Absa Group owns some 80% of Barclays Bank Mozambique and a majority of National Bank of Commerce in Tanzania. The company which also has representative offices in Namibia and Nigeria is taking steps to broaden its presence in its existing markets and the surrounding region. It acquired Global Alliance Seguros a Mozambique-based life and property/casualty insurer in 2011. Absa Group launched an insurance unit in Botswana that year as well.

In 2008 Absa Group acquired controlling interests in Meeg Bank and Woolworths Holdings' financial services operations further strengthening its presence in South Africa. The moves came after Absa Group canceled plans to buy Barclays' retail operations in Zimbabwe Zambia Kenya Botswana Ghana Tanzania the Seychelles and Mauritius. Additional acquisitions are expected.

The traditionally consumer-focused company is also making efforts to attract more commercial clients. During 2010 it established a corporate bank and invested in a transactional banking platform for commercial clients. Meanwhile the company is not ignoring consumers however as it retooled its retail franchise to focus more on value rather than volume. Absa Group has also used technology to simplify processes streamline customer service and improve access to banking.

Maria Ramos was named CEO of Absa Group in 2009 after former chief executive Steve Booysen retired after 20 years with the company.

EXECUTIVES

Deputy Group Chief Executive and Director, Louis L. von Zeuner, age 50
CEO Bancassurance, Willie T. Lategan, age 44
Executive Director Marketing and Communications, Happy Ntshingila, age 52
Group Chief Executive and Director, Maria Ramos, age 54
Finance Director and Board Member, David W. P. Hodnett, age 43
COO, N. Alfie Naidoo, age 45
Chief Executive Absa Capital, Stephen van Coller, age 47
Chief Executive Absa Africa, John Gachora
Director, Trevor S. Munday, age 63
Director, Robert Le Blanc, age 56
Deputy Group Chief Executive and Director, Louis L. von Zeuner, age 50
Director, Antony Jenkins
Director, Shauket A. Fakie, age 60
Director, Yolanda Z. Cuba, age 35
Director, Garth Griffin, age 63
Director, Eduardo C. Mondlane Jr., age 55
Director, Brand S.G. Pretorius, age 64
Director, Johan B. Willemse, age 57

Finance Director and Board Member, David W. P. Hodnett, age 43
Auditors: PricewaterhouseCoopersInc.

LOCATIONS

HQ: Barclays Africa Group Ltd
7th Floor, Absa Towers West, 15 Troye Street, Johannesburg 2001
Phone: (27) 11 350 5347 **Fax:** (27) 11 350 4009
Web: www.absa.co.za

PRODUCTS/OPERATIONS

2010 Sales

	% of total
Interest & similar	68
Net fee & commission	21
Net insurance premium	6
Gains from banking & trading	3
Other	2
Total	**100**

COMPETITORS

FirstRand
Nedcor
Sanlam
Standard Bank Group
Standard Chartered

HISTORICAL FINANCIALS

Company Type: Public

Income Statement

FYE: December 31

	ASSETS ($ mil.)	NET INCOME ($ mil.)	INCOME AS % OF ASSETS	EMPLOYEES
12/12	94,899	985	1.0%	0
12/11	97,146	1,194	1.2%	39,659
12/10	107,841	1,221	1.1%	43,239
12/09	96,981	924	1.0%	36,150
12/08	82,122	1,124	1.4%	37,828
Annual Growth	3.7%	(3.2%)	—	—

2012 Year-End Financials

Return on assets: 1.0%
Return on equity: 12.9%
Long-term debt ($ mil.): —
No. of shares (mil.): 717
Sales ($ mil): 9,391
Dividends
Yield: 4.1%
Payout: 1.7%
Market value ($ mil.): 27,974

	STOCK PRICE ($) FY Close	P/E High	P/E Low	PER SHARE ($) Earnings	Dividends	Book Value
12/12	38.98	0	0	1.37	1.61	10.95
12/11	34.85	0	0	1.66	0.03	10.73
12/10	42.00	0	0	1.70	1.16	11.82
12/09	34.85	0	0	1.30	0.02	9.54
12/08	21.95	0	0	1.60	0.02	(0.00)
Annual Growth	15.4%	—	—	(3.8%)	202.1%	—

Barclays Bank Plc

Barclays Bank is the flagship subsidiary of global financial group Barclays PLC. The bank is primarily active in the UK where it has some 1700 branches but also has significant retail and commercial operations in Europe Africa (it owns more than half of South African bank Absa Group) the Middle East and the US. Barclays Bank offers standard retail services such as deposit accounts and lending including Woolwich-brand mortgages. The bank also provides commercial money transfer services insurance products the Barclaycard line of credit cards and financial advisory services. Barclays Bank traces its roots to the late 17th century.

Barclays Bank has been building up its portfolio of global credit card accounts especially as other financial groups sell off noncore units during the economic recovery. In 2010 the company acquired the Italian credit card accounts of Citigroup in a deal that included some 197000 card accounts and approximately E234 million ($320 million) worth of assets. It previously bought Goldfish the struggling UK credit card unit of Discover Financial Services for some #46 million ($70 million). In 2011 Barclays acquired Egg UK's credit card portfolio which added more than 1 million accounts; it has agreed to buy more Citibank card accounts.

The bank has also been offloading some of its own holdings as part of an overall corporate restructuring. In 2010 Barclays sold its US subprime loan servicing business HomEq Servicing to Ocwen Financial. It also announced plans to abandon retail banking in certain international markets and instead focus on wholesale and commercial banking. In 2011 it shuttered its Indonesian retail unit Bank Akita which it had acquired only two years before. The company also sold its Russian retail and commercial operations to a group of investors citing difficulties competing in the market. Barclays will instead focus on its investment banking activities in the region.

In 2010 Barclays acquired Standard Life Bank from Standard Life for #226 million ($369 million). The deal added Standard Life's savings and mortgage books to the Barclays fold. Also as part of the deal Barclays and Standard Life entered into a partnership whereby Barclays markets pension products to its clients.

Despite challenges in the economy especially in regards to Europe's debt problems Barclays Bank's revenues grew 8% in 2011. Its Africa business performed relatively strongly with credit impairments improving as did Barclaycard thanks to the portfolio acquisitions which delivered profits. That year the bank closed nearly 150 European branches (largely located in Spain) the costs of which contributed to a 5% decline in net income.

EXECUTIVES

President Barclays PLC, Robert E. (Bob) Diamond Jr., age 61
Chairman, Sir David A. Walker, age 69
Chairman, Marcus Agius, age 66
Chief Operations and Technology Officer, Shaygan Kheradpir, age 52
CEO Barclaycard, Valerie (Val) Soranno-Keating
Chief Executive Americas, Hugh E. (Skip) McGee III
Chief Executive Barclays Wealth, Thomas L. (Tom) Kalaris
Group General Counsel, Mark Harding
Co-Chief Executive Corporate and Investment Banking, Thomas (Tom) King
CEO Retail and Business Banking, Ashok Vaswani
Co-Chief Executive Corporate and Investment Banking, Jerry del Missier
Chief Risk Officer, Robert Le Blanc, age 56
Director Human Resources, Cathy Turner
Group Chief Executive, Antony Jenkins
Group Finance Director and Board Member, Christopher (Chris) Lucas, age 52
Chief Executive Absa Group and Barclays Africa, Maria Ramos, age 54
Co-Chief Executive of Corporate and Investment Banking, Eric Bommensath
Co-Chief Executive Corporate and Investment Banking, Rich Ricci
Director Media Relations, Giles Croot
Head of Compliance and Government and Regulatory Relations, Sir Hector Sants
Group Financial Controller and Acting Chief Financial Officer, Peter Estlin
Group Finance Director, Tushar Morzaria
Group Chief Executive and Board Member, Robert E. (Bob) Diamond Jr., age 60
Director, Sir John M. Sunderland, age 67
Director, Fulvio Conti, age 65
Director, Sir Michael D. V. (Mike) Rake, age 65
Director, Alison J. Carnwath, age 60
Director, Reuben Jeffery III
Group Finance Director and Board Member, Christopher (Chris) Lucas, age 52
Director, David Booth, age 58
Director, Simon J. Fraser
Director, Dambisa Moyo, age 44
Auditors: PricewaterhouseCoopersLLP

LOCATIONS

HQ: Barclays Bank Plc
1 Churchill Place, London E14 5HP
Phone: (44) 20 7116 1000
Web: www.barclays.co.uk

PRODUCTS/OPERATIONS

2011 Assets

	% of total
Cash &	7
Trading portfolio	10
Financial assets designated at fair	2
Derivative financial	34
Loans &	31
Reverse purchase agreements & similar	10
Available for sale financial	4
Goodwill &	2
Total	**100**

2011 Sales

	% of total
Interest	48
Fees &	24
Net trading	18
Net investment	5
Net insurance premiums &	5
Total	**100**

COMPETITORS

Citibank
Credit Suisse
Deutsche Bank
HSBC
ING
Lloyds Banking Group
Nationwide Building Society
Royal Bank of Scotland
Standard Chartered

HISTORICAL FINANCIALS

Company Type: Public

Income Statement

FYE: December 31

	ASSETS ($ mil.)	NET INCOME ($ mil.)	INCOME AS % OF ASSETS	EMPLOYEES
12/12	2,402,885	(1,165)	—	139,200
12/11	2,415,227	5,586	0.2%	149,700
12/10	2,313,492	6,477	0.3%	151,300
12/09	2,233,641	16,184	0.7%	153,800
12/08	2,991,881	7,062	0.2%	156,300
Annual Growth	(5.3%)	—	—	(2.9%)

2012 Year-End Financials

Return on assets: (-0.0%)
Return on equity: (-1.1%)
Long-term debt ($ mil.): —
No. of shares (mil.): —
Sales ($ mil): 55,572
Dividends
Yield: —
Payout: —
Market value ($ mil.): —

	STOCK PRICE ($) FY Close	P/E High/Low		PER SHARE ($) Earnings	Dividends	Book Value
12/12	31.81	—	—	(0.00)	0.00	41.31
12/11	35.53	—	—	(0.00)	0.00	40.95
12/10	37.61	—	—	(0.00)	0.00	39.23
12/09	34.07	—	—	(0.00)	0.00	38.67
Annual Growth	(2.3%)	—	—	—	—	1.7%

Barclays PLC

Raising the bar for global finance Barclays owns one of Europe's largest banks a top market-making investment bank the top UK credit card and an international wealth management firm. Its flagship Barclays Bank has some 1700 branches in the UK as well as operations throughout Europe Africa the Middle East and the US. Its Barclaycard arm has more than 20 million credit cards and provides consumer lending and payment processing services primarily in Europe. Barclays Capital is one of the largest investment banks in the world (thanks largely to its acquisition of the North American operations of Lehman Brothers). Altogether Barclays serves more than 48 million customers in more than 50 countries.

Barclays' largest segment is the investment banking business Barclays Capital which represents nearly 40% of the group's income. Its second-largest segment UK Retail and Business Banking provides consumer and commercial banking Woolwich-branded mortgages insurance and money transmission services. Other segments include Barclaycard Europe Retail and Business Banking (active in France Spain Italy and Portugal) Africa Retail and Business Banking (including South African bank Absa). In addition to Barclays Capital the corporate and investment banking operations include Barclays Corporate Barclays Wealth and Investment Management (which oversees Barclays' 20% stake in BlackRock). There has been speculation that Barclays may regroup in a major way (a la Citigroup or RBS) in order to split off its riskier assets.

To weather the global economic crisis Barclays has already sold some businesses cut costs through branch closures and workforce reductions and restructured its credit market exposures. The company sold its African custody and securities business to Standard Chartered in 2010 and Barclays Capital wound down its Barclays Venture arm. The investment bank also sold Barclays Private Equity now Equistone Partners to that unit's management in an effort to raise more capital. Additionally Barclays has categorized its holding in BlackRock as available-for-sale after writing down the value of the stake in mid-2011.

To offset some of its exposure to the UK economy Barclays has been expanding its international business mostly in the US and in emerging markets. In 2011 the group sold its Russian retail business to focus on investment banking in that market. (Barclays found it difficult to compete in Russia where the majority of assets are held by state-owned banks.)

To boost its retail and commercial banking operations the company has sought opportunistic acquisitions as other financial groups sell off noncore units at discounted rates. In one such deal it bought Standard Life Bank from Scottish insurer Standard Life which exited the banking business for #226 million ($368.5 million) in 2010. The price was a significant discount from Standard Life Bank's net asset value. Barclays has been in talks to buy other businesses in similar transactions.

Barclays has also expanded its Barclaycard operations. Its 2008 acquisition of the money-losing Goldfish credit card operations from Discover Financial Services added some 1.7 million accounts and the follow-up purchases of Citibank's Portuguese and Italian credit card units added another 600000 accounts. In 2011 the company acquired the approximately 1.2 million UK card accounts held by Egg Banking at a discount. Continuing to build the card business the company bought some 60000 MBNA Europe Bank UK small business accounts from Bank of America. Barclays has also been an innovator with its money transfer operations introducing contactless cards and mobile phone person-to-person transfers.

With the help of the corporate shuffling the company's revenues grew by some 6% in 2011. Among the star performers that year were the UK Retail and Business Banking Barclaycard Africa Retail and Business Banking and Barclays Wealth segments which all saw double-digit growth in profits. Also in 2011 Barclay's European retail banking business returned to profitability after losing money the previous year. The tough economic climate though especially related to concerns over European sovereign debt brought down earnings in the investment bank's operations (which in turn proved a drag on overall performance). However Barclays believes it is on strong footing in terms of capital funding and liquidity.

More troubles hit Barclays in mid-2012 though as the company admitted to manipulating the London Interbank Offered Rate (LIBOR) a benchmark for daily global short-term interest rates. The bank repeatedly manipulated the LIBOR in order to make its funding position look stronger than it actually was; the rigging also helped the bank make money on credit derivatives. Chairman Martin Agius and CEO Bob Diamond both resigned as a result of the developments and the company paid US and UK regulators some #290 million ($453 million) in settlement fines. Shortly after the LIBOR scandal the UK's Serious Fraud Office launched an inquiry into payments Barclays made to sovereign investor Qatar Holding in 2008. That same year investment fund Qatar Investment Authority became the bank's largest shareholder with a 5% stake. Investigations for both the bid-rigging and bribery allegations continue.

HISTORY

Barclays first spread its wings in 1736 when James Barclay united his family's goldsmithing and banking businesses. As other family members joined the London enterprise it became known as Barclays Bevan & Tritton (1782).

Banking first became regulated in the 19th century. To ward off takeovers 20 banks combined with Barclays in 1896. The new firm Barclay & Co. began preying on other banks. Within 20 years it bought 17 including the Colonial Bank chartered in 1836 to serve the West Indies and British Guiana (now Guyana). The company renamed Barclays Bank Ltd. in 1917 weathered the Depression as the UK's #2 bank.

Barclays began expanding again after WWII and by the late 1950s it had become the UK's top bank. It had a computer network by 1959 and in 1966 it introduced the Barclaycard in conjunction with Bank of America's BankAmericard (now Visa).

In 1968 the UK's Monopolies Commission barred Barclays' merger with two other big London banks but had no objections to a two-way merger so Barclays bought competitor Martins.

Barclays moved into the US consumer finance market in 1980 when it bought American Credit 138 former Beneficial Finance offices and Bankers Trust's branch network.

During the 1980s London banks faced competition from invading overseas banks local building societies and other financial firms. Banking reform in 1984 led to formation of a holding company for Barclays Bank PLC.

To prepare for British financial deregulation in 1986 Barclays formed Barclays de Zoete Wedd (BZW) by merging its merchant bank with two other London financial firms. Faced with sagging profits Barclays sold its California bank in 1988 and its US consumer finance business in 1989.

In 1990 Barclays bought private German bank Merck Finck & Co. and Paris bank L'Europeenne de Banque. The company countered 1992's bad-loan-induced losses by accelerating a cost-cutting program begun in 1989. To appease stockholders chairman and CEO Andrew Buxton (a descendant of one of the bank's founding families) gave up his CEO title hiring Martin Taylor (previously CEO of textile firm Courtaulds) for the post.

The company sold its Australian retail banking business in 1994 then began trimming other operations including French corporate banking and US mortgage operations. However it bought the Wells Fargo Nikko Investment Company to boost Asian operations.

Barclays' piecemeal sale of BZW signaled its failure to become a global investment banking powerhouse. In 1997 it sold BZW's European investment banking business to Credit Suisse First Boston retaining the fixed-income and foreign exchange business. (Credit Suisse bought Barclays' Asian investment banking operations in 1998.)

Losses in Russia and a $250 million bailout of US hedge fund Long-Term Capital Management hit Barclays Capital in 1998. Taylor resigned that year in part because of his radical plans for the bank. Sir Peter Middleton stepped in as acting CEO; Barclays later tapped Canadian banker Matthew Barrett for the post. (Middleton also became chairman upon Buxton's retirement.)

Barclays in 1999 started a move toward online banking at the expense of traditional branches. The company announced free lifetime Internet access for new bank customers.

In 2000 the bank ruffled feathers when it announced the closure of about 170 mostly rural UK branches. Also in 2000 the company sold its Dial auto leasing unit to ABN AMRO and bought Woolwich plc. The following year Barclay's closed its own life insurance division opting instead to sell the life insurance and pension products of London-based Legal & General Group.

In 2004 chief executive Barrett was named Barclays' chairman succeeding Peter Middleton who became chairman of Centre for Effective Dispute Resolution (CEDR) and later chancellor of the University of Sheffield.

After exiting the South African market in 1987 over apartheid concerns Barclays returned in a big way in 2005 buying a majority stake (about 57%) in the Absa Group one of the country's largest retail banks. The deal also represented the largest-ever direct foreign investment there. The next year Barclays sold its South African businesses including corporate international retail and commercial operations to Absa.

The company entered the US credit card market when it bought Juniper Financial (now Barclays Bank Delaware) from Canadian Imperial Bank of Commerce (CIBC) in 2004. In a previous hook-up with CIBC Barclays merged its Caribbean banking business with CIBC's to create an 85-branch regional bank FirstCaribbean International Bank with each company owning 44%; Barclays sold its stake to CIBC in 2006.

In 2005 the bank sold its vendor finance businesses in the UK and Germany to CIT Group. Barclays said that the sale will allow it to focus on its commercial leasing business.

The bank moved to assimilate its Woolwich acquisition in 2006 when it closed 200 branches and consolidated Woolwich branches into existing Barclays locations. It retained the Woolwich mortgage brand but switched account holders to Barclays accounts.

The company and HSBC formed a joint venture that manages their cash handling operations in the UK. Named Vaultex the joint venture acquired Loomis Cash Management in 2007.

Marcus Agius succeeded the retiring Matthew Barrett as chairman in 2007.

Although the company withdrew its bid for Dutch banking giant ABN AMRO (narrowly escaping that troubled deal) in 2008 it bought Russian bank Expobank from Petropavlovsk Finance. Expobank was one of the largest ATM networks in Russia and part of the booming consumer banking industry there. Also that year Barclays sold noncore business Barclays Life and its portfolio of some 760000 life and pension policies to Swiss Re for #753 million ($1.5 billion).

The group chose not to participate in the UK's bank bailouts as the global financial crisis intensified in late 2008 but pursued its own capital-raising plan. Through the deal sovereign investment fund Qatar Investment Authority became the bank's largest shareholder with a 5% stake.

In 2009 it shut down US-based subprime mortgage lender EquiFirst which it had purchased from Regions Financial before it fell victim to the mortgage bust.

Later that year it sold a majority of Barclays Global Investors to American money manager BlackRock for #9.5 billion ($15 billion). In exchange it gained a 20% stake in the new BlackRock with some $3 trillion under management for institutional clients around the world. The deal provided the bank with much-needed cash and cleared the way for a commercial partnership with BlackRock.

Another major transaction was the #1 billion ($1.8 billion) acquisition of Lehman Brothers' North American operations a deal which made Barclays Capital one of the world's largest investment banks.

EXECUTIVES

Chairman, Sir David A. Walker, age 73
Chief Operations and Technology Officer, Shaygan Kheradpir, age 52
Deputy Chairman, Sir Michael D. V. (Mike) Rake, age 65
CEO Barclaycard, Valerie (Val) Soranno-Keating
Chief Executive Americas, Hugh E. (Skip) McGee III
Chief Executive Barclays Wealth Management and Executive Chairman of Barclays in the Americas, Thomas L. (Tom) Kalaris
Secretary, Lawrence Dickinson
Interim Chief Operations and Technology Officer, Darryl West
Head Corporate Communications and Media Relations New York, Michael O'Looney
Group General Counsel, Mark Harding
Co-Chief Executive Corporate and Investment Banking, Thomas (Tom) King
CEO Retail and Business Banking, Ashok Vaswani
President Barclays Capital and Co-CEO Corporate and Investment Banking, Jerry del Missier
Group Chief Risk Officer, Robert Le Blanc, age 55
Director Human Resources, Cathy Turner
Group Chief Executive and Director, Antony Jenkins
Group Finance Director and Director, Christopher (Chris) Lucas, age 52, $1,273,639 total compensation
Group Treasurer, Jon Stone
CEO Absa Group and Barclays Africa, Maria Ramos, age 54
CEO Barclays Commercial Bank, Eduardo Eguren
CEO Global Retail and Commercial Banking Emerging Markets, Vinit Chandra
Head Legal Operations, Cate Campany
Managing Director Egypt and North Africa, Khalid Elgibaly
Director Payment Innovations Barclaycard, Dan Salmons
Director Digital Banking UK, Sean Gilchrist
Managing Director Barclays Business, Steve Cooper
Co-Chief Executive Corporate and Investment Banking, Eric Bommensath
Managing Director and Head Business Strategy and Platforms Barclays Wealth Americas, Paul Morton
Head Global Research and Investment; Head Barclays Wealth Americas, Mitch Cox
CEO Corporate and Investment Banking, Rich Ricci
Head Debit Cards UK Retail Banking, Brian Cunnington
Finance Director, Tushar Morzaria
Director, Sir John M. Sunderland, age 67
Director, R. Leigh Clifford, age 64
Director, Fulvio Conti, age 66
Deputy Chairman, Sir Michael D. V. (Mike) Rake, age 65
Director, Alison J. Carnwath, age 59
Director, Sir Andrew Likierman, age 69
Group Chief Executive and Director, Antony Jenkins
Director, Reuben Jeffery III
Group Finance Director and Director, Christopher (Chris) Lucas, age 52
Director, David Booth, age 58
Director, Simon J. Fraser
Director, Dambisa Moyo, age 44
Auditors: PricewaterhouseCoopersLLP

LOCATIONS

HQ: Barclays PLC
1 Churchill Place, London E14 5HP
Phone: (44) 20 7116 1000
Web: www.barclays.com

2011 Sales

	% of total
UK	42
Americas	21
Africa & Middle	17
Europe	15
Asia	5
Total	**100**

PRODUCTS/OPERATIONS

2011 Sales by Segment

	% of total
Barclays	36
UK Retail & Business	16
Barclaycard	14
Africa Retail & Business	13
Barclays	10
Barclays	6
Europe Retail & Business	5
Investment	-
Total	**100**

COMPETITORS

AXA UK
Bank of New York Mellon
CIBC
Citigroup
Deutsche Bank
Grupo Santander
Lloyds Banking Group
Mitsubishi UFJ Financial Group
Mizuho Financial
RBC Financial Group
Royal Bank of Scotland
Standard Chartered
HSBC
Invesco
JPMorgan Chase
The Vanguard Group
UBS

HISTORICAL FINANCIALS

Company Type: Public

Income Statement

FYE: December 31

	ASSETS ($ mil.)	NET INCOME ($ mil.)	INCOME AS % OF ASSETS	EMPLOYEES
12/12	2,402,198	(1,677)	—	143,700
12/11	2,415,420	4,645	0.2%	141,100
12/10	2,312,882	5,533	0.2%	147,500
12/09	2,233,286	15,212	0.7%	144,200
12/08	2,991,809	6,385	0.2%	152,800
Annual Growth	(5.3%)	—	—	(1.5%)

2012 Year-End Financials

Return on assets: (-0.0%)
Return on ecuity: (-1.9%)
Long-term debt ($ mil.): —
No. of shares (mil.): —
Sales ($ mil): 55,810
Dividends
Yield: 2.1%
Payout: —
Market value ($ mil.): —

	STOCK PRICE ($) FY Close	P/E High/Low		PER SHARE ($) Earnings	Dividends	Book Value
12/12	17.32	—	—	(0.14)	0.38	7.06
12/11	10.99	215	81	0.37	0.89	7.04
12/10	16.52	187	119	0.44	0.27	6.48
12/09	17.60	79	8	1.32	0.07	6.71
12/08	9.80	200	27	0.84	2.64	6.37
Annual Growth	15.3%	—	—	—	(38.5%)	2.6%

BASF SE

The world is BASF's ester. BASF is the world's largest chemical company ahead of Dow and DuPont. It has more than 370 manufacturing facilities and does business worldwide through six business segments: plastics (polymers and polyurethanes) performance products (including dispersions and pigments adhesives and sealants personal care and pharma additives paper chemicals and lubricant additives) chemicals (plasticizers and solvents) oil and gas exploration and production (through subsidiary Wintershall AG) functional solutions (catalysts coatings and construction chemicals) and agricultural products (fungicides herbicides insecticides). BASF has divested most of its fertilizer operations.

BASF uses what it calls Verbund strategy throughout its facilities –plants are both customers and suppliers of each other. While the company still gets more than half its sales from Europe it continues to expand overseas particularly in Asia. It saw early on that the chemicals market in Asia would be the equal of that in Europe and wanted a healthy piece of the action. With a new unit based in the US it has begun positioning itself to become a leading supplier of battery materials for automotive battery applications –including cathode materials used to produce advanced lithium-ion batteries for electric vehicles.

In 2011 several events affected the growth of the company including the nuclear diaster in Japan Germany's decision to exit nuclear energy the suspension of crude oil in Libya and the debt crisis in Europe. Weak demand and an increase in the cost of raw materals also plagued BASF's two top divisions plastics and chemicals.

However BASF managed to surpass the record levels it set in 2010 in sales and earnings. After cutting costs and raising prices the company posted $98.7 billion in sales in 2011 up nearly 17% over the previous year as well as a net income of $8.3 billion up nearly 38%. But most of the increase was due to the sale of its 10% stake in K+S AG which began its exit from the fertilizer business. By 2012 BASF had sold most of its fertilizer operations including production plants in Antwerp Belgium and its share of the PEC-Rhin joint venture in France to Russia's EuroChem in a deal worth about $1.1 billion.

The company initiated several projects in 2011 including the startup of the first leg of the Nord Stream offshore gas pipeline that will eventually extend from Russia to Germany. Wintershall is involved in constructing the Nord Stream and South Stream gas pipelines to connect gas from Russia to Europe.

It also strengthened its presence in Asia that year by beginning the second expansion of its petrochemical site in Nanjing China with 50-50 joint venture partner Sinopec. And it founded BASF Hock Mining Chemical (China) Company with JiNing Hock Mining & Engineering Equipment Company. BASF holds a 75% stake in BASF Hock which makes cavity-filling products for the coal mining industry.

Much of the company's expansion has targeted the US market as well. In early 2012 the company halted its cultivation and development of genetically modified (GM) plants in Europe. Heavy resistance from European consumers farmers and politicians resulted in the company moving its plant science division from Limburgerhof Germany to Raleigh North Carolina. Some of its products for the European market included its Amflora starch potato for industrial use developed to be resistant to blight disease.

That year the company also strengthened its global crop protection operations by buying US-based Becker Underwood for $1.02 billion. The Iowa-based company provides biological seed treatment worldwide from 10 production sites. The BASF Crop Protection division plans to create Functional Crop Care a global business unit that will merge existing R&D and marketing activities in seed treatment crop protection and plant health with those of Becker Underwood.

BASF has also been collaborating with US-based Monsanto in the research and development of crops that have higher yields and better resistance to disease. For its GM products BASF focuses on markets in the Americas and Asia. It has not completely closed the door on Europe; it is still seeking authorizations to sell its potato products there.

In early 2012 BASF began a new global business unit Battery Materials to integrate its battery materials activities within an operating unit of New Jersey-based subsidiary BASF Catalysts. In moves to become a global leader in the supply of battery materials the company has made a series of acquisitions and licensing agreements to broaden its coverage of technology materials and components to serve cell and battery manufacturers worldwide. It has been licensed by the Argonne National Laboratory in Illinois to commercialize some of its advanced cathode materials used in hybrid and full-electric vehicles.

Adding to its battery operations again in 2012 BASF acquired Cleveland-based Novolyte Technologies from private equity group Arsenal Capital Partners for an undisclosed price. Novolyte manufactures electrolyte formulations for lithium-ion batteries and other specialty chemicals. It operates sites in the US and China. BASF will continue Novolyte's joint venture with Korean company Foosung which produces lithium hexafluorophospate a high-purity specialty salt used in producing lithium-iron battery electrolytes. The electrolytes are key components in lithium-ion batteries for the automotive consumer and industrial markets.

To expand its leadership position in polyurethane systems the company acquired US-based ITWC in 2012. ITWC manufactures cast elastomer polyurethane systems and polyester polyols in facilities in Iowa and California. The acquisition extends BASF's North American polyurethanes operations. Cast elastomers known for their abrasion resistance are used in several applications including industrial tires recreational wheels transportation gears and pulleys and sealants and adhesives.

The company's venture capital unit also poured $18.2 million into US-based renewable specialty chemicals company Allylix in 2012. Allylix owns a technology platform for developing terpenes and other chemicals for flavor and fragrance food ingredients cosmetics and other markets.

To expand its Nutrition and Health division in 2012 BASF acquired Equatec a UK-based supplier of omega-3 fatty acids for the pharmaceutical industry for an undisclosed price. Equatec which has a production site on the Isle of Lewis in Scotland will become part of BASF's Pharma Ingredients and Services unit.

BASF acquired inge watertechnologies a Germany-based provider of ultrafiltration membrane technology used to treat drinking water process water wastewater and seawater in 2011. The deal improves BASF's position in the water treatment industry and fits within its growth strategy for its chemicals and membrane filtration business.

After shelving previous efforts to exit the business in 2011 BASF formed a styrenics joint venture with INEOS called Styrolution. The venture produces styrene monomers polystyrene acrylonitrile butadiene styrene styrene-butadiene block copolymers and other styrene-based copolymers and copolymer blends. Styrolution is projected to have annual sales of $6.6 billion.

HISTORY

Originally named Badische Anilin & Soda-Fabrik BASF AG was founded in Mannheim Germany by jeweler Frederick Englehorn in 1861. Unable to find enough land for expansion in Mannheim BASF moved to nearby Ludwigshafen in 1865. The company was a pioneer in coal tar dyes and it developed a synthetic indigo in 1897. Its synthetic dyes rapidly replaced more expensive organic dyes.

BASF scientist Fritz Haber synthesized ammonia in 1909 giving BASF access to the market for nitrogenous fertilizer (1913). Haber received a Nobel Prize in 1918 but was later charged with war crimes for his work with poison gases. Managed by Carl Bosch another Nobel Prize winner BASF joined the I.G. Farben cartel with Bayer Hoechst and others in 1925 to create a German chemical colossus. Within the cartel BASF developed polystyrene PVC and magnetic tape. Part of the Nazi war machine I.G. Farben made synthetic rubber and used labor from the Auschwitz concentration camp during WWII.

After the war I.G. Farben was dismantled. BASF regained its independence in 1952 and rebuilt its war-ravaged factories. Strong postwar domestic demand for basic chemicals aided its recovery and in 1958 BASF launched a US joint venture with Dow Chemical. (BASF bought out Dow's half in 1978.) The company moved into petrochemicals and became a leading manufacturer of plastic and synthetic fiber.

In the US the company purchased Wyandotte Chemicals (1969) Chemetron (1979) and Inmont (1985) among others. To expand its natural gas business in Europe in 1991 the company signed deals with Russia's Gazprom and France's Elf Aquitaine. BASF bought Mobil's polystyrene-resin business and gained almost 10% of the US market.

BASF bought Imperial Chemical's polypropylene business in 1994 and became Europe's second-largest producer of the plastic. The next year the company paid $1.4 billion for the pharmaceutical arm of UK retailer Boots.

In 1997 BASF formed a joint venture with PetroFina (now TOTAL); in 2001 the venture opened the world's largest liquid steam cracker in Port Arthur Texas.

BASF made seven major acquisitions in 1998 including the complexing business of Ciba Specialty Chemicals. It also made six divestitures which included its European buildings-paints operations sold to Nobel N.V.

In 1999 the US fined the company $225 million for its part in a worldwide vitamin price-fixing cartel (in 2001 the European Commission fined it another $260 million bringing the total expected cost of fines out-of-court settlements and legal expenses to about $800 million). BASF also faced a class-action suit as a result of the scheme. That year the company moved into oil and gas exploration in Russia through a partnership agreement with Russia's Gazprom. BASF also merged its textile operations into Bayer and Hoechst's DyStar joint venture forming a $1 billion company that is a world-leading dye maker.

BASF completed its acquisition of Rohm and Haas' industrial coatings business in 2000 and bought the Cyanamid division (herbicides fungicides and pesticides) of American Home Products (now Wyeth). That year BASF expanded its superabsorbents business by paying $656 million for US-based Amcol International's Chemdal International unit.

Rather than attempt to compete in the rapidly consolidating pharmaceutical industry in 2001 BASF sold its midsized Knoll Pharmaceutical unit to Abbott Laboratories for about $6.9 billion. It also announced that it was closing 10 plants and cutting about 4000 jobs (4% of its workforce).

BASF sold its fibers unit in 2003 to focus on core chemical operations which it added to throughout the next few years. For example it bought a portion of Bayer's agchem businesses for $1.3 billion when European antitrust regulators mandated the Bayer divestment following its acquisition of Aventis CropScience. BASF also acquired Honeywell Specialty Materials' engineering plastics business in exchange for its fibers division. BASF's acquisition later that year of MSA's Callery Chemical Division strengthened BASF's line of inorganics which it planned to focus on providing to the pharmaceutical industry. Other acquisitions included Ticona's nylon 66 business and Sunoco's plasticizers unit.

That year also brought chairman Jurgen Hambrecht's announcement that the company would push forward with a restructuring of its North American business. The focus of the plan was to save more than $250 million over the next three years. Included among the steps were job cuts of approximately 1000 and the relocation of its North American headquarters (though remaining in New Jersey) in late 2004. (The move to smaller facilities was enabled by the sale of Knoll Pharmaceuticals in 2001 which reduced operations at the home base.)

BASF sold Basell its petrochemical JV with Shell in 2005. The two companies had announced in 2004 that they planned to exit the polyolefins business with the sale of Basell. The deal was finalized late the next year. Investment group Access Industries came in with the winning bid of about $5.7

billion. That company's name was changed to LyondellBasell after its 2007 acquisition of Lyondell Chemical Company.

The company opened two Verbund sites in Asia —one in Nanjing China and the other in Kuantan Malaysia. The Chinese site delivered its first product in early 2005 and began operating fully in the middle of that year. It's the centerpiece and primary operation of BASF-YPC a joint venture with Sinopec that was formed in 2000. BASF's goal is to achieve 70% of its sales in the region from local production by 2015; that figure hovered at about 60% in 2008.

The company also legally changed its name from BASF Aktiengesellschaft to BASF SE in 2008. The move made formal BASF's transition to a European company as opposed to one organized in Germany.

In 2009 BASF spent about $4 billion to acquire Swiss chemicals giant Ciba. Following a review phase of Ciba's operations and their fit within the structure of BASF the company began integrating Ciba into its performance products segment; this entailed the sale or closure of almost half of Ciba's 55 manufacturing facilities and the loss of about 3700 of its employees. As part of that strategy BASF SE sold the Regulatory and Safety Testing businesses of Ciba's Expert Services unit to London-based Intertek Group in 2010.

Also in 2010 BASF acquired specialty chemicals company Cognis GmbH in a $3.8 billion deal. Cognis gave BASF a boost in entering several high-margin business lines such as personal care and cosmetics.

EXECUTIVES

Deputy Chairman Supervisory Board, Michael Diekmann, age 59
President Performance Polymers, Wolfgang Hapke, age 58
Member Executive Board Crop Protection Coatings and Specialty Chemicals Research Division BASF Plant Science South America Regional Division, Stefan Marcinowski, age 61
Chairman Supervisory Board, Eggert Voscherau, age 70
Member Executive Board and CFO, Hans-Ulrich Engel, age 55
Chairman Executive Board, Kurt W. Bock, age 56
Member Executive Board Inorganics Petrochemicals Intermediates Chemicals Research and Engineering and BASF Future Business, Andreas Kreimeyer, age 59
SVP Investor Relations, Magdalena Moll
President Competence Center Specialty Chemicals Research, Harald Lauke, age 54
Head Corporate Media Relations, Michael Grabicki
President Market and Business Development Asia Pacific Hong Kong, Albert Heuser, age 58
President Polyurethanes, Wayne T. Smith
President South America, Alfred Hackenberger, age 62
President Care Chemicals Division, Gabriel Tanbourgi, age 58
Member Executive Board, Harald Schwager, age 54
President Performance Chemicals, Hans W. Reiners
Member Executive Board, Michael Heinz, age 49
Member Executive Board and and Industrial Relations Director, Margret Suckale, age 57
Deputy Chairman Supervisory Board, Robert Oswald, age 58
President Dispersions and Pigments, Markus Kramer
SVP Communications and Government Relations BASF Group, Elisabeth Schick, age 48
President Health and Safety Division, Ulrich von Deessen
President BASF Plant Science, Peter Eckes
President Asia Pacific, Saori Dubourg, age 42
Head of Research Chemicals, Friedrich Seitz, age 58
Vice Chairman Executive Board, Martin Brudermuller, age 52
President Paper Chemicals, Uwe Liebelt, age 47
VP Corporate Communications, Stefanie Wettberg
President Paper Chemicals, Fred Baumgartner
Independent Chairman of the Board, Vincenzo Pontolillo
President of the BASF Crop Protection division, Markus Heldt
Senior Vice President for Latin America, Eduardo Leduc
Deputy Chairman Supervisory Board, Michael Diekmann, age 59
Member Supervisory Board, Stephen K. Green, age 64
Member Supervisory Board, Max D. Kley, age 73
Member Supervisory Board, Michael Vassiliadis, age 49
Deputy Chairman Supervisory Board, Robert Oswald, age 58
Member Supervisory Board, Ralf-Gerd Bastian, age 57
Member Supervisory Board, Wolfgang Daniel, age 56
Member Supervisory Board, Prof Francois Diederich, age 59
Member Supervisory Board, Ralf Sikorski, age 52
Member Supervisory Board, Franz Fehrenbach
Member Supervisory Board, Denise Schellemans
Non-Executive Independent Director, Chiara Ruggieri
Non-Executive Director, Cosma Gelsomino
Non-Executive Independent Director, Lorenzo Idda
Auditors: KPMGDeutscheTreuhand-GesellschaftAG

LOCATIONS

HQ: BASF SE
Carl-Bosch-Strasse 38, Ludwigshafen D-67056
Phone: (49) 621 60 0 **Fax:** (49) 621 602525
Web: www.basf.com

2011 Sales by Region

	$ mil.	% of total
Europe		
Other countries	17	
Asia/Pacific	18	
Total	**0**	**100**

PRODUCTS/OPERATIONS

2011 Sales

	$ mil.	% of total
Performance Products	21	
Chemicals	18	
Oil & Gas	16	
Plastics	15	
Agricultural Solutions	6	
Total	**0**	**100**

Selected Products

Oil and Gas
- Crude oil and natural gas exploration
- Natural gas distribution and trading

Chemicals
- Inorganics
- Ammonia
- Formaldehyde
- Melamine
- Sulfuric acid
- Urea
- Intermediates
- Performance chemicals
- Water-based resins
- Petrochemicals
- Feedstocks
- Industrial gases
- Plasticizers
- Specialty chemicals

Plastics
- Engineering plastics
- Foams
- Polyamides and intermediates
- Polyurethanes
- Styrenics

Functional Solutions
- Catalysts
- Battery materials
- Chemical catalysts
- Coatings
  - Automotive coatings
  - Decorative paints
  - Industrial coatings
  - Pigments
- Construction chemicals

Performance Products
- Automotive fluids
- Care chemicals
- Paper chemicals
- Pharma ingredients
- Textile chemicals

Agricultural Solutions
- Crop protection
- Fungicides
- Herbicides
- Insecticides

COMPETITORS

3M
Air Products
Akzo Nobel
Albemarle
Ashland Inc.
BP
Bayer AG
Cargill
DSM
Dow Chemical
DuPont
Eastman Chemical
Evonik Degussa
Exxon Mobil
FMC
Formosa Plastics
Henkel
LANXESS
LG Group
Monsanto Company
Royal Dutch Shell
SABIC
TOTAL
Taminco

HISTORICAL FINANCIALS

Company Type: Public

Income Statement

FYE: December 31

	REVENUE ($ mil.)	NET INCOME ($ mil.)	NET PROFIT MARGIN	EMPLOYEES
12/12	103,768	6,430	6.2%	113,262
12/11	95,064	8,003	8.4%	111,141
12/10	85,485	6,098	7.1%	109,140
12/09	73,026	2,031	2.8%	104,779
12/08	87,106	4,071	4.7%	96,924
Annual Growth	4.5%	12.1%	—	4.0%

2012 Year-End Financials

Debt ratio: 8.6%
Return on equity: 19.9%
Cash ($ mil.): 2,342
Current ratio: 1.66
Long-term debt ($ mil.): —
No. of shares (mil.): 918
Dividends
Yield: 2.5%
Payout: —
Market value ($ mil.): 87,255

	STOCK PRICE ($) FY Close	P/E High/Low	PER SHARE ($) Earnings		
			Earnings	Dividends	Book Value
12/12	95.00	32 20	7.00	2.41	35.27
12/11	69.73	29 15	8.70	0.00	33.99
12/10	79.96	31 16	6.64	1.62	31.19
12/09	62.10	89 30	2.22	1.89	27.41
12/08	39.31	106 14	4.38	2.38	26.75
Annual Growth	24.7%	— —	12.5%	0.3%	7.2%

Bayer AG

You could get a headache trying to name all of Bayer's products. The company which created aspirin in 1897 makes pharmaceuticals OTC drugs and animal health care products through Bayer

HealthCare plastics and high-performance specialty materials via Bayer MaterialScience and crop protection and home garden care items through Bayer CropScience. Aside from Bayer Aspirin the company's best-known consumer brands include Aleve Alka-Seltzer and One-A-Day vitamins. Its top selling pharmaceuticals include multiple sclerosis treatment Betaseron and birth control pill YAZ. Also known as Bayer Group the firm has some 300 operating subsidiaries worldwide; it operates in the US through Bayer Corporation.

The majority of Bayer's sales come from European countries (roughly 40% of revenues) and North America (about 25% of sales) and most of the company's core manufacturing facilities are in Germany and the US. Bayer markets over 5000 products through a global sales and distribution network. Offerings from its largest division the HealthCare segment are distributed primarily through wholesalers and pharmacy chains while MaterialScience and CropScience products are sold through wholesalers and regional distributors.

Bayer is growing all three of its core businesses by enhancing its strong positions in key markets as well as by expanding into emerging geographic areas and investing in innovative technologies. Within its HealthCare division which accounts for just about half of its annual sales the company's growth strategy includes making targeted acquisitions entering into licensing and development deals with other pharmaceutical companies and performing in-house research and development. To counteract the effect of weakened sales in Europe and North America the HealthCare Pharmaceuticals segment is working to expand drug marketing efforts in China Brazil Mexico Russia and other high-growth markets. In 2010 the HealthCare segment also opened a new R&D center in China.

Acquisitions in the health arena include US subsidiary MEDRAD's 2011 purchase of Pathway Medical Technologies to expand its arterial disease therapies as well as the Animal Health division's purchase of New Zealand firm Bomac Group in 2010 to widen its drug offerings for agricultural animals. The company has high hopes for candidates in its internal R&D pipeline such as its newly introduced blood thinner Xarelto (which gained FDA approval in 2011) and several new women's health offerings. It has also entered into numerous collaboration agreements to boost its R&D programs in recent years including a partnership with Genzyme to co-develop and promote multiple sclerosis drugs and one with Onyx Pharmaceuticals to work on cancer medicines.

Bayer's growth measures in its two other core segments MaterialScience and CropScience include the construction of new manufacturing and production facilities in the US Europe and Asia. The MaterialScience unit expanded its distribution operations in Russia in 2011 through a joint venture with German firm ALBIS Group. The CropScience unit acquired Hornbeck Seed a maker of plant breeding products in 2011 and AgraQuest a California-based supplier of biological pest management solutions for $425 million in 2012. Bayer places a significant amount of focus on R&D efforts within its MaterialScience and CropScience divisions to be able to provide a broad range of crop solutions based on seeds traits chemical crop protection and biological pest and disease control.

All of the company's growth measures paid off when Bayer's sales rose in 2010 and 2011. The company also improved its net income figures in 2011; however declining income levels over the previous few years —caused by economic difficulties competitive conditions and other factors —have led Bayer to conduct some cost-control and restructuring measures. Such measures also include efforts to integrate a number of purchases made during a period of heavy acquisitive growth from 2005 through 2008.

After instituting some production expense cutbacks within its MaterialScience division in 2009 the unit returned to expected growth levels in 2010. However increased generic competition for branded HealthCare and CropScience products including the YAZ birth control pills and certain herbicides caused lower-than-expected results within those divisions in 2010. Additional restructuring efforts to resolve the troubles include 2011 measures to streamline and consolidate some of the Bayer HealthCare facilities especially in Germany and the US. In addition the firm has divested some noncore CropScience product lines.

HISTORY

Friedrich Bayer founded Bayer in Germany in 1863 to make synthetic dyes. Research led to such discoveries as Antinonin (synthetic pesticide 1892) aspirin (1897) and synthetic rubber (1915).

Under Carl Duisberg Bayer allegedly made the first poison gas used by Germany in WWI. During the war the US seized Bayer's US operations and trademark rights and sold them to Sterling Drug.

In 1925 Bayer BASF Hoechst and other German chemical concerns merged to form I.G. Farben Trust. Their photography businesses combined as Agfa also joined the trust. Between wars Bayer developed polyurethanes and the first sulfa drug Prontosil (1935).

During WWII the trust took over chemical plants of Nazi-occupied countries used slave labor and helped make Zyklon B gas used to kill people at Auschwitz. At war's end Bayer lost its 50% of Winthrop Laboratories (US) and Bayer of Canada (to Sterling Drug). The 1945 Potsdam Agreement called for the breakup of I.G. Farben and Bayer AG emerged in 1951 as an independent company with many of its original operations including Agfa.

After rebuilding in West Germany Bayer AG and Monsanto formed a joint venture (Mobay 1954); Bayer AG later bought Monsanto's share (1967). In the 1960s the company offered more dyes plastics and polyurethanes and added factories worldwide. Agfa merged with Gevaert (photography Belgium) in 1964; Bayer AG retained 60%. Over the next 25 years it acquired Miles Labs (Alka-Seltzer US 1978) the rest of Agfa-Gevaert (1981) Compugraphic (electronic imaging US 1989) and Nova's Polysar (rubber Canada 1990).

Bayer AG integrated its US holdings under the name Miles in 1992 (renamed Bayer Corporation in 1995). The next year it introduced its first genetically engineered product Kogenate hemophilia treatment. It regained US rights to the Bayer brand and logo in 1994 by paying SmithKline Beecham $1 billion for the North American business of Sterling Winthrop.

Bayer AG formed a joint venture with Swiss rival Roche Holding in 1996 to market over-the-counter Roche drugs in the US. In 1997 Bayer Baxter International Rhone-Poulenc Rorer and Green Cross agreed to a $670 million settlement over blood products that infected thousands of hemophiliacs with HIV during the 1980s.

In 1998 the company sold the food-ingredients arm of its Haarmann & Reimer unit to Tate & Lyle. Bayer bought US-based Chiron's diagnostics operations for $1.1 billion created a North American joint venture with Crompton & Knowles' seed-treatment unit and formed a research alliance with Millennium Pharmaceuticals. The firm spun off all but 30% of its photographic and electronic prepress business as Agfa-Gevaert (it plans to sell its remaining stake to Goldman Sachs).

Bayer Hoechst and BASF merged their textile activities in 1999 to form the world's largest dye-making company. The next year Bayer boosted its polyurethane business by paying $2.5 billion for US-based Lyondell Chemical's polyols unit. The company also formed a joint venture with Exelixis Pharmaceuticals to develop gene-based insecticides and announced it would develop an anti-impotence drug to rival Pfizer's Viagra (which drug launched in 2003 as Levitra).

In 2001 Bayer agreed to invest as much as $874 million on two drug-development deals with US genomics company CuraGen (Bayer will take a 7% stake).

The company's summer was marred by the one-two punch of sharply lower profits and the recall of Baycol (known as Lipobay in Europe) its popular cholesterol-lowering drug that has been linked to more than 100 deaths worldwide. Days after the recall Bayer announced that it would consider a pharmaceuticals deal in which its drug unit was the junior partner (possible partners included Merck & Co. Novartis Roche Eli Lilly Aventis and Sanofi-Synthelabo —the last two of which now form Sanofi-Aventis). Bayer announced in September 2001 that it was separating its health care and agrochemical operations from the chemicals and polymers businesses (in December it announced that it would do the same thing with the two units resulting in four independent operating units) but that it was keeping its pharmaceuticals business. Bayer did indicate an interest in forming a majority-owned joint venture preferably with a European partner for the pharmaceutical unit. The company finally decided against that move in late 2003 after failing to make a deal advantageous enough.

In a bid to bolster its agrochemical business Bayer acquired Aventis CropScience in 2002 for about $5 billion plus $2 billion in debt. The company was combined with Bayer Crop Protection to form Bayer CropScience.

That change precipitated a series of restructurings and realignments of Bayer's divisions. The company condensed seven units to four so that its health care agrochemical chemical and polymer operations would be able to operate with greater autonomy from one another. The successive restructurings were meant to pave the way for the sale of individual operations —such as its household insecticide business which Bayer sold to S.C. Johnson & Son in October 2002. In mid-2003 the company along with partner GlaxoSmithKline launched Levitra its rival to Pfizer's $1 billion-earning Viagra.

Late in 2003 Bayer announced that it planned to separate the chemicals business (combined with parts of Bayer MaterialScience) and spin it off to Bayer shareholders. The separation of its former chemicals subgroup was completed in 2005 when Bayer spun off the unit as a publicly traded company called LANXESS. Afterward Bayer began to concentrate on three core businesses: HealthCare CropScience and MaterialScience.

The company's OTC drugs unit got much larger in 2005 when Bayer bought Roche's consumer health unit for nearly $3 billion. The deal created one of the world's top three non-prescription drugs companies combining Bayer's aspirin Alka-Seltzer and Midol brands with Roche's Aleve pain relievers among others.

In 2006 Bayer acquired Schering AG for about $20 billion after a hostile bidding war with Merck. Bayer purchased Schering to strengthen its presence in the specialty pharmaceuticals business especially women's health. Schering AG was merged with Bayer's existing prescription drug business to create Bayer Schering Pharma AG (which was renamed Bayer Pharma AGand began operating as Bayer HealthCare Pharmaceuticals in 2011).

The Consumer Care unit acquired the Citracal line of calcium supplements in 2007 from Mission Pharmacal and it purchased OTC cough and cold remedies from Topsun Science and Technology for

$170 million to increase the group's standing in China in 2008. It also picked up the OTC business of Sagmel which it added to its Eastern European operations for some $410 million. The moves catapulted the company into the top five in the region.

Also in 2008 the HealthCare division grew again through equipment firm MEDRAD's acquisition of medical device maker Possis Medical for $360 million and Bayer HealthCare Pharmaceutical's purchase of biotech development firm DIREVO for $300 million. In the US Bayer netted itself two prescription dermatology product lines from SkinMedica (Desonate for dermatitis and NeoBenz for acne). The CropScience unit purchased AgroGreen's crop protection business that year as well.

In 2009 the company got a new CEO when Marijn Dekkers formerly head of Thermo Fisher Scientific was appointed to lead Bayer.

The MaterialScience division opened two new manufacturing plants for polyurethane ingredients in China in 2009 and 2010 while the CropScience division expanded its German and US production facilities in 2010. The unit also picked up US-based biotech company Athenix for which it paid about $365 million in 2009.

The MaterialScience unit also grew through the purchase of Artificial Muscle a California-based maker of electroactive polymers for consumer electronic applications in 2010.

EXECUTIVES

Chairman Board of Management, Marijn E. Dekkers, age 56
Chairman Supervisory Board, Manfred Schneider, age 75
Member Management Board Innovation Technology and Environment and Asia/Pacific, Wolfgang Plischke, age 62, $659,411 total compensation
Member Board of Management Bayer CropScience, Achim Noack, age 54
CEO Bayer CropScience, Sandra E. Peterson, age 55
Member Management Board Strategy and Human Resources and Americas Africa and Middle East, Richard Pott, age 60, $659,411 total compensation
President and CEO Bayer Corporation and Bayer MaterialScience LLC, Gregory S. (Greg) Babe, age 56
Deputy Chairman Supervisory Board, Thomas de Win, age 55
CEO Bayer MaterialScience, Patrick W. Thomas, age 56
CFO and Member Board of Management, Werner Baumann, age 51
COO CropScience, Lykele van der Broek, age 60
Head Investor Relations, Alexander Rosar
Manager Law Patents and Insurance, Roland Hartwig, age 59
Executive Committee Member Bayer HealthCare; Head Pharmaceuticals Division, Andreas Fibig, age 51
Chairman Bayer Business Services, Daniel Hartert
Head Communications, Michael Schade
Head Corporate Policy and Media Relations, Michael Preuss
Head Media Relations, Gunter Forneck
CEO Bayer HealthCare, Jorg Reinhardt, age 57
Managing Director Bayer Technology Services, Dirk Van Meirvenne, age 50
Head Public Policy/Environment, Dirk Frenzel
Member Supervisory Board, Clemens A. H. Borsig, age 64
Member Supervisory Board, Paul Achleitner, age 57
Member Supervisory Board, Ekkehard D. Schulz, age 72
Member Supervisory Board, Jurgen Weber, age 71
Member Supervisory Board, Klaus Sturany, age 67
Member Supervisory Board, Klaus Kleinfeld, age 55
Member Supervisory Board, Helmut Panke, age 67
Member Supervisory Board, Hubertus Schmoldt, age 69
Member Supervisory Board, Ernst-Ludwig Winnacker, age 72
Member Supervisory Board, Prof Hans-Olaf Henkel, age 73
Member Supervisory Board, Petra Kronen, age 49
Deputy Chairman Supervisory Board, Thomas de Win, age 55
Member Supervisory Board, Thomas Fischer, age 58
Member Supervisory Board, Willy Beuman, age 56
Member Supervisory Board, Reiner Hoffman, age 57
Member Supervisory Board, Peter Hausmann, age 60
Member Supervisory Board, Oliver Zuhlke, age 44
Member Supervisory Board, Andre Aich, age 43
Member Supervisory Board, Roswitha Su?elbeck, age 58
Auditors: PricewaterhouseCoopersAG

LOCATIONS

HQ: Bayer AG
Kaiser-Wilhelm Allee, Leverkusen D-51368
Phone: (49) 214 30 1 **Fax:** (49) 214 30 71985
Web: www.bayer.com

2010 Sales

	$ mil.	% of total
Europe	39	
Asia/Pacific	21	
Total	0	100

PRODUCTS/OPERATIONS

2010 Sales

	$ mil.	% of total
Health Care		
Consumer Health	17	
CropScience		
Environmental Science Bioscience	4	
Total	0	100

Selected Operations and Products

HealthCare
- Animal health products
- Diabetes care products
- Consumer care products (over-the-counter drugs)
- Pharmaceuticals

MaterialScience
- Coatings
- Colorants
- Plastics
- Polyurethanes

CropScience
- BioScience (biotechnology and seeds)
- Crop protection (insecticides and herbicides)
- Environmental science (lawn care and non-agricultural pesticides)

Selected Brands

HealthCare
- Adalat (cardiovascular medication)
- Advantage (animal health)
- Aleve/Flanax (analgesic)
- Alka-Seltzer (analgesic and antacid)
- Aspirin (analgesic)
- Aspirin Cardio (cardiovascular)
- Avalox/Avelox (antibiotic)
- Bepanthen/Bepanthol (skin care treatment)
- Betaferon/Betaseron (multiple sclerosis medication)
- Baytril (animal health infections)
- Breeze/Contour (diabetes care glucose meters)
- Canesten (antifungal)
- Cipro/Ciprobay (antibiotic)
- Glucobay (diabetes treatment)
- Iopamiron (diagnostic imaging)
- Kogenate (hematology/cardiology)
- Levitra (impotence drug)
- Magnevist (diagnostic imaging)
- Mirena (contraceptive)
- Nexavar (oncology)
- One-A-Day (vitamins)
- Supradyn (multivitamin)
- Ultravist (diagnostic imaging)
- Yasmin/Yasminelle/YAZ (contraceptive)

MaterialScience
- Baydur/Bayflex/Bayblend (polyurethane)
- Desmodur/Desmophen (isocyanates polyesters and polyols for polyurethanes)
- Makrolon (polycarbonate resin)

CropScience
- Betanal (herbicides)
- Confidor/Gaucho/Admire/Merit (insecticides/seed treatment)
- Decis (insecticides)
- Flint/Stratego/Sphere/Nativo (fungicides)
- Folicur/Raxil (fungicides/seed treatment)
- Poncho (seed treatment)
- Proline (fungicides)
- Puma (herbicides)

COMPETITORS

3M
Abbott Labs
Actavis Inc.
Akzo Nobel
AstraZeneca
BASF SE
Baxter International
Boehringer Ingelheim
Boston Scientific
Bristol-Myers Squibb
Celanese
DSM
Dow Chemical
DuPont
Eastman Chemical
Eli Lilly
Evonik Degussa
GE Healthcare
GlaxoSmithKline
Johnson & Johnson
Merck
Merck KGaA
Mitsubishi Chemical Holdings
Monsanto Company
Novartis
Pfizer
Ranbaxy Laboratories
Rhodia
Roche Holding
Sanofi
Syngenta
Teva

HISTORICAL FINANCIALS

Company Type: Public

Income Statement

FYE: December 31

	REVENUE ($ mil.)	NET INCOME ($ mil.)	NET PROFIT MARGIN	EMPLOYEES
12/12	52,405	3,223	6.2%	110,500
12/11	47,247	3,194	6.8%	111,800
12/10	46,960	1,741	3.7%	111,400
12/09	44,899	1,957	4.4%	108,400
12/08	46,022	2,410	5.2%	108,600
Annual Growth	3.3%	7.5%	—	0.4%

2012 Year-End Financials

Debt ratio: 5.6%
Return on equity: 12.9%
Cash ($ mil.): 2,234
Current ratio: 1.45
Long-term debt ($ mil.): —
No. of shares (mil.): 826
Dividends
Yield: 1.6%
Payout: 40.0%
Market value ($ mil.): 79,321

	STOCK PRICE ($) FY Close	P/E High/Low	PER SHARE ($) Earnings	Dividends	Book Value
12/12	95.92	57 33	3.90	1.56	29.44
12/11	63.80	55 29	3.87	3.06	30.05
12/10	73.36	99 56	2.10	1.34	30.48
12/09	79.80	103 47	2.45	1.37	32.92
12/08	59.40	89 37	3.10	1.63	29.75
Annual Growth	12.7%	— —	5.9%	(1.2%)	(0.3%)

Bayerische Landesbank (Germany)

Bayerische Landesbank (BayernLB) acts as the principal bank to the state of Bavaria and as the central clearing house for the 75 Bavarian sparkassen (savings banks). Also serving corporations national and local governments financial institutions and real estate firms the bank offers a variety of services including financing security underwriting and trading and risk management. It provides retail and private banking services for individuals through its Internet bank Deutsche Kreditbank which also targets infrastructure customers in eastern Europe. BayernLB is recovering after losing billions in the global economic crisis.

Gerd Hausler was named BayernLB's CEO in 2010. He succeeded Stefan Ermisch who served on an interim basis for four months following the resignation of Michael Kemmer. Hausler was most recently a manager and board member of financial investment firm RHJ International.

Michael Kemmer resigned after the company announced it would write off its investment in Austria's Hypo Alpe-Adria-Bank which was nationalized in late 2009 to prevent collapse. BayernLB had acquired a majority stake in the bank in 2007 as part of an ill-timed international expansion of its retail banking operations.

To regain a stable footing the bank has restructured to cut operating costs and sold risk assets and noncore units. It is also refocusing on its core financing operations in Bavarian and other German markets especially for midsized companies and large corporations. In 2010 it sold its 75%-owned Landesbank Saar subsidiary which operates in the German state of Saarland and in France. That year BayenLB also ended merger talks with WestLB another central bank in recovery. The combined entity would've become Germany's third-largest bank. However BayenLB's management didn't find that deal presented good enough advantages.

BayernLB is jointly owned by the state of Bavaria (94%) and the Association of Bavarian Savings Banks.

HISTORY

Bayerische Landesbank Girozentrale (the Bavarian regional bank clearinghouse) was formed by the government in 1972 from the merger of Bayerische Landesbodenkreditanstalt (the state authority for funding projects in Bavaria formed 1884) and Bayerische Gemeindebank (Girozentrale) Offentliche Bankanstalt (the central institution for local public authorities established 1914).

Amid the oil crisis of the 1970s the bank known as BayernLB joined with Commerzbank Dresdner Bank and other West German banks in a consortium to buy from Deutsche Bank a 25% stake in Daimler-Benz; then-Chancellor Helmut Schmidt wished to keep the automaker out of Iranian hands.

BayernLB began expanding outside Germany in the late 1970s; it opened an office in New York City by 1981. Three years later the bank joined with Westdeutsche Landesbank Commerzbank Deutsche Bank and Dresdner Bank to create the venture capital firm Deutsche Wagnisfinanzierung.

During the mid-1980s talk of merging West Germany's fragmented system of 11 Landesbanken and savings banks (a byproduct of post-WWII banking reforms) led BayernLB and Landesbank Stuttgart to consider merging to form a southern Landesbank. However by 1989 the bank had rallied against plans by the centralized Deutscher Sparkassen- und Giroverband to consolidate the operations of the various Landesbanken. That year it held indecisive merger talks with Landesbank Rheinland-Palatine.

Later the bank eschewed mergers and began looking eastward. In 1991 it acquired Czech bank Interbanka. BayernLB first sought out the Hungarian privatization authority in 1992 and by 1994 BayernLB purchased a one-quarter stake in the then-privatizing Hungarian Foreign Trade Bank (MKB; 75%-owned by 1999). The bank also looked to Asia opening an offshore banking branch in Malaysia in 1995. The bank gained assets closer to home by taking a 31% stake in the Austrian Bank fur Arbeit und Wirtschaft (Bawag; increased to nearly half by 1999).

BayernLB opened another offshore branch in Thailand in 1996 but two years later began to see negative consequences to its expansion in the East when the Asian currency crisis hit walloping the bank's normally stellar credit rating.

In 2000 the European Commission said it would take action against the German government over the role of the Landesbanken claiming a breach of antitrust laws. The legal threat laid the groundwork for strategic cooperation —and even talks of a merger –between BayernLB and Landesbank Hessen-Thuringen. Bavaria's government also pressured BayernLB raiding the bank in search of evidence related to alleged embezzlement in Singapore.

In 2001 BayernLB after much European Union antitrust scrutiny announced a partial privatization plan. The next year BayernLB changed its legal name from Bayerische Landesbank Girozentrale to simply Bayerische Landesbank.

When the global economy fell into crisis in 2008 BayernLB was the first German bank to take money from the country's bailout program. It received E4.5 billion ($6.9 billion) from the German government's E80 billion rescue fund and raised another E1 billion from two state-backed shareholders. The bank which has branches in Asia North America and other parts of Europe to complement its offices in Germany restructured in order to focus on its core European markets and cut approximately 30% of its workforce.

EXECUTIVES

CEO, Gerd Hausler, age 62
COO and CFO, Stephan Winkelmeier, age 45
Member Board of Management Head Corporate & Mittelstand, Michael Bucker, age 51
Chief Risk Officer, Marcus Kramer, age 49
Deputy CEO, Edgar Zoller, age 56
Member Management Board Markets, Nils Niermann, age 44
Chairman, Michael Schneider
Deputy Chairman, Walter Strohmaier
Auditors: KPMGDeutscheTreuhand-GesellschaftAG

LOCATIONS

HQ: Bayerische Landesbank (Germany)
Brienner Strasse 18, Munich D-80333
Phone: (49) 89 21 71 01 **Fax:** (49) 89 21 71 2 35 79
Web: www.bayernlb.de

PRODUCTS/OPERATIONS

Selected Subsidiaries

Banque LBLux S.A. (Luxembourg)
BayTech Venture Capital Beratungs GmbH
Bayern Consult Unternehmensberatung GmbH
Bayernimmo KG
BayernLB Private Equity
BayernInvest Luxembourg S.A.
Deutsche Kreditbank AG
MKB Bank Zrt (Hungary)

COMPETITORS

Aareal Bank
Commerzbank
DZ BANK
Deutsche Bank
Deutsche Postbank
KfW
Landesbank Baden-Wurttemberg
Landesbank Berlin
UniCredit Bank AG
WGZ BANK
WestLB
Wustenrot & Wurttembergische

HISTORICAL FINANCIALS

Company Type: Public

Income Statement

FYE: December 31

	ASSETS ($ mil.)	NET INCOME ($ mil.)	INCOME AS % OF ASSETS	EMPLOYEES
12/12	378,046	1,004	0.3%	9,932
12/11	399,862	134	0.0%	10,893
12/10	423,399	849	0.2%	10,853
12/09	488,090	(3,772)	—	11,821
12/08	589,232	(7,100)	—	20,285
Annual Growth	(10.5%)	—	—	(16.4%)

2012 Year-End Financials

Return on assets: 0.2%
Return on equity: 5.2%
Long-term debt ($ mil.): —
No. of shares (mil.): —
Sales ($ mil): 15,292
Dividends
Yield: —
Payout: —
Market value ($ mil.): —

Bayerische Motoren Werke AG

Bayerische Motoren Werke better known as BMW is among the top 10 automakers in the world. It manufactures premium brand cars and off-road vehicles under the BMW MINI and Rolls-Royce names as well as motorcycles under the BMW and Husqvarna names. Spare parts and accessories are also offered. Its vehicles and products are sold worldwide through company branches independent dealers subsidiaries and importers. BMW's financial services segment offers car leasing and credit financing for both retail and corporate fleet customers; dealer financing; insurance; and deposit banking.

Geographic Reach

BMW operates in more than 150 countries. It generates about half of its revenue in Europe while the remainder is well dispersed among the Americas (mainly the US) China and other parts of the world.

Operations

To support global markets BMW has 17 production facilities in Austria Germany the UK the US China and South Africa. It also has about 10 R&D centers in Austria Germany the US Japan and China. Some assembly is undertaken with external partners in emerging markets including India Malaysia Thailand and Russia.

Sales and Marketing

The company has a global sales network that spans more than 140 countries. BMW and MINI brand products are sold in Germany through the company's own branches and independent authorized dealers. Sales outside of Germany are carried out mainly by subsidiaries and in certain markets by independent importers. Rolls-Royce brand vehicles are sold in the US by a subsidiary and elsewhere by dealers. At year end 2012 BMW's car sales network was made up of 3300 BMW 1550 MINI and 110 Rolls-Royce dealerships worldwide.

Financial Performance

Fiscal 2012 was the most successful year in BMW's history in terms of financial performance as the company posted strong growth in sales volumes revenues and earnings for the year. The number of BMW MINI and Rolls-Royce vehicles delivered to customers was up about 11% over fiscal 2011 (itself previously a record year) and all three brands set new records thanks in part to increased demand for passenger vehicles in Asia and the Americas. Group revenues in 2012 grew by about 12% while group profit rose by some 4% despite greater investments in green and other technologies and higher personnel costs. Growth in its motorcycle and financial services segments also contributed to positive sales performance. BMW spent 2011 and 2010 getting the company back on track following the global economic crisis in 2008 and 2009.

Strategy

BMW is in the midst of what it call its Number ONE strategy an initiative begun in 2007 that continues today to boost profitability and enable expansion of its global production and sales networks. From 2007 to 2012 the company expanded from 23 production facilities to 29. More recent manufacturing plants have been opened in China through its BMW Brilliance joint venture with Brilliance China Automotive. BMW's goal is to sell more than two million BMW MINI and Rolls-Royce vehicles by 2016 –up from the 1.85 million cars it sold in fiscal 2012.

From an environmental perspective BMW's strategy is to invest in and develop technologies that support making its vehicle fleet more fuel efficient and reducing carbon dioxide emissions by 25% between 2008 and 2020. To this end it is increasing R&D expenditures in part to support continued development of a new fuel efficient engine family called Efficient Dynamics and improvement of a hybrid technology called ActiveHybrid. New vehicle models like the pure electric BMWi family are expected to launch in late 2013.

Additionally BMW looks for opportunities to partner with companies that are pushing developments in sustainable mobility. In early 2013 for instance BMW signed an agreement with one of the top automakers in the world Toyota to collaborate on fuel cells and lightweight construction technologies. BMW and Toyota also conduct joint research on lithium-air batteries the next generation of lithium-ion technology.

In other areas of its business BMW is dealing with contracting motorcycle markets worldwide and is therefore changing strategic course. In early 2013 it announced plans to sell its Husqvarna motorcycle business to Austrian company Pierer Industrie AG in order to focus in the future exclusively on the BMW motorcycle brand.

Ownership

Stefan Quandt and sister Susanne Klatten children of the late Herbert Quandt and both members of BMW's supervisory board together hold about a 28% stake in the company. Their mother Johanna Quandt also holds a certain share of voting rights. They are part of one of Germany's richest family dynasties.

HISTORY

BMW's logo speaks to its origin: a propeller in blue and white the colors of Bavaria. In 1913 Karl Rapp opened an aircraft-engine design shop near Munich. He named it Bayerische Motoren Werke (BMW) in 1917. The end of WWI brought German aircraft production to a halt and BMW shifted to making railway brakes until the 1930s. BMW debuted its first motorcycle the R32 in 1923 and the company began making automobiles in 1928 after buying small-car company Fahrzeugwerke Eisenach.

In 1933 BMW launched a line of larger cars. The company built aircraft engines for Hitler's Luftwaffe in the 1930s and stopped all auto and motorcycle production in 1941. BMW chief Josef Popp resisted and was ousted. Under the Nazis the company operated in occupied countries built rockets and developed the world's first production jet engine.

With its factories dismantled after WWII BMW survived by making kitchen and garden equipment. In 1948 it introduced a one-cylinder motorcycle which sold well as cheap transportation in postwar Germany. BMW autos in the 1950s were large and expensive and sold poorly. When motorcycle sales dropped the company escaped demise in the mid-1950s by launching the Isetta a seven-foot three-wheeled "bubble car."

Herbert Quandt saved the enterprise in 1959 by buying control for $1 million. Quandt's BMW focused on sports sedans and released the first of the "New Range" of BMWs in 1961. Success of the niche enabled BMW to buy automaker Hans Glas in 1966.

In the 1970s BMW's European exports soared and the company set up a distribution subsidiary in the US. The company also produced larger cars that put BMW on par with Mercedes-Benz.

Rapid export growth in the US Asia and Australia continued in the 1980s but Japanese bikes and poor demand hurt motorcycle sales. The launch of the company's luxury vehicles in 1986 heated up the BMW-Mercedes rivalry. US sales peaked that year and fell 45% by 1991. However in 1992 BMW outsold Mercedes in Europe for the first time and became the first European carmaker to operate a US plant since Volkswagen pulled out in 1988.

BMW teamed with the UK's Rolls-Royce aerospace firm in 1990 to make jet engines for planes that included executive business-travel jets such as the Gulfstream V.

The company bought UK carmaker Rover from British Aerospace and Honda in 1994 and introduced a cheaper vehicle the four-wheel-drive Discovery. It launched Highlander Land Rover in 1996 to meet a growing demand for 4x4 utility vehicles.

BMW offered to buy the luxury Rolls-Royce auto unit (including the Bentley) from UK-based Vickers in 1998 but lost out when Volkswagen (VW) countered with a higher offer. The company fared better however when aircraft engine maker Rolls-Royce sold the Rolls-Royce auto brand name and logo to BMW for $66 million. (VW got to use the name until 2003.) Also in 1998 BMW along with other German companies was hit by a class-action lawsuit brought by Holocaust survivors seeking compensation for their work as slave laborers during WWII. (BMW participated in a settlement agreement late the following year.)

In mid-1998 BMW began cutting jobs at its money-losing Rover unit. As Rover's plants continued their downward trend in 1999 BMW's board forced out chairman Bernd Pischetsrieder who spearheaded the Rover acquisition in 1994. The UK later pledged to help pay for renovations at Rover's Longbridge plant to save about 14000 jobs and prevent it from moving operations to Hungary.

The company in 2000 sold its Land Rover SUV operations to Ford in a deal worth about $2.7 billion. Also that year BMW handed over its Rover Cars operations and MG brand to the Phoenix Consortium a UK-based group led by former Rover CEO John Towers.

In 2001 BMW launched its MINI brand in the UK; other European markets soon followed. BMW brought the MINI Cooper to US shores in 2002. The following year BMW took control of the Rolls-Royce brand from Volkswagen and began making Rolls-Royce Phantoms in Goodwood in the south of England.

Despite selling the operations of Rover in 2000 BMW still retained the rights to the brand. In 2006 BMW agreed to sell the Rover brand to an unidentified buyer at an undisclosed price although Dow Jones Newswires reported the buyer was Shanghai Automotive Industry Corp. and the price was nearly $21 million. That deal however was derailed a month later when Ford Motor said it would exercise its right of first refusal agreement with BMW and take control of the brand for about $11 million.

Like its automotive OEM brethren BMW's activities were negatively impacted by the global recession. In 2009 and 2008 it saw consumer spending dip; more than 10% fewer BMW MINI and Rolls-Royce cars were sold than in 2008. BMW's automotive segment suffered an operating loss. Although international motorcycle demand eroded by about one-third BMW fared relatively better with volumes slumping by 14% from 2008. BMW's financial services operation edged up slightly despite weak new used and leased business as well as bad debt accounts. Year-over-year group sales tumbled about 5% in 2009 and earnings by more than 35%. BMW managed to generate a positive cash flow from operating activities albeit lower than 2008's level.

As a result of the economic crash BMW shifted direction in several areas. It trimmed vehicle production by more than 10% to align with lower demand reduced its workforce and cut back on R&D by some 8% and capital investments by 20%.

Even with the realignment and reductions BMW remained true to its green initiatives having rolled out 49 models in 2009 that meet the EU5 emissions standard. Its BMW 330d with BluePerformance technology was hailed as the first car on the market to comply with the EU6 emission standard effective in 2014. In 2009 BMW added numerous new car models including the MINI E which was launched on a trial basis giving BMW experience in delivering lithium-ion technology. Rolls-Royce got the Ghost a coupe version of the Phantom. The company made way for an inorganic sand core technology; the light alloy foundry method applies mineral binders that tout virtually no smell or emissions along with lower maintenance expenses and stronger yield.

As the company began recovering from the economic crisis BMW's joint venture with SGL Group gained momentum in 2010. SGL Automotive began investing $100 million to open a carbon fiber manufacturing plant in Washington's Moses Lake with production of lightweight carbon fiber reinforced plastics (CFRP) dedicated to BMW's Megacity Vehicle line. BMW announced in late 2010 that it would invested approximately ?530 million (more than $750 million) to launch the new Megacity Vehicle in 2013. Simultaneously BMW is working with SB Limotive a JV between Bosch and Samsung SDI to source the battery cells that will power the Megacity. The new facility and supply agreement are a strategic step in BMW's move to commercialize manufacture of CFRPs for future cars.

EXECUTIVES

Deputy Chairman Supervisory Board, Manfred Schoch, $148,852 total compensation

Chairman Supervisory Board, Joachim Milberg, age 70, $223,278 total compensation

Deputy Chairman Supervisory Board, Karl-Ludwig Kley, age 62

Deputy Chairman Supervisory Board, Stefan Quandt, $148,852 total compensation

Chairman Management Board, Norbert Reithofer, age 58, $1,183,980 total compensation

Member Management Board Sales and Marketing, Ian Robertson, age 56, $591,990 total compensation

Head Development ?Small Classes? Product Line and Member Supervisory Board, Anton Ruf, $71,538 total compensation
Member Management Board Production, Harald Kruger, age 49, $591,990 total compensation
Member Management Board Finance, Friedrich Eichiner, age 59, $591,990 total compensation
Member Management Board Purchasing and Supplier Network, Klaus Draeger, age 58, $581,876 total compensation
Member Management Board Production, Frank-Peter Arndt, age 57, $580,492 total compensation
Deputy Chairman Supervisory Board, Stefan Schmid, $161,909 total compensation
Member Management Board Development, Herbert Diess, age 56, $618,198 total compensation
General Counsel, Dieter Dieter Loechelt Loechelt
Member of the Management Board; Head of Human Resources; Industrial Relations Director, Harald Harald Krueger Krueger
Member Supervisory Board, Wolfgang Mayrhuber, age 66
Member Supervisory Board, Robert W. (Bob) Lane, age 63
Deputy Chairman Supervisory Board, Manfred Schoch
Deputy Chairman Supervisory Board, Karl-Ludwig Kley, age 62
Deputy Chairman Supervisory Board, Stefan Quandt
Member Supervisory Board, Franz M. Haniel
Member Supervisory Board, Susanne Klatten, age 50
Member Supervisory Board, Willibald Low
Member Supervisory Board, Werner Zierer
Member Supervisory Board, Bertin Eichler, age 61
Member Supervisory Board, Prof Renate Kocher, age 60
Head Development ?Small Classes? Product Line and Member Supervisory Board, Anton Ruf
Member Supervisory Board, Franz Oberlander
Deputy Chairman Supervisory Board, Stefan Schmid
Member Supervisory Board, Maria Schmidt
Member Supervisory Board, Reinhard Huttl
Member Supervisory Board, Horst Lischka
Member of the Supervisory Board; Employee Representative, Franz Franz Oberlaender Oberlaender
Member of the Supervisory Board, Henning Henning Kagermann Kagermann
Member of the Supervisory Board; Employee Representative, Juergen Juergen Wechsler Wechsler
Member of the Supervisory Board, Reinhard Reinhard Huettl Huettl
Member of the Supervisory Board, Renate Renate Koecher Koecher
Member of the Supervisory Board; Employee Representative, Willibald Willibald Loew Loew
Auditors: KPMGAGWirtschaftsprufungsgesellschaft

LOCATIONS

HQ: Bayerische Motoren Werke AG
Petuelring 130, Munich 80788
Phone: (49) 89 3 82 0 **Fax:** (49) 89 3895 5858
Web: www.bmwgroup.com

2012 Sales

	% of total
Europe	
Germany	16
Rest of	30
Americas	
US	17
Rest of	4
Asia	
China	19
Other	14
Total	**100**

PRODUCTS/OPERATIONS

2012 Sales

	% of total
Automobiles	77
Financial	21
Motorcycles	2
Total	**100**

Selected Products

Automobiles
- BMW
  - 1 Series3-door5-doorConvertibleCoupe
  - 3 SeriesConvertibleCoupeSedanTouring
  - 5 SeriesGran TurismoSedanTouring
  - 6 SeriesConvertibleCoupeGran Coupe
  - 7 SeriesSedan
  - X3 X5 X6 sports utility vehicles
  - M ModelsM3 ConvertibleM3 CoupeM3 SedanM6 ConvertibleM6 Coupe
  - Z4CoupeRoadster
- MINI
  - John Cooper Works (Hardtop Convertible Clubman)
  - MINI Cooper
  - MINI Cooper Clubman
  - MINI Cooper Convertible
  - MINI Cooper S
  - MINI Cooper S Clubman
  - MINI Cooper S Convertible
- Rolls-Royce
  - Ghost
  - Phantom
  - Phantom Coupe

Motorcycles
- BMW
- Husqvarna

COMPETITORS

Chrysler
Daimler
Ducati
Fiat
Ford Motor
General Motors
Harley-Davidson
Honda
Kawasaki Heavy Industries
Mazda
Mitsubishi Motors
Nissan
Porsche
Renault
Saab Automobile
Suzuki Motor
Toyota
Ultra Motorcycle
Volkswagen
Yamaha
Yamaha Motor

HISTORICAL FINANCIALS

Company Type: Public

Income Statement

FYE: December 31

	REVENUE ($ mil.)	NET INCOME ($ mil.)	NET PROFIT MARGIN	EMPLOYEES
12/12	101,289	6,716	6.6%	105,876
12/11	89,016	6,313	7.1%	100,306
12/10	80,940	4,306	5.3%	95,453
12/09	73,009	293	0.4%	96,230
12/08	74,374	452	0.6%	100,041
Annual Growth	8.0%	96.2%	—	1.4%

2012 Year-End Financials

Debt ratio: 69.4%
Return on equity: 17.7%
Cash ($ mil.): 11,032
Current ratio: 1.04
Long-term debt ($ mil.): 51,529
No. of shares (mil.): 602
Dividends
Yield: 2.0%
Payout: 11.0%
Market value ($ mil.): 19,625

	STOCK PRICE ($) FY Close	P/E High	P/E Low	PER SHARE ($) Earnings	Dividends	Book Value
12/12	32.60	7	5	10.24	0.67	66.33
12/11	22.23	9	5	9.64	0.76	58.09
12/10	26.09	10	5	6.57	0.08	51.30
12/09	15.19	126	45	0.45	0.09	47.63
12/08	10.55	44	26	0.69	0.00	47.06
Annual Growth	32.6%	—	—	96.6%	—	9.0%

BCE Inc.

BCE is Canada's Biggest Communications Enterprise. The company (BCE stands for Bell Canada Enterprises) owns Bell Canada the incumbent provider of long-distance and local telephone access in Ontario and Quebec with more than 9 million lines in service. It also provides broadband Internet access to about 3 million subscribers under the Bell Internet banner and digital video subscriptions to more than 2 million viewers via Bell TV. BCE's mobile holdings include wireless carrier Bell Mobility and subsidiary Virgin Mobile Canada (more that 7 million subscribers). It owns 44% of Bell Aliant which serves more than 2 million local phone and 840000+ broadband Internet customers in eastern Canada.

BCE's operating revenues were up about 2% in 2010 over 2009. Wireline revenue rose 0.3 while wireless was up more than 8%.

In response to the limited growth potential offered by its traditional wireline voice segment BCE said in 2011 that it plans to improve customer retention and increase sales of premium services through continued investment in its high-speed data network infrastructure. The company is extending the reach of DSL and fiber-optic broadband Internet connections to boost its capacity and is now providing such data-centric services as broadband television.

It also hopes to continue building its wireless lines. Efforts to entice more mobile users have included the addition of more than 30 new smartphones —21 of them offered only by BCE. The company is also adding streaming and downloadable mobile content such as music movies and sports programming through partnerships with such media providers as HBO and the NHL.

To help facilitate these improvements BCE has restructured its operations with an eye toward a more streamlined reporting structure. Recent measures for that goal have included combining wireless and residential wireline services under the same management. As another effort toward operational reorganization the company sold its stake in satellite communications provider SkyTerra (renamed LightSquared)to investment firm Harbinger Capital Partners in 2010 for $111 million.

BCE took a definitive place in Canada's broadcasting industry when it bought the 85% stake it did not already own in CTVglobemedia in 2011. The purchase which included broadcaster CTV Internet portal Sympatico and "The Globe and Mail" newspaper was made for about $1.5 billion in equity and $1.7 billion in debt from owners The Woodbridge Company Limited (the Toronto-based holding company of the Thomson family) Ontario Teachers Pension Plan and Torstar Corporation. CTV operates Canada's top television network with 27 stations nationwide and 30 specialty channels. The deal made CTV's video content available across BCE's TV Internet video and wireless delivery platforms and should improve the efficiency of its content and advertising operations. These broadcast and publishing assets became the cornerstone of BCE's newly-created Bell Media.

The media push continued in 2012 when the company announced that it would pay nearly $3.4 billion to acquire Montreal-based broadcaster Astral Media Canada's top pay TV provider. The deal will expand BCE's presence in Quebec's French-speaking market where BCE will gain 20 TV channels including MusiquePlus and Super Ecran. Additionally Astral Media owns more than 80 radio stations in 50 markets and it is Canada's number three outdoor advertising company.

Further diversifying its holdings that year Bell acquired a stake in Maple Leaf Sports & Entertainment (MLSE) giving it access to broadcast rights across a number of platforms for top professional sports teams in Toronto including the Maple Leafs Raptors Marlies and Toronto FC. The deal was part of Bell's strategy expand its content and outlets.

Bell is part of a group of Canadian investors that acquired MLSE from the Ontario Teachers Pension Plan. Bell and Rogers Communications jointly own a 75% equity stake in MLSE through a holding company. The remaining 25% is held by Kilmer Sports which is owned by Larry Tanenbaum chairman of MLSE and governor of the National Hockey League the NBA and Major League Soccer.

Late in 2012 it joined with Ontario Teachers' Pension Plan Providence Equity Partners and Madison Dearborn Partners in the C$1.1 billion purchase of data center services provider Q9 Networks.

HISTORY

Alexander Graham Bell experimented with the telephone in his native Canada before moving to the US in the mid-1870s. His father sold his Canadian patent rights to National Bell Telephone which combined with Canada's Hamilton District Telegraph to form Bell Telephone Company of Canada. Known as Bell Canada it received a charter in 1880 and settled in Montreal. By 1882 it had 40 exchanges. AT&T owned 48% of the company in 1890 but by 1925 Canadians owned 95% of Bell Canada. (AT&T severed all ties in 1975.)

As telecommunications needs grew the company began buying smaller exchanges (1954). It acquired a 90% stake in telecom equipment maker Northern Electric in 1957 and the rest in 1964. After Bell Canada reduced the stake in 1973 Northern became Northern Telecom in 1976 (now Nortel Networks). Bell Canada also invested in a satellite joint venture (Telesat 1970) and formed Bell Canada International (BCI) to provide international telecom consulting (1976).

In 1983 responding to proposed legislation that would have calculated manufacturing profits in phone rate formulas Bell created Bell Canada Enterprises (renamed BCE in 1988) as a holding company to separate unregulated businesses from phone carriers. BCE branched out with stakes in gas pipelines (1983) and real estate (1985) but dropped out of the ventures to focus on its core telecom business (1989). It began providing wireless phone service in 1985.

As deregulation rolled into Canada in the 1990s Bell Canada had to maintain high long-distance rates to subsidize its regulated local service. In 1993 it was denied a rate increase and took a large loss. In 1994 regulators allowed local rate increases. The next year BCE announced 10000 job cuts and began offering Internet access.

BCE took a loss in 1997 writing down assets in preparation for full competition. Also that year it floated part of BCI following contracts for cellular systems in Brazil and India. BCE began staging a comeback in 1998 when it sold its shares in Jones Intercable and C&W. It made new investments including 100% of Telesat Canada a part of fONOROLA's fiber network and more than 40% of computer consulting firm CGI Group. Insider Jean Monty (who had steered Nortel's turnaround) became CEO.

Through an alliance with MCI WorldCom (later WorldCom) the company gained access to a global network in 1999. Also that year Ameritech (which became SBC Ameritech) bought a 20% stake in Bell Canada. Bell Canada bought a 20% stake in Manitoba Telecom Services (MTS) that year (it sold its stake in MTS in 2004).

In 2000 Bell Canada spun off nearly all of its 40% Nortel stake to shareholders. That year it bought broadcaster CTV and went on to buy global broadband services provider Teleglobe in a $5 billion stock deal. BCE combined its broadcasting and Internet portal assets with Thomson's "The Globe and Mail" newspaper to form a new company Bell Globemedia (now CTVglobemedia) in 2001 (Thomson sold its stake in 2003).

BCE sold US-based long-distance operator Excel Communications to VarTec Telecom in 2002. BCE took full ownership of Internet portal Sympatico in 2002 acquiring the 29% formerly held by Lycos.

A lack of demand for its broadband services forced BCE to reconsider the value of its Teleglobe unit. In 2002 BCE discontinued long-term funding for Teleglobe which began working to restructure its debt under bankruptcy protection. As 2002 ended Teleglobe was sold to a unit of Ernst & Young the court-appointed creditors' monitor. BCE acquired the Canadian fiber network of 360networks including its GT Group Telecom unit in 2004.

Also that year BCE sold its 64% stake in e-commerce firm BCE Emergis in a spin-off to shareholders. It also sold its Bell Canada directories business to Kohlberg Kravis Roberts & Co. and a unit of the Ontario Teachers' Pension Plan. In the deal valued at C$3 billion BCE kept a 10% stake in the new company. BCE then used the proceeds from this sale to buy back the 16% of Bell Canada owned by AT&T Inc. It also bought the 40% of Bell West it did not own.

In an effort to return focus to its core phone business in late 2006 BCE sold its Telesat Canada unit to Loral Space & Communications and PSP Investments for approximately $3.42 billion. It also sold its stake in CTV globemedia in that year for $1.36 billion. Additionally BCE exited the IT services business when it sold its shares in CGI Group; most of the stake was sold back to CGI. The company sold its Telesat direct-to-home satellite television unit to Loral Space and Communications the following year for about $3 billion.

In 2007 BCE agreed to be acquired for about $50 billion in what would have been the largest leveraged buyout of a company in history. The buyer was an investment group led by Teachers Private Capital Providence Equity Partners and Madison Dearborn Partners. After some wrangling over the terms of the deal the consortium of banks (led by Citibank) which was slated to lend about $30 billion toward the purchase agreed to finance the buyout in mid-2008. The deal fell through later that year after it became clear that completion of the transaction would render BCE insolvent due to the devaluation of its stock amid the global credit crisis.

The company bought electronics chain The Source from bankrupt US-based retailer Circuit City in 2009 to bolster brand awareness and availability at the street level. The expanded retail presence gave BCE a boost in sales of wireless digital TV Internet and home phone services. The Source has about 750 stores located across Canada.

Late in 2010 BCE acquired the data hosting services business of Quebec-based Hypertec in order to expand its colocation and managed data center services business. Also that year BCE bought IT services provider xwave from subsidiary Bell Aliant for CAD $40 million in order to supplement its own technology infrastructure services business.

EXECUTIVES

Vice Chair Quebec, Martine Turcotte
President Bell Mobility and Residential Services, Wade Oosterman
President; Chief Executive Officer of the Company and Bell Canada; Director, George A. Cope, age 51, $900,000 total compensation
Executive Vice President Chief Financial Officer, Siim A. Vanaselja, $526,667 total compensation
President Bell Media, Kevin W. Crull, age 46
EVP Strategic Initiatives Bell Canada, Charles Brown
EVP and CIO Bell Canada, Michael Cole
Executive Vice President Field Operations, Mary Ann Turcke
EVP Corporate Services BCE and Bell Canada, David Wells
President Bell Business Markets, Tom Little
Head of Investor Relations, Thane Fotopoulos
Executive Vice President Customer Operations, John Watson
Executive Vice President Chief Technology Officer, Stephen Howe
Corporate Secretary, Alain Alain Dussault Dussault
Independent Chairman of the Board of the company and Bell Canada, Thomas Thomas ONeill ONeill
Executive Vice President and Chief Legal & Regulatory Officer, Mirko Bibic
Director, Brian M. Levitt, age 65
Director, Anthony S. Fell, age 74
Director, Paul M. Tellier, age 71
Director, Ronald A. (Ron) Brenneman, age 67
President; Chief Executive Officer of the Company and Bell Canada; Director, George A. Cope, age 51
Director, Andre Berard, age 71
Director, Edward C. Lumley, age 73
Director, Donna Soble Kaufman, age 68
Director, Carole S. Taylor, age 66
Director, Sophie Brochu, age 50
Director, Victor L. Young, age 67
Director, Robert E. (Bob) Brown, age 67
Director, Paul R. Weiss
Director BCE and Bell Canada, Rt. Hon. Jim Prentice
Independent Director, Andre Andre Berard Berard
Independent Director, Barry Barry Allen Allen
Independent Director, Robert Robert Simmonds Simmonds
Auditors: Deloitte&ToucheLLP

LOCATIONS

HQ: BCE Inc.
1 Carrefour Alexander-Graham-Bell, Building A, 8th Floor, Verdun, Quebec H3E 3B3
Phone: 514 786-8424 **Fax:** 514 766-8161
Web: www.bce.ca

PRODUCTS/OPERATIONS

2010 Sales

	% of total
Bell	
Bell	57
Bell	27
Bell	16
Total	**100**

COMPETITORS

Allstream
COGECO
Canada Payphone
Globalive
Primus Telecommunications
Quebecor
Rogers Communications
Shaw Broadcast Services
Shaw Communications
Skype
Sprint Nextel
TELUS
Vonage
Yak Communications

HISTORICAL FINANCIALS

Company Type: Public

Income Statement FYE: December 31

	REVENUE ($ mil.)	NET INCOME ($ mil.)	NET PROFIT MARGIN	EMPLOYEES
12/12	20,083	2,638	13.1%	55,500
12/11	19,112	2,177	11.4%	55,250
12/10*	18,107	2,087	11.5%	50,200
01/10	0	0	—	0
12/09	16,916	1,657	9.8%	50,662
Annual Growth	5.9%	16.8%	—	3.1%

*Fiscal year change

2012 Year-End Financials

Debt ratio: 39.3%
Return on equity: 18.9%
Cash ($ mil.): 127
Current ratio: 0.58
Long-term debt ($ mil.): 13,961

No. of shares (mil.): 775
Dividends
Yield: 5.1%
Payout: 65.4%
Market value ($ mil.): 33,295

	STOCK PRICE ($) FY Close	P/E High/Low		PER SHARE ($) Earnings	Dividends	Book Value
12/12	42.94	14	11	3.41	2.23	17.99
12/11	41.67	14	12	2.82	2.00	17.42
12/10*	35.46	13	9	2.75	1.74	13.53
01/10	27.61	—	—	(0.00)	1.50	(0.00)
12/09	27.61	12	6	2.01	1.41	22.41
Annual Growth	11.7%	—	—	19.2%	16.6%	(7.1%)

*Fiscal year change

Bertelsmann AG (Germany, Fed. Rep.)

This company is so big it takes up space on the bookshelf the magazine stand and on television. Bertelsmann is one of the world's leading media conglomerates with operations in publishing and TV. It owns about 90% of RTL Group Europe's #1 TV broadcaster with more than 40 channels operating in a dozen countries. Bertelsmann also owns Random House the world's top trade book publisher as well as 75% of magazine publisher Gruner + Jahr. In addition its arvato unit is a leading provider of distribution manufacturing and other business services to media companies. Carl Bertelsmann founded the company in 1835. His descendants the Mohn family control the business through the Bertelsmann Stiftung foundation.

One unique quality of Bertelsmann is that its divisions operate more like stand-alone businesses rather than being integrated with one another in a fashion similar to Time Warner or News Corporation. Within its home market of Germany Bertelsmann competes most directly with publisher Axel Springer and broadcaster ProSiebenSat.

Bertelsmann is certainly one of the largest but also one of the very few media conglomerates to dominate the European continent: While its TV and publishing businesses range across dozens of countries most of the company's nearest competitors restrict their activities to one or two countries.

But being a global powerhouse in publishing and broadcasting has made Bertelsmann vulnerable during the global recession. Advertising revenue has suffered steep declines in many markets while many of Gruner + Jahr's magazine titles struggle to hold on to readers in the age of digital distribution and expanding competition. Bertelsmann is also focused on managing its high level of debt in the face of declining revenue.

Bertelsmann is currently focused on exploiting new opportunities to turn its various businesses around. RTL Group is working to diversify away from commercial advertising by expanding its pay-TV and digital media operations. The broadcasting group is also buoyed by its FremantleMedia production unit responsible for spawning Pop Idol American Idol and all the other Idol competition programs around the world. Random House meanwhile is eyeing growth of electronic publishing thanks to popular reading devices such as the Kindle from Amazon.com and Apple's iPad tablet device.

Another growth area for the company is music publishing royalties. In 2008 Bertelsmann launched BMG Rights Management a joint venture with US-based private equity firm KKR which controls the rights to more than 75000 songs. BMG acquired US-based publisher Cherry Lane Music Publishing the following year. Bertelsmann had abandoned the music business earlier in 2008 when the company sold its 50% stake in Sony BMG Music Entertainment (now Sony Music Entertainment) to former joint venture partner Sony for $1.2 billion in cash. (The deal included $300 million from Sony Music's balance sheet.) In 2006 it sold BMG Music Publishing to Universal Music Group for $2.1 billion.

HISTORY

Carl Bertelsmann founded his publishing company C. Bertelsmann Verlag in Gutersloh Germany in 1835. The company primarily published hymnals and religious materials expanding into newspapers during the 1860s. Heinrich Mohn a fourth-generation descendant took over the company in 1921 and expanded its operations to include popular fiction which helped Bertelsmann expand to more than 400 employees by 1939.

During WWII the company published books and propaganda material for the German army but was closed by the Nazi government in 1944 as it was not considered important to the war effort. (The company had maintained for decades it was closed because it produced religious materials but contrary evidence was uncovered in 2000 by historians working at the behest of the company.) After WWII Mohn's son Reinhard (who had been captured by the Allies and interned in a Kansas POW camp) returned to Germany determined to rebuild the company.

Bertelsmann boosted book sales by launching book clubs in Germany during the 1950s and bought Germany's UFA (TV and film production) in 1964. It took a minority interest in publisher Gruner + Jahr in 1969 taking a controlling stake in 1973. In the US Bertelsmann bought 51% of Bantam Books in 1977 (and the rest in 1981) and Arista Records in 1979. In 1986 it took control of Doubleday Publishing and bought RCA Records (forming Bertelsmann Music Group the next year). Mohn transferred substantial non-voting shares in the company to the Bertelsmann Foundation (Bertelsmann Stiftung) in 1993.

The company teamed up with AOL in 1995 to form AOL Europe and with Luxembourg broadcaster CLT it launched CLT-Ufa in 1997. Bertelsmann acquired book publisher Random House the next year. The company also took a 50% stake in online bookseller barnesandnoble.com (retaining nearly 40% after an IPO in 1999). In addition Thomas Middelhoff became chairman and CEO in 1998. The next year Bertelsmann acquired some 85% of scientific publisher Springer Verlag. Also in 1999 Reinhard Mohn transferred his controlling shares in the company to Bertelsmann Verwaltungsgesellschaft a firm controlled by Bertelsmann executives and the Mohn family.

In 2000 Bertelsmann announced that it would sell its half-interest in AOL Europe back to AOL by mid-2002; it also spun off Lycos Europe (retaining 27% now about 20%). It later merged CLT-Ufa with Pearson TV to form RTL Group. (Bertelsmann got a 37% stake.) That year Bertelsmann bought online music retailer CDNOW and began negotiating a merger between BMG and EMI Group. (Those talks fell apart in 2001.) Late in 2000 the company formed an alliance with online music service Napster loaning the company start-up cash and allowing it to use the BMG music catalog to develop a subscription-based service. (Bertelsmann later tried to acquire Napster but a bankruptcy court quashed the deal. Napster went out of business shortly after although its name was acquired by Roxio now Napster.)

Bertelsmann bought Groupe Bruxelles Lambert 's 30% stake in RTL Group in 2001. As part of the deal Bruxelles gained a 25% stake in Bertelsmann —with the understanding that it would be able to float its interest to the public in four years. Bertelsmann combined RTL's Ufa Sports unit with French sports-rights company Jean-Claude Darmon in exchange for a 40% stake in the combined company now called Sportfive. Later that year it sold its stake in online music venture GetMusic to Universal Music Group. Also that year it bought Pearson's 22% stake in RTL Group.

The company's board fired Middelhoff in 2002 citing disagreements over the direction of the company. He was replaced by Gunter Thielen chairman of Bertelsmann's arvato business unit. The following year Bertelsmann sold its science publishing subsidiary BertelsmannSpringer. Music subsidiary BMG Entertainment merged with Sony Music in 2004 to create Sony BMG Music Entertainment a joint venture with Sony Corporation.

After a contentious few months in 2006 when Groupe Bruxelles Lambert almost forced an IPO of the notoriously private media firm the Mohn family bought out Lambert's interest in the company for $5.7 billion (leaving the Mohns with a 23% interest in Bertelsmann and the Bertelsmann Foundation owning the rest). Later that year the company sold BMG Music Publishing (which was not part of the BMG-Sony Music merger) to Universal Music Group for $2.1 billion.

Thielen stepped down as CEO of Bertelsmann at the beginning of 2008 and was replaced by Hartmut Ostrowski. Later that year Bertelsmann sold its stake in Sony BMG Music Entertainment to Sony for $1.2 billion in cash and stock. (The music business then changed its name to Sony Music Entertainment.)

EXECUTIVES

EVP Bertelsmann Digital Media Investments, Richard Sarnoff, age 53
Chairman and CEO Random House Group UK, Dame Gail Rebuck, age 61
Chairman and CEO Supervisory Board, Gunter Thielen, age 70
Chairman and CEO, Thomas Rabe, age 48
Board Member; Vice CEO Bertelsmann Stiftung and Chairwoman Bertelsmann Verwaltungsgesellschaft, Liz Mohn
EVP Legal Department, Urlich Koch
Chairman Executive Board and CEO, Hartmut Ostrowski, age 55
CFO Newspapers Coordination Business Magazines Worldwide Gruner + Jahr, Achim Twardy
EVP Bertelsmann US (BInc.), Rob Sorrentino

Chairman Arvato AG; Arvato Services international; Arvato Systems; InmediaONE; Arvato Print International, Rolf Eberhard Buch, age 48
Chief Financial Officer, Elmar Heggen, age 45
Executive Vice President Regional Operations & Business Development CEE and Asia, Andreas Rudas, age 59
EVP Tax Department, Michael Beisheim, age 48
EVP Human Resources, Immanuel Hermreck, age 40
President & CEO Random House of Canada, Brad Martin
Chairman and CEO Random House, Markus Dohle, age 44
EVP Corporate Treasury and Finance, Roger Schweitzer
CEO Direct Group, Fernando Carro, age 48
Senior Vice President Media Relations, Andreas Grafemeyer
EVP Corporate Communications, Thorsten Strau?
CFO Direct Group, Niklas Darijtschuk
CEO Gruner + Jahr AG, Bernd Buchholz, age 52
CEO Bertelsmann China Corporate Center; Managing Director Bertelsmann Asia Investments, Annabelle Yu Long
EVP Financial Reporting and Accounting, Martin Rembde
CEO Arvato Print CEE, Markus Schmedtmann
Deputy Head Press Office, Tobias Riepe
President Corporate Development and New Business, Thomas Hesse
Co-CEO RTL Group, Guillaume de Posch
Co-CEO RTL Group, Anke Schaferkordt
CEO Gruner + Jahr, Julia Jakel
CEO Be Printers Prinovis, Bertram Stausberg
CEO Arvato AG, Achim Berg
Chief Product Officer, Vorstand Produkt
Board Member, Joachim Milberg, age 69
Board Member, Karl-Ludwig Kley, age 61
Board Member, Wulf H. Bernotat, age 63
Board Member, Christoph Mohn, age 48
Board Member, Erich Ruppik
Board Member; Vice CEO Bertelsmann Stiftung and Chairwoman Bertelsmann Verwaltungsgesellschaft, Liz Mohn
Board Member, Kasper B. Rorsted, age 50
Board Member, Bodo Uebber, age 52
Board Member, Hans D. Potsch, age 61
Board Member, Ian Hudson
Board Member, Brigitte Mohn, age 48
Board Member, Lars R. S?rensen
Board Member, Kai Brettmann
Board Member, Christa Gomez
Auditors: KPMGDeutscheTreuhand-GesellschaftAG

LOCATIONS

HQ: Bertelsmann AG (Germany, Fed. Rep.)
Carl-Bertelsmann-Strasse 270, P.O. Box 111, Guetersloh D-33311
Phone: (49) 5241 80 0 **Fax:** (49) 5241 80 66 13
Web: www.bertelsmann.com

PRODUCTS/OPERATIONS

Selected Operations

arvato
DirectGroup
Gruner + Jahr
Random House
RTL Group

COMPETITORS

21st Century Fox
Amazon.com
Axel Springer
Bauer Verlagsgruppe
CANAL+
Cinram
Disney
Hearst Corporation
ITV
Lagardere
NBCUniversal
ProSiebenSat
Time Warner
Verlagsgruppe Georg
von Holtzbrinck
Viacom

HISTORICAL FINANCIALS

Company Type: Public

Income Statement FYE: December 31

	REVENUE ($ mil.)	NET INCOME ($ mil.)	NET PROFIT MARGIN	EMPLOYEES
12/12	21,489	637	3.0%	104,286
12/11	20,038	601	3.0%	100,626
12/10	21,330	639	3.0%	97,528
12/09	22,360	(118)	—	102,983
12/08	22,784	198	0.9%	106,083
Annual Growth	(1.5%)	33.9%	—	(0.4%)

2012 Year-End Financials

Debt ratio: 27.0%
Return on equity: 9.1%
Cash ($ mil.): 3,503
Current ratio: 1.40
Long-term debt ($ mil.): 4,760
No. of shares (mil.): 0
Dividends
Yield: —
Payout: —
Market value ($ mil.): —

BG Group Plc

BG Group exploits oil and gas assets far beyond Great Britain. In addition to conducting its core oil and gas exploration and production operations in 25 countries the integrated energy company is engaged in liquefied natural gas (LNG) production and gas transmission and distribution. In 2011 BG Group reported proved reserves of 12.8 trillion cu. ft. of natural gas 1.1 trillion barrels of oil and an annual production of 234 million barrels of oil equivalent. The group is one of the largest exploration and production companies in the North Sea and has also moved into the lucrative US shale gas market through an alliance with EXCO Resources.

A 2009 deal with EXCO entailed BG Group paying about $1.4 billion for what amounts to a half stake in EXCO's shale gas operations in Texas and Louisiana.

In 2010 BG Group entered another alliance with EXCO to develop that company's producing and non-producing natural gas assets in the Appalachian Basin. The partnership operates upstream assets and a 50-50 midstream joint venture company which invests in gathering and transportation in Pennsylvania and West Virginia. BG paid $835.2 million for its 50% stake in the joint venture.

BG Group is focusing on current and new exploration and production projects. In conjunction with its exploration operations it constructs gas infrastructure and develops gas markets.

As part of its strategy to develop gas markets around the world the company has acquired key gas distribution and transmission operations in Argentina Brazil and India. It owns stakes in the largest gas distributors in Argentina (MetroGas) and India (Gujarat Gas Company Limited and Mahanagar Gas Limited). It also owns 25% of the UK's Interconnector a pipeline system that links the industrial port of Bacton on the Norfolk coast of England to the Continental Europe energy markets.

To raise cash to pay down debt and invest in its core businesses in 2010 the company sold its 50% stake in UK-based power station company Seabank Power Limited to Electricity First Limited for $320 million and its Northern Ireland power station to AES for $150 million effectively exiting the power generation segment.

On the exploration and production front in 2011 the company was engaged in appraisal drilling in Brazil and reported oil and gas discoveries in Tanzania the UK and Norway and a large leasehold acquisition in Kenya.

In 2011 the recovering economy stronger demand for oil and gas and higher oil prices helped to lift BG Group's revenues by 23% in 2011 and its net income by more than 26%. In particular the company which is developing a major liquefied natural gas (LNG) plant in Australia saw demand for LNG spike in 2011 (LNG revenues grew by almost 30% that year). BG Group expects LNG demand from energy-hungry Japan China and India to continue to grow rapidly.

In 2012 to free up capital the BG Group agreed to sell its 60% in Comgas Brazil's largest gas distribution company for $1.8 billion. It also agreed to sell its 65% stake in India's Gujarat Gas Company.

That year it also signed a deal with Spectra Energy to develop a 525-mile pipeline from northeast British Columbia to serve BG Group's potential LNG export on the northwest coast of the province.

HISTORY

In 1792 William Murdock invented gas lighting for his Cornwall home. The Gas Light and Coke Company of London the world's first commercial gas company was formed in 1812. Sixteen years later 200 gas companies operated in the UK.

The UK's major industries were nationalized including the gas industry in 1949. Some 1050 gas suppliers were placed under the British Gas Council. In the 1960s the Gas Council promoted gas as a clean fuel. This effort was aided by the Clean Air Act of 1956 the discovery of an abundant supply of liquefied natural gas in the North Sea and OPEC oil price hikes in the 1970s. With the introduction of natural gas most gasworks were demolished and the British Gas Council (which became British Gas Corp. in 1973) began converting gas appliances to natural gas.

British Gas Corp. went public in 1986. Released from government-imposed limits British Gas began buying into international exploration and production companies. It also took a 25% stake in Natural Gas Clearinghouse (Dynegy) in 1994. By 1995 British Gas had exploration and production assets in 20 countries.

A year after the opening of the UK gas market in 1996 British Gas split into two public companies: Centrica (natural gas supply) and BG which got the Transco gas transportation monopoly and the international exploration and production operations.

In 1997 BG struck gas in three Indonesian wells and signed a 40-year production-sharing agreement with the Kazakhstan government. In 1998 a BG-led consortium won a 25-year franchise to develop gasworks in Egypt's Nile Valley. The following year BG and Royal Dutch Shell acquired a controlling stake in Comgas a subsidiary of Companhia Energetica de S?o Paulo and the largest natural gas distributor in Brazil for about $1 billion.

The company became BG Group in 1999 a holding company for BG Transco Holdings (gas transportation) and BG Energy Holdings (natural gas exploration and production and other operations). In 2000 the company reorganized again spinning off its telecommunications holdings and Transco. Also that year BG Group sold its stakes in Dynegy Russian oil company KomiArcticOil and its production assets in Qatar.

In 2001 BG Group sold 25% of UK distribution company Phoenix Natural Gas to East Surrey Investments. The company began its first commercial productions in Egypt that year. In 2002 the company demerged its distribution arm Lattice which became part of National Grid Transco. It also completed the purchase of oil and gas assets located in India from bankrupt energy group Enron that year.

To reinforce its LNG developments in Trinidad and Tobago and its LNG supply to US markets the company acquired the Elba Island LNG business from now-bankrupt El Paso Marketing for about $128 million in 2003.

The company expanded in Canada by purchasing El Paso Oil and Gas Canada from El Paso Corporation for $345.6 million in 2004. That year BG Group also acquired Shell's 40% interest in the Rosetta concession for exploration offshore Egypt. It disposed of its 50% interest in the Muturi project in Indonesia that year.

In 2006 BG Group entered the Alaska market acquiring oil and gas assets in the Foothills area of the North Slope.

In 2008 BG Group made a bold move into the Australian market with a $13 billion offer for Origin Energy but was rebuffed. Undeterred in 2008 it acquired AGL Energy's controlling stake in Queensland Gas Company (coal seam gas) for A$5.6 billion and in 2009 it completed a $796 million takeover of Australian coal seam gas producer Pure Energy Resources Ltd besting an existing offer from gas producer Arrow Energy Ltd. Further boosting its reserves in 2008 BG Group also made major oil and gas dicoveries in Iara and Guara in the Santos Basin in Brazil.

EXECUTIVES

Chairman, Andrew Gould, age 66
Chief Operating Officer and Executive Director, Martin Houston, age 55, $474,694 total compensation
Executive Vice President, Ashley Almanza, age 49, $1,063,457 total compensation
Chief Executive, Chris Finlayson, age 56
Executive Vice President Operations, Sami Iskander, age 46
Head Investor Relations, Chris Lloyd
EVP and Managing Director Australia, Catherine Tanna, age 50
Secretary, Keith Hubber, age 47
Media Relations Advisor, Paula Burton
General Counsel, Graham Vinter, age 56
EVP Policy and Corporate Affairs, Sir John Grant, age 58
Executive Vice President Human Resources, Robert Booker, age 46
Manager Media Relations, Jo Thethi
Manager Investor Relations, Damien Bird
Executive Director and Interim CFO, Den Jones
Executive Vice President Exploration, Malcolm Brown
Executive Vice President BG Advance, Chris Cox
Executive Vice President Global Energy Marketing and Shipping, Matt Schatzman
Director, Andrew Gould, age 65
Director, Jurgen Dormann, age 72
Director, Philippe Varin
CEO and Director, Frank Chapman, age 59
Chief Operating Officer and Executive Director, Martin Houston, age 55
Director, Peter Backhouse, age 61
Director, Baroness Sarah Hogg, age 66
Director, Patrick W. Thomas, age 55
Director, John Hood, age 60
Director, Mark Seligman
Director, Sir David G. Manning, age 62
Executive Director and Interim CFO, Den Jones
Auditors: PricewaterhouseCoopersLLP

LOCATIONS

HQ: BG Group Plc
100 Thames Valley Park Drive, Reading, Berkshire RG6 1PT
Phone: (44) 118 935 3222 **Fax:** (44) 118 935 3484
Web: www.bg-group.com

PRODUCTS/OPERATIONS

2011 Sales

	% of total
Exploration &	46
Liquefied natural	38
Transmission &	16
Total	**100**

COMPETITORS

BP
Bharat Petroleum
Eni
Exxon Mobil
GAIL
GDF SUEZ
Gas Natural SDG
Hess Corporation
Italgas
PETROBRAS
Royal Dutch Shell
TOTAL

HISTORICAL FINANCIALS

Company Type: Public

Income Statement FYE: December 31

	REVENUE ($ mil.)	NET INCOME ($ mil.)	NET PROFIT MARGIN	EMPLOYEES
12/12	18,933	4,519	23.9%	6,568
12/11	21,073	4,234	20.1%	6,625
12/10	17,166	3,351	19.5%	6,172
12/09	16,540	3,511	21.2%	6,079
12/08	18,312	4,556	24.9%	5,395
Annual Growth	0.8%	(0.2%)	—	5.0%

2012 Year-End Financials

Debt ratio: 23.7%
Return on equity: 14.4%
Cash ($ mil.): 4,434
Current ratio: 1.44
Long-term debt ($ mil.): 14,443
No. of shares (mil.): —
Dividends
Yield: 1.4%
Payout: 18.7%
Market value ($ mil.): —

	STOCK PRICE ($) FY Close	P/E High/Low	PER SHARE ($) Earnings	Dividends	Book Value
12/12	16.71	89 12	1.32	0.25	9.72
12/11	107.00	104 71	1.24	0.23	8.66
12/10	102.00	107 72	0.99	0.19	7.77
12/09	90.50	404212	1.04	0.20	6.81
12/08	71.15	419122	1.35	0.20	5.19
Annual Growth	(30.4%)	— —	(0.5%)	6.0%	17.0%

Bharat Petroleum Corp., Ltd. (India)

Although it carries the ancient Sanskrit name for India (Bharat) Bharat Petroleum Corporation Limited (BPCL) is a modern refining and distribution company. It vies with Hindustan Petroleum for the #2 slot behind Indian Oil. The company's refineries –in Mumbai Kochi and Numaligarh (62%-owned) –collectively process more than 24 million metric tons of crude oil per year. BPCL sells engine oils and gasolines liquefied petroleum gas (LPG) and kerosene. It has10000 gas stations a national network of kerosene dealers and more than 2450 LPG distributors. The company operates 50 LPG bottling plants and serves more than 30 million LPG customers across India.

With an eye to expanding BPCL's global hydrocarbon supply and lowering production costs BPCL's exploration and production unit Bharat PetroResources partners with major oil companies to develop oil and gas fields in India and abroad. In fiscal 2011 Bharat PetroResources reported five oil and gas discoveries in Brazil Indonesia and Mozambique.

BPCL is also modernizing and expanding its Indian refineries to handle increased demand. In fiscal 2011 it teamed up with Bharat Oman Refineries to develop a 6 million metric-ton-per-year refinery in Madya Pradesh to support BPCL's activities in the central and northern part of India. It also launched an expansion of its Kochi refinery to expand that plant's capacity from 7.5 million metric tons per year to 9.5 million metric tons per year.

It is also expanding its gas station network to meet growing domestic demand adding 600 retail outlets in fiscal 2011 with another 700 projected to be added in fiscal 2012. Depending on future growth BPCL may add up to 2500 gas stations by 2017.

Higher oil prices increased production and the expansion of its retail network helped to lift BPCL's revenues in fiscal 2011. Increased costs related to crude oil for resale and raw materials meant that net income was essentially flat for the year.

The Indian government owns 55% of the firm although it is considering eventually selling this stake as part of industrywide deregulation.

EXECUTIVES

Executive Director Corporate Finance, S. Varadarajan
General Manager Projects Kochi Refinery, K. N. Ravindran
Executive Director Kochi Refinery, E. Nandakumar
Chairman and Managing Director, R.K. Singh
Executive Director Gas, A.K. Bansal
General Manager International Trade, P.V. Kumar
Finance Director, S.K. Joshi
Human Resources Director, S. Mohan
General Manager Human Resources Mumbai Refinery, S. Vijayakumar
General Manager Sales Retail HQ, Sharad K. Sharma
General Manager Sales Strategy Retail HQ, V. Anand
Executive Director Refineries Finance, J. Ravichandran
Chief Vigilance Officer, I. Sasikala
Executive Director Pipelines, Anurag Deepak
Refineries Director, B.K. Datta
Executive Director Industrial and Commercial, D.M. Reddy
Executive Director Human Resources Development, Dipti Sanzgiri
Marketing Director, K.K. Gupta
Executive Director Planning, P. S. Bhargava
Executive Director International Trade, R. K. Mehra
General Manager Engineering and Advanced Services Kochi Refinery, Thomas Chacko
Executive Director Human Resources Services, S. P. Gathoo
Executive Director Engineering and Projects, S. P. Mathur
Executive Director Retail, S. Ramesh
Executive Director Audit, Sumita Bose Roy
General Manager Infrastructure and Services, A. K. Kaushik
General Manager Quality Control, Basudev Rana

General Manager Corporate Marketing, Brij Pal Singh
General Manager Lubes, George Paul
Chief Procurement Officer, Arun Singh
General Manager Logistics Retail, G. S. Wankhede
General Manager Marketing Gas, I. Srinivas Rao
General Manager Corporate Treasury, J. Dinaker
General Manager ERP - CC, K. B. Narayanan
General Manager Sales LPG HQ, K. P. Chandy
Executive Director Mumbai Refinery, K. V. Seshadri
General Manager Retail South, K. V. Shenoy
General Manager Operations Mumbai Refinery, Prasad K. Panicker
General Manager Pipeline Projects E&P, M. M. Chawla
General Manager Human Resources Kochi Refinery, M. P. Govindarajan
General Manager Urban Retailing, Monica Widhani
General Manager Engineering and Advanced Services Mumbai Refinery, Thomas Zachariah
General Manager Corporate Finance, P. Balasubramanian
General Manager Highway Retailing, P. C. Srivastava
Executive Director Retail East, Pallav Ghosh
General Manager Refinery Coordination, P. Padmanabhan
General Manager Retail North, Pramod Sharma
General Manager Finance Retail HQ, R. P. Natekar
General Manager Aviation, S. B. Bhattacharya
General Manager Legal, S. K. Agrawal
General Manager Rural Retailing and Real Estate, S. K. Mathur
General Manager Operations Kochi Refinery, Tomy Mathews
General Manager Talent Management, T. Somanath
Deputy General Manager Employee Satifaction Enhancement, Madhu Sagar
Deputy General Manager Brand and Public Relations, M. M. Somaya
Secretary, S.V. Kulkarni
General Manager Projects, P. Kumaraswamy

LOCATIONS

HQ: Bharat Petroleum Corp., Ltd. (India)
Bharat Bhavan, 4 & 6 Currimbhoy Road, Ballard Estate, Mumbai 400 001
Phone: (91) 22 2271 3000 **Fax:** (91) 22 2271 3688
Web: www.bharatpetroleum.in

PRODUCTS/OPERATIONS

Selected Operations

Aviation (jet fuel operations)
Exploration and production
Liquefied petroleum gas (Bharatgas cooking gas)
Lubricants (automotive and industrial lubricants)
Industrial and commercial (fuels and petrochemicals for industrial and commercial clients)
Refining (crude oil processing)
Retail (petrol diesel and kerosene retail outlets)

COMPETITORS

BG Group
BP
Bongaigaon Refinery
Exxon Mobil
GAIL
Hindustan Petroleum
Idemitsu Kosan
Indian Oil
Reliance Industries
Royal Dutch Shell
TOTAL

HISTORICAL FINANCIALS

Company Type: Public

Income Statement

FYE: March 31

	REVENUE ($ mil.)	NET INCOME ($ mil.)	NET PROFIT MARGIN	EMPLOYEES
03/12	41,698	153	0.4%	13,429
03/11	34,488	366	1.1%	13,915
03/10	29,241	383	1.3%	13,898
03/09	26,819	142	0.5%	14,016
03/08	27,961	476	1.7%	14,006
Annual Growth	10.5%	(24.7%)	—	(1.0%)

2012 Year-End Financials

Debt ratio: 0.7%
Return on equity: 4.9%
Cash ($ mil.): 260
Current ratio: 0.85
Long-term debt ($ mil.): 1,216
No. of shares (mil.): 361
Dividends
Yield: —
Payout: —
Market value ($ mil.): —

BHP Billiton Ltd.

Two heads (or headquarters) are better than one. Aussie minerals and oil company BHP Limited acquired UK miner Billiton plc in 2001. The result: a two-headquartered dual-listed company run as a single entity with the same board of directors and management. The Melbourne side is BHP Billiton Limited the London side is BHP Billiton Plc; collectively they are known as BHP Billiton. One of the largest diversified natural resources companies it ranks among the world's top producers of iron ore and coal (thermal and metallurgical). Other products include aluminum copper manganese nickel silver uranium and potash. BHP also has crude oil and natural gas holdings. The company may spin off its diamond assets.

The company has far-flung operations. In Canada's Saskatchewan province BHP produces potash a primary raw material used to manufacture fertilizers and a top priority for the global titans of mining. In Australia it operates a coal-producing joint venture with Mitsubishi that has mining projects in Australia. Its Australian minerals businesses include not only iron ore coal and potash but also copper and uranium. Its Chilean operations include a 58% stake in the Escondida mine one of the world's largest and lowest-cost copper producers. BHP's oil and gas operations are worldwide ranging from its Shenzi deepwater oil and gas field in the Gulf of Mexico to onshore natural gas production in Pakistan.

As a result of global demand for its resources BHP Billiton turned in a good performance for 2011. Strong demand from China and other developing countries helped contribute to BHP's sharp increase in revenue that year. The company recorded net sales of $71.7 billion (up 36% from 2010) and a net income of $23.7 billion (up 86%). It also achieved record production for most of its commodities including its 11th consecutive record in iron ore.

The company has created a diversified portfolio of tier one natural resources by investing in large high-quality low-cost assets. In addition to strategic acquisitions BHP seeks organic growth through investments in major projects for its segments. In 2011 it poured about $13 billion in 11 projects to help grow several of its businesses: natural gas iron ore coal copper and diamonds. The company expected its organic growth program to exceed more than $80 billion in new development spending by 2015.

With mineral prices falling rapidly in 2012 however the company may not meet its $80 billion spending target for investments and is reviewing its expansion plans. The price of iron ore for example has declined 29% since the company announced its plans for investments in early 2011.

Recent investments in on-shore shale assets in the US are also cause for concern. In 2011 BHP acquired Chesapeake Energy Corp.'s Fayetteville shale gas holdings in Arkansas for $4.75 billion. That year it also acquired Petrohawk Energy another US-based gas producer with projects in the Eagle Ford and Haynesville shale plays for $15.1 billion. In 2012 natural gas prices began to plummet. Although the company defended the long-term growth outlook for the shale assets it did not rule out a possible writedown later that year for those investments.

Following the Petrohawk announcement in 2011 BHP acquired three subsidiaries of HWE Mining a company owned by Leighton Holdings for $735 million. The HWE Mining subsidiaries provide contract iron ore mining services in Western Australia to BHP and the acquisition allows the company to both own and operate the mines.

BHP may also exit the diamonds business entirely. In 2012 it sold its 51% stake in the Chidliak diamond exploration project in Canada's Baffin Island to the project operator Peregrine Diamonds giving it full ownership. The sale follows BHP's review of its diamond businesses to determine whether they fit in its strategy. The company also owns an 80% stake in Canada's EKATI diamond mine which is still under review. The company could receive less than $500 million for the sale of the mine.

HISTORY

In 1883 Charles Rasp a boundary rider for the Mt. Gipps sheep station believed valuable ore lay in the Broken Hill outcrop in New South Wales Australia. He gathered a few young speculators and The Broken Hill Proprietary Company (BHP) was incorporated in 1885. BHP immediately found a massive lode of silver lead and zinc. None of the founders knew how to run a mine so they recruited US engineers William Patton and Herman Schlapp. From the beginning labor and management clashed. The founding directors set up the head office in Melbourne far from the mine and gambled with gold sovereigns in the boardroom. But the miners worked in dangerous conditions. An 1892 labor strike was the first of BHP's bitter strikes.

In 1902 the new general manager Guillaume Delprat invented a flotation process that recovered valuable metals from iron ore waste. Delprat also foresaw a future in steel although Australia had no steel industry. BHP commissioned the Newcastle steelworks in 1915 and soon became the country's largest steel producer. BHP's 1935 purchase of Australian Iron and Steel its only competitor gave it a virtual steel monopoly while high tariffs protected it from outside competition. Its exhausted Broken Hill mine was closed that year.

In the 1960s BHP got into oil when it partnered with Esso Standard the Australian subsidiary of Standard Oil of New Jersey for offshore exploration. In 1967 the partners found oil in the Bass Strait which soon supplied 70% of Australia's petroleum. In the 1960s and 1970s BHP began expanding its iron ore manganese and coal interests. Meanwhile public opposition mounted to BHP's market power and labor practices and in 1972 the government took steps to limit BHP's power removing some subsidies and tax breaks.

The weak steel market of the 1970s and 1980s caused BHP to lay off almost a third of its steelworkers in 1983 but with government intervention BHP radically improved its steel productivity. In 1984 BHP bought Utah International's mining assets from General Electric (including Chile's rich Escondida copper mine). In 1986 corporate raider Robert Holmes a Court took a run at BHP; BHP decided to become an international mining company to prevent further raids. Its acquisitions in the late 1980s included ERG Inc. and Monsanto Oil (combined into BHP Americas) Aquila Steel and Pacific Refining in Hawaii.

A peace deal with Holmes a Court gave BHP about 37% of Foster's Brewing but in 1992 BHP took a $700 million write-down after Foster's stock declined. BHP also bought Arizona-based Magma Copper in 1996 but plunging world copper prices forced a $420 million write-down.

With new worries over Asia's economic troubles BHP soon was struggling. In 1997 BHP sold most of its stake in Foster's and three senior executives resigned. In 1998 the company unloaded Pacific Refining which was acquired by Tesoro Petroleum for about $275 million.

As BHP's woes continued CEO John Prescott resigned; Paul Anderson was recruited from Duke Energy to succeed Prescott. In 1999 D. R. Argus took over as chairman replacing Jeremy Ellis. In a restructuring move the company sold its engineering power insurance and information technology businesses in 1999 and 2000. BHP began to sell $2 billion worth of steel operations (including its long product unit OneSteel). In 2000 the company shortened its official name to BHP Limited.

BHP acquired Billiton in 2001 forming BHP Billiton Ltd. and BHP Billiton plc. The combined BHP Billiton had sales of almost $20 billion and a market capitalization approaching $30 billion. In addition BHP paid $436 million for Dia Met Minerals which owned 29% of Canada's only producing diamond mine Ekati.

Also in 2001 BHP Billiton and Alcoa combined their North American metals distribution businesses as joint venture Integris Metals (subsequently sold and integrated into Ryerson). In order to focus on its minerals and oil and gas operations in 2002 BHP Billiton spun off its steel business as BHP Steel (now called Bluescope Steel).

In 2005 BHP Billiton acquired metals and minerals company WMC Resources which had been the subject of much takeover speculation and the target of the Swiss mining heavyweight Xstrata (since renamed Glencore Xstrata). Its offer of $7.3 billion surpassed Xstrata's and was accepted and endorsed by the WMC board which had turned down the two earlier proposals by Xstrata. The addition of WMC added significantly to BHP Billiton's copper nickel and uranium operations.

In 2008 BHP Billiton Mitsubishi Alliance (BMA) spent $2.4 billion to buy the Saraji East metallurgical coal project from New Hope Corporation. Each of BMA's owners paid $1.2 billion to New Hope for the project which lies adjacent to one of BMA's coal mines.

Though the global recession of 2008-2009 certainly pushed the company's fortunes down BHP Billiton experienced eyebrow-raising growth thanks in part to generally high commodity prices and the emerging Asian economies. China for example represented 20% of the company's total sales in 2007 doubling its share from just three years prior. The continent as a whole accounted for more than half of sales.

Due to the strong demand BHP Billiton increased production of iron ore coking coal and manganese. The shifting nature of the market though changed the company's highest-grossing segments. In 2009 high coal prices helped that business immensely while conversely the Base Metals business of copper lead zinc and precious metals mining suffered from low prices driving down the unit's revenues. On the petroleum side the company continued to acquire oil and gas exploration leases in the Gulf of Mexico.

Two failed deals by BHP Billiton occurred in 2010: a $39 billion takeover of Potash Corporation of Saskatchewan and a proposed joint venture with Rio Tinto Ltd. BHP Billiton's offer for Potash Corporation was first rejected by that company's board as inadequate and then by Canadian regulators who ruled the offer to be anticompetitive. After a $150 billion bid to buy Rio Tinto fell through due to the global economic meltdown the companies proposed a joint iron ore venture in Western Australia which also failed because of opposition from European regulatory authorities.

In 2010 BHP Billiton acquired Athabasca Potash Inc. (API) for about $320 million. API's projects are located in Saskatchewan close to BHP Billiton's own potash operations.

EXECUTIVES

Chairman, Jacques A. (Jac) Nasser, age 64
Group Executive and Chief Executive Ferrous and Coal, Marcus P. Randolph, age 57
Chief Executive Officer; Executive Director, Marius Kloppers, age 51, $1,677,070 total compensation
Group Executive and Chief People Officer, Karen J. Wood, age 57, $854,514 total compensation
Group Executive and Chief Executive Non-Ferrous, Andrew Mackenzie
Investor Relations Americas, Scott Espenshade
Group Company Secretary, Jane F. McAloon, age 49
President Iron Ore, Ian R. Ashby
CFO BHP Billiton Petroleum, David Powell
Group Executive and Chief Executive Petroleum, J. Michael (Mike) Yeager, age 61
Group Executive and Chief Commercial Officer, Alberto Calderon, age 54
Group Executive and CFO, Graham Kerr
Investor Relations United Kingdom and South Africa, Andre Liebenberg
Media Relations United Kingdom South Africa and Americas, Ruban Yogarajah
Group Executive and Chief Marketing Officer, Mike Henry
VP Human Resources BHP Billiton Petroleum, David J. Nelson
Investor Relations Australia, Brendan Harris
Investor Relations Australia, Leng Lau
Media Relations Australia, Kelly Quirke
Media Relations Australia, Fiona Martin
Investor Relations Contact Officer, James Agar
Deputy Company Secretary, Nicola Evans
President - Aluminium; Manganese and Nickel, Daniel Malchuk
President Copper, Peter BeavenBAcc
Director, Wayne W. Murdy, age 69
Director, Sir John G. S. Buchanan, age 69
Director, John M. Schubert, age 70
Director, Alan L. Boeckmann, age 65
Director, Keith C. Rumble, age 59
CEO and Director, Marius Kloppers, age 50
Director, Malcolm W. Broomhead, age 61
Director, Carolyn Hewson, age 58
Director, David A. Crawford, age 69
Group Company Secretary and Director, Jane F. McAloon, age 48
Director, Carlos Cordeiro, age 57
Director, Baroness Shriti Vadera
Independent Non-Executive Director, Lindsay Maxsted
Independent Non-Executive Director, Pat Davies
Auditors: KPMGAuditPlc

LOCATIONS

HQ: BHP Billiton Ltd.
BHP Billiton Centre, 171 Collins Street, Melbourne, Victoria 3000
Phone: (61) 3 9609 3333 **Fax:** (61) 3 9609 3015
Web: www.bhpbilliton.com

2011 Sales

	$ mil.	% of total
Asia		
China	20,261	28
Japan	9,002	13
Other countries	15,805	22
Europe (including UK)	9,413	13
North America	6,167	9
Australia	5,487	8
South America	2,592	4
Southern Africa	1,548	2
Other regions	1,464	2
Total	**71,739**	**100**

PRODUCTS/OPERATIONS

2011 Sales

	$ mil.	% of total
Iron ore	20,412	28
Base metals	14,152	20
Coal		
Energy coal	5,507	8
Petroleum	10,737	15
Stainless steel materials	3,861	5
Diamonds & specialty products	1,517	2
Total	**71,739**	**100**

Selected Divisions

Coal
- Metallurgical
- Energy

Iron ore
Petroleum
- Crude oil
- Ethane
- LPG
- Natural gas

Base metals
- Copper
- Gold
- Lead
- Silver
- Zinc

Aluminum
- Alumina
- Aluminum
- Bauxite

Manganese
Stainless steel materials
- Cobalt
- Ferrochrome
- Nickel

Diamonds and specialty products
- Diamonds
- Potash
- Titanium minerals

COMPETITORS

Alcoa
Anglo American
ArcelorMittal
BP
Chevron
Chinalco
Codelco
ConocoPhillips
Exxon Mobil
Fortescue Metals
Freeport-McMoRan
Koch Industries Inc.
Kumba Iron Ore
Marathon Oil
Newmont Mining
Nippon Steel & Sumitomo Metal Corporation
Norsk Hydro ASA
Repsol
Rio Tinto Limited
Royal Dutch Shell

TOTAL
Tata Europe
Teck
Vale
Xstrata

HISTORICAL FINANCIALS

Company Type: Public

Income Statement FYE: June 30

	REVENUE ($ mil.)	NET INCOME ($ mil.)	NET PROFIT MARGIN	EMPLOYEES
06/13	65,968	10,876	16.5%	49,496
06/12	72,226	15,417	21.3%	46,370
06/11	71,739	23,648	33.0%	40,757
06/10	52,798	12,722	24.1%	39,570
06/09	50,211	5,877	11.7%	40,990
Annual Growth	7.1%	16.6%	—	4.8%

2013 Year-End Financials

Debt ratio: 25.4%
Return on equity: 15.9%
Cash ($ mil.): 6,060
Current ratio: 0.97
Long-term debt ($ mil.): 29,862
No. of shares (mil.): —
Dividends
Yield: 0.0%
Payout: 111.9%
Market value ($ mil.): —

	STOCK PRICE ($) FY Close	P/E High	P/E Low	PER SHARE ($) Earnings	Dividends	Book Value
06/13	57.66	39	28	2.04	2.28	13.28
06/12	65.30	33	21	2.88	2.20	12.38
06/11	94.63	24	14	4.27	1.82	10.66
06/10	61.99	36	22	2.28	1.66	8.72
06/09	54.73	81	23	1.05	1.64	7.18
Annual Growth	1.3%	—	—	17.9%	8.6%	16.6%

BHP Billiton Plc

BHP Billiton Plc is one half of a dual-listed mining giant. It is headquartered in London; the other part of the company BHP Billiton Limited is based in Australia. Although they maintain separate listings the companies are managed as a single entity and have the same management team and board of directors. One of the largest diversified natural resources companies it ranks among the world's top producers of iron ore and coal (thermal and metallurgical). Other products include aluminum copper manganese nickel silver uranium and potash. BHP also has significant crude oil and natural gas holdings. For more information on the company refer to Hoover's BHP Billiton Limited profile.

In mid-2005 BHP Billiton acquired the Australian metals and minerals company WMC Resources which had been the subject of much takeover speculation and the target of the Swiss mining heavyweight Xstrata (since renamed Glencore Xstrata). BHP Billiton opened talks with WMC's board and made an offer for the Australian company in early 2005. The offer of $7.3 billion surpassed Xstrata's and was accepted and endorsed by the WMC board which had turned down the two earlier proposals by Xstrata.

The potential addition of WMC Resources adds significantly to BHP Billiton's copper nickel and uranium operations.

HISTORY

After starting out on its own in 1860 Billiton was subsequently bought first by Royal Dutch Shell and then by Gencor only to end up on its own once again. In 1860 a group of Dutch shareholders formed Billiton NV. The company bought the rich tin deposits of Billiton island (now part of Indonesia) for which it was named. The business grew to include tin and lead smelting in the Netherlands. Billiton NV began mining bauxite in the 1940s but WWII caused a production slowdown.

While demand for petroleum products exploded in the 1950s and 1960s in 1970 the industry nosedived. Royal Dutch Shell (formed from the merger of Royal Dutch and Shell Transport and Trading) responded by diversifying buying Billiton NV which it renamed Billiton International. Shell had gotten its start in commodities in the 1880s selling Russian oil of the Rothschilds to the Far East. Royal Dutch formed in 1890 after buying the rights to drill for oil in the Dutch East Indies. The two companies merged in 1907.

The 1970 Billiton purchase helped Royal Dutch Shell make up for the 1970s oil shortage and rationing that had resulted from OPEC's crude oil price hikes. Slow worldwide economic growth a major recession and oil and chemicals overcapacity impacted the company in the late 1970s and early 1980s.

Royal Dutch Shell sold Billiton in 1994 to Gencor which had been formed in 1980 by the merger of General Mining and Finance Corporation and Union Corporation. General Mining began mining gold in South Africa in the 1890s and Gencor continued its predecessors' metals and manufacturing operations. Gencor however spent the early 1980s focused on manufacturing because it anticipated a downturn in base metals. But the recession inflation and high interest rates stifled Gencor's success and the company became known as an unfocused conglomerate. In 1986 a newly appointed chairman separated Gencor's manufacturing and mining interests.

By 1989 Gencor had cut its staff and reorganized. That year it bought 31% of South Africa's Richards Bay aluminum smelter. Within two years Gencor had become a holding company with a primary interest in mining. In 1993 the firm unbundled its non-mining activities. With the end of apartheid in 1994 Gencor was able to expand abroad. Its purchase of Billiton catapulted its presence into 13 countries but in 1996 the metals market spiraled downward.

Billiton was spun off by Gencor in 1997. It took over all of Gencor's nonprecious metal interests including its aluminum titanium ferroalloy and coal assets. That year Billiton combined its nickel interests with QNI of Australia. Making good on its plan to buy new base metals assets Billiton entered a joint venture in 1998 to explore for lead and zinc with Ireland's Ennex. Billiton also sold its metals brokerage subsidiary to Metallgesellschaft AG (Germany).

In 1999 Billiton announced that it would invest in smaller companies with promising properties and limit its own in-house exploration operations. It entered joint ventures with PT Taraco Mining to explore for coal in Indonesia and with Comet Resources to develop the Ravensthorpe Nickel Project in Western Australia.

Billiton's offer for a 21% stake in the Gove bauxite-alumina project in Australia was bested by Alcan in 2000. The company agreed to pay Alcoa about $1.5 billion for its majority stake in the Worsley alumina refinery in Australia. With Anglo American and Glencore International (now Glencore Xstrata) it acquired a 50% stake in Colombia's Cerrejon Zona Norte coal mine for $384 million; it then bought Canadian mining company Rio Algom (copper molybdenum uranium and coal) for $1.2 billion.

In 2001 Billiton closed the purchase of Alcoa's share of the Worsley smelter. The same year Billiton agreed to be acquired by Aussie natural resources company BHP Ltd. to form a dual-listed entity —known collectively as BHP Billiton —consisting of BHP Billiton Limited (run from Melbourne) and BHP Billiton plc (run from London). The deal closed in June of 2001.

EXECUTIVES

CEO, Andrew Mackenzie
CFO, Alex Vanselow, age 50, $186,846 total compensation
Chairman BHP Billiton South Africa, Xolani Mkhwanazi, age 58
CFO BHP Billiton Petroleum, David Powell
President Copper, Peter Beaven
President Manganese, Tom Schutte
CFO, Graham Kerr
President Iron Ore, Jimmy Wilson
President Stainless Steel Materials, Glenn Kellow
President and COO New Mexico Coal, Jac Fourie
President Marketing & Technology, Mike Henry
President Diamonds and Specialty Products, Tim Cutt
President Aluminium Manganese & Nickel, Daniel Malchuk
President Coal, Dean Della Valle
Chairman of the UK Trustees for the Christchurch Earthquake appeal, Ondra Bank
President Aluminium Manganese & Nickel, Daniel MalchukBE
Director, Wayne W. Murdy, age 68
Director, John G. S. Buchanan, age 68
Director, John M. Schubert, age 69
Director, Alan L. Boeckmann, age 64
Director, Keith C. Rumble, age 58
CEO and Director, Marius Kloppers, age 50
Director, Malcolm W. Broomhead, age 59
Director, Carolyn Hewson, age 57
Director, David A. Crawford, age 68
Group Company Secretary and Director, Jane F. McAloon, age 48
Director, Carlos Cordeiro, age 56
Director, Baroness Shriti Vadera
Auditors: KPMGAuditPlc

LOCATIONS

HQ: BHP Billiton Plc
Neathouse Place, Victoria, London SW1V 1BH
Phone: (44) 20 7802 4000 **Fax:** (44) 20 7802 4111
Web: www.bhpbilliton.com

COMPETITORS

Alcoa	Norilsk Nickel
Anglo American	Norsk Hydro ASA
BP	Rio Tinto plc
Chevron	Vale
Newmont Mining	Xstrata

HISTORICAL FINANCIALS

Company Type: Public

Income Statement FYE: June 30

	REVENUE ($ mil.)	NET INCOME ($ mil.)	NET PROFIT MARGIN	EMPLOYEES
06/13	65,968	10,876	16.5%	49,496
06/12	72,226	15,417	21.3%	46,370
06/11	71,739	23,648	33.0%	40,757
06/10	52,798	12,722	24.1%	39,570
06/09	50,211	5,877	11.7%	40,990
Annual Growth	7.1%	16.6%	—	4.8%

2013 Year-End Financials

Debt ratio: 25.4%
Return on equity: 15.9%
Cash ($ mil.): 6,060
Current ratio: 0.97
Long-term debt ($ mil.): 29,862

No. of shares (mil.): —
Dividends
Yield: 0.0%
Payout: 111.9%
Market value ($ mil.): —

	STOCK PRICE ($)	P/E		PER SHARE ($)		
	FY Close	High/Low		Earnings	Dividends	Book Value
06/13	51.27	35	25	2.04	2.28	13.28
06/12	57.19	28	18	2.88	2.20	12.38
06/11	78.43	20	12	4.27	1.82	10.66
06/10	51.44	31	18	2.28	1.66	8.72
06/09	45.46	73	20	1.05	1.64	7.18
Annual Growth	3.1%	—	—	17.9%	8.6%	16.6%

BNP Paribas (France)

One of Europe's largest banks BNP Paribas operates about 7300 branches in more than 80 countries across Europe North America Africa and Asia. The company and its myriad subsidiaries specialize in retail banking corporate and investment banking and investment services. It operates in Italy through BNL banca commerciale. BNP Paribas also owns a majority stake in Belgium's BNP Paribas Fortis which operates more than 1000 branches in Europe and the US. In the western US the company owns BancWest (the parent of Bank of the West and First Hawaiian Bank). BNP Paribas earns more than half of its revenue outside its home country of France.

BNP Paribas' Investment Solutions division includes BNP Paribas Securities BNP Paribas Wealth Management and insurance firms BNP Paribas Cardif and Pinnacle Insurance (Cardif Pinnacle).

Other holdings include private bank BNP Paribas Banque Privee consumer lender Cetelem online brokerage Cortal Consors BNP Paribas Asset Management.

Major acquisitions in recent years have turned BNP Paribas into a leading bank in the euro zone and beyond. The company has expanded its operations into about a dozen countries since 2004.

In 2013 BNP agreed to buy Belgium's 25% share in its local consumer-banking unit for 3.25 billion euros ($4.37 billion) as the country works to cut public debt. It also acquired Poland's Bank BGZ from Rabobank Group in 2013.

Two of the most tranformative acquisitions include the deal to buy Italian bank BNL in 2006 and the 75% purchase of Fortis Bank (which also included a 25% stake in Fortis Insurance). Both deals boosted BNP Paribas' retail banking business across Europe. Retail banking is now responsible for some 50% of BNP Paribas' revenues.

In addition to the Fortis and BNL acquisitions BNP Paribas looked to grow in new markets. BNP Paribas acquired Sahara Bank in Libya and a 51% stake in UkrSibbank one of Ukraine's leading banks. In 2011 BNP Paribas continued its strategy of expanding in high growth markets and acquired a majority of South Africa's Cadiz Securities. BNP Paribas also owns Banque Internationale pour le Commerce et l'Industrie which is active in six African nations and a majority of Turk Ekonomi Bankasi in Turkey. BNP Paribas has been expanding in China Egypt Israel and Russia as well.

In 2010 BNP Paribas acquired US investment bank Hill Street Capital which became part of BNP Paribas Securities. The acquisition solidified the firm's mergers and acquisitions practices and other corporate advisory services in North and South America.

Despite all of this growth BNP Paribas has not been immune to difficulties in the banking sector especially in Europe where banks were exposed to sovereign debt. While retail banking remained strong BNP Paribas saw declines in its corporate and investment banking unit due to poor market conditions and losses on sales of sovereign bond debt. Like its peers the company announced job cuts in 2011. It also plans to cut some 10% of its total assets most of which will come from its investment and corporate banking operations. Also that year BNP Paribas sold its private investment management operations in the UK to Evolution Group's Williams de Broe.

The challenges of that year continued when BNP Paribas took a ?3 billion ($4.1 billion) hit after it marked down the value of its Greek debt by about 60%. It also reduced exposure to other European government debt in places such as Italy and Spain.

In 2012 the comany sold the bulk of its controlling stake in real estate firm Klepierre to US mall owner Simon for some ?1.5 billion (around $2 billion) to further raise its capital levels.

The Belgian government owns about 10% of BNP Paribas.

HISTORY

BNP Paribas Group's predecessor Banque Nationale de Paris (BNP) is the progeny of two state banks with parallel histories; each was set up to jump-start the economy after a revolution in 1848.

For a century Paris-based Comptoir National d'Escompte de Paris (CNEP) bounced between private and public status depending on government whim. It was the #3 bank in France from the late 19th century through the 1950s.

Banque National pour le Commerce et l'Industrie (BNCI) started in Alsace a region that was part of Germany from the Franco-Prussian War until WWI. BNCI served as an economic bridge between Germany and France which had to give the bank governmental resuscitation during the Depression. By the 1960s BNCI had passed CNEP in size.

French leader Charles de Gaulle expected banking to drive post-WWII reconstruction and in 1945 CNEP and BNCI were nationalized. In 1966 France's finance minister merged them and they became BNP. That year the company started an association with Dresdner Bank of Germany under which the two still operate joint ventures primarily in Eastern Europe.

By 1993 privatization was again in vogue and BNP was cut loose by the government. It expanded outside France to ameliorate the influences of the French economy and government. Even before it was privatized BNP was involved in such politically charged actions as the bailout of OPEC money repository Banque Arabe and the extension of credit to Algeria's state oil company Sonatrach.

The privatized BNP looked overseas in the late 1990s. In 1997 alone it won the right to operate in New Zealand bought Laurentian Bank and Trust of the Bahamas took control of its joint venture with Egypt's Banque du Caire and opened a subsidiary in Brazil.

BNP bought failed Peregrine Investment's Chinese operations in 1998. That year the bank also expanded in Peru opened an office in Algeria opened a representative office in Uzbekistan set up an investment banking subsidiary in India and bought Australian stock brokerage operations from Prudential.

After a decade of globe-trotting BNP brought it on home in 1999 and set off a year of tumult in French banking. As France's other two large banks (Societe Generale and Paribas) made plans to merge BNP decided it would absorb both banks as a means to get a bigger chunk of the to-be-privatized Credit Lyonnais and to protect France from Euro-megabank penetration by creating the globe's largest bank.

Executives at Societe Generale (SG) had other ideas forming a cartel called "Action Against the BNP Raid." Meanwhile BNP tried to boost to controlling stakes its holdings in the two banks. (In Europe's cross-ownership tradition the target banks also owned part of BNP.) France's central bank tried unsuccessfully to negotiate a deal (the government supported the triumvirate merger). A war of words was played out in the media and finally shareholders had to vote on the proposals. In the end BNP won control of Paribas but not SG. As BNP prepared to integrate a reluctant Paribas into its operations regulators ordered BNP to relinquish its stake in SG. The newly merged company was dubbed BNP Paribas Group.

In 2000 BNP Paribas and Avis Group launched a fleet-management joint venture. BNP also bought 150 shopping centers from French retailer Carrefour and the 40% of merchant bank Cobepa that it didn't already own. In 2001 BNP Paribas took full control of US-based BancWest. The company bought United California Bank from UFJ Holdings (now part of Mitsubishi UFJ Financial Group) the following year.

The bank opened up a second "home market" when it bought Italy's Banca Nazionale del Lavoro (BNL) for $11 billion in 2006.

In 2008 as the world's economies struggled to stay afloat the French government agreed to inject ?10.5 billion ($14 billion) into the nation's top six banks including BNP Paribas. The government didn't receive shares in the banks it assisted; rather the capital injections were meant to help reenergize lending activities in France. A year after receiving the cash BNP Paribas announced plans to repay the government's aid.

After a couple of false starts and a seven-month saga BNP Paribas acquired control of Fortis Banque (also known as Fortis Bank) in 2009. Fortis' Dutch operations were excluded from the transaction. The deal further cemented BNP Paribas as a top European bank. Fortis Bank was nationalized in October 2008 to prevent its collapse and the takeover by BNP Paribas was delayed and revised to satisfy Fortis shareholders and other interested parties. Upon the closing of the deal BNP Paribas became the market leader in Belgium and Luxembourg. The Belgian government gained more than 10% of BNP Paribas in the transaction.

BNP Paribas complimented its 2009 acquisition of Fortis with the purchase of private bank Insinger de Beaufort.

EXECUTIVES

Head Group Risk Management, Michel Konczaty
COO, Philippe Bordenave
COO Corporate & Investment Banking and Investment Solutions, Georges Chodron de Courcel, age 63, $803,412 total compensation
Chairman, Baudouin Prot, age 62, $1,324,710 total compensation
Managing Director and Head Compliance and Internal Control Coordinator, Jean Clamon, age 61, $648,370 total compensation
CEO and Director, Jean-Laurent Bonnafe, age 52
Global Head Information Technology and Processes, Alain Marbach, age 51
CEO and General Manager BNL, Fabio Gallia, age 49
Deputy Chief Operating Officer and Head of Investment Solutions Personal Finance and International Retail Banking, Jacques d'Estais

Deputy Chief Operating Officer and Head of Corporate and Investment Banking, Alain Papiasse, age 54
COO, Francois Villeroy de Galhau, age 54
Head of Asia-Pacific Region, Eric Raynaud
Head of Human Resources, Yves Martrenchar, age 56
Senior Latin American Economist, Nader Nazmi
Human Resources Director of Real Estate, Pascal Maury
Chief Executive Officer, Jean-Laurent Bonnafe
Director, Louis Schweitzer, age 70
Director, Claude Bebear, age 77
Director, Helene Ploix, age 67
Director, Denis Kessler, age 61
CEO and Director, Jean-Laurent Bonnafe, age 51
Director, Jean-Marie Gianno, age 60
Director, Prof Jean-Francois Lepetit, age 70
Director, Daniela Weber-Rey, age 55
Director, Meglena Kuneva, age 55
Auditors: Deloitte&Associes

LOCATIONS

HQ: BNP Paribas (France)
16, boulevard des Italiens, Paris 75009
Phone: (33) 1 40 14 45 46
Web: www.bnpparibas.com

PRODUCTS/OPERATIONS

2010 Sales by Segment

	% of total
Retail	54
Corporate and investment	27
Investment	14
Other	5
Total	**100**

COMPETITORS

ABN AMRO Group
BBVA
Banco Popular Espa?ol
Bank of America
Barclays
Citigroup
Credit Agricole
Deutsche Bank
HSBC
JPMorgan Chase
Natixis
Societe Generale
U.S. Bancorp
UBS
Wells Fargo

HISTORICAL FINANCIALS

Company Type: Public

Income Statement FYE: December 31

	ASSETS ($ mil.)	NET INCOME ($ mil.)	INCOME AS % OF ASSETS	EMPLOYEES
12/12	2,513,902	8,637	0.3%	188,551
12/11	2,541,999	7,825	0.3%	198,423
12/10	2,674,279	10,496	0.4%	205,348
12/09	2,964,257	8,401	0.3%	201,740
12/08	2,901,809	4,223	0.1%	173,188
Annual Growth	(3.5%)	19.6%	—	2.1%

2012 Year-End Financials

Return on assets: 0.3%
Return on equity: 8.1%
Long-term debt ($ mil.): —
No. of shares (mil.): 1,238
Sales ($ mil): 128,541
Dividends
Yield: 2.5%
Payout: 18.2%
Market value ($ mil.): 36,184

	STOCK PRICE ($) FY Close	P/E High/Low		PER SHARE ($) Earnings	Dividends	Book Value
12/12	29.21	10	5	6.79	0.75	91.38
12/11	19.65	16	6	6.22	2.72	81.80
12/10	31.95	13	6	8.46	1.87	83.57
12/09	40.16	18	5	7.49	1.64	84.52
12/08	21.45	40	12	4.28	2.59	81.95
Annual Growth	8.0%	—	—	12.2%	(26.7%)	2.8%

Boc Hong Kong Holdings Ltd

BOC Hong Kong (Holdings) is the parent of Bank of China (Hong Kong) which has about 300 branches in Hong Kong as well as on mainland China. The bank serves local businesses and consumers providing loans deposit accounts and other standard services as well as securities brokerage wealth management and project financing and syndication. It also prints currency. In addition Bank of China (Hong Kong) owns Nanyang Commercial Bank and some 70% of Chiyu Banking Corporation (both are also based in Hong Kong) as well as BOC Credit Card (International). Bank of China which is controlled by the Chinese government owns about two-thirds of BOC Hong Kong.

The company wants to diversify its revenue mix by focusing on increasing its business in wealth management insurance and corporate finance. It is looking to China for growth and has plans to expand to other parts of Asia as well.

EXECUTIVES

Vice Chairman, Changji Sun, age 70
Deputy Chief Executive, Yim Nam Lam, age 60
Company Secretary, Jason C. W. Yeung, age 58
Chairman, Xiao Gang, age 54
Vice Chairman and Chief Executive, Guangbei He, age 58
Executive Director and Deputy Chief Executive, Yingxin Gao, age 50
Chief Risk Officer, Alex Y. S. Cheung, age 51
CIO, Peter Y. K. Liu, age 61
Deputy Chief Executive, David S. H. Wong, age 61
Chief Financial Officer, Zhuo Chengwen
Senior Vice President General Manager Hong Kong & Macau, Chris Clark
Vice Chairman, Changji Sun, age 70
Vice Chairman and Chief Executive, Guangbei He, age 58
Auditors: PricewaterhouseCoopers

LOCATIONS

HQ: Boc Hong Kong Holdings Ltd
52nd Floor, Bank of China Tower, 1 Garden Road,
Phone: (852) 2846 2700 **Fax:** (852) 2810 5830
Web: www.bochk.com

COMPETITORS

AXA Asia Pacific
Bank of Communications
Bank of East Asia
CITIC International Financial
Chong Hing Bank
Citigroup
Dah Sing Financial Holdings Limited
HSBC
Hang Seng Bank
Standard Chartered

HISTORICAL FINANCIALS

Company Type: Public

Income Statement FYE: December 31

	ASSETS ($ mil.)	NET INCOME ($ mil.)	INCOME AS % OF ASSETS	EMPLOYEES
12/12	236,174	2,700	1.1%	14,638
12/11	223,804	2,630	1.2%	14,475
12/10	213,705	2,083	1.0%	13,806
12/09	156,400	1,769	1.1%	13,244
12/08	148,035	431	0.3%	0
Annual Growth	12.4%	58.2%	—	—

2012 Year-End Financials

Return on assets: 1.1%
Return on equity: 14.8%
Long-term debt ($ mil.): —
No. of shares (mil.): —
Sales ($ mil): 7,767
Dividends
Yield: 0.0%
Payout: 18.2%
Market value ($ mil.): —

	STOCK PRICE ($) FY Close	P/E High/Low		PER SHARE ($) Earnings	Dividends	Book Value
12/12	63.05	1	0	0.26	0.05	1.84
12/11	47.16	1	0	0.25	0.05	1.58
12/10	68.43	1	0	0.20	0.04	1.40
12/09	45.44	1	0	0.17	0.01	1.26
12/08	22.50	3	1	0.04	0.04	1.01
Annual Growth	29.4%	—	—	58.2%	4.8%	16.2%

Bombardier Inc.

Canada's Bombardier is the world's only manufacturer of both planes and trains (but no automobiles). The company's Aerospace division manufactures business (Learjet) commercial (CSeries) and amphibious military (Bombardier 415) aircraft while overseas its Germany-based Transportation division manufactures rail vehicles including monorails light rails metros commuter trains high-speed trains (including the very high speed ZEFIRO) and locomotives. Both are industry-leading businesses. A third division Flexjet offers fractional jet ownership and charter services. (In late 2013 Bombardier announced it was selling Flexjet.)

Strategy

Over the next decade industry forecasts show sustained growth in business and commercial aircraft markets. As a result Bombardier's Aerospace unit continues to invest in and develop new state-of-the art aircraft lines such as its CSeries commercial aircraft family which is aiming to be the world's greenest and most fuel efficient mainliner.

The Aerospace division made one of its largest business aircraft sales in its history in late 2012 when luxury aviation company VistaJet signed a deal for up to 142 Global family business jets for $7.8 billion if all options are exercised. Deliveries of these aircraft will begin in 2014. Prior to that in mid-2012 Bombardier Aerospace won another landmark business jet order from NetJets for a whopping $7.3 billion.

On the rail transportation side demand for sturdy and efficient trains continues to be driven by urban and suburban development worldwide as well as ongoing demand for reliable public transportation. In South America's largest metropolis Sao Paulo Brazil Bombardier's Transportation division is undertaking a notable project to build the world's largest largest mass transit monorail to deal with the city's congestion. The monorail is due to begin operating in early 2014. The project is part of a broader effort by Bombardier to gain a stronger foothold in emerging markets with high growth potential; others include China India and Russia.

Bombardier's Transportation division is actively involved in China's development of urban mass transit and advanced rail networks. Demand is strong there as the growing popularity of rail transportation is actually eating into the profits of regional aviation companies. Bombardier Transportation has three joint ventures in China as well as several wholly owned foreign enterprises and offices in Beijing Guangzhou Shanghai and Hong Kong. One of its key contracts is a $4 billion order from China's Ministry of Railways (MOR) to deliver of several different types of ZEFIRO very high speed trains.

Ownership

The company is controlled by the Bombardier family.

Company Background

Bombardier engineers and industrial designers spent two years designing the Vancouver 2010 Olympic torch. To ensure the flame would not extinguish in temperatures reaching minus 36 degrees Celsius (minus 96.8 degrees Fahrenheit) the company blended propane and isobutane a mixture that supports fire at extremely cold temperatures. It manufactured 12000 torches each with a side vent to allow the flame to unfurl like a flag.

HISTORY

Bombardier got its start in the 1920s when mechanic Joseph-Armand Bombardier began converting old cars into snowmobiles. He founded L'Auto-Neige Bombardier Limited in 1942 to make commercial snow vehicles. In 1959 Bombardier introduced the first personal snowmobile the Ski-Doo.

At age 27 Laurent Beaudoin became the company's president in 1966. Bombardier went public in 1969. When the bottom dropped out of the snowmobile business due to the energy crisis in 1973 Beaudoin diversified and in 1974 Bombardier won its first mass transit contract to build Montreal subway cars. Expanding further into mass transportation Bombardier merged with MLW-Worthington Limited a builder of diesel engines and diesel-electric locomotives. In 1978 the company became Bombardier Inc.

During the 1980s Bombardier continued to diversify. It expanded into military vehicles and became the leading supplier to the North American rail transit industry. The company entered the European railcar market in 1986 the same year it acquired Canadair Canada's largest aerospace company from the national government.

Founded in 1920 as the aircraft division of Canadian Vickers Canadair became a separate company producing military and civilian aircraft in 1944. Acquired by Electric Boat (which became part of General Dynamics) in 1947 it was nationalized by the Canadian government in 1976. In 1978 Canadair introduced its Challenger 600 business jet which became a major seller.

Bombardier began development of a commuter aircraft the Canadian Regional Jet (a 50-seat derivative of the Challenger) in 1989. In 1990 the company bought US-based Learjet and its service centers and two years later it acquired a stake in de Havilland a regional aircraft maker which it jointly owned with the Province of Ontario. The company bought German railroad equipment maker Waggonfabrik Talbot in 1995.

Amtrak selected an international consortium in 1996 headed by Bombardier to produce high-speed trains electric locomotives and train maintenance facilities. Also that year the Global Express business jet made its first flight.

Bombardier doubled the size of its European operations in 1998 by buying German railcar maker Deutsche Waggonbau. In 1999 Bombardier announced the launch of its all-new business jet the eight-passenger Continental.

The company sold its 50% stake in Shorts Missile Systems to Thomson-CSF (now Thales) in 2000. Also that year Bombardier landed an $817 million contract to supply Spanish carrier Air Nostrum with 44 planes. It also inked a $2 billion deal to make 94 regional jets for Delta Air Lines; the Delta order included options for an additional 406 aircraft through 2010.

Bombardier signed a deal with SkyWest in 2001 worth about $1.4 billion for 64 Canadair regional jets. It was also selected by a bankruptcy court as winning bidder for Outboard Marine's Evinrude and Johnson outboard marine engine assets. Completing an agreement made the year before Bombardier acquired DaimlerChrysler's Adtranz rail systems unit for about $725 million making it part of its Bombardier Transportation division. Later in the year the company announced that it would take a charge of about $600 million and lay off about 10% of its aerospace workforce (it also said that it would cut another 7% of that workforce if demand did not grow).

Bombardier sought about $870 million in damages in 2002 from DaimlerChrysler (now Daimler) over the Adtranz deal claiming that the level of equity in Adtranz was overstated and that the costs related to third-party contracts were higher than stated at the time of the deal. Later that year Bombardier temporarily suspended business jet production. Bombardier divested its Recreational Products unit (snowmobiles and personal watercraft) in 2003.

Bombardier announced in 2004 that it was considering building a family (CSeries) of 100- to 130-seat jets that would compete directly with Boeing and Airbus. The next year the company's board approved the larger CSeries planes but it deferred its final decision; in 2006 Bombardier announced that it would focus instead on 80- to 100-seat passenger planes. In 2007 the company announced the new project's official name —the CRJ1000. That same year Bombardier began a performance improvement project at its Transportation division. The project which aimed to improve performance by trimming costs —chiefly procurement costs — began to show signs of effectiveness in 2007. The company continued to seek the right mix of suppliers for parts including low-cost sources.

CEO Paul Tellier resigned in 2004 amid rumored boardroom differences with Laurent Beaudoin who assumed the CEO duties. A year later in 2005 the company sold its inventory finance division which provided equipment financing to GE Commercial Finance for $2.4 billion ($1.4 billion in cash and $1 billion in assumed liabilities).

Deliveries and orders were booming for Bombardier's line of business jets before the worldwide credit crisis and recession hit in 2008. The company had 232 deliveries for business jets in fiscal 2008 compared with 212 in 2007 and 197 in 2006.

Laurent Beaudoin maintained his role as chairman when in 2008 he handed over the president and CEO titles to his son Pierre.

The business and civil aircraft markets experienced their most turbulent conditions since the aftermath of September 11 due to the global recession and credit crisis in 2009. The perpetually dicey financial condition of the airline industry —due to fluctuating fuel prices and shifts in consumer spending —affected demand for commercial aircraft. Bombardier's limited number of customers many of which are government agencies or publicly held companies watched as their own revenues fell due to the recession.

Bombardier adapted by reducing its production of business jets and CRJ regional aircraft and reducing its workforce by 4700 (about 13%). The company also took the opportunity to build on its customer services opening a service center in Europe and a third service center in the US.

EXECUTIVES

SVP General Counsel and Assistant Secretary, Daniel Desjardins

Senior Vice President Bombardier Inc, Richard C. Bradeen

Vice Chairman, Jean-Louis Fontaine, age 74, $375,000 total compensation

Chairman, Laurent Beaudoin, age 75, $1,000,000 total compensation

President and COO Bombardier Aerospace, Guy C. Hachey, age 57

President Chief Operating Officer, Andre Navarri, age 61, $1,268,350 total compensation

President Chief Executive Officer, Pierre Beaudoin, age 55, $1,100,000 total compensation

SVP and CFO, Pierre Alary, $588,000 total compensation

President Bombardier Aircraft Service Centres, Michael McQuay

President Commercial Aircraft Bombardier Aerospace, Gary R. Scott

President Business Aircraft Bombardier Aerospace, Steven A. (Steve) Ridolfi

President Bombardier Specialized and Amphibious Aircraft, Michel Bourgeois

SVP Human Resources and Public Affairs, John Paul Macdonald

External Communications Bombardier Aerospace, Sylvie Gauthier

Public Relations and Communications Bombardier Aerospace, Marc Duchesne

Media Relations Commercial Aircraft Bombardier Aerospace, Bert Cruickshank

President Customer Services and Specialized &, James Hoblyn

President Rolling Stock Atlantic and Services, Laurent Troger

President North America, Raymond Bachant

Director Sales India Sales Commercial Aircraft, Sunder Venkat

Sales Director Asia/Pacific Sales Commercial Aircraft, Ryan DeBrusk

Media Relations Business Aircraft Bombardier Aerospace, Danielle Boudreau

Director Communications Canada, Isabelle Rondeau

Media Relations Commercial Aircraft Bombardier Aerospace, John Arnone

Communications and Public Affairs Europe, Alec McRitchie

Media Contact Flexjet, Erin Portman

Media Relations Nordic Countries, Heiner Spannuth

Media Relations Norway, Jonny Hedberg

Media Relations France, Anne Froger

Media Relations Spain Portugal and Greece, Luis Ramos

Chief Country Representative Belgium, Johan van den Bussche

Chief Country Representative Denmark, Klas Wahlberg

Director Sales South Asia Business Aircraft Bombardier Business Aircraft, Nilesh Pattanayak

Chief Country Representative Poland, Janusz Kucmin

Chief Country Representative Portugal, Mario Domingues

Chief Country Representative South Korea, Henry Kim

Chief Country Representative Spain, Alvaro Rengifo

Director Business Development Bombardier Customer Services Beijing, Gaetan Dureau

Regional VP Russia, Christophe Degoumois

President Flexjet, Deanna White

President Rail Control Solutions, Peter Cedervall

President Systems, Pierre Attendu

Director, Jean C. Monty, age 66

Director, Heinrich Weiss, age 71

Director, Thierry Desmarest, age 68

Director, Carlos E. Represas, age 68

Vice Chairman, Jean-Louis Fontaine, age 74

Vice Chairman, J.R. Andre Bombardier, age 69

Director, Jean-Pierre Rosso, age 73

Director, Andre Berard, age 71

President CEO and Director, Pierre Beaudoin, age 54

Director, Janine Bombardier, age 80
Director, Martha F. Brooks, age 53
Director, L. Denis Desautels, age 70
Director, Daniel Johnson, age 69
Auditors: Ernst&YoungLLP

LOCATIONS

HQ: Bombardier Inc.
800 Rene-Levesque Blvd. West, 29th Floor, Montreal, Quebec H3B 1Y8
Phone: 514 861-9481 **Fax:** 514 861-2420
Web: www.bombardier.com

2011 Aircraft Sales

	% of total
North America	
US	38
Europe	30
Asia/Pacific	17
Other	15
Total	**100**

2011 Transportation Sales

	% of total
Europe	65
Asia/Pacific	18
North	13
Other	4
Total	**100**

PRODUCTS/OPERATIONS

2011 Sales by Segment

	% of total
Transportation	51
Aerospace	49
Total	**100**

2011 Sales by Industry

	% of total
Manufacturing	73
Services	16
Other	11
Total	**100**

2011 Aerospace Sales by Market

	% of total
Business	44
Commercial	25
Services	18
Other	13
Total	**100**

2011 Transportation Sales by Market

	% of total
Rolling	70
Services	15
System and	15
Total	**100**

Selected Operations

Aerospace
Amphibious aircraft
415
415 MP
Business aircraft
Challenger
Global
Learjet
Commercial aircraft
CRJ Series
CSeries
Q-Series
Flying training
Military aircraft technical service
Specialized aircraft modified for special missions
Training and aircraft services
Maintenance
Parts
Technical support
Training
Flexjet
Fractional ownership
Whole aircraft ownership and management
Transportation
Customized transportation systems
Propulsion and controls
Rail control systems
Rail vehicles
Automated people movers
Commuter/regional trains
Intercity/high-speed trains
Light rail vehicles
Locomotives
Metros
Monorails
Rapid transit
Services
Fleet maintenance
Material management
Operations and maintenance
Vehicle refurbishment and modernization

COMPETITORS

ALSTOM
AeroCentury
Airbus
Beechcraft
Blue Star Jets
Boeing
COMAC
Cessna
Dassault Aviation
EADS
Embraer
Finmeccanica
Flight Options
Gulfstream Aerospace
Kawasaki Rail Car
Mitsubishi Heavy Industries
NetJets
Piper Aircraft
Siemens AG
Thales
XOJET

HISTORICAL FINANCIALS

Company Type: Public

Income Statement FYE: December 31

	REVENUE ($ mil.)	NET INCOME ($ mil.)	NET PROFIT MARGIN	EMPLOYEES
12/12	16,768	588	3.5%	71,500
12/11*	18,347	837	4.6%	70,000
01/11	17,712	755	4.3%	65,370
01/10	19,366	698	3.6%	62,900
01/09	19,721	1,008	5.1%	66,870
Annual Growth	(4.0%)	(12.6%)	—	1.7%

*Fiscal year change

2012 Year-End Financials

Debt ratio: 20.7%
Return on equity: 59.5%
Cash ($ mil.): 2,896
Current ratio: 1.07
Long-term debt ($ mil.): 5,360
No. of shares (mil.): 1,730
Dividends
Yield: 0.0%
Payout: 39.7%
Market value ($ mil.): 6,593

	STOCK PRICE ($) FY Close	P/E High/Low		PER SHARE ($) Earnings	Dividends	Book Value
12/12	3.81	15	9	0.32	0.13	0.77
12/11*	3.95	16	7	0.47	0.10	0.37
01/11	5.75	15	10	0.42	0.10	2.48
01/10	4.74	14	5	0.39	0.09	2.14
01/09	3.05	15	5	0.56	0.07	1.47
Annual Growth	5.7% (15.0%)	—	—	(13.1%)	17.0%	

*Fiscal year change

Bouygues S.A.

If all roads lead to Bouygues that's because the company built them. Bouygues (pronounced "bweeg") operates in three primary business areas: construction telecommunications and media. Its largest segment construction is involved in road work buildings and property development and accounts for some three-fourths of the group's sales. Subsidiaries include Colas (road construction and maintenance about 40% of sales) and Bouygues Construction (around 30%). Bouygues Immobilier is its property development arm with interests in commercial and residential development. The group owns 90% stake of Bouygues Telecom (France's #3 mobile phone carrier); it also owns more than 40% of TF1 (France's #1 TV channel).

Road builder Colas which accounts for about 40% of the group's sales provides construction and maintenance services as well as producing materials such as concrete and aggregates from its quarries and plants. Colas' sales declined by 1% in 2010 largely as a result of difficult market conditions in Central America. However the company saw growth in North America northern Europe and Asia that year. Colas is shifting its efforts in the regions accordingly.

Subsidiary Bouygues Construction is a force in itself with several subsidiaries performing civil construction and electrical/maintenance work. The group focuses on public-private partnerships those lucrative partnerships that governments use to build roads prisons schools and other infrastructure. Bouygues has increasingly participated in sustainable development projects with investments in training research and resources.

Bouygues Construction also is broadening its operations in electrical contracting and property development and expects to expand its presence in Europe as well. In 2010 the group acquired the UK division of Dutch builder Heijmans for E45 million ($59 million). Two years later the company bought Thomas Vale Group which is active in central England. Although tough economic conditions caused a cut in revenues in 2010 Bouygues has secured a number of lucrative international projects such as the Singapore Sports Hub and a rail tunnel in Hong Kong. It is also involved in its first North American projects.

Other Bouygues units have been busy too. TF1 holding company Television Francaise acquired additional stakes in channels TMC and NT1 in 2010 to diversify and its Eurosport International online and television platform has expanded to some 60 nations. In 2010 Bouygues Telecom added more than 700000 new mobile customers representing about a quarter of the net market growth. That year it introduced its Bbox fiber very-high-speed offering and in 2009 it launched the market's first quadruple play offering.

Bouygues also has a 30% stake in ALSTOM (making it the largest shareholder) which builds rail cars ships and power plants. After seeing a decline in revenue in 2009 and 2010 Alstom implemented some restructuring efforts which have paid off with rebounding sales. Key among its strategies is the focus shift from the developed world where demand for coal and gas power plants has weakened to emerging markets.

Chairman Martin Bouygues and his brother Olivier sons of the company's founder own about 20% of Bouygues through holding company SCDM; they control more than a quarter of the voting rights.

HISTORY

With the equivalent of $1700 in borrowed money Francis Bouygues son of a Paris engineer started Entreprise Francis Bouygues in 1952 as an industrial works and construction firm in the Paris region of France. Within four years his firm had expanded into property development.

By the mid-1960s Bouygues had entered the civil engineering and public works sectors and developed regional construction units across France. In 1970 it was listed on the Paris stock exchange. Four years later the company established Bouygues Offshore to build oil platforms.

In 1978 the firm built Terminal 2 of Paris' Charles de Gaulle airport. Three years later it won the contract to construct the University of Riyadh in Saudi Arabia (then the world's largest building project at 3.2 million sq. ft.) which was completed in 1984. That year Bouygues acquired France's #3 water supply company Saur and power transmission and supply firm ETDE.

Expansion continued in 1986 with the purchase of the Screg Group which included Colas France's top highway contractor. The next year the company led a consortium to buy 50% of newly privatized network Societe Television Francaise 1 (TF1). Bouygues became the largest shareholder with a 25% stake (increased to 40% by 1999). In 1988 the company began building the Channel Tunnel (completed 1994) and moved into its new ultra-modern headquarters dubbed Challenger in Saint-Quentin-en-Yvelines outside Paris.

After rumors of failing health Francis Bouygues resigned as chairman in 1989. His son Martin took over as chairman and CEO although the patriarch called France's "Emperor of Concrete" remained on the board until his death in 1993.

Despite fears that the group would suffer without its founder's leadership Bouygues continued to grow with the 1989 acquisition of a majority interest in Grands Moulins de Paris France's largest flour milling firm (sold 1998). In 1990 it purchased Swiss construction group Losinger.

The company entered the telecom industry in 1993 with a national paging network and added a mobile phone license a year later. In 1996 the group listed 40% of Bouygues Offshore's shares on the New York and Paris stock exchanges. Also that year it launched mobile phone operator Bouygues Telecom and entered a partnership with Telecom Italia.

By 1999 Bouygues Telecom had reached 2 million customers and Bouygues bought back a 20% share held by the UK's Cable and Wireless to increase its stake to nearly 54%. That year Bouygues Offshore bought Norwegian engineering firm Kvaerner and the group spun off its construction sector creating Bouygues Construction.

After word circulated that Deutsche Telekom wanted to acquire the group's telecom unit Bouygues became the target of takeover rumors. Francois Pinault France's richest businessman became Bouygues' largest non-family shareholder when he increased his stake to 14% (later reduced to about 2%). Pinault's biggest rival Bernard Arnault upped his stake to more than 9% of the group fueling speculation of a battle over control of the board.

In 2001 the company pulled out of France's auction for a third-generation wireless license and remained the only European incumbent mobile carrier without a major domestic investment in 3G technology (until 2009). The next year the company agreed to buy Telecom Italia's stake in Bouygues Telecom increasing Bouygues' ownership in the mobile operator from 54% to more than 65%. In 2002 the company sold its 51% stake in oil field platform construction unit Bouygues Offshore to Italian oil services group Saipem which announced plans to bid for the remaining shares.

However talks with German utility giant E.ON over the sale of Bouygues' Saur subsidiary failed that year after E.ON decided to focus instead on its electricity and gas operations.

In 2005 Bouygues was more successful when it sought to sell Saur piecemeal. It sold several divisions of the subsidiary (Coved Saur France Saur International and Stereau) to French private equity firm PAI Partners but retained the African and Italian (Sigesa-Crea) divisions of the firm.

Bouygues bought the French government's 21% stake in ALSTOM for $2.5 billion in 2006. The deal was approved on the condition that it not try to control the company for at least three years. Bouygues did build up its holding after the acquisition though.

In 2008 property developer Bouygues Immobilier expanded with the acquisition of Urbis a French rival. That year Colas bought the Gouyer Group of companies (distribution of construction materials) in Martinique and Guadeloupe while Bouygues Telecom acquired a fixed-line network that allowed it to launch the Bbox broadband router and Internet services that include VoIP e-mail Internet access and television; the telecom unit also gained the previously denied right to offer the iPhone 3G.

EXECUTIVES

Deputy CEO and Director, Olivier Bouygues, age 62, $920,000 total compensation
EVP Information Systems and New Technologies and Director, Alain Pouyat, age 69, $920,000 total compensation
Chairman and CEO, Martin Bouygues, age 61, $920,000 total compensation
Director; Chairman and CEO TF1, Nonce Paolini, age 64
Corporate Secretary, Jean-Francois Guillemin, age 61
Director; Chairman CEO and Director Bouygues Construction, Yves Gabriel, age 63, $850,000 total compensation
SVP Human Resources and Administration, Jean-Claude Tostivin, age 66
CEO and Director Bouygues Telecom, Olivier Roussat, age 49
CFO, Philippe Marien, age 57
Press Contact, Emilie Combe
Director, Jean Peyrelevade, age 74
Director; Chairman CEO and Director Colas, Herve Le Bouc, age 60
Deputy CEO and Director, Olivier Bouygues, age 62
EVP Information Systems and New Technologies and Director, Alain Pouyat, age 69
Director, Georges Chodron de Courcel, age 63
Director; Chairman and CEO TF1, Nonce Paolini, age 64
Director; Chairman CEO and Director Bouygues Immobilier, Francois Bertiere, age 62
Director, Pierre Barberis, age 71
Director, Lucien Douroux, age 80
Director, Patricia Barbizet, age 58
Director; Chairman CEO and Director Bouygues Construction, Yves Gabriel, age 63
Director, Francois-Henri Pinault, age 51
Director, Helman le Pas de Secheval, age 46
Auditors: Mazars&Guerard

LOCATIONS

HQ: Bouygues S.A.
32 avenue Hoche, Paris, Cedex 08 75378
Phone: (33) 1 44 20 10 00
Web: www.bouygues.com

2010 Sales

	% of total
Europe	
France	69
Other	14
North	7
Asia/Pacific	5
Africa & Middle	5
Central & South	-
Total	**100**

PRODUCTS/OPERATIONS

2010 Sales by Segment

	% of total
Construction	74
Telecoms	18
Media	8
Total	**100**

2010 Sales

	% of total
Colas	37
Bouygues	29
Bouygues	18
TF1	8
Bouygues	8
Other	-
Total	**100**

Selected Subsidiaries and Affiliates

Construction
- Autoroute de liaison Seine-Sarthe SA (33%)
- Bouygues Batiment Ile-de-France SA (99.9%)
  - Bati-Renov SA (99.3%)
- Bouygues Batiment International SA (99.9%)
  - Bouygues Thai Ltd (49%)
  - DTP Singapour Pte Ltd (99.9%)
  - Kohler Investment SA (Luxembourg 99.9%)
- Bouygues Construction SA (99.9%)
- ETDE SA (99.9%)
  - Exprimm IT (99.9%)
  - Icel Maidstone Ltd (UK 99.9%)
- Quille SA (99.9%)
- Westminster Local Education Partnership Ltd (UK 80%)

Media
- Metro France Publications (15%)
- Television Francaise 1 SA (TF1 43%)
- TF1 Video (43%)
- TV Breizh (43%)

Property
- Bouygues Immobilier
- Parque Empresearial Cristalia SL
- SNC Bouygues Immobilier Entreprises Ile-de-France

Roads
- Cofiroute (16%)
- Colas Guadeloupe (97%)
- Colas Hungaria (97%)
- Colas Polska (97%)
- Colas SA (96%)
- Spac (97%)

Telecommunications
- Bouygues Telecom SA (90%)

COMPETITORS

AMEC
Alarko
Anglian Water Group
Atlantia
Balfour Beatty
Bechtel
Bilfinger Berger
Bovis Lend Lease
CANAL+
CSCEC
Dragados
EIFFAGE
FCC Barcelona
Fluor
Foster Wheeler
GDF SUEZ
Groupe SNEF
HOCHTIEF
Hyundai Engineering and Construction
MWH Global
Orange
SFR
SUEZ Environnement
Severn Trent
Skanska
Technip
VINCI

HISTORICAL FINANCIALS

Company Type: Public

Income Statement

FYE: December 31

	REVENUE ($ mil.)	NET INCOME ($ mil.)	NET PROFIT MARGIN	EMPLOYEES
12/12	44,357	834	1.9%	133,780
12/11	42,483	1,383	3.3%	130,827
12/10	41,983	1,433	3.4%	133,456
12/09	45,366	1,900	4.2%	133,971
12/08	45,914	2,098	4.6%	145,150
Annual Growth	(0.9%)	(20.6%)	—	(2.0%)

2012 Year-End Financials

Debt ratio: 30.9%
Return on equity: 7.4%
Cash ($ mil.): 5,914
Current ratio: 0.99
Long-term debt ($ mil.): 9,888

No. of shares (mil.): 324
Dividends
Yield: —
Payout: 27.6%
Market value ($ mil.): —

	STOCK PRICE ($) FY Close	P/E High/Low		PER SHARE ($) Earnings	Dividends	Book Value
12/12	0.00	—	—	2.64	0.73	34.87
12/11	0.00	8	3	3.96	0.89	34.35
12/10	8.49	7	4	4.04	0.72	34.54
Annual Growth	—	—	—	(10.1%)	0.4%	0.2%

BP p.l.c.

BP is also BO (Big Oil). It is the world's #3 publicly traded integrated oil concern behind Exxon Mobil and Royal Dutch Shell. BP explores for oil and gas in 30 countries with proved reserves of 17 billion barrels of oil equivalent. It's the largest oil and gas producer in the US and a top refiner with 15 plants processing more than 2 million barrels of crude oil per day; it is also a major producer of petrochemicals. BP operates about 20000 BP Connect gas stations worldwide. The company took a major hit in 2010 when a Gulf of Mexico oil rig exploded and killed 11 workers. Millions of gallons of crude spilled into the Gulf and BP was forced to set aside $20 billion to pay for related damages in 2011 and 2012.

Company Background

The spill developed into a major political economic and public relations crisis for the company as it struggled to cap the leaking well clean up the massive spill and mollify Gulf Coast communities which saw their fishing industry decimated and their coastlines inundated by oil. To address the growing crisis in 2010 the company established an escrow account of $20 billion managed by a third party to reimburse claims from people and businesses financially damaged by the oil spill. (It settled with individual and business plaintiffs for $7.8 billion in 2012 but still faced federal state and local government charges). In a plea deal with the US government in 2012 BP plead guilty to criminal misconduct (12 felony counts) and in 2013 agreed to pay $4.5 billion in damages. The company has paid a total of about $40 billion related to the spill.

Financial Performance

Revenue was basically flat while profit plummeted 55% as the company paid off charges related to the Deepwater Horizon disaster.

Strategy

After the costly Gulf spill BP embarked on a "shrink to grow" strategy (set to run through 2014) of selling older oilfields around the world to generate cash for settlements and simplify its upstream operations. All told the company has sold about $37 billion in assets. Completed divestitures include one of the largest transactions in the Gulf of Mexico —BP's sale of a number of oil and gas fields in the deepwater Gulf of Mexico region to Plains Exploration & Production for $5.55 billion in November 2012. In July it sold assets in Canada Egypt and the Permian Basin in the US to fellow explorer Apache for about $7 billion. The deal included BP receiving a $5 billion cash advance. In 2011 BP sold its Colombian assets to Talisman Energy and Ecopetrol for $1.9 billion and properties in Venezuela and Vietnam to its Russian joint venture TNK-BP for $1.8 billion.

TNK-BP was BP's longtime drilling venture with several Russian partners. After years of feuding with those partners in 2013 BP sold that business to Russian state oil company Rosneft as part of a complex package of deals worth a whopping $55 billion. The transaction gave BP a nearly 20% stake in Rosneft and about $12.3 billion in cash allowing it to pursue offshore drilling opportunities in the Arctic Ocean and settle billions of dollars in US Gulf spill penalties. Several BP competitors Exxon Mobil Italy's Eni and Norway's Statoil already have Russian Arctic drilling deals.

On the renewables side of the business since 2006 BP has invested $7 billion (including $1.3 billion in 2009) to develop wind solar and other green energy sources.

HISTORY

The company which was formed in 1998 from the merger of British Petroleum and Amoco grew by buying Atlantic Richfield Company.

BP (formerly BP Amoco) was born on two sides of the Atlantic. In the US Amoco emerged from Standard Oil Trust organized by John D. Rockefeller in 1882. In 1886 he bought Lima (Ohio) oil a high-sulfur crude anticipating the discovery of a sulfur-removing process. Such a process was indeed patented in 1887 and in 1889 Standard organized Standard Oil of Indiana which later established such innovations as company-owned service stations and a research lab at the refinery.

Overseas British Petroleum (BP) was a twinkle in the eye of English adventurer William D'Arcy who began oil exploration of Persia in 1901. In 1908 bankrolled by Burmah Oil D'Arcy's firm was the first to strike oil in the Middle East. D'Arcy and Burmah Oil formed Anglo-Persian Oil in 1909 and the British government took a 51% stake in 1914.

Back in the US Standard was broken up into 34 independent oil companies in 1911. Standard Oil of Indiana kept its oil refining and US marketing operations. In 1925 it added a few Mexican and Venezuelan firms including Pan American Petroleum and Transport which held half of American Oil Co. known for Amoco antiknock gasoline. It began Amoco Chemicals in 1945.

Anglo-Persian took the BP name in 1954 and bought its own Standard Oil: After making a strike in Alaska in 1969 BP swapped Alaskan reserves for a 25% interest (later upped to 55%) in Standard Oil of Ohio (SOHIO). BP also struck North Sea oil in 1970. But falling oil and copper prices in the mid-1980s and a dry hole in the Beaufort Sea hurt earnings. Under Robert Horton SOHIO sold off units. BP also bought livestock feed producer Purina Mills (1986 sold 1998) and the rest of SOHIO (1987).

Standard Oil of Indiana had its own problems including being kicked out of Iran after the Islamic revolution and causing a major oil spill off the French coast in 1978. The firm which became Amoco in 1985 bought Canada's Dome Petroleum in 1988 making it the largest private owner of North American gas reserves but the big purchase proved hard to swallow.

In 1992 Amoco hurled itself into overseas oil exploration. It was the first foreign oil company to explore the Chinese mainland. But by 1995 production was down. That year John Browne often compared to Rockefeller became BP's CEO. In 1996 BP and Mobil merged their European fuel and lubricants operations and the British government sold its remaining stake in BP.

As oil prices tumbled in 1998 BP merged with Amoco in a $52 billion deal that formed BP Amoco. The new oil major agreed the following year to buy US-based Atlantic Richfield (ARCO) in a deal that closed in 2000. BP Amoco sold ARCO's Alaskan properties to Phillips (later ConocoPhillips) for $7 billion to gain regulatory approval for the purchase.

Its stake in Siberian oil fields was nearly taken away in a controversial 1999 bankruptcy sale before BP Amoco and Russia's Tyumen Oil agreed to cooperate. In 2000 BP Amoco and Shell Oil sold their stakes in Altura Energy to Occidental Petroleum for $3.6 billion. Also that year BP Amoco bought motor-oil maker Burmah Castrol for $4.7 billion. It paid $1.5 billion for the 18% of former ARCO exploration and production unit Vastar Resources that it didn't already own.

The company adopted BP as its main worldwide brand in 2000 and it officially shortened its name the next year.

In 2001 BP agreed to swap control of its stake in German natural gas supplier Ruhrgas plus $1.6 billion in cash and $950 million in assumed debt to German utility giant E.ON for a majority interest in Veba Oel owner of Germany's largest gas station chain. Regulators moved to keep E.ON from acquiring the Ruhrgas stake but BP agreed to make up the difference in cash if necessary and the deal proceeded. The agreement allowed BP to take full ownership of Veba Oel in 2002. To recoup some of its investment BP (with E.ON's consent) sold Veba Oel's exploration and production operations to Petro-Canada.

That year BP increased it stake in Russian oil and gas producer Sidanco from 10% to 25%.

In 2003 BP sold its Boqueron field and Desarrollo Zulia Occidental assets both located in Venezuela to Europe's Perenco. In late 2005 BP sold its petrochemical unit Innovene to INEOS for a reported $9 billion.

An explosion and fire in 2005 at BP's Texas City refinery killed 15 workers and injured many more.

In 2006 the company sold its remaining producing properties on the Outer Continental Shelf of the Gulf of Mexico to Apache Corporation for $845 million. That year BP sold its 28% stake in the Shenzi field in the Gulf of Mexico to Repsol for $2.2 billion. It also acquired a $1 billion stake in Rosneft.

In 2006 the discovery of corrosion in a major oil pipeline forced BP to close down part of its Prudhoe Bay oilfield (which represents 8% of daily US crude production) for several weeks.

That year the company also announced plans to invest $3 billion to reconfigure its Whiting Refinery in Indiana to process Canadian heavy crude oil.

In 2007 the company sold its Coryton refinery in the UK to Petroplus Holdings for $1.4 billion. That year BP acquired Chevron's 31% stake in a Netherlands-based refinery and other assets for $900 million.

BP's long-term chief executive John Browne was forced to step down in 2007 over a personal scandal and was replaced by BP veteran Tony Hayward. That year the company announced a major restructuring with a focus on core divisions Exploration & Production and Refining & Marketing and a new Alternative Energy unit dedicated to solar power wind energy and carbon capture technology.

In 2007 BP agreed to pay US authorities $373.5 million in fines relating to the 2005 Texas City refinery explosion the 2006 Alaska oil spill and a propane price-fixing scandal.

In 2008 the company signed a deal with Enbridge to pipe oil sands crude from Canada to the Texas Gulf Coast. Enbridge and BP will spend up to $2 billion to expand existing pipelines and build new connections to deliver up to 250000 barrels a day to Gulf Coast refiners by 2012. In another oil sands move BP and Husky Energy teamed up that same year to create an integrated North American oil sands business through two joint ventures BP-Husky Refinery LLC operated by BP and the Sunrise Oil Sands Partnership (SOSP) operated by Husky. BP committed $2.8 billion to create SOSP.

In 2008 BP acquired 90000 net acres of natural gas assets in the Arkoma Basin Woodford Shale play in the US from Chesapeake Energy for $1.75 billion. It subsequently bought a 25% stake in that company's Fayetteville Shale assets in Arkansas for $1.9 billion.

Boosting its North Sea assets in 2010 the company agreed to buy two oil fields in the Norwegian sector from TOTAL for $991 million. That year BP acquired Devon Energy's international assets for $7 billion in a deal that among other things gave BP a foothold in the emerging major oil play off the coast of Brazil. The company also gained properties in Azerbaijan and the Gulf of Mexico. (In 2010 it agreed to sell four of these mature deep-water oil and gas fields in Gulf of Mexico to Marubeni Oil and Gas for $650 million in order to pay down debt).

The global recession and the slump in demand for oil and gas products saw BP's revenues (along with those of its industry peers) plummet in 2009. Improved market conditions in 2010 lifted revenues. However the company reported a $4.9 billion loss for 2010 as a result of the Gulf oil spill and its aftermath the cost of which was pegged at almost $41 billion.

EXECUTIVES

CEO, Robert W. (Bob) Dudley, $1,160,100 total compensation
Company Secretary, David J. Jackson, age 60
Chairman, Carl-Henric Svanberg
EVP Corporate Business Activities and Director, Byron E. Grote, age 64, $2,754,894 total compensation
Group General Counsel, Rupert Bondy, age 51
Chief Executive Refining and Marketing, Iain C. Conn, $1,377,447 total compensation
EVP Strategy and Integration, Steve Westwell, age 54
President General Manager of BP Egypt, Hesham Mekawi
Press Officer, Robert Wine
Press Officer, Sheila Williams
EVP and Chief of Staff, Dev Sanyal
Director of Group Investor Relations, Jessica Mitchell
Head of North America Investor Relations, Nick Wayth
Manager Investor Relations, Gerry Bye
Chief Executive Upstream, H. Lamar McKay
Manager Investor Relations North America, Brian Sullivan
Director of Group Media, David Nicholas
Press Officer, Toby Odone
Head of Gulf Coast Restoration Organization, Mike Utsler
EVP Corporate Business Activities, Katrina Landis
President BP Wind Energy, John Graham
EVP Safety and Operational Risk, Mark Bly
COO Strategy and Regions Upstream, Andy Hopwood
EVP Exploration, Mike Daly
EVP Safety and Operational Risk, Bob Fryar
COO Production, Bernard Looney
EVP Group Human Resources Director, Helmut Schuster
Press Officer, Mark Salt
Manager Press Office, Carolyn Copland
Manager Investor Relations, Ruban Chandran
CFO, Brian Gilvary
Director, Cynthia B. Carroll, age 56
Director, George David, age 70
CEO and Director, Robert W. (Bob) Dudley, age 56
Director, Antony Burgmans, age 66
Director, Andrew B. Shilston, age 57
Director, Sir William M. (Bill) Castell, age 65
EVP Corporate Business Activities and Director, Byron E. Grote, age 64
Director, Ian E. L. Davis, age 62
Director, Paul M. Anderson, age 67
Chief Executive Refining and Marketing, Iain C. Conn, age 50
Director, Adm. Frank L. (Skip) Bowman
Director, Phuthuma F. Nhleko, age 53
Director, Brendan Nelson, age 63
CFO and Director, Brian Gilvary
Director, Dame Ann Dowling
Auditors: Ernst&YoungLLP

LOCATIONS

HQ: BP p.l.c.
1 St. James Square, London SW1Y 4PD
Phone: (44) 20 7496 4000 **Fax:** (44) 20 7496 4570
Web: www.bp.com

2012 Sales

	$ mil.	% of total
US	130,940	35
Other countries	244,640	65
Total	**375,580**	**100**

PRODUCTS/OPERATIONS

2012 Sales

	$ mil.	% of total
Refining & marketing	346,491	82
Exploration & production	71,940	17
Other	1,985	1
Adjustments	(44836)	-
Total	**375,580**	**100**

Major Operations
Refining and marketing
Marketing
Refining
Supply and trading
Transportation and shipping
Exploration and production
Field developmen
Gas processing and marketing
Oil and gas exploratio
Pipelines and transporta
Gas and power
Natural gas marketing and trading
Natural gas liquids
Chemicals
Chemical intermedia
Feedstock
Performance products
Polymers
Other
Coal mining
Solar power

Selected Subsidiaries

Atlantic Richfield Co
BP America Inc. (US)
BP Amoco Chemcal Company (US)
BP Oil Australia
BP Exploration Operating Company
BP Espa?a (Spain)
BP International
BP Norge (Norway)
BP Oil New Zealand
BP Shipping
BP Southern Africa (South Africa)
Burmah Castrol
The Standard Oil Company (US)

COMPETITORS

Apache
Ashland Inc.
BASF SE
BG Group
BHP Billiton
Chevron
ConocoPhillips
Dow Chemical
DuPont
Eni
Exxon Mobil
Hess Corporation
Huntsman International
Imperial Oil
Koch Industries Inc.
Marathon Oil
Norsk Hydro ASA
Occidental Petroleum
PEMEX
PETROBRAS
Petroleos de Venezuela
Repsol
Royal Dutch Shell
Sinclair Oil
Sunoco
TOTAL
Valero Energy

HISTORICAL FINANCIALS

Company Type: Public

Income Statement

FYE: December 31

	REVENUE ($ mil.)	NET INCOME ($ mil.)	NET PROFIT MARGIN	EMPLOYEES
12/12	381,589	11,582	3.0%	85,700
12/11	382,333	25,700	6.7%	83,400
12/10	302,545	(3,719)	—	79,700
12/09	243,965	16,578	6.8%	80,300
12/08	365,700	21,157	5.8%	92,000
Annual Growth	1.1%	(14.0%)	—	(1.8%)

2012 Year-End Financials

Debt ratio: 16.2%
Return on equity: 10.0%
Cash ($ mil.): 19,548
Current ratio: 1.43
Long-term debt ($ mil.): 38,767
No. of shares (mil.): —
Dividends
Yield: 4.7%
Payout: 217.5%
Market value ($ mil.): —

	STOCK PRICE ($) FY Close	P/E High/Low	PER SHARE ($) Earnings	Dividends	Book Value
12/12	41.64	79 60	0.60	1.98	6.19
12/11	42.74	36 26	1.34	1.68	5.87
12/10	44.17	— —	(0.20)	2.52	5.05
12/09	57.97	68 39	0.88	3.36	5.42
12/08	46.74	68 35	1.12	3.30	4.87
Annual Growth	(2.8%)	— —	(14.2%)	(12.0%)	6.1%

Bridgestone Corp. (Japan)

Bridgestone is one rolling stone that gathers no moss. Vying with Michelin to be the world's largest tire maker Bridgestone makes tires for a variety of vehicle types. In addition to passenger and commercial vehicle tires the company makes tires for construction and mining vehicles agricultural machinery and aircraft. It also manufactures a range of non-tire products including consumer products like golf balls and bicycles polyurethane foam for industrial applications and adhesive film for the solar industry. Bridgestone operates some 180 manufacturing plants in 25 countries and sells its products worldwide.

In response to declining consumer demand skyrocketing rubber prices and the unpredictable global economy the company has reworked its long-term growth strategy in an effort to streamline its operations and increase revenue in targeted business areas. The strategy - implemented in 2008 - focuses on closing and restructuring operations in certain businesses to cut costs (It sold two steel cord production facilities in Italy and China to Bekaert in 2010.) and increasing production at its plants in emerging markets. (For instance it is ramping up tire production in China India and Brazil to meet growing consumer demand in the regions.) Other key aspects of its strategy include bolstering its commercial and specialty passenger tire businesses particularly its runflat and UHP (ultra-high-performance) replacement passenger tires.

In 2010 tires accounted for more than 80% of Bridgestone's revenues; about three-quarters of its sales were earned overseas. After being hit hard by the economic downturn in 2008 and 2009 the company saw its sales and profits bounce back in

2010 an improvement that it attributes to its renewed strategic direction and an uptick in the global economy.

Bridgestone is also looking to its diversified products business segment to fuel its long-term growth. It is investing in the research and development of eco-friendly products such as adhesive films for solar cells which hold promise for growth as the renewable energy sector expands. The company is also rolling out an eco-friendly tire as well the ECOPIA which it markets in China India and other countries. In addition it continues to manufacture peripheral consumer products for Japan and elsewhere such as Bridgestone-branded golf balls and clubs as well as bicycles and related accessories.

The company operates through more than 50 major subsidiaries and affiliates. In the US subsidiary Bridgestone Americas operates the Bridgestone Retail Operations and Firestone Diversified Products businesses.

HISTORY

In 1906 Shojiro Ishibashi and his brother Tokujiro assumed control of the family's clothing business. They focused on making "tabi" traditional Japanese footwear and in 1923 began working with rubber for soles. In 1931 Shojiro formed Bridgestone (Ishibashi means "stone bridge" in Japanese) to make tires and during that decade the company began producing auto tires airplane tires and golf balls. Bridgestone followed the Japanese military to occupied territories where it built plants. The company's headquarters moved to Tokyo in 1937.

Although Bridgestone lost all of its overseas factories during WWII its Japanese plants escaped damage. The company began making bicycles in 1946 and signed a technical assistance pact with Goodyear five years later enabling Bridgestone to import badly needed technology. In the 1950s and 1960s Bridgestone started making nylon tires and radials and again set up facilities overseas mostly elsewhere in Asia. The company benefited from the rapid growth in Japanese auto sales in the 1970s. Shojiro died at age 87 in 1976.

In 1983 Bridgestone bought a plant in LaVergne Tennessee from tire maker Firestone. Five years later Bridgestone topped Italian tire maker Pirelli's bid and bought the rest of Firestone for $2.6 billion valuing the tire manufacturer at a lofty 26 times its earnings. Bridgestone/Firestone (currently Bridgestone Americas Holding and soon to be Bridgestone Americas Inc.) became Bridgestone's largest subsidiary. Harvey Firestone had founded his tire business in 1900 and expanded with the auto industry in the US. In the 1920s he leased 1 million acres in Liberia for rubber plantations and established a chain of auto supply and service outlets. After WWII Firestone started making synthetic rubber and automotive components expanded overseas and acquired US tire producers Dayton Tire & Rubber and Seiberling.

At the time of Firestone's purchase General Motors (GM) dropped it as a supplier. Bridgestone/Firestone compensated for this loss in volume by selling more tires through mass-market retailers. It began selling tires to GM's Saturn Corporation in 1990.

The following year new Bridgestone/Firestone chairman Yoichiro Kaizaki moved to cut production costs alienating union workers. He became company head in 1993. During the early 1990s Bridgestone bought Colonial Rubber Works a US roofing material manufacturer and America Off The Road Company which makes tires for heavy equipment. To improve its distribution in 1992 Bridgestone renamed its 1550 North American MasterCare auto service centers "Tire Zone at Firestone" and took the unheard-of step of selling rival Michelin's tires. It expanded operations in Brazil Indonesia Mexico Thailand and the US the next year.

Bridgestone's US operations have been plagued with problems such as disputes with the United Rubber Workers (URW) union. Tensions rose in 1995 when the company hired 2300 permanent replacement workers during a plant strike. In 1996 after URW members had become part of United Steelworkers of America the two sides approved a new contract.

In 1997 Bridgestone built a South Carolina plant to help reduce Japanese imports. Although sales remained almost steady that year net profit dropped nearly 50% when a change in accounting caused the company to write off costs associated with its Firestone purchase.

Bridgestone developed a "run-flat" tire in 1998 that remains functional for up to 50 miles without air. Expanding its markets Bridgestone opened a retail outlet in Moscow in 1999 and acquired a radial tire plant in China from South Korea's Kumho Industrial Company in 2000. That year the company recalled approximately 6.5 million Firestone ATX ATX II and Wilderness AT tires after dozens of incidents where the tires came apart at road speeds. The affected tires had been used on light trucks and SUVs since 1990 many of them as original equipment on the Ford Explorer. Not long after the recall Bridgestone/Firestone chairman and CEO Masatoshi Ono retired and was replaced by John Lampe. The fallout and ensuing blame-game (improper inflation guidelines/unstable vehicle vs. faulty tires) essentially ended Bridgestone's 95-year relationship with Ford (Bridgestone still does business with Ford outside the Americas).

In 2001 Bridgestone replaced president Yoichiro Kaizaki with SVP Shigeo Watanabe. Public bickering between Ford and Bridgestone over the cause of the multiple Firestone/Ford Explorer accidents continued unabated into the spring of 2001. Finally in May Bridgestone announced that it was ending its with Ford Motor which accounted for about 2% of sales. The two companies' founders —Henry Ford and Harvey Firestone —had been friends in the early days of mass automobile production. Then in June while revealing that it would face its first loss since listing 30 years previously Bridgestone announced that it would close the Decatur Illinois plant at which many of the recalled tires were made. The plant employed about 1500 workers. Later in the year the company announced that it would recall an additional 3.5 million tires at a cost of nearly $30 million.

Near the end of 2001 Bridgestone announced it would inflate its beleaguered Bridgestone/Firestone subsidiary with $1.3 billion in cash. The company also announced the restructuring of its Bridgestone/Firestone operations. The company established Bridgestone/Firestone Americas Holding Inc. (formerly known as Bridgestone/Firestone Inc.) to serve as a holding company for Bridgestone/Firestone North American Tire LLC (North American tire manufacturing and wholesale and original equipment sales). Bridgestone/Firestone Americas Holding also came to oversee the operations of newly created BFS Retail & Commercial Operations LLC (company-owned stores in the United States and Canada) and BFS Diversified Products LLC (non-tire operations in the Americas including building products synthetic and natural rubber and textiles).

Bridgestone and Continental AG entered into an agreement in early 2002 whereby the two companies will adapt run-flat technology to conventional wheel systems (conventional systems utilize special wheels). In early 2003 the company's US subsidiary changed its name from Bridgestone/Firestone Americas Holding to Bridgestone Americas Holding. Later in the year the company was awarded a contract to supply tires for the Airbus A380 aircraft; the deal was reportedly worth $84.3 million.

In 2005 Bridgestone purchased the Indonesian rubber plantations business (Goodyear Sumatra Plantations) of Goodyear Tire & Rubber for about $62 million.

Watanabe stepped down as chairman president and CEO the next year; he was replaced by EVP Shoshi Arakawa.

In 2007 Bridgestone purchased Bandag a retread company in the US with international production facilities. In late 2008 Bridgestone formed a joint venture with Indian auto parts maker Sundaram Industries part of TVS Group. The following year the company built a plant in Thailand to produce rubber parts for retread tires. The cost of the facility was approximately Y5.2 billion.

The company also sold off operations during this period. In 2010 Bridgestone sold two steel cord production facilities for approximately $100 million to Bekaert a steel cord producer based in Belgium. The manufacturing facilities in Italy and China generated approximately 10% of Bridgestone's total production capacity. In 2009 it closed factories in New Zealand and Adelaide Australia. (Steel cords are used to reinforce tires.)

To help with brand identification in 2009 the company changed the name of many of its subsidiaries (and in some cases dropped the name Firestone altogether). Bridgestone Americas Holding became Bridgestone Americas; Bridgestone Firestone North American Tire became Bridgestone Americas Tire Operations; BFS Retail & Commercial Operations became Bridgestone Retail Operations.

EXECUTIVES

SVP, Asahiko (Duke) Nishiyama
VP Senior Officer and Director, Kazuo Kakehi
COO, Kazuhisa Nishigai
VP Senior Officer and Chief Marketing Officer, Shuichi Ishibashi
VP Senior Officer and Director; Chairman President and CEO Bridgestone Europe, Toru Tsuda
Managing Director Tire Business Operations and Chief International Tire Business, Takashi Urano
VP Senior Officer and Director, Mikio Masunaga
Corporate Officer Deputy Human Resources Representative and the Central Research Institute, Hideki Yokoyama
VP and Senior Officer, Kiyoshi Nomura
Corporate Officer Bridgestone Americas Inc. (Akron) Dispatch, Hideo (Hank) Hara, age 62
Chairman and CEO, Masaaki Tsuya
SVP, Narumi (Nick) Zaitsu
Managing Director GLC, Yasumi Kawasaki
SVP and CTO, Yoshiyuki Morimoto
VP and Officer, Satoshi Tagomori
Corporate Officer Disaster Management Safety, Yoshiharu Inoue
VP and Officer, Natsuki Fujii
Corporate Officer Contact Corporate Communications, Naomi Eto
VP and Officer, Yasuo Ryuto
Corporate Officer Quality Staff, Yoichi Sato
VP and Officer, Isaku Motohashi
VP and Officer, Fumihiro Yanaga
VP and Senior Officer, Masato Hiruma
Corporate Officer and Group CEO, Hidekazu Ishibashi
Corproate Officer Tire Business Division, Shimizu Minoru
Corporate Officer Mamoru Tooru Hiroshi Toshi, Kunitoshi Takeda
VP; Chairman Bridgestone Europe, Eduardo Minardi

Managing Executive Officer; President and CEO of Subsidiary, Franco Annunziato
VP and Senior Officer; President and CEO Bridgestone Americas, Gary Garfield
Executive Officer; Chief Director of GLC Operation Planning, Masahito Tsuji
VP and Senior Officer; CEO Bridgestone Tire Japan, Minoru Shimizu
Executive Officer; Chief Director of Production Technology Basic Development, Seiichiro Kawai
Executive Officer, Tatsuro Hamada
VP Senior Officer and CIO, Yuichiro Takenami
VP, Akihiro Eto
VP and Senior Officer, Yasushi Ota
VP and Senior Officer, Masakazu Sekiguchi
VP Senior Officer and Director, Kazuo Kakehi
VP Senior Officer and Director, Kazuhisa Nishigai
VP Senior Officer and Director; Chairman President and CEO Bridgestone Europe, Toru Tsuda
VP Senior Officer and Director, Mikio Masunaga
VP Senior Officer Chief Risk Management Officer Chief Compliance Officer and Director; Acting Chairman Americas, Masaaki Tsuya
Director, Sakie Tachibana Fukushima
Director, Takao Enkawa
Independent Director, Kimiko Murofushi
Independent Director, Sakie Tachibana-Fukushima
Independent Director, Scott Davis
Auditors: DeloitteToucheTohmatsu

LOCATIONS

HQ: Bridgestone Corp. (Japan)
1-10-1 Kyobashi, Chuo-ku, Tokyo 104-8340
Phone: (81) 3 3563 6822
Web: www.bridgestone.co.jp

2010 Sales

	% of total
The	42
Japan	26
Europe	13
Other	19
Total	100

PRODUCTS/OPERATIONS

2010 Sales

	% of total
Tires	83
Diversified	17
Total	100

Selected Products

- Tires and tubes
  - Agricultural machinery
  - Aircraft
  - Buses
  - Cars
  - Commercial vehicles
  - Construction and mining vehicles
  - Monorails
  - Motorcycles
  - Race cars
  - Scooters
  - Trucks
- Diversified products
  - Bicycles and bicycle accessories
  - Chemical and industrial
    - Adhesive and anti-reflective film for glass and flat-panel displays
    - Conveyor belts
    - Electronic paper for still image display
    - High-performance films
    - Hydraulic hoses
    - Marine fenders
    - Panel type water tank
    - Polyurethane foam
    - Rubber tracks
    - Seismic isolators
    - Single crystal wafers for semiconductor devices
  - Sporting goods
    - Golf apparel
    - Golf balls
    - Golf clubs

COMPETITORS

3M
Acushnet
Callaway Golf
Continental AG
Cooper Tire & Rubber
Goodyear Tire & Rubber
Hankook Tire
Huffy Corporation
Kumho Tire
Marangoni
Michelin
Pirelli
Sime Darby
Sumitomo Rubber
Trelleborg
Yokohama Rubber

HISTORICAL FINANCIALS

Company Type: Public

Income Statement FYE: December 31

	REVENUE ($ mil.)	NET INCOME ($ mil.)	NET PROFIT MARGIN	EMPLOYEES
12/12	35,292	1,992	5.6%	143,448
12/11	39,081	1,330	3.4%	143,124
12/10	35,181	1,216	3.5%	139,822
12/09	28,108	11	0.0%	137,135
12/08	35,764	115	0.3%	137,981
Annual Growth	(0.3%)	104.0%	—	1.0%

2012 Year-End Financials

Debt ratio: 0.2%
Return on equity: 13.6%
Cash ($ mil.): 2,625
Current ratio: 1.66
Long-term debt ($ mil.): 3,889
No. of shares (mil.): 782
Dividends
Yield: 5.3%
Payout: —
Market value ($ mil.): 40,440

	STOCK PRICE ($) FY Close	P/E High/Low	PER SHARE ($) Earnings	Dividends	Book Value
12/12	51.67	— —	2.54	0.70	21.05
12/11	45.00	— —	1.70	0.00	19.25
12/10	38.73	— —	1.55	0.41	18.48
12/09	35.11	— —	0.01	0.40	15.47
12/08	30.20	— —	0.15	0.50	14.38
Annual Growth	14.4%	— —	103.8%	8.7%	10.0%

British American Tobacco Plc (United Kingdom)

When people pick up smoking British American Tobacco (BAT) picks up steam. BAT is the world's second-largest publicly-traded tobacco company by market share (after Philip Morris International). The company rolls more than 700 billion cigarettes a year sold in 180 countries. BAT's four global cigarette brands –Dunhill Kent Lucky Strike and Pall Mall –account for more than a third of group sales. BAT also produces loose tobacco and regional cigarette brands giving it a portfolio of more than 200 brands overall. It owns 42% of Reynolds American the #2 US cigarette maker created by the merger of BAT's Brown & Williamson unit with R.J. Reynolds Tobacco. BAT holds about 30% of India's ITC as well.

Driven by the strength of its four global brands and increased sales in the Asia-Pacific region BAT's group revenue increased 3% in 2011 vs. 2010 while adjusted group profit from operations increased 11% over the same period. Dunhill Kent Lucky Strike and Pall Mall together logged average volume growth of 9% while group volume dipped 0.4% to 705 billion cigarettes. BAT's market share increased amid declining industry volume. Industry volumes continued to fall in 2011 but the rate of decline appears to be moderating. In addition to economic uncertainty and the declining number of smokers in some markets expansion of the illicit trade in cigarettes also poses a growing threat to BAT and the industry overall.

BAT looks to acquisitions for further grow particularly in developing markets including Russia South Korea Vietnam Japan and Nigeria as well as Latin America. In fall 2011 it purchased Colombia's second-largest cigarette maker Productora Tabacalera de Colombia (Protabaco) for $452 million. Protabaco's brands include Mustang (the country's #2 selling cigarette) Premier and President. The deal elevates BAT from third place to second place in Colombia's cigarette market. (It also marked a setback for BAT rival Philip Morris International who abandoned a bid for the Colombian company earlier in the year.)

Going forward BAT has its eye on China which buys more than 40% of the five-and-a-half trillion cigarettes produced annually worldwide. Although plans for a factory in China are discussed the company has cut costs by closing and downsizing its operations in other countries including Italy Denmark Australia Poland as well as combining businesses in Belgium Luxembourg and the Netherlands. All told the cigarette maker has scaled back the number of factories it operates from 83 to 46 including acquisitions since 2000.

BAT has merged Indonesia's fourth-largest cigarette maker PT Bentoel Internasional Investama (acquired in 2009) with its Indonesian arm BAT Indonesia. The combination challenges the dominant players in the Indonesian market by securing a total market share of nearly 10%. (Indonesia is the world's fifth-largest tobacco market by volume.) BAT has also targeted opportunities in Africa and Middle East by acquiring the cigarette business assets of Tekel a Turkish state-owned tobacco company. However illicit trade in tobacco products which are cheaper albeit illegal remains an ongoing threat to BAT's stake in Turkey Romania and other developing regions.

BAT's portfolio is also evolving. In addition to cigarettes it offers cigars (such as Captain Black) and roll-your-own tobacco brands (the Dunhill Signed Range). Health concerns and lawsuits brought against the tobacco industry in the US have prompted BAT to test-market a Swedish smokeless product called snus a pasteurized tobacco product that resembles a small teabag. BAT markets snus as more than 100 times less harmful than cigarettes –selling it in South Africa under the Peter Stuyvesant brand and in Sweden under the Lucky Strike brand. Innovations in cigarette products aim to win more business too. New launches include Dunhill Reloc re-sealable packs and Kent Convertibles (with a crushable menthol-flavored capsule) in the Asia/Pacific region and Lucky Strike Click & Roll in the Americas and Europe.

HISTORY

After a year of vicious price-cutting between Imperial Tobacco (UK) and James Buchanan Duke's American Tobacco in the UK Imperial counterattacked in the US. To end the cigarette price war in the UK the firms created British American Tobacco (BAT) in 1902. The truce granted Imperial the British market American the US market and they jointly owned BAT in the rest of the world.

With Duke in control BAT expanded into new markets. In China it was selling 25 billion cigarettes a year by 1920. When the Communist revolution ended BAT's operations in China the company lost more than 25% of its sales (although China later reemerged as a major export market for the company's cigarettes).

A 1911 US antitrust action forced American to sell its interest in BAT and opened the US market to the company. BAT purchased US cigarette manufacturer Brown & Williamson in 1927 and continued to grow through geographic expansion until the 1960s. In 1973 BAT and Imperial each regained control of its own brands in the UK and Continental Europe. Imperial sold the last of its stake in BAT in 1980.

Fearing that mounting public concern over smoking would limit the cigarette market BAT acquired nontobacco businesses; it changed its name to B.A.T Industries in 1976. The acquisitions of retailers Saks (1973) Argos (UK 1979) Marshall Field (1982) and later insurance firms diversified the company's sales base. After a 1989 hostile takeover bid from Sir James Goldsmith it sold its retail operations and retained its tobacco and financial services.

In 1994 B.A.T acquired the former American Tobacco for $1 billion. In 1997 the company acquired Cigarrera de Moderna (with 50% of Mexico's cigarette sales) and formed a joint venture with the Turkish tobacco state enterprise Tekel.

B.A.T's tobacco operations were spun off in 1998 as British American Tobacco (BAT). The financial services operations were merged with Zurich Insurance in a transaction that created two holding companies: Allied Zurich (UK) and Zurich Allied (Switzerland). With the changes Martin Broughton became chairman of BAT.

The company in 1999 paid $8.2 billion to buy Dutch cigarette company Rothmans International (Rothmans Dunhill) from Switzerland's Compagnie Financiere Richemont and South Africa's Rembrandt Group –both controlled by Anton Rupert. With the purchase BAT received a controlling stake in Canada's Rothmans Benson & Hedges (RBH).

In early 2000 BAT bought the 58% of Canada's Imasco it didn't already own. Imasco sold off its financial services and BAT received Imasco's Imperial Tobacco unit (not related to the UK's Imperial Tobacco Group) in the deal. (Formerly called Imperial Tobacco Company of Canada Imasco was created in 1908 with help from BAT.) BAT also unloaded its share of RBH via a public offering.

In 2001 BAT bought the 40.5% of its BAT Australasia subsidiary (formed in 1999 through the Rothmans merger) it didn't already own. Broughton announced that year that the Chinese government had approved development plans that would allow the company to build a factory in China. The company also announced it would build the first foreign-owned cigarette factory in South Korea at that time the world's #8 tobacco market.

Increasing its Latin American regional presence BAT purchased a controlling stake in Peru's top tobacco company Tabacalera Nacional and several of its suppliers in 2003. However two months later BAT said it would not make the million-dollar investment in the company. The announcement came soon after Peru raised taxes on cigarettes. By the end of the year BAT had purchased tobacco manufacturer Ente Tabacchi Italiani S.p.A. from the Italian government. BAT sold the distribution end of its Italian business to Compa?ia de Distribucion Integral Logista in 2004 the same year that Broughton retired; the company named Jan du Plessis as chairman and Paul Adams as CEO.

In June 2009 the company acquired an 85% stake in Indonesia's fourth largest cigarette maker PT Bentoel Internasional Investama Tbk for #303 million ($494 million) from Rajawali Group. Later that year Richard Burrows became chairman; he replaced du Plessis who had become chairman of Rio Tinto. Replacing Adams Nicandro Durante became CEO in early 2011. BAT in fall 2011 acquired Colombia's second-largest cigarette maker Productora Tabacalera de Colombia (Protabaco) for $452 million.

EXECUTIVES

Director Corporate and Regulatory Affairs, Michael Prideaux, age 61
Chief Executive; Executive Director, Nicandro Durante, age 56, $516,791 total compensation
Legal Director and General Counsel, Neil Withington
President and CEO Imperial Tobacco Canada, Ian Muir
Chairman, Richard Burrows, age 67
CIO Director Finance and Board Member, Ben Stevens, age 52, $528,901 total compensation
Head Investor Relations, Ralph Edmondson
Chief Operating Officer; Executive Director, John P. Daly, age 55
Head Science and Regulation, Christopher (Chris) Proctor
Area Director Southern Cone South America, Benjamin (Benj) Kemball
Group Marketing Director, Jean-Marc Levy
Director Asia Pacific, David Fell, age 52
Director Latin America and Caribbean, Mark M. Cobben
Regional Director Africa and Middle East, Andrew Gray
Director Western Europe, Jack M. H. D. Bowles, age 49
Head Press Office, David Betteridge
Press Relations Manager, Catherine Armstrong
Operations Director, Des Naughton, age 46
Group Scientific Director, David Reilly
Group Human Resources Director, Giovanni Giordano
Board Member, Karen M. A. de Segundo, age 66
Board Member, Robert E. Lerwill, age 61
Board Member, Anthony (Thony) Ruys, age 65
Board Member, Sir Nicholas V. (Nick) Scheele, age 68
CEO and Director, Nicandro Durante, age 56
Chairman, Richard Burrows, age 67
CIO Director Finance and Board Member, Ben Stevens, age 52
Board Member, Ana Maria Llopis, age 63
Board Member, Kieran C. Poynter, age 63
Board Member, Christine Morin-Postel, age 66
COO and Board Member, John P. Daly, age 55
Board Member, Gerard Murphy
Non-Executive Director, Ann Godbehere
Non-Executive Independent Director, Christine Postel
Non-Executive Independent Director, Karen Segundo
Auditors: PricewaterhouseCoopersLLP

LOCATIONS

HQ: British American Tobacco Plc (United Kingdom)
Globe House, 4 Temple Place, London WC2R 2PG
Phone: (44) 20 7845 1000 **Fax:** (44) 20 7240 0555
Web: www.bat.com

2011 Sales

	% of total
Asia/Pacific	28
Eastern Europe Middle East &	26
Americas	23
Western	23
Total	**100**

PRODUCTS/OPERATIONS

2011 Cigarettes Sold

billion

Pall Mall		81
Kent		67
Dunhill		48
Lucky Strike		30
Other		479
Total	**0**	**705**

Selected Brands

Benson & Hedges (Asia/Pacific Middle East Africa)
Craven 'A'
Dunhill
John Player Gold Leaf
Kent
Kool
Lucky Strike
Pall Mall
Peter Stuyvesant
Player's Gold Lead
Rothmans
State Express 555
Viceroy
Vogue

COMPETITORS

Altria
Imperial Tobacco
Japan Tobacco
Lorillard
Philip Morris International
Reemtsma Cigarettenfabriken
Santa Fe Natural Tobacco
Swedish Match
Swisher International
Universal Corporation
Vector Group

HISTORICAL FINANCIALS

Company Type: Public

Income Statement

FYE: December 31

	REVENUE ($ mil.)	NET INCOME ($ mil.)	NET PROFIT MARGIN	EMPLOYEES
12/12	24,484	6,191	25.3%	87,485
12/11	23,789	4,781	20.1%	87,813
12/10	23,107	4,470	19.3%	92,285
12/09	23,011	4,393	19.1%	97,078
12/08	17,665	3,580	20.3%	96,381
Annual Growth	8.5%	14.7%	—	(2.4%)

2012 Year-End Financials

Debt ratio: 63.2%
Return on equity: 48.9%
Cash ($ mil.): 3,354
Current ratio: 1.13
Long-term debt ($ mil.): 14,640
No. of shares (mil.): 2,026
Dividends
Yield: 4.1%
Payout: 335.7%
Market value ($ mil.): 205,160

	STOCK PRICE ($) FY Close	P/E High/Low	PER SHARE ($) Earnings	Dividends	Book Value
12/12	101.25	140113	3.18	4.21	5.94
12/11	94.88	152114	2.41	9.68	6.23
12/10	77.70	138 87	2.24	3.17	7.06
12/09	64.66	132 74	2.21	2.73	6.09
12/08	53.11	192 83	1.79	2.63	5.00
Annual Growth	17.5%	— —	15.5%	12.5%	4.4%

BT Group Plc

Once BT Group's rivals could have fit into one of the company's signature red phone booths. Though competition has taken a toll BT still wears the crown as the UK's top telecommunications carrier. It offers local and long-distance phone service and provides Internet access and other data and IT services. BT Group operates through four divisions –corporate clients are served through its BT

Global Services unit while BT Retail oversees residential and small business service. The BT Wholesale and Openreach divisions are devoted to the broadband and local network needs of other carriers. BT which claims to be the world's oldest communications company is working to adapt to the age of mobile communications.

Geographic Reach

The UK is London-based BT Group's largest market accounting for more than three-quarters of its annual sales. Key European markets for the company include Italy Germany and Spain. In North America BT serves customers from offices in 25 cities. The firm also has a presence in high-growth regions in Asia Pacific Latin America the Middle East and Africa.

Operations

BT Global Services the group's enterprise telecommunications division is its largest segment by sales accounting for nearly 40% of revenue in fiscal 2013 (ended March). It provides voice and data communications as well as managed network and IT services to corporate and public sector customers in more than 170 countries; the UK government is the company's largest client. BT Global Services also operates customer contact and data centers and offers customer relationship management and managed network security.

Consumer services offered through BT Retail accounted for 37% of the group's fiscal 2013 revenue. BT Retail serves individual and small business customers (up to 1000 employees) in the UK with fixed-line broadband mobile broadband and Wi-Fi and digital television service. While it holds well over half of the domestic market for residential fixed-line service its number of access lines continues to drop as more people switch to cell phones. (Due to regulatory laws BT is unable to offer mobile cell phone service). Its growing pay TV brand BT Vision is seen in 575000 homes up from 423000 in 2009. BT Expedite BT Ireland and BT Redcare all operate as standalone businesses under BT Retail.

BT Wholesale provides network services to more than 1000 communications service providers in the UK. It operates the only network that covers the entire country and many competitors pay to use its network to enable their own services. BT Wholesale manages the network infrastructure for Virgin Media and KCOM while O2 and Vodafone use its fixed-line network for their business customers. Contracts typically run three to five years and 40% of its customers are signed to these long-term contracts.

Openreach is the group's smallest segment. It was created in 2006 as part of a settlement with regulatory agency Ofcom to ensure that other companies have full access to BT's network. About 500 communications service providers including BT divisions rely on Openreach for network communications.

Financial Performance

BT Group's revenue declined 5% in fiscal 2013 (ended March) versus the prior year to #18.2 billion. (Revenue and profit figures have not been adjusted for the effects of currency translation.) The decline reflected lower revenue from calls and lines difficult economic conditions in Europe and the financial sector and regulatory price reductions. The 8% drop in proceeds from calls and lines was caused by the continued migration from fixed-line calls to mobile broadband data and IP services. The decline was partially offset by a 7% annual increase in broadband and convergence revenue. Three of BT's four operating segments posted declines in fiscal 2013 with BT Global Services BT Retail and BT Wholesale down 8% 3% and 11% respectively. Broadband services unit Openreach with an 8% jump in revenue was the exception.

Net income grew 14% in fiscal 2013 versus 2012 while net cash outflow grew by #600 million over the same period.

Strategy

BT is pursuing new business in Turkey the Middle East Africa and high-growth areas of the Asia-Pacific Region. Investments in Asia have included adding sales marketing and operational staff and investing in network resources.

Notable contract wins for BT Global Services include its selection by the International Olympic Committee to provide communications services for the 2012 Olympic Games in London; an extension agreement with Unilever to continue supplying managed services to the company's global operations; and a deal with Swiss private banker UBS to provide voice and data telecom services worldwide.

As established carriers face mounting competition in the high-speed Internet space from the likes of Virgin and TalkTalk some have sought partnerships to shore up their online businesses. In 2010 BT took over management of the broadband network of France-based rival Orange's UK business which is experiencing a declining subscriber base.

BT is a very expensive company to operate - those cables don't lay themselves. It pays billions in taxes (around #3 billion annually) to the UK Exchequer. After being in business for more than 100 years it also spends a lot on pension payments.

Mergers and Acquisitions

In 2013 BT Group acquired the London-based technology group Tikit Group for #64.2 million ($103 million). The move was designed to strengthen BT Retail's position as a provider of ICT services to law firms in the UK. Tikit's clients include legal and accountancy firms.

Ownership

Asset manager Invesco owns about 10% of BT Group's stock.

HISTORY

In 1879 the British Post Office (now known as Royal Mail and formerly Consignia) got the exclusive right to operate telegraph systems. When private firms tried to offer phone service the government objected arguing in court that its telegraph monopoly was imperiled. The courts agreed and the Post Office was empowered to license private phone companies collect a 10% royalty and operate its own systems.

The private National Telephone Company emerged as the leading phone outfit competing with the Post Office. When National's license expired in 1911 the Post Office took over and became the monopoly phone company. In 1936 the phone system introduced its familiar red phone booths designed for King George V's jubilee.

Under a 1981 law telecommunications were split from the Post Office and placed under the new British Telecommunications (BT). The government also allowed competitor Mercury Communications —formerly One 2 One and now known as T-Mobile (UK) —to compete. The Thatcher government soon called for BT's privatization.

After the Telecommunications Act of 1984 BT went public in one of the largest UK stock offerings in history. The act set up the regulatory Office of Telecommunications (OFTEL). The next year Cellnet BT's joint venture with Securicor launched its mobile phone network. To become a multinational concern BT bought control of Canadian phone equipment maker Mitel (1986 sold in 1992) and 20% of firm McCaw Cellular (1989 sold to AT&T in 1994).

In 1990 the British government opened the UK to more phone competition and BT responded with improvements to its network and a workforce reduction. The government sold almost all of its remaining shares in BT in 1993. The next year the company bought a 20% stake in MCI the #2 US long-distance carrier and the two formed Concert a joint venture to compete in the international arena. BT's 1996 attempt to buy Cable and Wireless failed when the company asked for more than BT was willing to pay.

In 1996 BT announced a plan to buy out MCI but as losses mounted from MCI's expansion into the US local market BT in 1997 lowered its bid and lost MCI to upstart WorldCom. In 1998 BT bought the remaining 25% stake in Concert and found a new US partner in AT&T; the two agreed in 1999 to merge most of their international operations in a $10 billion global joint venture that took the Concert name (but after repeated losses the two parent companies dismantled the venture in 2002).

Also in 1999 BT expanded in continental Europe Latin America (a 20% stake in IMPSAT) Asia (with AT&T a 30% stake in Japan Telecom) and the US where it bought systems integration firm Syntegra (USA) (formerly Control Data Systems and now part of BT Americas) and Yellow Book USA. At home BT bought out Securicor's stake in Cellnet. UK regulators also ordered the company to upgrade its UK phone network and open it to rivals by 2001.

BT bought Ireland's Esat Telecom in 2000. That year the government sold its remaining stake in BT and the company bought Telenor's stake in VIAG Interkom; early the next year the company took full ownership of the German mobile phone company. Also in early 2001 BT sold its stakes in Japan Telecom and J-Phone Communications to Vodafone which later that year bought BT's Airtel Movil (now known as Vodafone Espa?a) interest.

BT Group countered increasing competition and mounting debt woes through restructuring that included the 2001 spinoff of its domestic and international wireless businesses combined under the mmO2 brand (formerly BT Wireless) which included BT Cellnet a leading UK mobile phone operator. The decision left BT Group as the only top-tier European telecom firm without a wireless network.

To further its restructuring the company in 2002 sold its Yellow Pages unit Yell to two buyout firms: Hicks Muse Tate & Furst (now HM Capital Partners) and Apax Partners. And in a further effort to cut debt it sold much of its property holdings and unloaded interests in the Pacific Rim.

The company also sold a 77% stake in Brightstar its technology incubator to private equity investment firm Coller Capital and New Venture Partners in a deal valued at $77 million. BT Group held a 23% stake and remained a limited partner in a new venture (NVP Brightstar) that continued to work closely with its BT Exact unit.

In 2002 BT dismantled Concert its failed business telecom services joint venture with AT&T that combined most of the companies' international operations. The company also sold its 26% stake in France's Cegetel to Vivendi Universal. It also has unloaded other noncore assets including its 21% stake in Hong Kong wireless carrier SmarTone Telecommunications in its continuing effort to reduce debt.

In a major reorganization BT Group turned itself into a holding company. Ordered to upgrade and open its domestic networks it split its UK fixed-line network operations into separate wholesale and retail businesses.

BT Group also expanded its information communications technology (ICT) services offered to multisite corporations in the US. It signed its largest IT services deal to date valued at $3 billion over eight-and-a-half years with the Reuters Group. BT Group also acquired financial services extranet provider Radianz from Reuters for $175 million.

The company in 2005 acquired Infonet a leading provider of corporate managed voice and data network services. The company renamed BT Infonet is part of the BT Global Services unit. That year BT Group also acquired SkyNet Systems a provider of Internet protocol-based LAN systems. To expand its global professional services offerings the company made several purchases in 2006 including US-based Counterpane Internet Security a provider of managed networked security services.

BT refocused its other international holdings to concentrate on Europe. It acquired Fiat's Italian telecom subsidiary Atlanet in early 2006 and later that year BT bought Fiat's Brazilian telecom business Telexis. It additionally acquired Indian Internet protocol communications services provider i2i Enterprise.

In 2007 the company purchased Comsat International a data communication services provider expanding its presence in Latin America. Also in 2007 BT bought the IT infrastructure division of France-based CS Communication & Systemes. Meanwhile it increased its North American presence with the acquisition of IT consulting and software provider International Network Services.

BT has responded to the growing global demand for business services with the acquisition of service providers from a range of disciplines in Europe and the US. In 2008 it bought German information technology firms Stemmer and SND from net AG to boost its presence in the region. The company also acquired UK online classified advertising specialist Ufindus which became part of BT's online directory business.

Also that year it bought US videoconferencing specialist Wire One Holdings to improve the capability and geographic reach of its conferencing unit and it picked up Silicon Valley-based integrated communications software developer Ribbit Corporation for $105 million as an addition to its existing software holdings.

EXECUTIVES

Regional Manager South West BT Regions, Michael Dunn
Head Data Centres BT Operate, David Edwards
Chief Executive and Board Member, Ian P. Livingston, age 48, $1,250,301 total compensation
Director Shared Services BT Global Services, Dave Mitchell
Regional Director BTLB Wales & West Midlands - BT Business BT Retail, Paul Evans
Chief Executive BT Wholesale, Sally Davis, age 59
Chief Procurement Officer, Neil Rogers
Country Manager BT Italia, Corrado Sciolla, age 50
Chairman, Sir Michael D. V. (Mike) Rake, age 65
CEO Openreach, Steve Robertson
Chief Executive BT Operate, Roel Louwhoff, age 49
Group Director London, Duncan Ingram
Director Client Business Development ? Managed Services BT Wholesale, Steve Edwards
Chief Executive, Gavin Patterson, age 46
President BT France, Olivier Huart, age 47
Director Group Public Policy, Dorothy Smith
CEO BT Northern Ireland and the Republic of Ireland, Graham Sutherland
Managing Director Retail Strategy, Sean M.G. Williams
CEO BT Germany, Karsten Lereuth
President Americas and Asia-Pacific, Michael Boustridge, age 50
President BT EMEA and Latin America, Luis ?lvarez
CEO BT Ireland, Chris Clark
Regional Director Yorkshire and the Humber, John Anderson
CEO Benelux, Bas Burger, age 42
Managing Director BT Consumer BT Retail, John Petter
Company Secretary, Andrew Parker, age 53
Group Finance Director and Board Member, Anthony E. A. (Tony) Chanmugam, age 59
VP European Affairs, Adrian Whitchurch
VP Global Portfolio BT Global Services, Neil Sutton
Chief Executive Officer - BT Wholesale, Nigel Stagg
Managing Director Customer Service BT Retail, Warren Buckley
Director Marketing and Brand, Suzi Williams
Regional Director ICT BT Business, John Dovey
Manager European Regulation, Henk Mannekens
Manager Public Affairs, Christine van der Steur
General Director BT Russia & CIS Countries, Richard van Wageningen
Regional Director East Midlands, Andrew Bacon
Leader Customers and Markets Venture - Strategic Research BT Innovate & Design East of England, John Seton
Chief Customer Innovation Officer BT Innovate & Design, Paul Excell
General Manager BT Openzone BT Retail, Chris Bruce
Director Service Operations BT Operate, Ashley Hannah
Regional Manager East of England BT Regions, Annette Thorpe
Head Data Network and ICT Sales (Midlands) BT Retail, Graham Wilkinson
Director Professional and Managed Services BT Engage IT BT Retail, Steve Alton
Regional Manager East Midlands BT Regions, Paul Bimson
Director Wireless Broadband BT Retail, David Hughes
General Manager London, Andrew Campling
General Manager Contact Delivery BT Retail, Julie Lowther
General Manager Digital Care BT Retail, Graeme Stoker
General Manager BT Supply Chain Operations North BT Procurement & Supply Chain, Chris Atkins
Head BT DWP Core Programmes BT Global Services, Chris Millman
Disruptive Futurist BT Global Services, Ian Neild
CEO BT South Tyneside BT Global Services, Margie Burdis
Regional Manager North East BT Regions, Simon Roberson
Director Central Government & Home Affairs BT Global Services, Mike Blackburn
Programme Director Manchester Communications Academy BT Global Services, Sue Webster
General Manager Product Development BT Innovate & Design, Steve Henderson
Head Sales Programmes and Alliance Partners-Shared Services BT Global Services, Sami Istephan
Director Retail North BT Global Services, Paul Skelt
Account Director BT Global Services, Mike Wrench
Regional Manager North West BT Regions, Peter Connor
Regional Director South East, Mike Gavin
Head PR and Communications BT Regions, Barbara Wise
Academies Project BT Global Services, Denise Westbury-Haines
Business Development Director - BT London 2012 BT Group, Jon Lane
Programme Manager Community Investment, Beth Courtier
General Manager ? CRM BT Wholesale, Stephen Hunt
Managing Director Research 21C CE & Technology Strategy BT Innovate & Design, Mike Galvin
Regional Manager South East BT Regions, Peter Cowen
Regional Director South West, Maj. Jon Reynolds
Head Business Improvement BT Global Services, Mike Buhagiar
Project Orchard BT Wholesale, Ranulf Scarborough
Senior Audit Manager, Jane Shipway
Head Commercial Management BT Retail, James Hennah
Manager Senior Client Business Development BT Retail, Liz King
Programme Manager BT Innovate & Design, Kelvin Blake
Head Learning and Development BT Operate, Mary Scarratt
Performance and Reporting Manager BT Group, Ian Wood
Service Director (BT Retail) Satellite MNS + OpenZone BT Operate, Keith Lawton
Regional Manager West Midlands BT Regions, Ian Binks
Programme Director BT Global Services, Zulfi Hussain
General Manager Market Development BT Wholesale, Peter Barnes
VP Global Services Transformation Programmes BT Innovate & Design, Jacqueline Steed
Head Marketing - GSUK Vertical Markets BT Global Services, Paul Woodman
Regional Manager Yorkshire and Humber BT Regions, Trevor Higgins
Director Wales, Ann Beynon
Regional Manager South Wales, Ceri Fitzpatrick
Director Sustainability Enablement BT Global Services, Sharanne Basham-Pyke
Managing Director Energy and Services MNC UK BT Global Services, Mark Rosson
Deputy General Manager ICT Solutions, Dai Jeremiah
Account Director BT Wholesale, Robert Milloy
Head HR COO and Public Sector BT Global Services, Mathew Davies
Director BT Scotland, Brendan Dick
General Manager Retail Custom Service Solutions BT Retail, Rosemary Calder
Head Customer Satisfaction BT Global Services, Robert Cole
Director Service Management BT Wholesale, Angus Flett
Director BT Devolved Government BT Global Services, Tom Kelly
Director Contracts Requirements BT Innovate & Design, Ed Lindsay
Director Human Resources Reward and Employee Relations BT Group, Jim McInally
Lead Consultant Devolved Government BT Global Services, Martin Southern
Senior Manager Media and Corporate Relations BT Group, Anna Steven
Director Next Generation Access Programme BT Design & Innovate, Ian Stirrat
Chief Architect, Howard Watson
Regional Business Development Director BT Global Services, Janice Hailwood
Head of strategic university research for BT, Jeff Patmore
Research Scientist, Jia-Yan Gu
Sales Manager BTB Mobility Solutions, Mark Barrow
President GB&FM and Sales & Marketing, Tom Regent
Group People Director, Clare Clare Chapman Chapman
CIO, Clive Selley
Chief Executive Officer - BT Global Services, Luis Alvarez
CEO BT Benelux, Joris van Oers
Chief Executive and Board Member, Ian P. Livingston, age 48

Independent Non-Executive Director, Phil Hodkinson, age 55
Board Member, J. Eric Daniels, age 61
Board Member; Chief Executive BT Retail, Gavin Patterson, age 45
Board Member, Rt. Hon. Patricia Hewitt, age 64
Group Finance Director and Board Member, Anthony E. A. (Tony) Chanmugam, age 59
Board Member, Tony Ball, age 57
Independent Non-Executive Director, Jasmine Jasmine Whitbread Whitbread
Non-Executive Director, Karen Karen Richardson Richardson
Independent Non-Executive Director, Nicholas Nicholas Rose Rose
Auditors: PricewaterhouseCoopersLLP

LOCATIONS

HQ: BT Group Plc
BT Centre, 81 Newgate Street, London EC1A 7AJ
Phone: (44) 20 7356 5000 **Fax:** (44) 20 7356 5520
Web: www.bt.com

2013 Sales

	% of total
Europe Middle East Africa	
UK	77
Other	14
Americas	6
Asia	3
Total	**100**

PRODUCTS/OPERATIONS

2013 Sales

	% of total
BT Global	39
BT	37
BT	14
Openreach	10
Total	**100**

2013 Sales by Market

	% of total
ICT & managed networks	34
Calls & lines	26
Broadband & convergence	17
Conveyance interconnectcircuits WLR global carrier& other wholesale	8
Transit	4
Other	11
Total	**100**

Selected Subsidiaries and Affiliates

Basilica Computing Limited (IT services)
British Telecommunications plc (telecommunication related services and products)
BT Americas Inc. (telecommunication related services and products US)
BT Australasia Pty Limited (telecommunication related services and products Australia)
BT Centre Nominee 2 Limited (property holding company)
BT Communications Ireland Limited (telecommunications services)
BT Conferencing Inc. (Audio video and Web conferencing services US)
BT Convergent Solutions Limited (communications related services and products)
BT ESPA?A Compa?ia de Servicios Globales de Telecomunicaciones S.A. (telecommunication related services and products Spain)
BT Fleet Limited (fleet management)
BT France SA (telecommunication related services and products)
BT Frontline Pte Ltd (communications related services and products Singapore)
BT (Germany) GmbH & Co. oHG (telecommunication related services and products)
BT Global Services Limited (international telecommunications network systems)
BT Holdings Limited (investment holding company)
BT Hong Kong Limited (telecommunication related services and products)
BT Infrastructures Critiques (IT systems and network services France)
BT INS Inc (Information telecommunication consulting and software US)
BT Italia SpA (telecommunications related services and products Italy 97%)
BT Limited (international telecommunication network systems provider)
BT Nederland NV (telecommunication related services and products The Netherlands)
BT US Investments Limited (investments holding company US)
Communications Global Network Services Limited (telecommunication related services and products Bermuda)
Communication Networking Services (UK) (telecommunication related services and products)
Infonet Services Corporation (global managed network services provider US)
Infonet USA Corporation (global managed network services provider US)
Radianz Americas Inc. (global managed network services provider US)

COMPETITORS

Accenture
BSkyB
COLT Group
Cable & Wireless
Capgemini
Deutsche Telekom
Easynet
IBM Global Services
KCOM Group
KPN
Orange
Orange
Orange Business Services
THUS Ltd.
TalkTalk
Telecom Italia
Telecom plus
Telefonica
Telenor
TeliaSonera
Verizon Enterprise Solutions
Virgin Media
Vodafone

HISTORICAL FINANCIALS

Company Type: Public

Income Statement

FYE: March 31

	REVENUE ($ mil.)	NET INCOME ($ mil.)	NET PROFIT MARGIN	EMPLOYEES
03/13	27,379	3,177	11.6%	87,900
03/12	30,280	3,208	10.6%	89,015
03/11	32,301	2,416	7.5%	92,600
03/10	31,634	1,559	4.9%	97,800
03/09	30,599	(118)	—	107,000
Annual Growth	(2.7%)	—	—	(4.8%)

2013 Year-End Financials

Debt ratio: 61.2%
Return on equity: 404.0%
Cash ($ mil.): 1,404
Current ratio: 0.61
Long-term debt ($ mil.): 12,577
No. of shares (mil.): —
Dividends
Yield: 0.0%
Payout: 828.6%
Market value ($ mil.): —

	STOCK PRICE ($) FY Close	P/E High/Low	PER SHARE ($) Earnings	Dividends	Book Value
03/13	42.03	380270	0.39	3.21	(0.05)
03/12	36.16	363245	0.39	3.00	0.25
03/11	30.08	420197	0.30	1.05	0.38
03/10	18.71	479182	0.20	0.50	(0.49)
03/09	11.17	— —	(0.02)	2.60	0.02
Annual Growth	39.3%	— —	—	5.4%	—

Bunge Ltd.

Bunge's businesses stretch from the farm field to your local supermarket shelf. A leading integrated agribusiness and food company Bunge produces stores and sells agricultural products such as oilseeds and grains which it turns into vegetable oils and protein meals. Customers include animal feed poultry and aquaculture producers. The agribusiness markets vegetable oils used in the biodiesel industry. The company's edible oil products segment sells packaged oils like shortening and margarine under brands Bunge Pro Floriol and Olek. A sugar and bioenergy unit produces sugar and ethanol which are sold primarily in Brazil. Bunge also mixes and distributes crop fertilizers to farmers in South America.

Geographic Reach

Bunge has operations in Africa Asia the Caribbean Europe the Middle East North and South America. Europe is the company's largest market accounting for nearly a third of total sales. The US represents about a quarter of sales while Asia accounts for nearly a fifth.

Operations

The integrated agribusiness and food company divides its operations into four divisions. Agribusiness is the largest accounting for nearly three-quarters of the company's sales. It's primarily involved in the purchase storage transport processing and ultimately the sale of agricultural commodities in North and South America Europe and Asia. Bunge's Food and Ingredients division houses edible oils products and milling products and includes businesses that produce and sell edible oils shortenings margarines mayonnaise and milled products such as wheat flours corn-based products and rice. The Sugar and Bioenergy segment produces and sells sugar and ethanol derived from sugarcane. The firm's shrinking Fertilizer arm makes blends and distributes fertilizer products for the agricultural industry primarily in South America.

Financial Performance

Bunge's sales approached $61 billion in 2012 a 4% increase versus 2011. Agribusiness and Edible Oil Products outperformed the company's other business segments posting sales increases of 15% and 7% respectively. The company's Sugar and Bioenergy operation's sales tumbled 20% in 2012 versus the prior year while sales of milling products declined by nearly 9%. Asia Canada and the US each posted double-digit annual sales comparisons while sales in Europe rose 6%. Brazil posted a 3% gain in 2012 sales while Argentina suffered a 16% decline. Overall 2012 marked the third consecutive year of increasing sales for Bunge although the rate of growth has slowed. Indeed in 2011 sales jumped 29% versus 2010.

Net income plunged 93% in 2012 its second year of steep decline due primarily to an after-tax charge related to the impairment of the Sugar & Bioenergy segment goodwill and a loss of $342 million for results of discontinued operations.

Strategy

Diversified Bunge is building some of its businesses while retrenching in others such as fertilizer. Indeed in 2013 the company sold its Brazilian fertilizer business to Yara International ASA for $750 million in cash. Also in 2012 the firm sold its 28% stake in Soloe LLC its joint venture with DuPont formed in 2003 for $440 million. Bunge will continue to supply fertilizer to farmers as part of its grain organization activities.

Bunge intends to fuel growth by investing in projects that strengthen its leadership in grains oilseeds and food ingredients.

Mergers and Acquisitions

In line with its focus on agriculture and environmental concerns Bunge in 2012 acquired London-based Climate Change Capital Group parent to Climate Change Capital (CCC) a UK-regulated sustainable asset manager and adviser. CCC makes investments in projects companies and technologies focusing on carbon finance private equity and property. Also in 2012 Bunge's subsidiary in India acquired the edible oils and fats business of Amrit Banaspati. The purchase which included the rights to the vanaspati (cooking oil) brand GAGAN furthers Bunge's presence in the Indian consumer foods market. The deal followed Bunge's purchase (through its North American subsidiary) of a pair of margarine production facilities and their assets from The C.F. Sauer Company in mid-2011. Bunge scooped up an assortment of low saturated and trans-fat products for its North American customers which include restaurants and food processors.

In April 2012 Bunge purchased the assets of MCN BioProducts a privately-held Canadian technology company. The purchase creates opportunities for Bunge to provide protein alternatives in existing and new markets.

HISTORY

In 2003 Bunge announced it acquired the India-based edible oils and fats businesses of Hindustan Lever as well as India oilseed-crushing business Prestige Foods Limited. That year it also sold its private-label retail bottled-oil business to ACH Food.

The company also sold the bakery business of its North American subsidiary to Dawn Food Products for about $82 million. The business included Bunge North America's frozen dough mixes syrups and toppings products. These changes allowed Bunge to continue its focus on its edible-oils business. In addition the acquisition of Cereol in 2003 made Bunge the world's largest oilseed producer.

The company is expanding into Eastern Europe and Asia. As part of that effort it purchased Poland's Kama Foods in 2004. Activity in Russia includes the purchase of a grain terminal in Rostov to handle the increase in Russian exports of wheat and barley. Taking its first step into China in 2005 Bunge purchased a controlling interest in a soybean crushing and refining plant in Shandong Province.

Bunge agreed to acquire Corn Products International (renamed Ingredion) in June 2008. In November 2008 Corn Products announced its board withdrew its support for its planned takeover without citing a reason. A week later Bunge issued a statement saying that although the company still believed the takeover was a good fit that it was not in its best interests to do pursue the takeover at that time. Falling corn prices and the weak economy are believed to be the deciding factors in the cancellation of the deal. Bunge is already the #3 agribusiness company in the global marketplace (after #1 Cargill and #2 Archer Daniels Midland). The acquisition of Corn Products would have given Bunge a much stronger presence in corn as well as greater access to markets in Asia and North and South America. Bunge did add to its holdings in 2008 when it acquired the international sugar trading and marketing division of European ingredients giant Tate & Lyle.

Founded in 1818 as a grain trading company in Amsterdam Bunge was held mostly by families descended from founder Johann Bunge until it went public in 2001.

EXECUTIVES

Executive Chairman of the Board, Alberto Weisser, age 57, $1,200,000 total compensation
Managing Director Global Government and Corporate Affairs, Carl L. Hausmann, age 66
Managing Director Bunge Global Agribusiness; CEO Bunge Product Lines, Raul Padilla, age 57
CEO Bunge Europe Middle East & Africa, Jean-Louis Gourbin, age 65
Deputy Chairman, L. Patrick Lupo, age 62
Chief Financial Officer; Global Operational Excellence Officer, Andrew J. (Drew) Burke, age 58, $500,000 total compensation
CEO Bunge Asia, Christopher S. White, age 60
Managing Director Food and Ingredients, Gordon Hardie
President and Chief Executive Officer; Bunge Brazil, Pedro Pullen Parente, age 60
Chief Personnel Officer, Vicente C. Teixeira, age 61
Chief Development Officer and Managing Director Sugar and Bioenergy, D. Benedict Pearcy, age 44, $427,490 total compensation
Chief Executive Officer; Director, Soren W. Schroder, age 51
Manager Exernal Communications, Susan Burns
CEO Bunge Argentina, Enrique Humanes
General Counsel Secretary Managing Director, Frank Jimenez
CEO Bunge EMEA, Tommy Jensen
Director, Larry G. Pillard, age 65
Director, Ernest G. Bachrach, age 60
Deputy Chairman, L. Patrick Lupo, age 62
Director, Michael H. Bulkin, age 73
Director, Jorge Born Jr., age 50
Director, Enrique H. Boilini, age 51
Director, Octavio Caraballo, age 69
Director, Francis Coppinger, age 61
Director, Bernard de La Tour d'Auvergne Lauraguais, age 68
Director, William Engels, age 53
Independent Director, Bernard Lauraguais
Independent Director, Kathleen Hyle
Independent Director, James Hackett
Auditors: Deloitte&ToucheLLP

LOCATIONS

HQ: Bunge Ltd.
50 Main Street, White Plains, NY 10606
Phone: 914 684-2800
Web: www.bunge.com

2012 Sales

	$ mil.	% of total
Europe	19,475	32
US	15,249	25
Asia	11,160	18
Brazil	8,583	14
Argentina	3,059	5
Canada	2,322	4
Other regions	1,143	2
Total	**60,991**	**100**

PRODUCTS/OPERATIONS

2012 Sales

	$ mil.	% of total
Agribusiness	44,561	73
Edible oil products	9,472	16
Sugar & bioenergy	4,659	8
Milling products	1,833	2
Fertilizer	466	1
Total	**60,991**	**100**

Selected Products and Services

Agribusiness
- Purchase storage transport processing and sale of agricultural commodities
  - Corn
  - Rapeseed (canola seed)
  - Soybeans
  - Sunflower seed
  - Wheat
- Sugar
- Sugar cane-based ethanol

Fertilizer
- Mining and processing of phosphate ore
- Production
  - Ammonia
  - Ammonium nitrate
  - Dicalcium phosphate
  - Monoammonium phosphate
  - Nitric acid
  - Phosphate rock
  - Phosphate-based animal feed ingredients
  - Phosphoric acid
  - Sulfuric acid
  - Triple superphosphate
  - Urea

Food and food ingredients
- Bulk oils
- Edible oils
  - Rapeseed (canola oil)
  - Soybean
  - Sunflower
- Margarines
- Mayonnaise
- Packaged vegetable oils
- Shortenings

Milling
- Brazil
  - Bakery mixes
  - Wheat flours
- North America
  - Corn oil
  - Corn-based animal feed
  - Corn/soy meal
  - Dry-milled cornmeal
  - Flours
  - Grits
  - Soy-fortified cornmeal

Selected Joint Ventures

Agribusiness
- AGRI-Bunge LLC (34% AGRI Industries grain origination and Mississippi river terminal operation)
- Biocolza-Oleos E Farinhas de Colza S.A. (40% joint venture with Tagol; rapeseed oil crushing and biodiesel production; Portugal)
- Biodiesel Bilbao S.A. (20% with Acciona Biocombustibles S.A.; biofuel production; Spain)
- Bunge-Ergon Vicksburg LLC (BEV; 50% with Ergon Ethanol Inc.; ethanol production)
- Diester Industries International S.A.S. (DII) (DII; 40% with Diester Industries a subsidiary of Sofiproteol; biodiesel production and marketing; Germany)
- Ecofuel S.A. (50% with AGD; biodiesel production; Argentina)
- Southwest Iowa Renewable Energy LLC (SIRE; 26% with agricultural producers located in Southwest Iowa; ethanol production)

Fertilizer
- Bunge Maroc Phosphore S.A. (50% with Office Cherifien Des Phosphates (OCP); ferlilizer production; Morocco)

Food Products
- Harinera La Espiga S.A. de C.V. (32% with Grupo Neva S.A. de C.V. and Cerrollera S.A. de C.V.; wheat milling and bakery dry mix production; Mexico)

Selected Subsidiaries

Argentina
- Fertimport S.A.
- Guide S.A.

Belgium
- Afrique Initiatives

Bulgaria
- Kaliakra A.D.

Canada
- CF Oils Investments Inc.
- Leblanc & Lafrance Inc.
- Neptune Bulk Terminals (Canada) Ltd.

China
- Bunge Sanwei Oil & Fat Co. Ltd.
- Taixing Zhenhua Oils & Fats Co. Ltd.

Cyprus
- Brea Commodities Limited

France
- Diester Industries International S.A.S.

Italy
- Escercizio Raccordi Ferroviari S.p.A.

Latvia
- Dan Store LSEZ SIA

Mexico
- Harinera La Espiga S.A. de C.V.
- Inmobiliaria A. Gil S.A.
- Inmobiliaria Gilsa S.A.

Poland
- Polska Trade Services S.p.z.o.o.
- Warsaw Mathematical Institute Sp z.o.o.
- Z.T. Kruszwica S.A.

Romania
- SC Interoil S.A.
- SC Muntenia S.A.
- SC Unirea S.A.

Russia
- LLC Bunge CIS
- OJS Kholmsky
- Rostov Grain Terminal LLC

Spain
- Biodiesel Bilbao S.L.
- Estacion de Descarga y Carga S.A. (Esdecasa)
- Huelva Belts S.L.
- Moyresa Girasol S.L.

Switzerland
- Ecoinvest Carbon S.A.
- Oleina S.A.

Ukraine
- Black Sea Industries Limited
- Suntrade S.E.

Uruguay
- Agritrade S.A.

US
- Biofuels Company of America LLC
- The Crete Mills Inc.
- Delphos Terminal Company Inc.
- International Produce Inc.
- Renewable Energy Group Inc.
- Solae Holdings LLC
- Southwest Iowa Renewable Energy LLC

Venezuela
- Almacen Terminal Santana C.A.

Vietnam
- Baria Joint Stock Company of Services for Import Export of Agro-Forestry Products and Fertilizer

COMPETITORS

ADM
Ag Processing Inc.
Associated British Foods
CHS
Cargill
ConAgra
Cosan
Danisco A/S
Dawn Food Products
General Mills
Ingredion
LifeLine
Louis Dreyfus Group
Mosaic Company
Potash Corp
Repsol
Rich Products
Sadia
Sudzucker
Tereos
Unilever
Ventura Foods
Wilmar

HISTORICAL FINANCIALS

Company Type: Public

Income Statement FYE: December 31

	REVENUE ($ mil.)	NET INCOME ($ mil.)	NET PROFIT MARGIN	EMPLOYEES
12/12	60,991	64	0.1%	36,000
12/11	58,743	942	1.6%	34,000
12/10	45,707	2,354	5.2%	33,021
12/09	41,926	361	0.9%	25,945
12/08	52,574	1,064	2.0%	24,787
Annual Growth	3.8%	(50.5%)	—	9.8%

2012 Year-End Financials

Debt ratio: 21.4%
Return on equity: 0.5%
Cash ($ mil.): 569
Current ratio: 1.49
Long-term debt ($ mil.): 3,532
No. of shares (mil.): 146
Dividends
Yield: 1.4%
Payout: 17.5%
Market value ($ mil.): 10,638

	STOCK PRICE ($) FY Close	P/E High/Low	PER SHARE ($) Earnings	Dividends	Book Value
12/12	72.69	389301	0.19	1.04	74.22
12/11	57.20	12 9	6.07	0.00	81.48
12/10	65.52	4 3	15.06	0.88	83.34
12/09	63.83	32 19	2.22	0.80	70.80
12/08	51.77	16 4	7.73	0.72	61.14
Annual Growth	8.9%	— —	(60.4%)	9.6%	5.0%

Byucksan Engineering & Construction Co Ltd

LOCATIONS

HQ: Byucksan Engineering & Construction Co Ltd
7-50 Songdo-dong, Yeonsoo-gu, Incheon 406-840
Phone: (82) 2 767 5114 **Fax:** (82) 2 767 5205
Web: www.beecco.co.kr

HISTORICAL FINANCIALS

Company Type: Public

Income Statement FYE: December 31

	REVENUE ($ mil.)	NET INCOME ($ mil.)	NET PROFIT MARGIN	EMPLOYEES
12/12	393,378	(343,330)	—	296
12/11	576	(72)	—	397
12/10	1,199	(212)	—	536
12/09	1,097	21	1.9%	0
12/08	865	(19)	—	0
Annual Growth	361.7%	—	—	—

2012 Year-End Financials

Debt ratio: —
Return on equity: (-1,284.5%)
Cash ($ mil.): 10,397
Current ratio: 1.39
Long-term debt ($ mil.): —
No. of shares (mil.): —
Dividends
Yield: —
Payout: —
Market value ($ mil.): —

Caixa Geral de Depositos, S.A.

Caixa Geral de Depositos (CGD) wants to hold what's left in Portuguese pockets and pocketbooks. As one of Portugal's largest banks CGD (along with its numerous subsidiaries and affiliates) offers a wide range of products and services in addition to commercial banking including investment banking venture capital asset management insurance and credit services. In the retail sector CGD concentrates on such traditional products as savings accounts mortgage loans and credit cards. The bank has about 850 Portuguese branches and another 465 branches in 23 other countries in Africa the Americas Asia and Europe. With more than 4 million customers in Portugal CGD has about $152 billion in assets.

Strategy

With the financial crisis in the eurozone striking Portugal especially hard CGD is focusing on its banking activity outside of Europe. Nevertheless the bank seeks to maintain and build upon its leadership position in Portugal to be ready to capitalize on recovery there.

EXECUTIVES

Chairman, Alvaro Jose Barrigas do Nascimento, age 47

Vice-Chairman and CEO, Jose Agostinho Martins de Matos

LOCATIONS

HQ: Caixa Geral de Depositos, S.A.
Av. Joao XXI, 63, Lisbon 1000-300
Phone: (351) 21 795 3000 **Fax:** (351) 21 790 5051
Web: www.cgd.pt

2012 Branches

	No.
Portugal	848
International	463
Total	**1,311**

COMPETITORS

Allianz S.p.A.
Assurances Generales de France
BBVA
BNP Paribas
Banco BPI
Banco Comercial Portugues
Banco Espirito Santo
Citigroup
Credit Suisse
Espirito Santo Investment Bank
Grupo Santander
UBS

HISTORICAL FINANCIALS

Company Type: Public

Income Statement FYE: December 31

	ASSETS ($ mil.)	NET INCOME ($ mil.)	INCOME AS % OF ASSETS	EMPLOYEES
12/12	154,022	(520)	—	22,964
12/11	155,945	(631)	—	23,135
12/10	168,450	335	0.2%	23,011
12/09	174,287	401	0.2%	22,164
12/08	155,272	641	0.4%	20,797
Annual Growth	(0.2%)	—	—	2.5%

2012 Year-End Financials

Return on assets: (-0.3%)
Return on equity: (-7.4%)
Long-term debt ($ mil.): —
No. of shares (mil.): 1,180
Sales ($ mil): 8,549
Dividends
Yield: —
Payout: —
Market value ($ mil.): —

Canadian Imperial Bank of Commerce

Canadian Imperial Bank of Commerce (CIBC) is both Canadian and imperial when it comes to growing its business. CIBC has more than 1000 domestic branches that offer a range of consumer and business financial services including deposits loans investments and insurance. It operates in two main segments: CIBC Retail Markets (consumer and small business banking credit cards wealth management) and wholesale banking arm CIBC World Markets (merchant and investment banking capital markets services and research for corporate institutional and government clients). Internationally CIBC owns a majority of FirstCaribbean International Bank.

CIBC also operates retail brokerage CIBC Wood Gundy and offers investment management services in Hong Kong and Singapore. Active mainly in North America CIBC World Markets has operations in Asia Australia and Europe as well. The unit has identified lending securitization foreign exchange and electronic trading as areas of possible growth.

CIBC is selling its stake in trust and custody services provider CIBC Mellon to its partner in the joint venture The Bank of New York Mellon for an undisclosed amount. The sale fits in with the company's goals of focusing on its core operations.

In 2011 CIBC bought a 41% stake in American Century Investments a US asset management company with $111 billion under management. The deal helps increase the firm's fee-based income and grows its asset management business internationally. The company is now buying the private wealth management business of MFS McLean Budden which oversees some $1.4 billion in assets for high-net-worth investors.

CIBC is looking to expand its wealth management business throughout North America. To that end in 2013 it acquired Atlanta-based Atlantic Trust from Invesco for $210 million. The purchase provides CIBC with entry into the US private wealth market where high-net-worth personal financial assets are growing 50% faster than those of the average US household and builds on the bank's recent purchase of MFS McLean Budden in Canada. Also CIBC is seeking a more substantial retail banking presence in the US like larger competitors Toronto-Dominion Bank of Montreal and Royal Bank of Canada. Though it is the smallest of Canada's Big Five banks (which also includes Scotiabank) the company is aiming to be among the top three in its home market. To that end it has been adding new products opening branches extending business hours and enhancing its technology. In 2010 it strengthened its credit card business in Canada through the acquisition of a $2 billion credit card portfolio from Citigroup. The deal made CIBC Canada's largest credit card issuer. Also thin 2010 the company acquired CIT's business credit operations in Canada to bolster its asset-based lending.

CIBC more than doubled its net income and earnings per share that year after economic conditions and losses in its structured credit business weighed on its bottom line in 2008 and 2009. The company experienced fewer loan write-offs thanks to improved performance in its credit card and personal lending portfolios.

CIBC made a move in 2011 that may signal that it is looking for acquisitions abroad as well. That year it bought more than 20% of Bermuda-based Bank of N.T. Butterfield. The acquisition may be small but it is a shift from CIBC's previous cost-cutting approach.

HISTORY

In 1858 Bank of Canada was chartered; Toronto financier William McMaster bought the charter in 1866 when investors failed to raise enough money to open it and changed the name to Canadian Bank of Commerce.

The firm opened in 1867 bought the Gore Bank of Hamilton (1870) and expanded within seven years to 24 branches in Ontario as well as Montreal and New York. Led by Edmund Walker the bank spread west of the Great Lakes with the opening of a Winnipeg Manitoba branch in 1893 and joined the Gold Rush with branches in Dawson City Yukon Territory and Skagway Alaska in 1898.

As the new century began the bank's purchases spanned the breadth of Canada from the Bank of British Columbia (1901) to Halifax Banking (1903) and the Merchants Bank of Prince Edward Island (1906). More buys followed in the 1920s; the bank's assets peaked in 1929 and then plunged during the Depression. It recovered during WWII.

In 1961 Canadian Bank of Commerce merged with Imperial Bank of Canada to become Canadian Imperial Bank of Commerce (CIBC). Imperial Bank was founded in 1875 by Henry Howland; it went west to Calgary and Edmonton and became known as "The Mining Bank." It bought Barclays Bank (Canada) in 1956.

As the energy and agriculture sectors declined in the early 1980s two of CIBC's largest borrowers Dome Petroleum and tractor maker Massey-Ferguson defaulted on their loans. Deregulation opened investment banking to CIBC which in 1988 bought a majority share of Wood Gundy one of Canada's largest investment dealers; CIBC also purchased Merrill Lynch Canada's retail brokerage business.

In 1992 CIBC added substantially to its loss reserves (resulting in an earnings drop of 98%) to cover real estate losses from developer Olympia & York and others. This launched more cost-cutting as the company reorganized by operating segments.

Deregulation allowed CIBC to begin selling insurance in 1993; the company built a collection of life credit personal property/casualty and nonmedical health companies.

In 1996 the bank formed Intria a processing and technical support subsidiary. The next year CIBC Wood Gundy became CIBC World Markets and CIBC bought securities firm Oppenheimer & Co. and added its stock underwriting and brokerage abilities to CIBC World Markets.

In 1998 increasing foreign competition prompted CIBC and Toronto-Dominion to plan a merger (as did Royal Bank of Canada and Bank of Montreal); the government halted both plans citing Canada's already highly concentrated banking industry.

Spurned the bank overhauled its operations to spark growth in the late 1990s. To cut costs it eliminated some 4000 jobs and sold its more than $1-billion real estate portfolio. It teamed with the Winn-Dixie (1999) and Safeway (2000) supermarket chains to operate electronic branches in the US. The firm scaled back its disappointing international operations and began selling its insurance units.

In 2000 CIBC created Amicus as a holding company for CIBC World Markets' retail electronic banking business. The following year the bank sold its merchant card services business to US-based Global Payments.

In 2002 the company snagged US-based Merrill Lynch's Canadian retail brokerage asset management and securities operations renaming it CIBC Asset Management Inc. That same year CIBC merged its Caribbean banking business with that of UK-based Barclays to create FirstCaribbean Bank.

The next year CIBC sold the Oppenheimer private client and asset-management divisions to Fahnestock Viner (now Oppenheimer Holdings). It sold Juniper Financial a Delaware-based credit card issuer to Barclays for some $293 million in 2004.

In 2004 and again in 2006 CIBC was sued by creditors of Internet telecommunications company Global Crossing stating that the bank had engaged in insider trading to the tune of $2 billion. Creditors demanded a return of the proceeds. CIBC denied the claims but in 2006 two units of the bank agreed to pay $17.4 million to investors in the ill-fated telecom.

More trouble came in 2005 when CIBC agreed to pay some $2.4 billion in an investor class-action suit to resolve claims that the company helped notorious energy trader Enron to conceal losses.

EXECUTIVES

Senior Executive Vice-President Managing Director, Richard E. Venn, age 63
SEVP and Chief Risk Officer, Tom D. Woods, age 61, $352,830 total compensation
President; Chief Executive Officer; Director, Gerald T. (Gerry) McCaughey, age 56, $849,500 total compensation
Chairman, Charles Sirois, age 58
SEVP; Group Head Wholesale International and Technology and Operations, Richard W. Nesbitt, age 58, $238,380 total compensation
Senior Executive Vice-President CIBC and Group, Victor Dodig
SEVP and Group Head Retail and Business Banking, J. David Williamson, age 53, $288,339 total compensation
Chief Financial Officer; Senior Executive Vice President, Kevin Glass
Vice Chairman and SEVP, Rt. Hon. Jim Prentice
Vice President of Legal Affairs and General Counsel, Alvaro Diaz
Vice President of Corporate Development, Andres Franco
Vice-President General Counsel, Charles Gerber
Vice President of Exploration, Christian Rios
Vice President - Legal, Corey M. Dean
Director, Gary F. Colter, age 66
Director, Ronald W. (Ron) Tysoe, age 59
President CEO and Director, Gerald T. (Gerry) McCaughey, age 56
Director, Linda S. Hasenfratz, age 45
Director, Robert J. (Bob) Steacy, age 62
Director, Dominic D'Alessandro, age 64
Director, Patrick D. Daniel, age 65
Director, Jane L. Peverett, age 54
Director, Brent S. Belzberg, age 61
Director, Leslie Rahl, age 61
Director, John P. Manley, age 62
Director, Katharine B. (Kate) Stevenson, age 50
Director, Gordon D. Giffin, age 62
Director, Nicholas D. Le Pan, age 60
Director, Luc Desjardins, age 59
Vice Chairman and SEVP, Rt. Hon. Jim Prentice
Auditors: Ernst&YoungLLP

LOCATIONS

HQ: Canadian Imperial Bank of Commerce
Commerce Court, Toronto, Ontario M5L 1A2
Phone: 416 980-3043 **Fax:** 416 980-7012
Web: www.cibc.com

PRODUCTS/OPERATIONS

2010 Sales

	% of total
Interest	
Loans	49
Securities &	12
Noninterest	
Deposit & payment	5
Mutual fund	5
Foreign exchange other than	4
Securitized	4
Trading	4
Commissions on securities	3
Investment management & custodial	3
Underwriting & advisory	3
Available-for-sale securities	3
Other	5
Total	**100**

COMPETITORS

BMO Financial Group
Barclays
Caisses centrale Desjardins
Citigroup
Goldman Sachs
JPMorgan Chase
National Bank of Canada
RBC Financial Group
Scotiabank
TD Bank

HISTORICAL FINANCIALS

Company Type: Public

Income Statement FYE: October 31

	ASSETS ($ mil.)	NET INCOME ($ mil.)	INCOME AS % OF ASSETS	EMPLOYEES
10/13	380,892	3,253	0.9%	43,039
10/12	394,456	3,340	0.8%	42,595
10/11	385,287	2,878	0.7%	42,239
10/10	345,577	2,406	0.7%	42,354
10/09	309,740	1,082	0.3%	41,941
Annual Growth	5.3%	31.7%	—	0.6%

2013 Year-End Financials

Return on assets: 0.8%
Return on equity: 19.3%
Long-term debt ($ mil.): —
No. of shares (mil.): 399
Sales ($ mil): 16,386

Dividends
Yield: 4.4%
Payout: 47.6%
Market value ($ mil.): 33,996

	STOCK PRICE ($) FY Close	P/E High	P/E Low	PER SHARE ($) Earnings	Dividends	Book Value
10/13	85.15	10	8	7.87	3.71	43.71
10/12	78.58	10	8	7.87	3.61	41.81
10/11	75.45	14	9	6.74	3.52	39.92
10/10	76.60	13	9	5.76	3.42	39.47
10/09	57.13	22	8	2.44	3.21	34.46
Annual Growth	10.5%	—	—	34.0%	3.7%	6.1%

Canon, Inc.

For Canon image is everything. The company makes printers multifunction document equipment and other computer peripherals for home and office use (more than half of sales). It also remains a force in the consumer and professional photography industry making still and video digital cameras LCD projectors lenses and binoculars. Canon also operates an industrial segment featuring such diverse products as semiconductor manufacturing equipment television broadcast lenses and devices used for eye examinations. Customers in its home country of Japan generate just 20% of the company's revenues.

Most of Canon's manufacturing is done in Japan but it also has plants in countries including Brazil France Germany the Netherlands China Malaysia Taiwan Thailand Vietnam and the US. Nearly 60% of Canon's revenues are divided between Europe which has the slightly larger share and the Americas served by subsidiaries including Canon U.S.A. and Canon Canada. The company circulates its products in those regions primarily through large distributors.

Like many companies Canon fell victim to the global recession with 2009 sales falling nearly one-quarter. Although the company recuperated with a 30% gain in 2010 it still hasn't returned to the level of growth it has typically had over the past decade. The deceptive 1% increase in revenues for 2011 when looked at in US currency reaching more than $45 billion was actually a 4% dip to Y3.6 trillion albeit by a less-dramatic drop than recession-addled 2009. Net profit of Y255 trillion (about $3.2 billion) is much closer to pre-recession levels though it's still essentially flat in domestic currency compared to 2010.

Canon-branded products are the company's primary source of revenue but it also sells equipment that is branded for its partners. Competitor Hewlett-Packard is among those customer-partners accounting for approximately 20% of sales. With the market relatively underpenetrated with color office products Canon and its competitors are pushing to shift customers away from monochrome products for growth in this segment.

While rivals such as Xerox may be digging deep into back office enterprise IT services Canon has stayed more focused on the front office. In 2011 however the company created the Canon Information and Imaging Solutions subsidiary under Canon U.S.A. to focus on the IT services market. The new company will look to cloud computing and other software and services for such areas as business process optimization security services and elements of enterprise resource planning. In 2012 Canon announced it would acquire Belgium-based document management and IT services company I.R.I.S. Group. Canon has partnered with the company for years and bought a 17% stake in it in 2009. Besides bringing in complementary products the purchase will fuel Canon's consultancy aspirations.

Perhaps still best known for its cameras Canon has seen its photographic business steadily decline as traditional camera manufacturers have started to directly compete with electronics manufacturers. However the company remains a leader in the digital camera market where it concentrates on high-end single-lens-reflex (SLR) devices which include professional video cameras used in broadcast and major motion picture production. Canon's third primary product group industry encompasses a diverse portfolio including semiconductor and LCD lithography equipment medical imaging equipment lenses micromotors and large-format printers.

Canon faces stiff competition in all of its segments all over the world. In Japan the digital camera market is particularly heated. Although the company's brand remains strong globally it faces intense rivalries with foes such as Sony Nikon and Panasonic. To increase its competitiveness Canon hopes to find ways to bring products and services to its customers via the cloud and boost its R&D activity in the US and Europe. It will also keep an eye out for acquisitions that could bring in new technologies. The company's sales efforts will focus on strengthening its group companies in developed countries and forging approaches in emerging markets according to the conditions in each region.

HISTORY

Takeshi Mitarai and a friend Saburo Uchida formed Seiki Kogaku Kenkyusho (Precision Optical Research Laboratory) in Tokyo in 1933 to make Japan's first 35mm camera. In 1935 the camera was introduced under the brand name Kwanon (after Quan Yin the Buddhist goddess of mercy) –but later renamed Canon. In response to a pre-WWII military buildup the company made X-ray machines for the Japanese.

In 1947 the company became Canon Camera Company as the brand name gained popularity. Canon opened its first overseas branch in New York in 1955. It diversified into business equipment by introducing the first 10-key electronic calculator (1964) and a plain-paper photocopier (1968) independent of Xerox's patented technology. Canon dropped "Camera Company" from its name in 1969.

The company invented the "liquid dry" copying system which used plain paper and liquid developer in 1972. It failed to produce new cameras and was surpassed by Minolta (now defunct) as Japan's top camera exporter. Sales were sluggish in the early 1970s and in 1975 Canon suspended dividends for the first time since WWII.

At that time Canon's managing director Ryuzaburo Kaku convinced Mitarai that the company's problems stemmed from indecisive leadership and weak marketing. Kaku turned Canon around unleashing the electronic AE-1 in a media blitz that in 1976 included the first-ever TV commercials for a 35mm camera. With automated features the AE-1 appealed to the clumsiest photographers. Its success catapulted Canon past Minolta as the world's #1 camera maker.

In 1979 Canon introduced the first copier to use a dry developer. As the copier market matured in the early 1980s Canon shifted to making other automated office equipment including laser printers and fax machines.

Mitarai died in 1984. Minolta the next year again displaced Canon as the world's #1 camera maker when it introduced a fully automated model. But Canon came back in 1987 with the electronic optical system (EOS) auto-focus camera which returned the company to preeminence in 1990. That year the company initiated an ink cartridge recycling program. Canon teamed up with IBM in 1992 to produce portable PCs. In 1993 Takeshi Mitarai's son Hajime who joined Canon in 1974 was named president and began expanding product development.

In 1995 Canon introduced the world's first color ferroelectric LCD designed to replace cathode ray tubes in computer and TV screens as the industry standard. When Hajime died that year cousin Fujio Mitarai a 34-year Canon employee who served as the head of Canon U.S.A. in the 1980s was named president and CEO. In 1996 the company made Canon Latin America a direct subsidiary of Canon U.S.A. with the "kyosei" idea that regionalized control would make the subsidiary more efficient.

Canon stopped making PCs in 1997. The next year the company unveiled its Hyper Photo System which combines a scanner PC server and printer to produce photo prints and expanded its copier remanufacturing operations. In 1999 after 16 years of production Canon stopped making optical memory cards. The company also opened a research and development facility in the US.

In 2000 Canon and Toshiba began working together to develop technology for flat-panel displays. Canon expanded its line of digital cameras in 2001; the company's sales in that segment almost doubled that year.

The next year the company announced that it would merge two of its office equipment subsidiaries Copyer and Canon Aptex in an effort to improve operating efficiency.

In 2004 Canon formed a joint venture with Toshiba to develop surface-conduction electron-emitter display (SED) products. Canon acquired Toshiba's stake in the company in 2007.

In 2010 Canon acquired Oce Europe's largest manufacturer of printers to solidify its position in that key geographic market. The company maintained the Oce brand following completion of the transaction operating the Dutch supplier of office machines as a division.

EXECUTIVES

Chairman President and CEO, Fujio Mitarai, age 78
EVP and CFO, Toshizo Tanaka, age 73
EVP; Group Executive Corporate Planning Development, Kunio Watanabe, age 69
Senior Managing Director; President and CEO Canon U.S.A., Yoroku (Joe) Adachi, age 66
Senior Managing Director; Chief Executive Peripheral Products Operations, Yasuo Mitsuhashi, age 64
EVP Canon USA, Seymour E. Liebman, age 64
Executive Officer Medical Equipment, Yukiaki Hashimoto

Senior Managing Director; Chief Executive Office Imaging Products Operations, Masaki Nakaoka, age 64
Senior Managing Director; Group Executive Device Technology Development, Shigeyuki Matsumoto, age 63
Group Executive Network Visual Solution Business Promotion, Masanori Yamada
President and CEO Canon Canada, Kazuto (Kevin) Ogawa
Senior Managing Director; Group Executive Production Engineering, Haruhisa Honda, age 65
Managing Director; Chief Executive Image Communication Products Operations, Masaya Maeda, age 61
President and CEO Canon France, Kenji Kobayashi
Senior Executive Officer; Group Executive Global Manufacturing, Sachio Kageyama
Group Executive Human Resources Management and Organization, Kazuto Ono
Deputy Chief Executive Peripheral Products Operations, Akio Noguchi
Group Executive Quality Management, Hiroyuki Suematsu
Director; Group Executive Digital Platform Technology Development, Yasuhiro Tani
EVP CTO and Board Member, Toshiaki Ikoma, age 72
President and CEO Canon Europe, Rokus van Iperen
Managing Director; President and CEO Canon (China), Hideki Ozawa
Deputy Chief Executive Image Communication Products Operations, Masato Okada
Senior Managing Director; Group Executive Procurement, Toshio Homma
Director; Group Executive Information and Communication Systems, Makoto Araki
Group Executive Corporate Intellectual Property and Legal, Kenichi Nagasawa
EVP Canon USA, Yuichi Ishizuka
Senior Vice President, Eliott Peck
Senior Vice President, Joseph G. Warren
Vice President General Manager Imaging Systems Group, Sam Yoshida
Chief Executive Optical Products Operations, Shigeyuki Uzawa
Chief Executive Inkjet Products Operations, Naoji Otsuka
Group Executive Public Affairs, Kazuhiko Noguchi
Group Executive Semiconductor Production Equipment Group, Hiroaki Takeishi
Group Executive R&D Project Group, Nobutoshi Mizusawa
EVP CFO and Board Member, Toshizo Tanaka, age 72
Senior Managing Director, Kunio Watanabe, age 68
Senior Managing Director; President and CEO Canon USA, Yoroku (Joe) Adachi, age 65
Senior Managing Director; Chief Executive Peripheral Products Operations, Yasuo Mitsuhashi, age 64
Managing Director; President and CEO Canon Europa, Ryoichi Bamba, age 65
Managing Director; Chief Executive Inkjet Products Operations, Katsuichi Shimizu, age 66
Managing Director, Tomonori Iwashita, age 63
Managing Director; Chief Executive Office Imaging Products Operations, Masaki Nakaoka, age 63
Senior Managing Director, Shigeyuki Matsumoto, age 63
Managing Director, Haruhisa Honda, age 65
Managing Director; Chief Executive Image Communication Products Operations, Masaya Maeda, age 61
Director; Group Executive Digital Platform Technology Development, Yasuhiro Tani
EVP CTO and Board Member, Toshiaki Ikoma, age 72
Managing Director, Masahiro Osawa, age 65
Managing Director; President and CEO Canon (China), Hideki Ozawa
Managing Director; Chief Executive L Printer Products Operations, Toshio Homma
Director; Group Executive Information and Communication Systems Headquarters, Makoto Araki
Auditors: Ernst&YoungShinNihon

LOCATIONS

HQ: Canon, Inc.
30-2, Shimomaruko 3-chome, Ohta-ku, Tokyo 146-8501
Phone: (81) 3 3758 2111
Web: www.canon.jp

2011 Sales

	% of total
Europe	31
Americas	27
Asia and	22
Japan	20
Total	**100**

PRODUCTS/OPERATIONS

2011 Sales

	% of total
Office	53
Consumer	36
Industrial &	11
Total	**100**

Selected Products

Office
- Copy machines
  - Office
  - Personal
  - Full-color
- Large format inkjet printers
- Laser printers
- Office imaging software
- Office network digital multifunction devices
- Toner Cartridges

Consumer
- Broadcasting equipment
- Cameras
  - SLR
  - Compact Digital
  - Video camcorders
- Inkjet and photo printers
- Lenses
- Liquid-crystal display projectors

Industrial and other
- Color label card printers
- Document scanners
- LCD Lithography Systems
- Medical equipment
  - Digital Radiography
  - Ophthalmic Equipment
- Semiconductor production equipment

COMPETITORS

ASML
Agfa
Barco
CASIO COMPUTER
Citizen
Eastman Kodak
Epson
FUJIFILM
Fujitsu
Hewlett-Packard
Hitachi
Hoya Corp.
IBM
JVC KENWOOD
Konica Minolta
Kyocera
Lexmark
NEC
Nikon
Oce
Oki Electric
Olympus
Panasonic Corp
Philips Electronics
Ricoh Company
SANYO
Samsung Electronics
Sharp Corp.
Sony
Toshiba
Xerox

HISTORICAL FINANCIALS

Company Type: Public

Income Statement

FYE: December 31

	REVENUE ($ mil.)	NET INCOME ($ mil.)	NET PROFIT MARGIN	EMPLOYEES
12/12	40,401	2,607	6.5%	196,968
12/11	45,969	3,212	7.0%	198,307
12/10	45,573	3,031	6.7%	197,386
12/09	34,734	1,424	4.1%	168,879
12/08	45,271	3,418	7.6%	166,980
Annual Growth	(2.8%)	(6.5%)	—	4.2%

2012 Year-End Financials

Debt ratio: 0.0%
Return on equity: 8.7%
Cash ($ mil.): 7,740
Current ratio: 2.47
Long-term debt ($ mil.): 24
No. of shares (mil.): 1,152
Dividends
Yield: 3.7%
Payout: 56.1%
Market value ($ mil.): 45,201

	STOCK PRICE ($) FY Close	P/E High/Low		PER SHARE ($) Earnings	Dividends	Book Value
12/12	39.21	0	0	2.22	1.49	26.17
12/11	44.04	0	0	2.64	0.00	27.44
12/10	51.34	0	0	2.46	1.23	26.48
12/09	42.32	0	0	1.15	1.15	23.57
12/08	31.40	0	0	2.72	1.07	23.82
Annual Growth	5.7%	—	—	(5.0%)	8.7%	2.4%

Carnival Corp.

Carnival offers a boatload of fun. The company is the world's #1 cruise operator boasting about a dozen cruise lines and about 100 ships with a total passenger capacity of more than 190000. Carnival operates in North America primarily through its Princess Cruise Line Holland America and Seabourn luxury cruise brand as well as its flagship Carnival Cruise Lines unit. Brands such as AIDA P&O Cruises and Costa Cruises offer services to passengers in Europe and the Cunard Line runs luxury trans-Atlantic liners. Carnival operates as a dual-listed company with UK-based Carnival plc forming a single enterprise under a unified executive team.

Operations

Carnival maintains its top position in the industry by leveraging its cruise lines to penetrate a number of different markets. Carnival Cruises a leading brand in the US and Princess both target families retirees and other upper middle class customers with competitively priced cruise packages. Its popular destinations include the Caribbean the Mexican Riviera and Alaska. P&O Cruises chases after a similar target customer in the UK with trips to the Mediterranean and Scandinavia. (P&O also operates out of Australia and New Zealand.) Holland America is known for its scenic getaways in New England Canada and along the Pacific coast. The company offers trips within the Asian market through its Costa Cruises. The line serves cruise-goers with Chinese-style food mah-jongg tables in its casino and luxury brands in its retail shops.

While Carnival has been known as the Fun Ship the cruiser also attracts those looking for a fine ship. Carnival's Seabourn brand operates luxury cruises to upscale travelers and caters to them with fine food personalized service and exotic destinations worldwide. Similarly its Swan Hellenic premium brand sails throughout Europe and Asia.

Of course luxury is the name of the game for Cunard which provides a variety of cruises in addition to its liner services.

Financial Analysis

On the heels of the global recession Carnival has enjoyed a gradual bump in revenues over the last three years. Total sales increased 9% from 2010 to 2011 mostly through an almost 10% uptick in passenger revenue. Passenger revenue typically represents about 77% of its revenue each year. Onboard and other cruise revenues jumped 8% and accounted for the remaining 23% in total sales for 2011.

North America is the most important region for Carnival representing half its total sales each year and increasing by 5% in 2011. European brands accounted for 38% of the company's total sales and increased by 7%.

Carnival's profits however decreased by 3% in 2011 as a result of higher fuel prices which cost the company an additional $535 million.

Another factor sure to affect the company's balance sheet is the tragic incident of the "Costa Concordia" grounding off the coast of Italy that occurred in January 2012. The ship remains grounded and partially submerged off the coast. Carnival estimated it suffered a first quarter 2012 loss of $139 million in conjunction with the accident.

Strategy

Fueled by optimism for the future Carnival has orders in place for 10 additional cruise ships which it will integrate into its fleet between 2012 and March 2016. The new additions are expected to result in a 32000 lower berth increase and a 16% increase in passenger capacity.

To fill its expanding inventory of passenger berths Carnival continues to spend heavily on marketing its cruises especially to consumers who have never taken to the high seas. While it relies on the traditional mediums such as television and magazines Carnival has been shifting its efforts from print media to online and social media utilizing Facebook YouTube Twitter Flickr and Podcasts. Its goal is to engage in two-way conversations with consumers and create brand fans. Also the company has expanded its number of homeports to put cruising possibilities closer to customers. Effective 2011 Carnival operates from 15 North American homeports.

The cruise firm is counting on Europe as well as Australia New Zealand Asia and South America for future growth as it believes these markets are relatively untapped.

Ownership

CEO Micky Arison and his family own about 30% of Carnival Corporation and control a 23% voting stake in the combined entity that consists of Carnival Corporation and Carnival plc. Arison one of the wealthiest people in Miami also owns the Miami Heat basketball team.

HISTORY

Israeli emigrant Ted Arison got into the cruise business in the mid-1960s forming Norwegian Caribbean Lines with shipping magnate Knut Kloster. After their partnership ended in 1971 Arison persuaded old friend Meshulam Riklis to bankroll his $6.5 million purchase of the "Empress of Canada" in 1972. Riklis owned (among other things) the Boston-based American International Travel Service (AITS). Arison set up Carnival Cruise Lines as an AITS subsidiary and renamed his ship the "Mardi Gras." Unfortunately she ran aground on her maiden voyage sending Carnival into red ink for three years.

Arison bought out Riklis in 1974 for $1 and assumed Carnival's $5 million debt. He envisioned a cruise line that would offer affordable vacation packages to young middle-class consumers and invented a new type of cruise ship featuring live music gambling and other entertainment on board. Carnival was profitable within a month and by the end of the following year Arison had paid off Carnival's debt and bought its second ship. Arison's son Micky became CEO in 1979. Despite the rising costs of shipbuilding and fuel prices Carnival continued to add to its fleet. The company grew to become the world's #1 cruise operator and the Arisons took Carnival public in 1987.

The company acquired luxury cruise business Holland America Line in 1989 and formed a joint venture with Seabourn Cruise Lines in 1992. Carnival changed its name to Carnival Corporation in 1994 to reflect its diversifying operations and it took a 50% stake in Seabourn the following year. Carnival stepped up its European expansion in 1996 by buying a stake in UK-based Airtours. The next year Carnival and Airtours jointly acquired an interest in European cruise giant Costa Crociere for about $275 million.

Carnival signed a deal with two shipyards in 1998 to build twelve more ships for the company by 2004 (six each for its Carnival and Holland America lines). It also bought a majority interest in the prestigious Cunard Line ("Queen Elizabeth 2") that year merged it with Seabourn and bought the remainder of the two cruise lines in 1999. An ugly lawsuit reared its head that year after a woman claimed to have been sexually assaulted while on a Carnival ship. Carnival acknowledged that it had received more than 100 similar complaints against its cruise employees dating back to 1995. (The suit was settled later that year.)

Carnival's bidding war with Genting Hong Kong Limited (formerly Star Cruises) for control of NCL Holding (parent of Norwegian Cruise Lines) came to an end in early 2000 when the two rivals agreed to undertake a joint takeover of the cruise line. However Carnival later backed out of the deal when the two firms couldn't agree on terms of the joint venture. Also that year the company canceled an agreement to buy time-share company Fairfield Communities because of Carnival's lagging share price. Later in 2000 Carnival acquired the remaining 50% of Costa Crociere from Airtours. The next year Carnival sold its 25% stake in Airtours (now known as MyTravel Group).

In an effort to make the airfares sold in connection with cruise packages more competitive the cruise line announced its plan in 2001 to cut travel agent commissions on the air-travel segment of cruise bookings. Also that year the company countered competitor Royal Caribbean's agreement to merge with P&O Princess Cruises with its own offer of #2.15 billion. P&O shareholders snubbed the offer but later softened and said it would consider a revised offer leaving the door open for a bidding war between Carnival and Royal Caribbean. That same year the company pleaded guilty to charges of polluting the ocean and falsifying oil-contaminated discharge records. It agreed to pay $18 million in fines and environmental costs hire overseers to monitor its ships and hire an environmental standards officer.

In 2003 Carnival succeeded in wooing P&O away from Royal Caribbean and the two corporations merged operations via a dual-listed company structure. Consequently P&O changed its name to Carnival plc. The dual-listing structure gave Carnival access to capital markets in both the US and the UK.

To expand its portfolio of ships Carnival entered a partnership with leading Spanish travel firm Orizonia in 2007 to form Ibero Cruises. The newer cruise line features a handful of Spanish ships sailing from Spain and Brazil.

In response to high early bookings for Queen Victoria (added to its fleet in 2007) Carnival inked a deal with Italy's state-owned shipbuilder Fincantieri in 2007 for a 2092-passenger liner (Queen Elizabeth) that launched in late 2010. To make room for its new order of cruise ships in November 2008 Carnival sold Cunard's 40-year-old Queen Elizabeth 2 to Dubai-based Istithmar for about $100 million.

EXECUTIVES

President and CEO Carnival Cruise Lines, Gerald R. (Gerry) Cahill, age 61, $750,000 total compensation
Vice Chairman and COO, Howard S. Frank, age 71, $780,000 total compensation
Chairman, Micky Arison, age 64, $880,000 total compensation
CEO Carnival Australia, Ann C. Sherry
President Seabourn; EVP Marketing Sales and Guest Programs Holland America Line Inc., Rick Meadows
President and CEO, Arnold W. Donald, age 58
COO, Alan B. Buckelew, age 65
CEO Carnival UK, David K. Dingle, age 56
Chairman Costa Crociere; Chairman and CEO Carnival Asia, Pier Luigi Foschi, age 66, $1,320,500 total compensation
SVP Shared Services, Richard D. Ames
Senior Vice President; General Counsel; Secretary, Arnaldo Perez, age 52
SVP and CFO, David Bernstein, age 56, $450,000 total compensation
President and CEO Holland America Line, Stein Kruse, age 55
President Seabourn and EVP Marketing Sales and Guest Programs Holland America, Richard D. (Rick) Meadows
Chief Executive Officer Costa Crociere S.p.A., Michael Thamm, age 47
President, Gianni Onorato
VP Public Relations Carnival Corporation and Carnival Cruise Lines, Tim Gallagher
Director Public Relations, Jennifer de la Cruz
VP Chief Accounting Officer and Controller, Larry Freedman, age 61
Senior Director Marketing, Bill Harber
Chief Executive Officer of AIDA Cruises, Michael Ungerer
senior Vice President of human resources, Bob Ihrie
senior Vice President General Counsel, Janet Saura
Senior Vice President General Counsel, Lee Reeves
senior Vice President Chief Accounting Officer, Matt Hollifield
Executive Vice President General Counsel Secretary, Robert B.?ri
Director, Randall J. Weisenburger, age 54
Director, Robert H. (Bob) Dickinson, age 70
Vice Chairman and COO, Howard S. Frank, age 71
Director, Laura A. Weil, age 56
Director, Stuart Subotnick, age 71
Director, Richard J. Glasier, age 67
Director, Peter G. Ratcliffe, age 65
President and CEO, Arnold W. Donald, age 58
Director, Sir John Parker, age 70
Chairman Costa Crociere; Chairman and CEO Carnival Asia, Pier Luigi Foschi, age 66
Director, Modesto A. Maidique, age 73
Director, Uzi Zucker, age 76
Director, Sir Jonathon Band, age 63
Non-Executive Director, Debra Kelly-Ennis
Auditors: PricewaterhouseCoopersLLP

LOCATIONS

HQ: Carnival Corp.
3655 N.W. 87th Avenue, Miami, FL 33178-2428
Phone: 305 599-2600
Web: www.carnivalcorporation.com

2011 Sales

North America Cruise Brands	8,921	56
Cruise support	90	1
Adjustments	(114)	-

2011 Sales

North America	7,835	50
Australia & Asia	1,528	9
Total	**15,793**	**100**

PRODUCTS/OPERATIONS

2011 Sales

Cruise		
Onboard & other	3,357	21
Total	**15,793**	**100**

Selected Cruise Ships

AIDA
- AIDAaura (launched in 2003; 1266 passengers)
- AIDAbella (2008; 2050)
- AIDAcara (1996; 1180)
- AIDAdiva (2007; 2050)
- AIDAvita (2002; 1266)

Carnival Cruise Lines
- Carnival Conquest (2002; 2966)
- Carnival Destiny (1996; 2634)
- Carnival Freedom (2007; 2966)
- Carnival Glory (2003; 2966)
- Carnival Legend (2002; 2118)
- Carnival Liberty (2005; 2966)
- Carnival Miracle (2004; 2118)
- Carnival Pride (2001; 2118)
- Carnival Spirit (2001; 2118)
- Carnival Splendor (2008; 2998)
- Carnival Triumph (1999; 2750)
- Carnival Valor (2004; 2966)
- Carnival Victory (2000; 2750)
- Ecstasy (1991; 2050)
- Elation (1998; 2050)
- Fantasy (1990; 2054)
- Fascination (1994; 2050)
- Holiday (1985; 1450)
- Imagination (1995; 2050)
- Inspiration (1996; 2050)
- Paradise (1998; 2048)
- Sensation (1993; 2050)

Costa Cruises
- Costa Allegra (1992; 784)
- Costa Atlantica (2000; 2114)
- Costa Classica (1991; 1302)
- Costa Concordia (2006; 2978; capsized off coast of Italy in January 2012)
- Costa Europa (1986; 1488)
- Costa Fortuna (2003; 2702)
- Costa Magica (2004; 2702)
- Costa Marina (1990; 762)
- Costa Mediterranea (2003; 2114)
- Costa Romantica (1993; 1344)
- Costa Serena (2007; 2978)
- Costa Victoria (1996; 1928)

Cunard Line
- Queen Mary 2 (2003; 2592)
- Queen Victoria (2007; 1980)
- Queen Elizabeth (2010; 2092)

Holland America Line
- Amsterdam (2000; 1380)
- Eurodam (2008; 2104)
- Maasdam (1993; 1258)
- Noordam (2006; 1918)
- Oosterdam (2003; 1848)
- Prinsendam (1988; 792)
- Rotterdam (1997; 1316)
- Ryndam (1994; 1260)
- Statendam (1993; 1258)
- Veendam (1996; 1258)
- Volendam (1999; 1432)
- Westerdam (2004; 1916)
- Zaandam (2000; 1432)
- Zuiderdam (2002; 1848)

Ibero Cruises
- Grand Celebration (1987; 1494)
- Grand Mistral (1999; 1244)
- Grand Voyager (2000; 834)

Ocean Village
- Ocean Village (1989; 1578)
- Ocean Village Two (1990; 1708)

P&O Cruises
- Arcadia (2005; 2016)
- Artemis (1984; 1200)
- Aurora (2000; 1870)
- Oceana (2000; 2016)
- Oriana (1995; 1818)
- Ventura (2008; 3078)

P&O Cruises Australia
- Pacific Dawn (1991; 1596)
- Pacific Sun (1986; 1480)

Princess Cruise Lines
- Caribbean Princess (2004; 3100)
- Coral Princess (2002; 1974)
- Crown Princess (2006; 3080)
- Dawn Princess (1997; 1998)
- Diamond Princess (2004; 2678)
- Emerald Princess (2007; 3080)
- Golden Princess (2001; 2598)
- Grand Princess (1998; 2592)
- Island Princess (2003; 1974)
- Pacific Princess (1999; 676)
- Royal Princess (2001; 710)
- Ruby Princess (2008; 3080)
- Sapphire Princess (2004; 2678)
- Sea Princess (1998; 2016)
- Star Princess (2002; 2598)
- Sun Princess (1995; 2022)
- Tahitian Princess (2000; 676)

Seabourn
- Seabourn Legend (1992; 208)
- Seabourn Pride (1988; 208)
- Seabourn Spirit (1989; 208)

COMPETITORS

Carlson Companies
Club Med
Disney
Fred. Olsen Energy
Genting Hong Kong
NCL
NYK Line
Royal Caribbean Cruises
Saga Group
TUI

HISTORICAL FINANCIALS

Company Type: Public

Income Statement FYE: November 30

	REVENUE ($ mil.)	NET INCOME ($ mil.)	NET PROFIT MARGIN	EMPLOYEES
11/13	15,456	1,078	7.0%	92,700
11/12	15,382	1,298	8.4%	89,700
11/11	15,793	1,912	12.1%	91,300
11/10	14,469	1,978	13.7%	89,200
11/09	13,157	1,790	13.6%	14,800
Annual Growth	4.1%	(11.9%)	—	58.2%

2013 Year-End Financials

Debt ratio: 23.8%
Return on equity: 4.4%
Cash ($ mil.): 462
Current ratio: 0.29
Long-term debt ($ mil.): 8,092
No. of shares (mil.): 776
Dividends
Yield: 0.0%
Payout: 107.9%
Market value ($ mil.): 28,021

	STOCK PRICE ($) FY Close	P/E High/Low		PER SHARE ($) Earnings	Dividends	Book Value
11/13	36.11	28	23	1.39	1.50	31.64
11/12	38.66	23	18	1.67	1.00	30.84
11/11	33.20	20	12	2.42	1.00	30.67
11/10	41.31	18	12	2.47	0.40	29.15
11/09	32.03	15	7	2.24	1.20	28.00
Annual Growth	3.0%	—	—	(11.2%)	5.7%	3.1%

Carrefour S.A.

At the junction of groceries merchandise and services you'll find Carrefour (which means "crossroads"). The world's second-largest retailer (behind Wal-Mart) Carrefour operates more than 9700 stores under various banners including hypermarkets (Carrefour) supermarkets (Carrefour Market formerly Champion) convenience stores (City Express Proxi) and cash-and-carry outlets (Promocash) in more than 30 countries in Europe Latin America and Asia. France with more than 4600 Carrefour stores accounts for 43% of the retailer's sales. Carrefour is struggling to reverse a decade-long sales slump at home while expanding in fast-growing emerging markets in Asia and Latin America.

Carrefour which pioneered the hypermarket format operates about 1450 of the huge general merchandise and grocery stores on three continents accounting for the majority of its sales. It also operates nearly 3000 supermarkets in 19 countries under the Carrefour market and other banners. The French retail giant also operates more than 5000 convenience stores 90% of which are operating under franchising agreements. Its cash & carry stores mostly in France combine wholesaling and hypermarkets offering larger quantities to cater to professionals. Carrefour also sells food and nonfood items online in France Brazil Spain and other countries. Carrefour sold its operations in Thailand in 2011 and spun off its Dia hard discount chain which is primarily located in Spain and listed it on the Madrid stock exchange in mid-2011.

France is Carrefour's largest market accounting for 43% of sales in 2011. Eight other countries in Europe including Belgium Greece Italy and Spain contribute 29% of sales. About 19% of the group's sales are rung up in Latin America (Argentina Brazil and Colombia) while Asia (including China) accounts for 9%. Emerging markets are growth driver for Carrefour.

Carrefour's sales increased by about 1% in 2011 compared with 2010 driven by growth in emerging markets in Asia and Latin America. Indeed sales in France fell more than 1% mainly due to weaker-than-expected performance of its hypermarkets. Challenging economic conditions in all of its other markets in Europe espeically Southern Europe (Greece Spain) resulted in a sales drop of more than 4% vs. the prior year. Latin America was a bright spot with sales up 10% while Asia posted a 5% gain driven by expansion in the region. Operating income across the group fell 19% in 2011 vs. the prior year because of the economic crisis in Greece poor hypermarket performance in France higher commodity prices and increased competition.

Carrefour is struggling to emerge from prolonged sales slump particularly in France. Increasingly shoppers are shunning its huge stores in favor of specialty shops and discount chains. To date attempts to right the business have failed and resulted in significant turnover in the executive suite. In May 2012 Georges Plassat took over as CEO. He is charged with leading an aggressive turnaround effort intended to reverse years of underperformance. To cut is exposure to ailing euro zone countries including Greece and Spain Carrefour in mid-2012 sold its stake in its joint venture Carrefour Marinopoulos –operator of Greece's leading supermarket chain –at a loss to its partner. It also spun off its Dia discount chain. The spinoff enables Carrefour to concentrate on restoring its weaker domestic operations. Carrefour also does not plan to use the proceeds from Dia's spinoff to cut its debt load; the company opted to pay out two special dividends to shareholders. The move to bolster stockholder returns came after urging by controlling investors Groupe Arnault (the investment company owned by Bernard Arnault head of LVMH Moet Hennessy Louis Vuitton) and Colony Capital. Other efforts to revive its retail business include the sale of $1.2 billion worth of assets –including its stores in Japan and Mexico –to lower prices and attract new shoppers.

The Halley family has ceded control of Carrefour to Blue Capital an investment vehicle jointly owned by Groupe Arnault and US private equity fund Colony Capital which is now Carrefour's largest shareholder.

HISTORY

Although its predecessor was actually a supermarket opened by Marcel Fournier and Louis Defforey in a Fournier's department store basement in Annecy France the first Carrefour supermarket was founded in 1963 at the intersection of five roads (Carrefour means "crossroads"). That year Carrefour opened a vast store dubbed a "hypermarket" by the media in Sainte-Genevieve-des-Bois outside Paris.

The company opened additional outlets in France and moved into other countries including Belgium (1969) Switzerland (1970 –the year it went public) Italy and the UK (1972) and Spain (1973). Carrefour stepped up international expansion during the mid-1970s after French legislation limited its growth within the country.

Carrefour exported its French-style hypermarkets to the US (Philadelphia) in 1988. Scant advertising limited selection and a union strike led Carrefour to close its US operations in 1993. Carrefour opened its first hypermarket in Taiwan in 1989. The next year it formed Carma a 50-50 joint venture with Groupama to sell insurance. Carrefour paid over $1 billion for two rival chains (the bankrupt Montlaur chain and Euromarche) in 1991.

Daniel Bernard replaced Michel Bon the hard-charging expansion architect in 1992 after a 50% drop in first-half profits. A year later Carrefour partnered with Mexican retailer Gigante to open a chain of hypermarkets in Mexico. (In 1998 Carrefour bought Gigante's share of the joint venture.) In 1996 the company bought a 41% stake in rival GMB (Cora hypermarket chain) and sold its 11% stake in US warehouse retailer Costco (it now owns 20% of Costco UK). The next year Carrefour allowed 16 hypermarkets owned by Guyenne et Gascogne Coop Atlantique and Chareton to operate under the Carrefour name. It expanded into Poland in 1997 and the Czech Republic in 1998.

Its biggest acquisition (at the time) came in 1998 when Carrefour acquired French supermarket operator Comptoirs Modernes (with about 800 stores under the Stoc Comod and Marche Plus flags). Carrefour also entered the Indonesian market that year.

In August 1999 Carrefour announced a deal even bigger than the one for Comptoirs Modernes –a $16.3 billion merger with fellow French grocer Promodes which operated more than 6000 hypermarkets supermarkets convenience stores and discount stores in Europe. Paul-Auguste Halley and Leonor Duval Lemonnier founded Promodes in Normandy France in 1961. Initially a wholesale food distributor Promodes opened its first supermarket in 1962. This was followed by a cash-and-carry wholesale outlet (1964) a hypermarket (1970) and convenience stores (Shopi and 8 a Huit during the 1970s). To gain regulatory approval for the acquisition Carrefour divested its stake in the Cora chain and sold nearly 40 other stores in France and Spain. The Promodes acquisition was completed in 2000.

The company joined with US retailer Sears and software maker Oracle among others to form Internet-based supply exchange GlobalNetXchange in early 2000. Also that year Carrefour bought Belgian retailer GB (about 500 stores).

In 2001 Carrefour sold its 74%-stake in Picard Surgeles (frozen food stores). Carrefour also opened its first Japanese grocery store near Tokyo that year.

The grocer sold its 10% stake in PetSmart Inc. in a public offering in July 2002. That December Carrefour acquired the remaining 20% of the shares of Centro Comerciales Carrefour its Spanish subsidiary it didn't already own in a public tender offer.

In February 2003 Carrefour acquired two hypermarkets in Italy from Hyparlo. In October it entered the Scandinavian market through a franchise partnership and supply agreement with Norwegian grocer NorgesGruppen. Soon after Carrefour Poland acquired two hypermarkets there from troubled Dutch retailer Royal Ahold. In late 2003 Carrefour's discount chain Ed acquired 44 Treff Marche shops in France from German retailer Edeka.

The company sold its seven-hypermarket Chilean division in January 2004 to Distribucion Y Servicio. In April Carrefour opened its first Champion supermarket in Beijing. In September it entered Norway with six Meny Champion discount supermarkets in Oslo in partnership with Norway's NorgesGruppen.

In February 2005 Luc Vandevelde the former chairman of troubled British retailer Marks and Spencer succeeded Daniel Bernard as non-executive chairman of Carrefour. Bernard had been with Carrefour for 13 years. No stranger to the company Vandevelde was chief executive of Promodes when it merged with Carrefour in 1999. Concurrently ex-CFO Jose-Luis Duran was named CEO. In March Carrefour sold its 29 hypermarkets in Mexico to Grupo Comercial Chedraui for an undisclosed sum. Also in March Carrefour exited the Japanese market with the sale of its eight hypermarkets there to Japanese retail giant AEON CO. On the plus side Carrefour completed the acquisition of Chris Cash & Carry of Cyprus through its Greek subsidiary Carrefour Marinopoulos. In November the French retailer acquired full ownership of three of its Chinese hypermarket joint ventures from its local partners: Kunming Department Store Co. a unit of China's Kunming Sinobright (Group) Co.; Hunan Yiyou Commercial Trade Co.; and Xinjiang Grandscape Investment Co. Also in 2005 Carrefour swapped 15 of its hypermarkets in Slovakia and the Czech Republic for five outlets in Taiwan operated by rival Tesco exiting both countries.

Carrefour increased its ownership stake in Groupe Hyparlo in late 2005 to 49% (up from 20% in 2004).

In 2006 the company pulled out of South Korea where it held a relatively weak market position. Carrefour sold its 32 stores there to local fashion retailer E.Land for about $1.9 billion. In July Carrefour acquired 98% of the share capital and 99% of the voting rights of Hyparlo which operates stores under the Carrefour banner in France and Romania. The retailer launched its own mobile phone service Carrefour Mobile at all 218 of its hypermarkets in France in late 2006. (Rival Auchan launched a similar product earlier in the year.)

Vandevelde resigned his position in 2007 as non-executive chairman after a falling out with the controlling Halley family. In July Carrefour acquired 250 Spanish discount supermarkets trading under the PLUS banner for about $275 million. About the same time it sold a dozen hypermarkets in Portugal to Sonae the country's largest retailer for about $920 million. In October Carrefour added to its holdings in Romania with the purchase of the Artima supermarket chain there from Polish-based private equity firm Enterprise Investors for about $87 million.

In March 2008 the Halley family split its 13% stake in Carrefour into two separate holding companies –Halley Participations SAS and Comet BV –thereby ceding control of the French retail giant to Blue Capital. In May Robert Halley stepped down as chairman of the company's supervisory board and was replaced by the deputy chairman Amaury de Seze. Blue Capital which recently was granted two seats on the company's supervisory board won a third with the appointment of Bernard Arnault.

Duran stepped down in January 2009 and Lars Olofsson took over as top executive. In June the company opened its first location in Russia: a hypermarket in Moscow. A second Russian store debuted in September.

In November 2010 Carrefour sold its 42 stores in Thailand to Casino Guichard-Perrachon's Big C affiliate there for some E868 million ($1.17 billion).

At Carrefour's annual meeting in June 2011 chairman Amaury de Seze stepped down and Olofsson added the chairman's title. Olofsson retired in May 2012 and was succeeded by Georges Plassat who joined Carrefour as COO in April 2012.

EXECUTIVES

Director Financial Communications and Investor Relations, Patrice Lambert-de Diesbach, age 56
Chairman and CEO, Georges Plassat
Group Marketing Director, Patrick Rouvillois
Group Chief Commercial Officer, Jose C. Gonzales-Hurtado, age 49
Executive Director China and Taiwan, Thierry Garnier, age 46
Vice Chairman, Sebastien Bazin, age 51
Executive Director Convenience Stores and Cash, Gerard Dorey
Chief Human Resources and Organization Officer, Jean-Christophe Deslarzes, age 49
Executive Director Group Merchandise, Eric Legros
Executive Director France, Noel Prioux, age 53
Executive Director Belgium, Gerard Lavinay
Executive Director Italy, Giuseppe Brambilla
Executive Director Group Supply Chain, Roberto Canevari, age 47
Executive Director Turkey, Guillaume de Colonges
Executive Director Poland, Jean Anthoine
Executive Director Brazil, Luiz Fazzio
Executive Director Hypermarkets France, Guillaume Vicaire
General Secretary, Pierre Alexandre Teulie
Group General Counsel, Franck Tassan
Executive Director Group Financial Control, Charles Desmartis
Executive Director Supermarkets France, Alexandre Falck
Executive Director Formats and Channels, Laurent Bendavid
Group Communications Director, Florence Baranes Cohen
Executive Director Group Strategy and Mergers & Acquisitions, Vincent Abello
Executive Director Europe (excluding France), Thomas M. Hubner, age 55
Chief Financial Officer, Pierre-Jean Sivignon
Executive Director Spain, Pascal Clouzard
Corporate Commercial Development Products & Offer Director, Dor Sela
Executive Director India, Jean-Noel Bironneau
Executive Director Argentina, Daniel Fernandez
Executive Director Taiwan, Patrick Ganaye
Executive Director Romania, Francois Melchior de Polignac
Executive Director International Partnerships, Stephane Thouin
Director, Rene Brillet, age 70
Director, Charles Edelstenne, age 76
Director, Thierry Breton, age 58
Director, Anne-Claire Taittinger, age 62
Director, Nicolas Bazire, age 56

Director, Jean-Laurent Bonnafe, age 51
Director, Amaury-Daniel de Seze, age 66
Vice Chairman, Sebastien Bazin, age 51
Director, Rene Abate, age 63
Director, Bernard Arnault
Director, Mathilde Lemoine
Auditors: KPMGAudit

LOCATIONS

HQ: Carrefour S.A.
33, avenue Emile Zola, TSA 55 555, Boulogne-Billancourt 92649
Phone:
Web: www.carrefour.com

2011 Sales

	% of total
Europe	
France	43
Other	29
Latin	19
Asia	9
Total	**100**

2011 Stores

	No.
Europe	
France	4,631
Other	3,964
Latin	583
Asia	380
Partner	213
Total	**9,771**

PRODUCTS/OPERATIONS

2011 Stores

	No.
Convenience	5,170
Supermarkets	2,995
Hypermarkets	1,452
Cash &	154
Total	**9,771**

2011 Sales

	% of total
Hypermarket	63
Supermarket	24
Other	13
Total	**100**

Selected Operations and Banners

Hypermarkets
  Carrefour
Supermarkets
  Champion
  GB
  Globi
  GS
  Marinopoulos
  Norte
  Super GB
  Super GS
  Unic
Hard discount stores
  Ed
  Minipreco
Other stores
  Cash-and-carry stores
  Docks Market
  Promocash
  Puntocash
Convenience stores
  8 a Huit
  Di per Di
  GB Express
  Marche Plus
  Proxi
  Shopi
Other Operations
Carfuel (petroleum products)
Comptoirs Modernes (supermarkets)
Costco UK (20% warehouse club)
Erteco (hard-discount stores)
Financiera Pryca (46% consumer credit Spain)
Fourcar B.V. (investments The Netherlands)
GlobalNetXchange (Internet-based supply exchange joint venture)
Ooshop (online shopping)
Prodirest (catering)
Providange (auto centers)
S2P (60% consumer credit)

COMPETITORS

AEON	Ito-Yokado
ALDI	La Rinascente
Auchan	Lianhua Supermarket
Brasileira de Distribuic?o	Lidl
Casino Guichard	Lotteshopping
China Nepstar	METRO AG
Dairy Farm International	Marui Group
Delhaize	Migros
E.Leclerc	REWE
Edeka Zentrale	Rallye
Eroski	Royal Ahold
Falabella	SHV Holdings
Galeries Lafayette	Super Indo
Globex Utilidades	Tengelmann
H&M	Tesco
ITM Entreprises	Wal-Mart
	WuMart
	Zara

HISTORICAL FINANCIALS

Company Type: Public

Income Statement FYE: December 31

	REVENUE ($ mil.)	NET INCOME ($ mil.)	NET PROFIT MARGIN	EMPLOYEES
12/12	103,414	1,625	1.6%	364,969
12/11	107,051	479	0.4%	371,003
12/10	122,478	579	0.5%	471,755
12/09	125,875	471	0.4%	475,976
12/08	123,346	1,778	1.4%	495,287
Annual Growth	(4.3%)	(2.2%)	—	(7.3%)

2012 Year-End Financials

Debt ratio: 32.3%	No. of shares (mil.): 686
Return on equity: 17.4%	Dividends
Cash ($ mil.): 8,663	Yield: 17.4%
Current ratio: 0.90	Payout: 8.9%
Long-term debt ($ mil.): 11,840	Market value ($ mil.): 3,533

	STOCK PRICE ($) FY Close	P/E High/Low		PER SHARE ($) Earnings	Dividends	Book Value
12/12	5.15	5	3	2.39	0.90	14.38
12/11	4.48	30	12	0.72	1.93	12.71
Annual Growth	15.0%	—	—	34.7%	(17.3%)	3.2%

Casino Guichard Perrachon S.A.

You won't hit the jackpot at Casino Guichard-Perrachon but odds are you'll go home with the groceries. One of the world's leading food retailers Casino Group owns and operates more than 11700 stores including hypermarkets (mostly Geant) supermarkets (Casino and Monoprix to name a few) restaurants (Casino Cafeteria) and discount stores (Leader Price). It is the third-largest food retailer (behind Carrefour and Auchan) and the #1 convenience store operator in France (primarily Petit Casino but other banners include Franprix Vival and Spar). Most of its stores are in France but it has outlets in 8 countries in Asia and South America including Brazil Colombia Thailand and Vietnam.

After a blip in 2009 when net sales dipped by just over 1% vs. the previous year Casino's sales (in local currency) rebounded by more than 8% in 2010. Profitability improved as well (up 7.5% for the year). With emerging economies in South America and Asia outperforming France Casino's international operation outperformed its domestic one with net sales overseas increasing by more than 22% while sales at home grew by less than 2%. Indeed international sales are a rapidly-growing part of Casino's revenue stream accounting for 48% of sales in 2011 up from 34% just two years ago. Key international markets for the French firm include Brazil where it operates more than 1500 stores Colombia Thailand and Vietnam.

More than 90% of Casino's growing international business comes from the fast-growing South American and Asian markets where the company is placing its bets. Brazil and Colombia together account for more than two-thirds of the company's overseas sales. Casino owns a 43% stake in Brazil's #1 retailer Companhia Brasileira de Distribuic?o (CBD) operator of the P?o de Acucar supermarket chain there. The French retailer also operates in the Indian Ocean region where it owns a majority stake in Vindemia an operator of supermarkets and hypermarkets in Asia and Africa. In Thailand Casino's Big C affiliate in late 2010 acquired about 40 stores (including 34 hypermarkets) from rival Carrefour for E868 million (about $1.17 billion). (Casino owns a 36% stake in that country's Big C Supercentre chain which is second in store count in Thailand to UK-owned Tesco Lotus.) The move doubled Big C's presence in Greater Bangkok.

At home price competition from discounters has hurt Casino and its rival Carrefour as French shoppers eschew their traditional hypermarkets and supermarkets for discount stores. In response Casino has strengthened its position in the convenience and discount store markets. Indeed convenience and discount stores are the retailer's most popular formats accounting for 60% of sales in France.

Casino shored up its balance sheet through a plan to dispose of some E1 billion ($1.3 billion) of assets by the end of 2010. The divestments included the sale of 42 superette Casino supermarket and Franprix-Leader price stores in 2008. Future divestments will include the sale of E334 million ($424 million) of soon-to-be-built real estate to Mercialys a property company spun off by Casino in 2006. Mercialys will pay for the properties in stock which will be redistributed to Casino shareholders as a dividend. Casino has been reducing its stake in Mercialys thereby raising E138 million ($182 million). It currently owns about 40% of the property company.

The company's 125-plus Geant hypermarkets (warehouse-style stores that sell groceries and other merchandise) and convenience stores together contribute more than 50% of revenues. Casino Cafeteria operates about 275 eating places in varying size and cuisines including Poncholito (Tex-Mex) and La Pastaria (Italian). Casino is also active in e-commerce (Cdiscount.com).

Casino is controlled by Euris which is controlled by Jean-Charles Naouri Casino's chairman and CEO.

HISTORY

Frenchman Geoffroy Guichard married Antonia Perrachon a grocer's daughter in 1889 in Saint-Etienne France. Three years later Geoffroy took over his father-in-law's general store (a converted "casino" or musical hall). In 1898 the company became Societe des Magasins du Casino. By 1900 when it became a joint stock company Casino had

50 stores; it opened its 100th store in 1904. That year the company introduced its first private-label product: canned sardines. In 1917 Guichard named his two sons Mario and Jean as managers.

By WWI there were about 215 branches more than 50 in Saint-Etienne. From 1919 to the early 1920s the company opened several factories to manufacture goods such as food soap and perfumes. In 1925 the elder Guichard retired leaving the day-to-day operations of Casino to his two sons. (Geoffroy died in 1940.) WWII took a heavy toll on the company: About 70 Casino stores were leveled and another 450 were damaged.

The company began opening cafeterias in 1967 and in 1976 it formed Casino USA to run them. Casino USA bought an interest in the California-based Thriftimart volume retailer in 1983 renaming the company after Thriftimart's Smart & Final warehouse stores.

Casino grew by acquiring companies across France including CEDIS (16 hypermarkets 116 supermarkets and 722 smaller stores in eastern France; 1985) and La Ruche Meridionale (18 hypermarkets and 112 supermarkets in southern France 1990). Casino bought nearly 300 hypermarkets and supermarkets from Rallye SA in 1992 giving Rallye about 30% of the company. The company opened its first hypermarket in Warsaw Poland in 1996.

Rival Promodes made a roughly $4.5 billion hostile takeover bid for Casino in 1997. Guichard family members voted against the Promodes offer instead backing a $3.9 billion friendly offer from Rallye (increasing their stake to nearly 50%). Casino also launched a massive counterattack – buying more than 600 Franprix and Leader Price supermarket stores from food manufacturer TLC Beatrice and acquiring a 21% stake in hypermarket chain Monoprix. Promodes withdrew its bid four months later.

Casino expanded internationally in the late 1990s acquiring stakes in food retailers in Argentina (Libertad) Uruguay (Disco) Colombia (Almacenes Exito SA) Brazil (Companhia Brasileira de Distribuic?o) and Thailand (Big C the country's largest retailer). It also opened its first hypermarket in Taichung Taiwan.

Expansion in France included a joint venture (called Opera) formed in 1999 with retailer Cora SA to buy food and nonfood goods for the Casino and Cora stores and the acquisition of 100 convenience stores (converted to the Petit Casino banner) in southwest France from retailer Guyenne et Gascogne.

Casino acquired 100 Proxi convenience stores in southeast France in 2000 from Montagne (most became Vival franchises) and more than 400 convenience stores (Eco Service and others) from Auchan. Casino also bought 51% of French online retailer Cdiscount.com (CDs videos CD-ROMs and DVDs) and upped its ownership in several of its international supermarket operations including gaining 100% ownership of Libertad. It also increased its ownership of Monoprix to 49%.

In July 2002 Casino bought a 38% stake in Laurus NV its financially troubled Dutch rival. Laurus operates nearly 2000 supermarkets in the Netherlands Spain and Belgium. (Soon after Casino sold Laurus's unprofitable stores in Spain and Belgium.) Also in 2002 the company sold its wine division Les Chais Beaucairois to wine and spirits company Marie Brizard for $22 million.

Chief executive Pierre Bouchut unexpectedly left Casino in March 2005. Jean-Charles Naouri the company's chairman and controlling shareholder replaced him. In May Casino took joint control of Brazil's leading food retailer Companhia Brasileira de Distribuic?o along with the family of Abilio Diniz. Previously Casino held a minority stake in the supermarket chain. Casino spun off some of its shopping center assets in an October IPO for part of its real estate assets in France including shopping mall properties adjacent to its hypermarket and supermarkets as well as the land under its cafeterias.

In 2006 the French supermarket operator spun off its property company Mercialys. (Following the IPO Casino holds about a 60% stake in Mercialys.) In January 2006 Casino increased its stake in Colombia's biggest retailer Exito to nearly 39%. The company in July sold its 19 hypermarkets in Poland to METRO AG its German rival for about $1.1 billion as part of its asset disposal program. In September Casino sold its 50% stake in its Taiwanese subsidiary Far Eastern Geant to its joint venture partner Far Eastern Department Stores.

Real estate sales continued in late 2007 with the announcement that Casino plans to sell nearly $930 million in assets including 255 grocery stores in France. The retailer says it plans to use the proceeds from the sale of these "mature" assets for high-potential projects in France and abroad. In May 2007 Casino sold its 55% stake of the California-based Smart & Final warehouse grocery chain to Apollo Management for $813 million thereby exiting the US market.

Casino acquired in July 2008 about 90% of the French textile maker International Textiles Associes (or INTEXA) from members of the Broyer family. Also Casino exercised its option in 2008 to increase its share in Dutch supermarket operator Super de Boer (formerly Laurus acquired in 2002) to a majority stake. However in December 2009 Casino sold its 57% stake in Super de Boer to Dutch rival Jumbo Groep Holding for E552.5 (nearly $800 million).

In November 2009 Casino acquired the remaining shares of Leader Price and Franprix chains from the Baud family bringing its ownership stake up to 100% in both chains.

EXECUTIVES

Chairman Chief Executive Officer, Jean-Charles Naouri, age 64
Finance Director, Antoine Giscard d'Estaing
Secretary, Jacques Dumas, age 61
Director, Frederic Saint-Geours
Director, Abilio dos Santos Diniz, age 77
Director, Marc Ladreit de Lacharriere, age 72
Director, Didier Carlier, age 62
Director, Philippe Houze, age 65
Director, Gerald de Roquemaurel, age 67
Director, David de Rothschild, age 71
Director, Jean-Marie Grisard, age 70
Director, Gilles Pinoncely, age 72
Director, Rose-Marie Van Lerberghe, age 73
Director, Henri M.E.V. Giscard d'Estaing, age 57
Director, Didier Leveque
Director, Michel Savart
Auditors: CabinetDidierKling&Associes

LOCATIONS

HQ: Casino Guichard Perrachon S.A.
1, Esplanade de France, B.P. 306, Saint-Etienne, Cedex 2 42008
Phone: (33) 4 77 45 31 31 **Fax:** (33) 4 77 45 38 38
Web: www.groupe-casino.fr

2011 Stores

	No.
France	9,450
International	
Brazil	1,571
Colombia	351
Thailand	221
Indian	53
Uruguay	52
Argentina	24
Vietnam	23
Total	**11,745**

PRODUCTS/OPERATIONS

2011 Stores (France)

	No.
Hypermarkets	127
Supermarkets	1,833
Discount	608
Superettes &	6,587
Other	295
Total	**9,450**

Selected Operations

Banque du Groupe Casino (60% financial services)
Big C (36% Thailand)
Casino Enterprise (non-food operations)
Cativen (66% Venezuela)
Cdiscount.com (67% e-commerce)
Companhia Brasileira de Distribuic?o (34% Brazil)
Devoto (97% supermarkets Uruguay)
Exito Colombia SA (55% supermarkets)
Franprix (supermarkets)
Geant (hypermarkets)
Imagica (photo and digital imaging processing)
Leader Price (supermarkets)
Libertad (hypermarkets Argentina)
Vindemia (supermarkets; Madagascar Mauritius Reunion)

COMPETITORS

ALDI
Auchan
Carrefour
E.Leclerc
Groupe Flo
Guyenne et Gascogne
IGA
ITM Entreprises
Kingfisher
METRO AG
Migros
Tesco
Wal-Mart Brazil

HISTORICAL FINANCIALS

Company Type: Public

Income Statement FYE: December 31

	REVENUE ($ mil.)	NET INCOME ($ mil.)	NET PROFIT MARGIN	EMPLOYEES
12/12	55,319	1,399	2.5%	316,711
12/11	44,444	734	1.7%	223,050
12/10	38,917	736	1.9%	170,248
12/09	38,545	851	2.2%	163,208
12/08	40,130	694	1.7%	173,367
Annual Growth	8.4%	19.1%	—	16.3%

2012 Year-End Financials

Debt ratio: 28.9%
Return on equity: 14.8%
Cash ($ mil.): 8,307
Current ratio: 1.05
Long-term debt ($ mil.): 12,381
No. of shares (mil.): 112
Dividends
Yield: 0.0%
Payout: 10.2%
Market value ($ mil.): 2,181

	STOCK PRICE ($) FY Close	P/E High	P/E Low	PER SHARE ($) Earnings	Dividends	Book Value
12/12	19.37	4	3	12.38	1.27	87.88
Annual Growth	—	—	—	—	—	—

Cathay Financial Holding Co

One of the largest financial services firms in Taiwan Cathay Financial Holding Co. owns companies involved in banking insurance brokerage and more. Its holdings include life accident and health insurer Cathay Life; property/casualty coverage provider Cathay Century; brokerage firm Cathay Securities; and Cathay United Bank which offers consumer banking services such as deposit accounts home mortgages credit cards and car loans as well as international banking and trust services. Cathay Financial Group also has units devoted to venture capital investing. All told the company has more than 700 locations and claims a customer base of more than ten million.

EXECUTIVES

Director; Chairman Cathay Insurance (China), Fa-Te Chang
Director; President Cathay Life Insurance, Ming-Ho Hsiung
Chairman Cathay Financial Holdings and Cathay Life Insurance, Hong-Tu Tsai
Vice Chairman; Chairman Cathay United Bank, Gregory K.H. Wang
President and Director, Chang-Ken Lee
CFO and First Deputy Spokesperson, Grace Chen
Director; Managing Director Cathay Life Insurance, Cheng-Ta Tsai
Director; Chairman Cathay Century Insurance, Cheng-Chiu Tsai
Director; Vice Chairman Cathay United Bank, Tsu-Pei Chen
Director; President Cathay Century Insurance, J. H. Hsu
EVP and Director; Chairman Cathay Securities Corporation, David P. Sun
EVP and Spokesperson, Alan Lee
Director; Chairman Cathay Insurance (China), Fa-Te Chang
Director; President Cathay Life Insurance, Ming-Ho Hsiung
Vice Chairman; Chairman Cathay United Bank, Gregory K.H. Wang
President and Director, Chang-Ken Lee
Director; Managing Director Cathay Life Insurance, Cheng-Ta Tsai
Director; Chairman Cathay Century Insurance, Cheng-Chiu Tsai
Director; Vice Chairman Cathay United Bank, Tsu-Pei Chen
Director; President Cathay Century Insurance, J. H. Hsu
EVP and Director; Chairman Cathay Securities Corporation, David P. Sun
Auditors: Ernst&Young

LOCATIONS

HQ: Cathay Financial Holding Co
No. 296, Sec. 4, Ren Ai Road, Da' an District, Taipei 106
Phone: (886) 2 2708 7698 **Fax:** (886) 2 2325 2488
Web: www.cathayholdings.com.tw

COMPETITORS

Bank of China
Chang Hwa Bank
Chinatrust Financial
E.Sun
First Financial Holding
Hua Nan Financial
Mega Financial
Shin Kong
SinoPac Holdings
Taishin
Taiwan Business Bank

HISTORICAL FINANCIALS

Company Type: Public

Income Statement FYE: December 31

	ASSETS ($ mil.)	NET INCOME ($ mil.)	INCOME AS % OF ASSETS	EMPLOYEES
12/12	187,283	587	0.3%	44,461
12/11	165,140	372	0.2%	43,904
12/10	161,137	148	0.1%	42,605
12/09	134,269	338	0.3%	43,340
12/08	114,306	60	0.1%	42,219
Annual Growth	13.1%	76.8%	—	1.3%

2012 Year-End Financials

Return on assets: 0.3%
Return on equity: 7.3%
Long-term debt ($ mil.): —
No. of shares (mil.): —
Sales ($ mil): 13,525
Dividends
Yield: —
Payout: —
Market value ($ mil.): —

	STOCK PRICE ($) FY Close	P/E High/Low	PER SHARE ($) Earnings	Dividends	Book Value
12/12	10.00	— —	0.05	0.00	0.79
12/11	10.60	— —	0.03	0.00	0.66
12/10	15.49	— —	0.01	0.00	0.70
12/09	19.92	— —	0.03	0.00	0.62
12/08	19.92	— —	0.00	0.00	0.41
Annual Growth	(15.8%)	— —	217.4%	—	18.1%

Celesio AG

Celesio likes being a middleman when it comes to pharmaceuticals. The company is one of Europe's largest drug wholesalers holding market-leading positions in several of the countries it serves. Its largest wholesale markets are France Germany and the UK. In addition to more than 130 wholesale distribution branches serving 65000 pharmacies Celesio owns retail chains consisting of 2200 pharmacies in Europe including Norway Italy and the UK. The company also offers marketing and logistics solutions to pharmaceutical makers through its manufacturer solutions division which includes the Pharmexx and Movianto units. Celesio which was founded in 1835 agreed to be acquired by McKesson in 2013.

Change in Company Type

McKesson struck an $8.3 billion deal to purchase Celesio in late 2013 to expand its operations into Europe. McKesson is purchasing a 50.01% stake in Celesio from German conglomerate Franz Haniel & Cie.; it is acquiring remaining shares in Celesio through a public share tender offer. Through an expanded global presence McKesson aims to increase globalization in a rapidly changing health care market; the combined entity is expected to benefit from increased purchasing power technology resources supply chain efficiencies and global sourcing capabilities. Following the purchase Celesio will continue to operate under the Celesio brand.

Operations

Celesio's wholesale pharmacy solutions segment operates in more than a dozen countries and accounts for more than half of annual revenues. Margins for the wholesale business however are continuously challenged by government price controls in many of the countries where Celesio operates especially in the core UK market. New legislation toughened things up in the German market in 2010 and competitive conditions have added challenges in the French market. As a result the company is working to reduce its operations in regulated markets where it largely depends on government reimbursement models.

As a result of distribution challenges the company has been aggressively expanding its patient and consumer solutions division which operates retail and mail-order pharmacies under a number of brands in about 10 countries including Lloydspharmacy in the UK and Apotheke DocMorris in Germany. The company has expanded the DocMorris mail-order pharmacy operations into the UK and Norway. It is also working to expand its DocMorris retail pharmacy franchise program into other European countries. It has some 4100 participants in its brand partnership programs.

Strategy

To expand its retail pharmacy franchise operations Celesio has introduced the DocMorris brand in countries including Ireland where it already operated its own chain of Unicarepharmacy locations. In 2010 Celesio began opening its own chain of DocMorris-branded pharmacies in Sweden following the implementation of a new law there that opened the door for private companies to establish pharmacies. In 2010 it started opening DocMorris pharmacies in Italy where it has additional pharmacy operations under the Admenta Italia brand.

As part of a program to maximize its portfolio assets in 2010 Celesio merged its Netherlands operations with those of rival distributor Phoenix Pharmahandel. Celesio has a 45% stake in the combined Dutch pharmacy unit Brocacef which has wholesale and retail pharmacy operations. Also in 2010 the company sold its minority stake in German wholesale firm Andreae-Noris Zahn (Anzag) to Anzag's majority shareholder Alliance Boots after deciding that the interest was no longer a strategic investment.

Celesio has also announced plans to diversify into new innovative fields of health care and manufacturer services citing the changing needs of markets undergoing reform measures and the increased competition and cost pressures faced by pharma manufacturers. It launched a patient services joint venture with Medco Health in 2010 to help manage prescription costs for patients with chronic conditions and it plans to move its mail-order operations under the Celesio Medco venture.

The company's growth program also outlines the streamlining of wholesale processes and the centralization of purchasing administration throughout the Celesio organization. All of the efforts are part of Celesio's plans to increase profitability and generate ?1 billion in EBITDA by 2015.

Mergers and Acquisitions

While Celesio already has subsidiaries and operations in more than 25 countries acquisitions have remained part of its growth strategy. To expand its activities in emerging growth markets outside of Europe Celesio acquired a majority stake in Panpharma Brazil's largest wholesale pharmaceuticals company in 2009. The deal includes the option for Celesio to increase its initial 54% holding at a later time. On the European front Celesio also expanded its Belgian operations by acquiring distribution firm Laboratoria Flandria and logistics firm Dirk Raes in 2009.

HISTORY

Merchant Franz Ludwig Gehe formed his Gehe & Co. chemist and dye wholesale business in Dresden in 1835. At a time when pharmaceuticals were a luxury Gehe supplied unprocessed raw materials to pharmacists to help make drugs more affordable. The company sold its products through traveling sales agents working around the world. Thirty years later the company opened its first factory.

In 1882 Gehe died and control of his firm passed to his nephew Rudolph Luboldt who had joined in 1859. Under the watch of Luboldt's successor son Walter Gehe & Co. published its first catalog of drugs in 1894. Almost 10 years later the firm became a joint-stock company. In 1910 it published a drug reference book for doctors and pharmacists.

Over the next 20 years the company opened offices in eastern Germany and Poland. It bought a Czech chemicals factory (1924) and set up subsidiaries in Germany Poland and Spain in the 1930s. After WWII it lost its Dresden headquarters and most of its branches (its eastern German operations eventually became Jenapharm a drug company owned by the East German government); Gehe & Co. rebuilt in West Germany moving its main office to Munich.

Gehe & Co. achieved record sales through most of the 1950s and 1960s. During this time it opened new offices and bought a few German rivals including Heitzer & Co. Growth continued in the 1970s; when family-owned conglomerate Franz Haniel & Cie. snapped up a majority holding in the firm in 1973 the firm acquired four of Haniel's existing wholesale units boosting its German market share. Gehe & Co. also began investing in technology as its industry automated.

Growth continued in the 1980s as it continued buying drug wholesalers. In 1981 the firm moved its headquarters again this time to Stuttgart and changed its name to GEHE AG. The company diversified when it bought mail-order office equipment firm Kaiser & Kraft Group in 1985; it supplemented this new division with further purchases. In 1989 GEHE returned to drug manufacturing when it bought a stake in generics maker Azuchemie.

The reunification of Germany also brought the company a reunification: In 1991 it bought Jenapharm bringing it back into the family. Two years later GEHE restructured becoming a holding company with divisions for its wholesale drug production and mail-order operations. Also in 1993 new German government regulations to control the soaring cost of public health care caused the firm's sales to plummet 20%. To escape price controls at home it focused on expanding in Europe in a big way. Among its purchases were leading wholesaler Office Commerciale Pharmaceutique (now OCP) and AAH which controlled 30%-40% of the wholesale market in Ireland and the UK. AAH brought with it a chain of retail pharmacies which GEHE grew by buying Lloyds Chemists in 1997.

As laws governing ownership of pharmacies in some European countries changed in the late 1990s the firm bought retail chains in Italy and the Czech Republic. In 1999 it opted to refocus on its pharmaceutical operations; GEHE spun off its Kaiser & Kraft mail-order business as TAKKT and sold its health care services (rehabilitation equipment). The next year it expanded into Austria when it bought wholesale market leader Herba Chemosan Apotheker. In 2001 GEHE extended its pharmacy operations into the Netherlands Norway Ireland and Belgium.

The company became Celesio AG after changing its name in 2003. The name change from GEHE to Celesio was made to distinguish the parent company from its similarly named subsidiaries. In 2005 Celesio advanced its pharmacy business by purchasing over 100 UK Cohens and Scholes pharmacies.

The company expanded into Denmark through its 2006 acquisitions of distribution companies K.V. Tjellesen and Max Jenne. It also enhanced its manufacturer solutions division which provides logistics and transportation services by acquiring Pharmexx a sales and marketing services provider.

In 2007 Celesio acquired Apotheke DocMorris a German retail and mail-order pharmacy company. DocMorris had built up partnerships with some 150 pharmacies in Germany.

In 2011 company CEO Fritz Oesterle stepped down from his executive post mid-year. Oesterle had led the company for 12 years and was a primary driver of Celesio's international growth efforts. Later in 2011 Markus Pinger a former member of the Beiersdorf AG management board was appointed to serve as Celesio's new CEO through August 2014.

EXECUTIVES

Deputy Chairman Supervisory Board, Ihno Goldenstein
Chairman of the Management Board and CEO, Markus Pinger, age 50
Chief Financial Officer, Christian Holzherr, age 50
Head Manufacturer Solutions and Head Global Strategic Marketing and Business Innovation Unit, Michael Lonsert
Head Corporate Communications, Rainer Berghausen
Supervisory Board Member, Hanspeter Spek, age 64
Supervisory Board Member, Klaus Trutzschler, age 63
Supervisory Board Member, Jorg Lauenroth-Mago
Supervisory Board Member, W. M. Henning Rehder
Deputy Chairman Supervisory Board, Ihno Goldenstein
Supervisory Board Member, Prof Julius Michael Curtius
Supervisory Board Member, Dirk-Uwe Kerrmann
Supervisory Board Member, Ulrich Neumeister
Group Managing Director Celesio Wholesale, Wolfgang Mahr, age 54
Supervisory Board Member, Hubertus Erlen
Supervisory Board Member, Klaus Borowicz
Supervisory Board Member, Susan Naumann
Auditors: Ernst&YoungAG

LOCATIONS

HQ: Celesio AG
Neckartalstrasse 155, Stuttgart D-70376
Phone: (49) 711 50 01 00 **Fax:** (49) 711 50 01 12 60
Web: www.celesio.com

2010 Sales

	% of total
France	29
UK	21
Germany	19
Other	31
Total	**100**

PRODUCTS/OPERATIONS

2010 Sales

	$ mil.	% of total
Pharmacy solutions		82
Manufacturing solutions		3

Selected Subsidiaries

Pharmacy Solutions (wholesale distribution division)
- AAH Pharmaceuticals Ltd. (UK)
- AFM S.p.A. (Italy)
- Cahill May Roberts Group Ltd (Ireland)
- GEHE Pharma Handel GmbH (Germany)
- GEHE Pharma Praha spol. S r.o. (Czech Republic)
- Herba Chemosan Apotheker AG (Austria)
- Kemofarmacija d.d. (Slovenia Romania and Croatia)
- Laboratoria Flandria NV (Belgian)
- Norsk Medisinaldepot AS (Norway)
- OCP Repartition (France)
- OCP Portugal Produtos Farmaceuticos SA (Portugal)
- Panpharma Participacoes S.A. (54% Brazil)
- Pharma Belgium SA
- Rudolf Spiegel GmbH (Germany)
- Tjellesen Max Jenne A/S (Denmark)

Patient and Consumer Solutions (retail pharmacies division)
- Admenta Italia S.p.A.
- Apotheke DocMorris (retail franchise)
- Brocacef (45% Netherlands)
- DocMorris Kooperationen GmbH (mail order)
- Lekarny Lloyds s.r.o. (Czech Republic)
- Lloyds Pharmacy Limited (UK)
- Lloydspharma SA (Belgium)
- Unicare Pharmacy Limited (Ireland)
- Vitusapotek AS (Norway)

Manufacturer Solutions (marketing logistics and services division)
- Celesio Medco
- Evolution Homecare
- Movianto
- pharmexx

COMPETITORS

Alliance Boots
Cardinal Health
Co-operative Group
Mawdsleys
Mediq
PHOENIX Pharma
Profarma Distribuidora
Sigma Pharmaceuticals
Superdrug
UDG Healthcare
Waymade

HISTORICAL FINANCIALS

Company Type: Public

Income Statement

FYE: December 31

	REVENUE ($ mil.)	NET INCOME ($ mil.)	NET PROFIT MARGIN	EMPLOYEES
12/12	29,354	(205)	—	28,877
12/11	29,783	2	0.0%	36,670
12/10	31,154	346	1.1%	36,411
12/09	30,969	(1)	—	46,095
12/08	30,520	(29)	—	37,746
Annual Growth	(1.0%)	—	—	(6.5%)

2012 Year-End Financials

Debt ratio: 34.6%
Return on equity: (-6.6%)
Cash ($ mil.): 690
Current ratio: 1.42
Long-term debt ($ mil.): 2,525
No. of shares (mil.): 170
Dividends
Yield: 1.2%
Payout: —
Market value ($ mil.): 570

	STOCK PRICE ($) FY Close	P/E High/Low	PER SHARE ($) Earnings	Dividends	Book Value
12/12	3.35	— —	(1.21)	0.04	16.75
12/11	3.11	977414	0.01	0.17	19.36
12/10	4.89	8 4	1.98	0.08	20.37
12/09	5.00	— —	(0.00)	0.09	19.77
12/08	5.45	— —	(0.17)	0.00	18.58
Annual Growth	(11.5%)	— —	—	—	(2.6%)

Cemex S.A.B. de C.V.

You certainly couldn't accuse CEMEX of being stuck in the mud. The building materials company is one of the top cement makers in the world (along with Lafarge and Holcim). The majority of its sales come from cement; the company has about 60 cement plants and an annual production capacity of about 95 million tons. It also produces markets and distributes ready-mix concrete aggregates and clinker (an intermediate product used to make cement). CEMEX operates in North America (through CEMEX Inc.) as well as in Africa Asia Europe the Middle East and South America. The

US Mexico and Europe account for more than 70% of revenues.

Fifty-five of CEMEX's 57 cement plants use the dry process of manufacturing which is more fuel efficient. The two plants that use the wet process are in Nicaragua and the United Kingdom. Most of the company's cement is distributed as a bagged branded product from a point near the site of its use. CEMEX also annually sells about 55 million cubic meters of ready-mix concrete a mixture of cement fine and coarse aggregates water and ingredients that affect such qualities as strength and setting time. Accordingly the operations for this product are often focused on the fulfillment of customers' unique needs.

CEMEX also annually sells about 160 million tons of aggregates including crushed stone sand and gravel obtained from quarries as well as rivers lakes and seabeds for use in the building of highways walkways and railways and as an ingredient in concrete asphalt and mortar. The company additionally sells more than 8 million tons of cement and clinker each year. CEMEX has paved more than 10000 kilometers of highways and roads in Mexico and has aided some of the nation's infrastructure projects such as the La Yesca Dam in Jalisco and Nayarit with custom services.

Supported by strong demand in the infrastructure and residential sectors CEMEX's revenue rose about 7% in 2011 compared with 2010. Looking at the company's major geographic segments we see Mexico's sales rising 1% in 2011 versus 2010 as a result in part of demand from the self-construction market. Likewise sales increased 1% during the same period in the US the company's second largest geographic segment owing mainly to an uptick in ready-mix concrete sales following the acquisition of complete ownership of a joint venture with Ready Mix USA. In the UK another important geographic segment sales increased about 7% over the same period on the back primarily of the infrastructure sector. Amid a rise in home and factory construction Germany's sales headed up about 12% in 2011 versus 2010. Sales in France also jumped 12% over the same period to meet demand for the construction of residences offices and warehouses.

The Rest of Northern Europe geographic segment which includes Austria the Czech Republic Finland Hungary Ireland Latvia Poland and Scandinavia enjoyed a 7% uptick in 2011 compared with 2010 to meet demand from the infrastructure sector among other factors. Columbia which comprises most of CEMEX's South American & the Caribbean segment enjoyed an uptick of 21% in 2011 versus 2010 to meet demand for the construction of middle and high income homes warehouses commercial buildings and roads.

CEMEX believes its focus on the sort of vertical integration that creates a more direct relationship with the end user has helped it grow from a concentration on its home country of Mexico to a major international player in the global construction sector. While continuing to integrate its business across the cement value chain and cut costs CEMEX also plans to focus on countries such as Colombia Mexico the Philippines Poland and the US that need to fill gaps in housing and infrastructure development.

Intending to serve all levels of the construction sector from homeowners self-constructing a residence to multinational firms the company is transitioning from a supplier of products to a turnkey service provider. Product development also takes a cue from this focus. For instance the company provides concrete for sidewalks and roadways that is porous enough to allow rainwater to seep back into the ground as well as concrete for coastal and marine areas that in turn resists water.

While siting terminals in strategic locations worldwide for better service to customers CEMEX has also created central management information systems for such functions as administration accounting purchasing customer service budgeting and control. Cost cutting efforts also include reduction of fossil fuels a major expense in the construction materials sector.

HISTORY

The foundation of CEMEX began with —what else? —cement. Lorenzo Zambrano founded Cementos Hidalgo in northern Mexico in 1906. In 1931 the company merged with Cementos Portland Monterrey and was renamed Cementos Mexicanos from which its current name CEMEX is derived.

During the 1960s the company expanded into the cities of Ciudad Valles and Torreon by building plants; it moved into Merida in 1966 by acquiring Cementos Maya. The founder's grandson also named Lorenzo Zambrano joined the company in 1968. CEMEX became a true national force during the 1970s by acquiring more plants including one in central Mexico.

CEMEX went public in 1976. With its acquisition of Cementos Guadalajara and its three plants it became Mexico's top cement maker. After serving in several engineering positions and as VP of operations Zambrano was named CEO in 1985. He had worked at CEMEX as a teenager in the early 1960s and claims he knew he wanted to work for CEMEX since he was 14.

Zambrano set about making CEMEX an international player. Already an exporter the company boosted its exporting business by purchasing Cementos Anahuac in 1987. Two years later CEMEX sealed its position as the top Mexican cement maker by acquiring that country's #2 cement company Cementos Tolteca. CEMEX then bought its first non-Mexican operations in 1992 adding Valenciana de Cementos and Sanson Spain's largest cement makers. Two years later CEMEX added Vencemos (Venezuela's top cement business) Cemento Bayano (Panama) and a plant in Texas.

The globalization of CEMEX helped the company weather several peso devaluations during the 1990s including one in late 1994. The company continued to expand abroad adding Cementos Nacionales (Dominican Republic) in 1995 and Cementos Diamante and Samper (both in Colombia) in 1996. Those deals made the company the world's third-largest cement producer.

After claiming more of the European and Latin American cement markets CEMEX turned its attention to the Pacific Rim where it made investments in Rizal Cement Company in the Philippines in 1997 and PT Semen Gresik in Indonesia in 1998 (it sold its 25% stake in 2006).

A booming US economy fueled residential and commercial construction in fiscal 1999 lifting CEMEX to record sales. In 2000 CEMEX gained significant size when it acquired US cement maker Southdown for $2.8 billion. The company sold its Kentucky and Missouri operations to Rinker Materials a unit of Australia's CSR Ltd in 2001.

In mid-2002 CEMEX bought Puerto Rican Cement Company (PRCC) for around $180 million. The next year CEMEX acquired Mineral Resource Technologies and Dixon-Marquette Cement in the US. In 2005 CEMEX added extensive European operations with the acquisition of UK-based ready-mix cement giant RMC Group. The deal worth about $5.8 billion instantly made CEMEX a leader in Europe.

The company also acquired Rinker Australia's biggest building material manufacturer for more than $14 billion in 2007. In 2008 CEMEX sold most of its stake in telecom company Axtel and later its Canary Islands operations garnering a combined $474 million for debt payments. In 2009 CEMEX (still struggling under the weight of debt and facing declining sales) sold its Australian operations to Holcim for nearly $2 billion. In 2011 CEMEX bought Ready Mix USA's interest in the companies' two joint ventures which have operations in the Southeast US.

EXECUTIVES

Chairman and CEO, Lorenzo H. Zambrano, age 69
General Counsel and Secretary, Ramiro G. Villarreal
EVP Finance and Administration and CFO, Fernando A. Gonzalez, age 56
President Northern Europe and Global Energy and Sustainability, Ignacio Madridejos
President USA, Karl Watson Jr., age 47
Vice Chairman of the Board of CEMEX Mexico; CEOs Consultant for Institutional Relations; Chairman of the Advisory Board of CEMEX Latinoamerican Region, Francisco Garza, age 56
President Mexico and Global Technology, Juan Romero, age 53
Media Relations, Jorge Perez
Investor Relations, Eduardo Rendon
Analyst Relations, Luis Garza
President Asia and Global Trading, Joaquin Estrada, age 48
Chief Comptroller, Rafael Garza
President South America Caribbean and Global Procurement, Jaime G. Elizondo, age 48
President Mediterranean, Jaime Muguiro
EVP Strategic Planning and New Business Development, Juan P. San Agustin
EVP Organization and Human Resources, Luis Hernandez
Executive Vice President of Finance and Administration; Chief Financial Officer, Fernando Olivieri
President of CEMEX Northern Europe Region; Director of Energy and Sustainability, Ignacio Fernandez
President of CEMEX Mediterranean Region, Jaime Dominguez
President of CEMEX South America and Caribbean Region; Director of Supply, Jaime Chapa
President of CEMEX Asia Region; Director of International Marketing, Joaquin Suarez
Executive Vice President of Strategic Planning and New Business Development, Juan Rubio
Executive Vice President of Organization and Human Resources, Luis Hern+index
President of CEMEX Mexico Region; Chief Technology Officer, Juan Torres
Controller, Rafael Lozano
Senior Vice President of Legal Affairs; Non-Member Secretary of the Board, Ramiro Morales
Executive Vice President of Human Resources and Organization, Luis Echavez
Executive Vice President of Organization and Human Resources, Luis Hernandez
Executive Vice President of Finance and Administration, Fernando A. Gonzalez
Director, Bernardo Quintana Isaac, age 70
Director, Jose A. Fernandez Carbajal, age 58
Director, Dionisio Garza Medina
Director, Alfonso C. Romo Garza, age 61
Director, Lorenzo Milmo Zambrano, age 75
Director, Roberto Zambrano Villarreal
Director, Jose M. Rincon Gallardo Puron, age 69
Director, Tomas Milmo Santos
Director, Armando J. Garcia Segovia, age 58
Director, Rafael Rangel Sostmann
Independent Director, Dionisio Medina
Independent Director, Jose Puron
Independent Director, Rafael Sostmann
Auditors: KPMGCardenasDosalS.C.

LOCATIONS

HQ: Cemex S.A.B. de C.V.
Avenida Ricardo Margain Zozaya 325, San Pedro Garza Garcia, Nuevo Leon 66265
Phone: (52) 81 8888 8888 **Fax:** (52) 81 8888 4417
Web: www.cemex.com

2011 Sales

	% of total
Mexico	21
US	16
Northern Europe	
Germany	8
United	8
France	7
Rest of Northern	7
South America & the	12
Mediterranean	
Egypt	3
Spain	4
Rest of	4
Asia	3
Rest of the	7
Total	**100**

PRODUCTS/OPERATIONS

2011 Sales

	% of total
Cement	47
Ready	37
Aggregates	15
Other	1
Total	**100**

Selected Subsidiaries

CEMEX Mexico S. A. de C.V.
CEMEX Espa?a S.A. (Spain)
Assiut Cement Company (Egypt)
Cement Bayano S.A. (Panama)
CEMEX Asia Holdings Ltd. (Singapore)APO Cement Corporation (Philippines)CEMEX (Thailand) Co. Ltd.Solid Cement Corporation (Philippines)
CEMEX Colombia S.A.CEMEX (Costa Rica) S.A.
CEMEX de Puerto Rico Inc
CEMEX Dominicana S.A. (Dominican Republic)
CEMEX France Gestion (S.A.S.)
CEMEX Corp. (US)
CEMEX Venezuela S.A.C.A.
CEMEX U.K.
CEMEX Austria AG
CEMEX Czech Republic s.r.o.
CEMEX Deutschland AG. (Germany)
CEMEX Holdings (Israel) Limited
CEMEX Investments Limited (UK)
CEMEX Polska sp. Z.o.o. (Poland)
CEMEX SIA (Latvia)
Readymix plc (Ireland)

COMPETITORS

Aggregate Industries
Ash Grove Cement
Buzzi Unicem USA
CRH
Cementos Portland Valderrivas
Eagle Materials
Essroc
HeidelbergCement
Holcim
Italcementi
Italmobiliare
Lafarge
Martin Marietta Materials
Siam Cement
Sumitomo Osaka Cement
TXI
Taiheiyo Cement
Tarmac
Trinity Industries
U.S. Concrete
Ube-Mitsubishi Cement
Vulcan Materials

HISTORICAL FINANCIALS

Company Type: Public

Income Statement

FYE: December 31

	REVENUE ($ mil.)	NET INCOME ($ mil.)	NET PROFIT MARGIN	EMPLOYEES
12/12	15,163	(914)	—	44,000
12/11	13,593	(1,774)	—	0
12/10	14,329	(1,087)	—	46,500
12/09	15,109	107	0.7%	47,000
12/08	17,552	164	0.9%	57,000
Annual Growth	(3.6%)	—	—	(6.3%)

2012 Year-End Financials

Debt ratio: 2.8%
Return on equity: (-8.0%)
Cash ($ mil.): 960
Current ratio: 1.18
Long-term debt ($ mil.): 13,663
No. of shares (mil.): —
Dividends
Yield: —
Payout: —
Market value ($ mil.): —

	STOCK PRICE ($) FY Close	P/E High/Low	PER SHARE ($) Earnings	Dividends	Book Value
12/12	9.87	— —	(0.03)	0.00	0.33
12/11	5.39	— —	(0.05)	0.00	0.35
12/10	10.71	— —	(0.03)	0.00	(0.00)
12/09	11.82	— —	0.00	0.00	0.57
12/08	9.14	— —	0.01	0.00	0.55
Annual Growth	1.9%	— —	—	—	(11.9%)

Central Bank of Ireland (Ireland)

LOCATIONS

HQ: Central Bank of Ireland (Ireland)
P.O. Box No. 559, Dame Street, Dublin 2
Phone: (353) 1 224 6278 **Fax:** (353) 1 671 6561
Web: www.centralbank.ie

HISTORICAL FINANCIALS

Company Type: Public

Income Statement

FYE: December 31

	ASSETS ($ mil.)	NET INCOME ($ mil.)	INCOME AS % OF ASSETS	EMPLOYEES
12/12	181,213	1,894	1.0%	1,394
12/11	227,966	1,552	0.7%	1,372
12/10	273,682	1,125	0.4%	1,226
12/09	179,922	1,345	0.7%	1,044
12/08	162,362	509	0.3%	1,023
Annual Growth	2.8%	38.9%	—	8.0%

Centrica Plc

Centrica is centered on integrated energy operations in the UK and North America through four major brands –British Gas Centrica Energy Centrica Storage and Direct Energy. The UK's largest gas supplier British Gas serves about 12 million homes and 1 million businesses with electricity gas and energy-related services in the UK. Through its Direct Energy unit Centrica supplies gas and power to residential customers in Canada and the US. Centrica is also engaged in gas exploration and production and storage operations. Other activities include gas and electricity production wholesale energy marketing international retail energy marketing drain cleaning services (the Dyno Group) and appliance sales.

Through Centrica Energy Centrica held proved and probable reserves of about 440 million barrels of oil equivalent in 2011. Centrica Storage handles the company's gas storage operations. Its Rough storage facility under the North Sea accounts for 70% of the UK's natural gas storage.

A major aspect of the company's strategy includes growing its core British Gas business and upstream operations (including gas supply storage and renewables) while establishing a leadership position as an integrated North American energy business. Centrica also intends to increase its gas production by 50% –to around 75 million barrels of oil equivalent over the next three to five years – by extending its geographic reach. The company also looks to investing in power generation using offshore wind nuclear and biomass technologies to supply its customers' needs. It plans to double the profitability of its business by 2014 through targeted acquisitions both upstream and downstream.

Centrica began in 2012 a program to save #500 million ($788 million) in costs over the next two years by identifying efficiencies. Although the company plans to continue investing for further growth it has already started cutting 2300 positions company-wide as well as implementing a pay freeze across much of the group. It set out to develop a better relationship with its customers by simplifying the purchase of gas and electricity. It also decided to make the cost of delivery more transparent by giving its customers a breakdown on their bill of the actual costs of providing the energy.

Through its aggressive acquisition strategy in North America the company has gained more than 6 million retail power and gas supply customers in less than a decade as part of its Direct Energy operations. Building on its portfolio of offerings in 2011 it acquired Illinois-based Home Warranty of America (HWA) for #30 million ($48 million). HWA provides whole home warranty plans to more than 70000 customers through a network of 4000 contractors.

Direct Energy also made three acquisitions in 2011 for its residential energy supply business in North America: Gateway Energy Services First Choice Power and Vectren Retail. The deals part of the company's strategy of acquiring smaller suppliers and buying in deregulated markets added more than 750000 customers.

In a major move to grow its upstream business and its Norwegian operations Centrica completed a #936 million ($1.5 billion) deal in 2012 to acquire Norwegian assets from Statoil and ConocoPhillips. Combined the new assets will increase the company's reserves by almost 40% and its production by more than 30%. The acquisition includes proved and probable reserves of 117 million barrels of oil equivalent and production of 34000 barrels of oil evalent per day. The buy also makes Centrica one of Norway's fastest growing companies with a third of its gas and oil production originating from that region. The company's upstream operations also have a presence in Trinidad and the Netherlands.

In spite of the growth of Centrica's gas assets the company decided to raise its gas and electricity prices by 17% in late 2011 to cover the rising wholesale commodity prices in the first half of the year. Mild weather that year led to a decline per household averaging 21% less in gas and 4% less in electricity consumption. With lower residential demand customer bills were 4% lower on average in 2011. Consumer complaints over higher prices for heating homes in the UK led to protests at the offices of utility companies and at town halls early in 2012.

The company's upstream businesses in the UK produced higher profits in 2011 especially the company's nuclear assets. Market conditions remained difficult for the gas-fired generation and gas storage businesses. An increase in taxation in the UK on upstream operations reduced the company's earnings in that segment. However in North America the company's Direct Energy unit showed a strong performance in 2011.

Centrica posted revenues of #22.8 billion ($36 billion) in 2011 a 2% hike over 2010 revenues primarily because of higher upstream revenue that year due to higher prices. The company also recorded earnings that year of #421 million ($662 million) plunging about 78% from the previous year due to a large one-off charge mild weather higher wholesale gas prices and a weak economy. The charge included costs for the revaluation of contracts pension changes and losses on the company's disposals.

HISTORY

William Murdock invented gas lighting in 1792. In 1812 the Gas Light and Coke Company of London was formed as the world's first gas supplier to the public and by 1829 the UK had 200 gas companies.

In the second half of the 19th century the gas industry began looking for new uses for the fuel. Gas stoves were introduced in 1851 the geyser water heater was invented in 1868 and in 1880 the first gas units to heat individual rooms were developed.

Gas companies countered the emerging electricity industry by renting gas stoves at low prices and installing gas fittings (stove pipe and lights) in poor homes with no installation charges or deposits. By 1914 the UK had 1500 gas suppliers.

The electricity industry soon made major strikes against the gas industry's dominance. In 1926 the government began reorganizing the fragmented electricity supply industry building a national power grid and establishing the Central Electricity Generating Board to oversee it.

The gas industry was nationalized in 1949 and 1050 gas suppliers were brought under the control of the British Gas Council. Still the gas industry was losing. Supplying gas was more expensive than generating electricity: Gas was seen as a power supply of the past. The Gas Council sought to change that image through an aggressive marketing campaign in the 1960s touting gas as a modern clean fuel. Other factors played a part in its re-emergence: The Clean Air Act of 1956 steadily reduced the use of coal for home heating liquefied natural gas was discovered in the North Sea and OPEC raised oil prices in the 1970s. When natural gas was introduced most of the old gasworks were demolished and the British Gas Council (which became the British Gas Corp. in 1973) set about converting free of charge every gas appliance in the UK to natural gas.

As Margaret Thatcher's government began privatizing state industries the British Gas Corp. was taken public in 1986. Freed from government control British Gas expanded its international exploration and production activities. When the US gas industry began deregulating British Gas formed joint venture Accord Energy in 1994 with US gas trader Natural Gas Clearinghouse (now NGC) to sell gas on the wholesale market.

With the opening of the UK gas-supply market (which began regionally in 1996 and went nationwide in 1998) British Gas split into two public companies to avoid a conflict of interest between its supply business and its monopoly transportation business. In 1997 it spun off Centrica the retail operations and BG (now BG Group) which received the transportation business and the international exploration and production operations.

The UK electricity supply market began opening up to competition in 1998 and Centrica won 750000 UK electricity customers most of them also gas customers. In 1999 it bought The Automobile Association which it sold to venture capitalists in 2004. In 2000 Centrica began offering telecom services in the UK.

Centrica moved into North America in 2000 by purchasing two Canadian companies: natural gas retailer Direct Energy Marketing and gas production company Avalanche Energy. It gained a 28% stake in US marketing firm Energy America through the Direct Energy transaction and purchased the remaining 72% from US firm Sempra Energy the next year. Continuing its non-domestic strategy Centrica bought a 50% interest in Belgium energy supplier Luminus.

The firm purchased 60% of the 1260-MW Humber Power station in 2001 its first domestic power plant interest. It also acquired the UK operations of Australia's One.Tel and it bought Enron's European retail supply business Enron Direct for $137 million.

In 2002 Centrica purchased the retail energy services business of Canadian pipeline company Enbridge for $637 million; it also agreed to acquire another Enron-controlled company US retail energy supplier NewPower Holdings for $130 million. But Centrica withdrew its offer to buy NewPower a month after the deal was announced because of concerns about NewPower's potential Enron-related liabilities. Later that year Centrica acquired 200000 retail customer accounts in Ohio and Pennsylvania from NewPower.

In 2004 the company brought all its UK upstream activities together under Centrica Energy.

In 2005 Centrica acquired Oxxio the Netherlands #4 energy supplier.

To pursue green energy options in 2007 British Gas launched British Gas New Energy.

In 2007 Centrica acquired Newfield Exploration's North Sea assets for $486 million and in 2008 it acquired its first gas and oil assets in the Norwegian North Sea for $375 million (from Marathon Oil).

Growing it retail business in 2008 Centrica acquired Electricity Direct a UK commercial retail supplier serving nearly 1 million customers.

In 2008 Centrica's British Gas unit acquired 40000 small and mid-sized business customers from UK retail energy provider BizzEnergy in the wake of the latter's sudden financial collapse.

EXECUTIVES

Chairman, Sir Roger M. Carr
CFO and Director, Nick Luff
Managing Director British Gas and Director, Phillip K. (Phil) Bentley, $700,744 total compensation
Chief Executive and Director, W. Samuel H. (Sam) Laidlaw
Managing Director International Downstream, Chris Weston
General Counsel and Company Secretary, Grant Dawson
Managing Director International Upstream, Mark Hanafin
Group Director Human Resources, Jill Shedden
Head of Group Media Relations, Greg Wood
CFO and Director, Nick Luff
Director, Ian K. Meakins
Managing Director British Gas and Director, Phillip K. (Phil) Bentley
Chief Executive and Director, W. Samuel H. (Sam) Laidlaw
Director, Andrew Mackenzie
Managing Director International Downstream, Chris Weston
Director, Paul Rayner, age 58
Managing Director International Upstream, Mark Hanafin
Director, Lesley Knox, age 59
Director, Margherita Della Valle
Director, Mary Francis, age 65
Independent Non-Executive Director, Margherita Margherita Della Valle Valle
Auditors: PricewaterhouseCoopersLLP

LOCATIONS

HQ: Centrica Plc
Millstream, Maidenhead Road, Windsor, Berkshire SL4 5GD
Phone: (44) 1753 494000 **Fax:** (44) 1753 494001
Web: www.centrica.com

2011 Sales

	% of total
UK	69
US	17
Canada	9
Other	5
Total	**100**

PRODUCTS/OPERATIONS

2011 Sales

	% of total
UK	
Downstream	
Residential energy	36
Business energy supply &	12
Residential	7
Upstream	
Gas	13
Power	6
Storage	1
North America	
Business energy	12
Residential energy	10
Residential & business	2
Upstream & wholesale	1
Total	**100**

COMPETITORS

AGL Resources
Community Energy
Constellation Energy Group
Dominion Resources
E.ON Ruhrgas
E.ON UK
EDF Energy
Electrabel
Gasunie
Green Mountain Energy
IBERDROLA
RWE npower
STASCO
Scottish and Southern Energy
Southern Company
United Utilities
Viridian Group
Western Power Distribution

HISTORICAL FINANCIALS

Company Type: Public

Income Statement FYE: December 31

	REVENUE ($ mil.)	NET INCOME ($ mil.)	NET PROFIT MARGIN	EMPLOYEES
12/12	38,591	2,051	5.3%	38,642
12/11	35,259	650	1.8%	39,432
12/10	34,814	3,004	8.6%	34,970
12/09	35,570	1,366	3.8%	34,125
12/08	31,106	(211)	—	32,817
Annual Growth	5.5%	—	—	4.2%

2012 Year-End Financials

Debt ratio: 39.1%
Return on equity: 22.0%
Cash ($ mil.): 1,500
Current ratio: 0.95
Long-term debt ($ mil.): 7,827

No. of shares (mil.): —
Dividends
Yield: 4.3%
Payout: 631.6%
Market value ($ mil.): —

	STOCK PRICE ($) FY Close	P/E High/Low	PER SHARE ($) Earnings	Dividends	Book Value
12/12	22.00	239173	0.39	0.96	1.84
12/11	17.82	702504	0.13	2.34	1.67
12/10	20.64	145 90	0.58	0.76	1.75
12/09	18.15	289177	0.27	2.61	1.32
12/08	15.20	— —	(0.05)	2.80	1.23
Annual Growth	9.7%	— —	—	(23.6%)	10.5%

Chiba Bank, Ltd

The Chiba Bank based in Japan's Chiba prefecture —located east of Tokyo —operates 175 branches and sub-branches across Japan. The bank has more than 39240 ATMs nationwide and operates international offices in Hong Kong London New York Shanghai and Singapore. Its lending focuses on home mortgages regional businesses and residential construction companies. In addition to providing traditional banking services to individuals and businesses The Chiba Bank offers investment trusts credit cards leasing financial consulting annuities and securities. Subsidiaries include Chibagin Accounting Service (cash and securities analysis) and Chibagin Capital (shareholders consultancy).

EXECUTIVES

President, Hidetoshi Sakuma, age 62
Senior Executive Officer, Tetsuya Koike
Senior Executive Officer, Toshikazu Okubo
Senior Executive Officer, Kyoichi Hanashima
Managing Executive Officer, Masao Morimoto
Managing Executive Officer, Osamu Kimura
Managing Executive Officer, Takeshi Kubo
Managing Executive Officer, Toru Nomura
Managing Executive Officer, Shoichi Hatano
Senior Executive Officer Chief Business Operation Unit and Director, Toshio Yoshii, age 61
Managing Executive Officer Treasury Division and Treasury Operation Division and Director, Hidetoshi Sakuma, age 61
Auditors: Ernst&YoungShinNihon

LOCATIONS

HQ: Chiba Bank, Ltd
1-2 Chiba-Minato, Chuo-ku, Chiba 260-8720
Phone: (81) 43 245 1111 **Fax:** (81) 43 242 9121
Web: www.chibabank.co.jp

COMPETITORS

Aozora Bank
Bank of Nagoya
Chiba Kogyo Bank
Chuo Mitsui Trust
Keiyo Bank
Mitsubishi UFJ Financial Group
Mizuho Financial
Mizuho Trust & Banking Ltd
Resona
Shizuoka Bank
Sumitomo Mitsui

HISTORICAL FINANCIALS

Company Type: Public

Income Statement

FYE: March 31

	ASSETS ($ mil.)	NET INCOME ($ mil.)	INCOME AS % OF ASSETS	EMPLOYEES
03/13	120,878	469	0.4%	4,454
03/12	133,082	497	0.4%	4,491
03/11	127,441	490	0.4%	4,490
03/10	109,857	402	0.4%	4,403
03/09	102,187	125	0.1%	4,266
Annual Growth	4.3%	39.0%	—	1.1%

2013 Year-End Financials

Return on assets: 0.4%
Return on equity: 6.4%
Long-term debt ($ mil.): —
No. of shares (mil.): 859
Sales ($ mil): 2,367

Dividends
Yield: —
Payout: —
Market value ($ mil.): —

	STOCK PRICE ($) FY Close	P/E High/Low	PER SHARE ($) Earnings	Dividends	Book Value
03/13	0.00	— —	0.54	0.00	9.01
03/12	29.50	— —	0.57	0.00	9.21
Annual Growth	—	— —	(1.2%)	—	(0.5%)

China Communications Construction Company Ltd

If you travel by car ship or train in China chances are you've used one of China Communications Construction Company's (CCCC) structures. One of China's largest infrastructure construction companies CCCC designs and builds sea ports roads bridges railways tunnels and other structures. In addition the company operates a dredging and reclamation business as well as a port machinery (mainly container cranes) and construction machinery manufacturing business. Although China constitutes its largest market CCCC also has substantial operations in Southeast Asia South America Africa and the Middle East. The company which operates through numerous subsidiaries was established in 2006.

Geographic Reach

Beyond China Beijing-based China Communications Construction Company has branches in Cuba Libya Saudi Arabia and Tanzania. The firm has overseas projects in Ethiopia Hong Kong Macao Malaysia Malta Sudan and Uzbekistan among other far flung locals.

Financial Performance

China Communications Construction Company's (CCCC) revenue grew by 8% in 2011 vs. 2010 while net income increased 24% over the same period. CCCC's design dredging and heavy machinery businesses each posted double-digit increases in revenue while construction which accounts for more than three-quarters of the company's total sales saw its revenue increase by a relatively-modest 7% year over year.

Strategy

As part of its growth strategy CCCC intends to bolster its dredging and port machinery manufacturing operations by acquiring and merging with related businesses. The company also plans to acquire businesses in emerging markets in order to grow its overseas business.

EXECUTIVES

President, Qitao Liu
CFO, Junyuan Fu
Auditors: PricewaterhouseCoopers

LOCATIONS

HQ: China Communications Construction Company Ltd
85 De Sheng Men Wai Street, Xicheng District, Beijing 100088
Phone: (86) 10 8201 6562 **Fax:** (86) 10 8201 6524
Web: www.ccccltd.cn

PRODUCTS/OPERATIONS

2011 Revenue

	% of total
Construction	77
Dredging	11
Heavy	7
Design	5
Other	2
Adjustment (2)	
Total	**100**

Selected Operations

Dredging
Infrastructure construction
- Bridge
- Port
- Railway
- Road
- Other projects

Infrastructure design
Heavy machinery manufacturing
Investment

COMPETITORS

Beijing Urban Construction
CRCC
CSCEC
China Railway Engineering
Shanghai Construction
Skanska
VINCI
Zhejiang Expressway

HISTORICAL FINANCIALS

Company Type: Public

Income Statement

FYE: December 31

	REVENUE ($ mil.)	NET INCOME ($ mil.)	NET PROFIT MARGIN	EMPLOYEES
12/12	47,370	1,964	4.1%	94,629
12/11	46,752	1,869	4.0%	90,674
12/10	41,376	1,496	3.6%	101,030
12/09	33,233	1,054	3.2%	100,461
12/08	26,216	890	3.4%	93,019
Annual Growth	15.9%	21.9%	—	0.4%

2012 Year-End Financials

Debt ratio: 5.3%
Return on equity: 15.5%
Cash ($ mil.): 10,826
Current ratio: 1.07
Long-term debt ($ mil.): 12,039

No. of shares (mil.): —
Dividends
Yield: 2.3%
Payout: 9.4%
Market value ($ mil.): —

	STOCK PRICE ($) FY Close	P/E High/Low	PER SHARE ($) Earnings	Dividends	Book Value
12/12	19.80	1 0	0.12	0.46	0.86
12/11	15.78	1 0	0.13	0.01	0.75
12/10	17.75	1 1	0.10	0.29	0.62
12/09	19.75	1 1	0.07	0.01	0.54
Annual Growth	0.1%	— —	14.5%	208.7%	12.4%

China Construction Bank Corp

LOCATIONS

HQ: China Construction Bank Corp
No. 25, Financial Street, Xicheng District, Beijing 100033
Phone: (86) 10 6621 5533 **Fax:** (86) 10 6621 8888
Web: www.ccb.com

HISTORICAL FINANCIALS

Company Type: Public

Income Statement FYE: December 31

	ASSETS ($ mil.)	NET INCOME ($ mil.)	INCOME AS % OF ASSETS	EMPLOYEES
12/12	2,241,301	30,986	1.4%	355,290
12/11	1,951,231	26,890	1.4%	329,438
12/10	1,640,014	20,456	1.2%	313,867
12/09	1,409,395	15,635	1.1%	301,537
12/08	1,107,269	13,570	1.2%	298,581
Annual Growth	19.3%	22.9%	—	4.4%

2012 Year-End Financials

Return on assets: 1.4%
Return on equity: 21.9%
Long-term debt ($ mil.): —
No. of shares (mil.): —
Sales ($ mil): 114,738
Dividends
Yield: 3.8%
Payout: 12.7%
Market value ($ mil.): —

	STOCK PRICE ($) FY Close	P/E High	P/E Low	PER SHARE ($) Earnings	Dividends	Book Value
12/12	16.23	1	0	0.12	0.62	0.60
12/11	13.94	1	0	0.11	0.01	0.52
12/10	18.30	2	1	0.08	2.47	0.42
12/09	42.66	2	1	0.07	0.53	0.35
Annual Growth	(27.5%)	—	—	16.4%	4.1%	14.8%

China International United Petroleum & Chemicals Co Ltd

LOCATIONS

HQ: China International United Petroleum & Chemicals Co Ltd
22 Chaoyangmen North Street, Chaoyang District, Beijing 100728
Phone: (86) 10 59966526 **Fax:** (86) 10 59966698
Web: www.sinopec.com

HISTORICAL FINANCIALS

Company Type: Public

Income Statement FYE: December 31

	REVENUE ($ mil.)	NET INCOME ($ mil.)	NET PROFIT MARGIN	EMPLOYEES
12/12	204,650	204	0.1%	0
12/11	175,374	72	0.0%	0
Annual Growth	16.7%	183.6%	—	—

2012 Year-End Financials

Debt ratio: 3.5%
Return on equity: 13.0%
Cash ($ mil.): 350
Current ratio: 1.04
Long-term debt ($ mil.): —
No. of shares (mil.): —
Dividends
Yield: —
Payout: —
Market value ($ mil.): —

	STOCK PRICE ($) FY Close	P/E High	P/E Low	PER SHARE ($) Earnings	Dividends	Book Value
12/12	0.00	—	—	(0.00)	0.00	(0.00)
12/11	0.00	—	—	(0.00)	0.00	(0.00)
/0.00	—	—	(0.00)	0.00	(0.00)	
Annual Growth	—	—	—	—	—	—

China Life Insurance Co Ltd

Life insurance nsk

EXECUTIVES

President, Ming Yang Wang

LOCATIONS

HQ: China Life Insurance Co Ltd
16 Financial Street, Xicheng District, Beijing 100033
Phone: (86) 10 63633333 **Fax:** (86) 10 66575722
Web: www.e-chinalife.com

PRODUCTS/OPERATIONS

HISTORICAL FINANCIALS

Company Type: Public

Income Statement FYE: December 31

	ASSETS ($ mil.)	NET INCOME ($ mil.)	INCOME AS % OF ASSETS	EMPLOYEES
12/12	304,594	1,774	0.6%	100,340
12/11	251,637	2,912	1.2%	100,319
12/10	213,996	5,101	2.4%	103,220
12/09	179,592	4,815	2.7%	96,698
12/08	153,122	3,118	2.0%	102,241
Annual Growth	18.8%	(13.1%)	—	(0.5%)

2012 Year-End Financials

Return on assets: 0.6%
Return on equity: 5.3%
Long-term debt ($ mil.): —
No. of shares (mil.): —
Sales ($ mil): 60,074
Dividends
Yield: 0.9%
Payout: —
Market value ($ mil.): —

	STOCK PRICE ($) FY Close	P/E High	P/E Low	PER SHARE ($) Earnings	Dividends	Book Value
12/12	49.69	3	2	0.06	0.47	1.25
12/11	36.97	2	1	0.10	0.02	1.08
12/10	61.17	1	1	0.18	1.37	1.12
12/09	73.35	1	1	0.17	1.32	1.09
12/08	46.40	2	1	0.11	0.89	0.94
Annual Growth	1.7%	—	—	(13.1%)	(14.5%)	7.6%

China Merchants Bank Co Ltd

China Merchants Bank (CMB) is out for the business of corporate and small-time merchants. The bank is one of China's top five banks and with 53 million credit cards its largest issuer. CMB offers businesses and individuals a range of financial services including credit cards savings accounts mortgage loans ATMs foreign exchange trading and on-line banking service. Corporate banking accounts for half of its operating income. CMB targets affluent markets through a network of more than 90 branches and 800 sub-branches and 2680 ATMs in more than 100 cities in China. It also maintains branches in New York City and London. CMB has relationships with more than 1600 banks worldwide.

Geographic Reach

CMB is headquartered in Shenzhen and primarily focuses on the Chinese domestic market. CMB operates a branch and a representative office in New York and also representative offices in London and Taipei.

Operations

CMB divides its operations into three main segments: corporate (or wholesale) banking retail banking and treasury. Corporate banking accounted for 63% of the bank's total revenue in 2011; retail banking 37%. The treasury operations lost money for the bank during its fiscal year 2011.

Financial Performance

Since the end of the global Great Recession CMB has seen four straight years of impressive growth. From 2010 to 2011 its net sales increased by 35% and its net income jumped by 40%.

The growth was attributed to a 34% increase in net interest which was mainly due to improvement in yield of interest-earning assets brought about by better risk pricing and positive re-pricing of assets as a result of rising interest rates and a steady expansion of the volume of interest-earning assets. Net fee and commission revenue also surged by 38% due to the increase in commissions from custody and other trustee businesses bank card commissions settlement and clearing fees and financial consultancy fees.

Net income in 2011 increased mainly due to the increase in net sales partially offset by a 25% increase in operating expenses. Staff costs and other general and administrative expenses increased by 27% due to increased headcounts along with business expansion.

EXECUTIVES

Vice Chairman, Wei Jiafu, age 62
Chairman, Yuning Fu, age 56
President CEO and Director, Ma Weihua
EVP and CFO, Li Hao

Executive Vice President, Tang Zhihong
Executive Vice President, Yin Fenglan
EVP, Zhang Guanghua
Executive Vice President, Ding Wei
CTO, Xu Lianfeng
Executive Vice President, Zhu Qi
Secretary, Lan Qi
Vice Chairman, Wei Jiafu, age 62
Director, Yinquan Li, age 58
Director, Sun Yueying, age 54
Director, Wang Daxiong
President CEO and Director, Ma Weihua
Director, Fu Junyuan
Director, Liu Hongxia
Director, Hong Xiaoyuan
Director, Yi Xiqun
Director, Yan Lan
Director, Chow (Edward) Kwong Fai

LOCATIONS

HQ: China Merchants Bank Co Ltd
7088 Shennan Boulevard, Futian District, Shenzhen, Guangdong Province 518040
Phone: (86) 755 83198888 **Fax:** (86) 755 83195109
Web: www.cmbchina.com

PRODUCTS/OPERATIONS

2011 Sales

Net interest income	79	
Other	5	
Total	**0**	**100**

2011 Sales

Corporate banking	63	
Total	**0**	**100**

COMPETITORS

Agricultural Bank of China
Bank of China
Bank of Communications
Bank of East Asia
China Construction Bank
China Development Bank
China Minsheng Banking
Chong Hing Bank
Chuo Mitsui Trust
HSBC
Hang Seng Bank
Hua Xia Bank
Industrial and Commercial Bank of China
Public Financial Holdings
Shanghai Pudong Development Bank

HISTORICAL FINANCIALS

Company Type: Public

Income Statement FYE: December 31

	ASSETS ($ mil.)	NET INCOME ($ mil.)	INCOME AS % OF ASSETS	EMPLOYEES
12/12	546,693	7,261	1.3%	59,340
12/11	444,040	5,739	1.3%	45,344
12/10	364,480	3,909	1.1%	43,089
12/09	302,861	2,670	0.9%	40,340
12/08	230,350	3,088	1.3%	36,916
Annual Growth	24.1%	23.8%	—	12.6%

2012 Year-End Financials

Return on assets: 1.4%
Return on equity: 24.7%
Long-term debt ($ mil.): —
No. of shares (mil.): —
Sales ($ mil): 28,387
Dividends
Yield: 2.4%
Payout: —
Market value ($ mil.): —

	STOCK PRICE ($) FY Close	P/E High/Low		PER SHARE ($) Earnings	Dividends	Book Value
12/12	2.18	0	0	0.34	0.27	1.49
12/11	2.08	0	0	0.27	0.00	1.21
12/10	2.46	0	0	0.19	0.00	0.94
12/09	2.54	0	0	0.14	0.00	0.71
12/08	1.76	0	0	0.16	0.00	0.61
Annual Growth	5.5%	—	—	20.2%	—	25.0%

China Minsheng Banking Corp Ltd

LOCATIONS

HQ: China Minsheng Banking Corp Ltd
No. 2, Fuxingmennei Avenue, Xicheng District, Beijing 100031
Phone: (86) 10 58560666 **Fax:** (86) 10 58560690
Web: www.cmbc.com.cn

HISTORICAL FINANCIALS

Company Type: Public

Income Statement FYE: December 31

	ASSETS ($ mil.)	NET INCOME ($ mil.)	INCOME AS % OF ASSETS	EMPLOYEES
12/12	515,218	6,025	1.2%	49,227
12/11	354,134	4,435	1.3%	40,820
12/10	276,675	2,667	1.0%	31,454
12/09	208,903	1,772	0.8%	26,039
12/08	154,517	1,155	0.7%	19,853
Annual Growth	35.1%	51.1%	—	25.5%

2012 Year-End Financials

Return on assets: 1.3%
Return on equity: 25.6%
Long-term debt ($ mil.): —
No. of shares (mil.): —
Sales ($ mil): 28,695
Dividends
Yield: 4.9%
Payout: 6.7%
Market value ($ mil.): —

	STOCK PRICE ($) FY Close	P/E High/Low		PER SHARE ($) Earnings	Dividends	Book Value
12/12	11.67	0	0	0.21	0.57	0.92
12/11	8.61	0	0	0.17	0.00	0.77
Annual Growth	35.5%	—	—	6.5%	—	4.6%

China Mobile Limited

China Mobile Limited sees unlimited potential. The company is China's (and the world's) leading wireless operator by subscribers which total more than 633 million. In terms of sales it trails UK-based global leader Vodafone Group. China Mobile offers domestic and international phone service text messaging and other mobile data services. In addition to its flagship postpaid GoTone brand the company targets the youth and budget-conscious markets with M-Zone and Easy Own prepaid services. State-controlled China Mobile Communications Corporation (CMCC) indirectly holds a majority stake of 74% through intermediary subsidiary China Mobile (Hong Kong) Group Limited.

Revenue rose more than 7% in 2010 over 2009 thanks mainly to upticks in voice usage volume and value-added business besides the more obvious factor of subscriber growth. In the company's main segment of usage and monthly fees (64% of revenue) revenue went up about 4% in 2010 over 2009 a trend that could continue because of tariff decreases that may bring more business. The value-added services segment (31% of revenue) enjoyed an increase of more than 15% in 2010 over 2009 owing mainly to the launch of new products and other business-development efforts.

Like any other major telecom company 3G (Third Generation) and LTE (Long Term Evolution) development have kept China Mobile Limited buzzing recently. After initiating 3G service in 2009 the company has signed up about 27 million customers for it. Efforts to keep 3G service up to speed could result in significant capital expenditures. In addition to that China Mobile has been helping its parent CMCC roll out the LTE network in six Chinese cities as well as installing a demonstration LTE network in Beijing.

Meanwhile China Mobile Limited's organic growth has been fueled in part by the adoption of mobile communications in rural areas that previously had no wired or wireless telephone services. Additionally the company has catered increasingly to corporate clients in a search for higher-margin contracts.

Other efforts to grow its business include the $35.9 million acquisition in 2011 of China Topssion Communication a seller of mobile phones and other electronic devices to build its distribution and retail operations. China Mobile bought state-run fixed-line carrier China Tietong Telecommunications in 2008 as part of a broader restructuring of the telecom industry in China which also involved former rival China Unicom selling its wireless operations to China Telecom. The previous year it grew globally as well with the acquisition of nearly 90% of Pakistani wireless company Paktel Ltd. for about $284 million.

These purchases continued the company's history of using acquisitions to expand operations. From 1998 to 2004 China Mobile purchased 29 regional telecom service providers. The company acquired China Resources Peoples Telephone (later renamed China Mobile Peoples Telephone) a Hong Kong-based telecom service provider for $436 million in 2006.

EXECUTIVES

Executive Director, Xu Long, age 55
CEO, Li Yue, age 54
VP and CFO, Xue Taohai, age 57
Chairman, Xi Guohua, age 62
Chairman and Executive Director, Wang Jianzhou, age 64
VP and Executive Director, Sha Yuejia, age 55
VP and Executive Director, Liu Aili, age 50
VP and Executive Director, Huang Wenlin, age 59
Director, Lo Ka Shui, age 66
Executive Director, Xu Long, age 55
CEO and Executive Director, Li Yue, age 53
VP and Executive Director, Lu Xiangdong, age 52
VP CFO and Executive Director, Xue Taohai, age 56
Director, Frank K. S. Wong, age 64
Director, Moses M. C. Cheng, age 62
VP and Executive Director, Sha Yuejia, age 54
VP and Executive Director, Liu Aili, age 49
VP and Executive Director, Xin Fanfei, age 55
VP and Executive Director, Huang Wenlin, age 58
Auditors: KPMG

LOCATIONS

HQ: China Mobile Limited
60th Floor, The Center, 99 Queen' s Road Central,
Phone: (852) 3121 8888 **Fax:** (852) 2511 9092
Web: www.chinamobileltd.com

PRODUCTS/OPERATIONS

2010 Sales

	% of total
Usage & monthly	64
Value-added services	31
Other	5
Total	**100**

COMPETITORS

China Telecom Corporation Limited
China Unicom
City Telecom
Hutchison Telecommunications
PCCW Ltd.
Vodafone

HISTORICAL FINANCIALS

Company Type: Public

Income Statement

FYE: December 31

	REVENUE ($ mil.)	NET INCOME ($ mil.)	NET PROFIT MARGIN	EMPLOYEES
12/12	89,892	20,736	23.1%	182,487
12/11	83,883	19,997	23.8%	175,336
12/10	73,613	18,150	24.7%	164,336
12/09	66,213	16,866	25.5%	350,192
12/08	60,429	16,530	27.4%	138,368
Annual Growth	10.4%	5.8%	—	7.2%

2012 Year-End Financials

Debt ratio: 0.4%
Return on equity: 18.7%
Cash ($ mil.): 11,373
Current ratio: 1.50
Long-term debt ($ mil.): 4,590
No. of shares (mil.): —
Dividends
Yield: 3.3%
Payout: 4.8%
Market value ($ mil.): —

	STOCK PRICE ($) FY Close	P/E High/Low		PER SHARE ($) Earnings	Dividends	Book Value
12/12	58.72	0	0	1.02	1.96	5.77
12/11	48.49	0	0	0.99	0.05	5.14
12/10	49.62	0	0	0.89	1.66	4.36
12/09	46.43	0	0	0.83	1.60	3.70
12/08	50.85	0	0	0.81	1.61	3.23
Annual Growth	3.7%	—	—	5.9%	5.0%	15.6%

China Petroleum & Chemical Corp. Inc

China Petroleum and Chemical Corporation (Sinopec Corp.) is China's largest producer and supplier of refined oil products and its second-largest crude oil producer. It is also China's largest petrochemicals producer and distributor and the world's fourth-largest ethylene producer. Operations include oil and gas exploration and production; crude oil processing; oil products trading transportation distribution and marketing; and petrochemicals manufacturing. In 2010 it reported proved reserves of 2.9 billion barrels of oil and 6.5 trillion cu. ft. of natural gas; it also owns more than 29600 gas stations and 34 refineries. China's government controls about 76% of the company through Sinopec Group.

Sinopec Corp. is committed to growing its oil and gas reserves to keep pace with the energy demands from China's booming industrial economy and growing population. The company operates 16 oil and gas production fields in China and also owns vast reserves in Africa. In 2010 the company produced an average of more than 1 billion barrels of oil equivalent per day. For the past few years it has been buying up resources across the globe as it competes with other developing countries for oil and gas reserves.

In late 2011 the company acquired Canada's Daylight Energy for $2.1 billion which gave it access to 69 oil and natural gas assets in the western provinces of British Columbia and Alberta. Daylight is being integrated within an indirect subsidiary of Sinopec Corp. and will operate as Sinopec Daylight Energy. The purchase was made on the heels of the acquisition of OPTI Canada in November by competitor CNOOC another Chinese state-owned company.

In 2013 it purchased a 50% undivided interest in 850000 of Chesapeake's net oil and natural gas leasehold acres in the Mississippi Lime play in northern Oklahoma (425000 acres net to Sinopec) for $1.02 billion.

The acquisitions follow several other purchases Sinopec has made since 2009 including shelling out $7.1 billion for Repsol's assets in Brazil $2.5 billion for Occidental Petroleum's assets in Argentina; $4.7 billion for ConocoPhillips' 9% stake in Syncrude; and $7.5 billion for Addax Petroleum which had reserves in Africa and the Middle East. In late 2010 the company also signed a deal with Chevron to help develop the $6 billion-plus Gendalo-Gehem deepwater natural gas project off the coast of Indonesia.

The shopping spree for oil and gas resources paid off in 2010 when Sinopec Corp. achieved record sales. The company's sales spiked 47% over the previous year and its net income grew by more than 20%. Its exploration and production operations not only grew exponentially but the official launch of the Sichuan-East China Gas project in 2010 also accelerated the company's growth. The pipeline has the capacity to produce about 12 billion cu. meters of gas per year.

Sinopec Corp.'s parent state-owned China Petrochemical (Sinopec Group) reorganized in 2000 and pooled the best of its assets as Sinopec Corp.

EXECUTIVES

Chairman, Su Shulin, age 50
Vice Chairman of the Board; President, Wang Tianpu, age 50, $106,214 total compensation
SVP and Director, Wang Zhigang, age 55, $92,216 total compensation
SVP and Director, Zhang Jianhua, age 48, $89,332 total compensation
SVP and Director, Cai Xiyou, age 51, $105,482 total compensation
Secretary, Chen Ge, age 50, $53,108 total compensation
SVP and Director, Dai Houliang, age 49, $105,482 total compensation
VP and Director General Engineering Department, Zhang Kehua, age 59, $73,681 total compensation
VP, Zhang Haichao, age 55, $65,047 total compensation
VP, Jiao Fangzheng, age 50, $67,148 total compensation
VP and Director General Development and Planning Department, Lei Dianwu, age 50, $52,961 total compensation
Vice Chairman, Zhang Yaocang, age 59
Chief Financial Officer, Wang Xinhua, age 57, $51,937 total compensation
Chairman of the Board of Directors, Fu Chengyu
Director, Liu Yun, age 56
Vice Chairman and President, Wang Tianpu, age 50
SVP and Director, Wang Zhigang, age 55
SVP and Director, Zhang Jianhua, age 48
SVP and Director, Cai Xiyou, age 51
Director, Li Chunguang, age 57
SVP and Director, Dai Houliang, age 49
Director, Ma Weihua
Director, Chen Xiaojin, age 68
Director, Li Deshui, age 69
Vice Chairman, Zhang Yaocang, age 59
Director, Cao Yaofeng, age 59
Director, Xie Zhongyu, age 69
Auditors: KPMGHuazhen

LOCATIONS

HQ: China Petroleum & Chemical Corp. Inc
22 Chaoyangmen North Street, Chaoyang District, Beijing 100728
Phone: (86) 10 5996 0028 **Fax:** (86) 10 5996 0386
Web: www.sinopec.com.cn

PRODUCTS/OPERATIONS

2010 Sales

	$ mil.	% of total
Exploration & production	43	
Marketing & distribution	28	
Chemicals	14	

COMPETITORS

BASF SE
BP
Bangchak Petroleum Public
CNOOC
CPC
Chevron
Exxon Mobil
Furmanite
PetroChina
Royal Dutch Shell
TOTAL

HISTORICAL FINANCIALS

Company Type: Public

Income Statement

FYE: December 31

	REVENUE ($ mil.)	NET INCOME ($ mil.)	NET PROFIT MARGIN	EMPLOYEES
12/12	446,893	10,246	2.3%	376,201
12/11	398,081	11,633	2.9%	377,235
12/10	290,245	10,892	3.8%	373,375
12/09	196,990	9,045	4.6%	371,333
12/08	212,808	4,362	2.1%	0
Annual Growth	20.4%	23.8%	—	—

2012 Year-End Financials

Debt ratio: 3.5%
Return on equity: 12.9%
Cash ($ mil.): 1,742
Current ratio: 0.71
Long-term debt ($ mil.): 26,004
No. of shares (mil.): —
Dividends
Yield: 4.8%
Payout: 4,999.1%
Market value ($ mil.): —

	STOCK PRICE ($) FY Close	P/E High/Low		PER SHARE ($) Earnings	Dividends	Book Value
12/12	114.92	6	4	0.09	4.25	0.73
12/11	105.05	4	3	0.10	0.06	0.67
12/10	95.69	4	3	0.10	2.47	0.56
12/09	88.07	4	2	0.08	2.07	0.49
12/08	61.79	11	4	0.03	2.01	0.43
Annual Growth	16.8%	—	—	26.9%	20.6%	14.2%

China Railway Construction Corp Ltd

LOCATIONS

HQ: China Railway Construction Corp Ltd
East, No. 40 Fuxing Road, Haidian District, Beijing 100855
Phone: (86) 10 5268 8600 **Fax:** (86) 10 5268 8302
Web: www.crcc.cn

HISTORICAL FINANCIALS

Company Type: Public

Income Statement FYE: December 31

	REVENUE ($ mil.)	NET INCOME ($ mil.)	NET PROFIT MARGIN	EMPLOYEES
12/12	77,685	1,360	1.8%	244,523
12/11	72,662	1,247	1.7%	241,621
12/10	69,230	544	0.9%	229,070
12/09	50,523	966	1.9%	209,103
12/08	32,155	534	1.7%	190,545
Annual Growth	24.7%	26.3%	—	6.4%

2012 Year-End Financials

Debt ratio: 2.7%
Return on equity: 12.3%
Cash ($ mil.): 14,801
Current ratio: 1.13
Long-term debt ($ mil.): 5,518
No. of shares (mil.): —
Dividends
Yield: —
Payout: —
Market value ($ mil.): —

	STOCK PRICE ($) FY Close	P/E High/Low		PER SHARE ($) Earnings	Dividends	Book Value
12/12	1.17	0	0	0.11	0.00	0.94
12/11	0.53	0	0	0.10	0.00	0.83
12/10	1.24	0	0	0.05	0.00	0.71
12/09	1.32	0	0	0.08	0.00	0.63
12/08	1.52	0	0	0.05	0.00	0.57
Annual Growth	(6.3%)	—	—	23.5%	—	13.3%

China Railway Group Ltd

LOCATIONS

HQ: China Railway Group Ltd
No. 1, Xinghuo Road, Fengtai District, Beijing 100070
Phone:
Web: www.crec.cn

HISTORICAL FINANCIALS

Company Type: Public

Income Statement FYE: December 31

	REVENUE ($ mil.)	NET INCOME ($ mil.)	NET PROFIT MARGIN	EMPLOYEES
12/12	74,688	1,179	1.6%	289,343
12/11	70,255	1,062	1.5%	294,761
12/10	69,194	1,136	1.6%	285,054
12/09	48,840	1,008	2.1%	276,150
12/08	32,978	197	0.6%	267,188
Annual Growth	22.7%	56.3%	—	2.0%

2012 Year-End Financials

Debt ratio: 4.7%
Return on equity: 9.7%
Cash ($ mil.): 10,865
Current ratio: 1.19
Long-term debt ($ mil.): 14,216
No. of shares (mil.): —
Dividends
Yield: 0.0%
Payout: —
Market value ($ mil.): —

	STOCK PRICE ($) FY Close	P/E High/Low		PER SHARE ($) Earnings	Dividends	Book Value
12/12	14.14	1	1	0.06	0.00	0.59
12/11	7.82	1	0	0.05	0.00	0.54
12/10	17.87	1	1	0.05	0.00	0.47
Annual Growth	(11.0%)	—	—	0.9%	(2.3%)	5.6%

China Shenhua Energy Co., Ltd.

China Shenhua Energy Company (CSEC) is an integrated coal mining company in China. CSEC operates four mining groups –two underground and two surface mining projects –in western and northern China. The Shendong Mines account for close to two-thirds of its total coal production which is more than 180 million tons a year. It also markets coal mined by other companies making a total of more than 230 million tons sold annually. CSEC owns and operates four railway lines and port facilities for the transportation of its coal. The company also operates more than a dozen power plants with a total installed capacity of close to 18000 MW. Shenhua Group holds about 75% of the company.

The group announced in early 2006 that it plans to funnel all of its coal-related activities into Shenhua Energy. Shenhua Group's other businesses include power station construction coal chemicals manufacturing and coal-to-oil production.

EXECUTIVES

Chairman, Zhang Xiwu, age 54
VP Safety Health and Environmental Management and Operational Coordination, Hao Gui, age 50
VP Strategic Planning and Coal Production, Wang Jinli, age 53
VP Transportation, Xue Jilian, age 58
VP Coal Sales and Marketing, Hua Zeqiao, age 61
VP Power Production, Wang Pingang, age 52
Secretary, Huang Qing, age 47
CFO, Zhang Kehui, age 49
Senior Vice President, Dong Li
Senior Vice President, Gui Hao
Vice President, Guiwu Zhai
Senior Vice President; Executive Director, Jianguo Han
Senior Vice President, Jilian Xue
Vice President, Jinli Wang
Chief Financial Officer, Kehui Zhang
Senior Vice President, Pingang Wang
Secretary of the Board, Qing Huang
President; Executive Director, Wen Ling
Senior Vice President, Xiaolin Wang
Chairman of the Board; Executive Director, Xiwu Zhang
Vice Chairman of the Board; Executive Director, Yuzhuo Zhang
Director, Zhang Yuzhuo, age 50
Director, Han Jianguo, age 54
Director, Huazhang Gong, age 67
Non-Executive Director, Benren Liu
Non-Executive Director, Dong Kong
Non-Executive Director, Hongsheng Chen
Independent Non-Executive Director, Peizhang Guo
Non-Executive Director, Songlin Xie
Independent Non-Executive Director, Xulitai Fan
Auditors: KPMG

LOCATIONS

HQ: China Shenhua Energy Co., Ltd.
Shenhua Tower, 22 Xibinhe Road, Andingmen, Dongcheng District, Beijing 100011
Phone: (86) 10 5813 3399 **Fax:** (86) 10 5813 1804
Web: www.csec.com

2008 Sales

	% of total
China	91
Other	9
Total	**100**

COMPETITORS

China Yangtze Power
Peabody Energy
Rio Tinto Limited
U.S. China Mining Group
Yankuang
Yanzhou Coal

HISTORICAL FINANCIALS

Company Type: Public

Income Statement FYE: December 31

	REVENUE ($ mil.)	NET INCOME ($ mil.)	NET PROFIT MARGIN	EMPLOYEES
12/12	40,142	7,837	19.5%	89,144
12/11	33,076	7,256	21.9%	82,260
12/10	23,069	5,784	25.1%	65,154
12/09	17,766	4,643	26.1%	62,286
12/08	15,700	3,904	24.9%	59,543
Annual Growth	26.5%	19.0%	—	10.6%

2012 Year-End Financials

Debt ratio: 2.3%
Return on equity: 20.2%
Cash ($ mil.): 8,281
Current ratio: 1.05
Long-term debt ($ mil.): 6,355
No. of shares (mil.): —
Dividends
Yield: 2.7%
Payout: 3.1%
Market value ($ mil.): —

	STOCK PRICE ($) FY Close	P/E High/Low		PER SHARE ($) Earnings	Dividends	Book Value
12/12	17.90	0	0	0.39	0.49	2.07
12/11	43.03	1	0	0.36	0.01	1.80
12/10	41.45	1	0	0.29	0.27	1.51
12/09	49.00	1	0	0.23	0.01	1.26
12/08	20.00	0	0	0.20	0.00	1.09
Annual Growth	(2.7%)	—	—	19.0%	—	17.5%

China Telecom Corp Ltd

China Telecom Corporation Limited is a leading provider of fixed-line (or wireline) phone and Internet broadband services in some 20 provinces and autonomous regions of China. Its principal operations are in four of the most economically developed regions in China including Shanghai and the provinces of Guangdong Jiangsu and Zhejiang. Services include local access domestic and international long-distance Internet access wireless service managed data services leased lines and about 15 million public phones. China Telecom counts 112 million residential landline customers 56 million wireless subscribers 53 million broadband subscribers and 32 million business wireless subscribers.

Revenues for residential landline customers continue to decrease as fewer households use landlines and instead make their primary phone a cell phone or VoIP service. The number of subscribers dropped 10% in 2009 and the company expects to lose about as many customers in 2010. Enterprise customers however such as corporations and government agencies still require wireline service and that business segment continues to grow by a few million new customers every year. As long as wireline customers switch to a wireless service with China Telecom the company isn't losing anything but the wireless service market is intensely competitive in China. Wireless customers currently make up about 10% of revenue.

Internet service accounts for a quarter of revenue and is the company's second-largest segment. Unlike the US where many customers use their television cable company as an Internet service provider China's television programming is largely state-controlled and thus service is offered through the phone company.

In 2008 the Ministry of Industry and Information the National Development and Reform Commission and the Ministry of Finance reformed the telecommunications industry in China by granting 3G network access to the three main providers — China Telecom China Mobile and China Unicom. As part of the deal China Telecom acquired the CDMA (code division multiple access) mobile communications business from China Unicom and was able to enter the wireless market in order to remain competitive.

China Telecom Corporation Limited is ultimately owned by the Chinese government. It is 71% controlled by the government-owned China Telecommunications Corporation. Chinese law forbids foreign investment and in order to trade on the New York Stock Exchange the company became an operating subsidiary.

EXECUTIVES

Chairman and CEO, Wang Xiaochu, age 55
Executive Director EVP and CFO, Andi Wu, age 58
Executive Director and EVP, Zhang Jiping, age 57
President COO and Director, Shang Bing, age 57
Director, Jianhua Miao, age 61
Executive Director and EVP, Yang Jie, age 51
Executive Director and EVP, Sun Kangmin, age 56
Chairman and General Manager Jiangxi Telecom Company Limited, Ke Ruiwen, age 49
Executive Director and EVP, Yang Xiaowei, age 49
Executive Director and EVP, Zhang Chenshuang, age 61
Director Corporate Strategic Department, Xu Cailiao, age 49
Director Audit Department, Han Fang, age 40
Senior Accountant, Zhu Lihao, age 72
Employee Representative Supervisor, Yuzhu Ma, age 60
Executive Director EVP and CFO, Andi Wu, age 58
Executive Director and EVP, Zhang Jiping, age 57
Director, Qin Xiao, age 66
President COO and Director, Shang Bing, age 57
Director, Jianhua Miao, age 61
Executive Director and EVP, Yang Jie, age 51
Executive Director and EVP, Sun Kangmin, age 56
Director, Aloysius H. Y. Tse, age 65
Executive Director and EVP, Yang Xiaowei, age 49
Executive Director and EVP, Zhang Chenshuang, age 61
Director, Prof Xu Erming, age 63
Director, Cha (Laura) May Lung, age 63
Director, Wu Jichuan, age 75
Auditors: KPMG

LOCATIONS

HQ: China Telecom Corp Ltd
31 Jinrong Street, Xicheng District, Beijing 100033
Phone: (86) 10 6642 8166 **Fax:** (86) 10 6601 0728
Web: www.chinatelecom-h.com

PRODUCTS/OPERATIONS

2009 Sales

	% of total
Wireline	38
Broadband	25
Wireless	10
Value-added services (Caller ID text messaging	10
Integrated information application	6
Other	6
Managed data and leased-line	5
Total	**100**

COMPETITORS

China Mobile Communications
China Netcom Hong Kong
China Tietong
China Unicom
Shanghai Mobile

HISTORICAL FINANCIALS

Company Type: Public

Income Statement FYE: December 31

	REVENUE ($ mil.)	NET INCOME ($ mil.)	NET PROFIT MARGIN	EMPLOYEES
12/12	45,406	2,394	5.3%	305,676
12/11	38,930	2,621	6.7%	309,799
12/10	33,355	2,390	7.2%	312,322
12/09	30,663	2,112	6.9%	312,520
12/08	27,376	129	0.5%	314,541
Annual Growth	13.5%	107.3%	—	(0.7%)

2012 Year-End Financials

Debt ratio: 2.9%
Return on equity: 5.7%
Cash ($ mil.): 4,809
Current ratio: 0.34
Long-term debt ($ mil.): 13,325
No. of shares (mil.): —
Dividends
Yield: 1.7%
Payout: —
Market value ($ mil.): —

	STOCK PRICE ($) FY Close	P/E High/Low		PER SHARE ($) Earnings	Dividends	Book Value
12/12	56.85	9	6	0.03	0.99	0.53
12/11	57.13	8	6	0.03	0.02	0.50
12/10	52.28	7	5	0.03	0.98	0.43
12/09	41.42	7	4	0.03	0.99	0.40
12/08	38.05	183	56	0.00	1.09	0.39
Annual Growth	10.6%	—	—	110.7%	(2.4%)	8.0%

China Unicom (Hong Kong) Ltd

China Unicom (Hong Kong) Limited has brought competition to the world's largest telecommunications market. The Chinese government set up China Unicom in 1994 as the first competitor to another government-owned telecommunications monopoly. The state-controlled company provides long-distance broadband data and mobile communications services in 31 provinces cities and other regions throughout China. It is the country's #2 mobile phone operator behind former monopoly China Mobile Communications.

Subsidiary China Netcom is China's #2 provider of fixed-line communications carrier behind China Telecom. It operates primarily in the northern provinces; major cities served include Beijing and Tianjin.

China Unicom became a full-service provider offering both wireless and wireline service after the 2008 acquisition of China Netcom for which it paid about $24 billion in stock. The deal expanded the company's resources and customer base to 31 provinces to better compete with both Chinese and regional rivals.

However the number of fixed-line customers continues to decrease as fewer households use landlines and instead make their primary phone a cell phone or VoIP service. Altogether China Unicom has about 62 million residential and 14 million business fixed-line subscribers. In addition it has about 19 million subscribers to its personal handyphone system (PHS). In China PHS is a cordless phone that has a wider roaming range but the country is phasing out the service; China Unicom hopes its subscribers will become wireless and/or wireline customers. Dial-up Internet service is also offered through the fixed-line segment; the company has about 38 million data customers growing about 30% a year. The company also maintains 8 million public pay telephones.

The company's wireless service has more customers and represents a growing segment compared to its fixed-line business but mobile service currently generates less revenue. Mobile service accounts for 47% of China Unicom's sales whereas landlines account for 53% of sales. The company has about 150 million mobile subscribers and enjoys a 20% market share in its service areas.

China Unicom sold its CDMA wireless business to China Telecom for about $16 billion in cash in 2008 while retaining its larger GSM-based wireless unit. GSM services accounted for almost two-thirds of the company's revenues in 2007.

Key international investors in China Unicom include Spanish telecom giant Telefonica which owns about 8% of the company.

EXECUTIVES

SVP and Director, Gang Li, age 55
SVP, Pei Aihua, age 63
CFO and Director, Tong Jilu, age 55
SVP and Director, Zuo Xunsheng, age 62
SVP, Zhao Jidong, age 62
Executive Chairman of the Board; Chief Executive Officer, Chang Xiaobing, age 56
SVP and Director, Li Jianguo, age 59
SVP and Director, Junan Zhang, age 56
President; Executive Director, Lu Yimin, age 49
SVP, Li Fushen
SVP, Jiang Zhengxin, age 57
Director, John L. Thornton, age 58
SVP and Director, Gang Li, age 55
CFO and Director, Tong Jilu, age 55
SVP and Director, Zuo Xunsheng, age 62
Director, Wu Jinglian, age 82
Director, Cheung Wing (Linus) Lam, age 63
Director, Cesareo (Cesar) Alierta Izuel, age 67
SVP and Director, Li Jianguo, age 59
SVP and Director, Junan Zhang, age 56
Director, Wong Wai Ming, age 54
President; Executive Director, Lu Yimin, age 49
Director, Timpson Chung Shui Ming, age 60
Auditors: PricewaterhouseCoopers

LOCATIONS

HQ: China Unicom (Hong Kong) Ltd
75th Floor, The Center, 99 Queen' s Road Central,
Phone: (852) 2121 3220 **Fax:** (852) 2121 3232
Web: www.chinaunicom.com.hk

PRODUCTS/OPERATIONS

2009 Sales

	% of total
Fixed-line	53
Mobile	47
Total	**100**

COMPETITORS

Beijing Mobile
China Mobile
China Mobile Communications
China Telecom Corporation Limited
China Tietong
Hunan Telecom
Hutchison Whampoa
Pacnet
Shanghai Mobile

HISTORICAL FINANCIALS

Company Type: Public

Income Statement FYE: December 31

	REVENUE ($ mil.)	NET INCOME ($ mil.)	NET PROFIT MARGIN	EMPLOYEES
12/12	39,928	1,138	2.9%	218,598
12/11	33,230	671	2.0%	297,210
12/10	25,987	584	2.2%	310,030
12/09	22,546	1,399	6.2%	321,772
12/08	21,822	4,969	22.8%	205,200
Annual Growth	16.3%	(30.8%)	—	1.6%

2012 Year-End Financials

Debt ratio: 4.4%
Return on equity: 3.4%
Cash ($ mil.): 2,932
Current ratio: 0.16
Long-term debt ($ mil.): 461
No. of shares (mil.): —
Dividends
Yield: 0.8%
Payout: 474.4%
Market value ($ mil.): —

	STOCK PRICE ($) FY Close	P/E High	P/E Low	PER SHARE ($) Earnings	Dividends	Book Value
12/12	16.29	2	1	0.05	0.14	1.43
12/11	21.13	3	2	0.03	0.00	1.39
12/10	14.25	2	1	0.02	0.47	1.33
12/09	13.11	1	0	0.06	0.26	1.28
12/08	12.20	0	0	0.21	0.29	1.27
Annual Growth	7.5%	—	—	(30.7%)	(16.0%)	2.8%

China United Network Communications Ltd

LOCATIONS

HQ: China United Network Communications Ltd
29th Floor, No. 1033, Changning Road, Changning District, Shanghai 200050
Phone: (86) 21 52732228 **Fax:** (86) 21 52732220
Web: www.chinaunicom-a.com

HISTORICAL FINANCIALS

Company Type: Public

Income Statement FYE: December 31

	REVENUE ($ mil.)	NET INCOME ($ mil.)	NET PROFIT MARGIN	EMPLOYEES
12/12	41,105	379	0.9%	0
12/11	34,239	224	0.7%	215,954
12/10	26,726	186	0.7%	215,815
12/09	23,194	459	2.0%	216,772
12/08	22,387	2,893	12.9%	204,354
Annual Growth	16.4%	(39.8%)	—	—

2012 Year-End Financials

Debt ratio: 3.2%
Return on equity: 3.3%
Cash ($ mil.): 2,938
Current ratio: 0.16
Long-term debt ($ mil.): 406
No. of shares (mil.): —
Dividends
Yield: —
Payout: —
Market value ($ mil.): —

Christian Dior SA

This is not your grandmere's Christian Dior. Under now former chief designer John Galliano the fashion house had gone from outfitting ladies who lunch to women who rock. The holding company's operating unit Christian Dior Couture designs and makes some of the world's most coveted haute couture as well as luxury ready-to-wear fashion and accessories for men and women. Christian Dior operates more than 235 boutiques worldwide with plans to open more. Don't let the pious name fool you though; Christian Dior is a wolf in very tight-fitting clothing due to its roughly 42% stake in luxury goods giant LVMH. Chairman and LVMH CEO Bernard Arnault and family control Christian Dior.

With the global economy apparently on the mend Dior enjoyed strong growth across all of its businesses in 2010. Indeed sales exceeded E21 billion (nearly $28 billion) an increase of 19% vs. 2009. The company's net profit increased by more than 70% over the same period. Even couture that most economically sensitive of businesses posted double-digit sales growth. Other strong performers included leather goods and men's and women's ready-to-wear apparel. Buoyed by the strong performance Dior plans to continue to open new boutiques and remodel existing shops.

Following its strong performance in 2010 Dior went through the trauma of separating itself from its famed money-making designer Galliano in March 2011. The move was spurred by allegations that he had racially abused Jewish patrons in a Parisian bar in February. Soon after the designer's ouster actress and the face of the Miss Dior Cherie perfume ad campaign Natalie Portman issued a statement that distanced herself from the designer.

In the wake of Galliano's firing Dior showed his latest (and possibly last) fall-winter 2011-2012 ready-to-wear collection in an uncharacteristically low-key presentation at a Paris townhouse in March. The event showcased just 19 looks –fewer than half of what would typically be shown on the catwalk. Viewed as a bold move letting Galliano go places Christian Dior in a position to search for yet another creative talent. Before Galliano came aboard in 1996 Christian Dior was known for its conservative cut. Galliano had quickly turned the staid fashion house on its head with his own brand of controversy –one Galliano line was based on the rags worn by homeless people.

Capitalizing on its brand's reputation for timeless elegance the company has been busy growing its network of swank boutiques in markets such as Russia Asia and the Middle East. It plans to continue building its presence in these regions specifically targeting China and Singapore.

HISTORY

Christian Dior a trained architect opened his own fashion house in 1947 with the backing of flamboyant textile king Marcel Boussac. Dior brightened up a bleak postwar Paris in 1948 when he launched his "New Look" designs. After years of slim cuts (to conserve fabric) and drab colors Dior's looks were feminine glamorous and opulent (skirts often used 40 or more yards of fabric).

Dior opened a store in New York in 1948 and pioneered the concept of licensing with hosiery and ties. Dior died unexpectedly from a stroke in 1957 and was succeeded by 21-year-old assistant Yves Saint-Laurent. By 1960 when Marc Bohan succeeded Saint-Laurent the house of Dior had dressed such famous women as Brigitte Bardot Marlene Dietrich and Eva Peron.

But mismanagement by Boussac took its toll and the company sold its trademark for perfume and cosmetics –potentially its most lucrative licenses –to Moet-Hennessy in 1972. Boussac drained the profits from Dior to finance his company's other struggling divisions and in 1978 the Boussac group was purchased by (also struggling) textile and retailing company Agache-Willot. Agache-Willot wound up in the hands of the French government with the dubious distinction of being France's largest bankruptcy since the war.

In 1984 ambitious but little-known real estate executive Bernard Arnault beat out several more prominent suitors to buy Agache-Willot from the French government; he put up $15 million of his own money and $45 million from investors and renamed the company Financiere Agache. He then laid off 9000 people sold factories and made the company profitable within three years.

Christian Dior SA was born in 1988 when Arnault sold 42% of it to the public to finance his victorious battle for control of newly formed luxury goods conglomerate LVMH Moet Hennessy Louis Vuitton. Meanwhile Arnault had to deal with the fact that Christian Dior's traditional business Dior Couture was losing its luster. Part of the problem was overlicensing –more than 250 licenses existed for everything Dior from sunglasses to sheets. What's more Dior Couture simply looked dowdy compared to other hot young designers.

To turn things around Arnault lured Beatrice Bongibault from Chanel and made her managing director of Dior Couture. She quickly cut nearly a quarter of the company's licenses and centralized control of those that remained improving quality and cutting costs. (Her techniques were quickly copied by other design houses.) She also replaced designer Bohan with Italian Gianfranco Ferre in 1989. Arnault ousted Bongibault in 1990. Dior Couture accused her of embezzlement but the parties settled out of court.

Dior Couture bought back most of its remaining licenses in 1994 and 1995. In 1996 Dior Couture turned to controversial designer John Galliano –already head of LVMH's house of Givenchy –to capitalize on the publicity that followed Galliano's eccentric sometimes bizarre creations.

Aided by its retail expansion Dior Couture bounced back from a 1997 loss with a profit in 1998. The fashion house opened 19 more boutiques in 2000 and introduced the Dior Homme collection of menswear –designed by Hedi Slimane –in January 2001 (now designed by Kris Van Assche).

In 2005 the company launched the perfume brands Miss Dior Cherie and Dior Homme. Christian Dior reclaimed the Baby Dior business in 2006 which had been operated under license. The fashion house celebrated its 60th anniversary in 2007.

In 2008 Christian Dior Couture acquired 87% of the shares of John Galliano SA a company specializing in the creation and concession of fashions and luxury items by the designer. To mark its entrance into the Chinese market the company hosted a major exhibition in Beijing.

Following allegations of anti-Semitic remarks made by its longtime and lucrative designer Christian Dior in March 2011 parted ways with Galliano.

EXECUTIVES

Chairman and CEO, Bernard Arnault, age 64
Vice Chairman, Eric Guerlain, age 73
Group Managing Director, Sidney Toledano, age 62
Vice Chairman, Eric Guerlain, age 73
Director, Denis Dalibot, age 67
Director, Antoine Bernheim, age 88
Group Managing Director, Sidney Toledano, age 62
Director, Segolene Gallienne
Director, Jaime de Marichalar Y Saenz De Tejada, age 49
Director, Pierre Gode, age 68
Director, Christian De Labriffe, age 65
Director, Alessandro Vallarino Gancia, age 45
Director, Renaud Donnedieu de Vabres, age 58
Auditors: Mazars&Guerard

LOCATIONS

HQ: Christian Dior SA
30, avenue Montaigne, Paris 75008
Phone: (33) 1 44 13 22 22
Web: www.dior-finance.com

2010 Sales

	% of total
Asia	
Japan	9
Rest of	25
Europe	
France	13
Rest of	22
US	22
Other	9
Total	**100**

PRODUCTS/OPERATIONS

Selective retailing	**25**				
Perfumes & cosmetics	15				
Wines & spirits		15			
Watches & jewelry			5		
Couture				4	
Total					100

Principal Holdings
Christian Dior Couture SA
- Accessories
- Haute couture
- Luxury ready-to-wear

LVMH Moet Hennessy Louis Vuitton (42%)
- Fragrances and cosmetics
- Leather and fashion
- Retailing
- Watches and jewelry
- Wine and spirits

COMPETITORS

Armani
Bill Blass
Calvin Klein
Chanel
Dolce & Gabbana
Escada
Estee Lauder
Gianni Versace
Hermes
Kering
Krizia
L' Oreal
Oscar de la Renta
Prada
Puig
Ralph Lauren
Richemont
Salvatore Ferragamo
Shiseido
Valentino Fashion
Vera Wang

HISTORICAL FINANCIALS

Company Type: Public

Income Statement

FYE: April 30

	REVENUE ($ mil.)	NET INCOME ($ mil.)	NET PROFIT MARGIN	EMPLOYEES
04/13	39,076	1,871	4.8%	108,546
04/12*	11,888	520	4.4%	100,755
12/11	31,855	1,654	5.2%	101,154
12/10	28,270	1,687	6.0%	86,818
12/09	25,562	1,001	3.9%	80,510
Annual Growth	15.2%	23.2%	—	10.5%

*Fiscal year change

2013 Year-End Financials

Debt ratio: 20.0%
Return on equity: 13.5%
Cash ($ mil.): 2,517
Current ratio: 1.41
Long-term debt ($ mil.): 6,146
No. of shares (mil.): 178
Dividends
Yield: 0.0%
Payout: 7.0%
Market value ($ mil.): 7,411

	STOCK PRICE ($) FY Close	P/E High/Low		PER SHARE ($) Earnings	Dividends	Book Value
04/13	41.50	10	9	10.33	0.73	80.29
04/12*	37.75	29	25	2.86	0.59	74.50
Annual Growth	9.9%	—	—	53.5%	7.3%	2.5%

*Fiscal year change

Chugoku Bank, Ltd. (The)

Chugoku Bank hopes to attract individuals and businesses who are looking to bank on the sunny side. The Japanese regional bank serves the Okayama prefecture (known as "the sunny land") and neighboring areas (Ehime Hiroshima Hyogo Kagawa and Tottori) through some 165 offices and a network of ATMs. The bank also has overseas operations with offices in China Hong Kong Singapore and the US. Chugoku Bank subsidiaries and affiliates are involved in such businesses as asset management credit cards credit guarantees financing leasing and pre-paid cards.

EXECUTIVES

Chairman, Fumihiro Izumi
Senior Managing Director, Hiromichi Tsuboi
President and Director, Masato Miyanaga
Managing Director, Hajime Aoyama
Managing Director, Yoshinori Yamamoto
Managing Director, Hiroyuki Hanazawa
Managing Director, Yoshimasa Asama
Auditors: KPMGAZSA&Co.

LOCATIONS

HQ: Chugoku Bank, Ltd. (The)
1-15-20 Marunouchi, Kita-ku, Okayama 700-8628
Phone: (81) 86 223 3111
Web: www.chugin.co.jp

COMPETITORS

Awa Bank
Hiroshima Bank
Hyakujushi Bank
Mitsubishi UFJ Financial Group
Mizuho Financial
Norinchukin Bank
Resona
Sumitomo Mitsui
Sumitomo Trust and Banking

HISTORICAL FINANCIALS

Company Type: Public

Income Statement

FYE: March 31

	ASSETS ($ mil.)	NET INCOME ($ mil.)	INCOME AS % OF ASSETS	EMPLOYEES
03/13	72,051	195	0.3%	3,570
03/12	77,278	232	0.3%	3,574
03/11	75,126	52	0.1%	3,583
03/10	64,948	109	0.2%	3,523
03/09	59,856	84	0.1%	3,442
Annual Growth	4.7%	23.4%	—	0.9%

2013 Year-End Financials

Return on assets: 0.2%
Return on equity: 4.5%
Long-term debt ($ mil.): —
No. of shares (mil.): 203
Sales ($ mil): 1,245
Dividends
Yield: —
Payout: —
Market value ($ mil.): —

Chuo Mitsui Trust & Banking Co., Ltd.

LOCATIONS

HQ: Chuo Mitsui Trust & Banking Co., Ltd.
1-4-1 Marunouchi, Chiyoda-ku, Tokyo 100-8233
Phone: (81) 3 3286 1111
Web: www.chuomitsui.co.jp

HISTORICAL FINANCIALS

Company Type: Public

Income Statement

FYE: March 31

	ASSETS ($ mil.)	NET INCOME ($ mil.)	INCOME AS % OF ASSETS	EMPLOYEES
03/12	150,528	246	0.2%	7,975
03/11	169,396	602	0.4%	7,938
03/10	158,302	508	0.3%	7,973
03/09	151,175	(969)	—	7,970
03/08	142,812	648	0.5%	8,230
Annual Growth	1.3%	(21.5%)	—	(0.8%)

2012 Year-End Financials

Return on assets: 0.1%
Return on equity: 2.7%
Long-term debt ($ mil.): —
No. of shares (mil.): —
Sales ($ mil): 3,494
Dividends
Yield: —
Payout: —
Market value ($ mil.): —

CNH Industrial N.V.

LOCATIONS

HQ: CNH Industrial N.V.
250 Via Nizza, Turin 10126
Phone: (39) 011 0062186 **Fax:** (39) 011 0061346
Web: www.cnhindustrial.com

HISTORICAL FINANCIALS

Company Type: Public

Income Statement FYE: December 31

	REVENUE ($ mil.)	NET INCOME ($ mil.)	NET PROFIT MARGIN	EMPLOYEES
12/12	33,985	1,067	3.1%	68,257
12/11	31,416	807	2.6%	66,998
12/10	28,563	456	1.6%	62,123
Annual Growth	9.1%	52.9%	—	4.8%

2012 Year-End Financials

Debt ratio: 69.8%
Return on equity: 17.0%
Cash ($ mil.): 6,077
Current ratio: 9.60
Long-term debt ($ mil.): 27,195
No. of shares (mil.): 1,222
Dividends
Yield: —
Payout: —
Market value ($ mil.): —

	STOCK PRICE ($) FY Close	P/E High/Low		PER SHARE ($) Earnings	Dividends	Book Value
12/12	0.00	—	—	0.87	0.00	5.32
12/11	0.00	—	—	0.63	0.00	5.39
Annual Growth	—	—	—	17.8%	—	(0.7%)

Cnooc Ltd.

CNOOC Limited manages China's offshore oil and gas exploration and production activities in partnership with international oil and gas firms. Under Chinese government-regulated production sharing contracts CNOOC Limited has the sole right to acquire up to 51% of any successful discovery offshore China made by foreign partners. CNOOC Limited has 2.6 billion barrels of oil equivalent in estimated proved reserves primarily in the South China Sea. CNOOC Limited is also engaged in oil refining natural gas processing and refined products marketing. The oil producer has a net production of 469.4 barrels of oil equivalent per day. To grow it global assets in 2012 the company agreed to buy Nexen for $15 billion.

The deal gives CNOOC access to major oil and gas plays including Canadian oil sands and conventional fields in western Canada the North Sea the Gulf of Mexico and Nigeria.

Growin its North American assets in 2010 the company paid about $1.1 billion for a one-third stake in Chesapeake Energy's 600000 oil and natural gas acres in the Eagle Ford shale project in South Texas. It boosted its shale holdings further in 2011 agreeing to spend $570 million to buy a one-third stake in Chesapeake Energy's drilling assets in a shale oil field in northeast Colorado and southeast Wyoming. It also bought oil sands producer OPTI Canada for $2.1 billion.

In another major expansion that year the company acquired a 33% stake in an onshore oilfield in Uganda from Tullow Oil for $1.5 billion.

CNOOC Limited is 64%-owned by China National Offshore Oil Corporation.

EXECUTIVES

Chairman, Chengyu Fu, age 62
Senior Vice President, Wei Chen, age 55
Vice Chairman, Yang Hua, age 52
EVP, Liu Jian, age 55
Compliance Officer and Executive Director, Guangqi Wu, age 56
Executive Vice President, Bi Chen, age 52
Vice President; General Manager - CNOOC International Limited, Zhi Fang, age 51
Executive Vice President, Guangyu Yuan, age 55
SVP and General Manager CNOOC China Limited Shanghai Branch, Guohua Zhang, age 54
Chief Geologist EVP and General Manager Exploration Department, Weilin Zhu, age 58
President; Chief Executive Officer; Executive Director, Fanrong Li, age 51
Company Secretary, Yongzhi Jiang
Chief Financial Officer; Joint Company Secretary, Hua Zhong
Joint Company Secretary, Sik Tsue
General Counsel, Liguo Zhao
Non-Executive Director, Shouwei Zhou, age 63
Vice Chairman, Yang Hua, age 52
Independent Non-Executive Director, Sung Hong Chiu, age 66
Compliance Officer and Executive Director, Guangqi Wu, age 56
Independent Non-Executive Director, Aloysius H. Y. Tse, age 65
Non-Executive Director, Xinghe Cao, age 64
Non-Executive Director, Zhenfang Wu, age 61
Independent Non-Executive Director, Edgar W. K. Cheng, age 70
Independent Non-Executive Director, Lawrence J. Lau, age 69
Independent Non-Executive Director, Tao Wang, age 83
President CEO and Director, Fanrong Li, age 50
Auditors: Ernst&Young

LOCATIONS

HQ: Cnooc Ltd.
65th Floor, Bank of China Tower, 1 Garden Road,
Phone: (852) 2213 2500 **Fax:** (852) 2525 9322
Web: www.cnoocltd.com

2007 Sales

	% of total
China	86
Other	14
Total	**100**

PRODUCTS/OPERATIONS

2007 Sales

	% of total
Production sharing	47
Independent	35
Trading	18
Total	**100**

Selected Subsidiaries

CNOOC China Limited (China)
CNOOC Finance (2002) Limited (British Virgin Islands)
CNOOC Finance (2003) Limited (British Virgin Islands)
CNOOC International Limited (British Virgin Islands)
CNOOC Offshore Oil (Singapore) Pte. Ltd.

COMPETITORS

Anadarko Petroleum
Apache
BP
Chevron
Exxon Mobil
PetroChina
Royal Dutch Shell
Sinopec Corp.

HISTORICAL FINANCIALS

Company Type: Public

Income Statement FYE: December 31

	REVENUE ($ mil.)	NET INCOME ($ mil.)	NET PROFIT MARGIN	EMPLOYEES
12/12	39,720	10,216	25.7%	10,063
12/11	38,279	11,161	29.2%	5,377
12/10	27,770	8,254	29.7%	4,650
12/09	15,406	4,318	28.0%	4,019
12/08	18,462	6,503	35.2%	3,584
Annual Growth	21.1%	12.0%	—	29.4%

2012 Year-End Financials

Debt ratio: 2.0%
Return on equity: 22.1%
Cash ($ mil.): 11,535
Current ratio: 2.07
Long-term debt ($ mil.): 4,660
No. of shares (mil.): —
Dividends
Yield: 2.2%
Payout: 2,169.1%
Market value ($ mil.): —

	STOCK PRICE ($) FY Close	P/E High/Low		PER SHARE ($) Earnings	Dividends	Book Value
12/12	220.00	4	3	0.23	4.99	1.11
12/11	174.68	4	2	0.25	0.14	0.94
12/10	238.37	4	3	0.18	4.74	0.73
12/09	155.45	5	2	0.10	4.64	0.57
12/08	95.24	4	1	0.15	4.75	0.53
Annual Growth	23.3%	—	—	11.9%	1.2%	20.6%

CNP Assurances S.A.

Running to the post office and the bank? Buy some insurance while you're out. CNP Assurances is France's top personal life insurer. In addition to life insurance and other savings products it sells health death and disability and other personal risk coverage and pensions. CNP sells its products primarily through the outlets of La Poste the French postal service and Groupe BPCE the state savings banks; together these two channels account for about 65% of CNP's sales. These partners are also shareholders in the company together owning about 35%. Another French paragovernmental organization Caisse des Depots et Consignations owns 40%.

The firm has distribution deals with France's Treasury and its civil service mutual insurance companies and such financial institutions as Mutualite Francaise the umbrella organization for France's mutual health insurers. CNP depends on these distribution networks to support sales of its retail savings offerings. It also seeks to maintain competitive pricing and product features to keep its domestic customer base stable. As economic instabilities in France and abroad have impacted the market for traditional savings life insurance products the company is working to increase sales of its higher-margin personal risk products such as long-term care funeral accident disability and illness policies.

While more than 80% of its premiums come from 14 million policyholders in the core market of Spain CNP also has operations in international markets serving another 14 million customers. It has taken stakes in neighboring countries' leading insurers as they are privatized primarily in Italy Spain and Portugal; it also has established significant operations in Brazil. The company is focusing its overseas growth gaze primarily on South America Southern Europe and the Mediterranean.

CNP is looking for both organic growth and acquisitions to meet its goals.

During 2009 CNP made good on its strategy moving into Cyprus and Greece. It paid E145 million ($191 million) for a majority stake in Marfin Insurance Holdings the insurance branch of Marfin Popular Bank Group Cyprus' second largest bank. Together the bank and CNP hold four companies with a total of more than 315 branches selling life and property insurance in the two island nations.

In 2010 the company sold stakes in one of its Portugal ventures Global Seguros to Portugese insurance company Rentipar Seguros SGPS. The move reflects CNP's focus on its bank-affiliated operations in Portugal which are conducted through a venture with Barclays Bank. The venture Barclays Vida y Pensiones also operates in Spain and Italy.

HISTORY

CNP Assurances traces its origins to three government insurance entities established in the mid-19th century. Caisse nationale d'assurance en cas d'accident ("accident insurance") was formed in 1868. Caisse nationale d'assurance en cas de deces ("death and disability insurance") was formed in 1848 while Caisse de retraite pour la vieillesse ("retirement pensions") followed two years later. These two organizations were merged in 1949 forming Caisse nationale d'assurance sur la vie. Ten years later it was merged with the government's accident insurance bureau to form Caisse Nationale de Prevoyance ("provident society"). CNP was put under the domain of the French government's investment banking arm Caisse des Depots et Consignations (CDC).

Over the years CNP earned a reputation for specializing in certain risks introducing a variety of life and personal risk insurance and pension and savings products. During the 1980s the company enjoyed a healthy growth rate around 20% annually as more French individuals and companies began investing in insurance products.

In 1987 CNP became a national public establishment making it independent from though still owned by the government. The next year the company teamed with Centre National des Caisses d'Epargne et de Prevoyance (now La Caisse Nationale des Caisses d'Epargne or Caisses d'Epargne) to form Ecureuil-Vie a joint venture to sell CNP's insurance and savings products in the national savings banks. That year it partnered with Portugal's Caixa Geral de Depositos to create new products.

In the early 1990s CNP was among several entities the government announced it would privatize. To prepare for the change the company reorganized and became CNP Assurances; the government sold a large chunk of the firm to CDC La Poste and Caisses d'Epargne reducing its stake to 42%. During this time CNP passed rival Union des Assurances de Paris (now part of AXA) to become France's top life insurer.

Privatization lurched along until 1995 when it was put on hold for elections; the Socialist government that came to power was less enthusiastic about the sale of government assets than its predecessor. The process hit another snag two years later when some workers protested fearing they'd lose their status as civil servants and the perks associated with it. Also in 1997 CNP became the major shareholder of Polish life insurer Polisa-Zycie when it raised its stake from 26% (purchased 1996) to 46%. By 1998 privatization was back on track and the government sold a 22% stake in CNP to the public. CDC La Poste and Caisses d'Epargne raised their interests to their current levels. Before the year's end CNP bought majority stakes in Portuguese insurers Global and Global Vida.

Expansion abroad continued in 1999 when CNP announced plans to set up operations in China. That year it teamed with the UK's Prudential for cobranded insurance products. In 2000 the company extended its selling arrangement with Caisses d'Epargne to 2005. In 2003 it sold off its share of Italian bancassurance company Carivita.

EXECUTIVES

CEO, Gilles Benoist, age 65
Director Management and Innovation, Jean-Pierre Walbaum, age 67
Director International Operations and Deputy CEO, Xavier Larnaudie-Eiffel
Director Finance and Deputy CEO, Antoine Lissowski
Director Redaction, Agathe Sanson
Head of Investor Relations, Jim Root
Manager Investor Relations, Jean-Yves Icole
Director Programmes Organisation and Information Systems and Deputy CEO, Michel Bois, age 53
Director Internal Auditing and Quality Mission and Secretary, Huguette Rellier, age 58
Auditors: KPMGAudit

LOCATIONS

HQ: CNP Assurances S.A.
4, place Raoul Dautry, Paris, Cedex 15 75716
Phone: (33) 1 42 18 97 73
Web: www.cnp.fr

2010 Premiums

	% of total
France	81
Italy	8
Brazil	8
Spain	2
Other	1
Total	**100**

PRODUCTS/OPERATIONS

2010 Revenues

Premiums	72	
Total	**0**	**100**

2010 Premiums

Life insurance	63
Financial instruments	29

Selected Subsidiaries

Barclays Vida y Pensiones (50% Spain)
Caixa Seguros (52% insurance Brazil)
CNP Europe Life Ltd (Ireland)
CNP Holding Brasil
CNP IAM
CNP Seguros de Vida (76% insurance Argentina)
CNP UniCredit Vita (57% insurance Italy)
CNP Vida (94% insurance Spain)
Global (83% insurance Portugal)
Global Vida (83% insurance Portugal)
ITV
La Banque Postale Prevoyance (50% insurance)
Marfin Insurance Holdings Ltd. (50% insurance Cyprus)
Previposte

COMPETITORS

AXA
Allianz
April Group
Assurances Generales de France
BNP Paribas
Credit Agricole
Eureko
Groupama
ING

HISTORICAL FINANCIALS

Company Type: Public

Income Statement FYE: December 31

	ASSETS ($ mil.)	NET INCOME ($ mil.)	INCOME AS % OF ASSETS	EMPLOYEES
12/12	465,555	1,253	0.3%	4,842
12/11	415,211	1,127	0.3%	3,077
12/10	427,755	1,405	0.3%	4,680
12/09	434,874	1,446	0.3%	4,628
12/08	376,875	1,021	0.3%	0
Annual Growth	5.4%	5.3%	—	—

2012 Year-End Financials

Return on assets: 0.2%
Return on equity: 7.2%
Long-term debt ($ mil.): —
No. of shares (mil.): 642
Sales ($ mil): 57,367
Dividends
Yield: 0.0%
Payout: 25.3%
Market value ($ mil.): 5,074

	STOCK PRICE ($) FY Close	P/E High	P/E Low	PER SHARE ($) Earnings	Dividends	Book Value
12/12	7.90	10	6	1.92	0.49	29.03
Annual Growth	—	—	—	—	—	—

Co-operative Bank p.l.c. (The) (United Kingdom)

LOCATIONS

HQ: Co-operative Bank p.l.c. (The) (United Kingdom)
1 Balloon Street, Manchester M60 4EP
Phone: (44) 161 832 3456 **Fax:** (44) 161 829 4475
Web: www.co-operativebank.co.uk

HISTORICAL FINANCIALS

Company Type: Public

Income Statement FYE: December 31

	ASSETS ($ mil.)	NET INCOME ($ mil.)	INCOME AS % OF ASSETS	EMPLOYEES
12/12	79,905	(820)	—	7,754
12/11	75,629	74	0.1%	8,528
12/10*	70,771	56	0.1%	8,746
01/09	22,796	20	0.1%	3,990
01/08	25,638	6	0.0%	4,071
Annual Growth	25.5%	—	—	13.8%

*Fiscal year change

2012 Year-End Financials

Return on assets: (-1.0%)
Return on equity: (-25.0%)
Long-term debt ($ mil.): —
No. of shares (mil.): —
Sales ($ mil): 2,641
Dividends
Yield: —
Payout: —
Market value ($ mil.): —

Colas SA Boulogne

Colas paves the way for drivers worldwide. The global road construction group was founded on and named after the creation of a revolutionary technical process —cold asphalt. Colas provides construction and maintenance services for infrastructure projects (roads airports ports railroads) urban redevelopment projects and recreation facilities around the world. In addition to its work on roads and related projects the company produces construction materials including concrete and aggregates from an international network of quarries gravel pits and asphalt plants. Colas also provides complementary services including design and engineering concessions and soil treatment. Bouygues owns 97% of Colas.

The group's largest business segment (about 80% of sales) is road construction and maintenance which includes work on highways airport runways bicycle paths ports and other project types. Colas also provides civil engineering services and environmental projects such as waterproofing of buildings soil remediation and industrial waste containment and recycling. Its Colas Rail subsidiary provides railway engineering construction and maintenance services primarily in France and the UK.

In addition to concrete and aggregates Colas produces emulsions and binders to complement its road building activities. Colas also develops new products. Among these are Rugosoft an asphalt concrete that cuts traffic noise; and Vegecol a binder that uses plant-based materials in place of bitumen.

The economic and building downturn had an impact on all construction companies and Colas was no exception. The available pool of projects dried up as funding became scarce especially in the public sector. Further exacerbating matters an atypically harsh winter shut down work on Colas' European jobs for two months in 2009. The company expects funding from government stimulus packages to begin kicking in to create new jobs. Colas has also continued to invest in its growth: In the past couple of years it has acquired a French bitumen refinery a Canadian road builder and stakes in other producers.

HISTORY

Colas got its start in 1924 as a division of Societe Generale d'Enterprises (SGE now known as VINCI) in a move to commercially exploit cold asphalt which had just been invented for use in road surfacing. Originally called Cold Spray it was later renamed Colas (short for cold asphalt) to differentiate it from imitations. Sales of the product quickly grew in France and demand spread to Algeria Poland Romania and Tunisia prompting SGE to open a new Colas production facility in Grand-Couronne in 1926.

Two years later it added five more in Bergerac Lyon Montlucon and Port St.-Louis-du-Rhone in France and in Algiers Algeria. The growth was more than SGE could handle so it teamed up with Royal Dutch Shell to form Societe Routiere Colas (SRC) in 1929. Led by Alexandre Giros the new company operated in France and French colonial territories while Shell worked to develop other Colas companies around the world.

Georges Mathieu replaced Giros as president in 1932. He expanded the company's operations beyond asphalt and emulsions manufacturing and invested the profits into research. SGE sold its shares in the company but Shell plowed its profits back into Colas enabling the company to double its capital by the mid-1930s. By the end of the decade Colas was offering a wide variety of roadwork services ranging from the supply and transport of raw materials to road construction.

Before the onset of WWII Colas had 19 factories in France and seven more in Algeria Morocco Senegal and Martinique. The company's Dutch ownership nearly caused its demise when the Germans invaded France. Colas was declared an enemy possession and its operations were shut down.

After the war Mathieu regained control of the company but the job of repairing was left to his successor Henry Forien who was named CEO in 1948. Forien added new facilities in France and northern Africa and turned branch operations into subsidiaries including Colas du Maroc (1949) and Colas d'Algerie (1950).

The company increased its road construction operations and developed new products and techniques during the 1950s. Shell sold a majority share to Societe Parisienne Raveau-Cartier which was led by Georges Raveau who took charge of Colas when Forien died in 1959. Under Raveau Colas went public on the Paris stock exchange in 1961. Through acquisitions the company began expanding beyond French-speaking countries during the mid-1960s including moves into Germany Kenya Nigeria and Spain. Its North American appearance came with the purchase of two Canadian companies in 1963; the two merged to become Sintra in 1974.

French construction company Bouygues took a majority stake in Colas during the 1980s and created a partnership with Shell that set the groundwork for the company to acquire the various other Colas operations formerly backed by Shell. The arrangement also aligned Colas with two of its French competitors Screg and Sacer both owned by Bouygues.

Colas acquired Sacer and its subsidiaries in 1993. The following year it acquired the remainder of the Shell-controlled companies with Colas trademarks. It purchased Screg in 1996. The company diversified into waterproofing and railroad works in 1999 with the purchase of Smac and Seco-Rail respectively. The following year Bouygues increased its stake in Colas to 96%. Also in 2000 Colas bolstered its position in North America with the purchase of three road construction companies.

The next year the company slowed down its acquisitions but did acquire Virginia-based road-building company Branscome and boosted its aggregates unit by acquiring a major quarry in France.

In 2007 the company acquired a 70% stake in Croatia-based road construction company Cesta-Varazdin. The purchase strengthened Colas' presence in central Europe a target market for growth.

EXECUTIVES

Board Member; Managing Director France, Thierry Genestar
President Colas Ile-de-France-Normandie, Jean-Paul Brossard
Chief Legal Officer, Alain Clotte
Finance, Laurent Le Boulc'h
President Colas Centre-Ouest, Serge Body
President Screg Ile-de-France-Normandie, Bruno Chambon
President Screg Sud-Est, Phillipe Guilmant
President Screg Est, Patrice Haltebourg
President Smac, Christian Lavedrine
Managing Director France, Christian de Pins
President Colas Rhone-Alpes, Philippe Decarnin
President Sacer Sud-Est, Jean-Pierre Belier
External Relations, Xavier Lepercq
President Colas Inc., Georges Ausseil
Managing Director North America, Louis Gabanna, age 58
President Colas Midi-Mediterranee, Daniel Ducroix
Accounting, Gilles Nicolle
President Sacer Paris-Nord-Est, Thierry Caussemille
Environment, Henri Molleron
President Screg Sud-Ouest, Philippe Durand
President Screg Nord-Picardie, Pascal Maridet
President Sacer Atlantique, Christian Raimondi
President Sintra, Normand Bedard
VP ColasCanada; President Works Alberta, Jacques Michel
Equipment, Phillippe Brissonneau
Managing Director Europe, Alain Benquet
President Terus Construction, Jean Vidal
President Aximum, Christophe Mitridati
Deputy Managing Director, Jacques Pastor
Human Resources, Philippe Tournier
Risk and Insurance, Jean-Yves Bignon
Building/Civil Engineering Techniques, Philippe Raffin
Corporate Communication, Sophie Sadeler
President Colas Nord-Picardie, Martine Bourdon
President Colas Est, Bernard Sala
President Colas Sud-Ouest, Christophe Da Poian
Chairman Chief Executive Officer of Bouygues Construction, Yves Gabriel
Board Member; Managing Director France, Thierry Genestar
General Secretary and Director, Thierry Montouche
Director, Olivier Bouygues, age 60
Director, Patrick Le Lay, age 70
Director, Christian Balmes
Director, Jean-Francois Guillemin, age 61
Director, Philippe Marien, age 56
Director, Francois Bertiere
Auditors: SalustroReydel

LOCATIONS

HQ: Colas SA Boulogne
7, place Rene-Clair, Boulogne-Billancourt, Cedex 92653
Phone: (33) 1 47 61 75 00 **Fax:** (33) 1 47 61 76 00
Web: www.colas.com

2009 Sales

	% of total
Europe	
Mainland	54
Overseas	4
Other	17
North	17
Other	8
Total	**100**

PRODUCTS/OPERATIONS

2009 Sales

	% of total
Roadworks	65
Materials	13
Civil engineering pipes &	7
Waterproofing	5
Railways	4
Safety &	3
Building	3
Total	**100**

COMPETITORS

CEMEX
EIFFAGE
FCC Barcelona
Ferrovial
Holcim
Italcementi
Lafarge
Peter Kiewit Sons'
Skanska
Tarmac
VINCI

HISTORICAL FINANCIALS

Company Type: Public

Income Statement FYE: December 31

	REVENUE ($ mil.)	NET INCOME ($ mil.)	NET PROFIT MARGIN	EMPLOYEES
12/12	17,205	398	2.3%	62,806
12/11	16,081	434	2.7%	62,680
12/10	15,630	299	1.9%	68,895
12/09	16,726	557	3.3%	71,318
12/08	17,880	685	3.8%	73,594
Annual Growth	(1.0%)	(12.7%)	—	(3.9%)

2012 Year-End Financials

Debt ratio: 9.3%	No. of shares (mil.): 32
Return on equity: 12.0%	Dividends
Cash ($ mil.): 573	Yield: —
Current ratio: 0.97	Payout: —
Long-term debt ($ mil.): 340	Market value ($ mil.): —

Commerzbank AG (Germany, Fed. Rep.)

Sprechen sie Commerz? The second-largest bank in Germany (behind Deutsche Bank) Commerzbank provides retail and commercial banking services from approximately 1200 branches nationwide and from offices in another 50 countries. The bank serves about 15 million customers primarily individuals and small to midsized businesses in Germany and abroad. Mortgage specialist Eurohypo provides commercial and residential real estate lending and public financing services in Europe and the US. Since Dresdner Bank merged into Commerzbank in 2009 the company has been retooling itself and focusing on its core banking operations.

It took two years for Commerzbank to fully integrate Dresdner Bank and its former Dresdner Kleinwort investment banking operations. It was the largest integration project in German banking history.

As a result of the merger Commerzbank scaled back some of its operations and is focused on becoming a leaner more efficient company. It is in the process of selling several private banking divisions including units acquired in the Dresdner Bank transaction. Units sold include Dresdner Bank of Switzerland Kleinwort Benson Private Bank Dresdner Monaco and Austria's Privatinvest Bank. Additionally Commerzbank has shut down or sold investment banking and securities lending units.

In 2010 the company continued to cut non-core assets selling its Montrada credit card processing unit to Equens and its Commerzbank International Trust Singapore fund management unit to Trident Trust. The company also is seeking buyers for Eurohypo (though finding a buyer for the troubled firm may be difficult).

The financial market and economic crisis dragged down performance of Commerzbank during the recession. However by 2010 Commerzbank returned to profit after posting losses in 2009. The increase in profit was attributed to net trading income and lower loan loss provisions. Charges connected to the integration of Dresdner Bank also were not a factor in 2010. With the integration behind Commerzbank it expects to realize synergies and reduce costs helping increase profits even more. The company also plans to reduce risk as a whole by scaling back its activity in commercial real estate and public finance.

As Commerzbank's performance improves one big goal is to repay the German government for the aid it received during the market turmoil. In 2008 the global economic crisis hit Germany and Commerzbank received a government bailout of E8 billion ($11 billion) to help stimulate lending and promote consumer confidence.

The government stepped in once again in early 2009 with an injection of some E10 billion ($14 billion) to help ensure the merger between Commerzbank and Dresdner Bank. As part of the intervention in which the government assumed one-fourth ownership of the company.

In 2011 Commerzbank started a two-step process to repay the government.

HISTORY

In 1870 a group of merchants and bankers formed Commerz- und Disconto-Bank in Hamburg. Germany boomed after the Franco-Prussian War and the bank expanded quickly into Frankfurt Berlin and London. Its 1905 purchase of Berliner Bank refocused the bank on the German capital.

After WWI hyperinflation led to a rash of mergers among crippled banks; Commerz absorbed regional players including Mitteldeutsche Privat-Bank (1920) and Mitteldeutsche Creditbank (1929). In the late 1920s the bank partnered with Chase National Bank to bring foreign money into Germany. As the Depression swept Europe the government bought a majority stake and merged it with Barmer Bank-Verein. Commerz became one of Germany's six "Berliner Grossbanken".

The bank took its current name after the government sold its stake in 1940. After WWII the Allies overhauled Germany's banking system and Commerzbank was split into three regional banks in 1952. In the late 1950s the rules barring large banks expired and the Commerz trio had regrouped by 1958 minus the company's prewar eastern German offices.

After rebuilding its domestic operations in the early 1960s Commerzbank expanded into Hong Kong the UK and the US among other countries. During the 1970s it acquired stakes in a variety of nonbanking companies spurred by a government fearful that Middle Eastern oil money would take control of the country's struggling industrial giants. It also diversified its services.

Overexpansion bad loans in Latin America and a bloated staff took their toll in the early 1980s. On the verge of failure Commerzbank brought in banker Walter Seipp to lead a recovery. He cut costs and focused on profit; the bank was back in shape by 1984. It then focused on creating an "allfinanz" group lining up with such firms as insurance provider DBV Versicherungen and savings and loan Leonberger Bausparkasse.

After the Berlin Wall fell in 1989 Commerzbank moved back into eastern Germany and made forays into other Eastern European countries. During the 1990s the bank focused on asset and investment management. It bought UK pension fund manager Jupiter Tyndall Group Martingale Asset Management (US) Montgomery Asset Management (US) and other firms and opened investment management offices in Frankfurt Hong Kong London New York and Tokyo. It added money market funds when they were introduced in Germany in 1994.

In 1996 the bank was embroiled in a tax evasion scandal when regulators charged that it had helped clients move assets to Luxembourg. The company was then hit hard by the Asian financial crisis of 1998 especially after the contagion spread to Russia. But as the situation eased in 1999 Commerzbank formed a joint venture with Bangkok Land to build a mall in Bangkok. That year the company announced an alliance with Assicurazioni Generali (which owns about 9% of Commerzbank) to cross-sell their banking and insurance products.

In 2000 Commerzbank and Dresdner Bank (on the rebound from a failed merger with Deutsche Bank) began merger talks. However after German regulators sought to prevent Commerzbank's largest single shareholder Cobra Beteiligungs from exercising its voting rights the bank's share price fell and the companies could not conclude the merger of equals. Amid swirling rumors of other potential alliances Commerzbank sought to strengthen its pan-European alliances and made connections with retail brokers in Japan. (German insurance giant Allianz bought Dresdner in 2001.)

Later in 2000 Commerzbank announced a restructuring plan that included closing about 150 branches and regrouping the bank's business divisions. The next year Commerzbank entered a strategic alliance with China-based China Southern Securities.

Commerzbank's mortgage bank RheinHyp merged with Dresdner Bank's Deutsche Hypothekenbank and Deutsche Bank's Eurohypo in 2002. The combined company was named Eurohypo.

As chief executive Klaus-Peter Muller launched a more performance-driven strategy for Commerzbank and implemented an Anglo-American style of management in an effort to make the bank competitive.

Commerzbank acquired the struggling SchmidtBank in 2004 in response to government pressure for consolidation in the banking industry.

In 2006 Commerzbank which owned about 32% of Eurohypo bought Deutsche Bank's 38% stake and Dresdner Bank's 28% interest for $6.9 billion in 2006 bringing Commerzbank's ownership in the venture to some 98%.

Commerzbank acquired rival Dresdner Bank from Allianz in 2009 cementing its position as Germany's second-largest bank. Commerzbank has boosted its Central and Eastern Europe business. It acquired 60% of Ukraine-based Bank Forum in 2009 and the following year increased its stake to 89%.

EXECUTIVES

Chairman, Klaus-Peter Muller, age 69
Chairman Managing Directors, Martin Blessing, age 50
Chief Risk Officer, Stefan Schmittmann, age 57
Managing Director Private Customers, Martin Zielke, age 50
Chief Operating Officer, Frank Annuscheit, age 51
Managing Director Human Resources and Integration, Ulrich Sieber, age 48
Managing Director Corporate and Markets, Michael Reuther, age 54
Managing Director Mittelstandsbank, Markus Beumer, age 49
Chief Financial Officer, Stephan Engels, age 51
Director, Sergio Balbinot, age 52
Director, Helmut Perlet, age 64
Director, Burckhard Bergmann, age 68
Director, Nikolaus von Bomhard
Director, Edgar Meister
Deputy Chairman, Uwe Tschage, age 43
Director, Otto Happel, age 64
Director, Astrid Evers, age 49
Director, Uwe Foullong, age 53
Director, Daniel Hampel, age 49
Director, Prof Ulrich Middlemann, age 66
Director, Marcus Schenck, age 48
Director, Karin van Brummelen, age 58
Director, Alexandra Krieger, age 40
Director, Barbara Priester, age 53

Director, Hans-Hermann Altenschmidt, age 50
Director, Prof Hans-Peter Keitel, age 63
Director, Beate Hoffmann, age 51
Director, Mark Roach, age 56
Auditors: PwCDeutscheRevisionAG

LOCATIONS

HQ: Commerzbank AG (Germany, Fed. Rep.)
Kaiserplatz, Frankfurt am Main D-60261
Phone: (49) 69 136 20 **Fax:** (49) 69 28 53 89
Web: www.commerzbank.com

PRODUCTS/OPERATIONS

2010 Sales

	% of total
Interest	81
Commissions	19
Total	**100**

2010 Sales by Segment

Private Customers	30
Corporates & Markets	19
Central & Eastern Europe	8
Portfolio restructuring unit	7
Consolidation & other	3

Selected Subsidiaries and Affiliates

AFOG GmbH & Co. KG
BRE Bank Hipoteczny SA (Poland)
comdirect bank Aktiengesellschaft
Commerz (East Asia) Ltd. (Hong Kong)
Commerzbank (Eurasija) SAO (Russia)
Commerzbank Inslandsbanken Holding GmbH
Erste Europaische Pfandbrief- und Kommunalkreditbank Aktiengesellschaft in Luxemburg
European Bank for Fund Services GmbH
OLEANDRA Grundstucks-Vermietungsgesellschaft mbH&Co. Objekt Jupiter KG

COMPETITORS

BayernLB	IKB
Credit Agricole	UBS
Credit Suisse	UniCredit Bank AG
Deutsche Bank	WestLB
Deutsche Postbank	

HISTORICAL FINANCIALS

Company Type: Public

Income Statement

FYE: December 31

	ASSETS ($ mil.)	NET INCOME ($ mil.)	INCOME AS % OF ASSETS	EMPLOYEES
12/12	838,118	7	0.0%	53,601
12/11	855,958	825	0.1%	58,160
12/10	1,009,532	1,913	0.2%	59,101
12/09	1,215,989	(6,535)	—	53,231
12/08	874,081	4	0.0%	43,169
Annual Growth	(1.0%)	17.2%	—	5.6%

2012 Year-End Financials

Return on assets: 0.0%
Return on equity: 0.0%
Long-term debt ($ mil.): —
No. of shares (mil.): 582
Sales ($ mil): 25,624
Dividends
Yield: —
Payout: —
Market value ($ mil.): 1,154

	STOCK PRICE ($) FY Close	P/E High/Low		PER SHARE ($) Earnings	Dividends	Book Value
12/12	1.98	—	—	(0.53)	0.00	59.13
12/11	1.69	9	1	2.33	0.00	60.98
12/10	7.36	2	1	16.19	0.00	318.29
12/09	8.45	—	—	(63.39)	0.00	317.36
12/08	9.71	—	—	(0.00)	0.00	372.53
Annual Growth	(32.8%)	—	—	—	—	(36.9%)

Commonwealth Bank of Australia

Commonwealth Bank of Australia (CBA) one of Australia's Big Four banks offers retail and commercial banking insurance and investment services including credit cards home loans deposit accounts and mutual funds. CBA's brands include Bankwest wealth manager Colonial First State master trust services provider FirstChoice online brokerage CommSec ASB Bank which provides banking investment and financial services in New Zealand. CBA has approximately 1100 branch offices in Australia (plus approximately 3700 Australia Post locations) as well as operations that reach Asia Europe and the US. CBA is also one of the largest life insurers in Australia and a leading provider of home loans there.

Geographic Reach

CBA has a growing international presence. It operates retail banks in New Zealand (ASB) and Indonesia (Commonwealth Bank of Indonesia). It has minority investments in two banks in China and one in Vietnam. It also has banking branch offices in London New York Tokyo Hong Kong Shanghai Singapore Auckland Ho Chi Minh City and Mumbai.

Operations

In addition to banking CBA has life insurance operations in New Zealand (Sovereign) Indonesia (Commonwealth Life) and a joint venture in China called BoCommLife. Its investment products include funds offered by CBA or through its master trust product FirstChoice the largest retail platform in Australia. CBA is one of the country's largest managers of Australian funds.

Strategy

CBA is expanding at home and abroad. Its acquisition of BankWestfrom HBOS in 2008 bolstered its position in western Australia. In 2010 CBA entered the Chinese insurance market with the launch of a joint venture with Bank of Communications. The following year the bank opened branches in China India and Indonesia and bought a 20% sake in Vietnam International Bank. The bank continued to strengthen its ties to China signing a referral agreement with Agricultural Bank of China in 2011 to capture potential customers.

Customer service and business banking are also areas of focus for the bank. To improve its banking offerings the company has been migrating its retail clients to a new core operating platform. CBA has also switched from overnight batch processing to real-time banking. In business banking new office openings and personnel have helped the company grow its market share from 12% (2006) to 18% (2011).

HISTORY

The Commonwealth Bank Act of 1911 allowed banks to conduct both savings bank and central bank functions and paved the way for the founding of the Commonwealth Bank of Australia the next year. The bank initially operated through a single main office and in nearly 500 post offices in Victoria; it spread out through the entire country over the next few years.

The young bank was drafted during WWI to help the federal government organize war loans and a merchant shipping fleet. In 1919 the bank took over responsibility for issuing notes from the Federal Treasury. In 1928 it created the Commonwealth Savings Bank from its savings department. Australia —heavily indebted to British lenders — was devastated by the Great Depression. As banks failed the Commonwealth Bank picked up several other institutions including the state banks in Western Australia and New South Wales. During those years Commonwealth took on more and more of the functions of a central bank.

During WWII the bank again came to the aid of its country acting as an agent for the federal government. After the war when the Australian economy stabilized the bank began offering home loans.

After years of controversy in 1959 two bank acts formally separated the Commonwealth Bank's central bank and savings functions. The Reserve Bank of Australia took over the central bank functions in 1960 and the trading and savings operations were taken over by the new Commonwealth Development Bank later renamed the Commonwealth Banking Corporation (a subsidiary of Commonwealth Bank of Australia).

The bank concentrated on expansion and diversification in the 1970s establishing travel home insurance and financing (CBFC 1978); it set its sights on technology in the 1980s expanding its credit card offerings and introducing electronic banking.

The US's 1987 stock market crash again affected Australia's banks which spent almost a decade recovering. Luckily for Commonwealth Bank it wasn't the hardest hit.

In 1988 Commonwealth Bank moved into life insurance and investment services forming subsidiaries Commonwealth Life and Commonwealth Management Services (now together known as CBA Financial Services). In 1989 the bank bought 75% of New Zealand-based ASB Bank.

Commonwealth faced a bevy of challenges including banking deregulation that began in 1982 foreign competition and 1990's banking-law amendments allowing banks to be publicly traded. All of these factors influenced Commonwealth's decision to reorganize. The government sold approximately 30% of its stake in 1991 in part to help Commonwealth fund its acquisition of the State Bank of Victoria. The government sold the rest of its stake in 1996.

That year the company's push into electronic banking bore fruit —some 60% of all its banking transactions were online; that figure later rose to 80%. The company moved into e-commerce in 1999 putting out a call for an overseas partner; Commonwealth's stated goal was to generate one-quarter of its income outside Australia. Also that year Commonwealth and a division of The Bank of Nova Scotia joined forces to form a commodities trading group specializing in metals. In 2000 the company bought Australian financial services firm Colonial Limited.

In late 2008 the company acquired Australia-based BankWest from British bank HBOS (now part of Lloyds Banking Group). The US$1.5 billion deal included insurer and asset manager St. Andrew's (which was later sold) and bolstered CBA's presence in western Australia.

EXECUTIVES

Chairman, David J. Turner, age 69
Chief Marketing Officer, Andrew Lark
Group Executive - Financial Services; Chief Financial Officer, David Craig
General Counsel, David Cohen
Company Secretary, John D. Hatton
Group Executive Institutional Banking and Markets, Ian Saines
Group Executive Business and Private Banking, Grahame A. Petersen, $395,776 total compensation
General Manager Media and Issues Management, Bryan Fitzgerald

Head of UK and Europe, Paul Orchart
Chief Executive Colonial First State Global Asset Management, Mark J. Lazberger
Company Secretary, Carla F. Collingwood
Group Executive Enterprise Services and CIO, Michael R. Harte, $85,763 total compensation
Chief Executive and Managing Director ASB, Barbara Chapman
Chief Executive Officer; Managing Director; Executive Director, Ian Narev, age 46
Regional Head Asia, Lindsay Mann
Regional General Manager Asia, Stephen Poon
Managing Partner Edinburgh, Stuart Paul
Managing Partner Edinburgh, Angus Tulloch
Group Head Strategy, Rob Jesudason
Chief Risk Officer, Alden Toevs
Group Executive Wealth Management, Annabel F. Spring
Group Executive International Financial Services, Simon Blair
Group Executive Retail Banking Services, Ross McEwan
Director Greater Asia Equities, M. Lau
Managing Director ASB Bank Limited, Charles Pink
China Chief Representative, Paul Au
General Manager China Life ? CMG Asia Life Assurance, Alan Wood
Chief Representative India, Ravi Kushan
President Director PT Bank Commonwealth Indonesia, Nursing Nursing
General Manager Japan, Richard Harris
General Director CBA HCMC Vietnam, Danny Armstrong
General Manager Americas, Ian Phillips
Investor Relations, Louise Amos
Group Executive - Retail Banking Services, Matt Comyn
Group Executive - Human Resources, Melanie Laing
Director, Andrew M. Mohl, age 57
Director, Jane S. Hemstritch, age 60
Director, S. Carolyn H. Kay, age 52
Director, Reginald J. (Reg) Clairs, age 73
Director, Colin R. Galbraith, age 64
Director, Sir John A. Anderson, age 68
Director, Fergus D. Ryan, age 71
Director, Harrison H. Young, age 68
Non-Executive Independent Director, Brian Long
Non-Executive Independent Director, Lorna Inman
Auditors: PricewaterhouseCoopers

LOCATIONS

HQ: Commonwealth Bank of Australia
Ground Floor, Tower 1, 201 Sussex Street, Sydney, New South Wales 2000
Phone: (61) 2 9378 2000 **Fax:** (61) 2 9118 7192
Web: www.commbank.com.au

PRODUCTS/OPERATIONS

2012 Sales by Segment

	% of total
Retail banking	45
Business & private	18
Institutional banking &	14
Bankwest	10
New	7
Other	6
Total	**100**

2012 Sales

	% of total
Banking	
Interest	77
Other	23
Total	**100**

Selected Brands

ASB (New Zealand)
Bankwest
Colonial First State
CommInsure
CommSec
FirstChoice
Sovereign

COMPETITORS

AMP Limited
AXA Asia Pacific
Asteron
Australia and New Zealand Banking
HSBC
Lloyds Banking Group
Macquarie Group
National Australia Bank
QBE
Suncorp-Metway
Westpac Banking

HISTORICAL FINANCIALS

Company Type: Public

Income Statement

FYE: June 30

	ASSETS ($ mil.)	NET INCOME ($ mil.)	INCOME AS % OF ASSETS	EMPLOYEES
06/13	695,355	7,081	1.0%	44,969
06/12	731,444	7,220	1.0%	44,844
06/11	715,933	6,853	1.0%	46,060
06/10	550,925	4,827	0.9%	45,025
06/09	505,429	3,847	0.8%	44,218
Annual Growth	8.3%	16.5%	—	0.4%

2013 Year-End Financials

Return on assets: 1.0%
Return on equity: 17.8%
Long-term debt ($ mil.): —
No. of shares (mil.): 1,605
Sales ($ mil): 40,531
Dividends
Yield: 0.0%
Payout: 81.9%
Market value ($ mil.): 101,731

	STOCK PRICE ($) FY Close	P/E High	P/E Low	PER SHARE ($) Earnings	Dividends	Book Value
06/13	63.35	15	10	4.28	3.51	25.82
06/12	53.69	14	9	4.41	3.44	26.37
06/11	54.70	17	9	4.24	3.01	25.38
06/10	41.65	12	8	3.02	0.86	19.37
Annual Growth	15.0%	—	—	9.1%	42.3%	7.4%

Compagnie de Saint-Gobain

One of the world's largest materials groups Compagnie de Saint-Gobain is in a glass by itself. The mega-group develops manufactures and distributes a wide variety of products for construction transportation industrial food storage and solar energy use. Saint-Gobain operates in four primary sectors: Building Distribution Construction Products (insulation roofing and other products) Innovative Materials (Flat Glass and High-Performance Materials such as polymers and glass fabrics) and Packaging (glass bottles). It owns notable brands such as Gyproc Dahl International and CertainTeed. Saint-Gobain dates to the 1660s when it made mirrors for the Palace of Versailles.

The global economy and slowdown in the construction market hurt Saint-Gobain's performance in 2008 and 2009 (when net income dropped by 85%). To weather the financial crisis the group cut costs and worked to improve operating efficiencies. The cost cutting (along with an increase in sales prices) helped. By 2010 the company began to recover. It returned to growth and reported an increase in sales.

Saint-Gobain which operates in about 65 countries around the world is focused on growing organically by constructing new manufacturing plants. It is keen on investing in emerging countries such as Asia Latin America Africa and the Middle East and Eastern Europe. In 2011 it made acquisitions in Turkey to expand it plasterboard business. It also bought a manufacturer of insulation in Russia and a float glass business in India.

Another key strategy is developing more sustainability technologies to take advantage of increasing interest in environmental issues. Some of its products include self-cleaning windows and green insulation systems and water supply systems. Saint-Gobain has a particular focus on solar power. Its solar unit is dedicated to solar-related products including photovoltaic panels and solar heating systems. The company plans to expand that business by more than ten-fold within five years; to that end Saint-Gobain acquired the 70% of solar roof tiles maker Solarwood Technology it didn't already own in 2010. It also bought the rest of photovoltaic panels maker Avancis from Shell. In another deal that year Saint-Gobain bought 50% of SAGE Electrochromics which manufactures tinted glass products. In 2011 Saint-Gobain agreed to acquire Solar Gard which specializes in manufacturing tinted films used to reduce energy consumption.

As part of a renewed focus on the construction sector Saint-Gobain plans to divest its Verallia packaging arm which makes bottles and jars for food and drinks. Verallia planned an initial public offering but that was delayed due to poor market conditions (and fears surrounding the Greek financial crisis). In another deal aimed at sharpening its focus on the construction sector Saint-Gobain sold its advanced ceramics unit to US specialty manufacturer CoorsTek for $245 million.

However construction isn't getting all of the attention. In 2011 Saint-Gobain announced plans to expand its building distribution segment (which represents more than 40% of sales) with the acquisition of the Build Center network from Wolseley. The deal will include 148 builders merchant branches in the UK as well as the French subsidiary Brossette. Saint-Gobain plans to blend the new locations in with its 500-store Jewson retail network

French holding company Wendel Investissement is Saint-Gobain's largest shareholder with a stake of 18%. Wendel also has three seats on the company's board of directors.

HISTORY

Originally called Dunoyer Saint-Gobain (named after the factory location) was founded in 1665 by order of the Sun King Louis XIV who needed mirrors to adorn his palaces. Because Venice had the monopoly on glass Louis lured Venetian artisans to Paris. Some were poisoned by Italian assassins but enough remained to teach Parisians their secrets. Saint-Gobain glass decorates the Palace of Versailles' Hall of Mirrors.

With its decreed glass monopoly in France the company grew steadily until the French Revolution interrupted its prosperity. By the early 1800s however Saint-Gobain was shining again. It set up a sales office in New York in 1830 and its first foreign subsidiary in Germany in 1857. Under chemist Joseph Gay-Lussac's direction Saint-Gobain began dabbling in chemicals in the mid-1800s.

Expanding to Italy (1889) and Spain (1904) the firm was Europe's leading glassmaker by 1913. Saint-Gobain pioneered the production of tempered security glass in the 1920s; it diversified into glass fiber in the 1930s.

Pilkington a UK competitor developed a glass-making method in 1959 that obviated the need for polishing and therefore slashed production costs. Saint-Gobain refit its factories to use the Pilkington method to keep its 50% EC market share. In 1968 the shareholding Suez Group forced Saint-Gobain to merge with Pont-a-Mousson (now Saint-Gobain Canalizacion) then the world's leading iron pipe maker. The merger led to a much-needed restructuring that included selling Saint-Gobain's chemical interests.

The company acquired a majority interest in US building-material maker CertainTeed in 1976. In 1982 it was forced to divest some of its interests when it was nationalized by France's new socialist government. Despite nationalization the company grew steadily during the 1980s investing in Compagnie Generale des Eaux the world's largest drinking-water distributor.

In 1986 after a change in France's political climate Saint-Gobain became the first company to be reprivatized. Three years later it purchased Generale Francaise de Ceramique (clay tile) and a controlling interest in Vetri (glass containers Italy).

Saint-Gobain bought Norton (the world's leader in abrasives) and UK glassmaker Solaglas in 1990. With the 1991 purchases of German glassmakers GIAG and Oberland Saint-Gobain became the world's #1 glass manufacturer within a year.

After the recession of the early 1990s Saint-Gobain sold its paper and packaging interests to Jefferson Smurfit in 1994 raising more than $1 billion for acquisitions. With Ball Corporation it formed a glass container joint venture Ball-Foster Glass in 1995; the next year it bought Ball's stake. Acquisitions in 1997 included industrial ceramics firms in Germany and France and UK abrasives maker Unicorn International. In 1998 Saint-Gobain bought Bird Corp. (roofing materials US) and CALMAR (plastic pump sprayers US). The next year it bought US-based Furon which was absorbed into a new unit Saint-Gobain Performance Plastics.

In 2000 Saint-Gobain acquired Meyer International (a UK building materials supplier) Raab Karcher (a German building materials distributor) and US-based polymer specialist Chemfab. The following year Saint-Gobain bolstered its ceiling systems operations with the acquisition of the Maars Group's metal ceiling grid business. In 2002 Saint-Gobain acquired the 25% of France-based Lapeyre (doors windows cabinetry) stock it didn't own.

The company's most notable deal of 2004 was the E686 million acquisition of Swedish plumbing products distributor Dahl International. Early in 2005 Saint-Gobain raised its stake in Hankuk Glass Industries a Korean glass maker with sales of more than $250 million from 46% to more than 80%.

In August 2005 the company made a hostile $6.5 billion bid for UK drywall/plasterboard maker BPB after friendly overtures were rejected. BPB with operations in some 60 countries rejected Saint-Gobain's initial offer as too low. Saint-Gobain came back with a sweetened $6.68 billion bid which BPB accepted. The transaction closed in 2006.

Also that year the company formed a joint venture with Owens Corning to merge their reinforcements and composites businesses. Owens Corning bought out Saint-Gobain's 40% stake in the venture for $640 million in 2007.

All told Saint-Gobain acquired around 70 companies in 2007. Its purchases that year included US vinyl siding manufacturer Norandex other building products distribution companies in Europe and the UK medical tubing products maker Consolidated Polymer Technologies (folded into its performance plastics group) and construction materials operations primarily in emerging countries. Perhaps its biggest deal was its acquisition of HeidelbergCement's industrial mortars division Maxit. The deal made Saint-Gobain the top producer in Germany and Scandinavia and strengthened its position in the rest of Europe.

Although it had embarked on a notable spending spree Saint-Gobain also sold noncore operations to refocus on its core products. In 2007 it sold 80% of its specialty bottle maker Desjonqueres to two investment funds Sagard and Cognetas. It planned to sell its packaging operations but halted those plans when the global financial markets crashed.

Saint-Gobain bought a 44% stake in Japanese insulation maker MAG in 2008. Later that year Saint-Gobain was fined nearly #900 million ($1.1 billion) by the European Union for alleged price fixing; it was one of the largest fines ever levied against a single firm.

Also in 2008 French holding company Wendel Investissement became Saint-Gobain's largest shareholder with a stake of approximately 20%. Wendel gained two board seats and a third seat in 2009.

EXECUTIVES

VP Construction Products Sector North America, Peter R. Dachowski
General Delegate North America, Gilles Colas
Corporate Secretary, Bernard Field, age 67
SVP and Director Audit and Internal Control, Jean-Francois Phelizon, age 67
Honorary Chairman, Jean-Louis Beffa, age 72, $1,298,696 total compensation
SVP Human Resources, Claire Pedini, age 49
General Delegate Central Europe and Northern Europe, Paul Neeteson
SVP; President Building Distribution Sector, Benoit Bazin, age 45
General Delegate United Kingdom Republic of Ireland and South Africa, Peter Hindle
SVP; President Packaging Sector, Jerome Fessard, age 59
SVP; Director Construction Products Sector, Claude Imauven, age 56
CFO, Laurent Guillot, age 44
SVP International Development; General Delegate Brazil Argentina and Chile, Jean-Claude Breffort, age 65
VP Research and Innovation, Didier Roux
Director; COO Saint- Gobain Eurocoustic, Bernard Cusenier, age 66
VP Communications, Sophie Chevallon
General Delegate for the Nordic and Baltic Countries, Thierry Lambert
SVP; President Innovative Materials Sector (Flat Glass and High-Performance Materials), Jean-Pierre Floris, age 65
VP Marketing, Gerard Aspar
General Delegate Eastern Europe, Olivier Lluansi
General Delegate India, Anand Mahajan
General Delegate Asia-Pacific Region, Emmanuel Normant
General Delegate Spain Portugal and Morocco, Ricardo de Ramon Garcia
General Delegate Mexico Venezuela and Colombia, Guy Rolli
General Delegate Italy Greece and Egypt, Gianni Scotti
VP Corporate Planning, David Molho
Corporate Secretary; Secretary of the Board of Directors; Member of the Management Committee and Executive Committee, Antoine Vignial
General Delegate to Brazil; Argentina and Chile, Benoit dIribarne
General Delegate to North America; Member of the Management Committee, John Crowe
Chairman of the Board and Chief Executive Officer; Member of the Management Committee and Executive Committee, Pierre-Andre Chalendar
General Delegate to Spain; Portugal and Morocco, Ricardo Garcia
General Delegate to Russia; Ukraine and CIS countries, Thierry Fournier
Director, Jean-Martin Folz, age 66
Director, Jean-Cyril Spinetta, age 70
Director, Isabelle Bouillot, age 63
Director, Robert Chevrier, age 69
Director, Gerhard Cromme, age 70
Director, Michel Pebereau, age 70
Director, Denis Ranque, age 61
Director, Gerard Mestrallet, age 64
Chairman and CEO, Pierre-Andre de Chalendar, age 54
Director, Bernard Gautier, age 53
Director, Lady Sylvia Jay, age 66
Director; COO Saint- Gobain Eurocoustic, Bernard Cusenier, age 66
Director, Yuko Harayama, age 62
Director, Frederic Lemoine, age 47
Director, Maj. Gilles Schnepp, age 54
Independent Director, Anne-Marie Idrac
Director - Representative of Employee Shareholders, Jacques Pestre
Independent Director, Olivia Qiu
Auditors: PricewaterhouseCoopersAudit

LOCATIONS

HQ: Compagnie de Saint-Gobain
Les Miroirs, 18, avenue d' Alsace, Courbevoie 92400
Phone: (33) 1 47 62 30 00
Web: www.saint-gobain.com

2010 Sales

	% of total
Western Europe	
France	28
Other	43
Asia & emerging	20
North	14
Total	**100**

PRODUCTS/OPERATIONS

2010 Sales by Market

	$ mil.	% of total
Renovation	45	
Construction	31	
Other	24	
Total	**0**	**100**

2010 Sales by Segment

	% of total
Building	43
Construction products	
Exterior	14
Interior	13
Innovative materials	
Flat	13
High-performance	10
Packaging &	7
Total	**100**

Selected Segments and Products

Construction products
- Exterior fittings
  - Asphalt roofing shingles
  - Siding
  - Vinyl fences
- Gypsum
  - Ceiling tiles
  - EPS insulation
  - Plaster
  - Plasterboard
- Industrial mortars
  - Flooring screed
  - Interior rendering
  - Masonry mortar
  - Tile adhesive and grouting
  - Wall rendering products

Insulation
- Glass wool
- Insulating foam
- Metal frames
- Rock wool
- Soundproof ceilings

Pipe
- Complete piping systems
- Ductile cast iron and steel manhole covers

Flat glass
- Construction glass
- Furniture glass
- Automotive glazing
- Photovoltaic systems
- Solar heating systems
- Specialty glass
  - Fireproof glass
  - Nuclear safety glass

High-performance materials
- Abrasives
  - Bonded abrasives
  - Superabrasives
  - Thin grinding wheels
- Ceramics
  - Advanced ceramics
  - Crystals
  - Diesel particulate filters
  - Grains and powders
- Performance plastics
  - Bearings and seals
  - Films foams and coated fabrics
  - Fluid control systems
- Textiles
  - Glass fiber yarn
  - Reinforcement fabrics for construction and manufacturing

Packaging
- Glass bottles and jars

COMPETITORS

3M
Anchor Glass
Asahi Glass
Ball Corp.
CRH
DuPont
Georgia-Pacific
Gerresheimer Glas
Grafton Group
Guardian Industries
Johns Manville
Knauf Insulation
Kubota
Kyocera
Lafarge
Nippon Electric Glass
Nitto Boseki
Owens-Illinois
PPG Industries
RHI
Rexam
Royal Group
SCHOTT
SIG plc
Travis Perkins
Wolseley

HISTORICAL FINANCIALS

Company Type: Public

Income Statement FYE: December 31

	REVENUE ($ mil.)	NET INCOME ($ mil.)	NET PROFIT MARGIN	EMPLOYEES
12/12	56,937	1,009	1.8%	192,781
12/11	54,475	1,660	3.0%	194,658
12/10	53,694	1,511	2.8%	189,193
12/09	54,433	291	0.5%	191,442
12/08	61,236	1,926	3.1%	209,175
Annual Growth	(1.8%)	(14.9%)	—	(2.0%)

2012 Year-End Financials

Debt ratio: 35.1%
Return on equity: 4.3%
Cash ($ mil.): 5,508
Current ratio: 1.31
Long-term debt ($ mil.): 12,637
No. of shares (mil.): 526
Dividends
Yield: —
Payout: —
Market value ($ mil.): 22,084

	STOCK PRICE ($) FY Close	P/E High/Low	PER SHARE ($) Earnings	Dividends	Book Value
12/12	41.95	58 33	1.91	0.00	43.66
12/11	38.00	53 25	3.13	0.00	43.79
12/10	51.50	42 27	2.90	0.00	45.49
12/09	58.10	294 95	0.62	0.00	45.08
12/08	45.73	52 16	5.12	0.00	52.79
Annual Growth	(2.1%)	— —	(21.8%)	—	(4.6%)

Compagnie Generale des Etablissements Michelin (France)

The Michelin Man may look like a marshmallow but what he's selling is tires. Behind that fluffy white figure is one of the world's top tire manufacturers Compagnie Generale des Etablissements Michelin which produces more than 175 million tires annually for all kinds of vehicles. The majority of its sales are made from supplying replacement tires to the passenger car and truck markets. It is also a world leader in aircraft and earthmover tires. Michelin sells to both consumers and vehicle manufacturers. Included in its stable are brands recognized regionally (Kleber in Europe Warrior in China) and worldwide (Michelin BF Goodrich). The company also publishes about 10 million maps and travel guides per year.

The company produces its tires at approximately 70 production sites across the Americas Asia Africa and Europe; its sales network is worldwide. North America is Michelin's second-largest market (with 18 manufacturing facilities) generating about one-third of the company's sales annually. With demand up in Europe and North America as well as in Asia and South America Michelin is building three high capacity plants in Brazil India and China; all of which are scheduled to begin production in 2012.

In fact with such a strong demand from these fast-growing emerging regions Michelin is realigning its business to emphasize the three countries. It is also bumping up its research and development investment from E1 billion (about $1.3 billion) to E1.6 billion (more than $2 billion) per year for the next five years. R&D will weigh the needs of the company's main emerging markets and will cater to the regions accordingly.

With its sights focused on China as a burgeoning region Michelin agreed in spring 2011 to form a joint venture (it will take a 40% stake) with China-based tire maker Double Coin and investment firm Shanghai Huayi to manufacture Warrior-brand car and truck tires for the Chinese market.

With resurging demand and new regional market interest Michelin's 2010 passenger and truck tire sales increased 18% and 26% respectively over 2009. With higher volumes sold and cost cutting measures in place the company realized a respectable overall revenue increase in 2010 of almost 12%; however its net income exceeded expectations at almost $1.4 billion representing an increase in excess of 800% over 2009. As tough as it was the company's Horizon 2010 plan did reduce costs and increased plant productivity by 35%; Michelin's cost-cutting measures and plans to improve efficiency showed up as positive cash flow. Higher prices for its tires and lower materials costs also helped the bottom line.

This positive showing comes not so long after the economic downturn that crushed the automotive industry particularly in North America and Europe. The US was at the forefront of the financial impact in 2009 when Michelin was forced to close its 1000-worker BF Goodrich plant in Opelika Alabama. Michelin chose to close the plant in order to focus on the Michelin brand which the company says is more resilient than other brands. Europe was hit hard as well and it suffered a similar fate with 1000 workers laid off in France; this was also part of a company-wide restructuring to focus on its best-selling brands.

HISTORY

After toying with making rubber balls Edouard Daubree and Aristide Barbier formed a partnership in Clermont-Ferrand France in 1863 and entered the rubber business in earnest. Both men soon died but Barbier in-law Andre Michelin a successful businessman took over the company in 1886. Andre recruited his brother Edouard a Parisian artist to run the company and in 1889 it was renamed Compagnie Generale des Etablissements Michelin.

That year Edouard found that air-filled tires made bicycling more comfortable. But pneumatic tires were experimental and because they were glued to the rims required hours to change. In 1891 Edouard made a detachable bicycle tire that took only 15 minutes to change.

The Michelins promoted their tires by persuading cyclists to use them in long-distance races where punctures were likely. They demonstrated the applicability of such tires for cars in an auto race in 1895. In 1898 Andre commented that a stack of tires would look like a man if it had arms a notion that led to the creation of Bibendum the Michelin Man. Andre launched the "Michelin Guide" for auto tourists in 1900.

Expansion followed as Michelin opened a London office (1905) and began production in Italy (1906) and the US (in New Jersey in 1908). Innovations included detachable rims and spare tires (1906) tubeless tires (1930) treads (1934) and modern low-profile tires (1937). During the Depression Michelin closed its US plant and accepted a stake in Citroen later converted into a minority stake in Peugeot in lieu of payment for tires.

Michelin patented radial tires in 1946. Expansion was largely confined to Europe in the 1950s but thanks to radials increased worldwide in the 1960s. Sears began selling Michelin radials in 1966. Radials took hold during the 1970s and Michelin returned to manufacturing in the US opening a plant in South Carolina in 1975.

Expanding aggressively (Michelin opened or bought a plant every nine months from 1960 to 1990) the company went into the red when economic conditions dipped in the early 1980s and in 1990 and 1991. The company's $1.5 billion purchase of Uniroyal Goodrich in 1990 contributed to the latter losses but improved Michelin's position in the US the world's largest auto market.

In response to the losses Michelin attacked its bloated infrastructure and reinvented itself along nine product lines (according to tire/vehicle type plus travel suspension and primary product manufacturing). It also consolidated facilities and cut about 30000 jobs. The company continued to focus on R&D bringing out new high-performance tires such as its "green" tire designed to help cars save fuel.

Michelin bought a majority interest in a Polish tire maker in 1995 and the next year it bought 90% of Taurus a Hungarian firm that produces most of that country's rubber. Michelin joined German competitor Continental in 1996 to make private-label tires for independent distributors. The next year Michelin introduced a run-flat tire –capable of traveling 50 miles after a puncture –for the automotive aftermarket. The company acquired Icollantas a Colombian tire group with two factories in Bogota and Cali in 1998.

After leading the company for more than 40 years patriarch Francois Michelin stepped down in 1999 leaving his youngest son Edouard in charge. Almost immediately Edouard announced a restructuring that would cut 7500 jobs in Europe including almost 2000 in France. The company benefited somewhat from Firestone's recall woes in 2000 but Michelin still faced rising material costs and difficult market conditions.

The European Commission fined Michelin nearly $20 million in 2001 claiming the company engaged in anticompetitive behavior by abusing its dominant position in Europe. In 2003 Michelin and TRW Automotive created EnTire Solutions a joint venture to develop a tire pressure monitoring system. Michelin announced a licensing agreement in 2004 for Toyo Tire to make sell and promote PAX system tires (run-flat tires).

Former co-managing partner Edouard Michelin the youngest son of patriarch Francois Michelin and the fourth generation of Michelins in the business was killed in a boating accident in May 2006.

The tire market made a huge shift during and after the Great Recession of 2009. While Europe and North American demand faltered emerging countries like China and India as well as countries in South America filled the gap in demand. To take advantage of the burgeoning Asian market Michelin increased its stake in South Korea-based Hankook Tires to about 10% in mid-2008.

EXECUTIVES

Member Supervisory Board, Benoit Potier, age 55
Member Supervisory Board, Louis Gallois, age 68
Member Supervisory Board, Francois Grappotte, age 76
Member Supervisory Board, Barbara M. Dalibard, age 54
Member Supervisory Board, Pierre Michelin, age 63
Member Supervisory Board, Pat Cox, age 59
Member Supervisory Board, Laurence Parisot, age 52
Auditors: PricewaterhouseCoopersAudit

LOCATIONS

HQ: Compagnie Generale des Etablissements Michelin (France)
23, place des Carmes-Dechaux, Clermont-Ferrand, Cedex 9 63040
Phone: (33) 4 73 32 20 00
Web: www.michelin.com

2010 Sales

	% of total
Europe	43
North	34
Other	23
Total	**100**

PRODUCTS/OPERATIONS

2010 Sales

	% of total
Passenger car & light truck tires & related	55
Truck tires & related	32
Specialty	13
Total	**100**

2010 Sales by Market

	% of total
Replacement	75
Original	25
Total	**100**

Selected Products and Services

Agricultural vehicle tires
Aircraft tires
Construction vehicle tires
Engineering consulting for constructors & equipment manufacturers
Heavy-goods vehicle tires
Motorcycle bicycle & scooter tires
Passenger car tires
Sports leisure & work accessories
Travel maps & guides
Truck tires

Selected Brands

BF Goodrich
Encore
Euromaster
Kleber
Kormoran
Michelin
Riken
Taurus
Tigar
Tyre Plus
Uniroyal
Warrior

Selected Subsidiaries

Compagnie Financiere Michelin (Switzerland)
Manufacture Francaise des Pneumatiques Michelin
Michelin Aircraft Tire Company (US)
Michelin Americas Research & Development Corporation (US)
Michelin Asia-Pacific Import-Export (HK) Limited (Hong Kong)
Michelin Corporation (US)
Michelin North America Inc. (US)
Michelin Gummi Compagni A/S (Denmark)

COMPETITORS

Avalon Travel Publishing
Bridgestone
Continental AG
Cooper Tire & Rubber
Fieldens
Goodyear Tire & Rubber
Kumho Tire
Pirelli
Sime Darby
Sumitomo Rubber
Toyo Tire & Rubber
Yokohama Rubber

HISTORICAL FINANCIALS

Company Type: Public

Income Statement FYE: December 31

	REVENUE ($ mil.)	NET INCOME ($ mil.)	NET PROFIT MARGIN	EMPLOYEES
12/12	28,303	2,069	7.3%	113,443
12/11	26,799	1,891	7.1%	115,000
12/10	23,944	1,402	5.9%	111,090
12/09	21,330	152	0.7%	109,193
12/08	22,939	503	2.2%	117,565
Annual Growth	5.4%	42.4%	—	(0.9%)

2012 Year-End Financials

Debt ratio: 20.1%
Return on equity: 18.8%
Cash ($ mil.): 2,448
Current ratio: 1.87
Long-term debt ($ mil.): 2,666
No. of shares (mil.): 182
Dividends
Yield: 2.7%
Payout: 8.0%
Market value ($ mil.): 3,503

	STOCK PRICE ($) FY Close	P/E High	P/E Low	PER SHARE ($) Earnings	Dividends	Book Value
12/12	19.19	4	2	11.08	0.53	61.36
12/11	11.72	5	2	10.31	0.93	58.19
12/10	14.34	5	3	8.89	0.75	61.57
12/09	15.40	52	15	1.02	0.28	53.66
12/08	10.55	9	5	3.44	0.00	49.25
Annual Growth	16.1%	—	—	34.0%	—	5.6%

Compass Group PLC (United Kingdom)

Look in almost any direction and you'll likely see a foodservice operation run by this company. Compass Group is the world's largest contract foodservices provider with operations in more than 50 countries. It provides hospitality and foodservice for a variety of businesses and such public-sector clients as cultural institutions hospitals and schools. It also offers vending catering concessions and security services for a number of events and sports venues. Its foodservice brands include Chartwells Crothall and Levy Restaurants. In addition Compass is a franchisee of such well-known chains as Burger King and Starbucks.

Compass became the leader in its industry through aggressive expansion and numerous acquisitions over the years. The company has been especially focused on boosting its presence internationally.

To this end in 2011 Compass acquired the remaining 50% of SOFRA its joint venture in Turkey and entered a deal to buy meal-delivery firm Obasan which serves business in Turkey Bursa and Istanbul. That same year Compass also acquired a pair of companies in India that provide facilities management and foodservice to businesses in Delhi. The twin purchases followed the acquisition of German education and health care foodservices provider Menke Menue for about E5 million (nearly $7 million) in cash and it snapped up a 90% stake in Japanese catering firm Chiyoda Food from Nippon Yusen Kabushiki Kaisha (which retained the remaining shares). In late 2011 Compass acquired UK-based Cygnet Foods a food and support services company for an undisclosed price.

In 2010 the company purchased Australia-based foodservices firm Life's A Party Group for #14 million ($22 million) and Denmark's IDA Service for #17 million ($27 million) from OKF Holding A/S and its management. Also that year Compass bought family-owned Tirumala Hospitality Services a leading caterer for corporate and industrial businesses in western India and France's Caterine Restauration a foodservices firm for the country's education and health care sectors.

The company continues to build on its operations back at home as well. Responding to the requests of its clients Compass extended its reach to the safety business in mid-2010 when it acquired VSG Group a security services firm from Lloyds Development Capital for $81 million. VSG supplies manned guarding electronic surveillance and support services to companies in the UK. VSG's security operations are complementary to Compass' cleaning and catering businesses as customers of these services often ask for security support.

While the global recession and credit crisis have caused hardships in many industries the contract foodservices segment has continued to grow as companies look for new ways to outsource and cut costs. As such Compass Group is focused on winning new services contracts and expanding its business relationships with existing customers. In 2009 and 2010 the company won new business from Visa Google Microsoft Nestle and Electrolux.

Compass Group has also been mindful of costs itself pulling out of some unprofitable global markets streamlining operations and strengthening financial controls throughout its expansive network of worldwide subsidiaries. The moves have helped the company to widen its margins.

HISTORY

Compass Group was formed in 1987 when management bought out the catering business of London-based food and spirits giant Grand Metropolitan (now Diageo) for $260 million. The company went public the next year listing on the London Stock Exchange. Gerry Robinson CEO at the time left in 1991 to take a position with British TV programming giant Granada Group (renamed ITV plc in 2004) where he helped that company diversify into food service operations. Finance director Francis Mackay took over as CEO.

Believing that real growth in the catering industry could come from size and economies of scale Mackay orchestrated a $2.5 billion acquisition plan over the next five years. In 1992 Compass bought Traveller's Fare (now Upper Crust) a railway caterer from British Rail. The company expanded into airports the following year with the acquisition of Scandinavian Airlines System's catering operations. Then in 1994 Compass bought Canteen Corporation the US's third-largest vending and food service company.

Compass achieved its goal of becoming the world's largest caterer in 1995 with the acquisition of France's Eurest International putting it ahead of Sodexho Alliance and Granada. Mackay calmed London investors nervous about the pace of Compass' acquisitions by selling off its hospital management operations and paying lip service to focusing on organic growth. Later that year Compass was awarded the world's largest food service contract a $250-million five-year deal with IBM.

By 1996 the company seemed to have forgotten all about organic growth buying Service America and then Daka International and France's SHRM in 1997. French subsidiary Eurest later snatched a $40 million contract from rival Sodexho (later Sodexo) to supply the staff restaurants at Euro Disney one of France's top three catering contracts. The next year Compass solidified its position in the airport markets with a five-year licensing deal for use of the T.G.I. Fridays brand joining Taco Bell Pizza Hut Burger King and Harry Ramsden's fish and chip shops in Compass' quiver of branded airport outlets.

In 1999 CEO Mackay became group chairman leaving the reins to Compass' chief of North American operations Michael Bailey. The company's US acquisitions quickly paid off that year with a contract to serve 90% of the food venues at the 2002 Winter Olympics in Salt Lake City. In 2000 the company merged with UK hospitality giant Granada Group (the combined firm became Granada Compass) which then spun off its media operations as a separate company Granada Media. Late that year it bought Boston-based bakery/cafe chain Au Bon Pain for about $108 million.

The new company got a quick divorce in 2001 when Granada Compass decided to demerge and make Compass Group public again. Compass Group later sold the Le Meridien hotel operations it gained from the Granada merger to Nomura International for nearly $3 billion. (The firm kept the Travelodge chain.) The company then began making purchases including Morrison Management Specialists for $563 million the 66% it didn't already own in Selecta Group UK vending machine company Vendepac and health care services management company Crothall Services. Compass lost seven operating sites during the September 11 terrorist attacks on the World Trade Center. Late in 2001 Compass strengthened its presence in Japan with the $277 million acquisition of Seiyo Food Systems that country's #2 food services group.

In 2002 Compass signed arguably the industry's largest contract ever a $200 million a year deal to feed Chevron employees around the world. In 2003 the company sold its Travelodge motel business and Little Chef diners to private equity firm Permira for $1.14 billion a 5% discount to the asking price. Compass became the first non-Chinese company to provide food in stations and on trains operated by the Shanghai Railway Administration in 2004. In addition the firm bought Creative Host Services in 2004.

In 2005 Compass sold a 75% stake in Au Bon Pain back to a management group retaining a 25% interest in the quick-casual chain. The following year the company sold its travel hospitality businesses including Select Service Partner (now SSP Group) and UK motorway operator Moto to private investors for more than $3 billion. Compass sold its European vending business Selecta to German financial giant Allianz for $1.5 billion in 2007.

In 2009 the firm added the US's Southeast Service Corporation which focuses on education catering for $65 million. Compass also purchased Germany's Plural which provides janitorial and related support services for corporate and health care clients and it took over the remaining 50% of shares it didn't already own in Brazil's GR SA. Touting its expertise in on-the-go food offerings Compass in 2009 purchased about 30 McColls retail locations in UK hospitals from Martin McColl.

EXECUTIVES

Chairman, Sir Roy A. Gardner, age 68
Group Chief Executive and Director, Richard J. Cousins, age 54, $313,000 total compensation
Group Managing Director USA and Canada and Director, Gary R. Green, age 56
General Counsel and Company Secretary, Mark J. White
Group Finance Director and Director, Andrew Martin, age 53, $461,000 total compensation
Director, Sir James R. Crosby, age 57
Group Chief Executive and Director, Richard J. Cousins, age 54
Group Managing Director USA and Canada and Director, Gary R. Green, age 56
Director, Sir Ian Robinson, age 71
Director, Steve Lucas, age 59
Director, Susan E. Murray, age 56
Group Finance Director and Director, Andrew Martin, age 53
Director, Don Robert
Auditors: DeloitteLLP

LOCATIONS

HQ: Compass Group PLC (United Kingdom)
Compass House, Guildford Street, Chertsey, Surrey KT16 9BQ
Phone: (44) 1932 573 000 **Fax:** (44) 1932 569 956
Web: www.compass-group.com

PRODUCTS/OPERATIONS

Selected Operating Units

All Leisure (sports and leisure venues)
Bon Appetit Management Company (on-site dining services)
Canteen (vending services)
Chartwells (education foodservices)
Crothall (health care facilities management)
ESS (offshore and remote foodservices)
Eurest (corporate foodservice)
FLIK (upscale foodservices)
Levy Restaurants (fine dining sports and leisure events)
Medirest (health care services)
Morrison Management Specialists (health care foodservice)
Restaurant Associates Managed Services (corporate dining and sporting and leisure events)
Scolarest (education foodservices)

COMPETITORS

ARAMARK
Autogrill
Centerplate
Delaware North
Elior
Farsight Security Services
Healthcare Services
Legion Group
Reliance Security
Securiplan
Sodexo

HISTORICAL FINANCIALS

Company Type: Public

Income Statement

FYE: September 30

	REVENUE ($ mil.)	NET INCOME ($ mil.)	NET PROFIT MARGIN	EMPLOYEES
09/13	28,340	692	2.4%	506,699
09/12	27,378	979	3.6%	508,714
09/11	24,662	1,133	4.6%	471,108
09/10	22,986	1,072	4.7%	428,202
09/09	21,662	944	4.4%	386,170
Annual Growth	6.9%	(7.5%)	—	7.0%

2013 Year-End Financials

Debt ratio: 40.0%
Return on equity: 14.2%
Cash ($ mil.): 1,623
Current ratio: 0.96
Long-term debt ($ mil.): 3,488
No. of shares (mil.): 1,804
Dividends
Yield: 2.1%
Payout: 201.2%
Market value ($ mil.): 24,734

	STOCK PRICE ($) FY Close	P/E High/Low	PER SHARE ($) Earnings	Dividends	Book Value
09/13	13.71	152118	0.38	0.30	2.49
09/12	11.05	96 62	0.52	0.71	2.82
09/11	8.02	67 50	0.60	0.27	2.87
09/10	8.50	61 43	0.57	0.19	2.58
09/09	6.18	56 26	0.51	0.16	2.20
Annual Growth	22.0%	— —	(7.2%)	16.3%	3.1%

Continental AG (Germany, Fed. Rep.)

Continental AG keeps rolling along as one of Europe's largest manufacturers of tires for cars trucks bicycles and agricultural products. Its Automotive Group is Continental's largest segment manufacturing brake and traction control systems passive safety products sensors and chassis and powertrain products. The Rubber Group comprises its Tires division (sold under the Continental Uniroyal and General brands) as well as its ContiTech division which produces vibration control and power transmission systems as well as conveyor belts. Germany-based bearing and clutch manufacturer Schaeffler controls 49% of Continental AG's shares.

Continental's Automotive Group generates about 60 % of total sales each year while its Rubber Group hauls in the remaining 40%. Automotive comprises the Interior Chassis and Safety and Powertrain segments. Each segment operates through about 50 to 60 production sites located throughout Australia Brazil China Europe India Japan Malaysia Mexico Russia Singapore South Korea Thailand the Philippines and the US.

The Rubber Group comprises Passenger and Light Truck Tires (50 locations spanning 35 countries) and Commercial Vehicle Tires (roughly 45 sites in more than 30 countries). Continental sells its tires to automakers such as BMW Daimler and Ford. Another division within the Rubber Group is ContiTech which operates out of almost 80 locations in some 25 countries. With its several business units ContiTech manufactures products that are also used on rail vehicles and in printing mining wind and power plant petrochemical and navigation markets. In its largest acquisition to date ContiTech acquired the auto air conditioning business owned by a division of Parker Hannifin in mid-2012. The deal gave ContiTech additional plants in China Mexico South Korea and the Czech Republic. In 2014 it inked a deal to buy US rubber and plastics maker Veyance Technologies from financial investment firm Carlyle for about EUR 1.4 billion (or US $1.9 billion) and fold the firm into its ContiTech business.

Like all players in the auto parts industry Continental was hit hard by the painful effects of the recession that decimated the auto construction and transportation sectors. From 2008 to early 2011 the company clamped down on its cost structure by closing plants restructuring reducing its research and development expenses and chipping away at its debt. As a result of an overall increase in demand in the automotive industry and its ability to diversify the product portfolio within its Automotive segment its net revenue rose 17% from 2010 to 2011. Although the 2011 Japan earthquake and European credit crisis negatively affected Continental the company was helped by increases in North American sales and other regions during 2011.

For its growth strategy Continental has identified about 25 of the fastest growing automotive groups including navigation systems turbochargers and systems used for reducing emissions. The decision to diversify product lines is also part of the company's strategy to keep its dependence on the automotive industry in check by generating additional sales in industries other than automotive. To that end ContiTech in late 2010 acquired Tianjin Xinbinhai Conveyor Belt a Chinese maker of conveyor-belts used in various industrial applications.

Continental also intends to tighten its grip in emerging markets in Asia where it already generates about 15% of its total sales. By 2015 the company plans to expand its tire manufacturing capacity by a combined total of more than 22 million tires. To achieve this in 2011 it established new tire plants in China Russia and the US; it also expanded existing ones in Brazil India and the US.

HISTORY

A group of financiers and industrialists with interests in the rubber industry founded Continental-Caoutchouc und Gutta-Percha Compagnie in Hanover Germany in 1871. The company's products included solid tires for carriages and bicycles rubberized fabrics and various consumer items.

In 1892 Continental was the first German maker of pneumatic bicycle tires. During this period the budding automobile and motorcycle industries created fresh demand for solid tires. Continental began producing pneumatic tires for automobiles in 1898.

By 1904 Continental was first to develop a treaded tire. Between 1905 and 1913 Continental expanded into Australia Denmark Italy Norway Romania Sweden and the UK by forming marketing subsidiaries. However the onset of WWI caused a shift to military production and the overseas sales network dissolved.

Poor overall economic conditions atrophied postwar tire industry growth and by the late 1920s the company merged several German rubber firms to create a much larger and stronger Continental. In 1929 the company changed its name to Continental Gummi-Werke AG. The Opel family which had sold its car unit to General Motors bought a substantial stake in the new company.

Emerging from the Great Depression total German tire production doubled between 1934 and 1938 as the Nazi government initiated a program to motorize Germany and reduce unemployment. During WWII the Nazis took over tire and rubber making to meet military needs.

After the war civilian production languished amid occupation and war-damaged factories. To get back on its feet Continental formed a technical assistance alliance with General Tire in 1948.

Between 1950 and 1965 the company tagged along as German car companies mostly Volkswagen expanded overseas. Continental established foreign subsidiaries in Brazil France Italy Portugal South Africa Spain and the UK.

The growth spurt was curtailed by the oil crisis of the 1970s. The company began making fan and conveyor belts in 1975. Continental bought the tire unit of US-based Uniroyal in 1979. In 1981 the company forged a deal with Toyo Rubber Industry Co. (now called Toyo Tire & Rubber Co.) to make Continental tires in Japan. The next year a similar deal was inked in the US with General Tire. By 1987 Continental owned General Tire buying it from GenCorp. The deal gave Continental four factories General's brands a new marketing network and lucrative OEM contracts; expansion into Africa Asia and South America made the deal even sweeter. That year the company's name changed to Continental AG.

In 1991 the company's industrial products segment was reorganized under the ContiTech name. ContiTech joined with Cooper Tire & Rubber in 1995 to collaborate on molded products extrusions and hoses. The following year the company secured the right to use the Uniroyal name in Europe.

Continental bought the automotive brake and chassis unit of ITT Industries for $1.93 billion in 1998; now Continental Teves it is part of Continental's Automotive Systems Group. The next year Continental formed a joint venture with Delco Remy International (now Remy International) to produce motors for integrated starter alternator damper (ISAD) systems.

In 2000 Continental announced that it would recall about 160000 tires fitted on Lincoln Navigators (Ford) in 1998 and 1999: The tires were reportedly prone to lose parts of their treads. The next year Continental announced that it would acquire (60% up front and the rest by 2005) Temic GmbH Daimler AG's automotive-electronics business in a deal worth around $550 million.

Continental announced in 2001 that it would sell off most of its ContiTech division. The same year Continental announced that it would supply Ford with more than 2 million Firestone-replacement tires. In July Ford dropped Continental's General Ameri* 550 AS tire after the NHTSA announced it was launching a probe into all 2.7 million of those tires made since 1995 because the model's tread failure rate was 124 per million (versus nine per million for Firestone's recalled Wilderness AT model).

In 2001 the company's Continental Teves subsidiary acquired a majority interest in Japan-based brake system manufactures Shin-Ei and ShinTec from Mazda Motor Corporation. CEO Stephan Kessel stepped down and was replaced by Manfred Wennemer in September of 2001. Wennemer had been head of ContiTech –Continental's most profitable division –which Kessel had wanted to sell. The German tire maker entered into an agreement in 2002 with Japan-based counterparts Bridgestone and Yokohama to explore run-flat technology. In early 2003 Continental acquired a 30% stake in Malaysia-based Sime Darby's tire business. CGS Tire acquired Continental's agricultural tire business in 2004.

Continental's 2004 acquisition of Phoenix AG strengthened the company's ContiTech division and contributed to its transformation to become a tier-one integrated automotive parts supplier. Likewise its 2006 acquisition of Motorola's automotive division for which it paid about $1 billion greatly expanded Continental's product portfolio with interior electronics controls sensors and telematics operations.

Continuing down the diversification road Continental acquired the 40% of Temic GmbH it didn't already own in 2005.

In 2007 Continental received EU approval to acquire a 51% stake in the conveyor belt tire and rubber machinery operations of Slovakia's Matador Group. Continental moved to enhance its brake offerings when later that year it agreed to buy Automotive Products Italia Srl (AP) from Australia's Pacifica Group for an undisclosed sum. AP which is one of Europe's leading makers of drum brakes had sales of about ?79 million in 2006.

Continental kept up its 2007 international buying spree when it agreed to purchase Zangjiang Fugang Heli Electronics Co. Ltd. a Chinese maker of cooling fan modules and window lift motors. The move marks Continental's first purchase in China the world's fastest-growing car market. The company has also announced plans to relocate a technical center to China as well as build new manufacturing operations in the country (a tire plant in Hefei and a hydraulic brake facility in Changshu).

In 2008 Continental acquired Siemens VDO Automotive (now known as VDO Automotive). The largest acquisition in Continental's 135-plus year history it made the company a top five global automotive supplier and the second largest German parts maker behind Robert Bosch.

Family owned Schaeffler made its hostile takeover bid in 2008; an agreement was made between the two companies in August 2008. As part of the deal changes were made at the top level Changes occurred not only to the business structure but to management as well. Continental CEO Manfred Wennemer stepped down at the end of August 2008. A decision to merge the two companies was abandoned years later and in 2011 Schaeffler lowered the amount of shares it owned in Continental to 49%.

EXECUTIVES

Member Executive Board and Head of Passenger and Light Truck Tires and Commercial Vehicle Tires Division Purchasing and Quality and Environment, Hans-Joachim Nikolin, age 57

Deputy Chairman Supervisory Board, Werner Bischoff, age 66

Head Corporate Quality and the Environment, Thorsten Reese

VP Media Relations, Hannes Boekhoff

SVP Corporate Communications, Felix Gress, age 52

Chairman Executive Board, Elmar Degenhart, age 55

Executive Board Member ContiTech Division, Heinz-Gerhard Wente, age 62

Member Executive Board Chassis and Safety, Ralf Cramer, age 48

Senior Vice President Chassis & Safety NAFTA, Samir Salman

VP Communications ContiTech, Anja Graf

Member Executive Board Interior, Helmut Matschi, age 50

Member Executive Board Tire Division, Nikolai Setzer, age 42

Head of Investor Relations, Rolf Woller

Chairman Supervisory Board, Prof Wolfgang Reitzle

Member Executive Board Finance Controlling Compliance Law and IT, Wolfgang Schafer, age 54
Member Executive Board Powertrain Division, Jose A. Avila, age 58
Vice President Communications, Nicole Geissler
Executive Vice President, Matthias Matic
Senior Vice President Systems & Technology, Peter Rieth
Senior Vice President Human Resources, Rainer Hetzer
Senior Vice President Finance Controlling & Law, Werner Volz
Executive Vice President Business Unit ADAS, Friedrich Angerbauer
Member Supervisory Board, Prof Siegfried Wolf, age 56
Member Supervisory Board, Michael Deister
Member Supervisory Board, Klaus Rosenfeld, age 47
Member Supervisory Board, Prof Hans-Olaf Henkel, age 73
Deputy Chairman Supervisory Board, Werner Bischoff, age 66
Member Supervisory Board, Hartmut Meine
Member Supervisory Board, Erwin Worle
Member Supervisory Board, Jorg Schonfelder
Member Supervisory Board, Michael Iglhaut
Member Supervisory Board, Gunter Dunkel
Member Supervisory Board, Hans Fischl
Member Supervisory Board, Jurgen Gei?inger
Member Supervisory Board, Jorg Kohlinger
Member Supervisory Board, Klaus Mangold
Member Supervisory Board, Dick Nordmann
Member Supervisory Board, Georg F. W. Schaeffler
Member Supervisory Board, Maria-Elisabeth Schaeffler
Member Supervisory Board, Bernd W. Voss, age 74
Auditors: KPMGDeutscheTreuhand-GesellschaftAG

LOCATIONS

HQ: Continental AG (Germany, Fed. Rep.)
Vahrenwalder Strasse 9, Hanover D-30165
Phone: (49) 511 938 01 **Fax:** (49) 511 938 8 17 70
Web: www.continental-corporation.com

2011 Sales

	$ mil.	% of total
Europe		
Other countries		33
Asia		17
Total	0	100

PRODUCTS/OPERATIONS

2011 Sales

	$ mil.	% of total
Automotive Group		
Chassis & safety		21
Rubber Group		
ContiTech		12
Total	0	100

Selected Automotive Group Products

Chassis and Safety
- Chassis components
- Electronic brake systems
- Hydraulic brake systems
- Passive safety and ADAS
- Sensors

Interior
- Body and security
- Commercial vehicles and aftermarket
- Connectivity
- Instrumentation and displays
- Interior modules
- Multimedia

Powertrain
- Engine systems
- Fuel supply
- Hybrid electric vehicle
- Sensors and actuators
- Transmissions

Selected Rubber Group Products

ContiTech
- Air spring systems
- Benecke-Kaliko group
- Conveyor belt group
- Elastomer coatings
- Fluid technology
- Power transmission group
- Vibration control

Tires
- Commercial vehicle
- Passenger and light truck

COMPETITORS

A.G. Simpson
AirBoss of America
Bridgestone
China Enterprises
Cooper Tire & Rubber
DENSO
Dana Holding
Delphi Automotive Systems
Gates Corp.
Goodyear Tire & Rubber
Hankook Tire
Johnson Controls
Kumho Tire
Lear Corp
Magna International
McLaren Performance
Meritor
Michelin
Nokian Tyres
Pirelli
Robert Bosch
Standard Motor Products
Sumitomo Rubber
Tomkins
Toyo Tire & Rubber
Trelleborg
Valeo
Visteon
Yokohama Rubber

HISTORICAL FINANCIALS

Company Type: Public

Income Statement FYE: December 31

	REVENUE ($ mil.)	NET INCOME ($ mil.)	NET PROFIT MARGIN	EMPLOYEES
12/12	43,147	2,482	5.8%	169,639
12/11	39,456	1,606	4.1%	163,788
12/10	34,860	770	2.2%	148,228
12/09	28,949	(2,375)	—	134,434
12/08	33,887	(1,570)	—	139,155
Annual Growth	6.2%	—	—	5.1%

2012 Year-End Financials

Debt ratio: 39.7%
Return on equity: 23.6%
Cash ($ mil.): 3,159
Current ratio: 0.99
Long-term debt ($ mil.): 5,510
No. of shares (mil.): 200
Dividends
Yield: 1.2%
Payout: 11.7%
Market value ($ mil.): 23,421

	STOCK PRICE ($) FY Close	P/E High/Low		PER SHARE ($) Earnings	Dividends	Book Value
12/12	117.10	22	12	12.42	0.29	57.78
12/11	62.00	33	14	8.03	0.00	46.21
12/10	78.10	59	25	3.85	0.73	39.21
12/09	53.00	—	—	(14.06)	0.00	32.16
12/08	39.65	—	—	(9.56)	0.49	43.56
Annual Growth	31.1%	—	—	—	(12.1%)	7.3%

Cosmo Oil Co., Ltd.

Cosmopolitan Cosmo Oil is one of Japan's top oil refiners and a major petroleum distributor. Cosmo Oil has four refineries; it markets its petroleum products through a network of almost 3500 gas stations. It has a refining and distribution joint venture with Nippon Oil that controls 40% of Japan's oil refining market. The company is also a major petrochemical producer. Cosmo Oil has exploration and production operations and imports crude oil from the Middle East and has affiliates in Singapore the UK and the US. Cosmo Oil has its refineries located near areas of large consumption: Tokyo Nagoya and Osaka.

Geographic Reach

The company serves petroleum product customers across Japan and petrochemical customers in Japan and South Korea.

In the United Arab Emirates and Qatar Cosmo Oil is engaged in oil exploration and production through Abu Dhabi Oil United Petroleum Development and Qatar Petroleum Development. The company is also conducting oil exploration in Australia.

Cosmo Oil operates through nine offices in Japan: Sapporo Sendai Tokyo Kanto-Minami Nagoya Osaka Hiroshima Takamatsu and Fukuoka.

Operations

The company's primary oil refining and petroleum product businesses is supported by two others: oil exploration and production and petrochemicals.

Cosmo Oil's petrochemical business with affiliate Maruzen Petrochemical produces ethylene and functional chemicals and subsidiaries CM Aromatics and Cosmo Matsuyama Oil produce mixed xylene. In addition Hyundai Cosmo Petrochemical a joint venture with Hyundai Oilbank produces and sales paraxylene. Petrochemical products are made and sold by Cosmo Matsuyama Oil CM Aromatics and Maruzen Petrochemical Co. Ltd. Also Hyundai Cosmo Petrochemical produces and sells petrochemical products in South Korea.

Its other businesses includes EcoPower Co. Ltd. which operates a wind power generation business in Japan and Cosmo Oil Group which is engaged in the construction of petroleum-related facilities leasing and insurance sales.

Financial Performance

The company's revenues increased by 12% in fiscal year 2012 thanks to positive results from its petroleum business. Product prices rose in tandem with an increase in the purchase price of crude oil. Higher fuel demand by thermal power plants following the shutting down of Japan's nuclear power plants led to an increase in sales volume of heavy fuel oil C used for electric power generation. Such growth was offset by sales volumes decline for gasoline kerosene naphtha jet fuel and heavy fuel oil A owing to the structural factors of improving fuel efficiency and the conversion to alternative fuels as well as the slow pace of economic recovery. The export volume of middle distillates (diesel fuel and jet fuel) declined due to the shutdown of the Chiba Refinery.

Cosmo Oil's net loss in fiscal 2012 (131% change over the previous year) which was attributed to The Great East Japan Earthquake which caused the shut down of the Chiba Refinery. Also tax system revisions led to a partial reversal of deferred tax assets.

Strategy

In 2013 the company diversified its business by entering into the mega-solar business with joint venture partners Showa Shell Sekiyu K.K and Development Bank of Japan. The new joint venture CSD Solar will operate and manage solar power generation facilities and sales of generated power to the general electricity utility companies. (Responding to the Japanese government's commitment to reduce carbon emissions and as part of its own push to diversify its operations in 2010 Cosmo made its first move into wind power buying Japan's #4 wind power company Eco Power which has 25 wind farms operating in Japan).

To further strengthen its competitiveness by expanding its network in Japan in 2012 Cosmo Oil bought 97% of Sojitz Energy from Sojitz Corporation. It is looking to leverage the numerous procurement sources loyal customers talented personnel and know-how of Sojitz Energy to beef up Cosmo Oil's domestic marketing strategy creating significant synergies in its supply stability and logistics network.

A major earthquake in 2011 badly damaged the Chiba refinery (40% of the company's total refining output) forcing Cosmo Oil to shut it down for repairs for an entire year.

To meet increased demand in Asia Cosmo Oil is investing more in these refineries and is expanding its petrochemical operations. The company is also looking to expand its operations in the Middle East where it has been involved in petroleum development in the United Arab Emirates for more than 30 years. In 2010 Cosmo Oil agreed to terms for renewing its license for three operating fields and gained a new concession area in Abu Dhabi. It is also looking to generate oil production from Australia.

The company is also pruning back its chain of service stations in order to be more efficient.

EXECUTIVES

Chairman, Yaichi Kimura
Chairman and Representative Director, Keiichiro Okabe
President, Keizo Morikawa
Managing Director, Kaoru Kawana
Senior Executive Officer Finance, Satoshi Miyamoto
Senior Executive Officer Refining and Technology Maintenance & Engineering and Safety and Environment Control, Hideto Matsumura
Senior Executive Officer General Affairs Affiliate Relations Information System Planning and Purchasing Center, Atsuto Tamura
Senior Executive Officer General Manager Chiba Refinery, Katsuhisa Ohtaki
Senior Executive Officer Petroleum E&P International V entures Crude Oil and Tanker and Petroleum Products Trading, Isao Kusakabe
General Manager Secretariat Office, Hideo Suzuki
Senior Executive Officer Sales Wholesale Marketing Industrial Fuel Marketing and Distribution, Hisashi Kobayash
President and Representative Director, Yaichi Kimura
Director, Mohamed D. Al Hamli
Director, Nasser A. Alsowaidi
EVP and Representative Director, Keizo Morikawa
Senior Executive Officer and Director, Satoshi Miyamoto
Senior Executive Officer Refining and Technology Maintenance & Engineering and Safety and Environment Control, Hideto Matsumura
Senior Executive Officer General Affairs Affiliate Relations Information System Planning and Purchasing Center, Atsuto Tamura
Senior Executive Officer and Director, Hisashi Kobayashi
Senior Executive Officer and Director, Isao Kusakabe
Auditors: KPMGAZSA&Co.

LOCATIONS

HQ: Cosmo Oil Co., Ltd.
1-1-1 Shibaura, Minato-ku, Tokyo 105-8528
Phone: (81) 3 3798 3243 **Fax:** (81) 3 3798 3237
Web: www.cosmo-oil.co.jp

PRODUCTS/OPERATIONS

2012 Sales

	% of total
Petroleum	94
Oil exploration &	3
Petrochemicals	1
Other	2
Total	**100**

COMPETITORS

Exxon Mobil
Idemitsu Kosan
JX Holdings
JX Nippon Oil & Energy
Showa Shell Sekiyu
Singapore Petroleum

HISTORICAL FINANCIALS

Company Type: Public

Income Statement FYE: March 31

	REVENUE ($ mil.)	NET INCOME ($ mil.)	NET PROFIT MARGIN	EMPLOYEES
03/13	33,655	(912)	—	6,496
03/12	37,909	(110)	—	6,247
03/11	33,469	349	1.0%	6,366
03/10	27,965	(114)	—	6,418
03/09	34,813	(938)	—	6,335
Annual Growth	(0.8%)	—	—	0.6%

2013 Year-End Financials

Debt ratio: 0.5%
Return on equity: (-31.3%)
Cash ($ mil.): 1,384
Current ratio: 1.18
Long-term debt ($ mil.): 5,991
No. of shares (mil.): 846
Dividends
Yield: —
Payout: —
Market value ($ mil.): 7,363

	STOCK PRICE ($) FY Close	P/E High/Low		PER SHARE ($) Earnings	Dividends	Book Value
03/13	8.70	—	—	(1.08)	0.00	3.23
Annual Growth	—	—	—	—	—	—

CPC Corporation, Taiwan

The Chinese petroleum handled by this company is in the other China –Taiwan. CPC (formerly Chinese Petroleum Corporation) is engaged in the exploration production refining storage transportation and the sale of oil and oil products in Taiwan. To supplement oil supply to hydrocarbon-poor Taiwan the state-owned monopoly has stakes in oil and gas exploration ventures in Australia Chad Ecuador Indonesia Libya the US and Venezuela. Its refineries produce natural gas kerosene fuel oil ethylene propylene and other refined products. CPC owns and operates more than 2030 gas stations as well as boat and aviation refueling stations. The Taiwanese government has CPC on track for privatization.

Geographic Reach

CPC has operations in Taiwan and in 21 active fields in seven countries including Block 16 and 17 in Ecuador; Sanga Sanga Bulungan Amborip VI and Sanga Sanga coal bed methane in Indonesia; Gulf of Paria East and Gulf of Paria West in Venezuela (negotiations are in progress in regard to confiscated prospects); Block AC/P21 and NT/P76 in Australia; Caviar Manahuilla Estrella Garden City Field and Hurricane Creek (Big Horn Shorts Creek Danub Yellowstone) Blocks in the USS; the Murzuq 162 Block in Libya; and the BCO III/BCS 11/BLT I Blocks in Chad. In tandem with CNPC it is also seeking to exploit the Agadem block in Niger.

Operations

In 2011 CPC sold a total of 15.28 billion cubic meters of natural gas mainly for power generation co-generation industrial and household use in Taiwan.

Financial Performance

In 2011 CPC's revenues increased by 10% and net income decreased by 302%.

Strategy

Because of its dependency of foreign oil and gas sources CPC plans to increase investment in domestic exploration and production in order to protect Taiwan from the rising costs of crude oil imports. In 2012 it signed a joint exploration and production agreement with Husky Energyto develop the deep water oil and gas reserve in the Tainan Basin in the Taiwan Strait southwest of Kaohsiung City.

Growing its marketing presence in 2012 CPC set up CPCI new subsidiary of the company's Overseas Petroleum and Investment Corporation (OPIC) Group as the first ever overseas oil trading unit in Singapore.

The company is also investing in upgrading its refinery infrastructure to increase its processing capacity and efficiency. To streamline refinery configuration and boost value-added profiles in 2012 CPC built a residue fluid catalytic cracking unit with a capacity of 80000 barrels per stream day. To meet the increase in ethylene demand by the local petrochemical industry that year CPC built a naphtha cracker unit with an annual capacity of 600000 metric tons of ethylene.

To comply with environmental regulations and to upgrade gasoline quality in 2011 CPC set up an alkylation unit with a capacity of 14000 barrels per stream day.

Company Background

Boosting its LNG supply base in 2008 CPC signed a deal whereby Woodside Petroleum agreed to supply 2-3 million tons per year for 15 to 20 years.

EXECUTIVES

Chairman, Sheng-Chung Lin
CEO Natural Gas Business Division, J. Y. Chen
President, Arthur H. Kung
VP; CEO Petrochemical Business Division, J. S. Yang
CEO Marketing Business Division, Cheng-Hsie Liu
CEO Solvent and Chemical Business Division, Jimmy Chang
VP, Ray-Chung Chang
VP, Shane S. I. Lin
VP, Ming-Huei Chen
CEO Exploration and Production Business Division, Jong-Chang Wu
CEO Refining Business Division, Ching-Yang Wu
CEO LPG Business Division, Jung-Lieh Lin
Acting CEO Lubricants Business Division, Ting Pang Chi
Director Refining & Manufacturing Research Institute, Vincent Y.S. Ho
Director Exploration & Development Research Institute, Shin-Tai Hu
Director Project & Construction Division and Acting Director LNG Project Division, Marc W.H. Lin
Director Green Technology Research Institute, Jung-Chung Wu
Director Material Testing & Certification Center, Ta-Tsung Yen
Auditors: DeloitteToucheTohmatsu

LOCATIONS

HQ: CPC Corporation, Taiwan
No. 3, Songren Road, Sinyi District, Taipei 11010
Phone: (886) 2 8789 8989 **Fax:** (886) 2 8789 9000
Web: www.cpc.com.tw

PRODUCTS/OPERATIONS

Selected Products

Industrial Oil
LNG Product
LPG Product
Lube Oil
Marine Oil
Motor Oil
RBU Product
SNC Product

COMPETITORS

BP
CNOOC
Cosmo Oil
Exxon Mobil
Formosa Plastics
Royal Dutch Shell
Sinopec Corp.
TOTAL

HISTORICAL FINANCIALS

Company Type: Public

Income Statement FYE: December 31

	REVENUE ($ mil.)	NET INCOME ($ mil.)	NET PROFIT MARGIN	EMPLOYEES
12/12	39,529	(1,158)	—	14,977
12/11	33,977	(1,070)	—	15,219
12/10	32,104	549	1.7%	14,871
12/09	22,974	1,176	5.1%	14,931
12/08	29,218	(3,678)	—	14,843
Annual Growth	7.8%	—	—	0.2%

2012 Year-End Financials

Debt ratio: 0.8%
Return on equity: (-13.0%)
Cash ($ mil.): 81
Current ratio: 0.89
Long-term debt ($ mil.): 6,080
No. of shares (mil.): —
Dividends
Yield: —
Payout: —
Market value ($ mil.): —

Credit Suisse Group

Credit Suisse is one of Switzerland's top financial services firms though a distant second to behemoth rival UBS. The group provides investment management private banking and asset management services to clients worldwide. Its investment banking offerings include debt and equity underwriting M&A advisory and other securities services. The group provides wealth management services in Switzerland through subsidiary Clariden Leu; internationally it operates under the Credit Suisse brand. Credit Suisse offers asset management services to individual institutional and government clients. With more than 200 retail branches in Switzerland it operates in more than 50 countries (including the US and UK).

Credit Suisse is working to rebound from the global economic meltdown. The group suffered hefty losses at the height of the crisis (in 2008) and subsequent legislation and market turmoil has continued to make it challenging for Credit Suisse. New regulation such as the Dodd-Frank Act enacted in 2010 to prevent risky activities in the financial industry impacted financial institutions like Credit Suisse by limiting proprietary trading and raising capital requirements. To this end the group has been reducing its investment banking operations and focusing on its client-focused businesses which are less volatile. In 2011 Credit Suisse exited proprietary trading and other businesses that were a drain on capital. In 2013 the firm also sold its exchange traded funds (ETFs) business to private equity giant BlackRock Inc.

Its three primary businesses —Private Banking Investment Banking and Asset Management —are increasingly collaborating to increase the group's efficiency. In 2011 Credit Suisse cut 3500 jobs (or 7% or its workforce) in an effort to reduce costs. It was part of a bigger plan to cut around 8% in total costs.

Credit Suisse's strategy as the economy recovers includes expanding its roster of high-net-worth customers around the world and in Switzerland adding commercial clients of all sizes. In investment banking Credit Suisse is focused on reducing its risky assets and cutting costs. In asset management the company is working in collaboration with its private banking and investment banking arms to grow revenues by expanding its product line. The asset management segment (which concentrates on alternative investments including private equity hedge funds and real estate) is growing in markets such as Brazil southeast Asia China and Russia.

The company continues to make strategic acquisitions in order to grow the business. In late 2010 the company acquired a 30% stake in US hedge fund York Capital Management. The following year it acquired Fortis' Nederland's Prime Fund Solutions business which will strengthen its hedge fund offerings. In 2012 the company acquired HSBC's private banking operations in Japan.

Results in 2011 were impacted by the struggling economy and new regulations within the financial services industry. Credit Suisse reported a 62% drop in net revenues in 2011. Results in the investment banking business were particularly hurt due to macroeconomic uncertainties political strife and regulatory changes. The company also is transitioning itself to operate within new global banking rules by ridding itself of risk and improving its capital ratios.

In 2012 Credit Suisse handed over information to the US government as part of an investigation into hidden Swiss bank accounts that are used by wealthy Americans to evade taxes. Credit Suisse was among other Swiss banks that were being investigated. Swiss privacy laws have typically protected wealthy individuals who funnel money through offshore accounts.

HISTORY

In 1856 shortly after the creation of the Swiss federation Alfred Escher opened Credit Suisse (CS) in Zurich. Primarily a venture capital firm CS helped fund Swiss railroads and other industries. It later opened offices in Italy and helped establish the Swiss Bank Corporation.

CS shifted its focus to commercial banking in 1867 and sold most of its stock holdings. By 1871 it was Switzerland's largest bank buoyed by the nation's swift industrialization. In 1895 CS helped create the predecessor of Swiss utility Electrowatt. Foreign activity grew in the 1920s. A run on banks in the Depression forced CS to sell assets at a loss and dip into reserves of unreported retained profits.

Trade declined in WWII but neutrality left Switzerland's institutions intact and made it a major banking center partly due to CS's role as a conduit for the Nazis' plundered gold. Foreign exchange and gold trading became important activities for CS after WWII. Mortgage and consumer credit acquisitions fueled domestic growth in the 1970s.

In 1978 the bank took a stake in US investment bank First Boston and with it formed London-based Credit Suisse-First Boston (CSFB). CS created 44%-owned holding company Credit Suisse First Boston to own First Boston CSFB and Tokyo-based CS First Boston Pacific.

The stock market crash of 1987 led a damaged First Boston to merge with CSFB the next year. In 1990 CS (renamed CS Holding) injected $300 million into CSFB and shifted $470 million in bad loans from its books becoming the first foreign owner of a major Wall Street investment bank.

In the early 1990s CS Holding strengthened its insurance business with a Winterthur Insurance alliance. In 1993 and 1994 acquisitions helped it gain share in its overbanked home market.

In 1996 CS Holding reorganized as Credit Suisse Group and grew internationally including further merging the daredevil US investment banking operations into Credit Suisse's more staid and relationship-oriented corporate banking. It bought Winterthur (Switzerland's #2 insurer) in 1997 as well as Barclays' European investment banking business.

Credit Suisse and other Swiss banks came under fire in 1996 for refusing to relinquish assets from Jewish bank accounts from the Holocaust era and for gold trading with the Nazi regime. In 1997 the banks agreed to establish a humanitarian fund for Holocaust victims. A stream of lawsuits by American heirs and boycott threats from US states and cities led in 1998 to a tentative $1.25 billion settlement (unpopular in Switzerland) with Credit Suisse on the hook for about a third of that.

CS in 1998 expanded its investment banking by buying Brazil's Banco de Investimentos Garantia; it also moved to expand US money management operations by allying with New York-based Warburg Pincus Asset Management. By 1999 that joint venture —which was to give the investment firm access to CS's mutual fund distribution channels in Europe and Asia —had morphed into CS's $650 million purchase of Warburg Pincus Asset Management.

Japan revoked the license of the company's financial products unit for obstructing an investigation (the harshest penalty ever given to a foreign firm at the time); it also accused the company of helping 60 others hide losses and cover up evidence.

In 2000 the company started a mortgage and home-buying Web site and decided to allow searches of Holocaust-era accounts. The next year as a part of its European expansion Credit Suisse acquired Spanish broker and asset manager General de Valores y Cambios.

Under former chairman and CEO Lukas Muhlemann the company expanded Credit Suisse First Boston when it bought US investment firm Donaldson Lufkin & Jenrette in 2000 and renamed it Credit Suisse First Boston (USA).

The collapse of Credit Suisse's share price along with what proved to be an over-ambitious acquisition strategy brought about the downfall of Muhlemann who was pressured out by shareholders in 2002.

In 2005 Credit Suisse merged with its Credit Suisse First Boston subsidiary creating a global Credit Suisse brand and in 2006 reorganized into three distinct operating segments —investment banking private banking and asset management along with insurance.

Credit Suisse sold insurance subsidiary Winterthur to AXA in 2006 for nearly $10 billion. A Winterthur sale had been on Credit Suisse's agenda for a while as a plan to divest noncore operations. Also that year Credit Suisse and General Electric jointly acquired a 50% stake in London City Airport which serves about 2 million travelers a year. The following year as a cost-saving measure Credit Suisse combined four private banks and one securities dealer into Clariden Leu.

The company named Brady Dougan CEO in 2007. Dugan was the first non-German speaker to hold the position.

Globally the investment banking industry was hit hard by the US subprime mortgage crisis and Credit Suisse was no exception. The company reported a net loss of ?5.4 billion in 2008 the worst in its history. Credit Suisse turned down a bailout offer from the Swiss government in 2008 but it did receive a capital injection of CHF10 billion ($8.7 billion) from private investors. However the capital infusion couldn't prevent losses as global credit markets froze and consumer and shareholder confidence fell.

The company cut more than 5000 jobs or some 11% of its workforce mostly from its investment banking unit. It also reviewed its results for 2007 and among its findings discovered rogue traders in its ranks a la the beleaguered Societe Generale. Credit Suisse reduced its results accordingly.

In 2008 it bought an 80% stake in US firm Asset Management Finance Corporation a division of National Bank of Canada. Also in 2008 it expanded its Middle East franchise when it bought majority ownership in joint venture Saudi Swiss Securities which it renamed Credit Suisse Saudi Arabia. It has added Shariah-compliant banking for Islamic clients and has expanded in other markets including Brazil Kazakhstan and Turkey.

The following year Credit Suisse sold certain fund management assets and businesses to Aberdeen Asset Management in exchange for about 25% of Aberdeen's shares.

EXECUTIVES

Chief Risk Officer, Tobias Guldimann, age 52
Vice Chairman, Peter Brabeck-Letmathe, age 69
Honorary Chairman of the Board of Directors, Rainer E. Gut, age 81
Independent Member of the Board, Walter B. Kielholz, age 62
CEO, Brady W. Dougan, age 54
Chief Talent Branding and Communications Officer, Pamela A. Thomas-Graham, age 50
Corporate Secretary, Pierre Schreiber
Head Private Banking and Wealth Management; CEO Region Americas, Robert S. (Rob) Shafir, age 56
Chairman, Urs Rohner, age 54
CEO Investment Bank; CEORegion Asia Pacific, Eric Varvel, age 50
CEO Private Banking and Credit Suisse Switzerland, Hans-Ulrich Meister
Chairman Private Banking, Walter Berchtold, age 51
CIO and Director, Karl Landert, age 55
CEO Europe Middle East and Africa, Fawzi Kyriakos-Saad
Chief Risk Officer Clariden Leu, Jean-Pierre Colombara
Head Mergers and Acquisitions Middle East and North Africa, Anthony Armstrong
CFO, David Mathers, age 49
General Counsel, Romeo Cerutti, age 51
CEO Americas, Antonio Quintella
CEO Asia Pacific, Osama Abbasi
Independent Member of the Board of Directors, Anton Anton van Rossum Rossum
Member of the Board of Directors, Jassim Jassim Al Thani Thani
Secretary of the Board, Joan Joan Belzer Belzer
Head Investment Banking; CEO Region Europe Middle East & Africa (EMEA), Gael de Boissard
Vice Chairman, Peter Brabeck-Letmathe, age 69
Director, Richard E. Thornburgh, age 62
Independent Member of the Board of Directors, Robert H. (Bob) Benmosche, age 68
Independent Member of the Board, Walter B. Kielholz, age 62
Director, Ernst Tanner, age 66
Director, Jean Lanier, age 67
Director, Anton van Rossum, age 67
Director, Aziz R.D. Syriani, age 70
Director, Andreas N. Koopmann, age 62
CIO and Director, Karl Landert, age 55
Director, Noreen Doyle, age 63
Director, David W. Syz, age 69
Director, Peter F. Weibel, age 71
Director, John Tiner, age 56
Auditors: KPMGAG

LOCATIONS

HQ: Credit Suisse Group
Paradeplatz 8, Zurich CH 8070
Phone: (41) 44 212 16 16 **Fax:** (41) 44 333 25 87
Web: www.credit-suisse.com

PRODUCTS/OPERATIONS

2011 Sales

	% of total
Interest and dividend	53
Commissions &	30
Trading	12
Other	5
Total	**100**

COMPETITORS

AEGON
Barclays
Citigroup
Deutsche Bank
Goldman Sachs
Grupo Santander
HSBC
ING
JPMorgan Chase
Mitsubishi UFJ Financial Group
Mizuho Financial
Morgan Stanley
Nomura Securities
TD Bank
UBS

HISTORICAL FINANCIALS

Company Type: Public

Income Statement FYE: December 31

	ASSETS ($ mil.)	NET INCOME ($ mil.)	INCOME AS % OF ASSETS	EMPLOYEES
12/12	1,008,171	1,617	0.2%	47,400
12/11	1,115,189	2,075	0.2%	49,700
12/10	1,102,816	5,447	0.5%	50,100
12/09	1,001,389	6,528	0.7%	47,600
12/08	1,100,225	(7,725)	—	47,800
Annual Growth	(2.2%)	—	—	(0.2%)

2012 Year-End Financials

Return on assets: 0.1%
Return on equity: 4.2%
Long-term debt ($ mil.): —
No. of shares (mil.): 1,293
Sales ($ mil): 26,143
Dividends
Yield: 3.3%
Payout: 173.9%
Market value ($ mil.): 31,776

	STOCK PRICE ($) FY Close	P/E High	P/E Low	PER SHARE ($) Earnings	Dividends	Book Value
12/12	24.56	39	20	0.98	0.82	30.04
12/11	23.48	41	18	1.45	1.82	29.33
12/10	40.41	15	9	4.16	1.78	30.30
12/09	49.16	11	3	4.99	0.09	31.15
12/08	28.26	—	—	(7.36)	2.78	26.09
Annual Growth	(3.4%)	—	—	—	(26.4%)	3.6%

CTBC Financial Holdings Ltd

Chinatrust Financial Holding (CFHC) is one of Taiwan's largest financial services groups. It operates Chinatrust Commercial Bank which has more than 140 domestic branches and more than 70 overseas. The group provides general banking services including corporate and consumer loans financial consulting checking and savings accounts letters of credit commercial drafts collections and payments and credit cards. It also offers property/casualty insurance life insurance investments and other related financial services. Overseas the bank operates subsidiaries in the US Canada the Philippines and Indonesia. The predecessor to the family-owned CFHC was founded in 1966.

EXECUTIVES

President Retail Banking Group, Oliver Shang
SVP, Miao-Chiu Hsu
President Institutional Banking Group and Director, James Chen
EVP; Managing Director Investment Banking Group, Larry Hsu
EVP; Managing Director Retail Banking Group, Su Kuo Huang
Managing Director General Administration, Thomas K. S. Chen
EVP; Managing Director Consumer Finance Group, Eric Wu
EVP; Managing Director Risk Management Group, Jack T. K. Cheng
EVP; Managing Director Audit Management Division, Julie L. Yang
EVP, Jason Wang
EVP, Albert Shiung
SVP, Connie Lin
Chief Executive Officer-Banking Business, DeNoma Michael
Chief Executive Officer-China Business, Lianfu Luo
Chairman of the Board, Liansong Gu
Chief Administrative Officer, Renjie Gao
Chief Information Officer, Rutian Zhang
Chief Risk Officer, Taike Zheng
Chief Executive Officer-Insurance Business, Yinbao Ling
President Institutional Banking Group and Director, James Chen
Director, Jeffrey L. S. Koo
Independent Director, Wenzhi Li
Independent Director, Zhihong Li

LOCATIONS

HQ: CTBC Financial Holdings Ltd
17F, No.3, Sung Shou Road, Taipei
Phone: (886) 2 2722 2002 **Fax:** (886) 2 2723 7883
Web: www.chinatrustgroup.com.tw

PRODUCTS/OPERATIONS

2007 Sales

	% of total
Institutional	38
Retail	34
Consumer	28
Total	**100**

COMPETITORS

Cathay Financial Holding
Fubon Financial
Hua Nan Financial

Chang Hwa Bank	Mega Financial
E.Sun	Shin Kong
East West Bancorp	SinoPac Holdings
First Financial Holding	Taishin
	Taiwan Business Bank

HISTORICAL FINANCIALS

Company Type: Public

Income Statement FYE: December 31

	ASSETS ($ mil.)	NET INCOME ($ mil.)	INCOME AS % OF ASSETS	EMPLOYEES
12/12	72,701	730	1.0%	13,107
12/11	66,632	603	0.9%	12,568
12/10	62,359	485	0.8%	11,562
12/09	55,032	76	0.1%	9,983
12/08	52,702	448	0.9%	10,113
Annual Growth	8.4%	12.9%	—	6.7%

2012 Year-End Financials

Return on assets: 1.0%
Return on equity: 12.3%
Long-term debt ($ mil.): —
No. of shares (mil.): —
Sales ($ mil): 3,272

Dividends
Yield: —
Payout: —
Market value ($ mil.): —

Dai Nippon Printing Co., Ltd.

A leading commercial printer Dai Nippon Printing (DNP) has diversified beyond the business of spreading ink on paper. The global firm still produces books and magazines dictionaries catalogs and business forms and it has added items such as CD-ROMs holograms and smart cards to the mix while subsidiary CHI Group sells e-books. Its Lifestyle and Industrial Supplies segment makes decorative materials for use in fixtures and furniture along with packaging for consumer products. Its Electronics segment's products include photomasks used in the manufacture of integrated circuits and color filters for LCD panels. DNP also has a Beverage unit through which it owns a majority of Hokkaido Coca-Cola Bottling.

DNP has about 60 production plants and 45 sales offices throughout Japan; it also operates about 10 plants and 20 sales offices in more than a dozen other countries. Like other leading printing companies DNP has branched out from publishing and commercial printing into such fields as environmentally friendly packaging decorative materials display-related products and electronics. In 2010 DNP's operating income improved in the Electronics and Lifestyle and Industrial Supplies segments because of a rebound in demand for flat-panel displays. As a result DNP's total earnings swung to a net income of some Y23 billion (about $275 million) in 2010 up from a loss of more than Y20 billion (about $239 million) in 2009.

In addition to a recovering economy that helped with increased sales the company has also benefitted from cost cutting efforts. On the manufacturing front DNP has been consolidating production systems in order to increase operating efficiencies. In fiscal year 2010 it integrated the domestic printing ink business of its Intec subsidiary with leading Japanese ink company DIC Corporation to form the joint venture DIC Graphics Corp.

Elsewhere in manufacturing DNP has expanded; in 2010 it opened a new plant in Taiwan to meet the overseas demand for photomasks. The company is responding to the recovery in the LCD market and Electronics had been DNP's fastest-growing business. Because it makes products for both the interior (photomasks) and exterior (displays) of high-tech equipment the company believes it is well-positioned for additional growth.

Adapting to the shrinking publishing market in Japan and beyond DNP has streamlined its books and magazine operations by merging several of its subsidiaries under a newly established holding company CHI Group Co. The group was formed in 2010 by the combination of DNP's bookstore chain Maruzen with library service provider TRC Inc. (TRC services include operational support and database management.) Bookseller Junkudo — which operates about 30 shops in major Japanese cities and which DNP acquired in 2009 —was also integrated into CHI Group. The group is the focus of DNP's strategy to introduce more e-books to the market. CHI is capitalizing on the fact that digital publishing is one of the few bright spots in an otherwise dismal publishing arena.

Another way in which DNP is working on digital publishing is by expanding its information security business. As part of these efforts in 2010 DNP acquired security system developer Intelligent Wave a Japanese firm engaged in network connection authorization and other processing systems for credit card payments. DNP and Intelligent Wave were already cooperating to provide security services to financial institutions and the acquisition strengthened DNP's resources for providing secure digital transactions.

The company's smallest business unit Hokkaido Coca-Cola Bottling accounts for less than 5% of sales. Beverage sales have lost their fizz as a result of a decrease in sales of tea and coffee drinks. The company is hoping that I LOHAS a new brand of water that uses "ecoru Bottle Shiboru" Japan's lightest PET (polyethylene terephthalate) plastic bottle will help boost the business.

HISTORY

In 1876 Shueisha the predecessor to Dai Nippon Printing (DNP) was established in central Tokyo. As the only modern printing firm in Japan it was well-positioned to attract the business of the emerging newspaper and book industries. The company originally used a movable-type hand printer but became the first private industry to use steam power in Japan when it updated its presses in 1884.

Following Japanese victories over China and Russia at the turn of the century Japan embarked on a period of military and economic expansion. This was matched by a growing demand for printing. In 1927 Japan published 20000 book titles and 40 million magazines. The country's first four-color gravure printing system was inaugurated the following year. In 1935 Shueisha changed its name to Dai Nippon Printing following its merger with Nisshin Printing.

The 1930s and 1940s were lean times for printers; Japan's repressive military government suppressed publishers and banned books. WWII devastated the publishing industry along with the rest of the Japanese economy but the publishing industry recovered soon after the end of the war. DNP was assisted in its recovery by government contracts; in 1946 it was designated by the Ministry of Finance to print 100-yen notes. In 1949 the company entered the securities printing business and in 1951 it expanded into packaging and decorative interiors production. DNP reemerged in 1958 as Japan's largest printing firm.

In 1963 DNP followed Toppan in setting up an office in Hong Kong. Both Hong Kong and Singapore had become havens for Shanghai printing entrepreneurs who had emigrated in the face of the Communist takeover of China in 1949. These cities became centers for low-cost high-quality color printing for British and American book publishers. In 1973 DNP overtook R. R. Donnelley as the world's largest printer. The next year the company set up a subsidiary in the US DNP (America) Inc.

DNP moved into the information processing business in the 1980s developing a credit card-sized calculator in 1985 a digital color printer system in 1986 and a Japanese-language word processor in 1987. The company launched Hi-Vision Static Pictures in 1989 to market a process that converted data into a form used by high-definition TV. In 1990 DNP bought a controlling stake in Tien Wah Press the #1 printer in Singapore.

The next year DNP completed the first construction stage of its Okayama plant dedicated to information media supplies (mainly transfer ribbons for color printers). The second stage specializing in interior decorative materials was completed in 1993.

In 1994 the company launched its Let's Go to an Amusement Park! virtual reality software system. Two years later DNP produced an integrated circuit card for about a tenth of current costs giving it a major competitive edge in the magnetic card market.

In 1999 the company began selling CD-ROMs online through subsidiary TransArt. The following year Dai Nippon formed partnerships or joint ventures with Toshiba (to develop printed circuit boards) Microsoft (to develop Windows-based smart cards) and Numerical Technologies (to develop advanced phase-shifted photomasks). In 2002 the company joined with Toshiba and Takara to develop and promote a lightweight educational computer called an Ex-Pad.

In 2006 the company renamed its Industrial Supplies operation to become Lifestyle Materials and made plans to expand that business. The following year it purchased a stake in bookstore chain Maruzen and invested in TRC Inc. a provider of library operation services. In 2008 TRC became a wholly owned subsidiary of DNP.

The company ramped up efforts to revitalize Japan's ailing book market through investments and acquisitions in 2009. Aiming to boost education and publishing operations DNP acquired a majority stake in bookseller Junkudo which operates about 30 shops in major Japanese cities. It also invested in Shufunotomo Co. a women's magazine publisher. DNP combined its resources and influence with three other Japanese publishers agreeing to acquire a roughly 30% stake in secondhand bookseller Bookoff. The chain operates through about 1000 stores across Japan.

EXECUTIVES

EVP, Koichi Takanami
EVP, Masayoshi Yamada
President, Yoshitoshi Kitajima
Senior Managing Director, Mitsuhiko Hakii
Senior Managing Director, Teruomi Yoshino
Senior Managing Director, Osamu Tsuchida
Corporate Officer, Masato Koike
EVP, Yoshinari Kitajima
Managing Director, Kazumasa Hiroki
Senior Managing Director, Yujiro Kuroda
Senior Corporate Officer, Tatsuya Nishimura, age 64
Senior Managing Director, Masahiko Wada
Managing Director, Tetsuji Morino
Managing Director, Kunikazu Akishige
Managing Director, Motoharu Kitajima
Managing Directors, Takao Shimizu
Senior Corporate Officer, Tatsuro Kitayuguchi
Senior Corporate Officer, Fujio Yamazaki
Senior Corporate Officer, Takashi Saito
Senior Corporate Officer, Shigemi Furuya

Corporate Officer, Jun-ichi Tsuchiya
Corporate Officer, Tokuji Kanda
Corporate Officer, Takashi Wada
Managing Director, Sakae Hikita
Corporate Officer, Ryuji Minemura
Corporate Officer, Masato Yamaguchi
Senior Corporate Officer, Tatsuo Komaki
Managing Director, Yoshiki Nozaka
Managing Director, Masaki Tsukada
Corporate Officer, Yasuo Takeda
Corporate Officer, Morihiro Muramoto
EVP and Director, Koichi Takanami
EVP and Director, Masayoshi Yamada
President and Director, Yoshitoshi Kitajima
EVP and Director, Satoshi Saruwatari
Senior Managing Director, Mitsuhiko Hakii
Senior Managing Director, Teruomi Yoshino
Senior Managing Director, Osamu Tsuchida
EVP and Director, Yoshinari Kitajima
Managing Director, Kazumasa Hiroki
Senior Managing Director, Yujiro Kuroda
Senior Managing Director, Masahiko Wada
Managing Director, Tetsuji Morino
Managing Director, Kunikazu Akishige
Managing Director, Yoshiaki Nagano
Managing Directors, Takao Shimizu
Managing Director, Sakae Hikita
Managing Director, Yoshiki Nozaka
Managing Director, Masaki Tsukada
Director, Tadao Tsukada
Auditors: MeijiAuditCorporation

LOCATIONS

HQ: Dai Nippon Printing Co., Ltd.
1-1-1 Ichigaya-Kagacho, Shinjuku-ku, Tokyo 162-8001
Phone: (81) 3 5225 8370 **Fax:** (81) 3 5225 8239
Web: www.dnp.co.jp

2010 Sales

	% of total
Japan	88
Other	12
Total	**100**

PRODUCTS/OPERATIONS

2010 Sales

	% of total
Information	46
Lifestyle & Industrial	34
Electronics	16
Beverages	4
Total	**100**

Selected Products and Services

Information Communication
- Bank notes
- Books
- Business forms
- Catalogs
- CD-ROMs and DVDs
- Direct mail
- Magazines
- Plastic cards
- Promotional publications

Lifestyle and Industrial Supplies
- Decorative materials
- Packaging

Electronics
- Color filters for liquid crystal displays
- Photomasks
- Projection TV screens
- Shadowmasks for color TVs

Beverages

COMPETITORS

3M
Asahi Breweries
Graphic Packaging Holding
Hitachi
LG Display
Photronics
Quad/Graphics
R.R. Donnelley
Sapporo
Siemens AG
Suntory Holdings
TSMC
Toppan Printing
Vesuvius

HISTORICAL FINANCIALS

Company Type: Public

Income Statement FYE: March 31

	REVENUE ($ mil.)	NET INCOME ($ mil.)	NET PROFIT MARGIN	EMPLOYEES
03/13	15,374	204	1.3%	39,445
03/12	18,374	(199)	—	39,986
03/11	19,193	302	1.6%	40,188
03/10	16,951	249	1.5%	39,643
03/09	16,093	(212)	—	40,317
Annual Growth	(1.1%)	—	—	(0.5%)

2013 Year-End Financials

Debt ratio: 0.1%
Return on equity: 2.1%
Cash ($ mil.): 2,270
Current ratio: 1.64
Long-term debt ($ mil.): 1,425
No. of shares (mil.): 643
Dividends
Yield: —
Payout: —
Market value ($ mil.): 6,087

	STOCK PRICE ($) FY Close	P/E High/Low	PER SHARE ($) Earnings	Dividends	Book Value
03/13	9.46	— —	0.32	0.00	15.48
03/12	10.17	— —	(0.31)	0.00	17.32
03/11	12.25	— —	0.47	0.37	17.87
03/10	13.58	— —	0.39	0.33	15.91
03/09	9.28	— —	(0.33)	0.38	14.83
Annual Growth	0.5%	— —	—	—	1.1%

Dai-Ichi Life Insurance Co., Ltd.

Trying its best to live up to its name (Dai-ichi means "first") Dai-ichi Life Insurance Company is one of Japan's top insurers. The firm sells individual and group life insurance annuities and supplemental medical coverage as well as individual and group pension products. Dai-ichi Life also provides nonlife insurance products through its partnership with Sompo Japan Insurance as well as cancer insurance through a partnership with Aflac. Other services include asset management and risk management. Dai-ichi Life sells its products through its network of thousands of sales representatives.

Sales and Marketing

Dai-ichi Life markets its products through sales representatives at a number of locations –including retail stores call centers and administration centers –as well as through online and direct mail programs.

Strategy

The company has responded to increased competition in the Japanese market by expanding its product offerings including lifetime supplemental medical coverage and annuity products. In expanding its financial services segment the company has become one of the top institutional investors in Japan.

Mergers and Acquisitions

Dai-ichi Life is also investing in overseas subsidiaries in a bid to increase its presence outside of Japan. In mid-2011 it strengthened its international presence by acquiring the balance of Tower Australia Group. (It first purchase a stake in the Australian life insurer in 2008.) Dai-Ichi Life has also made moves into Thailand and Vietnam.

Ownership

Previously named Dai-ichi Mutual Life Insurance the company jumped on the demutualization bandwagon and made its IPO on the Tokyo stock exchange in early 2010. The listing for the renamed Dai-ichi Life Insurance raised some Y1 trillion ($11 billion) and the proceeds were used to pad the company's coffers after the drop in value of its securities during the economic recession.

EXECUTIVES

Chairman, Katsutoshi Saito, age 70
Deputy President, Hideto Masaki
Senior Managing Executive Officer and Director, Shinsuke Kume
President, Koichiro Watanabe
Senior Managing Executive Officer, Ryoji Yajima
Senior Managing Executive Officer, Satoru Ueno
Senior Managing Executive Officer, Kazuma Ishii
Senior Managing Executive Officer, Shigeo Tsuyuki
Managing Executive Officer, Takahiro Inaba
Managing Executive Officer, Takehide Itonaga
Senior Managing Executive Officer, Norimitsu Horio
Managing Executive Officer and Director, Tomoyasu Asano
Managing Executive Officer and Director, Yoshio Takeyama
Executive Officer, Hiroshi Kanai
Executive Officer, Akio Tanaka
Executive Officer, Kenji Sakurai
Executive Officer, Morinobu Nagahama
Executive Officer, Hideo Teramoto
Executive Officer, Takashi Kawashima
Chairman Dai-ichi Life Insurance Company of Vietnam, Takashi Fujii
CEO and Managing Director Dai-ichi Life Australia, Jim Minto
Chairman Ocean Life Insurance, Kirati Assakul
Chief Representative Beijing, Zhao Ke Fei
Chief Representative Taipei, Hajime Namba
Executive Officer; Chief Director of Investment, Atsushi Nagayama
Executive Officer; Chief Director of Eastern Japan Sales, Atsushi Takahashi
Executive Officer; Chief Director of Underwriting; Director of Business Affaris Planning, Masao Taketomi
Executive Officer; President of Sapporo General Office; Director of Hokkaido Sales, Nobuyuki Akimoto
Executive Officer, Shinichi Aizawa
President Dai-ichi Life International (U.S.A.), Shigeru Mori
Managing Director Dai-ichi Life International (Europe), Shinichiro Masunaga
CEO Star Union Dai-ichi Life Insurance, Girish Kulkarni
Managing Director Dai-ichi Life International (AsiaPacific), Tatsusaburo Yamamoto
Chief Representative Shanghai, Tomoki Sugizaki
President and Board Member, Katsutoshi Saito, age 68
Senior Managing Executive Officer and Director, Hideto Masaki
Senior Managing Executive Officer and Director, Shinsuke Kume
Senior Managing Executive Officer and Director, Koichiro Watanabe
Director, Nobuya Minami
Managing Executive Officer and Director, Ryoji Yajima
Managing Executive Officer and Director, Kazuma Ishii
Managing Executive Officer and Director, Shigeo Tsuyuki

Managing Executive Officer and Director, Tomoyasu Asano
Senior Managing Executive Officer and Director, Kimio Oiso
Managing Executive Officer and Director, Yoshio Takeyama
Director, Haruo Funabashi
Independent Director, Michiko Miyamoto
Auditors: Ernst&YoungShinNihon

LOCATIONS

HQ: Dai-Ichi Life Insurance Co., Ltd.
1-13-1 Yuraku-cho, Chiyoda-ku, Tokyo 100-8411
Phone: (81) 3 3216 1211
Web: www.dai-ichi-life.co.jp

COMPETITORS

AXA Life Insurance	Meiji Yasuda Life
Asahi Mutual Life	Mitsui Life
Daido Life	Nippon Life Insurance
Fukoku Mutual	Sumitomo Life
Gibraltar Life Insurance	Taiyo Life

HISTORICAL FINANCIALS

Company Type: Public

Income Statement FYE: March 31

	REVENUE ($ mil.)	NET INCOME ($ mil.)	NET PROFIT MARGIN	EMPLOYEES
03/13	52,947	344	0.7%	60,771
03/12	55,775	248	0.4%	60,305
03/11	51,146	231	0.5%	59,356
03/10	53,009	595	1.1%	60,061
03/09	45,409	881	1.9%	55,883
Annual Growth	3.9%	(20.9%)	—	2.1%

2013 Year-End Financials

Debt ratio: 0.0%	No. of shares (mil.): 10
Return on equity: 2.4%	Dividends
Cash ($ mil.): 5,460	Yield: —
Current ratio: 0.14	Payout: —
Long-term debt ($ mil.): 1,642	Market value ($ mil.): 14,000

	STOCK PRICE ($) FY Close	P/E High/Low	PER SHARE ($) Earnings	Dividends	Book Value
03/13	1,400.00	— —	34.80	0.00	1,752.53
03/12	1,050.52	— —	25.13	0.00	1,209.00
Annual Growth	33.3%	— —	8.5%	—	9.7%

Daimler AG

Daimler's cars may stop on a dime but they cost a little more than that. Daimler's passenger car business Mercedes-Benz includes luxury brands Mercedes and Maybach as well as compact hybrid and electric models including its smart and B-Class F-Cell brands. Its Daimler Trucks North America unit manufactures heavy-trucks in the US and with its Fuso Mercedes-Benz and Sprinter brands Daimler is the world's leading maker of commercial vehicles. The Atego BlueTecHybrid truck was launched in 2011. The company holds a 22% stake in aerospace and defense consortium EADS and 60% in Formula One team Mercedes-Benz Grand Prix. Daimler sells its vehicles in 40 countries but Europe represents 40% of its sales.

What a difference a year makes. Daimler followed the global post-recession automotive trend with a 24% boost in its 2010 revenues over 2009. Its net income went from a negative E4.4 billion (more than $6 billion) to a positive E5.6 billion (almost $8 billion). China which is where Mercedes-Benz is the fastest growing premium brand posted a sales increase of almost 140% over 2009. Overall the company's vehicle sales increased by 27% trucks by 37% and vans 35% over 2009. Daimler expects a positive trajectory in 2011 sales but not at the level of 2010.

The global automotive markets started to recover in the second half of 2010 fueled by government incentive programs designed to stimulate car sales. Prior to that Daimler made certain that it was in the driver's seat when it came to navigating the economic gridlock of 2008 and 2009.

Daimler implemented restructuring and efficiency initiatives to bring production in line with demand. In addition it refined its strategy to develop environmentally friendly compact cars along with strengthening its luxury brand by engineering models adapted for regional markets such as Asia. Recognizing a change in investor behavior the company delisted and deregistered from the New York Stock Exchange (NYSE Euronext) and the SEC in mid-2010. Delisting saves on administrative expenses and fees for financial reporting.

Daimler also used 2010 to ally itself with companies to increase scale reduce expenses share in developing advanced technology as well as to expand geographically. To that end the company entered a partnership agreement with Nissan and Renault to share small-car technology and powertrains and work together to develop electric cars anticipating the ability to compete with global giants Toyota and VW. Through this alliance Daimler will also acquire technology for its next smart fortwo model (which will be developed alongside Renault's Twingo model) to help make the car profitable. The first jointly developed smart fortwo and Twingo models possibly including all-electric versions are expected to be launched in 2013. Additionally the company will have access to diesel engines and transmissions for its Mercedes-Benz Vito van. For its part Daimler will provide engines from its Mercedes division for use in Nissan's Infiniti luxury car model.

As part of the three-way deal the companies will take equity stakes in each other. Renault and Nissan will each acquire a 1.55% stake ; the combined 3.1% stake in Daimler is estimated to be worth about E1.2 billion ($1.6 billion). Daimler will acquire a 3.1% stake in each of Renault and Nissan. The equity investments are intended to encourage ongoing collaboration among the three companies.

Another way Daimler took advantage of the economic slowdown was to develop new products and get involved in markets with developing economies with a particular eye on Brazil China India and Russia. In mid-2010 the company formed a joint venture with Chinese automaker BYD to develop electric vehicles for the Chinese market. BYD's expertise in battery technology complements Daimler's knowledge of electric vehicle architecture. (Daimler has applied for more than 600 patents related to electric vehicle technology over the past 30 years.) The companies plan to launch the Chinese car by 2013. Daimler also partnered with China's Beiqi Foton Motor Co. to create a joint venture to produce heavy trucks.

On the Eastern front in late 2010 Daimler and Russian truck maker Kamaz expanded their existing partnership; Daimler supplies axles to Kamaz as well as makes Mercedes-Benz and Setra truck brands in Russia while Kamaz supplies axle components to Daimler. The two companies plan to invest about E50 million (more than $66 million) in axle production. Earlier Daimler's 89% owned Mitsubishi Fuso unit formed a joint venture with Kamaz to import produce and sell the light-duty Fuso Canter brand trucks. Daimler owns an approximate 15% stake in Kamaz.

On its heels Daimler formed a joint venture in 2010 with Uzavtosanoat an automotive holding company. The venture assembles and sells a range of bus models under the Mercedes-Benz brand to the Uzbekistan and neighboring markets. Subsidiary Mercedes-Benz Buses Central Asia holds a 51% interest in the partnership and Uzavtosanoat 49%.

India is another area of interest where Daimler is looking to go-it-alone with its commercial truck operations. To that end Daimler shed its approximate 5% state in Tata Motors Ltd. for an estimated $410 million in 2010. The deal provided a cash infusion for Daimler and repositioned the company to capture truck sales which are being fueled by a rise in government-backed urban renewal projects. India's Hero Group conglomerate withdrew from a truck-building partnership with another automotive maker transferring its 40% interest to Daimler. The company's trucks made in India are due to be released in 2012 and will carry the BharatBenz brand.

Domestically Daimler and Rolls-Royce announced plans in 2011 to acquire Tognum a Germany-based engine and powertrain supplier for distributed power generation and marine propulsion markets. Daimler is interested in the company's engines and powertrains for off-highway applications and for local power generators. After acquiring nearly a 60% stake Daimler and Rolls Royce upped the offer by just over 8% in mid-2011 with the goal of acquiring at least 75%. The takeover would give the companies rights to Tognum's intellectual property. If successful Daimler and Rolls Royce will own an equal stake in Tognum.

In the meanwhile Daimler for its part in developing more electric and hybrid automobiles is conducting large-scale field tests for electric vehicles — called e-mobility projects –in London (since 2007) and Berlin (since 2009) using battery-powered fortwo electric drive cars. In spring 2011 Daimler and Robert Bosch set up a 50/50 joint ventures to produce electrical vehicle engines that are to be used in Mercedes-Benz smart vehicles; production is set to start in 2012. In Berlin the company partnered with electricity provider RWE AG to set up 500 charging stations; Daimler is developing global standards for charging plugs and sockets for the power infrastructure. Daimler also plans to begin production of its own lithium-ion batteries for use by other automotive manufacturers with commercial production of the batteries scheduled for 2014.

Daimler in the same spirit made an equity investment in Tesla Motors the developer of an all-electric sports car taking a stake of nearly 10% in 2009. The companies previously collaborated on integrating Tesla's lithium-ion battery packs and charging electronics into the first 1000 units of Daimler's electric smart car. Although later that year Daimler sold part of its Tesla stake to Abu Dhabi-based Aabar Investments Daimler and Tesla continue to cooperate on development of battery systems electric drive and other projects.

In addition to Renault-Nissan's 3.1% stake in Daimler Aabar Investments holds an equity share of about 9% in the automaker making it the largest shareholder in Daimler. Aabar Investments also holds a 40% stake in Mercedes-Benz Grand Prix a UK-based Formula One racing team. The government of Kuwait owns almost 7% of the company.

After nearly 10 years of irreconcilable differences Daimler and Chrysler called it quits. They joined forces in 1998 in a $37 billion deal but the marriage never worked. In 2007 Daimler sold 80% of Chrysler to Cerberus Capital for $7.4 billion.

HISTORY

Daimler-Benz was formed by the merger of two German motor companies –Daimler and Benz –in 1926. Daimler-Benz bought Auto Union (Audi) in 1958 (sold to Volkswagen in 1966). The company's Mercedes cars gained international fame and sales expanded worldwide in the 1970s.

Daimler-Benz diversified in the 1980s buying aerospace heavy truck (Freightliner) and consumer and industrial electrical companies. Although diversification continued sales slowed. Losses at its aerospace unit forced Daimler-Benz into the red in 1995. Also that year the company and ABB Asea Brown Boveri (now ABB) formed joint venture Adtranz the #1 train maker in the world and Jurgen Schrempp became chairman of the management board (CEO).

In 1998 Daimler-Benz acquired Chrysler and introduced a subcompact car the smart in Europe. DaimlerChrysler rolled both companies' financial services units into DaimlerChrysler Interservices (DEBIS) and acquired the remaining shares of Adtranz in 1999.

North American influence in the company began to fade in 2000 with the exit of US management including co-chairman Robert Eaton. Prior to his retirement Eaton announced DaimlerChrysler's goal to become the world's #1 carmaker through partnerships or acquisitions.

In 2000 DaimlerChrysler agreed to buy a controlling $2.1 billion stake (34%) in Mitsubishi Motors (later upped to 37% when it acquired 3.3% from Volvo). It took a minority stake in South Korea-based Hyundai Motor (sold in 2004) and the two bid jointly on Daewoo Motor (now named GM Daewoo Auto & Technology; South Korea) but Ford was named exclusive bidder (although it later withdrew). DaimlerChrysler bought Canada-based truck maker Western Star Holdings for $456 million and paid about $473 million for the 79% of Detroit Diesel (heavy-duty truck engines) that it didn't already own. The company also agreed to sell its rail systems unit Adtranz to Bombardier (completed in 2001 for about $1.1 billion).

Also in 2000 in an effort to turn things around at its money-losing Chrysler division James Holden was replaced with Dieter Zetsche who immediately began making personnel changes. Days after Zetsche was installed billionaire investor Kirk Kerkorian filed an $8 billion lawsuit seeking to undo the 1998 Daimler-Benz/Chrysler merger on grounds that portraying the deal as a "merger of equals" was misrepresentative.

Zetsche announced early in 2001 that Chrysler would eliminate almost 26000 North American jobs over three years (largely through retirement and attrition) and make wholesale changes in the group's senior management positions overseeing the Chrysler and Mercedes divisions.

Early in 2003 in an effort to bolster its worldwide commercial vehicle ambitions DaimlerChrysler took a 43% stake in MFTBC. Mitsubishi Motors held a 20% stake and other Mitsubishi group companies controlled the rest of MFTBC. Early in 2004 DaimlerChrysler increased its stake in MFTBC to 65%.

Later that year mounting problems concerning poor quality and cover-ups plagued Mitsubishi and continued to cause problems at DaimlerChrysler when CEO Jurgen Schrempp's plan to infuse the ailing Japanese carmaker with $7 billion met with fierce resistance by many of Schrempp's fellow members of the management board including Schrempp's protege former Chrysler COO Wolfgang Bernhard. Bernhard had been slated to take over as chief of the Mercedes Group but his disloyalty to Schrempp and his heavy-handed management style blocked his promotion (soon afterward Bernhard left DaimlerChrysler and later was hired by VW).

In 2004 DaimlerChrysler created a joint venture with Magna International for the purposes of eventually selling DaimlerChrysler's driveline subsidiary New Venture Gear to Magna for about $435 million. The deal which received European Commission approval that year created a new company New Process Gear. Also in 2004 DaimlerChrysler sold its 10% stake in Hyundai Motor but the two companies said they would maintain a joint-development relationship on a project-by-project basis.

Late in 2004 DaimlerChrysler received Chinese regulatory approval to build cars in China with joint venture partner Beijing Automotive Industry Holding Co. Ltd. (BAIC).

Early in 2005 the problems with Mitsubishi came to a head when it was revealed that known truck defects at MFTBC had been covered up since 1974. A deal was struck whereby DaimlerChrysler got Mitsubishi Motors' 20% in MFTBC reducing Mitsubishi Motors' stake to zero. Also in 2005 joint venture Beijing Benz-DaimlerChrysler Automotive Co. Ltd. (with partner Beijing Automotive Industry Holding Company) got a license to build Mercedes-Benz C- and E- Class cars. Chinese Jeep production was also moved to this new facility. Late that year DaimlerChrysler sold its remaining 12% stake in Mitsubishi Motors to Goldman Sachs marking the end of the companies' previous cooperation. Goldman Sachs sold all but 0.01% of the stake on the open market the following day. DaimlerChrysler began offering passenger car and commercial vehicle financing in China through DaimlerChrysler Automotive Finance (China) Ltd. as 2005 wound down.

Early in 2006 DaimlerChrysler said it would eliminate 6000 administrative jobs or 20% of its worldwide administrative workforce in order to streamline operations. Later that year the company formed a joint venture with Chinese Fujian Motor Industry Group and Taiwanese China Motor Corporation for the manufacture of the Mercedes-Benz Sprinter and Vito vans for the Chinese market.

In early 2007 after Chrysler losses topping $1.5 billion in 2006 Daimler admitted for the first time that it was rethinking the wisdom of the merger with Chrysler and was looking at all options. Reports later emerged that Chrysler might be sold and that interested parties included General Motors Magna International and some private equity concerns including a team led by The Blackstone Group and Centerbridge Partners as well as Cerberus Capital Management. Through his investment firm Tracinda Corp. billionaire and former Chrysler and GM activist investor Kirk Kerkorian later threw his hat into the ring with a bid of $4.5 billion for Chrysler.

Cerberus won out over its rivals and struck a deal to buy roughly 80% of Chrysler for about $7.4 billion. Daimler retained about a 20% equity stake and the two companies continued to cooperate on alternative drive systems sales and financial services and purchasing outside North America. Daimler officially changed its name from DaimlerChrysler to Daimler AG two months after the Cerberus deal was completed.

The company reduced its 15% stake in EADS by selling 7% early in 2007 to German state-owned development bank KfW. Daimler however retained the stake's voting rights. In 2008 Daimler spent $1.5 billion to bring the smart fortwo minicar to the US. The cars are sold and serviced through Roger Penske's Penske Automotive Group (formerly United Auto Group) network of new-car franchises.

Despite negotiation with Cerberus to sell its remaining stake in Chrysler in 2008 Cerberus accused Daimler of concealing material facts about Chrysler –particularly the Chrysler Financial lending business –and the talks broke off. Daimler remained interested in selling its stake in Chrysler which received an emergency loan of $4 billion from the US government in early 2009 to continue operating. Chrysler –like Ford and General Motors –was struggling with too much capacity too few models that impress consumers and high costs for parts and labor. Ultimately in 2009 Daimler agreed to give up its remaining stake in Chrysler to Cerberus and to forgive loans to Chrysler. Cerberus and Chrysler in exchange agreed to waive any legal claims against Daimler. Chrysler and Daimler retained only a customer-supplier relationship for certain parts and technology. Daimler also agreed with the federal Pension Benefit Guaranty Corporation to make payments of $600 million over three years into Chrysler's pension plans.

To generate cash in 2009 Daimler sold an equity stake of about 9% to Aabar Investments for nearly E2 billion ($2.7 billion). Aabar controlled by the International Petroleum Investment Company (IPIC) of Abu Dhabi became Daimler's largest shareholder as a result overtaking the government of Kuwait which owns almost 7% of the automaker.

EXECUTIVES

Chairman Management Board; Head Mercedes-Benz Cars, Dieter Zetsche, age 60, $2,252,007 total compensation

Chairman Supervisory Board, Manfred Bischoff, age 71

Deputy Chairman Supervisory Board, Erich Klemm, age 59

Member of the Management Board; Mercedes-Benz Cars Production and Procurement; Mercedes-Benz Vans, Wolfgang Bernhard, age 53

Member Management Board Finance and Controlling Daimler Financial Services, Bodo Uebber, age 53, $874,632 total compensation

Member Management Board Group Research and Mercedes-Benz Cars Development, Thomas Weber, age 59, $802,185 total compensation

Member Management Board; Head Daimler Trucks, Andreas Renschler, age 55, $846,342 total compensation

Chairman Daimler Financial Services, Klaus Entenmann, age 57

Member Management Board Daimler Financial Services Africa and Asia/Pacific Region, Richard A. Howard

Sales and Marketing Mercedes-Benz Cars, Joachim Schmidt, age 64

Finance Controlling and Strategic Planning Mercedes-Benz Cars, Stephan Engels, age 51

Member Management Board Daimler Financial Services AG Europe Africa and Asia/Pacific, Alwin Epple, age 50

Member Management Board Daimler Financial Services Human Resources Sales and Financial Services, Dieter Buhl, age 57

Head Development Mercedes-Benz Vans, Sascha Paasche, age 56

Head Daimler Buses; CEO EvoBus GmbH, Hartmut Schick, age 50

Member Management Board Human Resources and Director Labor Relations, Wilfried Porth, age 55, $547,482 total compensation

Head Daimler Trucks Asia; President and CEO Mitsubishi Fuso Truck & Bus Corporation, Albert Kirchmann

Head Daimler Trucks North America, Martin Daum, age 53

Head Finance Controlling Business and Product Planning Daimler Trucks & Buses, Frank Lindenberg, age 49
Managing Director Mercedes-Benz Vans, Volker Mornhinweg, age 53
Member Management Board Intergrity and Legal Affairs, Christine Hohmann-Dennhardt, age 63
Senior Manager Institutional Investors and Analysts, Lutz Deus
Manager Institutional Investors and Analysts, Alexander Vollmer
Senior Manager Private Investors and Internet Investor Relations, Rolf Bassermann
Member of the Board of Management of Daimler AG, Hubertus Troska
Truck Product Engineering Daimler Trucks, Geor Weiberg
Procurement Trucks and Buses and Truck Powertrain Operations and Manufacturing Engineering, Stefan E. Buchner
Head Production Mercedes-Benz Vans, Heinrich Weiss
Head Sales and Marketing Mercedes-Benz Vans, Andreas Burkhart
Head Finance and Controlling Mercedes-Benz Vans, Martin Schad
Head Human Resources Mercedes-Benz Vans, Dietmar Meder
Head Procurement Mercedes-Benz Vans, Klaus Gritsch
Head Product Engineering Daimler Buses, Richard Averbeck
Head Marketing Sales and After Sales Daimler Buses, Holger Suffel
Member Supervisory Board, Lloyd G. Trotter, age 67
Member Supervisory Board, Clemens A. H. Borsig, age 64
Member Supervisory Board, Paul Achleitner, age 56
Member Supervisory Board, Sari M. Baldauf, age 57
Member Supervisory Board, Lynton R. Wilson, age 73
Member Supervisory Board, Bernhard Walter, age 70
Deputy Chairman Supervisory Board, Erich Klemm, age 59
Member Supervisory Board, Jurgen Hambrecht, age 66
Member Supervisory Board, Stefan Schwaab, age 61
Member Supervisory Board, Petraea Heynike, age 66
Member Supervisory Board, Jorg Hofmann, age 57
Member Supervisory Board, Gerard J. Kleisterlee, age 67
Member Supervisory Board, Heinrich Flegel, age 64
Member Supervisory Board, Thomas Klebe, age 65
Member Supervisory Board, Jurgen Langer, age 58
Member Supervisory Board, Valter Sanches, age 49
Member Supervisory Board, Uwe Werner, age 61
Member Supervisory Board, Ansgar Osseforth, age 66
Member Supervisory Board, Jorg Spies, age 51
Member of the Supervisory Board, Clemens Boersig Boersig
Auditors: KPMGDeutscheTreuhand-GesellschaftAG

LOCATIONS

HQ: Daimler AG
Mercedesstrasse 137, Stuttgart D-70327
Phone: (49) 711 17 97875 **Fax:** (49) 711 17 94075
Web: www.daimler.com

2010 Sales

	% of total
Western Europe	
Germany	20
Other	20
Americas	
US	21
Other	9
Asia	20
Other	10
Total	**100**

PRODUCTS/OPERATIONS

2010 Sales by Vehicle

	% of total
Mercedes-Benz	53
Daimler	22
Daimler Financial	12
Mercedes-Benz	8
Daimler	5
Total	**100**

2010 Sales by Segment

	% of total
Vehicles	86
Rental &	10
Daimler Financial	3
Automotive	1
Total	**100**

Selected Divisions and Brands

Mercedes-Benz Cars
- Maybach
- Mercedes-Benz
- smart

Daimler Trucks
- Freightliner
- Mitsubishi Fuso
- Mercedez-Benz
- Western Star Trucks

Daimler Financial Services
- Banking (Mercedes-Benz Bank)
- Fleet management
- Insurance
- Leasing and financing

Mercedes-Benz Vans

Daimler Buses
- Mercedes-Benz (city buses coaches interurban minibuses)
- Mercedes-Benz chassis
- Mitsubishi Fuso (large buses midi-sized buses minibuses)
- Orion (city buses)
- Setra (coaches interurban buses)
- Thomas Built Buses (hybrid school bus school and activity buses)

COMPETITORS

BMW
Fiat
Ford Motor
Fuji Heavy Industries
General Motors
Honda
Isuzu
Land Rover
MAN
Navistar International
Nissan
PACCAR
PROTON Holdings
Peugeot
Porsche
Renault
Saab Automobile
Scania
Toyota
Volkswagen
Volvo
ZAP

HISTORICAL FINANCIALS

Company Type: Public

Income Statement FYE: December 31

	REVENUE ($ mil.)	NET INCOME ($ mil.)	NET PROFIT MARGIN	EMPLOYEES
12/12	150,649	8,033	5.3%	275,087
12/11	137,804	7,329	5.3%	271,370
12/10	130,840	6,020	4.6%	260,100
12/09	113,695	(3,803)	—	256,407
12/08	134,039	1,884	1.4%	273,216
Annual Growth	3.0%	43.7%	—	0.2%

2012 Year-End Financials

Debt ratio: 61.6%
Return on equity: 14.5%
Cash ($ mil.): 14,493
Current ratio: 1.15
Long-term debt ($ mil.): 57,124
No. of shares (mil.): 1,067
Dividends
Yield: 4.0%
Payout: —
Market value ($ mil.): 58,686

	STOCK PRICE ($) FY Close	P/E High/Low		PER SHARE ($) Earnings	Dividends	Book Value
12/12	54.97	20	12	7.53	2.88	54.17
12/11	43.86	28	13	6.87	0.00	48.07
12/10	67.58	32	18	5.73	0.00	45.68
12/09	53.30	—	—	(3.79)	0.80	42.63
12/08	38.28	140	30	1.96	3.18	47.08
Annual Growth	9.5%	—	—	40.0%	(2.4%)	3.6%

Danone

You say Danone I say Dannon; let's call the whole thing one of the largest dairy food and water producers in the world. The company is organized around its core activities: fresh dairy products water and infant and medical nutrition. The company #1 maker of fresh dairy products worldwide offers dozens of worldwide and regional yogurt brands including the Dannon Activia and organic yogurt Stonyfield Farm. The company's Evian Volvic Aqua and other water brands make it #2 worldwide in bottled water. Danone became a player in the baby-food sector with its 2007 purchase of Royal Numico and is now the world's #2 baby nutrition company. Its medical nutrition products are #1 in Europe.

HISTORY

In 1965 Antoine Riboud replaced his uncle as chairman of family-run Souchon-Neuvesel a Lyons France-based maker of glass bottles. Antoine quickly made a mark in this field –he merged the firm with Boussois a major French flat-glass manufacturer creating BSN in 1966.

Antoine enlarged BSN's glass business and filled the company's bottles by acquiring well-established beverage and food concerns. In 1970 BSN purchased Brasseries Kronenbourg (France's largest brewer) Societe Europeenne de Brasseries (another French brewer) and Evian (mineral water France). The 1972 acquisition of Glaverbel (Belgium) gave BSN 50% of Europe's flat-glass market. The next year BSN merged with France's Gervais Danone (yogurt cheese Panzani pasta; founded in 1919 and named after founder Isaac Carasso's son Daniel). This moved the company into pan-European brand-name foods.

Increasing energy costs depressed flat-glass earnings so BSN began divesting its flat-glass businesses. In the late 1970s it acquired interests in brewers in Belgium Spain and Italy.

BSN bought Dannon the leading US yogurt maker (co-founded by Daniel Carasso who had continued making Danone yogurt in France until WWII) in 1982. It established a strong presence in the Italian pasta market by buying stakes in Ponte (1985) and Agnesi (1986). BSN also purchased Generale Biscuit the world's #3 biscuit maker (1986) and RJR Nabisco's European cookie and snack-food business (1989).

In a series of acquisitions starting in 1986 BSN took over Italy and Spain's largest mineral water companies and several European pasta makers and other food companies. Adopting the name of its leading international brand BSN became Groupe Danone in 1994.

Antoine's son Franck succeeded him as chairman in 1996 and restructured the company to focus on three core businesses: dairy beverages (specifically water and beer) and biscuits. By 1997

Danone had begun shedding non-core grocery products. The company simultaneously stepped up acquisitions of dairy beer biscuit and water companies in developing markets.

The 1998 purchase of AquaPenn Spring Water for $112 million doubled its US water-bottling production capacity. Danone in 1999 completed a merger and subsequent sale of part of its BSN Emballage glass-packaging unit to UK buyout firm CVC Capital Partners for $1.2 billion; Danone retained 44% ownership. Thirsty for the #2 spot in US bottled water sales Danone gulped down McKesson Water (the #3 bottled water firm in the US after Nestle and Suntory) for $1.1 billion in 2000.

Also in 2000 Danone's joint venture Finalrealm (which includes several European equity firms) along with Burlington Biscuits Nabisco and HM Capital Partners (then called Hicks Muse Tate & Furst) acquired 87% of leading UK biscuit maker United Biscuits. Danone then bought Naya (bottled water Canada) and sold its brewing operations (#2 in Europe) to Scottish & Newcastle (later acquired by Heineken and Carlsberg) for more than $2.6 billion.

During 2001 Danone announced restructuring would shutter two LU biscuit plants and eliminate about 1800 jobs; the move met with strikes and legal battles. That same year having been bumped to the #2 spot in the US yogurt market (after General Mills' Yoplait brand) Danone acquired 40% of Stonyfield Farm the #4 yogurt brand in the US and ultimately came to own 84% of the company.

The company launched 2002 with a series of beverage acquisitions including Frucor (New Zealand) and Zywiec Zdroj (the top brand of water in Poland). Danone then struck a deal handing Coca-Cola the distribution and marketing of Evian in North America and formed a joint venture with Coke to distribute its lower-end water brands. Antoine Riboud died that same year at the age of 83.

Danone divested noncore companies during 2002 including the sale of its Italian meat and cheese business Galbani and its Kro Beer Brands (Kronenbourg 1664 brands) to Scottish & Newcastle. Then typical of its consolidation strategy later in 2002 Danone acquired the home and office water delivery companies Chateaud'eau (France) Patrimoine des Eaux du Quebec (Canada) and Canada's Sparkling Spring (now Aquaterra).

In 2004 Danone sold its 10% interest in the Australian dairy firm National Foods. Later that year it announced an alliance with Japanese dairy group Yakult Honsha to focus both companies' efforts with probiotics. Danone is a 20% shareholder of Yakult and has agreed not to increase its share holdings of Yakult for five years and not to pursue majority control for another five. Also in 2004 Danone acquired the Mexican bottled water company Arco Iris.

While its dairy and water businesses bubbled along nicely Danone found its cookies crumbling. Opting for a new recipe in 2004 it joined with Argentine food giant ARCOR Group to merge both companies' biscuits operations in South America. Later that same year Danone sold off its W&R Jacob Ltd. biscuits operations in Ireland to local company Fruitfield Foods. It also sold Italaquae its Italian bottled water business to LGR Holding.

Long after its departure from brewing in 2004 Danone was fined E1.5 million for forming a beer distribution cartel along with Heineken in 1996. In 2005 Danone and Coca-Cola ended their 2002 water-distribution joint venture with Coke buying out Danone's 49% share for about $100 million.

In 2005 Danone got out of the brewing business altogether with the sale of its 33% stake in Spanish brewer Mahou. It sold its HP Foods Group including Amoy Lea & Perrins and HP sauce brands to Heinz and its biscuits businesses in the UK and Ireland. That year it sold its US home and office water-delivery company DS Waters of America to investment firm Kelso & Company. Danone has increased its ownership of Russian dairy and beverage company Wimm-Bill-Dann Foods to almost 20%.

Due to slow sales for its chilled products and competition from lower-priced brands in 2006 Danone introduced Senja (a soy-based yogurt) in France. It acquired Egyptian fresh dairy products company Olait (which it renamed Danone Dairy Egypt) and Algerian bottled water company Tessala. On the Asian front Danone acquired 23% of fruit-drink company China Huiyuan Juice Group and 51% of Wahaha. (It sold its interest in Huiyuan Juice in 2010.) In the Ukraine it bought fresh dairy company JSC Molochnyi Zavod. In the US it launched the Activia brand yogurt.

Because it wants to introduce more organic products in Europe in 2006 Danone announced the spending of $66 million on the expansion of its subsidiary Stonyfield Farm's New Hampshire production plant. (That year Stonyfield bought a 34% interest in Irish organic dairy Glenisk.)

In 2006 Danone sold its Amoy Asian sauce and chilled foods business to Ajinomoto exiting the sauce business altogether. It then sold virtually all of its grocery activities glass-container business its cheese and cured meat activities (Galbani) and its beer activities in Europe. It also sold New Zealand biscuits maker Griffins Food to investment firm Pacific Equity Partners.

Danone paid E12 billion (about $16 billion) for Numico maker of infant food and medical nutrition (nutritional bars and shakes) in 2007. The Numico products (Cow & Gate Dumex Mellin milupa NUTRICIA) joined Danone's bledina baby-food brand to create a wide array of well-known nutritional products for babies and adults. The purchase made Danone the largest baby-food maker in Europe.

Prior to announcing the Numico purchase Danone announced the sale of its cookie business to Kraft Foods; that deal closed in late 2007. At the time some analysts saw Danone as ripe for a takeover; hence the Numico deal was construed as a way for Danone to remain independent. (The acquisition was viewed as helping ward off predators who might have been attracted to the cash that Danone accrued as a result of the Kraft deal.) As part of its strategy to divest itself of all biscuit/cookie activities in 2009 the company ended its Indian joint venture with the Wadia Group. Danone sold its 50% interest in the operation ABI Holdings to Wadia.

Strengthening its business in Asia in 2007 Danone acquired all of the Japanese joint venture with Ajinomoto and Calpis that it did not already own. Renamed Danone Japan the operation manufactures fresh products for the expanding Japanese dairy market.

Saying it wanted to "regain room for maneuver[ing]" in 2007 it sold off its 20% stake in and terminated its distribution agreement with Shanghai-based Bright Dairy. Danone cited no specifics surrounding the move but the company has had legal disputes with various joint-venture partners in China and India recently relating to how its brands are marketed and produced.

In late 2007 the company exited its joint venture with Chinese company Mengniu Dairy Group citing time frame and other condition difficulties. (Both companies agreed to the termination of the venture which was initiated in 2006.) Turning to South America that same year Danone acquired a 70% holding in Chile's fresh dairy company Vialat.

Among its divestments in 2008 in order to fulfill European Union requirements for its acquisition of Numico the company sold off its French baby milk and baby drinks businesses to Groupe Lactalis. That year it also sold its subsidiary Frucor a maker of non-alcoholic beverages in New Zealand and Australia as well as its international brands V and Mizone (with the exception of in China and Indonesia) to Suntory for some E600 million ($780 million).

Danone took full control of its South African joint venture Danone Clover in 2009. It purchased Clover's 45% stake for R1085 ($145 million). (Clover is one of South Africa's largest dairy companies.) Other partnerships include a joint venture with Weight Watchers formed in 2008. The 51% Weight Watchers-49% Danone operation provides weight-management services to the People's Republic of China.

Following its acquisition of a controlling interest in a venture with Russia's Unimilk in 2010 Danone sold its 18.4% stake in Wimm-Bill-Dann Foods back to the Russian dairy and juice producer for $470 million.

EXECUTIVES

Vice Chairman and Co-COO, Jacques Vincent, age 66, $2,192,509 total compensation
Chairman and CEO, Franck Riboud, age 58, $3,494,439 total compensation
EVP Fresh Dairy Products, Thomas Kunz, age 56
Deputy General Manager and Co-COO; Director, Emmanuel Faber, age 50, $1,968,672 total compensation
Chairman President and CEO Stonyfield Farm, Gary Hirshberg
Deputy General Manager and Co-COO; Director, Bernard Hours, age 57, $4,036,272 total compensation
EVP Waters, Francisco Camacho, age 47
EVP Baby Nutrition, Felix Martin Garcia, age 53
General Manager Medical Nutrition, Flemming Morgan, age 57
Director Investor Relations, Antoine Guttinger
EVP Research and Development, Jean-Philippe Pare, age 55
Exec. VP Baby Nutrition; Member of the Executive Committee, Felix Garcia
Executive Vice President - Research & Development; Member of the Executive Committee, Jean-Philippe Pare
Executive VP HR and Chair of the Board of the Danone Ecosystem Fund; M. of Ex. Com., Muriel Penicaud
Chief Financial Officer; Member of the Executive Committee, Pierre-Andre Terisse
Vice Chairman and Co-COO, Jacques Vincent, age 66
Director, Michel David-Weill, age 81
Director, Bruno Bonnell, age 55
Director, Guylaine Saucier, age 67
Director, Benoit Potier, age 56
Director, Jean Gaston Pierre Marie Victor Laurent, age 68
Director, Baron Richard Goblet d'Alviella, age 65
Director, H?kan Mogren, age 69
Deputy General Manager and Co-COO; Director, Bernard Hours, age 57
Director, Christian Laubie, age 75
Director, Jacques-Alexandre Nahmias, age 65
Director, Naomasa Tsuritani, age 68
Independent Director, Richard dAlviella
Auditors: Mazars

LOCATIONS

HQ: Danone
17, Boulevard Haussmann, Paris 75009
Phone: (33) 1 44 35 20 20 **Fax:** (33) 1 44 35 26 95
Web: www.danone.com

2009 Sales

	% of total
Europe	60

Asia		12
Rest of the		28
Total		**100**

2009 Production Sites

No. of plants		
Europe		
Western	36	
Central	19	
Asia/Pacific	50	
Africa & Middle East	15	
North America	6	
Total	**0**	**126**

PRODUCTS/OPERATIONS

2009 Sales

	% of total
Fresh	57
Water	17
Baby	20
Medical	6
Total	**100**

Selected Products and Brands

Fresh dairy
- Africa (Clover)
- Argentina (La Serenissima Ser)
- China (Bright Dairy)
- France (Danette Danone Senja)
- International (Actimel Danone)
- Japan (Danone Yakult)
- Latin America (Corpus La Serenisima Mastellone)
- US (Activia Dannon Stonyfield Farm YoCream)

Bottled water
- Argentina (Villa del Sur)
- Asia/Pacific (Aqua)
- Canada (Crystal Springs Evian Labrador Naya)
- France (Badoit Salvetat Arvie)
- International (Evian Volvic)
- Mexico (Bonafont)
- Spain (Font Vella)
- Turkey (Hayat)
- US (Dannon Evian)

Baby nutrition
- Bebelac
- bledina
- Cow & Gate
- Dumex
- Gallia
- Mellin
- milupa
- NUTRICIA

Medical nutrition
- FortiCare
- Fortimel
- Fortisip
- Neocate
- Nutricia
- Nutrini

COMPETITORS

Abbott Nutrition
Ajinomoto
Arla Foods
Associated British Foods
Beech-Nut
Blue Bell
China Mengniu Dairy
Coca-Cola
Dairy Crest
Dairy Farm International
Dairygold
Dean Foods
Dr Pepper Snapple Group
Dreyer' s
Feihe
Fonterra
FrieslandCampina
General Mills
Gerber Products
Glanbia plc
Granarolo
HP Hood
Heinz
Irish Dairy Board
Kellogg
Kerry Group
Lactalis
Leche Pascual
Mead Johnson
Metagenics
Mondelez International
Nestle
Novartis
Parmalat
PepsiCo
Pfizer
Shanghai Bright Dairy & Food
Sodiaal
Unilever NV
Wells' Dairy
Wessanen
WhiteWave
Wimm-Bill-Dann
Yili Group

HISTORICAL FINANCIALS

Company Type: Public

Income Statement FYE: December 31

	REVENUE ($ mil.)	NET INCOME ($ mil.)	NET PROFIT MARGIN	EMPLOYEES
12/12	27,506	2,203	8.0%	102,401
12/11	24,986	2,161	8.7%	101,885
12/10	22,765	2,502	11.0%	100,995
12/09	21,582	1,960	9.1%	80,976
12/08	21,278	1,835	8.6%	80,143
Annual Growth	6.6%	4.7%	—	6.3%

2012 Year-End Financials

Debt ratio: 42.4%
Return on equity: 13.7%
Cash ($ mil.): 1,672
Current ratio: 0.81
Long-term debt ($ mil.): 8,364
No. of shares (mil.): 593
Dividends
Yield: 2.6%
Payout: 17.0%
Market value ($ mil.): 7,945

	STOCK PRICE ($) FY Close	P/E High	P/E Low	PER SHARE ($) Earnings	Dividends	Book Value
12/12	13.39	9	7	3.65	0.36	27.08
12/11	12.64	10	7	3.58	0.71	26.06
12/10	12.65	8	5	4.07	0.89	26.11
12/09	12.19	11	6	3.57	0.92	31.13
12/08	12.08	15	6	3.83	0.34	25.29
Annual Growth	2.6%	—	—	(1.2%)	1.4%	1.7%

Danske Bank AS (Denmark)

When you're the largest bank in Denmark there's nowhere to grow but out. Danske Bank serves consumers and businesses through a network of more than 300 branches in Denmark; it also has about 120 branches in Finland (where it operates Sampo Bank) some 50 branches each in Sweden (Ostgota Enskilda Bank) and Norway (Fokus Bank) and more than 100 branches in Ireland and Northern Ireland where it owns National Irish Bank and Northern Bank respectively. The company also has operations in Germany Poland Russia and the Baltic states. In addition to standard deposit and lending services Danske Bank offers asset management insurance leasing securities trading and research and real estate brokerage services.

The bank's Realkredit Danmark unit conducts mortgage financing while Danica Pension provides life insurance and retirement planning.

After a period of making expansions abroad Danske Bank retrenched amid the global economic turmoil. Revenues fell in 2009 and 2010 and net income (which plummeted in 2008) has been slowly on the rise. The bank isn't free from worries about the European sovereign debt crisis either with operations in Ireland and other afflicated nations. As such Danske Bank has focused internally on initiatives such as improving customer service and technology. Cost-cutting measures such as a 9% workforce reduction in late 2011 have also been implemented and further cost reductions could be in order if the crisis worsens.

Danish conglomerate A.P. Moller - Maersk and an associated Moller family fund together own more than 20% of Danske Bank.

HISTORY

Leathersmith-turned-stock trader Gottlieb Gedalia founded Den Danske Landmandsbank Hypothek- og Vexelbank i Kj?benhavn (The Danish Farmer's Bank Mortgage and Exchange Bank of Copenhagen. It would change its name four times before finally settling on the less-verbose Danske Bank.

Even in its early years Danske Bank never restricted itself to purely agricultural concerns preferring to offer a wide range of banking services that appealed to farmers merchants and businessmen alike. Isak Gluckstadt who managed the bank from 1872 until his death in 1910 guided the bank to prominence in Copenhagen's corporate landscape where it became a leading commercial bank. Gluckstadt's son Emil succeeded his father as managing director in 1910. Despite his best efforts Danske Bank could not cope with the strains of WWI and the Depression; the Danish government had to rescue the firm from bankruptcy. But the bank survived German occupation during WWII mostly unscathed.

During the 1960s and 1970s Denmark's government encouraged Danish banks to expand internationally. Danske Bank pounced on the opportunity by forming consortium banks with such Nordic neighbors as Skandinaviska Enskilda Banken (aka S-E-Banken). Danske Bank stayed ahead of its competitors through acquisitions including the purchase of two large Danish banks in 1990 making it Denmark's largest bank.

By 1990 the bank also had made its presence felt worldwide but Asian economic crises in the early 1990s caused the bank's international subsidiaries to fall short of expectations. After restructuring its international business the bank focused more energy on its Nordic customers. It bought Sweden's Ostgota Enskilda in 1998 and Norway's Fokus Bank in 1999. In 2000 Danske bought fellow Danish Bank BG Bank. Danske also added a Finnish asset management company and a majority interest in Pol-Can Bank of Poland in the same year. In 2001 Danske and BG trimmed down redundant branches.

Danske Bank bought the banking operations of Finnish insurer Sampo for more than $5 billion in 2007. The acquisition brought in more than 150 branches in Finland Estonia Latvia and Lithuania. It followed Danske Bank's 2005 acquisitions of National Irish Bank and Northern Bank from National Australia Bank for some $1.8 billion.

EXECUTIVES

EVP and Executive Board Secretariat, Erik Sevaldsen
SEVP International Banking, Mads Jacobsen
Chairman of Executive Board, Peter Straarup, age 62
Managing Director Sampo Bank, Ilkka Hallavo, age 57
Chairman home; CEO R?lkredit Danmark, Sven Holm
Head Danske Markets, Henrik Normann, age 59
Group CEO, Thomas F. Borgen, age 49
Chairman Nordania, Jakob Brogaard, age 66
Vice Chairman, Niels B. Christiansen, age 47
COO and Executive Board Member, Georg Schubiger
Executive Board Member and Head Group Credits, Per Damborg Skovhus, age 53
Member of the Executive Board and head of Personal Banking, Tonny Thierry Andersen, age 49
Head of Investor Relations, Martin Gottlob
Chief Executive National Irish Bank, Andrew Healy
Member of the Executive Board and head of Business Banking, Lars Stensgaard M?rch, age 41

Chairman of the Executive Board, Eivind Kolding, age 54
Group Treasury, Steen Blaafalk
SEVP Danske Capital; Chairman Dansk Bank International Luxembourg, Niels-Ulrik Mousten
Director; Chairman Dansk kreds, Per Alling Toubro, age 60
Personal Customer Advisor and Director, Charlotte Hoffmann, age 46
Chief Executive Northern Bank, Gerry Mallon
Member of the Executive Board and Chief Financial Officer, Henrik Ramlau-Hansen, age 57
Managing Director Danske Private Equity, John Danielsen
Managing Director Nordania, Henrik Bech-Hansen
Managing Director Danske Bank International Luxembourg, Klaus M. Pedersen
Chairman, Ole Gjesso Andersen, age 57
EVP, Lars Andreasen
SEVP and Head Credit Portfolio Management, Bo Sonne Ravn
EVP and Head Credit Methods and Process, Sune Visti Petersen
EVP and Head Credits Denmark, Henrik Hoffmann
Chief Actuary, Danske Bank
Member of the Board of Directors and Employee Representative, Carsten Carsten Eilertsen Eilertsen
Member of the Board of Directors and Employee Representative, Helle Helle Broendum Broendum
Head of Business Banking; Member of the Executive Board, Lars Lars Moerch Moerch
Member of the Executive Board and Head of Group Risk Management, Robert Endersby, age 54
Member of the Board of Directors and Employee Representative, Susanne Susanne Arboe Arboe
Director, Michael E. (Mike) Fairey, age 64
Director, Sten Scheibye, age 61
Director, Peter H?jland, age 62
Director, Prof Majken Schultz, age 54
Director, Prof Claus Vastrup, age 71
Director, Birgit Aagaard-Svendsen, age 57
Director; Chairman Dansk kreds, Per Alling Toubro, age 60
Assistant VP and Director, Verner Usbeck, age 62
Bank Clerk and Director, Helle Br?ndum, age 60
Personal Customer Advisor and Director, Charlotte Hoffmann, age 46
Director; Vice Chairman Dansk Kreds, Solveig ?rteby, age 47
Director, Mats Jansson, age 61
Auditors: GrantThornton

LOCATIONS

HQ: Danske Bank AS (Denmark)
Holmens Kanal 2-12, Copenhagen K DK-1092
Phone: (45) 33 44 00 00 **Fax:** 212 370-9564
Web: www.danskebank.com

PRODUCTS/OPERATIONS

2010 Sales

	% of total
Interest	51
Net	19
Net trading	17
Fee	8
Net income from insurance	5
Total	**100**

2010 Sales by Segment

	% of total
Banking	72
Danske	14
Danica	7
Danske	4
Other	3
Total	**100**

COMPETITORS

ABN AMRO Group
Citigroup
Credit Agricole
Credit Suisse
Deutsche Bank
DnB NOR
ING
Jyske
Nordea Bank
SEB AB
Svenska Handelsbanken
UniCredit Bank AG

HISTORICAL FINANCIALS

Company Type: Public

Income Statement FYE: December 31

	ASSETS ($ mil.)	NET INCOME ($ mil.)	INCOME AS % OF ASSETS	EMPLOYEES
12/12	615,733	838	0.1%	20,308
12/11	595,800	297	0.1%	21,320
12/10	577,066	657	0.1%	21,522
12/09	599,780	334	0.1%	22,093
12/08	664,976	189	0.0%	23,624
Annual Growth	(1.9%)	45.0%	—	(3.7%)

2012 Year-End Financials

Return on assets: 0.1%
Return on equity: 3.5%
Long-term debt ($ mil.): —
No. of shares (mil.): 1,001
Sales ($ mil): 22,503
Dividends
Yield: —
Payout: —
Market value ($ mil.): —

DBS Group Holdings Ltd.

DBS Group is the holding company for DBS Bank the largest bank in Singapore and a significant presence throughout Southeast Asia. DBS Bank offers personal and private banking in addition to commercial banking services to small and midsized companies through some 80 branches in its home country. The company also has around 50 locations in Hong Kong plus operations in China India Indonesia Malaysia The Philippines Taiwan and Thailand. DBS Group owns a 20% stake in the Bank of the Philippine Islands (that country's second-largest bank) as well. Other activities include capital markets brokerage fund management private equity and equipment and trade finance.

DBS intends to continue its expansion in Asia. It has opened new branches in India and Indonesia and was the first Singapore bank to establish a local subsidiary in China. In 2011 the company bought the retail and commercial banking operations of Royal Bank of Scotland in China and plans to more than double its presence in that country by 2013.

In 2012 DBS announced plans to acquire PT Bank Danamon Indonesia. The deal would greatly expand DBS' presence in Indonesia and add about 1400 branches.

In addition to expanding geographically DBS is also placing more emphasis on small and midsized businesses large corporations and affluent consumers. Areas of focus include transaction services treasury and markets and wealth management.

The Singapore government (through Temasek) owns more than a quarter of DBS Group.

EXECUTIVES

Managing Director and Head Capital Markets DBS Bank, Eric T. L. Ang
Group Executive Institutional Banking Group DBS Bank, Jeanette Wong
CFO DBS Bank, Chng Sok Hui
Vice Chairman DBS Bank (China) Limited, Teresa Lin
Managing Director and Head Group Strategic Marketing and Communications DBS Bank, Karen Ngui
CEO DBS Bank (Hong Kong); Managing Director & Head Wealth Management DBS Bank, Amy Yip
Chief Risk Officer DBS Bank, Elbert Pattijn
Managing Director and Head Enterprise Banking Singapore and South & SEA Corporate and Investment Banking DBS Bank, Edwin Khoo
President Director DBS Indonesia, Hendra Gunawan, age 43
CEO and Director, Piyush Gupta, age 53
Chairman, Peter L. H. Seah, age 66
Secretary, Linda Hoon
Managing Director and Head Group Technology and Operations DBS Bank, David Gledhill
Group Executive Treasury and Markets Wholesale Banking DBS Bank, Andrew Ng
President Commissioner PT Bank DBS Indonesia, Bernard Tan
Executive Director and CEO DBS Bank China, Melvin T. W. Teo
Managing Director and Head Wealth Management DBS Bank, Tan Su Shan, age 45
Director, Bart Joseph Broadman, age 52
Director, Euleen Y. K. Goh, age 57
Director, Christopher W. C. Cheng, age 65
Director, Kwa Chong Seng, age 66
CEO and Director, Piyush Gupta, age 53
Auditors: PricewaterhouseCoopersLLP

LOCATIONS

HQ: DBS Group Holdings Ltd.
6 Shenton Way, DBS Building Tower One, 068809
Phone: (65) 6878 8888 **Fax:** 213 627-0228
Web: www.dbs.com

PRODUCTS/OPERATIONS

Selected Subsidiaries

DBS Bank
- Bank of the Philippines Islands (20.3%)
- Cholamandalam DBS Finance Limited (37.4%)
- DBS Asia Capital Limited
- DBS Asset Management Ltd
- DBS Diamond Holdings Ltd
  - DBS Bank (Hong Kong) LimitedHutchison DBS Card Ltd (50%)
- DBSN Services Pte. Ltd.
- DBS Vickers Securities (Singapore) Pte Ltd
- The Islamic Bank of Asia Limited (50%)
- PT Bank DBS Indonesia (99%)

COMPETITORS

AmBank Group
Amara
Bangkok Bank
Bank Central Asia
Bank Mandiri
Bank Rakyat
Bank of China
HSBC
Hong Leong Finance
Maybank
Maybank Kim Eng
Metropolitan Bank and Trust
OCBC Bank
Standard Chartered
United Overseas Bank

HISTORICAL FINANCIALS

Company Type: Public

Income Statement FYE: December 31

	ASSETS ($ mil.)	NET INCOME ($ mil.)	INCOME AS % OF ASSETS	EMPLOYEES
12/12	288,638	3,114	1.1%	0
12/11	262,255	2,335	0.9%	0
12/10	221,253	1,272	0.6%	0
12/09	184,532	1,456	0.8%	0
12/08	177,795	1,335	0.8%	0
Annual Growth	12.9%	23.6%	—	—

2012 Year-End Financials

Return on assets: 1.0%
Return on equity: 12.5%
Long-term debt ($ mil.): —
No. of shares (mil.): —
Sales ($ mil): 8,972

Dividends
Yield: 3.5%
Payout: 89.7%
Market value ($ mil.): —

	STOCK PRICE ($) FY Close	P/E High/Low	PER SHARE ($) Earnings	Dividends	Book Value
12/12	49.06	21 15	1.28	1.74	10.66
12/11	35.42	25 15	0.97	1.08	9.47
12/10	44.94	39 29	0.53	1.62	9.01
12/09	44.00	25 8	0.62	5.46	7.96
12/08	26.85	25 8	0.84	2.26	9.02
Annual Growth	16.3%	— —	10.8%	(6.2%)	4.2%

Dekabank Deutsche Girozentrale

LOCATIONS

HQ: Dekabank Deutsche Girozentrale
Mainzer Landstrasse 16, Frankfurt 60325
Phone: (49) 69 7147 0 **Fax:** (49) 69 7147 1376
Web: www.dekabank.de

HISTORICAL FINANCIALS

Company Type: Public

Income Statement FYE: December 31

	ASSETS ($ mil.)	NET INCOME ($ mil.)	INCOME AS % OF ASSETS	EMPLOYEES
12/12	171,009	375	0.2%	4,040
12/11	172,983	337	0.2%	3,957
12/10	174,395	866	0.5%	3,683
12/09	192,003	556	0.3%	3,667
12/08	193,788	(113)	—	3,920
Annual Growth	(3.1%)	—	—	0.8%

2012 Year-End Financials

Return on assets: 0.2%
Return on equity: 8.2%
Long-term debt ($ mil.): —
No. of shares (mil.): 191
Sales ($ mil): 6,916

Dividends
Yield: —
Payout: —
Market value ($ mil.): —

Denso Corp. (Japan)

DENSO knows: When building cars the whole is very little without its parts. Among the world's largest automotive parts manufacturers DENSO supplies OEM and aftermarket components and systems for most of the world's carmakers. Its six product groups make systems for powertrain control information and safety electric electronic small motors and thermal systems. Its lines range from automotive air conditioning systems to radiators and spark plugs. The Information and Safety Systems arm develops car navigation and collision avoidance systems. Non-auto industrial systems and consumer products are also made; subsidiary DENSO WAVE makes bar code readers industrial robots and programmable logic controllers.

DENSO's holistic perspective is demonstrated in all aspects of its automotive business from product development and design to manufacturing and sales. The company touts collaborative efforts with local car manufacturers and suppliers that support each customer's specific regional requirements. Although the company has a global presence with more than 185 subsidiaries and operations in 35 countries more than half of its sales depend on Japanese manufacturers. US operations are overseen by DENSO International America which accounted for 14% of sales in fiscal 2011.

DENSO was spun off from Toyota Motor Corporation in 1949; its former parent remains the largest shareholder owning a 25% stake. Toyota Industries Corporation owns almost 9% while an affiliate of German auto parts giant Robert Bosch owns another 6%. Toyota Motor Corporation is also its largest customer accounting for about 30% of sales in 2011.

Like other auto parts manufacturers DENSO is looking to expand in emerging markets in Brazil China and India. It built a new plant for car air conditioners in Changchun a city in northeast China that is also home to the China FAW Group. The plant will supply AC units to Toyota and Volkswagen models built by China FAW and is expected to open by 2013. It also expanded its car air conditioner and radiator plant in Brazil to increase production capacity and established a joint venture with Indian air conditioning company Subros. It introduced four low-cost heat exchangers for the Indian market. Elsewhere DENSO bought CTR an Italian company that sells air conditioners to aftermarket customers and opened its first sales office in Dubai for customers in the Middle East and North Africa.

With international operations representing about a quarter of overall sales the company is pinning its future growth foremost on product research and development to boost fuel efficiency and reduce carbon dioxide emissions. New products include engines for hybrid and electric vehicles. DENSO is working on cutting costs and improving performance in key products such as inverters DC-DC converters battery monitoring units and electric compressors. It is also developing new products such as battery packs that integrate motor generators batteries battery monitoring units and cooling fans. Its intelligent sensing monitoring and navigation technologies are advancing too with components that promise to help reduce car accidents.

Cost-control measures are playing an equally dominant role in DENSO's operations. The company is shifting its concentration from products for mature markets and premium vehicles to producing low-cost lines that cater to rising demand in developing markets particularly for compact cars which are common in Asia. Business systems at DENSO are evolving as well; more projects are addressed on an interdepartmental basis allowing resources to be pooled and leveraged. The company set a goal to halve the manufacturing costs of 23 key products sold in emerging markets by buying local parts and materials. For fiscal 2011 DENSO managed to cut costs by 40%.

HISTORY

Originally the in-house parts supplier for Toyota Nippondenso Co. (the predecessor to DENSO) was spun off by Toyota in 1949 because Toyota no longer wanted the burden of Nippondenso's troubled financial performance. Nippondenso remained dependent upon Toyota for sales and members of Toyota's controlling family the Toyodas remained involved in management. Nippondenso established a technological partnership with Germany's Robert Bosch in 1953.

As part of its plan to become a major supplier to North American carmakers in 1966 Nippondenso established a sales office in Chicago and branch offices in Los Angeles and Detroit. It then turned to Europe establishing a branch office in Stuttgart Germany in 1970. The following year the company established its first overseas subsidiary Nippondenso of Los Angeles (now DENSO Sales California). In 1972 the company established three more foreign subsidiaries in Australia Canada and Thailand. A European subsidiary (now DENSO Europe) was established in the Netherlands in 1973.

Nippondenso began consignment production for what is now known as Asmo Co. a maker of electric motors in 1978. In 1984 the company joined with Allen Bradley Co. (US) to develop factory automation equipment. That year the predecessor to DENSO Manufacturing Michigan one of the company's largest international subsidiaries was established. Nippondenso expanded into Spain in 1989 by opening a plant in Barcelona.

In 1990 the company formed NDM Manufacturing (now DENSO Manufacturing UK) a joint venture (25%-owned) with Magneti Marelli of Italy for the manufacture of automotive air conditioning and heating systems. The following year Nippondenso and AT&T formed a joint venture for the development of integrated circuit (IC) cards.

Nippondenso established several Chinese manufacturing joint ventures during the mid-1990s. In 1994 the company was recognized by the "Guinness Book of Records" as the maker of the world's smallest car the DENSO Micro Car.

The company changed its name to DENSO CORPORATION in 1996. In 1999 it acquired the rotating machines business of Magneti Marelli. The next year DENSO agreed to buy out Magneti Marelli's share in the companies' automotive air conditioning and heating joint venture (the deal was completed in 2001).

In 2001 DENSO ceased production of wireless phones in order to focus on making onboard car information systems. Also in 2001 the company merged its industrial equipment subsidiaries (bar code scanners and factory automation robots) and spun them off as majority-owned subsidiary DENSO Wave.

DENSO joined forces with Robert Bosch GmbH in 2003 to form a joint venture for the development of car navigation and multimedia systems.

In 2006 DENSO added four new Chinese production facilities that make navigation systems air conditioner compressors instrument panels and oil filters. It has also established technical centers in China and Thailand.

EXECUTIVES

Managing Officer, Akio (Alex) Shikamura
EVP, Koji Kobayashi
EVP, Hiromi Tokuda
President and CEO, Nobuaki Katoh
Senior Managing Director Overall Production Affairs and Production Promotion Center and Board Member, Sojiro Tsuchiya
EVP, Hikaru Sugi
Managing Officer; President DENSO International Asia, Yasushi Nei
Managing Officer, Mitsuhiko Masegi
EVP, Masahiko Miyaki
Managing Officer, Haruya Maruyama
Managing Officer, Akio Tajima
Managing Officer, Yasushi Yamanaka
Senior Executive Directors Member of the Board, Michio Adachi
Managing Officer, Hiroyuki Wakabayashi
Managing Officer, Akihiro Yukawa
Managing Officer, Yoshihiro Saka
Managing Officer, Sadahiro Usui
Managing Officer; President and CEO DENSO International America, Yoshiki (Steve) Sekiguchi
Managing Officer, Hiroyuki Murayama
Managing Officer, Hitoshi Tasaka
COO DENSO International America, Kazumasa Kimura
Director, Shoichiro Toyoda, age 87
Senior Managing Director Overall Electronic Business and Director, Mitsuharu Kato
Senior Managing Director Corporate Center Procurement Group and North America Region and Board Member, Koji Kobayashi
EVP and Director, Hiromi Tokuda
EVP and Director, Kenji Ohya
Senior Managing Director Sales Group and Board Member, Kazuo Hironaka
Senior Managing Director Overall Production Affairs and Production Promotion Center and Board Member, Sojiro Tsuchiya
President, Hikaru Sugi
Senior Managing Director Electronic Systems Business Group and Board Member, Shinji Shirasaki
Auditors: DeloitteToucheTohmatsu

LOCATIONS

HQ: Denso Corp. (Japan)
1-1 Showa-cho, Kariya, Aichi 448-8661
Phone: (81) 566 25 5850 **Fax:** (81) 566 25 4913
Web: www.denso.co.jp

2011 Sales

	% of total
Japan	56
Rest of	17
North	14
Europe	11
Other	2
Total	**100**

PRODUCTS/OPERATIONS

2011 Sales

	% of total
Automotive	
Thermal	31
Powertrain control	25
Information & safety	17
Electronic	9
Electric	9
Small	7
Industrial systems & consumer	1
Total	**100**

Selected Products

Automotive
- Thermal systems
  - Air conditioning systems
  - Air purifiers
  - Cooling fans
  - Cooling modules
  - Front end modules
  - Oil coolers
  - Radiators
  - Truck refrigeration units
- Powertrain control systems
  - Diesel engine management systems
  - Gasoline engine management systems
  - Transmission control components
- Information and safety systems
  - Multi-information display
  - Radar system for detecting obstacles in front of vehicle
  - Remote touch controller
- Electronic systems
  - Car security systems
  - Instrument clusters
  - Integrated climate control panels
  - Rear and corner sonars
  - Remote keyless entry controllers
  - Smart keys
- Electric systems
  - ABS actuators
  - Airbag sensors
  - Alternators
  - Electric power steering motors
  - Starters
- Small motors
  - Power window motors
  - Windshield washer systems
  - Windshield wiper systems

Industrial and Consumer
- Bar code readers
- Industrial robots
- Programmable logic controllers

COMPETITORS

APM Automotive
Adept Technology
Aisin Seiki
Delphi Automotive Systems
Garmin
JTEKT
Johnson Controls
KUKA
Key Safety Systems
NGK SPARK PLUG
Prestolite Electric
Remy International
Robert Bosch
Standard Motor Products
TRW Automotive
Valeo
Visteon
Yazaki

HISTORICAL FINANCIALS

Company Type: Public

Income Statement

FYE: March 31

	REVENUE ($ mil.)	NET INCOME ($ mil.)	NET PROFIT MARGIN	EMPLOYEES
03/13	38,057	1,930	5.1%	0
03/12	38,456	1,088	2.8%	126,036
03/11	37,816	1,727	4.6%	123,165
03/10	31,868	786	2.5%	120,812
03/09	31,913	(853)	—	119,919
Annual Growth	4.5%	—	—	—

2013 Year-End Financials

Debt ratio: 0.1%
Return on equity: 8.4%
Cash ($ mil.): 7,069
Current ratio: 2.34
Long-term debt ($ mil.): 3,733
No. of shares (mil.): 795
Dividends
Yield: —
Payout: —
Market value ($ mil.): 16,894

	STOCK PRICE ($) FY Close	P/E High/Low	PER SHARE ($) Earnings	Dividends	Book Value
03/13	21.24	— —	2.41	0.00	32.43
03/12	16.82	— —	1.35	0.00	32.03
03/11	16.45	— —	2.14	0.21	31.06
03/10	118.51	— —	0.98	0.14	27.00
03/09	79.75	— —	(1.06)	0.28	23.95
Annual Growth	(28.2%)	— —	—	—	7.9%

Deutsche Bank AG

LOCATIONS

HQ: Deutsche Bank AG
Taunusanlage 12, Frankfurt am Main D-60325
Phone: (49) 69 9 10 00 **Fax:** (49) 69 910 34 225
Web: www.deutsche-bank.com

HISTORICAL FINANCIALS

Company Type: Public

Income Statement

FYE: December 31

	ASSETS ($ mil.)	NET INCOME ($ mil.)	INCOME AS % OF ASSETS	EMPLOYEES
12/12	2,652,349	312	0.0%	98,219
12/11	2,799,163	5,344	0.2%	100,996
12/10	2,550,442	3,091	0.1%	102,062
12/09	2,161,810	7,163	0.3%	77,053
12/08	3,079,188	(5,361)	—	80,456
Annual Growth	(3.7%)	—	—	5.1%

2012 Year-End Financials

Return on assets: 0.0%
Return on equity: 0.4%
Long-term debt ($ mil.): —
No. of shares (mil.): 929
Sales ($ mil): 66,023
Dividends
Yield: 1.6%
Payout: 19.3%
Market value ($ mil.): 41,154

	STOCK PRICE ($) FY Close	P/E High/Low	PER SHARE ($) Earnings	Dividends	Book Value
12/12	44.29	364175	0.33	0.92	76.60
12/11	37.86	28 12	5.56	0.00	76.34
12/10	52.05	48 27	3.91	0.93	71.13
12/09	70.91	23 5	10.93	0.70	85.13
12/08	40.69	— —	(10.64)	6.98	76.29
Annual Growth	2.1%	— —	—	(39.7%)	0.1%

Deutsche Bundesbank (Germany, Fed. Rep.)

Deutsche Bundesbank is not your local burg's bank. The central bank of Germany Deutsche Bundesbank is a major part of the European System of Central Banks (ESCB). Deutsche Bundesbank supervises the German banking system manages the country's monetary supply collects and publishes economic statistics advises the German government on monetary policy and settles cross-border euro transactions. With the ESCB it participates in monetary decisions for the European Union. Deutsche Bundesbank has nine regional offices and about 50 branches throughout Germany.

EXECUTIVES

Member Executive Board Controlling Accounting and Organisation Department, Hans Georg Fabritius
Member Executive Board Information Technology and Markets, Hans-Helmut Kotz
VP, Prof Franz-Christoph Zeitler

Member Executive Board Economics Department Statistics Department and the Economic Research Centre, Prof Hermann Remsperger
Member Executive Board, Hans Reckers
Chairman Executive Board and President, Jens Weidmann, age 44
VP, Sabine Lautenschlaeger-Peiter
Auditors: PricewaterhouseCoopersAGWirtschaftsprufungsgesellschaft

LOCATIONS

HQ: Deutsche Bundesbank (Germany, Fed. Rep.)
Wilhelm-Epstein-Strasse 14, Frankfurt am Main D-60431
Phone: (49) 69 9566 0 **Fax:** (49) 69 9566 3077
Web: www.bundesbank.de

COMPETITORS

Bank of England
Federal Reserve
Reserve Bank of Australia

HISTORICAL FINANCIALS

Company Type: Public

Income Statement FYE: December 31

	ASSETS ($ mil.)	NET INCOME ($ mil.)	INCOME AS % OF ASSETS	EMPLOYEES
12/12	1,351,404	875	0.1%	10,825
12/11	1,083,451	831	0.1%	9,743
12/10	898,394	2,952	0.3%	9,560
12/09	847,116	5,974	0.7%	9,822
12/08	856,418	8,753	1.0%	10,038
Annual Growth	12.1%	(43.8%)	—	1.9%

2012 Year-End Financials

Return on assets: 0.0%
Return on equity: 0.4%
Long-term debt ($ mil.): —
No. of shares (mil.): —
Sales ($ mil): 14,175
Dividends
Yield: —
Payout: —
Market value ($ mil.): —

Deutsche Lufthansa AG (Germany, Fed. Rep.)

Germany's air ambassador Deutsche Lufthansa rivals the world's largest airlines. Operating through some 400 subsidiaries and affiliated companies the global aviation group runs Europe's largest passenger airline. It operates a fleet of more than 700 aircraft flying passengers to some 280 destinations in more than 100 countries worldwide not counting those served by code-sharing. Its logistics segment is also a market leader in international airfreight transportation through Lufthansa Cargo. The group's other main business segments deal in maintenance repair and overhaul (MRO) services through Lufthansa Technik; airline catering services through LSG Sky Chefs; and IT services through Lufthansa Systems.

Lufthansa's passenger airline business segment consists of Lufthansa (which includes Lufthansa Regional and Lufthansa Italia) Austrian Airlines SWISS and Germanwings as well as equity stakes in Brussels Airlines JetBlue and SunExpress. The company is considered to be a leading European premium carrier with hubs in Brussels Frankfurt Munich Vienna and Zurich.

The company is quickly expanding the number of destinations that its passenger airlines reach through code-sharing partnerships with other airlines. It is a member of the Star Alliance a group of 27 member airlines and counting that together cover more than 1100 destinations across the globe and of Atlantic++ the largest transatlantic joint venture which was founded by Lufthansa Air Canada Continental Airlines and United Air Lines. With about 280 daily transatlantic flights Atlantic++ establishes a route network to North America from Europe the Middle East and Africa.

After being hit hard on all fronts by the global recession in fiscal 2010 Lufthansa began seeing clear signs of recovery as total revenues were the highest they had been in five years. Its passenger airline segment in particular saw passenger numbers rise sharply and it experienced strong performance in all regions. Capacity was up by about 20% in Europe (geographically its largest market) 17% in the Middle East and Africa regions and 8% in the Asia/Pacific region largely due to airline consolidation in those areas. Overall capacity was up 13% and total passenger airline sales were up roughly 15% for the fiscal period.

This positive uptick in passenger air travel is expected to help Lufthansa return to normal economic growth. A fleet modernization program may also prove fruitful over the long-term as Lufthansa ordered more than 50 new aircraft to be delivered starting in 2012. At the same time although it has a hedging strategy in place the company anticipates that it will continue to contend with ongoing increases in oil prices. It will also face a burdensome air traffic tax that the German and Austrian governments have introduced which may offset some of its growth.

Lufthansa Cargo one of the largest cargo airlines in the world is seeing a dramatic earnings turnaround due to the recovering global economy and a boom in German exports. With a fleet of about 18 freighters Lufthansa Cargo is adding freight capacity through its joint ventures AeroLogic (50/50 held with DHL Express) and Jade Cargo International (majority held by Shenzhen Airlines). The Asia/Pacific region is Lufthansa Cargo's most important sales market generating about half of its total traffic revenue. Outside of China Japanese airline JAL withdrew its freighter service as a result of the recession causing freighter service opportunities to Japan to expand substantially for other cargo carriers.

Lufthansa Technik serves its parent as one of the world's leading providers of MRO services for commercial aircraft. It provides maintenance aircraft overhaul technical support for engines components and landing gear and special maintenance services for VIP aircraft. Lufthansa Technik launched a multitude of products in 2010 including a new in-flight camera surveillance system and a kit that enables airlines to turn part of an aircraft cabin into an exclusive VIP compartment for VIP and business travel customers. Although it reported modest growth in 2010 Lufthansa Technik anticipates that the MRO market will continue to grow as a result of aircraft fleets being modernized and becoming larger around the world.

HISTORY

The Weimar government created Deutsche Luft Hansa (DLH) in 1926 by merging private German airlines Deutscher Aero Lloyd (founded 1919) and Junkers Luftverkehr (formed in 1921 by aircraft manufacturer Junkers Flugzeugwerke). DLH built what would become Europe's most comprehensive air route network by 1931. It served the USSR through Deruluft (formed 1921; dissolved 1941) an airline jointly owned by DLH and the Soviet government. In 1930 DLH and the Chinese government formed Eurasia Aviation Corporation to develop air transport in China.

DLH established the world's first trans-Atlantic airmail service from Berlin to Buenos Aires in 1934 and went on to develop air transport throughout South America. The outbreak of WWII ended operations in Europe and the Chinese government seized Eurasia Aviation in 1941. Klaus Bonhoeffer head of DLH's legal department led an unsuccessful coup against the Nazi leadership and was executed in 1945. Soon afterward all DLH operations ceased.

In 1954 the Allies allowed the recapitalization of Deutsche Lufthansa. The airline started with domestic routes returned to London and Paris (1955) and then re-entered South America (1956). In 1958 it made its first nonstop flight between Germany and New York and initiated service to Tokyo and Cairo. Meanwhile it started a charter airline with several partners in 1955. Lufthansa bought out its partners in 1959 and renamed the unit Condor two years later.

The carrier resumed service behind the Iron Curtain in 1966 with flights to Prague. The stable West German economy helped Lufthansa maintain profitability through most of the 1970s.

The reunification of Germany in 1990 ended Allied control over Berlin airspace allowing Lufthansa which had bought Pan Am's Berlin routes to fly there under its own colors for the first time since the end of WWII. The company began seeking international partners in 1991 but that year European air travel suffered its first-ever slowdown forcing Lufthansa into the red for the first time since 1973.

The company restructured in 1994 into a group of new business units: Lufthansa Technik Lufthansa Cargo and Lufthansa Systems. In 1995 the carrier began to face increased domestic competition from Deutsche BA a British Airways affiliate.

The airline formed a code-sharing agreement with Air Canada in 1996. In 1997 the Star Alliance was formed and Lufthansa signed a pact with Singapore Airlines. That year the German government sold its remaining 38% stake in Lufthansa. In 1998 Lufthansa and All Nippon Airways (later renamed ANA Holdings) formed a code-sharing alliance and Condor was combined with Karstadt's tour company NUR Touristic to form C&N Touristic. (After buying UK-based travel operator Thomas Cook in 2000 C&N Touristic changed its name to Thomas Cook in 2001.)

In a plan to gain more access to London's Heathrow Airport Lufthansa took a 20% stake in British Midland which was admitted into the Star Alliance in 2000 along with Mexicana Airlines. In 2001 the airline bought the 52% of Texas-based Sky Chefs it did not already own and formed a new unit LSG Sky Chefs International to hold its catering operations.

Lufthansa said goodbye to its 24% stake in delivery firm DHL when it sold its share to Deutsche Post in 2002. In 2004 the company sold its facilities management division Lufthansa Gebaudemanagement (LGM) to German construction company HOCHTIEF.

To facilitate international expansion and to respond to the acquisition of KLM by Air France in 2007 Lufthansa took full ownership of SWISS Switzerland's primary international airline. The carriers agreed to the deal in 2005 but issues related to international air traffic rights delayed the completion of the transaction. SWISS operates under its own brand and the carrier's Zurich headquarters became a third major hub for Lufthansa.

Lufthansa exited the leisure travel services business in 2006 by selling its 50% stake in Thomas Cook to German retailer Karstadt Quelle which owned the other half.

Lufthansa acquired a 45% stake in SN Airholding parent of Brussels Airlines in 2008. In 2009 Lufthansa completed its acquisition of UK-based airline bmi. It then sold it to International Airlines Group in 2012.

EXECUTIVES

Member Executive Board; Chief Officer Group Airlines and Corporate Human Resources; Chairman British Midland Airways, Stefan Lauer, age 58, $824,090 total compensation
Chairman Supervisory Board, Jurgen Weber, age 72
Honorary Chairman Supervisory Board, Wolfgang Roller
Chairman British Midland Airways, Nigel Turner
CEO, Christoph Franz, age 53, $453,215 total compensation
CEO Swiss International Air Lines, Harry Hohmeister, age 49
CEO British Midland Airways, Wolfgang Prock-Schauer, age 57
Deputy Chairman Supervisory Board, Frank Bsirske
Chairman LSG Lufthansa Service Holding, Walter N. Gehl, age 60
Operations and Sales LSG Lufthansa Service Holding, Thomas Nagel, age 63
Marketing and Sales Solutions LSG Lufthansa Service Holding, Jochen Muller, age 51
EVP Marketing and Sales Lufthansa Passenger Airlines, Thierry Antinori, age 51
Chief Executive Officer, Carsten Spohr, age 47
Member Executive Board; CFO and Head Aviation Services; Chairman LSG Lufthansa Service Lufthansa Cargo Lufthansa Technik, Stephan Gemkow, age 53, $824,090 total compensation
CEO Lufthansa Technik, August-Wilhelm Henningsen, age 63
Product and Service Lufthansa Technik, Thomas Stuger, age 57
CFO Lufthansa Technik, Peter Jansen, age 59
Marketing and Sales Lufthansa Systems, Gunter Kuchler
Group Representative and Head of Hub Management Munich, Thomas Kluhr, age 50
Director Public Affairs The Americas, Natalie A. Hartman
Chairman and CEO Cargo, Karl U. Garnadt, age 57
Director Corporate Communications The Americas, Martin Riecken
VP The Americas, Jens Bischof, age 48
Human Resources Lufthansa Technik, Uwe Mukrasch, age 52
EVP Operations Lufthansa Passenger Airlines, Jurgen Raps, age 62
General Director Argentina Chile Paraguay and Uruguay, Annette Taeuber
Regional Director Saint-Petersburg and North-Western Region of the Russian Federation, Bart Buyse, age 40
CEO Ukraine and Armenia, Harald Hahn
Manager Leisure and Specialist Sales UK and Ireland, Becky Schmidt
Chief Marketing and Strategy Officer Swiss International Air Lines, Christoph Beckmann
SVP and Head Corporate Communications, Klaus Walther
Head Media Relations, Andreas Bartels
Head Corporate Communications Europe, Aage Dunhaupt
Chairman Executive Board and CEO Lufthansa Systems, Stefan Hansen, age 49
Manager Media Communications North America, Christina Semmel
Member Supervisory Board, Klaus G. Schlede
Chairman Supervisory Board, Jurgen Weber, age 72
Member Supervisory Board, Werner Brandt, age 59
Member Supervisory Board, Michael Wollstadt
Member Supervisory Board, Jurgen Hambrecht, age 67
Member Supervisory Board, Jacques Aigrain, age 59
Deputy Chairman Supervisory Board, Frank Bsirske
Member Supervisory Board, Jurgen Erwert
Member Supervisory Board, Nicola Leibinger-Kammuller, age 54
Member Supervisory Board, Bernd Buresch
Member Supervisory Board, Jorg Cebulla
Member Supervisory Board, Dominique Hiekel
Member Supervisory Board, Eckhard Lieb
Member Supervisory Board, Simon Reimann
Member Supervisory Board, Matthias Wissmann
Member Supervisory Board, Stefan Ziegler
Member Supervisory Board, Marlies Rose
Auditors: PricewaterhouseCoopersAG

LOCATIONS

HQ: Deutsche Lufthansa AG (Germany, Fed. Rep.)
Lufthansa Aviation Center, Airportring, Frankfurt 60546
Phone: (49) 69 696 28008 **Fax:** (49) 69 696 90990
Web: www.lufthansa.com

2011 Sales

	% of total
Europe	65
Asia/Pacific	14
North	14
Middle	3
Africa	2
Central & South	2
Total	**100**

PRODUCTS/OPERATIONS

2011 Sales

	% of total
Passenger airline	75
Maintenance repair &	10
Logistics	8
Catering	6
IT	1
Total	**100**

COMPETITORS

AAR Corp.
Aer Lingus
Air Berlin
Air France-KLM
Alitalia
Amadeus IT
American Airlines Group
Aviall
British Airways
Delta Air Lines
Deutsche Bahn
Gate Gourmet
IAG
ITA Software
Japan Airlines
Jeppesen Sanderson
Korean Air
Qantas
Ryanair
SR Technics
TIMCO Aviation
Virgin Atlantic Airways
easyJet

HISTORICAL FINANCIALS

Company Type: Public

Income Statement FYE: December 31

	REVENUE ($ mil.)	NET INCOME ($ mil.)	NET PROFIT MARGIN	EMPLOYEES
12/12	39,868	1,304	3.3%	116,957
12/11	37,345	(16)	—	120,055
12/10	36,790	1,513	4.1%	117,019
12/09	32,424	(161)	—	117,521
12/08	35,019	837	2.4%	107,800
Annual Growth	3.3%	11.7%	—	2.1%

2012 Year-End Financials

Debt ratio: 32.0%	No. of shares (mil.): 459
Return on equity: 12.2%	Dividends
Cash ($ mil.): 1,892	Yield: 1.1%
Current ratio: 1.00	Payout: 13.4%
Long-term debt ($ mil.): 7,838	Market value ($ mil.): 8,872

	STOCK PRICE ($) FY Close	P/E High	P/E Low	PER SHARE ($) Earnings	Dividends	Book Value
12/12	19.29	15	8	2.85	0.22	23.61
12/11	11.78	—	—	(0.04)	1.22	22.45
12/10	21.76	18	8	3.31	0.00	24.09
12/09	16.90	—	—	(0.35)	0.65	19.17
12/08	15.95	49	15	1.82	1.50	20.93
Annual Growth	4.9%	—	—	11.9%	(38.0%)	3.1%

Deutsche Post AG

Deutsche Post has outgrown its mailbox origins. Doing business as Deutsche Post DHL the company divides its operations between delivering the mail in Germany (Deutsche Post) and being one of the world's leading providers of express delivery and logistics services (DHL). As Deutsche Post it delivers about 66 million letters a day to more than 42 million customers (about half of the German population). DHL handles the international express delivery freight forwarding global mail and supply chain business. Overall DHL-branded business activities account for the majority of Deutsche Post DHL's sales. The company's largest market is Europe which accounts for about two-thirds of sales.

Deutsche Post DHL operates through four divisions - Express Freight Forwarding Global Mail and Supply Chain. Deutsche Post only encompasses the group's German mail service. And as electronic communication grows the company is reevaluating its legacy operations. Demand for mail delivery has trended downward; and while that's good for the earth it's bad for business. In 2010 Deutsche Post's market share for German mail service fell slightly to 86.6%. In response Deutsche Post DHL is investing E750 million to modernize its parcel network in Germany to accommodate an uptick in e-commerce business. The company also plans to substitute mail shipped by air for less-costly ground transportation.

It also launched a new product in mid-2010 that uses email to send registered mail. The E-Postbrief is an electronic message that is also a binding legal document and costs the same to send as a normal letter. Companies such as insurance firms Allianz and Zurich Financial Services and software giant SAP have signed on to use the E-Postbrief which is delivered instantly saving time and resources but also generating revenue for Deutsche Post DHL.

The company expects the most growth to come from its DHL-branded services which handle the international express delivery freight forwarding global mail and supply chain business. Deutsche Post DHL drastically reduced its offerings in the US where FedEx and UPS lead the market to focus on emerging markets in Asia where much of the world's goods originate. In late 2008 it slashed 9500 US jobs –around 73% of its DHL Express (USA) workforce and closed hundreds of offices. DHL Express (USA) subsequently eliminated air and ground services within the US; maintains its international shipping services to and from the US and offers supply chain management through subsidiary Exel. (The company sold Exel's freight brokerage and intermodal services). It also sold its domestic express operations in France and the UK in 2009 and discontinued its bulk mail business in the Netherlands in 2011. The divestment followed a restructuring of the Express division in an attempt to make operations leaner and more streamlined.

With resources freed the company is looking to strengthen its international express services and its freight business. While revenues for the express division were down 4% in Europe in 2010 sales in Africa the Americas Asia Eastern Europe the Middle East experienced double-digit growth by as much as 30%. In China DHL-Sinotrans International Air Courier its joint venture with Sinotrans is one of the country's top express delivery firms but the company is selling its stake due to a change in China's legal framework. DHL Global Forwarding its air and sea freight business took over LifeConEx a joint venture it formed with Lufthansa in 2005. LifeConEx offers supply chain services for pharmaceutical and biotech companies. The company sees pharmaceutical shipping as a key growth area in both developed and emerging markets.

Deutsche Post evolved from a government-owned mail service to a publicly traded company with worldwide delivery and logistics operations. The German government controls a 31% stake in Deutsche Post DHL through KfW Bankengruppe.

HISTORY

The German postal system was established in the 1490s when German emperor Maximilian I ordered a reliable and regular messenger service to be set up between Austria (Innsbruck where the emperor had his court) and the farther reaches of his Holy Roman Empire: the Netherlands France and Rome. The von Tassis (later renamed Taxis) family of Italy was responsible for running the network. Family members settled in major cities across Europe to expand the postal business.

Although the family operated what was officially an exclusively royal mail service by the early 1500s the company was also delivering messages for private patrons. In 1600 a family member who served as general postmaster was authorized to collect fees for private mail deliveries. By the early 19th century Thurn und Taxis as the company was then called was the leading postal service in the Holy Roman Empire serving more than 11 million people.

The dissolution of the Holy Roman Empire prompted by Napoleon's military adventures led to the creation of a federation of 39 independent German states. Thurn und Taxis had to make agreements with members of the separate states including Austria and Prussia. After Austria's defeat in 1866 by Prussia the confederation was dissolved and all Thurn und Taxis postal systems were absorbed by Prussia. When Bismarck's Prussian-led German Reich was established in 1870 the new postal administration (Reichspostverwaltung) began issuing postage stamps valid across Germany.

After Germany was defeated in WWII and split into two nations in 1949 two postal systems were established: Deutsche Post (East Germany) and Deutsche Bundespost (West Germany). The fall of the Berlin Wall in 1989 preceded a reunion of the two German states in 1990. That year Deutsche Post led by chairman Klaus Zumwinkel was integrated into Deutsche Bundespost. The merger resulted in losses and a huge backlog of undelivered mail. Zumwinkel initiated the company's first steps to recovery by cutting 140000 jobs.

The heavy costs of reunification (it was 1994 before Deutsche Bundespost posted a profit again) prompted the German government to set the postal system on a course toward full privatization.

In 1995 the postal system was restructured as Deutsche Post AG and placed under the management of executives from the private sector.

In 1998 a new postal law reaffirmed Deutsche Post's monopoly on traditional letter delivery until 2002. However other special mail delivery options (such as same-day delivery of letters) were granted to private companies. That year Deutsche Post acquired shares in parcel delivery companies in Europe and the US including a stake of nearly 25% in DHL. In 1999 it acquired Deutsche Postbank the former retail banking arm of Deutsche Bundespost as part of a strategy to make it more attractive for an IPO.

Continuing its buying spree Deutsche Post grabbed Swiss-based logistics giant Danzas Holding Swedish freight forwarder ASG and the distribution and logistics unit of Dutch transport group Royal Nedlloyd. Undeterred by a European Commission probe into whether it received improper state subsidies Deutsche Post added more units in 2000 including US-based airfreight forwarder Air Express International which was integrated into Danzas. It also acquired New York-based QuickMAIL.

The German government sold a minority stake in Deutsche Post to the public in 2000. (Further share sales followed and by 2006 the government had reduced its stake in Deutsche Post to about 35%.)

In 2002 the company took full ownership of DHL and the next year Deutsche Post (through DHL) paid about $1 billion for the ground delivery network of US-based Airborne.

In its effort to move beyond mail Deutsche Post over the next few years gained control of express delivery and logistics operations across Europe and in the US. To eliminate overlaps in its operations Deutsche Post united its parcel and express delivery services (DHL and Euro Express) and logistics services (Danzas and Exel) under the DHL brand in 2005.

Klaus Zumwinkel resigned in February 2008 after he was questioned in connection with a government investigation into alleged tax evasion. Management board member Frank Appel succeeded him.

To focus on its core logistics operations as well as raise cash Deutsche Post in early 2009 sold a minority stake in its Deutsche Postbank unit to Deutsche Bank. The deal in which Deutsche Bank paid about $3.9 billion for nearly 30% of Postbank included options for both parties that could result in Deutsche Bank acquiring the remainder of Deutsche Post's shares in the financial services unit.

LOCATIONS

HQ: Deutsche Post AG
Charles-de-Gaulle-Strasse 20, Bonn D-53113
Phone: (49) 228 182 0 **Fax:** (49) 228 14 88 72
Web: www.dpwn.de

2010 Sales

	$ mil.	% of total
Europe		
Other countries	33	
Asia/Pacific	14	
Total	**0**	**100**

PRODUCTS/OPERATIONS

2010 Sales

	$ mil.	% of total
Mail	27	
Supply Chain	25	

Selected Services

Air freight
Contract logistics
Dialog marketing services
European road freight
International express
National and international mail and parcel services
Ocean freight
Outsourcing and system solutions for the mail business

HISTORICAL FINANCIALS

Company Type: Public

Income Statement FYE: December 31

	REVENUE ($ mil.)	NET INCOME ($ mil.)	NET PROFIT MARGIN	EMPLOYEES
12/12	73,167	2,185	3.0%	472,321
12/11	68,331	1,504	2.2%	467,188
12/10	68,900	3,400	4.9%	464,471
12/09	66,555	927	1.4%	488,518
12/08	76,159	(2,359)	—	512,536
Annual Growth	(1.0%)	—	—	(2.0%)

2012 Year-End Financials

Debt ratio: —
Return on equity: 14.4%
Cash ($ mil.): 3,163
Current ratio: 0.97
Long-term debt ($ mil.): —
No. of shares (mil.): 1,209
Dividends
Yield: 3.9%
Payout: 86.0%
Market value ($ mil.): 26,743

	STOCK PRICE ($) FY Close	P/E High/Low		PER SHARE ($) Earnings	Dividends	Book Value
12/12	22.12	28	19	1.74	0.87	13.03
12/11	15.42	40	22	1.24	1.63	11.78
12/10	17.09	19	11	2.81	0.76	11.64
12/09	19.40	82	28	0.76	0.76	9.74
Annual Growth	4.5%	—	—	22.9%	3.6%	7.5%

Deutsche Post RG

LOCATIONS

HQ: Deutsche Post RG
Charles-de-Gaulle-Str. 20, Bonn 53113
Phone: (49) 228 182 0 **Fax:** (49) 228 182 98 80
Web: www.dp-dhl.com

HISTORICAL FINANCIALS

Company Type: Public

Income Statement FYE: December 31

	REVENUE ($ mil.)	NET INCOME ($ mil.)	NET PROFIT MARGIN	EMPLOYEES
12/12	73,167	2,185	3.0%	473,626
12/11	68,331	1,504	2.2%	471,654
Annual Growth	7.1%	45.3%	—	0.4%

2012 Year-End Financials

Debt ratio: —
Return on equity: 14.4%
Cash ($ mil.): 3,163
Current ratio: 0.97
Long-term debt ($ mil.): —
No. of shares (mil.): 1,209
Dividends
Yield: —
Payout: 53.0%
Market value ($ mil.): —

	STOCK PRICE ($) FY Close	P/E High/Low		PER SHARE ($) Earnings	Dividends	Book Value
12/12	0.00	—	—	1.74	0.92	13.03
12/11	0.00	—	—	1.24	0.91	11.78
/0.00	—	—	(0.00)	0.00	(0.00)	
Annual Growth	—	—	—	—	—	—

Deutsche Postbank AG

Deutsche Postbank is claiming its post as one of Germany's leading retail banks. Spun off from postal service provider Deutsche Post in 2004 the bank offers deposits loans and mortgages asset management insurance and commercial finance including factoring and leasing services through more than 850 branches; it also offers some services through post office locations. The bank performs payment processing services as well with rivals including Deutsche Bank among its biggest customers. Outside Germany Deutsche Postbank offers banking services in Luxembourg and structured finance products to companies in North America. Deutsche Bank controls just over half of the bank.

In 2008 there was renewed interest in the acquisition of Deutsche Postbank as its former parent company Deutsche Post sought to sell the bank in order to focus on mail express deliveries and logistics. German banking giant Deutsche Bank acquired 25% of Deutsche Postbank for some $4 billion in 2009; it later upped its stake to more than 50% the next year.

Stefan Juette was named CEO of Deutsche Postbank in 2009. He followed Wolfgang Klein who resigned following a clash with members of the board. Juette was a Deutsche Postbank board member responsible for lending and credit management.

EXECUTIVES

Chairman Supervisory Board, Frank Appel, age 52
Member Management Board Human Resources Legal Affairs and Real Estate Management, Ralf Stemmer, $527,720 total compensation
Member Management Board Services, Mario Daberkow, age 44, $55,015 total compensation
Member Management Board Retail Sales, Hans-Peter Schmid, $571,653 total compensation
CFO and General Manager, Marc Hess
Member Management Board Product Marketing, Michael Meyer, age 49
Vice Chairman of the Supervisory Board, Frank Bsirske
Chairman of the Management Board, Frank Strauss
Member of the Management Board; Chief Risk Officer, Hanns-Peter Storr
Member of the Management Board; Responsible for Financial Markets; Treasurer, Horst Kuepker
Chairman of the Supervisory Board, Rainer Neske
Auditors: PricewaterhouseCoopersAG

LOCATIONS

HQ: Deutsche Postbank AG
Friedrich-Ebert-Allee 114-126, Bonn D-53113
Phone: (49) 228 920 0 **Fax:** (49) 228 920 35151
Web: www.postbank.com

2007 Sales

	% of total
Europe	
Germany	94
Other	4
US &	2
Total	**100**

PRODUCTS/OPERATIONS

2007 Sales by Segment

	% of total
Retail	77
Corporate	9
Transaction	8
Financial	6
Total	**100**

COMPETITORS

ABN AMRO Group
Commerzbank
DZ BANK
Deutsche Bank
Erste Bank
HSBC
UniCredit Bank AG

HISTORICAL FINANCIALS

Company Type: Public

Income Statement FYE: December 31

	ASSETS ($ mil.)	NET INCOME ($ mil.)	INCOME AS % OF ASSETS	EMPLOYEES
12/12	255,466	367	0.1%	18,599
12/11	248,319	143	0.1%	19,232
12/10	287,327	184	0.1%	20,361
12/09	326,446	109	0.0%	20,860
12/08	323,353	(1,147)	—	26,549
Annual Growth	(5.7%)	—	—	(8.5%)

2012 Year-End Financials

Return on assets: 0.1%
Return on equity: 4.6%
Long-term debt ($ mil.): —
No. of shares (mil.): 218
Sales ($ mil): 9,955
Dividends
Yield: —
Payout: —
Market value ($ mil.): 9,232

	STOCK PRICE ($) FY Close	P/E High/Low	PER SHARE ($) Earnings	Dividends	Book Value
12/12	42.20	57 52	1.69	0.00	37.98
12/11	30.10	113 99	0.66	0.00	33.73
12/10	34.52	112 71	0.84	0.00	34.40
12/09	33.00	233 47	0.50	0.00	34.55
12/08	21.65	— —	(6.81)	0.00	32.05
Annual Growth	18.2%	— —	—	—	4.3%

Deutsche Telekom AG

Operating the autobahn on the global information superhighway Deutsche Telekom (DT) is a leading telecom company in Europe and one of the largest carriers in the world. The company's core business is its services and products for fixed-network and mobile communications services as well as for enterprise information and communication technology (ICT). Germany's #1 fixed-line telephone operator it provides domestic and international long-distance voice services. It is a leading ISP offering other data and multimedia services such as its Entertain-branded Internet television. DT's T-Systems International delivers ICT services for businesses. About three-quarters of sales come from Europe.

Geographic Reach

Deutsche Telekom (DT) operates through its subsidiary in more than 50 countries worldwide. The company gets more than half of its revenue from outside Germany. While DT has an impressive global reach customers in Germany still comprise its largest single market accounting for almost 45% of sales; its customers in Europe are essentially in Eastern European countries.

Operations

DT offers goods & services through subsidiaries in 15 European countries including Austria Croatia the Czech Republic Greece (through a 30% stake in OTE) Hungary (Magyar Telekom) the Netherlands and Poland (Polska Telefonia Cyfrowa).

Outside Germany and Eastern Europe the company's key international wireless subsidiaries are T-Mobile USA and T-Mobile (UK). The UK is the group's third-largest market with about 17 million subscribers.

Financial Performance

Net revenue in fiscal 2012 was down by 1% compared with the prior year. Intense competition price changes imposed by regulatory authorities and the strained economic situation in most countries in its Europe operating segment had a negative effect.

Mergers and Acquisitions

In 2012 DT and MetroPCS Communications signed a definitive agreement to combine T-Mobile USA and MetroPCS. The transaction which is expected to close in mid-2013 will create a leading carrier in the US wireless marketplace.

Ownership

The German government and German state-owned development bank KfW together own about 32% of Deutsche Telekom.

HISTORY

Deutsche Telekom was formed by the 1989 separation of West Germany's telecommunications services from the nation's postal system Deutsche Post. Dating back to the 15th century (when the Thurn und Taxis private postal system was created for German principalities) the service expanded to cover Austria France the Netherlands and most of Germany by the 1850s. After the 1866 Austro-Prussian War it became part of the North German Postal Confederation. When the German Empire was formed in 1871 the postal operation became the Deutsche Reichspost (later the Bundespost). Shortly thereafter the newly invented telephone was introduced in Germany.

Post-WWI inflation shook the Bundespost and the government allowed it to try new organizational structures. A 1924 law allowed the state-run service to operate as a quasi-commercial company. After WWII the American-British zone returned postal authority to Germans and in 1949 the USSR established the state of East Germany.

Only by the 1960s did West Germany's postal and phone services meet modern standards. Privatization of the Bundespost became a political cause when many complained about the monopoly's cost and inefficiency. Efforts to privatize the agency (named Deutsche Telekom in 1989) intensified with the 1990 German reunification. Faced with updating the antiquated phone system of the former East Germany however political opposition to taking Deutsche Telekom public faded.

The company began operating T-D1 its mobile phone network in 1992 and the next year it launched T-Online now Germany's largest online service provider. In 1996 Deutsche Telekom finally went public and raised more than $13 billion in Europe's largest IPO. It also launched Global One with France Telecom (renamed Orange) and Sprint (now Sprint Nextel); as part of the partnership Deutsche Telekom took a 10% stake in Sprint.

In 1998 European Union (EU) member countries opened their phone markets to competition and Deutsche Telekom's long-distance market share quickly eroded. Under EU pressure in 1999 the company said it would sell its cable network which it divided into nine regional units.

Deutsche Telekom's plan to merge with Telecom Italia in 1999 blew up in its face: Olivetti butted in and took over Telecom Italia while an angry France Telecom filed a lawsuit claiming that Deutsche Telekom's merger plan violated their agreements (the case was settled in 2000).

Undaunted Deutsche Telekom forged ahead with its international expansion plans buying French fixed-line carrier SIRIS and UK wireless provider One 2 One (now T-Mobile UK). In 2000 the company sold its stake in Global One to France

Telecom as did Sprint. In the fallout from the unwinding of the Global One partnership Deutsche Telekom in 2001 sold its stake in Sprint PCS and its interest in France Telecom the next year.

T-Mobile International moved into the US mobile phone market in 2001 with the acquisitions of VoiceStream Wireless and Powertel now known as T-Mobile USA. The German government's stake in Deutsche Telekom decreased largely to accommodate US regulators for the VoiceStream and Powertel acquisitions.

With competition flourishing in Germany Deutsche Telekom worked hard to lose its bureaucratic image and reposition itself as a slimmer customer-friendly organization. To cut costs and eliminate debt it reduced its workforce by 22000 jobs nearly 10% over two years.

As the company's share price slumped amid the general telecom industry downturn CEO Ron Sommer was forced to resign in 2002. That year the company announced plans to sell its phone directory unit (DeTeMedien) saying it hoped to raise ?1 billion but reversed that decision a year later after making progress at reducing its debt burden. Also in 2003 the company announced plans to acquire the 51% of Polish wireless operator Polska Telefonia Cyfrowa (PTC) that it did not yet own from Vivendi and Elektrim. But the company pulled out of the deal which was valued at $1.26 billion after Elektrim officials sought a higher price. Nearly a decade later Vivendi and Deutsche Telekom closed an agreement that gave Deutsche Telekom full control of PTC in exchange for a payment of about ?1 billion (around $1.3 billion).

Until 2003 Deutsche Telekom was Germany's #1 cable provider through the company's six regional cable TV operations which it sold for nearly $2 billion to a group of US investors that included Apax Partners the Goldman Sachs Group and Providence Equity Partners. The deal represented a substantial discount from a 2001 agreement to sell the cable networks to US-based Liberty Media for about $5 billion. But German regulatory authorities blocked that sale. Deutsche Telekom previously sold controlling stakes in three other regional networks.

The company boosted its T-Mobile USA holdings through the acquisition in 2005 of wireless networks serving California and Nevada from Cingular Wireless (which became AT&T Mobility). The deal valued at $2.5 billion included the end of an agreement in which the two companies used each other's networks.

Faced with plummeting profits caused largely by operational inefficiencies Deutsche Telekom in 2007 began to reduce costs by cutting the pay and extending the hours of about 50000 or one-third of its employees. Also that year Deutsche Telekom sold is Ya.com unit to France Telecom for about $432 million. Acquisitions for the year included the cell phone unit of France Telecom and ISP Orange Netherlands.

Deutsche Telekom had previously said that it might combine IT services subsidiary T-Systems with a future acquisition. In 2008 it formed a partnership with US-based IT services provider Cognizant in order to cut operational costs and to expand T-Systems' potential European customer base for systems integration services. The deal included the transfer of staff from T-Systems' unit in India to Cognizant's Indian operations.

In 2009 T-Systems acquired about 90 hosting customers from enterprise applications giant and partner SAP. The deal saw T-Systems assume SAP software systems infrastructure and services support for these medium and large-sized corporate clients at its data centers. That year it also bought Strato the Web-hosting services unit of freenet for ?275 million (about $385 million) to boost its presence in the data network services market. The deal helped Deutsche Telekom to gain ground on market leader United Internet.

Also that year the company absorbed its T-Mobile International subsidiary which formerly oversaw the operations of its US and UK wireless businesses in a move to simplify both its corporate structure and its sales and marketing efforts. The reorganization resulted in the US and UK businesses coming under the direct supervision of Deutsche Telekom. Furthermore wireless operations in Germany were combined with the domestic landline operations T-Home unit under the simplified T brand early the next year.

In 2010 it bought UK-based online payment services provider ClickandBuy used by more than 16000 Web retailers.

EXECUTIVES

Member Management Board Data Privacy Legal Affairs and Compliance, Manfred Balz, age 69, $660,000 total compensation
SEVP Corporate Communications, Philipp Schindera, age 42
Director, Prof Ulrich Middelmann, age 67
Director, Hubertus von Grunberg, age 70
Director, Bernhard Walter, age 69
Director, Wulf H. Bernotat, age 63
Director, Lawrence H. Guffey, age 44
Director, Ulrich Hocker
Director, Monika Brandl
Director, Lothar Holzwarth
Director, Waltraud Litzenberger
Director, Michael Loffler
Director, Michael Sommer
Deputy Chairman, Lothar Schroder
Director, Hermann-Josef Becker
Director, Sylvia Kuhnast
Director, Ulrich Schroder, age 60
Director, Jorg Asmussen
Director, Hans Martin Bury
Director, Hans-Jurgen Kallmeier
Director, Sibylle Spoo
Auditors:
Ernst&YoungWirtschaftsprufungsgesellschaft

LOCATIONS

HQ: Deutsche Telekom AG
Unternehmenskommunikation, Postfach 2000, Bonn D-53105
Phone: (49) 228 181 4949 **Fax:** (49) 228 1 81 940 04
Web: www.telekom.com

2012 Sales

	$ mil.	% of total
Europe		
Other European countries		27
Other countries		1

PRODUCTS/OPERATIONS

2012 Sales

	$ mil.	% of total
Telecommunications	88	
Total	0	100

COMPETITORS

BT
Belgacom
COLT Group
Cable & Wireless
Freenet
HP Enterprise Services
Invitel
KPN
Orange
QSC
Swisscom
TDC
Tele Columbus
Tele2
Telecom Italia
Telefonica
Telefonica O2 Germany
Telekom Austria
Telenor
TeliaSonera
United Internet
Versatel
Vodafone
Vodafone D2

HISTORICAL FINANCIALS

Company Type: Public

Income Statement

FYE: December 31

	REVENUE ($ mil.)	NET INCOME ($ mil.)	NET PROFIT MARGIN	EMPLOYEES
12/12	76,669	(6,926)	—	229,686
12/11	75,864	720	0.9%	235,132
12/10	83,542	2,268	2.7%	246,777
12/09	93,063	508	0.5%	259,920
12/08	86,214	2,073	2.4%	227,747
Annual Growth	(2.9%)	—	—	0.2%

2012 Year-End Financials

Debt ratio: 54.4%
Return on equity: (-17.1%)
Cash ($ mil.): 5,306
Current ratio: 0.65
Long-term debt ($ mil.): 46,598
No. of shares (mil.): —
Dividends
Yield: 7.4%
Payout: —
Market value ($ mil.): —

	STOCK PRICE ($) FY Close	P/E High/Low	PER SHARE ($) Earnings	Dividends	Book Value
12/12	11.36	— —	(1.61)	0.85	7.91
12/11	11.45	246146	0.17	1.79	10.56
12/10	12.80	75 44	0.52	1.03	11.78
12/09	14.70	424254	0.12	1.04	12.01
12/08	15.30	139 64	0.48	0.95	12.83
Annual Growth	(7.2%)	— —	—	(2.8%)	(11.4%)

Diageo Plc

Diageo's company parties must be the talk of the town. It is the leading premium spirits business in the world by volume net sales and operating profit. The company produces and distributes eight of the world's top 20 spirits brands. It is also one of the few international drinks companies that span the entire beverage alcohol market offering beer wine and spirits. Diageo's well-known brands include Smirnoff vodka Baileys cream liqueur Johnnie Walker Scotch whisky Jose Cuervo tequila Tanqueray gin Captain Morgan rum Guinness beer and wines from Sterling Vineyards and Beaulieu Vineyard. Its products are sold worldwide.

Diageo owns 100-plus production facilities including malting distilleries breweries packaging maturation vineyards wineries and distribution. A Global Supply operation accounts for about 85% of production; the operation is divided among supply branches: Europe America Global Beer and Asia. Remaining production is integrated with distribution activities mainly in Africa.

Diageo has offices in 80 countries and production facilities in North America Latin America and Caribbean Europe Africa and the Asia/Pacific region. It sells products in 180 markets in these regions with subsidiary Diageo North America accounting for about one-third of the sales.

Even with challenging economic conditions at home and abroad Diageo has something to celebrate. Sales and profits (in pounds) jumped approximately 30% in fiscal 2011 over 2007. Results are driven by a strategic mix of premium global and local brands. Diageo's portfolio of global brands which are marketed worldwide and show the greatest earnings potential has grown to 14 labels. During 2011 they generated more than 65% of sales. Local brands (Crown Royal Canadian whiskey in North America Bundaberg rum in Asia and Gordon's gin in Europe) hold top positions in the particular market where they are distributed but have a smaller impact on total performance.

Diageo's geographic presence underpins the success of its premium brand portfolio. Although North American and European sales have remained flat to depressed as cash-strapped consumers traded down these regions accounted for a hefty two-thirds of sales in 2011. Developing markets (Africa Latin America and Asia) generate the remaining one-third of the company's sales.

Fundamental to its growth strategy Diageo aims to sell up to 50% of its products to developing markets by 2015. To that end Diageo has increased its stake in China's leading white spirits maker Shui Jing Fang to 53%. Shui Jing Fang produces of the country's most profitable and fastest-growing spirit Shanghai White vodka. During 2011 Diageo also boosted its interest to 53% in another Chinese white spirits maker Sichuan Chengdu Quanxing Group. (Quanxing owns roughly 40% of Shui Jing Fang making Diageo its largest indirect stakeholder.) In Vietnam Diageo ties up with Hanoi Liquor (Halico) the country's largest domestic branded spirits producer. As with its Chinese interests Diageo has inched up its control; in mid-2012 its total stake in Halico reached more than 45%.

Elsewhere in 2011 Diageo took over Mey Icki one of Turkey's leading vodka producers and the top seller of the country's Raki spirit. Diageo gained a market with a rising middle class. The company reached into Latin America too purchasing 50% of Rum Creations Products which owns the Zacapa rum brand.

Increasingly significant Diageo's African business generates nearly a third of its global beer sales. (All told beer sales represent more than 20% of Diageo's sales.) The company operates in Kenya through its 50% subsidiary East African Breweries (EAB). EAB owns Kenya Breweries which EAB gained full ownership from SABMiller in late 2011. Diageo taps Tanzanian thirst with a 51% stake in Serengeti Breweries (also owned through EAB). Serengeti Breweries claims more than 25% of the Tanzania's branded beer market. Diageo targeted Ethiopia in late 2011 by taking over one of the country's primary brewers Meta Abo Beer. Diageo's Guinness branded businesses lead in Nigeria and Cameroon.

Declining prices coupled with slow demand in the US and Europe has spurred Diageo to pare down Diageo Chateau & Estate Wines its US wine division as well as certain European wine businesses. It axed the Gilbeys wine distribution and wholesale drinks business in Ireland in 2011. The move followed the company's sale of Barton & Guestier wines to France's Castel Freres. In the US Diageo unloaded about 2000 acres of its vineyard properties as well as winemaking facilities in California's Napa Valley via a sale-leaseback deal with Realty Income Corporation; Diageo Chateau & Estate Wines continues to manage wine production on the properties.

HISTORY

Diageo –from the Latin word for "day" and the Greek word for "world" –was born from Guinness and GrandMet's 1997 merger to fight flat liquor sales and spirited competitors.

Guinness began business in 1759 when Arthur Guinness leased a small brewery in Dublin Ireland. Guinness began specializing in porters in 1799. Managed by the third generation of Guinnesses the company went public as a London-based firm in 1886.

In the 1950s managing director Hugh Beaver was credited with conceiving the "Guinness Book of World Records". During the 1970s Guinness bought more than 200 companies with disappointing results. Guinness refocused on brewing and distilling operations in the late 1980s by selling noncore businesses and acquiring firms such as Schenley (Dewar's). In 1988 and 1989 it bought 24% of LVMH Moet Hennessy Louis Vuitton (later exchanged for 34% of LVMH's wine and spirits business). More acquisitions followed in the 1990s capped by Guinness' 1997 announcement of its $19 billion merger with Grand Metropolitan.

GrandMet was established by Maxwell Joseph. In 1931 he began acquiring properties for resale but WWII slowed his progress. He started buying hotels in 1946 and by 1961 GrandMet had gone public.

Diversification began in 1970 with the purchases of catering firms restaurants and betting shops. In the early 1970s in what was the largest British takeover up to that time GrandMet bought brewer Truman Hanburg followed by Watney Mann which owned International Distillers & Vintners makers of Bailey's Bombay Gin and J&B.

GrandMet looked overseas through the 1970s taking over the Liggett Group a US cigarette maker (sold in 1986) whose Paddington unit was the US distributor of J&B Scotch. In 1987 it bought Heublein (Smirnoff Lancers Jose Cuervo). Two years later it bought The Pillsbury Company (Burger King and Green Giant) in a hostile takeover.

In 1997 Guinness and GrandMet combined creating Diageo and dividing the companies and brands among four divisions: The Pillsbury Company Burger King Guinness and United Distillers & Vintners.

In 2000 COO Paul Walsh a former Pillsbury CEO took over as CEO of both Diageo and its newly combined alcoholic beverage division Guinness/UDV. Also that year Diageo along with fellow wine and spirits producer Pernod Ricard agreed to pay $8.2 billion to Vivendi for the Seagram's drinks business that holds several brands including Crown Royal VO Canadian whiskies and Sterling Vineyards.

In 2001 Diageo sold its Guinness World Records business to media company Gullane Entertainment for $63 million. That year the company also completed its sale of Pillsbury to General Mills. After months of wrangling with the FTC Diageo finally won regulatory approval for the Seagram's drinks purchase from Vivendi in 2001. The company gained the Crown Royal and VO Canadian brands through this purchase.

In 2002 Diageo completed the sale of its Malibu rum brand to Allied Domecq for about $796 million; the deal also sealed Diageo's ownership of the Captain Morgan rum brand as Allied Domecq agreed to drop its lawsuit involving Captain Morgan. Diageo discontinued marketing its Captain Morgan Gold rum drink in the US later that year because of disappointing sales.

Also in 2002 Diageo sold Burger King for $1.5 billion to a group composed of Texas Pacific Group Bain Capital and Goldman Sachs Capital Partners. Diageo's decision to sell its Pillsbury unit and its Burger King business (the #2 burger chain after McDonalds) was part of the company's new focus on its spirits wine and beer businesses. The Pillsbury divestiture gave the company a 33% stake in General Mills (Diageo sold nearly half of its shares in October 2004). Also in 2002 Diageo and Pernod Ricard which together own rights to the Seagram's brand sold Seagram's line of nonalcoholic mixers to The Coca-Cola Company.

In 2003 Diageo and Jose Cuervo said they would jointly sell Don Julio and Tres Magueyes tequilas. Diageo also joined with Heineken to purchase 30% of InBev's (now Anheuser-Busch InBev's) Nambia Breweries in southern Africa. The brewery will make Heineken and Beck's beer.

Diageo said in 2003 that it would launch a low-alcohol version of its highly popular Baileys Irish Cream. Known as Baileys Glide the drink is made with Irish whiskey but Diageo said it would be manufactured in Germany. Also that year Diageo reopened the George Dickel distillery in Tullahoma Tennessee. That same year Diageo cut 150 jobs from its Guinness operation amid declining sales of the well-known stout.

In 2005 Diageo and Heineken formed a partnership for the production and distribution of Guinness in Russia. The company also acquired The Chalone Wine Group in 2005 for about $260 million. It added the winery into Diageo's current US wine operations which are organized under Diageo Chateau & Estate Wines. It also acquired Netherlands distiller Ursus Vodka for an undisclosed amount and added Bushmills Irish whiskey to its stable with the purchase of the brand from Pernod Ricard for $363 million. It also agreed to stay out of any negotiations regarding the takeover of Allied Domecq. (In 2005 Pernod Ricard acquired Allied Domecq.) That year it also disposed of its 4% holdings in General Mills saying the investment was not congruent with its business strategy.

In 2007 the company acquired about a 45% stake in Quanxing which distills the traditional premium Chinese liquor baijiu.

In 2008 Diageo formed a 50-50 joint venture with Dutch vodka maker Ketel One paying ?610 million ($900 million) for its interest. The partnership followed Diageo's abandoned plans to bid on Absolut vodka maker the V&S Group. (Ultimately the V&S Group was auctioned off to Pernod Ricard by its owner the Swedish government.) Also that year Diageo took full ownership of D Distribution the Russian distributor of the Smirnoff and Smirnov brands. It paid about $30 million for the remaining 25% stake held by Alfa Group.

Diageo saw its leadership change in 2008 when Lord James Blyth of Rowington stepped down as chairman. He was replaced by Dr. Franz Humer who previously served as CEO of F. Hoffmann-La Roche.

Meanwhile Diageo has signaled an interested in acquiring Moet Hennessy the spirits and wine subsidiary of French luxury conglomerate LVMH; however LVMH is not inclined to sell. Diageo owns about 35% of Moet Hennessy. Undeterred from building its liqueurs portfolio Diageo in mid-2010 increased its interest in the London Group which supplies the premium NUVO brand of liqueurs to a little more than 70%. London Group was created through a joint venture between Diageo and New York entrepreneur Raphael Yakoby.

EXECUTIVES

CEO and Director, Paul S. Walsh, age 58, $2,314,158 total compensation
Company Secretary, Paul D. Tunnacliffe, age 51
Chairman, Franz B. Humer, age 67, $797,760 total compensation
General Manager North and South LAC (Latin America and Caribbean) International, Alberto Gavazzi
Director Human Resources, Gareth Williams, age 59
Financial Director North America, Chris Davies
CEO, Ivan M. Menezes, age 52
Director Global Business Support, James N.D. (Jim) Grover, age 55
President - New Businesses, Andrew Morgan, age 57
President North America, Larry Schwartz, age 60
General Counsel, Timothy D. (Tim) Proctor, age 63
Global Brand Director Smirnoff, Simon Burch
President Africa Eastern Europe and Turkey, Nicholas B. (Nick) Blazquez, age 52
Chief Marketing Officer, Syl Saller

President and COO Africa, Andy Fennell, age 46
President; Diageo Asia-Pacific, Gilbert Ghostine, age 53
EVP Corporate Relations North America, Guy L. Smith, age 64
Head Financial Communications, James Crampton
Senior Director External Relations Diageo North America, Zsoka Mcdonald
President - Global Supply and Global Procurement, David Gosnell, age 56
Managing Director Diageo Latin America and Caribbean, John R. (Randy) Millian, age 60
President and Chief Marketing and Innovation Officer North America, Peter McDonough
Corporate Relations Director, Ian Wright, age 55
Managing Director Indian Operations, Roland Abella
Manager Supply Finance, Stephen Howe
CFO and Director, Dierdre A. Mahlan, age 51
Global Category Director Whiskey, David Gates
Global Category Director Vodka Gin and Rums, Edward Pilkington
Global Brand Director Johnnie Walker, Gavin Pike
Director Investor Relations, Nick Temperley
Director Investor Relations, Sarah Paul
Head Corporate PR, Rowan Pearman
Head Corporate Broadcast and Digital Media, Dominic Redfearn
Communications Manager Asia/Pacific, Jen Yap Hwee
Senior Manager Public Relations, Lisa Crane
COO Western Europe, John Kennedy
Managing Director Ireland, David Smith
Country Director Great Britain, Andrew Cowan
CEO and Director, Paul S. Walsh, age 58
Director, Betsy D. Holden, age 57
Director, Paul A. Walker, age 56
Director, Lord Clive R. Hollick, age 67
Director, H. Todd Stitzer, age 61
Director, Philip G. Scott, age 59
Director, Peggy B. Bruzelius, age 64
Director, Laurence Danon, age 58
Director, Lord E. Mervyn Davies of Abersoch, age 60
CFO and Director, Dierdre A. Mahlan, age 51
Non-Executive Director, KwonPing Ho
Auditors: KPMGAuditPlc

LOCATIONS

HQ: Diageo Plc
Lakeside Drive, Park Royal, London NW10 7HQ
Phone: (44) 20 8978 6000
Web: www.diageo.com

2013 Sales

	% of total
North	28
Western	24
Eastern Europe &	22
Asia/Pacific	15
Latin America &	11
Total	**100**

PRODUCTS/OPERATIONS

2013 Sales

	% of total
Spirits	71
Beer	19
Ready-to-drink	6
Wine	3
Other	1
Total	**100**

Selected Brands

Strategic brands
- Baileys Original Irish Cream liqueur
- Buchanan' s De Luxe Scotch whiskey
- Bushmills Irish whiskey
- Captain Morgan rum
- Ciroc vodka
- Crown Royal Canadian whisky
- Guinness stout
- J&B Scotch whiskey
- Johnnie Walker Scotch whisky
- Ketel One vodka
- Smirnoff vodka
- Tanqueray London Dry and Tanqueray No. TEN gin
- Windsor Premier Scotch whisky

Other beer
- Bell lager
- Harp lager
- Kilkenny
- Red Stripe lager
- Senator Keg
- Serengeti
- Smithwick' s ale
- Tusker lager
- Windhoek lager

Other spirits
- Brandy
  - Bertrams VO
- Cognac
  - Hennessy
- Gin
  - Gordon's
- Liqueurs
  - Romana Sambuca
  - Sheridan's
- Rum
  - Bundaberg
  - Cacique
  - Myers's
  - Pampero
  - Zacapa
- Schnapps
  - Archers
- Spirit drink
  - Pimm's
  - Pimm's Winter
- Tequila
  - Don Julio
- Whiskey
  - Malt ScotchCaol IlaCardhuClynelishCragganmoreDalwhinnieGlen ElginGlenkinchieKnockandoLagavulinObanRoyal LochnagarThe SingletonSingleton of DufftownSingleton of GlendullanTalisker
  - ScotchBell'sBuchanan'sDimple/PinchOld ParrVAT 69White Horse
  - WhiskeyBulleit bourbon

Wine
- Blossom Hill
- Chalone
- Dom Perignon champagne
- Justerini & Brooks
- Moet & Chandon champagne
- Piat d' Or
- Rosenblum Cellars
- Sterling Vineyards
- Vignobles Internationaux

COMPETITORS

Angostura
Anheuser-Busch
Anheuser-Busch InBev
Asahi Breweries
Asia Pacific Breweries
Bacardi
Bavaria S.A.
Beam Global Spirits & Wine
Blavod
Brown-Forman
Cabo Wabo
Campari
Carlsberg A/S
Cervecerias Unidas
Constellation Brands
E. & J. Gallo
FEMSA
Grupo Modelo
Heaven Hill Distilleries
Heineken
Kirin Holdings Company
Lion
Martini & Rossi
Maxxium
Molson Coors UK
Paramount Distillers
Pernod Ricard
Quinsa
Remy Cointreau
SABMiller
Sapporo
Sidney Frank Importing
Skyy
The Trump Organization
Tsingtao
Yuengling & Son

HISTORICAL FINANCIALS

Company Type: Public

Income Statement FYE: June 30

	REVENUE ($ mil.)	NET INCOME ($ mil.)	NET PROFIT MARGIN	EMPLOYEES
06/13	17,426	3,787	21.7%	28,410
06/12	16,791	3,030	18.0%	25,698
06/11	15,915	3,043	19.1%	24,020
06/10	14,689	2,446	16.7%	23,521
06/09	15,464	2,692	17.4%	24,270
Annual Growth	3.0%	8.9%	—	4.0%

2013 Year-End Financials

Debt ratio: 61.3%
Return on equity: 39.3%
Cash ($ mil.): 2,700
Current ratio: 1.55
Long-term debt ($ mil.): 12,548
No. of shares (mil.): —
Dividends
Yield: 0.0%
Payout: 446.8%
Market value ($ mil.): —

	STOCK PRICE ($) FY Close	P/E High/Low	PER SHARE ($) Earnings	Dividends	Book Value
06/13	114.95	299244	1.50	6.72	3.89
06/12	103.07	337229	1.21	6.57	3.17
06/11	81.87	295198	1.22	2.49	3.05
06/10	62.74	267196	0.98	2.33	2.19
06/09	57.25	378145	1.08	2.28	1.94
Annual Growth	19.0%	— —	8.6%	31.1%	19.0%

DNB ASA

Financial services 'n real estate are what DnB NOR is for. One of the largest banks in Norway the company serves retail and corporate clients at more than 200 locations that operate under the DnB NOR Bank Nordlandsbanken and Postbanken banners. In addition to traditional banking services such as deposits and loans it also provides life and pension insurance (through its Vital subsidiary) credit cards (through Cresco) and mutual funds and institutional asset management in Norway and Sweden (through DnB NOR Asset Management) as well as real estate brokerage and capital markets services.

DnB NOR also has banking and insurance operations in Sweden where it operates through Svensk Fastighetsformedling and SalusAnsvar. Elsewhere it provides banking services in Poland Denmark and the Baltic States through DnB NORD and in Russia through DnB NOR Monchebank. The group's strategy for international growth is focused on large corporate clients particularly in the energy shipping and seafood industries. DnB NOR also has limited operations in the US and Asia.

The company acquired the 49% it didn't already own in DnB NORD from German venture partner Norddeutsche Landesbank Girozentrale (NordLB) in late 2010. NordLB had considered buying out DnB NOR in the Baltic venture which had been hit hard by the global economic crisis but ultimately chose not to. DnB NOR instead took over the unit. DnB NORD is still reeling from the downturn but its 2010 losses were about a third of 2009's.

To strengthen the group's identity and streamline operations DnB NOR is uniting itself under one brand. Among its planned changes is the eventual phasing out of the Postbanken name.

Also DnB NOR discontinued its mortgage lending business in Sweden in 2011. It sold its retail customer mortgage loan portfolio to SEB that year.

The Norwegian government owns about a third of DnB NOR.

EXECUTIVES

Group EVP Retailing, ?smund Sk?r, age 54, $507,375 total compensation
Head Investor Relations and Long-Term Funding, Per Sagbakken
Director; Chairman DnB NOR Bank, Bent Pedersen, age 71
Group Audit, Harald J?gtnes
Director; Chairman DnB NOR Bank, Bent Pedersen, age 71
Director, Trine S?ther Romuld, age 46
Director, J?rn O. Kvilhaug, age 63
Director, Per Hoffmann, age 63
Auditors: PricewaterhouseCoopersAS

LOCATIONS

HQ: DNB ASA
Dronning Eufemias gate 30, Oslo NO-0021
Phone: (47) 915 03000 **Fax:** 212 681-4121
Web: www.dnb.no

PRODUCTS/OPERATIONS

2010 Sales by Segment

	% of total
Retail Banking	47
Large Corporates & International	24
DnB NOR Markets	14
DnB NORD	5
Insurance & Asset Management	10
Total	**100**

COMPETITORS

ABN AMRO Group
BNP Paribas
Credit Suisse
Danske Bank
Deutsche Bank
Grupo Santander
HSBC
Nordea Bank
SEB AB
Svenska Handelsbanken
UBS

HISTORICAL FINANCIALS

Company Type: Public

Income Statement

FYE: December 31

	ASSETS ($ mil.)	NET INCOME ($ mil.)	INCOME AS % OF ASSETS	EMPLOYEES
12/12	404,904	2,441	0.6%	13,291
12/11	353,609	2,158	0.6%	13,620
12/10	319,028	2,538	0.8%	13,021
12/09	316,505	1,490	0.5%	13,317
12/08	261,601	1,315	0.5%	14,057
Annual Growth	11.5%	16.7%	—	(1.4%)

2012 Year-End Financials

Return on assets: 0.6%
Return on equity: 11.0%
Long-term debt ($ mil.): —
No. of shares (mil.): 1,628
Sales ($ mil): 17,777
Dividends
Yield: 2.6%
Payout: 25.2%
Market value ($ mil.): 210,651

	STOCK PRICE ($) FY Close	P/E High/Low		PER SHARE ($) Earnings	Dividends	Book Value
12/12	129.33	1	0	1.49	3.42	14.05
12/11	95.00	1	0	1.33	0.33	12.03
12/10	130.45	0	0	1.48	0.69	11.70
Annual Growth	(0.4%)	—	—	0.2%	49.5%	4.7%

DZ Bank AG Deutsche Zentral-Genossenschaftsbank

DZ BANK is the central institution for some 1100 local cooperative banks which serve 30 million customers from a combined 12000 branch offices across Germany. It provides administrative services for its member banks which are also the company's owners. Additionally DZ BANK provides corporate banking services including commercial lending for small to midsized businesses investment banking structured financing and private banking. GZ-Bank and DG Bank –Germany's primary central institutions for cooperative lenders – merged in 2001 to create today's DZ BANK.

Subsidiary Union Investment is one of Germany's top fund managers and has some E177 million (approximately $2324 million) in assets under management. ReiseBank another unit provides foreign cash exchange and transfers from about 100 locations around Germany. Other divisions offer credit processing for financial companies and specialist consumer financing.

In the aftermath of the global financial crisis DZ BANK has renewed its focus on its core business –serving the cooperative bank network. It has thus started reducing its corporate banking and structured finance activities. As a result pre-tax profits rose in 2010 and the following fiscal year improved even more. As a result of heightened capital and liquidity requirements amid concerns surrounding European sovereign debt the company has also improved its capital base levels.

In 2009 DZ BANK and WGZ BANK the second-largest central institution for Germany's cooperative banking network postponed merger discussions for the fourth time in three years. The deal would have created the third-largest bank in Germany. However the two companies have combined certain operations such as their investment advisory and private banking units.

HISTORY

Created as a public entity in 1895 DG Bank began as the Preussische Central Genossenschafts-Kasse (Preussenkasse). The bank controlled liquidity and also managed cashless payment transfers and securities business for central cooperative banks. By 1905 regional co-op banks had taken equity stakes in the Preussenkasse. In the years that followed more central banks began to work with the company and its influence spread to all areas of the cooperative movement as well as outside Prussian borders.

Even the German government took an interest in the Preussenkasse and by 1932 had taken it under its control and renamed it the Deutsche Zentralgenossenschaftskasse. The partition of Germany following WWII affected the bank in two ways: assets of companies in the Soviet zone were seized and the bank's headquarters located in the Soviet-occupied portion of Berlin had to be moved. The bank operated from Marburg and Hamburg until a new headquarters was chosen in 1949. This new bank was based in Frankfurt and called Deutsche Genossenschaftskasse. The entity had a similar structure and public mandate to Preussenkasse and Deutsche Zentralgenossenschaftskasse.

In the following decades the bank started accepting deposits and received trust investment status (1954) began issuing securities (1957) and expanded its investment portfolio. The Deutsche Genossenschaftsbank Act of 1975 formalized the company's development into a commercial bank and gave it the new name Deutsche Genossenschaftsbank to reflect this.

Throughout the late 1980s the bank underwent mergers that expanded its abilities as a cooperative central institution. During this time the bank arose as the central bank of Bavaria northern Germany and parts of Hesse. In 1987 the bank approached the trade union-owned Volksfursorge Group about merging with the R&V Versicherungsgruppe to form an insurance group in an effort to boost bank and insurance cross-marketing. The next year DG solicited a possible merger among West Germany's five cooperative banks. It also took a stake in its Spanish counterpart Cajas Rurales. Both offers fell through in 1989 as some of the other cooperatives dissented and management decided against acquiring a 75% stake in Volksfursorge.

In 1990 several French banks cried outrage over $3.5 billion in bonds that had sunk in value by about $350 million. Inflation and fears over the currency integration with East Germany were the culprits for the devaluation. A vice chairman of the company took responsibility for the dispute and resigned. By 1991 three key DG Bank executive had left or announced their resignations from the company. Bernd Thiemann took the helm to restore credibility to the company which had alienated itself from other cooperative banks and whose plans to be a universal bank made it overextend itself.

With the reunification of Germany in the early 1990s DG assumed the role of the central bank for former East German cooperatives as well as East Germany's Bank fur Landwirtschaft und Nahrungsguterwirtschaft der DDR (Agriculture and Food Industry Bank).

In 1995 the bank started to look outside Germany for expansion and by 1997 it was ready to open an office in Hong Kong. In addition DG purchased a majority stake in Magyar Takarekszovethezeti Bank of Hungary. That year DG Bank along with other state-owned banks in Germany came under fire from the European Commission for receiving illegal public aid.

DG became a publicly traded company in 1998. Early that year the bank began discussions with Rabobank and Credit Agricole (similarly organized banks in the Netherlands and France) about establishing a European cooperative bank.

In 2000 DG Bank began to securitize mortgages originated by its DG Hypothekenbank unit and scrapped its planned merger with the Netherlands-based Rabobank. DG Bank then found a merger partner in the fellow German cooperative bank GZ Bank. They formed DZ BANK in 2001.

EXECUTIVES

Managing Director, Albrecht Merz
CEO, Wolfgang Kirsch
Managing Director, Thomas Duhnkrack
President DZ Financial Markets, Gerhard Summerer
General Manager London, Holger Wessling
General Manager Singapore, Klaus G. Borig
Managing Director DZ BANK Ireland, Mark Jacob
Chairman of the Supervisory Board, Rolf Hildner
Managing Director and Head of Project and Structured Finance Europe Middle East and Africa, Jonathan Bullock
Global Product Head Project Finance, Bill Roos
Managing Director DZ BANK Ireland, Tilmann Gerhards
General Manager DZ PRIVATBANK Schweiz, Richard Manger

General Manager DZ PRIVATBANK Schweiz, Marion Pester
Divisional Head Communication and Marketing, Martin Roth
Deputy Chairman of the Supervisory Board, Helmut Gottschalk
Managing Director, Frank Westhoff, age 52
Founder of the commercial cooperative system, Hermann Schulze-Delitzsch
Deputy Chairman of the Supervisory Board, Wolfgang Apitzsch
Deputy Chairman of the Supervisory Board, Helmut Gottschalk
Auditors: Ernst&YoungGmbH

LOCATIONS

HQ: DZ Bank AG Deutsche Zentral-Genossenschaftsbank
Platz der Republik, Frankfurt am Main 60265
Phone: (49) 69 7447 01 **Fax:** (49) 69 7447 1685
Web: www.dzbank.com

PRODUCTS/OPERATIONS

2011 Sales

	% of total
Insurance premiums	58
Net	16
Fees &	13
Gains on trading	2
Other	11
Total	**100**

Selected Subsidiaries

Bausparkasse Schwabisch Hall
Deutsche Genossenschafts-Hypothekenbank AG (DYG HYP)
DZ PRIVATBANK Group
R+V Versicherung AG
TeamBank
Union Investment Group
VR LEASING

COMPETITORS

BNP Paribas
Barclays
BayernLB
Citibank
Commerzbank
Deutsche Bank
HSBC
KBC
UniCredit Bank AG
WGZ BANK
WestLB

HISTORICAL FINANCIALS

Company Type: Public

Income Statement

FYE: December 31

	REVENUE ($ mil.)	NET INCOME ($ mil.)	NET PROFIT MARGIN	EMPLOYEES
12/12	34,534	910	2.6%	28,227
12/11	31,051	497	1.6%	27,825
12/10	33,971	1,160	3.4%	26,800
12/09	35,870	193	0.5%	25,636
12/08	30,892	(1,691)	—	24,642
Annual Growth	2.8%	—	—	3.5%

2012 Year-End Financials

Debt ratio: —
Return on equity: 9.6%
Cash ($ mil.): 3,291
Current ratio: —
Long-term debt ($ mil.): —
No. of shares (mil.): 1,215
Dividends
Yield: —
Payout: —
Market value ($ mil.): —

E.ON SE

E.ON has transformed itself from a regional conglomerate into a multi-utility and a global player with 26 million customers. Its diversified business consists of power generation natural gas energy trading retail and distribution operations. Subsidiary E.ON Energie is one of Germany's top two power companies (running neck and neck with RWE) with some 17 million electricity gas and water customers; the unit also has about 69000 MW of electric generating capacity across Germany and Central Europe. E.ON operates E.ON Ruhrgas Germany's #1 natural gas supplier. Non-German utility subsidiaries include E.ON UK and E.ON Nordic.

Geographic Reach

E.ON operates in Bulgaria the Czech Republic France Germany Hungary Italy the Netherlands Romania Russia Slovakia Spain Sweden and the UK.

Financial Analysis

In 2011 the company reported revenue growth of 22% thanks to a 2% increase in Generation revenue as a result of higher sales volume higher average transfer prices and positive currency-translation effects in Sweden's Nuclear sales. Other factors included high Fossil segment sales a 26% increase in the Renewables segment and an 8% increase in the Gas segment as a result of positive energy price developments. There was also a 50% jump in the Trading segment as a result of an increase in trading activity in power and gas and a 29% increase in Russian sales as a result of a growth in generating capacity coupled with higher power prices.

E.ON has a net loss of 130% in 2011 attributable to the 58% decrease in Net book gains compared to 2010 and E3 billion ($4.2 billion) in impairment charges on assets and goodwill mainly at its generation businesses. It also had impairment charges of E1.9 billion ($2.7 billion) in Spain and Italy due to poor regional economic forecasts for the long-term development of power prices regulatory intervention and reduced use of gas-fired and coal-fired power stations.

Strategy

The company is focusing on realigning its businesses to create greater efficiencies putting more emphasis on developing its renewable power operations and reducing its debt.

In response to tightening European regulations regarding carbon emissions E.ON has announced plans to obtain 24% of its generating capacity from renewable energy sources by 2030.

In 2012 the company started building the Wysoka (Wysoka 1 und 2) onshore wind farm in Poland growing E.ON's position as one of the leading players on the Polish wind energy market.

Creating a foothold in Brazil in 2012 the company formed a power generation joint venture with Brazilian company MPX to develop 20000 MW of capacity in Brazil and Chile.

E.ON is seeking to generate about E15 billion ($21 billion) through divestments by the end of 2013. Paying down debt in 2012 E.ON sold Open Grid Europe its gas transmission company in Germany to a consortium led by Macquarie European Infrastructure Fund 4 for about E3.2 billion ($4.5 billion).

In 2011 it sold its Italian natural gas distribution network unit (E.ON Rete) to a group of Italian and French investors for EUR290 million (US$392.3 million). It also sold its UK-based Central Networks unit to PPL for $5.7 billion

HISTORY

VEBA (originally Vereinigte Elektrizitats-und Bergwerks AG) was formed in 1929 in Berlin to consolidate Germany's state-owned electricity and mining interests. These operations included PreussenElektra an electric utility formed by the German government in 1927; Hibernia a coal mining firm founded in 1873; and Preussag a mining and smelting company founded in 1923.

In the 1930s VEBA produced synthetic gasoline (essential to the German war machine) from coal at its Hibernia plant. In 1938 the company and chemical cartel I. G. Farben set up Chemische Werke Huls to make synthetic rubber. After WWII VEBA's assets in western Germany were transferred to the government and several executives were arrested. Preussag was spun off in 1959.

In 1965 the government spun off VEBA to the public. That year the company entered trading and transportation by buying Stinnes one of West Germany's largest industrial companies. In 1969 VEBA transferred its coal mining interests to Ruhrkohle and a few years later moved into oil exploration and development. The company shortened its name to VEBA in 1970.

The West German government sold its remaining stake in VEBA in 1987. In a changed regulatory environment large investors were able to accumulate big portions of stock and their dissatisfaction with the company's lackluster results made it a takeover target. In response new chairman Ulrich Hartmann began cutting noncore businesses and reducing staff.

In 1990 VEBA began accumulating mobile communications networking and cable TV companies. It allied with the UK's Cable and Wireless (C&W) in 1995 to develop a European mobile phone business but in 1997 C&W sold its interest to VEBA (as part of the deal VEBA gained a 10% stake in C&W which it sold in 1999). In anticipation of the 1998 deregulation of the German telecom market VEBA and RWE merged their German telecom businesses in 1997.

VEBA acquired a 36% stake in Degussa a specialty chemicals company in 1997; two years later Degussa merged with Huls to form a separately traded chemical company called Degussa-Huls in which VEBA took a 62% stake. VEBA sold a 30% stake in Stinnes to the public in 1999. The company's telecom venture sold its fixed-line telephone business its cable TV unit and its stake in mobile phone operator E-Plus.

These moves however were just the prelude to a bigger deal: a $14 billion merger agreement between VEBA and fellow German conglomerate VIAG. The partners announced plans to dump noncore businesses and beef up their energy and chemicals holdings. VEBA and VIAG completed their merger in 2000 and the combined company adopted the name E.ON. The companies' utilities businesses were combined into E.ON Energie and their chemicals units were brought together as Degussa.

To gain regulatory approval to form E.ON VEBA and VIAG agreed to sell their stakes in German electric utilities Bewag and VEAG and coal producer LAUBAG. E.ON sold its VEAG and LAUBAG interests along with semiconductor and electronics distribution units in 2000 and sold Bewag in 2001.

In 2001 E.ON agreed to acquire UK electricity generator Powergen (now E.ON UK) and it sold off nonutility operations including Degussa and Veba Oel. E.ON swapped a 51% stake in Veba Oel for BP's 26% stake in German natural gas supplier Ruhrgas (now E.ON Ruhrgas). E.ON also sold Klockner to UK steel trader Balli and sold its stake in silicon wafer maker MEMC to buyout firm Texas Pacific Group.

In 2002 E.ON sold its VAW Aluminum unit to Norwegian conglomerate Norsk Hydro in a $2.8 billion deal. Regulators moved to prevent E.ON from acquiring BP's stake in Ruhrgas in 2002 but BP agreed to pay for the Veba Oel stake in cash if necessary and the swap was completed later that year. E.ON also acquired Vodafone and ThyssenKrupp's stakes in Ruhrgas in 2002 and it sold its remaining stake in Veba Oel to BP.

Also in 2002 E.ON completed its purchase of Powergen (which included its US subsidiary LG&E Energy) for about $8 billion and it sold its 65% stake in logistics company Stinnes to German railroad operator Deutsche Bahn. In late 2002 E.ON acquired the UK energy supply and generation businesses of TXU Europe in a $2.5 billion deal.

The following year E.ON swapped its majority stake in chemical maker Degussa with coal group RAG for RAG's 18% interest in Ruhrgas. It completed its acquisition of Ruhrgas by purchasing the combined 40% stake held by Royal Dutch Shell Exxon Mobil and TUI (formerly Preussag). It also sold subsidiary Viterra's energy services unit (gas and water meters) to CVC Capital Partners.

In 2005 the company acquired the Enfield power station in the UK for $250.2 million.

In 2007 E.ON acquired Ireland-based wind farm company Airtricity for $1.4 billion.

Pursuing growth in new geographic markets in 2007 E.ON acquired Russia-based power utility OGK-4 for almost $6 billion. Outmaneuvered by its rivals in 2008 it dropped its $56 billion bid to buy Endesa S.A. Spain's largest electric utility settling for the purchase of a number of Endesa's generation assets in Spain and Italy.

In 2009 to counter EDF's acquisition of British Energy E.ON and RWE formed a joint venture to develop 6000 MW of nuclear power capacity in the UK.

That year prompted by the regulatory requirements of the European Commission E.ON and GDF SUEZ agreed to swap generating assets to allow for more competition in their major markets. It sold 860 MW of Germany-based conventional power plants 132 MW of hydroelectric plants and access to 770 MW of nuclear power. In return GDF SUEZ sold to E.ON a similar amount of power generation capacity in France and the Benelux countries. In 2010 also to meet EU anti-monopoly regulations it sold grid operator Transpower to Dutch giant TenneT for $1.1 billion and it swapped 5000 MW of generation capacity with EDF and EnBW.

In 2010 the company sold E.ON U.S. which operates Kentucky's two major utilities for $7.6 billion. Its US assets were no longer considered a core part of its growth strategy and the sale helped to pay down debt. To raise cash that year it also sold its 3.5% stake in Gazprom to Russian investment bank Vnesheconombank for $4.4 billion.

EXECUTIVES

Chairman Supervisory Board, Werner Wenning, age 67
EVP Corporate Responsibility and Health Safety & Environment, Peter Blau
Press Spokesperson, Josef Nelles
SVP Investor Relations, Sascha Bibert
Chief Commercial Officer E.ON Energy Tradign, Gareth Griffiths
Chairman Chief Executive Officer CEO, Johannes Teyssen, age 54
CEO E.ON UK, Tony Cocker
Member Board of Management Regional Units Distribution & Retail, Bernhard Reutersberg, age 59
Member Board of Management Group Human Resources IT Group Procurement Legal and Compliance Corporate Incident and Crisis Management Real Estate/Mining Facility Management and E.ON Academy, Regine Stachelhaus, age 58
Member Board of Management Finance Accounting Controlling and Corporate Planning Mergers & Acquisitions Tax, Marcus Schenck, age 48
Sales E.ON Energie, Stefan Vogg, age 51
Member Board of Management Research and Development New Build and Technology Corporate Responsibility Health/Safety and Environment, Klaus-Dieter Maubach, age 51
CEO E.ON Sverige, Jonas Abrahamsson
Member of the Board of Management Commercial Operations & Analysis Optimization & Trading Exploration & Production, J?rgen Kildahl, age 50
CEO E.ON Espa?a; President E.ON Italia, Miguel Anto?anzas
Chairman E.ON Energie, Ingo Luge, age 55
VP Corporate Responsibility, Anette Bickmeyer
Press Spokesperson, Carsten Thomsen-Bendixen
Member of the Board of Management Corporate Incident & Crisis Management Health/Safety & Environment Engineering & Major Projects Technology & Innovation, Michael (Mike) Winkel, age 42
CEO E.ON Climate & Renewables, Steve Trenholm
Director, Ulrich Lehner, age 67
Director, Henning Schulte-Noelle, age 71
Director, Rene Obermann, age 49
Director, Baroness Denise Kingsmill, age 66
Director, Gabriele Gratz
Director, Werner Bartoschek
Director, Ulrich Hocker
Director, Hubertus Schmoldt, age 69
Director, Klaus-Dieter Raschke, age 57
Director, Georg Freiherr von Waldenfels
Director, Hans Wollitzer
Director, Theo Siegert
Director, Hans Prufer
Deputy Chairman, Erhard Ott
Director, Karen de Segundo
Director, B?rd Mikkelsen
Director, Sven Bergelin
Director, Walter Reitler
Director, Oliver Biniek
Auditors: PricewaterhouseCoopersAG

LOCATIONS

HQ: E.ON SE
E.ON-Platz 1, Duesseldorf D-40479
Phone: (49) 211 45 79 0 **Fax:** (49) 211 45 79 5 01
Web: www.eon.com

2011 Sales

	% of total
Europe	
Germany	42
UK	28
Sweden	4
Other	25
Other	1
Total	**100**

PRODUCTS/OPERATIONS

2011 Sales

	% of total
Electricity	53
Gas	41
Other	6
Total	**100**

Selected Business Areas

Power Generation
Energy Mix
Coal
Natural Gas and Oil
Nuclear
Water
Wind
Solar
Bio Energy
Gas Supply & Production
Exploration & Production
LNG
Sources of Supply
Security of Supply
Gas Storage & Transportation
Underground Storage Facilities
Nord Stream Pipeline
Trading
Power and Emissions Trading
Gas and Oil Trading
Coal Biofuels and Freight Trading
Market Activity
Market Development
Distribution
Power Distribution
Gas Distribution
Technology of the Future

COMPETITORS

BASF SE
Bayer AG
Business Group Benelux
Deutsche Telekom
Dow Chemical
DuPont
EVN
Electricite de France
EnBW
Endesa S.A.
Enel
Eni
GDF SUEZ
Orange
RWE
Vattenfall

HISTORICAL FINANCIALS

Company Type: Public

Income Statement FYE: December 31

	REVENUE ($ mil.)	NET INCOME ($ mil.)	NET PROFIT MARGIN	EMPLOYEES
12/12	174,687	2,922	1.7%	72,083
12/11	146,751	(2,870)	—	78,889
12/10	125,181	7,833	6.3%	83,105
12/09	118,691	12,095	10.2%	88,227
12/08	122,061	1,769	1.5%	93,538
Annual Growth	9.4%	13.4%	—	(6.3%)

2012 Year-End Financials

Debt ratio: 24.3%
Return on equity: 6.2%
Cash ($ mil.): 8,627
Current ratio: 1.20
Long-term debt ($ mil.): 28,914
No. of shares (mil.): 1,906
Dividends
Yield: 5.1%
Payout: 110.3%
Market value ($ mil.): 35,818

	STOCK PRICE ($) FY Close	P/E High/Low	PER SHARE ($) Earnings	Dividends	Book Value
12/12	18.79	38 25	1.53	0.96	24.16
12/11	21.39	— —	(1.50)	3.04	24.26
12/10	30.41	27 14	4.11	1.40	29.26
12/09	41.75	21 10	6.35	1.48	30.50
12/08	40.75	231 77	0.95	1.66	25.30
Annual Growth	(17.6%)	— —	12.6%	(12.7%)	(1.1%)

Ecopetrol SA

Ecopetrol (formerly Empresa Colombiana de Petroleos) performs crude oil and natural gas exploration production refining and transportation. The largest company in Colombia and one of the largest integrated oil firms in Latin America Ecopetrol has two large refineries (Barrancabermeja and Cartagena) strategically located to supply the domestic market and to export oil and oil products to the southern US. Ecopetrol explores for oil and gas across Colombia and is expanding internationally through exploration partnerships in Brazil Peru and the US Gulf of Mexico. In 2010 the company reported proved reserves of more than 1.6 billion barrels of oil equivalent.

Of its two largest refineries Ecopetrol has updated its oldest in Cartagena. The refinery was built in 1956 and produces about 20% of the company's exports. Ecopetrol also has a pipeline transportation network that extends 5000 miles.

The company has ambitious expansion plans. Its 2015 goals include the production of 1 million barrels of oil per day the doubling of refining capacity and the emergence of Ecopetrol as a leader in biofuels production. (In 2008 the company entered the ethanol market teaming up with subsidiary Bioenergy S.A. to build a sugar cane-based ethanol plant in the province of Meta capable of producing up to 2000 barrels of ethanol per day).

It is growing its upstream and midstream assets. In 2009 Ecopetrol acquired Maurel & Prom's Hocol an oil explorer working in Colombia in a deal worth $748 million. It also spent C$535 million ($420 million) to buy Enbridge's quarter stake in Colombian pipeline operator Oleoducto Central S.A. (OCENSA). The deal increased Ecopetrol's stake in the pipeline to 60%.

Riding the wave of a recovering global economy in 2010 the company reported a robust growth in revenues fueled by greater industrial demand and much higher oil prices. Its export sales of crude oil and petroleum products almost doubled that year.

Moving to take advantage of BP's need to shed assets to pay for that company's oil spill in the Gulf of Mexico in 2011 the company in tandem with Talisman Energy purchased BP Exploration Company (Colombia) Limited for about $1.8 billion. The unit (renamed Equion Energia Limited) produces about 25000 barrels per day and has proved reserves of 95 million barrels of oil equivalent.

In 2010 the company formed a new subsidiary Ecopetrol Transportation Investments Ltd. as an investment vehicle.

The Colombian government owns 90% of Ecopetrol.

EXECUTIVES

President of the Board, Fabio Echeverri Correa, age 80
General Secretary, Margarita Obregon Triana
Executive Vice President of Exploration and Production, Hector Manosalva Rojas
VP Legal, Mauricio Echeverry Gutierrez, age 57
VP Exploration, Enrique Velazquez Convers, age 60
EVP Downstream, Pedro Alfonso Rosales Navarro, age 50
VP Refining and Petrochemicals, Federico Maya Molina
President, Javier G. Gutierrez Pemberthy, age 62
CFO, Adriana M. Echeverri, age 42
VP Strategy and Growth, Camilo Marulanda, age 34
VP Human Talent, Martha Cecilia Casta?o
VP Transporation, Alvaro Castaneda Caro
Disciplinary Control Office, Adriana Marcela Neira
VP Production, Hector Castano Aristizabal, age 51
VP Services and Technology, Oscar A. Villadiego, age 49
VP Supply and Marketing, Claudia L. Castellanos R.
President of the Board, Fabio Echeverri Correa, age 80
Director, Ignacio Sanin Bernal, age 64
Director, Joaquin Moreno, age 64
Director, Maria E. Velasquez, age 55
Director, Amilkar Acosta Medina, age 60
Director, Mauricio Cardenas, age 51
Director, Carlos Rodado Noriega
Director, Hernando J. Gomez
Auditors: Ernst&YoungAudit

LOCATIONS

HQ: Ecopetrol SA
Carrera 13 No. 36 ? 24, Bogota
Phone: (57) 1 234 5190 **Fax:** (57) 1 234 5628
Web: www.ecopetrol.com.co

2010 Sales

	% of total
Colombia	40
Other	60
Total	**100**

PRODUCTS/OPERATIONS

2010 Sales

	% of total
Crude	52
Refined petroleum products and	48
Total	**100**

COMPETITORS

Apco Oil and Gas International
BP
Exxon Mobil
Gran Tierra Energy
HKN
Houston American Energy
Hunt Oil
Nexen
Pacific Rubiales
Petrobank Energy and Resources
Royal Dutch Shell
Talisman Energy

HISTORICAL FINANCIALS

Company Type: Public

Income Statement FYE: December 31

	REVENUE ($ mil.)	NET INCOME ($ mil.)	NET PROFIT MARGIN	EMPLOYEES
12/12	38,801	8,328	21.5%	9,701
12/11	33,928	7,973	23.5%	8,729
12/10	21,097	4,095	19.4%	7,575
12/09	14,858	2,508	16.9%	7,395
12/08	15,016	5,152	34.3%	0
Annual Growth	26.8%	12.8%	—	—

2012 Year-End Financials

Debt ratio: 0.0%
Return on equity: 24.6%
Cash ($ mil.): 4,474
Current ratio: 0.99
Long-term debt ($ mil.): 6,462
No. of shares (mil.): —
Dividends
Yield: 6.6%
Payout: —
Market value ($ mil.): —

	STOCK PRICE ($) FY Close	P/E High/Low	PER SHARE ($) Earnings	Dividends	Book Value
12/12	59.67	— —	0.20	4.38	0.89
12/11	44.52	— —	0.20	0.00	0.69
12/10	43.62	— —	0.10	0.93	0.51
12/09	24.26	— —	0.06	2.05	0.39
12/08	18.37	— —	0.13	0.48	0.38
Annual Growth	34.2%	— —	12.3%	73.8%	23.7%

EDF Trading Ltd

LOCATIONS

HQ: EDF Trading Ltd
Third floor, Cardinal Place, 80 Victoria Street, London SW1E 5JL

HISTORICAL FINANCIALS

Company Type: Public

Income Statement FYE: December 31

	REVENUE ($ mil.)	NET INCOME ($ mil.)	NET PROFIT MARGIN	EMPLOYEES
12/12	212,057	412	0.2%	697
12/11	220,255	549	0.2%	918
Annual Growth	(3.7%)	(25.0%)	—	(24.1%)

2012 Year-End Financials

Debt ratio: —
Return on equity: 12.7%
Cash ($ mil.): 116
Current ratio: 1.26
Long-term debt ($ mil.): —
No. of shares (mil.): 81
Dividends
Yield: —
Payout: —
Market value ($ mil.): —

	STOCK PRICE ($) FY Close	P/E High/Low	PER SHARE ($) Earnings	Dividends	Book Value
12/12	0.00	— —	(0.00)	0.00	43.28
12/11	0.00	— —	(0.00)	0.00	35.78
/0.00	—	—(0.00)	0.00	(0.00)	
Annual Growth	—	— —	—	—	—

EDP Energias de Portugal S.A.

If you live in Portugal or Brazil you can plug into EDP - Energias de Portugal a state-controlled holding company for utilities that generate transmit and distribute electricity. EDP's distribution unit serves customers across Portugal and has stakes in Brazilian power distributors. EDP serves more than 9.9 million electric customers. Other operations include a majority stake in Spanish utility HC Energia gas distribution (more than 1 million customers) utility metering and billing engineering and water and wastewater projects. EDP (a major wind energy player) has a combined generating capacity of more than 22000 MW from its domestic hydroelectric fossil-fueled and wind-powered plants.

Branching out across the peninsula EDP has grown its interests in HC Energia from 40% to 97% by purchasing the shares owned by German utility Energie Baden-Wurttemberg and Spanish banks Cajastur and Caser. It also controls 95% of Spanish gas utility Naturgas (acquiring 25% in 2010 for $803 million).

The company is looking to grow its generating capacity primarily through the development of wind-powered generating plants through its EDP Renovaveis unit. By the end of 2010 the company had a total wind power installed capacity of 6437 MW located in eight countries including the US.

Increased wind power capacity help to lift the company's revenues in 2010 along with higher power demand stemming from the recovering global economy.

Since 2007 the company has sold much of its holdings in other firms to pay down debt. Divestment deals include a 30% stake in Portugal's national transmission grid operator Rede Electrica Nacional (REN); a 40% stake in TURBOGAS - Produtora Energetica the company behind the construction of gas power station Tapada do Outeiro; and a 27% stake in PORTUGEN - Energia which is in charge of operating Tapada do Outeiro. In

2011 it agreed to sell a 7.7% stake in Brazil's Ampla Energia to a subsidiary of Spain's Endesa for E85 million ($121 million).

The Portuguese government controls about 26% of EDP.

HISTORY

EDP - Energias de Portugal has its roots in the several power enterprises that sprouted throughout the country during the infancy of electricity. The first recorded event in Portugal's electrification was the import of six voltaic arc lamps in 1878. The nation's first large-scale project saw the light in 1893 when the city of Braga was illuminated by the Sociedade de Electricidade do Norte de Portugal.

Electricity grew throughout the 1900s in the form of municipal concession contracts for distribution and government-licensed power plants. Large-scale power stations were not in effect in Portugal until after 1947 when Companhia Nacional de Electricidade was formed to interconnect the small generating systems dotting the nation. From the 1950s to mid-1970s new companies were formed to bring electricity to various parts of Portugal.

The original Electricidade de Portugal was founded in the wake of a leftist revolution during the 1970s in Portugal. In what became known as the Captain's Revolution military officers overthrew the Portuguese government which had been a dictatorship since 1933. The new government dominated by Marxists nationalized Portugal's industries including its generation transmission and distribution companies in 1975. The next year the Portuguese government created Electricidade de Portugal to unify the recently nationalized companies.

A new Social Democrat government came to power in 1987 and decided to denationalize Portuguese industry including EDP. The company reorganized into four major sectors in 1994: production (headed by its CPPE subsidiary) transmission distribution and services (led by its REN subsidiary which operated the national grid four regional utilities and 10 services units). EDP was the holding company.

Seeking opportunities opened up by the privatization of Brazil's state-owned electricity distributor EDP joined a consortium with Spain's Endesa and Chile's Chilectra to buy 70% of Rio de Janeiro distributor CERJ in 1996. The next year EDP gained a license to help build a hydro plant in Brazil. By 1998 the Endesa-led consortium had gained control of another Brazilian distributor Coelce.

The Portuguese government floated 30% of EDP in 1997 raising $1.76 billion. In a joint venture with the UK's PowerGen and Germany's Siemens EDP formed Turbogas to operate a power plant that would produce 20% of Portugal's electricity.

In 1998 EDP forged an alliance with Spain's Iberdrola and bought 80% of Guatemalan utility EEGSA. That year EDP and S?o Paulo utility CPFL gained control of S?o Paulo distributor Bandeirante. In 1999 EDP acquired stakes in two other Brazilian distributors. It also joined the UK's Thames Water to develop projects in Portugal Chile and Brazil and bought 45% of Chilean water and sewage company Essel. (EDP exchanged its stake in Essel for Thames Water's interest in the Portuguese joint venture in 2002.) The Portuguese state reduced its stake in EDP to about 50% in 1999.

Stepping up its telecommunications activities in 2000 EDP made its telecom unit Onitelecom (ONI) fully operational and agreed to share a fiber-optic network on the Iberian Peninsula with Spain's Iberdrola. (In 2006 however the company sold its stake in ONI.) Also in 2000 the Portuguese government acquired a majority stake in EDP's REN unit and EDP combined its four power distribution utilities into one unit (EDP Distribuic?o).

In 2001 EDP and Spanish savings bank Cajastur jointly bid to buy Hidrocantabrico one of Spain's leading utilities. EDP won control of 20% of Hidrocantabrico while German utility Energie Baden-Wurttemberg (EnBW) won control of 60%. The following year after a fierce bidding war the two companies agreed that EDP would control the majority share (40%) while EnBW would own only 35%.

The company changed its name from EDP - Electricidade de Portugal to EDP - Energias de Portugal in 2004.

EXECUTIVES

Director Consolidation Accounting Control and Taxation, Miguel Ribeiro Ferreira
Director Organisational Development, Rui Ferin Cunha
Chairman, Eduardo e Almeida Catroga, age 70
Executive Director, Ana Maria M. Fernandes, age 50
Executive Director, Jorge M. Pragana da Cruz Morais, age 57
Executive Director and CFO, Nuno M. Pestana de Almeida Alves, age 55
Director Investor Relations, Miguel Viana
Director Brand and Communication, Paulo C. Costa
Director Management Planning and Control, Nuno Chung
Director Internal Audit, Azucena Vi?uela
Member of the General and Supervis. Bd.; China International Water & Electric Corps Representative, Guojun Lu
Independent Member of the General and Supervisory Board, Ilidio Pinho
Member of the Executive Board of Directors, Joao Manso
Member of the Executive Board of Directors, Joao Cruz
Independent Member of the General and Supervisory Board, Jorge Macedo
Member of the General and Supervisory Board, Jose Ricciardi
Member of the General and Supervisory Board; Jose de Mello Energia SAs Representative, Luis Pereira
Independent Member of the General and Supervisory Board, Manuel Monteiro
Independent Member of the General and Supervisory Board, Maria Cardona
Company Secretary, Maria Pereira
Member of the Executive Board of Directors, Miguel Andrade
Independent Member of the General and Supervisory Board, Alberto Castro
Chairman of the Executive Board of Directors; Chief Executive Officer, Antonio Mexia
Member of the Executive Board of Directors, Antonio Abreu
Independent Member of the General and Supervisory Board, Antonio Mota
Member of the General and Supervisory Board; China Three Gorges Corporations Representative, Dingming Zhang
Independent Chairman of the General and Supervisory Board, Eduardo Catroga
Member of the General and Supervisory Board; Cajastur Inversiones SAs Representative, Felipe Fernandez
Independent Member of the General and Supervisory Board, Fernando Herrero
Member of the General and Supervisory Board; Senfora SARLs Representative, Mohamed Fahim
Member of the Executive Board of Directors, Nuno Alves
Mb. of the Gen. and Superv. Bd.; China Three Gorges International (Europe) Limiteds Representative, Shengliang Wu
Independent Member of the General and Supervisory Board, Vasco Vieira
Independent Member of the General and Supervisory Board, Vitor Goncalves
Member of the General and Supervisory Board; China Three Gorges New Energy Co Ltds Representative, Ya Yang
Director, Manuel Menendez Menendez, age 51
Director, Vasco M. G. Jose de Mello, age 54
CEO EDP - Energias do Brasil, Antonio M. Pita de Abreu, age 62
CEO EDP International EDP Soluc?es Comerciais and EDP Distribuic?o, Antonio F. Melo Martins da Costa, age 56
Director, Jo?o M. Manso Neto, age 53
Director, Manuel F. de Macedo Alves Monteiro, age 56
Director, Vitor D. Seabra Franco, age 60
Director, Prof Vitor F. de Conceicao Goncalves, age 56
Director, Diogo C. B. de Lacerda Machado, age 50
Director, Prof Vital M. Moreira, age 66
Director, Jose M. E. Santo Silva Ricciardi, age 56
Director, Antonio F. B. de Sousa Gomes, age 75
Independent Member of the General and Supervisory Board, Paulo T. Pinto, age 52
Director, Mohamed Meziane
Director, Rui Pena
Director, Miguel Stilwell de Andrade
Auditors: KPMG&AssociadosSROCSA

LOCATIONS

HQ: EDP Energias de Portugal S.A.
Praca Marques de Pombal 12, Lisbon 1250-162
Phone: (351) 21 001 25 00 **Fax:** (351) 21 001 14 03
Web: www.edp.pt

2010 Sales

	$ mil.	% of total
Europe		
Americas		
Brazil		13
US		2

PRODUCTS/OPERATIONS

2010 Sales

	$ mil.	% of total
Electricity	89	
Other	1	

COMPETITORS

AES
Cemig
E.ON
ELETROBRAS
Electrabel
Electricite de France
Endesa S.A.
Enel
IBERDROLA
Jazztel
RWE

HISTORICAL FINANCIALS

Company Type: Public

Income Statement

FYE: December 31

	REVENUE ($ mil.)	NET INCOME ($ mil.)	NET PROFIT MARGIN	EMPLOYEES
12/12	21,536	1,334	6.2%	12,275
12/11	19,558	1,454	7.4%	12,305
12/10	18,965	1,444	7.6%	12,096
12/09	17,572	1,474	8.4%	12,096
12/08	19,425	1,526	7.9%	12,245
Annual Growth	2.6%	(3.3%)	—	0.1%

2012 Year-End Financials

Debt ratio: 63.4%
Return on equity: 12.3%
Cash ($ mil.): 2,234
Current ratio: 0.93
Long-term debt ($ mil.): 22,032

No. of shares (mil.): —
Dividends
Yield: 5.3%
Payout: 749.5%
Market value ($ mil.): —

	STOCK PRICE ($) FY Close	P/E High/Low	PER SHARE ($) Earnings	Dividends	Book Value
12/12	30.66	196120	0.37	1.65	2.98
12/11	31.10	255159	0.40	3.51	2.89
12/10	33.25	298157	0.40	1.56	2.90
12/09	44.45	362188	0.40	1.52	2.90
12/08	38.20	491164	0.42	1.54	2.46
Annual Growth	(5.3%)	— —	(3.1%)	1.7%	4.9%

Endesa S.A.

Endesa provides power to more than 24 million customers in 11 countries (50% Spanish customers) on three continents. A subsidiary of Italian power giant Enel Endesa is Spain's #1 electric utility and has a generating capacity of 39700 MW from nuclear fossil-fueled hydroelectric and renewable energy plants. Endesa is the primary electricity company in Chile Argentina Colombia and Peru and also operates in Brazil. It is a major player in the Mediterranean region especially Italy and is active in other countries. Endesa serves more than 397200 natural gas customers in Spain. The company is also investing heavily in renewable energy to meet Spain's commitment to greenhouse gas reduction.

In 2009 Endesa had a generating capacity of more than 3700 MW of wind power or about 10% of the Spanish wind power market. In another major move to promote renewable energy in 2010 the company agreed to develop about 550 recharging locations in Barcelona Madrid and Seville to power electric cars.

The company found itself the target of takeover bids by other European power companies seeking to bulk up in the wake of the deregulation of the European power and gas markets. In 2007 E.ON and Gas Natural made bids of $47-plus billion and $26-plus billion respectively for Endesa. That year Enel and Acciona jumped into the fray buying about 70% and 25% of the company respectively when Gas Natural dropped out of the bidding. E.ON dropped out in 2008 in return for buying some power plants and shareholdings in Italy Spain and France from Endesa. In 2009 Enel bought Acciona's stake.

Formerly a state-owned firm Endesa branched out into new territories to prepare for the deregulation of Spain's electric utility market which took full effect in 2003.

HISTORY

When dictator Francisco Franco set about rebuilding Spain after the Civil War Empresa Nacional de Electricidad (Endesa) was formed in 1944 under the state-run Instituto Nacional de Industria (INI). The nation's lack of power facilities sparked the company into building hydroelectric plants. In the 1950s the US fighting the Cold War financed Spain's industrial boom which Endesa aided by building coal-fired plants including Compostilla (on line in 1961).

When inflation plagued Spain in the late 1950s the government cut off INI's funding. INI and its companies then borrowed heavily from banks. Spain then passed the Stabilization Act in 1959 to make INI companies self-financing though they were still government-owned. In the 1960s many of Spain's rural areas were undeveloped so the government instituted and funded a plan to build power infrastructure.

In 1972 Endesa acquired the As Pontel and Teruel facilities where it began constructing fossil fuel plants. However the energy crisis of the early 1970s kept the plants from operating until 1976 and 1979 respectively.

After Franco's death in 1975 King Juan Carlos moved Spain into Europe's free market union. In preparation for the liberalization of the energy markets INI and Endesa reorganized in 1983 and shifted INI's holdings in regional electric utilities (Eneco Enher Gesa and Unelco) to Endesa.

After the government halted its nuclear power program in 1984 many private electric companies were left with bad investments. Endesa was brought in to bail them out by taking over power plants; to repay Endesa they were forced to buy Endesa's electricity. The 1985 asset swaps also brought regional power companies Erz and Fecsa into Endesa's grasp.

In 1986 Spain joined the European Community; two years later the government sold 20% of Endesa to the public. In the early 1990s Endesa went into coal production when it purchased ENCASUR (1990) and it continued buying interests in private power companies including Viesgo and Sevillana.

The government floated more of the company in 1997 and the utility became Endesa S.A. Its eye on Latin American opportunity Endesa bought a 29% stake in Chile's largest power company Enersis. It also branched into telecommunications by grabbing a small stake in Retevision.

Endesa was fully privatized in 1998 the year Spain's deregulation process began. The next year Endesa paid some $2.6 billion to buy the outstanding shares of its regional units and merge them into the company as part of its larger effort to reorganize and cut its costs and workforce. Endesa also increased its stake in Enersis to more than 60%.

In 2000 Endesa began restructuring its regional electric utilities into separate generation and distribution units. Also that year Endesa Telecom Italia and Union Fenosa combined their Spanish telecom holdings to form the Auna joint venture. (Telecom Italia later sold its stake to Santander Central Hispano.) Endesa also agreed to acquire rival Spanish utility Iberdrola but the companies cancelled the transaction in 2001.

In 2001 Endesa completed the purchase of a 30% interest in French generation company SNET. The company also acquired one of Italian utility Enel's power production units (Elettrogen). Endesa sold its New Viesgo unit (a spinoff composed of regional electric utility Electra de Viesgo which served 500000 customers and had 2400 MW of generation assets) to Enel in 2002.

In 2005 Endesa sold its major stake in Auna to France Telecom (since renamed Orange).

EXECUTIVES

Director, Valentin Montoya Moya, age 58
CEO and Director, Rafael Miranda Robredo, age 63
Director, Andrea Brentan, age 63
Director, Claudio Machetti, age 54
Director, Fernando d'Ornellas Silva, age 55
Director and Deputy CEO, Esteban Morras Andres, age 54
Director, Maria del Carmen Becerril Martinez
Director, Luigi Ferraris, age 50
Auditors: DeloitteSL

LOCATIONS

HQ: Endesa S.A.
calle Ribera del Loira, 60, Madrid 28042
Phone: (34) 91 213 10 00 **Fax:** (34) 91 563 81 81
Web: www.endesa.es

2009 Sales

	% of total
Europe	
Spain &	68
Latin	32
Total	**100**

COMPETITORS

AES
Business Group Benelux
E.ON
Edison
Electricite de France
Energias de Portugal
Gas Natural SDG
HC Energia
IBERDROLA
International Power
PPL Corporation
RWE
Red Electrica de Espa?a
Sempra Energy
Telefonica
Tractebel Engineering
Vattenfall

HISTORICAL FINANCIALS

Company Type: Public

Income Statement

FYE: December 31

	REVENUE ($ mil.)	NET INCOME ($ mil.)	NET PROFIT MARGIN	EMPLOYEES
12/12	44,725	2,680	6.0%	22,807
12/11	42,277	2,861	6.8%	22,877
12/10	41,726	5,526	13.2%	24,732
12/09	37,011	4,941	13.4%	26,305
12/08	31,926	10,022	31.4%	26,587
Annual Growth	8.8%	(28.1%)	—	(3.8%)

2012 Year-End Financials

Debt ratio: 24.3%
Return on equity: 10.1%
Cash ($ mil.): 2,617
Current ratio: 1.33
Long-term debt ($ mil.): 13,030

No. of shares (mil.): 1,058
Dividends
Yield: —
Payout: —
Market value ($ mil.): 24,073

	STOCK PRICE ($) FY Close	P/E High/Low	PER SHARE ($) Earnings	Dividends	Book Value
12/12	22.74	21 12	2.53	0.00	25.71
12/11	19.75	33 16	2.70	0.00	23.57
12/10	25.05	17 9	5.22	0.00	22.47
12/09	34.00	23 11	4.67	0.00	19.36
12/08	38.75	18 7	9.47	0.00	22.56
Annual Growth	(12.5%)	— —	(28.1%)	—	3.3%

ENI S.p.A.

It's not teeny it's Eni —and it's huge. One of Italy's largest companies Eni operates in the oil and natural gas petrochemicals and oil field services industries and has expanded into power generation. Its main subsidiaries and affiliates include EniPower (power generation) Italgas (natural gas transmission) Saipem (oil field services) pipeline operator Snam Rete Gas and Snamprogetti (contracting engineering). As one of the world's leading oil enterprises in 2010 Eni had proved reserves of 6.8 billion barrels of oil equivalent most of it in Italy and in Africa. The Italian government owns 27% of Eni.

The company's oil and gas holdings and exploration and production efforts extend into more than 30 countries on five continents. Eni has expanded outside its traditional bases of Africa and Italy with ventures in the Americas the Asia/Pacific region Europe and the Middle East.

In response to the opening up of Italy's energy markets Eni is increasing its natural gas holdings and adding electricity generating power units. In 2007 the company bought Dominion Resources' US oil and gas assets in the Gulf of Mexico for $4.75 billion. To expand its Asian and Algerian holdings in 2008 Eni acquired Burren Energy and First Calgary Petroleums. It was able to benefit from SUEZ's acquisition of Gaz de France by buying up GDF SUEZ's majority stake in Belgian gas company Distrigas. Eni now owns 100% of Distrigas.

In 2009 to raise cash to pay down debt the company sold its 20% stake in Gazprom Neft to strategic partner Gazprom for $4.2 billion. To save operating costs that year Eni consolidated its gas divisions and sold Italgas and Stogit (gas storage) to subsidiary Snam Rete Gas.

Expanding its Central European market share in 2010 it acquired Exxon Mobil's 135 gas stations and other downstream assets in Austria.

In the wake of the global recession the company saw its revenues and income bounce back in 2010 thanks to higher commodity prices and stronger demand. The unrest in Libya in 2011 had a material impact of Eni which gets 15% of it production from the North African country. To compensate the company is investing heavily in growing production in other areas. Looking to expand in China in 2011 Eni signed a strategic alliance with Chinese oil major PetroChina.

In order to comply with an EU anti-trust ruling in 2011 the company sold its 89% stake in the TAG Pipeline (which transports gas from Russia to Italy) to Cassa Depositi e Prestiti for $986 million.

HISTORY

Although the Italian parliament formed Ente Nazionale Idrocarburi (National Hydrocarbon Agency) in 1953 Enrico Mattei is the true father of Eni. In 1945 Mattei a partisan leader during WWII was appointed northern commissioner of Agip a state-owned petroleum company founded in 1926 by Mussolini and ordered to liquidate the company. Mattei instead ordered the exploration of the Po Valley where workers found methane gas deposits in 1946.

When Eni was created in 1953 Mattei was named president. His job was to find energy resources for an oil-poor country. He initiated a series of joint ventures with several Middle Eastern and African nations offering better deals than his large oil company rivals which he dubbed the Seven Sisters.

Mattei didn't stick to energy: By the time he died in a mysterious plane crash in 1962 Eni had acquired machinery manufacturer Pignone finance company Sofid Milan newspaper "Il Giorno" and textile company Lane Rossi. Eni grew during the 1960s partly because of a deal made for Soviet crude in 1958 and a joint venture with Esso in 1963. It also expanded its chemical activities.

By the early 1970s losses in Eni's chemical and textile operations the oil crisis and the Italian government's dumping of unprofitable companies on Eni hurt its bottom line. Former finance minister Franco Reviglio took over in 1983 and began cutting inefficient operations.

EniChem merged with Montedison Italy's largest private chemical company in 1988 but clashes between the public agency and the private company made Montedison sell back its stake in 1990. Eni became a joint stock company in 1992 but the government retained a majority stake.

Franco Bernabe took over Eni following a 1993 bribery scandal and began cutting noncore businesses. The Italian government began selling Eni stock in 1995. In 1996 Eni signed on to develop Libyan gas resources and build a pipeline to Italy. A year later the company merged its Agipa exploration and production subsidiary into its main operations. Eni also took a 35% stake in Italian telecom company Albacom (which has since been sold to British Telecom Group).

The government cut its stake in Eni from 51% to 38% in 1998. That year Vittorio Mincato a company veteran succeeded Bernabe as CEO. In 1999 Eni and Russia's RAO Gazprom the world's largest natural gas production firm agreed to build a controversial $3 billion natural gas pipeline stretching from Russia to Turkey. Eni agreed to invest $5.5 billion to develop oil and gas reserves in Libya; it also sold interests in Saipem and Nuovo Pignone as well as some of its Italian service stations.

In 2000 Eni paid about $910 million for a 33% stake in Galp a Portuguese oil and gas company that also has natural gas utility operations. Also that year Eni bought British-Borneo Oil & Gas in a $1.2 billion deal and in 2001 it paid $4 billion for UK independent exploration and production company LASMO topping a bid by US-based Amerada Hess.

The Italian government sold off another 5% of Eni in 2001 reducing its stake to about 30% and announced that it was considering selling its entire investment. In an effort to reduce noncore holdings the company sold property management subsidiary Immobiliare Metanopoli to Goldman Sachs. Also that year Eni sold a minority stake in its gas pipeline unit Snam Rete Gas to the public.

In 2002 Eni entered discussions to acquire Enterprise Oil but lost out to a rival bid from Royal Dutch Shell. Later that year Eni's oil field services unit Saipem gained control of Bouygues Offshore.

In 2006 Eni and Gazprom formed an international alliance to launch joint mid and downstream gas projects and collaborate in upstream and in technological activities.

EXECUTIVES

CEO, Paolo Scaroni, age 67
COO, Salvatore Sardo, age 62
CFO, Alessandro Bernini, age 53
SEVP Public Affairs and Communication, Stefano Lucchini, age 51
EVP External Communication, Gianni Di Giovanni
SEVP Corporate Affairs and Governance and Secretary, Roberto Ulissi, age 51
COO Gas and Power, Umberto Vergine, age 56
SEVP Legal Affairs and General Counsel, Massimo Mantovani, age 50
COO Exploration and Production Division, Claudio Descalzi, age 58
COO Refining and Marketing, Angelo Fanelli, age 62
Chairman, Giuseppe Recchi, age 49
Chairman Syndial, Leonardo Bellodi
SEVP Midstream, Marco Alvera
EVP Research and Technological Innovation, Salvatore Meli
EVP Internal Audit, Marco Petracchini
Senior Vice President Media Relations, Camilla Palladino
Director of Human Resources and Organization, Pierluigi Pierluigi Renzi Renzi
Executive Assistant to the Chief Executive Officer, Raffaella Raffaella Leone Leone
CFO, Massimo Mondazzi
Director, Alberto Clo, age 65
Director, Francesco Taranto, age 73
Director, Mario Resca, age 68
Director, Pierluigi Scibetta, age 54
Director, Marco Reboa, age 58
Director, Paolo Andrea Colombo, age 53
Director, Paolo Marchioni, age 44
Independent Director, Alessandro Alessandro Lorenzi Lorenzi
Independent Director, Alessandro Alessandro Profumo Profumo
Independent Director, Carlo Carlo Gatto Gatto
Independent Director, Roberto Roberto Petri Petri
Auditors: RecontaErnst&YoungS.p.A.

LOCATIONS

HQ: ENI S.p.A.
1, piazzale Enrico Mattei, Rome 00144
Phone: (39) 2 52041730 **Fax:** (39) 2 52041765
Web: www.eni.com

2010 Sales

	% of total
Europe	
Italy	49
Other EU	21
Other	4
Africa	13
Americas	7
Asia	6
Total	**100**

PRODUCTS/OPERATIONS

2010 Sales

	% of total
Refining &	42
Gas &	29
Exploration &	13
Engineering &	9
Petrochemicals	6
Corporate &	1
Total	**100**

Selected Subsidiaries and Affiliates

Distrigas NV (gas Belgium)
EniPower SpA (power generation)
Italgas SpA (natural gas supply)
Saipem SpA (42.9% oil field services)
Snam Rete Gas SpA (52.5% gas pipeline)
Snamprogetti SpA (contracting and engineering)

COMPETITORS

A2A
Ashland Inc.
BASF SE
BG Group
BP
Chevron
ConocoPhillips
ERG S.p.A.
Edison
Exxon Mobil
Hellenic Petroleum
Marathon Oil
Occidental Petroleum
PEMEX
PETROBRAS
Petroleos de Venezuela
Royal Dutch Shell
Sunoco
TOTAL

HISTORICAL FINANCIALS

Company Type: Public

Income Statement FYE: December 31

	REVENUE ($ mil.)	NET INCOME ($ mil.)	NET PROFIT MARGIN	EMPLOYEES
12/12	169,719	10,264	6.0%	77,838
12/11	142,954	8,873	6.2%	78,686
12/10	133,139	8,455	6.4%	79,941
12/09	121,504	6,290	5.2%	78,417
12/08	152,207	12,338	8.1%	78,880
Annual Growth	2.8%	(4.5%)	—	(0.3%)

2012 Year-End Financials

Debt ratio: 23.0%
Return on equity: 13.5%
Cash ($ mil.): 10,234
Current ratio: 1.43
Long-term debt ($ mil.): 25,410
No. of shares (mil.): —
Dividends
Yield: 4.3%
Payout: 89.7%
Market value ($ mil.): —

	STOCK PRICE ($) FY Close	P/E High/Low		PER SHARE ($) Earnings	Dividends	Book Value
12/12	49.14	40	27	2.83	2.14	21.54
12/11	41.27	55	30	2.44	3.67	19.81
12/10	43.74	60	33	2.33	1.87	18.92
12/09	50.61	97	47	1.74	2.37	18.32
12/08	47.82	76	27	3.40	4.24	17.15
Annual Growth	0.7%	—	—	(4.4%)	(15.7%)	5.9%

Ergo Versicherungsgruppe AG

ERGO Insurance Group thinks logically: people need insurance ergo they sell it! The company comprises a number of firms specializing in life health property casualty and legal expenses insurance as well as pensions. Property/casualty and life policies are offered under the ERGO brand while health legal and travel insurance are provided through the DKV D.A.S. and ERV divisions. The company targets individuals and small to midsized businesses. ERGO is controlled by reinsurance giant Munich Re; the two companies have formed joint venture MEAG MUNICH ERGO AssetManagement to provide financial services.

ERGO sells its products through a vast network of self-employed agents direct sales employees and brokers. ERGO's marketing efforts target private individuals who account for the lion's share of premiums.

In 2009 the company consolidated its property/casualty and life operations under the ERGO brand withdrawing the Victoria and Hamburg-Mannheimer brands from the German market. ERGO also renamed its majority-owned KarstadtQuelle Insurance subsidiary which provides insurance and financial advice to department stores and mail-order customers through a partnership with Arcandor (formerly Karstadt Quelle) as ERGO Direct. ERGO also has cooperative agreements with banker HVB.

ERGO's health insurance and legal expenses products are its biggest sellers in Germany and Europe. In 2009 the company introduced a new product in those markets the "Home and Walkies" insurance package which covers liabilities related to dogs (such as fights with others' dogs while out for a walk or doggie messes left on apartment rugs or hotel floors).

ERGO has been strengthening its foreign operations through acquisitions and joint ventures. The company operates in approximately 30 countries; focus areas for growth include Eastern Europe including Poland and Turkey as well as Asian countries such as India and China. To that end ERGO acquired a majority stake in Turkish insurer ISVICRE and formed an Indian joint venture HDFC Ergo General Insurance with Housing Development Finance Corporation.

It expanded its Baltic States operations in 2008 by forming a European Public Company to offer health insurance and then merging its existing life insurance operations into the new company becoming the first non-government health insurer in the Baltics. The company operates in Estonia and Lithuania.

HISTORY

In 1843 Otto Crelinger applied for a royal license to create a railway insurance company in Prussia; King Friedrich Wilhelm IV of Prussia granted it 10 years later. By 1861 the company was selling life insurance as well and in 1875 it took the name VICTORIA.

VICTORIA was the first German company to offer life insurance to the public without the need to see a doctor (a plan modeled after Prudential's operations in the UK) and it gradually extended its reach to several other European countries and expanded into other areas of insurance including property casualty and automobile. By 1900 it was Germany's largest insurance company and on the eve of WWI it was the largest in Europe.

The war took a severe toll on VICTORIA but careful planning kept it on its feet. By 1927 it was back to prewar asset levels. In 1932 the company accounted for 80% of foreign premiums collected by German insurance companies.

WWII would prove to be an even more trying period for VICTORIA. Among the company's many misfortunes was the destruction of its main offices in Berlin. However cautious planning again kept the company afloat. By 1953 it was back on top of its game now mainly operating from Dusseldorf.

West Germany's economy flourished in the 1960s. During this decade VICTORIA bought D.A.S. then a relatively small legal expenses insurer that would grow to be the leader in its market. The 1970s saw a downturn in the world economy but VICTORIA weathered the decade well even expanding into the health insurance market.

In 1997 German reinsurer Munich Re decided to bring together three insurance companies in which it held stakes: VICTORIA Hamburg-Mannheimer (primarily a life and accident insurer) and DKV (a health insurer). The group instantly became Germany's second-largest insurer behind Allianz. All of these companies served mostly individual customers in Germany and abroad with secondary focuses on small to midsized businesses and some government institutions. Munich Re owned about 54% of the new holding company which was called ERGO Insurance Group (Versicherungsgruppe). ERGO shares went public in February 1998. Later that year Munich Re increased its stake to about 63%.

The new insurance conglomerate continued strengthening its international presence acquiring Spain's fifth-largest insurer Previasa. In 1999 ERGO acquired the Netherlands' health insurer Levob and Spain's Nordica. In 2000 the company acquired Italy's Bayerische Vita (life insurance) and Bayerische Assicurazioni (property and casualty insurance) an additional Netherlands insurer and majority stakes in Poland's Compensa Zycie (a life insurer) and a new life and accident insurer in Slovakia.

Also in 2000 the company's joint venture with Munich Re MEAG MUNICH ERGO AssetManagement began providing financial services and ERGO forged a strategic partnership with Deutsche Telekom to develop an online marketplace for insurance and financial services. The company together with affiliate Osterreichische Volksbanken also made a bid for the Austrian Post Office Savings Bank.

In 2001 ERGO took a majority stake in PREVENTA Lithuania's third biggest insurer.

Since then the company has been focused on continuing to grow its foreign operations primarily through acquisitions. To that end the company has made about five major buys over the past few years.

EXECUTIVES

Chairman Supervisory Board, Nikolaus von Bomhard
Chairman Management Board, Torsten Oletzky
Chief Investment Officer, Daniel von Borries
Management Board Member Composite Segment; Chairman Victoria Versicherung and Hamburg-Mannheimer Sachversicherungs, Christian Diedrich, age 57
COO and Managing Director ITERGO Informations-technologie GmbH, Ina Kirchhof, age 50
Chief Information Officer, Bettina Anders
CFO, Christoph Jurecka
Deputy Chairman Supervisory Board, Michael David
Supervisory Board Member, Gerhard Jooss
Supervisory Board Member, Heiner Hasford
Supervisory Board Member, Lothar Meyer, age 70
Supervisory Board Member, Klaus L. Wubbenhorst, age 56
Supervisory Board Member, Theo Siegert, age 64
Supervisory Board Member, Markus Miele
Supervisory Board Member, Karin Dorrepaal, age 50
Supervisory Board Member, Klaus Roth
Supervisory Board Member, Waltraud Baier
Supervisory Board Member, Gunter Bayerle
Supervisory Board Member, Hans-Peter Clau?en
Supervisory Board Member, Frank Fassin
Supervisory Board Member, Gunter Greisinger
Supervisory Board Member, Marco Norenberg
Supervisory Board Member, Reinhard Pasch
Supervisory Board Member, Prof Bernd Raffelhuschen
Supervisory Board Member, Richard Sommer
Supervisory Board Member, Volker Kalle
Supervisory Board Member, Prof Beatrice Weder di Mauro
Auditors: KPMGBayerischeTreuhandgesellschaftAG

LOCATIONS

HQ: Ergo Versicherungsgruppe AG
Victoriaplatz 2, Duesseldorf D-40198
Phone: (49) 211 477 0 **Fax:** (49) 211 477 1500
Web: www.ergo.de

2009 Sales

	$ mil.	% of total
Germany		70
Total		**100**

PRODUCTS/OPERATIONS

2009 Sales

	% of total
Health	31
Life	29
Direct/travel	23
Property/casualty	17
Total	**100**

COMPETITORS

AEGON
AOK
AWD
AXA
Ageas Insurance International
Allianz
Generali
Generali Deutschland
Helvetia Group
Prudential plc
Vienna Insurance Group
Zurich Insurance Group

HISTORICAL FINANCIALS

Company Type: Public

Income Statement FYE: December 31

	ASSETS ($ mil.)	NET INCOME ($ mil.)	INCOME AS % OF ASSETS	EMPLOYEES
12/12	194,027	363	0.2%	29,768
12/11	180,237	432	0.2%	31,311
12/10	186,373	460	0.2%	32,997
12/09	195,233	232	0.1%	33,152
12/08	186,012	104	0.1%	21,709
Annual Growth	1.1%	36.5%	—	8.2%

2012 Year-End Financials

Return on assets: 0.1%	Dividends
Return on equity: 6.8%	Yield: —
Long-term debt ($ mil.): —	Payout: —
No. of shares (mil.): 75	Market value ($ mil.): —
Sales ($ mil): 34,636	

Ericsson

Ericsson opens all lines of communication. The world's leading maker of mobile broadband infrastructure gear provides the equipment that telecom carriers use to build and expand their networks. The company also provides wireline broadband metro area Ethernet LTE modems and optical transport equipment. Its services unit handles operations ranging from systems integration to network deployment and management. Ericsson's multimedia arm provides content-related products including Internet television systems. The company traces its roots back to 1876 when Lars Magnus Ericsson opened up a telegraph repair shop in Stockholm.

Operations

Ericsson's core business comprises three segments: networks professional services and support solutions. The networks segment which accounts for more than half of the company's sales develops and deploys the latest generation of mobile broadband networks (LTE) and maintains and refines older networks (GSM WCDMA etc.) for its network operator customers. The segment also provides equipment for Internet protocol (IP) microwave transport and core networks including IP routers core routers and switches cables and interconnect products microwave radio links optical transport components radio base stations and wireline network access equipment.

Serving network operators Ericsson's professional services segment supports its customers network operations through its consulting customer support network design and integration and training services. The segment also offers managed services like application hosting and network operations. The growing professional services unit is supported by four global service centers in India China Mexico and Romania. The services segment accounts for about 40% of the company's net sales.

The company's multimedia support solutions segment offers software for consumer-facing applications including mobile and Internet television messaging and music as well as billing support systems for telecommunications network operators.

Financial Performance

For 2012 Ericsson reported modest revenue growth and a 50% drop in its net income from 2011 levels. While its networks segment struggled its growing professional services segment finished strong in 2012. The company attributed the group-wide drop in profitability to operating losses in its ST-Ericsson joint venture (which it dissolved in late 2013) as well as to high research and development and other costs tied to the ongoing modernization of its networks product line. Geographically North America and northeast Asia were Ericsson's strongest markets where demand for mobile products continues to climb.

Strategy

Capitalizing on the booming mobile communications industry Ericsson's is focusing on growing its broadband network equipment and services businesses while divesting non-core businesses. In 2012 Ericsson sold its 50% stake in Sony Ericsson to Sony for more than ?1 billion (about $1.5 billion) in cash. Ericsson which is now focused on global wireless connectivity surrendered the handset portion of the Sony Ericsson business to Sony. Sony and Ericsson plan to work together on a wireless connectivity initiative Ericsson's primary expertise and a pivotal component of Sony's device convergence strategy.

In 2013 semiconductor manufacturer STMicroelectronics (ST) sold its stake in ST-Ericsson a now-dissolved joint venture with Ericsson. The two companies split the joint venture's assets with Ericsson taking over the development and sales of the newer LTE multimedia thin modems (which complement its mobile broadband business) and ST taking a portion of the existing ST-Ericsson modem product line. Other assets including a global navigation satellite system were sold to third parties.

Mergers and Acquisitions

Ericsson is using acquisitions to bolster its product portfolio and expand further into international markets to capitalize on demand for the mobile broadband services that its equipment supports and fuel the growth of its global services organization. The company bought New Jersey-based Telcordia in 2012 for more than $1 billion in cash to expand its mobile broadband and business communications software holdings particularly in the areas of operations support systems and business support systems applications and to further expand its North American business. Telcordia brought in about $740 million in revenue for its 2011 fiscal year.

Ericsson kept pouring money into boosting its wireless portfolio with the 2012 purchase of BelAir Networks which provides carrier-grade Wi-Fi equipment in North America. Ericsson also established a stronger presence as a provider of managed services for broadcasters that year when it bought a related division from Technicolor for nearly ?20 million (about $25 million). The acquisition extended its reach beyond Sweden into France the Netherlands and the UK and became a leading provider in Europe.

HISTORY

Lars Magnus Ericsson opened a telegraph repair shop in Stockholm in 1876 the same year Alexander Graham Bell applied for a US patent on the telephone. Within two years Ericsson was making telephones. His company grew rapidly supplying equipment first to Swedish phone companies and later to other European companies. In 1885 Ericsson crafted a combination receiver-speaker in one handset.

In 1911 Ericsson and SAT the Stockholm telephone company merged under the Ericsson banner. The company adopted its present name in 1926. In 1930 international financier Ivar "The Match King" Kreuger owner of the Swedish Match Co. won control of Ericsson. His triumph was short-lived. Krueger committed suicide in 1932 and one of his creditors Sosthenes Behn's ITT took over.

ITT in 1960 sold its interest in Ericsson to the top Swedish industrialist family the Wallenbergs. In 1975 Ericsson introduced its computer-controlled exchange called AXE. Buoyed by AXE's success the company unveiled the "office of the future" in the early 1980s diversifying into computers and office furniture.

However Ericsson's timing was off: The demand for office automation never materialized and profits plunged. Electrolux chairman Hans Werthen was recruited to split his time between the two companies and rescue Ericsson. The company sold its computer business to Nokia in 1988 and refocused on telephone equipment. It dusted off its aging AXE system for the burgeoning cellular market and quickly won key contracts.

The company and aircraft maker Saab merged their military aviation electronics operations as Ericsson Saab Avionics in 1996. (It was dissolved in 1998.) In 1998 manager Sven-Christer Nilsson was appointed CEO. He reorganized the company and laid off 14000 workers.

After Ericsson fought bitterly with rival QUALCOMM over wireless standards and patents the companies settled in 1999 agreeing to push for the standardization of third-generation technology based on QUALCOMM's code-division multiple access (CDMA) technology. As a part of the deal Ericsson purchased QUALCOMM's infrastructure business. To expand its Internet offerings Ericsson bought Internet router maker Torrent and Internet telephony company Touchwave.

By 1999 Nilsson was pushed out for moving too slowly on restructuring plans and was replaced as CEO by chairman Lars Ramqvist who put many of the duties on president Kurt Hellstrom. Hellstrom immediately set out to simplify the company's managerial and accounting structure trim its workforce and slow-growth businesses and push new phone models to market.

The next year Ericsson sold noncore businesses including its private radio systems power supply and equipment shelter operations. The company also agreed to develop a standard for secure wireless transactions with Nokia and Motorola and formed a joint venture with Web router maker Juniper Networks to sell routers for mobile Internet applications.

Fierce competition an industrywide slowdown in handset sales and manufacturing glitches led Ericsson to outsource the manufacture of its phones to Flextronics and form a joint venture (Sony Ericsson Mobile Communications) with Sony to link the development and marketing of their handsets in 2001. Ericsson also sold its direct enterprise sales and service unit outsourced IT operations in Europe to Electronic Data Systems (which later became HP Enterprise Services) and cut more than 20000 jobs that year. Hellstrom became CEO in 2001.

Chairman Ramqvist became honorary chairman in 2002; Electrolux CEO Michael Treschow was named as the acting chairman. Ericsson announced 20000 more layoffs in 2002. That year the company sold its semiconductor unit to Infineon for about $380 million.

Ericsson sold its optoelectronic components business in 2003. Hellstrom retired later that year and Carl-Henric Svanberg former CEO of Assa Abloy was appointed as company president and CEO. In 2005 Ericsson acquired certain telecom hardware assets from troubled Marconi (later renamed telent) for about $2.1 billion.

The company acquired seven companies in 2007 the largest of which were Redback Networks ($1.9 billion) and TANDBERG Television ($1.4 billion). The Redback buy gained Ericsson broadband IP routers while the TANDBERG Television purchase brought software and services for the cable television market. It also picked up fiber-access technology company Entrisphere in an effort to expand its broadband access offerings in North America.

Looking to broaden its multimedia offerings the company purchased Mobeon a Swedish provider of IP-based voice and video mail. Other 2007 acquisitions included German customer care software provider LHS Swedish mobile service deliver platform developer Drutt and Spanish IPTV specialist HyC. In an effort to refocus its multimedia operations on key areas such as service delivery and provisioning Ericsson sold its enterprise PBX products business to Aastra Technologies for about $100 million in 2008.

To expand its North American business Ericsson bought bankrupt Nortel Network's CDMA and LTE-based wireless business there in 2009 for $1.1 billion. The deal significantly boosted its profile as a provider of mobile networking gear to wireless carriers on the continent. The company's other acquisitions that year complemented its manufacturing and services activities. These purchases included the manufacturing operations of Estonian electronics maker Elcoteq as well as Turkish systems integrator Bizitek.

In 2010 EVP/CFO Hans Vestberg took over as president and CEO of Ericsson succeeding Carl-Henric Svanberg who resigned to become chairman of BP.

EXECUTIVES

VP and CTO Sony Ericsson, Jan Uddenfeldt
Chairman, Leif Johansson, age 62
SVP and Head Sales and Marketing, Jan Wareby, age 57
Deputy Chairman, Jacob Wallenberg, age 58
EVP and Head Global Services, Magnus Mandersson, age 51
VP Investor Relations, Gary Pinkham
President CEO and Director, Hans Vestberg, age 48, $2,321,550 total compensation
VP Communications Americas, Kathy Egan Wummer
President Sony Ericsson Mobile Communications, Bert Nordberg
Head North America Region; President and CEO Ericsson North America, Angel Ruiz
Head Human Resources China and North East Asia, Marita Hellberg, age 57
Deputy Chairman, Sverker Martin-Lof, age 71
Head Middle East, Anders Lindblad
EVP and CFO, Jan Frykhammar, age 48
SVP and Head Strategy, Douglas L. Gilstrap, age 50
SVP; Head of Business Unit Support Solutions, Per G. Borgklint, age 38
VP and Head Investor and Analyst Relations, ?se Lindskog
Head Corporate Public and Media Relations, Ola Rembe
Head Greater China and North East Asia, Mats H. Olsson, age 59
Deputy Chairman, Marcus Wallenberg, age 57
Head Vodafone Global Customers, Torbjorn Possne, age 59
Head Western and Central Europe, Anders Runevad
EVP and Head Networks, Johan Wibergh, age 50
Senior Vice President Strategic Projects, Rima Qureshi, age 48
Head Sub-Saharan Africa, Lars Linden
Head South East Asia and Oceania, Arun Bansal
Head Latin America, Sergio Quiroga da Cunha
Head Mediterranean, Nunzio Mirtillo
SVP and Head Human Resources and Organization, Bina Chaurasia
SVP General Counsel and Head Legal Affairs, Nina Macpherson
SVP CTO and Head Technology and Portfolio Management, Ulf Ewaldsson
SVP and CIO; Head Group Function Business Excellence and Common Functions, Anders Thulin
Director, Roxanne S. Austin, age 52
Director, Carl-Henric Svanberg
Deputy Chairman, Jacob Wallenberg, age 58
President CEO and Director, Hans Vestberg, age 48
Director, Jan Hedlund, age 67
Director, Ulf J. Johansson, age 68
Director, Nancy McKinstry, age 54
Director, Sir Peter L. Bonfield, age 68
Deputy Chairman, Sverker Martin-Lof, age 71
Director, Anders Nyren, age 58
Director, E. Borje Ekholm, age 49
Deputy Chairman, Marcus Wallenberg, age 57
Director, Kristina Davidsson, age 58
Director, Karin ?berg, age 53
Director, Michelangelo (Mike) Volpi, age 47
Director, Pehr Claesson, age 47
Auditors: PricewaterhouseCoopersAB

LOCATIONS

HQ: Ericsson
Torshamnsgatan 23, Kista, Stockholm SE-164 83
Phone: (46) 10 719 0000
Web: www.ericsson.com

2012 Sales

	% of total
North	25
China & North East	16
Mediterranean	10
Latin	10
Western & Central	8
Middle	7
South East Asia &	7
Northern Europe & Central	6
Sub-Saharan	5
India	3
Other	3
Total	**100**

PRODUCTS/OPERATIONS

2012 Sales

	% of total
Networks	51
Services	43
Support	6
Total	**100**

COMPETITORS

Accenture
Alcatel-Lucent
Amdocs
Cisco Systems
Comverse Technology
HP Enterprise Services
HTC Corporation
Harmonic
Huawei Technologies
IBM
Juniper Networks
LG Electronics
Motorola Mobility
Nokia Siemens Networks
Oracle
QUALCOMM
Samsung Electronics
Sharp Corp.
Tata Consultancy
Tech Mahindra
Technicolor
ZTE

HISTORICAL FINANCIALS

Company Type: Public

Income Statement — FYE: December 31

	REVENUE ($ mil.)	NET INCOME ($ mil.)	NET PROFIT MARGIN	EMPLOYEES
12/12	34,964	886	2.5%	110,255
12/11	32,901	1,768	5.4%	104,525
12/10	30,325	1,662	5.5%	90,261
12/09	28,991	515	1.8%	82,493
12/08	26,752	1,443	5.4%	78,740
Annual Growth	6.9%	(11.5%)	—	8.8%

2012 Year-End Financials

Debt ratio: 1.6%
Return on equity: 4.1%
Cash ($ mil.): 6,858
Current ratio: 1.98
Long-term debt ($ mil.): 3,668
No. of shares (mil.): —
Dividends
Yield: 3.4%
Payout: 52.6%
Market value ($ mil.): —

	STOCK PRICE ($) FY Close	P/E High/Low		PER SHARE ($) Earnings	Dividends	Book Value
12/12	10.10	0	0	0.27	0.35	6.52
12/11	10.13	0	0	0.55	0.00	6.46
12/10	11.53	0	0	0.52	0.28	6.76
12/09	9.19	0	0	0.16	0.23	6.15
12/08	7.81	0	0	0.45	0.42	5.55
Annual Growth	6.6%	—	—	(11.8%)	(4.7%)	4.1%

Erste Group Bank AG

First there was Erste. Erste Group Bank is the holding company of Erste Bank which is Austria's oldest banks dating back to 1819. However the company has grown beyond its home country and has some 3200 branches in eight Central and Eastern European nations. The company has operating subsidiaries in Austria Croatia the Czech Republic Romania Serbia Slovakia Slovenia Hungary and Ukraine. Erste Group banks provide financial services such as savings and lending to individuals and small to medium-size businesses.

As Austrian banks consolidated the group increased its presence in surrounding nations. Since the early 2000s the holding company has expanded its market by purchasing stakes in or acquiring outright banks in Austria Bosnia Russia and the Ukraine. Each of its subsidiaries is focused on local operations.

Erste Group slowed its acquisitions during the economic downturn and focused instead on cutting costs and making good lending decisions. The choices helped the company weather the financial crisis rather well. Over the long term Central and Eastern European countries are expected to record economic growth. Erste Group expects loan growth and an increased demand for asset management services in those emerging countries.

The company has sharpened its focus on its core banking activities by selling non-core insurance subsidiaries. It sold most its insurance brokerage operations to Austrian firm GrECo International in 2010.

In 2011 Erste Group made its first acquisitions in several years when it took control of Intermarket Bank —the largest factoring bank in Austria. Erste Group already owned more than 20% of Intermarket Bank and it acquired an additional 56%. The transaction was part of Erste Group's strategy to offer broad services to corporate customers. Also in 2011 Erste offered to buy the rest of majority-held Romanian unit Banca Comerciala Romana it doesn't already own.

HISTORY

In 1819 a bank was born and its name was Erste oesterreichische Spar-Cassa. Called Die Erste for short the bank was Austria's first commercial and savings bank. Unlike Austria's community savings banks Die Erste was independent —not backed by government guarantees.

For more than 150 years Die Erste operated as a local savings bank serving Vienna. Then in 1979 the Austrian government passed a law that would alter the face of the banking industry in that country. The Banking Act of 1979 placed banks and savings institutions in direct competition with each other by allowing them both to take part in all aspects of the banking business. As a result of the enhanced competition Die Erste began expanding its domestic branch network.

Meanwhile the Austrian savings banks had established their own central institution in 1937 and called it Girovereinigung der osterreichischen Sparkassen or Girozentrale for short. Girozentrale focused on managing the liquidity reserves of the savings banks and helping them with their syndication and securities businesses. The bank also endeavored to improve the non-cash payment system and to promote mortgage savings. Concentrating on international and investment banking rather than retail banking Girozentrale eventually became the country's third-largest bank.

Throughout the late 1980s and into the 1990s rumors began to spread about a possible merger between Girozentrale and Die Erste (both were associated with the nation's conservative People's Party). In 1992 Girozentrale merged with Osterreichisches Credit-Institut (OCI) to create GiroCredit giving the central savings bank a branch network for the first time. But it also made GiroCredit a direct competitor with its two largest shareholders — Bank Austria (now part of HypoVereinsbank) and Die Erste who were also fierce competitors with each other.

Between 1992 and 1994 Die Erste and Bank Austria struggled to find a solution to the problem of GiroCredit's ownership. In 1994 Bank Austria emerged the victor by winning the majority stake in GiroCredit in a move that was characterized by Die Erste as "unfriendly."

Throughout the next two years Die Erste attempted to secure a stake in Creditanstalt Austria's second-biggest bank as the Austrian government began moves to privatize it. Die Erste acted as a part of a consortium of Austrian German and Italian entities interested in obtaining stakes in the bank. But in 1997 Bank Austria won that battle too managing to take over Creditanstalt. In turn Die Erste bought Bank Austria's majority stake in GiroCredit. The resulting company was given the name Erste Bank which went public that year in the largest stock issue in Austrian history. In 1998 it became the first major Austrian company to allow for the election of small shareholder representatives to its supervisory board.

In 2000 Erste Bank bought a majority stake in Ceska Sporitelna the largest retail bank in the Czech Republic from the Czech government. Later in the year the Slovak government allowed Erste Bank to become a major shareholder in the previously state-owned Slovenska sporitel'na. Erste Bank was also one of several Austrian banks to be accused by the European Commission of fixing foreign exchange fees.

In 2001 Erste Bank took control of Slovenska Sporitel'na and acquired majority ownership of Tiroler Sparkasse Bank AG. The following year Erste Bank took full control of Czech Republic-based Czeska Sporitelna. Ever acquisitive in 2005 the company completed its acquisition of Serbia's Novosadska banka.

Erste in 2006 acquiered Romanian bank Banca Comerciala Romana the largest bank in that country and previously state-owned.

Erste switched to a holding company structure in 2008. That year the company also sold most of its insurance business to Vienna Insurance Group.

EXECUTIVES

Deputy Chairman Management Board and Deputy CEO, Franz Hochstrasser, $1,115,030 total compensation
Chairman Management Board and CEO, Andreas Treichl, $1,452,791 total compensation
Second VP Supervisory Board, Theresa Jordis, age 64
Member of the Management Board and Chief Risk Officer, Bernhard Spalt, $93,670 total compensation
Member Management Board Corporate and Investment Banking, Gernot Mittendorfer, age 49
Member Management Board and COO, Herbert Juranek
First VP Supervisory Board, Georg Winckler, age 70
Head of Investor Relations, Thomas Sommerauer
Chairman of the Management Board, Pavel Kysilka
Member Supervisory Board, Wilhelm G. Rasinger
Second VP Supervisory Board, Theresa Jordis, age 64
Member Supervisory Board, Juan Maria Nin Genova, age 59
First VP Supervisory Board, Georg Winckler, age 70
Member Supervisory Board, Brian D. O'Neill
Member Supervisory Board, Friedrich Rodler
Member Supervisory Board, John James Stack
Member Supervisory Board, Werner Tessmar-Pfohl
Auditors: Sparkassen-PrufungsverbandAuditingAgency

LOCATIONS

HQ: Erste Group Bank AG
Milchgasse 1, Vienna A-1010
Phone: (43) 50100 17 693 **Fax:** (43) 50100 9 13112
Web: www.erstegroup.com

PRODUCTS/OPERATIONS

2010 Sales

	% of total
Interest	69
Fees and commissions	25
Trading and other	6
Total	**100**

Selected Subsidiaries

Banca Comerciala Romana S.A. (BCR)
Ceska Sporitelna (Czech Republic)
Erste Bank a.d. Novi Sad (Serbia)
Erste Bank Croatia (Erste & Steiermarkische Bank d.d.)
Erste Bank der oesterreichen Sparkassen AG
  Autoleasing EBV
  Sparkasse Salzburg
  Wohnbaubank
Erst Bank Hungary Nyrt.
Erste Bank Ukraine (formerly Bank Prestige)
Slovenska sporitelna a.s. (Slovakia)

COMPETITORS

BAWAG
Banca Comerciala Romana
Bank Austria
Credit Suisse
Deutsche Bank
Deutsche Post
Deutsche Postbank
Erste & Steiermarkische Bank
Investkredit
OTP Bank
Oberbank AG
RZB Group
UBS
UniCredit Bank AG

HISTORICAL FINANCIALS

Company Type: Public

Income Statement FYE: December 31

	ASSETS ($ mil.)	NET INCOME ($ mil.)	INCOME AS % OF ASSETS	EMPLOYEES
12/12	281,830	637	0.2%	49,381
12/11	271,633	(929)	—	50,452
12/10	275,621	1,359	0.5%	50,272
12/09	290,577	1,301	0.4%	50,488
12/08	281,633	1,201	0.4%	52,648
Annual Growth	0.0%	(14.7%)	—	(1.6%)

2012 Year-End Financials

Return on assets: 0.2%
Return on equity: 3.8%
Long-term debt ($ mil.): —
No. of shares (mil.): 375
Sales ($ mil): 14,977
Dividends
Yield: —
Payout: —
Market value ($ mil.): 6,030

	STOCK PRICE ($) FY Close	P/E High	P/E Low	PER SHARE ($) Earnings	Dividends	Book Value
12/12	16.05	32	15	1.15	0.00	45.10
12/11	8.65	—	—	(2.95)	0.00	41.92
12/10	23.77	20	10	3.11	0.00	50.23
12/09	18.84	21	3	3.41	0.00	51.54
12/08	11.35	31	5	3.83	0.00	39.07
Annual Growth	9.0%	—	—	(26.0%)	—	3.7%

Espirito Santo Financial Group S.A. (Luxembourg)

Espirito Santo Financial Group (ESFG) wields its earthly powers via two main entities: Banco Espirito Santo (BES) and Companhia de Seguros Tranquilidade one of Portugal's top insurance firms. BES is the largest commercial bank in Portugal where it has a 20% market share. Its Banco Espirito Santo de Investimento offers investment banking; Espirito Santo Activos Financeiros is a fund management firm. Although most of its operations are in Portugal ESFG has financial services and insurance interests across Europe Africa Brazil the Caribbean the Middle East and the US where it owns Espirito Santo Bank in Florida. Entities associated with the founding Espirito Santo family are ESFG's major shareholders.

In 2008 ESFG established a partnership with Danish company Saxo Bank acquiring a 5% stake in the bank with an option to buy an additional 5%. Saxo Bank specializes in online trading and will partner with ESFG's majority owned asset management trading firm Banco BEST to provide integrated products and services.

The group provides private banking services primarily in Switzerland (through Banque Privee Espirito Santo) the US and Portugal. Its ES Bankers (Dubai) unit offers asset management services in the United Arab Emirates.

HISTORY

The Espirito Santo financial empire traces its roots to a bank founded by Jose Maria de Espirito Santo Silva in Lisbon in 1884. After WWI Portugal underwent a major banking expansion and in 1920 the Espirito Santo family established Banco Espirito Santo which grew rapidly thanks to postwar expansion and speculation.

After Jose Maria's oldest son Jose fled the bank and the country in scandal his brother Ricardo led the massive growth of both the bank and the family's fortune. During the 1930s the Espirito Santos acquired a major interest in insurance company Tranquilidade and in 1937 Banco Espirito Santo merged with Banco Comercial de Lisboa (founded 1875) to create Banco Espirito Santo e Comercial de Lisboa.

The family's fortunes were aided by dictator Antonio de Oliveira Salazar who came to power in

1933. During WWII Salazar declared Portugal neutral and the country became a sanctuary for many of Europe's elite who brought the Espirito Santos business and contacts.

The Espirito Santo empire was fostered by Salazar's postwar protectionist policies. Banco Espirito Santo became one of Portugal's largest banks and Tranquilidade one of its largest insurance companies. The family also acquired large coffee sugar and palm-oil plantations in Portugal's colonies Angola and Mozambique. At their peak the Espirito Santo holdings were valued at $4 billion.

But the family's fortunes turned with political upheaval in Portugal during the 1970s. In 1974 the military overthrew Salazar's successor Marcelo Caetano. A year later the leftist government nationalized Portugal's major corporations including Banco Espirito Santo and Tranquilidade.

The family fled to London and pooled their savings to create a new company in Luxembourg Espirito Santo Financial Holding (ESFH). In the late 1970s they got a banking license in Brazil and later set up a fund management company in Switzerland and banks in Miami and Paris. The family's name attracted business and investors.

The Portuguese government reprivatized financial services organizations in 1986. That year ESFH and France's Credit Agricole opened Banco Internacional de Credito in Portugal. After raising money on the Eurobond market ESFH bought back control of Tranquilidade in 1990. A year later the company and a group of investors including Credit Agricole reacquired control of Banco Espirito Santo.

In 1993 ESFH reduced its interest in Banco Internacional de Credito to 47% (it regained 100% control in 1997). Since then the company has concentrated on Portugal. In the early 1990s recession rocked the economy –and the company. But in the mid-1990s despite poor commercial demand consumer-related services rebounded.

ESFH expanded its commercial banking network in 1995 and 1996. In 1997 the company and Brazil's Monteiro Aranha bought more than 60% of that country's Banco Boavista. The company also dropped "Holding" in favor of "Group" and the next year ESFG in a vote of confidence in Brazil moved to raise its holdings in Banco Boavista.

In 1999 amid a flurry of speculation about Spanish/Portuguese banking mergers the company agreed to buy a majority interest in Spanish brokerage Benito y Monjardin. The company also moved to bolster its asset management operations by inking a deal to buy Portugal-based fund manager Gescapital.

In 2000 ESFG bought the majority stake of French credit institution Via Banque from BNP Paribas (it acquired the rest of Via Banque in 2001). The next year ESFG in conjunction with Portugal Telecom launched Banco Electronico de Servico Total (Banco Best) as a technologically integrated banking investment and brokerage service.

ESFG had sold the lion's share of Tranquilidade's insurance pension and investment products through its bank offices but the company reorganized in 2006 to separate the bank and non-bank distribution networks. The two bancassurance distribution units BES Vida (life insurance) and BES Seguros (non-life insurance) are now controlled and managed by Credit Agricole. Tranquilidade's non-life insurance business that is not distributed through banks remains with ESFG.

EXECUTIVES

Vice Chairman, Jose Manuel Pinheiro Espirito Santo Silva, age 67
Director, Patrick Monteiro de Barros, age 67
Director, Robert Studer, age 74
Director, Manuel Guerrero Peman, age 63
Director, Mario Mosqueira do Amaral, age 80
Director, Manuel Fernando de Moniz Galv?o Espirito Santo Silva, age 54
Director, Jackson B. Gilbert, age 80
Director, Philippe Guiral, age 64
Director, Manuel Antonio Ribeiro Serzedelo de Almeida, age 69
Director, Jose Maria Espirito Santo Silva Ricciardi, age 58
Director, Pedro Guilherme Beauvillain de Brito e Cunha, age 61
Director, Carlos Augusto Machado de Almeida Freitas, age 62
Director, Anibal da Costa Reis Oliveira, age 77
Director, Juan Villalonga Navarro, age 59
Director, Othman Benjelloun, age 80
Director, Jose Pedro Torres Garcia Caldeira da Silva, age 53
Director, Fernando Pedro Braga Pereira Coutinho, age 65
Director, Yves Alain Marie Morvan, age 73
Director, Alexandre da Paix?o Coelho, age 70
Controller and Director, Jose Carlos Cardoso Castella, age 63
Director, Horacio Lisboa Afonso, age 63
Director, Bernard Basecqz, age 67
CEO and Director, Gerard Laffineur Petracchini, age 50
Auditors: KPMG

LOCATIONS

HQ: Espirito Santo Financial Group S.A. (Luxembourg)
22-24 Boulevard Royal, Luxembourg L-2449
Phone: 212 270-3400 **Fax:** 212 980-1777
Web: www.esfg.com

PRODUCTS/OPERATIONS

Selected Subsidiaries

AdvanceCare - Gest?o de Servicos (health insurance)
Banco Espirito Santo de Investimento SA (investment bank)
Banco Espirito Santo SA (BES) (commercial bank)
Banque Privee Espirito Santo S.A. (private bank in Switzerland)
BES Investimento do Brasil (investment bank branch in Brazil)
Companhia de Seguros Tranquilidade SA (non-life insurance)
ES Bankers (Dubai) Limited (private bank in Dubai)
Espirito Santo Activos Financeiros (asset management)
Espirito Santo Saude (private health care provider in Portugal)
Seeguros LOGO (non-life insurance)
T-Vida (life insurance)

COMPETITORS

BBVA
BNP Paribas
Banco Comercial Portugues
Caixa Geral de Depositos
Citigroup
Credit Suisse
Deutsche Bank
Grupo Santander
Itausa
JPMorgan Chase
Societe Generale
UBS
Zurich Insurance Group

HISTORICAL FINANCIALS

Company Type: Public

Income Statement

FYE: December 31

	ASSETS ($ mil.)	NET INCOME ($ mil.)	INCOME AS % OF ASSETS	EMPLOYEES
12/12	115,426	413	0.4%	12,036
12/11	108,675	156	0.1%	14,889
12/10	116,639	163	0.1%	14,813
12/09	122,905	226	0.2%	13,758
12/08	109,260	107	0.1%	13,491
Annual Growth	1.4%	40.0%	—	(2.8%)

2012 Year-End Financials

Return on assets: 0.3%
Return on equity: 18.0%
Long-term debt ($ mil.): —
No. of shares (mil.): 207
Sales ($ mil): 8,857
Dividends
Yield: —
Payout: —
Market value ($ mil.): 1,408

	STOCK PRICE ($) FY Close	P/E High/Low		PER SHARE ($) Earnings	Dividends	Book Value
12/12	6.80	6	6	2.45	0.00	14.00
12/11	6.55	15	4	3.25	0.00	15.60
12/10	18.30	29	26	1.39	0.00	26.50
12/09	20.90	30	14	2.30	0.00	28.70
12/08	12.25	50	17	1.76	0.00	23.03
Annual Growth	(13.7%)	—	—	8.6%	—	(11.7%)

Etablissements Delhaize Freres et Cie Le Lion S.A. (Belgium)

This Belgian's roar can be heard from Brussels to Bali to Baltimore. Food retailer Delhaize Group runs about 3400 stores –including flagship banner Delhaize Le Lion –in the US Southeastern Europe and Asia. Food retailing accounts for a lion's share of the company's profits but it also engages in food wholesaling and the sale of pet food and pet products in Belgium. Delhaize Group's sales network consists of company-operated affiliated and franchised stores 85% of which conform to the supermarket format. Other store formats include neighborhood convenience and specialty stores. US subsidiary Delhaize America is one of the largest supermarket operators on the East Coast from Maine to Florida.

The operation of retail supermarkets accounts for nearly 90% of Delhaize Group's sales. Its US subsidiary Delhaize America is the third-largest operator of grocery stores along the East Coast of the US where it operates some 1650 stores in 17 states from Maine to Florida. Stores banners include Food Lion Hannaford Sweetbay and Harveys. It also operates two of fast-growing off-price formats: Bloom and the Bottom Dollar chain of limited-assortment discount supermarkets. In its home market of Belgium (including the Grand Duchy of Luxembourg) Delhaize operates a multi-format network of about 820 stores under about a half a dozen banners. It does business in Greece through some 250 Alfa-Beta stores and in five Balkan countries through the recently-acquired Delta Maxi chain of supermarkets. In Indonesia its 51%-owned PT Lion Super Indo chain operates stores on the island of Java where it has about an 11% share of the retail food market. Beyond retailing Delhaize supplies food to affiliated stores and independent customers. The company also sells pet food and pet products at about 135 Tom & Co. stores in Belgium.

Brussels-based Delhaize rings up nearly two-thirds of its sales and earns more than 60% of its operating profit in the US where it operates about 1650 supermarkets. Belgium and Luxembourg account for more than 20% of sales with Southern Europe (Albania Bosnia and Herzegovina Bulgaria Greece Montenegro Romania and Serbia) and Indonesia making up the rest.

Despite continued shaky economic conditions in Europe (including an economic catastrophe in Greece) and parts of the US Delhaize Group rang up more than E21 billion ($29.4 billion) in sales in 2011 a 1.3% increase vs. 2010. The company's operating profit fell 21% over the same period. The US operation outperformed Belgium with sales up more than 2% vs. 1% respectively. While growth in the US was modest it was an improvement over the past few years when Delhaize America posted declining annual sales comparisons. Delhaize's Southeastern Europe and Asia segment saw sales climb by nearly a third driven by the acquisition half way through the year of Delta Maxi's 485 retail stores in the Baltic states and expansion in Indonesia. Looking ahead Delhaize expects Delta Maxi to generate approximately E1.3 billion in revenues in 2012.

To grow Delhaize Group is setting its sights on newer and faster growing opportunities. The purchase of the Delta Maxi stores in Southeastern Europe fits the bill. Delhaize in July 2011 it acquired Serbia's leading food retail chain for about E630 million (nearly $875 million) from businessman Miroslav Miskovic. Delta Maxi operates about 485 retail stores in Albania Bosnia Bulgaria Montenegro and Serbia. Combined with its existing operations in Greece where it owns the #2 food retailer Alfa-Beta and Romania (Mega Image) the Belgian retailer is now a leading player with about 850 grocery stores in the seven countries. Fast-growing Indonesia is another focus of growth for the Belgian retailer. In 2011 the company added 16 new stores bringing the total to about 90 supermarkets there. Other growth formats include limited-assortment low-cost supermarkets: Bottom Dollar in the US and Red Market (launched in 2009) in Europe.

HISTORY

Two brothers and a brother-in-law —all teachers —founded Delhaize in 1867 in Charleroi Belgium. A professor of commercial sciences Jules Delhaize wanted to try out his ideas about food retailing such as creating a network of stores and a centralized warehouse and charging set prices for items. He enlisted the aid of his brother Edouard and his brother-in-law Jules Vieujant. The trio picked the symbol that has become synonymous with the company —the lion because it represented strength and it was the emblem of their native country. A third brother Adolphe later started his own food-retailing operation also with multiple branches. (His operations were merged into Delhaize in 1950.)

The company moved to Brussels in 1871. In the early 1880s the company moved closer to a rail line for better transportation services opened a large warehouse and other operations and began setting up factories to produce its own brand-name foods and beverages.

Although it still had stores only in Belgium (more than 500 by 1914) the company had an international presence because of its appearance at exhibitions such as the St. Louis World's Fair in 1904. After WWI the company began investigating possibilities for international trade by sending a delegation to the US and Canada.

At the beginning of WWII Delhaize had 744 branches and 1500 affiliated shops including several in the Belgian Congo. At war's end Delhaize started closing some of its factories although it kept a few.

Taking a page from the American supermarkets it had been studying Delhaize in 1957 opened Europe's first full self-serve supermarket complete with pre-packaged meat frozen foods and fresh produce and the look of American stores —bright colors checkout stands and fluorescent lighting. Delhaize went public in 1962 as S.A. Delhaize Freres et Cie "Le Lion."

In 1972 Jacques LeClercq the great-grandson of Jules Delhaize persuaded the Delhaize board that future opportunities for growth lay in the US. Two years later with the enactment of "padlock laws" to halt the spread of hypermarkets in Belgium and similar restrictions occurring elsewhere in Europe the company bought 32% of Food Town an American chain with 19 stores. (Delhaize bought a controlling interest in Food Town in 1976.) A few years later Delhaize bought Food Giant in Atlanta and began expanding beyond the supermarket in Belgium setting up the Di body care shops and in 1981 the AD (Delhaize Affiliates) chain to offer wholesale and management advice services.

Food Town became Food Lion in 1983. Two years later Delhaize opened a new chain Cub Food in Atlanta. In 1989 it set up Caddy-Home a home-delivery service and Tom & Co stores selling pet foods and supplies.

International expansion was the byword for the 1990s. Delhaize set up Delvita in 1991 in the Czech Republic. Further acquisitions included controlling interests in Alfa-Beta Vassilopoulos (Greece 1992) the Kash n' Karry chain (US 1996) and interests in supermarket chains in Thailand and Indonesia (1997). Acquisitions in 1999 included 49% of Shop n Save (Singapore) and 28 Farmer Jack stores (US).

Expansion continued in 2000 with further acquisitions in Thailand and Romania and the mid-year US acquisition of Hannaford Bros. In April 2001 Delhaize acquired all of Delhaize America merging its US operations and listing on the New York Stock Exchange (the only Belgian company on that august body). In late 2001 the company shut down its Atlanta-based joint venture 19 Super Discount Markets in which it held a 60% ownership stake.

In October 2003 Delhaize Group completed the acquisition of 43 Harveys supermarkets in Florida and central and southern Georgia filling in an area where Food Lion has a limited presence. Following the acquisition Harveys became the Delhaize Group's fourth US banner. In November Delhaize agreed to sell its 49% stake in Singapore food retailer Shop N Save to Cold Storage Singapore for E21.9.

Delhaize Group shut down its Food Lion Thailand operation in August 2004 with the sale of 20 stores there to Central Food Retail Co. and the closure of its remaining locations. In November the company —through its US subsidiary Hannaford Bros. —acquired the 19-store Victory Super Markets chain Massachusetts and New Hampshire for $175 million. At year end Baron Gui de Vaucleroy retired down as chairman of the board and was succeeded by Georges Jacobs.

In May 2005 Delhaize Group completed the acquisition of Cash Fresh a chain of 43 supermarkets mainly in northeastern Belgium for about E169 million (including real estate). In June the company sold all 11 Delvita stores in Slovakia to Germany's Rewe exiting that market.

Stiff competition in its home market from discounters including ALDI Lidl and French hypermarket operator Carrefour led Delhaize Group to cut prices on some 1000 items in early 2006.

The following year the Belgian grocer sold its Delvita stores in the Czech Republic also to Rewe. Also the last of the company's Kash n' Karry stores in Florida were converted to the Sweetbay banner.

In April 2008 Delhaize through its Alfa-Beta subsidiary in Greece acquired 34 Plus Hellas supermarkets there from Germany's Tengelmann for about $108 million. Mega Image in 2008 nearly doubled its store network through acquisitions including the purchase of the 14-store La Fourmi chain for E19 million (about $26 million).

To streamline its European operations the company in July 2009 sold its four stores in Germany to rival REWE. (Delhaize entered the German market in 2003.)

In 2010 the company added 110 new stores: 40 in the US 28 in Belgium 14 in Greece 21 in Romania and seven in Indonesia. Delhaize acquired all of the minority shares in Alfa-Beta and delisted the company from the Athens Stock Market in 2010.

In July 2011 Delhaize acquired Serbia's Delta Maxi chain of stores from businessman Miroslav Miskovic for about E630 million (nearly $875 million). Delta Maxi is Serbia's #1 food retailer with 365 stores there. The grocery chain operates about 100 other stores in Bulgaria Bosnia and Herzegovina Montenegro and Albania.

EXECUTIVES

Executive Vice President General Counsel and General Secretary, Maura Abeln Smith, age 57
EVP; President and CEO Delhaize America, Roland C. Smith, age 58
Executive Vice President and Chief Financial Officer, Pierre B. Bouchut, age 58
President and CEO, Frans W.H. Muller, age 52
EVP Human Resources and Organizational Development, Nicolas Hollanders, age 52
Chairman, Mats Jansson, age 62
Vice President Delhaize America, Greg Amoroso
Vice President Treasury Delhaize Group, Miguel Gonzales
Executive Vice President of Delhaize Group and Chief Executive Officer Southeastern Europe, Kostas Macheras
Board Member, Jack J. Stahl, age 59
Board Member, Claire H. Babrowski, age 54
Board Member, Robert J. Murray, age 70
Group President CEO and Board Member, Pierre-Olivier Beckers, age 52
Board Member, Hugh G. Farrington, age 67
Board Member, Didier Smits, age 50
Board Member, Jacques de Vaucleroy, age 51
Board Member, Baron Luc Vansteenkiste, age 65
Auditors: DeloitteBedrijfsrevisorenBV

LOCATIONS

HQ: Etablissements Delhaize Freres et Cie Le Lion S.A. (Belgium)
Square Marie Curie 40, Brussels 1070
Phone: (32) 2 412 22 11 **Fax:** (32) 2 412 22 22
Web: www.delhaizegroup.com

2011 Sales

	% of total
US	65
Belgium &	23
Southeast Europe &	12
Total	**100**

2011 Stores

	No.
US	1,650
Belgium &	821
Greece	251
Romania	105

Indonesia	89
Serbia	366
Bosnia and	44
Bulgaria	42
Montenegro	22
Albania	18
Total	**3,408**

PRODUCTS/OPERATIONS

2011 Sales

	% of total
Retail	
Perishable	38
Non-perishable	36
Nonfood	15
Wholesale	11
Total	**100**

Selected Store Banners

Belgium
- AD Delhaize
- Delhaize Le Lion
- Proxy Delhaize
- Red Market
- Shop 'n Go
- Tom & Co

Greece
- Alfa-Beta

Indonesia
- Super Indo

Romania
- La Fourmi
- Mega Image

Serbia
- Delta Maxi

US
- Bloom
- Bottom Dollar Food
- Food Lion
- Hannaford Bros. Co.
- Harveys Supermarket
- Sweetbay Supermarket

COMPETITORS

ALDI
Ahold U.S.A.
Albertsons
Auchan
BI-LO
Carrefour
Casino Guichard
Coop
Costco Wholesale
DeMoulas Super Markets
Golub
Harris Teeter
ITM Entreprises
Kroger
METRO AG
Migros
Publix
REWE
Royal Ahold
Shaw' s
Tengelmann
Tesco
Wal-Mart
Winn-Dixie

HISTORICAL FINANCIALS

Company Type: Public

Income Statement FYE: December 31

	REVENUE ($ mil.)	NET INCOME ($ mil.)	NET PROFIT MARGIN	EMPLOYEES
12/12	29,968	138	0.5%	158,000
12/11	27,316	614	2.2%	160,000
12/10	27,905	768	2.8%	138,622
12/09	28,722	740	2.6%	138,119
12/08	26,597	652	2.5%	140,992
Annual Growth	3.0%	(32.1%)	—	2.9%

2012 Year-End Financials

Debt ratio: 34.7%
Return on equity: 1.9%
Cash ($ mil.): 1,228
Current ratio: 1.15
Long-term debt ($ mil.): 3,855
No. of shares (mil.): 100
Dividends
Yield: 4.0%
Payout: 34.7%
Market value ($ mil.): 4,091

	STOCK PRICE ($) FY Close	P/E High/Low		PER SHARE ($) Earnings	Dividends	Book Value
12/12	40.55	96	50	1.37	1.62	67.82
12/11	56.35	36	20	6.05	3.50	69.56
12/10	73.71	27	20	7.60	1.46	67.45
12/09	76.72	33	19	7.32	1.56	63.32
12/08	62.99	41	16	6.42	1.67	58.12
Annual Growth	(10.4%)	—	—	(32.0%)	(0.8%)	3.9%

European Investment Bank

The biggest international lovefest since Esperanto the European Investment Bank (EIB) is the financial backbone of the European Union (EU). Led by finance ministers from EU countries the bank makes loans for trans-European enterprise and infrastructure projects focusing on less-developed EU countries. About 90% of the loans go to projects located within the EU; major loan categories are transportation and energy. The bank also offers development aid to some non-European countries. The EIB owns a majority of the European Investment Fund (EIF) which invests in venture capital funds and debt financing for small businesses in the EU.

The EIB provides loans and finances the development of infrastructure and businesses according to the policies of the EU. Loan categories also include health care organizations educational ventures and housing throughout the EU and beyond. Most of the 150 non-European countries it makes loans to are former colonies of European countries. The EIB which loans more money annually than the World Bank has lending policies geared to foster economic integration and social cohesion among current and potential EU member nations.

A board of governors (consisting of EU member states' finance ministers) appoints a 28-person board of directors (along with 18 alternates) to manage the bank's affairs. One director and one alternate represent the European Commission. The board of directors meets once a month to approve loans review policies and suggest changes in the EIB's credit policy. The EIB also employs an audit committee and a management committee to oversee daily functions. The bank's president chairs the management committee's meetings.

Although the EIB enjoys unique legal and financial autonomy within the EU it must also remain competitive with private banks in the international market. The bank's concerns for economic parity among member nations sometimes pit it against the EU which seeks to bring Europe's poorer cousins of the east into the Union's political fold. Watchdog groups have called for the bank to be more open in its decision-making process and policies arguing that large infrastructure projects funded by EIB loans have a substantial environmental impact.

The EIB's clients include public entities EU and non-EU governments and large private corporations.

HISTORY

The European Investment Bank (EIB) has its roots in the Messina Conference of 1955 when the soon-to-be members of the European Economic Community (EEC) proposed a central public body to oversee the spread of wealth between rich and poor European nations.

In 1958 the Treaty of Rome established the EEC and the EIB was founded to make and guarantee loans that helped develop infrastructure and improvements in member countries. The six founding countries were Belgium France Italy Luxembourg the Netherlands and West Germany.

The Yaounde (Cameroon) Convention of 1963 saw the EIB expand its lending activities to 17 African former colonies of European countries. Under the Yaounde Convention these nations were provided financial aid and trading advantages.

In 1973 the UK Denmark and Ireland joined the EEC and the EIB grew in size assets and lending power. The Lome (Togo) Convention of 1975 expanded the Yaounde Convention to include 70 more African Caribbean and Pacific countries. Meanwhile the EEC continued to grow adding Greece (1981) and Spain and Portugal (1986). It became the more fully integrated European Union (EU) in 1993 (Finland Austria and Sweden were added in 1995). The bank's loans first exceeded those of the World Bank in 1992.

In 1994 the European Investment Fund (EIF) was created by the EIB the EU and private European banks to invest in venture capital funds and to guarantee financed debt.

Environmental groups denounced the EIB for loans they considered ecologically damaging in the mid-1990s; those included loans for a Sweden-Denmark bridge a gold mine in Papua New Guinea a water project in Lesotho (Africa) and a gas pipeline between Bolivia and Brazil.

In 2000 EIF realigned itself as the EIB's specialist risk capital arm while the EIB raised its stake to more then 50% of the fund.

EXECUTIVES

Chairman and President, Philippe Maystadt, age 65
Director General Credit Risk, Pierluigi Gilibert
Director General Lending Operations - Other Countries, Jean-Louis Biancarelli
VP, Philippe de Fontaine Vive Curtaz, age 54
Chairman Board of Governors, Charilaos Stavrakis, age 57
VP, Ploutarchos K. Sakellaris
VP, Dario Scannapieco, age 46
VP, Simon Brooks, age 59
VP, Carlos da Silva Costa
VP, Matthias Kollatz-Ahnen
VP, Eva Srejber
VP, Marta Gajecka
Auditors: KPMGAuditS.a.r.l.

LOCATIONS

HQ: European Investment Bank
98-100, Boulevard Konrad Adenauer, Luxembourg L-2950
Phone: (352) 43 79 1 **Fax:** (352) 43 77 04
Web: www.eib.org

The EIB has offices in Australia Austria Belgium Egypt Finland France the French Caribbean Germany Greece Italy Kenya Luxembourg Morocco Poland Portugal Romania Senegal South Africa Spain Tunisia and the UK.

COMPETITORS

BNP Paribas
Banco Comercial Portugues
Banco Popular Espa?ol
Citigroup
Deutsche Bank
National Bank of Greece
Royal Bank of Scotland
UniCredit Bank AG

HISTORICAL FINANCIALS

Company Type: Public

Income Statement

FYE: December 31

	REVENUE ($ mil.)	NET INCOME ($ mil.)	NET PROFIT MARGIN	EMPLOYEES
12/12	34,262	3,611	10.5%	0
12/11	32,346	2,964	9.2%	0
12/10	26,578	3,539	13.3%	2,077
12/09	19,156	(3,285)	—	1,896
12/08	27,416	8,885	32.4%	1,744
Annual Growth	5.7%	(20.2%)	—	—

2012 Year-End Financials

Debt ratio: —	No. of shares (mil.): —
Return on equity: 5.5%	Dividends
Cash ($ mil.): 23,224	Yield: —
Current ratio: 1.53	Payout: —
Long-term debt ($ mil.): —	Market value ($ mil.): —

Fiat SPA

The country that gave us Sophia Loren and Leonardo da Vinci also gave us the century-old Fiat. The group's cars range from models like the popular Fiat Nuova 500 to the Alfa Romeo Ferrari (85% owned) and Maserati brands. Fiat holds a 53% stake in Chrysler and has management control of the US carmaker. Fiat reorganized its operations in early 2011 and sent its agricultural and construction equipment (led by 89% owned CNH Global) commercial vehicles (Iveco) and most of the rest of its nonautomobile operations to the newly created Fiat Industrial.

Reinvented and free of its industrial operations "New Fiat" aims to drive an unadulterated auto company able to manufacture six million cars by 2014. Its primary brands will include Fiat Alfa Lancia Maserati and Ferrari. If successful Fiat could possibly shop around for a buyer for its Magneti Marelli (power train operations) and boost its ownership in Chrysler. Fiat through its sale of stock is also looking to invest in current and new factories and equipment in Asia Europe and North and South America. To that end the company's Fiat Powertrain unit got the greenlight by the European Commission in spring 2011 to acquire Penske Corporation's 50% stake in VM Motori an Italy-based diesel engines; General Motors (GM) has owned the other 50% since 2007. In addition to expanding Fiat's diesel engine offerings the VM Motori deal should enhance the company's new V-6 engine.

Fiat earlier reached a deal with Chrysler and its majority owner at the time Cerberus Capital Management on a broad cooperative agreement that would give the Italian carmaker a 20% equity stake in Chrysler. In January 2011 Fiat upped its stake to 25% when Chrysler agreed to build a Fiat four-cylinder engine in a US factory. The stake was increased to 30% after Fiat fulfilled its second goal set forth by the US government –to market one or more Chrysler vehicles in Brazil and Europe. Fiat obtained an additional 16% stake when Chrysler paid the $7 billion it owed to the governments of Canada and the US; Fiat then upped its stake from 46% to 53% in mid-2011. Fiat's increased ownership may negate the need for Chrysler to conduct an IPO. Fiat will provide technology and vehicle platforms to the American carmaker allowing Chrysler to build and sell smaller more fuel-efficient cars in North America.

President Obama said the US government would require Chrysler to repay the bailout loans it received from the US Department of the Treasury before allowing Fiat to take a majority stake in the company. Chrysler was able to complete new agreements with its labor unions and most of its lenders were willing to swap their debt for a cash payout proposed by the Obama administration's auto task force. A group of lenders held out on the deal however and Chrysler filed for Chapter 11 protection from creditors along with 24 of its US subsidiaries.

Chrysler and Fiat went forward with their plans when the American carmaker exited from bankruptcy reorganization six weeks after its filing. Fiat appointed three of the nine directors on Chrysler's new board. Fiat CEO Sergio Marchionne became the CEO of Chrysler Group (as the restructured company is known) succeeding Robert Nardelli and initiated a wide-ranging management reorganization.

Fiat subsequently picked up niche car maker Carrozzeria Bertone and plans to manufacture Chrysler vehicles at the Bertone plants. The Bertone name associated with such fast plates as the Alfa Romero Giulietta Sprint and the Lamborghini Countach highlights Marchionne's focus on producing Chrysler models outside of North America.

The Italian car company also has plans to return to the US for the first time in over 25 years. As part of the planned return Chrysler has begun assigning Fiat franchises in about 120 US markets with expectations of that number going as high as 200 by 2011. The Fiat 500 minicar (subcompact) should reach dealer showrooms in early 2011. Also debuting in 2011 is a Chrysler-built Fiat-based sedan which will carry the Dodge brand.

After two failed attempts Fiat is again looking to expand into China. In 2009 the company set up a E400 million ($570 million) joint venture with Guangzhou Automobile Group to make cars and engines for the Chinese market. Its first China-made model is planned for a 2011 launch of a yet-to-be-unveiled brand of economical family sedan.

An earlier agreement with Chery Automobile of China to make and sell Fiat Alfa Romeo and Chery cars was called off when the companies discovered that their models would be in direct competition. A deal with Fiat's first partner Nanjing Auto ended when Fiat couldn't agree on a licensing fee for its technology; Nanjing Auto was subsequently taken over by Shanghai Automotive Industry Corporation (SAIC).

Although Fiat has not made any public statement regarding its intention to sell Alfa Romeo VW chairman Ferdinand Piech has made public his desire to acquire the brand. Some see the deal making sense after Alfa Romeo sales dropped about 1% in 2009 compared to the previous year when Fiat expected a dramatic increase.

Fiat is also looking for growth in other emerging markets such as India Russia and South America. Fiat's joint venture with India's Tata Motors builds passenger cars engines and transmissions in India. That JV is part of a larger cooperative agreement that also has the companies making Tata trucks at a Fiat plant in Argentina.

The company is in partnership with Russia-based car maker Sollers to assemble as many as 25000 vehicles a year of three Fiat models. Desiring to increase the manufacturing number to 500000 vehicles per year Fiat and Sollers signed a memorandum of understanding (MoU) in early 2010 to set up a joint venture for the manufacture of cars and SUVs at a new Russian plant. Viewed as a key joint venture Prime Minister Vladimir Putin attended the ceremony when the news was announced; however during 2010 the financial funding of the partnership came into question. When talks ended between Fiat and Sollers in early 2011 Ford took the opportunity to arrive on the scene with its own offer; Ford and Sollers subsequently signed an MoU. Fiat plans to go it alone carving out a presence in Russia through its own independent strategies.

The founding Agnelli family through holding company EXOR owns about 30% of Fiat.

HISTORY

Ex-cavalry officer Giovanni Agnelli founded Fabbrica Italiana di Automobili Torino (Fiat) in 1899. The automaker expanded into trucks railcars aviation and tractors between 1903 and 1918. Protected by tariffs Fiat became Italy's dominant auto company.

WWII boosted Fiat's fortunes but bombs damaged many of its plants. With US support Fiat rebuilt and survived by exporting and by building plants abroad. As growth in Italy resumed Fiat began making steel and construction equipment.

After the European Community forced Italy to lower tariffs in 1961 Fiat lost market share although foreign sales helped offset its woes. Giovanni Agnelli II (the founder's grandson) became chairman in 1966. Fiat bought high-end Italian carmakers Lancia and Ferrari in 1969.

The company formed Fiat Auto S.p.A. in 1979 bringing together the Fiat Lancia Autobianchi Abarth and Ferrari lines. The next year Cesare Romiti became managing director and cut 23000 jobs and broke union influence at Fiat. The company closed its unprofitable US car operations in 1983. Fiat and British Ford combined their truck operations in 1986 and Fiat also bought Alfa Romeo that year.

In 1989 Fiat purchased 49% of luxury carmaker Maserati (it bought the rest in 1993). Fiat and Ford merged their farm and construction equipment divisions in 1991 to form Fiat subsidiary New Holland (renamed CNH Global in 1999). After posting its biggest loss in 1993 Fiat restructured.

Slow car sales in Italy prompted Fiat to temporarily lay off about 74000 workers in 1996 and chairman Agnelli stepped down. In 1997 Romiti and financial director Paolo Mattioli were convicted of falsifying records and illegally financing political parties. They were barred from employment at Fiat.

Paolo Fresco former vice chairman of General Electric replaced Romiti as head of Fiat in 1998. Challenged with slumping car sales in Italy and South America the company sold its chemicals and telecom businesses. Car-price wars in Europe contributed to a stark downward shift in 1998 profits.

Deals abounded in 1999. Fiat's New Holland subsidiary bought agricultural and construction equipment maker Case Corporation for around $4.3 billion and changed its name to CNH Global. Also Fiat began making light commercial trucks in China with Yuejin Motor. Fiat's truck-making division agreed in 1999 to buy vehicle-leasing company Fraikin for $596 million.

Other deals in 1999 included Fiat's Comau robotics unit's purchase of a 51% stake in France-based Renault Automation; the two began a bus-making joint venture and combined their foundry operations under Fiat subsidiary Teksid. Also Fiat bought Progressive Tool & Industries (automated welding equipment US) for $350 million.

To expand its auto business outside Europe Fiat agreed in 2000 to trade a 20% stake in its car unit for a 5.1% stake in GM. That year ALSTOM agreed to buy a 51% stake in Fiat's rail unit (Fiat Ferrovia). Also in 2000 Fiat began selling off the divisions of Magneti Marelli. These included heating and cooling (to Denso of Japan) rearview mirrors (to Ficosa of Spain) and lubricants (to Doughty

Hanson & Co. Ltd. of the UK). The company's bid (with a consortium including Electricite de France) of about $5.5 billion for control of agro-energy group Montedison was accepted in July.

Toward the end of 2001 Fiat announced that it would postpone selling off any more of Magneti Marelli due to the economic downturn. Fiat then announced it would reorganize Fiat Auto into four business units (Fiat/Lancia Alfa Romeo International Development and Services) in order to fully take advantage of brand valuation.

In 2002 Fiat sold the aluminum components division of its Teksid casting subsidiary to a group of funds including JP Morgan Partners Questor Management Company and Italy's Private Equity Partners.

As 2002 came to a close Fiat announced it would lay off as many as 5600 workers and it sold its entire stake in GM to an unnamed investment bank for nearly $1.2 billion. A provision of the 2000 deal that gave GM 20% (later reduced to 10%) of Fiat Auto also gave the Italian automaker the option to force GM to buy the remaining 90% as early as 2004 (or as late as 2009). The "put option" was later backed off by Fiat to 2005 (or as late as 2010). Gianni Agnelli Fiat's honorary chairman and grandson of the company's founder died at the age of 81 in early 2003. Later that year Fiat sold its Fiat Avio aviation unit to The Carlyle Group and Italian defense group Finmeccanica for about $1.8 billion.

Fiat chairman Umberto Agnelli died in late May of 2004 plunging the company into management chaos. When the board named Ferrari and Maserati chairman Luca Cordero di Montezemolo chairman of Fiat instead of Fiat CEO Giuseppe Morchio Morchio suddenly quit. The company quickly named turnaround specialist Sergio Marchionne as Fiat S.p.A.'s fifth CEO in two years.

In 2005 GM claimed the previously negotiated put option was rendered invalid when Fiat Auto restructured and GM's stake was reduced to 10%. Fiat insisted GM's claim was false. After a month of very private negotiations GM finally agreed to pay Fiat $2 billion to settle the dispute and thereby avoided having to buy Fiat Auto. After the messy divorce from General Motors Fiat replaced the CEO of beleaguered Fiat Auto Hebert Demel with Fiat CEO Sergio Marchionne marking the first time since 1899 that a single person ran both the Fiat holding company and Fiat Auto. Marchionne also became the fourth executive to run Fiat Auto in a little more than three years.

In 2008 Fiat ended a joint venture with Cummins when it acquired the US-based diesel engine manufacturer's share of European Engine Alliance.

In mid-2009 Fiat took a 20% stake in Chrysler assuming management control of the US carmaker. Fiat had reached a deal with Chrysler and its majority owner at the time Cerberus Capital Management on a broad cooperative agreement that would give the Italian carmaker a 20% equity stake in Chrysler which it could increase to 35% once certain milestones were reached. Reeling from turmoil in the auto industry in the midst of a global economic downturn Chrysler sought loans from the US government's auto task force to hold it over until the deal with Fiat could be completed. While most of Chrysler's lenders agreed to swap their debt for a cash payout from the US administration a group of lenders held out on the deal; Chrysler filed for Chapter 11 bankruptcy protection early in 2009. Fiat and Chrysler were able to complete the deal when Chrysler emerged from bankruptcy six weeks after its filing. Fiat CEO Sergio Marchionne took over as CEO of Chrysler Group (as the restructured company is known).

EXECUTIVES

VP Brand Promotion Fiat Auto, Lapo Elkann
Head International Operations and Fiat Professional, Lorenzo Sistino
Statutory Auditor, Piero Locatelli
CEO and Director; CEO Fiat Group Automobiles; CEO Chrysler Group LLC, Sergio Marchionne, age 60
Director, Vittorio Mincato, age 76
Director, Ratan N. Tata, age 74
Director, Tiberto Ruy Brandolini d'Adda, age 64
Director, Pasquale Pistorio, age 75
Director, Virgilio Marrone, age 66
Secretary and Director, Franzo Grande Stevens
Director, Luca Garavoglia, age 43
Director, Roland Berger, age 75
Director, Rene Carron, age 70
Director, Gian Maria Gros-Pietro, age 70
Director, Mario Zibetti, age 73
Director, Carlo Sant'Albano, age 48
Director, Andrea Agnelli, age 37
Auditors: Deloitte&ToucheS.p.A.

LOCATIONS

HQ: Fiat SPA
250 Via Nizza, Turin I-10126
Phone: (39) 011 00 61111 **Fax:** (39) 011 00 63796
Web: www.fiatspa.com

2009 Sales

	% of total
Europe	
Italy	25
Other	35
South	20
North	10
Other	10
Total	**100**

PRODUCTS/OPERATIONS

2009 Sales

	% of total
Automobiles	
Core (Fiat Lancia Alfa	46
Ferrari	3
Maserati	1
Agricultural & Construction Equipment	18
Trucks & Commercial Vehicles	13
FPT Powertrain	9
Components (Magneti	8
Production Systems	1
Metallurgical Products	1
Total	**100**

Selected Brands

Abarth
500
  Grande Punto
Alfa Romeo
  8C
147
159
  Brera
  GT
  MiTo
  Spider
Ferrari
  Eight Cylinder
    430 Scuderia
    F430 Spider
    Ferrari California
  12 Cylinder
    599 GTB Fiorano
    612 Scaglietti
    FXX
Fiat
500
600
  Bravo
  Grande Punto 3
  Multipla
  Nuova Croma
  Panda
  Punto Classic
  Qubo
  Sedici
  Ulysse
Lancia
  Delta
  Musa
  Phedra
  Thesis
  Ypsilon
Maserati
  Gran Turismo
  Gran Turismo S
  Quattroporte
  Quattroporte S
  Quattroporte Sport GT S

COMPETITORS

BMW
Daimler
Delphi Automotive Systems
Faurecia
Ford Motor
General Motors
Honda
Ingersoll-Rand
Isuzu
Kia Motors
Mazda
Meritor
Nissan
PROTON Holdings
Peugeot
Porsche
Renault
Saab Automobile
Suzuki Motor
Tata Motors
Toyota
Volkswagen

HISTORICAL FINANCIALS

Company Type: Public

Income Statement

FYE: December 31

	REVENUE ($ mil.)	NET INCOME ($ mil.)	NET PROFIT MARGIN	EMPLOYEES
12/12	110,659	458	0.4%	214,836
12/11	77,036	1,725	2.2%	197,021
12/10	48,020	695	1.4%	199,924
12/09	72,175	(1,207)	—	190,014
12/08	83,018	2,253	2.7%	198,348
Annual Growth	7.4%	(32.8%)	—	2.0%

2012 Year-End Financials

Debt ratio: 44.7%
Return on equity: 3.9%
Cash ($ mil.): 23,272
Current ratio: 4.57
Long-term debt ($ mil.): 36,759
No. of shares (mil.): 1,215
Dividends
  Yield: —
  Payout: —
Market value ($ mil.): 6,140

	STOCK PRICE ($) FY Close	P/E High	P/E Low	PER SHARE ($) Earnings	Dividends	Book Value
12/12	5.05	39	25	0.37	0.00	9.82
12/11	4.51	33	7	1.37	0.00	9.95
12/10	20.50	87	39	0.55	0.00	13.63
12/09	15.06	—	—	(0.98)	0.00	13.09
12/08	7.05	41	11	1.80	0.00	12.77
Annual Growth	(8.0%)	—	—	(32.4%)	—	(6.4%)

Finmeccanica S.p.A.

Italy's largest engineering and aerospace/defense group Finmeccanica makes helicopters military aircraft defense systems satellites and much more. The company operates through some 100 subsidiaries in Italy and elsewhere. While the aerospace and defense businesses account for more than 80% of sales all is not fight or flight. Finmeccanica's Ansaldo Energia subsidiary is an energy producer and also builds generation and transmission components turbines cogeneration plants and nuclear power plants. The company's transportation operations manufacture buses railway vehicles and trolleys as well as signaling and control systems.

The company operates through seven segments: Defense Electronics and Security Helicopters Aeronautics Transportation Defense Systems Space Energy and Other. Defense Electronics and Security operates through several units. The segment's New Jersey-based DRS Technologies is focused on infrared technology persistent surviellance battle management power technology satellite networks communications infrastructures and other technologies. Other units in the segment include SELEX Galileo (sensors defensive aids tracking targetting navigation simulation) SELEX Elsag (serving avionics logistics automation and other functions) and SELEX Sistemi Integrati (large systems for homeland security systems and radar sensors for air defense air traffic control).

The Helicopter segment works through AgustaWestland which boasts expertise in all aspects of helicopter production including avionics flight control and mission management systems. Aeronautics' main unit is Alenia Aermacchi a maker of unmanned aerial vehicles (UAVs) and aerostructures as well as military and civilian aircraft.

The Transportation segment includes Ansaldo STS which provides rail and metro signaling and traffic monitoring systems AnsaldoBreda (rail and metro rolling stock) and bus maker BredaMenarinbus. Defense Systems concentrates on missile systems torpedoes naval artillery and armored vehicles.

The Space segment offers satellite management through Telespazio and produces satellite systems through Thales Alenia Space. Both units are joint ventures with Thales. Besides Ansaldo Energia the Energy segment operates through FATA which constructs gas-turbine power plants. FATA EPC Powers works with Ansaldo Energia in turnkey projects.

Struggling with budget cuts in its client sectors of the military and security the company weathered a revenue decrease of 7% in 2011 compared with 2010. Finmeccanica also contended with a 22% drop in new orders in 2011 versus 2010. By segment Defense Electronics and Security's revenue fell 15% as a result in part of the conclusion of some US military programs.

Helicopters increased 7% thanks in part to a strong performance from product support which rose 18%. Challenged by a decline in the EFA and B787 programs Aeronautics decreased about 5%. Transportation went down 4% due in part to fewer orders for signalling after some Italian projects were completed and Libyan orders were stalled.

Defense Systems rose 1% on the back of strong business from the land sea and air weapons systems market while Space jumped 8% supported by demand in several markets including commercial and military telecommunications and orbital infrastructure. Struggling with lower orders for turbine parts and spare parts Energy plummeted 31%. The Other segment soared 26%.

Amid worldwide defense budget cuts Finmeccanica is looking to seek new markets for its defense technology capabilities. These include security environmental monitoring and protection cyber security and smart cities. By segment the company is looking to the civil aircraft market for growth in Aeronautics. The Space segment is also optimistic about growth in the civilian sector. While governments are cutting back on defense they continue to increase demand for satellite operations. And despite cuts in defense spending Finmeccanica expects that its defense operations will enjoy demand as emerging markets upgrade their fleets among other factors. The company's defense operations are also poised to meet more demand for lighter and more easily maneuverable land vehicles.

The company foresees demand from both the civilian and military markets for its Helicopter segment until 2015-2016 when new helicopter deliveries should stabilize. The company's defense and security operations are also focused on the civilian security market in the face of defense cuts. The Energy segment is counting on more demand for coal-fired plants in China and gas plants in the West. Transportation is positioned for more growth in the developing world especially Brazil and China.

Formerly run by the government-operated Istituto per la Ricostruzione Industriale Finmeccanica was privatized by a plan that called for the group's various businesses to form joint ventures with multiple international partners. (The Italian state continues to hold a 30% stake.)

HISTORY

Italian dictator Benito Mussolini created Istituto per la Ricostruzione Industriale SpA (IRI Institute for Industrial Reconstruction) in 1933 to rehabilitate and manage industrial enterprises that were controlled by banks which were themselves put under state control in the midst of Italy's banking crisis. The idea was to create a temporary state company to provide stability in the midst of an economic depression. As Mussolini tightened his grip on the country and Italy headed toward war the temporary intent of IRI dissolved.

In 1947 Finmeccanica was formed as a holding company for IRI's engineering firms but after WWII IRI became a safety net for faltering Italian businesses. Troubled Italian companies would appeal to be "IRI-ized" and brought into the IRI fold. Many appeals were granted and IRI grew into a lumbering badly run institution. Because of the transitory nature of the Italian government (more than 50 different postwar administrations) change in the institution was not forthcoming. By the 1960s IRI controlled about half of Italy's large companies. The oil woes of the 1970s and competition of the 1980s led more and more companies to plead for IRI-ization.

Finally in the early 1990s as Italy's debt grew well past the size of its economy and European countries began to unify the Italians began working toward privatizing many of Italy's government-run organizations.

EFIM another government-run holding company was declared insolvent in 1993. EFIM's assets included seven defense companies: Agusta SpA (helicopters); OTO Melara (missile systems army and naval weapons); Agusta Sistemi Agusta OMI Officine Galileo SpA (fire control systems electro-optics guidance systems); Breda Meccanica Bresciana SpA (anti-aircraft and anti-missile weapon mountings anti-tank weapons turrets); and SMA (radar systems displays). These assets were transferred to Finmeccanica.

Plans to sell Finmeccanica whole were shelved after a huge loss in 1997 and it was restructured into separate companies under a holding company.

In 1998 Finmeccanica and General Electric Company (GEC —later Marconi and now telent) formed Alenia Marconi Systems a radar air traffic management missile simulation and control systems joint venture. That year the company agreed to a joint military and communications satellite venture with Daimler Aerospace GEC and Lagardere. Finmeccanica formed an alliance with GKN Westland Helicopters in 1999 and entered talks with British Aerospace (now BAE SYSTEMS) which bought GEC's defense electronics businesses.

Talks between Finmeccanica's Alenia Aerospazio unit and Astrium (75% owned by EADS 25% by BAE) fell through in 2000. Alenia Aerospazio had been expected to join the consortium but reportedly balked at accepting a minority role in the venture. In 2001 after almost three years of negotiating the company announced the completion of a merger between its Agusta helicopter unit and GKN's Westland helicopter unit forming AgustaWestland. The next year Finmeccanica acquired Marconi Mobile (mobile communications) from Marconi and Telespazio SpA (satellite and space services) from Telecom Italia.

Finmeccanica bought out GKN's stake in helicopter joint venture AgustaWestland in 2004 for about $2 billion.

Early in 2008 Finmeccanica acquired SELEX Systems Integration (formerly VEGA Group PLC) of the UK. SELEX is a provider of engineering and technology consulting services in the areas of aerospace and defense simulation and training. SELEX is involved in a number of high-profile European aerospace and defense projects including the Eurofighter and Galileo (the European satellite navigation program).

Also in 2008 the company announced an agreement for several joint ventures with Russian manufacturer Russian Technologies. The two agreed to make carbon fiber components for the aerospace industry. Finmeccanica already had an agreement in place to assist Russian Railways with signaling safety and communications.

Additionally in 2008 the company acquired DRS Technologies a US-based military contractor for $5.2 billion including about $1.6 billion in assumed debt. Not only will the DRS purchase give Finmeccanica a greater presence in the US but it could potentially also act as a springboard for other US military contracts. Finmeccanica will also increase the scope of business it does with Lockheed Martin due to the working relationship DRS has with Lockheed Martin Missiles and Fire Control.

The company's Defense business got a boost in 2009 from a deal to supply the United Arab Emirates (UAE) air force with transonic trainer jet aircraft. In addition to 48 planes the contract won by Finmeccanica's subsidiary Alenia Aermacchi included a joint venture in the UAE that included a final assembly line. Later in 2009 Finmeccanica signed a contract for over $10 million to supply ground intelligence and surveillance system services to the US Army.

In 2011 Finmeccanica sold a 45% stake in Ansaldo Energia to US fund First Reserve Corp. The deal netted a E450 million ($624.2 million) capital gain for the Italian defense company and enabled it to preserve majority ownership and operating control.

EXECUTIVES

General Manager, Giorgio Zappa
CEO SELEX Communications, Giancarlo Grasso
Chairman and CEO, Pier Francesco Guarguaglini, age 76
Co-General Manager and CFO, Alessandro Pansa, age 51
VP Investor Relations, John D. Stewart
CEO AgustaWestland, Giuseppe Orsi
CEO Alenia Aeronautica, Giuseppe Giordo, age 49
Investor Relations Officer, Raffaella Luglini
CEO Thales Alenia Space, P. Seznec
Chief Executive Officer, L. Pasquali
CEO WASS, R. Lunardi
CEO MBDA, A. Bouvier
CEO and General Manager MBDA ITALIA, A. Perfetti
CEO Ansaldo STS, S. De Luca
Independent Chairman of the Board, Jean Lafleur
IR Contact Officer, Michael DAmico
Auditors: PricewaterhouseCoopersSpA

LOCATIONS

HQ: Finmeccanica S.p.A.
4 Piazza Monte Grappa, Rome I-00195
Phone: (39) 06 324 731 **Fax:** (39) 06 320 8621
Web: www.finmeccanica.com

2011 Sales

	% of total
Europe	
Italy	20
UK	12
Rest of	27
North	23
Rest of the	18
Total	**100**

PRODUCTS/OPERATIONS

2011 Sales

	% of total
Defense Electronics &	34
Helicopters	22
Aeronautics	15
Transportation	11
Defense	7
Space	5
Energy	5
Other	1
Total	**100**

Selected Products

Defense electronics
- Air traffic management
- Avionics
- Command and control systems
- Communications equipment
- Electronic systems
- Radar
- Simulators
- Unmanned aerial vehicles

Helicopters
- A109 Light Utility Helicopter
- A109 Power
- A119 Koala
- A129
- AW139
- BA609
- EH 101
- Grand Light Utility Helicopter
- NH90
- Super Lynx 300

Aeronautics
- Control surfaces
- Fuselage components
- Horizontal stabilizers
- Mechanical parts
- Winglet

Transportation
- Chopper and inverter drives
- Converters
- DC AC and multi-voltage locomotives
- DC and AC motors
- Electric multiple units
- High-speed trains
- Light and heavy metropolitan railways
- Trambuses
- Trolley buses

Defense systems
- Airborne and naval weaponry
- Armored vehicles
- Main battle tanks
- Missile systems
- Naval systems
- Weapons systems

Energy
- Boilers
- Cogeneration plants
- Combined cycle generators
- Geothermal generators
- Hydrogenerators
- Nuclear power plants
- Steam and gas turbines
- Turbogas generators

Space
- Modules
- Satellites

Selected Operations

Alenia Aermacchi
Alenia Aeronautica (aerospace)
SELEX Sistemi Integrati SpA (formerly Alenia Marconi Systems)
Ansaldo Energia (energy)
AgustaWestland (helicopters)
DRS Technologies (military data systems)
MBDA (25% with EADS and BAE SYSTEMS)

COMPETITORS

ABB	General Dynamics
Alliant Techsystems	Goodrich Corp.
Arianespace	Invensys
BAE SYSTEMS	Kaman
Beechcraft	Lockheed Martin
Bell Helicopter	Magellan Aerospace
Boeing	Northrop Grumman
Bombardier	Raytheon
DIRECTV	Robinson Helicopter
Daimler	Rockwell Automation
Elbit Systems	Schneider Electric
Embraer	Siemens AG
Eurocopter	Sikorsky
GE	

HISTORICAL FINANCIALS

Company Type: Public

Income Statement FYE: December 31

	REVENUE ($ mil.)	NET INCOME ($ mil.)	NET PROFIT MARGIN	EMPLOYEES
12/12	23,788	(1,091)	—	67,408
12/11	23,111	(3,033)	—	70,474
12/10	25,639	659	2.6%	75,197
12/09	27,594	942	3.4%	73,056
12/08	22,412	798	3.6%	73,398
Annual Growth	1.5%	—	—	(2.1%)

2012 Year-End Financials

Debt ratio: 26.6%
Return on equity: (-21.4%)
Cash ($ mil.): 2,816
Current ratio: 0.96
Long-term debt ($ mil.): 5,679
No. of shares (mil.): 578
Dividends
Yield: —
Payout: —
Market value ($ mil.): 1,648

	STOCK PRICE ($) FY Close	P/E High	P/E Low	PER SHARE ($) Earnings	Dividends	Book Value
12/12	2.85	—	—	(1.89)	0.00	7.75
12/11	1.78	—	—	(5.25)	0.35	9.62
12/10	5.70	19	9	1.14	0.17	15.79
12/09	7.95	18	9	1.63	0.19	15.86
12/08	6.10	8	8	1.81	0.00	14.46
Annual Growth	(17.3%)	—	—	—	—	(14.4%)

First Commercial Bank

First Commercial Bank makes it its business to lend a financial hand to growing businesses. Operating from a single location First Commercial offers commercial loans and deposit services to small and midsized businesses in the Minneapolis/St. Paul area. The bank targets the commercial real estate market often lending to projects involving multi-family residences small-scale shopping centers and office developments. First Commercial also serves other business markets and provides private banking lending and deposit services to high-net-worth individuals. Founded in 1999 the bank is headed by CEO Bradley K. Meier and is privately owned.

First Commercial's range of banking offerings includes standard deposit accounts and remote deposit-capture services.

LOCATIONS

HQ: First Commercial Bank
30, Chung-King S. Road, Sec. 1, Taipei 100-05
Phone: (886) 2 2348 1111 **Fax:** (886) 2 2361 0036
Web: www.firstbank.com.tw

PRODUCTS/OPERATIONS

HISTORICAL FINANCIALS

Company Type: Public

Income Statement FYE: December 31

	ASSETS ($ mil.)	NET INCOME ($ mil.)	INCOME AS % OF ASSETS	EMPLOYEES
12/12	71,316	357	0.5%	7,255
12/11	67,153	284	0.4%	7,279
12/10	68,812	217	0.3%	7,178
12/09	60,059	64	0.1%	7,094
12/08	53,870	273	0.5%	7,202
Annual Growth	7.3%	6.9%	—	0.2%

2012 Year-End Financials

Return on assets: 0.5%
Return on equity: 8.5%
Long-term debt ($ mil.): —
No. of shares (mil.): —
Sales ($ mil): 1,175
Dividends
Yield: —
Payout: —
Market value ($ mil.): —

Flextronics International Ltd.

Having factories on four continents would make you flexible too. Flextronics International offers turnkey manufacturing services to the world's leading electronics companies including Apple Cisco Ericsson HP Huawei Lenovo Microsoft BlackBerry and Xerox. The company's services range from design engineering through manufacturing and assembly to distribution and warehousing. It manufactures and assembles printed circuit boards electromechanical components subsystems and complete systems for a wide range of makers of networking and telecommunications equipment computers consumer electronics and medical instrumentation.

Flextronics has reorganized its market segments into four areas: high-reliability solutions (automotive aerospace and defense medical) high-velocity solutions (game consoles mobile handsets and smartphones printers enterprise PC manufacturing) industrial and emerging industries (clean technology including solar industrial semiconductor capital equipment) and integrated network solutions (connected home data networking servers and storage and telecommunications infrastructure equipment). The company has exited the original design manufacturing (ODM) personal computers business which generated $1.6 billion in sales and $113 million in losses. It continues to provide ODM products —where customers buy products designed and manufactured by Flextronics —in the automotive industrial infrastructure medical and power supply sectors among others.

Flextronics maintains facilities in more than 30 countries. Much of its manufacturing capacity is located in regions with lower labor costs including Brazil China Hungary India Malaysia Mexico Poland and Ukraine. China (38% of sales) and Mexico (14%) lead the way among Flextronics's manufacturing operations. Sales outside the US account for 90% of sales.

Overall sales were $29.4 billion in fiscal 2012 an increase of around 3% over 2011. Flextronics recorded growth across nearly all of its product groups as the company benefited from an improved global economy and more balanced portfolio of products. Net income was down 18% for the year due in part to an out-of-period adjustment to cost of sales (the errors were related to one of its foreign locations for fiscal periods 2009-2011) and a writedown of inventory related to one of its solar customers. While sales to customers in its high velocity solutions (HVS) market segment make up 40% of sales Flextronics is looking to further shift its product balance to non-HVS businesses with a target of 70% of sales coming from non-HVS businesses.

The majority of Flextronics' growth in fiscal 2012 was organic.The company mirrors its customers to align with changes in their marketing strategy and to take advantage of changes in outsourcing trends. Flextronics has also diversified its business across and within many different end markets in order to protect against shifts in demand and to expand the range of opportunities available in each market. Like many contract electronics manufacturers the company is increasingly offering more aftermarket supply chain services including product order fulfillment refurbishment repair recycling and warranty management.

Flextronics' continuous expansion has elevated it into the top ranks of the consolidating contract electronics manufacturing business. The company has to be able to expand capacity during periods of high demand while keeping costs low enough to maintain profitability in a low-margin industry. New facilities were opened during 2011 for the company's medical and logistics business operations. Flextronics Medical is a contract manufacturer for medical devices (customers include Insulet and Waters Corporation) and Flextronics Global Services offers post-manufacturing supply chain logistics. A medical equipment plant in Romania was expanded to better serve the emerging market of Eastern Europe. Flextronics Global Services added facilities in India and Turkey. The Indian facility provides repair services to a smartphone manufacturer and the Turkish facility is the new inbound distribution hub for a computer manufacturer. Also that year Flextronics and solar company SunPower joined together to open a small solar panel assembly plant in California.

In 2012 Flextronics acquired Stellar Microelectronics an EMS provider based in California that specializes in custom packaging services for the aerospace defense and medical manufacturing markets. The move is part of the company's plan to expand services in those markets which often have to meet specific regulations for product manufacturing. It also acquired Michigan-based EMS provider Saturn Electronics & Engineering that year. The following year in a move that underscores its commitment to expand its services to the healthcare market Flextronics acquired RIWISA a European provider of injection molding and other services for medical consumer and industrial applications.

Part of expanding is a willingness to part with assets that are not core to future growth. In 2012 Flextronics sold its Vista Point camera module business to DigitalOptics a subsidiary of Tessera Technologies. The sale included the brand intellectual property and China-based manufacturing assets. Flextronics retained part of Vista Point's assets but plans to use them to expand other manufacturing services.

HISTORY

Flextronics International formed in 1990 followed two earlier contract manufacturers named Flextronics formed in 1969 and 1980. The latter iteration used acquisitions to expand throughout Asia and the US. In 1988 it opened the first US-managed contract electronics plant in China and that year sales topped $200 million.

But acquisitions burdened Flextronics with debt and left it with disparate operations. It divested its US-based manufacturing operations and laid off 75% of its workforce. The company brought in a management team to sell its healthy Asian operations to pay off debt. These operations formed the current incarnation of Flextronics International.

A revitalized Flextronics based in Singapore went public in 1994. It quickly joined the industry rush toward consolidation and globalization. Acquisitions included nCHIP (California 1996) FICO Plastics (Hong Kong 1997) Neutronics Electronic Industries (Austria 1997) and Kyrel EMS Oyj (Finland and France 1999).

In 2000 Flextronics acquired rival The DII Group which propelled the company to the #4 spot in contract manufacturing (behind Solectron SCI Systems and Celestica). The company was also selected by Microsoft to build the software juggernaut's Xbox video game console. Later that year Motorola and Flextronics signed one of the largest outsourcing deals ever worth an estimated $30 billion over five years. The company expanded further in Asia when it acquired JIT Holdings a Singapore-based electronics manufacturer.

In 2001 Flextronics announced a deal with telecommunications giant Ericsson; under the pact Flextronics assumed management of Ericsson's mobile phone manufacturing operations worldwide. Later that year the company announced that it would cut its workforce by about 10% and that the multibillion-dollar deal with Motorola unraveled due to a continuing market slowdown. Flextronics also repurchased Motorola's 5% stake in the company.

Also that year Flextronics bought Telcom Global Solutions a supplier of planning and design services for telecommunications providers. Flextronics later announced a deal with Xerox to acquire Xerox facilities in Brazil Canada Malaysia and Mexico for about $220 million and to provide manufacturing services to Xerox for five years. Later that year the company laid off 10000 workers — about 15% of its staff –in a cost-cutting move. Flextronics also acquired a 91% stake in Orbiant a telephone network services spinoff of Swedish telecom giant Telia for $100 million in cash (along with future payments pegged to the unit's performance).

In 2002 the company made a deal with CASIO COMPUTER under which Flextronics bought two CASIO plants in Asia then supplied the Japanese electronics maker with finished products in a three-year pact. Also that year the company significantly expanded its presence in southern China with the purchase of Hong Kong-based NatSteel Broadway (printed circuit boards plastic and metal components) for about $367 million.

In 2004 Flextronics took over optical wireless and enterprise manufacturing as well as optical design operations from Nortel Networks in a four-year supply deal generating about $2.5 billion in annual revenues. Flextronics later closed several former Nortel facilities in Canada France and Northern Ireland.

Flextronics also acquired a majority ownership stake in India-based software services provider Hughes Software Systems (HSS) in 2004. The following year Flextronics purchased Agilent's mobile communications camera module business. The company sold its semiconductor division to AMIS Holdings (now part of ON Semiconductor) and its Flextronics Network Services division was merged with a company called Telavie and renamed Relacom; Flextronics retained a 30% stake.

Flextronics set plans in 2005 to build an industrial park in Chennai India to supplement its existing operations on the subcontinent where it previously employed more than 5000 people. The development added to the two manufacturing facilities and three design centers Flextronics had in India.

To focus on its core electronics manufacturing services business in 2006 Flextronics sold its Flextronics Software Systems business (renamed Aricent) to an affiliate of KKR for about $900 million in cash and notes. Flextronics retained a 15% equity interest in the software development business which was primarily based in India (it sold the remaining stake in 2009). Divestitures of its software and semiconductor businesses took a small chunk out of the company's revenues —$278 million in fiscal 2006.

Flextronics then acquired International DisplayWorks a contract manufacturer of small LCDs and LCD modules for cell phones and other consumer electronics for stock valued at approximately $243 million. International DisplayWorks became a wholly owned subsidiary of Flextronics operating within the company's Components Group. Also in 2006 nLight Corp. acquired the assets of Flextronics Photonics including a line of fiber-coupled and hybrid microelectronic devices.

In 2007 Flextronics purchased rival contract manufacturer Solectron in a deal valued at $3.6 billion. The combination vaulted the company into the position of the second-largest contract electronics manufacturer in the world trailing only Hon Hai Precision Industry the maker of products for Apple Dell and many other companies.

The next year it bought contract disposable device maker Avail Medical Products a private company with around $250 million in sales to further the expansion of its Flextronics Medical segment. Also in 2008 Flextronics inked a deal to acquire Elcoteq's ZAO Elcoteq subsidiary and plant in St. Petersburg Russia. Flextronics however later terminated the transaction and was forced to pay a fee for noncompletion.

In 2009 it sold its stake in Aricent a privately held communications software company to investment firms KKR and CPP Investment Board for about $250 million. The sale was part of a plan to sell noncore assets as Flextronics tried to bolster its balance sheet during the economic downturn. At the end of the year it bought SloMedical S.R.O. a leading maker of disposable medical devices for the European market. In addition to adding disposable devices for the medical and surgical market in Eastern Europe SloMedical (based in Slovenia) gave Flextronics an FDA-compliant clean room-enabled production site with low production costs.

In 2012 Flextronics acquired Stellar Microelectronics an EMS provider based in California that specializes in custom packaging services for the aerospace defense and medical manufacturing markets as part of a plan to expand services for the highly regulated markets. Also that year Flextronics sold its Vista Point camera module business to Tessera Technologies' subsidiary DigitalOptics; the sale included the brand intellectual property and China-based manufacturing assets.

EXECUTIVES

Chairman, H. Raymond Bingham, age 67
Executive Vice President; General Counsel, Jonathan S. (Jon) Hoak, age 63
Chief Executive Officer; Director, Michael M. (Mike) McNamara, age 56, $1,250,000 total compensation
Executive Vice President of Human Resources of Flextronic, Peter A. Stickler
CFO, Christopher (Chris) Collier, age 45, $375,000 total compensation
President Multek, Werner Widmann, age 61, $464,753 total compensation
Chief Financial Officer, Paul Read, age 48, $600,000 total compensation
President - Global Operations & Components, Francois Barbier, age 54, $499,838 total compensation
VP Investor Relations, Kevin Kessel
Chief Marketing Officer, Catherine Hernandez-Blades
SVP and CIO, David E. Smoley
Executive Vice President - Human Resources; President - High Reliability Solutions, Paul Humphries
Director, Willy C. Shih, age 61
Director, Daniel H. (Dan) Schulman, age 55
Director, James A. (Jim) Davidson
Director, William D. (Bill) Watkins, age 61
CEO and Director, Michael M. (Mike) McNamara, age 56
Director, Robert L. Edwards, age 57
Director, Lip-Bu Tan, age 53
Auditors: Deloitte&ToucheLLP

LOCATIONS

HQ: Flextronics International Ltd.
2 Changi South Lane, 486123
Phone: (65) 6876 9899
Web: www.flextronics.com

2012 Sales

	$ mil.	% of total
China	11,148	38
Mexico	4,005	14
US	3,006	10
Malaysia	2,869	10
Hungary	2,123	7
Other countries	6,234	21
Total	**29,387**	**100**

PRODUCTS/OPERATIONS

2012 Sales by Market

	$ mil.	% of total
High velocity solutions	11,645	40
Integrated network solutions	11,358	39
Industrial & emerging industries	3,989	13
High reliability solutions	2,394	8
Total	**29,387**	**100**

Selected Services

- Assembly and manufacturing
  - Box build (complete systems)
  - Complex electromechanical components
  - Printed circuit boards (PCBs)
  - Subsystems (including those that incorporate PCBs)
- Engineering
  - Design
  - Prototyping
  - Test development
- Materials procurement and management
  - Planning
  - Purchasing
  - Warehousing
- Network support
  - Installation and maintenance of telecommunications systems and corporate networks
- Packaging
- Plastic and metal components
- Product distribution
- Recycling and refurbishment
- Testing of PCBs subsystems and systems
- Warranty repair

COMPETITORS

ASUSTeK
Benchmark Electronics
Cal-Comp Electronics
Celestica
Changhong Electric
Compal Electronics
Fabrinet
Hana Microelectronics
Hon Hai
IBM Canada
Ingram Micro
Jabil
Kimball International
MiTAC
Nam Tai
Plexus
Quanta Computer
SYNNEX
Sanmina
TTM Technologies
Tech Data
Universal Scientific
Venture Corp.
Viasystems
WBL Corp.
Wistron

HISTORICAL FINANCIALS

Company Type: Public

Income Statement

FYE: March 31

	REVENUE ($ mil.)	NET INCOME ($ mil.)	NET PROFIT MARGIN	EMPLOYEES
03/13	23,569	277	1.2%	149,000
03/12	29,387	488	1.7%	159,000
03/11	28,679	596	2.1%	176,000
03/10	24,110	18	0.1%	165,000
03/09	30,948	(6,086)	—	160,000
Annual Growth	(6.6%)	—	—	(1.8%)

2013 Year-End Financials

Debt ratio: 19.5%	No. of shares (mil.): 638
Return on equity: 12.2%	Dividends
Cash ($ mil.): 1,587	Yield: —
Current ratio: 1.26	Payout: —
Long-term debt ($ mil.): 1,650	Market value ($ mil.): 4,319

	STOCK PRICE ($) FY Close	P/E High/Low	PER SHARE ($) Earnings	Dividends	Book Value
03/13	6.76	17 13	0.41	0.00	3.52
03/12	7.22	11 8	0.67	0.00	3.34
03/11	7.47	11 6	0.75	0.00	3.03
03/10	7.84	412145	0.02	0.00	2.44
03/09	2.89	— —	(7.41)	0.00	2.27
Annual Growth	23.7%	— —	—	—	11.6%

Fomento de Construcciones y Contratas, S.A.

The Spanish building giant with a flamboyant past Fomento de Construcciones y Contratas (FCC) is one of Spain's largest construction groups. Its many companies build and engineer the infrastructure of modern cities: highways airports dams harbors railways and oil and gas pipelines. It is also engaged in infrastructure maintenance water purification residential and commercial building and toll road and tunnel concessions. The group's largest segments are its construction environmental services water management renewable energy production and cement production businesses. Esther Koplowitz daughter of the group's founder controls FCC.

The company is active in more than 50 countries around the world and its international business accounts for about half of all sales. FCC has also sought to expand outside of its traditional markets including renewable energy.

A fixture in Spanish urban areas FCC is a market leader in municipal waste management services in Spain. It provides water and sewage services manages parking lots maintains highways manages bus lines disposes of industrial waste and handles airline cargo among other services. FCC-owned companies also make urban fixtures (bus shelters and signposts) and traffic signals.

The group operates cement production facilities in the US through subsidiary Cementos Portland Valderrivas of which it owns some 70%. Other holdings include stakes in Realia (real estate) and Versia (logistics urban furniture).

HISTORY

Fomento de Construcciones y Contratas (FCC) resulted from the 1992 merger of two top construction companies: Construcciones y Contratas (Conycon) founded in 1944 in Madrid and Fomento de Obras y Construcciones (FOCSA) formed in 1900 in Barcelona.

Conycon though younger controlled FOCSA at the time of the merger. Conycon's history is tied to Ernesto Koplowitz a Jew who escaped Nazi persecution in his native Poland. Madrid was still rebuilding after the Civil War so in 1944 Koplowitz borrowed money from a friend and founded a small building firm specializing in reconstruction. This became Conycon. In 1950 Koplowitz —who already had two out-of-wedlock children with Isabel Amores Herrera —married a wealthy marquess Esther Romero de Joseu y Armenteros and had two daughters Esther and Alicia. (Wife and mistress sat on Conycon's board of directors.)

In 1962 Koplowitz fell from a horse and died. He left one-third of Conycon to his oldest children Ernest and Isabel Clara a stake they later sold to their half-sisters who held the balance.

Family friend Ramon Areces ran Conycon moving it into department store development during the building boom of the 1960s. He also drew up the marriage contracts of the Koplowitz sisters: Alicia married Alberto Cortina a Spanish ambassador's son and Esther married the ambassador's cousin Alberto Alcocer. By the early 1980s the two cousins nicknamed "Los Albertos" were heading the company.

Conycon began buying up other firms including cement manufacturer Portland Valderrivas and in 1986 it acquired 47% of Catalonian rival FOCSA a major player in the waste disposal market. Los Albertos also diversified the company's holdings with the purchase of Banco Zaragazano. But the pair overreached when they tried to take over one of Spain's financial strongholds Banco Central in 1989.

Esther and Alicia divorced their husbands and took over the reins of Conycon in 1990. In 1992 they merged FOCSA and Conycon into FCC creating Spain's largest construction firm which began trading on the Madrid Stock Exchange in 1994. FCC sought growth opportunities throughout the decade taking on contracts that included building motorways in Canada and providing urban services in the UK. In 1996 it formed a venture with competitor Dragados y Construcciones to bid on international projects but in 1998 Dragados exited the deal.

Tired of publicity Alicia sold her 28% stake in FCC to Esther that year. In 1999 French conglomerate Vivendi got European Union permission to buy that stake from Esther who sold 28% to Vivendi Universal (which later transferred the shares to subsidiary Veolia Environnement (formerly Vivendi Environnement) in 2000 on the condition she would have the option to buy it back from Vivendi.

As part of the Xfera Consortium FCC was the first to be awarded a wireless license from the Spanish government that year. Also that year FCC announced plans to float its construction business which would mark the company's exit from construction services. Plans for the flotation were abandoned however the next year.

After sales of cement materials proved to be FCC's most profitable earner in 2001 FCC announced plans the next year to merge with its 48%-owned Portland Valderrivas unit by taking over the 52% it didn't already own through a share swap.

Also in 2002 Vivendi Universal indicated its intention to decrease its construction and utility holdings and reduce its stake in Veolia Environnement. Spanish newspapers reported that if Vivendi Universal reduced its stake Esther Koplowitz would exercise her option to buy back the 28% stake in Veolia Environnement owned in FCC. Ms. Koplowitz later resigned from Vivendi Universal's board and reportedly agreed to not exercise her option in Veolia Environnement.

Then in 2004 rival Acciona acquired a 15% stake in FCC with an eye on swallowing the entire firm. Koplowitz thwarted Acciona's plan by acquiring Veolia Environnement's controlling stake after all.

In 2005 FCC acquired logistics company Grupo Logistico Santos and folded it into its Versia subsidiary. The company acquired privately held Austrian builder Alpine Mayreder Bau for $604 million in 2006. The following year it bought Hydrocarbon Recovery Services and International Petroleum Corp. from Siemens Water Technologies. Those two deals made it one of the largest waste management companies in the US.

After its failed attempt to buy FCC Acciona sold its 15% stake in FCC real estate holding company Inmobiliaria Colonial in 2006. Two years later Inmobiliaria Colonial announced plans to sell its stake in the company.

EXECUTIVES

Director General Human Resources, Antonio Perez Colmenero
Chairman and Managing Director, Baldomero (Baldo) Falcones Jaquotot, age 64
Secretary, Francisco Vicent Chulia
Auditors: Deloitte

LOCATIONS

HQ: Fomento de Construcciones y Contratas, S.A. Federico Salmon, 13, Madrid 28016
Phone: (34) 91 343 7181
Web: www.fcc.es

PRODUCTS/OPERATIONS

2009 Sales

	% of total
Construction	57
Evironmental	28
Cement	8
Versia	6
Energy	1
Total	**100**

COMPETITORS

ACS
Abengoa
Abertis
Acciona
Aguas de Barcelona
Andrade Gutierrez
Autoroutes du Sud de la France
Balfour Beatty
Bechtel
Befesa
Bilfinger Berger
Black & Veatch
Bouygues
CEMEX Espa?a
Cintra
Colas
Corporacion GEO
Dragados
Duro Felguera
Elecnor
Empresas ICA
Ezentis
Ferrovial
Grupo San Jose
Hanson Limited
Holcim Canada
INYPSA
Impregilo
Italmobiliare
Itinere Infraestructuras
Mondragon Corporacion
OHL
Odebrecht
Sacyr Vallehermoso
Tecnicas Reunidas
VINCI

HISTORICAL FINANCIALS

Company Type: Public

Income Statement — FYE: December 31

	REVENUE ($ mil.)	NET INCOME ($ mil.)	NET PROFIT MARGIN	EMPLOYEES
12/12	15,363	(1,354)	—	85,959
12/11	15,690	140	0.9%	91,291
12/10	16,776	403	2.4%	92,293
12/09	18,882	442	2.3%	93,666
12/08	20,239	471	2.3%	93,863
Annual Growth	(6.7%)	—	—	(2.2%)

2012 Year-End Financials

Debt ratio: 63.0%
Return on equity: (-56.3%)
Cash ($ mil.): 1,537
Current ratio: 0.87
Long-term debt ($ mil.): 6,729
No. of shares (mil.): 127
Dividends
Yield: —
Payout: —
Market value ($ mil.): —

Fomento Economico Mexicano, S.A.B. de C.V.

From soda pop to shops FEMSA is quenching Mexico's thirsty throats. Fomento Economico Mexicano or FEMSA is a top soft drink bottler and convenience store operator in Latin America. Its Coca-Cola FEMSA subsidiary is the world's largest Coca-Cola bottler. FEMSA bottles Coca-Cola Sprite other soft drinks juices and water in nine Latin American countries. FEMSA also owns 9000 OXXO convenience stores in 31 Mexican states primarily in the northern part of the country through its FEMSA Comercio subsidiary. FEMSA was a major beer brewer in Mexico and Brazil as well through its former FEMSA Cerveza subsidiary. It brewed Carta Blanca Indio Sol and Tecate beer until the unit was sold to Heineken in 2010.

In early 2010 Heineken acquired FEMSA Cerveza for E3.8 billion (about $5.4 billion). The all-stock deal gave FEMSA a 20% stake in Heineken. As a result the company plans to borrow against the stake and use the money to make acquisitions for its Coca-Cola FEMSA unit as well as extend the reach of its OXXO convenience store chain.

In 2011 Coca-Cola FEMSA expanded into dairy products and made two other acquisition offers while FEMSA Comercio grew its number of OXXO stores to 9000. First Coca-Cola FEMSA bought Grupo Industrias Lacteas a Panamanian company that sells juice milk yogurt and ice cream under the brands De Oro Del Prado Estrella Azul Plamosa Vaquita and Vita Slim. Next it offered to buy Grupo Tampico for 6.55 billion pesos ($555 million) in stock and rival bottler Grupo CIMSA for 11 billion pesos ($825 million) in stock and debt. The CIMSA offer includes a 13.2% stake in sugar company Promotora Industrial Azucarera S.A. de C.V.

FEMSA Coca-Cola and all of the other Mexican and Brazilian Coke bottlers together own the Mexican juice company Jugos del Valle as a joint venture. FEMSA's ownership stake is approximately 20%. It also owns 83% of Brazilian brewer Cervejarias Kaiser.

Swayed by renewable energy FEMSA joined investment firm Macquarie Capital in purchasing a wind farm in southern Mexico for $89 million in early 2011. FEMSA owns 45% of the wind-power project and Macquarie owns the balance. The wind farm is equipped with more than 130 wind turbines that churn out 396 megawatts of power. FEMSA and its parent plan to use the power generated by the farm at its area operations for the next 20 years.

The company also operates a packaging subsidiary that produces coolers refrigeration equipment aluminum cans tops bottle caps glass bottles and other related materials.

The founding Garza family and a number of board members and their heirs belong to a trust that owns some 75% of FEMSA.

HISTORY

FEMSA's 2005 purchase of Panamerican Beverages (Panamco) through its Coca-Cola subsidiary gave the company access to markets in Brazil Colombia Costa Rica Guatemala Nicaragua Panama and Venezuela.

EXECUTIVES

CEO Coca-Cola FEMSA, Carlos Salazar Lomelin, age 62
VP Corporate Development, Federico Reyes Garcia, age 68
CEO FEMSA Comercio, Eduardo Padilla Silva, age 56
VP Administration and Corporate Control, Jose Gonzalez Ornelas, age 62
EVP Human Resources Procurement and IT, Alfonso Garza Garza, age 51
Director Corporate Affairs, Genaro Borrego Estrada, age 64
Chairman and CEO, Jose Antonio Fernandez Carbajal
Corporate VP, Javier Gerardo Astaburuaga Sanjines
General Vice President of Corporate Affairs, Genaro Estrada
Chief Accounting Officer, Jos Ornelas
Director, Lorenzo H. Zambrano, age 69
Director, Roberto Servitje, age 84
Director, Robert E. Denham, age 67
Director, Helmut Paul, age 72
Director, Consuelo Garza de Garza, age 82
Director, Jose Manuel Canal Hernando, age 71
Director, Armando Garza Sada, age 54
Director, Alexis E. Rovzar de la Torre, age 61
Director, Jose Fernando Calderon Rojas, age 57
Director, Max Michel Suberville, age 79
Director, Alberto Bailleres, age 80
Director, Francisco Javier Fernandez Carbajal, age 56
Director, Ricardo Guajardo Touche, age 63
Director, Alfredo Livas Cantu, age 60
Director, Carlos Salguero, age 82
Director, Paulina Garza de Marroquin, age 40
Director, Barbara Garza Laguera Gonda, age 52
Director, Eva Garza Laguera Gonda, age 54
Director, Mariana Garza Laguera Gonda, age 42
Auditors: ManceraS.C.

LOCATIONS

HQ: Fomento Economico Mexicano, S.A.B. de C.V.
General Anaya 601 Poniente, Colonia Bella Vista, Monterrey, Nuevo Leon 64410
Phone: (52) 81 8328 6000 **Fax:** (52) 81 8328 6080
Web: www.femsa.com

COMPETITORS

Andina
Arca Continental
Danone Water
Dr Pepper Snapple Group
Embotelladoras Unidas
Empresas Polar
Nestle Waters
Pepsi Amercias Beverages

HISTORICAL FINANCIALS

Company Type: Public

Income Statement FYE: December 31

	REVENUE ($ mil.)	NET INCOME ($ mil.)	NET PROFIT MARGIN	EMPLOYEES
12/12	18,340	1,593	8.7%	182,260
12/11	14,427	1,097	7.6%	177,470
12/10	13,688	3,246	23.7%	153,809
12/09	15,050	756	5.0%	127,179
12/08	12,126	484	4.0%	122,981
Annual Growth	10.9%	34.7%	—	10.3%

2012 Year-End Financials

Debt ratio: 0.9%
Return on equity: 13.7%
Cash ($ mil.): 2,810
Current ratio: 1.56
Long-term debt ($ mil.): 2,204
No. of shares (mil.): —
Dividends
Yield: 1.3%
Payout: 775.4%
Market value ($ mil.): —

	STOCK PRICE ($) FY Close	P/E High/Low		PER SHARE ($) Earnings	Dividends	Book Value
12/12	100.70	0	0	0.18	1.40	0.67
12/11	69.71	0	0	0.12	0.01	0.58
12/10	55.92	—	—	0.00	0.62	0.53
12/09	47.88	—	—	0.08	0.36	0.35
12/08	30.13	—	—	0.05	0.46	0.28
Annual Growth	35.2%	—	—	34.8%	32.1%	24.5%

Formosa Petrochemical Corp

Formosa Petrochemical Corporation (FPCC) is second only to Chinese Petroleum Corporation for oil refining in Taiwan. The company produces refined petroleum products (jet fuel liquid petroleum gas and gasoline) and petrochemicals (ethylene propylene and butadiene) from its naphtha cracking operations. It owns gas stations through subsidiary Formosa Oil. FPCC also sells electricity and steam from its co-generation plants. Its engineering and maintenance divisions carry out planning construction and daily maintenance services on behalf of group companies.

Geographic Segment

FPCC sells its products worldwide. In 2011 Taiwan accounted for 58% of the company's revenues.

Sales and Marketing

In 2011 Formosa Chemicals & Fibers accounted for 19% of sales; Formosa Plastics 13%.

Financial Performance

FPCC's revenues increased by 7% in 2011 and its net income decreased by 45%.

Strategy

In 2011 the company restarted its 700000 tons-per-year No. 1 naphtha cracker after a four-month shutdown due to a fire.

Ownership

Formosa Plastics owns 29% of FPCC; affiliates Formosa Chemicals & Fibers and Nan Ya Plastics also own 25% and 24% respectively.

Company Background

The three group companies formed FPCC in 1992 to build and run a giant integrated petrochemicals facility called the No. 6 Naphtha Cracking Project.

EXECUTIVES

Executive Director, Wilfred Wang
Senior Vice President Hang, C. Y. Su
SVP and Director, Han-Ting Chen
Vice President President's Office, Keh-Yen Lin
Chief Financial Officer, Ming-Hsiung Shih
Vice President of Engineering, Ja-Tao Huang
Vice President of Maintenance, Tsai-Shan Kao
Chairman, Chen Bao-Lang
SVP and Director, Han-Ting Chen
Director, Chi-Tong Lo
Director, C. P. Chang
Auditors: DiwanErnst&Young

LOCATIONS

HQ: Formosa Petrochemical Corp
1-1, Formosa Plastics Group Industrial Zone, Mailiao, Yunlin
Phone: (886) 5 6812345
Web: www.fpcc.com.tw

2011 Sales

	% of total
Taiwan	58
Singapore	8
China	3
Korea	1
Other	30
Total	**100**

PRODUCTS/OPERATIONS

2011 Sales

	% of total
Petrochemical	29
Diesel	25
Gasoline	15
Jet	6
Electricity	3
Steam	2
Other petrochemical	20
Total	**100**

COMPETITORS

BASF-YPC
CPC
ExxonMobil Chemical
OCI Company
Total Petrochemicals

HISTORICAL FINANCIALS

Company Type: Public

Income Statement FYE: December 31

	REVENUE ($ mil.)	NET INCOME ($ mil.)	NET PROFIT MARGIN	EMPLOYEES
12/12	30,818	93	0.3%	6,507
12/11	26,405	742	2.8%	6,426
12/10	25,736	1,406	5.5%	5,604
12/09	19,867	1,225	6.2%	6,275
12/08	26,763	463	1.7%	6,027
Annual Growth	3.6%	(32.9%)	—	1.9%

2012 Year-End Financials

Debt ratio: 1.4%
Return on equity: 1.2%
Cash ($ mil.): 728
Current ratio: 2.49
Long-term debt ($ mil.): 5,416
No. of shares (mil.): —
Dividends
Yield: —
Payout: —
Market value ($ mil.): —

Fresenius SE & Co KGaA

Fresenius SE takes a free hand with dialysis and infusion products and services. The company offers a wide range of health products and services through its four core business segments: Fresenius Medical Care Fresenius Kabi Fresenius Helios and Fresenius Vamed. The company's Medical Care division specializes in treating chronic kidney failure at some 2800 dialysis clinics worldwide. Fresenius Kabi provides nutrition infusion and IV therapies and related equipment. Fresenius Helios operates private hospitals in Germany while Fresenius Vamed offers facility management project development and other services to hospitals and health facilities. Fresenius SE has operations in about 100 countries.

The company has been aggressively expanding its core operating segments through both organic growth and acquisitions. Its majority owned Fresenius Medical Care subsidiary which accounts for 60% of the firm's revenues has expanded its dialysis service and its equipment manufacturing operations through acquisitions. Though Fresenius Medical Care primarily grows through purchases of single clinics or small dialysis groups it occasionally makes larger acquisitions. For instance in 2010 the business acquired Asia Renal Care which operates about 100 clinics throughout Asia. It also added 70 European clinics in 2011 by purchasing International Dialysis Centers (IDC) and it acquired some 260 clinics in the US through the 2012 purchase of Liberty Dialysis (including the Renal Advantage unit). The division is also widening its operations in the fields of home dialysis and renal pharmaceuticals.

Fresenius has also expanded Fresenius Kabi's operations through a number of acquisitions in recent years. In 2012 for instance Kabi agreed to purchase Fenwal a developer and manufacturer of blood collection separation and transfusion technologies for some $1.1 billion. In addition Fresenius Kabi is working to expand in the generic injectables market by developing and releasing new IV pharmaceutical products and expanding distribution of existing drugs both in the US and international markets. Kabi is also working to increase its offerings of infusion and nutrition equipment such as feeding tubes and drug delivery pumps.

In the acute care business Fresenius Helios is an operator of about 60 hospitals while Fresenius Vamed provides hospitals with engineering equipment planning and other upkeep-related services. Helios is seeking to increase brand recognition and add more facilities as Germany's hospitals become increasingly privatized while Vamed is focused on growth of engineering and other specialty services.

In a move that would have created the largest private hospital operator in Germany in 2012 Fresenius made a voluntary public takeover offer of E3.1 billion ($3.9 billion) for hospital firm Rhon-Klinikum with the intention of merging it with its Helios unit. However Fresenius dropped its efforts later that year after two competitors purchased minority stakes in Rhon-Klinikum to prevent Fresenius from gaining majority control. The deal would have added more than 50 hospitals to the Helios network.

This action followed steps taken in 2011 when the Helios unit expanded its hospital network by acquiring a majority stake in the Damp Hospital Group in northern Germany. The purchase added seven acute care hospitals and four rehabilitation hospitals with a total of more than 4100 beds to the Helios network. A maximum care hospital in Duisburg was also added to the regional network that year.

Outside of its four core operating divisions Fresenius SE provides healthcare information technology services and solutions through its Fresenius Netcare subsidiary. The company also develops and markets drugs to treat various cancers and suppress immune functions for organ transplants through its Fresenius Biotech unit.

HISTORY

Fresenius was founded as the Hirsch Pharmacy in 1462. The Fresenius family took over its ownership in the 18th century and converted it into a pharmaceutical manufacturing entity in 1912.

Fresenius entered the dialysis equipment market in 1966. The company formed its Fresenius Medical Care unit in 1996 when it merged its dialysis systems division with National Medical Care (NMC).

In 1999 Fresenius formed its Fresenius Kabi division by combining its infusion pharmaceutical operations with the former infusion solution business of drugmaker Pharmacia & Upjohn which it acquired the previous year.

The company conducted a number of expansion efforts within the Kabi division in the following decade including the 2007 purchase of IV drug manufacturing firms Labesfal (Portugal) and Filaxis (Argentina) as well as German medical device maker Clinico. Also that year the company bought the artificial colloid product business of Kyorin to build up a presence in the Tokyo market.

It then purchased Indian oncology drug manufacturer Dabur Pharma in 2008. Also that year the unit expanded its reach in the US market for injectable drugs by acquiring US generics maker APP Pharmaceuticals for $3.7 billion plus debt.

Following the acquisition of German private clinic operator Helios Kliniken Fresenius refreshed its acute care operations by separating its hospital division (Fresenius ProServe) into two business segments Fresenius Helios and Fresenius Vamed in 2008.

EXECUTIVES

Deputy Chairman, Gerhard Rupprecht, age 65
CEO Fresenius Medical Care, Ben J. Lipps, age 73
SVP Investor Relations, Birgit Grund
Chairman Managing Board, Ulf M. (Mark) Schneider, age 48
CEO Fresenius Kabi, Rainer Baule, age 65
Chairman, Dieter Schenk, age 61
SVP Corporate Communications and Public Affairs, Joachim Weith
CFO, Stephan Sturm, age 50
CEO Fresenius Helios, Francesco De Meo, age 50
CEO Fresenius Vamed, Ernst Wastler, age 54
Director of Corporate Communications, Matthias Link
Vice President Investor Relations, Leslie Iltgen
Member of the Management Board; CEO Fresenius Helios, Francesco Meo
Chief Legal and Compliance Officer; Labor Relations Director; Member of the Management Board, Juergen Goetz
Deputy Chairman of the Supervisory Board; Employee Representative, Niko Stumpfoegger
Deputy Chairman, Gerhard Rupprecht, age 65
Director, Gerhard Roggemann
Director, Klaus-Peter Muller
Deputy Chairman, Niko Stumpfogger
Director, H. C. Roland Berger
Director, Dario Ilossi
Director, Konrad Kolbl
Director, Stefan Schubert
Director, Rainer Stein
Director, D. Michael Albrecht
Director, Dieter Reu?
Member of the Supervisory Board, Dieter Reuss
Member of the Supervisory Board, Klaus-Peter Mueller
Member of the Supervisory Board, Konrad Koelbl
Auditors: KPMGDeutscheTreuhand-GesellschaftAG

LOCATIONS

HQ: Fresenius SE & Co KGaA
Else-Kroener-Strasse 1, Bad Homburg D-61352
Phone: (49) 6172 608 0 **Fax:** (49) 6172 608 2488
Web: www.fresenius.com

2009 Sales

	% of total
North	43
Europe	42
Asia	8
Latin America & other	7
Total	**100**

PRODUCTS/OPERATIONS

2009 Sales

	% of total
Fresenius Medical Care	57
Fresenius Helios	17
Total	**100**

Selected Services

Fresenius Medical Care
- Dialysis facility operation
- Disease management
- Disposable dialysis supplies
- Hemodialysis equipment
- Peritoneal dialysis equipment

Fresenius Kabi
- Blood volume replacement
- Enteral nutrition
- Infusion and IV devices
- Infusion therapies
- IV generic drugs
- Parenteral nutrition
- Tranfusion products

Fresenius Helios
- HELIOS Kliniken Group (61 private hospitals Germany)

Fresenius Vamed
- Construction management
- Facility planning
- Maintenance services
- Operational management
- Project development
- Staff recruitment and training

COMPETITORS

Asahi Kasei
B. Braun Melsungen
Baxter International
Becton Dickinson
Ben Venue
Bio-Reference Labs
DaVita
Dialysis Clinic Inc
Hospira
Johnson & Johnson
NxStage
Ranbaxy Laboratories
Renal Advantage
Terumo
Teva

HISTORICAL FINANCIALS

Company Type: Public

Income Statement

FYE: December 31

	REVENUE ($ mil.)	NET INCOME ($ mil.)	NET PROFIT MARGIN	EMPLOYEES
12/12	25,425	1,220	4.8%	169,324
12/11	21,370	892	4.2%	149,351
12/10	21,376	832	3.9%	127,552
12/09	20,404	711	3.5%	130,510
12/08	17,246	377	2.2%	118,668
Annual Growth	10.2%	34.1%	—	9.3%

2012 Year-End Financials

Debt ratio: 47.3%
Return on equity: 14.3%
Cash ($ mil.): 1,166
Current ratio: 1.56
Long-term debt ($ mil.): 13,575
No. of shares (mil.): 178
Dividends
Yield: 0.6%
Payout: 17.9%
Market value ($ mil.): 2,566

	STOCK PRICE ($) FY Close	P/E High	P/E Low	PER SHARE ($) Earnings	Dividends	Book Value
12/12	14.40	5	3	6.97	0.10	56.46
12/11	11.70	5	5	5.41	0.00	47.31
Annual Growth	23.1%	—	—	6.6%	—	4.5%

Fuji Heavy Industries, Ltd.

Fuji Heavy Industries (FHI) is the parent of Subaru of America the automotive company known for its all-wheel-drive (AWD) technology found in cross-over vehicles (a sedan drive with SUV looks) such as the Forester and Outback and in the Impreza Legacy and Tribeca models. Through some 70 subsidiaries FHI has manufacturing operations in China Japan Taiwan and the US where it operates through Subaru of America. Other FHI businesses include Aerospace (aircraft and structural components) Industrial Products (general-purpose engines) and Eco Technologies (sanitation trucks and wind power systems). However automobiles account for more than 90% of sales.

The company had been recovering nicely from the economic crisis that saw sales drop in 2009 until the devastating earthquake struck Japan in March 2011. Sales were back up and FHI returned to profitability in fiscal 2010 and 2011 after instituting a management plan whereby directors gave up bonuses and compensation with other senior management accepting 10% reductions. The company cut shifts and redundant jobs at Japan plants and reduced its car output by tens of thousands of units. Instead of building a new plant for the Subaru BRZ sports car (jointly developed with Toyota) FHI used an existing plant. Subaru also decided in 2011 to stop making minicars (called kei cars) which were only sold in Japan.

With production in Japan shut down for a month because of the earthquake FHI was well aware that it needs to focus on overseas sales specifically in China and the US in order to grow. Overall the company sold about 657000 Subarus in fiscal 2011 up 17% from 563000 in 2010. And for the first time overseas sales accounted for the majority (61%) of revenue in 2011. In the US its top market FHI sold 279000 vehicles up from 227000 in 2010 from the country's 620 dealerships. Japan is the company's second-largest market and in China its third-largest market FHI sold 62000 cars up from 49000 in 2010. The company plans to open 250 dealerships in China by 2015. It also entered into the Korean market in 2010 with an initial sales goal of 600 Forester Legacy and Outback models and signed an agreement in mid-2011 with Tan Chong to produce and distribute Subarus in Malaysia.

The company continues to develop and refine its AWD technology focusing on new technology like the Boxer diesel engine which runs cleaner and with less vibration. The Boxer made its debut in the Impreza and Forester which were launched in 2009 and the Subaru XV crossover vehicle still in its conceptual phase. Additionally FHI is developing a clean diesel engine to hit the market in 2011 as well as a gasoline-electric hybrid model for release in 2012. The company's electric Stella came out in Japan in 2009 but is limited to corporate users. In preparation for a broader line of electric vehicles FHI allied with Nissan Mitsubishi Motors and Tokyo Electric Power to develop rapid rechargers for electric vehicles.

The company has entered into an alliance with Toyota and Daihatsu to strengthen the companies' competitiveness through shared technology R&D and product supply. Toyota doubled its stake in Subaru to over 16% improving the capital on hand for Subaru in return for taking advantage of some of Subaru's engineering. Toyota builds Camrys at Subaru's US plant in Indiana and together the two are developing and marketing the Subaru BRZ a compact rear-wheel-drive sports car which is expected to be released in 2012.

Fuji Industrial Products holds a large share in the global general-purpose engine market with more than 2000 models one of which is the Robin engine which is sold in more than 70 countries. Fuji's Eco Technologies supplies vehicles (Fuji Mighty sanitation truck) used to collect and transport waste products as well as wind-power systems. Its Clean Robot division was the first to commercialize floor-cleaning robots for high-rise buildings.

Fuji Aerospace manufactures main wings and other structural aircraft components. It is the primary contractor of the AH-64D combat helicopter to the Japan Defense Agency (JDA). Fuji Aerospace also supplies JDA with fixed-wing aircraft and primary trainers and manufactures components for Boeing aircraft (767/777); its center wing box is part of the Boeing 787 Dreamliner. Other technology includes unmanned aircraft and development of a Fuji Aerial Robot (FABOT) system that uses GPS navigation and handles takeoffs and landings by small fixed-wing aircraft.

HISTORY

Chikuhei Nakajima started the Aircraft Research Laboratory north of Tokyo in 1917 renaming it the Nakajima Aircraft Company in 1931. Amid the ashes of WWII Nakajima formed Fuji Sangyo to make products with aircraft technology in 1945. His motor scooters used bomber tail wheels and he later added buses with unibody frames. Nakajima died in 1949.

Fuji Sangyo joined four other firms in 1953 and Fuji Heavy Industries was born. The Subaru car division debuted in 1958 and FHI went public two years later. The firm expanded product lines throughout the 1960s and in 1968 Nissan Motor invested in FHI. The relationship lasted more than 30 years.

Subaru expanded to the US in 1968 with the help of furniture retailer Harvey Lamm. Lamm visiting Japan saw Subaru's utilitarian front-wheel-drive station wagon and recognized its potential. He convinced FHI to make him its US importer and he set up Subaru of America. Lamm ultimately became chairman and CEO of the US subsidiary.

In 1975 FHI exported the four-wheel-drive Subaru GF to the US; it was the country's first four-wheel-drive car for the mass market. High energy prices and the appeal of a four-wheel-drive car drove sales in the 1970s and early 1980s. By 1986 Subaru achieved 12 straight years of record sales and profits.

The next year however a rising yen boosted Japanese car prices and sales dips fueled round after round of incentives. Profits tanked and Subaru responded by expanding trim levels and power train choices. The misstep confused shoppers and sales nose-dived.

Also in 1987 FHI and Isuzu teamed up to build an assembly plant (Subaru-Isuzu Automotive) in Indiana while other makers introduced minivans and sport utility vehicles. Focusing on cars Subaru missed the start of the SUV boom. Even the arrival of the Legacy in 1989 failed to jumpstart sales. Lamm left Subaru in 1990 and two years later Subaru's US arm posted a record loss of $250 million.

Veteran CFO George Muller took over as president and COO of Subaru of America in 1993. Saddled with inventory plummeting sales and a poor brand image he promptly launched one of the greatest turnarounds in US automotive history.

Muller refined the niche Lamm carved out in the 1970s. He cut every product from the lineup that lacked all-wheel-drive. Enlisting the Legacy a car-SUV hybrid (Outback) was created in 1995 by lifting the body a few inches and adding beefy-looking body attachments.

Muller took aggressive steps at the corporate level to cut costs and build a culture of risk-taking initiative and speed. By 1999 profits were back to record levels. In Japan though trouble at parent FHI overshadowed Subaru's rejuvenation.

In 1998 revelations surfaced that FHI bribed legislator Yojiro Nakajima (a former official in Japan's defense agency and grandson of Chikuhei) to secure government contracts for a sea rescue aircraft. FHI had also illegally funneled cash to Nakajima to help his 1996 election bid. Nakajima along with FHI's chairman and several former executives was arrested. He later committed suicide and FHI was barred from bidding on defense contracts for one year.

GM bought 20% of FHI for $1.5 billion in 1999. The deal included the 4% held by FHI's largest investor Nissan. GM won access to FHI's all-wheel-drive technology and provided FHI resources to develop more-efficient fuel systems. Midway through 2000 Muller resigned from Subaru.

FHI struck a deal with Airbus in 2001 develop the company's new Airbus A380 airliner. Subaru and GM also unveiled plans to jointly produce an all-wheel-drive sport wagon to be built at the Subaru-Isuzu plant in the US.

FHI announced in 2002 that it would cease production of bus bodies and railway cars by March 2003. Later that year FHI bought Isuzu Motors' 49% stake in the companies' carmaking joint venture Subaru-Isuzu Automotive. FHI renamed the company Subaru of Indiana Automotive.

That same year FHI implemented sweeping changes in an effort to focus on its core business —building cars. The Fuji Dynamic Revolution-1 plan (FDR-1) aimed to increase sales by 35% by 2007 and to remake Subaru as a luxury brand. Part of the original plan was for the company to leverage its relationship with GM to reduce procurement and purchasing costs. GM however decided largely to terminate its relationship with FHI and has sold its 20% stake in the Japanese manufacturer about 9% of it going to Toyota Motor. It sold the remaining 11% through Fuji's open-market share-buyback program and through regular market sales.

In the first product tie-up since Toyota became FHI's largest shareholder the two companies announced in early 2006 that Toyota Camrys would be built at FHI's Subaru of Indiana plant. That production began the following year.

In 2006 FHI made a few adjustments to its FDR-1 plan. The company restructured its sales networks and layed off about 700 workers to meet its cost reduction goals. The notion of transforming into a luxury brand however was deemed to be infeasible from a cost standpoint. FDR-1's successes were mixed. FHI managed to increase sales but profits were hurt by poor sales at home in Japan and meager sales of higher-end Subaru models in the US which were likely slowed by high fuel prices.

In 2007 FHI established its Overseas Sales and Marketing Divisions I & II. The first overseas division is dedicated to centralizing control of manufacturing and sales activities in the US. The move aimed to bring refinement and sophistication to the Subaru brand in the US while capitalizing on its reputation of offering affordable compelling AWD vehicles.

EXECUTIVES

SEVP and Representative Director, Hiroshi Komatsu
EVP and Director, Hiroyuki Oikawa
Chairman and CEO, Ikuo Mori
EVP and Director, Jun Kondo
EVP and Director, Kazushige Okuhara
EVP and Director, Masatsugu Nagato
SVP, Yoshio Hasunuma
SVP, Naoto Muto
President COO and Director, Yasuyuki Yoshinaga
SVP, Tamaki Kamogawa
VP, Masakazu Kimura
SVP, Akira Mabuchi
SVP, Tomohiko Ikeda
VP, Takeshi Tachimori
SVP, Hisashi Nagano
SVP and CFO, Mitsuru Takahashi
VP, Motokiyo Nomura
SVP, Motohisa Miyawaki
VP, Masahiro Kasai
VP, Naoto Arai
VP, Yasuo Ueno
VP, Hidetoshi Kobayashi
VP, Yoshio Hirakawa
VP, Ryoichi Shimokawa
VP, Tatsuhiko Mukawa
VP, Yasuo Kosakai
Senior Managing Executive Officer; Chief Director of 2nd Subaru Overseas Sales, Mitsuru Takada
Senior Managing Executive Officer; Director of Business Planning, Shuzo Haimoto
Executive Officer, Tsuyoshi Tsuyoshi Nakai Nakai
Executive Officer; Chief Director of Subaru Cost Planning Management, Yasunobu Nogai
Executive Officer; President of Subsidiary, Masaki Ohkawara
Executive Officer; Chief Director of Subaru Domestic Sales, Masami Iida
SEVP and Representative Director, Hiroshi Komatsu
EVP and Director, Hiroyuki Oikawa
EVP and Director, Jun Kondo
EVP and Director, Kazushige Okuhara
EVP and Director, Masatsugu Nagato
President COO and Director, Yasuyuki Yoshinaga
Auditors: KPMGAZSA&Co.

LOCATIONS

HQ: Fuji Heavy Industries, Ltd.
1-7-2 Nishi-Shinjuku, Shinjuku-ku, Tokyo 160-8316
Phone: (81) 3 3347 2005 **Fax:** (81) 3 3347 2295
Web: www.fhi.co.jp

2011 Sales

	% of total
Japan	30
North	46
Other	9
Europe	8
Rest of	7
Total	**100**

2011 Sales by Unit

	% of total
US	278,959
Japan	158,105
China	62,412
Europe	48,244
Australia	41,150
Canada	28,059
Russia	11,320
Other	28,715
Total	**656,964**

PRODUCTS/OPERATIONS

2011 Sales

	% of total
Automobiles	91
Aerospace	5
Industrial	2
Other	2
Total	**100**

2011 Sales by Unit

	% of total
Legacy	248,061
Forester	189,138
Impreza	107,250
Minicars	89,971
OEM	8,295
Exiga	7,859
Tribeca	5,643
Other	747
Total	**656,964**

Selected Products and Divisions

Aerospace
- AH-64D combat helicopter
- Center-wing section (Boeing B-777)
- Design and training simulators
- Fixed-wing aircraft
- T-1 Trainer
- Unmanned aircraft

Automobiles
- Dex
- Dias Wagon
- Exiga
- Forester
- Impreza (wagon sedan)
- Legacy (touring B4 Outback)
- Outback (sport wagon sedan)
- Sambar (van truck wagon)
- Stella (R1 R2 Pleo)
- Tribeca

Eco Technologies
- Clean Robot floor-cleaning system
- Intermediate refuse collection systems
- Maintenance and sanitation vehicles
- Refuse management systems
- Special purpose vehicles
- Sweepers and scrubbers
- Wind-power systems

Industrial Products
- Agricultural machinery
- Construction machinery
- Forestry machinery
- General-purpose engines (Robin)
- Other machine tools and their components

Selected Subsidiaries:

Fuji Heavy Industries U.S.A. Inc.
Fuji Machinery Co. Ltd. (Japan)
Subaru Canada Inc.
Subaru of China Ltd.
Subaru Europe N.V./S.A. (Belgium)
Subaru of America Inc. (US)
Subaru of Indiana Automotive Inc.

COMPETITORS

Chrysler
Daimler
Ford Motor
General Motors
Honda
Kawasaki Heavy Industries
MPM Technologies
Mazda
Mitsubishi Heavy Industries
Mitsubishi Motors
Nissan
Sumitomo Heavy Industries
Suzuki Motor
Toyota
Volvo Trucks

HISTORICAL FINANCIALS

Company Type: Public

Income Statement

FYE: March 31

	REVENUE ($ mil.)	NET INCOME ($ mil.)	NET PROFIT MARGIN	EMPLOYEES
03/13	20,330	1,270	6.3%	27,509
03/12	18,494	468	2.5%	27,123
03/11	19,087	607	3.2%	27,296
03/10	15,295	(176)	—	27,586
03/09	14,681	(710)	—	27,659
Annual Growth	8.5%	—	—	(0.1%)

2013 Year-End Financials

Debt ratio: 0.2%
Return on equity: 22.8%
Cash ($ mil.): 3,030
Current ratio: 1.44
Long-term debt ($ mil.): 2,137
No. of shares (mil.): 780
Dividends
Yield: —
Payout: —
Market value ($ mil.): 24,708

	STOCK PRICE ($) FY Close	P/E High/Low	PER SHARE ($) Earnings	Dividends	Book Value
03/13	31.66	— —	1.63	0.00	8.13
03/12	16.18	— —	0.60	0.00	7.05
03/11	64.74	— —	0.78	0.54	6.41
03/10	51.55	— —	(0.23)	0.00	5.25
03/09	33.15	— —	(0.93)	0.47	5.14
Annual Growth	(1.1%)	— —	—	—	12.1%

FUJIFILM Holdings Corp

FUJIFILM doesn't focus only on the negatives. Its imaging solutions unit is its smallest by far making photographic films and papers digital cameras photofinishing equipment and chemicals. It still leads the film market in Japan and has hammered away at rival Kodak in the US. FUJIFILM's main businesses each more than 40% of sales are document operations and information-related products and services. Its document business includes joint venture Fuji Xerox offering copy machines printers and production services. The information unit provides medical imaging large-scale printing recording media optical and flat panel display devices and components. Customers in Japan account for more than 45% of sales.

Similar to Xerox and other rivals FUJIFILM has expanded into the professional global services business. The company's production services and global services together represent more than a quarter of FUJIFILM's largest segment document solutions. At about 45% of the holding company's sales document solutions makes the rest of its money from office products (more than half of the segment) and office printers (16%).

Close behind the document segment is the information unit. Medical and life sciences systems are that segment's largest business at about one-third of the segment. Information offerings also include products and services for graphic arts applications (about a quarter of the segment) flat panel displays (about a fifth) industrial products and electronic materials (nearly a tenth) with the remainder of the segment about evenly divided between recording media and optical devices.

Imaging is a much smaller slice of FUJIFILM's pie now about 15% of sales though the company is still a major global force there. Photo imaging retains the lion's share of this segment bringing in nearly two-thirds of its sales through film paper chemicals photo finishing and lab services. Electronic imaging (digital cameras) accounts for the rest. That split has been shifting however with photo dwindling as electronic offerings increase.

In 2012 FUJIFILM announced it would expand capacity for certain products with two new facilities. It's investing Y2.3 billion (about $30 million) to build a factory in the Philippines that will work on optical lenses meant for digital cameras projectors and surveillance cameras. That facility will begin operation in mid-2013. On the document side Fuji Xerox will spend Y9 billion (nearly $115 million) to build a manufacturing site in northern Vietnam with plans to be operational late in 2013. It will focus on digital color multifunction devices and small form-factor LED printers as well as related components.

Revenue for fiscal 2012 (ended March) was just about even with the previous year sliding less than 1% to Y2.2 trillion ($26.8 billion). Net income took a bigger hit falling more than 30% to Y43.8 billion (nearly $535 million) as expenses grew instead of falling like sales. The sales miss was attributed to the appreciation of the yen the major earthquake in Japan and flooding in Thailand. Only the document solutions segment saw a slight increase though information solutions joined it in turning an operating profit.

FUJIFILM still sees the economic climate as harsh and will be exceptionally focused on profitability. For growth it considers its greatest opportunities to be in emerging countries and in its medical and life sciences systems the global and production services from its document solutions unit and materials for electronics industrial and flat-panel displays. Emerging geographic regions it considers most fertile are BRIC (Brazil Russia India and China) Turkey the Middle East and Southeast Asia. Geographically in 2011 and 2012 it opened local companies in the Ukraine South Korea Indonesia and South Africa.

FUJIFILM has used acquisitions to help further its strategic goals particularly in the health care sector. To develop more business in medical equipment it acquired bedside and point-of-care ultrasound company SonoSite for nearly $1 billion in 2012. In 2011 the company acquired the Merck BioManufacturing Network a provider of contract manufacturing and development services for the biopharmaceutical industry for Y40 billion (nearly $500 million). It was renamed Fujifilm Diosynth Biotechnologies.

Other health care-related acquisitions included Turkish endoscopy product direct-seller Filmed Tibbi Cihazlar Pazarlama in 2011 and the Brazil-based X-ray film dealer NDT Comercial in 2010. FUJIFILM is the 51% owner of a joint venture with Indian pharmaceuticals maker Dr. Reddy's Laboratories to develop and market generic drugs in Japan expected to introduce its first products by 2015.

As part of its information solutions business the company established a joint venture with SVA Electron of China to make color filters used in thin film transistor LCDs widely used in flat-screen monitors and televisions. FUJIFILM formed another joint venture equally owned with Kyowa Hakko Kirin to assert its presence in biosimilar pharmaceuticals (pharmaceutical "copies" often less expensive of original products whose patents have expired).

HISTORY

Mokichi Morita president of Japan's leading celluloid maker (Dainippon Celluloid Company founded 1919) decided to start making motion picture film in the early 1930s. Movies were becoming popular in Japan but there was no domestic film supplier. Working with a grant from the government Dainippon Celluloid established Fuji Photo Film Co. an independent company in 1934 in Minami Ashigara Village near Mount Fuji.

At first the company had trouble gaining acceptance in Japan as a quality film producer. However German emulsion specialist Dr. Emill Mauerhoff helped Fuji overcome its product deficiencies producing black-and-white photographic film (1936) and the first Japanese-made color film (1948). In the meantime Fuji added 35mm photographic film 16mm motion picture film and X-ray film to its product line. By the early 1940s the company was operating four factories and a research laboratory in Japan. Its first overseas office opened in Brazil in 1955 was followed by offices in the US (1958) and Europe (1964).

Fuji continued to expand its product line adding magnetic tape in 1960. Two years later it formed Fuji Xerox a Japanese joint venture with Xerox to sell copiers in Japan and the Pacific Rim. It operated as a private-label film supplier in the US and did not market its products under its own brand name until 1972.

International marketing VP Minoru Ohnishi became Fuji's youngest president in 1980 at age 55. To decrease dependence on Japanese film sales he built sales in the US (agreeing to sponsor the 1984 Los Angeles Olympics after Eastman Kodak refused to was key) and pumped money into the production of videotapes floppy disks and medical diagnostic equipment. Fuji introduced Fujicolor Quicksnap the world's first 35mm disposable camera in 1986. It began establishing manufacturing operations in the US two years later.

The company created the FUJIFILM Micro-devices subsidiary to produce image-processing semiconductors in 1990. In 1992 Fuji scientists completed a crude artificial "eye" (a possible forerunner of more efficient eyes for robots). The following year it launched the Pictrostat instant print system which produces color prints in one minute from photos slides and objects.

Fuji was forced to temporarily raise US prices in 1994 after Kodak accused it of illegally dumping its photographic paper exported to the US. But Fuji skirted the problem in 1995 by making the paper at its US plant. That year Kodak asked for economic sanctions against Fuji and the Japanese government saying that the government encouraged Fuji to use exclusive contracts to control film distribution thus keeping Kodak from selling film in many stores. (The case was rejected by the World Trade Organization in 1997.)

The firm unveiled the Advanced Photo System (co-developed with Kodak and three other companies) in 1996 combining conventional photography with digital-image processing and printing technology. Also that year Fuji bought six off-site wholesale photofinishing plants from Wal-Mart (the largest US provider of photofinishing services) and won contracts to provide supplies to all of Wal-Mart's in-store one-hour photo labs.

In 1997 it chopped film prices in the US and began making film at its US plant. In 1999 Fuji introduced a high-quality image sensor for digital cameras (Super CCD) and Instax an instant picture camera. Fuji and Sony launched HiFD a floppy disk with 140 times the storage capacity of traditional disks in early 2000. Fuji later announced plans to develop more efficient low-cost ink jet printers through an alliance with Xerox and Sharp Corp.

In March 2001 Fuji acquired half of Xerox's 50% stake in the companies' Fuji Xerox joint venture. In 2002 the company acquired Japanese film processing company Jusphoto Co. and in 2003 purchased additional shares of Process Shizai Co. renaming it Fujifilm Graphic Systems Co. Ltd.

It bought Sericol from Saratoga Partners in 2005 for $230 million and Avecia Inkjet in 2006 for $260 million. Also that year the company adopted a new holding company structure and changed its name to FUJIFILM Holdings. Also that year the firm acquired US-based Problem Solving Concepts a manufacturer of medical imaging information systems for cardiology; TSR Holding S.A. a medical equipment service and maintenance supplier; and the remaining shares of Fuji Medical Systemes France S.A. a medical imaging products distributor.

In January 2008 FUJIFILM Holdings acquired Germany's IP Labs GmbH a developer of online photo service systems. The consolidation of Toyama Chemical into a consolidated subsidiary in March marked the holding company's entry into the pharmceutical business. In November it purchased Empiric Systems LLC a US-based maker of radiology information systems.

EXECUTIVES

Corporate Auditor, Kiichiro Furusawa, age 74
Chairman and CEO, Shigetaka Komori
President and COO, Shigehiro Nakajima
Corporate VP, Kouichi Tamai
Corporate VP, Toshiaki Suzuki
Corporate VP and Director, Nobuaki Inoue
Corporate Auditor, Daisuke Ogawa
Corporate Auditor, Toshimitsu Kawamura
Corporate VP, Kouichi Suematsu
Corporate VP, Kazuhiko Furuya
President FUJIFILM Holdings America Corporation and President and CEO FUJIFILM North America Corporation, Ryutaro (Ray) Hosoda
Director, Teisuke Kitayama
Chairman Chief Executive Officer, Shigetaka Komori
Director, Tadahito Yamamoto
EVP CFO and Director, Toshio Takahashi
Director, Tadashi Sasaki
Director, Yuzo Toda
Corporate VP and Director, Nobuaki Inoue
Director, Teisuke Kitayama
Auditors: Ernst&YoungShinNihon

LOCATIONS

HQ: FUJIFILM Holdings Corp
9-7-3 Akasaka, Minato-ku, Tokyo 107-0052
Phone: (81) 3 6271 1111
Web: www.fujifilmholdings.com

2012 Sales

	% of total
Japan	46
Americas	17
Europe	12
Rest of the	25
Total	**100**

PRODUCTS/OPERATIONS

2012 Sales

	% of total
Document	45
Information	40
Imaging	15
Total	**100**

2012 Sales

	% of total
Sales	85
Rentals	15
Total	**100**

Selected Products

Document
- Business process outsourcing
- Digital color printers
- Digital multifunction printer/copiers
- Digital photo printers
- On-demand publishing systems

Imaging
- Color photo printing paper and chemicals
- Digital cameras and accessories
- Electronic imaging systems
- Film processing services
- Motion picture films
- Photo lab equipment
- Photographic films

Information
- Data storage media
- LCD materials
- Medical imaging systems and films
- Nutraceuticals
- Pharmaceuticals
- Plate-making supplies films and chemicals
- Printer inks
- X-ray films

COMPETITORS

Agfa
Bayer AG
Brother Industries
Canon
Datapulse Technology
Eastman Kodak
Electronics for Imaging
GlaxoSmithKline
Hewlett-Packard
Hitachi
IBM
Imation
Iomega
Konica Minolta
Kyocera
Kyocera Document Solutions
Lexmark
Mitsubishi Paper Mills
NEC
Nikon
Novartis
Olympus
Panasonic Corp
Pfizer
Philips Electronics
Ricoh Company
Samsung Electronics
Sharp Corp.
Sony
Toshiba
Xerox

HISTORICAL FINANCIALS

Company Type: Public

Income Statement FYE: March 31

	REVENUE ($ mil.)	NET INCOME ($ mil.)	NET PROFIT MARGIN	EMPLOYEES
03/13	23,537	576	2.5%	80,322
03/12	26,762	533	2.0%	81,691
03/11	26,774	771	2.9%	78,862
03/10	23,356	(411)	—	74,216
03/09	24,720	106	0.4%	76,252
Annual Growth	(1.2%)	52.4%	—	1.3%

2013 Year-End Financials

Debt ratio: 0.1%
Return on equity: 3.0%
Cash ($ mil.): 4,772
Current ratio: 2.86
Long-term debt ($ mil.): 3,375
No. of shares (mil.): 481
Dividends
Yield: 0.0%
Payout: 0.0%
Market value ($ mil.): 9,464

	STOCK PRICE ($) FY Close	P/E High/Low		PER SHARE ($) Earnings	Dividends	Book Value
03/13	19.64	0	0	1.15	0.00	41.22
03/12	23.51	0	0	1.06	0.00	43.57
03/11	31.01	0	0	1.46	0.32	43.19
03/10	34.35	—	—	(0.84)	0.27	38.27
03/09	21.97	0	0	0.21	0.35	36.51
Annual Growth	(2.8%)	—	—	52.1%	(88.6%)	3.1%

Fujitsu Ltd.

Fujitsu Limited's supply of high-tech offerings seems almost limitless. The company provides customers worldwide with products ranging from computers and electronic components to air conditioners and bar code scanners. Fujitsu's computer products include PCs servers storage systems and peripherals. One of the top IT services firms in the world it provides consulting infrastructure management and systems integration. Other lines include a wide range of software telecommunications transmission equipment consumer electronics and semiconductors. Fujitsu also owns Nifty one of Japan's leading ISPs. The company gets the vast majority of its sales in Japan.

Already struggling amid the global economic slump –with a year-over-year decline in net sales of 3% in 2010 –Fujitsu booked an extraordinary loss of Y11.6 billion ($150.8 million) and operating income fell Y13 billion ($169 million) primarily as a result of the Great East Japan Earthquake in March 2011. Year-over-year net sales were again down 3% in 2011 but rose 1.4% to $55.4 billion the following year.

The company's Technology Solutions unit generates the largest portion of its revenue. In addition to consulting and outsourcing this division provides systems integration application development hardware installation and other services. Fujitsu Services is among the company's key IT services subsidiaries. Fujitsu's software offerings include customer relationship management (CRM) supply chain management (SCM) and enterprise resource planning (ERP) applications. Revenue for technology solutions declined about 4% in 2011.

Fujitsu's ubiquitous solutions division includes PCs tablets mobile phones and audio and navigation equipment. Ubiquitous solutions (22% of sales) rose 0.5% in 2011. The device solutions segment which includes LSI devices and electronic components and represents 12% of revenue rose 7% in 2011.

In 2012 Fujitsu spun off its access network business as a new company called Access Network Technology Ltd. The venture is 52.8% owned by Fujitsu with the remainder held by NTT DoCoMo (19.9%) NEC (17.8%) and Fujitsu Semiconductor (9.5%). The joint venture will develop chips that control wireless communications and signals but will outsource production of those chips. The move is intended to take take on industry leader QUALCOMM in the fast-growing market for mobile communications chips used smartphones and tablets.

The Access Network Technology venture was the result of a failed attempt by the company to establish a partnership with NTT Docomo Fujitsu Semiconductor NEC Panasonic Mobile Communications and Samsung Electronics earlier in 2012. Intended to give the companies a way to develop and market their own cellphone chips the venture was abandoned after the partners were unable to come to an agreement over details.

In 2010 the company combined its cell phone business with that of key rival Toshiba in hopes that the new business (anticipated to be the largest cell phone maker in Japan) would be better able to compete with global industry leaders. Fujitsu carried an 80% stake in the new company Fujitsu Toshiba Mobile Communications Limited until it bought Toshiba's remaining 20% in 2012 making the company a subsidiary Fujitsu Mobile Communications Limited.

Fujitsu generates most of its revenues in Japan but its growth strategy includes strengthening its international operations with a goal of increasing the percentage of sales outside Japan to 40%. To increase its international operations the company acquired KAZ Group the IT arm of Australian telecom Telstra in 2009. It also bought out Siemens' stake in their European computer joint venture Fujitsu Siemens for E450 million ($570 million) in 2009. The unit is now called Fujitsu Technology Solutions.

Fujitsu's efforts to strengthen its North American operations have included consolidating a number of its subsidiaries in the region. In 2009 the company combined three of its US-based subsidiaries –Fujitsu Consulting Fujitsu Computer Systems and Fujitsu Transaction Solutions –to form Fujitsu America.

HISTORY

Furukawa Electric and Siemens created Fuji Electric in 1923 to produce electrical equipment. Fuji Electric spun off Fujitsu its communications division in 1935. Originally a maker of telephone equipment Fujitsu produced anti-aircraft weapons during WWII. After the war it became one of four major suppliers to state-owned monopoly Nippon Telegraph and Telephone (NTT) and continued to benefit from Japan's rapid economic recovery in the 1950s and 1960s.

With encouragement from Japan's Ministry of International Trade and Industry (MITI) Fujitsu developed the country's first commercial computer in 1954. MITI erected trade barriers to protect Japan's computer industry and in the early 1960s sponsored the production of mainframe computers directing Fujitsu to develop the central processing unit. The company expanded into semiconductor production and factory automation in the late 1960s. Its factory automation business was spun off as Fujitsu Fanuc in 1972.

Fujitsu gained badly needed technology when it bought 30% of IBM-plug-compatible manufacturer Amdahl in 1972. By 1979 Fujitsu had passed IBM to become Japan's #1 computer manufacturer. In Europe Fujitsu entered into computer marketing ventures with Siemens (1978) and UK mainframe maker ICL (1981). In the US it teamed with TRW to sell point-of-sale systems (1980) assuming full control of the operation in 1983. Fujitsu released its first supercomputer in 1982.

Fujitsu bought 80% of ICL (from the UK's Standard Telephones & Cables) in 1990 for $1.3 billion. In 1993 it formed a joint venture with Advanced Micro Devices to make flash memory products.

The company doubled its share of Japan's PC market in 1995 to more than 18% and the next year expanded its PC business globally. In 1997 Fujitsu paid about $878 million for the 58% of Amdahl it didn't already own. The next year it bought the 10% of ICL it didn't own. Fujitsu's 1998 earnings suffered from a slump in the semiconductor market Amdahl-related expenses and a weak Asian economy.

Also in 1998 Naoyuki Akikusa son of a former NTT president became head of Fujitsu. He began trimming some operations while ramping up the company's Internet activities. Fujitsu in 1999 became full owner of online services provider Nifty Serve making it Japan's largest Internet service provider. It merged Nifty with the operations of another ISP called InfoWeb. Also that year Siemens and Fujitsu combined their European computer operations in a 50-50 joint venture (Fujitsu Siemens Computers) as one part of a larger global alliance. A restructuring of Fujitsu's semiconductor operations caused losses for 1999.

Akikusa's reorganization continued in 2000. Fujitsu overhauled its server business (subsidiary Amdahl ceased production of IBM-compatible mainframes) and accelerated production of flash memory. Responding to a global slump in its markets in 2001 Fujitsu announced that it would cut more than 16000 jobs –about 10% of its workforce –to control costs. Soon after it announced the cutting of an additional 4500 jobs.

In 2002 Fujitsu moved to outsource its semiconductor test and assembly operations when it agreed to sell its Kyushu Fujitsu Electronics subsidiary to Amkor Technology; the deal was terminated however when Amkor and Fujitsu were unable to agree to terms.

In 2003 the company formed a joint venture with AMD called Fujitsu AMD Semiconductor Ltd. or FASL to manufacture flash memory. (Renamed Spansion in 2004 the company went public in 2005 filed for Chapter 11 in 2009 and emerged from bankruptcy reorganization in 2010.)

In 2005 Fujitsu sold Hitachi its stake in Fujitsu Hitachi Plasma Display a company it formed with Hitachi to develop plasma display panels for televisions. Fujitsu sold its LCD business Fujitsu Display Technologies to Sharp in 2005.

Fujitsu spun off its advanced semiconductor business as a separate subsidiary Fujitsu Microelectronics (now Fujitsu Semiconductor) in 2008. The following year it sold its hard-disk drive business to Toshiba but retained about a 20% stake in the business which was renamed Toshiba Storage Device. Late in 2010 Toshiba bought Fujitsu's remaining shares.

EXECUTIVES

Chairman, Michiyoshi Mazuka, age 70
EVP, Kazuhiko Kato
President and CEO Fujitsu America, Anthony P. (Tony) Doye, age 55
SVP, Akira Yamanaka
President, Masami Yamamoto, age 60
EVP, Rod Vawdrey
CEO UK & Ireland, Duncan Tait
EVP, Hirokazu Uejima
Corporate Executive Vice President Director, Kenji Ikegai
SVP, Tsuneo Kawatsuma
SVP, Masaaki Hamaba
SEVP, Masami Fujita
SVP, Takashi Mori
SEVP, Hideyuki Saso
SVP, Bunmei Shimojima
SVP, Kazuhiro Igarashi
SVP, Norihiko Taniguchi
EVP, Chikafumi Urakawa
SVP, Noriyuki Toyoki
CEO Fujitsu Australia and New Zealand, Mike Foster
SVP, Yoshihiko Hanada
Vice Chairman, Masahiro Koezuka
SVP, Nobuo Otani
EVP and Director, Masahiro Koezuka
Executive Officer; Chief Director of Social Base System, Atsuo Atsuo Yatagai Yatagai
Executive Officer; Chief Director of IA Server Business, Hiroaki Hiroaki Kondo Kondo

Executive Officer; Chief Director of Health Care Solution Business, Hirofumi Hirofumi Goda Goda
Executive Officer; Chief Director of Mobile Phone Business, Katsumi Katsumi Takada Takada
Executive Officer, Kazuhiko Kazuhiko Ogawa Ogawa
Executive Officer; Chief Director of Cloud Platform Development, Kazuo Kazuo Imada Imada
Senior Manager of Corporate Affairs, Koji Koji Shiseki Shiseki
Executive Officer; Chief Director of Automobile Business, Motoyuki Motoyuki Ozawa Ozawa
Managing Executive Officer, Nobuo Nobuo Ohtani Ohtani
Executive Officer; Chief Director of Network Service Business, Shingo Shingo Kagawa Kagawa
Executive Officer; Chief Director of Network Business Group Business Planning, Tango Tango Matsumoto Matsumoto
EVP, Yoshikazu Kudo
Executive Officer; Chief Director of Solution Business Promotion, Yoshiki Yoshiki Kondo Kondo
Executive Vice President, Ryosuke Mori
Executive Vice President Enterprise Business Services, Alexandre Attal
Sr. Vice President Operations Fujitsu America, David Berry
Executive Vice President Platform Products, Bill King
Corporate Vice President, Jiro Otsuki
Chief Information Officer, Timothy L. Branham
CEO President Fujitsu America, Robert D. Pryor
Senior Vice President Chief Financial Officer, Richard Deranleau
Director, Hiroshi Oura, age 77
EVP and Director, Kazuhiko Kato
SEVP and Director, Kazuo Ishida
Independent Director, Takashi Okimoto
Director, Haruo Ito
SEVP and Director, Masami Fujita
Director, Yoko Ishikura
Vice Chairman, Masahiro Koezuka
Director, Ryosei Kokubun
EVP and Director, Masahiro Koezuka
Independent Director, Shotaro Yachi
Auditors: Ernst&YoungShinNihon

LOCATIONS

HQ: Fujitsu Ltd.
Shiodome City Center, 1-5-2 Higashi-Shimbashi, Minato-ku, Tokyo 105-7123
Phone: (81) 3 6252 2220
Web: www.fujitsu.com

2011 Sales

	% of total
Asia/Pacific	
Japan	65
Other	9
EMEA	19
Americas	7
Total	**100**

PRODUCTS/OPERATIONS

2011 Sales

	% of total
Technology solutions	
Services	53
System	12
Ubiquitous solutions	
Personal computers & mobile	16
Mobileware	6
Device solutions	
LSI	6
Electronic	6
Other	1
Total	**100**

Selected Products and Services

Technology Solutions
- Services
  - Infrastructure services
  - Systems integration
- System platforms
  - Network products
  - System products

Ubiquitous Product Solutions
- Hard disk drives
- Mobile phones
- PCs

Device Solutions
- Electronic components
- LSI devices

COMPETITORS

Alcatel-Lucent
CASIO COMPUTER
Canon
Cisco Systems
Dell
EMC
Epson
Ericsson
FUJIFILM
Hewlett-Packard
Hitachi
IBM
Infineon Technologies
Intel
Micron Technology
Microsoft
Mitsubishi Electric
Motorola Solutions
NCR
NEC
NTT DATA
Nokia
Nortel Networks
Oki Electric
Oracle
Panasonic Corp
Philips Electronics
Ricoh Company
STMicroelectronics
Samsung Electronics
Seagate Technology
Sharp Corp.
Siemens AG
Sony
TDK
Texas Instruments
Toshiba
Unisys
Western Digital

HISTORICAL FINANCIALS

Company Type: Public

Income Statement

FYE: March 31

	REVENUE ($ mil.)	NET INCOME ($ mil.)	NET PROFIT MARGIN	EMPLOYEES
03/13	46,568	(774)	—	168,733
03/12	54,462	520	1.0%	173,155
03/11	54,686	665	1.2%	172,336
03/10	50,097	996	2.0%	172,438
03/09	47,656	(1,141)	—	165,612
Annual Growth	(0.6%)	—	—	0.5%

2013 Year-End Financials

Debt ratio: 0.2%
Return on equity: (-8.9%)
Cash ($ mil.): 2,152
Current ratio: 1.10
Long-term debt ($ mil.): 2,890
No. of shares (mil.): 2,069
Dividends
Yield: —
Payout: —
Market value ($ mil.): 43,557

	STOCK PRICE ($) FY Close	P/E High/Low	PER SHARE ($) Earnings	Dividends	Book Value
03/13	21.05	— —	(0.37)	0.00	4.67
03/12	26.44	— —	0.25	0.00	5.69
03/11	28.00	— —	0.31	0.57	5.57
03/10	32.63	— —	0.45	0.33	4.92
03/09	18.95	— —	(0.55)	0.63	4.55
Annual Growth	2.7%	— —	—	—	0.7%

Fukoku Mutual Life Insurance Co (Japan)

Fukoku Mutual Life Insurance Company is one of Japan's major life insurers. As part of its business it sells products through a network of nearly 11000 agents as well as through more than 60 branch locations and about 470 field offices. It operates primarily through half a dozen subsidiaries that extends its reach to London New York and Singapore. Fukoku Mutal sells both face-to-face in the field and through call centers offering life and nonlife insurance products (such as medical and nursing care insurance) as well as a variety of financial products and services. Fukoku Mutal's typical clients include private individuals and business owners. Fukoku Mutual was founded in 1923.

Fukoku Mutual's traditional strategies –investing conservatively and targeting government agencies as customers –have earned it a reputation as one of the more stable insurers in an industry experiencing heavy losses primarily stemming from the weak economy and slumping stock markets. As Japan's economy recovers Fukoku Mutual and other insurers have been increasing their exposure to riskier investments including real estate.

EXECUTIVES

Chairman, Tomofumi Akiyama
Deputy President and Executive Officer, Katsumasa Furuya
President and CEO, Yoshiteru Yoneyama
Director and Managing Executive Officer, Hitoshi Sakai
Director and Managing Executive Officer, Toshihiro Hayashi
Director and Managing Executive Officer, Kenji Hirai
Director and Managing Executive Officer, Tadashi Akikawa
Deputy President and Executive Officer, Mikio Yamamoto
Deputy President and Executive Officer, Katsumasa Furuya
President and CEO, Yoshiteru Yoneyama
Director and Managing Executive Officer, Hitoshi Sakai
Director and Managing Executive Officer, Toshihiro Hayashi
Director and Managing Executive Officer, Kenji Hirai
Director and Managing Executive Officer, Tadashi Akikawa
Auditors: KisaragiAuditCorporation

LOCATIONS

HQ: Fukoku Mutual Life Insurance Co (Japan)
2-2-2 Uchisaiwaisho, Chiyoda-ku, Tokyo 100-0011
Phone: (81) 3 3508 1101 **Fax:** (81) 3 3591 6446
Web: www.fukoku-life.co.jp

PRODUCTS/OPERATIONS

Selected Subsidiaries and Affiliates

Fukoku Capital Management Inc.
Fukoku Information Systems Co. Ltd.
Fukoku Life International (America) Inc.
Fukoku Life International (U.K.) Limited
Fukoku Shinyo Hosho Company Limited
Fukokushinrai Life Insurance Company

COMPETITORS

Asahi Mutual Life
Dai-ichi Life
Daido Life
Gibraltar Life Insurance
Meiji Yasuda Life
Mitsui Life
Nippon Life Insurance
Sony Financial
Sumitomo Life
T&D Holdings
Taiyo Life

HISTORICAL FINANCIALS

Company Type: Public

Income Statement FYE: March 31

	ASSETS ($ mil.)	NET INCOME ($ mil.)	INCOME AS % OF ASSETS	EMPLOYEES
03/13	80,122	0	—	13,488
03/12	85,745	0	—	13,502
03/11	80,553	0	—	13,702
03/10	65,177	0	—	14,207
03/09	57,985	0	—	13,836
Annual Growth	8.4%	—	—	(0.6%)

2013 Year-End Financials

Return on assets: —
Return on equity: —
Long-term debt ($ mil.): —
No. of shares (mil.): —
Sales ($ mil): 11,405

Dividends
Yield: —
Payout: —
Market value ($ mil.): —

Gas Natural SDG, S.A.

A latter-day Spanish "conquistador" Gas Natural is venturing into markets in both the Old World and the New. Gas Natural operates a group of energy companies that supply natural gas and electricity serving 20.2 million customers primarily in Spain but also in France Italy and Latin America. The largest natural gas supplier in Spain Gas Natural is also a leading liquefied natural gas (LNG) supplier. The company has a generating capacity of 17800 MW (including 4400 MW in Latin America). In 2009 Gas Natural greatly expanded its power business acquiring Spanish utility Union Fenosa in a $26 billion deal and in 2010 adopted Gas Natural Fenosa as its new corporate brand name.

The Union Fenosa purchase boosted the company's profile as an integrated gas and power enterprise and extended Gas Natural's operations to more than 20 countries. In order to comply with antirust regulations the terms of the deal included having the company selling 600000 gas customer connections 2000 MW of installed power capacity and its remaining stake in Enagas Spain's gas transportation and storage enterprise. At the end of 2009 the company supplied energy to 10.1 million gas meters and 8.7 million gas meters.

To help pay down debt related to the Union Fenosa acquisition in 2009 the company sold power assets in Mexico to Mitsui and Tokyo Gas for $1.2 billion. The merger went ahead in a tough economic environment. Despite the global recession the company's hedging strategies and balanced portfolio allowed it to post both improved revenues and income in the face of lower commodity prices and weakened demand for power and gas.

In response to the deregulation of Spain's retail gas market Gas Natural has been working to become a multi-utility though such initiatives as LNG projects domestic fiber-optic telecommunications and electricity generation and supply operations. The company has also turned to the Americas for growth: Gas Natural has steadily acquired interests in gas suppliers and distributors in Argentina Brazil Colombia Mexico and Puerto Rico. It also trades natural gas in Europe operates a gas pipeline in Morocco and an Italian gas marketing unit.

HISTORY

Gas Natural SDG was created in 1992 when Spanish oil giant Repsol and the bank La Caixa merged their interests in natural gas distributors Catalana de Gas (of Barcelona) and Gas Madrid into a national company and gave it Repsol's gas pipelines. Catalana de Gas' leader Pere Duran Farell who in the 1960s had led efforts to introduce natural gas to Spain became chairman (serving until 1997).

Repsol's formation was the result of Spain's efforts to organize its fragmented energy industry. After an era of dependency on foreign investment before and during Francisco Franco's dictatorship (1939-75) Spain in 1979 set up the Instituto Nacional de Hidrocarburos (INH) which placed all state-owned gas and oil firms under one agency in 1981.

Spain entered the European Economic Community (or EEC which became the European Union) in 1986. A year later Repsol was created to bring the state oil companies into a unified company to meet European liberalization goals. Repsol offered a 26% stake to the public in 1989.

Under pressure from the EEC to open up Spain's markets to foreign competition Repsol and La Caixa formed Gas Natural in 1992 to create a gas distributor big enough to compete effectively. Gas Natural had a 40% market share. The European Union subsidized its pipeline construction and the Spanish government assisted its rapid growth by promoting natural gas as electric utility fuel in lieu of imported oil.

Gas Natural became a fully integrated company in 1995 when it acquired Empresa Nacional de Gas (Enagas) the country's national gas grid operator from INH. The purchase of the much larger Enagas which was building expensive pipelines was made possible only by INH taking on part of the pipeline cost. Enagas was the sole industrial supplier and Gas Natural the largest commercial and residential supplier; the two combined became the #3 gas distributor in Europe behind British Gas (now BG) and Gaz de France.

In 1997 Gas Natural which had acquired Gas de Buenos Aires Norte when it was newly formed won the bid for Rio de Janeiro gas utilities auctioned off by Brazil's government. It also won concessions in Colombia and Mexico.

That year electric utility Iberdrola Repsol and Gas Natural agreed to build power plants jointly. But Gas Natural was forced out of the partnership when other power companies for whom Gas Natural was the sole gas supplier complained.

In 1998 as the Hydrocarbons Law kicked off a liberalization plan for the Spanish gas market Gas Natural planned to build two power plants much to the chagrin of the electric companies. Gas Natural cut a deal with the leading electric company Endesa under which Endesa agreed to buy gas from Gas Natural in return for participating in Gas Natural's power projects. The two also agreed to combine some of their gas utilities and pursue international projects together.

The next year Repsol which had gained control of giant Argentine oil company YPF became Repsol YPF. Gas Natural also made plans in 1999 to restructure operations and unbundle its services in compliance with the Hydrocarbons Law. In 2000 Gas Natural made an unsolicited bid to buy Spanish utility Iberdrola which instead agreed to be acquired by Endesa. The following year Gas Natural signed an agreement with Italian energy giant Enel to explore joint marketing and sales negotiations for liquefied natural gas internationally.

In 2002 Repsol YPF sold a 23% interest in Gas Natural to institutional investors (it retained a 24% stake in the company). Later that year Gas Natural spun off 65% of Enagas in an IPO. In September 2005 Gas Natural made a E22.5 billion (more than $26 billion) takeover bid for Endesa. To ease some concerns authorities may have about that bid Gas Natural divested its distribution and transport operations in October 2005.

In a more ambitious plan in 2005 Gas Natural created a liquefied natural gas (LNG) joint venture with Repsol YPF with a marketing capacity of 12 million metric tons of LNG a year.

EXECUTIVES

General Director of Gas Regulated Business, Antoni Mingot
General Director of Strategy and Development, Antonio Tena
Vice Chairman of the Board, Antonio Niubo
Chief Corporate Officer; General Director of Resources, Antonio Gabas
Chief Financial-Economy Officer, Carlos Fernandez
General Director of Energy Retail Business, Daniel Jorda
General Director of Communication and Chairmans Office, Jordi Tabernero
General Director of Regulated Power Business, Jose Lopez
General Director of Generation Division, Jose Martinez
General Director of Energy Planning, Jose Krauel
General Director of Energy Wholesale Business, Manuel Alvarez
General Director of Legal Services, Manuel Cobaleda
Chief Executive Officer; Director, Rafael Marco
General Director of Latin America Unit, Sergio Moreno
CEO and Director, Rafael Villaseca Marco, age 61
Vice Chairman, Antonio Brufau Niubo, age 64
Independent Director, Carlos Marrodan
Independent Director, Emiliano Achurra
Independent Director, Miguel Maseda
Independent Director, Santiago Cobo
Auditors: PricewaterhouseCoopersAuditoresS.L.

LOCATIONS

HQ: Gas Natural SDG, S.A.
Placa del Gas, 1, Barcelona 08003
Phone: (34) 93 219 9199 **Fax:** (34) 93 402 5870
Web: www.gasnatural.com

2009 Sales

	% of total
Europe	
Spain	63
Other	6
Latin	27
North America	
USA	2
Puerto	1
Other	1
Total	**100**

PRODUCTS/OPERATIONS

2009 Sales

	% of total
Wholesale &	39
Electricity	25
Gas	20
Electricity	11
Upstream &	2
Other	3
Total	**100**

COMPETITORS

BG Group
BP
CEPSA
Endesa S.A.
HC Energia
IBERDROLA
Italgas
MetroGAS
Royal Dutch Shell
TGS

HISTORICAL FINANCIALS

Company Type: Public

Income Statement FYE: December 31

	REVENUE ($ mil.)	NET INCOME ($ mil.)	NET PROFIT MARGIN	EMPLOYEES
12/12	32,824	1,899	5.8%	15,959
12/11	27,260	1,713	6.3%	16,202
12/10	26,272	1,607	6.1%	17,347
12/09	21,434	1,721	8.0%	18,314
12/08	18,935	1,477	7.8%	6,757
Annual Growth	14.7%	6.5%	—	24.0%

2012 Year-End Financials

Debt ratio: 56.7%
Return on equity: 11.0%
Cash ($ mil.): 5,844
Current ratio: 1.48
Long-term debt ($ mil.): 23,481
No. of shares (mil.): 1,000
Dividends
Yield: 0.0%
Payout: 12.8%
Market value ($ mil.): 3,502

	STOCK PRICE ($) FY Close	P/E High	P/E Low	PER SHARE ($) Earnings	Dividends	Book Value
12/12	3.50	4	2	1.91	0.25	17.47
12/11	3.51	6	4	1.80	0.11	16.68
12/10	3.00	7	4	1.74	0.26	16.53
12/09	4.30	6	5	2.13	0.50	16.69
Annual Growth	(6.6%)	—	—	(2.7%)	(16.4%)	1.1%

Gazprom Neft

One of Russia's largest integrated oil companies Gazprom Neft (formerly Siberian Oil Company or Sibneft) is engaged in exploration production refining and marketing of petroleum products. Retail operations include about 760 gas stations. The company with proved reserves of 4 billion barrels of oil equivalent controls refineries in Moscow Mozyr Noyabrsk and Omsk that produce more than 32.7 million tonnes of oil products per year. The company also shares ownership with NOVATEK of a major natural gas project SeverEnergia. Russian gas giant Gazprom owns 79% of Gazprom Neft having Gazprom acquired Italian energy titan ENI's 20% share in the company in 2009.

HISTORY

In the aftermath of the fall of the Soviet Union in the early 1990s Sibneft was formed in 1995 as part of Russia's privatization of state industries. Sibneft included western Siberian oil producer Noyabrskneftegas and the Omsk oil refinery. The Russian government was to retain a 51% stake for three years while limiting foreign ownership to 15%. Finance Oil Company (FNK) controlled by business oligarch Boris Berezovsky the man reportedly behind Sibneft's formation gained a controlling stake in Sibneft. The new integrated oil company's prize asset was the Omsk refinery. Built in the mid-1980s it was Russia's largest and most modern refinery.

In 1997 Sibneft became the first Russian company to issue a Eurobond. Despite an economic crisis in 1998 Sibneft continued to service all of its financial obligations. That year Sibneft made plans to merge with rival oil company Yukos (controlled by oligarch Mikhail Khodorkovsky) but falling oil prices led the two firms to scuttle the proposed union.

Also in 1998 Sibneft published a corporate governance charter compiled by leading European experts to bring the company in line with international practices. This move was followed up with the appointment of three non-executives to the company's board of nine directors. A year later Sibneft became the first major Russian oil company to publish its financial accounts (audited by Arthur Andersen) according to US generally accepted accounting principles. In 1999 Sibneft also formed alliances with two Western oil services firms US-based Schlumberger and Canadian-based BJ Services to enhance its extraction of oil and gas.

During the 1999 Russian Duma elections reclusive oligarch Roman Abramovich (who had acquired a 12% stake in Sibneft in 1996) claimed to control Sibneft whereas Berezovsky (also elected to the Duma) was said to have only a background role in Sibneft.

The company announced plans in 2000 to invest $52 million to modernize the Omsk refinery upgrading its capacity to produce lead-free gasoline. That year Sibneft also agreed to acquire majority stakes in two refined products retailers in the Urals region which together controlled 132 service stations and 20 storage sites.

Sibneft lost out in its bid to gain control of Onako another former state-owned oil company that was privatized in 2000. Sibneft had teamed up with two other oil companies Yukos and Stroitransgaz (a unit of Russian gas giant Gazprom) to bid for Onako but lost out to rival Tyumen Oil Co. (TNK). However Sibneft which had gained control of a 40% stake in Onako's main oil producing subsidiary Orenburgneft reportedly made an arrangement with TNK to swap its Orenburgneft shares for a minority stake in Onako. Also in 2000 Sibneft and other Russian oil companies were investigated by Russian authorities after allegations of tax evasion.

In 2001 the company announced plans to search for oil in the Chukotka autonomous district. (Abramovich is the governor of Chukotka). This unexplored area has a similar geological structure to Alaska's oil-rich North Slope. Later that year Sibneft acquired a 36% stake in a Moscow refinery from oil giant LUKOIL allowing the company to supply markets in European Russia.

In 2002 Sibneft opened its first gas station in Moscow.

Gazprom Neft (as Sibneft) was once controlled by UK-residing Chelsea soccer club-owning Russian oligarch Roman Abramovich through investment company Millhouse Capital. In 2005 Gazprom bought its majority stake in Sibneft from Millhouse Capital for $11 billion. The company changed its name to Gazprom Neft the next year and ENI acquired 20% of Gazprom Neft in 2007 following the bankruptcy of Yukos. Gazprom had the option to buy ENI's stake within two years and exercised that right in 2009 paying just more than $4 billion to ENI. Gazprom now directly owns or indirectly controls through subsidiaries about 95% of Gazprom Neft.

EXECUTIVES

Chairman, Alexey B. Miller, age 52
Deputy CEO Corporate Communications, Alexander Dybal, age 47
CEO and Director, Alexander V. Dyukov, age 46
Deputy Chairman and Deputy CEO for Logistics Processing and Sales, Anatoly Cherner, age 60
Deputy CEO Foreign Asset Management, Kirill Kravchenko, age 37
CFO, Vadim Yakovlev, age 43
Deputy General Director for Legal and Corporate Affairs, Elena A. Ilyukhina, age 45
Head Investor Relations, Anna Sidorkina
Executive Vice President Strategy and Business Development, Mikhail Slobodin
Director, Vasiliy Podyuk, age 65
Director, Andrey V. Kruglov, age 45
Director, Kirill Gennadievich Seleznev, age 39
Director, Olga P. Pavlova, age 60
CEO and Director, Alexander V. Dyukov, age 46
Director, Claudio Descalzi, age 57
Director, Dubik Nikolai Nikolaevich
Director, Valery Golubev, age 61
Director, Marco Alvera, age 37
Auditors: ZAOPricewaterhouseCoopersAudit

LOCATIONS

HQ: Gazprom Neft
Galernaya, 5, Let. A, A, St. Petersburg 190000
Phone: (7) 812 363 31 52 **Fax:** (7) 812 363 31 51
Web: www.gazprom-neft.ru

2007 Sales

	% of total
Refining marketing &	99
Exploration &	1
Total	**100**

COMPETITORS

BP
Devon Energy
Exxon Mobil
JX Nippon Oil & Energy
LUKOIL
Mitsui
Occidental Petroleum
Rosneft
Royal Dutch Shell
Surgutneftegas
TOTAL
Tatneft
Transneft

HISTORICAL FINANCIALS

Company Type: Public

Income Statement FYE: December 31

	REVENUE ($ mil.)	NET INCOME ($ mil.)	NET PROFIT MARGIN	EMPLOYEES
12/12	40,415	5,791	14.3%	0
12/11	44,172	5,352	12.1%	0
12/10	32,772	3,148	9.6%	0
12/09	24,166	3,013	12.5%	0
12/08	33,075	4,658	14.1%	48,000
Annual Growth	5.1%	5.6%	—	—

2012 Year-End Financials

Debt ratio: 0.5%
Return on equity: 40.9%
Cash ($ mil.): 2,497
Current ratio: 1.87
Long-term debt ($ mil.): 5,466
No. of shares (mil.): —
Dividends
Yield: 4.0%
Payout: 0.0%
Market value ($ mil.): —

	STOCK PRICE ($) FY Close	P/E High	P/E Low	PER SHARE ($) Earnings	Dividends	Book Value
12/12	23.76	0	0	1.23	0.95	5.81
12/11	23.33	24	15	1.13	0.66	4.98
12/10	20.95	44	24	0.67	0.47	3.96
12/09	27.35	47	15	0.64	0.74	3.42
12/08	9.95	41	8	0.98	0.70	2.96
Annual Growth	24.3%	—	—	5.8%	8.2%	18.4%

Gazprom OAO

Gazprom Russia's largest company has proved and probable oil and gas reserves of 29.2 billion tons of coal equivalent and produces about 513 billion cu. meters of natural gas a year. With 18% of the world's gas reserves it is also the world's largest gas producer. The company is engaged in oil and gas exploration processing transport and marketing. It operates Russia's domestic gas pipeline network and delivers gas to countries across Central Asia and Europe. Gazprom relies heavily on Western exports. It also holds stakes in Russian financial institutions a polypropylene plant and its own telecom network and produces 17% of Russia's electricity. Gazprom accounts for about 25% of Russia's tax revenues.

Exports to Europe are critical to Gazprom which is burdened by debt because of the insolvency of Russian consumers and hordes of nonpaying customers. Gazprom holds strategic partnerships with Western energy companies including Germany's E.ON Ruhrgas. Other partners include Royal Dutch Shell Eni of Italy and Finland's Fortum. In addition Gazprom has a deal with German chemical conglomerate BASF that grants BASF minority shares in both the proposed North Europe Gas Pipeline and the West Siberia field that will feed it. The company is also working on the South Stream Pipeline a massive project aimed at linking Russia's southern gas fields to Western markets via Bulgaria.

In addition to natural gas Gazprom holds a 5% global share of the production of liquefied natural gas (LNG). It also holds 79% of oil producer Gazprom Neft. It also holds stakes in Russian financial institutions a polypropylene plant and its own telecom network and produces 17% of Russia's electric power.

Gazprom exports gas to more than 30 countries within and beyond the borders of the former Soviet Union. The company has offices in Algiers Astana Ashkhabad Bishkek Dokha Ekaterinburg Kiev Kishinev Krasnodar Minsk Moscow Novy Urengoy Peking Riga Rio de Janeiro Samara St. Petersburg Tehran Tomsk Khabarovsk and Yuzhno-Sakhalinsk.

In 2011 Gazprom reported a 29% spike in revenues (in local currency) driven by expanded capacity higher oil and gas prices and by a 16% jump in demand for gas from former Soviet Union countries (where the company has invested heavily in building infrastructure). Net profit rose further to 30% as rapid revenue growth outstripped an increase in operating costs and other expenses. An improving economy and a related increase in the volume and price of natural gas also drove up revenues and operating profits in 2010.

To expand its gas supply in 2012 the company announced that it planned to spend 43 billion rubles (US $1.4 billion) that year to develop gas infrastructure projects (gas fields and pipelines) in the Sakhalin region of Eastern Russia. In 2011 Gazprom acquired TNK-BP's east Siberian Kovykta gas field for about $770 million. The purchase opens up the possibility of a major supply agreement with China.

While natural gas is its core asset the company is also ramping up its other segments as part of a diversification drive to broaden its revenue base and enhance its profile as an integrated energy producer. In 2011 it installed 1.9 GW of combined heat and power generation units and deployed an offshore production platform at the Prirazlomnoye oil field in the Pechora Sea in the Arctic.

Expanding its energy footprint in 2011 Gazprom agreed to acquire power generation KES Holding (which owns four power companies) to create Russia's largest power company. KES Holding will hold 25% of the new joint venture.

In 2010 the company made its first entry into the US gas market when it began trading and marketing natural gas though Gazprom Marketing & Trading USA. It also signed a strategic partnership with Royal Dutch Shell to develop oil and gas assets in Russian Siberia and the Far East and process and market products in Russia and Europe.

To raise cash to pay down debt in 2010 the company sold its controlling stake in SeverEnergia (a natural gas project partly owned by ENI) to a joint venture owned by Gazprom Neft and OAO Novatek for $1.5 billion. To raise cash it sold 9% of its 19% stake in Novatek to Gazprombank for $2.8 billion.

Over time the Russian government has boosted its stake in Gazprom from 38% to more than 50%.

HISTORY

Following the breakup of the Soviet Union in the early 1990s one of the first priorities of the Russian government was to move some state monopolies toward a free-market economic system. A presidential decree in 1992 moved the company toward privatization by calling for the formation of a Russian joint-stock company to explore for and produce gas gas condensates and oil; provide for gas processing; operate gas wells; and build gas pipelines and storage facilities.

By 1993 the government had converted its natural gas monopoly Gazprom into a joint-stock company; the company had dated back to the 1940s and the USSR Ministry of the Gas Industry had kept all of its assets when it became a corporation in 1989.

The new Gazprom was 15%-owned by Gazprom workers and 28% by people living in Russia's gas-producing regions. The state retained about a 40% share (boosted to 51% in 2003). The company inherited all of the former Soviet republics' export contracts to Western and Central Europe.

Thanks to the power of Viktor Chernomyrdin (Gazprom's former Soviet boss and gas industry minister who became Russia's prime minister in 1992) the company was able to enjoy large tax breaks and maintain its role as a monopoly —even as other industries were being more deeply privatized. However the privatization of Gazprom was later attacked as being manipulated to profit the company's top management including Chernomyrdin. Top managers were rumored to have each received 1%-5% of shares —holdings potentially worth $1.2 billion-$10 billion each.

Needing to raise cash in 1996 Gazprom offered 1% of its stock to foreigners the first sale of stock to foreign investors. In 1997 Gazprom and Royal Dutch/Shell formally became partners. That year Gazprom began building its Blue Stream pipeline across the Black Sea to Turkey. Italian group Eni helped back the project and became a partner by 1999.

In 1998 Gazprom acquired a stake in Promostroibank Russia's fourth-largest financial institution. German energy powerhouse Ruhrgas acquired a 3% stake in Gazprom in 1998 which it increased to nearly 4% the next year. Also in 1999 Gazprom started building its Yamal-Europe pipeline which was to stretch to Germany for exports to Europe.

The next year an attempt by Gazprom to muscle into Hungary's chemicals sector by offering cheaper raw materials was blocked by Hungary's TVK and Borsodchem and their allies. Also in 2000 Gazprom became embroiled in a politically controversial issue when it called for the country's leading private media holding group Media-MOST to sell shares to the gas giant in order to settle millions of dollars of debt. Because Media-MOST held NTV television a major critic of Russian President Vladimir Putin the deal was alleged to have been directed by the Kremlin. A government probe into the deal was later ordered. (By 2002 Gazprom owned a significant stake in NTV which it sold that year so it could focus on its core energy businesses.)

The alignment of Gazprom's board changed in 2000 after the annual shareholder's meeting. For the first time in Gazprom's history company managers did not have a majority of seats. A new chairman Dmitri Medvedev second in command to Putin was elected to replace Chernomyrdin. In 2001 the board fired CEO Rem Vyakhirev and replaced him with Deputy Energy Minister Alexei Miller a Putin ally.

Gazprom had announced plans in 2004 to acquire Rosneft (effectively giving the Russian government control of Gazprom) though the deal was complicated by Rosneft's acquisition of the Yugansk assets acquired from YUKOS. In 2005 Gazprom abandoned plans to merge with Rosneft and acquired Sibneft in an effort to add significant oil operations to its business. Millhouse Capital a holding company controlled by Russian oligarch Roman Abramovich sold its majority stake in what was then a major exploration and production company called Sibneft (now Gazprom Neft) to Gazprom for a reported $13 billion. At the time Sibneft was Russia's fifth-largest oil company.

In 2006 Gazprom signed long-term contracts for gas deliveries with Austrian energy giant OMV. That year Royal Dutch/Shell agreed to give control of the $22 billion Sakhalin-2 project (run by Sakhalin Energy Investment) in Russia's Far East to Gazprom.

Former Gazprom chairman Dmitri Medvedev was elected president of Russia in 2008.

The company became embroiled in a pricing dispute with neighbor Ukraine in 2009 resulting in the disruption of gas supplies to Ukraine and because of its transnational pipelines to dozens of other countries in Europe.

Wanting to expand its Russian and international assets and diversify its profile in 2009 Gazprom acquired Italian energy titan ENI's 20% share in oil producer Gazprom Neft raising the Russian giant's direct ownership to 79%. ENI had acquired its stake in 2007 following the bankruptcy of YUKOS. Gazprom had the option to buy ENI's stake within two years and exercised that right in 2009 paying just more than $4 billion to ENI. Gazprom directly owns or indirectly controls through subsidiaries about 95% of Gazprom Neft.

EXECUTIVES

Deputy Chairman and CEO, Alexey B. Miller, age 52
Deputy Chairman Management Committee; Director General OOO Gazprom export, Alexander I. Medvedev, age 58
Deputy Chairman Management Committee and Chief Accountant, Elena A. Vasilyeva, age 54
Deputy Chairman Management Committee and Head Finance and Economics Department, Andrey V. Kruglov, age 45
Deputy Chairman Management Committee, Valery A. Golubev, age 61
Member Management Committee; Head Strategic Development Department, Vlada V. Rusakova, age 60
Member Management Committee; Head Marketing and Processing of Gas and Liquid Hydrocarbons Department; Director General OOO Mezhregiongaz, Kirill Gennadievich Seleznev, age 39
Director; Deputy Chairman and Head Administration Management Committee, Mikhail L. Sereda, age 43
Deputy Chairman Management Committee, Alexander N. Kozlov, age 61
Member Management Committee; Head Legal Department, Nikolay N. Dubik, age 42
Chairman, Victor A. Zubkov, age 72
Deputy Chairman Management Committee; Director General Gazprom Corporate Security Service, Sergey F Khomyakov

Member Management Committee; Director General OOO Gazprom komplektatsiya, Igor Y. Fyodorov, age 48
Member Management Committee; Head Investment and Construction Department, Yaroslav Y. Golko, age 52
Head Information Policy Department, Alexander D. Bespalov, age 63
Member Management Committee and Head Department Gas Transportation Underground Storage and Utilization Department, Oleg E. Aksyutin
Head Central Production and Dispatch Department, Boris S. Posyagin, age 69
Head Technological Process Control Systems Automation Department, Nikolai F. Stolyar, age 61
Director General Gazprom dobycha Krasnoyarsk, Mikhail Sirotkin, age 41
Deputy Chairman Management Committee, Vitaly Markelov, age 50
Member Management Committee; Head Gas Gas Condensate and Oil Production, Vsevolod Cherepanov, age 47
Member Management Committee; Head Dept. of Goverment Relations, Vladimir Markov, age 58
Member Management Committee; Head Asset Management and Corporate Relations, Elena Mikhailova, age 36
Deputy Chairman of the Management Board, Aleksandr Kozlov
Deputy Chairman of the Management Board, Aleksandr Medvedev
Chairman of the Management Board; Deputy Chairman of the Board; General Director, Aleksey Miller
Member of Management Board; Head of Asset Management and Corporate Relations Department, Elena Mikhaylova
Deputy Chairwoman of the Management Board; Chief Accounting Officer, Elena Vasileva
Management Board Member, Igor Fedorov
Chairman of the Board, Viktor Zubkov
Head of the Department for Pricing and Economic Expert Analysis Department; Director, Yelena Karpel
Director, Burckhard Bergmann, age 67
Deputy Chairman and CEO, Alexey B. Miller, age 52
Director; Deputy Chairman Management Committee, Alexander G. Ananenkov, age 59
Director; Deputy Chairman and Head Administration Management Committee, Mikhail L. Sereda, age 43
Director, Farit R. Gazizullin, age 67
Director, Elena E. Karpel, age 69
Director, Igor K. Yusufov, age 57
Chairman, Victor A. Zubkov, age 72
Director, Elvira Nabiullina, age 49
Director, Valery A. Musin, age 74
Director, Sergey I. Shmatko, age 46
Auditors: ZAOPricewaterhouseCoopersAudit

LOCATIONS

HQ: Gazprom OAO
16 Nametkina St., Moscow 117997
Phone: (7) 495 719 3001 **Fax:** (7) 495 719 8333
Web: www.gazprom.com

PRODUCTS/OPERATIONS

2011 Sales

	% of total
Gas	59
Oil & refined	27
Gas transportation power &	14
Total	**100**

COMPETITORS

BP
Centrica
E.ON Ruhrgas
Gasunie
LUKOIL
Qatar Petroleum
Rosneft
Sakhalin Energy
Surgutneftegas
Tatneft

HISTORICAL FINANCIALS

Company Type: Public

Income Statement FYE: December 31

	REVENUE ($ mil.)	NET INCOME ($ mil.)	NET PROFIT MARGIN	EMPLOYEES
12/12	156,607	38,850	24.8%	417,000
12/11	143,741	40,490	28.2%	401,000
12/10	118,085	31,741	26.9%	393,000
12/09	98,941	25,717	26.0%	386,000
12/08	119,680	25,267	21.1%	456,000
Annual Growth	7.0%	11.4%	—	(2.2%)

2012 Year-End Financials

Debt ratio: 0.4%
Return on equity: 14.8%
Cash ($ mil.): 13,782
Current ratio: 1.62
Long-term debt ($ mil.): 38,696
No. of shares (mil.): —
Dividends
Yield: 4.6%
Payout: 0.0%
Market value ($ mil.): —

	STOCK PRICE ($) FY Close	P/E High/Low		PER SHARE ($) Earnings	Dividends	Book Value
12/12	9.73	0	0	1.69	0.46	12.00
12/11	10.68	0	0	1.76	0.00	10.06
12/10	25.44	0	0	1.38	0.12	8.91
12/09	25.05	0	0	1.09	0.15	7.65
12/08	14.25	0	0	1.07	0.00	6.61
Annual Growth	(9.1%)	—	—	12.1%	—	16.1%

GDF SUEZ

GDF SUEZ channels its energy as Europe's top power gas and infrastructure players. It is engaged in the purchasing production and marketing of natural gas and electricity; the development and maintenance of major natural gas and electricity infrastructures; and the creation and marketing of energy and environmental services. With operations in about 70 countries power producer GDF SUEZ had 118200 MW of installed capacity in 2011. It is Europe's top importer of liquefied natural gas (LNG) its largest supplier of natural gas the continent's leading supplier of multi-technical energy services and a leading global supplier of water and waste management services.

Geographic Reach

GDF SUEZ operates around the world. Europe accounted for 80% of the company's revenues in 2011.

Operations

The company has expertise in four key sectors: liquefied natural gas energy efficiency services independent power production and environmental services. Its environmental services segment offers water management and waste treatment and recovery through its subsidiary SUEZ Environnement.

In 2011 GDF SUEZ operated more than 1200 water production sites producing around 4.5 billion metric meters of drinking water in 2011. In sanitation services it biologically treated around 3.2 billion metric meters of waste water. Internationally in the waste segment it operates 120 composting platforms 48 incineration sites (including 45 that recover energy) 645 sorting and transfer stations and 130 storage centers.

In the renewable energy sector GDF SUEZ had an installed capacity of 16121 MW at the end of 2011. At 11332 MW the company is a hydroelectric operator in France and Brazil where it is continuing to develop large-scale projects. It also has a production capacity of 918 MW in biomass and biogas in Europe the US and Latin America. Wind energy is also a priority with capacity of 3792 MW making the Group the leading operator on the French and Belgian markets and the second in Portugal.

Financial Performance

Despite unfavorable weather conditions and flat natural gas prices in France the company's revenues grew by 7% in 2011. In Europe water revenues increased by 3% and waste by 7.1%. Internationally sales from both of these sectors went up by 3.7% that year.

Strategy

GDF SUEZ is looking to harness its global size and its presence in a mix of energy areas (nuclear natural gas LNG coal and renewables) with its water sanitation and waste management expertise to deliver energy in a way that preserves the environment. The company is constructing 11800 MW of installed power-production capacity. (To raise capital to help fund its expansion between 2011 and 2013 the company sold stakes in power projects in Slovakia Canada and the UK and elsewhere).

In 2013 GDF SUEZ announced the construction of the 300 MW Tarfaya wind farm in Morocco which will be the largest wind project in Africa. The project is owned in partnership with Nareva Holding a Moroccan energy company. GDF SUEZ is also developng Cyberjaya Malaysia's premier cybercity through a joint venture with local partner Cyberview Sdn Bhd of Cyberjaya's district cooling network.

In 2012 GDF SUEZ and its International Power subsidiary expanded its power generation of Tihama power sites in Saudi Arabia by 532 MW following an award from Saudi Aramco.

Dramatically boosting its power generation assets in 2011 the company's GDF SUEZ Energy International merged with UK-based International Power. The $21.5 billion deal created one of the world's largest global independent power generation companies. GDF SUEZ held 70% of International Power which has generation capacity of 66000 MW in 2011 and bought out the other 30% in 2012 for about $2.2 billion to gain full ownership.

Later than year International Power formed a joint venture with Supreme Energy and Marubeni Corporation to develop the Rantau Dedap geothermal project located in Sumatra.The 220 MW geothermal plant is part of the Indonesian government's long-term plan meet its country's needs with renewable power.

Ownership

In 2012 the French government owned about 37% of GDF SUEZ.

HISTORY

The first canal in Egypt was dug in the 13th century BC but it was Napoleon who revived the idea of a shorter trade route to India: a canal through Egypt linking the Gulf of Suez with the Mediterranean. Former French diplomat and engineer Ferdinand de Lesseps formed Compagnie Universelle du Canal Maritime de Suez in 1858 to build and eventually operate the canal which opened 11 years later. Egypt's modernization had pushed it into debt and increased its ties to the British government which by 1875 had acquired a 44% stake in the company.

For more than 80 years the Suez Canal was a foreign enclave protected by the British Army since 1936. After Egypt's puppet government fell and as Gamal Abd Al-Nasser assumed power in 1956 British troops exited the Canal Zone which Egypt quickly nationalized. Israel Britain and France attacked but the United Nations arranged a truce and foreign forces withdrew leaving the Suez in Egypt's control.

With no canal to operate Universelle du Canal Maritime de Suez became Compagnie Financiere de Suez in 1958. A year later it created a bank (which became Banque Indosuez in 1974).

In 1967 Financiere de Suez became the largest shareholder in Societe Lyonnaise des Eaux et de L'Eclairage a leading French water company. Formed in 1880 Lyonnaise des Eaux had stakes in water (Northumbrian Water) and energy (Elyo). After France's energy firms were nationalized in 1946 Lyonnaise des Eaux dipped deeper into the water industry by acquiring Degremont (now Ondeo-Degremont) in 1972. It also purchased stakes in waste management (SITA 1970) and heating systems (Cofreth 1975).

In the 1980s Lyonnaise des Eaux expanded in Spain the UK and the US and diversified into cable TV (1986) and broadcast TV (1987). It merged with construction firm Dumez in 1990.

Meanwhile Financiere de Suez became a financial power when it won a controlling stake in Societe Generale de Belgique (SGB) in 1988 and bought Groupe Victoire in 1989. But the two buys left the firm (renamed Compagnie de Suez in 1990) deeply in debt.

Losing money Compagnie de Suez disposed of Victoire (1994) and then the valuable Banque Indosuez (1996). In 1996 the company bought a controlling stake in Belgium's top utility Tractebel (now SUEZ-TRACTEBEL). Compagnie de Suez and Lyonnaise des Eaux merged in 1997 to create Suez Lyonnaise des Eaux. The following year Suez Lyonnaise acquired the rest of SGB and bought the European and Asian operations of waste management giant Browning-Ferris Industries; it also began divesting noncore operations.

Suez Lyonnaise in 1999 expanded its core businesses primarily in the US. The company bought Calgon (water treatment US) and Nalco Chemical (water treatment chemicals US) then merged Calgon into Nalco to form Ondeo Nalco. (The company's name was changed back to Nalco when it was divested in 2003.)

In 2000 Suez Lyonnaise bought United Water Resources (now United Water) and acquired the rest of SITA. Through its Elyo subsidiary Suez Lyonnaise bought out minority shareholders in US-based Trigen Energy. The company also merged its construction unit Groupe GTM with French construction rival VINCI; Suez Lyonnaise then sold the VINCI shares that it received from the transaction.

The next year the company shortened its name to Suez (later modified to SUEZ) as part of a global rebranding effort. It also united its water services operations under the ONDEO brand. In 2002 SUEZ made Tractebel a wholly owned subsidiary by purchasing the remaining publicly held shares. Also in 2002 SUEZ sold minority stakes in communications equipment manufacturer Sagem (now SAFRAN) steelmaker Arcelor and motorway operator Autopistas Concesionaria Espa?ola (ACESA).

SUEZ divested most of its 11% stake in Belgian insurance firm Fortis for nearly $2 billion in 2003. It also sold its 79% stake in cable company Coditel that year. In 2003 the company merged Tractebel and SGB (Tractebel's former holding company) to form SUEZ-TRACTEBEL. Gaz de France was founded in 1946 by the French government to consolidate the more than 500 (mostly coal-fired) gas works that had existed before WWII. From 1949 on Gaz de France focused on upgrading gas plants and local transmission networks. Its first long-distance pipeline was built in 1953 linking Paris to the Lorraine coal gas fields. With the development of the Lacq gas field in southwestern France annual gas sales increased by 300% between 1957 and 1962.

By 1965 nearly half of the French population was supplied with natural gas. Spurred on by the loss of its Algerian colony which held major oil and gas assets the French government pushed for new gas supplies to supplement its Lacq resources. Gaz de France was able to secure a contract with Algerian natural gas supplier Sonatrach in 1965 and in 1967 it signed an import contract with Dutch supplier Gasunie. The company also diversified in the 1960s helping to build a natural gas liquefaction plant in Algeria and a receiving terminal in Le Havre. It also helped pioneer gas storage engineering.

Following the price shock of the Arab oil embargo of the early 1970s Gaz de France stepped up its search for alternative suppliers including contracts with Russia's largest gas producer Soyouzgazexport (in 1976 1980 and 1984) and four separate Norwegian producers Efofisk (1977) Stafjord (1985) Heimdal (1986) and Gullfaks (1987). The company also renewed contracts with its Dutch and Algerian suppliers.

During the 1990s Gaz de France expanded its international operations as deregulation in the industry accelerated. In 1994 the company gained a foothold in eastern Germany's gas sector by buying gas production and storage company Erdgas Erdol GmbH (EEG). Three years later Gaz de France acquired Italian heating and related services firm Agip Servizi and was awarded a joint venture contract to distribute gas in Berlin in 1997 and in the suburbs of Mexico City in 1998.

Through contracts for North Sea oil and gas with Elf Aquitaine (now owned by TOTAL FINA ELF) British-Borneo and Ruhrgas in 1999 the company increased its natural gas supplies. It also established new gas supply contracts with Nigeria and Qatar.

For the first time in its history Gaz de France became an offshore field operator in 2000 by acquiring exploration and production company TransCanada International Netherlands and a 39% stake in Noordgastransport BV an offshore gas pipeline operator.

In 2001 through the purchase of a 10% interest in Petronet LNG Gaz de France embarked on a project to import liquefied natural gas from Qatar to India.

France's energy and environmental services giants came together when SUEZ merged with Gaz de France in 2008 to form GDF SUEZ. As part of the merger agreement and in order to clear hurdles set up by the EU competition policy SUEZ then spun off its waste and water unit SUEZ Environnement.

Following the 2008 merger of Gaz de France with SUEZ in a move to expand geographically GDF SUEZ acquired a 90% stake in Izmit Gaz Dagitim San Ve Tic AS (Turkey's third-largest natural gas distributor) for $232 million.

In 2009 the company made further geographic realignments prompted by the regulatory requirements of the European Commission for GDF SUEZ and Germany's E.ON to allow for more competition in their major markets by swapping some generation capacity. It acquired from E.ON 860 MW of Germany-based conventional power plants 132 MW of hydroelectric plants and through subsidiary Electrabel access to 770 MW of nuclear power. In return GDF SUEZ sold to E.ON a similar amount of power generation capacity in France and the Benelux countries.

Ramping up its nuclear assets in 2011 GDF SUEZ formed a joint venture with IBERDROLA and Scottish and Southern Energy. NuGeneration planned to develop up to 3600 MW of nuclear power in the UK. Late in 2011 SSE announced plans to sell its 25 percent in NuGen to GDF SUEZ and IBERDROLA and return to its renewable energy strategy.

EXECUTIVES

Executive Vice-President Energy Service, Jerome Tolot, age 62
Executive Member Senior Managers Department, Emmanuel van Innis, age 65
President Energy Policy Committee, Jean-Pierre Hansen, age 64
EVP Global Gas and LNG Business Line, Jean-Marie Dauger, age 61
Executive Vice-President Communications Marketing and Sustainable Development, Valerie Bernis, age 55
Chairman and CEO; Chairman SUEZ-TRACTEBEL GDF SUEZ Energy Services and SUEZ Environnement, Gerard Mestrallet, age 64
Executive Vice-President Energy International Business, Dirk Beeuwsaert, age 66
Executive Member Human Resources, Philippe Saimpert, age 59
Executive Member Energy Europe and International, Pierre Clavel, age 53
Executive Member Business Strategy and Sustainable Development, Alain Chaigneau, age 61
Executive Member and General Secretary, Yves de Gaulle, age 61
Executive Vice-President Environment Business, Jean-Louis Chaussade, age 62
Vice Chairman and President, Jean-Francois Cirelli, age 55
Executive Vice-President Chief Financial Officer, Isabelle Kocher, age 46
CEO of GDF SUEZ Energy International, Willem van Twembeke, age 48
Executive Member Audit and Risks, Philippe Jeunet, age 59
Executive Vice-President Group Human Resources, Henri Ducre, age 57
Executive Vice-President Infrastructures, Jean-Claude Depail, age 65
Chief Executive Officer, Activites Nucleaires
Director of Group Purchasing, Claire Brabec-Lagrange
Director of the Group Sales and Marketing, Jean-Louis Blanc
Director of Information Systems, Veronique Durand-Charlot
Vice-President in charge of Group Human Resources, Henri Ducra
Director, Jean-Louis Beffa, age 71
Director, Anne Lauvergeon, age 53
Director, Paul Desmarais Jr., age 58
Director, Edmond Alphandery, age 69
Director, Baron Albert Frere, age 86
Director, Aldo Cardoso, age 57
Director, Rene Carron, age 70
Director, Jean-Paul Bailly, age 66
Director, Pierre Graff, age 65
Vice Chairman and President, Jean-Francois Cirelli, age 55
Director, Thierry de Rudder, age 63
Director, Pierre-Franck Chevet, age 51
Director, Ramon Fernandez, age 45
Director, Alain Beullier, age 49
Director, Patrick Petitjean, age 60
Director, Anne-Marie Mourer, age 54
Director, Gabrielle Prune, age 56
Director, Olivier Bourges, age 46
Director, Lord Simon of Highbury, age 73
Director, Pierre Mongin, age 58
Auditors: Mazars

LOCATIONS

HQ: GDF SUEZ
1, place Samuel de Champlain, Courbevoie 92400
Phone: (33) 1 44 22 00 00
Web: www.gdfsuez.com

2011 Sales

	% of total
Europe	80
Asia Pacific & Middle	8
North	6
Latin	5
Africa	1
Total	1

PRODUCTS/OPERATIONS

2011 Sales

	% of total
Electricity	33
Environmental	33
Natural gas &	34
Total	100

COMPETITORS

BG Group
Bouygues
CANAL+
Centrica
Covanta
Dragados
E.ON
Electricite de France
Electricite de Strasbourg
Enel
Eni
Gas Natural SDG
Gasunie
Gazprom
Italgas
National Grid
RWE
SABESP
United Utilities
Vattenfall
Veolia Environnement

HISTORICAL FINANCIALS

Company Type: Public

Income Statement

FYE: December 31

	REVENUE ($ mil.)	NET INCOME ($ mil.)	NET PROFIT MARGIN	EMPLOYEES
12/12	127,900	2,042	1.6%	236,156
12/11	117,281	5,177	4.4%	240,303
12/10	113,063	6,177	5.5%	236,116
12/09	115,113	6,449	5.6%	242,714
12/08	94,963	6,790	7.2%	234,653
Annual Growth	7.7%	(25.9%)	—	0.2%

2012 Year-End Financials

Debt ratio: 36.6%
Return on equity: 2.5%
Cash ($ mil.): 15,003
Current ratio: 1.07
Long-term debt ($ mil.): 59,637
No. of shares (mil.): —
Dividends
Yield: 14.2%
Payout: 371.8%
Market value ($ mil.): —

	STOCK PRICE ($) FY Close	P/E High/Low		PER SHARE ($) Earnings	Dividends	Book Value
12/12	21.04	73	47	0.88	3.00	33.41
12/11	27.17	44	23	2.33	3.75	36.77
12/10	36.04	41	22	2.81	3.07	37.43
12/09	42.80	49	25	2.92	3.09	39.19
12/08	49.45	49	19	4.12	1.06	37.63
Annual Growth	(19.2%)	—	—	(32.0%)	29.6%	(2.9%)

GlaxoSmithKline Plc

GlaxoSmithKline (GSK) gives anxiety asthma and other ailments the ax. One of the top five pharmaceutical firms in the world GSK's bestsellers include respiratory neurological cardiovascular and dermatology drugs as well as vaccines and antivirals. Its top product is asthma medication Advair (aka Seretide) which combines two of its other asthma products Flovent and Serevent. Other bestsellers include epilepsy treatment Lamictal cholesterol medicine Lovaza prostate enlargement drug Avodart and antibiotic Augmentin as well as Cervarix and Pediarix vaccines. The company's consumer products include Tums dental care products Aquafresh and Sensodyne and smoking-cessation products NicoDerm and Nicorette.

The company markets its products directly to hospitals pharmacies doctors and other health care consumers; it also uses wholesale distributors in some markets and serves customers in more than 100 countries overall. Pharmaceuticals account for two-thirds of sales with vaccines and consumer health products making up the remainder of revenues. Respiratory drugs are the company's largest sales category primarily due to blockbuster Advair which brings in more than #5 billion ($6.7 billion) annually. GSK also has a strong presence in the central nervous system cardiovascular urogenital dermatology (through its Stiefel division) virology infectious disease oncology and metabolism treatment markets.

As sales in GSK's largest market the US account for more than a third of pharmaceutical sales maintaining a rich portfolio of US patent-protected products can make or break the company's future. Examples of GSK drugs that have experienced sales slumps due to patent losses include its bestselling herpes drug Valtrex which began facing generic competition in 2009 and accounted for a 5% to 10% drop in US and European pharmaceutical sales in both 2010 and 2011. Other recent patent losses include cardiovascular drug Arixtra and oncology drug Hycamtin both of which began facing generic competition in 2011.

The development of new potential blockbusters is the best way to alleviate these losses and GSK's development efforts include about 100 different clinical stage projects. Its major R&D centers are located in the UK the US Spain Belgium and China. GSK has some 30 candidates in late-phase trials for conditions such as HIV pulmonary conditions Parkinson's disease type-2 diabetes heart disease and various cancers. One candidate Benlysta became the first lupus therapy approved by the FDA in more than 50 years in 2011; the drug was developed with Human Genome Sciences(HGS) and was also approved in Europe that year. Other drugs launched in 2011 include epilepsy treatment Potiga (also known as Trobalt) and restless leg syndrome medication Horizant.

GSK is also working to pump potential new blockbusters into its pipeline by acquiring promising research firms and forming development agreements with other drug companies. For instance the company is developing cancer drug Arzerra for additional indications with biotech firm Genmab. It also has development deals with OncoMed (for new cancer treatments) and Theravance (respiratory drugs). GSK is also working with Pfizer on HIV medications; many of the company's HIV and vaccine development programs aim to provide affordable disease preventions and treatments to developing countries.

To further solidify its R&D relationships in 2012 the company increased its minority stake in development partner Theravance from 19% to 27% acquired a 15% stake in companion diagnostic test provider and partner Response Genetics Inc. (RGI) and fully acquired HGS for some $3 billion. In acquiring HGS GSK gained full access to Benlysta and other partnered development candidates.

A major trend among pharmaceutical companies is to focus on growing in emerging markets which represent an opportunity for big sales because of a relatively untapped consumer base. Towards that end GSK owns a minority stake (about 20%) in South African generic drugmaker Aspen Pharmacare; it has also established a presence in select Asian African Latin American and Middle Eastern nations. In 2010 the company spent about #174 million ($250 million) to expand in Latin America with the buy of Laboratorios Phoenix an Argentinean drug manufacturer and marketer.

GSK also expanded its Asian operations by acquiring Nanjing MeiRui Pharma a Chinese manufacturer of allergy and urology products in 2010 and by buying out its Chinese partner Neptunus in a joint venture to manufacture influenza vaccines in 2011. The following year GSK formed a joint venture with Daiichi Sankyo to make and sell vaccines in Japan a market where GSK has seen rapid growth in recent years.

CEO Andrew Witty is intent on keeping the company focused on small strategic acquisitions and expansion in fast-growing markets including vaccines biopharmaceuticals and consumer health products. He is also carrying forth the company's ongoing cost-cutting measures which aim to reduce operational expenses through measures such as simplifying its administrative infrastructure narrowing its R&D programs and consolidating its drug development and manufacturing sites. To focus on its top selling drugs and R&D investments the company is also divesting assets where it sees fit.

For instance GSK sold a penicillin manufacturing site in Bristol Tennessee to Dr. Reddy's Laboratories for an undisclosed price in 2011. The sale also included the rights to the Augmentin and Amoxil brands in the US. GSK kept the rights to those brands outside the US. The firm also sold its minority stake (about 20%) in laboratory services firm Quest Diagnostics (which provides clinical trial testing to GSK) for some #585 million ($1.1 billion) and it sold North American rights back to Valeant Pharmaceuticals for antiviral cream Zovirax.

Still in the mood to divest GSK also announced plans to sell some noncore consumer health brands. In early 2012 it completed the sale of a portfolio of North American OTC brands including BC Beano Ecotrin Fiber Choice Goody's and Tagamet to Prestige Brands Holdings for some #426 million ($660 million). Later in 2012 GSK reached agreements to sell its noncore OTC offerings in Europe and other international markets including Solpadeine and Zantac; European rights will go to Omega Pharma for some #391 million ($614 million) and rights in other international markets will be sold to Aspen Pharmacare for some #164 million ($263 million). GSK also plans to divest global rights to its OTC weight loss product alli.

The company has faced some trouble in recent years over diabetes drug Avandia which was linked to heart attack risks in 2007. GSK has since withdrawn sales of the drug in most markets; the European Medicines Agency suspended marketing authorization for Avandia in 2010 and the FDA placed use of the drug under a strict risk evaluation and mitigation strategy (REMS) program that same year. In addition the firm is working to settle a large number of patient lawsuits related to Avandia.

GSK paid $3 billion in 2012 to settle numerous fraud charges by the US Justice Department and other federal and state autorities including for failing to report safety data on Avandia. The agreement which was the largest such drugmaker settlement to date also covered lawsuits over improper sales and marketing practices for several other products as well as improper Medicaid reimbursement activities.

Overall revenues declined 1% in 2011 to #27.4 billion ($43.4 billion) as GSK worked to stabilize its operations following the Valtrex patent loss. (Sales had decreased 3% the previous year largely due to the increase in generic competition.) Other factors impacting the firm's revenues in 2010 and 2011 include decreased sales of Avandia and a drop in demand for pandemic flu vaccines and flu-related antivirals. Net income also fell in 2010 to some #1.6 billion ($2.5 billion) due to legal expenses but in 2011 profits bounced back to previous levels of more than #5 billion ($8 billion). Sales from new product launches as well as increased revenues in emerging and Asian markets have helped to offset the impact of competition and other factors causing flat or decreased sales in the US and Europe.

HISTORY

Englishman Joseph Nathan started an import-export business in New Zealand in 1873. He obtained the rights to a process for drying milk and began making powdered milk in New Zealand selling it as baby food Glaxo.

Nathan's son Alec dispatched to London to oversee baby food sales in Britain increased Glaxo's name recognition by publishing the Glaxo Baby Book a guide to child care. After WWI the company began distribution in India and South America.

In the 1920s Glaxo launched vitamin D-fortified formulations. It entered the pharmaceutical business with its 1927 introduction of Ostelin a liquid vitamin D concentrate and continued to grow globally in the 1930s introducing Ostermilk (vitamin-fortified milk).

Glaxo began making penicillin and anesthetics during WWII; it went public in 1947. A steep drop in antibiotic prices in the mid-1950s led Glaxo to diversify; it bought veterinary medical instrument and drug distribution firms.

In the 1970s the British Monopolies Commission quashed both a hostile takeover attempt by Beecham and a proposed merger with retailer and drugmaker Boots. Glaxo launched US operations in 1978.

Glaxo shed nondrug operations in the 1980s to concentrate on pharmaceuticals. A 1981 marketing blitz launched antiulcer drug Zantac (to vie with SmithKline's Tagamet) in the US where Glaxo's sales had been small. The company boosted outreach by contracting to use Hoffmann-La Roche's sales staff. The Zantac sales assault gave Glaxo leadership in US antiulcer drug sales.

Under CEO Sir Richard Sykes Glaxo in 1995 made a surprise bid for UK rival Wellcome. Founded in 1880 by Americans Silas Burroughs and Henry Wellcome to sell McKesson-Robbins' products outside the US Burroughs Wellcome and Co. began making its own products two years later. By the 1990s the company which fostered Nobel Prize-winning researchers led the world in antiviral medicines. Its primary drug products were Zovirax (launched 1981) and Retrovir (1987).

Though an earlier bid by Glaxo had been rejected Sykes won the takeover with backing from Wellcome Trust Wellcome's largest shareholder.

In 1997 the company formed a new genetics division buying Spectra Biomedical and its gene variation technology. That year the company pulled diabetes drug Romozin (Rezulin in the US) from the UK market over concerns that it caused liver damage.

Glaxo in 1998 ended its joint venture with Warner-Lambert (begun 1993) selling its former partner the Canadian and US marketing rights to acid blocker Zantac 75.

In 1999 Glaxo trimmed its product line pulling hepatitis treatment Wellferon because of slow sales and selling the US rights to several anesthesia products. It also cut some 3400 jobs (half from the UK). Also that year Glaxo threatened to leave the UK after the National Health Service opted not to cover antiflu inhalant Relenza claiming the drug is not cost-effective.

The FDA in 2000 approved Glaxo's Lotronex for irritable bowel syndrome but several hospitalizations linked to the drug prompted the FDA to ask the company to withdraw it from the US market. Later that year Glaxo completed its merger with former UK rival SmithKline Beecham to create GlaxoSmithKline (GSK); Jean-Pierre Garnier took over as CEO.

Although GSK has largely escaped the flurry of patent worries afflicting other druggernauts in 2001 a US court declared invalid three patents protecting Augmentin from generics until 2017 and opened the door for cheaper rivals.

GSK returned European and international marketing rights for erectile dysfunction drug Levitra back to its developer Bayer HealthCare in late 2004 after it umm failed to perform. (It still markets the drug with Schering-Plough in the US.)

In 2005 the company expanded its vaccine operations through the acquisition of Corixa; that purchase gained the company a factory engaged in producing Monophosphoral Lipid A a key ingredient in a number of the company's vaccines and vaccine-related products. Later its acquisition of ID Biomedical a Canadian vaccine producer bolstered GSK's influenza vaccine production capability. The company also increased its flu vaccine capacity five-fold by building a new production facility in Dresden Germany; a $633 million production facility in France; and a vaccine plant in Singapore.

The fall of 2005 saw the sale of the company's US dermatology business (part of GlaxoSmithKline Consumer Healthcare) to the PharmaDerm division of ALTANA Inc. (which later became Nycomed US and then Fougera Pharmaceuticals); products involved in the deal included Alcovate Cutivate Emgel Oxistat and Temovate. In 2006 GSK sold its unbranded generic drug businesses in Spain and Italy to India's pharma giant Ranbaxy.

In 2006 GSK settled a tax dispute with the IRS for $3.1 billion the largest single tax payment in IRS history over international profit allocation in taxes filed by Glaxo Wellcome (prior to the 2001 Glaxo Wellcome/ SmithKline Beecham merger) from 1989 through 2000. The payment also includes taxes owed from 2001 through 2005.

GSK boosted its development pipeline in 2006 with the acquisition of the research operations of PLIVA Eastern Europe's largest pharmaceutical maker (the remainder of which was bought by Barr Pharmaceuticals) which focused on research into macrolide antibiotics (it developed blockbuster antibiotic Zithromax sold by Pfizer). That same year GSK acquired private biotech Domantis Ltd which specialized in laboratory-engineered monoclonal antibodies. The additions which cost the company more than $450 million nearly doubled the size of GSK's research capabilities. GSK also expanded its consumer products operations by purchasing CNS the maker of Breathe Right nasal strips in late 2006.

Tykerb an orally administered breast-cancer treatment gained FDA approval in 2007 and EU approval the following year. Human papillomavirus (HPV) vaccine Cervarix was also approved for sale in the EU in 2007.

Diabetes treatment Avandia another new drug that was a top seller in 2006 experienced a decrease in sales in 2007 after its safety was disputed by scientific studies that linked the drug to a risk of heart attack. GSK updated Avandia's warning labels and began conducting further studies on the drug. As a result of Avandia's troubles and increased generic competition GSK announced a cost-cutting program towards the end of 2007 to streamline manufacturing operations and marketing programs.

GSK acquired Reliant Pharmaceuticals for $1.65 billion to expand its cardiovascular product line (including coronary artery disease treatment Lovaza) in December 2007; GSK integrated Reliant's operations shortly after.

The company launched an operational excellence restructuring program in 2007 that aimed to reduce costs across the GSK organization. In 2008 Jean-Pierre Garnier was replaced as CEO by Andrew Witty who had been with the company for over 20 years and was previously president of GSK's European pharmaceuticals division.

In 2008 GSK acquired biotech firm Sirtris Pharmaceuticals for #362 million ($720 million). Following the purchase the acquired firm operated as an independent drug discovery subsidiary focused on the areas of metabolism immunology inflammation and neurology.

GSK's added a line of dermatology products when it acquired Stiefel Laboratories from the Stiefel family and other investors (including the Blackstone Group) for some $2.9 billion in 2009. The acquisition added prescription and over-the-counter medications for conditions including acne psoriasis dandruff and fungal infections. Stiefel was combined with the existing GSK prescription dermatology and OTC operations into a new business unit under the Stiefel name. Also in 2009 GSK acquired a portfolio of international prescription products from UCB for some #477 million to expand in Africa the Middle East Latin America and the Asia/Pacific region.

GSK sold US marketing rights to antidepressant Wellbutrin XL in 2009 after it began facing generic competition in 2006 and has thus seen lower sales volumes to fellow drugmaker Valeant Pharmaceuticals (formerly Biovail) for $510 million. GSK retained international marketing rights for the drug.

A highlight for GSK's development and commercialization programs in 2009 came from its pandemic vaccine program which delivered vaccines for H1N1 or swine flu. (It also previously developed a vaccine for H5N1 avian bird flu.) GSK also pooled its HIV/AIDS assets with Pfizer's in 2009 to form ViiV Healthcare a joint venture aiming to develop and sell affordable HIV therapies.

EXECUTIVES

Chairman, Sir Christopher Charles (Chris) Gent, age 65
President Asia Pacific and Japan, Marc Dunoyer
CEO and Director, Sir Andrew Witty, age 49, $1,230,205 total compensation
President Global Manufacturing and Supply, David Pulman
SVP Human Resources, Claire Thomas
President Consumer Healthcare Worldwide, Emma Walmsley
President North America Pharmaceuticals, Deirdre P. Connelly, age 52
SVP Governance Ethics and Assurance, Simon M. Bicknell
SVP Global Communications, Philip (Phil) Thomson
Chairman Research and Development and Director, Moncef Slaoui, age 53, $825,000 total compensation
President - Pharmaceuticals R&D, Patrick Vallance
President Emerging Markets and Asia Pacific, Abbas Hussain
SVP Core Business Services and Chief Information Officer, Bill Louv
President Pharmaceuticals Europe, Eddie Gray
Chief Strategy Officer, David Redfern
SVP and General Counsel, Dan Troy
CFO and Director, Simon Dingemans

Senior Vice President Global Communications, Phil Thomson
Senior Vice President; General Counsel, Daniel Troy
President - Global Manufacturing & Supply, Roger Connor
President - Vaccines, Christophe Weber
Director, Sir Deryck Maughan, age 65
Director, James R. Murdoch, age 40
Director, Tom de Swaan, age 68
Director, H. Lawrence (Larry) Culp Jr., age 50
Director, Judy C. Lewent, age 64
Director, Sir Robert P. Wilson, age 70
Director, Stacey Cartwright, age 49
Director, Stephanie A. Burns, age 58
CEO and Director, Sir Andrew Witty, age 49
Chairman Research and Development and Director, Moncef Slaoui, age 53
Director, Daniel K. Podolsky, age 59
Director, Sir Roy Anderson, age 66
CFO and Director, Simon Dingemans
Auditors: PricewaterhouseCoopersLLP

LOCATIONS

HQ: GlaxoSmithKline Plc
980 Great West Road, Brentford, Middlesex TW8 9GS
Phone: (44) 20 8047 5000 **Fax:** (44) 20 8047 7807
Web: www.gsk.com

2011 Sales

	% of total
US	32
Emerging markets	19
Asia/Pacific	7
Other	4
Total	**100**

PRODUCTS/OPERATIONS

2011 Sales

	% of total
Pharmaceuticals	
Cardiovascular & urogenital	10
ViiV Healthcare (HIV)	6
Antibacterials	5
Dermatology	4
Antivirals (non-HIV)	3
Oncology & emesis	2
Other	4
Consumer Healthcare	
OTC medicines	9
Oral health care	6
Nutritional health care	4
Total	**100**

Selected Products

Pharmaceuticals
- Respiratory
  - Beconase (allergies)
  - Becotide/Beclovent (asthma and chronic obstructive pulmonary disease)
  - Flixonase/Flonase (allergies)
  - Flixotide/Flovent (asthma and chronic obstructive pulmonary disease)
  - Seretide/Advair (asthma and chronic obstructive pulmonary disease)
  - Serevent (asthma and chronic obstructive pulmonary disease)
  - Ventolin (asthma and chronic obstructive pulmonary disease)
  - Veramyst/Avamys (rhinitis)
- Cardiovascular and urogenital
  - Arixtra (deep vein thrombosis and pulmonary embolism)
  - Avodart (prostatic hyperplasia)
  - Benlysta (systemic lupus erychematosus with HGS)
  - Coreg CR (heart failure and hypertension)
  - Fraxiparine (deep vein thrombosis and pulmonary embolism)
  - Levitra (erectile dysfunction with Bayer)
  - Lovaza (coronary heart disease)
  - Vesicare (overactive bladder)
  - Volibris (pulmonary hypertension)
- Central nervous system disorders
  - Horizant (post-herpetic neuralgia or restless leg syndrome)
  - Imigran/Imitrex (migraines)
  - Lamictal (epilepsy and bipolar disorder)
  - Potiga/Trobalt (epilepsy and partial seizures)
  - Requip (Parkinson's disease)
  - Seroxat/Paxil (depression)
  - Treximet (migraine)
  - Wellbutrin SR (depression)
- ViiV Healthcare (HIV with Pfizer)
  - Combivir/Biovir (reverse transcriptase inhibitor for HIV/AIDS)
  - Epivir/3TC (reverse transcriptase inhibitor for HIV/AIDS)
  - Epizicom/Kivexa (combination of Epivir and Ziagen for HIV/AIDS)
  - Lexiva/Telzir (protease inhibitor for HIV/AIDS)
  - Selzentry (HIV)
  - Trizivir (three reverse transcriptase inhibitors for HIV/AIDS)
- Antibacterials
  - Amoxil and Augmentin (antibiotics non-US only)
- Dermatology
  - Bactroban (skin infections)
  - Duac (acne vulgaris)
  - Zovirax (herpes infections shingles chicken pox and cold sores)
- Antivirals
  - Relenza (influenza)
  - Hepsera (hepatitis B)
  - Valtrex/Zelitrex (shingles and genital herpes)
  - Zeffix/Septavir/Heptodin/Epivir HBV (hepatitis B)
- Vaccines
  - Cervarix (human papilloma virus)
  - Fluarix (influenza)
  - FluLaval (influenza)
  - Infanrix/Pediarix (diphtheria tetanus pertussis polio and hepatitis B)
  - Rotarix (rotavirus)
  - Synflorix (pneumonia)
  - Twinrix (hepatitis A and hepatitis B)
- Metabolic
  - Avandia Avandamet (type 2 diabetes)
  - Boniva/Bonviva (osteoporosis with Roche)
- Oncology and emesis
  - Arzerra (refractory chronic lymphocytic leukemia)
  - Hycamtin (ovarian cervical and small cell-lung cancers)
  - Promacta/Revolade (blood therapy)
  - Tykerb/Tyverb (advanced and metastatic breast cancer)
  - Votrient (metastatic renal cell carcinoma)

Consumer products
- Over-the-counter medicines
  - Abreva (cold sores)
  - alli (weight loss)
  - Breathe Right (nasal strips)
  - Citrucel (laxative)
  - Commit (smoking-cessation)
  - Contac (respiratory product)
  - Nicabate/NicoDerm/NiQuitin CQ (smoking-cessation)
  - Nicorette (smoking-cessation)
  - Panadol (analgesic)
  - Tums (antacid)
- Oral care
  - Aquafresh (toothpaste and toothbrushes)
  - Corega (denture care)
  - Dr Best (toothbrushes)
  - Macleans (toothpaste)
  - Odol (toothpaste)
  - Polident (denture cleaner)
  - Poli-Grip (denture adhesive)
  - Sensodyne (toothpaste)
- Nutritional health care
  - Horlicks (milk-based malted food and chocolate drinks)
  - Lucozade (glucose energy drink)
  - Ribena (line of juice drinks rich in vitamin C)

COMPETITORS

Abbott Labs
Amgen
AstraZeneca
Bayer AG
Biogen Idec
Bristol-Myers Squibb
Colgate-Palmolive
Dr. Reddy' s
Elan
Eli Lilly
Forest Labs
Gilead Sciences
Johnson & Johnson
Merck
Mylan
Novartis
Novo Nordisk
Pfizer
Procter & Gamble
Ranbaxy Laboratories
Reckitt Benckiser
Roche Holding
Sanofi
Takeda Pharmaceutical
Teva
UCB

HISTORICAL FINANCIALS

Company Type: Public

Income Statement

FYE: December 31

	REVENUE ($ mil.)	NET INCOME ($ mil.)	NET PROFIT MARGIN	EMPLOYEES
12/12	42,603	7,358	17.3%	99,488
12/11	42,308	8,127	19.2%	97,389
12/10	44,082	2,537	5.8%	96,461
12/09	45,944	8,957	19.5%	99,913
12/08	35,488	6,706	18.9%	99,003
Annual Growth	4.7%	2.3%	—	0.1%

2012 Year-End Financials

Debt ratio: 71.1%
Return on equity: 65.7%
Cash ($ mil.): 6,744
Current ratio: 0.99
Long-term debt ($ mil.): 23,647
No. of shares (mil.): —
Dividends
Yield: 5.7%
Payout: 168.5%
Market value ($ mil.): —

	STOCK PRICE ($) FY Close	P/E High/Low	PER SHARE ($) Earnings	Dividends	Book Value
12/12	43.47	133115	1.47	2.48	1.91
12/11	45.63	109 85	1.59	5.53	2.46
12/10	39.22	337225	0.50	2.00	2.66
12/09	42.25	106 56	1.75	1.85	2.86
12/08	37.27	176 79	1.28	2.14	2.04
Annual Growth	3.9%	— —	3.5%	3.7%	(1.6%)

Glencore Xstrata PLC

LOCATIONS

HQ: Glencore Xstrata PLC
Baarermattstrasse 3, P.O. Box 777, Baar CH-6341
Phone: (41) 41 709 2000 **Fax:** (41) 41 709 3000
Web: www.glencore.com

PRODUCTS/OPERATIONS

Proforma	2,012 $ mil.	Revenues % of total
Marketing activities	190,000	80
Industrial activities	47,000	20
Total	**237,000**	**100**

Selected Operations

Agricultural Products
- Barley
- Corn
- Meals
- Rice
- Sugar
- Wheat

Energy Products
- Coal
- Oil

Metals and Minerals
- Copper
- Ferroalloys
- Lead
- Nickel
- Zinc

Selected Mergers and Acquisitions

2013
Xstrata ($41 billion; Switzerland; diversified metals miner)
2012
Viterra ($6.2 billion; Canada; grain merchant)

HISTORICAL FINANCIALS

Company Type: Public

Income Statement FYE: December 31

	REVENUE ($ mil.)	NET INCOME ($ mil.)	NET PROFIT MARGIN	EMPLOYEES
12/12	214,436	1,004	0.5%	0
12/11	186,152	4,048	2.2%	0
12/10	144,978	1,291	0.9%	0
12/09	106,364	983	0.9%	0
Annual Growth	26.3%	0.7%	—	—

2012 Year-End Financials

Debt ratio: 36.1%
Return on equity: 3.3%
Cash ($ mil.): 2,782
Current ratio: 1.15
Long-term debt ($ mil.): 19,028
No. of shares (mil.): —
Dividends
Yield: 2.6%
Payout: —
Market value ($ mil.): —

	STOCK PRICE ($) FY Close	P/E High/Low		PER SHARE ($) Earnings	Dividends	Book Value
12/12	5.80	55	33	0.14	0.15	4.40
12/11	6.04	11	8	0.69	0.00	4.23
12/10	0.00	—	—	8,606.00	0.00	36,160.00
Annual Growth	—	—	—	(97.5%)	—	(95.0%)

Great-West Lifeco Inc.

Great-West writes policies for the Great White North and beyond. Holding company Great-West Lifeco majority-owned by Power Financial is one of Canada's largest insurance organizations but its reach extends to the US and to Europe. Through subsidiaries (including Great-West Life Assurance in Canada and Great-West Life & Annuity in the US) the company offers a range of individual and group life and health insurance retirement savings and investment products reinsurance and services to financial institutions. Great-West Life Assurance's two major subsidiaries Canada Life and London Life Insurance provide individual insurance and wealth-management products in Canada Germany Ireland and the UK.

Operations

In the US Great-West Life & Annuity (GWL&A) provides retirement savings plans to employers. Great-West Lifeco's companies also provide reinsurance to niche markets in the US and Europe.

Strategy

To further its strategy of focusing on and expanding its financial services operations in the US in 2008 Great West Lifeco sold Great-West Healthcare which offers self-funded employee benefits plans to Cigna for $1.5 billion. However the global financial crisis hit the company's books and caused it to slow its expansion efforts that same year. By 2009 the combination of cost-cutting measures and a nascent credit market recovery eased the downward pressure. After weathering the storm the company said in mid-2010 that it was ready to resume acquisitions focusing on the US and Europe.

Mergers and Acquisitions

In 2013 Great-West Lifeco agreed to acquire Irish Life Group Limited for some E1.3 billion ($1.75 million) from the Irish government. The purchase will give Great-West a leading position in life insurance pension and investment management markets in Ireland. Following the transaction Great-West Lifeco will combine its existing Irish subsidiary Canada Life (Ireland) into the Irish Life division.

EXECUTIVES

President and CEO Putnam Investments, Robert L. (Bob) Reynolds, age 61
Chairman of the Board; Chairman of the Board Great-West Life; London Life Canada Life; Great-West Life and Annuity, Raymond L. McFeetors, age 67
Chairman, R. Jeffrey Orr
Chief Financial Officer; Executive Vice President, William W. Lovatt
President CEO and Director; President and CEO Great-West Life Assurance London Life Insurance and Canada Life Assurance, D. Allen Loney
President and CEO Great-West Life & Annuity Insurance, Mitchell T. G. Graye, age 57
Senior Vice President & General Counsel; Canada & Europe, Andrew D. Brands
Senior Vice President and Chief Risk Officer, Alexandre J. Guertin
SVP and General Counsel US, Richard G. Schultz, age 52
EVP Capital Management, Arshil Jamal
VP and Corporate Secretary, Laurie A. Speers
President and CEO, Paul A. Mahon
Senior Vice President - Capital Management, Garry MacNicholas
Senior Vice President and Chief Internal Auditor; SVP & Chief Internal Auditor of Great-West; London Life & Canada Life, Helen Kasdorf
Chief Compliance Officer; Canada, Anne Toal
Senior Vice-President and Chief Internal Auditor, Douglas Tkach
President and COO Canada of Great -West Life London Life and Canada Life, J. Dave Johnston
Director, R. Jeffrey Orr
Corporate Director, Marcel R. Coutu, age 59
Director, Andre R. Desmarais, age 55
Corporate Director, Raymond Royer, age 74
Director, Michel Plessis-Belair, age 70
Director, Paul Desmarais Jr., age 59
Corporate Director, David A. Nield, age 74
President CEO and Director; President and CEO Great-West Life Assurance London Life Insurance and Canada Life Assurance, D. Allen Loney
Director, Henri-Paul Rousseau, age 64
Director, Michael L. Hepher, age 70
Director, Rt. Hon. Donald F. (Don) Mazankowski, age 76
Director, Jerry E. A. Nickerson, age 77
Director, Emoke J. E. Szathmary
Director, Brian E. Walsh, age 59
Director, Philip K. Ryan, age 56
Director, H. David Graves
Director, Chaviva M. Hosek
Corporate Director, George S. Bain
Independent Director, Emoke Szathmary
Independent Director, Michel Plessis-Belair
Auditors: Deloitte&ToucheLLP

LOCATIONS

HQ: Great-West Lifeco Inc.
100 Osborne Street North, Winnipeg, Manitoba R3C 1V3
Phone: 204 946-1190 **Fax:** 204 946-4139
Web: www.greatwestlifeco.com

PRODUCTS/OPERATIONS

2009 Premiums

	% of total
Proprietary mutual funds	38
Life insurance guaranteed annuities & insured health	32
Segregated deposits	
Group	15
Individual	11
Self-funded premium equivalents (ASO	4
Total	**100**

Selected Subsidiaries & Affiliates

The Great-West Life Assurance Company
Canada Life Financial Corporation
The Canada Life Assurance CompanyCanada Life Capital Corporation Inc.The Canada Life Group (U.K.) LimitedCanada Life International Re LimitedCanada Life Irish Holding Company Limited
Crown Life Insurance Company
Laketon Investment Management Ltd.
London Insurance GroupLondon Life Insurance CompanyLondon Reinsurance Group Inc.
GWL&A Financial Inc. (US)
Great-West Life & Annuity Insurance Company
Advised Assets Group LLC
FASCore LLC

COMPETITORS

AXA Financial
CIBC
Industrial Alliance Insurance and Financial Servic
John Hancock Financial Services
Liberty Mutual
Manulife Financial
Nationwide Financial
Prudential
RBC Financial Group
RBC Insurance
Sun Life

HISTORICAL FINANCIALS

Company Type: Public

Income Statement FYE: December 31

	ASSETS ($ mil.)	NET INCOME ($ mil.)	INCOME AS % OF ASSETS	EMPLOYEES
12/12	255,102	1,940	0.8%	17,870
12/11	234,062	2,076	0.9%	17,350
12/10	229,909	1,704	0.7%	17,450
12/09	122,442	1,620	1.3%	18,150
12/08	105,984	1,183	1.1%	19,000
Annual Growth	24.6%	13.1%	—	(1.5%)

2012 Year-End Financials

Return on assets: 0.7%
Return on equity: 13.3%
Long-term debt ($ mil.): —
No. of shares (mil.): 950
Sales ($ mil): 30,225
Dividends
Yield: 0.0%
Payout: 64.7%
Market value ($ mil.): 23,214

	STOCK PRICE ($) FY Close	P/E High/Low		PER SHARE ($) Earnings	Dividends	Book Value
12/12	24.42	14	10	1.91	1.24	15.95
12/11	20.04	14	8	2.07	1.21	14.32
12/10	26.50	17	12	1.70	1.23	13.49
12/09	25.48	14	4	1.64	1.17	13.12
12/08	17.01	19	7	1.27	0.98	11.42
Annual Growth	9.5%	—	—	10.8%	6.0%	8.7%

Gunma Bank, Ltd. (The) (Japan)

Gunma Bank hopes that you have more than just a yen for its services. Through more than 140 branches The Gunma Bank provides banking services in the Gunma prefecture and surrounding areas of Japan through some 150 branches. The Gunma Bank also operates a subsidiary in Hong Kong and a branch in New York City. As the company's name might imply the Gunma prefecture (known for its industry and agriculture-based economy) accounts for more than 80% of deposits. Besides deposits Gunma Bank's services include loans to companies individuals and the government securities insurance and exchange. The Gunma Bank was founded in 1932.

Auditors: Ernst&YoungShinNihon

LOCATIONS

HQ: Gunma Bank, Ltd. (The) (Japan)
194 Motosoja-machi, Maebashi, Gunma 371-8611
Phone: (81) 27 252 1111
Web: www.gunmabank.co.jp

COMPETITORS

77 Bank
Hachijuni Bank
Ito-Yokado
Japan Post

HISTORICAL FINANCIALS

Company Type: Public

Income Statement FYE: March 31

	ASSETS ($ mil.)	NET INCOME ($ mil.)	INCOME AS % OF ASSETS	EMPLOYEES
03/13	72,746	218	0.3%	3,405
03/12	78,760	228	0.3%	3,399
03/11	75,207	209	0.3%	3,347
03/10	66,031	194	0.3%	3,359
03/09	60,136	111	0.2%	3,311
Annual Growth	4.9%	18.4%	—	0.7%

2013 Year-End Financials

Return on assets: 0.3%
Return on equity: 4.9%
Long-term debt ($ mil.): —
No. of shares (mil.): 473
Sales ($ mil): 1,383
Dividends
Yield: —
Payout: —
Market value ($ mil.): —

	STOCK PRICE ($) FY Close	P/E High/Low	PER SHARE ($) Earnings	Dividends	Book Value
03/13	0.00	— —	0.46	0.00	10.01
03/12	5.46	— —	0.47	0.00	10.21
03/11	5.73	— —	0.43	0.00	9.43
03/10	5.57	— —	0.39	0.00	8.15
Annual Growth	—	— —	3.9%	—	5.3%

Hachijuni Bank, Ltd. (Japan)

The Hachijuni Bank operates more than 150 branches in Japan primarily in the central prefecture of Nagano. It serves individuals and businesses with traditional products as deposit services and loans. The bank also owns subsidiaries active in financial services including leasing consumer loan guarantee investment advisory venture capital for high-tech firms and credit cards. Overseas Hachijuni has a branch in Hong Kong and representative offices in China Singapore and Thailand. The company was founded in Nagano City in 1931.

The Hachijuni Bank is looking to expand both through opening additional offices and through beefing up its offerings in such areas as investment production sales and consultation services.

EXECUTIVES

President and Director, Yoshiyuki Yamaura
Managing Director, Yoshio Horigome
Deputy President and Director, Sadayuki Koide
Managing Director, Tadashige Maeyama
Managing Director, Yoshio Horigome
Deputy President and Director, Sadayuki Koide
Managing Director, Tadashige Maeyama
Auditors: DeloitteToucheTohmatsu

LOCATIONS

HQ: Hachijuni Bank, Ltd. (Japan)
178-8 Aza Okada, Oaza Nakagosho, Nagano 380-8682
Phone: (81) 26 227 1182
Web: www.82bank.co.jp

COMPETITORS

Daishi Bank
Gunma Bank
Hokuetsu Bank Ltd.
Mitsubishi UFJ Financial Group
Mizuho Financial
Musashino Bank
Resona
Sumitomo Mitsui
Towa Bank

HISTORICAL FINANCIALS

Company Type: Public

Income Statement FYE: March 31

	ASSETS ($ mil.)	NET INCOME ($ mil.)	INCOME AS % OF ASSETS	EMPLOYEES
03/13	77,105	235	0.3%	3,756
03/12	80,473	211	0.3%	3,800
03/11	76,006	244	0.3%	3,862
03/10	65,939	180	0.3%	3,851
03/09	61,677	4	0.0%	3,711
Annual Growth	5.7%	163.2%	—	0.3%

2013 Year-End Financials

Return on assets: 0.3%
Return on equity: 4.3%
Long-term debt ($ mil.): —
No. of shares (mil.): 506
Sales ($ mil): 1,727
Dividends
Yield: —
Payout: —
Market value ($ mil.): 30,098

	STOCK PRICE ($) FY Close	P/E High/Low	PER SHARE ($) Earnings	Dividends	Book Value
03/13	59.46	— —	0.46	0.00	11.83
03/12	58.85	— —	0.41	0.00	11.75
03/11	57.56	— —	0.47	0.75	10.99
03/10	56.60	— —	0.34	0.54	9.53
03/09	58.50	— —	0.01	0.64	7.86
Annual Growth	0.4%	— —	166.1%	—	10.7%

Hang Seng Bank Ltd.

Hang Seng Bank whose name means "ever-growing" in Chinese is one of Hong Kong's largest banks. It has more than 220 branches and automated banking centers —including one in every subway station —throughout the city plus more than 45 outlets in mainland China and locations in Macao Singapore and Taiwan. The bank provides corporate and retail banking services including deposit accounts credit cards mortgages business and personal loans insurance and investment products and services such as securities trading and mutual funds. It also offers personal wealth management and private banking services.

EXECUTIVES

Chairman, Raymond K. F. Ch'ien, age 60
Director and Head of Personal Banking, William Wing Cheung Leung, age 58
Director; Vice Chairman and Chief Executive Hang Seng Bank (China) Limited, Dorothy K. Y. P. Sit, age 61
General Manager and Head Investment and Insurance, Andrew H. C. Fung
Vice Chairman and CEO, Margaret K. M. Y. Leung, age 62
Deputy General Manager and CFO, Andrew Leung, age 50
Director, Alexander A. (Sandy) Flockhart, age 61
Director and Head of Personal Banking, William Wing Cheung Leung, age 58
Director; Vice Chairman and Chief Executive Hang Seng Bank (China) Limited, Dorothy K. Y. P. Sit, age 61
Director, Iain J. Mackay, age 51
Vice Chairman and CEO, Margaret K. M. Y. Leung, age 62
Director, Tung Shun (Peter) Wong
Director, Yat Sun (Richard) Tang, age 60
Director, Hong Sui (Vincent) Lo
Director, LI Ka (Eric) Cheung, age 59
Director, Ting Chang (Peter) Lee, age 58
Director, Jenki Hui, age 68
Director, Kin Tung (Marvin) Wong, age 65
Director, Cho Chak (John) Chan, age 70
Auditors: KPMG

LOCATIONS

HQ: Hang Seng Bank Ltd.
83 Des Voeux Road Central,
Phone: (852) 2198 1111 **Fax:** (852) 2868 4047
Web: www.hangseng.com

COMPETITORS

Bank of China (Hong Kong)
Bank of Communications
Bank of East Asia
CITIC International Financial
China Development Bank
China Merchants Bank
China Minsheng Banking
Chong Hing Bank
Dah Sing Financial Holdings Limited
Public Financical Holdings
Shanghai Pudong Development Bank
Standard Chartered

HISTORICAL FINANCIALS

Company Type: Public

Income Statement FYE: December 31

	ASSETS ($ mil.)	NET INCOME ($ mil.)	INCOME AS % OF ASSETS	EMPLOYEES
12/12	138,949	2,506	1.8%	9,680
12/11	125,572	2,147	1.7%	9,834
12/10	117,967	1,919	1.6%	9,642
12/09	106,516	1,704	1.6%	9,342
12/08	98,346	1,819	1.8%	9,764
Annual Growth	9.0%	8.3%	—	(0.2%)

2012 Year-End Financials

Return on assets: 1.8%
Return on equity: 22.6%
Long-term debt ($ mil.): —
No. of shares (mil.): 1,911
Sales ($ mil): 6,353
Dividends
Yield: 4.6%
Payout: —
Market value ($ mil.): 29,614

	STOCK PRICE ($) FY Close	P/E High/Low		PER SHARE ($) Earnings	Dividends	Book Value
12/12	15.49	0	0	1.31	0.72	6.23
12/11	11.80	0	0	1.12	0.01	5.30
12/10	16.49	0	0	1.00	0.60	4.71
12/09	14.88	0	0	0.89	0.74	3.93
12/08	13.26	0	0	0.95	0.74	3.48
Annual Growth	4.0%	—	—	8.4%	(0.5%)	15.6%

Hannover Rueckversicherung SE

Who insures insurance companies over and over? Hannover! Hannover Ruck (Hannover Re) is the second-largest German reinsurance company (Munich Re is #1) and the fourth-largest such company in the world. Through more than 100 subsidiaries the company provides property and casualty (Hannover Re's largest segment) financial life and health reinsurance products in about 150 countries worldwide. Financial reinsurance is provided through Hannover Re Advanced Solutions a Dublin-based consortium managed jointly with HDI Reinsurance (Ireland); both Hannover Re and HDI Reinsurance (Ireland) are subsidiaries of HDI Haftpflichtverband der Deutschen Industrie.

Hannover Re is 50%-owned by German mutual insurance group Talanx AG part of HDI Haftpflichtverband der Deutschen Industrie.

Like nearly all other insurers Hannover Re saw its investment income for 2008 shrink significantly. But an uptick in demand for reinsurance in 2009 along with a decrease in catastrophe losses and a more than 300% increase in investment returns put group results back in line with pre-financial crisis levels. In the second quarter of 2010 however the company experienced higher-than-expected major losses with the sinking of the Deepwater Horizon oil rig operated by BP.

The property/casualty unit of the ever-diversifying Hannover Re accounts for more than 55% of all premiums and is geared toward markets in the US Germany and Japan. Its life/health business is marketed through subsidiary Hannover Life Re and focuses on treaty (groups of risks) rather than facultative (individual risk) policies.

To boost its presence in the US the company purchased a portfolio of life reinsurance from Scottish Re in 2009. The deal gave Hannover a business it attempted to buy from ING Groep in 2004 but lost out to Scottish Re. In 2011 Scottish Re offloaded another chunk of life reinsurance which Hannover Re readily purchased.

While Hannover Re's traditional "brot und butter" has been property and casualty reinsurance the firm has expanded its life and health lines which are contributing closer and closer to half of all premiums. Hannover Re has also adopted American accounting practices and become more transparent in order to remain a compelling stock in investors' eyes.

HISTORY

Hannover Re was founded in 1966 as the Aktiengesellschaft fur Transport und Ruckversicherung (ATR) by the Feuerschadenverband Rheinisch-Westfaelischer Zechen (FSV) a mutual insurer specializing in fire damage in the town of Bochum. Within five years ATR had expanded into international reinsurance markets. In 1970 FSV merged with another mutual HDI Haftpflichtverband der Deutschen Industrie which owned reinsurer Eisen und Stahl Ruckversicherungs-AG. ATR's headquarters relocated to Hannover and six years later it was renamed Hannover Ruckversicherungs-Gesellschaft.

Jointly managed by HDI Hannover Re and Eisen und Stahl operated separately until 1996: Hannover Re targeted international markets while Eisen und Stahl operated mostly within Germany.

Hannover Re maintained its foreign focus throughout the 1970s and 80s expanding in Europe and South Africa and making its first forays into the US. In 1990 the firm acquired US life insurer Reassurance Company of Hannover.

Hannover Re went public in 1994 selling 25% of its stock. Also that year the firm formed an Australian subsidiary. The next year Hannover Re acquired Eisen und Stahl (renamed E+S Ruck 1996) which then assumed total control of the company's domestic business.

In 1998 Hannover Re became the first reinsurer to securitize life insurance business (reinsurers often securitize non-life policies to protect against natural catastrophe risks) through an agreement with Interpolis an Irish reinsurance subsidiary of the Netherlands' Rabobank. Also that year the firm expanded its financial reinsurance business reorganizing the Irish consortium it formed with another subsidiary of HDI into Hannover Re Advanced Solutions.

As various natural disasters offset earnings in Hannover Re's property & casualty division in 1998 and 1999 its life and health segment boomed. To facilitate further growth the firm restructured these operations into a new subsidiary Hannover Life Re. Also in 1999 the firm acquired the Clarendon Insurance Group of New York. In 2001 Hannover Re joined Inreon an online reinsurance trading exchange set up by rivals Munich Re and Swiss Re. Also in 2001 the company established a Bermuda-based subsidiary focused on catastrophe business. The following year Hannover Re split its stock in order to stimulate demand and become a more widely held company.

Like many other insurers the company was hit hard by the attacks of September 11 2001 falling stock markets and in 2005 damages in the Gulf of Mexico caused by hurricanes Katrina and Rita.

Late in 2006 China loosened its regulation of a number of industries and insurance was one of them —Hannover Re was one of the first to gain permission to enter the Chinese market for life and health reinsurance.

At about the same time the company announced plans to cut down on its noncore business operations. The first move in this direction was the sale of its US-based Praetorian Group subsidiary to QBE's US-based subsidiary for a sum in excess of $800 million. Hannover Re used the proceeds to shore up its property/casualty and life/health reinsurance businesses.

EXECUTIVES

CEO Hannover Life Re, Wolf Becke, age 66
Deputy Chairman Supervisory Board, Klaus Sturany, age 67, $67,254 total compensation
Executive Board Member Non-life, Michael Pickel, age 53
Executive Board Member Non-Life, Andre Arrago, age 64
Chairman of the Executive Board, Ulrich Wallin, age 52
Chief Public Relations Manager, Gabriele Handrick
CFO, Roland Vogel
Senior Manager Investor Relations, Klaus Paesler
Head Corporate Communications, Karl Steinle, age 43
Executive Board Member Hanover Life Re Northern and Central Europe, Klaus Miller, age 53
Chief Risk Officer, Eberhard Muller
CFO, Elke A. K?nig
Member of the Executive Board, Claude Chevre
Member of the Executive Board, Juergen Graeber
Chief Executive Officer, Nick Parr
Director, Herbert K. Haas, age 59
Director, Karl H. Midunsky
Director, Immo Querner
Deputy Chairman Supervisory Board, Klaus Sturany, age 67
Director, Uwe Kramp
Director, Otto Muller
Director, Erhard Schipporeit
Director, Gert Wachtler
Member of the Supervisory Board, Andrea Pollak
Member of the Supervisory Board; Employee Representative, Gert Waechtler
Member of the Supervisory Board; Employee Representative, Otto Mueller
Member of the Supervisory Board, Wolf-Dieter Baumgartl
Auditors: KPMGAGWirtschaftsprufungsgesellschaft

LOCATIONS

HQ: Hannover Rueckversicherung SE
Karl-Wiechert-Allee 50, Hannover D-30625
Phone: (49) 511 5604 0 **Fax:** (49) 511 5604 1188
Web: www.hannover-re.com

2009 Premiums Written

	% of total
Europe	
Germany	13
UK	17
France	5
Other	12
North America	
US	28
Other	4
Asia	8
Australia	4
Africa	3
Other	6
Total	**100**

COMPETITORS

Everest Re
General Re
Lloyd' s
Munich Re Group
PartnerRe
Reinsurance Group of America
SCOR
Swiss Re
XL Group plc

HISTORICAL FINANCIALS

Company Type: Public

Income Statement FYE: December 31

	ASSETS ($ mil.)	NET INCOME ($ mil.)	INCOME AS % OF ASSETS	EMPLOYEES
12/12	72,244	1,131	1.6%	2,312
12/11	64,500	783	1.2%	2,217
12/10	62,535	1,002	1.6%	2,192
12/09	60,884	1,053	1.7%	2,069
12/08	53,129	(177)	—	1,812
Annual Growth	8.0%	—	—	6.3%

2012 Year-End Financials

Return on assets: 1.6%
Return on equity: 15.5%
Long-term debt ($ mil.): —
No. of shares (mil.): 120
Sales ($ mil): 18,484

Dividends
Yield: 2.5%
Payout: 10.2%
Market value ($ mil.): 4,695

	STOCK PRICE ($) FY Close	P/E High/Low		PER SHARE ($) Earnings	Dividends	Book Value
12/12	38.93	10	6	9.38	0.98	66.19
12/11	24.82	12	7	6.49	2.35	53.31
12/10	26.70	8	5	8.31	0.96	50.04
12/09	23.60	9	4	8.73	0.00	44.34
12/08	16.15	—	—	(1.47)	1.39	32.81
Annual Growth	24.6%	—	—	—	(8.3%)	19.2%

HDFC Bank Ltd

HDFC Bank may not fulfill your spiritual needs but it can help with your finances. The bank provides a variety of wholesale retail and depository financial services through more than 1700 branches and some 5000 ATMs throughout India. Established by financial institution Housing Development Finance Corporation in 1994 the bank offers deposit accounts loans credit cards insurance investments and related services. Subsidiary HDFC Securities provides online brokerage services. HDFC Bank targets individual customers in the middle and upper-class as well as trusts small businesses and not-for-profit organizations in the country.

The company is the second-largest private sector bank in India after ICICI. Housing Development Finance owns about a quarter of HDFC Bank.

EXECUTIVES

Managing Director, Aditya Puri, age 62
Head Wholesale Banking and Director, Harish Engineer, age 64
Head Audit Compliance Vigilance, G. Subramanian, age 65
Head Credit and Market Risk and Human Resources and Director, Paresh Sukthankar, age 50
Head Equities and Private Banking, Abhay Aima, age 50
Head Wholesale Credit Market Risk and Retail Risk Policy, Kaizad Bharucha, age 47
Head Retaill Assets, Pralay Mondal, age 47
Member of Senior Management, Bhavesh Zaveri, age 47
Head Branch Banking, Navin Puri, age 54
Member of Senior Management, Jimmy Tata, age 46
Head Finance, Sashi Jagdishan, age 48
Member of Senior Management, Rajender Sehgal, age 57
Treasury, Ashish Parthasarthy, age 45
Head Retail Liabilities Marketing and Phone Banking, Rahul N. Bhagat, age 49
Executive Vice President - Legal; Compliance Officer; Company Secretary, Sanjay Dongre
Member of Senior Management, Anil Jaggia
Director, Arvind Pande, age 70
Managing Director, Aditya Puri, age 62
Director, Keki M. Mistry, age 58
Director, Renu S. Karnad, age 60
Head Wholesale Banking and Director, Harish Engineer, age 64
Head Credit and Market Risk and Human Resources and Director, Paresh Sukthankar, age 50
Director, Ashim Samanta, age 58
Director, C.M. Vasudev, age 69
Director, Pandit Palande, age 51
Director, Partho Datta
Non-Executive Independent Director, Bobby Parikh
Non-Executive Independent Director, Anami Roy
Auditors: Haribhakti&Co.

LOCATIONS

HQ: HDFC Bank Ltd
HDFC Bank House, Senapati Bapat Marg, Lower Parel, Mumbai 400 013
Phone: (91) 22 66521000 **Fax:** (91) 22 24960737
Web: www.hdfcbank.com

PRODUCTS/OPERATIONS

2010 Sales By Segment

	% of total
Retail	51
Wholesale	27
Treasury	15
Other	7
Total	**100**

COMPETITORS

Bank of Baroda
Bank of India
Canara Bank
ICICI Bank
Industrial Development Bank of India
State Bank of India

HISTORICAL FINANCIALS

Company Type: Public

Income Statement FYE: March 31

	ASSETS ($ mil.)	NET INCOME ($ mil.)	INCOME AS % OF ASSETS	EMPLOYEES
03/13	80,517	1,138	1.4%	69,065
03/12	70,194	978	1.4%	66,076
03/11	0	924	****************%	55,752
03/10	49,549	656	1.3%	51,888
03/09	36,049	442	1.2%	52,687
Annual Growth	22.2%	26.6%	—	7.0%

2013 Year-End Financials

Return on assets: 1.5%
Return on equity: 14.3%
Long-term debt ($ mil.): —
No. of shares (mil.): —
Sales ($ mil): 7,719
Dividends
Yield: 0.0%
Payout: 0.0%
Market value ($ mil.): —

	STOCK PRICE ($) FY Close	P/E High/Low		PER SHARE ($) Earnings	Dividends	Book Value
03/13	37.42	0	0	0.48	0.00	3.63
03/12	34.10	0	0	0.42	0.00	3.31
03/11	169.94	0	0	0.39	0.15	(0.00)
03/10	139.39	—	—	0.30	0.12	2.09
03/09	60.93	—	—	0.21	0.11	1.40
Annual Growth	(11.5%)	—	—	23.2%	(84.3%)	26.9%

HeidelbergCement AG

HeidelbergCement believes in concrete results. The company is one of the world's leading producers of cement and clinker (more than 100 million tons annually) and concrete; it is the largest cement producer in Germany. Cement concrete and aggregates together account for more than 90% of the company's sales. HeidelbergCement also has group services which manage fossil fuels and electricity for its operations and trade internationally in cement and clinker (an intermediate product used to make portland cement). The company has operations in 40 countries in Africa Asia Australia Europe and North America. Subsidiary Hanson is a top building materials company in the UK.

The worldwide economic downturn and a decline in the construction industry as a whole hit HeidelbergCement in 2009. To help ease losses in sales and reduce debt the company began cutting costs and selling non-core businesses.

HeidelbergCement also made cost reductions during the recession. It adjusted plant production especially in North America and cut jobs worldwide by nearly 15%.

The changes (along with a return to economic growth) helped the company fare better in 2010 (sales increased by more than 28%). Moving forward Heidelberg is looking to keep a tight lid on expenses. But it also wants to make targeted investments to improve cement capacities in emerging markets (which generate some 35% of sales).

Those growing markets include Asia Africa and Central Europe. As a result of the accelerated growth in Asia HeidelbergCement has primarily looked east for expansion. The company also has created joint ventures in China –China Century Cement and Jidong Heidelberg Cement Company.

Heidelberg also has grown in Africa. Through an agreement with International Finance Corporation which is part of the World Bank it added cement capacity in Africa in 2010. By doing so the company is helping expand infrastructure in places such as Liberia and Ghana. Heidelberg also acquired three cement plants in the Democratic Republic of Congo. In Central Europe HeidelbergCement is planning to open a new plant in Moscow and increase capacity at other plants

Ludwig Merckle and his family (one of Germany's wealthiest) owns some 25% of HeidelbergCement. Family patriarch Adolf Merckle reportedly killed himself in 2009 after he accumulated a mountain of debt. The family which once held a 70% stake in HeidelbergCement later sold a large chunk (some 45%) of the company.

HISTORY

HeidelbergCement AG's history began in 1872 when Johann Philipp Schifferdecker a wealthy brewer went to Heidelberg Germany where his son was studying chemistry. Once there he bought a bankrupt cement plant located on the Neckar River near Heidelberg in 1873. Schifferdecker named the firm Portland-Cement-Werk Heidelberg Schifferdecker & Sohne OHG.

The company's first year of operation 1875 ended in a loss. The raw materials used to make its cement contained too much magnesium. To correct the problem Schifferdecker leased a new limestone mine to obtain higher-quality raw materials. Transport presented a problem and in 1883 Schifferdecker built a railroad to transport limestone to the plant. With these problems solved the company built a second plant in 1888 the year that Schifferdecker died. The company went public the next year and Schifferdecker's heirs renamed the firm Portland-Cementwerk Heidelberg vormals Schifferdecker & Sohne.

A fire destroyed the company's plant in 1895 but the Schifferdeckers used the disaster as an opportunity to modernize the plant. The construction boom sparked at the turn of the century increased cement sales and the enterprise continued to expand. In 1901 the company merged with its rival Mannheimer Portland-Cement-Fabrik AG to create Portland-Cementwerke Heidelberg und Mannheim AG.

Heidelberg-Mannheimer's plans for expansion died in WWI. From 1916 to 1923 the German government took control of the entire German cement industry. During that time the company merged with Stuttgarter Immobilien- und Bau-

Geschaft AG to create Portland-Cementwerke Heidelberg-Mannheim-Stuttgart AG.

After the war peace did not bring prosperity to Germany. Hyperinflation made German cement 765 times more expensive than it had been in 1914. By 1926 the German economy had recovered and one year later the company converted its plants to electrical operations. The good times did not last long however. As the Great Depression strangled the German economy the company's cement shipments dropped by two-thirds from 1927 levels.

Just before WWII the company renamed itself Portland-Zementwerke Heidelberg AG. During the war the German cement industry was highly regulated by the German government. The destructive WWII years all but assured the renewed growth of the German cement industry and Portland-Zementwerke Heidelberg grew steadily during the 1940s and 1950s. Annual shipments of 6 million tons were reached by 1965.

Peter Schumacher took over the company in 1971 and transformed it into an international enterprise with the 1977 acquisition of Pennsylvania-based Lehigh Portland Cement Company. That year the company adopted the name Heidelberger Zement AG. (Schumacher who led the company for 25 years died in 2002.)

During the 1980s Heidelberger Zement bought Atlas Cement Company and founded Addiment Inc. in Georgia to market its building chemicals. The company also boosted its operations in Italy and France. It expanded into Eastern Europe in the early 1990s and by 1997 had broadened its geographic reach to include acquisitions in countries such as China and Turkey.

Heidelberger Zement purchased Scancem a Scandinavian cement operation in 1999 to open up new markets in Africa the Baltic States and the UK. It also bolstered its building materials segment by increasing its stake in maxit Group a Germany-based leader in the dry mortar business. In 2001 the company acquired majority stakes in regional cement makers Indocement Tunggal Prakarsa (Indonesia) Cesla (Russia) and Kryvyi Rih (Ukraine).

In 2003 the company moved its entire Heidelberg Building Materials Europe division under the maxit Group unit.

Spohn Group run by long-time HeidelbergCement board members the Merckle family acquired a majority stake in 2005.

In 2007 HeidelbergCement acquired UK's Hanson one of the largest producers of aggregates in the world. The E9 billion ($12 billion) acquisition helped position HeidelbergCement as a global integrated supplier of building materials and strengthened its materials base for aggregates.

Adolf Merckle committed suicide in 2009. His family later sold a large stake in HeidelbergCement.

EXECUTIVES

Member of the Managing Board Northern and Western Europe Mediterranean Africa Group Services and Environmental Sustainability, Daniel Gauthier, age 54
Member Managing Board Asia-Oceania and Heidelberg Technology Center, Albert Scheuer, age 52
Chairman of the Managing Board, Bernd Scheifele, age 52
Member of the Managing Board Finance Group Accounting Controlling Taxes Insurance and Corporate Risk Management IT Shared Service Center and Logistics, Lorenz Nager, age 50
Member of the Managing Board Central Europe Central Asia Sales and Marketing, Andreas Kern, age 52
Chairman of the Supervisory Board, Fritz-Jurgen Heckmann
Member Managing Board North America Purchasing Worldwide Coordination of Competence Center Materials, Dominik von Achten, age 45
Deputy Chairman, Heinz Schmitt
Group Communication and Investor Relations, Andreas Schaller
Member of the Supervisory Board, Max D. Kley, age 70
Member of the Supervisory Board, Herbert Lutkestratkotter, age 60
Member of the Supervisory Board, Ludwig Merckle
Member of the Supervisory Board, Robert Feiger, age 48
Member of the Supervisory Board, Josef Heumann
Member of the Supervisory Board, Hans G. Kraut
Member of the Supervisory Board, Tobias Merckle
Deputy Chairman, Heinz Schmitt
Member of the Supervisory Board, Frank-Dirk Steininger
Member of the Supervisory Board, Werner Schraeder
Member of the Supervisory Board, Alan Murray
Auditors: Ernst&YoungGmbHWirtschaftsprufungsgesellschaft

LOCATIONS

HQ: HeidelbergCement AG
Berliner Strasse 6, Heidelberg D-69120
Phone: (49) 6221 481 13227 **Fax:** (49) 6221 481 13217
Web: www.heidelbergcement.com

2010 Sales

	% of total
Western and Northern	31
North	25
Asia-Pacific	21
Eastern Europe-Central	9
Africa-Mediterranean	8
Group	6
Total	**100**

PRODUCTS/OPERATIONS

2010 Sales

	% of total
Aggregates	66
Cement and	22
Other Building	12
Total	**100**

Selected Products

Cement
- Binders for geotechnology environmental technology and road construction
- Decorative concrete
- Fast-hardening cement
- Masonry cement
- Specialty cements for hydraulic engineering sewage works construction soil injection and masonry repair and waste dump sealing

Concrete
- Light heavy and aerated concrete building blocks
- Pavers
- Prefab ceilings walls cellar units and sewage works units

Building Materials
- Building chemicals
- Dry mortar
- Environmental technology
- Expanded clay
- Limestone and lime products
- Sand-lime bricks
- Special gypsums

Aggregates

Other
- Plaster
- Self-compacting concrete
- Steel-fiber concrete

COMPETITORS

Aggregate Industries
BPB
BUZZI UNICEM
CEMEX
CRH
Eagle Materials
FLSmidth
Franz Haniel
Holcim
Italcementi
Lafarge
Tarmac
Titan Cement
U.S. Concrete
USG
Vicat
Vulcan Materials
Wienerberger

HISTORICAL FINANCIALS

Company Type: Public

Income Statement FYE: December 31

	REVENUE ($ mil.)	NET INCOME ($ mil.)	NET PROFIT MARGIN	EMPLOYEES
12/12	18,546	397	2.1%	51,966
12/11	16,737	450	2.7%	0
12/10	15,755	458	2.9%	53,437
12/09	15,677	61	0.4%	53,302
12/08	19,971	2,528	12.7%	60,841
Annual Growth	(1.8%)	(37.0%)	—	(3.9%)

2012 Year-End Financials

Debt ratio: 40.3%
Return on equity: 2.3%
Cash ($ mil.): 1,943
Current ratio: 1.18
Long-term debt ($ mil.): 9,421
No. of shares (mil.): 187
Dividends
Yield: 0.4%
Payout: —
Market value ($ mil.): 2,271

	STOCK PRICE ($) FY Close	P/E High/Low		PER SHARE ($) Earnings	Dividends	Book Value
12/12	12.11	13	8	2.12	0.06	88.68
12/11	8.41	15	6	2.41	0.08	87.04
12/10	12.61	14	10	2.45	0.00	86.09
Annual Growth	(2.0%)	—	—	(3.5%)	—	0.7%

Heineken N.V. (Netherlands)

Smaller brewers are green with envy. Heineken one of the world's brewing giants sells its namesake beer in a signature green bottle in just about every country on the planet. The Dutch brewer operates more than 140 breweries in 70-plus countries. Its other well-known brands include Amstel and Kingfisher. In addition to its own brands the company boasts about 170 international regional and specialty beers including Murphy's Irish Red (Europe) Cordoba (Argentina) and Tiger (Asia). As part of its business Heineken also distributes wine soft drinks and other beverages. To get a leg up in Latin America Heineken acquired the Mexican brewer of Sol and Tecate beers –FEMSA Cerveza –in 2010.

Heineken paid Cerveza's former parent company Fomento Economico Mexicano E3.8 billion (about $5.4 billion) in an all-share deal. As a result Heineken became a stronger more competitive player in the Latin American beer market –one of the most profitable and fastest growing market niches in the world. The deal added Cerveza's beer brands including Dos Equis Sol and Tecate to Heineken's global platform and brand portfolio.

As for sales in Western and Central and Eastern Europe sales accounted for some 65% of sales in 2010. The company showed a strong presence in Western Europe especially in the UK France Italy and the Netherlands. Heineken also has a stronghold in Central and Eastern Europe with countries like Greece Austria Slovakia Bulgaria and Macedonia.

Even though the company is the largest brewer in Europe in 2010 it faced challenges especially in Central and Eastern Europe which were affected by poor economic conditions and higher excise duties. To offset these economic challenges the company plans to leverage brands such as Desperados Strongbow and Dos Equis and invest in premium beers.

As Heineken continues to invest in its core beer market it is selling other assets. To that end in 2010 it sold its UK drinks distribution unit WaverleyTBS to private investment firm Manfield Partners. (The WaverleyTBS subsidiary United Wine Merchants operating in Northern Ireland was not included in the sale and remained part of Heineken UK.) Following the sale WaverleyTBS retained its commercial distribution agreements with Heineken. In early 2011 Heineken and joint venture partner APB sold their roughly 20% share of China-based Kingway Brewery to the brewer's controlling shareholder Guangdong Holdings Group for Y1 billion (about $205 million). Heineken is looking to devote its resources to more profitable beverage lines now that its investment in Kingway has been disposed of. The company in 2012 gave conglomerate Fraser and Neave some $4 billion in cash to in 2013 acquire its remaining 40% share in Asia Pacific Breweries (APB) maker of Tiger beer and give it full rights to the brand. Heineken made its move for APB after Thai Beverage agreed to purchase a 22% stake in Fraser and Neave. Brewers have been eyeing Asia as it has become the largest beer-drinking region in the world by volume.

In addition the Americas segment accounted for roughly 20% of sales in 2010. Beer consumption primarily grew in the Caribbean Canada Chile and Argentina offsetting lower consumption in the US. Heineken's position was strengthened by the acquisition of FEMSA which helped with solid brands such as Sol Dos Equis and Tecate. The company's joint venture with Chilean-based Companias Cervecerias Unidas and its positions in Argentina and Chile helped with higher beer volumes and profitability. Heineken also benefited from Brazil's thriving economy and a more willing consumer to spend.

During the past few years political unrest has impeded Heineken's growth in Africa an emerging beer market. However things are looking up for the top brewer who in early 2011 acquired controlling interests in a handful of breweries in Nigeria. It now controls Nigerian breweries Sona IBBI Benue Life and Champion and their brands such as Goldberg Williams Dark Ale and Malta Gold. That same year Heineken added to its interests in Africa by acquiring Bedele and Harar breweries from the government of Ethiopia for around $163 million. The two breweries have a combined market share of about 18% in the Ethiopian beer market. Brands include Bedele Premium Bedele Special Harar Hakim Stout and Hara Sofi.

In a deal that launched Heineken to a leading position as a pub operator in the UK the brewer acquired the Galaxy Pub Estate there from The Royal Bank of Scotland for E480 million ($634 million) in late 2011. Galaxy operates more than 900 pubs which will be combined with Heineken's existing portfolio of 460-plus outlets.

The founding Heineken family controls the company.

HISTORY

Every Sunday morning Gerard Heineken's mother was appalled by crowds of drunken Dutchmen who had consumed too much gin the night before. Heineken who wanted his mother's financial backing insisted that drunkenness would decrease if people drank beer instead of gin and pointed out that there were no good beers in Holland. His strategy worked. In 1863 Heineken's mother put up the money to buy De Hooiberg (The Haystack) a 271-year-old brewery in Amsterdam.

Gerard proved his aptitude for brewing and within 10 years had established a brewery in Rotterdam. He named the business Heineken in 1873 and launched the company's lucrative foreign trade by exporting beer in 1876 to France. (By the 1950s half the beer brewed by the company was for export.) The company perfected a yeast strain (Heineken A-yeast) in 1886 that is still in use today.

In 1917 Gerard's son Dr. Henri Pierre Heineken inherited the firm and expanded operations to the US. Making a voyage to that country Henri Pierre met Leo van Munching a ship's bartender who displayed a remarkable knowledge of beer. Recognizing van Munching's talent Henri Pierre hired him as Heineken's US importer. Prohibition killed the US operations although the company entered new markets elsewhere; after repeal Heineken was the first foreign beer to re-enter the US market.

After WWII Henri Pierre sent his son Alfred to learn the business under van Munching who had created a national distribution system in the US. Alfred succeeded his father in 1953 and stepped down in 1989.

Heineken bought the Amstel Brewery in Holland (founded 1870) in 1968. Two years later it became a producer of stout through the acquisition of James J. Murphy in Cork Ireland. Facing a consolidation of the European market Heineken launched a campaign in the 1980s to expand its European beer operations purchasing breweries in France Greece Ireland Italy and Spain.

In 1991 Heineken bought the van Munching US import business and a majority interest in Hungarian brewer Komaromi Sorgyar its first Eastern European investment. Two years later Karel Vuursteen was appointed chairman.

The firm cut more than 1300 jobs in 1993 and sold its spirits and wine operations the next year. In 1995 Heineken began a major spending spree acquiring Interbrew Italia and 66% of Zlaty Bazant the largest Slovakian brewery and maltworks (it acquired the rest in 1999). The company bought Birra Moretti Italy's third-largest brewery in 1996. It also purchased interests in two African breweries. All the acquisitions led to high integration costs and lower profits.

To boost its sales in Poland in 1998 Heineken raised its stake in brewer Zaklady Piwowarskie W. Zywcu (Zywiec) to 75% bought a minority stake in Brewpole and merged the companies to create the largest Polish brewer. That year Heineken bought about 25% of Pivara Skopje the largest brewery in the former Yugoslav republic of Macedonia through its Brewinvest joint venture. In 1999 the company bought about 18% of Israel's leading brewer Tempo (Goldstar and Maccabee beers).

In 2000 Heineken bought 99% of Spanish brewer Cruzcampo most of it from Diageo. Cruzcampo later merged with Heineken's Spanish brewer El Aguila to create Heineken Espa?a. In February 2001 Heineken created a joint venture BrauHolding International with Bayerische BrauHolding to sell Paulaner Weiss beer and to give Heineken access to two German beer makers.

VP Anthony Ruys replaced Vuursteen as CEO in 2002. Heineken also announced it would launch its premium Heineken beer in the UK in 2003 and eventually withdraw its Heineken Cold Filtered and Heineken Export beers from that market. It also signed a deal allowing Belgium's Interbrew (now Anheuser-Busch InBev) to brew and sell Murphy's Irish Stout in Britain. Heineken also gained EU approval that year to buy a stake in German brewer Karlsberg.

Also in 2002 Heineken agreed to buy stakes in two Central American breweries: Costa Rica's Florida Ice and Farm Company (FIFCO) and Nicaragua's Consorcio Cervecero Centroamericano (COCECA). With FIFCO and Coca-Cola bottler Panamerican Beverages Heineken purchased Cervecerias Brau-Panama the country's second-largest brewer for $138 million. The company later purchased Russian brewer Bravo International (which changed its name to Heineken Brewery in 2003). Heineken also bought a controlling stake in Egyptian brewer Al Ahram Beverages in 2002. Ak Agram produces Fayrouz a nonalcoholic beer favored by Muslims. The brewer also agreed to increase its stake in Lebanese brewer Almaza from 10% to 79%.

In 2003 Heineken purchased Austrian brewer BBAG Osterreichische Brau-Beteiligungs-AG for $1.7 billion. It combined its regional operations with BBAG creating Brau Union AG. That year Heineken sold all of its shares (15% of outstanding shares) in Quilmes to Beverage Associates Corp. (BAC); AmBev (now InBev) acquired 8.6% of the Quilmes shares from BAC.

Making a strong play for the growing US Hispanic market Heineken inked a three-year deal with FEMSA Cerveza in 2004 making it the sole importer of FEMSA's Mexican beers Tecate Sol Dos Equis Carta Blanca and Bohemia. Heineken recognized the growing number of people using online music stores. That year it entered a joint venture with Lion Nathan Limited to sell its flagship brand in Australia. Heineken also began an aggressive push into Russia that year when it purchased Sobol Beer in West Siberia and the Volga and Shikhan breweries. Heineken also grew steadily in new markets such as Asia and South America. In 2004 it joined its Chinese operations with those of Asia Pacific Breweries to form Heineken Asia Pacific Breweries China (HAPBC) and that year HAPBC bought an approximate 21% stake in China's Kingway Brewery.

In order to compete with competitors' low-calorie low-carb beers in 2005 the company introduced Heineken Premium Light in select markets in the US market. Also in 2005 the company formed a partnership with Diageo to produce and distribute Guinness in Russia. It also acquired approximately 91% of German brewer Wurzburger Hofbrau.

In 2006 the company focused on growth in Indo-China. Its Asian joint venture with Fraser and Neave Asia Pacific Breweries made a number of strategic acquisitions including the Fosters brewing assets in Vietnam and the Quang Nam Brewery in Vietnam. In addition it announced an acquisition in Laos and acquired shares in Tunisian distribution company Societe de Production et de Distribution des Boissons.

Heineken was one of three Dutch brewers (along with Grolsch and Bavaria Brewery) that in 2007 were fined by the European Commission for price fixing surrounding sales to Dutch bars and restaurants in the late 1990s. Heineken's fine amounted to E219 million (about $297 million).

In 2008 Heineken and Denmark's Carlsberg acquired Scottish & Newcastle (S&N) which it renamed Heineken UK. The $15.3 billion takeover resulted in Heineken owning the US Indian (37% of United Breweries maker of Kingfisher beer) UK and other European operations of the noted Irish brewer. Carlsberg took over 100% ownership of

Baltic Beverage Holdings (BBH) the 50-50 joint venture it had with S&N as well as its Chinese French Greek and Vietnamese operations. As if that weren't enough for the its bean counters the company added more operations in 2008 as well. Upping its presence in the Czech market Heineken acquired Drinks Union and its national brand Zlatopramen among others. Other notable wheeling and dealing included an agreement to buy the beverage operations of Swiss company Eichhof Holding and the purchase of Romanian brewer Bere Mures.

EXECUTIVES

Chairman of the Executive Board and CEO, Jean-Francois M. L. van Boxmeer, age 51, $1,103,925 total compensation
Executive Board Member and CFO, Rene Hooft Graafland, age 58, $809,545 total compensation
President Americas, John R. Nicolson, age 60
Regional President Central and Eastern Europe, Nico Nusmeier, age 51
President Western Europe, Didier Debrosse, age 57
President Africa and the Middle East, Siep Hiemstra, age 57
Chief Supply Chain Officer, Marc Gross, age 56
Chief Business Services Officer, Frans Eusman
Director Group Corporate Relations, Sean O'Neill, age 49
Chairman Supervisory Board, Cees van Lede, age 71
Director Group Control and Accounting, Floris van Woerkom, age 50
Secretary Treasurer, Robin H. von Konijnenburg
Managing Director Scottish and Newcastle UK, Stefan Orlowski, age 46
Chief Human Resources Officer, Michael O?Hare, age 47
Chairman and General Manager Heineken Slovensko, Door Plantenga
Chief Commercial Officer, Alexis Nasard, age 48
President Asia Pacific, Theo de Rond
Vice Chairman Supervisory Board, Jose Antonio Fernandez Carbajal
President Central and Eastern Europe, Jan Derck van Karnebeek
Member Supervisory Board, Christophe Navarre, age 56
Member Supervisory Board, Maarten M. Das, age 66
Member Supervisory Board, Michel de Carvalho, age 70
Member Supervisory Board, Jan-Michiel Hessels, age 70
Member Supervisory Board, Mary E. Minnick, age 54
Member Executive Board and CFO, Rene Hooft Graafland, age 57
Member Supervisory Board, Jan M. de Jong, age 68
Member Supervisory Board, Lord Ian C. MacLaurin, age 75
Member Supervisory Board, Annemiek Fentener van Vlissingen, age 52
Director, Charlotte Kwist, age 44
Vice Chairman Supervisory Board, Jose Antonio Fernandez Carbajal
Member Supervisory Board, Javier Gerardo Astaburuaga Sanjines
Member Supervisory Board, Hans Wijers
Auditors: KPMGAccountantsN.V.

LOCATIONS

HQ: Heineken N.V. (Netherlands)
Tweede Weteringplantsoen 21, Amsterdam 1017 ZD
Phone: (31) 20 5239 239 **Fax:** (31) 20 627 9684
Web: www.theheinekencompany.com

2010 Sales

	% of total
Western	47
The	21
Central & Eastern	19
Africa & the Middle	12
Asia/Pacific	1
Total	**100**

PRODUCTS/OPERATIONS

Selected Brands

- The Americas
  - Argentina
    - Cordoba
    - Dos Equis
    - Heineken
    - Rosario
    - Salta
    - Santa Fe
    - Schneider
    - Sol
  - Bahamas
    - Guinness
    - Heineken
    - Kalik
    - Vitamalt
  - Brazil
    - Bavaria
    - Dos Equis
    - Heineken
    - Kaiser
    - Santa Cerva
    - Sol
    - Summer
    - Xingu
  - Chile
    - Christal
    - Escudo
    - Heineken
  - Costa Rica
    - Bavaria
    - Heineken
    - Imperial
    - Pilsen
    - Rock Ice
  - Dominican Republic
    - Heineken
    - Presidente
  - Haiti
    - Guinness
    - Malta
    - Prestige
  - Jamaica
    - Dragon Stout
    - Guinness
    - Heineken
    - Red Stripe
  - Martinique
    - Lorraine
    - Malta
    - Porter
  - Netherlands Antilles
    - Amstel
    - Amstel Bright
    - Malta
  - Nicaragua
    - Bufalo
    - Tona
    - Victoria
  - Panama
    - Cristal
    - Guinness
    - Panama
    - Soberana
  - Saint Lucia
    - Guinness
    - Heineken
    - Piton
  - Surinam
    - Heineken
    - Parbo
- Africa and the Middle East
  - Burundi
    - Amstel
    - Primus
  - Cameroon
    - Amstel
    - Dynamalt
    - Mutzig
  - Congo
    - Amstel
    - Guinness
    - Maltina
    - Mutzig
    - Primus
    - Turbo King
  - Egypt
    - Birell
    - Fayrouz
    - Heineken
    - Meister
    - Sakara
    - Stella
  - Ghana
    - Amstel Malta
    - Guinness
    - Gulder
    - Maltina
    - Star
  - Israel
    - Gold Star
    - Heineken
    - Maccabee
    - Malt Star
    - Nesher
  - Jordan
    - Amstel
  - Lebanon
    - Almaza
    - Amstel
    - Laziza
  - Morocco
    - Amstel
    - Heineken
  - Namibia
    - Beck's
    - Guinness
    - Heineken
    - Killkenny
    - Windhoek
  - Nigeria
    - "33" Export
    - Amstel Malta
    - Gulder
    - Heineken
    - Hi-Malt
    - Legend
    - Maltina
    - Star
  - Republic of Congo
    - Amstel
    - Guinness
    - Maltina
    - Mutzig
    - Ngok
    - Primus
    - Turbo King
  - Reunion
    - Bourbon
    - Dynamalt
  - Rwanda
    - Amstel
    - Guinness
    - Mutzig
    - Primus
  - Sierra Leone
    - Guinness
    - Heineken
    - Maltina
    - Star
- Asia/Pacific
  - Cambodia
    - ABCStout
    - Anchor
    - Gold Crown
    - Tiger
  - China
    - Anchor
    - Aoke
    - Heineken
    - Kingway
    - Reeb
    - Tiger
  - Indonesia
    - Bintang
    - Bintang Zero
    - Green Sands
    - Guinness
    - Heineken
  - Malaysia
    - Anchor Ice
    - Baron's

Guinness
Heineken
Kilkenny
Tiger
New Caledonia
Havannah
Number One
New Zealand
Amstel
DB Draft
Export Gold
Heineken
Monteith's
Tui
Papua New Guinea
Niugini Ice Beer
South Pacific Export lager
SP Lager
Singapore
ABC Stout
Anchor
Baron's
Heineken
Tiger
Thailand
Heineken
Tiger
Vietnam
Anchor Draft
Bivina
Heineken
Tiger
Europe
Austria
Edelweiss
Gosser
Heineken
Kaiser
Puntigamer
Schlossgold
Schwechater
Wieselburger
Zipfer
Belgium
Affligem
Bulgaria
Amstel
Ariana
Grimbergen
Heineken
Maes
Stolichno
Zagorka
Croatia
Desperados
Heineken
Karlovacko
Czech Republic
Heineken
Hostan
Starobrno
Zlaty Bazant
France
33 Export
Adelscott
Amstel
Buckler
Desperados
Dorelei
Fisher tradition
Heineken
Kriska
Murphy's Irish Stout
Pelforth
St. Omer
Germany
Arnegger
Baren Pilsner
Desperados
Edel-Weizen
Export
Furstenberg
Goldkopfle
Grape
Hacker-Pschorr
Hefe Weisbier
Hoepfner
Judelbier
Karslberg
Keller-Weisbier
Krausen
Kulmbacher
Leicht
Maibock
Mixery
Monchshof
Paulaner
Porter
QOWAZ
Radler
Riegeter
Sternquell
UrPils
Greece
Alfa
Amstel
Buckler
Desperados
Fischer
Heineken
McFarland
Murphy's Irish Stout
Zorbas
Hungary
Amstel
Buckler
Gosser
Heineken
Kaiser
Schlossgold
Soproni Aszok
Talleros
Zlaty Bazant
Italy
Amstel
Birra Messina
Birra Moretti
Budweiser
Classica von Wunster
Dreher
Heineken
Ichnusa
McFarland
Murphy's Irish Stout
Prinz
Sans Souci
Kazakhstan
Amstel
Heineken
Tian Shan
Macedonia
Amstel
Gorsko
Heineken
Skopsko
The Netherlands
Amstel
Heineken
Lingen's Blond
Murphy's Irish Red
Vos
Wieckse
Poland
Heineken
Krolewskie
Kujawiak
Lezajsk
Specjal
Strong
Tatra
Warka Jasne Pelne
Zywiec
Romania
Bucegi
Ciuc
Gambrinus
Golden Brau
Gosser
Heineken
Schlossgold
Silva
Russia
Botchkarov
Heineken
Lowenbrau
Ochota
Okskoye
Rusich
Sedoy Ural
Shikan
Sobol
Solyanaya Pristan
Volga
Zhigulevskoye
Slovakia
Amstel
Corgon
Gemer
Heineken
Kelt
Martiner
Zlaty Bazant
Spain
Amstel
Buckler
Cruzcampo
Guinness
Heineken
Kaliber
Legado de Yuste
Murphy's Irish Red
Switzerland
Amstel
Calanda
Haldengut
Heineken
Murphy's Irish Red
UK
Amstel
Coors Light
Foster's
Heineken
Jacques
John Smiths
Kronenbourg
McEwan's
Murphy's Irish Stout
Newcastle
Strongbow (apple cider)

COMPETITORS

Anheuser-Busch InBev
Asahi Breweries
Asia Pacific Breweries
Bavaria S.A.
Boston Beer
Carlsberg A/S
Cervecerias Unidas
Constellation Brands
Danone Water
Diageo
FEMSA
Grolsch
Holsten-Brauerei
Kingway Brewery
Kirin Holdings Company
Lion
Mendocino Brewing
Molson Coors
Nestle Waters
SABMiller
San Miguel Corporation
Sapporo
Taiwan Tobacco & Wine

HISTORICAL FINANCIALS

Company Type: Public

Income Statement FYE: December 31

	REVENUE ($ mil.)	NET INCOME ($ mil.)	NET PROFIT MARGIN	EMPLOYEES
12/12	24,229	3,886	16.0%	76,191
12/11	22,147	927	4.2%	64,252
12/10	21,591	963	4.5%	65,730
12/09	21,177	1,466	6.9%	55,301
12/08	20,019	292	1.5%	56,208
Annual Growth	4.9%	91.0%	—	7.9%

2012 Year-End Financials

Debt ratio: 49.4%
Return on equity: 35.6%
Cash ($ mil.): 1,366
Current ratio: 0.71
Long-term debt ($ mil.): 15,074
No. of shares (mil.): 288
Dividends
Yield: —
Payout: —
Market value ($ mil.): 9,669

	STOCK PRICE ($) FY Close	P/E High/Low	PER SHARE ($) Earnings	Dividends	Book Value
12/12	33.57	11 11	6.75	0.00	53.50
Annual Growth	—	— —	—	—	—

Henkel AG & Co KGAA

Home and hearth are at the heart of Henkel. The company makes branded products for laundry and homecare (Persil Purex Pril) cosmetics and toiletries (Schwarzkopf Dial Syoss) and many adhesives (Loctite Ceresit UniBond). Henkel's business is centered in Europe with a growing presence in developing economies such as Asia Africa and the Middle East and Latin America. It owns The Dial Corporation anchoring its US market. Henkel owns subsidiaries in some 75 countries with offices located nearly everywhere. Started in 1876 the company is owned by descendants of the founding Henkel family. Amid a global economic downturn Henkel initiated a turnaround strategy with financial targets that extend into 2012.

Henkel's business is divided among three units: laundry and homecare which generates more than one quarter of sales; cosmetics and toiletries approximately 20% of sales and adhesive technologies 50% of sales. Each unit claims a large share of their market through established brands. All told the company's top 10-brands account for more than 40% of sales. In cosmetics and toiletries 90% of sales are driven by the business unit's top-10 brands; in laundry and homecare more than 80% and in adhesive technologies about 55%.

Laundry and homecare and cosmetics and toiletries are primarily sold in Europe and North America and certain developing regions. The company's adhesive technologies have gained a worldwide presence. In 2011 emerging markets (Eastern Europe Africa/Middle East Latin America and Asia excluding Japan) generated more than 40% of Henkel's sales with Western Europe contributing more than one third and North America roughly 15%.

Henkel manufactures products at 180 facilities dotting 56 countries. Its largest plant located in Dusseldorf Germany makes detergents and household cleaning products as well as adhesives for consumers craftsmen and industrial customers. The company's cosmetics and toiletries are produced at eight plants with the largest located in Wassertrudingen Germany.

Given a steep decline in 2009 profits coupled with the ongoing economic environment Henkel's financial targets are ambitious. Among them the company aims for between 3% and 5% organic sales growth per year through 2012. (Organic sales are sales not related to acquisitions.) In 2011 organic sales increased by roughly 6% over the prior year. All business units contributed to the uptick led by Henkel's adhesive technologies (up some 8%). Emerging markets for the first time fueled a major share of the growth. The top line also reflected higher selling prices spurred by an increase in raw material costs. The company cited higher sales coupled with cost savings as driving a 12% jump in year-over-year earnings.

The company is concentrating on its higher-performing brands simultaneous with strengthening customer service and creating a more global and knowledgeable workforce by expanding a share services model for corporate functions. Henkel's strategy includes acquisitions and divestments to engineer a balanced growth portfolio. In 2012 the company extended its reach in the Central American laundry and home care market by buying Colgate-Palmolive's laundry cleaning business including the Fab brand. To supplement its adhesives business that year Henkel acquired Cytec Industries' pressure sensitive adhesives (PSA) product business. The deal followed Henkel's investment in constructing its largest adhesives plant in Shanghai.

In 2011 Henkel gained a direct presence in the US hair salon market by acquiring California-based Schwarzkopf Inc. Henkel also sold off its lack luster Irish detergent unit (Henkel Ireland Detergents) to a German investment fund and its interest in Indian laundry and homecare products maker Henkel India Ltd. picked up by Jyothy Laboratories.

HISTORY

In 1876 Fritz Henkel a chemical plant worker started Henkel & Cie in Aachen Germany to make a universal detergent. He moved the business to Dusseldorf in 1878 and launched Henkel's Bleaching Soda one of Germany's first brand-name products. In the 1880s the company began making water glass an ingredient of its detergent which differs from soap in the way it emulsifies dirt. Henkel debuted Persil a detergent that eliminated the need for rubbing or bleaching clothes in 1907. Persil became a leading detergent in Germany.

Henkel set up an Austrian subsidiary in 1913. In response to a postwar adhesives shortage the company started making glue for its own packaging and soon became Europe's leading glue maker. Henkel began making cleansers with newly developed phosphates in the late 1920s.

When Fritz died in 1930 Henkel stock was divided among his three children. In the 1930s the company sponsored a whaling fleet that provided fats for its products and by 1939 the firm had 16 plants in Europe.

During WWII Henkel lost most of its foreign plants and made unbranded soap in Germany. After the war the company retooled its plants branched out into personal care products and competed with Unilever Procter & Gamble and Colgate-Palmolive for control of the German detergent market. (By 1968 Henkel dominated with close to a 50% share.)

In 1960 Henkel bought its first US company Standard Chemicals (renamed Henkel Corp. in 1971). Konrad Henkel who took over in 1961 modernized the company's image by making changes in management structure and marketing techniques. Henkel patented a substitute for environmentally harmful phosphates acquired 15% of Clorox in 1974 and bought General Mills' chemical business in 1977.

Henkel owned at the time by 66 family members went public with nonvoting shares in 1985. It bought US companies Nopco (specialty chemicals) and Parker Chemical (metal surface pretreatment) in 1987 and Emery the #1 US oleochemicals maker in 1989.

Henkel reorganized its product lines in 1991 by selling several noncore businesses. That year Henkel formed a partnership with Ecolab (of which it owned 24% –later expanded to 50%); acquired interests in Hungary Poland Russia and Slovenia; and introduced Persil in Spain and Portugal. In 1994 Henkel expanded into China and bought 25% of a Brazilian detergent maker.

The company's 1995 acquisition of Hans Schwarzkopf GmbH made Henkel the #1 hair-coloring manufacturer in Germany. The company bought Novamax Technologies a US-based maker of metal-surface treatments in 1996. The next year Henkel paid $1.3 billion for US adhesive giant Loctite its biggest purchase to date. In 1998 it bought Ohio-based adhesive maker Manco to combine its US and Canadian consumer adhesive businesses (parts of Loctite and LePage respectively) under Manco. Henkel pushed into the US toiletries market in 1998 by paying $93 million for DEP and creating a new subsidiary Schwarzkopf & DEP Inc.

In 1999 Henkel created chemicals unit Cognis to focus primarily on palm kernel- and coconut oil-based products. To strengthen Cognis Henkel bought Laboratoires Serobiologiques a French producer of ingredients for the cosmetic and food industries and divested specialty-paper chemicals operations. Henkel also formed a joint venture with soap maker Dial (Dial/Henkel LLC); the joint venture later bought the Custom Cleaner home dry cleaning business from Creative Products Resource.

Henkel picked up Yamahatsu Sangyo a Japanese maker of hair colorants in 2000. The company sold its Substral unit (fertilizer and plant care) to Scotts Company (now Scotts Miracle-Gro). In 2001 Henkel bought TOTAL's metal-treatment chemicals business. In addition the company sold its Cognis specialty chemicals unit to private equity funds Schroeder Ventures and Goldman Sachs Capital Partners for about $2.2 billion. Also in 2001 Henkel said it would cut 2500-3000 jobs (about 5% of its workforce) over the next two years.

In 2003 Henkel purchased a majority stake in La Luz S.A. a Central American manufacturer and marketer of detergents and household cleaners. (Henkel entered the Latin American detergents market via Mexico in 2000.)

Henkel strengthened its adhesives business in Russia and North Central and Eastern Europe when it acquired Makroflex from YIT Construction Ltd. in July 2003. Makroflex located in Finland and Estonia developed and made old sealants and insulation materials for the construction industry.

In 2004 Henkel acquired Alberto-Culver's Indola European professional hair care business which had logged about $55 million in recent annual sales. That year Henkel and US bleach giant Clorox agreed to a deal (in the form of an asset swap) that dissolved Henkel's nearly 30% stake in Clorox. The $2.8 billion transaction involved Henkel's purchase of Clorox's 20% stake in Henkel Iberica a joint venture between the two in Portugal and Spain. Henkel also bought Clorox's stake in a pesticide company as part of the transaction and added Combat insecticides and Soft Scrub bathroom cleaner to its brand portfolio.

Henkel acquired Advanced Research Laboratories in 2004 and folded the company into its existing Schwarzkopf & Dep subsidiary based in California. The deal boosted the company's share of the US hairstyling market. Henkel bought US-based Dial Corporation (Dial soap Purex laundry products Renuzit air fresheners) in 2004 for $2.9 billion in cash.

Also in 2004 Henkel bought 70% of Coventry's Chemtek an independent firm that specializes in formulating and manufacturing liquid cleaners. The balance of the share is owned by Chartered-brands of Edinburgh.

To strengthen its foothold in the electronics market in China Henkel in late 2005 bought a majority stake in Huawei Electronics Co. Ltd. a maker of epoxy molding compounds for semiconductors.

In 2006 the company sold its rubber-to-substrate bonding and rubber coating business to North Carolina-based LORD Corporation. Also that year Dial added the Right Guard Soft & Dri and Dry Idea brands previously owned by Procter & Gamble and Gillette for about $420 million. Henkel sold Dial's Armour-branded products (Treet Vienna sausages) corn starch and boxed pizza to Pinnacle Foods Group for $183 million.

Henkel in 2008 sold its roughly 30% stake in Minnesota-based Ecolab through a public offering. Ecolab itself paid Henkel $300 million for a portion of the shares. The selloff ended a partnership that began in 1989. Also that year Henkel sold its industrial water treatment unit to BK Giulini part of Israel Chemical. Henkel considered the unit noncore in light of its plans to focus on home care personal care and adhesives and sealants. To that end the company purchased the adhesives and electronic materials units of National Starch and Chemical Company from Akzo Nobel in 2008 for about $5 billion.

In early 2011 the company sold Henkel Ireland Detergent to an investment fund as part of its strategy to focus on its core business. (Henkel Ireland Detergents' sales in 2009 exceeded E35 million.)

EXECUTIVES

SVP Information Technology, Peter Wroblowski
CEO, Kasper B. Rorsted, age 51
EVP Purchasing Information Technology Legal and CFO, Lothar Steinebach, age 65
Chief Communications Officer, Carsten Tilger, age 45
SVP Adhesive Technologies and Global Electronic Materials Business, Alan Syzdek
EVP Beauty Care, Hans Van Bylen, age 52
SVP Laundry & Home Care Business Development and MENA Asia-Pacific Central America Regions, Alain Bauwens
Head Communications and Information Headquarters Dusseldorf and Germany, Lars Witteck
Chairwoman Supervisory Board, Simone Bagel-Trah
SVP Finance and Controlling, Wolfgang Beynio
SVP Industrial Adhesives SBU, Jean Fayolle
SVP and Chief Compliance Officer, Dirk-Stephan Koedijk
EVP Laundry & Home Care, Friedrich Stara, age 64
SVP Infrastructure Services, Andreas Bruns
SVP Laundry & Home Care Research and Development Technology and Supply Chain, Thomas Muller-Kirschbaum
SVP Consumer Goods North America, Stefan Sudhoff
SVP Consumer and Craftsmen Adhesives and Building Adhesives SBUs Adhesive Technologies Western Europe Central Easterern Europe and MEA Regions, Enric Holzbacher
SVP Schwarzkopf Professional, Norbert Koll
SVP SBU Hair Skin and Oral Care, Tina Muller
Financial Director Laundry & Home Care, Marcus Kuhnert
EVP Adhesive Technologies, Jan-Dirk Auris, age 44
SVP Adhesive Technologies North America, Julian Colquitt
EVP Finance CFO and Purchasing & Integrated Business Solutions, Carsten Knobel
EVP Laundry and Home Care, Bruno Piacenza, age 46
SVP Adhesive Technologies and Financial Director, Matthias Schmidt
EVP HR and Infrastructure Service, Kathrin Menges
Member Supervisory Board, Bernhard Walter, age 70
Member Supervisory Board, Hans Dietrichs, age 68
Member Supervisory Board, Bernd Hinz, age 60
Member Supervisory Board, Michael Vassiliadis, age 48
Member Supervisory Board, Michael Kaschke, age 56
Member Supervisory Board, Thierry Paternot, age 64
Member Supervisory Board, Andrea Pichottka, age 53
Member Supervisory Board, Friderike Bagel, age 40
Member Supervisory Board, Engelbert Ba?ler, age 60
Member Supervisory Board, Rolf Zimmermann, age 58
Member Supervisory Board, Thomas Manchot, age 47
Member Supervisory Board, Konstantin von Unger, age 46
Member Supervisory Board, Jutta Bernicke, age 51
Member Supervisory Board, Fritz Franke, age 57
Member Supervisory Board, Birgit Helten-Kindlein, age 49
Member Supervisory Board, Ulf Wentzien, age 49
Member Supervisory Board, Johann-Christoph Frey, age 58
Member Supervisory Board, Theo Siegert, age 42
Member Supervisory Board, Stefan Hamelmann, age 50
Auditors: KPMGDeutscheTreuhand-GesellschaftAG

LOCATIONS

HQ: Henkel AG & Co KGAA
Henkelstrasse 67, Duesseldorf D-40191
Phone: (49) 211 797 0 **Fax:** (49) 211 798 4040
Web: www.henkel.com

2011 Sales

	% of total
Emerging Regions (Eastern Europe Africa/Middle East Latin America & Asia excluding	42
Western	36
North	17
Japan/Australia/New	4
Corporate	1
Total	**100**

PRODUCTS/OPERATIONS

2011 Sales

	% of total
Adhesive	50
Laundry & home	27
Cosmetics &	22
Corporate	1
Total	**100**

Selected Brands

Adhesives technologies
- Ariasana
- Ceresit
- Elch
- Fster
- LePage
- Loctite
- Metylan
- Pattex
- Ponal
- Pritt
- Rubson
- Sellotape
- Sista
- Solvite
- Tangit
- Technomelt
- Teroson
- Thomsit
- UniBond

Cosmetics and toiletries
- Antica Erboristeria
- Aok
- Bac
- Barnangen
- Citre Shine
- Clynol viton
- Coast
- Denivit
- Dep
- Diadermine
- Dial
- Dry Idea
- Fa
- Indola Professional
- L.A. Looks
- La Toja
- Licor del Polo
- Mon Saint Michel
- Natural & Easy
- Neutromed
- Right Guard
- Schwarzkoph
- Seborin
- Smooth 'N Shine
- Soft & Dri
- Syoss
- Theramed
- Thicker Fuller Hair
- Tone
- Vademecum
- Zero Frizz

Laundry and homecare
- Bref
- Dixan
- Mir
- Persil
- Perwoll
- Pril
- Pur
- Purex
- Sil
- Soft Scrub
- Somat
- Spee
- Vernel

COMPETITORS

3M
Alticor
Avon
BASF SE
Bayer AG
Beiersdorf
Church & Dwight
Clorox
Colgate-Palmolive
Dow Chemical
DuPont
Estee Lauder
H.B. Fuller
Johnson & Johnson
Kimberly-Clark
L' Oreal
Procter & Gamble
Reckitt Benckiser
S.C. Johnson
Sara Lee
Shiseido
Unilever

HISTORICAL FINANCIALS

Company Type: Public

Income Statement

FYE: December 31

	REVENUE ($ mil.)	NET INCOME ($ mil.)	NET PROFIT MARGIN	EMPLOYEES
12/12	21,761	1,990	9.1%	46,610
12/11	20,184	1,620	8.0%	47,753
12/10	20,198	1,496	7.4%	48,141
12/09	19,552	867	4.4%	51,361
12/08	19,756	1,707	8.6%	55,142
Annual Growth	2.4%	3.9%	—	(4.1%)

2012 Year-End Financials

Debt ratio: 25.4%
Return on equity: 16.7%
Cash ($ mil.): 1,631
Current ratio: 1.31
Long-term debt ($ mil.): 3,234
No. of shares (mil.): 259
Dividends
Yield: 1.0%
Payout: —
Market value ($ mil.): 21,402

	STOCK PRICE ($) FY Close	P/E High/Low	PER SHARE ($) Earnings	Dividends	Book Value
12/12	82.38	42 27	4.57	0.73	47.57
12/11	57.91	47 31	3.71	0.00	43.02
12/10	62.10	46 28	3.43	0.48	40.49
12/09	51.80	84 30	1.99	0.46	35.90
12/08	32.15	41 15	3.90	0.00	34.89
Annual Growth	26.5%	— —	4.1%	—	8.1%

Hennes & Mauritz AB

H&M Hennes & Mauritz targets the Hip & Modish. The firm designs cheap yet chic clothing mainly for men and women ages 18 to 45 children's apparel and its own brands of cosmetics. Fast-growing H&M operates some 2470 stores in some 35 countries and offers online shopping in eight countries. Germany is its #1 market accounting for more than 20% of sales. The firm doesn't own factories but buys its goods from suppliers primarily in Asia and Europe. H&M opened its first women's clothing store in 1947 as Hennes (Swedish for "hers"); it later bought the hunting and men's clothing store Mauritz Widforss. H&M is controlled by the family of chairman Stefan Persson (the billionaire son of founder Erling Persson).

H&M's cheap-chic strategy and global retail presence has largely insulated the company from the global economic downturn. Indeed fiscal 2010 (ends November) sales were up 7% vs. the prior year after climbing 15% in the previous annual comparison. (The retailer also enjoyed double-digit sales growth in 2008 vs. 2007.) International expansion has been the hallmark of H&M's business plan in recent years. Indeed the fast-growing chain added about 220 stores in 2010 including its first locations in South Korea Israel and Turkey. Also in 2010 H&M launched an e-commerce site in the UK H&M's second-largest market. Going forward H&M plans to stick to its ambitious target to increase the number of stores by 10% to 15% per year. Despite its rapid growth H&M has been overtaken by Spain's Inditex owner of the Zara chain as Europe's largest apparel retailer.

Taking a page from Inditex which also operates Zara Home the Swedish retailer in early 2009 quietly launched a catalog and Internet H&M Home business in Austria Germany the Netherlands and the Nordic region. Longer-term the H&M Home brand of pillows towels curtains and other home textiles may support retail stores. Moving up market H&M has launched a chain called COS —for Collection of Style. Aimed at the premium market the first COS store debuted in London in 2007. The chain has since grown to about 35 locations in Belgium Denmark France Ireland Germany the Netherlands Spain and the UK.

In late 2010 H&M acquired the remaining 40% of the shares in FaBric Scandinavien AB which runs the store chains Weekday and Monki as well as the Cheap Monday brand. The brands will continue to operate as separate retail concepts.

H&M generates "buzz" and drives shoppers to its stores through tie ups with big name designers and celebrities. The company's latest collaboration is with the Italian brand Marni and its founder and creative director Consuelo Castiglioni. Marni will design a spring collection for H&M in 2012. Previous design partners have included Karl Lagerfeld Stella McCartney Comme des Garcons Jimmy Choo Lanvin and Versace.

Women's clothing accounts for 60% of sales; private-label brands include Hennes L.O.G.G. (Label of Graded Goods) and the plus-size BiB (Big is Beautiful) line.

HISTORY

Swedish salesman Erling Persson visited the US in 1947 and returned intrigued by the low-price high-turnover clothing store he saw on his trip. That year Persson opened his first Hennes store (Swedish for "hers" because it only sold women's apparel) in Vaster?s Sweden. The company expanded opening its first foreign stores in Norway in 1964 and Denmark in 1967. As it grew and increased volume the retailer was able to offer lower prices. The company bought hunting and men's clothing shop Mauritz Widforss in 1968 and began offering men's clothing in Mauritz stores.

The firm took its fashions to a different market in 1974 when its stock was listed on the Swedish stock exchange. H&M Hennes & Mauritz introduced cosmetics in 1975 and began opening stores in London the following year. Also in 1976 the company introduced its teenage clothing stores under the Impulse banner.

By the end of the 1970s the company had moved into Switzerland (1978) and Germany (1980) and introduced baby clothes. In 1980 H&M also purchased mail-order company Rowell.

Stefan Persson took over as CEO from his father Erling in 1982. He expanded throughout northern Europe and H&M boasted 200 stores in 1985. By 1988 the company was sustaining annual sales growth rates of 25%-30% to the delight of investors. H&M saw fashion globalization coming and knew that more and more people would be dressing similarly even if they lived in different countries. At the same time however the company maintained local flavor in its stores so shoppers would feel as if they were shopping with a hometown merchant rather than a foreign company.

The firm's European expansion continued and by 1998 H&M had entered six more countries including France Austria Finland and the Benelux countries. By this time the company had also consolidated its men's women's children's and teens' stores under the H&M banner. Stefan gave up his CEO position and became executive chairman of the board in 1998. The company's purchasing director Fabian M?nsson succeeded him as CEO. In 1998 and 1999 H&M began selling online first in Sweden then in Denmark and Finland.

The company moved into the US and Spain in 2000. The openings considered a success by H&M put a strain on earnings which sent the stock into a dive. Before the drop the company had the second-largest market cap on the Swedish exchange. In a move the company said was unrelated M?nsson resigned and was replaced by Danish subsidiary CEO Rolf Eriksen.

In 2001 the company said it was planning to have 85 stores in the US by 2003 but it scaled back its US expansion plans somewhat in early 2002. In October founder Erling Persson died at the age of 85.

In 2004 Gap Inc. sold H&M the entirety of its German operations including ten stores which were later converted to H&M stores. That fall H&M hired fashion industry giant Karl Lagerfeld best known for his bringing back the Chanel brand for a collection of 30 pieces. The following year the Swedish retailer enlisted Stella McCartney to design a one-time women's collection of some 40 items under the label "Stella McCartney for H&M."

In November 2005 H&M opened a pair of stores in San Francisco the company's first on the West Coast. Overall in 2005 the company opened 145 stores and closed 20; new markets included Ireland and Hungary with a major expansion in Spain.

In September 2006 the company opened its first two stores in Dubai in the Mall of the Emirates as well as its first store in Southern California (in Pasadena). In 2007 the retailer expanded in Asia with stores in Hong Kong and Shanghai. In 2008 H&M added more than 230 shops worldwide. H&M also acquired a 60% share in FaBric Scandinavien AB in 2008. (The company exercised its option to buy the remaining 40% of FaBric in late 2010.)

Karl-Johan Persson —son of chairman Stefan Persson —took the helm at H&M in July 2009 when CEO Rolf Eriksen retired. Persson is a member of the board and served in the executive post responsible for expansion and business development. Also in 2009 the chain opened its first store in Russia.

EXECUTIVES

Head Human Resources, Sanna Lindberg
Chairman, Stefan Persson, age 66
Head Production, Karl Gunnar Fagerlin
Head Communications, Kristina Stenvinkel
Head Investor Relations, Nils Vinge
Chief Accountant, Anders Jonasson
Managing Director and Chief Executive Officer, Karl-Johan Persson, age 38
Head Buying, Madeleine Persson
Head IT, Kjell-Olof Nilsson
Head Logistics, Jonas Guldstrand
Head Design, Ann-Sofie Johansson
Chief Financial Officer, Jyrki Tervonen
Sales Officer, Stefan Larsson
Head Business Development, Bjorn Magnusson
Head Marketing, Anna Tillberg Pantzar
Marketing/Brand Officer, Anna Anna Pantzar Pantzar
Security Officer, Cenneth Cenneth Cederholm Cederholm
Sustainability Officer, Helena Helena Helmersson Helmersson
Head Buying, Stina Westerstad
Board Member, Melker Schorling, age 65
Board Member, Lottie Knutson, age 49
Board Member, Sussi Kvart, age 57
Chairman of the Auditing Committee, Bo Lundquist, age 71
Board Member, Stig Nordfelt, age 72
Board Member, Mia Brunell Livfors, age 48
Board Member, Margareta Welinder, age 51
Board Member, Marianne Broman, age 68
Board Member, Agneta Ramberg, age 67
Board Member, Tina Jaderberg, age 38
Independent Director, Anders Anders Dahlvig Dahlvig
Independent Director, Christian Christian Sievert Sievert
Director; Deputy Employee Representative, Marie Marie Bjorstedt Bjorstedt
Independent Director, Melker Melker Schorling Schorling
Director; Deputy Employee Representative, Tina Tina Jaderberg Jaderberg
Auditors: Ernst&YoungAB

LOCATIONS

HQ: Hennes & Mauritz AB
Master Samuelsgatan 46A, Stockholm SE-106 38
Phone: (46) 8 796 55 00 **Fax:** (46) 8 796 55 44
Web: www.hm.com

2010 Stores

	No.
Germany	377
US	208
UK	192
Sweden	168
France	151
Spain	122
The	112
Norway	101
Denmark	87
Poland	76
Switzerland	75
Italy	72
Austria	66
Belgium	64
Canada	55
China	47
Finland	43
Czech	22
Portugal	21
Greece	18
Hungary	15
Ireland	12
Russia	11
Slovenia	11
Luxembourg	10
Japan	10
Slovakia	7
South	2
Turkey	1
Franchise	50
Total	**2,206**

2010 Sales

	% of total
Euro	54
Nordic	16
Rest of	30
Total	**100**

PRODUCTS/OPERATIONS

Selected Banners

Cheap Monday
COS
H&M
H&M Home
Monki
Weekday

Selected Brands

Baby Baby
Beauty Box
BiB
Chiboogi
Clothes
Clothes Men
Conwell
Divided
DUbbSTER
Face of Beauty
Hennes
L.O.G.G.
L.O.G.G. Sport
Mama
RESQ

COMPETITORS

Abercrombie & Fitch	LVMH
Arcadia	Marks & Spencer
Benetton	Maxeda
Bleach Group	Monsoon
Brice	NEXT plc
C&A	Naf Naf
Cortefiel	New Look
Etam Developpement	Otto Group
Fast Retailing	Ralph Lauren
Forever 21	SCF
French Connection	Target Corporation
Hanna Andersson	Ted Baker
Inditex	The Gap
Kooperativa Forbundet	Vivarte
	Zannier

HISTORICAL FINANCIALS

Company Type: Public

Income Statement

FYE: November 30

	REVENUE ($ mil.)	NET INCOME ($ mil.)	NET PROFIT MARGIN	EMPLOYEES
11/12	18,170	2,537	14.0%	72,276
11/11	15,988	2,299	14.4%	64,874
11/10	15,402	2,652	17.2%	59,440
11/09	14,576	2,355	16.2%	53,476
11/08	10,905	1,884	17.3%	53,430
Annual Growth	13.6%	7.7%	—	7.8%

2012 Year-End Financials

Debt ratio: —
Return on equity: 38.2%
Cash ($ mil.): 2,128
Current ratio: 2.66
Long-term debt ($ mil.): —

No. of shares (mil.): 1,655
Dividends
Yield: 4.2%
Payout: 0.3%
Market value ($ mil.): 10,621

	STOCK PRICE ($) FY Close	P/E High/Low		PER SHARE ($) Earnings	Dividends	Book Value
11/12	6.42	0	0	1.53	0.27	3.98
11/11	6.25	0	0	1.39	0.31	3.87
11/10	6.74	0	0	1.60	0.41	3.79
11/09	11.83	0	0	1.42	0.39	3.53
11/08	7.35	0	0	1.14	0.00	2.75
Annual Growth	(3.3%)	—	—	7.7%	189.9%	9.7%

Heraeus Holding GmbH (Germany Fed. Rep.)

Precious metals are priority at Heraeus Holding. The family-owned company processes precious and specialty metals into products used in the aerospace automobile chemical electronics and pharmaceutical industries. Among Heraeus Holding's 100 other subsidiaries and affiliates are Heraeus Dental Heraeus Dental Heraeus Quarzglas (equipment and optics made from quartz glass) Heraeus Electro-Nite (temperature sensors used in the steel and auto industries and appliances) and Heraeus Noblelight (infrared ultraviolet and other specialty light sources).

Geographic Reach

The company operates globally with Asia accounting for more than half of sales.

Operations

Heraeus holds more than 5900 patents. Precious Metals contributes about 40% of the company's overall revenues

Financial Performance

The company's revenues increased by 16% in 2011 due to organic growth in all segments. The precious metals' sales increase was due to an expanding market for products for the photovoltaic industry. The materials and technologies business group saw growth because of the demand for products for the automotive industry and the improved economic situation in Asia. The dental products business group logged only slight growth reflecting a weak market for dental consumables.

By expanding its marketing activities especially in Asia the biomaterials and medical products business group boosted revenues. The quartz glass division profited from strong demand in the solar and semiconductor markets in the first half of the year as well as from sustained high demand in the market for optical fibers for the telecommunications industry.

Heraeus' net income increased by 17% in 2011 due to higher revenues primarily as the result of growth in the US and Germany.

Operations

The company is focused on growing organically and through acquisitions responding to market trends in energy health communication mobility and the environment.

In 2013 to strengthen Heraeus' position as a solar paste Heraeus Precious Metals business group bought Ferro's solar paste business unit.

During 2011 Heraeus divided the former precious metals business group (W. C. Heraeus) into two business groups (precious metals and materials and technologies) in order to spur growth as individual units.

That year it also began construction on the Heraeus Asia Center located in Tuas the first complete facility in the Asia/Pacific region for silver conductive pastes for the photovoltaics sector. That year Heraeus Metals Shanghai Co. Ltd. commenced trading. (The Trading Division of Heraeus Precious Metals is represented at four locations: Shanghai Hong Kong Hanau (Germany) and New York.

Ownership

The Heraeus family owns the company.

HISTORY

The origin of Heraeus Holding can be traced back to the 1600s when the Heraeus family owned Einhorn-Apotheke (the Unicorn Pharmacy) in Hanau Germany. The pharmacy was passed from generation to generation and reached pharmacist Wilhelm Carl Heraeus in 1851. In addition to his chemical experiments for the pharmacy Wilhelm began to experiment with platinum waste and successfully melted platinum in 1856. The following year the company began exporting its processed platinum and in 1859 it sold a total of 59 kg of platinum products. The company's platinum production reached 1000 kg in 1888.

Facing low supplies of platinum from Russia the company began to diversify its line of unfinished platinum products and started to produce gold and platinum vessels used in the chemical industry. Between 1891 and 1896 the company built platinum-processing plants on the outskirts of Hanau. Also in the 1890s Heraeus created its ceramics division which developed heat-resistant precious metals. It also began melting rock crystal to form quartz glass for laboratory equipment. In 1901 the company formed the Heraeus quartz-melting facility and in 1904 Heraeus began producing resistance thermometers. The family-owned company began producing melting furnaces in 1910.

During WWI the company continued to add new products including platinum catalyst gauzes for the chemical industry (1914) and vacuum induction furnaces (1917). Following the war the company faced additional problems with the supply of platinum but it managed to weather the tough period and continued to expand and diversify its product line.

Throughout the 1930s the company was successful in developing techniques to melt other metals (titanium tantalum and zirconium) that have high melting temperatures. Following WWII Heraeus Edelmetalle was created in 1947 to handle its growing dental products business.

During the 1950s Heraeus began producing operating-room light systems and in 1958 the company established its first foreign sales subsidiaries in France and Italy. Additional foreign subsidiaries were created in Switzerland and the Netherlands by 1964. In 1969 the company acquired several laboratory equipment companies. Heraeus established subsidiaries and affiliates in Japan the UK and the US in 1972 and built a precious metals refinery in Hanau in 1976.

The company made a major push in the 1980s to establish itself as an international company. It bought US-based Cermalloy (thick film) in 1980 and Pacific Platers Hong Kong in 1982. In 1985 Heraeus Holding was officially created as a holding company. It acquired Belgium's Electro-Lite International and its worldwide subsidiaries (metal-melt measuring systems) and the surgical lasers division of US-based Cooper Laser Sonics in 1988.

The company was organized into its present divisional structure in 1990. It acquired Bayer's dental business in 1995 and opened a semiconductor products plant in the Philippines the following year. Heraeus bought US-based Jelenko a maker of dental amalgams in 1997. Through the merger of Heraeus Instruments and Sorvall Laboratory Products (US) the company formed Kendro Laboratory Products the next year. In 2000 Heraeus purchased PGP Industries (US) a recycler of precious metals; it also sold its Singapore-based lead-frame business (used in the semiconductor industry) to Jade Technologies.

The increase in precious metal prices (mainly platinum) helped boost the company's sales in 2000. In 2001 the company had a reversal in fortune with a slowing economy and falling platinum prices which ultimately affected its bottom line. Heraeus spun off its fiber-optics business as Heraeus Tenevo in 2001 (it was reintegrated into the company in 2003). The next year it sold its Heraeus Med GmbH unit to Sweden-based medical technology company Getinge. In 2003 a Medical

Components division was created upon the acquisition of the medical unit from Metalor Technologies.

In 2010 Heraeus sold its ceramic color business to Ferro while acquiring Ferro's precious metal preparation and lustres operations. The two-way deal will enable both companies to focus on their core businesses. Also that year Heraeus made two more strategic acquisitions buying Clevios the conductive polymers business of HC Starck GmbH and a majority stake in South Korean dental products distributor Huden Dental.

Since 2008 it has added to its business with acquisitions in three areas: medical components quartz and ceramic colors. Heraeus bought business units from the likes of Synovis Life Technologies BASF Catalysts Saint-Gobain and Kulicke & Soffa.

EXECUTIVES

Vice Chairman of the Supervisory Board, Hans Ostermeier
Managing Director W. C. Heraeus, Roland Gerner, age 59
Chairman of the Management Board, Frank Heinricht, age 51
Managing Director Heraeus Quarzglas, Heinz Fabian, age 52
Managing Director Heraeus Quarzglas, Wolfgang Stang, age 57
Managing Director Heraeus Electro-Nite International, Jan Doets, age 54
Auditors: KPMGAGWirtschaftsprufungsgesellschaft

LOCATIONS

HQ: Heraeus Holding GmbH (Germany Fed. Rep.)
Heraeusstrasse 12-14, Hanau 63450
Phone: (49) 61 81 35 5100 **Fax:** (49) 61 81 35 42 42
Web: www.heraeus.com

PRODUCTS/OPERATIONS

Selected Operations

Haraeus Precious Metals (precious and specialty metals alloys and products)
Haraeus Materials Technology (high-tech industrial products using precious metals)
Haraeus Dental (prosthetics)
Haraeus Medical (medical products)
Heraeus Electro-Nite (sensors used in industrial medical and household applications; Belgium)
Heraeus Quarzglas (quartz glass used to make semiconductors and optical communications products)
Heraeus Noblelight (specialty lighting sources including ultraviolet and infrared used in medical and industrial instrumentation printing water purification and surface treatments)

COMPETITORS

3M
ArcelorMittal South Africa
BASF Catalysts
CONMED Corporation
Danaher
Haynes International
Johnson Matthey
MAN
Umicore
Vesuvius

HISTORICAL FINANCIALS

Company Type: Public

Income Statement FYE: December 31

	REVENUE ($ mil.)	NET INCOME ($ mil.)	NET PROFIT MARGIN	EMPLOYEES
12/12	26,646	304	1.1%	13,615
12/11	33,866	399	1.2%	13,323
12/10	29,478	341	1.2%	12,931
12/09	23,366	167	0.7%	12,340
12/08	22,248	232	1.0%	12,830
Annual Growth	4.6%	6.9%	—	1.5%

2012 Year-End Financials

Debt ratio: 12.9%
Return on equity: 10.1%
Cash ($ mil.): 393
Current ratio: 3.97
Long-term debt ($ mil.): 523
No. of shares (mil.): —
Dividends
Yield: —
Payout: —
Market value ($ mil.): —

Hindustan Petroleum Corp., Ltd. (India)

Hindustan Petroleum is one of India's top oil refiners (along with Indian Oil and Bharat Petroleum) and accounts for 10% of the country's total refining requirements. The company has two major refineries –one in Mumbai the other in the southern Indian city of Vishakhapatnam –and produces lubricants aviation fuel liquefied petroleum gas and light diesel oil. Hindustan Petroleum also holds a 17% stake in a refinery at Mangalore. Other businesses include pipelines a lube refinery (with a 40% share of the lube oil market) and more than 11250 retail outlets nationwide. The Indian government owns 51% of the company.

Geographic Reach

The company's marketing network consists of 13 zonal offices in major cities and 101 regional offices. It has a major refinery in Mumbai on India's west coast and in Vishakhapatnam on the east coast and 17% of Mangalore Refinery & Petrochemicals Limited in the south of India and a joint venture refinery in the Punjab in the north.

Operations

Hindustan Petroleum has a refining capacity of more than 15 million metric tonnes per year. Its refineries produce a wide variety of petroleum fuels and specialty products. Its supply and distribution infrastructure includes terminals pipeline networks aviation service stations LPG bottling plants inland relay depots and retail outlets lube and LPG distributorships.

Financial Performance

Higher prices and demand help to lift the company's revenues by 33% in 2011.

Net income decreased by 90% in 2011 due to increase in depreciation and amortization expenses other expenses transshipping expenses purchase in stock-in-trade and cost of materials consumed.

Strategy

Hindustan Petroleum in addition investing heavily in the modernization and expansion of its major refineries is opening new retail outlets to keep up with the growing population. In 2011 the company commissioned 1056 retail outlets including 329 in rural areas.

To stay competitive the company has been diversifying by entering into exploration and production as well as into the supply of liquefied natural gas (LNG) and compressed natural gas (CNG). In 2011 the company held minority stakes in oil and gas fields in Australia Egypt India and Oman.

Ownership

The company is controlled by the Government of India.

EXECUTIVES

Chairman and Managing Director, S. Roy Choudhury
Human Resources Director, V. Vizia Saradhi
Finance Director, Bhaswar Mukherjee
Refineries Director, K. Murali
Marketing Director, Nishi Vasudeva
Auditors: B.K.Khare&Co.

LOCATIONS

HQ: Hindustan Petroleum Corp., Ltd. (India)
Petroleum House, 17, Jamshedji Tata Road, Mumbai 400 020
Phone:
Web: www.hindustanpetroleum.com

COMPETITORS

Bharat Petroleum
Essar Group
Exxon Mobil
Indian Oil

HISTORICAL FINANCIALS

Company Type: Public

Income Statement FYE: March 31

	REVENUE ($ mil.)	NET INCOME ($ mil.)	NET PROFIT MARGIN	EMPLOYEES
03/12	36,620	34	0.1%	11,226
03/11	31,397	382	1.2%	11,248
03/10	25,235	328	1.3%	11,291
03/09	25,548	148	0.6%	11,246
03/08	27,805	339	1.2%	10,949
Annual Growth	7.1%	(43.6%)	—	0.6%

2012 Year-End Financials

Debt ratio: 0.8%
Return on equity: 1.3%
Cash ($ mil.): 144
Current ratio: 0.85
Long-term debt ($ mil.): 2,721
No. of shares (mil.): 338
Dividends
Yield: —
Payout: —
Market value ($ mil.): —

Hino Motors, Ltd.

Hino Motors introduced Japan's first truck in 1918 long before Godzilla was throwing vehicles all over Tokyo. These days the company not only manufactures medium- and heavy-duty diesel trucks but it also makes buses special-purpose vehicles and industrial diesel engines. Hino Motors dominates Japan's domestic truck market beating out such competitors as Mitsubishi Motors and Isuzu Motors. Manufacturing vehicles and service parts for Toyota Motor represents more than 35% of the company's sales. Asia accounts for nearly 90% of sales. Toyota Motor owns more than 50% of the company.

Although both commercial and light-duty truck sales in Japan saw dramatic declines in 2009 the company was buoyed by sales of the Toyota-branded land Cruiser and FJ Cruiser in the US. The company also entered the emergency vehicle market in the US with the introduction of an ambulance chassis in early 2010. Hino will continue to look to foreign markets for vehicle sales as commercial truck sales in Japan are not expected to recover in 2011.

HISTORY

Hino Motors was founded in 1910 as a unit of the Tokyo Gas Industry Company. It was established to build trucks for the emerging Japanese industrial economy. By 1918 the company was mass-producing the A-Type truck. The pace of industrialization increased in Japan in the early 1930s. To survive automotive companies had to maximize economies of scale. Finding safety in numbers many merged their operations.

In 1937 Tokyo Gas combined its auto unit with Automobile Industry Company and Kyodo Kokusan. The new enterprise was called Tokyo Automobile Industry Company.

Japan's occupation of China during the late 1930s had opened new markets but it also brought a trade embargo from the US in 1941. Japan did not back down however. Instead the Japanese government continued a program of military buildup that greatly benefited companies such as Tokyo Automobile. Later in 1941 the company changed its name to Diesel Motor Industry Company.

By 1942 Japan was at war with the US and Britain and Diesel Motor was split into two companies. The larger company retained the Diesel Motor name (eventually it became Isuzu Motors) and the smaller one became Hino Heavy Industry Company.

Most of Hino's Tokyo facilities escaped damage during the war until an American bomb hit a Hino factory in 1945. After the war the factory was converted into a barracks for occupying forces. A year after the end of the war Hino introduced a new truck the massive T10-20 that found immediate popularity. In 1947 the company launched a bus based on the T10-20 frame –the 96-passenger T11-B-25. Hino was listed on the Tokyo Stock Exchange in 1949.

Demand for trucks by United Nations forces during the Korean War prompted Hino to open an additional production line. Taking notice of Japan's demand for foreign passenger cars Hino began to look for a manufacturing partner and eventually decided on Renault. Hino began producing Renault 4CV cars in Japan in 1953.

Struck by the fact that much of Japan was being rebuilt with pricey foreign dump trucks Hino resolved to build a similar truck to compete with imports. Hino introduced the 13.5 ton ZG and it soon became Japan's leading dump truck. In 1959 the company changed its name to Hino Motors Ltd.

Hino introduced its own car the Contessa 900 in 1961. However the company was not yet ready to ride solo. In 1966 Hino linked its carmaking operations with those of Toyota and began making Toyotas on a large scale.

By the mid-1970s Hino was ready to embark on an aggressive export campaign. It set up a sales network in Southeast Asia and opened parts depots in Latin America and Europe. Hino's products were a hit overseas and in 1980 the company opened a new factory to meet demand. During the 1980s Hino established offices in Pakistan and an assembly plant in Taiwan. Hino entered the US market in 1984 with the introduction of a cab-over engine (COE) medium duty truck.

With the US and Japanese economies in recession the early 1990s were tough for Hino although the company managed to continue to expand into new markets. It entered a joint venture to produce buses in China (1993) and teamed with the Vietnamese government to make trucks and buses in Vietnam (1996). Toyota turned its manufacturing of two-ton-sized trucks over to Hino and increased its stake in the company from 11% to 16% in 1997 and to 20% the next year.

In 1999 Hino made plans to combine its bus-making operations with those of Isuzu by 2002 in hopes of capturing 50% of the Japanese market (these plans were later postponed due to the worldwide drop in truck demand). Toyota increased its stake to 34% in 2000. Toyota Motor further increased its stake in Hino to more than 50% in 2001.

EXECUTIVES

Chairman, Masakazu Ichikawa
EVP, Seiei Okazaki
EVP, Kenji Wagu
President, Yasuhiko Ichihashi, age 61
President Hino Motor Sales, Sumio Fukaya
President, Yoshio Shirai
EVP, Koichi Ojima
President Hino Motors Manufacturing USA, Yasuo Tanigawa
Vice President of Marketing for Hino Trucks, Glenn Ellis
EVP and Board Member, Masakazu Ichikawa
Senior Managing Director and Board Member, Seiei Okazaki
EVP and Board Member, Takahiko Yamamoto
Senior Managing Director and Board Member, Toshiki Inoue
Senior Managing Director and Board Member, Kenji Wagu
Senior Managing Director and Board Member, Shinji Fujimoto
Senior Managing Director and Board Member, Manabu Kasai
Senior Managing Director and Board Member, Tsunehiko Fujii
Senior Managing Director and Board Member, Akimasa Yamamoto
Auditors: ChuoAoyamaPricewaterhouseCoopers

LOCATIONS

HQ: Hino Motors, Ltd.
3-1-1 Hinodai, Hino, Tokyo 191-8660
Phone: (81) 42 586 5111
Web: www.hino.co.jp

2010 Sales

	% of total
Asia	
Japan	66
Other	22
North	6
Oceania	3
Latin	2
Other	1
Total	**100**

PRODUCTS/OPERATIONS

2010 Sales

	% of total
Automobiles	
Hino	41
Toyota	27
Parts	7
Other	25
Total	**100**

Selected Overseas Subsidiaries and Affiliates

Hino Motor Sales Australia Pty. Ltd.
Hino Motor Sales U.S.A. Inc.
Hino Motors (Malaysia) Sdn. Bhd.
Hino Motors Sales (Thailand) Ltd.
Hinopak Motors Ltd. (Pakistan)
Shenyang Shenfei Hino Automobile Manufacturing Co. Ltd. (China)

COMPETITORS

Ashok Leyland
China Yuchai
Cummins
Daimler
General Motors
Isuzu
Mitsubishi Fuso Truck & Bus
Navistar International
PACCAR
Peterbilt
Renault
Scania
UD Trucks
Volvo

HISTORICAL FINANCIALS

Company Type: Public

Income Statement — FYE: March 31

	REVENUE ($ mil.)	NET INCOME ($ mil.)	NET PROFIT MARGIN	EMPLOYEES
03/13	16,381	506	3.1%	27,705
03/12	16,025	198	1.2%	25,820
03/11	15,007	(121)	—	24,934
03/10	10,957	(32)	—	24,785
03/09	10,860	(627)	—	24,492
Annual Growth	10.8%	—	—	3.1%

2013 Year-End Financials

Debt ratio: 0.2%
Return on equity: 20.1%
Cash ($ mil.): 288
Current ratio: 1.02
Long-term debt ($ mil.): 436
No. of shares (mil.): 571
Dividends
Yield: —
Payout: —
Market value ($ mil.): 62,838

	STOCK PRICE ($) FY Close	P/E High/Low	PER SHARE ($) Earnings	Dividends	Book Value
03/13	110.00	— —	0.89	0.00	5.56
03/12	70.28	— —	0.35	0.00	5.02
03/11	47.90	— —	(0.21)	0.00	4.59
03/10	42.40	— —	(0.06)	0.00	4.27
03/09	22.15	— —	(1.10)	0.98	3.89
Annual Growth	49.3%	— —	—	—	9.4%

Hiroshima Bank, Ltd. (The) (Japan)

Few banks have deeper roots in the Hiroshima Prefecture than the Hiroshima Bank. Established in 1878 the bank serves Japan's Chugoku and Shikoku regions through more than 175 offices and 830 ATMs. Hiroshima organizes its business approach into three distinct areas: financial intermediation risk management assistance and information provision. It offers the traditional array of financial services including investment and private banking products real estate appraisal banking software venture capital support and assistance with corporate restructuring.

EXECUTIVES

President, Isao Sumihiro
Executive Officer, Hideo Yamashita
Executive Officer, Makoto Tsukamoto
Executive Officer, Hironori Kawasaki
Executive Officer, Hiroshi Matsushige
Auditors: KPMGAZSA&Co.

LOCATIONS

HQ: Hiroshima Bank, Ltd. (The) (Japan)
1-3-8 Kamiya-cho, Naka-ku, Hiroshima 730-0031
Phone: (81) 82 247 5151 **Fax:** (81) 82 247 5234
Web: www.hirogin.co.jp

COMPETITORS

Aozora Bank
Chugoku Bank
Higo Bank
Mitsubishi UFJ Financial Group
Miyazaki Bank
Shizuoka Bank

HISTORICAL FINANCIALS

Company Type: Public

Income Statement FYE: March 31

	ASSETS ($ mil.)	NET INCOME ($ mil.)	INCOME AS % OF ASSETS	EMPLOYEES
03/13	75,050	184	0.2%	3,207
03/12	81,075	168	0.2%	3,274
03/11	77,165	166	0.2%	3,371
03/10	68,151	118	0.2%	3,385
03/09	63,244	72	0.1%	3,392
Annual Growth	4.4%	26.2%	—	(1.4%)

2013 Year-End Financials

Return on assets: 0.2%
Return on equity: 5.5%
Long-term debt ($ mil.): —
No. of shares (mil.): 619
Sales ($ mil): 1,407

Dividends
Yield: —
Payout: —
Market value ($ mil.): —

	STOCK PRICE ($) FY Close	P/E High/Low	PER SHARE ($) Earnings	Dividends	Book Value
03/13	0.00	— —	0.30	0.00	6.28
Annual Growth	—	— —	—	—	—

Hitachi, Ltd.

Hitachi which means "risen sun" is looking for a new dawn of profits from its galaxy of businesses. The company's Information & Telecommunications Systems (semiconductors servers mainframes ATMs) brings in the most revenue followed by Social Infrastructure (elevators escalators industrial machinery) and High Functional Materials (wire cables specialty steel circuit boards). Its Electronic Systems & Equipment segment includes specialized manufacturing equipment and power tools. The company is a world leader in consumer goods ranging from TVs to washing machines and in power generation equipment. Hitachi also has operations in financial services automotive systems and construction machinery.

Operations

Responding to such IT changes as cloud computing and business globalization the company announced it would merge Information & Telecommunication Systems' units Hitachi Electronics Services (HES) and Hitachi Information Systems (Hitachi Joho) to create Hitachi Systems. Effective in 2011 the combination is designed to strengthen the company's data center services business in Japan. The move follows Hitachi's efforts to focus on its most profitable segments and streamline sector management.

Financial Analysis

When the company announced fiscal 2011 results it showed improved revenue on the strength of an increase in global demand amid economic recovery and the company's restructuring and cost-cutting measures. Revenue had declined 10% the prior year due to falling demand though belt tightening in 2009 had begun to have a positive effect on net income.

Strategy

Hitachi plans to put many of its eggs in the Social Innovation basket where its Social Infrastructure unit works with its other four leading business units –Information & Telecom Power Construction Machinery and High Functional Materials –to create IT power and transportation systems for urban and industrial segments. The eggs in the basket are about Y2.6 trillion in capital expenditures strategic investments and R&D spending on Social Innovation through fiscal 2014. Other targets include improving Hitachi's overall business structure and expanding globally especially in China Germany and the US.

In a move aimed at improving its ability to compete in an increasingly global marketplace in early 2011 Hitachi formed an alliance with Mitsubishi Heavy Industries (MHI) and Mitsubishi Electric Corp to spin off and integrate their hydroelectric power businesses. The joint venture 98% owned by Hitachi with 1% for each of the other partners is tentatively named HM Hydro. The companies' variable-speed technology could give them an advantage over other power players if smart grids continue to expand in global markets. The joint venture is a way for Hitachi and its partners to better compete for international projects against market leaders such as Toshiba and Voith Hydro (a joint venture between Voith and Siemens). The domestic market for hydroelectric power systems in Japan has stopped growing which has forced companies there to rely on maintenance services to stay afloat.

An increasingly competitive climate along with expected growth in the small and midsized display market prompted another alliance in this case with Sony and Toshiba. Each of the three companies will integrate their businesses in this niche under a new company to be set up and run by Innovation Network Corporation of Japan (INCJ). INCJ will hold 70% of the voting stock in the company while the remaining shares will be evenly divided among the other three companies.

As part of its strategy to refocus on its infrastructure businesses in 2012 Hitachi sold its Hitachi Global Storage Technologies (HGST) disk drive subsidiary to Western Digital in a $4.3 billion cash and stock transaction. The deal gave Hitachi a 10% stake in Western Digital and board representation along with an estimated $3.5 billion in cash. Hitachi originally planned on an IPO for HGST which became profitable in 2011 after five years of losses. HGST was not considered core to ongoing operations. Also in 2012 Hitachi's display business was folded into a new joint venture with Sony and Toshiba called Japan Display Inc. The company was launched on the same day as South Korea-based rival Samsung Display Co. Ltd. and focuses on small and midsized displays for mobile devices automotive and industrial applications.

Mergers and Acquisitions

In 2012 Hitachi announced it would buy the UK Horizon nuclear project from Germany's E.ON and RWE for $1.12 billion to build four to six new nuclear power stations. It hopes to have the first of the 1300 megawatt (MW) nuclear power plants operations by the mid-2020s. Together the plants could provide electricity to 14 million homes for more than 60 years. Hitachi along with British companies Babcock International and Rolls-Royce will use Horizon to create a strong and permanent base of nuclear skills in the UK.

HISTORY

Namihei Odaira an employee of Kuhara Mining in the Japanese coastal city of Hitachi wanted to prove that Japan did not have to depend on foreigners for technology. In 1910 he began building electric motors in Kuhara's engineering and repair shop. Japanese power companies were forced to buy Odaira's generators when WWI made imports scarce. Impressed they reordered and in 1920 Hitachi (meaning "risen sun") became an independent company.

During the 1920s acquisitions and growth turned Hitachi into a major manufacturer of electrical equipment and machinery. In the 1930s and 1940s Hitachi developed vacuum tubes and light bulbs and produced radar and sonar for the Japanese war effort. Postwar occupation forces removed Odaira and closed 19 Hitachi plants. Reeling from the plant closures war damage and labor strife Hitachi was saved from bankruptcy by US military contracts during the Korean War.

In the 1950s Hitachi became a supplier to Nippon Telegraph and Telephone (NTT) the state-owned telecommunications monopoly. Japan's economic recovery led to strong demand for the company's communications and electrical equipment. Hitachi began mass-producing home appliances radios TVs and transistors. The group spun off Hitachi Metals and Hitachi Cable in 1956 and Hitachi Chemical in 1963.

With the help of NTT the Ministry of International Trade and Industry and technology licensed from RCA (bought by General Electric in 1986) Hitachi produced its first computer in 1965. Hitachi built factories in Southeast Asia and started manufacturing integrated circuits.

Hitachi launched an IBM-compatible computer in 1974. The company sold its computers in the US through Itel until 1979 when Itel was bought by National Semiconductor and afterward through National Semi's National Advanced Systems (NAS) unit. In 1982 FBI agents caught Hitachi staff buying documents allegedly containing IBM software secrets. Settlement of a civil lawsuit required Hitachi to make payments to IBM for eight years as compensation for the use of IBM's software.

When the rising Japanese yen hurt exports Hitachi focused on its domestic market and invested heavily in factory automation in the late 1980s. But a recession at home caused earnings to fall. In 1988 the company and Texas Instruments joined in the costly development and production of 16-megabyte DRAMs. In 1989 Hitachi bought 80% of NAS giving it direct control of its US distribution.

Despite its rivalry with IBM in 1991 Hitachi began to resell IBM notebook PCs under its own name in Japan. In a major move to combat sluggish consumer electronics sales in 1994 Hitachi merged with its marketing subsidiary Hitachi Sales Corp. Hitachi used joint ventures to beef up its international presence including a 1995 agreement with India's Tata Group.

Tokyo police in 1997 began investigating Hitachi charging that the company and others had paid off a corporate racketeer. A slump in semiconductor prices coupled with the Asian economic turmoil hurt Hitachi in 1998. Etsuhiko Shoyama became president the next year replacing Tsutomu Kanai who became chairman. Hitachi posted its then-worst loss in history in 1999; the firm combined some subsidiaries and announced layoffs. It also formed a joint venture with Fujitsu to make plasma display panels. The JV was called Fujitsu Hitachi Plasma Display (FHP).

Hitachi spun off its DRAM business into Elpida Memory a joint venture with NEC that began operations in 2000. That year Hitachi launched the Internet & Network Services Group to focus on Internet business development; in 2001 it joined with NEC to develop semiconductors for LCD panels and cell phone displays.

Hitachi teamed with Sun Microsystems in 2002 in a multibillion-dollar storage software distribution and cross-licensing agreement. The company also formed a joint venture with IBM for Hitachi to acquire IBM's disk drive operations which was launched the following year as Hitachi Global Storage Technologies.

In 2002 Hitachi merged its system chip unit with that of Mitsubishi Electric to form a new company Renesas Technology.

In early 2003 the company unveiled a three-year program to reorganize its businesses known as Hitachi Plan II. The plan called for the company to exit certain businesses and to focus on targeted businesses using a process it called "future inspiration value."

In 2003 the company unveiled a finger vein authentication system for use in confirming user identities. Hitachi also increased its investment in Elpida Memory by $80 million along with NEC and added Intel as an investor in the memory semiconductor business. Intel put in $100 million. Later that year Hitachi merged Hitachi netBusiness (established 2000) with Hitachi Information Systems.

It sold its Hitachi Printing Solutions subsidiary to Ricoh in 2004. To strengthen its automotive business Hitachi merged its TOKICO affiliate with its Hitachi Unisia Automotive subsidiary consolidating the operations within the company. Hitachi also announced plans for an LCD television joint venture with Toshiba and Matsushita Electric in 2004 and a plasma television JV with Matsushita Electric in 2005. It collaborated with NEC again on forming another ALAXALA Networks to make backbone routers and switches for communications networks. Hitachi took a 60% interest in ALAXALA.

In early 2005 Hitachi assumed control of Fujitsu Hitachi Plasma Display by buying 30% of FHP from Fujitsu leaving Hitachi with 80% of the JV. That year the company sold shares in Elpida Memory reducing its ownership to nearly 20%. Hitachi launched a computer server systems business in North America as part of Hitachi America. Hitachi Plant Engineering & Construction Hitachi Kiden Kogyo and Hitachi Industries merged in 2006 along with part of Hitachi's Industrial Systems Group to become Hitachi Plant Technologies. Hitachi Mobile in which Hitachi held an equity stake of about 65% became a wholly owned subsidiary of Hitachi. Hitachi Mobile was established in 1950 to repair automobiles and to sell car parts; it later offered auto and mobile communication equipment.

Hitachi Renesas and Toshiba set up a joint-venture planning company in early 2006 to study whether the three chip makers should go into the silicon foundry business (contract manufacturing of semiconductors) together. By midyear however Hitachi concluded that such a move was not feasible under industry conditions at the time. The three chip makers along with NEC Electronics agreed on standardizing technology among them for fabricating semiconductors with features as small as 45 nanometers.

Etsuhiko Shoyama president and CEO of Hitachi since mid-2003 became chairman of the company in early 2006. EVP Kazuo Furukawa was promoted to president and CEO at the same time.

In late 2006 Hitachi took control of Clarion a manufacturer of audio and navigation systems for motor vehicles. In 2000 the company had established a joint venture with Clarion HCX and in 2004 Hitachi became Clarion's largest shareholder buying nearly 15% of the company. Through a tender offer Hitachi increased its ownership to nearly 64% spending almost Y32 billion (about $260 million). The acquisition was expected to strengthen its position in the car information systems market.

Hitachi decided to exit the consumer PC market in late 2007. The company scaled back production of PCs at its factory in Toyokawa Japan to focus on manufacturing computer servers for business applications. Hitachi had previously contracted out some PC production to Hewlett-Packard. According to MM Research Institute Hitachi was eighth in the Japanese PC market with a share of only 4.5% well behind competitors Dell Fujitsu NEC and Toshiba.

The economic downturn and slow recovery forced change across Hitachi's businesses. In 2009 Renesas Technology Corp. a joint venture between Hitachi and Mitsubishi Electric merged with NEC Electronics. Yasushi Akao Renesas president took the reins as president of the merged company. It also created a joint venture with NEC Corp. and CASIO COMPUTER to compete in the growing global cell phone market.

Continuing the streamlining in 2009 Hitachi established new units designed to take advantage of synergies. It created a Battery Systems Division bringing together its work in lithium-ion batteries and a Renewable Energy & Smart Grid Division both in the Power Systems Group. The company launched a Material Resource Recycling Office in the Business Incubation Division for recycling home appliances and other products. It also merged communication subsidiaries in the US to create Hitachi Communication Technologies America.

In 2012 Hitachi sold its Hitachi Global Storage Technologies disk drive subsidiary to Western Digital in a cash and stock deal valued at around $4.3 billion. The move was part of Hitachi's plan to focus on its social infrastructure businesses.

EXECUTIVES

Chairman, Takashi Kawamura, age 74
SVP and Executive Officer, Shinjiro Iwata, age 65
SVP and Executive Officer, Masahide Tanigaki, age 63
Representative Executive Officer and President General Manager, Hiroaki Nakanishi, age 67
SVP and Executive Officer, Makoto Ebata, age 63
EVP and Executive Officer, Kazuhiro Mori, age 64
EVP Representative Executive Officer and Director, Takashi Miyoshi, age 65
EVP and Representative Executive Officer, Junzo Nakajima, age 65
EVP and Representative Executive Officer, Koji Tanaka
VP and Executive Officer, Toshiaki Higashihara
Executive Vice President and Executive Officer, Toyoaki Nakamura, age 61
Senior Vice President and Executive Officer, Toshiaki Kuzuoka, age 59
VP and Executive Officer; Management Strategies, Toshikazu Nishino
VP and Executive Officer; Information and Telecommunication Systems Business, Kaichiro Sakuma, age 59
Executive Vice President and Executive Officer, Shigeru Azuhata, age 64
EVP and Representative Executive Officer, Nobuo Mochida, age 66
SVP and Executive Officer, Yutaka Saito, age 59
VP and Executive Officer; Information and Telecommunication Systems Business, Yoshihiko Mogami, age 60
VP and Executive Officer, Ryuichi Kitayama, age 61
VP and Executive Officer; Urban Planning and Development Systems Business, Toshio Ikemura
VP and Executive Officer; Power Systems Business, Tatsuro Ishizuka
VP and Executive Officer, Yoshifumi Kanda
VP and Executive Officer, Kazuhiro Kurihara
VP and Executive Officer; Government and External Relations, Yasuo Tanabe
VP and Executive Officer; Power Systems Business (Nuclear Power Systems Business Promotion), Masaharu Hanyu
VP and Executive Officer; Human Capital, Naoki Mitarai
Vice President and Executive Officer, Shinichiro Omori
Vice President and Executive Officer, Hiroshi Nakayama
Vice President and Executive Officer, Kaoru Kawano
Vice President and Executive Officer, Masaya Watanabe
Vice President and Executive Officer, Keiji Kojima
Vice President and Executive Officer, Yoshihito Kitamatsu
Director, Mitsuo Ohashi, age 77
Director, Isao Ono
President Representative Executive Officer and Director, Hiroaki Nakanishi, age 67
EVP Representative Executive Officer and Director, Takashi Miyoshi, age 65
Director, Sir Stephen Gomersall, age 65
Director, Tohru Motobayashi, age 75
Auditors: Ernst&YoungShinNihon

LOCATIONS

HQ: Hitachi, Ltd.
1-6-6 Marunouchi, Chiyoda-ku, Tokyo 100-8280
Phone: (81) 3 3258 1111
Web: www.hitachi.co.jp

2011 Sales

	% of total
Asia/Pacific	
Japan	57
Other	22
Europe	8
North	8
Other	5
Total	**100**

PRODUCTS/OPERATIONS

2011 Sales

	% of total
Information & Telecom	16
High Functional Materials &	13
Social Infrastructure & Industrial	11
Electronic Systems &	10
Digital Media & Consumer	9
Components &	8
Power	8
Automotive	7
Construction	7
Financial	4
Other	7
Total	**100**

Selected Products and Services

Digital media and consumer products
- Batteries
- Fluorescent lamps
- Kitchen appliances
- LCD projectors
- Mobile phones
- Refrigerators
- Room air conditioners
- TVs
- VCRs
- Videotapes
- Washing machines

Electronic devices
- LCDs
- Medical electronics equipment
- Memories
- Multipurpose semiconductors
- Semiconductor manufacturing equipment
- System LSIs
- Testing and measurement equipment

Financial services
- Insurance services
- Leasing
- Loan guarantees

High-functional materials and components
- Cables
- Carbon products
- Chemical products
- Components
- Copper products
- Electrical insulating materials
- Fine ceramics
- Magnetic materials
- Malleable cast-iron products
- Printed circuit boards
- Specialty steels
- Synthetic resins
- Wires

Information and telecommunication systems

Computer peripherals
Fiber-optic components
Mainframes
Servers
Software
Switches
Systems integration

Power and industrial systems
Air-conditioning equipment
Automotive equipment
Construction machinery
Elevators
Environmental control systems
Escalators
Hydroelectric power plants
Industrial machinery and plant construction
Nuclear power plants
Rolling stock
Thermal power plants

Logistics services and other
General trading
Property management
Transportation

Selected Acquisitions

Mica-AVA (Guangzhou) Material Co. (2011 75% advanced laminate products)
Aptivo Consulting S.A. (2011; financial- public sector- and telecom-focused IT consulting)
Sierra Atlantic (2011 offshore IT outsourcing)
Telco Construction Equipment Co. Ltd. (2010; 60%; hydraulic excavators backhoe loaders wheel loaders)
Wenco International Mining Systems Ltd. (2009 fleet management systems)
Aqua-Tech Engineering and Supplies Pte. Ltd. (2009 water-treatment systems)
Astral Meditech GmbH (2008 70% ultrasound probe cables)
M-Tech Information Technology Inc. (2008 67% identity management software)
Tanaka Kogyo (2007 power generation equipment)
Clarion (2006 64% audio and navigation systems for motor vehicles)

COMPETITORS

ALSTOM
AREVA
Alcatel-Lucent
Applied Materials
Babcock & Wilcox
Canon
Dell
Ericsson
Fluor
Fujitsu
GE
Hewlett-Packard
IBM
Johnson Controls
Kyocera
LG Group
McDermott
Micron Technology
Mitsubishi Electric
Mitsubishi Heavy Industries
NEC
Nippon Steel & Sumitomo Metal Corporation
Nokia
Nortel Networks
Oki Electric
Panasonic Corp
Philips Electronics
SANYO
Samsung Group
Sharp Corp.
Siemens AG
Sony
TDK
Texas Instruments
Toshiba
Truly International
Unisys
United Technologies
Whirlpool

HISTORICAL FINANCIALS

Company Type: Public

Income Statement FYE: March 31

	REVENUE ($ mil.)	NET INCOME ($ mil.)	NET PROFIT MARGIN	EMPLOYEES
03/13	96,087	1,863	1.9%	374,775
03/12	117,833	4,232	3.6%	369,722
03/11	112,500	2,884	2.6%	406,149
03/10	96,015	(1,145)	—	399,308
03/09	101,552	(7,995)	—	403,893
Annual Growth	(1.4%)	—	—	(1.9%)

2013 Year-End Financials

Debt ratio: 0.2%
Return on equity: 9.1%
Cash ($ mil.): 5,607
Current ratio: 1.31
Long-term debt ($ mil.): 13,887
No. of shares (mil.): —
Dividends
Yield: 0.0%
Payout: 0.0%
Market value ($ mil.): —

	STOCK PRICE ($) FY Close	P/E High	P/E Low	PER SHARE ($) Earnings	Dividends	Book Value
03/13	57.90	0	0	0.39	0.00	4.58
03/12	64.69	0	0	0.88	0.00	4.66
03/11	51.63	0	0	0.60	0.59	3.85
03/10	37.19	—	—	(0.31)	0.00	3.07
03/09	27.45	—	—	(2.41)	0.60	3.21
Annual Growth	20.5%	—	—	—	(87.2%)	9.3%

Hochtief AG

HOCHTIEF is a giant in Germany and beyond. In addition to doing business throughout Europe the construction-related services provider operates in the Americas and the Asia/Pacific region and is among the world's largest general builders. US subsidiaries Turner and Flatiron provide building and infrastructure construction. Leighton Holdings based in Australia provides engineering and construction services for the infrastructure and mining industries. The group also operates in European countries including the Czech Republic Poland Russia and the UK. HOCHTIEF focuses all of its business around the world in four areas: Americas Asia Pacific Europe and concessions.

Spanish construction group Actividades de Construcciones y Servicios (ACS) is HOCHTIEF's largest shareholder controlling more than 45% of its capital (and more than 50% voting rights); a Qatar sovereign wealth fund owns some 10%. ACS has been building up its ownership for several months and in late 2010 bid to buy the company outright. HOCHTIEF management initially fought off the acquisition but gave up the fight in 2011 clinching the takeover. Then-chairman and CEO Herbert Lutkestratkotter stepped down as did CFO Burkhard Lohr and four supervisory board members. ACS board member Frank Stieler succeeded Lutkestratkotter.

HOCHTIEF aims to provide services that span the lifecycle of a construction project. The company is known for building private projects such as warehouses and retail complexes. But its growing concessions and public-private partnership (PPP) division works on major federal state and municipal projects such as power plants toll roads tunnels and water treatment facilities. HOCHTIEF is continually growing and has its sights set on areas of growth especially in places where the PPP market is expanding as it is in North America. Other growth areas include the wind power market. Geographically HOCHTIEF plans to expand into India.

Through its concessions division the group also is active in airport projects and it runs public buildings such as schools hospitals and prisons. HOCHTIEF AirPort has grown to become one of the world's largest independent airport managers. The division also takes ownership stakes in projects; its portfolio encompasses principal airports in Athens; Budapest Hungary; Dusseldorf and Hamburg Germany; Sydney; and Tirana Albania. HOCHTIEF in 2013 agreed however to sell its airport portfolio to Public Sector Pension Investment Board of Canada. The deal values the business at 1.5 billion Euros ($2 billion) giving HOCHTIEF about 1.1 billion Euros after its other business partners are paid. Also in 2011 HOCHTIEF sold several of its Leighton mining assets in Australia as a way to boost profit.

The company's former real estate and services divisions merged into the Europe division in 2011. The restructuring helped streamline business and save the company money. The Europe division includes HOCHTIEF Solutions which plans develops and markets large real estate properties such as hotels office buildings and retail and residential projects in Europe.

In addition to building and developing properties HOCHTIEF also makes sure those properties stay running. Its services division includes facility management and energy management providers. The division specializes in servicing the automotive industry chemical and pharmaceutical plants financial services facilities airports and health care and event facilities.

HISTORY

Brothers Philipp and Balthasar Helfmann mill and farm workers from Kelsterbach Germany started construction company Fa. Gebr. Helfmann Bauunternehmer in Frankfurt am Main in 1875. The firm primarily built houses until 1878 when it was contracted to build the university at Giessen.

In 1884 the company was made a general partnership. Projects of this era included Frankfurt's Hotel Continental and Wiesbaden's Hotel Kaiserhof. When Balthasar died in 1896 Philipp converted the business to a joint stock company and renamed it Actien-Gesellschaft fur Hoch- und Tiefbauten. Three years later with new capital for expansion the company won its first contract abroad —construction of a pneumatic conveyer-equipped granary in the harbor at Genoa (its first reinforced-concrete project).

Philipp Helfmann died in 1899 but the company continued operating. The battlefields of WWI took away most of the workforce and construction slowed to a near halt. But in the years following the war the company grew. In 1921 German industrialist Hugo Stinnes began buying stakes in the company and was its major shareholder by 1923. The company decided in 1922 to relocate to Essen closer to the Stinnes Group's operations and in 1923 it was renamed HOCHTIEF Aktiengesellschaft fur Hoch- und Tiefbauten vorm. Gebr. Helfmann.

Stinnes died in 1924 and two years later his empire collapsed. But German banks helped keep HOCHTIEF alive and operating as an independent company. That year Rheinisch-Westfalische-Elektrizitatswerke AG (RWE) the electric utility that Stinnes helped create became the main shareholder in HOCHTIEF with a 31% stake.

Many of RWE's facilities were damaged during WWII including its Essen headquarters and the RWE staff used the HOCHTIEF building until 1961. Postwar reconstruction kept the company active including Germany's first nuclear reactor built by HOCHTIEF and commissioned in 1966.

After the war RWE began increasing its stake in HOCHTIEF until it became the majority shareholder (56%) in 1989.

As a division of the RWE Group HOCHTIEF began acquiring former state-owned companies throughout Germany. By 1996 it had added financing and operation of major projects to its services. That year it led a consortium to build and operate an international airport in Athens. In 1997 it teamed with Ireland's Aer Rianta to build new terminals and manage the airport in Dusseldorf Germany. The next year HOCHTIEF won a bid to build and operate Berlin's new airport but a rival's allegations of bidding irregularities led to a raid by prosecutors on HOCHTIEF's headquarters. Charges were dismissed but the company was disqualified from the project.

The company sought to expand internationally with an agreement to take a 49% stake in the US holdings of its main rival Philipp Holzmann (1997). But when these plans failed and HOCHTIEF was blocked by regulators from increasing its 20% stake in the competitor (held since 1981) it lost interest and relinquished its shares.

HOCHTIEF like many of its competitors expanded abroad in 1999 by helping engineer Canadian firm Armbro's takeover of rival BFC (and then grabbing a 49% share in the merged firm now Aecon Group) and by acquiring US construction giant Turner. The company suffered a $75 million operating loss in 2000 because of a slowdown in the German construction industry and expenses related to acquisitions.

It secured a contract to build a rail tunnel under the River Thames in London in 2001. Also that year it merged its building and civil units into HOCHTIEF Construction and made plans to join former rival IVG Immobilien to bid on building Berlin's new airport Berlin-Brandenburg. HOCHTIEF reorganized in 2001 to reflect its increasingly international operations.

By 2002 Philipp Holzmann was in insolvency and HOCHTIEF initially made plans to bid on its former rival's technical services group HSG. However after reviewing the unit's prospectus HOCHTIEF withdrew from the bidding.

Longtime shareholder and German energy giant RWE sold its 56% stake in HOCHTIEF in 2004 to European and US institutional investors. It was the largest such transaction involving a German stock.

HOCHTIEF subsidiary Leighton and joint venture partner Downer EDI won a ?100 million contract to build a four-lane highway in New Zealand in 2006. The project is expected to be finished in 2010.

In 2007 the company acquired the energy contracting business of Vattenfall Europe adding to its existing service portfolio of energy contracting and management operations. Also that year HOCHTIEF acquired Flatiron Construction from Royal BAM Group. That deal provided the group with entry into infrastructure PPP markets in the US and Canada.

EXECUTIVES

President and CEO Turner Construction, Peter J. Davoren, age 58
CEO Flatiron Construction, John A. DiCiurcio, age 58
Chairman and CEO, Marcelino F. Verdes, age 57
CEO Flatiron Construction, Tom Rademacher
CFO and Member Executive Board, Peter Sassenfeld, age 47
Chief Executive Officer CEO, Rainer Eichholz, age 57
CEO Leighton Holdings Limited, Hamish G. Tyrwhitt, age 49
Head Investor Relations, Ulrike Kroner
Senior Vice President Corporate Communications, Bernd Putter
Chairman of the Executive Board CEO of HOCHTIEF Solutions AG, Rainer Eicholz
Head of Investor Relations, Ulrike Ulrike Kroener Kroener
Member Supervisory Board, Angel Garcia Altozano
Member Supervisory Board, Gerrit Pennings
Member Supervisory Board, Marcelino F. Verdes
Member Supervisory Board, Klaus Wiesehugel
Member Supervisory Board, Gregor Asshoff
Deputy Chairman Supervisory Board, Ulrich Best
Member of the Supervisory Board, Abdulla Abdulla Al-Subaie Al-Subaie
Member of the Supervisory Board, Eggert Eggert Voscherau Voscherau
Member of the Supervisory Board; Employee Representative, Johannes Johannes Howorka Howorka
Member of the Supervisory Board, Jose Jose Luis del Valle Perez Perez
Member of the Supervisory Board; Employee Representative, Klaus Klaus Wiesehuegel Wiesehuegel
Member of the Supervisory Board; Employee Representative, Nikolaus Nikolaus Graf von Matuschka Matuschka
Member of the Supervisory Board; Employee Representative, Olaf Olaf Wendler Wendler
Member of the Supervisory Board, Pedro Pedro Jose Lopez Jimenez Jimenez
Auditors: Deloitte&ToucheGmbH

LOCATIONS

HQ: Hochtief AG
Opernplatz 2, Essen D-45128
Phone: (49) 201 824 0 **Fax:** (49) 201 824 2777
Web: www.hochtief.com

2010 Sales

	% of total
Australia	41
Americas	34
Europe	
Germany	8
Other	5
Asia	12
Total	**100**

2009 Sales

	% of total
Americas	37
Australia	35
Europe	
Germany	12
Other	6
Asia	10
Total	**100**

PRODUCTS/OPERATIONS

2010 Sales

	% of total
Asia/Pacific	54
Americas	29
Europe	11
Services	3
Real	2
Concessions	1
Total	**100**

Selected Subsidiaries and Associates

Airport
HOCHTIEF AirPort Capital Verwaltungs GmbH & Co. KG
HOCHTIEF AirPort GmbH
Construction Services Americas
Flatiron Construction Corp. (US)
HOCHTIEF Americas GmbH
HOCHTIEF do Brasil S.A. (92%)
The Turner Corporation (US)
Construction Services Asia Pacific
HOCHTIEF Asia Pacific GmbH
Construction Services Europe
DURST-BAU GmbH (Austria)
HOCHTIEF Construction AG
Development
Deutsche Bau-und Siedlungs-Gesellschaft mbH
HOCTHIEF Aurestis Beteiligungsgesellschaft mbH

COMPETITORS

Acciona
Avionic Services International
BAA
Bechtel
Bilfinger Berger
Bouygues
Cheung Kong Infrastructure
Dragados
Fluor
KBR Building Group
PCL Employees Holdings
Parsons Corporation
Peter Kiewit Sons'
STRABAG SE
Skanska
Tutor Perini
VINCI

HISTORICAL FINANCIALS

Company Type: Public

Income Statement FYE: December 31

	REVENUE ($ mil.)	NET INCOME ($ mil.)	NET PROFIT MARGIN	EMPLOYEES
12/12	33,767	208	0.6%	79,987
12/11	29,928	(207)	—	75,449
12/10	27,187	385	1.4%	70,657
12/09	26,215	281	1.1%	66,178
12/08	26,707	244	0.9%	64,527
Annual Growth	6.0%	(3.9%)	—	5.5%

2012 Year-End Financials

Debt ratio: 31.7%
Return on equity: 6.0%
Cash ($ mil.): 3,314
Current ratio: 1.35
Long-term debt ($ mil.): 3,600
No. of shares (mil.): 77
Dividends
Yield: —
Payout: —
Market value ($ mil.): 903

	STOCK PRICE ($) FY Close	P/E High/Low	PER SHARE ($) Earnings	Dividends	Book Value
12/12	11.73	9 9	2.83	0.00	45.20
12/11	11.39	— —	(2.82)	0.00	43.65
Annual Growth	3.0%	— —	—	—	0.9%

Hokuhoku Financial Group Inc

Short on cash and passing through the Hokuriku or Hokkaido districts of Japan? You might want to check in with this group. The Hokuhoku Financial Group's core business is banking primarily through its chief subsidiaries: The Hokuriku Bank and The Hokkaido Bank. Through both banks' approximately 325 branches the financial services group targets the Toyama Ishikawa and Fukui Prefectures. In addition to banking Hokuhoku Financial Group provides credit cards leasing services venture capital and financing products. Hokuriku Bank (founded in 1877) merged with Hokkaido Bank in 2004 to form Hokuhoku Financial Group which today operates in the Hokuriku and Hokkaido district and Tokyo Osaka and Nagoya.

EXECUTIVES

President Hokuhoku Financial Group and The Hokuriku Bank, Shigeo Takagi
Chairman, Yoshihiro Sekihachi
Senior Managing Director The Hokuriku Bank, Tatsuya Kaseda
President, Eishin Ihori
Senior Managing Director The Hokuriku Bank, Tetsuji Mitsuzuka
Senior Managing Director The Hokuriku Bank, Takashi Nakano

LOCATIONS

HQ: Hokuhoku Financial Group Inc
1-2-26 Tsutsumicho-dori, Toyama 930-8637
Phone: (81) 76 423 7331
Web: www.hokuhoku-fg.co.jp

2013 Branches

	No.
Hokuriku	149
Hokkaido	158
Other major metro	17
Other	4
Total	**328**

PRODUCTS/OPERATIONS

Selected Subsidiaries and Affiliated Companies

Hokugin Lease Co. Ltd.
Hokugin Software Co. Ltd.
Hokuriku Capital Co. Ltd.
Hokuriku Card Co. Ltd.
Hokuriku Hosho Services Co. Ltd.
Nihonkai Services Co. Ltd.
The Hokkaido Bank Ltd.
  Dogin Business Service Ltd.
  Dogin Card Co. Ltd.
The Hokuriku Bank Ltd.
  Hokugin Business Services Co. Ltd.
  Hokugin Corporate Co. Ltd.
  Hokugin Office Services Co. Ltd.
  Hokugin Real Estate Services Co. Ltd.
  Hokugin Shisankanri Co. Ltd.
  Hokuriku International Cayman Limited

COMPETITORS

Bank of Nagoya
Hachijuni Bank
Hokkoku Bank
Hyakujushi Bank
Mitsubishi UFJ Financial Group
Sapporo Hokuyo

HISTORICAL FINANCIALS

Company Type: Public

Income Statement

FYE: March 31

	ASSETS ($ mil.)	NET INCOME ($ mil.)	INCOME AS % OF ASSETS	EMPLOYEES
03/13	116,686	192	0.2%	5,569
03/12	129,578	172	0.1%	5,573
03/11	127,828	222	0.2%	5,447
03/10	108,205	205	0.2%	5,044
03/09	100,828	376	0.4%	4,843
Annual Growth	3.7%	(15.4%)	—	3.6%

2013 Year-End Financials

Return on assets: 0.1%
Return on equity: 3.8%
Long-term debt ($ mil.): —
No. of shares (mil.): 1,339
Sales ($ mil): 2,116
Dividends
  Yield: —
  Payout: —
Market value ($ mil.): —

	STOCK PRICE ($) FY Close	P/E High/Low	PER SHARE ($) Earnings	Dividends	Book Value
03/13	0.00	— —	0.13	0.00	3.82
03/12	1.91	— —	0.11	0.00	3.95
03/11	1.84	— —	0.15	0.00	3.71
03/10	2.10	— —	0.13	0.00	3.18
Annual Growth	—	— —	(0.1%)	—	4.7%

Holcim Ltd

What do you use to build a modern colossus? Cement of course. Holcim is one of the world's largest cement makers (along with CEMEX and Lafarge) with an annual production capacity of more than 215 million tons. The company operates in some 70 countries around the world; its international subsidiaries include Holcim (US) St. Lawrence Cement in Canada Aggregate Industries in the UK Holcim (Australia) and Holcim Apasco in Mexico. Although geographically diverse Holcim sticks to the basics when it comes to products: cement clinker concrete aggregates and lime. The company also offers research import/export trading consulting and management services for the construction industry.

Geographic Reach

Zurich-based Holcim has production sites in around 70 countries and boasts a market presence on every continent making the Swiss firm more geographically diversified than its rivals. Holcim's largest market is the Asia-Pacific region (39% of sales) which recently surpassed Europe as the firm's leading market.

Financial Performance

Holcim's 2011 sales declined by 4% vs. 2010 while net income fell by 58% over the same period. 2011 was characterized markedly varied economic conditions across Holcim's global markets. While construction activity in mature markets including Europe and North America was sluggish Asia and Latin America performed better. Holcim sold more cement in four of its five regional groups (Asia-Pacific Europe Latin America and North America). Only Africa Middle East saw a decline in volume sales. Ready-mix concrete sales were strong in North America as a result of acquisitions.

Strategy

Holcim's business strategy is based on continuous growth in both developed economies as well as high-growth emerging markets. Indeed emerging markets represent about 75% of the firm's operational capacity and account for almost half of its net sales. In emerging markets Holcim is focused on building and expanding cement production. In more mature markets the firm is focused on vertical integration and establishing ready-mix concrete businesses in major urban areas.

Holcim is growing through acquisitions and by increasing its stakes in its holdings throughout the world including the Asia/Pacific region Latin America and Eastern Europe in recent years. Significant purchases include Aggregate Industries (2005) which gave the Swiss firm an instant presence in the UK and US markets. The company bought CEMEX's Australian business now Holcim (Australia) in 2009. That purchase included some 350 plants and quarries and aligned with Holcim's strategic expansion plans in Australia –a country that has been rather resilient during the economic downturn. The following year its ACC unit –India's largest cement maker by capacity – acquired Encore Cement & Additives boosting its operations in southern India. Now a wholly owned unit of ACC Encore Cement has a 200000 metric ton-capacity grinding plant in Andhra Pradesh state.

Ownership

Director and former chairman Thomas Schmidheiny is Holcim's largest shareholder with about 20% of the company's stock. Eurocement Holding AG owns nearly 11% of the shares.

HISTORY

Cement company Aargauische Portlandcementfabrik Holderbank-Wildegg was founded near Zurich in 1912. Two years later Ernst Schmidheiny bought a stake in the company. His son and namesake later expanded the company beyond Switzerland then grouped its interests under holding company "Holderbank" Financiere Glaris Ltd. in 1930. By WWII Holderbank had operations in Belgium Egypt Greece Lebanon and South Africa.

After the war Holderbank expanded into the Americas. It purchased Canada-based St. Lawrence Cement in 1953 and was listed on the Zurich stock exchange in 1958.

In 1970 the company swapped some assets with rival Swiss Cement-Industrie-Gesellschaft in a deal that increased Holderbank's presence in Costa Rica Lebanon Mexico and West Germany. The company also converted several of its minority stakes into majority shareholdings. Thomas Schmidheiny became chairman of Holderbank's executive committee in 1978 and chairman of the board in 1984 upon his father's (Ernst's brother Max) retirement.

During a late-1980s market slump Holderbank bought stakes in several US cement companies. It became the #1 US cement maker by purchasing Ideal Basic Industries in 1986. As the decade closed Holderbank consolidated in Europe and in 1990 placed many of its US operations under holding company Holnam.

Holderbank then pushed into Central and Eastern Europe where it gained production capacity in Hungary among other countries. The company bought a 51% stake in Morocco-based Les Ciments de l'Oriental (CIOR) in 1993. Geographic diversity helped Holderbank weather depressed periods in regional markets such as in Mexico where profits dropped 83% from 1994 to 1995 during an economic crisis there.

The company picked up major acquisitions in Malaysia the Philippines Sri Lanka and Thailand during a crippled economic period in Asia in the late 1990s. It also added capacity in the booming US market. Holderbank sought to invest in India in 1999 but the fragmented market there prevented it from finding a sizable company. Meanwhile Holderbank continued searching for investments in China to expand its presence there. The following year the company became the majority shareholder of Indonesian cement company PT Semen Cibinong (now PT Holcim Indonesia). Its joint bid (with Portugal's Secil) for CIMPOR the largest Portuguese cement manufacturer got stuck in regulatory issues however.

Holderbank changed its name to Holcim Ltd. in 2001. The name is derived from "Holderbank" (where it was founded) and "ciment" (French for cement). In 2002 Holcim's Thai subsidiary Siam City Cement acquired a controlling stake in TPI Polene beating out rival CEMEX for the deal. Holcim acquired Spain-based Cementos de Hispania and disposed of Eternit AG business in 2003.

That year when operations in Europe and North America showed little growth the company looked toward emerging markets in Africa Asia and Latin America. Holcim tightened its hold on Holcim Apasco in Mexico by increasing its stake in the company from 69% to 93% in 2004; it later took full ownership.

In 2005 Holcim acquired UK-based construction products provider Aggregate Industries. The deal gave the group more than 140 quarries in the UK and US. It followed that up the following year with the purchases of aggregates producer Foster Yeoman in the UK and ready-mix concrete maker Meyer Material in the US.

In 2007 Holcim acquired control of Ambuja Cements in India; took a majority stake in the Croatian Plovanija Kamen cement plant and stone quarry; and bought building materials supplier Jurong Cement in Singapore.

The company acquired Tarmac Iberia from Anglo American for some E148 million ($228 million) in 2008. The deal added about 50 ready-mixed concrete plants in Spain.

EXECUTIVES

CEO St. Lawrence Cement Canada, Paul Ostrander
Executive Committee Belgium France the Netherlands Germany Switzerland and Italy, Patrick Dolberg, age 58
Executive Committee South Asia & ASEAN (excluding the Philippines), Paul Hugentobler, age 65
Executive Committee North America UK Norway Mediterranean Iberian Peninsula and International Trade, Benoit-H. Koch, age 61
CEO and Director, Markus Akermann, age 66
CFO, Theophil H. Schlatter, age 63
Regional General Manager Germany Switzerland and Italy, Carlo Gervasoni
Chairman, Rolf Soiron, age 69
Country Manager Bulgaria, Todor Kostov
President and CEO Holcim US and Area Manager, Bernard Terver
Country Manager France Holcim France Benelux, Gerard Letellier, age 61
CEO Holcim Germany, Leo Mittelholzer
CEO Holcim Morocco, Dominique Drouet
CEO Siam City Cement Thailand, Philippe Arto
Regional General Manager Mexico, Eduardo Kretschmer
Deputy Chairman, Andreas von Planta, age 59
Area Manager Andes nations Central America Caribbean, Andreas Leu
Corporate Communications, Roland Walker
Country Manager Switzerland, Kaspar Wenger
Country Manager Hungary, Richard Skene
CEO Cemento de El Salvador, Ricardo A. Chavez Caparroso
CEO Holcim Costa Rica and Holcim Nicaragua, Sergio Egloff
CEO Societe de Ciments et Materiaux Ivory Coast, Johan Pachler
CEO Holcim Lebanon, Vincent Bouckaert
CEO Aden Cement Enterprises Republic of Yemen, Jaafar Skalli
Area Manager Mediterranean Indian Ocean and West Africa, Javier de Benito, age 55
Manager Cement Manufacturing Services, Jacques Bourgon, age 55
Manager Corporate Strategy and Risk, Roland Kohler, age 60
CEO Philippines, Roland van Wijnen
Area Manager Vietnam Malaysia Singapore Bangladesh, Aidan Lynam
CEO Ciments de Guinee Guinea, Mohamed Ali Bensaid
Country Manager Serbia, Gustavo Navarro
Country Manager Italy, Domenico Salvadore
Country Manager Azerbaijan, Horia Adrian
Country Manager France Holcim Western Europe, Vincent Lefebvre
Country Manager Belgium Holcim Western Europe, Lukas Epple
CEO Panama Cement Holding, Rodolfo Montero
CEO Holcim Sri Lanka, Stefan Huber
Chief Executive Officer, Rajnish Kapur
CEO Holcim Malaysia, Mahanama Ralapanawa
General Manager Holcim Singapore, Sujit Ghosh
Member Executive Committee East Asia Philippines Oceania and South and East Africa, Ian Thackwray, age 55
CEO Holcim New Zealand, Jeremy Smith
Director, Robert F. Spoerry, age 58
CEO and Director, Markus Akermann, age 66
Director, Thomas Schmidheiny, age 68
Director, Peter Kupfer, age 68
Director, Erich Hunziker, age 60
Director, Wolfgang Schurer, age 66
Director, Dieter Spalti, age 51
Deputy Chairman, Andreas von Planta, age 59
Director, Adrian Loader, age 65
Director, H. Onno Ruding, age 73
Director, Christine Binswanger, age 49
Auditors: Ernst&YoungLtd.

LOCATIONS

HQ: Holcim Ltd
Zuercherstrasse 156, Jona 8645
Phone: (41) 58 858 86 00 **Fax:** (41) 55 222 87 19
Web: www.holcim.com

2011 Sales

	% of total
Asia/Pacific	39
Europe	30
Latin	16
North	14
Africa & Middle	5
Adjustment (4)	
Total	**100**

PRODUCTS/OPERATIONS

2011 Sales

	% of total
Aggregates	45
Cement	38
Ready-mix	13
Asphalt	3
Mineral	1
Total	**100**

Selected Subsidiaries

ACC Ltd. (50.1% India)
Aggregate Industries UK Ltd.
Alpha Cement J.S.C. (81% Russia)
Ambuja Cements Ltd. (50.01% India)
Aden Cement Enterprises Ltd. (Yemen)
Cement Australia Holdings Pty Ltd (75%)
Cemento de El Salvador S.A. de C.V. (92%)
Cemento Polpaico S.A. (54% Chile)
Ciments de Guinee S.A. (60% Guinea)
Holcim (Australia) Holdings Pty Ltd
Holcim (Canada) Inc. (formerly St. Lawrence Cement Inc.)
Holcim (Ecuador) S.A. (92%)
Holcim (Srbija) a.d. (Serbia)
Holcim (US) Inc.
Holcim (Singapore) Pte. Ltd
Holcim Trading SA (Spain)
Holcim (Vietnam) Ltd. (65%)
Juan Minetti S.A. (80% Argentina)
Lafarge Cement Egypt S.A.E. (formerly Egyptian Cement Company S.A.E. 44%)
PT Holcim Indonesia Tbk. (78%)
Siam City Cement (Public) Company Limited (37% Thailand)

COMPETITORS

Boral
CEMEX
CRH
Dyckerhoff
Franz Haniel
HeidelbergCement
Italcementi
Lafarge
Martin Marietta Materials
Sumitomo Osaka Cement
Taiheiyo Cement
Tarmac
Titan Cement
Vicat

HISTORICAL FINANCIALS

Company Type: Public

Income Statement

FYE: December 31

	REVENUE ($ mil.)	NET INCOME ($ mil.)	NET PROFIT MARGIN	EMPLOYEES
12/12	23,501	678	2.9%	78,103
12/11	22,049	292	1.3%	80,967
12/10	23,138	1,263	5.5%	80,310
12/09	20,516	1,428	7.0%	81,498
12/08	23,649	1,675	7.1%	86,713
Annual Growth	(0.2%)	(20.2%)	—	(2.6%)

2012 Year-End Financials

Debt ratio: 26.0%
Return on equity: 3.6%
Cash ($ mil.): 3,430
Current ratio: 1.00
Long-term debt ($ mil.): 10,808
No. of shares (mil.): 325
Dividends
Yield: 1.3%
Payout: 11.3%
Market value ($ mil.): 4,747

	STOCK PRICE ($) FY Close	P/E High	P/E Low	PER SHARE ($) Earnings	Dividends	Book Value
12/12	14.59	9	6	2.09	0.20	56.83
12/11	10.60	25	13	0.91	0.37	55.94
12/10	15.04	5	3	3.94	0.43	60.46
12/09	15.54	3	1	4.79	0.28	57.71
Annual Growth	(2.1%)	—	—	(18.7%)	(7.8%)	(0.4%)

Hon Hai Precision Industry Co., Ltd.

Hon Hai Precision Industry may be the biggest electronics company you never heard of. The company more commonly known by its trade name Foxconn is the world's largest contract electronics manufacturer. It manufactures computers consumer electronics communications and other products including connectors cable assemblies enclosures flat-panel displays game consoles motherboards servers and televisions. Hon Hai also provides design engineering and mechanical tooling services. The global company's customers include Apple Cisco Dell Nokia and Sony. Chairman Terry Gou founded Hon Hai in 1974 to make plastic switches for TVs.

Hon Hai's operations are closely tied to consumer demand for computers and consumer electronics. Because of its size the company is able to take on significant new orders in a relatively short time. The company was tapped by Microsoft in 2009 to supply Xbox consoles for the holiday shopping season shortly after Hon Hai landed the contract to provide Sony with PS3 consoles. The company's sales also increased after Microsoft released its Windows 7 operating system. It also makes several products for Apple –the iPod Nano music player the iPhone the iPad and the iMac – all products that are in greater demand during the holiday season.

After having a 30% growth rate for years in 2010 the company lowered its growth forecasts. Computer sales are predicted to slow throughout 2011 and demand for iPhones and iPads has not offset shrinking PC sales. In 2011 the company's sales were up just 11% to $113 billion and its net income rose a mere 2%.

Hon Hai has tried to expand its focus beyond consumer electronics with biotechnology nanotechnology and media content mentioned as industries the company is interested in as it tries to sustain growth. The company is also targeting the budding automotive market in China (the company makes automotive connectors) smartbooks (mini-laptops that use smartphone technology) and e-book readers for the Taiwan market. (Hon Hai already makes about 80% of e-book readers made globally including the Amazon Kindle reader.)

In another move aimed at expanding its reach Hon Hai has tried to reach a deal with Sharp which is spiraling downward along with prices for flat-panel TVs. Sharp which has had too narrow a focus on TVs in the last few years also makes displays for Hon Hai's Apple products something Hon Hai is eager to get its hands on. In 2012 Hon Hai offered to buy nearly 10% of Sharp for around $1.7 billion. But Sharp's market value plummeted as it later widened expectations for a record loss and its credit was downgraded to junk status. Hon Hai wants to renegotiate the initial deal including lowering the price and having a hand in Sharp's operations. Chairman Gou left negotiations in Japan a day early and without a deal when Sharp's management balked at the idea. Hon Hai is also looking at buying plants in Mexico and China from Sharp; the two companies are joint owners in the Sakai LCD panel factory which has been running below capacity and contributed to the losses at Sharp.

Hon Hai focuses more on internal development than growth through acquisitions stating that it had paid too much for some acquisitions. The company has expanded its product lines and design capabilities through a number of select acquisitions including Finland-based Eimo renamed Foxconn Oy which makes plastic moldings for cell phone components. It also bought Taiwan-based Ambit Microsystems for $1.1 billion; Ambit makes routers modems and networking equipment. Hon Hai has also boosted its manufacturing capacity through acquisitions such as its purchase of the PC manufacturing assets in Hungary Mexico and the US with associated logistics services from rival Sanmina-SCI which is getting out of the PC-making business.

Hon Hai subsidiary INNOLUX Display acquired flat-panel display manufacturer Chi Mei Optoelectronics through a share swap in 2010 creating a company called Chimei Innolux. Through Chimei Innolux Hon Hai will compete with big display makers in South Korea and Taiwan which dominate the market.

Outside of acquisitions Hon Hai grows organically by investing in new manufacturing facilities as it prepares to enter new markets. The company is investing about $1 billion to build a new manufacturing facility in China as part of its environmental protection technology initiative. The plant will develop and make products for the alternative energy market including LED (light-emitting diode) backlights and LCD display modules. Hon Hai subsidiary Foxsemicon is working with semiconductor manufacturing equipment maker Applied Materials to develop products for solar energy manufacturing equipment.

A spate of suicides by workers at its Shenzhen production facilities sent Hon Hai reeling in 2010. The company responded by increasing wages at its largest facilities and relocating some production facilities inland closer to the hometowns of much of the workforce. It has also hired a significant number of employees (in 2011 the number of employees rose by 85%) and restricted the number of hours that can be worked. The moves increased production costs for Hon Hai not all of which could be recouped by raising the prices charged to manufacturers. After reports of poor working conditions at some facilities Apple took heat for continuing to source products from Hon Hai.

A Hon Hai affiliate Foxconn International Holdings (FIH) has struggled after handset orders from major clients declined. The company makes handsets for companies including Nokia which are losing market share to smartphones like the iPhone and devices based on Google's Android operating system. FIH which began relocating some of its Chinese facilities in 2007 also moved some production to northern China and to India to lower costs.

In 2013 Hon Hai embarked on an extensive restructuring effort to create more nimble business units and streamline decision-making. The company may spin off one or more of its business units as part of the initiative.

EXECUTIVES

Chairman, Terry T.M. Gou
Investor Relations Contact, Arthur Huang
Auditors: PricewaterhouseCoopers

LOCATIONS

HQ: Hon Hai Precision Industry Co., Ltd.
No. 2, Tzu Yu Street, Tucheng Industrial Area, Tucheng, Taipei County
Phone: (886) 2 2268 3466
Web: www.foxconn.com.tw

PRODUCTS/OPERATIONS

Selected Products

Cable assemblies
CD-ROMs
Connectors
E-book readers
Enclosures
Flat-panel displays
Game consoles
Handsets
Keyboards
LCD (liquid-crystal display) TVs
Mobile phones
Motherboards
Personal computers
Servers
Smartphones
Switches
Tablets
Thermal products

COMPETITORS

ASUSTeK
Amphenol
BenQ
Cal-Comp Electronics
Celestica
First International Computer
Flextronics
Hosiden
Inventec
Jabil
MiTAC
Molex
Nam Tai
Quanta Computer
Sanmina
TPV Technology
Universal Scientific
Venture Corp.
WBL Corp.
Wistron

HISTORICAL FINANCIALS

Company Type: Public

Income Statement FYE: December 31

	REVENUE ($ mil.)	NET INCOME ($ mil.)	NET PROFIT MARGIN	EMPLOYEES
12/12	134,567	3,162	2.4%	1,290,000
12/11	113,912	2,703	2.4%	961,000
12/10	103,000	2,593	2.5%	836,000
12/09	61,239	2,387	3.9%	611,000
12/08	59,513	1,729	2.9%	486,000
Annual Growth	22.6%	16.3%	—	27.6%

2012 Year-End Financials

Debt ratio: 0.2%
Return on equity: 14.1%
Cash ($ mil.): 17,418
Current ratio: 1.23
Long-term debt ($ mil.): 3,641
No. of shares (mil.): —
Dividends
Yield: —
Payout: —
Market value ($ mil.): —

	STOCK PRICE ($) FY Close	P/E High/Low	PER SHARE ($) Earnings	Dividends	Book Value
12/12	5.82	— —	0.25	0.00	1.80
12/11	5.27	— —	0.20	0.00	1.57
12/10	8.00	— —	0.20	0.06	1.37
12/09	9.25	— —	0.18	0.09	1.16
12/08	3.40	— —	0.13	0.07	0.95
Annual Growth	14.4%	— —	17.2%	—	17.5%

Honda Motor Co., Ltd.(Honda Giken Kogyo Kabushiki Kaisha) (Japan)

According to Honda you might be in your Element if you do you Civic duty and get Fit. Honda Motor is Japan's #2 automaker (after Toyota) and the world's largest motorcycle producer. The company's car models include the Accord CR-V Civic Element and Fit; gasoline-electric hybrid versions of the Civic and Accord; and seven models of the luxury Acura line. Honda's line of motorcycles includes everything from scooters to superbikes. The company also makes a line of ATVs and personal watercraft. Honda's power products division makes commercial and residential machinery (lawn mowers snow blowers and tillers); portable generators; and outboard motors. Almost 70% of Honda Motor sales come from outside Japan.

The company's strong sales in fiscal 2011 left the days of the global economic recession in Honda's rearview mirror. Sales were down in both fiscal 2009 and 2010 while the automotive industry took a hit. However as the economy improved and the value of the Japanese yen grew stronger Honda saw its overall sales grow 4% in its native currency and 16% in US dollars. The company sold 3.5 million passenger vehicles (up 3%) and more than 11 million motorcycles (up 18%) in fiscal 2011. To top it off profits doubled to $6 billion.

Unfortunately fiscal 2012 was affected by two major natural disasters in Asia. The tsunami and earthquake that rattled Japan in March 2011 killed one worker and injured more than a dozen others. Honda and other car manufacturers in the country were forced to cease production for about a month before resorting to operating at reduced capacity due to a shortage of parts. Then in October its auto parts manufacturing plants in Thailand were damaged by floods. The Thai plant supplied parts to the US and Canada and Honda had to reduce North America production until the damage in Thailand could be assessed and the plants can be repaired. Production was down more than 30% for the first half of 2012.

Like its rival Toyota Honda is facing questions about the quality of its cars. The company recalled some 2.5 million vehicles in August 2011 over software in the automatic transmission that could cause the vehicle to stall and make it difficult to put the car into park.

Automotive sales account for more than 75% of Honda's revenues. In its home region of Asia Honda's automotive focus is the same as everyone else's –China and India. Unit sales in the region for 2011 grew by 32% and revenue increased more than 20%. To meet the increasing demand Honda added capacity to one of its Chinese factories and opened new facilities in both India and Thailand. Its Dongfeng Honda Automobile unit a 50/50 joint venture with Dongfeng Motor is building a second factory in China to keep up with surging demand. The plant which is expected to open sometime in 2012 is expected to produce 100000 units a year by 2012. The car company's 50/50 joint venture with Denway Motors known as Guangqi Honda Automobile should produce 480000 units annually by the end of 2011. Altogether Honda's total production capacity in China will reach 890000 vehicles by 2013.

With a desire to concentrate on its own growth strategy in the India market Honda sold its 26% stake in Hero Honda Motors (renamed Hero MotoCorp Ltd. in mid-2011) a joint venture between Honda and Hero Group which is run by the Munjal family. Though the exact amount of the 2011 transaction was not reported Hero indicated earlier in the year that it would buy the shares for approximately $853 million. Hero Group now owns about 52% of Hero MotoCorp.

Honda is enjoying brisk motorcycle sales particularly in Asia where motorcycles are a popular mode of transportation. Motorcycle sales account for almost 15% of revenues. The company is beefing up production capacity in India to keep up with demand. Honda is adding on to its two existing Indian factories and is building a third one. Indonesia is the world's third-largest market for motorcycles (after China and India). Although high gas prices triggered inflation in Indonesia and the ensuing credit crunch put a damper on sales demand for motorcycles in the region remains high. To that end Honda has announced plans to expand its plant and increase motorcycle production in Indonesia to 4 million in 2012. The company is also expanding its plant in Vietnam to produce 2 million bikes. Motorcycle sales in South America (particularly Brazil) are zooming along; however sales in North America and Europe slowed in 2011. North American motorcycle sales were hurt by rising gas prices and interest rates. Sales of ATVs also declined in North America as economic jitters prompted consumers to postpone purchases of expensive recreational goods.

HISTORY

Soichiro Honda spent six years as an apprentice at Tokyo service station Art Shokai before opening his own branch of the repair shop in Hamamatsu in 1928. He also raced cars and in 1931 received a patent for metal spokes that replaced wood in wheels.

Honda started a piston ring company in 1937. During WWII the company produced metal propellers for Japanese bombers. When bombs and an earthquake destroyed most of his factory Honda sold it to Toyota in 1945.

In 1946 Honda began motorizing bicycles with war-surplus engines. When this proved popular Honda began making engines. The company was renamed Honda Motor Co. in 1948 and began producing motorcycles. Soichiro Honda hired Takeo Fujisawa in 1949 to manage the company so Honda could focus on engineering. Honda's innovative overhead valve design made its early 1950s Dream model a runaway success. In 1952 the smaller Cub sold through bicycle dealers accounted for 70% of Japan's motorcycle production.

Funded by a 1954 public offering and Mitsubishi Bank Honda expanded capacity and began exporting. American Honda Motor Company was formed in Los Angeles in 1959 accompanied by the slogan "You meet the nicest people on a Honda" in a campaign crafted to counter the stereotypical biker image. Honda added overseas factories in the 1960s and began producing lightweight trucks sports cars and minicars.

The company began selling its tiny 600 model in the US in 1970 but it was the Civic introduced in 1973 that first scored with the US car market. Three years later Honda introduced the Accord which featured an innovative frame adaptable for many models. In 1982 Accord production started at the company's Ohio plant.

Ex-Honda engineer Nobuhiko Kawamoto was named president in 1990 a year before Soichiro Honda died. Kawamoto cut costs and continued to expand the company internationally. That year the Big Three US automakers (General Motors Ford and Chrysler) clamoring for trade sanctions against Japanese carmakers threw Honda out of the US carmakers' trade association.

In 1997 Honda bought Peugeot's plant in Guangzhou China and boosted its US vehicle production by opening an all-terrain vehicle (ATV) plant in South Carolina in 1998. American Honda agreed in 1998 to pay $330 million to settle a class-action lawsuit filed by 1800 dealers who accused Honda of delivering popular models only to dealers who paid bribes (18 executives from American Honda were convicted). That year Hiroyuki Yoshino an engineer with US management experience succeeded Kawamoto as CEO.

Honda and GM agreed in 1999 to a deal in which Honda would supply low-emission V6 engines and automatic transmissions to GM while Isuzu a GM affiliate would supply Honda with diesel engines. True to Honda's go-it-alone style the deal had no equity component.

In 2000 Honda announced that its super-low-emission engine (as called for by US regulators) would make its mass-market debut in 2001 well ahead of competitor versions. Also Honda recalled 500000 cars in Japan due to problems with audio systems and engine oil seals.

Honda announced in 2001 that it would introduce diesel-powered vehicles in Europe by 2003. Later that year Honda's R&D unit set up a solar-powered hydrogen production station in California as part of its efforts to develop renewable-energy fuel-cell vehicles.

In 2006 Honda announced it would enter the aviation market with the introduction of what Honda CEO Takeo Fukui called the "Honda Civic of the sky." Honda began taking orders for the six-passenger twin-engine HondaJet that year and the planes became available in 2011 through Honda Aero.

In 2008 Honda's car sales especially diesel models in Eastern Europe and Russia surpassed those from the previous year. Two years earlier diesel engines officially became the European preference when diesels outsold gas engines for the first time. Honda began shipping diesel-equipped Accords to Europe in 2004 and is working to keep up with demand (Honda has since added diesel versions of the CR-V the FR-V and the Civic).

As vehicle sales slowed in 2008 however Honda cut production by 12% in Japan and North America. The company also quit its participation in Formula One racing to devote corporate resources to its core car business.

Honda began marketing its FCX Clarity a zero-emissions hydrogen fuel cell sedan in 2008. It also introduced the Insight Hybrid at the Paris Motor Show that year. The Insight is Honda's answer to Toyota's popular Prius. Honda executives are acting on their belief that dedicated hybrid vehicles like the Insight will perform better than hybridized current models. The company began selling the Insight in Europe Japan and the US in 2009.

In 2009 Honda increased its commitment to hybrid vehicles by signing a joint venture contract with GS Yuasa to establish a new company Blue Energy. GS Yuasa Power Supply a wholly owned subsidiary of GS Yuasa owns a 51% stake and Honda Motor owns a 49% stake. The two companies decided that Blue Energy will manufacture lithium-ion batteries and drive sales and R&D. Lithium-ion batteries are lighter and hold almost double the energy of a standard battery which may optimize the performance of next-generation hybrid vehicles. With the increasing interest in low-emission vehicles worldwide and many governments' plans to promote green efforts by automakers the venture spurs Honda's lineup of hybrid vehicles as well as its position in the US market for its Insight model.

EXECUTIVES

Chairman, Koichi Kondo, age 66
Corporate Auditor, Toru Onda, age 64
President and CEO, Takanobu Ito, age 60
Senior Managing Director and Board Member; President and Director Honda Motor Europe; COO Regional Operations (Europe Middle East and Africa), Shigeru Takagi, age 61
EVP Executive Officer and Director; COO Production Operations, Akio Hamada, age 65
EVP; President Honda North America, Tetsuo Iwamura, age 62
Senior Managing Director and Board Member; COO Motorcycle Operations; Chief Officer of Driving Safety Promotion Center, Tatsuhiro Oyama, age 63
Chairman, Fumihiko Ike, age 61
Corporate Auditor, Koukei Higuchi, age 77
Corporate Auditor, Fumihiko Saito, age 68
Senior Managing Officer, Takashi Yamamoto
Managing Officer; EVP and Director Honda Motor Europe; President and Director; Honda U.K. Manufacturing, Suguru Kanazawa
Managing Officer; President Honda Motor Europe, Manabu Nishimae
Managing Director COO Purchasing Operations and Board Member, Masaya Yamashita, age 60
Managing Officer; President Asian Honda Motor, Hiroshi Kobayashi, age 59
Senior Managing Officer, Sho Minekawa, age 59
Senior Managing Officer; President and CEO Honda North America Services, Hidenobu Iwata
Managing Officer Quality Certification and Regulation Compliance, Koichi Fukuo
Managing Executive Officer, Takuji Yamada, age 57
Operating Officer; President and CEO Honda Engineering, Hiroshi Sasamoto
Corporate Auditor, Hideki Okada, age 60
COO Automobile Operations and Board Member, Tsuneo Tanai, age 56
Executive Officer; President of Subsidiary, Takashi Sekiguchi
COO Business Management Operations and Board Member, Yoichi Hojo, age 57
Managing Executive Officer; President Honda South America, Masahiro Takedagawa
Managing Officer; President Honda Motor India, Yoshiyuki Matsumoto
Operating Officer; President and Director Honda Engineering, Eiji Okawara
Operating Officer and General Manager Saitama Factory of Production Operations, Ko Katayama
COO Business Support Operations and Board Member, Masahiro Yoshida, age 56
Operating Officer; President Honda Motor (China) Investment, Seiji Kuraishi, age 55

Operating Officer; President and Director Honda Siel Cars India and Honda Motor India, Takashi Nagai
Operating Officer; General Manager Kumamoto Factory of Production Operations, Katsushi Watanabe
Operating Officer; President Guangqi Honda Automobile, Toshiaki Mikoshiba
Operating Officer Production Operations and Production for Regional Operations (China), Yoshi Yamane
Operating Officer General Manager Automobile Purchasing Division 2 in Purchasing Operations, Takahiro Hachigo
Managing Executive Officer, Chitoshi Yokota
Operating Officer; President Honda Aircraft, Michimasa Fujino
Managing Director and Board Member; President and Director Honda R&D, Tomohiko Kawanabe, age 61
Corporate Auditor, Yuji Matsuda, age 62
Senior Managing Officer; President and CEO Honda R&D, Yoshiharu Yamamoto
Operating Officer; President Honda R&D Europe (U.K.), Soichiro Takizawa
Operating Officer; COO Motorcycle Operations, Shinji Aoyama
Board Member, Takeo Fukui, age 69
Board Member, Nobuo Kuroyanagi, age 72
President CEO and Director; COO Automobile Operations, Takanobu Ito, age 59
Senior Managing Director Government and Industrial Affairs and Compliance Officer and Board Member, Mikio Yoshimi, age 65
Senior Managing Director and Board Member; President and Director Honda Motor Europe; COO Regional Operations (Europe Middle East and Africa), Shigeru Takagi, age 61
Board Member, Kensaku Hogen, age 72
Senior Managing Director and Board Member; President and Director Honda North America; COO Regional Operations North America, Tetsuo Iwamura, age 62
Senior Managing Director and Board Member; COO Motorcycle Operations; Chief Officer of Driving Safety Promotion Center, Tatsuhiro Oyama, age 63
Board Member; President and Director Asian Honda Motor COO Regional Operations Asia and Oceania, Fumihiko Ike, age 60
Managing Director COO Purchasing Operations and Board Member, Masaya Yamashita, age 60
Board Member; COO Regional Sales Operations (Japan), Hiroshi Kobayashi, age 59
Board Member; COO Regional Operations Latin America; President and Director Honda South America Moto Honda da Amazonia and Honda Automoveis do Brasil, Sho Minekawa, age 59
Managing Executive Officer, Takuji Yamada, age 57
COO Automobile Operations and Board Member, Tsuneo Tanai, age 56
COO Business Management Operations and Board Member, Yoichi Hojo, age 57
COO Business Support Operations and Board Member, Masahiro Yoshida, age 56
Board Member, Seiji Kuraishi, age 55
Board Member, Hiroyuki Yamada, age 57
Managing Director and Board Member; President and Director Honda R&D, Tomohiko Kawanabe, age 61
Auditors: KPMGAZSA&Co.

LOCATIONS

HQ: Honda Motor Co., Ltd.(Honda Giken Kogyo Kabushiki Kaisha) (Japan)
1-1, Minami-Aoyama 2-chome, Minato-ku, Tokyo 107-8556
Phone: (81) 3 3423 1111 **Fax:** (81) 3 5412 1515
Web: www.honda.co.jp

2011 Sales

	% of total
North	37
Asia	
Japan	32
Other	16
Europe	6
Other	9
Total	**100**

PRODUCTS/OPERATIONS

2011 Sales

	% of total
Automobiles	76
Motorcycles	14
Financial	6
Power products &	4
Total	**100**

Selected Acura Models

CSX (Canada)
MDX
RDX
RL
TL
TSX
ZDX

Selected Honda Car and Truck Models

Passenger cars
- Accord
- City
- Civic
- Insight
- Inspire
- Legend

Minivans Multi-wagons Sport Utility Vehicles
- Airwave
- Crossroad
- CR-V
- CR-Z
- Element
- Elysion
- Fit
- FREED
- FR-V
- Jazz
- Odyssey
- Partner Pilot
- Ridgeline
- Step Wagon
- Stream

Mini cars
- Acty
- Life
- Vamos
- Zest

Selected Motorcycle Models

CBR600RR
CBR1000RR
Elite (scooter)
Fury
Gold Wing
Interstate
NT700V
Nighthawk
PCX (scooter)
Ruckus (scooter)
Sabre
SH150i (scooter)
Shadow RS
Silver Wing (scooter)
Stateline
ST1300
VFR1200F

Selected ATVs

Utility ATVs
- FourTrax Foreman 4x4
- FourTrax Rancher
- FourTrax Rancher AT
- FourTrax Recon
- FourTrax Rincon

Multipurpose Utility Vehicles
- Big Red

Selected Personal Watercraft

AquaTrax F-15
AquaTrax F-15X

Selected Power Products

Cogeneration Units
Commercial mowers
Engines
Lawn mowers
Marine motors
Portable generators
Pumps
Snowblowers
Tillers

COMPETITORS

BMW
Briggs & Stratton
Brunswick Corp.
Caterpillar
Chrysler
Daihatsu
Daimler
Deere
Exmark Manufacturing
Fiat
Ford Motor
Fuji Heavy Industries
General Motors
Harley-Davidson
Hyundai Motor
Indian Motorcycle
Isuzu
Kawasaki Heavy Industries
Kia Motors
Land Rover
Mahindra Renault
Mazda
Mitsubishi Motors
Nissan
Peugeot
Renault
Saab Automobile
Suzuki Motor
Tata Motors
Textron
Toro Company
Toyota
Triumph Motorcycles
Viper Motorcycle
Volkswagen
Volvo
Yamaha Motor

HISTORICAL FINANCIALS

Company Type: Public

Income Statement

FYE: March 31

	REVENUE ($ mil.)	NET INCOME ($ mil.)	NET PROFIT MARGIN	EMPLOYEES
03/13	104,981	3,902	3.7%	190,338
03/12	96,892	2,578	2.7%	187,094
03/11	107,924	6,449	6.0%	179,060
03/10	91,846	2,873	3.1%	176,815
03/09	101,662	1,391	1.4%	181,876
Annual Growth	0.8%	29.4%	—	1.1%

2013 Year-End Financials

Debt ratio: 0.3%
Return on equity: 7.7%
Cash ($ mil.): 12,818
Current ratio: 1.30
Long-term debt ($ mil.): 28,810
No. of shares (mil.): 1,802
Dividends
Yield: 0.0%
Payout: 0.0%
Market value ($ mil.): 68,956

	STOCK PRICE ($) FY Close	P/E High	P/E Low	PER SHARE ($) Earnings	Dividends	Book Value
03/13	38.26	0	0	2.17	0.00	29.71
03/12	38.43	0	0	1.43	0.00	29.78
03/11	37.51	0	0	3.57	0.60	29.82
03/10	35.29	0	0	1.58	0.37	25.54
03/09	23.70	0	0	0.77	0.75	22.43
Annual Growth	12.7%	—	—	29.6%	(89.0%)	7.3%

HSBC Bank Canada

HSBC Bank Canada is one of the largest foreign-owned banks in Canada. Through approximately 250 locations including some 140 bank branches it provides a range of commercial and retail financial services including deposit accounts loans and mortgages import and export financing equipment leasing and investment capital financing. Through subsidiaries the bank also offers brokerage services insurance mutual funds merchant banking trust services and portfolio management and investment counseling. HSBC Bank Canada is controlled by one of the largest banks on the planet UK-based financial services heavyweight HSBC Holdings.

The bank's loan portfolio is dominated by residential mortgages and real estate loans to businesses and government entities. Nearly half of all the bank's loans are originated in British Columbia.

HSBC Bank Canada's operations fall into four segments: retail banking and wealth management commercial banking global banking and markets and consumer finance (which is being wound down). The retail banking and wealth management segment has seen growth by providing specialized services for high-net-worth individuals and families. In commercial banking the company's growth centers around clients including small businesses and midsized Canadian companies doing business overseas. HSBC Banks Canada's global banking and markets segment is also focused on international growth offering trading and investment banking services.

The final segment consumer finance provided products including mortgages loans specialty insurance and credit cards through subsidiary HSBC Financial. In 2012 as part of parent HSBC's restructuring efforts to create a leaner group HSBC Bank Canada announced plans to wind down the consumer finance segment. The decision was made after no buyer could be found for the business.

The closure follows the 2011 sale of the full-service investment advisory business of HSBC Securities (Canada) to National Bank of Canada. Both divestitures reflect the group's strategy to focus on commercial banking retail banking and wealth management.

HSBC Bank Canada's profits rose 14% from 2010 to 2011 as the company reported lower loan impairment charges and fee income grew. The growth was slightly offset by decreased interest income (primarily due to lower interest rates) and net trading income. The company also recorded a one-time charge for a write down in the value of investment property which lowered its other operating income by about half.

EXECUTIVES

Chairman, Samuel (Sam) Minzberg, age 63
President and CEO, Paulo Maia
VP Corporate Affairs, Ernest Yee
Assistant VP Public Affairs, Sharon Wilks
EVP Commercial Banking; Regional President Central and Eastern Canada, Linda Seymour
COO, Sandra Stuart
EVP Personal Financial Services and Wealth Management, Margaret Willis
Co-Head Global Markets, Jason Henderson
Chief Risk Officer, Ralph Hilton
Senior Administrative Assistant, Edith Ho
Director of Operations, Craig Shearer
CFO, Jacques Fleurant
Director, Michael A. Grandin, age 68
Director, Timothy R. (Tim) Price, age 71
Director, Beth Horowitz
Director, Caleb Chan
Auditors: KPMGLLP

LOCATIONS

HQ: HSBC Bank Canada
885 West Georgia Street, Vancouver, British Columbia V6C 3E8
Phone: 604 685-1000 **Fax:** 604 641-3098
Web: www.hsbc.ca

PRODUCTS/OPERATIONS

2011 Sales

	% of total
Interest	
Loans	47
Financial	12
HSBC Financial	10
Noninterest	
Fees	22
Net trading	5
Net gains from financial	1
Other	3
Total	**100**

Selected Subsidiaries

Household Trust Company
HSBC Capital (Canada) Inc.
HSBC Financial Corporation Limited
HSBC Global Asset Management (Canada) Limited
HSBC Investment Funds (Canada) Inc.
HSBC Loan Corporation (Canada)
HSBC Mortgage Corporation (Canada)
HSBC Securities (Canada) Inc.
HSBC South Point Investments (Barbados) LLP
HSBC Trust Company (Canada)

COMPETITORS

BMO Financial Group
CIBC
Canadian Western Bank
IGM Financial
Laurentian Bank
National Bank of Canada
RBC Financial Group
Scotiabank
TD Bank

HISTORICAL FINANCIALS

Company Type: Public

Income Statement FYE: December 31

	ASSETS ($ mil.)	NET INCOME ($ mil.)	INCOME AS % OF ASSETS	EMPLOYEES
12/12	81,154	693	0.9%	0
12/11	78,418	620	0.8%	7,900
12/10*	78,183	532	0.7%	8,200
01/10	74,882	0	—	0
12/09	68,043	481	0.7%	8,400
Annual Growth	6.0%	12.9%	—	—

*Fiscal year change

2012 Year-End Financials

Return on assets: 0.8%
Return on equity: 13.6%
Long-term debt ($ mil.): —
No. of shares (mil.): 498
Sales ($ mil): 3,264
Dividends
Yield: 4.8%
Payout: —
Market value ($ mil.): 13,347

	STOCK PRICE ($) FY Close	P/E High/Low	PER SHARE ($) Earnings	Dividends	Book Value
12/12	26.77	20 19	1.39	1.26	10.35
12/11	26.85	22 20	1.24	1.62	9.78
12/10*	27.72	27 25	1.06	1.22	8.89
01/10	26.80	— —	(0.00)	1.14	(0.00)
12/09	26.90	30 27	0.86	1.12	8.35
Annual Growth	(0.1%)	— —	17.4%	4.1%	7.4%

*Fiscal year change

HSBC Bank Plc (United Kingdom)

LOCATIONS

HQ: HSBC Bank Plc (United Kingdom)
8 Canada Square, London E14 5HQ
Phone: (44) 20 7991 8888 **Fax:** (44) 20 7992 4880
Web: www.hsbc.co.uk

HISTORICAL FINANCIALS

Company Type: Public

Income Statement FYE: December 31

	ASSETS ($ mil.)	NET INCOME ($ mil.)	INCOME AS % OF ASSETS	EMPLOYEES
12/12	1,314,446	3,842	0.3%	74,190
12/11	1,279,092	3,597	0.3%	80,013
12/10	1,239,773	4,594	0.4%	77,932
12/09	1,217,808	5,007	0.4%	82,296
12/08	1,346,882	5,014	0.4%	87,492
Annual Growth	(0.6%)	(6.4%)	—	(4.0%)

2012 Year-End Financials

Return on assets: 0.2%
Return on equity: 7.5%
Long-term debt ($ mil.): —
No. of shares (mil.): 796
Sales ($ mil): 32,959
Dividends
Yield: —
Payout: —
Market value ($ mil.): —

HSBC Holdings Plc

HSBC would be a real alphabet soup if the company's name reflected its geographic diversity. One of the world's largest banking groups by assets (and the leader in customer deposits with more than $1 trillion) HSBC Holdings owns subsidiaries throughout Europe Hong Kong and the rest of the Asia/Pacific region the Middle East and Africa and the Americas. All told the company has some 7200 locations in more than 80 countries. Its activities include consumer and commercial banking credit cards private banking investment banking and leasing. Its North American operations include HSBC USA HSBC Bank Canada HSBC Bank Bermuda and Grupo Financiero HSBC in Mexico.

Operations

HSBC has always had a bent towards international expansion even from its inception. Founded in Hong Kong in 1865 HSBC owns all or parts of The Hongkong and Shanghai Banking Corporation HSBC France The Saudi British Bank and Hong Kong's Hang Seng Bank. The company was also one of the first foreign banks to receive regulatory approval to incorporate in China. It owns about 20% of Bank of Communications one of the largest commercial banks in the country.

Strategy

With market instability prevalent in the US and Europe HSBC has been increasingly looking toward emerging markets in Asia and Latin America for growth. The company believes that over the next few decades the global economy will shift towards those markets and it plans to be in place to provide them with cross-border services.

However the global financial crisis is forcing HSBC to rethink its expansion strategy and make some big cuts in some markets. In early 2013 HSBC reported that it had sold or closed nearly 50 businesses around the world since CEO Stuart Gulliver set out a new strategy for the bank in May 2011. The strategy involves cutting costs (including 30000 jobs) and trimming low-growth markets. In Latin America for instance HSBC is focusing on its core growth markets of Brazil Argentina and Mexico after a series of disposals in other countries in the region.

In Asia HSBC sold its private banking operations in Japan to Credit Suisse in 2012. It also shut down its retail banking operations in Japan though it continues to offer corporate banking there.

HSBC sold its US credit card portfolio worth some $30 billion to Capital One in 2012 and is selling 195 US bank branches mainly in upstate New York to First Niagara Financial Group for #613 million ($1 billion).

In the private equity realm HSBC is divesting five of its private equity fund management businesses to their management teams in order to conform to new regulations that put limits on banks' trading activities. The first to go was HSBC's Private Equity (Asia) now Heartland Capital Partners which the company sold to unit's management.

Financial Performance

They're the latest moves the company has made to recover from bad loans in the US. The belt tightening paid off in 2010 as HSBC turned a profit in each of its geographic regions and business lines for the first time in four years including North America and Personal Financial Services which had been weighed down by the consumer credit woes. Earnings continued to recover in 2011 with 26% growth in revenues and 15% growth in profits before taxation. However factors such as concerns over European sovereign debt and the possibility of a double-dip recession on the continent have had a negative impact on the group's trading revenues.

HISTORY

Scotsman Thomas Sutherland and other businessmen in 1865 opened the doors to Hongkong & Shanghai Bank financing and promoting British imperial trade in opium silk and tea in East Asia. It soon established a London office and created an international branch network emphasizing China and East Asia. It claims to have been the first bank in Thailand (1888).

War repeatedly disrupted but never demolished the bank's operations. During WWII the headquarters were temporarily moved to London. (They moved back on a permanent basis in 1991.) The bank's chief prewar manager Sir Vandeleur Grayborn died in a Japanese POW camp. After the Communists took power in China in 1949 the bank gradually withdrew; by 1955 only its Shanghai office remained and it was later closed. The bank played a key role in Hong Kong's postwar growth by financing industrialists who fled there from China.

In the late 1950s Hongkong & Shanghai Bank's acquisitions included the British Bank of the Middle East (founded 1889; now The Saudi British Bank) and Mercantile Bank (with offices in India and Southeast Asia). In 1965 the company bought 62% of Hang Seng Hong Kong's #2 bank. It also added new subsidiaries including Wayfoong (mortgage and small-business finance 1960) and Wardley (investment banking Hong Kong 1972).

In the late 1970s and into the 1980s China began opening to foreign business. The bank added operations in North America to capitalize on business between China and the US and Canada. Acquisitions included Marine Midland Bank (US 1980) Hongkong Bank of Canada (1981) 51% of treasury securities dealer Carroll McEntee & McGinley (US 1983) most of the assets and liabilities of the Bank of British Columbia (1986) and Lloyds Bank Canada (1990).

Following the 1984 agreement to return Hong Kong to China Hongkong & Shanghai Bank began beefing up in the UK buying London securities dealer James Capel & Co. (1986) and the UK's #3 bank Midland plc (1992). In 1993 the company formed London-based HSBC Holdings and divested assets most notably its interest in Hong Kong-based Cathay Pacific Airways.

HSBC then began expanding in Asia again particularly in Malaysia where its Hongkong Bank Malaysia became the country's first locally incorporated foreign bank. The company returned to China with offices in Beijing and Guangzhou. It also added new European branches.

Latin American banks acquired in 1997 were among the non-Asian operations that cushioned HSBC from the worst of 1998's economic crises. Nonetheless The Hong Kong Monetary Authority took a stake in the bank to shore up the stock exchange and foil short-sellers.

In 1999 China's government made HSBC a loan for mainland expansion. That year the company was foiled in its attempt to buy South Korea's government-owned Seoulbank but did buy the late Edmond Safra's Republic New York Corporation and his international bank holding company Safra Republic Holdings (it negotiated a $450 million discount on the $10 billion deal after a Japanese probe of Republic's securities division caused delays).

The company unveiled several online initiatives in 2000 including Internet ventures with Cheung Kong (Holdings) and Merrill Lynch and bought CCF (then called Credit Commercial de France now HSBC France). However HSBC's plans to buy a controlling stake in Bangkok Metropolitan Bank fell through before the year's end.

In 2001 HSBC agreed to pick up Barclays Bank's fund management operations in Greece. Later in response to the slowing economy it froze the salaries of 14000 employees. Argentina's 2001 peso devaluation cost the company half a billion dollars in currency conversion losses alone. Total charges pertaining to Argentina equaled more than $1 billion that year.

HSBC expanded its consumer finance operations with the purchase of US-based Household International (now HSBC Finance) in 2003.

The next year HSBC acquired The Bank of Bermuda as well as Marks and Spencer Financial Services (aka M&S Money) one of the UK's leading credit card issuers. It bought US credit card company Metris the following year.

HSBC's Latin American operations at this point were primarily in Argentina Brazil and Mexico. The company expanded its presence in Central America and the Caribbean with the 2006 purchase of Panama-based Banistmo a banking group with offices in the Bahamas Colombia Costa Rica El Salvador Honduras and Nicaragua.

HSBC asold its regional banking operations in France to Banque Populaire in 2008. The deal included eight banks with around 400 branches. Also that year the company canceled its proposed $6 billion acquisition of Lone Star's 51% stake in Korea Exchange Bank a deal that had been held up for months by an investigation by the South Korean government. HSBC cited weakened asset values in the global financial markets for the cancellation.

Beset by mortgage defaults the group closed its Decision One US-based wholesale subprime lending unit in 2007. In 2009 it shuttered its North American consumer lending business placing related portfolios (excluding credit cards) in run-off. To further reduce its exposure to consumer credit it sold a $4 billion car loan portfolio and servicing platform to an affiliate of Santander USA.

The company acquired a majority stake in Indonesian lender Bank Ekonomi in 2009 doubling its presence in the nation.

In 2010 HSBC sold HSBC Insurance Brokers to Marsh & McLennan in a #135 million ($218 million) cash-and-stock deal. As part of the transaction the companies entered into a strategic partnership under which Marsh markets insurance and risk management services to HSBC's corporate and private clients ahead of other providers.

In late 2011 the Financial Services Authority (the UK regulator of financial services providers) fined HSBC #10.3 million after it was found that salespeople at its NHFA Limited subsidiary had sold inappropriate and unsuitable five-year bonds to nearly 3000 elderly customers. HSBC which had alerted the FSA once it was made aware of the issue closed NHFA to new business that year.

EXECUTIVES

Group Company Secretary; Group General Manager, Ralph G. Barber, age 62

Chairman, Douglas J. Flint, age 58, $1,237,440 total compensation

Group General Manager and Group General Counsel, R. E. T. Bennett, age 61

Chairman of the Board Chief Executive Officer, Patrick J. (Pat) Burke, age 51

Group Managing Director and Global Head Personal Financial Services and Marketing; Chairman HSBC Bank A.S., Alexander C. (Alex) Hungate, age 46

Group Chief Executive; Group Managing Director; Executive Director, Stuart T. Gulliver, age 53, $1,236,240 total compensation

CEO Global Private Banking, Krishna Patel, age 64

Group Managing Director and Chief Executive Global Banking, Samir Assaf, age 53

Group Press Office, Patrick McGuinness

Group Managing Director; CEO HSBC North America, Niall S. K. Booker, age 54

Group General Manager and Head Operational Risk, M. J. W. King, age 56

Group Managing Director; Chief Executive of HSBC Bank plc, Brian Robertson, age 58

Group Managing Director; CEO Retail Banking and Wealth Management, Paul A. Thurston, age 59

Group General Manager and Director Communications, Richard S. Beck, age 47

Group Managing Director; Chief Executive Asia Pacific; Chairman HSBC Bank (China), Peter T. S. Wong, age 62

CEO HSBC France, Christophe de Backer, age 48

Group General Manager; CEO Continental Europe; Deputy Chairman HSBC France, Peter W. Boyles, age 57

Group General Manager; Chairman HFC Bank, David C. Budd, age 59

Deputy CEO and Director HSBC UK, Joe D. Garner, age 43

Deputy Chairman, Sir Simon Robertson, age 71

Group Managing Director and Chief Risk Officer, Marc Moses

EVP Corporate Affairs North America, Lisa M. Sodeika, age 49

Co-Head Global Banking, Kevin Adeson, age 49

Co-Head Global Markets, Spencer Lake, age 53

Group General Manager and Group Head Audit, Paul J. Lawrence, age 51

CEO Asia Pacific Asset Management, Joanna Munro

Group Director Finance, Iain J. Mackay, age 51

Director, Laura M. L. Cha, age 63

Group General Manager and Head of Global Transaction Banking, Andrew P. Long, age 57

Group Managing Director and Head Latin America and the Caribbean, Emilson Alonso, age 57

Group Managing Director and Group Head Human Resources, Ann Almeida, age 56
Group General Manager; President and CEO HSBC Bank USA, I. M. Dorner, age 58
Group Managing Director and Global Head Commercial Banking, Alan M. Keir, age 54
Group General Manager; CEO Hang Seng Bank, Margaret K. M. Y. Leung, age 62
Group General Manager; Deputy CEO Continental Europe, A. M. Mahoney, age 50
SEVP and Chief Auditor, Mark Martinelli, age 53
President and CEO HSBC Bank Canada, Paulo Maia
General Manager and Head of Global Markets, S. Assaf, age 53
Group General Manager; Chairman and CEO HSBC Egypt, A. S. El Anwar, age 67
Group General Manager and Group Head Insurance, D. L. Fried, age 52
CEO HSBC Hong Kong, Anita Y. M. Fung, age 53
Group General Manager; Head HSBC Amanah; CEO Malaysia, M. M. Hussain, age 53
Head Group Public Affairs Asia, David Hall
Head Public Affairs Mexico, Roy Caple
Head Marketing and Communications HSBC Private Bank (UK), Tony Joyce
Manager Investor Relations, Alastair Brown
Head Investor Relations Asia, Hugh Pye
Senior Manager External Relations Asia-Pacific/Hong Kong, Gareth Hewett
Deputy CEO Continental Europe, Tony Mahoney
U.S Chief Economist Global Banking and Markets, Kevin Logan
CEO China, Helen Wong
Director Marketing and Communications HSBC Private Bank (UK), John Dore
Senior Media Relations Manager Global Banking & Markets, Charles Clarke
Global Head Media Relations Global Banking & Markets, Jezz Farr
Communications Director Brazil, Helio Duarte
Communications Manager Regional Communications Middle East, Ahmad Othman
CEO Global Asset Management, John Flint
CEO Europe Asset Management, Rudolf Apenbrink
COO Asia Pacific Asset Management, Edmund Stokes
Co-Head Global Banking, Robin Phillips, age 55
Co-Head Global Markets, Jose-Luis Guerrero, age 48
Head of Commercial Banking Asia Pacific, Noel Quinn
Chief Investment Officer Global Asset Management Asia, Bill Maldonado
Head of Human Resources, Udi Agnon
Head of Private Banking, Raz Lerman
Head of Marketing, Michal Karnibad
Head of Treasury, Harel Cordova
Head of Legal and Compliance, Mira Gladstone
Chief Risk Officer, Bentzi Guetta
Chief Financial Officer Israel, Alon Jannai
Head of Corporate Banking, Carol Shaked
Head of Turkish Desk, Emmanuel Lion
Head Of Operations, Erik Wedborn
Head of Trade, Liliana Drozdovsky
Investor Relations Manager, Guy Lewis
Chief Legal Officer; Group Managing Director, Stuart Levey
Director; Chairman HSBC North America Holdings, John L. Thornton, age 59
Director, Rona A. Fairhead, age 51
Director, Gwyn Morgan, age 67
Director, Alexander A. (Sandy) Flockhart, age 61
Director, James W. J. Hughes-Hallett, age 63
Director, Safra A. Catz, age 51
CEO and Director, Stuart T. Gulliver, age 52
Director, W. Samuel H. (Sam) Laidlaw
Director, Rachel Lomax, age 67
Director, Sir Brian Williamson, age 68
Director, Marvin K.T. Cheung, age 65
Director, John D. Coombe, age 68
Deputy Chairman, Sir Simon Robertson, age 71
Director, Laura M. L. Cha, age 63
Director, N. R. Narayana Murthy, age 67
Independent Non-Executive Director, Joachim Faber
Independent Non-Executive Director, John Lipsky
Auditors: KPMGAuditPlc

LOCATIONS

HQ: HSBC Holdings Plc
42nd Floor, 8 Canada Square, London E14 5HQ
Phone: (44) 20 7991 8888 **Fax:** (44) 20 7992 4880
Web: www.hsbc.com

PRODUCTS/OPERATIONS

2011 Sales

	% of total
Interest	57
Fees	19
Net earned insurance	12
Net trading	6
Other	6
Total	**100**

2011 Sales by Segment

	% of total
Retail banking & wealth	42
Global banking &	20
Commercial	19
Global private	7
Other	12
Total	**100**

Selected Subsidiaries

Hang Seng Bank Limited (62% Hong Kong)
The Hong Kong and Shanghai Banking Corporation Limited
HSBC Asset Finance (UK) Ltd.
HSBC Bank Argentina S.A. (99.9%)
HSBC Bank A.S. (Turkey)
HSBC Bank Australia Limited
HSBC Bank Bermuda Limited
HSBC Bank Brasil S.A. - Banco Multiplo
HSBC Bank Canada
HSBC Bank (China) Company Limited
HSBC Bank Egypt S.A.E. (95%)
HSBC Bank International Limited (Jersey)
HSBC Bank Malaysia Berhad
HSBC Bank Malta p.l.c. (70%)
HSBC Bank Middle East Limited
HSBC Bank (Panama) S.A.
HSBC Bank plc
HSBC Bank USA N.A.
HSBC Finance Corporation (US)
HSBC France
HSBC Mexico S.A. Institucion de Banca Multiplo Grupo Financiero HSBC (99.9%)
HSBC Private Banking Holdings (Suisse) S.A. (Switzerland)
HSBC Securities (USA) Inc.
HSBC Trinkaus & Burkhardt AG (80% Germany)
Marks and Spencer Retail Financial Services Holdings Limited

COMPETITORS

BBVA
Bank of America
Bank of China
Barclays
CIBC
Citigroup
Credit Suisse
Deutsche Bank
Hutchison Whampoa
Intesa Sanpaolo
JPMorgan Chase
Lloyds Banking Group
Mitsubishi UFJ Financial Group
Mizuho Financial
Prudential plc
RBC Financial Group
Royal Bank of Scotland
Standard Chartered
UBS

HISTORICAL FINANCIALS

Company Type: Public

Income Statement FYE: December 31

	ASSETS ($ mil.)	NET INCOME ($ mil.)	INCOME AS % OF ASSETS	EMPLOYEES
12/12	2,692,538	14,027	0.5%	270,000
12/11	2,555,579	16,797	0.7%	298,000
12/10	2,454,689	13,159	0.5%	307,000
12/09	2,364,452	5,834	0.2%	302,000
12/08	2,527,465	5,728	0.2%	325,000
Annual Growth	1.6%	25.1%	—	(4.5%)

2012 Year-End Financials

Return on assets: 0.5%
Return on equity: 8.3%
Long-term debt ($ mil.): —
No. of shares (mil.): —
Sales ($ mil): 108,851
Dividends
Yield: 4.7%
Payout: 277.0%
Market value ($ mil.): —

	STOCK PRICE ($) FY Close	P/E High/Low		PER SHARE ($) Earnings	Dividends	Book Value
12/12	53.07	72	52	0.74	2.50	9.48
12/11	38.10	64	39	0.91	1.95	8.88
12/10	51.04	81	61	0.72	1.70	8.35
12/09	57.09	188	69	0.34	1.70	7.37
12/08	48.67	187	97	0.47	4.65	7.73
Annual Growth	2.2%	—	—	12.0%	(14.4%)	5.2%

Hutchison Whampoa Ltd.

Hutchison Whampoa has a hand in just about everything in Hong Kong. The company one of Hong Kong's oldest "hongs" (trading companies) has extensive holdings in retailing (A.S. Watson & Co) ports energy (Hongkong Electric Husky Energy) telecommunications (3G mobile phone and paging services) and infrastructure (power plants toll roads and construction materials). In addition Hutchison Whampoa owns hotels and a sizable portfolio of Hong Kong properties. Outside Hong Kong the company has operations in about 55 countries including China and elsewhere in the Asia/Pacific region as well as in Europe and the Americas. Hutchison Whampoa is controlled by Li Ka-shing one of the world's wealthiest men.

Although it took awhile the global recession and concurrent decline in consumer demand and trade caught up with Hutchison Whampoa in 2009. Total revenue at the diversified company declined 14% in 2009 vs. 2008. With the exception strong performances from the property and hotels business (up 33%) and its telecommunications business in Hong Kong (up 6%) all of its other businesses declined. Retail the company's largest business segment was down just 2%. The poor performance in 2009 was a reversal from 2008 and 2007 when the company was propped up by strong demand and growth in China and the Asia/Pacific region.

Hutchison Whampoa's retail and manufacturing subsidiary A.S. Watson & Co. (ASW) accounts for more than 45% of revenues (from established businesses) with more than 8900 retail stores spread among a dozen chains. Operations include supermarkets (Park'N Shop) health and beauty stores (Watson's Your Personal Store Drogas Kruidvat)

Fortress electrical appliance stores in Hong Kong soft drink and water bottling operations and wine retailing (Watson's Wine Cellar). Already the world's largest operator of health and beauty stores (by store count) with outlets throughout Europe and Asia ASW has expanded its health and beauty business with the acquisition of the French retail perfume chain Marionnaud Parfumeries and the 120-door The Perfume Shop chain in the UK. Its Chinese retail arm Watsons China operates about 400 stores in some 65 cities on the Mainland.

Hutchison Port Holdings (HPH) is the world's leading port investor developer and operator with 300-plus berths in some 50 ports. HPH operates in about 25 countries and in six of the nine busiest container ports in the world including three key ports on Britain's east coast and ports on both ends of the Panama Canal. In addition to owning a controlling interest in Hongkong International Terminals which handles traffic passing through Hong Kong's container port HPH has large investments in terminal operations in southern China. In March 2011 Hutchison launched an IPO for its port operations in the Pearl River Delta which includes Hong Kong and Shenzhen in an initial public offering of Hutchison Port Holdings Trust. Hutchison says it expects to raise as much as $5.8 billion in the offering and will use the proceeds to retire debt and for possible acquisitions and growth within its diverse businesses.

Hutchison Whampoa is a leading competitor in mobile telecommunications offering wireless service to some 16 million customers throughout Australia Europe and Hong Kong. Subsidiary company Hutchison Telecommunications International Limited (HTIL) provides fixed-line and mobile communications services to customers primarily in Southeast Asia (Indonesia Sri Lanka Thailand and Vietnam). Its services include voice calling and broadband Internet access as well as the sale of wireless handsets and accessories. Hutchison Whampoa HTIL's biggest shareholder took the business private in mid-2010.

In an effort to shore up its share value the company's Husky Energy division announced plans to spin off its oil and gas assets in Southeast Asia into a separate publicly traded firm. (Hutchison Whampoa owns a 34% stake in Husky Energy; the division's largest shareholder L.F. Investments holds a 36% share.) The plan however is in an early stage of development. The move could raise up to $1 billion for the spinoff unit which is valued at about $4 billion.

Hutchison Whampoa has strong connections to the Chinese government thanks to its rags-to-riches chairman Li who has spent years building business relationships inside China. His Cheung Kong (Holdings) Limited is a substantial shareholder in Hutchison Whampoa. In turn Hutchison Whampoa owns about 85% of Cheung Kong Infrastructure.

HISTORY

Hongkong and Whampoa Dock was the first registered company in Hong Kong. The enterprise was founded in 1861 when it bought dry docks in Whampoa (near present-day Guangzhou China) after the kidnapping and disappearance of the docks' owner John Couper during the Second Opium War (1856-60). It bought docks in Hong Kong in 1865.

Founded in 1880 by John Hutchison Hutchison International became a major Hong Kong consumer goods importer and wholesaler. It took control of Hongkong and Whampoa Dock and of A.S. Watson (drugstores supermarkets soft drinks) during an acquisition spree in the 1960s. The purchases entailed a complex web of deals that fell apart in the mid-1970s. To save Hutchison International the Hongkong & Shanghai Bank took a large stake in the company and brought in Australian turnaround specialist Bill Wyllie. Wyllie slashed expenses sold 103 companies in 1976 and bought the rest of Hongkong and Whampoa Dock in 1977. The company became Hutchison Whampoa that year.

In a surprise move in 1979 Hongkong & Shanghai Bank sold its 23% stake in Hutchison to Cheung Kong Holdings: Cheung Kong founder Li Ka-shing who began his career at age 14 by selling plastic flowers became the first Chinese to control a British-style "hong". Wyllie left in 1981.

In the 1980s Hutchison redeveloped its older dockyard sites which had become prime real estate. The company's International Terminals unit grew with Hong Kong's container traffic into the world's largest privately owned container terminal operator. In the 1980s the firm diversified into energy (buying stakes in utility Hongkong Electric and Canada-based Husky Oil) and precious metals and mining. It also moved into telecommunications buying Australian paging and UK mobile telephone units in 1989.

The following year the "hong" launched the AsiaSat I satellite in a venture with Cable & Wireless (C&W) and China International Trust & Investment. More acquisitions followed including European mobile phone businesses and telecom equipment makers. In 1996 the firm reorganized its Hong Kong telecom operations into Hutchison Telecommunications and launched its European wireless operations as a new public company Orange. In 1998 Hutchison Telecommunications made a move into the US when it bought a 20% stake in Western Wireless' digital PCS unit VoiceStream.

In 1999 the company and C&W sold their stakes in AsiaSat. Hutchison Whampoa also traded its stake in Orange to Mannesmann acquiring 10% of the German conglomerate which was later acquired by Vodafone. It recorded a profit that year of more than $15 billion on its investment in Orange. Also in 1999 Hutchison Whampoa and Global Crossing formed a $1.2 billion telecom joint venture to build a fiber-optic network in China (in 2002 the company purchased the remaining 50% of the venture from the beleaguered telecommunications company and renamed it Hutchison Global Communications).

Hutchison Whampoa Dutch phone company KPN and Japanese mobile phone giant NTT DoCoMo (which had purchased a 19% stake in Hutchison Whampoa in 1999) formed an alliance in 2000 to bid on next-generation mobile phone licenses in Europe.

In 2001 Hutchison Whampoa sold its 18% stake in US-based mobile phone operator VoiceStream to Deutsche Telekom for $5.1 billion in cash and stocks and purchased a 15% stake in travel Web site priceline.com. The next year its A.S. Watson Group bought the Netherlands-based health-and-beauty retail chain Kruidvat Group which operates about 1900 stores in six European countries. Also in 2002 supermarket chain PARKnSHOP opened four large stores in southern China.

In April 2003 Hutchison Telecommunications backed out of a joint bid to invest $125 million in bankrupt Global Crossing citing regulatory difficulties. In November the company sold $5 billion worth of bonds (a record global bond sale) to finance its heavy investment in high-speed mobile phone networks in Europe. In March 2004 Hutchison Whampoa sold its Hong Kong fixed-line business to Vanda Systems & Communications Holdings. In June the company sold the remaining 20% stake in its joint venture in China with household-products-giant Procter & Gamble to P&G for $1.8 billion.

In March 2004 Hutchison Whampoa's fixed-line telecommunications group acquired Vanda Systems and became a listed company on the Hong Kong Stock exchange under the new name Hutchison Global Communications Holdings (HGCH). In October the company combined its 52% stake in HGCH with its interests in the 2G cellular businesses under a single parent company Hutchison Telecommunications International Limited (HTIL) and took it public on the Hong Kong and New York stock exchanges. In the interim Hutchison Whampoa's retail arm the A.S. Watson Group acquired a leading health and beauty chain in Latvia and Lithuania Drogas in June marking its entry into the Baltic region. In August Watson acquired a 40% stake in German health and beauty chain Rossmann which operates more than 1100 stores throughout the Czech Republic Germany Hungary and Poland.

In May 2008 Hutchison Whampoa launched a new division Hutchison Water a provider of water production and treatment solutions.

EXECUTIVES

Group Finance Director and Executive Director, Frank J. Sixt, age 61
Executive Director; Deputy Managing Director Cheung Kong (Holdings); Group Managing Director Cheung Kong Infrastructure Holdings; President and CEO CK Life Sciences International, Kam Hing Lam, age 67
Deputy Group Managing Director and Executive Director, Susan M. F. Chow Woo, age 59
Deputy Chairman and Executive Director, Victor T. K. Li, age 49
Chairman, Li Ka-shing, age 84
Executive Director; Deputy Chairman Hutchison Harbour Ring;, Dominic K. M. Lai, age 59
Company Secretary, Edith Shih, age 60
Corporate Communications, Laura Cheung
Corporate Communications, Hans Leung
Deputy Group Managing Director; Executive Director, Mo Woo
Group Finance Director and Executive Director, Frank J. Sixt, age 61
Executive Director; Deputy Managing Director Cheung Kong (Holdings); Group Managing Director Cheung Kong Infrastructure Holdings; President and CEO CK Life Sciences International, Kam Hing Lam, age 67
Deputy Group Managing Director and Executive Director, Susan M. F. Chow Woo, age 59
Deputy Chairman and Executive Director, Victor T. K. Li, age 49
Group Managing Director and Executive Director, Canning K. N. Fok, age 60
Director, Sir Michael D. Kadoorie, age 72
Director, George C. Magnus, age 78
Director, William E. Mocatta, age 60
Director, William Shurniak, age 81
Director, Holger Kluge, age 71
Director, Wong Chung Hin, age 79
Director, Margaret K. M. Y. Leung, age 62
Non-Executive Independent Director, May Ko
Auditors: PricewaterhouseCoopers

LOCATIONS

HQ: Hutchison Whampoa Ltd.
22nd Floor, Hutchison House, 10 Harcourt Road,
Phone: (852) 2128 1188 **Fax:** (852) 2128 1705
Web: www.hutchison-whampoa.com

2010 Sales

	% of total
Europe	41
Hong	18
Asia &	13
Americas & other	16
China	12
Total	**100**

PRODUCTS/OPERATIONS

2010 Sales

	% of total
Retail	38
320	
Husky	14
Ports & related	11
Cheung Kong	5
Property &	5
Hutchison Telecommunications Hong	3
Hutchison Asia	1
Finance &	1
Other	2
Total	**100**

Selected Subsidiaries and Affiliates

Retail
- A/S Drogras (Latvia)
- A.S. Watson & Company Limited
- Dirk Rossmann GmbH (40% Germany)
- Fortress Limited
- Guangzhou Watson's Food and Beverages Co. Ltd. (95% China)
- Kruidvat Retail B.V. (The Netherlands)
- Marionnaud Parfumeries SA (perfumes France)
- Nuance-Watson (Singapore) Pte Ltd. (50% duty-free shops)
- Park' N Shop Limited (supermarkets)
- The Perfume Shop Limited (UK)
- Savers Health and Beauty Limited (UK)
- Superdrug Stores plc (UK)
- Watson's Personal Care Stores (Taiwan) Co. Limited

Energy and infrastructure
- Cheung Kong Infrastructure Holdings Limited (85%)
- Hongkong Electric Holdings Limited (33% utility)
- Husky Energy Inc. (35% oil and gas investment Canada)

Ports and related services
- Hongkong International Terminals Limited (53% container terminal operations)
- Hongkong United Dockyards Limited (50% ship repair and general engineering)
- Shanghai Mingdong Container Terminals Limited (40% China)
- Yantian International Container Terminals Limited (38% China)

Telecommunications
- 3 Italia S.p.A. (97% 3G mobile multimedia services)
- Hutchison 3G UK Limited (3G mobile multimedia services)
- Hutchison Telecommunications (Australia) Limited (52% holding company and multimedia services)
- Hutchison Telecommunications (Hong Kong) Limited (60%)

Property and hotels
- Harbour Plaza Hotel Management (International) Limited (50%)
- Hutchison Whampoa Properties Limited (holding company)

Finance and investments
- Hutchison Whampoa (Europe) Limited (consulting services UK)

Other
- TOM Group Limited (24% Internet portal)

COMPETITORS

AT&T
Aldeasa
Alliance Boots
BT
Cable & Wireless
Carrefour
China Mobile
China Unicom
DFS Group
DP World
Dairy Farm International
Deutsche Telekom
Hopewell Holdings
Jardine Matheson
KP
Orange
Orange
Orient Overseas
PCCW Ltd.
PSA International
Road King Infrastructure
Schlecker
Sime Darby
SkyTel
Sprint Communications
Swire Pacific
Verizon
Wharf

HISTORICAL FINANCIALS

Company Type: Public

Income Statement

FYE: December 31

	REVENUE ($ mil.)	NET INCOME ($ mil.)	NET PROFIT MARGIN	EMPLOYEES
12/12	31,359	3,370	10.7%	250,000
12/11	30,084	7,211	24.0%	250,000
12/10	26,912	2,578	9.6%	240,000
12/09	26,927	1,827	6.8%	0
12/08	30,382	2,279	7.5%	0
Annual Growth	0.8%	10.3%	—	—

2012 Year-End Financials

Debt ratio: 4.1%
Return on equity: 6.9%
Cash ($ mil.): 13,925
Current ratio: 1.57
Long-term debt ($ mil.): 28,437
No. of shares (mil.): —
Dividends
Yield: 2.2%
Payout: —
Market value ($ mil.): —

	STOCK PRICE ($) FY Close	P/E High/Low		PER SHARE ($) Earnings	Dividends	Book Value
12/12	21.18	0	0	0.79	0.48	11.85
12/11	16.58	0	0	1.69	0.01	10.86
12/10	51.41	0	0	0.60	0.43	9.34
12/09	34.40	0	0	0.43	0.43	8.58
12/08	25.21	0	0	0.53	0.43	8.22
Annual Growth	(4.3%)	—	—	10.3%	2.8%	9.6%

Hyundai Heavy Industries Co., Ltd.

Not afraid to play the heavy Hyundai Heavy Industries (HHI) is the world's largest shipbuilder and among the top five manufacturers in other heavy industries. Started in 1972 HHI's shipbuilding division (15% global market share) builds containerships tankers bulk/petrochemical carriers drillships and specialty vessels. HHI also offers offshore construction and exploration services and has expanded into robotic systems and large industrial pumps and presses. Additionally HHI makes diesel engines and engine parts for industrial and marine applications. Other HHI offerings include electric systems (circuit breakers switchgear transformers) and construction equipment (excavators forklifts and loaders).

Operations

HHI operates through seven business divisions: Construction Equipment Electro Electric System Engine and Machinery Green Energy Industrial Plant and Engineering Offshore and Engineering and its bread and butter Shipbuilding.

The Construction Equipment segment is capitalizing on China's infrastructure market flooded with government stimulus funding. HHI's excavators claim more than a 10% share of China's excavator market. The company operates manufacturing plants in China as well as India that position HHI to capture an increasing share of the countries' construction equipment growth.

The Offshore and Engineering business operates a 230-acre offshore yard and fabrication shop for engineering and construction of offshore oil and gas facility projects. The Industrial Plant and Engineering business works on industrial plant projects for power generation desalination and oil and gas processing and capitalizes on bourgeoning work in the Middle East and South America. Despite a drop in marine engine and power engine demand pressured by the slow economy the Engine and Machinery business continues to benefit from HHI's move into China India and other developing markets.

Another small business of HHI is its Electro Electric Systems segment which manufactures and installs electrical systems in power plants locomotives subways and marine vessels. The business' performance is buoyed by the increase in replacement electrical equipment for renovating and upgrading power transformers and other facilities in North America as well as building new facilities in the Middle East and other rapidly modernizing regions.

Financial Performance

Research and development is also bolstering HHI's reach into profitable niche markets related to its established presence. Shipbuilding HHI's largest business represents roughly 40% of sales and revenues. From 2010 to 2011 its revenues increase by 44% but its net income decreased by 38% during that same time period.

Strategy

Responding to slow economy the company is diversifying its vessel offerings by concentrating resources on specialized energy-related vessels such as FSRU (floating storage and regasification unit) drillships and LNG and LNG-FPSO (floating production storage and offloading) facilities. (HHI introduced the world's largest FPSO in late 2010.) In addition it is partnering with shipbuilders around the world in an effort to court local relationships.

EXECUTIVES

Director, Jin-won Park
Director, Jae-kye Lee
Director, Young-june Park
Director, Man-woo Lee
Auditors: KPMGSamjongAccountingCorp.

LOCATIONS

HQ: Hyundai Heavy Industries Co., Ltd.
#1 Jeonha-dong, Dong-gu, Ulsan 682-792
Phone: (82) 52 202 2114 **Fax:** (82) 52 202 3432
Web: www.hhi.co.kr

PRODUCTS/OPERATIONS

Selected Divisions Products and Services

Construction Equipment
- Excavators
- Forklifts
- Skid loaders
- Wheel loaders

Electro Electric Systems
- Low- and Medium-voltage circuit breakers
- Power electronics and control systems
- Rotating machinery
- Transformers gas insulated switchgear switchgear

Engine and Machinery
- Diesel and gas power plant engines
- Industrial and marine pumps industrial robots side thrusters
- Propellers and crankshafts
- Presses conveyor systems steel strip process lines
- Steam turbines and turbochargers
- Two-stroke diesel engines four-stroke (HiMSEN) engines

Green Energy

Industrial Plant and Engineering
- Plant equipment
- Power plants
- Process plants

Offshore and Engineering
- Floating units
- Fix platforms
- Land-based modules
- Offshore installations

Pipelines and subsea facilities
Shipbuilding
Containerships bulk carriers OBO carriers
Drillships
LNG carriers LPG carriers
Ro-pax ships ro-ro ships pure car carriers tankers/VLCCs
Submarines destroyers frigates
VLCCs tankers product carriers chemical tankers

COMPETITORS

ALSTOM
Aker Solutions
Babcock & Wilcox
Baltija Shipbuilding
Bechtel
Bharat Heavy Electricals
Caterpillar
China State Shipbuilding
China Yuchai
Crown Equipment
DSME
Doosan Infracore
Ebara
Evergreen Marine
General Dynamics
Gulf Island Fabrication
Hanjin Heavy Industries & Construction
Harbison-Fischer
Hitachi Zosen
Huntington Ingalls
KBR
Kawasaki Heavy Industries
Komatsu
McDermott
Mitsubishi Heavy Industries
Mitsui Engineering & Shipbuilding
NASSCO
Oceaneering International
Samsung Heavy Industries
Siemens Industry Automation
Stolt-Nielsen
Sumitomo Heavy Industries
Technip USA

HISTORICAL FINANCIALS

Company Type: Public

Income Statement FYE: December 31

	REVENUE ($ mil.)	NET INCOME ($ mil.)	NET PROFIT MARGIN	EMPLOYEES
12/12	51,487	921	1.8%	26,255
12/11	46,355	2,208	4.8%	24,948
12/10	33,303	3,704	11.1%	24,222
12/09	25,283	1,850	7.3%	24,982
12/08	21,652	1,775	8.2%	25,240
Annual Growth	24.2%	(15.1%)	—	1.0%

2012 Year-End Financials

Debt ratio: 0.0%
Return on equity: 5.9%
Cash ($ mil.): 1,037
Current ratio: 1.14
Long-term debt ($ mil.): 5,902
No. of shares (mil.): 61
Dividends
Yield: —
Payout: —
Market value ($ mil.): —

Hyundai Motor Co., Ltd.

Hyundai vehicles run the gamut from budget cars to luxury sedans to commercial trucks. South Korea's leading carmaker Hyundai Motor produces compact and luxury cars SUVs minivans trucks buses and other commercial vehicles. Its cars are sold in 180 countries through some 6000 dealerships. Hyundai generates about half of its sales in South Korea but its vehicles are also popular in emerging markets such as China and India. The company operates a dozen manufacturing plants in China the Czech Republic India Russia South Korea Turkey and the US. It sold 3.6 million passenger cars in 2010 but only 500000 in the US where it does business as Hyundai Motor America. Hyundai also owns a 34% stake in Kia Motors.

Although South Korea accounts for half of Hyundai's sales and vehicle production capabilities the company is focused on growth in other markets. China's two plants now account for about 20% of production and construction on a third plant began in 2011. The plant a 50/50 joint venture with Beijing Automotive Industry Holding Co. Ltd. will be the company's largest in China capable of producing 400000 small and mid-size vehicles specifically designed for the Chinese market. (Hyundai's other two plants can make 300000 cars per year each). When the plant opens in 2012 Hyundai will be manufacturing 1 million cars a year in China.

Hyundai also established a second 50/50 joint venture in spring 2011 to begin making commercial trucks and buses in China. Both Hyundai and Sichuan Nanjun Automobile are investing about $275 million each to build Sichuan Hyundai a plant with an annual production capacity of 160000 units (150000 trucks and 10000 buses) starting in 2013. Sichuan Hyundai will make two types of trucks –value models sold under the Nanjun brand and higher-priced models sold under the Hyundai brand. Still the market for commercial vehicles in China is very tight and Hyundai only expects to sell 160000 trucks and buses per year by 2015 for a market share of 3%. A previous joint venture with Baotou Bei Ben Heavy-Duty Truck signed in late 2009 fell through.

To keep pace with markets in Europe Hyundai has manufacturing plants in the Czech Republic Russia and Turkey. The Russian plant opened in early 2011 and can manufacture 150000 Solaris sedans a model specifically designed to withstand Russia's cold climate. Hyundai exports another 10 models to Russia including the Elantra sedan the Sonata sedan and the Santa Fe SUV. Together the company's plants in the Czech Republic and Turkey produce about 7% of Hyundai's vehicles while all of Europe accounts for about 15% of sales.

The company is also setting up shop in Brazil to target the fast-growing Latin American market. Construction on a $600 million manufacturing plant began in early 2011 with the government providing Hyundai with free land and tax breaks. The plant will first produce a small hatchback specifically designed for the market with a goal of manufacturing 150000 ethanol flex-fuel cars per year. Currently top models for the Brazilian market include the compact i30 the Azera and Sonata sedans and the Veracruz and ix35 SUVs.

Hyundai is a leading brand in India as well trailing domestic players Maruti Suzuki India and Tata Motors. India accounts for more than 15% of the company's total production and is the company's international base for economy vehicles. Its newest compact vehicle for India the Eon launched in October 2011.

HISTORY

Hyundai Motor Company was established in 1967 and it initially began manufacturing cars and light trucks through a technology collaboration with Ford's UK operations. By the early 1970s Hyundai was ready to build cars under its own nameplate. The company debuted the subcompact Hyundai Pony in 1974 at Italy's annual Turin Motor Show.

The Pony was an instant domestic success and soon propelled Hyundai to the top spot among South Korea's carmakers. During the mid-1970s the company began exporting the Pony to El Salvador and Guatemala.

By the 1980s Hyundai was ready to shift into high gear and begin high-volume production in anticipation of penetrating more overseas markets. The company began exporting to Canada in 1983.

Hyundai introduced the Hyundai Excel in 1985. That year the company established its US subsidiary Hyundai Motor America. By 1986 Hyundai was exporting Excels for sale in the US. Sales of the Excel soared the next year so Hyundai decided to build a factory in Bromont Quebec.

But by the time the factory was finished in 1989 consumers were tiring of the aging compact car and the quality problems that came with it. Hyundai closed the plant after just four years of operation.

The company introduced its first sports car the Scoupe in 1990. The following year it developed the first Hyundai-designed engine called the Alpha. Two years later the carmaker unveiled its second-generation proprietary engine the Beta.

By 1998 Hyundai was beginning to feel the pinch of the Asian economic crisis as domestic demand dropped drastically. However the decrease in Korean demand was largely offset by exports. That year Hyundai took a controlling stake in Korean competitor Kia Motors.

In hopes of increasing its share of the Asian automotive market Daimler AG took a 10% stake in Hyundai in 2000 (sold 2004). The deal included the establishment of a joint venture to manufacture commercial vehicles as well as an agreement among Hyundai Daimler and Mitsubishi Motors to develop small cars for the global market.

In 2001 Hyundai decreased its stake in Kia Motors to about 46%.

The following year Daimler announced it would exercise its option to take a 50% stake in Hyundai's heavy truck business.

In 2004 Hyundai CEO Kim Dong-Jin was indicted in South Korea on charges that he violated campaign finance laws and engaged in managerial negligence. The charges stemmed from a general crackdown on campaign finance violations during which more than a dozen members of South Korea's parliament were either indicted or detained. Later in 2004 Kim was convicted of the charges against him and sentenced to a suspended two-year prison term.

To increase its presence in the US Hyundai completed construction of a new manufacturing plant Hyundai Motor Manufacturing Alabama in 2005. The plant's annual production was about 300000 cars.

In 2006 Hyundai's legal woes persisted when two executives were arrested as part of a Korean bribery investigation. The pair were accused of creating a slush fund that was allegedly used to fund a lobbyist who sought favors for Hyundai from the South Korean government. Officials were also investigating whether the slush fund was created at the behest of Hyundai chairman Chung Mong-Koo.

Chung then was indicted and arrested on charges that he embezzled Hyundai company cash to finance bribes for Korean government officials in exchange for corporate favors. After two months of incarceration Chung was released from jail on $1 million bail.

He was convicted early in 2007. Under Korean law Chung faced a potential life sentence but received only a three-year prison term as the judge in the case said Chung contributed hugely to the development of the Korean economy. During his trial Chung admitted some wrongdoing when he said "I admit to my guilt to some extent." However

Chung appealed the conviction. Three other Hyundai officials were also convicted but they received suspended sentences. Chung's son Kia Motors boss Chung Eui-Sun also was under investigation but prosecutors did not indict him.

Later in 2007 Chung's three-year prison sentence was suspended by an appeals court with a three-judge panel citing his importance to Korea's economy. The appellate judges however required the Hyundai executive to maintain a clean record for five years to avoid prison and to fulfill a promise he made to donate $1.1 billion of his personal assets to society.

EXECUTIVES

Chairman, Chung Mong-Koo, age 64
Vice Chairman, Chung Eui-Sun, age 42
President CEO and Director, Kim Eok-Jo
Vice Chairman, Chung Eui-Sun, age 42
Director, Kwang-Nyun Kim
Director, Il-Hyung Kang
Director, Young-chul Yim
Director, Sung-Il Nam
Director, Young-Rok Lim
President CEO and Director, Kim Eok-Jo
Auditors: DeloitteAnjinLLC

LOCATIONS

HQ: Hyundai Motor Co., Ltd.
231 Yangjae-dong,Seocho-gu, Seoul 137-938
Phone: (82) 2 3464 1114 **Fax:** (82) 2 3463 3484
Web: www.hyundai-motor.com

2010 Sales

	% of total
South	49
North	22
Rest of	15
Europe	14
Total	**100**

PRODUCTS/OPERATIONS

2010 Sales

	% of total
Automotive	95
Financial	5
Total	**100**

Selected Models

Commercial vehicles
- Aero (large city bus)
- Aero Town (medium bus)
- County (small bus)
- e-Mighty (light commercial truck)
- Super Aero City (bus)
- Universe (large coach bus)

Passenger cars
- Accent (compact coupe)
- Atos Prime (subcompact)
- Avante XD
- Azera (sedan)
- Elantra (sedan)
- Entourage (minivan)
- Equus/Centennial (premium sedan)
- Genesis (premium coupe)
- Getz (compact sedan)
- Santa Fe (SUV)
- Sonata (sedan)
- Tiburon (coupe)
- Tucson (SUV)
- Trajet (SUV)
- Veracruz (SUV)

COMPETITORS

BYD
Chery Automobile
Chrysler
Daihatsu
Daimler
Dongfeng Motor
Honda
Isuzu
Maruti Suzuki
Mazda
Nissan
Peugeot
Fiat
Ford Motor
GM Korea
General Motors
Hindustan Motors
Renault
Ssangyong Motor
Tata Motors
Toyota
Volkswagen

HISTORICAL FINANCIALS

Company Type: Public

Income Statement

FYE: December 31

	REVENUE ($ mil.)	NET INCOME ($ mil.)	NET PROFIT MARGIN	EMPLOYEES
12/12	79,113	8,018	10.1%	59,831
12/11	67,142	6,607	9.8%	57,105
12/10	59,740	4,964	8.3%	56,137
12/09	79,048	2,569	3.3%	55,984
12/08	62,819	675	1.1%	56,020
Annual Growth	5.9%	85.6%	—	1.7%

2012 Year-End Financials

Debt ratio: 0.0%
Return on equity: 21.0%
Cash ($ mil.): 6,330
Current ratio: 1.67
Long-term debt ($ mil.): 28,578
No. of shares (mil.): 209
Dividends
Yield: —
Payout: —
Market value ($ mil.): 6,309

	STOCK PRICE ($) FY Close	P/E High	P/E Low	PER SHARE ($) Earnings	Dividends	Book Value
12/12	30.15	—	—	29.52	0.00	197.10
12/11	25.25	—	—	24.34	0.00	153.06
12/10	27.69	—	—	18.30	0.00	(0.00)
12/09	17.00	—	—	9.46	0.00	89.55
12/08	6.68	—	—	1.97	0.00	71.80
Annual Growth	45.7%	—	—	96.8%	—	28.7%

Iberdrola SA

Once just a force in Spain IBERDROLA has established itself as a major global player in the power industry over the past few years. In 2012 it was serving 31 million customers in Europe and the Americas and it owned hydroelectric fossil-fueled nuclear and renewable power generation facilities with a capacity of about 46590 MW (56% of which was derived from hydrolectric or other green energy sources). It also has gas distribution operations in Spain. The company is putting a major focus on being the world leader in developing renewable energy plants primarily wind power facilities and had some 13000 MW of installed capacity in 2011 and a project pipeline of more than 62610 MW.

IBERDROLA owns hydroelectric fossil-fueled nuclear and renewable power generation facilities. It also has gas distribution operations in Spain.

In 2012 the company's installed electric generating capacity included 25700 MW in Spain 7250 MW in the UK 6380 MW in the US and 5880 MW in Latin America.

In 2011 IBERDROLA reported a 4% rise in revenues (in Euros). A weakening of regional economies led to 3% lower power demand in Spain and the UK. US demand stayed flat while Brazil reported a 3% rise in power use. However higher power pricing enabled the company to produce a gain in revenues. Net profits fell by 2% (in Euros) due to higher operating and fuel costs and higher taxation. In a move to improve its financial condition in 2011 the company took its IBERDROLA RENOVABLES subsidiary private (citing that unit's underperformance on the stock market since its was spun off in 2007 and assimilated it).

The company's long term strategy is to focus on the development on its portfolio of clean energy plants and to upgrade its network of transmission and distribution grids to more efficiently harness the new power coming online. It is also focusing on strengthening its presence in Brazil Mexico the US and the UK. With Spain's economy in a serious slump the company needs growth markets in North and South America to sustain its financial performance.

Growing its green energy portfolio in 2011 it acquired 20% of US-based Westec Environmental Solutions which develops carbon dioxide capture and storage technologies. As part of its renewable energy push that year the company announced plans to invest about $2.6 billion in its first offshore wind farm located off the west coast of England. The wind farm (with about 390 MW capacity) is scheduled to come online in 2014.

A possible merger between IBERDROLA and German power player RWE fell through in 2011 due to market and political concerns (resistance to the reduction of competition in the EU market).

In 2010 IBERDROLA secured a contract with partner Vattenfall to build one of the world's largest marine wind farms in the world (in offshore UK) with a capacity of 7200 MW capable of supplying clean energy to 5 million homes. Further boosting in presence in the UK in 2010 the company formed NuGeneration a nuclear joint venture (with GDF SUEZ and Scottish and Southern Energy) which aims to develop up to 3600 MW of nuclear power. (In late 2011 SSE withdrew from the joint ventures as it returned to its renewable energy strategy). In 2012 NuGeneration applied for a license to generate power in the UK.

HISTORY

The 1992 merger of two private utilities –Hidroelectrica Espa?ola (Hidrola) and Hidroelectrica Iberia Iberduero —created IBERDROLA. Iberduero's forebear Hidroelectrica Iberica was born in 1901 in Spain's industrialized north; its first power plant began operations in 1904.

In 1918 Saltos del Duero began producing hydroelectric power along the Duero River. The two companies merged to become Iberduero in 1944 five years after the reign of Gen. Francisco Franco began. Neither Iberduero nor Hidrola (founded in 1907 to electrify Madrid and Valencia) grew much during Spain's isolationist years.

Hoping to make friends the US pumped money into Spain in the 1950s. As industrial production picked up both Hidrola and Iberduero completed construction on several large power plants between 1957 and 1969.

Dependent on imported oil Spain was shaken by the 1970s oil crisis. In 1975 a few months before Franco died the government began to promote nuclear energy. Both firms invested heavily in nukes but by 1984 overcapacity high building costs and inflation led the government to freeze nuclear construction. Hidrola Iberduero and other private utilities were left deeply in debt.

In the late 1980s the government arranged nuclear and hydro asset swaps to spread the debt around. Ultimately more power was shifted to the state utility Endesa. In 1992 with Endesa gobbling up smaller utilities and European deregulation in the wings Iberduero and Hidrola merged in self-defense. The result was IBERDROLA Spain's largest privately owned utility and Endesa's only real competition. IBERDROLA and Endesa stayed at odds particularly over stranded costs from the stalled nuclear program and the government's mandate that the private utilities buy Endesa's energy to repay Endesa for taking over their power plants. Finally in 1996 the government agreed to issue bonds to cover most of the debt.

IBERDROLA began piling up Latin American interests in 1992 by buying stakes in Argentina's Gas Litoral and the Guemes power plant. It soon grabbed holdings in Bolivian electricity distributors Electropaz and Elfeo (1995) two Chilean utilities (1996) gas and electric companies in Brazil and a gas company in Colombia (1997).

To create a more horizontal business structure in 1995 IBERDROLA created Iberinco an engineering firm and Iberener to manage Latin American energy holdings. It formed telecom joint venture Utilitel with Telefonica in 1997 and founded data management firm Iberdrola Sistemas in 1998.

IBERDROLA agreed to cooperate with oil company Repsol on developing energy projects in 1997 a year before Spain's deregulation began. With Electricidade de Portugal and the US's TECO Energy it acquired Guatemala's Empresa Electrica in 1998 and with Telefonica bought interests in Brazilian wireless phone companies.

In 1999 IBERDROLA took over US company Energy Works (which managed electricity buys for industrial customers) allied with German giant RWE to compete throughout Europe and made plans to exit the Utilitel venture.

IBERDROLA bought Brazilian electric distributor CELPE for $1 billion in 2000. Later that year the company itself agreed to be acquired by rival Endesa for $12.9 billion but the deal was abandoned in 2001. Also in 2001 IBERDROLA sold its Latin American telecommunications interests to Telefonica.

In 2002 the company sold controlling stakes in its Spanish water utilities (Pridesa and Ondagua) to RWE's Thames Water unit for $96 million. IBERDROLA also sold its power transmission assets to Infraestructuras de Alta Tension (INALTA) which is owned by CVC Capital Partners (75%) and Red Electrica de Espa?a (25%).

IBERDROLA expanded in Latin America to include electric generation and distribution companies in Brazil Bolivia Chile Guatemala and Mexico.

The company sold off noncore assets including some domestic water utility and real estate assets its Latin American gas businesses and two Chilean hydroelectric plants. Spanish construction giant ACS acquired 10% of IBERDROLA in 2006 for $2.7 billion. That year the company acquired two UK-based wind power projects with a combined power capacity of more than 20MW its first such acquisition in the UK.

IBERDROLA became a major global force in 2007 with the friendly takeover of Scottish Power for $22.5 billion. Scottish Power was the third-largest electricity distributor and largest wind power producer in the UK. In 2008in a major move into the US power market IBERDROLA acquired Energy East (now Iberdrola USA) for $4.5 billion. Iberdrola USA distributes and markets power and natural gas to Connecticut Maine Massachusetts New Hampshire and New York.

EXECUTIVES

CFO, Jose Sainz Armada
Director Development, Pedro Azagra Blazquez
Chief Executive Officer of Iberdrola Ingenier?a, Alberto Sicre
Head Renewables, Xabier Viteri
Head Non Energy Business, Pedro Velasco
Director Iberia and Latin America, Jose Luis San Pedro
Board Member, Braulio Medel Camara, age 65
Board Member, Jose I. Berroeta Echevarria, age 73
Board Member, Julio de Miguel Aynat, age 70
Board Member, Sebastian Battaner Arias, age 73
Board Member, Xabier de Irala Estevez, age 66
Board Member, I?igo V. de Oriol Ibarra, age 50
Board Member, Ines Macho Stadler, age 53
Vice Chairman, Victor de Urrutia Vallejo, age 70
Board Member, Ricardo Alvarez Isasi, age 73
Board Member, Jose Luis Olivas Martinez, age 62
Board Member, Samantha Barber, age 43
Board Member, Santiago Martinez-Lage, age 68
Board Member, Maria Helena Antolin Raybaud, age 46
Auditors: Ernst&YoungS.L.

LOCATIONS

HQ: Iberdrola SA
Tomas Redondo, 1, Madrid 28033
Phone: (34) 91 784 2742 **Fax:** (34) 91 784 2977
Web: www.iberdrola.es

2011 Sales

	% of total
Europe	
Spain	48
UK	27
Other	1
South	14
US	10
Total	**100**

PRODUCTS/OPERATIONS

2011 Sales

	% of total
Deregulated	67
Network	16
Renewables	5
Other	12
Total	**100**

COMPETITORS

AES
CEPSA
Cemig
Constellation Energy Group
E.ON UK
ELETROBRAS
Edison
Electricite de France
EnBW
Endesa S.A.
Enel
Energias de Portugal
Enersis
Ezentis
Gas Natural SDG
HC Energia
International Power
Navitas Energy
PPL Corporation
Plambeck Neue Energien
Red Electrica de Espa?a
Sempra Energy
Tractebel Engineering

HISTORICAL FINANCIALS

Company Type: Public

Income Statement FYE: December 31

	REVENUE ($ mil.)	NET INCOME ($ mil.)	NET PROFIT MARGIN	EMPLOYEES
12/12	45,078	3,744	8.3%	31,338
12/11	40,935	3,627	8.9%	31,885
12/10	40,728	3,842	9.4%	31,344
12/09	35,378	4,068	11.5%	32,711
12/08	35,226	3,999	11.4%	28,096
Annual Growth	6.4%	(1.6%)	—	2.8%

2012 Year-End Financials

Debt ratio: 46.2%
Return on equity: 8.5%
Cash ($ mil.): 4,012
Current ratio: 1.13
Long-term debt ($ mil.): 38,027
No. of shares (mil.): —
Dividends
Yield: 4.6%
Payout: —
Market value ($ mil.): —

	STOCK PRICE ($) FY Close	P/E High/Low	PER SHARE ($) Earnings	Dividends	Book Value
12/12	21.32	96 45	0.60	0.99	7.25
12/11	24.10	148 81	0.62	0.00	7.23
12/10	30.65	143 70	0.71	2.26	7.10
12/09	37.85	154 72	0.80	1.48	7.31
12/08	36.00	248 75	0.82	1.42	6.53
Annual Growth	(12.3%)	— —	(7.2%)	(8.6%)	2.6%

ICICI Bank Ltd (India)

You see ICICI Bank is India's #2 bank (after State Bank of India) and its largest private bank with some Rs. 6 trillion in assets. The bank has some 2700 branches nationwide; it also has locations in about 20 other countries. The retail banking group offers lending and deposit services to small businesses and individuals; larger businesses are served by the corporate banking group which offers finance services and treasury products. The rural and government banking unit offers microloans and agricultural banking. Foreign operations as well as services related to international trade finance and expatriate Indians fall under international banking. The bank also offers life and property/casualty insurance.

Key subsidiaries include ICICI Prudential Life Insurance (the largest private sector life insurer in the country) ICICI Lombard General Insurance (property/casualty coverage) ICICI Prudential Asset Management (mutual funds) ICICI Securities (investment banking and brokerage) and ICICI Venture Funds Management (venture capital).

Consumer loans including mortgages auto loans credit card receivables and commercial business loans account for more than half of the bank's lending portfolio. The company also offers commercial and agricultural loans and leasing. It extends credit to small business and entrepreneurs especially rural residents requiring micro-financing.

Although it has seen a rise in nonperforming loans ICICI Bank remained relatively unscathed from the global financial crisis. At the height of the crisis the company focused on cutting costs and tightening its lending practices. Since then it has again worked on building up its loan portfolio especially with such assets as mortgages project finance and secured retail loans. The growth has helped stimulate the company's earnings: In 2012 the bank's revenues grew 8% and net income grew 26% largely due a 21% increase in net interest income and a 45% decrease in loan loss provisions. However noninterest income fell 9% as insurance and brokerage earnings dipped.

Founded by the World Bank as a development financial institution in the 1950s ICICI has since become a full-fledged financial services company offering a range of products and services. Its insurance business which recently turned its first profit has helped ICICI as it broadens its revenue streams. The company's growth strategy includes seeking ways to enhance its retail and corporate banking operations while strengthening its insurance securities and asset management units. ICICI is also a leader in technology innovation: It was India's first bank to offer mobile banking services and it plans to continue driving the growth of that offering.

The bank also has large cash reserves and knows how to use them: It plans on making strategic international investments over the next few years but will focus largely on its domestic banking and related operations. In particular retail lending including credit cards and secured loans are a key to ICICI's long-term growth. In 2010 the company acquired Bank of Rajasthan expanding its retail network by about 500 branches.

Deutsche Bank Trust owns 27% of ICICI Bank.

EXECUTIVES

Chairman, Kundapur V. (K. V.) Kamath, age 66, $394,454 total compensation
Deputy Managing Director Rural Banking Government Banking and Global Markets and Director, Nachiket Mor, age 51, $258,600 total compensation
Chief Financial Officer; Wholetime Director, N. S. Kannan, age 48, $72,340 total compensation
Executive Director and Chief Human Resources Officer, Krishnaswamy Ramkumar, age 52, $233,443 total compensation
CTO and Director, Pravir Vohra, age 60, $234,686 total compensation
Group Executive Wholesale Banking, Zarin Daruwala
Group Compliance Officer; Company Secretary; Senior General Manager, Sandeep Batra, age 48, $38,700 total compensation
Joint General Manager, Rajiv Arora, age 47, $76,675 total compensation
Head of Cards Product Group, Sachin Khandelwa
Head of Corporate Communications, Charudatta Deshpande
Investor Relations, Rupesh Kumar
Executive Director, Rajiv Sabharwal
President, Vijay Chandok
Investor Relations Officer, Rakesh Mookim
Director, Lakshmi N. Mittal, age 62
Director, M. S. Ramachandran, age 68
Executive Director and Chief Human Resources Officer, Krishnaswamy Ramkumar, age 52
Director, Prof Marti G. Subrahmanyam, age 65
Director, Sridar A. Iyengar, age 66
CTO and Director, Pravir Vohra, age 60
Director, V. Sridar
Director, Homi R. Khusrokhan
Director, Mahendra Kumar Sharma, age 66
Director, T. S. Vijayan, age 59
Managing Director and CEO ICICI Life and Board Member, Sandeep Bakhshi, age 52
Director, Anup K. Pujari, age 67
Director, Prof Marti Gurunath, age 66
Independent Director, Swati Piramal
Independent Director, Tushaar Shah
Auditors: KPMGLLP

LOCATIONS

HQ: ICICI Bank Ltd (India)
ICICI Towers, Bandra-Kurla Complex, Mumbai 400 051
Phone: (91) 22 2653 1414 **Fax:** (91) 22 2653 1122
Web: www.icicibank.com

PRODUCTS/OPERATIONS

2012 Sales by Segment

	% of total
Treasury	29
Wholesale	25
Retail	19
Life	17
General	4
Venture Fund	-
Other	3
Other	3
Total	**100**

2012 Sales

	% of total
Interest	
Advances & Investments	37
Investments	17
Other	3
Noninterest	
Premium & other insurance	31
Commissions exchange &	9
Other	3
Total	**100**

COMPETITORS

BNP Paribas
Bank of Baroda
Bank of India
Canara Bank
Citigroup
GE Money India
HSBC
ING
Industrial Development Bank of India
Punjab National Bank
Standard Chartered
State Bank of India
UCO Bank

HISTORICAL FINANCIALS

Company Type: Public

Income Statement FYE: March 31

	ASSETS ($ mil.)	NET INCOME ($ mil.)	INCOME AS % OF ASSETS	EMPLOYEES
03/13	124,309	1,769	1.4%	62,065
03/12	118,759	1,502	1.3%	58,276
03/11	119,719	1,366	1.1%	79,978
03/10	108,994	1,040	1.0%	74,056
03/09	94,876	703	0.7%	73,362
Annual Growth	7.0%	25.9%	—	(4.1%)

2013 Year-End Financials

Return on assets: 1.5%
Return on equity: 14.7%
Long-term debt ($ mil.): —
No. of shares (mil.): 1,153
Sales ($ mil): 13,572
Dividends
Yield: —
Payout: —
Market value ($ mil.): 49,493

	STOCK PRICE ($) FY Close	P/E High/Low	PER SHARE ($) Earnings	Dividends	Book Value
03/13	42.90	— —	1.53	0.00	10.98
03/12	34.87	— —	1.30	0.00	10.45
03/11	49.83	— —	1.19	0.52	10.77
03/10	42.70	— —	0.93	0.97	10.25
03/09	13.29	— —	0.63	0.52	8.32
Annual Growth	34.0%	— —	24.7%	—	7.2%

Idemitsu Kosan Co Ltd

As long as Japanese drive Toyotas there will be a role for Idemitsu Kosan. The company is the #2 oil refiner in Japan (behind Nippon Oil). At its four refineries in Japan (processing 640000 barrels per day) Idemitsu Kosan produces petroleum products such as gasoline and other fuels kerosene and lubricants. It markets its fuel products through a network of 4600 service stations. Idemitsu Kosan sells heavy oil and jet fuels to industries and kerosene and liquefied petroleum gas (LPG) to the residential sector. The company also has interests in oil exploration and production as well as coal and uranium.

Operations

Idemitsu Kosan has three reportable segments: Its petroleum products business includes fuel oil and petrochemical products. Its petrochemical products operations consist of the basic chemicals business which jointly operates an ethylene complex with Mitsui Chemicals and the functional materials business which develops functional flexible polypropylene. The company's resources businesses is engaged in exploration activities to expand its oil reserves.

In addition to its oil and gas businesses the company has a number of New Growth activities including agro-business (pesticides) and green energy (wind solar and geothermal). Idemitsu Kosan is also developing electronic materials (organic light-emitting diode luminous materials with Sony Corporation) and lithium battery development.

Geographic Reach

Idemitsu Kosan has offices in Africa Asia (East South East and South West) Australia Europe (including Russia) the Middle East and North and South America.

Financial Performance

In 2012 the company's revenues increased by 18% due to increases in the prices of crude oil and naphtha significant rises in coal prices and an increase in the volume of products sold. Japan accounted for 84% of the company's revenues that year.

Net income increased by 6% in 2012 thanks to higher revenues and the result of progress in streamlining activities in production sales and distribution as well as improved product margins for petrochemical products despite a contraction of margins for petroleum products.

Business Strategy

To meet increased demand Idemitsu Kosan is enhancing its petroleum products business in the growing overseas markets centered on the Pacific Rim. As part of this process in 2012 it acquired Freedom an independent Australian petroleum products distributor that sells petroleum products wholesale and operates about 40 gas stations on Australia's east coast.

That year it also opened an office in China formed a joint venture in Taiwan and set up a lubricant manufacturing and sales company in Vietnam.

Idemitsu Kosan unified its ethylene production with Mitsui Chemicals in 2010 to promote efficiency.

Company Background

Pooling their LPG resources and expertise in 2006 Idemitsu Kosan merged its LPG operations with those of Mitsubishi to form Astomos Energy.

EXECUTIVES

Chairman, Akihiko Tembo
EVP, Kenichi Matsui
President, Kazuhisa Nakano, age 65
Managing Director, Seiji Fukunaga
Managing Director, Akiro Nishiyori
Managing Director, Junjiro Kuramochi
EVP, Takashi Tsukioka
Managing Director, Yasunori Maeda
Managing Director, Osamu Kamimae
EVP, Yoshihisa Matsumoto
Managing Executive Officer, Kiyotsugu Suita
Executive Officer, Yasuo Kushihashi
Executive Officer, Hiroaki Muko
Executive Officer, Daisuke Seki
Executive Officer, Hiroshi Seki
Executive Officer, Kiyonobu Kobayashi
Executive Officer, Sakugoro Matsuda
Executive Officer, Yasuhiro Haba
Executive Officer, Ryuhei Masumoto
Executive Officer, Shigeki Nakajima
Managing Director, Kenichi Matsui
President and Director, Kazuhisa Nakano, age 65
EVP and Director, Shuichi Omiya
Managing Director, Takahisa Hiruma
Managing Director, Yoshinori Kawamoto
Managing Director, Zenichi Suda
Managing Director, Seiji Fukunaga
Managing Director, Akiro Nishiyori
Director, Mitsuru Soneda
Director, Junjiro Kuramochi

Director, Takashi Tsukioka
Director, Yasunori Maeda
Director; President Idemitsu Snorre Oil Development, Osamu Kamimae
Auditors: DeloitteToucheTohmatsuLLC

LOCATIONS

HQ: Idemitsu Kosan Co Ltd
3-1-1 Marunouchi, Chiyoda-ku, Tokyo 100-8321
Phone: (81) 3 3213 3150
Web: www.idemitsu.co.jp

2012 Sales

	% of total
Japan	84
Asia &	8
North	5
Europe	2
Other	1
Total	**100**

PRODUCTS/OPERATIONS

2012 Sales

	% of total
Petroleum	83
Petrochemical	12
Resources	4
Other	1
Adjustments	-
Total	**100**

Selected Subsidiaries

Apollo Service Co. Ltd.
Idemitsu Apollo Corp. (US)
Idemitsu Engineering Co. Ltd.
Idemitsu International (Asia) Pte. Ltd. (Singapore)
Idemitsu International (Europe) PLC (UK)
Idemitsu Oil & Gas Co. Ltd.
Idemitsu Oil Development Co Ltd.
Idemitsu Oita Chinetsu Co. Ltd.
Idemitsu Petrochemical Co. Ltd.
IS Electrode Materials Co. Ltd.
Munakata Shipping Co. Ltd.

COMPETITORS

Cosmo Oil
JX Holdings
JX Nippon Mining & Metals
JX Nippon Oil & Energy
SK Innovation
Showa Shell Sekiyu

HISTORICAL FINANCIALS

Company Type: Public

Income Statement

FYE: March 31

	REVENUE ($ mil.)	NET INCOME ($ mil.)	NET PROFIT MARGIN	EMPLOYEES
03/13	46,493	533	1.1%	8,684
03/12	52,545	784	1.5%	8,243
03/11	44,190	732	1.7%	8,201
03/10	33,319	63	0.2%	8,330
03/09	38,573	33	0.1%	7,826
Annual Growth	4.8%	99.4%	—	2.6%

2013 Year-End Financials

Debt ratio: 0.3%
Return on equity: 8.0%
Cash ($ mil.): 1,241
Current ratio: 1.11
Long-term debt ($ mil.): 5,461
No. of shares (mil.): 79
Dividends
Yield: —
Payout: —
Market value ($ mil.): —

	STOCK PRICE ($) FY Close	P/E High/Low	PER SHARE ($) Earnings	Dividends	Book Value
03/13	0.00	— —	6.67	0.00	91.42
03/12	73.25	— —	9.81	0.00	93.66
03/11	73.25	— —	9.16	0.00	81.67
Annual Growth	—	— —	(7.6%)	—	2.9%

Imperial Oil Ltd.

Imperial Oil Canada's second-largest oil integrated company behind Suncor Energy holds sway over a vast empire of oil and gas resources. Imperial is one of Canada's top natural gas producers a leading refiner and marketer of petroleum products and a major supplier of petrochemicals. It sells petroleum products including gasoline heating oil and diesel fuel under the Esso name and other brand names. In 2010 it reported proved reserves of 57 million barrels of oil 1.7 billion barrels of bitumen 681 million barrels of synthetic oil and 576 billion cu. ft. of natural gas. Most of the company's production comes from fields in Alberta and the Northwest Territories. Exxon Mobil owns about 70% of Imperial.

The company sells gasoline to motorists at 1850 Esso gas stations (510 company-owned or leased) across Canada.

Imperial's petroleum products and chemicals business operates four refineries (with a collective capacity to process 500000 gallons a day) and has an extensive network of wholesale outlets (in addition to its gas station chain) in every region of Canada. The company's chemicals segment operates a manufacturing plant in Sarnia Ontario and a number of distribution centers across Canada.

In addition to its conventional oil operations Imperial owns 25% of Syncrude Canada which operates the world's largest oil sands development with synthetic oil and bitumen/heavy oil end products.

At Cold Lake Alberta the company uses steam to recover very heavy crude and related products from oil sands deposits (115000 net barrels per day in 2010). Management is seeking to boost production from its plentiful oil sands holdings; its research laboratories in Ontario and Alberta are focused on developing technology for finding better ways to recover heavy oil.

In 2009 the company reported depressed earnings an effect of the global recession that reduced oil and gas prices and demand. A recovering economy higher commodity prices and increased demand for oil and gas products helped to lift Imperial's revenues and net income in 2010.

HISTORY

London Ontario boomed from the discovery of oil in the 1860s and 1870s but when the market for Canadian kerosene became saturated in 1880 16 refiners banded together to form the Imperial Oil Company.

The company refined sulfurous Canadian oil nicknamed "skunk oil" for its powerful smell. Imperial faced tough competition from America's Standard Oil which marketed kerosene made from lighter less-odorous Pennsylvania crude. Guided by American expatriate Jacob Englehart Imperial built a better refinery and hired a chemist to develop a process to clean sulfur from the crude.

By the mid-1890s Imperial had expanded from coast to Canadian coast. Cash-starved from its expansion the company turned to old nemesis Standard Oil which bought a controlling interest in Imperial in 1898. That interest is today held by Exxon Mobil.

After the turn of the century Imperial began producing gasoline to serve the new automobiles. The horseless carriages were spooking the workhorses at the warehouse where fuel was sold so an Imperial manager in Vancouver opened the first Canadian service station in 1907. The company marketed its gas under the Esso banner borrowed from Standard Oil.

An Imperial crew discovered oil in 1920 at Norman Wells in the remote Northwest Territories. In 1924 a subsidiary sparked a new boom with a gas well discovery in the Turner Valley area northeast of Edmonton. But soon Imperial's luck ran as dry as the holes it was drilling; it came away empty from the next 133 consecutive wells. That string ended in 1947 when it struck oil in Alberta at the Leduc No. 1. To get the oil to market Imperial invested in the Interprovincial Pipe Line from Alberta to Superior Wisconsin.

The company began research in 1964 to extract bitumen from the oil sands in Cold Lake Alberta. During the 1970s oil crisis Imperial continued to search for oil in northern Canada. It found crude on land near the Beaufort Sea (1970) and in its icy waters (1972). The company formed its Esso Resources Canadian Ltd. subsidiary in 1978 to oversee natural resources production.

In 1989 Texaco (acquired by Chevron in 2001) still reeling from a court battle with Pennzoil sold Texaco Canada to Imperial. To diminish debt and comply with regulators Imperial agreed to sell some of Texaco Canada's refining and marketing assets in Atlantic Canada its interests in Interhome Energy and oil and gas properties in western Canada.

Imperial reorganized in 1992 centralizing several units and in 1993 closed its refinery at Port Moody British Columbia. It sold most of its fertilizer business in 1994 disposed of 339 unprofitable gas stations in 1995 and the next year closed down Canada's northernmost oil refinery at Norman Wells.

In 1997 Imperial announced an ambitious program to expand Syncrude's oil sands bitumen upgrading plant. In 1998 Exxon agreed to buy Mobil which had substantial Canadian oil assets. In 1999 Canada preapproved the potential merger of Imperial Oil and Mobil Canada. Later that year Exxon completed its purchase of Mobil to form Exxon Mobil.

Expanding its exploration and production assets in 2007 Imperial and ExxonMobil Canada acquired exploration rights for a development parcel in the Beaufort Sea and in 2008 in the Horn River area of northeastern British Columbia.

EXECUTIVES

Vice President; General Counsel; Corporate Secretary, Brian W. Livingston, $349,191 total compensation
Chairman President and CEO, R. M. (Rich) Kruger
Chairman President Chief Executive Officer, Bruce H. March, age 56, $392,299 total compensation
Controller, Sean R. Carleton
Director Corporate Planning, George E. Bezaire
VP; General Manager Fuels Marketing, Simon M. Smith, $334,880 total compensation
Investor Relations, Mark Stumpf
Senior Vice President - Finance and Administration; Controller, Paul J. Masschelin, age 58
Senior Vice President - Resources, T. G. (Glenn) Scott
Vice President and General Manager - Refining and Supply, Gilles Courtemanche
Treasurer, Phil Dranse
Director, Roger Phillips, age 73
Director, Sheelagh D. Whittaker, age 66
Director, Krystyna T. Hoeg, age 63
Director, Victor L. Young, age 68
Director, J. M. (Jack) Mintz, age 62
Chairman President Chief Executive Officer, Bruce H. March, age 56
Director, Robert C. Olsen, age 63
Independent Director, David Sutherland
Auditors: PricewaterhouseCoopersLLP

LOCATIONS

HQ: Imperial Oil Ltd.
237 Fourth Avenue S.W., Calgary, Alberta T2P 3M9
Phone: 416 968-8145 **Fax:** 416 968-5345
Web: www.imperialoil.ca

PRODUCTS/OPERATIONS

2010 Sales

	% of total
Refining &	78
Exploration &	17
Chemicals	4
Total	**100**

COMPETITORS

Abraxas Petroleum
Ashland Inc.
BHP Billiton
BP
Barnwell Industries
Canadian Natural
ConocoPhillips
Devon Energy
Dominion Resources
DuPont
Encana
Eni
Hunting
Husky Energy
Koch Industries Inc.
Marathon Oil
Murphy Oil
Occidental Petroleum
PEMEX
PETROBRAS
Petroleos de Venezuela
Pioneer Natural Resources
Royal Dutch Shell
Suncor
Sunoco
TOTAL
Talisman Energy

HISTORICAL FINANCIALS

Company Type: Public

Income Statement

FYE: December 31

	REVENUE ($ mil.)	NET INCOME ($ mil.)	NET PROFIT MARGIN	EMPLOYEES
12/12	31,358	3,786	12.1%	5,100
12/11	30,108	3,304	11.0%	5,085
12/10	25,145	2,214	8.8%	4,970
12/09	20,410	1,506	7.4%	5,015
12/08	25,730	3,159	12.3%	4,850
Annual Growth	5.1%	4.6%	—	1.3%

2012 Year-End Financials

Debt ratio: 4.0%
Return on equity: 25.2%
Cash ($ mil.): 484
Current ratio: 0.69
Long-term debt ($ mil.): 1,181
No. of shares (mil.): 847
Dividends
Yield: 1.1%
Payout: 10.8%
Market value ($ mil.): 36,447

	STOCK PRICE ($) FY Close	P/E High	P/E Low	PER SHARE ($) Earnings	Dividends	Book Value
12/12	43.00	11	8	4.44	0.48	19.43
12/11	44.48	14	8	3.87	0.43	15.41
12/10	40.52	17	13	2.60	0.41	13.21
12/09	38.66	21	12	1.76	0.38	10.62
12/08	33.72	12	4	3.55	0.31	8.59
Annual Growth	6.3%	—	—	5.8%	11.6%	22.6%

Imperial Tobacco Group Plc

The UK's #1 cigarette maker Imperial Tobacco Group eyes an even larger throne. The group has lavished billions on brand-building acquisitions — including Spain's Altadis (2008) Commonwealth Brands in the US (2007) and Germany's Reemtsma (Davidoff and West cigarettes 2002) — to extend its reign across Europe Africa the Middle East and Asia/Pacific region and North America. In addition to Davidoff major brands include Gauloises JPS Rizla Montecristo cigars and Skruf snus. Imperial Tobacco operates some 50 cigarette and tobacco product and processing plants worldwide as well as a logistics business. Products are sold in 160-plus countries; emerging markets account for 60% of cigarettes sold.

An expanding global reach helped the group post a slight uptick in net tobacco revenue in 2011 over 2010 albeit less than previous years. It managed nonetheless a rough 125% bounce in earnings over the prior year thanks to significantly lower finance costs among various factors. Sales in emerging markets on top of demand for fine-cut tobacco and Habanos cigars and price hikes also fueled momentum amid a decline in smoking in the group's mature markets. In Spain Imperial Tobacco holds more than a quarter of the market but a ban on smoking in public places and a rise in taxes on already cash-strapped Spaniards hurt sales. Market sales further deteriorated when rival British American Tobacco (BAT) slashed prices sparking a price war. In England a ban on tobacco sales from vending machines threatens to reduce cigarette purchases. (The move was unsuccessfully challenged by Sinclair Collis Imperial Tobacco's vending machine subsidiary.)

Known largely for its premium brands (Davidoff West and Gauloise) Imperial Tobacco's strategy includes diversifying its portfolio in order to boost revenues through sales of lower-priced tobacco products in mature markets. (In a troubled economy Imperial Tobacco saw an improving trend as more smokers traded down in order to maintain their habit.) The group controls almost half of the shrinking UK cigarette market which accounts for 10% of the tobacco giant's sales volumes.

Concurrently Imperial Tobacco is rolling out regional and local luxury tobacco brands with some success in emerging markets particularly the Asia/Pacific region but also Eastern Europe Africa and the Middle East. In China Imperial Tobacco has signed a 10-year pact to produce and sell cigarettes. Snus brands Skruf and Knox hold more than 5 % of total snus sales volumes in Sweden and Norway.

Size however remains a strategic advantage. The addition of Altadis owner of the world's largest cigar maker to the group's portfolio created the fourth-largest tobacco company worldwide by volume (behind BAT). Imperial Tobacco boasts some of the most popular cigar brands in the US including Romeo y Julieta and Montecristo which have a loyal following despite the recession and their extreme regulation. As part of the deal for Altadis Imperial Tobacco disposed of its fine cut tobacco brand Interval and several other brands to Philip Morris International. Proceeds were used in part to reduce debt a top priority for the group.

Government regulation in the UK and abroad coupled with rising health concerns are spurring the group to broaden its horizons. Like competitors BAT and Gallaher (now owned by Japan Tobacco) Imperial Tobacco is eager to distance itself from litigious tobacco issues. The group opened a smoking balcony at Birmingham Airport in mid-2012 as part of its Smoking Allowed campaign. In a follow-on purchase to Altadis Imperial Tobacco acquired separately listed distribution unit Cia. de Distribucion Integral Logista bolting on a new business segment to support activities. Logista delivers tobacco and other products for international manufacturers to tobacconists and other retail outlets across Southern Europe.

Imperial Tobacco has stayed relevant as well by acquiring Sweden's Skruf snus business (2005) a product positioned toward younger men as less harmful. Since then Imperial Tobacco has gained an impressive share of the smokeless tobacco market.

HISTORY

Imperial Tobacco Group was formed in 1901 to fight American Tobacco's invasion of the UK. American Tobacco had become the dominant US tobacco company partly by using a large cash reserve to undercut competitors. When it bought UK tobacco and cigarette factory Ogden's that year 13 UK tobacco firms responded by registering as The Imperial Tobacco Company. The firms (including Wills Lambert & Butler and John Player & Sons) continued to make and sell their products separately.

As expected American Tobacco cut prices and Imperial fought back acquiring the Salmon & Cluckstein tobacco shop chain and offering bonuses to retailers that sold its products. When Imperial threatened US expansion in 1902 American Tobacco surrendered: It gave Ogden's to Imperial and halted its Ireland and Great Britain business in exchange for Imperial's pledge to stay out of the US (except for buying tobacco leaf). The two formed the British American Tobacco Company (BAT) to sell both firms' cigarettes overseas. But when American Tobacco split into four companies in 1911 and sold its BAT interest the agreement was modified to let Imperial sell some of its brands in the US.

By the 1950s Imperial controlled more than 80% of the UK tobacco market but its share decreased during the 1960s due to competition from Gallaher Group (Benson & Hedges). Imperial diversified buying companies such as Golden Wonder Crisps snack food (1961) and the Courage & Barclay brewery (1972).

In 1973 BAT and Imperial agreed that each firm would control its own brands in the UK and Continental Europe. Imperial sold the last of its stake in BAT in 1980. Conglomerate Hanson Trust paid $4.3 billion for Imperial in a 1986 hostile takeover. Hanson reduced Imperial's tobacco brands from more than 100 to five brand families (a move that decreased its UK market share to 33% by 1990). It also sold Imperial's drinks unit including Courage and John Smith beer to Elders IXL (now Foster's Brewing). Between 1986 and 1993 Hanson cut Imperial's tobacco operations from five factories and 7500 employees to three factories and 2600 employees; it also sold Imperial's restaurant and food operations.

As UK cigarette consumption dropped Imperial began expanding overseas in 1994. By 1996 exports had risen to 15% of sales. That year Gareth Davis became CEO of Imperial.

Facing further declining UK cigarette sales and a government tax hike Imperial bought the world's #1 cigarette paper brand Rizla (1997) and Sara Lee's cut-tobacco unit Douwe Egberts Van Nelle (1998) which it renamed Van Nelle Tabak. That acquisition added Drum hand-rolling tobacco and Amphora pipe tobacco to Imperial's brands. In 1999 the company added a bevy of Australian and New Zealand brands (Horizon Brandon Flagship Peter Stuyvesant) from BAT.

In 2000 Imperial acquired paper maker EFKA (Germany Canada) and tobacco maker Baelen (Belgium). That year Imperial tripled its cigarette vending operations by acquiring Mayfield Vending (27000 UK locations).

Imperial expanded operations in Africa in 2001 with the acquisition of 75% of Tobaccor. It also began distributing the Marlboro brand in the UK.

The company bought 90% of Reemtsma in 2002; the deal at the time was valued at $5.1 billion.

In 2004 Imperial cut 940 jobs as it closed manufacturing plants in Hungary Slovakia and Slovenia. The company shifted production to Germany and Poland. In 2005 Imperial restructured its European production resulting in the closure of its operations in Dublin Ireland and nearly 100 job cuts. In late 2005 Imperial acquired the Swedish snus manufacturer Skruf to get a foothold in the popular niche of the tobacco market) and Norwegian tobacco product distributor Gunnar Stenberg.

In February 2007 Imperial Tobacco acquired the Commonwealth Brands cigarette division of Houchens Industries for $1.9 billion. Commonwealth Brands which makes 14 billion cigarettes each year rang up nearly $350 million in sales in 2006.

In January 2008 the company completed the purchase of Altadis for $18.2 billion. In May it completed the purchase of Altadis's Logista tobacco and tobacco products distribution business. In April Imperial sold its nearly 50% stake in the Aldeasa a duty-free retailer based in Spain to Autogrill Espana for about E355 million ($496 million).

In May 2010 Alison Cooper succeeded the retiring Gareth Davis as CEO of the company.

EXECUTIVES

Finance Director and Director, Robert (Bob) Dyrbus, age 62, $1,098,038 total compensation
Chief Executive and Director, Alison J. Cooper, age 47, $791,831 total compensation
Group Corporate Legal Affairs Director Secretary and Director, Matthew Phillips, age 43
Director Corporate Communications, Alex Parsons
Chairman, Iain J. G. Napier, age 64, $859,614 total compensation
Director Investor Communications, Gerry Gallagher
Company Secretary, John Downing
Director, Michael H. C. Herlihy, age 60
Director, Pierre H. Jungels, age 68
Finance Director and Director, Robert (Bob) Dyrbus, age 62
Director, Susan E. Murray, age 56
Director, Ken Burnett, age 61
Chief Executive and Director, Alison J. Cooper, age 47
Director, Mark Williamson, age 55
Group Corporate Legal Affairs Director Secretary and Director, Matthew Phillips, age 43
Director, Berge Setrakian, age 64
Independent Non-Executive Director, David Haines
Independent Non-Executive Director, Malcolm Wyman
Auditors: PricewaterhouseCoopersLLP

LOCATIONS

HQ: Imperial Tobacco Group Plc
121 Winterstoke Road, Bristol BS3 2LL
Phone: (44) 117 963 6636 **Fax:** (44) 117 933 7430
Web: www.imperial-tobacco.com

2011 Tobacco Sales

	% of total
EU	
Germany	13
UK	12
Spain	8
Other	22
Americas	11
Other	34
Total	**100**

PRODUCTS/OPERATIONS

2011 Sales

	% of total
Tobacco (manufacturing marketing &	88
Logistics (distribution of tobacco & other	12
Total	**100**

2011 Sales (volumes)

	% of total
White stick	50
Cigarettes	44
Fine cut	6
Total	**100**

Selected Products and Brands

Cigarettes
- Balkan Star
- Bonus
- Classic
- Davidoff (global strategic cigarette brand)
- Drum (roll-your-own tobacco)
- Ducados Rubio
- Excellence
- Fine
- Fortuna
- Gauloises Bondes (global strategic cigarette brand)
- Gitanes
- Golden Virginia
- John Player Special (JPS)
- Lambert & Butler (discount brand)
- Marquise
- Maxim
- Paramount
- Richmond (discount brand)
- Rizla (rolling paper)
- Route 66 (American blend sold in France Belgium and Eastern Europe)
- Sonoma
- Style
- USA Gold
- West (global strategic cigarette brand)
- Windsor Blue

Cigars
- Antonio y Cleopatra
- Cadena
- Castella
- Classic
- Cohiba
- Dutch Masters cigarillos
- Farias
- Hav-A-Tampa
- Montecristo
- Phillies cigarillos
- Panama
- Romeo y Julieta

Rolling paper and tobacco
- Amphora
- Drum
- Rizla (rolling paper)
- St Bruno

Snus
- Knox
- Skruf

COMPETITORS

Altria
British American Tobacco
General Cigar
Gudang Garam
JT International
Japan Tobacco
Lorillard
Philip Morris International
Reynolds American
Swedish Match
Swisher International
UST llc

HISTORICAL FINANCIALS

Company Type: Public

Income Statement

FYE: September 30

	REVENUE ($ mil.)	NET INCOME ($ mil.)	NET PROFIT MARGIN	EMPLOYEES
09/13	45,631	1,512	3.3%	35,300
09/12	46,277	1,098	2.4%	37,200
09/11	45,520	2,797	6.1%	38,200
09/10	44,759	2,391	5.3%	38,300
09/09	42,726	1,068	2.5%	38,381
Annual Growth	1.7%	9.1%	—	(2.1%)

2013 Year-End Financials

Debt ratio: 63.2%
Return on equity: 16.1%
Cash ($ mil.): 2,920
Current ratio: 0.76
Long-term debt ($ mil.): 12,684
No. of shares (mil.): 969
Dividends
Yield: 4.5%
Payout: 554.8%
Market value ($ mil.): 71,869

	STOCK PRICE ($) FY Close	P/E High/Low	PER SHARE ($) Earnings	Dividends	Book Value
09/13	74.15	221170	1.55	3.38	9.31
09/12	74.04	323241	1.10	7.78	9.87
09/11	67.10	105 79	2.75	2.86	11.80
09/10	59.40	119 77	2.35	2.35	10.97
09/09	58.99	297145	1.05	1.89	10.36
Annual Growth	5.9%	— —	10.2%	15.6%	(2.6%)

Indian Oil Corp., Ltd. (India)

LOCATIONS

HQ: Indian Oil Corp., Ltd. (India)
3079/3, Sadiq Nagar, J.B. Tito Marg, New Delhi 110 049
Phone: (11) 262 60000 **Fax:** (91) 22 2642 7384
Web: www.iocl.com

HISTORICAL FINANCIALS

Company Type: Public

Income Statement

FYE: March 31

	REVENUE ($ mil.)	NET INCOME ($ mil.)	NET PROFIT MARGIN	EMPLOYEES
03/12	80,378	830	1.0%	34,233
03/11	69,484	1,756	2.5%	34,105
03/10	58,567	2,449	4.2%	34,363
03/09	56,638	470	0.8%	33,998
03/08	58,626	2,129	3.6%	31,945
Annual Growth	8.2%	(21.0%)	—	1.7%

2012 Year-End Financials

Debt ratio: 0.7%
Return on equity: 7.1%
Cash ($ mil.): 161
Current ratio: 0.95
Long-term debt ($ mil.): 3,599
No. of shares (mil.): —
Dividends
Yield: —
Payout: —
Market value ($ mil.): —

Industria De Diseno Textil (Inditex) SA

Industria de Dise?o Textil (Inditex) makes disposable chic fashions that are here today and gone tomorrow. The Spanish designer-cum-retailer uses technology and an armada of designers to master cheap chic. Inditex sells on a global scale with some 4900 shops in about 75 countries under eight different banners: Zara Oysho Massimo Dutti Pull and Bear Bershka Stradivarius Zara Home and Uterque. Located mostly in Europe the firm's stores answer to popular trends by telling designers in Spain what customers are asking for locally. Inditex responds in about two weeks with new designs. Amancio Ortega Gaona Spain's wealthiest businessman founded Zara in 1975 and later created Inditex as a holding company.

Inditex's worldwide presence and low-price selling strategy have served it well during the global recession and the nascent recovery. Sales were up 9% (at constant exchange rates) in fiscal 2010 (ends January) after rising 12% in fiscal 2009 while those of many other retailers fell. Indeed while competitors were closing stores Inditex added about 340 new shops (an 8% increase in selling space) across its varied banners in fiscal 2010. Recent stops on the retailer's world tour included New Delhi and Mumbai India where the company has begun opening Zara stores in partnership with Trent Ltd. (part of India's Tata Group). In 2011 the partnership was extended to set up Massimo Dutti stores there.

Inditex is focusing its expansion efforts on China and in Europe in such countries as Italy Turkey France Germany Poland and Russia. The Spanish firm is growing quickly in China with some 110 shops there since entering the market in 2006. It also has more than 55 stores in Japan and about 90 others in Indonesia Malaysia Singapore South Korea Thailand and the Philippines.

More than two-thirds of the company's sales are made outside of Spain where Inditex operates more than 1900 stores. Beyond Europe Inditex operates stores in Asia the Americas the Middle East and North Africa. Inditex's US presence is slight (only about 50 Zara stores) compared to its massive European footprint. After a seemingly splashy US debut the company has decided to grow slowly there while it focused on expanding in Europe. However a deal Inditex inked in early 2011 indicates that the holding company has big plans for its Zara banner. Inditex is investing in retail space on swanky Fifth Avenue in Manhattan to be "one of Zara's most emblematic flagships worldwide." The company has agreed to pay $400 million to occupy a 32000-sq.-ft. retail space at 666 Fifth Avenue that once was an NBA store. The deal includes the purchase price plus fewer than three years left on NBA's lease.

The company's fashion-forward flagship Zara chain navigates the prevailing winds of the fickle fashion world with an army of about 1485 stores in more than 70 countries. Zara's team of more than 200 designers produces 20000 items each year. In order to respond to popular demand and draw repeat business new merchandise is sent to Zara stores twice each week. Zara controls prices through vertical integration. Indeed Zara's low prices and rapid response to fashion trends has positioned it to challenge Gap Inc. for top ranking among global clothing vendors.

Capitalizing on Zara's success Inditex has launched two brand extensions: Zara Home and Zara Kids as well as an e-commerce site for Zara Home in Europe. Zara Home which has grown to about 270 stores in some 25 countries sells home furnishings tableware and linens for the table bedroom and bathroom. Overall Zara sales account for nearly two-thirds of its parent company's total revenue.

Inditex designs manufactures and distributes garments to clothe all kinds of customers: Zara (fashion forward apparel for men women and kids) Oysho (lingerie) Pull and Bear (urban youth ages 14 to 28) Massimo Dutti (upscale fashion boutiques) and two brands targeted at young women Stradivarius and Bershka. The company's newest banner is Uterque (launched in 2008) which sells leather goods numbers about 70 shops in 15 countries worldwide.

HISTORY

Holding company Industria de Dise?o Textil (Inditex) got its start as Confecciones Goa in 1963 making women's lingerie and housecoats in La Coru?a Spain.

Founder Amancio Ortega learned the rag trade as a boy when at age 13 he made deliveries for a shirtmaker. Managing a tailor shop when he was a young man Ortega spied an expensive negligee for sale and he thought he could make copies and sell them for half the price. From there he made nightshirts and pajamas before he opened the first Zara store in La Coru?a in 1975 where Ortega began expanding his offerings for women.

Ortega formed Inditex as a holding company for his growing operations in 1985. Inditex ran nearly 100 Zara stores before venturing out of the country to Portugal in 1988. New York City and Paris stores opened in 1989.

The company created the Pull & Bear clothing chain in 1991. About that time Inditex purchased a 65% stake in the Massimo Dutti group. (Inditex owns it all now.) The group continued to open stores around the globe: Mexico in 1992 Greece in 1993 Belgium and Sweden in 1994 Malta and Cyprus in 1996 and Israel and Norway in 1997.

In 1998 Inditex opened the Berksha chain to lure young females. The company further expanded that year into Argentina Japan Lebanon the UK and Venezuela.

Inditex then acquired 90% of Stradivarius a young women's chain with about 80 stores mostly in Spain. Meanwhile that year Inditex moved into nine more countries: Bahrain Brazil Canada Chile Germany the Netherlands Poland Saudi Arabia and Uruguay.

In 2000 the company announced it would open 150 new stores in the next two years including perhaps 40 in the US. Later in the year however the company said it would hold off on US expansion to concentrate on European growth. To fuel the growth of its Zara chain Inditex floated 26% of the company in a public offering in May 2001.

Over the course of 2001 Inditex entered six new markets: the Czech Republic Iceland Ireland Jordan Luxembourg and Puerto Rico.

In 2003 the first Zara Home stores opened and Inditex entered new markets in Malaysia Russia Slovakia and Slovenia. The following year the group surpassed the 2000 store count and entered Estonia Hungary Latvia Lithuania Morocco Panama and Romania.

Early in 2005 Inditex stopped selling fur items in all of its stores worldwide. In June Pablo Isla Alvarez de Tejera succeeded Jose Maria Castellano Rios as chief executive of the Spanish fashion giant. Castellano remained a non-executive vice chairman of the company until September when he resigned unexpectedly following a disagreement with Inditex's chairman Amancio Ortega over his failed bid for Fenosa a Spanish utility company. Castellano's departure ended a 31-year partnership between the two men.

Overall Inditex opened about 450 stores in 2005 and in the process became Europe's largest apparel retailer ahead of Sweden's H&M Hennes & Mauritz.

In February 2006 the first Zara store opened its doors in Shanghai the first Inditex shop in China.

In 2007 80% of new stores opened were located outside of Spain. Overall the group added 560 stores in some 50 countries. Also in 2007 the group's Kiddy's Class business segment combined operations with Zara Childrenswear. In October Zara Home launched an online shopping site. The online portal is a first for Inditex which has focused on the international expansion of its fashion chains.

In 2009 Inditex signed a joint venture with the Tata Group to open stores in India beginning in 2010. Also in 2009 the firm opened its first stores in Syria.

EXECUTIVES

Second Deputy Chairman, Carlos Espinosa de los Monteros, age 68
General Counsel Secretary and Director, Antonio Abril Abadin, age 54
Director, Juan Manuel Urgoiti y Lopez-Oca?a, age 72
First Deputy Chairman and CEO, Pablo Isla Alvarez de Tejera, age 48
Director, Francisco Luzon Lopez, age 64
Director, Irene R. Miller, age 59
Director, Flora Perez Marcote
Director, Jose Luis Vazquez Mari?o, age 68

LOCATIONS

HQ: Industria De Diseno Textil (Inditex) SA
Avda. de la Diputacion s/n, Edificio INDITEX, La Coruna, Arteixo 15142
Phone: (34) 98 118 5400
Web: www.inditex.es

2010 Sales

	% of total
Europe	
Spain	32
Other	46
America	10
Asia & other	12
Total	**100**

2010 Stores

	No.
Europe	
Spain	1,916
Other	2,006
Americas	390
Asia & other	595
Total	**4,907**

PRODUCTS/OPERATIONS

2010 Stores

	No.
Zara	1,483
Bershka	698
Pull &	663
Stradivarius	573
Massimo	519
Oysho	422
Zara	272
Zara	205
Uterque	72
Total	**4,907**

2010 Sales

	% of total
Zara	64
Bershka	11
Massimo	7
Pull &	7
Stradivarius	6
Oysho	3
Zara	2
Uterque	-
Total	**100**

COMPETITORS

Adolfo Dominguez
Arcadia
Benetton
Carrefour
Cortefiel
Diesel SpA
El Corte Ingles
Fast Retailing
French Connection
H&M
IKEA
Kering
L Brands
LVMH
NEXT plc
Prada
Selfridges
The Gap

HISTORICAL FINANCIALS

Company Type: Public

Income Statement FYE: January 31

	REVENUE ($ mil.)	NET INCOME ($ mil.)	NET PROFIT MARGIN	EMPLOYEES
01/13	21,613	3,199	14.8%	120,314
01/12	18,180	2,546	14.0%	109,512
01/11	17,128	2,368	13.8%	100,138
01/10	15,366	1,822	11.9%	92,301
01/09	13,324	1,604	12.0%	89,112
Annual Growth	12.9%	18.8%	—	7.8%

2013 Year-End Financials

Debt ratio: 0.0%
Return on equity: 29.6%
Cash ($ mil.): 5,208
Current ratio: 1.92
Long-term debt ($ mil.): 5
No. of shares (mil.): 623
Dividends
Yield: 1.2%
Payout: —
Market value ($ mil.): 17,391

	STOCK PRICE ($) FY Close	P/E High	P/E Low	PER SHARE ($) Earnings	Dividends	Book Value
01/13	27.90	14	7	5.13	0.35	18.37
01/12	17.45	12	8	4.09	0.35	15.68
01/11	15.05	12	6	3.80	0.24	14.01
01/10	12.50	13	5	2.93	0.42	11.85
01/09	7.50	7	6	2.58	0.00	9.70
Annual Growth	38.9%	—	—	18.8%	—	17.3%

Industrial and Commercial Bank of China Ltd

In the event not every young man wants to go west Industrial and Commercial Bank of China (ICBC) is able to finance trips elsewhere. The firm is one of China's biggest banks –and one of the largest in the world. ICBC manages more than 16000 domestic branches and more than 200 overseas branches and offices. The bank's financial services offered in Chinese renminbi and foreign currencies include wholesale retail and international banking for more than 4 million corporate clients and some 280 million individuals. It oversees about a quarter of the total domestic assets owned by China's commercial banks. The Chinese government controls about 70% of ICBC.

ICBC makes more than half of its earnings through its corporate banking segment. To support the world's sluggish financial recovery the bank has increased its lending activities for large corporate concerns as well as small to micro businesses. The bank has also made significant inroads into expansion abroad and now has some 1700 correspondent banks around the world.

The company has been gaining steadily since its record-setting 2006 IPO. In 2011 ICBC's operating income grew 24% from the previous year while profits rose 26%. Both interest and noninterest earnings grew –net fee and commission income grew by nearly 40% that year. Assets have also been growing and the bank is considered the world's largest by market capitalization and customer deposits. Conversely ICBC's portfolio of non-performing loans has been shrinking.

Although it doesn't have the international presence of fellow Chinese group Bank of China ICBC does have its eyes on growth abroad. In 2011 the bank established operations in about a dozen new international markets. The bank's targeted markets for growth include Russia Vietnam Pakistan the Middle East and the Americas. ICBC owns most of Bank Halim Indonesia a minority stake in South Africa-based Standard Bank Group and an approximately 80% stake in ICBC (Macau). In 2010 the company bought a 70% stake in Bank of East Asia's Canadian unit –now ICBC (Canada); it upped its stake to 80% the following year. The bank also opened a Malaysian subsidiary indicative of growing trade between China and Malaysia.

ICBC ventured into the US broker-dealer business in 2010 when it acquired the Prime Dealer Services unit of Fortis Securities from BNP Paribas. The company again hooked up with Bank of East Asia in 2012 when it bought a majority of that company's US operations including more than a dozen bank branches in New York and California. The deal marked the first time that a US retail bank was acquired by a Chinese company.

ICBC also has plans to establish operations in Peru and Brazil. In 2011 it arranged to buy 80% of Standard Bank's three Argentinean businesses further boosting its presence in the Americas. (South America has a growing Chinese population which the bank hopes to take advantage of.)

EXECUTIVES

VP and Director, Li Xiaopeng, age 54
Chairman and Executive Director, Jiang Jianqing, age 60
President and the vice chairman of ICBC, Yang Kaisheng, age 64
VP and Director, Zhang Furong, age 61
VP and Director, Zhang Qu, age 66
VP and Director, Wang Lili, age 62
President ICBC Beijing, Yi Huiman, age 49
Chief Risk Officer, Wei Guoxiong, age 58
SEVP, Zhang Hongli
VP and Director, Li Xiaopeng, age 54
Vice Chairman and President, Yang Kaisheng, age 63
VP and Director, Zhang Furong, age 61
VP and Director, Zhang Qu, age 66
VP and Director, Wang Lili, age 62
Director, Song Zhigang, age 62
Auditors: Ernst&YoungHuaMing

LOCATIONS

HQ: Industrial and Commercial Bank of China Ltd
No. 55 Fuxingmennei Avenue, Xicheng District, Beijing 100140
Phone: (86) 10 66108608 **Fax:** (86) 10 66107571
Web: www.icbc-ltd.com

PRODUCTS/OPERATIONS

2011 Sales

	% of total
Interest	
Loans &	59
Financial	17
Other	7
Noninterest	
Fees &	16
Other	1
Total	**100**

2011 Sales by Segment

	% of total
Corporate	53
Personal	31
Treasury	15
Other	1
Total	**100**

COMPETITORS

Agricultural Bank of China
Bank of China
Bank of Communications
CITIC International Financial
China Construction Bank
China Merchants Bank
HSBC
Hua Xia Bank

HISTORICAL FINANCIALS

Company Type: Public

Income Statement FYE: December 31

	ASSETS ($ mil.)	NET INCOME ($ mil.)	INCOME AS % OF ASSETS	EMPLOYEES
12/12	2,813,847	38,261	1.4%	427,356
12/11	2,458,831	33,087	1.3%	408,859
12/10	2,041,783	25,055	1.2%	397,339
12/09	1,725,989	18,840	1.1%	389,827
12/08	1,429,932	16,244	1.1%	385,609
Annual Growth	18.4%	23.9%	—	2.6%

2012 Year-End Financials

Return on assets: 1.4%
Return on equity: 22.8%
Long-term debt ($ mil.): —
No. of shares (mil.): —
Sales ($ mil): 135,669
Dividends
Yield: 3.6%
Payout: —
Market value ($ mil.): —

	STOCK PRICE ($) FY Close	P/E High	P/E Low	PER SHARE ($) Earnings	Dividends	Book Value
12/12	0.71	0	0	0.11	0.53	0.52
12/11	0.59	0	0	0.09	0.00	0.44
12/10	0.75	0	0	0.07	1.75	0.36
12/09	0.82	0	0	0.06	1.07	0.30
12/08	0.54	0	0	0.05	0.00	0.26
Annual Growth	7.1%	—	—	22.1%	—	18.2%

Industrial Bank Co., Ltd.

There's nothing average about Industrial Bank. Founded in 1988 Industrial Bank is one of China's first joint stock commercial banks. Through some 80 branches and more than 650 sub-branches across China Industrial Bank offers standard deposit loan wealth management credit card and e-banking products and services to personal and commercial banking customers. Fujian Finance Department a government institution controls about a fifth of Industrial Bank while Hong Kong's Hang Seng Bank owns more than 10%.

EXECUTIVES

President, Li Renjie, age 58
VP, Kang Yukun, age 59
VP, Chen Dekang, age 59
Secretary of the Board; Director, Bin Tang
Head of Bank; Director, Renjie Li
Vice President Industrial Bank Co. Ltd, Jiang Yunming
Independent Director, Bin Xu
Independent Director, Bingkun Lin
Independent Director, Qinye Zhou
Independent Director, Ruoshan Li
Independent Director, Shusong Ba

LOCATIONS

HQ: Industrial Bank Co., Ltd.
154 Hudong Road, Fuzhou, Fujian Province 350003
Phone: (86) 591 87824863 **Fax:** (86) 591 87842633
Web: www.cib.com.cn

COMPETITORS

Bank of China
Bank of East Asia
Bank of Shanghai
China Construction Bank
China Merchants Bank
China Minsheng Banking
Shanghai Pudong Development Bank

HISTORICAL FINANCIALS

Company Type: Public

Income Statement FYE: December 31

	ASSETS ($ mil.)	NET INCOME ($ mil.)	INCOME AS % OF ASSETS	EMPLOYEES
12/12	521,470	5,568	1.1%	0
12/11	382,689	4,052	1.1%	0
12/10	280,610	2,809	1.0%	0
12/09	195,102	1,945	1.0%	0
12/08	149,615	1,668	1.1%	0
Annual Growth	36.6%	35.2%	—	—

2012 Year-End Financials

Return on assets: 1.2%
Return on equity: 24.3%
Long-term debt ($ mil.): —
No. of shares (mil.): —
Sales ($ mil): 13,997
Dividends
Yield: —
Payout: —
Market value ($ mil.): —

ING Bank N.V. (Netherlands)

LOCATIONS

HQ: ING Bank N.V. (Netherlands)
Bijlmerplein 888, Amsterdam 1102 MG
Phone: (31) 20 5639111 **Fax:** (31) 20 5760950
Web: www.ing.com

HISTORICAL FINANCIALS

Company Type: Public

Income Statement FYE: December 31

	REVENUE ($ mil.)	NET INCOME ($ mil.)	NET PROFIT MARGIN	EMPLOYEES
12/12	86,064	4,105	4.8%	66,879
12/11	90,271	5,180	5.7%	71,175
12/10	99,292	6,015	6.1%	71,287
12/95	5,884	672	11.4%	0
12/94	4,551	536	11.8%	0
Annual Growth	(3.5%)	(2.5%)	—	—

2012 Year-End Financials

Debt ratio: —
Return on equity: 8.7%
Cash ($ mil.): 20,359
Current ratio: —
Long-term debt ($ mil.): —
No. of shares (mil.): 465
Dividends
Yield: —
Payout: —
Market value ($ mil.): —

ING Groep N.V.

ING Groep is a Dutch hybrid of banking insuring and asset-managing services. One of the world's largest banking and financial services companies its operations are focused on its home Benelux market as well as the rest of Europe and in the Americas and Asia. The company's banking operations include wholesale and retail banking mortgage lending and online retail banking (ING Direct). Key insurance products include life insurance pensions and retirement services. ING provides asset management for individuals and institutions through both its insurance and banking units. The firm is selling off insurance operations as well as some banking and investment businesses to repay government bailout loans.

Geographic Reach

ING operates in about 40 countries in Europe North America South America Asia and the Asia/Pacific region. North America is the largest segment accounting for 38% of revenues in 2012 with the Netherlands accounting for about one-third of sales.

Operations

Amid the global financial crisis of 2008 ING accepted a ?10 billion (about $13 billion) bailout loan from the Dutch government to shore up its capital position and reassure wary investors. Since then ING has been focused on repaying the loan and enacting strategic measures to further offset losses including layoffs and asset sales. Under requirements for the bailout funds ING is also working to separate its banking and insurance operations through the sale of the insurance assets (as well as some banking assets). Through its restructuring measures and stock rights issuances the company was able to repay half of the funds received through the Dutch government bailout at the end of 2009. By the end of 2012 it had reduced the funds owed to about ?2 billion.

The company is focused on its European banking operations –including divisions in the Netherlands Belgium and Germany –which provide a full range of services including savings and investment products. Due to the restructuring efforts banking operations now account for 70% of revenues (insurance was previously the core business). Remaining insurance operations are primarily located in the Benelux region and in the US.

Sales and Marketing

ING uses a multi-channel distribution model to reach customers including individuals families small business entities large corporations government agencies and institutions. Marketing and sales methods include Internet banking mobile banking call centers mailings and branch and outbound sales representative efforts.

Financial Performance

ING's revenues fell 7% in 2012 to ?91.1 billion largely due to asset disposal efforts. Net income also fell by 31% to ?3.3 billion on lower revenues and increased restructuring costs and banking operational expenses.

Strategy

ING's restructuring plan encompasses the sale or spinoff of all of its insurance operations which have included life insurance and non-life insurance businesses in Europe the Americas and the Asia/Pacific. The plan also includes the divestiture of the company's insurance-related investment management operations as well as select noncore banking operations. Through its restructuring measures ING aims to improve finances streamline its portfolio and repay state aid. The company is focusing its business efforts on building strong domestic retail and commercial banking units as well as strong banking positions in other Central and Eastern European markets.

The company is focused on selling insurance operations in Asia. In late 2013 ING sold its investment management business in South Korea to Macquarie Group an Australian global financial services provider. It sold its Malaysian insurance operations to AIA Group for ?1.3 billion in 2012. It also sold its insurance assets in Hong Kong Macau and Thailand to Pacific Century Group for ?1.6 billion ($2.1 billion) as well as its 33% stake in China Merchants Fund (investment management venture) to partner China Merchants Bank for ?100 million. From 2009 to 2011 the company sold off a number of insurance and investment management businesses in North America Latin America the Asia/Pacific region and Europe.

To narrow the focus of its banking operations in early 2012 the group sold its ING Direct USA banking business to Capital One for $6 billion in cash and a 10% ownership stake in Capital One; ING sold the Capital One shares for some $3 billion later that year. The ING Direct Canada unit was sold to Scotiabank for some ?2.4 billion in 2012 and in 2013 ING completed the sale of its ING Direct UK division to Barclays. In 2014 ING exited its equity investment management business in the Middle East and North Africa.

Some of ING's divestitures will be conducted through public offerings. In late 2012 ING U.S. filed a registration statement to complete an IPO; the offering was completed in May 2013 to raise some $1.3 billion. ING retained a 75% stake in ING U.S. which holds ING's remaining US-based life insurance retirement and investment management operations. The company plans to reduce its stake through future share offerings; it also plans to rename ING U.S. as Voya Financial. ING also plans to conduct an IPO of its European life insurance and investment management operations.

Company Background

Prior to the economic meltdown ING took aim at becoming a financial services player in all four corners of the world and made acquisitions accordingly. Along with much of the insurance industry it shifted its base from traditional life insurance products to investment-backed products which favor companies that can sell through banks. ING utilized its owns banks to distribute such products. The company also targeted expansion in growing economies such as South Korea Turkey and Thailand to meet anticipated consumer demand for new banking and retirement options. In more mature markets like North America and Europe the company had the aging population in its sights and placed retirement planning and pensions as sources of future growth.

HISTORY

HCING Groep's roots go back to 1845 when its earliest predecessor the Netherlands Insurance Co. was founded. The firm began expanding geographically; in 1903 it added life insurance. In 1963 it merged with the century-old Nationale Life Insurance Bank to form Nationale-Nederland (NN). Over the next three decades the company grew primarily through acquisitions in Europe North America and Australia. In 1986 NN became the first European life insurance company to be licensed in Japan.

Another predecessor the Rijkspostspaarbank was founded in 1881 to provide Dutch citizens with simple post office savings accounts. In 1918 the Postcheque-en Girondienst (giro) system was established to allow people to use vouchers drawn on their savings accounts to pay bills. This system became the main method of settling accounts (instead of bank checking accounts).

Rijkspostspaarbank and Postcheque merged in 1986 to become Postbank. Postbank merged in 1989 with the Nederlandse Middenstandsbank (founded 1927) to become NMB Postbank. The vast amounts of cash tied up in the post office savings and giro systems fueled NMB's business.

In 1991 as the European economic union became a reality and barriers between banking and insurance began to fall NN merged with NMB Postbank to form Internationale Nederland Groep (ING). ING began cutting costs shedding redundant offices and unprofitable operations in both its segments. In the US where insurance and banking were legally divided the company "debanked" itself in order to keep its more lucrative insurance operations (but retained the right to provide banking services to those operations).

ING sought to increase its investment banking and finance operations in the 1990s. In 1995 it took over UK-based Barings Bank (personal banker to the Queen of England) after Nicholas Leeson a trader in Barings' Singapore office lost huge sums of money in derivatives trading. The acquisition gave the firm a higher profile but cost more than anticipated and left it embroiled in lingering legal actions.

In 1996 ING bought Poland's Bank Slaski (the company had first entered Poland in 1994). The next year it expanded its securities business by acquiring investment bank Furman Selz doubled its US life insurance operations by purchasing Equitable of Iowa and listed on the NYSE. In 1998 ING's acquisition strategy again involved Europe and North America: It bought Belgium's Banque Bruxelles Lambert and Canadian life insurer Guardian Insurance Co. (from Guardian Royal Exchange now part of AXA UK).

ING turned eastward in 1999 kicking off asset management operations in India and buying a minority stake in South Korea's HC&B (formerly Housing & Commercial Bank). In 2000 the company bulked up its North American operations with the purchase of 40% of Savia SA a Mexican insurance concern. It also bought US firm ReliaStar Financial in a $6 billion deal and Charterhouse Securities from CCF (then called Credit Commercial de France).

In 2004 ING realigned its management structure dividing the company's operations into six business lines: Insurance Americas Insurance Europe Insurance Asia-Pacific Wholesale Banking Retail Banking and ING Direct. ING boosted its North American insurance operations with the acquisition of Allianz's Canadian property and casualty operations.

The company struggled with investment banking arm ING Barings. The unit was reorganized and streamlined for cost-savings purposes but ultimately was put on the block. Its Asian equities operations were sold to Macquarie Bank in 2004. Barings Private Equity Partners unit was sold to its management. The Barings investment management operations were sold to MassMutual in 2005 while Northern Trust bought up its fund administration trust and custody operations.

ING sold most of ING BHF-Bank to Sal. Oppenheim during 2004. The next year ING turned over its US life reinsurance operations to Scottish Re and sold subsidiary Life Insurance Company of Georgia to Jackson National Life.

During 2005 ING acquired a 20% stake in the Bank of Beijing as part of a strategic alliance. In 2006 the company sold off its UK brokerage business Williams de Broe to The Evolution Group.

In 2008 the company acquired CitiStreet a leading US administrator of defined-contribution retirement savings pension health and other plans; it paid about $900 million for the firm.

After the global financial crisis hit in 2008 ING accepted a ?10 billion (more than $13 billion) bailout loan from the Dutch government. The bailout was intended to shore up the company's capital position and reassure wary investors. Strategic measures to further offset losses and repay debt were enacted in 2009 including layoffs and asset sales. CEO Michael Tilmant stepped down and was replaced by former chairman Jan Hommen. By the end of 2009 job cuts totaled about 10% of its workforce. The company also outlined plans to split the company in half by separating its insurance and banking operations.

Prior to the bailout ING has already been working to simplify and streamline its operations through a "Back to Basics" strategy. Restructuring measures under the strategy include the refocusing of ING's banking operations on (mostly Central) Europe and the reduction of the company's US financial product offerings.

In early 2009 the company sold its ING Canada property/casualty business which was then renamed Intact Financial. ING sold its life insurance joint venture stake in Australia and New Zealand to partner ANZ and offloaded its noncore annuity and mortgage businesses in Chile to life insurer Corp Group Vida Chile in late 2009. The company also sold its Taiwanese life insurance business to Fubon Financial Holding in a deal worth ?447 million ($600 million) in mid-2009. ING gained a 5% stake in Fubon through the deal which it sold the following year for another ?395 million ($522 million).

In early 2010 ING completed sales of the company's Swiss Private Banking unit to Julius Baer for $506 million and its Asian Private Banking unit (operating in Hong Kong the Philippines and Singapore) to OCBC Bank for nearly $1.5 billion. In addition the company sold its North American reinsurance operations to RGA and most of its US insurance brokerage operations to Lightyear Capital in early 2010. ING has also agreed to sell its stake in one of its Chinese life insurance ventures (Pacific Antai with China Pacific Insurance) to China Construction Bank.

In 2011 ING sold its Asian and European real estate investment management (REIM) operations as well as select US REIM assets for about $940 million to broker CBRE Group (formerly CB Richard Ellis Group). The firm sold its remaining US REIM assets to Lightyear Capital for some $100 million. Also that year the firm agreed to sell its Australian investment management business to UBS for an undisclosed sum.

Farther south in 2011 the company sold its Latin American insurance operations to Columbian insurer GrupoSura for $3.7 billion. The sale included insurance savings and investment management operations in Chile Colombia Mexico Uruguay and Peru. It also sold ING Car Least to BMW.

EXECUTIVES

Chairman Executive Board, Jan H. M. Hommen, age 71
Vice Chairman Supervisory Board, Peter A. F. W. Elverding, age 66
CEO ING Investment Management, Gilbert Van Hassel
COO Insurance; Management Board Insurance, Thomas J. (Tom) McInerney, age 57, $579,013 total compensation
CEO Retail Banking Direct and International, Eli P. Leenaars, age 52, $396,996 total compensation
CEO Commercial Banking; Vice Chairman Management Board Banking, Eric Boyer de la Giroday, age 61, $1,278,414 total compensation
Head of Operations and Information Technology Banking, Steve Van Wyk
CEO Retail Banking Benelux, Hans van der Noordaa, age 52, $396,996 total compensation
CEO ING Insurance U.S., Robert G. (Rob) Leary
Vice Chairman Management Board Banking, J. V. (Koos) Timmermans, age 54, $978,813 total compensation
Head Media Relations, Peter Jong
Head Group Investor Relations, Dorothy Hillenius, age 44
CEO Nationale-Nederlanden, Lard Friese, age 50
Member Executive Board and CFO, Patrick G. Flynn, age 52, $650,673 total compensation
Chief Administrative Officer, Matthew J. Rider
CEO ING Bank Slaski, Malgorzata Kolakowska
Chief Risk Officer, Wilfred F. Nagel, age 58
Head of Media Relations, Raymond Vermeulen
Chairman of the Supervisory Board, Jeroen Veer
Member Supervisory Board, Aman Mehta, age 68
Vice Chairman Supervisory Board, Peter A. F. W. Elverding, age 66
Member Supervisory Board, Piet C. Klaver, age 69
Member Supervisory Board, Henk W. Breukink, age 64
Member Supervisory Board, Lodewijk J. de Waal, age 64
Member Supervisory Board, Tineke J.P. Bahlmann, age 64
Member of the Supervisory Board, Joost Kuiper
Member of the Supervisory Board, Lodewijk Waal
Member of the Supervisory Board, Robert Reibestein
Member of the Supervisory Board, Sjoerd Keulen
Member of the Supervisory Board, Yvonne Rooy
Auditors: Ernst&YoungAccountants

LOCATIONS

HQ: ING Groep N.V.
Bijlmerplein 888, Amsterdam 1102 MG
Phone: (31) 20 563 6710
Web: www.ing.com

2012 Sales

	% of total
Europe	
The	33
Belgium	10
Other	16
North	38
Asia	2
Australia	1
Total	**100**

PRODUCTS/OPERATIONS

2012 Sales

	% of total
Banking	
Commercial	22
Retail	20
Retail	11
Retail other & corporate line	17
Insurance	30
Total	**100**

COMPETITORS

ABN AMRO Group
AEGON
AIG
AXA
Achmea
Ageas Insurance International
Allianz
Aviva
Barclays
CNP Assurances
Citigroup
Credit Suisse
Delta Lloyd
Deutsche Bank
Deutsche Bundesbank
Generali
HSBC
KBC
Legal & General Group
Lincoln Financial Group
MetLife
Nationwide
Principal Financial
Prudential
Prudential plc
RSA Insurance
Rabobank
Swiss Life
The Hartford
UBS
Zurich Financial Services

HISTORICAL FINANCIALS

Company Type: Public

Income Statement FYE: December 31

	ASSETS ($ mil.)	NET INCOME ($ mil.)	INCOME AS % OF ASSETS	EMPLOYEES
12/12	1,531,742	4,295	0.3%	92,572
12/11	1,647,314	6,130	0.4%	104,419
12/10	1,663,388	3,716	0.2%	106,139
12/09	1,671,020	(2,049)	—	110,325
12/08	1,861,786	(1,019)	—	125,285
Annual Growth	(4.8%)	—	—	(7.3%)

2012 Year-End Financials

Return on assets: 0.2%
Return on equity: 6.6%
Long-term debt ($ mil.): —
No. of shares (mil.): —
Sales ($ mil): 118,467
Dividends
Yield: 0.0%
Payout: —
Market value ($ mil.): —

	STOCK PRICE ($) FY Close	P/E High/Low		PER SHARE ($) Earnings	Dividends	Book Value
12/12	9.49	25	13	0.91	0.00	17.95
12/11	7.17	30	12	1.10	0.00	15.18
12/10	9.79	35	19	0.83	0.00	15.35
12/09	9.81	—	—	(1.08)	0.00	13.58
12/08	11.10	—	—	(0.50)	2.36	18.52
Annual Growth	(3.8%)	—	—	—	—	(0.8%)

International Consolidated Airlines Group SA

A member of the royal family of European airlines British Airways (BA) carries passengers and cargo to more than 160 destinations in some 75 countries from hubs at London's Heathrow Gatwick and London City airports. The carrier operates a fleet of more than 250 aircraft (with another 20 on order) consisting mainly of Airbus and Boeing jets. BA extends its network to more than 400 total destinations via joint business agreements and code-sharing relationships with AMR's American Airlines and members of the Oneworld alliance such as Qantas. In 2011 BA merged with Spain's #1 airline Iberia forming International Airlines Group (IAG).

Operations

Upon its formation IAG joined the wave of multinational air carriers namely Air France-KLM and Lufthansa (which owns Austrian Brussels and SWISS). Although BA and Iberia continue to fly under their own names the merger created Europe's third largest scheduled airline by revenue and one of the world's top five airline groups. The deal also marked the end of more than two decades of trading under the British Airways name. Under the merger's terms BA owns 56% and Iberia holds the remaining 44% of IAG. In addition to its brand name each carrier maintains its own hub.

The Passenger segment which includes both scheduled and unscheduled services accounts for nearly 90 percent of revenue. The Cargo segment operated with scheduled passenger services represents 7% of revenue. The Passenger and Cargo segments are operated as one business unit. The Other segment accounts for 5% of revenue.

Financial Performance

BA's revenue increased slightly (8%) due to increased ticket prices and a boost from the purchase of British Midland Airways (bmi). However continued high fuel costs contributed to a 110% increased in net loss. The company also disposed of two of bmi's subsidiaries adding to the loss. Consequently cash flow was down more than 170%.

Strategy

To compensate for the rise of fuel cost which accounts for one-third of expenses BA has been focusing on working with suppliers to drive down controllable costs. The company also cushions itself against the high price of fuel by buying oil derivatives in forward markets.

To further hedge its bets on fuel and go a little green BA has partnered with Solena Group to build a sustainable jet fuel plant where fuel will be created from waste biomass. The facility which is the first of its kind in Europe is expected to be in operation by 2015.

To stand out from its competition in a soft market the company is investing more than #5 billion to purchase new Airbus A380 and Boeing 787 aircraft upgrade its cabins and lounges and new technology all in an effort to persuade air travelers to choose BA.

Mergers and Acquisitions

IAG acquired British Midland Airways from Lufthansa in 2012 and began integrating it with BA's operations. Also BA Iberia and American Airlines rolled out a transatlantic joint venture a step up from their code-sharing alliance that defends their routes between the US and UK. Other transatlantic joint ventures include SkyTeam (including Delta and Korean Air Lines) and Star Alliance (United Continental and Lufthansa among its members).

HISTORY

British Airways has a jet trail winding back to 1916 and its biplane-flying ancestor Aircraft Transport and Travel which in 1919 launched the world's first daily international air service (between London and Paris). Concerned about subsidized foreign competition British authorities in 1924 merged Aircraft Transport and Travel successor Daimler Airways with other fledgling British carriers –British Air Marine Navigation Handley Page and Instone Air Line –to form Imperial Airways.

Imperial pioneered routes from London to India (1929) Singapore (1933) and –in partnership with Qantas Empire Airways –Australia (1934). Competition on European routes emerged in the 1930s from upstart British Airways; in 1939 the government troubled by the threat to Imperial nationalized and merged the two airlines to form British Overseas Airways Corporation (BOAC).

After WWII BOAC continued as the UK's international airline but state-owned British European Airways (BEA) took over domestic and European routes. In 1972 the government combined the duo to form British Airways (BA).

BA and Air France jointly introduced supersonic passenger service in 1976 with the Concorde –a PR victory that contributed to years of losses. Colin Marshall became CEO in 1983 and reduced manpower and routes.

In 1987 the government sold BA to the public and the airline bought chief UK rival British Caledonian. Hoping to become a globe-spanning carrier in 1992 BA tried to gain a 44% stake in USAir (which became US Airways). American Airlines United and Delta strongly objected demanding equal access to UK markets. BA settled for a 25% stake the maximum foreign ownership allowed by US law in 1993. It also bought 25% of Qantas.

That year BA settled a libel suit brought by UK competitor Virgin Atlantic Airways which accused BA of waging a smear campaign against it. The settlement cost BA about $5 million and Virgin Atlantic followed with a $1 billion antitrust suit in the US (dismissed in 1999). In 1994 BA paid out $4 million to settle yet another Virgin Atlantic suit this one claiming BA had done sloppy maintenance on Virgin aircraft. BA also sold British Caledonian.

In 1996 Marshall turned over the CEO job to Bob Ayling who had joined BA in 1985. BA and American Airlines agreed to coordinate prices and schedules and to share market data for their transatlantic routes. Though the deal met regulatory obstacles from the start in 1997 BA sold its stake in US Airways. BA and American also took the lead in forming the Oneworld global alliance (which took effect in 1999).

The next year BA launched low-fare European carrier Go. In 1999 BA and American all but abandoned plans for their comprehensive transatlantic linkup after US regulators denied antitrust immunity. Meanwhile as fuel prices rose and passenger numbers fell BA announced it would cut unprofitable routes and use smaller planes.

Ayling resigned in 2000 and Marshall stepped in as temporary CEO before Rod Eddington a veteran of Cathay Pacific and Ansett was appointed. Also that year BA took a 9% stake in Iberia and sold its interest in France's Air Liberte.

BA grounded its Concordes in 2000 (flights resumed in 2001) three weeks after the crash of an Air France Concorde outside Paris in which 113 people were killed. The airline put its no-frills carrier Go up for sale that year and in 2001 sold the airline to venture capital firm 3i Group. Also in 2001 BA and American announced plans to once again seek regulatory approval for a code-sharing partnership.

That year BA laid off 5200 employees as a result of decreased demand for air travel after the terrorist attacks in New York and Washington DC. The layoffs were on top of 1800 job cuts the airline made earlier in the year reducing BA's workforce by 10%.

BA's long-negotiated trans-Atlantic alliance with American Airlines received tentative approval from the US Department of Transportation in 2002. But the airlines chose to abandon the deal rather than accept regulators' terms which called for BA and American to give up more landing slots at London's Heathrow airport than they were willing to relinquish. The next year the carriers won approval for an extensive code-sharing agreement that did not include routes between London and US cities.

The year 2003 also saw the retirement of the BA's Concorde fleet a longtime symbol of the airline's trans-Atlantic dominance. That year the carrier acquired four additional slots at London's Heathrow Airport from rival United Airlines which was reorganizing under bankruptcy protection.

BA sold its 19% stake in Qantas in 2004 to help cut down on its debt. Eddington stepped down as CEO in 2005 and former Aer Lingus chief Willie Walsh was named to replace him.

In 2006 BA was a target of an investigation by US and UK government agencies into alleged price-fixing on fuel surcharges by airlines. Two company officials commercial director Martin George and communications head Iain Burns were placed on leave and then resigned in connection with the inquiry. The next year BA settled the charges by agreeing to pay fines of about $300 million to the US and about $247 million to the UK.

As early as 2007 BA has started working steadily to cut costs throughout its business and eliminate unprofitable operations in order to focus on core long-haul offerings. Toward that end the company sold most of the operations of its money-losing BA Connect regional business to rival Flybe.

BA moved to augment its transatlantic service in June 2008 by launching a new carrier OpenSkies. The startup which began operations by flying between Paris and New York was inspired by the Open Skies treaty between the US and the EU which allows European airlines to serve city pairs that don't include their home countries and enables US airlines to directly serve more European destinations. OpenSkies which uses a custom-configured Boeing 757 from the BA fleet hopes to simultaneously differentiate itself from its parent and benefit from BA's strong brand and deep pockets. To strengthen OpenSkies BA in July 2008 paid about $107 million for French startup carrier L'Avion which also uses 757s to provide business-class service between Paris and Newark New Jersey. L'Avion's operations were integrated into those of OpenSkies.

In the meantime BA attempted to merge with leading Australian airline Qantas. In December 2008 BA announced it was in talks with Qantas but the talks quickly fizzled out. Among other hurdles BA disagreed with Qantas owning more than 50% of the combined firm. (Australian law states that Qantas has to remain majority-owned by Australian investors with its head office residing in Australia.) Qantas also was apprehensive about BA's merger talks with Iberia occurring at the same time it was trying to reach an agreement with Qantas.

In 2008 BA reach a long-awaited milestone when it moved its Heathrow operations to a new facility Terminal 5. The new terminal was seen as a major step up both for passengers and for employees; functions such as security and baggage handling for example were designed to be easier to manage. However Terminal 5's opening was marred as not all of the bugs had been worked out of the new baggage-handling system. Hundreds of flights were canceled during the first week of operations because of problems with the baggage system —causing BA's reputation for customer service to suffer. In late 2009 BA announced it would merge with Iberia.

British Airways faced ongoing difficulties in 2010 with the eruption of the Iceland volcano Eyjafjallajokull in April. The airline sustained millions of pounds in losses a day due to the airspace closure.

EXECUTIVES

Director Investments and Alliances, Roger P. Maynard, age 71
Chairman, Sir Martin F. Broughton, age 67
Secretary, Alan K. Buchanan, age 55
Chief Information Officer, Paul Coby, age 57
Director People and Organizational Effectiveness, Tony McCarthy
Director Strategy and Business Units, Robert Boyle, age 49
CEO and Director, Keith Williams, age 58
Director Engineering, Garry Copeland
CFO, Nick Swift, age 48
Director Corporate Communications, Julia Simpson
Customer Director, Silla Maizey
Manager Investor Relations, Robert French
Director Operations, Andy Lord
Director Sales and Marketing, Andrew Crawley
Director, James A. (Jim) Lawrence, age 61
Director, Maarten A. van den Bergh, age 71
Director, Alison Reed, age 57
Director, Baroness Denise Kingsmill, age 65
Director, Baroness Elizabeth C. Symons, age 61
CEO and Director, Keith Williams, age 58
Director, Ken Smart, age 68
Director, Rafael Sanchez-Lozano Turmo, age 55
Auditors: Ernst&Young

LOCATIONS

HQ: International Consolidated Airlines Group SA
2 World Business Centre, Newall Road, London Heathrow Airport, Hounslow TW6 2SF
Phone: (44) 20 8564 2800
Web: www.iairgroup.com

2012 Sales

	% of total
Europe	
UK	44
Continental	16
Americas	
US &	20
Rest of the	3
Africa Middle East and Indian	10
Far East &	7
Total	**100**

PRODUCTS/OPERATIONS

2012 Sales

	% of total
Passenger	88
Cargo	7
Other	5
Total	**100**

COMPETITORS

ANA Holdings
Air Berlin
Air Europa
Air France
Air France-KLM
Alitalia
British Midland
Continental Airlines
Delta Air Lines
Flybe
Japan Airlines
KLM Royal Dutch Airlines
Lan Airlines
Lufthansa
Ryanair
SAS
Singapore Airlines
Spanair
TAM SA
US Airways
United Air Lines
United Continental
Virgin Atlantic Airways
easyJet

HISTORICAL FINANCIALS

Company Type: Public

Income Statement FYE: December 31

	REVENUE ($ mil.)	NET INCOME ($ mil.)	NET PROFIT MARGIN	EMPLOYEES
12/12	23,879	(1,242)	—	59,574
12/11	20,828	726	3.5%	56,791
12/10*	8,944	210	2.3%	39,828
03/10	12,123	(671)	—	41,494
03/09	12,863	(536)	—	44,987
Annual Growth	16.7%	—	—	7.3%

*Fiscal year change

2012 Year-End Financials

Debt ratio: 31.8%
Return on equity: (-18.5%)
Cash ($ mil.): 3,834
Current ratio: 0.66
Long-term debt ($ mil.): 5,440
No. of shares (mil.): 1,855
Dividends
Yield: —
Payout: —
Market value ($ mil.): 28,665

	STOCK PRICE ($) FY Close	P/E High/Low	PER SHARE ($) Earnings	Dividends	Book Value
12/12	15.45	— —	(0.67)	0.00	3.38
12/11	11.38	133 57	0.38	0.00	3.75
12/10*	21.15	507216	0.18	0.00	2.55
03/10	36.65	— —	(0.58)	0.00	2.51
03/09	20.39	— —	(0.47)	0.49	2.04
Annual Growth	(6.7%)	— —	—	—	13.4%

*Fiscal year change

Internetq Plc, London

LOCATIONS

HQ: Internetq Plc, London
St. Botolph Building, 138, Houndsditch, London EC3A 7AR,
Phone: (44) 20 35 19 5250
Web: www.internetQ.com

HISTORICAL FINANCIALS

Company Type: Public

Income Statement FYE: December 31

	REVENUE ($ mil.)	NET INCOME ($ mil.)	NET PROFIT MARGIN	EMPLOYEES
12/12	96,786	7,910	8.2%	91
12/11	64,771	3,131	4.8%	137
Annual Growth	49.4%	152.6%	—	(33.6%)

2012 Year-End Financials

Debt ratio: 4.6%
Return on equity: 15.2%
Cash ($ mil.): 12,298
Current ratio: 2.78
Long-term debt ($ mil.): 316
No. of shares (mil.): 34
Dividends
Yield: —
Payout: —
Market value ($ mil.): —

Intesa Sanpaolo S.P.A.

Ciao money! Intesa Sanpaolo provides retail and commercial banking services in Italy through its Banca dei Territori division. The company operates from approximately 5800 branches throughout Italy and an additional 1700 locations in Central and Eastern Europe as well as the Mediterranean basin. Intesa Sanpaolo also performs investment banking public and infrastructure finance factoring and trade financing services. The company offers life property and casualty insurance through EurizonVita and other insurance subsidiaries. Asset management is handled by Eurizon Capital and its Banca Fideuram arm provides financial planning services.

Intesa Sanpaolo is the result of the 2007 mega-merger between Banca Intesa and Sanpaolo IMI. After the merger the company reshuffled its assets and sold off some branches in order to comply with antitrust orders and raise capital.

The company also sold its securities services arm to US money manager State Street in 2010 and has been exploring a possible sale or spinoff of Fideuram.

Intesa Sanpaolo is working to strengthen its retail banking operations and maintain a diversified presence in international markets. For now its focus is on the Banca dei Territori division which handles domestic commercial banking and is responsible for retail customers individual customers and small businesses. In mid-2011 it bought a majority stake in Banca Monte Parma which operates some 70 branches in central Italy.

While Italy is the company's main focus it is also strategically expanding in foreign markets which have been less severly impacted by the economic downturn. Intesta Sanpaolo will look to grow organically in countries where the group already has a presence. It also will look to other favorable markets such as Polan Czech Republic and Turkey. In 2008 it opened its first branch in Dubai and entered the Ukraine market for the first time. Intesa Sanpaolo has one branch in the US –a banking location in New York City.

Intesa Sanpaolo's financial results were affected by the global economic crisis from 2008 through 2010. While the economy began to recover in 2010 there continued to be tension in the European market thanks to government debt and creditworthiness. Intesa Sanpaolo's strategy going forward is to reduce its risks increase liquidity and strengthen its capital base.

HISTORY

In Italy charity begins at home and often heads to the financial institutions. In 1563 Turin citizens founded Compagnia di San Paolo a foundation that provided education and dowries to orphaned girls and aid to impoverished nobility. In 1579 the organization began a pawn shop the Monte di Pieta or Mountain of Mercy (founded in 1519 and reopened by the Compagnia). The foundation grew over the next 200 years fattened by bequests and inheritances from wealthy Piedmontese families.

The French Republican government in Piedmonte gradually took control of the foundation's operations and closed it in 1802. The Monte di Pieta was reopened in 1804 and under the French influence became more bank-like. In 1848 the charitable and financial operations were formally divided.

Industrialization came slowly to Italy after its unification in the 1860s (the country remained largely agricultural until after WWII) and the organization survived a banking crisis from 1887 to 1894 by operating conservatively. It contributed to the WWI effort by purchasing government bonds. In 1928 the foundation separated Monte di Pieta's credit and pawn operations and adopted the name Istituto di San Paolo di Torino - Beneficenza e Credito (San Paolo).

Specialized institutions were founded in the 1920s to finance utilities and transportation; one of them La Centrale Societa per il Finanziamento di Imprese Elettriche e Telefoniche was formed in 1925 to help finance Italy's energy and telecommunications industries. In 1965 this entity enlarged its focus and changed its name to La Centrale Finanziaria Generale a forerunner of Banca Intesa.

La Centrale's interests in energy were transferred to ENEL the state holding company in 1985 leaving it with banking finance and insurance holdings. That year the bank merged with Nuovo Banco Ambrosiano formerly Banco Ambrosiano.

Banco Ambrosiano was founded in 1896 by Guiseppi Tovino whose good works and sturdy faith made him a saint (he was beatified in 1998). Betraying his legacy in 1981 chairman Roberto Calvi was found hanging under the Blackfriars Bridge in London. Calvi called "God's Banker" for his connections to the Vatican left behind a tangle of debt phony holding companies and fraud that implicated the Catholic Church brought down an archbishop and involved a secretive Masonic lodge. Banco Ambrosiano was taken over by a group of creditor banks and its name was changed to Nuovo Banco Ambrosiano.

In 1989 Nuovo Banco Ambrosiano merged with its subsidiary Banco Cattolica del Veneto and became known as Banco Ambroveneto. It bought La Cassa di Risparmio delle Provincie Lombarde (Cariplo) Italy's biggest savings bank in 1997; they merged to form Banca Intesa the following year. Cariplo was founded by the Austro-Hungarian government in 1823 when the region was still recovering from Napoleon's depredations. Count Giovanni Pietro Porro wanted to allow artisans and day laborers to set aside money and the company remained true to that mission throughout Italy's unification and two world wars.

Italy began its race toward privatization in 1990 to counter the growing interest of foreign banks in the Italian market and help the nation meet the criteria for joining the European Union. In 1992 San Paolo was one of the first banks to sell a 20% stake in itself (it sold another 20% in 1997). The bank bought several regional and national banks over the next few years and in 1998 merged with investment bank Istituto Mobiliare Italiano or IMI (founded 1931) to form Sanpaolo IMI.

Banca Intesa was the product of a combination of the staid Cassa di Risparmio delle Provincie Lombarde (Cariplo) and the somewhat more colorful Banco Ambroveneto whose history helped inspire the plot of "The Godfather Part III". It took over Banca Commerciale Italiana (BCI or Comit) in 2000 creating one of Italy's largest banks. Banca Intesa integrated BCI to form IntesaBci the following year and then in late 2002 rebranded as Banca Intesa.

Banca Intesa and Sanpaolo IMI merged in 2007. After the deal antitrust authorities ordred the company to sell some 200 branches to France-based Credit Agricole. In late 2008 the Italian banking group sold 36 branches to Veneto Banca for E274 million ($401 million).

A good portion of its branches were acquired in 2007 when Intesa Sanpaolo increased its stake in Banca CR Firenze to some 60% in preparation for taking over the bank outright. Banca CR Firenze added about 550 locations in Tuscany and surrounding regions to Intesa Sanpaolo's network.

The next year the bank upped its stake in Cassa dei Risparmi di Forli e della Romagna to about 70% increasing its influence in northern Italy. During more reshuffling of assets Intesa Sanpaolo sold a 30% stake in Cassa di Risparmio di Fano to Credito Valtellinese in 2009.

EXECUTIVES

Chairman, Giovanni Bazoli, age 81
Chief Risk Officer, Bruno Picca, age 64
Deputy Chairman Management Board, Orazio Rossi, age 81
Chairman Management Board, Enrico Salza, age 76
CEO, Enrico T. Cucchiani, age 63
Head Corporate Affairs, Piero Luongo, age 58
Head Retail Marketing Banca dei Territori Division, Marina Tabacco, age 58
Head of Administration and Tax, Ernesto Riva
CFO, Carlo Messina, age 52
Managing Director and General Manager Finance Banca Infrastrutture Innovazione e Sviluppo, Mario Ciaccia, age 67
Head of Internal Auditing, Renato Dalla Riva
Head Legal Affairs, Elisabetta Lunati
Head International Subsidiary Banks Divisions, Giovanni Boccolini, age 60
Head of Research, Gregorio de Felice
Head Operations Intesa Sanpaolo Group Services, Maurizio Manzotti
Manager Banca dei Territori Division Milano and Province, Franco Ceruti
Manager Banca dei Territori Division Lazio Sardegna and Sicilia, Franco Gallia
Head of Corporate Relationship Management and International Network, Giuseppe Castagna
Head of Merchant Banking Corporate Division, Marco Cerrina Feroni
Deputy CEO and General Manager; Head of the Banca dei Territori Division, Marco Morelli
Manager Banca dei Territori Division Toscana and Umbria, Luciano Nebbia
Managing Director and General Manager Banca Fideuram, Matteo Colafrancesco, age 63
COO, Pier Luigi Curcuruto, age 63
Chief Lending Officer, Eugenio Rossetti, age 58
Head ICT Systems Intesa Sanpaolo Group Services, Silvio Fraternali
Head Real Estate and Procurement Intesa Sanpaolo Group Services, Luca Tedesi
Head Media Relations, Matteo Fabiani
Corporate and Investment Banking Media Relations, Simone Blasi
Head Human Resources, Marco Vernieri
Head External Relations, Vittorio Meloni
Treasurer, Stefano Del Punta
Head Planning and Control, Lucia Ariano
Head Compliance, Piero Boccassino
Head Risk Management, Davide Alfonsi
Head Organization and Security Intesa Sanpaolo Group Services, Marco Cesareo
Head Loan Recovery, Stefano Marchetti
Head Investor Relations, Andrea Tamagnini
Head Rating Agencies, Marco Delfrate
Head SME Marketing Banca dei Territori Division, Carlo Berselli
Manager Banca dei Territori Division Piemont Valle d'Aosta and Liguria, Adriano Maestri
Manager Banca dei Territori Division Lombardia, Bruno Bossina
Manager Banca dei Territori Division Veneto Friuli-Venezia Giulia and Trentino-Alto Adige, Fabio Innocenzi
Manager Banca dei Territori Division Emilia-Romagna Marche Abruzzo and Molise, Giuseppe Feliziani
Manager Banca dei Territori Division Campania Basilicata Calabria and Puglia, Antonio Nucci
Deputy Chairman, Mario Bertolissi, age 65
Deputy Chairwoman, Elsa Fornero, age 65
Chief Risk Officer of Intesa Sanpaolo, Bruno Paesana
Chief Operating Officer of Intesa Sanpaolo, Francesco Roma
Chief Executive Officer of Intesa Sanpaolo, Enrico Milano
Chief Lending Officer of Intesa Sanpaolo, Eugenio Roma
Board Member, Marco Mangiagalli, age 64
Board Member, Jean-Paul Fitoussi, age 71
Board Member, Rosalba Casiraghi
Board Member, Franco Dalla Sega, age 54
Board Member, Gianluca Ferrero, age 51
Board Member, Pietro Garibaldi, age 46
Board Member, Giulio Lubatti, age 66
Board Member, Gianluca Ponzellini, age 67
Board Member, Gian Guido Sacchi Morsiani, age 79
Board Member, Ferdinando Targetti, age 68
Board Member, Livio Torio, age 70
Board Member, Riccardo Varaldo, age 78
Deputy Chairman, Mario Bertolissi, age 65
Deputy Chairwoman, Elsa Fornero, age 65
Board Member, Gianni Marchesini, age 54
Board Member, Fabio Pasquini, age 60
Board Member, Marco Spadacini, age 75
Board Member, Luigi A. Bianchi, age 55
Auditors: RecontaErnst&YoungS.p.A.

LOCATIONS

HQ: Intesa Sanpaolo S.P.A.
Piazza San Carlo, 156, Torino 10121
Phone: (39) 11 5551
Web: www.intesasanpaolo.com

2010 Sales

	% of total
Italy	77
Other	22
Total	**100**

PRODUCTS/OPERATIONS

2010 Sales

	% of total
Banca dei	58
Corporate & Investment	20

International Subsidiary	13
Banca	4
Public	2
Eurizon	1
Total	**100**

COMPETITORS

BBVA
BNL bc
Banca Popolare di Milano
Banco Popolare
Dexia
Mediobanca
Monte dei Paschi di Siena
UniCredit

HISTORICAL FINANCIALS

Company Type: Public

Income Statement FYE: December 31

	ASSETS ($ mil.)	NET INCOME ($ mil.)	INCOME AS % OF ASSETS	EMPLOYEES
12/12	887,669	2,115	0.2%	96,170
12/11	826,801	(10,593)	—	100,118
12/10	881,662	3,620	0.4%	102,501
12/09	900,131	4,040	0.4%	103,718
12/08	889,371	3,569	0.4%	108,310
Annual Growth	(0.0%)	(12.3%)	—	(2.9%)

2012 Year-End Financials

Return on assets: 0.2%
Return on equity: 3.3%
Long-term debt ($ mil.): —
No. of shares (mil.): —
Sales ($ mil): 46,919
Dividends
Yield: 2.6%
Payout: 355.2%
Market value ($ mil.): —

	STOCK PRICE ($) FY Close	P/E High/Low	PER SHARE ($) Earnings	Dividends	Book Value
12/12	10.64	223 99	0.13	0.28	4.22
12/11	9.94	— —	(0.72)	2.19	3.93
12/10	16.22	258106	0.28	0.41	6.05
12/09	27.10	279 85	0.32	0.00	6.40
12/08	21.57	516136	0.28	2.59	5.78
Annual Growth	(16.2%)	— —	(17.1%)	(42.6%)	(7.5%)

Investec plc

Investec plc is the UK arm of Investec a dual-listed financial services firm providing private banking asset management brokerage and investment banking primarily to wealthy clients. (Partner Investec Limited is based in South Africa.) The firm's capital markets unit offers specialized lending structured derivatives and securitization while its asset and wealth management unit has some #54 billion ($88 billion) under management. It also has units devoted to property and private equity funds and institutional research. Investec is primarily active in the UK South Africa and Australia but operates elsewhere in Europe and in the Americas. In late 2011 it acquired financial services group Evolution.

The company won a battle with Canaccord for boutique investment bank Evolution which accepted Investec's #233 million all-share offer. In addition to boosting Investec's investment banking operations the deal also boosted its wealth management business: Evolution brought its Williams de Broe business to the table. The deal also included Evolution's brokerage operations.

With its beginnings as a South African leasing company Investec expanded into the UK in 2002. It has expanded to provide banking and related services both organically and through acquisitions. In 2010 it acquired UK asset manager Rensburg Sheppards boosting its funds under management by about half. The group has also been expanding its geographic reach into select markets.

EXECUTIVES

Managing Director, Bernard Kantor, age 63
Group Risk and Finance Director, Glynn R. Burger, age 56
Company Secretary, David Miller
Joint Non-Executive Chairman of the Board, David Prosser
Joint Non-Executive Chairman of the Board, Fani Titi
Senior Non-Executive Independent Director, George Alford
Executive Director, Hendrik Toit
Managing Director, Bernard Kantor, age 63
Group Risk and Finance Director, Glynn R. Burger, age 56
Non-Executive Director, Bradley Fried
Non-Executive Independent Director, Cheryl Carolus
Non-Executive Independent Director, Haruko Fukuda
Non-Executive Director, Ian Kantor
Non-Executive Director, Mangalani Malungani
Non-Executive Independent Director, Peregrine Crosthwaite
Non-Executive Independent Director, Peter Thomas
Non-Executive Independent Director, Samuel Abrahams
Auditors: Ernst&YoungLLP

LOCATIONS

HQ: Investec plc
2 Gresham Street, London EC2V 7QP
Phone: (44) 20 7597 4000 **Fax:** (44) 20 7597 4491
Web: www.investec.com

PRODUCTS/OPERATIONS

Selected Segments

Asset and wealth management
- Asset Management
- Private Wealth

Specialist bank
- Capital Markets
- Investment Banking
- Private Banking
- Property Activities

COMPETITORS

Barclays
Citigroup
Grupo Santander
HSBC
ING
Invesco Perpetual
Lloyds Banking Group
Prudential plc
Royal Bank of Scotland

HISTORICAL FINANCIALS

Company Type: Public

Income Statement FYE: March 31

	ASSETS ($ mil.)	NET INCOME ($ mil.)	INCOME AS % OF ASSETS	EMPLOYEES
03/13	77,499	482	0.6%	8,151
03/12	82,605	396	0.5%	7,781
03/11	37,111	264	0.7%	7,237
03/10	33,188	195	0.6%	6,123
03/09	53,080	417	0.8%	5,951
Annual Growth	9.9%	3.7%	—	8.2%

2013 Year-End Financials

Return on assets: 0.6%
Return on equity: 8.5%
Long-term debt ($ mil.): —
No. of shares (mil.): 594
Sales ($ mil): 5,441
Dividends
Yield: —
Payout: —
Market value ($ mil.): 4,164

	STOCK PRICE ($) FY Close	P/E High/Low	PER SHARE ($) Earnings	Dividends	Book Value
03/13	7.00	54 38	0.47	0.00	9.52
03/12	6.20	84 49	0.39	0.00	10.07
03/11	7.65	— —	(0.00)	0.00	5.74
03/10	8.30	— —	(0.00)	0.00	(0.00)
03/09	4.40	58 23	0.52	0.00	7.78
Annual Growth	12.3%	— —	(2.6%)	—	5.2%

Isuzu Motors, Ltd. (Japan)

Isuzu Motors has been trucking along since 1916 as one of Japan's first automobile manufacturers. The company is one of the world's top commercial truck makers with heavy- medium- and light-duty models. Isuzu is also a leading diesel engine manufacturer for such automakers as Adam Opel and GM; its engines are used in automotive as well as industrial and marine applications. Other vehicle products include sightseeing and private buses passenger pickup trucks and SUVs. Its D-MAX pickup is particularly popular in Thailand and South America. Isuzu Motors has a worldwide distributor network across almost every major continent though it has stopped selling passenger vehicles in the US.

The company once a pioneer in the American SUV market announced it would stop selling its pickups and SUVs in the US in early 2009 after an eight-year slide in US sales. Longtime partner GM produced the Ascender SUV and the i-Series pickups Isuzu had been selling in the US but it struggled against automakers with stronger brands and dealer networks. (GM had gradually sold off its holding in Isuzu; Mitsubishi currently holds 9% and Toyota 6%.) Isuzu said it would continue to provide parts and service for those vehicles in the US and would continue to sell its two main products –commercial vehicles and diesel engines –in an effort to gain market share in the US and around the world.

Commercial truck and bus demand is forecast to grow in developing markets specifically China Russia and India (where Isuzu has established a production facility via a joint venture with Sumitomo Corp. and local companies). In 2010 Isuzu set up a truck sales joint venture in China with Qingling Motors. The venture builds on a manufacturing tie-up started in 1985 which fostered co-production of trucks sport utility vehicles and diesel engines and sales on behalf of Isuzu by Qingling Motors. Through the sales venture Isuzu took the wheel in setting prices and selecting models with the hope of building China into its largest market. It plans to double its annual capacity of trucks in China to 200000 units by around 2015. The company is also building new sales facilities in South America and a plant in Saudi Arabia to build medium-duty trucks.

At home it is maintaining a strong domestic market position especially with its N Series light-duty line of trucks. Isuzu is also attempting to hold on to if not surpass its spot as the world's #4 manufacturer of diesel engines (by production volume) by continuing to invest in research and development of advanced diesel technology. The sluggish economy in Japan has hampered any real growth though.

Like the rest of the automotive industry Isuzu has been buffeted by the global recession. Sales peaked in 2008 but have declined since as demand plummeted. The company did manage to turn around its $273 million net income loss from 2009 to show positive $90 million net income in 2010 by increasing sales through pushing into new markets and streamlining operations. It plans to more than double net income for fiscal 2011.

HISTORY

After collaborating on car and truck production for 21 years Tokyo Ishikawajima Shipbuilding and Engineering and Tokyo Gas and Electric Industrial formed Tokyo Motors Inc. in 1937. The partners began producing the A truck (1918) and the A9 car (1922) under licenses from Wolseley (UK).

Tokyo Motors made its first truck under the Isuzu nameplate in 1938. It spun off Hino Heavy Industries in 1942. By 1943 the company was selling trucks powered by its own diesel engines mostly to the Japanese military.

By 1948 the company was Japan's premier maker of diesel engines. It was renamed Isuzu (Japanese for "50 bells") in 1949. With generous public- and private-sector financing and truck orders from the US Army during the Korean War Isuzu survived and refined its engine- and truck-making prowess. A pact with the Rootes Group (UK) enabled Isuzu to enter automaking. Beginning in 1953 Isuzu built Rootes' Hillman Minx in Japan.

Despite its strong reputation as a truck builder Isuzu suffered financially and by the late 1960s its bankers were shopping the company around to more stable competitors. GM after witnessing rapid Japanese progress in US and Asian auto markets bought about 34% of Isuzu in 1971. During the 1970s Isuzu launched the popular Gemini car and gained rapid entry to the US through GM exporting such vehicles as the Chevy Luv truck and the Buick Opel.

As exports to GM waned Isuzu set up its own dealer network in the US in 1981. That year GM CEO Roger Smith told a stunned Isuzu chairman Toshio Okamoto that Isuzu lacked the global scale GM was seeking. Smith asked Okamoto for help in buying a piece of Honda. After Honda declined and GM settled for 5% of Suzuki Isuzu extended its GM ties building the Geo Storm and establishing joint production facilities in the UK and Australia.

Despite a high-profile advertising campaign featuring Joe Isuzu the company suffered in the 1980s in its efforts to gain any kind of significant share of the US passenger car market. Post-1985 yen appreciation hurt exports. Subaru-Isuzu Automotive a joint venture with Fuji Heavy Industries initiated production of Rodeos in Lafayette Indiana in 1989.

After Isuzu lost nearly $500 million in 1991 and 1992 it called on GM for help. GM responded by sending Donald Sullivan a strategic business planning expert to become Isuzu's #2 operations executive.

Isuzu signed a joint venture with Jiangxi Automobile Factory and ITOCHU in 1993 to build light-duty trucks in China. In 1994 Nissan and Isuzu agreed to cross-supply vehicles.

Isuzu weathered a public relations storm in 1996 when "Consumer Reports" magazine claimed that the top-selling Trooper sport utility vehicle was prone to tip over at relatively low speeds. Isuzu dismissed the report as unscientific and the National Highway Traffic Safety Administration sided with the automaker. In 1997 the company sued the magazine for defamation. (Isuzu lost the case in 2000.) Also in 1997 Isuzu agreed to develop GM's diesel engines and began constructing a plant in Poland to supply engines to GM's Germany-based subsidiary Opel AG.

The next year GM and Isuzu announced a joint venture to make diesel engines in the US. Also in 1998 Isuzu announced restructuring plans that included cutting 4000 jobs and reducing the number of its domestic marketing subsidiaries. In 1999 the plant in Poland opened and GM boosted its stake in Isuzu to 49%. Isuzu also agreed to form a joint venture with Toyota to manufacture buses.

Amid mounting losses and pressure from GM Isuzu announced a management shake-up in 2001 that included naming GM chairman John Smith Jr. as special advisor and installing Randall Schwarz (GM truck group) as VP. Days later Isuzu announced its "Isuzu V plan" its sweeping cost-savings scheme that included job cuts and the closure of one factory.

The Isuzu V plan was revised in 2002 when the company announced GM would write off its entire stake while infusing Isuzu with about $84 million. Near the close of 2002 Isuzu agreed to sell its 49% stake in carmaking joint venture Subaru-Isuzu Automotive Inc. to Fuji Heavy Industries (FHI). When the deal was completed in January 2003 FHI renamed the company Subaru of Indiana Automotive Inc.

Isuzu had some rocky going in the early part of the 21st century. The company asked its creditor banks to forgive 100 billion yen (about $750 million) in debt in exchange for stakes in the company. As part of the plan GM wrote off its entire stake in Isuzu and reinfused the ailing carmaker with $84 million. The deal resulted in a recapitalized Isuzu and reduced GM's stake to 8%. Early in 2006 GM sold its 8% stake in Isuzu to entities including Mitsubishi Corporation ITOCHU Corporation and Mizuho Corporate Bank.

As 2006 wound near its close Toyota Motor picked up a 6% stake in Isuzu Motors from Mitsubishi and ITOCHU. The two companies agreed to cooperate on engine technologies with Isuzu focusing on small diesel engines and diesel emission controls and Toyota concentrating on environmental improvements to gasoline engines and alternative fuels.

EXECUTIVES

EVP, Ryozo Tsukioka
Senior Executive Officer and Director, Ryo Sakata, age 62
President, Susumu Hosoi
Senior Executive Officer and Director, Tsutomu Yamada
Managing Executive Officer, Masanori Katayama
President of Subsidiary; Director, Chikao Mitsuzaki
Managing Executive Officer, Toshio Sasaki
Senior Executive Officer and Director, Katsumasa Nagai
Senior Executive Officer, Kazuhiko Ito
Executive Officer, Yoshifumi Komura
Executive Officer, Makoto Kawahara
Senior Executive Officer, Hiroyoshi Sakai
Executive Officer, Takashi Kikuchi
Executive Officer, Kengo Baba
Executive Officer, Satoru Kaga
Executive Officer, Masashi Harada
Executive Officer, Jun Motoki
Senior Executive Officer and Director, Haruki Mizutani
EVP, Takanobu Furuta
Managing Executive Officer, Naoto Hakamata
Executive Officer, Susumu Kawahata
Leader of General Affairs Group in General Affairs and Human Resources Unit, Yasuo Fujikake
Vice President; Chief Director of Sales; Director, Ryozo Tsukioka
President and Director, Susumu Hosoi
EVP and Representative Director, Yoshihiro Tadaki
Senior Executive Officer and Director, Tsutomu Yamada
Managing Executive Officer and Director, Masanori Katayama
Director; President Isuzu Motors Sales, Chikao Mitsuzaki
Managing Executive Officer and Director, Toshio Sasaki
Senior Executive Officer and Director, Katsumasa Nagai
Senior Executive Officer and Director, Haruki Mizutani
Managing Executive Officer and Director, Takanobu Furuta
Auditors: Ernst&YoungShinNihon

LOCATIONS

HQ: Isuzu Motors, Ltd. (Japan)
6-26-1 Minami-Oi, Shinagawa-ku, Tokyo 140-8722
Phone: (81) 3 5471 1141
Web: www.isuzu.co.jp

2010 Sales

	$ mil.	% of total
$ mil	% of total	
Asia		
Japan	8,713	65
Rest of Asia	3,537	27
North America	567	4
Other regions	535	4
Total	**13,353**	**100**

PRODUCTS/OPERATIONS

Selected Vehicles and Brands

Buses
- Erga heavy-duty bus
- Erga Mio medium-duty bus

Commercial vehicles
- C&E Series heavy-duty trucks & tractors
- F Series medium-duty trucks
- N Series light-duty trucks

Diesel engines
- Automotive
- Industrial
- Marine

Pickup trucks & SUVs
- D-MAX
- MU-7 (Thailand)
- Panther (Indonesia)

Selected Subsidiaries and Affiliates

Anadolu Isuzu Otomotiv Sanayi Ve Ticaret AS (Turkey)
DMAX Ltd. (US)
Isuzu Australia Limited
Isuzu Motors Europe N.V. (Belgium)
Isuzu (China) Holding Co. Ltd.
Isuzu Commercial Truck of America Inc.
Isuzu Commercial Truck of Canada Inc.
Isuzu Motors America LLC
Isuzu Motors Asia Ltd. (Singapore)
Isuzu Motors Co. (Thailand) Ltd.
Isuzu Motors Germany GmbH
Isuzu Motors Polska Sp. zo. o. (Poland)
Isuzu Philippines Corporation
Isuzu Truck (UK) Ltd.
P.T. Isuzu Astra Motor Indonesia
Qingling Motors Co. Ltd. (China)

COMPETITORS

Ashok Leyland
China Yuchai
Cummins
Daimler
Daimler Trucks North America
MAN
Mitsubishi Fuso
Navistar International
PACCAR
Renault
Scania

Ford Motor	UD Trucks
General Motors	Volkswagen
Hino Motors	Volvo

HISTORICAL FINANCIALS

Company Type: Public

Income Statement FYE: March 31

	REVENUE ($ mil.)	NET INCOME ($ mil.)	NET PROFIT MARGIN	EMPLOYEES
03/13	17,595	1,025	5.8%	26,102
03/12	17,067	1,112	6.5%	24,656
03/11	17,094	623	3.6%	24,461
03/10	11,572	89	0.8%	24,440
03/09	14,467	(272)	—	24,257
Annual Growth	5.0%	—	—	1.8%

2013 Year-End Financials

Debt ratio: 0.1%	No. of shares (mil.): 1,694
Return on equity: 20.4%	Dividends
Cash ($ mil.): 1,963	Yield: —
Current ratio: 1.30	Payout: —
Long-term debt ($ mil.): 857	Market value ($ mil.): 102,217

	STOCK PRICE ($) FY Close	P/E High/Low		PER SHARE ($) Earnings	Dividends	Book Value
03/13	60.33	—	—	0.61	0.00	3.90
03/12	58.66	—	—	0.66	0.00	3.45
03/11	40.16	—	—	0.37	0.00	2.76
03/10	26.85	—	—	0.05	0.00	2.24
03/09	11.97	—	—	(0.16)	0.00	1.99
Annual Growth	49.8%	—	—	—	—	18.3%

Itau Unibanco Holding S.A.

Itau Unibanco is one way of saying "really big bank." The Brazilian bank offers a variety of standard retail and commercial banking services as well as consumer credit financial management leasing foreign exchange and trade financing. It is one of the largest credit card issuers in Brazil. Itau Unibanco also provides investment banking securities brokerage and insurance services. In addition to a network of approximately 5000 branches in Brazil the company has operations in other South America countries and in North America the Caribbean Asia and Europe. The bank has used acquisitions to expand its presence abroad as well as at home. Banco Itau merged with Unibanco to become Itau Unibanco in 2009.

The deal to combine the two Brazilian megabanks established the largest private financial conglomerate in South America. Itau Unibanco is now better equipped to compete on an international level as it expands its global presence. The merger also allowed the bank to expand credit and increase its range of products and services. Since joining forces the group has more than doubled its earnings.

In 2012 the bank agreed to buy the 49.99% it doesn't already own in card payment processing firm Redecard for some R11.8 billion (approximately $6.8 billion). The deal will help boost earnings from credit and debit card usage; it should also help Redecard compete in the growing payment-processing sector.

Itau Unibanco is controlled by holding company IUPAR itself controlled by the Egydio de Souza Aranha family. The Moreira Salles family which previously controlled Unibanco holds a stake of about 25% of the bank. Together the families have board representation with five company directors (including president and CEO Egydio Setubal).

EXECUTIVES

Vice Chairman President and CEO, Roberto Egydio Setubal, age 58
Investor Relations Officer and Director, Alfredo Egydio Setubal, age 54
Director, Henri Penchas, age 66
EVP and Director, Candido Botelho Bracher, age 53
Director, Alcides Lopes Tapias, age 70
Director, Ricardo Villela Marino, age 38
Director, Gustavo Jorge Laboissiere Loyola, age 59
Vice Chairman and EVP, Alfredo Egydio Arruda Villela Jr.
Director, Fernando Roberto Moreira Salles, age 66
Director, Francisco Eduardo de Almeida Pinto
Director, Israel Vainboim, age 68
Director, Pedro Luiz Bodin de Moraes, age 56
Auditors: PricewaterhouseCoopersAuditoresIndependentes

LOCATIONS

HQ: Itau Unibanco Holding S.A.
Praca Alfredo Egydio de Souza Aranha, 100, Sao Paulo 04344-902
Phone: (55) 11 5019 1267
Web: www.itau-unibanco.com

PRODUCTS/OPERATIONS

2010 Sales

	% of total
Interest	
Loans &	47
Trading	7
Other	17
Noninterest	
Fees &	15
Insurance premiums &	6
Other	8
Total	**100**

COMPETITORS

Banco Bradesco	Banco do Brasil
Banco Frances	Caixa Economica Federal
Banco Santander	

HISTORICAL FINANCIALS

Company Type: Public

Income Statement FYE: December 31

	ASSETS ($ mil.)	NET INCOME ($ mil.)	INCOME AS % OF ASSETS	EMPLOYEES
12/12	468,153	6,179	1.3%	96,977
12/11	438,678	7,419	1.7%	104,542
12/10	438,241	7,053	1.6%	0
12/09	343,415	8,073	2.4%	101,640
12/08	172,153	2,079	1.2%	71,354
Annual Growth	28.4%	31.3%	—	8.0%

2012 Year-End Financials

Return on assets: 1.4%	Dividends
Return on equity: 16.8%	Yield: 3.3%
Long-term debt ($ mil.): —	Payout: 40.9%
No. of shares (mil.): —	Market value ($ mil.): —
Sales ($ mil): 74,367	

	STOCK PRICE ($) FY Close	P/E High/Low		PER SHARE ($) Earnings	Dividends	Book Value
12/12	16.46	2	1	1.36	0.51	16.22
12/11	18.56	3	1	1.64	0.19	17.32
12/10	24.01	4	2	1.55	0.45	17.44
12/09	22.84	2	1	1.86	0.24	8.77
12/08	11.60	5	1	0.63	0.56	4.54
Annual Growth	9.1%	—	—	21.1%	(2.4%)	37.5%

ITOCHU Corp. (Japan)

If you drive it eat it fly it or wear it there's a good chance this company is involved with it. ITOCHU Corporation is a leading Japanese "sogo shosha" (general trading company) along with Mitsui & Co. and Mitsubishi and has business interests in such diverse areas as aerospace equipment manufacturing food distribution and clothing production. It also has interests and operations in chemicals energy and mining financial services and retailing. The conglomerate has approximately 130 offices in 67 countries and operates through some 500 subsidiaries and affiliated companies around the world.

In 2011 ITOCHU began rebounding from a flat fiscal 2010 caused by sagging prices for raw materials and energy and a downturn in the economy. It saw its revenues jump to $43.9 billion in 2011 nearly 7% over the previous year despite the effects of the earthquake that hit Japan in 2011. Driving the hike was higher sales in several divisions higher prices for mineral resources and oil and gas operations returns from its strategic investments and higher volumes of transactions in its chemicals businesses. It also saw net income increase nearly 26% to about $2 billion following ITOCHU's jettisoning of inefficient assets and the tidying up of pending problems on its balance sheet by March 2011.

In what it calls its "Brand-new Deal 2012" ITOCHU believes it is financially ready to seek new opportunities and expand the scale of its operations. Among targets it has set for 2012 are to increase its net income by 49% over 2011 expand operations in China increase assets in the machinery-related sector and expand its natural resources operations. It also will seek acquisitions in regions besides China based on the strategies of its individual divisions.

ITOCHU has invested the past few years in streamlining its business divisions and focusing on growth industries. It is looking to expand its involvement in new energy resources pharmaceutical marketing and environmental services as well as communications logistics and technology services. Geographically the company continues to increase its presence in China and North America; however its domestic operations still account for some three-quarters of its revenue.

Following its strategy ITOCHU formed a joint venture in 2011 in China with Toho Holdings and Jointown Pharmaceutical Group to distribute Japanese-made wholesale drugs and medical equipment in China. Based in Wuhan in Hubei province the venture will sell over-the-counter medicines and daily goods —such as disposable pocket warmers —to local drugstores. It will also market prescription drugs and medical equipment such as X-ray machines to hospitals. Toho holds 41% of the venture with ITOCHU holding 10% and Jointown the balance.

In another move to expand its overseas operations in 2011 ITOCHU acquired UK auto repair business Kwik-Fit (GB) Ltd. from European private equity firm PAI Partners for about $1 billion. The purchase which boosts ITOCHU's presence in Europe's auto services market was something of a bargain —PAI Partners paid about $1.5 billion in 2005 after a bidding war for the company.

ITOCHU also agreed to acquire a 20% stake in a Colombian coal mine in a joint venture with US miner Drummond Co. The $1.5 billion deal will tie up the two companies in a mine with about 2 billion tons of provable and probable coal reserves. The deal fits ITOCHU's strategy of raising its equity share in coal mining operations to about 20 million tons per year by 2015.

To raise cash in 2011 the company sold US-based diesel engine marketer and distributor EMDSI - Hunt Power to Stewart & Stevenson for an undisclosed price. That year it also unloaded subsidiary Cieco Energy Ventures which held oil and gas properties in the Gulf of Mexico to Houston-based Tammany Oil & Gas for an undisclosed price.

HISTORY

Chubei Itoh was only 18 when he organized his own wholesale linen business C. Itoh & Co. in 1858. As Japan opened to foreign trade in the 1860s the company prospered and was one of Osaka's largest textile wholesalers by the 1870s. C. Itoh established a trade office in San Francisco in 1889.

By 1919 C. Itoh had trading offices in New York Calcutta Manila and four cities in China. Although it was not one of the "zaibatsu" (industrial groups) that flourished in Japan during the period between the world wars C. Itoh benefited from the general increase in trade.

C. Itoh merged in 1941 with two other trading operations Marubeni and Kishimoto into a new company Sanko Kabushiki Kaisha. C. Itoh and Marubeni were separated in 1949. C. Itoh supplied UN troops with provisions during the Korean War; profits were used to diversify into petroleum machinery aircraft and automobiles.

After the oil crisis of 1973 demonstrated Japan's vulnerability to oil import disruptions C. Itoh actively participated in the development of petroleum production technology. To prevent the failure of Japan's 10th-largest trading company Ataka the Japanese government arranged a merger in 1977 making C. Itoh the third-largest "sogo shosha."

The company established Japan Communications Satellite (JCSAT) with Mitsui and Hughes Communications in 1985. JCSAT launched its first two satellites in 1989 and 1990. The following year C. Itoh and Toshiba joined Time Warner in a limited partnership Time Warner Entertainment Company to produce and distribute movies and television programs and to operate cable TV systems in the US. C. Itoh Time Warner and Toshiba formed another joint venture to distribute Warner Bros. films and develop amusements parks in Japan.

C. Itoh changed its name to ITOCHU a transliteration of its Japanese name in 1992. After sales dropped the next year ITOCHU began selling poorly performing subsidiaries reducing its investment portfolio by more than one-third.

In 1996 the company formed an alliance with US oil company Atlantic Richfield to buy Coastal Corp.'s western US coal operations and it took a stake in a massive project led by Amoco and British Petroleum to develop oil and gas deposits in the Caspian Sea. That year PerfecTV! (a joint venture with Sumitomo and other Japanese companies) began satellite broadcasting. Also in 1996 ITOCHU bought stakes in the Asia Broadcasting and Communications Network a satellite communications company.

To help cover its losses from the Asian currency crisis the company sold 40% of its stake in Time Warner in 1998; in 1999 ITOCHU sold its remaining stake. ITOCHU also sold low-performing real estate investments and laid plans to divest about one-third of its subsidiaries.

Two of ITOCHU's agricultural subsidiaries were liquidated in 2000. The company also sought out partnerships in order to offset costs incurred in new ventures: it joined with Japan's other top trading companies and Brazil's Petrobras to develop oil fields in South America. And in response to the rapid consolidation of Japan's steel industry ITOCHU and Marubeni agreed to integrate their steel operations in 2001 to better compete.

In 2002 ITOCHU formed a partnership with Bally International to expand the European fashion brand's presence in Japan. In 2004 the company sold its interest in Utah-based Canyon Fuel Co. to Arch Coal Inc. for $112 million and dissolved its subsidiary ITOCHU Coal International Inc. Also that year the company formed a joint venture with Ishimori Shotaro Pro Inc. to establish Ishimori Entertainment which produces movies television programs and publications based on Shotaro Ishimori titles including the popular MASKED RIDER.

ITOCHU established a fund with Turner Broadcasting to finance Japanese animation in 2005. It also acquired two US medical-device-distribution companies Products for Surgery and Flanagan Instruments marking ITOCHU's first step into that market.

In 2008 the company partnered with BayCorp Holdings and Energy Management to form American Renewables to develop build and operate biomass-fueled power-generation facilities in the US. Also that year it acquired 41% of Medical Collective a Japanese company that provides marketing assistance to pharmaceutical companies.

In 2010 ITOCHU bought China-based daily goods wholesaler Hangzhou New Huahai Business & Trading boosting its presence in that market. That same year ITOCHU agreed to acquire a 15% stake in Kalahari Minerals PLC which holds uranium gold copper and other base metal interests in Namibia.

Also that year ITOCHU made deals to move into the US energy market joining Chubu Electric Power in a joint venture to buy five natural-gas fired power plants from Tenaska and acquire a 25% interest in the Niobrara shale oil mining project in southeastern Wyoming. With the latter transaction ITOCHU became the first Japanese company to participate in a US shale oil project. The company had acquired 85% of US-based solar power systems maker Solar Net LLC in 2009.

Masahiro Okafuji was named president of ITOCHU in 2010. He replaced Eizo Kobayashi who was named the company's chairman. Okafuji was previously ITOCHU's EVP.

EXECUTIVES

EVP, Yoichi Kobayashi
Chairman, Eizo Kobayashi, age 64
President and CEO, Masahiro Okafuji, age 63
President and CEO ITOCHU International, Eiichi Yonekura
President Machinery, Takao Shiomi
Senior Managing Executive Officer; President Food, Yoshihisa Aoki
CEO ITOCHU East Asia Bloc, Shuichi Koseki
President Metals and Minerals, Ichiro Nakamura
President General Products and Realty, Tomofumi Yoshida
Senior Managing Executive Officer, Koji Takayanagi
EVP and CFO, Tadayuki Seki
President Textile, Hitoshi Okamoto
President Energy and Chemicals, Yuji Fukuda
CEO Oceania ASEAN and South West Asia Bloc, Junichi Sasaki
CEO ITOCHU Europe, Masahiro Imai
Director, Uichiro Niwa, age 73
Senior Managing Director; President Energy Metals and Minerals Company and Director, Yoichi Kobayashi
EVP and Director, Toshihito Tamba
Chief Officer Human Resources General Affairs Legal and Chief Compliance Officer and Director, Yoshio Akamatsu
Director, Tohru Matsushima
Director, Takanobu Furuta
President Food Company and Director, Yoshihisa Aoki
President ICT Aerospace and Electronics Company and Director, Hiroo Inoue
Managing Executive Officer and Director, Kenji Okada
Chief Corporate Planning Officer CIO and Director, Koji Takayanagi
President Chemicals Forest Products and General Merchandise Company and Director, Satoshi Kikuchi
CFO and Director, Tadayuki Seki
Director, Hitoshi Okamoto
Auditors: DeloitteToucheTohmatsu

LOCATIONS

HQ: ITOCHU Corp. (Japan)
3-1-3 Umeda, Kita-ku, Osaka 530-8448
Phone: (81) 6 7638 2121
Web: www.itochu.co.jp

2011 Sales

	$ mil.	% of total
Japan		74
Australia		6
Total		**100**

COMPETITORS

Altria
Balli
Dow Chemical
Exxon Mobil
Fluor
Ito-Yokado
JX Nippon Mining & Metals
Kanematsu
LG Group
Marubeni
Marui Group
Mitsubishi Corp.
Mitsui
NTT
Nippon Steel & Sumitomo Metal Corporation
Nippon Television
Panasonic Corp
Rio Tinto plc
Samsung Group
Sharp Corp.
Sojitz
Sumitomo
Sumitomo Metal Mining
Tokyo Broadcasting System
Yahoo Japan

HISTORICAL FINANCIALS

Company Type: Public

Income Statement FYE: March 31

	REVENUE ($ mil.)	NET INCOME ($ mil.)	NET PROFIT MARGIN	EMPLOYEES
03/13	48,673	2,978	6.1%	98,272
03/12	52,066	3,663	7.0%	94,366
03/11	44,074	1,943	4.4%	84,589
03/10	36,577	1,371	3.8%	84,695
03/09	34,720	1,679	4.8%	77,236
Annual Growth	8.8%	15.4%	—	6.2%

2013 Year-End Financials

Debt ratio: 0.4%	No. of shares (mil.): 1,577
Return on equity: 17.9%	Dividends
Cash ($ mil.): 6,054	Yield: 0.0%
Current ratio: 1.44	Payout: 0.0%
Long-term debt ($ mil.): 26,015	Market value ($ mil.): 38,635

	STOCK PRICE ($) FY Close	P/E High	P/E Low	PER SHARE ($) Earnings	Dividends	Book Value
03/13	24.49	0	0	1.88	0.00	11.89
03/12	21.85	0	0	2.32	0.00	10.54
03/11	20.90	0	0	1.23	1.24	8.84
03/10	87.15	0	0	0.87	0.34	7.45
03/09	49.45	0	0	1.06	0.40	5.47
Annual Growth	(16.1%)	—	—	15.6%	(86.0%)	21.4%

J. Sainsbury PLC

J Sainsbury's trolley is filled with more than groceries. The UK's third-largest food retailer (after Tesco and ASDA) operates the Sainsbury's Supermarkets chain of some 570 stores throughout the UK. Its Sainsbury's online home delivery shopping service covers more than 90% of the UK population. In addition to supermarkets it operates a fast-growing convenience store business with 440 shops under the Sainsbury's Local banner. The firm also owns half of Sainsbury's Bank (in a 50-50 joint venture with Lloyds Banking Group) and a pair of property joint ventures. Sainsbury also sells apparel and home goods including cookware and bedding in its supermarkets and online. In 2011 it acquired Global Media Vault.

Sainsbury bought the online entertainment company from MBL Group plcfor #1 billion ($1.57 billion) in October. The grocery chain which launched its own entertainment Web site in late 2010 said the acquisition will support its drive into the growing online and digital entertainment market. Global Media Vault's digital database includes more than three million music film and game assets for the UK market.

After losing the #2 slot in the UK grocery market years ago to Wal-Mart-owned ASDA Sainsbury has made a strong comeback battling back and forth with ASDA for second place. Currently with a market share of more than 16% Sainsbury trails ASDA by about a percentage point. The two rivals are enmeshed in an ongoing price war with market leader Tesco and other domestic and foreign food retailers including deep-discounters such as ALDI and Lidl. (Sainsbury enjoys an even stronger position in populous London with about 25% of the market.)

Despite pricing pressures Sainsbury has seen its total sales grow by about 40% over the past five years with nonfood sales growing three times as fast as food sales. In fiscal 2012 (ends March) Sainsbury's retails sales and profit both rose nearly 7% vs. the previous year. Sales got a boost from the addition of more than 75 new stores in fiscal 2012 most of which were convenience stores. The company expects to open one to two convenience stores per week throughout the coming year.

Sainsbury also attributes its recent strong performance to growing demand for fresh food and its own private-label brand products which now number more than 5000 items. The grocery chain has also cut prices and stepped up promotions in a bid to lure cash-strapped shoppers from more upscale rivals such as Marks & Spencer and Waitrose. The company's TU clothing brand for women and children has been a big success. Launched in 2004 TU has grown into the seventh-largest apparel retailer in the UK market by volume where it competes with ASDA's George line of apparel Marks & Spencer and others.

Qatar Holdings LLC controls about a 26% of Sainsbury's voting shares.

HISTORY

Newlyweds John James and Mary Ann Sainsbury established a small dairy shop in their London home in 1869. Customers flocked to the clean and efficient store a far cry from most cluttered and dirty London shops. They opened a second store in 1876. By 1914 115 stores had been opened and the couple's sons had entered the business.

During WWI the company's stores established grocery departments to meet demand for preserved products such as meat and jams which were sold under the Sainsbury's label.

Mary Ann died in 1927 and John James the next year. Son John Benjamin wholly devoted to the family business took charge. (He is reported to have said on his deathbed "Keep the stores well lit.") In the 1930s he engineered the company's first acquisition the Thoroughgood stores.

Sales dropped by 50% during WWII and some shops were destroyed by German bombing. Under third-generation leader Alan John Sainsbury the company opened its first self-service store in 1950 in Croydon. The 75000-sq.-ft. store opened in 1955 in Lewisham was considered to be the largest supermarket in Europe.

J Sainsbury went public in 1973. It established a joint venture with British Home Stores in 1975 forming the Savacentre hypermarkets (the company bought out its partner in 1989).

Sainsbury partnered with Grand Bazaar Innovation Bon Marche of Belgium in 1979 to establish Homebase a do-it-yourself chain. (It bought the remaining 25% in 1996 and then sold the company in 2001 retaining only 18%.)

By 1983 most of Sainsbury's 229 stores were clustered in the south of England. A mature market and stiff competition forced the company to look elsewhere –both overseas and close to home. It began buying out US-based Shaw's Supermarkets in New England and in 1984 opened its first Scottish hypermarket. By 1987 the grocer owned 100% of Shaw's which had 60 stores in Massachusetts Maine and New Hampshire.

In 1991 Sainsbury came under competitive pressure from Tesco and the Argyll Group (later renamed Safeway plc) which also began building superstores. It responded with an expansion drive of its own including opening its first Scottish supermarket (in Glasgow) the next year.

In 1994 the company purchased a $325 million stake in Maryland-based Giant Food. Sainsbury bought home improvement retailer Texas Homecare from UK leisure concern Ladbroke in 1995 and integrated it into its Homebase unit. The following year it bought 12 supermarkets in Connecticut from Dutch retailer Royal Ahold (the purchase lowered its profits for the year) and entered Northern Ireland.

A year later the company opened Sainsbury's Bank. Royal Ahold bought Giant Food including Sainsbury's 20% stake in 1998. David Sainsbury —a great-grandson of the founders —retired as chairman in 1998 to pursue politics marking the first time a Sainsbury had not headed up the company in its more-than-a-century history.

As a cost-cutting effort in 1999 Sainsbury cut 2200 jobs more than half in management. It also launched its convenience store concept called Sainsbury's Local. Also that year Sainsbury bought the 53-store Star Markets chain of Massachusetts merging it into its Shaw's operations. In March 2000 Sir Peter Davis took over as CEO of Sainsbury's Supermarkets replacing David Bremner.

In 2001 Sainsbury acquired 19 Grand Union stores in the US (17 of which were converted to the Shaw's banner) and opened 25 new stores in the UK. The company also exited the Egyptian market and sold its home-and-garden chain Homebase to private equity firm Permira.

In 2002 Shaw's Supermarkets bought control of 18 stores in New England from bankrupt discounter Ames.

In November 2003 Sainsbury reached a #2 million out-of-court settlement with designer Jeff Banks over termination of his contract to revamp its clothing line in a bid to emulate rival ASDA's success with its George line of apparel.

In January 2004 the grocery chain acquired Swan Infrastructure (an Accenture affiliate) the company that ran its information technology systems for about $1 billion. The move brought the grocers information technology operations which were outsourced in 2000 back in-house.

In February 2004 Sainsbury acquired 54 Bells convenience stores. (Bells Stores was founded in 1968 by Les Bell and was owned by the Bell family until its acquisition.) Justin King (formerly of Marks & Spencer) joined Sainsbury as its CEO in March 2004 succeeding Sir Peter Davis who became chairman of the board. In April Sainsbury sold JS USA Holdings which operated 203 Shaw's and Star Markets stores in New England to US grocery chain Albertson's in a deal worth about $2.4 billion. The retailer also disposed of JS Developments its property development operation in fiscal 2004. Davis stepped down as chairman of Sainsbury on July 1 2004 one year ahead of schedule and following a prolonged dispute with investors that culminated in a fight over his compensation.

Philip Hampton (former finance director of Lloyds TSB (now Lloyds Banking Group) BT Group and BG Group) joined Sainsbury as its new chairman on July 19 2004. Hampton's appointment and experience with mergers and acquisitions fueled speculation that the struggling grocery chain may become a takeover target. In August Sainsbury acquired Jacksons Stores Ltd. and its wholly owned subsidiary Jacksons Stores 2002 Ltd. for about #100 million. In September Sainsbury agreed to pay ex-chairman Davis #2.6 million despite shareholder protests in July that forced the grocery retailer to withdraw a similar offer. At that time Lord Levene of Portsoken and Keith Butler-Wheelhouse both non-executive directors of the company and members of the remuneration committee resigned from the board.

In October 2004 Sainsbury said it was writing off #140 million against information technology systems and an another #120 million linked to ineffective supply chain equipment as a result of a huge infrastructure investment program instituted by ex-chairman Davis that failed. In November the company acquired JB Beaumont a convenience store chain with six stores in the East Midlands. In 2005 the grocery chain acquired the five-store SL

Shaw chain in southeastern England. Sainsbury renamed the shops Sainsbury's Local. The acquisitions pushed Sainsbury's convenience store count to nearly 300 outlets throughout the UK giving the company a 2% share of the convenience market.

The company sold 5% of its majority stake in Sainsbury's Bank in February 2007 to its joint venture partner HBOS for about #21 million ($40 million). As a result the bank became a 50-50 joint venture between the two firms. Also in 2007 the company shutdown its online entertainment division Sainsbury's Entertain You which offered books CDs DVDs videos computer games and a DVD rental service citing stiff competition in the online arena. The company removed hydrogenated fats from its branded products in 2007.

In mid-2008 Qatar Holding-backed real estate investment group Delta Two increased its stake in Sainsbury to about 25% fueling speculation that it may attempt to take over the British grocer. (In 2007 Delta Two made a bid to buy the remainder of the company but withdrew the offering in November amid turmoil in the credit markets.) Delta Two was the second suitor to leave the grocery chain at the altar. The company and key shareholders from the founding Sainsbury family rebuffed a group of private equity investors led by CVC Capital earlier in the year.

In mid-2009 the grocery chain launched online sales of some 8000 non-food items such as kitchenware and furniture. It also extended its online home grocery delivery service to an additional 200 stores. The company welcomed David Tyler formerly chairman of Logica as its new chairman in November 2009. Tyler succeeded Sir Philip Hampton.

In November 2010 the company launched Sainsbury's Entertainment a digital download service that provides customers with access to more than 150000 books DVDs Blu-rays CDs and games to purchase online.

EXECUTIVES

Chairman, David A. Tyler, age 60
MD of General Merchandise Clothing & Logistics, Roger Burnley
Chief Executive Officer, Justin King, age 51, $700,000 total compensation
Human Resources Director, Imelda Walsh
Group Development Director, Darren Shapland, age 46, $261,000 total compensation
Executive Chef, John Wood
Company Secretary, Tim Fallowfield
Customer Director, Gwyn Burr
Retail Director, Helen Buck
Manager Agriculture, Annie Graham
Managing Director Non-Food, Luke Jensen
Director Commercial Services, Neil Sachdev
Chief Financial Officer, John Rogers
Head - Investor Relations, Adam Adam Katsibas Katsibas
IT Director, Rob Fraser
Marketing Director, Sarah Warby
Group Commercial Director, Mike Coupe
Director, Robert J. (Bob) Stack, age 61
Director, John D. G. McAdam, age 65
Director, Gary Hughes, age 51
Director, Valerie F. (Val) Gooding, age 61
Commercial Director, Michael (Mike) Coupe, age 51
CEO and Director, Justin King, age 50
Group Development Director, Darren Shapland, age 46
Director, Anna Ford, age 69
Director, Mary E. Harris, age 47
CFO and Director, John Rogers
Director, Matthew (Matt) Brittin
Auditors: PricewaterhouseCoopersLLP

LOCATIONS

HQ: J. Sainsbury PLC
33 Holborn, London EC1N 2HT
Phone: (44) 20 7921 6000
Web: www.j-sainsbury.co.uk

PRODUCTS/OPERATIONS

2012 Stores

	No.
Sainsbury's	572
Convenience	440
Total	**1,012**

COMPETITORS

ALDI
ASDA
Alliance Boots
Co-operative Group
Costcutter Supermarkets
Iceland Foods
Lidl
METRO AG
Marks & Spencer
Musgrave Retail Partners
One Stop Stores
SNAX 24
SPAR (UK)
Tesco
Waitrose
Wm Morrison Supermarkets

HISTORICAL FINANCIALS

Company Type: Public

Income Statement FYE: March 16

	REVENUE ($ mil.)	NET INCOME ($ mil.)	NET PROFIT MARGIN	EMPLOYEES
03/13	35,322	930	2.6%	105,000
03/12	35,079	940	2.7%	101,900
03/11	34,073	1,033	3.0%	99,300
03/10	30,247	886	2.9%	97,300
03/09	27,400	418	1.5%	148,500
Annual Growth	6.6%	22.1%	—	(8.3%)

2013 Year-End Financials

Debt ratio: 33.2%
Return on equity: 10.8%
Cash ($ mil.): 783
Current ratio: 0.61
Long-term debt ($ mil.): 3,966
No. of shares (mil.): 1,892
Dividends
Yield: 0.0%
Payout: 506.0%
Market value ($ mil.): 41,343

	STOCK PRICE ($) FY Close	P/E High/Low	PER SHARE ($) Earnings	Dividends	Book Value
03/13	21.84	173125	0.49	2.46	4.59
03/12	19.10	193121	0.50	2.46	4.70
03/11	22.60	190121	0.55	2.13	4.68
03/10	19.94	184116	0.48	2.16	4.04
03/09	17.85	538192	0.24	2.50	3.61
Annual Growth	5.2%	— —	19.6%	(0.4%)	6.2%

Japan Tobacco Inc.

Japan Tobacco (JT) has plenty to puff about. The company secures about 55% of the Japanese cigarette market –the fourth largest worldwide. It holds eights of the country's top 10 brands including Mild Seven Seven Stars and Caster. Globally JT is the #3 tobacco maker trailing Philip Morris International and BAT. Driving growth its JT International arm which owns Britain's Gallaher Group makes and markets Camel Salem and Winston brands outside the US (once made by Reynolds American's RJR Tobacco) and others. JT also has holdings in the food and pharmaceutical industries. In 1985 the company shifted from a state monopoly to a public company; some 50% of JT is held by Japan's Minister of Finance.

Japan Tobacco operates six cigarette manufacturing plants and four factories that make tobacco related products across Japan. Outside its home country it operates 28 factories that make cigarettes and other tobacco and tobacco-related products. Foreign subsidiaries of the company include UK-based Gallaher Ltd. (acquired in 2007) and Liggett-Ducat in Russia. Beyond tobacco which accounts for more than 90% of the company's sales the company is engaged in the production of processed foods and beverages through its JT Beverage and TableMark Co. subsidiaries. Japan Beverage makes canned coffee drinks (under the Roots brand) and operates beverage vending machines. TableMark which makes and sells frozen and other processed foods is exiting the processed fishery products business. The company is also active in the research and development of new drugs through a pharmaceutical arm Torii Pharmaceutical Co. Ltd.

Japan accounts for more than 50% of the company's sales. International markets include Africa Brazil Europe Malaysia North America and Russia. Japan Tobacco's total tobacco sales volume at home and abroad comes to about 534 billion cigarettes per year representing nearly 9% of the global market.

Japan Tobacco saw its adjusted net fiscal 2012 (ends March) sales decline at home by more than 3% vs. the prior year while international sales increased less than 1% over the same period. In Japan sales volume declined as a result of the contracting adult population stricter anti-smoking laws higher taxes and the impact of the massive earthquake that struck eastern Japan in March 2011. Still profits increased at home due to price increases. Indeed the company shipped 534 billion cigarettes in fiscal 2012 compared with 563 billion in 2011. The company's pharmaceutical business posted a nearly 8% gain in 2012 sales while the food and beverage sales declined for the third consecutive year.

Faced with a contracting market at home Japan Tobacco is looking to Africa Asia Eastern Europe and Russia for growth. To that end in late-2011 it paid $450 million to acquire the Haggar Cigarette & Tobacco Factory of Sudan and South Sudan. Haggar produces the Bringi brand of cigarettes and boasts more than 80% market share in Sudan. Its sales volume in 2010 was reportedly more than 4.5 billion cigarettes. Indeed the international business is the profit growth engine for the group. Through additional acquisitions on ongoing investment in foreign markets Japan Tobacco hopes to grow its market share in many key markets. Among other threats to its tobacco business JT faces volatile prices for various crops which cause leaf tobacco costs to stay high. The company has moved to increase its control over both the price and quality of its tobacco leaf supply through a series of acquisitions and alliances. In 2009 the company acquired UK-based Tribac Leaf and two Brazilian firms in a deal valued at about $230 million. Tribac Leaf has growing operations in Malawi Zambia China and India and the Brazilian units operate in their home country. Separately JT formed a new tobacco sourcing company –called JTI Leaf Services –with US leaf suppliers Hail & Cotton and J.E.B. International.

HISTORY

In 1898 roughly 325 years after tobacco was introduced in Japan the nation's Ministry of Finance formed a bureau to monopolize its production to fund military and industrial expansion.

During WWII Japan's tobacco leaf imports from North and South America grew scarce and led to cigarette rationing. In 1949 the government began operating the tobacco production bureau as a business: the Japan Tobacco and Salt Public Corporation (in 1905 the bureau also became responsible for a salt monopoly).

The company launched Hope the first Japanese-made filter cigarette in 1957 and it became the world's best seller a decade later. In 1972 it began printing mild packaging "warnings": "Be careful not to smoke excessively for your health."

Japan Tobacco and Salt began selling Marlboro cigarettes licensed from Philip Morris in 1973. The Mild Seven brand (its current best-seller) went on sale in 1977; it became the world's #1 cigarette in 1981 but dropped to #2 (behind Marlboro) in 1993.

When its tobacco monopoly ended in 1985 the government established the firm as Japan Tobacco (a government-owned joint stock company). As competition from foreign imports increased the firm came up with new means of making yen. It formed Japan Tobacco International (cigarette exports mainly to the US and Southeast Asia) moved into agribusiness and real estate operations and in 1986 created JT Pharmaceutical. In 1987 cigarette import tariffs ended and importers lowered prices to match the company's; its sales and market share subsequently declined. During the late 1980s it introduced HALF TIME beverages and its first low-tar cigarettes (Mild Seven Lights is now the world's #1 light cigarette).

In 1992 Japan Tobacco bought its first overseas production facility Manchester Tobacco (closed in 2001). Former Ministry of Finance official Masaru Mizuno became CEO that year —and soon took up smoking. Also in 1992 the company and Agouron Pharmaceuticals agreed to jointly develop immune system drugs; in 1994 they added antiviral drugs. The government sold about 20% of the firm's stock to the public in 1994 and 13% in 1996. The firm began operating Burger King restaurants in Japan in 1996. Japan Tobacco bought Pillsbury Japan in 1998.

Japan Tobacco in 1999 paid nearly $8 billion for R.J. Reynolds International the international tobacco unit of what was then RJR Nabisco. The company then renamed the unit which has operations in 70 countries worldwide JT International. It also bought the food products division of Asahi Chemical Torii Pharmaceutical from Asahi Breweries and the Unimat vending machine company.

Slowing sales prompted Japan Tobacco to announce in 2000 that it would reduce its workforce by 6100 by 2005. Company exec Katsuhiko Honda became CEO that year (Mizuno remained as chairman) and said he'd push the government to sell its stake. Honda retired in 2006. In February 2001 the company announced plans to sell parts of its OTC drugs and health care businesses to Nichiiko Pharmaceutical to concentrate on prescription drugs. It also intends to sell all 25 of its Burger King outlets. In May Mizuno stepped down as chairman and was replaced by Takashi Ogawa.

In December 2001 Japan's Ministry of Finance recommended that it cut its holdings in the company from 66% to 50%; it would also allow the company to sell additional shares which could further dilute the government's stake to as little as 33%. In 2002 Japan Tobacco completed the sale of its 25 Burger King outlets and its OTC drug business.

In January 2004 the company unveiled six new brands: Mild Seven One Menthol Box Bitter Valley Fuji Renaissance Fuji Renaissance 100's Hi-Lite Menthol and BB Slugger. An added brand Hope Menthol currently being tested in the marketplace also will see expanded availability. Japan Tobacco's Canadian subsidiary filed for bankruptcy protection in August 2004 following a billion-dollar smuggling claim by the Canadian government. Canada said that the company owed $1.4 billion in Canadian back taxes for allegedly smuggling cigarettes in 1998 and 1999.

Japan Tobacco in 2005 ended its agreement with Philip Morris to make and sell Marlboro cigarettes. The company closed 13 of its 25 manufacturing plants and six of its 30 sales branches by early 2006 as part of an effort to increase profits. These reductions slashed as many as 4000 jobs from company payrolls as demand for cigarettes partly depressed by higher taxes continues to decline. Japan Tobacco is also using its own line of premium smokes to fill the gap left in the product line by the absence of Marlboro cigarettes. The company's deal with Philip Morris to sell Marlboro lapsed in 2005.

In April 2007 JT acquired Britain's Gallaher Group for about $15 billion. The purchase which added Silk Cut and Benson & Hedges cigarette brands to its products portfolio was the largest foreign acquisition by a Japanese company.

In January 2008 the company acquired a majority stake in Katokichi Co. for about $900 million. It then sold a 49% stake in the business to Nissin Foods forming a joint venture. In April JT entered the seasonings business acquiring a controlling stake in Fuji Foods.

At the end of 2008 Japan Tobacco placed Hans Group its Australia-based chilled foods venture and its subsidiaries into administration under the care of KordaMetha.

In 2009 Japan Tobacco acquired the UK's Tribac Leaf and Brazil-based leaf suppliers Kannenberg & Cia and Kannenberg Barker Hail & Cotton Tabacos.

EXECUTIVES

Chairman, Hiroshi Kimura, age 58
President, Mitsuomi Koizumi
SVP; President Pharmaceutical Business, Muneaki Fujimoto
Executive Deputy President, Yasushi Shingai
SEVP, Kenji Iijima
Executive Deputy President, Noriaki Okubo
SEVP, Mutsuo Iwai
Executive Deputy President; President Tobacco Business, Akira Saeki
Standing Auditor, Hisao Tateishi
EVP, Shinichi Murakami
SVP and Head China Division Tobacco Business, Atsuhiro Kawamata
SVP and Head Central Pharmaceutical Research Institute Pharmaceutical Business, Junichi Haruta
SVP and Head of Soft Drink Business Division Food Business, Ryoko Nagata
Executive Deputy President, Hideki Miyazaki
SEVP, Ryoji Chijiiwa
SVP and CFO, Naohiro Minami
President CEO and Director, Hiroshi Kimura, age 57
Executive Deputy President; President Tobacco Business; and Director, Mitsuomi Koizumi
Director, Yasushi Shingai
SEVP; President Pharmaceutical Business; and Director, Noriaki Okubo
Executive Deputy President and Chief Communications Officer Assistant to CEO in CSR and General Administration and Director, Masakazu Shimizu
EVP; President Food Business; and Director, Sadao Furuya
Executive Deputy President and Assistant to CEO in Compliance Finance and Food Business and Director, Munetaka Takeda
Executive Deputy President and Assistant to CEO in Strategy HR Legal and Operational Review and Business Assurance and Director, Masaaki Sumikawa
Auditors: DeloitteToucheTohmatsu

LOCATIONS

HQ: Japan Tobacco Inc.
2-2-1 Toranomon, Minato-ku, Tokyo 105-8422
Phone: (81) 3 3582 3111 **Fax:** (81) 3 5572 1441
Web: www.jti.co.jp

2012 Sales

	% of total
Japan	52
Other	48
Total	**100**

PRODUCTS/OPERATIONS

2012 Sales

	% of total
Tobacco	
Japanese	53
International	40
Food	6
Pharmaceutical	1
Others	-
Total	**100**

Selected Cigarette Brands

BB Slugger
Benson & Hedges
Bitter Valley
Cabin and Cabin Mild
Camel (outside the US)
Caster and Caster Mild
Frontier
Fuji Renaissance
Glamour
Hi-Lite Menthol
Hope Menthol
LD
Marlboro (outside the US)
Mild Seven
Pianissimo (includes Lucia and Icene)
Russian Style
Salem (outside the US)
Seven Stars
Silk Cut
Sobranie
Winston (outside the US)

COMPETITORS

Ajinomoto
Altadis
Asahi Breweries
British American Tobacco
Coca-Cola
Imperial Tobacco
Mitsubishi Chemical
Nestle
Nisshin Seifun Group
Philip Morris International
Reemtsma Cigarettenfabriken
Suntory Holdings
Unilever
Vector Group

HISTORICAL FINANCIALS

Company Type: Public

Income Statement FYE: March 31

	REVENUE ($ mil.)	NET INCOME ($ mil.)	NET PROFIT MARGIN	EMPLOYEES
03/13	22,533	3,651	16.2%	49,507
03/12	24,793	3,911	15.8%	48,529
03/11	24,869	2,938	11.8%	48,472
03/10	65,676	1,482	2.3%	49,665
03/09	69,381	1,253	1.8%	47,977
Annual Growth	(24.5%)	30.7%	—	0.8%

2013 Year-End Financials

Debt ratio: 0.0%
Return on equity: 19.9%
Cash ($ mil.): 1,516
Current ratio: 1.09
Long-term debt ($ mil.): 2,873
No. of shares (mil.): 1,817
Dividends
Yield: —
Payout: —
Market value ($ mil.): 58,341

	STOCK PRICE ($) FY Close	P/E High	P/E Low	PER SHARE ($) Earnings	Dividends	Book Value
03/13	32.10	0	0	1.92	0.00	10.56
03/12	5,550.00	0	0	2.05	0.00	10.46
03/11	3,600.00	0	0	1.53	0.00	9.67
03/10	3,550.00	—	—	154.69	0.00	1,925.79
03/09	3,050.00	—	—	130.79	0.00	1,721.76
Annual Growth	(68.0%)	—	—	(65.2%)	—	(72.0%)

Jardine Matheson Holdings Ltd.

LOCATIONS

HQ: Jardine Matheson Holdings Ltd.
Jardine House, 33-35 Reid Street, Hamilton
Phone: (441) 292 0515 **Fax:** (441) 292 4072
Web: www.jardines.com

HISTORICAL FINANCIALS

Company Type: Public

Income Statement FYE: December 31

	REVENUE ($ mil.)	NET INCOME ($ mil.)	NET PROFIT MARGIN	EMPLOYEES
12/12	39,593	1,688	4.3%	0
12/11	37,967	3,449	9.1%	0
12/10	30,053	3,084	10.3%	0
12/09	22,501	1,604	7.1%	0
12/08	22,362	666	3.0%	0
Annual Growth	15.4%	26.2%	—	—

2012 Year-End Financials

Debt ratio: 18.1%
Return on equity: 9.8%
Cash ($ mil.): 4,298
Current ratio: 1.46
Long-term debt ($ mil.): 7,896
No. of shares (mil.): 300
Dividends
Yield: 1.9%
Payout: 25.6%
Market value ($ mil.): 18,668

	STOCK PRICE ($) FY Close	P/E High	P/E Low	PER SHARE ($) Earnings	Dividends	Book Value
12/12	62.23	14	10	4.62	1.19	59.34
12/11	47.51	6	5	9.46	1.10	54.89
12/10	44.26	6	3	8.34	0.91	46.32
12/09	30.45	7	4	4.44	0.72	33.83
12/08	18.95	19	8	1.88	0.65	28.25
Annual Growth	34.6%	—	—	25.2%	16.1%	20.4%

Jardine Strategic Holdings Ltd (Bermuda)

Jardine Strategic Holdings (JSH) invests in multinational businesses with a focus on Asia. Its primary interests include stakes in retail firm Dairy Farm International with 5000 locations hotel group Mandarin Oriental with 45 hotels holding firm Jardine Cycle & Carriage financial services firm Rothchilds Continuation and real estate developer Hongkong Land. Jardine Cycle's main holding Astra International is the largest vehicle engine manufacturer in Indonesia. JSH and its Hong Kong-based affiliate Jardine Matheson Holdings Ltd share these interests and are operated together in a complex ownership structure. Jardine Matheson also provides management and legal resources for JSH and owns about 80% of JSH's stock.

The company was originally formed in the wake of the breakup of the East India Company's tea trade monopoly in 1832. Following Jardines' founding it was a key company that promoted the founding of Hong Kong.

EXECUTIVES

Managing Director and Director, Anthony J. L. Nightingale
Chairman, Henry Keswick
CFO, James Riley
Company Secretary, C. H. Wilken
Director, Simon L. Keswick, age 70
Managing Director and Director, Anthony J. L. Nightingale
Director, Percy Weatherall
Director, Lord C. G. Rodney Leach, age 78
Director, Jenkin Hui
Director, R. C. Kwok
Director, George C.G. Koo
Director, P.L.A. Jamieson
Auditors: PricewaterhouseCoopersLLP

LOCATIONS

HQ: Jardine Strategic Holdings Ltd (Bermuda)
Jardine House, 33-35 Reid Street, Hamilton
Phone:
Web: www.jardines.com

COMPETITORS

Accor
China Resources Enterprise
Continental Automotive Group
Daiei
HSBC
Hopewell Holdings
Hutchison Whampoa
Hyatt
ITOCHU
Marriott
Marubeni
McDonald' s
Royal Ahold
Swire Pacific

HISTORICAL FINANCIALS

Company Type: Public

Income Statement FYE: December 31

	REVENUE ($ mil.)	NET INCOME ($ mil.)	NET PROFIT MARGIN	EMPLOYEES
12/12	33,098	1,839	5.6%	0
12/11	31,049	3,943	12.7%	0
12/10	25,498	3,535	13.9%	0
12/09	18,905	1,844	9.8%	0
12/08	18,455	692	3.7%	0
Annual Growth	15.7%	27.7%	—	—

2012 Year-End Financials

Debt ratio: 17.6%
Return on equity: 8.9%
Cash ($ mil.): 3,947
Current ratio: 1.53
Long-term debt ($ mil.): 7,661
No. of shares (mil.): 200
Dividends
Yield: 2.3%
Payout: 3.5%
Market value ($ mil.): 3,552

	STOCK PRICE ($) FY Close	P/E High	P/E Low	PER SHARE ($) Earnings	Dividends	Book Value
12/12	17.76	23	5	2.99	0.42	106.72
12/11	54.92	11	8	6.34	0.10	98.26
12/10	55.20	10	6	5.54	0.37	78.99
12/09	36.00	12	6	2.93	0.09	56.73
12/08	20.25	34	16	1.12	0.34	46.88
Annual Growth	(3.2%)	—	—	27.8%	5.5%	22.8%

JBS S.A.

Carnivores have a friend in JBS. With a daily slaughter capacity of 86000 head of cattle JBS is the world's biggest beef (and pork poultry and lamb) processor and exporter. In addition to fresh and processed beef and pork (it is the #3 pork producer in the US) JBS offers cooked and canned meats ready-to-eat meals as well as hides and dairy products. JBS sells beef domestically under the Friboi brand. It also owns control of US poultry giant Pilgrim's Pride. The company exports products worldwide; top markets include Japan the Middle East and Africa and Mexico. Positioned as an integrated food company JBS is expanding in the US and Australia. The Batista family through FB Participac?es owns 47% of JBS.

Managing its growth strategy is challenging the company's already full plate of activities. JBS posted almost a 60% increase in year-over-year revenues in 2010 fueled in part by its business acquisitions and marking it as Brazil's third largest company by revenue. Earnings before interest and taxes soared too. Nonetheless net earnings plummeted to roughly a $180 million loss eroded by debt which swelled by more than 20% and other costs. Among them the cost to restructure its US operations (including consolidation of Pilgrim's Pride) simultaneous with incorporating Bertin (a Brazilian meatpacker taken over in late 2009) with the JBS Mercosul food division has taken a toll on working capital resulting in higher financial expenses.

Adding to its frustration after two unsuccessful runs at Sara Lee in 2011 and late 2010 JBS ended its attempt to buy the iconic cheesecake maker. A takeover of Sara Lee's packaged meat business (Ball Park Jimmy Dean) would have consolidated JBS's power as a global integrated meat producer rivaling US-based Tyson Foods and Smithfield Foods. Following JBS's second failed bid Wesley Batista succeeded his brother Joesley as company CEO. Wesley formerly head of JBS USA Holdings has more than two decades of experience in the company.

Under Joesley Batista JBS undertook an aggressive international expansion strategy culminating in alliances and acquisitions in Argentina Australia Europe and the US. Late 2010 JBS entered a 50/50 joint venture with Jack Link's Beef Jerky a maker of the top US meat snack brand. Concurrently Jack Link's purchased a beef jerky manufacturing plant from JBS and JBS agreed to supply raw meat to Jack Link's for processing packaging and distribution.

Significant acquisitions have included taking over the ailing Pilgrim's Pride (2009). The deal marked JBS's entry into the US poultry industry and rank as the #2 poultry producer in the world with a daily slaughtering capacity of 7.9 million birds. After acquiring its initial stake in Pilgrim's Pride JBS upped its holding to more than 67% in late 2010.

JBS also bought out US beef producer Swift Foods (2007) now JBS USA. To diversify its funding resources and raise money for acquisitions the company in 2009 filed to take JBS USA public. It delayed the IPO and paid an approximately $315 million penalty for its inaction (which added to the company's loss in 2010). In early 2011 JBS withdrew the IPO.

HISTORY

After nearly two decades in operation JBS began to expand its business significantly and steadily during the 1970s by purchasing independent slaughterhouses and cattle processing facilities throughout Brazil. These acquisitions continued through the end of the century at which point JBS also began to turn an acquisitive eye toward Argentina.

In 2005 the Brazilian meat giant took its first step abroad buying 85% of Swift Armour Argentina's largest beef processor for $200 million. In 2007 the company acquired US-based Swift Foods for $225 million and assumed its heavy debt load estimated at more than $1 billion a few months after going public on the Sao Paulo Stock Exchange.

In 2008 JBS acquired Australian-based beef producer Tasman Group for $107 million in cash. Also that year it bought US processor Smithfield Beef from Smithfield Foods for $565 million. In Europe it formed a 50:50 joint venture with Italy's Cremonini and subsidiary Inalca with plants in Italy Russia and Africa for $328 million.

In 2009 JBS filed with US regulators to hold a $2 billion initial public offering for JBS USA Holdings (It withdrew the proposed IPO in 2011.) Also in 2009 JBS acquired a 64% stake in restructured US poultry producer Pilgrim's Pride for $800 million. Prior to declaring bankruptcy in 2008 Pilgrim was the #1 US chicken producer and despite selling off some of its operations was still a huge poultry operation. Other than saying it hoped to increase Pilgrim's competitiveness both domestically and internationally JBS made no other statement as to Pilgrim's future. In late 2009 JBS acquired Australia's Tatiara Meat Company from the Dutch company VION Food Group for $28 million. Tatiara is Australia's largest exporter of fresh lamb meat; it also offers value-added lamb products. It was integrated into JBS's Swift Australia operations. At home JBS bought #2 Brazilian beef producer Bertin with 38 plants at home and abroad in an all-stock deal in 2009.

Eyeing acquisitions on the other side of the globe JBS in September 2010 bought Australia's Rockdale Beef from joint owners Itoham Foods and Mitsubishi Corporation. The deal valued at about $38 million boosted the firm's processing capacity by some 550 cattle per day and secured its foothold in the country. In February 2011 Wesley Batista succeeded his brother Joesley Batista as CEO of the company. Wesley formerly head of the company's US subsidiary is a 22-year veteran of JBS. Joesley Batista continued as chairman. In March JBS terminated its joint venture with Italy's Cremonini after a protracted dispute by selling its 50% stake in Inalca back to Cremonini for $304 million.

EXECUTIVES

Chairman, Joesley Mendonca Batista, age 39
President CEO and Director, Wesley Mendonca Batista, age 41
Director Legal, Franciso de Assis
Investor Relations Officer, Jeremiah A. (Jerry) O'Callaghan, age 58
President CEO and Director, Wesley Mendonca Batista, age 41
Director, Jose Batista Sobrinho
Director, Jose Batista Jr.
Director, Marcus Vinicius Pratini de Moraes
Director, Wagner Pinheiro de Oliveira
Auditors: GrantThornton

LOCATIONS

HQ: JBS S.A.
Avenida Marginal Direita do Tiete, 500, Sao Paulo, SP 05118-100
Phone: (55) 11 3144 4000 **Fax:** (55) 11 3144 4171
Web: www.jbs.com.br

2010 Sales

	% of total
Domestic	70
Export	30
Total	**100**

2010 Export Sales

	% of total
Africa & Middle	18
Mexico	14
Japan	12
Russia	10
EU	8
Hong	7
South	5
Canada	4
China	4
USA	3
Taiwan	2
Indonesia	1
Other	12
Total	**100**

PRODUCTS/OPERATIONS

2010 Sales

	% of total
Beef	64
Chicken	22
Pork	9
Other	5
Total	**100**

Selected Products and Brands

Agricultural inputs (animal nutrition sanitation and management)
Beef jerky
Biodiesel
  JBS Biodiesel
  Bertin
Biolins (thermoelectric plant)
Cans
  JBS Latas
Casings (for sausage salamis hotdogs)
Collagen
  Novaprom
Confinements (livestock fencing structures)
Dairy products
  Amelia
  Bertin
  Carmelita
  Danubio
  Faixa Azul
  Franciscano
  Leco
  Mesa
  Serrabella
  Vigor
Leather
  JBS Couros
Oleochemicals
Pet feed
  Bertin
Protein (beef pork chicken sheep)
  Anglo
  Apeti
  Bertin
  Bordon
  Caba?a Las Lilas
  Friboi
  Maturatta
  Organic Beef
  Pilgrim's Pride
  Swift
Recycling (HDPE LDPE LDLPE and PP resins)
Shipping
  JBS Transportadora
Trade (vegetal oils chemicals animal fat)
Vegetables
  Anglo
  Bordon
  Swift

COMPETITORS

Agri Beef
AzTx Cattle
Bachoco
Birchwood Meat & Provision
Brasil Foods
Cactus Feeders
Campofrio Foopd
Cargill Meat Solutions
Danish Crown
Eleva
Ellison Meat Company
Golden Belt Feeders
Greater Omaha Packing
HKScan
Hormel
Kepak Group
King Ranch
Lykes Bros.
Marfrig
Minerva sa
Moksel
National Beef Packing
Perdue Incorporated
Pilgrim' s Pride
Rosen' s Diversified
Sam Kane Beef Processors
Sanderson Farms
Seara Alimentos
Smithfield Foods
Tejon Ranch
Tyson Foods
U.S. Premium Beef
VION N.V.

HISTORICAL FINANCIALS

Company Type: Public

Income Statement FYE: December 31

	REVENUE ($ mil.)	NET INCOME ($ mil.)	NET PROFIT MARGIN	EMPLOYEES
12/12	37,024	351	0.9%	0
12/11	33,134	(40)	—	0
12/10	33,166	(182)	—	0
12/09	19,668	74	0.4%	0
12/08	13,013	11	0.1%	55,000
Annual Growth	29.9%	137.1%	—	—

2012 Year-End Financials

Debt ratio: 20.1%
Return on equity: 3.4%
Cash ($ mil.): 2,632
Current ratio: 1.68
Long-term debt ($ mil.): 7,038
No. of shares (mil.): —
Dividends
  Yield: —
  Payout: —
Market value ($ mil.): —

	STOCK PRICE ($) FY Close	P/E High	P/E Low	PER SHARE ($) Earnings	Dividends	Book Value
12/12	6.00	0	0	121.22	0.00	3.54
12/11	6.31	—	—	(14.89)	0.00	3.74
12/10	8.67	—	—	(73.16)	0.02	4.25
12/09	11.11	—	—	(0.00)	0.00	4.13
12/08	4.40	—	—	(0.00)	0.00	(0.00)
Annual Growth	8.1%	—	—	—	—	—

JFE Holdings Inc

JFE Holdings has an iron will unmatched in Japan and much of the rest of the world. The "J" in JFE stands for Japan; "F" is for Fe the chemical symbol for iron; and "E" stands for engineering. JFE Holdings' steel business unit JFE Steel accounts for about 85 % of total sales and manufactures steel products such as bars pipes steel frames tubes and stainless steel for the automotive construction and petroleum industries. JFE is among the world's largest steel companies ranking behind ArcelorMittal Japan's Nippon Steel & Sumitomo Metal and China's Hebei Iron and Steel and Baosteel.

Geographic Reach

While most of its steel production facilities are in Japan JFE's reach is global and it has offices in 12 other countries.

Operations

JFE's engineering unit makes designs and builds facilities such as gasifying and melting furnaces water purification plants steelworks plants and equipment and steel structures used in the energy environmental and steel structural sectors. Its shipbuilding unit constructs both merchant and military vessels in several Japanese ports including Kyoto and Yokahama. JFE's urban development unit develops large-scale condominium complexes using large plots of undeveloped land while its microelectronics (LSI) division includes Kawasaki Microelectronics which produces integrated circuits for digital cameras.

Financial Performance

The company's revenues decreased by a marginal 1% (in local currency) in fiscal year 2012 to a decrease in sales in the steel urban development and LSI segments due to a decline in demand which was partially offset by an increase in sales in the engineering and shipbuilding segments.

However its net income decreased by 163% in local currency in fiscal year 2012 due to a drop in operating income and ordinary income and a loss on the valuation of overseas investments.

Strategy

The company buys and sell steel companies and other assets as it seeks to deliver the best returns for its shareholders.

In 2012 JFE Steel agreed to acquire threading business and related assets of US-based Benoit Machine LLC through holding company Benoit Holding jointly owned by JFE Steel and Kanematsu USA a subsidiary of Kanematsu. The deal will enable JFE Steel and Kanematsu to establish a total supply chain for the manufacture threading and distribution of oilfield tubing and downhole accessories and thereby meet diversified needs in the oil and gas industry and capture growing demand for oilfield tubing going

On the other side of the ledger in 2012 JFE Steel sold part of its stake in South Korean steelmaker Hyundai Hysco to the Hyundai Group for an undisclosed amont. The stake was cut to below 8%. JFE Steel supplies hot-rolled steel sheet to Hyundai Hysco for the construction and automobile industries but Hyundai has stepped up its steel production and reduced the need for imports.

In 2010 JFE Steel acquired all shares of Toyohira Steel it did not already own taking full control of the company. Toyohira a Sapporo-based electronic furnace steelmaker is a wholly owned subsidiary of JFE Steel.

That same year JFE Steel acquired a 24% stake in Pancheng Yihong Pipe Co. a China-based maker of seamless pipes for oilfields in a stock-purchase deal. Following the investment JFE jointly owns the company along with China's Chengdu Steel & Vanadium Co. (51%) and another Japanese company Marubeni-Itochu Steel (25%).

EXECUTIVES

CEO and Board Member, Fumio Sudo, age 71
Director and EVP, Toshikuni Yamazaki
President JFE Engineering, Sumiyuki Kishimoto
President JFE Steel Corporation, Eiji Hayashida
President and CEO JFE Shoji Trade Corporation, Tsutomu Yajima
EVP Finance Investor Relations and Corporate Planning, Shinichi Okada
SVP General Administration, Sakio Sasamoto
Director; President JFE Steel, hajime Yamazaki
President and CEO, Hajime Bada, age 64
CEO and Board Member, Fumio Sudo, age 71
Director and EVP, Toshikuni Yamazaki
Director; President JFE Engineering, Sumiyuki Kishimoto
Director and SVP Corporate Planning and Controller, Eiji Hayashida
Director; President JFE Steel, hajime Yamazaki
Director, Shigeo Asai
Auditors: Ernst&YoungShinNihon

LOCATIONS

HQ: JFE Holdings Inc
2-2-3 Uchisaiwai-cho, Chiyoda-ku, Tokyo 100-0011
Phone: (81) 3 3597 4321
Web: www.jfe-holdings.co.jp

PRODUCTS/OPERATIONS

2012 Sales

	% of total
Steel	85
Engineering	8
Shipbuilding	6
LSI	1
Total	**100**

COMPETITORS

ArcelorMittal
Baosteel
BlueScope Steel
Kobe Steel
Nippon Steel & Sumitomo Metal Corporation
Nippon Yakin
Nisshin Steel
Severstal
Shougang Corp.
Sumitomo Metal Industries
United States Steel

HISTORICAL FINANCIALS

Company Type: Public

Income Statement FYE: March 31

	REVENUE ($ mil.)	NET INCOME ($ mil.)	NET PROFIT MARGIN	EMPLOYEES
03/13	33,894	420	1.2%	57,044
03/12	38,601	(446)	—	54,133
03/11	38,590	707	1.8%	54,400
03/10	30,451	488	1.6%	53,892
03/09	39,688	1,972	5.0%	56,547
Annual Growth	(3.9%)	(32.0%)	—	0.2%

2013 Year-End Financials

Debt ratio: 0.4%
Return on equity: 2.6%
Cash ($ mil.): 686
Current ratio: 1.48
Long-term debt ($ mil.): 13,082
No. of shares (mil.): 576
Dividends
Yield: —
Payout: —
Market value ($ mil.): 11,625

	STOCK PRICE ($) FY Close	P/E High/Low	PER SHARE ($) Earnings	Dividends	Book Value
03/13	20.15	— —	0.76	0.00	29.41
03/12	22.05	— —	(0.84)	0.00	32.97
03/11	29.60	— —	1.32	0.00	33.62
03/10	39.25	— —	0.92	0.00	29.67
03/09	21.50	— —	3.44	0.00	26.44
Annual Growth	(1.6%)	— —	(31.5%)	—	2.7%

Johnson Matthey Plc (United Kingdom)

Johnson Matthey is truly a golden oldie. The company which dates to 1817 is an established world leader in the refining and distribution of gold silver and platinum group metals (about 70% of sales). It is the sole marketing arm for Anglo Platinum the world's largest platinum producer through its Precious Metal Products division. Johnson Matthey's Environmental Technologies Catalysts division produces emission control products fuel cells and process catalysts. Its Fine Chemicals division makes base and precious metals catalysts and chemicals as well as active pharmaceutical ingredients (API) sold to pharmaceuticals manufacturers. Johnson Matthey operates in 30 countries on six continents.

Active worldwide the company has been concentrating on expanding its business in China and India. In the former Johnson Matthey focuses on catalysts that will control nitrogen oxide emissions from China's massive coal industry. The company has set a long-term strategy of focusing on leading-edge catalysts using technology as a differentiator keeping platinum group metals (PGMs) as a major part of its operations and concentrating on organic growth.

The marketing and refining agent for Anglo American Platium since 1931 Johnson Matthey also ranks as one of the largest PGM traders and marketers as well as one of the largest suppliers of PGMs for industrial use. It supplies about 5 million ounces of PGMs per year.

The company's revenues were up 27% in 2011 over the previous year resulting from high metal prices and high sales volumes. Its Precious Metals unit increased 33% for the year because of higher metal prices and strong demand while Environmental Technologies advanced 31% due to global growth in light-duty vehicle production and more diesel cars produced in Europe that year. Its Fine Chemicals unit saw an increase of 14% over the previous year's revenues marked by good sales by its API business. Underlying profit before tax was up 36% from the previous year.

HISTORY

Percival Johnson set up an assayer's shop in London in 1817. Using chemical and physical tests he determined the amount of gold in a given bar and guaranteed his results by offering to buy the bars he assayed. Johnson then set up a gold refinery in the early 1830s and developed a method for extracting platinum group metals. As part of that process he produced vitreous colors for pottery and glass refined nickel and silver nitrate for medical use and later for photographic uses.

George Matthey joined the company in 1838 and championed the platinum business securing a steady supply of platinum from Russia. The company thrived on business generated by gold rushes in California (1849) and Australia (1851). It built a silver refinery to melt down European coinage and extract component metals and in 1870 it bought a company that produced magnesium antimony vanadium and aluminum. In 1891 the company became Johnson Matthey & Co. Limited. Around the turn of the century it bought rolling mills and began forming metals into sheet tube and wire to better serve jewelers.

During WWI Johnson Matthey & Co. provided platinum catalysts and magnesium powder for explosives and in WWII the company was appointed the government's agent for controlling platinum stocks. Johnson Matthey & Co. expanded its international operations rapidly during the post-war boom adding holdings in Australia India North America and South Africa. It established subsidiaries in France and the Netherlands (1956) Italy (1959) Sweden (1960) Belgium (1961) and Austria (1962). The company also began conducting research on automotive catalytic converters to reduce pollution. It formed Johnson Matthey Bankers (JMB) to carry out its banking and trading activities.

A foray into the US jewelry business led to big losses in 1980 and the company pressed JMB to make higher-risk loans. JMB's contribution to profits went from less than 25% in 1981 (the year the company took its present name) to more than 60% in 1983. The bank ended up with so many bad loans that the Bank of England had to arrange a bailout in 1984. Gene Anderson who became CEO in 1985 cut 3000 jobs and reduced the number of divisions from 78 to 4. Profits rebounded but Anderson resigned in 1989 after failing to persuade the board to diversify away from platinum.

During the 1990s the company invested heavily in its electronics division which had been doing well since the 1989 acquisition of Cominco Electronic Materials (ultra-pure metals for microchips). By 1995 the division was responsible for about a third of Johnson Matthey's profits. In 1998 it bought Cookson Group's 50% share of its ceramics joint venture.

In 1998 Johnson Matthey shifted its focus to three core businesses: catalysts colors and coatings and precious metals. The next year it sold its electronic materials business Johnson Matthey Electronics to US-based AlliedSignal (now Honeywell International) and began looking for takeover opportunities in its core markets. In 2001 the company acquired pharmaceuticals manufacturers Meconic (now Macfarlan Smith; it's the UK's only maker of medical opiates –cocaine and heroin) and Pharm-Eco then used these acquisitions as the basis for a fourth division: Pharmaceutical Materials (now a part of its Fine Chemicals and Catalysts Division).

In 2002 the company acquired Cascade Biochem Limited to strengthen its Pharmaceutical Materials division and metal catalyst company Synetix. CEO Chris Clark retired in 2003. He was succeeded by Neil Carson former executive director of the precious metals and catalysts operations.

Following the sale of its Pigments & Dispersions unit to Rockwood Pigments in 2004 Johnson Matthey restructured its Colours and Coatings division by closing several of its manufacturing sites and transferring some operations to its Precious Metal Products division. The moves created what became the Ceramics division the 2007 sale of which was the last in the dismantling of the Colours and Coatings division.

At the beginning of 2008 the company acquired the Argillon Group which manufactured catalysts and advanced ceramic materials from Ceramics Luxembourg (owned by KKR). Later that year Johnson Matthey sold the acquired ceramic insulators alumina business for about $40 million.

In 2010 a Johnson Matthey subsidiary formed a joint venture with Aoxing Pharmaceutical to manufacture ingredients for narcotics and neurological drugs for the Chinese market. That same year Johnson Matthey acquired Intercat a supplier of fluid catalytic cracking services for the petroleum refining industry for $56 million. It became part of Johnson Matthey's Process Technologies division's Ammonia Methanol Oil and Gas unit.

EXECUTIVES

Executive Director Environmental Technologies Division and Director, Larry C. Pentz, age 58, $444,506 total compensation
Chairman, Tim E. P. Stevenson, age 64
Chief Executive and Board Member, Neil A. P. Carson, age 56, $1,218,910 total compensation
Director Group Systems and Environment Health and Safety and Human Resources, I. F. Stephenson
Chairman of Johnson Matthey, Sir John Banham, age 72
Group Treasurer, G. J. Coates
Group Legal Director and Secretary, S. Farrant
IR Contact Officer, Ian D. Godwin
Director Technology Centre, B. A. Murrer
Group Finance Director, Robert MacLeod, age 49, $294,000 total compensation
Division Finance Director Emission Control Technologies, S. M. Christley
Division Director Catalysts Chemicals and Refining, G. P. Otterman
Director Group Business Development, F. K. Sheffy
Executive Director Precious Metal Products, W. F. (Bill) Sandford, $209,000 total compensation
Division Finance Director Precious Metals, B. M. O'Connell
Director Marketing Precious Metals, M. Bedford
Deputy Director Group Environment Health and Safety and Human Resources, P. C. Framp
President Pharmaceutical Materials and Services, J. B. Fowler
Group Reporting Controller, V. E. Gough
Division Director and Head Corporate Development, N. P. H. Garner
Managing Director Emission Control Technologies Europe, J. F. Walker
Director Technology and Business Development Emission Control Technologies, D. W. Prest
General Manager Noble Metals Europe, C. C. Howlett
General Manager Noble Metals North America, J. D. Malanga
Division Finance Director Catalysts Chemicals and Refining, T. Hassan
Managing Director Tracerco and Vertec, A. C. Hurst
President Global Research Chemicals, B. C. Singelais
President Davy Process Technology, D. J. Tomlinson
General Manager Gold North America, A. J. McCullough
Managing Director Emission Control Technologies Asia, J. V. Zubrickas
Divisional Finance Director Process Technologies, G. L. McGregor
Managing Director Colour Technologies, R. L. P. J. van der Heijden
Director Tax, S. P. Robinson
Chief Scientist, M. V. Twigg
Technology and Business Development Director Emission Control Technologies, C J Bennett
Business Development Director Process Technologies, A. Bordet
Managing Director Refineries and Gas Processing, J.K. Dunleavy
Managing Director Syngas and Gas to Products, A. Wright
Division Finance Director Fine Chemicals, M. Gaffney
Board Member, Robert J. W. (Rob) Walvis, age 66
Executive Director Environmental Technologies Division and Director, Larry C. Pentz, age 58
Board Member, Michael J. (Mike) Roney, age 58
Chief Executive and Board Member, Neil A. P. Carson, age 56
Board Member, Dorothy Thompson, age 52
Board Member, Sir Thomas Harris, age 68
Board Member, Alan M. Thomson, age 66
Independent Non-Executive Director, Alan Ferguson
Non-Executive Director, Colin Matthews
Auditors: KPMGAuditPlc

LOCATIONS

HQ: Johnson Matthey Plc (United Kingdom)
5th Floor, 25 Farringdon Street, London EC4A 4AB
Phone: (44) 20 7269 8400 **Fax:** (44) 20 7269 8433
Web: www.matthey.com

PRODUCTS/OPERATIONS

2011 Sales

Precious Metals	74
Fine Chemicals & Catalysts	2

COMPETITORS

BASF Catalysts
GEA Group
Heraeus Holding
Heraeus Precious Metals
IBIDEN
Impala Platinum
Kyocera
Metalor USA Refining
Mitsui Mining and Smelting
OM Group
Showa Denko
Sud-Chemie
Umicore
Vesuvius

HISTORICAL FINANCIALS

Company Type: Public

Income Statement FYE: March 31

	REVENUE ($ mil.)	NET INCOME ($ mil.)	NET PROFIT MARGIN	EMPLOYEES
03/13	16,303	420	2.6%	10,498
03/12	19,266	506	2.6%	10,058
03/11	16,065	293	1.8%	9,742
03/10	11,888	249	2.1%	8,949
03/09	11,226	249	2.2%	8,540
Annual Growth	9.8%	14.0%	—	5.3%

2013 Year-End Financials

Debt ratio: 40.1%
Return on equity: 18.9%
Cash ($ mil.): 106
Current ratio: 1.37
Long-term debt ($ mil.): 927
No. of shares (mil.): 204
Dividends
Yield: 0.0%
Payout: 56.4%
Market value ($ mil.): 14,314

	STOCK PRICE ($) FY Close	P/E High/Low	PER SHARE ($) Earnings	Dividends	Book Value
03/13	69.85	155111	2.03	1.14	10.34
03/12	73.17	128 79	2.35	0.00	11.43
03/11	59.92	196112	1.37	0.00	10.53
03/10	53.00	179 84	1.17	0.00	8.83
03/09	30.17	289 49	1.17	0.00	7.83
Annual Growth	23.4%	— —	14.6%	—	7.2%

Joyo Bank, Ltd.

Tracing its roots back to 1938 The Joyo Bank offers regional banking services for Japan's Ibaraki Prefecture and its surrounding regions. Backed by more than 170 branches Joyo offers deposits loans investment portfolios international business and other traditional retail banking products. Subsidiaries and affiliated companies include Joyo Computer Service Co. (calculation software) Joyo Lease Co. (machinery and equipment leasing) Joyo Credit Guarantee Co. (housing loans credit) and

Joyo Cash Service Co. (ATM and CD management and maintenance).

EXECUTIVES

President, Kazuyoshi Terakado
Auditors: Ernst&YoungShinNihon

LOCATIONS

HQ: Joyo Bank, Ltd.
2-5-5 Minami-machi, Mito, Ibaraki 310-8604
Phone: (81) 29 231 2151 **Fax:** (81) 29 231 2193
Web: www.joyobank.co.jp

COMPETITORS

Aozora Bank
Iyo Bank
Mitsubishi UFJ Financial Group
Miyazaki Bank
Norinchukin Bank
Shizuoka Bank
Towa Bank

HISTORICAL FINANCIALS

Company Type: Public

Income Statement FYE: March 31

	ASSETS ($ mil.)	NET INCOME ($ mil.)	INCOME AS % OF ASSETS	EMPLOYEES
03/13	87,871	241	0.3%	3,766
03/12	97,589	221	0.2%	3,783
03/11	89,827	168	0.2%	3,793
03/10	79,401	150	0.2%	3,863
03/09	75,291	52	0.1%	3,790
Annual Growth	3.9%	46.4%	—	(0.2%)

2013 Year-End Financials

Return on assets: 0.2%
Return on equity: 4.7%
Long-term debt ($ mil.): —
No. of shares (mil.): 750
Sales ($ mil): 1,599
Dividends
Yield: —
Payout: —
Market value ($ mil.): 3,729

	STOCK PRICE ($) FY Close	P/E High/Low	PER SHARE ($) Earnings	Dividends	Book Value
03/13	4.97	— —	0.32	0.00	7.17
03/12	6.05	— —	0.29	0.00	7.16
03/11	6.05	— —	0.22	0.00	6.69
03/10	6.05	— —	0.19	0.00	5.93
03/09	6.05	— —	0.07	0.00	4.92
Annual Growth	(4.8%)	— —	47.6%	—	9.9%

JX Holdings, Inc.

Japan's JX Holdings is an integrated energy holding company that combines the businesses of two of the country's top oil refiners Nippon Oil and Nippon Mining Holdings which merged to become a powerhouse with diverse operations in petroleum refining and marketing oil and natural gas exploration and production and metals (mainly copper). JX Holdings produces 128000 barrels of oil equivalent form its exploration and production asserts in ficscal year 2012. Its refineries have the capacity to process roughly 1.7 million barrels of crude oil per day representing more than a quarter of the total amount of crude oil processed per day in Japan. It also operates a metal business mainlu focued on copper proudction.

Operations

JX Holding operates through three major subsidiaries: JX Nippon Oil & Energy; JX Nippon Oil & Gas Exploration; and JX Nippon Mining & Metals.

The company's petroleum refining and marketing business accounted for 85 % of total revenues in fiscal 2012. Among its refined petroleum products are gasoline and gas oil for automobiles and trains; jet fuel for aircraft; kerosene for heating homes; lubricant oil for machinery and engines; naphtha for production of petrochemicals; petrochemicals for manufacturing synthetic fibers paints and plastics; and fuel oils and other heavy oils for heating buildings and operating heavy machinery.

Geographic Reach

The company markets refined products across Japan; is engaged in exploration development and production of oil and gas in 14 countries around the world; and has stake in a copper mine in Chile. In fiscal year 2012 Japan accounted for 87% of JX Holdings' revenues.

Financial Performance

Revenues increased by 11% (in local currency) in fiscal year 2012 due to a 13% increase in the Petroleum Refining and Marketing Business thanks to higher prices and increased demand and a 26% increase in the Oil and Natural Gas E&P Business thanks to higher sales prices outpacing lower production volume at existing oil and gas fields and the sale of assets in the US. In addition the company reported a 6% increase in the Metals Business due to higher prices for precious metals and increased collection of recycled materials.

JX Holdings' net income decreased by 45% in fiscal year 2012 due to an increase in selling general and administrative expenses.

Strategy

The merger of Nippon Oil and Nippon Mining in 2010 was spurred on by changes in the Japanese oil industry including excess refining capacity due to the continued decline in domestic demand for refined petroleum products a growing consumer awareness of environmental issues and alternative energy options and a sluggish Japanese economy. Such trends prompted the two to consider restructuring and integrating their businesses to strengthen competitiveness. Following the merger JX Nippon set up upstream oil business JX Nippon Oil & Gas Exploration and metals unit JX Nippon Mining and Metals as operating subsidiaries.

Petroleum refining and marketing will continue to be a core segment that JX Holdings plans to expand further throughout Asia and arpund the world. However it may also look for future opportunities to engage in new energy markets such as fuel cells and photovoltaic power generation to keep up with the growing green trend.

In 2012 the company's wholly owned subsidiary JX Nippon Exploration and Production (U.K.) Limited signed sale and purchase agreements to acquire an extensive portfolio of non-operated oil and gas assets in the UK Continental Shelf from ENI. The assets give JX a substantial long-term oil and gas production base in the UK.

LOCATIONS

HQ: JX Holdings, Inc.
2-6-3 Otemachi, Chiyoda-ku, Tokyo 100-8161
Phone: (81) 3 6275 5009
Web: www.hd.jx-group.co.jp

HISTORICAL FINANCIALS

Company Type: Public

Income Statement FYE: March 31

	REVENUE ($ mil.)	NET INCOME ($ mil.)	NET PROFIT MARGIN	EMPLOYEES
03/13	119,239	1,694	1.4%	25,569
03/12	130,730	2,079	1.6%	24,236
03/11	116,348	3,764	3.2%	24,691
Annual Growth	1.2%	(32.9%)	—	1.8%

2013 Year-End Financials

Debt ratio: 0.3%
Return on equity: 8.6%
Cash ($ mil.): 2,658
Current ratio: 1.13
Long-term debt ($ mil.): 12,889
No. of shares (mil.): —
Dividends
Yield: —
Payout: —
Market value ($ mil.): —

	STOCK PRICE ($) FY Close	P/E High/Low	PER SHARE ($) Earnings	Dividends	Book Value
03/13	11.39	— —	0.68	0.00	9.93
03/12	11.80	— —	0.84	0.00	10.02
03/11	13.75	— —	1.51	0.00	9.16
/0.00	—	—(0.00)	0.00	(0.00)	
/0.00	—	—(0.00)	0.00	(0.00)	
Annual Growth	—	— —	—	—	—

Kansai Electric Power Co., Inc. (Kansai Denryoku K. K.) (Japan)

LOCATIONS

HQ: Kansai Electric Power Co., Inc. (Kansai Denryoku K. K.) (Japan)
3-6-16 Nakanoshima, Kita-ku, Osaka 530-8270
Phone: (81) 6 6441 8821
Web: www.kepco.co.jp

HISTORICAL FINANCIALS

Company Type: Public

Income Statement FYE: March 31

	REVENUE ($ mil.)	NET INCOME ($ mil.)	NET PROFIT MARGIN	EMPLOYEES
03/13	30,385	(2,587)	—	33,537
03/12	34,273	(2,953)	—	32,961
03/11	33,448	1,487	4.4%	32,418
03/10	27,905	1,361	4.9%	32,083
03/09	28,327	(89)	—	30,490
Annual Growth	1.8%	—	—	2.4%

2013 Year-End Financials

Debt ratio: 0.5%
Return on equity: (-17.6%)
Cash ($ mil.): 1,662
Current ratio: 0.65
Long-term debt ($ mil.): 38,530
No. of shares (mil.): 893
Dividends
Yield: —
Payout: —
Market value ($ mil.): 4,063

	STOCK PRICE ($) FY Close	P/E High/Low	PER SHARE ($) Earnings	Dividends	Book Value
03/13	4.55	— —	(2.90)	0.00	15.21
03/12	7.65	— —	(3.31)	0.00	20.88
03/11	12.66	— —	1.66	0.00	24.78
03/10	45.60	— —	1.50	0.00	21.26
Annual Growth	(53.6%)	— —	—	—	(8.0%)

KB Financial Group, Inc.

KB Financial Group holding company for Kookmin Bank provides commercial and consumer banking services in South Korea. It offers asset management and life insurance through alliances with Netherlands-based ING Groep. The bank's lending activities mainly entail residential mortgages home equity loans consumer loans and corporate loans. Kookmin Bank has more than 1200 branches in its home country where it claims some 26 million customers or about half of the population of South Korea. The bank provides corporate services such as foreign exchange and securities trading from offices at home and abroad in New York London Hong Kong Tokyo and Auckland New Zealand.

KB Financial became a bank holding company in 2008 and made no bones about its ambitions to stretch its wings with acquisitions. It has been eyeing brokerage firms as well as other financial services companies.

It is reportedly interested in acquiring troubled Korea Exchange Bank. This is the second time KB Financial has wanted to buy KEB; in 2006 its $7 billion offer was stymied by KEB's parent US-based private equity firm Lone Star Funds. In 2008 the South Korean government blocked HSBC's acquisition of KEB putting the bank in play once more.

A proposed KEB acquisition is just one part of KB Financial's strategy. Seeking strategic opportunities in emerging markets the bank has opened representative offices in Kazakhstan the Ukraine and Vietnam and is mulling moves into other Central and Southeast Asian nations. In 2008 it bought a 30% stake in Kazakhstan bank JSC Bank CenterCredit; it eventually intends to build up to a controlling stake of that bank.

In the meantime the company sold its nearly 14% stake in PT Bank International Indonesia to Malayan Banking Berhad for some $309 million.

Kookmin Bank spun off its credit card business in 2011 and KB Financial took it over. The new company KB Kookmin Card Co. will focus on credit card/telecommunications services and include a mobile credit card. Other services include consumer financing and insurance.

In 2006 erstwhile Kookmin Bank CEO Kim Jung-tae resigned in the face of disciplinary sanctions imposed by financial regulators after he was accused of accounting irregularities. Some South Korean newspapers speculated that a disciplinary warning issued by the Financial Supervisory Commission was retaliation for Kim's opposition to government-led bailouts of financially troubled companies.

Citigroup owns around 17% of KB Financial.

EXECUTIVES

SEVP Capital Markets and Treasury Group, Young Han Choi, age 55
Chairman and CEO, Yoon-Dae Euh, age 68
Director, Jacques P.M. Kemp, age 63
Director, Dam Cho, age 60
SEVP Strategy Planning Group and Director, Ki Hong Kim, age 55
Director, Bo Kyung Byun, age 59
SEVP Strategy Group and Director, In Gyu Choi, age 56
Director, Suk Sig Lim, age 59
Director, Sang Moon Hahm, age 60
Director, Han Kim, age 59
Director, Chan Soo Kang, age 51
Chief Audit Executive and Director, Yong Hwa Cheong, age 59
Director, Chee Joong Kim, age 57
Auditors: SamilPricewaterhousecoopers

LOCATIONS

HQ: KB Financial Group, Inc.
5th Floor ~ 7th Floor, 9-1, 2-ga, Namdaemoon-ro, Jung-gu, Seoul 100-703
Phone: (82) 2 2073 2844 **Fax:** (82) 2 2073 2848
Web: www.kbfng.com

PRODUCTS/OPERATIONS

Selected Subsidiaries

KB Asset Management Co. Ltd. (80%)
KB Credit Information Co. Ltd. (99.7%)
KB Data Systems Co. Ltd. (99.99%)
KB Futures Co. Ltd. (99.98%)
KB Investment Co. Ltd. (99.99%)
KB Real Estate Trust Co. Ltd. (99.99%)
Kookmin Bank
Kookmin Bank Hong Kong Ltd.
Kookmin Bank International Ltd.

COMPETITORS

Busan Bank
Citigroup
Daegu Bank
Hana Bank
Industrial Bank of Korea
Korea Exchange Bank
SHC Management
Samsung Life Insurance
Shinhan Financial
Woori

HISTORICAL FINANCIALS

Company Type: Public

Income Statement FYE: December 31

	ASSETS ($ mil.)	NET INCOME ($ mil.)	INCOME AS % OF ASSETS	EMPLOYEES
12/12	264,124	1,594	0.6%	157
12/11	239,580	2,048	0.9%	148
12/10	230,781	130	0.1%	155
12/09	226,584	466	0.2%	100
12/08	210,785	482	0.2%	96
Annual Growth	5.8%	34.9%	—	13.1%

2012 Year-End Financials

Return on assets: 0.6%
Return on equity: 7.1%
Long-term debt ($ mil.): —
No. of shares (mil.): 386
Sales ($ mil): 16,457
Dividends
Yield: 1.7%
Payout: 14.6%
Market value ($ mil.): 13,870

	STOCK PRICE ($) FY Close	P/E High/Low	PER SHARE ($) Earnings	Dividends	Book Value
12/12	35.90	— —	4.12	0.64	59.42
12/11	31.34	— —	5.56	0.00	51.19
12/10	52.89	— —	0.38	0.21	42.70
12/09	50.85	— —	1.43	0.00	39.93
12/08	26.20	— —	1.68	0.00	34.99
Annual Growth	8.2%	— —	25.1%	—	14.1%

KBC Group NV

Neither a purveyor of fried chicken nor an ominous Russian spy shop KBC Groep (or KBC Group as its known in the US) is actually one of Belgium's largest financial services firms. The company operates 845 bank branches in Belgium and more than 1100 in Central and Eastern Europe. It has other operations in Western Europe the US and Southeast Asia although much of the company's international operations are being scaled back. KBC caters to individuals small and mid-sized businesses and private banking clients. It also offers insurance and asset management. The group is organized into four business units: Belgium; Central and Eastern Europe banking; merchant banking; and shared services and operations.

Following the global economic meltdown KBC Groep has sharpened its focus on regional European financial services and worked to lower its risk profile. The global financial crisis took a big toll on the company which received three government bailouts with a combined value of some ?30 billion ($40 billion) by 2009. KBC attributed its losses to bad loans but its business margins began to recover by 2010 thanks to an increase in fee and commission income generated by its asset management business and rigorous cost cutting. KBC also saw lower impairment charges on its loan portfolio in 2010.

The company is selling off assets. It is scaling down non-core activities and focusing more on its main Belgium and Central European business units. (It's Belgium unit accounted for more than 60% of KBC's profit in 2010). KBC also is reducing its risk profile. Those initiatives should help the company pay back the aid it received from the government.

Many of KBC's divestments have been made overseas as the company aims to significantly cut back its presence in markets outside of its core geographic home. To that end in 2013 it sold its Russian banking business Absolut Bank to a group of Russian companies for about ?300 million ($388.5). Much of KBC's international loan portfolio and investment banking activities also are being scaled back. KBC sold its global convertible bond and Asian equity derivatives operations to Daiwa Securities Group for ?790 million ($1 billion). It also sold a ?5 billion ($7 billion) portfolio of life settlement insurance policies to Fortress Investment Group. In a much smaller deal it sold KBC Asset Management to RHJ International for ?23.7 million ($29 million). KBC also sold UK-based investment bank subsidiary Peel Hunt to the unit's management and other investors. There are also plans to shut down its Russia business and withdraw from countries such as Serbia. As part of its strategy KBC in early 2013 sold its remaining 22% stake in NLB to the Republic of Slovenia.

The group planned to sell KBL its European private banking network to the Hinduja Group for some ?1.35 billion ($1.69 billion) but that deal was blocked by Luxembourg regulators in 2011. Instead the company sold the private banking operations to Qatari investors Precision Capital.

Some non-core assets in Belgium also are being sold. In 2011 KBC sold savings bank subsidiary Centea (Belgium) to Credit Agricole for ?527 million ($737 million). The deal freed up capital for the company.

KBC took on its current form when KBC Bank and Insurance acquired its parent company Almanij in 2005. The companies merged to streamline their operations and provide a more appealing stock offering for investors.

HISTORY

KBC Group traces its roots back to 1931 when a commercial bank named Algemeene Bankvereeniging responded to the global financial crisis by restructuring. The bank decided to regroup its assets in Belgium and Hungary and create a new holding company Algemene Maatschappij voor Nijverheidskrediet –or Almanij for short.

In 1935 Almanij helped organize a new bank Kredietbank in exchange for a majority stake in the company. Within the next few years Almanij managed to accrue a large debt to Kredietbank; in order to pay it back the company was forced to sell its shares in other firms. The debt was finally cleared by 1945.

Kredietbank quickly grew to be one of Belgium's leading banks. In 1949 it set up private bank KB Luxembourg which would later operate as an independent company majority-controlled by Almanij. In the ensuing years Almanij benefited from Belgium's ability to bounce back after WWII relative to the rest of Europe.

Fears that the Belgian government would like the French nationalize the country's banks led Almanij to make some changes in 1978. The company sliced Kredietbank and KB Luxembourg into two firms and refocused its investments into three major branches: Kredietbank KB Luxembourg and insurance and leasing entities such as the insurer Fidelitas. Though the 1980s were a shaky time for Belgian banks Almanij endured and industry conditions improved toward the end of the decade.

In 1991 the Banking and Finance Commission in Brussels announced changes in the regulations for Belgian banks; these changes included the stipulation that the main shareholders of banks make up the majority on their boards. The new regulations allowed holding companies like Almanij to have more influence over banks' strategies while also forcing them to drum up more capital for the banks.

Almanij acquired a majority stake in investment firm Gevaert in 1997. The following year it hit the big time with the creation of KBC Bank and Insurance Holding Company which went on to become one of the top financial services firms in Belgium. In 1999 Almanij formed Almafin a wholly owned consulting services subsidiary.

Almanij ran into some trouble in 2000 when the government began investigating Kredietbank and KBC Bank and Insurance for possible tax fraud. That year Cera Holding spun off most of its stake in Almanij in the form of a new holding company called Almancora.

Late in 2004 KBC Bank and Almanij announced that KBC would acquire Almanij to streamline operations; the deal which created KBC Group was completed early in 2005.

The company then expanded through a variety of deals. It acquired the Czech-based Ceskoslovenska Obchodni Banka (CSOB Bank) which it later split into two entities separately serving the Czech Republic and Slovakia. KBC also acquired complete ownership of Hungary-based K&H Bank. Other deals included acquisitions in Romania and Bulgaria. In 2008 the group bought Slovakia's eighth largest bank Istrobanka which it merged into CSOB Bank.

EXECUTIVES

President CEO and Director, Jan Vanhevel, age 64
Director, Jo Cornu, age 68
Director, Philippe Naert, age 69
Director, Paul Bostoen, age 73
Director, Luc Debaillie, age 72
Director, Noel Devisch, age 69
Director, Dirk Heremans, age 69
Director, Alain Tytgadt, age 56
CEO European Private Banking and Director, Etienne Verwilghen, age 65
Vice Chairman, Philippe Vlerick, age 57
Director, Frank Donck, age 47
Director, Paul Borghgraef, age 58
Director, Germain Vantieghem, age 67
Director, Franky Depickere, age 53
Director, Theodoros Roussis, age 58
Director, Hendrik Soete, age 62
Director, Marc Wittemans, age 55
Director, Charles Van Wymeersch
Director, Lode Morlion, age 52
Director, Ghislaine Van Kerckhove, age 49
Auditors: Ernst&YoungReviseursd'EntreprisesSCC

LOCATIONS

HQ: KBC Group NV
Havenlaan 2, Brussels 1080
Phone: (32) 2 429 49 16 **Fax:** (32) 2 429 44 16
Web: www.kbc.com

PRODUCTS/OPERATIONS

Selected Subsidiaries

KBC Bank NV
- Antwerp Diamond Bank NV (Belgium)
- CBC Banque SA (universal bank serving French-speaking region of Belgium)
- CIBANK (Bulgaria)
- CSOB (Slovakia)
- CSOB (Czech Republic)
- K&H Bank Rt. (Hungary)
- KBC Asset Management NV
- KBC Bank Nederland NV
- KBC Finance Ireland
- Kredyt Bank (Poland)

KBC Insurance
- A. Banka A.D. (Russia)
- Assurisk SA (Luxembourg)
- CSOB Poist' ovna (Slovakia)
- CSOB Pojist' ovna (Czech Republic)
- DZI Insurance (Bulgaria)
- Fidea NV (Belgium)
- K&H Insurance (Hungary)
- TUiR WARTA SA (Poland)
- VAB Group (Belgium)

KBL EPB
- Brown Shipley & Co. Limited (UK)
- KBL Richelieu Banque Privee (France)
- KBL European Private Bankers (Luxembourg)
- KBL (Switzerland) Ltd.
- Merck Fink & Co. (Germany)
- Puilaetco Dewaay Private Bankers SA (Belgium)
- Theodoor Gilissen Bankiers NV (99.9% Netherlands)
- VITIS Life SA (Luxembourg)

COMPETITORS

BNP Paribas
Commerzbank
Credit Suisse
Deutsche Bank
Dexia
ING
Natixis
Rabobank
SEB AB

HISTORICAL FINANCIALS

Company Type: Public

Income Statement FYE: December 31

	ASSETS ($ mil.)	NET INCOME ($ mil.)	INCOME AS % OF ASSETS	EMPLOYEES
12/12	338,588	806	0.2%	37,083
12/11	369,127	16	0.0%	47,530
12/10	429,380	2,489	0.6%	50,494
12/09	467,077	(3,552)	—	54,185
12/08	496,765	(3,472)	—	59,279
Annual Growth	(9.1%)	—	—	(11.1%)

2012 Year-End Financials

Return on assets: 0.2%
Return on equity: 3.8%
Long-term debt ($ mil.): —
No. of shares (mil.): 416
Sales ($ mil): 21,742
Dividends
Yield: 0.0%
Payout: —
Market value ($ mil.): 7,435

	STOCK PRICE ($) FY Close	P/E High/Low		PER SHARE ($) Earnings	Dividends	Book Value
12/12	17.83	—	—	(1.44)	0.01	49.31
12/11	6.10	—	—	(2.50)	0.69	61.01
12/10	17.39	11	8	4.98	0.00	70.49
Annual Growth	1.3%	—	—	—	—	(8.5%)

KDDI Corp

LOCATIONS

HQ: KDDI Corp
3-10-10 Iidabashi, Chiyoda-ku, Tokyo 102-8460
Phone: (81) 3 6678 0712
Web: www.kddi.com

HISTORICAL FINANCIALS

Company Type: Public

Income Statement FYE: March 31

	REVENUE ($ mil.)	NET INCOME ($ mil.)	NET PROFIT MARGIN	EMPLOYEES
03/13	38,922	2,566	6.6%	20,238
03/12	43,546	2,908	6.7%	19,680
03/11	41,476	3,080	7.4%	18,418
03/10	36,850	2,277	6.2%	18,301
03/09	35,516	2,261	6.4%	16,967
Annual Growth	2.3%	3.2%	—	4.5%

2013 Year-End Financials

Debt ratio: 0.2%
Return on equity: 11.2%
Cash ($ mil.): 1,030
Current ratio: 1.43
Long-term debt ($ mil.): 7,496
No. of shares (mil.): 764
Dividends
Yield: —
Payout: —
Market value ($ mil.): 15,900

	STOCK PRICE ($) FY Close	P/E High/Low		PER SHARE ($) Earnings	Dividends	Book Value
03/13	20.80	—	—	3.07	0.00	32.30
03/12	16.24	—	—	3.45	0.00	33.95
03/11	62.18	—	—	3.51	0.37	30.89
03/10	51.80	—	—	2.56	0.32	24.98
03/09	47.83	—	—	2.54	0.00	21.45
Annual Growth	(18.8%)	—	—	4.9%	—	10.8%

Kia Motors Corp. (South Korea)

During tough economic times a generous warranty coupled with lower-than-Japan and Detroit prices translates into sales for South Korea's #2 carmaker (behind Hyundai Motor). Kia Motors produces more than 2 million vehicles a year at 13 manufacturing and assembly plant in eight countries. Its compact Kia picanto is the second-best selling car in South Korea. Other popular models include the Forte the Sorento and the Soul. Kia also makes a number of commercial vehicles. Its high-capacity plants outside Korea are in the US Slovakia and China. After Korea Kia's second-largest market is the US. Part of the Hyundai Kia Automotive Group Kia operates as an affiliate of Hyundai Motor which owns about a third of its stock.

Kia and its controlling sister company Hyundai account for the majority of South Korea's car sales. Together they form the world's sixth-largest automotive group by sales. 2010 was a record year for Kia as sales jumped more than 35% due to strong demand from the domestic and international market. In terms of the number of vehicles sold sales grew more than 25% as the company passed the 2 million mark. That year Kia doubled the number of vehicles it sold in Eastern Europe; China grew almost 40% and North America grew 18%.

Kia's best-selling model overseas in 2010 was the Forte which comes in a sedan coupe or five-door hatchback with more than 400000 units sold. Kia's Sportage SUV and compact Rio followed with more than 200000 units sold each. The Sorento mid-size CUV came in fourth with almost 175000 units sold while the Soul urban crossover vehicle launched in 2009 with accolades for its unique design rounded out the top five with more than 135000 units sold.

Kia is focused on edging out the competition with its stylish design that doesn't come with a European price tag. Its Chief Design Officer is Peter Schreyer the man who invented the Audi TT. Schreyer has been key in transforming Kia from a budget lineup to one that can still claim a small sticker price but offer a 100000-mile powertrain warranty at the same time. By strengthening its platform to smaller lighter cars Kia aims to rapidly respond to changes in consumer demand. The company markets its value in design esthetics and fuel efficiency. None of its vehicles are gas guzzlers and its Optima sedan came with a hybrid engine option for the 2012 model year. Most of its vehicles have a gasoline direct injection (GDI) engine that results in better fuel economy and the company is working on two electric concept cars the TAM for the domestic market and the POP for export.

Kia has established manufacturing plants in key regions two in China (set up as joint partnerships with Yueda and Dongfeng Motor) a Slovakia assembly plant in Eastern Europe (that also produces Hyundai vehicles) and one in the US in Georgia. The US plant opened in late 2009 with an annual production capacity of 300000 Sorento SUVs. The $1 billion project neighbors Hyundai's Alabama facility and benefits from the south's tax incentives and laws that make it easier to build a largely nonunion work force. Demand was so strong that Kia expanded the plant in 2011 to begin producing 60000 Optima sedans a year.

In addition Kia announced plans to build a third manufacturing plant in China where the company is one of the top 10 automakers. The plant its second joint venture with Dongfeng Motor will have a production capacity of 300000 vehicles boosting its total production capacity in China to 730000. Kia plans to manufacture new vehicle models developed specifically for the Chinese market. (China is its fourth-largest market behind South Korea the US and Europe). The plant is expected to open in 2014.

HISTORY

Kia's conglomerate ownership is also fundamental to its operation. Favoring its founding family former president of Kia Hyundai Motors vice chairman Chung Eui-sun is the son of Hyundai Kia Automotive Group chairman Chung Mong-koo. The elder Chung is the son of Hyundai's founder and controls the car company through a series of cross-holdings involving auto-parts maker Hyundai Mobis and steelmaker Hyundai Steel. In 2010 he stepped down from Kia Motors' board. To fill his vacancy the role of CEO was jointly held by Kia vice chairman Chung Sung-eun and Kia president Seo Young-jong until late 2010 when Chung Sung-eun resigned amidst the recall of some 100000 automobiles. President and COO Lee Hyoung-keun was named as Chung's replacement.

Leadership has had other rough patches as well. A court found then-chairman Chung guilty of embezzlement and fraud in a slush fund scandal that passed corporate control and wealth from father to son hurting shareholders' value. An appeals court suspended the chairman's prison sentence to community service citing the executive's irreplaceable role in the company and country's economic well-being. He was subsequently pardoned by the South Korean president.

EXECUTIVES

Chairman and CEO, Chung Mong-Koo, age 64
Chief Designer Kia Europe Design Center, Gregory Guillaume
Chief Design Officer, Peter Schreyer, age 59
Chairman and Group CEO Kia Motors America and Kia Motors Manufacturing Georgia; President and CEO Kia Motors America Inc., Byung Mo Ahn
Vice Chairman, Hyoung-Keun (Hank) Lee
President and Director, Chung Euisun
Deputy General Manager International Public Relations Overseas Communications Team, Michael Choo
Senior Executive Vice President COO, Thomas Oh
Director, Cho Dong-Sung
Director, Shin Keon-Soo
Director, Lee Doo-Hee
Director, Hong Hyun-Kook
Head Finance Division and Director, Lee Jae-Rok
Vice Chairman, Hyoung-Keun (Hank) Lee
CEO President and Director, Seo Young-Jong
President and Director, Chung Euisun
Director, Park Young-Soo
Vice Chairman, Jeong Seung-Eun
Auditors: KPMGSamjongAccountingCorp.

LOCATIONS

HQ: Kia Motors Corp. (South Korea)
231 Yangjae-dong, Seocho-gu, Seoul 137-938
Phone: (82) 2 3464 1114 **Fax:** (82) 2 3464 6813
Web: www.kia.co.kr

2010 Sales

	% of total
South	23
Europe	19
US	17
China	16
Rest of	25
Total	**100**

PRODUCTS/OPERATIONS

Selected Models

Commercial vehicles
- K2700/Strong/3000s/2500TCI
- K4000G

Passenger cars
- Cadenza
- cee'd
- cee'd_sw
- Cerato/Forte
- Cerato/Forte Koup
- Optima
- Picanto
- pro_cee'd
- Rio
- Soul

SUV & MPV
- Borrego/Mohave
- Carens/Rondo
- Carnival/Sedona
- Sorento
- Sportage
- Venga

COMPETITORS

BYD
Chery Automobile
China FAW
Chrysler
Daimler
Fiat
Ford Motor
Fuji Heavy Industries
GM Korea
General Motors
Honda
Isuzu
Mazda
Nissan
Peugeot
Renault
Shanghai Automotive
Ssangyong Motor
Suzuki Motor
Toyota
Volkswagen

HISTORICAL FINANCIALS

Company Type: Public

Income Statement FYE: December 31

	REVENUE ($ mil.)	NET INCOME ($ mil.)	NET PROFIT MARGIN	EMPLOYEES
12/12	44,247	3,619	8.2%	32,756
12/11	37,275	2,947	7.9%	32,411
12/10	31,951	2,392	7.5%	32,599
12/09	25,448	846	3.3%	32,616
12/08	17,503	(71)	—	32,720
Annual Growth	26.1%	—	—	0.0%

2012 Year-End Financials

Debt ratio: 0.0%
Return on equity: 25.3%
Cash ($ mil.): 1,782
Current ratio: 1.11
Long-term debt ($ mil.): 2,299
No. of shares (mil.): 404
Dividends
Yield: —
Payout: —
Market value ($ mil.): —

Kingfisher PLC

Kingfisher is a big fish in do-it-yourself (DIY) retail. Europe's leading home improvement retail group and the third-largest in the world Kingfisher operates more than 950 home improvement stores in eight countries in Europe and Asia. The company's DIY portfolio includes: B&Q stores in the UK Ireland and China; and Castorama and Brico Depot in France Poland and Russia. Kingfisher's other DIY stores include Brico Depot in Spain and 50%-owned Koctas in Turkey. Its Screwfix business is the UK's largest direct and online supplier of tools to the trade. Economic gloom and weak sales in its home market have led Kingfisher to seek growth beyond Britian.

Kingfisher's group sales increased more than 3% in fiscal 2012 (ends January) vs. the prior year after posting a flat previous annual comparison. On a regional basis sales in the UK and Ireland were essentially unchanged (up just 0.1%) but rose by more than 6% in France. Elsewhere sales rose nearly 6%. As a result of France's strong performance it overtook the UK and Ireland as Kingfisher's largest market. Indeed the London-based DIY retailer rang up 42% of its sales and 48% of its profits in France in 2012 vs. 40% of sales and just 31% of profits at home. French consumers are much less indebted than the British who are facing a double-dip recession. After adding stores in France in recent years there are currently about 100 Castorama and 100 Brico Depot outlets throughout France.

Russia is another growth market on Kingfisher's global itinerary. The company currently has nearly 20 Castorama stores there but plans to build many more including a smaller "city store" format in Moscow. To that end Kingfisher has appointed a former IKEA executive Peter Partma as the country manager for Castorama Russia. Kingfisher hopes to replicate its success in Poland where it has grown quickly to number about 65 outlets in Russia.

After expanding rapidly and then stumbling in China Kingfisher is cutting its loses. The company reduced the number of B&Q outlets there by about a third from more than 60 to 40 at present. It's also downsizing about half of the remaining locations in an attempt to cut its losses and right the business. It's remerchandising its China stores to focus more on home decor soft furnishings and accessories to cater to the growing population of apartment dwellers there.

At home Kingfisher is attempting to reverse the slump in DIY sales brought on by the recession and housing market crash. To that end Kingfisher is remodeling 110 of its biggest B&Q warehouse stores in Britain. It also upped its store count by acquiring more than 30 stores in 2011 from ailing rival Focus (DIY). The company's also looking to expand its considerable acreage within the UK with plans to expand its building trade-oriented chain that would bring its French Brico into the country as well as drilling in deeper with Screwfix. In addition to the websites of its banners Kingfisher reels in more business online through Screwfix Direct which operates a website that offers next-day delivery of tools and other hardware products.

Kingfisher owns about a fifth of Hornbach Holding the parent company of German's #1 DIY warehouse retailer Hornbach-Baumarkt with some 120 stores across Europe.

HISTORY

The beginning of Kingfisher is directly tied to the former US Woolworth chain (now Foot Locker). With the success of F.W. Woolworth general merchandise stores in the US founder Frank Woolworth expanded overseas first to Canada then in 1909 to Liverpool England. By 1914 Woolworth's UK subsidiaries had 31 stores.

Growing quickly the company went public in 1931 with its US parent retaining a 53% stake. The company spent most of the postwar years rebuilding bombed stores and had 762 stores by 1950.

The company opened its first Woolco Department Store modeled after the US Woolco stores of its parent in 1967. However other retailers had cut into sales and by 1968 it lost its place as Britain's leading retailer to Marks and Spencer. In 1973 it opened Shoppers World a catalog showroom. It made its first takeover in 1980 buying B&Q a chain of 40 do-it-yourself stores.

An investment group acquired Woolworth in 1982 using the vehicle Paternoster Stores. (The US parent sold its stake in Woolworth.) The company renamed Woolworth Holdings closed unprofitable Woolworth stores and sold its Shoppers World stores in 1983 and its Ireland Woolworth stores in 1984. It also acquired Comet a UK home electronics chain and continued to expand B&Q.

Two years later all of its F.W. Woolworth stores were renamed Woolworths and food and clothing lines were abandoned. Also in 1986 the company sold its Woolco stores and bought record and tape distributor Record Merchandisers (later renamed Entertainment UK). The next year Woolworth Holdings acquired Superdrug a chain of 297 discount drugstores. Adding to its Superdrug chain in 1988 the company acquired and integrated two UK pharmacy chains: 110-store Tip Top Drugstores and 145-store Share Drug.

To reflect its growing diversity of businesses the company was renamed Kingfisher in 1989. Also that year it bought drug retailer Medicare with 86 stores. Expanding further into electronics in 1993 Kingfisher acquired Darty with 130 stores. Adding music retail to music distribution that year the firm founded Music and Video Club (MVC).

In 1998 Kingfisher increased its presence in France by taking control of electronics chain BUT. It also merged its B&Q chain with the do-it-yourself stores of France's Castorama in 1998 and gained a 55% stake in the new group (though as part of the deal Kingfisher received only 50% of the group's voting rights).

Following the lead of rival Dixons in 1999 Kingfisher launched its own free Internet access service in France called Libertysurf. Soon thereafter Libertysurf acquired 70% of Objectif Net and its website Nomade.fr. Kingfisher's planned purchase of food retailer ASDA Group collapsed in June 1999 after being outbid by Wal-Mart Stores.

Kingfisher sold its 35% stake in Libertysurf to Italian ISP Tiscali in 2001 and it sold its Superdrug chain to Kruidvat a Dutch health and beauty group. Kingfisher demerged Woolworths Group the same year in a public offering. With Woolies went electronic entertainment companies EUK MVC VCI and Streets Online. Also in 2001 Kingfisher bought 25% plus one share of the unlisted ordinary voting shares of Germany's Hornbach Holding a family-owned group that owns 80% of one of Germany's leading DIY chains Hornbach-Baumarkt.

In 2002 Kingfisher acquired the remainder of Castorama and bought 17.4% of Hornbach's listed non-voting preference shares (which with the 2001 purchase represents a 21.2% stake in Hornbach). Kingfisher additionally bought 5.5% of the ordinary shares of Hornbach-Baumarkt.

CEO Geoffrey Mulcahy stepped down in 2002 and was replaced by Gerry Murphy formerly CEO for Carlton (now ITV plc) in 2003. Kingfisher sold its 20 retail parks for $1.1 billion to a consortium that includes real estate firms Pillar Property and Capital & Regional Properties the same year. Also in 2003 Kingfisher sold ProMarkt with about 190 stores in Germany to its former owners Michael and Matthias Wegert.

To focus on DIY Kingfisher floated its electrical businesses as a new company Kesa Electricals in 2003. Kesa Electricals includes Darty France's leading electrical retailer with more than 180 stores and Comet with some 260 stores in the UK. Kingfisher sold two home-improvement chains that year. Reno-Depot which operates about 20 home-improvement stores in Canada was sold to RONA. NOMI with about 40 stores in Poland was acquired by Enterprise Investors.

And in 2003 Kingfisher sold Dubois Materiaux a French building materials dealer to Saint-Gobain Building Distribution.

In June 2005 the company acquired its biggest competitor in Asia OBI Asia which added about a dozen stores in China and its first outlet in South Korea. The next year Kingfisher entered its 11th market Russia with its first Castorama store there. In May Sir Francis Mackay retired as chairman of the company and was succeeded by Peter Jackson.

Kingfisher named Ian Cheshire as its new chief executive in 2008 succeeding Gerry Murphy who resigned in late 2007. Cheshire joined B&Q in 1998. Also in 2008 Kingfisher sold its Italian Castorama business to France's Groupe ADEO for $871 million. In addition the company sold its Castorama business in Spain in search of higher returns elsewhere in Europe. The retailer also closed its unprofitable Trade Depot format in the UK.

Daniel Bernard took over the chairman's seat from Jackson in 2009.

EXECUTIVES

Chairman, Daniel Bernard, age 67
Group Finance Director and Board Member, Kevin O'Byrne, age 48
CEO and Director, Ian Cheshire, age 53, $888,555 total compensation
Group Communications Director, Ian Harding, age 48
CEO UK Division, Euan A. Sutherland, age 44
CEO France, Phillippe Tible, age 61
Head Communications, Nigel Cope
Director Corporate Affairs, Nick Folland, age 47
CEO International, Peter H?gsted, age 44
CEO Screwfix, Steve Willett
Head Investor Relations, Sarah Gerrand
Group Property Director, Ian Playford
Group Innovation Director, Andy Wiggins
Group Commercial Director, Veronique Laury-Deroubaix
Finance Director, Karen Witts
Chief Financial Officer, Rene Lemesre
Group Sourcing Director, Anthony Anthony Sutcliffe Sutcliffe
Director - Group Internal Communications, Benedikt Benedikt Benenati Benenati
Group HR Director, Evelyn Evelyn Gleeson Gleeson
Chief Executive; Kingfisher B&Q; Director, Kevin Kevin OByrne OByrne
Senior Non-Executive Independent Director, Mark Mark Seligman Seligman
Group IT Director, Mike Mike Bell Bell
Director, Andrew R. J. Bonfield, age 50
Director, Anders Dahlvig
Director, Clare M. Chapman, age 53
Director, Michael L. Hepher, age 68
Group Finance Director and Board Member, Kevin O'Byrne, age 48
CEO and Director, Ian Cheshire, age 53
Director, John Nelson, age 65
Director, Janis Kong, age 62
Non-Executive Director, Pascal Pascal Cagni Cagni
Auditors: PricewaterhouseCoopersLLP

LOCATIONS

HQ: Kingfisher PLC
3 Sheldon Square, Paddington, London W2 6PX
Phone: (44) 20 7372 8008 **Fax:** (44) 20 7644 1001
Web: www.kingfisher.com

2012 Sales

	% of total
France	42
UK &	40
Rest of Europe &	18
Total	**100**

2012 Stores

	No.
UK &	572
France	205
Poland	67
China	40
Turkey	36
Russia	18
Spain	17
Total	**955**

COMPETITORS

Grafton Group
Grafton Merchanting
Homebase Limited
Leroy Merlin
METRO AG
MPS Builders and Merchants
Praktiker
Saint-Gobain Building Distribution
Tengelmann
Travis Perkins
Wolseley

HISTORICAL FINANCIALS

Company Type: Public

Income Statement FYE: February 2

	REVENUE ($ mil.)	NET INCOME ($ mil.)	NET PROFIT MARGIN	EMPLOYEES
02/13*	16,739	892	5.3%	77,000
01/12	17,012	1,005	5.9%	77,000
01/11	16,644	786	4.7%	78,000
01/10	16,786	620	3.7%	80,000
01/09	14,635	305	2.1%	85,000
Annual Growth	3.4%	30.8%	—	(2.4%)

*Fiscal year change

2013 Year-End Financials

Debt ratio: 6.8%	No. of shares (mil.): —
Return on equity: 9.3%	Dividends
Cash ($ mil.): 630	Yield: 0.0%
Current ratio: 1.07	Payout: 179.5%
Long-term debt ($ mil.): 525	Market value ($ mil.): —

	STOCK PRICE ($) FY Close	P/E High/Low		PER SHARE ($) Earnings	Dividends	Book Value
02/13*	8.64	105	80	0.38	0.68	4.10
01/12	8.02	88	63	0.42	0.55	3.79
01/11	8.04	105	64	0.33	0.36	3.67
01/10	6.75	133	42	0.26	0.38	3.35
01/09	3.95	198	69	0.13	0.46	2.96
Annual Growth	21.6%	—	—	30.5%	10.0%	8.5%

*Fiscal year change

Kirin Holdings Co Ltd

You might say this company makes good-luck beer. Named for a unicorn which is a Japanese symbol of good fortune Kirin Holdings is a top beer maker in Japan through its Kirin Brewery Co. In addition to its domestic Kirin-branded beers the company owns brewers that serve overseas markets such as Australia's Lion and Philippines-based San Miguel Brewery. The beer brewer also makes soft drinks (coffee tea drinks and mineral water) the alcoholic fruit drink chu-hi and owns Japanese wine producer Mercian Corporation. Beyond beverages Kirin also has operations in health and dairy foods and pharmaceutical-manufacturing sectors. In 2013 the company agreed to sell its Food Science Business to Mitsubishi.

Kirin is looking to expand outside Japan because of the country's unfavorable demographics (i.e. a declining birth rate). Indeed Japan's beer market has shrunk by about 15% in terms of shipment volumes over the past decade. Reflecting the trend Kirin's sales three-quarters of which are generated in Japan dipped slightly in 2009 from the prior year.

The company has set a goal of generating more than 30% of its sales outside its home country in 2015. One focus for Kirin is the Asia-Oceania region where it aims to build on recent acquisitions. Kirin took 100% control of Lion Nathan paying A$3.5 billion (about $3.2 billion) to acquire the 54% of Australia's #2 brewer that it did not already own. Australia presents Kirin with a stable customer base and was one of the few countries that avoided the recessionary conditions that rocked the global economy in 2009. In the same vein Kirin also acquired all of the shares of Filipino beer maker San Miguel Brewery in 2009 a 15% stake in Singapore-based Fraser & Neave (which has breweries and soft drink operations) in 2010 and a more than 55% stake in Vietnamese soft drink producer Interfood Shareholding in early 2011.

The company also has its eye on the emerging market of Brazil. Kirin in late 2011 acquired all of the remaining shares of Schincariol the second-largest brewer in Brazil for $1.3 billion after a three-month battle with shareholders opposed to the deal. Previously Kirin purchased an approximate 50.5% stake for $2.3 billion. Schincariol is poised for growth as Brazil's economy continues to expand; the country is the third-largest beer market in the world and about double the size of Japan (in sixth place). The Brazilian brewer has been family run since its founding in 1939 and operates more than a dozen breweries in the country. Its beers carry the Nova Schin label; Schincariol also rolls out Schin-branded sodas.

China is another attractive market for Kirin. In 2011 the company established a 40:60 joint venture with China Resources Enterprise –producer of China's top-selling Snow beer brand –to make and distribute non-alcoholic beverages including bottled water and soft drinks in China. Kirin plans to invest about $400 million in the joint venture and will transfer ownership of four local subsidiaries in Shanghai and Beijing to the partnership. To fund this move while reorganizing its production in China Kirin's selling its 25% stake in Dalian Daxue Brewery to Anheuser-Busch InBev.

At home after calling off merger talks with rival Japanese brewer Suntory Holdings in 2009 the company is focusing on organic growth while not ruling out domestic acquisitions. Indeed in the aftermath of its failed deal with Suntory Kirin teamed up with Japanese confectioner and snack food maker Ezaki Glico. Co. in the chilled-beverage field in a bid to step up its domestic operations.

Outside Japan Kirin has established local operations in China Taiwan the US and Europe. In the US it owns soft-drink bottler Coca-Cola Bottling Company of Northern New England and bourbon maker Four Roses Distillery in Kentucky.

Kirin Holdings is also involved in potato growing and cut-flower production. The company's pharmaceutical products include treatments for renal anemia and leucopenia; in the development pipeline are treatments for kidney-cell cancer and other kidney diseases.

HISTORY

American William Copeland went to Yokohama Japan in 1864 and five years later established the Spring Valley Brewery the first in Japan to provide beer for foreign nationals. Lacking funds to continue the brewery Copeland closed it in 1884. The next year a group of foreign and Japanese businessmen reopened it as Japan Brewery. The business created the Kirin label in 1888 and was soon profitable.

The operation was run primarily by Americans and Europeans at first but by 1907 Japanese workers had filled the ranks and adopted the Kirin Brewery Company name. Sales plummeted during WWII when the government limited brewing output. After the war the US occupation forces inadvertently assisted Kirin when they split Dai Nippon Brewery (Kirin's main competitor) into two companies (Asahi and Sapporo Breweries) while leaving Kirin intact. The company became Japan's leading brewer during the 1950s.

During the 1970s Kirin introduced several soft drinks and in 1972 branched into hard liquor through a joint venture with Seagram (Kirin-Seagram).

The firm bought several Coca-Cola bottling operations in New England and Japan in the 1980s. Kirin also entered the pharmaceuticals business in part through a joint venture with US-based Amgen. In 1988 the brewer signed an agreement with Molson to produce Kirin beer for the North American market. In 1989 Kirin bought Napa Valley's Raymond Vineyards.

In 1991 Kirin formed a partnership to market Tropicana drinks in Japan. It also entered an alliance with Sankyo (Japan's #2 drug company) in 1991 to market Kirin's medication for anemia which it had developed with Amgen.

Chairman Hideyo Motoyama resigned in 1993 after four company executives were arrested for allegedly paying a group of racketeers who had threatened to disrupt Kirin's annual meeting. Joint venture Kirin-Amgen won the rights to make thrombopoietin (TPO) a blood platelet growth stimulator in 1995.

Yasuhiro Satoh became president of Kirin in 1996. The brewer moved into China that year through an agreement with China Resources (Shenyang) Snowflake Brewery. To brew its beers in the US the company formed Kirin Brewery of America also in 1996.

In response to losing market share to Asahi Kirin cut its workforce in 1998 and introduced Tanrei a cheaper low-malt beer that quickly captured half its market. Building on its presence in China Kirin bought 46% of brewer Lion Nathan (based in Australia and New Zealand) for $742.5 million that year. It became a licensed brewer of Anheuser-Busch in 1999.

Like other Japanese brewers Kirin struggled against dwindling demand for its most expensive brews in 2000. Koichiro Aramaki was named president of the company the following year and began to expand and diversify Kirin's operations to overcome slow growth domestically. In 2002 the company bought 15% of Philippine food and drink giant San Miguel for about $530 million. It also boosted ties with beverage giant Pernod Ricard by purchasing 32% of SIFA a French food services firm for an estimated $155 million. In 2002 Kirin also formed Flower Season Ltd. a joint venture with Dole Food Company to sell flowers to Japanese retailers. Also in 2002 Kirin launched its new Pure Blue brand of "shochu" distilled liquor.

In 2006 Aramaki stepped down as president (he remained chairman) and turned the reins over to former managing director Kazuyasu Kato. The following year Kirin reorganized as a holding company.

The company added to its international dairy holdings with its 2007 acquisition of Australian milk and cheese producer National Foods. The following year National Foods acquired Australian dairy company Australian Co-operative Foods Limited (dba Dairy Farmers) for about $763 million. With some 2000 members Dairy Farmers is one of the biggest dairy product makers in Australia. These acquisitions made Kirin a top player in the Oceania dairy sector which is part of the company's larger strategy to focus and grow in the Asian and Oceania markets.

In May 2009 Kirin acquired a 100% interest in San Miguel Brewery of the Philippines. Following Kirin's successful tender offer to acquire the remainder of Lion Nathan's shares in October 2009 Lion Nathan and National Foods were consolidated under Kirin's Australian holding company which was renamed Lion Nathan National Foods.

Early in 2010 company veteran Senji Miyake was named president and CEO of the Japanese brewer (among other top management changes). Miyake joined Kirin Brewery Company in 1970. In December Kirin made Mercian Corp. a wholly-owned subsidiary following a scandal at Mercian's fish feedstuffs division.

EXECUTIVES

Managing Director, Hirotake Kobayashi

Chairman, Kazuyasu Kato, age 69
President and CEO, Senji Miyake
Managing Director and CFO, Yoshiharu Furumoto
Managing Director, Yoshinori Isozaki, age 59
Auditor, Kazuo Tezuka
Auditor, Teruo Ozaki
Managing Director, Hajime Nakajima
Managing Director, Hiroshi Ogawa
CFO, Masahito Suzuki
Managing Director, Toru Suzuki
Director, Satoru Kishi, age 82
Director, Yuzuru Matsuda
EVP and Director, Kazuhiro Sato
President and CEO, Senji Miyake
Managing Director and CFO, Yoshiharu Furumoto
Director, Akira Genma
Auditors: KPMGAZSA&Co.

LOCATIONS

HQ: Kirin Holdings Co Ltd
2-10-1 Shinkawa, Chuo-ku, Tokyo 104-8288
Phone: (81) 3 5540 3455 **Fax:** (81) 3 5540 3550
Web: www.kirinholdings.co.jp

2009 Sales

	% of total
Japan	77
Asia/Oceania	20
Other	3
Total	**100**

PRODUCTS/OPERATIONS

2009 Sales

	% of total
Alcoholic	48
Food & soft	32
Pharmaceuticals	9
Other	11
Total	**100**

COMPETITORS

Anheuser-Busch InBev
Asahi Breweries
Asia Pacific Breweries
Carlsberg
Chugai
Coca-Cola
Diageo
E. & J. Gallo
FEMSA
Fonterra
Heineken
ITOCHU
Kokubu
LVMH
Megmilk Snow Brand
Mercian
Molson Coors
Nippon Beet Sugar
Novartis
Pabst
PepsiCo
Red Bull
SABMiller
Sapporo
Suntory Holdings
Taiwan Tobacco & Wine
Takara
Tsingtao

HISTORICAL FINANCIALS

Company Type: Public

Income Statement FYE: December 31

	REVENUE ($ mil.)	NET INCOME ($ mil.)	NET PROFIT MARGIN	EMPLOYEES
12/12	25,382	652	2.6%	41,246
12/11	26,771	95	0.4%	40,348
12/10	26,774	140	0.5%	31,966
12/09	24,661	532	2.2%	35,150
12/08	25,472	886	3.5%	36,554
Annual Growth	(0.1%)	(7.4%)	—	3.1%

2012 Year-End Financials

Debt ratio: 0.3%
Return on equity: 6.2%
Cash ($ mil.): 974
Current ratio: 1.10
Long-term debt ($ mil.): 8,923
No. of shares (mil.): 961
Dividends
Yield: 2.8%
Payout: —
Market value ($ mil.): 11,278

	STOCK PRICE ($) FY Close	P/E High/Low	PER SHARE ($) Earnings	Dividends	Book Value
12/12	11.73	— —	0.67	0.34	13.93
12/11	12.00	— —	0.09	0.00	14.08
12/10	14.09	— —	0.15	0.27	14.81
12/09	16.09	— —	0.56	0.24	13.61
12/08	13.15	— —	0.93	0.22	13.32
Annual Growth	(2.8%)	— —	(8.0%)	10.8%	1.1%

Komatsu, Ltd.

Depsite a name that means "little pine tree" Komatsu produces an evergreen lineup of big equipment. The company is the world's #2 construction equipment maker behind Caterpillar. Komatsu builds and sells building and mining equipment from bulldozers and wheel loaders to dump trucks and debris crushers. Komatsu also produces industrial machinery such as laser-cutting tools wire saws and sheet-metal presses. Other lines include generators light armored vehicles and diesel engines. Its engineering and construction arm supplies prefabricated structures contracting real estate sales and leasing services. Komatsu America represents its chief operations in North America.

Komatsu operates through 180 companies (among this total are some 140 subsidiaries). The company's core segment —Construction Mining and Utility Equipment —generated 88 % of total sales in 2012. Industrial Machinery and Others accounted for the remainder of revenue.

Komatsu has more than 40 manufacturing plants primarily in Brazil China Germany Japan India Indonesia Italy Russia Sweden Thailand the UK and the US. The Asia/Pacific region accounts for almost 60% of its total sales with Japan representing 20% of that amount.

Despite a strained global economy and the March 2011 Great East Japan Earthquake disaster Komatsu saw an increase in demand for its machinery products in both its operating segments for its fiscal year ending March 2012. As a result from 2011 to 2012 its consolidated net revenues increased by 7.5% while operating income spiked by 15%. Decreases in the demand for construction equipment in China were offset by higher demand in Japan other regions within Asia and North America. Komatsu also enjoyed an increase in its parts sales and service revenues in the mining equipment sector as the total number of its mining equipment in operations went up in 2012.

In early 2011 the company absorbed its Komatsu Utility subsidiary in an effort to streamline operations and reduce redundancies. Komatsu's recessionary measures also included reorganizing its hub plants for global production and consolidating sales and service networks. In Japan North America and Europe the company trimmed eliminated and or consolidated facilities to further curb operating expenses as well as balance inventory levels.

In a more environmentally conscious world Komatsu's blueprint for growth involves introducing products that feature lighter environmental impact. The Dantotsu line for example is touted as 25% more fuel efficiency with lower CO2 emissions than previous models. The hybrid hydraulic excavator Komatsu's flagship product promises to scoop up sales in China and other strategic international sectors. The company is also expanding its hybrid electric forklift truck line and aims to combine its production with building compact construction equipment lines.

Komatsu's future relies heavily on integrating information and communication technologies (ICT) with its products and parts. Its ICT focus led to the development of the Komatsu Machine Tracking System (KOMTRAX) now standard on its construction equipment. It also spurred introduction of the world's first Autonomous Haulage System (AHS); copper mining giant Codelco uses the remote-control system to run huge dump trucks at its copper mine in Chile. Komatsu's AHS is used at a mine in Australia too. The company looks to further leverage other ICT applications to its portfolio.

HISTORY

Komatsu's roots reach back to the Takeuchi Mining Company founded in Japan in 1894. The company grew during WWI and in 1917 it created an in-house ironworks to make machine tools and mining equipment. The ironworks was separated in 1921 to create Komatsu Manufacturing.

The firm grew into one of Japan's major makers of machine tools and pumps by adding new products to its line. Komatsu introduced its first metal press in 1924 and in 1931 made Japan's first crawler-type farm tractor. Komatsu began making high-grade casting and specialty steel materials in 1935.

During WWII Komatsu made munitions and bulldozers for the Japanese Navy. After the war it began making construction machinery and industrial vehicles as Japan rebuilt its infrastructure. The company began building diesel engines in 1948. Komatsu continued to expand during the 1950s. In 1952 it began producing motor graders which became its first construction equipment to be exported (to Argentina) in 1955.

During the 1960s Komatsu entered joint ventures with US manufacturers including Cummins Engine (1961) Bucyrus Erie (1963) and International Harvester (now Navistar 1965). Komatsu established its first overseas subsidiary Komatsu Europe in Belgium in 1967 and introduced the world's first radio-controlled bulldozer.

The company changed its name to Komatsu Limited in 1970. International expansion continued as subsidiaries were established in the US Brazil and Germany (1970) Singapore (1971) and Panama (1972). Komatsu began making bulldozers in Mexico (1976) and opened an Australian subsidiary (1978).

In the 1980s Komatsu pushed further into the US market going head-to-head with Caterpillar. A strong dollar helped Komatsu undercut Caterpillar's prices by as much as 30%. In 1986 the company opened its first US factory in Chattanooga Tennessee. In 1988 it merged American construction equipment-making operations with those of Dresser Industries creating Komatsu Dresser.

Komatsu partnered with semiconductor giant Applied Materials in 1993 and entered the LAN market the next year with a print server and two types of hubs. The company expanded its construction equipment operations outside Japan in the mid-1990s when it formed a joint venture in Vietnam and opened plants in China. Demand for construction equipment in Japan plunged soon after.

In 1997 Komatsu set up a joint venture with India's Larsen & Toubro to make hydraulic excavators. A semiconductor industry downturn prompted Komatsu to close some of its US silicon wafer operations in 1998.

Hammered by low demand for construction equipment in Japan (down nearly 80% over three years) Komatsu recorded its first loss in fiscal 1999 and closed plants. The company backed out of its joint venture with Applied Materials selling its stake back to Applied Materials for $87 million in cash. Former GM manager Keith Sheldon was hired to overhaul the company's ailing global finances and prepare the company for listing on the New York Stock Exchange. In March 2000 the company sold its machine vision systems business to Cognex Corporation. Komatsu reached profitability in fiscal 2001 thanks to a new growth strategy focused on its construction and mining equipment businesses. Later the same year –as the economy swooned –Komatsu announced that it expected losses and was cutting about 2200 jobs in Japan.

Komatsu's reorganization plans launched during the last quarter of 2001 carried over through 2002 and 2003. The company implemented its new growth strategy for the construction and mining equipment business reduced fixed costs and restructured its electronics business. In 2003 the company showed an increase of 5.2% in consolidated net sales over the previous year. That year the company decided to dissolve its Komatsu Metal Ltd. subsidiary.

Also in 2003 Komatsu acquired KONE Corporation's Partek Forest AB and Partek Forest Holdings (collectively known as Partek Forest); the additions became a part of Komatsu Forest AB.

In 2005 the company sold a 75% stake in its US subsidiary Advanced Silicon Materials to Renewable Energy Corporation. Advanced Silicon Materials made polycrystalline silicon for use in semiconductors. The company provided nearly $140 million in annual sales.

The company finished the construction of three new plants –Ibaraki Plant Kanazawa Plant (Japan) and Chennai Plant (India) –in 2007. In 2009 Komatsu focused on restructuring its Japanese sales and service teams for construction equipment by launching Komatsu Construction Equipment Sales and Service Japan Ltd.

Komatsu's performance during the recession continued to decline. Year-over-year sales in 2009 and 2010 fell by almost 10% and 30% respectively. Revenues however from China (the only region to sustain year-over-year improvement) grew by 24% in 2009 over 2008 and by more than 14% in 2010. Even with the increase Komatsu's earnings during the same period plummeted by about 62% and 57%.

EXECUTIVES

President CEO and Director, Kunio Noji, age 66
Chairman of the Board, Masahiro Sakane, age 72
EVP; President Construction & Mining Equipment Marketing Division, Yoshinori Komamura, age 65
Senior Executive Officer; President Utility Equipment Division, Mamoru Hironaka
Senior Executive Officer; President Development Division, Nobukazu Kotake
Executive Officer; President Procurement Division, Tetsuro Kajiya
Executive Officer; General Manager Construction Equipment Technical Center 2 and Development Division, Nobuki Hasegawa
Senior Executive Officer CFO and Director, Mikio Fujitsuka
Senior Executive Officer and Director; President Production Division Supervising Production and e-KOMATSU, Tetsuji Ohashi
Senior Executive Officer; President Defense Systems Division, Shinichirou Komiya
Senior Executive Officer; President Development Division Supervising Research, Fujitoshi Takamura
Senior Executive Officer and VP Production Division, Yoshisada Takahashi
Senior Executive Officer; President Industrial Machinery Division and Komatsu Industries Corporation, Tadashi Okada
Executive Officer; President Procurement Division, Masahiro Uegaki
President Global Mining Business Division, Kazunori Kuromoto
Executive Vice President Chief Technical Officer, Mitsuru Ueno
President of the Japanese Society for Quality Control, Noriaki Kano, age 73
Senior Executive Officer; Supervising Corporate Communications CSR and General Affairs, Fusao Seki
Senior Executive Officer; President Rental and Used Equipment Business, Noriyuki Sudo
President Construction Equipment Marketing Division, Hisashi Shinozuka
Vice President Industrial Machinery Division, Katsushi Momoi
President Research Division, Kikuo Ejima
President Information Strategy Division, Kosuke Yamane
President Japanese Domestic Marketing, Takenori Tokunaga
President Business Planning & Strategy Division, Akira Akira Sugiki Sugiki
President Aftermarket Business Division, Hidetaka Hidetaka Kita Kita
President Quality Assurance Division, Yasuhiro Yasuhiro Matsuo Matsuo
President CEO and Director, Kunio Noji, age 66
Director, Morio Ikeda, age 76
Senior Executive Officer Senmu; Supervisor Environment Research and Design Quality Assurance and Director, Masao Fuchigami, age 63
Senior Executive Officer and Director; President Industrial Machinery, Yasuo Suzuki, age 64
Senior Executive Officer and Director; President Production Division Supervising Production and e-KOMATSU, Tetsuji Ohashi
Director, Noriaki Kano, age 72
Auditors: KPMGAZSA&Co.

LOCATIONS

HQ: Komatsu, Ltd.
2-3-6 Akasaka, Minato-ku, Tokyo 107-8414
Phone: (81) 3 5561 2604 **Fax:** (81) 3 3586 0374
Web: www.komatsu.co.jp

2012 Sales

Asia/Pacific	
China	14
The Americas	23
Europe & Commonwealth of Independent States (CIS)	11

PRODUCTS/OPERATIONS

2012 Sales

Construction Mining & Utility Equipment	88	
Total	**0**	**100**

Products and Services
Construction and mining equipment
Backhoe loaders
Crawler dozers
Crawler excavators
Diesel engines and power generators
Dump trucks
Forest machines
Hydraulic equipment
Mini excavators
Minimal swing radius excavators
Mobile crushers/r
Motor graders
Skid steer loaders
Vibratory rollers
Wheel excavators
Wheel loaders
Industrial machinery vehicles and other
Crankshaft millers
Forging presses
Forklift trucks
Large presses
Press brakes
Recycling plants
Shears
Small and midsized presses
Electronics
Excimer lasers
Mobile tracking and communication terminals
Network information terminals
Semiconductor manufacturing-related thermoelectric devices
Thermoelectric modules
Vehicle controller

COMPETITORS

Barloworld
CLARK Material Handling
CNH Global
Caterpillar
Coherent Inc.
Comau
Cymer
Deere
Deere-Hitachi
Doosan Infracore
Furukawa
Hitachi Construction Machinery
Hyundai Heavy Industries
JLG Industries
John Deere Thibodaux
Kubota
Kuraki
Mahindra
Manitowoc
Metso Minerals
Mitsubishi Heavy Industries
Mitsubishi Materials
Mitsui
Nisshinbo
P & H Mining
RAG AG
Rasa Industries
Sumitomo
Terex
Toyota
Victor L. Phillips
Volvo Construction Equipment
Wowjoint

HISTORICAL FINANCIALS

Company Type: Public

Income Statement FYE: March 31

	REVENUE ($ mil.)	NET INCOME ($ mil.)	NET PROFIT MARGIN	EMPLOYEES
03/13	20,033	1,342	6.7%	46,730
03/12	24,158	2,036	8.4%	44,206
03/11	22,258	1,820	8.2%	41,059
03/10	15,326	359	2.3%	38,518
03/09	20,530	800	3.9%	39,855
Annual Growth	(0.6%)	13.8%	—	4.1%

2013 Year-End Financials

Debt ratio: 0.2%
Return on equity: 11.4%
Cash ($ mil.): 997
Current ratio: 1.80
Long-term debt ($ mil.): 3,654
No. of shares (mil.): 952
Dividends
Yield: 0.0%
Payout: 0.0%
Market value ($ mil.): 22,638

	STOCK PRICE ($) FY Close	P/E High	P/E Low	PER SHARE ($) Earnings	Dividends	Book Value
03/13	23.76	0	0	1.41	0.00	13.31
03/12	28.75	0	0	2.11	0.00	12.93
03/11	34.00	0	0	1.88	0.30	11.53
03/10	21.09	0	0	0.37	0.28	9.22
03/09	44.24	0	0	0.81	0.43	8.55
Annual Growth	(14.4%)	—	—	14.8%	(88.6%)	11.7%

Koninklijke Ahold NV

A tattered prince of global food retailing Royal Ahold owns or has an interest in more than 5600 supermarkets and specialty stores in Europe and the US. While its status as one of the world's largest grocery retailers has been greatly diminished it still ranks as a leading supermarket operator along the East Coast of the US under names including Giant Food and Stop & Shop which account for about 60% of its total sales. Royal Ahold also operates Albert Heijn (the #1 food retailer in The Netherlands) as well as stores in Portugal the Baltic states the Czech Republic and Slovakia. Other interests include the US online grocery ordering and delivery service Peapod and Gall & Gall liquor stores.

HISTORY

Albert Heijn and his wife took over his father's grocery store in Ootzaan Netherlands in 1887. By the end of WWI the company had 50 Albert Heijn grocery stores in Holland and at WWII's end it had almost 250 stores. In 1948 the company went public.

It opened its first self-service store in 1952 and its first supermarket in 1955. Growing into the #1 grocer in the Netherlands Albert Heijn opened liquor and cosmetic stores in 1973. (It changed its name to Ahold that year to better reflect its range of businesses.) Ahold expanded outside the Netherlands in 1976 when it founded supermarket chain Cadadia in Spain (sold 1985).

Ahold entered the US in 1977 by purchasing BI-LO and furthered its expansion in 1981 by adding Pennsylvania-based Giant Food Stores. In 1987 in honor of its 100th anniversary Ahold was granted the title Koninklijke (Dutch for "royal"). In 1988 it bought a majority stake in Dutch food wholesaler Schuitema.

The company added New York-based TOPS Markets in 1991. That year Royal Ahold founded food retailer and distributor Euronova (now called Ahold Czech Republic) and in 1992 it acquired 49% of Portuguese food retailer Jeronimo Martins Retail. In 1993 Cees van der Hoeven was promoted to chief executive and Royal Ahold was listed on the NYSE.

Other acquisitions included New England grocery giant The Stop & Shop Companies in 1996. That year saw the beginning of several Asian joint ventures that gave Royal Ahold stores in Singapore Malaysia and Thailand. It also formed a joint venture in 1998 with Argentina's Velox Retail Holdings (owner of about 90% of supermarket operators DISCO and Santa Isabel) and Royal Ahold added Maryland-based grocer Giant Food Inc. (unrelated to Royal Ahold's Giant Food Stores).

Royal Ahold's moves in 1999 included the acquisition of several Spanish supermarket chains (with a total of about 200 stores) the purchase of Dutch institutional food wholesaler Gastronoom and the acquisition of 50% of Sweden's top food seller ICA AB. In Central America it acquired half of La Fragua an operator of supermarkets and discount stores. However North American expansion plans hit a snag when Royal Ahold backed out of a deal to buy Pathmark Stores.

In 2000 Royal Ahold acquired Spanish food retailer Kampio+ #2 and #4 foodservice distributors U.S. Foodservice and PYA/Monarch US convenience store chains Sugar Creek and Golden Gallon and all of the voting stock of Brazilian retailer Bompreco. In June the firm bought a 51% stake in online grocer Peapod. Royal Ahold took over food retailer Superdiplo which runs more than 300 stores in Spain (including the Canary Islands) in late 2000.

In March 2001 Royal Ahold began buying the remaining outstanding shares of Bompreco with the intention of delisting the company from the Brazilian Luxembourg and New York stock exchanges (which it did in late December). Chicago-based Peapod became a wholly owned Royal Ahold subsidiary in 2001. The retailer also expanded its bricks-and-mortar US presence in 2001 by purchasing Alliant Exchange parent of Alliant Foodservice which distributes food to more than 100000 customers and Bruno's Supermarkets which operates more than 180 stores in the Southeast. In December Ahold also agreed to buy the 32-store G. Barbosa supermarket chain which would add to its holdings in Brazil.

Royal Ahold reported its first net loss in nearly 30 years in the second quarter of 2002. In August 2002 Royal Ahold assumed full control of Disco Ahold International Holdings its former joint venture company with Velox Retail Holdings. Soon after the company increased its ownership stake in Chilean grocery chain Santa Isabel from 70% to 97% in a tender offer. In October the company integrated its Polish Czech and Slovak operations under the umbrella of Ahold Central Europe (ACE). ACE will manage more than 400 Albert supermarkets and Hypernova hypermarkets in Central Europe. In late 2002 subsidiary U.S. Foodservice agreed to buy Allen Foods a major independent foodservice distributor in the Central Plains region.

In February 2003 CEO Cees van der Hoeven and CFO Michiel Meurs resigned following an announcement that the grocery giant would restate its financial results by at least $500 million because of accounting irregularities at U.S. Foodservice. (van der Hoeven is facing charges by Dutch prosecutors in connection with the scandal at U.S. Foodservice.) Chairman Henny de Ruiter became acting CEO of the company and Dudley Eustace a British national who serves as a director of several Dutch companies was named interim CFO in March. In May 2003 IKEA veteran Anders Moberg became acting CEO; de Ruiter remained chairman. Soon after Ahold said it would restate earnings downward by $880 million (much more than the original $500 million projection) because of the accounting scandal at U.S. Foodservice. Further accounting investigations uncovered about $29 million in irregularities at the company's TOPS Markets US subsidiary.

In May Ahold completed the sale of its De Tuinen natural product stores to NBTY's British subsidiary Holland & Barrett Europe. In June it sold its Jamin chain of candy stores to Jamin management. The Santa Isabel chain in Chile was sold in July to Cencosud for about $95 million far less than the $150 million originally discussed. Adding to its woes in July the public prosecutor in Amsterdam launched a criminal investigation into possible falsification of accounts by the company. Soon after Ahold completed the sale of 22 stores in Indonesia to PT Hero Supermarket as well as its Malaysian retail business. In September the board of directors of Royal Ahold approved the appointment of Moberg and Ryopponen as CEO and CFO respectively. Later in the month the global grocer sold its operations in Paraguay (Supermercados Stock S.A.) to A.J. Vierci for about $4 million.

In October 2003 Royal Ahold published its long-awaited 2002 results revealing a $1.27 billion loss which the retailer attributed to special charges related to overstated profits at U.S. Foodservice. That month the company completed the sale of its 138-store Golden Gallon convenience chain to The Pantry for about $187 million and de Ruiter resigned and was succeeded by Karel Vuursteen previously a board member. In November Royal Ahold sold two hypermarkets in Poland to Carrefour Poland as part of its overall strategy to restructure its retail portfolio. In December the Peruvian operations of its Santa Isabel chain were sold to Grupo Interbank and other investors led by Nexus Group.

In March 2004 Royal Ahold sold its 118-store Bompreco chain in Brazil to Wal-Mart Stores and its credit card business (Hipercard) there to Unibanco S.A. for a combined price of about $500 million. Also in March the Dutch chain sold its stake in CRC Ahold operating in Thailand to its partner the Central Food Retail Co. completing the company's withdrawal from Asia. At a shareholders meeting in March Ahold placed the blame for the accounting scandal which nearly bankrupted the company in 2003 squarely on the shoulders of Jim Miller the former CEO of U.S. Foodservice. (Later Miller and Ahold agreed in late 2007 to settle litigation related to the matter with Miller paying Ahold $8 million.) In August Karel Vuursteen resigned as chairman of the supervisory board for personal reasons as was succeeded by Rene Dahan. In September Ahold reached a settlement with the Dutch public prosecutor in which the company agreed to pay ?8 million. In return the Dutch prosecutor agreed not to undertake proceedings against Royal Ahold. In October the company reached a settlement with the US Securities and Exchange Commission that imposed no fines on Royal Ahold due in part to its "extensive co-operation" with the investigation. The company also finalized a deal to increase its stake in its Scandinavian retail joint venture ICA AB. It paid its ?811 million for a 20% stake in the partnership sold by Canica. In December Ahold completed the sale of its retail activities in Spain and the Canary Islands (nearly 600 stores) to the Permira Funds.

In January 2005 the grocery giant sold its BI-LO and Bruno's chains in the southeastern US to an affiliate of Lone Star Funds for some $660 million. In February the Dutch retailer completed the sale of a dozen Hypernova hypermarkets in Poland to rival Carrefour followed by the sale of a single large hypermarket to a local Polish firm two months later. Also in April Royal Ahold completed its exit from Brazil with the sale of 32 G. Barbosa hypermarkets there to ACON Investments a US-based investment firm. In May the company announced completion of the sale of its 50% stake in Spanish winery Bodegas Williams & Humbert (formerly known as Luis Paez) to its joint venture partner Jose Medina y Cia SA for an undisclosed sum. In June Ahold completed the sale of its chain of 198 Wilson Farms and Sugarcreek convenience stores part of its TOPS Markets subsidiary in the US to WFI Acquisition for an undisclosed sum. In September Ahold sold its Deli XL foodservice operation in Belgium and the Netherlands to a subsidiary of South Africa-based The Bidvest Group for about ?140 million.

CFO Hannu Ryopponen resigned at the end of August 2005 to join Stora Enso an integrated paper packaging and forest products company. In October Royal Ahold completed the acquisition of 56 stores in the Czech Republic from Julius Meinl a.s. In November the company settled a US class action lawsuit by paying $1.1 billion to shareholders who purchased stock between July 3 1999 and February 23 2003; just before the 2003 accounting scandal broke. Concurrently the company reached an agreement to settle litigation with the Dutch Shareholders' Association.

The grocery chain also sold 13 large Hypernova hypermarkets in Poland to Carrefour and a local operator in early 2005. The company also moved its corporate headquarters from Zaandam to Amsterdam later in the year.

In 2006 the company sold three shopping centers in Poland and the Czech Republic for about ?108 million. In April Jose Alvarez was named president and CEO of the combined Stop & Shop/Giant-Landover organization succeeding Marc Smith who retired. In September Royal Ahold was reported to be in talks with its Belgian counterpart Delhaize regarding a possible merger. However negotiations were later suspended. In November the Dutch grocer completed the acquisition of 27 Konmar stores in the Netherlands from Laurus B.V. for about $130 million.

More than three years after teetering on the brink of bankruptcy as a result of one of Europe's largest financial scandals a Dutch court found former CEO Cees van der Hoeven and former CFO Michael Meurs guilty of fraud. Van der Hoeven and Meurs were accused of improperly booking sales from four subsidiaries in Scandinavia Argentina and Brazil. Both men were fined and given suspended sentences. Former executive board member Jan Andreae who headed Ahold's European operations was sentenced to four months in jail suspended for two years and fined.

CEO Anders Moberg left the company in July 2007. Also in July U.S. Foodservice was finally sold to a consortium of Clayton Dubilier & Rice and Kohlberg Kravis Roberts & Co. for about $7.1 billion. In November John Rishton Ahold's CFO who had been serving as interim chief executive since Moberg's departure was named to the post permanently. In December Royal Ahold sold its underperforming TOPS Markets chain to Morgan Stanley Private Equity for about $310 million.

In June 2008 the company completed sold its 73% stake in Schuitema N.V. to private equity firm CVC Capital Partners in return for cash and the transfer of 50-plus Schuitema stores to Ahold.

In 2009 Royal Ahold's Albert/Hypernova business in the Czech Republic and Slovakia closed 23 underperforming stores and downsized a dozen hypermarkets. It also finished converting its Hypernova stores to the Albert brand in the Czech Republic.

In February 2010 Ahold acquired 25 Ukrop's Super Market stores inventory equipment and leases in a $140 million transaction. The Ukrop's chain became part of Ahold USA's Giant-Carlisle division.

In March 2013 the company sold its 60% stake in the Sweden's largest food retailer ICA AB to Sweden's Hakon Invest for SEK 21.2 billion ($3.3 billion) in cash to better stick to its strategy of focusing on businesses it controls.

EXECUTIVES

Vice Chairman, Tom de Swaan, age 67
Chairman, Rene Dahan, age 72
CEO, A. Dick Boer, age 56, $828,250 total compensation
COO Europe, Sander van der Laan, age 44
Division President Giant Food Stores, Rick Herring
CFO, Jeff Carr, age 52
COO Ahold USA, James McCann, age 44
President and CEO Albert and Hypernova, Jan Van Dam, age 41
EVP and Chief Corporate Governance Counsel, Lodewijk Hijmans van den Bergh, age 49
General Manager Gall & Gall, Marit van Egmond
Vice Chairman, Tom de Swaan, age 67
Director, Derk C. Doijer, age 63
Director, Judith A. (Judy) Sprieser, age 59
Director, Ben J. Noteboom, age 55
Director, Stephanie M. Shern, age 65
Director, Rob F. van den Bergh
Director, Mark G. McGrath, age 66
Auditors: DeloitteAccountantsB.V.

LOCATIONS

HQ: Koninklijke Ahold NV
Piet Heinkade 167-173, Amsterdam 1019 GM
Phone: (31) 88 659 5100
Web: www.ahold.com

2012 Stores

	No.
Europe	2,302
US	772
Total	**3,074**

2012 Sales

	% of total
US	61
Europe	
The	34
Other	5
Total	**100**

PRODUCTS/OPERATIONS

2012 Stores

	No.
Albert Heijn Etos Gall &	1,996
Stop & Shop New England & Metro	403
Giant-Carlisle &	369
Albert/Hypernova	306
Total	**3,074**

Selected Operations

Retail
Europe
Albert (supermarkets Czech Republic and Slovakia)
Albert Heijn (supermarkets convenience stores)
bol.com (e-commerce nonfood)
Etos (drugstores online shopping)
Feira Nova (hypermarkets Portugal)
Gall & Gall (liquor stores)
Hypernova (hypermarkets Slovakia)
Pingo Doce (supermarkets Portugal)
US
Giant-Carlisle (supermarkets & superstores)
Giant-Landover (supermarkets)
Stop & Shop (supermarkets)
Peapod (online grocery shopping)

COMPETITORS

A&P
ALDI
BJ' s Wholesale Club
Big Y Foods
Carrefour
Costco Wholesale
Delhaize
Golub
Kooperativa Forbundet
Kroger
Lidl
METRO AG
NorgesGruppen
Safeway
Shaw' s
Target Corporation
Tesco
Wal-Mart
Wegmans
Whole Foods

HISTORICAL FINANCIALS

Company Type: Public

Income Statement

FYE: December 30

	REVENUE ($ mil.)	NET INCOME ($ mil.)	NET PROFIT MARGIN	EMPLOYEES
12/12*	43,286	1,090	2.5%	225,000
01/12	39,154	1,315	3.4%	218,000
01/11	39,475	1,140	2.9%	213,000
01/10	40,136	1,284	3.2%	206,000
12/08	36,163	1,509	4.2%	203,000
Annual Growth	4.6%	(7.8%)	—	2.6%

*Fiscal year change

2012 Year-End Financials

Debt ratio: 28.3%
Return on equity: 13.9%
Cash ($ mil.): 2,485
Current ratio: 1.00
Long-term debt ($ mil.): 4,095
No. of shares (mil.): 1,038
Dividends
Yield: 0.0%
Payout: 73.4%
Market value ($ mil.): 13,843

	STOCK PRICE ($) FY Close	P/E High/Low	PER SHARE ($) Earnings	Dividends	Book Value
12/12*	13.33	32 23	1.03	0.76	7.61
01/12	13.45	29 21	1.15	0.66	7.17
01/11	13.19	36 27	0.96	0.44	6.90
01/10	13.25	40 24	1.06	0.34	6.62
12/08	12.40	38 18	1.25	0.43	5.59
Annual Growth	1.8%	— —	(4.8%)	15.0%	8.0%

*Fiscal year change

Koninklijke KPN NV

Koninklijke KPN which is also known as Royal KPN is the leading provider of telecommunications services in the Netherlands where it has more than 4 million fixed-line phone customers. The company's core business however is KPN Mobile which serves more than 34 million subscribers in the Netherlands Germany Belgium Spain and France. Through its ownership of several European ISPs KPN also provides broadband Internet access to 2+ million customers and it offers business network services and data transport. Subsidiary Getronics provides a wide range of IT services to clients throughout the world. In the US the company operates iBasis which trades in international voice traffic.

Revenue was down 0.8% in 2010 compared with 2009. Cost reduction efforts throughout 2010 included cutting thousands of jobs.

After launching interactive TV in 2010 KPN is focusing on further growth of its television service which now serves more than a million customers while also promoting SIM-only products particularly in France and Spain. For operations as a whole the company is upgrading its networks with VDSL and fiber to provide faster bandwidth and enable more services such as triple play packages (telephone Internet television). Outside traditional telecom markets the company is focusing on communication products for the healthcare sector including bedside terminals and smart-metering products for the utility sector.

KPN sold KPN France which serves about 180000 mobile customers to Bouygues Telecom late in 2011.

HISTORY

Koninklijke KPN is a descendant of the Dutch PTT –a traditional European state-owned postal telegraph and telephone monopoly. The PTT traces its roots to the 1700s when the Dutch provinces began taking over postal operations from the cities. Under Napoleonic rule in 1799 mail delivery was organized under one national service.

In 1877 postal and telegraph services were assigned to the new ministry for water commerce and industry. The operation became an independent administration called Postal Services and Telegraphy (P&T) in 1893.

The telephone made its Dutch debut in 1881 with Netherlands Bell Telephone and several private operators and P&T soon entered the business. After building its first local phone exchange in 1911 P&T became the Staats Bedrijf der Posterijen Telegraphie & Telephony (PTT) in 1928. In 1941 during the Nazi occupation all independent phone operators were folded into PTT.

After WWII business began to boom for PTT which had fully automated its phone systems by 1962. Despite inflation and the government's practice of siphoning off PTT funds in the 1970s the company stuck to a course of investment and new services. It launched a packet data network in 1982 and an analog mobile phone network in 1985.

Following years of debate PTT became an independent corporation called PTT Nederland NV in 1989 but the state was its only shareholder. Momentum was building within Europe for liberalizing telecom services and the door was opened to competition for some postal and telecom services. Fearing competition from the likes of British Telecom (now BT Group) PTT joined Sweden's Televerket (renamed Telia in 1993 and later TeliaSonera) to form Unisource a global communications provider. Swisscom joined Unisource in 1993 and AT&T began working with the venture the next year.

Meanwhile KPN launched a digital GSM (global system for mobile communications) mobile phone network in 1994 and Dutch mobile use began to take off. The company now called Koninklijke PTT Nederland NV (or KPN; "Koninklijke" means "royal") launched its long-awaited IPO that year; the state sold a 30% share. Also in 1995 the firm began offering Internet access.

KPN's mail delivery and logistics businesses were finally spun off in 1998 as TNT Post Group (KPN bought express carrier TNT in 1996). The company began to focus squarely on telecom and adopted the name Royal KPN. AT&T abandoned the unsuccessful Unisource venture that year and the others decided to sell its assets. Wireless subsidiary KPN Mobile was formed in 1999 and took a 77% interest in German GSM operator E-Plus (BellSouth bought the remaining 23% then sold it to KPN in 2002).

KPN announced it would take KPN Mobile public in 2001 and entered merger talks with Belgacom Belgium's leading telecom company but the companies could not come to terms.

Also in 2001 KPN raised $4.6 billion in a public offering that reduced the Dutch government's stake in the company to 35%. The same year KPN sold its stake in Ireland's eircom.

The next year the company dissolved KPN Qwest its bankrupt joint venture formed in 1999 with US-based Qwest Communications which operated a pan-European data communications network with connections to North America. The venture became another victim of the overdevelopment of broadband infrastructure and a general economic downturn in the telecom sector.

Also in 2002 KPN began searching for a buyer for its stake in the European wireless services joint venture with NTT DoCoMo and Hutchison Whampoa (formed in 2000). Additionally that year the company sold its share in Hungarian mobile phone operator Pannon GSM. The next year the company sold its directory unit to private equity firm 3i Group and investment bank Veronis Suhler Stevenson Partners in a deal valued at $503 million. Also in 2003 the company sold its 16% stake in Ukrainian Mobile Communications for $55 million to Mobile Telesystems of Russia. The same year it additionally sold its stake in Czech phone company Cesky Telecom and its Belgian ISP Planet Internet Belgium. In 2004 KPN bought HubHop a wireless Internet (Wi-Fi) services provider and Freeler a small ISP in the Netherlands. The next year the company sold its stake in US-based Infonet.

To expand its IP-based services it acquired Dutch telecom firm Enertel from Greenfield Capital in a 2006 deal valued at E10 million. The company further strengthened its Dutch IT business in 2007 with the acquisition of Getronics for $1 billion. The company in 2007 sold its international voice wholesale business KPN Global Carrier Services to US-based VoIP carrier iBasis. The deal gave KPN a 51% stake in iBasis.

In 2008 the company bought 65% of Belgium-based Ortel Mobile from its founders to strengthen its position in the prepaid wireless services segment in the Netherlands Germany and Belgium. KPN sold the public sector portion of Getronics which provided IT services to the Dutch government and health care customers to Total Specific Solutions in 2009.

Also in 2009 KPN bought out the minority shareholders of iBasis in a bid to strengthen its position in North America and the VoIP computer telephony market. It acquired the remaining 35% of Ortel that it did not already own in 2010.

Also in 2010 KPN sold its business and carrier services network operations in Belgium to Belgian mobile carrier Mobistar.

The following year it acquired Dutch cable service provider Caiway. The deal added more than 150000 television broadband and Internet phone subscribers.

EXECUTIVES

Chairman Supervisory Board, Joseph B.M. (Jos) Streppel, age 63
Chairman Management Board and CEO, Eelco Blok, age 56, $669,593 total compensation
Director Corporate Market, Steven van Schilfgaarde, age 48
Managing Director The Netherlands, Joost Farwerck, age 48
CEO KPN Mobile International, Thorsten Dirks
Director Consumer Residential and Mobile, Jesper T. Eriksen, age 45
Managing Director Consumer Segment, Marco Visser, age 50
Chief Strategy Innovation & Technology Officer, Erik Hoving, age 50
CEO BASE, Libor Voncina
Member Management Board and Managing Director Netherlands, Baptiest Coopmans, age 48, $570,203 total compensation
CFO, Eric Hageman, age 42
CEO Getronics, Erik van der Meijden, age 53
Director Business Market, John van Vianen
Director NetCo, Eric Kuisch
CEO KPN Group Belgium, Jos Donvil
Member Supervisory Board, Manfred Bischoff, age 71
Member Supervisory Board, Rob J. Routs, age 65
Member Supervisory Board, A. H. J. (Ton) Risseeuw, age 76
Member Supervisory Board, Marike E. van Lier Lels, age 53
Member Supervisory Board, C.M. Colijn-Hooymans, age 61
Member Supervisory Board, D. J. Haank, age 60
Auditors: PricewaterhouseCoopersAccountantsN.V.

LOCATIONS

HQ: Koninklijke KPN NV
Maanplein 55, The Hague 2516 CK
Phone: (31) 70 343 43 43
Web: www.kpn.com

COMPETITORS

BT	TDC
Belgacom	Tele2
COLT Group	Tele2 Netherlands
Deutsche Telekom	TeliaSonera
Magyar Telekom	Vodafone
Orange	Vodafone Libertel
Orange Business Services	

HISTORICAL FINANCIALS

Company Type: Public

Income Statement FYE: December 31

	REVENUE ($ mil.)	NET INCOME ($ mil.)	NET PROFIT MARGIN	EMPLOYEES
12/12	16,355	910	5.6%	26,156
12/11	16,843	2,003	11.9%	30,941
12/10	17,832	2,399	13.5%	30,599
12/09	19,377	3,137	16.2%	33,148
12/08	20,170	1,862	9.2%	40,288
Annual Growth	(5.1%)	(16.4%)	—	(10.2%)

2012 Year-End Financials

Debt ratio: 81.7%	No. of shares (mil.): 1,431
Return on equity: 25.8%	Dividends
Cash ($ mil.): 1,695	Yield: 15.3%
Current ratio: 0.53	Payout: —
Long-term debt ($ mil.): 16,302	Market value ($ mil.): 7,129

	STOCK PRICE ($) FY Close	P/E High	P/E Low	PER SHARE ($) Earnings	Dividends	Book Value
12/12	4.98	42	17	0.65	0.76	2.22
12/11	11.92	31	18	1.37	0.00	2.65
12/10	14.67	30	17	1.54	0.82	3.01
12/09	17.05	30	17	1.92	0.76	3.43
12/08	14.73	56	25	1.06	0.86	3.07
Annual Growth	(23.7%)	—	—	(11.7%)	(2.9%)	(7.8%)

Koninklijke Philips N.V.

In the beginning Royal Philips Electronics created an array of products to shed some light. It now produces light bulbs (#1 worldwide) LED lighting and lamps as well as audio/multimedia entertainment electronics electric shavers and toothbrushes coffee makers and other kitchen appliances. It also makes a slew of medical equipment for disease diagnosis treatment and management. Amid a down economy and weak markets Philips has dumped noncore businesses such as its stakes in TSMC LG Display and music giant PolyGram as it acquires and forms JVs in its fast-growing businesses: healthcare consumer lifestyle and lighting. The company's presence in developing markets generates about one-third of its sales.

HISTORY

Gerard Philips (later joined by brother Anton) founded Philips & Co. in the Dutch city of Eindhoven in 1891. Surviving an industry shakeout Philips prospered as a result of Gerard's engineering and Anton's foreign sales efforts. The company had become Europe's #3 light bulb maker by 1900. It adopted the name Philips Gloeilampenfabrieken (light bulb factory) in 1912.

The Netherlands' neutrality during WWI allowed Philips to expand and integrate into glass manufacturing (1915) and X-ray and radio tubes (1918). The company set up its first foreign sales office in Belgium in 1919; it started building plants abroad in the 1930s to avoid trade barriers and tariffs.

During WWII Philips created US and British trusts to hold majority interests in North American Philips (NAP) and in Philips' British operations. Following the war the company established hundreds of subsidiaries worldwide. It repurchased its British businesses in 1955; NAP operated independently until it was reacquired in 1987.

The company started marketing televisions and appliances in the 1950s. Philips introduced audiocassette VCR and laser disc technology in the 1960s but had limited success with computers and office equipment. Despite its development of new technologies in the 1970s Philips was unable to maintain market share against an onslaught of inexpensive goods from Japan. Meanwhile NAP acquired Magnavox (consumer electronics US) in 1974. NAP also purchased GTE Television in 1981 and Westinghouse's lighting business in 1983. In 1986 it provided $60 million in seed money to start Taiwan Semiconductor Manufacturing with the Taiwanese government.

Philips' successful PolyGram unit (formed in 1972) went public in 1989 and bought record companies Island (UK) that year and A&M (US) the next. In 1991 the company changed its name to Royal Philips Electronics.

Ill-timed product introductions contributed to huge losses in the early 1990s. Philips cut some 60000 jobs and sold money-losing businesses including its computer business. Cor Boonstra a former Sara Lee executive was named chairman and president in 1996. The company sold its cellular communications business in 1996 to AT&T and merged its systems integration unit with BSO/Origin to form Origin B.V. Continuing to focus on core businesses it sold its 75% stake in PolyGram to Seagram and bought US-based medical instruments maker ATL Ultrasound in 1998. Also that year Philips sold its optoelectronics unit to Uniphase Corp.

The company formed an alliance with Sun Microsystems and Sony in 1999 to develop appliances that use the Internet. Philips then launched a hostile takeover of microchip maker VLSI Technology and after negotiations bought VLSI for nearly $1 billion. It also bought a 50% stake in LG LCD a subsidiary of LG Group for $1.6 billion. It was renamed LG.Philips LCD Co. soon thereafter. Since then Philips has begun to slowly reduced its stake in LG.Philips LCD to some 20%. In one move Philips in October 2007 sold the equivalent of $2.2 billion in LG.Philips LCD (some 46.4 million shares) or a 13% stake.

In 2000 the company formed TriMedia Technologies with Sony to create embedded processor core designs and software. Also that year Philips divested its 24% stake ($3.8 billion) in semiconductor equipment maker ASML Holding. In late 2000 Philips bought 60% of top medical transcription service MedQuist and agreed to buy Adac Laboratories (nuclear imaging technology) for $426 million.

In 2001 amid a large decline in profits Philips announced plans to trim its semiconductor spending by up to 50%. Also that month Boonstra retired and COO Gerard Kleisterlee became chairman and president. In August 2001 Philips completed its acquisition of the Healthcare Solutions Group of Agilent Technologies for $1.7 billion and in October the firm acquired Marconi Medical Systems a distributor of medical imaging systems.

Since 2001 Philips has cut more than 35000 jobs; the reductions are the result of support staff job eliminations and the sale of noncore businesses (Communication Security and Imaging unit to Robert Bosch GmbH; contract manufacturing services to Jabil Circuit; healthcare products group to Platinum Equity Holdings). The company also dissolved its components division (maker of screens for mobile phones and optical storage products) and transferred Mexican production of computer monitors to China.

In 2003 Fidelio Acquisition Company (an investor firm led by Philips along with Sony Corporation of America) acquired InterTrust Technologies a manufacturer of digital copy-protection software for $450 million.

The company sold 80% of its aerospace division to Italian firm the Avio Group who renamed it DutchAero.

In a transaction valued at $2 billion Philips in 2005 sold its computer-monitor manufacturing operations and a portion of its flat screen TV business to Hong Kong-based TPV Technology making that company the world's largest manufacturer of PC monitors.

Also that year Frits Philips son of founder Anton Philips and the last member of the Philips family to manage the company (he retired in 1977) and who helped develop audio cassettes and the compact disc died at the age of 100.

The company focused on strengthening its presence in its core lighting industry during 2005. It extended its reach into LEDs with the purchase of Agilent Technologies that year.

It also focused on developing its presence in health care. Philips purchased personal emergency response service Lifeline Systems in 2006 and rolled the Lifeline operations into its medical systems unit. Also that year it acquired Intermagnetics General Corporation a US manufacturer of magnetic resonance imaging (MRI) scanners for about $1.3 billion in cash. The deal allows Philips to flex its muscle in the MRI niche of the medical imaging and equipment industry and gives the company a leg up in fast-growing radio frequency coils which are sold to hospitals and imaging centers. (Intermagnetics was folded into the company's medical systems division; its headquarters in Latham New York became the worldwide base for Philips' MRI business.)

Philips Electronics sold 80% of its semiconductor division in 2006 to a group of private equity firms including Kohlberg Kravis Roberts & Co. Silver Lake Partners and AlpInvest Partners for about $4.3 billion. The deal created a stand-alone company called NXP (for Next Experience) based in Eindhoven the Netherlands. NXP supplies chips to improve the performance of next generation consumer devices including digital TVs and cell phones rather than personal computers. Philips also sold its Philips Sound Solutions (PSS) business to Japan's D&M Holdings. PSS supplied speaker systems primarily to the automotive industry.

In 2007 the company announced a reorganization of its top units in order to simplify structure. The company established three core units: Philips Lighting Philips Consumer Lifestyle and Philips Healthcare.

Extending its reach into the home health and baby care arenas in 2007 the company acquired personal emergency-response service Health Watch Holdings for $130 million and UK baby care products maker Avent for about $860 million. The move was part of a Philips strategy to solidify its baby products presence in Europe with an eye toward expansion of Avent into Asia.

Philips and China Electronics Corporation (CEC) inked a deal in 2007 that transferred Philips' remaining mobile phone activities to CEC. As a result of the deal CEC took over the responsibility for Philips' mobile phone business.

In order to gain its own share in growing light-emitting diode (LED) sector Philips in 2007 acquired Color Kinetics which caters to the professional LED niche for some $690 million as well as Canada's TIR Systems for about $70 million. (Following the acquisition of Color Kinetics Philips changed the unit's name to Philips Solid-State Lighting Solutions.)

In 2008 Philips purchased Respironics a leading medical alert system in North America for $4.9 billion. Respironics also develops medical devices for treating sleep apnea and other respiratory disorders a growing healthcare issue. The deal gained a foothold in the home health care solutions market a new line of business for the Dutch conglomerate. Philips' other significant acquisition in 2008 was Genlyte Group bought for nearly $3 billion. The addition later renamed Philips Lighting Business Unit Professional Luminaires North America boosted Philips' place in the lighting industry which accounts for approximately one-third of its sales.

Building on its health care information technology holdings Philips in 2008 also acquired VISICU which develops remote patient-monitoring systems for about E300 million (about $430 million) and cardiac data monitoring company TOMCAT Systems. Concurrently Philips unloaded the final shares in Taiwan Semiconductor Manufacturing Company one of the largest contract semiconductor manufacturers in the world. The company recorded a profit of E260 million (nearly $400 million) from the sale.

To better focus on its core businessesPhilips in 2009 sold its nearly 15% stake in LG Display for about E630 million (about $900 million). LG Display originally a joint venture with LG Electronics was formed when the two firms merged their LCD businesses. The company built on its emergency care offerings in 2009 through the purchase of InnerCool Therapies a developer of temperature management products from Cardium Therapeutics. The deal was worth about $10 million and included the transfer of some $1.5 million in trade payables.

Philips paid E170 million ($241.5 million) to acquire the Italian espresso machine maker Saeco International Group in 2009. Following the purchase Saeco became part of the domestic appliances unit of the Philips Consumer Lifestyle business.

Among its 11 acquisitions in 2010 Philips purchased specialized lighting company Burton Medical Products Corporation. Burton's lineup is mainly used in healthcare facility lighting. It also acquired China-based Shanghai Apex Electronics Technology (Apex). Supporting Philips' lead in the medical equipment market Apex manufactures ultrasound equipment. The Consumer Lifestyle arm of Phillips gained Discus Holdings a maker of professional tooth-whitening products.

Frans van Houten was named president/CEO and chairman of the company's management board in April 2011.

EXECUTIVES

VP Member of Management Board and Chief Exec, Stephen H. (Steve) Rusckowski, age 57
EVP; CEO Philips Lighting, Rudy S. Provoost, age 54
President; Chief Executive Officer; Chairman of the Board of Management and Executive Committee, Frans van Houten, age 54
EVP and CFO, Ron H. Wirahadiraksa
EVP; CEO Philips Consumer Lifestyle, Pieter Nota, age 49
EVP; CEO Greater China, Patrick S. Kung
EVP; CEO Philips Healthcare, Deborah DiSanzo
Member Group Management Committee Chief Strategy Officer and Group Controller, Gerard Ruizendaal, age 55
Member Group Management Committee and CTO, Rick Harwig, age 64
Head External Communications, Gerd Gotz
SVP and General Manager Global Business Unit Hospitality, Paul Peeters, age 50
EVP and Chief Legal Officer, Eric Coutinho, age 62
Member Group Management Committee and Global Head Human Resources Management, Hayko Kroese, age 58
Member Group Management Committee CIO and Global Head Purchasing, Maarten de Vries
Director Corporate Communications, David L. Wolf
Head Investor Relations, Stewart McCrone
Chief Press Officer, Arent Jan Hesselink
Senior Press Officer, Shai Dewan
Vice Chairman Supervisory Board, John M. Thompson, age 70
Manager Investor Relations, Pim Preesman
Communications Manager Healthcare, Andre Manning
Communications Manager Philips Design, Ange Dunselman
Communications Manager Consumer Lifestyle, Jurn Hageman

Communications Manager Philips Corporate Technologies, Ellen de Vries
Communications Manager Lighting, Marike Westra
Communications Manager Philips Intellectual Property and Standards, Bjorn Teuwsen
Communications Manager Asia Pacific, Donough Foley
Communications Manager Latin America, Fabiano Lima
EVP Chief Strategy Officer and Chief Innovation Officer, Jim Andrew, age 52
EVP and Chief Human Resources Officer, Carole Wainaina, age 48
Executive Vice President & Chief Market Leader; Member of Executive Committee, Ronald Jong
CEO of Philips Healthcare, DiSanzo Deborah
Member of the Management Board and Chief Executive Officer Philips Lighting Division, Eric Rondolat
Chairman of the Supervisory Board, Jeroen Veer
Director, James J. (Jim) Schiro, age 67
Director, Cornelis J. A. (Cees) van Lede, age 71
Director, Ewald Kist, age 69
Director, Heino von Prondzynski, age 63
Director, Jackson P. Tai, age 62
Member of the Supervisory Board, Christine A. (Chris) Poon, age 60
Vice Chairman Supervisory Board, John M. Thompson, age 70
Member of the Supervisory Board, Cornelis Lede
Member of the Supervisory Board, Heino Prondzynski
Member of the Supervisory Board, Neelam Dhawan
Auditors: KPMGAccountantsN.V.

LOCATIONS

HQ: Koninklijke Philips N.V.
Breitner Center, Amstelplein 2, Amsterdam 1096 BC
Phone: (31) 20 59 77 777
Web: www.philips.com

2011 Sales

	% of total
US	28
China	9
Germany	6
France	5
Japan	4
Brazil	3
Netherlands	3
Other	41
Total	**100**

PRODUCTS/OPERATIONS

2011 Sales

	% of total
Healthcare	39
Lighting	34
Consumer	26
Group management & services	1
Total	**100**

2011 Sales

	% of total
Goods	85
Services	13
Licenses and	2
Total	**100**

Selected Business Areas

Consumer
- Audio video multimedia and accessories
- Coffee
- Domestic appliances
- Health and wellness
- Personal care

Healthcare
- Home healthcare
- Imaging systems
- Patient care and clinical informatics
- Customer services

Lighting
- Automotive
- Home luminaries and systems
- Lamps
- Lighting systems and controls
- Lumileds
- Professional luminaries and systems
- Special lighting applications

Philips Group
- Healthcare Incubators
- Philips Design
- Philips Innovation Campus
- Philips Innovation Services
- Philips Intellectual Property and Standards
- Philips Research

COMPETITORS

BSH Bosch und Siemens Hausgerate
Covidien
De' Longhi
Fujitsu
GE
GE India
Harman International
Invacare
LG Electronics
Mitsubishi Electric
OSRAM
Panasonic Corp
Pioneer Corporation
ResMed
SANYO
Samsung Group
Sharp Corp.
Siemens AG
Siemens Corp.
Sony
Spectrum Brands
Technicolor
Texas Instruments
Toshiba

HISTORICAL FINANCIALS

Company Type: Public

Income Statement FYE: December 31

	REVENUE ($ mil.)	NET INCOME ($ mil.)	NET PROFIT MARGIN	EMPLOYEES
12/12	32,671	297	0.9%	118,087
12/11	29,204	(1,675)	—	125,241
12/10	34,020	1,935	5.7%	119,001
12/09	33,405	590	1.8%	115,924
12/08	36,888	(260)	—	121,398
Annual Growth	(3.0%)	—	—	(0.7%)

2012 Year-End Financials

Debt ratio: 20.5%
Return on equity: 1.9%
Cash ($ mil.): 5,053
Current ratio: 1.26
Long-term debt ($ mil.): 4,909
No. of shares (mil.): 914
Dividends
Yield: 3.0%
Payout: 250.3%
Market value ($ mil.): 24,273

	STOCK PRICE ($) FY Close	P/E High/Low	PER SHARE ($) Earnings	Dividends	Book Value
12/12	26.54	187113	0.32	0.80	16.05
12/11	20.95	— —	(1.76)	0.00	17.26
12/10	30.70	42 29	2.05	0.79	21.28
12/09	29.44	138 55	0.66	0.80	22.67
12/08	19.87	— —	(0.27)	1.09	24.60
Annual Growth	7.5%	— —	—	(7.5%)	(10.1%)

Korea Electric Power Corp

Korea Electric Power (KEPCO) is slowly relinquishing its status as South Korea's electric utility monopoly. The company is still the country's primary power distributor serving 12 million households. It generates 87% of Korea's power supply with an installed capacity of more than 65380 MW (primarily from thermal and nuclear plants). KEPCO also buys capacity from independent power producers. Industrial demand accounts for more than 50% of the company's annual output. In response to deregulation the company plans to divest more than half of its Korean-based generation assets while it builds an extensive power plant portfolio in other countries. The Korean government controls 51% of KEPCO.

In a government effort to restructure the power industry KEPCO is required to spin off all of its fossil-fueled power generation operations which have been split up into five new subsidiaries; the utility will retain its nuclear and hydroelectric plants. However due to market conditions the privatization plans have been delayed. The government looked at options to allow competition in the country's power distribution market but these plans have also been suspended.

KEPCO is looking to become both a leader in the use of green technology (pushing "smart" grid deployment and cleaner burning power plants and wind farms). With power use beginning to plateau in Korea KEPCO is looking to become a global power player (a "Global Top Five Energy and Engineering Company by 2020"). In 2010 the company was engaged in power plant and related projects in a wide range of countries including Australia China Egypt Nigeria the Philippines Russia and the US and had more than 5420 MW of installed capacity outside of Korea. All told it was involved in 84 international projects in nuclear hydro and thermal power plants transmission and distribution projects and energy resources development initiatives.

To improve its coal self-sufficiency in 2010 KEPCO acquired the Bylong coal mine in Australia from Anglo American PLC for $340 million.

The reviving economy higher commodity prices and increased energy demand helped to lift sales and net income in 2010.

In 2011 the company agreed to set up a 66%-owned joint venture with Germany's Uhde GmbH. Kepco-Uhde Inc. will work on joint projects in Korea relating to integrated gasification combined cycle and synthetic natural gas.

EXECUTIVES

President CEO and Director, Ssang-Su Kim, age 67
EVP Chief Nuclear Project Officer and Director, Jun-Yeon Byun, age 56
EVP COO and Director, Woo-Kyum Kim, age 58
Controller Auditor General and Director, Dae-Soo Han
EVP CFO and Director, In-Kook Cho, age 57
EVP Chief Human Resources Officer and Director, Jong-Ho Kim
EVP CTO and Director, Chong-Young Kim
President CEO and Director, Ssang-Su Kim, age 67
EVP Chief Nuclear Project Officer and Director, Jun-Yeon Byun, age 56
Director, Tae-Sik Lee, age 66
Director, Seog-Hoon Kang, age 47
Director, Jung-Kook Kim, age 65
Director, Kyung-Min Kim, age 56
Director, Il-Soon Shin, age 63
Director, Dong-Rack Chung
Director, Gi-Pyo Lee
EVP COO and Director, Woo-Kyum Kim, age 58
Controller Auditor General and Director, Dae-Soo Han
EVP CFO and Director, In-Kook Cho, age 57
EVP Chief Human Resources Officer and Director, Jong-Ho Kim
EVP CTO and Director, Chong-Young Kim
Director, Hae-Joo Chung
Auditors: DeloitteAnjinLLC

LOCATIONS

HQ: Korea Electric Power Corp
167 Samseong-dong, Gangnam-gu, Seoul 135-791
Phone: (82) 2 3456 3114 **Fax:** (82) 2 3456 4299
Web: www.kepco.co.kr

PRODUCTS/OPERATIONS

2010 Sales

	% of total
Electricity	97
Other	3
Total	**100**

Selected Subsidiaries

Korea-based companies
- Korea East-West Power Co. Ltd. (EWP power generation)
- Korea Hydro & Nuclear Power Co. Ltd. (KHNP power generation)
- Korea Midland Power Co. Ltd. (KOMIPO power generation)
- Korea South-East Power Co. Ltd. (KOSEP power generation)
- Korea Southern Power Co. Ltd. (KOSPO power generation)
- Korea Western Power Co. Ltd. (KOWEPO power generation)

KEPCO Austrailia Pty. Ltd.
KEPCO International Hong Kong Ltd.
KEPCO Middle East Holding Company
KEPCO Philippines Corporation

COMPETITORS

AES
CLP Holdings
EGAT
Huaneng Power
International Power
National Power
Power Assets
Taiwan Power
Tokyo Electric
Tractebel Engineering

HISTORICAL FINANCIALS

Company Type: Public

Income Statement FYE: December 31

	REVENUE ($ mil.)	NET INCOME ($ mil.)	NET PROFIT MARGIN	EMPLOYEES
12/12	46,287	(2,965)	—	19,568
12/11	37,570	(2,908)	—	19,579
12/10	35,233	(106)	—	19,927
12/09	29,379	(83)	—	20,170
12/08	24,864	(2,328)	—	20,970
Annual Growth	16.8%	—	—	(1.7%)

2012 Year-End Financials

Debt ratio: 0.0%
Return on equity: (-6.1%)
Cash ($ mil.): 1,830
Current ratio: 0.74
Long-term debt ($ mil.): 43,130
No. of shares (mil.): 623
Dividends
Yield: —
Payout: —
Market value ($ mil.): 8,704

	STOCK PRICE ($) FY Close	P/E High/Low	PER SHARE ($) Earnings	Dividends	Book Value
12/12	13.97	— —	(4.76)	0.00	75.00
12/11	10.98	— —	(4.67)	0.00	73.79
12/10	13.51	— —	(0.17)	0.00	81.38
12/09	14.54	— —	(0.13)	0.00	56.95
12/08	11.61	— —	(3.74)	0.77	51.83
Annual Growth	4.7%	— —	—	—	9.7%

Korea Gas Corp. (South Korea)

As the world's largest importer of liquefied natural gas (LNG) KOGAS single-handedly helps South Koreans stay warm and chill out. The company is the sole provider of LNG to the country (about 25 million tons imported annually) operating three terminals and a nationwide pipeline network. KOGAS supplies LNG to power plants and utility companies throughout South Korea and produces and supplies LNG products to domestic and overseas markets. It imports come around the world including from Indonesia Malaysia Myanmar Oman Qatar and Russia. KOGAS development initiatives include natural gas vehicles LNG chiller/heater systems for homes and fuel cells.

Operations

KOGAS operates three LNG terminals and a nationwide pipeline network spanning over 3022 km. The company imports LNG and distributes it to consumers across South Korea. Ten power generation companies (17 power generation plants) supply the gas to their end users within their respective regions.

It major business lines include: Construction and Operation of LNG Terminals and Natural Gas Distribution Network; Exploration and Import/Export of Natural Gas and LNG; Production and Distribution of Natural Gas (including Purification and Sales of By-products); and Research and Technical Development.

Financial Performance

In 2011 KOGAS' revenues increased by 25% and its net income by 134%.

Strategy

It has expanded its research and development's core competencies in upstream businesses new energy and future growth engines and is expanding its network by adding domestic and overseas energy research and development institutes.

Seeking future LNG supply it is also active in global gas supply and LNG projects. In 2011 KOGAS signed on to an LNG joint development project in Indonesia and in 2010 it secured development and production rights in the oil and gas fields in Zubair and Badra in Iraq and an equity partnership in Australia's Gladstone LNG project.

Ownership

The Korean government owns about 27% of the company KEPCO 24.5%.

Company Background

KOGAS was incorporated by the Korean government in 1983.

In 2006 KOGAS acquired an 8% interest in China Gas Holdings as a strategic partner. The deal paved the way for further expansion in China's gas distribution market. KOGAS additionally acquired four LNG tankers in a joint venture with three other South Korean companies. The move pointed to a broadening of its overall LNG business.

EXECUTIVES

CEO, Kangsoo Choo
Auditors: AnjinDeloitteLLC

LOCATIONS

HQ: Korea Gas Corp. (South Korea)
215 Jeongja-dong, Bundang-gu, Seongnam, Gyeonggi-do 463-754
Phone: (82) 31 710 0114 **Fax:** (82) 31 710 0399
Web: www.kogas.or.kr

COMPETITORS

BP
Exxon Mobil
GS Caltex
JX Nippon Oil & Energy
SK Innovation

HISTORICAL FINANCIALS

Company Type: Public

Income Statement FYE: December 31

	REVENUE ($ mil.)	NET INCOME ($ mil.)	NET PROFIT MARGIN	EMPLOYEES
12/12	32,809	343	1.0%	2,999
12/11	24,591	156	0.6%	2,815
12/10	20,280	246	1.2%	2,797
12/09	16,889	206	1.2%	2,790
12/08	18,446	258	1.4%	2,806
Annual Growth	15.5%	7.4%	—	1.7%

2012 Year-End Financials

Debt ratio: 0.0%
Return on equity: 4.4%
Cash ($ mil.): 229
Current ratio: 1.16
Long-term debt ($ mil.): 16,314
No. of shares (mil.): 72
Dividends
Yield: —
Payout: —
Market value ($ mil.): —

Kuehne & Nagel International AG

Pass it on –Kuehne + Nagel International is one of the world's top freight forwarding and logistics groups. Kuehne + Nagel (pronounced "KOO-nuh and NAH-gel") provides sea freight and airfreight forwarding arranges the transportation of goods by road and rail and offers customs brokerage services. The company's contract logistics unit offers warehousing and distribution services and it manages more than 7 million sq. meters of warehouse space. Overall Kuehne + Nagel operates from about 900 locations in more than 100 countries worldwide. Executive chairman Klaus-Michael Kuehne grandson of the company's co-founder owns a controlling stake in Kuehne + Nagel.

Operations in Europe account for about two-thirds of the company's sales. Understandably continued growth in Europe is one of the chief destinations on Kuehne + Nagel's roadmap for success. In 2011 it moved to bolster its road and rail operations outside of its primary target (southern and eastern Europe) by making good on its acquisition strategy. It plans to take over Brazil trucking company Grupo Eichenberg for $52 million. The deal follows Kuehne + Nagel's acquisitions of Translago in Columbia and UK-based RH Freight (Rennies Investment). The latter transaction (for an undisclosed sum) extends Kuehne + Nagel's overland network with 17 hubs in the UK and two in Finland as well as its sea- and airfreight and contract logistics capacity.

In 2010 the company opened new distribution centers in France Germany Spain and Latvia. Other stops along the way include Asia and the Middle East; Kuehne + Nagel added 18 new shipping routes to Asia in late 2010 and relocated the hub for its Middle East operations from Istanbul to Dubai. In early 2009 the company acquired France-based Alloin Group a logistics aggregator operating more than 50 cross-docking terminals. The group manages 20000 shipments per day.

The company's US arm Kuehne + Nagel Inc. specializes in contract logistics services. Kuehne + Nagel has gained revenue in the US and Canada as customers based elsewhere have expanded their operations in North America. Kuehne + Nagel agreed to pay a $9.87 million fine in late 2010 to settle charges that the Sherman Act was violated when the logistics company established surcharges for international freight forwarding services to the US.

As it works to gain market share Kuehne + Nagel transitioned its leadership team in early 2009 when CEO Klaus Herms retired after more than 40 years with the company. Deputy CEO Reinhard Lange a veteran of Kuehne + Nagel's freight forwarding business replaced him.

HISTORY

Kuehne + Nagel (also Kuhne + Nagel) was founded in 1890 in Bremen Germany by shipping veterans August Kuehne and Friedrich Nagel. The forwarding and commissioning agency's initial contracts were for glassware and cotton. Kuehne + Nagel convinced Hamburg sugar refiners to use its services to transport sugar by rail to the ice-free port of Bremen when the refiners' major export route the Weser River was frozen. By 1902 Kuehne + Nagel had an office in Hamburg. Nagel died in 1907.

Rebuilding after WWI Kuehne + Nagel acquired the Weber & Freund import company in the early 1920s and expanded into Austria Czechoslovakia Switzerland and the Balkans. In 1932 when August Kuehne died sons Alfred and Werner became sole owners of Kuehne + Nagel. (Werner left the company in 1951.)

Kuehne + Nagel's headquarters in Bremen was destroyed in WWII. As postwar German trade recovered Kuehne + Nagel grew rapidly opening a subsidiary in Canada in 1953 and setting up branches across Germany including Frankfurt (1949) Bonn and Hanover (1950) Wuppertal (1961) and Nuremberg (1963).

After the European Economic Community was founded Kuehne + Nagel established a network of forwarding agents and subsidiaries across Europe including offices in Antwerp Belgium and Rotterdam the Netherlands in 1954 and offices in Basel and Zurich Switzerland in 1963. Kuehne + Nagel took control of Greek forwarder Proodos in 1963 and set up an Italian subsidiary a year later.

Alfred Kuehne died in 1981. Heavy losses resulting from the expansion of the shipping fleet of Kuehne + Nagel prompted it to sell half of the company to British conglomerate Lonrho (renamed Lonmin in 1999). Alfred's son Klaus-Michael Kuehne and Lonrho's Roland "Tiny" Rowland were appointed as joint chief executives.

In 1985 Kuehne + Nagel began expanding its transportation warehousing and distribution network by acquiring stakes in leading freight companies including Domenichelli (Italy) Hollis Transportation (UK) and Van Vliet (the Netherlands). The Kuehne family expanded Kuehne + Nagel's presence in Switzerland (seen as a pan-European center) during the 1970s and 1980s and in 1992 Kuehne + Nagel moved its global headquarters to Schindellegi near Zurich.

In the early 1990s after German reunification and the fall of the Soviet Union Kuehne + Nagel acquired former East German state-owned forwarder VEB Deutrans. It also signed deals with local freight-forwarding operators in Russia and across Eastern Europe.

In 1992 Klaus-Michael Kuehne bought out Lonrho's stake and later sold a 33% stake to German conglomerate VIAG (later part of E.ON) which sold it back to Kuehne + Nagel in 1999. In 1994 Kuehne + Nagel went public.

To expand its rail network the company in 1997 acquired a 51% stake in Swiss rail forwarder Ferroviasped a major player in freight services for national railroads in Denmark France Spain and Switzerland.

To stay competitive in a rapidly consolidating industry Kuehne + Nagel formed an alliance in 1999 with French freight forwarder GEFCO a subsidiary of Peugeot S.A. A year later Kuehne + Nagel formed an alliance with Singapore-based SembCorp Logistics which later acquired a 20% stake in Kuehne + Nagel. In return Kuehne + Nagel bought 5% of SembCorp Logistics.

In 2000 Kuehne + Nagel also made plans to expand operations in the US. The company followed through the next year when it bought Connecticut-based USCO Logistics for $300 million. USCO Logistics was renamed Kuehne + Nagel Logistics in 2004.

Also in 2004 Kuehne + Nagel and SembCorp Logistics terminated their alliance in order to proceed independently.

Kuehne + Nagel expanded its operations in Europe by acquiring ACR Logistics in January 2006. Later that year the company bought HSBC Export Services a UK-based provider of sea freight and road freight forwarding and export documentation and credit management services.

EXECUTIVES

Chairman, Klaus-Michael Kuehne, age 73, $410,700 total compensation
CFO, Gerard van Kesteren, age 61
CEO, Reinhard Lange, age 61
Vice Chairman, Bernd Wrede, age 67
COO Road and Rail Logistics, Xavier Urbain, age 53
EVP Contract Logistics, Dirk Reich, age 47
Head of Corporate Communications, Inge Lauble-Meffert
Manager Corporate Communications, Robert Cathomas
CIO, Martin Kolbe, age 49
Assistant Corporate Communications, Andrea Zander
Managing Director Kuehne + Nagel KG; Regional Manager Central Europe, Hans-Georg Brinkmann
EVP Sea and Air Logistics, Peter Ulber, age 50
Managing Director Poland, Tobias Jerschke
Chief Human Resources Officer, Lothar A. Harings, age 50
Assistant Investor Relations, Andrea Kobei
IR Contact, Andrea Kobi
Member of the Management Board; Chief Financial Officer, Gerard Kesteren
Member of the Management Board; Executive Vice President Seafreight, Horst Schacht
Member of the Management Board; Executive Vice President Airfreight, Tim Scharwath
Director, Hans Lerch, age 61
Vice Chairman, Bernd Wrede, age 67
Director, Georg Obermeier, age 69
Director, Joachim Hausser, age 66
Director, Thomas Staehelin, age 63
Director, Wolfgang Peiner, age 66
Director, Karl Gernandt, age 50
Director, Juergen Fitschen, age 62
Director, Hans-Joerg Hager, age 62
Non-Executive Director, Joerg Wolle
Non-Executive Director, Renato Fassbind
Auditors: KPMGAG

LOCATIONS

HQ: Kuehne & Nagel International AG
Kuehne & Nagel House, P.O. Box 67, Schindellegi CH-8834
Phone: (41) 44 786 95 11 **Fax:** (41) 44 786 95 95
Web: www.kuehne-nagel.com

2009 Sales

	$ mil.	% of total
Europe		67
Asia/Pacific		8
Total		**100**

PRODUCTS/OPERATIONS

2009 Sales

	$ mil.	% of total
Sea freight	44	
Airfreight	16	
Insurance brokerage & real estate	1	

COMPETITORS

APL Logistics
Agility Holdings
Bollore
C.H. Robinson Worldwide
CEVA Logistics
DB Mobility Logistics
DHL Global Forwarding
Damco
Expeditors
GEFCO
Geodis
Hellmann Worldwide Logistics
Menlo Worldwide
Nippon Express
Norbert Dentressangle
Panalpina
Ryder System
Sinotrans
UPS Supply Chain Solutions
UTi Worldwide
Wincanton

HISTORICAL FINANCIALS

Company Type: Public

Income Statement FYE: December 31

	REVENUE ($ mil.)	NET INCOME ($ mil.)	NET PROFIT MARGIN	EMPLOYEES
12/12	18,675	529	2.8%	63,248
12/11	17,238	638	3.7%	63,110
12/10	18,014	642	3.6%	57,536
12/09	13,918	453	3.3%	54,680
12/08	16,913	549	3.3%	53,823
Annual Growth	2.5%	(1.0%)	—	4.1%

2012 Year-End Financials

Debt ratio: 1.1%
Return on equity: 20.2%
Cash ($ mil.): 1,181
Current ratio: 1.26
Long-term debt ($ mil.): 34
No. of shares (mil.): 119
Dividends
Yield: 1.9%
Payout: 12.7%
Market value ($ mil.): 2,913

	STOCK PRICE ($) FY Close	P/E High	P/E Low	PER SHARE ($) Earnings	PER SHARE ($) Dividends	PER SHARE ($) Book Value
12/12	24.33	8	6	4.43	0.48	21.83
12/11	22.35	7	5	5.35	0.00	21.22
Annual Growth	8.9%	—	—	(4.6%)	—	0.7%

L'Air Liquide S.A. (France)

Forget the outer planets the earth has its own gaseous giant in the form of L'Air Liquide. Also known as Air Liquide the company jockeys with Linde to be the world's largest industrial gas supplier. Its gases include argon carbon dioxide helium hydrogen nitrogen and oxygen. Industrial gases are used by almost every major market in their production processes while medical gases such as oxygen are used by hospitals and other health care providers. Air Liquide has more than a hundred subsidiaries in 75 countries with a clear strength in Europe. The company operates in the US its second-largest segment through American Air Liquide. It also serves customers in Asia Africa and the Middle East.

With an established footprint in mature markets and production units all over the world a key driver in the group's plan for long-term growth is seizing on opportunities to both acquire and build production facilities in emerging economies with a focus on five regions: China India Russia Latin America and the Middle East. Those regions open opportunities to reduce its overall cost base and to train and develop a new generation of personnel.

L'Air Liquide saw a small increase in revenues in 2010 up on the strength of a recovering global economy. The company's strongest performance was in developing economies where it showed a significant increase. Its Gas & Services unit led segment growth followed by Large Industries Electronics and Healthcare units. Net income also increased a modest amount over the previous year.

New facilities are typically designed and built by Air Liquide's own global engineering and construction division. That division also offers design/build services to third-party customers in need of production facilities equipped with specialized technologies such as adsorption permeation and cryogenics. In addition to engineering and construction other services Air Liquide offers include gas cylinder rental and residual gas disposal for customers that deal in toxic corrosive or inflammable gases.

On the R&D side of its strategy Air Liquide strives to improve gas production technology and develop new applications for gases. It maintains eight research centers in France Germany Japan and the US focused on developing products that anticipate and meet evolving customer demands. The R&D group tackles three major project areas that Air Liquide believes are driving the world forward: a sustainable environment high-tech communications and health care. The teams study ways in which gases can enhance everything from photovoltaics and electronics to medical inhalation therapies. More than 60% of its R&D budget is dedicated to environmental work.

In 2009 Air Liquide expanded its Middle Eastern operations with the acquisition of Saudi company Al Khafrah Industrial Gases. It also added new production units in the US China South Korea and Malaysia.

HISTORY

Just after the turn of the century French chemist Georges Claude discovered a method for liquefying acetylene. He obtained financing from two acquaintances Paul Delorme and Frederic Gallier and L'Air Liquide (Air Liquide) was incorporated in 1902. Delorme became president of the company and served in that capacity until 1945.

After a few bumpy years the company expanded opening plants in Belgium and Brazil in 1906. Claude applied for a patent for neon tubes in 1907 and the company began producing oxygen in 1908. Before WWI Air Liquide had plants in Canada Japan Spain and Sweden. Between the wars the company continued to expand opening plants in Greece Hong Kong Malaysia and Portugal. After WWII Claude was accused of collaborating with the Nazis on the development of the infamous V-1 and V-2 "buzz bombs." A French court sentenced him to life in prison but he was released in 1950.

Despite sales declines in the 1960s Paul Delorme's son Jean resisted the gas industry's trend toward diversification choosing instead to sell the company's less profitable units. In 1969 the company opened for business in the US. Air Liquide's US operations grew and it had about a 14% market share in 1986. That year it acquired Texas-based Big Three Industries in a $1.6 billion deal becoming the second-largest industrial gas producer in the US.

The recession of the early 1990s prompted cost-cutting and a restructuring that decentralized decision making to regional groups. Also the company and the industry showed increased interest in small on-site production units specially designed for individual customers. In 1996 two large iron and steel contracts in Poland garnered a foothold there. In 1999 Air Liquide and Air Products and Chemicals agreed to jointly take over UK-based British Oxygen Corporation (BOC) in an $11.2 billion deal. Air Liquide had purchased BOC's operations in Belgium the Netherlands and Germany earlier that year.

In 2000 Air Liquide and Air Products and Chemicals shelved their plan to acquire BOC when it became clear that the deal could not gain approval by the US Federal Trade Commission because of antitrust concerns. The following year Air Liquide spurned acquisition offers by French utilities group Suez.

Air Liquide took advantage of the break-up of Messer Griesheim in 2004 buying a large portion of that company's operations –in Germany the UK and the US –for more than $3 billion. Analysts deemed the price a bit high but Air Liquide wanted to act before rivals Praxair and Air Products and Chemicals jumped into the fray. Praxair was able to benefit from the Messer Griesheim firesale in any event. Late in the year Air Liquide sold some of its German assets to Praxair for about $650 million; the sale was mandated to satisfy antitrust and regulatory restrictions.

EXECUTIVES

Senior Executive Vice-President, Pierre Dufour, age 58
Executive Vice-President, Jean-Pierre Duprieu, age 62
Group VP Finance and Operations Control, Fabienne Lecorvaisier, age 52
Group VP Large Industries World Business Line, Ron LaBarre, age 63
Finance Director Director Treasury & Corporate Finance, John Glen, age 54
SVP Engineering Construction Research and Technology, Francois Darchis, age 58
Investor Relations, Virginia Jeanson
Director External Relations, Corinne Estrade-Bordry
Vice-President Western Europe, Guy Salzgeber, age 56
VP Human Resources, Augustin de Roubin, age 61
Senior Vice-President, Michael J. (Mike) Graff, age 58
VP North-East Asia, Mok Kwong Weng
Investor Relations, Annie Fournier
Team Coordinator Investor Relations, Martine Fitoussi
Vice-President Human Resources, Francois Abrial
Vice President homecare business, Olivier Petit
Senior Vice-President, Jean-Marc Royere
Vice-President North-East and South-East Asia, Mok Weng
Vice-President South America, Augustin Roubin
Director, Karen L. Katen, age 64
Director, Thierry Desmarest, age 68
Director, Jean-Claude Buono, age 70
Director, Alain Joly, age 75
Director, Gerard de La Martiniere
Director, Prof Rolf Krebs, age 74
Director, Paul D. Skinner, age 68
Director, Thierry Peugeot
Director, Beatrice Majnoni d'Intignano, age 69
Director, Cornelis van Lede, age 72
Director, Jean Paul Agon
Auditors: Mazars&Guerard

LOCATIONS

HQ: L' Air Liquide S.A. (France)
75, quai d' Orsay, Paris 75007
Phone: (33) 1 40 62 55 55
Web: www.airliquide.com

2010 Sales

	% of total
Europe	52
Americas	23
Asia/Pacific	22
Africa & Middle	3
Total	**100**

PRODUCTS/OPERATIONS

2010 Sales

	% of total
Gas &	89
Engineering &	6
Other	5
Total	**100**

2010 Sales by Business Line

	% of total
Industrial	40
Large	34
Health	16
Electronics	10
Total	**100**

Selected Products

Acetylene
Argon
Carbon dioxide
Carbon monoxide
Gas mixtures
Helium
Hydrogen
Liquid chemicals
Nitrogen
Oxygen
Silane
Synthesis gas

COMPETITORS

Air Products
Airgas
Iwatani International
Messer Group
Praxair
Taiyo Nippon Sanso
The Linde Group

HISTORICAL FINANCIALS

Company Type: Public

Income Statement

FYE: December 31

	REVENUE ($ mil.)	NET INCOME ($ mil.)	NET PROFIT MARGIN	EMPLOYEES
12/12	20,378	2,121	10.4%	49,500
12/11	18,879	1,985	10.5%	46,200
12/10	18,225	1,878	10.3%	43,600
12/09	17,515	1,771	10.1%	42,300
12/08	18,319	1,705	9.3%	43,000
Annual Growth	2.7%	5.6%	—	3.6%

2012 Year-End Financials

Debt ratio: 38.3%
Return on equity: 16.0%
Cash ($ mil.): 1,521
Current ratio: 1.03
Long-term debt ($ mil.): 7,630
No. of shares (mil.): 311
Dividends
Yield: 2.2%
Payout: 14.6%
Market value ($ mil.): 7,922

	STOCK PRICE ($) FY Close	P/E High	P/E Low	PER SHARE ($) Earnings	Dividends	Book Value
12/12	25.45	9	6	6.79	0.58	43.24
12/11	24.60	12	8	6.36	1.13	40.59
12/10	25.55	11	7	6.05	0.80	38.31
12/09	23.89	12	6	6.16	1.01	37.77
12/08	18.40	16	6	5.94	0.84	33.59
Annual Growth	8.4%	—	—	3.4%	(9.0%)	6.5%

Landesbank Baden-Wurttemberg

Landesbank Baden-Wurttemberg (LBBW) acts as the central bank to savings banks in the German states of Baden-Wurttemberg Rhineland Palatinate and Saxony. The bank handles large transactions (wholesale banking financial securities foreign exchange) too costly for the smaller state savings banks. Through its regional banks Baden Wurttembergische Bank and Sachsen Bank and Rheinland-Pfalz Bank LBBW also provides traditional retail banking services such as real estate and commercial loans and portfolio management at more than 200 branches. Other subsidiaries provide leasing factoring venture capital and equity financing services.

LBBW operates offices worldwide that assist export-oriented companies and other German-based customers. LBBW has offices in New York London Singapore Seoul and Mexico City. Those operations are supplemented by four German Centres of Industry in Beijing Mexico City Singapore and India.

Banks all over the world felt the impacts of the global financial crisis and LBBW was not immune. Solid income from its corporate financial markets and private customer segments was not enough to protect the bank from overall losses due to a slowdown in the banking sector and exposure to toxic assets in 2008 and 2009.

In order to strengthen its capital base and provide LBBW with enough liquidity for it to continue functioning as a financing partner the company's government owners pumped in about E5 billion ($6.5 billion) to the bank in 2009. The state of Baden-Wurttemberg also provided a E13 billion ($16.5 billion) protection guarantee against risks. As a condition of the bailout the European Commission ordered LBBW to undergo restructuring.

Under the plan the bank was forced to scale back its credit substitute business and cut costs by selling equity investments and eliminating 2500 jobs. At the end of the restructuring LBBW will be smaller and more focused on its core business with corporations private customers and savings banks. It also plans to grow its financial markets and real estate financing business.

As part of the restructuring LBBW agreed to sell its LBBW Securities to Guggenheim Partners in 2010. LBBW Securities is the US broker/dealer for LBBW and handles repurchase agreements securities lending and other financing transactions.

The Savings Banks Association of Baden-Wurttemberg owns about 40% of LBBW. The state of Baden-Wurttemberg its capital of Stuttgart and Landesbeteilgungen Baden-Wurttemberg each controls about 20%.

HISTORY

Landesbank Baden-Wurttemberg traces its roots to three German institutions. The oldest Landesgirokasse - Offentliche Bank und Landessparkasse was founded in 1818 in Stuttgart Germany and eventually grew to be a medium-sized regional savings bank.

Landeskreditbank Baden-Wurttemberg was formed in 1924 and throughout the rest of the 20th century Landeskreditbank operated as a public-sector bank serving the western German state of Baden-Wurttemberg.

Sudwestdeutsche Landesbank Girozentraler (SudwestLB) was formed in 1988 by the merger of Badische Kommunale Landesbank Girozentrale (Bakola) and Landesbank Stuttgart Girozentrale (formerly Wurttembergische Kommunale Landesbank Girozentrale).

SudwestLB established itself as the first Landesbank to be wholly owned by the state's savings banks. In 1990 SudwestLB became the first regional bank to take a stake in WestDeutsche Landesbank at the time Germany's largest public-sector financial institution; the move was intended to increase SudwestLB's presence abroad. SudwestLB then joined with WestDeutsche Landesbank Girozentrale in 1992 to purchase Chartered WestLB a pan-European corporate finance company.

In 1998 SudwestLB agreed to merge with Landesgirokasse and the commercial banking unit of Landeskreditbank. The merger which took effect on January 1 1999 resulted in the formation of Landesbank Baden-Wurttemberg (LBBW). LBBW immediately became one of the top public-sector banks in Germany.

In 2005 LBBW focused on growing its retail banking business. It acquired Baden Wurttembergische Bank (BW Bank) in Landesbank Rheinland-Pfalz (renamed Rheinland-Pfalz Bank). Three years later LBBW looked to broaden its retail banking reach in Central Germany. It acquired Sachsen LB in 2008 which was integrated under the name Sachsen Bank.

EXECUTIVES

Chairman Board of Managing Directors, Siegfried Jaschinski
Deputy Chairman Board of Managing Directors, Michael Horn
Member Board of Managing Directors, Joachim E. Schielke
Member Board of Managing Directors, Bernhard Walter
Head of Capital Markets Trading and Sales, Ralf Winkelmann
Member Board of Managing Directors and Head of International Funding and Investor Relations, Peter A. Kaemmerer
Head of Strategic Debt Distribution, Karl Haeling
Head of Group Communications and Marketing, Michael Pfister
Head of Press Office, Christian Potthoff
Auditors: PricewaterhouseCoopersAGWirtschaftsprufungsgesellschaft

LOCATIONS

HQ: Landesbank Baden-Wurttemberg
Am Hauptbahnhof 2, Stuttgart D-70173
Phone: (49) 7 11 127 0 **Fax:** (49) 7 11 127 43544
Web: www.LBBW.de

PRODUCTS/OPERATIONS

Select Subsidiaries and Affiliates

Baden-Wurttembergische Equity Gesellschaft mit beschrankteter Haftung
Baden-Wurttembergische L-Finance
BW Capital Markets Inc.
BWK GmbH
Cellent AG
Cellent Finance Solutions AG
Deutsche Mittelstandsinformatik GmbH
Landesbank Baden-Wurttembergische Capital Markets plc
LBBW Asset Management Investmentgesellschaft mbH
LBBW Bank CZ a.s.
LBBW Dublin Management GmbH
LBBW Equity Partners GmbH & Co. KG
LBBW Immobilien GmbH
LBBW Leasing GmbH
LBBW Pensionsmanagement GmbH
LBBW Structured Investment LLC
LBBW (Schweiz) AG
LBBW Venture Capitala GmbH
LHI Leasing GmbH
MKB Mittelrheinische Bank GmbH
SudFactoring GmbH
Sud Beteiligungen GmbH
SudWERT Wohnungsprivatisierungsgesellschaft mbH
Vorarlberger Landes- und Hypothekendbank AG

COMPETITORS

BayernLB
Commerzbank
DZ BANK
Deutsche Bank
UniCredit Bank AG

HISTORICAL FINANCIALS

Company Type: Public

Income Statement FYE: December 31

	ASSETS ($ mil.)	NET INCOME ($ mil.)	INCOME AS % OF ASSETS	EMPLOYEES
12/12	443,294	525	0.1%	11,642
12/11	482,533	113	0.0%	12,231
12/10	501,103	(464)	—	13,906
12/09	593,073	(2,136)	—	14,292
12/08	626,249	(2,839)	—	13,369
Annual Growth	(8.3%)	—	—	(3.4%)

2012 Year-End Financials

Return on assets: 0.1%
Return on equity: 4.0%
Long-term debt ($ mil.): —
No. of shares (mil.): —
Sales ($ mil): 55,190
Dividends
Yield: —
Payout: —
Market value ($ mil.): —

Landesbank Berlin - Gironzentrale (Germany, Fed. Rep.)

LOCATIONS

HQ: Landesbank Berlin - Gironzentrale (Germany, Fed. Rep.)
Alexanderplatz 2, Berlin D-10178
Phone: (49) 30 86 95 00 **Fax:** (49) 30 86 98 30 74
Web: www.lbb-holding.de

HISTORICAL FINANCIALS

Company Type: Public

Income Statement FYE: December 31

	ASSETS ($ mil.)	NET INCOME ($ mil.)	INCOME AS % OF ASSETS	EMPLOYEES
12/12	155,922	130	0.1%	5,802
12/11	169,668	(107)	—	5,931
12/10	175,965	357	0.2%	5,985
12/09	207,204	370	0.2%	6,009
12/08	203,241	23	0.0%	5,999
Annual Growth	(6.4%)	53.1%	—	(0.8%)

2012 Year-End Financials

Return on assets: 0.0%
Return on equity: 3.9%
Long-term debt ($ mil.): —
No. of shares (mil.): —
Sales ($ mil): 5,730
Dividends
Yield: —
Payout: —
Market value ($ mil.): —

Landesbank Berlin Holding AG (Berlin)

Landesbank Berlin Holding (LBB Holding) provides comprehensive banking services to its core market of Berlin and adjoining areas. Formerly Bankgesellschaft Berlin LBB Holding operates through several subsidiaries namely Berliner Sparkasse a leading German savings bank for retail customers with about 150 branches and Landesbank Berlin AG a regional corporate banking center for small and medium-sized businesses. LBB Holding also offers services in capital markets which help private investors with trading and sales and commercial real estate financing which support institutional investors and residential developers. Erwerbsgesellschaft der S-Finanzgruppe mbH & Co. KG owns 88% of LBB Holding.

Erwerbsgesellschaft der S-Finanzgruppe mbH & Co. KG became a majority shareholder when the state of Berlin finalized the sale of its 81% interest in mid-2007.

LBB Holding holds about 40% of Berlin's market share. It continues to solidify that standing by increasing sales activities in consumer loans and securities and by cross-selling certain products to acquire new customers.

HISTORY

Landesbank Berlin Holding predecessor Berliner Bank was formed in 1950 by the city of West Berlin. Although the bank was legally a private institution it was owned by the city. After more than 30 years of keeping Berliner Bank funded (in the early 1980s it was hit hard by bad loans to Polish and German companies that failed) in 1984 the city floated a portion of the bank on the West German stock market cutting its stake to about 75%. Two years later West Germany's Gothaer insurance group claimed a 17% share. Before the insurer could raise its stake the Berlin Wall came tumbling down.

After buying Berliner Stadtbank its East Berlin counterpart in 1991 Berliner Bank was in talks with other Berlin banking institutions to form a financial services group in the city. By the end of 1992 a deal had been arranged: Berliner Bank would merge with Berliner Hypotheken und Pfandbriefbank (Berlin Hyp) a property financing specialist and Landesbank Berlin the central bank for the region's "sparkassen" (savings banks). The banks would be managed by a public company BGB. Both Berlin Hyp and Landesbank Berlin were state-owned and the new group was the first blending of private and public entities.

BGB began operations in 1994. The city of Berlin claimed a 68% stake in the bank Gothaer owned 10% and private investors owned the rest. To win the growing mortgage sector in eastern and northern Germany the group partnered with Norddeutche Landesbank Girozentrale (Nord LB) and sold it a 10% stake that year.

BGB stumbled early when its bottom line was hit hard by loans to businesses many located in the former East Germany that went bankrupt. In 1996 it cut some 1000 jobs to reduce costs and its struggle to remain competitive in overbanked Germany led to merger talks with Nord LB. Discussions resulted not in a merger (BGB's bad loans made it too risky) but in an agreement to become closer allies.

In 1997 BGB opened its Berliner Bank (Polska) subsidiary in Poland. At home the group was still struggling with losses; it reorganized along business lines and trimmed 10% of its employees. BGB continued to grow outside Germany buying a majority stake in Zivnostenska banka a leading Czech bank and entering a project finance deal with Bank of Moscow. Merger talks with Nord LB began again and in early 1998 they announced plans of a union.

The engagement was short-lived. BGB once again found itself in loan trouble (bad property loans in Berlin and eastern Germany made by Berliner Bank were largely to blame) and when its stock tumbled in late 1998 Nord LB split. Jilted in 1999 the group consoled itself with yet another reorganization to try to stem its losses. It closed a number of branches in eastern Germany with banking giant Deutsche Bank taking over the accounts and sold its direct banking unit. The next year BGB announced plans to expand in Eastern Europe; as part of this move it increased its stake in Zivnostenska banka to about 80% and considered upping its 5% stake in Poland's BIG Bank Gdanski.

In 2001 the EU approved a state-sponsored bailout plan for Bankgesellschaft Berlin mandating that the government sell its stake in the bank by the end of 2007 (the deal with Deutscher Sparkassen- und Giroverband was completed in August 2007). In 2006 BGB changed its name to Landesbank Berlin Holding AG.

As one of Germany's top credit card issuers the company boosted its consumer credit operations in early 2008 with the acquisition of Deutsche Postbank subsidiary BHW's loan business.

EXECUTIVES

Chairman of the Supervisory Board, Heinrich Haasis
Managing Director Retail Banking Landesbank Berlin, Johannes Evers
Managing Director Regional Corporate Banking Landesbank Berlin, Hans Jurgen Kulartz
Deputy Chairwoman Supervisory Board, Barbel Wulff
Managing Director Risk Controlling Controlling Compliance Lending Business Risk Management and BankenService Landesbank Berlin, Martin K. Mueller
Member of the Management Board, Jan Bettink
Member of the Management Board, Patrick Tessmann
Member of the Management Board, Serge Demoliere
Deputy Chairwoman Supervisory Board, Barbel Wulff
Director, Dietmar P. Binkowska
Director, Gregor Bohmer
Director, Dagmar Brose
Director, Hans Jorg Duppre
Director, Christina Forster
Director, Artur Grzesiek
Director, Jurgen Hilse
Director, Claus Friedrich Holtmann
Director, Thomas Mang
Director, Peter Schneider
Director, Friedrich Schubring-Giese
Director, Harald Vogelsang
Member of the Supervisory Board; Employee Representative, Christina Foerster
Member of the Supervisory Board; Employee Representative, Daniel Kasteel
Member of the Supervisory Board; Employee Representative, Frank Meysel
Member of the Supervisory Board; Employee Representative, Frank Wolf
Member of the Supervisory Board; Employee Representative, Gerald Herrmann
Member of the Supervisory Board, Gerhard Grandke
Member of the Supervisory Board; Employee Representative, Gerhard Henschel
Member of the Supervisory Board, Hans Duppre
Member of the Supervisory Board; Employee Representative, Heiko Barten
Member of the Supervisory Board, Helmut Schleweis
Member of the Supervisory Board; Employee Representative, Michael Dutschke
Member of the Supervisory Board; Employee Representative, Michael Jaenichen
Member of the Supervisory Board; Employee Representative, Peter Mohr
Member of the Supervisory Board; Employee Representative, Sabine Garzon
Member of the Supervisory Board; Employee Representative, Sascha Haendler
Member of the Supervisory Board; Employee Representative, Wolfgang Pansegrau
Auditors: PwCDeutscheRevisionAG

LOCATIONS

HQ: Landesbank Berlin Holding AG (Berlin)
Alexanderplatz 2, Berlin D-10178
Phone: (49) 30 86 95 00 **Fax:** (49) 30 86 98 30 74
Web: www.llb-holding.de

PRODUCTS/OPERATIONS

2007 Sales

	% of total
Retail	39
Regional corporate	13
Capital	17
Real estate	31
Total	**100**

COMPETITORS

BayernLB
Commerzbank
DZ BANK
Deutsche Bank
Landesbank Baden-Wurttemberg
Nordea Bank
UniCredit Bank AG
WestLB

HISTORICAL FINANCIALS

Company Type: Public

Income Statement FYE: December 31

	ASSETS ($ mil.)	NET INCOME ($ mil.)	INCOME AS % OF ASSETS	EMPLOYEES
12/12	155,922	130	0.1%	5,802
12/11	169,668	(107)	—	5,931
12/10	175,965	357	0.2%	5,985
12/09	207,204	370	0.2%	6,009
12/08	206,036	24	0.0%	0
Annual Growth	(6.7%)	52.6%	—	—

2012 Year-End Financials

Return on assets: 0.0%
Return on equity: 3.9%
Long-term debt ($ mil.): —
No. of shares (mil.): —
Sales ($ mil): 5,783
Dividends
Yield: —
Payout: —
Market value ($ mil.): —

Landesbank Hessen-Thueringen Girozentrale (Helaba) (Germany, Fed. Rep.)

LOCATIONS

HQ: Landesbank Hessen-Thueringen Girozentrale (Helaba) (Germany, Fed. Rep.)
Neue Mainzer Strasse 52-58, Frankfurt am Main D-60311
Phone: (49) 69 91 32 01 **Fax:** (49) 69 29 15 17
Web: www.helaba.de

HISTORICAL FINANCIALS

Company Type: Public

Income Statement FYE: December 31

	ASSETS ($ mil.)	NET INCOME ($ mil.)	INCOME AS % OF ASSETS	EMPLOYEES
12/12	262,688	417	0.2%	6,284
12/11	212,106	513	0.2%	5,748
12/10	222,496	400	0.2%	6,180
12/09	244,754	466	0.2%	5,890
12/08	258,048	(62)	—	5,815
Annual Growth	0.4%	—	—	2.0%

2012 Year-End Financials

Return on assets: 0.1%
Return on equity: 5.1%
Long-term debt ($ mil.): —
No. of shares (mil.): —
Sales ($ mil): 8,505
Dividends
Yield: —
Payout: —
Market value ($ mil.): —

Landwirtschaftliche Rentenbank (Germany, Fed. Rep.)

LOCATIONS

HQ: Landwirtschaftliche Rentenbank (Germany, Fed. Rep.)
Hochstrasse 2, Frankfurt am Main D-60313
Phone: (49) 69 2107 0 **Fax:** (49) 69 2107 6444
Web: www.rentenbank.de

HISTORICAL FINANCIALS

Company Type: Public

Income Statement FYE: December 31

	ASSETS ($ mil.)	NET INCOME ($ mil.)	INCOME AS % OF ASSETS	EMPLOYEES
12/12	116,512	321	0.3%	250
12/11	114,958	(89)	—	239
12/10	112,132	203	0.2%	227
12/09	112,145	(110)	—	218
12/08	125,969	647	0.5%	206
Annual Growth	(1.9%)	(16.1%)	—	5.0%

2012 Year-End Financials

Return on assets: 0.2%
Return on equity: 11.5%
Long-term debt ($ mil.): —
No. of shares (mil.): —
Sales ($ mil): 5,152
Dividends
Yield: —
Payout: —
Market value ($ mil.): —

Legal & General Group PLC (United Kingdom)

Legal & General Group is one of the UK's biggest life insurers. The holding company operates four main divisions: investment management risk savings and international. Its investment management arm generates more than 50% of revenues as the UK's largest pension fund manager serving institutional and retail investors. Its risk businesses provide groups and individuals with life insurance annuities and homeowners insurance. Personal savings products include unit trusts investment bonds and savings accounts. International offers life insurance group benefits and wealth management products. The firm operates in the US as Banner Life Insurance Company and William Penn Life Insurance Company of New York.

As part of its distribution network Legal & General's Mortgage Club serves as a marketplace for mortgage advisors to shop for lenders and other services.

The company serves more than 7 million individual corporate and institutional customers. It mainly distributes its insurance products in the UK through retail independent financial advisers (IFAs) and employee benefit consultants which make up more than 70% of it distribution mix. Banks and building societies including Sainsbury's Bank and Barclays also distribute its products.

Strategically Legal & General is focused on broadening its core product offerings finding new markets building its brand recognition and widening its distribution network to provide a variety of ways to access its products. Additionally the company is pursuing growth opportunities both domestically and overseas to expand its global reach in response to customer demand particularly in North America the Gulf and Asia. Other key strategic goals include improving customer engagement by 2014 increasing cash generation and delivering strong return on equity results through capital management and improving organizational production responsiveness and diversity. Achieving positive results toward its objectives has put the company in a postion of strength in the midst of economic uncertainties and regulatory changes.

Legal & General managed to serve up positive results in 2011 with across-the-board increases in its sales operational cash generation and operating profits in each of its divisions even though its revenues of #18.3 million ($28.5 million) for the year represented a decrease of more than 50% from 2010 and its net income fell nearly 12% to #0.7 million ($1.1 million) mainly due to a 63% drop in investment returns.

HISTORY

The Legal in Legal & General's name comes from its founding mission –to provide life insurance to members of the legal profession. The company was started in 1836 by six lawyers as the Legal & General Life Assurance Society; its first customer solicitor Thomas Smith ill-manneredly died four years later after paying less than 200 pounds on a 1000-pound policy.

Throughout that century and into the next the company made loans to individuals and corporations; it also moved into real estate. After struggling under claims during WWI and the 1918 flu pandemic it moved into fire and accident coverage in 1920. It opened membership to nonlawyers in 1929. The company took over the UK operations of the US firm Metropolitan Life (MetLife) in 1933.

In 1934 Legal & General bought Gresham Life Assurance and Gresham Fire and Accident to gain a presence in Australia. During WWII the company was hit hard by German air attacks both physically (it had to relocate away from London for a time) and at the bottom line.

The postwar years were a time of expansion as the company moved into South Africa and also broadened its operations at home. In 1949 it moved into marine insurance and in 1956 inaugurated life insurance in Australia.

The company began expanding its product offerings in the 1970s with managed pension funds and retail unit trusts. It established a direct sales force for life and pensions in 1977. The company also formed alliances with several European insurance companies and sold its Gresham life subsidiary. In 1979 it formed Legal & General Group Limited as a holding company for its now-separate insurance international and investment management operations.

In 1981 Legal & General bought US auto insurer GEICO's two-thirds interest in Government Employees Life Insurance Company changing the subsidiary's name to Banner Life. Three years later it bought the Dutch operations of Unilife Assurance and created a subsidiary in the Netherlands. Despite all this activity however the company's performance during the 1980s was poor and it brought in David Prosser (who became CEO in 1991) to goose its asset management operations.

In 1989 the company bought William Penn Life Insurance from Continental Corp. and opened its first real estate agency –just in time for the real estate market crash. Legal & General and other mortgage guarantee insurers were also squeezed by the resulting increase in mortgage default rates as homebuyers were caught between high interest rates and high unemployment.

The company formed a joint venture with Woolwich Building Society to provide Woolwich customers with insurance products in 1995. The next year it followed the insurance industry trend by establishing a bank of its own.

With each succeeding merger of its rivals Legal & General became the target of rumors about its own fate. The company has remained adamantly independent with Prosser claiming that Legal & General could instead benefit by picking up business left behind by the new entities.

In 1998 the British insurance industry was stung by scandalous revelations regarding improper pension sales in the late 1980s and early 1990s. Legal & General set aside about $1 billion to compensate victims; it also sold its Australian operations. In 1999 banking company National Westminster and Legal & General talked takeover but the deal fell through. (NatWest was eventually bought by Royal Bank of Scotland.)

In 2001 Legal & General announced a deal with UK-based Barclays to provide the bank's customers with life insurance and pension products. In 2002 Legal & General extended its marketing agreement with UK financial services company Alliance & Leicester.

The company then discontinued its health insurance offerings and reduced its venture capital investment operations. In 2005 the company sold its Gresham Insurance subsidiary to Barclays Bank.

EXECUTIVES

Vice Chairman, Henry E. Staunton, age 64
Chief Executive and Director, Nigel Wilson, age 57
Chairman, John M. Stewart, age 64
Group Executive Director Risk and Director, John Pollock, age 54, $738,631 total compensation
Executive Director Savings and Director, Mark Gregory, age 49
Group M&A and Strategy Director and Interim Group CFO, Wadham Downing
Group Executive Director LGIM, Mark Zinkula
Director, Nicholas E. T. (Nick) Prettejohn, age 52
Director, Rudy H. P. Markham, age 66
Director, Michael E. (Mike) Fairey, age 63
Director, Dame Clara H. F. Furse, age 54
Vice Chairman, Henry E. Staunton, age 64
Chief Executive and Director, Nigel Wilson, age 57
Group Executive Director Risk and Director, John Pollock, age 54
Director, Julia Wilson
Executive Director Savings and Director, Mark Gregory, age 49
Director, Stuart Popham
Auditors: PricewaterhouseCoopersLLP

LOCATIONS

HQ: Legal & General Group PLC (United Kingdom)
One Coleman Street, London EC2R 5AA
Phone: (44) 20 3124 2000 **Fax:** (44) 20 3124 2500
Web: www.legalandgeneralgroup.com

PRODUCTS/OPERATIONS

2011 Revenues by Segment

	% of total
Investment	52
Risk (life & property	33
Savings	9
International	6
Group capital &	-
Total	**100**

2011 Distribution Channels

	% of total
Retail independent financial advisers	37
Employee benefit	35
Bancassurance	23
Direct	3
Tied	2
Total	**100**

Selected Acquisitions

2012
Bechtel House ($66.7 million; London; office building - Investment management)

Selected Subsidiaries

Banner Life Insurance Company Inc - long-term business; US
First British American Reinsurance Company II - reinsurance; US
First British Bermudan Reinsurance Company II Limited - reinsurance; Bermuda
First British Vermont Reinsurance Company II - reinsurance; US
First British Vermont Reinsurance Company - reinsurance; US
Legal & General (France) SA - long-term business
Legal & General (Portfolio Management Services) Limited - institutional fund management
Legal & General (Unit Trust Managers) Limited - unit trust management
Legal & General Assurance (Pensions Management) Limited - long-term business
Legal & General Assurance Society Limited - long-term and general insurance
Legal & General Bank (France) SA - financial services
Legal & General Finance PLC1 - treasury operations
Legal & General Insurance Limited - general insurance
Legal & General International (Ireland) Limited - long-term business
Legal & General Investment Management America Inc - institutional fund management
Legal & General Investment Management Limited - institutional fund management
Legal & General Nederland Levensverzekering Maatschappij NV - long-term business; Netherlands
Legal & General Partnership Services Limited - provision of services
Legal & General Pensions Limited - reinsurance
Legal & General Property Limited - property management
Legal & General Resources Limited1 - provision of services
Legal & General Risques Divers (France) SA - insurance company
LGV Capital Limited - private equity
Nationwide Life Limited - long-term business
Suffolk Life Annuities Limited - long-term business
Suffolk Life Pensions Limited - long-term business
William Penn Life Insurance Company of New York Inc - long-term business; US

COMPETITORS

AEGON	MetLife
AXA	Prudential
Allianz	Prudential plc
Aviva	Royal London Mutual
Friends Provident	Standard Life
ING	Zurich Insurance Group
Lloyds Banking Group	

HISTORICAL FINANCIALS

Company Type: Public

Income Statement FYE: December 31

	ASSETS ($ mil.)	NET INCOME ($ mil.)	INCOME AS % OF ASSETS	EMPLOYEES
12/12	558,191	1,310	0.2%	9,864
12/11	504,733	1,121	0.2%	9,138
12/10	502,858	1,273	0.3%	8,662
12/09	481,086	1,397	0.3%	9,324
12/08	374,128	(1,554)	—	9,777
Annual Growth	10.5%	—	—	0.2%

2012 Year-End Financials

Return on assets: 0.2%
Return on equity: 15.2%
Long-term debt ($ mil.): —
No. of shares (mil.): —
Sales ($ mil): 56,376
Dividends
Yield: 3.9%
Payout: 570.8%
Market value ($ mil.): —

	STOCK PRICE ($) FY Close	P/E High/Low	PER SHARE ($) Earnings	Dividends	Book Value
12/12	12.42	227144	0.22	0.49	1.49
12/11	7.95	211129	0.19	0.95	1.37
12/10	7.67	153 82	0.22	0.27	1.28
12/09	6.50	137 25	0.24	0.23	1.16
12/08	5.90	— —	(0.26)	0.54	0.89
Annual Growth	20.5%	— —	—	(2.3%)	13.8%

Lenovo Group Ltd

Workhorse Lenovo is the second-largest PC vendor in the world today behind #1 HP and ahead of #3 Dell. Although Lenovo is a global supplier of Think-branded commercial PCs and Idea-branded consumer PCs it holds a dominant position in China. The company makes tablets smartphones laptops desktops workstations servers software and accessories and it is developing and launching mini ultrabooks and ideapads. Lenovo offers services for enterprise small business and home office markets. Certain products and services are geared specifically at the growing education government and health care verticals. Lenovo formed out of the acquisition of IBM's Personal Computing division in 2005.

Operations

Lenovo has operations in more than 60 countries across the globe. It has headquarters in the tech hubs of Beijing and North Carolina and manufacturing sites in the US Mexico Brazil China and India. With a substantial portion of revenues coming from China it's no surprise that it also maintains major research centers in Beijing Shanghai and Shenzhen as well as in Japan and the US.

Aiming to boost sales growth Lenovo in 2013 began producing PCs in North Carolina at a new assembly plant. As part of this effort the company is devoting more investment dollars to domestic manufacturing.

Geographic Reach

Lenovo serves customers in more than 160 countries. The company generates nearly half of its revenues in China where it holds more than 30% market share in PCs. Lenovo is also increasing sales in other emerging markets.

Strategy

Between 2011 and 2012 Lenovo jumped from being the world's fourth-largest PC vendor to the second-largest. In 2012 and 2011 it outgrew the worldwide PC market in unit shipments and gained market share in all geographies products and customer segments. Today it is the #1 PC company in China and in Japan. It is also the top PC company in the world for large enterprises and the public sector. Lenovo used a different growth strategy than most of its big competitors to reach this market spot expanding East to West. New products are introduced in China then spread across the globe.

Although it has long been the leader in China Lenovo does not rest on its laurels when it comes to increasing additional share in the Asia/Pacific region. To maintain supremacy in this market Lenovo's Hefei China-based joint venture with Compal Electronics began mass producing notebooks in 2013. Lenovo which holds a 51% stake and Compal which owns the remaining 49% will invest a total of $300 million in the JV's expansion.

In Japan Lenovo leverages the strength of that country's #1 PC company NEC through a joint venture called NEC Lenovo Japan Group. That JV of which Lenovo holds a majority stake is the dominant PC maker in Japan with about a 25% share of the market. Prior to the JV's formation in 2011 NEC had been the market leader in Japan but was not turning a profit when it made the deal. The JV helps give NEC access to cheaper Chinese supplies and manufacturing.

Mergers and Acquisitions

In the last two years Lenovo has made acquisitions to beef up its hardware offerings and support expansion in select markets. In January 2014 it agreed to pay more than $5 billion to acquire two new major product lines. First it announced plans to buy IBM's low-end x86 server business for $2.3 billion. The business includes System x BladeCenter and Flex System blade servers and switches x86-based Flex integrated systems NeXtScale and iDataPlex servers and associated software blade networking and customer service operations. The 7500 employees who work for IBM are expected to be transferred to Lenovo. The acquisition frees up IBM to focus on its cloud computing business.

A few weeks later it agreed to pay $2.9 billion for Motorola Mobility. Google bought Motorola's smartphone business in 2012 with big plans for its Android phones. However the division continued to suffer losses in the highly competitive smartphone market and Motorola Mobility was forced to cut staff and close locations. As part of the deal Lenovo will own the brands Moto X Moto G and the DROID Ultra series while Google will own the patent portfolio.

In 2012 the company acquired US-based Stoneware to expand its secure cloud computing portfolio. The deal add new technologies and added capabilities for both commercial and consumer cloud offerings particularly the ability to provide secure content across multiple devices in education and government. Also in September of that year Lenovo made strides in Latin America by acquiring Brazil's CCE a regional leader in PCs and consumer electronics. It added manufacturing facilities; an extensive selection of consumer products such as PCs tablets smartphones and televisions; and a robust supply chain.

Across the Atlantic Lenovo's growth in Europe was supported by a majority stake acquisition in mid-2011 of Germany-based computer and electronics reseller MEDION. The MEDION buy doubles Lenovo's market share in Germany and makes it the third-largest PC company in Europe's largest PC market.

Ownership

Legend Holdings which is controlled by the Chinese government owns more than 40% of Lenovo. IBM which has over the years decreased its ownership from 19% to about 4% finally sold its remaining stake for around $265 million in 2011.

HISTORY

Liu Chuanzhi an engineer at the Chinese Academy of Sciences who wrote industry research reports established Legend Group Holdings Co. in 1984 in Beijing. Backed by a modest investment from the academy Liu who went on to become something of an entrepreneurial hero in China and 10 other engineers were given a green light to form a retail business. They first bought and sold items ranging from TVs to roller skates but later focused on distributing computer products and eventually moved into manufacturing PCs for AST Research. Legend introduced its first proprietary product a Chinese character system for PCs in 1985.

In 1988 the company formed Legend Holdings Limited which was originally a Hong Kong-based PC distributor. The following year the parent company began designing and manufacturing motherboards and added systems integration services to its offerings. In 1990 China reduced import tariffs a move that opened the trade door for companies such as IBM and Compaq. That year Legend Group Holdings began making its own brand of PCs.

Legend Holdings went public in 1994 and the following year began absorbing operations from its parent company which retained approximately 60% ownership in the subsidiary. By 1996 it was tied with IBM for PC market share in China; it became the country's top brand the following year.

In 1998 parent company Legend Group Holdings transferred Beijing Legend Group to its Hong Kong-based subsidiary. The following year Microsoft looking to extend its operating system dominance into China teamed up with Legend Holdings to create set-top boxes. In 2000 the company partnered with Pacific Century CyberWorks to provide broadband Internet services. The following year Legend spun off its distribution business Digital China as a separate public company. In 2001 Yang Yuanqing was named CEO of the company.

In 2002 Legend Holdings changed its English company name to Legend Group Limited. The company launched a corporate brand Lenovo the following year and in 2004 it officially adopted Lenovo as its English name. It also sold its non-telecom IT services business to AsiaInfo Holdings renamed AsiaInfo-Linkage in 2004.

Lenovo acquired IBM's worldwide PC operations for approximately $1.75 billion in 2005. IBM executive Stephen Ward was named CEO of Lenovo at the time of the merger but he was replaced by William Amelio before year's end. Amelio headed Dell's Asia/Pacific operations before joining Lenovo. In 2006 Lenovo launched a unit called Lenovo Services.

In 2007 Lenovo stopped using the IBM PC brand to which it still held the rights and began offering only Lenovo-branded machines. The following year it sponsored and supported the Olympic Summer Games in Beijing providing more than 30000 pieces of equipment and 600 engineers.

Looking to focus on its core PC operations Lenovo sold its mobile phone business Lenovo Mobile Communications to Hony Capital in 2008. Hony the private equity arm of Legend Holdings paid $100 million for the unit.

A year later Lenovo bought back the mobile communications business for about $200 million in cash and stock. The company cited the growth of the mobile Internet market and the increasing convergence between the PC and wireless handset sectors for the about-face in product strategy. Lenovo's move came as Dell introduced a mobile phone for the Chinese market.

Citing a flagging economy Lenovo announced a restructuring plan in 2009 that included a workforce reduction of 11% executive pay cuts and the consolidation of its China and the Asia/Pacific units. The company also initiated a management shakeup including its chairman taking over as CEO. The change may in part have reflected a strategy shift for Lenovo. With corporate spending flagging particularly in the US the company planned to focus on China and other emerging markets with an emphasis on consumers.

EXECUTIVES

SVP and Chief Marketing Officer, David A. Roman
Vice Chairman, Ma Xuezheng, age 60, $114,000 total compensation
Chairman, Liu Chuanzhi, age 69
Chairman and CEO, Yuanqing Yang, age 50, $894,000 total compensation
SVP and CTO, George Z. Q. He, age 51
SVP WW Services and CIO, Xiaoyan Wang, age 52
SVP; President Consumer Business Group, Jun Liu, age 45
SVP and Chief Procurement Officer, Qiao Song, age 45
SVP; Acting CEO and President Lenovo Mobile, Lu Yan
senior Vice President Emerging Markets, Chen Shaopeng, age 44
VP Corporate Strategy and Planning, Qiao Jian
SVP; Group President Lenovo China, Xudong Chen
SVP E-Commerce and Chief Marketing Officer, Deepak Advani, age 49
General Manager Large Customer, Tong Fuyao
senior Vice President Human Resources, Kenneth A. (Ken) DiPietro, age 54
General Manager China, Xia Li
SVP EMEA President, Gianfranco Lanci, age 58
Senior Vice President ; THINK Product, Francis K. (Fran) O'Sullivan, age 54
SVP Think Business Group, Peter D. Hortensius, age 53
Managing Director Lenovo India, Amar Babu
SVP and CFO, Wai Ming Wong, age 55
VP Investor Relations, Gary Ng
SVP Operations Mature Markets, David Schmoock, age 44
SVP; President Asia Pacific, Milko Van Duijl, age 51
President and COO; Acting President Latin America Group, Rory Read, age 51
SVP; President Americas, Gerry P. Smith, age 50
VP Diversity, Yolanda Conyers
SVP and General Counsel, Michael J. O'Neill, age 56
Executive Director External Communications, Raymond (Ray) Gorman
Managing Director Lenovo Ireland, Fiona O'Brien
VP Worldwide Notebook Product Marketing, Sam Dusi
Regional Director Transactional Business, Ali Al Amine
VP Corporate Identity and Design, David Hill
SVP Global Services, Peter Bartolotta
Senior Manager Investor relations, William Li
General Manager Hong Kong and Macau Operationso, Alice N. L. Ong
senior Vice President Human Resources, Jian Gina
Senior Vice President General Counsel, Michael Oneill
Senior Vice President Legal, Jay Clemens
Vice Chairman, Ma Xuezheng, age 60
Director, James G. (Jim) Coulter, age 53
Director, William O. Grabe, age 75
Director, Prof Woo Chia-Wei, age 76
Director, Tian Suning, age 49
Director, Zhu Linan, age 51
Director, Ting Lee Sen, age 70
Director, Nicholas C. Allen, age 58
Director, Wu Yibing, age 45
Auditors: PricewaterhouseCoopers

LOCATIONS

HQ: Lenovo Group Ltd
23rd Floor, Lincoln House, Taikoo Place, 979 King' s Road, Quarry Bay,
Phone: (852) 2590 0228 **Fax:** (852) 2516 5384
Web: www.lenovo.com

2011 Sales

	$ mil.	% of total
Emerging markets		
China	10,015	46
Other	3,859	18
Mature markets	7,719	36
Total	**21,594**	**100**

PRODUCTS/OPERATIONS

2011 Sales

	$ mil.	% of total
Personal computer		
Notebook	12,990	60
Desktop	7,307	34
Mobile phone	804	4
Others	492	2
Total	**21,594**	**100**

COMPETITORS

ASUSTeK
Acer
Apple Inc.
BlackBerry
Dell
Digital China
Founder Holdings
Fujitsu
Great Wall Technology
HTC Corporation
Hedy Holding
Hewlett-Packard
Hitachi
IBM
LG Electronics
Microsoft
NEC
Nokia
Panasonic Corp
Positivo Informatica
Samsung Electronics
Siemens AG
Sony
Toshiba
Wipro

HISTORICAL FINANCIALS

Company Type: Public

Income Statement FYE: March 31

	REVENUE ($ mil.)	NET INCOME ($ mil.)	NET PROFIT MARGIN	EMPLOYEES
03/13	33,873	635	1.9%	35,026
03/12	29,574	472	1.6%	27,000
03/11	21,594	273	1.3%	27,039
03/10	16,604	129	0.8%	22,205
03/09	14,901	(226)	—	22,511
Annual Growth	22.8%	—	—	11.7%

2013 Year-End Financials

Debt ratio: 2.8%
Return on equity: 26.3%
Cash ($ mil.): 3,454
Current ratio: 1.02
Long-term debt ($ mil.): 303
No. of shares (mil.): —
Dividends
Yield: —
Payout: —
Market value ($ mil.): —

	STOCK PRICE ($) FY Close	P/E High/Low		PER SHARE ($) Earnings	Dividends	Book Value
03/13	1.01	19	11	0.06	0.00	0.24
03/12	0.90	20	11	0.05	0.00	0.23
03/11	0.56	28	18	0.03	0.00	0.18
03/10	0.68	54	14	0.01	0.00	0.16
03/09	0.22	—	—	(0.03)	0.00	0.14
Annual Growth	46.2%	—	—	—	—	13.4%

LG Electronics Inc

LG Electronics (LGE) makes the products that have tech-savvy consumers chomping at the bit in the kitchen in the media room and on the go. A leader in consumer electronics mobile communications and home appliances LGE operates through more than 80 subsidiaries worldwide that design and make flat panel TVs audio and video products mobile handsets air conditioners washing machines refrigerators and more. Asia and North America are its two largest markets each contributing about 30% of sales. LGE owns Zenith Electronics (acquired in 1995) and LG Display. Founded in 1958 as Goldstar LGE established a North American headquarters in 2004. South Korea's LG Corp. owns about one-third of LGE.

LGE is investing heavily in brand marketing in a bid to position itself as one of the world's top three electronics brands in 2010. Its goal is to sell 8 million LCD TV units as well as 2.5 million plasma TV units. LGE is also focused on boosting sales of its commercial air conditioners drum washing machines and side-by-side (aka French door) refrigerators. LGE and US rival Whirlpool have been trading patent infringement claims over refrigerator technology. In 2009 LGE claimed that Whirlpool infringed on its patent for the "ice-making system in the fresh food compartment." Previously Whirlpool had claimed that LGE violated five of its refrigerator patents but subsequently withdrew four of the infringement claims.

To bolster production of large-scale air conditioning systems both in South Korea and abroad LGE acquired the A/C business of industrial machinery manufacturer LS Mtron for $134 million in early 2011. The deal included a factory in Jeonju South Korea as well as a research and development team. LS Mtron operated as part of LG Group until 2003 when its operations were spun off.

Amid rising competition from electronics makers and tough economic times in many key markets LGE is teaming up with other companies to make a name for itself in noncore businesses such as water processing and solar energy technology. It is moving into the water treatment business agreeing in mid-2011 to form a joint venture with Hitachi Plant Technologies in Japan. The joint venture called LG-Hitachi Water Solutions will be 51%-owned by LGE and 49%-owned by Hitachi Plant Technologies. LGE aims to build the water treatment business into a $6 billion sales generator by 2020. In 2011 the company added Daewoo ENTEC a Korean water treatment firm to its portfolio water treatment businesses. Solar cell technology is also a focus for LGE. In 2009 it partnered with Germany's Conergy to form a joint venture to manufacture solar cells. As part of the agreement LGE acquired a 75% stake in Conergy's Frankfurt solar cell plant. The company also decided to convert its plasma panel manufacturing line in Gumi Korea into a solar cell production line with plans for two solar cell production lines at a later date.

LGE is focusing on boosting its mobile communication handset business and enhancing its share of the LCD TV market. Indeed the company is looking to sell about 20% more cell phones. To that end in September 2009 LGE announced the launch of three new Windows phones. The three smartphones are the first of 13 LG-branded Windows phones slated to launch globally before the end of 2010. The new smartphones build on previous offerings including the Shine phone launched in 2007 as a follow-up product to its popular Chocolate phone.

The company is also focusing on the organic light-emitting diode (OLED) business. In 2009 LGE acquired the OLED division of Eastman Kodak which pioneered the technology in the 1970s but lacked the investment capability to see it through. OLEDs are commonly used in screens and monitors and are recognized for their energy efficiency and vivid display quality. As part of the agreement LG's OLED patents and developments will be accessible to Kodak as they pertain to its own product line.

LGE is closely watching the digital television market. In 2009 it agreed to develop core digital TV chips and semiconductors with Samsung Electronics. As part of the agreement LGE will design the electronic units and Samsung will make and test them. The firms expect to save about $240 million over three years through the development deal and generate about as much by exporting its products.

It's also partnering with other suppliers in the industry to extend its reach into other niches. The company has created a device that allows Netflix users to watch downloaded movies on their TV screens.

LGE in 2009 consolidated its home appliance and consumer electronics businesses in the US to align its sales and marketing divisions for LG Electronics USA. The company's also restructuring its manufacturing facilities in Mexico. As a result LG Electronics plans to invest some $1 million through 2012 to improve its plants in Mexico the production hub for North America.

EXECUTIVES

CEO, Bon Joon Koo, age 61
EVP and CEO Home Appliance, Moon-Bum Shin
CEO LG Corp.; Vice Chairman, Yu-Sig Kang
Public Relations and Corporate Communications, Judy Pae
EVP CFO and Director, David Jung
President and CEO Mobile Communications Company, Skott Ahn
President and CEO Air Conditioning & Energy Solution Company, Hwan Yong Nho, age 58
President Home Entertainment, Havis Kwon
EVP and CEO Mobile Communications, Jong-Seok Park
CEO LG Corp.; Vice Chairman, Yu-Sig Kang
EVP CFO and Director, David Jung
Director, In Ki Joo
Director, Kyu Min Lee
Director, Jong Nam Joo
Auditors: SamilPricewaterhousecoopers

LOCATIONS

HQ: LG Electronics Inc
LG Twin Towers, 20 Yeouido-dong, Yeongdeungpo-gu, Seoul 150-721
Phone: (82) 2 3777 1114 **Fax:** (82) 2 3777 3428
Web: www.lge.com

2009 Sales

	% of total
North	28
Europe	20
China & Asia-	19
South & Central	9
Korea	8
Middle East &	7
Other	9
Total	**100**

PRODUCTS/OPERATIONS

2009 Sales

	% of total
Home	35
Mobile	32
Home	17
Air	8
Business	8
Total	**100**

Selected Major Products & Services

Home Entertainment (LCD TVs plasma TVs audio video & optical storage)
Mobile Communication (mobile handsets mobile accessory)
Home Appliance (washing machines refrigerators cooking appliances vacuum cleaners built-in appliances)
Air Conditioning (residential air conditioners commercial air conditioners home solution compressors)
Business Solutions (monitors commercial displays car infotainment security business)

COMPETITORS

BSH Home Appliances
Electrolux
GE Appliances & Lighting
Haier Group
Motorola Solutions
Panasonic Corp
Philips Electronics
SANYO
Samsung Electronics
Sony
Technicolor
Whirlpool

HISTORICAL FINANCIALS

Company Type: Public

Income Statement FYE: December 31

	REVENUE ($ mil.)	NET INCOME ($ mil.)	NET PROFIT MARGIN	EMPLOYEES
12/12	47,728	62	0.1%	36,376
12/11	46,825	(405)	—	35,286
12/10	49,723	1,094	2.2%	32,972
12/09*	47,959	1,977	4.1%	29,554
01/09	0	0	—	0
Annual Growth	—	—	—	—

*Fiscal year change

2012 Year-End Financials

Debt ratio: 0.0%	No. of shares (mil.): 162
Return on equity: 0.5%	Dividends
Cash ($ mil.): 1,766	Yield: —
Current ratio: 1.14	Payout: —
Long-term debt ($ mil.): 4,145	Market value ($ mil.): —

Linde AG (Germany, Fed. Rep.)

Linde's business is lighter than air and bigger than everyone else's. Operating in more than 100 countries it is the world's largest producer of industrial and medical gases. Linde also has an engineering unit that builds process plants for companies in the petrochemical pharmaceutical and gas manufacturing industries; the gases unit accounts for more than three-quarters of its sales. A third division provides logistics and supply chain services to a broad range of commercial and industrial sectors including electronics grocery retail and gas. The company still does about half of its business in Europe but its presence is growing in emerging markets in Asia and Africa.

Linde operates through a number of subsidiaries including Eibl Homecare GmbH Linde BOC Process Plants African Oxygen Spectra Gases Hoek Loos Linde Medical Devices GmbH and Linde Finance. Linde's business is organized in three divisions: Industrial Gases and Healthcare Engineering and Gist. Industrial Gases and Healthcare is Linde's largest division and has operating segments in Europe the Americas Asia and Africa. Its Engineering division specializes in constructing plants for the production of hydrogen oxygen and olefins. It also builds plants for natural gas treatment. Linde's Gist division provides supply chain services for businesses that include Marks & Spencer British Airways Carlsberg and Dairy Crest.

Acquisitions and joint ventures play a key role in Linde's efforts to grow. On the health care side 2012 was a big year for acquisitions by the company. Linde acquired US-based homecare health company Lincare Holdings for $4.6 billion and it acquired Air Products' homecare business in continental Europe for $751 million. The latter's oxygen- sleep- and infusion-therapy operations serve more than 250000 patients in Belgium France Germany Portugal and Spain. Linde expects to double its sales from this area which would make it one of Europe's top suppliers of homecare respiratory products.

Additionally joint ventures are allowing it to gain entry into emerging markets such as China. In 2011 the company formed a joint venture to build and operate a large gas plant with Chongqing Chemical & Pharmaceutical Holding Company in China. Based in Chongqing the plant will produce carbon monoxide hydrogen and synthesis gas to the production facilities of BASF SE. It will be operational by 2014.

The following year in mid-2012 Linde made a major stride in Southeast Asia by winning a long-term contract to supply Vietnamese steel company POSCO SS-Vina (PSSV) with industrial gases. As part of the deal Linde will invest in and build the country's largest air separation unit in the Vung Tau province. The unit is slated to commence production also in 2014.

Linde's sales increased 7% in fiscal 2011 reaching E13.7 billion ($16.7 billion). Its Gases and Healthcare Division's sales rose 8% that year following an increase in global demand for gases. Its net income also rose nearly 16% in fiscal 2011 to E1.2 billion ($1.5 billion). Sales in the Gases division grew most significantly in the emerging economies of Asia as well as in South America. The division achieved strong growth in its on-site business which supplies gases on site to major customers. Its Engineering Division experienced a 3% increase over the previous year and saw a higher number of orders from the Gases Division than the previous year.

HISTORY

German engineer Karl von Linde perfected the ammonia-compression refrigeration machine in 1876. For the first time ice could be produced commercially instead of being cut in blocks from lakes. In 1879 Gesellschaft fur Linde's Eismaschinen was founded to sell the machines. Its first customers were brewers who wanted to make beer in the summer; the company later designed a refrigerator for the home.

Von Linde granted technology licenses to foreign firms but many licensees couldn't create working systems. Von Linde bought his patents back and in 1885 he set up his first affiliate outside of Germany the Linde British Refrigeration Company which built a London ice factory.

A decade later Von Linde a pioneer in cryogenics patented a process for the liquefaction of air — he had discovered the means to mass produce liquid oxygen. At the same time a similar process was developed by a Frenchman George Claude. To beat his rival Von Linde built an oxygen factory near Munich in 1902 and set up Linde Air Products (now Praxair) in the US in 1907.

After Germany's defeat in WWI the overseas businesses were seized. In the 1920s Linde's Eismaschinen bought German engine manufacturers including Guldner-Motoren-Gesellschaftin (1929). Von Linde died in 1934 at the age of 92. Then came WWII and in the aftermath the company again lost its industrial rights and investments overseas. (In the US Air Products had supplied oxygen to Allied fighter pilots.)

The recovering company launched Hydrocar the first platform truck with a hydrostatic drive in 1955. In 1958 Guldner began making forklift trucks and hydraulic equipment.

Renamed Linde AG in 1965 the firm won its first industrial construction contract to build a petrochemical plant. Switching gears Linde sold its home appliances business to AEG in 1967 and in 1969 Guldner stopped building tractors and diesel engines in favor of materials handling equipment and hydraulics. The forklift operations expanded further with the acquisition of SE Fahrzeugwerke (now STILL) in 1973.

Linde established branches to make industrial gases in Brazil and Australia (1974) and bought forklift manufacturers: Fenwick in France (1984); UK firm Lansing (1989); and a 51% stake in Italy's FIAT OM Carrelli Elevatori (1992). In 1992 it also increased its holding in Hoek's Machine-en Zuurstoffabriek (aka Hoek Loos) the Netherland's largest industrial gases supplier to 60%. Other major acquisitions followed including Italian supplier Caracciolossigeno (1994) Czech gases firm Technoplyn (1995) and US engineering firm Pro-Quip (1996).

The company also built up its lines of refrigerated cases. It had taken a stake in CRIOSBANC an Italian manufacturer in 1992 (buying the rest in 1998). Linde acquired UK supplier Radford Retail Systems in 1997 and the next year gained controlling stakes in Brazilian supplier Seral do Brasil and in European distributor Chief Group.

In 1998 Linde also bought Thyssen Krupp Stahl's air separation plants in Duisburg-Ruhrort. A year later Linde reorganized its gases division as a separate operating company (Linde Technische Gase) and in 2000 it acquired Swedish industrial gases giant AGA in a deal that made Linde the world's #4 gas supplier. That year after abandoning plans to take over rival Messer Griesheim's gas operations Linde inked a deal with Japan's Komatsu Forklift for global collaboration. The demise of the Messer Griesheim merger led Linde to restructure its gas and engineering business segment and its refrigeration operations in 2001.

In 2004 Linde sold its refrigeration equipment and cooling systems business to Carrier (a subsidiary of United Technologies Corporation) for $400 million.

Linde became the world's largest gas manufacturer ahead of France's L'Air Liquide in the mid-2000s after it acquired UK gas producer BOC Group. Following the BOC acquisition Linde separated its material handling division and sold it to Kohlberg Kravis Roberts and Goldman Sachs Capital Partners for about $5 billion.

EXECUTIVES

President and CEO, Wolfgang H. Reitzle, age 64, $2,590,728 total compensation
Second Deputy Chairman, Michael Diekmann, age 58
Chairman Supervisory Board, Manfred Schneider, age 74
Member of the Executive Board, Aldo Belloni, age 62, $951,696 total compensation
SVP Communications and Investor Relations, Harry Roegner
Deputy Chairman, Hans-Dieter Katte
Member of the Executive Board, Sanjiv Lamba, age 49
Member of the Executive Board, Georg Denoke, age 47, $745,495 total compensation
Head External Communications, Uwe Wolfinger
Head Investor Relations, Thomas Eisenlohr
Supervisory Board Member, Clemens A. H. Borsig, age 65
Second Deputy Chairman, Michael Diekmann, age 58
Supervisory Board Member, Klaus-Peter Muller, age 67
Supervisory Board Member, Matthew F. C. Miau, age 66
Deputy Chairman, Hans-Dieter Katte
Supervisory Board Member, Thilo Kammerer
Supervisory Board Member, Jens Riedel
Supervisory Board Member, Josef Schregle
Supervisory Board Member, Xaver Schmidt
Auditors: KPMGDeutscheTreuhand-GesellschaftAG

LOCATIONS

HQ: Linde AG (Germany, Fed. Rep.)
Klosterhofstrasse 1, Munich D-80331
Phone: (49) 89 35757 01 **Fax:** (49) 89 35757 1075
Web: www.linde.com

2011 Sales

	$ mil.	% of total
Europe		
Other countries		34
North America		14
Africa		6
South America		5

PRODUCTS/OPERATIONS

2011 Sales

	$ mil.	% of total
Linde Gas		78
Linde Engineering		18
Total	**0**	**100**

COMPETITORS

Air Products
Fluor
GEA Group
L' Air Liquide
Praxair

HISTORICAL FINANCIALS

Company Type: Public

Income Statement FYE: December 31

	REVENUE ($ mil.)	NET INCOME ($ mil.)	NET PROFIT MARGIN	EMPLOYEES
12/12	20,139	1,647	8.2%	61,965
12/11	17,832	1,518	8.5%	50,417
12/10	17,222	1,345	7.8%	48,430
12/09	16,150	851	5.3%	47,731
12/08	17,704	1,002	5.7%	51,908
Annual Growth	3.3%	13.2%	—	4.5%

2012 Year-End Financials

Debt ratio: 39.8%
Return on equity: 10.0%
Cash ($ mil.): 1,605
Current ratio: 0.98
Long-term debt ($ mil.): 11,680
No. of shares (mil.): 185
Dividends
Yield: 1.2%
Payout: 4.2%
Market value ($ mil.): 3,276

	STOCK PRICE ($) FY Close	P/E High/Low		PER SHARE ($) Earnings	Dividends	Book Value
12/12	17.69	5	3	9.19	0.22	93.19
12/11	14.91	5	3	8.82	0.39	87.74
12/10	15.15	5	3	7.84	0.16	85.25
12/09	12.11	8	3	5.01	0.00	74.51
Annual Growth	13.5%	—	—	16.3%	—	5.8%

Lloyds Banking Group Plc

Don't confuse Lloyds Banking Group with that "other" Lloyds. Unrelated to Lloyd's of London Lloyds Banking Group was formed by the 2009 merger of UK banks Lloyds TSB and HBOS. Its retail banking services include deposit accounts credit cards loans and wealth management. Lloyds Banking Group is also one of the nation's top home mortgage lenders. Other products include insurance and investment services through Scottish Widows and wholesale and international banking for UK corporate clients and multinationals. Lloyds Banking Group which operates under the brands Lloyds TSB Halifax and Bank of Scotland has some 2900 branches with representative offices in the Middle East Asia and the Americas.

The UK government owns slightly less than 40% of Lloyds after bailing it out in 2008. After the bailout the company embarked on one of the largest-ever capital raisings in Europe. Although the merger with HBOS nearly destroyed Lloyds – HBOS had a much higher risk tolerance than Lloyds and the company has faced billions in losses since the deal –the combined company controls some 30% of the UK's mortgage market and half of the savings market.

The company has been compelled by European authorities to sell the 600 retail banking branches associated with the Lloyds TSB brand along with a large part of its Cheltenham & Gloucester network. It has received some interest from Virgin Money; another option would be spinning them off to the public. Lloyds Banking Group has divested some noncore businesses such as its fund management arm Insight which was sold to Bank of New York Mellon for #235 million ($386 million); its Irish retail unit which lost billions in toxic loans and its Australian and New Zealand property and corporate loans for $684 million. The company also may spin off its private equity unit Lloyds TSB Development Capital. In late 2013 the company sold its remaining stake in St. James's Place Plc for about 680 pounds ($1.1 billion) to focus on its primary retail and commercial businesses.

As part of its strategic review and after some layoffs related to the ill-fated HBOS acquisition the company announced another round of job cuts in 2011 (mostly back-office and middle management positions). Lloyds has already shed 27500 jobs and will cut another 15000 in the process. The group's strategy for growth include simplifying operations (it completed the integration of HBOS in 2011) while investing in core areas and strenghtening its balance sheet and liquidity position.

The restructuring efforts have helped to cut the company's losses. In 2011 Lloyds lost #342 million before taxes a large improvement over the 2010 losses of #2.9 billion. Net interest grew 1% to #12.7 million a modest increase as retail lending markets remained pressured. However revenues declined that year 32% to #17.2 billion largely due to the ongoing economic challenges in the UK and Ireland. Fees and commissions as well as net trading income declined in 2011. The wholesale business' profits decreased by 67% that year as a result of lower asset balances and losses on asset disposals. Earnings were also affected by some #3.6 billion in provisions including a #375 million provision for the mis-selling of payment protection insurance to customers from 2007 to 2011.

HISTORY

In 1765 John Taylor and Sampson Lloyd II founded Taylors and Lloyds bank in Birmingham England; five years later their sons opened a London agency. In 1852 the last Taylor involved with the bank died. In 1865 the bank converted to joint stock form and became Lloyds Banking Company Ltd. Over the next half century it grew by merging with some 50 banks becoming one of England's largest banks by the turn of the century.

Despite the post-WWI roller-coaster economy the bank acquired Capital and Counties Bank (1918 bringing foreign connections); Fox Fowler & Company (1921); and Cox & Company (1923). During both wars deposits grew while lending dropped. After WWII growth was hampered by high inflation.

Lloyds added branches and products in the 1960s. By 1971 it had branches in 43 countries. It moved into insurance (1972) home mortgages (1979) real estate agency services (1982) and merchant banking (1986).

In 1987 Latin American bank defaults pummeled Lloyds. Refocusing on domestic operations the bank sold overseas subsidiaries (including Lloyds Bank Canada in 1990) and acquired 58% of life insurer Abbey Life (1988) and Cheltenham & Gloucester Building Society (1994). HSBC outbid Lloyds for Midland Bank in 1992; Lloyds bought TSB Group in 1995.

TSB Group evolved from the trustee savings banks (TSBs) formed in the 1800s. By 1860 there were 600 such banks mainly in northern England and Scotland. During WWI many TSBs consolidated or closed. By WWII about 100 remained and the mergers continued.

In the 1960s TSBs began offering checking accounts and trust services. Loans credit cards and other services came in 1973. In 1986 the four remaining TSBs (TSB Channel Islands TSB England and Wales TSB Northern Ireland and TSB Scotland) agreed to merge and go public in order to gain equal footing with stock banks. TSB Group was born.

Flush with cash from its offering TSB group defied the late 1980s recession to buy Target Group (life insurance sold 1993) Hill Samuel (merchant banking) and other units; the purchases sent TSB sprawling.

As debt rose in the 1990s TSB Group refocused on banking and insurance. TSB and Lloyds merged in 1995 linking their geographically complementary branch networks to fend off competition.

After the merger Lloyds TSB focused on loans and insurance and dabbled in consumer finance including the sale and delivery of big-ticket items (cars large appliances). Returning overseas it bought the consumer finance unit of Brazil's Banco Multiplic.

In late 1997 and 1998 the bank overhauled its operations to eliminate redundancies and began rebranding under one green and blue banner. In 1999 Lloyds TSB bailed out Abbey Life which had nearly been bankrupted by the cost of settling pension mis-selling claims.

The bank in 2000 bought Scottish Widows to boost its fund management services. It sold the Abbey Life name and its new business to Zurich Financial Services' Allied Dunbar; Abbey Life continued to service existing business for Lloyds. Also that year Lloyds TSB bought consumer and auto finance unit Chartered Trust from Standard Chartered. After a yearlong battle to buy London-based mortgage lender Abbey National the UK government in 2001 blocked the merger attempt because of concerns for the consumer.

Earlier in 2001 Lloyds TSB closed Bahamas-based subsidiary British Bank of Latin America because of alleged money-laundering links revealed in a US Senate report.

Lloyds TSB's asset finance operations bought First National Vehicle Holdings and Abbey National Vehicle Finance from Abbey National plc in 2002. The division also acquired Chartered Trust and Dutton-Forshaw Group a car dealership. Lloyds TSB sold National Bank of New Zealand to Australia and New Zealand Bank Group in 2003.

Commerzbank unit Comdirect Bank sold its UK subsidiary Comdirect Ltd to Lloyds TSB unit Executive Services Group in 2004.

The company sold its Abbey Life unit to Deutsche Bank for nearly $2 billion in 2007. (The life insurer had been closed to new business since 2000.) The group also sold Lloyds TSB Registrars and car dealership The Dutton-Forshaw Group which were noncore units of its wholesale and international business.

The global economic crisis was a difficult time for Lloyds. The UK government took a 40% stake in the company after bailing it out along with seven other top banks in 2008. Lloyds accepted some #17 billion ($25 billion) in taxpayer money. The government hoped the infusion of cash would loosen up credit markets and restore confidence in the financial system. As part of a restructuring plan (and to repay the UK government) Lloyds Banking Group launched one of the largest-ever capital raisings in Europe which included a #9 billion ($13 billion) debt exchange and a nearly #14 billion ($20 billion) rights issue.

Around the same time of the government bailout Lloyds TSB agreed to take over struggling HBOS the UK's top mortgage lender. The controversial #12 billion ($22 billion) deal was announced after HBOS shares fell dramatically amid rising concerns surrounding the vitality of financial services companies worldwide. The combined bank served about one of every three UK consumers and controlled more than a quarter of the

UK residential mortgage market. The UK government further capitalized the deal to ensure its viability.

Within weeks though Lloyds Banking Group revealed that HBOS had incurred some #11 billion ($18 billion) in losses and shareholder unrest grew concerning the billions of pounds in toxic assets gained with the acquisition. The merger meant drastic cost cuts and job losses as the company announced more than 42000 job cuts.

Needless to say not everyone was happy with the HBOS merger. At Lloyds Banking Group's annual meeting in 2009 a large group of shareholders loudly criticized the company's board for the HBOS deal demanding resignations and threatening lawsuits over the merger. In 2010 one group of disgruntled shareholders launched legal action in order to recoup up to #14 billion ($20 billion) that they claim they lost as a result of the merger.

Lloyds Banking Group defended the merger though saying it helped improve the company's strategic position by improving its market position (it controlled about half of the savings market) brand recognition and expanding its customer base. Although the deal brought short-term costs company leaders were convinced that it was better positioned for future growth.

EXECUTIVES

Chairman, Sir Winfried F. W. (Win) Bischoff, age 72
Vice Chairman, David L. Roberts, age 50
Group Director Finance and Director, George Culmer, age 50
Group Chief Executive and Director, Antonio Horta-Osorio, age 49
Director, Anita M. Frew, age 54
Vice Chairman, David L. Roberts, age 50
Group Director Finance and Director, George Culmer, age 50
Director, Martin A. Scicluna, age 61
Director, Anthony (Tony) Watson, age 67
Director, T. Timothy Ryan Jr., age 67
Group Chief Executive and Director, Antonio Horta-Osorio, age 49
Auditors: PricewaterhouseCoopersLLP

LOCATIONS

HQ: Lloyds Banking Group Plc
25 Gresham Street, 5th Floor, London EC2V 7HN
Phone: (44) 20 7626 1500
Web: www.lloydsbankinggroup.com

PRODUCTS/OPERATIONS

2011 Sales

	% of total
Interest	64
Insurance	20
Net fees & Other	9 7
Total	100

2011 Sales by Division

	% of total
Retail	47
Wholesale	21
Insurance	13
Wealth & Commercial	10 9
Total	100

Selected Brands

Bank of Scotland
Cheltenham & Gloucester
Clerical Medical
Halifax
Lloyds TSB
Scottish Widows

COMPETITORS

Barclays
Grupo Santander
HSBC
Invesco
Northern Rock (Asset Management)
Northern Rock plc
Royal Bank of Scotland
Standard Life Bank
Woolwich

HISTORICAL FINANCIALS

Company Type: Public

Income Statement FYE: December 31

	ASSETS ($ mil.)	NET INCOME ($ mil.)	INCOME AS % OF ASSETS	EMPLOYEES
12/12	1,490,254	(2,300)	—	92,788
12/11	1,499,351	(696)	—	98,538
12/10	1,539,557	(496)	—	104,230
12/09	1,663,722	4,578	0.3%	107,144
12/08	635,431	1,193	0.2%	58,756
Annual Growth	23.8%	—	—	12.1%

2012 Year-End Financials

Return on assets: (-0.1%)
Return on equity: (-3.1%)
Long-term debt ($ mil.): —
No. of shares (mil.): —
Sales ($ mil): 88,336
Dividends
Yield: 0.0%
Payout: —
Market value ($ mil.): —

	STOCK PRICE ($) FY Close	P/E High/Low		PER SHARE ($) Earnings	Dividends	Book Value
12/12	3.20	—	—	(0.03)	0.16	1.01
12/11	1.57	—	—	(0.01)	0.00	1.03
12/10	4.11	—	—	(0.01)	0.00	1.05
12/09	3.27	272	68	0.12	2.28	1.10
12/08	7.70	1574	219	0.10	2.67	1.12
Annual Growth	(19.7%)	—	—	—	(50.4%)	(2.7%)

Loblaw Cos. Ltd.

LOCATIONS

HQ: Loblaw Cos. Ltd.
1 President' s Choice Circle, Brampton, Ontario L6Y 5S5
Phone: 905 459-2500 **Fax:** 905 861-2206
Web: www.loblaw.ca

HISTORICAL FINANCIALS

Company Type: Public

Income Statement FYE: December 29

	REVENUE ($ mil.)	NET INCOME ($ mil.)	NET PROFIT MARGIN	EMPLOYEES
12/12	31,776	653	2.1%	134,000
12/11*	30,634	753	2.5%	135,000
01/11	30,916	676	2.2%	136,000
01/10	29,224	623	2.1%	138,000
01/09	25,554	452	1.8%	139,000
Annual Growth	5.6%	9.6%	—	(0.9%)

*Fiscal year change

2012 Year-End Financials

Debt ratio: 36.8%
Return on equity: 10.4%
Cash ($ mil.): 1,084
Current ratio: 1.24
Long-term debt ($ mil.): 5,024
No. of shares (mil.): 281
Dividends
Yield: 0.0%
Payout: 37.2%
Market value ($ mil.): 11,605

	STOCK PRICE ($) FY Close	P/E High/Low		PER SHARE ($) Earnings	Dividends	Book Value
12/12	41.20	19	13	2.29	0.85	22.91
12/11*	37.82	17	12	2.66	0.82	20.93
01/11	40.50	18	13	2.39	0.84	20.02
01/10	32.10	12	7	2.26	0.80	21.60
01/09	28.58	15	7	1.65	0.70	17.64
Annual Growth	9.6%	—	—	8.6%	5.2%	6.7%

*Fiscal year change

LVMH Moet Hennessy Louis Vuitton

LVMH Moet Hennessy Louis Vuitton is the world's largest luxury goods company with brands that are bywords for the good life and everything showy. LVMH makes wines and spirits (Dom Perignon Moet & Chandon Veuve Clicquot and Hennessy) perfumes (Christian Dior Guerlain and Givenchy) cosmetics (Bliss Fresh and BeneFit) fashion and leather goods (Donna Karan Givenchy Kenzo and Louis Vuitton) and watches and jewelry (TAG Heuer Ebel Chaumet and Bulgari). LVMH's selective retail division includes Sephora cosmetics stores Le Bon Marche Paris department stores and 61% of DFS Group (duty-free shops). Chairman Bernard Arnault and his family through Groupe Arnault own about 47% of LVMH.

With the market for luxury goods on a tear –especially in fast-growing markets in Asia –LVMH is flush with cash for acquisitions. Putting that cash to use in late 2011 the French luxury goods firm completed a ?3.7 billion ($5 billion) tender offer for the shares of Rome-based jeweler Bulgari. Bulgari is the smallest of the major luxury jewelry and watch makers and the deal doubles LVMH's watch and jewelry business. The Bulgari deal was announced soon after LVMH acquired a pair of niche brands: Ole Henriksen and Nude skin care. In late 2010 LVMH bought more than 20% of the shares of its rival Hermes International. While LVMH described the move as friendly and said it would not launch a takeover bid for Hermes it nevertheless led to speculation regarding further consolidation in the luxury goods industry as LVMH is known for its predatory nature.

LVMH expanded its products portfolio in mid-2013 when it purchased an 80% stake in Italian cashmere company Loro Piana for $2.57 billion more than three times the $900 million in sales the company had expected to post in 2013. LVMH values Loro Piana for its products' unique quality and craftsmanship and its six generations of leadership. As part of the transaction the cashmere company's owners will retain a stake in the business.

LVMH's Louis Vuitton unit has continued the acquisition streak purchasing Swiss timepiece maker La Fabrique du Temps in mid-2011. La Fabrique has been Louis Vuitton's manufacturing partner since 2007; the deal helps the luxury leather goods firm to lessen its dependence on external suppliers –similar to moves made by competitors. Additionally LVMH in late 2011 acquired 100% of the shares of ArteCad a top maker of Swiss watch dials. (Shortly before the acquisition PPR –later renamed Kering –took control of Sowind Group another Swiss watchmaker.)

The rebound in luxury goods sales comes after a turbulent 2009 for LVMH during which revenue dipped about 1% overall and profit fell more than 7% vs. 2008. LVMH adopted a cautious approach in 2010 given the ongoing financial uncertainty caused by the financial crisis in Greece concern about the fiscal health of other countries in Europe and up-and-down stock market in the US. Still it continued to invest in promising markets such as Brazil China the Middle East (Qatar and Bahrain) and Russia (it owns a majority stake of Russian retailer Ile de Beaute). China is a huge emerging market for luxury goods and a pillar of growth for the French company. To that end LVMH opened two stores there in 2010 timed to coincide with the Shanghai World Expo.

The company has been focusing on controlling as much of its distribution as possible. LVMH has more than 2400 retail outlets (about 85% are outside France). Nearly half are fashion and leather goods stores led by Louis Vuitton and also including Fendi boutiques and hundreds of other shops under the Celine Givenchy Donna Karan Thomas Pink Pucci and Marc Jacobs brands among others. LVMH's namesake Louis Vuitton brand as well as Fendi and Marc Jacobs are proving resilient in Europe despite the economic slowdown there and posting strong revenue gains in Asia.

Striking out in a new direction the luxury goods firm is venturing into the hotel business via a partnership with Egypt's Orascom Development Holding. Together the two plan to develop upmarket resorts in Egypt and Oman with LVMH overseeing the design and running of the hotels which are slated to open in 2012. With LVMH investing no capital in the hotel venture (it will be paid a management fee) the deal could prove less risky than its 2008 purchase of Dutch yacht maker Royal van Lent and the financial newspaper Les Echos.

HISTORY

Woodworker Louis Vuitton started his Paris career packing dresses for French Empress Eugenie. He later designed new types of luggage and in 1854 he opened a store to sell his designs. In 1896 Vuitton introduced the LV monogram fabric that the company still uses. By 1900 Louis Vuitton had stores in the US and England and by WWI Louis' son Georges had the world's largest retail store for travel goods.

Henry Racamier a former steel executive who had married into the Vuitton family took charge in 1977 repositioning the company's goods from esoteric status symbols to designer must-haves. Sales soared from $20 million to nearly $2.5 billion within a decade. Concerned about being a takeover target Racamier merged Louis Vuitton in 1987 with Moet Hennessy (which made wines spirits and fragrances) and adopted the name LVMH Moet Hennessy Louis Vuitton.

Moet Hennessy had been formed through the 1971 merger of Moet et Chandon (the world's #1 champagne maker) and the Hennessy Cognac company (founded by Irish mercenary Richard Hennessy in 1765). Moet Hennessy acquired rights to Christian Dior fragrances in 1971.

Racamier tried to reverse the merger when disagreements with chairman Alain Chevalier arose. Racamier invited outside investor Bernard Arnault to increase his interest in the company. Arnault gained control of 43% of LVMH and became chairman in 1989. Chevalier stepped down but Racamier fought for control for another 18 months and then set up Orcofi a partner of cosmetics rival L'Oreal.

LVMH increased its fashion holdings with the purchases of the Givenchy Couture Group (1988) Christian Lacroix (1993) and Kenzo (1993). The company also acquired 55% of French media firm Desfosses International (1993) Celine fashions (1996) the Chateau d'Yquem winery (1996) and duty-free retailer DFS Group (1996). Next LVMH bought perfume chains Sephora (1997) and Marie-Jeanne Godard (1998). In 1998 LVMH integrated the Paris department store Le Bon Marche which was controlled by Arnault.

LVMH accumulated a 34% stake in Italian luxury goods maker Gucci in early 1999 and planned to buy all of it. Fellow French conglomerate Pinault-Printemps-Redoute (PPR) later thwarted LVMH by purchasing 42% of Gucci.

Through its LV Capital unit in 1999 LVMH began acquiring stakes in a host of luxury companies including a joint venture with fashion company Prada to buy 51% of design house Fendi (LVMH bought Prada's 25.5% stake for $265 million in November 2001). It has since upped its Fendi stake to about 70%. LVMH later added the Ebel Chaumet and TAG Heuer brands to its new watch division.

In early 2000 LVMH bought Miami Cruiseline Services which operates duty-free shops on cruise ships auction house L'Etude Tajan and 67% of Italian fashion house Emilio Pucci. The company later purchased 35% of French video game retailer Micromania and 51% of department store Samaritaine. In late 2000 LVMH acquired Gabrielle Studio which owns all Donna Karan licenses. In 2001 the company bought Donna Karan International.

LVMH bought in 2001 the Newton and MountAdam vineyards for about $45 million. It then began marketing De Beers diamond jewelry in a 50-50 joint venture with the diamond powerhouse. In March LVMH prompted the investigation of a Dutch court into the PPR-Gucci alliance. The company sold its stake in Gucci to PPR for $806.5 million in October.

In October 2002 LVMH ceased trading on the Brussels and Nasdaq exchanges to concentrate on its Euronext investors. In October 2003 the company sold Canard-Duchene to the Alain Thienot Group. LVMH shed several of the less productive of its 50 brands in 2003 including auction house Phillips de Pury & Luxemborg and fashion brand Michael Kors.

LVMH opened its biggest store —a four-story emporium on New York's Fifth Avenue —in February 2004. A few months later the company added whisky-maker Glenmorangie PLC to its subsidiary roster. LVMH also made its debut in the South African market in October 2004 opening its first sub-Saharan boutique in Johannesburg. Also during the year Bliss spas was sold off.

In early 2004 LVMH won a landmark lawsuit against Morgan Stanley alleging that the firm had used biased research in misstatements about the financial health of LVMH that caused damage to the company's image. The presiding Parisian court ordered Morgan Stanley to pay 100 million euros (about $38 million) in damages. Morgan Stanley appealed the ruling later that year.

In late 2005 LVMH opened its largest store to date on the Champs-Elysees in Paris and the De Beers brand was introduced in the US with stores in New York and Los Angeles. Also that year LVMH was the winning bidder for whisky maker Glenmorangie PLC for which it paid #300 million. On the sell side LVMH divested fashion design house Christian Lacroix SNC.

In May 2007 LVMH acquired a 55% stake in Chinese distillery Wenjun for an undisclosed amount. (Jiannanchun the distillery's previous owner retained a 45% stake in Wenjun.) In December 2007 the luxury goods firm acquired the French newspaper Les Echos from publisher Pearson. LVMH controls Les Echos' rival the financial daily La Tribune but has agreed to sell it. Group Les Echos deal includes the newspaper Web site business magazine Enjeux and other financial information services.

In late 2008 Sephora SA acquired a 45% stake in the Russian perfume and cosmetics chain Ile de Beaute. (The agreement which gave Sephora the option to become a majority shareholder allowed LVMH to up its share to 65% in mid-2011.) The firm acquired the luxury yacht-maker Royal Van Lent.

In August 2009 LVMH acquired 50% stakes in two French wine makers: privately-held Cheval Blanc; and La Tour du Pin owner of the Chateau Quinault l'Enclose estate.

In early 2010 LVMH acquired a 40% stake in Dondup an Italian apparel and denim brand for more than $43 million (or 30 million euros). Its plans are to expand Dondup's business internationally. Later in 2010 the company purchased a 70% stake in the Brazilian fragrance and cosmetics retailer Sack's. The acquisition estimated to be worth R$250 million is a move on LVMH's part to expand its Sephora beauty chain in Brazil one of the fastest-growing beauty markets in the world.

Adding to its vast portfolio of luxury brands in February 2011 LVMH acquired Ole Henriksen a leading luxury botanical skincare company founded and owned by its namesake. Later that same week LVMH bought a 70% stake in Nude Brands skin care as the company continues to acquire niche brands. The four-year-old line - described as "biocompatible luxury skin care" - was founded by Bryan Meehan and Ali Hewson wife of U2 front man Bono. In March LVMH fired Dior star designer John Galliano amid charges of anti-Semitism. In September LVMH completed its tender offer from Rome-based Bulgari acquiring about 98% of the shares.

EXECUTIVES

Chief Executive Officer, Bernard Arnault, age 64
President Watches & Jewelry, Francesco Trapani, age 56
Group Managing Director and Board Member, Antonio (Toni) Belloni
CEO Bulgari, Jean-Christophe Babin, age 54
Member Executive Committee Human Resources, Chantal Gaemperle
Board Member, Nicholas C. Worms
Executive Committee Member Development and Acquisitions and Board Member, Nicolas Bazire, age 55
Board Member, Yves-Thibault de Silguy, age 63
Board Member, Charles F. W. de Croisset, age 69
Group Managing Director and Board Member, Antonio (Toni) Belloni
Board Member, Baron Albert Frere, age 86
Board Member, Felix G. Rohatyn, age 84
Vice Chairman, Antoine Bernheim, age 88
Board Member, Gilles Hennessy
Board Member, Patrick Houel
Board Member, Antoine Arnault
Vice Chairman, Pierre Gode, age 68
Board Member, Hubert Vedrine
Board Member, Lord Powell of Bayswater
Board Member, Delphine Arnault
Board Member, Bernadette Chirac
Auditors: Deloitte&Associes

LOCATIONS

HQ: LVMH Moet Hennessy Louis Vuitton
22, avenue Montaigne, Paris 75008
Phone: (33) 1 44 13 22 22 **Fax:** (33) 1 44 13 22 23
Web: www.lvmh.com

2012 Stores

	No.
Europe	
France	412
Other	910

Asia	
Japan	370
Other	670
US	644
Other	198
Total	**3,204**

2012 Sales

	% of total
Europe	
France	11
Other	20
Asia	
Japan	8
Other	28
US	23
Other	10
Total	**100**

PRODUCTS/OPERATIONS

2012 Sales

	% of total
Fashion & leather	35
Selective retailing	**28**
Wines & spirits	15
Perfumes & cosmetics	13
Watches & jewelry	10
Adjustment	(1)
Total	100

Selected Brands and Operations

Fashion and leather goods
- Berluti
- Celine
- Donna Karan
- Emilio Pucci
- Fendi
- Gabrielle Studio (Donna Karan label)
- Givenchy
- Kenzo
- Loewe
- Loro Piana
- Louis Vuitton
- Marc Jacobs
- Thomas Pink

Retailing
- DFS Group
- La Samaritaine
- Le Bon Marche
- Miami Cruiseline Services (duty-free shops)
- Sephora

Fragrances and cosmetics
- Aqua di Parma
- BeneFit
- Bliss
- Fresh
- Guerlain
- Kenzo Parfums
- Make Up For Ever
- Marc Jacobs Fragrances
- Nude skin care
- Ole Henriksen
- Parfums Christian Dior
- Parfums Givenchy

Spirits and wines
- 10 Cane
- Belvedere
- Canard-Duchene
- Chandon Estates
- Chateau d' Yquem
- Dom Perignon
- Hennessy
- Krug
- Mercier
- Moet & Chandon
- MountAdam
- Newton
- Ruinart
- Veuve Clicquot

Watches and jewelry
- Bulgari
- Chaumet
- De Beers
- Ebel
- Fred
- Omas
- TAG Heuer
- Zenith

Media (Desfosses International Group)
- Investir
- La Tribune
- Les Echos
- Radio Classique

Other
- Royal van Lent (luxury yachts)

COMPETITORS

Armani
Asprey
Avon
Bacardi
Brown-Forman
Calvin Klein
Chanel
Douglas Holding
E. & J. Gallo
Escada
Estee Lauder
Galeries Lafayette
Gianni Versace
Harry Winston
Hermes
Hugo Boss
Inditex
Kering
Kirin Holdings Company
L' Oreal
MacAndrews & Forbes
Oscar de la Renta
Patek Philippe
Prada
Puig
Ralph Lauren
Remy Cointreau
Richemont
Rolex
Shiseido
Swatch
Taittinger
Tiffany & Co.
Unilever
Vera Wang

HISTORICAL FINANCIALS

Company Type: Public

Income Statement

FYE: December 31

	REVENUE ($ mil.)	NET INCOME ($ mil.)	NET PROFIT MARGIN	EMPLOYEES
12/12	37,041	4,513	12.2%	106,348
12/11	30,601	3,964	13.0%	97,559
12/10	27,195	4,057	14.9%	83,542
12/09	24,566	2,528	10.3%	77,302
12/08	24,037	2,832	11.8%	77,087
Annual Growth	11.4%	12.3%	—	8.4%

2012 Year-End Financials

Debt ratio: 17.9%
Return on equity: 14.5%
Cash ($ mil.): 2,894
Current ratio: 1.51
Long-term debt ($ mil.): 5,056
No. of shares (mil.): 500
Dividends
Yield: 2.0%
Payout: 14.6%
Market value ($ mil.): 18,845

	STOCK PRICE ($) FY Close	P/E High	P/E Low	PER SHARE ($) Earnings	Dividends	Book Value
12/12	37.69	9	7	8.99	0.76	64.75
12/11	28.10	11	7	8.06	1.11	58.29
12/10	33.15	10	5	8.46	0.50	48.08
12/09	22.45	13	5	5.33	0.45	41.90
12/08	13.15	24	4	5.96	0.33	38.12
Annual Growth	30.1%	—	—	10.8%	23.2%	14.2%

LyondellBasell Industries NV

LOCATIONS

HQ: LyondellBasell Industries NV
Stationsplein 45, Rotterdam 3013 AK
Phone: (31) 30 275 5500
Web: www.lyondellbasell.com

HISTORICAL FINANCIALS

Company Type: Public

Income Statement

FYE: December 31

	REVENUE ($ mil.)	NET INCOME ($ mil.)	NET PROFIT MARGIN	EMPLOYEES
12/12	45,352	2,848	6.3%	13,500
12/11	51,035	2,147	4.2%	14,000
12/10*	27,684	1,587	5.7%	14,000
04/10	13,467	8,564	63.6%	0
12/09	30,828	(2,865)	—	0
Annual Growth	13.7%	—	—	—

*Fiscal year change

2012 Year-End Financials

Debt ratio: 18.1%
Return on equity: 26.1%
Cash ($ mil.): 2,732
Current ratio: 2.41
Long-term debt ($ mil.): 4,304
No. of shares (mil.): 572
Dividends
Yield: 7.3%
Payout: 121.7%
Market value ($ mil.): 32,656

	STOCK PRICE ($) FY Close	P/E High	P/E Low	PER SHARE ($) Earnings	Dividends	Book Value
12/12	57.09	11	7	4.92	4.20	19.47
12/11	32.49	12	6	3.74	5.05	18.61
12/10*	34.40	12	5	2.78	0.00	20.43
04/10	22.30	—	—	(0.00)	0.00	(0.00)
Annual Growth	36.8%	—	—	—	—	—

*Fiscal year change

Macquarie Group Ltd

One of the few domestically owned investment banks in the Land Down Under Macquarie Group does business at home in Australia and beyond. The holding company for Macquarie Bank and other subsidiaries it operates an investment banking practice that performs financing trading strategic advisory equities research and other services for corporate and government clients. Other operations include fund management retail banking and lending and wealth management. Macquarie has jumped headfirst into the international private-equity market as well focusing on the energy sector through its Macquarie Energy arm. Founded in 1969 Macquarie has more than 70 offices around the world.

Macquarie's business activities are divided into six operating groups: Banking and Financial Services; Corporate and Asset Finance; Fixed Income Currencies and Commodities; Macquarie Capital; Macquarie Funds; and Macquarie Securities.

The company aims to be a global organization and its strategy is to not only build upon assets in Australia but to also enter markets abroad (mostly in the US and Europe). Most of its focus is on the energy renewables resources financial services and infrastructure sectors. The company's main strategy is to build diversity and expand its global platform.

Most recently Macquarie has been acquiring several North America-based financial services companies including investment bank Fox-Pitt Kelton Cochran Caronia Waller. In 2010 Macquarie expanded upon its individual and institutional asset management business when it acquired US-based Delaware Investments. It also bought the Canadian investment dealing business of Blackmont Capital and rebranded it as Macquarie Private Wealth.

Two more US acquisitions were designed to enhance Macquarie Capital's advisory business. In 2010 Macquarie bought US-based specialist Presidio Partners which performs real estate advisory and capital raising advisory services. Macquarie also bought Los Angeles-based investment bank Regal Capital Advisors a specialist in strategic and financial advice for the gaming lodging and leisure industries. Macquarie's recent US shopping spree has helped boost revenues brought in from the US. That market now contributes about 30% of the company's revenues.

Next on the acquisition radar is Europe. Macquarie acquired the cash equities sales and research business of German private bank Sal. Oppenheim Jr. & Cie. in 2010. The acquisition broadened Macquarie's European business bolstering its presence in several key markets. Macquarie is looking to buy trading and investment banking businesses in Europe.

Macquarie is known as a specialist in the Asia/Pacific market. The firm has expanded in that sector and worked on some of the largest transactions in the region such as the IPO of Agricultural Bank of China. The company also manages several funds in Asia most of them focused on infrastructure.

Macquarie also has been focusing on the energy market. In 2009 it acquired Canadian boutique investment bank Tristone Capital which serves the oil and gas industry. Macquarie also acquired the downstream natural gas trading operations of Constellation Energy. The company then combined that business with its Macquarie Cook Energy business to form Macquarie Energy a larger North American wholesale gas company. In 2010 Macquarie Energy acquired the wholesale electric marketing and trading portfolio of Integrys Energy Services in a deal that more than doubled Macquarie Energy's customer base and strengthened its position in key North American power markets. Also that year subsidiary Macquarie Aerospace agreed to purchase a portfolio of 53 aircraft from AIG unit International Lease Finance Corporation.

But acquisitions aren't the only tricks up Macquarie's sleeves. The company has created investment funds and management companies out of acquired assets ranging from tollways to office buildings to water treatment systems and unleashed them on public markets around the globe. These include Macquarie Infrastructure Company in the US and Macquarie Infrastructure Group in Australia.

In 2012 a fund managed by Macquarie Group acquired WCA Waste Corp. The deal will expand and diversity Macquarie's North American portfolio.

While the energy and financial services sectors seem to be Macquarie's main focus other parts of the company's business are being reshuffled as a result of the global financial crisis. The group restructured several of its property-related subsidiaries in 2008 merging its property advisory division with the investment bank's real estate group which covers funds management and development finance. The company also scaled back its mortgage business. In 2010 Macquarie sold the majority of its Australian real estate management platform to the Charter Hall property group.

David Clarke resigned as chairman of Macquarie Group and Macquarie Bank in 2011. After 40 years with the company Clarke stepped down due to health issues. He died shortly afterwards. Former director Kevin McCann was appointed the new chairman.

EXECUTIVES

Head Risk Management Group, Stephen Allen
Head Banking and Financial Services Group, Peter J. Maher, $455,273 total compensation
Managing Director Chief Executive Officer, Nicholas W. Moore, age 54, $474,459 total compensation
Head Fixed Income Currencies and Commodities, Andrew J. Downe, $479,234 total compensation
Head Corporate Affairs Group, Greg C. Ward
Chairman, H. Kevin McCann, age 72
Executive Chairman Macquarie Capital, Michael Carapiet, $383,387 total compensation
Head Macquarie Funds Group, Shemara Wikramanayake
Head Macquarie Securities Group and Macquarie Capital, Roy Laidlaw
CEO Macquarie Capital (USA), Tim Bishop
Head Corporate and Asset Finance Group, Garry Farrell
Head Cash Equities Macquarie Securities Group, Stevan Vrcelj
Country Head - United States of America, M. McLaughlin
Assistant Company Secretary, Nigel Donnelly
Assistant Company Secretary, Paula Walsh
Deputy Head - Global Oil and Gas; Executive Director, Sandy Edmonstone
Chief Operating Officer, Nicole Sorbara
Director, Michael J. (Mike) Hawker, age 53
Director, Peter M. Kirby, age 65
Managing Director Chief Executive Officer, Nicholas W. Moore, age 54
Director, John R. Niland, age 72
Director, Helen M. Nugent, age 62
Director, Catherine B. Livingstone, age 57
Director, Peter H. Warne, age 57
Independent Non-Executive Director, Diane Grady
Independent Non-Executive Director, Michael Coleman
Auditors: PricewaterhouseCoopers

LOCATIONS

HQ: Macquarie Group Ltd
No. 1, Martin Place, Sydney, New South Wales 2000
Phone: (61) 2 8232 3333 **Fax:** (61) 2 8232 4330
Web: www.macquarie.com.au

2011 Sales

	% of total
Australia	54
Americas	23
Europe Middle East	16
Asia/Pacific	7
Total	**100**

PRODUCTS/OPERATIONS

2011 Sales

	% of total
Banking & financial	21
Fixed income currencies &	17
Macquarie Funds	14
Corporate & asset	13
Macquarie Securities	12
Corporate	12
Macquarie	11
Total	**100**

2011 Sales

	% of total
Lending	30
Financial	29
Capital	21
Asset & wealth	20
Total	**100**

COMPETITORS

Citigroup
Deutsche Bank
Goldman Sachs
HSBC
Merrill Lynch
Morgan Stanley
UBS Investment Bank

HISTORICAL FINANCIALS

Company Type: Public

Income Statement FYE: March 31

	ASSETS ($ mil.)	NET INCOME ($ mil.)	INCOME AS % OF ASSETS	EMPLOYEES
03/13	157,029	886	0.6%	13,663
03/12	159,857	759	0.5%	14,202
03/11	163,063	989	0.6%	15,556
03/10	133,547	960	0.7%	14,657
03/09	103,217	602	0.6%	12,716
Annual Growth	11.1%	10.1%	—	1.8%

	STOCK PRICE ($) FY Close	P/E High/Low		PER SHARE ($) Earnings	Dividends	Book Value
03/13	38.72	18	10	2.56	0.00	34.96
03/12	30.22	21	9	2.11	0.00	33.44
03/11	38.04	16	9	2.86	0.00	34.03
03/10	43.10	14	4	2.90	0.00	29.86
03/09	18.75	13	1	2.14	0.00	21.15
Annual Growth	19.9%	—	—	4.7%	—	13.4%

Magna International Inc.

Through its various subsidiaries and divisions Magna International makes just about everything needed to put together a motor vehicle. Magna Steyr its largest division offers vehicle engineering and assembly. Magna's interior and exterior systems division makes trim lighting sealing systems instrument and door panels and sound insulation. Cosma International makes body and chassis systems. Magna Powertrain offers transaxles transmission systems and engine parts while Magna Mirrors makes mirrors and driver assistance products. Other Magna operations include Seating E-Car Systems Electronics Roof and Closures. Its geographic markets include North America Europe Africa and Asia.

Geographic Reach

The company operates through almost 310 manufacturing operations and roughly 90 product development engineering and sales centers in nearly 30 countries. Magna follows a decentralized mode of operation meaning its businesses operate independently.

The company has restructured itself along geographic lines to be more responsive to customers' needs and is paying particular attention to the "Rest of World" market that encompasses developing regions such as Africa Asia Eastern Europe and South America.

Sales and Marketing

BMW Daimler Fiat/Chrysler Ford GM and VW accounted for approximately 83% of Magna's total sales in 2012.

Financial Performance

Magna has enjoyed sizable growth over the years as the global automotive sector recovers. Its total sales were up by 7% from $28.8 billion to $30.8 billion during 2011 to 2012. Profits also skyrocketed by 41% from $1 billion to $1.4 billion during that same time period. Both these revenue and profit totals represented historical milestones for the company.

The company attributes the growth in 2012 to an increase in light vehicle production in North America (18%) and western Europe (7%). It also was helped by a 33% increase in Rest of World production sales and by acquisitions it made in 2012.

Strategy

Magna International seeks expansion opportunities in the Eastern European and Russian markets by strengthening its ties to the GAZ Group Russia's largest auto maker. Magna has several facilities in Russia including a plant in Kaluga that makes parts for Volkswagen (VW) Skoda Renault and Peugeot. It also has facilities in the St. Petersburg area.

Farther East Magna's Cosma International formed a joint venture in 2011 with China-based Guangzhou Automobile Group Component Co. (GACC). The business entity Changsha Cosma Automotive manufactures major body and chassis components and structural assemblies from a new facility in Changsha City in the Hunan Province. The company also opened new facilities in India and South Korea.

Looking to the Western Hemisphere Magna Seating acquired Germany-based Vogelsitze GmbH in early 2011. Vogelsitze makes seats for buses and passenger trains. A year later Magna obtained Verwaltungs GmbH a maker of automotive vacuum engine and transmission pumps with two facilities in Germany and one in each of China and Bulgaria.

Strengthening its automotive pump operations even further in 2012 Magna purchased the remaining 50% interest it didn't already own of STT Technologies. STT makes transmission and engine related pumps and caters to the North American market.

HISTORY

Magna International is rooted in a tool and die shop founded by Frank Stronach and friend Tony Czapka in Ontario Canada in 1957. Austrian-born Stronach immigrated to Canada in 1954. By the end of 1957 the business called Multimatic had 10 employees. Multimatic delved into car parts when it landed a contract in 1960 to make sun visor brackets for a General Motors division in Canada.

To go public Multimatic underwent a reverse merger in 1969 with Magna Electronics a publicly traded maker of components for aerospace defense and industrial markets. (Stronach retained control of the company.) Annual sales reached $10 million that year. The company expanded its automotive operations during the early 1970s by adding more stamped and electronic components. Magna was renamed Magna International in 1973.

With sales increasing steadily among its auto parts businesses Magna sold its aerospace and defense business (now part of Heroux-Devtek) in 1981. The new Magna consisted of five distinct automotive divisions that made seat tracks door latches electronic components and other auto parts. During the 1980s the company expanded by adding factories and product lines. It also capitalized on car makers' penchant for outsourcing labor and bypassing unions. By 1987 when sales reached $1 billion the company was producing systems for every area of the automobile. Stronach didn't spend all his time on cars however; he owned race horses and restaurants. He had opened restaurants tried various publishing ventures (which failed) and even made an unsuccessful run for a Canadian parliament seat in 1988.

Aggressive expansion during the 1980s eventually caught up with the company and in 1989 Magna began to restructure selling assets to pay off its debt. The company also was bailed out in part by two of its principal customers –General Motors and Chrysler. Having recovered somewhat Magna began acquiring small auto parts companies in Europe in 1992.

Magna expanded its European presence with the purchase of Austria-based Steyr-Daimler-Puch in 1998 adding about $1 billion in annual sales. The deal steered Magna into the auto assembly business. Stronach also added Santa Anita Park to his holdings that year. In late 1999 the company's racetrack interests were spun off as Magna Entertainment with Magna retaining a 78% stake. Stronach's horse Red Bullet won the 2000 Preakness. Later that year Magna sold its 50% stake in Webasto Sunroofs to privately-owned German auto parts maker Webasto.

Early in 2001 Stronach's daughter Belinda was named vice chairman and CEO. The company then prepared to spin off Magna Steyr and Intier (now Magna's interiors and seating divisions) as public companies; Intier was spun off later in 2001.

Magna acquired rival automotive mirror maker Donnelly in 2002 in a stock-and-debt deal worth $320 million. The company divested its stake in Magna Entertainment in 2003.

Belinda Stronach stepped down as president CEO and director in order to make a bid for the leadership of Canada's new Conservative Party. Her father assumed the role of interim president in early 2004. Ms. Stronach's bid for the leadership of the Conservative Party was not successful. Mr. Stronach ran the company until 2005 when Magna adopted a co-CEO management structure with Donald Walker and Siegfried Wolf at the helm.

Magna and Daimler announced in 2004 that Magna would buy Daimler's drivetrain manufacturing subsidiary New Venture Gear for about $435 million. After approval by the European Commission New Venture Gear was acquired by a newly created joint venture called New Process Gear with Magna holding an 80% interest; Daimler held 20% until 2007 when Magna bought out its stake.

Russian conglomerate Basic Element led by Russian aluminum magnate Oleg Deripaska spent about $1.5 billion to purchase 20% of Magna in 2007. The transaction gave Magna entry to the Russian market but late in 2008 Deripaska's bank BNP Paribas made a margin call that forced the businessman to give up his shares. In 2008 Magna International acquired Technoplast a Russia-based manufacturer of plastic automotive interior and exterior parts which bolstered its capacity in Eastern Europe and Russia.

On the heels of the General Motors bankruptcy filing in 2009 the German government selected Magna International as a partner for Adam Opel and agreed to provide about ?1.5 billion (around $2 billion) in bridge loans while GM and Magna finalized the contract. A trusteeship for Opel was arranged to keep European operations separate from the Chapter 11 proceedings of GM.

Magna teamed up with Russian banking firm Sberbank to purchase a 55% interest in Opel and its UK-based Vauxhall unit. While GM initially agreed to the sale in September 2009 it backed out in November. The GM board decided to restructure Opel and its European operations instead because business conditions were improving and the Opel brand was important to its global strategy. In Europe the decision was met with demands by the German government that its ?1.5 billion in bridge loans be returned as well as protests and planned work stoppages by the German labor union.

The GM bankruptcy was brought on by the economic crisis of 2008 and 2009. Magna responded by implementing cost cutting measures which included reducing its headcount by approximately 11500 representing a 14% cutback between 2007 and 2009. It also sold off some of its non-core assets.

Founder and chairman Frank Stronach stepped down in 2010 citing the trend toward more regulatory limitations on company management as one of the reasons. He gave up his controlling share in the company and with it his voting control. The company purchased and cancelled all of its Class B shares held by the Stronach Group and issued Class A Common shares. This capital transaction ended the company's dual class stock structure. The former premier of Ontario Mike Harris took Stronach's place. Co-CEO Siegfried ("Sigi") Wolf also resigned which made co-CEO Donald Walker the sole CEO of Magna International as of mid-2011.

EXECUTIVES

Chief Executive Officer; Director, Donald J. Walker, age 57

Executive Vice-President and Chief Financial Officer, Vincent J. Galifi, $110,500 total compensation

Executive Vice President; Chief Legal Officer, Jeffrey O. Palmer

Executive Vice President - Global Human Resources, Marc J. Neeb

Chief Operating Officer, Tom Skudutis, $110,500 total compensation

EVP and Chief Strategy Officer, Herbert Demel, age 60

Executive Vice President, Alon Ossip

Chairman of the Board, William L. Young, age 57

President Magna Europe, Guenther Apfalter

VP and Secretary, Bassem A. Shakeel

Chief Marketing Officer and President Magna Asia, James J. (Jim) Tobin Sr.

CTO, Burkhard Goeschel, age 66

Director Corporate Communications and Media Relations, Tracy Fuerst

Executive Vice-President Corporate Engineering & R&D, Seetarama Kotagiri

Vice President Sales & Marketing, Hubert H?dl

CEO and Director, Donald J. Walker, age 56

Director, Donald Resnick, age 84

Director, Rt. Hon. Franz Vranitzky, age 74

Director, Lawrence D. Worrall, age 71

Director, Michael D. (Mike) Harris, age 67

Independent Director, Kurt Lauk

Independent Director, Trevor Eyton

Auditors: Ernst&YoungLLP

LOCATIONS

HQ: Magna International Inc.
337 Magna Drive, Aurora, Ontario L4G 7K1

Phone: 905 726-2462

Web: www.magna.com

2012 Sales

North America	53
Other regions	6

PRODUCTS/OPERATIONS

2012 Sales

	$ mil.	% of total
Exterior & interior systems	11,673	38
Body systems & chassis systems	7,123	23
Powertrain systems	3,825	12
Complete vehicle assembly	2,561	8
Tooling engineering & other	2,317	8
Vision & electronic systems	2,132	7
Closure systems	1,206	4
Total	**30,837**	**100**

2012 Sales by Customer

General Motors	19
Fiat/Chrysler	13
Volkswagen	12
Other	17

Selected Operations Products and Services

Cosma International Inc. - body and chassis systems
- Body systems
- Chassis systems
- Design and engineering
- Finishing
- Metal forming technologies
- Stampings

Decoma International - exterior and interior systems
- Body side systems
- Bumper systems (front and rear)
- Cargo management
- Carpet and loadspace
- Cockpit systems
- Engineered glass
- Exterior trim
- Greenhouse systems
- Lighting systems
- Plastic body panels
- Polymeric glazing systems
- Sealing systems
- Vehicle enhancement packages

Magna Car Top Systems - roof systems
- Soft tops
- Removable roof systems
- Retractable hard tops
- Sliding roof systems

Magna Closures - closure systems
- Door modules
- Driver controls
- Handle assemblies
- Power closures and latching systems
- Window systems

Magna E-Car Systems
- Battery cells and packs
- Hybrid and electric vehicle development and production

Magna Electronics - electronic systems
- Body electronics
- Driver assistance and safety systems
- Engine electronics
- Intelligent power systems
- Lighting systems
- Liquid sensors

Magna Mirrors - vision systems
- Actuators
- Electronic vision systems
- Exterior and interior mirrors

Magna Powertrain - powertrain systems
- Automatic overdrives
- Die castings
- Differentials
- Engine systems
- Fluid pressure and controls
- Power take-offs
- Stampings
- Transaxles
- Transfer cases
- Transmission systems

Magna Seating - seating systems
- Seat mechanism systems
- Seating systems

Magna Steyr - complete vehicle manufacturing and OEM engineering
- Energy storing systems
- Fuel systems

COMPETITORS

A.G. Simpson
Aisin Seiki
American Axle & Manufacturing
Benteler Automotive
BorgWarner
Calsonic Kansei
Commercial Vehicle
DENSO
DURA Automotive
Dana Holding
Delphi Automotive Systems
Eaton
Faurecia
Ficosa
GKN
Gentex
Haldex
Hella
Johnson Controls
KUO
Lacks Enterprises
Lear Corp
Linamar Corp.
Meritor
Plastic Omnium
Prodrive
Robert Bosch
Tenneco
Textron
Torotrak
Tower International
Toyota Auto Body
Valeo
Visteon
ZF Friedrichshafen

HISTORICAL FINANCIALS

Company Type: Public

Income Statement

FYE: December 31

	REVENUE ($ mil.)	NET INCOME ($ mil.)	NET PROFIT MARGIN	EMPLOYEES
12/12	30,837	1,433	4.6%	119,000
12/11	28,748	1,018	3.5%	108,275
12/10	24,102	973	4.0%	96,600
12/09	17,367	(493)	—	72,500
12/08	23,704	71	0.3%	0
Annual Growth	6.8%	112.0%	—	—

2012 Year-End Financials

Debt ratio: 2.5%
Return on equity: 16.2%
Cash ($ mil.): 1,522
Current ratio: 1.37
Long-term debt ($ mil.): 112
No. of shares (mil.): 233
Dividends
Yield: 2.2%
Payout: 18.6%
Market value ($ mil.): 11,662

	STOCK PRICE ($) FY Close	P/E High	P/E Low	PER SHARE ($) Earnings	Dividends	Book Value
12/12	50.02	8	5	6.09	1.10	40.44
12/11	33.31	14	7	4.20	1.00	35.04
12/10	52.00	24	11	4.18	0.42	33.25
12/09	50.58	—	—	(2.21)	0.36	32.66
12/08	29.93	259	75	0.31	0.63	32.69
Annual Growth	13.7%	—	—	110.5%	15.0%	5.5%

Malayan Banking Berhad

Malaysia's largest bank Malayan Banking Berhad (better known as Maybank) and its subsidiaries operate some 500 branches mostly in Malaysia but also in Singapore Indonesia the Philippines and elsewhere throughout Southeast Asia. Its core services consist of deposits mortgages and other loans and credit cards to individuals and businesses. Other offerings include investment banking asset management online banking brokerage insurance unit trusts and other investments and corporate finance. Amanah Raya a trust company controlled by the Malaysian government owns more than 45% of Maybank.

Maybank called off plans to pursue the acquisition of fellow Malaysian lender RHB Capital in mid-2011. The company was vying along with rival CIMB for a merger with RHB Capital but both companies called off talks within weeks. Competition among the Malaysian banks became heated after another rival Hong Leong Bank acquired Eon Capital.

One of Maybank's fastest growing segments is banking services and Takaful (insurance) that adhere to Islamic law which prohibits the collection of interest but allows profit-sharing and the sale and buy-back of homes (instead of the origination of mortgages). Serving Muslim individuals organizations and businesses the company is opening branches at home and abroad that offer such services.

Maybank has also targeted Indonesia as a growth market. The bank completed its acquisition of the 250-branch Bank Internasional Indonesia (BII) in 2008. The deal had stalled when banking regulator Bank Negara Malaysia prohibited the transaction but that decision was reversed and the acquisition was ultimately allowed. Maybank plans to add 200 new branches to BII's network by 2013.

The company has made other moves to expand its international presence. It acquired minority stakes in Pakistan's MCB Bank and Vietnam's An Binh Bank (ABBank) in 2008; it also bought Kookmin Bank's minority stake in PT Bank International Indonesia. In 2011 the company acquired 100% of Singapore brokerage Kim Eng Holdings. The addition boosts Maybank's international profile and expands its distribution capabilities.

EXECUTIVES

President Chief Executive Officer, George Martirez
President & CEO, Abdul Farid Alias
President; Chief Executive Officer; Non-Independent Executive Director, Abdul Abdul Wahid bin Omar Omar
Acting President Director - PT Bank Internasional Indonesia Tbk, Bapak Bapak Alimhamzah Alimhamzah
Head - Enterprise Transformation Services, Geoffrey Geoffrey Stecyk Stecyk
Head - Insurance & Takaful; Chief Executive Officer - Mayban Ageas Holdings Berhad, Hans Hans De Cuyper Cuyper
Group Chief Risk Officer, Hin Hin Hock Lee Lee
Independent & Non-Executive Director, Johan Johan bin Ariffin Ariffin
Chairman, Megat Zaharuddin Megat Mohd Nor
General Counsel; Company Secretary; Head of Corporate & Legal Services, Mohd Mohd Nazlan bin Mohd Ghazali Ghazali
Independent Non-Executive Vice Chairman of the Board, Mohd Mohd Salleh bin Harun Harun
Head Islamic Banking; Chief Executive Officer Maybank Islamic Berhad, Muzaffar Hisham
Head - Group Human Capital, Nora Nora Abd Manaf Manaf
Chief Strategy & Transformation Officer, Seong Seong Yew Foong Foong
Chief Executive Officer - Maybank Singapore, Sim Sio Hoong
Head - Investment Banking; Chief Executive Officer - Maybank Investment Bank Bhd, Zafrul Zafrul Abd Aziz Aziz
CFO, Mohamed Merican
Deputy President & Head Community Financial Services, Lim Hong Tat
Chief Executive Officer Etiqa, Kamaludin Ahmad
Director, Spencer Lee Tien Chye
Director, Datuk Syed Tamin Syed Mohamed
President CEO and Director, Abdul Wahid bin Omar, age 48
Director, Wai Tan Tat, age 66
Director, Ismail Shahudin, age 62
Director, Hadenan Jalil, age 67
Director, Abidin Jamal Zainal
Independent Non-Executive Director, Alister Alister Maitland Maitland
Independent Non-Executive Director, Erry Erry Riyana Hardjapamekas Hardjapamekas
Independent Non-Executive Director, Mohaiyani Mohaiyani binti Shamsudin Shamsudin
Independent Non-Executive Director, Tat Tat Wai Tan Tan
Independent Non-Executive Director, Teik Teik Seng Cheah Cheah
Non-Independent Non-Executive Director, Zainal Zainal Abidin bin Jamal Jamal
Auditors: Ernst&Young

LOCATIONS

HQ: Malayan Banking Berhad
14th Floor, Menara Maybank, 100, Jalan Tun Perak, Kuala Lumpur 50050
Phone: (60) 3 2070 8833 **Fax:** (60) 3 2032 4775
Web: www.maybank.com

COMPETITORS

AmBank Group
Bank Muamalat
Bank of China
Bank of East Asia
Hang Seng Bank
Hong Leong Bank
Malaysian Industrial Development Finance
OCBC Bank
Public Bank
RHB Capital
Standard Chartered

HISTORICAL FINANCIALS

Company Type: Public

Income Statement FYE: December 31

	ASSETS ($ mil.)	NET INCOME ($ mil.)	INCOME AS % OF ASSETS	EMPLOYEES
12/12	161,627	1,876	1.2%	47,233
12/11*	142,407	815	0.6%	45,000
06/11	136,387	1,473	1.1%	42,000
06/10	103,108	1,169	1.1%	40,000
06/09	88,414	196	0.2%	39,684
Annual Growth	16.3%	75.7%	—	4.4%

*Fiscal year change

2012 Year-End Financials

Return on assets: 1.2%
Return on equity: 15.1%
Long-term debt ($ mil.): —
No. of shares (mil.): —
Sales ($ mil): 7,551
Dividends
Yield: 6.8%
Payout: 12.8%
Market value ($ mil.): —

	STOCK PRICE ($) FY Close	P/E High	P/E Low	PER SHARE ($) Earnings	Dividends	Book Value
12/12	6.11	1	1	0.24	0.42	1.63
12/11*	5.65	2	1	0.11	0.03	1.38
06/11	5.60	1	1	0.20	0.31	1.39
06/10	4.00	2	0	0.17	0.01	1.21
06/09	3.25	3	1	0.03	0.31	1.00
Annual Growth	17.1%	—	—	62.4%	8.0%	13.0%

*Fiscal year change

Man SE

This venerable old MAN still shows all the right moves. For more than 250 years MAN SE and its subsidiaries have manufactured transport- and energy-related equipment from trucks and buses to diesel engines for ships. MAN Nutzfahrzeuge is one of Europe's largest truck and commercial vehicle makers as well as a giant supplier of vehicle boat and power generation engines. MAN Diesel & Turbo makes a variety of compressors expanders and gas and steam turbines as well as leads the world market for shipboard diesel engines and is second in stationary engines. It also provides parts and service. Although MAN's reach is global Europe accounts for over 60% of sales. Volkswagen (VW) owns more than 30% of MAN.

Once VW secured a majority stake in MAN in mid-2011 a mandatory takeover bid was triggered which is in accordance with Germany's takeover rules. The share register indicates that VW has grasped voting stock in excess of 50%. The majority stake was made possible when MAN's share price temporarily fell below VW's offer price. VW values MAN at approximately ?13.7 billion (almost $20 billion).

Management shake-ups and scandal have rattled MAN SE as of late. CEO Hakan Samuelsson resigned unexpectedly in late 2009. Although the company has been the subject of an internal corruption probe there were no allegations made against Samuelsson who had served as CEO since 2005. Bribery charges were subsequently filed against former head of the MAN Turbo unit Heinz Juergen Maus. Georg Pachta-Reyhofen who had previously served as head of MAN Diesel replaced Samuelsson. Some industry insiders have speculated that Samuelsson's leaving was due to VW's desire to create a truck alliance between MAN SE and Sweden-based Scania. Samuelsson however was opposed to the integration of Scania and MAN SE. VW made it known in early 2011 that it would seek the remaining shares of MAN.

Like many industrial manufacturers MAN is looking for ways to streamline its operations. Beginning in 2010 MAN Diesel's operations merged with those of MAN Turbo to create MAN Diesel & Turbo. Together their products offer an impressive portfolio of large-bore diesel engines compressors and turbines. The merger also reduces the manufacturing and overhead costs of MAN's Power Engineering business by combining complementary operations. Moreover MAN Diesel ranked as the only provider of diesel engines for both marine propulsion and power plants. MAN Turbo was among the world's largest makers of thermal turbo-machines. Its slate of products and services from design to manufacture and assembly fueled MAN SE's reach into more than 120 countries.

MAN's commercial vehicle business segment (MAN Nutzfahrzeuge and MAN Latin America) which accounts for about 65% of group revenues is countering the weak economy by expanding into developing regions. In fall 2009 it acquired a 25% stake in China-based Sinotruk a state-owned truck maker which MAN will use to produce a new series of heavy trucks. Through the $800 million partnership MAN will license engine chassis axles and other technologies to Sinotruk which will manufacture the series at its plants in China. MAN also stepped up its efforts in Latin America. In 2009 it bought blue chip brand VW Truck & Bus VW's vehicle manufacturing operations in Brazil. MAN increased its stake to 50% in an India-based joint venture with Force Motors Ltd. in 2008 as well.

Domestically MAN raised its stake in EURO-Leasing GmbH to approximately 50% in 2009 snatching up majority control in the truck leasing company. The deal widens MAN Nutzfahrzeuge's access to the truck rental market and provides synergies in repair sales and after-sales service for used trucks and trailers. EURO-Leasing operates a fleet of about 2600 trailers and 8000 semitrailers. At the same time the company is streamlining non-core operations. MAN sold its 70% stake in industrial services group MAN Ferrostaal to International Petroleum Investment Co. a state-owned United Arab Emirates company. Negotiations to buy the remaining 30% broke down in 2011 after a bribery investigation involving Ferrostaal when it was still owed by MAN.

HISTORY

MAN grew out of a company started by Carl August Reichenbach and Carl Buz who leased an engineering plant in Augsburg Germany in 1844. Reichenbach whose uncle had invented the flatbed printing press began producing printing presses in 1845. On the same premises Buz began manufacturing steam engines and industrial drive systems and he soon added rotary printing presses water turbines pumps and diesel engines. In 1898 the company took the name MAN (Maschinenfabrik Augsburg-Nurnberg) after merging with a German engineering company of the same name.

Another German heavy-industry company Gutehoffnungshutte Aktienverein AG (GHH with roots stretching to 1758) bought a majority interest in MAN in 1921. Through acquisitions and internal growth MAN emerged from the world wars as one of Germany's major heavy-industry companies with added interests in commercial vehicles shipbuilding and plant construction. By 1955 MAN's commercial vehicles were a major division destined to dominate the company's sales; MAN moved the division's headquarters to Munich that year.

During the 1970s an overseas recession caused the sales of some operations to slump although MAN's commercial vehicles and printing-equipment businesses held steady. When economic hardship reached Europe in the 1980s MAN sought markets outside its home region especially targeting Asia the Middle East and the US. Late in the decade the company dropped its less-profitable products (lifts pumps heavy cranes) and began licensing more of its technology and subcontracting out more work. MAN moved its corporate headquarters to Munich in 1985 and merged with GHH in 1986.

After a fast start in the 1990s Europe's economy again faltered taking a toll on the company's sales. MAN's profits slumped in fiscal 1994. It laid off about 10% of its workforce between 1993 and 1995. As the economy recovered so did MAN and by fiscal 1998 its stagnant profits had rebounded.

Early in 2000 MAN purchased truck makers ERF Holdings (UK) and STAR (Poland). Later that year MAN picked up ALSTOM's diesel engine business. MAN acquired the Neoplan bus-making business of Gottlob Auwarter GmbH in 2001 as well as the turbomachinery business of Switzerland's Sulzer. After discovering accounting irregularities that year the company suspended the CEO (John Bryant) and CFO (Klaus Wagner) of the newly acquired ERF. In 2002 the company began implementing its Truck Generation A (TG-A) technology into all of its commercial vehicles. In 2003 MAN sold its 51% stake in SMS AG.

In 2005 the MAN Group sold off its MAN Wolffkran subsidiary to private investors. The business sold and rented tower cranes a.k.a. cherry pickers for the building industry; the sale was part of the company's effort to pare down its operations to what are considered to be its core divisions. MAN also restructured its financial services division to prepare it for expansion; the company was renamed MAN Finance International financing activities in seven countries including France Germany Italy and Spain.

In 2006 MAN sold MAN TAKRAF Fordertechnik to Germany's VTC Industrieholding. TAKRAF Fordertechnik acquired by MAN in 1994 built equipment systems and complete facilities for open-pit mining harbor and crane technology and bulk cargo handling.

Also that year the company sold MAN Roland Druckmaschinen its printing press business to a new venture put together by Allianz Capital Partners for ?624 million (about $790 million). MAN kept a 35% equity stake in the business following the transaction.

EXECUTIVES

Deputy Chairman Supervisory Board, Ekkehard D. Schulz, age 72
Chairman Supervisory Board, Ferdinand K. Piech, age 75
Chief Executive Officer, Georg Pachta-Reyhofen, age 58
Chief Human Resources Officer and Member Management Board, Jorg Schwitalla, age 52
Member Management Board; President MAN Latin America, Antonio R. Cortes, age 58
Deputy Chairman Supervisory Board, Thomas Otto
VP Investor Relations, Silke Glitza-Stamberger
Manager Investor Relations, Florian Feick
CEO MAN Diesel & Turbo SE, Rene Umlauft, age 48

Chief Procurement Officer, Ulf Berkenhagen
CFO and Member Management Board, Frank H. Lutz
General Counsel, Wolfgang Betz
Head Corporate Communications, Andreas Lampersbach
Manager Public Relations, Stefan Straub
Chief Human Resources Officer, Jochen Schumm
Deputy Chairman Supervisory Board, Ekkehard D. Schulz, age 72
Member Supervisory Board, Rudolf Rupprecht, age 74
Member Supervisory Board, Heiner Hasford
Member Supervisory Board, Rupert Stadler, age 50
Deputy Chairman Supervisory Board, Thomas Otto
Member Supervisory Board, Michael Behrendt
Member Supervisory Board, Marek Berdychowski
Member Supervisory Board, Detlef Dirks
Member Supervisory Board, Jurgen Dorn
Member Supervisory Board, Jurgen Kerner
Member Supervisory Board, Renate Kocher
Member Supervisory Board, Gerhard Kreutzer
Member Supervisory Board, Nicola Lopopolo
Member Supervisory Board, Erich Schwarz
Member Supervisory Board, Ulf Berkenhagen
Auditors: KPMGAGWirtschaftsprufungsgesellschaft

LOCATIONS

HQ: Man SE
Ungererstrasse 69, Munich 80805
Phone: (49) 89 36098 111 **Fax:** (49) 89 36098 382
Web: www.man.eu

2009 Sales

	% of total
Europe	
Germany	23
Other European	32
Other	7
America	16
Asia	16
Africa	5
Australia &	1
Total	**100**

PRODUCTS/OPERATIONS

2009 Sales

	% of total
Commercial vehicles	
MAN	53
MAN Latin	12
MAN	20
MAN	12
Other	3
Total	**100**

Selected Operating Units

MAN Nutzfahrzeuge (commercial vehicles produced in Europe)
MAN Latin America (commercial vehicles produced in South America)
MAN Diesel & Turbo (large-bore diesel engines and turbomachinery for marine and stationary applications)
RENK AG (76%; transmissions slide bearings flexible couplings and industrial and marine gears)

COMPETITORS

ALSTOM
Baldwin Technology
China Yuchai
Cummins
DEUTZ
Daimler
Dana Holding
Dresser-Rand
Federal-Mogul
GE Energy
GEA Group
Goss International
Hanjin Heavy Industries & Construction
Heidelberger Druckmaschinen
ITT Corp.
Kawasaki Heavy Industries
Koenig & Bauer
Meritor
Mitsubishi Heavy Industries
Navistar International
PACCAR
Renault
Scania
Siemens AG
Sumitomo Heavy Industries
TUI
Voith
Volvo

HISTORICAL FINANCIALS

Company Type: Public

Income Statement

FYE: December 31

	REVENUE ($ mil.)	NET INCOME ($ mil.)	NET PROFIT MARGIN	EMPLOYEES
12/12	20,788	233	1.1%	52,481
12/11	21,305	307	1.4%	50,178
12/10	19,640	954	4.9%	45,693
12/09	17,324	(388)	—	47,743
12/08	20,894	1,723	8.3%	51,329
Annual Growth	(0.1%)	(39.3%)	—	0.6%

2012 Year-End Financials

Debt ratio: 35.0%
Return on equity: 3.1%
Cash ($ mil.): 1,800
Current ratio: 1.02
Long-term debt ($ mil.): 3,909
No. of shares (mil.): 140
Dividends
Yield: 3.7%
Payout: 22.1%
Market value ($ mil.): 1,494

	STOCK PRICE ($) FY Close	P/E High	P/E Low	PER SHARE ($) Earnings	Dividends	Book Value
12/12	10.60	20	12	1.58	0.40	51.89
12/11	8.79	17	7	2.10	0.35	50.72
12/10	11.85	5	2	6.49	0.02	56.34
12/09	7.78	—	—	(2.65)	0.00	51.90
Annual Growth	10.9%	—	—	—	—	(0.0%)

Manulife Financial Corp.

Manulife the holding company for The Manufacturers Life Insurance Company and John Hancock Financial Services has gone mano a mano with its competitors. Manulife provides individual life insurance group life and health group pension products variable annuities wealth management and financial products in nearly two dozen countries and territories worldwide. North America and Asia make up its largest operations. Manulife's reinsurance division provides life health and accident reinsurance and was one of North America's top life retrocessionaires (firms that reinsure reinsurers) until it sold that division in 2011. The company also provides investment management real estate and lending services.

Geographic Reach

Sales in the US still make up about a third of Manulife's annual revenue (though the market there has shrunk in response to the flagging economy); Canada and Asia each account for about 30% of Manulife's premium income. Its efforts to grow in China through partnerships have paid off with the company's sales there challenging those in Canada (formerly its second-largest market after the US).

Operations

Along with its John Hancock subsidiary Manulife is one of the top five life insurers in North America and is a top 10 global life insurer based on market capitalization. North American financial products are offered primarily under the John Hancock brand while life insurance is offered through Manufacturers Life. Other brands and subsidiaries include Portland Investment Counsel (mutual funds retail investment funds) and Pottruff & Smith (travel insurance).

Strategy

Besides building up its more successful offerings and divesting those with higher risks Manulife's strategy for growth includes maintaining a diversified mix and hedging its in-force public equity and interest rate risks over time. The company's objective is to increase its earnings to $4 billion by 2015.

Manulife also grows through collaborations such as its partnership with Edward Jones which helped the company expand its sales network in the US and add agents to increase its distribution presence in Asia. Its Manulife-Sinochem (MSL) partnership with Sinochem has also allowed the company to deepen its reach in China. With operations in 50 Chinese cities MSL has the broadest geographic footprint of any foreign invested joint venture firm in that country. Manulife also has a 49% interest in ABN AMRO TEDA Fund Management in China. The Manulife-TEDA partnership allows the company to expand in China's wealth management market.

Further expansion in China is in the company's plans as is increasing sales of wealth management products. In 2012 for example Manulife Asset Management procured licensure to provide institutional asset management services in Korea's fast-growing market.

Mergers and Acquisitions

Manulife continues to invest in acquisitions in the near-term specifically as they relate to bolstering its mutual fund business as that is an area Manulife is making great effort to grow. To that end it purchased Wellington West Financial Services from National Bank Financial Group in 2012 for an undisclosed price adding about 40 advisors and some $900 in assets under management to its Canadian investment unit (Manulife Securities) in the deal.

In 2013 Manulife expanded in Canada's mortgage creditor insurance market through the purchase of Benesure Canada. Benesure provides distribution and third-party administration of life and disability creditor policies to mortgage brokerage entities.

In 2011 Manulife continued to diversify and grow different arms of its business. Its global real estate arm Manulife Real Estate made acquisitions valued at $555 million in the key markets of metropolitan New York San Diego and Toronto bringing its total real estate assets to C$7.5 billion ($7.3 billion). This unit is also expanding its multi-family residential holdings having recently acquired properties in New Brunswick New Jersey and Alexandria Virginia.

Manulife sold its life retrocession business to Pacific Life Insurance in 2011 because it didn't align with the firm's future growth strategy of focusing on its other insurance offerings: individual and group life health and group pension. Additionally Manulife wanted to avoid the more restrictive Canadian regulatory requirements for the life retrocession business.

Company Background

Manulife acquired US financial services giant John Hancock in a $10 billion deal in 2004 bringing Manulife into the top ranks of US and global life insurers. Manulife subsequently rebranded its US financial products with the more-recognizable John Hancock name and logo. Manulife also consolidated John Hancock's Canadian subsidiary Maritime Life Assurance Company into its flagship subsidiary The Manufacturers Life Insurance Company.

EXECUTIVES

Vice Chairman, Richard B. DeWolfe, age 69
President; Chief Executive Officer; Director, Donald A. Guloien, $738,340 total compensation
Senior Executive Vice President and General Manager; Asia, Robert A. (Bob) Cook
EVP Individual Wealth Management Canadian Division; Chairman and CEO Elliott and Page Limited, J. Roy Firth
EVP and Chief Strategy Officer, Beverly S. Margolian
Chairman, Gail C. A. Cook-Bennett, age 72
President and CEO Manulife Canada, Paul L. Rooney
SEVP and Chief Investment Officer; Chairman Manulife Asset Management, Warren A. Thomson, age 58
SEVP Corporate Development and General Counsel, Jean-Paul (J-P.) Bisnaire
SEVP and General Manager Canadian Division, Marianne Harrison
President and CEO Indonesia, Alan Merten
Media Relations Canada, Tom Nunn
Public Affairs Corporate, Laurie Lupton
President John Hancock Financial Services, Craig Bromley
EVP General Account Investments, Scott Hartz
Public Affairs Corporate, David Paterson
Media Relations Canada, Jasmine Mangalaseril
Corporate Communications John Hancock Financial, Roy Anderson
Corporate Communications John Hancock Financial, Leslie Uyeda
Media Relations Asia, Juliana Gittler
Media Relations Manulife-Sinochem Life Insurance Co. Ltd. (China), Lillian Li
Director Marketing and Communications PT Asuransi Jiwa Manulife Indonesia, Kumala D. Ruslie
Media Relations Hong Kong, Helena Lee
Media Relations Hong Kong, Lily Chan
Media Relations Manulife Insurance (Malaysia) Berhad, Susan Ong
Media Relations The Manufacturers Life Insurance Co. (Philippines), Lils Liwanag
Media Relations Manulife (Singapore) Pte Ltd., Cindy Cheng
Media Relations Manulife (International) Limited Taiwan Branch, Suzanne Lee
Media Relations Manulife (Vietnam) Limited, Hang Luu
Communications Japan, Minoru Shimizu
Media Relations Real Estate Division Canada, Tina Acranis
Media Relations MFC Global Investment Management, Brian Carmichael
VP and Head Agency Sales Hong Kong, Kareen Chow
VP and CFO Hong Kong, Nigel Ke
Senior Vice President, Paul Lorentz
President CEO, Doug Conick
Manager Sales Midwest John Hancock Retirement Plan Services (RPS), Cheney L. Hunt III
Head Fixed Income Manulife Asset Management (Singapore), Pang Cheng Duan
President and CEO Singapore, Annette King
Head Institutional Sales North Asia, Edwina Ho
EVP Human Resources and Communications, Stephani E. Kingsmill
Chief Actuary; Executive Vice President, Cindy Forbes
Assistant VP and Head Sales and Marketing Employee Benefits Sales Manulife (International) Limited, Doris Chan
EVP and Chief Risk Officer, Rahim Hirji
SEVP and CFO, Steve Roder
COO, Paul L. Rooney
Director, Thomas E. (Tom) Kierans, age 72
Director, Scott M. Hand, age 71
Vice Chairman, Richard B. DeWolfe, age 69
President CEO and Director, Donald A. Guloien
Director, Lino J. Celeste, age 74
Director, John M. Cassaday, age 60
Director, Pierre Y. Ducros, age 72
Director, Hugh W. Sloan Jr., age 72
Director, Lorna R. Marsden, age 71
Director, Robert J. (Bob) Harding, age 55
Director, Donald R. (Don) Lindsay, age 55
Director, Linda B. Bammann
Director, Robert E. Dineen Jr., age 72
Director, Gordon G. Thiessen, age 73
Director, Thomas P. d'Aquino, age 72
Director, Luther S. Helms
Director, John R. V. Palmer
Director, Joseph P. Caron
Director, Tsun-yan Hsieh
Director, Andrea Rosen
Director, Sheila Fraser
Auditors: Ernst&YoungLLP

LOCATIONS

HQ: Manulife Financial Corp.
200 Bloor Street East, North Tower 10, Toronto, Ontario M4W 1E5
Phone: 416 926-3427 **Fax:** 416 926-5657
Web: www.manulife.com

2010 Revenues

US	32	
Canada	30	
Total	**0**	**100**

PRODUCTS/OPERATIONS

2010 Revenues

Premiums	
Annuities & pensions	12
Other	17

Selected Subsidiaries & Affiliates

Elliott & Page Limited
FNA Financial Inc.
John Hancock Financial Network Inc. (US)
John Hancock Financial Services Inc. (US)
John Hancock Investment Management Services LLC (US)
John Hancock Life Insurance Company (U.S.A.)
John Hancock Life Insurance Company of New York
Manulife International Holdings Limited (Bermuda)
Manulife (Singapore) Pte. Ltd.
Manulife (Vietnam) Limited
Manulife Bank of Canada
Manulife Life Insurance Company (Japan)
Manulife Sinochem Life Insurance Co. Ltd. (China)
NAL Resources Management Limited
P.T. Asuransi Jiwa Manulife Indonesia
The Manufacturers Investment Corporation (US)
The Manufacturers Life Insurance Co. (Philippines) Inc.
The Manufacturers Life Insurance Company

COMPETITORS

AEGON
AIG
Allianz
Canada Life
China Life Insurance
Dai-ichi Life
Fairfax Financial Holdings
Generali
Great-West Lifeco
ING
Industrial Alliance Insurance and Financial Servic
Liberty Mutual
Meiji Yasuda Life
MetLife
Nationwide
New York Life
Nippon Life Insurance
Power Financial
Principal Financial
Prudential
Sun Life
Swiss Re
T&D Holdings
The Hartford
Tokio Marine

HISTORICAL FINANCIALS

Company Type: Public

Income Statement FYE: December 31

	ASSETS ($ mil.)	NET INCOME ($ mil.)	INCOME AS % OF ASSETS	EMPLOYEES
12/12	488,707	1,745	0.4%	28,000
12/11	452,995	126	0.0%	26,000
12/10	425,672	(1,666)	—	25,000
12/09	195,669	1,354	0.7%	24,000
12/08	171,942	404	0.2%	24,000
Annual Growth	29.8%	44.1%	—	3.9%

	STOCK PRICE ($) FY Close	P/E High/Low		PER SHARE ($) Earnings	Dividends	Book Value
12/12	13.59	16	11	0.88	0.52	14.08
12/11	10.62	962467		0.02	0.51	13.32
12/10	17.18	—	—	(0.99)	0.51	13.68
12/09	18.34	27	6	0.78	0.67	15.68
12/08	17.03	106	28	0.26	0.94	13.89
Annual Growth	(5.5%)	—	—	35.7%	(13.7%)	0.3%

Mapfre SA

To whom do you turn when your vehicle intersects with the "Running of the Bulls?" Through its subsidiaries MAPFRE provides customers with property/casualty (especially auto) coverage life insurance and reinsurance. The firm does business primarily in its home country of Spain where it is a top insurer and in about 45 other nations including many in North and South America. Individual and group offerings include funeral home medical and agricultural insurance. It additionally provides financial services such as investment and pension funds. MAPFRE also maintains a very successful alliance with Spanish banking company Caja Madrid through which the companies cross-market each other's products.

Geographic Reach

MAPFRE operates a network of 15000 branches half of which are located in Spain. Of the international locations about 2000 offices are located in Latin American countries. International operations account for about 60% of MAPFRE's annual revenues.

Operations

MAPFRE conducts its operations through about 240 subsidiaries. The group's activities are divided into four segments: life direct motor direct other non-life direct and reinsurance and other activities.

Sales and Marketing

MAPFRE's products are primarily marketed through distribution agreements with third parties especially banks; it also has direct sales operations in Spain. The company has relationships with some 9700 bank branches and other retail outlets. MAPFRE and Caja Madrid run CCM Vida Y Pensiones a 50/50 joint venture to develop and sell life and pension insurance at the bank and banking products through insurance agents. The company also markets products through a network of 70000 agents and brokers in the Americas.

Financial Performance

MAPFRE achieved 15% revenue growth and doubled net income in 2011. Progress was attributed to its diversification activities and strong returns from the international direct insurance and reinsurance operations. Efforts to strengthen the distribution network in Spain also led to stabilization of sales in the domestic auto life and homeowner's insurance markets. The company has also attributed growth to its prudent financing and investment strategies. MAPFRE has reported increased revenues each year since 2007.

Strategy

MAPFRE is focused on expanding its operations through geographic diversification and continued acquisitions in high-growth markets are key to MAPFRE's expansion plans as domestic markets contract. In South America it has moved to become one of the largest non-life insurers in countries including Brazil and Argentina. The company has a partnership with Banco do Brazil to collaborate on the marketing of property insurance in the Brazilian market. Other areas of expansion have included the emerging markets of India Panama and Ecuador.

North America has been another area of focus for MAPFRE's international expansion strategy. Its MAPFRE U.S.A. unit sells car insurance in Massachusetts and more than a dozen other states.

To increase efficiencies and streamline operations in 2011 the company reorganized its domestic distribution network to focus on retail and corporate customers. It is also revamping its international sales networks to maximize returns.

To increase direct sales in Spain the company launched its VERTI internet and phone sales organization in 2011 for home and auto insurance products. MAPFRE also formed a joint venture with Euler Hermes to market credit and surety products in Spain Portugal and Latin America in 2011.

EXECUTIVES

Secretary, Jose Manuel Gonzalez Porro
Vice Chairman, Filomeno Mira Candel
Chairman and CEO, Jose Manuel Martinez Martinez
Secretary, Jose Manuel Gonzalez Porro
Vice Chairman, Filomeno Mira Candel
Auditors: Ernst&YoungS.L.

LOCATIONS

HQ: Mapfre SA
Paseo de Recoletos, 25, Madrid 28004
Phone: (34) 91 581 1100 **Fax:** (34) 91 581 1143
Web: www.mapfre.es

PRODUCTS/OPERATIONS

2011 Sales

	% of total
International	60
Spain	
Life	19
Non-life	18
Commercial	3
Total	**100**

COMPETITORS

AEGON
AXA
Allianz
Allstate
Arbella Insurance
BUPA
Banco Popular Espa?ol
Catalana Occidente
El Corte Ingles
GEICO
Generali
Grupo Santander
ING
Markel International
Munich Re Group
Progressive Corporation
Safety Insurance
Triple-S Management

HISTORICAL FINANCIALS

Company Type: Public

Income Statement FYE: December 31

	ASSETS ($ mil.)	NET INCOME ($ mil.)	INCOME AS % OF ASSETS	EMPLOYEES
12/12	75,106	877	1.2%	34,962
12/11	70,953	1,245	1.8%	32,798
12/10	65,141	1,249	1.9%	35,704
12/09	62,096	1,335	2.2%	34,326
12/08	58,285	1,259	2.2%	32,927
Annual Growth	6.5%	(8.6%)	—	1.5%

Marks & Spencer Group PLC

The sun never sets on Marks and Spencer (M&S). The British retail icon operates about 345 M&S department stores and some 385 Simply Food shops throughout the UK. Beyond Britain it boasts about 385 locations mostly franchises in about 40 countries including China India Indonesia Russia and South Korea. Its department stores sell mid-priced apparel food and household items under the company's private label brands including Autograph Classic per una and Portfolio. About 90% of the company's sales are made in its home country where it is the #1 provider of womenswear lingerie and menswear. The retailer also sells goods online. M&S has been in business for more than 125 years.

While total group sales increased by just 2% in fiscal 2012 (ends March) vs. the prior year some of M&S's businesses outperformed others. Standouts included online sales (up 18%) international sales (up nearly 6%) and UK food sales (up a more modest 4%). By comparison sales of clothing and home goods in the UK declined by nearly 1%. Given the turbulent state of Britain's economy it's not surprising the retailer's international arm outperformed the domestic operation. (Priority markets for M&S include China India and the Middle East where it enjoyed double-digit sales growth in 2012.) The company's recent financial results are in line with its business strategy (adopted in 2009) to grow by focusing on increasing online sales and its international presence.

To that end M&S lured away the chief executive of rival Tesco PLC's online business to lead a #1 billion ($1.6 billion) Internet sales initiative. In mid-2011 Laura Wade-Gery joined M&S as executive director of the company's Multi-channel E-commerce division. M&S CEO Marc Bolland has said he aims to lift e-commerce sales from #400 million to #800 million to #1 billion by 2013-2014. Soon after Wade-Gery joined the business M&S launched its first international website in fall 2011 serving customers across France. The French-language e-commerce launch was followed by the opening in November of a shop on the Champs-Elysees in Paris that marked the retailer's return to France. (Two more stores are planned for Paris and M&S is looking for suitable sites for its Simply Food stores in the French capital.)

At home the growth story for M&S is its food business which is helping to sustain the company while the general merchandise business struggles. Indeed food now accounts for a greater share of the company's sales than general merchandise. In addition to fresh produce the stores also sell prepared foods such as its popular (and high-margin) ready-to-go meals. The company has more than 385 small Simply Food outlets around the UK located mainly on high streets or within railway stations and airports. M&S is scouting for locations to build larger supermarket-sized (up to 30000 square feet) Simply Food stores.

Its core womenswear business struggled in recent years losing sales to rival ASDA's George clothing line. Overall M&S has about an 12% share (by volume) of the UK clothing and footwear market and is the leading lingerie retailer in Britain with about 25% of the market. M&S has taken a number of steps to defend its UK apparel business. It has upgraded its women's Classic range and launched a petite line. The company has pared its menswear offering from eight brands to three (Autograph Blue Harbour and Collezione). The clothing retailer has also launched a new underwear collection for men and women. Building on the success of its per una clothing line M&S launched per una due (designed by high-street legend George Davies) an edgy clothing line targeted at women in their late teens to early 30s.

HISTORY

Fleeing anti-Semitic persecution in Russian Poland 19-year-old Michael Marks immigrated to England in 1882. Eventually settling in Leeds Marks eked out a meager existence as a traveling peddler until he opened a small stall at the town market in 1884. Because he spoke little English Marks laid out all of his merchandise and hung a sign that read "Don't Ask the Price It's a Penny" unaware at the time that self-service would eventually become the retailing standard. His methods were so successful that he had penny bazaars in five cities by 1890.

Finding himself unable to run the growing operation alone Marks established an equal partnership with Englishman Tom Spencer a cashier for a local distributor forming Marks and Spencer in 1894. By the turn of the century the company had 36 branches. Following the deaths of Spencer (1905) and Marks (1907) management of the company did not return to family hands until 1916 when Marks' 28-year-old son Simon became chairman.

Marks and Spencer broke with time-honored British retailing tradition in 1924 by eliminating wholesalers and establishing direct links with manufacturers. In 1926 the firm went public and two years later it launched its now famous St Michael brand. The company turned its attention to pruning unprofitable departments to concentrate on goods that had a rapid turnover. In 1931 the Marks & Spencer stores (M&S) introduced a food department that sold produce and canned goods.

The company sustained severe losses during WWII when bombing damaged approximately half of its stores. Marks and Spencer rebuilt and in 1964 Simon's brother-in-law Israel Sieff became chairman. The company expanded to North America a decade later by buying three Canadian chains: Peoples (general merchandise sold 1992) D'Allaird's (women's clothing sold 1996) and Walker's (clothing shops converted to M&S). Sieff's son Marcus Sieff became chairman in 1972. It opened its first store in Paris in 1975.

Derek Rayner replaced Marcus Sieff as chairman in 1984 becoming the first chairman hired from outside the Marks family since 1916. Under Rayner Marks and Spencer moved into financial services by launching a charge card in 1985. The company purchased US-based Kings Super Markets and Brooks Brothers (upscale clothing stores) in 1988. Rayner retired in 1991 and CEO Richard Greenbury became chairman. During the 1990s M&S opened new stores in Germany Hong Kong Hungary Spain and Turkey.

In 1997 it paid Littlewoods $323 million for 19 UK stores which it converted to M&S. Greenbury facing criticism that the company was too slow to expand and embrace new ideas was succeeded in 1999 as CEO by handpicked heir Peter Salsbury. That year continued poor sales led Marks and Spencer to cut 700 jobs close its 38 M&S stores in Canada and part ways with its clothing supplier of 30 years William Baird. In early 2000 Marks and Spencer dodged a takeover attempt by investor Philip Green. Chairman Luc Vandevelde took over as CEO in September when Salsbury resigned.

In spring 2001 Marks and Spencer announced a recovery plan to salvage its struggling M&S chain by selling off many of its global operations including its profitable US businesses (Brooks Brothers and Kings Super Markets). Unhappy with the company's direction and its departure from older values Marks and Spencer board members Sir David Sieff (the last remaining founder member) Sir Ralph Robins and Sir Michael Perry left the board in July 2001. Marks and Spencer sold Brooks Brothers to Retail Brand Alliance for $225 million (a loss from the $750 million the company paid for it in 1988) in November 2001 and nearly managed to sell its Kings Super Markets business to New York supermarket operator D'Agostino in July 2002 but the deal fell through later in the year due to a lack of financing.

Also in July 2002 Vandevelde –who is credited with masterminding the M&S turnaround –announced he would give up his role as CEO and hand the reins to managing director Roger Holmes. Vandevelde became the company's part-time chairman in January 2003.

In May 2004 both Vandevelde and Holmes left M&S. Stuart Rose formerly head of Arcadia was named CEO; non-executive board member Paul Myners was named interim chairman of the company. Prior to the shift in management billionaire entrepreneur Philip Green (who owns Arcadia and Bhs in the UK) confirmed that he would mount a takeover bid for the retail group. Ultimately Green's final proposal (the third he made for the retailer in a five week period) was rejected by the M&S board in July 2004. In October M&S bought the Per Una brand from designer George Davies for about #126 million and moved its head office from the old Baker Street location to Waterside House by the Grand Union Canal in London. In November Rose ousted more than a handful of company executives including Maurice Helfgott Mark McKeon Laurel Powers-Freeling Jean Tomlin Jack Paterson and 20-year veteran Alison Reed who stepped down as CFO in April 2005.

M&S relaunched its Home catalogue in early 2005. In February of that year the company announced the sale of its former Baker Street headquarters Michael House to real estate company London & Regional Properties for #115 million. M&S which is in a profit squeeze said it plans to used the proceeds for "general corporate purposes." In August M&S sold its Lifestore in Gateshead to Active Asset Investment Management for #43 million. In December M&S won a ruling by the European Court of Justice that resulted in the company receiving a #30 million tax windfall from the Treasury.

In April 2006 M&S completed the sale of its 26-store Kings Super Markets chain in the US for about $61.5 million. Lord Burns a former chairman of Abbey National took up the post of chairman in July 2006 after joining Marks and Spencer as deputy chairman in 2005. Burns succeeded interim chairman Paul Myners.

In 2007 M&S opened three stores in Taiwan. (Marks & Spencer Taiwan is 60%-owned by the British retailer and 40% by President Chain Store.) The following year M&S opened its first store on the mainland in Shanghai.

In June 2008 Lord Burns stepped down as chairman of the company and was succeeded by CEO Stuart Rose who became executive chairman. David Michels was appointed deputy chairman as well. Rose stepped down as CEO in May 2010 to make way for Marc Bolland thus decoupling the roles of chairman and chief executive at the firm.

EXECUTIVES

Executive Director Marketing & Business Development, Patrick Bousquet-Chavanne, age 55
Deputy Chairman, Sir David M. C. Michels, age 66
Director Communications and Investor Relations, Dominic Fry, age 52
CEO and Board Member, Marc J. (M. J.) Bolland, age 53
Executive Director Multi-Channel E-Commerce, Laura Wade-Gery, age 47
Executive Director General Merchandise and Board Member, Kate Bostock, age 56, $63,811 total compensation
Executive Director Marketing and Board Member, Steven (Steve) Sharp, age 62, $1,066,843 total compensation
Director Human Resources, Tanith Dodge
Executive Director Food, Steve Rowe
Chairman, Robert Swannell, age 62
Director Property, Clem Constantine
Director Information Technology and Logistics, Darrell Stein
Executive Director General Merchandise, John Dixon
Director Store Environment and Product Presentation, Nayna McIntosh, age 49
Group Secretary Head of Corporate Governance and Board Member, Amanda Mellor
IR Contact Officer, Majda Rainer
IR Contact Group Secretariat, Lesley Brownett
IR Contact Group Secretariat, Anthony Clarke
IR Contact Group Secretariat, Andrew Green
CFO, Alan Stewart, age 53
Director International, Jan Heere
Style Director, Belinda Belinda Earl Earl
Senior Independent Non-Executive Director, Jan Jan du Plessis Plessis
Executive Director - Multi-channel E-commerce; Director, Laura Laura Wade-Gery Wade-Gery
Corporate Director - Strategy Implementation and Business Development, Patrick Patrick Bousquet-Chavanne Bousquet-Chavanne
Director Supply Chain, Dirk Lembregts
Director Retail, Sacha Berendji
Vice President General Manager Aramis International, Estee Lauder
Board Member, Martha Lane Fox, age 40
Deputy Chairman, Sir David M. C. Michels, age 66
Board Member, Steven J. (Steve) Holliday, age 56
Board Member, Jan P. du Plessis, age 58
CEO and Board Member, Marc J. (M. J.) Bolland, age 53
Board Member, Jeremy Darroch, age 50
Board Member, Louise A.V.C. Patten, age 59
Executive Director General Merchandise and Board Member, Kate Bostock, age 56
Executive Director Marketing and Board Member, Steven (Steve) Sharp, age 62
Executive Director General Merchandise, John Dixon
Group Secretary Head of Corporate Governance and Board Member, Amanda Mellor
Independent Non-Executive Director, Manvinder Manvinder Banga Banga
Independent Non-Executive Director, Martha Martha Fox Fox
Independent Non-Executive Director, Miranda Miranda Curtis Curtis
Auditors: PricewaterhouseCoopersLLP

LOCATIONS

HQ: Marks & Spencer Group PLC
Waterside House, 35 North Wharf Road, London W2 1NW
Phone: (44) 20 7935 4422
Web: www.marksandspencer.com

2012 Sales

	% of total
UK	89
International	11
Total	**100**

2012 Stores

	No.
UK	731
International	
Rest of	157
Middle East & North	122
Asia	108
Total	**1,118**

PRODUCTS/OPERATIONS

2012 UK Stores

	No.
High	243
Simply Food	220
Simply Food (company	168
Outlet	47
Major	42
Premiere	11
Total	**731**

2012 Sales

	% of total
UK	
Food	47
General	42
International	11
Total	**100**

COMPETITORS

ASDA
Arcadia
Benetton
Berwin & Berwin
Burberry
Carrefour
Co-operative Group
Debenhams
Fortnum & Mason
Gap UK
H&M
Harrods
Harvey Nichols
House of Fraser
J Sainsbury
John Lewis
Kingfisher
Mothercare
NEXT plc
New Look
Pret A Manger
Primark
Shop Direct
T.K. Maxx
Tesco
Topshop
Zara

HISTORICAL FINANCIALS

Company Type: Public

Income Statement

FYE: March 31

	REVENUE ($ mil.)	NET INCOME ($ mil.)	NET PROFIT MARGIN	EMPLOYEES
03/13	15,236	709	4.7%	81,734
03/12*	15,918	822	5.2%	81,208
04/11	15,630	982	6.3%	78,169
04/10	14,503	800	5.5%	76,267
03/09	12,956	726	5.6%	77,864
Annual Growth	4.1%	(0.6%)	—	1.2%

*Fiscal year change

2013 Year-End Financials

Debt ratio: 45.9%
Return on equity: 17.6%
Cash ($ mil.): 293
Current ratio: 0.57
Long-term debt ($ mil.): 2,624
No. of shares (mil.): 1,613
Dividends
Yield: 0.0%
Payout: 268.5%
Market value ($ mil.): 19,092

	STOCK PRICE ($) FY Close	P/E High/Low	PER SHARE ($) Earnings	Dividends	Book Value
03/13	11.83	109 77	0.44	1.18	2.36
03/12*	12.06	107 71	0.52	1.30	2.78
04/11	10.83	90 55	0.62	1.09	2.71
04/10	11.37	101 59	0.50	1.10	2.08
03/09	7.48	140 38	0.46	2.03	1.89
Annual Growth	12.1%	— —	(1.2%)	(12.6%)	5.8%

*Fiscal year change

Marubeni Corp.

Marubeni's name combines the Japanese words for "circle" and "red" and Marubeni hopes the comprehensive range of products manufactured and traded by its circle of operating units will keep the company out of the red. One of Japan's largest "sogo shosha" (general trading companies) Marubeni has a broad range of operating segments: Chemicals; Energy; Finance Logistics & IT Business; Food; Forest Products; Lifestyle; Metals & Mineral Resources; Real Estate Development; Plant & Industrial Machinery; Power Projects & Infrastructure; and Transportation Machinery.

In 2011 the trading company simplified its reporting structure into four broad segments: Machinery (Plant & Industrial Machinery Power Projects & Infrastructure and Transportation Machinery); Resources (Energy and Metals & Mineral Resources); Materials (Chemicals Forest Products and General Merchandise); and Consumer Products (Finance Logistics & IT Business Food Lifestyle and Real Estate Development.)

Marubeni has hundreds of operating companies in 70 countries.

A recovering economy and a robust growth in commodity prices lifted Marubeni's revenues and income in 2012. In fiscal 2012 the company reported a 19% increase in revenues driven by a 17% jump in the volume of Marubeni's trading transactions especially from higher oil prices. Energy accounted for 29 % of total trading volume in 2012 and was 22% greater in actual volume than in 2011. Marubeni's higher overall revenues in 2012 outpaced increased expenses enabling the trading house to post a 26% jump in net income.

The group has been particularly active in Asia where its diversity has enabled it to develop local industries and to help build utility and industrial infrastructures such as telephone systems power plants and water systems. The company has championed international expansion since the mid-1990s but Japan's credit crunch and the Asian economic crisis have hurt the company's production and processing operations across Southeast Asia. Marubeni has been reducing debt controlling operating costs and investing in commodity trading natural resources projects and international power generation schemes.

Growing its commodity business in 2012 the company agreed to acquire US-based grain fertilizer and energy commodities distribution and natural gas network Gavilon for $3.6 billion.

Taking advantage of BP's need to raise cash in the wake of its Gulf of Mexico oil disaster in 2011 Marubeni bought four mature producing deepwater oil and gas fields in Gulf from BP for $650 million. In 2013 it also agreed to acquire a 49% stake in Williams Partners' floating production platform project for Tubular Bells Field in the Gulf of Mexico.

In 2011 Marubeni formed a joint venture with Supreme Energy and International Power to develop the Rantau Dedap geothermal project located in Sumatra. The 220 MW geothermal plant is part of the Indonesian government's long-term plan meet its country's needs with renewable power.

It also entered a new market that year airplane leasing with a deal with Deucalion Limited to set up a company in Singapore to invest into aircraft assets.

In 2011 the company announced a medium-term growth plan focusing on natural resources (primarily copper) infrastructure environmental products (especially water businesses) and essential living commodities (building up its grain position in China).

HISTORY

Marubeni's origins are closely linked to those of another leading Japanese trading company. ITOCHU founder Chubei Itoh set up Marubeni Shoten K. K. in 1858 as an outlet in Osaka for his textile trading business (originally C. Itoh & Co.). The symbol for the store was a circle ("maru") drawn around the Japanese word for red ("beni"). As C. Itoh's global operations expanded the Marubeni store served as headquarters.

Marubeni was split off from C. Itoh in 1921 to trade textiles although it soon expanded its operations to include industrial and consumer goods. To mobilize for WWII the Japanese government re-united Marubeni and C. Itoh in 1941 merging them with another trading company Kishimoto into a new entity Sanko Kabushiki Kaisha. In 1944 Sanko Daido Boeki and Kureha Spinning were ordered to consolidate into a larger entity to be called the Daiken Co. but the war ended before all operations were fully integrated.

Spun off from Daiken in 1949 Marubeni began trading internationally. It opened a New York office in 1951 and diversified into food metals and machinery. During the Korean War Marubeni benefited from the UN's use of Japan as a supply base.

In 1955 Marubeni merged with Iida & Company and changed its name to Marubeni-Iida. It received a government concession to supply silicon steel and iron sheets critical to the growing Japanese auto and appliance industries. The company expanded into engineering –building factories aircraft and a nuclear reactor for the Japan Atomic Energy Research Institute –and into petrochemicals fertilizers and rubber products.

Marubeni-Iida was behind the Fuyo "keiretsu" formed in the early 1960s. Fuyo (another word for Mt. Fuji) is a powerful assemblage of some 150 companies including Canon Hitachi and Nissan that form joint ventures and develop think tanks.

The firm became Marubeni Corp. in 1972 and a year later it bought Nanyo Bussan another trading company. In 1973 Marubeni's image was tarnished by allegations that it had hoarded rice for sale on the Japanese black market.

In the 1990s Marubeni won several major construction contracts. Among them Marubeni formed a venture in 1998 with John Laing and Turkey's Alarko Alsim to rebuild three airports in Uzbekistan.

Marubeni had begun offering Internet access in 1995 and two years later it launched an Internet-based long-distance telephone service. In 1999 the trading house formed two ventures with US firm Global Crossing one to start operating Pacific Crossing One (the Japan-US cable) and another to lay a cable network in Japan.

That year Marubeni tied up with fellow trading company ITOCHU to integrate their steel processing subsidiaries in China to try to keep their Chinese businesses afloat. In 2000 ITOCHU and Marubeni formed an online steel trading joint venture with US-based e-commerce company MetalSite. The two companies also integrated their entire steel divisions in 2001 forming the Marubeni-Itochu Steel joint venture among the largest steel companies in Japan.

Taking responsibility for the sharp downturn in Marubeni's financial performance chairman Iwao Toriumi announced in 2001 that he would step down. The company launched a major restructuring effort the next year that was designed to give more autonomy to the managers of individual business units.

In 2005 Marubeni launched a large power and water project in Abu Dhabi.

In 2007 Marubeni entered into the finance leasing industry in the US launching subsidiary CoActiv Capital Partners.

In 2008 Marubeni acquired US-based The PIC Group Inc. an independent global provider of services and programs focused on power generation and other industrial facilities and services. In 2009 it acquired 49% of Invenergy Thermal Financing LLC which owns three natural-gas fired power plants (with 1014 MW of generating capcity) in the US.

In 2009 the company completed the Laffan Refinery in Qatar which began commercial operations that year. It also signed a $2 billion deal to build the Shuweihat S2 Independent Water and Power Producer project in the United Arab Emirates.

EXECUTIVES

Chairman, Nobuo Katsumata
Chairman, Teruo Asada
Corporate Auditor, Hideyuki Yasue
President and CEO, Fumiya Kokubu
Managing Executive Officer and Director, Takafumi Sakishima
Managing Executive Officer and Director, Michihiko Ota
Regional CEO Chairman, Shinji Kawai
Corporate Auditor, Hiroshi Kudo
Senior Managing Executive Officer, Shigeru Yamazoe
Senior Managing Executive Officer, Mitsuru Akiyoshi
Executive Officer, Chihiro Shikama
Executive Officer, Masahiro Enoki
Senior Managing Executive Officer, Yutaka Nomura
Executive Officer, Naoya Iwashita
Executive Officer, Shoichi Ikuta
Managing Executive Officer, Shoji Kuwayama
Managing Executive Officer, Daisuke Okada

Executive Officer, Shingo Tsuda
Executive Officer, Keizo Torii
Managing Executive Officer, Kazuaki Tanaka
Managing Executive Officer, Yukihiko Matsumura
Executive Officer, Hiroshi Ikuno
Executive Officer, Kaoru Iwasa
General Manager Human Resources Dept, Kaoru Kuzume
General Manager Finance Dept, Nobuhiro Yabe
Regional COO for North & Central America, Yoshiaki Mizumoto
Managing Executive Officer, Masumi Kakinoki
President CEO and Director, Teruo Asada
Managing Executive Officer and Director, Toshinori Umezawa
Managing Executive Officer and Director, Takafumi Sakishima
Managing Executive Officer and Director, Michihiko Ota
Managing Executive Officer and Director, Hisashi Sunaoshi
Managing Executive Officer and Director, Shinji Kawai
Director, Toshiyuki Ogura
Director, Shigeaki Ishikawa
Auditors: Ernst&Young

LOCATIONS

HQ: Marubeni Corp.
1-4-2 Ohtemachi, Chiyoda-ku, Tokyo 100-8088
Phone: (81) 3 3282 2111 **Fax:** (81) 3 3282 4241
Web: www.marubeni.co.jp

2012 Sales

	% of total
Japan	68
US	17
Singapore	6
Other	9
Total	**100**

PRODUCTS/OPERATIONS

2012 Sales

	% of total
Consumer	44
Materials	22
Resources	21
Machinery	13
Total	**100**

COMPETITORS

ITOCHU
Jardine Matheson
Kanematsu
LG Group
Largo Vista
Mitsubishi Corp.
Mitsubishi International
Mitsui
Nissan Chemical
Rio Tinto plc
Samsung Group
Seika
Showa Denko
Sime Darby
Sojitz
Sojitz Corporation of America
Sumikin Bussan
Sumitomo
Sumitomo Heavy Industries

HISTORICAL FINANCIALS

Company Type: Public

Income Statement FYE: March 31

	REVENUE ($ mil.)	NET INCOME ($ mil.)	NET PROFIT MARGIN	EMPLOYEES
03/13	51,665	2,186	4.2%	42,937
03/12	53,521	2,098	3.9%	41,503
03/11	44,487	1,648	3.7%	38,700
03/10	35,114	1,020	2.9%	29,604
03/09	40,642	1,129	2.8%	30,426
Annual Growth	6.2%	18.0%	—	9.0%

2013 Year-End Financials

Debt ratio: 0.5%
Return on equity: 20.7%
Cash ($ mil.): 10,125
Current ratio: 1.36
Long-term debt ($ mil.): 25,681
No. of shares (mil.): 1,736
Dividends
Yield: 0.0%
Payout: 0.0%
Market value ($ mil.): 132,772

	STOCK PRICE ($) FY Close	P/E High/Low		PER SHARE ($) Earnings	Dividends	Book Value
03/13	76.48	0	0	1.26	0.00	6.93
03/12	72.50	0	0	1.21	0.00	5.98
03/11	72.43	0	0	0.95	0.00	5.38
03/10	62.55	0	0	0.59	0.70	4.60
03/09	31.50	0	0	0.65	1.41	3.32
Annual Growth	24.8%	—	—	18.0%	(87.4%)	20.2%

Mazda Motor Corp. (Japan)

Mazda and its Zoom-Zoom spirit races alongside the top automakers in Japan. Selling more than 1.2 million vehicles annually Mazda makes passenger cars commercial vehicles and crossover SUVs. It comprises more than 50 subsidiaries including sales companies: Mazda Motor of America Europe and Australia. The company manufactures in Japan China and Thailand. Models include the Mazda 2 3 6 and 8 passenger vehicles; MX-5 (Miata) RX-8 sports cars; E-series commercial vehicles; and B-Series pickup trucks. Mazda added crossover SUVs to its lineup with the Tribute Mazda5 (Premacy) Verisa Biante CX-7 and CX-9. Ford Motor holds a 3.5% stake in Mazda.

Just as the automotive industry was getting back on course natural catastrophe in the form of the Great Tohoku Kanto Earthquake and subsequent tsunamis struck Japan in March 2011. Many industries ground to a halt temporarily including Mazda's manufacturing facilities in Hiroshima and Hofu —limited production continued through the end of the month picking up to full production in April. Compounding factors to this event include political unrest in various regions of the world and rising oil prices. Still the company experienced sales increases in certain regions particularly in North America (10% increase) as well as emerging markets such as Russia China and other Asian countries. Mazda realized a 7% increase in overall sales for 2011 but this total was offset by sluggish sales in Japan and European countries as well as a strong yen. Before the fiscal year ended the earthquake struck and Mazda felt the aftershock to its 2011 bottom line posting an almost 60% loss over 2010.

Mazda had started on the road to recovery after the economic crisis in 2009. It weathered the worst of the downturn by implementing cost-saving measures —its workforce was reduced temporary workers' contracts were not renewed and inventory adjustments were made to match demand. Additionally Mazda executives agreed to take a 20% salary cut.

As a result of the recession Mazda's business plan revised target numbers and put an emphasis on brand and technology. Both areas are being served through new models and features. With an added emphasis on innovative technologies Mazda introduced its SKYACTIV technologies in 2011 with the claim that it will improve the fuel efficiency of its vehicles 30% by 2015. The SKYACTIV vision includes the redesign of Mazda's transmissions bodies and chassis for inclusion in its upcoming models. The SKYACTIV-G is a direct-injection gas engine that can achieve 30% fuel economy without the use of an electric motor; it is scheduled for release in Australia in 2011. The Demio (Mazda2) sporting the new engine was released in Japan early in 2011. Prior technology releases included Mazda's Smart Idle Stop System (iStop) which automatically shuts down the engine when the vehicle is stationary. The Mazda Premacy Hydrogen RE (Rotary Engine) Hybrid vehicle is the first of its kind to be made available through leasing; the RX-8 Hydrogen RE was introduced to Norway in 2009.

Ford once held a majority stake in Mazda but it cut its 33% interest to 13% in 2008 because it needed cash. As of 2011 Ford held only 3.5% of Mazda. Following the independence from Ford Takashi Yamanouchi took over as president and CEO of Mazda in 2008 assuming the responsibility of shoring up tumbling profits caused by an unstable yen and a decrease in demand. Former president Hisakazu Imaki continues serving as chairman but plans to retire in the near future; insiders report that Yamanouchi will assume the chairmanship. The management shakeup means Yamanouchi who is a proponent of expanding into the Chinese automobile market may speed up the process of the company's independent development strategy in China.

HISTORY

Ingiro Matsuda founded cork producer Toyo Cork Kogyo in Hiroshima in 1920. The company changed its name to Toyo Kogyo in 1927 and began making machine tools. Impressed by Ford trucks used in 1923 earthquake-relief efforts Matsuda had the company make a three-wheel motorcycle/truck hybrid in 1931.

During the 1930s the company supplied products to the Sumitomo industrial conglomerate. The Sumitomo Bank became a major shareholder of Toyo Kogyo.

The second Sino-Japanese War forced Toyo Kogyo to make rifles and cut back on its truck production. Although the company built a prototype passenger car in 1940 the outbreak of WWII refocused it on weapons. The August 1945 bombing of Hiroshima killed more than 400 Toyo Kogyo workers but the company persevered producing 10 trucks that December. By 1949 it was turning out 800 per month.

The company launched the first Mazda a two-seat minicar in 1960. The next year Toyo Kogyo licensed AUDI's new rotary engine technology. After releasing a string of models the company became Japan's #3 automaker in 1964. Toyo Kogyo introduced the first Mazda powered by a rotary engine Cosmo/110S in 1967 followed by the Familia in 1968.

The company grew rapidly and began exporting to the US in 1970. However recession high gas prices and concern over the inefficiency of rotary engines halted growth in the mid-1970s. Sumitomo Bank bailed out Toyo Kogyo. The company shifted emphasis back to piston engines but managed to launch the rotary engine RX-7 in 1978.

Ford's need for small-car expertise and Sumitomo's desire for a large partner for its client led to Ford's purchase of 25% of Toyo Kogyo in 1979. The company's early 1980s GLC/323 and 626 models were sold as Fords in Asia Latin America and the Middle East.

Toyo Kogyo changed its name to Mazda Motor Corporation in 1984. ("Mazda" is loosely derived from Matsuda's name but the carmaker has never discouraged an association with the Zoroastrian god of light Ahura Mazda.) The company opened a US plant in 1985 but a strong yen expensive increases in production capacity and a growing number of models led to increased overhead soaring debt and shrinking margins. By 1988 Mazda had begun to focus on sporty niche cars launching the hot-selling Miata in 1989.

The company faced more problems with the early 1990s recession. In 1992 Mazda introduced a new 626 model. That year Mazda also sold half its interest in its Flat Rock Michigan plant to Ford. As the yen development costs and prices for its cars in the US all rose sales in the US fell. In 1993 Mazda reorganized subsidiary Mazda of America by cutting staff.

Ford sank $481 million into Mazda in 1996 increasing its stake to 33%. That year the Ford-appointed former EVP of Mazda Henry Wallace became Mazda's president making history as the first non-Japanese to head a major Japanese corporation. In 1997 Wallace resigned to become CFO of Ford's European operations and former Ford executive James Miller replaced him. That year Mazda consolidated four US operations into Mazda North American Operations.

Restructuring continued in 1998 as Mazda consolidated some European operations and closed a plant in Thailand. In 1999 Mazda sold its credit division to Ford and its Naldec auto parts unit to Ford's Visteon unit. It announced plans to sell its stake in South Korean carmaker Kia Motors. Later in the year another American Ford's Mark Fields took over as president.

In 2000 Mazda recalled 30000 of that year's MPV minivans to fix a powertrain control module and asked owners of all 2000 MPVs to bring in their vehicles for front-bumper reinforcement. Mazda also announced plans to close about 40% of its North American dealership outlets over the next three years. The following year Mazda completed a program to assume direct control over distribution in some European markets including France Italy Spain and the UK.

In 2007 Mazda opened a new vehicle assembly plant in Nanjing China and also began building its passenger vehicle plant in Thailand. To strengthen its sales in Japan the company introduced the Mazda Advantage Loan in 2007 in cooperation with PRIMUS Financial Services. Mazda acquired a 40% stake in PRIMUS in March 2008 to strengthen its auto financing business.

Ford's 33% stake in the company was reduced to about 13% in 2008 after the cash-starved company sold off approximately 20% of its holdings. A consortium of Hiroshima Bank Panasonic (both Mazda business partners) and Mazda itself paid a combined sum of about $540 million to bring control of the company back to Japan.

EXECUTIVES

Chairman, Hisakazu Imaki
Chairman, Takashi Yamanouchi
EVP Research and Development Production Purchasing and Quality and Director, Masaharu Yamaki
Senior Managing Executive Officer Global Marketing Global Sales and Customer Service, Masazumi Wakayama
EVP, Akira Marumoto
Managing Executive Officer; President and CEO Mazda Motor Manufacturing de Mexico, Keishi (Keith) Egawa
Senior Managing Executive Officer, Nobuhide Inamoto
Representative Director Senior Managing Executive Officer and CFO Corporate Planning Profit Control and Financial Services and Cost Innovation, Kiyoshi Ozaki
Managing Executive Officer; President and CEO Mazda Motor of America, James J. (Jim) O'Sullivan
Senior Managing Executive Officer Research and Development Quality and Powertrain Development and Electric Drive System Development and Director, Nobuhiro Hayama
Managing Executive Officer Quality Assurance; General Manager Quality Division, Satoshi Tachikake
Managing Executive Officer; President and CEO Mazda Motor Europe, Jeffrey H. Guyton
Managing Executive Officer; Assistant to the Officer in charge of Research and Development; President Toyo Advanced Technologies, Yasuto Tatsuta
Vice Chairman, Seita Kanai
Managing Executive Officer Vehicle Development and Technical Research Center, Hirotaka Kanazawa
President and CEO, Masamichi Kogai
Managing Executive Officer Customer Service; President Mazda Parts, Kozo Kawakami
Managing Executive Officer China Business; Chairman and CEO Mazda Motor China, Noriaki Yamada
Executive Officer and President AutoAlliance Thailand, Toshinori Kusuhashi
Senior Managing Executive Officer; President Mazda South East Asia, Yuji Nakamine
Executive Officer and General Manager Hiroshima Plant, Masafumi Nakano
Executive Officer and Assistant to the Officer in charge of Corporate Planning; Corporate Liaison; Oversight of Tokyo Office, Minoru Mitsuda
General Manager Sales Planning Deptartment and Deputy General Manager Domestic Business Division, Raita Nishiyama
General Manager Product Quality, Yusuke Watanuki
Managing Executive Officer Purchasing; Assistant to the Officer in charge of Cost Innovation; General Manager Purchasing Division, Kazuki Imai
Executive Officer Fleet Sales in the Domestic Business; President Mazda Chuhan, Hiroshi Yamamoto
Senior Managing Executive Officer, Koji Kurosawa
Senior Managing Executive Officer, Yuji Harada
Executive Officer Product Planning and Powertrain Development; General Manager Product Planning, Kiyoshi Fujiwara
General Manager Powertrain Development Division, Mitsuo Hitomi
General Manager Hiroshima Inspection Department, Toru Utamura
Executive Officer and General Manager Production Engineering, Kiyotaka Shobuda
Managing Executive Officer, Masahiro Moro
Executive Vice President, Akira Koga
Executive Officer and General Manager Hofu Plant, Nariaki Uchida
Executive Officer and General Manager Research and Development Liaison Office, Paul R. Randle
Managing Executive Officer, Takashi Furutama
Executive Officer COO Sales and Marketing Mazda Motor Europe, Philip J. Waring
General Manager Purchasing Div, Kazuhisa Fujikawa
President CEO, Takao Hotta
General Manager Human Resources Office, Takeshi Fujiga
Managing Executive Officer; President Mazda Engineering & Technology, Takahisa Sori
Executive Officer; CEO Mazda Motor (China), Nobuhiko Watabe
Executive Officer; President and CEO Mazda Powertrain Manufacturing (Thailand), Hidenori Kawakami
President CEO and Director, Takashi Yamanouchi
EVP Research and Development Production Purchasing and Quality and Director, Masaharu Yamaki
Senior Managing Executive Officer Global Marketing Global Sales and Customer Service, Masazumi Wakayama
Senior Managing Executive Officer Corporate Planning Product Strategy and Profit Control; Assistant to the Officer in charge of Cost Innovation and Director, Akira Marumoto
Representative Director Senior Managing Executive Officer and CFO Corporate Planning Profit Control and Financial Services and Cost Innovation, Kiyoshi Ozaki
Senior Managing Executive Officer Research and Development Quality and Powertrain Development and Electric Drive System Development and Director, Nobuhiro Hayama
President In charge of promoting Mono Tsukuri Innovation, Seita Kanai
Senior Managing Executive Officer CSR Environment and Corporate Communications and Director, Yuji Harada
Auditors: KPMGAZSA&Co.

LOCATIONS

HQ: Mazda Motor Corp. (Japan)
3-1 Shinchi, Fuchu-cho, Aki-gun, Hiroshima 730-8670
Phone: (81) 82 282 1111 **Fax:** (81) 82 287 5237
Web: www.mazda.co.jp

2011 Sales

	% of total
Japan	59
North	19
Europe	13
Other	9
Total	**100**

PRODUCTS/OPERATIONS

2011 Sales

	% of total
Vehicles	74
Parts	9
Knockdown parts	6
Other	11
Total	**100**

Selected Models

B-Series (pickup)
E-Series (vans and commercial vehicles)
CX-7 (crossover SUV)
CX-9 (crossover SUV)
Mazda 2 (Demio)
Mazda 3 (Axela hatchback sedan)
Mazda 5 (Premacy minivan)
Mazda 6 (sport sedan)
Mazda 8 (MPV)
Mazda Biante (minivan)
Mazda Tribute
MX-5 Miata (roadster)
RX-8 (sports car)
Tribute (SUV)

Selected Subsidiaries and Affiliates

Mazda Australia Pty. Ltd.
Mazda Motor Logistics Europe NV (Belgium)
Mazda Motor of America Inc.

COMPETITORS

BMW
Chrysler
Daimler
Fiat
Ford Motor
Fuji Heavy Industries
General Motors
Honda
Isuzu
Kia Motors
Nissan
Peugeot
Renault
Saab Automobile
Suzuki Motor
Toyota
Volkswagen

HISTORICAL FINANCIALS

Company Type: Public

Income Statement

FYE: March 31

	REVENUE ($ mil.)	NET INCOME ($ mil.)	NET PROFIT MARGIN	EMPLOYEES
03/13	23,437	364	1.6%	37,745
03/12	24,784	(1,313)	—	37,617
03/11	28,085	(725)	—	38,117
03/10	23,166	(69)	—	38,987
03/09	25,751	(725)	—	39,852
Annual Growth	(2.3%)	—	—	(1.3%)

2013 Year-End Financials

Debt ratio: 0.3%	No. of shares (mil.): —
Return on equity: 7.1%	Dividends
Cash ($ mil.): 3,200	Yield: —
Current ratio: 1.35	Payout: —
Long-term debt ($ mil.): 5,493	Market value ($ mil.): —

	STOCK PRICE ($) FY Close	P/E High/Low		PER SHARE ($) Earnings	Dividends	Book Value
03/13	2.95	—	—	0.12	0.00	1.82
03/12	1.78	—	—	(0.70)	0.00	1.93
03/11	2.23	—	—	(0.41)	0.00	2.94
03/10	2.77	—	—	(0.05)	0.00	3.08
03/09	1.85	—	—	(0.53)	0.00	3.21
Annual Growth	12.4%	—	—	—	—	(13.2%)

Mediobanca Banca Di Credito Finanziario SpA

There's not much room for mediocrity at Mediobanca. A leading Italian investment bank the firm offers underwriting M&A support wholesale banking and financial advisory to corporate clients. It also offers private banking factoring credit management and leasing services. CheBanca! (formerly Micos Banca) operates about 40 retail banking branches mostly in Italy. Mediobanca has expanded domestically and internationally: It opened some 20 new branches in Italy Germany Spain and the UK in 2008. The bitter fights that plagued Mediobanca in the early part of the decade have simmered down and the bank is less-often called secretive and Machiavellian following the 2003 departure of CEO Vincenzo Maranghi.

The firm has been strengthening its position as the primo Italian corporate underwriter a reputation shaken in recent years amid shareholder disputes that would have had the late CEO Enrico Cuccia spinning in his grave. Vincenzo Maranghi who replaced Cuccia in 2000 was forced out of the company after shareholders questioned his operating methods.

Mediobanca has holdings in some of Italy's most powerful companies including broadband provider Telecom Italia and insurer Assicurazioni Generali.

HISTORY

In 1946 the three Italian "banks of national interest" Banca Commerciale Italiana (Comit) Credito Italiano (now Unicredito Italiano) and Banco di Roma (now part of Banca di Roma) founded Mediobanca to offer medium-term credit a market they were barred from.

Enrico Cuccia was with Comit at the time Mediobanca was formed and moved over to head the new institution. In 1955 he created the shareholder structure that later caused a twin uproar in Italian banking and politics: Although the state owned well more than half of the bank's shares a group of wealthy shareholders who together owned less than 10% of the bank wielded the power.

Over the next several decades Cuccia and Mediobanca operated on the behalf of these powerful shareholders and their family businesses devising deals on terms that other companies could not get. Mediobanca also created a web of crossholdings in other banks which made money for the bank by selling its funds and other services.

In the 1960s and 1970s the bank was at the center of a number of deals not all of which were stellar successes. The bank engineered a merger between Pirelli and Dunlop which fizzled and also pushed the merger of chemical companies Montecatini and Edison into Montedison which took a beating in the marketplace.

In 1982 Cuccia ostensibly retired taking the title of honorary chairman. However his influence never waned and the 1980s brought a war for the soul of Italian business. In 1985 Romano Prodi head of IRI the state-run organization (liquidated in 2000) that owned nearly 60% of the bank planned to privatize the bank. Instead the noble wing came up with its own privatization plan: The private shareholders requested that the state bring its stake in Mediobanca to below 50% by selling some of its shares to the Mediobanca cabal. In 1988 the privatization went through but as part of the pact it was stipulated that the new shareholders would share decision-making powers with the "Ala Nobile."

If the 1980s were wild the 1990s were out of control. Italy's banking industry hampered by red tape and old alliances was left behind the rest of Europe. Many of Italy's banks became stock companies when banking laws changed and many merged to compete in the European Union. Many of those deals threatened Mediobanca's hegemony so it tried to block them. The bank nixed Unicredito's 1998 bid for Comit (which instead merged with Banca Intesa) as well as Sanpaolo IMI's 1999 offer for Banca di Roma.

In 2000 the bank still keeping a grip on the wheels of finance orchestrated investment firm Compart's buyout of Montedison (the merged entity took the Montedison name). That year the company launched an online private banking joint venture with Mediolanum.

Also in 2000 its 46-year relationship with Lazard ended when the international investment banker announced plans to sell back to Mediobanca its 4% stake in the company along with its nearly 5% stake in Assicurazioni Generali.

After Cuccia's death in 2000 successor Vincenzo Maranghi battled such controlling shareholders as the Agnelli and Pirelli families and Deutsche Bank over the bank's future. These shareholders wanted to bring Mediobanca into the modern world by possibly merging it with another top Italian bank or even separating its investment management operations from its investment banking which generates a large majority of Mediobanca's profits.

However in a bid to stick to the old ways Maranghi arranged for backing (in exchange for a small stake in Mediobanca) from Swiss Life. Maranghi was blamed in part for the bank's decline: He forced out some of the investment banking division's top talent in the late 1990s and eventually resigned in 2003

Despite efforts to become more open some of the mystery surrounding Mediobanca remains. The shareholder dispute erupted after the death of Cuccia (whose body was subsequently robbed from its grave and later found).

Maranghi's replacement Gabriele Galateri di Genola had his work cut out for him repairing cracks in Mediobanca's image but he saw profits rise considerably. Under his watch the group has made its first foray into operations abroad opening an office in Paris. By 2004 the company posted improved financial results for a second consecutive year including a 20% increase in investment banking fees.

Galateri di Genola resigned from Mediobanca in 2007 after he lost the support of the supervisory board. He was succeeded by Alberto Nagel the company's general manager.

EXECUTIVES

Managing Director, Alberto N. Nagel, age 48
Manager Investor Relations, Jessica Spina
Media Relations, Lorenza Pigozzi
Head Financial Reporting, Massimo Bertolini
Chairman, Marco T. Provera
Management Board Member, Maurizio Cereda
Management Board Member, Massimo Di Carlo
Management Board Member, Francesco Saverio Vinci
Deputy Chairman and Interim Chairman, Dieter Rampl, age 65
Board Member, Ennio Doris, age 73
Board Member, Gilberto Benetton, age 72
Board Member, Vincent Bollore, age 61
Board Member, Pietro Ferrero, age 49
Board Member, Jonella Ligresti, age 46
Board Member, Fabrizio Palenzona, age 60
Board Member, Roberto Bertazzoni, age 71
Board Member, Carlo Pesenti, age 50
Board Member, Antoine Bernheim, age 89
Board Member, Eric Strutz, age 47
Board Member, Luigi Zunino, age 53
Board Member, Jean Azema, age 59
Board Member, Francesco Denozza, age 66
Board Member, Giancarlo Cerutti, age 59
Board Member, Tarak Ben Ammar, age 64
Board Member, Angelo Caso'
Board Member, Eugenio Pinto
Chairman, Marco T. Provera
Board Member, Gabriele Villa
Auditors: RecontaErnst&YoungS.p.A.

LOCATIONS

HQ: Mediobanca Banca Di Credito Finanziario SpA
Piazzetta Enrico Cuccia 1, Milan 20121
Phone: (39) 02 8829 1 **Fax:** (39) 02 882 9367
Web: www.mediobanca.it

2008 Sales

	% of total
Italy	92
Other	8
Total	**100**

COMPETITORS

Banca Carige	Goldman Sachs
Banca Popolare di Milano	Interbanca
Banco di Desio	Intesa Sanpaolo
CREDEM	Lazard
Credit Suisse	Morgan Stanley
Deutsche Bank	UBS Investment Bank
Gemina	UniCredit
	Vontobel

HISTORICAL FINANCIALS
Company Type: Public

Income Statement FYE: June 30

	ASSETS ($ mil.)	NET INCOME ($ mil.)	INCOME AS % OF ASSETS	EMPLOYEES
06/13	95,201	(235)	—	3,673
06/12	99,026	101	0.1%	3,652
06/11	109,031	533	0.5%	3,452
06/10	93,870	491	0.5%	3,242
06/09	104,444	3	0.0%	3,105
Annual Growth	(2.3%)	—	—	4.3%

2013 Year-End Financials

Return on assets: (-0.2%)
Return on equity: (-2.6%)
Long-term debt ($ mil.): —
No. of shares (mil.): 844
Sales ($ mil): 4,047
Dividends
Yield: 0.0%
Payout: —
Market value ($ mil.): —

	STOCK PRICE ($) FY Close	P/E High/Low	PER SHARE ($) Earnings	Dividends	Book Value
06/13	0.00	— —	(0.26)	0.07	10.76
Annual Growth	—	— —	—	—	—

Mega International Commercial Bank Co Ltd

LOCATIONS

HQ: Mega International Commercial Bank Co Ltd
No. 100 Chi-lin Road, Taipei 10424
Phone: (886) 2 2563 3156 **Fax:** (886) 2 2356 8936
Web: www.megabank.com.tw

HISTORICAL FINANCIALS
Company Type: Public

Income Statement FYE: December 31

	ASSETS ($ mil.)	NET INCOME ($ mil.)	INCOME AS % OF ASSETS	EMPLOYEES
12/12	84,154	666	0.8%	5,763
12/11	76,711	495	0.6%	5,803
12/10	76,068	383	0.5%	5,608
12/09	69,152	333	0.5%	5,722
12/08	63,046	104	0.2%	5,815
Annual Growth	7.5%	58.9%	—	(0.2%)

2012 Year-End Financials

Return on assets: 0.8%
Return on equity: 11.2%
Long-term debt ($ mil.): —
No. of shares (mil.): —
Sales ($ mil): 1,976
Dividends
Yield: —
Payout: —
Market value ($ mil.): —

Metallurgical Corp China Ltd

LOCATIONS

HQ: Metallurgical Corp China Ltd
MCC Tower, 28 Shuguang Xili, Chaoyang District, Beijing 100028
Phone: (86) 10 59868666 **Fax:** (86) 10 59868999
Web: www.mccchina.com

HISTORICAL FINANCIALS
Company Type: Public

Income Statement FYE: December 31

	REVENUE ($ mil.)	NET INCOME ($ mil.)	NET PROFIT MARGIN	EMPLOYEES
12/12	35,468	(1,115)	—	0
12/11	36,496	674	1.8%	127,746
12/10	31,312	807	2.6%	126,987
12/09	24,167	653	2.7%	120,385
12/08	23,138	461	2.0%	0
Annual Growth	11.3%	—	—	—

2012 Year-End Financials

Debt ratio: 5.4%
Return on equity: (-15.5%)
Cash ($ mil.): 5,487
Current ratio: 1.14
Long-term debt ($ mil.): 9,153
No. of shares (mil.): —
Dividends
Yield: —
Payout: —
Market value ($ mil.): —

	STOCK PRICE ($) FY Close	P/E High/Low	PER SHARE ($) Earnings	Dividends	Book Value
12/12	0.00	— —	(0.06)	0.00	(0.00)
12/11	4.79	1 1	0.03	0.00	0.40
Annual Growth	—	— —	—	—	—

Metro AG

A ride on this METRO could be a shopper's delight. Germany's uber retailer the company ranks fourth in the world (behind Wal-Mart Carrefour and Tesco). METRO owns and operates more than 2200 wholesale stores supermarkets hypermarkets department stores and the fast-growing Media Markt and Saturn consumer electronics chains. More than 930 of its shops are in Germany but METRO also has stores in more than 30 other countries including China Egypt France India Russia and Vietnam. Store banners include METRO and Makro Cash & Carry wholesale outlets Real hypermarkets and Galeria Kaufhof department stores. METRO is also launching e-commerce platforms for each of its retail businesses.

The German retail group comprises five units: Metro Cash & Carry self-service wholesale stores; Media Markt and Saturn consumer electronics stores; Real hypermarkets; Galeria Kaufhof department stores in Germany and Belgium; and METRO Properties the group's international real estate arm with properties in 33 countries. METRO Cash & Carry and Makro wholesale outlets which sell food and other grocery and non-grocery items to businesses and institutional customers account for 47% of group sales while Media-Saturn is Europe's #1 seller of consumer electronics with about 900 locations in 16 countries.With about 140 department stores Galeria Kaufhof is a leading Germany department store chains. Real operates about 425 hypermarkets mostly in Germany but also in Eastern Europe including Poland Romania and Russia.

Germany is METRO AG's largest market accounting for 39% of sales in 2011. About 25 other countries in Western and Eastern Europe account for 56% of sales while Asia and Africa make up the rest.

The debt crisis in the euro zone negatively impacted METRO AG's operations in 2011. Against a backdrop of high unemployment and weak consumer confidence group sales totaled E66.7 billion in 2011 vs. E67.3 billion in 2010. Western Europe suffered a 3% decline in sales in 2011 vs. the prior year while Germany (Europe's strongest economy) saw sales fall 1%. Asia and Africa were bright spots with sales in the region posting an 11% gain. The group's core Metro Cash & Carry business saw its sales eke up 0.2% while department store chain Galeria Kaufhof's sales fell nearly 4% and METRO's consumer electronics chains Media Markt and Saturn saw sales decline 1%.

Economic uncertainty has slowed METRO's historically rapid store development plans. But while the company has trimmed its store count at home it continues to grow abroad. Its focus is on Eastern Europe (especially Poland and Russia) and Asia. China is METRO's most promising new market. Media Markt which opened six locations in Shanghai in 2011 after entering the market in 2010 saw its sales in China increase to E92 million from E 9 million in 2010.

METRO AG's largest shareholders are German conglomerate Franz Haniel and the Schmidt-Ruthenbeck and Beisheim families which together control METRO with about 60% of the voting rights and are actively involved in the management of the company.

HISTORY

Otto Beisheim founded METRO SB-Grossmarkte in the German town of Mulheim in 1964. A wholesale business serving commercial customers it operated under the name METRO Cash & Carry. Three years later Beisheim received backing from the owners of Franz Haniel & Cie (an industrial company founded in 1756) and members of the Schmidt-Ruthenbeck family (also in wholesaling). This allowed METRO to expand rapidly in Germany and in 1968 into the Netherlands under the name Makro Cash & Carry via a partnership with Steenkolen Handelsvereeniging (SHV). During the 1970s the company expanded its wholesaling operations within Europe and moved into retailing.

METRO's foray into retailing was aided during the next decade by the acquisition of department store chain Kaufhof AG. By the 1980s the rise of specialty stores had many department stores on the defensive and Kaufhof's owners sold it to METRO and its investment partner Union Bank of Switzerland.

As METRO's ownership interest in Kaufhof rose above 50% the chain began converting some of its stores from department stores into fashion and sporting goods sellers. Kaufhof began acquiring a stake in computer manufacturer and retailer Vobis in 1989. In 1993 METRO now operating as METRO Holding AG acquired a majority interest in supermarket company Asko Deutsche Kaufhaus which owned the Praktiker building materials chain. The reclusive Beisheim retired from active management the following year.

To cut costs and prepare for expansion into Asia in 1996 METRO Holding merged its German retail holdings –Kaufhof; Asko; another grocery operation Deutsche SB Kauf; and its German cash-and-carry operations –into one holding company METRO AG. The new subsidiary purchased 58 Wirichs home improvement centers in Germany that year to complement its Praktiker chain.

In 1998 METRO bought the 196-store Makro self-service wholesale chain from Dutch-based SHV. METRO also added to its German food operations by acquiring the 94-store German Allkauf hypermarket chain and then by purchasing the 20-store Kriegbaum hypermarket chain.

Later that year METRO transferred its interests in non-core businesses including office supply stores footwear stores discount stores computer operations (including Vobis) and 25 unprofitable Kaufhof department stores to its Divaco (formerly Divag) unit. Divaco then sold 165 German Tip discount stores to Tengelmann Group.

Hans-Joachim Korber became METRO's CEO in 1999. In 2000 the company transferred 290 hypermarkets and department stores in Germany Greece Hungary Luxembourg and Turkey to a joint venture company (51% owned by Westdeutsche Landesbank) to raise cash for the expansion and remodeling of its wholesale outlets. Expanding on the Internet METRO acquired control of German e-commerce business Primus Online.

In 2001 METRO AG redistributed all of its shares held by METRO Holding AG to its top three shareholders for tax purposes. At the end of the year the first two Cash & Carry stores in Russia and one in Croatia opened.

In August 2002 METRO sold its entire stake in Primus Online to Beisheim Holding Schweiz AG. Overall in 2002 METRO opened 61 stores –53 of which were Metro Cash & Carry outlets –including new stores in China Bulgaria and Russia (one each) and Vietnam (two outlets). In April 2003 the company opened its first store in St. Petersburg (its fourth in Russia). In July a third METRO Cash and Carry store opened in Vietnam. The German retailer opened a global sourcing headquarters in Hong Kong in September that covers all markets outside the European Union.

As part of its international expansion plan in October 2003 METRO opened the first of two cash-and-carry distribution centers in Bangalore India. In December 2003 METRO sold its 49% stake in Divaco in a buyout led by Divaco's management. Divaco was originally founded together with financial investors as a joint venture with the objective of optimally divesting noncore METRO Group activities.

Gunther Hulse stepped down as chairman of METRO's supervisory board for personal reasons in June 2004. Hulse was succeeded by Theo Siegert a member of the management board of Franz Haniel & Cie a German wholesale drug distribution company. The German retailer added two new nations to its roster in 2004: Russia and Moldova. On the technology front METRO began using radio frequency identification (RFID) tags throughout the supply chain in November 2004.

METRO closed three of its Kaufhof stores in Germany in early 2005 amid slumping sales in its department store business. In late 2005 METRO took its DIY home improvement chain Praktiker Bau- und Heimwerkermarkte public. Following the IPO METRO retained a 40% stake in its former subsidiary. (It sold the remainder of its shares less 5% in April 2006.)

In February 2006 Theo Siegert stepped down as chairman of the supervisory board and was succeeded by Eckhard Cordes. In the first half of the year METRO completed the conversion of 85 stores acquired from Wal-Mart Germany and 20 stores purchased from France's Casino Guichard-Perrachon to the Real banner. In a follow-up deal METRO agreed to buy express-delivery provider DHL's SCM logistics unit which supplied the stores acquired from Wal-Mart for an undisclosed sum.

In 2007 the retailer opened more than 130 new stores including 84 Media Markt and Saturn consumer electronics shops and a single Galeria Kaufhof department store.

Continuing its global tour METRO entered Kazakhstan and Egypt with Makro stores in those markets in 2009 and 2010 respectively.

In July 2012 METRO sold its UK wholesale business Makro Self Service Wholesalers Ltd. (aka Makro UK) to Booker Group. Under the terms of the deal Booker acquired all 30 of Makro UK's wholesale stores and METRO received 10% of Booker's shares plus #15.8 million (~25 million).

EXECUTIVES

CEO Metro Cash and Carry (Asia/New Markets) Advertising, Frans W.H. Muller, age 52
Head Human Resources, Heiko Hutmacher, age 56
Chairman Management Board, Olaf Koch, age 43
CEO METRO Cash & Carry Germany, John Rix
Sales Director METRO Cash & Carry Germany, Arnd Riehl
Managing Director Food Division METRO Cash & Carry Germany, Jorg Ossenberg-Engels
CFO, Mark Frese, age 49
CEO of Booker, Charles Wilson
Chairman of the Supervisory Board, Franz Haniel
Director, Klaus J. Mangold, age 67
Director, Hans-Jurgen Schinzler, age 72
Director, Wulf H. Bernotat, age 63
Director, Marie-Christine Lombard, age 53
Director, M. P. M. (Theo) de Raad, age 67
Director, Ulrich Dalibor
Director, Bernd Pischetsrieder
Director, Werner Klockhaus
Director, Rainer Kuschewski
Director, Peter Stieger
Director, Hubert Frieling
Director, Andreas Herwarth
Director, Xaver Schiller
Director, Angelika Will
Director, Uwe Hoepfel
Auditors: KPMGDeutscheTreuhand-GesellschaftAG

LOCATIONS

HQ: Metro AG
Schluterstrasse 1, Duesseldorf 40235
Phone: (49) 211 6886 0 **Fax:** (49) 211 68 86 20 00
Web: www.metrogroup.de

2011 Sales

	% of total
Western Europe	
Germany	39
Other	31
Eastern	25
Africa &	5
Total	**100**

2011 Stores

	No.
Western Europe	
Germany	937
Other	619
Eastern	531
Asia &	100
Total	**2,187**

PRODUCTS/OPERATIONS

2011 Sales

	% of total
Cash &	47
Consumer	31
Food	17
Department	5
Other	-
Total	**100**

2011 Stores

	No.
Media Markt &	893
METRO Cash &	728
Real	426
Galeria	140
Total	**2,187**

Selected Operations

Wholesale Stores
Makro
Metro Cash & Carry (wholesale stores)
Food
Extra (supermarkets)
Real (hypermarkets)
Nonfood Specialty Stores
Media Markt (consumer electronics)
Saturn (consumer electronics)
Department Store
Galeria Kaufhof
Other Operations
Dinea Gastronomie (restaurants/catering)
METRO MGE Einkauf (purchasing)
METRO MGI Informatik (IT services)
METRO Real Estate Management (construction services)
METRO Werbegesellschaft (advertising)
METRO Online AG (Internet retailer)
MGB METRO Buying Group Hong Kong Ltd.
(purchasing Asia and Non-European Union countries)

COMPETITORS

ALDI
Best Buy
Carrefour
Casino Guichard
Darty
Delhaize
Dixons Retail
Edeka Zentrale
Lidl
Marktkauf
Maxeda
REWE
Royal Ahold
Tengelmann
Tesco
Wal-Mart

HISTORICAL FINANCIALS

Company Type: Public

Income Statement

FYE: December 31

	REVENUE ($ mil.)	NET INCOME ($ mil.)	NET PROFIT MARGIN	EMPLOYEES
12/12	87,965	3	0.0%	536,744
12/11	86,275	816	0.9%	533,233
12/10	90,016	1,137	1.3%	283,280
12/09	94,399	551	0.6%	286,091
12/08	95,008	563	0.6%	290,940
Annual Growth	(1.9%)	(71.1%)	—	16.5%

2012 Year-End Financials

Debt ratio: 32.4%
Return on equity: 0.0%
Cash ($ mil.): 6,984
Current ratio: 0.87
Long-term debt ($ mil.): 8,878
No. of shares (mil.): 324
Dividends
Yield: 0.0%
Payout: 2,877.9%
Market value ($ mil.): 1,815

	STOCK PRICE ($) FY Close	P/E High/Low	PER SHARE ($) Earnings	Dividends	Book Value
12/12	5.60	1444832	0.01	0.38	24.50
12/11	7.81	15 7	2.50	0.49	25.40
Annual Growth	(28.3%)	— —	(73.0%)	(6.3%)	(0.9%)

Migros-Genossenschafts-Bund (Switzerland)

The Swiss have a name for diversification: Federation of Migros Cooperatives (Migros or FCM). With more than two million members it is Switzerland's biggest cooperative and the #1 retailer (ahead of Coop). Migros comprises 10 regional cooperatives and owns about 20 food and beverage manufacturing plants. With stores in France and Germany Migros' retail empire spans supermarkets specialty stores and gas stations under the Migros Globus and Ex Libris banners. Its business also includes banking (Migros Bank) hotels (Hotelplan) oil (Migrol) and wholesaling of its consumer goods. Migros was founded in 1925 and transformed into a cooperative by the late consumer rights advocate Gottlieb Duttweiler.

Migros operates through five strategic business units (SBUs): Cooperative Retailing (60% of sales); Commerce; Industry & Wholesaling; Financial Services; and Travel. The SBUs centralize activities and companies in similar markets. (Cooperative Retail is the exception in that the regional cooperatives are legally independent and only indirectly managed by Migros.) The cooperative's retailing operations are extensive with more than 600 stores that include supermarkets and convenience stores to department stores men's apparel stores bookshops furniture shops sporting goods stores and DIY home and garden centers. It also operates Switzerland's largest online supermarket (LeShop.ch) as well as language schools fitness centers and public golf courses. On the manufacturing front the Industry segment makes some 20000 food products for Migros supermarkets and export. True to its Swiss roots Migros is a force in chocolate. Through its Chocolat Frey brand the company produces chocolates gums and other confections.

Zurich-based Migros rings up about 95% of its sales at home in Switzerland. The remainder is contributed by its retail operations in neighboring countries including Austria France Germany and Italy.

The sick European economy has put a lid on Migros's sales growth. The coop's sales dipped less than 1% in 2011 vs. 2010 the third consecutive year of flat or declining sales. Profits also declined in 2011 for the second year in a row. Price reductions on all goods sold in its supermarkets and specialty stores and on manufactured products such as chocolate depressed profit margins across the business. The coop's travel business shrunk as well in 2011 with sales down more than 6% vs. the prior year.

In its foreign food markets including France and Germany Migros faces tough competition from homegrown retailers. France's Carrefour and German discounters ALDI and Lidl have likewise been fierce rivals in the Swiss market. Increased competition from discounters and the soft economy have put great pressure on Migros to cut prices or risk losing shoppers. Indeed in 2011 the Swiss coop invested CHF 600 million (~$647 million) in price reductions in Cooperative Retailing alone. It's also wringing discounts from its suppliers to defend its hold on the Swiss market. Still Migros in 2011 saw its market share in Switzerland dip slightly to 15.2% from 15.4% the previous year. Beyond Switzerland in early 2011 Migros took control of German retailer Gries Deco the operator of about 225 stores in Germany and Austria that sell home accessories and decor and small furniture. The Hotelplan group acquired a 26% stake in a Germay's Inter Chalet a marketer of holiday homes.

HISTORY

Switzerland's largest employer — Migros-Genossenschafts-Bund –started off simply enough. In 1925 founder Gottlieb Duttweiler outfitted five Model-T Ford trucks with sugar coffee macaroni rice shortening and laundry soap (presumably to get all the cooking stains out). The trucks patrolled village streets hawking their wares and undercutting the prices of the local stores.

Those were the rowdy roaring 1920s for what would become a cooperative of more than 600 stores firmly rooted at home and stretching to points on the globe selling groceries and consumer goods publishing newspapers financing elections and sponsoring concerts educational programs and community improvement projects.

In 1926 Duttweiler opened a store in Zurich but the trucks kept running. Then in 1933 still aggressively underpricing his goods relative to other stores' prices Duttweiler founded the first Migros cooperative in Tessin. Taking his brand of consumer advocacy a giant step further he established the Alliance of Independents political party to combat the retail forces marshalling against his cooperatives which had begun to flourish. The Federation of Migros Cooperatives was organized in 1941. Its charter set aside half of one percent of the federation's sales for community improvement.

Throughout the 1940s Migros dodged charges of anti-competitive practices by other retailers and suppliers while it continued to invest in the communities which it served. Migros established a magazine founded adult learning clubs and a language school (French German and Italian all are spoken in Switzerland) and funded charities. By the 1950s Migros had grown to include a bank an insurance company and a petroleum cooperative to sell oil and gasoline.

For the next two decades Migros enjoyed rapid growth through customer loyalty spawned from competitive prices and the federation's social activism. By the 1980s Migros had swollen into a federation of 10 regional cooperatives throughout Switzerland and it talked of foreign investment. But public sentiment and the Swiss government balked as did the majority of Migros' directors. Not until 1993 would Migros launch a retail center outside of Switzerland. It did so in Thoiry France.

Following openings in France Germany and Austria Migros launched M-Online in 1998 an e-commerce Web site in German and French. Rapid expansion and price competition led to declines in sales growth in 1999 and 2000.

Sales recovered but profits fell 32% in 2001 dragged down by reorganization costs in its convenience and ABM department store operations and declining income from its bank. In February 2002 fire destroyed chocolate Easter rabbits and eggs worth nearly $12 million at a Migros distribution center north of Zurich. Globus cut the number of Au Bon Marche discount department stores from 50 to 28 in 2002.

In 2007 Migros acquired a 70% stake in the Swiss discount supermarket chain Denner. The purchase was a defensive move designed to prevent rivals such as ALDI and Lidl from doing so.

EXECUTIVES

Head HR Cultural and Social Affairs Leisure, Gisele Girgis
Head Industry Departement, Walter Huber, age 53
Manager Bischofszell Food Ltd., Mark Aegler
Manager Seba Aproz Ltd., Michel Charbonnet
Manager Riseria Taverne Ltd., Ernst Amstutz
Manager Estavayer Lait Ltd. and Mifroma Ltd., Gilles Oberson
Manager Mifa Ltd., Luigi Pedrocchi
Manager Micarna SA, Albert Baumann, age 54
Chairman and CEO, Herbert Bolliger
Head Marketing, Oskar Sager
Head Trading Departement, Ernst Dieter Berninghaus
Manager Frey-Chocolate Ltd. and Delica Ltd., Hansruedi Christen
Manager Scana Food Services Ltd., Walter Brandenberger
Auditors: PricewaterhouseCoopersAG

LOCATIONS

HQ: Migros-Genossenschafts-Bund (Switzerland)
Limmatstrasse 152, P.O. Box, Zurich CH-8031
Phone: (41) 1 277 21 11 **Fax:** (41) 1 277 25 25
Web: www.migros.ch

2011 Sales

	% of total
Switzerland	95
Other	5
Total	**100**

PRODUCTS/OPERATIONS

2011 Sales

	% of total
Retail	60
Commerce	19
Industry &	16
Travel	4
Financial	-
Other	1
Total	**100**

COMPETITORS

ALDI
Carrefour
Casino Guichard
Coop
Lidl
Nestle
REWE
Tengelmann
UBS

HISTORICAL FINANCIALS

Company Type: Public

Income Statement FYE: December 31

	REVENUE ($ mil.)	NET INCOME ($ mil.)	NET PROFIT MARGIN	EMPLOYEES
12/12	26,967	1,084	4.0%	87,461
12/11	26,096	702	2.7%	86,393
12/10	26,469	952	3.6%	83,616
12/09	23,970	957	4.0%	83,780
12/08	23,941	659	2.8%	84,096
Annual Growth	3.0%	13.2%	—	1.0%

2012 Year-End Financials

Debt ratio: —
Return on equity: 6.4%
Cash ($ mil.): 4,746
Current ratio: —
Long-term debt ($ mil.): —
No. of shares (mil.): 2
Dividends
Yield: —
Payout: —
Market value ($ mil.): —

Mitsubishi Chemical Holdings Corp

Mitsubishi Chemical Holdings is the largest chemical manufacturer in Japan. Subsidiary Mitsubishi Chemical Corporation produces a wide variety of petrochemicals specialty chemicals and the like. Another unit Mitsubishi Plastics manufactures plastics and films data storage devices such as CDs and DVDs as well as chemicals for semiconductor manufacturing. Mitsubishi Tanabe Pharma makes pharmaceutical products for central nervous system cardiovascular and gastrointestinal disorders in addition to OTC and anti-inflammatory drugs. Mitsubishi Rayon as its fourth business unit.

Mitsubishi Chemical Holdings serves customers in the performance products health care and industrial material markets. Its major products include optical recording media polymer films plastics pharmaceuticals purified terephthalic acid synthetic fibers and a range of polymers. It has more than 340 consolidated subsidiaries and more than 60 affiliated companies.

The company has major operations in Australia India North Asia Southeast Asia Europe and the US.

In Fiscal 2012 Mitsubishi Chemical Holdings reported a 1% drop in revenues (in local currency) as the company's growth in production was offset by weak economic conditions in Japan (still recovering from the major earthquake in 2011) the appreciation of the yen Europe's economic slowdown and the industrial disruption caused by floods in Thailand. However it posted a 36% drop in net income (in local currency) largely due to higher current and deferred taxes.

In 2010 Mitsubishi Chemical Holdings spent $2.4 billion to purchase Mitsubishi Rayon a manufacturer of monomers and polymers which became the holding company's fourth line of business. It is also the world's #1 maker of methyl methacrylate (a common and versatile plastic also known as MMA) through its 2008 acquisition of Lucite.

Earlier the company merged the former Mitsubishi Pharma with the former Tanabe Seiyaku to form Mitsubishi Tanabe of which it owns about half. In 2008 the company split off its Performance Products segment into a separate operating subsidiary.

Mitsubishi Chemical Holdings was formed in 2005 as the parent of Mitsubishi Chemical Corporation. The company is a subsidiary of Mitsubishi Corporation.

EXECUTIVES

President and CEO, Yoshimitsu Kobayashi
Deputy CEO, Shotaro Yoshimura
Senior Managing Executive Officer, Noboru Tsuda
Managing Executive Officer, Noriyoshi Ohira
Managing Executive Officer, Masanori Karatsu
Auditors: Ernst&YoungShinNihon

LOCATIONS

HQ: Mitsubishi Chemical Holdings Corp
1-1-1 Marunouchi, Chiyoda-ku, Tokyo 100-8251
Phone: (81) 3 6748 7115
Web: www.mitsubishichem-hd.co.jp

2012 Sales

	% of total
Japan	73
Other	27
Total	**100**

PRODUCTS/OPERATIONS

2012 Sales

	% of total
Chemicals	31
Polymers	22
Designed	21
Health	16
Electronics	4
Other	6
Total	**100**

COMPETITORS

Asahi Kasei
Astellas
BASF SE
Bayer AG
Chugai
Daicel Chemical
Daiichi Sankyo
Dainippon Sumitomo Pharma
DuPont
Evonik Degussa
Hitachi Chemical
Kyowa Hakko Kirin
Mitsui Chemicals
Nissan Chemical
SABIC Innovative Plastics
Sinopec Group
Sumitomo Chemical
Takeda Pharmaceutical
Tokai Carbon
Tokuyama

HISTORICAL FINANCIALS

Company Type: Public

Income Statement FYE: March 31

	REVENUE ($ mil.)	NET INCOME ($ mil.)	NET PROFIT MARGIN	EMPLOYEES
03/13	32,825	197	0.6%	55,131
03/12	39,109	432	1.1%	53,979
03/11	38,243	1,009	2.6%	53,882
03/10	26,925	137	0.5%	53,907
03/09	29,540	(682)	—	41,480
Annual Growth	2.7%	—	—	7.4%

2013 Year-End Financials

Debt ratio: 0.3%
Return on equity: 2.3%
Cash ($ mil.): 1,232
Current ratio: 1.16
Long-term debt ($ mil.): 6,942
No. of shares (mil.): 1,474
Dividends
Yield: —
Payout: —
Market value ($ mil.): 6,562

	STOCK PRICE ($) FY Close	P/E High/Low	PER SHARE ($) Earnings	Dividends	Book Value
03/13	4.45	— —	0.13	0.00	8.67
03/12	6.80	— —	0.28	0.00	9.46
03/11	7.30	— —	0.65	0.52	9.12
03/10	5.00	— —	0.09	0.00	8.06
03/09	2.70	— —	(0.50)	0.00	6.94
Annual Growth	13.3%	— —	—	—	5.7%

Mitsubishi Corp

In Japanese "mitsubishi" means "three diamonds" and Mitsubishi Corporation is one of Japan's crown jewels. The "sogo shosha" or trading company operates through six main business groups: living essentials (agricultural products food and beverages textiles and construction materials); metals; machinery (power generation equipment electrical systems automobiles); energy (liquefied natural gas crude oil); and chemicals (petrochemicals fertilizers plastics). Its other main business group is industrial finance which handles banking asset management construction and logistics. The company generated most of its fiscal 2012 gross profit from living essentials (42%) metals (24%) and machinery (16%).

Mitsubishi Corporation is part of the Mitsubishi "keiretsu" a network of affiliated companies that has no official status as a group but within which there is some cross-ownership and considerable business activity. Other affiliates include Mitsubishi Heavy Industries The Bank of Tokyo-Mitsubishi Mitsubishi Electric Mitsubishi Motors and Nikon.

Mitsubishi operates a network of more than 500 group companies in about 90 countries.

Buoyed by higher energy commodity prices and earlier investments in its chemicals segment the company posted an 8% rise in revenues in fiscal 2012. However lower metals income (due in part to a strike which disrupted coal operations in Australia) and lower automobile manufacturing production (due to flooding in Thailand) dragged down Mitsubishi's net income by 2%.

The Sendai earthquake and tsunami in 2011 severely disrupted the Japanese economy and affected Mitsubishi's operations and domestic revenues and net income that year (limited as it occurred late in the fiscal year). Nevertheless Mitsubishi was able to post an overall growth in revenues and net income thanks to a stronger global economy and an increase in demand for steel products and higher oil prices among other factors.

Mitsubishi has set about strengthening its financial position and devised a strategic growth plan that involves focusing on new operational initiatives including new energy sources and on environment and financial services.

Energy plans include the development of biofuels solar and wind energy technologies as industrial emissions-reducing technologies. It is also looking to ramp up its holdings in the global water business to meet growing water infrastructure demand from emerging economies.

On the financial front Mitsubishi is leveraging the group's financial assets and sheer size to facilitate the financing of its own as well as other companies' growth efforts. With its financial services operations the group is targeting real estate development aircraft and other industrial leasing services and it is considering strategic acquisitions of additional financial services assets.

Growing its metals assets in 2011 Mitsubishi acquired nearly 25% of Anglo American Sur a Chile-based copper mining and smelting company owned by Anglo American plc. Anglo American Sur's copper assets include the Los Bronces mine El Soldado mine and Chagres smelter. The purchase is expected to boost Mitsubishi's attributable copper production to 250000 metric tons per year.

To further expand its metals operations Mitsubishi agreed in 2012 to invest about $95 million to acquire a 25% stake in Stillwater Mining's Marathon PGM (platinum group metals) project in Ontario Canada. The project is expected to produce about 200000 ounces of PGMs and 17000 metric tons of copper per year for about 11 1/2 years. Mitsubishi also has the option to purchase up to 100% of the PGM production. PGMs are used in applications such as automobile catalysts electronic devices and fuel cells.

In 2012 Mitsubishi along with Indian fertilizer company Zuari Industries acquired a 30% stake in Fasfatos del Pacifico (FOSPAC) from a Peruvian cement manufacturer Cementos Pacasmayo. Pacasmayo explores for and produces rock phosphate in Peru and the investment will allow the companies to acquire FOSPAC's rock phosphate production (after fulfillment of local demand) for 20 years. The initial production capacity is expected to be about 2.5 million metric tons per year.

That year the company entered the Indonesian geothermal power market through the acquisition of 20% of Star Energy Geothermal Pte Ltd. Mitsubishi is looking to become further involved in geothermal power generation in countries that possess promising geothermal resources including Japan.

Growing another segment in 2013 the company agreed to buy Kirin's Food Science Business.

To raise cash in 2011 Mitsubishi sold its subsidiary Jicoux Datasystems Inc. to NEC Corp. Jicoux offers a fleet management service for commercial vehicles that includes automatic creation of daily reports based on speed route and distance data collected from in-vehicle devices over the internet. NEC plans to absorb the Jicoux's employees and operations and liquidate the company.

Along with the rest of the Mitsubishi companies Mitsubishi Corporation has been hurt by Japan's persistent economic stagnation. The company has restructured and reduced its workforce in the past decade and it has divided the operations of its former information technology and electronics business among its other groups.

HISTORY

Yataro Iwasaki's close ties to the Japanese government (along with subsidies and monopoly rights) ensured the success of his shipping and trading company Mitsubishi. Founded in 1870 Mitsubishi diversified into mining (1873) banking (1885) and shipbuilding (1887); it began to withdraw from shipping in the 1880s. During the next decade it invested in Japanese railroads and property.

In 1918 the Mitsubishi "zaibatsu" (conglomerate) spun off its central management arm Mitsubishi Trading (the forerunner of Mitsubishi Corporation). By WWII the group was a huge amalgam of divisions and public companies. During the war it made warplanes ships explosives and beer.

The "zaibatsu" were dissolved by US occupation forces and Mitsubishi was split into 139 entities. After the occupation the Japanese government encouraged many of the former business groups to reunite around the old "zaibatsu" banks. In 1954 Mitsubishi Trading became the leader of the Mitsubishi Group and established Mitsubishi International (US) which became a leading exporter of US goods.

The 1964 merger of three Mitsubishi companies created Mitsubishi Heavy Industries a top Japanese maker of ships aircraft plants and heavy machinery. Mitsubishi Kasei separated from Asahi Glass and Mitsubishi Rayon by a US fiat became Japan's #1 chemical concern. Mitsubishi Electric emerged as one of the country's leading electrical equipment and electronics manufacturers. In 1971 Chrysler invested in Mitsubishi Motors which began making cars for the US automaker. That year Mitsubishi Trading was renamed Mitsubishi Corporation.

Through the 1980s Japan seemed economically invincible. Then its "bubble economy" burst. The group fell behind in electronics and autos in the US consumer demand dried up at home and Mitsubishi Bank was left with a heavy burden of bad loans. Group members which traditionally provided materials supplies and sales outlets for each other began loosening old "keiretsu" ties during Japan's recession of the 1990s.

In 1993 Chrysler sold its stock in Mitsubishi Motors and two years later the companies severed production ties. This loss and declining demand in the US for Mitsubishi cars hurt auto sales.

Mitsubishi Bank merged with Bank of Tokyo in 1996 to form the biggest bank in the world The Bank of Tokyo-Mitsubishi (BTM). In 1997 several Mitsubishi companies admitted paying off a corporate racketeer setting off a wave of executive resignations.

By 1999 BTM had tumbled from the top spot and was unable to keep the money freely flowing to fellow Mitsubishi members.

Hit hard by the Asian economic crisis all the struggling Mitsubishi companies had to look outside of the "keiretsu" for help. In 1999 Mitsubishi Motors found a foreign partner Volvo for its truck making operations. Mitsubishi Oil merged with an outsider Nippon Oil to form Nippon Mitsubishi Oil (later renamed Nippon Oil). In 2000 Daimler-Chrysler (now Chrysler and Daimler) acquired a controlling stake in Mitsubishi Motors for $2.1 billion.

Executives at Mitsubishi Motors were charged in 2001 after they allegedly kept the lid on thousands of reported defects in Mitsubishi cars instead of issuing recalls. Stung by this and the after-effects of scandals from the previous decade Mitsubishi unveiled a new corporate philosophy as part of a strategy to revive the group's reputation.

In 2003 Mitsubishi disbanded its information technology and electronics business unit. The unit's operations were divided between the new business and machinery groups. In 2004 the company formed an alliance with GE Yokogawa Medical Systems (GEYMS) to provide GEYMS with help in developing its presence in the Japanese diagnostic imaging market.

In 2004 the company formed a food distribution joint venture with five Japanese food wholesalers comprising national wholesaler Meidi-ya and four regional companies. The joint venture called Alliance Network became one of Japan's largest food wholesalers. Mitsubishi had a 51% stake in Alliance Network. Later in 2004 Mitsubishi acquired the food beverage additive and pharmaceutical active and excipient businesses of Ashland Distribution.

In 2006 Mitsubishi bolstered its automotive operations when it acquired shares in Isuzu from General Motors; Mitsubishi ended up with a 10% stake in Isuzu. Mitsubishi and Isuzu soon after formed a European joint venture to market light-duty trucks throughout the continent. Later that year Mitsubishi bought the Avon Automotive subsidiary of Avon Rubber in a deal worth $120 million.

The following year Mitsubishi bought majority control of Nosan Corporation a manufacturer of livestock feed. In late 2007 the company acquired the majority interest in Kentucky Fried Chicken Japan.

On the medical health care front Mitsubishi shifted the focus of certain of its subsidiaries to providing services to hospitals and nursing care facilities. It established the Trinity Healthcare Fund in 2007 to provide management support for the restructuring of hospitals and other medical institutions. Other Mitsubishi subsidiaries focused on medical services include ProCure which is a medical equipment wholesale distributor and Apprecia which provides hospital construction consulting services.

During 2007 the group began investing in energy-related assets as part of this strategy. It acquired nearly 40% of Encore Energy Pte. which in turn owns 51% of Medco Energy an Indonesian oil and gas concern. The deal was valued at about $350 million and gave Mitsubishi a 20% stake in Medco. Mitsubishi was already working with Medco on an Indonesian gas plant and the two companies plan to pursue further international energy partnerships.

In 2009 it entered the solar energy business buying 34% of a subsidiary of Spanish renewable energy firm Acciona SA

Mitsubishi in 2010 it merged subsidiaries Mitsubishi Corporation Unimetals and Mitsubishi Shoji Light Metal Sales Corporation. The resulting company was named Mitsubishi Corporation Unimetals and remained a subsidiary of Mitsubishi. The merger was made to concentrate the company's management expertise in the non-ferrous metals industry.

EXECUTIVES

Chairman, Yorihiko Kojima
EVP; Group CEO Industrial Finance Logistics and Development Group, Eiichi Tanabe
EVP; General Manager Nagoya Branch, Ichiro Ando
Executive Vice President; Representative Director, Ryoichi Ueda
SEVP, Hideto Nakahara
EVP; Regional CEO Asia and Oceania, Toru Moriyama
SVP; Division COO Isuzu Business Division, Morikazu Chokki
EVP; Regional CEO Latin America, Seiji Shiraki
EVP; Group CEO Energy Business Group, Seiji Kato
President and CEO, Ken Kobayashi
SEVP and CIO, Hideyuki Nabeshima
SEVP, Jun Yanai
EVP; General Manager Nagoya Branch, Shosuke Yasuda
SEVP, Jun Kinukawa
EVP; Group CEO Global Environment and Infrastructure Business Group, Nobuaki Kojima
SEVP, Takahisa Miyauchi
EVP; Regional CEO Middle East and Central Asia, Shigeaki Yoshikawa
SVP; Chairman and Managing Director Mitsubishi Corporation India, Keiichi Nakagaki
SVP; Division COO Development and Construction Project Division, Ichiro Miyahara
EVP, Yasuo Nagai
EVP; Group CEO Machinery Group, Kozo Shiraji
EVP; President Americas, Yasuyuki Sugiura
EVP and CFO, Shuma Uchino
EVP; Group CEO Business Service Group, Toshimitsu Urabe
EVP; Regional CEO East Asia, Shunichi Matsui
SVP; Division COO Non-Ferrous Metals Division, Kenji Tani
EVP; Group CEO Living Essentials Group, Takehiko Kakiuchi
SVP; Division COO Infrastructure Project Division, Kazushi Okawa
SVP; Division COO Petroleum Business Division, Hajime Hirano
SVP; Division COO Asset Finance and Business Development Division, Yuichi Hiromoto
SVP; Division COO Commodity Chemicals Division A, Tatsuya Kiyoshi
Vice President Treasurer, Yuzo Nouchi
Vice President Secretary, Jason Stevens
Senior Vice President Chief Technology Officer, Jeffrey W. Daley
Vice President Director of Human Resources, Jil Galloway
Senior Vice President, Makoto Okawara
Vice President, Masakazu Horikawa
Senior Vice President Energy, Masatsugu Kurahashi
Senior Vice President Chemicals, Nobuhiko Otomo
Vice President, Ryugo Izumida
Vice President, Ryuji Watanabe
Senior Vice President, Tsunehiko Yanagihara
Vice President, Gosuke Nakae
Senior Vice President, Shinichiro Kawazoe
Vice President, Tadashi Takasugi
Senior Vice President Machinery, George Takahashi
General Manager Finance Department, Yoichi Shimoyama
Senior Vice President Metals, Daiju Mita
EVP, Kazuyuki Mori
Senior Vice President Metals Group, Hideki Nakagawa
Senior Vice President Corporate Staff Group, Katsuhiro Ito

EVP Audits and Internal Control and Director, Kiyoshi Fujimura
Director, Tamotsu Nomakuchi
Director, Mikio Sasaki
SEVP Resources and Energy Strategies and Director, Hisanori Yoshimura
SEVP Food Agricultural Resources and Consumer Market Strategies Customer Relations Management Regional Strategy (Japan) and Director, Takeshi Inoue, age 66
Director, Kazuo Tsukuda
SEVP CFO and Director, Ryoichi Ueda
EVP Corporate Administration Legal and Human Resources and Director, Tsuneo Iyobe
EVP Global Strategy Regional Development and Director, Hideto Nakahara
Director, Tomio Tsutsumi
SEVP; Group CEO Living Essentials Group and Director, Masahide Yano
Director, Kunio Ito
President CEO and Director, Ken Kobayashi
SEVP; Group CEO Business Service Group and Director, Hideyuki Nabeshima
EVP; Regional Strategy Japan and Director, Yasuo Nagai
Director, Ryozo Kato
Director, Hidehiro Konno
Auditors: DeloitteToucheTohmatsu

LOCATIONS

HQ: Mitsubishi Corp
2-3-1 Marunouchi, Chiyoda-ku, Tokyo 100-8086
Phone: (81) 3 3210 2121
Web: www.mitsubishicorp.com

2011 Sales

	% of total
Japan	73
Australia	10
Thailand	7
Other	10
Total	**100**

PRODUCTS/OPERATIONS

Selected Products and Services

Metals
- Bullion and metals futures
- Fabricated steel structures
- Metallurgical and thermal coal
- Nonferrous metal products
- Nonferrous metals
- Nuclear fuel and components
- Precious metals
- Raw materials for steel
- Semifinished products
- Steel materials
- Specialty steel

Living Essentials
- Apparel
- Canned foods
- Ceramic materials
- Cigarettes
- Coffee beans coffee and beverages
- Confections and snacks
- Contract food services
- Dairy foods and processed foods
- Fabrics
- Feedstuffs
- Fresh and frozen foods
- Grains and agricultural products
- Marine products
- Meat and livestock
- Mineral water
- Oils and fats
- Photosensitized materials
- Pulp paper and packaging materials
- Soft drinks
- Sweeteners
- Textile raw materials
- Textiles for industrial use
- Tires
- Wood wood products and construction materials

Machinery
- Automobiles
- Commercial aviation
- Defense systems and equipment
- Electronics products
- Industrial agricultural construction and other general machinery
- Plant and machinery for power generation electricity oil/gas/chemicals steel/cement and environmental protection
- Project development and construction
- Satellite communications
- Ships
- Space systems
- Transportation systems

Energy
- Carbon materials and products
- Crude oil
- LNG
- LPG
- Orimulsion
- Petroleum products

Industrial Finance Logistics and Development
- Commerce services
- Consumer services
- Financial services
- Logistics

Chemicals
- Fertilizers
- Fine and specialty chemicals
- Inorganic chemicals
- Petrochemicals
- Plastics

COMPETITORS

ITOCHU	Samsung Group
Marubeni	Sime Darby
Mitsui	Sumitomo

HISTORICAL FINANCIALS

Company Type: Public

Income Statement

FYE: March 31

	REVENUE ($ mil.)	NET INCOME ($ mil.)	NET PROFIT MARGIN	EMPLOYEES
03/13	63,435	3,826	6.0%	83,891
03/12	67,851	5,532	8.2%	82,792
03/11	62,879	5,593	8.9%	77,494
03/10	48,620	2,924	6.0%	78,146
03/09	62,415	3,756	6.0%	77,877
Annual Growth	0.4%	0.5%	—	1.9%

2013 Year-End Financials

Debt ratio: 0.4%	No. of shares (mil.): 1,646
Return on equity: 9.3%	Dividends
Cash ($ mil.): 14,302	Yield: 0.0%
Current ratio: 1.44	Payout: 0.0%
Long-term debt ($ mil.): 47,811	Market value ($ mil.): 61,803

	STOCK PRICE ($) FY Close	P/E High	P/E Low	PER SHARE ($) Earnings	PER SHARE ($) Dividends	PER SHARE ($) Book Value
03/13	37.53	0	0	2.32	0.00	26.97
03/12	46.76	0	0	3.36	0.00	25.99
03/11	55.33	0	0	3.39	1.08	24.12
03/10	52.60	0	0	1.78	0.72	19.29
03/09	26.50	0	0	2.28	1.31	14.73
Annual Growth	9.1%	—	—	0.4%	(89.1%)	16.3%

Mitsubishi Electric Corp.

If it has an "on" switch chances are Mitsubishi Electric makes it or makes a part for it. The company part of the Mitsubishi Corporation operates across five primary sectors: Energy and Electric Systems (power generation plants supervisory systems and escalators); Industrial Automation Systems (programmable controllers measurement and control systems); Home Appliances (air-conditioning systems TVs and Blu-ray disc recorders); Information and Communication Systems (satellites wireless systems and network systems); and Electronic Devices (power devices LCD displays). Mitsubishi Electric has operations in about 40 countries but it earns the majority of its sales from Japan.

Energy and Electric Systems representing 25% of sales which the company terms its social infrastructure business includes building systems with elevators and escalators. The AXIEZ elevator features LED lighting and speed-adjustment technology that reduces waiting time. The segment also installs power plants for operations that range from utility companies to the individual sites of companies seeking in-house power generation.

Industrial Automation Systems making up 23% of sales provides such products as programmable logic controllers under the MELSEC brand; the MELSERVO-J4 used for the manufacturing of semiconductors flat panel display equipment and industrial machinery; no-fuse circuit breakers and earth leakage circuit breakers for wiring protection and short-circuit protection; and electrical discharge machines for the manufacturing of automobiles home electronics and IT-related devices. Home Appliances accounting for 20% of sales includes KIRIGAMINE air conditioners photovoltaic generation heat pumps LED lighting RakuRakuUD technology that enhances the performance of appliances as well as products that go beyond the domestic market such as digital signage and other visual equipment.

Information and Communication Systems 12% of sales offers services that include information systems monitoring server integration and such products as satellite platforms vehicle-mounted satellite communication equipment broadband optical access systems and digital closed-circuit TV systems. Electronic Devices 5% include products for cutting power losses and power consumption integrated circuits for electric vehicles high-electron mobility transistor amplifiers and LCD modules for high brightness and contrast. The company's Other segment 15% of sales mainly comprises materials procurement and engineering.

Mitsubishi Electric has more than 20 manufacturing plants in Japan as well as factories in other countreis that include China Malaysia Thailand the US and the UK.

Consolidated net sales were flat year-over-year from 2011 to fiscal 2012 falling a fraction of a percentage point. By segment Energy and Electric Systems' net sales were also flat falling likewise a fraction of a percentage point. The segment struggled with falling orders in the Japanese public utility and rolling-stock equipment markets.

Supported by demand in the Asian smartphone and tablet markets as well as the automotive equipment markets in the developing world and North America Industrial Automation Systems' sales headed up about 6% in fiscal 2012 compared with 2011. Home Appliances was down 8% in fiscal

2012 versus 2011 as a result in part of lower demand for photovoltaic systems in Europe and weak demand for hot water supply and induction heating cooking systems.

Thanks in part to large orders for submarine line terminal equipment and demand for communications infrastructure systems integration network and system operations and electronics Information and Communication Systems increased 6% over the period between 2011 and fiscal 2012. Electronic Devices rose 14% in fiscal 2012 versus 2011 to meet a strong demand for power modules in the industrial commercial automotive and railcar markets. The Other segment headed up just a fraction of a percentage point in 2012 versus 2011. During that period the company's net income declined about 10% mainly due to a tax adjustment.

Looking ahead each segment has specific goals for product development. The Energy and Electric Systems segment is focused on research and development to improve rotating machines for generators electric motors switches and transformers transportation systems and elevators and escalators. The segment is also concentrating its R&D efforts on IT for supervision and control power information systems and building management systems.

Industrial Automation Systems is focused on improving motors mechatronics equipment automotive components electric power steering and auto multimedia systems. Information and Communication Systems is emphasizing network systems for telecommunication operators and space systems.

Electronic Devices is tasked with product development in semiconductors while Home Appliances is focused on energy saving recycling universal design and digital imaging systems. The Other segment is focused on work that helps the entire group. This segment's accomplishments include a robot system for bulk components and a multiband power amplifier.

Each segment has also enjoyed some significant capital expenditures. Energy and Electric Systems received investments for more production capacity. Factory automation systems and automotive equipment operations were the focus for Industrial Automation. Home Appliance spending favored increasing production capacity for air-conditioning equipment. Improving research and development received the most capital expenditure focus in Information and Communication Systems and the Other segment. Electronic Devices concentrated on improvements for its power device operations.

In 2012 Mitsubishi Electric acquired the Messung Group which makes programmable logic controllers and human machine interfaces and had served as a sales and distribution partner in India.

HISTORY

Mitsubishi Electric was among 10 companies fined in 2007 by the European Commission (EC) for allegedly conspiring to fix prices for gas-insulated switchgear industrial equipment used by electric utilities. Along with Fuji Electric Hitachi Toshiba and other Japanese manufacturers the company was accused of colluding with ALSTOM AREVA Schneider Electric and Siemens to reserve European markets for Europe-based manufacturers while European companies generally stayed out of the Japanese market. Mitsubishi Electric was fined a mere E118.5 million ($1 million) for its part in the price-fixing cartel.

EXECUTIVES

Executive Officer Accounting and Finance; Director, Hiroki Yoshimatsu
Chairman, Setsuhiro Shimomura, age 69
Executive Officer Energy & Industrial Systems, Yoshiaki Nakatani
EVP, Mitsuo Muneyuki
Executive Officer Living Environment & Digital Media Equipment, Hiroyuki Umemura
Executive Officer Auditing Government & External Relations Legal Affairs Export Control and Intellectual Property, Tsuyoshi Nakamura
President and CEO, Kenichiro Yamanishi, age 63
SVP Global Strategic Planning & Marketing, Takashi Sasakawa
SVP Factory Automation Systems, Hideyasu Nonaka
Executive Officer Communication Systems, Yasuyuki Nakanishi
Executive Office Public Utility Systems, Susumu Shikata
Executive Officer Total Productivity Management and Environmental Programs, Masaharu Moriyasu
EVP, Masaki Sakuyama
Senior Vice President, Noritomo Hashimoto
Executive Officer Purchasing, Shoichi Sakata
Executive Officer, Kazuhiko Tsutsumi
Managing Executive Officer, Hideyuki Ohkubo
Section Chief of Accounting Unit, Homare Ikeda
Managing Executive Officer, Isao Iguchi
Managing Executive Officer, Masayuki Ichige
Managing Executive Officer; Director, Nobuyuki Ohkuma
Executive Officer, Takayuki Sueki
Managing Executive Officer, Toru Yoshinaga
Managing Executive Officer, Yutaka Ohashi
Executive Officer, Akihiro Matsuyama
Director, Mikio Sasaki
Director, Shigemitsu Miki, age 78
Executive Officer Accounting and Finance; Director, Hiroki Yoshimatsu
Director, Kazuo Sawamoto
Executive Officer General Affairs Human Resources and Public Relations; Director, Noritomo Hashimoto
Director, Hiroyoshi Murayama
Director, Shunji Yanai
Director, Osamu Shigeta
Independent Director, Fujiatsu Makino
Independent Director, Mitoji Yabunaka
Auditors: KPMGAZSA&Co.

LOCATIONS

HQ: Mitsubishi Electric Corp.
2-7-3 Marunouchi, Chiyoda-ku, Tokyo 100-8310
Phone: (81) 3 3218 2272
Web: www.mitsubishielectric.co.jp

2012 Sales

	$ mil.	% of total
Asia		
Japan	38,862	74
Other Asia	7,108	13
Europe	3,780	7
North America	2,714	5
Rest of the World	490	1
Eliminations	(8571)	-
Total	**44,383**	**100**

PRODUCTS/OPERATIONS

2012 Sales

	$ mil.	% of total
Energy & electric systems	12,526	25
Industrial automation systems	11,931	23
Home appliances	10,357	20
Information & communication systems	6,297	12
Electronic devices	2,449	5
Other	7,458	15
Eliminations	(6635)	-
Total	**44,383**	**100**

Selected Products

Energy and Electric Systems
- Elevators
- Nuclear power plant equipment
- Power distribution systems
- Power generation systems
- Propulsion control systems
- Smart grids
- Substation systems
- Train information systems
- Train vision systems
- Visual information systems

Home Appliances
- Air-conditioning systems
- Blu-ray disc players
- Televisions

Industrial Automation Systems
- Automotive equipment
- Circuit breakers
- Factory automation systems
- Industrial robots
- Power meters

Information and Communication Systems
- Antenna technology
- Closed-circuit television systems
- Radar system technology
- Space systems
- Wireless systems

Electronic Devices
- High frequency & optical devices
- LCD displays
- Power devices

COMPETITORS

Autoliv
Continental AG
DENSO
Delphi Automotive Systems
Ericsson
Fujitsu
Hella
Hitachi
Intel
Johnson Controls
KONE
Lear Corp
Magneti Marelli
Meritor
Motorola Solutions
NEC
Oki Electric
Panasonic Corp
Philips Electronics
Raytheon
Robert Bosch
Rockwell Collins
SANYO
Samsung Electronics
Sanken Electric
Schindler Holding
Schneider Electric
Sharp Corp.
Siemens AG
Sony
Spirit AeroSystems
Sumitomo Electric
TRW Automotive
ThyssenKrupp
Toshiba
United Technologies
Valeo
Visteon
Yokogawa Electric

HISTORICAL FINANCIALS

Company Type: Public

Income Statement FYE: March 31

	REVENUE ($ mil.)	NET INCOME ($ mil.)	NET PROFIT MARGIN	EMPLOYEES
03/13	37,911	738	1.9%	120,958
03/12	44,367	1,366	3.1%	117,314
03/11	44,022	1,503	3.4%	114,443
03/10	35,899	302	0.8%	109,565
03/09	37,218	123	0.3%	106,931
Annual Growth	0.5%	56.4%	—	3.1%

2013 Year-End Financials

Debt ratio: 0.1%
Return on equity: 5.7%
Cash ($ mil.): 3,176
Current ratio: 1.50
Long-term debt ($ mil.): 3,248
No. of shares (mil.): 2,143
Dividends
Yield: 0.0%
Payout: 0.0%
Market value ($ mil.): 35,158

	STOCK PRICE ($) FY Close	P/E High	P/E Low	PER SHARE ($) Earnings	Dividends	Book Value
03/13	16.40	0	0	0.34	0.00	6.45
03/12	17.78	0	0	0.64	0.00	6.44
03/11	23.85	0	0	0.70	0.00	5.92
03/10	93.50	0	0	0.14	0.04	4.82
03/09	44.51	0	0	0.06	0.26	4.02
Annual Growth	(22.1%)	—	—	56.4%	(89.2%)	12.5%

Mitsubishi Motors Corp. (Japan)

Mitsubishi Motors is a small fish in the big pond of global car manufacturing. The company sells about a million cars per year (far below rival Toyota) in more than 160 countries worldwide. The 20 models of cars trucks minivans and SUVs are made at its plants in Asia Europe and the US. Mitsubishi products include the Lancer Galant Eclipse and Outlander; about eight models are limited to Japanese sales only. The company's R&D facilities are in the US Germany and Japan. Mitsubishi Corporation and Mitsubishi Heavy Industries together own about a 30% stake in Mitsubishi Motors which traces its roots to Heavy Industries' 1917 "Mitsubishi Model A" project. About 80% of sales come from outside of Japan.

Mitsubishi sees its future in electric vehicles which it has been developing since 1966. The company develops plug-in hybrids and other electric vehicles through its research and development facilities and through joint ventures with other auto makers. In 2011 it announced it would partner with Nissan to develop and manufacture new electric minicars. Vehicles produced from the joint venture would be launched in 2013.

Mitsubishi already has an electric minicar the i-MiVE on the market in Japan and Europe. (Minicars are a popular vehicle class in the Japanese and European markets and are gaining popularity in other parts of the world.) While it sells in Japan under its own brand the MiVE is sold in Europe through an agreement with French car maker Peugeot S.A. which buys and resells MiVE under a different brand. Peugeot and Mitsubishi are also working to develop an electric delivery van; additionally the two companies co-own a manufacturing plant in Russia that among other vehicles produces Mitsubishi cars and SUVs rebranded as Peugeot and Citroen.

As it has in years past the company also continues to turn to emerging markets to increase its sales and boost profits. It has been targeting its products to customers in emerging markets like China Russia the Ukraine and other countries in Asia and Eastern Europe. Other sales-boosting initiatives include construction of a compact car factory in Thailand (scheduled to open in 2012) renewing key joint ventures in China and designing a new SUV product in Russia.

While it has suffered in recent years from the global economic downturn and plummeting automotive sales worldwide Mitsubishi benefited from what it deemed to be a mild recovery in the global economy in 2010 and an uptick in auto sales across the industry. The recovery along with its successful expansion into emerging markets drove an increase in overall sales and profits for the company that year.

The company intends to improve its bottom line by finding ways to cut operational personnel and other expenses. Joint ventures with Peugeot and Nissan are a key part of its strategy in part because such partnerships allow Mitsubishi to share research and development manufacturing and other costs while earning revenue in markets where it does not directly compete with other car makers. The company also plans to boost profits by seeking more expansion opportunities in China Russia and other emerging markets.

HISTORY

Mitsubishi Motors Corporation was created in 1970 when Mitsubishi Heavy Industries spun off its motor vehicle division. Mitsubishi Heavy Industries was created in 1934 by the merger of Mitsubishi Aircraft and Mitsubishi Shipbuilding (which had been making cars since 1917).

Mitsubishi Motors immediately focused on exports. In 1971 Chrysler took a 15% stake in Mitsubishi Motors and began marketing its cars in the US –the cars were sold as Dodge Colts and Plymouth Arrows. By the mid-1970s the company's relationship with Chrysler had become tense –Mitsubishi Motors felt Chrysler meddled too much in its decision-making processes. In 1977 the company began setting up its own Colt dealerships in Europe. Despite direct competition in the subcompact car market the two companies continued to cooperate with Chrysler marketing Mitsubishi cars in the US and Mitsubishi Motors lending engineering expertise to Chrysler.

In 1980 Mitsubishi Motors joined with Mitsubishi Corporation to buy Chrysler Australia. The new company was named Mitsubishi Motors Australia Ltd. Mitsubishi Motors entered the US under its own name in 1982 introducing the Starion Cordia and Tredia car models.

Mitsubishi Motors and Chrysler teamed again in 1985 to form Diamond-Star Motors. Diamond-Star began to build Chryslers in the US using Mitsubishi engines and transmissions. Mitsubishi Motors went public in 1988. Mitsubishi Heavy Industries reduced its stake in the company to 25% while Chrysler raised its share to 20%. The money raised by the offering was used to pay down debt and to expand the company's operations in the Philippines Malaysia and Thailand.

By the end of the 1980s Mitsubishi Motors had begun a major push into the US. It embarked on a plan to expand its US dealer network by 40%. The Diamond-Star venture began to take off with Chrysler selling the Mitsubishi-made Plymouth Laser.

While most US carmakers were scaling back operations because of poor sales the company added a number of models in 1991. Its strategy was to target customers leaning toward Japanese or European cars and offer models at lower prices than its competitors. Later in 1991 Mitsubishi Motors bought out Chrysler's share in Diamond-Star Motors. About this time Chrysler dropped its stake in Mitsubishi Motors to about 11%.

By focusing on the lower end of the auto market Mitsubishi Motors surpassed other Japanese carmakers for most of the early 1990s. Chrysler reduced its stake in the company to less than 3% in 1992 before selling it all off in 1993. The two companies maintained working relations however with Chrysler supplying engines for Diamond-Star and Mitsubishi Motors continuing to market Chryslers in Japan.

In 1994 Mitsubishi Motors Mitsubishi Corporation and the Vietnamese government formed VIETRANSIMEX to assemble buses in Vietnam. Mitsubishi Motors established a joint venture to build engines in China in 1997. The next year it began building and selling buses in Egypt.

Mitsubishi Motors and Volvo bought small stakes in each other in 1999 to cement a vehicle-building alliance. In 2000 it came to light that Mitsubishi Motors had been concealing customer complaints regarding safety for several years. Also in 2000 Mitsubishi Motors instituted a turnaround program aimed at focusing exclusively on car operations.

Early in 2001 Mitsubishi announced that it was recalling about 1.35 million cars – including 950000 cars in the US –to fix a ball joint in the front suspension that can cause stalling. The recall also included about 110 000 cars already recalled in 2000. Soon afterward it was reported that the company would cut about 9500 jobs and streamline production. Mitsubishi then bought AB Volvo's 3.3% stake.

Later in 2001 in the effort to further cut costs Mitsubishi announced plans to spin off its automatic transmission unit and combine it with Nissan Motor subsidiary Jatco TransTechnology. Nissan will take an 80% stake in the new venture; Mitsubishi will own 20%. The deal was completed the following year.

In early 2003 Mitsubishi Motors spun off its truck business as Mitsubishi Fuso Truck and Bus Corp (MFTBC). Daimler purchased a 43% stake in the new enterprise Mitsubishi Motors retained 42% while other Mitsubishi group firms hold the remaining 15% (Daimler later increased its stake to 65% reducing Mitsubishi Motors' stake to 20%).

The new venture was plagued by quality problems including a recall involving wheels that suddenly fly off and an attempt to cover the whole mess up. Mitsubishi and Daimler later agreed to a settlement surrounding the cover-ups at MFTBC that gave Daimler Mitsubishi Motor's remaining 20% stake (reducing Mitsubishi's stake to zero). The deal also gave Daimler a cash payment of about $200 million.

After suffering heavy losses and quality problems Mitsubishi closed one of its Japanese plants in the Spring of 2004 to cut costs. Production at the Gifu prefecture plant was shifted to another of Mitsubishi's plants in Japan. German-born CEO Rolf Eckrodt resigned shortly after Daimler announced that it would not infuse any money into Mitsubishi.

As if Mitsubishi didn't have enough problems just days after Daimler cut off any future support the Japanese transport ministry said it would not certify new trucks made by Mitsubishi Fuso Truck and Bus thus making it impossible to sell the trucks in Japan until their safety could be verified. The move by the Japanese transport ministry came after several former Mitsubishi executives were arrested for covering up details surrounding an accident in which a Japanese woman was killed by a runaway truck wheel. The arrests also prompted the transport ministry to ban Mitsubishi from bidding on any Japanese government contracts.

The bad news kept on coming in 2004 when Mitsubishi Fuso Truck and Bus announced another recall of 200000 trucks for faulty clutch parts that caused several accidents including one wreck that killed a truck driver.

Early in 2005 Mitsubishi group companies (including Mitsubishi Heavy Industries Mitsubishi Corporation and Mitsubishi UFJ Financial Group) said they would infuse their ailing car affiliate with another $2.6 billion through the purchase of common and preferred shares. Fresh bank loans gave Mitsubishi another $2.4 billion. Daimler's stake in Mitsubishi Motors was thereby reduced to about 12%. Mitsubishi also announced Chairman Yoichiro Okazaki had stepped down taking responsibility for the company's turnaround failures. Mitsubishi Heavy Industries Chairman Takashi Nishioka was named as his successor.

Then late in 2005 Daimler sold its 12% stake to Goldman Sachs for an undisclosed price.

EXECUTIVES

Chairman, Takashi Nishioka
EVP and Representative Director, Hiizu Ichikawa
Executive Officer Corporate General Manager Design, Akinori Nakanishi
Executive OfficerCorporate General ManagerCorporate Affairs, Keizo Fuchita
President and Representative Director, Osamu Masuko

Managing Director Chief Business Ethics Officer and Board Member, Shuichi Aoto
Managing Director Production Group and Board Member, Tetsuro Aikawa
EVP and Representative Director, Hiroshi Harunari
Executive Officer; Corporate General Manager CSR Promotion Office, Yoshikazu Nakamura
Executive Officer; Corporate General Manager Planning Office, Shuma Uchino
Managing Director Domestic Sales and Board Member, Seiichi Ohta
Senior Executive Officer President & Chief Executive Manufacturing?Mitsubishi Motors North America, Shiro Futaki
President and CEO Mitsubishi Motors North America, Shinichi Kurihara
Head Development Group and Director, Ryugo Nakao
Executive Officer President's Assistant Vice Corporate General Manager Customer Service and Promotion, Masao Ohmichi
Executive Officer Plant General Manager Nagoya, Yasuo Ohyama
Executive Officer Corporate General Manager Asia and ASEAN, Toshihiko Hattori
Senior Executive Officer Managing Director Assistant, Masahide Konishi
Executive Officer Corporate General Manager Finance General Manager Financial Planning Department, Kazuya Matsushita
Executive Officer Plant General Manager Powertrain, Shuzo Muramoto
Executive Officer President?Mitsubishi Motors Thailand Co, Michiro Imai
EVP and Representative Director, Gayu Uesugi
Head Quality Affairs and Director, Takitaro Fukuda
President COO of Mitsubishi Motor Sales of America, Pierre Gagnon
Director, Mikio Sasaki
EVP and Representative Director, Hiizu Ichikawa
Director, Hidetoshi Yajima
President and Representative Director, Osamu Masuko
Managing Director Chief Business Ethics Officer and Board Member, Shuichi Aoto
Managing Director Production Group and Board Member, Tetsuro Aikawa
EVP and Representative Director, Hiroshi Harunari
Managing Director Domestic Sales and Board Member, Seiichi Ohta
Head Development Group and Director, Ryugo Nakao
EVP and Representative Director, Gayu Uesugi
Head Quality Affairs and Director, Takitaro Fukuda
Auditors: Ernst&YoungShinNihon

LOCATIONS

HQ: Mitsubishi Motors Corp. (Japan)
5-33-8 Shiba, Minato-ku, Tokyo 108-8410
Phone: (81) 3 3456 1111
Web: www.mitsubishi-motors.com

2010 Sales

	% of total
Europe	26
Japan	20
Asia	20
Oceania	10
North	10
Other	14
Total	**100**

PRODUCTS/OPERATIONS

Selected Models

Challenger
Colt
Diamante
Eclipse
Eclipse Spyder
Endeavor
Galant
i MiEV
Lancer
Lancer Evolution
Mirage
Outlander
Raider

COMPETITORS

BMW
Caterpillar
Chrysler
Daihatsu
Deere
Fiat
Ford Motor
Fuji Heavy Industries
General Motors
Hino Motors
Honda
Isuzu
Kia Motors
Land Rover
Mazda
Nissan
Peugeot
Remy International
Renault
Suzuki Motor
Toyota
Volkswagen
Volvo
smart GmbH

HISTORICAL FINANCIALS

Company Type: Public

Income Statement FYE: March 31

	REVENUE ($ mil.)	NET INCOME ($ mil.)	NET PROFIT MARGIN	EMPLOYEES
03/13	19,290	403	2.1%	29,822
03/12	22,032	291	1.3%	30,777
03/11	22,081	188	0.9%	30,709
03/10	15,476	50	0.3%	31,003
03/09	20,041	(557)	—	31,905
Annual Growth	(0.9%)	—	—	(1.7%)

2013 Year-End Financials

Debt ratio: 0.2%	No. of shares (mil.): —
Return on equity: 12.7%	Dividends
Cash ($ mil.): 4,352	Yield: —
Current ratio: 1.12	Payout: —
Long-term debt ($ mil.): 1,210	Market value ($ mil.): —

Mitsubishi UFJ Financial Group Inc

Mitsubishi UFJ Financial Group (MUFG) is the largest banking group in Japan (ahead of Mizuho Financial and Sumitomo Mitsui Financial) and one of the largest in the world. The group provides retail banking corporate banking and trust services in more than 40 countries. Subsidiary The Bank of Tokyo-Mitsubishi UFJ operates about 500 branches across Japan and another 80 overseas. Mitsubishi UFJ Trust and Banking oversees some Y27 trillion ($343 billion) in assets under management. Other holdings include investment bank Mitsubishi UFJ Securities California-based Union Bank and a more than 20% stake in Morgan Stanley. MUFG was formed in the 2005 merger of Mitsubishi Tokyo Financial Group and UFJ Holdings

The group also includes credit card company Mitsubishi UFJ NICOS and Mitsubishi UFJ Lease & Finance. The company is targeting the latter unit for growth; it also plans to expand its corporate investment banking practice in North America Japan and the rest of Asia.

Japan's weakened economy in which loan demand remains soft and consumer spending is down has negatively impacted MUFG's earnings. Its NICOS consumer loan portfolio has contracted recently due to regulatory reforms in Japan thereby lowering the bank's interest income. In fiscal 2012 the bank's revenues fell 5% while profits fell 8%. Although overall interest earnings grew (largely due to the conversion rate related to the conversion of Morgan Stanley's preferred stock into common stock) noninterest earnings including fees and commissions declined that year. That decline could be primarily attributed to the securities business as well as a reduction of business volume all of which reflectes the slowly recovering economy.

With the stagnant Japanese economy the company has increasingly looked to emerging markets in Asia Latin America and Central and Eastern Europe (among its most recent targets: Turkey) for growth. In the US subsidiary Union Bank has been expanding through the acquisition of other community banks.

MUFG is also looking towards its alliance with Morgan Stanley to grow its global investment banking operations. The two companies combined their Japanese brokerage operations in 2010; to help fund that deal MUFG raised more than $10 billion through a stock offering. The company then got approval from the US Federal Reserve to up its stake in Morgan Stanley to nearly 25% in 2011. The partnership could ultimately prove very lucrative for MUFG although the bank does not have any control over Morgan Stanley's business operations.

On a much smaller scale MUFG has been expanding its reach by acquiring stakes in firms in other parts of the world. In 2010 it became the first Japanese bank to acquire an interest in a Chinese asset manager when it bought out BNP Paribas Asset Management's 33% stake in a joint venture with Shenyin & Wanguo Securities. The following year it acquired some 15% of AMP Limited in Australia. The moves should allow it to expand its investment services to pension funds and other institutional investors as part of a plan to expand its trust operations.

MUFG is a member of the Mitsubishi group a melange of about 30 different companies –active in manufacturing transportation insurance and other industries –that shared common ownership before WWII but have been operated autonomously since.

HISTORY

Mitsubishi Bank emerged from the exchange office of the original Mitsubishi "zaibatsu" (industrial group) in 1885. It evolved into a full-service bank by 1895 and became independent in 1919 though its primary customers were Mitsubishi group companies. The bank survived WWII but a US fiat dismantled the "zaibatsu" after the war. Mitsubishi Bank reopened as Chiyoda Bank in 1948. After reopening offices in London and New York the bank readopted the Mitsubishi name.

In the 1950s Mitsubishi Bank became the lead lender for the reconstituted Mitsubishi group ("keiretsu"). In the 1960s it followed its Mitsubishi partners overseas helping finance Japan's growing international trade. In 1972 it acquired the Bank of California and began doing more business outside the group.

Japan's overinflated real estate market of the 1980s devastated many of the country's banks including Nippon Trust Bank of which Mitsubishi owned 5%. Japan's Ministry of Finance (MoF) urged Mitsubishi to bail Nippon out; as a reward for raising its stake in Nippon to 69% and assuming a mountain of unrecoverable loans the MoF allowed Mitsubishi to begin issuing debt before other Japanese banks. In 1995 Mitsubishi Bank and Bank of Tokyo agreed to merge.

Bank of Tokyo (BOT) was established in 1880 as the Yokohama Specie Bank; the Iwasaki family founders of the Mitsubishi group served on its board. With links to the Imperial family the bank was heavily influenced by government policy. With Japan isolated after the Sino-Japanese War its international operations suffered greatly even before WWII. Completely dismantled after WWII the bank was re-established in 1946 as the Bank of Tokyo a commercial city bank bereft of its foreign exchange business. During the 1950s the government restored it as a foreign exchange specialist but regulations limited its domestic business.

BOT evolved into an investment bank in the 1970s; its reputation as the leading foreign exchange bank brought in international clients and successful derivatives trading and overseas banking. By the time BOT and Mitsubishi Bank agreed to merge BOT had 363 foreign offices (only 37 in Japan) with more foreign than Japanese employees.

The two banks merged in 1996 to form The Bank of Tokyo-Mitsubishi (BTM); Mitsubishi was the surviving entity. Their California banks merged to create Union Bank of California (UnionBanCal). The next year BTM reorganized its operations but had problems assimilating its disparate corporate cultures.

In 1998 Japanese banking regulators doled out nearly $240 billion to the industry to prop up failing banks and to strengthen healthier ones. Also that year BTM was fined for bribing MoF officials with entertainment gifts and posted a huge loss after writing off $8.4 billion in bad debt. Losses continued in 1999 and the bank responded by reorganizing operationally cutting jobs and offices and selling stock in UnionBanCal.

In 2000 BTM announced plans to form a financial group with Mitsubishi Trust Bank and Nippon Trust Bank. The following year the three banks unified and formed Mitsubishi Tokyo Financial Group. Before rolling into Mitsubishi Trust Financial Group BTM paid back the money showered upon it by the Japanese government in 1998.

In 2004 MTFG introduced a new organizational structure that focused on its three core markets — retail corporate and trust asset businesses. The company planned to unify business within each division and to improve decision-making companywide. The group also introduced a new executive officer system with the idea of separating company oversight and business execution. A mechanism for credit risk control was also added.

It was all to change in 2005 however. During this time Mitsubishi Tokyo Financial Group merged with UFJ Holdings emerging (at that time) as the world's largest bank by assets. As a result of the merger the group was renamed Mitsubishi UFJ Financial Group (MUFG).

As with most of its peers MUFG was not immune to the global credit crisis that began in 2007. Its NICOS consumer lending subsidiary had a disappointing year due to the credit crunch. The unit sold its installment credit car loan and car leasing businesses to JACCS in 2008. In 2009 MUFG announced plans to close 50 branches and cut nearly 1000 jobs as a part of a long-term restructuring plan. In addition the bank shut down some 200 ATMs and relocated another 1000 employees.

In 2008 the group bought the rest of UnionBanCal and Mitsubishi UFJ NICOS it didn't already own and acquired a stake in bulge-bracket firm Morgan Stanley. MUFG also bought a 10% stake in UK-based Aberdeen Asset Management that year. (It later upped its interest to around 17%.)

EXECUTIVES

President CEO and Representative Director, Katsunori Nagayasu, age 66
Chairman, Takamune Okihara, age 62
Deputy Chairman, Kinya Okauchi, age 61
President and CEO, Nobuyuki Hirano, age 62
Managing Officer, Takehiko Nemoto, age 59
Senior Managing Director, Taihei Yuki, age 61
Deputy President, Masaaki (Masa) Tanaka, age 60
Executive Officer, Muneaki Tokunari
Executive Officer, Saburo Araki
Deputy President and Representative Director, Tatsuo Tanaka
Deputy Chairman, Tatsuo Wakabayashi
Managing Director, Akihiko Kagawa
Director, Ryuji Araki, age 74
President CEO and Representative Director, Katsunori Nagayasu, age 66
Director, Takuma Otoshi, age 65
Managing Director and Representative Director, Ichiro Hamakawa
Director, Takashi Oyamada, age 57
Deputy Chairman, Kinya Okauchi, age 61
Deputy President and Representative Director, Nobuyuki Hirano, age 61
Senior Managing Director and Representative Director, Taihei Yuki, age 60
Managing Director and Representative Director, Masao Hasegawa
Deputy President and Representative Director, Tatsuo Tanaka
Deputy Chairman, Tatsuo Wakabayashi
Auditors: DeloitteToucheTohmatsu

LOCATIONS

HQ: Mitsubishi UFJ Financial Group Inc
2-7-1 Marunouchi, Chiyoda-ku, Tokyo 100-8330
Phone: (81) 3 3240 8111 **Fax:** (81) 3 3240 8203
Web: www.mufg.jp

2012 Sales

	% of total
Asia/Oceania	
Japan	69
Other	9
US	12
Europe	7
Other	3
Total	**100**

PRODUCTS/OPERATIONS

2012 Sales

	% of total
Interest	
Loans including	36
Investment	9
Trading account	6
Other	1
Noninterest	
Fees &	22
Net trading account	14
Other	12
Total	**100**

COMPETITORS

Aozora Bank
BNP Paribas Bangkok
Chuo Mitsui Trust
Citigroup
HSBC
Ito-Yokado
Japan Post
Mizuho Financial
Mizuho Trust & Banking Ltd
ORIX
Resona
Shinsei Bank
Sony
Sumitomo Mitsui

HISTORICAL FINANCIALS

Company Type: Public

Income Statement FYE: March 31

	ASSETS ($ mil.)	NET INCOME ($ mil.)	INCOME AS % OF ASSETS	EMPLOYEES
03/13	2,450,358	11,362	0.5%	112,100
03/12	2,623,454	5,074	0.2%	110,500
03/11	2,449,821	5,576	0.2%	113,000
03/10	2,142,061	9,205	0.4%	115,300
03/09	1,964,959	(14,907)	—	78,500
Annual Growth	5.7%	—	—	9.3%

2013 Year-End Financials

Return on assets: 0.4%
Return on equity: 11.1%
Long-term debt ($ mil.): —
No. of shares (mil.): —
Sales ($ mil): 39,675
Dividends
Yield: 0.0%
Payout: 0.0%
Market value ($ mil.): —

	STOCK PRICE ($) FY Close	P/E High	P/E Low	PER SHARE ($) Earnings	Dividends	Book Value
03/13	6.00	0	0	0.79	0.00	7.97
03/12	4.98	0	0	0.34	0.00	7.40
03/11	4.60	0	0	0.38	0.14	7.13
03/10	5.23	0	0	0.73	0.12	6.72
03/09	4.92	—	—	(1.40)	0.14	5.44
Annual Growth	5.1%	—	—	—	(89.2%)	10.0%

Mitsui & Co., Ltd.

Part of a network of companies that was founded by a samurai centuries ago Mitsui & Co. now does battle in the marketplace. Mitsui & Co. spearheads the Mitsui Group one of Japan's largest "keiretsu" (companies loosely connected through cross-ownership). A leading Japanese general trading firm (sogo shosha) Mitsui & Co. has about 320 subsidiaries in a wide range of industries. Its major business units are engaged in the production and sale of chemicals electronics and information energy foods iron and steel nonferrous metals textiles and machinery. The company's largest revenue generators are its trading activities in the energy and chemical sectors.

Geographic Reach

The company maintains a global network of 151 offices in 67 countries as well as about 320 subsidiaries in a wide range of industries and associated companies worldwide.

Operations

Mitsui & Co.'s operating units include Americas; Asia Pacific; Basic Chemicals; Consumer Service; Energy; Europe the Middle East and Africa; Financial & New; Food Products & Services; Food Resources; Infrastructure Projects; Iron & Steel Products; IT; Marine & Aerospace; Mineral & Metal Resources; Motor Vehicles & Construction Machinery; Performance Chemicals; and Transportation Logistics.

Financial Performance

After a decline in its revenues in fiscal years 2010 over 2009 due to the impact of the recession and the major tsunami Mitsui & Co. experienced significant growths in revenues in both fiscal years 2011 and 2012. In fiscal year 2012 the company's revenues increased by 12% and profits grew by 42%. The increase in the revenues was due to the positive impact of the recovering global economy. The growth in profits was due to the increases in commodity prices including crude oil gas iron ore and coal as well as the reversal effect of the previous year's settlement payment related to the Deepwater Horizon oil spill incident in the Gulf of Mexico. (Mitsui & Co. had a minority interest in the doomed rig. Mitsui's energy sector through its MOEX Offshore 2007 subsidiary saw impairment losses on property equipment and mineral rights from its involvement with the massive oil rig fire and subsequent oil spill in the Gulf of Mexico during the summer of 2010).

Strategy

Mitsui & Co.'s strategic role as a sogo shosha brings together marketing financing logistics risk management and IT and process development functions on behalf of its many subsidiaries. It grows through acquisitions and by forming joint ventures and strategic partnerships.

In 2013 Mitsui & Co. agreed to acquire Total E&P Energia Italia S.r.l which owns a 25% stake in the Tempa Rossa onshore oil field in the Gorgoglione concession in Italy. That year the company also formed a joint venture with JGC Corporation and Chongqing Liangjiang New Area Development & Investment Group Co. Ltd. The joint venture company will produce an urban development master plan for the Yulin Business Park to be developed in the Chongqing Liangjiang New Area and will also be involved in promotional activities for inward investment for the Business Park. Liangjiang New Area Development & Investment will hold a 50% stake in the joint venture company and Mitsui and JGC will own 25% respectively.

Mitsui & Co. entered a 50-50 joint venture with Dow Chemical in 2010 to build and operate a membrane chlor-alkali facility located at Dow's Freeport Texas complex. The new facility is expected to begin operations in mid-2013. Mitsui formed yet another joint venture with Dow in 2011 to develop biofuels and biopolymers or organic plastics in Brazil. The 50-50 operation will use Dow's sugar cane production to develop ethanol and packaging materials offering a "green alternative" and replacement product for the flexible packaging hygiene and medical markets.

In 2011 Mitsui & Co. raised its stake in Brazilian grain broker Multigrain SA to almost 90% by buying a 44% stake from US grain company CHS Inc. for $480 million. Mitsui which hopes to improve its competitiveness on the global grain market previously owned about half of the company.

Also that year Mitsui & Co. entered a joint venture with Russian automaker Sollers to construct Toyota vehicles in a production facility in Vladivostok. The venture would be the first Japanese auto assembly operation in Russia's Far East region. The deal calls for the the Mitsui/Sollers JV to manufacture about 30000 vehicles a year and distribute them throughout the Russian Federation via the Trans-Siberian Railway.

Mitsui & Co. also acquired Mercian Corporation's pharmaceutical and chemical businesses in 2011. Mercian's drug and chemical businesses known as MBS Company utilize fermentation technology. Mitsui aims to boost its business in substances such as anti-cancer bioagents and will position MBS as part of its core group.

HISTORY

In the 17th century unemployed samurai (warrior nobleman) Sokubei Mitsui opened a sake and soy sauce brewery at the urging of his wife Shuho. After parental encouragement their youngest son Hachirobei went to Edo (now Tokyo) and opened a dry goods store in 1673. Breaking with Japanese retailing tradition the store offered merchandise at fixed prices on a cash-and-carry basis.

Hachirobei in 1683 opened a currency exchange that evolved into Mitsui Bank. The bank became the Osaka government's official money changer in 1691 and was the first bank to offer money orders in Japan. Before his death in 1694 Hachirobei drafted a unique succession plan to hand down control of the company to every related family not just the eldest son's side.

The shogun's government called upon Mitsui in the mid-1800s to help finance its war against rebels. The family hired Rizaemon Minomura an outsider with influence in the government to protect the company from increasing demands for money. Mitsui became the bank of the Meiji government after Minomura astutely switched support to the winning rebels. Government industrialization pushed Mitsui into textiles paper goods and machinery. Minomura emphasized foreign trade and banking creating Mitsui Bussan (now Mitsui & Co.) and Mitsui Bank in 1876. In the late 1800s Mitsui Bussan profited from a Japanese military buildup formed a shipping line to take on Mitsubishi's monopoly and bought coal mines. The Mitsui family withdrew from Mitsui Bussan management in 1936 following attacks by right-wing terrorists who opposed its democratic leanings.

Mitsui prospered during the 1930s as Japan's military prepared for war. After the defeat occupation forces disbanded Japan's "zaibatsu" industrial groups slicing Mitsui into more than 200 separate entities. By 1950 more than two dozen leaders of the former Mitsui companies began gathering the Mitsui Group back together. Trading firm Mitsui & Co. was established in 1959. The oil crises of the 1970s stalled the oil-dependent Japanese economy prompting Mitsui companies to expand operations overseas and move into industries such as technology and aluminum.

The mammoth Sakura Bank was formed in 1990 with the merger of Mitsui Bank and Taiyo Kobe Bank. Other major ventures were to follow: In 1992 Mitsui & Co. joined with Marathon and Royal Dutch Shell and others to search for oil and gas off Russia's Sakhalin Island; and Mitsui & Co. and other Japanese traders were enlisted by Oman in 1993 for a $9 billion liquefied natural gas transport venture. As cable TV emerged in Japan Mitsui & Co. teamed up the next year with National Media Corp. to launch a home-shopping network.

In anticipation of deregulation in Japan's financial markets four Mitsui Group firms' pension funds –Sakura Bank Mitsui Marine & Fire Insurance Mitsui Mutual Life Insurance and Mitsui Trust and Banking –were linked in 1998. The next year Sakura Bank set aside old loyalties and agreed to merge with Sumitomo Bank the Sumitomo "keiretsu's" main bank; the deal closed in 2001. The group's Mitsui Trust and Banking merged with Chuo Trust and Banking to form Chuo Mitsui Trust and Banking part of Mitsui Trust Holdings.

Mitsui & Co. was implicated in bid-rigging and bribery scandals in 2002 and the company's chairman and CEO resigned. In 2003 the company moved into the German pesticide market by acquiring an 80% stake in Spiess-Urania Chemical a subsidiary of Norddeutsche Affinerie. Later that year it entered the biotechnology market by creating TM Cell Research a 35%-owned joint venture created with Toyobo. The company also entered the telecommunications market by acquiring a 30% stake in Shineedotcom from Shin Corp.

In 2003 Mitsui turned its focus back to the expansion of its current operations. The company acquired a 15% stake in Valepar a holding company of Brazilian-based iron ore producer Companhia Vale do Rio Doce. Mitsui and International Power completed the acquisition of the 1200 MW gas-fired Saltend Power plant in the UK from Calpine Corporation. In 2005 Mitsui acquired a stake in Gas Participac?es (Gaspart) a Brazil-based gas distribution company.

To help pay down debt related to its purchase of Union Fenosa in 2009 Gas Natural sold power assets in Mexico to Mitsui and Tokyo Gas for $1.2 billion.

Mitsui sold its share of the TAMCO steel mini-mill joint venture to Gerdau Ameristeel in 2010 for about $40 million. Its other partners Ameron and Tokyo Steel also sold their shares in the project to Gerdau.

Eyeing opportunities in the North American gas market Mitsui in 2010 announced plans to invest $1.4 billion to develop a shale gas project in Pennsylvania with Anadarko Petroleum. It also teamed up with Penn West Energy Trust to form an $850-million natural-gas joint venture to develop an oil shale play in British Columbia.

Also in 2010 Mitsui teamed up with US fertilizer company Mosaic for a joint venture in a phosphorus ore development project in Peru. Mitsui will spend $275 million to acquire a 25% stake and voting rights in a subsidiary of Vale while Mosaic will hold a 24% stake. Mitsui is seeking to obtain a steady supply of phosphate which is used in its fertilizer production operations.

Mitsui entered the water infrastructure business in China in 2010 through a 50-50 joint venture with Singapore's Hyflux Ltd. a major provider of integrated water management services. Mitsui plans to do business with local governments and in areas with many industrial complexes by leveraging Hyflux's technological expertise and its own business network.

EXECUTIVES

Chairman, Shoei Utsuda, age 70
Corporate Auditor, Satoru Miura, age 66
Representative Director; EVP, Ken Abe, age 64
EVP CFO and Representative Director, Junichi Matsumoto, age 65
EVP; COO Asia/Pacific Business Unit, Toshimasa Furukawa, age 64
Corporate Auditor, Motonori Murakami, age 64
Senior Executive Managing Officer; COO EMEA Business Unit, Koji Nakamura, age 65
Managing Officer; President Mitsui & Co. (Canada), Terukazu Okahashi
President and CEO, Masami Iijima, age 63
EVP, Seiichi Tanaka, age 61
Senior Executive Managing Officer; COO Americas Business Unit; President and CEO Mitsui USA, Masaaki Fujita
Managing Officer; Deputy COO Americas Business Unit, Katsumi Ogawa
Representative Director; Senior Executive Managing Officer Energy Business Unit I; Energy Business Unit II; Financial Markets Business Unit; Domestic Offices and Branches; Chairman of Environment and New Energy Committee, Norinao Iio, age 62
Senior Executive Managing Officer and CFO, Joji Okada, age 75
Managing Officer; COO Foods & Retail Business Unit, Takashi Fukunaga
Senior Managing Executive Officer, Takashi Yamauchi
Managing Officer; COO IT Business Unit, Shuji Nakura
Managing Executive Officer; Chief Director of America, Mitsuhiko Kawai
Senior Executive Managing Officer, Daisuke Saiga, age 58
Senior Executive Managing Officer CIO and Chief Privacy Officer, Masayuki Kinoshita
Executive Managing Officer; Chief Representative Mitsui & Co. Ltd. China, Atsushi Oi

Representative Director; Senior Executive Managing Officer Infrastructure Projects Business Unit; Motor Vehicles Business Unit; Consumer Service Business Unit; IT Business Unit, Takao Omae, age 63
Representative Director; Senior Executive Managing Officer Iron & Steel Products Business Unit; Marine & Aerospace Business Unit; and Foods & Retail Business Unit, Masayoshi Komai, age 64
Executive Managing Officer; Deputy COO EMEA Business Unit, Noriaki Sakamoto
EVP, Fuminobu Kawashima
Executive Officer; Vice President of Kansai Office, Katsunori Aikyo
Managing Executive Officer; President of Subsidiary, Makoto Suzuki
Senior Executive Managing Officer, Shintaro Ambe
Representative Director; EVP, Ken Abe, age 64
EVP CFO and Representative Director, Junichi Matsumoto, age 65
Director, Toshiro Muto, age 70
President CEO and Representative Director, Masami Iijima, age 62
EVP CIO Chief Privacy Officer and Representative Director, Seiichi Tanaka, age 60
Director, Ikujiro Nonaka, age 78
Director, Hiroshi Hirabayashi, age 73
Director, Nobuko Matsubara, age 73
Representative Director; Senior Executive Managing Officer Energy Business Unit I; Energy Business Unit II; Financial Markets Business Unit; Domestic Offices and Branches; Chairman of Environment and New Energy Committee, Norinao Iio, age 62
Representative Director; Executive Managing Officer and Chief Compliance Officer, Daisuke Saiga, age 58
Representative Director; Senior Executive Managing Officer Infrastructure Projects Business Unit; Motor Vehicles Business Unit; Consumer Service Business Unit; IT Business Unit, Takao Omae, age 63
Representative Director; Senior Executive Managing Officer Iron & Steel Products Business Unit; Marine & Aerospace Business Unit; and Foods & Retail Business Unit, Masayoshi Komai, age 64
Auditors: DeloitteToucheTohmatsu

LOCATIONS

HQ: Mitsui & Co., Ltd.
2-1 Ohtemachi 1-chome, Chiyoda-ku, Tokyo 100-0004
Phone: (81) 3 3285 1111 **Fax:** (81) 3 3285 9821
Web: www.mitsui.com

COMPETITORS

ITOCHU
Kanematsu
Komatsu
Marubeni
Mitsubishi Corp.
Samsung Group
Sojitz
Sumitomo

HISTORICAL FINANCIALS

Company Type: Public

Income Statement FYE: March 31

	REVENUE ($ mil.)	NET INCOME ($ mil.)	NET PROFIT MARGIN	EMPLOYEES
03/13	52,200	3,272	6.3%	61,898
03/12	64,020	5,296	8.3%	64,218
03/11	56,510	3,703	6.6%	59,404
03/10	43,855	1,602	3.7%	60,961
03/09	55,900	1,803	3.2%	39,864
Annual Growth	(1.7%)	16.1%	—	11.6%

2013 Year-End Financials

Debt ratio: 0.4%
Return on equity: 10.5%
Cash ($ mil.): 15,196
Current ratio: 1.52
Long-term debt ($ mil.): 33,849
No. of shares (mil.): 1,825
Dividends
Yield: 0.0%
Payout: 0.0%
Market value ($ mil.): 509,223

	STOCK PRICE ($) FY Close	P/E High/Low		PER SHARE ($) Earnings	Dividends	Book Value
03/13	279.00	0	0	1.79	0.00	18.53
03/12	330.63	0	0	2.90	0.00	17.64
03/11	359.10	0	0	2.03	7.20	15.66
03/10	335.71	0	0	0.88	1.58	13.08
03/09	202.37	0	0	0.99	9.60	10.49
Annual Growth	8.4%	—	—	16.1%	(88.6%)	15.3%

Mitsui Life Insurance Co., Ltd.

LOCATIONS

HQ: Mitsui Life Insurance Co., Ltd.
1-1-20 Aomi, Koto-ku, Tokyo 135-8222
Phone: (81) 3 6831 8000
Web: www.mitsui-seimei.co.jp

HISTORICAL FINANCIALS

Company Type: Public

Income Statement FYE: March 31

	ASSETS ($ mil.)	NET INCOME ($ mil.)	INCOME AS % OF ASSETS	EMPLOYEES
03/13	76,823	81	0.1%	11,552
03/12	87,382	167	0.2%	12,118
03/11	87,242	171	0.2%	12,610
03/10	80,300	49	0.1%	13,868
03/09	74,998	(1,855)	—	13,284
Annual Growth	0.6%	—	—	(3.4%)

2013 Year-End Financials

Return on assets: 0.1%
Return on equity: 2.7%
Long-term debt ($ mil.): —
No. of shares (mil.): 278
Sales ($ mil): 10,181
Dividends
Yield: —
Payout: —
Market value ($ mil.): —

MOL Hungarian Oil and Gas Plc

The downstream operations of MOL Magyar Olaj-es Gazipari Rt. (Hungarian Oil and Gas Company or MOL) have moved it up to become Hungary's biggest company and one of Central Europe's top refiners. MOL's refineries produce 90400 barrels of oil equivalent per day and it operates 1500 gas stations in Croatia the Czech Republic Hungary Italy Poland Romania Slovakia Slovenia and the Ukraine. Other activities include exploration and production in Hungary Russia and other areas of Central and Eastern Europe. The company has proved and probable reserves of 434.2 million barrels of oil equivalent.

In addition to expanding its refining and marketing operations across Central Europe the company has restructured its exploration and production activities to focus on the development of oil fields in Russia.

In 2007 MOL acquired two refining and marketing companies –IES in Italy and Tifon in Croatia. Also that year MOL announced plans to merge with Austria's OMV though those plans were abandoned the next year due to regulatory concerns from the European Commission. In 2009 OMV sold its 21% stake in MOL to Russian oil company Surgutneftegas. Eyeing new areas of exploration that year MOL also acquired a 10% stake in Pearl Petroleum giving it access to gas-condensate fields in Iraq.

In 2011 the Hungarian government acquired Surgutneftegas' 21% stake in MOL for about EUR 1.9 billion (US$2.6 billion).

HISTORY

The oil refining industry in Hungary dates to the 1880s when refineries were opened in Fiume (1882) and Budapest (1883). By 1913 Hungary had 28 plants.

Following Hungary's defeat in WWI the country's refining industry fell into decline as new national boundaries placed most of its former oil refineries and oil-producing regions outside its borders. By 1921 Hungary had only six operational refineries.

British and American investors set up the European Gas and Electric Company (EUROGASCO) in the US in 1931 to acquire oil and gas concessions in Central Europe and to build power plants. By 1937 EUROGASCO (controlled by Standard Oil of New Jersey) was producing oil. A year later Standard Oil set up the Hungarian-American Oil Industry Shareholding Co. (MAORT) to develop the fields and in 1940 MAORT's production was meeting all of Hungary's oil needs.

During WWII MAORT requisitioned all oil assets. The oil industry boomed as Hungary served as a major supplier for the German war machine. But by 1944 with German armies in retreat from the Eastern Front much of Hungary's oil machinery and plants were dismantled. The remaining plants suffered heavy bombing from Allied forces or had equipment confiscated by Russian and Romanian troops.

After the war the Hungarian Soviet Crude Oil Co. began rebuilding Hungary's oil industry and started drilling on the Great Hungarian Plain in 1946. MAORT also ramped up oil production in the Trans-Danubian fields. In 1949 following charges of sabotage against MAORT managers MAORT was nationalized and broken up into five national companies which re-merged in 1952 with Hungarian Soviet Oil Co. (successor to Hungarian Soviet Crude Oil Co.).

In 1957 all operations of the Hungarian crude oil industry were consolidated under Crude Oil Trust which took over the gas industry by 1960. That year the company was renamed National Crude Oil and Gas Trust (OKGT) and the focus of exploration soon shifted from Trans-Danubian fields to the Great Plain. By 1970 the Great Plain accounted for 67% of oil production and 96% of natural gas production.

Hungary began allowing foreign gasoline distributors to compete in domestic markets during the 1980s. Moving toward privatization the Hungarian government founded MOL in 1991 as the successor to OKGT which comprised nine oil and gas enterprises. In 1993 the socialist government sold 8%

of MOL to the public. By 1998 the government had sold all but 25% of MOL.

During the 1990s the company also expanded in Central Europe. With Austria's OMV in 1994 it began building a 120-km pipeline linking Austria and Hungary which gave it access to natural gas from Western Europe for the first time. MOL also opened up service stations in neighboring countries beginning with one in Romania in 1996. By 2000 the company was operating about 80 stations in Romania 18 in Slovakia three in Ukraine and two in Slovenia in addition to its 330 stations in Hungary. MOL also acquired about 20% of chemical processor TVK in 1999 and upped the stake to nearly 33% by 2000. That year MOL also acquired 36% of Slovnaft Slovakia's only oil refiner and its major retailer.

In 2003 MOL concluded a long-term crude oil supply agreement with Russian oil giant YUKOS.

The company agreed in 2004 to sell its gas businesses to E.ON Ruhrgas for about $1 billion. (After much scrutiny by Hungarian and EU regulators the deal was completed in 2006.)

In 2005 MOL acquired the Romanian subsidiary of Royal Dutch Shell including the purchase of 59 Shell filling stations. Royal Dutch Shell also sold MOL its Romania-based lubricants aviation and commercial businesses.

EXECUTIVES

Group CEO and Director; Chairman TVK, Gyorgy Mosonyi, age 62
Chairman and CEO, Zsolt Hernadi, age 49
Group Chief Executive Officer (GCEO), Jozsef Molnar, age 55
SVP Petrochemicals; CEO TVK, Arpad Olvaso, age 53
EVP Retail, Laszlo Piry, age 45
EVP Exploration and Production, Sandor Fasimon, age 43
EVP Refining and Marketing Division and MOL Downstream, Ferenc Horvath, age 48
Vice Chairman, Sandor Csanyi, age 56
Group CFO, Jozsef Simola, age 43
President Management Board INA d.d., Zoltan Aldott, age 43
CEO Romania, Szabolcs I. Ferencz, age 44
Managing Director Lubes Division, Ferenc Denes, age 58
Managing Director Health Safety and Environmental Protection Division, Bela Cseh
Corporate Counsel, Pal Kara, age 39
Managing Director Natural Gas Transmission Division, Janos Zsuga
Director Investor Relations, Richard Benke
EVP Strategy and Business Development, Lajos Alacs, age 48
Director Investor Relations, Zsuzsanna Kun
Communications Director, Dora Somlyai, age 39
Director and Chairman and CEO Slovnaft a.s., Oszkar Vilagi
Group CEO and Director; Chairman TVK, Gyorgy Mosonyi, age 62
Vice Chairman, Sandor Csanyi, age 56
Director and Chairman and CEO Slovnaft a.s., Oszkar Vilagi
Auditors: Ernst&YoungKft

LOCATIONS

HQ: MOL Hungarian Oil and Gas Plc
Oktober huszonharmadika u. 18, Budapest H-1117
Phone: (36) 1 209 0000
Web: www.mol.hu

PRODUCTS/OPERATIONS

2009 Sales

	% of total
Refining &	74
Petrochemicals	9
Exploration &	9
Gas &	7
Other	1
Total	**100**

COMPETITORS

BG Group
BP
CEPSA
Eni
Hellenic Petroleum
Norsk Hydro ASA
OMV
PKN ORLEN
Repsol YPF
Royal Dutch Shell
TOTAL

HISTORICAL FINANCIALS

Company Type: Public

Income Statement FYE: December 31

	REVENUE ($ mil.)	NET INCOME ($ mil.)	NET PROFIT MARGIN	EMPLOYEES
12/12	25,006	686	2.7%	29,298
12/11	22,118	636	2.9%	31,471
12/10	20,692	500	2.4%	32,394
12/09	17,194	617	3.6%	34,090
12/08	18,681	747	4.0%	17,213
Annual Growth	7.6%	(2.1%)	—	14.2%

2012 Year-End Financials

Debt ratio: 0.1%
Return on equity: 9.0%
Cash ($ mil.): 1,442
Current ratio: 1.17
Long-term debt ($ mil.): 3,091
No. of shares (mil.): 79
Dividends
Yield: 2.3%
Payout: —
Market value ($ mil.): 3,275

	STOCK PRICE ($) FY Close	P/E High/Low	PER SHARE ($) Earnings	Dividends	Book Value
12/12	41.35	— —	6.75	0.97	97.18
12/11	36.18	— —	6.37	0.00	86.34
12/10	47.00	— —	5.82	0.00	87.22
12/09	46.84	— —	7.23	0.00	88.46
12/08	28.00	— —	4.31	2.99	80.78
Annual Growth	10.2%	— —	11.9%	(24.5%)	4.7%

Morrison (Wm.) Supermarkets Plc

Wm Morrison Supermarkets moved up the UK food chain with the acquisition of its larger rival Safeway plc. The UK's fourth-largest grocery chain Morrison runs about 475 stores throughout England and Scotland up from just 125 when it beat out UK supermarket giants Tesco (the UK's #1 food retailer) and Wal-Mart-owned ASDA in a highly-contested takeover battle. Morrison's supermarkets offer a variety of food and nonfood items most notably through its Market Street specialty departments. About 300 of the locations sell gas. The Safeway purchase transformed Wm Morrison into a national chain with about a 13% share of the UK grocery market. Wm Morrison was founded by its namesake in 1899.

Morrison has been a good steady performer in recent years despite the recession government austerity measures and continued fierce price competition among grocery chains in the UK. In fiscal 2012 (ends January) its sales increased by 7% helped by the addition of 37 new stores including the company's first three convenience stores. The 7% rise followed a similar 7% increase and 6% increase in fiscal years 2011 and 2010 respectively. The launch of its new M savers brand for budget conscious shoppers helped drive sales despite a tough economic backdrop.

As England's fourth-largest chain Morrison feels it has plenty of room to grow. With shops ranging in size from 11000 to more than 40000 sq. ft. it can be flexible when selecting sites. It is also growing by making acquisitions. To that end in early 2011 Morrison acquired 16 former Netto UK stores from rival ASDA which recently bought the Netto chain. Morrison paid some #28 million ($44 million) for the stores the first of which began trading under the Morrison banner in May. The 16 Netto conversions accounted for nearly half the new stores opened in fiscal 2012. To boost the flower offering in its supermarkets the grocer in mid-2011 acquired flower importer and distributor Flower World.

Under CEO Dalton Philips who joined the business from Loblaw in Canada in 2010 Morrison has made some interesting moves. It opened its first convenience stores –under the M local banner –in 2011 and is finally set to launch an online offering in 2012. (Morrison is the only major UK supermarket without an online business.) To this end in February 2011 it acquired Kiddicare a multichannel online retailer of baby products for GBP70 million ($112 million). Morrison plans to run the company separately and leverage Kiddicare's technology platform and management team. Soon after Morrison bought a 10% stake in the US online grocer Fresh Direct. The #35 million ($56 million) investment will give Morrison access to Fresh Direct's profitable model and help the UK grocer develop its own online food offering which is slated to debut shortly and will target Londoners. Morrison will take on Ocado and Waitrose in the online space.

Morrison has steadily increased its share of the UK grocery market from just under 12% in 2007 to 12.8% in fiscal 2012. The chain is strongest in Yorkshire with a 22% share of the market in the North and in Scotland where is claims in excess of 16% of the market. Morrison's focus on its in-store specialty shops known as Market Street has boosted meat bakery pre-packed fresh food and convenience food sales. To compete with discounters including rival ASDA and limited assortment ALDI and appeal to cash-strapped shoppers the firm has been cutting thousands of prices despite its own rising costs. While nonfood items account for a small percentage of overall sales Morrison is looking to expand its general merchandise offering by adding clothing and other goods. To that end it has begun adding Peacocks concessions to some of its larger stores.

The chain is known as the master of small to medium-sized supermarkets as most of the company's stores fall into the 25000-to-40000 sq. ft. range. The shops are noted for their Market Street departments a collection of in-store specialty shops that ring the perimeter of the store. They include a bakery butcher shop and deli. Market Street departments also offer pizza pies and curry. Outlets also have in-store cafes. Morrison is vertically integrated including operating facilities for processing packing and distributing meat and produce. Its Farmers Boy unit supplies its stores with fresh food including pizzas cooked meats and other prepared foods. It also operates three bakeries. Morrison is one of the UK's top food producers.

HISTORY

A former grocer's apprentice William Morrison founded his company in Bradford UK in 1899 as a wholesale seller of eggs and butter. Named William Morrison (Provisions) the business eventually expanded into retail by opening grocery stalls and by the 1920s was operating counter service shops as well.

Self-service stores became popular in the UK during the late 1940s and 1950s and the company began opening self-service outlets during that time. William's son Ken (born when William was 57 years of age) joined the company in 1950 and became chairman in 1956. The chain opened its first supermarket in Bradford in 1962 by converting an abandoned cinema. Wm Morrison Supermarkets went public five years later.

In 1979 Wm Morrison moved into Lancashire by purchasing the 10-store grocery chain Whelans Discount founded by Dave Whelan an ex-football star who also founded JJB Sports. Two years later it bought the Mainstop chain. The company's sales grew by a factor of 10 during the 1980s and 1990; it added about 50 stores in the 1990s. In 1993 Wm Morrison began opening stores on Sundays and in 1997 it teamed up with Midland Bank to offer in-store banking.

The company had operated mostly in northeastern England but a new distribution center that opened in 1996 in Cheshire allowed it to handle more distribution duties and gave it the base to expand west. Wm Morrison also turned south opening superstores in three southern regions (Oxford Essex and Kent) in 1998. The retailer also acquired two stores from Food Giant and three superstores (one near London) from Co-operative Retail Services that year. Wm Morrison expanded its Farmers Boy food processing operations by opening a new 180000-sq.-ft. facility in 1999. It opened four new stores in 2000 and bought three others.

The company's highly regarded Managing Director John Dowd resigned in March 2002 because of ill health. Soon after Marie Melnyk and Robert Stott were promoted to the positions of joint managing director. Morrison added six stores in fiscal year 2003 (ended January 2003).

On January 9 2003 Morrison made an offer of 1.32 Morrison shares for each share of Safeway plc. In March the company's bid for its rival lapsed after the Office of Fair Trading referred the bid to the Competition Commission.

Following clearance from Britain's High Court the company's acquisition of Safeway closed on March 8 2004. (Morrison shareholders own 60% of the enlarged company with Safeway shareholders left with 40%.)

In June 2006 the company named Marc Bolland formerly COO of brewer Heineken as CEO succeeding Bob Stott who retired. Stott became CEO in 2005.

Sir Kenneth Morrison retired as chairman in March 2008 after 55 years with the company. Morrison who was named honorary president was succeeded by former deputy chairman Sir Ian Gibson. The grocery chain opened eight new supermarkets in fiscal 2008.

In 2009 Morrisons acquired about 40 Co-operative Group and former Somerfield stores for about #220 million (about $330 million). In November Bolland resigned to join Marks and Spencer. He was succeeded by Dalton Philips who joined the business in March 2010.

In 2011 Morrisons acquired about 18 Netto UK stores from ASDA. In June it bought Flower World an importer and wholesaler of flowers in the UK in a bid to improve the flower offering at its supermarkets.

EXECUTIVES

Manufacturing Director, M. Fletcher
Corporate Services Director, Martyn Jones, age 54, $679,235 total compensation
Retail Projects Director, P. J. Pleasance
Trades Specialist Director, T. Robinson
Regional Director, A. Downey
Public Relations Director, G. Hall
Group Retail Director, Mark D. Harrison
Security Director, A. Hudson
Construction Director, D. N. Wade
Chairman, Sir Ian Gibson, age 66, $596,880 total compensation
Group Finance Director and Director, Richard Pennycook, age 49, $1,076,374 total compensation
Marketing Director, M. Bates
Regional Director, S. Eastwood
Regional Director, David Gardner
Regional Director, I. Grace
Purchasing Director, K. L. Johnson
Stores Director (South), C. Taylor
MIS Director, G. Barr
Managing Director Morrisons.com, Simon Thompson
Chief Executive; Executive Director, Dalton T. Philips, age 45
Logistics Director, Neal Austin
Corporate Affairs Director, Richard Taylor
Licensed Trades Director, Grant Eastwood
Director Investor Relations and Financial Planning, Niall Addison
Secretary, Greg McMahon
Human Resources Director, Norman Pickavance
Group Property Director, Terry Hartwell
Corporate Services Director, Martyn Jones, age 54
Director, Philip G. Cox, age 62
Director, Penelope L. (Penny) Hughes, age 54
Group Finance Director and Director, Richard Pennycook, age 49
Director, Nigel Robertson, age 53
Director, Brian Flanagan, age 60
Director, Johanna Waterous, age 55
Auditors: KPMGAuditPlc

LOCATIONS

HQ: Morrison (Wm.) Supermarkets Plc
Hilmore House, Gain Lane, Bradford BD3 7DL
Phone: (44) 845 611 5000
Web: www.morrisons.co.uk

PRODUCTS/OPERATIONS

2012 Sales

	% of total
Food & general	76
Fuel	23
Total	**100**

COMPETITORS

ALDI
ASDA
Alliance Boots
BP
Co-operative Group
Exxon Mobil
J Sainsbury
John Lewis
Marks & Spencer
Musgrave Retail Partners
Royal Dutch Shell
SPAR (UK)
Tesco

HISTORICAL FINANCIALS

Company Type: Public

Income Statement — FYE: February 3

	REVENUE ($ mil.)	NET INCOME ($ mil.)	NET PROFIT MARGIN	EMPLOYEES
02/13*	28,681	1,024	3.6%	128,705
01/12	27,743	1,083	3.9%	131,207
01/11	26,247	1,006	3.8%	132,074
01/10	24,629	955	3.9%	133,744
02/09	21,207	671	3.2%	124,530
Annual Growth	7.8%	11.1%	—	0.8%

*Fiscal year change

2013 Year-End Financials

Debt ratio: —
Return on equity: 11.9%
Cash ($ mil.): 419
Current ratio: 0.57
Long-term debt ($ mil.): —
No. of shares (mil.): —
Dividends
Yield: 0.0%
Payout: 479.0%
Market value ($ mil.): —

	STOCK PRICE ($) FY Close	P/E High/Low	PER SHARE ($) Earnings	Dividends	Book Value
02/13*	19.74	231186	0.42	2.02	3.53
01/12	22.89	244194	0.41	2.20	3.35
01/11	20.97	257178	0.37	1.42	3.25
01/10	23.59	293158	0.36	1.14	2.98
02/09	19.00	279199	0.25	0.08	2.51
Annual Growth	1.0%	—	— 13.8%	120.9%	8.9%

*Fiscal year change

MS&AD Insurance Group Holdings

LOCATIONS

HQ: MS&AD Insurance Group Holdings
1-3-7 Yaesu, Chuo-ku, Tokyo 103-0028
Phone: (81) 3 6202 5270
Web: www.ms-ad-hd.com

HISTORICAL FINANCIALS

Company Type: Public

Income Statement — FYE: March 31

	REVENUE ($ mil.)	NET INCOME ($ mil.)	NET PROFIT MARGIN	EMPLOYEES
03/13	45,785	888	1.9%	36,643
03/12	45,775	(2,065)	—	36,929
03/11	40,878	65	0.2%	36,538
03/10	20,903	402	1.9%	21,908
03/09	20,665	83	0.4%	21,336
Annual Growth	22.0%	80.8%	—	14.5%

2013 Year-End Financials

Debt ratio: 0.0%
Return on equity: 4.7%
Cash ($ mil.): 17,630
Current ratio: 0.22
Long-term debt ($ mil.): 3,094
No. of shares (mil.): 621
Dividends
Yield: —
Payout: —
Market value ($ mil.): 6,853

	STOCK PRICE ($) FY Close	P/E High/Low	PER SHARE ($) Earnings	Dividends	Book Value
03/13	11.02	— —	1.43	0.00	34.55
03/12	10.26	— —	(3.32)	0.00	29.64
03/11	11.27	— —	0.10	0.31	31.72
03/10	13.77	— —	0.96	0.29	33.83
03/09	11.67	— —	0.20	0.15	24.78
Annual Growth	(1.4%)	— —	64.0%	—	8.7%

Muenchener Rueckversicherungs-Gesellschaft AG (Germany)

Some companies live with risk... Munchener Ruckversicherungs-Gesellschaft (Munich Re) on the other hand "thrives" on risk. Reinsurance coverage (insurance for insurers) includes fire life motor and liability policies on both a facultative (individual risk) and treaty (categorized risk) basis. The company also provides direct insurance including life health and property coverage through Germany-based ERGO and other subsidiaries and it provides asset management services through MEAG MUNICH ERGO. Through Munich Re America Munich Re enjoys greater access to the US market. As one of the world's largest reinsurance and risk management firms the company operates in some 160 countries.

Geographic Reach

Europe is Munich Re's biggest market (accounting for about 55% of premiums in 2011) and the company has expanded its European presence over the years through acquisitions and internal growth programs. North America is the second-largest market accounting for about 30% of premiums (up from 25% in 2010 due to acquisitions and organic growth in the US).

Operations

Munich Re's reinsurance and primary insurance segments respectively account for about 50% and 40% of annual premiums. After focused growth efforts in the primary insurance segment the ERGO division has grown to insure clients in 30 countries in Europe and Asia.

The company's health insurance operations are handled through the company's Deutsche Krankenversicherung unit (DKV a subsidiary of ERGO) in Germany and through the Munich Health division (which also holds Munich Re's health reinsurance operations) in international countries. The MEAG asset management unit holds some E200 billion ($260 billion) in investments.

Financial Performance

Munich Re reported E61 billion ($79 billion) in revenues in 2011 down 7% from results in 2010. Net income was E712 million ($922 million) down 71%.

Munich Re suffered a significant natural catastrophe loss (estimated at some E1.5 billion or $2.1 billion) in the first quarter of 2011 due to the earthquake and tsunami that struck Japan in March. The subsequent damage to the Japanese infrastructure led to one of the largest levels of commercial coverage claims for Munich Re. The firm also experienced high catastrophe losses in 2010; however such losses are part and parcel for reinsurance companies who rely on the less-disastrous years to even out those creating heavy burdens.

Strategy

Though reinsurance is its largest operating segment the company hopes to continue the growth of its traditional insurance segment in the core German market and other European markets focusing on personal lines. As part of this strategy the company is widening the presence of the ERGO brand across its insurance operations in its European markets (especially in Germany).

Additionally Munich Re is working to extend the ERGO brand into new markets especially in emerging markets in Eastern Europe and parts of Asia. In 2011 ERGO formed a joint venture with Assets Investment Holding to sell life insurance in China; it also entered the Vietnamese market that year. However ERGO has also been selling off select international operations in noncore markets; it exited operations in Portugal and South Korea in 2011 and 2012.

In the North American market Munich Re is expanding in the specialty property/casualty and health insurance markets primarily through acquisitions. It is also working to expand its presence in the growing health care insurance arena in emerging markets like India.

Mergers and Acquisitions

To expand its global health insurance operations in 2011 Munich Re's Munich Health North America division acquired Windsor Health Group a US provider of Medicare services for some $131 million.

Ownership

Billionaire investment mogul Warren Buffett who controls a number of insurance and reinsurance players through Berkshire Hathaway has taken notice of Munich Re. Buffett increased his stake in the company to 10% in 2010.

HISTORY

Investors Carl Thieme and Theodor Cramer-Klett founded Munich Re in 1880. Within a month Munich Re opened offices in Hamburg Berlin Vienna and St. Petersburg establishing treaties with German and Danish insurers. In 1888 Munich Re went public; two years later it opened an office in London and helped finance the creation of Allianz which would soon come to dominate the German insurance industry. In 1892 the firm opened a branch in the US (it incurred severe losses from the 1906 San Francisco earthquake).

WWI interrupted Munich Re's UK and US operations. The company recovered after 1918 only to be hobbled again by the Great Depression. In 1933 Munich Re executive Kurt Schmitt became minister of economic affairs for the Nazis. Objecting to the evolving policies of National Socialism he left after a year returning to Munich Re where he became chief executive in 1938.

Hitler's ignition of WWII wasn't quite the boom Munich Re needed; its international business was again disrupted. After the war the Allies further limited overseas operations. Because of his involvement with the Nazi government Schmitt was replaced by Eberhard von Reininghaus in 1945. The division of Germany further hampered the company's recovery.

Jump-started by the Marshall Plan in 1950 the West German "Wirtschaftswunder" (economic miracle) kicked into high gear as the devastated country rebuilt. Relaxation of occupation-era trading limits also helped as the company rebuilt its foreign business. By 1969 Munich Re's sales topped DM 2 billion. Amid the global oil crisis and a rash of terrorist acts in Germany the firm reported its first-ever reinsurance loss in 1977.

German reunification in 1990 provided new markets for Munich Re but advantages from new business in the East were wiped out by claims arising from that year's harsh winter.

In 1992 an investigation by the German Federal Cartel Office prompted a realignment in the insurance business —Allianz ceded its controlling interests in three life insurers (Hamburg-Mannheimer Versicherungs Karlsruher Lebensversicherung and Berlinische Lebensversicherung) to Munich Re bringing it into direct insurance. Munich Re took over Deutsche Krankenversicherung (DKV) in 1996. Also that year Munich Re acquired American Re.

During the 1990s reinsurance sales dwindled as competition increased forcing lower premiums and alternatives to insurance and reinsurance became more common. Munich Re looked to direct insurance particularly individual property/casualty and life insurance to compensate. In 1997 it merged Hamburg-Mannheimer and DKV with another insurer Victoria AG to form ERGO Versicherungsgruppe. Within a year ERGO's insurance income accounted for half of all revenues.

Munich Re and ERGO launched asset management firm MEAG Munich ERGO AssetManagement in 1999. That year Munich Re experienced its worst year ever after natural disasters hit its reinsurance business hard. To recoup its losses the next year the firm expanded both its reinsurance and primary insurance operations into key markets in Europe North and South America and Asia. Also in 2000 Munich Re bought CNA Financial's life reinsurance operations. Together with Swiss Re the company launched Inreon an online reinsurance exchange in 2001.

As one of the companies hit hardest financially by the World Trade Center tragedy Munich Re paid out some $2 billion in claims. In 2003 Allianz and Munich Re terminated their cooperation agreement as their shareholdings in each other fell to under 15%. (The two companies gradually sold off nearly all of their ownership interests in following years.)

In 2004 Munich Re entered its first Asian market by forming a joint venture in China.

In 2005 Munich Re took a nearly 75% hit on its profit margin due to re-investment in its American Re subsidiary whose internal reserves required a $1.6 billion injection for expected claims related to asbestos and environmental claims on policies mostly written between 1997 and 2002. The firm also suffered a large natural catastrophe loss that year due to Hurricane Katrina's devastating effects on the US Gulf Coast; Munich Re paid some $1.6 billion in claims as a result of the disaster.

The company expanded in the European market in 2007 when it bought British underwriting management group Bell & Clements Group in an effort to bolster its bottom line with profit-making basic services. It also purchased MSP Underwriting UK parent of Lloyd's Syndicate 318 manager Beaufort Underwriting Agency.

To further its US property/casualty operations in 2008 the company acquired US specialty insurance provider The Midland Company for $1.3 billion; Midland's American Modern Insurance Group subsidiaries became part of the Munich Re America organization. Munich Re also bought Aon subsidiary Sterling Life Insurance for $352 million to expand its life and health insurance provisions in the US. Sterling Life became part of the newly formed Munich Health unit in 2009.

In 2009 Munich Re America expanded again by purchasing specialty insurance and reinsurance provider HSB Group from American International Group for $739 million in cash (plus $76 million in debt assumptions). The acquisition expanded

Munich Re's niche insurance and risk management offerings in North America.

The company launched a re-branding program in 2009 to increase the presence of its ERGO brand across its insurance operations included the retiring of some older German monikers and in 2010 a widespread marketing program was launched to make the ERGO brand more familiar to German consumers.

EXECUTIVES

Member Board of Management Chairman Reinsurance Committee, Torsten Jeworrek, age 52, $791,580 total compensation
Member Board of Management Europe and Latin America, Georg Daschner, age 64, $699,152 total compensation
Head Group Communications, Christian Lawrence
Member Board of Management Services Germany Asia/Pacific and Africa, Ludger Arnoldussen, age 51, $588,760 total compensation
Member Board of Management Special and Financial Risks Reinsurance Investments and Central Procurement, Thomas Blunck, $571,678 total compensation
Member Board of Management Health and Human Resources and Labor Relations Director, Wolfgang Strassl, age 56, $571,678 total compensation
Spokesperson US; VP and Head Marketing Communications Munich Reinsurance America, Terese Rosenthal
Member Board of Management Global Clients and North America, Peter Roder, age 53, $462,630 total compensation
Member Board of Management Life, Joachim Wenning, age 48, $300,000 total compensation
Head Media Relations, Johanna Weber
Deputy Head Media Relations, Michael Able
Media Relations Solvency II and Human Resources, Irmgard Joas
Media Relations Reinsurance Life Munich Health Primary Insurance Issues Munich Re (Group), Regine Kaiser
Media Relations Reinsurance Property, Anke Rosumek
Spokesperson Asia, Nikola Kemper
Chief Financial Officer, Greg Guelfand
Chief Risk Officer, Joachim Oechslin
President Chief Executive Officer, Kenneth B. Irvin
President Chief Executive Officer, Mary Forrest
Chief Executive Officer, Peter Goschl
Executive Director Chairman, Tony Medniuk
Head of Investor & Rating Agency Relations, Christian Christian Becker-Hussong Becker-Hussong
Deputy Chairman of the Supervisory Board; Employee Representative, Hans Hans Claussen Claussen
Chairman of the Management Board; Chief Investment Officer, Nikolaus Nikolaus von Bomhard Bomhard
Member of the Management Board, Peter Peter Roeder Roeder
Chief Financial Officer, Jorg Schneider
Member Supervisory Board, Wolfgang Mayrhuber, age 66
Member Supervisory Board, Thomas Wellauer, age 57
Member Supervisory Board, Ron Sommer, age 64
Member Supervisory Board, Herbert Bach
Member Supervisory Board, Henning Kagermann, age 66
Member Supervisory Board, Anton van Rossum, age 68
Member Supervisory Board, Bernd Pischetsrieder
Member Supervisory Board, Peter Loscher, age 55
Deputy Chairman Supervisory Board, Hans-Peter Clau?en
Member Supervisory Board, Frank Fassin
Member Supervisory Board, Reinhard Pasch
Member Supervisory Board, Richard Sommer
Member Supervisory Board, Peter Gruss, age 64
Member Supervisory Board, Dina Bosch
Member Supervisory Board, Christian Fuhrmann
Member Supervisory Board, Silvia Muller
Member Supervisory Board, Marco Norenberg
Member Supervisory Board, Andres Ruiz Feger
Supervisory Board Member, Benita Ferrero-Waldner, age 65
Member of the Supervisory Board; Employee Representative, Andres Andres Ruiz Feger Feger
Member of the Supervisory Board, Annika Annika Falkengren Falkengren
Member of the Supervisory Board, Anton Anton van Rossum Rossum
Member of the Supervisory Board; Employee Representative, Dina Dina Boesch Boesch
Member of the Supervisory Board; Employee Representative, Marco Marco Noerenberg Noerenberg
Member of the Supervisory Board, Peter Peter Loescher Loescher
Member of the Supervisory Board; Employee Representative, Silvia Silvia Mueller Mueller
Auditors: KPMGBayerischeTreuhandgesellschaftAG

LOCATIONS

HQ: Muenchener Rueckversicherungs-Gesellschaft AG (Germany)
Koeniginstrasse 107, Munich D-80802
Phone: (49) 89 38 91 0 **Fax:** (49) 89 39 90 56
Web: www.munichre.com

2011 Premiums

	% of total
Europe	55
North	30
Asia &	10
Latin	3
Africa Near & Middle	2
Total	**100**

PRODUCTS/OPERATIONS

2011 Sales

	% of total
Reinsurance	
Property/casualty	31
Life	17
Primary insurance	
Life	18
Health	13
Property/casualty	10
Munich	10
Asset	1
Total	**100**

Selected Brands

ERGO (primary insurance)
- Deutscher Automobil Schutz (D.A.S. auto insurance)
- Deutsche Krankenversicherung (DKV)
- ERV

ERGO Direkt (commercial customer consulting)
DKV (domestic health insurance)
Munich Health (international health insurance domestic and international health reinsurance)
Munich Re
Munich Re America
- American Modern Insurance (specialty property/casualty insurance life insurance reinsurance)
- Hartford Steam Boiler (HSB specialty property/casualty insurance and reinsurance)

COMPETITORS

ACE Limited
AEGON
AIG
AXA
Allianz
Allstate
Manulife Financial
MetLife
Nippon Life Insurance
OdysseyRe
PartnerRe
Prudential plc
Baloise-Holding
Berkshire Hathaway
Everest Re
General Re
Hannover Re
Helvetia Group
ING
Reinsurance Group of America
RenaissanceRe
Swiss Re
Transatlantic Holdings
XL Group plc

HISTORICAL FINANCIALS

Company Type: Public

Income Statement

FYE: December 31

	ASSETS ($ mil.)	NET INCOME ($ mil.)	INCOME AS % OF ASSETS	EMPLOYEES
12/12	340,531	4,211	1.2%	45,437
12/11	320,232	908	0.3%	47,206
12/10	316,335	3,241	1.0%	46,915
12/09	321,840	3,631	1.1%	47,429
12/08	301,172	2,101	0.7%	44,209
Annual Growth	3.1%	19.0%	—	0.7%

2012 Year-End Financials

Return on assets: 1.2%
Return on equity: 12.6%
Long-term debt ($ mil.): —
No. of shares (mil.): 179
Sales ($ mil): 87,956
Dividends
Yield: 3.0%
Payout: —
Market value ($ mil.): 3,234

	STOCK PRICE ($) FY Close	P/E High	P/E Low	PER SHARE ($) Earnings	Dividends	Book Value
12/12	18.03	2	1	23.70	0.55	199.76
12/11	12.28	8	5	5.10	1.14	166.33
12/10	15.11	2	1	17.48	0.54	161.79
12/09	15.50	3	1	18.66	0.51	165.51
12/08	15.80	5	3	10.46	0.00	149.82
Annual Growth	3.4%	—	—	22.7%	—	7.5%

National Australia Bank Ltd.

National Australia Bank (NAB) is one of Australia's Big Four banks (along with ANZ Westpac and Commonwealth Bank of Australia). It operates in Australia New Zealand Asia the UK and the US through subsidiaries that provide banking wealth management and investment banking services. NAB also offers debt risk management and investment products for institutional clients. The company and its subsidiaries have more than 1800 branches and service centers. Subsidiaries Clydesdale Bank and Yorkshire Bank operate offices in the UK. In New Zealand NAB operates as Bank of New Zealand and in the US the company's Great Western Bank includes 200 branches.

NAB's main strategy is to develop a diverse business portfolio. The company often looks to expand its geographic reach in addition to its service offerings through acquisitions and organic growth.

Australia is at the core of NAB and the company works to improve its business banking personal banking and wealth businesses as well as drive mortgage and deposit growth at home. In 2011 the company's net profits were up 24% from the previous year. The increase was largely due to strong growth in its Australian business and personal banking segments (which saw net operating growth of 7% and 10% respectively.)

In 2011 NAB acquired Challenger Financial Service's mortgage management business (rebranded as Advantage). NAB also launched UBank a branchless direct bank that specializes in home loans. Both deals expanded the company's retail banking business.

While NAB works to develop its portfolio in Australia expansion abroad (including its branch network in the US and in Asia) is a main focus. In 2009 NAB expanded its asset management business in Asia when it acquired Hong Kong-based Calibre Asset Management. In 2010 Great Western further established its presence in the US Midwest (and increased agriculture lending) when it acquired F&M Bank with its 10 Iowa branches and TierOne Bank in Nebraska.

The company also is building up its offerings for high-net-worth customers. In 2009 it bought the Australian life and pensions business of British insurance giant Aviva for $A825 million ($650 million) increasing its position in the life insurance market. It also acquired a majority stake in Goldman Sachs' Australia and New Zealand wealth management operations. Goldman Sachs retained ownership of about 20% of the unit which operates under the JBWere brand.

NAB is reviewing its UK operations and it is expected to retool the structure of its Clydesdale and Yorkshire bank brands which represent 330 retail branches and 70 service centers. The economic recession and slow recovery in the UK banking sector lowered profits for NAB. Poor performance in business lending was mostly to blame. NAB saw net operating income drop 7% in the UK in 2011.

HISTORY

Formed in 1858 in Melbourne National Bank of Australasia (NBA) just missed the peak of the Victoria gold rush. The bank expanded across the territory and was one of the first to lend to farmers and ranchers using land deeds as security. In the late 1870s drought imperiled Victoria. Seeking greener pastures NBA entered New South Wales in 1885 then headed into Western Australia. Economic instability continued; in 1893 the bank experienced its first panic and was shuttered for eight weeks. NBA reopened only to close a quarter of its branches between 1893 and 1896.

During the Australian commonwealth's early years Western Australia was the bank's salvation as the economies in Victoria and South Australia stagnated. NBA helped fund Australia's WWI efforts through public loans. A postwar consolidation wave in banking swept up NBA which made acquisitions in 1918 and 1922.

Overdue farm and ranch loans weakened the bank during the Depression. As WWII raged the Commonwealth Bank (established in 1912) took greater control of Australia's banks. With competition among banks primarily limited to branch growth NBA acquired Queensland National Bank in 1948 and Ballarat Banking Co. in 1955. The bank diversified into consumer finance through acquisition. In the 1960s Australia experienced an economic boom as immigration and industrialization grew. The boom went bust in the 1970s as the world sunk into recession. Still under the Commonwealth Bank's tight control the banks watched business that had once been theirs lost to building societies merchant banks and credit unions.

The 1980s brought banking deregulation. To vie with foreign banks entering Australia NBA in 1981 merged with Commercial Banking Co. of Sydney and became the National Commercial Banking Corp. of Australia in 1982. (It took its present name in 1984.) Throughout the 1980s the bank diversified and moved into the US and Japan. It invested in property and made loans to foreign countries. All too quickly though property values sank and countries defaulted on loans.

To fight recession NAB looked abroad for opportunities. In 1987 it bought Clydesdale Bank Northern Bank and National Irish Bank from Midland Bank Group (now part of HSBC Holdings). Three years later NAB bought Yorkshire Bank then turned the four banks around by linking them and tightening loan operations. In 1992 it bought the troubled Bank of New Zealand again tightening loan operations. Three years later NAB claimed Michigan National in the US.

After the mid-1990s economic recovery NAB bought HomeSide to try to adapt the US mortgage firm's efficient operations for all its banks.

NAB in 2000 bought Lend Lease's MLC fund management group. It also announced plans to launch a separate stock for its European businesses fueling speculation it might be on the prowl to buy or merge with a large UK bank. The Australian Competition and Consumer Commission (ACCC) that year accused NAB of credit card transaction price-fixing; the bank faced a possible fine of nearly $6 million but the ACCC dropped litigation against the group the following year.

Also in 2001 NAB sold US-based Michigan National Bank to ABN AMRO and sold mortgage lender HomeSide International to Washington Mutual the following year. In fiscal year 2002 the bank cut some 2000 jobs mostly in back-office operations.

During fiscal year 2003 the company booked pre-tax losses of some $360 million due to unauthorized trading in the company's foreign currency options department. By the end of March 2004 chairman Charles Allen chief executive Frank Cicutto and the heads of global markets and foreign exchange had resigned. Three more executives and at least five traders were fired. The fallout continued the next year as the company struggled to regroup.

NAB sold its Irish banks —National Irish Bank and Northern Bank —to Danske Bank in 2005. It retained its UK banks Yorkshire Bank (England) and Clydesdale Bank (Scotland).

In 2006 NAB sold its Custom Fleet vehicle leasing division to GE Capital as well as its Asian life insurance and wealth management operations. The downsizing was part of the company's move to streamline operations.

To establish a foothold in the US NAB acquired Great Western Bancorporation for $A836 million (nearly US$800 million) in 2008.

Also that year NAB took a 20% stake in Chinese property trust Union Trust and Investment. The deal made NAB the first foreign bank to buy into a Chinese trust firm.

EXECUTIVES

Group Executive People Communications & Governance, Michaela J. Healey, age 46
Group Executive Product & Markets, Rick Sawers
Chairman, Michael A. Chaney, age 63
Managing Director & CEO Bank of New Zealand, Andrew Thorburn
CEO and Director, Cameron A. Clyne, $903,998 total compensation
Group Executive Personal Banking, Gavin R. Slater
Group Chief Risk Officer, Bruce Munro
Group Executive Business Banking, Joseph Healy
Executive Director Finance, Mark A. Joiner, $823,837 total compensation
Group Executive Enterprise Services and Transformation, Lisa Gray
Group Executive NAB Wealth, Andrew Hagger
General Manager China Banking, Danny Armstrong
Group Executive Finance & Strategy, Craig Drummond
Director, Sir Malcolm Williamson, age 73
Director, Paul J. Rizzo, age 66
Director, Geoffrey A. (Geoff) Tomlinson, age 65
CEO and Director, Cameron A. Clyne
Director, John G. Thorn, age 64
Director, Patricia Cross, age 53
Director, Daniel T. (Danny) Gilbert, age 60
Director, Jillian S. Segal, age 55
Executive Director Finance, Mark A. Joiner
Director, John Waller
Director, Anthony K. T. Yuen
Auditors: Ernst&Young

LOCATIONS

HQ: National Australia Bank Ltd.
800 Bourke Street, Docklands, Melbourne, Victoria 3008
Phone: (61) 3 8641 9083 **Fax:** (61) 3 8641 4927
Web: www.nabgroup.com

PRODUCTS/OPERATIONS

2011 Cash Earnings

	% of total
Business	44
Personal	17
wholesale	12
New Zealand	11
MLC & NAB	10
UK	3
Great Western	3
Total	**100**

Selected Subsidiaries

Calibre Asset Management
Great Western Bancorporation
nabCapital (formerly Institutional Markets & Services)
National Australia Group Europe Limited
  Clydesdale Bank PLC
    Yorkshire Bank Home Loans Limited
    Yorkshire Bank Investments Limited
  National Australia Group Europe Services Limited
National Australia Group (NZ) Limited
  Bank of New Zealand
    BNZ International Funding Limited
National Australia Trustees Limited
National Wealth Management Holdings Limited
MLC Limited
  National Wealth Management International Holdings Limited

COMPETITORS

Australia and New Zealand Banking
Barclays
Commonwealth Bank of Australia
HSBC
Lloyds Banking Group
Northern Rock (Asset Management)
Royal Bank of Scotland
Westpac Banking

HISTORICAL FINANCIALS

Company Type: Public

Income Statement FYE: September 30

	ASSETS ($ mil.)	NET INCOME ($ mil.)	INCOME AS % OF ASSETS	EMPLOYEES
09/12	796,373	4,260	0.5%	0
09/11	732,251	5,070	0.7%	0
09/10	664,069	4,089	0.6%	0
09/09	576,719	2,282	0.4%	0
09/08	528,353	3,648	0.7%	0
Annual Growth	10.8%	3.9%	—	—

2012 Year-End Financials

Return on assets: 0.5%
Return on equity: 9.4%
Long-term debt ($ mil.): —
No. of shares (mil.): —
Sales ($ mil): 49,200
Dividends
Yield: 0.0%
Payout: 101.3%
Market value ($ mil.): —

	STOCK PRICE ($) FY Close	P/E High/Low		PER SHARE ($) Earnings	Dividends	Book Value
09/12	26.43	18	12	1.82	1.85	20.35
09/11	21.15	14	8	2.25	1.65	19.03
09/10	24.54	14	8	1.85	1.27	18.07
09/09	27.01	17	5	1.08	1.21	16.28
09/08	19.45	57	4	2.10	1.74	15.75
Annual Growth	8.0%	—	—	(3.5%)	1.6%	6.6%

National Bank of Abu Dhabi

LOCATIONS

HQ: National Bank of Abu Dhabi
P.O. Box 4, Abu Dhabi
Phone:
Web: www.nbad.com

HISTORICAL FINANCIALS

Company Type: Public

Income Statement FYE: December 31

	ASSETS ($ mil.)	NET INCOME ($ mil.)	INCOME AS % OF ASSETS	EMPLOYEES
12/12	81,833	1,179	1.4%	0
12/11	69,606	1,009	1.5%	0
12/10	57,560	1,002	1.7%	4,216
12/09	53,588	822	1.5%	3,753
12/08	44,825	821	1.8%	3,666
Annual Growth	16.2%	9.5%	—	—

2012 Year-End Financials

Return on assets: 1.5%
Return on equity: 15.0%
Long-term debt ($ mil.): —
No. of shares (mil.): —
Sales ($ mil): 3,057
Dividends
Yield: —
Payout: —
Market value ($ mil.): —

National Bank of Canada

What's the bank for the Quebecois? The National Bank of Canada says "C'est moi!" Also known as National Bank Financial Group the company offers personal and commercial banking services through about 450 branches in Canada primarily in Quebec. The bank's offerings include deposits mortgages loans and credit cards. Through subsidiaries it also provides insurance trust services wealth management online brokerage and private banking. The company with $185 billion in assets manages more than 50 proprietary mutual funds under the National Bank Omega and Altamira banners. Its Natbank unit has two branches in Florida for snowbirds.

Through some 85 locations the company's National Bank Financial subsidiary offers investments portfolio management and group insurance plans. The unit manages more than $50 billion of client assets. It also performs investment banking and brokerage services such as mergers and acquisitions advice institutional trading securities clearing and corporate finance.

To boost its institutional services business National Bank of Canada agreed in late 2013 to acquire The Toronto-Dominion Bank's TD Waterhouse Institutional Services business for $250 million.

In 2012 National Bank of Canada sold its Natcan Investment Management arm to Fiera Sceptre (since renamed Fiera Capital) for more than $309 million. As part of the deal the bank received voting shares representing about 35% of Fiera. National Bank of Canada's strategy is to develop partnerships to grow in the wealth management business. In years prior the bank had been growing its wealth management segment hoping to capitalize on an aging Canadian populace investing toward retirement.

National Bank of Canada has benefited from a relatively strong Canadian economy and a rebound in employment in Quebec in particular. It reported more than $1 billion in net income in 2010 and enjoys one of the lowest loan loss ratios among financial institutions in the country. The company is focusing on referrals between its banking and financial markets segments to foment growth.

EXECUTIVES

President CEO and Director, Louis Vachon, age 51, $838,000 total compensation
EVP Finance Risk and Treasury and CFO, Patricia Curadeau-Grou, $330,800 total compensation
SVP Finance Taxation and Investor Relations, Jean Dagenais, age 55, $174,311 total compensation
Chairman, Jean Douville, age 70
EVP Human Resources and Corporate Affairs, Lynn Jeanniot
VP and Corporate Secretary, Linda Caty
EVP Finance and Treasury and CFO, Ghislain Parent
EVP Wealth Management; Co-President and Co-CEO National Bank Financial, Luc Paiement, $279,750 total compensation
VP Corporate Marketing and Communications, Sylvie Roy
SVP Information Technology Sourcing and Organizational Performance, John B. Cieslak
EVP Financial Markets; Co-President and Co-CEO National Bank Financial, Ricardo Pascoe, $279,750 total compensation
President and CEO Natcan Investment Management, Pascal Duquette
President National Bank Direct Brokerage, Nicolas Milette
EVP Risk Management, William Bonnell
Senior Advisor Public Relations, Joan Beauchamp
Manager Branding and Advertising, Alison Marks
Senior Manager Branding and Advertising, Lise-Anne Amyot
VP Operations National Bank General Insurance, Denis Blackburn
President and CEO Natbank, Marie-Claude Lebel
Senior Manager Public Affairs, Claude Breton
Vice Chairman, Luc Bertrand
EVP Personal and Commercial Banking, Diane Giard
Executive Vice President - Operations, France Maffe
Executive Vice President - Personal and Commercial Banking, Rejean Levesque
EVP Marketing, Karen Leggett
EVP Information Technology and Organizational Performance, Dominique Fagnoule
EVP Operations, Stephane Bilodeau
President CEO and Director, Louis Vachon, age 51
Director, Jean R. Gaulin, age 69
Director, Paul Gobeil, age 70
Director, Pierre Bourgie, age 55
Director, Andre Caille, age 68
Director, Lawrence S. Bloomberg, age 70
Director, Marcel Dutil, age 69
Director, Shirley A. Dawe, age 65
Director, Marc P. Tellier, age 43
Director, Gerard Coulombe, age 65
Director, Roseann Runte, age 65
Director, Bernard Cyr, age 65
Director, Nicole Diamond-Gelinas, age 67
Director, Louise Laflamme, age 60
Director, Gillian H. (Jill) Denham, age 52
Vice Chairman, Luc Bertrand
Independent Director, Andre Caille
Independent Director, Pierre Thabet
Auditors: SamsonBelair/Deloitte&Touchesencrl

LOCATIONS

HQ: National Bank of Canada
600 De La Gauchetiere Street West, 7th Floor,
Montreal, Quebec H3B 4L2
Phone: 866 517-5455 **Fax:** 514 394-6196
Web: www.nbc.ca

PRODUCTS/OPERATIONS

2010 Sales

	% of total
Interest	
Loans	37
Securities &	18
Noninterest	
Trust services & mutual	7
Securities brokerage	6
Securitization	5
Underwriting & advisory	5
Deposit & payment service	4
Lending	3
Other	15
Total	**100**

Selected Subsidiaries

Natbank (banking US)
NATCAN (75% portfolio management and investments)
National Bank Direct Brokerage (online brokerage)
National Bank Financial (investment banking)
National Bank General Insurance (home and auto coverage)
National Bank Insurance Firm (insurance brokerage)
National Bank Life Insurance Company
National Bank Securities (mutual funds)
National Bank Trust (trust services)

COMPETITORS

BMO Financial Group
CIBC
Caisses centrale Desjardins
Laurentian Bank
RBC Financial Group
Scotiabank
TD Bank

HISTORICAL FINANCIALS

Company Type: Public

Income Statement FYE: October 31

	ASSETS ($ mil.)	NET INCOME ($ mil.)	INCOME AS % OF ASSETS	EMPLOYEES
10/13	179,938	1,375	0.8%	19,691
10/12	178,387	1,522	0.9%	19,920
10/11*	167,519	1,141	0.7%	19,431
11/10	151,807	0	—	0
10/10	142,633	1,015	0.7%	15,298
Annual Growth	8.1%	10.7%	—	8.8%

*Fiscal year change

2013 Year-End Financials

Return on assets: 0.7%
Return on equity: 18.7%
Long-term debt ($ mil.): —
No. of shares (mil.): 325
Sales ($ mil): 6,811
Dividends
Yield: 7.5%
Payout: 80.8%
Market value ($ mil.): 28,344

	STOCK PRICE ($) FY Close	P/E High/Low		PER SHARE ($) Earnings	Dividends	Book Value
10/13	86.95	18	14	4.21	3.35	23.88
10/12	77.36	18	12	4.67	3.06	22.44
10/11*	72.47	25	17	3.47	2.77	20.27
11/10	65.26	—	—	(0.00)	2.40	(0.00)
10/10	65.26	22	16	2.92	2.43	21.73
Annual Growth	7.4%	—	—	13.0%	11.2%	3.2%

*Fiscal year change

National Bank Of Greece S A

Like the ancient ruins that dominate the landscape of Greece National Bank of Greece (NBG) dominates the banking landscape of the Mediterranean. In addition to holding the top position at home NBG has taken a leading position in the Balkans by acquiring controlling stakes in banks throughout the region. The bank offers such services as commercial and consumer banking asset management investment banking financing and insurance. It has more than 500 domestic branches and another 1200 in a dozen outside countries. NBG once served as the Greek central bank but the government sold its stake in the company in 2004.

Geographic Reach

In addition to Greece NBG operates banks in Albania Bulgaria Cyprus Egypt Macedonia Romania Serbia South Africa and Turkey.

HISTORY

The National Bank of Greece (NBG) can trace its banking heritage back to Pasion a metic (non-Greek) former slave living in Athens in the fourth century BC. To help his former master rebuild after one of Greece's many wars he obtained a small private bank that had been formed a few decades earlier and became one of Athens' greatest bankers.

The bank as it exists today though was established in 1841 and for most of its existence served as Greece's central bank. It listed on the Athens Stock Exchange in 1880. NBG survived WWI and Germany's occupation of Greece during WWII. It weathered the civil war in the late 1940s the military coup that overthrew the constitutional monarchy in the 1960s and democratic reformation in the 1970s.

As the 1980s dawned and Andreas Papandreou's socialist government came to power in Greece the bank launched a joint venture in Paris with Credit Lyonnais and other investors. NBG caused plenty of problems for its privately owned competitors during the early part of the decade — as deposits declined profits shrank and labor costs rose the bank was able to undercut competitors thanks to its government backing.

A banking scandal involving NBG and Papandreou helped topple the socialist government in the late 1980s. The bank's US subsidiary Atlantic Bank of New York was one of two Greek banks charged with money laundering to the tune of $700 million. Rival political parties called for Papandreou already ailing to resign. (In 1992 the former leader was acquitted of corruption charges stemming from the scandal.)

Under the leadership of a different government in the early 1990s the bank looked to shake up its holdings to improve profits. It sold off a number of subsidiaries including a chain of luxury hotels an insurance unit and Traders Credit Bank a small commercial bank. These divestitures were just the beginning as the Greek government looked to privatize a number of its holdings. Turmoil in the Greek economy in the mid-1990s forced the bank to limit withdrawals hike interest rates and take other conservative measures as the government tried to prevent a devaluation of the native currency.

In the late 1990s Greece looked to join the Euro zone and its institutions began shaping up. Doing its part NBG took measures to clean up its balance sheet writing off a number of bad loans it had been pressured to make by the government. The bank focused on retail operations absorbed the National Mortgage Bank and transformed its ETEVA development banking subsidiary into a full-fledged investment bank. It began shoring up flagging overseas operations listed on the NYSE (1999) and looked to expand in the Balkans.

In 1997 the bank opened offices in Albania and three years later bought controlling interests in Macedonia's Skopanska Banka and United Bulgarian Bank. As the 20th century drew to a close NGB won more freedom from the Greek government when the finance ministry announced it would no longer appoint the bank's executive officers instead allowing NGB's board of directors and shareholders to make the decisions.

In 2000 the company launched subsidiary NBG Venture Capital which concentrates on Greece southeast Europe and the eastern Mediterranean. The government sold 10% of its stake in the bank in 2003 as part of its privatization program. Although the move dropped its holdings to 30% the government retained management control. The state divested its interest in the company in 2004.

EXECUTIVES

Head of Human Resources, Andreas Vranas
Deputy CEO, Petros Christodoulou, age 53, $405,545 total compensation
General Manager Risk Management, Michael Oratis, age 56, $405,994 total compensation
CEO; Chairman of the Executive Committee, Alexandros G. Tourkolias, age 67, $514,114 total compensation
Deputy CEO and Member of the Executive Committee, Anthimos C. Thomopoulos, age 52, $529,985 total compensation
General Manager of Strategy & International Activities Chief Economist of the Group, Paul Mylonas, age 55, $367,008 total compensation
Chairman, Prof Vassilios T. Rapanos, age 66
General Manager International Activities, Agis Leopoulos, age 45, $311,960 total compensation
Chief Risk Officer, Demetrios Lefakis, age 53, $482,980 total compensation
CEO and Director, Apostolos S. Tamvakakis, age 56
General Manager of Corporate Banking Chairman of the Board of Directors at Ethniki Insurance Co, Dimitrios G. Dimopoulos, age 67, $305,636 total compensation
General Manager of Retail Banking, Nelly Tzakou-Lambropoulou, age 52, $294,213 total compensation
General Manager Investment Banking, Lambros Papakonstantinou, age 48
General Manager Real Estate, Aristotelis Karytinos, age 58, $494,215 total compensation
General Manager Treasury and Global Markets, Leonidas Fragkiadakis, age 48, $346,367 total compensation
Chief Financial Officer, Paula N. Hadjisotiriou, age 56
Chairman, George P. Zanias, age 58
Manager Investor Relations, Gregory Papagrigoris
Assistant General Manager and Supervisor Operational Procedures Ethnodata S.A., Demetrios Vrailas, age 62, $176,103 total compensation
Assistant General Manager Retail Banking, Ioanna Katzilieri-Zour, age 52, $212,286 total compensation
Deputy CFO, Ioannis Kyriakopoulos, age 54, $169,249 total compensation
Assistant General Manager Corporate Banking, Theofanis Panagiotopoulos, age 58, $96,248 total compensation
Assistant General Manager Financial and Operations, Garyfallia Spyriouni, age 50, $346,019 total compensation
Deputy CEO and Member of the Executive Committee, Leonidas Theoklitos
Assistant General Manager and Chief Audit Officer, Petros Fourtounis
General Manager, Maria-Ioanna Politopoulou
General Manager Retail Banking, Antreas Athanassopoulos
General Manager Corporate Banking, Dimitrios G. Dimopoulos
CFO, Babis Mazarakis
General Manager Group Retail Collections, Marianna Politopoulou
General Counsel, Miltiadis Stathopoulos
Assistant General Manager Branch Network, Spyros Asimopoulos
Chief of Operations, Damianos Charalampidis
Chief Credit Officer, Dimitris Frangetis
Group CIO, Nikos Christodoulou
Head of Human Resources, Andreas Vranas
Non-Executive Director, Petros K. Sabatacakis, age 67
Deputy CEO and Member of the Executive Committee, Alexandros Tourkolias, age 67
Deputy CEO and Member of the Executive Committee, Anthimos C. Thomopoulos, age 52
Non-Executive Director, Alexandra Papalexopoulou-Benopoulou, age 47
Non-Executive Director, H. E. the Metropolitan of Ioannina Theoklitos
Non-Executive Director, Stefanos C. Vavalidis, age 67
Director, Ioannis C. Giannidis, age 63
CEO and Director, Apostolos S. Tamvakakis, age 56
Director, Ioannis P. Panagopoulos, age 58
Non-Executive Director, Alexandros Makridis, age 51
Non-Executive Director, George P. Zanias, age 58
Non-Executive Director, Vassilios Konstantakopoulos, age 78
Director, Avraam Triandafyllidis
Deputy CEO and Member of the Executive Committee, Leonidas Theoklitos
Director, Maria (Marily) Frangista

LOCATIONS

HQ: National Bank Of Greece S A
86 Eolou St., Athens 10232
Phone: (30) 210 334 1000 **Fax:** (30) 210 334 2235
Web: www.nbg.gr

COMPETITORS

Agricultural Bank of Greece
Alpha Bank
Bank of Cyprus
Citibank
EFG Eurobank Ergasias
Emporiki Bank
HSBC
Piraeus Bank S.A.
Royal Bank of Scotland

HISTORICAL FINANCIALS

Company Type: Public

Income Statement FYE: December 31

	ASSETS ($ mil.)	NET INCOME ($ mil.)	INCOME AS % OF ASSETS	EMPLOYEES
12/10	161,601	542	0.3%	36,866
12/09	163,352	1,329	0.8%	36,314
12/08	142,379	2,161	1.5%	36,589
12/07	133,009	2,391	1.8%	34,623
12/06	101,064	1,306	1.3%	31,622
Annual Growth	12.5%	(19.7%)	—	3.9%

2010 Year-End Financials

Return on assets: 0.3%
Return on equity: 4.2%
Long-term debt ($ mil.): —
No. of shares (mil.): 95
Sales ($ mil): 10,555

Dividends
Yield: —
Payout: —
Market value ($ mil.): 160

	STOCK PRICE ($) FY Close	P/E High	P/E Low	PER SHARE ($) Earnings	Dividends	Book Value
12/10	1.68	2	1	6.16	0.00	141.08
12/09	5.21	1	0	21.32	0.00	212.99
12/08	3.81	1	0	40.96	0.00	211.76
12/07	13.79	1	1	47.38	0.00	248.01
12/06	9.30	1	1	29.04	0.00	228.77
Annual Growth	(34.8%)	—	—	(32.1%)	—	(11.4%)

National Grid plc

It's not gridlock but a lock on the Grid that is a good thing for National Grid. It is the sole owner and operator of the electricity transmission system in England and Wales. It transmits electricity through about 4500 miles of overhead and underground lines to distribution utilities serving more than 52 million people. National Grid also operates the UK natural gas transmission and distribution system (serving 11 million homes and businesses) through its National Grid Gas subsidiary. However it is the company's Northeastern US gas distribution and power generation transmission and distribution operations led by National Grid USA that bring in the bulk of the company's revenues.

In the US the company distributes power to about 3.3 million customers in Massachusetts New Hampshire New York and Rhode Island and natural gas to 3.4 million clients in those states. It also manages the electricity distribution network in Long Island.

The company's long-term strategy is to focus on large-scale power and gas systems in the UK and the US and to better integrate its various operations. In 2010 a National Grid and TenneT joint venture began laying the first section of a high-voltage cable that will link the power grids in the UK and the Netherlands bolstering power supply in both countries. The project due for completion by 2012 will help the companies meet environmental goals by facilitating power flows from low-carbon generation plants.

With an eye on meeting ambitious European Union goals for carbon emission reductions in 2009 National Grid released a report that by 2020 half of the UK's heating needs could be provided by biogas (converted from sewage and injected into the national gas distribution system) compensating for a decline in North Sea gas supply. In 2010 the company had one renewable gas plant under development in the US and two in the UK.

The company reported a major jump in revenues and income in 2010 primarily driven by a rebounding economy (prompting increased demand for power and gas) and by improved rates in the US market. Revenues grew by 40% in 2011 and net income by 30% thanks to strong demand and higher prices in the UK and increased rates in the US.

In 2011 National Grid announced plans to save $200 million in a restructuring of its US operations including cutting 1200 jobs. Late in 2011 the company sold the Seneca-Upshur Petroleum subsidiary for approximately $152 million. The deal is a further move to return to core business operations in gas and electricity distribution. That year it also agreed to sell its non-regulated metering business in the UK (Onstream) to Macquarie Bank for about $440 million.

HISTORY

The National Grid Company was formed in 1990 as part of the privatization of the electricity industry in England and Wales. Until then the Central Electricity Generating Board (CEGB) a state monopoly responsible for power generation in England and Wales owned the national power grid (transmission system) and sold power to 12 area boards the regional authorities that distributed electricity to customers.

The Electricity Act of 1989 paved the way for competition; in 1990 the CEGB was split into The National Grid Company and three power-generating firms: National Power PowerGen and Nuclear Electric. The 12 area boards transferred their assets to 12 regional companies which jointly owned National Grid. The company keeping its monopoly status was charged to develop and operate an efficient coordinated and economical transmission system and to facilitate competition among power producers.

The company moved outside the UK when it invested in Citelec in 1993. An international consortium Citelec controlled Transener the surviving transmission system after Argentina privatized its electric utilities.

Also in 1993 National Grid set up Energis as a telecommunications firm to provide service to businesses. Piggybacking its fiber-optic lines on National Grid's transmission network Energis introduced national services in 1994 and by 1996 it had won several major customers including the BBC and Microsoft.

In 1995 National Grid went public as The National Grid Group. It also secured concessions to build transmission lines in Pakistan but in 1997 a new Pakistani government put the project on hold. That year it also upped its stake in Citelec from 15% to 41% which increased its control over the development of Argentina's transmission system. With partner CINergy Global it also acquired 80% of the Power Division of Zambia Consolidated Copper Mines in 1997 and it was chosen as a joint venture partner by India's Karnataka Electricity Board to build a transmission line in that state.

The company sold 26% of Energis in 1997; in 1998 it announced plans to sell the rest of Energis and launch a new company under the National Grid banner to set up telecom firms overseas. That year it laid plans to enter the US by agreeing to acquire New England Electric System (NEES). (The $3.2 billion purchase closed in 2000.)

In 1999 the company cut its stake in Energis to 46% and announced plans to shop for more US energy holdings. A deal was struck to purchase New York Utility Niagara Mohawk Holdings the following year. (The deal was completed in 2002.) Also in 2000 and 2001 the company continued to slim its stake in Energis (33%).

National Grid sold some noncore businesses in 2001 including UK metering company Datum Services and US energy marketer Allenergy and pulled out of the transmission project in India. It also agreed to manage the Alliance Regional Transmission Organization (RTO) in the US. In 2002 National Grid sold Niagara Mohawk's 50% interest in Canadian Niagara Power to Canadian utility Fortis.

The firm changed its name to National Grid Transco in 2002 upon completion of its acquisition of Lattice Group in a $21.5 billion deal.

In 2005 National Grid Transco sold four of its regional gas distribution networks; the North England network was acquired by a consortium that includes United Utilities and Cheung Kong Infrastructure; the South of England and Scotland networks were sold to Scottish and Southern Energy Borealis Infrastructure and Ontario Teachers' Pension Plan; and the Wales & West distribution network was purchased by a consortium managed by Macquarie Bank Limited. The company dropped Transco from its name in 2005.

National Grid dramatically boosted its North American assets in 2007 by acquiring gas distributor KeySpan for more than $7 billion. To comply with federal regulations connected to the KeySpan deal in 2008 National Grid sold its 2480-MW Ravenswood Generating Station in New York City to TransCanada for $2.9 billion.

In the second half of the decade to raise cash and narrow its operational focus the company jettisoned a number of noncore operations. National Grid sold its stakes in the alternative telecommunications network industry. The company also sold its telecom interests in Chile Argentina and Poland and wrote off its 33% stake in bankrupt UK telecommunications firm Energis which uses fiber-optic cable strung along National Grid's power lines. National Grid also sold former Lattice Group subsidiary 186k (fiber-optic networking) to Hutchison Whampoa and exited its telecom venture in Brazil. It also sold its electricity interconnector linking Australia to the island state of Tasmania.

EXECUTIVES

Executive Director Electricity Distribution and Generation and Board Member, Thomas B. (Tom) King, age 51, $1,308,321 total compensation
Finance Director and Board Member, Andrew R. J. Bonfield, age 50
Chief Executive; Executive Director, Steven J. (Steve) Holliday, age 57, $1,819,845 total compensation
Group Company Secretary General Counsel and Director, Helen M. Mahy, age 52
Executive Director Transmission and Board Member, Nick Winser, age 53, $727,142 total compensation
CIO, David W. Lister
Director Investor Relations U.S., George Laskaris
Chairman, Sir Peter Gershon, age 66
Manager Investor Relations, Victoria Davies
Manager Investor Relations, Andy Mead
Global Director Strategy and Business Development, Alison Wood
Director Corporate Affairs, George Mayhew
Executive Director Electricity Distribution and Generation and Board Member, Thomas B. (Tom) King, age 51
Director, George W. Rose, age 61
Director, Philip S. (Phil) Aiken, age 65
Director, Stephen R. Pettit, age 60
Finance Director and Board Member, Andrew R. J. Bonfield, age 50
Chief Executive; Executive Director, Steven J. (Steve) Holliday, age 57

Group Company Secretary General Counsel and Director, Helen M. Mahy, age 52
Director, Kenneth G. (Ken) Harvey, age 73
Executive Director Transmission and Board Member, Nick Winser, age 53
Deputy Chairman, Sir Peter Gershon, age 64
Executive Director Gas Distribution and Board Member, Mark Fairbairn, age 53
Director, Maria C. Richter, age 59
Director, Linda Adamany, age 60
Director, John M. Allan, age 63
Non-Executive Director, Nora Brownell
Auditors: PricewaterhouseCoopersLLP

LOCATIONS

HQ: National Grid plc
1-3 Strand, London WC2N 5EH
Phone: (44) 20 7004 3000 **Fax:** (44) 20 7004 3004
Web: www.nationalgrid.com

2011 Sales

	% of total
US	61
UK	39
Total	**100**

PRODUCTS/OPERATIONS

2011 Sales

	% of total
Gas	37
Electricity distribution &	32
Transmission	27
Other	4
Total	**100**

COMPETITORS

Con Edison
Enterprise Group
HomeServe
IBERDROLA
Northeast Utilities
Northern Electric
Northern Ireland Electricity
Northern Powergrid
Scottish and Southern Energy

HISTORICAL FINANCIALS

Company Type: Public

Income Statement FYE: March 31

	REVENUE ($ mil.)	NET INCOME ($ mil.)	NET PROFIT MARGIN	EMPLOYEES
03/13	21,820	3,487	16.0%	25,224
03/12	22,164	3,262	14.7%	25,645
03/11	23,077	3,473	15.1%	27,089
03/10	21,213	2,101	9.9%	28,106
03/09	22,350	1,350	6.0%	27,886
Annual Growth	(0.6%)	26.8%	—	(2.5%)

2013 Year-End Financials

Debt ratio: 78.0%
Return on equity: 23.5%
Cash ($ mil.): 1,019
Current ratio: 1.29
Long-term debt ($ mil.): 37,454
No. of shares (mil.): —
Dividends
Yield: —
Payout: —
Market value ($ mil.): —

	STOCK PRICE ($) FY Close	P/E High/Low		PER SHARE ($) Earnings	Dividends	Book Value
03/13	58.01	229	186	0.95	0.00	4.24
03/12	50.48	241	204	0.91	0.00	4.15
03/11	48.04	199	139	1.02	7.03	4.00
03/10	48.75	254	149	0.85	2.89	2.58
03/09	38.64	549	196	0.55	3.00	2.34
Annual Growth	10.7%	—	—	14.7%	—	16.0%

National Westminster Bank Plc

One of the retail banking arms of The Royal Bank of Scotland (RBS) National Westminster Bank (NatWest) provides banking and financial services to individual and small business clients in the UK. The bank offers deposits mortgages credit cards and personal loans through a network of 1500 bank branches. It also offers phone and Internet banking as well as a network of cash machines and mobile banking units. Subsidiary Ulster Bank has some 240 branches across the island of Ireland. Other offerings include life insurance pensions private banking services carbon offsets and other more prosaic business services as well as investment and retirement management.

NatWest was formed by the 1968 merger of National Provincial Bank (established in 1833) and Westminster Bank (1836). RBS acquired the company in 2000 in the UK's largest bank takeover to date.

The bank has struggled through the global financial crisis which deeply crippled parent RBS. RBS became 84% owned by the UK government after it received a series of bailouts in 2008 and 2009. NatWest reported a loss in 2010 as the result of lower gains on redemption of own debt higher costs and higher impairment losses.

As part of RBS' agreement with the European Commission the company is selling more than 300 of its branches and locations including seven NatWest branches in Scotland to Spanish bank Santander. The transaction (aimed at cutting costs) is expected to close in 2012.

EXECUTIVES

Chief Executive, Stephen A. M. Hester, age 52
Chairman, Sir Philip Hampton, age 60
Auditors: Deloitte&Touche

LOCATIONS

HQ: National Westminster Bank Plc
135 Bishopsgate, London EC2M 3UR
Phone: (44) 131 626 4099 **Fax:** (44) 131 626 3081
Web: www.natwest.com

PRODUCTS/OPERATIONS

2010 Sales

	% of total
Net interest	39
Non interest	61
Total	**100**

COMPETITORS

AIB
Barclays
Clydesdale Bank
Grupo Santander
HSBC
Lloyds Banking Group
Yorkshire Bank

HISTORICAL FINANCIALS

Company Type: Public

Income Statement FYE: December 31

	ASSETS ($ mil.)	NET INCOME ($ mil.)	INCOME AS % OF ASSETS	EMPLOYEES
12/12	612,451	(5,280)	—	24,100
12/11	567,814	(5,950)	—	26,900
12/10	569,092	(3,502)	—	27,300
12/09	568,032	1,836	0.3%	29,700
12/08	468,112	652	0.1%	32,600
Annual Growth	6.9%	—	—	(7.3%)

2012 Year-End Financials

Return on assets: (-0.8%)
Return on equity: (-17.7%)
Long-term debt ($ mil.): —
No. of shares (mil.): 1,678
Sales ($ mil): 16,597
Dividends
Yield: 7.8%
Payout: —
Market value ($ mil.): 41,585

	STOCK PRICE ($) FY Close	P/E High/Low		PER SHARE ($) Earnings	Dividends	Book Value
12/12	24.78	—	—	(0.00)	1.94	19.88
12/11	16.78	—	—	(0.00)	4.81	14.85
12/10	21.73	—	—	(0.00)	1.94	13.93
12/09	17.35	—	—	(0.00)	1.94	13.70
12/08	9.90	—	—	(0.00)	1.94	10.54
Annual Growth	25.8%	—	—	—	(0.0%)	17.2%

NEC Corp

NEC knows a little something about Networking Electronics and Computers. The Japanese tech giant provides a broad range of IT products and services through five business groups. IT Services offers consulting integration and support services. Personal Solutions oversees personal computers monitors mobile handsets and Internet service. Carrier Network supplies network infrastructure equipment for telecom carriers. The Platform business supplies network systems such as servers supercomputers storage equipment and IP telephony systems while the Social Infrastructure segment provides broadcasting systems satellites CCTV surveillance and other security systems. NEC does most of its business domestically.

NEC has suffered declining revenues since the onset of the global economic recession that began in late 2008. Sales dropped again in fiscal 2011 by about 13% which was less severe than the 15% decline of the previous year. Unlike 2010 when the company was able to earn a profit by cutting Y320 billion ($3.4 billion) in operating costs mostly by reducing headcount of outsourced engineers and administrative expenses NEC lost money in 2011.

In addition to a slow recovery in the Japanese IT market and the catastrophic 2011 earthquake in eastern Japan the company cited the 2010 spin off of its Electron Devices semiconductor business segment as the key contributor to lower sales in 2011. It divested NEC Electronics which was combined with Renesas Technology to form Renesas Electronics a specialist in semiconductor systems for mobile phones and automotive appications. The merging of NEC Electronics and Renesas created one of the largest chip makers in Japan rivaling Toshiba Semiconductor. The move was prompted by intense competition in the mobile handset sector particularly outside Japan; NEC decided that getting out of the global chip business would enable it to better concentrate on its core domestic sales efforts.

NEC continues to pursue a strategy that includes efforts to address the growing market for products and services that support corporate cloud computing and attempts to expand its global business. To further its cloud computing strategy the company's IT Services division has revamped its core IT system into a hosted service platform and developed systems to enable customers to provide their own cloud computing services from its data centers. As part of this NEC announced in 2011 that it would form a joint venture with ST Electronics the electronics unit of Singapore Technologies Engineering to offer Software-as-a-Service (SaaS) capabilities from a new data center to clients in Asia. NEC will own a 60% stake in the business which will be known as NEC STEE Cloud Services.

In 2012 NEC bought the IT services (managed services enterprise services and consulting) business of CSG Limited extending its reach in Australia. The acquired business will be an independent business unit within NEC Australia.

NEC enlisted even more help on its business support and cloud expansion hopes in 2012 when its NetCracker subsidiary bought Massachusetts-based Convergys' information management business for about $450 million. The unit made business support systems software designed for the communications utilities and logistics industries among others. The products were integrated into NetCracker's operations.

The IT Services unit's other core services are systems integration consulting and maintenance. It supports public sector and health care IT and digital records systems; banking and broadcast systems for financial services telecom carriers and media companies; production and sales management systems for manufacturers; and inventory and distribution systems for retail and consumer services companies.

NEC restructured its Personal Solutions division in 2011 by breaking out its domestic PC business to become part of a new joint venture with Hong Kong-based PC maker Lenovo. Known as NEC Lenovo Japan Group the business markets personal computers in Japan. Lenovo contributed its Tokyo-based Lenovo Japan subsidiary and $175 million in stock to the new enterprise which is the largest PC seller in Japan giving it 51% ownership. NEC Lenovo Japan Group competes with other Japanese companies (Fujitsu and Toshiba) as well as US-based vendors (Dell and HP). Personal Solutions continues to handle international PC sales as well as peripherals mobile devices and BIGLOBE one of Japan's top Internet service providers.

NEC's Carrier Network unit provides enterprise and carrier-grade communications infrastructure and access networking equipment including optical systems switching gear wireless base stations satellite systems broadcasting transmitters studio equipment and IP telephony systems. It also provides operational and systems support services. Telecom companies make up a large segment of the division's customers.

Together NEC's IT Services Personal Solutions and Carrier Network divisions accounted for 70% of sales in 2011 (up from nearly two-thirds the previous year).

Formerly the company's largest segment (representing almost a quarter of sales in 2009) NEC's Network business was renamed as the Platform unit in 2010 when the company reorganized and disbanded Electron Devices. Platform sells enterprise computing products such as workstations servers thin clients mainframes enterprise software supercomputers storage systems and networking equipment. Due to decreased demand for hardware the segment accounted for only 12% of sales in 2011.

To diversify its business in 2011 NEC bought Jicoux Datasystems a unit of Mitsubishi that offers fleet management services for commercial vehicles. NEC wants to develop information services that automatically exchange information between commercial and privately owned vehicles. Vehicle-to-vehicle communications systems —also called automotive telematics —are hoped to help ease traffic congestion.

As for its global business sales outside Japan make up 15% of revenues. In recent years NEC has consolidated a number of its hundreds of international subsidiaries across Asia and in the US including the merger of NEC Infrontia and NEC Unified Solutions into NEC America. In 2011 the company established a Latin American headquarters in Sao Paulo Brazil to act as the hub for all of its business in the region; it also has operations in Argentina Chile Colombia and Mexico. NEC also has partnerships with Alcatel-Lucent EMC and Philips to develop products specifically aimed at markets outside Japan.

With Fujitsu Fujitsu Semiconductor Panasonic Mobile Communications and Samsung Electronics the company attempted to establish a joint venture that would develop and market semiconductor products for mobile devices but it was abandoned after being unable to come to an agreement over details by the deadline in 2012.

HISTORY

A group of Japanese investors led by Kunihiko Iwadare formed Nippon Electric Company (NEC) in a joint venture with Western Electric (US) in 1899. Starting as an importer of telephone equipment NEC soon became a maker and a major supplier to Japan's Communications Ministry. Western Electric sold its stake in NEC in 1925. The company became affiliated with the Sumitomo "keiretsu" (industrial group) in the 1930s and went public in 1949.

After Nippon Telegraph and Telephone (NTT) was formed in 1952 NEC became one of its four leading suppliers. The post-WWII need to repair Japan's telephone systems and the country's continuing economic recovery resulted in strong demand from NTT for NEC's products. In the 1950s and 1960s NTT business represented more than half of sales even though NEC expanded overseas diversified into home appliances and formed a computer alliance with Honeywell. NTT which began acquiring shares in the company decades earlier and owned as much as 59% of NEC sold its stake in the 1960s.

In the 1970s Honeywell's lagging position in computers hurt NEC; the company recovered through in-house development efforts and a mainframe venture with Toshiba. In 1977 CEO Koji Kobayashi articulated his revolutionary vision of NEC's future as an integrator of computers and communications through semiconductor technology.

NEC invested heavily in R&D and expansion becoming the world's largest semiconductor maker in 1985. Despite its proprietary operating system NEC garnered more than 50% of the Japanese computer market in the 1980s. NEC entered into a mainframe computer partnership with Honeywell and France's Groupe Bull in 1987.

By the early 1990s NEC lost its status as the world's largest semiconductor maker to Intel. NEC bought 20% of US computer maker Packard Bell in 1995 and merged most of its PC business outside Japan with that company creating Packard Bell NEC in 1996. Also in 1996 NEC created US subsidiary Holon Net Corp. to make hardware and software for Internet and intranet markets.

NEC took control of Packard Bell NEC in 1998 upping its stake to 53%. A sluggish Japanese economy and slumping memory prices contributed to NEC's drop in income for fiscal 1998. A defense contract scandal involving overbilling and improper hiring by an NEC unit forced the resignation of chairman Tadahiro Sekimoto and later president Hisashi Kaneko.

President Koji Nishigaki the first at NEC without an engineering background led a sweeping reorganization to cut 10% of the company's workforce —15000 employees —over three years. He revamped NEC operations around Internet application hardware software and services. In 1998 NEC formed a rare pact with a Japanese rival allying with Hitachi to consolidate memory chip operations. The restructuring of Packard Bell NEC (NEC by then owned 88%) helped cause a $1.3 billion loss for fiscal 1999 NEC's worst-ever drop. NEC folded up its Packard Bell NEC division later that year imposing layoffs of about 80% of its staff divesting it from the US retail market and excising the historic Packard Bell brand name in that region.

NEC restructured again in 2000 splitting into more autonomous units and streamlining its PC operations. That year the company launched an aggressive spending program in a move to lead the broadband mobile networking market. In 2001 NEC ended a long-running dispute with Cray investing $25 million in the company and granting distribution rights to its vector supercomputers in North America —a deal contingent upon Cray's dropping an antidumping suit that led to heavy import taxes being placed on NEC supercomputers sold in the US.

Nishigaki became vice chairman in 2004 and Akinobu Kanasugi was named president. Kanasugi held the post just two years until poor health forced him to turn the reins over to SVP Kaoru Yano. Yano stepped down as president in April 2010 but retained his position as chairman. SVP Nobuhiro Endo who has been with the company since 1981 was promoted to president.

In 2004 NEC took public its DRAM joint venture Elpida Memory thereby reducing its stake in the company and the volatile memory sector. NEC also sold its plasma display business to Pioneer that same year. In 2005 the company dissolved its monitor joint venture with Mitsubishi and took full ownership of the unit (NEC Display Solutions). The next year it sold its European PC operations Packard Bell to Lap Shun "John" Hui a co-founder of eMachines.

The company joined with Sumitomo Electric Industries in 2008 to acquire fiber-optic submarine cable manufacturer OCC Holdings; NEC and Sumitomo acquired 75% and 25% stakes respectively.

Kaoru Yano stepped down as president of NEC in 2010 but retained his position as chairman. SVP Nobuhiro Endo who has been with the company since 1981 was promoted to president.

EXECUTIVES

Chairman, Kaoru Yano, age 69
SEVP Chief Supply Chain Officer and Director, Junji Yasui, age 63
President and Director, Nobuhiro Endo, age 60
Associate SVP, Masaki Kidowaki
Associate SVP, Takayuki Morita
Executive Vice President Chief Marketing Officer, Toshiyuki Mineno, age 62
Associate SVP, Naoki Yoshimura
SVP and Director, Manabu Kinoshita, age 59
Senior Executive Vice President CSO Chief Strategy Officer CIO Chief Information Officer, Takashi Niino
SVP and Associate SVP, Tomonori Nishimura
SVP, Takayuki Okada

Senior Executive Vice President and Member of the Board Re, Yukihiro Fujiyoshi, age 64
SVP, Masaki Fukui
SVP, Kuniaki Okada
Associate SVP, Takashige Mouri
SVP, Masato Yamamoto
SVP, Fujio Okada
Associate SVP, Masamichi Imai
Associate SVP, Nobuyuki Yanaginuma
Associate SVP, Masahiro Annaka
Associate SVP, Shunichiro Tejima
Associate SVP, Masao Wada
Associate SVP, Hirokazu Takahara
Associate SVP, Takaaki Shimizu
Associate SVP, Masanobu Yamaguchi
Associate SVP, Takemi Hosaka
Associate SVP, Takao Maruyama
Associate SVP, Yasushi Abe
Associate SVP, Kunio Kondo
Associate SVP, Katsumi Emura
Associate SVP, Yasuyuki Nakae
SVP and Director, Takemitsu Kunio, age 59
Associate SVP and CFO, Isamu Kawashima
Associate Senior Vice President, Shinya Oda
Director, Kenji Miyahara, age 78
Director, Yoshinari Hara, age 70
Director, Hideaki Takahashi, age 65
Director, Toshio Morikawa, age 79
SEVP Chief Marketing Officer and Director, Toshimitsu Iwanami, age 63
SEVP Chief Supply Chain Officer and Director, Junji Yasui, age 63
Director, Sawako Nohara, age 56
President and Director, Nobuhiro Endo, age 60
SVP and Director, Toshiyuki Mineno, age 61
SVP and Director, Manabu Kinoshita, age 59
SEVP CIO and Director, Yukihiro Fujiyoshi, age 64
SVP and Director, Takemitsu Kunio, age 59
Auditors: Ernst&YoungShinNihon

LOCATIONS

HQ: NEC Corp
5-7-1 SHiba, Minato-ku, Tokyo 108-8001
Phone: (81) 3 3454 1111
Web: www.nec.co.jp

2011 Sales

	% of total
Asia	
Japan	85
Other	5
Europe	3
Other	7
Total	**100**

PRODUCTS/OPERATIONS

2011 Sales

	% of total
IT	26
Personal	25
Carrier	19
Platform	12
Social	10
Other	8
Total	**100**

Selected Products

IT Services
- Consulting
- Maintenance
- Outsourcing
- Support
- Systems integration

Personal Solutions
- Internet service (NEC BIGLOBE)
- Mobile handsets
- Peripherals (floppy and optical drives monitors printers projectors)
- Personal computers

Carrier Network
- Access Networking systems (broadband and mobile microwave communication systems)
- Backbone networking systems (SDH systems WDM systems routers/switching systems)
- Network control platform systems
- Network infrastructure (fixed-line and mobile communication systems)
- Network service delivery platform systems

Platform Business Systems
- Enterprise computing (workstations servers storage systems mainframes supercomputers)
- Enterprise network systems (IP telephony routers/switching systems wireless LAN)
- Networking equipment (enterprise carrier)
- Software (application middleware operating systems)
- Storage products

Social Infrastructure
- Aerospace and defense systems
- Broadcasting systems and video equipment
- Control systems
- Fire and disaster prevention systems
- Transportation and public systems

COMPETITORS

AMD
Acer
Alcatel-Lucent
Apple Inc.
Avaya
BlackBerry
CASIO COMPUTER
Canon
Cisco Systems
Citizen
Dell
Emerson Electric
Epson
Ericsson
FUJIFILM
Fujitsu
Harris Corp.
Hewlett-Packard
Hitachi
Huawei Technologies
IBM
Intel
Kyocera
Lenovo
Lexmark
Micron Technology
Microsoft
Mitsubishi Electric
Motorola Solutions
NTT DATA
Nokia
Nortel Networks
Oki Electric
Panasonic Corp
Philips Electronics
Ricoh Company
SCSK
STMicroelectronics
Samsung Electronics
Sharp Corp.
Siemens AG
Sony
Sony Mobile
Texas Instruments
Toshiba
UTStarcom
Unisys
ZTE

HISTORICAL FINANCIALS

Company Type: Public

Income Statement FYE: March 31

	REVENUE ($ mil.)	NET INCOME ($ mil.)	NET PROFIT MARGIN	EMPLOYEES
03/13	32,644	323	1.0%	102,375
03/12	37,020	(1,344)	—	109,102
03/11	37,622	(151)	—	115,840
03/10	38,360	122	0.3%	142,358
03/09	42,808	(3,012)	—	143,327
Annual Growth	(6.6%)	—	—	(8.1%)

2013 Year-End Financials

Debt ratio: 0.2%
Return on equity: 4.4%
Cash ($ mil.): 1,852
Current ratio: 1.35
Long-term debt ($ mil.): 4,219
No. of shares (mil.): —
Dividends
Yield: —
Payout: —
Market value ($ mil.): —

	STOCK PRICE ($) FY Close	P/E High	P/E Low	PER SHARE ($) Earnings	Dividends	Book Value
03/13	2.55	—	—	0.12	0.00	3.42
03/12	1.95	—	—	(0.52)	0.00	3.65
03/11	2.12	—	—	(0.06)	0.04	4.07
03/10	2.40	—	—	0.05	0.00	3.84
03/09	2.75	—	—	(1.49)	0.07	3.94
Annual Growth	(1.9%)	—	—	—	—	(3.5%)

Nedbank Group Ltd

LOCATIONS

HQ: Nedbank Group Ltd
Nedbank Sandton, 135 Rivonia Road, Sandown, Sandton 2196
Phone: (27) 11 294 4444 **Fax:** (27) 11 294 6540
Web: www.nedbankgroup.co.za

HISTORICAL FINANCIALS

Company Type: Public

Income Statement FYE: December 31

	ASSETS ($ mil.)	NET INCOME ($ mil.)	INCOME AS % OF ASSETS	EMPLOYEES
12/12	80,221	878	1.1%	28,748
12/11	80,032	764	1.0%	28,494
12/10	91,622	724	0.8%	27,525
12/09	77,113	652	0.8%	27,037
12/08	60,180	680	1.1%	27,570
Annual Growth	7.5%	6.6%	—	1.1%

2012 Year-End Financials

Return on assets: 1.1%
Return on equity: 14.4%
Long-term debt ($ mil.): —
No. of shares (mil.): 457
Sales ($ mil): 7,285
Dividends
Yield: 3.2%
Payout: 0.5%
Market value ($ mil.): 10,308

	STOCK PRICE ($) FY Close	P/E High	P/E Low	PER SHARE ($) Earnings	Dividends	Book Value
12/12	22.54	0	0	1.87	0.73	13.86
12/11	17.66	0	0	1.66	0.01	13.28
12/10	40.34	0	0	1.58	1.18	14.80
12/09	34.05	0	0	1.50	1.20	12.30
12/08	20.75	0	0	1.65	1.61	9.04
Annual Growth	2.1%	—	—	3.1%	(17.8%)	11.3%

Nestle S.A.

With instant coffee baby food and bottled water in the mix Nestle crunches more than just chocolate. The world's #1 food and drinks company in terms of sales Nestle is also the world leader in coffee (Nescafe). It also makes coffee for the home-brewing system Nespresso. Nestle is one of the world's top bottled water makers (Nestle Waters) one of the biggest frozen pizza makers (DiGiorno) and a big player in the pet food business (Friskies Purina). Its most well-known global food brands include Buitoni Dreyer's Maggi Milkmaid Carnation and Kit Kat. The company owns Gerber Products and Jenny Craig. North America is Nestle's most important market.

Geographic Reach

The Americas (particularly North America) is Nestle's largest market accounting for nearly 45% of sales. Europe contributes nearly 30% while the company's fast-growing business in Asia Oceania & Africa accounts for just over 25%. China is delivering the strongest sales growth. The Swiss-based food giant has operations in 194 countries worldwide and factories in about 85 countries.

Operations

In addition to being the world's biggest food company Nestle operates several joint ventures including one with L'Oreal called Galderma which makes nutritional supplements aimed at improving skin hair and nails. Other JVs include Cereal Partners Worldwide with General Mills and Beverage Partners Worldwide with Coke. Nestle also owns approximately 30% of cosmetics giant L'Oreal.

Financial Performance

Despite a challenging year particularly in Europe Nestle's sales topped $100 billion in 2012 an increase of 13.5% versus 2011. The increase was driven by organic growth price increases and favorable foreign exchange rates. The company posted a net profit of $11.6 billion over the same period. The maker of Nescafe Perrier Haagen Dazs and Carnation reported broad-based growth across all product ranges and regions. In 2012 Asia Oceania & Africa outperformed the Americas and Europe posting an organic growth rate of 10% versus 6% and 2% for the Americas and Europe respectively. Among Nestle's vast product portfolio the best sellers were powdered and liquid beverages and pet care. For the year developed markets contributed 57% of Nestle's sales with the rest originating in emerging markets such as Brazil and China.

Strategy

Nestle is attempting to reposition itself away from reliance on processed foods toward higher-margin products with a "nutrition health and wellness" profile. The company operates according to a strategic roadmap that leverages its huge product and brand portfolio strong R&D and product launch capabilities and an expansive geographic presence. It uses these strengths to build its nutrition and health and wellness businesses and position products in emerging markets. In late 2012 for instance Nestle boosted its infant nutrition portfolio by purchasing Pfizer's nutrition business for about $11.8 billion in cash. About 85% of Pfizer's nutrition sales come from emerging markets such as Asia Africa and the Middle East.

Hoping to repeat the considerable success of its Nespresso coffee machines business Nestle in 2011 launched a spinoff product for baby formula called BabyNes. The new system initially available only in Switzerland features powdered milk capsules that are fed into a machine which heats and adds water preparing a bottle is less than 30 seconds. The cost of the formula capsules is about four times that of a Nespresso coffee capsule. Nespresso launched in 1986 has become one of Nestle's biggest and most profitable brands with 2010 sales exceeding $3.4 billion.

Looking to rid its portfolio of underperforming businesses Nestle in late 2013 agreed to sell the Jenny Craig weight-control business to the Connecticut-based private equity firm North Castle Partners.

Mergers and Acquisitions

Nestle's $11.8 billion acquisition of Pfizer's nutrition business in 2012 is one of several key deals the company has made in recent times. To boost its presence in China it acquired a 60% stake in Chinese food maker Yinlu Foods Group expanding its instant food offering in a key growth market. Family-owned Yinlu is a major distributor of ready-to-drink peanut milk and instant canned rice pudding. The deal extends cooperation between the two companies as Yinlu is a co-producer of Nestle's Nescafe coffee in China. In late 2011 Nestle paid $2.1 billion for a 60% interest in China-based confectionery Hsu Fu Chi. The deal put Nestle at the helm of China's second-largest confectionery. The purchase ranked as one of the largest foreign takeovers of a Chinese company.

On the health and wellness side Nestle is embracing the concept of science-based nutrition which emphasizes using food to treat chronic conditions and diseases. In early 2011 Nestle acquired CM&D Pharma a London-based firm that has formulated Fostrap chewing gum to aid kidney disease sufferers and Eviendep dietary fiber mix to slow the development of colon polyps. Many of CM&D's "medical foods" are in trial stages but none have been introduced to the public. CM&D is the first addition to Nestle Health Science (NHS) a subsidiary created at the start of 2011 to affirm Nestle's interest in science-based nutrition.

HISTORY

Henri Nestle purchased a factory in Vevey Switzerland in 1843 that made products ranging from nut oils to rum. In 1867 he developed a powder made from cow's milk and wheat flour as a substitute for mother's milk. A year earlier Americans Charles and George Page had founded the Anglo-Swiss Condensed Milk Company in Cham Switzerland using Gail Borden's milk-canning technology. In 1875 Nestle sold his eponymous company then doing business in 16 countries. When Anglo-Swiss launched a milk-based infant food in 1878 Nestle's new owners responded by introducing a condensed-milk product. In 1905 a year after Nestle began selling chocolate the companies ended their rivalry by merging under the Nestle name. Hampered by limited milk supplies during WWI the company expanded into regions less affected by the war such as the US. In 1929 it acquired Cailler the first company to mass-produce chocolate bars and Swiss General inventor of milk chocolate. An investment in a Brazilian condensed-milk factory during the 1920s paid an unexpected dividend when Brazilian coffee growers suggested the company develop a water-soluble "coffee cube." Released in 1938 Nescafe instant coffee quickly became popular. Other new products included Nestle's Crunch bar (1938) Quik drink mix (1948) and Taster's Choice instant coffee (1966). Nestle expanded during the 1970s with acquisitions such as Beringer Brothers wines (sold in 1995) Stouffer's and Libby's. Moving beyond foods in 1974 Nestle acquired a 49% stake in Gesparal a holding company that controls the French cosmetics company L'Oreal. It acquired pharmaceutical firm Alcon Laboratories three years later. Helmut Maucher was named chairman and CEO in 1981. He began beefing up Nestle's global presence. Boycotters had long accused Nestle of harming children in developing countries through the unethical promotion of infant formula and Maucher acknowledged the ongoing boycott by meeting with the critics and setting up a commission to police adherence to World Health Organization guidelines. Nestle bought Carnation in 1985. Maucher doubled the company's chocolate business in 1988 with the purchase of UK chocolate maker Rowntree (Kit Kat). Also in the 1980s Nestle acquired Buitoni pastas. The company expanded in the 1990s with the purchases of Butterfinger and Baby Ruth candies Source Perrier water Alpo pet food and Ortega Mexican foods. Company veteran Peter Brabeck-Letmathe succeeded Maucher as CEO in 1997. He cleaned out Nestle's pantry by selling non-core businesses (Contadina tomato products Libby's canned meat products) but restocked with San Pellegrino (mineral water) and Dalgety's Spillers (pet food) in 1998. By 1999 the company started rolling out its Nestle Pure Life bottled water. It also sold its Findus brand (fish vegetables) and its non-instant US coffee brands. That year Nestle merged its US novelty ice-cream unit with operations of Pillsbury's Haagen-Dazs to form Ice Cream Partners USA. In 2000 Nestle purchased snack maker PowerBar. In 2001 it bought Ralston Purina for $10.3 billion making it the world's largest pet food maker. To win FTC approval the companies agreed to sell Meow Mix and Alley Cat dry cat food brands to Hartz Mountain. In a deal that gives Nestle a 99-year license to use the Haagen-Dazs brand in the US the company agreed to pay $641 million to General Mills (which has bought Pillsbury from Britain's Diageo) for the other half of Ice Cream Partners. In 2002 Nestle acquired German ice-cream maker Schoeller Holding Group as well as US food company Chef America maker of Hot Pockets and Lean Pockets. That same year Nestle also spun off eyecare subsidairy Alcon Laboratories but retained about 75% ownership of it. The company renamed its water unit from Perrier Vittel SA to Nestle Waters and bought Russian bottled water company Saint Springs. The company sold its savory flavor business Food Ingredients Specialties (FIS) to Swiss flavoring company Givaudan and its UK and Ireland ambient foods business to HM Capital Partners (then named Hicks Muse Tate & Furst). It also formed a joint venture with New Zealand dairy co-op Fonterra to produce and distribute dairy products in the Americas. Nestle and Cadbury Schweppes (now Cadbury) made a joint $10.5 billion bid for The Hershey Company in 2002 but Hershey called the sale off later that year. While Nestle already owned 30% of US ice cream powerhouse Dreyer's in 2002 it proposed a merger of its US ice cream businesses. After months of antitrust scrutiny the final deal gave Nestle 67% of Dreyer's. Seeking to further strengthen its position in the worldwide ice cream market Nestle acquired the ice cream and related products of Movenpick a Swiss food company 2003. The acquisition brought Nestle licensing agreements with companies in Egypt Finland Germany Norway Sweden and Saudi Arabia. Other transactions in 2003 included the Nestle USA unit selling its Ortega brand Mexican food products to B&G Foods and the parent company selling Mont Blanc France's leading dessert brand to French investment firm Activa Capital. Also that year the company added to its bottled-water business by acquiring Hutchison Whampoa's Powwow which operates in Denmark France Germany Italy the Netherlands Portugal and the UK. In addition it acquired Clear Water a bottled-water home-and-office delivery company located in Russia. In line with its strategy to concentrate on value-added products in 2004 Nestle sold its cocoa-processing facilities in Germany and the UK to Cargill. Also in 2004 the company acquired Finnish dairy company Valid's Valiojaatelo ice cream business and increased its stake in Israeli bakery company Osem to 53%. In addition Nestle sold its German frozen food distributor Eastman that year and Nestle Espa?a bought Nestle Portugal for about $682 million. Nestle was ordered by the Brazilian government to sell its Chocolates Garoto in 2004 on the grounds that ownership of Garoto presented unfair market competition. Later that same year CEO Peter Brabeck-Letmathe announced he was considering reducing the number of outside directorships that he held because of increased demands as the leader of Nestle. At the time Brabeck-Letmathe sat on the boards of Alcon Credit Suisse Dreyer's Grand Ice Cream L'Oreal Roche Holding and "Winterthur" Swiss Insurance Company. (He has since left the "Winterthur" board.) And that year in a tangle with a French union over retirement benefits Nestle threatened to sell Perrier or produce its popular water from another source. However the company reached a settlement with the union and the production of Perrier continued. Long-time chairman Rainer Gut retired in 2005 and Brabeck-Letmathe replaced him. In 2005 it became a 90% owner of Dreyer's Grand Ice Cream. The next year Nestle became the owner of more than 90% of Dreyer's as the result of an exercise of a Put Right whereby Nestle was required to purchase certain shareholders' Class A Callable Puttable Common Stock (or Class A shares). As a result of this "short form merger" Dreyer's ceased trading on the Nasdaq stock exchange. In keeping with its strategy to concentrate on value-added products during 2006 Nestle sold its cocoa processing facilities in Germany and the UK to Cargill. Adding to its dominance in the European ice cream sector the company acquired Finnish dairy company Valid's Valiojaatelo's ice cream business and Greece's Delta Ice cream which has operations in Bulgaria Greece Macedonia Montenegro Romania and Serbia. Later that year Nestle bought the Australian breakfast cereal snack and soup operations of Uncle Tobys from Burns Philp for $670 million. The cereal portion was integrated into Cereal Partners Worldwide. In another streamlining move the company agreed to sell its canned liquid milk businesses in Southeast Asia to Singapore-based Fraser and Neave. Hedging its bets considering its food products (candy bars ice cream) are on the opposite end of the waistline wars Nestle acquired Jenny Craig for $600 million in 2006. In 2007 the company purchased the medical-nutrition business of Novartis for ?1.88 billion ($2.5 billion). The business which has operations in 40 countries worldwide makes food for hospital patients. The purchase was seen as a move by Nestle to concentrate on higher-margin products. Brands in the acquisition included Boost and Resource nutritional supplements and Optifast dieting products. Nestle divested some operations in France and Spain in order to settle competitive concerns surrounding the deal voiced by the European Commission. On the food front Nestle subsidiary Dreyer's purchased the Eskimo Pie and Chipwich brands from Canadian ice cream maker CoolBrands in 2007 for almost $19 million. Nestle spooned out $5.5 billion in cash to purchase Gerber Products from Novartis in 2007. The deal made Nestle the world's largest baby food company.

Due to the increased workload as chairman Peter Brabeck-Letmathe stepped down as CEO in 2008; he remained in an active role as board chairman. Paul Bulcke former head of Zone Americas for Nestle replaced Brabeck-Letmathe as CEO.

The company it added to its "out of home food and beverage" operations (i.e. foodservice) in 2009 with the purchase of Tampa-based Vitality Foodservice. Vitality provides commercial and non-commercial beverage services worldwide.

In August 2010 Nestle acquired Liverpool-based Vitaflo a maker of clinical nutrition products for people with metabolic disorders. Also in August it completed the sale of Alcon to Novartis. The pharmaceutical maker acquired Nestle's stake in Alcon in two steps beginning with the sale of a 25% stake for $11 billion in July 2008. Novartis exercised its option to buy Nestle's remaining percentage of Alcon for $28 billion in 2010.

In November 2011 Nestle acquired the Oscar stocks and sauces business from Paulig Group building Nestle Professional's presence in the culinary flavors sector.

EXECUTIVES

Chairman, Peter Brabeck-Letmathe, age 69, $1,514,880 total compensation
SVP Corporate Governance Compliance and Corporate Services, David P. Frick, age 48
EVP Zone Americas, Chris Johnson, age 52
EVP; Chairman and CEO NestlT Waters, John J. Harris, age 63
EVP CTO and Head Innovation Technology and Research and Development, Werner J. Bauer, age 63
Deputy EVP Nestle Professional, Marc Caira, age 59
Head of Investor Relations, Roddy Child-Villiers
Member of the Executive Board; Deputy Executive Vice President Nestle Nutrition, Kurt T. Schmidt, age 56
CEO, Paul Bulcke, age 59, $1,893,600 total compensation
Member of the Executive Board; Executive Vice President Strategic Business Units; Marketing; Sales and Nespresso, Patrice Bula
EVP and CFO, Wan Ling Martello
Member of the Management Board; Chief Financial Officer; Executive Vice President, James Singh, age 67
EVP Europe, Laurent Freixe
Executive Vice President, Martial C. Rolland
Deputy EVP Human Resources and Centre Administration, Jean-Marc Duvoisin, age 54
Member of the Executive Board; Deputy Executive Vice President Nestle S.A.; Head of Nestle Nutrition, Nandu Nandkishore
Second Vice Chairman of the Board, Rolf Haenggi
Second Vice Chairman, Rolf Hanggi, age 68
Board Member, Jean-Pierre Meyers, age 65
Board Member, Jean-Rene Fourtou, age 73
Board Member, Daniel V. Borel, age 63
Board Member, Jean-Pierre Roth, age 67
Board Member, Andre Kudelski, age 52
First Vice Chairman, Andreas N. Koopmann, age 61
Board Member, Beat W. Hess, age 64
Board Member, Carolina Muller-Mohl, age 43
Board Member, Steven G. Hoch, age 59
Board Member, Naina L. Kidwai, age 55
Board Member, Titia de Lange
Second Vice Chairman of the Board, Rolf Haenggi
Auditors: KPMGS.A.

LOCATIONS

HQ: Nestle S.A.
Avenue Nestle 55, Vevey CH-1800
Phone: (41) 21 924 2111 **Fax:** (41) 21 924 4800
Web: www.nestle.com

2012 Factories

	No.
Americas	171
Europe	153
Asia Oceania &	144
Total	**468**

2012 Sales

	% of total
Americas	44
Europe	29
Asia Oceania &	27
Total	**100**

PRODUCTS/OPERATIONS

2012 Product Sales

	% of total
Powdered & liquid	22
Milk products & ice	20
Prepared dishes & cooking	15
Pet	12
Nutrition & health	12
Confectionery	11
Water	8
Total	**100**

Selected Products and Brands

Bouillons soups seasonings pasta and sauces
- Buitoni
- Maggi
- Thomy
- Winiary

Chilled Nestle
- Chiquitin
- La Laitiere
- La Lechera
- LC1
- Molico
- Ski
- Sveltesse
- Svelty
- Yoco

Chocolate confectionery and biscuits
- Aero
- Baci
- Butterfinger
- Cailler
- Crunch
- Galak/Milkybar
- Kit Kat
- Nestle
- Polo
- Smarties

Coffee
- Bonka
- Loumidis
- Nescafe
- Nespresso
- Ricore Ricoffy
- Taster' s Choice
- Zoegas

Foodservice and professional products
- Chef
- Davigel
- Minor' s
- Santa Rica

Frozen foods (prepared dishes pizzas)
- Buitoni
- California Pizza Kitchen (licensed)
- Delissio (Canada only)
- Hot Pockets
- Jack' s Pizza
- Lean Cuisine
- Maggi
- Stouffer' s
- Tombstone

Healthcare and nutrition
- Clinutren
- Modulen
- Nutren
- Peptamen

Ice cream
- Antica Gelateria del Corso
- Chipwich
- Dreyer' s
- Drumstick/Extreme
- Edy' s
- Eskimo Pie
- Haagen-Dazs
- Maxibon/Tandem
- Mega
- Movenpick
- Parar
- Sin Parar/Sem

Infant food and nutrition
- Beba
- Cerelac
- Gerber
- Good Start
- Guigoz
- Lactogen
- Nan
- Neslac
- Nestle
- Nestogen
- Nestum

Other beverages
- Carnation
- Caro
- Libby' s
- Milo
- Nescau
- Nesquik
- Nestea

Performance nutrition
- PowerBar
- Pria

Pet care
- Alpo
- Beneful
- Cat Chow
- Dog Chow
- Fancy Feast
- Felix
- Gourmet
- Pro Plan
- Purina Friskies
- Purina ONE
- Tidy Cats

Refrigerated products (cold meat products dough pasta pizzas sauces)
- Buitoni

Herta
Nestle
Toll House
Shelf-stable products
Bear Brand
Carnation
Coffee-Mate
Gloria
Klim
La Lechera
Milkmaid
Moca
Molico
Nestle Omega
Nido
Ninho
Svelty
Water
Acqua Panna
Al Manhal
Arrowhead
Contrex
Deer Park
Hepar
Ice Mountain
Levissima
Nestle Aquarel
Nestle Pure Life
Nestle Vera
Ozarka
Perrier
Poland Spring
Quezac
S.Pellegrino
San Bernardo
Vittel
Zephyrhills

Selected Subsidiaries Joint Ventures and Affiliates

Beverage Partners Worldwide (50% with The Coca-Cola Company US)
Cereal Partners Worldwide (50% with General Mills US)
Galderma and Laboratoires inneov (29% with L' Oreal cosmetic and nutritional supplement products)
Gerber Products Company (infant nutrition US)
Jenny Craig Inc. (weight-loss centers and foods US)
Uncle Tobys (soups breakfast cereal snacks Australia)

COMPETITORS

Abbott Labs
Associated British Foods
Atkins Nutritionals
Bally Total Fitness
Barilla
Beech-Nut
Campbell Soup
Coca-Cola
ConAgra
Danone
Danone Water
Dean Foods
Dreyer' s
Ferrara Pan Candy
Fit America
GNC
General Mills
Goya
HMG
Heinz
Hershey
Indofood
Kellogg
Kent Gida
Kerry Group
Lindt & Sprungli
Mars Incorporated
Medifast
Mondelez International
Nutrisystem
PepsiCo
Procter & Gamble
Revlon
Russell Stover
Sara Lee
Slim-Fast
Smucker
Starbucks
Suntory Holdings
Tata Global Beverages
United Biscuits
Weight Watchers International
Wimm-Bill-Dann
World' s Finest Chocolate
eDiets.com
maxingvest

HISTORICAL FINANCIALS

Company Type: Public

Income Statement FYE: December 31

	REVENUE ($ mil.)	NET INCOME ($ mil.)	NET PROFIT MARGIN	EMPLOYEES
12/12	100,713	11,575	11.5%	339,000
12/11	89,041	10,084	11.3%	328,000
12/10	117,250	36,581	31.2%	281,005
12/09	104,483	10,124	9.7%	278,165
12/08	103,322	16,958	16.4%	283,000
Annual Growth	(0.6%)	(9.1%)	—	4.6%

2012 Year-End Financials

Debt ratio: 23.8%
Return on equity: 17.9%
Cash ($ mil.): 10,281
Current ratio: 0.91
Long-term debt ($ mil.): 9,827
No. of shares (mil.): —
Dividends
Yield: 3.2%
Payout: 69.5%
Market value ($ mil.): —

	STOCK PRICE ($) FY Close	P/E High/Low		PER SHARE ($) Earnings	Dividends	Book Value
12/12	65.17	24	19	3.62	2.11	20.85
12/11	57.71	31	20	3.15	2.47	19.03
12/10	58.82	7	4	10.81	1.38	20.30
12/09	48.35	17	8	2.83	1.24	13.68
12/08	39.70	25	5	4.55	1.15	13.20
Annual Growth	13.2%	—	—	(5.5%)	16.3%	12.1%

Nippon Life Insurance Co. (Japan)

Nippon Life Insurance also known as Nissay is a top life insurer in Japan. The company which has some 10 million policyholders uses a door-to-door sales corps and other representatives to peddle its traditional insurance products including individual and group life and annuity policies to Japanese consumers. In addition to its life insurance products the company administers pension plans and medical coverage plans and provides asset management services. Through its affiliates and subsidiaries the company also sells auto and other property/casualty insurance in Japan and it has some international life insurance operations as well as select real estate and financial service assets.

Geographic Reach

Nippon Life operates about 50 subsidiaries and affiliates and has some 120 branch locations. It operates in China India Japan Continental Europe the UK and the US.

Operations

In addition to the core insurance operations other Nippon Life subsidiaries and affiliates are involved in real estate investment mortgage lending and investment advisory among other financial services activities. Its operating group includes subsidiaries NLI Insurance Tokyo Agency of Nippon NLI Properties Nissay Asset Management and Nissay Capital.

Sales and Marketing

Nippon Life primarily sells policies through its dedicated field sales force as well as through retail store locations call centers and online. It also sells through select insurance brokerages and via partnerships with financial services firms including banks.

Financial Performance

Nippon Life increased revenues by 7% to Y7.2 trillion ($87 billion) in 2012 due to higher insurance and reinsurance premiums and lower than expected policy payouts (related to the massive tsunami/earthquake events in 2011) despite reporting lower investment income levels that year. Net income decreased slightly due to decreased gains on asset disposals and change in security investment prices. Nippon Life has increased revenues steadily over the past few years.

Strategy

Nippon Life along with its competitors in Japan is faced with several market challenges including a declining population (meaning a smaller customer pool) an aging population (meaning more payouts on claims) and an uneven economic recovery (which translates to cutbacks in personal expenditures).

To combat some of these problems Nippon Life has been broadening its sales channels to include an agency network and partnerships with financial services firms. (Deregulation has allowed sales of some insurance products at banks.)

Nippon Life has also been adding more medical coverage products to appeal to older consumers and is working to offer more comprehensive and flexible life insurance coverage options. Nippon Life is also investing in information technology system improvements to enhance customer service and it is expanding its international operations particularly in China India and the US.

In response to a decline in policies in force the company launched an new integration strategy in 2012. The project focuses on combining innovative insurance policies with stronger IT infrastructure and sales force resources.

Mergers and Acquisitions

Nippon Life acquired minority stakes in two affiliates Reliance Life Insurance Company Limited and Reliance Capital Asset Management Limited during 2011 and 2012. The purchases were part of a strategic collaboration with Reliance Capital formed in 2011 through which Nippon Life aims to increase its operations in India.

HISTORY

Nippon Life known as Nissay was a product of the modernization that began after US Commodore Matthew Perry opened Japan's ports to foreigners in 1854. Industry and trade were Japan's first focus but financial infrastructure soon followed. The country's first insurer (Meiji Mutual) opened in 1881. In 1889 Osaka banker Sukesaburo Hirose founded Nippon Life as a stock company. It grew and opened branches in Tokyo (1890) and Kyushu (1895).

In the 20th century the company developed a direct sales force and began lending directly to businesses. Lending remained the backbone of its asset strategy through most of the century. The insurance market in Japan grew quickly until the late 1920s but had already slowed by the eve of the Depression.

After WWII the company reorganized as a mutual and began mobilizing an army of women to build its sales of installment-premium basic life policies. In 1962 the company began automating its systems and established operations in the US (1972) and the UK (1981).

As interest rates rose in the wake of oil price hikes in the 1970s the company began offering term life and annuities and slowly moved to diversify its asset holdings from mostly government bonds (whose yields declined as rates rose) to stocks. This movement accelerated in the 1980s as the businesses that traditionally borrowed from Nippon Life turned directly to capital markets to raise money through debt issues. Seeking to replace its shrinking lending business the company began investing in US real estate and businesses whose values rose in the mid-1980s. The company reached its zenith in 1987; it owned about 3% of all the stocks on the Tokyo Exchange held more real estate than Mitsubishi's real estate units and had bought 13% of US brokerage Shearson Lehman from American Express.

By the end of the year thanks to the US stock market crash the value of the Shearson investment had fallen 40%. But the company felt confident enough of its importance as the world's largest insurance company (by assets) to crow its intentions to strong-arm Japan's Ministry of Finance into letting it diversify into trust and securities operations.

Then its bubble burst. In 1989 real estate crashed and the stock market lost more than half its value. Japan's economy failed to improve and Nippon Life was left struggling with nonperforming loans and assets whose value had declined. The company suffered further from policy cancellations and from the Ministry of Finance's focus on buoying banks. In 1997 the ministry asked Nippon Life to convert its subordinated debt from Nippon Credit Bank (now Aozora Bank) to stock. That year Nippon Life formed an alliance with Marsh & McLennan's Putnam Investments subsidiary to help manage its assets; the relationship deepened in 1998 when they began developing investment trust products.

The next year Nippon Life faced a shareholder lawsuit over its involvement in the collapse of Nippon Credit Bank; the company claims the Ministry of Finance tricked it into bailing out the bank even though it was beyond rescue. In 2001 the company merged its Nissay General subsidiary with Dowa Fire & Marine creating nonlife insurer Nissay Dowa.

In 2003 joint venture Nissay-SVA Life Insurance was formed with consumer electronics manufacturer SVA (Group) Ltd.

The company made a $1.2 billion real estate investment in 2009 when it purchased the Japan headquarters of ailing US insurer AIG.

EXECUTIVES

Chairman, Kunie Okamoto, age 69
Vice Chairman, Sadao Kato, age 65
Senior Managing Executive Officer, Kazuo Kobayashi
President, Yoshinobu Tsutsui
EVP, Takeshi Furuichi
EVP, Kenichi Kobayashi
Senior Managing Executive Officer, Koji Aiba
Senior Managing Executive Officer, Yasuomi Matsuyama
Senior Managing Executive Officer, Masami Kuroda
President and CEO Nippon Life Benefits, Toshihiro Nakashima
SVP; CFO Nippon Life Benefits, Bruce Walker
Executive Vice President Chief Operating Officer, Francine Young
Vice President Chief Business Development Officer, Joe McLaughlin
Vice President General Counsel Secretary, Tess Leopold
President Chief Executive Officer, Takayuki Murai
Vice Chairman, Sadao Kato, age 63
Managing Executive Officer and Director, Kazuo Kobayashi
Senior Managing Executive Officer and Director, Hiroshi Manabe
EVP and Director, Kiyoshi Ujihara
President and Director, Yoshinobu Tsutsui
Senior Managing Executive Officer and Director, Takeshi Furuichi
EVP and Director, Kenichi Kobayashi
Senior Managing Executive Officer and Director, Yasuomi Matsuyama
Managing Executive Officer and Director, Masami Kuroda
Managing Executive Officer and Director, Yoshinori Terajima
Executive Officer and Director, Nobusuke Matsui
Executive Officer and Director, Shohei Miki
Executive Officer and Director, Hiroyuki Nishi
Auditors: Tohmatsu&Co.

LOCATIONS

HQ: Nippon Life Insurance Co. (Japan)
3-5-12, Imabashi, Chuo-ku, Osaka 541-8501
Phone: (81) 6 6209 4500 **Fax:** 212 906-1933
Web: www.nissay.co.jp

PRODUCTS/OPERATIONS

Selected Products and Services

Products for Individuals
- Annuities
- Asset management
- Cancer Medical Insurance
- Dread Disease Insurance
- Endowment Insurance
- General Medical Insurance
- Limited Injury Insurance
- Non-life Insurance Products
- Nursing Care Insurance
- Physical Disability Insurance
- Products for Children
- Single-payment Products
- Term Life Insurance
- Term Life Insurance with Survival Benefits
- Whole Life Insurance

Products for Businesses
- Disability coverage
- Home buying preparation
- Medical coverage
- Retirement coverage
- Survivor coverage
- Various life plans

COMPETITORS

AIG
AXA
AXA Life Insurance
Allianz
American Life Insurance
Asahi Mutual Life
Dai-ichi Life
Daido Life
Fukoku Mutual
Gibraltar Life Insurance
ING
Meiji Yasuda Life
MetLife
Mitsui Life
Sompo Japan Insurance
Sumitomo Life
Taiyo Life
The Hartford
Tokio Marine

HISTORICAL FINANCIALS

Company Type: Public

Income Statement FYE: March 31

	ASSETS ($ mil.)	NET INCOME ($ mil.)	INCOME AS % OF ASSETS	EMPLOYEES
03/13	586,294	2,635	0.4%	70,004
03/12	623,756	2,741	0.4%	69,620
03/11	603,214	2,721	0.5%	70,002
03/10	522,981	2,608	0.5%	67,438
03/09	467,097	1,544	0.3%	66,074
Annual Growth	5.8%	14.3%	—	1.5%

2013 Year-End Financials

Return on assets: 0.4%
Return on equity: 7.6%
Long-term debt ($ mil.): —
No. of shares (mil.): —
Sales ($ mil): 77,167
Dividends
Yield: —
Payout: —
Market value ($ mil.): —

Nippon Steel & Sumitomo Metal Corp

When it comes to steel Nippon Steel & Sumitomo Metal rates as Japan's heavy lifter. The company the world's second-largest steelmaker after ArcelorMittal manufactures pig iron and ingots steel bars plates sheets pipes and tubes as well as specialty processed and fabricated steel products. Nippon Steel & Sumitomo Metal's annual crude steel output is 48 million tons. The company's operations include engineering construction chemicals nonferrous metals ceramics electricity supply information and communications and urban development (theme parks and condominiums). In 2012 Nippon Steel acquired fellow Japanese steel maker Sumitomo Metal Industries to form a global metals giant.

The $24 billion acquisition of Sumitomo Metal Industries mating Japan's #1 and #3 steelmakers boosted the expended company's market share against ArcelorMittal and other Asian rivals in an increasingly competitive marketplace. Similar consolidation has been happening in other countries —particularly China and Russia —aimed at elevating their steel industries to compete in the international market.

Nippon Steel & Sumitomo Metal makes a range of products including pig iron and ingots steel bars plates sheets pipes and tubes and specialty processed and fabricated steel items. Other operations include engineering construction chemicals nonferrous metals ceramics electricity supply information and communications and urban development. It also provides energy finance and insurance services.

Nippon Steel & Sumitomo Metal's primary operations are in Japan but it also has major subsidiaries in Australia Brazil China Indonesia Thailand and the US.

Prior to the acquisition in fiscal 2012 (FYE March 31 2012) Nippon Steel reported flat revenues (in local currency). Increased demand from industrial machinery and carmakers in Japan was offset by a slump in demand from flood-ravaged Thailand and the slowing of other Asian economies. Nippon Steel reported a 37% drop in net income (in local currency) that year as higher selling general and administrative expenses and steeper losses on securities significantly outpaced revenues.

The company has experienced steady growth in its overall business over the past several years due to an increase in exports primarily to East Asia and more specifically China. The rising demand for steel has brought its own challenges such as bottlenecked production.

Part of its strategy to meet demand calls for alliances with other major steelmakers including one with POSCO where Nippon Steel & Sumitomo Metal has transferred its direct-melting gasification technology. Nippon Steel & Sumitomo Metal has also formed an alliance with Kobe Steel to acquire equity stakes in East Asia United Steel which will share semi-finished products. The then Nippon Steel and Sumitomo Metal Industries integrated their building products units (structural steel sheet) and civil engineering materials operations creating two new joint ventures.

In 2013 ArcelorMittal formed a joint venture with Nippon Steel & Sumitomo Metal to buy ThyssenKrupp Steel USA from ThyssenKrupp for $1.5 billion. The deal is expected to deliver $60 million in annual savings.

The company set up a joint venture in 2011 with China's Wuhan Iron & Steel Co. to make and sell tin plate in China. Nippon and Wuhan China's third-largest steelmaker will each take a 50% stake in the $293 million venture. When operational in 2013 the Hubei province-based plant will have a 400000-ton-per-year annealing and processing line and a 200000-ton-per-year electrolytic tinning line. It also increased its holding in a joint venture with Baosteel to make steel sheets for China's booming automotive market. ArcelorMittal agreed to sell its 12% stake in Baosteel-NSC/Arcelor Automotive Steel Sheets Co. (known as BNA) to Nippon Steel in 2011 making the then Nippon Steel a 50% owner.

Nippon Steel and Ternium agreed to form a joint venture in Monterrey Mexico in 2010 to manufacture and sell hot-dip galvanized and galvannealed steel sheets to serve the Mexican automobile market. Production at the $350 million Tenigal SRL de CV facility is set to begin in 2013.

HISTORY

As Japan prepared for war the government in 1934 merged Yawata Works its largest steel producer and other Japanese steelmakers into one giant company —Japan Iron & Steel. During postwar occupation Japan Iron & Steel was ordered to dissolve. Yawata Iron & Steel and Fuji Iron & Steel emerged from the dissolution and with Western assistance the Japanese steel industry recovered from the war years. In the late 1960s Fuji Steel bought Tokai Iron & Steel (1967) and Yawata Steel took over Yawata Steel Tube Company (1968).

Yawata and Fuji merged in 1970 and became Nippon Steel the world's largest steelmaker. In the 1970s the Japanese steel industry was criticized in the US; American competitors complained that Japan was "dumping" low-cost exports. Meanwhile Nippon Steel aggressively courted China.

The company diversified in the mid-1980s to wean itself from dependence on steel. It created a New Materials unit in 1984 retraining "redundant" steelworkers to make silicon wafers and forming an Electronics Division in 1986. Nippon Steel began joint ventures with IBM Japan (small computers and software) Hitachi (office workstations) and C. Itoh (information systems for small and midsized companies) in 1988 as increased steel demand for construction and cars in Japan's "bubble economy" took the company to new heights.

In an atmosphere of economic optimism the company spent more than four times the expected expense to build an amusement park capable of competing with Tokyo Disneyland. The company plowed ahead spending some $230 million on the park. Space World amusement park opened on the island of Kyushu in 1990. The company's bubble burst that year. (The theme park declared bankruptcy in May 2005 and was sold to Kamori Kanko later that year.)

In response Nippon Steel cut costs and intensified its diversification efforts by targeting electronics information and telecommunications new materials and chemicals markets. Seeking to remake its steel operations the company began a drastic phased restructuring in 1993 that included a step most Japanese companies try to avoid —cutting personnel. A semiconductor division was organized that year as part of the company's diversification strategy.

Upgrading its steel operations Nippon Steel and partner Mitsubishi in 1996 introduced the world's first mass-production method for making hot-rolled steel sheet directly from smelted stainless steel. Profits were hurt that year by a loss-making project in the information and communications segment and by a steep decline in computer memory-chip prices.

The company began operation of a Chinese steelmaking joint venture Guangzhou Pacific Tinplate in 1997. The next year its Singapore-based joint venture with Hitachi Ltd. began mass-producing computer memory chips in hopes of stemming semiconductor losses. But falling prices convinced Nippon Steel to get out of the memory chip business and in 1999 it sold its semiconductor subsidiary to South Korea's United Microelectronics.

That year the US imposed antidumping duties on the company's steel products. The next year Nippon Steel agreed to form a strategic alliance with South Korea-based Pohang Iron and Steel (POSCO) at that time the world's #1 steel maker. The deal called for the exploration of joint ventures shared research and joint procurement as well as increased equity stakes in each other (at 2%-3%). Also in 2000 Nippon Steel agreed to provide Sumitomo Metal Industries and Nisshin Steel Co. with stainless steel products.

Early in 2001 Nippon Steel formed a cooperative alliance —focused on automotive sheet products —with French steel giant Usinor (now a part of ArcelorMittal). At the end of the year Nippon Steel decided to form an alliance with Kobe Steel to pare down costs and share in distribution and production facilities. In 2002 the company continued its series of comprehensive alliances by forming alliances with Japanese steelmaker Nippon Metal Industry to exchange its semi-finished stainless steel technologies and with POSCO to build environment-related businesses.

The company reported a loss of Y51.69 billion ($430 million) for fiscal 2003 due to securities valuation losses and group restructuring charges. In 2004 Nippon Steel formed a joint venture with Baoshan Iron & Steel and Arcelor to manufacture high-grade automotive steel sheets.

Nippon Steel moved into the South American market in 2006 forming alliances with steelmaker Usiminas and iron miner CVRD. And the next year it created a JV with Baosteel and ArcelorMittal that produces automotive steel sheets.

The company joined up with Sumitomo Metal Industries in 2009 when the two companies agreed to form a joint venture that will combine their arc-welded stainless steel pipe and tube operations. Sumitomo will own 60% of the JV. The operations that make up the new company which will be called Sumikin & Nippon Steel Stainless Steel Pipe Co. achieved sales of more than $250 million in 2008.

EXECUTIVES

President and COO, Hiroshi Tomono, age 68
Chairman and CEO, Shoji Muneoka, age 67
EVP, Syuichiro Kozuka, age 65
EVP and Representative Director, Shinichi Taniguchi, age 63
EVP, Masakazu Iwaki, age 64
EVP Director Technical Development and Representative Director, Norio Katsuyama
EVP, Kosei Shindo
EVP, Shinya Higuchi
EVP, Katsuhiko Ota
EVP, Akihiro Miyasaka
President and Board Member, Shoji Muneoka, age 65
Managing Director General Manager Personnel and Labor Relations and Board Member, Kizo Hirayama, age 63
EVP and Representative Director, Kozo Uchida, age 63
EVP and Representative Director, Shinichi Taniguchi, age 63
EVP and Representative Director, Masakazu Iwaki, age 63
Managing Director and Board Member, Yasuo Hamamoto, age 61
EVP Director Technical Development and Representative Director, Norio Katsuyama
EVP and Representative Director, Kosei Shindo
Auditors: KPMGAZSA&Co.

LOCATIONS

HQ: Nippon Steel & Sumitomo Metal Corp
2-6-1 Marunouchi, Chiyoda-ku, Tokyo 100-8071
Phone: (81) 3 6867 4111 **Fax:** (81) 3 6867 5607
Web: www.nsc.co.jp

2012 Sales

	% of total
Asia	
Japan	67
Other	24
Other	9
Total	**100**

PRODUCTS/OPERATIONS

2012 Sales

	$ mil.	% of total
Steelmaking & Steel Fabrication		84
Chemicals		4
Urban Development		2
Total	**0**	**100**

Selected Products and Services

Steelmaking and Steel Fabrication
- Fabricated and processed steels
- Pig iron and ingots
- Pipes and tubes
- Plates and sheets
- Sections
- Specialty sheets

Engineering and Construction
- Building construction
- Civil engineering
- Marine construction
- Plant and machinery
- Technical cooperation

Chemicals
- Aluminum products
- Ammonium sulfate
- Cement
- Ceramic products
- Coal tar
- Coke
- Ferrite
- Metallic foils
- Slag products

System Solutions
- Communications services
- Computers and equipment
- Data processing
- Systems development and integration

Urban Development
- Condominiums
- Theme parks

New Materials
- Semiconductor bonding wire
- Silicon wafers
- Titanium products
- Transformers

Other operations
- Services
  - Energy services
  - Financial services
  - Insurance services
- Transportation
  - Loading and unloading
  - Marine and land transportation
  - Warehousing

Selected Subsidiaries and Affiliates

Subsidiaries
- Nippon Steel & Sumikin Coated Sheet Corporation
- Nippon Steel & Sumikin Metal Products Co. Ltd.
- Nippon Steel & Sumikin Stainless Steel Corporation
- Nippon Steel & Sumikin Welding Co. Ltd.
- Nippon Steel Australia Pty. Limited
- Nippon Steel Blast Furnace Slag Cement Co. Ltd.
- Nippon Steel Drum Co. Ltd. 1654
- Nippon Steel Logistics Co. Ltd.
- Nippon Steel Shipping Co. Ltd.
- Nippon Steel Transportation Co. Ltd.

Nippon Steel U.S.A. Inc.
Nittetsu Cement Co. Ltd.
Nittetsu Elex Co. Ltd.
Nittetsu Finance Co. Ltd.
Nittetsu Steel Pipe Co. Ltd. 4832
Nittetsu Tokai Steel Wire Co. Ltd.
NS Preferred Capital Limited
Osaka Steel Co. Ltd.
Siam Nippon Steel Pipe Co. Ltd.
The Siam United Steel (1995) Co. Ltd.

Affiliates
Daiwa Can Company
Geostr Corporation
Godo Steel Ltd.
Japan Casting & Forging Corporation
Krosaki Harima Corporation
Mitsui Mining Co. Ltd.
Nichia Steel Works Ltd.
Nippon Steel Trading Co. Ltd.
Sanko Metal Industrial Co. Ltd.
Sanyo Special Steel Co. Ltd.
Sanyu Co. Ltd.
Suzuki Metal Industry Co. Ltd.
Taihei Kogyo Co. Ltd.
Topy Industries Ltd.

COMPETITORS

ArcelorMittal	POSCO
BlueScope Steel	Tata Europe
JFE Holdings	ThyssenKrupp Steel
Kobe Steel	United States Steel
Marubeni	Vale
Mitsubishi Corp.	Yamato Kogyo

HISTORICAL FINANCIALS

Company Type: Public

Income Statement

FYE: March 31

	REVENUE ($ mil.)	NET INCOME ($ mil.)	NET PROFIT MARGIN	EMPLOYEES
03/13	46,655	(1,323)	—	83,187
03/12	49,871	712	1.4%	60,508
03/11	49,631	1,125	2.3%	59,183
03/10	37,338	(123)	—	52,205
03/09	48,436	1,574	3.3%	50,077
Annual Growth	(0.9%)	—	—	13.5%

2013 Year-End Financials

Debt ratio: 0.3%
Return on equity: (-5.9%)
Cash ($ mil.): 949
Current ratio: 1.07
Long-term debt ($ mil.): 19,877
No. of shares (mil.): —
Dividends
Yield: —
Payout: —
Market value ($ mil.): —

	STOCK PRICE ($) FY Close	P/E High/Low	PER SHARE ($) Earnings	Dividends	Book Value
03/13	25.42	— —	(0.17)	0.00	3.44
03/12	27.50	— —	0.11	0.00	4.55
03/11	32.10	— —	0.18	0.00	4.58
03/10	39.02	— —	(0.02)	0.00	3.98
03/09	26.95	— —	0.24	0.00	3.52
Annual Growth	(1.5%)	— —	—	—	(0.5%)

Nippon Telegraph & Telephone Corp. (Japan)

Nippon Telegraph and Telephone (NTT) executed an AT&T-style breakup but unlike Ma Bell's gang the family stuck together. One of the world's largest telecom companies NTT owns a controlling stake in Japan's dominant cellular carrier NTT DoCoMo (60 million subscribers) and it is a holding company for regional phone companies NTT East and NTT West which enjoy de facto monopolies in their respective markets. NTT provides long-distance international and data networking services through subsidiary NTT Communications. The company also operates an ISP and provides IT services through majority-owned NTT DATA. NTT has foreign holdings in Europe the Pacific Rim and the US. The Japanese state owns 34% of the company.

Like most large carriers NTT is investing in upgrades to its landline and mobile networks to improve and expand existing services and enable new functionality. The company has extended the reach of its domestic broadband Internet network and fiber optic video services as landline voice subscriptions continue to decline. While sales from NTT's wireless business have slipped due to decreased voice revenue the company has added mobile subscribers and improved profits by offering more robust data services and improving customer retention.

NTT does business principally in Japan although the company has investments and operations throughout the Pacific Rim –including holdings in Australia Hong Kong Malaysia the Philippines Singapore –as well as in Europe Latin America and the US. The company is investing in its international operations particularly in the areas of data networking and IT services through strategic partnerships and acquisitions primarily to address the needs of its globalized corporate clientele.

NTT's key Asian holdings include minority stakes in Philippine Long Distance Telephone and Mumbai-based Tata Teleservices. The company operates in the US through enterprise communications services subsidiary NTT America and it owns Colorado-based Web-hosting and data services provider Verio. NTT also operates a submarine communications system known as Pacific Crossing which directly links NTT's network in Japan with carriers in the US. The company does business in Europe through UK-based NTT Europe and Germany-based itelligence Cirquent and Integralis.

Pressing further into Asia in search of growth NTT established the first of a series of fiber-optic networks in Indonesia in 2012 to better serve commercial customers. It also acquired about three-quarters of India-based Netmagic Solutions to expand its data services outsourcing business in the country and support the cloud-based services such as managed hosting and Internet connectivity that it provides to clients across the region. NTT picked up seven datacenters in major Indian cities such as Mumbai Chennai and Bangalore as part of the deal.

NTT bought US-based Keane in 2011 through NTT DATA to expand its IT services business in the US and better compete with larger rivals like IBM. The deal expanded NTT's global IT business and added expertise in developing and managing complex technology systems. The company acquired South Africa-based Dimension Data the previous year for about $3.2 billion. Both purchases were key components of NTT's growing focus on providing integrated communications and IT services to globally distributed corporations. The company has its eye set on further investments in IT service businesses in South America China and Southeast Asia and in 2012 announced 012 that it would establish a subsidiary in Myanmar to expand its offshore development capability in support of clients in Japan.

NTT's sales rose slightly in fiscal 2011. While voice-related services declined (voice telephone subscriptions shrank from 30.2 million in 2010 to 27.5 million in 2011) the company cited increased sales of data services as well as greater revenue from its systems integration business driven by the acquisitions of Keane and Dimension Data.

HISTORY

In 1889 the Japanese Ministry of Communications began telephone service operated as a monopoly after 1900. In 1952 the ministry formed Nippon Telegraph and Telephone Public Corporation (NTT). Regulated by the Ministry of Posts and Telecommunications NTT was charged with rebuilding Japan's war-ravaged phone system. Another company Kokusai Denshin Denwa (now KDD) was created in 1953 to handle international phone service.

Japanese authorities cast NTT in the image of AT&T but prohibited it from manufacturing to encourage competition among equipment suppliers. Nonetheless NTT bought most equipment from favored Japanese vendors. By the late 1970s NTT was a large bureaucracy perceived as inefficient and corrupt. NTT's president quipped that the only equipment the firm would buy overseas was telephone poles and mops but in 1981 NTT was forced to allow US companies to bid. The phone firm spent heavily in the 1980s installing a nationwide fiber-optic network and high-speed ISDN lines.

In 1985 Japan privatized NTT as a precursor to deregulation. At its IPO NTT became the world's most valuable public company. NTT International was established to provide overseas telecom engineering and NTT Data Communications Systems Japan's largest systems integrator was formed in 1988.

As Japan's stock market bubble burst in 1990 NTT chose AT&T Motorola and Ericsson to develop a digital mobile phone system and the next year formed NTT Mobile Communications Network (NTT DoCoMo) as its mobile carrier. Following the deregulation of Japan's cellular market NTT launched its Personal Handyphone Service (PHS) in 1995.

The Japanese government unveiled a plan to break up NTT in 1996 a year before the World Trade Organization spearheaded a historic agreement to open international telecom markets. Meanwhile the government forced NTT to allow rivals to connect to its new all-digital systems. Overseas NTT made its first significant investment in the US by buying a 12.5% stake in local carrier Teligent (later reduced).

In 1998 tiny Tokyo Telecommunications Net (a Tokyo Electric Power affiliate) offered discount phone rates spurring NTT to do the same. NTT spun off DoCoMo in the world's largest IPO at the time.

NTT lost its 1999 bidding war with the UK's Cable and Wireless for International Digital Communications. That year NTT split into three carriers two near-monopoly regional local phone providers –NTT East and NTT West –and a long-distance and international carrier called NTT Communications. Unlike AT&T's breakup in 1984 this split featured a holding company –the new NTT – that owns the three carriers. Criticized for continuing to promote last-generation ISDN as the key to high-speed Internet access NTT in 1999 began to test higher-speed digital subscriber line (DSL) service and planned to cut 21000 jobs at NTT West and NTT East over three years.

The company pressed forward with international investments taking a 49% stake in HKNet of Hong Kong and a 49% stake in Davnet Telecommunications a subsidiary of Australia's Davnet Limited (both were later increased to 100%). In 2000 the Japanese government said it would sell another 6% of NTT. That year NTT paid $5.5 billion for the 90% of US Web-hosting firm Verio that it didn't already own.

NTT purchased mobile phone application developer Panasonic Mobile Communications from parent Panasonic Corporation (formerly Matsushita Electric) in 2008.

In 2010 the company acquired a 70% stake in Singapore-based Emerio GlobeSoft in a further effort to boost its international technology services business. Active primarily in the Asia/Pacific region Emerio specialized in custom software development and support IT network support and business process outsourcing services such as account processing. Additionally NTT established a wireless subsidiary in China through NTT DoCoMo to tap into the booming market there.

EXECUTIVES

Chairman, Norio Wada, age 73
SEVP CTO CIO and Board Member, Noritaka Uji, age 64
President and CEO, Hiroo Unoura, age 65
Chairman, Satoshi Miura, age 69
President NTT DoCoMo, Ryuji Yamada, age 65
President and CEO America, Kazuhiro Gomi
President and CEO Verio, Kiyoshi Maeda
SEVP Risk Management and International Standardization Chief Compliance Officer and Board Member, Kaoru Kanazawa, age 68
SVP Director Finance and Accounting Department and Board Member; President NTT Capital UK, Toshio Kobayashi, age 61
SEVP CIO and CTO, Yasuyoshi Katayama, age 62
SEVP and CFO, Hiroki Watanabe, age 60
EVP, Hiromichi Shinohara, age 59
Board Member, Takashi Imai, age 83
Board Member, Yotaro Kobayashi, age 80
SEVP CTO CIO and Board Member, Noritaka Uji, age 64
SEVP Business Strategy CFO Director Strategic Business Development Division and Board Member, Hiroo Unoura, age 64
President CEO and Board Member, Satoshi Miura, age 69
SEVP Risk Management and International Standardization Chief Compliance Officer and Board Member, Kaoru Kanazawa, age 68
SVP Director Finance and Accounting Department and Board Member; President NTT Capital UK, Toshio Kobayashi, age 61
EVP Director Technology Planning Department and Next Generation Network Office and Board Member, Yasuyoshi Katayama, age 61
EVP Director Corporate Strategy Planning Department and Board Member, Hiroki Watanabe, age 60
SVP Director General Affairs Department and Internal Control Office and Board Member, Tetsuya Shouji
SVP Director Research and Development Planning Department and Board Member, Hiromichi Shinohara
Auditors: KPMGAZSA&Co.

LOCATIONS

HQ: Nippon Telegraph & Telephone Corp. (Japan)
3-1 Ohtemachi 2-chome, Chiyoda-ku, Tokyo 100-8116
Phone: (81) 3 5205 5581 **Fax:** (81) 3 5205 5589
Web: www.ntt.co.jp

PRODUCTS/OPERATIONS

2011 Sales

	% of total
IP/packet	32
Fixed-line	21
Mobile	20
Systems	13
Telecom	8
Other	6
Total	**100**

COMPETITORS

AT&T
BT
Cable & Wireless
Deutsche Telekom
EMOBILE
Fujitsu
Hikari Tsushin
Internet Initiative Japan
Jupiter Telecommunications
KDDI
KEPCO
Pacnet
SOFTBANK MOBILE
Telstra
Tokyo Electric

HISTORICAL FINANCIALS

Company Type: Public

Income Statement FYE: March 31

	REVENUE ($ mil.)	NET INCOME ($ mil.)	NET PROFIT MARGIN	EMPLOYEES
03/13	113,726	5,569	4.9%	324,713
03/12	128,091	5,701	4.5%	313,586
03/11	124,446	6,154	4.9%	302,226
03/10	108,999	5,270	4.8%	271,253
03/09	105,776	5,470	5.2%	266,769
Annual Growth	1.8%	0.5%	—	5.0%

2013 Year-End Financials

Debt ratio: 0.2%
Return on equity: 6.4%
Cash ($ mil.): 10,218
Current ratio: 1.33
Long-term debt ($ mil.): 34,762
No. of shares (mil.): 1,185
Dividends
Yield: 0.0%
Payout: 0.0%
Market value ($ mil.): 25,770

	STOCK PRICE ($) FY Close	P/E High/Low		PER SHARE ($) Earnings	Dividends	Book Value
03/13	21.74	0	0	4.60	0.00	74.59
03/12	22.62	0	0	4.47	0.00	78.52
03/11	22.49	0	0	4.65	0.69	73.21
03/10	21.02	0	—	3.98	0.62	63.01
03/09	19.03	0	—	4.07	0.51	56.01
Annual Growth	3.4%	—	—	3.1%	(87.6%)	7.4%

Nishi-Nippon City Bank Ltd.

The Nishi-Nippon City Bank is more of a community bank. It operates about 200 branches in the Kyushu region of southern Japan (poplation 14.5 million) for a customer base of mainly individuals and small and midsized businesses. Nishi-Nippon City Bank offers traditional banking services such as checking and savings accounts as well as securities credit guarantees credit cards and credit management and business consulting services. In addition to the parent bank it operates through eight subsidiaries. It also maintains representative offices in Hong Kong Seoul and Shanghai. Tracing its roots back to 1944 the bank took its current form in 2004 when Nishi-Nippon Bank acquired Fukuoka City Bank.

EXECUTIVES

Chairman, Masahiro Honda
President and Director, Isao Kubota
Deputy President and Director, Kazushige Higuchi
Executive Director, Seiji Isoyama
Executive Director, Hiromichi Tanigawa
Executive Director, Shigeru Urayama
Managing Director, Sadamasa Okamura
Managing Director, Kiyota Takata
Executive Director, Soichi Kawamoto
Managing Director, Yasuyuki Ishida
Managing Director, Hiroyuki Irie
Managing Director, Michiharu Kitazaki
President and Director, Isao Kubota
Deputy President and Director, Kazushige Higuchi
Executive Director, Seiji Isoyama
Executive Director, Hiromichi Tanigawa
Executive Director, Shigeru Urayama
Managing Director, Sadamasa Okamura
Managing Director, Kiyota Takata
Executive Director, Soichi Kawamoto
Managing Director, Yasuyuki Ishida
Managing Director, Hiroyuki Irie
Managing Director, Michiharu Kitazaki

LOCATIONS

HQ: Nishi-Nippon City Bank Ltd.
3-1-1 Hakata-ekimae, Hakata-ku, Fukuoka 812-0011
Phone: (81) 92 476 1111
Web: www.ncbank.co.jp

COMPETITORS

Aozora Bank
Awa Bank
Bank of Kyoto
Bank of Yokohama
Chiba Bank
Chugoku Bank
Chuo Mitsui Trust
Eighteenth Bank Ltd.
Fukuoka Financial Group
Hokkoku Bank
Hokuhoku Financial Group
Mitsubishi UFJ Financial Group
Nanto Bank
Norinchukin Bank
Shiga Bank
Shinsei Bank
Shizuoka Bank
Sumitomo Mitsui
Suruga Bank
Tokyo Tomin Bank
Towa Bank

HISTORICAL FINANCIALS

Company Type: Public

Income Statement FYE: March 31

	ASSETS ($ mil.)	NET INCOME ($ mil.)	INCOME AS % OF ASSETS	EMPLOYEES
03/13	82,627	195	0.2%	4,392
03/12	93,513	219	0.2%	4,534
03/11	89,386	644	0.7%	4,677
03/10	78,022	233	0.3%	4,688
03/09	73,199	148	0.2%	4,709
Annual Growth	3.1%	7.2%	—	(1.7%)

2013 Year-End Financials

Return on assets: 0.2%
Return on equity: 5.0%
Long-term debt ($ mil.): —
No. of shares (mil.): 795
Sales ($ mil): 1,661
Dividends
Yield: —
Payout: —
Market value ($ mil.): —

Nissan Motor Co., Ltd.

Nissan Motor one of Japan's leading automakers wants to get big by going small. Through its small-car initiative the company primarily produces low-cost and fuel-efficient small cars with standard comfort safety style and performance. Nissan's models include Maxima and Sentra cars and Altima and Infiniti upscale sedans as well as pickups SUVs and sports cars. It is also one of the world's largest manufacturers of forklifts. Renault holds a 43% stake in Nissan Motor and Nissan has a 15% stake in Renault constituting the Renault-Nissan Alliance.

Nissan manufactures in about 20 countries and sells and services products in more than 160 countries.

Revenue rose around 7% in fiscal 2012 compared with 2011. Despite such challenges as the Great East Japan Earthquake Nissan enjoyed record sales in fiscal 2012. It sold more than 4.8 billion units in 2012 which was about a 16% increase from the previous year. It also grew its market share by 0.6 points to more than 6%. The company's strong sales were supported by demand for the Serena and Juke in Japan; the Sunny Teana Sylphy Qashqai and Tiida in China; and the Altima Rogue and Versa in North America. The company expects to enjoy double-digit sales growth in fiscal 2013 as a result in part of demand in China the company's largest market.

The Nissan Power 88 plan calls for attaining 8% global market share and an 8% operating profit margin by 2017. A major element of Power 88 is the development of about 90 new technologies including a next-generation XTRONIC continuously variable transmission technology. The plan additionally includes investing 70% of research and development expenses into green technology.

Nissan responded to the 2008 financial crisis by initiating what it calls a localization strategy that stresses a balance of manufacturing and sourcing with sales operations. As a result of the strategy Nissan has implemented local manufacturing and sales of the V-platform car in China India Mexico and Thailand. China is not only Nissan's largest market but also the location of its biggest manufacturing site the Huada facility –where the Tiida hatchback is made –with the ability to produce some 600000 units a year. Nissan spearheads its business development efforts in China through a joint venture with Dongfeng Motor.

Nissan also has set a goal of increasing the percentage of fully built units that are locally made in the Americas to 85% by 2015. New plants in Brazil and Mexico are tasked with increasing production in the Americas from 1.2 million units a year in 2011 to 2 million units annually by 2014. The Great East Japan of Earthquake of 2011 and other contingencies also lead the company to create more efficient business continuity procedures for parts purchasing.

HISTORY

In 1911 US-trained Masujiro Hashimoto established Tokyo-based Kwaishinsha Motor Car Works to repair import and manufacture cars. Kwaishinsha made its first car sporting its DAT ("fast rabbit" in Japanese) logo in 1913. Renamed DAT Motors in 1925 and suffering from a strong domestic preference for American cars the company consolidated with ailing Jitsuyo Motors in 1926. DAT introduced the son of DAT in 1931 –the Datsun minicar ("son" means "damage or loss" in Japanese hence the spelling change).

Tobata Casting (cast iron and auto parts) bought Datsun's production facilities in 1933. Tobata's Yoshisuke Aikawa believed there was a niche for small cars and the car operations were spun off as Nissan Motors that year.

During WWII the Japanese government limited Nissan's production to trucks and airplane engines; Nissan survived postwar occupation in part due to business with the US Army. The company went public in 1951 and signed a licensing agreement the next year with Austin Motor (UK) which put it back in the car business. A 40% import tax allowed Nissan to compete in Japan even though it had higher costs than those of foreign carmakers.

Nissan entered the US market in 1958 with the model 211 using the Datsun name; it established Nissan Motor Corporation in Los Angeles in 1960. Exports rose as factory automation led to higher quality and lower costs. In the 1970s Nissan expanded exports of fuel-efficient cars such as the Datsun B210. The company became the leading US car importer in 1975.

The company's name change in the US from Datsun to Nissan during the 1980s confused customers and took six years to complete. In 1986 Nissan became the first major Japanese carmaker to build its products in Europe. It launched its high-end Infiniti line in the US in 1989.

Nissan and Japanese telecom firm KDDI Corporation set up cellular phone operations in 1992. Japan's recession resulted in a $450 million loss the next year. The company cut costs in 1993 and sold $200 million in real-estate holdings in 1994.

Nissan suffered its fourth straight year of losses posting an $834 million loss for 1996. Fiscal 1997 brought profits for Nissan –its first since 1992 –in part the result of cost-cutting moves sales to countries with currencies stronger than the yen and the launching of new models. In 1998 Nissan received an $827 million loan from the government-owned Japan Development Bank to restructure its debt.

Suffering under an estimated $30 billion in debt in 1999 Nissan invited major carmakers to buy into the company. Renault took a 37% stake and a 15% stake in affiliate Nissan Diesel Motor for $5.4 billion. The stake gave Renault veto power and enabled it to install its chief cost-cutter Carlos Ghosn (nicknamed "Le Cost Killer" based on his talent for turning red ink black) as COO. Ghosn began plans to slash the number of suppliers close five plants and cut its workforce by 14% by 2002.

Under the watchful eye of Ghosn Nissan went from a doubtful future to a corporate success story in just a few years. The company announced its Nissan Revival Plan (NRP) in 1999. The plan called for the closing of inefficient factories workforce reductions curbing purchasing costs sharing operations with Renault and introducing new products. By 2001 Nissan was again making a profit –one year earlier than the NRP predicted.

Not satisfied with this Nissan then launched a three-year business scheme called Nissan 180 aiming to grow annual sales by 1 million units generate an 8% operating profit margin and eliminate automotive debt. Nissan made good on all these goals. In fact the company's operating margin exceeded 10% every year since the plan was initiated (making it the envy of most of the world's carmakers). Nissan not only managed to erase automotive debt it piled up cash reserves of about $1.65 billion. Meanwhile Nissan sold its interests in nine mobile-phone companies and its powder metallurgy business.

In 2000 Nissan sold its stake in Fuji Heavy Industries. That year Ghosn became president of Nissan; Nissan's former president Yoshikazu Hanawa remained as CEO and chairman. Nissan also announced that it was developing a full-sized truck for the US market and that it and Renault were combining their European sales and marketing operations. Late in the year the company announced plans to build a $930 million manufacturing plant in the US.

Ghosn was named CEO (in addition to president) in 2001. Later in 2001 Nissan announced it would take a 15% stake in Renault while the French carmaker would increase its stake in Nissan to 44%. These steps along with the French government's decision to reduce its interest in Renault from 44% to 25% were aimed at further strengthening the bond between the two companies. In 2002 Nissan and Renault completed their planned equity swap.

The following year Nissan rolled out the most dramatic new lineup of vehicles it had introduced in years. The company debuted the Murano urban SUV the full-size Titan pickup and the full-size Armada SUV.

In mid-2005 Nissan announced that it had selected its assembly plant in Tennessee for production of its first hybrid vehicle. The following year Nissan began talks with AB Volvo and the Chinese authorities for the sale of Nissan's 50% stake in Dongfeng Motor –China's largest maker of commercial trucks.

Later in 2006 billionaire General Motors investor Kirk Kerkorian (who owned about a 10% stake in GM at the time) proposed that the beleaguered US automaker should form a three-way alliance with Nissan and Renault. The three companies' boards subsequently held hasty meetings to ponder the idea. The companies later announced they'd decided there would be no alliance. Also in 2006 Nissan sold its remaining 6% stake in Nissan Diesel Motor to AB Volvo for about $69 million.

Nissan hit its first series of speed bumps in 2006 after a long stretch of smooth road. Sales hiccups in Japan the US and Europe prompted a few tweaks. After a surge of new products in 2005 Nissan rode out the product in-between time in the US until freshened versions of the Altima and Sentra were unveiled in late 2006. Nissan also made production adjustments at its plants in the US and Japan.

Just as some observers began to suggest a dearth of hybrids might also be causing sales doldrums at Nissan the company devised an ambitious hybrid scheme. Late in 2006 Nissan announced plans to introduce a hybrid based on Nissan-developed technology in fiscal 2010. The move was part of the self-described "Nissan Green Program 2010." The plan also called for bringing clean diesel engines to Europe in fiscal 2007 with the US China and Japan getting them sometime after April 2010.

The company also planned to expand the availability of flex-fuel vehicles (capable of burning gasoline and ethanol-derived E85) in 2007 with the debut of a flex-fuel Armada (the flex-fuel Titan was introduced in 2004). The Nissan Green plan also called for reducing CO_2 plant emissions to 7% less than 2005 levels by 2010 the vague launching of an electric car sometime in the next decade the introduction of a three-liter car that will go more than 60 miles on less than a gallon of gas and entering the lithium-ion battery market.

In a deal completed in 2008 Nissan agreed to build a small car for Chrysler; in return a Chrysler manufacturing facility in Mexico would make the replacement for the Nissan Titan truck scheduled to debut in 2011. However in 2009 both parties decided to freeze the project and reassess the profitability of the venture. Chrysler admitted that having Fiat on board (Fiat had invested in Chrysler in 2009) to develop small cars had a bearing in the decision.

EXECUTIVES

Chairman President and CEO, Carlos Ghosn, age 59
Vice Chairman, Toshiyuki Shiga
EVP Manufacturing and SCM, Hidetoshi Imazu
EVP and CFO, Joseph G. (Joe) Peter, age 50
EVP, Mitsuhiko (Mike) Yamashita
EVP and Chief Competitive Officer, Hiroto Saikawa, age 60
Corporate VP Infiniti Product Development Vehicle Test Technology Development, Tsuyoshi Yamaguchi
EVP, Kimiyasu Nakamura
SVP; President Infiniti Global, Johan de Nysschen, age 48
SVP External and Government Affairs and Intellectual Asset Management, Hitoshi Kawaguchi
SVP Technology Development Division, Minoru Shinohara
SVP Office of CEO, Greg Kelly
Corporate VP, Toshifumi Hirai
Corporate VP, Atsushi Hirose
EVP, Takao Katagiri
Executive Vice President; Chairman & President of Subsidiaries; Director, Colin Dodge
Corporate VP, Asako Hoshino
Corporate VP and CIO, Celso Guiotoko
SVP Production Engineering Division, Shigeaki Kato
Fellow, Haruyoshi Kumura
EVP and Chief Planning Officer, Andy Palmer
Corporate VP, Gilles Normand
SVP Product Development Division Nissan PV Product Development Division No.2 and Nissan LCV Product Development Division, Atsushi Shizuta
Corporate VP, Joji Tagawa
SVP Purchasing, Yasuhiro Yamauchi
SVP Japan Marketing and Sales, Massaaki Nishizawa
Fellow, Kimio Tomita
Corporate VP, Shohei Kimura
Corporate VP, Shunichi Toyomasu
Corporate VP, Yusuke Takahashi
Corporate VP, John Martin
Corporate VP, Vincent Cobee
Corporate VP, Takao Asami
Corporate VP, Makoto Yoshimoto
Corporate VP, Hideyuki Sakamoto
Corporate VP, Hideto Murakami
Corporate VP Global Control Budget and Accounting, Hiroshi Karube
Corporate VP, Shuichi Nishimura
Auditor, Toshiyuki Nakamura
EVP, Jose Munoz
SVP Manufacturing and Industrial Engineering, Akira Sakurai
Director Customer and Sales Satisfaction, William (Billy) Hayes
IR Contact Officer, Minoru Tagami
Executive Officer, Rakesh Kochhar
Managing Executive Officer, Toshiaki Ohtani
EVP and Chief Performance Officer, Trevor Mann
SVP; President Dongfend Motor, Jun Seki
Corporate VP, Roel De Vries
Director, Jean-Baptiste Duzan, age 67
SVP Design and Brands Champion, Shiro Nakamura
Vice Chairman, Toshiyuki Shiga
EVP Manufacturing and SCM and Director, Hidetoshi Imazu
EVP Research and Development and Total Customer Satisfaction Function and Director, Mitsuhiko (Mike) Yamashita
EVP Japan Asia/Pacific Industrial Machinery Marine Administration for Affiliates Purchasing and Director, Hiroto Saikawa, age 59
EVP Americas Operations and Director; Chairman Americas, Carlos Tavares, age 53
EVP Europe Africa Middle East India and New Project and Director, Colin Dodge
Auditors: Ernst&YoungShinNihon

LOCATIONS

HQ: Nissan Motor Co., Ltd.
1-1-1 Takashima, Nishi-ku, Yokohama 220-8686
Phone: (81) 45 523 5523
Web: www.nissan-global.com

PRODUCTS/OPERATIONS

Selected Products

Forklifts
- Engine-powerd forklifts
- Electric-powered forklifts
- Warehouse products
  - Order pickers
  - Pallet stackers
  - Pallet transporters
  - Reach trucks

Infiniti
- Infiniti G
- Infiniti G convertible
- Infiniti G coupe
- Infiniti M
- Infiniti EX
- Infiniti FX
- Infiniti JX
- Infiniti QX

Nissan
- Altima
- Altima coupe
- Altima hybrid
- Armada
- Cube
- Frontier
- GT-R
- Maxima
- Murano
- Pathfinder
- Rogue
- Sentra
- Titan
- Versa
- Xterra

Nissan Marine outboard motors

COMPETITORS

BMW
CLARK Material Handling
Chrysler
Crown Equipment
Daihatsu
Daimler
Deere
Fiat
Ford Motor
Fuji Heavy Industries
General Motors
Honda
Hyundai Motor
Isuzu
Kia Motors
Mazda
Mitsubishi Motors
NACCO Industries
Peugeot
Saab Automobile
Suzuki Motor
Tata Motors
Toyota
Volkswagen
Volvo
Volvo Car Corp.

HISTORICAL FINANCIALS

Company Type: Public

Income Statement

FYE: March 31

	REVENUE ($ mil.)	NET INCOME ($ mil.)	NET PROFIT MARGIN	EMPLOYEES
03/13	102,342	3,639	3.6%	160,530
03/12	114,701	4,162	3.6%	157,365
03/11	105,946	3,855	3.6%	155,098
03/10	80,478	453	0.6%	151,698
03/09	85,676	(2,373)	—	155,659
Annual Growth	4.5%	—	—	0.8%

2013 Year-End Financials

Debt ratio: 0.4%
Return on equity: 9.9%
Cash ($ mil.): 7,341
Current ratio: 1.67
Long-term debt ($ mil.): 32,455
No. of shares (mil.): —
Dividends
Yield: —
Payout: —
Market value ($ mil.): —

	STOCK PRICE ($) FY Close	P/E High/Low	PER SHARE ($) Earnings	Dividends	Book Value
03/13	19.20	— —	0.87	0.00	9.64
03/12	21.47	— —	1.00	0.00	9.37
03/11	17.65	— —	0.92	0.12	8.82
03/10	17.20	— —	0.11	0.00	7.36
03/09	7.25	— —	(0.58)	0.60	6.78
Annual Growth	27.6%	— —	—	—	9.2%

NKSJ Holdings, Inc.

NKSJ Holdings was created to hold two insurance companies: Sompo Japan and Nipponkoa Insurance. While already strong players in Japan's property/casualty (called non-life in Japan) and life insurance markets when merger mania hit the industry they didn't want to be left out and formed the joint holding company in 2010. Eventually the two companies will merge into one entity Sompo Japan Nipponkoa Insurance but until then the two company brands remain separate. NKSJ's businesses includedomestic property/casualty and life insurance as well as overseas insurance asset and risk management services pension plans and some supplemental health insurance products.

Geographic Reach

NKSJ has operations in 200 cities in some 30 countries. It earns about 90% of revenues in the Japanese market.

Strategy

Why merge in the first place? The company cites pressures on its industry from several sources including the country's declining birthrate its rapidly aging population and the effects of climate change. While those are real challenges to the industry the Sompo/Nipponkoa merger also took place at the same time as several other large mergers among Japanese insurance companies. When the dust settles there will be fewer but larger companies elbowing each other to claim market share.

NKSJ is gradually integrating the operating units of Sompo and Nipponkoa. In 2011 it combined the two firm's life insurance divisions Sompo Japan Himawari Life and Nipponkoa Life into a new unit named NKSJ Himawari Life Insurance.

After natural disasters impacted NKSJ's earnings in 2011 the company accelerated its integration plans. In early 2012 it announced it would merge the remaining non-life operations of Sompo and Nipponkoa into one administrative company (though the Sompo and Nipponkoa brands would continue to be used).

At the same time it is integrating NKSJ is working to improve operational efficiencies in order to improve profits. It is also working to expand its life and non-life operations through organic measures and acquisitions. For instance it opened its first Chinese branch in 2012.

Mergers and Acquisitions

Since the merger NKSJ has been working to expand its operations outside the saturated Japanese market. The company purchased Singapore property/casualty firm Tenet Insurance for about Y6.4 billion ($70 million) in mid-2010 and it acquired Turkish non-life insurer Fiba Sigorta for some

Y27.4 billion ($338 million) later that year. In 2011 the company purchased an underwriting agency Nateus Nederland in the Netherlands.

LOCATIONS

HQ: NKSJ Holdings, Inc.
1-26-1 Nishi-Shinjuku, Shinjuku-ku, Tokyo 160-8338
Phone: (81) 3 3349 3000
Web: www.nksj-hd.com

HISTORICAL FINANCIALS

Company Type: Public

Income Statement FYE: March 31

	REVENUE ($ mil.)	NET INCOME ($ mil.)	NET PROFIT MARGIN	EMPLOYEES
03/13	30,071	463	1.5%	35,481
03/12	33,881	(1,124)	—	35,542
03/11	31,517	(156)	—	34,203
Annual Growth	(2.3%)	—	—	1.9%

2013 Year-End Financials

Debt ratio: 0.0%
Return on equity: 3.8%
Cash ($ mil.): 6,195
Current ratio: 1.12
Long-term debt ($ mil.): 2,779
No. of shares (mil.): 414
Dividends
Yield: —
Payout: —
Market value ($ mil.): 9,103

	STOCK PRICE ($) FY Close	P/E High/Low		PER SHARE ($) Earnings	Dividends	Book Value
03/13	21.95	—	—	1.11	0.00	32.89
03/12	22.66	—	—	(2.71)	0.00	29.40
03/11	0.00	—	—	(0.38)	0.00	31.40
/0.00	—	—(0.00)		0.00	(0.00)	
Annual Growth	—	—	—	—	—	—

Noble Group Ltd

LOCATIONS

HQ: Noble Group Ltd
18th Floor, MassMutual Tower, 38 Gloucester Road,
Phone: (852) 2861 3511 **Fax:** (852) 2527 0282
Web: www.thisisnoble.com

HISTORICAL FINANCIALS

Company Type: Public

Income Statement FYE: December 31

	REVENUE ($ mil.)	NET INCOME ($ mil.)	NET PROFIT MARGIN	EMPLOYEES
12/12	94,045	471	0.5%	15,000
12/11	80,732	431	0.5%	14,000
12/10	56,696	605	1.1%	8,000
12/09	31,183	556	1.8%	4,900
12/08	36,090	577	1.6%	4,800
Annual Growth	27.1%	(4.9%)	—	33.0%

2012 Year-End Financials

Debt ratio: 28.6%
Return on equity: 9.6%
Cash ($ mil.): 751
Current ratio: 1.42
Long-term debt ($ mil.): 4,466
No. of shares (mil.): —
Dividends
Yield: 1.5%
Payout: 438.9%
Market value ($ mil.): —

	STOCK PRICE ($) FY Close	P/E High/Low	PER SHARE ($) Earnings	Dividends	Book Value
12/12	18.81	351237	0.07	0.30	0.79
12/11	17.55	543235	0.07	0.46	0.71
12/10	33.35	340309	0.10	0.70	0.66
Annual Growth	(24.9%)	— —	(9.3%)	(19.4%)	4.7%

Nokia Corp.

Nokia is not a plea to boycott the South Korean car manufacturer –it's one of the world's leading makers of cell phones. First incorporated in the Finnish city it's named after Nokia's business consists of mobile device manufacturing and services primarily running Microsoft's Windows mobile platform as well as NAVTEQ (digital map content and services). Nokia also operates the Nokia Siemens Networks in partnership with Munich-based Siemens; the joint venture is a leading player in the telecom infrastructure and services market. With products in more than 160 countries. Nokia has agreed to sell its largest business Devices & Services (51% of 2012 sales) to US software giant Microsoft.

Geographic Reach

By region Europe is Nokia's largest contributor to sales representing nearly 30% in 2012. Its business in the US generates less than 5% of sales behind six other countries by percentage of Nokia's sales. Key R&D and software development locations are in China Finland Germany and the US.

Strategy

In a surprise move Nokia has agreed to sell substantially all of its Devices & Services business (51% of 2012 sales) which includes the Mobile Phones and Smart Devices business units and license its patents to software giant Microsoft for ?5.44 billion ($7.2 billion) in cash. The deal is expected to close in early 2014. At that time Nokia CEO Stephen Elop (a former Microsoft executive who joined Nokia as its first non-Finnish CEO in 2010) will rejoin the US firm.

Once dominant in the cell phone device market Nokia has faced increasing competition both on the device side and the operating system side. While the company is still a top three player in devices (behind only Samsung Electronics and Apple) its Symbian OS has long-since been eclipsed by the two main juggernauts. A key move to combat this in 2011 Nokia began a major partnership with Microsoft which includes a shift away from Symbian to focus on Microsoft's more competitive Windows smartphone OS. The company expects that transition to take about two years. The company further paved this road that year by outsourcing its Symbian software development and support to Accenture effective through 2016 which included a transfer of 2300 employees to the outsourcer. Nokia's partnership with Microsoft will also touch developments in other areas such as Nokia's location and commerce business.

Strengthening Nokia Siemens Networks' global presence particularly in the US and Japan the company picked up Motorola Solutions' networks business in 2011 for nearly $1 billion. The acquired assets include the company's GSM CDMA WCDMA WiMAX and LTE products and services. Besides the improved global visibility the purchase also boosted its position with service providers such as China Mobile KDDI Clearwire Sprint and Verizon Wireless.

To gain ground in the US against device competitors Nokia increased its focus on its core handset business by selling its wireless modem operations to Renesas Electronics in 2010 for about $200 million. The deal included the transfer of more than 1000 employees to Renesas and plans for the two companies to cooperate in developing high-speed modem technology.

Earlier in 2010 the company fueled its location and commerce business when it acquired geographic data and mapping software maker MetaCarta as part of its ongoing investment in technology to support location-based mobile services for wireless phones. Also that year Nokia it acquired Novarra a developer of a browser and service platform for mobile devices. Nokia uses the Novarra software on its Series 40 platform and other handset manufacturers employ Novarra's mobile software products as well. It later bought US-based mobile application tracking and reporting service provider Motally to further enhance the wireless Web-browsing functionality of its mobile devices.

HISTORY

Nokia got its start in 1865 when engineer Fredrik Idestam established a mill to manufacture pulp and paper on the Tammerkoski rapids of the Nokianvirta River in Finland. Although Nokia flourished within Finland the company was not well known to the rest of the world until it attempted to become a regional conglomerate in the early 1960s. French computer firm Machines Bull selected Nokia as its Finnish agent in 1962 and Nokia began researching radio transmission technology. In 1967 with the encouragement of Finland's government Nokia merged with Finnish Rubber Works (a maker of tires and rubber footwear formed in 1898) and Finnish Cable Works (a cable and electronics manufacturer formed in 1912) to form Nokia Corporation.

The oil crisis of 1973 created severe inflation and a large trade deficit for Finland. Nokia reassessed its heavy reliance on Soviet trade and shifted its focus to consumer and business electronics. Nokia's basic industries –paper chemicals electricity and machinery –were modernized and expanded into robotics fiber optics and high-grade tissues.

The company acquired a 51% interest in the state-owned Finnish telecom company in 1981 and named it Telenokia. The next year Nokia designed and installed (in Finland) the first European digital telephone system. Also in 1982 Nokia acquired interests in Salora Scandinavia's largest maker of color televisions and Luxor the Swedish state-owned electronics and computer firm.

Nokia acquired control of Sahkoliikkeiden Finland's largest electrical wholesaler in 1986. It then created the largest information technology (IT) group in Scandinavia Nokia Data by purchasing Ericsson's Data Division in 1988. Sales soared but profits plunged because of stiff price competition in consumer electronics.

To raise cash the company sold Nokia Data to IT services company ICL in 1991 and bought UK mobile phone maker Technophone which had been #2 in Europe after Nokia. Under the leadership of Jorma Ollila (appointed CEO in 1992 and chairman in 1999) Nokia intensified its focus on telecommunications and sold its noncore power (1994) televisions and tire and cable machinery (1995) units.

It also began selling digital phones at the end of 1993. The company expected to sell 400000; it shipped 20 million in 1995. The company rode the phones' success to a billion-dollar profit in 1997.

Nokia sold more than 40 million mobile phones in 1998 to surpass Motorola and became the world's #1 mobile phone company. Extending its push into Internet capability Nokia that year bought several small companies that develop e-commerce and telephony technologies. In 1999 Nokia penned deals to put its wireless application protocol (WAP) software into Hewlett-Packard's and IBM's network servers.

The company which also unveiled several WAP-enabled phones designed to access the Internet widened its lead as the world's top seller of mobile phones and made several acquisitions to strengthen its Internet protocol networks business.

Although Nokia was leaps and bounds ahead of its rivals with digital phones and dominated the European global system for the mobile communications (GSM) market it lagged in the US market where many big carriers adopted QUALCOMM's CDMA standard. Nokia in 2000 began to cover the bases for the third generation by offering products to bridge the gap between generations.

In 2001 Nokia added Internet security appliances to its product line-up with the acquisition of Ramp Networks. Later that year as part of an initiative to build up its line of network infrastructure products the company bought US-based router maker Amber Networks. Nokia began working with other equipment makers and wireless service providers that year to develop a global standard for 3G phone software. The company also outsourced the management of some of its infrastructure operations centers in the US China and Singapore to Hewlett-Packard.

Nokia formed a subsidiary Vertu in 2002 to sell "luxury" mobile phones and accessories made of precious metals.

In an effort to jumpstart slowing handset sales as the cell phone market in the West and Japan flirted with saturation Nokia in 2003 teamed with other phone makers and wireless service providers to develop a common global standard for 3G phone software. The effort was also backed by Motorola Sony Ericsson and Japan's NTT DoCoMo. After inking several new deals in Europe and Asia Nokia was a supplier to half of the world's commercial 3G networks by the end of 2003.

The mobile phone unit introduced new products in 2003 across a range of market niches and the company rolled out new business and consumer models and introduced a unit capable of English and Chinese text recognition to be sold by vendors in China. The company also introduced the N-Gage mobile gaming device.

Acquisitions for 2007 reflected the company's invesment in multimedia software and services. It bought photo-sharing Web site Twango mobile advertising software and services provider Enpocket and wireless Internet file sharing specialist Avvenu.

Nokia in 2008 restructured its business from four divisions into three following the break out of its network products business into Nokia Siemens Networks and the acquisition of digital mapping and navigation software provider NAVTEQ. The $8.1 billion acquisition served to further improve the company's ability to enhance the feature set of its mobile devices in response to increased competition in the smart phone market where navigation features have become standard on more devices.

Other acquisitions for the year were also geared toward building out Nokia's mobile device and service functionality. These purchases included Montreal-based messaging software developer OZ Communications and subscriber network database specialist Apertio. Nokia ended 2008 by acquiring the 52% in UK-based mobile software licensing company Symbian that it did not already own for about $410 million in cash. Following its purchase of Symbian Nokia in 2009 reorganized the software maker as a not-for-profit foundation that licenses its mobile OS on a royalty-free basis to other cell phone manufacturers instead of charging for usage as it once did.

Nokia also divested certain operations including the sale of its Identity Systems software business to data integration software developer Informatica (Identity Systems specialized in identity resolution applications) in 2008 and the sale of its security appliance business to Check Point Software Systems in 2009.

EXECUTIVES

President and Chief Executive Officer; Chairman of Nokia Leadership Team; Director, Stephen A. Elop, age 50
VP North American Sales, Ian G. A. Laing, age 54
Vice Chairman, Dame Marjorie M. Scardino, age 67, $220,785 total compensation
Chairman, Jorma Ollila, age 63, $580,492 total compensation
Executive Vice President of Operations; Member of Nokia Leadership Team, Juha Putkiranta
EVP Mobile Phones, Mary T. McDowell, age 49, $673,649 total compensation
EVP and Chief Marketing Officer, Jerri L. DeVard, age 54
EVP and General Manager Markets, Niklas Savander, age 51
Director South East Asia Pacific and Japan and Korea Communications, Ai Fong Wong
VP Markets and Regional Communications, Thomas Jonsson
CEO Nokia Siemens Networks, Rajeev Suri, age 46
EVP Devices, Kai Oistamo, age 49, $677,074 total compensation
EVP Human Resources, Juha Akras, age 49
SVP Corporate Communications, Arja Suominen
Head Communications Middle East and Africa, Marianne Holmlund
Executive Vice President; HERE; Member of Nokia Leadership Team, Michael Halbherr
Head Corporate Alliances and Business Development, Robert Andersson, age 53
President Nokia North America, Mark Louison
EVP Corporate Relations and Responsibility, Esko Aho, age 59
EVP and CFO, Timo Ihamuotila, age 47, $568,730 total compensation
EVP Sales, Colin Giles
Director General Russia, Niels Nielsen
General Manager Nokia Taiwan, Michael Hsu
VP and Head Nokia Nseries, Jonas Geust
Director Communications North America, Laurie Armstrong
EVP Solutions, Alberto Torres, age 48
Director Corporate Development Communications, Mark Durrant
Director Investor Relations US, Matt Shimao
Manager Investor Relations US, Deirdre Collins
Senior Manager Investor Relations Europe, Jussi Havu
Director Devices and Services Communications, Douglas Dawson
Head Communications Europe, Ingrid Peura
Director Communications China, Louise Ingram
Head Eurasia Communications, Victoria Eremina
Director India Communications, Poonam Kaul
Director Communications Latin America, Vivian Kobeh de Palacio
SVP Marketing Go-To-Market Operations, Charmaine Eggberry
CEO NAVTEQ, Larry Kaplan
Executive Vice President; Chief Technology Officer; Member of Nokia Leadership Team, Henry Tirri
Executive Vice President; Design; Member of Nokia Leadership Team, Marko Ahtisaari
Executive Vice President; Chief Legal Officer; Member of Nokia Leadership Team, Louise Pentland
Executive Vice President; Chief Development Officer; Member of Nokia Leadership Team, Kai Oistamo
Executive Vice President; Human Resources; Member of Nokia Leadership Team, Juha Akras
Executive Vice President; Smart Devices; Member of Nokia Leadership Team, Jo Harlow
Executive Vice President of Sales & Marketing; Member of the Leadership Team, Chris Weber
Executive Vice President; Mobile Phones; Member of Nokia Leadership Team, Timo Toikkanen
Vice Chairman, Dame Marjorie M. Scardino, age 67
Director, Risto Siilasmaa, age 47
Director, Georg Ehrnrooth, age 73
Director, Henning Kagermann, age 66
Director, Keijo Suila, age 68
Director, Bengt Holmstrom, age 64
Director, Per Karlsson, age 58
Director, Lalita D. Gupte, age 65
Director, Isabel Marey-Semper, age 46
Auditors: PricewaterhouseCoopersOy

LOCATIONS

HQ: Nokia Corp.
Nokia House, Keilalahdentie 4, Espoo 02150
Phone: (358) 7 1800 8000 **Fax:** (358) 7 1803 8503
Web: www.nokia.com

2012 Sales

	% of total
Europe	29
Asia/Pacific	27
Greater	10
Middle East &	14
Latin	13
North	7
Total	**100**

PRODUCTS/OPERATIONS

2012 Sales

	% of total
Devices &	51
Nokia Siemens	45
HERE (formerly Location &	4
Total	**100**

Selected Products

Accessories
- Bluetooth headsets
- Wireless charging stations
- Wireless speakers

Phones
- Asha
- Belle
- Lumia
- N9-00

COMPETITORS

Accenture
Alcatel-Lucent
Amdocs
Apple Inc.
BlackBerry
Cisco Systems
Ericsson
Fujitsu
Garmin
HP Enterprise Group
HTC Corporation
Huawei Technologies
IBM
Kyocera
LG Group
Microsoft
Motorola Mobility
NEC
Oki Electric
Oracle
Panasonic Mobile Communications
QUALCOMM
SANYO
Samsung Electronics
Sony Mobile
Tellabs
TomTom
ZTE

HISTORICAL FINANCIALS

Company Type: Public

Income Statement FYE: December 31

	REVENUE ($ mil.)	NET INCOME ($ mil.)	NET PROFIT MARGIN	EMPLOYEES
12/12	39,773	(4,093)	—	97,798
12/11	50,003	(1,505)	—	130,050
12/10	56,808	2,475	4.4%	132,427
12/09	59,040	1,283	2.2%	123,553
12/08	70,897	5,575	7.9%	128,529
Annual Growth	(13.5%)	—	—	(6.6%)

2012 Year-End Financials

Debt ratio: 24.4%
Return on equity: (-31.0%)
Cash ($ mil.): 4,618
Current ratio: 1.43
Long-term debt ($ mil.): 6,704
No. of shares (mil.): —
Dividends
Yield: 6.3%
Payout: —
Market value ($ mil.): —

	STOCK PRICE ($) FY Close	P/E High/Low	PER SHARE ($) Earnings	Dividends	Book Value
12/12	3.95	— —	(1.11)	0.25	2.86
12/11	4.82	— —	(0.40)	1.10	4.10
12/10	10.32	57 26	0.67	0.49	5.14
12/09	12.85	141 66	0.35	1.04	5.03
12/08	15.60	75 20	1.47	1.80	5.23
Annual Growth	(29.1%)	— —	—	(38.8%)	(14.0%)

Nomura Holdings Inc

Nomura Holdings is the parent company of Nomura Securities Japan's leading investment bank and brokerage house. The company performs trading equity and bond underwriting research and mergers and acquisitions (M&A) advisory services. It also makes private equity and venture capital investments. Subsidiary Nomura Asset Management is Japan's largest asset management company in terms of assets under management in investment trusts which it offers to retail investors and through institutional funds. It oversees some Y71 trillion in retail client assets. Nomura Holdings has operations in more than 30 countries; Nomura Securities International is the company's US trading and investment banking unit.

Nomura operates through three business divisions: retail (investment consultation services) asset management (investment trusts and investment advisory services) and wholesale (corporate and institutional products and services). On the retail side Nomura Securities serves individuals and businesses from nearly 200 locations in Japan. The group controls about 20% of Japan's public mutual fund market. Additional units include Nomura Trust & Banking big-ticket financing firm Nomura Babcock & Brown and the Nomura Institute of Capital Markets Research.

Nomura's earnings have improved significantly since fiscal 2009 when the group lost more than $7 billion. Revenues grew 37% in 2012 from the prior year despite challenges that faced the financial sector. During that fiscal year Japan was recovering from a major earthquake and tsunami which caused disruptions to industry in the country and led to a reduction in the nation's real gross domestic product. Nomura's retail profits slipped that year by 11% primarily because of a decline in brokerage and investment trust commissions. Although the company saw declines in earnings it saw increases in client accounts and client asset inflows. Wholesale profits also slipped in 2012 by 12% to Y555.9 billion. Those declines were largely attributed to market weaknesses related to the sovereign debt crisis in Europe.

The group's strategy for growth in its retail business includes providing a variety of delivery channels for services including online and telephone centers. Nomura continues to open new retail branches and in 2011 launched Nomura Net & Call to provide non-face-to-face services. Nomura is also focused on providing a diverse product offering.

Internationally Nomura is well-positioned to take advantage of expected growth in other Asian nations. It manages funds that invest in several countries including Thailand India Taiwan and Korea.

In the wake of 2011's record earthquake and tsunami disaster Nomura marketed stock-based loans to consumers. The niche product generally provides customers with access to cash more quickly than they would be able to get via traditional bank loans. As a result of the marketing push and the demand for liquid capital Nomura's retail lending jumped by 50% within weeks.

HISTORY

Tokushichi Nomura started a currency exchange Nomura Shoten in Osaka in 1872 and began trading stock. His son Tokushichi II took over and in 1910 formed Nomura's first syndicate to underwrite part of a government bond issue. It established the Osaka Nomura Bank in 1918. The bond department became independent in 1925 and became Nomura Securities. The company opened a New York office in 1927 entering stock brokerage in 1938.

The firm rebuilt and expanded retail operations after WWII. It encouraged stock market investing by promoting "million ryo savings chests" –small boxes in which people saved cash (ryo was an old form of currency). When savings reached 5000 yen savers could buy into investment trusts. Nomura distributed more than a million chests in 10 years.

Nomura followed clients overseas in the 1960s helped underwrite a US issue of Sony stock and opened a London office. It became Japan's leading securities firm after a 1965 stock market crash decimated rival Yamaichi Securities. The firm grew rapidly in the 1970s ushering investment capital in and out of Japan and competing with banks by issuing corporate debt securities.

As the Japanese economy soared in the 1980s the company opened Nomura Bank International in London (1986) and bought 20% of US mergers and acquisitions advisor Wasserstein Perella (1988 sold 2001).

Then the Japanese economic bubble burst. Nomura's stock toppled 70% from its 1987 peak and underwriting plummeted. In 1991 and 1992 amid revelations that Nomura and other brokerages had reimbursed favored clients' trading losses the firm was accused of manipulating stock in companies owned by Japanese racketeers. Nomura's chairman and president –both named Tabuchi –resigned admitting no wrongdoing.

The firm trimmed staff and offices and focused on its most efficient operations. From 1993 to 2000 it seesawed from red to black and back again.

Junichi Ujiie became president after the payoff scandal; he restructured operations to prepare for Japan's financial deregulation. Nomura invested in pub chain Inntrepreneur and William Hill a UK betting chain. It also created an entertainment lending unit to lend against future royalties or syndication fees and spun off a minority stake in its high-risk US real estate business which ceased lending altogether the next year.

In 1998 Nomura was dealt a double blow when Asian economies collapsed and Russia defaulted on its debts. Incurring substantial losses the firm refocused on its domestic market and reduced overseas operations. That year it teamed with Industrial Bank of Japan for derivatives sales in the UK and pension plan consulting in Japan.

In 1999 Nomura bailed out ailing property subsidiary Nomura Finance which had been crippled by the sinking Japanese real estate market. It also invested heavily in UK real estate and bought 40% of the Czech beer market with South African Breweries.

The next year the firm agreed to buy the business services arm of Welsh utilities firm Hyder; it also bought 114000 flats in Germany with local government authorities its first European deal outside the UK. Also in 2000 Nomura sold its assets in pachinko parlors and "love" hotels Japanese cultural traditions with less-than-sparkling reputations. British authorities that year fined Nomura traders in relation to charges of trying to rig Australia's stock market in 1996.

The company converted to a holding company structure in 2001 and months later made its debut on the NYSE. It made two big deals in the UK that year buying hotel chain Le Meridien and becoming the nation's largest pub owner via the purchase of some 1000 locations from Bass. The company also bought a stake in Thomas Weisel Partners to increase its participation in M&A action between US and Japanese firms. In 2002 the company decided to sell the network of more than 4100 pubs to a consortium of private investors for some $3 billion.

In 2007 Nomura acquired global agency brokerage Instinet. The deal allowed the company to begin offering electronic trading services.

In 2008 Japanese regulators chose a consortium led by Nomura to take control of troubled Ashikaga Bank from the government; Nomura's private equity arm took a stake of about 45% in Ashikaga. The deal marked Nomura's first foray into retail banking.

The global financial crisis heavily impacted Nomura which reported steep declines in 2008 and 2009. The company lost some Y208 billion ($2 billion) in 2009 alone on trading and equity investments. The US subprime mortgage bust further hurt the group which lost money on mortgage-backed securities.

In response Nomura cut operating costs and fine-tuned its offerings. The following year the company boosted its global investment banking capabilities by acquiring parts of the fallen bulge-bracket firm Lehman Brothers including operations in Asia Europe and the Middle East as well as the India-based back office operations. (In its post-acquisition transition the company laid off some 11% of its UK workforce or about 1000 employees in its London office.) In an effort to boost its domestic asset management business Nomura bought NikkoCiti Trust and Banking from Citigroup in 2009. The company also exited the US residential mortgage-backed securities business entirely.

The Lehman Brothers acquisition helped boost Nomura's profile in European equities and fixed-income trading. Adding on to that purchase Nomura bought London-based Tricorn Partners –a move that further complements its UK corporate finance advisory business.

Nomura Asset Management also bought a 35% stake in LIC Mutual Fund Asset Management Company of India. The deal gave Nomura a larger foothold in the Indian market and strengthened its credentials as an international asset manager.

EXECUTIVES

President and COO, Atsushi Yoshikawa, age 59
Senior Managing Director, Paul Spanswick
Senior Managing Director; Regional Co-CEO Europe Middle East and Africa, Yasuo Kashiwagi
CFO, Shigesuke Kashiwagi, age 54
Senior Managing Director, Akihito Watanabe, age 56
Senior Managing Director, Hiromasa Yamazaki
Senior Managing Director, Naoki Matsuba
Executive Managing Director, Shoichi Nagamatsu, age 62
Senior Managing Director, Noriaki Nagai, age 56
Senior Managing Director, Yuji Nakata
CEO; President Nomura Securities, Koji Nagai
Senior Managing Director; Regional CEO Asia except Japan, Minoru Shinohara
Joint Head Global Investment Banking, William Vereker
Chief Risk Officer and Senior Managing Director, David Benson
Senior Managing Director Advisory Fund Management Nomura Asset Management, Kunio Watanabe
Senior Managing Director, Kentaro Okuda
Senior Managing Director, Junko Nakagawa
Head of Regional Property Research, Paul Louie
Senior Partner Chairman, Edward Tse
Senior Managing Director; Regional CEO Americas, David Findlay
Senior Managing Director, Steven Ashley
Senior Managing Director; Regional CEO Europe Middle East and Africa, Jeremy Bennett
Senior Managing Director; Regional Co-CEO Americas, Toshiya Hasegawa
Senior Managing Director, Masaru Konno
Senior Managing Director, Eiji Miura
Senior Managing Director, Hisato Miyashita
Executive Managing Director, Toshio Morita
Senior Managing Director, Lewis O'Donald
Senior Managing Director and CIO, Naohiro Sako
Senior Managing Director, Chie Toriumi
Deputy President COO and Director Nomura Holdings and Nomura Securities; Chairman Wholesale, Takumi Shibata, age 59
President CEO and Director; President CEO and Director Nomura Securities, Kenichi Watanabe, age 59
Director, Masahiro Sakane, age 71
Director, Masaharu Shibata, age 75
Director, Masanori Itatani
Director, Hideaki Kubori, age 68
Director, Haruo Tsuji, age 80
Director, Fumihide Nomura, age 78
Director, Yoshifumi Kawabata, age 60
Executive Managing Director and Merchant Banking CEO; Director and President Nomura Principal Finance; Senior Managing Director Nomura Securities, Soichi Nagamatsu, age 61
Executive Managing Director Group Compliance Head Head Global Operations and CIO; Senior Corporate Managing Director Nomura Securities, Hiroshi Tanaka, age 56
Director, Tsuguoki Fujinuma
Auditors: Ernst&YoungShinNihon

LOCATIONS

HQ: Nomura Holdings Inc
9-1 Nihonbashi 1-chome, Chuo-Ku, Tokyo 103-8645
Phone: (81) 3 5255 1000
Web: www.nomuraholdings.com

PRODUCTS/OPERATIONS

2012 Sales

	% of total
Interest &	24
Commissions	19
Net gain on	15
Asset management & portfolio service	8
Fees from investment	3
Gain on private equity	1
Gain on investments in equity	-
Other	30
Total	**100**

COMPETITORS

Bank of America
Barclays
Boom Securities
Daiwa Securities Group
Deutsche Bank
Goldman Sachs
HSBC
SMBC Nikko Securities
UBS Investment Bank

HISTORICAL FINANCIALS

Company Type: Public

Income Statement

FYE: March 31

	ASSETS ($ mil.)	NET INCOME ($ mil.)	INCOME AS % OF ASSETS	EMPLOYEES
03/13	403,248	1,139	0.3%	27,956
03/12	435,172	141	0.0%	34,395
03/11	443,117	346	0.1%	26,871
03/10	345,052	725	0.2%	26,374
03/09	252,224	(7,191)	—	25,626
Annual Growth	12.4%	—	—	2.2%

2013 Year-End Financials

Return on assets: 0.2%
Return on equity: 4.8%
Long-term debt ($ mil.): —
No. of shares (mil.): —
Sales ($ mil): 8,595
Dividends
Yield: 0.0%
Payout: 0.0%
Market value ($ mil.): —

	STOCK PRICE ($) FY Close	P/E High/Low		PER SHARE ($) Earnings	Dividends	Book Value
03/13	6.17	0	0	0.30	0.00	6.57
03/12	4.41	0	0	0.04	0.00	7.01
03/11	5.20	0	0	0.09	0.09	6.98
03/10	7.33	0	0	0.23	0.13	6.21
03/09	5.03	—	—	(3.72)	0.25	6.00
Annual Growth	5.2%	—	—	—	(93.0%)	2.3%

Nordea Bank AB

Nordea Bank is one of the largest financial services groups in the Nordic and Baltic Sea regions. Sweden is its home but Nordea also is active in Denmark Finland Norway Estonia Latvia Lithuania Poland and Russia. The bank splits its operations into three main divisions: retail banking wholesale banking and wealth management. The bank also provides life and pension products. It operates through a network of about 1400 branches and serves some 11 million customers including about 700000 corporate clients –a key customer segment for Nordea. About 60% of its lending activity is to corporations. Its Internet bank claims nearly 6 million users.

Nordea Bank also has an international network present in some 20 countries around the world. Additional offices are located in major cities such as New York London and Frankfurt. In addition Nordea has various agreements with banks in places such as Asia and Latin America where customers are able to be served through representative offices.

Growth in new European markets has been a focus for Nordea. The company purchased a 75% stake in Russian bank JSB Orgresbank. It bought the remaining stake in 2009 and the bank was rebranded OJSC Nordea Bank. Nordea also bought the Polish life insurance operations of Finnish banking group Sampo doubling Nordea's customer base in Poland. However Nordea put the breaks on aggressive growth and completely halted branch expansion in Russia and the Baltic countries in light of the global financial crisis.

The worldwide economic slowdown began affecting Nordea in 2008 as the bank saw an increase in loan losses. Nordea announced a "middle-of-the-road approach" in 2009 and slowed acquisition growth to focus on doing more business with existing customers and attracting new customers with good credit.

By 2010 Nordea emerged from the financial crisis and started looking to grow again. The company is mostly focused on organic growth in order to attract new customers. It launched several initiatives to increase customer activity income and profit. That year Nordea also opened 45 new branches in Poland which is one of the most important growth markets for the company. Other growth strategies include expanding the company's corporate merchant banking business in Sweden in addition to investing in technical infrastructure.

In 2011 Nordea reorganized itself in order to focus on capital and cost efficiency. The reshuffling was done in effort to adapt to new government regulations that require banks to hold more capital. That year company chairman Hans Dalborg stepped down from the post. He was replaced by Bjorn Wahlroos.

Sampo owns more than 20% of Nordea. The Swedish government held a nearly 20% stake in the bank but reduced that to 13% in 2011 as part of its plan to raise capital. It plans to sell more and possibly all of its Nordea stake over time.

HISTORY

Nordea traces its roots to 1974 when two Swedish government-owned banks Postbanken and Sveriges Kreditbank merged to form the country's largest bank Post-och Kreditbanken (PKbanken) in order to compete with S-E-Banken and Svenska Handelsbanken.

PKbanken didn't hold on to the top spot long. By the early 1980s a recession and languid profits sank the company to third. However the firm did expand teaming with Norway's Christiana Bank og Kreditkasse to open joint offices in Hong Kong Houston London S?o Paolo and Singapore.

As regulatory restrictions in Sweden eased the government spun off 15% of its interest in the company on the Stockholm Stock Exchange in 1984.

PKbanken pulled out of its deal in London with Christiana Bank in 1986 but it bought a stake in London-based English Trust Group to expand its merchant banking services. In 1988 PKbanken acquired government-owned Carnegie Fondkommission Sweden's largest brokerage and in 1989 purchased the state-controlled Swedish Investment Bank a provider of funding to small and midsized businesses.

A year later PKbanken acquired regional Swedish bank Nordbanken and assumed the smaller firm's name. Soon after the government axed the combined firm's top officers and installed new management. The purging didn't help as another recession and a real estate market crash hammered the company's bottom line. In 1992 the Swedish government intervened again acquiring all of the outstanding shares of Nordbanken that it did not already own. The company rebounded quickly after selling bad loans to the state and cutting staff by a fifth.

In 1994 the Swedish government transferred its ownership of Gota Bank to Nordbanken. The company resumed trading on the Stockholm Stock Exchange the following year.

Across the border in Finland rivals Union Bank of Finland and Kansallis-Osake-Pankki merged in 1995 to create Merita Bank the country's largest.

In 1997 Nordbanken and Merita Bank combined to form MeritaNordbanken but their parents Nordbanken Holdings and Merita Ab remained separate. In 2000 the company bought Danish bank Unidanmark. MeritaNordbanken's holding companies united and assumed the name Nordic Baltic Holding. Later the company changed its name to Nordea an amalgamation of "Nordic" and "idea."

In 2001 Nordea bought Christiania Bank og Kreditkasse and later that year attached the Nordea Bank name to its banking subsidiaries in Denmark Finland Norway and Sweden.

By 2003 the company composed primarily of the four national banking groups –Nordea Bank Denmark Nordea Bank Finland Nordea Bank Norway and Nordea Bank Sweden –decided to change its complex legal structure and create one European company under the Nordea Bank banner.

Nordea acquired Denmark's Fionia Bank in 2009 including the bank's staff and its 29 branches but excluding some 2000 troubled corporate customers. The Denmark government had taken control of the failing bank earlier in the year.

EXECUTIVES

Vice Chairman, Timo Peltola, age 67, $167,377 total compensation
President and CEO, Christian Clausen, age 58, $1,408,087 total compensation
Chairman, Bjorn Wahlroos, age 61
EVP and CFO; Head Group Corporate Centre; Country Senior Executive Sweden, Fredrik Rystedt, age 49
Head Banking Sweden, Hans Jacobson
Head Planning and Control and Investor Relations, Johan Ekwall
Executive Vice President Chief Risk Officer Head Group Risk Management Country Senior Executive Finland, Ari Kaperi, age 53
Head of Banking Products and Group Operations, Michael Rasmussen, age 49
Head of Banking Denmark, Anders Jensen
Chief Press Officer Denmark, Claus Christensen
Chief Press Officer Finland, Kati Tommiska
Chief Press Officer Norway, Thomas Sevang
Press Officer Poland Russia Baltic Region and International, Anders Edlund
Head of Household Management Denmark, Ken Adrian
Chief Economist Denmark, Helge J. Pedersen
Head of Nordea Finance Denmark, Lars Bang
Head of Legal Denmark, Niels B. J?rgensen
Director Marketing Denmark, Kim Grue
Head of Corporate Merchant Banking Finland, Olli-Petteri Lehtinen
Managing Director Nordea Investment Fund Company Finland; Head of Asset Management Products Finland, Jari Kivihuhta
Head European Affairs, Leena Morttinen
Deputy Head of Banking Norway, Jon Brenden
Chief Economist Norway, Steinar Juel
Head of Global Sales and Research Norway, Jan Pollestad
Director Marketing Norway, Arne Lambech
Head of Household Management Sweden, Petra Eklund
Chief Economist Sweden, Annika Winsth
Head of Global Sales and Research Sweden, Mads Jakobsen
Head of Investment Funds Sweden, Erik Feldt
Head of Life and Pensions Sweden, Britta Burreau
Head of Private Banking Sweden, Inga-Lill Carlberg
Head of New European Markets Sweden, Thomas Neckmar
Investor Relations Officer, Andreas Larsson
Head Group Identity and Communications, Jan Larsson
Chief Economist Finland, Martti Nyberg, age 47
Deputy Chairman, Marie Ehrling, age 59
Head of Strategic Customer Events Sweden, Tomas Bjorklund
Head Private Banking Nordic, Niklas Ekvall
Executive Vice President Head of Wholesale Banking, Casper von Koskull
Executive Vice President Head of Wealth Management Country Senior Executive in Norway, Gunn W?rsted, age 58
Executive Vice President Head of Retail Banking Country Senior Executive in Sweden, Lennart Jacobsen, age 47
Head of Group Corporate Centre and Group CFO, Torsten Hagen J?rgensen
Executive Vice President Chief Operating Officer of Wholesale Banking Country Senior Executive in Denmark, Peter Nyegaard, age 50
Director, Svein S. Jacobsen, age 62
Director, Lars G. Nordstrom
Vice Chairman, Timo Peltola, age 67
Director, Heidi M. Petersen, age 54
Director, Marie Ehrling, age 58
Auditors: KPMGAB

LOCATIONS

HQ: Nordea Bank AB
Smalandsgatan 17, Stockholm SE-105 71
Phone: (46) 8 614 78 00 **Fax:** (46) 8 10 50 69
Web: www.nordea.com

2010 Sales

	% of total
Denmark	26
Sweden	22
Finland	17
Norway	14
New European	7
Other	14
Total	**100**

PRODUCTS/OPERATIONS

2010 Sales

	% of total
Banking	55
Capital markets	22
Savings products and asset	7
Life and	4
Other	12
Total	**100**

COMPETITORS

BNP Paribas
Citigroup
Danske Bank
Deutsche Bank
HSBC
JPMorgan Asset Management
KBC
SEB AB
Schroders
Skandia
Svenska Handelsbanken

HISTORICAL FINANCIALS

Company Type: Public

Income Statement FYE: December 31

	ASSETS ($ mil.)	NET INCOME ($ mil.)	INCOME AS % OF ASSETS	EMPLOYEES
12/12	892,873	4,111	0.5%	31,466
12/11	926,375	3,397	0.4%	33,068
12/10	777,378	3,556	0.5%	33,809
12/09	731,152	3,333	0.5%	0
12/08	662,798	3,734	0.6%	34,008
Annual Growth	7.7%	2.4%	—	(1.9%)

2012 Year-End Financials

Return on assets: 0.4%
Return on equity: 11.4%
Long-term debt ($ mil.): —
No. of shares (mil.): —
Sales ($ mil): 23,131
Dividends
Yield: 3.6%
Payout: 59.0%
Market value ($ mil.): —

	STOCK PRICE ($) FY Close	P/E High/Low		PER SHARE ($) Earnings	Dividends	Book Value
12/12	9.61	22	15	1.03	0.35	9.23
12/11	7.82	34	18	0.84	0.75	8.32
Annual Growth	22.9%	—	—	5.2%	(17.6%)	2.6%

Nordea Bank Denmark A/S

LOCATIONS

HQ: Nordea Bank Denmark A/S
Strandgade 3, PO Box 850, Copenhagen C DK-0900
Phone: (45) 33 33 33 33 **Fax:** (45) 33 33 63 63
Web: www.nordea.com

HISTORICAL FINANCIALS

Company Type: Public

Income Statement FYE: December 31

	ASSETS ($ mil.)	NET INCOME ($ mil.)	INCOME AS % OF ASSETS	EMPLOYEES
12/12	892,873	4,111	0.5%	31,466
12/11	926,375	3,397	0.4%	33,068
12/10	777,378	3,556	0.5%	33,809
12/09	731,152	3,333	0.5%	33,347
12/08	662,798	3,734	0.6%	34,008
Annual Growth	7.7%	2.4%	—	(1.9%)

2012 Year-End Financials

Return on assets: 0.4%
Return on equity: 11.4%
Long-term debt ($ mil.): —
No. of shares (mil.): —
Sales ($ mil): 23,131
Dividends
Yield: —
Payout: —
Market value ($ mil.): —

North Pacific Bank, Ltd.

Sapporo Hokuyo Holdings supposes it has what customers need in the way of banking and financial services. The company was formed in 2001 to serve as the holding company for North Pacific Bank and The Sapporo Bank; together the regional banks have some 230 offices in Hokkaido as well as an office in Tokyo and two offices in China. North Pacific Bank which is the largest bank in Hokkaido accounts for most of the holding company's sales; the bank traces its roots to 1917. The company also has subsidiaries active in credit cards and leasing; bank subsidiaries engage in such activities as financing.

LOCATIONS

HQ: North Pacific Bank, Ltd.
3-7 Odori Nishi, Chuo-ku, Sapporo, Hokkaido 060-0042
Phone: (81) 11 261 1311 **Fax:** (81) 11 261 2280
Web: www.hokuyobank.co.jp

COMPETITORS

Hokkoku Bank
Hokuhoku Financial Group
Hyakujushi Bank
Mitsubishi UFJ Financial Group
Mizuho Financial
Resona
Sumitomo Mitsui

HISTORICAL FINANCIALS

Company Type: Public

Income Statement FYE: March 31

	ASSETS ($ mil.)	NET INCOME ($ mil.)	INCOME AS % OF ASSETS	EMPLOYEES
03/13	83,029	206	0.2%	3,808
03/12	93,947	294	0.3%	3,886
03/11	89,384	148	0.2%	3,941
03/10	79,164	339	0.4%	4,107
03/09	73,422	(2,177)	—	4,117
Annual Growth	3.1%	—	—	(1.9%)

2013 Year-End Financials

Return on assets: 0.2%
Return on equity: 6.0%
Long-term debt ($ mil.): —
No. of shares (mil.): 398
Sales ($ mil): 1,724
Dividends
Yield: —
Payout: —
Market value ($ mil.): —

	STOCK PRICE ($) FY Close	P/E High/Low	PER SHARE ($) Earnings	Dividends	Book Value
03/13	0.00	— —	0.29	0.00	10.69
03/12	2.99	— —	0.48	0.00	10.53
03/11	2.99	— —	0.27	0.00	9.90
Annual Growth	—	— —	1.6%	—	1.9%

Novartis AG Basel

Although it's based in neutral Switzerland Novartis has been aggressive in attacking illnesses on multiple fronts including pharmaceuticals vaccines and consumer health. Its largest division Pharmaceuticals develops and manufactures prescription drugs for blood pressure cancer and other ailments. Novartis' Sandoz subsidiary produces generic drugs and active pharmaceutical ingredients while the Vaccine and Diagnostics segment makes immune health and blood-screening tools. Its Alcon division makes ophthalmic drugs surgery systems and contact lenses. The Consumer Health unit includes OTC medications such as Excedrin and Theraflu as well as agricultural animal and pet care products.

Geographic Reach

Novartis has operations in 140 countries around the world including sales administrative research and manufacturing locations. The US is the company's largest geographic market accounting for about one-third of revenues followed by Japan Germany and France (each accounting for less than 10% of sales).

Operations

Prescription drugs account for more than half of Novartis' annual revenues. Its blockbusters include high blood pressure treatment Diovan leukemia drug Gleevec/Glivec age-related macular degeneration drug Lucentis and Zometa an intravenous treatment for bone tumors caused by prostate lung and breast cancers. Other strong products include hormone balancing drug Sandostatin Exelon for Alzheimer's disease and Femara which is used to treat postmenopausal women with early and advanced breast cancer.

The company's Sandoz and Alcon units each account for nearly 20% of sales. Sandoz is currently among the largest manufacturers of generic drugs in the world while Alcon is a leader in cataract and vision correction surgical equipment.

Financial Analysis

Novartis' steady growth pace has produced rising revenues over the past decade including a 15% increase to some $59 billion in 2011. The annual sales increase was largely attributed to the acquisition of Alcon as well as to positive currency impacts and sales of newly launched products. However net income dropped 7% to $9.1 billion in 2011 due to acquisition and restructuring costs as well as increased sales marketing manufacturing and other operational expenses.

Like most large drugmakers Novartis is facing increasing pressure to keep its operations lean and develop new blockbusters in the face of patent expiration and rising levels of generic competition. Several of the company's former best sellers including Famvir (antiviral) Lotrel (high blood pressure) and Trileptal (epilepsy treatment) are experiencing dwindling sales due to launches of generic versions in recent years. The company is especially hurting as top seller Diovan which previously accounted for more than $6 billion in sales (or 20% of the firm's annual pharmaceutical revenues) lost patent protection in the US market in 2012 and in Europe in 2011.

To balance out the reduced sales from off-patent products Novartis is conducting cost-cutting programs including a number of workforce reduction plant closure divestiture and outsourcing measures announced in 2011 and 2012.

Strategy

To ward off competitive pressures and support its prescription drug business Novartis maintains a healthy drug pipeline with about 140 candidates in clinical development stages. Novartis relies upon a steady regimen of internal development partnerships and acquisitions to keep its pipeline up and running. R&D programs are focused on core therapeutic areas including cardiology metabolism oncology neurology respiratory ophthalmic and infectious disease. The company is especially focused on increasing its development of biologic (protein and gene-based) drugs. Recently launched products in the US market include chronic obstructive pulmonary disease (COPD) treatment Arcapta in 2011. In addition oncology drug Afinitor gained FDA approval to treat pancreatic tumors and breast cancer in 2012.

In addition Novartis is counting on its new drug for multiple sclerosis Gilenya (licensed from Mitsubishi Tanabe) to be a big revenue earner in the coming years. Gilenya was launched in the US market in 2010 and is the first oral treatment for MS. It is also among the most expensive drugs for the disease. The drug was approved in the European Union market in 2011.

Though the Alcon Sandoz consumer health and vaccines and diagnostics units are smaller than the core pharmaceuticals business Novartis maintains strong acquisition and internal research programs in those divisions as well. For instance to further its goals in personalized medicine Novartis is working to develop more sensitive molecular diagnostics that can be used to monitor patients and determine which medicines will most effectively treat their ailments.

Mergers Acquisitions & Divestitures

Along with new drugs the company's other pharma growth efforts are conducted through numerous acquisitions. Making a bold move in the eye-care market Novartis made ocular drug and vision care company Alcon a wholly owned subsidiary in 2011 after a drawn-out series of share purchases: Novartis first acquired about 77% of Alcon from Nestle for some $39 billion (through two transactions in 2008 and 2010). Then in early 2011 Novartis acquired the remaining shares in Alcon through a public tender offer worth nearly $13 billion. Novartis then combined its existing CIBA Vision eye care unit into Alcon which became Novartis' fifth operating segment.

To expand its Sandoz division Novartis completed a $1.5 billion deal to acquire generic drugmaker Fougera Pharmaceuticals in 2012. The purchase strengthened Sandoz's position in the global dermatology medication market.

Additionally the company periodically divests underperforming or noncore assets to focus on its key areas of growth. For instance in 2011 the company sold global rights to eczema treatment Elidel to Meda for some $420 million.

HISTORY

Johann Geigy began selling spices and natural dyes in Basel Switzerland in 1758. A century later the Geigy family began producing synthetic dyes. About that time Alexander Clavel also entered the synthetic dye trade in Basel forming the Gesellschaft fur Chemische Industrie Basel (Ciba). Ciba was Switzerland's #1 chemical firm at century's end.

After WWI Ciba Geigy and Sandoz (a Basel synthetic dye maker founded in 1886) formed the Basel AG cartel to compete with German rival I.G. Farben. Basel used its profits to diversify into pharmaceuticals and other chemicals and to gain a foothold in the US. In 1929 Basel merged with its German and later French and British counterparts but WWII shattered the so-called Quadrapartite Cartel in 1939 leaving only Basel AG intact.

Basel scientist Paul Muller won a Nobel Prize in 1948 for inventing DDT. Basel AG voluntarily dissolved itself back into its component parts in 1951.

Ciba Geigy and Sandoz continued to diversify. Finding new markets in agricultural chemicals Geigy had passed Ciba in sales by 1967. That year Sandoz bought the Wander group of companies (dietetic products). Ciba and Geigy merged in 1970 and began a series of US acquisitions including Funk Seeds in 1974. Sandoz bought Minneapolis-based Northrup King & Co. (1976) and Dutch seed company Zaadunie (1980).

Ciba-Geigy and US biotech company Chiron started a joint venture in 1986 to produce and market genetically engineered vaccines (Ciba-Geigy acquired 50% of Chiron in 1994). Sandoz also bought shares in US biotechnology companies including Genetic Therapy and SyStemix in 1991. It bought Gerber (founded 1927) in 1994.

Ciba-Geigy and Sandoz rejoined to form Novartis in 1996. To win approval for the merger Sandoz (whose Daniel Vasella became CEO of the new company) sold its corn herbicide and US animal health businesses. Novartis spun off its specialty chemicals unit in 1997 and bought Merck's insecticide and fungicide operations.

In 1998 the company merged its OTC health and nutrition businesses into a new consumer health division and in the following year sold several units including cracker maker Wasa to focus the new division's operations. Chairman Alex Krauer who had overseen the formation of Novartis stepped down that year leaving the post to Vasella.

To boost its market share CIBA Vision bought colored contact lens maker Wesley Jessen VisionCare in 2000. Novartis spun off its crop protection and seed units merging them with AstraZeneca's Agrochemicals unit to create Syngenta.

Novartis Ophthalmics split off from the CIBA Vision division to become a separate eye health care unit under the Pharmaceutical Division of Novartis in 2001. The firm's joint venture with BioTransplant successfully cloned genetically altered pigs whose organs would be more suitable for human transplants. Attempting to refine the company's focus on pharmaceuticals Novartis made several acquisitions in 2002 including two animal vaccine companies Grand Laboratories and Immtech Biologies and generic manufacturer Lek Pharmaceuticals while divesting its food and beverage division to Associated British Foods. The remaining assets including sports nutrition health and weight loss products were grouped under the Nutrition & Sante banner and were sold to management in 2004.

Novartis engineered one of the largest deals in European pharma in 2004 when it acquired the rights to a prospective inhaled chronic obstructive pulmonary disease (COPD) treatment from UK drug concerns Arakis and Vectura Group.

Novartis' consumer health business got a Boost literally when it purchased Mead Johnson's adult nutrition business in 2004. The buy included brands such as Boost nutritional drinks and feeding tube products Isocal and Ultracal. In a move to further bolster its consumer offerings that same year the company purchased the US and Canadian consumer products division of Bristol-Myers Squibb which brought headache remedy Excedrin cold and flu treatment Comtrex and Keri moisturizers into the company's consumer products stable.

To bulk up Sandoz (which had refocused strictly on generic pharmaceuticals over the years) in 2004 Novartis bought a Canadian maker of generic injectable drugs and a Danish generics maker to increase market share in key regional markets. In 2005 the firm acquired Hexal AG one of Germany's top generics makers and a controlling stake in Hexal's sister firm Eon Labs a US generics manufacturer.

The constant appetite of its drug pipeline was briefly sated in mid-2006 when Novartis acquired NeuTec Pharma a UK-based biopharmaceutical company with two drug candidates that target otherwise drug-resistant "superbugs." That year Novartis spent $5.1 billion to acquire struggling vaccine and biopharmaceuticals products maker Chiron despite Chiron's board rebuffing an earlier offer. Novartis then created a Vaccine and Diagnostics division composed of its existing vaccine operations and Chiron's diagnostics.

Putting its focus entirely on health care Novartis sold off the last of its non-health care businesses in 2007 when Nestle purchased Novartis' medical nutrition business for $2.5 billion and its Gerber baby products business for $5.5 billion. Also in 2007 Novartis formed a new unit to focus on biologic drug development which already made up 25% of its preclinical research pipeline.

In 2008 Novartis purchased Speedel the Swiss biotech drugmaker with which it developed blood pressure medication Rasilez (known as Tekturna in the US) for $888 million. It also completed a $400 million acquisition of US biopharmaceutical development company Protez Pharmaceuticals which added a late-stage candidate for drug-resistant Staphylococcus infections. Later that year the company also acquired the pulmonary drug delivery R&D business of Nektar Therapeutics for $115 million. The two companies had already collaborated on the development of an inhaled powder therapy for lung infections and the deal brought that treatment fully under Novartis' roof.

Also in 2008 Novartis struck a deal with Nestle to acquire its majority stake (about 77%) in eye care firm Alcon. The deal took place over the course of two years and included a $10.4 billion purchase in mid-2008 and a $28.3 billion transaction in mid-2010.

In 2009 it completed a $1.3 billion acquisition of the specialty generic injectables arm of Austrian-based Ebewe Pharma. The buy gave Sandoz a line of oncology drugs that are widely considered to be essential to adhering to standard-of-care guidelines for treating a range of cancers.

To increase the capacity of its Vaccine and Diagnostics division Novartis opened a new vaccine plant in North Carolina in 2009 and in 2010 the company launched Menveo a new meningitis vaccine.

Novartis conducted an executive management shift in early 2010 when Daniel Vasella stepped down as CEO after holding the job for 14 years but remained chairman. Joe Jimenez moved from his position as head of the company's pharmaceutical division to become CEO.

Schizophrenia treatment Fanapt was approved by the FDA in early 2010. Novartis added some late-stage heart failure drugs to its pipeline that year by acquiring privately held drug developer Corthera for $120 million plus up to $500 million in potential milestones. The firm also sold the US rights to overactive bladder treatment Enablex to Warner Chilcott for $400 million in 2010.

EXECUTIVES

Vice Chairman, Ulrich Lehner, age 67
Chairman, Daniel L. Vasella, age 59, $3,188,700 total compensation
General Counsel, Felix R. Ehrat
Chief Executive Officer; Member of the Executive Committee, Joseph (Joe) Jimenez Jr., age 54, $1,054,050 total compensation
President Novartis Institutes for BioMedical Research, Mark C. Fishman, age 62, $963,333 total compensation
CEO Novartis Pharmaceuticals, David R. Epstein, age 52
Public Relations US, Pamela (Pam) McKinlay
Head Human Resources, Juergen Brokatzky-Geiger, age 61, $534,459 total compensation
CEO Consumer Health Division; Head Novartis Animal Health Business Unit, George Gunn, age 63
Division Head Alcon, Kevin J. Buehler, age 55
Head Corporate Communications, Sheldon Jones
Chief Financial Officer; Member of the Executive Committee, Jonathan R. (Jon) Symonds, age 53
Director Global Media Relations, Eric Althoff
CEO Sandoz Division, Jeffrey (Jeff) George, age 39
CEO Vaccines and Diagnostics Division, Andrin Oswald
Head Public Relations Switzerland, Michael Schiendorfer
Head Novartis Group Quality, Juan Andres
Head Group Country Management and External Affairs, Kim Stratton
President Novartis Corporation, Andre (Andy) Wyss
Head OTC Division, Naomi Kelman
Chief Compliance Officer of Novartis, Peter Kornicker
Corporate Secretary, Charlotte Pamer-Wieser
Vice President Internal Audit, Yves Teirlynck
Vice President Ethics & Compliance, Julie Kane
Chief Procurement Officer, Phillip Duncan
Vice Chairman, Ulrich Lehner, age 67
Director, Alexandre F. Jetzer-Chung, age 72
Director, Ann M. Fudge, age 61
Director, Wendelin Wiedeking, age 61
Director, Pierre Landolt, age 66
Director, Rolf M. Zinkernagel, age 69
Director, Srikant M. Datar, age 60
Director, Andreas von Planta, age 59
Director, Marjorie M. T. Yang, age 61
Director, William Brody, age 68
Director, Enrico Vanni
Auditors: PricewaterhouseCoopersAG

LOCATIONS

HQ: Novartis AG Basel
Lichtstrasse 35, Basel CH-4056
Phone: (41) 61 324 1111
Web: www.novartis.com

2011 Sales

	% of total
US	33
Japan	9
Germany	7
France	5
Switzerland	1
Other	45
Total	**100**

PRODUCTS/OPERATIONS

2011 Sales

	% of total
Pharmaceuticals	56
Alcon	17
Sandoz	16
Consumer	8
Vaccines &	3
Total	**100**

Selected Acquisitions

2012
- Fougera Pharmaceuticals ($1.5 billion; Melville New York; generic dermatology medications)

2011
- Alcon ($52 billion over three years; contact lenses vision pharmaceuticals surgery equipment)
- Genoptix ($470 million; Carlsbad California; laboratory services and molecular diagnostics)
- Zhejiang Tianyuan ($194 million; China; vaccines)

2010
- Corthera ($120 million; late-stage heart failure candidate)
- Oriel Therapeutics (respiratory drug development)

Selected Products

Pharmaceuticals
- Afinitor/Votubia (breast cancer pancreatic tumors brain tumors)
- Arcapta/Onbrez (pulmonary inhalation medicine)
- Clozaril/Leponex (schizophrenia)
- Comtan/Stalevo (Parkinson's disease)
- Diovan/Co-Diovan (hypertension)
- Estraderm/Estragest (menopause and osteoporosis)
- Exelon/Exelon Patch (Alzheimer's disease)
- Exforge (hypertension)
- Exjade (iron chelator)
- Extavia (multiple sclerosis)
- Famvir (antiviral for herpes)
- Fanapt (schizophrenia)
- Femara (advanced breast cancer)
- Foradil (asthma chronic obstructive pulmonary disease)
- Galvus (diabetes)
- Gilenya (multiple sclerosis)
- Gleevec/Glivec (chronic myeloid leukemia and gastrointestinal tumor treatment)
- Lescol (cholesterol)
- Lotrel (hypertension)
- Lucentis (age-related macular degeneration)
- Miacalcin/Miacalcic (osteoporosis)
- Myfortic (transplant)
- Neoral/Sandimmun (transplant rejection preventative)
- Ritalin/Focalin (attention deficit hyperactivity disorder)
- Reclast/Aclasta (osteoporosis)
- Sandostatin (acromegaly)
- Tasigna (chronic myeloid leukemia)
- Tekturna/Rasilez (blood pressure)

Tegretol (epilepsy acute mania and bipolar affective disorders)
Trileptal (epilepsy)
Visudyne (wet age-related macular degeneration pathological myopia)
Voltaren (antirheumatic for inflammation and pain)
Xolair (asthma)
Zaditor/Zaditen (allergic conjunctivitis)
Zometa (cancer complications)
Sandoz generic pharmaceuticals
Acetylcysteine (respiratory)
Amlodipine/Benazepril (hypertension)
Amoxicillin (antibiotic)
Enoxaparin sodium (anti-coagulant)
Fentanyl (pain)
Lansoprazole (proton pump inhibitor)
Losartan (hypertension)
Omeprazole (heartburn and ulcer)
Paclitaxel (cancer)
Simvastatin (cholesterol)
Tacrolimus (transplant)
Tiamulin (statin)
Vancomycin (antibiotic)
Zarzio/Filgrastim Hexal (cancer)
Consumer Health
Animal health
Atopica (atopic dermatitis management)
Denaguard (antimicrobial for pigs)
Deramaxx (pain relief for dogs and cats)
Sentinel/Milbemax/Interceptor (intestinal parasite and heart worm control)
OTC
Benefiber (fiber supplements)
Excedrin (systemic analgesic)
Lamisil AT Cream (athlete's foot treatment)
Nicotinell (or Habitrol smoking cessation patch)
Prevacid/Pantoloc (heartburn)
Theraflu/NeoCitran (flu treatment)
Triaminic/Otrivin (cough and cold remedies)
Voltaren Emulgel (topical analgesic)
Vaccines and Diagnostics
Flu vaccines (Agrippal AgriFlu Fluad Fluvirin Optaflu)
HIV hepatitis and West Nile tests (Procleix)
Meningitis vaccines (Menveo Menjugate)
Pediatric vaccines (Polioral Quinvaxem)
Traveling vaccines (Encepur Ixiaro Rabipur)
Alcon
Ophthalmic drugs
Azopt/Azarga (glaucoma)
Ciprodex Otic (anti-infective)
Patanase/Pantanol (allergy)
TobraDex (ophthalmic suspension)
Travatan/DuoTrav (glaucoma)
Vigamox (antibiotic)
Surgical
Allegretto (laser surgery system)
AcrySof (intraocular lenses for cataract surgery)
Infiniti (cataract lens removal system)
WaveLight (refractive laser)
Vision Care
Air Optix (monthly contact lenses)
Aquify (contact lens cleaning solution)
Cibasoft (contact lenses)
Clear Care (aka Aosept contact lens cleaning system)
Dailies (disposable contact lenses)
FreshLook (tinted contact lenses)
ICAPS (vitamins)
Opti-Free (cleaning solution)
Systane (eye drops)

COMPETITORS

Abbott Labs
Allergan
Amgen
AstraZeneca
Bausch & Lomb
Baxter International
Bayer AG
Biogen Idec
Bristol-Myers Squibb
Carl Zeiss Meditec
Dr. Reddy' s
Eli Lilly
Essilor International
GlaxoSmithKline
Johnson & Johnson
Merck
Novo Nordisk
Perrigo
Pfizer
Ranbaxy Laboratories
Roche Holding
Sanofi
Teva

HISTORICAL FINANCIALS

Company Type: Public

Income Statement FYE: December 31

	REVENUE ($ mil.)	NET INCOME ($ mil.)	NET PROFIT MARGIN	EMPLOYEES
12/13	58,831	9,175	15.6%	0
12/12	57,561	9,505	16.5%	127,724
12/11	59,375	9,113	15.3%	123,686
12/10	51,561	9,794	19.0%	119,418
12/09	45,103	8,400	18.6%	99,834
Annual Growth	6.9%	2.2%	—	—

2013 Year-End Financials

Debt ratio: 14.2%
Return on equity: 12.7%
Cash ($ mil.): 6,687
Current ratio: 1.16
Long-term debt ($ mil.): 11,242
No. of shares (mil.): —
Dividends
Yield: 3.0%
Payout: 65.4%
Market value ($ mil.): —

	STOCK PRICE ($) FY Close	P/E High	P/E Low	PER SHARE ($) Earnings	Dividends	Book Value
12/13	80.38	21	17	3.70	2.43	30.64
12/12	63.30	16	13	3.89	2.48	28.54
12/11	57.17	17	13	3.78	2.36	27.36
12/10	58.95	14	10	4.26	1.95	27.60
12/09	54.43	15	9	3.69	1.71	25.34
Annual Growth	10.2%	—	—	0.1%	9.1%	4.9%

Novo-Nordisk A/S

Until there is a cure for diabetes Novo Nordisk will stay busy and as long as diabetes is on the rise it will likely stay profitable. It is one of the world's leading producers of human insulin insulin analogues injection devices and education materials. It makes modern insulin analogues Levemir and NovoLog (which mimic natural insulin regulation more closely than human insulin) and the FlexPen a pre-filled injection tool. The firm also has products in the areas of hemostasis management (blood clotting) human growth hormone and estrogen replacement therapy. The not-for-profit Novo Nordisk Foundation through its Novo A/S subsidiary controls the voting power in Novo Nordisk.

The company operates production facilities around the globe but keeps the production of its active pharmaceutical ingredients close to home in Denmark. As with most biopharmaceutical enterprises Novo Nordisk engages in alliances with medical institutions and other drug companies to further its research and marketing activities.

Drawing upon its familiarity in working with chronic disorders Novo Nordisk has built up a stable group of non-diabetic biopharmaceuticals. NovoSeven is used to treat hemophilia in patients who have developed inhibitors to other treatments and to treat patients who develop hemophilia later in life. Norditropin is the company's liquid human growth hormone which is given to children and adults with a growth hormone deficiency. It has extended the line of products to include easier-to-use injection devices. Its line of female hormone replacement therapies are used to reduce symptoms of menopause.

Diabetes care accounts for some 75% of the company's sales and with the steady increase of numbers of diabetic patients the future looks especially good for Novo Nordisk. The company is growing on the strength of its insulin product lines. In particular increased demand for prefilled cartridges and insulin analogues or modern insulins is contributing to strong results. The company's Victoza has been approved in more than 45 countries as a once-daily injection to control blood sugar levels in patients with type 2 diabetes. Victoza is an analog of a hormone involved in glucose regulation and is used to support oral antidiabetic treatments. Novo Nordisk is banking on Victoza to become one its lead products.

The company markets its drugs in nearly 200 countries with Europe and North America as its largest markets. North America has shown the most growth in recent years overtaking Europe as Novo Nordisk's number one market thanks to strong sales of Levemir NovoLog and NovoLog Mix. The company is looking to grow in developing markets including China and Turkey. However it is also cautiously watching as economic instability is forcing some European governments to cut back on reimbursement of medical expenses including some of the costlier new diabetes products. At the same time generic versions of NovoNorm have begun to erode sales and European patent expirations on NovoLog could prove costly if biosimilar (generic) versions are created and approved.

The company's pipeline includes candidates in areas such as inflammation and obesity. It is also developing additional treatments for hemophilia and type 2 diabetes. Novo Nordisk runs clinical trials in more than 50 countries

HISTORY

Novo Nordisk was formed by the 1989 merger of Danish insulin producers Novo and Nordisk.

Soon after Canadian researchers first extracted insulin from the pancreases of cattle Danish researcher August Krogh (winner of the 1920 Nobel Prize in physiology) and physician Marie Krogh his wife teamed up with H. C. Hagedorn also a physician to found Nordisk Insulinlaboratorium. One of their lab workers was an inventor named Harald Pedersen and in 1923 Nordisk hired Pedersen's brother Thorvald to analyze chemicals. The relationship was unsuccessful however and the brothers left the company.

The Pedersens decided to produce insulin themselves and set up operations in their basement in 1924. Harald also designed a syringe that patients could use for their own insulin injections. Within a decade their firm Novo Terapeutisk Laboratorium was selling its product in 40 countries.

Meanwhile Nordisk introduced a slow-acting insulin in 1936. NPH insulin launched in the US in 1950 soon became the leading longer-acting insulin. Nordisk later became a major maker of human growth hormone.

During WWII Novo produced its first enzyme trypsin used to soften leather. It began producing penicillin in 1947 and during the 1950s developed Heparin a trypsin-based drug used to treat blood clots. The company unveiled more industrial enzymes in the 1960s.

In 1981 Novo began selling its insulin in the US through a joint venture with E. R. Squibb (now part of Bristol-Myers Squibb). The next year Novo was the first to produce human insulin (actually a modified form of pig insulin) and in 1983 Nordisk introduced the Nordisk Infuser a pump that constantly released small quantities of insulin. Two years later Novo debuted the NovoPen a refillable injector that looked like a fountain pen.

Novo was the world's #2 insulin maker (and the world's largest maker of industrial enzymes) when it merged with #3 Nordisk in 1989. By combining their research and market share they were better able to compete globally with then-#1 Eli Lilly.

After the merger Novo Nordisk introduced the NovoLet the world's first prefilled disposable insulin syringe.

Novo Nordisk introduced drugs for depression (Seroxat 1992) epilepsy (Gabitril 1995) and hemophilia (NovoSeven 1995). The company entered a joint marketing alliance with Johnson & Johnson subsidiary LifeScan the world's #1 maker of blood glucose monitors in 1995. It also began working with Rhone-Poulenc Rorer on estrogen replacement therapies.

Eli Lilly raised a new challenge in 1996 with the FDA approval of Humalog (the US's first new insulin product in 14 years) which is absorbed faster giving users more flexibility in their injection schedule. (Novo Nordisk's own fast-acting insulin product NovoLog received FDA approval four years later.) A 1998 marketing pact with Schering-Plough signaled Novo Nordisk's desire to boost sales of its diabetes drugs in the US where Eli Lilly had historically dominated.

In 2000 Novo Nordisk split its health care and enzymes businesses; the split left Novo Nordisk with all the health care operations while a new company Novozymes was formed to carry out the enzyme business. It bought out the remaining shares in its Brazilian subsidiary Biobras in 2001. In 2002 the company spun off its US-based biotechnology firm ZymoGenetics. It retained a one-third of the company until selling its shares to Bristol-Myers Squibb in 2010.

In 2008 the company halted development on its AERx inhaled insulin product believing that the product could not provide significant benefits over existing therapies. The decision came soon after Pfizer's much-publicized failure with Exubera its own inhaled insulin which had not sold well. Novo Nordisk had been working on AERx with drug delivery specialist Aradigm.

EXECUTIVES

EVP and CFO, Jesper Brandgaard, age 50, $707,070 total compensation
EVP and Chief Science Officer, Mads K. Thomsen, age 53, $707,070 total compensation
Senior Vice President Regulatory Affairs Management, Peter Bonne Eriksen
Senior Vice President Quality Management, Mariann Strid Christensen
President and CEO, Lars Rebien S?rensen, age 59, $1,142,190 total compensation
Executive Vice President Chief Information Officer CIO, Lars A. J?rgensen, age 65
Corporate Vice President, Per Valstorp
Member Senior Management Board Legal Affairs, Ole Ramsby
Member Senior Management Board Global Quality, Lars Guldb?k Karlsen
Member Senior Management Board Europe, Martin H. Soeters, age 59
Member Senior Management Board NNE Pharmaplan, Hans Ole Voigt
EVP and Chief of Staffs, Lise Kingo, age 52, $554,400 total compensation
Member Senior Management Board Diabetes Research, Peter Kurtzhals
Chief Medical Officer, Alan C. Moses
Member Senior Management Board CMC Supply, Jesper B?ving
Senior Vice President Global Support, Kim Tosti
Vice Chairman, Goron Ando, age 64
Senior Director Corporate Communications US, Lori Moore
Member Senior Management Board Liraglutude, Jakob Riis
Chairman, Sten Scheibye, age 62
Member Senior Management Board Corporate Finance, Lars Green
Member Senior Management Board IT and Corporate Development, Lars F. J?rgensen
Member Senior Management Board Corporate People and Organisation, Lars Christian Lassen
VP Corporate Communications, Mike Rulis
Associate Director Corporate Communications US, Sean Clements
Director Investor Relations North America, Hans Rommer
Member Senior Management Board Japan and Korea, Claus Eilersen
Member Senior Management Board Global Development, Peter Kristensen
Director Media Relations, Katrine Sperling
Manager Investor Relations, Kasper Roseeuw Poulsen
Investor Relations Coordinator, Celena Lund Pedersen
Manager Communication, Rachel Curtis Gravesen
Media Relations Officer, Mette Kruse Danielsen
Media Relations Officer, Tania Sabroe
Media Relations Officer, Elin K. Hansen
SVP Biopharmaceuticals Research Unit, Per Falk
Senior Vice President Devices & Sourcing, Susanne Hundsb?k-Pedersen
Corporate Vice President Global Stakeholder Engagement, Charlotte Ersb.ll
Vice President Occupational, Henrik Salomonsen
Senior Vice President Corporate People & Organisation, Lars Chr
President Chief Executive Officer CEO, Lars S?rensen
Vice President Corporate Responsibility Management, Elin Schmidt
Vice President Corporate, Peter Gerhardsson
President and CEO, Lars Rebien S?rensen, age 59
Board Member, Kurt Anker Nielsen, age 68
Board Member, Pamela J. Kirby, age 60
Board Member, Hannu Ryopponen, age 61
Vice Chairman, Goron Ando, age 64
Board Member, Henrik Gurtler, age 59
Board Member, Johnny Henriksen, age 63
Board Member, Anne Marie Kverneland, age 57
Board Member, S?ren Thuesen Pedersen, age 49
Board Member, Stig Str?b?k, age 48
Board Member, J?rgen Wedel, age 64
Auditors: PricewaterhouseCoopers

LOCATIONS

HQ: Novo-Nordisk A/S
Novo Alle, Bagsvaerd DK-2880
Phone: (45) 4444 8888 **Fax:** (45) 4449 0555
Web: www.novonordisk.com

2011 Sales

	% of total
North	40
Europe	29
Japan &	9
China	8
Other	14
Total	**100**

PRODUCTS/OPERATIONS

2011 Sales

	$ mil.	% of total
Diabetes care		
Human insulin		16
Oral antidiabetic products		4
Biopharmaceuticals		
Norditropin		8
Other products		1

Selected Products

Diabetes products
- Human insulins
  - Actrapid
  - Insulatard
  - Mixtard 30
- Glucagon-like Peptide-1
  - Victoza
- Modern insulins
  - Levemir
  - NovoMix
  - NovoRapid
- Oral antidiabetic agents
  - NovoNorm
  - PrandiMet

Biopharmaceuticals
- NovoSeven (recombinant hemophilia therapy)
- Norditropin (human growth hormone)
- Hormone replacement therapy
  - Activelle
  - Estrofem
  - Novofem
  - Vagifem

COMPETITORS

Amylin Pharmaceuticals
Animas
Baxter International
Becton Dickinson
Biogen Idec
Eli Lilly
Genentech
GlaxoSmithKline
MannKind
Marina Biotech
Medtronic
Merck Serono
Novartis
Pfizer
Sanofi
Wockhardt

HISTORICAL FINANCIALS

Company Type: Public

Income Statement

FYE: December 31

	REVENUE ($ mil.)	NET INCOME ($ mil.)	NET PROFIT MARGIN	EMPLOYEES
12/13	15,424	4,647	30.1%	37,978
12/12	13,785	3,786	27.5%	34,286
12/11	11,543	2,974	25.8%	32,632
12/10	10,912	2,586	23.7%	30,483
12/09	9,887	2,084	21.1%	28,809
Annual Growth	11.8%	22.2%	—	7.2%

2013 Year-End Financials

Debt ratio: 0.0%
Return on equity: 60.5%
Cash ($ mil.): 1,979
Current ratio: 1.74
Long-term debt ($ mil.): —
No. of shares (mil.): —
Dividends
Yield: 6.1%
Payout: 145.9%
Market value ($ mil.): —

	STOCK PRICE ($) FY Close	P/E High/Low		PER SHARE ($) Earnings	Dividends	Book Value
12/13	184.76	1	1	1.73	2.26	2.94
12/12	163.21	1	0	1.37	1.83	2.65
12/11	115.26	1	0	1.04	0.01	2.35
12/10	112.57	1	0	0.88	0.98	2.32
12/09	63.85	1	0	0.69	0.78	2.35
Annual Growth	30.4%	—	—	25.8%	30.5%	5.7%

NTT DOCOMO, Inc.

The Japanese yen for mobility means business for NTT DoCoMo. The mobile phone carrier is one of the world's largest wireless network operators in terms of subscribers behind global leader Vodafone. NTT DoCoMo has about 56 million subscribers to its FOMA-branded wireless voice network in Japan (giving it about half of market share) while about 49 million customers subscribe to its i-mode mobile Internet services. The company also sells wireless telephone handsets under the DoCoMo brand and it provides emergency satellite services primarily for maritime use. NTT DoCoMo is the wireless spinoff of Japan's leading telecommunications carrier Nippon Telegraph and Telephone (NTT); NTT owns two-thirds of NTT DoCoMo.

The company saw sales slip in 2010 mainly due to the decline of its core voice segment. Meanwhile NTT DoCoMo improved its profits for the year due to decreased costs of equipment and reduced network costs. The company has said that it expects profits to increase in 2011 due to ongoing efforts to further bring down costs as well as initiatives to drive customer usage of data services by offering reduced pricing options and expanded mobile services such as original content delivery and wireless Internet tethering between wireless devices and portable computers.

DoCoMo means "anywhere" and NTT DoCoMo is everywhere in the Japanese market for mobile communication services. However faced with a mature market and stiff competition at home NTT DoCoMo has renewed its efforts to tap into growth markets abroad particularly in the Asia/Pacific region.

In 2011 the company agreed to a deal with JG Summit that gives it the option to buy additional shares in Philippine Long Distance Telephone (PLDT) for around $263 million. NTTDoCoMo already owns about 10% of PLDT.

Its largest purchase in this overseas push was the 2009 acquisition of about one-quarter of India-based Tata Teleservices for about $2.7 billion. The company hopes to tap into the burgeoning Indian market through this alliance with the telecommunications arm of the Tata Group. Also that year NTT DoCoMo bought a 35% stake in US multimedia software maker PacketVideo to bolster its internal efforts to develop applications for mobile video services. It acquired the rest of the company from parent NextWave Wireless for about $115 million in 2010.

NTT DoCoMo's efforts to garner higher subscription fees from its existing customer base in Japan and improve retention have included an increase in the variety of mobile services it offers the introduction of cell phones offering a broader set of features (email music playback and gaming) and ongoing investments in its network infrastructure to enable bandwidth-hungry streaming content such as video programming. The company is counting on increased data usage to fuel profits as sales of voice services decline.

With Fujitsu Fujitsu Semiconductor NEC Panasonic Mobile Communications and Samsung Electronics the company attempted to establish a joint venture that would have developed and marketed semiconductor products for mobile devices but abandoned it after being unable to come to an agreement over details by the deadline in 2012.

HISTORY

Formed in 1952 by the Japanese Ministry of Communications to rebuild Japan's war-ravaged phone system Nippon Telegraph and Telephone (NTT) enjoyed a monopoly on phone services for more than four decades.

NTT first went into mobile communications with a maritime phone service in 1959 and in 1968 the company began offering paging services. Other telecommunications services followed: car phone service (1979) in-flight phone service (1986) and mobile phone service (1987).

In 1991 NTT established a subsidiary to adopt these wireless segments; it launched operations in 1992 as NTT Mobile Communications Network under the leadership of NTT executive Kouji Ohboshi. The firm quickly took on the DoCoMo nickname. The year closed with slightly more than a million analog mobile phone users in Japan —a market DoCoMo shared with upstart telecom companies DDI and IDO (later bought by DDI). Paging service was more popular and DoCoMo won more than 3 million customers.

DoCoMo in 1993 launched digital mobile phone service based on a scheme called PDC (personal digital cellular) —a system incompatible with the digital standards that would take root in Europe and the US. Liberalization of the cellular phone market in 1994 triggered unexpected growth: Customers who previously had to lease mobile phones from the network operators could now buy them at retail stores. Further competition emerged in 1995 with the launch of personal handyphone services or PHS (parent company NTT was among the companies providing PHS) but DoCoMo's subscriber count passed 3.5 million mobile phone users —about half the market.

DoCoMo's pager business peaked in 1996 before commencing a long-term decline; the mobile phone market where DoCoMo had more than 8 million subscribers overtook it. The company launched a satellite-based mobile phone system that year to serve customers beyond the range of cell sites reaching ships and mountainous regions.

Financial crises rocked the Pacific Rim in 1997 and Japan's Fair Trade Commission rocked NTT by ordering it to cut its 95% ownership of DoCoMo. Customers continued to flock to mobile phones despite economic turmoil and DoCoMo passed the 15-million-subscriber mark. In 1998 DoCoMo gave hope to Japan's low-flying market when it left the nest: Its mammoth IPO raised more than $18 billion.

Meanwhile DDI (now KDDI) had become the first Japanese carrier to launch a digital mobile phone network based on CDMA (code division multiple access) technology. Though DoCoMo still used PDC it redoubled its efforts to help develop and standardize a next-generation wideband version of CDMA.

In 1999 DoCoMo took over NTT's unprofitable PHS unit and rolled out a high-speed data service over the PHS network. That year it acquired a 19% stake in the telecom unit of Hong Kong's Hutchison Whampoa but failed expectations led the company to sell its stake in Hutchison 3G UK to Hutchison Whampoa in 2005 for E120 million.

In 2000 the company adopted NTT DoCoMo as its corporate name. To promote its new data services NTT DoCoMo launched a joint venture in Japan with Microsoft (Mobimagic). It took the i-mode service international in 2001 when the company teamed up with Telecom Italia Mobile to introduce the 3G service in Europe. The next year NTT DoCoMo became the largest shareholder in America Online Japan but it sold the more than 40% stake to America Online in 2003.

The company staked its claim in the US too by paying $9.8 billion for a 16% stake in AT&T Wireless in 2001. NTT DoCoMo sold its stake following the 2004 takeover of AT&T Wireless by rival Cingular Wireless (now AT&T Mobility) in a deal valued at $41 billion.

The company in 2002 took full ownership of its eight majority-owned regional operating subsidiaries and began consolidating operations. The company also has liquidated several other subsidiaries including an operating unit in Brazil and it has reorganized its European holdings under a single subsidiary DoCoMo Europe Ltd.

It also continued to advance digital wireless technologies through partnerships that include an alliance (formed in 2000) with Hutchison Whampoa and Dutch mobile phone company KPN Mobile to bid on European operating licenses. It also paid $4.5 billion for a 15% stake in KPN Mobile. (The stake was reduced to 2% then sold back to parent firm KPN. An i-mode affiliation continues however.)

After the number of paging service subscribers fell to less than 300000 from a high of 6.5 million (in 1996) NTT DoCoMo ended the service in early 2007. It additionally dissolved allucher a marketing and consulting services provider to mobile phone users and its animation-related Web portal management and marketing business known as Hive. NTT DoCoMo also discontinued its Personal Handyphone Service (PHS) and its CITYPHONE digital mobile service in 2008.

NTT DoCoMo in 2008 bought stakes in operators in Bangladesh (TM International 30%) and the Philippines (PLDT 20%). Additionally the company has i-mode network technology licensing agreements with about a dozen GSM network operators in Europe including Russia and Greece as well as in the Asia/Pacific region.

EXECUTIVES

President and CEO PacketVideo, Mark Tapling
SEVP Multimedia Services and Technology and Board Member, Kiyoyuki Tsujimura, age 63
EVP Consumer Sales, Takashi Tanaka, age 58
EVP Consumer Sales and Director, Bunya Kumagai, age 60
SEVP Global Business and Board Member, Masatoshi Suzuki, age 61
SVP and Managing Director Hokkaido Regional Office, Hiroaki Nishioka, age 64
SEVP Chief Privacy Officer and Chief Information Security Officer, Fumio Iwasaki, age 60
President CEO and Board Member, Ryuji Yamada, age 64
EVP Managing Director Research and Development and Board Member, Mitsunobu Komori, age 60
EVP and Managing Director Tokai Regional Office, Toru Kobayashi
SEVP and CFO, Kazuto Tsubouchi, age 61
SVP and Managing Director Credit Card Business, Masaki Yoshikawa
SVP and Managing Director Chugoku Regional Office, Akiko Ide
SVP and Managing Director Advertising and Promotion, Yuji Araki
EVP and Managing Director Network, Kiyoshi Tokuhiro
EVP and CIO, Seiji Nishikawa
SVP Managing Director General Affairs and Corporate Citizenship and Board Member, Katsuhiro Nakamura, age 60
SVP and Managing Director Global Business, Toshinari Kunieda
EVP Marketing, Tsutomu Shindou
EVP and Managing Director of Corporate Strategy & Planning Department, Kazuhiro Yoshizawa
SVP and Managing Director Product, Kiyohito Nagata
SEVP and Board Member, Hiroshi Matsui, age 66
President and CEO, Kaoru Kato, age 62
EVP and Managing Director Corporate Marketing, Akio Oshima
EVP and Deputy Managing Director Corporate Marketing, Haruhide Nakayama
EVP and Managing Director Kansai Regional Office, Shozo Nishimura
SVP and Managing Director Business Process Improvement Office, Tooru Azumi
SVP and Managing Director Shikoku Regional Office, Masaaki Sado
SVP and General Manager Kanagawa Branch, Yasuhiro Taguchi
EVP and CTO, Seizo Onoe
SVP and Managing Director Hokuriku Regional Office, Tadashi Kitamura
SVP and Managing Director Tohoku Regional Office, Tetsuya Suzuki
SVP and Deputy Managing Director Research and Development, Yoshiyuki Takeda
EVP Multimedia Services, Hiroyasu Asami

SVP Managing Director Public Relations and Deputy Managing Director Mobile Society Research Institute, Yoshikiyo Sakai
SVP and Managing Director Communication Device Support, Tomohiro Kurosawa
CEO, Isao Moriyasu
President CEO Director Oricon Inc, Koh Koike
Executive Vice President, Masaaki Shintaku
SEVP Multimedia Services and Technology and Board Member, Kiyoyuki Tsujimura, age 63
SVP Managing Director Human Resources Management and Board Member, Takashi Tanaka, age 58
EVP Consumer Sales and Director, Bunya Kumagai, age 60
SEVP Global Business and Board Member, Masatoshi Suzuki, age 61
SVP Managing Director Kyushu Regional Division and Board Member, Fumio Iwasaki, age 60
President CEO and Board Member, Ryuji Yamada, age 64
EVP Managing Director Research and Development and Board Member, Mitsunobu Komori, age 60
EVP CFO Managing Director Accounts and Finance and Board Member, Kazuto Tsubouchi, age 61
SVP Managing Director General Affairs and Corporate Citizenship and Board Member, Katsuhiro Nakamura, age 59
SEVP and Board Member, Hiroshi Matsui, age 66
President CEO, Kaoru Kato, age 62
Board Member, Hiroshi Tsujigami, age 54
Board Member, Akio Oshima
Auditors: KPMGAZSA&Co.

LOCATIONS

HQ: NTT DOCOMO, Inc.
Sanno Park Tower, 11-1, Nagata-cho 2-chome, Chiyoda-ku, Tokyo 100-6150
Phone: (81) 3 5156 1111 **Fax:** (81) 3 5156 0271
Web: www.nttdocomo.co.jp

PRODUCTS/OPERATIONS

2010 Sales

	% of total
Wireless services	
Cellular	
Voice	44
Packet	37
Other	6
Equipment	13
Total	**100**

Selected Services

Cellular
i-mode (wireless Internet access)
In-flight telephone
Mobile multimedia
Satellite mobile communications
Third-generation (3G) wireless (W-CDMA)
World Call (direct international calling)

Selected Regional Operating Subsidiaries

DOCOMO Business Net Inc.
DOCOMO Engineering Chugoku Inc.
DOCOMO Engineering Hokkaido Inc.
DOCOMO Engineering Hokuriku Inc.
DOCOMO Engineering Inc.
DOCOMO Engineering Kansai Inc.
DOCOMO Engineering Kyushu Inc.
DOCOMO Engineering Shikoku Inc.
DOCOMO Engineering Tohoku Inc.
DOCOMO Engineering Tokai Inc.
DOCOMO I Kyushu Inc.
DOCOMO Mobile Inc.
DOCOMO Mobile Tokai Inc.
DOCOMO Mobile Media Kansai Inc.
DOCOMO Service Chugoku Inc.
DOCOMO Service Hokkaido Inc.
DOCOMO Service Hokuriku Inc.
DOCOMO Service Inc.
DOCOMO Service Kansai Inc.
DOCOMO Service Kyushu Inc.
DOCOMO Service Shikoku Inc.
DOCOMO Service Tohoku Inc.
DOCOMO Service Tokai Inc.
DOCOMO Support Inc.
DOCOMO Systems Inc.
DOCOMO Technology Inc.

COMPETITORS

BT
China Mobile
EMOBILE
Hutchison Telecommunications
KDDI
Optus
SK Telecom
SOFTBANK MOBILE
Telstra
Vodafone

HISTORICAL FINANCIALS

Company Type: Public

Income Statement FYE: March 31

	REVENUE ($ mil.)	NET INCOME ($ mil.)	NET PROFIT MARGIN	EMPLOYEES
03/13	47,507	5,267	11.1%	35,426
03/12	51,688	5,655	10.9%	32,244
03/11	51,013	5,923	11.6%	31,157
03/10	45,867	5,297	11.5%	29,266
03/09	45,168	4,791	10.6%	21,831
Annual Growth	1.3%	2.4%	—	12.9%

2013 Year-End Financials

Debt ratio: 0.0%
Return on equity: 9.4%
Cash ($ mil.): 5,246
Current ratio: 1.98
Long-term debt ($ mil.): 1,817
No. of shares (mil.): —
Dividends
Yield: 303.3%
Payout: 48.5%
Market value ($ mil.): —

	STOCK PRICE ($) FY Close	P/E High/Low		PER SHARE ($) Earnings	Dividends	Book Value
03/13	14.87	0	0	1.27	0.62	13.91
03/12	16.67	0	0	1.36	0.66	14.88
03/11	17.59	0	0	1.42	0.59	14.13
03/10	15.20	0	0	1.27	0.54	11.93
03/09	13.65	0	0	1.13	0.47	10.56
Annual Growth	2.2%	—	—	2.9%	7.1%	7.1%

Obayashi Corp. (Japan)

Obayashi's buildings shake rattle and roll —but they don't fall. A leading global contractor and one of Japan's top four general contractors the company is a pioneer in the development of earthquake-resistant building techniques. Obayashi serves as architect consultant engineer and systems designer for buildings and large-scale civil engineering projects worldwide. Projects have included the Dubai Urban Rail Transit System; the bobsled and luge runs used in the 1998 Winter Games in Nagano; the Ted Williams tunnel in Boston; and restoration of port facilities in Kobe Japan damaged by a 1995 earthquake.

Shaken by the Asian economic crisis Obayashi cut costs reducing subcontracting fees and personnel expenses to counter the severe downturn in Japan's construction industry. Although the nation's economy has not fully recovered and orders are still slow Obayashi has benefited from an increase in urban redevelopment projects.

To counter the downturn in Japan's construction industry Obayashi has ventured into environmental services including hazardous and radioactive waste containment. It has also committed itself to green building practices and counts the US among its most promising markets for growth.

HISTORY

With the first wave of Japanese modernization in 1892 Yoshigoro Ohbayashi opened a small construction operation in Osaka. He won the bid for construction of the Abe Paper Mill. In 1898 he joined with partner Kamezo Shirasugi to lay the foundations for the Obayashi Corporation.

Obayashi's first big contract came in 1901 for the construction of buildings for Osaka's Fifth National Industry Fair. During the Russo-Japanese War the young corporation built 100 barracks in three weeks a feat that helped it win a contract to build Tokyo Station (completed 1914). Obayashi executives were invited to the US by the Fluor Company in the early 1920s to study advanced construction techniques. After a 1923 earthquake and firestorm leveled much of Tokyo Obayashi applied the technology it learned from Fluor to build quake-resistant fireproof buildings.

Like many Japanese companies Obayashi is quiet about its history in the years leading up to WWII and the rebuilding that followed. However the Korean War increased demand for company projects such as the Tokyo Station annex the Japan Broadcasting Corporation building and the first of 50 major dam projects.

In the 1960s Obayashi became the first Japanese construction firm to build an internal R&D facility. Its Technical Research Institute developed the OWS-Soletanche Diaphragm Wall Construction Method which it used on the New Osaka building in 1961 and has adapted to many other buildings since. In 1965 the company began its first major civil engineering project overseas doing its part in a 32-year-long excavation in Singapore that reclaimed about 3% of that country's land mass from the sea. Also that year Obayashi completed the first high-rise in Japan Yokohama's 21-story Hotel Empire.

Expo '70 in Osaka showcased Obayashi's air-membrane dome and roof lift-up method. During the 1970s the company played key roles in Japan's massive highway-building projects. In 1979 it was the first Japanese construction company to be awarded a public works contract in the US.

Obayashi completed thousands of projects during the 1980s. It helped build the Tsukuba Expo '85 and restored the Katsura Rikyu Detached Palace a national treasure.

In 1994 two former Obayashi executives were found guilty of giving a 10 million yen (about $100000) bribe to the mayor of Sendai two years earlier. The company was one of several major construction companies involved in the scandal.

In the 1990s Obayashi "mole" machines chewed through the earth to create the Tokyo Bay Aqualine tunnel. In 1996 the company developed anti-earthquake construction methods for structures built on soft ground (almost a fifth of buildings in Tokyo).

Obayashi was hard hit in 1998 and 1999 as financial crises created turmoil in Japan's construction industry. The company responded by reducing its workforce by about 5% taking advantage of economies of scale in materials purchasing and working with subcontractors to cut costs. Beefing up its project orders is another key strategy. New projects secured by Obayashi in 2000 included the Taiwan North-South High Speed Rail Project and a new head office for Japanese advertising giant Dentsu.

In 2002 the group completed the NHK Osaka Broadcasting Station and the renovation of Kobe Wing Stadium a site for part of the 2002 World

Cup soccer finals. Obayashi and Kobe Steel won the contract to operate the stadium for 15 years.

Obayashi was caught in a building scandal in its home country in 2005 when it came to light that an outside architect had falsified documents regarding earthquake resistance for one of its projects a hotel. Obayashi said that the falsifications were too skillfully done to catch at the construction stage.

EXECUTIVES

President, Toru Shiraishi, age 66
EVP, Tadahiko Noguchi, age 66
EVP, Makoto Kanai, age 65
Senior Managing Executive Officer, Makoto Kishida, age 61
EVP, Shozo Harada, age 63
Senior Managing Executive Officer, Akihisa Miwa, age 61
Chairman, Takeo Obayashi, age 59
Senior Managing Executive Officer, Kenichi Shibata, age 63
Senior Managing Executive Officer, Nao Sugiyama, age 63
EVP CFO and Director, Eiji Noma
EVP and Director, Shigeyoshi Cho, age 66
EVP and Director, Masashi Honjo, age 68
Senior Managing Director, Yuji Nakamura, age 68
President CEO and Director, Toru Shiraishi, age 65
Senior Managing Director, Ryuichi Irahara, age 67
Senior Managing Director, Takehiko Totsuka
Senior Managing Director, Tadahiko Noguchi
Managing Director, Makoto Kanai
Managing Director, Makoto Kishida
Managing Director, Shozo Harada
Managing Director, Akihisa Miwa
Director, Takeo Obayashi
Auditors: Ernst&YoungShinNihon

LOCATIONS

HQ: Obayashi Corp. (Japan)
2-15-2 Konan, Minato-ku, Tokyo 108-8502
Phone: (81) 3 5769 1017
Web: www.obayashi.co.jp

PRODUCTS/OPERATIONS

Selected Subsidiaries and Affliates

Atelier G&B Co. Ltd.
E.W. Howell Co. Inc. (US)
James E. Roberts-Obayashi Corporation (50% housing projects US)
Mutsuzawa Green Co. Ltd. (golf club and restaurant operations)
Naigai Technos Corporation
Obayashi Real Estate Corporation
Obayashi Road Corporation
OC Finance Corporation
OC Real Estate Management LLC (US)
SOMA Environment Service Corporation
Taiwan Obayashi Corporation
Thai Obayashi Corporation Limited (49%)

COMPETITORS

ABB
Bechtel
CSCEC
Fluor
Hazama
Hyundai Engineering and Construction
ITOCHU
Kajima
Kumagai Gumi
Parsons Corporation
Penta-Ocean Construction
Shimizu
TOA
Taisei
Takenaka

HISTORICAL FINANCIALS

Company Type: Public

Income Statement FYE: March 31

	REVENUE ($ mil.)	NET INCOME ($ mil.)	NET PROFIT MARGIN	EMPLOYEES
03/13	15,392	140	0.9%	12,838
03/12	15,186	62	0.4%	12,870
03/11	13,668	186	1.4%	14,639
03/10	14,361	(571)	—	14,476
03/09	17,085	111	0.7%	15,150
Annual Growth	(2.6%)	5.9%	—	(4.1%)

2013 Year-End Financials

Debt ratio: 0.2%
Return on equity: 3.6%
Cash ($ mil.): 1,059
Current ratio: 1.01
Long-term debt ($ mil.): 2,549
No. of shares (mil.): 718
Dividends
Yield: —
Payout: —
Market value ($ mil.): 3,383

	STOCK PRICE ($) FY Close	P/E High/Low	PER SHARE ($) Earnings	Dividends	Book Value
03/13	4.71	— —	0.20	0.00	6.14
03/12	4.45	— —	0.09	0.00	6.20
03/11	4.58	— —	0.26	0.00	5.90
03/10	4.30	— —	(0.79)	0.00	5.48
03/09	4.95	— —	0.15	0.00	5.59
Annual Growth	(1.2%)	— —	6.0%	—	2.4%

Oil and Natural Gas Corp. Ltd.

The crown jewel of India's oil and gas assets state-owned Oil & Natural Gas Corporation (ONGC) is India's largest exploration and production company. It is also the country's largest multinational corporation. In a country reliant on imported fuels ONGC which has estimated proved and probable reserves of 6.4 billion metric tonnes of oil equivalent accounts for the 78% of India's oil and gas production. ONGC operates a more than 15000-km. pipeline network and owns nearly 72% of Mangalore Refinery & Petrochemicals Ltd. (MRPL). International exploration and production subsidiary ONGC Videsh has established exploration activities in 17 countries. India's government owns 74% of ONGC.

ONGC has been searching for ways to expand its stakes in oil patches around the world.

Through its ONGC Videsh subsidiary the company joined rival China National Petroleum Corporation (CNPC) to acquire a 38% stake in Syria's largest oil company from Petro-Canada. The Syrian company Al Furat Petroleum is 62%-owned by Royal Dutch Shell. ONGC had lost out to CNPC in an earlier bid in 2005 for PetroKazakhstan.

In 2006 ONGC acquired Exxon Mobil's 30% stake in a field in the Campos Basin of Brazil for $1.4 billion. Other partners in the field are the state-owned Petrobras and Royal Dutch Shell which each own 35%. ONGC had lost out to Chinese rivals in previous bids for assets in South America.

In 2008 ONCG Videsh announced plans to acquire Imperial Energy for $2.6 billion giving it a foothold in the Siberian oil market.

EXECUTIVES

Chairman and Managing Director, R. S. Sharma
Director Human Resources, A. K. Balyan
Director Onshore, A. K. Hazarika
Director Offshore, N. K. Mitra
Director Exploration, N. K. Pande
Director Technology and Field Services, U N Bose
Director Finance, D. K. Sarraf
Director Operations, Shyamal Bhattacharya
Director Human Resources, A. K. Balyan
Director Onshore, A. K. Hazarika
Director Offshore, N. K. Mitra
Director Exploration, N. K. Pande
Director Technology and Field Services, U N Bose
Director Finance, D. K. Sarraf

LOCATIONS

HQ: Oil and Natural Gas Corp. Ltd.
Tel Bhavan, Dehradun, Uttaranchal 248 003
Phone: (91) 135 275 9561 **Fax:** (91) 11 2331 6413
Web: www.ongcindia.com

COMPETITORS

BP
Cairn Energy
Exxon Mobil
Occidental Petroleum
Royal Dutch Shell
TOTAL
Talisman Energy

HISTORICAL FINANCIALS

Company Type: Public

Income Statement FYE: March 31

	REVENUE ($ mil.)	NET INCOME ($ mil.)	NET PROFIT MARGIN	EMPLOYEES
03/12	298,969	55,319	18.5%	32,909
03/11	277,788	50,366	18.1%	33,273
03/10	23,838	4,394	18.4%	32,826
03/09	21,486	3,962	18.4%	33,035
03/08	25,266	5,037	19.9%	32,996
Annual Growth	85.5%	82.0%	—	(0.1%)

2012 Year-End Financials

Debt ratio: 0.1%
Return on equity: 22.3%
Cash ($ mil.): 54,819
Current ratio: 1.19
Long-term debt ($ mil.): 10,238
No. of shares (mil.): —
Dividends
Yield: —
Payout: —
Market value ($ mil.): —

Oil Co Lukoil

Russians look to LUKOIL for their energy needs. Russia's #1 integrated oil company produces refines and sells oil and oil products; it accounts for 16% of Russia's crude oil production. In 2012 LUKOIL reported proved reserves of 17.3 billion barrels of oil equivalent the majority of which is located in Russia. The company explores for oil and gas in Russia and in about a dozen other countries in Eastern Europe the Middle East Asia and South America. It owns refineries in five countries and marketing and distribution assets in nearly 30 including about 6000 gas stations. In addition LUKOIL has power generation assets in Russia Bulgaria Romania and the Ukraine.

Operations

It operates five refineries in Russia one each in Ukraine Bulgaria Romania the Netherlands and Italy; LUKOIL's gas stations are located in Russia the Baltic states Central and Eastern Europe and the US.

LUKOIL Russia's second-largest company behind natural gas monopoly Gazprom is steadily transforming itself from a top-heavy bureaucratic enterprise into a decentralized entrepreneurial company competing in free markets through joint ventures and strategic relationships.

Financial Performance

The company has seen a few years of robust growth in revenues and net income due in part to the expansion of its activities (including increased hydrocarbon production and the growth of its gas station network) but largely because of the recovering global economy's effect on increasing demand and lifting commodity prices.

Ownership

LUKOIL president Vagit Alekperov controls about 20% of the company. ING Bank Eurasia holds about 70% of LUKOIL's shares on behalf of other investors.

HISTORY

LUKOIL was formed from the combination of three major state-owned oil and gas exploration companies –Langepasneftegaz Uraineftegaz and Kogalymneftegaz –that traced their origins to the discovery of oil in western Siberia in 1964. More than 25 years later after the Soviet Union broke up the oil and gas sector was one of the first industries marked for privatization.

In 1992 the government called for Langepasneftegaz Uraineftegaz and Kogalymneftegaz to merge and LUKOIL was created the next year. (The LUK of LUKOIL comes from the initials of the three companies.) Russian president Boris Yeltsin appointed Siberian oil veteran Vagit Alekperov as the company's first president. The Russian government also formed several other large integrated oil companies including Yukos Surgutneftegaz Sidanco and Sibneft.

LUKOIL went public on the fledgling Russian Trading System in 1994. The next year the company absorbed nine other enterprises including oil exploration companies Astrakhanneft Kaliningradmorneftegaz and Permneft. That year LUKOIL became the first Russian oil company to set up an exploration and production trading arm. In 1996 LUKOIL acquired a 41% stake in "Izvestia" Russia's major independent newspaper.

Chevron and LUKOIL with seven other oil and gas companies and three governments agreed in 1996 to build a 1500-kilometer pipeline to link the Kazakhstan oil fields to world markets.

In 1997 LUKOIL became the first Russian corporation to sell bonds to international investors and the government sold 15% of its stake in the company. That year LUKOIL's 50%-owned Nexus Fuels unit opened its first gas stations located in the parking lots of US grocery stores (the partnership dissolved and Nexus went bankrupt in 2000).

LUKOIL began a partnership with Conoco (later ConocoPhillips) in 1998 to develop oil and natural gas reserves in Russia's northern territories. LUKOIL also acquired 51% of Romania's Petrorel refinery. In 1999 it acquired control of refineries in Bulgaria and Ukraine and in a petrochemical firm in Saratov. It also acquired oil company KomiTEK in one of Russia's largest mergers.

The government sold a 9% stake in LUKOIL to a Cyprus-based unit Reforma Investments held in part by LUKOIL's "boss of bosses" Vagit Alekperov (gained at the bargain price of $200 million). Critics cited the sale as Yeltsin's bid to gain Alekperov's political support.

The company announced the first major oil find in the Russian part of the Caspian Sea in 2000 and formed a joint venture (Caspian Oil Company) with fellow Russian energy giants Gazprom and Yukos to exploit resources in the Caspian. The next year LUKOIL acquired more than 1300 gas stations on the East Coast of the US when it bought Getty Petroleum Marketing.

That year LUKOIL also acquired Bitech a Canadian oil exploration and production firm with operations in the Republic of Komi in the Russian Federation. In 2002 the company sold its oil service business a move that cut its overall workforce by some 20000 and resulted in savings of $500 million annually.

With an appetite for expansion the company upped its production with refinery acquisitions and invested heavily in new oil patches such as the Caspian Sea. In 2005 LUKOIL acquired Finland-based Oy Teboil AB and Suomen Petrooli Oy affiliated refined oil products companies for an undisclosed amount. LUKOIL also acquired Nelson Resources which had oil and gas interests in Western Kazakhstan for about $2 billion.

The next year the company acquired Marathon Oil's assets in Khanty-Mansiysk Autonomous Region –Yugra of Western Siberia –for $787 million. LUKOIL also acquired 376 European gas stations from ConocoPhillips in 2006.

In 2007 LUKOIL signed a strategic exploration and production agreement with Qatar Petroleum.

In 2008 the company diversified its operations further creating a power generation segment which encompasses its own generators at well sites and a number of generating units in Bulgaria Romania and Ukraine.

In 2008 it began to re-engage in Iraq where it had held oil concessions prior to the US-led invasion in 2003. It also acquired a retail network in Turkey in 2008 for $500 million.

EXECUTIVES

First VP Economics and Finance, Sergei P. Kukura, age 60
First EVP Exploration and Production, Ravil U. Maganov, age 59
President; Chairman of the Management Board; Director, Vagit Y. Alekperov, age 62
VP General Affairs Corporate Security and Communications, Anatoly A. Barkov, age 64
VP Strategic Development, Leonid A. Fedun, age 56
SVP Finance, Alexander K. Matytsyn, age 52
First VP Refining Marketing and Distribution, Vladimir I. Nekrasov, age 56
Chairman, Valery Grayfer, age 84
Vice-President Chief Accountant, Lyubov Khoba, age 56
VP HR Corporate Structure Development, Anatoly Moskalenko, age 53
Secretary and Head of the Board's Office, Evgueni Havkin, age 48
VP Technologies Oil and Gas Fields Development, Vladimir Mulyak, age 57
VP Sales and Supplies, Valery Subbotin, age 38
SVP Oil and Gas Production, Azat Shamsuarov, age 50
Vice-President OAO ?LUKOIL? Chief of Staff, Evgeny Khavkin
Head of Business Development, Graham Marshall
VP Petroleum Products Sales Coordination, Vadim Vorobyev
Vice-President General Counsel, Ivan Maslyaev
First EVP Exploration and Production and Director, Ravil U. Maganov, age 58
President and Director, Vagit Y. Alekperov, age 62
Director, Alexander Shokhin, age 61
Director, Sergei Mikhailov, age 55
Director, Donald E. (Don) Wallette Jr., age 53
Director, Herman Gref, age 49
Director, Igor Belikov, age 57
Director, Igor Ivanov, age 68
Director, Victor Blazheev, age 52
Director, Mark Mobius
Auditors: ZAOKPMG

LOCATIONS

HQ: Oil Co Lukoil
11 Sretensky Boulevard, Moscow 101000
Phone: (7) 495 627 4444 **Fax:** (7) 495 625 7016
Web: www.lukoil.com

2012 Sales

	$ mil.	% of total
Russia	64,725	36
Other countries	114,001	64
Adjustments	(39555)	-
Total	**139,171**	**100**

PRODUCTS/OPERATIONS

2012 Sales

	$ mil.	% of total
Refined products	103,407	95
Crude oil 27	670	3
Gas & gas products	3,477	2
Petrochemicals	1,410	-
Sales of energy & related services	1,394	-
Other	1,813	-
Total	**139,171**	**100**

COMPETITORS

Ashland Inc.
BP
Exxon Mobil
Gazprom Neft
Imperial Oil
Norsk Hydro ASA
Occidental Petroleum
PEMEX
PETROBRAS
Petroleos de Venezuela
Rosneft
Royal Dutch Shell
Surgutneftegas
TOTAL
Tatneft

HISTORICAL FINANCIALS

Company Type: Public

Income Statement FYE: December 31

	REVENUE ($ mil.)	NET INCOME ($ mil.)	NET PROFIT MARGIN	EMPLOYEES
12/12	139,171	11,004	7.9%	0
12/11	133,650	10,357	7.7%	0
12/10	104,956	9,006	8.6%	0
12/09	81,083	7,011	8.6%	0
12/08	107,680	9,144	8.5%	0
Annual Growth	6.6%	4.7%	—	—

2012 Year-End Financials

Debt ratio: 6.6%
Return on equity: 15.5%
Cash ($ mil.): 2,914
Current ratio: 1.95
Long-term debt ($ mil.): 5,963
No. of shares (mil.): 754
Dividends
Yield: 4.5%
Payout: 21.5%
Market value ($ mil.): 50,953

	STOCK PRICE ($) FY Close	P/E High	P/E Low	PER SHARE ($) Earnings	Dividends	Book Value
12/12	67.50	5	4	14.17	3.05	96.98
12/11	53.20	6	4	13.04	1.71	87.34
12/10	57.22	6	4	10.94	1.39	75.76
12/09	56.40	8	4	8.28	1.38	66.13
12/08	33.10	10	2	10.88	1.31	59.45
Annual Growth	19.5%	—	—	6.8%	23.5%	13.0%

Old Mutual Plc

The name belies its demutualized status: Financial services group Old Mutual provides banking insurance and asset management services in about 30 nations in southern Africa Europe Asia and the

Americas. Founded in 1845 Old Mutual owns a majority stake of South Africa's Nedbank Group which provides commercial banking finance investment banking and other services. It also owns Old Mutual (US) Holdings also known as Old Mutual Asset Management (US) or OMAM (US). Skandia Insurance offers insurance products and mutual funds primarily in the UK and Sweden. Old Mutual has some #262 billion (some $357 billion) in funds under management.

Geographic Reach

London-based Old Mutual generated more than 40% of its fiscal 2012 revenue from emerging markets. This includes business in Africa operations in Colombia and Mexico and joint ventures in India and China.

Operations

Old Mutual operates through several business lines: long-term savings and investments US asset management banking and short-term insurance. Long-term savings and investments accounted for 70% of the company's fiscal 2012 revenue.

Old Mutual's Asset Management arm offers clients access to more than 115 investment strategies through its affiliated investment firms.

Sales and Marketing

The financial firm boasts more than 14 million customers worldwide. Clients buy products directly from Old Mutual or indirectly through an intermediary such as an independent financial advisor. Old Mutual reaches out to customers through a combined strategy of tied agents and independent financial advisors as well as via the Internet and call center functionality.

Strategy

Old Mutual aims to expand in South Africa Africa and other selected emerging markets. In 2013 the firm purchased a majority stake in Ghana-based Provident Life Assurance Company Limited and entered a strategic partnership with Faulu Kenya DTM LTD by buying a controlling stake in its emerging marketing business. To boot Old Mutual acquired Oceanic Life the life assurance operations of the former Oceanic Bank of Nigeria to extend its reach into the Nigerian market. Focused on strengthening its distribution capabilities in Latin America Old Mutual in 2012 acquired AIVA Business Platforms (AVIA) one of the largest financial groups globally.

It's also working to develop and grow its Old Mutual Wealth and US Asset Management businesses even including a partial IPO of its US Asset Management unit when economic conditions are favorable. For its Nedbank business Old Mutual is focused on boosting non-interest revenue growing the retail business via client-centered strategies and effective risk management and shifting the focus of its portfolio on profit-enhancing products and services.

Stung in the US Old Mutual has been restructuring its operations to recover from the financial crisis. To this end it exited several underperforming markets and sold noncore businesses. The group sold its US life insurance operations to Harbinger Group for $350 million in 2011. Old Mutual also sold its Skandia's business in the Nordic region and rebranded its remaining Skandia units Old Mutual Wealth to unify its brand. By divesting certain businesses Old Mutual can concentrate on its core long-term savings and investments operations. Proceeds from the sales are being used to reduce debt.

Not content with just making divestitures Old Mutual remains as aggressive as practical in target areas such as developing new investment products for distribution in emerging markets. The company has also seen marked improvements in returns due to an upswing in the economy. By streamlining its expansive structure while investing in growth Old Mutual is positioning itself to take advantage of the expected economic recovery.

HISTORY

Old Mutual was founded in 1845 as the Mutual Life Assurance Society of the Cape of Good Hope to sell life insurance in the Cape Colony. When South Africa gained self-governance from the UK in 1910 Old Mutual chairman John Merriman became the colony's first premier. In 1927 the company made its first international expansion into Zimbabwe (then called Rhodesia).

Life insurance remained the firm's sole line of business until 1948 when it acquired a controlling stake in what would become Mutual & Federal a general insurer. To better administer its mutual fund and trust businesses the firm formed the South African Mutual Unit Trust Company in 1966.

Old Mutual diversified in 1986 buying a controlling stake in the Nedcor banking group. Also that year the firm made its first major acquisition outside Africa buying UK life insurer Providence Capitol. In 1995 the firm expanded into Hong Kong and the US where it opened Old Mutual Investment Advisers in Boston. Seeking a way into the UK financial services market the company acquired asset managers Capel-Cure Myers and Albert E Sharp in 1997 and 1998 respectively merging them into Capel-Cure Sharp.

The firm further globalized its asset management operations in 1999 establishing an alliance with Japanese insurer Sumitomo Life to cross-market trust and investment services. Also that year its Nedcor banking subsidiary launched a hostile takeover bid for Standard Bank Investment Corporation (of which Old Mutual already owned 20%); the merger would have created South Africa's largest bank but government regulators nixed the deal.

Old Mutual demutualized in 1999 listing on both the London and Johannesburg stock exchanges. In 2000 the company sold its UK insurance operations to XL Mid Ocean Reinsurance and Century Group then acquired UK brokerage Gerrard Group and started an infrastructure investment joint venture with Australia's Macquarie Bank. Old Mutual also bought US-based United Asset Management (selling its Murray Johnstone Holdings subsidiary to Aberdeen Asset Management). Meanwhile Nedcor (now Nedbank) bought 50.1% of Imperial Bank a South African bank with a large vehicle finance business.

While the firm's Old Mutual (US) operations proved successful other areas of growth were less salutary. Three years after forming Gerrard Limited in 2000 as part of a bid to boost the UK business the asset manager was sold to Barclays.

Old Mutual gained control of insurer and mutual fund manager Skandia Insurance in 2006 through a nearly #4 billion ($7 billion) hostile takeover bid. The acquisition brought more life insurance asset management and banking to Old Mutual and gave it deeper access into Asia Europe Latin America and the UK.

Satisfied with the results of its asset management operations in the US the company began expanding its asset management services in South Africa and the UK. In a shift from operating its businesses regionally the company took to grouping them by their primary operations.

EXECUTIVES

Group Company Secretary, Martin C. Murray
Group Finance Director, Philip Broadley, age 53, $796,015 total compensation
President Asia Pacific, Steffen Gilbert, age 51
CEO Nedbank Group, Michael W. T. (Mike) Brown, age 46
Regional Director Old Mutual Europe, Robert M. (Bob) Head, age 54
Interim CEO and COO Old Mutual Asset Management, Linda T. Gibson
CEO Long-Term Savings; Chairman Old Mutual South Africa, Paul Hanratty, age 52
Managing Director Mutual & Federal, Keith N. Kennedy
CEO Skandia Nordic, Bertil Hult, age 57
CEO South Africa, Kuseni Dlamini, age 45
CEO US Life Business, Christopher (Chris) Chapman
CEO Skandia UK, Peter Mann
Director Group Risk and Actuarial, Andrew Birrell, age 43
Head Strategy Development, Donald I. (Don) Hope, age 56
Head Strategic Implementation, Paul Maddox, age 52
Group Human Resources Director, Don Schneider, age 56
Manager Corporate Communications, Julie Hutchins
Head Corporate Responsibility, Helen Wilson
Group Investor Relations Manager, Aleida White
Director External Communications, Patrick Bowes
Managing Director Customer Solutions South Africa, Mike Harper, age 58
Managing Director Retail (Mass Market) South Africa, Marshall Rapiya, age 61
Director Corporate Affairs Media and Marketing South Africa, Crispin Sonn
Managing Director African Operations South Africa, Johannes Gawaxab, age 57
Group Finance Director South Africa, Diane Radley
Managing Director Old Mutual Service Technology and Administration South Africa, Rose Keanly
Managing Director Fairbairn Private Bank, Greg J. Horton
Executive General Manager Human Resources Mutual & Federal, Basetsana Magano
CEO Old Mutual Bermuda, Andrew Darfoor
CEO Namibia, Gregg MacIntyre
Group CEO Zimbabwe, Luke Ngwerume
CEO Skandia Retail Europe, Jonas Jonsson
Chief Executive and Chief Investment Officer Old Mutual Asset Management UK, Peter Baxter
Director Investor Relations, Deward Serfontein
Media Contact Finsbury, Don Hunter
Treasurer, James Simpson
Chief Executive Officer, Ralph Mupita
Group Strategy Director, Ian Gladman
Chairman of the Board, Patrick OSullivan
President and Chief Executive Officer - US Asset Management, Peter Bain
Chief Risk Officer, Sue Kean
Director, Richard A. Pym, age 64
Chief Executive and Director, Julian V. F. Roberts, age 54
Director, Nigel D. T. Andrews, age 66
Director, Alan R. Gillespie, age 62
Director, Russell P. Edey, age 71
Director, Reuel Khoza, age 63
Director, Michael (Mike) Arnold, age 65
Director, Lars Otterbeck, age 71
Director, Bongani Nqwababa, age 47
Independent Non-Executive Director, Eva Castillo
Independent Non-Executive Director, Nonkululeko Nyembezi-Heita
Independent Non-Executive Director, Roger Marshall
Auditors: KPMGAuditPlc

LOCATIONS

HQ: Old Mutual Plc
5th Floor, Millennium Bridge House, 2 Lambeth Hill, London EC4V 4GG
Phone:
Web: www.oldmutual.com

Selected Subsidiaries

Old Mutual (South Africa) Ltd
Old Mutual Africa Holdings (Pty) Ltd
Old Mutual Life Assurance Company (South Africa) Ltd
Old Mutual Investment Group (South Africa) (Pty) Ltd
Nedbank Group Ltd
Nedbank Ltd
Mutual & Federal Insurance Company Ltd
Old Mutual Life Assurance Company (Namibia) Ltd
Old Mutual (US) Holdings Inc
Old Mutual (Bermuda) Ltd
Acadian Asset Management LLC
Barrow Hanley Mewhinney & Strauss LLC
Rogge Global Partners plc
OM Group (UK) Ltd
Old Mutual Wealth Management Limited

PRODUCTS/OPERATIONS

2012 Revenue

	% of total
Long-term savings	
Emerging	43
Old mutual	27
NedBank	25
M&F	3
US Asset	2
Total	**100**

COMPETITORS

Absa
Alliance Trust
Allianz
Aviva
Fidelity Worldwide Investment
FirstRand
Investec
PineBridge Investments
Russell
Sanlam
Standard Bank Group

HISTORICAL FINANCIALS

Company Type: Public

Income Statement

FYE: December 31

	ASSETS ($ mil.)	NET INCOME ($ mil.)	INCOME AS % OF ASSETS	EMPLOYEES
12/12	231,298	1,890	0.8%	54,368
12/11	250,861	1,030	0.4%	57,430
12/10	300,516	(437)	—	55,730
12/09	265,297	(550)	—	53,706
12/08	211,814	642	0.3%	56,546
Annual Growth	2.2%	31.0%	—	(1.0%)

2012 Year-End Financials

Return on assets: 0.7%
Return on equity: 14.3%
Long-term debt ($ mil.): —
No. of shares (mil.): —
Sales ($ mil): 31,942
Dividends
Yield: 0.0%
Payout: 127.4%
Market value ($ mil.): —

	STOCK PRICE ($) FY Close	P/E High/Low	PER SHARE ($) Earnings	Dividends	Book Value
12/12	23.00	244141	0.37	0.47	2.58
12/11	16.88	372221	0.18	0.00	2.26
12/10	15.25	— —	(0.09)	0.00	2.44
12/09	14.25	— —	(0.13)	0.00	2.48
12/08	6.25	918122	0.12	0.00	2.04
Annual Growth	38.5%	— —	33.3%	—	6.0%

OMV AG (Austria)

Oil and chemicals group OMV is Austria's largest industrial company. A leading oil and gas company in Central and Eastern Europe it explores for natural gas and crude oil; refines crude oil; and imports transports and stores gas. In 2012 OMV reported proved reserves of 1.2 billion barrels of oil equivalent; it produced about 303000 barrels of oil equivalent per day and sold 13 billion cu. ft. of gas. The bulk of OMV's sales come from refining and marketing with the company operating five refineries and more than 4500 gas stations in 13 countries.

Operations

The company operates in three major segments. OMV Exploration and Production's core countries in Romania and Austria OMV is focusing on reducing the natural decline and on enhancing the recovery rates from mature fields. It is looking to find new growth areas within the Caspian Middle East and Africa regions..

OMV Gas and Power ensures the supply of natural gas to its customers via a 2000 km gas pipeline in Austria. Its natural gas network serving about 90% of Austria's natural gas demand draws gas supplies from Russia Norway and Germany as well as from domestic reserves. Austria's gas market now dominated by OMV is slated for full competition and OMV is among state-controlled companies set for full privatization.

OMV Refining and Marketing serves about 1.5 million people a day through retail gas stations in 13 countries and is the market leader in Central and South Eastern Europe.

A fourth segment OMV Solutions is the integrated shared service center for all of the OMV Group companies. Its portfolio spans IT financial services and human resources administration.

Financial Performance

OMV's revenue increased by 28% in 2012 thanks to higher oil prices increased demand and the sale of higher volumes of oil and petroleum products.

However net income decreased by more than 11% in 2012 (before the restatement of 2011 results).

Strategy

Exploration and production is the growth driver of OMV and in 2013 the company announced plans to direct more than two-thirds of future investments towards exploration and production of oil and gas. It also plans to grow its integrated natural gas assets and restructure its downstream business by selling non-core refining and marketing assets.

In 2012 the company sold its gas station subsidiary in Croatia. That year it boosted it E&P assets entering Abu Dhabi and acquiring natural gas assets in Norway.

In a further push to grow in the Middle East in 2011 the company acquired two Tunisia-based exploration and production units from Pioneer Natural Resources for $866 million. It also boosted its footprint in Pakistan acquiring Petronas Carigali (Pakistan) Ltd. in 2011.

The Refining and Marketing portfolio will be adjusted in response to falling demand for crude oil products in Europe. The restructuring of the R&M portfolio will prioritize highquality products the integration with petrochemicals and improved performance.

The aquisition of full control (in 2010) of Petrol Ofisi Turkey's leading filling station and retail business with the only nationwide filling station network in the country (approximately 2300 stations) built a strategic bridge in the growth market of Turkey.

Ownership

OMV's largest shareholders are Austrian state holding company OIAG (32%) and the International Petroleum Investment Company (IPIC) of Abu Dhabi (20%).

HISTORY

Oil exploration began in Austria in the 1920s largely as joint ventures with foreign firms such as Shell and Socony-Vacuum. Full-scale production did not get underway until 1938 when the Anschluss (the absorption of Austria by Germany) paved the way for Germany to exploit Austria's natural resources to fuel its growing war machine. In the division of spoils following WWII Russia gained control of Austria's oil reserves.

The Russian-administered oil assets were transferred to the new Austrian government in 1955 which authorized the company Osterreichische Mineralolverwaltung (OMG) in 1956 to control state oil assets. OMG state-controlled by the Austrian Mineral Oil Administration set about building a major refinery in 1960 and acquiring marketing companies Martha and OROP in 1965.

In 1968 OMG became the first Western company to sign a natural gas supply contract with Russia. In 1974 the company commissioned the Trans-Austria Gas Pipeline which enabled the supply of natural gas to Italy. That year OMG changed its name to OMV Aktiengesellschaft (OMV became OMV in 1995 for international markets).

During the 1970s OMV expanded its crude supply arrangements tapping supplies from Iran Iraq Libya and other Middle Eastern countries. It moved into oil and gas exploration in the mid-1980s forming OMV Libya (acquiring 25% of Occidental's Libyan production) and OMV UK.

With Austria moving toward increasing privatization in 1987 about 15% of OMV's shares were sold to the public. The government sold another 10% two years later. In 1989 OMV acquired PCD Polymere. With the aim of merging state-owned oil and chemical activities OMV acquired Chemie Linz in 1990. The company also opened its first OMV-branded service station that year. In 1994 OMV reorganized itself as an integrated oil and gas group based in Central Europe with international exploration and production activities and with other operations in the chemical and petrochemical sectors.

In 1995 OMV acquired TOTAL-AUSTRIA expanding its service stations by 59. The company introduced OMV lubricants to the Greek market in 1996. It also expanded its OMV service station network in Hungary to 66 stations after acquiring 31 Q8 (Kuwait) sites. In 1997 the Stroh Company's retail network in Austria was merged into OMV.

Expanding its retail network even farther OMV acquired BP's retail network in the Czech Republic Slovakia and Hungary in 1998. It also sold its stake in Chemie Linz and acquired a 25% stake in major European polyolefin producer Borealis which in turn acquired PCD Polymere. In 1999 the company pushed its retail network into Bulgaria and Romania. That year OMV also acquired Australian company Cultus Petroleum.

OMV and Shell agreed to develop North Sea fields together in 2000. That year OMV also formed a joint venture with Italy's Edison International to explore in Vietnam and acquired more than 9% of Hungarian rival MOL. It upped that stake to 10% in 2001.

In 2002 OMV opened its first gas station in Serbia and Montenegro. It also increased its German gas station count from 79 to 151 with the purchase of 32 units from Royal Dutch Shell and 40 stations from Martin GmbH & Co.

In 2003 the company acquired Preussag Energie's exploration and production assets for $320 million. That year the company moved into Bosnia-Herzegovina opening nine gas stations.

During 2004 the company bought up 51% of Romania's Petrom making it the top oil and gas producer in Central Europe. As part of the deal OMV chose to divest itself of its quarter-chunk of Rompetrol.

In 2006 Russian energy giant Gazprom signed long-term contracts for gas deliveries with OMV.

In a major consolidation move in 2006 OMV agreed to buy Austrian power firm Verbund for $17 billion but the move was rebuffed by government regulators. The next year the company announced plans to merge with Hungary's energy powerhouse MOL but those plans were called off as well due to European Commission regulatory concerns in 2008.

After plans to merge with Hungary's MOL went south OMV the next year sold its 21% stake in it to Russian oil company Surgutneftegas for E1.4 billion ($1.85 billion). Also in 2009 in keeping with its focus on retail markets in the Danube region southeastern Europe and the Black Sea region OMV sold subsidiary OMV Italia; San Marco Petroli acquired the network of about 100 gas stations in the northern Italian region of Triveneto.

OMV has been disposing of some of its heating oil operations. In 2008 it unloaded Bayern GmbH and it plans to sell its OMV Warme VertriebsgmbH by the end of 2010. At that point the sale of heating oil to private clients will be handled by partners but OMV will continue to service corporate customers.

Eyeing new areas of exploration that year OMV also acquired a 10% stake in Pearl Petroleum giving it access to gas-condensate fields in Iraq.

In 2010 the company boosted its share of Turkey-based oil products company Petrol Ofisi (renamed OMV Petrol Ofisi) from 42% to 96% by acquiring a 54% stake from Doan Holding for about $1.4 billion. The deal gave OMV access to not only Turkey but the Caspian region and the Middle East.

EXECUTIVES

Deputy Chairman Supervisory Board, Wolfgang C. G. Berndt, age 70
Deputy Chairman Executive Board, David C. Davies, age 59, $1,096,338 total compensation
Executive Board Member, Jaap Huijskes, age 49
Chairman Supervisory Board, Markus Beyrer, age 48
CEO, Doris Bures
Chairman of the Intergovernmental Panel on Climate Change, Rajendra Pachauri
Deputy Chairwoman of the Supervisory Board, Alyazia Kuwaiti
Deputy Chairman of the Supervisory Board, Khadem Qubaisi
Head of Investor Relations, Lacramiorara Diaconu
Member of the Executive Board, Manfred Leitner
Deputy Chairman Supervisory Board, Wolfgang C. G. Berndt, age 70
Director, Helmut Draxler, age 63
Director, Herbert Stepic, age 67
Member of the Supervisory Board, Wolfram Littich
Director, Herbert Werner, age 66
Director, Norbert Zimmermann, age 66
Director, Alyazia Ali Saleh Al Kuwaiti, age 37
Deputy Chairman Supervisory Board, Khadem A. Al Qubaisi, age 41
Member of the Supervisory Board, Elif Bilgi-Zapparoli
Member of the Supervisory Board; Employee Representative, Ferdinand Nemesch
Member of the Supervisory Board; Employee Representative, Franz Kaba
Member of the Supervisory Board; Employee Representative, Leopold Abraham
Member of the Supervisory Board; Employee Representative, Martin Rossmann
Member of the Supervisory Board; Employee Representative, Wolfgang Baumann

LOCATIONS

HQ: OMV AG (Austria)
Trabrennstrasse 6-8, Vienna 1020
Phone: (43) 1 40440 0 **Fax:** (43) 1 40440 27900
Web: www.omv.com

2012 Sales

	% of total
Europe	
Central & Europe	
Austria	37
Germany	16
Turkey	13
Romania	11
Other	15
Other	8
Total	**100**

PRODUCTS/OPERATIONS

2012 Sales

	% of total
Refining &	62
Gas &	25
Exploration &	12
Corporate &	1
Total	**100**

COMPETITORS

BP	MOL
Eni	PKN ORLEN
Exxon Mobil	Royal Dutch Shell
Hellenic Petroleum	Unipetrol

HISTORICAL FINANCIALS

Company Type: Public

Income Statement

FYE: December 31

	REVENUE ($ mil.)	NET INCOME ($ mil.)	NET PROFIT MARGIN	EMPLOYEES
12/12	56,213	1,796	3.2%	28,658
12/11	44,046	1,375	3.1%	29,800
12/10	31,215	1,232	3.9%	31,398
12/09	25,811	823	3.2%	34,676
12/08	35,710	1,921	5.4%	41,282
Annual Growth	12.0%	(1.7%)	—	(8.7%)

2012 Year-End Financials

Debt ratio: 20.6%	No. of shares (mil.): 326
Return on equity: 11.8%	Dividends
Cash ($ mil.): 1,617	Yield: 2.8%
Current ratio: 1.30	Payout: 32.6%
Long-term debt ($ mil.): 5,816	Market value ($ mil.): 11,971

	STOCK PRICE ($) FY Close	P/E High	P/E Low	PER SHARE ($) Earnings	Dividends	Book Value
12/12	36.70	17	10	5.50	1.05	48.09
12/11	30.38	26	15	4.36	1.95	43.52
12/10	41.80	30	16	4.11	1.51	40.67
12/09	44.10	51	23	2.75	2.00	39.05
12/08	26.63	43	9	6.43	1.48	34.63
Annual Growth	8.3%	—	—	(3.9%)	(8.1%)	8.6%

Orange

For many in Europe and elsewhere the telecom landscape has an Orange glow. Formerly France Telecom Orange provides fixed-line and mobile voice and data services to consumers and commercial clients around the world. The company serves some 230 million customers in more than 30 countries. It is a leading European wireless operator and broadband service provider with more than 170 million mobile customers and some 15 million broadband subscribers. Orange's services for corporate clients are provided by its Orange Business Services unit which offers a wide range of managed business networking and data services. The company had been coalescing around its Orange brand since 2006 culminating in the mid-2013 name change.

Geographic Reach

Orange divides up its primary business –mobile and fixed-line telephony along with Internet access services –by region with France comprising nearly half of total operations. Spain and Portugal are its other two major regions with these services. The rest of the world makes up nearly a fifth of total revenues. The remaining business about 15% of sales is largely the company's enterprise services operations.

Financial Performance

The company increased its number of customers by 8% in 2011 but intense pricing competition kept revenues essentially flat dipping less than 1% to ?45.3 billion ($58.6 billion). Africa and the Middle East continue to be the company's key growth region and it picked up 16 million subscribers there in the year. Orange's enterprise services segment saw double digit growth in emerging countries. Net income was down a steeper 22% mainly because the previous year enjoyed a tax benefit from discontinued operations.

Strategy

Orange has become more active partners with Deutsche Telekom (DT) in recent years. In 2010 the companies formed Everything Everywhere a 50/50 joint venture that combined the UK mobile and broadband Internet businesses of both. The joint venture competes with major players such as BT Group Virgin Media TalkTalk and BSkyB all of which have considerably more market share in the region. In 2011 Orange and DT formed another equally-owned joint venture called Buyin a procurement operation based in Belgium that will focus on handsets and network equipment.

The company's near-term strategy includes efforts to simplify its products and services by focusing on customer-facing improvements and marketing. It also continues to look beyond France for new business including doubling revenues in Africa and the Middle East by 2015 and expanding in Europe. That expansion will not only benefit Orange's core business but also its enterprise services success.

Mergers and Acquisitions

In 2011 it helped that plan along when it bought Congo Chine Telecom (CCT) from ZTE and the government of Congo for $17 million. Orange sees Congo as an underpenetrated market with considerable growth potential and will make a multi-installment capital investment in CCT of $185 million.The company in 2010 paid $840 million for a 40% stake in Moroccan network operator Meditel in a move to push further into emerging markets. The deal put the company in direct competition in that country with fellow French rival Vivendi which owns a controlling stake in former Moroccan telecom monopoly Maroc Telecom.

Also that year Orange bought submarine communications cable laying and maintenance specialist Elettra from Telecom Italia to expand its capacity to install and service undersea networks. The company combined the operations of Elettra including its two cable ships with its existing cable laying subsidiary.

In 2012 it expanded in Egypt by completing the purchase of Orascom Telecom's wireless services provider Mobinil Egypt's biggest wireless carrier. Also that year to focus on higher growth areas in Europe Orange sold Orange Switzerland for ?1.6 billion ($2.1 billion) to investment firm Apax Partners.

Ownership

The French government owns more than one-quarter of Orange.

HISTORY

Shortly before he abdicated King Louis Philippe laid the groundwork for France's state-owned telegraphic service. Established in 1851 the operation became part of the French Post Office in the 1870s about the time Alexander Graham Bell invented the telephone. The French government licensed three private companies to provide telegraph service and during the 1880s they merged into the Societe Generale de Telephones (SGT). In 1883 the country's first exchange was initiated in Rheims. Four years later an international circuit was installed connecting Paris and Brussels. The government nationalized SGT in 1889.

By the turn of the century France had more than 60000 phone lines and in 1924 a standardized telephone was introduced. Long-distance service improved with underground cabling and phone exchanges in Paris and other leading cities became automated during the 1930s.

WWII proved a major setback to the French government's telephone operations Direction Generale des Telecommunications (DGT) because a large part of its equipment was destroyed or damaged. For the next two decades France lagged behind other nations in telephony infrastructure development. An exception to this technological stagnation was Centre National d'Etudes des Telecommunications (CNET) the research laboratory formed in 1944 that eventually became France Telecom's research arm.

In 1962 DGT was a key player in the first intercontinental television broadcast between the US and France via a Telstar satellite. The company began to catch up with its peers when it developed a digital phone system in the mid-1970s. In 1974 CNET was instrumental in the launch of France's first experimental communications satellite. In another technological advance DGT began replacing its paper directories with the innovative Minitel online terminals in 1980.

The French government created France Telecom in 1988. In 1993 France Telecom and Deutsche Telekom (DT) teamed up to form the Global One international telecommunications venture and Sprint joined the next year. Global One was formally launched in 1996. Also that year France Telecom began providing Internet access though Minitel still reigned as the country's top online service.

In 1997 the government sold about 20% of France Telecom to the public. With Europe's state telephone monopolies ending in 1998 France Telecom reorganized and brought prices in line with those of its competitors.

France Telecom paid $4.3 billion to DT and Sprint in 2000 to take full ownership of Global One. Later that year it snatched up UK mobile phone operator Orange in a $37.5 billion cash and stock deal after Vodafone was forced to divest the company before merging with Mannesmann. France Telecom also invested $4.5 billion in UK cable operator NTL and sold its stake in Mexican telecom giant Telmex.

In 2001 the company sold its 49.9% stake in Noos France's #1 cable-TV operator. It sold its nearly 11% stake in Greek mobile carrier Vodafone-Panafon to Vodafone Group for ?311 million the following year.

France Telecom took full ownership of Orange and Wanadoo a European directory publisher and ISP in 2004. In 2006 the company sold its 54% stake in directories business PagesJaunes Groupe to Kohlberg Kravis Roberts (now KKR) in a deal valued at about $4.2 billion. Also that year it acquired the remaining shares that it did not already own of Dutch-based carrier Equant; it subsequently changed the name to Orange Business Services.

The company in 2007 sold the mobile phone unit of France Telecom Espa?a to Deutsche Telekom in return for that company's Ya.com Internet unit. It also acquired a controlling stake in security network specialist Silicomp.

EXECUTIVES

SEVP Communication and Brand, Xavier Couture, age 62
EVP Group Human Resources, Bruno Mettling, age 55
Deputy CEO Quality Corporate Social Responsibility, Jean-Philippe Vanot, age 61
SEVP Marketing and Innovation, Jean-Paul Cottet, age 58
EVP Group General Secretary and France Carriers Division, Pierre Louette, age 50
EVP Africa the Middle-East and Asia, Marc Rennard, age 56
SEVP Enterprise Communication Services, Vivek Badrinath, age 42
SEVP Events Cultural and Institutional Partnerships and Philanthropy, Christine Albanel, age 57
SEVP Networks and Carriers and Research and Development, Thierry Bonhomme, age 56
SEVP Strategy and Development, Elie Girard, age 33
SEVP Europe, Benoit Scheen, age 45
Executive Vice President - Group Strategy & Development; Member of the Executive Committee, Elie Girard
Executive Vice President Marketing and Innovation; Member of the Executive Committee, Jean Cottet
Executive Vice President - Operations in Europe (excluding France); Member of the Executive Committee, Benoit Scheen
Deputy Chief Executive Officer - Orange France; Member of the Executive Committee, Delphine Delphine Ernotte Cunci Cunci
Director, Charles-Henri Filippi, age 60
Director, Jose-Luis Duran, age 47
Director, Marcel Roulet, age 79
Director, Gilles Michel, age 56
Director, Henri Martre, age 84
Director, Bernard Dufau, age 71
Director, Jean Simonin, age 67
Director, Stephane Tierce, age 43
Director, Claudie Haignere, age 54
Director, Bruno Bezard, age 48
Director, Pascal Faure, age 50
Director, Caroline Angeli, age 55
Director, Ghislaine Coinaud, age 56
Director, Daniel Guillot, age 55
Director, Marc Maouche, age 48
Director, Patrick Roussel
Director, Thierry Franchi
Independent Director, Claudie Haignere
Independent Director, Jean Severino
Independent Director, Jose Duran
Independent Director, Muriel Penicaud
Auditors: Deloitte&Associes

LOCATIONS

HQ: Orange
78 rue Olivier de Serres, Paris 75015
Phone: (33) 1 44 44 21 05
Web: www.orange.com

PRODUCTS/OPERATIONS

2011 Sales

	% of total
Personal and communicat	
France	47
Spain	9
Poland	8
Enterprise	15
International operators and shared	2
Rest of the	19
Total	**100**

2011 Mobile Customers

	$ mil.	% of total
France	27	16
Poland	14	9
UK	13	8
Spain	12	8
Rest of the world	99	60
Total	**167**	**100**

2011 Broadband Customers

	$ mil.	% of total
France	9	67
Poland	2	16
Spain	1	9
UK	0	2
Rest of the world	0	6
Total	**14**	**100**

Selected Operations

Audience and advertising (Internet advertising business)
Content (partnerships with content providers and development of related technology platforms)
Enterprise communication services (communication services to companies)
Health (services to the health care industry)
Home communication services (residential communication services especially fixed-line broadband)
Personal communication services (communication services for individuals using mobile devices)

COMPETITORS

AT&T
BSkyB
BT
Belgacom
Bouygues
COLT Group
Cable & Wireless
Deutsche Telekom
Equinix Group
HP Enterprise Services
Hutchison Whampoa
IBM Global Services
Jazztel
KPN
Maroc Telecom
SFR
TalkTalk
Tele2
Telecom Italia
Telefonica
Telefonica Europe
Tiscali
Unisys
Virgin Mobile
Vivendi
Vodafone

HISTORICAL FINANCIALS

Company Type: Public

Income Statement FYE: December 31

	REVENUE ($ mil.)	NET INCOME ($ mil.)	NET PROFIT MARGIN	EMPLOYEES
12/12	57,009	1,080	1.9%	170,531
12/11	58,438	5,038	8.6%	171,949
12/10	60,881	6,531	10.7%	168,694
12/09	66,218	4,317	6.5%	167,148
12/08	74,486	5,688	7.6%	182,793
Annual Growth	(6.5%)	(34.0%)	—	(1.7%)

2012 Year-End Financials

Debt ratio: —
Return on equity: 3.1%
Cash ($ mil.): 10,967
Current ratio: 0.65
Long-term debt ($ mil.): —
No. of shares (mil.): —
Dividends
Yield: 0.1%
Payout: 704.7%
Market value ($ mil.): —

	STOCK PRICE ($) FY Close	P/E High/Low		PER SHARE ($) Earnings	Dividends	Book Value
12/12	11.05	90	56	0.41	2.88	12.19
12/11	15.66	31	17	1.89	3.66	13.54
12/10	21.08	27	15	2.44	2.87	14.70
12/09	25.24	52	34	1.63	4.00	14.16
12/08	28.07	51	25	2.15	6.01	14.81
Annual Growth	(20.8%)	—	—	(34.0%)	(16.8%)	(4.7%)

Orix Corp. (Japan)

An international financing leviathan ORIX is one of Japan's largest public financial services firms. The company finances leases of everything from computers and measuring equipment to aircraft and ships; it rents out some 22000 different items and is adding more. ORIX also engages in consumer and corporate finance investment banking brokerage car rental and property development and management services in Japan and more than 20 other countries. Its retail offerings include banking life insurance credit cards and trust services. ORIX even has its own professional baseball team the Kobe-based ORIX Buffaloes.

The company operates around 1200 offices in Japan (where it earns more than 80% of its revenues) and 260 more overseas. ORIX USA acts as the holding company for the firm's operations in the US which ORIX is targeting for growth. Among its holdings are Los Angeles-based investment bank Houlihan Lokey which specializes in middle-market mergers and acquisitions.

ORIX is also looking to build its fee-based business in Japan and abroad. Asia and China in particular are additional areas of focus for the company. It also plans to continue to expand its already diverse array of offerings by moving into energy and environmental products. ORIX has been able to remain profitable during the global credit crunch but the stagnant economy as well the company's internal deleveraging have been a drag on its bottom line.

ORIX invested some Y10 billion ($111 million) into regional bank Tokyo Star in 2010. It will also work to help the struggling bank restabilize itself for which it should receive advisory commissions as well as dividend returns. If Tokyo Star successfully turns around ORIX may consider similar transactions in the future.

The company in 2009 sold a 51% stake in ORIX Credit Corporation to Sumitomo Mitsui Financial Group. The following year ORIX sold its Orix Securities brokerage unit to online brokerage Monex Group in a stock swap. Through the deal ORIX became Monex's largest shareholder with a nearly 25% stake.

EXECUTIVES

President ORIX Baseball Club, Hiroaki Nishina, age 69
Chairman and CEO, Yoshihiko Miyauchi, age 78
Deputy President and CIO, Tamio Umaki, age 65
Corporate EVP, Shintaro Agata, age 63
Corporate EVP, Yuki Oshima, age 66
Deputy President and CFO, Haruyuki Urata, age 59
EVP; President ORIX Real Estate, Yoshiyuki Yamaya, age 57
SVP; President ORIX Auto, Katsunobu Kamei
EVP; President NS Lease, Katsutoshi Kadowaki
President and COO, Mikoto Inoue, age 61
Corporate EVP, Kazuo Kojima
SVP; President ORIX Credit, Masatoshi Kemmochi
Vice Chairman; Chairman ORIX Real Estate Corporation, Hiroaki Nishina, age 68
Director, Yoshinori Yokoyama, age 70
Director, Takeshi Niinami
Director, Hirotaka Takeuchi, age 66
Deputy President CFO and Director, Haruyuki Urata, age 58
President COO and Director, Makoto Inoue, age 60
Director, Takeshi Sasaki, age 70
Director, Eiko Tsujiyama
Director, Robert Feldman
Auditors: KPMGAZSA&Co.

LOCATIONS

HQ: Orix Corp. (Japan)
Mita NN Building, 4-1-23 Shiba, Minato-ku, Tokyo 108-0014
Phone: (81) 3 5419 5042 **Fax:** (81) 3 5419 5901
Web: www.orix.co.jp

2011 Sales

	% of total
Japan	85
Asia Europe &	9
Americas	6
Total	**100**

PRODUCTS/OPERATIONS

2011 Sales

	% of total
Operating	27
Interest on loans &	19
Life insurance premiums & related	11
Real estate	7
Direct financing	6
Gain on sales of real estate under operating	2
Other	28
Total	**100**

Selected Subsidiaries and Segments

ORIX Aircraft (aircraft leasing)
ORIX Asset Management & Loan Services Corporation (commercial mortgage servicing)
ORIX Auto (car rental and leasing)
ORIX Baseball Club (professional baseball team)
ORIX Life Insurance
ORIX Real Estate (real estate development and investment)
ORIX Real Estate Investment Advisors (asset management)
ORIX Rentec (rental operations)
ORIX Trust and Banking
ORIX USA
SUN Leasing Corporation (medical equipment leasing)

COMPETITORS

CIT Group
GE Capital
ILFC
Mitsubishi UFJ Financial Group
Mizuho Financial
Rentokil Initial
Sumitomo

HISTORICAL FINANCIALS

Company Type: Public

Income Statement

FYE: March 31

	ASSETS ($ mil.)	NET INCOME ($ mil.)	INCOME AS % OF ASSETS	EMPLOYEES
03/13	89,696	1,189	1.3%	19,043
03/12	101,851	1,050	1.0%	17,488
03/11	103,634	812	0.8%	17,578
03/10	82,860	404	0.5%	17,725
03/09	84,993	222	0.3%	18,920
Annual Growth	1.4%	52.0%	—	0.2%

2013 Year-End Financials

Return on assets: 1.3%
Return on equity: 7.3%
Long-term debt ($ mil.): —
No. of shares (mil.): 1,221
Sales ($ mil): 11,325
Dividends
Yield: 0.0%
Payout: 0.0%
Market value ($ mil.): 77,659

	STOCK PRICE ($) FY Close	P/E High/Low		PER SHARE ($) Earnings	Dividends	Book Value
03/13	63.58	0	0	0.93	0.00	14.30
03/12	48.25	0	0	0.82	0.00	15.83
03/11	46.57	0	0	0.64	0.40	14.82
03/10	44.11	0	0	0.34	0.36	(0.00)
03/09	16.47	0	0	0.24	0.26	13.26
Annual Growth	40.2%	—	—	40.6%	(86.9%)	1.9%

Otto Versand (GmbH & Co.) (Germany, Fed. Rep.)

Otto Group will sell you the goods and deliver them too. One of the world's leading multichannel retailers Otto sells merchandise in Germany and about 20 countries in Europe North America and Asia through more than 600 print catalogs the Internet and more than 350 stores worldwide. It sells products from apparel to appliances to sporting goods. Otto also owns a majority stake in the Crate & Barrel housewares chain. Otto's Hermes Logistik unit supports the group's own retail businesses and those of other clients. Overall Otto operates more than 120 companies including travel and financial services firms. The family of chairman Michael Otto owns the majority of the company.

Otto's core business is multichannel retail which accounts for around 85% of the group's total sales. The company operates more than 350 bricks-and-mortar stores and some 50 online shops and it boasts more than 1800 catalog titles. Already a giant in catalogs Otto has been actively expanding its e-commerce operations which accounted for more than 53% of sales in fiscal 2012 (ends February). Indeed e-commerce is the company's key growth engine. The company has seen increased traffic to group brands such as OTTO Bonprix Baur and Witt and the NaDom Group.

The company's services business which includes logistics and sourcing entities accounted for close to 10% of the group total sales. Sales increased throughout Germany and the UK. Through its 14000 plus shops Hermes Logistik Gruppe Deutschland is one of Germany's largest independent B2C parcel delivery service. The Hermes Transport Logistics business provides parcel and customs clearance delivery in Europe and the Hermes Fulfilment business handles logistics. Otto Freizeit und Touristik Group provides travel services through more than 350 Reiseland and Travel Overland travel agencies and travel portals in Germany.

On the financial services front EOS Group is a leading provider of financial services such as consumer loans and liquidity management in Europe. The group also operates Hanseatic Bank in partnership with France's Societe General. The company started new financial service companies in Brazil Canada and France which helped booster overall sales. Overall the EOS Group operates around 50 businesses in just about 25 countries.

Otto has grown largely through its acquisitions and diversification tactics (entering non-mail-order businesses). The firm derives more than 55% of its sales in Germany and customers there can get same-day delivery of many of Otto's wares. North America accounted for around 10% of overall sales.

Otto is targeting the BRIC nations (Brazil Russia India and China) as growth markets. In 2011 the company entered the Russian mail order business through German-based 3Pagen. The company has also entered the Brazilian mail order market with subsidiaries Bonprix and Arqueonautas which will target Otto's e-commerce initiatives in South America. Overall Otto has expanded into Brazil within its three operating segments.

HISTORY

East German refugee Werner Otto founded Otto Versand (German for "dispatch") in Hamburg West Germany in 1949. It distributed its first catalog in 1950; 300 hand-bound copies offered only shoes but in 28 styles. Instead of being required to pay upon delivery customers received bills with their orders; this was new for mail orders. By 1956 the firm employed 500 people; by 1958 the catalog had expanded to 200 pages offering low-cost women's fashions and other products to 200000 potential customers.

In 1963 Otto Versand began taking phone orders. Its catalog grew to 800 pages and 1 million copies by 1967. The following year it published the Post Shop Magazine its first special-interest catalog which targeted fashion-conscious youth. In 1969 Otto Versand formed Hanseatic Bank to offer customers monthly payment plans; three years later it formed the Hermes Express Package delivery service.

The firm began a shopping spree in the 1970s by investing in mail-order companies 3 Suisses International (France 1974) Heinrich Heine (luxury clothes and household goods West Germany 1974) and Hanau (West Germany 1979).

Werner's son Michael succeeded him as chairman in 1981 and in 1982 he led the acquisition of low-cost women's apparel firm Spiegel. Michael immediately revamped Spiegel into an upscale retailer. The ownership of Spiegel was restructured in 1984 but the Otto family remained in control of the US company.

Throughout the 1980s the firm continued investing in European companies (entering the UK in 1986 and Austria in 1988) and began Otto-Sumisho in Japan (a joint venture 1986). Its combined catalog circulation reached 200 million in 1987.

Otto Versand launched 24-hour delivery service in 1990; that year it expanded to the Polish market by forming joint venture Otto-Epoka. In 1991 it began 24-hour phone sales and acquired a majority stake in Grattan (the UK's fourth-largest mail-order firm). Acquisitions continued during the early and mid-1990s including Margareta (Hungary) Postalmarket (Italy's largest mail-order firm) and Otto-Burlingtons (Germany-India joint venture).

Otto Versand acquired a majority stake in Reiseland's 60 travel agencies in 1993 and bought two UK collection agencies in 1994. In 1994 it became Germany's first mail-order firm to offer an interactive CD-ROM catalog.

The firm bought a majority stake in US housewares retailer Crate & Barrel in 1998 and bought German computer wholesaler Actebis Holding. It then formed Zara Deutschland a joint venture in Germany (with Spain's Inditex) to sell clothing in a new chain of outlets. Otto Versand added to its travel business (about 140 locations) in 1998 with the purchase of 25 offices from American Express Germany. It closed Postalmarket that year because of problems with the Italian postal service.

In 1999 Otto Versand acquired the Freemans catalog business (nearly $900 million in 1998 sales) from the UK's Sears PLC. The deal nearly doubled the company's UK mail-order market share from 8% to 15%. In late 1999 the firm formed a joint venture with Harrods to sell fancy English goods online.

In early 2000 Otto Versand set up a joint venture with America Online and Deutsche Bank 24 to offer online banking Internet service and PCs. In October 2001 the company entered into a joint venture with US Internet travel service provider Travelocity.com to form Travelocity Europe.

In 2003 Otto Versand changed its name to Otto GmbH & Co KG.

In 2005 Otto sold its longstanding controlling interest in US catalog company Spiegel as well as a 75% stake in Hanseatic Bank to French banking giant Societe General.

In mid-2007 the company sold its information technology distribution subsidiary Actebis Holding to German equity investment firm Arques.

EXECUTIVES

Supervisory Board Chairman, Michael Otto, age 71
Executive Board Vice Chairman Otto Group; Executive Board Member Marketing Sales E-Commerce OTTO, Rainer Hillebrand, age 57
VP Corporate Communications, Thomas Voigt
Executive Board Member Human Resources and Controlling OTTO, Alexander Birken
Executive Board Format and Category Management OTTO, Michael Heller
Executive Board Chairman Baur Versand (GmbH & Co. KG), Marc Opelt
VP Corporate Responsibility, Johannes Merck
Sustainability, Isabella Grindel
E-Commerce, Katrin Steinmann
Chief Financial Officer CFO, Jurgen Schulte-Laggenbeck
Supervisory Board Chairman, Michael Otto, age 69
Board Member, Michael E. Crusemann
Board Member, Peer Witten, age 63
Board Member, Hans Jorg Hammer
Executive Board Vice Chairman Otto Group; Executive Board Member Marketing Sales E-Commerce OTTO, Rainer Hillebrand, age 55
Board Member, Siegfried Kockmann
Board Member, Michael Lichtenauer
Deputy Chairman, Uwe Rost
Board Member, Annette Adam
Board Member, Thomas Armbrust
Board Member, Anita Beermann
Board Member, Horst Bergmann
Board Member, Olaf Brendel
Board Member, Thomas Finne, age 53
Board Member, Herta Heuberger
Board Member, Frank Leibig
Board Member, Ulrich Meinecke
Board Member, Alexander Otto
Board Member, Lars-Uwe Rieck
Board Member, Monika Vietheer-Grupe
Division Manager Corporate Benefits and Policies Otto (GmbH & Co KG) and Board Member, Mechtild Wigger
Auditors: KPMGAG

LOCATIONS

HQ: Otto Versand (GmbH & Co.) (Germany, Fed. Rep.)
Wandsbeker Strasse 3-7, Hamburg D-22172
Phone: (49) 40 64 61 0 **Fax:** (49) 40 64 61 85 71
Web: www.ottogroup.com

2012 Sales

	% of total
Europe	
Germany	57
France	12
Russia	4
Other	14
North	10
Asia	2
Other	1
Total	**100**

PRODUCTS/OPERATIONS

2012 Sales

	% of total
Multichannel	86
Services	8
Financial	6
Total	**100**

Selected Operations

3 Suisses International Group (multichannel retail)
ALBA MODA GmbH (multichannel retail)
Crate & Barrel (multichannel retail)
EOS Group (financial services)
Frankonia (multichannel retail)
Grattan (multichannel retail)
Handelsgesellshaft Heinrich Heine GmbH (multichannel retail)
Hanseatic Bank GmbH (consumer loans)
Hermes Logistik Group (logistics services)
Mondial Relay (logistics services)
myToys.de Gmbh (multichannel retail)
Otto Freizeit und Touristik Group (tourism services)
Parcelnet (logistics services)
Reiseland (travel agencies)
Witt (multichannel retail)

COMPETITORS

Amazon.com
American Express
Bed Bath & Beyond
Deutsche Post
Fast Retailing
Hammacher Schlemmer & Co.
Hanover Direct
J. C. Penney
Kering
L.L. Bean
Lands' End
METRO AG
Macy' s
Maxeda
Orchard Brands
Pier 1 Imports
Provell
Rakuten
Shop Direct
TAKKT AG
TUI
Williams-Sonoma

HISTORICAL FINANCIALS

Company Type: Public

Income Statement FYE: February 28

	REVENUE ($ mil.)	NET INCOME ($ mil.)	NET PROFIT MARGIN	EMPLOYEES
02/13	15,454	188	1.2%	53,823
02/12	15,585	30	0.2%	53,103
02/11	15,772	250	1.6%	49,721
02/10	13,797	272	2.0%	47,952
02/09	12,816	407	3.2%	49,539
Annual Growth	4.8%	(17.5%)	—	2.1%

2013 Year-End Financials

Debt ratio: 34.0%	No. of shares (mil.): —
Return on equity: 9.6%	Dividends
Cash ($ mil.): 555	Yield: —
Current ratio: 1.40	Payout: —
Long-term debt ($ mil.): 1,724	Market value ($ mil.): —

Oversea-Chinese Banking Corp. Ltd. (Singapore)

Singapore bank Oversea-Chinese Banking Corporation (OCBC Bank) operates more than 470 branches and offices in 15 countries including some 350 offices in Indonesia through its Bank OCBC NISP subsidiary. The company offers traditional banking services for individuals and businesses as well as financial services such as brokerage and asset management. Private banking for high-net-worth families is offered through the Bank of Singapore while Great Eastern Holdings which provides life and property/casualty insurance is the largest insurance company in Singapore and Malaysia. OCBC Bank was founded in 1912 to serve the Chinese business community of Singapore and other parts of Asia but now serves the general public.

Geographic Reach

The bank's main operations are in its home country of Singapore which accounts for 60% of business. Malaysia where it operates as OCBC Bank Malaysia and offers Islamic banking services through OCBC Al-Amin Bank accounts for about 20% of business. Indonesia and China each account for less than 10% of business.

In addition to its core markets OCBC also has a presence in Australia Brunei Dubai Hong Kong Japan The Philippines South Korea Taiwan Thailand the UK the US (in New York and Los Angeles) and Vietnam through branches and representative offices.

Strategy

With Singapore's population only 5 million people the bank has targeted China Indonesia and Malaysia as international growth markets. It plans to increase its Islamic banking and insurance operations in Malaysia home to almost 30 million people. In Indonesia (population 247 million) the bank consolidated its banking subsidiaries in order to grow the OCBC NISP brand there. And in China with 1.3 billion people the bank plans to cater to wealthy citizens by offering private banking services through the Bank of Singapore.

EXECUTIVES

Chairman, Cheong Choong Kong, age 71
Director and CEO OCBC Bank Malaysia, Jeffrey S. T. Chew, age 48
CEO and Director, David P. Conner
SVP Group Corporate Communications, Koh Ching Ching, age 45
Chief Operating Officer, Ching Wei Hong, age 53
EVP Group Investment Banking, George L. W. Lee, age 60
EVP Group Audit, Lai Teck Poh, age 68
EVP Group Human Resources, Cynthia G. H. Tan, age 62
EVP Group Quality and Service Excellence, Teng Soon Lang, age 62
Company Secretary, Peter B. A. Yeoh, age 58
Group Chief Executive Officer, Samuel N. (Sam) Tsien, age 58
EVP Enterprise Banking and Financial Institutions, Linus T. L. Goh, age 50
SVP Group Property Management, Vincent Soh, age 57
SVP Group Transaction Banking, Neo Bock Cheng, age 48
Senior Executive Vice President Head of Global Treasury, Lam Kun Kin, age 50
EVP International, Na Wu Beng, age 56
EVP Group Risk Management, Gilbert Kohnke, age 54
Chairman OCBC Bank China, Leong Wai Leng, age 47
Head Group Operations and Technology, Lim Khiang Tong, age 53
Head of Audit, Kng Tin
General Counsel, Loretta Yuen
Executive Vice President, Cynthia Hiang
Executive Vice President, Gan Kim
Chief Financial Officer, Darren T.S. Peng, age 42
Head of Global Commercial Banking, Linus G.T. Liang, age 50
Executive Vice President Head of Global Corporate Banking, George L.L. Wah
Chief Executive Officer Bank of Singapore, Renato de Guzman
CEO OCBC Bank China, Kng Hwee Tin
CEO and Director, David P. Conner
Director, Bobby Chin, age 61
Director, Lee Seng Wee, age 81
Director, Lee Tih Shih, age 49
Director, Prof Neo Boon Siong, age 55
Director, Patrick K. H. Yeoh, age 74
Director, Pramukti Surjaudaja, age 50
Auditors: KPMGLLP

LOCATIONS

HQ: Oversea-Chinese Banking Corp. Ltd. (Singapore)
65 Chulia Street 09-00 OCBC Centre, 049513
Phone: (65) 6318 7222 **Fax:** (65) 6533 7955
Web: www.ocbc.com

2012 Sales

	% of total
Singapore	63
Malaysia	20
Indonesia	7
China	7
Rest of	2
Rest of	1
Total	**100**

PRODUCTS/OPERATIONS

2012 Sales

	% of total
Interest	59
Noninterest	
Fees &	12
Life	7
General	1
Rental	1
Dividends	1
Other	19
Total	**100**

Selected Subsidiaries

Banking
Bank of Singapore Limited
OCBC Al-Amin Bank Berhad
OCBC Bank (Malaysia) Berhad
Singapore Island Bank Limited
Insurance
Great Eastern Life Assurance (Malaysia) Berhad
Overseas Assurance Corporation (Malaysia) Berhad
The Great Eastern Life Assurance Company Limited
The Overseas Assurance Corporation
Asset management
Lion Global Investors Limited
Great Eastern Holdings Limited
Stockbroker
OCBC Securities Private Limited

COMPETITORS

ABN AMRO Group
AmBank Group
BNP Paribas
Bank Central Asia
Bank Danamon Indonesia
Bank Mandiri
Bank Rakyat
Citigroup
DBS Group Holdings
HSBC
Hong Leong Finance
Maybank
Standard Chartered
United Overseas Bank

HISTORICAL FINANCIALS

Company Type: Public

Income Statement

FYE: December 31

	ASSETS ($ mil.)	NET INCOME ($ mil.)	INCOME AS % OF ASSETS	EMPLOYEES
12/12	241,962	3,264	1.3%	24,628
12/11	213,713	1,779	0.8%	22,892
12/10	178,808	1,757	1.0%	21,585
12/09	138,624	1,400	1.0%	19,561
12/08	125,621	1,211	1.0%	19,876
Annual Growth	17.8%	28.1%	—	5.5%

2012 Year-End Financials

Return on assets: 1.3%	Dividends
Return on equity: 16.4%	Yield: —
Long-term debt ($ mil.): —	Payout: —
No. of shares (mil.): —	Market value ($ mil.): —
Sales ($ mil): 16,365	

	STOCK PRICE ($) FY Close	P/E High	P/E Low	PER SHARE ($) Earnings	Dividends	Book Value
12/12	7.92	5	3	0.92	0.00	6.15
12/11	6.18	8	5	0.50	0.00	5.05
12/10	7.72	7	5	0.51	0.00	4.86
12/09	6.20	5	2	0.42	0.00	4.19
12/08	3.05	6	3	0.38	0.00	3.55
Annual Growth	26.9%	—	—	25.1%	—	14.8%

Panasonic Corp

Panasonic has been one of the world's most prolific electronics manufacturers since 1919. It operates worldwide through about 600 companies under brands Panasonic Quasar Technics and others. The company spans multiple fields: Its consumer business consists of AVC (audio video and communications) equipment along with hardware and software for linking it together and home appliances (washing machines vacuum cleaners personal grooming aids and commercial HVAC). In the field of devices Panasonic covers multimedia and eco-car equipment industrial electronic components and batteries. The company's solutions equipment targets environmentally conscience businesses manufacturers and health care firms.

Geographic Reach

The company sells its products and services in Asia Europe and North and South America. Japan accounts from just over 50% of net sales. While North and South America accounts for over 10% of net sales. Europe also represents some 10% of net sales.

Operations

Within the company's businesses are eight segments: digital AVC networks appliances eco solutions industrial devices systems and communications automotive systems energy and other.

Panasonic is weighing the sale of its medical products unit to shore up its balance sheet.

Panasonic is financially diversified across its segments with the digital AVC networks segment consisting of imaging equipment AVC network equipment such as flat-panel TVs blu-ray disc recorders digital cameras notebook PCs projectors and in-flight entertainment systems. Its appliances segment manufactures products like air conditioners refrigerators washing machines and other home appliances. Its eco solutions group includes four business groups which include the lighting (lamps devices and equipment) energy systems (distribution panelboards energy management products and wiring equipment) housing systems (home and building products) and environmental systems (air quality appliances and solutions).

Financial Performance

Panasonic's overall sales for fiscal 2012 (ends March 31) came in at Y7.8 trillion (about $97 billion) a decrease of 10% from Y8.7 trillion (about $105.7 billion) in fiscal 2011. The company reported a net loss of Y77.2 billion (about $9.6 billion) in fiscal 2012 compared to a net income of Y74 billion (about $946 million) in fiscal 2011. The affects of the Great East Japan Earthquake flooding in Thailand the European financial crisis and the high yen resulted in lower sales and net income.

In fiscal 2012 the company's business tumbled in the wake of supply chains affected by the flooding in Thailand and the unwavering European financial crisis. In the US business remained sluggish but emerging markets such as China and India provided a relative boost to the company's bottom line.

Strategy

Panasonic however along with other Japanese consumer electronics makers is struggling to make money on products like TVs VCRs and DVD players. To compensate Panasonic's management has announced a three-year plan called the "Green Transformation 2012" designed to accelerate the company's push toward becoming #1 in green technology in the electronics industry. SANYO Electric fits neatly into this strategy. Purchased for 400 billion-plus yen ($4.6 billion) in 2011 SANYO Electric repositioned Panasonic as Japan's second-largest electronics company after Sony. In addition the deal gave Panasonic the keys to the growing hybrid car battery market; SANYO Electric is the world's largest maker of rechargeable batteries and Volkswagen's partner in developing lithium-ion batteries.

During 2012 Panasonic has moved to reposition SANYO's operations including the rechargeable battery business as part of its global branding strategy. The change follows the transfer of SANYO Electric's low-margin washing machine and refrigerator business to China-based Haier Group. The deal valued at about $130 million is intended to allow Panasonic to concentrate on SANYO's more profitable and greener operations. Panasonic expects to have unified all of its branding by April 2013.

As one of the conditions for the deal Chinese officials urged Panasonic to decrease its stake in its hybrid-car-battery joint venture with Toyota Motor Corporation. To this end Panasonic exited its Primearth EV joint venture (formerly Panasonic EV Energy Co.) but acquired a 2% stake in Tesla Motors to co-develop electric vehicle batteries with the US car maker. The deal follows a previous agreement with Tesla under which Panasonic supplies lithium ion batteries for Tesla's electric cars. Also Panasonic sold its automotive nickel hydride battery business to a Chinese firm for about JPY500 million ($6 million).

HISTORY

Grade school dropout Konosuke Matsushita took $50 in 1918 and went into business making electric plugs (with his brother-in-law Toshio Iue founder of SANYO). His mission to help people by making high-quality low-priced conveniences while providing his employees with good working conditions earned him the sobriquet "god of business management." Matsushita Electric Industrial grew by developing inexpensive lamps batteries radios and motors in the 1920s and 1930s.

During WWII the Japanese government ordered the firm to build wood-laminate products for the military. Postwar occupation forces prevented Matsushita from working at his firm for four years. Thanks to unions' efforts he rejoined his namesake company shortly before it entered a joint venture with Dutch manufacturer Philips in 1952. The following year it moved into consumer goods making televisions refrigerators and washing machines and later expanding into high-performance audio products. Matsushita bought a majority stake in Victor Company of Japan (JVC originally established by RCA Victor) in 1954. Its 1959 New York subsidiary opening began Matsushita's drive overseas.

Sold under the National Panasonic and Technics names the firm's products were usually not cutting-edge but were attractively priced. Under Masaharu Matsushita the founder's son-in-law who became president in 1961 the company became Japan's largest home appliance maker introducing air conditioners microwave ovens stereo components and VCRs in the 1960s and 1970s. JVC developed the VHS format for VCRs which beat out Sony's Betamax format.

Matsushita built much of its sales growth on new industrial and commercial customers in the 1980s. The company expanded its semiconductor office and factory automation auto electronics audio-visual housing and air-conditioning product offerings that decade. Konosuke died in 1989.

The next year Matsushita joined the Japanese stampede for US acquisitions buying Universal Studios' then-owner MCA. In 1993 Yoichi Morishita was named president and the company acquired Philips' stake in their joint venture. Two years later when cultural incompatibility depressed MCA's performance Matsushita sold 80% of the company (now Universal) to liquor mogul Seagram resulting in a fiscal 1996 loss. That year Matsushita pushed the technology envelope introducing the first DVD player.

Declining sales forced the firm to rethink its strategy; it began a multiyear restructuring including a buildup in parts of Asia with cheaper labor and job cuts. In 1997 Matsushita consolidated most of its business units into basic categories: consumer products industrial products and components. The downside of Matsushita's move into emerging Asian markets became apparent that year as many Southeast Asian countries suffered currency crises.

In fiscal years 1998 and 1999 the company's income dropped partly due to a slow domestic economy. A lagging market led Matsushita to close its North American semiconductor operations in late 1998. Also that year the company bought a stake in Mobile Broadcasting (a digital satellite broadcasting venture of nine companies) and introduced digital TVs.

Matsushita in 1999 bought a 9% stake in Symbian a venture created by the makers of 85% of the world's mobile phones (including Motorola and Nokia).

In June 2000 Yoichi Morishita became chairman and Kunio Nakamura took the reins as president of Matsushita. The next December following a year with a three-fold increase in expenditures on chip-making ($1.2 billion) the company began making chips for cell phones digital cameras and digital TVs.

In early 2002 Matsushita announced plans to turn around its financial slump by cutting 13000 local jobs (through early retirement) and trimming directors' salaries. The company also reclassified its former consumer industrial and components categories into four new divisions: AVC networks home appliances industrial equipment and components and devices.

In April 2002 Matsushita teamed up with Chinese home appliance manufacturer TCL Holdings; the move was intended to help Matsushita increase its presence in China's growing consumer electronic market. That month the firm established a joint venture with Toshiba for the manufacture and sale of liquid crystal display (LCD) panels and next-generation display devices.

The company launched a global brand consolidation strategy in 2003 rebranding all home appliance products in non-Japanese markets to Panasonic from National. (The National brand continues to be used along with the Panasonic brand in Japan.) It further expanded the Panasonic brand's reach in 2004 when it increased its stake (to 60%) in Indonesian manufacturing PT Panasonic Gobel a joint venture between Matsushita and the Gobel family. The transaction allowed Matsushita to assume control of Panasonic sales in that country.

In early 2004 Matsushita acquired affiliate Matsushita Electric Works (MEW) a company in which it previously held a 32% share. MEW which makes lighting security systems and kitchen and bathroom fittings was spun off from Matsushita in 1935. The acquisition makes Matsushita the largest Japanese electronic and electrical equipment manufacturer. Many of the two companies' overlapping research and development sales marketing and manufacturing capabilities have been combined so that a unified brand V-products is presented to the public. In late 2004 the company closed down its MT Picture Display Corporation of America operations which made CRTs (cathode ray tubes) for TVs. The unit was part of the Matsushita Toshiba Picture Display family a joint venture of MEI and Toshiba.

In 2005 Matsushita continued to collaborate with other companies to create new products. That January the company agreed to work with Olympus to develop new digital cameras. It also announced a deal with Hitachi to produce plasma display panels.

In June 2006 senior managing director Fumio Ohtsubo was named president succeeding Kunio Nakamura who became chairman of the company's board of directors.

In a rather large shift to leverage the strength of its Panasonic brand name Matsushita in October 2008 changed the name of its company to Panasonic Corporation. The company also adopted the Panasonic name worldwide for its brands including the National brand it uses in Japan. Matsushita's founder's name means "lucky man under the pine tree."

In late 2009 Panasonic purchased a 51% stake in rival SANYO Electric after about a year of battling antitrust regulators across the globe. The deal put Panasonic in the driver's seat in the hybrid car battery market.

In October 2010 Panasonic completed a tender offer for SANYO Electric's shares raising its stake in the company to more than 80% and making SANYO Electric a wholly-owned subsidiary. At the same time it completed another tender offer which raised its stake in Panasonic Electric Works from 51% to 84%.

EXECUTIVES

Chairman, Kunio Nakamura, age 74
EVP, Yasuo Katsura, age 66
Vice Chairman, Masayuki Matsushita, age 68
Chairman, Fumio Ohtsubo, age 68
Senior Managing Director and President Automotive and Industrial Systems Company, Yoshihiko (Yoshi) Yamada, age 62
President, Kazuhiro Tsuga
Managing Executive Officer; President Panasonic Electronic Devices, Toshiaki Kobayashi
Managing Executive Officer and Director Corporate Management Division for Asia and Oceania; Managing Director Panasonic Asia Pacific Pte. Ltd., Ikuo Miyamoto
Managing Executive Officer and Head China and Northeast Asia, Hidetoshi Osawa
Executive Officer; Director Corporate Management Division for North America; Chairman and CEO North America, Joseph M. (Joe) Taylor
Managing Director; President AVC Networks Company, Yoshiyuki Miyabe
Senior Managing Director and President Appliances Company, Kazunori Takami, age 59
Managing Director Accounting and Finance, Hideaki Kawai
Managing Executive Officer and Chairman and CEO Panasonic Europe, Laurent Abadie
EVP and President Eco Solutions Company, Shusaku Nagae
Managing Executive Officer and Head Asia the Middle East and Africa, Yorihisa Shiokawa
Managing Director Technology Intellectual Property and Information Systems, Mamoru Yoshida
President Panasonic Healthcare Co. Ltd., Kenji Yamane
President CEO*, Patrick D. O'Brien
Chairman, Kunio Nakamura, age 73
EVP and Representative in Tokyo Director Corporate Division for Government and Public Affairs and Board Member, Yasuo Katsura, age 65
Vice Chairman, Masayuki Matsushita, age 68
Board Member, Ikuo Uno, age 77
Board Member, Masayuki Oku, age 68
Chairman, Fumio Ohtsubo, age 68
EVP Domestic Consumer Marketing General Director Consumer Products Marketing Domestic Customer Satisfaction and Design and Board Member, Toshihiro Sakamoto, age 66
Managing Director Industrial Sales and Board Member, Yoshihiko (Yoshi) Yamada, age 61
Senior Managing Director Overseas Operations and Board Member, Hitoshi Otsuki, age 65
EVP Corporate Division for Promoting System & Equipment Business and Electrical Supplies Sales Project Sales and Building Products Sales and Board Member, Takahiro Mori, age 65
Executive Officer Manufacturing Innovation Facility Management Quality Administration FF Customer Support and Management and Environmental Affairs and Board Member, Masashi Makino, age 64
Senior Managing Director and Board Member; President AVC Networks Company, Ken Morita, age 64
Senior Managing Director Intellectual Property and Board Member, Ikusaburo Kashima, age 64
Senior Managing Director Corporate Division for Promoting Energy Solutions Business and Board Member, Junji Nomura, age 65
Managing Director Accounting Finance and Information Systems and Board Member, Makoto Uenoyama, age 59
Managing Director and Board Member; President Home Appliances Company In Charge Of Lighting Company, Kazunori Takami, age 58
Board Member; President System Networks Company and Panasonic System Networks Co. Ltd., Takashi Toyama, age 57
Managing Director Personnel General Affairs Social Relations and e-Work Promotion Office and Board Member, Masatoshi Harada, age 57
Auditors: KPMGAZSA&Co.

LOCATIONS

HQ: Panasonic Corp
1006 Oaza Kadoma, Kadoma, Osaka 571-8501
Phone: (81) 6 6908 1121
Web: www.panasonic.co.jp

2012 Sales

	% of total
Japan	53
North & South	12
Europe	10
Asia &	25
Total	**100**

PRODUCTS/OPERATIONS

2012 Sales

	% of total
AVC	17
Appliance	15
Eco	15
Industrial	14
Systems &	8
Automotive	7
Energy	6
Other	18
Total	**100**

Selected Segments and Products

AVC Networks
- Camcorders
- Computer drives (CD-ROM DVD-ROM/RAM)
- Computers (PCs)
- Digital cameras
- DVD players and recorders
- Fax machines
- Printers
- Telephones
- TVs (color LCD plasma display)

PEW and PanaHome
- Automation controls
- Beauty and personal care products
- Electronic and plastic materials
- Home security systems
- Interior furnishings

Home appliances
- Air conditioners and purifiers
- Dishwashers
- Dryers
- Fans
- Refrigerators
- Vacuum cleaners
- Water heaters
- Washing machines

Components and devices
- Batteries (dry rechargeable)
- Displays (CRTs LCDs PDPs)
- Electric motors
- General components (capacitors resistors printed circuit boards)
- Magnetic recording heads
- Semiconductors

Selected Brands

National
Panasonic
Quasar
Technics
Victor

COMPETITORS

A123 Systems
Apple Inc.
BSH Bosch und Siemens Hausgerate
BYD
Canon
Konica Minolta
LG Electronics
Motorola Solutions
NEC
Nokia
Olympus
Dell
Eastman Kodak
Electrolux
Fujitsu Technology Solutions
GE Appliances & Lighting
Haier Group
Hewlett-Packard
IBM
Intel
Philips Electronics
Procter & Gamble
Samsung Electronics
Sharp Corp.
Sony
TE Connectivity
Technicolor
Toshiba
Truly International
Whirlpool
Yuasa Battery Thailand

HISTORICAL FINANCIALS

Company Type: Public

Income Statement

FYE: March 31

	REVENUE ($ mil.)	NET INCOME ($ mil.)	NET PROFIT MARGIN	EMPLOYEES
03/13	77,615	(8,016)	—	293,742
03/12	95,650	(9,413)	—	330,767
03/11	104,975	893	0.9%	366,937
03/10	79,415	(1,107)	—	384,586
03/09	78,857	(3,848)	—	292,250
Annual Growth	(0.4%)	—	—	0.1%

2013 Year-End Financials

Debt ratio: 0.2%
Return on equity: (-47.2%)
Cash ($ mil.): 5,292
Current ratio: 0.96
Long-term debt ($ mil.): 7,047
No. of shares (mil.): —
Dividends
Yield: 0.0%
Payout: —
Market value ($ mil.): —

	STOCK PRICE ($) FY Close	P/E High/Low	PER SHARE ($) Earnings	Dividends	Book Value
03/13	7.33	— —	(3.47)	0.00	5.85
03/12	9.25	— —	(4.07)	0.00	10.18
03/11	12.59	0 0	0.43	0.11	14.93
03/10	15.32	— —	(0.53)	0.14	14.44
03/09	11.03	— —	(1.85)	0.40	13.65
Annual Growth	(9.7%)	— —	—	(93.3%)	(19.1%)

Pegatron Corp

LOCATIONS

HQ: Pegatron Corp
5/F., No. 76, Ligong Street, Beitou District, Taipei 112
Phone: (886) 2 8143 9001 **Fax:** (886) 2 2893 9366
Web: www.pegatroncorp.com

HISTORICAL FINANCIALS

Company Type: Public

Income Statement

FYE: December 31

	REVENUE ($ mil.)	NET INCOME ($ mil.)	NET PROFIT MARGIN	EMPLOYEES
12/12	30,387	343	1.1%	177,948
12/11	19,793	109	0.6%	112,318
12/10	18,231	364	2.0%	104,608
12/09	16,819	329	2.0%	96,534
Annual Growth	21.8%	1.4%	—	22.6%

2012 Year-End Financials

Debt ratio: 0.3%
Return on equity: 8.0%
Cash ($ mil.): 2,072
Current ratio: 1.31
Long-term debt ($ mil.): 943
No. of shares (mil.): —
Dividends
Yield: —
Payout: —
Market value ($ mil.): —

PetroChina Co Ltd

If you want petroleum in China or elsewhere then PetroChina is your company. A subsidiary of state-owned China National Petroleum Corporation (CNPC) PetroChina produces two-thirds of China's oil and gas. The company has proved reserves of 11.3 billion barrels of oil and 63.2 trillion cu. ft. of natural gas. In China it owns more than 50620 kilometers of natural gas and refined products pipeline and operates 26 refineries and 13 chemical plants. PetroChina also owns or has interests in more than 17260 gas stations. The company was created in 2000 as a separate company to initially manage the domestic operations –and in recent years some key international assets –of CNPC.

PetroChina is taking advantage of the growing consumption of natural gas in China by expanding its transmission infrastructure. It is also expanding its oil reserves and refining operations through the purchase of international oil fields and refineries including several assets from its parent.

In 2009 the company acquired Keppel's 45% stake in Singapore Petroleum Company in a $1.5 billion deal that enables PetroChina (which plans to acquire all of SPC) to expand into refining and marketing in Southeast Asia. It followed this up with a deal to own 49% of Nippon Oil's Osaka refinery.

As part of its global expansion drive in 2010 PetroChina acquired 60% of two oil sands project in western Canada from Athabasca Oil Sands for $1.9 billion. It has also signed a 20-year deal with Royal Dutch Shell to purchase a supply of up to 40 million tons of liquefied natural gas (LNG). The company also (with Shell) jointly acquired Australia-based LNG producer Arrow Energy for about $3.5 billion.

PetroChina signed an agreement also in 2010 for a joint venture between Air Products and Technip to build a hydrogen production facility in Sichuan China. It will be the first time a state-owned refinery in China has outsourced its hydrogen production. The plant will produce more than 90 million cu. ft. per day of hydrogen when it is operational in 2012.

In the Chinese market in 2008 PetroChina acquired oil assets in Liaoning Jilin Tianjin Hebei Sichuan and Shaanxi provinces from state-owned parent CNPC. In 2009 it also agreed to buy two oil pipelines in Western China from CNPC for $1.4 billion. In 2010 PetroChina subsidiary Kunlun Energy Company bought a 60% stake in Beijing Gas Pipeline also a PetroChina subsidiary for $2.85 billion.

Looking to boost its financial assets to expand in China and internationally in 2011 the company signed a strategic alliance with Italian oil heavyweight Eni. That year it agreed to pay $5.4 billion to Encana for a 50% stake in a Canadian shale gas project and buy 50% of INEOS refinery operations in France and Scotland for $1 billion. However the Encana deal fell through in June 2011 when the parties could not come to terms.

PetroChina has been laying out cash ($7 billion in acquisitions since 2010) to buy oil and gas reserves globally in Africa Australia Canada Iraq and Qatar.

In 2011 PetroChina was 86%-owned by the Chinese government.

EXECUTIVES

Chairman, Jiang Jiemin, age 57
General Accountant; Director, Wang Guoliang, age 60
Chairman of the Board; President, Zhou Jiping, age 60
VP and Deputy General Manager and Safety Director; Director, Liao Yongyuan, age 50
VP, Li Hualin, age 50
Supervisor, Wen Qingshan, age 54
VP and General Manager Exploration and Production, Zhao Zhengzhang, age 56
Chief Geologist and General Manager Changqing Oilfield, Wang Daofu, age 57
Chief Engineer and General Manager Natural Gas and Pipelines, Huang Weihe, age 55
VP, Sun Longde, age 51
VP, Liu Hongbin, age 50
Supervisor, Li Yuan, age 67
Supervisor, Sun Xianfeng, age 61
Supervisor, Wang Daocheng, age 73
CFO, Zhou Mingchun, age 45
Chief Engineer, Lin Aiguo, age 54
VP and General Manager China National Oil and Gas Exploration and Development Corporation, Qiliang Bo, age 50
VP and General Manager Trans-Asia Gas Pipeline Company Limited, Bo Sun, age 52
Chairman, Jiang Jiemin, age 56
General Accountant; Director, Wang Guoliang, age 60
Deputy General Manager; Director, Wang Fucheng, age 61
Director, Franco Bernabe, age 64
Chairman of the Board; President, Zhou Jiping, age 60
Director, Zeng Yukang, age 61
VP and Deputy General Manager and Safety Director; Director, Liao Yongyuan, age 50
Director, Chee-Chen Tung, age 69
Director, Liu Hongru, age 81
Director, Li Yongwu, age 68
Director, Li Xinhua, age 59
Director, Cui Junhui, age 68
Director, Jiang Fan, age 49
Auditors: PricewaterhouseCoopers

LOCATIONS

HQ: PetroChina Co Ltd
No. 9 Dongzhimen North Street, Dongcheng District, Beijing 100007
Phone: (86) 10 5998 6223 **Fax:** (86) 10 6209 9557
Web: www.petrochina.com.cn

2009 Sales

	% of total
China	78
Other	22
Total	**100**

PRODUCTS/OPERATIONS

2009 Sales

	% of total
Marketing	72
Refining &	12
Exploration &	10
Natural gas &	6
Total	**100**

COMPETITORS

Bangchak Petroleum Public
CNOOC
Chevron
Exxon Mobil
Sinopec Shanghai Petrochemical

HISTORICAL FINANCIALS

Company Type: Public

Income Statement FYE: December 31

	REVENUE ($ mil.)	NET INCOME ($ mil.)	NET PROFIT MARGIN	EMPLOYEES
12/12	352,134	18,498	5.3%	548,355
12/11	318,353	21,123	6.6%	552,810
12/10	222,315	21,237	9.6%	552,698
12/09	149,278	15,141	10.1%	539,168
12/08	156,978	16,770	10.7%	477,780
Annual Growth	22.4%	2.5%	—	3.5%

2012 Year-End Financials

Debt ratio: 3.2%
Return on equity: 11.1%
Cash ($ mil.): 6,960
Current ratio: 0.72
Long-term debt ($ mil.): 47,122
No. of shares (mil.): —
Dividends
Yield: 0.0%
Payout: 111.8%
Market value ($ mil.): —

	STOCK PRICE ($) FY Close	P/E High	P/E Low	PER SHARE ($) Earnings	Dividends	Book Value
12/12	143.78	6	5	0.10	0.11	0.93
12/11	124.31	5	4	0.12	0.12	0.87
12/10	131.49	4	3	0.12	0.08	0.78
12/09	118.96	5	2	0.08	0.08	0.68
12/08	88.98	6	2	0.09	0.08	0.63
Annual Growth	12.7%	—	—	2.3%	7.9%	10.2%

Petroleo Brasileiro S.A.

PETROLEO BRASILEIRO (PETROBRAS) isn't brash but it is Brazil's top company and has assets in 30 countries. The integrated energy company explores for oil and gas and produces refines and transports oil and gas products. With extensive assets in offshore Brazil in 2011 PETROBRAS reported proved reserves of 12.9 billion barrels of oil equivalent. In Brazil it also operates 12 refineries an extensive oil and gas pipeline network and more than 7300 gas stations. Petrobras Distribuidora is Brazil's #1 retailer of oil products and fuel alcohol. Petrobras Argentina is a top Argentine oil firm. Other units operate electricity (10 power plants) petrochemicals and natural gas assets.

Petrobras Internacional also known as Braspetro conducts exploration worldwide including in Angola Nigeria Tanzania Portugal the US and across Latin America.

The bulk of PETROBRAS' production comes from its operations in Brazilian waters; the company is recognized as a leader in offshore drilling technology and deepwater wells. In 2011 it was operating more than 130 production platforms. PETROBRAS has made a number of major offshore oil discoveries in offshore Brazil since 2000 including the Tupi field (found in 2007) and which has the potential to boost Brazil's oil reserves by 40%. In 2010 PETROBRAS announced another major discovery a 3.7 to 15 billion-barrels-of-oil-reserves find (offshore of Rio de Janeiro) that could double Brazil's known reserves.

PETROBRAS is also a major ethanol producer and plans (through Petrobras Transporte S.A. which oversees oil and derivatives ethanol biofuels and natural gas transportation and storage activities) to invest billions of dollars in biofuel development to ensure Brazil's fuel independence as its economy and population grows.

The global recession hurt the company's financial performance in 2009 as low commodity prices and weak sales pulled down revenues and income. However PETROBRAS is well positioned for economic growth. In 2010 the company raised $70 billion to develop its lucrative offshore oilfields in the world's largest ever public share offerings.

That year PETROBRAS reported robust revenues and income growth fueled by a growing economy higher commodity prices and increased production.

Streamlining its Petrobras Argentina operations in 2011 the company acquired that unit's Brazilian petrochemicals business (Innova SA) for $332 million.

In 2012 it teamed up with GE Oil & Gas in a $1.1 billion deal through which the GE unit will supply 380 subsea wellhead systems to a number of PETROBRAS' oil and gas fields in offshore Brazil.

Brazil's government owns more than 55% of PETROBRAS.

HISTORY

O petroleo e nosso!"“

"The oil is ours!" proclaimed the Brazilian nationalists' slogan in 1953 and President Getulio Vargas approved a bill creating a state-run monopoly on petroleum discovery development refining and transport. The same year that PETROLEO BRASILEIRO (PETROBRAS) was created a team led by American geologist Walter Link reported that the prospects of finding petroleum in Brazil were slim. The report outraged Brazilian nationalists who saw it as a ploy for foreign exploitation. PETROBRAS proved it could find oil but Brazil continued to import crude oil and petroleum products. By 1973 the company produced about 10% of the nation's needs.

When oil prices soared during the Arab embargo the government instead of encouraging exploration for domestic oil pushed PETROBRAS into a program to promote alcohol fuels. The company was forced to raise gasoline prices to make the more costly gasohol attractive to consumers. During the 1979 oil crunch the price of gasohol was fixed at 65% of gasoline. But during the oil glut of the mid-1980s PETROBRAS' cost of making gasohol was twice what it cost to buy gasoline —in other words PETROBRAS lost money.

PETROBRAS soon began overseas exploration. In 1980 it found an oil field in Iraq an important trading partner during the 1980s. The company also drilled in Angola and through a 1987 agreement with Texaco in the Gulf of Mexico.

In the mid-1980s PETROBRAS began production in the deepwater Campos basin off the coast of Rio de Janeiro state. Discoveries there in 1988 in the Marlim and Albacora fields more than tripled its oil reserves. It plunged deep into the thick Amazon jungle in 1986 to explore for oil and by 1990 Amazon wells were making a significant contribution to total production. That year to ease dependence on imports PETROBRAS launched a five-year $16.9 billion plan to boost crude oil production. It also began selling its mining and trading assets.

Before the invasion of Kuwait Brazil relied heavily on Iraq trading weapons for oil. After the invasion spawned increases in crude prices PETROBRAS raised pump prices but yielding to the government's anti-inflation program still did not raise them enough to cover costs. It lost $13 million a day.

The company sold 26% of Petrobras Distribuidora to the public in 1993 and privatized several of its petrochemical and fertilizer subsidiaries. A 1994 presidential order bent on stabilizing Brazil's 40%-per-month inflation cut the prices of oil products. In 1995 the government loosened its grip on the oil and gas industry and allowed foreign companies to enter the Brazilian market. In the wake of this reform PETROBRAS teamed up with a Japanese consortium to build Brazil's largest oil refinery.

In 1997 PETROBRAS appealed a $4 billion judgment from a 1992 shareholder lawsuit; the suit alleged PETROBRAS had undervalued shares during the privatization of the loss-making Petroquisa affiliate. (The appeal was granted in 1999.)

As part of an effort to boost oil production PETROBRAS also began to raise money abroad in 1999. The next year PETROBRAS and Spanish oil giant Repsol YPF agreed to swap oil and gas assets in Argentina and Brazil in a deal worth more than $1 billion.

In 2000 the company announced plans to change its corporate name to PETROBRAX but fierce political and popular reaction forced the company to abort this plan in 2001. In an even greater public relations disaster that year one of PETROBRAS' giant rigs sank off of Brazil and 10 workers were killed. In 2001 PETROBRAS announced that it was going to spend as much as $3 billion to buy an oil company in order to increase its production in the Gulf of Mexico.

In 2002 the company expressed an interest in buying Argentina's major oil company (YPF) from Spanish/Argentine energy giant Repsol YPF. That year PETROBRAS bought control (59%) of Argentine energy company Perez Companc in a deal valued at $1 billion. PETROBRAS also reported its first oil find in Argentina in 2002.

In 2006 the company acquired a 50% stake in a deepwater block in Equatorial Guinea from a private group of companies for an undisclosed sum.

The company also restructured the Brazilian petrochemical industry to make it more efficient. Its actions included the purchase of the petrochemical assets of the Ipiranga Group in 2007 and Suzano Petroquimica a leader in Latin American polypropylene resin production in 2008.

In 2007 PETROBRAS announced a major offshore oil discovery in the Tupi. In 2008 it reported it had discovered a major natural gas field near the Tupi find.

EXECUTIVES

Chief Downstream Officer, Paulo R. Costa, age 59
CFO and Chief Investor Relations Officer, Almir G. Barbassa, age 66
Chairman, Guido Mantega, age 64
Chief International Officer, Jorge L. Zelada, age 56
Exploration and Production Officer; Member of the Executive Board, Guilherme Guilherme de Oliveira Estrella Estrella
Chief Executive Officer; Member of the Executive Board; Director, Maria Maria das Gracas Silva Foster Foster
Services Officer; Member of the Executive Board, Renato Renato de Souza Duque Duque
Director, Jorge Gerdau Johannpeter, age 75
Director, Josue Christiano Gomes da Silva
Director, Luciano Galv?o Coutinho, age 66
CEO and Director, Maria das Gracas Silva Foster, age 59
Director, Francisco Roberto de Albuquerque, age 75
Director, Sergio F. Quintella, age 78
Director, Marcio Pereira Zimmermann, age 57
Director, Miriam Aparecida Belchior
Auditors: Ernst&YoungAuditoresIndependentesS/C

LOCATIONS

HQ: Petroleo Brasileiro S.A.
Avenida Republica do Chile, 65, Rio de Janeiro 20031-912
Phone: (55) 21 3224 4477
Web: www.petrobras.com.br

2010 Sales

	% of total
Brazil	74
Other	28
Total	**100**

PRODUCTS/OPERATIONS

2010 Sales

	% of total
Refining transportation &	46
Exploration &	26
Distribution	18
International	6
Gas &	4
Total	**100**

Selected Subsidiaries

Downstream Participac?es S.A. (asset exchanges between Petrobras and Repsol-YPF)
Petrobras Argentina (59%; oil and gas Argentina)
Petrobras Comercializadora de Energia Ltda
Petrobras Distribuidora SA (BR; distribution and marketing of petroleum products fuel alcohol and natural gas)
Petrobras Gas SA (Gaspetro management of the Brazil-Bolivia pipeline and other natural gas assets)
Petrobras Internacional SA (Braspetro; overseas exploration and production marketing and services)
Petrobras International Finance Company PIFCO (oil imports)
Petrobras Negocios Eletronicos S.A.
Petrobras Quimica SA (Petroquisa petrochemicals)
Petrobras Transporte SA (Transpetro oil and gas transportation and storage)

COMPETITORS

Ashland Inc.
BHP Billiton
BP
Chevron
Devon Energy
Eni
Exxon Mobil
Imperial Oil
Koch Industries Inc.
Marathon Oil
Norsk Hydro ASA
Occidental Petroleum
PEMEX
Petroleos de Venezuela
Royal Dutch Shell
Sunoco
TOTAL

HISTORICAL FINANCIALS

Company Type: Public

Income Statement FYE: December 31

	REVENUE ($ mil.)	NET INCOME ($ mil.)	NET PROFIT MARGIN	EMPLOYEES
12/12	144,103	11,034	7.7%	85,065
12/11	145,915	20,121	13.8%	81,918
12/10	120,052	19,184	16.0%	80,492
12/09	91,869	15,504	16.9%	74,240
12/08	118,257	18,879	16.0%	74,240
Annual Growth	5.1%	(12.6%)	—	3.5%

2012 Year-End Financials

Debt ratio: 28.9%
Return on equity: 6.4%
Cash ($ mil.): 13,520
Current ratio: 1.70
Long-term debt ($ mil.): 88,570
No. of shares (mil.): —
Dividends
Yield: 4.4%
Payout: 54.6%
Market value ($ mil.): —

	STOCK PRICE ($) FY Close	P/E High/Low		PER SHARE ($) Earnings	Dividends	Book Value
12/12	19.47	38	21	0.85	0.86	12.87
12/11	24.85	27	14	1.54	0.93	13.48
12/10	37.84	25	16	1.94	0.99	24.39
12/09	47.68	30	13	1.77	1.05	18.54
12/08	24.49	61	7	2.15	0.80	12.20
Annual Growth	(5.6%)	—	—	(20.7%)	2.0%	1.3%

Petroliam Nasional Berhad (Malaysia)

LOCATIONS

HQ: Petroliam Nasional Berhad (Malaysia)
Tower 1, Petronas Twin Towers, Kuala Lumpur City Centre, Kuala Lumpur 50088
Phone: (60) 3 **Fax:** (60) 3
Web: www.petronas.com

HISTORICAL FINANCIALS

Company Type: Public

Income Statement FYE: December 31

	REVENUE ($ mil.)	NET INCOME ($ mil.)	NET PROFIT MARGIN	EMPLOYEES
12/12	95,035	16,130	17.0%	46,145
12/11*	70,305	15,419	21.9%	43,266
03/11	79,744	18,131	22.7%	41,628
03/10	66,332	12,348	18.6%	40,992
03/09	72,459	14,412	19.9%	39,236
Annual Growth	7.0%	2.9%	—	4.1%

*Fiscal year change

2012 Year-End Financials

Debt ratio: 2.8%
Return on equity: 16.6%
Cash ($ mil.): 35,187
Current ratio: 2.34
Long-term debt ($ mil.): 10,468

No. of shares (mil.): 100
Dividends
Yield: —
Payout: —
Market value ($ mil.): —

Peugeot S.A. (France)

Peugeot S.A. enjoys its space under L'Arc de Triomphe besting rival Renault to claim the top spot in the battle for auto sales in France. Peugeot makes cars and light commercial vehicles under the Peugeot and Citroen brands. Peugeot is among the top manufacturers in European passenger car and commercial vehicle sales. Also part of Peugeot's automotive operations are Faurecia (auto parts) GEFCO (transportation and logistics) and Banque PSA Finance (financial services for dealers and customers). Other group products include motorcycles and scooters. Peugeot makes most of its sales in Europe. The Peugeot family controls about 38% of the voting stock.

The Peugeot brand rolled out more than 2.1 million vehicles in 2011. Sales outside Europe accounted for 48% of the total. Peugeot models include the Peugeot 508 RXH the Peugeot 3008 crossover and the RCZ coupe. Citroen sold more than 1.4 million cars in 2011. Citroen models include the DS4 DS5 C3 Picasso C4 and C-Crosser. Both brands boast electric cars the Peugeot iOn and the Citroen C-ZERO as well as electric commercial vehicles the Peugeot Partner Origin and Citroen Berlingo First. The company has sold about 4000 electric vehicles and has orders for more than 6000.

Financing vehicle sales as well as vehicle and replacement part inventories at dealers Banque PSA Finance operates in more than 20 countries. It annually provides financing for more than 840000 vehicles. Deriving about 38% of its sales from non-Peugeot clients Gefco provides upstream and downstream logistics services in about 150 countries. Peugeot plans to sell all or part of Gefco in 2012. Faurecia 57% owned by Peugeot focuses its automotive equipment operations on automotive seating emissions control technologies interior systems and automotive exteriors. Faurecia operates at about 240 locations and about 40 research and development centers in more than 30 countries.

Peugeot's consolidated sales and revenue rose about 7% in 2011 compared with 2010. By segment the automotive division's consolidated revenue increased 3% over the same period. New vehicle sales similarly went up about 3%. By region the division responded to strong demand in Latin America China and Russia. Also the percentage of premium cars sold rose from 13% in 2010 to 18% in 2011.

Faurecia soared 17% in 2011 versus 2010. Sales of the division's catalytic converter monoliths rose about 24% while sales of R&D tooling and prototypes headed up 19%. The division also enjoyed strong sales in all regions. European sales were up 11 while North America jumped about 33% Asia headed up 15% South America surged about 15% and the rest of the world increased about 31%.

Gefco jumped about 13% in 2011 versus 2010 supported by the acquisition of 70% of the Italy-based Mercurio group which transports vehicles worldwide in May 2011. The Mercurio acquisition boosted the segment's business in downstream logistics. Services for external customers rose 19%.

Banque PSA Finance inched up about 3%. The segment financed about 28% of all new Peugeot and Citroen cars in 2011. It enjoyed especially strong demand in Argentina Brazil and Russia.

While Peugeot is anticipating a contraction of auto sales in the European auto market it expects to see strong growth in China Latin America and Russia. In China where the company has a market share of more than 3% the Peugeot brand boasts more than 500 sales outlets while Citroen has about 860. To boost Latin American sales the company has launched two locally produced models the Peugeot 408 and Citroen C3 Picasso. In Russia the two brands operate more than 140 sales outlets that cover 90% of the country.

In 2012 Peugeot and General Motors announced that they would form an alliance to share vehicle platforms components and modules and to establish a global purchasing joint venture. The companies hope the partnership will create annual savings of $2 billion within five years. As part of the deal GM will pay $400 million to $470 million (depending on market conditions) for a 7% stake in Peugeot. The company's engine partnership with BMW gave birth to a 50/50 joint venture in 2011 to produce powertrain components such as battery packs power electronics and software for hybrid vehicles. The main components used in BMW's and Peugeot's hybrid vehicles will be standardized thus saving manufacturing and development costs for both car companies.

HISTORY

In 1810 brothers Frederic and Jean-Pierre Peugeot made a foundry out of the family textile mill in the Alsace region of France and invented the cold-roll process for producing spring steel. Bicycle production began in 1885 at the behest of avid cyclist Armand Peugeot Jean-Pierre's grandson.

Armand turned to automobiles and built Peugeot's first car a steam-powered three-wheeler in 1889. A gas-fueled Peugeot tied for first place in the 1894 Paris-Rouen Trials the earliest auto race on record. That year the budding carmaker built the first station wagon followed in 1905 by the first compact the 600-pound "Le Bebe."

Peugeot built factories in France including one in Sochaux (1912) that remains the company's main plant. It made the first diesel passenger car in 1922. The 1929 introduction of the reliable 201 model was followed by innovations such as synchromesh gears in 1936. The company suffered heavy damage in WWII but quickly bounced back and began expanding overseas after the war.

In 1954 CEO Roland Peugeot rebuffed a board proposal calling for global expansion that would place the company in competition with US automakers. By 1976 the French government persuaded Peugeot to merge with Citroen.

Andre Citroen founded his company in 1915 and in 1919 it became the first in Europe to mass-produce cars. Citroen hit the skids during the Depression and in 1934 handed Michelin a large block of stock in lieu of payment for tires. Citroen never fully recovered though by 1976 the company's line ranged from the 2CV minicar (discontinued in 1990) to limousines.

In 1978 Peugeot bought Chrysler's aging European plants and withering nameplates including Simca (France) and Rootes (UK). Peugeot changed the nameplates to Talbot but sales continued to slide. It lost nearly $1.2 billion from 1980 to 1984.

Jacques Calvet took over as CEO in 1984. He cut 30000 jobs and spent heavily on modernization. Aided by the strong launch of the 205 superminicar Peugeot returned to profitability in 1985 and by 1989 had halved its production break-even point. In the 1980s Peugeot inked production deals with Renault (industrial vehicles motors gearboxes) and Fiat (light trucks) and introduced a reasonably priced electric van in 1990.

Peugeot withdrew from the US in 1991 after five years of declining sales. A year later Renault and Peugeot developed electric cars and set up servicing centers throughout France. Citing an economic slump in 1993 Peugeot suffered its first loss ($239 million) since 1985. A French government incentive to replace cars more than 10 years old boosted 1994 sales.

Peugeot and rival Renault together introduced a V6 engine in 1996. Jean Martin Folz replaced Calvet as managing board chairman in 1997; Folz headed up Peugeot for 10 years and was replaced by Christian Streiff in 2007. In 1998 the company began building Peugeots and Citroens in the same plants and created its Faurecia unit when its ECIA subsidiary merged with car parts maker Bertrand Faure. In an effort to capitalize on the growing South American car market the company purchased more than 80% of Argentina's Sevel and built a plant in Brazil. In 1999 the company sold its flight systems supplier SAMM to TRW's Lucas Aerospace unit.

With demand for its cars falling steeply in South America due to the region's continuing economic crisis Peugeot restructured its Brazil operations in 2000 and formed a new subsidiary Citroen do Brasil.

In 2001 Peugeot announced that it was building an engine plant in Brazil and agreed to produce a subcompact car for the European market with Toyota. The following year Peugeot formed an alliance with BMW to develop and build a line of small diesel engines for use in vehicles made by both companies.

In 2005 Peugeot achieved a major milestone when for the first time it sold more than 1 million units outside its traditional market of Western Europe or 30% of total sales. Large gains were made in South America and even more so in China. In 2006 the company repeated the feat. With Western Europe a mature market Peugeot was looking to three key emerging markets to drive future growth: China the Mercosur region (Argentina Brazil Paraguay and Uruguay) and Central and Eastern Europe.

EXECUTIVES

Vice Chairman, Jean-Philippe Peugeot
Chairman, Thierry Peugeot
Executive Vice-President of Human Resources at PSA Peugeot Citro, Philippe Dorge
Vice Chairman, Jean-Louis Silvant
Director, Robert Peugeot
Director, Jean-Paul Parayre, age 75
Director, Joseph F. Toot Jr.
Vice Chairman, Jean-Philippe Peugeot
Director, Marc Freidel, age 64
Director, Jean-Louis Masurel
Director, Marie-Helene Roncoroni
Director, Henri-Philippe Reichstul, age 63
Director, Ernest-Antoine Seilliere
Director, Geoffroy Roux de Bezieux
Auditors: PricewaterhouseCoopers

LOCATIONS

HQ: Peugeot S.A. (France)
75, avenue de la Grande-Armee, Paris 75116
Phone: (33) 1 40 66 55 11 **Fax:** (33) 1 40 66 54 14
Web: www.psa-peugeot-citroen.com

2011 Sales

	% of total
Europe	73
Latin	9
Asia	5
Russia	3
Rest of the	10
Total	**100**

PRODUCTS/OPERATIONS

2011 Sales

% of sales

Automotive division	66	
Faurecia	25	
Gefco	6	
Banque PSA Finance	3	
Total	**0**	**100**

2011 Sales

Units	% of total	
Peugeot brand	2,114,000	60
Citroen brand	1,436,000	40
Total	**3,550,000**	**100**

Selected Subsidiaries

Citroen
Peugeot
Banque PSA Finance
Faurecia (57% automotive components)
GEFCO (transportation and logistics services)

COMPETITORS

BMW
CRCAM IDF CCI
Chrysler
Daimler
Fiat
Ford Motor
General Motors
Honda
Isuzu
Kia Motors
Mazda
Nissan
Norbert Dentressangle
Piaggio & Co.
Renault
Saab Automobile
Suzuki Motor
Toyota
Volkswagen
Volvo Car Corp.
Yamaha Motor

HISTORICAL FINANCIALS

Company Type: Public

Income Statement FYE: December 31

	REVENUE ($ mil.)	NET INCOME ($ mil.)	NET PROFIT MARGIN	EMPLOYEES
12/12	73,080	(6,603)	—	204,287
12/11	77,493	760	1.0%	0
12/10	75,030	1,517	2.0%	198,220
12/09	69,748	(1,672)	—	186,220
12/08	75,994	(479)	—	201,700
Annual Growth	(1.0%)	—	—	0.3%

2012 Year-End Financials

Debt ratio: 66.1%
Return on equity: (-42.2%)
Cash ($ mil.): 8,977
Current ratio: 1.04
Long-term debt ($ mil.): 10,317
No. of shares (mil.): 342
Dividends
Yield: 53.9%
Payout: —
Market value ($ mil.): 2,548

	STOCK PRICE ($) FY Close	P/E High	P/E Low	PER SHARE ($) Earnings	Dividends	Book Value
12/12	7.45	—	—	(20.56)	4.02	37.85
12/11	15.62	33	10	3.31	2.97	82.52
12/10	38.10	16	7	6.65	0.00	81.58
12/09	34.00	—	—	(7.38)	0.00	78.18
12/08	17.25	—	—	(2.11)	2.31	81.00
Annual Growth	(18.9%)	—	—	—	14.8%	(17.3%)

PICC Property and Casualty Co Ltd

PICC Property and Casualty (PICC P&C) is the leading property and casualty (P&C) insurer in bustling China. Founded in 1949 as the state-owned People's Insurance Company of China (now known as PICC Holding) PICC P&C was spun off in 2003. (Another unit PICC Asset Management was created as a life insurance provider.) It operates throughout most of China with more than 4000 branch offices providing primarily auto insurance (nearly 70% of sales). Additional types of coverage include commercial property liability accident and homeowners insurance.

Founded just 20 days after ceremonies marking the founding of China PICC P&C has survived a twenty-year suspension of insurance activities within China to control 70% of the P&C market in spite of increasing competition both from China-based insurers and from foreign companies entering the burgeoning marketplace.

EXECUTIVES

Chairman, Wu Yan, age 48
Vice Chairman and President, Wang Yincheng, age 48
EVP Board Secretary and Director, Liu Zhenghuan, age 59
EVP, Guo Shengchen, age 54
EVP, Zhao Shuxian, age 56
EVP, Jia Haimao, age 55
EVP, Wang He, age 52
Chief Compliance Officer, Wang Yueshu, age 53
EVP, Wang Dedi, age 51
EVP, Jiang Caishi, age 44
Secretary, Man Kam Ching
Vice Chairman and President, Wang Yincheng, age 48
EVP Board Secretary and Director, Liu Zhenghuan, age 59
Director, Zhou Shurui, age 56
Director, Edmund S.W. Tse, age 71
Director, Christopher W. C. Cheng, age 60
Director, Lu Zhengfei, age 46
Director, Peter K. Y. Luk, age 68
Director, Ding Ningning, age 61
Auditors: Ernst&Young

LOCATIONS

HQ: PICC Property and Casualty Co Ltd
Tower 2, No. 2 Jianguomenwai Avenue, Chaoyang District, Beijing 100022
Phone: (86) 10 85176084 **Fax:** (86) 10 85176084
Web: www.piccnet.com.cn

PRODUCTS/OPERATIONS

2005 Sales

	% of total
Motor	68
Commercial	13
Cargo	4
Liability	4
Accidental	4
Homeowners	2
Other	5
Total	**100**

COMPETITORS

AIG
Allianz Guangzhou
CNinsure
China Life Insurance
China Pacific Property Insurance
Chubb Corp
Ping An Insurance

HISTORICAL FINANCIALS

Company Type: Public

Income Statement FYE: December 31

	ASSETS ($ mil.)	NET INCOME ($ mil.)	INCOME AS % OF ASSETS	EMPLOYEES
12/12	46,585	1,669	3.6%	156,364
12/11	42,203	1,275	3.0%	140,942
12/10	30,612	790	2.6%	60,629
12/09	24,221	261	1.1%	60,202
12/08	22,400	7	0.0%	59,669
Annual Growth	20.1%	288.5%	—	27.2%

2012 Year-End Financials

Return on assets: 3.7%
Return on equity: 25.7%
Long-term debt ($ mil.): —
No. of shares (mil.): —
Sales ($ mil): 26,122
Dividends
Yield: 0.0%
Payout: —
Market value ($ mil.): —

	STOCK PRICE ($) FY Close	P/E High	P/E Low	PER SHARE ($) Earnings	Dividends	Book Value
12/12	32.21	1	1	0.14	0.02	0.59
12/11	25.30	2	1	0.11	0.04	0.46
Annual Growth	27.3%	—	—	5.8%	(17.5%)	6.9%

Ping An Insurance (Group) Co of China Ltd.

Ping An Insurance is China's second-largest life insurance company (after China Life Insurance Company) and offers a variety of products including fire marine cargo and accident insurance as well as a home protection plan. The company also provides stock trading equity investment funds and bonds property leasing and asset management services through Ping An Trust; and its Shenzhen Ping An Bank subsidiary offers retail banking and other consumer services such as credit card and mortgage lending. In addition Ping An Insurance founded in 1988 has launched Ping An Health Insurance Company of China.

While insurance is still the company's main staple it is hoping to secure a prime spot in China's developing asset management industry.

London-based HSBC Holdings which has had operations in China for more than 140 years doubled its stake in Ping An to about 20% in 2006 through a $1 billion deal with shareholders Goldman Sachs Group and a unit of the private equity business of Morgan Stanley.

In 2008 Ping An agreed to acquire half of the asset management business of Fortis in an attempt to diversify its operations and make them more global in scope. However the deal valued at nearly $3.4 billion was terminated when Fortis foundered in late 2008.

Meanwhile the company's insurance arm set to investigating and paying claims from the 2008 earthquake and aftershocks in the Sichuan province. By 2009 the company had already paid out its largest claim ever: $105 million to Lafarge Shui Cement the worlds' largest cement manufacturer for damages to several cement plants it operated in that area.

EXECUTIVES

Chairman and CEO, Peter M. Z. Ma, age 56
President, Alex H. C. Ren, age 43
Chief Legal Officer and Joint Secretary, Jun Yao, age 46
Chief Finance Business Officer, Richard Jackson, age 56
SVP, Liping Wang, age 55
SVP and General Manager, Kexiang Chen, age 54
SVP and CIO, Sai Lai Lo, age 49
Investor Relations, Shaoliang Jin
Investor Relations, Zhang Xuewu
EVP Vice Chief Executive Officer and Director, Jianyi Sun, age 59
SVP and Chief Investment Officer, John Pearce, age 49
SVP, Shifan Cao, age 56
Director, Louis C. Y. Cheung, age 48
EVP Vice Chief Executive Officer and Director, Jianyi Sun, age 59
Director, Lijun Lin, age 49
Director, Peter T. S. Wong, age 60
Director, Sing Yip Ng, age 61
Director, Hongyi Zhang, age 66
Director, Su Chen, age 54
Director, Liping Xia, age 74
Auditors: Ernst&Young

LOCATIONS

HQ: Ping An Insurance (Group) Co of China Ltd.
Offices at 15, 16, 17, 18 Floors, Galaxy Development Center, Fu Hua No. 3 Road, Futian District, Shenzhen, Guangdong Province 518048
Phone: (86) 400 8866 338 **Fax:** (86) 755 8243 1029
Web: www.pingan.com

PRODUCTS/OPERATIONS

2007 Revenues

	% of total
Life	56
Property/casualty	11
Banking	8
Securities	8
Other	17
Total	**100**

Selected Subsidiaries & Affiliates

China Ping An Insurance Overseas (Holdings) Limited
China Ping An Insurance (Hong Kong) Company Limited (75%)
Ping An of China Asset Management (Hong Kong) Company Limited
China Ping An Trust & Investment Co. Ltd.
Ping An Securities Co. Ltd.
Ping An Annuity Insurance Company of China Ltd.
Ping An Health Insurance Company of China Ltd.
Ping An Life Insurance Company of China Ltd.
Ping An Property & Casualty Insurance Company of China Ltd.
Shenzhen Ping An Bank Co. Ltd.

COMPETITORS

CNinsure
China Insurance
China Life Insurance
China Pacific Insurance
China Pacific Property Insurance
Chubb Corp
PICC Property

HISTORICAL FINANCIALS

Company Type: Public

Income Statement FYE: December 31

	ASSETS ($ mil.)	NET INCOME ($ mil.)	INCOME AS % OF ASSETS	EMPLOYEES
12/12	456,232	3,216	0.7%	190,284
12/11	363,088	3,094	0.9%	175,136
12/10	177,745	2,626	1.5%	128,808
12/09	137,040	2,033	1.5%	100,267
12/08	110,605	39	0.0%	82,808
Annual Growth	42.5%	200.8%	—	23.1%

2012 Year-End Financials

Return on assets: 0.7%
Return on equity: 13.7%
Long-term debt ($ mil.): —
No. of shares (mil.): —
Sales ($ mil): 54,408
Dividends
Yield: 0.5%
Payout: 0.6%
Market value ($ mil.): —

	STOCK PRICE ($) FY Close	P/E High	P/E Low	PER SHARE ($) Earnings	Dividends	Book Value
12/12	17.19	0	0	0.41	0.10	3.23
12/11	13.11	0	0	0.40	0.00	2.63
12/10	22.45	0	0	0.35	0.11	2.22
12/09	17.59	0	0	0.28	0.08	1.69
12/08	9.10	11	3	0.01	0.00	1.66
Annual Growth	17.2%	—	—	188.5%	128.9%	18.2%

Piraeus Bank SA

Greece is the word and Piraeus has most certainly heard. Piraeus Bank provides retail banking investment banking leasing and insurance services in the Mediterranean and in Central and Eastern Europe. Its network of branches across Greece is approaching 1000 plus it has about 500 more in Albania (Tirana Bank) Romania Bulgaria Serbia the Ukraine and the US (New York's Marathon Bank). Piraeus Bank also provides its services through its electronic Winbank business which includes ATMs Internet and phone banking. The company maintains a diverse loan portfolio with energy and transportation loans making up 30% of its portfolio. Piraeus Bank was founded in 1916 and was under state control until 1991.

Since Piraeus Bank was privatized it has grown rapidly through acquisitions of other banks in Greece. The company also has expanded internationally into Central and Eastern Europe and elsewhere in the Mediterranean. It acquired Bulgarian Eurobank (now Piraeus Bank Bulgaria) Atlas Bank (renamed Piraeus Bank Beograd) Egyptian Commercia Bank (Piraeus Bank Egypt) Share Capital of International Commerce Bank in the Ukraine and the Cyprus branch network of Arab Bank (Piraeus Bank Cyprus).

In 2009 Piraeus Bank teamed with BNP Wealth Management to begin offering wealth management services. In another partnership that year the company signed an agreement with Victoria General Insurance Group in order to offer insurance. Piraeus Bank continues to seek investments for further growth.

EXECUTIVES

Chairman Board of Director and Executive Board, Michalis G. Sallas, age 64
Board Member and Managing Director; Chairman Romania and Beograd, Stavros M. Lekkakos, age 61
Board Member and Managing Director Chairman Piraeus Securities, Alexandros S. Manos
Board Member and Deputy Managing Director Retail Branch Network and Medium-Sized Enterprises, Christodoulos G. Antoniadis, age 58
Board Member and Deputy Managing Director International Banking, Ilias D. Milis
Board Member and Deputy Manager Director Retail Lending and Business Development, Spyros A. Papaspyrou, age 53
Director-Representative of the Hellenic Financial Stability Fund, Ekaterini Mperitsi
Chief Risk Officer, Georgios Mantakas
Chief Financial Officer; General Manager of Financial Management and Strategic Planning, Georgios Poulopoulos
Non-Executive Vice Chairman of the Board, Ioannis Vardinogiannis
Assistant General Manager, Konstantinos Paschalis
Non-Executive Vice Chairman of the Board, Panagiotis Roumeliotis
Director-Representative of the Hellenic Financial Stability Fund, Solomon Beracha
Board Member, Iakovos G. Georganas, age 81
Board Member, Georgios P. Alexandridis, age 80
Board Member and Managing Director; Chairman Romania and Beograd, Stavros M. Lekkakos, age 61
Board Member, Chariklia A. Apalagaki, age 54
Board Member, Vassilios S. Fourlis, age 53
Board Member, Stilianos D. Golemis
Board Member and Managing Director Chairman Piraeus Securities, Alexandros S. Manos

Board Member and Deputy Managing Director Retail Branch Network and Medium-Sized Enterprises, Christodoulos G. Antoniadis, age 58
Board Member and Deputy Managing Director International Banking, Ilias D. Milis
Board Member and Deputy Manager Director Retail Lending and Business Development, Spyros A. Papaspyrou, age 53
Board Member, Theordoros P. Mylonas, age 64
Director; Representing the Greek State, Athanasios Tsoumas
Non-Executive Member of the Board, Eftychios Vasilakis
Non-Executive Director, Jiri Smejc
Non-Executive Director, Konstantin Yanakov
Non-Executive Independent Member of the Board, Stylianos Gkolemis

LOCATIONS

HQ: Piraeus Bank SA
4 Amerikis str., Athens 105 64
Phone: (30) 210 333 5000 **Fax:** (30) 210 333 5080
Web: www.piraeusbankgroup.com

PRODUCTS/OPERATIONS

Selected Subsidiaries

ATEbank
ETBA Industrial Areas S.A.
Marathon Bank of New York (USA)
OJSC Piraeus Bank ICB (Ukraine)
Picar S.A.
Piraeus Asset Management Mutual Funds S.A.
Piraeus Bank AD Beograd (Serbia)
Piraeus Bank Bulgaria AD
Piraeus Bank (Cyprus) Ltd
Piraeus Bank Egypt SAE
Piraeus Capital Management
Piraeus Card Services
Piraeus Direct Services S.A.
Piraeus Insurance and Reinsurance Brokerage S.A.
Piraeus Insurance Agency S.A.
Piraeus Factoring S.A.
Piraeus Leaases SA
Piraeus Leasing Bulgaria
Piraeus Bank Romania S.A.
Piraeus Leasing Romania
Piraeus Private Equity
Piraeus Real Estate S.A.
Piraeus Securities S.A.
Piraeus Wealth Management
Tirana Bank S.A. (Albania)
Tirana Leasing (Albania)

COMPETITORS

Alpha Bank
Bank of Cyprus
EFG Eurobank Ergasias
Emporiki Bank
National Bank of Greece

HISTORICAL FINANCIALS

Company Type: Public

Income Statement

FYE: December 31

	ASSETS ($ mil.)	NET INCOME ($ mil.)	INCOME AS % OF ASSETS	EMPLOYEES
12/12	92,798	(671)	—	18,872
12/11	63,834	(8,554)	—	12,806
12/10	77,038	(27)	—	13,320
12/01	10,922	45	0.4%	0
12/00	10,513	133	1.3%	0
Annual Growth	19.9%	—	—	—

2012 Year-End Financials

Return on assets:
Return on equity: ***,***.*%
Long-term debt ($ mil.): —
No. of shares (mil.): —
Sales ($ mil): 5,458
Dividends
Yield: —
Payout: —
Market value ($ mil.): —

	STOCK PRICE ($) FY Close	P/E High/Low	PER SHARE ($) Earnings	Dividends	Book Value
12/12	6.45	— —	(0.58)	0.00	(1.30)
12/11	6.45	— —	(7.91)	0.00	(1.08)
12/10	6.45	— —	(0.04)	0.00	10.20
Annual Growth	(0.0%)	— —	—	—	—

POSCO (South Korea)

POSCO has steeled itself for any set of business conditions. The company makes hot- and cold-rolled steel products (plate steel stainless steel electrical steel and wire rods) which it sells to the auto shipbuilding home appliance engineering and machinery industries. It produces more than 39 million tons of steel a year making it the world's #3 steelmaker behind ArcelorMittal and Nippon Steel. Majority-owned POSCO Engineering & Construction builds industrial facilities such as steel plants and energy plants. POSCO Energy is Korea's largest private power generator and subsidiary Daewoo International is a global steel and raw materials trading company. Most of POSCO's sales are to Korean markets.

POSCO's hot- and cold-rolled products segments account for about two-thirds of sales. Hot-rolled products are used in the construction of automobile chassis buildings and bridges industrial pipes and tanks and railway rolling stocks. The company's cold-rolled products such as cold-rolled coils and galvanized cold-rolled products are used in the automotive industry to manufacture car body panels and for other uses like household goods electrical appliances and engineering and metal parts. It produces most of its steel at its integrated steel facilities Pohang Works and Gwangyang Works. POSCO also engages in steel and raw materials trading and invests in energy and mineral development projects around the world though its Daewoo International unit.

South Korea has little native iron ore and POSCO has had to look elsewhere for its raw materials. It purchases iron ore or coal from Australia Brazil Canada South Africa and the US from companies such as Vale Rio Tinto and BHP Billiton. To expand its production operations POSCO has developed joint ventures with companies in China Southeast Asia and Latin America.

In 2011 the company reported an 11% rise in revenues (a more than 40% increase in local revenues) thanks in part to higher selling prices for its steel and wire rod products but primarily because of a 200%-plus growth in trading revenues as the result of the Daewoo acquisition in 2010. However POSCO reported a drop of 13% in net income for the year as major cost increases related to the Daewoo purchase outpaced revenue growth.

To geographically expand its operations POSCO has an alliance with long-time rival Nippon Steel whereby each has taken a small stake in the other; it has also formed a joint venture with Steel Authority of India and plans to establish agreements with other steelmakers in China and Europe.

POSCO is looking to expand into the energy industry market for steel plate (used in the construction oil platforms). In 2012 it secured a steel supply contract from rig maker Samkang M&T for North Sea rigs and has set its sights on getting a 10% global share of the oil and gas industry's steel plate market by 2020.

In 2011 POSCO entered a $6 billion joint venture with Vale's Mozambique operations to mine coal in the southern part of that country. The mine expected to produce 11 million tons of metallurgical coal a year will help POSCO maintain a steady supply of raw materials for its steel mills. At the same time POSCO agreed to set up a similar joint mining venture in neighboring Zimbabwe with Anchor Holdings to develop chrome coal iron ore and other minerals.

That same year POSCO acquired a 20% stake in US-based graphene company XG Sciences in a move to diversify its business. Graphene is a raw material used to manufacture high-tension nanocarbon. POSCO also moved to acquire all of Thailand-based stainless steel producer Thainox Stainless pcl in 2011. POSCCO already owned a 16% stake but had waited for political stability to return to Thailand before acquiring the balance.

HISTORY

After the Korean War South Korea the US and its allies wanted to rebuild South Korea's infrastructure as quickly as possible. Steel was given a high priority and before long about 15 companies were making various steel products. Quality was a problem though as the companies used dated production processes.

With the backing of South Korean president Chung Hee Park momentum for a large steel plant grew in the late 1960s. In 1967 the South Korean government and Korean International Steel Associates (KISA) —a consortium of seven Western steelmakers - signed an agreement that called for the completion of an integrated mill by 1972. Pohang Iron & Steel Co. (POSCO) the operating company was incorporated in 1968. Efforts to raise the necessary capital failed however and KISA was dissolved in 1969.

Undaunted the South Koreans turned to the Japanese who arranged loans covering most of the mill's costs and the early phases of planning and construction. The Japanese also transferred the technology needed to run such a plant. Slow and deliberate planning resulted in a plant far away from Seoul (part of a plan to locate industries throughout the country) and a design that lent itself to future expansion. The first stage including a blast furnace and two steel converters was completed in 1973. By the time the fourth stage of construction began in 1979 the Koreans had gained enough confidence to take over many of the tasks. When the last stage was completed in 1981 the plant had an annual capacity of 8.5 million tons.

To ensure steel of acceptable quality POSCO focused first on plain high-carbon steel for general construction rather than on specialized (and difficult to produce) varieties. The company gradually broadened its specialized offerings.

In 1985 POSCO began construction on a second integrated steel plant located in Kwangyang. That plant was also built in four stages; its annual production capacity when it was completed in 1992 was 11.4 million tons. By 1987 POSCO was exporting almost 3 million tons of steel a year and using its knowledge to assist in plant construction projects in other countries.

By the mid-1990s POSCO was exporting 6 million tons of steel annually. The South Korean government sold a 5% stake in POSCO to the public in 1998 and vowed to open up the primary steelmaking industry to competition. However facing a severe downturn in steel demand that year because of sluggishness in Asian and domestic markets the company canceled two projects in China and suspended two in Indonesia. In 1999 POSCO merged its two subsidiaries Pohang Coated Steel and Pohang Steel Industries to create Pohang Steel Co. That same year POSCO Machinery & Engineering POSEC-HAWAII and P.T. Posnesia Stainless Steel Industry were joined to form POSCO Machinery Co. The South Korean government continued selling off its 13% stake in 1999.

In 2000 POSCO sold its 51% stake in telecommunications company Shinsegi Telecom to SK Telecom in exchange for cash and a 6.5% stake in SK Telecom. It also formed a strategic alliance –exploration of joint ventures shared research and joint procurement –with Nippon Steel the world's #1 steelmaker. The deal also calls for each to take increased equity stakes (2% or 3%) in the other. After about 30 years of government control the South Korean government sold its remaining shares of POSCO in 2001.

In June 2002 Chairman Yoo was indicted for influencing POSCO subsidiaries and contractors to buy inflated shares of Tiger Pools International (South Korea's sole sports lottery business) for Kim Hong-Gul the third son of South Korean President Kim Dae-Jung. That same year Pohang Iron & Steel Co. officially changed its company name to POSCO to try and strengthen brand recognition.

In 2003 Yoo resigned ahead of the company's shareholder meeting amid his possible involvement in illegal stock transactions.

The company invested in its Mexican operations in 2006 announcing a joint venture coil processing facility with Daewoo International to serve local carmakers. In 2010 POSCO acquired a majority stake in Daewoo International. Daewoo shareholders voted to put the company's depressed shares up for sale after the South Korean government gave its approval for the deal early in 2010.

EXECUTIVES

CEO, Joon-Yang Chung, age 66
EVP and Head of Growth and Investment Division, Yoon Yong-Won, age 61
President Chief Financial and Planning Officer and Director, Choi Jong-Tae, age 62
CEO and Director, Joon-Yang Chung, age 64
Director, Sun Wook, age 67
Director, Charles Ahn, age 50
Director, Yoo Jang-Hee, age 71
Director, Han Joon-Ho, age 66
Director, Kim Byung-Ki, age 32
Director, Lee Chang-Hee, age 52
Director, Park Sang-Yong, age 61
Auditors: KPMGSamjongAccountingCorp.

LOCATIONS

HQ: POSCO (South Korea)
1, Goedong-dong, Nam-gu, Pohang, Gyeongsangbuk-do 790-300
Phone: (82) 54 220 0114 **Fax:** (82) 54 220 6000
Web: www.posco.co.kr

2011 Sales

	$ mil.	% of total
Asia/Pacific		
China	9	
Other Asia	4	
Other regions	4	

PRODUCTS/OPERATIONS

2011 Sales

	$ mil.	% of total
Steel	57	
Construction	8	
Total	0	100

COMPETITORS

ArcelorMittal
Baosteel
Bechtel
Fluor
Hitachi
Hyundai Steel
JFE Holdings
Kobe Steel
Mitsubishi Steel Mfg.
Nippon Steel & Sumitomo Metal Corporation
Samsung Group
Severstal
Tata Steel
ThyssenKrupp Steel
United States Steel

HISTORICAL FINANCIALS

Company Type: Public

Income Statement FYE: December 31

	REVENUE ($ mil.)	NET INCOME ($ mil.)	NET PROFIT MARGIN	EMPLOYEES
12/12	59,571	2,305	3.9%	0
12/11	59,496	3,148	5.3%	17,553
12/10	42,707	3,661	8.6%	16,390
12/09	31,852	2,781	8.7%	16,516
12/08	32,886	3,449	10.5%	16,707
Annual Growth	16.0%	(9.6%)	—	—

2012 Year-End Financials

Debt ratio: 0.0%
Return on equity: 6.3%
Cash ($ mil.): 4,383
Current ratio: 1.60
Long-term debt ($ mil.): 13,498
No. of shares (mil.): 77
Dividends
Yield: 2.5%
Payout: 7.0%
Market value ($ mil.): 6,346

	STOCK PRICE ($) FY Close	P/E High/Low		PER SHARE ($) Earnings	Dividends	Book Value
12/12	82.15	—	—	29.85	2.09	478.38
12/11	82.10	—	—	40.76	0.00	428.55
12/10	107.69	—	—	48.09	1.97	423.45
12/09	131.10	—	—	36.28	1.57	346.78
12/08	75.25	—	—	45.70	2.59	284.64
Annual Growth	2.2%	—	—	(10.1%)	(5.2%)	13.9%

Power Corp. of Canada

Founded in the 1920s to develop hydroelectric power Power Corporation of Canada now generates cash not electricity. Through its majority stake in Power Financial the company controls one of Canada's leading mutual fund firms (IGM Financial) one of its largest life insurers (Great-West Lifeco) and other insurance firms. It also owns Gesca which publishes Montreal's "La Presse" and six other daily newspapers in Quebec and Ontario and a majority of Pargesa Group which has stakes in large companies involved in energy (TOTAL) utilities (GDF SUEZ) construction (Lafarge) wines and spirits (Pernod Ricard) and other sectors in Europe through a controlling stake in Groupe Bruxelles Lambert.

In addition Power Corporation has investments in hedge funds private equity fund managers in France and the US and companies involved in biotechnology clean tech digital media and television production. Through Great-West Lifeco the company owns US-based mutual fund manager Putnam which it acquired from insurance brokerage Marsh & McLennan in 2007. The nearly $4 billion deal gave Power Corporation a significant presence in the US.

The company proved to be rather resilient during the economic downturn as its portfolio companies for the most part performed relatively well. Earnings were up in 2010 as IGM Financial and Great-West Lifeco reported higher sales. Power Corporation continues to focus on its core asset management and retirement planning operations and build the online presence of its media holdings. In 2011 the company made a move to enter China's fast-growing fund management sector by arranging to buy a 10% state in China Asset Management.

Former chairman Paul Desmarais (whose sons Paul and Andre are co-CEOs) owns more than 60% of Power Corporation of Canada.

EXECUTIVES

VP and Controller, Denis Le Vasseur
Director; Vice Chairman Power Financial, Raymond L. McFeetors, age 68
Director; President and CEO Power Financial, R. Jeffrey Orr
VP, Peter Kruyt, age 58
SVP General Counsel and Secretary, Edward Johnson
SVP, Arnaud Vial, age 61, $452,627 total compensation
Executive Vice President, John A. Rae, $426,128 total compensation
Deputy Chairman, Robert Gratton, age 69
Chairman and Co-CEO; Co-Chairman Power Financial, Paul Desmarais Jr., age 59, $952,900 total compensation
EVP and CFO Power Corporation of Canada and Power Financial, Gregory D. Tretiak
Vice Chairman Power Corporation of Canada and Power Financial, Henri-Paul Rousseau, age 64
Treasurer, Isabelle Morin
VP, Daniel Friedberg
VP and Assistant General Counsel, Stephane Lemay
VP and Head Corporate Finance, Richard Pan
VP, Luc Reny
Vice President; Controller, Denis Vasseur
Vice President, Pierre Larochelle
Vice President, Yuhong Liu
Vice President; General Counsel; Secretary, Stephane Lemay
Director; Vice Chairman Power Financial, Raymond L. McFeetors, age 68
Director; President and CEO Power Financial, R. Jeffrey Orr
EVP and Director, John A. Rae
Deputy Chairman President and Co-CEO; Co-Chairman Power Financial, Andre R. Desmarais, age 55
Director, Isabelle Marcoux, age 43
Vice Chairman, Michel Plessis-Belair, age 70
Deputy Chairman, Robert Gratton, age 69
Vice Chairman Power Corporation of Canada and Power Financial, Henri-Paul Rousseau, age 64
Director, James R. Nininger
Director, Paul Desmarais Sr., age 85
Director, Pierre Beaudoin, age 55
Director, Rt. Hon. Donald F. (Don) Mazankowski, age 78
Director, Laurent Dassault, age 60
Director, Anthony R. Graham, age 56
Director, Jerry E. A. Nickerson, age 77
Director, Emoke J. E. Szathmary
Director, Robert Parizeau
Director, Guy Fortin
Independent Director, Emoke Szathmary
Independent Director, Marcel Coutu
Auditors: Deloitte&ToucheLLP

LOCATIONS

HQ: Power Corp. of Canada
751 Victoria Square, Montreal, Quebec H2Y 2J3
Phone: 514 286-7400 **Fax:** 514 286-7484
Web: www.powercorporation.com

2010 Sales

	% of total
Canada	52
Europe	28
US	20
Total	**100**

PRODUCTS/OPERATIONS

2010 Sales

	% of total
Premium	54
Net investment	29
Fees & media	17
Total	**100**

2010 Sales by Segment

	% of total
Great-West	91
IGM	8
Other	1
Total	**100**

Selected Investments

Communications
- Gesca Ltee (newspaper publisher)
- Square Victoria Communications Group Inc.
  - Square Victoria Digital Properties Inc.

Financial Services
- Great-West Lifeco Inc. (68%)
  - The Canada Life Assurance Company
  - Great-West Life & Annuity Insurance Company
  - The Great-West Life Assurance Company
  - London Life Insurance Company
  - Putnam Investments LLC
- IGM Financial Inc. (57%)
  - Investment Planning Counsel (91%)
  - Investors Group
  - Mackenzie Financial Corporation
- Power Financial Corporation (66%)
- Victoria Square Ventures Inc.

Other
- Pergesa Holding S.A. (Switzerland)

COMPETITORS

AGF Management
Berkshire Hathaway
Brookfield Asset Management
CI Financial
CPP Investment Board
Caisse de depot et placement du Quebec
Counsel Corporation
Dundee Corp.
Loews
Manulife Financial
Onex
Ontario Teachers' Pension Plan

HISTORICAL FINANCIALS

Company Type: Public

Income Statement

FYE: December 31

	ASSETS ($ mil.)	NET INCOME ($ mil.)	INCOME AS % OF ASSETS	EMPLOYEES
12/12	273,127	50	0.0%	30,900
12/11	250,461	40	0.0%	30,700
12/10	248,053	41	0.0%	31,126
12/09	136,405	650	0.5%	30,744
12/08	117,062	707	0.6%	31,700
Annual Growth	23.6%	(48.4%)	—	(0.6%)

2012 Year-End Financials

Return on assets: 0.0%
Return on equity: 0.5%
Long-term debt ($ mil.): —
No. of shares (mil.): 411
Sales ($ mil): 33,207

Dividends
Yield: 0.0%
Payout: 64.8%
Market value ($ mil.): 10,517

	STOCK PRICE ($) FY Close	P/E High/Low		PER SHARE ($) Earnings	Dividends	Book Value
12/12	25.58	16	11	1.80	1.17	24.70
12/11	23.33	13	8	2.27	1.14	23.43
12/10	27.79	19	14	1.57	1.16	23.06
12/09	27.68	19	6	1.34	1.11	56.40
12/08	18.19	19	5	1.47	0.91	47.47
Annual Growth	8.9%	—	—	5.3%	6.5%	(15.1%)

Power Financial Corp

Power Financial gets a charge out of insurance and investments. The holding company seeks controlling stakes in financial services companies in the US the UK and Canada. Core investments include 68%-owned Great-West Lifeco (subsidiaries include Great-West Life Assurance Canada Life and London Life Insurance leading providers of insurance in Canada). Lifeco's US subsidiary Great-West Life & Annuity Insurance provides employee benefits and retirement plans. Boston-based fund manager Putnam Investments is also part of the family. Power Financial owns about half of IGM Financial which owns Investors Group and Mackenzie Financial distributors of mutual funds and other investment products and services.

Power Financial also is a 50% partner in Dutch holding company Parjointco with the Frere-Bourgeois and CNP groups the joint venture that owns a 54% stake in Pargesa which invests in building materials utilities minerals and energy companies (with Groupe Bruxelles Lambert it owns stakes in Imerys and TOTAL).

In 2007 Power Financial surprised many when it purchased the once-venerable but recently disgraced Putnam Investments. Speculation turned to I-told-you-so the following year when Putnam like most money managers was slammed by the subprime mortgage and credit market collapse. In mid-2008 Power Financial brought in long-time Fidelity Investments COO Robert Reynolds as president and CEO of Putnam. The new leader trimmed staff tied pay to performance and started two new funds to attract fresh money.

Power Corporation of Canada the country's fifth largest firm by revenue owns two-thirds of Power Financial. Canada's well-known billionaire Desmarais family controls Power Corporation.

EXECUTIVES

VP and Controller, Denis Le Vasseur
Vice Chairman, Raymond L. McFeetors, age 68, $1,821,767 total compensation
President Chief Executive Officer, R. Jeffrey Orr, $2,880,391 total compensation
Senior Vice-President, Arnaud Vial, age 61, $132,548 total compensation
SVP General Counsel and Secretary, Edward D. Johnson
Co-Chairman, Paul Desmarais Jr., age 59, $408,900 total compensation
Vice Chairman, Henri-Paul Rousseau, age 64
Human Resources Director, Luc Reny
Managing Director Power Financial Europe, Jocelyn Lefebvre, age 56
Treasurer, Isabelle Morin
Executive Vice-President Chief Financial Officer, Gregory D. Tretiak
Vice-President Controller, Denis Vasseur
Vice President, Richard Pan
Vice President; General Counsel; Secretary, Stephane Lemay
Vice Chairman, Raymond L. McFeetors, age 68
President CEO and Director, R. Jeffrey Orr
Co-Chairman, Andre R. Desmarais, age 55
Director, Raymond Royer, age 74
Director, Michel Plessis-Belair, age 70
Director, Robert Gratton, age 69
Vice Chairman, Henri-Paul Rousseau, age 64
Director, Paul Desmarais Sr., age 85
Director, Rt. Hon. Donald F. (Don) Mazankowski, age 76
Director, J. Brian Aune, age 72
Director, Louise Roy
Director, Anthony R. Graham, age 56
Director, Gerald Frere, age 61
Director, Jerry E. A. Nickerson, age 75
Director, Emoke J. E. Szathmary
Director, V. Peter Harder, age 60
Director, Marc A. Bibeau
Director, Amaury de Seze
Independent Director, Emoke Szathmary
Independent Director, Gerald Frere
Auditors: Deloitte&ToucheLLP

LOCATIONS

HQ: Power Financial Corp
751 Victoria Square, Montreal, Quebec H2Y 2J3
Phone: 514 286-7400 **Fax:** 514 286-7484
Web: www.powerfinancial.com

2010 Revenues

Canada	52
US	20

PRODUCTS/OPERATIONS

2010 Revenues

Great-West Lifeco	70
Pargesa	7

Selected Subsidiaries & Affiliates

Great-West Lifeco Inc. (68%)
- Great-West Life & Annuity Insurance Company (US)
- Great-West Life Assurance Company
  - Canada Life Financial Corporation
  - London Insurance Group Inc.
- Putnam LLC

IGM Financial Inc. (57%)
- Investment Planning Counsel (94%)
- Investors Group Inc.
- Mackenzie Financial Corporation

COMPETITORS

AXA Financial
Allstate
CIGNA
Industrial Alliance Insurance and Financial Servic
Manulife Financial
Prudential
RBC Financial Group
State Farm
Sun Life

HISTORICAL FINANCIALS

Company Type: Public

Income Statement

FYE: December 31

	ASSETS ($ mil.)	NET INCOME ($ mil.)	INCOME AS % OF ASSETS	EMPLOYEES
12/12	270,058	1,634	0.6%	17,870
12/11	247,698	1,688	0.7%	29,100
12/10*	245,165	1,471	0.6%	0
01/10	222,678	0	—	0
12/09	133,757	1,372	1.0%	0
Annual Growth	26.4%	6.0%	—	—

*Fiscal year change

2012 Year-End Financials

Return on assets: 0.6%
Return on equity: 11.7%
Long-term debt ($ mil.): —
No. of shares (mil.): 709
Sales ($ mil): 32,723

Dividends
Yield: 0.0%
Payout: 60.8%
Market value ($ mil.): 19,351

	STOCK PRICE ($) FY Close	P/E High	P/E Low	PER SHARE ($) Earnings	PER SHARE ($) Dividends	PER SHARE ($) Book Value
12/12	27.29	13	10	2.31	1.41	19.89
12/11	25.07	14	9	2.36	1.37	18.72
12/10*	30.84	16	12	2.06	1.37	18.13
01/10	29.49	—	—	(0.00)	1.33	17.27
12/09	29.49	14	5	1.82	1.24	17.85
Annual Growth	(1.9%)	—	—	8.3%	4.3%	3.7%

*Fiscal year change

Prudential Plc

When it comes to life insurance a little prudence goes a long way. Working through its subsidiaries Prudential is the UK's largest life insurer and the largest European insurer operating in Asia. In addition to insurance Prudential UK's products include pensions annuities investment bonds and fund management. Other businesses include UK fund manager M&G. In Asia the company sells life insurance savings and investment products in about a dozen countries through its Prudential Corporation Asia unit. In the US Prudential owns Jackson National Life Insurance which offers annuities and life insurance. Prudential plc was formed in 1848 to offer life insurance and loans to the middle class.

Operations

Prudential serves more than 24 million policyholders through its global insurance divisions and it has a total of some #405 million in assets under management. About 13 million customers are in Asian markets.

The company's operations are divided into four segments: Jackson National in the US Prudential Corporation Asia and Prudential UK and M&G based in the UK market. Operating subsidiaries within the UK-based divisions include Prudential Assurance Prudential Annuities Prudential Retirement and Prudential Assurance Singapore.

Insurance revenues account for more than 90% of annual earnings while asset management services provided by the M&G division make up the remainder of annual revenue.

Geographic Reach

Through its UK-based businesses Prudential has about 50 branch locations in the UK other European countries and India. Jackson National distributes products in all 50 US states from about 20 regional offices. In Asia Prudential has about 30 businesses that are spread over 14 markets.

Sales and Marketing

Prudential conducts sales through independent brokers and agents institutional product distributors regional brokers captive agents banks and investment advisors.

In addition to joint ventures with banks in China (with CITIC Group) and India (with ICICI Bank) Prudential has bank distribution agreements in other Asian markets. It life accident and health insurance policies are sold in Singapore Indonesia and Thailand through the more than 500 branches of United Overseas Bank.

Financial Performance

Rises in earned premiums and investment returns led to a 54% revenue increase to some #55.5 billion ($89.6 billion) in 2012. The company reported premium growth in all three core markets (the US Asia and the UK).

However sales declined in both 2010 and 2011 after a large jump in 2009. Prudential has seen volatile earnings in recent years due to the fact that the company relies on investment returns for more than 40% of its insurance income (in addition to premiums and fees) which makes it vulnerable to changes in market conditions.

Profits rose 55% to #2.2 billion ($3.6 billion) in 2012 due to higher revenues. Prudential has seen steadily climbing net income over the past five years as revenues outweigh expenses.

Strategy

A key part of Prudential's growth strategy and differentiation from its competitors is its presence in Asia particularly in markets including Southeast Asia Singapore and Hong Kong. The company entered the new Asian market of Cambodia in 2013. It is especially working to increase sales of savings and insurance products to the emerging group of middle class individuals in Asian markets.

Another strategic area of focus is retirement savings products (such as variable annuities) in the US. Its Jackson National Life Insurance takes advantage of the fact that the US has the largest market for retirement-related financial products. Prudential is also focused on strengthening existing life insurance operations in the US. In the UK the company is maximizing its asset management operations and focusing on core insurance markets.

Prudential also looks to diversify its earnings and offerings by making bolt-on acquisitions when opportunities emerge.

Mergers and Acquisitions

In 2013 the company widened its operations in Southeast Asia through the purchase of Thailand-based Thanachart Life Assurance from Thanachart Bank for some #368 million; the transaction also included a deal in which Prudential distributes policies through Thanachart's banking branches. To expand in the US market Prudential acquired SRLC America a US division of Swiss Re for some #370 million ($587 million) in 2012. The purchase diversified Jackson's life insurance underwriting activities in the US market.

Ownership

Capital Group International owns about 10% of the company.

HISTORY

Actually prudence almost killed Prudential before it ever got started. Founded in 1848 as Prudential Mutual Assurance Investment and Loan Association the firm initially insured middle-class customers. The Dickensian conditions of the working poor made them too risky for insurers. Unfortunately the company found few takers of the right sort and by 1852 Prudential was in peril.

Two events saved Prudential: The House of Commons pressed for insurance coverage for all classes and Prudential's own agents pushed for change. The company expanded into industrial insurance a modest coverage for the working poor. In 1864 to quell criticism of the insurance industry Prudential brought in independent auditors to confirm its soundness. This soon became a marketing tool and business took off. The Pru as it came to be known became the leading industrial insurer by the 1880s. It covered half the country's population by 1905. The firm's salesmen were known for making personal visits to customers (the "Man from the Pru" became a ubiquitous icon in the 1940s and was revived in 1997).

During the two world wars Prudential boosted its reputation by honoring the policies of war victims when it could have legally denied them. Between wars the company added fire and accident insurance in Europe.

The 1980s were volatile for insurance companies especially in the wake of Britain's financial deregulation in 1986. Therefore in 1982 under the direction of CEO Brian Corby the Pru reorganized product lines and in 1985 entered the real estate business. In 1986 it entered the US market by buying US-based Jackson National Life Insurance.

Prudential which had considered selling Mercantile and General Reinsurance in the early 1990s (purchased in 1969) sold the reinsurer back to Swiss Re in 1996. It also formed Prudential Bank and created an Asian emerging-market investment fund that year.

Insurance regulators reprimanded the company for mis-selling financial products in 1997. In 1998 Jackson National bought a California savings and loan enabling it to sell investment products in the US. Also that year the Pru sold its Australian and New Zealand businesses and Prudential Bank launched its pioneering Internet bank Egg Banking.

In 1999 Prudential bought investment manager M&G Group. The company then changed its name to Prudential plc and began talks with the Prudential Insurance Company of America to resolve confusion of their similar names as they expanded into new markets. Also in 1999 the Pru joined forces with the Bank of China to offer pension and asset management in Hong Kong.

The company announced plans in 2000 to sell a chunk of its institutional fund management business as well as its traditional balanced pension business to Deutsche Bank. That year the company spun off 20% of Egg (it sold the rest in 2007).

Entering the Japanese life insurance market Prudential bought Orico Life in 2001. Prudential's hopes of capturing the lucrative annuities market by acquiring American General were dashed that year as American General instead embraced American International Group leaving the Pru with a $600 million break-up fee. To consolidate operations the firm sold its general insurance business in 2001 to Swiss insurer Winterthur (a subsidiary of Credit Suisse).

In early 2006 Prudential rejected a takeover offer from larger rival Aviva valued at nearly $30 billion.

After helping oversee the shift in focus that brought the company growth in Asia and stability during the 2008 economic downturn CEO Mark Tucker stepped down at the end of September 2009. The company chose CFO Tidjane Thiam to replace him. Thiam a native of Ivory Coast became the first black CEO of a FTSE 100 company.

In early 2010 the company expanded its operations in Singapore by acquiring United Overseas Bank's life insurance unit for S$428 million ($307 million). Along with becoming owner of UOB Life Assurance Ltd. Prudential entered into an agreement through which UOB sells Prudential's life accident and health insurance policies for 12 years at the bank's more than 400 branches in Singapore Indonesia and Thailand giving Prudential a greater presence in those markets. In 2011 Prudential targeted the business of Singapore's class of "rising rich" individuals as an important area for growth.

Prudential made a splashy bid on AIG's Hong Kong-based American International Assurance (AIA) business in 2010. The $35.5 billion deal ($25 billion in cash $8.5 billion in securities and $2 billion in stock) would have made Prudential the largest life insurer in Hong Kong and allowed AIG to pay off a chunk of its debt to the US government. However Prudential's shareholders were not impressed and raised a ruckus over the deal. To appease them Prudential attempted to reduce its offer to $30 billion –which AIG coolly refused –and then simply withdrew its entire offer.

EXECUTIVES

COO M&G Group, Martin Lewis
Executive Director; President and CEO Jackson National Life, Michael A. (Mike) Wells, age 52
Chief Risk Officer Prudential UK and Europe, Marcia Cantor-Grable
Executive Director; Chief Executive Prudential UK and Europe, Robert A. (Rob) Devey, $109,889 total compensation
COO Prudential Property Investment Managers (PRUPRIM) M&G, Malcolm Smith
Deputy Chief Executive Prudential UK and Europe, Barry O'Dwyer
Deputy Chief Executive Prudential UK and Europe, Andrew M. (Andy) Crossley
Chief Actuary Prudential UK, David Belsham
Chief Executive Fund Management Prudential Corporation Asia, Graham Mason
Director Human Resources Prudential UK and Europe, Catherine (Cathy) Lewis
Managing Director Prudential Property Investment Managers (PRUPRIM) M&G, Martin R. Moore
Group Chief Risk Officer and Director, John Foley, age 56
Director, Michael W.O. Garrett, age 70
Director, Kathleen A. O'Donovan, age 54
Executive Director; Chief Executive The M&G Group, Michael G.A. McLintock, age 51
Director, James H. Ross, age 74
Director, Keki B. Dadiseth, age 66
Director, Bridget A. Macaskill, age 62
Director, Ann F. Godbehere, age 56
Executive Director; President and CEO Jackson National Life, Michael A. (Mike) Wells, age 52
Director, Sir Howard J. Davies, age 61
Director, Paul Manduca, age 60
Director, Lord Andrew Turnbull, age 67
Group Chief Executive and Director, Tidjane C. Thiam, age 49
CFO and Director, Nicolaos (Nic) Nicandrou
Executive Director; Chief Executive Prudential UK and Europe, Robert A. (Rob) Devey
Group Chief Risk Officer and Director, John Foley, age 55
Auditors: KPMGAuditPlc

LOCATIONS

HQ: Prudential Plc
Laurence Pountney Hill, London EC4R 0HH
Phone: (44) 20 7548 3640
Web: www.prudential.co.uk

2012 Sales

	% of total
US	27
Asia	15
UK	14
Investment	44
Total	**100**

PRODUCTS/OPERATIONS

2012 Sales

	% of total
Insurance	96
Asset	4
Total	**100**

COMPETITORS

AEGON
AIA Group
AIG
Lincoln Financial Group
Lloyds Banking Group
AXA
Allianz
Aviva
BlackRock
Canada Life
Cathay Life Insurance
China Life Insurance
China Pacific Insurance
Citigroup
FMR
Friends Provident
Great Eastern Holdings
HSBC
ING
Invesco Perpetual
Jupiter Fund Management
Legal & General Group
Manulife Financial
MetLife
Mitsui Sumitomo Insurance
Nationwide Financial
New York Life
Nippon Life Insurance
Ping An Insurance
Prudential
RSA Insurance
Resolution Ltd
Samsung Life Insurance
Schroders
Sompo Japan Insurance
Standard Life
State Farm
TIAA-CREF
The Hartford
Tokio Marine
Zurich Insurance Group

HISTORICAL FINANCIALS

Company Type: Public

Income Statement FYE: December 31

	ASSETS ($ mil.)	NET INCOME ($ mil.)	INCOME AS % OF ASSETS	EMPLOYEES
12/12	500,086	3,541	0.7%	27,619
12/11	422,641	2,301	0.5%	25,414
12/10	404,937	2,221	0.5%	25,992
12/09	368,866	1,094	0.3%	27,389
12/08	314,109	(577)	—	29,683
Annual Growth	12.3%	—	—	(1.8%)

2012 Year-End Financials

Return on assets: 0.7%
Return on equity: 22.5%
Long-term debt ($ mil.): —
No. of shares (mil.): —
Sales ($ mil): 89,419
Dividends
Yield: 2.8%
Payout: 149.1%
Market value ($ mil.): —

	STOCK PRICE ($) FY Close	P/E High/Low		PER SHARE ($) Earnings	Dividends	Book Value
12/12	28.55	89	57	1.39	0.81	6.53
12/11	19.74	113	66	0.91	2.00	5.53
12/10	20.86	94	57	0.88	0.60	4.90
12/09	20.39	218	47	0.44	0.61	4.01
12/08	12.65	—	—	(0.23)	0.70	2.95
Annual Growth	22.6%	—	—	—	3.6%	22.0%

PT Resource Alam Indonesia TBK

LOCATIONS

HQ: PT Resource Alam Indonesia TBK
Bumi Raya Group Building, Jl. Pembangunan I No. 3, Jakarta Pusat 10130
Phone: (62) 21 633 3036 **Fax:** (62) 21 633 7006
Web: www.raintbk.com

HISTORICAL FINANCIALS

Company Type: Public

Income Statement FYE: December 31

	REVENUE ($ mil.)	NET INCOME ($ mil.)	NET PROFIT MARGIN	EMPLOYEES
12/12	214,901	23,591	11.0%	172
12/11	234	49	21.2%	175
12/10	107	18	17.1%	95
12/09	43	3	7.9%	117
12/94	30	3	10.1%	170
Annual Growth	(10.3%)	(10.3%)	—	(0.0%)

2012 Year-End Financials

Debt ratio: 0.4%
Return on equity: 6.4%
Cash ($ mil.): 7,654
Current ratio: 1.95
Long-term debt ($ mil.): —
No. of shares (mil.): 990
Dividends
Yield: —
Payout: —
Market value ($ mil.): —

PTT Public Co Ltd.

Thailand fills its tanks thanks to integrated oil company PTT the nation's largest company. Its PTT Oil transportation and marketing unit operates more than 1200 gas stations. PTT Gas procures processes transports and distributes natural gas. PTT owns 49% of the nation's largest refiner Thai Oil. Other PTT units engage in oil and gas exploration and production (in Thailand and elsewhere) produce petrochemicals and mine coal. It is also has major oil and gas trading operations. The company is majority-owned by the Government of Thailand.

Operations

PTT's core businesses are Exploration & Production and Gas and Oil.

PTT Exploration and Production Public Company Limited (PTTEP). PTT has also invested in natural gas-related corporations both in Thailand and abroad.

The Gas Business Group engages in natural gas supply procurement pipeline transmission separation and distribution.

The Oil Business Group engages in distribution of refined fuel and lubricating products covering retail marketing run through PTT service stations wholesale marketing and commercial marketing for government agencies industry sector airlines and oil vessels.

The International Trading Business Group covers procurement and import-export trading of crude oil condensate petroleum and petrochemical products .

On the investment side PTT invests in a wide range of its related businesses with an emphasis on petrochemical and oil refining businesses.

Financial Performance

The company's revenues increased by 28% in 2011 with a jump in profits of 25% reflected the success in natural gas procurement to meet growing demand efficiency improvement of gas separation plants (GSPs) and the commercial operation of GSP unit 6 (Rayong) which boosted production capacity.

Other factors include PTTEP's production increase (especially from the oil sands KKD project in Canada); production capacity expansion in the petrochemical group; improved returns from portfolio risk management investment and development programs; and pricing risk management for PTT and PTT group.

Strategy

The company sees its role as being the lead player in Thailand's oil and gas development and revenue production. PTT is relying on the synergy between various downstream businesses to add business value and reduce operating costs.

Ownership

The Government of Thailand owns 51% of PTT.

Company Background

Thailand which created PTT to secure energy supplies during the oil crunch of the late 1970s sold a third of the company in a 2001 IPO.

In 2008 as part of PTT's energy diversification drive the company opened the world's largest NGV (natural gas vehicle) gas station in Thailand to respond to the growing number of NGV vehicles in the country.

EXECUTIVES

President CEO Secretary and Director, Pailin Chuchottaworn
Chairman, Norkun Sitthiphong
Director Chairman of the Audit Committee, Chulasingh Vasantasingh
Auditors: OfficeoftheAuditorGeneralofThailand

LOCATIONS

HQ: PTT Public Co Ltd.
555 Vibhavadi-Rangsit Road, Chatuchak, Bangkok 10900
Phone: (66) 2 537 2000 **Fax:** (66) 2 537 3498
Web: www.pttplc.com

PRODUCTS/OPERATIONS

2011 Sales

	% of total
International	53
Oil	21
Natural	16
Exploration &	6
Petrochemical	3
Coal	1
Other	-
Total	**100**

Selected Subsidiaries and Affiliates:

PetroAsia (Huizhou) Co. Ltd. (25%)
PTT Exploration and Production Public Co. Ltd. (66%)
PTT Mart Co. Ltd. (49%)
PTT Natural Gas Distribution Co. Ltd. (58%)
Star Petroleum Refining Co. Ltd. (36%)
Thai Lube Blending Co. Ltd. (49%)
Thai Oil Plc. (50%)

COMPETITORS

BP
Chevron
Salamander Energy

HISTORICAL FINANCIALS

Company Type: Public

Income Statement FYE: December 31

	REVENUE ($ mil.)	NET INCOME ($ mil.)	NET PROFIT MARGIN	EMPLOYEES
12/12	91,301	3,420	3.7%	20,816
12/11	77,158	3,345	4.3%	18,240
12/10	63,259	2,766	4.4%	9,015
12/09	47,611	1,787	3.8%	7,952
12/08	57,513	1,486	2.6%	7,989
Annual Growth	12.2%	23.2%	—	27.1%

2012 Year-End Financials

Debt ratio: 0.9%
Return on equity: 17.9%
Cash ($ mil.): 4,474
Current ratio: 1.24
Long-term debt ($ mil.): 12,991

No. of shares (mil.): —
Dividends
Yield: —
Payout: —
Market value ($ mil.): —

	STOCK PRICE ($) FY Close	P/E High/Low		PER SHARE ($) Earnings	Dividends	Book Value
12/12	10.79	0	0	1.20	0.00	6.93
12/11	9.50	0	0	1.17	0.00	6.18
12/10	10.20	0	0	0.97	0.00	5.74
12/09	4.50	0	0	0.63	0.00	4.55
12/08	6.00	0	0	0.52	0.00	3.90
Annual Growth	15.8%	—	—	22.9%	—	15.4%

QBE Insurance Group Ltd.

QBE Insurance Group may be one of Australia's leading insurers but it also has a hefty global reach. The company offers a variety of insurance and reinsurance through offices in about 50 countries. QBE provides general property/casualty policies as well as liability auto marine aviation energy accident workers' compensation and professional indemnity coverage. The company writes both individual and commercial insurance policies and also administers reinsurance coverage. It sells its products through direct and independent representative agencies. QBE Insurance Group earns about three-fourths of its revenue outside of Australia.

QBE has expanded its presence around the world through acquisitions. Large and small purchases have especially helped to boost its underwriting operations in Europe and the Americas each of which account for about a third of sales. The company has also been working to expand its direct distribution network by acquiring insurance agencies in select regions including the US Central Europe and Australia.

QBE has been steadily making buys in key markets of North America. After making a number of purchases in 2007 and 2008 the company slowed its US acquisition pace due to economic turmoil in 2009. But once the markets stabilized a bit it resumed its habits through the 2010 purchase of US crop insurer NAU Country Insurance for $565 million. It also paid some $275 million to acquire the US insurance operations of RenaissanceRe. The purchase added to QBE'S US crop insurance and other specialty lines. In 2011 the company acquired certain property/casualty operations of Bank of America for about $700 million. The acquisition included portfolio and distribution rights of Bank of America's Balboa Insurance Company subsidiary and affiliated entities.

International buys in 2012 included the general insurance businesses of HSBC Argentina Holdings and Hang Seng Bank both of which are subsidiaries of HSBC Holdings for $420 million and Puerto-Rico-based Optima Insurance Group (motor casualty and property risks) including Optima Insurance Co. (property/casualty) Colonial Insurance Agency (a managing general agent) and New Century Financial Corp. (premium financing for clients of Optima and Colonial).

European acquisitions have included purchases of the 2010 purchase of Belgium-based reinsurance firm Secura NV for some E267 million ($335 million). Secura provides reinsurance services to a number of property/casualty providers across Europe and is now part of QBE's London-based European reinsurance division. In 2012 QBE gained the potential to control 5% of the UK market in 2013 by purchasing the renewal rights of Brit Insurance's regional operations.

In addition the company has been seeking to solidify and grow its position in the Asia/Pacific region including its home market of Australia. QBE expanded its Australian underwriting and marketing footprint in 2011 by acquiring the Australian business of US-based CUNA Mutual Group which provides policies to credit unions and other small financial institutions.

After sifting through the fallout of a record number of catastrophes across the globe in 2011 QBE's net profit dropped 45% from a year earlier to $704 million. The company's balance sheets began to recover in 2012 and through acquisitions QBE plans to meet its premium growth expectations for the year.

HISTORY

QBE Insurance Group was formed through a series of mergers. One predecessor North Queensland Insurance Company Limited (the "Q" in QBE) was founded by Scottish immigrant James Burns in 1886. Burns who owned interests in a variety of businesses in Australia formed the company to insure the shipping fleets of Burns Philp his conglomerate. The two companies would share cross-holdings for more than 100 years. Four years after its founding the insurance company (which later dropped the "North" from its name) had nearly 40 agencies with operations in New Zealand Hong Kong Singapore and London.

Bankers' and Traders' Insurance Company the "B" in QBE was formed in 1921. Almost 40 years later Queensland bought the "E" in QBE The Equitable Probate and General Insurance Co. Limited (which later took the name Equitable Life and General Insurance Company). In 1973 QBE Insurance Group came into being when Queensland Insurance bought Bankers' and Traders'. The new entity listed that year on the Australian Stock Exchange.

The next year Australia suffered one of its worst natural disasters; Cyclone Tracy battered the Northern Territory city of Darwin and hammered QBE and its rivals' bottom lines. Throughout the 1970s and 1980s the Australian insurance industry suffered through a number of natural disasters –floods fires cyclones and other acts of God –that led its players to tighten operations to weather these storms.

In the 1980s QBE began a series of acquisitions that expanded its presence around the globe. Among its purchases were Sequoia Insurance in the US in 1986 (which nearly doubled the company's overseas operations) and Universal Insurance Company of Ireland (now QBE Insurance & Reinsurance (Europe) Limited) in 1988.

Exposure to natural disasters in Australia as well as to earthquakes and wildfires in California and massive storms in the UK helped make 1990 one of QBE's worst years. But the company wasn't the only one suffering and as the weaker players faltered QBE bought them. In 1991 it ended its shareholder relationship with Burns Philp by then primarily a food and hardware group selling their cross-holdings to focus on expanding their respective businesses. Soon thereafter QBE went on another buying spree to shore up its operations: Purchases included American Royal Reinsurance (now Sydney Reinsurance) in 1993. The company also concentrated on its presence in Asia establishing joint ventures in Thailand and Indonesia and eyeing entry into China and India.

In 1995 QBE sold Sequoia Insurance which had for many years been its top contributor to international sales when the company found US regulation of primary insurance difficult. Two years later the firm entered the export credit insurance market when it bought 75% of Trade Indemnity Australia; the niche market had only 20 or so players. In the late 1990s it moved into Central and Eastern Europe buying insurance firms or teaming with local companies in such countries as Ukraine Bulgaria and Hungary. QBE also entered China in 1998.

At the close of the century it continued to strengthen its operations both at home and abroad: The firm teamed with domestic rival Mercantile Mutual to cross-sell their insurance products and it announced plans to grow through further acquisitions overseas. In 2000 QBE acquired UK-based insurer Limit which was integrated into QBE's Lloyd's operations. It followed up with the purchase of Lloyd's Syndicate 980 a commercial motor portfolio managed by Ensign in 2003.

In 2005 the company acquired Greenhill Underwriting which expanded its operations in France Germany and Spain.QBE added its QBE Agri business through the purchase of One Beacon Agriculture in the US in 2006.

The company doubled the size of its US business in 2007 by acquiring Hannover Re's US-based specialty insurance subsidiary Praetorian Group for about $800 million and the US property/casualty holdings of AXA Winterthur (renamed QBE Regional) for about $1.2 billion. QBE also acquired Mexico-based insurer Seguros Cumbre (now named QBE Mexico Seguros) that year.

Not content with simply doubling its US sales through acquisitions made in 2007 the company continued on its buying streak by purchasing North Pointe Holdings for $146 million in 2008; the deal expanded QBE's general underwriting and distribution operations in the southeastern US. Later in 2008 QBE bought US mortgage policy agent ZC Sterling (later renamed Sterling National and then QBE FIRST) for $575 million.

After a failed hostile takeover attempt to acquire Insurance Australia Group (IAG) in 2008 QBE successfully snapped up PMI Australia the Australian arm of beleaguered US-based mortgage insurer PMI Group for $920 million later that year. The deal handed QBE 40% of Australia's mortgage insurance market and allowed PMI Australia to protect its valuable ratings from the woes of its former parent. QBE purchased Hong Kong-based PMI Asia shortly after and the two businesses were renamed QBE Lenders' Mortgage Insurers.

Though QBE suffered some losses due to economic conditions and a downturn in the global financial marketplace in 2008 the company quickly rebounded to previous levels of profitability in 2009.

QBE paid about $A315 million ($265 million) in 2009 to buy Elders Insurance a subsidiary of Australian rural and financial services company Elders Limited. It also gained a stake in the Elders Insurance Agency business through the deal and gave Elders a much-needed infusion of cash.

In 2009 the firm also purchased Endurance a property/casualty insurance provider in the UK and Carlife an auto warranty broker in Central Europe.

EXECUTIVES

Chief Financial Officer, Neil Drabsch, age 65
CEO and Director, Frank O'Halloran, age 66
COO, Vince McLenaghan, age 54
Group General Manager Investments, Mark ten Hove, age 56
CEO European Operations, Steven Burns, age 55
Chief Executive Officer, John Neal, age 49
Chief Actuarial Officer, Blair Nicholls, age 46
Global Head Distribution, Terry Ibbotson, age 68
CEO Asia-Pacific, Michael Goodwin, age 54
Group Executive Officer People and Communications, Jenni Smith, age 51
Chairman, Belinda J. Hutchinson, age 60
Group Chief Risk Officer, George Thwaites, age 48
President and CEO The Americas, John Rumpler, age 53
President Equator Re, Des Fogarty, age 52
Chief Executive Officer; Australian and New Zealand Operations, Colin Fagen
General Counsel; Company Secretary, Duncan Ramsay
Chief Executive Officer - Latin American Operations, Jose Sojo
Deputy Company Secretary, P. Smiles
Member of the Group Executive; Global Head of Investor Relations and Communications, Tony Jackson
Director, Charles Irby, age 68
CEO and Director, Frank O'Halloran, age 66
Director, Isabel Hudson, age 54
Director, Duncan Boyle, age 62
Director, Len Bleasel, age 71
Director, Irene Lee, age 60
Non-Executive Director, John Graf
Non-Executive Director, John Green
Auditors: PricewaterhouseCoopers

LOCATIONS

HQ: QBE Insurance Group Ltd.
Level 2, 82 Pitt Street, Sydney, New South Wales 2000
Phone: (61) 2 9375 4444 **Fax:** (61) 2 9235 3166
Web: www.qbe.com

2011 Earned Premiums by Regional Operations

	% of total
North	42
Europe	26
Australia	24
Latin	4
Asia/Pacific	4
Total	**100**

PRODUCTS/OPERATIONS

2011 Earned Premiums by Product

	% of total
Property	33
Motor & motor	14
Agricultural &	13
Public/product	12
Marine energy &	7
Workers'	7
Financial &	5
Professional	4
Accident &	4
Other	1
Total	**100**

Selected Acquisitions
2011
Balboa (lender-placed homeowners business US)
CUNA Mutual Australia (credit general insurance and term life)
Renaissance Re's US Operations (mainly crop)

COMPETITORS

AEGON
AIG
AMP Limited
AXA
AXIS Capital Holdings
Allianz
Allstate
Assurances Generales de France
Australia and New Zealand Banking
Aviva
Commonwealth Bank of Australia
GEICO
Generali
ING
Insurance Australia
Loews
Munich Re Group
National Australia Bank
Nationwide
RSA Insurance
Samsung Fire & Marine
Standard Chartered
State Farm
Suncorp-Metway
Swiss Re
Travelers Companies
Westpac Banking

HISTORICAL FINANCIALS

Company Type: Public

Income Statement FYE: December 31

	ASSETS ($ mil.)	NET INCOME ($ mil.)	INCOME AS % OF ASSETS	EMPLOYEES
12/12	50,762	761	1.5%	0
12/11	46,737	704	1.5%	0
12/10	42,188	1,278	3.0%	0
12/09	36,841	1,771	4.8%	0
12/08	33,350	1,281	3.8%	0
Annual Growth	11.1%	(12.2%)	—	—

2012 Year-End Financials

Return on assets: 1.5%
Return on equity: 6.9%
Long-term debt ($ mil.): —
No. of shares (mil.): 1,194
Sales ($ mil): 17,031
Dividends
Yield: 5.5%
Payout: 103.1%
Market value ($ mil.): 13,647

	STOCK PRICE ($) FY Close	P/E High/Low	PER SHARE ($) Earnings	Dividends	Book Value
12/12	11.43	23 16	0.62	0.64	9.51
12/11	13.25	32 18	0.61	0.58	9.34
Annual Growth	(13.7%)	— —	0.1%	2.3%	0.5%

Quanta Computer Inc

Quanta Computer is an original design manufacturer (ODM) serving some of the leading names in computer hardware including Dell Apple and HP. It is one of the world's largest manufacturers of notebook computers and also produces network servers television set-top boxes monitors LCD TVs and smartphones. Quanta Computer's other business units include Quanta Storage (data storage products) and RoyalTek Company (personal navigation devices and other GPS products). While well known for its notebooks and their smaller computer cousins the netbooks Quanta Computer is diversifying into other consumer electronics and IT products.

Geographic Reach The company is based in Taiwan with additional facilities in Asia Europe and North and South America.

Financial Performance Quanta Computer's 2011 revenue fell just over 1% to NT$1.1 trillion (around $37 billion). Its net income however rose by 22% for the same period to NT$23 billion (about $780 million) as a result of strict cost controls it put in place. The company is focused on inventory reductions and yield rate improvements among other measures.

Strategy The company is focusing its R&D efforts on cloud computing connectivity and client devices. All three areas are part of a broader cloud computing initiative that involves the design and manufacture of data storage products and servers (for providing cloud-computing services) next-generation data networking products (for enabling uninterrupted cloud-computing connections and service coverage) and client devices (for accessing cloud networks). Outside of notebooks other areas of focus include mobile devices automotive electronics high-definition video conferencing and satellite technology.

Auditors: KPMG

LOCATIONS

HQ: Quanta Computer Inc
No. 188, Wen Hwa 2nd Road, Kuei Shan Hsiang, Taoyuan
Phone: (886) 3 327 2345 **Fax:** (886) 3 327 1511
Web: www.quantatw.com

COMPETITORS

ASUSTeK	Hon Hai
BenQ	Inventec
Celestica	MiTAC
China Techfaith	Pegatron
Compal Electronics	Super Micro Computer
First International Computer	Tatung
Flextronics	TriGem
Foxconn International	Wistron

HISTORICAL FINANCIALS

Company Type: Public

Income Statement FYE: December 31

	REVENUE ($ mil.)	NET INCOME ($ mil.)	NET PROFIT MARGIN	EMPLOYEES
12/12	35,061	806	2.3%	121,917
12/11	36,612	775	2.1%	108,872
12/10	38,651	664	1.7%	68,720
12/09	26,250	729	2.8%	64,719
12/08	24,981	644	2.6%	60,900
Annual Growth	8.8%	5.8%	—	18.9%

2012 Year-End Financials

Debt ratio: 0.1%
Return on equity: 18.3%
Cash ($ mil.): 6,481
Current ratio: 1.22
Long-term debt ($ mil.): 641
No. of shares (mil.): —
Dividends
Yield: —
Payout: —
Market value ($ mil.): —

	STOCK PRICE ($) FY Close	P/E High/Low	PER SHARE ($) Earnings	Dividends	Book Value
12/12	0.00	— —	0.20	0.00	1.17
12/11	0.00	— —	0.20	0.00	1.06
12/10	7.75	— —	0.16	0.00	1.07
Annual Growth	—	— —	5.5%	—	2.4%

Rallye S.A.

Retail giant Rallye musters its businesses around not just the French flag but around flags worldwide. Rallye's Casino Guichard-Perrachon subsidiary operates more than 9000 hypermarkets supermarkets and convenience stores in Europe (mostly France) Asia/Pacific and Latin America. It also has a foothold in the sporting goods and athletic shoe department with Groupe Go Sport which runs about 400 shops. In addition to retailing the company is active in real estate development banking and a variety of investment vehicles. Fonciere Euris controls about 58% of Rallye and nearly 75% of the voting rights.

Rallye's Casino subsidiary is a leading supermarket chain in France and operates in about 10 countries worldwide. Store banners include Casino Franprix Geant Leader Price and Monoprix. Casino is the #1 convenience store operator in France with stores under the Petit Casino Spar and Vival names. Casino has grown by purchasing stakes in supermarket hypermarket and convenience store companies with international locations. It plans to continue expanding globally focusing on South America and Asia/Pacific.

While Rallye exited the footwear retail business in the US with its sale of The Athlete's Foot the company plans to continue to expand Groupe Go Sport in Europe. The retailer was formed when Rallye merged two subsidiaries: Go Sport (France's #2 sporting goods retailer) with about 150 stores and Courir (France's #1 sports and leisure footwear retailer) with more than 200.

Rallye has increased its e-commerce activities through its majority stake of Cdiscount.com a French online retailer of CDs videos and more. Cdiscount belongs to the non-food group which also includes Mercialys (retail real estate development) Casino Cafeteria (corporate cafeterias) and Banque Casino (consumer lending).

In order to strengthen its financial flexibility the company plans to significantly reduce its debt. To this end Rallye looks to dispose of commercial real estate and private equity investments valued at more than $1 billion by the end of 2010. Its supermarket group anticipates saving about $200 million in 2009 by making store operations more efficient and lowering supply chain and overhead costs.

HISTORY

Rallye has its roots in Casino Guichard-Perrachon which was formed after Geoffroy Guichard took over his father-in-law's general store in 1892.

In the early 1920s the company which would later become a Rallye holding opened factories to produce items that included food and soap. In 1924 Rallye was formed as a food retailer. Also that year a food distribution group that would become an important acquisition for Rallye in the 1990s Genty was founded (renamed Genty Cathiard in 1959).

By WWII Casino had 215 branches. During the war Casino's troubles included 70 stores leveled and 450 damaged in bomb attacks.

The firm launched its first supermarket (Grenoble) in 1960 and its first cafeteria in 1967. It expanded to Geant hypermarkets (Marseille) in 1970 and formed Casino USA in 1976.

Rallye entered sporting goods in 1981 through the purchase of France's 11-unit Athletic Attic chain and the acquisition of a minority stake of US sports footwear and apparel retailer The Athlete's Foot Group. Rallye then acquired majority control of Athlete's Foot in 1984.

Rallye's sales reached $4.4 billion in 1989. The next year it acquired the food distribution group Genty Cathiard which included retail units Go Sport (sporting goods) and Courir (sports footwear). The acquisition moved Rallye from #8 to #5 in French supermarket groups.

By 1991 Rallye operated 51 hypermarkets and 227 supermarkets. That year Euris headed by Jean-Charles Naouri bought a stake in Rallye which had heavy debt after borrowing funds to acquire Genty Cathiard. Rallye traded its food retail operations (close to 300 hypermarkets and supermarkets) with food giant Casino in exchange for a 30% stake in Casino in 1992.

Rallye merged with subsidiary Genty Cathiard in 1993 when the company went public. Also in 1993 Rallye began a major restructuring for Go Sport that lasted until 1996.

French supermarket chain Promodes made a hostile takeover attempt on Casino and Rallye in 1997 which would have made Promodes France's largest retailer. Rallye (which still had 30% of Casino and about 40% of voting rights) made a friendly counter bid; Promodes backed out and Rallye took control of Casino. By 1998 The Athlete's Foot Group had grown to more than 260 US outlets (company-owned) and more than 400 franchises (about 180 in the US).

Franchises were also located in 38 countries including Australia Canada France and Hong Kong. Go Sport operated 80 outlets in France and six in Belgium and there were more than 100 Courir stores (France) by the beginning of 1998. Rallye spun off nearly 20% of Courir in 1999.

Casino expanded its international markets in 1999 by acquiring stakes in food retailing companies in countries that included Brazil Colombia Thailand and Venezuela. Go Sport grew in 1999 by launching new stores in France Belgium and Poland –a new market.

In 2000 Casino bought a 51% stake in French online CD retailer Cdiscount.com. Although Rallye as a whole nearly doubled its net profit in 2000 Athlete's Foot suffered a loss of almost $29 million that year and began a three-year restructuring plan that included the closure of 84 unprofitable stores. Conversely 100 new Athlete's Foot franchises opened in 2001 including the first stores in Mexico and Hungary.

In June 2002 Casino acquired a nearly 40% stake in Laurus a leading retailer in the Netherlands.

In December 2003 Rallye sold its interest in The Athlete's Foot (TAF) to the chain's managers in a management-led buyout for an undisclosed sum. Accounting for less than 1% of Rallye's sales TAF had closed nearly 100 branches since 2001 but was still unprofitable.

Francois de Montaudouin resigned as managing director of Rallye in January 2004 and was succeeded by Chairman Jean-Charles Naouri.

In 2005 the company held an initial public offering for its shopping center real estate development company Mercialys.

LOCATIONS

HQ: Rallye S.A.
83, rue du Faubourg Saint-Honore, Paris 75008
Phone: (33) 1 44 71 13 73 **Fax:** (33) 1 44 71 13 70
Web: www.rallye.fr

2009 Sales

	% of total
France	67
Latin	24
Asia	6
Other	3
Total	**100**

PRODUCTS/OPERATIONS

2009 Sales

	$ mil.	% of total
Food & general retailing		97
Total		**100**

HISTORICAL FINANCIALS

Company Type: Public

Income Statement FYE: December 31

	REVENUE ($ mil.)	NET INCOME ($ mil.)	NET PROFIT MARGIN	EMPLOYEES
12/12	56,231	322	0.6%	321,385
12/11	45,344	19	0.0%	227,995
12/10	39,856	9	0.0%	175,380
12/09	39,583	145	0.4%	168,046
12/08	41,170	(120)	—	178,327
Annual Growth	8.1%	—	—	15.9%

2012 Year-End Financials

Debt ratio: 45.2%	No. of shares (mil.): 48
Return on equity: 14.1%	Dividends
Cash ($ mil.): 8,344	Yield: —
Current ratio: 1.01	Payout: —
Long-term debt ($ mil.): 15,460	Market value ($ mil.): —

Randstad Holding N.V.

Randstad Holding has the supply to meet nearly any demand. The company is one of the largest temporary staffing and employment services agencies in the world (behind Adecco). It operates primarily in Europe but also in Asia and North America under the Randstad brand and several others including Sapphire Technologies (IT staffing) Yacht (industrial staffing) and Tempo-Team (general staffing). Through almost 4200 locations in more than 40 countries Randstad supplies temporary workers for small assignments as well as large-scale deployments. It also offers permanent placement and HR project management and consultancy services. Randstad Holding was established in 1960.

Randstad's operations are divided across four business segments: staffing professionals HR solutions (payroll services HR consulting and vendor management services) and in-house services (works onsite with clients primarily residing in the manufacturing and logistics sectors).

While Randstad is a global staffing leader it has been working to improve its position in the lucrative North America market. In 2011 it bought SFN Group a staffing and technology services provider based in Florida. Randstad paid about $770 million in a deal that improved its ability to provide administrative finance and accounting services. SFN Group serves 8000 clients through more than 550 locations in Canada and the US.

In perhaps the most significant milestone in its history Randstad acquired rival Vedior for about $5.1 billion in 2008. The acquisition created a staffing services juggernaut adding thousands of branch offices to Randstad's already vast network and expanding its geographic scope into an additional 30 countries. Specifically the deal enhanced Randstad's position in the lucrative markets of France and the UK and led to the formation of subsidiary Randstad CPE which specializes in recruiting services for the construction property and engineering fields.

Despite the expansion through Vedior due to weak demand and the slumping economy Randstad was forced to close about 85 branch offices in France in early 2009. Its profits also took a major hit in 2008 but the company has since bounced back. From 2008 to 2010 its net income skyrocketed from $25 million to $382 million.

Believing that the Japanese market is one of the largest staffing markets in the world Randstad is looking to the country as an important location for achieving growth. Randstad initially improved its market position in the country in 2008 when it acquired 10% of FujiStaff Holdings a staffing firm owning some 85 locations throughout the country. In late 2010 Randstad acquired a majority share in FujiStaff upping its stake to 95%.

Frits Goldschmeding the founder and former president and CEO of Randstad owns about 30% to 40% of the company's shares.

HISTORY

Frits Goldschmeding founded Randstad Holding as Uitzendbureau Amstelveen near Amsterdam in 1960.

Originally part of a student project the company turned a small profit its first year and was renamed Randstad Uitzendbureau in 1964. ("The Randstad" is the densely populated area including Amsterdam Rotterdam and the Hague.)

It launched its first operation outside the Netherlands the next year establishing Interlabor Interim in Belgium. By 1970 Randstad had 32 branches in four countries including Germany and the UK.

Continuing its expansion across Europe (it entered France in 1973) the company was recast as Randstad Holding in 1978. The next year it opened its 100th branch and launched its Randon security business in the Netherlands in 1980. In 1985 Randstad celebrated its silver anniversary with 250 branches.

The company went public in 1990 listing its shares on the Amsterdam Stock Exchange. That year it moved its headquarters to the Amsterdam suburb of Diemen.

In 1993 Randstad entered the US market when it bought Atlanta-based Temp Force and later acquired Nashville-based Jane Jones Enterprises. It also expanded its staffing business into Spain that year. Randstad's US business later scored a coup when it became a sponsor of the 1996 Olympic Games in Atlanta. The company placed more than 16000 temporary employees to help out during the games. By 1997 the company had more than 1000 branches in Europe and North America.

Founder and CEO Goldschmeding resigned his post in 1998 and was replaced by Hans Zwarts. That year Randstad bought Strategix Solutions the commercial staffing unit of US-based AccuStaff (later MPS Group) for $850 million. The next year the company bought Germany's Time Power Personal-Dienstleistungen and Spain's Tempo Grup. Randstad and Dutch publisher VNU announced plans to create an online employment site covering Europe in 2000 (the site was closed in 2001).

The following year Randstad bought Spanish staffing firm Umano giving the company 150 additional locations throughout Spain. It also sold its security and cleaning businesses in 2001. Zwarts retired in 2002 and was replaced by 30-year company veteran Cleem Farla. In 2003 Ben Noteboom took over as CEO. In 2004 Randstad opened an office in Poland and bought staffing firm Take Air.

In 2007 Randstad almost doubled Randstad Switzerland's revenue through the acquisition of Job One. The Swiss staffing firm operated about two dozen branches and focuses on the technology health care and construction industries. In the biggest acquisition in its company's history Randstad acquired rival staffing agency Vedior in mid-2008. The deal catapulted Randstad ahead of other staffing rivals making it one of the largest in the world.

Striving to improve its position in Canada and the US Randstad purchased rival SFN Group for about $770 million in 2011.

EXECUTIVES

Vice Chairman, Leo M. van Wijk, age 65
Chairman Supervisory Board, Fritz W. Frohlich, age 70
CEO and Chairman Executive Board, Ben J. Noteboom, age 54, $1,171,632 total compensation
CFO and Vice Chairman Executive Board, Robert-Jan van de Kraats, age 52, $726,251 total compensation
Executive Board Member, Leo J.M.V. Lindelauf, age 61, $731,534 total compensation
Managing Director Group Accounting, Rob Fenne
Managing Director Nordics and Eastern Europe, Paul P. M. van de Kerkhof
Managing Director Group Marketing and Communications, Frans Cornelis
Managing Director Social and Public Affairs, Sieto de Leeuw
Managing Director Yacht, Peter J. Hulsbos
Executive Board Member, Jacques van den Broek, age 52, $731,534 total compensation
Managing Director Group Consultancy, C. H. (Cor) Versteeg
President Randstad North America, Linda Galipeau
Executive Board Member, Brian Wilkinson, age 56, $539,868 total compensation
Managing Director Randstad Staffing and Professionals Germany, Eckard Gatzke
Group CIO; Managing Director Business Concept Development and Innovation, Hans E. Wanders
Managing Director Randstad and Tempo-Team Belgium and Luxembourg, Herman Nijns
Managing Director Group Human Resources, Marielle de Macker
Managing Director Randstad Denmark and Sweden, Jeroen Tiel
Executive Board Member, Greg A. Netland, age 50, $674,835 total compensation
Managing Director Randstad Group France, Francois Beharel
Managing Director Randstad Netherlands, Chris Heutink
Managing Director Mailprofs, Theo Das
Managing Director Otter-Westelaken, Gerard de Kock
Managing Director Gulp, Michael Moser
CEO Randstad Australia and New Zealand, Fred van der Tang
Managing Director Group Legal, James King
Managing Director Randstad Spain, Rodrigo Martin Velayos
Managing Director Portugal, Mario Costa
Managing Director Randstad Italy, Marco Ceresa
Managing Director Tempo-Team, Kees Stroomer
Managing Director Randstad Switzerland, Richard Jager
President Randstad Professionals USA, Dan Foley
President Randstad Canada, Jan Hein Bax
Managing Director Randstad Mexico, Alejandro Alvarez Blanco
Managing Director Randstad Asia Pacific, Debbie Loveridge
Managing Director Randstad India, E. Balaji
Managing Director Randstad/FujiStaff Japan, Marcel Wiggers
Managing Director Group Control Strategy and Mergers and Acquisitions, Han Kolff
Managing Director Group Tax, Hans van der Kroon
Managing Director Group Professional Concepts, Robbin Brugman
Managing Director Randstad Holding UK, Mark Bull
Managing Director Yacht/Teccon, Stephanie Vonden
Managing Director Tempo-Team Germany, Uwe Beyer
Managing Director Tempo-Team Belgium, Marc de Braekeleer
Managing Director Tempo-Team Luxembourg, Marios Paras
Managing Director Randstad Poland, Kajetan Slonina
General Manager Randstad China, George Wang
Regional Director Randstad Singapore and Malaysia, Karin Clarke
Managing Director Chief Information Officer, Alan Stukalsky
Managing Director, Ben Elliott
Division President of National accounts, Traci Fiatte
Vice Chairman, Leo M. van Wijk, age 65
Supervisory Board Member, Beverley C. Hodson, age 60

Supervisory Board Member, Robert (Rob) Zwartendijk, age 73
Supervisory Board Member, Giovanna Kampouri Monnas, age 55
Supervisory Board Member, Henri M.E.V. Giscard d'Estaing, age 55
Supervisory Board Member, Jaap Winter
Auditors: PricewaterhouseCoopersN.V.

LOCATIONS

HQ: Randstad Holding N.V.
Diemermere 25, Diemen 1100 AP
Phone: (31) 20 569 59 11 **Fax:** (31) 20 569 55 20
Web: www.randstad.com

COMPETITORS

Adecco
Allegis Group
CDI
Kelly Services
ManpowerGroup
Robert Half
Technical Aid Corporation
Volt Information

HISTORICAL FINANCIALS

Company Type: Public

Income Statement FYE: December 31

	REVENUE ($ mil.)	NET INCOME ($ mil.)	NET PROFIT MARGIN	EMPLOYEES
12/12	22,521	39	0.2%	611,020
12/11	20,986	231	1.1%	605,500
12/10	18,977	385	2.0%	546,980
12/09	17,862	98	0.6%	493,240
12/08	19,626	25	0.1%	583,830
Annual Growth	3.5%	11.6%	—	1.1%

2012 Year-End Financials

Debt ratio: 24.9%
Return on equity: 1.0%
Cash ($ mil.): 252
Current ratio: 0.79
Long-term debt ($ mil.): —
No. of shares (mil.): 172
Dividends
Yield: 3.4%
Payout: 509.6%
Market value ($ mil.): 3,201

	STOCK PRICE ($) FY Close	P/E High/Low	PER SHARE ($) Earnings	Dividends	Book Value
12/12	18.60	201127	0.22	0.65	20.87
12/11	14.80	54 22	1.29	1.30	21.93
12/10	26.36	33 18	2.18	0.00	22.44
12/09	25.25	153 71	0.52	0.41	21.16
Annual Growth	(9.7%)	— —	(18.9%)	12.3%	(0.3%)

Reliance Industries Ltd

India and Reliance Industries rely on each other. The company is India's largest petrochemical firm and among the country's largest companies (along with Indian Oil and Tata Group) accounting for 14% of India's total exports and 4% of its total market capitalization. Oil refining and the manufacture of polyolefins and related chemicals account for the bulk of Reliance Industries' sales. It also makes textiles and explores for oil and gas. Reliance Industries operates more than a dozen manufacturing plants in India. The company has fully integrated its oil and gas refining subsidiary Reliance Petroleum in an effort to consolidate the company's position as a major player in the global refining business.

Reliance Industries' diverse portfolio includes the exploration and production of oil and gas petroleum refining and marketing and petrochemicals (including the production of polyester fiber intermediates plastics and chemicals) as well as textiles retail telecommunications and special economic zones.

In India the company has manufacturing plants in Allahabad Barabanki Dahej Hazira Hoshiarpur Jamnagar Nagothane Nagpur Naroda Patalganga Silvassa and Vadodara. Relaince Industries has operations around the world including in Kenya the Netherlands Singapore the UAE the US (oil and gas) and the UK (retail).

In Fiscal 2012 the company reported a 35% spike in revenues driven by a jump in oil prices and increased demand from petroleum products in developing countries coupled with an increase in Indian domestic demand for textiles chemicals and petroleum products. However its net income dipped by 1% due to a spike in current taxation charges. Buoyed by a recovering global economy the expansion of its own operations and higher oil prices in 2011 Reliance Industries posted a 30% rise in revenues.

Reliance Industries operates in the retail sector through subsidiary Reliance Retail Limited. That unit has big ideas about starting an Indian retail revolution with supermarket outlets across the country under the name Reliance Fresh. It operates a joint venture with UK retail legend Marks & Spencer that hopes to open 50 retail locations by 2014. Moving into the financial services sector in 2011 the company formed a joint venture with US-based investment firm D. E. Shaw.

Reliant Industries is targeting oil and gas as a key growth segment. Seeking funds and expertise to boost its oil and gas exploration and production operations in India in 2011 the company sold BP a 30% stake in 23 oil and gas blocks for about $7.2 billion.

The company is also growing its oil and gas exploration and production assets outside of India. In 2010 it also got a strong foothold in the North American gas market by forming a $1.7 billion Marcellus Shale joint venture with Atlas Energy. Atlas Energy is the development operator for the Appalachian joint venture. In return Reliance Industries owned 40% of Atlas Energy's core Marcellus Shale acreage. In 2011 Chevron stepped in and paid $4.3 billion to acquire Atlas and take over its joint venture with Reliant.

In 2010 Reliance Industries formed a 60%-owned joint venture with Carrizo Oil & Gas which acquired 104400 additional acres in the Marcellus Shale play. That same year Reliance Industries acquired a 45% share in a Pioneer Natural Resources tract in southern Texas for $1.35 billion.

The company began to further diversify in 2010. Reentering the telecommunications sector the company acquired 95% of Infidel Broadband Services a national broadband provider for about $1.02 billion. Infotel was the only company to secure a nationwide license to offer wireless broadband service across India a market with 600 million cell phone users. The deal marked Reliance Industries' return to the telecom market after a 5-year hiatus.

Following a prolonged dispute among the founding Ambani family after the death of patriarch Dhirubai Ambani the company demerged into separate entities –including Reliance Capital (financial services) Reliance Communications (telecommunications) and Reliance Energy (utilities) –in 2006. Mukesh Ambani took control of Reliance Industries and Indian Petrochemicals while his brother Anil took over Reliance Capital Reliance Communications and Reliance Energy.

Mukesh Ambani controls almost half of Reliance Industries.

EXECUTIVES

Executive Director, Hital R. Meswani, $34,530 total compensation
Executive Director, Nikhil R. Meswani, $37,590 total compensation
Chairman and Managing Director, Mukesh D. Ambani, age 56, $11,510 total compensation
Executive Director, P.M.S. Prasad
Executive Director, Pawan K. Kapil
Vice President Corporate Secretarial, S Sudhakar
Executive Director, Hital R. Meswani
Executive Director, Nikhil R. Meswani
Director, Prof Dipak C. Jain, age 55
Executive Director, P.M.S. Prasad
Director, Ramniklal H. Ambani
Director, Mansingh L. Bhakta
Director, Yogendra P. Trivedi
Director, Prof Ashok Misra
Director, Dharam V. Kapur
Director, Mahesh P. Modi
Director, Raghunath Anant Mashelkar
Executive Director, Pawan K. Kapil
Auditors: Chaturvedi&Shah

LOCATIONS

HQ: Reliance Industries Ltd
3rd Floor, Maker Chambers IV, 222, Nariman Point, Mumbai 400 021
Phone: (91) 22 2278 5000 **Fax:** (91) 22 2278 5111
Web: www.ril.com

PRODUCTS/OPERATIONS

2012 Sales

Petroleum	72	
Oil & Gas	4	
Total	**0**	**100**

Selected Products

Chemicals
- Benzene
- Linear alkyl benzene
- Solvents
- Toluene
- Xylenes

Fiber Intermediates
- Di-Ethylene Glycol
- Mono ethylene glycol (MEG)
- Purified terephalic acid (PTA)
- Tri-Ethylene Glycol

Oil and Gas
- Crude oil
- Natural gas

Polyester
- Polyester filament yarn (PFY)
- Polyester staple fiber (PSF)

Polymers
- Polyethylene (HDPE & LLDPE)
- Polypropylene
- Polyvinyl chloride

Textiles
- Furnishings fabrics
- Sleep products
- Texturized yarns

COMPETITORS

Adani Enterprises
Asahi Kasei
Bharat Petroleum
Chargeurs
DuPont
Eastman Chemical
Essar Group
ExxonMobil Chemical
Hindustan Petroleum
Indian Oil
LyondellBasell
Milliken
Reliance Communications
Shell Chemicals
Tata Group

HISTORICAL FINANCIALS

Company Type: Public

Income Statement FYE: March 31

	REVENUE ($ mil.)	NET INCOME ($ mil.)	NET PROFIT MARGIN	EMPLOYEES
03/12	70,467	3,876	5.5%	23,166
03/11	59,618	4,327	7.3%	22,661
03/10	49,127	5,457	11.1%	23,365
03/09	30,546	2,942	9.6%	24,679
03/08	36,028	4,863	13.5%	25,487
Annual Growth	18.3%	(5.5%)	—	(2.4%)

2012 Year-End Financials

Debt ratio: 0.5%	No. of shares (mil.): —
Return on equity: 12.1%	Dividends
Cash ($ mil.): 8,006	Yield: —
Current ratio: 1.82	Payout: 0.0%
Long-term debt ($ mil.): 12,845	Market value ($ mil.): —

Renault S.A. (France)

In Renault's road race against rival Peugeot Citroen to be France's dominant automaker second place will have to deux. Renault manufactures and markets small to midsize cars and light trucks under three brands: Renault Dacia and Renault Samsung Motors (Renault holds 80% Samsung 20%). The company owns Automobile Dacia (Romania's leading automaker) and holds just under half of the Renault-Nissan Alliance (and 43% of Nissan). It also participates in an alliance with Russian car maker AvtoVAZ and helps Germany's Daimlerbuild smart cars. Renault which has become an international brand operates nearly 40 manufacturing facilities in more than 15 countries and sells into 118 nations.

The synergies between Renault and Nissan have produced a reciprocal benefit — Renault has adopted a better production system with Nissan's support and Nissan has embraced better cost-control measures practiced by Renault. The Alliance gives both companies a competitive edge over other automotive companies through shared technologies and platforms. For example Nissan can use Renault's research when developing a diesel engine and Renault can benefit from Nissan's battery technology. By sharing production facilities — which the companies do in Mexico South Africa South Korea and Spain –they save on production purchasing and related costs. The Alliance also allows Renault and Nissan to tackle projects such as electric vehicles the cost of which would be prohibitive if each company had to bear it separately. As is both companies have invested E4 billion (almost $5 billion) into research and development and the manufacturing of vehicles and batteries. The Renault-Nissan Alliance is making a tandem expansion into emerging countries such as Russia India and Brazil. In an attempt to get a larger piece of the growing car market in India Renault has made a point of introducing a steady stream of new models there. To get a larger chunk of the rapidly growing Russian car market Renault-Nissan forged an alliance with Russian carmaker AvtoVAZ. Renault holds about 50% of the company and has invested heavily in upgrading its production plants.

Like most other carmakers Renault-Nissan is investing heavily in Asia. In China the Alliance is principally represented by Nissan which has a partnership with local carmaker Dongfeng Motor. The joint venture plans to produce 40000 vehicles annually. The Alliance is also making concerted steps to expand in India where it has a plant in Chennai. Renault-Nissan entered yet another collaborative agreement in early 2010 when it joined up with Daimler to give Toyota and Volkswagen a run for their money. Renault will provide its small-car technology to Daimler for use in some of its models. As part of the deal Renault and Nissan each took a 1.55% share in Daimler while Daimler has a 3.1% stake in each of them. The company expects the partnership to provide a benefit of about E2 billion ($3.6 billion) to Renault-Nissan by 2015.

Going forward Renault is focusing on the mass marketing of electric vehicles with plans to produce 500000 by 2015. Not just content to make electric cars Renault and Nissan together with German power utility RWE set up 1000 charging stations in Germany to help sell its cars.

The French government and Nissan each hold about 15% of Renault though Nissan has agreed not to exercise the voting control associated with its shares.

HISTORY

In the Paris suburb of Billancourt in 1898 21-year-old Louis Renault assembled a motorized vehicle with a transmission box of his own design. Louis and his brothers Marcel and Fernand established Renault Freres and produced the world's first sedan in 1899. Marcel died in a racing accident (1903) and Fernand left the business (1908) leaving Louis in sole possession of the company. He renamed it La Societe Louis Renault in 1908.

In 1914 a fleet of 600 Paris taxis shuttled French troops to fight the Germans in the Battle of the Marne. Renault also built light tanks and airplane engines. Between world wars Renault expanded into trucks tractors and aircraft engines. Renault sustained heavy damage in WWII but Louis Renault operated the remaining Paris facilities for the Germans during their occupation of France. After the liberation of Paris he was accused of collaboration and died in prison while awaiting trial in 1944. The de Gaulle government nationalized Renault in 1945 and gave the company its present name.

Worldwide economic growth aided Renault's postwar comeback. The company achieved its greatest success in high-volume low-cost cars such as the 4 CV in the late 1940s and 1950s the Renault 4 in the 1960s and 1970s and the Renault 5 in the 1970s and 1980s.

In 1979 Renault acquired 46% of American Motors Corporation (AMC). In the early 1980s AMC fared poorly and Renault suffered from a worldwide slump in auto sales an aging product line and stiff competition from Japanese carmakers. Decreasing sales an unwieldy bureaucracy and above-average wages contributed to a $1.5 billion loss in 1984.

Georges Besse took over Renault in 1985 and trimmed employment by 20000. When Besse was assassinated by Red Army Faction terrorists in 1986 Raymond Levy assumed his role and continued his policies laying off 30000 more workers and selling AMC to Chrysler (1987).

Renault and AB Volvo agreed to extensive cross-ownership and cooperation in 1990. In 1994 Renault swapped its 25% stake in Volvo's car division for the latter's 45% stake in Renault's troubled truck unit. (Volvo sold its remaining 11% stake in 1997.)

The French government reduced its share of the firm from 80% to 52% in 1995 and to 44% the following year. In 1997 it shut down a Belgian plant that employed more than 3000 workers and fired a similar number of employees in France. Renault paid a $13 million civil penalty to the EPA in 1998 to settle allegations that its Mack Trucks unit cheated on its diesel engine emissions tests.

Renault and Fiat struck several deals in 1999. They combined their bus-making operations under the name Irisbus and their foundry operations into jointly owned Teksid. Renault sold a 51% stake in Renault Automation to Fiat's Comau robotics unit. Also that year Renault bought a 51% stake in Romanian automaker Automobile Dacia SA and paid $5.4 billion for a 37% stake in Nissan and a 15% (later increased to 23%) stake in truck affiliate Nissan Diesel Motor.

Early in 2000 the company announced that it would spend around $100 million to build an SUV factory in Brazil and announced plans to trim almost $3 billion in costs between 2001 and 2003. The same year Renault agreed to buy a 70% stake in Samsung Motors' automobile business for around $550 million. It also sold its Mack truck unit to Volvo in exchange for a 15% stake in the Swedish truck maker. Renault planned to buy another 5% of Volvo on the open market. Renault and Nissan also announced plans to save about $1 billion by combining their European sales and marketing operations.

Renault sold its Renault V.I. subsidiary and its Mack Trucks unit to Volvo in return for a 20% stake in the Swedish truck maker.

Later in 2001 Renault furthered strengthen ties with Nissan. The plan increased Renault's stake in Nissan to 44% while granting Nissan a 15% stake in Renault. The French Finance Ministry also announced that it would reduce the French government's stake in Renault from 44% to 25% through a public offering. The two deals were completed in 2002. In 2003 the French government further reduced its stake in Renault from 25% to about 15%.

Early in 2005 Renault sold its 18% stake in Nissan Diesel Motor Co. Ltd. to J.P. Morgan Securities Ltd. who in turn sold the shares on the open market.

The following year Renault called an emergency board meeting to ponder a proposal put forth in writing by billionaire General Motors investor Kirk Kerkorian (he owned about a 10% stake in GM at the time). Kerkorian suggested GM Renault and Nissan form a three-way global automotive alliance but the parties decided otherwise and announced at the Paris Auto Show in 2006 that no such alliance would be formed.

In 2005 Carlos Ghosn was appointed as CEO; he also remained as CEO with Nissan. Ghosn had been Renault's chief cost cutter since 1999. Ghosn made public his plans to revamp Renault by slashing the number of suppliers close five plants and cut its workforce by 14%. While not in the same precarious position as its North American counterparts Chrysler Ford and GM Renault's 2005 profits fell by more than 35% from the previous year and its lineup of products is growing stale.

In 2006 Renault formed a car manufacturing joint venture with India's Mahindra & Mahindra which produced the no-frills midsized Logan model sedan. In 2010 Renault sold its 49% interest in the venture to Mahindra but continued to supply key engine and transmission components. Sales of the Logan never reached expected levels and Renault stated it would rather focus on more profitable alliances in the region including its Renault-Nissan alliance.

EXECUTIVES

President of Renault, Louis Schweitzer, age 71
Chairman Chief Executive Officer, Carlos Ghosn, age 59
EVP and Leader Asia Africa Management Committee, Katsumi Nakamura, age 60
SVP Global Supply Chain, Michel Faivre-Duboz, age 62

Chairman Renault Sport and Renault F1 Team, Bernard Rey, age 67
EVP Engineering and Quality, Jean-Michel Billig, age 50
Leader Euromed Region Management Committee, Jacques Chauvet, age 64
EVP Engineering and Quality, Odile Desforges, age 62
Executive Vice President Corporate Planning, Philippe Klein, age 56
Advanced Process Design Engineer and Director, Yves Audvard, age 60
Document Manager Quality and Director, Alain Champigneux, age 59
Chief Operating Officer for Renault, Carlos Tavares, age 54
EVP Sales and Marketing & Light Commercial Vehicles, Jerome Stoll, age 59
SVP Pre-Engineering Projects and Requirements, Michel Balthazard, age 59
Executive Vice President Chief Financial Officer Chairman CEO, Dominique Thormann, age 59
SVP Corporate Design, Laurens G. van den Acker, age 47
SVP and Alliance Managing Director Global Logistics, Christian Mardrus, age 53
Corporate Controller, Eric Nicolas, age 53
EVP Human Resources, Marie-Francoise Damesin, age 56
SVP Global Marketing, Stephen Norman, age 59
EVP and Chairman France Operations, Gerard Leclercq, age 65
SVP Powertrain Engineering, Jacques Prost, age 60
Cost Control - Technocentre Guyancourt and Director, Patrick Biau, age 56
SVP Vehicle Engineering, Nadine Leclair, age 56
SVP Market Area France, Bernard Cambier, age 60
Managing Director Russia; Chairman Eurasia Region, Bruno Ancelin, age 57
SVP Purchasing; Chairman RNPO, Christian Vandenhende, age 53
SVP Quality, Jean-Pierre Vallaude, age 61
SVP Light Commercial Vehicles, Jean-Christophe Kugler, age 52
Expert Fellow, Christian Deleplace
SVP and Chairman Americas Region, Denis Barbier, age 55
Chief Executive Renault Samsung Motors, Francois Provost
Director of Investor Relations, Thierry Huon
EVP Manufacturing and Supply Chain, Thierry Bollore
EVP and Chairman Europe Region, Stefan Mueller
Director, Alain J. P. Belda, age 69
Director, Thierry Desmarest, age 67
Director, Franck Riboud, age 57
Director, Jean-Pierre (JP) Garnier, age 65
Director, Marc Ladreit de Lacharriere, age 72
Director, Charles F. W. de Croisset, age 69
Director, Hiroto Saikawa, age 59
Director, Pascale Sourisse
Director, Philippe Lagayette, age 69
Advanced Process Design Engineer and Director, Yves Audvard, age 60
Document Manager Quality and Director, Alain Champigneux, age 59
Director, Dominique de La Garanderie, age 69
Director, Takeshi Isayama
Director, Luc Rousseau
Cost Control - Technocentre Guyancourt and Director, Patrick Biau, age 56
Head Sociotechnics UET and Director, Michel Sailly
Director, Alexis Kohler
Director, Bernard Delpit, age 47
Auditors: Deloitte&Associes

LOCATIONS

HQ: Renault S.A. (France)
13-15, quai Le Gallo, Boulogne-Billancourt, Cedex 92513
Phone: (33) 1 76 84 04 04
Web: www.renault.com

2010 Sales

	% of total
Europe	70
Americas	10
Asia &	10
Euromed (Algeria Morocco Romania	7
Eurasia (former Soviet	3
Total	**100**

PRODUCTS/OPERATIONS

2010 Sales

	% of total
Automobiles	95
Sales	5
Total	**100**

COMPETITORS

BMW
Chrysler
Daimler
Fiat
Ford Motor
General Motors
Honda
Isuzu
Kia Motors
Mahindra
Mazda
Peugeot
Saab Automobile
Suzuki Motor
Tata Motors
Toyota
Volkswagen
Volvo Car Corp.

HISTORICAL FINANCIALS

Company Type: Public

Income Statement FYE: December 31

	REVENUE ($ mil.)	NET INCOME ($ mil.)	NET PROFIT MARGIN	EMPLOYEES
12/12	54,395	2,335	4.3%	127,086
12/11	55,137	2,705	4.9%	128,322
12/10	52,157	4,577	8.8%	124,749
12/09	48,564	(4,501)	—	124,307
12/08	52,835	798	1.5%	129,068
Annual Growth	0.7%	30.8%	—	(0.4%)

2012 Year-End Financials

Debt ratio: 57.7%
Return on equity: 7.3%
Cash ($ mil.): 14,735
Current ratio: 1.04
Long-term debt ($ mil.): 8,728
No. of shares (mil.): 291
Dividends
Yield: —
Payout: —
Market value ($ mil.): 16,173

	STOCK PRICE ($) FY Close	P/E High	P/E Low	PER SHARE ($) Earnings	Dividends	Book Value
12/12	55.45	15	9	8.57	0.00	109.78
12/11	35.27	16	7	9.93	0.00	106.82
12/10	56.82	8	4	17.00	0.00	101.63
12/09	50.55	—	—	(17.47)	0.00	82.10
12/08	25.65	130	16	3.10	0.00	95.98
Annual Growth	21.3%	—	—	28.9%	—	3.4%

Repsol S.A.

The sun shines on Repsol (formerly Repsol YPF) Spain's largest oil company. A fully integrated oil and gas company it operates in Latin America the Middle East and North Africa. Repsol operates five refineries in Spain and one in Peru and produces chemicals plastics and polymers. It sells gas under the brands Campsa Petronor and Repsol at 4500 service stations in Europe and Latin America. It is one of Spain's largest sellers of liquefied petroleum gas and liquefied natural gas. Repsol has proved reserves of 2.2 billion barrels of oil equivalent. Affiliate YPF conducts exploration production refining logistics marketing and chemicals in Argentina. Repsol also owns 30% of Gas Natural Fenosa.

Change in Company Type

In 2012 the Argentine government shocked the company when it seized control of subsidiary YPF as part of a nationalization drive.

Repsol had owned YPF Argentina's #1 oil company since 1999. However the Fernandez government took back a 51% stake in YPF. The bid reflects a growing trend towards nationalization of key industries (airlines private pension funds) that have drawn warnings from Argentina's trading partners.

Geographic Reach

Repsol operates globally and has major assets primarily in Spain and Argentina. In 2011 Europe accounted for 63% of company's revenues.

Operations

Repsol upstream's division is engaged in oil and natural gas exploration and production activities based on key traditional regions located in Latin America (mainly Trinidad and Tobago Peru Venezuela Bolivia Colombia and Ecuador) and in North Africa (Algeria and Libya). Strategic areas for short and medium-term growth include the US Gulf of Mexico and offshore fields in Brazil.

The company's LNG activities include the liquefaction transportation marketing and regasification of liquefied natural gas in addition to electricity generation activities in Spain at the Bahia de Bizkaia Electricidad plan and natural gas marketing in North America.

Repsol's downstream business includes the supply and trading of crude and other products oil refining marketing of oil products and LPG and the production and marketing of chemicals.

Financial Performance

Higher oil prices and increased demand lifted Repsol's revenues by 6% in 2011. Net income decreased by 53% in 2011 due to the impact on revenues of the depreciation of the dollar against the euro and increase in personnel expense.

Strategy

Repsol plans to invest more than E21 billion (more than $26 billion) over the next few years in its operations particularly in exploration and production including its Spanish refineries which will receive an investment of about E4 billion (more than $4 billion).

To raise cash and to rebalance its global portfolio in 2011 Repsol sold about 4% of its stake in YPF to Lazard Asset Management for $639 million.

Repsol created the New Energies Business Unit in 2010 assigned to the Downstream Division to promote and new cleaner energy initiatives to reduce carbon dioxide emissions.

HISTORY

Repsol officially created in 1987 is actually the result of efforts that began as early as the 1920s to organize Spain's fragmented energy industry.

Following an era of dependency on foreign investment prior to and during Francisco Franco's dictatorship (1939-75) Spain began reorganizing its energy industry. In 1979 it set up the Instituto Nacional de Hidrocarburos which in 1981 incorporated all public-sector firms involved in gas and oil under one government agency.

Repsol was formed six years later to provide central management to a Spanish oil company that could compete in the unified European market. The government chose the name Repsol after a well-known brand of Spanish lubricant products. The firm was charged with pursuing a global strategy to bring together all levels of the industry.

In 1989 Repsol offered 26% of the firm on the Madrid and New York stock exchanges raising more than $1 billion. That year Repsol increased its marine fleet with the purchase of the Naviera Vizcaina shipping company and bought Carless Refining & Marketing a UK business with a chain of 500 service stations operating mainly under the Anglo brand. Although Spain was opening its doors to foreign investment the Spanish government maintained control over the country's energy industry including a tightly guarded distribution network under state-controlled Campsa. Campsa oversaw a marketing/logistics system of pipelines storage terminals and sales outlets.

The European Community demanded that Spain open its markets to other EC members forcing Campsa in 1991 to divide its 3800 gasoline stations among its four major shareholders: Cepsa (Spain's largest private refiner) Petromed Ertoil and Repsol. Repsol gained 66% of the logistical network and use of the Campsa brand name.

Repsol and Spanish bank La Caixa merged their interests in natural gas in 1992 to create Gas Natural a new gas distributor. That year the Spanish government began reducing its majority holding and by 1996 its stake had dwindled to 10%. (It sold its remaining stock in 1997.)

Expanding its South American operations Repsol acquired control of Argentinian oil company Astra CAPSA and a Peruvian oil refinery in 1996. That year Repsol purchased a 30% stake in the Tin Fouye Tabankort field in Algeria.

In 1999 Repsol paid $2 billion for a 15% stake in giant oil company YPF which was auctioned off by Argentina's government. After acquiring another 83% of YPF for $13.2 billion Repsol changed its name to Repsol YPF. To help pay down debt incurred in the acquisition Repsol YPF sold its UK North Sea oil and gas operations to US independent Kerr-McGee for $555 million in 2000. That year the company (as part of its commitment to Argentina's government after acquiring YPF) agreed to swap some of its Argentine refining and marketing assets for Brazilian oil and gas operations owned by Petrobras.

In 2002 Repsol YPF sold oil and gas assets in Indonesia to CNOOC for about $585 million. Former chairman of Spain's top gas supplier Gas Natural S.A. Antonio Brufau replaced Alfonso Cortina de Alcocer in 2004 as chairman of Repsol.

In 2006 the company acquired BP's 28% stake in the Shenzi field in the Gulf of Mexico. The next year Repsol YPF began selling minority stakes in YPF to generate cash to support the Argentine company's growth.

EXECUTIVES

Executive Managing Director YPF, Antonio Gomis Saez
Executive Managing Director Downstream, Pedro Fernandez Frial
Executive Managing Director Upstream, Nemesio Fernandez-Cuesta Luca de Tena
General Counsel Secretary and Director, Luis Suarez de Lezo Mantilla, age 63
CFO, Miguel Martinez San Martin
Executive Managing Director HR and Organization, Cristina Sanz Mendiola
Executive Director Communications and Chairman's Office, Bego?a Elices Garcia
Deputy Director National International and Financial Media, Maria Ritter
International and Financial Media Manager, Kristian Rix
Media Director, Juan Valdemoro
General Director of Exploration and Production, Luis Cabra
General Counsel; General Secretary; Secretary of the Board; Executive Director, Luis Mantilla
Director of Investor Relations, Maria Zingoni
General Director of Economics and Finance; Director, Miguel Barrio
Chief Financial and Economic Officer; General Director of Subsidiaries; Affiliates and Development, Miguel Martin
Chief Operating Officer; Business Director, Nemesio Tena
Executive Director of Commercial Area, Pascual Olmos
General Director of Strategy and Control, Pedro Frial
Executive Director of Resources, Andreu Punet
Executive President; Chief Executive Officer; Chairman of the Board; Executive Director, Antonio Niubo
General Manager of YPF SA, Antonio Saez
General Director of Communication and Chairmans Office; Director, Begona Garcia
Executive Director of GNL, Benjamin Palomo
Director of Human Resources and Organization, Cristina Mendiola
Executive Director of Trading and Transport, Ignacio Egea
Vice Chairman of the Board, Isidro Casas
General Director of Industrial Area and New Energies, Josu Miguel
Vice Chairman of the Board, Juan Gallo
Vice Chairman, Isidro Faine Casas, age 70
Director, Juan Maria Nin Genova, age 59
General Counsel Secretary and Director, Luis Suarez de Lezo Mantilla, age 63
Director, Carmelo de las Morenas Lopez, age 74
Director, Henri-Philippe Reichstul, age 64
Vice Chairman, Juan Abello Gallo, age 71
Director, Paulina Beato Blanco, age 68
Director, Artur Carulla Font, age 66
Director, Luis Carlos Croissier Batista, age 64
Director, Angel Durandez Adeva, age 71
Director, Javier Echenique Landiribar, age 61
Director, Jose Manuel Loureda Manti?an, age 75
Director, Maria Isabel Gabarro Miquel, age 58
Director, Jose M. Carrera Panizzo
Independent Director, Mario Pelaz
Independent Director, Javier Landiribar
Director; Representative of Pemex Internacional Espana SA, Jose Panizzo
Auditors: DeloitteSL

LOCATIONS

HQ: Repsol S.A.
Mendez Alvaro, 44, Madrid 28045
Phone: (34) 91 75 38 100 **Fax:** (34) 902 303 145
Web: www.repsol.com

PRODUCTS/OPERATIONS

2011 Sales

	% of total
Downstream	63
YPF	17
Gas Natural	10
Upstream	6
LNG	4
Corporate	-
Total	**100**

COMPETITORS

Anadarko Petroleum
Apco Oil and Gas International
BHP Billiton
BP
Devon Energy
Murphy Oil
Noble Energy
Norsk Hydro ASA
Occidental Petroleum
PEMEX
PETROBRAS
Endesa S.A.
Eni
Exxon Mobil
IBERDROLA
Imperial Oil
Koch Industries Inc.
Marathon Oil
Petrobras Argentina
Petroleos de Venezuela
Pioneer Natural Resources
RasGas
Royal Dutch Shell
TOTAL

HISTORICAL FINANCIALS

Company Type: Public

Income Statement FYE: December 31

	REVENUE ($ mil.)	NET INCOME ($ mil.)	NET PROFIT MARGIN	EMPLOYEES
12/12	77,152	2,715	3.5%	29,985
12/11	80,848	2,836	3.5%	46,575
12/10	75,018	6,280	8.4%	43,298
12/09	68,241	2,245	3.3%	41,014
12/08	82,987	3,790	4.6%	36,302
Annual Growth	(1.8%)	(8.0%)	—	(4.7%)

2012 Year-End Financials

Debt ratio: 38.7%
Return on equity: 8.1%
Cash ($ mil.): 7,780
Current ratio: 1.51
Long-term debt ($ mil.): 20,166
No. of shares (mil.): 1,192
Dividends
Yield: 6.1%
Payout: 142.5%
Market value ($ mil.): 24,928

	STOCK PRICE ($) FY Close	P/E High/Low		PER SHARE ($) Earnings	Dividends	Book Value
12/12	20.90	32	13	2.24	1.29	29.51
12/11	30.51	38	24	2.33	2.08	27.71
12/10	27.94	14	8	5.14	0.93	26.46
12/09	26.66	48	20	1.86	1.65	23.54
12/08	21.51	43	13	3.12	1.23	23.02
Annual Growth	(0.7%)	—	—	(7.9%)	1.2%	6.4%

Resona Holdings Inc
Osaka

Resona Holdings resonate in Japan's retail banking market. As the holding company of Resona Bank and the smaller regional banks Kinki Osaka Bank and Saitama Resona Bank Resona Holdings focuses on consumer and small business banking in the greater Tokyo area and Kansai region. Resona Bank provides corporate pension management banking and trust services. Personal banking services at each bank include loans for individuals asset management and estate planning. The company also provides corporate banking services such as loans pension management and real estate services. Altogether Resona Holdings has more than 1400 branches (600 manned and 800 unmanned) throughout Japan.

EXECUTIVES

Chairman and Representative Executive Officer; Chairman Resona Bank, Eiji Hosoya, age 68
President and Representative Executive Officer, Kazuhiro Higashi, age 56
Director President and Representative Executive, Seiji Higaki
Executive Officer; Representative Director and President Resona Bank, Naoki Iwata
Executive Officer; Representative Director President and Executive Officer The Kinki Osaka Bank, Kazuyoshi Ikeda

President Saitama Resona Bank, Masahito Kamijo
Representative Executive Officer, Toshiki Hara
Representative Executive Officer, Tetsuya Kan
President The Kinki Osaka Bank, Koji Nakamae
Deputy President Representative Executive Officer and Director; Executive Officer of Resona Bank, Kazuhiro Higashi, age 56
President Representative Executive Officer and Director, Seiji Higaki
Director, Kaoru Isono
Auditors: DeloitteToucheTohmatsu

LOCATIONS

HQ: Resona Holdings Inc Osaka
1-5-65 Kiba, Koto-ku, Tokyo 135-0042
Phone: (81) 3 6704 3111
Web: www.resona-gr.co.jp

PRODUCTS/OPERATIONS

Selected Subsidiaries

Daiwa Guarantee Co. Ltd. (credit guarantee)
Resona Bank Ltd. (bank)
Resona Guarantee Co. Ltd. (credit guarantee)
Saitama Resona Bank Ltd. (bank)
Kinki Osaka Shinyo Hosho Co. Ltd. (credit guarantee)
The Kinki Osaka Bank Ltd. (bank)
P.T. Bank Resona Perdania (bank)
Resona Kessai Service Co. Ltd. (collections agency)
Resona Card Co. Ltd. (credit cards)
Resona Capital Co. Ltd. (private equity)
Resona Research Institute Co. Ltd. (consulting)
Resona Business Service Co. Ltd. (staffing)

COMPETITORS

Aozora Bank
Bank of Yokohama
Chiba Bank
Chugoku Bank
Chuo Mitsui Trust
Citigroup
Fukuoka Financial Group
Gunma Bank
Hachijuni Bank
Hokuhoku Financial Group
Iyo Bank
Joyo Bank
Juroku Bank
Mitsubishi UFJ Financial Group
Mizuho Financial
NORTH PACIFIC BANKLTD.
Nishi-Nippon City Bank
Shinsei Bank
Shizuoka Bank
Sumitomo Mitsui
Yamaguchi Financial Group

HISTORICAL FINANCIALS

Company Type: Public

Income Statement

FYE: March 31

	ASSETS ($ mil.)	NET INCOME ($ mil.)	INCOME AS % OF ASSETS	EMPLOYEES
03/13	458,175	2,924	0.6%	16,826
03/12	526,633	3,092	0.6%	16,881
03/11	515,742	1,933	0.4%	16,941
03/10	436,191	1,415	0.3%	16,756
03/09	404,804	1,258	0.3%	16,498
Annual Growth	3.1%	23.5%	—	0.5%

2013 Year-End Financials

Return on assets: 0.6%
Return on equity: 14.4%
Long-term debt ($ mil.): —
No. of shares (mil.): —
Sales ($ mil): 8,856
Dividends
Yield: —
Payout: —
Market value ($ mil.): —

	STOCK PRICE ($) FY Close	P/E High	P/E Low	PER SHARE ($) Earnings	Dividends	Book Value
03/13	5.47	—	—	0.77	0.00	9.49
03/12	4.42	—	—	0.83	0.00	9.17
03/11	5.86	—	—	0.50	0.00	7.85
03/10	11.16	—	—	0.57	0.00	21.14
03/09	14.00	—	—	0.55	0.00	20.56
Annual Growth	(20.9%)	—	—	9.0%	—	(17.6%)

Ricoh Co., Ltd.

Ricoh may be best known for its imaging equipment but the company is more than just another copycat. One of the world's leading manufacturers of copiers and supplies Ricoh also makes fax machines scanners and printers. Other products from the company which operates about 235 subsidiaries and affiliates in more than 180 countries include digital cameras servers software for its products semiconductors printed circuit boards thermal paper labels and optical equipment. Ricoh is represented in the US and across the Americas by its Ricoh Americas subsidiary.

Geographic Reach

Sales outside Japan account for about 45% of the company's revenues. The company plans to increase its sales in Asia/Pacific outside Japan from 7% in 2011 to 17% by 2014.

Strategy

Although printers and office equipment are Ricoh's biggest moneymakers the company has moved beyond its core products into related services including managed document services document outsourcing services logistics financing leasing and IT service. The company is investing $300 million in its managed document services infrastructure through 2014. Ricoh leases its equipment through a separate publicly traded company in Japan named Ricoh Leasing.

To boost more business in the consumer market Ricoh formed PENTAX RICOH IMAGING out of the 2011 acquisition of Hoya's PENTAX Imaging Systems Business. The PENTAX unit focuses on digital cameras and binoculars as well as lenses for security cameras.

HISTORY

Ricoh began in 1936 as the Riken Kankoshi Company making photographic paper. With founder Kiyoshi Ichimura at the helm the company soon became the leader in Japan's sensitized paper market. It changed its name to Riken Optical Company in 1938 and started making cameras. Two years later it produced its first camera under the Ricoh brand.

By 1954 Ricoh cameras were Japan's #1 seller and also popular abroad. The next year it entered the office machine market with its compact mimeograph machine. Ricoh followed that in 1960 with an offset duplicator.

Ricoh built its business in the 1960s with a range of office machines including reproduction and data processing equipment and retrieval systems. The company began establishing operations overseas including US subsidiary Ricoh Industries U.S.A. in 1962. The US unit started marketing cameras but found greener pastures in the copier industry where Ricoh's products were sold under the Pitney Bowes and Savin brand names. It changed its name to Ricoh Company in 1963. Two years later Ricoh entered the emerging field of office computers and introduced an electrostatic copier. In 1968 Ichimura died and Mikio Tatebayashi took over as president for the next eight years.

During the 1970s Ricoh debuted the first high-speed fax machine and began consolidating its network outside Japan. In 1973 it established a second US subsidiary —Ricoh Electronics —to assemble copier supplies and parts becoming the first Japanese company to produce copiers in the US. It released a plain-paper copier in 1975 followed the next year by a daisy wheel printer and its first word processor. Tatebayashi died in 1976 and was replaced by Takeshi Ouye as president. Subsidiary Rapicom was established in 1978 in Japan to develop fax products.

Throughout the 1970s Savin and Pitney Bowes continued to brand and sell Ricoh-made products in the US but in the early 1980s Ricoh started marketing products under its own name. It introduced a PC and its first laser printer in 1983. By the next year Ricoh had 7% of the US copier market. Other products introduced in the 1980s included a color copier minicomputers developed with AT&T and (in Japan) a digital copier that could also be used as an input/output station for electronic filing systems. Ricoh's overseas sales continued to grow in the late 1980s and for a while exceeded its domestic sales. In 1983 Ouye turned over leadership of the company to Hiroshi Hamada.

Ricoh founded Tailien Optical (Shenzhen) Co. Ltd. in 1992 to make compact camera parts. As the 1990s progressed the company increasingly pushed products based on digital technologies.

Ricoh won licensing fees from Samsung Electronics in a 1995 dispute over fax machine patents. Seeking to boost international sales it bought Savin in the US and Gestetner Holdings (later renamed NRG Group) in Europe that year. The next year Hamada became chairman and CEO and Masamitsu Sakurai took over as president.

The company's push during the mid-1990s to increase overseas sales paid off. Amid an Asian economic crisis Ricoh's overall sales remained relatively stable while sales of its copiers outside Japan increased 20% and 9% for 1998 and 1999 respectively.

In 2000 the company reorganized its US operations and consolidated its European distribution centers. Early the following year Ricoh boosted its push into the US market with its acquisition of office equipment supplier Lanier Worldwide for about $250 million. Despite shaky world economic conditions in fiscal 2002 Ricoh saw growth in sales and profits with strong overseas sales making up for slightly lowered revenues from Japan.

Ricoh augmented its printer business by acquiring Hitachi Printing Solutions in 2004. Two years later Shiro Kondo became president and CEO of Ricoh and Hamada stepped up to the chairmanship.

In 2007 the company's Ricoh Europe subsidiary acquired the European operations of Danka Business Systems. The purchase included 16 companies in 12 countries. The following year NRG Group was integrated into Ricoh UK.

For the consumer market in 2009 Ricoh launched an online storage service called quanp short for "quantum paper." The service which includes a Windows-based client program that enables visual search tools lets users upload store and access digital photos and other content.

To further streamline its global operations Ricoh consolidated seven sales companies and its corporate marketing group into one subsidiary called Ricoh Japan Corporation in 2010.

Also in 2010 Ricoh took complete control of Ricoh Production Print Solutions formerly Info-Print Solutions a manufacturer and distributor of high-volume production printers which began as a joint venture with IBM.

EXECUTIVES

Chairman, Masamitsu Sakurai, age 71
SVP; Chairman Ricoh Electronics Devices Shanghai; General Manager Research and Development Group, Terumoto Nonaka, age 65
President CEO and Director, Shiro Kondo, age 63
EVP Internal Management and Control Division CFO CIO Chief Strategy Officer and Director; General Manager CRGP Office Global Marketing Support Division and Trade Affairs and Export and Import Administration Division, Zenji Miura, age 63
EVP and Director; Chairman Ricoh Software Research Center (Beijing); General Manager Corporate Technology Development Group, Hiroshi Kobayashi, age 65
VP; General Manager Legal and Intellectual Property Division, Yutaka Ebi, age 63
Corporate Auditor, Takao Yuhara, age 67
EVP and Director; General Manager MFP Business Group, Yoshimasa Matsuura, age 66
Group Executive Officer; Executive President & CEO of Subsidiary, Sadahiro Arikawa, age 64
EVP and Director; Chairman Ricoh Europe and Ricoh Europe (Netherlands); General Manager Europe Marketing Group, Shiro Sasaki, age 63
SVP; General Manager Production Business Group, Kenichi Kanemaru, age 60
VP; President and CEO InfoPrint Solutions Company, Daisuke Segawa, age 59
VP; General Manager RS Product Division of Production Business Group, Kenichi Matsubayashi, age 65
SVP; General Manager Corporate Planning Division, Shoichi Nagamatsu, age 62
SVP; General Manager Platform Development Center of Imaging Engine Development Division, Yohzoh Matsuura, age 57
VP; President Ricoh Asia Pacific; General Manager Asia Pacific Marketing Group, Nobuaki Majima, age 61
Corporate Auditor, Tsukasa Yunoki, age 70
VP; General Manager Quality and Engineering Process Innovation Center of Quality Management Division, Katsumi Kurihara, age 57
VP; General Manager GJ Design & Development Division, Junichi Matsuno, age 59
VP; General Manager Finance and Accounting Division, Kunihito Minakawa, age 59
VP; General Manager Printer Business Group and Controller Development Division, Seiji Sakata, age 55
Corporate Executive Vice President, Yoshinori Yamashita, age 56
Executive Officer; Chief Director of Printer Business; Manager of Business Strategy Center, Hidenobu Endo
Executive Officer; Chief Director of Imaging Engine Development, Hisao Murayama
Executive Officer; President of Electric Equipment Unit Company, Kazuo Nishinomiya
Executive Officer; Chief Director of Production Business, Masayuki Ishihara
Executive Officer; Chairman of Subsidiaries, Yasutomo Mori
Executive Officer; President of Electronics Devices Company; Chairman of Subsidiary, Masahiro Nakamura
Director, Eiji Hosoya, age 68
EVP Corporate Social Responsibility Chief Human Resources Officer and Director; General Manager Personnel Division, Takashi Nakamura, age 66
President CEO and Director, Shiro Kondo, age 63
EVP Internal Management and Control Division CFO CIO Chief Strategy Officer and Director; General Manager CRGP Office Global Marketing Support Division and Trade Affairs and Export and Import Administration Division, Zenji Miura, age 63
EVP Chief Marketing Officer and Director; General Manager Global Marketing Group, Kazunori Azuma, age 63
EVP and Director; General Manager MFP Business Group, Yoshimasa Matsuura, age 66
EVP and Director; President Ricoh Institute of Sustainability and Business, Nobuo Inaba, age 62
Director, Mochio Umeda, age 53
Independent Director, Kunio Noji
Auditors: KPMGAZSA&Co.

LOCATIONS

HQ: Ricoh Co., Ltd.
8-13-1 Ginza, Chuo-ku, Tokyo 104-8222
Phone: (81) 3 6278 5241 **Fax:** (81) 3 3543 9086
Web: www.ricoh.co.jp

2011 Sales

	% of total
Japan	45
The	27
Europe	21
Other	7
Total	**100**

PRODUCTS/OPERATIONS

2011 Sales

	% of total
Imaging solutions	
Imaging	74
Network system	15
Industrial	5
Other	6
Total	**100**

Selected Products

Imaging and Solutions
- Imaging Solutions
  - Diazo copiers
  - Digital duplicators
  - Digital monochrome and color copiers
  - Fax machines
  - Imaging supplies and consumables
  - Wide-format copiers
  - Printing systems (laser multifunction)
  - Scanners
- Network System Solutions
  - Document management software
  - Networking and applications software
  - Network systems
  - Personal computers
  - Servers
  - Services and support

Industrial
- Electronic components
- Measuring equipment
- Optical equipment
- Semiconductor devices
- Thermal media

Other
- Digital cameras and other photographic equipment
- Financing and logistics services
- Optical disks

COMPETITORS

3M
Brother Industries
CASIO COMPUTER
Canon
Dell
Eastman Kodak
Epson
FUJIFILM
Fuji Xerox
Hewlett-Packard
Lexmark
NEC
Nikon
Oce
Oki Electric
Olympus
Panasonic Corp
SANYO
Sharp Corp.
Toshiba
Hitachi
Konica Minolta
Kyocera Document Solutions
Xerox

HISTORICAL FINANCIALS

Company Type: Public

Income Statement FYE: March 31

	REVENUE ($ mil.)	NET INCOME ($ mil.)	NET PROFIT MARGIN	EMPLOYEES
03/13	20,453	345	1.7%	107,431
03/12	23,204	(543)	—	109,241
03/11	23,452	237	1.0%	109,014
03/10	21,586	298	1.4%	108,525
03/09	21,240	66	0.3%	108,477
Annual Growth	(0.9%)	51.0%	—	(0.2%)

2013 Year-End Financials

Debt ratio: 0.3%
Return on equity: 3.7%
Cash ($ mil.): 1,244
Current ratio: 1.61
Long-term debt ($ mil.): 5,062
No. of shares (mil.): 725
Dividends
Yield: 0.0%
Payout: 0.0%
Market value ($ mil.): 39,406

	STOCK PRICE ($) FY Close	P/E High	P/E Low	PER SHARE ($) Earnings	Dividends	Book Value
03/13	54.35	0	0	0.48	0.00	13.16
03/12	49.38	—	—	(0.75)	0.00	13.83
03/11	58.59	0	0	0.32	1.90	15.48
03/10	78.70	0	0	0.40	1.73	14.36
03/09	59.26	0	0	0.09	1.74	13.65
Annual Growth	(2.1%)	—	—	52.1%	(90.1%)	(0.9%)

Rio Tinto Ltd

Rio Tinto is on the lookout for pay dirt. Rio Tinto Limited one of the world's largest mining operations (along with BHP Billiton and Vale) is the Australian half of dual-listed sister companies with Rio Tinto plc taking up residence in London. Although each company trades separately the two Rio Tintos operate as one business. Rio Tinto explores for a variety of commodities: bauxite coal copper diamonds gold iron ore minerals (borates and titanium dioxide) nickel and potash. Iron ore makes up about 44% of the group's sales. It also produces aluminum through its Rio Tinto Alcan unit. Most of its businesses are in Australia and North America but it is expanding its operations in China and Mongolia.

By focusing on a strategy of developing large-scale long-term mining operations and businesses Rio Tinto has tried to weather commodity prices that have dipped and risen over several years. The mining industry is affected by both oversupply and rising costs in raw materials. Like its rivals the company continues to seek acquisitions that will grow shareholder value as it cuts costs and improves productivity.

Despite a year of challenges including six fatalities at its mining sites and flooding that disrupted production in Australia Rio Tinto recorded revenues of $60.5 billion in 2011. Net income however fell about 59% –from $15.3 billion in 2010 to $6.8 billion in 2011. The company attributes an $8.9 billion impairment charge related to its aluminum assets as the cause of its precipitous fall in net earnings that year.

The company's iron ore business also contributed 78% of the group's net income in 2011. Rio Tinto is the world's second-largest supplier of iron ore which is used in steelmaking operations. Its key iron ore operations are in the Pilbara region of Western Australia and in Quebec in Canada.

In 2011 the company started trimming its aluminum operations. It placed 13 assets on the chopping block allowing Rio Tinto Alcan to focus on its high-quality tier one assets (mostly in Canada) and improve performance. The company also planned to transfer its stakes in six Australian and New Zealand operations to a new business unit Pacific Aluminium that would be managed and reported separately from Rio Tinto Alcan.

In 2011 to raise cash the company sold its talc business to Imerys for $340 million. That year Rio Tinto also increased its stake to 49% in Canada-based Ivanhoe Mines which manages the Oyu Tolgoi mine in Mongolia one of the world's largest undeveloped copper-gold projects. In 2012 it upped its holding in Ivanhoe Mines to 51% to become the majority owner. Commercial production at the mine may be delayed however because an agreement to supply electricity has not yet been reached between China and Mongolia.

In another strategic move in 2011 Rio Tinto made an all-cash offer for Canada-based uranium producer Hathor Exploration valued at $578 million after rival Cameco Corp. made a takeover bid for the company. In 2012 Rio Tinto was successful in acquiring Hathor which supplies about a fifth of the world's uranium.

In the first half of 2011 the company completed the acquisition of the Riversdale coal mine which has now been renamed Rio Tinto Coal Mozambique.

In 2012 the company began an overview of operations and announced that it may sell its diamond business. The company operates diamond mines in Canada Zimbabwe and Australia. At its Argyle mine in Australia the company unearthed a rare pink diamond in the rough in 2012. The Argyle mine is undergoing a $2.1 billion expansion and is the world's largest producer of pink diamonds. However in 2011 diamond operations made up only 2% of the company's total earnings before interest tax depreciation and amortization. Argyle's lower production also helped lead to an 86% drop in overall earnings for its diamonds unit that year.

Slimming down further in 2012 the company agreed to sell one of its noncore US operations Atlanta-based wire and cable business Alcan Cable to Kentucky-based General Cable for $185 million. General Cable makes and distributes copper aluminum and fiber-optic wire and cable products. Alcan Cable serves the energy and construction markets.

HISTORY

Rio Tinto Limited began life as the Zinc Corporation in 1905 to recover zinc from the tailings of the silver and lead mines around Australia's mineral-rich Broken Hill area. The company expanded steadily extending its operations into a wide range of mining and metallurgical activities primarily in Australia. By 1914 it had changed its name to Consolidated Zinc Corporation. The company discovered the world's largest deposit of bauxite (1955) and formed Hamersley Holdings with Kaiser Steel (1962) to mine iron ore.

Rio Tinto plc (UK) began with mining operations in Spain in 1873. It sold most of its Spanish holdings in 1954 and branched out to Australia Africa and Canada. In 1962 Rio Tinto and Australia's Consolidated Zinc merged to form RTZ. The companies merged their Australian interests as a partially owned subsidiary CRA (from Conzinc Riotinto of Australia).

In 1968 RTZ bought U.S. Borax which was built on one of the earth's few massive boron deposits. (The use of boron in cleansers was widespread in the late 19th century.) A 1927 discovery in the Mojave Desert led to development of a large boron mine. Until its Turkish mine was nationalized RTZ controlled the world's boron supply. It sold U.S. Borax's consumer products operations in 1988.

RTZ opened a large copper mine at Bougainville in Papua New Guinea in 1969. Subsidiary CRA discovered diamonds in Western Australia's Argyle region three years later. CRA then opened Australia's largest thermal-coal development at Blair Athol in 1984.

RTZ bought Kennecott Corporation in 1989 and expanded its copper operations. Kennecott had been formed by Stephen Birch and named for Robert Kennicott (a typo altered the spelling of the company's name); it had begun mining at Bingham Canyon Utah in 1904. Kennicott had died in Alaska while trying to establish an intercontinental telegraph line. Backed by J.P. Morgan and the Guggenheims Birch also built a railroad to haul the ore. Kennecott merged its railroad and mine operations in 1915. Kennecott consolidated its hold on Chile's Braden copper mine (1925) and on the Utah Copper Company (1936) and other US mines. When copper prices slumped British Petroleum's Standard Oil of Ohio subsidiary bought Kennecott (1981). In 1989 RTZ purchased British Petroleum's US mineral operations including Kennecott.

By the 1990s RTZ and CRA (by then 49%-owned by RTZ) were increasingly competing for mining rights to recently opened areas of Asia and Latin America. RTZ sold the last of its nonmining holdings (building products group) in 1993. In 1995 RTZ brought CRA into its operations. Through Kennecott RTZ purchased US coal mine operators Nerco Cordero Mining Company and Colowyo Coal Company. Also in 1995 the company acquired 13% of Freeport-McMoRan Copper & Gold (sold in 2004).

The RTZ and CRA company names were changed to Rio Tinto plc and Rio Tinto Limited respectively in 1997. Rio Tinto bought a Wyoming coal mine from Kerr-McGee for about $400 million in 1998. The next year Rio Tinto bought 80% of Kestrel (coal Australia) increased its ownership of Blair Athol from 57% to 71% and increased its stake in Comalco (aluminum) to 72%.

In 2000 CEO Leon Davis retired; his position passed to energy group executive Leigh Clifford. In a move that sparked an outcry from union officials Davis accepted a position as non-executive deputy chairman (he retired from the board in 2005). Later that year Rio Tinto acquired both North Limited and Ashton Mining. The company also bought Comalco's outstanding shares and the Peabody Group's Australian subsidiaries.

Rio Tinto sold its Norzink Zink Smelter to Outokumpu in 2001. It also increased its holdings in Queensland Alumina Coal & Allied Industries and Palabora Mining and it began developing the Hail Creek Coal Project in Australia which is based on one of the largest coking coal deposits in the world. In 2003 Rio Tinto sold its 25% stake in Minera Alumbrera (Argentina) and Peak Gold Mine (Australia) to Wheaton River Minerals for around $210 million.

Rio Tinto had owned 14% of Lihir Gold but divested its stake in the company. Prior to that decision the company had controlled Lihir and its management. In late 2005 though Rio Tinto reliquished its management rights and decided to sell its entire stake in Lihir.

Tom Albanese succeeded Clifford in 2007.

In 2007 Rio Tinto swooped in and made a successful $38 billion offer to buy Alcan then the world's #3 aluminum producer. That came not long after Alcoa #2 in the world had offered $33 billion. The deal combined Rio Tinto's own aluminum operations with Alcan's to form the new world leader Rio Tinto Alcan based in Canada. Rio Tinto's operations were located in Australia New Zealand and Africa as well as in Italy and the UK. Alcan's geographic strengths were in North America throughout Europe and in the Asia/Pacific region.

After that acquisition Rio Tinto announced a major divestment program saying it wanted to sell off $15 billion worth of assets. In early 2008 it began that program selling stakes in two North American properties to Hecla Mining and Barrick Gold. The properties had been a part of Kennecott Minerals and netted Rio Tinto about $2.5 billion. Later that year the company spun off most of its North American coal operations into a company called Cloud Peak Energy which it spun off through a public offering in 2009 using the almost $750 million it received to help recoup expenses from the purchase of Alcan. A major step in the divestment plan was taken in early 2009 when the company sold its undeveloped potash assets and a Brazilian iron ore mine to Vale for about $1.5 billion.

The company's most significant deals though have been the ones that didn't happen. In 2008 BHP Billiton approached Rio Tinto with an offer to buy its Anglo-Australian rival at a price that valued the company at nearly $150 billion. Rio Tinto's Board rejected the notion but BHP Billiton kept up its pursuit. The combination would have created the world's largest minerals company and one of the largest companies of any sort in terms of market cap. Months later though at the end of a year mired by the global economic meltdown BHP Billiton announced that the deal no longer provided value to its shareholders and called it off.

In an effort to obstruct BHP Billiton's takeover bid for Rio Tinto in 2008 Alcoa and Aluminum Corporation of China (Chinalco) had acquired 14% of Rio Tinto for $14 billion. Early the next year Chinalco stepped in with an offer to assist Rio Tinto out of a portion of its debt which was considerable. The complicated arrangement would have given Rio Tinto $19.5 billion through investments in aluminum copper and iron ore joint ventures as well as through convertible bonds. Chinalco's stake in Rio Tinto would have been raised to 19% and the Chinese company would have had the right to name two members to Rio Tinto's Board.

However the transaction —never popular with domestic investors –fell through by mid-2009. Rio Tinto instead went with a rights issue hoping to raise $15 billion and an agreed-upon joint venture with BHP Billiton that would have combined the two companies' iron ore projects in Western Australia. However that deal fell through also after German authorities ruled in 2010 that it was anti-competitive.

In late 2010 Rio Tinto made a $3.5 billion tender offer for Australian coal producer Riversdale Mining Ltd. but ran into problems convincing two large institutional shareholders to sell their stakes. Rio Tinto upped the offer to about $4 billion in early 2011 but India's Tata Steel and Brazil's CSN —which together held about 47% of Riversdale — were still not willing to part with their shares. A couple of deadline extensions and price bumps later Rio Tinto acquired both the CSN and Tata stakes to control close to 100% of Riversdale's shares.

EXECUTIVES

Chief Executive Aluminum, Oscar Y. L. Groeneveld, age 58, $1,261,000 total compensation
Chairman, Jan P. du Plessis, age 59
CEO and Board Member, Tom Albanese, age 55, $1,664,000 total compensation
Finance Director and Board Member, Guy R. Elliot, age 57, $1,239,000 total compensation
Chief Executive Iron Ore, Sam Walsh, age 63, $1,245,000 total compensation
Company Secretary, Stephen Consedine, age 51
Group Executive Business Support and Operations, Bret Clayton, age 51, $680,000 total compensation
Managing Director Australia, David Peever
Chief Executive Technology and Innovation, Preston Chiaro, age 59, $714,000 total compensation
Global Head Legal, Debra A. Valentine, age 59, $548,000 total compensation
Company Secretary, Ben Mathews, age 46
Global Practice Leader Media Relations, Christina Mills
Group Executive Technology and Innovation, Grant Thorne, age 63, $773,000 total compensation
Managing Director; President Simandou, David Smith
Chief Executive Copper, Andrew Harding, age 47
Country Manager Mozambique; CEO Riversdale Mining, Eric Finlayson
Chief Executive Energy, Doug Ritchie, age 57
Managing Director China, Ian Bauert
Chief Executive - Copper, Jean-Sebastien Jacques
Board Member, Richard R. Goodmanson, age 65
Board Member, Andrew Gould, age 66
Board Member, Paul M. Tellier, age 73
Board Member, John S. Varley, age 56
Board Member, Sir Roderick I. (Rod) Eddington, age 62
CEO and Board Member, Tom Albanese, age 55
Finance Director and Board Member, Guy R. Elliot, age 57
Board Member, Lord John O. Kerr of Kinlochard, age 71
Board Member, Ann F. Godbehere, age 57
Board Member, Robert E. (Bob) Brown, age 67
Board Member, Vivienne Cox, age 53
Board Member, Michael Fitzpatrick, age 60
Board Member, Yves Fortier, age 75
Auditors: PricewaterhouseCoopers

LOCATIONS

HQ: Rio Tinto Ltd
Level 33, 120 Collins Street, Melbourne, Victoria 3000
Phone: (61) 3 9283 3333 **Fax:** (61) 3 9283 3707
Web: www.riotinto.com

2011 Sales by Destination

	$ mil.	% of total
Asia		
Japan	17	
Other countries	16	
US	14	
Canada	3	
UK	1	
Australia	2	
Total	**0**	**100**

PRODUCTS/OPERATIONS

2011 Sales

	$ mil.	% of total
Iron Ore	44	
Aluminum	18	
Copper	11	
Energy	10	
Other	12	

Selected Holdings

Aluminum
- Bell Bay
- Boyne Island (59% smelting)
- Queensland Alumina Ltd. (80%)
- Tiwai Point (79% New Zealand)
- Weipa (Australia)

Iron Ore
- Hamersley Iron Pty. Ltd.
  - Channar (60%)
  - Marandoo mine (Pilbara Australia)
  - Nammuldi
- Iron Ore Co. of Canada (59%)
- Robe River Iron Associates (53%)

Energy & Minerals
- Coal
  - Bengalla (30% Australia)
  - Blair Athol Coal (71%)
  - Hail Creek Coal (82%)
  - Hunter Valley Operations (76%)
  - Kestrel (80%)
  - Mt Thorley (61%)
  - Warkworth (42%)
- Rio Tinto Diamonds & Minerals
  - Rio Tinto Diamond (diamonds Australia Canada Zimbabwe)
  - Rio Tinto Minerals (borates titanium dioxide Argentina/Australia/US)

Copper Products
- Escondida (30% Chile)
- Grasberg (40% Indonesia)
- Kennecott Utah Copper (US)
- Northparkes (80%)
- Palabora (58% South Africa)

Gold
- Barneys Canyon (US)
- Bingham Canyon (US)
- Escondida (30% Chile)
- Rawhide (51% US)

COMPETITORS

ALROSA	Glencore Xstrata
ASARCO	Goldcorp
Alcoa	Grupo Mexico
Anglo American	ITOCHU
AngloGold Ashanti	Kaiser Aluminum
BHP Billiton	Marubeni
Barrick Gold	Newmont Mining
CONSOL Energy	Norsk Hydro ASA
Cliffs Natural Resources	RUSAL
Codelco	Recylex
Fortescue Metals	Southern Copper
Freeport-McMoRan	Teck
	Vale

HISTORICAL FINANCIALS

Company Type: Public

Income Statement FYE: December 31

	REVENUE ($ mil.)	NET INCOME ($ mil.)	NET PROFIT MARGIN	EMPLOYEES
12/12	50,967	(2,990)	—	61,305
12/11	60,537	5,826	9.6%	56,965
12/10	56,576	14,324	25.3%	69,002
12/09	41,825	4,872	11.6%	95,608
12/08	54,264	3,676	6.8%	98,723
Annual Growth	(1.6%)	—	—	(11.2%)

2012 Year-End Financials

Debt ratio: 22.8%
Return on equity: (-6.0%)
Cash ($ mil.): 7,082
Current ratio: 1.39
Long-term debt ($ mil.): 24,591
No. of shares (mil.): 1,861
Dividends
Yield: —
Payout: —
Market value ($ mil.): 126,669

	STOCK PRICE ($) FY Close	P/E High/Low		PER SHARE ($) Earnings	Dividends	Book Value
12/12	68.06	—	—	(1.62)	0.00	25.18
12/11	61.46	30	18	3.01	0.00	27.81
12/10	86.52	12	7	7.26	0.00	29.73
12/09	65.75	24	10	2.75	0.00	22.37
12/08	24.00	52	8	2.85	0.00	16.07
Annual Growth	29.8%	—	—	—	—	11.9%

Rio Tinto Plc

You aren't seeing double. Rio Tinto plc one of the world's largest mining operations (along with BHP Billiton and Vale) is the British half of dual-listed companies. Its Australian counterpart is Rio Tinto Limited with headquarters in Melbourne. Rio Tinto explores for a variety of commodities: bauxite coal copper diamonds gold iron ore minerals (borates and titanium dioxide) nickel and potash. Iron ore makes up about 44% of the group's sales. The company also produces aluminum through its Rio Tinto Alcan unit. Rio Tinto may sell its diamond business. For more information see Hoover's Rio Tinto Limited profile.

By focusing on a strategy of developing large-scale long-life mining operations Rio Tinto has tried to weather commodity prices that have dipped and risen over several years. Like its rivals the company continues to seek strategic acquisitions as it cuts costs and improves productivity. Rio Tinto's tight-fisted operating style while providing exceptional margins for its industry has drawn the ire of unions which have been critical of the company's employment and environmental records.

Following a tough 2009 in which the global recession depressed commodity prices Rio Tinto rebounded strongly in 2010 posting a 35% increase in overall revenues due primarily to increased sales volumes and prices generated by the beginnings of an economic recovery. Leading the pack for Rio Tinto was its Iron Ore segment which saw an increase of 91% over the previous year followed by the Copper segment with a hike of 24% and the Energy unit with 15%. Profitability soared in 2010 as net income jumped more than 184% due to lower operating costs and significant reductions in debt.

Despite its failed effort the previous year to hike its 9% stake in Rio Tinto to 19% Aluminum Corporation of China (Chinalco) formed a joint venture with Rio Tinto in 2010 to operate an iron ore project in Guinea West Africa. A Chinalco subsidiary will hold 47% of Rio Tinto's Simandou project which is expected to begin producing up to 70 million tons of ore per year by 2015.

In 2011 Rio Tinto and Chinalco teamed up again on a new joint venture that will focus on mineral exploration in China. Chinalco is seeking to find and develop domestic sources of copper coal and potash to offset the cost of importing those raw materials. Chinalco will hold a 51% interest in the joint venture Chinalco Rio Tinto Exploration with Rio Tinto holding the remaining 49%.

One of the world's largest producers of copper Rio Tinto operates the Oyu Tolgoi project in Mongolia along with Canada's Ivanhoe Mines and the Mongolian government. Vancouver-based Ivanhoe controlled one of the world's largest untapped copper and gold deposits in Mongolia and Rio Tinto expects the mine to be one of the world's top 10 copper producers as well as one of the top gold producers by 2018. In 2012 Rio Tinto upped its holding in Ivanhoe from 49% to 51% to become the majority owner.

Also in early 2012 Rio Tinto completed its offer for Canada-based uranium producer Hathor Exploration valued at $578 million after rival Cameco Corp. made a takeover bid for the company in 2011. Hathor supplies about a fifth of the world's uranium.

In 2011 the company also started slimming its aluminum operations. It placed 13 assets on the chopping block allowing Rio Tinto Alcan to focus on its high-quality tier one assets (mostly in Canada) and improve performance. The company also planned to transfer its stakes in six Australian and New Zealand operations to a new business unit Pacific Aluminium.The new unit managed and reported separately from Rio Tinto Alcan would include the company's Gove bauxite mine and alumina refinery Boyne Smelters and Gladstone Power Station Tomago smelter and Bell Bay smelter in Australia. In New Zealand it would include the New Zealand Aluminium Smelters.

For at least a while longer the company is holding on to seven noncore assets managed by Rio Tinto Alcan including operations in France Germany the UK and the US. The company is in no hurry to sell and may wait until the economy improves before divesting certain operations. Rio Tinto has tried a similar divestment strategy before. It embarked on a divestment plan in the mid-2000s with the long-term goal of turning out $15 billion from its divestments. By 2010 the company had gained more than $10 billion from the divestment program.

EXECUTIVES

Chief Executive, Sam Walsh, age 63
CFO and Director, Guy Elliott, age 57
Group Executive Business Support and Operations, Bret Clayton, age 51
Group Executive Technology and Innovation, Preston Chiaro, age 59
Group Executive Legal and External Affairs, Debra A. Valentine, age 59
Chief Executive Rio Tinto Alcan, Jacynthe Cote, age 55
Chief Executive Copper, Andrew Harding, age 47
Group Executive People and Organisation, Hugo Bague, age 52
Chief Executive Energy, Harry Kenyon-Slaney
Chairman, Jan du Plessis
Chief Executive Diamonds and Minerals, Alan Davies
Director, Richard R. Goodmanson, age 65
Chief Executive and Director, Tom Albanese, age 53
Chief Executive Iron Ore and Australia and Director, Sam Walsh, age 61
CFO and Director, Guy Elliott, age 57
Director, Vivienne Cox, age 53
Director, Michael Fitzpatrick, age 60
Director, Lord Kerr Kinlochard, age 70
Non-Executive Independent Director, Christopher Lynch
Non-Executive Independent Director, John Kerr
Auditors: PricewaterhouseCoopersLLP

LOCATIONS

HQ: Rio Tinto Plc
2 Eastbourne Terrace, London W2 6LG
Phone: (44) 20 7781 2000 **Fax:** (44) 20 7781 1800
Web: www.riotinto.com

2011 Sales by Destination

Asia	
China	31
Japan	17
Other countries	16
US	14
Canada	3
Europe	
UK	1
Other countries	11
Australia	2
Total	**100**

PRODUCTS/OPERATIONS

2011 Sales	
Iron ore	44
Copper	11
Energy	10
Diamonds & minerals	5
Total	**100**

COMPETITORS

ALROSA
ASARCO
Alcoa
Anglo American
AngloGold Ashanti
BHP Billiton
Barrick Gold
CONSOL Energy
Cliffs Natural Resources
Codelco
DeBeers
Fortescue Metals
Freeport-McMoRan
Glencore Xstrata
Goldcorp
Grupo Mexico
ITOCHU
Kaiser Aluminum
Marubeni
Newmont Mining
Norsk Hydro ASA
RUSAL
Southern Copper
Teck
Vale

HISTORICAL FINANCIALS

Company Type: Public

Income Statement FYE: December 31

	REVENUE ($ mil.)	NET INCOME ($ mil.)	NET PROFIT MARGIN	EMPLOYEES
12/12	50,967	(14)	—	71,219
12/11	60,537	939	1.6%	67,930
12/10	56,576	860	1.5%	76,894
12/09	41,825	463	1.1%	101,994
12/08	54,264	933	1.7%	105,785
Annual Growth	(1.6%)	—	—	(9.4%)

2012 Year-End Financials

Debt ratio: —
Return on equity: (-0.0%)
Cash ($ mil.): 7,082
Current ratio: 1.39
Long-term debt ($ mil.): —
No. of shares (mil.): 1,411
Dividends
Yield: 2.8%
Payout: —
Market value ($ mil.): 81,980

	STOCK PRICE ($) FY Close	P/E High	P/E Low	PER SHARE ($) Earnings	Dividends	Book Value
12/12	58.09	—	—	(1.62)	1.66	33.21
12/11	48.92	25	14	3.01	1.17	36.57
12/10	71.66	34	5	7.26	0.88	38.22
12/09	215.39	80	29	2.75	6.38	28.76
12/08	88.91	194	21	2.85	1.52	20.68
Annual Growth	(10.1%)	—	—	—	2.2%	12.6%

Roche Holding Ltd.

Roche is on a medicinal roll. The company operates two segments pharmaceuticals and diagnostics and sells its products in some 180 countries. Roche's prescription drugs include cancer therapies MabThera/Rituxan and Avastin anemia treatment NeoRecormon/Epogin hepatitis drug Pegasys transplant drug CellCept macular degeneration therapy Lucentis and Tamiflu which is used to prevent and treat influenza (including pandemic strains). The company markets many of its bestsellers through subsidiary Genentech and affiliate Chugai Pharmaceutical. Roche's diagnostics arm offers clinical lab supplies genetic tests diabetes monitoring supplies and point-of-care diagnostics for health care providers.

Operations

Roche's pharmaceuticals division accounts for more than three-fourths of annual revenues with oncology drugs making the largest sales contribution (45% of revenues). The smaller yet faster-growing diagnostics segment is a leading maker of in vitro clinical diagnostic tests through its professional diagnostics segment; it is also an established provider of diabetes tests and glucose monitors.

Geographic Reach

The largest geographic markets for the pharma segment are the US and Western Europe. Product marketing efforts in the US are conducted through Roche's main US subsidiary Genentech which is one of the world's largest biotech companies. The company also has a solid stance in the Japanese drug market through its 60% stake in Chugai Pharmaceutical and it is experiencing growth in Latin America and Asia.

Financial Analysis

As one of the top 10 global pharmaceutical companies Roche has steadily grown its revenues and profits over the last decade. But while the company reported net income growth of 13% to more than $10 billion in 2011 largely attributed to its cost-control and efficiency programs (including workforce reductions and facility consolidation efforts) its revenues took a 9% dip to about $47 billion due to poor currency exchange rates for the Swiss Franc. However Roche reported a group sales increase of 1% at constant exchange rates due to increased returns from sales of key pharmaceutical and diagnostic products.

Key drivers for growth in 2011 included rising global sales of Lucentis Actemra/RoActemra Mircera (for anemia in kidney disease patients) and four of the top cancer drugs (MabThera/Rituxan Herceptin Tarceva and Xeloda). However sales of one top selling cancer drug –Avastin –fell after the FDA revoked its indication for breast cancer. Revenues from bestseller Tamiflu also declined in 2010 and 2011 following a sharp rise in demand from flu pandemics and resulting government stockpiling in previous years. Growth in the smaller diagnostics business segment is attributed to increased sales of clinical laboratory supplies and cancer diagnostic products.

Strategy

In order to expand its pharmaceutical product offerings and stave off revenue losses from patent expirations and other competitive pressures Roche invests heavily in internal research and development programs to expand its pipeline of small-molecule and biotechnology drug candidates. The company has about 100 drugs in clinical development stages the bulk of which aim to treat oncology cardiovascular metabolic viral inflammatory autoimmune and central nervous system disorders. New drugs that have emerged from Roche's pipeline include Zelboraf a melanoma medicine marketed in partnership with Daiichi Sankyo and launched in 2011 Perjeta (pertuzumab) a new Genentech-developed breast cancer drug approved by the FDA in 2012.

The firm has also widened its R&D programs by forming partnerships with other drugmakers such as Biogen Idec and Pharmasset as well as through acquisitions. In addition to new drug formulas Roche conducts R&D programs on existing drugs to gain regulatory approval for new indications which typically helps to extend a drug's patent protection and increase sales volumes.

Not one to neglect its smaller division Roche has been aggressively adding to its diagnostic testing stable through R&D partnership and acquisition efforts. In addition to clinical and diabetes tests focus areas for the diagnostics division include tissue-based cancer diagnostics (through its Ventana Medical Systems subsidiary) life science (gene sequencing) technologies and molecular diagnostics which include personalized (or companion) tests that are used to determine the best treatment regimen for a specific patient.

Mergers and Acquisitions

Acquisitions are also key elements in Roche's R&D growth strategy and have expanded its pharmaceutical segment in focused therapeutic areas. For instance the 2011 purchase of drug developer

Anadys Pharmaceuticals expanded its hepatitis C virus (HCV) development portfolio.

In the diagnostics segment the company would have become a market leader in the gene sequencing market in 2012 had it been successful in its hostile attempts to acquire research equipment maker Illumina. Past purchases have expanded its professional and cancer testing operations.

In 2013 it enhanced its diagnostics business and strengthened its hematology offerings with the $220 million purchase (plus contingent payments) of Constitution Medical Investors which makes tests for blood diseases.

Ownership

Descendants of the founding Hoffmann and Oeri families own about half of Roche. In addition fellow Swiss drugmaker Novartis owns 33% of the company.

HISTORY

Fritz Hoffmann-La Roche backed by family wealth began making pharmaceuticals in a lab in Basel Switzerland in 1894. At the time drug compounds were mixed at pharmacies and lacked uniformity. Hoffmann was not a chemist but saw the potential for mass-produced standardized branded drugs.

By WWI Hoffman had become successful selling Thiocal (cough medicine) Digalen (digitalis extract) and other products on four continents. During the war the Bolsheviks seized the firm's St. Petersburg Russia facility and its Warsaw plant was almost destroyed. Devastated Hoffmann sold company shares outside the family in 1919 and died in 1920.

As WWII loomed Roche divided its holdings between F. Hoffman-La Roche and Sapac which held many of Roche's foreign operations. US operations became more important during the war. Roche synthesized vitamins C A and E (eventually becoming the world's top vitamin maker) and built plants and research centers worldwide.

Roche continued to develop such successful products as tranquilizers Librium (1960) and Valium (1963) –the world's best-selling prescription drug prior to anti-ulcer successors Tagamet (SmithKline Beecham now part of GlaxoSmithKline) and Prilosec (AstraZeneca). Roche made its first fragrance and flavor buy Givaudan in 1963.

In the 1970s after several governments accused it of price-gouging on Librium and Valium Roche agreed to price restraints. The company was fined for vitamin price-fixing in 1976. It was also rapped that year for its slow response to an Italian factory dioxin leak that killed thousands of animals and forced hundreds of families to evacuate.

Roche became one of the first drugmakers to sell another's products when it agreed to sell Glaxo's Zantac ulcer treatment in the US in 1982. The move let Roche maintain its large US sales force at the time when Valium went off patent decimating the company's drug sales.

Roche acquired a product pipeline when it bought a majority stake in genetic engineering firm Genentech in 1990. In 1994 it bought the struggling Syntex solidifying its position in North America. The company gained Aleve and other products in 1996 when it bought out its joint venture with Procter & Gamble and also acquired Cincinnati-based flavors and fragrances firm Tastemaker.

In its biggest acquisition ever Roche bought Corange in 1998 for $10.2 billion; its subsidiary Boehringer Mannheim was renamed Roche Molecular Biochemicals. In 1999 Roche announced it had located the gene that causes osteoarthritis. The company began to market anti-obesity pharmaceutical Xenical in the US that year despite reports of some unpleasant side effects.

Also in 1999 Roche agreed to a record-setting fine to end a US Justice Department investigation into Roche's role in an alleged vitamin price-fixing cartel; in 2000 it agreed to pay out again (to 22 states) to settle a lawsuit regarding the cartel. A related European Union probe the following year also found Roche guilty and levied heavy fines against the firm. In 1999 and 2000 Roche squeezed cash out of its high-flying biotech progeny; it bought the 33% of Genentech it didn't own in 1999 then raised a total of almost $8 billion by reselling 42% of Genentech in three public offerings in 1999 and 2000.

Influenza drug Tamiflu failed to win European Union approval in 2000 but breast cancer drug Herceptin was OK'd there. Also that year the company spun off its fragrances and flavors unit Givaudan SA and divested its BASILEA Pharmaceutica biotech division which focused on infectious disease and skin disorder drugs. Two long-time Roche leaders chairman Fritz Gerber and CFO Henri Meier retired that year; both remained on Roche's board for a brief time thereafter.

In 2001 rival Swiss pharmaceuticals firm Novartis bought a 20% stake in Roche from financier Martin Ebner's BZ Gruppe Holding. The company sold its fine chemicals business to DSM in 2003 to further narrow its focus and in 2005 Roche sold its consumer health business which included vitamins the analgesic Aleve and antacid Rennie to Bayer HealthCare.

In 2006 Roche received approval for the application of its cancer drug MabThera (known as Rituxan in the US) in treating rheumatoid arthritis throughout the EU. It also put its post-menopausal osteoporosis treatment Boniva out on the EU and US markets at that time.

One major acquisition came with the $3.4 billion purchase of Ventana Medical Systems a diagnostic firm focusing on cancers in 2008. The purchase expanded the company's operations into tissue-based diagnostics.

The company added to its oncology R&D efforts in 2008 through the $160 million acquisition and integration of UK biotech research firm Piramed and the purchase of Canadian antibody developer ARIUS Research (later integrated into Roche Canada). Roche also expanded its neurology pipeline through the purchase of Memory Pharmaceuticals in 2008 for $50 million to gain access to the company's memory loss and cognition therapies.

In a move to secure its global presence in 2008 Roche upped its stake in Japan's Chugai Pharmaceutical from 50.1% to about 60% through a shareholder tender offer worth some $900 million.

Roche also began making attempts to take full control of Genentech in late 2008 when the company made a $44 billion offer to purchase the 44% of Genentech that it didn't already own; however Genentech rejected the takeover offer as undervalued. In early 2009 Roche issued a hostile $42 billion tender offer but after a tepid response from Genentech shareholders Roche upped the offer to its final value of about $47 billion. The deal was completed later that year. While Roche and Genentech already shared rights to numerous commercial and development-stage drugs (including some bestselling cancer therapies) Roche wanted Genentech as a wholly owned subsidiary to gain full access to its drugs and keep its pipeline full of new biotech development projects for years to come. Roche also cut costs and increased efficiencies through the acquisition by combining certain functions of Genentech with its existing US operations (while at the same time aiming to keep Genentech's innovative identity and culture intact). As a result in 2010 Genentech became Roche's US sales marketing manufacturing and administrative headquarters

Roche gained marketing approval for Actemra (or RoActemra in some markets) a rheumatoid arthritis medicine in the EU in 2009 and in the US in 2010.

As a result in 2010 Genentech became Roche's US sales marketing manufacturing and administrative headquarters taking over those roles from the previous main location in Nutley New Jersey (operating as Hoffman-La Roche Inc.).

On top of the Genentech integration efforts in late 2010 the company announced plans to cut some 6% of its global workforce (about 4800 jobs) primarily in its manufacturing and sales and marketing organizations to improve operational efficiency and production levels.

EXECUTIVES

Chairman, Franz B. Humer, age 67, $5,709,204 total compensation
Chairman President and CEO Chugai, Osamu Nagayama, age 66
Head Genentech Research and Early Development, Richard H. Scheller, age 60
Vice Chairman, Prof Bruno Gehrig, age 67
CEO Genentech, Ian T. Clark, age 53
Chief Financial and IT Officer, Alan Hippe, age 46
General Counsel, Gottlieb A. Keller, age 59, $1,420,200 total compensation
Head Human Resources, Silvia Ayyoubi, age 60, $686,434 total compensation
Vice Chairman, Andre Hoffman, age 55
CEO, Severin Schwan, age 46, $2,722,052 total compensation
Head CEO Office and Secretary to the Corporate Executive Committee, Per-Olof Attinger, age 53
COO Pharmaceuticals, Daniel O'Day, age 49
Head Group Communications, Stephan Feldhaus
COO Diagnostics, Roland Diggelmann
Head of Roche Pharma Research & Early Development, Mike Burgess
Head of Roche Partnering, Sophie Kornowski-Bonnet
Director, Lodewijk J.R. de Vink, age 67
Director, Pius Baschera, age 62
Director, DeAnne S. Julius, age 63
Vice Chairman, Prof Bruno Gehrig, age 67
Director, Sir John Irving Bell, age 60
Vice Chairman, Andre Hoffman, age 55
Director, Andreas Oeri, age 63
Director, Prof Beatrice Weder di Mauro, age 47
Auditors: KPMGKlynveldPeatMarwickGoerdelerSA

LOCATIONS

HQ: Roche Holding Ltd.
Grenzacherstrasse 124, Basel CH-4070
Phone: (41) 61 688 1111 **Fax:** (41) 61 691 93 91
Web: www.roche.com

2011 Sales

	% of total
North	36
Europe	35
Asia	19
Latin	7
Africa Australia &	3
Total	**100**

PRODUCTS/OPERATIONS

2011 Sales

	% of total
Pharmaceuticals	
Oncology	45
Inflammatory autoimmune &	7
Virology	6
Metabolic &	5
Ophthalmology	4
Respiratory	2
Renal	2
Cardiovascular	2

Central nervous	2
Infectious	1
Other	1
Diagnostics	23
Total	**100**

Selected Products

Top 20 Products (listed alphabetically)
- Actemra/RoActemra (rheumatoid arthritis)
- Activase/TNKase (cardiovascular)
- Avastin (colorectal cancer non-small cell lung cancer breast cancer kidney cancer)
- Bonviva/Boniva (osteoporosis)
- CellCept (transplantation)
- Herceptin (HER2-positive breast cancer)
- Lucentis (wet age-related macular degeneration diabetic macular edema)
- MabThera/Rituxan (non-Hodgkin' s lymphoma rheumatoid arthritis chronic lymphocytic leukemia)
- Madopar (Parkinson's disease restless leg syndrome)
- Mircera (predialysis)
- NeoRecormon/Epogen (anemia oncology)
- Neutrogin/Neupogen (neutropenia associated with chemotherapy)
- Nutropin (growth hormone deficiency)
- Pegasys (hepatitis B and C)
- Pulmozyme (cystic fibrosis)
- Tamiflu (treatment and prevention of influenza)
- Tarceva (advanced non-small cell lung cancer advanced pancreatic cancer)
- Valcyte/Cymevene (cytomegalovirus infection)
- Xeloda (colorectal cancer breast cancer colon cancer)
- Xolair (asthma)

Other Products
- Anaprox (pain fever and inflammation)
- Bactrim (anti-infective)
- Bondronat (bone disease in breast cancer patients)
- Dilatrend (hypertension)
- Dormicum (sedation)
- Erivedge (basal cell carcinoma)
- Fuzeon (HIV)
- Invirase (HIV)
- Kytril (nausea and vomiting induced by chemotherapy or radiation therapy)
- Lariam (malaria)
- Perjeta (breast cancer)
- Roaccutane/Accutane (acne)
- Rocaltrol/Calcitriol (osteoporosis)
- Rocephin (bacterial infections)
- Roferon-A (hepatitis C hairy cell leukemia AIDS-related Kaposi's sarcoma)
- Toradol (acute pain)
- Valium (anxiety disorders)
- Vesanoid (leukemia)
- Viracept (HIV)
- Xenical (weight loss weight control)
- Zelboraf (metastatic melanoma)
- Zenapax (transplant rejection)

Selected Acquisitions

2011
- Anadys Pharmaceuticals ($230 million; San Diego California; virology drugs)
- mtm laboratories AG (E190 million or $265 million; Germany; cervical cancer testing)
- PVT (E85 million or $120 million; Germany and US; in vitro diagnostic tests and lab equipment)

2010
- BioImagene ($100 million; tissue-based cancer diagnostics for personalized tests)
- Medingo (up to $200 million; Israel; insulin pump manufacturing)

COMPETITORS

Abbott Labs
Actavis Inc.
Amgen
Astellas
AstraZeneca
Bayer AG
Becton Dickinson
Biogen Idec
Bristol-Myers Squibb
Eisai
Eli Lilly
Gilead Sciences
GlaxoSmithKline
Johnson & Johnson
Merck
Merck KGaA
Novartis
Pfizer
Ranbaxy Laboratories
Sanofi
Siemens Healthcare Diagnostics
Takeda Pharmaceutical
Teva

HISTORICAL FINANCIALS

Company Type: Public

Income Statement

FYE: December 31

	REVENUE ($ mil.)	NET INCOME ($ mil.)	NET PROFIT MARGIN	EMPLOYEES
12/12	51,755	10,405	20.1%	82,089
12/11	46,889	9,930	21.2%	80,129
12/10	52,540	9,260	17.6%	80,653
12/09	49,661	7,557	15.2%	81,507
12/08	45,033	8,431	18.7%	80,080
Annual Growth	3.5%	5.4%	—	0.6%

2012 Year-End Financials

Debt ratio: 41.3%
Return on equity: 71.5%
Cash ($ mil.): 4,941
Current ratio: 1.55
Long-term debt ($ mil.): 19,483
No. of shares (mil.): 160
Dividends
Yield: 1.8%
Payout: 18.1%
Market value ($ mil.): 8,080

	STOCK PRICE ($) FY Close	P/E High	P/E Low	PER SHARE ($) Earnings	Dividends	Book Value
12/12	50.50	5	4	12.17	0.92	98.82
12/11	42.55	6	3	11.67	2.03	80.35
12/10	36.65	5	3	10.80	0.70	63.24
12/09	42.20	8	2	8.76	0.33	44.70
12/08	76.55	9	5	9.62	0.56	261.34
Annual Growth	(9.9%)	—	—	6.1%	13.1%	(21.6%)

Rolls Royce Holdings Plc

Rolls-Royce Holdings doesn't make cars so luxurious you'll cry (see Motor Cars) but it sure can make an aircraft engine whine. One of the world's largest aircraft engine makers Rolls-Royce through its Civil and Defense Aerospace businesses makes commercial and military engines for a broad customer base including airlines corporate and utility aircraft and helicopter operators and armed forces around the world. Beyond aviation its Energy unit supplies gas turbine power generation to the oil and gas industry while its Marine segment makes propulsion systems that power 70 navies worldwide. Rolls-Royce has operations in North America Europe and Asia with an emerging presence in the Middle East.

The company supports its geographic markets with manufacturing and service facilities in 50 countries and recent expansion includes construction of a manufacturing and assembly facility in the US (Crosspointe Virginia) as well as an assembly and manufacturing plant in Singapore. The company which addresses four global markets –Civil Aerospace Defense Aerospace Marine and Energy (including nuclear) –keeps its business plans long-term. The lifecycle of Rolls-Royce's products and services averages 40 to 50 years so the company bases its investments in technology programs on forecasts of up to 20 years. Its performance is best viewed by decades rather than individual years. With that in mind the company was nonplussed by the lack of sales growth in 2011 and continues to follow a strategy it has had in place for years that includes investing in technology and infrastructure; growing market share and installed product base; and adding value with product related services.

This strategy has resulted in a company that shelters itself through diversity. The company achieves diversity not only in its regional markets but also in its balanced offering of products and services as well as its product portfolio and the diverse end-markets that it serves. The different geographies product selections and customers mitigate for one another in the event of a market swing. After recognizing a marked increase in revenue from its engine aftercare services the company has boosted its offerings to include aftermarket repair and overhaul as well as field maintenance and fleet data management. All these factors along with its cost savings measures and operational improvements allow the company to forecast its revenue as doubling in a decade (by organic growth alone).

Consistent investments in research and development as well as the occasional acquisition represent part of the company's strategy in action. In early 2011 Rolls-Royce together with Daimler announced plans to acquire Tognum a German engine and powertrain supplier for distributed power generation and marine propulsion markets. This follows the company's strategy to increase market share for its marine products. With a 95% stake in Tognum the two companies can further develop the business jointly. The sizeable hold gives the companies rights to Tognum's intellectual property in the form of patents.

In 2010 subsidiary Rolls-Royce Marine bought Norwegian engineering firm ODIM ASA. The purchase added automated handling systems for seismic and offshore drilling vessels that complement Rolls-Royce's ship design and power systems for the offshore drilling industry. Outside of Norway ODIM has operations in Canada Singapore and Vietnam.

The company's Marine business also boasts an extensive range of products and services from ship design to power systems and controls to aftermarket support services. It is benefitting from defense contracts in the US and the UK where its engines power US Marine Corps and Royal Navy ships respectively. Rolls-Royce's merchant marine operations are headquartered in Shanghai taking strategic advantage of its proximity to the shipbuilding centers of China Japan and Korea –these countries when combined account for a majority of the world's commercial shipbuilding.

These actions come as no surprise after the civil aerospace sector took a beating during the economic crisis and with a recovery slow to materialize. Despite the difficult conditions some regions are showing promise. For example: the Middle East signed a long-term services contract with Emirates Airline (part of The Emirates Group) for more than $2 billion. Singapore Airlines made its $1 billion order for Trent 700 engines in mid-2011 around the same time that Brazil's TAM air carrier signed a contract valued at more than $2 billion for Trent XWB engines. Rolls-Royce engines power some 30 types of civil aircraft from small executive jets to large passenger aircraft. Several of the company's customers saw their aircraft take flight in 2009. Those aircraft powered by Rolls-Royce engines included the Boeing 787 Dreamliner Gulfstream G650 Airbus A400M Embraer Legacy 650. The company also signed an exclusive deal to power the Airbus 350-1000 aircraft.

On the defense side Rolls-Royce commands approximately one-quarter of the world's military engine manufacturing market share. Its portfolio covers all major sectors – combat helicopters unmanned and tactical aircraft training and transport. While the defense budgets for the US and UK have called for funding cuts to certain projects the US government approved funding for the F-35 Joint Strike Fighter so that Rolls-Royce can move ahead in collaboration with General Electric to develop the F136 engine for that aircraft.

Rolls-Royce's Energy (including nuclear) business holds a global position as a leading supplier of power and compression equipment such as industrial gas turbines to the oil and gas industry especially to offshore oil rigs and platforms. With a plan to expand its civil nuclear power generation activities the company established a civil nuclear business unit in 2009 and will build a factory in the UK to assemble test systems and components for nuclear power stations. While Rolls-Royce's traditional markets are showing weak demand emerging economies such as India and Venezuela are showing opportunities for long-term growth for the company's gas turbines and reciprocating engines.

Although Rolls-Royce shares its name with the luxury car the two parted ways when the British government split them in 1971. Since 1996 Sir John Rose has been the driving force behind Rolls-Royce's transformation increasing revenues more than three-fold. He retired in spring 2011 and is succeeded by another John –John F. Rishton –former finance director at British Airways and chief executive of Royal Ahold a Dutch retailer. Rishton began in a non-executive director role at Rolls-Royce in 2007.

HISTORY

In 1906 automobile and aviation enthusiast Charles Rolls and engineer Henry Royce unveiled the Silver Ghost an automobile that earned Rolls-Royce a reputation as maker of the best car in the world.

A year after Rolls' 1910 death in a biplane crash Royce suffered a breakdown. From his home Royce continued to design Rolls-Royce engines such as the Eagle its first aircraft engine in 1914 and other engines used to power airplanes during WWI –but management of the company fell to Claude Johnson who remained chief executive until 1926.

Although the company returned primarily to making cars after WWI its engines were used in several history-making flights and in 1931 set world speed records for land sea and air. Rolls-Royce bought the Bentley Motor Company that year. In 1933 it introduced the Merlin engine which powered the Spitfire Hurricane and Mustang fighters of WWII. Rolls-Royce began designing a jet engine in 1938 and over the years it pioneered the turboprop engine turbofan and vertical takeoff engine.

Realizing that it had to break into the lucrative US airliner market to stay alive Rolls-Royce bought its main British competitor Bristol-Siddley Engines in 1966. With Bristol-Siddley came its contract to build the engine for the Anglo-French Concorde in 1976 and a US presence.

Lockheed ordered the company's RB211 engine for its TriStar in 1968 but Rolls-Royce underestimated the project's technical and financial challenges and entered bankruptcy in 1971. The British government stepped in and nationalized the aerospace division and sold the auto group. The RB211 entered service on the TriStar in 1972 and on the Boeing 747 in 1977.

Rolls-Royce was reprivatized in 1987. In a diversification effort two years later the company bought mining marine and power plant specialist Northern Engineering Industries. In the early 1990s the aerospace market was hurt by military spending cutbacks and a recession; the company cut more than 18000 jobs.

A joint venture with BMW launched the BR710 engine for Gulfstream and Canadair's long-range business jets in 1990. The company bought Allison Engine in 1995.

Rolls-Royce sold Parsons Power Generation Systems to Siemens in 1997. Also that year it won a contract to supply Trent 892 engines for Boeing 777 jets being built for American Airlines (a subsidiary of AMR Corporation) in a deal worth $1 billion.

In 1998 the British government approved a repayable investment of about $335 million in the company to develop a new model of Trent aircraft engines. Narrowing its focus the company sold its power transmission and distribution business to Austria-based VA Technologie.

Rolls-Royce pumped up its gas and oil equipment business in 1999 by buying the rotating compression equipment unit of Cooper Cameron (now Cameron International); it became one of the world leaders in marine propulsion by acquiring Vickers. The company then bought the aero and industrial engine repair service of First Aviation Services and took full control of its aircraft-engine joint venture with BMW; in return BMW received a 10% stake in Rolls.

In 2000 subsidiary Rolls-Royce Energy Systems India Private was awarded its first order: producing a Bergen gas engine for Garden Silk Mills for powering a textile plant in India. That year Rolls-Royce won a contract to supply engines for Israel's El Al airline's Boeing 777s. Late in 2000 it was reported that the company would cut about 5000 jobs over three years.

Early in 2001 Rolls-Royce sold most of its Vickers Turbine Components business. In October the company cut about 11% of its workforce in response to the worldwide crisis in the commercial jet business.

In 2002 the company announced that it had inked a 10-year $2 billion deal to supply engines to Gulfstream Aerospace. That year Rolls-Royce sold its Vickers Defence Systems unit which made tanks and armored vehicles to Alvis Plc. In 2003 Sir Ralph Robins who had been executive chairman for more than a decade retired from his post.

Early in 2004 Rolls-Royce and GE Aircraft Engines were picked to supply engines for Boeing's upcoming 787 Dreamliner. Rolls-Royce was also selected to supply engines for Airbus' upcoming behemoth A380.

In late 2007 it scored one of its largest contracts a $42 million project to provide steering gear and deck machinery for Chinese shipbuilder Sinopacific.

In 2008 it entered into a joint venture with Goodrich Corporation called Aero Engine Controls to produce engine controls for Rolls-Royce aircraft. It also partnered with France's AREVA to construct the first new nuclear reactors built in the UK in more than 20 years.

In 2009 the company focused on developing four advanced manufacturing research centers in the US the UK and Singapore. Rolls-Royce invested #300 million (more than $450 million) in its UK factories as part of its almost #2 billion (over $3 billion) capital replacement plan to be carried out over a period of 10 years. That same year Rolls-Royce engines allowed the BAE Systems' Mantis UAV and AgustaWestland's Lynx Wildcat helicopter to take flight.

Rolls-Royce's nuclear market was strengthened in 2009 by its agreement with electric service provider EDF Energy (formerly known as London Electricity Group) to enter into a joint venture with EDF Energy giving support to the UK facility. The following year the company introduced its STOVL (short take-off and vertical landing) Rolls-Royce LiftSystem.

The bell of financial crisis knelled in 2008 causing the company to implement cost-cutting measures which included headcount reductions of almost 10%. The company in partnership with GE Aviation continued development of the F136 engine for the F-35 Joint Strike Fighter and its Trent 1000 engine took its first flight in the Boeing 787 Dreamliner. Also in 2008 Rolls-Royce established its civil nuclear business to tap a growing global market.

EXECUTIVES

President and CEO North America, James M. (Jim) Guyette, $732,916 total compensation
President Marine and Nuclear, Lawrie Haynes
COO and Board Member, Mike J. Terrett, age 54, $998,150 total compensation
SVP Corporate Communications North America, Mia K. Walton
Chief Executive and Board Member, John F. Rishton, age 55
Executive Vice President Communications Nuclear, Paul Vallance
Chairman, Ian E. L. Davis, age 62
President - Civil Aerospace, Mark King
Director Manufacturing, Mike Lloyd
Chairman, Sir Simon Robertson, age 71
Director Global Corporate Development, Miles A. Cowdry
President Defence Aerospace, Daniel G. (Dan) Korte, age 52
President Deutschland; COO Corporate and Regional Engines, Michael Haidinger
President India, Anil Shrikhande
Head Corporate Communications, Josh Rosenstock
President Marine and Industrial Power Systems, John Paterson
Director Engineering and Technology; Board Member, Colin P. Smith, age 58, $664,074 total compensation
Chief Procurement Officer, Mike Orris
Operations Director, Alain Michaelis, age 47
Director Corporate Affairs, Peter Morgan
President Helicopters, Kenneth (Ken) Roberts
Head Communications Civil Aerospace, Ian Bustin
Head Communications Energy, Gary Hyman
Head Communications Defence Aerospace, Jane Terry
Director Financial Communications, Mark Alflatt
President Aerospace, Tony Wood
SVP Asia Pacific and Africa Civil Aerospace, Jim Sheard
President Offshore and Marine Services, Anders Almestad
SVP Ship Technology Offshore, J?rn Heltne
Head Communications Middle East, Saad Hakim
Head Communications Asia and Marine, Jonathan Webster
Chief Scientific Officer, Paul Stein
EVP Civil Nucler India, Atul Tandon
Head of Communications Europe, Frank-Martin Hein
Senior Communications Manager External Communications, Steffi Anders
Director Investor Relations, Simon Goodson
Head of Corporate Communications South America, Rodrigo Barbosa
Vice President Communications North America, Laura Catalano
Communications Manager - Singapore, Karun Arya
Assistant Director Investor Relations, Jilinda Crowley
Communications Director, George McLaren
Head of Asia Pacific Communications, Erin Atan
Communications Officer, Stephanie Watters
Vice President Communications & Public Affairs, Ashmita Sethi
Executive Vice President Human Resources, Kirk Larson
CFO, Mark Morris
Executive Vice President Government Business, Stephen B. Plummer
Executive Vice President General Counsel, Thomas P. Dale

Executive Vice President Supply Management, Beverly J. Gaskin
Director - Human Resources, Kath Durrant
President Energy, Andrew Heath
Company Secretary, Nigel Goldsworthy
General Counsel & Head of Risk, Robert Webb
President - Naval, Don S. Roussinos
President Defense, Thomas A. Bell
Executive Vice President Crosspointe Rolls-Royce North America Inc, Thomas O. Loehr
Board Member, John D. G. McAdam, age 65
President and CEO North America, James M. (Jim) Guyette
Board Member, Ian C. Strachan, age 70
Finance Director and Board Member, Andrew B. Shilston, age 56
Board Member, Dame Helen Alexander, age 57
Board Member, Peter J. Byrom, age 69
COO and Board Member, Mike J. Terrett, age 54
Chief Executive and Board Member, John F. Rishton, age 55
Board Member, Iain C. Conn
Board Member, Prof Peter J. Gregson, age 55
Board Member, John M. Neill, age 66
Director Engineering and Technology; Board Member, Colin P. Smith, age 58
Auditors: KPMGAuditPlc

LOCATIONS

HQ: Rolls Royce Holdings Plc
65 Buckingham Gate, London SW1E 6AT
Phone: (44) 20 7222 9020 **Fax:** (44) 20 7227 9170
Web: www.rolls-royce.com

2011 Sales

	% of total
Europe	
UK	12
Other	18
North America	
US	32
Canada	3
Asia	29
Africa	2
Australasia	2
Other	2
Total	**100**

PRODUCTS/OPERATIONS

2011 Sales (by market)

	% of total
Civil	49
Marine	20
Defense	20
Energy	11
Total	**100**

2011 Sales

	% of total
Aftermarket	53
Original	47
Total	**100**

Selected Products and Services

Aircraft engines
Automation and control equipment
Bearings and seals
Diesel and gas turbine engines
Electric propulsion systems
Engine support services
Helicopter engines
Fuel cells
Generators
Offshore drilling equipment
Overhaul and repair services
Ship designs
Technical publications
Training

Selected Subsidiaries

Civil aerospace
Optimized Systems and Solutions Limited (OSyS) (advanced controls and predictive data management)
Rolls-Royce Leasing Limited (engine leasing)
Rolls-Royce Total Care Services Limited (aftermarket support services)
Corporate
Rolls-Royce International Limited (international support and commercial information services)
Rolls-Royce Power Engineering plc (power generation and marine systems)
Energy
Rolls-Royce Fuel Cell Systems Limited (fuel cell system development)
Rolls-Royce Power Development Limited (project development)
Tidal Generation Limited (development of tidal generation systems)
Marine
ODIM ASA (offshore drilling naval and power generation equipment)
Rolls-Royce Marine Electrical Systems Limited (marine electrical systems)
Rolls-Royce Power Development Limited (generation of electricity from independent power projects)
Rolls-Royce Marine Power Operations Limited (nuclear submarine propulsion systems)
Rolls-Royce Power Engineering plc (energy and marine systems)p>#

COMPETITORS

Emerson Electric
GE Aviation
GE Honda Aero Engines
HEICO
Honeywell Aerospace
IHI Corp.
Kawasaki Heavy Industries
McDermott
Pratt & Whitney
SAFRAN
Siemens AG
Volvo

HISTORICAL FINANCIALS

Company Type: Public

Income Statement FYE: December 31

	REVENUE ($ mil.)	NET INCOME ($ mil.)	NET PROFIT MARGIN	EMPLOYEES
12/12	19,601	3,676	18.8%	42,800
12/11	17,184	1,313	7.6%	40,400
12/10	17,211	836	4.9%	38,900
12/09	16,866	3,597	21.3%	38,500
12/08	13,235	(1,952)	—	39,000
Annual Growth	10.3%	—	—	2.4%

2012 Year-End Financials

Debt ratio: 12.3%
Return on equity: 42.9%
Cash ($ mil.): 4,166
Current ratio: 1.33
Long-term debt ($ mil.): 1,989
No. of shares (mil.): 1,872
Dividends
Yield: 1.9%
Payout: 14.3%
Market value ($ mil.): 134,413

	STOCK PRICE ($) FY Close	P/E High/Low	PER SHARE ($) Earnings	Dividends	Book Value
12/12	71.79	155114	1.96	1.39	5.24
12/11	57.73	315232	0.70	0.25	3.73
12/10	48.68	454304	0.45	1.14	3.30
12/09	39.01	93 32	1.93	1.16	3.30
12/08	24.70	— —	(1.07)	1.30	1.99
Annual Growth	30.6%	— —	—	1.6%	27.3%

Rosneft Oil Co OJSC (Moscow)

LOCATIONS

HQ: Rosneft Oil Co OJSC (Moscow)
26-1 Sofiyskaya embankment, 1, GSP-8, Moscow 115998
Phone: (7) 495 777 44 42 **Fax:** (7) 495 777 44 44
Web: www.rosneft.com

HISTORICAL FINANCIALS

Company Type: Public

Income Statement FYE: December 31

	REVENUE ($ mil.)	NET INCOME ($ mil.)	NET PROFIT MARGIN	EMPLOYEES
12/12	101,114	11,202	11.1%	166,110
12/11	84,202	9,789	11.6%	160,837
12/10	62,888	9,602	15.3%	159,771
12/09	46,826	6,514	13.9%	0
12/08	68,991	11,120	16.1%	0
Annual Growth	10.0%	0.2%	—	—

2012 Year-End Financials

Debt ratio: 0.8%
Return on equity: 15.9%
Cash ($ mil.): 9,723
Current ratio: 2.15
Long-term debt ($ mil.): 27,758
No. of shares (mil.): —
Dividends
Yield: 0.0%
Payout: 0.0%
Market value ($ mil.): —

	STOCK PRICE ($) FY Close	P/E High/Low	PER SHARE ($) Earnings	Dividends	Book Value
12/12	8.85	0 0	1.19	0.00	0.01
Annual Growth	—	— —	—	—	—

Royal Bank of Canada

Royal Bank of Canada is Canada's #1 bank by assets and market capitalization and is a leading North American financial services company. Royal Bank of Canada and its subsidiaries operate under the brand name RBC providing a diversified set of personal and commercial banking wealth management insurance investor and wholesale banking services globally. RBC serves large and small personal business public sector and institutional clients through offices in Canada the US and about 49 other countries including the UK and other select parts of Europe and Asia/Pacific.

Geographic Reach

Canada is RBC's largest market accounting for more than two-thirds of total revenue. The remainder of revenue is balanced between the US and other international markets (which include Europe and Asia).

Operations

In fiscal 2012 RBC realigned its business segments into five units. It eliminated its International Banking segment and created a new Investor & Treasury Services segment which offers advisory custodial and financing services to safeguard assets and manage risk to institutional investors. That segment includes RBC Investor Services the largest custodian in Canada and formerly a joint venture called RBC Dexia. Concurrently RBC created a Personal & Commercial Banking segment which includes personal and business banking operations and certain investment businesses in Canada the US and the Caribbean.

Wholesale banking business Capital Markets continues to provide a full suite of products and services —including corporate and investment banking equity and debt origination and structuring and trading –to public and private companies institutional investors governments and central banks. Rounding out RBC's business segments are Wealth Management and Insurance which remain unchanged from previous years.

Financial Performance

RBC reported record earnings in fiscal 2012 up 17% from the previous year thanks in large part to record earnings in its Personal & Commercial Banking Capital Markets and Insurance business segments. Aggressive management of costs relative to revenue growth is also helping RBC to reinvest in its businesses and carry them through slower economic periods.

Strategy

With Canada generating more than two-thirds of RBC's revenue it's no surprise that the company's strategy in that market is to remain the undisputed leader in financial services. In support of that goal RBC acquired the Canadian auto finance and deposit business of Ally Financial in early 2013 in a deal valued at $1.4 billion. The deal positions RBC as a leader in the Canadian auto finance business.

Outside of Canada in an effort to be a leading provider of capital markets and wealth management services the company is focusing on high-net-worth corporate and institutional clients in the US the UK and key emerging markets like Hong Kong and Singapore. In mid-2012 RBC acquired the Latin American Caribbean and African private banking business of Coutts the wealth management division of Royal Bank of Scotland to increase market share with high-net-worth clients. (It sold its Jamaican banking operations in 2014 to Sagicor Group Jamaica Ltd.)

RBC in 2012 also shed its money-losing US retail bank operations RBC Bank (USA) and a US credit card business selling them to PNC Financial for $3.6 billion. RBC said those operations lacked the scale to accomplish what the company wanted to do in the US. RBC had also been struggling with credit losses in the US following the economic downturn. The company continues to serve its US wealth management client base however as wealth management continues to be a key growth business. RBC is the sixth-largest global wealth manager by assets under management.

Other initiatives the company is undertaking to achieve its growth strategy are tightly managing costs deepening client relationships increasing price competitiveness and investing in technology.

HISTORY

Royal Bank of Canada (RBC) has looked south of the border ever since its 1864 creation as Merchants Bank in Halifax Nova Scotia a port city bustling with trade spawned by the US Civil War. After incorporating in 1869 as Merchants Bank of Halifax the bank added branches in eastern Canada. Merchants opened a branch in Bermuda in 1882. Gold strikes in Canada and Alaska in the late 1890s pushed it into western Canada.

Merchants opened offices in New York and Cuba in 1899 and changed its name to Royal Bank of Canada in 1901. RBC moved into new Montreal headquarters in 1907 and grew by purchasing such banks as Union Bank of Canada (1925). In 1928 it moved into the 42-story Royal Bank Building then the tallest in the British Empire.

The bank faltered during the Depression but recovered during WWII. After the war RBC financed the expanding minerals and oil and gas industries. When Castro took power in Cuba RBC tried to operate its branches under communist rule but sold out to Banco Nacional de Cuba in 1960.

RBC opened offices in the UK in 1979 and in West Germany Puerto Rico and the Bahamas in 1980. As Canada's banking rules relaxed RBC bought Dominion Securities in 1987. The US Federal Reserve approved RBC's brokerage arm for participation in stock underwriting in 1991.

The bank faced a $650 million loss in 1992 after backing the Reichmann family's Olympia & York property development company which failed under the weight of its UK projects. The next year an ever-diversifying RBC bought Royal Trustco Canada's #2 trust company and Voyageur Travel Insurance its largest retail travel insurer. A management shakeup in late 1994 ended with bank president John Cleghorn taking control of the company.

In 1995 RBC listed on the New York Stock Exchange and the next year joined with Heller Financial (an affiliate of Japan's Fuji Bank) to finance trade between Canada and Mexico. It began offering PC home banking in 1996 and Internet banking in 1997. That year RBC became one of the world's largest securities-custody service providers with its acquisition of The Bank of Nova Scotia's institutional and pension custody operations.

The company and Bank of Montreal agreed to merge in 1998 but Canadian regulators fearing the concentration of banking power seen in the US rejected the merger. In response the bank trimmed its workforce and orchestrated a sale-leaseback of its property portfolio (1999).

In the late 1990s RBC grew its online presence by purchasing the Internet banking operations of Security First Network Bank (now Security First Technologies 1998) the online trading division of Bull & Bear Group (1999) and 20% of AOL Canada (1999). It also bought several trust and fiduciary services businesses from Ernst & Young.

It acquired US mortgage bank Prism Financial and the Canadian retail credit card business of BANK ONE in 2000. RBC also sold its commercial credit portfolio to U.S. Bancorp. The company agreed to pay a substantial fine after institutional asset management subsidiary RT Capital Management came under scrutiny from the Ontario Securities Commission for alleged involvement in illegal pension-fund stock manipulation. RBC ended up selling RT Capital to UBS AG the following year.

Also in 2001 RBC made another US purchase: North Carolina's Centura Banks (now RBC Centura Banks). It sold Houston-based home lender RBC Mortgage to New Century Financial in 2005. Also that year it acquired private bank Abacus Financial which adding locations in the UK and Amsterdam.

RBC spent the decade prior to the global recession building up its US operations. The company moved into the US trust business in 2006 when it purchased American Guaranty & Trust a unit of National Life Insurance Company. In 2007 it bought the electronic brokerage business of New York boutique Carlin Financial Group. Other acquisitions made during that period include debt securities investor Access Capital Strategies energy advisory firm Richardson Barr and DC-area investment bank Ferris Baker Watts.

In 2008 RBC acquired community banks in Alabama Georgia and Florida including Alabama National BanCorporation. That same year RBC agreed to buy back some $850 million in auction-rate securities and pay the New York State attorney general's office a nearly $10 million fine. Auction-rate securities were sold to investors as a low-risk investment but as the economy worsened in 2007 and 2008 banks canceled the regular auctions rendering the securities worthless. Customers and regulators claimed that banks continued to sell them the securities even though they knew the investments had become very high risk.

Also in 2008 RBC Bank expanded its finance operations when it bought the Canadian commercial leasing business of ABN AMRO. It renamed the unit RBC Equipment Finance Group.

To cement its place among the world's 10 largest wealth managers RBC bought UK-based fixed income specialist BlueBay Asset Management for some $1.5 billion in 2010. Also that year it bought BNP Paribas Fortis' Hong Kong wealth management business.

In 2010 it also sold Liberty Life its US life insurance subsidiary that had posted losses for two years to Apollo affiliate Athene Holding. To boost brand recognition of another US unit the company changed the name of Voyageur Asset Management to RBC Global Asset Management (US).

EXECUTIVES

Group Head International Banking and Insurance; Chairman and CEO RBC Bank (USA), W. James (Jim) Westlake, $559,500 total compensation
Chairman, David P. O'Brien, age 71
President Chief Executive Officer, Gordon M. Nixon, age 56, $1,466,500 total compensation
Chief Administrative Officer Chief Financial Officer, Janice R. Fukakusa, $547,844 total compensation
Co-Group Head Capital Markets; Chairman and Co-CEO RBC Capital Markets, A. Douglas (Doug) McGregor, age 57, $165,400 total compensation
Group Head Wealth Management; President and CEO RBC Asset Management, M. George Lewis
SVP & Chief Economist, Craig Wright
Chief Operating Officer, Barbara G. Stymiest, $652,750 total compensation
Co-Group Head Capital Markets; President and Co-CEO RBC Capital Markets, Mark A. Standish, age 52, $178,946 total compensation
Chief Risk Officer, Morten N Friis
Regional President Atlantic Provinces, Greg Grice
Group Head Canadian Banking, David I. (Dave) McKay, age 50, $413,500 total compensation
Chief Human Resources Officer, Zabeen Hirji
President RBC Asset Management, Douglas (Doug) Coulter
Head RBC Global Asset Management Institutional Client Group; President Phillips Hager & North, Damon Williams
CEO RBC Global Asset Management, John S. Montalbano
Regional VP Newfoundland and Labrador, Sean Munro
CEO Caribbean Banking, Suresh Sookoo
Executive Vice President, Charlie Coffey
Independent Chairman of the Board, David OBrien
Director, Douglas T. (Doug) Elix, age 63
Director, Alice D. Laberge, age 57
Director, J. Pedro Reinhard, age 68
Director, Richard L. (Rick) George, age 62
Director, Michael H. McCain, age 54
Director, John T. Ferguson, age 70
Director, Jacques Lamarre, age 70
President CEO and Director, Gordon M. Nixon, age 55
Director, Timothy J. (Tim) Hearn, age 68
Director, Brandt C. Louie, age 70
Director, Paule Gauthier, age 69
Director, Heather E. L. Munroe-Blum, age 63
Director, W. Geoffrey (Geoff) Beattie, age 53
Director, Kathleen P. (Katie) Taylor, age 56
Director, Victor L. Young, age 68
Director, Edward Sonshine, age 67
Director, Bridget van Kralingen

Director, David Denison
Independent Director, Bridget Kralingen
Auditors: Deloitte&ToucheLLP

LOCATIONS

HQ: Royal Bank of Canada
200 Bay Street, Toronto, Ontario M5J 2J5
Phone: 416 974-5151 **Fax:** 416 955-7800
Web: www.rbc.com

2012 Sales

	% of total
Canada	67
US	16
Other	17
Total	**100**

PRODUCTS/OPERATIONS

2012 Sales

	% of total
Personal & commercial	56
Capital	22
Wealth	11
Insurance	10
Investor & treasury	1
Total	**100**

COMPETITORS

AGF Management
BMO Financial Group
Bank of America
Barclays
CI Financial
CIBC
Caisse de depot et placement du Quebec
Caisses centrale Desjardins
Canadian Western Bank
Central 1 Credit Union
Citigroup
Deutsche Bank
Dundee Corp.
Goldman Sachs
Great-West Lifeco
Guardian Capital Group
HSBC Bank Canada
JPMorgan Chase
Laurentian Bank
National Bank of Canada
Nomura Securities
Power Financial
Scotiabank
TD Bank
UBS

HISTORICAL FINANCIALS

Company Type: Public

Income Statement

FYE: October 31

	ASSETS ($ mil.)	NET INCOME ($ mil.)	INCOME AS % OF ASSETS	EMPLOYEES
10/13	823,013	7,965	1.0%	0
10/12	827,347	7,462	0.9%	80,000
10/11	796,996	6,368	0.8%	74,000
10/10	712,875	5,127	0.7%	79,000
10/09	603,899	3,557	0.6%	20,876
Annual Growth	8.0%	22.3%	—	—

2013 Year-End Financials

Return on assets: 0.9%
Return on equity: 17.9%
Long-term debt ($ mil.): —
No. of shares (mil.): 1,440
Sales ($ mil): 37,063
Dividends
Yield: 3.7%
Payout: 48.1%
Market value ($ mil.): 96,765

	STOCK PRICE ($) FY Close	P/E High	P/E Low	PER SHARE ($) Earnings	Dividends	Book Value
10/13	67.18	11	9	5.30	2.48	32.22
10/12	57.03	12	8	4.94	2.27	30.72
10/11	48.92	16	10	4.21	2.13	27.71
10/10	53.38	18	12	3.40	1.96	26.87
10/09	50.40	19	6	2.37	1.84	24.04
Annual Growth	7.4%	—	—	22.3%	7.7%	7.6%

Royal Bank of Scotland Group Plc

If you have overdraft protection for your checking account you can thank The Royal Bank of Scotland (RBS) which introduced the service in 1728. Today RBS is one of Europe's largest banking groups. Through subsidiaries Royal Bank of Scotland and National Westminster Bank it has the UK's largest bank network of more than 2000 branches. RBS offers private banking and insurance products through Coutts Group and Adam & Company. Other divisions include Ulster Bank which operates in Ireland and Northern Ireland; Citizens Financial which operates as Citizens Bank and Charter One in the US; and US transaction processor RBS Lynk. After a series of bailouts in 2008 and 2009 the UK government owns 81% of RBS.

The group was crippled by both the global financial crisis and its ambitious international expansion primarily its disastrous 2007 investment in Dutch bank ABN AMRO. In late 2008 the UK took a 60% stake in RBS but the bank still ended up reporting an annual loss of some #28 billion ($41 billion) –the largest loss in British corporate history. The government has since stepped in twice more to help RBS manage its debt and interest payments.

The government intervened with the contingency that RBS make significant efforts to get back on solid ground. Toward that end the group is cutting costs and selling operations to refocus on its core banking business. In 2010 it sold more than 300 branches and offices to Banco Santander for some #1.65 billion ($2.6 billion). RBS is also selling noncore asset management units to Aberdeen Asset Management for a gain of #84.7 million ($135 million). RBS sold its factoring and invoice financing unit to GE Capital and its payment services unit Global Merchant Services to Advent International and Bain Capital. It also sold its interest in RBS Sempra Commodities. In 2012 the company sold the international private banking business of Coutts to Royal Bank of Canada. Other divisions are simply being wound down and closed.

RBS also is scaling back on the international growth that weakened the group during the economic fallout. In 2009 the group sold its 4% stake in Bank of China for some #1.6 billion ($2.4 billion); it also sold most of its operations in Southeast Asia to Australia and New Zealand Banking Group for about $550 million. RBS divested units in Argentina Colombia Chile the United Arab Emirates Kazakhstan and Pakistan –all assets gained as part of its ABN AMRO transaction. In 2012 RBS sold all of the related investment banking operations in the Netherlands back to the reformed ABN AMRO. Additionally HSBC has agreed to buy the group's retail and commercial banking operations in India; DBS Group is buying those operations in China. Scotiabank bought the bank's business in Chile.

The five-year plan to restore RBS has made some progress. The bank has somewhat narrowed its losses for the past three years although it still reported a nearly #2 billion (some $3.2 billion) loss in 2011. RBS has been diligently reducing its exposure to riskier assets and strengthening its core business. However the company has been hurt by a number of factors including a #1.1 billion impairment on Greek sovereign debt in 2011 and its exposure to bad loans from its Irish operations. Total revenues fell some 9% that year largely due to lower interest and trading earnings and the group's reduced size and scope.

More changes were announced in 2012 as the company continues to exit or downsize certain activities. It restructured its wholesale banking operations into two divisions –markets and international banking –and plans to stop doing business in cash equities corporate brokering equity capital markets and mergers and acquisitions. Its markets business is focused on fixed income while the international banking unit provides debt financing risk management and payments services.

RBS was ordered by the Federal Reserve in 2011 to improve its US operations or risk losing permission to do business in America. RBS must strengthen oversight management and risk management.

HISTORY

Royal Bank of Scotland was founded in 1727 but its roots go back to the Darien Company a merchant expedition that was established to set up a Scottish trading colony in Panama. The Darien expedition ended disastrously in 1699. In 1707 England voted to compensate Scottish creditors for the colony's failure (in part because England had promised support then reneged contributing to the collapse) and a small industry sprang up around paying creditors and loaning them money. In 1727 the Equivalent Company the combined entity of these organizations was granted a banking charter and became Royal Bank of Scotland.

In 1826 the Parliament voted to take away Scottish banks' right to issue banknotes for less than five pounds which would have required banks to use gold or silver. Few banks had such reserves and the move sparked an outcry. Novelist Sir Walter Scott's "The Letters of Malachi Malagrowther" which defended the Scottish one-pound note helped shoot down the proposal.

RBS expanded throughout Scotland over the next 50 years. It opened a London branch in 1874; it didn't establish a branch outside London until it bought Williams Deacon's Bank which had a branch network in North England. RBS continued to use the Williams Deacon's name as it did with Glyn Mills & Co. which it purchased in 1939.

In 1968 RBS took on its modern persona as a public company when it merged with National Commercial Bank. The company moved overseas during the 1970s establishing offices in Hong Kong and major US cities.

RBS spent the next 20 years trying to achieve another merger of the same scale as National Commercial. In 1981 the bank was wooed by Standard Chartered Bank and Hongkong and Shanghai Bank (now part of HSBC Holdings) but British regulators denied both suitors.

The bank moved into telephone operations in 1985 when it set up Direct Line for selling car insurance. In 1988 RBS bought New England bank Citizens Financial. In 1989 the company entered into an alliance with Banco Santander (now Santander Central Hispano) Spain's largest banking group. The alliance created a cross-pollination of ideas and strategies that boosted both banks' operations. The first fruit of the alliance came in 1991 with the launch of Interbank On-line Systems (IBOS) which connected several European banks and allowed for instantaneous money transfers.

In the 1990s RBS was linked with a variety of partners. It even made a bid for the much larger bank Barclays in a move regarded as cheeky but was rebuffed. In 1997 it announced a joint venture with Richard Branson's Virgin Group called Virgin Direct to offer personal banking. The company also bought Angel Trains Contract a rolling stock leasing company and established a transatlantic banking transfer system (similar to IBOS) with US bank CoreStates (now owned by First Union).

In 2000 RBS acquired NatWest after a prolonged takeover battle with rival Bank of Scotland (now part of HBOS plc). The bank sold Gartmore Investment Management its fund management unit to Nationwide Mutual Insurance Company. Royal Bank also sold the assets of NatWest's Equity Partners unit and launched NatWest Private Banking to target wealthy investors.

In 2004 RBS made several acquisitions to boost its US presence: It paid about $360 million for the credit card business of Connecticut-based People's Bank and bought payments processor Lynk Systems (now RBS Lynk) while Citizens Financial bought Cleveland-based bank Charter One Financial. Also that year Ulster Bank bought Ireland-based retail financial services provider First Active.

In 2007 RBS led the consortium that acquired the Dutch bank for ?71 billion in a deal that was called the largest ever in the banking industry. The buyers carved ABN AMRO into pieces; RBS took the global wholesale and international retail operations in Asia Eastern Europe and the Middle East. The ambitious takeover preceded the global economic crisis though and RBS was among the hardest hit financial groups.

The troubled company made several moves to try and raise capital. Early in 2008 the company announced a #12 billion rights issue. RBS also tried but failed to find a buyer for its insurance arm. However other assets were divested that year. The company sold rolling stock leasing firm Angel Trains to Babcock & Brown and others and it sold its joint venture Tesco Personal Finance back to supermarket giant Tesco. The efforts proved inadequate though. The government took a controlling stake in the group in 2008 the same year that RBS reported the largest corporate loss in British history.

Also as part of the government rescue RBS went through a management shakeup. Fred Goodwin the architect of the bank's international expansion was removed as CEO. He was replaced by Stephen Hester formerly the CEO of British Land Company. Johnny Cameron chairman of the group's global banking and markets segment (which lost the group's most money in 2008) was also ousted and chairman Tom McKillop retired early.

RBS also shuffled its corporate structure in 2009. It split its UK retail and commercial banking division into three segments (retail commercial and wealth) and made Ulster Bank its own segment. The group folded its operations support division into other arms and established a segment to manage the selling and runoff of noncore operations. RBS retained the Global Banking & Markets Global Transaction Services US Retail & Commercial and RBS Insurance (including Churchill Insurance) segments although several of their components were transferred to the noncore segment.

In October 2012 RBS sold a 30% stake in Direct Line Group part of its insurance group in an IPO valued at #2.6 billion ($4.2 billion).

EXECUTIVES

CFO and Director, Bruce W. Van Saun, age 55, $530,336 total compensation
Group Chief Executive and Director, Stephen A. M. Hester, age 52, $1,765,706 total compensation
Head Human Resources, Neil Roden
Global Head Global Restructuring Group, Derek S. Sach, age 58
Chief Executive - Citizens and Head of Americas, Ellen Alemany, age 57
President Global Banking and Markets, Suneel Kamlani
Chairman, Sir Philip Hampton, age 60, $1,114,820 total compensation
Chief Administration Officer, Ron Teerlink, age 52
Head Group Corporate Affairs, Andrew Wilson, age 42
Head Restructuring and Risk, Nathan Bostock, age 52
Group Treasurer, John Cummins
CEO UK Corporate Banking Division, Chris Sullivan, age 55
Co-Head Global Banks and Markets Americas; Head Fixed Income Trading for Americas, Michael Lyublinsky
Head Investor Relations, Richard O'Connor
Chairman Asia, John McCormick
Group Chief Economist and Head Communications, Andrew McLaughlin
Head Finance Europe Middle East and Africa, John McIntyre
Co-Head Global Banking and Markets Americas; Head North America Corporate Coverage and Advisory, Bob McKillip
Director, Baroness Sheila V. Noakes, age 63
CEO Global Banking and Markets, John Hourican, age 42
Global Head Markets, Peter Nielsen
Chief Administrative Officer Markets, Jeremy Wright
CEO RBS Insurance, Paul Geddes, age 43
Chief Executive UK Retail, Ross McEwan
Chief China Economist, Ben Simpfendorfer
COO Group Manufacturing, Richard Hemsley
Deputy CEO Global Banking and Markets, Marco Mazzuchelli
Head Group Media Centre, Jason Knauf
Senior Assistant Secretary, Jan Cargill
Group Secretary, Aileen Taylor
Group General Counsel, Chris Campbell
CEO UK Corporate and Institutional Banking, Mark Catton
Head Noncore Division and Asset Protection Scheme, Rory Cullinan
Global Head Securitized Products and Head of US Credit Global Banking & Markets Division, Scott Eichel
Chairman and CEO China, Sherry Liu
Regional Head Global Banking, Matthew Kirkby
Head West Register, Helen Gordon
Owner of a start-up business, Josh Parker
Group Finance Director; Executive Director, Bruce Saun
Vice President and he, Gao Qi
CFO and Director, Bruce W. Van Saun, age 55
Director, Joseph P. (Joe) MacHale, age 61
Director, Arthur F. (Art) Ryan, age 70
Group Chief Executive and Director, Stephen A. M. Hester, age 52
Director, John McFarlane, age 65
Director, Sir Sandy Crombie, age 64
Director, Philip G. Scott, age 59
Director, Penelope L. (Penny) Hughes, age 54
Director, Alison Davis, age 51
Director, Anthony (Tony) Di Iorio, age 69
Director, Baroness Sheila V. Noakes, age 63
Director, Brendan Nelson, age 63
Independent Non-Executive Director, Tony Iorio
Auditors: Deloitte&ToucheLLP

LOCATIONS

HQ: Royal Bank of Scotland Group Plc
P.O. Box 1000, Gogarburn, Edinburgh EH12 1HQ
Phone: (44) 131 556 8555 **Fax:** (44) 131 626 3081
Web: www.rbs.com

2011 Sales

	% of total
UK	67
Rest of	11
US	18
Other	4
Total	**100**

PRODUCTS/OPERATIONS

2011 Sales by Segment

	% of total
Global banking &	21
UK	20
RBS	15
UK	14
US retail &	11
Global transaction	8
Wealth	4
Ulster	3
Other	4
Total	**100**

2011 Sales

	% of total
Net	42
Fees &	21
Insurance net premium	14
Other	23
Total	**100**

Selected Subsidiaries

Citizens Financial Group Inc. (banking US)
Coutts & Co (private banking)
Direct Line Insurance Group plc
National Westminster Bank Plc
The Royal Bank of Scotland plc
Ulster Bank Limited (Northern Ireland)

COMPETITORS

AIB
Bank of America
Bank of Ireland
Barclays
Citigroup
HSBC
ING Direct UK
JPMorgan Chase
Lloyds Banking Group
PNC Financial
Santander UK
Standard Chartered
Standard Life
permanent tsb

HISTORICAL FINANCIALS

Company Type: Public

Income Statement

FYE: December 31

	ASSETS ($ mil.)	NET INCOME ($ mil.)	INCOME AS % OF ASSETS	EMPLOYEES
12/12	2,115,244	(9,600)	—	137,200
12/11	2,327,889	(3,085)	—	142,600
12/10	2,256,880	(1,717)	—	145,500
12/09	2,747,596	(5,749)	—	159,700
12/08	3,499,930	(34,306)	—	173,000
Annual Growth	(11.8%)	—	—	(5.6%)

2012 Year-End Financials

Return on assets: (-0.4%)
Return on equity: (-8.3%)
Long-term debt ($ mil.): —
No. of shares (mil.): —
Sales ($ mil): 41,752
Dividends
Yield: —
Payout: —
Market value ($ mil.): —

	STOCK PRICE ($) FY Close	P/E High/Low	PER SHARE ($) Earnings	Dividends	Book Value
12/12	10.79	— —	(0.88)	0.00	1.92
12/11	6.37	— —	(0.28)	0.00	10.49
12/10	12.32	— —	(0.08)	0.00	10.66
12/09	9.39	— —	(1.02)	0.00	22.34
12/08	15.17	— —	(21.23)	2.81	21.75
Annual Growth	(8.2%)	— —	—	—	(45.5%)

Royal Bank of Scotland plc

LOCATIONS

HQ: Royal Bank of Scotland plc
36 St Andrew Square, Edinburgh EH2 2YB
Phone: (44) 131 556 8555
Web: www.rbs.co.uk

HISTORICAL FINANCIALS

Company Type: Public

Income Statement FYE: December 31

	REVENUE ($ mil.)	NET INCOME ($ mil.)	NET PROFIT MARGIN	EMPLOYEES
12/12	40,424	(6,210)	—	111,000
12/11	42,138	(2,541)	—	113,700
12/10	47,931	(1,510)	—	113,600
12/09	56,029	(385)	—	0
12/08	48,547	(13,927)	—	0
Annual Growth	(4.5%)	—	—	—

2012 Year-End Financials

Debt ratio: —
Return on equity: (-6.3%)
Cash ($ mil.): 120,122
Current ratio: —
Long-term debt ($ mil.): —
No. of shares (mil.): —
Dividends
Yield: —
Payout: —
Market value ($ mil.): —

	STOCK PRICE ($) FY Close	P/E High/Low	PER SHARE ($) Earnings	Dividends	Book Value
12/12	27.70	— —	(0.00)	0.00	14.46
12/11	24.06	— —	(0.00)	0.00	14.43
12/10	25.82	— —	(0.00)	0.00	13.39
Annual Growth	3.6%	— —	—	—	1.9%

Royal Dutch Shell Plc

Royal Dutch Shell which sits on an oil and gas throne that is only slightly lower than that of #1 oil company Exxon Mobil has worldwide proved reserves of 14.2 billion barrels of oil equivalent. Most of the oil giant's crude is produced in Nigeria Oman the UK and the US. Royal Dutch Shell is also investing heavily in the Athabasca Oil Sands Project which converts oil sands in Alberta to synthetic oil. The company operates 43000 gas stations (the world's largest retail fuel network). Royal Dutch Shell which operates in more than 80 countries also produces refined products and chemicals at more than 30 refineries transports natural gas trades gas and electricity and develops renewable energy.

While committed to developing clean energy as a way to reduce carbon emissions Royal Dutch Shell is focusing on clean oil production technology (such as carbon sequestration) and biofuels which are more in line with its core oil and gas competencies rather than on wind power and solar energy. In 2010 the company formed a $12 billion joint venture with Brazil's Cosan to ramp up ethanol production.

Boosting its core oil and gas businesses that year Royal Dutch Shell announced that its gas-to-liquids plant and liquefied natural gas (LNG) project in Qatar (which came onstream in 2011) will add $4 billion a year to the company's cash flow. The two projects will deliver 350000 barrels of oil equivalent per day or 10% of the company's total production and make Qatar a core region for Royal Dutch Shell's future growth.

Higher commodity prices and a recovering global economy led to large increase in production and product sales in 2011 boosting the company's revenues by 28% and net income by 54%.

Expanding its Canadian oil and gas production activities in 2012 Royal Dutch Shell announced plans to ramp up production at its Athabasca Oil Sands project in Alberta and to develop shale gas and an LNG export terminal in British Columbia. It also agreed to buy Hess' stake in the North Sea Beryl area fields and the Scottish Area Gas Evacuation System for $525 million.

That year Royal Dutch Shell also backed out of the race to acquire UK-based Cove Energy after a six-month bidding war with Thailand's PTT Exploration and Production. Cove Energy holds about a 9% stake in Anadarko Petroleum's huge gas reserves off the coast of Mozambique and the acquisition would have allowed Shell to extend its presence in East Africa.

In a move to expand its position as a provider of shallow water drilling services in Asia Africa and the Middle East in 2012 it formed Shell Drilling Holdings which bought 37 jackup drilling rigs one swamp barge and associated operations from Transocean for $1.05 billion.

HISTORY

In 1870 Marcus Samuel inherited an interest in his father's London trading company which imported seashells from the Far East. He expanded the business and after securing a contract for Russian oil began selling kerosene in the Far East.

Standard Oil underpriced competitors to defend its Asian markets. Samuel secretly prepared his response and in 1892 unveiled the first of a fleet of tankers. Rejecting Standard's acquisition overtures Samuel created "Shell" Transport and Trading in 1897.

Meanwhile a Dutchman Aeilko Zijlker struck oil in Sumatra and formed Royal Dutch Petroleum in 1890 to exploit the oil field. Young Henri Deterding joined the firm in 1896 and established a sales force in the Far East.

Deterding became Royal Dutch's head in 1900 amid the battle for the Asian market. In 1903 Deterding Samuel and the Rothschilds (a French banking family) created Asiatic Petroleum a marketing alliance. With Shell's non-Asian business eroding Deterding engineered a merger between Royal Dutch and Shell in 1907. Royal Dutch shareholders got 60% control; "Shell" Transport and Trading 40%.

After the 1911 Standard Oil breakup Deterding entered the US building refineries and buying producers. Shell products were available in every state by 1929. Royal Dutch/Shell joined the 1928 "As Is" cartel that fixed prices for most of two decades.

The post-WWII Royal Dutch/Shell profited from worldwide growth in oil consumption. It acquired 100% of Shell Oil its US arm in 1985 but shareholders sued maintaining Shell Oil's assets had been undervalued in the deal. They were awarded $110 million in 1990.

Management's slow response to two 1995 controversies —environmentalists' outrage over the planned sinking of an oil platform and human rights activists' criticism of Royal Dutch/Shell's role in Nigeria –spurred a major shakeup. It began moving away from its decentralized structure and adopted a new policy of corporate openness.

In 1996 Royal Dutch/Shell and Exxon (now Exxon Mobil) formed a worldwide petroleum additives venture. Shell Oil joined Texaco (now part of Chevron) in 1998 to form Equilon Enterprises combining US refining and marketing operations in the West and Midwest. Similarly Shell Oil Texaco and Saudi Arabia's Aramco combined downstream operations on the US's East and Gulf coasts as Motiva Enterprises.

In 1999 Royal Dutch/Shell and the UK's BG plc acquired a controlling stake in Comgas a unit of Companhia Energetica de S?o Paulo and the largest natural gas distributor in Brazil for about $1 billion.

In 2000 the company sold its coal business to UK-based mining giant Anglo American for more than $850 million. To gain a foothold in the US power marketing scene Royal Dutch/Shell formed a joint venture with construction giant Bechtel (called InterGen). The next year the company agreed to combine its German refining and marketing operations with those of RWE-DEA. Royal Dutch/Shell tried to expand its US natural gas reserves in 2001 by making a $2 billion hostile bid for Barrett Resources but the effort was withdrawn after Barrett agreed to be acquired by Williams for $2.5 billion.

In 2002 in connection with Chevron's acquisition of Texaco Royal Dutch/Shell acquired ChevronTexaco's (now Chevron) stakes in the underperforming US marketing joint ventures Equilon and Motiva. That year the company through its US Shell Oil unit acquired Pennzoil-Quaker State for $1.8 billion. Also that year Royal Dutch/Shell acquired Enterprise Oil for $5 billion plus debt. In addition it purchased RWE's 50% stake in German refining and marketing joint venture Shell & DEA Oil (for $1.35 billion).

In 2004 the group signed a $200 million exploration deal with Libya signaling its return to that country after a more than decade-long absence. Also that year the company reported that it had overestimated its reserves by 24%. The bad news resulted in the ouster of the chairman and CFO.

The Anglo-Dutch entity restructured to stay competitive. Revelations of overestimated oil reserves in 2004 prompted a push for greater transparency in the company's organizational structure. This led to the 2005 merger of former publicly traded owners Royal Dutch Petroleum and The "Shell" Transport and Trading Company into Royal Dutch Shell.

Searching for new oil assets in 2006 the company acquired a large swath of oil sands acreage in Alberta Canada. Further boosting its oil sands business in 2007 the company acquired the 22% of Shell Canada that it did not already own. The company also began investing some $12 billion (in addition to the $2.6 billion already spent) in offshore projects near Dubai. In 2008 Royal Dutch Shell expanded its exploration assets in Alaska by acquiring 275 lease blocks in the Chukchi Sea for $2.1 billion.

In 2009 the company made significant oil discoveries in the deepwater eastern Gulf of Mexico at West Boreas Vito and the Cardamom Deep and in 2010 at the Appomattox prospect in the Mississippi Canyon block. The finds expanded Shell Oil's long-term development plans in the area.

Further expanding its unconventional natural gas resources in 2010 the company spent $4.7 billion to acquire East Resources which holds 1 million acres of Marcellus Shale one of the fastest-growing shale plays in the US.

On the conventional side of the oil business the Gulf of Mexico produces 370000 barrels of oil per day or about 15% of Royal Dutch Shell's worldwide production. In 2010 the company claimed an industry record starting production at the deepest floating drilling and production platform in the world. The Perdido Development operates in 8000 ft. of water in the Gulf of Mexico. In response to the BP oil rig disaster in the Gulf of Mexico the company joined forces with Exxon Mobil Chevron and ConocoPhillips to form a $1 billion rapid-response joint venture that will be able to better manage and contain future deepwater spills.

With an eye toward raising cash and focusing on its majority holdings and joint ventures rather than on minority held businesses in 2010 Royal Dutch Shell sold 10% of its 34% in Australian oil and gas enterprise Woodside Petroleum for $3.3 billion. Royal Dutch Shell also announced that it would seek to sell the rest of its stake in Woodside Petroleum over time. (Earlier in the year the company formed a $3.5 billion joint venture with PetroChina which acquired Arrow Energy a company with major natural gas assets in Northern Australia).

As part of its strategy of selling noncore downstream assets to raise cash in 2010 Royal Dutch Shell sold its Finnish and Swedish operations (including a refinery in Gothenburg and 565 gas stations) to Finland-based St1 for $640 million. In 2011 it sold its UK-based Stanlow refinery to India's Essar Group for $350 million.

EXECUTIVES

Chairman, Jorma Ollila, age 63
Downstream Director, Mark Williams, age 62
Chief Financial Officer, Simon Henry, age 52, $643,507 total compensation
Chairman Shell Companies in Australia, Russell R. Caplan, age 66
Chief Executive Officer, Peter R. Voser, age 55, $1,815,864 total compensation
Chairman Shell U.K. Limited, James Smith
Vice President Global Business Environment, Jeremy B. Bentham
Deputy Chairman, Lord John O. Kerr of Kinlochard, age 71
President Director Upstream Americas Shell Oil Company; Chairman Shell Canada, Marvin E. Odum, age 55
Company Secretary, Michiel Brandjes, age 58
President Shell Energy North America (US), Mark Quartermain
EVP Russia and Caspian Region, Charles Watson
EVP Upstream Australia, Ann Pickard
EVP Americas Shell Gas & Power, Curtis R. Frasier
VP Shell Canada, Thomas G. Zengerly
EVP Shell Canada, John Abbott
President and Country Chair Shell Canada, Lorraine Mitchelmore
VP Shell Canada, Stephanie Sterling
Chair and Managing Director Shell Petroleum Development Company Nigeria; VP Production Africa, Mutiu Sunmonu
Head Group Media Relations, Stuart Bruseth
VP Downstream Australia, Andrew Smith, age 49
Finance Manager Shell Development Australia, Michael Carey
Technical VP Europe, John Gallagher, age 53
General Manager UK Retail, Melanie Lane
VP Human Resources UK Ireland and Nordics, Paul Milliken
Head UK Government Relations, Kate Smith
VP Corporate and UK Country Controller, Graham Talbot
Vice President Global Media Relations, Andy Norman
Vice President Investor Relations, Ken Lawrence
Board Member, Charles O. (Chad) Holliday Jr., age 66
Board Member, Josef Ackermann, age 65
CFO and Board Member, Simon Henry, age 52
Board Member, Jeroen van der Veer, age 65
Chief Executive Officer, Peter R. Voser, age 55
Board Member, Guy Elliott, age 56
Board Member, G. J. (Hans) Wijers, age 62
Executive Director Upstream International and Board Member, Malcolm Brinded, age 59
Deputy Chairman, Lord John O. Kerr of Kinlochard, age 71
Board Member, Wim Kok, age 74
Board Member, Christine Morin-Postel, age 66
Board Member, Gerard J. Kleisterlee, age 67
Independent Director, Martha Piper
Auditors: PricewaterhouseCoopersLLP

LOCATIONS

HQ: Royal Dutch Shell Plc
Carel van Bylandtlaan 30, The Hague 2596 HR
Phone: (31) 70 377 9111 **Fax:** (44) 20 7934 5153
Web: www.shell.com

2011 Sales

	$ mil.	% of total
Europe	187,498	40
Africa Asia Australia/Oceania	148,260	31
US	91,946	20
Other Americas	42,467	9
Adjustments	14,318	-
Total	**484,489**	**100**

PRODUCTS/OPERATIONS

2011 Sales

	$ mil.	% of total
Downstream	427,864	91
Upstream	42,260	9
Corporate & other	47	-
Adjustments	14,318	-
Total	**484,489**	**100**

COMPETITORS

7-Eleven
Ashland Inc.
BHP Billiton
BP
Chevron
ConocoPhillips
Dow Chemical
DuPont
Eastman Chemical
Eni
Exxon Mobil
FEC Resources
Hess Corporation
Huntsman International
Imperial Oil
Koch Industries Inc.
Marathon Oil
Norsk Hydro ASA
Occidental Petroleum
PEMEX
PETROBRAS
PetroKazakhstan
Petroleos de Venezuela
Repsol
Sinopec Shanghai Petrochemical
Sunoco
TOTAL

HISTORICAL FINANCIALS

Company Type: Public

Income Statement FYE: December 31

	REVENUE ($ mil.)	NET INCOME ($ mil.)	NET PROFIT MARGIN	EMPLOYEES
12/12	481,700	26,592	5.5%	87,000
12/11	484,489	30,918	6.4%	90,000
12/10	378,152	20,127	5.3%	97,000
12/09	285,129	12,518	4.4%	101,000
12/08	458,361	26,277	5.7%	102,000
Annual Growth	1.2%	0.3%	—	(3.9%)

2012 Year-End Financials

Debt ratio: 10.4%
Return on equity: 14.8%
Cash ($ mil.): 18,550
Current ratio: 1.18
Long-term debt ($ mil.): 29,921
No. of shares (mil.): —
Dividends
Yield: 4.9%
Payout: 80.6%
Market value ($ mil.): —

	STOCK PRICE ($) FY Close	P/E High	P/E Low	PER SHARE ($) Earnings	Dividends	Book Value
12/12	68.95	17	14	4.24	3.42	29.77
12/11	73.09	16	12	4.98	3.36	27.10
12/10	66.78	21	15	3.28	3.36	23.93
12/09	60.11	31	19	2.04	3.32	21.86
12/08	52.94	20	10	4.26	3.12	20.39
Annual Growth	6.8%	—	—	(0.1%)	2.3%	9.9%

RWE AG

RWE doesn't stand for Runs With Electricity but it could. RWE is one of Germany's top two electricity suppliers (along with E.ON). Through its subsidiaries the energy conglomerate provides electricity and gas to residential and business customers primarily in Central and Western Europe. It also owns major UK-based utilities and German-based electricity and gas supplier RWE npower. RWE owns oil and gas exploration and production unit RWE-DEA; other businesses include companies engaged in gas transportation and storage power generation (including wind) energy trading information technology and coal mining. In 2011 RWE served 17 million electricity customers and 8 million gas customers.

Geographic Reach

RWE operates in Germany the Netherlands/Belgium the UK and in Central Eastern and South Eastern Europe. Germany accounted for more than 50% of the company's revenues in 2011.

Operations

In addition to generating power and distributing electricity and gas in its core geographic markets the company also develops renewable power through RWE Innogy; explores for and produces oil and gas through RWE-DEA; and engages in energy trading and gas midstream activities through RWE Supply & Trading.

Financial Performance

The company's revenues decreased by 3% in 2011 due to a drop in revenues from the Germany power generation Netherlands/Belgium and Trading/Gas Midstream segments. Power generation revenues declined due to the German government's shift in energy policy (exiting nuclear power) following the reactor disaster at Fukushima. Netherlands/Belgium revenues declined due to a drop in Essent's gas midstream business caused by a drop in electricity generation margins. Trading/Gas Midstream revenues declined due to a drop in the realization of successful forward transactions and in some of its gas purchase contracts.

The company's net income decreased by 45% in 2011 due to a decrease in revenues and operating income caused by an increase in the costs of material depreciation amortization and impairment losses and other operating expenses.

Strategy

RWE plans its investments in power stations networks and raw material production facilities in terms of decades not in terms of years. It is looking to compete more effectively in the deregulated German power and gas markets order by restructuring its regional energy businesses. The company's former German utility unit RWE Energie lost its regional monopoly status because of deregulation and RWE has responded by splitting its domestic power generation distribution and supply operations into new units. RWE has also responded by acquiring utilities and energy services companies in the Czech Republic Hungary Poland and Slovakia and by targeting expansion in Europe.

RWE is also focusing on the expansion of renewable energy in Germany the UK the Netherlands Poland Spain and Italy.

In 2011 the company acquired Energy Resources Holding B.V. which has owns 30 % of EPZ a Dutch electricity generator.

To meet antitrust requirements in 2011 RWE sold its 75% stake in the German natural gas transmission grid business (Thyssengas) to Macquarie Group. To pay down debt in 2011 it also sold its German long-distance power grid to a consortium of five pension funds of German and Swiss insurers for $1.4 billion. RWE retained operational control of the grid.

A possible merger between RWE and Spanish power giant IBERDROLA fell through in 2011 due to market and political concerns.

HISTORY

Founded at the end of the 19th century RWE mirrored the industrialization of Germany in its growth. It was formed as Rheinisch-Westfalisches Elektrizitatswerk in 1898 by Erich Zweigert the mayor of Essen and Hugo Stinnes an industrialist from Mulheim to provide electricity to Essen and surrounding areas. The company began supplying power in 1900.

Stinnes persuaded other cities –Gelsenkirchen and Mulheim –to buy shares in RWE in 1905. In 1908 RWE and rival Vereinigte Elektrizitatswerk Westfalen (VEW) agreed to divide up the territories that each would supply.

Germany's coal shortages caused by WWI prompted RWE to expand its coal operations and it bought Rheinische Aktiengesellschaft fur Braunkohlenbergbau a coal producer in 1932. RWE also built a power line network completed in 1930 to connect populous northern Germany with the south. By 1939 as WWII began the company had plants throughout most of western Germany. However the war destroyed much of its infrastructure and RWE had to rebuild.

The company continued to rely on coal for most of its fuel needs in the 1950s but in 1961 RWE and Bayern Atomkraft sponsored the construction of a demonstration nuclear reactor the first of several such projects at Gundremmingen. The Gundremmingen plant was shut down in 1977 and to replace it RWE built two 1300-MW reactors that began operation in 1984.

RWE began to diversify and in 1988 it acquired Texaco's German petroleum and petrochemical unit which became RWE-DEA. By 1990 RWE's operations also included waste management and construction. RWE reorganized creating RWE Aktiengesellschaft as a holding company for group operations.

RWE-DEA acquired the US's Vista Chemical in 1991 and RWE's Rheinbraun mining unit bought a 50% stake in Consolidation Coal from DuPont. (The mining venture went public in 1999 as CONSOL Energy.) RWE led a consortium that acquired major stakes in three Hungarian power companies in 1995.

Hoping to play a role in Germany's telecommunications market RWE teamed with VEBA in 1997 to form the o.tel.o joint venture and RWE and VEBA gained control of large German mobile phone operator E-Plus. The nation's telecom market was deregulated in 1998 but Mannesmann and former monopoly Deutsche Telekom proved to be formidable competitors. In 1999 RWE and VEBA sold o.tel.o's fixed-line business (along with the o.tel.o brand name) and cable-TV unit Tele Columbus. The next year the companies sold their joint stake in E-Plus.

Faced with deregulating German electricity markets RWE Energie had begun restructuring as soon as the market opened up in 1998. It agreed to buy fellow German power company VEW in a $20 billion deal that closed in 2000. RWE also joined with insurance giant Allianz and France's Vivendi in a successful bid for a 49.9% stake in state-owned water distributor Berliner Wasserbetriebe (Vivendi later spurned an RWE offer to buy its energy businesses).

After taking advantage of deregulating markets in Germany RWE moved to pick up other European utilities: It acquired UK-based Thames Water (later renamed RWE Thames Water) in 2000 and bought a majority stake in Dutch gas supplier Intergas the next year. In 2002 the company issued an exchange offer to acquire UK electricity supplier Innogy (later renamed RWE npower) for a total of about $4.4 billion in cash and $3 billion in assumed debt. It also completed a $3.7 billion purchase of Czech Republic gas supplier Transgas.

In a move to further streamline operations RWE sold its 50% stake in refinery and service station subsidiary Shell & DEA Oil to Deutsche Shell and Shell Petroleum. To do battle in an increasingly competitive utility industry RWE is acquiring stakes in other European utilities. In 2003 RWE also acquired North American utility American Water Works which was combined with the US operations of RWE Thames Water for $4.6 billion in cash and $4 billion in assumed debt.

Recognizing that its international acquisitions of water utilities in the early 2000s had left it overextended RWE has been to selling its water assets in order to save cash and streamline its operations around its core power businesses. Overextended in 2006 the company sold its Thames Water unit to Kemble Water Limited a consortium led by Macquarie Bank's European Infrastructure Funds. It spun off its American Water unit in 2008.

The company saw its revenues drop in 2009 as the global recession hammered gas prices. However the same lower gas prices helped RWE to save costs enabling it to post an improved net income that year.

After being outmaneuvered by EDF in its plan to grow its Pan-European power footprint by acquiring British Energy RWE in 2009 acquired top Dutch power utility Essent for $10.7 billion. The deal boost its position as one of the top electricity and gas utilities in Europe.

Growing its energy sources in 2009 it also formed a joint venture with E.ON to develop 6000 MW of nuclear power capacity in the UK. In a move to reduce its dependency on the wholesale gas markets in 2009 RWE acquired 70% of the Breagh North Sea gas field for about $350 million.

The company announced CEO Jurgen Gro?mann who fought Germany's decision to phase out nuclear power stepped down in July 2012. Gro?mann was replaced by Peter Terium the CEO of Essent. COO Rolf Martin Schmitz was named Deputy CEO.

EXECUTIVES

Chairman Supervisory Board, Manfred Schneider, age 74
CFO and Member Executive Board, Rolf Pohlig, age 60
Deputy Chairman, Frank Bsirske
Chief Human Resources Officer, Alwin Fitting, age 60
Chairman Executive Board, Peter Terium, age 49
Manager Investor Relations Retail Shareholders, Cornelia Rath
Chief Commercial Officer, Leonhard Birnbaum, age 46
COO, Rolf Martin Schmitz, age 56
Manager Investor Relations Germany Switzerland and Asia, Martin Vahlbrock
Manager Investor Relations Scandinavia and Fixed Income, Oliver van der Mond
VP Investor Relations, Stephan Lowis
Executive Vice President of RWE Power AG, Matthias Hartung
Member of the Supervisory Board, Carl-Ludwig Boehm-Bezing
Director, Christine Merkamp
Director, Dagmar Muehlenfeld
Director, Frithjof Kuehn
Director, Manfred Holz
Director, Roger Graef
Director, Ullrich Sierau
Member of the Supervisory Board, Wolfgang Schuessel
Director, Dieter Zetsche, age 59
Director, Paul Achleitner, age 56
Director, Ekkehard D. Schulz, age 72
Chairman Supervisory Board, Manfred Schneider, age 74
Director, Carl Ludwig von Boehm-Bezing
Director, Werner Bischoff, age 65
Deputy Chairman, Frank Bsirske
Director, Dieter Faust
Director, Wolfgang Reiniger
Director, Gunter Reppien
Director, Uwe Tigges
Director, Heinz Buchel
Director, Dagmar Schmeer
Director, Dagmar Muhlenfeld
Director, Gerhard Langemeyer
Director, Andreas Henrich
Director, Manfred Weber
Director, Frithjof Kuhn
Director, Hans-Peter Lafos
Director, Wolfgang Schussel
Member of the Supervisory Board, Carl-Ludwig Boehm-Bezing
Director, Christine Merkamp
Director, Dagmar Muehlenfeld
Director, Frithjof Kuehn
Director, Manfred Holz
Director, Roger Graef
Director, Ullrich Sierau
Member of the Supervisory Board, Wolfgang Schuessel
Auditors: PricewaterhouseCoopersAG

LOCATIONS

HQ: RWE AG
Opernplatz 1, Essen 45128
Phone: (49) 201 12 00 **Fax:** (49) 201 12 15199
Web: www.rwe.com

2011 Sales

	% of total
Germany	53
UK	17
Netherlands	11
Czech	5
Hungary	4
Other	10
Total	**100**

PRODUCTS/OPERATIONS

2011 Sales

	% of total
Geographic Divisions	
Germany (64% see divisions)	
Central Eastern & South Eastern	17
UK	5
Netherlands &	4
Operating Divisions	
Power generation	40
Supply & distribution	22
Gas & oil	10
Renewables	2
Trading & gas	-
Other	-
Total	**100**

Selected Divisions and Subsidiaries

RWE Energy (German and continental European downstream energy operations)
RWE npower (affiliated with RWE Innogy electricity and gas supply UK)
RWE Supply & Trading (power gas coal and oil trading)
RWE-DEA AG (oil and gas exploration production and storage)
RWE Power (upstream energy operations)

COMPETITORS

BP
Centrica
Enel
Exxon Mobil

E.ON	Royal Dutch Shell
Electricite de France	Vattenfall
Endesa S.A.	

HISTORICAL FINANCIALS

Company Type: Public

Income Statement FYE: December 31

	REVENUE ($ mil.)	NET INCOME ($ mil.)	NET PROFIT MARGIN	EMPLOYEES
12/12	66,918	1,721	2.6%	70,208
12/11	63,577	2,335	3.7%	72,068
12/10	68,151	4,427	6.5%	70,856
12/09	66,907	5,144	7.7%	70,726
12/08	66,694	3,576	5.4%	65,908
Annual Growth	0.1%	(16.7%)	—	1.6%

2012 Year-End Financials

Debt ratio: 29.8%	No. of shares (mil.): 575
Return on equity: 8.5%	Dividends
Cash ($ mil.): 3,521	Yield: 4.6%
Current ratio: 1.02	Payout: 119.0%
Long-term debt ($ mil.): 20,320	Market value ($ mil.): 23,974

	STOCK PRICE ($) FY Close	P/E High	P/E Low	PER SHARE ($) Earnings	Dividends	Book Value
12/12	41.64	40	27	2.81	1.93	33.94
12/11	34.93	39	16	4.33	6.90	35.37
12/10	66.39	31	17	8.30	3.42	44.20
12/09	96.90	31	16	9.65	4.29	37.26
12/08	91.15	64	24	6.64	3.92	30.95
Annual Growth	(17.8%)	—	—	(19.4%)	(16.2%)	2.3%

S-Oil Corp

S-Oil aims to become the most S-uccessful refiner in South Korea and beyond. The company is one of its country's leading refiners and a major provider of lubricants and gasoline. S-Oil is capable of producing 669000 barrels per day at its Onsan refinery and its product menu includes gasoline kerosene diesel lube base oil automotive and industrial oils and petrochemical products such as benzene and toluene. S-Oil operates a naphtha reforming plant with a daily capacity of 45000 barrels and a BTX production plant with an annual capacity of 900000 tons. Its joint venture with Saudi Arabia's Aramco –signed in 1991 –ensures a steady supply of crude oil.

Operations

The company operates the Onsan Refinery and other facilities at that location that can produce petrochemicals and lube base oil. S-Oil produces and supplies high quality oil products based on the world-class Bunker-C Cracking Center and the xylene Center a paraxylene plant with the world's highest production capacity for a single facility.

Geographic Reach

S-Oil exports more than 60% of its annual production to about 30 countries around the world.

Financial Performance

Thanks to high oil prices and the expansion of its refining capacity S-Oil's 2011 revenues increased by 56% and its net income by 69%.

Business Strategy

The company's long-term strategy includes further investment in the refining business integration with the petrochemical business and growing its renewable energy business.

Buoyed by increasing demand for petroleum products from China and other Asian countries in 2011 S-Oil completed its Onsan refinery expansion project. The expansion doubles the plant's production of paraxylene and benzene to 2.4 million tons a year. It also increased its refining capacity from 580000 barrels per day to 669000 barrels per day.

Company Background

S-Oil began commercial operations in 1980. The company broke off from SsangYong Group in 1999 and changed its name to S-Oil a year later.

EXECUTIVES

CFO, Yul Ryu, age 53
Account Manager, T.H. Kang
Director CEO, Nasser Al-Mahasher

LOCATIONS

HQ: S-Oil Corp
63 building, 60 Yeouido-dong, Youngdeungpo-gu, Seoul 150-607
Phone: (82) 2 3772 5151 **Fax:** (82) 2 783 9546
Web: www.s-oil.com

COMPETITORS

GS Caltex	SK Group
LG International	

HISTORICAL FINANCIALS

Company Type: Public

Income Statement FYE: December 31

	REVENUE ($ mil.)	NET INCOME ($ mil.)	NET PROFIT MARGIN	EMPLOYEES
12/12	32,521	548	1.7%	2,671
12/11	27,542	1,027	3.7%	2,622
12/10*	18,292	633	3.5%	2,551
01/10	0	0	—	0
12/09	15,169	198	1.3%	2,473
Annual Growth	28.9%	40.3%	—	2.6%

*Fiscal year change

2012 Year-End Financials

Debt ratio: 0.0%	No. of shares (mil.): 112
Return on equity: 11.0%	Dividends
Cash ($ mil.): 406	Yield: 0.0%
Current ratio: 1.37	Payout: 0.0%
Long-term debt ($ mil.): 630	Market value ($ mil.): 5,742

	STOCK PRICE ($) FY Close	P/E High	P/E Low	PER SHARE ($) Earnings	Dividends	Book Value
12/12	51.00	—	—	4.73	0.00	44.72
12/11	40.75	—	—	8.85	0.00	40.06
12/10*	29.23	—	—	5.46	0.00	(0.00)
01/10	22.81	—	—	(0.00)	0.00	(0.00)
12/09	22.81	—	—	1.70	0.00	30.09
Annual Growth	22.3%	—	—	40.5%	—	14.1%

*Fiscal year change

SABMiller Plc (United Kingdom)

Thanks to this beer maker "It's 5 O'Clock Somewhere." SABMiller is one of the world's largest brewers producing more than 200 international national and local beer brands spanning the globe. Its big brands include Grolsch Miller Peroni Nastro and Pilsner Urquell and many local favorites such as Castle Lager the #1 beer in Africa. In Latin America it owns Bavaria and Cerveceria Nacional; in the US the company owns 58% of MillerCoors a joint venture with Molson Coors. SABMiller acquired Australian rival Foster's in 2011. Beyond brewing SABMiller is one of the world's top bottlers of Coca-Cola products. Altria owns more than 25% of SABMiller and Colombia-based Santo Domingo Group almost 15%.

SABMiller owns more than 100 breweries and 40 bottling plants. It also produces at plants owned and operated through several strategic alliances and joint ventures. Production is organized among six regions: Latin America Europe North America Africa Asia/Pacific and South Africa. In fiscal 2012 (ends March) beverage and lager volumes increased 5% and more over the prior year. Beverages are marketed under local brands brews typically produced and consumed in their hometowns and global brands brews demonstrating worldwide appeal. Soft drinks volumes were up 8%. In addition to bottling products for The Coca-Cola Company it has hotel and gaming interests through Tsogo Sun Holdings South Africa's largest gaming group doing business as Gold Reef Resorts.

SABMiller has offices and facilities in more than 75 countries dotting Latin America Europe North America Africa the Asia/Pacific region and South Africa. Approximately 90% of its beverages are sold in markets in which it is the #1 or #2 beer maker. Africa led by South Africa accounted for more than one-third of the company's earnings before interest and taxes in 2012.

Despite the impact of the economic downturn on sales in North America and more so in Europe group sales have maintained a positive trajectory from fiscal 2007 through 2012 fueled by consumer demand in most developing regions notably the Asia/Pacific. Earnings which dipped slightly in 2009 from 2008 have since regained momentum soaring roughly 75% year-over-year in 2012 buoyed by selective price increase cost cuts and operating synergies from combined facilities as well as acquisitions.

The beer maker's strategy for growth includes targeted acquisitions international partnerships and a stream of brand introductions. SABMiller has concurrently boosted its customer base by broadening its geographic footprint including entering developing regions where bottled beverage consumption notably beer is accelerating as well as more mature markets where consumption is significant.

With an eye toward the future SABMiller pursued Australia's oldest and biggest brewer Foster's Group. Although its unsolicited takeover offer was rebuffed in fall 2011 SABMiller upped its bid to approximately $12.3 billion for Foster's following a three-month long frosty face-off during which the Miller beer-maker took its initial $9.5 million offer directly to shareholders. The acquisition –SABMiller's largest ever –closed late 2011 giving the company an approximate 50% share of the prized Australian beer market. (The acquisition is also the beer industry's biggest since AB InBev's $52 billion takeover of Anheuser-Busch in 2008.)

Africa is an equally significant market due to a hefty brewing and beverage presence in more than 15 African countries albeit largely South Africa and an additional 19 countries through an alliance with African beer maker Castel. Looking for a larger share of the local alcoholic beverage market SABMiller has eliminated most of its African cross-shareholdings with Diageo.

Meanwhile SABMiller has signaled the launch of Miller Genuine Draft into Kenya through the beverage business of Crown Foods a resident water and juice company acquired in partnership with Castel in late 2010. SABMiller also owns the leading water company in Uganda –Rwenzori; the move further strengthens the beer maker's local resources. In Uganda SABMiller has built a malt facility as well as opened new breweries in a number of other African countries.

Latin American consumers are SABMiller's second largest market generating more than 20% of sales. It has expanded its reach by purchasing local Argentine brewer CASA Isenbeck which has distribution extending into Paraguay southern Brazil and Uruguay. Entry the Argentine beer market represents SABMiller's most significant addition in Latin America a region dominated by Anheuser-Busch InBev. SABMiller's position in the region is also supported by bottling arrangements for Coke products in El Salvador and Honduras and Pepsi products in Panama for PepsiCo International.

The company's business in the US is perhaps the most challenging due to the presence of arch rival Anheuser-Busch (now part of the world's #1 brewer AB InBev). Taking market share away SABMiller formed MillerCoors with Molson Coors in 2008 adding the popular domestic labels Miller and Coors; imports including Molson Canadian and Pilsner Urquell; and craft brews such as Leinenkugel's and Blue Moon to its US offerings. (SABMiller acquired Miller Brewing in 2002.) The venture has proven a success for SABMiller: It is now the second-largest brewer in the US with a 30% market share.

Asia (comprising mainly China and India) may be SABMiller's smallest in terms of revenue but next to Africa the region is its fastest growing. The brewer produces the popular Snow beer brand through China Resources Snow Breweries a joint venture with China Resources Enterprise. SABMiller owns a 49% interest and China Resources 51%. To better compete with rival Tsingtao as well as build a national presence in China's still-fragmented beer industry Snow Breweries has been an active acquirer of regional Chinese breweries. Indeed in 2013 SABMiller and CR Snow agreed to acquire Kingway Brewery Holdings for $864 million. The deal would bolster CR Snow's position in Guangdong province.

HISTORY

British sailor Frederick Mead purchased the Castle Brewery in Johannesburg in 1892 about 15 years after gold was discovered in South Africa. Mead took his brewing operation public as South African Breweries (SAB) in 1895. The company launched its flagship Castle Lager three years later and survived the Anglo-Boer War (1899-1902) as South Africa's fastest-growing non-industrial firm. Mead died in 1915.

The brewer acquired the Grand Hotel in Cape Town in 1921 and a stake in Schweppes (carbonated drinks) in 1925. In the late 1940s SAB began an extensive expansion program involving its breweries small hotels and pubs. In 1951 it acquired the Hotel Victoria in Johannesburg. An increase in beer taxes during the 1950s led SAB to start producing liquors. With beer demand slackening South Africa's three largest brewers –SAB Ohlsson's and United Breweries –merged in 1956. The new company which took the SAB name controlled about 90% of the beer market. Beer taxes continued to pressure sales and in 1960 SAB acquired control of Stellenbosch Farmers' Winery to extend its product range. In 1962 the restriction prohibiting alcohol consumption by blacks was lifted opening an enormous market. SAB continued to extend its range of beer brands during the 1960s by adding licenses to brew Amstel and Carling Black Label.

Further diversifying SAB formed Barsab (an investment venture with Thomas Barlow & Sons) in 1966. The company launched its hotel division Southern Sun Hotels three years later by merging its hotels with those owned by the Sol Kerzner family. The Barsab venture was dissolved in 1973 leaving SAB with furniture and footwear businesses. The following year it acquired the South African bottling business of Pepsi (converted to Coca-Cola in 1977). The company added the beer interests of the Rembrandt Group and a 49% stake in Appletiser a fruit drinks company in 1979. (It gained control of it in 1982.)

SAB moved into apparel retailing with its purchase of the Scotts Stores (1981) and Edgars (1982). After forming a joint venture with Ceres Fruit Juices (1986) SAB made a number of investments in South Africa including Lion Match Company (1987) Da Gama Textiles (1989) and Plate Glass (1992).

In the 1990s the company expanded internationally. It acquired stakes in breweries in Hungary (1993) Tanzania and China (1994) and Poland and Romania (1996). Graham Mackay (now CEO) became managing director in 1996.

Before moving its main listing to the London Stock Exchange in 1999 SAB sold its Amalgamated Retail unit (furniture appliances) Lion Match Company and a large stake in Edgars. It then bought controlling interests in Czech brewers Pilsner Urquell and Radegast to become the largest brewer in Central Europe and sold its 68% interest in Plate Glass to Dibelco (a D'Ieteren and Copeba joint venture). Bevcon (a consortium of three South African companies) sold its 27% interest in SAB in 1999.

The continuing woes of the South African economy in 2000 fueled SAB's desire to continue expanding its international base. In 2001 SAB announced its China Resources Breweries Ltd joint venture in the Sichuan province of China. It also became the first international brewer with a presence in Central America spending more than $500 million on breweries in Honduras and El Salvador.

In 2002 SAB bought Miller Brewing from Philip Morris (now Altria Group) for $5.6 billion making it the world's second-largest brewer at the time. SAB then changed its name to SABMiller plc. SABMiller moved into Western Europe in 2003 with the $270 million purchase of Italian brewer Birra Peroni.

Similar to rival Anheuser-Busch SABMiller is particularly interested in growing its base in China which has the world's largest market for alcohol. SABMiller has invested heavily in China Resources Breweries. It had hoped to purchase control of the Harbin Brewery Group but was spurned by Anheuser-Busch which successfully outbid SABMiller for control of the brewery in 2004. Several months later SABMiller and China Resources Breweries purchased the Chinese brewing assets of Lion Nathan Limited.

In 2005 SABMiller acquired almost 97% of Bavaria S.A. the second-largest brewer in South America. Bavaria's brands include Aguila Atlas Cristal and Pilsener. In 2006 it announced a joint venture with Vietnam Dairy Products Joint Stock Company (Vinamilk) to establish a brewery in Vietnam. It also acquired citrus-flavored malt beverage Sparks and lager Steel Reserve from contract brewer McKenzie River Corporation for $215 million.

In an attempt to gain market share SABMiller formed MillerCoors with Molson Coors in 2008 adding the popular domestic labels Miller and Coors as well as imports including Molson Canadian and Pilsner Urquell and craft brews such as Leinenkugel's and Blue Moon to its US offerings.

In 2008 it acquired Dutch brewer Royal Grolsch for about $1.2 billion. That same year it entered the growing Ukrainian beer market with the purchase of CJSC Sarmat one of that country's largest brewers.

EXECUTIVES

Chairman and Managing Director SAB Ltd., Norman J. Adami, age 58, $323,375 total compensation
Executive Chairman, E.A. G. (Graham) Mackay, age 63, $2,283,244 total compensation
Chief Executive, Alan Clark, age 53
Deputy Chairman, John Manser, age 73
Director, Helen A. Weir, age 51
Director Human Resources and Supply Chain, Tony van Kralingen, age 55
CEO MillerCoors, Tom Long, age 54
Director Marketing, Nick Fell, age 59
CFO MillerCoors, Gavin Hattersley
Managing Director SABMiller Europe, Sue Clark, age 49
Corporate Affairs Director, Catherine May
SVP Investor Relations, Gary Leibowitz
Senior Manager Investor Relations Latin America, Katie Close
Group Treasurer, David Mallac
President Ursus Breweries, Andrew Highcock
President SABMiller Latin America, Karl Lippert, age 52
Managing Director SABMiller Africa, Mark J. Bowman, age 46
Group Company Secretary and General Counsel, John Davidson, age 54
CFO and Director, James (Jamie) Wilson, age 53
Managing Director SABMiller Asia Pacific and Chief Executive Officer Carlton and United Breweries, Ari Mervis, age 49
Business Media Relations Manager, Richard Farnsworth
Manager Corporate Media Relations, Bianca Shevlin
Senior Manager Investor Relations Europe, Richard Mather
Senior Manager Investor Relations South Africa and Asia, Henry Rudd
Senior Media Relations Executive, Alisa Charkova
Corporate Finance and Development Director, Domenic De Lorenzo, age 49
Group Chief Brewer, Katherine Smart
General Manager Royal Grolsch, Tom Verhaegen, age 40
Managing Director Asia, Harald Harvey
Vice President Global Industry Affairs, Kristin Wolfe
Director, Geoffrey C. (Geoff) Bible, age 75
CEO and Director, E.A. G. (Graham) Mackay, age 62
Director, Robert (Rob) Pieterse, age 69
Director, Mark H. Armour, age 58
Chief Executive, Alan Clark, age 53
Deputy Chairman, John Manser, age 73
Director, Helen A. Weir, age 51
Director, John A. Manzoni, age 53
Director, Dinyar S. Devitre, age 66
Director, Howard A. Willard III, age 50
Director, Lesley Knox, age 59
Director, Miles Morland, age 70
Director, M. Cyril Ramaphosa, age 60
Director, Carlos Alejandro Perez Davila, age 50
Director, Alejandro Santo Domingo Davila, age 36
CFO and Director, James (Jamie) Wilson, age 53
Director, Dambisa Moyo, age 44
Auditors: PricewaterhouseCoopersLLP

LOCATIONS

HQ: SABMiller Plc (United Kingdom)
One Stanhope Gate, London W1K 1AF
Phone: (44) 20 7659 0100 **Fax:** (44) 20 7659 0111
Web: www.sabmiller.com

2012 Brewing Operations

No. Breweries

Africa		
South Africa	7	
Other countries	32	
Europe	17	
Latin America	17	
Asia/Pacific	23	
North America	8	
Total	**0**	**104**

2012 Sales

	% of total
Africa	
South	20
Other	12
Latin	23
Europe	17
North	17
Asia/Pacific	11
Total	**100**

PRODUCTS/OPERATIONS

Selected Brands

- Beer
  - Africa
    - South AfricaAppletiserBrutal FruitCarling Black LabelCastle LiteCastle Milk StoutHansa PilsenerRedd'sSaritaSkelter's Straight
    - Other Africa2MBalimiBaron'sBohlinger'sCastleChairman'sChibukiClub LagerEagleFusionImpalaKilimanjaroLaurentinaLion LagerMalutiManicaMosiNdovuN'GOLANile SpecialRaizRwenzoriSafariSibebeStoneSt LouisTrophyTuskerVolticWhite BullZ
  - Asia/Pacific
    - Bluetongue
    - Bondi Blonde
    - Carlton Draught
    - Cascade
    - Crown Lager
    - Fat Yak
    - Foster's
    - Haywards 5000
    - Huadan Dry Beer
    - Indus Pride
    - Knock Out
    - Lowen
    - New Three Star
    - Pure Blonde
    - Royal Challenge
    - Shengquan
    - Singo
    - Snow
    - Victoria Bitter
    - Zero
    - Zorok
  - Europe
    - Amsterdam
    - Arany Aszok
    - Ciucas
    - Dbowe Mocne
    - Dorada
    - Dreher
    - Essa
    - Frisco
    - Gambrinus
    - Gingers
    - Gran Riserva
    - Grolsch
    - Kbanyai Sor
    - Kozel
    - Ksiazece Tyskie
    - Lech
    - Moya Kaluga
    - Peroni
    - Pilsner
    - Radegast
    - Raffo
    - Saris
    - Siroco
    - St Stefanus
    - Smadny Mnich
    - Stejar
    - Timisoreana
    - Topvar
    - Tri Bogatyrya Svetloye
    - Tropical
    - Tyskie
    - Ursus Premium
    - Velkopopovicky Kozel
    - Wojak
    - Wuhrer
    - Zolotaya Bochka
    - ubr
  - Global Brands
    - Grolsch
    - Miller Genuine Draft
    - Peroni Nastro Azzurro
    - Pilsner Urquell
  - Latin America
    - Aguila
    - Arequipe?a
    - Atlas
    - Balboa
    - Barena
    - Club
    - Conquer
    - Coste?a
    - Cristal
    - Cusque?a
    - Golden Light
    - Imperial
    - Isenbeck
    - Pilsen
    - Pilsener
    - Poker
    - Pony Malta
    - Port Royal
    - Regia Extra
    - Rhino
    - Salva Vida
    - San Juan
    - Suprema
  - North America (Miller Brewing Company and MillerCoors LLC joint venture)
    - Blue Moon
    - Coors
    - Hamm's
    - Henry Weinhard's
    - Icehouse
    - Keystone Light
    - Leinenkugel's
    - MGD 64
    - Mickey's
    - Miller
    - Miller Lite
    - Milwaukee's Best
    - Olde English
    - Steele Reserve
- Hotels and gaming (South Africa)
  - Tsogo Sung Group (39.7% shareholder)
    - Gold Reef Resorts Ltd.
- Soft drinks and juice
  - Appletiser (South Africa)
  - Coca-cola (licensed El Salvador Honduras Angola; South Africa and 20 other African markets)
  - Club (Ghana)
  - Malta Vigor (Panama)
  - Maltizz (Columbia)
  - Pepsi (licensed Panama)
  - Tropical (Honduras)
- Water
  - Ambo (Ethiopia)
  - Rwenzori (Uganda)
  - Voltic (Ghana Nigeria)

COMPETITORS

AmBev
Andina
Anheuser-Busch InBev
Asahi Breweries
Asia Pacific Breweries
Boston Beer
Brau Union
Carlsberg A/S
Constellation Brands
Cuauhtemoc Moctezuma
Danone Water
Diageo
E. & J. Gallo
FEMSA
Fuller' s
Grupo Modelo
Heineken
Kingway Brewery
Kirin Holdings Company
Nestle Waters
Pabst
PepsiCo
Pernod Ricard
Quinsa
San Miguel Corporation
Sapporo
Suntory Holdings
Tsingtao
UB Group

HISTORICAL FINANCIALS

Company Type: Public

Income Statement FYE: March 31

	REVENUE ($ mil.)	NET INCOME ($ mil.)	NET PROFIT MARGIN	EMPLOYEES
03/13	23,213	3,274	14.1%	70,486
03/12	21,760	4,221	19.4%	71,144
03/11	19,408	2,408	12.4%	69,212
03/10	18,020	1,910	10.6%	70,131
03/09	18,703	1,881	10.1%	68,635
Annual Growth	5.5%	14.9%	—	0.7%

2013 Year-End Financials

Debt ratio: 32.9%
Return on equity: 12.7%
Cash ($ mil.): 2,171
Current ratio: 0.67
Long-term debt ($ mil.): 16,079
No. of shares (mil.): 1,602
Dividends
Yield: 0.0%
Payout: 44.5%
Market value ($ mil.): 84,744

	STOCK PRICE ($) FY Close	P/E High/Low		PER SHARE ($) Earnings	Dividends	Book Value
03/13	52.89	26	18	2.04	0.91	16.46
03/12	40.49	16	12	2.64	0.79	15.75
03/11	35.79	23	18	1.52	0.67	13.87
03/10	29.21	25	12	1.22	0.54	12.03
03/09	14.75	21	10	1.25	0.53	9.70
Annual Growth	37.6%	—	—	13.0%	14.6%	14.1%

Safran S.A.

SAFRAN strives to keep civilians and military personnel safe in the air and on land. The company has returned to its aerospace roots while building up its defense and security segments. It restructured its operations to three divisions: Aerospace manufactures aircraft/rocket/space engines and propulsion systems for fixed wing as well as rotorcraft; Defense develops and builds navigation systems drones and optronics; and Security offers biometric identification and access control systems. SAFRAN's segments serve both the civilian and military sectors working alone or in partnership with other major companies. SAFRAN is a product of the Sagem and Snecma merger.

Reporting its results in four segments Safran split its Aerospace division into two segments Aerospace Propulsion and Aircraft Equipment. The largest of SAFRAN's segments is Aerospace Propulsion which accounts for more than half of overall sales. The segment's operations include an alliance with General Electric through CFM International a 50/50 joint venture contracted through 2040. CFM develops and markets the CFM56 turbofan engine for single-aisle commercial jets. In the military sector Aerospace Propulsion makes engines for combat training and transport aircraft. The segment also has made more than 50000 helicopter turbine engines for some 2200 customers in about 150 countries.

The Aircraft Equipment segment accounts for 26% of sales. The segment supplies engine nacelles and thrust reversers for the Airbus A380. It also provides landing systems for the A380 and the Airbus Military A400M the Boeing 787 Dreamliner and the Dassault Aviation Rafale. The segment's wheels and carbon brakes have been installed in more than 3500 planes used by some 300 airlines.

Defense 11% of sales provides inertial navigation systems for use on military transport and combat aircraft helicopters warships armored vehicles and other systems. The segment also provides products for digital combat including technology for vehicle digitization and encryption. Security 11% of sales offers multibiometric identification technologies that can identify persons through fingerprints iris face and vein recognition. It also offers explosive detection systems and smart cards. The segment's systems have been implemented in more than 100 countries.

Safran's revenue increased 9% in 2011 compared with 2010 thanks in part to lower costs and more demand from OEM and aftermarket customers in the aerospace market. Adjusted net income was up 27%. By segment revenue for Aerospace Propulsion rose 9% in 2011 compared with 2010 thanks in part to more demand for CFM and high-thrust engines and helicopter turbines from the civilian aftermarket. OEM customers also bought more CFM56 engines. Sales for Aircraft Equipment also went up 9% in 2011 vs. 2010 to meet more demand for nacelles wheels and brakes from OEMs and civil aerospace services.

Defense inched up 2% in 2011 compared with 2010. The segment enjoyed healthy demand for the Felin soldier integrated equipment suites from the French army and long-range infra-red goggles for export. Security surged about 20% over the same period. The segment did well with e-Documents in the Latin American telecommunications and banking markets and identification products in emerging countries.

The company's new Leading Edge Aviation Propulsion (LEAP) engine for single-aisle commercial jets intended as a replacement of the best-selling CFM56 engine received more than 3000 orders from Airbus Boeing and the Commercial Aircraft Corp. of China (Comac) in 2011 that will bring even more revenue down line through maintenance. Also in 2011 CFM International the Safran-GE joint venture received 1500 –a record number –orders for the CFM56 totaling about $52 billion from civilian and military customers. These orders are also expected to bring more revenue in the future through orders for spare parts and other maintenance services. To meet the challenge of fulfilling demand for the LEAP among other goals Safran hired 6000 new employees –half of them in France –in 2011 and stated plans to hire about as many in 2012.

In 2011 SAFRAN wrapped up its acquisition of US-based L-1 Identity Solutions for more than $1 billion and changed the company's name to MorphoTrust USA. The operating and holding company of MorphoTrust which specializes in biometrics and ID management joined SAFRAN's MorphoTrak security business. The deal positioned SAFRAN as the world's leader in providing biometric identity systems and services. (MorphoTrust's intelligence services group was picked up earlier by BAE SYSTEMS plc.) In 2009 SAFRAN acquired Motorola's biometric operations; the deal included Motorola's Printrak fingerprint identification system. Subsequently Printrak and Sagem Securite's subsidiary Sagem Morpho were united as MorphoTrak. The business offers biometric and identification management products and services to federal state and local governments and commercial markets.

The Aerospace Propulsion segment expanded in spring 2011 when SAFRAN acquired the propellants and explosives arm of SNPE SNPE Materiaux Energentiques (SME). The deal pockets SME its subsidiaries and a 50% stake in Roxel a maker of solid rocket motors and 40% stake in Regulus a maker of space launcher propellants. In 2012 SME's operations were merged with Snecma Propulsion Solide (a solid propellant rocket engine business of the Aerospace segment) to form a new subsidiary called Herakles one of the world's leading solid rocket propulsion providers.

The French government is SAFRAN's largest shareholder with a 30% stake.

HISTORY

The Societe d'Applications Generale d'Electricite et de Mecanique (Sagem) was founded in 1924 to make equipment and parts for the Michelin tire company. After WWII the company developed military electronics including navigation and attack systems for the French navy's Super Etendard fighter plane.

As Sagem expanded its heavy manufacturing offerings including automotive and coal mining equipment the company continued to design military electronics. By the mid-1980s it was one of Europe's top military suppliers. Employees led a leveraged buyout of the company in 1985.

In 1991 the French secret service discovered that Sagem had sold guidance systems to Iraq that were used in Scud missiles fired at coalition troops and Israel during the Persian Gulf War. After the uproar subsided Sagem orchestrated another big military deal in 1995 when it sold 34 unmanned Sparrow Hawk reconnaissance planes to the Netherlands. Three years later the company streamlined its defense operations by reabsorbing its 75%-owned SAT subsidiary which specialized in military communications.

In 1999 Sagem rolled out its wireless Internet mobile phones to rave reviews. In 2000 it won a $330 million contract to develop 750 missile guidance systems for the French Ministry of Defense.

Early in 2001 the company's longtime chairman and CEO Pierre Faurre died unexpectedly forcing Sagem to reorganize its management structure. The board of directors became the supervisory board headed by Sagem CFO Mario Colaiacovo. Alcatel executive Gregoire Olivier was named chairman of the executive board and CEO.

However in the years to come the management structure was due to change even further. In late 2004 Sagem acquired France-based aircraft engine maker Snecma (hoping to expand its aerospace product offerings). Shortly after the company rebranded itself as SAFRAN a French word for the rudder blade on a boat; the newly merged company hoped this new moniker would reflect its ambition for movement strategy and direction. After the merger all the group's subsidiaries located in over 30 countries worldwide maintained their names.

The company decided to get out of the communications business. Early in 2008 it sold Sagem Communications which provided broadband services to The Gores Group a US-based private equity firm. Shortly after SAFRAN sold its Sagem Mobiles operation (mobile phone manufacturing) to French venture capital firm Sofinnova. SAFRAN retained a 10% equity stake in the business which was renamed Sagem Wireless.

In 2008 SAFRAN formed a joint venture with GE to build nacelles for single-aisle aircraft. The new company combined SAFRAN's Aircelle subsidiary and GE's Middle River Aircraft Systems subsidiary. Both subsidiaries had complementary operations and focused on thrust reversers fan cowls acoustic treatment and thermal protection products among other aspects of engine nacelles.

Also in 2008 SAFRAN acquired Sdu Identification which developed secure ID documents from investment firms AAC Capital Partners and Advantage Capital Partners.

Addressing defense on a more domestic level SAFRAN has been working to expand the scope of its Security unit's products. In 2009 SAFRAN acquired an 81% majority stake in GE Homeland Protection which makes explosives and narcotics detection equipment for about $580 million; GE retained a 19% share in the unit.

SAFRAN sold its Cinch Connectors business to Bel Fuse in 2010 for about $39 million. Cinch made a wide range of interconnect devices for aerospace communications computing military and transportation applications.

EXECUTIVES

EVP Strategy and Development, Jean-Pierre Cojan, age 59
Chairman and CEO, Jean-Paul Herteman
EVP Operations, Marc Ventre
EVP International, Bruno Cotte
EVP Social Legal and Institutional Affairs, Dominique-Jean Chertier
EVP Economic and Financial Affairs, Ross McInnes, age 59
Board Member, Michel Toussan
Board Member, Bernard Vatier
Board Member, Jean-Marc Forneri, age 54
Board Member, Christophe Burg
Board Member, Shemaya Levy, age 67
Board Member, Francois Polge de Combret
Board Member, Yves Guena
Board Member, Christian Halary
Board Member, Michele Monavon
Board Member, Jean-Bernard Pene
Board Member, Jean Rannou
Board Member, Armand Dupuy
Board Member, Patrick Gandil
Board Member, Pierre Aubouin
Auditors: ConstantinAssocies

LOCATIONS

HQ: Safran S.A.
2, boulevard du General Martial-Valin, Paris, Cedex 15 75724
Phone: (33) 1 40 60 80 80 **Fax:** (33) 1 40 60 81 02
Web: www.safran-group.com

Selected Subsidiaries

Heracles (aerospace propulsion)
Hispano-Suiza (aircraft equipment)
Labinal (aircraft equipment)
Messier-Bugatti-Dowty (aircraft equipment)
Microturbo (aerospace propulsion)
Morpho (defense/security)
Sagem (defense/security)
Snecma (aerospace propulsion)
Techspace Aero (aerospace propulsion)
Turbomeca (aerospace propulsion)

PRODUCTS/OPERATIONS

2011 Sales

	% of total
Aerospace	52
Aircraft	26
Defense	11
Security	11
Total	**100**

Selected Products

- Aerospace
  - Aerospace Propulsion
    - Ballistic missiles & space
    - Civil aviation
    - Helicopter engines
    - Military aviation
  - Aircraft Equipment
    - Electrical systems & engineering
    - Engine systems
    - Landing systems
- Defense (air land and sea)
  - Helicopter flight controls
  - Inertial navigation
  - Optronic systems
  - Tactical Drones
- Security
  - Automated Fingerprint Identification Systems

Biometric ID documents
Explosive detection systems
Gaming terminals
Identification systems
Multibiometric technology
Smart cards
Trace detection equipment

COMPETITORS

BAE Systems Inc.
Boeing
Elbit Systems
GE Aviation
General Dynamics
Goodrich Corp.
Honeywell International
Lockheed Martin
Pratt & Whitney
Rockwell Collins
Rolls-Royce
Siemens AG
United Technologies

HISTORICAL FINANCIALS

Company Type: Public

Income Statement FYE: December 31

	REVENUE ($ mil.)	NET INCOME ($ mil.)	NET PROFIT MARGIN	EMPLOYEES
12/12	19,515	1,716	8.8%	62,558
12/11	16,000	618	3.9%	59,805
12/10	15,294	277	1.8%	54,256
12/09	15,398	923	6.0%	54,872
12/08	15,353	(286)	—	54,493
Annual Growth	6.2%	—	—	3.5%

2012 Year-End Financials

Debt ratio: 18.2%
Return on equity: 23.5%
Cash ($ mil.): 2,890
Current ratio: 1.13
Long-term debt ($ mil.): 2,977
No. of shares (mil.): 415
Dividends
Yield: 8.0%
Payout: 35.6%
Market value ($ mil.): 17,988

	STOCK PRICE ($) FY Close	P/E High/Low	PER SHARE ($) Earnings	Dividends	Book Value
12/12	43.25	24 16	4.13	0.87	19.21
12/11	30.20	68 40	1.53	1.92	15.70
12/10	31.45	119 67	0.68	0.76	15.17
12/09	18.20	26 24	2.30	0.48	15.69
12/08	19.00	— —	(0.71)	1.10	13.07
Annual Growth	22.8%	— —	—	(5.7%)	10.1%

SAIC Motor Corp Ltd

LOCATIONS

HQ: SAIC Motor Corp Ltd
No. 489, Weihai Road, Jingan District, Shanghai 200041
Phone: (86) 21 22011138 **Fax:** (86) 21 22011199
Web: www.saicmotor.com

HISTORICAL FINANCIALS

Company Type: Public

Income Statement FYE: December 31

	REVENUE ($ mil.)	NET INCOME ($ mil.)	NET PROFIT MARGIN	EMPLOYEES
12/12	77,151	3,328	4.3%	0
12/11	69,077	3,212	4.7%	5,379
12/10	47,541	2,082	4.4%	5,536
12/09	20,450	965	4.7%	4,373
12/08	15,518	96	0.6%	4,173
Annual Growth	49.3%	142.6%	—	—

2012 Year-End Financials

Debt ratio: 0.3%
Return on equity: 18.4%
Cash ($ mil.): 9,760
Current ratio: 1.21
Long-term debt ($ mil.): 151
No. of shares (mil.): —
Dividends
Yield: —
Payout: —
Market value ($ mil.): —

Saipem S.p.A.

Saipem doesn't mind being in deep water or in a lonely desert. The Milan-based company provides construction and drilling services to oil and gas companies worldwide. It is organized into major two business units: Engineering and Construction (which generates the bulk of its revenues) and Drilling. To help oil and gas companies with field development the company installs fixed platforms and floating production systems. Saipem is a leader in providing engineering procurement project management and construction services with a bias toward large scale offshore and onshore projects. The company has three major drilling vessels 10 offshore rigs and a construction fleet of about 40 units.

The company has strategically focused on providing oil and gas exploration and production and related construction activities in remote land areas and in deepwater locations. It conducts offshore drilling and cosntruction activities off the coasts of northern Europe West Africa and northern India. Saipem's onshore activities are primarily in Algeria Egypt India Italy Kazakhstan Nigeria Peru Russia Saudi Arabia and Venezuela.

To expand further into deepwater exploration the company has invested $1 billion to strengthen its position in the market. Saipem is also building new towers on its barges that will allow it to lay pipeline in deeper waters and has invested in state-of-the-art drilling units including an ultra-deepwater rig (Saipem 10000) that can drill to a depth of 10000 ft.

In 2008 Sonatrach awarded Saipem an onshore contract worth more than $1 billion to build an LPG processing plant at the Hassi Messaoud oil and gas complex in central Algeria. In 2009 among its several new contracts the company won a $1 billion award for offshore drilling in Kazakhstan.

The company saw its revenues pick up in 2010 as the global economy rebounded and demand for oil increased and oil prices rose. Saipem reported a 33% rise in offshore revenues thanks to higher fleet use and new rigs commencing operations. Offshore revenues grew by 24% thanks to rigs coming online in South America and the Congo and to the upgrade of two rigs working in Kazakhstan.

Responding to the increased demand for oil and gas infrastructure in 2011 Saipem was awarded contracts worth more than $3.2 billion for offshore engineering and construction work in Saudi Arabia(for EPIC) China (for Husky Oil)and Brazil (for PETROBRAS).

Saipem is 43%-owned by Italian energy giant Eni.

HISTORY

Saipem has been operating as part of energy giant Eni since 1953 when the Italian government formed Ente Nazionale Idrocarburi (National Hydrocarbon Agency or Eni). Eni's mission was to reduce Italy's dependence on international energy companies and sources. The agency began to emphasize oil field services and engineering activities in the late 1950s primarily through Saipem and its subsidiaries.

The company was incorporated in 1969 as an international contractor offering a full range of services (including subsea pipelaying platform installation and drilling services) to the oil and gas industry. Saipem was first listed on the Milan stock exchange in 1984 and on the Paris stock exchange a year later.

As part of the Italian government's strategy to privatize its state industries during the 1990s Eni became a joint stock company in 1992 with the government retaining a majority stake. During 1998 and 1999 Eni cut its holding in Saipem to 43%. In 2000 Saipem appointed Pietro Franco Tali a former Saipem CFO as chairman and CEO.

Delays in the development of large oil and gas fields in deep waters off of Brazil the Gulf of Mexico and West Africa caused a drop in Saipem's 2000 revenues despite robust oil prices.

In 2001 the company secured two contracts in Saudi Arabia (including the conversion of an oil pipeline into a gas pipeline for Saudi Aramco) worth $180 million.That year it also started construction on a major Turkish gas pipeline.

Saipem bought a 51% stake in French oil field construction contractor Bouygues Offshore in 2002. Later that year the company increased its stake to 96.8%. In 2003 Saipem acquired International Development Process and Engineering which was previously set to be acquired by Bouygues Offshore.

EXECUTIVES

COO Offshore Business Unit, Yves Inbona
Chairman, Marco Mangiagalli, age 63
Deputy CEO and Director, Hugh J. (James) O'Donnell, age 61
CFO and Company Affairs, Giulio Bozzini
Human Resources and Organization, D. Gallinari
Multi Business Engineering, G. Franco
Legal Affairs, P. Galizzi
Internal Audit, A. Riva
Quality Health Safety and Environment, S. de Sanctis
Procurement, P. Daleffe
Risk Opportunity and Knowledge Management, A. Gebbia
Integrated Projects, S. Bianchi
COO Onshore Business Unit, P. Varone
COO Drilling Business Unit, G. Caselli
Chief Executive Officer, Hugh ODonnell
Vice President Investor Relations, Salvatore Colli
Director, Pierantonio Nebuloni, age 60
Deputy Chairman and CEO, Pietro Franco Tali, age 63
Deputy CEO and Director, Hugh J. (James) O'Donnell, age 61
Director, Salvatore Sardo, age 61
Director, Ian Wybrew-Bond, age 71
Director, Anna Maria Artoni
Director, Luca Anderlini
Auditors: PricewaterhouseCoopersSpA

LOCATIONS

HQ: Saipem S.p.A.
Via Martiri di Cefalonia 67, San Donato Milanese, MI I-20097
Phone: (39) 02 5201 **Fax:** (39) 02 52054295
Web: www.saipem.it

2010 Sales

	% of total
Africa	
West	24
North	23
Asia	
CIS	11
Other	18
Europe	
Italy	7
Other	10
Americas	6
Other	1
Total	**100**

PRODUCTS/OPERATIONS

2010 Sales

	% of total
Onshore	48
Offshore	40
Offshore	7
Onshore	5
Total	**100**

Selected Subsidiaries

Intermare Sarda S.p.A.
Saipem Energy International S.p.A.
Saipem FPSO S.p.A
Saipem s.a
Saipem International B.V.

COMPETITORS

ASCO
Diamond Offshore
Halliburton
Hyundai Engineering and Construction
McDermott
Noble
Oceaneering International
Pride International
Schlumberger
Subsea 7
Technip
Tidewater Inc.
Transocean

HISTORICAL FINANCIALS

Company Type: Public

Income Statement

FYE: December 31

	REVENUE ($ mil.)	NET INCOME ($ mil.)	NET PROFIT MARGIN	EMPLOYEES
12/12	17,643	1,188	6.7%	42,554
12/11	16,337	1,191	7.3%	40,388
12/10	14,958	1,129	7.6%	38,428
12/09	14,865	1,054	7.1%	36,224
12/08	14,173	1,277	9.0%	34,493
Annual Growth	5.6%	(1.8%)	—	5.4%

2012 Year-End Financials

Debt ratio: 43.5%
Return on equity: 17.7%
Cash ($ mil.): 1,746
Current ratio: 1.03
Long-term debt ($ mil.): 4,669
No. of shares (mil.): 439
Dividends
Yield: 1.5%
Payout: 19.1%
Market value ($ mil.): 8,569

	STOCK PRICE ($) FY Close	P/E High/Low		PER SHARE ($) Earnings	Dividends	Book Value
12/12	19.50	22	15	2.70	0.31	16.21
12/11	21.15	26	13	2.70	0.55	13.90
12/10	24.60	23	12	2.57	0.22	12.41
12/09	17.50	22	19	2.39	0.00	11.21
Annual Growth	3.7%	—	—	3.1%	—	9.7%

Samsung Electronics Co., Ltd.

Samsung Electronics is an electronics Samson. One of the world's largest semiconductor manufacturers Samsung Electronics is also South Korea's top electronics company. It makes many kinds of consumer devices including DVD players digital TVs and digital still cameras; computers color monitors LCD panels and printers; semiconductors such as DRAMs static RAMs flash memory and display drivers; and communications devices ranging from wireless handsets and smartphones to networking gear. The company which is the flagship member of Samsung Group also makes microwave ovens refrigerators air conditioners and washing machines. Nearly half of sales come from the Asia/Pacific region.

The company operates through business units that operate independently: Visual Display Mobile Communications Telecommunications Systems Digital Appliances IT Solutions Digital Imaging Memory System LSI (mobile application processors and CMOS image processors) and LCD. Over the long term Samsung Electronics is looking to grow in key product areas including mobile devices (phones and tablets) LCD panels flat-panel TVs system LSI chips IT products and home appliances. It is also promoting future growth centered around software and service opportunities while continuing to lay the foundation for future businesses particularly in the solar cell and health and medical equipment markets.

LCD technology is gradually being replaced by the similar but competing OLED (organic light-emitting diode) technology. Although OLED has some of the drawbacks of LCD (e.g. narrower viewing angle than plasma) it also offers improvements such as lower power consumption deeper black levels thinner and lighter panels and are cheaper to produce. In light of that in 2012 the LCD business was spun off as a subsidiary (Samsung Display Co. Ltd.) of Samsung Electronics. The spin-off is meant to give its display business better traction with more focused strategy faster decision-making and investment and fortified technological competitiveness. With those objectives in mind it will also consider combining it with its Samsung Mobile Display operations which works on OLED displays and the S-LCD joint venture it recently agreed to acquire from Sony. Samsung will also shift its stake in the Samsung Corning Precision Materials joint venture with Corning to the new subsidiary.

Samsung Electronics' reported record overall sales and net income in 2010. The company's three primary strategies for 2011 are to solidify its market leadership by focusing on product differentiation in each business unit; identify businesses that will sustain growth over the next five to ten years; and prepare management to anticipate and respond to business risks during times of global market uncertainty. Certain businesses such as telecommunications and semiconductor products continued to see strong growth rates in 2011 while others experienced slower demand over the course of the year.

Sales of the company's mobile phone product line rose by 23% in 2010 over 2009. One strategy employed by Samsung Electronics —that of supporting products with software and services —has paid off in increased sales and market share for its smartphones and tablet PCs. The company has focused on more than simply increasing sales of its flagship Galaxy S smartphone models and GALAXY Tab tablets (both based on the Android operating system). Supporting the phones with content Samsung Apps —its mobile and TV applications store —reached 100 million downloads in early 2011; the app store opened in mid-2010. The content includes more than 13000 applications and services tailored to meet local needs in 120 countries. By adding content and services to its smart mobile devices Samsung Electronics is taking direct aim at Apple's market dominance.

In addition Samsung Electronics is a leader in producing many of the chips at the heart of its products. The company has been the leader in the worldwide memory market for more than a decade and has a significant share of the global market for CMOS image sensors for mobile phones. Its Green Memory strategy revolves around developing memory products that use less power considered essential to powering smart mobile devices.

Looking to increase its share of the fast-growing e-reader market in 2011 Samsung Electronics bought Netherlands-based Liquavista. The company has developed a new type of display technology called electrowetting which has a faster response time and uses less battery power than existing displays used in e-readers mobile phones media players and similar mobile devices. It can also be manufactured by modifying LCD production lines rather than requiring new equipment providing cost-savings in the manufacturing process.

While tending to its industry-leading memory chip business Samsung Electronics has spent millions on boosting production of system LSI semiconductors. The move puts Samsung deeper into the silicon foundry business where companies with silicon wafer fabrication plants make chips on a contract basis for chip firms without fabs. Samsung has a major contract to make chips for QUALCOMM the giant designer of semiconductors for cell phones and other mobile electronics which is a fabless company.

With Fujitsu Fujitsu Semiconductor NEC Panasonic Mobile Communications and NTT DoCoMo the company attempted to establish a joint venture that would develop and market semiconductor products for mobile devices but abandoned it after being unable to come to an agreement over details by the deadline in 2012.

Samsung Electronics has formed a number of alliances with other high-tech titans. A partnership with IBM Microelectronics allows Samsung to share chip-making technology with the computing giant and its S-LCD Corp. joint venture with Sony produces large LCD television screens. In 2011 Samsung agreed to pay Sony about $935 million for its stake in the S-LCD joint venture which was formed to ensure a steady supply of flat screens for Sony. The deal came after an earlier announcement (in 2011) that S-LCD would reduce its capital structure by $555 million. Sony is facing its seventh straight year of losses in its TV business as well as shrinking demand for LCDs as the more energy-efficient organic light-emitting diode (OLED) displays begin to take hold. After Sony divests its stake in S-LCD it will form a new partnership with Samsung Electronics to buy flat screens. For its part Samsung Electronics continues to invest in both LCD and OLED technology.

Samsung Electronics is also ridding itself of operations considered non-core. In 2011 Samsung Electronics sold its disk drive business to Seagate for about $1.4 billion in cash and stock. The deal gave Samsung Electronics a nearly 10% stake in Seagate and a spot on the company's board. As part of the transaction Seagate will supply Samsung Electronics with disk drives for its consumer electronics products while Samsung Electronics will provide Seagate with flash memory chips for storage devices. The two companies have teamed up before. In 2009 they began to jointly develop solid-state drives (SSDs) which are faster and more energy efficient than hard-disk drives and have become the storage technology of choice for mobile devices such as tablets netbooks and smartphones.

Conversely Samsung Electronics is investing in industries it isn't traditionally known for. In 2011 the company bought the Nexus division of cardiac point-of-care testing products company ITC Nexus Holding. Earlier in the year Samsung bought diagnostic ultrasound manufacturer Medison. These purchases are part of the company's goal to inject 1.2 trillion won (about $1 billion) into its strategy to grow as a healthcare technology player.

Samsung Electronics settled a memory chip price-fixing complaint brought by the European Commission in 2010 agreeing to pay a penalty of E145.7 million (about $180 million). The case was concluded under the regulatory body's fast-track settlement procedures which allow members of alleged cartels to settle complaints with a 10% discount on their fines.

In a case with potentially wide-ranging implications in August 2012 Samsung Electronics lost a patent infringement lawsuit with Apple in an ongoing copyright battle between the two. Samsung was found to have violated several Apple patents including the "bounce back" effect and the physical design of the iPhone but argued that the design similarities were not copying but benchmarking (a practice used by companies to keep up with rivals on details such as battery life screen size and other core features). Apple was awarded $1 billion in damages (the company originally sought $2.75 billion) but Samsung plans to appeal. The verdict is complicated by a decision the same week in a South Korean court that each company had infringed on the others' patents that resulted in bans and fines for both parties. Samsung continues to be nonetheless a major supplier of components for Apple products including the iPhone.

EXECUTIVES

Chairman, Yoon-Woo Lee, age 67
Vice Chairman and CEO, Oh-Hyun Kwon
Vice Chairman and CEO, Gee-Sung Choi, age 61
President of Samsung Telecommunications America STA, Dale Sohn
CFO, Sang-Hoon Lee, age 58
President Samsung Austin Semiconductor, Woosung Han
President and CEO Samsung Electronics North America, Yangkyu Y.K. Kim
President and CEO Samsung Semiconductor Inc., Charlie Bae
President and CEO Samsung Telecommunications America, Gregory Lee
Director, In-Ho Lee, age 69
Vice Chairman and CEO, Gee-Sung Choi, age 61
CFO and Director, Ju-Hwa Yoon, age 60
Director, Chae-Woong Lee, age 71
Director, Oh-Soo Park, age 60
Auditors: SamilPricewaterhousecoopers

LOCATIONS

HQ: Samsung Electronics Co., Ltd.
416, Metan 3-dong, Yeongtong-gu, Suwon, Kyeonggi-do 443-742
Phone: (82) 31 200 1114 **Fax:** (82) 31 200 7538
Web: www.samsung.com

2010 Sales

	% of total
Asia/Pacific	
South	17
China	16
Other	16
America	28
Europe	23
Total	**100**

PRODUCTS/OPERATIONS

2010 Sales

	% of total
Digital	37
Telecom	27
Semiconductor	24
LCD	19
Others (7)	
Total	**100**

Selected Products

Computers and Peripherals
- All-in-One PCs
- Hard disk drives
- Monitors
- Notebook PCs
- Personal digital assistants
- Printers
- Servers
- Storage
- Tablet PCs

Consumer Electronics
- Blu-ray Disc players
- Digital cameras and camcorders
- DVD players/recorders
- Portable audio devices
- TVs (analog and digital)

Home Appliances
- Air conditioners
- Gas ovens and ranges
- Microwave ovens
- LED lighting
- Refrigerators
- Washing machines

Networking Equipment
- Ethernet hardware
- Fiber-optic cable and hardware
- Modems (cable and DSL)
- Multiplexers
- Switches
- Transceivers

Semiconductors
- Application-specific integrated circuits (ASICs)
- Communications chips (baseband and radio-frequency)
- Memory
  - DRAMs
  - Electrically erasable programmable read-only memories (EEPROMs)
  - Flash memories
  - Mask ROMs
  - SRAMs
- Microcontrollers
- Smart card ICs

Telecommunications
- Enterprise communications systems
- Internet-based phones and systems
- Mobile phones
- Smartphones
- Wireless communications infrastructure

COMPETITORS

AMD
AU Optronics
Apple Inc.
Canon
Chimei Innolux
Cisco Systems
Corning
Dalian Daxian
Elpida Memory
Ericsson
Fujitsu
HTC Corporation
Hewlett-Packard
Hitachi
IBM
Infineon Technologies
Intel
JDS Uniphase
Kyocera
LG Display
LG Electronics
Lenovo
Micron Technology
Mitsubishi Electric
Motorola Solutions
NEC
Nokia
Nortel Networks
Panasonic Corp
Philips Electronics
QUALCOMM
SANYO
SK Hynix
Sharp Corp.
Silicon Valley Analog
Sony
Sony Mobile
Spansion
Toshiba
Truly International

HISTORICAL FINANCIALS

Company Type: Public

Income Statement

FYE: December 31

	REVENUE ($ mil.)	NET INCOME ($ mil.)	NET PROFIT MARGIN	EMPLOYEES
12/12	188,351	21,715	11.5%	90,700
12/11	142,403	11,529	8.1%	101,970
12/10	137,905	14,090	10.2%	95,659
12/09*	117,820	8,272	7.0%	85,085
01/09	0	0	—	0
Annual Growth	—	—	—	—

*Fiscal year change

2012 Year-End Financials

Debt ratio: 0.0%
Return on equity: 21.5%
Cash ($ mil.): 17,599
Current ratio: 1.86
Long-term debt ($ mil.): 5,106
No. of shares (mil.): 130
Dividends
Yield: —
Payout: —
Market value ($ mil.): 176,645

	STOCK PRICE ($) FY Close	P/E High	P/E Low	PER SHARE ($) Earnings	Dividends	Book Value
12/12	1,350.00	—	—	144.19	0.00	838.14
12/11	835.00	—	—	76.80	0.00	646.02
12/10	660.00	—	—	94.24	0.00	587.88
12/09*	655.80	—	—	55.82	0.00	(0.00)
01/09	626.41	—	—	(0.00)	0.00	(0.00)
Annual Growth	21.2%	—	—	—	—	—

*Fiscal year change

San Miguel Corp

A household name because of its brewery biz San Miguel Corporation (SMC) is one of the largest food-to-power conglomerates in the Philippines. It operates more than 100 facilities in Southeast Asia and China. The company's flagship unit is San Miguel Brewery (beer and liquor) while its Pure Food unit manufactures a variety of staples including meats dairy products and coffee. SMC also has packaging operations. It owns a major stake in the country's biggest oil refiner Petron a 33% interest in Manila Electric and a joint venture with Qatar Telecom that operates mobile and broadband businesses in the Philippines. SMC has other investments in energy telecommunications mining construction and banking.

SMC's operations consist of five units: Beverages includes five domestic breweries and one each in Indonesia Vietnam Thailand and two in China and two distillers (mostly gin). The unit claims 90% of the Philippine beer market but also produces ready-to-drink tea and juices. It generated 16% and 30% of SMC's 2011 sales and operating profits respectively.

Food San Miguel Pure Foods and subsidiaries comprises manufacture of national food brands Magnolia Monterey and Pure Foods among several supported by partnerships with international companies such as Hormel Foods. The unit represented 16% of sales and 11% of operating profits.

Packaging includes a handful of domestic plants plus 10 foreign plants dotting Southeast Asia. Facilities make glass and polyethylene terephthalate (PET) plastic paper and metal containers for SMC as well as local manufacturers of food pharmaceutical chemical beverages and personal care products. The unit drove 4% of sales and 5% of operating profits.

SMC's Power segment representing 13% and 31% of sales and operating profits respectively consists of the Philippines biggest electricity producer. The unit owns three power plants (coal-fired hydro-electric and one natural gas-fired) and three coal mining companies.

SMC owns some 68% of Petron. The country's largest refiner of crude oil and marketer and distributor of refined petroleum products accounted for 50% of SMC's sales and 24% of its operating profits.

Geographically SMC's activities are concentrated in the Philippines. In 2011 international business represented about 5% of consolidated sales and a deficit 2% of SMC's earnings.

In fiscal 2011 (ends December) SMC reported an 18% increase in net income (calculated in local currency) on sales that more than doubled over the prior year. Results reflected sales and operating income growth across the company's business segments coupled with a more than 60% contribution in sales from acquired power and fuel and oil businesses. Earnings' momentum was hampered by both higher selling and administrative expenses and financing charges.

Strategically SMC is in the process of further diversifying into heavy industry banking infrastructure telecommunications and energy (power fuel and oil). It is doing so in order to improve profitability stating that businesses in those markets will provide even greater returns than those from the food and beverage markets it already dominates.

In spring 2012 SMC acquired a 49% interest in Philippine Airlines and its affiliate budget carrier. During 2009 through 2011 SMC snapped up coal mines toll road projects and power plants. It also purchased stakes in three telecommunications businesses and a bank as well as a 93% stake in Trans Aire Development Holdings (formerly known as Caticlan International Airport) and in Indophil Resources which owns an indirect interest in the Tampakan gold and copper mine in southern Philippines.

In order to fund such acquisition efforts in 2009 SMC sold 48% of its San Miguel Brewery to Japan's Kirin for a whopping $1.2 billion. SMC is likely to try to sell other beverage food and packaging assets as well.

SMC's largest shareholder is investment firm Top Frontier Investment Holdings which owns more than half of the company's common stock. A group of 44 companies associated with chairman Eduardo Cojuangco owns roughly 20%.

HISTORY

Don Enrique Barretto y de Ycaza opened La Fabrica de Cerveza de San Miguel a brewery in Manila in 1890. By 1900 the European-styled beers of San Miguel were outselling imported brands five to one. The company became a corporation in 1913. By WWI the brewery was selling beer in Hong Kong Shanghai and Guam.

Andres Soriano y Roxas joined San Miguel in 1918 and in the 1920s established the Royal Soft Drinks Plant (1922) the Magnolia Ice Cream Plant (1925) and the first non-US national Coca-Cola bottling and distribution franchise (1927). After WWII the company added additional facilities and factories as it modernized and expanded.

In the 1960s the firm changed its name to San Miguel Corporation (SMC). After the death of Andres in 1964 his son Andres Soriano Jr. became president. He decentralized operations into product segments. SMC continued to diversify in the 1970s.

A family feud erupted in 1983 when members of the controlling Soriano and Zobel families engaged in a proxy battle. Realizing he couldn't win the proxy fight Enrique Zobel sold all of his shares (about 20% of SMC) to Eduardo Cojuangco a Ferdinand Marcos ally and president of United Coconut Planters Bank. Upon Soriano's death in 1984 Cojuangco became chairman.

Cojuangco's estranged cousin Corazon Aquino won the 1986 national election and her government claimed assets associated with Marcos and his followers including Cojuangco's share of SMC. Cojuangco left the country with Marcos and Andres Soriano III became CEO. Cojuangco returned to the Philippines in 1989 to reclaim his share of the company. In mid-1998 immediately following Cojuangco-backed Joseph Estrada's election as president of the Philippines Andres Soriano III stepped down and Cojuangco returned to SMC's helm.

SMC sold Coca-Cola Bottlers Philippines to Sydney-based Coca-Cola Amatil (CCA) in 1995 in exchange for a 25% stake in CCA. Four years later SMC flirted with plans to sell its interest in CCA and then went on a buying binge. SMC and a company it majority owns La Tonde?a Distillers jointly bought Filipino juice maker Sugarland. SMC then bought Australian brewer J. Boag & Son in 2000.

Estrada announced the government's plan to sell a 27% stake in SMC but those plans were altered dramatically after Estrada's ouster in early 2001. His successor President Gloria Arroyo said the government would seize 47% of the company's shares controlled by United Coconut Planters Bank (27%) and Cojuangco (20%).

Meanwhile company expansion continued. San Miguel agreed to buy the Philippines' largest processed-meat maker Pure Foods. The company bought 65% of bottler Coca-Coca Philippines from CCA in July giving up its stake in CCA as part of the deal. In August 2001 SMC then acquired 83% of rival RFM's Cosmos Bottling the Philippines' #2 soft drink company further consolidating its domestic beverage dominance. In September the company transferred its 49% stake in Sugarland to La Tonde?a Distillers which then became the sole owner of the juice maker.

In 2002 Japanese brewer Kirin paid $530 million for 15% of San Miguel. Following an announced expansion plan into Asia San Miguel purchased a Thailand industrial complex for $20 million in September 2003 and Thai Amarit Brewery in April 2004. SMC snapped up a majority stake in Singapore-based ice-cream producer King's Creameries the following year and acquired control of Australia's National Foods for $1.45 billion.

In 2007 it sold its 65% stake in Coca-Cola Bottlers Philippines to The Coca-Cola Company which had previously owned 35% of the Philippine bottler. The deal was worth $590 million. SMC also sold National Foods a leading supplier of milk cheese and other dairy products in Australia to Kirin Holdings for about $2.6 billion in 2007.

EXECUTIVES

Vice Chairman President and COO, Ramon S. Ang, age 60
Chairman and CEO, Eduardo M. (Danding) Cojuangco Jr., age 78
CFO Treasurer and Director, Ferdinand K. Constantino, age 62
VP Corporate Affairs Office, Ramon A. Santiago
President Petron Corporation and Director, Eric O. Recto, age 50
Vice Chairman President and COO, Ramon S. Ang, age 60
Director, Roberto V. Ongpin, age 76
CFO Treasurer and Director, Ferdinand K. Constantino, age 62
President Petron Corporation and Director, Eric O. Recto, age 50
Director, Winston F. Garcia, age 55
Director, Joselito D. Campos Jr.
Director, Estelito P. Mendoza, age 83
Director, I?igo Zobel, age 57
Director, Menardo R. Jimenez, age 81
Director, Leo S. Alvez, age 71
Director, Hector L. Hofile?a
Director, Carmelo L. Santiago, age 70
Director, Alexander J. Poblador
Director, Reynato S. Puno
Auditors: ManabatSanagustin&Co.

LOCATIONS

HQ: San Miguel Corp
40 San Miguel Avenue, Mandaluyong City, Metro Manila 1550
Phone: (63) 2 632 3000 **Fax:** (63) 2 632 3099
Web: www.sanmiguel.com.ph

2011 Sales

	% of total
Philippines	95
Indonesia	1
China	1
Vietnam	1
Other	2
Total	**100**

PRODUCTS/OPERATIONS

2011 Sales

	% of total
Petron	50
Beverages	16
Food	16
Power	13
Packaging	5
Total	**100**

COMPETITORS

Amcor
Anheuser-Busch InBev
Asahi Breweries
Ayala
Ball Corp.
Banco de Oro
Cargill
Coca-Cola
Dairy Farm International
Danone
Del Monte Pacific
Diageo
First Pacific
Fonterra
Heineken
Indofood
International Paper
JG Summit Holdings
Metro Pacific
Nestle
PepsiCo
SABMiller
Tsingtao
Tyson Foods

HISTORICAL FINANCIALS

Company Type: Public

Income Statement FYE: December 31

	REVENUE ($ mil.)	NET INCOME ($ mil.)	NET PROFIT MARGIN	EMPLOYEES
12/12	17,041	672	3.9%	18,275
12/11	12,237	400	3.3%	12,566
12/10	5,637	460	8.2%	16,682
12/09	3,770	1,250	33.2%	14,893
12/08	3,542	407	11.5%	15,000
Annual Growth	48.1%	13.3%	—	5.1%

2012 Year-End Financials

Debt ratio: 1.3%
Return on equity: 11.4%
Cash ($ mil.): 3,063
Current ratio: 1.39
Long-term debt ($ mil.): 9,769
No. of shares (mil.): —
Dividends
Yield: 1.1%
Payout: 0.0%
Market value ($ mil.): —

	STOCK PRICE ($) FY Close	P/E High/Low		PER SHARE ($) Earnings	Dividends	Book Value
12/12	25.25	0	0	0.22	0.29	2.59
12/11	25.50	0	0	0.11	0.00	2.21
12/10	37.60	0	0	0.14	1.07	2.12
12/09	14.85	0	0	0.41	0.00	2.02
12/08	8.50	0	0	0.13	0.00	1.00
Annual Growth	31.3%	—	—	14.2%	672.5%	26.8%

Sandvik AB (Sweden)

When it comes to engineered tools Sandvik knows the drill. The company is a global manufacturer whose largest segment specializes in mining and construction equipment for drilling crushing and loading applications. Its tooling segment makes metal cutting tools and components made from cemented carbide and other hard materials for the general engineering automotive and aerospace industries. Its materials technology business makes heating materials and tube strip and wire products made of special alloys and stainless steel. Sandvik also controls metal cutting group Seco Tools. Sandvik operates in more than 130 countries worldwide. Its top markets are the US Australia and Germany.

Coming off a difficult couple of years due to the economic downturn and recession Sandvik is bouncing back having reported increases in sales productivity and profitability in fiscal 2010. Although sales were about 10% below the group's level prior to the downturn in 2008 the global economy is experiencing recovery and Sandik's initiatives aimed at consolidating its operations and reducing costs are beginning to pay off.

There was a sharp improvement in demand for Sandvik's tooling products in particular as industrial production is beginning to pick up again around the world. The strongest markets here are North America and Europe as well as in the Asian markets of China India and South Korea. The company's mining and construction business also noted a strong positive demand trend in 2010 which is being driven by a rise in metal consumption and higher prices for metals and coal. But despite the introduction of stimulus packages the construction industry continues to display weak development.

Despite these conditions Sandvik sees China as a major investment opportunity and in 2011 it acquired Shanghai Jianshe Luqiao Machinery Co. a Chinese mining and construction company that supplies crushing equipment and consumables among its products and services. In addition Sandvik is coordinating logistics and opening new production plants in China. Other key investments include expanding its production of tubing for the nuclear power industry.

Elsewhere in the Asia/Pacific region Sanvik's mining and construction group signed a major contract in 2011 with Boral a global building and construction materials supplier in Australia. The order includes the design supply installation and commissioning of a new quarrying plant for a Boral site in New South Wales. The project is expected to be completed in 2013. Australia is one of Sandvik's single largest markets.

Demand for materials technology was also positive for the year especially in the energy and mining industries in Europe and Asia. To strengthen is position in powder technology and materials used by the energy sector Sandvik's materials technology business entered into a strategic partnership with Carpenter Technology.

AB Industrivarden owns about a 12% stake in Sandvik.

HISTORY

Sandvik's origins go back to 1862 when a steelworks called Hogbo Stal & Jernwerks was founded by Goran Fredrik Goransson in Sandviken Sweden. Its products in the 1860s included steam hammers and rock drills. Hogbo Stal & Jernwerks' primary financial backer Johan Holm had money problems that left him and the company financially ruined; the company went bankrupt in 1866. Hogbo Stal & Jernwerks was reorganized and renamed Sandvikens Jernwerks AB and Anders Henrik Goransson the founder's son took over as the new manager.

By the 1890s the company's steel products included cold-rolled steel rod and strip and seamless tubing. It also made manufactured products such as saws boiler tubes for steamships and railway engines and wire for umbrellas. Sandvikens Jernwerks was listed on the Stockholm stock exchange in 1901.

WWI put a damper on exports but strong domestic demand for steel picked up the slack. By 1920 steel was the company's dominant product line; manufactured products only accounted for 6% of sales. Karl Fredrik Goransson grandson of the founder became managing director in 1920 and chairman in 1929.

During WWII Sandvik entered the cemented-carbide business. Cemented carbide made by combining tungsten carbide powder with cobalt powder is pressed into the desired shape and subjected to extreme heat. The cobalt melts and acts as a binding agent. The resulting substance is extremely hard and resistant to wear making it ideal for the manufacture of cutting tools. Cemented carbide was developed in Germany in the 1920s by Fried. Krupp AG. Krupp's domination of the market disappeared during the war leaving the gate open for new participants.

Sandvik teamed with Atlas Copco to develop ready-made cemented-carbide tools for rock drilling. Previously cemented carbide was sold in blanks. The rock drills were an instant hit. The technology later was applied to metalworking tools and by 1956 they also gained wide acceptance. The collaboration with Atlas Copco lasted until 1988.

In 1957 Swedish investment firm Kinnevik acquired a stake in the company putting an end to Goransson family control. By 1971 sales of cemented-carbide products surpassed steel products for the first time. To reflect the change the company changed its name from Sandvikens Jernwerks AB to Sandvik AB the following year.

During the 1970s and 1980s Sandvik managed to compete against larger steel companies by making specialty products such as surgical needles scalpels and artificial hip joints. This also was a period of global expansion through acquisitions. Between 1970 and 1979 the company expanded into France Germany Spain the UK and the US. In 1980 Swedish construction company Skansa AB bought Kinnevik's stake in the company amassing a 37% share.

Acquisitions continued through the 1980s and included GE's Carboloy division in 1987 and Metinox Steel Ltd. (stainless steel medical products) in 1989.

Despite the recession of the early 1990s Sandvik made 10 acquisitions in 1991. Two years later the company formed a Chinese subsidiary to make cemented-carbide tools.

In 1997 Sandvik acquired Tamrock (rock drilling equipment Finland) Kanthal (high-temperature metallic and ceramic materials) and Precision Twist Drill (drill bits US). That year Skanska sold the bulk of its stake in the company. Sandvik sold its saws and hand tools business to US-based Snap-On in 1999. The company also restructured into three business segments: tooling mining and construction and specialty steels. The following year Sandvik sold its metal casting subsidiary Guldsmedshytte Bruks to the Windcast Group of Norway.

Sandvik gained complete control of India-based Choksi Tube Company when it acquired the 49% it did not already own in 2001. That year Sandvik agreed to acquire a controlling stake in Germany-based industrial tool company WALTER AG and acquired certain assets of Swedish rock processor Svedela when Metso was forced to divest crushing and screening units in Sweden and France to gain regulatory approval. In 2002 the company sold its 50% stake in dental technology firm Procera-Sandvik AB to Nobel Biocare. Sandvik bought Milacron's North American tool business the same year.

Sandvik added to its European mining equipment operations with the acquisition of certain Svedala assets including its crushing and screening units in Sweden and France. In 2004 it acquired Technical Tooling a precision tool manufacturer for the beverage can industry from Federal Signal.

Also in 2004 Sandvik announced that German engineering group DEPO would come under the Sandvik umbrella of companies by the beginning of the following year. However in 2005 the businesses announced jointly that current market conditions did not favor such a move. As a result DEPO remained independent and the two companies continued their business relationship as before.

The company acquired five firms in 2006. One of those acquisitions Hagby-Asahi AB of Nora Sweden had a construction division that made equipment for drilling and grinding of concrete with diamond tools. Sandvik decided in 2008 that this division was not core to its business interests and sold the construction division to Husqvarna Construction Products Sweden AB.

The global recession forced the company to reorganize its operations in 2009 closing 20 production units and combining its Valenite and Walter branded tools. As part of that and a company-wide shakeup Sandvik cut about 11000 positions or 20% of its workforce across its steel IT and tooling divisions.

Even a down year didn't stop the acquisitive nature of Sandvik though. The same year as the cuts it picked up Austrian tungsten producer Wolfram Bergbau- und Hutten-GmbH (WBH). Sandvik had already been using WBH's tungsten carbide to produce its cemented carbide.

EXECUTIVES

President Sandvik Venture, Anders Thelin, age 63
EVP and General Counsel, Bo Severin, age 59
Group Assurance, Bernth Nilsson
President and CEO, Olof Faxander, age 43
President Sandvik Construction, Thomas Schulz, age 48
Executive Vice President Group Communications Sandvik AB, Jan Liss?ker
Vice President Group Communication, Anders Wallin
EVP Human Resources, Anna Vikstrom Persson
President Sandvik Materials Technology, Jonas Gustavsson, age 46
Auditor, Caj Nackstad
Real Estate, Carl Larsson
EVP and Head IT, Tomas Nordahl, age 45
President Sandvik Mining, Gary Hughes, age 55

President Sandvik Machining Solutions, Andreas Evertz, age 44
Chairman of the Board, Anders Nyren
Executive Vice President Group Communications, Jan Lissaker
Head of Research and Development, Olle Wijk
Head of External Communications, Par Altan
Chief Financial Officer; Executive Vice President, Emil Nilsson
President of Sandvik Materials Technology, Petra Einarsson
President of Sandvik Construction, Andy Taylor
President Sandvik Materials Technology +46 26 26 36 36, Petra Einersson
Director, Lars Westerberg, age 65
Director, Egil Myklebust, age 71
Director, Fredrik Lundberg, age 63
Director, Georg Ehrnrooth, age 73
Director, Simon R. Thompson, age 54
Director, Hanne de Mora, age 53
Director, Tomas Karnstrom, age 46
Director, Jan Kjellgren, age 61
Director, Bo Westin, age 64
Director, Alicia del Carmen Espinosa, age 47
Independent Director, Hanne Mora
Independent Director, Johan Karlstrom
Director; Employee Representative, Tomas Karnstrom
Auditors: KPMGBohlinsAB

LOCATIONS

HQ: Sandvik AB (Sweden)
Storgatan 2, Sandviken SE-811 81
Phone: (46) 26 26 00 00 **Fax:** (46) 26 26 10 22
Web: www.sandvik.com

North America		
US	12	
Canada	3	
Asia/Pacific		
Australia	9	
China	7	
India	3	
Japan	2	
Europe		
Germany	8	
Sweden	5	
France	4	
Italy	3	
Russia	3	
UK	3	
South & Central America	6	
Africa	5	
Other countries	27	
Total	**0**	**100**

PRODUCTS/OPERATIONS

2010 Sales

	% of total
Sandvik Mining and	42
Sandvik	29
Sandvik Materials	22
Seco	7
Total	**100**

2010 Sales by Customer

	% of total
Mining	36
Engineering	19
Automotive	12
Construction	12
Energy	11
Consumer-related	4
Aerospace	3
Other	3
Total	**100**

COMPETITORS

Alfa Laval
ArcelorMittal
Astec Industries
Atlas Copco
Kennametal
Kyocera
Metso
Mitsubishi Heavy Industries
BOHLER-UDDEHOLM
Boart Longyear
Caterpillar
Furukawa
Hitachi
Joy Global
SKF
Terex
Tubacex
Universal Stainless
Volvo

HISTORICAL FINANCIALS

Company Type: Public

Income Statement FYE: December 31

	REVENUE ($ mil.)	NET INCOME ($ mil.)	NET PROFIT MARGIN	EMPLOYEES
12/12	15,124	1,244	8.2%	48,742
12/11	13,641	797	5.8%	50,030
12/10	12,326	989	8.0%	47,064
12/09	10,100	(372)	—	44,355
12/08	11,864	956	8.1%	50,028
Annual Growth	6.3%	6.8%	—	(0.6%)

2012 Year-End Financials

Debt ratio: 5.1%	No. of shares (mil.): 1,254
Return on equity: 23.5%	Dividends
Cash ($ mil.): 2,122	Yield: 2.9%
Current ratio: 2.27	Payout: 1.0%
Long-term debt ($ mil.): 4,952	Market value ($ mil.): 20,258

	STOCK PRICE ($) FY Close	P/E High	P/E Low	PER SHARE ($) Earnings	Dividends	Book Value
12/12	16.15	0	0	1.00	0.47	4.42
12/11	12.20	0	0	0.67	0.01	3.97
12/10	19.50	0	0	0.83	0.13	4.10
12/09	12.08	—	—	(0.31)	0.38	3.43
12/08	6.44	0	0	0.81	1.10	3.84
Annual Growth	25.8%	—	—	5.5%	(19.3%)	3.6%

Sanofi

Sanofi is out to make all the world's creatures a little healthier. The company formerly known as Sanofi-Aventis develops and manufactures prescription and over-the-counter drugs and vaccines for mankind and man's best friend. Sanofi's pharmaceutical division is its biggest revenue generator with top sellers that include blood thinners Plavix and Lovenox cancer drug Taxotere and insulin brand Lantus. US consumers will recognize at least one of the brands produced by subsidiary Chattem (Gold Bond Icy Hot and Selsun Blue to name a few). Sanofi also operates Merial one of the world's largest animal health firms. Subsidiary Sanofi Pasteur makes vaccines while its Genzyme unit makes biopharmaceuticals.

The company operates worldwide marketing its products through direct sales representatives and through partnering firms. For example Sanofi co-markets cardiovascular drugs Plavix and Aprovel with Bristol-Myers Squibb (BMS). It also has agreements with Warner Chilcott to market osteoporosis drug Actonel and with Teva Pharmaceuticals for Copaxone. Products are distributed via large wholesalers and to retail chains and health care organizations. Europe and North America are the firm's largest markets.

Sanofi has worked hard to diversify its operations in the wake of and ahead of patent expirations for some of its biggest sellers. Its allergy blockbuster Allegra and sleep aid Ambien have both lost their patent protection in recent years (as has Lovenox) clearing the way for generic competition. Another top seller Plavix lost patent protection in the US in 2012 (resulting in reduced royalties from marketing partner BMS) as did blood pressure drug Avapro. Sanofi's diversification strategy hinges mainly upon making strategic acquisitions in its core therapeutic areas as well as in new markets and emerging regions poised for growth.

To boost offering of delicate biopharmaceuticals Sanofi acquired prescription drug firm Genzyme in 2011 for some $20.1 billion after months of negotiation including a lower hostile bid failed. The deal included an additional $3.8 billion that is contingent on the future performance of Genzyme's lead drug candidates (including multiple sclerosis candidate Lemtrada) and its manufacturing facilities. The purchase of Genzyme gives Sanofi a portfolio of products focused on rare inherited disorders kidney disease orthopedics transplant and immune disease cancer and diagnostic testing. Its top product is rare disease treatment Cerezyme for Gaucher's disease. Following the acquisition Genzyme became the headquarters of the parent's rare disease program. Once Genzyme was formally part of its structure the company chose to simplify the collective organization's identity by shortening its name from Sanofi-Aventis to simply Sanofi.

Another area in which the company has been particularly focused on growing is the worldwide OTC market largely through its US Chattem division which converted Allegra to an OTC product in 2011 following its patent expiration. Also in 2011 Sanofi acquired BMP Sunstone a US-based firm that markets vitamins and mineral supplements and cough and cold medicines in China for about $520 million. Through its majority owned India unit Aventis Pharma Sanofi also expanded its portfolio by buying the marketing and distribution business of Universal Medicare which makes more than 40 branded nutraceutical formulations in India.

Not one to miss an opportunity Sanofi decided it too would take advantage of patent expirations by growing its generics business especially in the European generics market where it maintains the Winthrop brand. It has also established a generic presence in emerging markets (another growth area for the company) in the Middle East Latin America and Asia.

In 2010 Sanofi took its plan to reduce its reliance on prescription drugs one step further by entering the market for medical devices. The company joined forces with medical equipment maker Agamatrix to develop blood sugar monitoring devices for diabetes patients. Sanofi already has a solid presence in the diabetes market with its insulin products Apidra and Lantus. The blood glucose monitoring systems designed to work in conjunction with the company's existing diabetes treatments were launched in European markets under the BGStar and iBGStar brands in 2011.

The next year Sanofi agreed to acquire Pluromed a medical device company that developed proprietary polymer technology used in injectable plugs for improving the safety efficacy and costs of medical interventions. The company also makes LeGoo gel a product used in surgery for temporary endovascular occlusion of blood vessels in the US and Europe.

While it has been growing some operations the company has taken a different approach to its research and development business. Beginning in 2009 Sanofi began cutting back on its pipeline of drug candidates in an effort to save on R&D costs narrowing its focus on the most promising candidates in targeted areas including cancer diabetes cardiology neurology vaccines and biologics. As of early 2011 it had about 55 candidates in its drug pipeline with about a dozen of them in late stages of clinical development. In 2009 it successfully launched a new atrial fibrillation (irregular heart beat) medicine Multaq and in 2010 it introduced prostate cancer drug Jevtana.

The company is also increasingly relying on partnerships and licensing agreements with other firms and academic institutions to support its research efforts. For instance in 2010 Sanofi formed a major outsourcing agreement with contract research organization (CRO) Covance. The deal worth up to $2.2 billion included Covance's purchase of two Sanofi R&D facilities in Europe. Covance will provide drug development services to the company through a ten-year contract.

Though it is streamlining its internal development operations the company still pursues acquisitions to bolster its late-stage pipeline in core research areas. In 2010 the company boosted its pipeline with treatments for leukemia and certain blood disorders by buying privately held TargeGen for $75 million (plus up to $485 million in potential future milestone payments).

In the vaccines market Sanofi's biggest sellers include pediatric combination vaccines and the cervical cancer vaccine Gardasil (marketed through an agreement with Merck). Subsidiary Sanofi Pasteur is also a top maker of flu vaccines and has received a boost from growing concerns over the possibility of an influenza pandemic. While its vaccine business only makes up about 10% of the company's sales Sanofi has made small acquisitions to keep its pipeline pumping.

Sanofi's animal health operations are conducted through its Merial subsidiary which was formerly a 50-50 joint venture with Merck. Sanofi acquired Merck's share of Merial (as Merck prepared for its acquisition of drugmaker Schering-Plough) in 2009 for about $4 billion. The two exercised an option to strike a fresh venture early the next year and announced plans to combine Merial with Merck's animal health business Intervet; however after spending a year planning the merger the two companies ended the agreement in 2011 citing complexities arising from anticipated divestitures to satisfy antitrust regulators. Sanofi has stated that it will instead grow its animal health operations through smaller bolt-on acquisitions.

While the company has been aggressively expanding its product offerings and R&D pipeline of potential blockbusters to help ward off the threat of generic competition it has also been pursuing cost-cutting measures as a means of offsetting future patent losses. In 2011 for instance Sanofi announced that it was reviewing options to divest its US dermatology business Dermik and later that year it sold the unit to Valeant Pharmaceuticals for some $425 million. In addition in 2010 the company downsized certain manufacturing and sales operations to reduce inefficiencies and prepare for lower production and sales volumes of selected products going off-patent. It has also conducted some layoffs.

HISTORY

The Sanofi group got its start in 1973 when French oil conglomerate Elf Aquitaine (later part of TOTAL) merged several health care cosmetics and animal nutrition companies into one subsidiary. In 1977 Sanofi set up a Japanese subsidiary through which it developed joint ventures with Japan's Meiji Seika Kaisha and Taisha Pharmaceutical firms. In 1979 Elf spun off Sanofi although it retained ownership of more than half of the company. Almost from its founding Sanofi grew through acquisitions and alliances. During the 1980s it used a massive war chest to buy stakes and set up joint ventures such as one with American Home Products in 1982.

The company bought "couturier et parfumier" Nina Ricci in 1988; such well-known fragrances as L'Air du Temps put it among the industry's top perfume houses. But Sanofi overreached the next two years and was outbid by American Home Products for AH Robins (the drug firm bankrupted by lawsuits over deaths from its Dalkon Shield IUD) and by Rhone-Poulenc (now part of Aventis) for Rorer. A chastened Sanofi and Kodak subsidiary Sterling Drug in 1991 entered into an alliance that didn't involve an exchange of cash.

In 1993 Sanofi made a splash when it bought the perfume business of fashion designer Yves Saint-Laurent. The next year it bought out much of the pharmaceutical joint venture with Kodak. Sanofi began divesting such noncore businesses as veterinarian and biotech operations in 1995. After suffering a loss in its perfume and beauty division in 1996 it sold Nina Ricci. The rest of its beauty division was sold in 1999 in preparation for the Synthelabo merger.

Synthelabo was founded in 1970 when drug firms Laboratoires Dausse and Laboratoires Robert et Carriere merged. In 1973 it became a 53%-owned subsidiary of beauty products maker L'Oreal. In 1980 drug firm Metabio-Jouillie became a part of Synthelabo making it the #3 drug company in France. In 1983 Synthelabo and US drugmaker Searle created Lorex to market the French firm's products in the UK. (Synthelabo bought Searle's interest 10 years later.)

Throughout the 1980s Synthelabo acquired merged and formed joint ventures including some in Japan with Mitsubishi Chemical Fujisawa Pharmaceutical (1985) and Tanabe Seiyaku (1987). The company continued its acquisitive ways in the 1990s buying several French rivals.

Synthelabo openly admitted its quest for a large international presence in 1996 announcing it wanted 80% of its sales to come from such foreign markets as Asia and the US. That year the company entered an alliance with Genset to research cancer-causing genes; it also signed on with SmithKline Beecham (now GlaxoSmithKline) and Human Genome Sciences to fund genetic research. Synthelabo's Hungarian subsidiary began planning to make drugs for the first time rather than just selling its parent's products as in the past. The next year Synthelabo bought Pharmacia & Upjohn's German generic drug subsidiary Sanorania Pharma.

As Synthelabo and Sanofi merged in 1999 the new company's concentration on pharmaceuticals dictated several changes including the sale of the company's interests in joint venture Pasteur Sanofi Diagnostics as well as its beauty division home to such well-known perfume lines as Yves Saint Laurent. It also sold its veterinary and animal feed division to what is now BNP Paribas.

Sanofi-Synthelabo made good on its plans to target the US in 2000 expanding its sales force there. But the merger wasn't without its problems: Former Synthelabo CEO Herve Guerin was ousted as vice chairman and COO of Sanofi-Synthelabo after he and chairman Jean-Francois Dehecq butted heads. In 2002 the company boosted its pipeline by entering into an alliance with Immuno-Designed Molecules a biotechnology firm focusing on cancer drugs. Also that year the FDA approved the firm's colorectal cancer drug Eloxatine in record time.

Sanofi-Synthelabo acquired Aventis —and with it the Allegra franchise and Merial joint venture — in 2004. Following the merger the company changed its name to Sanofi-Aventis.

Even though key patents for Plavix weren't scheduled to expire until 2011 generics maker Apotex introduced a generic version in 2006 that flooded the US market. An injunction issued by US courts halted Apotex's manufacturing of the drug (though not sales of already distributed products) but the episode still reduced Sanofi-Aventis' Plavix sales in the US by about 16% compared to the previous year. Both companies pursued litigation.

The company received EU approval in 2006 for the use of its weight-loss drug rimonabant which entered the market under the brand name Acomplia. However in 2008 Sanofi-Aventis suspended marketing efforts for Acomplia due to reports of psychiatric side effects; the company canceled all clinical trials for the drug later that year.

In 2008 the company acquired the Australian vitamin and mineral supplements business of Symbion (now part of Primary Health Care) for $480 million. It also purchased vaccine-maker Acambis which had a history of working with Sanofi Pasteur and brought with it an approved smallpox vaccine and a solid pipeline of vaccines in development.

In late 2009 it shelled out nearly $2 billion to acquire Chattem which not only gave it a hefty line of well-known consumer products but also increased Sanofi's presence in the US (which accounted for about 30% of the company's annual sales in 2009). As part of that deal Sanofi decided to convert Allegra from a prescription to an OTC drug (following its patent expiration) and transfer it to Chattem to market. The company also expanded its presence in Asia by forming a joint venture with Chinese nutritionals firm Minsheng Pharmaceutical in 2009.

In 2009 the company paid some $1.5 billion to acquire the remaining shares of Czech generics maker Zentiva in which it already held a 25% stake. Zentiva brought with it generic operations in emerging markets including Turkey and Russia. Sanofi also expanded its Asian generics operations by forming a joint venture with Japan's Nichi-Iko Pharmaceuticals and it became sizeable in South America when it bought top Brazilian generic drug manufacturer Medley for $663 million in 2009.

In 2009 it acquired US development firm BiPar Sciences in a deal worth up to $500 million adding potential therapies for breast ovarian and other cancers; it also purchased ophthalmology development firm Fovea Pharmaceuticals for $540 million.

EXECUTIVES

Senior Vice President President Sanofi France, Christian Lajoux, age 66
President Global Operations, Hanspeter Spek, age 64
Chairman, Serge Weinberg, age 62
Chief Executive Officer, Christopher A. (Chris) Viehbacher, age 53
SVP Vaccines, Wayne F. Pisano, age 59
President Global Research and Development, Elias A. Zerhouni, age 61
Senior Vice President Secretary, Philippe Peyre, age 63
SVP Corporate Social Responsibility, Gilles Lhernould, age 58
SVP Pharmaceutical Operations Intercontinental, Antoine Ortoli, age 60
Chairman Strategic Development and Scientific Advisory Council, Richard D. Klausner
SVP Global Diabetes, Pierre Chancel, age 57
VP Media Relations and Corporate Communications, Jean-Marc Podvin
Senior Vice President Global Services, Gregory (Greg) Irace, age 54
SVP Human Resources, Roberto Pucci, age 49
SVP Industrial Development and Innovation, Jean-Philippe Santoni, age 59
SVP Legal Affairs and General Counsel, Karen Linehan, age 55
SVP Industrial Affairs, Philippe Luscan, age 50
Senior Vice President Corporate Communications, Laure Thibaud, age 54

SVP Pharmaceutical Customer Solutions, Jean-Francois Brin, age 48
SVP and Chief Medical Officer, Jean-Pierre Lehner, age 65
SVP Global Oncology, Debasish Roychowdhury, age 51
VP External and Scientific Communications, Pascal Barollier
President North America, Anne C. Whitaker
Chief Strategy Officer, David-Alexandre Gros
Senior Vice President Chief Medical Officer, Paul Chew
Director, Robert Castaigne, age 65
Director, Thierry Desmarest, age 68
Director, Gerard Van Kemmel, age 73
Director, Lindsay Owen-Jones, age 67
Director, Igor Landau, age 69
Director, Jean-Rene Fourtou, age 73
Director, Lord Douro, age 67
Director, Christian Mulliez, age 53
Director, Klaus Pohle, age 76
CEO and Director, Christopher A. (Chris) Viehbacher, age 53
Director, Uwe Bicker, age 67
Director, Claudie Haignere, age 54
Director, Partick de la Chaevardiere, age 55
Auditors: PricewaterhouseCoopersAudit

LOCATIONS

HQ: Sanofi
54, Rue La Boetie, Paris 75008
Phone: (33) 1 53 77 40 00 **Fax:** (33) 1 53 77 43 03
Web: www.sanofi.com

2010 Sales

	$ mil.	% of total
Emerging Markets	30	
Western Europe (including France)	30	
Other regions & countries (including Japan)	11	

PRODUCTS/OPERATIONS

2010 Sales

	% of total sales
Prescription pharmaceut	
Lantus	12
Lovenox	9
Taxotere	7
Plavix	7
Aprovel	4
Ambien/Stilnox/Myslee	3
Allegra	2
Copaxone	2
Amaryl	2
Eloxatin	1
Tritace	1
Other prescription	25
Vaccines	13
Consumer health	7
Generics	5
Total	**100**

Selected Products

Prescription pharmaceuticals
- Actonel (osteoporosis)
- Acomplia/Zimulti (obesity)
- Allegra/Telfast (allergies)
- Amaryl (diabetes)
- Ambien/Stillnox/Myslee (insomnia)
- Apidra (diabetes)
- Aprovel/Avapro (hypertension)
- Copaxone (multiple sclerosis)
- Depakine (epilepsy)
- Eloxatine (colorectal cancer)
- Jevtana (prostate cancer)
- Lantus (long-acting insulin for diabetes)
- Lovenox/Clexane (deep vein thrombosis other cardiovascular conditions)
- Multaq (atrial fibrillation and atrial flutter)
- Nasacort (allergic rhinitis)
- Plavix (arterial blood clots)
- Taxotere (breast and ovarian cancer)
- Tritace (hypertension)
- Vaxigrip (influenza vaccine)
- Xatral (benign prostatic hypertrophy)

Vaccines
- Adacel (diphtheria tetanus and pertussis adult booster vaccine)
- Fluzone (influenza vaccine)
- Insuman (diabetes)
- Menactra (meningitis and pneumonia vaccine)
- Pentaxim/Pentacel (Polio pertussis and HIB pediatric combination vaccine)

Consumer health
- Doliprane (pain)
- Enterogermina (intestinal health)
- Essentiale (liver therapy)
- Gold Bond (athlete's foot)
- Icy Hot (pain)
- Selsun Blue (dandruff)
- Unisom (sleep aid)

Animal health
- Frontline (antiparasitic)
- Heartgard (parasiticide)
- Ivomec (parasiticide)

Acquired Genzyme products
- Aldurazyme (genetic disease)
- Campath (oncology)
- Cerezyme (genetic disease)
- Clolar (oncology)
- Elaprase (genetic disease)
- Fabrazyme (genetic disease)
- Hectorol (kidney disease)
- Leukine (oncology)
- Mozobil (oncology)
- Myozyme/Lumizyme (genetic disease)
- Renagel/Renvela (kidney disease)
- Thymoglobulin (organ rejection)
- Thyrogen (endocrinology)

COMPETITORS

Abbott Labs
Actavis Inc.
Amgen
Amicus Therapeutics
Apotex
Astellas
AstraZeneca
Bayer AG
Biogen Idec
Boehringer Ingelheim
Bristol-Myers Squibb
Eli Lilly
Fresenius
GlaxoSmithKline
Insulet Corporation
Johnson & Johnson
LifeScan
Medtronic Limited
Merck
Merck KGaA
Novartis
Novo Nordisk
Pfizer
Procter & Gamble
Roche Holding
Shire
Sunovion
Takeda Pharmaceutical
Teva

HISTORICAL FINANCIALS

Company Type: Public

Income Statement FYE: December 31

	REVENUE ($ mil.)	NET INCOME ($ mil.)	NET PROFIT MARGIN	EMPLOYEES
12/12	47,393	6,546	13.8%	111,974
12/11	45,345	7,363	16.2%	113,719
12/10	42,874	7,316	17.1%	101,575
12/09	44,296	7,584	17.1%	104,867
12/08	40,288	5,384	13.4%	98,213
Annual Growth	4.1%	5.0%	—	3.3%

2012 Year-End Financials

Debt ratio: 19.0%	No. of shares (mil.): 1,323
Return on equity: 8.7%	Dividends
Cash ($ mil.): 8,410	Yield: 3.5%
Current ratio: 1.65	Payout: 70.8%
Long-term debt ($ mil.): 14,128	Market value ($ mil.): 62,693

	STOCK PRICE ($) FY Close	P/E High/Low	PER SHARE ($) Earnings	Dividends	Book Value
12/12	47.38	22 14	4.93	1.69	57.12
12/11	36.54	18 12	5.55	3.23	54.93
12/10	32.23	19 11	5.59	1.47	54.46
12/09	39.27	21 11	5.81	3.06	53.03
12/08	32.16	34 15	4.11	1.63	48.05
Annual Growth	10.2%	— —	4.6%	1.0%	4.4%

SAP AG

SAP's software wants to sap all the problems from your business processes. The company is the leading provider of enterprise resource planning (ERP) software used to integrate back-office functions such as distribution accounting human resources and manufacturing. Its clients are mainly in the service manufacturing and consumer industries but also in public services and financial services. The backbone of SAP's products is its on-premise offerings spearheaded by its Business Suite which includes ERP and CRM software among others. It also offers implementation and training services. The EMEA region (Europe the Middle East and Africa) makes up half of sales while the US brings in a quarter.

SAP's revenues have rebounded after its customers' pocketbooks dried up in the heat of the global recession. In 2010 businesses began investing more in IT than they had since 2007. Growth among its served markets in 2011 was greatest in its largest customer set discrete manufacturing (makers of products that go directly to consumers) which was up nearly 20% while most other sectors also had double digit growth. Geographically its non-US Americas sales came mainly from Canada Brazil and Mexico. Though still only 5% of sales Japan grew the most rising more than a quarter over 2010. SAP's top line improvement came from both increased volume and prices.

The return to form has also been driven by a focus on improving its development process better tying those teams in with customers to speed up go-to-market times on new products. That has become particularly important as SAP feels the pressure to innovate to maintain its leading position. That process reorganization led the company to divide its target industries into nine customer sets instead of six. While the company reviews revenue by industry geography and sales type its products are more strategically divided into five market categories: applications analytics cloud database and technology and mobile.

SAP has leveraged its position as the enterprise software leader in the ERP market to expand into related fields including business intelligence CRM software database products and mobile infrastructure tools. The most important trends by which it expects to supplement its core on-premise arsenal are cloud computing which it supports with its Business ByDesign product; business analytics championed by its in-memory computing technology through its HANA (High Performance Analytic Appliance) platform which impacts all five market categories; the mobile on-device space; social networking; and "big data."

Like many large software providers SAP is making much of its software available as hosted on-demand applications as more customers move from traditional client/server installed software to distributed software in cloud-computing environments. While some competitors make cloud their entire focus SAP works to distinguish itself by in part accommodating different installation arrangements including a combination of on-premise on-demand and on-device. It also works to tailor its offerings for more targeted industries (including financial services and retail) and expanding its products for small and midsized businesses.

Geographic expansion also remains pivotal. SAP has earmarked $2 billion through 2015 for growth in China. The company established a development lab in Moscow and plans additional market investments in other regions.

In 2011 the company bought a disclosure management product line from SAP systems integrator cundus AG. The deal added the information-Collector application which is designed to work with business intelligence and enterprise performance management products from SAP expanding the company's portfolio of finance tools. SAP also acquired security identity and access management software assets from Swiss IT security software and services provider SECUDE that year.

SAP also bought Munich-based business-to-business integration company Crossgate to offer enterprise-level networking applications used to help businesses share data and more easily communicate with various operational stakeholders.

In 2012 SAP completed the $3.4 billion purchase of cloud-based human capital management firm SuccessFactors. Also that year SAP bought enterprise visualization software company Right Hemisphere which provided product and enterprise asset modeling in 2-D and 3-D and related information integration. SAP immediately launched three related offerings after the purchase.

Again in 2012 SAP bolstered its education software offerings with the acquisition of datango AG a provider of workforce performance support software. datango's software –used to develop translate and deploy content for documentation training and user support functions –was rebranded as SAP Workforce Performance Builder. That year SAP also bought Syclo a developer of enterprise asset management software used to enable management of field services inventory and other functions from wireless devices. The deal extended SAP's mobile abilities and added customers in the utilities energy life sciences and manufacturing industries. The company also announced in 2012 it would pay about $4.3 billion for Ariba.

In 2013 SAP agreed to buy Swiss CRM supplier Hybris AG. The company is working to boost its offerings in that area as it has seen US rival salesforce.com move to the top of the CRM market.

Three of SAP's founders –Hasso Plattner Dietmar Hopp and Klaus Tschira –collectively control nearly 25% of the company.

HISTORY

Former IBM software engineers Hasso Plattner Hans-Werner Hector Dietmar Hopp Claus Wellenreuther and Klaus Tschira started SAP in 1972 when the project they were working on for IBM was moved to another unit.

While rival software firms made many products to automate the various parts of a company's operations these engineers decided to make a single system that would tie a corporation together. In 1973 they launched an instantaneous accounting transaction-processing program called R/1. By 1979 they had adapted the program to create R/2 mainframe software that linked external databases and communication systems.

The company went public in 1988. That year Plattner began a project to create software for the computer network market. In 1992 as sales of its R/2 mainframe software lagged SAP introduced its R/3 software which would later become its flagship SAP ERP.

In 1996 Hector decided to sell holdings amounting to about 10% of SAP's stock a move that possibly undermined hostile-takeover barriers; he left the company after a dispute with Hopp.

In 1998 SAP listed its stock on the NYSE. In 1999 the company expanded on the Internet unveiling a Web-based exchange (mySAP.com) supporting online transactions and other services. The company's longstanding resistance to employee stock options weakened in 2000 when SAP approved an option program to offset the loss of more than 200 key US managers in an 18-month period. Later that year SAP launched a US subsidiary (SAP Markets) and increased its minority stake in software maker Commerce One.

In 2001 SAP acquired enterprise portal software provider Top Tier Software renaming it SAP Portals. It also invested additional money in Commerce One raising its ownership stake to about 20%. The company reabsorbed its SAP Portals and SAP Markets subsidiaries in 2002 integrating their offerings into its mySAP product family.

The next year SAP announced it was acquiring the public stake in SAP SI as part of a plan to fold that company into its services operations. Following Oracle's acquisition of ERP rival PeopleSoft SAP acquired TomorrowNow a PeopleSoft support firm in an effort to lure customers away from Oracle. Ironically that company was shuttered in 2008 due to corporate theft charges brought against it by Oracle for which the SAP competitor was awarded $1.3 billion in 2010.

In 2005 SAP agreed to acquire retail software specialist Retek but it was eventually outbid by Oracle. Later in the year SAP acquired point-of-sale software provider Triversity as well as KhiMetrics a developer of pricing and forecasting software for the retail market.

SAP's acquisition of business intelligence software provider Business Objects for $6.8 billion in 2008 expanded its product line and bolstered its business intelligence offerings but was also a response in part to competitive pressure from Oracle Microsoft Hewlett-Packard and IBM.

In 2009 the company bought France-based Highdeal a developer of transaction automation and service provisioning applications which fit well with SAP's existing transaction software portfolio.

Among its larger acquisitions was the $5.8 billion purchase of enterprise database management company Sybase in 2010. The Sybase purchase added both database products and tools for transmitting and managing data to smartphones and other mobile devices. It also increased SAP's competition with Oracle. An altered form of Sybase became a fourth reportable segment for SAP.

EXECUTIVES

Co-CEO, William R. (Bill) McDermott, age 51, $395,200 total compensation
COO OnPremise Delivery, Gerhard Oswald, age 59, $602,966 total compensation
Chairman, Prof Hasso Plattner, age 69
CFO, Werner Brandt, age 59, $403,039 total compensation
Head Global On-Demand Sales and Go-to-Market, Greg Tomb
SVP and Head Global Retail Industry Business, Lori Mitchell-Keller, age 46
President and Corporate Officer, Sanjay Poonen
President Global Ecosystem and Channels, Eric Duffaut
SVP and General Manager Strategic Industries SAP North America, Patrick (Pat) Bakey
President and General Manager U.S. Sales, Gregory (Greg) McStravick
Chief Marketing Officer, Jonathan D. Becher
President SAP North America, Geraldine McBride
SVP Ecosystem and Channels SAP North America, Kevin J. Gilroy, age 57
CTO, Vishal Sikka, age 45
Co-CEO, Jim Hagemann Snabe, age 47, $227,500 total compensation
President SAP Europe, Jose Duarte
President SAP Americas, Rodolpho Cardenuto
COO SAP North America, Steven M. (Steve) Winter
EVP North America Field Services SAP North America, Ross Wainwright
Managing Director SAP Canada, Mark Aboud
Vice President Communications, Emile Lee
SVP and General Manager Central Region SAP North America, Maj. Paul Carreiro
CFO SAP North America, Joel Bernstein
SVP Strategic Ecosystem Partners SAP North America, Michael Schulze
SVP Business Analystics SAP North America, John Schweitzer
Head of Innovation Sales SAP Americas, Chris Ball
CIO, Oliver Bussmann
President SAP Public Services, Jennifer Morgan
Head Line of Business OnDemand Solutions, Kevin Nix
President Global Sales and Interim President North America, Rob Enslin
COO SAP North America, John Graham
Chief Human Resources Officer; Labor Relations Director, Luisa Deplazes Delgado
CEO Cloud Business Unit, Lars Dalgaard
SVP and General Manager Ecosystems Group, Troy K. Richardson
Deputy Chairman of the Supervisory Board; Employee Representative, Lars Lars Lamade Lamade
Vice President Human Resources, Brigette McInnis-Day
Senior Vice President General Counsel, Mary Hanss
President Managing Director, Andrew Barkla
Board Member, Joachim Milberg, age 69
Board Member, Pekka Ala-Pietila, age 55
Board Member, Klaus Wucherer, age 68
Board Member, Bernard Liautaud, age 49
Board Member, Hartmut Mehdorn, age 70
Board Member, Erhard Schipporeit, age 64
Developer and Board Member, Willi Burbach, age 49
Board Member, Wilhelm Haarmann, age 61
Manager Development Project and Board Member, Gerhard Maier, age 58
Deputy Chairman and Project Manager Service and Support, Lars Lamade, age 40
Manager Project Development and Board Member, Stefan Schulz, age 42
Support Expert and Board Member, Panagiotis Bissiritsas, age 43
Industry Business Development Expert and Board Member, Peter Koop, age 45
COO Operations and Board Member, Thomas Bamberger, age 44
Deputy Chairperson Works Council and Board Member, Christiane Kuntz-Mayr
Member of the Supervisory Board, Hans-bernd Hans-bernd Meier Meier
Member of the Supervisory Board, Pekka Pekka Ala-Pietila Ala-Pietila
Auditors: KPMGAG

LOCATIONS

HQ: SAP AG
Dietmar-Hopp-Allee 16, Walldorf D-69190
Phone: (49) 6227 74 74 74 **Fax:** (49) 6227 75 75 75
Web: www.sap.com

2011 Sales

	% of total
Europe Middle East Africa	
Germany	16
Other	33
Americas	
US	26
Other	10
Asia/Pacific	
Japan	5
Other	10
Total	**100**

PRODUCTS/OPERATIONS

2011 Sales by Type

	% of total
Software & service	
Support	49
Software	28
Subscription & other software-related	3

Professional and service	
Consulting	16
Other	4
Total	**100**

2011 Sales by Market

	% of total
Manufacturing	
Discrete	18
Process	10
Services	15
Energy & natural	14
Consumer	10
Public	10
Retail &	9
Financial	9
Health care & life	5
Total	**100**

2011 Sales by Segment

	% of total
Product	70
Consulting	21
Sybase	6
Training	3
Total	**100**

Selected Customers

Aigo
City of Cape Town South Africa
Danone
Beaumont Health System
McLaren Group

Selected Software

SAP Business All-in-One
SAP Business ByDesign
SAP Business One
SAP Business Suite
SAP ERP
SAP HANA
SAP NetWeaver

Selected Services

Application hosting
Business consulting
Custom development
Financing
Implementation
Maintenance
Training

Selected Acquisitions

SuccessFactors (2012; cloud-based workforce management)
Right Hemisphere (2012; enterprise visualization)
TechniData (2010; environmental health and safety)
Sybase (2010 business intelligence and database management)
Clear Standards (2009 environmental)
Highdeal (2009 billing)
Visiprise (2008 manufacturing process management)
Business Objects (2008 business intelligence)
OutlookSoft (2007 business performance management)
Pilot Software (2007 business performance management)

COMPETITORS

BMC Software
CA Inc.
CDC Software
Electronic Data Processing
Epicor Software
Hewlett-Packard
IBM
Lawson Software
MicroStrategy
Microsoft
Oracle
Software AG
Workday Inc.
salesforce.com

HISTORICAL FINANCIALS

Company Type: Public

Income Statement — FYE: December 31

	REVENUE ($ mil.)	NET INCOME ($ mil.)	NET PROFIT MARGIN	EMPLOYEES
12/12	21,382	3,720	17.4%	64,422
12/11	18,409	4,446	24.2%	55,765
12/10	16,681	2,423	14.5%	53,513
12/09	15,373	2,518	16.4%	48,471
12/08	16,168	2,611	16.2%	51,638
Annual Growth	7.2%	9.3%	—	5.7%

2012 Year-End Financials

Debt ratio: 25.7%
Return on equity: 20.9%
Cash ($ mil.): 3,264
Current ratio: 1.05
Long-term debt ($ mil.): 5,860
No. of shares (mil.): 1,192
Dividends
Yield: 1.2%
Payout: 54.8%
Market value ($ mil.): 95,827

	STOCK PRICE ($) FY Close	P/E High/Low		PER SHARE ($) Earnings	Dividends	Book Value
12/12	80.38	60	38	3.12	1.02	15.66
12/11	52.95	45	28	3.74	1.10	13.80
12/10	50.61	66	45	2.03	0.42	11.05
12/09	46.81	77	39	2.12	0.50	10.27
12/08	36.22	82	33	2.20	0.61	8.51
Annual Growth	22.1%	—	—	9.2%	13.7%	16.5%

Saudi Basic Industries Corp - SABIC (Saudi Arabia)

SABIC is the acronym for Saudi Basic Industries Corporation but it could also stand for "seriously a big industrial company." Saudi Arabia's largest non-oil company SABIC operates through six units: chemicals performance chemicals polymers (polyolefins PVC and polyester) plastics (including US-based SABIC Innovative Plastics) fertilizers and metals (mostly steel along with stakes in aluminum companies). SABIC is one of the world's largest makers of polyethylene and polypropylene. It operates 60 manufacturing and compouding plants around the world as well as numerous distribution centers offices and storage facilities. SABIC it is majority owned (70%) by the Saudi government.

A leading industrial player in Saudi Arabia the company primary leverages by-products of oil production to create value-added export commodities (chemicals polymers and fertilizers) and provides the commodity and financial basis for industrial diversification (such as steel production) within and outside the Kingdom.

EXECUTIVES

Vice Chairman and CEO, Mohamed H. Al-Mady
Chairman, Prince Saud bin Abdullah bin Thenayan Al-Saud
EVP Strategic Planning, Abdullah Bazid, age 57
EVP Corporate Strategy and Planning, Yousef Al-Zamel
EVP Fertilizers, Khaled Al-Mana
EVP Corporate Human Resources, Fahad Al-Sheaibi
EVP Polymers, Mosaed Al-Ohali
EVP Corporate Finance, Mutlaq Al-Morished
EVP Corporate Control, Homood A. Al-Tuwaijri
EVP Innovative Plastics, Keith J. Smith
EVP Chemicals, Yousef A. Al-Benyan
EVP Metals, Abdulaziz S. Al-Humaid
EVP Performance Chemicals, Jacobus van Haasteren
EVP Performance Chemicals, Abdullah S. Al-Rabeeah
VP Corporate Communications, Samir A. Al-Abdrabbuh
EVP Technology and Innovation, Ernesto Occhiello
EVP Shared Services, Omar A. Al-Amoudi
EVP Manufacturing, Awadh Al-Maker
Vice Chairman and CEO, Mohamed H. Al-Mady
Director, Mohammed S. Abanumay
Director, Abdullah M. Al-Issa
Auditors: Ernst&Young

LOCATIONS

HQ: Saudi Basic Industries Corp - SABIC (Saudi Arabia)
P.O. Box 5101, Riyadh 11422
Phone: (966) 1 225 8000 **Fax:** (966) 1 225 9000
Web: www.sabic.com

PRODUCTS/OPERATIONS

Selected Subsidiaries & Affiliates

Al-Jubail Petrochemical Co
Aluminum Bahrain
Arabian Industrial Fibers Co
Arabian Petrochemical Co
Eastern Petrochemical Co
Gulf Aluminum Rolling Mill Co
Gulf Petrochemical Industries Co
Jubail Fertilizer
Jubail United Petrochemical Co
Maaden Phosphate Co.
National Chemical Carrier Company
National Chemical Fertilizer Co
National Industrial Gases Co
National Methanol Co
SABIC Innovative Plastics
Saudi Arabian Fertilizer Co
Saudi Iron & Steel Co
Saudi Kayan Petrochemical Co
Saudi Methanol Co
Saudi Organometallic Chemicals Co
Saudi Petrochemical Co
Saudi Specialty Chemicals Co
Saudi-Yanbu Petrochemical Co
Saudi-European Petrochemical Co
Sinopec SABIC Tianjin Petrochemical Co
Yanbu National Petrochemical

COMPETITORS

A. Schulman
ArcelorMittal
BASF SE
Bayer MaterialScience
Dow Chemical
DuPont
ExxonMobil Chemical
INEOS
INEOS AG
Lucite
LyondellBasell
Nippon Steel & Sumitomo Metal Corporation
POSCO
Shell Chemicals
Sumitomo Chemical

HISTORICAL FINANCIALS

Company Type: Public

Income Statement FYE: December 31

	REVENUE ($ mil.)	NET INCOME ($ mil.)	NET PROFIT MARGIN	EMPLOYEES
12/12	50,400	6,607	13.1%	40,000
12/11	50,639	7,797	15.4%	33,000
12/10	40,524	5,740	14.2%	33,000
12/09	27,476	2,419	8.8%	33,000
12/08	40,247	5,879	14.6%	0
Annual Growth	5.8%	3.0%	—	—

2012 Year-End Financials

Debt ratio: 7.5%
Return on equity: 17.2%
Cash ($ mil.): 13,713
Current ratio: 2.82
Long-term debt ($ mil.): 21,230

No. of shares (mil.): —
Dividends
Yield: —
Payout: —
Market value ($ mil.): —

Sberbank Russia

LOCATIONS

HQ: Sberbank Russia
19 Vavilova St., Moscow 117997
Phone: (7) 495 500 55 50 **Fax:** (7) 495 957 5731
Web: www.sberbank.ru

HISTORICAL FINANCIALS

Company Type: Public

Income Statement FYE: December 31

	REVENUE ($ mil.)	NET INCOME ($ mil.)	NET PROFIT MARGIN	EMPLOYEES
12/12	45,370	11,458	25.3%	286,019
12/11	31,876	9,795	30.7%	266,187
12/10	31,689	5,968	18.8%	262,779
12/09	32,164	804	2.5%	260,805
Annual Growth	12.1%	142.4%	—	3.1%

2012 Year-End Financials

Debt ratio: —
Return on equity: 24.1%
Cash ($ mil.): 42,403
Current ratio: —
Long-term debt ($ mil.): —

No. of shares (mil.): —
Dividends
Yield: 1.5%
Payout: 0.0%
Market value ($ mil.): —

	STOCK PRICE ($) FY Close	P/E High/Low	PER SHARE ($) Earnings	Dividends	Book Value
12/12	12.56	0 0	0.53	0.19	2.35
12/11	9.94	0 0	0.45	0.00	1.82
12/10	0.00	— —	0.28	0.00	1.49
Annual Growth	—	— —	24.0%	—	16.4%

Schlumberger Ltd.

LOCATIONS

HQ: Schlumberger Ltd.
42 Rue Saint-Dominique, Paris 75007
Phone: 713 375-3400
Web: www.slb.com

HISTORICAL FINANCIALS

Company Type: Public

Income Statement FYE: December 31

	REVENUE ($ mil.)	NET INCOME ($ mil.)	NET PROFIT MARGIN	EMPLOYEES
12/13	46,459	6,732	14.5%	123,000
12/12	42,321	5,490	13.0%	118,000
12/11	39,669	4,997	12.6%	113,000
12/10	28,931	4,267	14.7%	108,000
12/09	22,975	3,134	13.6%	77,000
Annual Growth	19.2%	21.1%	—	12.4%

2013 Year-End Financials

Debt ratio: 19.6%
Return on equity: 18.1%
Cash ($ mil.): 8,370
Current ratio: 1.94
Long-term debt ($ mil.): 10,393

No. of shares (mil.): 1,307
Dividends
Yield: 1.3%
Payout: 25.9%
Market value ($ mil.): 117,804

	STOCK PRICE ($) FY Close	P/E High/Low	PER SHARE ($) Earnings	Dividends	Book Value
12/13	90.11	19 14	5.05	1.25	30.19
12/12	69.30	19 14	4.10	1.10	26.16
12/11	68.31	26 16	3.67	1.00	23.44
12/10	83.50	25 15	3.38	0.84	22.94
12/09	65.09	27 13	2.59	0.84	16.00
Annual Growth	8.5%	— —	18.2%	10.4%	17.2%

Schneider Electric S.A.

If you're hungry for power this company can help. Schneider Electric is a leading global manufacturer of equipment for electrical power distribution and for industrial control and automation. The company helps power generators distribute electricity; designs automation systems for the automobile and water treatment industries; builds electric networks and utility management systems for energy water treatment oil and gas and marine applications; and manages electric power in residential industrial and commercial buildings. It sells its products to the construction electric power industrial and infrastructure markets.

Schneider Electric operates through five operating segments. The Power segment accounting for 37% of sales serves industrial and office buildings as well as residences through operations that include low voltage equipment installation and control systems renewable energy and electric vehicle charging. Infrastructure 22% of sales and formerly operating as Energy focuses on medium voltage operations including disconnectors circuit breakers and transformers.

The Industry segment representing 20% of sales supplies industrial firms and OEMS with products that include programmable logic controllers automation platforms contactors overload relays and motor circuit breakers. The company's smallest segments are Information Technology accounting for 14% of sales and Buildings 7% of sales. Information Technology provides critical power and cooling services especially for finance and other information technology companies. Focused on technical building management Buildings aids in the lowering of energy use and maintenance expenses among other services.

Deriving about two-thirds of its sales from outside Western Europe Schneider Electric distributes its products in some 190 countries.

Leveraging organic growth and acquisitions and focusing on areas with strong economies and on its energy management business Schneider Electric increased its revenue 14.3% at current scope and exchange rates in 2011 compared with 2010. Revenue for the power segment rose 7% on an actual basis and 7.6% at constant scope and exchange rates. The segment's uptick was supported in part by strong performance in the manufacturing and infrastructure sectors and more business development in emerging markets. Infrastructure headed up about 13% on an actual basis but 7.5% at constant scope and exchange rates. The segment did well with oil and gas and mining and metals as well as infrastructure in emerging markets.

Industry revenue enjoyed an uplift of 10.5% on an actual basis and 10.4% at constant scope and exchange rates. Machine manufacturing in emerging markets drive systems for the mining oil and gas and cement markets energy efficiency and industrial services helped boost the segment's results. Benefiting in part from demand for data centers the Information Technology sector's revenue surged about 18% on an actual basis and 10.3% at constant scope and exchange rates. Meeting demand for advanced and installed base services security systems and energy efficiency Buildings' revenue was raised 10.7% on an actual basis and 4.8% at constant scope and exchange rates. Net income rose 6% in 2011 compared with 2010 reaching a record level.

The company's Connect strategy which is being implemented from 2012 to 2014 includes four main elements: Connect to Customers Connect Everywhere Connect People and Connect for Efficiency. Connect to Customers targets opportunities for partners and distributors and improvements in the supply chain to meet the unique manufacturing and delivery needs of customers. Connect Everywhere is tasked with developing business for electric vehicle charging home automation and carbon management in mature markets and with seeking opportunities in second-tier cities in emerging markets.

Connect People is focused on workforce development including cross-business opportunities. Connect for Efficiency intends to use information technology and other functions to increase production and and to leverage research and development which now represents 5% of sales for product growth. Connect takes off from the One strategy implemented between 2008 and 2011 to organize the company around one brand served by customer segments. One was intended to position the company for opportunities in emerging markets and for more demand for energy efficiency.

In 2011 Schneider acquired Telvent GIT for about E1.4 billion ($2 billion) to expand its holdings in Spain and diversify its product line. The same year Schneider acquired US-based Summit Energy a provider of energy procurement services that complement Schneider's energy auditing and monitoring offerings. The company offers services that include energy efficiency projects risk advisory planning supply analysis contract negotiation and utility bill auditing.

Additionally in 2011 Schneider acquired India-based Luminous Power Technologies to tap growth in demand in the country for inverters and secured power products. Also in 2011 Schneider acquired Uniflair a manufacturer of precision cooling systems and other products used to cool building data centers and telecommunications facilities. The deal strengthens Schneider's presence in Europe and expands its reach in China and India. Uniflair is joining Schneider's Building segment.

HISTORY

Schneider Electric's predecessor was founded in 1782 to make industrial equipment. After the upheavals of the French Revolution and the Napoleonic Wars the company came under the control of brothers Adolphe and Eugene Schneider in 1836. Within two years they had built the first French locomotive (the country's first rail line opened in 1832).

Schneider became one of France's most important heavy industry companies branching into a variety of machinery and steel operations. However the country's industrial development continued to trail that of Britain and Germany due to recurrent political strife including the revolution of 1848 and the Franco-Prussian War. France also possessed fewer coal and iron deposits.

During WWI Schneider was a key part of France's war effort. It entered the electrical contracting business in 1929 and fought off nationalization attempts in the mid-1930s.

The blitzkrieg of 1939 brought much of France under Nazi occupation and the Schneider factories that were not destroyed were commandeered by the Germans. The company rebuilt after the war aided by the French government. It was restructured as a holding company and its operating units were split into three subsidiaries: civil and electrical engineering industrial manufacturing and construction. Charles Schneider the last family member to lead the company died in 1950.

In 1963 Schneider concluded an alliance with the Empain Group of Belgium and by 1969 three years after Schneider went public the two companies merged to become Empain-Schneider. It was a period when the company made numerous noncore acquisitions entering such fields as ski equipment fashion publishing and travel.

Schneider began reorganizing in 1980. The effort entered its final phase in 1993 with a major recapitalization that saw the merger of its former parent company Societe Parisienne d'Entreprises et de Participations with Schneider SA and the issue of new stock to existing stockholders. The company also streamlined operations. Merlin Gerin (acquired 1975) and Telemecanique (1988) became Schneider Electric in Europe and their North American operations were merged into Square D after its acquisition in 1991.

Schneider's 1994 takeover of two Belgian subsidiaries led Belgium's government to charge then-CEO Didier Pineau-Valencienne with fraud in the valuation of the stock. (A Belgian newsmagazine reported in 1997 that the government turned down an offer to settle out of court.)

In 1996 Schneider established the Schneider Electric (China) Investment Co. in Beijing China's first totally French-owned firm. The next year the company sold Spie Batignolles its electrical contracting subsidiary. Cost-cutting measures and strong sales in France and North America combined to boost the company's 1998 income.

In 1999 Schneider agreed to pay $1.1 billion for Lexel a joint venture owned by Finland's Ahlstrom and Denmark's NKT Holding to broaden its electrical equipment offerings for the household. That year the company changed its name to Schneider Electric and its main subsidiary's name to Schneider Electric Industries. Looking to add more machinery makers to its list of customers the company acquired France-based Crouzet Automatismes and Switzerland-based Positec in 2000.

Although Schneider announced in early 2001 that it would buy Legrand (a deal valued at about $6.4 billion) EU regulators blocked the acquisition in October. (In 2007 the European Court of Justice's Court of the First Instance ruled that the European Commission wrongly denied Schneider's bid to buy Legrand and ordered the EC to pay damages to Schneider for losses incurred as a result of the stymied acquisition.)

As part of the UN's "Oil for Food" program Schneider received an order from Iraq in 2002 for nearly 16000 circuit breakers to be used in that country's power grid. In September 2003 the company acquired TAC Limited (building automation and security controls). Earlier that year Schneider Electric's North American division and US-based Leviton Manufacturing inked a joint technology agreement to develop prototype voice-data-image products.

In 2004 Schneider acquired the Kavlico sensor business of Solectron for nearly $200 million and the US-based Andover Controls (building automation and security controls) from Balfour Beatty for about $400 million. Schneider continued with the purchase of France-based optoelectronics maker Dinel later that year.

The following year Schneider acquired electronic sensor specialist BEI Technologies for about $562 million. After buying the European and Middle Eastern operations of Invensys Building Systems for $150 million in 2005 Schneider in 2006 acquired the Asian and US operations of Invensys Building Systems for nearly $300 million in cash.

Also in 2006 Schneider bought the Napac subsidiary of L'Air Liquide. The French firm made intelligent remote management products for the infrastructure market allowing engineers and operators to run refineries water systems refrigerated warehouses power plants and other facilities from a distance. Napac was integrated into Schneider's Sorhodel Bardin subsidiary. That same year the company acquired GET Group a UK manufacturer of wiring devices and other electrical products. GET made lighting fixtures HVAC equipment and security systems among other offerings.

In 2007 Schneider bought video security systems specialist Pelco for $1.22 billion in cash adding to its Building Automation business. The company paid another $320 million in cash for a tax benefit held by Pelco increasing the value of the transaction to $1.54 billion. Earlier that year Schneider acquired American Power Conversion (APC) for about $6.1 billion in cash widening the company's portfolio in uninterruptible power supply systems. Schneider merged APC with the US subsidiary of its MGE UPS SYSTEMS power supplies business.

In 2008 Schneider acquired Xantrex Technology for about $500 million in cash to strengthen its product portfolio in power inverters for solar and wind energy products. Also that year the company purchased Wessen a Russia-based maker of switches sockets and other wiring devices that complements Schneider's existing wiring portfolio. Other acquisitions in 2008 included two US-based companies: RAM Industries (control systems for energy-efficiency) and Intelligent Motion System (integrated motor control and drive products). On the flip side Schneider sold its Selectron Systems AG subsidiary (automation systems for the rail industry) in 2008 as part of a change in market focus.

Reaching into Latin America in 2009 the multinational company acquired Brazil's #3 maker of UPS (uninterruptible power supplies) power protection voltage regulators and accessories Microsol Tecnologia. The purchase opened up new retail channels and local government support.

Also that year the company acquired two Indian companies: Conzerv Systems active in the Indian industrial and commercial energy market with strength in energy audits and energy management systems and Bangalore-based Meher Capacitors which became Schneider's R&D and manufacturing hub for capacitors in the region.

Schneider rang in 2010 by acquiring Cimac a Dubai-based control and system integrator. The acquisition increased the company's geographic footprint in the Gulf countries. The same year Schneider purchased Australia's SCADAgroup for A$200 million (about E140 million or around $191 million). With operations in North America and the UK in addition to Australia SCADAgroup makes telemetry products for customers in electric power generation oil and gas production and water and wastewater treatment. Its products allow end users to remotely control measure and monitor widely scattered systems.

Also in 2010 Schneider Electric and ALSTOM acquired AREVA's power transmission and distribution business (moving electricity long distances to homes and businesses). General Electric and Toshiba were ousted as potential buyers in favor of the two French companies which promised not to lay off workers and to offer positions to AREVA employees in their respective geographic areas.

EXECUTIVES

Chief Marketing Officer, Aaron L. Davis, age 47
Vice Chairman, Leo Apotheker, age 60
EVP Global Supply Chain, Annette K. Clayton, age 50
Executive Vice-President Finance, Emmanuel Babeau, age 42
Executive Vice-President Custom Sensors & Technologies Business * 1, Eric Pilaud, age 56
Secretary, Philippe Bougon
EVP Power North America and Buildings Businesses, Christopher B. (Chris) Curtis, age 56
President and CEO, Jean-Pascal Tricoire, age 50
EVP Power Global and EMEAS Business, Julio Rodriguez, age 50
Executive Vice-President IT Business, Daniel Doimo
EVP Infrastructure Business, Michel Crochon, age 62
EVP Power Asia/Pacific Business, Eric Rondolat, age 47
Executive Vice-President Customers & Alliances, Christian Wiest, age 64
EVP IT Business, Laurent Vernerey, age 53
EVP Global Human Resources, Karen Ferguson, age 49
Chairman, Henri Lachman, age 74
EVP Strategy and Innovation, Philippe Delorme, age 42
President Power Buildings and Energy US, Jeff Drees
EVP Finances, Emmauel Babeau, age 47
Chief Information Officer, Herve Coureil, age 43
EVP Industry Business, Clemens Blum, age 58
Executive Vice President China Operations 1, Zhu Hai
Executive Vice-President Global Operations 1, Julio Rodriguez
Executive Vice-President IT Business, Laurent Verneray
Director, Noel Forgeard, age 66
Director, Serge Weinberg, age 62
Director, Willy R. Kissling, age 68
Vice Chairman, Leo Apotheker, age 60
Director, Gordon R. Thoman, age 68
Director, Jerome Gallot, age 53
Director, Anand G. Mahindra, age 57
Director, Cathy Kopp, age 63
Director, Gerard de La Martiniere, age 68
Director, Claude Briquet, age 52

Director, Claude Bebear, age 76
Director, Dominique Senequier, age 60
Auditors: Ernst&YoungetAutres

LOCATIONS

HQ: Schneider Electric S.A.
35 rue Joseph Monier, Rueil-Malmaison, Cedex 92506
Phone: (33) 1 41 29 70 00 **Fax:** (33) 1 41 29 71 00
Web: www.schneider-electric.com

2011 Sales

	% of total
Western	32
Asia/Pacific	27
North	23
Rest of the	18
Total	**100**

PRODUCTS/OPERATIONS

2011 Sales

	% of total
Power	37
Infrastructure	22
Industry	20
Information	14
Buildings	7
Total	**100**

Selected Products

Advanced human-machine interface terminals
Camera sensors
Centralized building management systems
Circuit breakers
Customized sensors
Disconnectors
Electric vehicle charging infrastructure
Electrical panels
Indicator lights
InRow Cooling Systems
Installation & control systems
Medium voltage cells
Network power control
Optimum temperature control
Power supply
Programmable regulators
Renewable energies integration
Security monitoring equipment
Server cabinets
Software for the integrated management of mission critical infrastructure
Supervision Control & Data Acquisition (SCADA) management systems
Transformers
Uninterruptable power supply
  Monophase
  Three-phase

COMPETITORS

ABB
ALSTOM
Alcatel-Lucent
Bechtel
Beghelli
Bharat Heavy Electricals
Checkpoint Systems
Danaher
EMCOR
Eaton
Electricite de France
Emerson Electric
Endress + Hauser
Finmeccanica
Fluor
GE
Itron
Johnson Controls
Legrand
Measurement Specialties
Mitsubishi Electric
Nissin Electric
Rockwell Automation
Roper Industries
Sentry Technology
Siemens AG
Technology Research Corp.
Transtector
Vicon Industries
Woodhead Industries
Yokogawa Electric

HISTORICAL FINANCIALS

Company Type: Public

Income Statement

FYE: December 31

	REVENUE ($ mil.)	NET INCOME ($ mil.)	NET PROFIT MARGIN	EMPLOYEES
12/12	31,562	2,425	7.7%	152,384
12/11	28,956	2,354	8.1%	140,491
12/10	26,205	2,302	8.8%	123,482
12/09	22,750	1,227	5.4%	116,065
12/08	25,600	2,351	9.2%	126,481
Annual Growth	5.4%	0.8%	—	4.8%

2012 Year-End Financials

Debt ratio: 29.6%
Return on equity: 11.2%
Cash ($ mil.): 4,925
Current ratio: 1.51
Long-term debt ($ mil.): 8,443
No. of shares (mil.): 546
Dividends
  Yield: 2.9%
  Payout: 16.3%
Market value ($ mil.): 8,088

	STOCK PRICE ($) FY Close	P/E High	P/E Low	PER SHARE ($) Earnings	PER SHARE ($) Dividends	PER SHARE ($) Book Value
12/12	14.79	8	5	4.43	0.43	40.11
12/11	10.51	10	5	4.33	0.88	38.10
12/10	15.34	9	5	4.38	0.25	37.00
12/09	11.85	15	6	2.47	0.49	32.81
12/08	7.60	7	3	4.89	0.00	31.78
Annual Growth	18.1%	—	—	(2.5%)	—	6.0%

Seven & i Holdings Co. Ltd.

Japan's biggest retail conglomerate Seven & i Holdings caters to six of the so-called seven deadly sins (saving wrath for its competition). The "seven" of the company's title reflects the seven areas of business that it is involved with: convenience stores general merchandise and department stores restaurants supermarkets banks and IT services. The "holding" part of the firm's name consists of its subsidiaries: Seven-Eleven Japan (parent of 7-Eleven in the US) Ito-Yokado Sogo & Seibu Co. Seven & i Food Systems Seven Bank and York-Benimaru. Created in 2005 after stock-transfer agreements absorbing its subsidiaries into the company took effect Seven & i operates some 41900 stores worldwide.

After two years of decline the holding company's fiscal 2011 (ends February) total sales inched up a bit while net income more than doubled vs. the previous year. Seven & i's convenience stores posted a sales gain while sales at its superstores and department stores were flat. Already the world's #1 convenience store operator Seven & i's worldwide network of c-stores topped 40000 in fiscal 2011. (Convenience stores account for about 40% of the group's total worldwide sales.) By March 2014 the company is planning to open a record 1500 c-stores (for a net gain of more than 900) as it works to cater to "housewives and the elderly."

While Seven & i rings up more than two-thirds of its total sales at home the holding company oversees about 100 operating companies in 15 other countries in Asia North America and Europe. With the Japanese economy in a prolonged slump and reeling from the effects of the massive earthquake in March 2011 it's looking beyond its borders for growth opportunities. China is an important emerging market for Seven & i Holdings: It currently operates more than 4800 stores and restaurants in Taiwan and supermarkets stores and restaurants in Beijing Chengdu and Shanghai. Indeed in early 2009 Seven & i Food Systems formed a joint venture company with a large Chinese corporation to establish the family restaurant chain "AllDay's" there.

Seeking to further expand its retail empire the company and Ain Pharmaciez formed Seven Health Care which plans to open drugstores inside superstores and shopping malls operated by Seven & i Holdings and to develop generic drugs. Seven Health Care is jointly owned by Seven & i Holdings (10%) and its subsidiaries Ito-Yokado (50%) and Seven-Eleven Japan (10%) as well as Ain Pharmaciez (30%). More recently the company also boosted its entertainment holdings by doubling its stake in Tower Records Japan in 2011 to about 45%. The move made Seven & i the largest shareholder in the music retail chain (ahead of NTT DoCoMo with 42%).

While the global appetite for convenience store fare is growing the hunger for department store merchandise is not. As the Japanese department store industry struggles with weak personal consumption the company rearranged its department store holdings when it merged holding company Millennium Retailing with Sogo and Seibu department stores to form Sogo & Seibu Co. in August 2009. The merger was effected to capitalize on the well-known Sogo and Seibu names reduce costs and to foster collaboration with Seven & i.

The "i" of Seven & i Holdings stands for "innovation" as well as for the similar-sounding Japanese word for "love."

EXECUTIVES

President and COO, Noritoshi Murata, age 69
Chairman and CEO, Toshifumi Suzuki, age 81
President and COO Seven-Eleven Japan, Ryuichi Isaka
Chairman Seven Bank, Takashi Anzai
President and COO York-Benimaru, Zenko Ohtaka
Managing Executive Officer and Chief Administrative Officer, Katsuhiro Goto
President and COO Ito-Yokado, Atsushi Kamei
Executive Officer, Masao Eguchi
Executive Officer, Yoshihiro Tanaka
Executive Officer, Yasuo Takaha
Executive Officer, Kazuo Otsuka
Executive Officer and CFO, Kunio Takahashi
Executive Officer, Masayuki Sato
Executive Officer, Akira Miyakawa
President Sogo & Seibu, Ryu Matsumoto
President Seven & i Food Systems, Tsuneo Okubo
Director, Takashi Anzai
Director, Zenko Ohtaka
Chief Administrative Officer and Director, Katsuhiro Goto
Director, Noritaka Shimizu
Director, Scott T. Davis
Director, Atsushi Kamei
CFO and Director, Kunio Takahashi
Director, Tsuyoshi Kobayashi
Director, Ryuchi Isaka
Director, Ikujiro Nonaka
Auditors: KPMGAZSA&Co.

LOCATIONS

HQ: Seven & i Holdings Co. Ltd.
8-8 Niban-cho, Chiyoda-ku, Tokyo 102-8452
Phone: (81) 3 6238 3000
Web: www.7andi.com

2011 Stores

	No.
Asia Oceania	

Japan	14,088
China	1,734
Other	16,454
North	8,356
Europe	506
Hawaii	55
Total	**41,193**

2011 Sales

	% of total
Japan	69
North	29
Other	2
Total	**100**

PRODUCTS/OPERATIONS

2011 Sales

	% of total
Convenience	39
Superstores	38
Department	18
Financial	2
Food	2
Other	1
Total	**100**

Selected Subsidiaries

Convenience stores
- 7-Eleven Inc.
- Seven-Eleven (Beijing) Co. (65%)
- Seven-Eleven China Co.
- Seven-Eleven (Hawaii) Inc.
- Seven-Eleven Japan Co.

Superstores
- Chengdu Ito-Yokado (74%)
- Hua Tang Yokado (76%)
- Ito-Yokado
- York Mart
- York-Benimaru

Department stores
- Gottsuo Bin Co.
- The Loft Co. (71%)
- Shell Garden Co.
- Sogo & Seibu Co.

Financial services
- K.K. York Insurance
- Seven & i Financial Center
- Seven Bank (49%)
- Seven Card Service (96%)

Food services
- Seven & i Food Systems
- Seven & i Restaurant (Beijing) Co. (75%)

COMPETITORS

A.S. Watson
AEON
Asahi Kasei
Carrefour
Couche-Tard
Daiei
Dairy Farm International
FamilyMart
Fast Retailing
Isetan Mitsukoshi
J. Front
Kirin Holdings Company
Kokubu
LAWSON
McDonald' s
Nisshin Seifun Group
Seiyu
Takashimaya
Uny
Yamazaki Baking

HISTORICAL FINANCIALS

Company Type: Public

Income Statement FYE: February 28

	REVENUE ($ mil.)	NET INCOME ($ mil.)	NET PROFIT MARGIN	EMPLOYEES
02/13	54,169	1,498	2.8%	55,011
02/12	59,516	1,614	2.7%	51,888
02/11	62,535	1,367	2.2%	50,765
02/10	57,514	504	0.9%	52,814
02/09	57,882	945	1.6%	54,486
Annual Growth	(1.6%)	12.2%	—	0.2%

2013 Year-End Financials

Debt ratio: 0.2%
Return on equity: 7.5%
Cash ($ mil.): 7,715
Current ratio: 1.08
Long-term debt ($ mil.): 5,626
No. of shares (mil.): 883
Dividends
Yield: 2.7%
Payout: —
Market value ($ mil.): 51,597

	STOCK PRICE ($) FY Close	P/E High/Low	PER SHARE ($) Earnings	Dividends	Book Value
02/13	58.40	— —	1.69	1.59	24.50
02/12	55.21	— —	1.83	1.47	26.19
02/11	55.83	— —	1.54	1.29	24.56
02/10	44.86	— —	0.56	0.00	22.34
02/09	43.10	— —	1.03	0.00	21.10
Annual Growth	7.9%	— —	13.3%	—	3.8%

Sharp Corp. (Japan)

Sharp can give a its peers pointers on innovation. Best known for its consumer electronics the company is a top maker of electronic components and computer hardware and peripherals. Its flagship components business makes LCDs (used in everything from airplane cockpits to PCs to pinball machines) flash memory laser diodes and optical sensors. Sharp also makes printers and cell phones; consumer audio and video products such as Blu-ray disc players and LCD TVs; and a variety of appliances such as air purifiers and steam ovens. The 100-year-old company is also one of the world's largest manufacturers of photovoltaic solar cells.

Sharp gets more than half of sales from customers located outside of Japan. The company has established regional headquarters in the Americas China and in Europe as it looks to expand internationally. It plans to establish a regional center in Asia in 2014.

Sharp's sales fell by more than 16% to Y2455 billion (about $30 billion) for 2012 primarily due to continued declines in prices for LCD TVs. In Japan there was a particularly steep drop in demand for flat-panel TVs and large-size LCD panels along with slumping demand for solar cells. Slower growth in China and other emerging economies and the ongoing European debt crisis were also cited by the company as reasons for the dismal results. Most likely a combination of many factors Sharp recorded a 2012 annual net loss of Y376 billion (around $4.7 billion) the largest in its history.

Part of the problem was that in 2011 looking to keep sales strong Sharp focused on the development of more business for LCDs and solar products. The company has also relied on Japanese supplies for its components rather than looking to buy cheaper parts made elsewhere raising its production costs. Sharp's new strategy is to return to the development of unique products –talking vacuum cleaner anyone? –that by their very nature spur demand. It is the strategy that the company has relied on for growth and revitalization during most of its 100 year history.

Sharp's focus on large LCD panels caused problems at its Sakai site after domestic TV demand fell. For much of 2012 the factory operated below capacity making the displays produced there even more expensive. Sharp and Hon Hai have joint ownership in the Sakai production plant the world's most advanced LCD plant. Hon Hai chairman Terry Gou purchased a 38% stake in the plant and wants to invest another $1 billion to boost capacity at Sakai looking to secure a source of the advanced LCD panels that could give it an advantage in keeping the contract for the Apple iPhone and iPad it currently manufactures. (Sharp is one of three LCD panel suppliers for Apple. The other two are Samsung Electronics and LG Electronics.)

Shares in Sharp plummeted after the company reported its 2012 financial results putting the debt-ridden company in a financial bind. Sharp's debt is estimated at around Y1.25 trillion it has mortgaged nearly all of its offices and factories in Japan and its credit ratings have been downgraded to junk. Sharp was looking to an agreement with Hon Hai to provide cash to pay the bills. As its shares continued to slide Hon Hai insisted the companies renegotiate the terms of the cash-and-stock deal.

Hon Hai initially agreed to pay Y67 billion (about $856 million) in exchange for a 9.9% stake in Sharp. At the time Sharp was trading at Y550 per share. The shares then dropped to less than Y200 a share in August and Hon Hai chairman Terry Gou demanded that the deal include a management role –and a say in its business strategy – in addition to the stake and further cooperation in Sharp's small LCD display business. Gou made a trip to Japan in late August and expectations were that an agreement would be concluded at that time; instead Gou returned home early before a scheduled meeting with Sharp executives and the meeting has not been rescheduled.

Sharp's lenders have stepped in. Mizuho Financial Group and Mitsubishi UFJ Financial Group are working to arrange financing for up to Y300 billion ($3.87 billion) to keep the electronics giant afloat. Sharp is also cutting costs planning to slash 5000 jobs (about 10% of its global workforce and its first layoffs in 60 years) as well as trim the salaries of managers by 10% and institute an across-the-board wage cut for its other workers. It also cancelled its centennial celebrations

HISTORY

Tokuji Hayakawa got started in manufacturing in 1912 when he established Hayakawa Electric Industry to make a type of belt buckle he had designed. Three years later he invented the first mechanical pencil named the Ever-Sharp which was a commercial success. After an earthquake leveled much of Tokyo in 1923 including Hayakawa's business he moved to Osaka and sold the rights to his pencil to finance a new factory. He introduced Japan's first crystal radio sets in 1925 and four years later debuted a vacuum tube radio.

Following WWII Hayakawa Electric developed an experimental TV which it began mass-producing in 1953. The company was ready with color TVs when Japan initiated color broadcasts in 1960. Hayakawa Electric grew tremendously during the 1960s introducing microwave ovens (1962) solar cells (1963) the first electronic all-transistor-diode calculator (1964) and the first gallium arsenide LED (1969). The firm opened a US office in 1962.

In 1970 the company began to make its own semiconductor devices and changed its name to Sharp Corporation a nod to the name of its first product. It began mass production of LCDs in 1973. Sharp later introduced the first electronic calculator with an LCD (1973) solar-powered calculators (1976) and a credit card-sized calculator (1979).

The company began producing VCRs in the early 1980s and in 1984 Sharp introduced its first color copier. That year the firm introduced a fax machine and began concentrating its marketing efforts on small businesses (while its competitors were scrambling for large corporate accounts). Haruo Tsuji became president in 1986. He restructured the company and concentrated research on

LCDs. Sharp blitzed the market with a new line of creative products in the late 1980s including a high-definition LCD color TV (1987) and a notebook-sized PC (1988).

Sharp introduced a cordless pocket telephone in 1992 that operated continuously for over five hours as well as a low-cost high-definition television (HDTV). That year the company announced strategic alliances with Apple to build the Newton personal digital assistant (which flopped) and with the Shanghai Radio and Television to make air conditioners fax machines copiers and printers (Shanghai Sharp Electronics began production in 1994). During the mid-1990s Sharp's ViewCam camcorder and Zaurus personal digital assistant were both big sellers.

In 1996 Sharp formed partnerships with Alcatel (now Alcatel-Lucent) Advanced Micro Devices (AMD) Fujitsu Intel and Nanjing Panda Electronics (China's second-largest TV maker). More joint ventures followed in 1997 including a partnership with Sony to develop flat-panel displays.

Katsuhiko Machida became president in 1998 as the company attempted to pump younger blood into its veins; Tsuji became company adviser. That year the company restructured around three business areas: home appliances and consumer electronics information and communications and components. Restructuring in its LCD operations reduced profits by 80% in 1999. The company rebounded the next year but a downturn in the global economy and competitive pricing in the LCD business again put Sharp's profits under pressure in 2001. The company reduced its workforce and simplified its organizational structure reorganizing its operations from 42 divisions into 24.

Also in 2001 Sharp introduced its AQUOS flat-panel TV which became a popular model among consumers; it had made 10 million AQUOS TVs by mid-2006. It set plans to build its Mihara Plant for manufacturing electronic components and agreed to collaborate on home appliances with SANYO Electric.

In 2002 Sharp built a plant for large-screen LCD TVs in Kameyama City in Japan's Mie prefecture. It began production of system LCDs at the Tenri Plant. Later that year Sharp broke ground on a new plant in Kameyama.

The following year the company began production of system LCDs at the Mie Plant No. 3. Sharp joined with eight other manufacturers of consumer electronics in forming the Blu-ray Disc Founders (later the Blu-ray Disc Association) an industry organization promoting a next-generation technology format for DVDs. SAP and Sharp agreed on partnering for mobile business applications. The company initiated production of photovoltaic modules in Europe.

Sharp launched an online music distribution service Any Music in 2004. The company built a printed circuit board manufacturing facility at the Mihara Plant and set plans to construct a second plant and technical center in Wuxi China. IBM Japan and Sharp collaborated on developing an IC card with a new operating system. Sharp and Sony Ericsson started working together on a 3G FOMA mobile phone for the Japanese market.

In 2005 the company acquired Fujitsu's LCD subsidiary Fujitsu Display Technology.

Construction finally began on Plant No. 2 in Kameyama in mid-2005; about a year later the plant started turning out LCD panels for flat-screen TVs. Later that year Sharp and the University of Tokyo established Todai-Sharp Laboratories for advanced R&D on flexible electronics.

In 2006 Sharp recalled 28000 battery packs made by Sony for laptop computers in the Japanese market because the lithium-ion batteries were at risk of overheating and catching fire. Fujitsu and other PC makers also recalled the Sony-made batteries.

Sharp spent about Y6 billion (more than $50 million) on building an LCD module assembly plant in Poland. The facility began production in 2007 providing LCD modules for TVs being sold into European markets.

Katsuhiko Machida was promoted to chairman in 2007. Succeeding him as president of the company was Mikio Katayama a corporate director since 2003 who had joined Sharp in 1981.

Also in 2007 the company teamed up with rival Pioneer to work together on developing consumer electronics products such as car navigation systems displays DVD players and home networking equipment. As part of the cooperative agreement Sharp made an equity investment in Pioneer taking a stake of 14% and becoming Pioneer's biggest shareholder (Sharp now holds more than 9%). The business and capital alliance was intended to help both companies compete better with bigger vendors such as Panasonic Samsung Electronics and Sony.

In late 2008 Sharp pleaded guilty to fixing prices on LCD panels under charges brought by the US Department of Justice and agreed to pay a fine of $120 million. Federal prosecutors and antitrust regulators previously investigated alleged price fixing in the semiconductor industry with mixed results. They found multiple violations in the DRAM business but none in the markets for graphics processing chips and cards and for static RAMs.

In 2010 Sharp and Sony formed a joint venture –Sharp Display Products Corporation –to operate an LCD panel plant in Sakai City. Sony owns about 7% of the JV with Sharp holding the remaining stake. Sony was going to invest Y100 billion ($926 million) in the LCD JV and increase its holding in the venture to 34% but weak sales of flat-panel TVs led the company to abandon the plans.

Also in 2010 the company announced two joint ventures aimed at the solar market. The first is a thin-film solar cell production venture between Sharp STMicroelectronics and Enel Green Power (EGP) a unit of Italian utility giant (and Sharp partner) Enel S.p.A. The three companies made equal initial investments of up to E70 million to construct a plant in the Catania province of the Sicily region in Italy which began operations in 2011. Solar cells produced at the plant are marketed by Sharp and EGP in Europe the Middle East and Africa. In the second agreement Sharp and EGP set up Enel Green Power & Sharp Solar Energy S.r.l. (ESSE) with plans to build multiple independent power plants with a total generating capacity of more than 500 MW by the end of 2016. ESSE completed construction of its first plant in Southern Italy in early 2011. The initial market for the power produced will be Mediterranean countries including Italy France and Spain; ESSE uses solar cells from the Catania plant.

EXECUTIVES

President, Kozo Takahashi
President and COO, Mikio Katayama, age 55
Group General Manager Global Market Development Group?Emerging Markets Asia Oceania, Takashi Okuda, age 59
Group General Manager Health and Environment Systems Group, Noboru Fujimoto
General Manager Corporate Strategy and Management Planning Board, Toshihiko Fujimoto, age 58
EVP and CTO, Shigeaki Mizushima, age 58
General Manager Liquid Crystal Display Business; Group General Manager Liquid Crystal Display Group, Yoshisuke Hasegawa, age 58
Group General Manager Audio-Visual Systems Development Group, Masatsugu Teragawa, age 61
Group General Manager Production Technology Development Group, Toshihiko Hirobe, age 57
Group General Manager Human Resources Group and Director, Nobuyuki Taniguchi, age 55
Director; Group General Manager China Group; Chairman Sharp Electronics Sales (China) Co. Ltd., Nobuyuki Sugano, age 65
General Manager Domestic Sales and Marketing; Group General Manager Domestic Sales and Marketing Group, Moriyuki Okada
Group General Manager Corporate Sales Group, Kazutaka Ihori
Senior Executive Managing Officer, Fujikazu Nakayama
General Manager Information and Communication Systems Business; Group General Manager Communication Systems Group, Masami Ohbatake
Group General Manager CS Promotion Group, Motohiko Hayashi
Group General Manager Environmental Protection Group, Hiroshi Morimoto
Director, Kunio Ito
Group General Manager CSR Promotion Group; General Manager Legal Affairs Division, Kazutoshi Goto
Operations Director, Christine Wenner
President Sharp Electronics Marketing, Akira Atarashi
IR Contact Officer, Hiroshi Hiroshi Sato Sato
Executive Officer; Chief Director of Solar System Business, Kazushi Kazushi Mukai Mukai
Executive Officer; Chief Director of Brand Strategy Promotion, Keiko Keiko Okada Okada
Executive Officer; Chief Director of AV System Business, Masayuki Masayuki Mori Mori
Executive Officer; Chief Director of Research Development, Mototaka Mototaka Taneya Taneya
Executive Officer; Chief Director of Electronic Device Sales, Noboru Noboru Yamazawa Yamazawa
Senior Executive Managing Officer, Norikazu Hoshi
Executive Officer; Chief Director of Europe & Central and Eastern Europe; President of Subsidiary, Paul Paul Molyneux Molyneux
Executive Officer; Chief Director of Electronic Device Business, Ryutaro Ryutaro Egawa Egawa
Senior Executive Managing Officer, Tetsuo Onishi
Executive Officer; Chief Director of Environment Security, Tetsuro Tetsuro Muramatsu Muramatsu
Executive Officer; Chief Director of America; President & Chairman of Subsidiary, Toshiyuki Toshiyuki Osawa Osawa
EVP and Director; Chief Officer General Administration and Solar Business and Group General Manager Global Brand Strategy Group, Toshishige Hamano, age 66
Senior Executive Managing Officer and CTO; Group General Manager Intellectual Property Group, Kenji Ohta, age 64
EVP Electronic Components and Devices Business and Director; Group General Manager Sales and Marketing Group?Electronic Components and Devices, Yoshiaki Ibuchi, age 65
EVP Audio-Visual Systems Business and Director, Masafumi Matsumoto, age 64
President and COO, Mikio Katayama, age 55
EVP Chief Legal Affairs Officer and Director; Group General Manager Tokyo Branch, Toshio Adachi, age 64
Group General Manager Human Resources Group and Director, Nobuyuki Taniguchi, age 55
Director; Group General Manager China Group; Chairman Sharp Electronics Sales (China) Co. Ltd., Nobuyuki Sugano, age 65
Director, Kunio Ito
Director, Katsuaki Nomura
Independent Director, Makoto Makoto Kato Kato
Auditors: KPMGAZSA&Co.

LOCATIONS

HQ: Sharp Corp. (Japan)
22-22 Nagaike-cho, Abeno-ku, Osaka 545-8522
Phone: (81) 6 6621 1221
Web: www.sharp.co.jp

2012 Sales

	% of total
Japan	48
China	20
The	12
Europe	11
Other	9
Total	**100**

PRODUCTS/OPERATIONS

2012 Sales

	% of total
Audiovisual & communication	43
LCDs	17
Health & environmental	12
Information	11
Solar	9
Other electronic	8
Total	**100**

Selected Products

Consumer/information products
- Audiovisual and communication equipment
  - Audio amplifiers
  - Blu-ray disc players
  - Digital cameras
  - High-definition televisions
  - Liquid crystal display DVD televisions
  - Liquid crystal display televisions
  - Liquid crystal display video projectors
  - Mobile phones
  - Video cameras
- Information equipment
  - Calculators
  - Digital copiers
  - Fax machines
  - Mobile business tools
  - Personal computers
  - Printers
- Home appliances
  - Air cleaning systems
  - Superheated steam ovens

Electronic components
- Flash memory
- Integrated circuits
- Laser diodes and other optoelectronic devices
- Radio-frequency components
- Satellite broadcasting components
- Solar cells and other photovoltaic devices

COMPETITORS

AU Optronics
Avago Technologies
BP Solar
CASIO COMPUTER
Canon
Dell
Eastman Kodak
Electrolux
Epson
Ericsson
FUJIFILM
First Solar
Fuji Xerox
Fujitsu
GE
Hewlett-Packard
Hitachi
IBM
JDI
Konica Minolta
Kyocera
LG Electronics
Lexmark
Mitsubishi Electric
Motorola Solutions
NEC
Oki Electric
Panasonic Corp
Philips Electronics
Pioneer Corporation
Q-Cells
Ricoh Company
SANYO
Samsung Electronics
Siemens AG
SolarWorld
Sony
SunPower
Suntech Power
TCL
TPV Technology
Tatung
Toshiba
Xerox
Yingli

HISTORICAL FINANCIALS

Company Type: Public

Income Statement

FYE: March 31

	REVENUE ($ mil.)	NET INCOME ($ mil.)	NET PROFIT MARGIN	EMPLOYEES
03/13	26,342	(5,795)	—	50,647
03/12	29,938	(4,584)	—	56,756
03/11	36,494	234	0.6%	55,580
03/10	29,504	47	0.2%	53,999
03/09	28,913	(1,277)	—	54,144
Annual Growth	(2.3%)	—	—	(1.7%)

2013 Year-End Financials

Debt ratio: 0.5%
Return on equity: (-145.3%)
Cash ($ mil.): 2,039
Current ratio: 0.73
Long-term debt ($ mil.): 2,477
No. of shares (mil.): 1,166
Dividends
Yield: —
Payout: —
Market value ($ mil.): 3,242

	STOCK PRICE ($) FY Close	P/E High/Low		PER SHARE ($) Earnings	Dividends	Book Value
03/13	2.78	—	—	(5.21)	0.00	1.23
03/12	7.38	—	—	(4.17)	0.00	7.15
03/11	9.83	—	—	0.20	0.23	11.51
03/10	12.40	—	—	0.04	0.15	10.37
03/09	8.05	—	—	(1.16)	0.28	9.68
Annual Growth	(23.3%)	—	—	—	—	(40.3%)

Shenzhen Development Bank Co., Ltd.

Shenzhen Development Bank (SDB) has international character. It was the first Chinese bank to receive significant foreign investment and its chairman and CEO Frank Newman is a former deputy secretary of the US Treasury. SDB has more than 250 bank branches in economic centers including Beijing Shanghai and Tianjin; it has correspondent branches in more than 70 international regions. The bank offers standard deposit and lending services to commercial and individual customers. It also trades in foreign and domestic securities and offers a mix of financial services including trust services and investment banking. Ping An Insurance built its ownership of SDB to more than 50% in mid-2011.

LOCATIONS

HQ: Shenzhen Development Bank Co., Ltd.
Shenzhen Devolopment Bank Building, No. 5047, Shennan East Road, Shenzhen, Guangdong Province 518001
Phone: (86) 755 82080387 **Fax:** (86) 755 82080386
Web: www.sdb.com.cn

HISTORICAL FINANCIALS

Company Type: Public

Income Statement

FYE: December 31

	ASSETS ($ mil.)	NET INCOME ($ mil.)	INCOME AS % OF ASSETS	EMPLOYEES
12/12	257,695	2,149	0.8%	0
12/11	199,888	1,632	0.8%	0
12/10	110,384	953	0.9%	0
12/09	86,088	736	0.9%	0
12/08	69,530	89	0.1%	10,381
Annual Growth	38.8%	121.1%	—	—

2012 Year-End Financials

Return on assets: 0.9%
Return on equity: 16.9%
Long-term debt ($ mil.): —
No. of shares (mil.): —
Sales ($ mil): 6,391
Dividends
Yield: —
Payout: —
Market value ($ mil.): —

Shinhan Financial Group Co. Ltd.

Shinhan Financial Group one of South Korea's largest financial companies in terms of assets provides retail and corporate banking credit cards insurance investment management securities brokerage and credit reporting services. Its primary subsidiary is Shinhan Bank which with more than 1000 locations has one of the largest branch networks in the country. Shinhan Financial Group has international operations in about a half-dozen Asian countries Europe and the US. Other units include Shinhan Investment Corp. (formerly Goodmorning Shinhan Securities with more than 80 offices) and Shinhan Life Insurance (about 140 offices).

Shinhan Financial Group has a joint venture with Australia's Macquarie Bank to provide project financing and corporate advisory services primarily for infrastructure-related projects. Established in 2005 Shinhan Macquarie Financial Advisory has grown to be a leading infrastructure-related financial services company in South Korea

Shinhan makes acquisitions in order to strengthen its position in South Korea's financial services market. It has made several big deals over the years to add to its operations and capabilities. In 2011 Shinhan agreed to acquire ailing Tomato Savings Bank.

EXECUTIVES

Director; CEO Shinhan Bank, Jin Won Suh, age 62
Deputy President, Jae Gwang Soh, age 52
Deputy President and CFO, Jung Kee Min, age 54
Deputy President, Dong Hwan Lee, age 54
Deputy President, Buhmsoo Choi, age 57
Chairman and CEO, Dong Woo Han, age 65
Vice President, Se Se Yil Oh Oh
Deputy President, Sung Ho Wi, age 55
IR Contact Officer, Seung Seung Heon Ryu Ryu
Deputy President, Sin Gee Lee, age 57
Director; CEO Shinhan Bank, Jin Won Suh
Chairman CEO and Director, Dong Woo Han
Director, Ke Sup Yun, age 67
Director, Yoji Hirakawa, age 59
Director, Philippe Aguignier, age 54
Non-Executive Independent Director, Gi Gi Yeong Kim Kim

Non-Executive Independent Director, Gye Gye Seop Yoon Yoon
Non-Executive Independent Director, Haruki Haruki Hirakawa Hirakawa
Non-Executive Independent Director, Hun Hun Namgoong Namgoong
Non-Executive Independent Director, Jae Jae Geun Yoo Yoo
Non-Executive Independent Director, Sang Sang Gyeong Lee Lee
Non-Executive Independent Director, Seok Seok Won Kim Kim
Non-Executive Independent Director, Tae Tae Eun Gwon Gwon
Auditors: KPMGSamjongAccountingCorp.

LOCATIONS

HQ: Shinhan Financial Group Co. Ltd.
120, 2-ga, Taepyung-ro, Jung-gu, Seoul 100-102
Phone: (82) 2 6360 3071 **Fax:** (82) 2 6360 3082
Web: www.shinhangroup.com

PRODUCTS/OPERATIONS

Selected Subsidiaries

Good Morning Shinhan Securities Co. Ltd.
Jeju Bank (62%)
Shinhan Bank
Shinhan Capital Co. Ltd.
Shinhan Card Co. Ltd.
Shinhan Credit Information Co. Ltd.
Shinhan Life Insurance Co. Ltd.
Shinhan Macquarie Financial Advisory (51%)

COMPETITORS

KB Financial Group
Korea Exchange Bank
Samsung Life Insurance
Woori

HISTORICAL FINANCIALS

Company Type: Public

Income Statement FYE: December 31

	ASSETS ($ mil.)	NET INCOME ($ mil.)	INCOME AS % OF ASSETS	EMPLOYEES
12/12	281,771	2,175	0.8%	155
12/11	248,656	2,675	1.1%	158
12/10	239,510	2,394	1.0%	145
12/09	220,404	1,128	0.5%	135
12/08	208,001	1,590	0.8%	98
Annual Growth	7.9%	8.1%	—	12.1%

2012 Year-End Financials

Return on assets: 0.7%
Return on equity: 9.1%
Long-term debt ($ mil.): —
No. of shares (mil.): 474
Sales ($ mil): 16,792
Dividends
Yield: 1.8%
Payout: 29.3%
Market value ($ mil.): 17,375

	STOCK PRICE ($) FY Close	P/E High/Low	PER SHARE ($) Earnings	Dividends	Book Value
12/12	36.64	— —	4.39	0.66	51.97
12/11	68.21	— —	5.03	0.00	44.40
12/10	93.82	— —	4.53	0.71	46.52
12/09	74.28	— —	1.98	0.82	37.77
12/08	47.16	— —	3.44	1.85	35.01
Annual Growth	(6.1%)	— —	6.3%	(22.7%)	10.4%

Shinsei Bank Ltd. (Japan)

Shinsei Bank provides financial services from about 40 branches throughout Japan. The company organizes its business into three segments: Institutional Banking Consumer and Commercial Finance and Retail Banking. Shinsei used to focus on financing Japan's large industrial firms but has been cultivating its retail and small business banking operations. It offers services such as deposits mortgages and investments. Institutional activities include asset management bond sales and underwriting and trust services as well as real estate finance and public sector finance. Founded as the Long-Term Credit Bank of Japan in 1952 the company was reborn as Shinsei (Japanese for "new birth") Bank in 2000.

The Japanese government nationalized Shinsei Bank's debt-ridden Long-Term Credit Bank in 1998. It sold the bank to an international group led by US-based Ripplewood Holdings in 2000 making it one of the few major Japanese banks to come under foreign control. Ripplewood spun off the bank in 2004 placing it on the Tokyo Stock Exchange.

Today investment firm J.C. Flowers is Shinsei's largest shareholder with a 33% stake; the Japanese government owns some 25%. The company is still working to repay public funds received when it was nationalized.

In 2010 Shinsei Bank sold Shinsei Asset Management its Mumbai-based asset management operation to Daiwa Bank. The company will use the proceeds to pay down its debt.

Shinsei has been battered by its exposure to toxic assets including loans to failed Lehman Brothers and structured asset-backed securities. It has also taken a hit in the domestic real estate market in which the company has been a significant lender. Record losses reported for 2008 sparked rumors that Shinsei would merge with Aozora Bank another struggling midsized bank that was nationalized in 2001. The two banks reached a merger agreement in 2009 but called those plans off due to strategic differences.

Also as part of its restructuring efforts the company is realigning its retail and consumer finance operations. It it building up its stakes in majority-owned consumer lender APLUS which it may eventually spin off to another subsidiary Shinsei Financial.

In 2007 Shinsei acquired a minority stake in global advisory firm Duff & Phelps. The following year it acquired GE's consumer finance business in Japan consisting of credit card personal lending and mortgage operations.

EXECUTIVES

President and CEO, Shigeki Toma, age 65
Senior Managing Executive Officer, Hitomi Sato, age 65
Senior Managing Executive Officer and Group CIO, Michiyuki Okano, age 53
Senior Managing Executive Officer, Sanjeev Gupta, age 53
Deputy President, Yukio Nakamura, age 59
Senior Managing Executive Officer and CFO, Shigeru Tsukamoto, age 62
Managing Executive Officer, Norio Funayama, age 56
Managing Executive Officer, Toru Myochin, age 48
Head of Structured Finance Sub-Group, Yoshiaki Kozano
Managing Executive Officer, Yoshiaki Kozano, age 51
Managing Executive Officer, Hideyuki Kudo, age 50
Managing Executive Officer, Hironobu Satou, age 53
Managing Executive Officer, Shinichirou Seto, age 52
Managing Executive Officer, Masashi Yamashita, age 55
Director, J. Christopher Flowers, age 55
President CEO and Director, Shigeki Toma, age 64
Director, Shigeru Kani, age 69
Director, Oki Matsumoto, age 48
Director, Hiroyuki Takahashi, age 76
Senior Managing Executive Officer Head Risk Management Chief Risk Officer and Director, Yukio Nakamura, age 58
Auditors: DeloitteToucheTohmatsu

LOCATIONS

HQ: Shinsei Bank Ltd. (Japan)
2-4-3 Muro-machi, Nihonbashi, Chuo-ku, Tokyo 103-8303
Phone: (81) 3 6880 7000
Web: www.shinseibank.com

PRODUCTS/OPERATIONS

2008 Sales

	% of total
Interest	
Loans &	61
Dividends on	9
Other	2
Noninterest	
Fees &	12
Other	16
Total	**100**

COMPETITORS

Aozora Bank
Bank of Yokohama
Chuo Mitsui Trust
Mitsubishi UFJ Financial Group
Mizuho Financial
Mizuho Trust & Banking Ltd
Resona
Sumitomo Mitsui
Sumitomo Trust and Banking

HISTORICAL FINANCIALS

Company Type: Public

Income Statement FYE: March 31

	ASSETS ($ mil.)	NET INCOME ($ mil.)	INCOME AS % OF ASSETS	EMPLOYEES
03/13	95,962	542	0.6%	4,863
03/12	104,957	78	0.1%	4,830
03/11	123,559	515	0.4%	5,718
03/10	121,797	(1,500)	—	6,116
03/09	121,342	(1,453)	—	7,006
Annual Growth	(5.7%)	—	—	(8.7%)

2013 Year-End Financials

Return on assets: 0.5%
Return on equity: 8.6%
Long-term debt ($ mil.): —
No. of shares (mil.): —
Sales ($ mil): 4,115
Dividends
Yield: —
Payout: —
Market value ($ mil.): —

	STOCK PRICE ($) FY Close	P/E High/Low	PER SHARE ($) Earnings	Dividends	Book Value
03/13	2.33	— —	0.20	0.00	2.74
03/12	1.28	— —	0.03	0.00	2.88
03/11	1.34	— —	0.26	0.00	2.78
03/10	1.15	— —	(0.76)	0.00	3.46
03/09	1.14	— —	(0.74)	0.06	3.97
Annual Growth	19.6%	— —	—	—	(8.9%)

Shizuoka Bank, Ltd. (Japan)

The Shizuoka Bank is one of Japan's largest regional banks. It has more than 190 branches in and around Shizuoka prefecture a major manufacturing region southwest of Tokyo. The bank specializes in commercial and industrial loans to businesses such as manufacturers wholesalers and retailers within Shizuoka. Other offerings include deposit accounts consumer loans asset management and investment banking services. Shizuoka Bank also boasts about a dozen major subsidiaries that are devoted to leasing credit cards mortgages securities brokerage and management consulting. It has representative offices and branches in Belgium Hong Kong China Singapore and the US.

EXECUTIVES

Chairman, Yasuo Matsuura, age 71
President and CEO, Katsunori Nakanishi, age 60
COO and Director, Tohru Sakurai
Chairman, Seiya Ito
Deputy Chairman, Kazuhiro Satomi
Deputy President and COO, Masahiro Goto
Senior Managing Executive Officer, Toshihiko Yamamoto
Senior Managing Executive Officer, Akihiro Nakamura
Senior Executive Officer, Itsuro Hitosugi
Senior Executive Officer, Hiroki Saito
Director, Masakazu Oishi, age 68
COO and Director, Tohru Sakurai
CFO and Director, Seiya Ito
Deputy Chairman, Kazuhiro Satomi
Deputy Chairman, Moritaka Nakamura
Senior Executive Officer and Director, Masahiro Goto
Senior Executive Officer and Director, Toshihiko Yamamoto
Senior Executive Officer and Director, Akihiro Nakamura
Director, Toshiaki Sugiyama
Auditors: DeloitteToucheTohmatsu

LOCATIONS

HQ: Shizuoka Bank, Ltd. (Japan)
1-10 Gofuku-cho, Aoi-ku, Shizuoka 420-8761
Phone: (81) 54 261 3131
Web: www.shizuokabank.co.jp

COMPETITORS

Bank of China
Chuo Mitsui Trust
HSBC
Mitsubishi UFJ Financial Group
Mizuho Financial
Norinchukin Bank
Shimizu Bank
Sumitomo Mitsui
Sumitomo Trust and Banking
Suruga Bank

HISTORICAL FINANCIALS

Company Type: Public

Income Statement FYE: March 31

	ASSETS ($ mil.)	NET INCOME ($ mil.)	INCOME AS % OF ASSETS	EMPLOYEES
03/13	109,624	605	0.6%	4,269
03/12	118,194	453	0.4%	4,257
03/11	114,025	436	0.4%	4,252
03/10	96,783	350	0.4%	4,210
03/09	92,558	132	0.1%	4,130
Annual Growth	4.3%	46.3%	—	0.8%

2013 Year-End Financials

Return on assets: 0.5%
Return on equity: 7.4%
Long-term debt ($ mil.): —
No. of shares (mil.): 648
Sales ($ mil): 2,309
Dividends
Yield: —
Payout: —
Market value ($ mil.): 6,465

	STOCK PRICE ($) FY Close	P/E High/Low	PER SHARE ($) Earnings	Dividends	Book Value
03/13	9.97	— —	0.93	0.00	13.29
03/12	9.34	— —	0.69	0.00	13.96
03/11	8.65	— —	0.64	0.00	12.76
03/10	8.65	— —	0.50	0.00	11.06
03/09	8.05	— —	0.19	0.00	9.49
Annual Growth	5.5%	— —	48.9%	—	8.8%

Showa Shell Sekiyu K.K.

Show and tell? When is comes to oil and petroleum products Showa Shell Sekiyu has plenty to show and talk about. Showa Shell 35%-owned by Royal Dutch Shell and 15% by Saudi Aramco is one of Japan's leading oil refiners. The company imports refines and distributes petroleum products. The firm's three local refining affiliates Showa Yokkaichi Toa Oil and Seibu Oil have a collective refining capacity of 395000 barrels a day. Showa Shell markets its products through 3800 gas stations; it also has solar power electricity city gas (liquefied petroleum gas) and property businesses.

Operations

The company operates the Yokkaichi Refinery of Showa Yokkaichi Sekiyu Co. Ltd. (210000 barrels per day) the Keihin Refinery of Toa Oil Co. Ltd. (65000 barrels per day) and the Yamaguchi Refinery of Seibu Oil Co. Ltd. (120000 barrels per day). These refineries produce fuel oils such as gasoline; diesel oil; kerosene; basic materials for petrochemical products such as mixed xylene benzene and propylene; lubricants; asphalt; and other products.

Showa Shell markets its products through 3800 gas stations;

The company has developed the technology for manufacturing next-generation CIS thin-film solar panels.

It also operates Ohgishima Power which has two natural gas-fired power plants as a joint venture with Tokyo Gas. Electricity produced at the plants is sold primarily to customers in or near Tokyo.

Sales and Marketing

Showa Shell sells petroleum products in Japan primarily through its gas station network. Products sold include gasolines kerosene and a range of automotive lubricants. The company also directly sells fuel oil gas oil naphtha lubricants bitumen and LP gas to construction firms electric power and gas utilities fishing fleets manufacturers and shipping companies. Showa Shell's international sales include aviation fuel to airlines and marine bunker fuels and lubricants to shipping firms.

Financial Performance

Showa Shell's revenues increased by 18% in 2011 due to a 17% hike in prices on petroleum products which rose in tandem with higher crude oil prices pushing up sales for the oil business. The increase in crude oil prices also had a positive effect on inventory valuation. In addition the sales volume increased for kerosene and other middle distillates; and 128% increase in Energy Solution Businesses due to the greater scale of sales in the solar business stemming from the start of operations at the third Miyazaki Plant.

Net income increased by 45% in 2011 thanks to higher prices on petroleum products and higher net sales. It also benefited from increased demand for heating fuels due to particularly cold weather at the beginning of the year as well as a recovery in petroleum product margins.

Strategy

In addition to growing its core refining and petroleum products businesses the company is expanding its solar energy assets. In 2011 it launched the Kunitomi Plant its Solar Frontier unit's third Miyazaki plant and one of the largest solar plants in the world.

Ownership

Showa Shell is 35%-owned by Royal Dutch Shell and 15% by Saudi Aramco.

Company Background

The company was founded in 1985 through a merger between Japan's Showa Oil and Royal Dutch Shell's Shell Sekiyu.

EXECUTIVES

Senior Managing Director Solar Business Center; President Solar Frontier K.K., Shigeaki Kameda
Senior Executive Officer, Tomonori Okada
COO, Jun Arai, age 54
Senior Executive Officer, Atsuhiko Hirano
Chairman and CEO, Shigeya Kato
EVP; President Solar Frontier, Hiroto Tamai
Corporate Executive Officer Group Functions (Public Affairs Secretariat and HSSE), Kiyotaka Yamada
Executive Officer Group Functions (Legal and Personal Data Protection), Yuri Inoue
Corporate Executive Officer Oil Business Center (New Business Promotion); Group Functions (Corporate Planning (Including Corporate Governance), Misao Hamamoto
Corporate Executive Officer Solar Business Center (Executive Officer Solar Frontier K.K.; Miyazaki Plant and Procurement), Tomoaki Itou
Executive Officer Solar Frontier K.K. (Communications and Operations), Brooks Herring
Executive Officer Oil Business Center (Supply Oil Products Crude Oil & Marine and Marine), Masayuki Kobayashi
Executive Officer Group Functions (Finance & Control and Credit & Financial Risk Management), Tsutomu Yoshioka
CFO, Douglas Wood
President and Director, Jun Arai, age 54
VP CFO and Director, Richard A. Carruth
Auditors: ChuoAoyamaAuditCorporation

LOCATIONS

HQ: Showa Shell Sekiyu K.K.
2-3-2 Daiba, Minato-ku, Tokyo 135-8074
Phone: (81) 3 5531 5591 **Fax:** (81) 3 5531 5598
Web: www.showa-shell.co.jp

PRODUCTS/OPERATIONS

2011 Sales

	% of total
Oil	97
Energy Solution	3
Total	**100**

COMPETITORS

Cosmo Oil
Exxon Mobil
Idemitsu Kosan
JX Holdings
JX Nippon Mining & Metals
JX Nippon Oil & Energy
SK Innovation

HISTORICAL FINANCIALS

Company Type: Public

Income Statement FYE: December 31

	REVENUE ($ mil.)	NET INCOME ($ mil.)	NET PROFIT MARGIN	EMPLOYEES
12/12	30,526	11	0.0%	5,848
12/11	35,812	298	0.8%	5,947
12/10	28,843	196	0.7%	5,761
12/09	21,890	(623)	—	5,439
12/08	36,189	(179)	—	5,229
Annual Growth	(4.2%)	—	—	2.8%

2012 Year-End Financials

Debt ratio: 0.2%
Return on equity: 0.4%
Cash ($ mil.): 211
Current ratio: 1.04
Long-term debt ($ mil.): 1,843
No. of shares (mil.): 376
Dividends
Yield: —
Payout: —
Market value ($ mil.): 2,165

	STOCK PRICE ($) FY Close	P/E High/Low		PER SHARE ($) Earnings	Dividends	Book Value
12/12	5.75	—	—	0.03	0.00	8.44
12/11	10.75	—	—	0.79	0.00	9.58
12/10	9.56	—	—	0.52	0.00	8.59
12/09	9.56	—	—	(1.66)	0.00	7.41
12/08	8.50	—	—	(0.48)	0.00	9.65
Annual Growth	(9.3%)	—	—	—	—	(3.3%)

Siam Commercial Bank Public Co., Ltd. (The)

One of Thailand's largest commercial bank by total assets deposits and loans The Siam Commercial Bank (SCB) hails from royal beginnings. It is the country's oldest bank established by King Rama V in 1906 in response to the proliferation of foreign financial institutions in Thailand. Today the bank offers an array of financial services that include corporate and personal lending retail and wholesale banking credit cards life insurance foreign currency trading international trade financing cash management and investment banking. SCB operates through a network of about 1150 branches and nearly 9000 ATMs; it is expanding regionally starting with Mekong countries such as Myanmar.

EXECUTIVES

Senior Executive Vice President Group Head Retail Banking Group, Yol Phokasub
Chairman of Executive Committee and Director, Vichit Suraphongchai
Chairman, Anand Panyarachun
SEVP General Counsel and Director, Bodin Asavanich
President and Executive Director, Kannikar Chalitaporn
Senior Executive Vice President Chief Financial Officer & Head Finance Group and Change Program, Deepak Sarup
EVP, Kannika Ngamsopee
Senior Executive Vice President Chief Risk Officer, Yokporn Tantisawetrat
EVP, Sutharntip Phisitbuntoon
Senior Executive Vice President and Group Head Business Banking Group, Sirichai Sombutsiri
Senior Executive Vice President Division Head Special Assets Group, Sarunthorn Chutima
EVP, Grish Attagrish
EVP, Somchai Sanyalaksiri
EVP, Narong Srichukrin
EVP, Rungruang Sukkirdkijpiboon
EVP, Ongorn Abhakorn Na Ayuthaya
EVP, Amrit Laorakpong
SEVP and Group Head Human Resources, Manoon Sunkunakorn
Senior Executive Vice President Group Head Wholesale Banking Group, Arthid Nanthawithaya
Senior Executive Vice President Group Head Technology and Operations Group, Banesh Prabhu
Chairman of Executive Committee and Director, Vichit Suraphongchai
Director, Chirayu Isarangkun Na Ayuthaya
Director, Maris Samaram
SEVP General Counsel and Director, Bodin Asavanich
Director, Sumate Tanthuwanit, age 67
Director, Mom Rajawongse Disnadda Diskul
Director, Khunying Jada Wattanasiritham
President and Executive Director, Kannikar Chalitaporn
Director, Chumpol Na Lamlieng
Director, Supa Piyajitti
Auditors: DeloitteToucheTohmatsuJaiyos

LOCATIONS

HQ: Siam Commercial Bank Public Co., Ltd. (The)
9 Ratchadapisek Road, Jatujak, Bangkok 10900
Phone: (66) 2 544 1111 **Fax:** (66) 2 544 2658
Web: www.scb.co.th

COMPETITORS

Bangkok Bank
Bank of Ayudhya
KASIKORNBANK
TMB Bank
Thanachart Capital

HISTORICAL FINANCIALS

Company Type: Public

Income Statement FYE: December 31

	ASSETS ($ mil.)	NET INCOME ($ mil.)	INCOME AS % OF ASSETS	EMPLOYEES
12/12	74,179	1,314	1.8%	20,994
12/11	59,670	1,152	1.9%	19,566
12/10	49,168	805	1.6%	18,097
12/09	38,842	623	1.6%	0
12/08	35,691	615	1.7%	0
Annual Growth	20.1%	20.9%	—	—

2012 Year-End Financials

Return on assets: 1.9%
Return on equity: 19.8%
Long-term debt ($ mil.): —
No. of shares (mil.): —
Sales ($ mil): 6,006
Dividends
Yield: 0.0%
Payout: —
Market value ($ mil.): —

	STOCK PRICE ($) FY Close	P/E High/Low		PER SHARE ($) Earnings	Dividends	Book Value
12/12	23.65	0	0	0.39	0.00	2.10
Annual Growth	—	—	—	—	—	—

Siemens AG (Germany)

For Siemens one of the largest electronics and industrial engineering companies in the galaxy everything comes down to four main objectives: Industry Energy Healthcare and City Infrastructure. Siemens' operations which encompass some 750 subsidiaries and associated companies around the globe make everything from automation equipment and building technologies for manufacturers and construction companies to diagnostic and imaging systems for hospitals and clinics. Other key products include power generation and distribution equipment for the oil and gas and renewable energy sectors. Siemens Energy Siemens Healthcare Siemens Industry and Siemens Infrastructure & Cities are its primary targeted segments.

HISTORY

In 1847 electrical engineer Werner von Siemens and craftsman Johann Halske formed Siemens & Halske. The firm's first major project linked Berlin and Frankfurt with the first long-distance telegraph system in Europe (1848). In 1870 it completed a 6600-mile telegraph line from London to Calcutta India and in 1874 it made the first transatlantic cable linking Ireland to the US.

The company's history of firsts includes Europe's first electric power transmission system (1876) the world's first electrified railway (1879) and one of the first elevators (1880). In 1896 it patented the world's first X-ray tube and completed the first European subway in Budapest Hungary.

By the next century it had formed light-bulb cartel OSRAM with German rivals AEG and Auer (1919) and created a venture with Furukawa Electric called Fuji Electric (1923). It developed radios and traffic lights in the 1920s and began producing electron microscopes in 1939.

Siemens & Halske played a critical role in Germany's war effort in WWII and suffered heavy losses. During the 1950s it recovered by developing data processing equipment silicates for semiconductors and the first implantable pacemaker. It moved into the nuclear industry in 1959 when its first reactor went into service at Munich-Garching. In 1966 the company reincorporated as Siemens AG. It formed joint ventures with Bosch (BSH Bosch und Siemens Hausergate appliances 1967) and AEG (Kraftwerk Union nuclear power 1969) among others. AEG dropped out of Kraftwerk Union (later Siemens Power Generation) in 1977.

In 1981 Karlheinz Kaske became the first CEO from outside the von Siemens family. Under his lead the firm entered joint ventures with Philips Intel and Advanced Micro Devices. In 1988 and 1989 it made several buys including Bendix Electronics (US) and was a willing buyer when IBM wanted to unload ROLM (then the #1 maker of PBXs). It had acquired all of ROLM's businesses by 1992. That year Heinrich von Pierer replaced Kaske as CEO.

The 1990s saw more consolidation: Siemens and German computer maker Nixdorf combined computer businesses to form Siemens Nixdorf Informationssysteme (SNI 1990); the firm acquired Sylvania's North American lamp business from GTE and merged it with the OSRAM companies in North America to form OSRAM SYLVANIA (1993).

The Asian economic crisis combined with other factors to make 1998 the worst year in the company's 150-year history. That year Siemens sold its defense electronics operations to British Aerospace (now BAE SYSTEMS) and Daimler-Benz (now Daimler) and bought CBS's power generation business (formerly Westinghouse Electric).

SNI's operations were juggled in a 1999 revamping of the company's information and communications units. That year Siemens held an IPO for its passive components and electron tubes unit. It spun off its semiconductor operations into Infineon Technologies but kept a 71% stake after Infineon's IPO in 2000. Siemens also sold its electromechanical components unit to Tyco International and its fiber-optic cable and hardware businesses to Corning.

In 2000 BSH paid $9.2 billion for the engineering and automotive parts unit Atecs Mannesmann. Also that year Siemens boosted its IT Service unit in the US by purchasing information services company ENTEX and it merged its nuclear business with that of Framatome (the combined business is known as AREVA NP).

Siemens shares began trading on the New York Stock Exchange in 2001. The company bought Dallas-based Efficient Networks for $1.5 billion that year. The slump in the telecommunications industry hurt Siemens that year and the company cut 9700 jobs.

Late in 2001 Siemens cut its stake in Infineon Technologies to less than 50% and in 2002 it announced an additional 6500 jobs to be cut from its telecom unit. The company continued to trim its information and communications holdings with the July 2002 sale of Unisphere Networks to Juniper Networks. Later that year the company sold seven non-core subsidiaries (including Mannesmann Plastics Machinery Stabilus Demag Cranes & Components and Gottwald Port Technology) to buyout firm Kohlberg Kravis Roberts (now KKR) for $1.7 billion.

Siemens in 2004 bought the equipment treatment and technology components of US Filter for more than $990 million in cash as part of its expansion into the US. The purchase the company's largest since the 2001 acquisition of Efficient Networks was intended to strengthen its presence in the industrial water treatment and supply equipment market and to help it better compete against General Electric.

At the beginning of 2005 Klaus Kleinfeld who headed Siemens' US operations was named CEO; von Pierer became chairman of the company's supervisory board.

Also in 2005 Siemens bought medical-imaging equipment maker CTI Molecular Imaging in a deal valued at about $1 billion; it bolstered its financial services division especially in the medical equipment financing sector with the acquisition of UK-based financial services firm Broadcastle; and it purchased Flender Holding a German supplier of gear systems from a unit of Citigroup in a deal valued at $1.5 billion.

In 2005 Siemens sold its mobile phone business to Taiwanese electronics manufacturer BenQ (BenQ Mobile filed for insolvency the following year). Siemens restructured its entire communications group in 2006; its enterprise communications unit became a standalone company and its wireless modules business became part of the Siemens Group Automation and Drives division. It streamlined its telecommunications product line by discontinuing its enterprise networks business and selling its mobile phone operations. Later in 2006 the company announced that it was combining its carrier-related network operations with those of Nokia creating a joint venture called Nokia Siemens Networks. Each company took a 50% stake in the joint venture which commenced operations in 2007. The company also exited the auto parts market; Siemens sold its VDO Automotive unit to Continental for $16.7 billion in 2007.

The company augmented the automation and drives part of its Industry division when it bought UGS a developer of product lifecycle management software for about $3.5 billion in 2007. The company also grew its Healthcare division with major acquisitions. It purchased Diagnostic Products Corporation (DPC) a maker of immunodiagnostic systems for about $1.9 billion in 2006. On the heels of the DPC buy the company acquired the diagnostics division of Bayer for more than $5 billion. In 2007 the company purchased Dade Behring Holdings a provider of diagnostic testing kits for $7 billion.

Siemens attracted unwanted attention in 2006 when it was accused of making improper payments to secure contracts in Eastern Europe and the Middle East; embezzlement and tax evasion were also among the charges levied against the company. Siemens which was involved in a number of bribery cases prior to 2006 uncovered more than $500 million worth of suspicious transactions made over a seven-year period with its own probe. The investigation led to the arrest of several Siemens managers and in 2007 Heinrich von Pierer the chairman of Siemens' supervisory board who served as the company's CEO from 1992 to 2005 announced his resignation. German authorities later filed civil proceedings against von Pierer seeking damages. Siemens' CEO Klaus Kleinfeld then stepped down. Peter Loscher a veteran of General Electric and Merck succeeded Kleinfeld. After cooperating with various investigations by the SEC the US Department of Justice and other prosecutors and regulators around the world as a result of the corruption cases Siemens settled the claims in late 2008. The company agreed to pay record-setting fines of $1.6 billion to American and European authorities (including $450 million to the Justice Department $350 million to the SEC and $540 million to German prosecutors). Siemens pleaded guilty to US federal charges that it violated a law banning the use of corrupt practices in foreign business dealings but it avoided pleading guilty to bribery charges allowing it to remain a potential government contractor in the US and elsewhere.

Soon after Loscher took over Siemens announced its reorganization. Though its holdings remain vast the Siemens group initiated a significant shift in its operations. In 2009 the company designated Industry Energy and Healthcare as its primary business divisions while its IT Solutions and Financial Services segments filled supportive functions across its three main divisions in addition to growing their own customer bases. In 2011 the company announced its plans to divest its IT Solutions and Services unit to French IT company Atos Origin for approximately ?850 million (more than $1 billion).

Starting in 2008 it began divesting non-core operations including its majority stake (51%) in Siemens Enterprise Communications to the US management firm The Gores Group; an over 80% stake in Siemens Home and Office Communication Devices to ARQUES Industries; OSRAM's Global Tungsten & Powders unit; and its Wireless Modules Business.

In 2009 it continued its restructuring plan set in motion in 2008 by divesting a number of non-core operations. Fujitsu bought Siemens' 50% share in Fujitsu Siemens Computers (now Fujitsu Technology Solutions) for about ?450 million. In the latter part of the year the company sold its airfield lighting company ADB Airfield Solutions to UK-based Montagu Private Equity. Siemens also spun off its Munich-based Electronic Device Manufacturing (EDM) unit and subsequently withdrew from its joint venture Areva NP by selling its interest to Areva S.A. In 2010 the company shed its 35% stake in Hydro Power a joint venture with Voith. Hong Kong's ASM Pacific Technology acquired Siemens Electronics Assembly Systems a manufacturer of surface-mount technology equipment in early 2011. In an agreement to support the loss-making business which is burdened by ?160 million ($208 million) in loans Siemens shelled out ?29 million (about $38 million) to ASM Pacific.

The company sold its IT Solutions and Services unit (part of Siemens Industry business) to France-based Atos (formerly Atos Origin) for approximately ?850 million (more than $1 billion). Siemens accepted a 15% stake in Atos.

EXECUTIVES

EVP Head Corporate Legal and Compliance; Member Managing Board and General Counsel Siemens AG, Peter Y. Solmssen, age 59, $1,061,580 total compensation

CEO Energy Service Division; President and CEO Siemens Energy, Randy H. Zwirn

Second Deputy Chairman, Josef Ackermann, age 66, $96,616 total compensation

Chairman, Gerhard Cromme, age 70, $285,240 total compensation

CEO BSH Bosch und Siemens Hausgerate GmbH, Kurt-Ludwig Gutberlet, age 57

First Deputy Chairman, Berthold Huber, age 64, $113,984 total compensation

CEO OSRAM Division, Wolfgang Dehen, age 60, $1,126,710 total compensation

CEO Clinical Products Division USA, Norbert Gaus

CFO Siemens Building Technologies, Heribert Stumpf

President and CEO, Peter Loscher, age 55, $2,860,110 total compensation

CEO Industry Solutions Division, Jens M. Wegmann

EVP Head Supply Chain Management Chief Sustainability Officer and Member Managing Board, Barbara Kux, age 59, $982,741 total compensation

Head Corporate Supply Chain Management, Bernd Regendantz

President and CEO, Joe Kaeser, age 56, $1,126,710 total compensation

CEO Building Technologies Division, Johannes Milde

CFO Siemens Austria, Reinhard Pinzer, age 61

CFO Energy Sector, Ralf Guntermann

CEO Power Transmission Division, Udo Niehage

COO Osram, Martin Goetzeler, age 50

Chief Compliance Officer, Hans-Jorg Grundmann

CFO Siemens IT Solutions and Services, Martin Bentler, age 52

CFO Mobility Division, Michael Schulz-Drost

CEO Siemens IT Solutions and Services, Christian Oecking

CEO Financial Services, Roland W. Chalons-Browne, age 57

Head Mergers Acquistions Post Closing Management, Karl-Heinz Seibert, age 54

CEO Rail Automation, Jochen Eickholt, age 51

Member of the Managing Board; Chief Executive Officer of Healthcare Sector, Hermann Requardt, age 59, $1,126,710 total compensation

Member of the Managing Board; Chief Executive Officer of Industry Sector, Siegfried Russwurm, age 50, $1,061,580 total compensation

CEO Infrastructure and Cities Sector, Roland Busch, age 49

CEO Customer Solutions Division, Thomas (Tom) Miller

CFO Imaging and Therapy Divisions, Jochen Schmitz

CEO Siemens IT Solutions and Services US and Canada, John E. Evers Jr., age 52

CEO Siemens UK, Andreas J. Goss, age 49

Head Corporate Communications and Government Affairs, Stephan Heimbach, age 52

CEO Imaging & Therapy Systems, Bernd Montag

CFO Industry Sector, Ralf P. Thomas, age 51

Head Corporate Press Office Media Relations, Constantin Birnstiel, age 41

CFO Fossil Power Generation Division, Michael Becker

CFO Renewable Energy Division, Michael Axmann

CFO Oil and Gas Division, Volker Walprecht

CFO Energy Services Division USA, Steve Conner

CEO Power Distribution Division, Ralf Christian
CFO Power Distribution Division, Matthias Platsch
Head Corporate Information Technology, Norbert Kleinjohann
CFO Siemens Financial Services, Peter Moritz
CFO Industry Solutions Division, Wolfgang Hermann
CFO Healthcare Sector, Michael Sen, age 45
CEO VAI Metals Technologies, Werner Auer
CEO Oil and Gas Division, Tom Blades, age 57
CEO Fossil Power Generation, Roland Fischer, age 51
Chief Diversity Officer, Denice Kronau, age 54
CFO OSRAM, Thomas Schaffer
CFO Drive Technologies Division, Thomas Rathmann
CTO and Member Managing Board Siemens AG, Klaus Helmrich, age 55
CEO Industry Automation Division, Anton S. Huber
CFO Industry Automation Division, Miguel-Angel Lopez
Member of the Managing Board; Chief Executive Officer Energy Sector, Michael Suess, age 50
CFO Customer Solutions Division, Wolfgang Beitz
CEO Corporate Unit Finance and Controlling Head of the Project Stand-alone READINESS, Hannes Apitzsch
CEO Siemens Real Estate, Zsolt Sluitner
CEO Audiologische Technik, Roger Radke
President and CEO Siemens Corporation, Eric A. Spiegel
CEO Siemens Austria, Wolfgang Hesoun, age 53
Head Corporate Human Resources Director Labor and Member Managing Board of Siemens AG, Brigitte Ederer, age 57
CEO Siemens Regional Company Indonesia, Josef Winter
Chief Counsel Compliance, Klaus Moosmayer
Head EU Affairs Berlin and Brussels, Peter Witt
CEO Diagnostics Division USA, Michael Reiterman
Head Smart Grid Applications Sector Energy, Richard Hausmann
CFO Clinical Products Division, Klaus-Armin Kiesel
Head Corporate Unit Corporate Sustainability Office, Siegmar Proebstl
Head Siemens Corporate Research and Technologies, Reinhold Achatz
Head Corporate Development Siemens One, Pedro Miranda
Head Corporate Development Executives, Nicolas von Rosty
Head HR Governance Germany, Walter Huber
Head Taxes, Christian Kaeser
CEO Industry Solutions Division and CEO Customer Services Division., Dirk Hoke, age 43
CEO Drive Technologies, Ralf-Michael Franke, age 55
Chief Financial Officer, Klaus P. Stegemann
Vice President Sustainability, Alison Taylor
Vice President Corporate Affairs, Camille Johnston
Vice President and Chief Intellectual Property Counsel, Daniel J. Staudt
Senior Vice President Siemens Government Affairs, Kathleen A. Ambrose
Senior Vice President General Counsel Secretary, Rose Glazer
Sr. Vice President Communications & Marketing, Jim Whaley
President of the Managing Board; Chief Executive Officer, Peter Peter Loescher Loescher
Senior Vice President Manufacturing Engineering Software, Zvi Feuer
Senior Vice President General Manager Mainstream Engineering Software, Karsten Newbury
Senior Vice President Chief Information Officer, Craig J. Berry
Senior Vice President of Human Resources, Dan Malliet
senior Vice President of Industry Strategy for Siemens PLM Software, Stephen M. Bashada
Senior Vice President Lifecycle Collaboration Software, Eric Sterling
Senior Vice President Product Driven Services, Kevin Eustace
Senior Vice President Product Engineering Software, Jim Rusk
Senior Vice President Strategy Initiatives, Raj Khoshoo
Senior Vice President, Steve Luby
Board Member, Michael Diekmann, age 59
Board Member, Jean-Louis Beffa, age 72
Second Deputy Chairman, Josef Ackermann, age 66
Board Member, Lord Iain D. T. Vallance of Tummel, age 70
First Deputy Chairman, Berthold Huber, age 64
Board Member, Lothar Adler, age 64
Board Member, H?kan Samuelsson, age 62
Board Member, Hans-Jurgen Hartung, age 61
Board Member, Nicola Leibinger-Kammuller, age 53
Board Member, Dieter Scheitor, age 63
Board Member, Gerd von Brandenstein, age 71
Board Member, Hans Michael Gaul, age 71
Board Member, Peter Gruss, age 64
Board Member, Bettina Haller, age 54
Board Member, Harald Kern, age 53
Board Member, Werner Monius, age 58
Board Member, Rainer Sieg, age 65
Board Member, Birgit Steinborn, age 53
Board Member, Sibylle Wankel, age 49
Member of the Supervisory Board, Gerd Brandenstein
Member of the Supervisory Board, Iain Tummel
Member of the Supervisory Board, Nicola Leibinger-Kammueller
Member of the Supervisory Board; Employee Representative, Werner Moenius
Auditors: Ernst&YoungWirtschaftsprufungsgesellschaft

LOCATIONS

HQ: Siemens AG (Germany)
Wittelsbacherplatz 2, Munich D-80333
Phone: (49) 89 636 00 **Fax:** (49) 89 636 34242
Web: www.siemens.com

2010 Sales

	% of total
Europe CIS Africa Middle	55
Germany	15
Other	40
Americas	27
US	19
Other	8
Asia	18
China	8
India	3
Other	7
Total	**100**

PRODUCTS/OPERATIONS

2010 Sales

	% of total
Industry	44
Energy	33
Health	16
Other	7
Total	**100**

Selected Operations

Industry
- Building technology (heating and ventilation security fire safety systems)
- Industry automation (manufacturing and process automation)
- Industry solutions (systems integration for industrial plants)
- Mobility (transportation systems)
- Motion control (converters drives motors numerical control systems)
- OSRAM (light-emitting diodes light bulbs)

Energy
- Fossil power generation (gas and steam turbines and generators power plants)
- Oil and gas (extraction conversion and transportation systems)
- Power distribution (powergrid automation switch gear components)
- Power transmission (high-voltage equipment)
- Renewable energy (wind energy)
- Service rotating equipment (power plant services and operation)

Health care
- Diagnostics (immune diagnostics molecular analysis)
- Imaging and IT (imaging systems and networking)
- Workflow and solutions (health care systems and services)

Other
- BSH Bosch und Siemens Hausgerate (equity investment)
- ELIN GmbH & Co. (equity investment)
- Enterprise Network Holdings (equity investment)
- Financial services (cross-sector)
- Krauss-Maffei Wegmann GmbH & Co. (equity investment)
- Nokia Siemens networks (equity investment)
- Real estate (cross-sector)
- Information Technology

Selected Key Subsidiaries

Siemens Corp. (US)
Siemens Energy (Germany and US)
Siemens Enterprise Communications GmbH (Germany)
Siemens Financial Services GmbH (Germany)
Siemens Healthcare (Germany and US)
Siemens Holdings plc (UK)
Siemens Industry Automation (US; subsidiary of Siemens Industry)
Siemens Industry Inc. (US)
Siemens Industry Inc. (US)
Siemens Ltda. (Brazil)
Siemens Osakeyhtio Group (Finland)
Siemens Product Lifecycle Management Software Inc. (US; subsidiary of Siemens Industry)
Siemens Water Technologies Corp.(US; subsidiary of Siemens Industry)

COMPETITORS

ABB
ALSTOM
AREVA
Abbott Labs
Affiliated Computer Services
Alcatel-Lucent
Avaya
BP Solar
Beckman Coulter
Bharat Heavy Electricals
Bombardier
Capgemini
Cerner
Computer Sciences Corp.
Danfoss Turbocor
Danieli
Dassault
Dresser-Rand
Eaton
Emerson Electric
FANUC
GE
GN ReSound
Gamesa
Hitachi
Hologic
Honeywell International
Huawei Technologies
Johnson Controls
MAN
McKesson
Mitsubishi Electric
Mitsubishi Heavy Industries
Nichia
Nortel Networks
OSRAM
Philips Electronics
Philips Healthcare
REpower Systems
Roche Diagnostics
Rockwell Automation
Schneider Electric
Sonova
Toshiba
Tyco
United Technologies
Varian Medical Systems
Veolia Environnement
Vestas Wind Systems

HISTORICAL FINANCIALS

Company Type: Public

Income Statement FYE: September 30

	REVENUE ($ mil.)	NET INCOME ($ mil.)	NET PROFIT MARGIN	EMPLOYEES
09/13	102,419	5,782	5.6%	362,400
09/12	101,236	5,764	5.7%	370,000
09/11	99,176	8,290	8.4%	350,500
09/10	103,544	5,313	5.1%	405,000
09/09	112,197	3,354	3.0%	405,000
Annual Growth	(2.3%)	14.6%	—	(2.7%)

2013 Year-End Financials

Debt ratio: 27.0%
Return on equity: 14.5%
Cash ($ mil.): 12,403
Current ratio: 1.24
Long-term debt ($ mil.): 24,982
No. of shares (mil.): 843
Dividends
Yield: 4.9%
Payout: 87.6%
Market value ($ mil.): 101,590

	STOCK PRICE ($) FY Close	P/E High/Low		PER SHARE ($) Earnings	Dividends	Book Value
09/13	120.51	44	33	6.79	5.95	45.01
09/12	100.15	40	25	6.52	4.75	46.41
09/11	89.79	42	23	9.39	2.70	48.65
09/10	105.40	47	31	6.05	1.63	44.41
09/09	92.96	79	31	3.85	1.53	45.02
Annual Growth	6.7%	—	—	15.2%	40.4%	(0.0%)

Sistema JSFC

LOCATIONS

HQ: Sistema JSFC
13 Mokhovaya Street, Moscow 125099
Phone: (7) 495 730 66 00
Web: www.sistema.com

HISTORICAL FINANCIALS

Company Type: Public

Income Statement FYE: December 31

	REVENUE ($ mil.)	NET INCOME ($ mil.)	NET PROFIT MARGIN	EMPLOYEES
12/12	34,240	946	2.8%	0
12/11	32,981	218	0.7%	0
12/10	28,098	918	3.3%	0
12/09	18,749	1,643	8.8%	0
Annual Growth	22.2%	(16.8%)	—	—

2012 Year-End Financials

Debt ratio: 35.0%
Return on equity: 10.9%
Cash ($ mil.): 1,872
Current ratio: 0.99
Long-term debt ($ mil.): 12,462
No. of shares (mil.): —
Dividends
Yield: —
Payout: —
Market value ($ mil.): —

	STOCK PRICE ($) FY Close	P/E High/Low		PER SHARE ($) Earnings	Dividends	Book Value
12/12	0.00	—	—	0.10	0.00	1.00
Annual Growth	—	—	—	—	—	—

SK Holdings Co Ltd

LOCATIONS

HQ: SK Holdings Co Ltd
99 SK Building, Seorin-dong, Jongro-gu, Seoul 110-728
Phone: (82) 2 2121 5114 **Fax:** (82) 2 2121 7001
Web: www.sk.co.kr

HISTORICAL FINANCIALS

Company Type: Public

Income Statement FYE: December 31

	REVENUE ($ mil.)	NET INCOME ($ mil.)	NET PROFIT MARGIN	EMPLOYEES
12/12	112,088	982	0.9%	196
12/11	95,985	1,443	1.5%	145
12/10	80,741	824	1.0%	300
12/09	71,018	232	0.3%	298
12/08	69,979	224	0.3%	279
Annual Growth	12.5%	44.6%	—	(8.4%)

2012 Year-End Financials

Debt ratio: 0.0%
Return on equity: 9.4%
Cash ($ mil.): 6,692
Current ratio: 1.13
Long-term debt ($ mil.): 16,798
No. of shares (mil.): 40
Dividends
Yield: —
Payout: —
Market value ($ mil.): —

SK Innovation Co Ltd

SK Innovation (formerly known as SK Energy) is the energy lubricants and chemicals affiliate of South Korea's SK Group. Korea's largest oil refiner SK Innovation controls about 34% of Korea's fuel retailing market. The firm holds stakes in 30 oil exploration and production projects in 16 countries and has proved reserves of more than 500 million barrels of oil equivalent. It imports liquid petroleum gas (LPG) and claims a 44% share of the Korean LPG market. SK Innovation supplies natural gas to Seoul and other cities in Korea. The company also makes lubricants low-pollutant gasoline petrochemicals and batteries for electric vehicles.

In 2011 in order to be a more flexible organization in dealing with a rapidly changing marketplace SK Innovation spun off its refining unit as SK Energy its chemical operations as SK Global Chemicals and its lubricant oil business as SK Lubricants. All the units are wholly-owned subsidiaries. A part of the innovative push the company's new corporate name claims the company is looking to expand in the field of alternative energy including pursuing new battery and carbon capture technologies.

SK Innovation is focusing on strengthening its overseas oil exploration and production operations. It has formed strategic alliances with other global oil concerns such as Nippon Oil and PERTAMINA to in order to expand activities in China Vietnam and Indonesia.

In 2010 it formed a joint venture with KBR to market and license SK Innovation's petrochemical and related process technologies. That same year it agreed to sell its Brazilian oil interests to Denmark's Maersk Oil for $2.4 billion. SK Innovation plans to use the proceeds either to invest in developing oil and gas fields or to buy other international oil companies. That year the company signed a contract to operate and maintain Vietnam's first petrochemical plant.

On the innovative technology side of the ledger in 2010 Korea launched its first electric car a vehicle powered by an SK Innovation lithium-ion battery.

In 2008 the company merged with subsidiary SK Incheon Oil a major Korean refiner allowing the company to further its plans to be a major oil and fuels exporter to the growing China market.

EXECUTIVES

EVP Ethics Management Office and Director, Joon Ho Kim
Chairman and CEO, Tae-Won Chey
CEO President Corporate Planning and Global Technology and Director, Ja-Young Koo
EVP Ethics Management Office and Director, Joon Ho Kim
Director, Soon Cho
Director, Young-Suk Han
Director, Dae-Woo Nam
Director, Sei-Jong Oh
Director, Tai-Yoo Kim
Director, Myung-Hae Choi
Director, Hoon-Kyu Lee
Director, In-Goo Han
CEO President Corporate Planning and Global Technology and Director, Ja-Young Koo
Auditors: Ernst&YoungHanYoung

LOCATIONS

HQ: SK Innovation Co Ltd
99 Seorin-dong, Jongro-gu, Seoul 110-728
Phone: (82) 2 2121 5114 **Fax:** (82) 2 2121 5114
Web: www.skenergy.com

2009 Sales

	% of total
Korea	41
Other	59
Total	**100**

PRODUCTS/OPERATIONS

2009 Sales

	% of total
Petroleum	68
Petrochemicals	27
Lubricants	3
Exploration & production &	2
Total	**100**

COMPETITORS

BHP Billiton
Daewoo International
Exxon Mobil
GS Caltex
Hyundai Corporation
Idemitsu Kosan
Nippon Oil
Royal Dutch Shell

HISTORICAL FINANCIALS

Company Type: Public

Income Statement FYE: December 31

	REVENUE ($ mil.)	NET INCOME ($ mil.)	NET PROFIT MARGIN	EMPLOYEES
12/12	68,680	1,110	1.6%	1,881
12/11	59,007	2,734	4.6%	1,642
12/10	47,911	1,015	2.1%	5,457
12/09	37,913	578	1.5%	5,582
12/08	41,445	699	1.7%	5,629
Annual Growth	13.5%	12.2%	—	(24.0%)

2012 Year-End Financials

Debt ratio: 0.0%	No. of shares (mil.): 91
Return on equity: 7.8%	Dividends
Cash ($ mil.): 2,649	Yield: —
Current ratio: 1.49	Payout: —
Long-term debt ($ mil.): 4,312	Market value ($ mil.): —

SK Telecom Co Ltd (South Korea)

SK Telecom a member of the SK Group chaebol is the #1 wireless communication services provider in South Korea in terms of subscribers. The company serves 26 million mobile customers (50% of the domestic market share). In addition to cellular and wireless data services SK Telecom provides broadband Internet access through a controlling stake in the #2 South Korean alternative local-exchange carrier and ISP SK Broadband. It also offers international long distance computer and business phone services (SK Telink); mobile satellite video broadcasting (TU Media); and it operates Internet portal NATE.com. SK Telecom has international offices in Beijing Ho Chi Minh City Jakarta London and Tokyo.

SK Telecom is using investments and acquisitions to improve its position in the consumer telecom services market. The company acquired a 49% stake in the credit card unit of Hana Bank in late 2009 to improve its ability to offer emerging mobile services such as payment by cell phone. That year the company introduced the T-Cash wireless payment service which lets mobile subscribers make electronic retail transactions that are tied to their cell phone accounts.

Since SK Telecom dominates the domestic wireless market the company is looking to maintain its market share by offering value-added services to its customers. Its MelOn music service allows users to stream or download music while 11th Street is its online shopping mall. T Store is the company's app store and its Cyworld is a popular social networking site with 25 million users in South Korea and 55 million in China. In mid-2011 SK Telecom announced it was considering spinning off its mobile content businesses called its platform business into a separate company.

In a move to give a boost to its broadcast business SK Telecom announced a joint venture with Disney in 2010 to bring Disney programming to South Korea over cable direct-to-home satellite computer television and mobile formats. SK Telecom owns a controlling 51% stake in the venture. It also announced a joint venture that year with China Railway No. 2 Engineering Group to build the infrastructure for a commercial and residential development in Cheungdu China; SK Telecom will own 60% of the venture and provide technology consulting and system support services.

Meanwhile SK Telecom continues to integrate the marketing and operational activities of its wireless business with those of SK Broadband so that it can more easily combine its mobile and fixed line products into packages that appeal to a broader range of customers.

In another industry semiconductors SK Telecom bought a 21% stake in Hynix Semiconductor for more than $3 billion in 2012 becoming the largest shareholder and renamed the flash memory chip maker SK Hynix.

HISTORY

SK Telecom was South Korea's first wireless telecommunications service provider. Its new product front generated buzz in 2005 when it announced a new service that allows customers to repel mosquitoes within a range of one meter using their cell phones. The service –introduced in South Korea in 2004 –was rolled out to a smattering of Southeast Asian countries.

Through its WitherThan.com mobile phone content unit SK Telecom established new offices in the UK and Indonesia in 2005 to expand its cell phone Internet business abroad. A month later it announced plans to invest $490 million in building third-generation mobile phone networks utilizing a European standard. The networks would be installed in 84 cities around South Korea.

The company decided to sell its stake in handset manufacturer SK Teletech to Pantech (South Korea's second-largest handset maker) in 2005. The $299.1 million deal sealed the sale of a 60% interest held by SK Telecom and helped SK Teletech avoid government regulation. The company was prevented from selling more than 1.2 million handsets per year because it was a unit of SK Telecom previously a wireless monopoly. Regulators simultaneously fined the company $90 million for offering illegal handset subsidies.

SK Telecom also jointly launched a mobile phone production plant in China with Pantech in 2005 to help expand its market position in that country.

Legal troubles hounded the company in 2005. The Korea Baseball Organization sued over unauthorized broadcasts of baseball games on its mobile TV service. The organization claimed TU Media a unit of SK Telecom broadcasted the games for its mobile TV subscribers without permission. It was also fined $1.4 million for discriminating against other Internet portal companies in opening its wireless network to them.

Aiming for improved network quality SK Telecom said in 2005 it would invest $152.4 million to upgrade its mobile phone network infrastructure by year's end. The company also began exploring opportunities in the entertainment industry. It announced plans to set up a joint $74.9 million fund with investment companies that would invest in entertainment-related ventures. The company also unveiled plans to open a research and development center in China.

In 2006 SK Telecom invested $1 billion in China Unicom taking a small stake in the company. The investment was seen as an endorsement of the advanced wireless technology known as CDMA2000.

SK Telecom effectively ended its activities in the North America when it sold its stake in joint wireless venture HELIO in 2008. The company had entered the US market in early 2005 when it formed HELIO with EarthLink to market wireless voice and data services. HELIO did not meet with the reception its parent companies had hoped however and both SK Telecom and Earthlink sold their interests in the struggling business to Virgin Mobile USA for about $39 million in 2008; SK Telecom took a 17% stake in Virgin Mobile USA as part of the deal. It eventually sold those shares to Sprint Nextel in late 2009.

The company in 2008 bought a stake in hanarotelecom which subsequently changed its name to SK Broadband; the company increased its stake in SK Broadand to just over 50% in 2009. The deal added broadband Internet and fixed-line telephone services to the company's portfolio enabling it to better compete with the country's largest fixed line carrier KT Corporation SK Telecom bought the leased line business of affiliate SK Networks later that year to improve the quality of its fixed-line voice calling.

EXECUTIVES

President and CEO, Man Won Jung
Chief Financial Officer, Seung Ahn
Director, Man-Won Jung, age 62
Director, Jae-Won Chey
Director, Dal Sup Shim
Director, Rak Yong Uhm
Director, Jay Young Chung
Director, Jae Ho Cho
Director, Ki Haeng Cho
Director, Hyun Chin Lim
Auditors: DeloitteHanaAnjinLLC

LOCATIONS

HQ: SK Telecom Co Ltd (South Korea)
11 Euljiro 2-ga, Jung-gu, Seoul 100-999
Phone: (82) 2 6100 2114 **Fax:** (82) 2 6100 7830
Web: www.sktelecom.com

PRODUCTS/OPERATIONS

2010 Sales

	% of total
Wireless	83
Fixed-line service (through SK	14
Other	3
Total	**100**

COMPETITORS

KT Corp.
LG Group
NTT DoCoMo

HISTORICAL FINANCIALS

Company Type: Public

Income Statement

FYE: December 31

	REVENUE ($ mil.)	NET INCOME ($ mil.)	NET PROFIT MARGIN	EMPLOYEES
12/12	15,266	1,078	7.1%	4,074
12/11	13,798	1,391	10.1%	3,955
12/10	13,911	1,642	11.8%	4,421
12/09	12,579	1,077	8.6%	4,441
12/08	11,046	957	8.7%	4,411
Annual Growth	8.4%	3.0%	—	(2.0%)

2012 Year-End Financials

Debt ratio: 0.0%	No. of shares (mil.): 69
Return on equity: 9.7%	Dividends
Cash ($ mil.): 861	Yield: 5.7%
Current ratio: 0.86	Payout: 7.1%
Long-term debt ($ mil.): 5,009	Market value ($ mil.): 1,103

	STOCK PRICE ($) FY Close	P/E High/Low	PER SHARE ($) Earnings	Dividends	Book Value
12/12	15.83	— —	15.12	0.92	159.31
12/11	13.61	— —	19.18	0.00	144.41
12/10	18.63	— —	22.24	0.93	142.13
12/09	16.26	— —	14.73	0.78	133.26
12/08	18.18	— —	13.05	1.06	115.68
Annual Growth	(3.4%)	— —	3.8%	(3.7%)	8.3%

Skandinaviska Enskilda Banken

Snow banks are a common winter sight in Sweden; SEB banks are easy to spot year-round. Skandinaviska Enskilda Banken (SEB) provides merchant banking retail banking wealth management and life insurance in some 20 nations primarily in Northern Europe. Its merchant banking division targets large corporate clients and other financial institutions for whom it provides lending debt capital markets trading finance and custody services. Its retail division provides business services including loans and card services. SEB Wealth Management offers asset management and private banking services to institutional and wealthy clients. The group traces its roots back to 1856.

Sweden accounts for more than half of SEB's sales. The company has focused on growth in the Nordic and Baltic nations where it hopes to become the top financial services provider. Norwegian bank DnB NOR which decided to exit Sweden's mortgage market sold its portfolio of mortgage loans to SEB in 2011. Germany has been another target growth market for the group. It developed a retail branch network there but sold those operations to Banco Santander in early 2011. SEB is still dedicated to its wholesale business in Germany.

The divestiture of SEB's German branches will cut into the group's interest income. Additionally the group's fees into a nationwide banking fund have doubled to SEK 600 million ($95 million). The fund was established to maintain stability in — and prevent the collapse of —Sweden's economy. However the Nordic region is one of Europe's strongest so the company enjoys an added level of financial security.

In 2011 SEB announced plans to sell its Ukrainian retail banking operations to Eurobank Group for 250 million kronor ($37 million). The deal will include 60 branches.

The wealthy Wallenberg family controls about 21% of SEB (through holding company Investor and a family foundation).

HISTORY

Skandinaviska Enskilda Banken (SEB) was incorporated in 1972 as a result of the merger between Stockholm's Enskilda Bank (founded in 1856 by the Wallenberg family) and Skandinaviska Banken (founded in 1864 and a pioneer in commercial lending in Scandinavia). By 1974 SEB had begun expanding its operations forming an investment management subsidiary. It then became one of the first Swedish banks to go international when it took a stake in the German Deutsch-Skandinavische Bank in 1976. By the end of the 1970s SEB had reached halfway around the world establishing a subsidiary in Singapore to handle Southeast Asian operations.

By the early 1980s SEB was leading the nation in industrial as well as private accounts largely due to deregulation and the introduction of new financial instruments including Swedish treasury bills a commercial paper market and market-rate state bonds. The bank continued to expand opening branches in the Cayman Islands Hamburg London and New York; it also began cross-border banking in Scandinavia through a regional alliance with Bergen Bank of Norway Privatbanken of Denmark and Union Bank of Finland.

In another step toward deregulation the Swedish government lifted the ban on foreign banking in 1985. Within a year a dozen international banks had established themselves in Sweden but SEB continued to expand; its investment banking subsidiary Enskilda Securities opened branches in Hong Kong London New York Paris and Singapore in the latter half of the 1980s.

In 1990 the bank acquired an option to buy about a third of Skandia Sweden's largest private insurance company. But facing strong resistance from Skandia's management SEB accepted defeat and sold most of its option to two Scandinavian insurance companies. Winds of change blew through Sweden in the early 1990s as the country suffered a severe economic recession. Deregulation in the mid-1980s followed by excessive lending to the property market led to inflated real estate prices and then a collapse of the market. Banks investing in property experienced huge losses; many banks (including SEB) had to turn to the government for help to strengthen their capital bases. The mid-1990s saw the bank still trying to recover selling several of its subsidiaries including a vehicle finance unit to GE Capital.

1997 saw SEB acquire Trygg-Hansa (now SEB Trygg Liv) one of Sweden's major insurers. The bank remained acquisitive in 1998 expanding aggressively into the Baltic by buying major stakes in banks in Estonia (Eesti Uhlspank) Latvia (Latvija Unibanken) and Lithuania (Vilniaus Bankas).

In 1999 the bank further emphasized its Internet business making it a separate unit. Also that year SEB sold Trygg-Hansa's non-life business to Denmark's Codan Insurance in exchange for Codan's banking subsidiary and other assets. In 2000 the bank acquired Germany's almost 200-branch BfG Bank from Credit Lyonnais; it then used BfG to create a cross-selling and Internet alliance with German insurer Gerling. Also in 2000 SEB upped its stake in Eesti Uhispank Vilniaus Bankas and Latvijas Unibanka.

The following year SEB announced plans to acquire fellow Swedish bank ForeningsSparbanken to create SEB SwedBank. EU regulators investigated the proposal and demanded significant concession. As a result the two banks dropped plans for the merger later in 2001.

SEB continued to boost its offerings and services —largely through acquisitions —during the early years of the 21st century. Purchases included Europay in Norway (2002) Danish life insurer Codan Pension (2004) Ukraine's Bank Agio (2005) and Russia's PetroEnergoBank (2006). In 2007 it acquired nearly all of Factorial Bank adding 65 branches in Eastern Ukraine. The following year it bought London-based hedge fund Key Asset Management.

EXECUTIVES

Deputy Chairman, Urban Jansson, age 68
Deputy Chairman, Jacob Wallenberg, age 58
Executive Vice President Chief Financial Officer, Jan Erik Back, age 52
President CEO and Director, Annika Falkengren, age 51
Chairman, Marcus Wallenberg, age 58
Executive Vice President Head of Merchant Banking, Magnus Carlsson, age 57
Head Group Communications, Viveka Hirdman-Ryrberg, age 51
Deputy President Deputy CEO and Head Group Staff and Business Support, Bo Magnusson, age 50
Head Group Strategy and Business Development, Hans Larsson, age 52
Head Group Human Resources, Ulf Peterson, age 53
Executive Vice President Head of Retail Banking, Mats Torstendahl
Head of Life & Wealth Management, Anders Johnsson, age 54
Chief Risk Officer, Johan Johan Andersson Andersson
Executive Vice President Head of Business Support, Martin Johansson, age 51
Country Manager SEB Denmark and Head of Merchant Banking Denmark, Peter H?ltermand, age 50
Head of Baltic, David Teare, age 50
Country Manager SEB Norway, William Paus, age 46
Director, Carl Wilhelm Ros, age 71
Deputy Chairman, Urban Jansson, age 68
Director, Jesper Ovesen, age 55
Deputy Chairman, Jacob Wallenberg, age 58
Deputy Chairman, Tuve Johannesson, age 70
President CEO and Director, Annika Falkengren, age 51
Director, Christine Novakovic, age 49
Independent Director, Birgitta Birgitta Kantola Kantola
Director; Employee Representative, Cecilia Cecilia Martensson Martensson
Director; Employee Representative, Goran Goran Lilja Lilja
Independent Director, Johan Johan Andresen Andresen
Independent Director, Signhild Signhild Arnegard Hansen Hansen
Independent Director, Tomas Tomas Nicolin Nicolin
Auditors: PricewaterhouseCoopersAB

LOCATIONS

HQ: Skandinaviska Enskilda Banken
Kungstradgardsgatan 8, Stockholm SE-106 40
Phone: (46) 771 62 10 00
Web: www.sebgroup.com

2010 Sales

	% of total
Scandinavia	
Sweden	55
Norway	13
Denmark	12
Finland	6
Baltics	
Lithuania	5
Estonia	4
Latvia	3
Germany	2
Total	**100**

PRODUCTS/OPERATIONS

2010 Sales by Segment

	% of total
Merchant	53
Retail	19
Life	13
Wealth	10
Baltic	5
Total	**100**

COMPETITORS

Citigroup Global Markets
Danske Bank
Deutsche Bank
DnB NOR
Goldman Sachs
KBC
Morgan Stanley
Nordea Bank
Skandia
Storebrand ASA
Svenska Handelsbanken
Swedbank AB
UBS Investment Bank

HISTORICAL FINANCIALS

Company Type: Public

Income Statement FYE: December 31

	ASSETS ($ mil.)	NET INCOME ($ mil.)	INCOME AS % OF ASSETS	EMPLOYEES
12/12	376,613	1,785	0.5%	18,168
12/11	342,561	1,610	0.5%	18,912
12/10	325,075	1,005	0.3%	20,717
12/09	324,096	156	0.0%	21,640
12/08	321,488	1,285	0.4%	22,311
Annual Growth	4.0%	8.6%	—	(5.0%)

2012 Year-End Financials

Return on assets: 0.4%
Return on equity: 10.6%
Long-term debt ($ mil.): —
No. of shares (mil.): —
Sales ($ mil): 14,204

Dividends
Yield: —
Payout: —
Market value ($ mil.): —

	STOCK PRICE ($) FY Close	P/E High/Low		PER SHARE ($) Earnings	Dividends	Book Value
12/12	8.54	0	0	0.81	0.00	7.66
12/11	5.78	0	0	0.73	0.00	7.20
12/10	7.65	0	0	0.46	0.00	6.75
12/09	7.05	0	0	0.08	0.00	6.36
12/08	7.56	0	0	1.88	0.00	15.57
Annual Growth	3.1%	—	—	(18.9%)	—	(16.2%)

Skanska AB

Skanska lays out a healthy smorgasbord of construction services. Scandinavia's largest construction and property development group Skanska provides building financing development and management services for commercial residential and civic projects in Europe the US and Latin America. Its areas of expertise include office buildings industrial plants single- and multifamily residences hospitals bridges and highways. The group's US divisions include Skanska USA Civil and Skanska USA Building. Skanska has completed work for clients such as Boeing IKEA Volvo and PETROBRAS. The company traces its roots to the 1887 founding of concrete manufacturer Aktiebolaget Sk?nska Cementgjuteriet.

Skanska's largest single market is the US where it ranks among the largest construction companies. The group has participated in such US projects as the $1 billion renovation of the United Nations headquarters the $1 billion Meadowlands football stadium in New Jersey and the $2.2 billion Croton Water Filtration Plant in the Bronx. The latter is Skanska's largest US project ever.

The company's largest segment by far is its construction business. Its construction units are active in Central Europe Latin America Scandinavia the UK and the US. Skanska's development segments (residential commercial and infrastructure) are primarily active in Europe. The company participates in public-private-partnership (PPP) projects including highways hospitals utilities and public schools.

Like all construction firms Skanska took a hit in the building downturn especially in its residential and infrastructure development arms. The group responded by cutting costs and curtailing new investments instead focusing on completing and selling existing developments and securing new contracts. The strategy helped Skanska weather the economic recession relatively unscathed and it has designs on growing its residential operations. The group is seeing an increase in infrastructure projects as a result of various government stimulus packages (particularly in the US and Central Europe). Skanska has also begun offering commercial development services in the US.

Marking a turnaround in the economy Skanska has begun making new investments. It acquired Slovakian concrete structures firm SkyBau in late 2010. At around the same time it bought Swedish HVAC contractor TKI. Also in 2010 Skanska was awarded its largest-ever contract: the design and construction of Karolinska Solna a 600-inpatient-bed university hospital and Sweden's first health care PPP project. It followed those deals up with the 2011 purchase of Polish construction company PUDiZ which specializes in road projects.

In 2011 Skanska announced its acquisition of Industrial Contractors in the US. The deal will help reduce Skanska's dependence on the public sector and boost its position in the industrial and energy sectors.

Another area of focus for the group is green construction. The company delivered Europe's first Green Building-certified project in the Czech Republic. In the US Skanska redesigned and retrofitted the 32nd floor of the Empire State Building (where Skanska USA is now housed) in a LEED Platinum-certified project. The company has also built an apartment building in Sweden offering solar energy panels as part of its sustainable urban living program.

HISTORY

In 1887 Rudolf Fredrik Berg a young engineer founded Aktiebolaget Sk?nska Cementgjuteriet initially devoted to manufacturing decorative concrete fittings for churches and public buildings. The company soon diversified its services by making construction components and performing construction work. Skanska received its first order from abroad within 10 years.

Great Britain's National Telephone bought 62 miles of hollow concrete blocks used for holding phone cables which represented Skanska's further expansion in the building materials market and its first foray into the telecom arena. The company then began producing concrete pipes in 1902 at a St. Petersburg factory in Russia. The pipes replaced the old wooden sewers used throughout the Russian empire.

Skanska reached a milestone in 1927 when it constructed Sweden's first asphalt-paved road. It garnered another record in 1943 constructing what was then the world's longest concrete arch-span bridge Sweden's 264-meter-long Sando Bridge. Until the 1960s the Sando stood as the longest such bridge in the world.

Achieving a breakthrough in construction technology Skanska in 1952 developed its Allbetong method which allowed off-site production of some prefabricated components. By the mid-1950s Skanska had become a major player in international markets.

Listed on the Stockholm Stock Exchange A-list in 1965 Skanska entered markets in the Middle East and Africa in the late 1960s and moved into Poland and the Soviet Union during the 1970s. In 1974 Skanska completed the 750-room Forum Hotel in Warsaw its first turnkey-hotel project outside Sweden.

To reflect its global presence the company dropped its original name in 1984 and became simply Skanska AB. In 1994 Skanska already entrenched in the New York area doubled its US presence by buying Atlanta-based Beers Construction one of the largest construction companies in the Southeast.

In 1995 a Skanska-led consortium was awarded a contract to build the 10-mile-long Oresund Link between Sweden and Denmark the first fixed road and rail connections between the Scandinavia peninsula and the rest of Europe (completed 2000). Three years later a Skanska-led consortium won a contract to design and build the AirTrain light rail link between JFK airport and New York City (completed 2003).

At the beginning of 1999 Skanska acquired Argentine construction company SADE firmly establishing the company's presence in Latin America. By year's end in alliance with US firm MasTec Skanska obtained a $1.4 billion contract to construct a fiber-optic network for US telecom company RCN. Other contracts that followed included football stadiums in Houston and Boston and the Brooklyn-Queens Expressway.

In 2000 the company bought Norwegian company Kvaerner's construction unit and the US-based construction management companies Barclay White and Baugh Enterprises. The company fine-tuned its organizational structure in 2001 to place more focus on client relations. Late that year the company's US-based group began projects related to the reconstruction of Ground Zero in New York City.

Skanska's success in the US may have prompted the company to look there for leadership. In 2002 the group selected Stuart Graham who had been president of Skanska USA as its new president and CEO replacing Claes Bjork. Graham had been with Skanska since it acquired Sordoni Construction in 1990.

Also in 2002 Skanska gained a nationwide footprint in US infrastructure by acquiring California-based civil engineering firm Yeager Construction which it merged with Skanska USA Civil. The parent company also decided to consolidate the co-branded companies of Skanska USA Building (Barclay White Skanska Etkin Skanska Sordoni Skanska and Baugh Skanska as well as Beers Skanska) under the single Skanska name.

The Swedish competition authority imposed fines in 2003 on 11 companies that it alleged had participated in an illegal cartel to inflate asphalt contract prices. Skanska and rival NCC received the stiffest penalties but Skanska countered that only one of its employees had confessed to price-fixing and that the company had cooperated fully with authorities.

Skanska took a $56 million charge in 2004 for a federal government project that subsidiary USA Building was overseeing. The write-down led to a new company policy of generating new business through negotiated contracts instead of from lump-sum bidding in the US.

In 2005 Skanska completed the Cooper River Bridge in South Carolina the longest cable-stayed bridge in North America one year ahead of schedule. The following year it bought UK transportation and utilities contractor McNicholas plc for #50 million ($96 million).

Graham stepped down as CEO in 2008. Johan Karlstrom formerly the president of Skanska USA Building was named his successor.

EXECUTIVES

President Skanska Commercial Development USA, Mats Johansson, age 55

President and Chief Executive Officer; Director, Johan Karlstrom, age 57, $1,159,200 total compensation

EVP Residential Development Nordic and IT, Tor Krusell, age 49

Executive Vice President Chief Financial Officer, Peter Wallin, age 46

Executive Vice President, Mats Williamson

Chairman, Stuart E. (Stu) Graham, age 68, $316 total compensation

President Skanska Norway, Petter Eiken, age 58

SVP Risk Management, Thomas Alm, age 64

Executive Vice President, Claes Larsson, age 48

Press Officer, Peter Gimbe

CFO Skanska Sweden, Anders Lilja

President of Skanska USA Civil, Richard (Rich) Cavallaro

President Skanska UK, Michael C. (Mike) Putnam, age 53

Executive Vice President and President CEO of Skanska USA Inc, Michael (Mike) McNally, age 59

President of Skanska USA Building, William (Bill) Flemming

Senior Vice President; Sustainability and Green Construction, Noel Morrin
President Skanska Latin America, Hernan Morano
Executive Vice President, Karin Lepasoon, age 46
Executive Vice President and President of Skanska Norway, Anders Danielsson
President of Skanska Czech and Slovak Republics, Dan Tok
SVP Investor Relations, Pontus Winqvist
Executive Vice President, Richard Hultin
Executive Vice President Skanska Czech Republic and Skanska Poland, Roman Wieczorek
President of BoKlok Housing, Jonas Spangenberg
President of Skanska Financial Services, Magnus Paulsson
Human Resources Manager Venezuela, Karina Valero
President of Skanska Poland, Krzysztof Andrulewicz
Executive Vice President Human Resources, Veronica Rorsg?rd, age 40
President Skanska Commercial Property Development Nordic, Jan Odelstam
SVP Reporting, Katarina Bylund
President of Skanska Infrastructure Development, Steve Sams
SVP Internal Audit, Anders Blomqvist, age 52
Senior Vice President of Legal Affairs, Ann-Marie Hedbeck
Chairman, Friends Provident
Senior Vice President Communications Sweden, Katarina Gronwall
Vice Chairman, Svenska Handelsbanken
Senior Vice President, Kevin Hutchinson
Senior Vice President; Risk Management, Christel Christel Akerman Akerman
Chief Executive Officer; President; Director, Johan Johan Karlstrom Karlstrom
President Skanska Finland, Kenneth Nilsson
Senior Vice President; Controlling, Louise Louise Hallqvist Hallqvist
President of Skanska Residential Development UK, Magnus Magnus Andersson Andersson
Skanska Residential Development Czech Republic, Mikael Mikael Matts Matts
President Skanska Commercial Development Europe, Nicklas Lindberg
Senior Vice President; Safety, Niel Niel Moore Moore
President Skanska Sweden, Pierre Olofsson
Senior Vice President, Staffan Staffan Schele Schele
Executive Vice President; Human Resources, Veronica Veronica Rorsgard Rorsgard
President Skanska Norway, St?le R?d
President Skanska Latin America, Alfredo Collado
President Skanska Residential Development Poland, Michal Melaniuk
Vice President - Operations, Kerim Evin
Vice President - Business Development, Laura Onessimo
Senior Vice President - Preconstruction, Mark Johnson
Executive Vice President General Manager, Paul Hewins
Director, Fredrik Lundberg, age 62
President CEO and Director, Johan Karlstrom, age 55
Vice Chairman, Stuart E. (Stu) Graham, age 66
Director, Sir Adrian A. Montague, age 65
Director, Inge Johansson, age 62
Director, Lars Pettersson, age 59
Director, Matti Sundberg, age 70
Director, Richard Horstedt, age 49
Director, Jessica Karlsson, age 37
Director, Roger Karlstrom, age 64
Director, Josephine Rydberg-Dumont, age 57
Director, Charlotte Stromberg, age 53
Director, Anders Fogelberg, age 62
Director, Thomas Larsson
Vice Chairman, Svenska Handelsbanken
Independent Director, Charlotte Charlotte Stromberg Stromberg
Director; Employee Representative, Roger Roger Karlstrom Karlstrom
Auditors: KPMGAB

LOCATIONS

HQ: Skanska AB
Rasundavagen 2, Solna SE-169 83
Phone: (46) 10 448 00 00 **Fax:** (46) 8 755 12 56
Web: www.skanska.se

2010 Sales

	% of total
Europe	
Sweden	23
Other Nordic	16
Other	28
US	28
Latin	5
Total	**100**

PRODUCTS/OPERATIONS

2010 Sales

	% of total
Construction	90
Residential	6
Commercial	4
Total	**100**

COMPETITORS

Bechtel
Bilfinger Berger
Bouygues
Bovis Lend Lease
Colas
EIFFAGE
Fluor
Foster Wheeler
HOCHTIEF
Jacobs Engineering
NCC
PCL Constructors
Parsons Corporation
Peter Kiewit Sons'
Technip
Uhde
VINCI

HISTORICAL FINANCIALS

Company Type: Public

Income Statement FYE: December 31

	REVENUE ($ mil.)	NET INCOME ($ mil.)	NET PROFIT MARGIN	EMPLOYEES
12/12	19,855	437	2.2%	56,618
12/11	17,215	1,100	6.4%	52,557
12/10	18,227	599	3.3%	51,645
12/09	19,208	508	2.6%	52,931
12/08	18,397	397	2.2%	57,815
Annual Growth	1.9%	2.5%	—	(0.5%)

2012 Year-End Financials

Debt ratio: —
Return on equity: 14.7%
Cash ($ mil.): 885
Current ratio: 1.17
Long-term debt ($ mil.): —
No. of shares (mil.): 419
Dividends
Yield: 0.0%
Payout: 1.8%
Market value ($ mil.): 6,702

	STOCK PRICE ($) FY Close	P/E High/Low		PER SHARE ($) Earnings	Dividends	Book Value
12/12	15.96	0	0	1.06	0.02	7.01
12/11	16.65	0	0	2.65	0.04	6.70
12/10	18.85	0	0	1.44	0.00	7.35
Annual Growth	(8.0%)	—	—	(7.4%)	—	(1.2%)

Societe Generale

Societe Generale wants to be top brass in the French banking industry. The bank (more familiarly known as SocGen) commands a three-pronged campaign with operations entailing domestic retail banking (including regional bank Credit du Nord and majority-owned online bank and brokerage Boursorama) international retail banking and corporate and investment banking. Other key activities include specialized finance consumer finance and insurance and investment management private banking and securities services. Altogether SocGen has more than 3200 branches in France and nearly 4000 additional locations in more than 75 countries worldwide.

SocGen has international banking operations in nearly 40 countries. Key markets for the segment are Russia Central and Eastern Europe the Mediterranean basin sub-Saharan Africa and Asia particularly China India and Vietnam. The company's asset management operations include two joint ventures with fellow French banking giant Credit Agricole: Amundi (25% owned) and brokerage Newedge (50%).

SocGen reported a 3% decline in net banking income for 2011 but a nearly 40% decrease in profits from E3.9 billion to E2.4 billion (approximately $5 billion to $3.1 billion). The company attributed its results in part to a decline in corporate and investment banking earnings amid turbulent markets as well as restructuring changes and the write down of goodwill and Greek sovereign debt.

SocGen's primary strategic initiatives include controlling risk and improving customer service. Some of the ways the bank is achieving its goals include streamlining its loan application process increasing capital reserves and reducing its exposure to sovereign debt of troubled countries such as Ireland Italy Portugal and Spain. To help improve its capital position SocGen announced plans to sell US asset manager TCW Group to The Carlyle Group in 2012. It's also partnering with Tikehau Group to take over French investment company Salvepar.

HISTORY

In 1864 French steel magnate Joseph Schneider along with a group of Parisian bankers incorporated Societe Generale pour Favoriser le Developpement du Commerce et de l'Industrie en France. The bank which for obvious reasons came to be known as Societe Generale had the duty "to encourage the development of trade and industry in France." It took deposits from the public and offered lines of credit to companies. The bank also helped organize businesses and invested in them.

By the 1890s Societe Generale's branches placed shares with the public and issued private unsecured loans in France and Russia.

The bank counted 14000 shareholders in 1895 and 18 years later the number had boomed to 122000. The bank continued its brisk growth through the first decades of the 20th century opening more than 1400 branches by 1933.

Although Societe Generale managed to move into Africa and America in the 1930s the Depression and WWII forced the bank to reduce its size and close branches at home.

After WWII the bank was nationalized by the French government to help rebuild the war-ravaged country. Societe Generale (already active in New York) was well-positioned to distribute the US-sponsored postwar reconstruction initiative aka the Marshall Plan. For 30 years the bank grew steadily under state control.

The 1960s were a boom time for French exports. The decade brought the bank greater expansion both geographically (Europe Latin America) and economically thanks to the specialization of credit investment banking finance leasing for companies and home mortgages for retail customers. Societe Generale also began dealing in Eurocurrencies (money deposited outside the investing company or government's home country).

In 1973 a new law in France allowed the bank to sell up to 25% of its shares to its staff and a limited circle of institutional investors.

A year later amid the oil crisis low-quality Eurocurrency market loans came back to haunt Societe Generale. In one case the bank had unwisely lent Eurodollars to the United States National Bank of San Diego which failed and cost Societe Generale $7.5 million.

In 1975 the bank launched Agrifan an export-based food products trading company to great success. Agrifan was followed by two more companies specializing in food-industry equipment and medical supplies.

Conservatives regained power in the French government in 1986. The next year Societe Generale was officially privatized.

In 1998 the bank extended the reach of its financial services by acquiring Barr Devlin a US-based investment banker and adviser and Yamaichi Capital Management in Japan.

The next year Societe Generale undertook a friendly merger with fellow French banking gargantuan Paribas only to have Banque Nationale de Paris swoop in and steal the prize to form BNP Paribas.

Societe Generale had to satisfy itself with a piecemeal expansion. By 2000 it had hammered out an ambitious strategic alliance with Spain-based Santander Central Hispano. The French bank also snapped up 30% of Italian insurer Societa Assicuratrice Industriale's Banca SAI subsidiary giving it access to SAI's 3 million customers. The buying spree continued into 2001 with Societe Generale acquiring Deutsche Bank's leasing and vehicle-fleet businesses Gefa and ALD. The bank then bought a controlling stake in LA-based fund manager TCW Group.

SocGen sold its South American retail banking unit Banco Societe Generale Argentina to Argentine banking group Banco Banex in 2005. The following year SocGen spun off US-based investment bank Cowen Group.

In 2008 SocGen uncovered fraud by one of its traders in one of the world's largest-ever instances of trading fraud. Soon after the company began raising funds to help cover the estimated $7.1 billion cost of the fraud and also initiated legal proceedings against the (by then former) employee. The Banking Commission of France fined the company $6.3 billion for breaches in internal controls.

Additionally chairman and then-CEO Daniel Bouton and co-CEO Philippe Citerne each gave up a half-year's salary to compensate for the company's losses. Although Bouton's offers to resign amidst the firestorm were twice rejected by SocGen's board of directors he eventually did step down. CFO Frederic Oudea succeeded him in both positions. Didier Alix and Severin Cabannes replaced Citerne as deputy CEOs.

The company spent years building up its portfolio in banks in Central and Eastern Europe including majority stakes in Russia's Rosbank in 2008 and in Macedonia's Ohridska Banka and Bauritanian Bank Banque in 2007. SocGen also expanded its private banking operations. In 2008 its SG Private Banking unit acquired a 37% stake in US-based wealth manager Rockefeller Financial Services and in 2007 it bought ABN AMRO's London private banking unit.

In 2008 SocGen merged the brokerage activities of subsidiary Fimat with Credit Agricole Corporate and Investment Bank (formerly Calyon) creating a joint venture named Newedge. The following year SocGen merged its asset management business with that of Credit Agricole creating a combined firm called Amundi with more than E690 billion ($1 trillion) of assets under management. SocGen owns 25% of the joint venture while Credit Agricole holds the other 75%.

EXECUTIVES

Director, Robert Castaigne, age 64
Director, Jean-Martin Folz, age 65
Vice Chairman, Anthony B. Wyand, age 69
Director, Luc Vandevelde, age 61
Director, Michel Cicurel, age 65
Director, Kenji Matsuo, age 63
Director, Jean Azema, age 59
Director, Elisabeth Lulin, age 46
Director, Gianemilio Osculati, age 64
Director, Nathalie Rachou
Director, Patrick Delicourt
Director, France Houssaye
Director, Jean-Bernard Levy
Auditors: Ernst&YoungAudit

LOCATIONS

HQ: Societe Generale
29, Boulevard Haussmann, Paris 75009
Phone: (33) 1 42 14 20 00
Web: www.societegenerale.com

PRODUCTS/OPERATIONS

2011 Income by Segment

	% of total
French	32
Corporate & Investment	23
International Retail	20
Specialized Financial Services &	14
Global Investment Management &	9
Corporate &	2
Total	**100**

Selected Subsidiaries and Affiliates

ALD (vehicle leasing and fleet management)
Banco Cacique (consumer finance Brazil)
Banco Pecunia (consumer finance Brazil)
Bank Republic (Georgia)
Banque de Polynesie (72% French Polynesia)
BDK Bank (consumer finance Germany)
BelRosbank (Belarus)
BFV-Societe Generale (banking Madagascar)
Boursorama SA (56% online banking and brokerage)
BRD-Groupe Societe Generale (banking Romania)
CGI (consumer finance)
CredAgoria (consumer finance Portugal)
Credit du Nord (banking France)
DeltaCredit (banking Russia)
ESSOX (consumer finance Czech Republic)
Eurobank (consumer finance Poland)
Fiditalia (consumer finance Italy)
Geniki Bank (54% Greece)
Komercni Banka (60% Czech Republic)
Lyxor (investment management)
Mobiasbanka (Moldova)
National Societe Generale Bank (Egypt)
Ohridska Banka (Macedonia)
Rosbank (Russia)
SG Mumbai (India)
SeABank (Vietnam)
SG VietFinance (Vietnam)
SKB Banka (Slovenia)
Societe Generale Albania
Societe Generale Algerie (banking Algeria)
Societe Generale Bank Cyprus
Societe Generale Benin
Societe Generale de Banque - Jordanie (Jordan)
Societe Generale de Banque au Liban (Lebanon)
Societe Generale de Banques au Cote d'Ivoire
Societe Generale de Banques au Senegal
Societe Generale Burkina Faso
Societe Generale (China) Limited
Societe Generale Expressbank (Bulgaria)
Societe Generale Maroc (Morocco)
Societe Generale - Splitska Banka (Croatia)
Societe Generale Tchad (Chad)
SOGECAP (life insurance)
Union Internationale de Banques (Tunisia)

COMPETITORS

BBVA
BNP Paribas
CIC
CRCAM IDF CCI
Caisse des Depots et Consignations
Credit Agricole
Credit Foncier de France
Credit Suisse
Deutsche Bank
HSBC France
Natixis
Union Financiere de France

HISTORICAL FINANCIALS

Company Type: Public

Income Statement FYE: December 31

	ASSETS ($ mil.)	NET INCOME ($ mil.)	INCOME AS % OF ASSETS	EMPLOYEES
12/12	1,648,479	1,020	0.1%	154,009
12/11	1,528,048	3,084	0.2%	159,616
12/10	1,515,133	5,242	0.3%	155,617
12/09	1,474,712	976	0.1%	156,681
12/08	1,579,847	2,810	0.2%	163,082
Annual Growth	1.1%	(22.4%)	—	(1.4%)

2012 Year-End Financials

Return on assets: 0.0%
Return on equity: 1.5%
Long-term debt ($ mil.): —
No. of shares (mil.): 754
Sales ($ mil): 107,290
Dividends
Yield: —
Payout: —
Market value ($ mil.): 5,896

	STOCK PRICE ($) FY Close	P/E High	P/E Low	PER SHARE ($) Earnings	Dividends	Book Value
12/12	7.82	22	9	0.84	0.00	87.07
12/11	4.36	8	2	4.11	0.92	81.50
12/10	10.87	6	2	6.61	0.86	85.68
12/09	14.05	76	19	0.65	1.13	84.58
12/08	10.40	18	4	4.70	1.56	89.97
Annual Growth	(6.9%)	—	—	(34.9%)	—	(0.8%)

Sodexo

This company has a lot of mouths to feed. Formerly Sodexho Alliance Sodexo is the world's #2 contract foodservice provider (after Compass Group) with operations in about 80 countries. Its subsidiaries offer corporate foodservice and hospitality services vending services and foodservices for educational institutions and other public-sector clients. Other operations include event concessions health care foodservices and such outsourced on-site service solutions as cleaning groundskeeping and laundry. Its US-based subsidiary Sodexo Inc. is one of the largest contract foodservice providers in North America. The company has some 33900 service sites worldwide.

In addition to its core foodservice and facilities management services Sodexo is a leading provider of voucher cards in Europe and Latin America used to buy groceries clothing and other basic necessities. The company operates voucher systems for both employers that use the cards as a form of employee benefits as well as for government welfare programs. Vouchers include restaurant gift and childcare passes. (Sodexo refers to its voucher operations as motivation solutions.)

Sodexo's business strategy includes the following: to become a world leader in on-site service solutions and motivation solutions and to maintain its leadership in the foodservice sector. It sets forth these basic goals in order to meet challenges such as the recent and on-going worldwide economic turndown and the aging of the population (particularly in North America). It also faces diminishing sources of and rising costs of its raw materials (ex: energy and food). And finally as the world population continues to grow and at the same time societies' wealth grows Sodexo must to deal with quality-of-life issues with regard to the goods and services it provides.

Working to fulfill these strategies the company won the contract for organizing the 2010 Winter Olympics in Vancouver. During 2009 it increased its contract obligations with France's Ministry of Justice to deliver service solutions to 27 additional prisons. It also won the Microsoft Europe contract and renewed its contract with Procter & Gamble for which Sodexo provides a wide range of services at 38 sites in 13 European countries. It also signed a 30-year contract to design construct and manage a military training center for The Defense Training Review in the UK. (Sodexo hopes to realize E30 billion in revenue over the life of the contract.) In addition Sodexo made acquisitions in high-growth markets in 2009 including Zehnacker in Germany RKHS in India and Comfort Keepers in the US. Following that trend into 2011 the company acquired the Brazilian based Puras do Brazil for approximately E525 million mid year.

During 2008 it signed contracts to provide services to GlaxoSmithKline in Canada and Societe Generale in France. The company has also been making targeted acquisitions to expand both its services and geographical reach. It purchased a 90% stake in Zehnacker Group a facilities management services provider in Germany for more than E170 million ($234 million) in 2008. That same year it acquired Score Groupe in France.

The company changed its name in 2008 to Sodexo dropping both the word "Alliance" and the "h" as part of a global rebranding effort. The name change was intended to raise the company's profile and recognition by focusing on the singular name (that it also hopes is easier to spell and pronounce without the extra letter).

Chairman Pierre Bellon and his family own about 38% of the company.

HISTORY

The Bellon family had been luxury ship hospitality specialists since the turn of the century 60 years before Pierre Bellon founded Sodexho in 1966. By 1971 Bellon had his first contract outside France to provide foodservice to a Brussels hospital. Sodexho continued to expand its services into the late 1970s entering remote site management in Africa and the Middle East in 1975 and starting its service vouchers segment in Belgium and Germany in 1978.

Sodexho jumped the pond in 1980 expanding its businesses into North and South America. The company went public on the Paris Bourse exchange in 1983. Two years later it bought Seiler a Boston vending machine company-turned-restaurateur. Sodexho then bought San Francisco's Food Dimensions in 1987. After beefing up its American operations with four other US acquisitions the company merged Food Dimensions and Seiler in 1989. Sodexho's US river cruise company Spirit Cruises –an echo of the Bellon family's original calling –was also included in the merger. The merged US companies were renamed Sodexho USA in 1993.

The 1990s proved an era of growth and acquisitions for Sodexho. The company expanded into Japan Africa Russia and five Eastern European countries in 1993. The company acquired a 20% stake in Corrections Corporation of America the following year and virtually doubled its size with the acquisition of the UK's Gardner Merchant in 1995. The largest catering company in that region Gardner Merchant had holdings that spanned Australia Asia northern Europe the UK and the US — generally markets where Sodexho did not have a strong presence. That year the company also acquired Partena a Swedish security and care company from Volvo's Fortos.

Gardner Merchant's US business was officially merged with Sodexho USA in 1996 to make it the #4 foodservice company in the US. Also that year Sodexho acquired Brazilian service voucher company Cardapio. After a year of legal wrangling Sodexho also lost a fight for control of Accor's Eurest France to rival caterer Compass Group and sold off its minority interest. The next year Sodexho acquired 49% of Universal Ogden Services renamed Universal Services an American remote site manager. To signify its efforts to maintain the individuality of the companies it acquires Sodexho changed its name to Sodexho Alliance in 1997.

Marriott International merged its foodservice branch with Sodexho's North American foodservice operations in 1998. With a 48% stake Sodexho Alliance became the largest shareholder; former Marriott International stockholders took the rest with the Marriott family controlling 9%. Before the merger Sodexho USA was less than one-fourth the size of Marriott International's foodservice division. Sodexho acquired GR Servicios Hoteleros in 1999 thereby becoming the largest caterer in Spain. The following year it agreed to merge its remote site management operations with Universal Services and rename it Universal Sodexho (later Sodexo Remote Sites).

In 2001 its initial $900 million bid to buy the 52% of Sodexho Marriott Services it didn't already own was rebuffed by its subsidiary's shareholders. Sodexho Alliance made a better offer (about $1.1 billion) and finally reached an agreement to purchase the rest of Sodexho Marriott Services. The deal was completed later that year and Sodexho Marriott Services changed its name to Sodexho Inc. Also that year the company agreed to pay some $470 million for French rival Sogeres and US-based food management firm Wood Dining.

In 2002 the company announced it had detected accounting and management errors in its UK operations causing the value of its stock to fall by nearly one-third. In addition the company replaced its UK management team because of poor performance there.

Admitting no wrongdoing Sodexho settled an $80 million race-bias lawsuit just before it was to go to trial in 2005. The suit brought by the African-American employees of its American subsidiary Sodexho Inc. charged that African-Americans were routinely passed over for promotions and were segregated within the company. In addition to paying the monetary award Sodexho agreed to increase company diversity through promotion incentives monitoring and training.

In 2005 Bellon 75 stepped down as company CEO but remained chairman. He was replaced by Sodexho veteran Michel Landel. The company changed its name to Sodexo in 2008 a rebranding effort that eliminated both the word "Alliance" and the "h" from its name.

EXECUTIVES

Chief Executive Officer, Michel Landel, age 62, $1,082,058 total compensation
Group EVP Chief Human Resources Officer and Internal Communications Officer, Elisabeth Carpentier, age 59
Chairman, Pierre Bellon, age 81, $386,053 total compensation
Group COO; CEO Remote Sites Asia/Australia and On-site Service Solutions, Nicholas Japy, age 57
President Chief Executive Officer of Sodexo North America, George Chavel
Vice Chairman, Robert Baconnier, age 73
Group EVP and Chief Marketing Officer Client Retention Offer Marketing Supply Chain and Sustainable Development, Damien Verdier, age 57
Group COO CEO Europe and President Motivation Solutions, Pierre Henry, age 62
Executive Vice President Strategic Planning and, Aurelien Sonet, age 39
Human Resources Director, Natalie Bickford
Chief Information Officer, Mark Mitchelson
Group CEO Executive Committee President and Director, Michel Landel, age 61
Director, Peter M. Thompson, age 66
Director, Paul Jeanbart, age 74
Director, Astrid Bellon, age 44
Director, Bernard Bellon, age 78
Director, Francois-Xavier Bellon, age 48
Director, Sophie Clamens, age 52
Director, Nathalie Szabo, age 50
Vice Chairman, Robert Baconnier, age 73
Director, Patricia Bellinger, age 53
Auditors: PricewaterhouseCoopers

LOCATIONS

HQ: Sodexo
255, quai de la Bataille de Stalingrad, Issy-les-Moulineaux, Cedex 9 92866
Phone: (33) 1 30 85 75 00
Web: www.sodexo.com

COMPETITORS

ARAMARK
Accor
Autogrill
Berendsen
Cintas
Compass Group
Delaware North
Elior
Healthcare Services
ISS A/S
SSP
SSP America
UniFirst

HISTORICAL FINANCIALS

Company Type: Public

Income Statement FYE: August 31

	REVENUE ($ mil.)	NET INCOME ($ mil.)	NET PROFIT MARGIN	EMPLOYEES
08/13	24,357	581	2.4%	427,921
08/12	22,959	660	2.9%	421,391
08/11	23,183	651	2.8%	391,148
08/10	19,350	518	2.7%	379,137
08/09	20,959	561	2.7%	379,749
Annual Growth	3.8%	0.9%	—	3.0%

2013 Year-End Financials

Debt ratio: 27.8%
Return on equity: 14.6%
Cash ($ mil.): 1,783
Current ratio: 0.87
Long-term debt ($ mil.): 2,509
No. of shares (mil.): 151
Dividends
Yield: —
Payout: —
Market value ($ mil.): 13,348

	STOCK PRICE ($) FY Close	P/E High/Low		PER SHARE ($) Earnings	Dividends	Book Value
08/13	88.10	57	44	3.81	0.00	25.81
08/12	78.85	40	31	4.34	1.90	25.36
08/11	73.55	57	36	4.25	0.00	24.30
08/10	57.69	44	32	3.34	1.73	22.37
08/09	57.85	56	28	3.61	1.63	20.99
Annual Growth	11.1%	—	—	1.4%	—	5.3%

Softbank Corp. (Japan)

SOFTBANK's investment strategy is anything but soft. Under the leadership of founder chairman and CEO Masayoshi Son (sometimes referred to as the Bill Gates of Japan) the company makes investments in a variety of ventures. Its portfolio holdings span mobile and fixed-line telecommunications Internet commerce and content technology services marketing broadband infrastructure and more. The company also provides venture capital to technology-related concerns in Asia Europe and the US. Interests in SOFTBANK MOBILE SOFTBANK TELECOM and Yahoo Japan along with a minority stake in Yahoo! comprise the bedrock of SOFTBANK's holdings. The firm has stakes in more than 60 companies in all.

Mergers & Acquisitions

In order to boost its position as a global player SOFTBANK is betting big on the US wireless service market. It has entered into an agreement to acquire 78% of Sprint Nextel. If completed the deal would be the largest acquisition of a US technology company by a Japanese business in history. Under the agreement SOFTBANK will invest a whopping $21.6 billion (raised from $20.1 billion after DISH Network made an unsolicited bid) in Sprint of which $16.6 billion will be distributed to Sprint stockholders and $5 billion will be used to strengthen Sprint's balance sheet. SOFTBANK brings both cash and expansion experience to Sprint. It also allows SOFTBANK to grow its expertise in smartphones and next-generation high speed networks. The closing of the transaction is expected to occur in mid-2013.

Strategy

SOFTBANK often uses joint ventures to accomplish its goal of increasing its foothold as a global player. In the Asia/Pacific market for example it announced a joint venture with PayPal in 2012 to establish a digital payments business in Japan. The company also works with website operator Alibaba.com (of which it controls about a third) to develop mobile Internet services and an online shopping market in China and Japan. Additionally SOFTBANK participates in a joint venture with wireless network giants China Mobile Verizon Wireless and Vodafone to develop similar services.

Other strategic areas of focus for SOFTBANK include enhancing its networks sales structure and branding. Despite a soft spot for all things technological SOFTBANK also has holdings outside of the wired world: It owns the Fukuoka SOFTBANK HAWKS (formerly the Fukuoka Daiei Hawks) a professional baseball team it acquired in 2005.

Ownership

Masayoshi Son owns approximately 30% of SOFTBANK which he started in 1981 as a distributor of packaged software. In 2010 the company launched SOFTBANK Academia a program designed to identify and train potential successors to Son as CEO.

HISTORY

Ethnic Korean Masayoshi Son grew up in Japan using the name Yasumoto to conform with the Japanese policy of assimilation. In the early 1970s the 16-year-old came to the US and began using his Korean name. Son entered the University of California at Berkeley and while there invented the prototype for the Sharp Wizard handheld organizer.

Bankrolled by the nearly $1 million that Sharp paid him for his patent Son returned to Japan and founded software distributor SOFTBANK in 1981. The company got its first big break when it inked a distribution agreement with Joshin Denki one of Japan's largest consumer electronics retailers that year. Son used this agreement to gain exclusive distribution rights for much of the software he distributed.

SOFTBANK went public in 1994. That year as part of an evolving plan to control digital data delivery Son bought the trade show division of Ziff-Davis Publishing augmenting it in 1995 with the purchase of COMDEX the trade show operations of the Interface Group. The next year SOFTBANK bought the rest of Ziff-Davis. It also bought 80% of Kingston Technology (sold 1999) and a stake in Yahoo! —which laid the cornerstone for its Internet empire.

SOFTBANK accelerated its Internet investment pace in 1997 taking stakes in dozens of Web companies. That year it filed suit against Yell Publishing a Japanese firm that published a book accusing SOFTBANK of issuing phony financial statements among other improprieties.

In 1998 the firm moved into financial services entering a joint venture with E*TRADE to offer online stock trading in Japan. SOFTBANK also took Ziff-Davis public (it retained a majority stake).

Internal changes marked 1999 when SOFTBANK merged with MAC Son's private asset management company and transformed itself into a holding company focused on Internet-related companies. It teamed with the National Association of Securities Dealers to create a Japanese version of the Nasdaq stock market (launched in 2000; closed in 2002). SOFTBANK also partnered with Microsoft and Tokyo Electric Power to launch SpeedNet a Japanese Internet service provider.

In 2000 the nearly decimated Ziff-Davis announced it would transform its online arm ZDNet from a tracking stock into a stand-alone company and adopt the ZDNet name; later CNET Networks (now a part of CBS Interactive) bought both companies instead. That year SOFTBANK formed venture capital funds focusing on areas such as Latin America Japan Europe the UK and emerging markets.

The company reorganized in 2000 and placed most of its non-Japan-based holdings under a new unit called SOFTBANK Global Ventures. Sharpening its focus on Internet investments SOFTBANK sold its stake in antivirus software maker Trend Micro. Branching into banking SOFTBANK headed a consortium that paid $932 million for Japan's failed Nippon Credit Bank. SOFTBANK's share of the bank (renamed Aozora) stood at nearly 49%. The firm's stock price tumbled in 2000 and it considered taking several holding companies public.

In 2001 Cisco bought a nearly 2% stake in SOFTBANK in exchange for the firm's 12% stake in the hardware company's Japanese unit. The company also sold its SOFTBANK Forums Japan an Internet trade show company to MediaLive International. In 2002 Nasdaq Japan announced its plans to close after two loss-making years. SOFTBANK owned 43%.

In an attempt to create a larger domestic market for its e-commerce and Internet companies SOFTBANK moved aggressively into the broadband market providing asymmetric digital subscriber line (ADSL) services.

EXECUTIVES

SEVP, Ken Miyauchi, age 64
Chairman and CEO, Masayoshi Son, age 56
President SOFTBANK Holdings, Ronald D. (Ron) Fisher, age 65
President Fukuoka SoftBank Hawks Marketing, Kazuhiko Kasai
Managing Partner, Kabir Misra
VP Finance and Operations, Josh Lubov
VP Technology, Phil Shevrin
VP Fund Operations, Melanie Dyer
COO and Director, Ken Miyauchi
Director; President and Director SOFTBANK Holdings, Ronald D. (Ron) Fisher, age 64
Director, Tadashi Yanai, age 63
Director and Director Softbank Mobile, Kazuhiko Kasai
Director, Jun Murai
Director, Mark Schwartz
Director, Yun Ma
Auditors: ChuoAoyamaPricewaterhouseCoopers

LOCATIONS

HQ: Softbank Corp. (Japan)
1-9-1 Higashi-Shinbashi, Minato-ku, Tokyo 105-7303
Phone: (81) 3 6889 2290
Web: www.softbank.co.jp

COMPETITORS

3i Group
Accel Partners
Alloy Ventures
Benchmark Capital
Hummer Winblad
ICG Group
IVP
JAFCO
Kleiner Perkins
Mayfield Fund
Menlo Ventures
NEA
Sequoia Capital
Sevin Rosen
Trinity Ventures

HISTORICAL FINANCIALS

Company Type: Public

Income Statement FYE: March 31

	REVENUE ($ mil.)	NET INCOME ($ mil.)	NET PROFIT MARGIN	EMPLOYEES
03/13	35,904	3,075	8.6%	24,598
03/12	39,039	3,824	9.8%	22,710
03/11	36,285	2,291	6.3%	21,799
03/10	29,584	1,035	3.5%	21,885
03/09	27,144	438	1.6%	21,048
Annual Growth	7.2%	62.7%	—	4.0%

2013 Year-End Financials

Debt ratio: 0.4%
Return on equity: 23.1%
Cash ($ mil.): 14,551
Current ratio: 1.00
Long-term debt ($ mil.): 17,173
No. of shares (mil.): 1,191
Dividends
Yield: —
Payout: —
Market value ($ mil.): 27,166

	STOCK PRICE ($) FY Close	P/E High/Low		PER SHARE ($) Earnings	Dividends	Book Value
03/13	22.80	—	—	2.70	0.00	18.79
03/12	14.87	—	—	3.40	0.00	15.93
03/11	19.78	—	—	2.04	0.00	9.81
Annual Growth	7.4%	—	—	7.3%	—	17.6%

Sojitz Corp

Sojitz Corporation is trading in all kinds of places. The company's 500-plus subsidiaries trade in a wide array of businesses ranging from steel and automobile parts to apparel making it one of the largest trading houses in Japan. Sojitz's other major businesses include aerospace foods oil and gas chemicals and plastics retail property development and construction materials. Its North American unit Sojitz Corporation of America is a major contributor to its overseas trading operations. In addition it has operations in Africa China Europe the Middle East Oceania and Russia. Sojitz was formed by the 2003 merger of two Japanese trading powerhouses Nissho Iwai and Nichimen Corporation.

Revenues at Sojitz dropped in 2010 hampered by the slow pace of the global economic recovery. Net sales decreased in all four major business segments with Energy and Metals the biggest loser down more than 42%. Net income also dropped significantly over the previous year. In 2011 the company announced plans going forward to reduce inventories in its weaker segments (such as automotive and real estate) while concentrating resources in markets with high growth potential including energy minerals and fertilizers.

In 2011 Sojitz formed a joint venture with Archean Chemical Industries in India to produce sulphate of potash a key element in many fertilizers. Production will be at Archean's facility in Gujarat. Sojitz is providing most of the funding ($216 million) and will market the product globally. Operations are set to begin in 2012.

The company also formed a joint venture with United Africa Group and Korea Midland Power to implement Namibia's first wind power project. The 44MW project in Luderitz in southwest Namibia will also be the first such project in sub-Saharan Africa with a Japanese firm participating. Operations are set to begin in 2013.

Sojitz also began searching in 2010 for sources other than China for rare earth metals. It signed a contract in mid-year with Lynas Corporation in Australia to purchase about 8500 tons a year some 30% of Japan's annual demand. It also entered a joint venture with Toyota Tusho to import another 3000 tons from Vietnam. Shipments from China which mines and sells most of the world's rare earth metals were delayed in 2010 in a move Japan said was a de facto blockade. Rare earth metals such as palladium are a key element in the production of electronic components and lithium-ion batteries.

The company formed a subsidiary in China in 2009 to enter key businesses such as the automotive ball bearing textiles and plastics industries. That year it transferred its domestic foodstuffs business to a wholly owned subsidiary called Sojitz Foods Corporation.

HISTORY

The Nissho and Iwai companies got their acts together as Nissho Iwai in 1968 but each company dates back to the middle of the 19th century. In 1863 Bunsuke Iwai opened a shop in Osaka to sell imported goods such as glass oil products silk and wine. The Meiji government which came to power in 1868 encouraged modernization and industrialization a climate in which Iwai's business flourished. In 1877 Iwajiro Suzuki established a similar trading concern Suzuki & Co. that eventually became Nissho.

After cotton spinning machines were introduced in Japan in the 1890s both Iwai and Suzuki imported cotton. Iwai began to trade directly with British trader William Duff & Son (an innovation in Japan where the middleman or shokan played the paramount role in international trade). Iwai became the primary agent for Yawata Steel Works in 1901 and was incorporated in 1912. Meanwhile Suzuki solely engaged in the import trade emerged as one of the top sugar brokers in the world and established an office in London.

To protect itself from foreign competition Iwai established a number of companies to produce goods in Japan including Nippon Steel Plate (1914) and Tokuyama Soda (1918). Stagnation after WWI forced Suzuki to restructure. In 1928 the company sold many of its assets to trading giant Mitsui and reorganized the rest under a new name Nissho Co.

Both Iwai and Nissho subsequently grew as they helped fuel Japan's military expansion in Asia in the 1930s. But Japan's defeat in WWII devastated the companies. When the occupation forces broke up Mitsui and other larger trading conglomerates both companies took advantage of the situation to move into new business areas. In 1949 Nissho established Nissho Chemical Industry Nissho Fuel and Nijko Shoji (a trading concern). It also opened its US operations Nissho American Corp. in 1952.

Poor management by the Iwai family led the company into financial trouble in the 1960s and prompted the Japanese government to instruct the profitable Nissho to merge with Iwai in 1968.

In 1979 Nissho Iwai was accused of funneling kickbacks from US aircraft makers to Japanese politicians. The scandal led to arrests the resignation of the company's chairman and the suicide of another executive. Nissho Iwai exited the aircraft marketing business in 1980.

Despite Japan's recession in the 1990s Nissho Iwai managed to make some significant investments. In 1991 the company teamed up with the Russian government to develop a Siberian oil refinery. A year later Nissho acquired a stake in courier DHL International and in 1995 it set up a unit to process steel plates in Vietnam.

However in the late 1990s rough economic conditions caught up with the firm. It dissolved its NI Finance unit (domestic financing) in 1998 after its disastrous performance. The large trading firm or sogo shosha also began a major restructuring effort to get back on track.

In 1999 Nissho Iwai sold its headquarters its 5% stake in DHL International and its stake in a Japanese ISP Nifty. CEO Masatake Kusamichi resigned. He was replaced by Shiro Yasutake who took charge of the firm's restructuring. In 2000 the company's ITX Corp. acquired five IT-related affiliates of Nichimen Corp.

As part of the group's streamlining efforts in 2001 Nissho Iwai spun off its nonferrous marketing unit (Alconix) and agreed to merge the group's LNG operations with Sumitomo's LNG business. The next year Hidetoshi Nishimura replaced Yasutake as CEO.

In 2003 Nissho Iwai merged with the smaller Nichimen Corp. to form Nissho Iwai-Nichimen Holdings. Hidetoshi Nishimura president and CEO of Nissho Iwai and Toru Hambayashi president of Nichimen became co-CEOs of the new holding company. Former board member Akio Dobashi took over the reins as president and sole CEO early in 2004; in April he moved over to the chairman's seat and Yutaka Kase assumed the president and CEO titles. In June the company changed its name from Nissho Iwai-Nichimen Holdings to Sojitz Holdings Corporation.

As part of its ongoing reorganization in 2005 the company renamed itself again when it merged the holding company into Sojitz Corporation.

EXECUTIVES

Chairman, Akio Dobashi
President Machinery and Aerospace, Kazunori Teraoka
President and CEO Americas, Jun Matsumoto
EVP, Shinichi Taniguchi
EVP, Joji Suzuki
Managing Executive Officer and CIO, Tetsuya Konoda
CFO and Chief Administrative Officer Americas, Junichi Hamatsuka
Chairman, Yutaka Kase
President and CEO, Yoji Sato
President and CEO Europe Russia and NIC; President Sojitz Europe plc and Sojitz UK plc, Kazuhiko Nakajima
EVP, Shigeki Dantani
Senior Managing Executive Officer and CFO, Yoshio Mogi
President Energy and Metal Division, Masahiro Komiyama
President Chemicals Division, Satoshi Mizui
SVP and General Manager Machinery and Aerospace Automotive Unit, Tatsunobu Sako
President and CEO China, Kazuhiko Kawasaki
SVP Consumer Lifestyle Business Division and Senior General Manager Foods Unit, Takashi Ikeda
President Sojitz (Shanghai), Masao Goto
SVP Machinery and Aerospace Division and Senior General Manager Information and Industrial Machinery Unit, Yoshihisa Suzuki
Auditor, Yukio Machida
President and CEO The Americas, Shinichi Teranishi
Human Resources and General Affairs, Masayuki Hanai
President and CEO China, Shigeru Ohno
Senior Vice President Chemicals Division, Tsutomu Tanaka
Senior Vice President Machinery Division, Takeshi Yoshimura
Senior Vice President Consumer Lifestyle Business Division, Masato Takei
Senior Vice President Energy & Metal Division, Masashi Shinohara
Senior Vice President Machinery Division, Hideto Maruta
Senior Vice President Machinery Division, Yoshizumi Kurata
Senior Vice President Chemicals Division, Yoshihiro Tamura
Vice Chairman, Takashi Hara
President Machinery Division, Toshihiko Kita
President Consumer Lifestyle Business Division, Hideaki Kato
President Sojitz (China), Yukio Matsuki
President and CEO Asia and Oceania, Toshiharu Yoshimura
Director, Yoshihiko Miyauchi, age 77
EVP and Director, Hiroyuki Tanabe
Vice Chairman, Masaki Hashikawa
Director, Shigeo Muraoka
Chairman, Yutaka Kase
EVP CFO and Director, Yoji Sato
Auditors: KPMGAZSA&Co.

LOCATIONS

HQ: Sojitz Corp
2-1-1 Uchisaiwai-cho, Chiyoda-ku, Tokyo 100-8691
Phone: (81) 3 6871 5500
Web: www.sojitz.com

2010 Sales

	$ mil.	% of total
Asia & Oceania		
Other countries		10
North America		2
Total	**0**	**100**

PRODUCTS/OPERATIONS

2010 Sales

	$ mil.	% of total
Energy & Mineral Resources		26
Machinery & Aerospace		21
Overseas subsidiaries		11
Other		2

COMPETITORS

Chori
ITOCHU
Kanematsu
Marubeni
Mitsubishi Corp.
Mitsui
Sekisui House
Sumitomo
Toyota Tsusho
Xstrata

HISTORICAL FINANCIALS

Company Type: Public

Income Statement FYE: March 31

	REVENUE ($ mil.)	NET INCOME ($ mil.)	NET PROFIT MARGIN	EMPLOYEES
03/13	18,574	142	0.8%	15,963
03/12	24,462	(12)	—	17,039
03/11	48,482	192	0.4%	16,456
03/10	41,157	94	0.2%	17,331
03/09	52,461	192	0.4%	17,524
Annual Growth	(22.9%)	(7.2%)	—	(2.3%)

2013 Year-End Financials

Debt ratio: 0.5%
Return on equity: 3.7%
Cash ($ mil.): 4,510
Current ratio: 1.52
Long-term debt ($ mil.): 8,700
No. of shares (mil.): 1,250
Dividends
Yield: —
Payout: —
Market value ($ mil.): 1,939

	STOCK PRICE ($) FY Close	P/E High/Low	PER SHARE ($) Earnings	Dividends	Book Value
03/13	1.55	0 0	0.11	0.00	3.25
03/12	1.86	— —	(0.01)	0.00	3.22
03/11	1.90	— —	0.15	0.00	3.43
03/10	1.75	— —	0.08	0.00	3.23
03/09	1.15	— —	0.16	0.00	2.93
Annual Growth	7.7%	— —	(7.4%)	—	2.7%

Solvay S.A.

Survey says: Solvay is one of top 10 largest chemical manufacturers worldwide. The company joined those ranks after acquiring Rhodia in 2012. Today the company produces and sells a balanced portfolio of plastics (specialty polymers and vinyls) and chemicals (basic and specialty). About one-third of that portfolio are products used in sustainable development. End markets for its products are diverse and include agriculture automotive consumer goods construction electronics energy environment and water. With some 110 plants in 55 countries Europe is Solvay's largest market followed by North America Latin America and Asia/Pacific.

Mergers and Acquisitions

Solvay had a pivotal year in 2011 when it acquired France's Rhodia in a friendly tender offer for $4.8 billion. The deal doubled the size of Solvay's business and strengthened its presence in fast-growing emerging markets like Brazil China and India.

Operations

The company today operates in three major segments: Rhodia Plastics and Chemicals. Rhodia is a global leader in the development and production of specialty chemicals such as cellulose acetate engineering plastics and fluorinated compounds. The group's Plastics segment is a major producer of specialty polymers and vinyls. Its Chemicals segment is the largest producer of soda ash hydrogen peroxide and sodium bicarbonate.

Financial Analysis

Buoyed by the Rhodia acquisition the company's proforma group sales grew by 14% (in local currency) in 2011. The increase represented steady growth in sales volumes for each of the group's activities (Chemicals up 4%; Plastics up 2%; and Rhodia up 3%). Solvay's net income plunged to E296 million in 2011 compared to E1.8 billion in 2010 a figure that was boosted by the sale of the company's pharmaceuticals unit as acquisition and restructuring costs took their toll.

Strategy

With the acquisition of Rhodia and the sale of its pharmaceutical activities in 2011 Solvay is setting itself up to be a major player in sustainable chemistry. It is taking steps to strengthen its footprint in fast-growing countries and develop greener value-added products through capital investments acquisitions joint ventures and R&D partnerships.

In 2011 for example Solvay sought growth in the Asia/Pacific region by establishing a partnership to create a soda ash plant in China; setting up a joint R&D center in South Korea to test a new fluorine technology that can reduce emissions during solar cell and semiconductor manufacturing; and commissioning the world's largest hydrogen peroxide plant in Thailand. In the Middle East plans to build a similar hydrogen peroxide megaplant are under way through a joint venture with Saudi Arabia's Sadara Chemical Company —a JV between Saudi Aramco and Dow Chemical.

In Russia Solvay and Russian firm SIBUR formed a joint venture called Ruspav in 2012 to produce surfactants and oilfield process chemicals. The venture's plant to be located located near SIBUR's petrochemicals operations east of Moscow is expected to be up and running in 2015.

Meanwhile to increase its leadership in energy efficiency and emissions reduction Solvay acquired Societe Generale's stake in Orbeo formerly a 50/50 joint venture between the two companies that focused on carbon-trading markets. Orbeo is now a subsidiary of Rhodia Energy and is called Orbeo Climate Care. The acquisition is meant to speed up development of projects to curb greenhouse gas emissions.

HISTORY

Solvay began in the 1860s when founder Ernest Solvay perfected a method that created soda ash at a lower cost than the prevailing Leblanc process. In 1886 the company began to diversify into manufacturing chlorine and expanded beyond Belgium into the France Germany Russia the UK and the US. By the 1900s Solvay had reduced the price for soda ash by two-thirds what it had been before his entry into the field.

The company lost its Russia-based plants during the Russian Revolution. Ernest Solvay died shortly thereafter in 1922. To overcome its Russian losses the company modernized its remaining plants and added new businesses such as potassium mining.

During the 1930s and 1940s the company began to switch its plants to the electrolysis process and expanded into Italy Greece and other countries. Because of their locations the firm's plants suffered during WWII and the company lost several as the Iron Curtain descended across East Europe. The company rebuilt what facilities it could and once again diversified its product base.

Solvay began making plastic (polyvinyl chloride PVC) in 1949 at its plant in Jemeppe Belgium and throughout the 1950s and 1960s the company developed into a major manufacturer of bulk chemicals. In the late 1960s Baron Rene Boel who had married into the family managed the company; he took it public in 1971. Boel hired executives from outside the family and modernized the company's management structure. These changes kept the company financially healthy until 1976 when US companies began manufacturing soda ash from trona rock mine. Cheaper and more environmentally friendly the process forced Solvay to close its soda ash plants. (The company later returned to making soda ash.)

Despite these problems Solvay continued expansion during the 1980s which included creating Solvay America a holding company for its US companies. Recognizing its vulnerability from a reliance on bulk chemicals the company began to diversify into drug production.

In 1993 Solvay recorded a $198 million loss its first in more than a decade. Analysts questioned whether the company could compete against companies such as Akzo (now Akzo Nobel) which produced nothing but pharmaceuticals. Under the leadership of CEO Baron Daniel Janssen Solvay tried to kill off its reputation as an industrial dinosaur. With the fall of the Berlin Wall Solvay recovered many of the plants it had lost during WWII and the Cold War. It renovated them closed many of its unprofitable operations and sold off noncore businesses such as its animal health units to American Home Products (renamed Wyeth in 2002). To improve profits it teamed up with companies such as US pharmaceutical giant Upjohn (Pharmacia & Upjohn).

By 1996 Solvay concentrated on chemicals plastics pharmaceuticals and processing (manufacturing finished products such as pipes and fittings). In 1998 Solvay veteran Alois Michielsen replaced Daniel Janssen who retired as executive committee chairman and CEO. The appointment marked the first time a non-family member was tapped to run the company. Michielsen went to work on improving the company's old-fashioned image which he considered partially to blame for depressing the firm's stock price.

The company's plastic division in 1999 suffered from low PVC prices which rebounded within the year when EVC International NV (now INEOS Vinyls) shut down its PVC plant in Italy. Solvay bought US-based Unimed Pharmaceuticals and a strategic stake in generic prescription drugmaker Duramed that year. In 2000 Solvay entered into a 50/50 venture with Plastic Omnium (plastics processing) called Inergy Automotive Systems; the new company is the largest maker of plastic fuel tanks in the world. In 2002 the company acquired Ausimont from Montedison and Longside International for about $1.1 billion. It also has acquired pharmaceuticals makers and products including hypertension medications Aceon and Teveten.

In 2008 Solvay acquired Egyptian chemicals maker Alexandria Sodium Carbonate Company (ASCC) for $130 million. The company viewed the acquisition as an entry not only into the Egyptian market but also into the greater Middle East and Northern African regions. Solvay began doubling the capacity at ASCC's manufacturing facility.

Solvay sold its manufactured pharmaceuticals unit to US-based Abbott Labs in 2010 for $7.6 billion.

EXECUTIVES

CEO and Director, Christian Jourquin, age 66

Group General Manager Plastics Sector, Jacques van Rijckevorsel, age 64
Vice Chairman, Denis Solvay, age 56
Group General Manager Rhodia Sector, Gilles Auffret, age 66
Group General Manager Human Resources, Daniel Broens
Deputy CEO, Jean-Pierre Clamadieu, age 55
Head of Investor Relations, Patrick Verelst
Group General Manager Chemicals Sector, Vincent De Cuyper, age 53
Group General Manager Technology Research Services and Procurement, Jean-Michel Mesland, age 57
Group General Counsel, Dominique Dussard
Regional Manager Asia Pacific, Roger Kearns, age 51
Group Corporate Secretary, Michel Defourny
Region General Manager Europe, Alexis Brouhns
Corporate Press Officer, Erik De Leye
External and Financial Communication Officer, Marie-Jeanne Marchal
Head Future Businesses & Corporate Platforms, Leopold Demiddeleer
General Manager Strategic Business Unit Peroxides, Eric Mignonat
Head of the PR and Communication Department, Violeta Targova
Director de Comunica+.ao, Mario Branco
Chief Financial Officer, Bernard Laguiche
Chairman of the Solvay Board of Directors, Nicolas Bo+?l
Member of the Executive Committee; Group General Manager of Chemicals Sector, Vincent Cuyper
Member of the Executive Committee; Group General Manager of Plastics Sector, Jacques Rijckevorsel
Director, Jean-Martin Folz, age 66
CEO and Director, Christian Jourquin, age 66
Director, Bernhard Scheuble, age 60
Vice Chairman, Denis Solvay, age 56
Director, Anton van Rossum, age 68
Director, Jean-Marie Solvay, age 57
Director, Guy de Selliers de Moranville, age 61
Director, Nicolas Boel, age 49
CFO and Director, Bernard de Laguiche, age 52
Director, Jean van Zeebroeck, age 70
Director, Charles Casimir-Lambert, age 46
Director, Baron Herve Coppens d'Eeckenbrugge, age 56
Director, Petra Mateos-Aparicio Morales
Director, Evelyn du Monceau
Independent Director, Yves-Thibault Silguy
Independent Director, Anton Rossum
Independent Director, Evelyn Bergendal
Independent Director, Guy Moranville
Independent Director, Herve dEeckenbrugge
Independent Director, Jean Zeebroeck
Independent Director, Petra Morales
Auditors: DeloitteReviseursd'EntreprisesSCs.f.d.SCRL

LOCATIONS

HQ: Solvay S.A.
Rue de Ransbeek, 310, Brussels 1120
Phone: (32) 2 264 2111 **Fax:** (32) 2 264 3061
Web: www.solvay.com

2011 Sales

	% of total
Europe	43
North	17
Latin	14
Asia & other	26
Total	**100**

PRODUCTS/OPERATIONS

2011 Sales

	% of total
Rhodia	49
Plastics	29
Chemicals	22
Total	**100**

2011 Sales by End Market

	% of total
Consumer	28
Construction	18
Automobile	15
Electricity & Energy	7
	5
Environment	4
Agriculture forestry & Paper	4
	2
Other	18
Total	**100**

COMPETITORS

A. Schulman
Akzo Nobel
Arkema
Celanese
FMC
Honeywell Specialty Materials
INEOS ChlorVinyls
Occidental Chemical
PolyOne

HISTORICAL FINANCIALS

Company Type: Public

Income Statement

FYE: December 31

	REVENUE ($ mil.)	NET INCOME ($ mil.)	NET PROFIT MARGIN	EMPLOYEES
12/12	16,389	769	4.7%	29,103
12/11	10,488	319	3.0%	29,121
12/10	9,514	2,378	25.0%	16,785
12/09	12,223	743	6.1%	28,204
12/08	13,267	566	4.3%	0
Annual Growth	5.4%	8.0%	—	—

2012 Year-End Financials

Debt ratio: 26.2%
Return on equity: 9.4%
Cash ($ mil.): 2,330
Current ratio: 1.91
Long-term debt ($ mil.): 4,377
No. of shares (mil.): 82
Dividends
Yield: 0.0%
Payout: 4.6%
Market value ($ mil.): 1,183

	STOCK PRICE ($) FY Close	P/E High/Low		PER SHARE ($) Earnings	Dividends	Book Value
12/12	14.26	4	2	9.31	0.43	97.73
12/11	8.31	10	5	3.92	0.50	98.06
12/10	9.95	1	1	29.18	0.00	105.98
Annual Growth	19.7%	—	—	(24.9%)	—	(2.0%)

Sony Corp

Sony is synonymous with consumer electronics. It's especially big in TVs and game consoles like the new PlayStation4. Officially named Sony Kabushiki Kaisha the company designs develops makes and sells a host of electronic equipment instruments and devices for consumer professional and industrial markets. Professional products include semiconductors and components. A top global media conglomerate Sony boasts additional assets in the areas of music (Sony Music Entertainment) film (Sony Pictures Entertainment and Sony Digital Production) DVDs (Sony Pictures Home Entertainment) and TV (Sony Pictures Television). Sony also has several financial services businesses and an advertising agency in Japan.

Geographic Reach

Sony's primary manufacturing facilities are located in Asia including Japan where it is headquartered. Japan is also its single largest market by sales (32% in fiscal 2012 ends March). The US China and Europe are also key markets.

Operations

Sony realigned its reportable segments in 2012 as part of a reorganization. The operations of the former Consumer Professional & Devices (CPD) and Networked Products & Services (NPS) segments are now part of the Consumer Products & Services (CPS) –the company's largest segment by sales –and Professional Device & Solutions (PDS) segments. CPS includes LCD televisions Blu Ray disc and DVD players digital and video cameras PCs and gaming consoles. Certain PlayStation products are marketed and distributed by Sony Computer Entertainment LLC and Sony Computer Entertainment Europe Ltd. PDS the company's second largest segment includes broadcast and other B2B products as well as semiconductors and components.

A smaller business segment Sony Ericsson was renamed Sony Mobile Communications in 2012. As a result of a reorganization that Sony is undertaking plans to even further realign its business segments are under way.

Sales and Marketing

Sony's products are marketed worldwide by sales subsidiaries and unaffiliated distributors as well as direct online sales.

Financial Performance

Sony's fiscal 2012 (ends March) sales fell 9% vs. the prior year while net income continued its steep decline. Indeed the company marked its fourth consecutive year of unprofitability in 2012 as its losses widened.

Sony's consumer products and services segment CPS remains the company's bread and butter accounting for 45% is its fiscal 2012 sales. But competition is fierce in this industry with Apple paving the way in music players with the iPod and Microsoft (Xbox 360) and Nintendo (Wii) jockeying for dominance in game console sales globally.

The rising Yen decreasing demand for its products pricing pressures and the lingering global economic crisis has sidelined Sony in recent years. After logging a record profit in 2007 the company has seen its business stall as consumers tightened their belts.

Strategy

The most pressing part of Sony's current strategy is turning around its electronics businesses. With a new management team established in April 2012 the company moves forward with a plan to strengthen certain core areas: digital imaging game and mobile. Sony is trying to develop new products expand its hardware and software offerings and integrate the operations of its smartphone business (operated by Sony Mobile) with its tablet and PC businesses. Another aspect of this strategy is to turn around its TV business to improve profitability there; TVs generate a large chunk of sales within the CPS segment.

The company may have a hit on its hands with the new PlayStation4 (PS4) which went on sale in North America in November 2013. Indeed Sony sold more than 1 million PS4s in the first 24 hours of sales. The new games console is the centerpiece of the new management team's turnaround strategy for Sony's consumer electronics and film businesses.

Sony also has been consolidating manufacturing facilities selling off businesses and facilities and reducing headcounts. Divestments include its TV production assets.

In a very competitive electronics environment Sony is simultaneously trying to innovate and launch products in new markets such as it is doing with medical peripherals like printers monitors cameras and recorders. The company is drawing on its audio and visual expertise to build a 4K technology product lineup. 4K is said to deliver more than four times the resolution of full HD.

On the music side Sony's wholly owned subsidiary Sony Corporation of America (SCA) in 2012 led a group of investors in a high-profile high-dollar deal. Alongside the Estate of Michael Jackson David Geffen and Blackstone Group SCA acquired EMI Music Publishing for $2.2 billion from Citigroup. The company's Sony/ATV Music Publishing which owns more than 750000 copyrights now oversees EMI Music Publishing and its 1.3 million copyrights on behalf of the investor group. (Sony/ATV Music Publishing is co-owned by subsidiaries of SCA and trusts formed by the Estate of Michael Jackson.)

HISTORY

Akio Morita Masaru Ibuka and Tamon Maeda (Ibuka's father-in-law) started Tokyo Telecommunications Engineering in 1946 with funding from Morita's father's sake business. The company produced the first Japanese tape recorder in 1950. Three years later Morita paid Western Electric (US) $25000 for transistor technology licenses which sparked a consumer electronics revolution in Japan. His firm launched one of the first transistor radios in 1955 followed by the first Sony-trademarked product a pocket-sized radio in 1957. The next year the company changed its name to Sony (from "sonus" Latin for "sound" and "sonny" meaning "little man"). It beat the competition to newly emerging markets for transistor TVs (1959) and solid-state videotape recorders (1961).

Sony launched the first home video recorder (1964) and the first solid-state condenser microphone (1965). Its 1968 introduction of the Trinitron color TV tube began another decade of explosive growth. Sony bet wrong on its Betamax VCR (1976) which lost to rival Matsushita's (now Panasonic Corp.) VHS as the industry standard. However 1979 brought another success the Walkman personal stereo.

Pressured by adverse currency rates and competition worldwide Sony used its technology to diversify beyond consumer electronics and began to move production to other countries. In the 1980s it introduced Japan's first 32-bit workstation and became a major producer of computer chips and floppy disk drives. The purchases of CBS Records in 1988 ($2 billion) and Columbia Pictures in 1989 (a $4.9 billion deal which included TriStar Pictures) made Sony a major force in the rapidly growing entertainment industry.

The firm manufactured Apple's PowerBook but its portable CD player Data Discman was successful only in Japan (1991). In the early 1990s Sony joined Nintendo to create a new kind of game console combining Sony's CD-ROM drive with the graphic capabilities of a workstation. Although Nintendo pulled out in 1992 Sony released PlayStation in Japan (1994) and in the US (1995) to great success. Two years later in a joint venture with Intel it developed a line of PC desktop systems.

Rather than support an industry-wide standard in 1997 Sony teamed up with Philips Electronics to make another recording media called Super Audio CD which could replace videotapes and CDs. (Sony and Philips created the CD and continue to receive royalties from it.)

In 1998 Sony shipped its first digital high-definition TV to the US folded TriStar into Columbia Pictures merged its Loews Theatres unit with Cineplex Odeon and launched its Wega flat-screen TV.

Philips Sun Microsystems and Sony formed a joint venture in early 1999 to develop networked entertainment products. Also in 1999 Nobuyuki Idei became CEO and the company introduced a Walkman with the capability to download music from the Internet.

In 2000 Sony formed PlayStation.com Japan to sell game consoles and software online; it also introduced its 128-bit PlayStation 2 which plays DVD movies and connects to the Internet. The company later restructured placing all of its US entertainment holdings under a newly-formed umbrella company called Sony Broadband Entertainment.

In early 2001 Sony started an online bank with Japan's Sakura Bank and JP Morgan Chase. Struggling to coordinate its content units (music movies games etc.) with its manufacturing operations (TVs VCRs radios etc.) Sony announced yet another corporate restructuring plan; that move placed all electronics units under one upper-management group.

Adverse market conditions in 2001 aggravated by the September 11 attacks led Sony Pictures Entertainment to consolidate its two domestic television operations folding Columbia TriStar Network Television into Columbia TriStar Domestic Television (CTDT).

In February 2002 an investment group led by Onex Corporation acquired its Loews Theatres unit (which filed for bankruptcy in February 2001). In the course of the fiscal year ending March 2002 Sony laid off about 13700 employees primarily in its electronics and music businesses.

In an attempt to capitalize on the strength of its own brand Sony Pictures Entertainment renamed its Columbia TriStar Domestic Television (CTDT) and Columbia TriStar International Television (CTIT) divisions in September 2002 designating them as Sony Pictures Television (SPT) and Sony Pictures Television International (SPTI) respectively. In October 2002 Sony transformed its Aiwa unit into a wholly-owned subsidiary and absorbed the struggling firm in December 2002.

In 2003 Sony adopted a US-style corporate governance model (made possible by a revision in Japan's Commercial Code) and acquired CIS Corp. a Japanese information system consulting firm. In an effort to cut costs through manufacturing consolidation Sony closed its audio equipment plant in Indonesia that year.

Sony unveiled the Vaio Pocket in 2004 a portable music player designed to compete with Apple's iPod; Vaio Pocket debuted in the US later that year. Sony also introduced a similar product Network Walkman –its first Walkman with a hard drive –in 2004. In October 2004 the company launched a music download system in Japan dubbed MusicDrop. The system utilizes Microsoft's Windows Media Player.

To manage its financial units (Sony Life Insurance Company Sony Assurance and Sony Bank) it created Sony Financial Holdings in 2004. The company announced in 2005 that Idei would be succeeded by foreigner Howard Stringer who had been in charge of Sony's entertainment unit. In 2005 Sony sold its minority stake in music club Columbia House to BMG Direct a subsidiary of Germany's Bertelsmann. In December 2005 the company spun off Sony Communication Network the subsidiary that operates So-Net Internet service (which has nearly 3 million subscribers) through an IPO.

In June 2006 Sony created a holding company for its Japanese-based retail operations (Sony Plaza Sony Family Club B&C Laboratories CP Cosmetics Maxim's de Paris and Lifeneo) and sold 51% of the holding company to investment firm Nikko Principal Investments Japan.

In late 2008 Sony bought out NEC's 45% stake in joint venture Sony Optiarc.

The company in 2010 sold the measuring equipment business of Sony Manufacturing Systems to Mori Seiki a Japan-based precision tool maker in a deal valued at about Y6 billion (nearly $70 million). It also sold off its 90% stake in Sony Baja California its main TV factory in North America located in Tijuana Mexico to Taiwanese company Hon Hai Precision Industry. It generated $217 million for its share in HBO Latin America which it sold to Time Warner.

In February 2012 Sony acquired Telefonaktiebolaget LM Ericsson's 50% stake in Sony Ericsson Mobile Communications AB marking the completion of the previously announced transaction. As a result Sony Ericsson became a wholly-owned subsidiary of Sony and was renamed "Sony Mobile Communications."

EXECUTIVES

CEO Sony Corporation of America and Chairman and CEO Sony Pictures Entertainment, Michael M. Lynton, age 54

Chairman, Sir Howard Stringer, age 71

Co-Chairman Sony Pictures Entertainment, Amy Pascal, age 55

Vice President Chief Financial Officer, Masaru Kato

President Sony Ericsson Mobile Communications AB, Bert Nordberg

EVP and General Counsel; President Sony Corporation of America (SCA), Nicole Seligman, age 57

Executive Deputy President, Hiroshi Yoshioka, age 61

EVP and Chief Strategy Officer, Tadashi (Tan) Saito

Vice Chairman; CEO Product Quality and Safety and Environmental Affairs, Ryoji Chubachi, age 66

EVP Intellectual Property and Disc Manufacturing, Keiji Kimura, age 61

SVP New Business Professional Solutions Group, Hiromasa Otsuka, age 63

SVP External Relations and Kansai Region and Device Sales Consumer Professional and Devices Group, Tsugie Miyashita

President and CEO; Chairman Sony Corporation of America, Kazuo (Kaz) Hirai, age 53

Executive Deputy President Manufacturing Logistics and Procurement, Yutaka Nakagawa, age 68

SVP Environment and Technology Policy and Relations, Kiyoshi Nishitani

SVP Technology (System) Semiconductor Business Group, Norihisa Shirota

EVP, Shoji Nemoto

VP Product Marketing Sony Computer Entertainment America, Scott A. Steinberg

EVP China, Akira Kubota

SVP; President Advanced Materials Laboratories Core Device Development Group Research and Development and Common Software Platform, Osamu Kumagai

SVP Products Quality and Safety, Makoto Kogure

EVP, Tomoyuki Suzuki

SVP Technologies Networked Products and Services Group, Masaaki Tsuruta

SVP Japan Sales Professional Solutions Group Consumer Professional and Devices Group, Shinji Hanatani

EVP Human Resources and Corporate Workplace Solutions, Kunitaka Fujita

Chairman Sony Music Entertainment, Masao Morita, age 58

President and Group Chief Executive, Andrew House

President and CEO Sony Computer Entertainment America, Jack Tretton
President and General Manager Sony Discovery Communications and IMAX Joint Venture 3D Television Network, Tom Cosgrove
SVP Publisher Relations Sony Computer Entertainment America, Robert Dyer
VP Human Resources Sony Computer Entertainment America, Sally Buchanan
SVP and CFO Sony Computer Entertainment America, Jim Bass
VP Operations Sony Computer Entertainment America, Glenn Nash
SVP Business Development Sony Computer Entertainment America, Philip Rosenberg
EVP, Kunimasa Suzuki, age 53
SVP and Chief Transformation Officer, George Bailey
SVP; President Home Entertainment and Sound Business Group, Masashi Imamura
CFO Sony Ericsson, William A. (Bill) Glaser Jr.
President and COO Sony Electronics, Phil Molyneux
CEO Sony Music Entertainment, Doug Morris
President and CEO Sony Computer Entertainment Europe, Jim Ryan
SVP and Chief Information Security Officer, Philip R. Reitinger
Director, Yorihiko Kojima
Director, Fujio Cho, age 75
Director, Roland A. Hernandez, age 55
Director, Sir Peter L. Bonfield, age 68
Vice Chairman; CEO Product Quality and Safety and Environmental Affairs, Ryoji Chubachi, age 66
Director, Yukako Uchinaga, age 67
Director, Yoshiaki Yamauchi, age 76
Director, Ryuji Yasuda, age 67
Director, Mitsuaki Yahagi, age 65
Director, Tsun-Yan Hseih, age 59
Director, Yuichiro Anzai
Auditors: PricewaterhouseCoopersAarata

LOCATIONS

HQ: Sony Corp
7-1, KONAN 1-CHOME, MINATO-KU, Tokyo 108-0075
Phone: (81) 3 6748 2111 **Fax:** (81) 3 6748 2244
Web: www.sony.co.jp

2012 Sales

	% of total
Japan	32
Europe	19
US	19
Asia/Pacific (except Japan and China	10
China	8
Other	12
Total	**100**

PRODUCTS/OPERATIONS

2012 Sales

	% of total
Consumer Products & Services	45
Professional Device & Solutions	19
Financial	13
Pictures	10
Music	6
Sony	1
Other	6
Total	**100**

Selected Products

Consumer Products & Services (CPS)
- Digital imaging
- Game hardware and software
- Home audio and video
- Personal and mobile products
- Televisions

Professional Device & Solutions (PDS)
- Broadcast and professional-use products
- Semiconductors
- Components

COMPETITORS

Apple Inc.
Bertelsmann
Dell
Disney
Eastman Kodak
Fujitsu
Hewlett-Packard
IBM
Intel
Kyocera
LG Electronics
Microsoft
Motorola Solutions
Nintendo
Nokia
Panasonic Corp
Philips Electronics
Pioneer Corporation
SANYO
Samsung Group
Sharp Corp.
Technicolor
Universal Studios

HISTORICAL FINANCIALS

Company Type: Public

Income Statement FYE: March 31

	REVENUE ($ mil.)	NET INCOME ($ mil.)	NET PROFIT MARGIN	EMPLOYEES
03/13	72,278	457	0.6%	146,300
03/12	79,156	(5,566)	—	162,700
03/11	86,723	(3,134)	—	168,200
03/10	77,231	(436)	—	167,900
03/09	78,497	(1,004)	—	171,300
Annual Growth	(2.0%)	—	—	(3.9%)

2013 Year-End Financials

Debt ratio: 0.0%
Return on equity: 2.0%
Cash ($ mil.): 8,782
Current ratio: 0.85
Long-term debt ($ mil.): 9,973
No. of shares (mil.): 1,010
Dividends
Yield: 0.0%
Payout: 0.0%
Market value ($ mil.): 17,590

	STOCK PRICE ($) FY Close	P/E High	P/E Low	PER SHARE ($) Earnings	Dividends	Book Value
03/13	17.40	0	0	0.43	0.00	23.11
03/12	20.77	—	—	(5.55)	0.00	24.65
03/11	31.83	—	—	(3.12)	0.28	30.66
03/10	38.32	—	—	(0.44)	0.27	31.64
03/09	20.63	—	—	(1.00)	0.44	30.00
Annual Growth	(4.2%)	—	—	—	(90.2%)	(6.3%)

SSE PLC

SSE (formerly Scottish and Southern) sees a powerful future. One of the UK's top energy firms the integrated company distributes power and gas and other services to more than 10 million customers via subsidiaries Southern Electric Scottish Hydro Electric SWALEC and Atlantic Electric and Gas and others. Regulated assets include 79300 miles of power transmission and distribution lines that serve 3.5 million end-users. SSE has more than 11300 MW of generating capacity. It also owns 50% of Scotia Gas Networks which delivers gas to 5.7 million customers. Other operations include gas exploration energy trading wind farms electrical and environmental contracting gas storage and retail appliance sales.

In response to energy deregulation in the UK SSE is looking to increase its generating capacity expand its customer base and diversify its operations. This has included moving into gas storage and fiber-optic cable operations and developing wind farms in Scotland.

In 2010 the company (as Scottish and Southern) changed its corporate name to a less geographically limiting name (SSE). That year the company acquired the ATLAS Connect fiber telecommunications network (7000 miles) which spans six business parks across Scotland. It also bought the 32 MW Calliachar wind farm project (on which construction is due to start in 2012) from I & H Brown.

SSE is also moving to boost its natural gas sources signing a deal with explorer Faroe Petroleum in 2010 to develop oil and gas fields in the North Sea. In 2011 it acquired natural gas assets and infrastructure in three regions of the North Sea from Hess Limited for $324 million.

That same year SSE acquired the Keadby Wind Farm in North Lincolnshire UK from Renewable Energy Systems Group. The 34-turbine project still in the development stage will produce between 68 and 84 MW of non-polluting energy when it is completed in 2014.

To grow its UK nuclear power assets in 2010 the company (with partners GDF SUEZ and IBERDROLA) formed NuGeneration a nuclear joint venture which aims to build up to 3600 MW of new nuclear power plants. However the Japanese nuclear plant accident in 2011 forced the global nuclear power plant industry to hit the pause button while it reviewed the safety and viability of current and future plants. In late 2011 the company announced plans to sell its 25% stake in NuGeneration to GDF SUEZ and IBERDROLA in a move to focus more on renewable energy.

The company reported a strong growth in revenues (40%) in Fiscal 2011 as a result of expanded capacity and services the acquisition of 310000 new retail customers and a generally favorable price environment. Net income also rose by about 30% due to increased demand and higher rates.

In 2012 through its Airtricity Energy Supply (Northern Ireland) unit the company acquired Phoenix Supply a regulated supplier of natural gas to 130000 customers in Northern Ireland from Phoenix Energy Holdings.

HISTORY

SSE (as Scottish and Southern Energy) was formed by the 1998 merger of Scottish Hydro-Electric and Southern Electric both of which had been created by the privatization of the UK electricity industry.

In the 1980s the Thatcherite government opened up state-owned industries to private capital and management. The electricity industry (except for nuclear power) was privatized by the Electricity Act of 1989. The next year the Central Electricity Generating Board (CEGB) the state monopoly was dismantled and CEGB's 12 regional boards transferred their assets to 12 regional electricity companies (RECs). One of these Southern Electric (first incorporated in 1989) went public in 1990.

Because the government planned to fully deregulate the industry Southern Electric expanded beyond its core electricity supply business. In 1992 it formed Southern Electric Power Generation to invest in independent power projects and the firm moved into natural gas marketing through a joint venture with Phillips Petroleum. It also developed Southern Electric Contracting an electrical contractor and formed a retail appliance company E & S Retail in alliance with fellow REC Eastern Electricity (now a unit of TXU Europe); another REC East Midlands Electricity later came onboard. The retail business renamed Powerhouse Retail lost money and was sold to the Hanson conglomerate in 1995.

That year a wave of takeovers began to swamp the privatized RECs especially by US utilities itching to try out a competitive market. Only Southern Electric was left standing after the government blocked a bid by UK power generator National Power in 1996. To avoid being run over by larger rivals in 1997 Southern Electric allied with British Energy in Sabre Power a venture to build small gas-fired plants to supply industrial customers.

Meanwhile to the north of Southern Electric Scottish Hydro-Electric had been founded in 1943 when less than 20% of northern Scotland's homes were electrified. Originally called the North of Scotland Hydro-Electric Board it built eight hydropower plants in the 1950s and by the mid-1960s most of the region had received electricity.

Like Southern Electric Hydro-Electric was incorporated in 1989 and it was taken public in 1991. However unlike its English counterpart Hydro-Electric remained integrated and encompassed power generation distribution and supply. In the 1990s it diversified into combined-cycle gas turbine plants (more efficient than coal-fired units) and cogeneration plants (producing both heat and power) in England through several joint ventures.

To prepare for deregulation of the retail power market (completed in 1999) Southern Electric acquired Hydro-Electric in 1998 in a $4.8 billion deal and formed Scottish and Southern Energy. Hydro-Electric's Lord Wilson took the chairman position and Southern's Jim Forbes became chief executive. The new company began investing in small-scale generating projects. The next year it introduced affordable renewable energy products and Internet-based billing.

In 2000 Scottish and Southern began building fiber-optic networks in southern England and Scotland. Later in 2000 the company bought British Energy's SWALEC a Wales-based electricity and gas supplier for about $315 million.

In 2002 Jim Forbes retired and Ian Marchant took his place as chief executive. The following year Scottish and Southern agreed to purchase fellow UK utility Midlands Electricity from Aquila (which held 80% of Midlands) and FirstEnergy (which held the remaining 20%); however the deal was canceled later that year.

In 2004 Scottish and Southern completed the acquisition of two power plants in the UK (2000 MW of capacity) from American Electric Power for $456 million.

Scottish and Southern considered a merger with Glasgow rival Scottish Power (acquired by IBERDROLA in 2007) to prevent that company's takeover by Germany's utility group E.ON.

Acquisitions in 2008 included Slough Heating and Power (integrated energy business) Airtricity Holdings (renewable energy) and Seeboard Trading (street lighting projects). That year the company also moved into the Irish power supply market with the purchase of CHP Supply.

EXECUTIVES

Chairman, Lord Robert Smith, age 68, $627,314 total compensation
COO Lead Director Health and Safety and Board Member, Colin Hood, age 59, $1,097,019 total compensation
Energy Supply Director and Board Member, Alistair Phillips-Davies, age 46, $688,565 total compensation
Company Secretary, Vincent Donnelly
Finance Director and Board Member, Gregor Alexander, age 51, $688,565 total compensation
Manager Investor Relations, Sally Fairbairn
Director Offshore, Jim Smith
General Manager of Solutions, Andrew Blincow
General Manager, Paul Cooley
Head of Strategy, Pamela Walsh
Chief Executive Officer, Kevin Greenhorn
Board Member, Nick Baldwin, age 61
Chief Executive and Board Member, Ian Marchant, age 51
Board Member, Rene Medori, age 55
COO Lead Director Health and Safety and Board Member, Colin Hood, age 59
Energy Supply Director and Board Member, Alistair Phillips-Davies, age 46
Finance Director and Board Member, Gregor Alexander, age 51
Board Member, Richard D. Gillingwater, age 57
Board Member, Thomas Thune Andersen, age 58
Board Member, Susan Rice, age 68
Non-executive Director, Jeremy Beeton
Auditors: KPMGAuditPlc

LOCATIONS

HQ: SSE PLC
Inveralmond House, 200 Dunkeld Road, Perth PH1 3AQ
Phone: (44) 17 38456000 **Fax:** (44) 17 38457005
Web: www.sse.com

2011 Sales

	% of total
UK	98
Ireland & Continental	2
Total	**100**

PRODUCTS/OPERATIONS

2011 Sales

	% of total
Generation &	93
Power	3
Other	4
Total	**100**

Selected Subsidiaries and Divisions

SSE Contracting Limited
- Southern Electric Contracting Limited (electrical contracting)
- SSE Utility Services plc (utility contracting)
- Thermal Transfer Limited (environmental control systems)

SSE Energy Supply Limited
- Atlantic Electric and Gas (electricity and gas supply)
- Scottish Hydro-Electric (electricity and gas supply Scotland)
- Southern Electric (electricity and gas supply England)
- SWALEC (electricity and gas supply Wales)

SSE Gas Storage
- SSE Hornsea Limited (gas storage)

SSE Generation (power generation)
SSE Network Solutions (asset management)
SSE Power Distribution (regulated electricity transmission and distribution assets)
- S+S Limited (electricity connections)

SSE Retail Limited (Hienergyshop appliance sales and services)
SSE Telecommunications Limited (business-to-business telecommunications services)
- SSE Neosnetworks Limited (Neos telecommunications networking services)

COMPETITORS

BG Group
Centrica
E.ON UK
EDF Energy
Edison International
International Power
National Grid
Northern Powergrid
RWE npower
United Utilities
Viridian Group
Western Power Distribution

HISTORICAL FINANCIALS

Company Type: Public

Income Statement FYE: March 31

	REVENUE ($ mil.)	NET INCOME ($ mil.)	NET PROFIT MARGIN	EMPLOYEES
03/13	43,012	647	1.5%	19,795
03/12	50,835	316	0.6%	19,489
03/11	45,588	2,420	5.3%	20,249
03/10	32,682	1,873	5.7%	20,177
03/09	36,370	160	0.4%	18,795
Annual Growth	4.3%	41.7%	—	1.3%

2013 Year-End Financials

Debt ratio: 44.9%
Return on equity: 8.4%
Cash ($ mil.): 818
Current ratio: 0.89
Long-term debt ($ mil.): 6,899
No. of shares (mil.): 964
Dividends
Yield: 0.0%
Payout: 438.9%
Market value ($ mil.): 21,899

	STOCK PRICE ($) FY Close	P/E High/Low	PER SHARE ($) Earnings	Dividends	Book Value
03/13	22.71	132107	0.68	2.98	8.74
03/12	21.51	292224	0.34	2.97	7.78
03/11	20.47	33 21	2.61	1.38	8.93
03/10	16.68	37 26	2.03	1.01	5.13
03/09	16.25	686226	0.18	1.02	4.63
Annual Growth	8.7%	— —	38.7%	30.6%	17.2%

Standard Chartered Plc

While the British Empire isn't as global as it used to be that hasn't stopped Standard Chartered. The UK-based banking group known as Stanchart primarily operates in its target markets of Asia the Middle East and Africa which offer some of the world's fastest-growing economies. It also operates in Europe and the Americas. In all Stanchart has more than 1700 offices in more than 70 countries. The company operates through two business segments: consumer banking (deposit accounts loans cards and investment products) and wholesale banking (capital markets cash management international trade custody and clearing services). Stanchart traces its roots back more than 150 years.

Geographic Reach

Based in London Stanchart operates globally in the Asia/Pacific region as well as in Africa the Middle East Europe and the Americas.

Sales and Marketing

Looking to reinforce its commitment to making a positive impact in the communities where it operates Stanchart in 2012 rolled out an international advertising campaign that spanned multiple media such as TV print outdoor and digital.

Financial Performance

Stanchart logged revenue increases of 4% in 2012 as compared to 2011 fueled by interest income and income from other operating income. Contributing to the interest income gains were revenue from treasury bills loans and advances to customers and unlisted debt securities. Its other operating income gains came from fewer losses on the disposal of financial assets and gains on the repurchase of subordinated liabilities.

Positive income growth across all its markets helped Stanchart post revenue growth during the reporting period. India was an exception however as it was impacted by depreciation of the Indian rupee against the US dollar.

Net income meanwhile dropped by $697 million in 2012 vs. 2011 thanks to declines in cash provided by financing activities attributable to more cash used to repay subordinated liabilities and less cash generated from the gross proceeds from the issue of senior debts.

Consumer banking income rose 6% in 2012 to $7.2 billion representing double-digit growth in Other Asia Africa and Americas UK and Europe. It saw strong growth in cards personal loans and unsecured lending (CCPL).

Wholesale banking revenue came in 9% higher at $11.77 billion. Stanchart points to its well diversified revenue streams for the boost.

Strategy

Africa and the Middle East are among Stanchart's targeted areas for growth. It owns First Africa Group which provides mergers and acquisitions advisory services to companies wanting to invest in Africa. Stanchart bought Barclays Bank's custody business in 2010 adding operations in eight African nations.

The Asia/Pacific region also remains a key focus for Stanchart and the company has raised capital to fund acquisitions there. It owns midsized investment bank Standard Chartered Securities (Hong Kong) as well as the Hong Kong consumer finance business of GE Capital and GE's consumer finance operations in Singapore. Other growth markets for Stanchart include India Indonesia Korea Thailand and Taiwan. In late 2011 for example the company bought the performing segment of Barclays' credit card business in India at a discount. The company's growth in India has been rapid as that nation's economy has expanded. Stanchart was the first foreign bank to receive a license to open a branch in Iran after that country's Islamic Revolution in 1979.

Stanchart has been pursuing a new strategy in its consumer banking business shifting to a customer-focused business model and standardizing its processes. It has entered new segments such as private banking. It has used its 2008 acquisition of American Express's international banking business to not only boost its private banking operations but strengthen its presence in key markets in Asia and the Middle East. Stanchart has also aggressively added more branches and ATMs to its retail network and invested in making improvements to its online and mobile capabilities.

Mergers and Acquisitions

Helping to position Stanchart as a top South African custodian the company in 2013 acquired the South African custody and trustee business of Absa Bank. Since 2011 the group has developed a profitable custody model across more than 20 sub-Saharan African countries.

Stanchart also purchased Credit Agricole Yatirim Bankasi Turk A.S. (CAYBT) a fully-owned subsidiary of Credit Agricole Corporate and Investment Bank. The 2012 deal has allowed Stanchart to expand its wholesale banking business in Turkey.

HISTORY

Standard Chartered began in 1853 as the Chartered Bank of India Australia and China to finance trade between the UK and its Asian colonies. It began establishing offices in 1858. Over the next 40 years The Chartered Bank expanded throughout Asia. In the 20th century the bank opened branches in Germany and the US. In 1957 Chartered entered the Middle East by acquiring Eastern Bank. In 1969 it agreed to merge with Standard Bank.

In 1862 schoolmaster John Paterson established the Standard Bank of British South Africa Ltd. to fund trade with mining businesses. Within two years the bank had 15 branches. Like Chartered Standard had moved into Germany and the US by 1905 and operated in central and southern Africa by 1912.

In 1962 the bank was renamed The Standard Bank Ltd. Three years later it expanded into Gambia Ghana Nigeria and Sierra Leone but the end of colonialism meant instability; business was threatened and ruling parties often nationalized Standard's banks. In 1969 the bank agreed to merge with Chartered Bank.

Asian and Middle Eastern business flourished in the early 1970s while South African branches struggled under growing international pressure on the country's apartheid regime. In response the company diversified into metals trading and consumer finance. It also expanded in the US market with the purchase of Union Bancorp of California.

Standard Chartered failed in a 1981 attempt to gain entry to the UK market through purchasing Royal Bank of Scotland. Four years later that bank went public.

In 1986 Lloyds Bank tried to take over Standard Chartered but investors Robert Holmes a Court Yue-Kong Pao and Khoo Teck Puat acquired enough of the company to block the play. Meanwhile overseas financial deregulation brought more competition and Hong Kong Singapore and Malaysia sank into recession.

Hit by trade sanctions against South Africa the bank in 1987 sold its operations there. As the world tumbled deeper into recession Standard Chartered's loan losses climbed. But the bank began to recover the next year as it trimmed its US bank holdings.

Scandal hit the bank in the 1990s. In 1992 Standard Chartered paid $515 million in restitution after a broker in its Mumbai India office embezzled some $1.2 billion from Indian banks. In 1994 executives with Mocatta were convicted of bribery and the Hong Kong government banned Standard Chartered Securities (sold in 1996) from underwriting stock offerings for nine months after it falsified six IPOs.

In 1997 Standard Chartered refocused on retail banking with its 1998 purchase of what is now Banco Standard Chartered in Latin America and its bank/insurance tie-ups with CGU (now CGNU) and Prudential plc. The promotion of Rana Talwar to CEO brought a strategic focus on emerging markets from which other banks were withdrawing.

Standard Chartered in 1999 bought Thailand's Nakornthon Bank and the non-Swiss trade financing operations of UBS AG and expanded into China through a pact with the Bank of China. In 2000 the company bought Australia and New Zealand Banking Group's Grindlays operations in South Asia and the Middle East. The following year Stanchart began cutting 20% of its workforce. It also folded Grindlay's operations into its own while retaining the brand's name.

In 2004 Stanchart bought the majority of Australia and New Zealand Banking Group's project finance business which is headquartered in London. The business which cost Stanchart about $1.5 billion operates in four regions: the UK the US the Middle East and South Asia (especially India).

In 2005 the bank acquired Korea First Bank (now SC First Bank); the deal was the biggest foreign investment ever for South Korea's financial sector. The following year Stanchart paid about $1.2 billion for Taiwan's Hsinchu Bank making it the first foreign bank owner in that country. Also in 2006 the bank acquired 20% of China Bohai Bank.

In 2008 the UK government responded to the global financial crisis by investing #50 billion ($87.9 billion) in the nation's top banks including Stanchart. It agreed to guarantee another #250 billion ($438 billion) in bonds and provide additional liquidity of at least #200 billion ($350 billion) to the banks. The bailout plan was initiated to provide capital directly to the banks in order to revitalize lending activities.

Also in 2008 the company made some acquisitions for further international expansion. It bought Asia Trust and Investment Corporation which added some 10 branches in the lucrative Taipei market. Stanchart also bought some of the Brazil operations of Lehman Brothers after that company filed for bankruptcy protection.

EXECUTIVES

Chairman, Sir John W. Peace, age 64

Global Head Credit Risk Review Wholesale Banking, Andrew Willans

Group Chief Executive, Peter A. Sands, age 52, $1,002,000 total compensation

Group Finance Director and Board Member, Richard H. Meddings, age 55, $841,000 total compensation

Regional CEO South East Asia, Neeraj Swaroop, age 53

Director People Property and Assurance, Timothy J. (Tim) Miller, age 55

Group Executive Director and CEO Asia, Jaspal Singh Bindra, age 53

Group Head of People Compliance Communications and Culture; Director, Tracy J. Clarke, age 46

Group Executive Director and CEO Wholesale Banking, Alun M. G. (Mike) Rees, age 57

Group Chief Risk Officer, Richard F. Goulding, age 53

Global Head Private Banking, Shayne K. Nelson

Chairperson Greater China Standard Greater China, Katherine Tsang, age 56

CEO Standard Chartered Afghanistan, Joseph Silvanus

CEO Standard Chartered Bangladesh, Osman Morad

CEO Standard Chartered South Africa, Ebenezer Essoka

CEO Standard Chartered Nigeria, Christopher Knight

CEO Standard Chartered Nepal, Sujit Mundul

CEO Standard Chartered Nigeria, Simon J. Millett

CEO Standard Chartered Indonesia, Simon Morris

Group Head Strategy Corporate Development and Corporate Secretariat, Annemarie Durbin

CEO Standard Chartered Botswana, David D. Cutting

CEO Standard Chartered Qatar and Egypt, Tom Aaker

CEO Standard Chartered Zimbabwe, Washington Matsaira

Group Executive Director and CEO Consumer Banking, Stefano Paolo (Steve) Bertamini, age 48

Group Head Origination and Client Coverage, Sean Wallace

Head Investor Relations, Stephen Atkinson

CEO Standard Chartered Bank Oman, Ravneet Chowdhury

CEO Standard Chartered Vietnam, Ashok Sud

CEO and Executive Vice Chairman Standard Chartered China, Lim Cheng Teck

CEO Standard Chartered Kenya, Richard Etemesi

Head of Corporate Affairs Americas, Elaine Chin

Group Executive Director and CEO Europe Middle East Africa and Americas, Viswanathan (Shankar) Shankar, age 55

CEO Standard Chartered Saadiq, Afaq Khan

Chief Economist and Group Head Global Research, Gerard Lyons, age 52

Managing Director and Regional Head Global Markets Americas, Mohammed Grimeh

Chief Information Officer and Group Head of Group Technology and Operations, Jan Verplancke, age 49
Head Corporate Communications, Tim Baxter
External Communications Manager, Yuki Finch
Global Head Sales and Financial Markets, David Carr
Global Head Financial Institutions Sales Financial Markets, Adrian Walkling
Group Head Financial Markets, Lenny Feder
CEO Standard Chartered Bahrain, Jonathan Morris
CEO Standard Chartered UK and Europe, Richard W. Holmes
CEO Standard Chartered Cameroon, Mathieu Mandeng
Chief Executive Officer, Jeremy Awori
CEO Standard Chartered Mauritius, Sridhar Nagarajan
Head of Media Relations, Jonathan Tracey
President and CEO Korea and First Bank Korea; President and CEO Standard Chartered First Bank, Richard Hill
Regional Credit Officer Wholesale Banking; Country Chief Risk Officer Americas, Peter Shaw
Head Consumer Banking Southeast Asia, Ajay Kanwal
CEO Americas, Julio Rojas
Regional CEO India and South Asia, Sunil Kaushal
Board Member, Rudy H. P. Markham, age 67
Board Member, Jamie F. T. Dundas, age 62
Board Member, Valerie F. (Val) Gooding, age 62
Board Member, Paul D. Skinner, age 69
Board Member, Oliver Stocken, age 71
Board Member, John Paynter, age 58
Board Member, Ruth Markland, age 60
Group Chief Executive, Peter A. Sands, age 52
Group Finance Director and Board Member, Richard H. Meddings, age 55
Board Member, Gareth R. Bullock, age 59
Group Executive Director and CEO Asia, Jaspal Singh Bindra, age 53
Group Executive Director and CEO Wholesale Banking, Alun M. G. (Mike) Rees, age 57
Group Executive Director and CEO Consumer Banking, Stefano Paolo (Steve) Bertamini, age 48
Group Executive Director and CEO Europe Middle East Africa and Americas, Viswanathan (Shankar) Shankar, age 55
Board Member, Seung-Soo Han
Board Member, Richard Delbridge
Auditors: KPMGAuditPlc

LOCATIONS

HQ: Standard Chartered Plc
1 Aldermanbury Square, London EC2V 7SB
Phone: (44) 20 7885 8888
Web: www.standardchartered.com

2012 Sales

	% of total
Asia/Pacific	
Hong	18
Singapore	11
Korea	10
Other	21
India	8
Middle East & other South	12
Americas UK &	12
Africa	8
Total	**100**

PRODUCTS/OPERATIONS

2012 Sales

	% of total
Interest	68
Noninterest	
Fees &	17
Net trading	11
Other	4
Total	**100**

COMPETITORS

Bank of America
Bank of China
Bank of East Asia
Barclays
Citigroup
DBS Group Holdings
Deutsche Bank
Grupo Santander
HSBC
Hang Seng Bank
Lloyds Banking Group
Maybank
OCBC Bank
Royal Bank of Scotland
Standard Bank Group
State Bank of India
United Overseas Bank
Woori

HISTORICAL FINANCIALS

Company Type: Public

Income Statement FYE: December 31

	ASSETS ($ mil.)	NET INCOME ($ mil.)	INCOME AS % OF ASSETS	EMPLOYEES
12/12	636,518	4,887	0.8%	89,058
12/11	599,070	4,849	0.8%	86,865
12/10	516,542	4,332	0.8%	85,231
12/09	436,653	3,380	0.8%	77,326
12/08	435,068	3,408	0.8%	73,802
Annual Growth	10.0%	9.4%	—	4.8%

2012 Year-End Financials

Return on assets: 0.7%
Return on equity: 11.3%
Long-term debt ($ mil.): —
No. of shares (mil.): —
Sales ($ mil): 26,932
Dividends
Yield: —
Payout: —
Market value ($ mil.): —

Standard Life Assurance Co. (United Kingdom)

LOCATIONS

HQ: Standard Life Assurance Co. (United Kingdom)
Standard Life House, 30 Lothian Road, Edinburgh EH1 2DH
Phone: (44) 131 225 2552 **Fax:** (44) 131 245 7990
Web: www.standardlife.com

HISTORICAL FINANCIALS

Company Type: Public

Income Statement FYE: December 31

	ASSETS ($ mil.)	NET INCOME ($ mil.)	INCOME AS % OF ASSETS	EMPLOYEES
12/12	280,627	1,125	0.4%	8,458
12/11	247,366	460	0.2%	8,789
12/10	239,286	670	0.3%	9,254
12/09	237,451	344	0.1%	9,752
12/08	199,621	145	0.1%	9,959
Annual Growth	8.9%	66.7%	—	(4.0%)

2012 Year-End Financials

Return on assets: 0.4%
Return on equity: 16.7%
Long-term debt ($ mil.): —
No. of shares (mil.): —
Sales ($ mil): 31,001
Dividends
Yield: —
Payout: 93.2%
Market value ($ mil.): —

Standard Life Plc

Trying to set the standard for life insurance and financial services both at home and abroad Standard Life plc is a leading UK insurance asset management and pension firm. The holding company does business through subsidiaries including Standard Life Assurance Limited which provides life and pension products to 4 million customers in the UK market. Other divisions include Standard Life Investments (retail and institutional investment management). Standard Life established in 1825 has 6 million customers in the UK and abroad. In Canada its second largest market the company offers insurance pensions and asset management.

Geographic Reach

Standard Life's operations cover markets in North America Europe Asia and the Middle East. In addition to the UK (65% of sales) and Canada other international operations include subsidiaries and offices in Austria Australia Bermuda Germany Hong Kong Korea Ireland Singapore the United Arab Emirates and the US. It operates joint ventures in China and India. In all of these markets Standard Life offers life insurance and pension products to individuals and corporate clients.

Operations

The company's operating divisions provide investment protection and savings products; benefit and pension plans; and asset management services to corporations and individuals. Its Standard Life Investments division manages some #180 billion in assets around the globe. Altogether Standard Life's subsidiaries administer some #230 billion in assets (as of mid-2013). Due to the nature of the company's businesses investment returns often account for a larger percent of annual revenues than do insurance premiums and product fees and commissions.

Sales and Marketing

Standard Life distributes products directly to customers as well as through partnerships with banks. It formed a new partnership with RBS in 2012 to provide investment solutions to RBS banking customers.

Financial Performance

Revenue increased 111% in 2012 due to higher investment returns premiums and fee and commission income. Investment returns were up on equity security gains while fee and commission income received a boost from reclassified income. Net income rose 134% on higher revenues.

Strategy

The company is focused on maximizing profits to provide dividend growth and to reinvest in business growth. In the Standard Life Investments business the firm is focused on growing geographically and increasing investment capabilities. It opened new offices in Singapore and the Middle East and launched a new savings product in Germany in 2012. The company is also expanding its Standard Life Wealth division in the domestic market. In addition the Standard Life organization aims to increase customer and shareholder value and provide long-term savings and investment propositions.

Standard Life at one time had a few more eggs in its basket but pressures from the global economic downturn induced the company to simplify its holdings and focus more carefully on insurance long-term savings and investment management. The company sold off its Standard Life Bank (mortgages and savings products) subsidiary to Barclays in early 2010 for in #226 million ($369 million); Standard Life and Barclays entered a partnership to offer retail investment offerings following the deal. Also in 2010 the company sold its

Standard Life Healthcare (now part of PruHealth) to South African insurance and finance firm Discovery Holdings for #138 million ($205 million).

Mergers and Acquisitions

To enhance its wealth management operations in 2011 the company acquired financial software and consulting firm Focus Solutions. In 2013 the Standard Life Wealth division further widened its operations through the purchase of the Newton Private Clients division of Newton Management.

HISTORY

The Life Insurance Company of Scotland opened in Edinburgh in 1825 as a subsidiary of The Insurance Company of Scotland a fire insurance firm. In 1832 the subsidiary became a separate business received a royal charter and began anew as The Standard Life Assurance Company. In 1833 Standard Life opened its first overseas agency in Canada and continued to grow by acquisitions.

Company executives established Colonial Life Assurance as a sister company in 1846 to insure clients across the far-flung British empire. When Colonial's success became a threat to Standard Life's own business at home Standard bought Colonial.

In 1869 Standard Life moved into India and China (although only to insure Europeans). It moved into Scandinavia Argentina and South Africa in the 1890s.

After the turn of the century however the company began to spin off foreign offices and focus on its domestic business. Standard Life became a customer-owned mutual company in 1925.

The company was expanding again by the 1990s. It bought health insurer Prime Health (now Standard Life Healthcare) in 1994. The next year it formed a joint venture with India-based Housing Development Finance Corporation to sell insurance. In 1998 it expanded its financial services with the opening of Standard Life Bank and Standard Life Investments.

Expanding globally Standard Life was granted a license in 2000 to sell policies in the huge Indian market. The company opened up an office in Hong Kong in 2001. Just like many other companies Standard Life wanted to do business in China so it set up a joint venture and was granted a license to sell there in 2005.

After long resisting the worldwide trend for demutualization Standard Life's board eventually succumbed to the necessity of such an action. Faced with lackluster equity markets and regulatory criticism of its capital-reserves accounting in 2004 the company announced plans to restructure. The firm's transformation from a mutual organization into a holding company was completed through a public offering in mid-2006; the IPO was the London Stock Exchange's biggest in five years. The company's name was changed from The Standard Life Assurance Company to Standard Life plc.

In 2007 the company made a failed attempt to take over fellow UK insurance firm Resolution plc.

To enhance growth back home the company formed a UK wealth management unit in 2008 and launched additional initiatives to strengthen its corporate offerings and online services. To further this goal it acquired employee benefits management software maker Vebnet in 2008.

At the start of 2010 long-time executive Sir Sandy Crombie stepped down from his post as CEO of Standard Life. Crombie led the company through many challenges including its successful demutualization. David Nish who previously held the title of finance director at Standard Life took over the role of CEO.

EXECUTIVES

Group Chief Executive, David Nish, age 56
Chairman, Gerry E. Grimstone, age 63
Managing Director Information Systems, Keith Young
President and CEO Standard Life Canada, Charles Guay
Executive Director and Chief Executive Standard Life Investments Limited, Keith Skeoch, age 67
Group Company Secretary; General Counsel, Malcolm Wood
Chief Executive Europe, Nathan Parnaby
Head Media Relations, Barry Cameron
Public Relations Manager, Nicola McGowan
Chief Marketing Officer, Simon Gulliford
Group Human Resources Director, Mike Conway
Chief Executive U.K., Paul Matthews
Chief Financial Officer, Jackie Hunt, age 45
Affairs Manager, Claire Burston
Affairs Manager, Nicki Lundy
Senior Non-Executive Independent Director, John John Paynter Paynter
UK Chief Information Officer, Mark Dixon
Group Marketing Director, Bruce Kelsall
Director, Crawford Gillies
Board Member, Colin Buchan, age 58
Group Chief Executive, David Nish, age 56
Director, Sheelagh D. Whittaker, age 66
Board Member, Lord Norman Blackwell, age 60
Board Member, Kent Atkinson, age 68
Executive Director and Chief Executive Standard Life Investments Limited, Keith Skeoch, age 67
Board Member, Baroness Margaret J. McDonagh, age 52
Independent Non-Executive Director, David David Grigson Grigson
Non-Executive Director, Lynne Lynne Peacock Peacock
Non-Executive Director, Noel Noel Harwerth Harwerth
Non-Executive Director, Pierre Pierre Danon Danon
Auditors: PricewaterhouseCoopersLLP

LOCATIONS

HQ: Standard Life Plc
Standard Life House, 30 Lothian Road, Edinburgh EH1 2DH
Phone: (44) 131 225 2552
Web: www.standardlife.com

2012 Premiums

	% of total
UK	65
Canada	18
International	17
Total	**100**

PRODUCTS/OPERATIONS

2012 Revenues

	% of total
Investment	73
Earned	22
Fee & commission	5
Total	**100**

Selected Products

Life insurance
Pension products
- Active Money Personal Pension (AMPP)
- Self Invested Personal Pension (SIPP)
- Stakeholder pension
- Starting a pension for a child

Retirement products
- Compulsory Purchase Annuity
- Immediate Vesting Personal Pension
- Immediate Vesting Personal Pension Select
- Impaired Life Annuity
- Income Drawdown

Savings and investment products
- International Bond
- Investment funds
- Other Onshore Bonds
- Stocks and Shares ISA
- Tailored Investment Bond

COMPETITORS

AXA UK	Power Financial
Aviva	Prudential plc
Canada Life	ReAssure
Equitable Life	Royal London Mutual
Friends Provident	Schroders
Great-West Lifeco	Scottish Equitable
Legal & General Group	Skandia UK
Liverpool Victoria	St. James' s Place plc
Phoenix Group	Sun Life
	permanent tsb

HISTORICAL FINANCIALS

Company Type: Public

Income Statement

FYE: December 31

	REVENUE ($ mil.)	NET INCOME ($ mil.)	NET PROFIT MARGIN	EMPLOYEES
12/12	30,923	1,125	3.6%	8,458
12/11	14,036	460	3.3%	8,789
12/10	28,830	670	2.3%	9,254
12/09	28,237	344	1.2%	9,752
12/08	22,719	145	—	10,394
Annual Growth	—	66.7%	—	(5.0%)

2012 Year-End Financials

Debt ratio: —
Return on equity: 16.7%
Cash ($ mil.): 16,025
Current ratio: —
Long-term debt ($ mil.): —

No. of shares (mil.): —
Dividends
Yield: —
Payout: —
Market value ($ mil.): —

	STOCK PRICE ($) FY Close	P/E High/Low		PER SHARE ($) Earnings	Dividends	Book Value
12/12	5.30	50	26	0.48	0.00	2.98
12/11	3.15	80	52	0.20	0.00	2.60
12/10	3.30	48	29	0.30	0.19	2.65
12/09	3.35	103	43	0.16	0.00	2.50
12/08	2.93	333	132	0.07	0.00	2.28
Annual Growth	16.0%	—	—	63.2%	—	6.9%

Statoil ASA

The status of Statoil is that it is Norway's top integrated oil and gas company. Statoil operates in 40 countries focusing its upstream activities in more than 10 of them primarily on the Norwegian continental shelf the North Sea the Caspian Sea Western Africa North America and South America. In 2010 Statoil reported proved reserves of 5.3 billion barrels of oil equivalent. It indirectly operates a network of more than 2280 gas stations in Russia Scandinavia Poland and the Baltic States. (77% of these stations are in Scandinavia). Statoil also operates natural gas pipelines supplies electricity in Norway and Sweden and is engaged in green energy development (wind and biofuels).

Statoil manages the Norwegian state's direct financial interest (known as SDFI) in oil and gas partnerships active on the Norwegian continental shelf. It also owns the world's largest offshore gas platform the Aasgard B off Norway's west coast.

The company's strategy is to develop new oil and gas assets (based on its ongoing success in the Norwegian Continental Shelf) in four focus areas:

deepwater harsh environment gas value chains and heavy oil.

Beefing up its global infrastructure in 2009 the company bought a crude oil terminal in the Bahamas (and a 50% interest in a related tugboat business) from World Point Terminals for $263.2 million.

The company reported a downturn in revenues and income in 2009 primarily as the result of the impact of the global recession on lowering commodity prices and weakening oil and gas demand.

In 2010 in a move to generate cash to pay down debt and to invest in its higher-return core exploration and production assets Statoil spun off its retail network of gas stations (including a chain of 200 automated outlets) in eight north European countries. Statoil retained more than 50% of the unit (Statoil Fuel and Retail) following the spin off. It also sold a 40% stake in its Peregrino oil field (offshore Brazil) to Sinochem for $3 billion and a 40% stake in its Canadian oil sands project to PTT Exploration and Production for $2.3 billion. In 2011 it also sold its 24% stake in the Gassled Pipeline joint venture to investment firms for $3.3 billion. That year it increased its presence in Alaska (where it is the fourth largest explorer) by acquiring a 25% stake in 50 Conoco Phillips oil leases located in the Chukchi Sea.

Higher oil and gas price and increased demand coupled with its strategic acquisitions divestments and reorganizations helped to lift Statoil's revenue sand net income in 2010.

Building its exploration and production position in the US in 2011 the company expanded its holdings in shale assets buying Brigham Exploration in a $4.4 billion deal. Thanks to new drilling technologies US gas shale has emerged as a lucrative growth market and Brigham Exploration had well-established shale plays in the Rockies.

To raise cash and focus on its core exploration and production activities in 2012 the company agreed to sell its 54% stake in Statoil Fuel and Retail to Alimentation Couche-Tard for $2.8 billion.

The Norwegian government owns 67% of Statoil.

HISTORY

To exert greater control over exploration and production of the Norwegian continental shelf (NCS) the government of Norway set up Den norske stats oljeselskap (Statoil) in 1972.

A decade earlier three geologists had visited Norway on behalf of Phillips Petroleum (later renamed ConocoPhillips) to apply for sole rights to explore on the NCS. The government initially refused drilling rights to foreign companies and in 1963 Norway claimed sovereignty over the NCS. Two years later the government began allowing exploration. Phillips' major discovery in the Ekofisk field in 1969 prompted Norway to set up its own oil company. After Statoil's formation in 1972 the company garnered funds to expand through taxation of multinationals production limits leasing contracts and other measures.

In 1974 a giant discovery was made in the North Sea's Statfjord field and Statoil was given a 50% stake. A year later Statoil began exploring for oil and gas exporting oil and commissioning its first subsea oil pipeline the Norpipe which extended to the UK. In 1986 Statoil's gas pipeline system the Statpipe began transporting gas from the North Sea to the mainland.

Moving into retailing Statoil acquired Esso's service stations and other downstream operations in Sweden and Denmark in 1985 and 1986. The next year cost overruns stemming from the extension of Statoil's Mongstad oil refinery led to the ousting of the company's first president Arve Johnsen and many of his deputies. Harald Norvik was appointed CEO in 1988.

In 1990 Statoil and BP teamed up to develop international operations and in 1992 Statoil acquired BP's service stations in Ireland. Statoil and Neste Chemicals (later part of Industri Kapital) formed the Borealis petrochemicals group in 1994.

The company in 1995 acquired Aran Energy moving into exploration of offshore Ireland and the UK. Statoil brought its field projects in China and Azerbaijan onstream in 1997. That year Statoil spun off its shipping operations as Navion partly owned by Norway's Rasmussen group. It also contracted with Kvaerner to build a giant offshore gas platform for the Aasgard field in the Norwegian Sea.

The Aasgard field project resulted in cost overruns in 1999 again leading to a Statoil board shakeup and CEO resignation. Norvik who had advocated partial privatization of Statoil was replaced by Olav Fjell former head of Norway's Postbanken (who resigned in 2003). That year Statoil helped Norsk Hydro take over rival Saga in return for some of Saga's assets.

As part of a major restructuring in 2000 Statoil sold most assets of US unit Statoil Energy. Political opposition that year postponed Statoil's plans for partial privatization but the government proceeded with an IPO in 2001 raising about $3 billion.

In 2002 Statoil sold its oil and gas assets in the Danish North Sea to Dong the Danish state oil company for about $120 million. That year the company also acquired the Polish unit of Sweden's Preem Petroleum which owned 79 gas stations in Poland.

In 2003 Statoil sold its Navion unit to shipping group Teekay for about $800 million. That year it also acquired two Algerian natural gas projects from BP for $740 million. A bribery scandal involving an Iranian oil contract forced the resignation of the chairman CEO and another top executive in 2003.

Statoil sold its 50% stake in petrochemicals venture Borealis in 2005.

In 2006 the company acquired three oil prospects in the Gulf of Mexico from Plains Exploration & Production for $700 million. It also acquired offshore assets in the Gulf of Mexico from Anadarko Petroleum for $901 million.

Expanding its upstream midstream and downstream assets in 2007 the company acquired $4.2 billion of subsea equipment from Aver Kvaerner Canada's North American Oil Sands Corporation for $1.96 billion and 274 gas stations in Scandinavia from ConocoPhillips.

In a major expansion that gave it a major international profile (including a strong presence in the deepwater Gulf of Mexico) in 2007 Statoil acquired the oil and gas exploration and production operations of Norsk Hydro in a $30 billion deal and became StatoilHydro.

In 2008 Statoil acquired ConocoPhillips' Jet gas station chain in Norway Sweden and Denmark.

Growing its exploration and production asset base in 2008 paid about $1.8 billion to acquire holdings in heavy-oil and deep-water projects in Brazil and the Gulf of Mexico from Anadarko Petroleum. That year it also teamed up with Chesapeake Energy to jointly explore unconventional gas opportunities around the world including in the Marcellus Shale play in the US.

EXECUTIVES

VP Media Relations North America, Jannik Lindb?k, age 73
EVP Development and Production International, Peter Mellbye, age 63, $631,293 total compensation
President; Chief Executive Officer, Helge Lund, age 50, $1,072,974 total compensation
SVP Corporate Human Resources, Jens R. Jenssen, age 59
Chairman, Svein Rennemo, age 65
EVP Exploration, Tim Dodson, age 53
Deputy Chairman, Marit Arnstad, age 50
SVP Investor Relations, Lars Troen S?rensen
VP Media Relations, Ola M. Aanestad
President StatoilHydro Brazil, Kjetil Hove
Public Affairs Manager, Kai Nielsen
Investor Relations, Morten S. Johannessen
EVP Development and Production International, Lars C. Bacher
EVP Development and Production North America, Bill Maloney, age 58
EVP Global Strategy and Business Development, John Knight, age 55
EVP and CFO, Torgrim Reitan
EVP and Chief Staff Officer, Tove Stuhr Sj?blom, age 47
President Canada, Stale Tungesvik
Executive Vice President; Marketing; Processing and Renewable Energy, Eldar Saetre
Executive Vice President; Technology; Projects and Drilling, Margareth Ovrum
Director, Lady Barbara T. Judge, age 66
Director, Lill-Heidi Bakkerud, age 49
Director, Grace Reksten Skaugen, age 59
Director, Morten Svaan, age 56
Deputy Chairman, Marit Arnstad, age 50
Director, Roy Franklin, age 59
Director, Jakob Stausholm, age 45
Director, Einar A. Iversen, age 51
Director, Bjorn T. Godal
Auditors: Ernst&YoungAS

LOCATIONS

HQ: Statoil ASA
Forusbeen 50, Stavanger N-4035
Phone: (47) 51 99 00 00 **Fax:** (47) 51 99 00 50
Web: www.statoil.com

2010 Sales

	% of total
Norway	78
US	10
Sweden	4
Denmark	3
Other	5
Total	**100**

PRODUCTS/OPERATIONS

2010 Sales

	% of total
Manufacturing &	52
Exploration &	28
Natural	11
Fuel &	9
Total	**100**

COMPETITORS

BP
Exxon Mobil
OMV
Royal Dutch Shell
TOTAL

HISTORICAL FINANCIALS

Company Type: Public

Income Statement FYE: December 31

	REVENUE ($ mil.)	NET INCOME ($ mil.)	NET PROFIT MARGIN	EMPLOYEES
12/12	129,328	12,317	9.5%	23,028
12/11	111,467	13,103	11.8%	31,715
12/10	90,766	6,526	7.2%	30,344
12/09	80,787	3,178	3.9%	28,739
12/08	93,692	6,179	6.6%	29,500
Annual Growth	8.4%	18.8%	—	(6.0%)

2012 Year-End Financials

Debt ratio: 2.7%
Return on equity: 22.9%
Cash ($ mil.): 11,656
Current ratio: 1.12
Long-term debt ($ mil.): 18,056
No. of shares (mil.): —
Dividends
Yield: 4.2%
Payout: 26.3%
Market value ($ mil.): —

	STOCK PRICE ($) FY Close	P/E High/Low		PER SHARE ($) Earnings	Dividends	Book Value
12/12	25.04	0	0	3.86	1.07	17.95
12/11	25.61	0	0	4.11	0.03	14.58
12/10	23.77	0	0	2.05	0.92	11.83
12/09	24.91	0	0	1.00	1.14	10.82
12/08	16.66	0	0	1.94	1.65	9.60
Annual Growth	10.7%	—	—	18.8%	(10.4%)	16.9%

Storebrand ASA

If you're planning for your golden years in Norway you may want to shop with Storebrand. The company provides insurance and financial services in the Nordic region and other areas of Europe including life insurance policies property/casualty coverage health insurance asset management and banking. Its largest unit Storebrand Life offers pension savings occupational pension and life insurance products while its Storebrand P&C division provides property protection policies to individuals and businesses. The Storebrand Bank subsidiary is a commercial bank that focuses on the retail and corporate markets. The Storebrand Asset Management unit manages mutual funds and client portfolios.

EXECUTIVES

Chairman, Birger Magnus, age 58, $44,918 total compensation
CEO and Managing Director, Odd Arild Grefstad, age 48, $471,038 total compensation
Executive Vice President Corporate Communications, Egil Thompson, age 49, $338 total compensation
EVP Operative Processes, Roar Thoresen, age 56, $502,876 total compensation
Chief Marketing Officer, Anders R?ed, age 45, $308,299 total compensation
EVP SPP, Sarah McPhee, age 59, $511,653 total compensation
EVP Insurance and Risk, Gunnar Rogstad, age 58, $336,283 total compensation
Executive Vice President Corporate Responsibility, Elin M. Myrmel-Johansen, age 40
Head Investor Relations, Trond Finn Eriksen
EVP Bank, Truls Nergaard
Chief Operating Officer, Heidi Skaaret, age 53
Managing Director of Storebrand Livsforsikring AS, Geir Holmgren
Managing Director; Storebrand Asset Management, Hans Aasnaes
Chief Financial Officer, Lars Loddesol
Director, Halvor Stenstadvold, age 69
Director, Birgitte Nielsen, age 50
Director, Jon Arnt Jacobsen, age 56
Director, John Staunsbjerg Dueholm, age 63
Director, Camilla Marianne Grieg, age 48
Director, Annika Lundius, age 60
Director, Knut Dyre Haug, age 58
Director, Erik Haug Hansen, age 57
Director, Ann-Mari Gj?stein, age 49
Director; Employee Representative, Ann-Mari Gjostein
Director; Employee Representative, Kirsti Valborgland
Auditors: DeloitteAS

LOCATIONS

HQ: Storebrand ASA
Professor Kohtsvei 9, P.O. Box 500, Lysaker NO-1327
Phone: (47) 22 31 50 50 **Fax:** (47) 22 48 98 90
Web: www.storebrand.no

COMPETITORS

AXA
Allianz
Danske Bank
Eureko
ING
Nordea Bank
SEB AB
Skandia
Swedbank AB
Zurich Insurance Group
ageas SA/NV

HISTORICAL FINANCIALS

Company Type: Public

Income Statement FYE: December 31

	ASSETS ($ mil.)	NET INCOME ($ mil.)	INCOME AS % OF ASSETS	EMPLOYEES
12/12	75,119	179	0.2%	2,250
12/11	66,767	112	0.2%	2,221
12/10	66,905	252	0.4%	2,206
12/09	63,555	161	0.3%	2,280
12/08	53,219	(318)	—	2,516
Annual Growth	9.0%	—	—	(2.8%)

2012 Year-End Financials

Return on assets: 0.2%
Return on equity: 5.2%
Long-term debt ($ mil.): —
No. of shares (mil.): 449
Sales ($ mil): 9,384
Dividends
Yield: —
Payout: —
Market value ($ mil.): 4,276

	STOCK PRICE ($) FY Close	P/E High/Low		PER SHARE ($) Earnings	Dividends	Book Value
12/12	9.50	0	0	0.40	0.00	7.88
12/11	12.05	0	0	0.25	0.01	6.89
12/10	14.16	0	0	0.57	0.19	6.95
12/09	11.05	0	0	0.36	0.00	6.58
Annual Growth	(4.9%)	—	—	2.7%	—	4.6%

Sumitomo Chemical Co., Ltd.

Sumitomo Chemical makes chemicals for almost everything made and grown under the sun. About one-third of the company's sales come from petrochemicals and plastics such as polypropylene ethylene and elastomers. Sumitomo's other major units make pharmaceuticals agricultural chemicals (insecticides herbicides and fertilizers) and basic chemicals such as caustic soda and methanol. The company also makes chemicals for electronics and fine chemicals. A part of Japan's Sumitomo Group the company has 146 subsidiaries and 35 affiliates. Its pharmaceutical business operates through Dainippon Sumitomo Pharma. Sumitomo ranks among Japan's top three chemical producers along with Mitsubishi Chemical and Asahi Kasei.

In fiscal 2011 Sumitomo Chemical reported net sales of nearly Y2 trillion up 22% from the previous year. Its international sales alone jumped 45% from the previous year surpassing the company's domestic sales. A series of international coups during the past two years contributed to those gains. Recently acquired subsidiary Sunovion launched a new antipsychotic agent in the US under the brand name LATUDA in 2011 to treat schizophrenia. The company also benefited from its 20% stake in Australian agrochemicals group Nufarm that it acquired in 2010 as well as from a partnership in crop protection with giant US agrochemicals group Monsanto.

Sumitomo Chemical also entered a joint venture in 2011 with Korea's Samsung Electronics to manufacture wafers that would be used to ultimately produce light-emitting diodes or LEDs. The operation scheduled to begin production in 2012 will make the "sapphire wafers" primarily for the flat-screen television market.

To boost its market share in India in 2010 Sumitomo Chemical acquired India-based agrochemicals and drug maker New Chemi Industries. Established in 1961 New Chemi has been a partner in Sumitomo Chemical's manufacturing joint venture company in India since 2000. It has a large portfolio of crop protection products that complement Sumitomo Chemical's product lines currently distributed in India.

HISTORY

The story of Sumitomo Chemical begins in 1590 with the Sumitomo family's founding of a copper refinery in Japan. For three hundred years generations of the family nurtured the copper business. Early in the 20th century noxious sulfur dioxide emissions at the company's Nihama copper smelter began to endanger the local population. To halt the pollution the company built a plant in 1913 to convert the sulfur dioxide to sulfuric acid and calcium superphosphate products Sumitomo used to make fertilizer. In 1925 the chemical plant at the Nihama smelter was spun off as an independent company and renamed Sumitomo Fertilizer Manufacturing.

The company broadened its product line in the 1930s by adding ammonia-related chemicals (also used to make fertilizer) to its production. In 1934 the company changed its name to Sumitomo Chemical.

During WWII Sumitomo Chemical grew rapidly as it provided chemicals for military use. The company absorbed Japan Dyestuff Manufacturing (dyes and pharmaceuticals) in 1944. When the war ended in 1945 nearly half of Sumitomo Chemical's plants lay in ruins. Even battered the company managed to enter the postwar period as Japan's largest chemical company.

Following the war the Allied occupation authority forced Sumitomo Chemical to separate from Sumitomo and change its name to Nisshin Chemical Industries. Nisshin Chemical bought Sumitomo Aluminum Reduction another former affiliate of the Sumitomo group in 1949.

The Korean War created a need for chemicals in the region and led to the relaxation of restrictive commercial laws. In 1952 Nisshin Chemical changed its name back to Sumitomo Chemical and once again affiliated with Sumitomo. Continuing to build its product line the company constructed one of Japan's first petrochemical plants in 1958. Sumitomo Chemical's second petrochemical complex was built near Tokyo in 1965.

The company's metals division grew to a point that in 1976 Sumitomo Chemical converted it into an independent subsidiary called Sumitomo Aluminum Smelting. Market conditions began to deteriorate and Sumitomo Chemical failed to respond adequately. As a result Mitsubishi Chemical soon surpassed Sumitomo Chemical as Japan's largest chemical producer.

The company's response was to consolidate its petrochemical operations during the 1980s and to form a partnership with the Singaporean government to operate a nationalized chemical complex. Sumitomo Chemical merged its pharmaceutical businesses with those of Inabata & Company in 1984 and spun off those operations as Sumitomo Pharmaceuticals. Also during this time the company expanded into North America and moved its aluminum smelting operations out of Japan (1986).

A prolonged recession in Japan during the 1990s and monetary crises in Asian countries led to decreases in demand and prices for the company's products. These forces contributed to Sumitomo Chemical's increased emphasis on globalization. In 1997 the company expanded its petrochemical complex in Singapore and the next year it formed chemical subsidiaries in Australia and China. Continuing its overseas expansion in 1999 Sumitomo Chemical formed Philagro South Africa (agricultural chemicals and hygiene products).

The company added US-based Abbott Laboratories' agricultural products business in 2000. In March 2003 the company called off a planned merger with Mitsui Chemicals Japan's #4 chemical maker at the time after more than two years of negotiations. The combined company would have been Japan's largest.

In 2005 Sumitomo formed a joint venture called SUMATION with Cambridge Display Technology to develop and supply advanced polymer materials called polymer-organic light emitting diodes which are used to deliver fine resolution for televisions and in lighting applications. Two years later the company acquired Cambridge Display taking full ownership of the JV in the process for $285 million. It also acquired Dow Chemical's LUMATION light-emitting polymers business.

In 2009 the company swooped in to take advantage of Australian agrochemical company Nufarm's uncertainty regarding a proposed offer to buy that company from Chinese giant Sinochem. When Sinochem revised its bid lower Sumitomo Chemical stepped in to take a 20% stake in Nufarm (completed in 2010). Also in 2009 subsidiary Dainippon Sumitomo acquired US pharmaceutical firm Sunovion (the former Sepracor) which holds a patent to the insomnia drug Lunesta.

The pharmaceuticals unit was formed through the 2005 merger of the company's pharma operations with Dainippon Pharmaceuticals. Sumitomo Chemical still owns just more than half of the company whose products include medications for cardiovascular disease and gastrointestinal disorders as well as anti-allergy pharmaceuticals.

EXECUTIVES

Chairman, Hiromasa Yonekura
Vice Chairman, Osamu Ishitobi
EVP, Yoshimasa Takao
President, Masakazu Tokura
Senior Managing Executive Officer, Yoshihiko Okamoto
Senior Managing Executive Officer, Toshihisa Deguchi
Managing Executive Officer, Kunio Nozaki
EVP and Director, Naoya Kanda
EVP and Director, Osamu Ishitobi
Senior Managing Executive Officer Basic Chemicals Sector and Director, Yasuo Kamei
Senior Managing Executive Officer Petrochemicals and Plastics Sector and Director, Yoshitsugu Sakamoto
President and Director, Hiroshi Hirose
Senior Managing Executive Officer Fine Chemicals Sector and Director, Takatsugu Enami
Senior Managing Executive Officer and Director, Kiyohiko Nakae
Senior Managing Executive Officer and Director, Yoshimasa Takao
Senior Managing Executive Officer IT-related Chemicals Sector and Director, Masakazu Tokura
Senior Managing Executive Officer Agricultural Chemicals Sector and Director, Kenjiro Fukubayashi
Auditors: KPMGAZSA&Co.

LOCATIONS

HQ: Sumitomo Chemical Co., Ltd.
2-27-1 Shinkawa, Chuo-ku, Tokyo 104-8260
Phone: (81) 3 5543 5265
Web: www.sumitomo-chem.co.jp

2011 Sales

	$ mil.	% of total
Total	0	100

PRODUCTS/OPERATIONS

2011 Sales

	$ mil.	% of total
Petrochemicals & Plastics	33	
Pharmaceuticals	18	
Basic Chemicals	13	
Agricultural Chemicals	11	
Other	5	

COMPETITORS

Asahi Kasei
BASF SE
Dow Chemical
DuPont
Hitachi Chemical
Lucite
Marubeni
Mitsubishi Chemical
Mitsubishi Gas Chemical
Mitsui Chemicals
Nippon Kayaku
Nissan Chemical
Sinopec Group
Ube

HISTORICAL FINANCIALS

Company Type: Public

Income Statement FYE: March 31

	REVENUE ($ mil.)	NET INCOME ($ mil.)	NET PROFIT MARGIN	EMPLOYEES
03/13	20,750	(542)	—	30,396
03/12	23,745	68	0.3%	29,839
03/11	23,940	295	1.2%	29,382
03/10	17,353	157	0.9%	27,828
03/09	18,159	(600)	—	26,902
Annual Growth	3.4%	—	—	3.1%

2013 Year-End Financials

Debt ratio: 0.4%
Return on equity: (-10.3%)
Cash ($ mil.): 796
Current ratio: 1.27
Long-term debt ($ mil.): 7,515
No. of shares (mil.): 1,634
Dividends
Yield: —
Payout: —
Market value ($ mil.): 25,711

	STOCK PRICE ($) FY Close	P/E High/Low	PER SHARE ($) Earnings	Dividends	Book Value
03/13	15.73	— —	(0.33)	0.00	4.86
03/12	21.18	— —	0.04	0.00	5.38
03/11	24.75	— —	0.18	0.18	5.61
Annual Growth	(20.3%)	— —	—	—	(3.5%)

Sumitomo Corp. (Japan)

Sumitomo Corporation specializes in the general. A Japanese "sogo shosha" (general trading company) Sumitomo is active in a wide range of commercial ventures. Through some 800 subsidiaries and affiliates it imports and exports raw materials and goods including metals machinery electronics fuels chemicals and food products. It also participates in finance logistics and real estate development. The group's auto finance and media holdings are among its fastest-growing operations. Sumitomo Corporation is part of the Sumitomo "keiretsu" a group of companies loosely linked by cross-ownership. Other group companies include Sumitomo Mitsui Banking Sumitomo Life Insurance and electronics maker NEC.

Never one to sit still Sumitomo occupies much of its time trading on its own behalf. The company searches for opportunities to take advantage of market trends and secure new lines of revenue. For example it was one of a number of foreign groups to move into Australia's agricultural sector when it bought half of Emerald Group in 2010. (It acquired the remaining 50% in 2014.) Emerald Group is one of Australia's largest grain trading firms; Japan also happens to be a major importer of Australian wheat. Sumitomo also invested some $100 million in rare earth producer Molycorp giving it access to a reliable source of manufacturing minerals.

Also that year the company increased its stake in Jupiter Telecommunications (J:COM) Japan's largest cable television operator from 27% to 40%. It had tried unsuccessfully to buy out J:COM's largest owner Liberty Media. Instead Liberty sold its 38% stake to KDDI Corporation one of Japan's largest telecommunications companies.

In late 2012 KDDI and Sumitomo agreed to acquire all outstanding shares of J:COM and merge it with Japan's #2 cable operator Japan Cablenet (owned by KDDI); the resulting entity will control half of Japan's cable market.

Sumitomo has been building up its metals and mining business. In 2010 Sumitomo bought a 30% stake in the iron ore unit of Brazilian steelmaker Usiminas. Due to increasing copper demand especially from China Sumitomo has increased its copper mining operations in Indonesia. The company has also invested in a nickel mine in Madagascar with partners Korea Resources Sherritt International and SNC Lavalin. In 2011 Sumitomo and its Sumitomo Metal unit acquired Standard Steel in the US. The deal allowed Sumitomo to expand its railway business by tapping into the growing demand for train wheels in North America.

As part of a consortium Sumitomo purchased an oil and gas operation in the UK North Sea from Paris-based Wendel in 2009. The company Oranje-Nassau Energie owns six oil blocks capable of producing some 7000 barrels worth of oil and gas a day through 2030. The deal was worth about $900 million. Also that year Sumitomo acquired a 42%-stake in a US wind farm from American International Group; the group already had wind farms in Japan and China in its fold.

In 2008 Sumitomo took full control over its 24-hour home shopping network Jupiter Shop Channel when it bought a 30% equity stake from IAC for Y46 billion ($493 million). The acquisition provided the company with more flexibility in running the retail business and to implement a multi-channel strategy. Sumitomo also plans to leverage its existing media and lifestyle business portfolio via the channel.

HISTORY

Around 1630 Masatomo Sumitomo a Buddhist priest from the Kyoto area opened a medicine shop/bookstore after the dissolution of his sect. His descendants preserved his writings on business ethics and he is considered the spiritual founder of the Sumitomo Group. The commercial founder of the "keiretsu" however was Riemon Soga Sumitomo's brother-in-law. Soga researched and duplicated a Western copper-smelting technique that enabled him to build a prosperous copper company. After Soga died in 1636 his son Tomomochi married into the Sumitomo family and became its head.

Tomomochi Soga combined the families' businesses and moved to Osaka. By 1693 the family had turned a dilapidated copper mine into one of Japan's top producers. By the mid-1800s however the company's biggest mine was aging and output had dropped. The family mortgaged its assets to modernize the mine imported French technology and bought ships for copper transport. Production soared.

Sumitomo Bank was created from existing family operations in 1895. A copper wire business founded in 1897 evolved into Sumitomo Electric and Sumitomo Metal Industries. The family formed Sumitomo Chemical in 1913 and in 1925 began selling life insurance.

Nippon Electric Company (NEC) was managed by Sumitomo from 1932 until post-WWII occupation forces split the "zaibatsu" (family-run conglomerate) into numerous independent pieces. Employees of the old Sumitomo group migrated to a real estate and trading company today's Sumitomo Corporation. Sumitomo companies began regrouping in the 1950s at the behest of the Japanese government.

Sumitomo companies went on a buying spree during the "bubble economy" of the 1980s and early 1990s. Purchases included Dunlop's tire operations investments in Phelps Dodge's (now Freeport-McMoRan) Candelaria copper and gold mine in Chile and one-third of Satellite Japan. The Sumitomo Bank bought 13% of US investment house Goldman Sachs. In 1990 however bank chairman Ichiro Isoda resigned in an illegal-loan scandal.

Sumitomo Metal Industries invested about $200 million in LTV in 1993 to shore up its US supply of high-quality steel. Ironically LTV was one of several US steel companies that campaigned against Japanese steel imports in 1998.

In its first loss in 50 years Sumitomo Bank took a $2.8 billion hit in 1995 because of bad loans (the legacy of the economy's bubble burst of 1992). The next year Sumitomo Corporation announced that its head copper-trader Yasuo Hamanaka had engaged in unauthorized trading over the previous decade –first attempting to corner the market then trying to cover his own deficit. Hamanaka pleaded guilty and went to jail. Sumitomo Corporation chairman Tomiichi Akiyama resigned in 1997. By 1998 the company had suffered $3 billion in trading losses fines and restitutions. (Sumitomo Corporation sued four investment banks alleging they had aided Hamanaka; separately Merrill Lynch settled a dispute over its role in the scandal by agreeing in 2000 to pay the company $275 million.)

In 1999 Sumitomo Rubber Industries and Goodyear Tire formed an alliance: Sumitomo Rubber got cash and control of Goodyear's Japanese operations and Goodyear gained control of Sumitomo Rubber's business in the US and Europe. Sumitomo Bank in 1999 announced plans to merge with Sakura Bank; the deal was completed in 2001.

That year Sumitomo Corporation agreed to buy Nomura Trading's steel-related operations; the deal was completed in 2002. Adding to one of its core businesses that year Sumitomo bought the steel products businesses of Nichimen (now Sojitz). Also in 2002 Sumitomo Corporation moved to expand its activities in China.

The year 2004 was a big one for the company: Sumitomo purchased US-based life science venture capital firm Oxford Finance embarked upon a joint venture with Australia-based glove manufacturer Ansell and fabric manufacturer Shinwa to make gloves and other products launched a credit-card subsidiary and acquired Nissin Sugar Manufacturing. In other deals it purchased US pet care products maker Hartz Mountain for $364 million; acquired Kiriu Corp a disc and drum brake-maker with operations in Asia and North America; and took controlling stakes of Sumisho Computer Systems Corp and movie theater chain United Cinemas.

Late in 2005 Sumitomo expanded its retailing operations again when its Sumitomo Corporation of America subsidiary acquired tire distributor TBC Corporation in a $1.1 billion deal. TBC's operations included National Tire & Battery Tire Kingdom and Merchant's Tire & Auto. It also owned the Big O Tires franchise business.

In 2008 the company increased its focus on upstream oil development and the trading of crude oil and petroleum products. To that end it sold its shares in domestic oil distribution unit Sumisho Oil to Idemitsu Kosa. The group also acquired 20% of Abu Dhabi-based energy and desalinated water supplier Shuweihat CMS International Power Company. The deal included a 50% stake in the company's operation and maintenance partnership.

Sumitomo exits or sells divisions that are less profitable. In 2008 it dissolved diamond distribution company FB Jewelry and began the dissolution of GeoFocus a developer of communication systems. The group cited poor performances of both units for the closures.

EXECUTIVES

Chairman, Motoyuki Oka
President and CEO, Susumu Kato
Senior Managing Executive Officer and General Manager Transportation & Construction Systems Business Unit, Naoki Hidaka
Executive Officer; General Manager Internal Auditing, Makoto Nakamura
Senior Managing Executive Officer and President Sumitomo Corporation of America, Kazuhiro Takeuchi
Chairman, Kazuo Ohmori
CFO Senior Managing Executive Officer and Director; General Manager Financial Resources Management Group, Toyosaku Hamada
Senior Managing Executive Officer and General Manager Americas; President and CEO Sumitomo Corporation North America Group; Director & President Sumitomo Corporation of America, Takashi Kano
President and CEO, Kuniharu Nakamura
EVP and General Manager Media Network Lifestyle Related Goods & Services Business Unit, Shinichi Sasaki
EVP and General Manager Human Resources General Affairs & Legal Group, Takuro Kawahara
Senior Managing Executive Officer and Director; General Manager Media Network and Lifestyle Retail Business Unit, Yoshio Osawa
EVP and General Manager Metal Products Business Unit, Kazuhisa Togashi
Senior Managing Executive Officer and General Manager Mineral Resources Energy Chemical & Electronics Business Unit, Toru Furihata
Managing Executive Officer and Director; General Manager Corporate Planning and Coordination, Masayuki Doi
Senior Managing Executive Officer and CFO, Hiroyuki Inohara
Senior Managing Executive Officer and General Manager Kansai Regional Business Unit, Masaru Nakamura
Managing Executive Officer and President and CEO Sumitomo Corporation Asia & Oceania Group, Kohei Hirao
Senior Managing Executive Officer and General Manager Corporate Planning & Coordination Group, Yasuyuki Abe
Senior Managing Executive Officer and General Manager Environment & Infrastructure Business Unit, Michihiko Kanegae
Executive Officer; General Manager Automotive Division No.2, Kiyomi Machida
Executive Officer; Assistant General Manager Financial Resources Management Group; General Manager Corporate Risk Management, Hideki Iwasawa
Executive Officer; EVP and CFO Sumitomo Corporation North America Group; General Manager Corporate Coordination Group Sumitomo Corporation North America Group; EVP and CFO Sumitomo Corporation of America; Assistant General Manager Americas, Masato Sugimori
Executive Officer; General Manager Mineral Resources Division No.1, Akira Takeuchi
Executive Officer; General Manager Accounting Controlling, Koichi Takahata
Executive Officer; General Manager Legal, Kiyoshi Ogawa
Executive Officer and President and CEO Sumitomo Corporation Kyushu Co. Ltd., Hiroaki Mizobuchi
Executive Officer; General Manager Non-Ferrous Products and Metals, Masao Sekiuchi
Executive Officer; General Manager Planning and Administration and Transportation and Construction Systems, Yutaka Sekine
Executive Officer and President and CEO Sumitomo Corporation (Shanghai) Limited, Fumihiro Koba
President and CEO, Susumu Kato
EVP and Director; General Manager Transportation and Construction Systems Business Unit, Kazuo Ohmori
CFO Senior Managing Executive Officer and Director; General Manager Financial Resources Management Group, Toyosaku Hamada
EVP and Director; General Manager Infrastructure Business Unit, Takahiro Moriyama
EVP and Director; General Manager Metal Products Business Unit, Shunichi Arai
Senior Managing Executive Officer and Director; General Manager Mineral Resources Energy Chemical & Electronics Business Unit, Kuniharu Nakamura
Senior Managing Executive Officer and Director; General Manager General Products and Real Estate, Shinichi Sasaki

Senior Managing Executive Officer and Director; General Manager Human Resources General Affairs and Legal Group, Takuro Kawahara
Senior Managing Executive Officer and Director; General Manager Media Network and Lifestyle Retail Business Unit, Yoshio Osawa
Managing Executive Officer and Director; General Manager Corporate Planning and Coordination, Masayuki Doi
Senior Managing Executive Officer Director and General Manager New Industry Development and Cross-function Business Unit, Yasuyuki Abe
Auditors: KPMGAZSA&Co.

LOCATIONS

HQ: Sumitomo Corp. (Japan)
1-8-11 Harumi, Chuo-ku, Tokyo 104-8610
Phone: (81) 3 5166 5000 **Fax:** (81) 3 5166 6203
Web: www.sumitomocorp.co.jp

PRODUCTS/OPERATIONS

2010 Sales by Segment

	% of total
Media Network & Lifestyle	21
Overseas Subsidiaries &	20
Transportation & Construction	17
Mineral Resources Energy Chemical &	13
General Products & Real	11
Metal	8
Domestic Regional Business Units &	4
New Industry Development &	3
Infrastructure	3
Total	**100**

Selected Subsidiaries

General Poducts & Real Estate
S.C. Cement Co. Lt.
TBC Corporation (US wholesale and retail tires)
Infrastructure
MobiCom Corporation (34% telecommunications in Mongolia)
Media Network & Lifestyle Retail
Jupiter Telecommunications Co. Ltd. (28%)
Montrive Corporation (luxury fabrics)
Metal Products
Asian Steel Company Ltd. (steel plates)
SC Pipe Services Inc. (US)
Mineral Resources Energy Chemical and Electronics
Cantex Inc. (pipes)
The Hartz Mountain Corporation (US pet products)
LNG Japan Corporation (50%)
Nusa Tenggara Mining Corporation (Indonesia 74%)
Sumisho Coal Australia Pty. Ltd.
Sumitronics Corporation (electronics)
New Industry Development and Cross-Function
Bluewell Corporation (insurance agency)
Overseas
Sumitomo Corporation Europe Holding Ltd.
Sumitomo Corporation of America
Transportation and Construction Systems
P.T. Summit Oto Finance (99.6% motorcycle financing)
Sumisho Mitsui Auto Service Company Limited (60%)

COMPETITORS

ITOCHU
Kanematsu
Komatsu
Marubeni
Mitsubishi Corp.
Mitsui
Samsung C&T America
Samsung Group
Sojitz
TOTAL

HISTORICAL FINANCIALS

Company Type: Public

Income Statement FYE: March 31

	REVENUE ($ mil.)	NET INCOME ($ mil.)	NET PROFIT MARGIN	EMPLOYEES
03/13	32,056	2,470	7.7%	73,953
03/12	39,753	3,055	7.7%	72,087
03/11	37,438	2,417	6.5%	64,886
03/10	30,797	1,770	5.7%	72,030
03/09	35,659	2,184	6.1%	91,729
Annual Growth	(2.6%)	3.1%	—	(5.2%)

2013 Year-End Financials

Debt ratio: 0.5%
Return on equity: 12.4%
Cash ($ mil.): 9,825
Current ratio: 1.63
Long-term debt ($ mil.): 33,645
No. of shares (mil.): 1,250
Dividends
Yield: 0.0%
Payout: 0.0%
Market value ($ mil.): 15,768

	STOCK PRICE ($) FY Close	P/E High/Low		PER SHARE ($) Earnings	Dividends	Book Value
03/13	12.61	0	0	1.97	0.00	17.45
03/12	14.52	0	0	2.44	0.00	16.47
03/11	14.33	0	0	1.93	0.36	15.17
03/10	11.53	0	0	1.42	0.26	13.13
03/09	8.70	0	—	1.75	0.38	10.99
Annual Growth	9.7%	—	—	3.1%	(87.9%)	12.2%

Sumitomo Electric Industries, Ltd. (Japan)

You might say that Sumitomo Electric Industries (SEI) produces the wide world of wire. The company which has more than 320 subsidiaries and affiliates around the globe is Japan's largest producer of wire and cable. SEI's automotive segment about half of sales makes automotive wiring harnesses wires wheel speed sensors and dash boards. Next in sales is the electric wire and cable division which makes power and industrial cables as well as magnetic and hybrid products. Other units produce optical fiber cables fiber-optic components industrial cables printed circuits ultrafine wire and semiconductors. SEI was formed in 1897 as Sumitomo Copper Rolling Works.

With nearly half the company's sales coming from the automotive segment SEI's 2009 books took a hit when the global recession eroded demand for autos and all the wiring and other components that go into them. A similar drop in demand for cell phones and other consumer electronics compounded the problem. The company also paid high prices for raw copper in 2008 and then saw the price for finished copper products plummet in 2009. Add a strong yen taking a bite out of export profits and it really got ugly. All told net income for fiscal 2009 dropped 84%.

SEI responded by cutting bonuses and other costs and reducing its Japanese workforce. It also acquired Fujitsu's 50% equity stake in Eudyna Devices making Eudyna a wholly owned subsidiary. The company's moves along with a gradual rebound in auto sales increased smart phone sales and growth across all sectors in China lead to improved results for 2010 and 2011 (a 11% sales growth). The improvements were tempered by weakened domestic demand due to The Great East Japan Earthquake and tsunami that hit the country in early 2011 as well as a higher yen that lead to decreased exports. SEI redoubled its overseas expansion (four new Asian plants) and cost cutting efforts to double operating income and improve net income by 250%.

Because of the number of SEI's customers moving to China the company is expanding its presence in that region. In mid-2010 it formed a joint venture with Chinese partner Nanjing Putian Telecommunications to manufacture fiber-optic equipment to connect Chinese consumers to fiber-optic networks. SEI is investing Y530 million ($5.72 million) in the venture.

HISTORY

Sumitomo Electric Industries as a part of the Sumitomo group business began nearly 400 years ago with the paired talents of spiritual founder Masatomo Sumitomo (who had received training as a Buddhist priest) and his disciple and brother-in-law Riemon Soga. Sumitomo wrote treatises on the conduct of commercial activity and Soga applied his technological skill in extracting silver from copper ore improving upon traditional Western methods and opened a copper business in Kyoto in 1590 that soon transformed the copper refining industry in Japan.

Soga's prosperous copper business became the founding company of the Sumitomo group. After Soga died in 1636 his son Tomomochi married Masatomo's daughter (entering into the Sumitomo family) and became the company's leader.

By the late 1600s the family was one of Japan's top copper producers. The house of Sumitomo entered several other businesses by the mid-1800s in order to insulate itself from waning copper production. The family established the Sumitomo Copper Rolling Works in 1897 to produce bare copper wire.

In 1909 production of cable for Japan's telecommunications industry began and in 1920 the family took their company public renaming it Sumitomo Electric Wire & Cable Works. The next year the company added high-carbon steel wire manufacturing. Its name changed to Sumitomo Electric Industries (SEI) in 1939.

The company began making rubber products for use in aircraft fuel tanks in 1943. The decade drew to a close with the addition of overhead transmission cable engineering operations.

SEI continued to move into new businesses in the 1960s. In 1960 SEI took a 25% stake in Sumitomo 3M a three-way joint venture with NEC (25%) and 3M (50%) to produce industrial cable in Japan. To capitalize on the boom in Japan's automobile and industrial equipment industries SEI introduced disc brakes to its lineup in 1963. Also SEI formally entered into management participation in Japan's Dunlop Tire Company which was then renamed Sumitomo Rubber Industries. (It had initially invested in the tire maker in 1960.)

SEI hit pay dirt with its automotive businesses producing brakes for manufacturers of passenger cars commercial vehicles motorcycles construction and industrial equipment and railcars. In the late 1960s SEI added traffic control systems.

With the introduction of compound semiconductors (used in wireless transmitters and electronic control devices) and cable television systems the 1970s brought SEI into the arena of value-added high-tech products. SEI began producing optical-fiber cable in 1974.

SEI expanded further into fiber optics when it introduced its first LAN in 1981 and set up its US-based Sumitomo Electric Lightwave unit in 1983.

In 1987 the company began producing antilock brakes (ABS) and invested $45 million in an evenly split ABS manufacturing US joint venture (Lucas

Sumitomo) with a unit of Lucas Varity. Lucas Varity was later bought by TRW and Sumitomo eventually acquired its remaining 50%. SEI closed out the 1980s by adding satellite navigation systems to its growing automobile product offerings.

The 1990s saw wider global expansion through more alliances and acquisitions. In 1990 SEI teamed up again with Lucas Varity to establish a joint venture in the UK to make automobile wiring harnesses. (SEI together with one of its own affiliates bought Lucas' half share in the company in 1999.) That year SEI through its Sumitomo Electric Wiring Systems unit formed AutoNeural Systems a joint venture with Ford-affiliated Visteon for automobile wiring harnesses.

In 2000 SEI set up ExceLight Communications (spun off from Sumitomo Electric Lightwave) to make optical components and subsystems for telecommunications cable TV and broadband equipment industries. The company restructured its electric power cable operations in early 2001 forming a manufacturing joint venture with Hitachi Cable and shutting one of its plants in Japan. Early the following year SEI acquired the Japan-based Calsonic Kansei Corporation's wiring harness business. SEI closed its electric furnaces in Japan and spun off its Sumitomo Steel Wire Corp. in late 2002. In early 2003 the company joined efforts with Hitachi Cable and Tatsuta Electric Wire & Cable to form Sumiden Hitachi Cable Ltd. a company that specialized in the manufacture of low-voltage power cables.

In 2006 the company acquired the former Volkswagen Bordnetze (now called Sumitomo Electric Bordnetze) a Germany-based manufacturer of wire harnesses from its previous joint owners Volkswagen and VDO Automotive.

Continuing to strengthen its European operations the company along with subsidiary Sumitomo Electric Sintered Alloy acquired Germany-based Cloyes Europe a sintered parts maker in 2007. SEI will use this acquisition to supply Japanese auto parts makers that have manufacturing facilities in Europe.

Also in 2007 as part of a group realignment SEI increased its ownership in Nissin Electric to more than 50% and it acquired affiliate Toyokuni Electric Cable. The acquisitions are part of the company's efforts to position itself as a global player.

EXECUTIVES

President and CEO, Masayoshi Matsumoto
EVP, Hiroyuki Takenaka
EVP, Fumikiyo Uchioke
Managing Director, Shigeru Noda
Senior Managing Director, Shigeru Tanaka
Managing Director, Atsushi Yano
Managing Executive Officer, Akito Kubo
Executive Officer, Masamichi Yokogawa
Executive Officer, Hisashi Takada
Senior Managing Director, Hideaki Inayama
Executive Officer, Makoto Tani
Senior Managing Director, Mitsuo Nishida
Managing Executive Officer, Seizo Takamuku
Managing Executive Officer, Masanori Yoshikai
Executive Officer, Fumiyoshi Kawai
Executive Officer, Yoshihiro Minato
Executive Officer, Naoyuki Yamabayashi
Executive Officer, Satoru Ogura
Managing Executive Officer; Chief Director of Special Cable Business, Hiroyasu Torii
Executive Officer, Jun Ito
Executive Officer; Deputy Chief Director of Automobile Business, Kazuhiko Hayashi
Executive Officer; Deputy Chief Director of Automobile Business, Kenichi Urushibata
Executive Officer; Deputy Chief Director of Advanced Material Business, Mamoru Moritani
Managing Executive Officer; Chief Director of Advanced Material Business, Nozomi Ushijima
Executive Officer; Deputy Chief Director of Electronics Business, Shigeo Saito
Managing Executive Officer; Chief Director of Network Sales, Shosuke Hongo
Executive Officer; Deputy Chief Director of Electric Wire & Machine Parts & Energy Business, Takahiro Nakano
Executive Officer; Deputy Chief Director of Production Technology, Takashi Yoshioka
Executive Officer; Deputy Chief Director of Optical Network Business, Yasushi Kida
Executive Officer; Deputy Chief Director of Production Technology, Yoshitomo Kasui
President CEO and Director, Masayoshi Matsumoto
Senior Managing Director, Toshihide Kimura
Managing Director, Akira Nishimura
Managing Director, Yuji Hamasaki
Managing Director, Atsushi Yano
Managing Director, Mitsuo Nishida
Auditors: KPMGAZSA&Co.

LOCATIONS

HQ: Sumitomo Electric Industries, Ltd. (Japan)
Sumitomo Bldg., 4-5-33 Kitahama, Chuo-ku, Osaka 541-0041
Phone: (81) 6 6220 4141 **Fax:** (81) 6 6222 3380
Web: www.sei.co.jp

2010 Sales

	% of total
Asia	
Japan	56
China and other Asian	22
Americas	12
Europe & other	10
Total	**100**

PRODUCTS/OPERATIONS

2010 Sales

	% of total
Automotive	47
Electric wire & cable	22
Information &	10
Electronics	8
Industrial materials &	13
Total	**100**

COMPETITORS

Alcatel-Lucent
American Superconductor
Amphenol
Asia Pacific Wire & Cable
Belden
CommScope
Corning
DENSO
Delphi Automotive Systems
Finisar
Fujikura Ltd.
Furukawa Electric
General Cable
Hitachi Cable
LEONI
Lear Corp
Magna International
Mitsubishi Electric
Nexans
OFS BrightWave
Robert Bosch
SWCC SHOWA
Southwire
Superior Essex
Tatung
Tokyo Rope Mfg.
Tyco
Valeo

HISTORICAL FINANCIALS

Company Type: Public

Income Statement FYE: March 31

	REVENUE ($ mil.)	NET INCOME ($ mil.)	NET PROFIT MARGIN	EMPLOYEES
03/13	22,955	403	1.8%	206,323
03/12	25,104	717	2.9%	194,734
03/11	24,561	852	3.5%	182,773
03/10	19,659	307	1.6%	157,203
03/09	21,548	175	0.8%	152,547
Annual Growth	1.6%	23.2%	—	7.8%

2013 Year-End Financials

Debt ratio: 0.2%
Return on equity: 3.6%
Cash ($ mil.): 1,834
Current ratio: 1.70
Long-term debt ($ mil.): 3,140
No. of shares (mil.): 793
Dividends
Yield: —
Payout: —
Market value ($ mil.): 93,790

	STOCK PRICE ($)	P/E	PER SHARE ($)		
	FY Close	High/Low	Earnings	Dividends	Book Value
03/13	118.25	— —	0.51	0.00	16.68
03/12	138.50	— —	0.90	0.00	17.51
03/11	132.75	— —	1.08	0.00	16.64
03/10	122.00	— —	0.39	1.54	14.37
03/09	74.25	— —	0.22	0.00	12.98
Annual Growth	12.3%	— —	23.8%	—	6.5%

Sumitomo Life Insurance Co. (Japan)

Sumitomo Life is one of Japan's biggest mutual life insurers (along with Nippon Life). The firm sells individual group life and specialized health policies through about 70 branch offices and 1500 district offices. Along with its sales force Sumitomo Life sells its products through a network of financial institutions and affiliates. It also administers pension and employee benefit plans and offers brokerage and consulting. The company has a total of some 7 million policyholders. Sumitomo Life which has operations in other Asian and North American countries is part of the Sumitomo Mitsui keiretsu –a group of firms linked by cross-ownership.

Geographic Reach

In addition to Japan Sumitomo Life has operations in China and the US.

Sales and Marketing

The company's principal selling channels are its sales force of 30000 representatives banks and a third party distribution channel formed through sales agreements with Japan Post Group. It also has some online and retail sales operations.

Strategy

As part of the company's push into Southeast Asia Sumitomo Life has agreed to buy a 40% stake in PT BNI Life Insurance the life insurance unit of Bank Negara Indonesia. The move valued at more than 4 trillion rupiah ($351 million) makes Sumitomo Life the second-largest shareholder in BNI Life.

Financial Performance

Sumitomo Life reported decreased revenues in fiscal 2012 through 2010 due to decreased new business. The decrease in 2012 was attributed to intentional decreased sales of new single-premium life insurance policies as well as lower levels of investment income.

EXECUTIVES

Chairman, Shinichi Yokoyama
President and CEO, Yoshio Sato
Senior Managing Executive Officer, Koichi Suzaki
Senior Managing Executive Officer, Haruo Urata
Senior Managing Executive Officer, Masahiro Hashimoto
President CEO and Director, Yoshio Sato
Senior Executive Officer and Director, Fumio Tokubutsu
Senior Executive Officer and Director, Ikunori Kato
Senior Executive Officer and Director, Norio Takamatsu
Managing Executive Officer and Director, Yutaka Amino
Senior Executive Officer and Director, Koichi Suzaki
Managing Executive Officer and Director, Haruo Urata
Managing Executive Officer and Director, Michihisa Tanimoto
Managing Executive Officer and Director, Masahiro Hashimoto
Director, Tsuguoki Fujinuma
Managing Executive Officer and Director, Yukio Noro
Managing Executive Officer and Director, Masaya Honjo
Director, Yosaku Fuji
Director, Hiroyuki Kamano
Auditors: KPMGAZSA&Co.

LOCATIONS

HQ: Sumitomo Life Insurance Co. (Japan)
1-4-35 Shiromi, Chuo-ku, Osaka 540-8512
Phone: (81) 6 6937 1435 **Fax:** 212 750-7930
Web: www.sumitomolife.co.jp

COMPETITORS

AIG
AXA
AXA Life Insurance
American Life Insurance
Asahi Mutual Life
Dai-ichi Life
Daido Life
Fukoku Mutual
Gibraltar Life Insurance
Meiji Yasuda Life
Mitsui Life
Nippon Life Insurance
T&D Holdings
Taiyo Life

HISTORICAL FINANCIALS

Company Type: Public

Income Statement FYE: March 31

	ASSETS ($ mil.)	NET INCOME ($ mil.)	INCOME AS % OF ASSETS	EMPLOYEES
03/13	282,347	1,146	0.4%	42,098
03/12	292,984	1,316	0.4%	42,953
03/11	286,871	1,315	0.5%	42,366
03/10	247,005	1,197	0.5%	45,281
03/09	230,175	1,058	0.5%	44,546
Annual Growth	5.2%	2.0%	—	(1.4%)

2013 Year-End Financials

Return on assets: 0.4%
Return on equity: 10.2%
Long-term debt ($ mil.): —
No. of shares (mil.): —
Sales ($ mil): 45,886
Dividends
Yield: —
Payout: —
Market value ($ mil.): —

Sumitomo Mitsui Financial Group Inc Tokyo

Sumitomo Mitsui Financial Group (SMFG) is the holding company for Sumitomo Mitsui Banking which is one of Japan's largest banks (along with Mitsubishi UFJ and Mizuho). The bank's operations include retail corporate and investment banking; asset management; securities trading; and lending. Sumitomo Mitsui Banking has some 500 domestic branches and another 20 branches abroad. Other units of SMFG include credit card company Sumitomo Mitsui Card brokerage SMBC Friend Securities management consulting firm Japan Research Institute and Sumitomo Mitsui Finance and Leasing. In the US it operates the California-based Manufacturers Bank. SMFG listed its shares on the NYSE in late 2010.

The NYSE listing was timed to help SMFG in its efforts to become a leading global financial group. The group operates in more than 50 countries; its targeted areas of growth include Asia/Pacific nations with emerging and developing economies (such as Korea Taiwan Singapore and Thailand). It is also establishing trading and securities offices in the US and the UK.

The company has also been aggressively pursuing opportunities in the financing industry. In 2009 it combined three of its credit card units –OMC Card Central Finance and QUOQ –into one Cedyna Financial to operate along with Sumitomo Mitsui Card. The move cuts overhead costs helping SMFG meet its goal of becoming the nation's largest credit card company. Also that year it acquired a 51% stake in Orix Credit Corporation a consumer lending unit of ORIX. In late 2011 its auto service unit bought a 49% stake of Hitachi subsidiary Hitachi Capital Auto Lease.

SMFG acquired Nikko Cordial Securities and other assets of Nikko Citi Holdings in Japan from Citigroup in another 2009 deal. On the heels of that deal SMFG and Daiwa Securities Group terminated their Daiwa Securities SMBC joint venture. Citing differences of opinion in strategy SMFG sold its 40% stake in the investment bank. The following year SMFG and Daiwa dismantled their Daiwa SB Investments asset management venture. The two companies remain open to possible future partnerships.

EXECUTIVES

Chairman Sumitomo Mitsui Banking Corporation, Teisuke Kitayama
Chairman, Masayuki Oku, age 69
Head of Corporate Banking Unit International Banking Unit Global Advisory Department Sumitomo Mitsui Banking Corporation, Yoshinori Kawamura
Director; President Sumitomo Mitsui Banking, Takeshi Kunibe
Director; Senior Managing Director Human Resources Dept. Human Resources Development Dept. Quality Management Dept. General Affairs Dept. Legal Dept. and Administrative Services Dept. Sumitomo Mitsui Banking Corporation, Junsuke Fujii
Senior Managing Director IT Planning; Senior Managing Director IT Planning Dept. IT Business Promotion Dept. Operations Planning Dept. and Operations Support Dept. Sumitomo Mitsui Banking Corporation, Hideo Shimada
Senior Managing Director Investment Banking Planning; Senior Managing Director Sumitomo Mitsui Banking Corporation, Tetsuya Kubo
Senior Managing Director Consumer Planning Department; Senior Managing Director Consumer Banking Unit Sumitomo Mitsui Banking Corporation, Satoru Nakanishi
Corporate Auditor, Yoji Yamaguchi
Corporate Auditor Sumitomo Mitsui Financial Group and Sumitomo Mitsui Banking Corporation, Ikuo Uno
President, Koichi Miyata
Director, Ken Kubo
Director, Yujiro Ito
Managing Director, Jun Ohta
Managing Director, Yasuyuki Kawasaki
Managing Director, Fumiaki Kurahara
Director, Yoshinori Yokoyama, age 71
Director, Hiroki Nishio
Director, Yoshiaki Yamauchi, age 75
Director, Yoichiro Yamakawa
Deputy President Corporate Risk Management and Director Sumitomo Mitsui Financial Group and Sumitomo Mitsui Banking Corporation, Wataru Ohara
Senior Managing Director IT Planning; Senior Managing Director IT Planning Dept. IT Business Promotion Dept. Operations Planning Dept. and Operations Support Dept. Sumitomo Mitsui Banking Corporation, Hideo Shimada
Senior Managing Director Investment Banking Planning; Senior Managing Director Sumitomo Mitsui Banking Corporation, Tetsuya Kubo
Senior Managing Director Audit Department, Fumihiko Tanizawa
Senior Managing Director Consumer Planning Department; Senior Managing Director Consumer Banking Unit Sumitomo Mitsui Banking Corporation, Satoru Nakanishi
Managing Director Card Business Department; Managing Director Sumitomo Mitsui Banking Corporation; President SMFG Card and Credit, Kazuya Jono
Auditors: KPMGAZSA&Co.

LOCATIONS

HQ: Sumitomo Mitsui Financial Group Inc Tokyo
1-1-2 Marunouchi, Chiyoda-ku, Tokyo 100-0005
Phone: (81) 3 3282 8111
Web: www.smfg.co.jp

PRODUCTS/OPERATIONS

2011 Sales

	% of total
Interest	
Loans &	46
Investment	5
Other	1
Noninterest	
Fees &	24
Trading	10
Other	14
Total	**100**

COMPETITORS

Bank of Yokohama
Chuo Mitsui Trust
Citigroup
Credit Saison
Mitsubishi UFJ Financial Group
Mizuho Financial
Norinchukin Bank
Resona
Shinsei Bank

HISTORICAL FINANCIALS

Company Type: Public

Income Statement FYE: March 31

	ASSETS ($ mil.)	NET INCOME ($ mil.)	INCOME AS % OF ASSETS	EMPLOYEES
03/13	1,580,333	8,439	0.5%	64,635
03/12	1,743,755	6,321	0.4%	64,225
03/11	1,664,157	5,747	0.3%	61,555
03/10	1,318,519	2,907	0.2%	57,888
03/09	1,214,899	(3,792)	—	48,079
Annual Growth	6.8%	—	—	7.7%

2013 Year-End Financials

Return on assets: 0.5%
Return on equity: 13.7%
Long-term debt ($ mil.): —
No. of shares (mil.): 1,353
Sales ($ mil): 45,984
Dividends
Yield: —
Payout: —
Market value ($ mil.): 11,048

	STOCK PRICE ($) FY Close	P/E High/Low		PER SHARE ($) Earnings	Dividends	Book Value
03/13	8.16	—	—	6.23	0.00	66.28
03/12	6.64	—	—	4.56	0.00	65.46
03/11	6.25	—	—	4.07	0.00	62.35
03/10	3.25	—	—	2.61	0.00	53.65
03/09	3.48	—	—	(5.05)	0.00	60.90
Annual Growth	23.7%	—	—	—	—	2.1%

Sumitomo Mitsui Trust Holdings Inc

Chuo Mitsui Trust Holdings entailed Chuo Mitsui Trust and Banking Company (retail trust banking real estate and stock transfer services) and Chuo Mitsui Asset and Banking Company (pension and securities trusts) which also owned investment trust and private equity managers Chuo Mitsui Asset Management and Chuo Mitsui Capital. The group had units in the US the UK Singapore the Cayman Islands and China. Chuo Mitsui Trust Holdings and Sumitomo Trust and Banking merged in 2012 to form Sumitomo Mitsui Trust Bank one of Japan's largest asset management groups. The two firms had previously discussed a merger in 2001 and again in 2005.

HISTORY

Before world markets were rocked by the shock waves of the US real estate and financial markets crash CMHD received about Y430 billion ($4.4 billion) in government support. The company had been making steady payments since 2006 and planned to pay the remaining Y200 before the August 2009 deadline for the conversion of the government's preferred shares into ordinary shares. But mid-year the bank along with several of its Japanese mid-level peers announced it would be unable to meet the goal due to poor earnings.

Once the crisis passes the company's strategy includes a focus on real estate lending long a mainstay of business and improving its position in the investment trust and real estate investing markets.

EXECUTIVES

Chairman, Hitoshi Tsunekage, age 59
Managing Executive Officer and Director, Shinji Ochiai, age 58
Managing Executive Officer and Director, Tetsuo Ohkubo, age 57
President and Representative Director, Kazuo Tanabe
Director, Jun Okuno, age 62
Deputy President and Representative Director, Kiyoshi Mukohara, age 60
Senior Managing Executive Officer and Director, Nobuo Iwasaki, age 57
Managing Executive Officer and Director, Junichi Sayato, age 57
Deputy President and Representative Director, Kunitaro Kitamura, age 60
Managing Executive Officer and Director, Shinji Ochiai, age 58
Managing Executive Officer and Director, Tetsuo Ohkubo, age 57
Auditors: DeloitteToucheTohmatsu

LOCATIONS

HQ: Sumitomo Mitsui Trust Holdings Inc
1-4-1 Marunouchi, Chiyoda-ku, Tokyo 100-6611
Phone: (81) 3 6256 6000
Web: www.smth.jp

COMPETITORS

Aozora Bank
Mitsubishi UFJ Financial Group
Mizuho Trust & Banking Ltd
Resona
Sumitomo Trust and Banking

HISTORICAL FINANCIALS

Company Type: Public

Income Statement FYE: March 31

	ASSETS ($ mil.)	NET INCOME ($ mil.)	INCOME AS % OF ASSETS	EMPLOYEES
03/13	400,714	1,421	0.4%	20,189
03/12	419,068	2,007	0.5%	20,305
03/11	171,859	570	0.3%	8,846
03/10	160,350	501	0.3%	8,872
03/09	153,200	(934)	—	8,828
Annual Growth	27.2%	—	—	23.0%

2013 Year-End Financials

Return on assets: 0.3%
Return on equity: 7.2%
Long-term debt ($ mil.): —
No. of shares (mil.): —
Sales ($ mil): 11,920
Dividends
Yield: —
Payout: —
Market value ($ mil.): —

	STOCK PRICE ($) FY Close	P/E High/Low		PER SHARE ($) Earnings	Dividends	Book Value
03/13	4.67	—	—	0.33	0.00	6.72
03/12	3.14	—	—	0.47	0.00	6.86
Annual Growth	48.8%	—	—	(8.3%)	—	(0.5%)

Sun Life Financial Inc

Sun Life tries to stay on the sunny side of life and life insurance. The company offers insurance and wealth management products to individuals and business entities primarily in Canada and the US. It also has operations in Asia Europe and the UK. Sun Life's products include individual and group life and health insurance individual annuities group pensions mutual funds and asset management services. The US subsidiaries include Massachusetts Financial Services (or MFS Investment Management). Sun Life's products and services are distributed through direct and independent sales agents as well as banks and consultants.

In its home market Sun Life is a key player in individual life insurance employee benefits products as well as mutual funds. Its Asian operations are focused on the growing middle class customers in China India and the Philippines.

Having developed an allergy to equity volatility and low interest rates in late 2011 the company decided to reduce its exposure in its US operations. It announced that it would quit selling variable annuities and individual life insurance products in the US and instead is choosing to focus on its employee benefits and voluntary benefits business. Sun Life had already quit selling plain vanilla universal life insurance products in the US citing their status as commodities with low margins. In late 2012 it agreed to sell its US annuity business to Delaware Life Holdings for some $1.35 billion.

In the wake of the global financial crisis Sun Life has steadily adjusted its goals and worked to "de-risk" its products. It made an effort to build up its sales to individual customers in Canada tightened up its distribution system and expanded direct sales channels in Asia including China and its joint venture in India. To perk up its branding the company purchased the naming rights to the sports stadium in Miami and rolled out fresh ad campaigns in key markets.

The company is slowly regaining its acquisition groove after the financial crisis. It paid some C$359 million to buy up Lincoln National (UK) from Lincoln National in 2009. It merged the business with its existing UK operations doubling the number of policies the company holds there. In 2011 it agreed to acquire 49% of Grepalife Financials a bancassurance insurance provider in the Philippines for an undisclosed sum.

Sun Life demutualized in 2000 and the money it raised as a publicly traded company helped finance growth. During the first ten years of its public status it grew through a steady pace of acquisitions beginning with its buy of Clarica Life in 2002. Clarica's products were later rebranded with the Sun Life name. International acquisitions have included Genworth's US employee benefits group (2007) and insurance and pension operations in Hong Kong from Commonwealth Bank of Australia (2005).

Sun Life has disposed of businesses including the 2008 sale of Sun Life Retirement Services unit a US business that provided 401k administrative services to Hartford Financial Services. At the close of 2010 the company sold off its life reinsurance business to Berkshire Hathaway for an undisclosed sum. Proceeds from the asset sale were earmarked to fund growth efforts in other business areas.

After selling off a minority ownership in a Canadian mutual fund provider in 2008 Sun Life did an about-face and reentered the Canadian mutual fund market in 2010 by forming a new standalone mutual fund company: Sun Life Global Investments (Canada). Sun Life launched the new company and a family of funds in 2010 sold through Sun Life Financial advisers. The new funds came from the company's MFS affiliate in the US McLean Budden in Canada and Biria Sun Life Asset Management in India.

EXECUTIVES

EVP Corporate Development and General Counsel, Thomas A. Bogart
President Sun Life Financial US, Westley V. (Wes) Thompson, age 59

Senior Managing Director and Head of North American Private Fixed Income, Thomas J. Robinson
Chairman, James H. (Jim) Sutcliffe, age 56
SVP Group Retirement Services Sun Life Financial Canada, Thomas G. Reid
SVP and General Manager Individual Insurance Sun Life Financial U.S. and International, Janet V. Whitehouse
President Sun Life Financial Canada and Sun Life Global Investments, Kevin P. Dougherty, $1,019 total compensation
SVP and Chief Credit Risk Officer, Candace G. Shaw
Chairman and CEO MFS Investment Management Sun Life Global Investments, Robert J. (Rob) Manning
EVP and CFO, Colm J. Freyne, $318,598 total compensation
SVP and General Counsel Sun Life Financial Canada, William R. Minucci
EVP Actuarial and Risk Management, Claude A. Accum
Vice-President Human Resources, Sean N. Woodroffe
EVP and Chief Investment Officer, Stephen C. Peacher, $106,187 total compensation
SVP Client Solutions Sun Life Financial Canada, Brigitte Parent
SVP and General Counsel Sun Life Financial US and International, Scott M. Davis
Chairman and CEO MFS McLean Budden Limited Sun Life Global Investments, Martin E. (Marty) Beaulieu
President CEO and Director, Dean A. Connor, $538,354 total compensation
SVP Individual Insurance and Investments Sun Life Financial Canada, Kevin D. Strain
SVP and CFO Sun Life Financial Canada, Paul O. Petrelli
Media Contact Philippines, Mariquit Lintag
SVP Tax, Michael J. O'Connor
VP Human Resources Sun Life Financial Canada, Sandra L. Delamere
SVP Operations Sun Life Financial Canada, Jim Giesinger
SVP Group Benefits Sun Life Financial Canada, Stuart Monteith
Head of Human Resources Sun Life Financial Asia, Michelle Li
President Sun Life Global Investments (Canada), Rick Headrick
VP Investor Relations, Philip G. (Phil) Malek
EVP and CIO, Mark S. Saunders
SVP Enterprise Infrastructure and CTO, Stevan Lewis
VP Corporate Communications, Frank T. Switzer
SVP Application Services, Philip Armstrong
President Sun Life Financial Quebec, Isabelle Hudon
VP Associate General Counsel and Corporate Secretary, Dana J. Easthope
VP Voluntary Benefits Sun Life Financial U.S. and International, Robert E. Klein
Media Contact Canada, Andrea Zviedris
Media Contact United Kingdom, James Terry
Executive Vice-President Human Resources, Carolyn Blair
Executive Vice President; Chief Marketing Officer and Public & Corporate Affairs, Mary Paoli
Director, Mitchell M. (Mitch) Merin, age 60
Director, William D. (Bill) Anderson, age 64
Director, Jon A. Boscia, age 59
Director, David W. Kerr, age 70
Director, Hugh D. Segal, age 62
Director, Martin J. G. Glynn, age 61
Director, Prof Idalene F. (Idie) Kesner, age 56
Director, David A. Ganong, age 70
Director, Krystyna T. Hoeg, age 63
Director, Bertin F. Nadeau, age 71
President CEO and Director, Dean A. Connor
Director, John H. Clappison, age 67
Independent Director, Richard Booth
Auditors: Deloitte&ToucheLLP

LOCATIONS

HQ: Sun Life Financial Inc
150 King Street West, Toronto, Ontario M5H 1J9
Phone: 416 979-9966 **Fax:** 416 979-3209
Web: www.sunlife.com

PRODUCTS/OPERATIONS

2010 Revenues

Premiums		
Health insurance	18	
Net investment income	32	
Total	**0**	**100**

2010 Revenues

	% of total
SLF	46
SLF	33
SLF	7
MFS	6
Corporate	8
Total	**100**

COMPETITORS

AGF Management
AIA Group
Aviva
Canada Life
China Life Insurance
Fairfax Financial Holdings
Great-West Life Assurance
Great-West Lifeco
Industrial Alliance Insurance and Financial Servic
Manulife Financial
MetLife
Prudential
Standard Life
The Hartford

HISTORICAL FINANCIALS

Company Type: Public

Income Statement FYE: December 31

	ASSETS ($ mil.)	NET INCOME ($ mil.)	INCOME AS % OF ASSETS	EMPLOYEES
12/12	227,013	4,627	2.0%	14,880
12/11	213,730	(196)	—	15,000
12/10*	210,695	1,502	0.7%	14,755
01/10	192,293	0	—	0
12/09	114,538	593	0.5%	14,500
Annual Growth	25.6%	98.3%	—	0.9%

*Fiscal year change

2012 Year-End Financials

Return on assets: 2.0%
Return on equity: 28.2%
Long-term debt ($ mil.): —
No. of shares (mil.): 587
Sales ($ mil): 17,654
Dividends
Yield: 5.4%
Payout: 55.3%
Market value ($ mil.): 15,594

	STOCK PRICE ($) FY Close	P/E High/Low		PER SHARE ($) Earnings	Dividends	Book Value
12/12	26.53	11	7	2.60	1.44	28.65
12/11	18.52	—	—	(0.51)	1.41	26.23
12/10*	30.10	13	9	2.40	1.39	28.02
01/10	28.72	—	—	(0.00)	1.37	(0.00)
12/09	28.72	33	9	0.90	1.28	29.43
Annual Growth	(2.0%)	—	—	42.7%	3.9%	(0.9%)

*Fiscal year change

Suncor Energy Inc.

Suncor Energy takes a shine to the cold of Canada. That country's largest energy company explores for processes and markets oil and natural gas. In 2012 it reported net proved and probable reserves of 1.8 billion barrels of synthetic oil 163 million barrels of bitumen 159 million barrels of oil and 619 billion cu. ft. of natural gas. Suncor Energy was first company to produce commercial crude oil from Canada's Athabasca oil sands. It also holds 12% of Syncrude. Its Sunoco unit refines crude oil and processes and distributes fuels petrochemicals and heating oils and invests in renewable energy. Suncor Energy also operates a nationwide network of gas stations primarily under the Petro-Canada brand.

Geographic Reach

The company has operations in Canada Germany Libya the Netherlands Norway Syria the UK and the US. In 2012 Canada accounted for 79% of Suncor Energy's revenues.

Operations

Suncor Energy is one of Canada's largest oil sands producers. It oil sands assets include a 36% interest in the Joslyn North mine 41% in the Fort Hills mine and 51% of the Voyageur upgrader project as well as a 12% stake in the Syncrude oil sands mining venture.

The company also has conventional natural gas assets as well as international and offshore oil exploration and production holdings. In addition to its production refining and marketing operations across Canada (and in Colorado) the company has exploration assets in Libya Norway Syria and the UK. (In 2011 Suncor Energy suspended its operations in Syria in light of international sanctions imposed against that country).

The company has four refineries (in Alberta Ontario Quebec and Colorado —460000 barrels of combined capacity per day) and a network of 1460 Petro-Canada retail gas stations.

To meet clean air regulations the company is also investing in green energy. It has six wind power projects (255 MW) and operates Canada's largest biofuel plant (412 million liters of ethanol per day) at St.Clair Ontario.

Financial Performance

Suncor Energy's revenues declined by $176 million in 2012 as a result of lower product stemming from planned off-station maintenance programs at Terra Nova and related delays in get back online planned maintenance at White Rose oilfield in Nova Scotia the suspension of oil and gas operations in Syria and declines in production from the North America Onshore segment. These factors were partially offset by the resumption of operations in Libya. Oil Sands oil prices declined in 2012 due primarily to lower premiums for sweet crude oil and wider light/heavy differentials that impacted prices for sour crude oil and bitumen.The company reported a $35% drop in net income in 2012 due to lower reveneus and an increase in operating expenses.

Strategy

Oil sands which hold deposits of heavy bitumen make up nearly a third of Canada's oil production and Suncor Engery's long term business focus is developing synthetic oil from its oil sands holdings in Alberta. Suncor Energy plans to produce 1 million barrels per day of oil equivalent from its oil sands holdings by 2020.

To focus on its growth markets and to pay down debt in 2013 the company agreed to sell its conventional natural gas business in Western Canada to a Centrica and Qatar Petroleum partnership for $1 billion.

Company Background

To further develop its oil sands assets in 2010 the company formed a strategic alliance with TOTAL. As part of the deal France-based TOTAL paid Suncor Energy about $1.7 billion to acquire 19% of Suncor Energy's 60% interest in the Fort Hills mining project and a 49% stake in the Voyageur Upgrader project near Fort McMurray. Suncor Energy acquired about 37 % of total's stake in the Joslyn project.

Boosting its profile as an integrated energy company in 2009 the company acquired Petro-Canada in a $15 billion deal. The acquisition created an energy behemoth with extensive holdings in oil sands solid conventional exploration and production assets and a major refining and retailing network. Following the Petro-Canada deal the company divested about $1.5 billion of non-core assets in Western Canada the US Trinidad and Tobago and the North Sea. In 2010 Suncor Energy sold its North Sea exploration assets (of Petro Canada Netherlands) to Dana Petroleum for $393 million. Later that year it sold a pair of natural gas properties in Alberta to a subsidiary of Abu Dhabi National Energy Company for $285 million. It also sold its Wildcat Hills assets which produce some 80 million cu. ft. of natural gas per day to Direct Energy for about $360 million.

EXECUTIVES

Senior Vice President General Counsel Corporate Secretary, Janice B. Odegaard
CEO and Director, Richard L. (Rick) George, age 61, $1,115,708 total compensation
Executive Vice President - Refining and Marketing, Boris J. Jackman, $711,926 total compensation
Chairman, John T. Ferguson, age 72
President; Chief Executive Officer; Non-independent Director, Steven W. (Steve) Williams, $698,514 total compensation
SVP Exploration and Production, Francois Langlois
CFO, Bart W. Demosky, $288,472 total compensation
Executive Vice President - Oil Sands Ventures, Steve D. L. Reynish
Executive Vice President - Major Projects, Mike MacSween
EVP Oil Sands and In Situ, Mark Little
Executive Vice President - Business Services, Eric Axford
SVP Human Resources, Paul Gardner
SVP Supply Trading and Corporate Development, Kris Smith
Director, John R. Huff, age 67
Director, Eira M. Thomas, age 45
Director, Michael W. (Mike) O'Brien, age 69
CEO and Director, Richard L. (Rick) George, age 61
Director, Dominic D'Alessandro, age 65
Director, Mel E. Benson, age 65
Director, W. Douglas (Doug) Ford, age 69
President COO and Director, Steven W. (Steve) Williams
Director, Maureen McCaw, age 59
Director, James W. (Jim) Simpson, age 69
Independent Director, Dominic Alessandro
Independent Director, Michael Brien
Auditors: PricewaterhouseCoopersLLP

LOCATIONS

HQ: Suncor Energy Inc.
150 - 6th Avenue S.W., Calgary, Alberta T2P 3E3
Phone:
Web: www.suncor.com

2012 Sales

	% of total
Canada	79
Other	21
Total	**100**

PRODUCTS/OPERATIONS

2012 Sales

Refining & marketing	63
Exploration & production	11

COMPETITORS

Anadarko Petroleum	Husky Energy
BP NGL	Imperial Oil
Canadian Natural	Murphy Oil
Devon Energy	Nordex
Dominion Resources	Shell Canada
Encana	Talisman Energy

HISTORICAL FINANCIALS

Company Type: Public

Income Statement FYE: December 31

	REVENUE ($ mil.)	NET INCOME ($ mil.)	NET PROFIT MARGIN	EMPLOYEES
12/12	38,826	2,798	7.2%	13,932
12/11	39,005	4,219	10.8%	13,026
12/10*	32,673	3,837	11.7%	12,076
01/10	0	0	—	0
12/09	24,303	1,093	4.5%	12,978
Annual Growth	16.9%	36.8%	—	2.4%

*Fiscal year change

2012 Year-End Financials

Debt ratio: 14.5%
Return on equity: 7.1%
Cash ($ mil.): 4,416
Current ratio: 1.48
Long-term debt ($ mil.): 9,992
No. of shares (mil.): 1,523
Dividends
Yield: 1.5%
Payout: 27.7%
Market value ($ mil.): 50,230

	STOCK PRICE ($) FY Close	P/E High/Low		PER SHARE ($) Earnings	Dividends	Book Value
12/12	32.98	21	14	1.80	0.50	25.89
12/11	28.83	18	8	2.62	0.42	24.28
12/10*	38.29	16	11	2.44	0.38	22.53
01/10	35.31	—	—	(0.00)	0.19	(0.00)
12/09	35.31	38	14	0.91	0.18	20.86
Annual Growth	(1.7%)	—	—	25.7%	39.3%	7.5%

*Fiscal year change

Suncorp Group Ltd.

Suncorp-Metway (aka Suncorp Group) wants to be a rising star in Australia's insurance and banking sectors. The group owns Suncorp Insurance which operates one of the country's largest general insurance companies as well as a small but growing life insurance and wealth management business. The general insurance business sells personal and commercial property/casualty insurance under its Suncorp AAMI GIO Vero and Shannons brands. In addition to its insurance business Suncorp also runs Suncorp Bank an operator of some 170 branches in eastern Australia. Among other products the bank offers personal and commercial banking accounts financial planning and loans to consumers and small to midsized businesses.

The year 2010 marked significant changes for Suncorp-Metway which proposed to rework its corporate structure by organizing its general insurance life insurance and banking business under a new non-operating entity Suncorp Group Ltd. Suncorp-Metway is looking to restructure in order to in part facilitate simpler acquisitions divestitures and other corporate transactions. The company is also responding to its ever-growing insurance business which has in recent years grown larger than its banking business. Under its current structure Suncorp-Metway also doubles as the group's banking operations; a reorganization would allow it to update its ownership structure to reflect the larger insurance business.

In 2010 Suncorp-Metway also whittled down its life insurance and wealth management business (which operate under the same division) after selling funds management subsidiary Tyndall Investments to Japanese firm Nikko Asset Management. The sale –part of the company's restructuring effort –served to refocus the company's life insurance division on insurance by scaling back its wealth management offerings.

EXECUTIVES

CEO and Director, Patrick Snowball, age 62
Chairman, John D. Story, age 66
Group Executive Banking, David Foster
Group Executive Personal Insurance, Mark Milliner
CEO and Director, Patrick Snowball, age 62
Auditors: KPMG

LOCATIONS

HQ: Suncorp Group Ltd.
Level 18 Suncorp Centre, 36 Wickham Terrace, Brisbane, Queensland 4000
Phone: (61) 7 3362 1222 **Fax:** (61) 7 3135 2940
Web: www.suncorpgroup.com.au

PRODUCTS/OPERATIONS

2010 Sales

	% of total
General Insurance	
Personal	31
Commercial	24
Banking	28
Life and Wealth	13
New Zealand General	4
Total	**100**

Selected Subsidiaries

Asteron Group Ltd. (life insurance)
GIO General Ltd (general insurance products)
Suncorp Life & Superannuation Limited life (insurance products)
Suncorp Metway Insurance Ltd (general insurance products)
Suncorp Metway Investment Management Limited (investment schemes and provides investment management services)
Vero Insurance Ltd. (New Zealand general insurance)

COMPETITORS

AMP Limited	Insurance Australia
AXA Asia Pacific	Macquarie Group
Australia and New Zealand Banking	National Australia Bank
Commonwealth Bank of Australia	Westpac Banking

HISTORICAL FINANCIALS

Company Type: Public

Income Statement FYE: June 30

	ASSETS ($ mil.)	NET INCOME ($ mil.)	INCOME AS % OF ASSETS	EMPLOYEES
06/13	88,481	452	0.5%	0
06/12	97,829	737	0.8%	0
06/11	102,355	485	0.5%	0
06/10	81,266	664	0.8%	0
06/09	79,405	283	0.4%	0
Annual Growth	2.7%	12.4%	—	—

2013 Year-End Financials

Return on assets: 0.5%
Return on equity: 3.5%
Long-term debt ($ mil.): —
No. of shares (mil.): 1,286
Sales ($ mil): 14,929

Dividends
Yield: 0.0%
Payout: 160.2%
Market value ($ mil.): 13,972

	STOCK PRICE ($) FY Close	P/E High/Low		PER SHARE ($) Earnings	Dividends	Book Value
06/13	10.86	33	20	0.35	0.57	10.01
06/12	8.29	18	12	0.57	0.39	11.17
06/11	7.97	27	18	0.38	0.32	11.66
06/10	7.07	10	7	0.51	0.10	9.27
Annual Growth	15.4%	—	—	(8.8%)	55.8%	2.0%

Suzuki Motor Corp. (Japan)

Suzuki Motor Corporation is a leading Japanese carmaker and a global motorcycle manufacturer competing head-to-head with rivals Honda and Yamaha. Suzuki's passenger car models include the Alto Grand Vitara Swift Splash and SX4. Its motorcycle products include cruiser motocross offroad scooter street and touring models as well as ATVs. Suzuki Motor's non-vehicle products include outboard motors for boats and motorized wheelchairs. It builds its lineup on its own and through numerous subsidiaries and joint ventures overseas. Japan accounts for nearly 45% of sales. Suzuki entered the US car market in 1985 with the Samurai the country' first compact SUV.

Geographic Reach

The company has man production facilities in 22 countries and serves more than 200 countries. Outside of Japan (around 45% of its total sales) Asian consumers represent nearly 35% of its sales whereas North American and European purchases combined account for nearly 15%. Suzuki subsidiary Maruti Suzuki India is India's largest passenger car company.

Operations

Suzuki divides its operations into four reportable segments. The Automobile segment generated 88% of the company's total sales for 2012 while its motorcycle operations accounted for 10%. The other segments –marine and power products; and financial services –accounted for the remaining 2%.

Financial Performance

Suzuki's balance sheet has been up and down over the years. After posting increases in both revenue and net income in 2011 the company saw its revenues decrease by 4% in 2012. The lower revenue was attributed to a 1% decrease in its motorcycle segment and a 4% dip in its automobile segment. The company however did recognize a 19% increase in its net income for 2012 due to lower expenses related to sales marketing and promotions.

Strategy

Suzuki is expanding its vehicle lineup in China through Suzuki China which imports and sells Japanese-made cars. The company imports and exports Suzuki-brand vehicles through Suzuki Automobile (Thailand) a joint venture with Siam International Corp. Demand in Vietnam the Philippines and Malaysia has continued to grow modestly too.

In 2012 Suzuki began construction of a new motorcycle plant in Rohtak Haryana of India and a second plant through Chongqing Changan Suzuki Automobile Co. Ltd. (Changan Suzuki) an automobile manufacturing and sales joint venture company in China. The Indian motorcycle market in 2011 exceeded 13 million units and Suzuki expects continuous growth in the region. To capitalize on the expanding Chinese automobile market and to establish an annual capacity of 500000 units Suzuki has decided to construct its second plant in the area next to its current plant.

HISTORY

In 1909 Michio Suzuki started Suzuki Loom Works in Hamamatsu Japan. The company went public in 1920 and continued producing weaving equipment until the onset of WWII when it began to make war-related products.

Suzuki began developing inexpensive motor vehicles in 1947 and in 1952 it introduced a 36cc engine to motorize bicycles. The company changed its name to Suzuki Motor and launched its first motorcycle in 1954. Suzuki's entry into the minicar market came in 1955 with the Suzulight followed by the Suzumoped (1958) a delivery van (1959) and the Suzulight Carry FB small truck (1961).

Suzuki's triumph in the 1962 50cc-class Isle of Man TT motorcycle race started a string of racing successes that brought international prominence to the Suzuki name. The company established its first overseas plant in Thailand in 1967.

In the 1970s Suzuki met market demand for motorcycles with large engines. Meanwhile a mid-1970s recession and falling demand for low-powered cars in Japan led the minicar industry there to produce two-thirds fewer minicars in 1974 than in 1970. Suzuki responded by pushing overseas beginning auto exports and expanding foreign distribution. In 1975 it started producing motorcycles in Taiwan Thailand and Indonesia.

Suzuki boosted capacity internationally throughout the 1980s through joint ventures. Motorcycle sales in Japan peaked in 1982 then tapered off but enjoyed a modest rebound in the late 1980s. In 1988 the company agreed to handle distribution of Peugeot cars in Japan.

Suzuki and General Motors began their longstanding relationship in 1981 when GM bought a small stake in Suzuki. The company began producing Swift subcompacts in 1983 and sold them through GM as the Chevy Sprint and later the Geo Metro. In 1986 Suzuki and GM of Canada jointly formed CAMI Automotive to produce vehicles including Sprints Metros and Geo Trackers (Suzuki Sidekicks) in Ontario; production began in 1989.

Although sales via GM increased through 1990 US efforts with the Suzuki nameplate faltered shortly after Suzuki formed its US subsidiary in Brea California in 1986. A 1988 "Consumer Reports" claim that the company's Samurai SUV was prone to rolling over devastated US sales. The next year Suzuki's top US executives quit apparently questioning the company's commitment to the US market.

Suzuki established Magyar Suzuki a joint venture with Hungarian automaker Autokonszern Rt. C. Itoh & Co. and International Finance Corporation in 1991 to begin producing the Swift sedan in Hungary. The company expanded a licensing agreement with a Chinese government partner in 1993 becoming the first Japanese company to take an equity stake in a Chinese carmaking venture. The next year Suzuki introduced the Alto van Japan's cheapest car at just over $5000 and the Wagon R miniwagon which quickly became one of Japan's top-selling vehicles.

In a case that was later overturned a woman was awarded $90 million from Suzuki after being paralyzed in a Samurai rollover in 1990. The company sued Consumers Union publisher of "Consumer Reports" in 1996 charging it had intended to fix the results in the 1988 Samurai testing.

GM raised its 3% stake in Suzuki to 10% in 1998. The company teamed up with GM and Fuji Heavy Industries (Subaru) in 2000 to develop compact cars for the European market. It was also announced that GM would spend about $600 million to double its stake in Suzuki to 20%. In 2001 Suzuki announced that it had agreed to cooperate with Kawasaki in the development of new motorcycles scooters and ATVs.

The following year Suzuki agreed to take control of Maruti Udyog Ltd. the state-owned India-based car manufacturer in an $80 million rights issue deal.

GM sold almost all of its 20% stake in Suzuki in early 2006 to raise cash for its own beleaguered operations. GM divested the remaining 3% stake in late 2008 for about $230 million as it endured a dire cash crisis.

EXECUTIVES

Chairman and CEO, Osamu Suzuki
EVP, Toshihiro Suzuki
EVP, Minoru Tamura
EVP, Osamu Honda
EVP, Yasuhito Harayama
Managing Officer, Takashi Iwatsuki
EVP and Director, Toshihiro Suzuki
Senior Managing Officer and Director, Masanori Atsumi
Senior Managing Officer and Director, Shinzo Nakanishi
EVP and Director, Minoru Tamura
Senior Managing Officer and Director, Naoki Aizawa
Senior Managing Officer and Director, Eiji Mochizuki
Senior Managing Officer and Director, Toyokazu Sugimoto
EVP and Director, Osamu Honda
EVP and Director, Yasuhito Harayama
Auditors: SeimeiAuditCorporation

LOCATIONS

HQ: Suzuki Motor Corp. (Japan)
300 Takatsuka-cho, Hamamatsu, Shizuoka 432-8611
Phone: (81) 53 440 2030
Web: www.suzuki.co.jp

2012 Sales

Asia		
Other countries		34
North America		4
Total	**0**	**100**

PRODUCTS/OPERATIONS

2012 Sales

Automobiles	88
Other products	2

List of Items
Automobiles
Alto/CELERIO
APV
Grand Vitara SUV
Jimny
Kizashi sport sedan
Splash
Swift
SX4 Crossover Sport SportBack
Motorcycles/ATV
Cruiser
Dual purpose
Motocross
Offroad
Scooter

Sport Enduro Tourer
Street
Supersport
Outboard motors
Carburetor series (4-stroke)
Electronic fuel injection series (4-stroke)
Kerosene Outboards (2-stroke)

COMPETITORS

BMW
Bajaj Auto
Brunswick Corp.
Chrysler
Daimler
Ducati
Ek Chor China Motorcycle
Ford Motor
General Motors
Harley-Davidson
Honda
Hyundai Motor
Kawasaki Heavy Industries
Mahindra
Mazda
Nissan
Piaggio & Co.
Polaris Industries
Renault
Tata Motors
Toyota
Triumph Motorcycles
Volkswagen
Yamaha Motor

HISTORICAL FINANCIALS

Company Type: Public

Income Statement FYE: March 31

	REVENUE ($ mil.)	NET INCOME ($ mil.)	NET PROFIT MARGIN	EMPLOYEES
03/13	27,402	854	3.1%	55,948
03/12	30,625	656	2.1%	54,484
03/11	31,497	545	1.7%	52,731
03/10	26,433	309	1.2%	51,503
03/09	30,514	278	0.9%	50,613
Annual Growth	(2.7%)	32.3%	—	2.5%

2013 Year-End Financials

Debt ratio: 0.1%
Return on equity: 7.5%
Cash ($ mil.): 2,965
Current ratio: 1.76
Long-term debt ($ mil.): 2,342
No. of shares (mil.): 560
Dividends
Yield: —
Payout: —
Market value ($ mil.): 50,771

	STOCK PRICE ($) FY Close	P/E High/Low	PER SHARE ($) Earnings	Dividends	Book Value
03/13	90.52	— —	1.40	0.00	24.61
03/12	96.10	— —	1.08	0.00	24.16
03/11	85.50	— —	0.89	0.00	23.83
03/10	87.20	— —	0.59	0.00	20.94
Annual Growth	1.3%	— —	24.0%	—	4.1%

Svenska Handelsbanken

Svenska Handelsbanken is Swedish for universal banking. The group provides corporate and individual clients with deposit products loans credit cards and other banking services. Subsidiaries operate in several related areas including life insurance mortgages pensions fund management and Internet banking. The bank has more than 730 branches mostly in Sweden and the rest of Scandinavia the UK and other countries; it has a presence in countries including Austria China Hong Kong Russia and the US. Subsidiaries include corporate financing unit Handelsbanken Finans Handelsbanken Asset Management and Handelsbanken Liv (asset management and pension products).

The bank has been growing its retail operations both at home and overseas; it has opened some 150 new branches in the past few years. Handelsbanken usually opts for organic growth as a basic strategy. However it does make some acquisitions. It also recently launched operations in Lithuania; it already had a presence in the Balkans in Estonia and Latvia.

As it grows the company also is reconfiguring its nonbank operations selling some and in the case of its Internet bank Stadshypotek Bank merging it into the parent so as to streamline its brands. It also sold its SPP occupational pensions subsidiary to Storebrand of Norway.

HISTORY

Svenska Handelsbanken (roughly translated as The Swedish Commercial Bank) was founded as Stockholms Handelsbank in 1871 by former directors of Stockholms Enskilda Bank who lost an internal power struggle. Industrialization in the latter stages of the 19th century saw Stockholms Handelsbank expand nationwide with the bank pursuing an aggressive lending policy. Larger companies required larger financing resulting in smaller local banks running into trouble and forcing them to merge with bigger ones. Through a series of mergers of this kind Stockholms Handelsbank exploded in size and branches increased from seven (all Stockholm-based) to 250 nationwide by 1919. To reflect this growth the company changed its name to Svenska Handelsbanken the same year.

Sweden remained neutral during WWI allowing business to prosper but the depression hit hard. The bank had to write off millions in bad loans and additions to its reserves. During the 1930s Handelsbanken regained stability largely thanks to its geographical diversity; operations in areas with high economic activity made up for struggling regions.

Sweden once again remained neutral during WWII but political uncertainty kept deposits high and it became difficult to maintain profitable loan volumes. In the 1940s Svenska Handelsbanken divested many of its industrial holdings and began to rededicate itself to small- and medium-scale lending.

Through a string of purchases in the 1950s and 1960s the bank became the largest bank in Scandinavia and began looking to expand internationally. Joint ventures and acquisitions saw the company move into other parts of Europe and the US in the 1970s. Nordic American Banking a US subsidiary was set up to handle import and export financing for North and South American clients doing business with Scandinavian countries. The 1980s saw the company establish a merchant-banking subsidiary in London and enter the Asian market forming Svenska Handelsbanken Asia (based in Singapore).

The bank remained acquisitive during the first half of the 1990s including a purchase of life insurance company RKA (later renamed Handelsbanken Liv) and parts of the Finnish Skopbank. In 1996 Handelsbanken acquired Swedish mortgage company Stadshypotek.

During the latter half of the 1990s it ventured into e-business and increased its presence in the Nordic countries and the UK. In 1999 the company acquired the Norwegian Bergensbanken after having been beaten by MeritaNordbanken in the chase for Christiania Bank (which was Norway's second-largest at the time). The next year Handelsbanken acquired Spartacus a Danish consumer finance company. In 2001 it made another Danish purchase Midtbank making it one of Denmark's largest bankers. That year it also acquired Swedish life insurance company SPP.

In 2004 Handelsbanken bought Swedish fund manager XACT Fonder from OMHEX (now OMX).

The company bought Lokallbanken in Denmark in 2008. The deal added about 15 branches to Handelsbanken's network.

EXECUTIVES

Vice Chairman, Fredrik Lundberg, age 61
Director, Goran Ennerfelt, age 72
Director, Jon F. Baksaas, age 58
Director, Bente Rathe, age 58
Director, Jan C. Johansson, age 58
Director, Sverker Martin-Lof, age 69
Vice Chairman, Anders Nyren, age 58
President and Group CEO, Par Boman, age 51
Director, Ulrika Boethius, age 51
Director, Tommy Bylund, age 53
Director, Lone F. Schroeder, age 52
Auditors: KPMGBohlinsAB

LOCATIONS

HQ: Svenska Handelsbanken
Kungstradgardsgatan 2, Stockholm SE-106 70
Phone: (46) 8 701 10 00
Web: www.handelsbanken.com

PRODUCTS/OPERATIONS

2010 Sales by Segment

	% of total
Branch operations	
Sweden	56
Other	28
Capital	15
Other	1
Total	**100**

COMPETITORS

BNP Paribas
Citigroup
Credit Agricole
Danske Bank
Deutsche Bank
Nordea Bank
SEB AB
Societe Generale

HISTORICAL FINANCIALS

Company Type: Public

Income Statement FYE: December 31

	ASSETS ($ mil.)	NET INCOME ($ mil.)	INCOME AS % OF ASSETS	EMPLOYEES
12/12	366,543	2,233	0.6%	11,192
12/11	355,859	1,786	0.5%	11,184
12/10	321,154	1,644	0.5%	10,850
12/09	298,066	1,438	0.5%	10,821
12/08	276,426	1,553	0.6%	10,833
Annual Growth	7.3%	9.5%	—	0.8%

2012 Year-End Financials

Return on assets: 0.6%
Return on equity: 14.4%
Long-term debt ($ mil.): —
No. of shares (mil.): 632
Sales ($ mil): 11,232
Dividends
Yield: 4.0%
Payout: 0.4%
Market value ($ mil.): 11,410

	STOCK PRICE ($) FY Close	P/E High/Low	PER SHARE ($) Earnings	Dividends	Book Value
12/12	18.03	0 0	3.47	0.72	25.93
12/11	13.43	0 0	2.81	0.02	21.96
12/10	16.30	0 0	2.60	0.01	21.14
12/09	14.15	0 0	2.24	1.12	18.72
Annual Growth	8.4%	— —	11.5%	(10.5%)	8.5%

Swedbank A B

From Scandinavia to the Baltics one common denominator might be the institution with which people entrust their money. Swedbank serves more than 10 million private and corporate customers through 315 branches in Sweden and more than 200 branches in the Baltic countries. The bank also has an international presence in countries such as China Russia and Ukraine. Swedbank offers the usual banking staples –checking savings accounts credit cards electronic banking and loans –but also runs the gamut from investment business in the commodity stock and money markets to real estate brokerage and life insurance. The bank was formed by the 1997 merger of Foreningsbanken and Sparbanken Sverige.

After enduring some rather big losses as a result of the global economic crisis and (more specifically) bad loans in the Baltics Swedbank is trying to pick up the pieces and move forward. The company was able to recover in 2010 and reported a profit. The improvement was due to economic growth in Sweden and improving financial conditions in the Baltics. Swedbank also received backing from the Swedish government and moved to reduce costs. Conditions continued to improve (along with higher interest rates) in 2011 and net interest income rose by 17%. However profit dipped drastically in the final quarter of 2011 (down 65%) prompting the company to continue cutting costs.

Despite the stumbling block created by the global crash Swedbank maintains its vision to become an international banking group with a Swedish base. The bank is looking to build its business in Estonia Latvia and Lithuania. Estonia entered the eurozone at the end of 2010 which will help reduce business risk and boost the country's economy.

However the European debt crisis which struck in 2011 impacted growth prospects. Swedbank is scaling back some of its international ambitions and is focusing more on its home markets. The company had positioned itself for growth in Russia and Ukraine. However in 2010 Swedbank chose to shift its focus in Russia and Ukraine away from private customers and to target only corporate customers in the bank's home markets. The private customer offering will be gradually phased out and the number of branches reduced.

Swedbank is placing more emphasis on its corporate customers. Large corporates and institutions is a major contributor to Swedbank's income and the company's goal is to be the primary provider of financial advice and capital market products in its core markets. The company is working to broaden customer relations and attract new corporate and institutional clients. One way it is doing this is by growing its Norwegian brokerage First Securities which offers equity trading and research corporate finance and fixed-income trading. In 2010 Swedbank bought the half of First Securities it already didn't own.

Swedbank's smallest business segment is also its newest. Born out of the global economic meltdown Ektornet manages and develops Swedbank's repossessed assets and tries to recover as much value as possible. The real estate segment seeks to reduce costs and minimize impairment losses for the company.

EXECUTIVES

Head of Group Human Resources, Marie Hallander Larsson, age 52
Chairman, Anders Sundstrom, age 61
Head of Retail, Catrin Fransson, age 50
Deputy Chair, Lars Idermark, age 57
President and CEO, Michael Wolf, age 50
Head of Corporate Affairs, Thomas Backteman, age 48
Chief Risk Officer, H?kan Berg, age 58
Head of Group Business Support, Mikael Bjorknert, age 48
Head Baltic Banking, Birgitte Bonnesen, age 58
CFO, Goran Bronner, age 52
President CEO, Ulrika Born
Head of Baltic Institutes for Private Finances, Erika Pahne
Independent Vice Chairman of the Board, Anders Anders Sundstrom Sundstrom
Head of Russia & Ukraine, Annika Annika Wijkstrom Wijkstrom
Member of the Board of Directors, Charlotte Charlotte Stromberg Stromberg
Head of Large Corporates & Institutions, Magnus Geeber, age 44
Head of Group Human Resources, Marie Marie Hallander Larsson Larsson
Head of Group Business Support, Mikael Mikael Bjorknert Bjorknert
Head of Group HR, Lars Friberg
Head of South region, Stojko Gjurovski, age 51
Head of North region, Ulf Ejelov
Head of East region, Marie Halling, age 50
Head of Region Stockholm, Bjorn Elfstrand, age 49
CIO, Mats Engstrand, age 49
Chief Risk Officer, Anders Karlsson, age 47
Head of Group Treasury, Jonas Erikson
Head of West region, Lena Smeby-Udesen
Head of Central Region, Johan Smedman, age 49
Director, Ulrika Francke, age 56
Independent Director, Anders Anders Igel Igel
Independent Director, Helle Helle Kruse Nielsen Nielsen
Director; Employee Representative, Jimmy Jimmy Johnsson Johnsson
Independent Director, Karl-Henrik Karl-Henrik Sundstrom Sundstrom
Director; Employee Representative, Kristina Kristina Janson Janson
Independent Director, Olav Olav Fjell Fjell
Independent Director, Pia Pia Rudengren Rudengren
Independent Director, Siv Siv Svensson Svensson
Auditors: DeloitteAB

LOCATIONS

HQ: Swedbank A B
Brunkebergstorg 8, Stockholm SE-105 34
Phone: (46) 8 585 900 00 **Fax:** (46) 8 796 80 92
Web: www.swedbank.se

PRODUCTS/OPERATIONS

2011 Income

	% of total
Retail	54
Large corporations and	20
Baltic	17
Asset	5
Russia and	2
Other	2
Total	**100**

COMPETITORS

Danske Bank
Jyske
MDM Bank
Nordea Bank
SEB AB
Sberbank
Sistema
Storebrand ASA
Svenska Handelsbanken
ZAO Citibank

HISTORICAL FINANCIALS

Company Type: Public

Income Statement FYE: December 31

	ASSETS ($ mil.)	NET INCOME ($ mil.)	INCOME AS % OF ASSETS	EMPLOYEES
12/12	283,511	2,216	0.8%	16,088
12/11	269,256	1,702	0.6%	18,716
12/10	255,858	1,110	0.4%	20,639
12/09	251,990	(1,475)	—	23,696
12/08	231,981	1,394	0.6%	21,280
Annual Growth	5.1%	12.3%	—	(6.8%)

2012 Year-End Financials

Return on assets: 0.7%
Return on equity: 14.1%
Long-term debt ($ mil.): —
No. of shares (mil.): 917
Sales ($ mil): 11,162
Dividends
Yield: 3.9%
Payout: 0.9%
Market value ($ mil.): 18,167

	STOCK PRICE ($) FY Close	P/E High	P/E Low	PER SHARE ($) Earnings	Dividends	Book Value
12/12	19.80	0	0	1.87	0.78	17.75
12/11	12.85	0	0	1.38	0.01	15.66
12/10	14.06	0	0	0.96	1.99	14.87
12/09	10.00	—	—	(1.50)	2.26	13.39
12/08	5.75	0	0	2.11	1.77	21.42
Annual Growth	36.2%	—	—	(3.0%)	(18.6%)	(4.6%)

Swiss Re Ltd.

LOCATIONS

HQ: Swiss Re Ltd.
Mythenquai 50/60, PO Box, Zurich 8022
Phone: (41) 43 285 2121 **Fax:** (41) 43 285 2999
Web: www.swissre.com

HISTORICAL FINANCIALS

Company Type: Public

Income Statement FYE: December 31

	REVENUE ($ mil.)	NET INCOME ($ mil.)	NET PROFIT MARGIN	EMPLOYEES
12/12	33,624	4,257	12.7%	11,193
12/11	28,083	2,626	9.4%	10,788
12/10	28,835	1,980	6.9%	10,362
Annual Growth	8.0%	46.6%	—	3.9%

2012 Year-End Financials

Debt ratio: 9.2%
Return on equity: 13.3%
Cash ($ mil.): 10,837
Current ratio: 18.16
Long-term debt ($ mil.): 16,286
No. of shares (mil.): 343
Dividends
Yield: 4.5%
Payout: 29.7%
Market value ($ mil.): 24,811

	STOCK PRICE ($) FY Close	P/E High	P/E Low	PER SHARE ($) Earnings	Dividends	Book Value
12/12	72.30	6	4	11.06	3.29	99.08
12/11	50.55	8	5	7.49	0.00	86.33
12/10	0.00	—	—	2.43	0.00	73.97
/0.00	—	—	(0.00)	0.00	(0.00)	
Annual Growth	—	—	—	—	—	—

T&D Holdings Inc

No mystery in a name here: T&D Holdings serves as the holding company for Japanese insurance companies Taiyo Life and Daido Life. Combined the companies constitute one of Japan's top life insurers. Taiyo Life gears its products to individuals while Daido Life's products are targeted towards small businesses. Another subsidiary T&D Financial Life sells whole life policies through financial institutions. Other businesses under the T&D umbrella include T&D Asset Management T&D Customer Services (administrative services) and T&D Information Systems (computer processing).

Operations

T&D Holdings' Taiyo Life division which accounts for half of the holding company's annual revenues serves households with comprehensive life products including death benefits and medical or nursing care coverage. Meanwhile the Daido Life unit (40% of sales) focuses on the sale of term life insurance and illness policies through business accounts. The third-largest business unit T&D Financial Life sells whole life policies.

Sales and Marketing

The operating units of T&D Holdings use targeted sales techniques. With a focus on selling to housewives and middle-aged women Taiyo Life employs a sales force made up of women (similar in age to their target market base) who visit homes to present tailor-made coverage options. Daido Life gears its marketing efforts towards small and midsized businesses by partnering with enterprise associations (such as the National Federation of Corporate Taxpayers Association). The company's T&D Financial Life unit markets through a network of some 80 agencies including financial institutions.

Financial Performance

T&D Holdings reported revenue increase of 6% to Y2104 billion ($26 billion) in 2012 due to increased policy premium income and investment income. Higher sales in 2012 followed two years of decline in 2010 and 2011 due to high claims volumes. Net income also rose in 2012 by 12% to Y27 billion ($325 million) due to a reversal of outstanding claims reserves (related to reserves posted in 2011 from the earthquake/tsunami events that occurred).

Strategy

T&D Holdings is seeking to grow by branching out beyond its traditional market segments. Its Taiyo Life unit is working to expand policy sales by marketing policies geared at men and children. Daido Life is adding products for business owners such as living protection coverage while T&D Financial Life is introducing new products for bereaved families and retirees.

T&D Holdings is also growing its operations into the provision of short-term small-amount policies for pet shops. The company seeks to expand in new and existing business fields through alliances and acquisitions as well.

Company Background

T&D Holdings was formed through the merger of Taiyo Life and Daido Life in 2004. The companies first began working together through an alliance formed in 1999.

EXECUTIVES

Chairman, Naoteru Miyato, age 70
President and Representative Director, Kenji Nakagome, age 60
Senior Executive Officer and Director, Tamiji Matsumoto, age 59
Senior Executive Officer and Director, Tsutomu Igarashi, age 62
EVP and Director, Sonosuke Usui
Director; President Daido Life, Tetsuhiro Kida, age 60
Managing Executive Officer and Director T&D Holdings and Taiyo Life, Terunori Yokoyama, age 60
Executive Officer, Hirohisa Uehara, age 52
President and Representative Director, Kenji Nakagome, age 60
Senior Executive Officer and Director, Tamiji Matsumoto, age 59
Senior Executive Officer and Director, Tsutomu Igarashi, age 62
EVP and Director, Sonosuke Usui
Director; President Daido Life, Tetsuhiro Kida, age 60
Managing Executive Officer and Director T&D Holdings and Taiyo Life, Terunori Yokoyama, age 60
Auditors: Ernst&YoungShinNihon

LOCATIONS

HQ: T&D Holdings Inc
1-2-3 Kaigan, Minato-ku, Tokyo 105-0022
Phone: (81) 3 3434 9151 **Fax:** (81) 3 3434 9055
Web: www.td-holdings.co.jp

PRODUCTS/OPERATIONS

2012 Sales

Taiyo Life	51
T&D Financial Life	5
Other	1

COMPETITORS

Aflac
American Life Insurance
Asahi Mutual Life
Dai-ichi Life
Fukoku Mutual
Gibraltar Life Insurance
Meiji Yasuda Life
Mitsui Life
Nippon Life Insurance
Sumitomo Life

HISTORICAL FINANCIALS

Company Type: Public

Income Statement FYE: March 31

	ASSETS ($ mil.)	NET INCOME ($ mil.)	INCOME AS % OF ASSETS	EMPLOYEES
03/13	145,269	677	0.5%	20,497
03/12	156,784	326	0.2%	20,982
03/11	153,861	288	0.2%	21,732
03/10	137,877	260	0.2%	21,975
03/09	126,921	(904)	—	21,499
Annual Growth	3.4%	—	—	(1.2%)

2013 Year-End Financials

Return on assets: 0.4%
Return on equity: 7.9%
Long-term debt ($ mil.): —
No. of shares (mil.): 674
Sales ($ mil): 25,711
Dividends
Yield: —
Payout: —
Market value ($ mil.): 3,979

	STOCK PRICE ($) FY Close	P/E High/Low	PER SHARE ($) Earnings	Dividends	Book Value
03/13	5.90	— —	1.00	0.00	14.50
03/12	5.43	— —	0.48	0.00	12.39
03/11	12.21	— —	0.42	0.00	11.03
Annual Growth	(30.5%)	— —	24.1%	—	7.1%

Taiwan Cooperative Bank

Taiwan Cooperative Bank is Taking Care of Business. Known as TCB for short the bank was founded in 1946 during the Japanese occupation of Taiwan to foster the country's burgeoning cooperative system. Today the bank still provides financing for economic development particularly for cooperative enterprises and small and middle-market businesses with a focus on the fishing and farming sectors. It also provides standard banking services such as deposits and financial management to businesses and consumers. TCB has more than 300 branches in its home country plus six offices in the US China Belgium and Philippines. The Taiwanese government owns nearly 40% of the bank.

In late 2009 TCB formed a life insurance joint venture with BNP Paribas. The program strengthened the bank's foothold in the insurance market by taking advantage of its branch network. The deal expanded TCB's offerings to include savings-linked insurance products and mortgage insurance. Shortly afterwards TCB and BNP announced plans for another joint venture –this time focused on asset management services. TCB's stake in both ventures is 51% to BNP's 49%.

EXECUTIVES

EVP, Chung-Dea Hsieh
EVP, Shu-Chang Chou
SVP and General Manager Information Technology Division, Hsiang Hu
President, Chiu-Jung Tsai
EVP, Yang-Jan Fan
VP and General Manager Treasury Department, Pe-Chu Wu
SVP and General Manager Electronic Banking Department, Chun-Lung Chou
SVP and General Manager Loan Assets Management Department, Cheng-Kang Chen
SVP and General Manager Secretariat Department, Fei-Ling Hu
SVP and General Manager Accounting Division, Chen-Tsai Chou
SVP and General Manager Risk Management Division, Shiaw-Yen Lun
SVP and General Manager Human Resources Division, Sue-Chuan Wang
Auditors: Deloitte&Touche

LOCATIONS

HQ: Taiwan Cooperative Bank
No. 77, Kuanchien Road, Jhongjheng District, Taipei 100
Phone: (886) 2 2311 8811 **Fax:** (886) 2 2375 2954
Web: www.tcb-bank.com.tw

COMPETITORS

Chang Hwa Bank
Fubon Financial
Hua Nan Financial
SinoPac Holdings
Taiwan Business Bank

HISTORICAL FINANCIALS

Company Type: Public

Income Statement FYE: December 31

	ASSETS ($ mil.)	NET INCOME ($ mil.)	INCOME AS % OF ASSETS	EMPLOYEES
12/12	98,419	259	0.3%	8,563
12/11	90,932	250	0.3%	8,697
12/10	91,985	264	0.3%	8,803
12/09	80,937	212	0.3%	0
12/08	76,494	225	0.3%	0
Annual Growth	6.5%	3.6%	—	—

2012 Year-End Financials

Return on assets: 0.2%
Return on equity: 6.0%
Long-term debt ($ mil.): —
No. of shares (mil.): —
Sales ($ mil): 1,141
Dividends
Yield: —
Payout: —
Market value ($ mil.): —

Taiwan Semiconductor Manufacturing Co., Ltd.

If you're absolutely fabless this company is for you. Taiwan Semiconductor Manufacturing Company (TSMC) is the first and largest dedicated silicon foundry (contract semiconductor manufacturer) in the world with nine plants in Asia and one in the US. Logic semiconductors make up about 70% of sales while mixed-signal products represent most of the rest. Largely a wafer fabricator TSMC makes chips for fabless semiconductor and systems companies (accounting for about 80% of sales) such as AMD Broadcom NVIDIA and QUALCOMM while remaining sales come from integrated device manufacturers including STMicroelectronics and Texas Instruments. The company gets about 60% of its sales from customers in the US.

While wafer manufacturing makes up about 90% of sales TSMC's remaining sales come mainly from fabricating masks –a kind of silkscreen used to expose silicon wafers to a certain light pattern –and it also provides services such as design probing and testing and assembly. Constituting its largest-selling product logic semiconductors are standard logic devices such as microprocessors microcontrollers digital signal processors graphic chips and chip sets. The bulk of its remaining business mixed-signal semiconductors is used in systems for data storage and program instructions such as SRAM DRAM and flash memory.

TSMC continues to increase the capacity and improve the efficiency of its wafer fabrication processes but it is also seeking long-term growth opportunities outside the traditional foundry business model. To that end TSMC formed two new subsidiaries in 2011: TSMC Solid-State Lighting (TSMC SSL manufacturing such products as light-emitting diodes (LEDs)) and TSMC Solar. So far TSMC has one LED production plant in Taiwan in the same commercial technology park as the company headquarters and a number of its traditional fabrication plants. On the solar side it acquired and has built up a stake of more than 23% in Stion which makes thin-film photovoltaic modules in the US. TSMC Solar became ready for production in 2012 at one of TSMC's sites in Taiwan after receiving certification from Underwriters Laboratories and the International Electrotechnical Commission. Among the company's other subsidiaries is Washington State US-based WaferTech which began as a joint venture with US investors to create a $1.2 billion foundry in the US.

After seeing revenues rebound by about 50% in 2010 growth in 2011 was a tamer 2% (by domestic currency) rising to nearly NT$430 billion (more than $14 billion). Net income however dropped by about 20% to less than NT$140 billion ($4.4 billion) though that was still about 50% better than 2009 profit. The company's 10 largest customers account for more than half of sales; the top three represent a third of total revenue.

The government of Taiwan is among the stakeholders of TSMC holding more than 6% of the company.

HISTORY

The big foundries –including TSMC's Taiwanese archrival United Microelectronics Corporation (UMC) –played a major role in the growth of the worldwide fabless semiconductor industry in the 21st century. Foundries aim to save clients the costs and time associated with building expensive wafer fabrication plants (fabs) of their own. Their services are especially vital for fabless companies whose entire business model is predicated on outsourcing all manufacturing.

Morris Chang learned early to adapt to rapid change. The future founder and chairman of Taiwan Semiconductor Manufacturing Company (TSMC) lived in six cities before age 18 as his family fled the ravages of the Sino-Japanese War and WWII in China. Chang immigrated to the US to attend MIT and Stanford where he ultimately earned a Ph.D. in electrical engineering.

In 25 years at Texas Instruments (TI) Chang worked his way up from the ranks of technical management into the executive suite. In 1983 he resigned from TI to become CEO of General Instrument but in 1985 the Taiwanese government recruited him to head its Industrial Technology Research Institute (ITRI). He remained chairman of ITRI from 1988 to 1994.

Working from his position at ITRI Chang became chairman of contract electronics manufacturer United Microelectronics Corporation (UMC) in 1987. Also that year he founded TSMC as the world's first dedicated contract semiconductor manufacturer –the first silicon foundry. Chang's pioneering role in the foundry industry has earned him many accolades including the first-ever Robert N. Noyce Medal of the Institute of Electrical and Electronics Engineers and the first-ever Exemplary Leadership award (subsequently named in his honor) of the Fabless Semiconductor Association (now the Global Semiconductor Alliance). Known for his analytical mind Chang was once ranked among the top 1000 players of contract bridge in the world.

TSMC became profitable within 15 months of its founding. Throughout the 1990s it continued to be among industry leaders both in production capacity and in deployment of cutting-edge technology.

The company opened its first US office in 1992 and its first European office in 1993. During the early 1990s it opened a series of fabs in the Hsinchu industrial zone in northwestern Taiwan.

In 1997 TSMC broke ground on the first of a series of fabs in the Tainan industrial zone in southern Taiwan and in 1998 the company opened its first office in Japan. The following year TSMC and Philips began construction on their Systems on Silicon Manufacturing Company (SSMC) foundry joint venture in Singapore.

TSMC made a series of acquisitions in 2000 as it enjoyed a string of record sales months: It bought out Acer's majority share in their Taiwan-based joint venture it bought out three minority partners in the US-based WaferTech joint venture and it acquired outright Taiwan's #3 chip foundry Worldwide Semiconductor Manufacturing. Also in 2000 TSMC's 25%-owned Vanguard International Semiconductor stopped making DRAM chips to become a full-time chip foundry.

Despite a broad industry downturn in 2001 the company continued its rollout of cutting-edge manufacturing processes for 300mm silicon wafers and for 0.13-micron chip circuitry designs. The company weathered a dismal 2001 –by consensus the worst year in the chip industry's history –better than its smaller rivals and by 2002 TSMC began efforts to expand its manufacturing reach into mainland China where it established an office.

In 2003 a strong earthquake rattled the island of Taiwan; the temblor didn't disrupt production at TSMC's fabs in the northern part of Taiwan and only temporarily halted work at Fab 6 in southern Taiwan.

Also in 2003 TSMC filed a lawsuit against Semiconductor Manufacturing International Corp. (SMIC) its up-and-coming rival on the Chinese mainland alleging patent infringement and misappropriation of trade secrets. The competitors reached a legal settlement in 2005 with SMIC agreeing to pay $175 million to TSMC over six years.

Morris Chang stepped aside as CEO in 2005 while remaining chairman. Rick Tsai who was TSMC's president and COO was promoted to CEO. F. C. Tseng previously the company's deputy CEO became vice chairman. Chang returned to the CEO position when Tsai left the company in 2009.

The TSMC-SMIC legal dispute flared up again in 2006 as TSMC filed suit against its mainland competitor and claimed that SMIC breached the 2005 settlement agreement. SMIC denied the allegations and filed a countersuit against TSMC.

In November 2009 TSMC won a legal battle against its rival when SMIC was found guilty of stealing trade secrets from TSMC related to its manufacturing processes. The dispute has been going on since 2003 when TSMC filed suit against SMIC for patent infringement; though SMIC disputed the allegations it agreed to a settlement in 2005 that included a $175 million fine and the rights to use TSMC patents. The following year TSMC filed another suit alleging that SMIC violated the terms of the agreement by continuing to steal trade secrets. TSMC is receiving $200 million as well as an unknown amount of stock and warrants in damages.

TSMC founded the New Businesses group in 2009 before crystallizing that into the solid-state lighting and solar subsidiaries. In February 2010 it acquired a 20% stake (for nearly $195 million) in Motech Industries a solar-cell manufacturer. The acquisition made TSMC the largest shareholder in Motech and expanded its presence in the alternative energy sector. Later that year TSMC announced it would invest nearly $260 million on phase one of its first thin-film solar R&D center and fab. The company planned to begin initial volume production in 2012 with a second phase planned to expand production and staff. In March 2010 the company committed to entering the fast growing LED lighting sector when it broke ground on its LED lighting R&D center and fab.

EXECUTIVES

VP Operations/Affiliate Fabs, M. C. Tzeng

SVP Research and Development, Shang-Yi Chiang

Vice Chairman, F. C. Tseng, $153,303 total compensation

Chairman and CEO, Morris Chang, age 81, $156,070 total compensation

Senior Vice President of Worldwide Sales and Marketing of TSMC, Jason C. S. Chen

Chairman Chief Executive Officer of two TSMC wholly-owned subsidiaries, Rick Tsai
President TSMC Japan, Makoto Onodera
SVP Operations, Mark Liu
SVP and General Counsel, Richard (Dick) Thurston
SVP and CIO, Stephen T. (Steve) Tso
Chief Financial Officer, Lora Ho
President TSMC Europe, Maria Marced
VP Human Resources, L.C. Tu
Corporate Communications Director, Elizabeth Sun
VP Research and Development, Burn J. Lin
VP and President TSMC North America, Rick Cassidy, age 61
VP Operations and Manufacturing Technology, Wei-Jen Lo
VP Research and Development and CTO, Jack Sun
VP Design and Technology Platform, Cliff Hou
VP Operations and Product Development, Y. P. Chin
VP Quality and Reliability, N. S. Tsai
Production Equipment Procurement Division Director, Handy Ko
VP Operations/Mainstream Fabs, J.K. Lin
VP Operations/300mm Fabs, J.K. Wang
VP Corporate Planning, Irene Sun
President TSMC China, C.H. Chen
Vice President Corporate Staff, Haynes Boone
Director, Thomas J. (Tom) Engibous, age 60
Director, Stan Shih, age 69
Vice Chairman, F. C. Tseng
President and CEO TSMC Solar Ltd. and TSMC Solid State Lighting Ltd.; Director, Rick Tsai
Director, Sir Peter L. Bonfield, age 68
Director, Gregory C. Chow
Director, Kok-Choo Chen
Director, Johnsee Lee
Auditors: Deloitte&Touche

LOCATIONS

HQ: Taiwan Semiconductor Manufacturing Co., Ltd.
No. 8, Li-Hsin Road 6, Hsinchu Science Park, Hsinchu 300
Phone: (886) 3 563 6688 **Fax:** (886) 3 563 7000
Web: www.tsmc.com

2011 Sales by Location of Client Headquarters

	% of total
North	69
Asia/Pacific	14
Europe	9
Japan	4
China	4
Total	**100**

2011 Sales by Billed Regions

	% of total
US	59
Asia	
Taiwan	12
Other	18
Europe	11
Total	**100**

PRODUCTS/OPERATIONS

2011 Sales by Customer

	% of total
Fabless semiconductor companies/systems	81
Integrated device	19
Total	**100**

2011 Sales

	% of total
Wafer	90
Mask	6
Other	4
Total	**100**

2011 Sales

	% of total
CMOS	
Logic	69
Mixed-signal	29
Memory	1
BiCMOS	1
Total	**100**

Selected Services

Semiconductor photomasks (circuit pattern guides)
- Design
- Manufacturing

Semiconductor wafers (integrated circuits and other semiconductor devices)
- Computer-aided design
- Manufacturing
- Packaging
- Testing

Selected Customers

Fabless semiconductor companies
- Advanced Micro Devices
- Altera
- Broadcom
- Marvell
- MediaTek
- NVIDIA
- QUALCOMM

Integrated device manufacturers
- LSI Corp.
- STMicroelectronics
- Texas Instruments

COMPETITORS

Advanced Semiconductor Engineering
Advanced Semiconductor Manufacturing
ChipMOS
Dai Nippon Printing
Dongbu HiTek
GLOBALFOUNDRIES
Grace Semiconductor
IBM Microelectronics
MagnaChip
Photronics
SK Hynix
SMIC
Samsung Electronics
Shanghai Hua Hong NEC
Silterra
Toppan Photomasks
Tower Semiconductor
UMC
Winbond Electronics
X-FAB Silicon Foundries

HISTORICAL FINANCIALS

Company Type: Public

Income Statement FYE: December 31

	REVENUE ($ mil.)	NET INCOME ($ mil.)	NET PROFIT MARGIN	EMPLOYEES
12/12	17,443	5,725	32.8%	39,267
12/11	14,090	4,427	31.4%	35,457
12/10	14,417	5,553	38.5%	33,232
12/09	9,244	2,788	30.2%	24,466
12/08	10,165	3,049	30.0%	24,834
Annual Growth	14.5%	17.1%	—	12.1%

2012 Year-End Financials

Debt ratio: 0.4%
Return on equity: 24.5%
Cash ($ mil.): 4,941
Current ratio: 1.77
Long-term debt ($ mil.): 2,829
No. of shares (mil.): —
Dividends
Yield: 2.3%
Payout: 221.0%
Market value ($ mil.): —

	STOCK PRICE ($) FY Close	P/E High	P/E Low	PER SHARE ($) Earnings	Dividends	Book Value
12/12	17.16	0	0	0.22	0.40	0.96
12/11	12.91	0	0	0.17	0.00	0.80
12/10	12.54	0	0	0.21	0.37	0.76
12/09	11.44	0	0	0.11	0.36	0.60
12/08	7.90	0	0	0.12	0.39	0.56
Annual Growth	21.4%	—	—	17.4%	0.7%	14.2%

Talanx AG

Talanx Group offers its customers an army of protection. The Germany-based insurance group is the third-largest in the country. Talanx operates in property/casualty insurance life insurance and financial services as well as reinsurance in both the property/casualty and life categories. Brands include HDI Direkt and HDI-Gerling which provide insurance policies to both private and industrial customers; Aspecta a provider of individual insurance and investment products; Hannover Re (of which Talanx owns 51%) one of the world's largest reinsurers; and fund guarantor and asset manager AmpegaGirling among others. Talanx has operations in 150 countries worldwide.

Major operations outside of Germany are located in Austria Hungary Italy Spain Poland Russia and Turkey. The company also has operations in the Americas Africa and the Asia/Pacific region. Talanx prefers to operate semi-independent businesses in local markets and expands by acquiring or opening divisions in new territories.

Japanese insurer Meiji Yasuda Life Insurance has laid out plans to expand into Europe using Talanx as a springboard. In 2010 the two companies agreed to establish a joint venture using a Talanx subsidiary as the framework to grow into the Central and Eastern European markets.

In 2008 the company completed the integration of the former operations of Gerling a German insurance provider acquired in 2006 into its existing Ampega and HDI divisions. In addition the company absorbed BHW Lebensversicherung and BHW Pensionskasse two life insurance firms acquired in 2007.

On the sale side Talanx divested Gerling's former German real estate holdings. Another asset sale occurred in 2007 when majority owned Hannover Re sold its non-life reinsurance subsidiary Praetorian Financial Group to Australia-based QBE Insurance Group for about $800 million.

The company traces its roots back over a century but began operating as a holding company under the name HDI Beteilgung AG in 1996. In 1998 it was renamed Talanx which is a blend of the words "talent" and "phalanx" (a Greek word referring to a battle formation).

EXECUTIVES

Chairman Management Board, Herbert K. Haas, age 59
Member Management Board, Immo Querner
Member Management Board Reinsurance, Ulrich Wallin, age 52
Chairman Supervisory Board, Wolf-Dieter Baumgartl, age 70
Deputy Chairman Management Board, Christian Hinsch, age 58
Deputy Chairman Supervisory Board, Prof Eckhard Rohkamm
Head Communications, Thomas von Mallinckrodt
Head Investor Relations, Wolfram Schmitt, age 55
Member Management Board, Thomas Noth
Deputy Chairman Supervisory Board, Ralf Rieger
Member Management Group Retail Germany, Heinz-Peter Ro?
Member Supervisory Board, Michael Rogowski, age 74
Member Supervisory Board, Hans-Dieter Petram, age 70
Member Supervisory Board, Erhard Schipporeit, age 65
Deputy Chairman Supervisory Board, Prof Eckhard Rohkamm
Member Supervisory Board, Gerald Herrmann
Member Supervisory Board, Thomas Lindner

Member Supervisory Board, Otto Muller
Deputy Chairman Supervisory Board, Ralf Rieger

LOCATIONS

HQ: Talanx AG
Riethorst 2, Hannover 30659
Phone: (49) 511 3747 0 **Fax:** (49) 511 3747 2525
Web: www.talanx.com

PRODUCTS/OPERATIONS

2008 Premiums

	% of total
Property/casualty	31
Life	30
Non-life	24
Life/health	15
Total	**100**

COMPETITORS

AEGON
AXA
Allianz
ERGO
General Re
Generali
ING
Munich Re Group
Swiss Re
Zurich Insurance Group

HISTORICAL FINANCIALS

Company Type: Public

Income Statement

FYE: December 31

	REVENUE ($ mil.)	NET INCOME ($ mil.)	NET PROFIT MARGIN	EMPLOYEES
12/12	35,406	830	2.3%	22,180
12/11	31,411	672	2.1%	18,314
12/10	31,363	294	0.9%	18,006
12/09	30,534	757	2.5%	18,038
12/08	24,498	261	1.1%	16,541
Annual Growth	9.6%	33.5%	—	7.6%

2012 Year-End Financials

Debt ratio: —
Return on equity: 9.7%
Cash ($ mil.): 2,792
Current ratio: —
Long-term debt ($ mil.): —
No. of shares (mil.): 252
Dividends
Yield: —
Payout: —
Market value ($ mil.): —

Tata Motors Ltd

Tata Motors enjoys giant-sized growth thanks to its Nano cars. The company –India's largest automobile maker by sales –makes buses trucks tractor-trailers passenger cars (Indica Indigo Jaguar Land Rover Safari Sumo and the popular micro car Nano) light commercial vehicles and utility vehicles. It also makes construction equipment and provides IT services. Tata Motors sells through more than 1000 dealers in India as well as exports vehicles to countries in Africa Asia Europe the Middle East and South America. In addition the company distributes Fiat-brand cars in India through its Tata-Fiat dealer network.

Geographic Reach

Through subsidiaries and affiliated companies Tata Motors has operations in India the UK South Korea Thailand Spain and South Africa. India is its largest market representing 34% of its total sales. China the UK and the US follow with 18% 11% and nearly 10 % of total sales respectively. Other European countries account for nearly 12 % of total sales while the rest of the world contributes roughly 18%.

Operations

Tata Motors' business segments are primarily its automotive operations which develop design manufacture assemble and sell vehicles and provide financing. The automotive segment is divided into Tata and other brand vehicles as well as Jaguar Land Rover. Other operations include information technology or IT services and machine tools and factory automation products and services.

Tata Motors also has franchisee and joint venture assembly operations in Bangladesh Ukraine and Senegal.

Sales and Marketing

Tata Motors' vehicles are sold through a network of authorized dealers and service centers across the Indian market and a network of distributors and local dealers in international markets.

Financial Performance

Tata Motors has seen significant growth over the last four years with 2012 representing its best year to date. From 2011 to 2012 its total revenues in rupees increased by 35% (or 18% when converted into US dollar) and its net income skyrocketed by 58% (37% in US dollar).

The company has been helped by increases in volumes across all its markets particularly a 29% surge in the premium car segment and impressive growth in the Chinese market. Revenues in China increased 155% and accounted for 18% of the company's net revenues in 2012.

Strategy

Tata Motors is a leader in one of the only growth areas for the automotive market in recent years – India –which gives it a slight edge over competitors in the region. It is also extending its commercial vehicles penetration into countries like Bangladesh Nepal Sri Lanka and Bhutan.

During the Great Recession the Jaguar and Land Rover lines created financial pressure for Tata Motors as consumers bought smaller more fuel efficient cars. However by mid-2010 interest in luxury cars returned spurring the company to secure some $1.5 billion to support the expansion of Jaguar and Land Rover manufacturing facilities over the next four years. This allowed the luxury brands to remain in the UK and quickly cut costs tightened up efficiencies and improved its cash management. Now the well-known British brands are recapturing some of their lost luster generating rising sales from important markets like Shanghai to London.

Company Background

In 2008 Tata Motors bought the Jaguar and Land Rover brands from Ford for about $2.3 billion. It took over the two struggling businesses in an effort to diversify its customer base by expanding its product portfolio from commercial and small passenger vehicles to premium cars.

Ownership

Tata Sons Limited and Subsidiaries own 26% of the company while Citibank N owns 16%.

EXECUTIVES

Director; CEO Jaguar and Land Rover, Ralf Speth, age 57
Managing Director, Karl Slym, age 51
President and Head Engineering Research Centre, Tim Leverton
Vice Chairman, Ravi Kant, $625,903 total compensation
President and CFO, C. Ramakrishnan, $326,378 total compensation
Executive Director and Head Commercial Vehicles Business Unit, Ravindra Pisharody, $154,989 total compensation
Executive Director and Head Quality, Satish B. Borwankar, $164,951 total compensation
Chairman, Cyrus P. Mistry
President and Head Passenger Vehicles Business Unit, Ranjit Yadav
SVP and Head Purchasing and Supply Chain, Venkatram Mamillapalle
Sr. Vice President Chief Human Resources Officer, Prabir Jha
SVP and Head Commercial Passenger Vehicle Business Unit, Ankush Arora
Director; CEO Jaguar and Land Rover, Ralf Speth, age 57
Vice Chairman, Ravi Kant, age 69
Managing Director Indian Operations and Board Member, Prakash M. Telang, age 58
Director, Subodh Bhargava, age 70
Director, Nusli N. Wadia, age 69
Director, S. M. (Sam) Palia, age 74
Director, Jamshed J. (JJ) Irani, age 76
Director, Ramesh A. Mashelkar, age 69
Director, Nasser M. Munjee, age 60
Director, V. K. Jairath, age 54
Director, Ranendra Sen, age 68
Auditors: DeloitteHaskins&Sells

LOCATIONS

HQ: Tata Motors Ltd
Bombay House, 24, Homi Mody Street, Mumbai, Maharashtra 400 001
Phone: (91) 22 6665 8282 **Fax:** (91) 22 6665 7799
Web: www.tatamotors.com

2012 Sales

	$ mil.	% of total
India		34
China		18
UK		11
US		9
Total	**0**	**100**

Selected Subsidiaries

Concorde Motors (India) Limited
Jaguar Land Rover PLC-UK
PT Tata Indonesia
Sheba Properties Ltd-India
TAL Manufacturing Solutions Ltd-India
Tata Daewoo Commercial Vehicle Co Ltd- South Korea
Tata Hispano Motors Carrocera SA- Spain
Tata Marcopolo Motors Ltd-India.
Tata Motors (SA) Proprietary Ltd South Africa.
Tata Motors European Technical center PLC UK
Tata Motors Finance Ltd India
Tata Motors Insurance Broking and Advisory Services Ltd-India
Tata Motors(Thailand) Ltd
Tata Precision Industries Pts Ltd-Singapore
Tata Technologies Ltd-India
TML Distribution Company Ltd-India
TML Drivelines Ltd-India
TML Holdings Pte Ltd- Singapore

PRODUCTS/OPERATIONS

Selected Products and Services

Light commercial vehicles
- Ace
- Magic
- Winger

Medium and heavy commercial vehicles
- Paradiso
- Prima

Passenger cars
- Indica
- Indica Vista
- Indigo eCS
- Indigo Manza
- Jaguar
- Nano

Utility vehicles
- Aria
- Land Rover
- Range Rover
- Sumo
- Safari
- Venture
- Xenon XT

COMPETITORS

BMW
Bajaj Auto
Caterpillar
Chrysler
Daimler
Fiat
Ford Motor
Fuji Heavy Industries
General Motors
Hindustan Motors
Honda
Hyundai Motor
Isuzu
Kia Motors
Komatsu
Mahindra
Mazda
Nissan
Renault
Saab Automobile
Suzuki Motor
Toyota
Volkswagen
Volvo

HISTORICAL FINANCIALS

Company Type: Public

Income Statement

FYE: March 31

	REVENUE ($ mil.)	NET INCOME ($ mil.)	NET PROFIT MARGIN	EMPLOYEES
03/13	34,813	1,633	4.7%	62,716
03/12	32,724	2,273	6.9%	58,618
03/11	27,635	1,646	6.0%	26,214
03/10	20,631	847	4.1%	0
03/09	14,100	(484)	—	23,638
Annual Growth	25.4%	—	—	27.6%

2013 Year-End Financials

Debt ratio: 0.6%
Return on equity: 25.3%
Cash ($ mil.): 3,409
Current ratio: 0.88
Long-term debt ($ mil.): 5,995
No. of shares (mil.): —
Dividends
Yield: 0.0%
Payout: 0.0%
Market value ($ mil.): —

	STOCK PRICE ($) FY Close	P/E High/Low		PER SHARE ($) Earnings	Dividends	Book Value
03/13	24.41	0	0	0.51	0.00	2.14
03/12	26.97	0	0	0.71	0.00	2.03
03/11	27.79	0	0	0.11	0.30	1.48
03/10	18.46	0	0	0.06	0.10	(0.00)
03/09	4.93	—	—	(0.45)	0.35	0.45
Annual Growth	49.2%	—	—	—	(86.7%)	47.3%

Telecom Italia SPA

Telecom Italia's wireline unit is Italy's #1 telephone operator with some 4.1 million fixed access lines. It serves Italian customers through millions of broadband and wireless connections. While Telecom Italia does most of its business in Italy Latin America is a key international market. The company provides wholesale network access in South America as well as Italy. Its TIM Brasil subsidiary is a leader in the Brazilian wireless market with more than 64.1 million subscribers; its Argentina subsidiaries cater to 1.6 million broadband subscribers and 18.2 million mobile subscribers.

Geographic Reach

Telecom Italia has a presence in Italy Latin America North America Europe Africa and Asia. It generates about 64% of its revenue from its domestic market (Italy) and the remaining 36% derive from Brazil and Argentina.

Operations

The operating segments of Telecom Italia are organized according to the relative geographical location for the telecommunications business and relative to the specific businesses for the other segments. The market of its main business unit is focused mainly in serving customers in Europe Asia and South America.

In addition subsidiary Telecom Italia Media produces and distributes TV and Web content and Olivetti provides office equipment such as ink-jet printer heads mostly for the banking industry.

Financial Performance

Thanks to growth in foreign markets the company's revenues increased by 9% from 2010 to 2011. Revenues from Brazil were up by 18% as a result of a 26% increase in the market share of mobile lines. Revenue from Argentina increased by 27% in 2011 due to the growth of customers in the fixed and broadband businesses as well as mobile businesses.

Despite this growth Telecom Italia recorded a net loss for 2011 due to the acquisition of goods and services and net impairment losses on noncurrent assets.

Strategy

Over the last few years the company has been selling off interests not related to its businesses in Italy or Brazil. These deals were also part of Telecom Italia's ongoing effort to sell non-core businesses in order to reduce debt.

Outside Italy the company is focused on bolstering its operations only in Brazil an emerging market that now accounts for almost 20% of revenue. In 2011 it bought AES Atimus a Brazilian subsidiary of US power company AES. AES Atimus operates a 3400-mile fiber optic network in Rio de Janeiro and Sao Paulo. The deal ?700 million ($1 billion) was Telecom Italia's largest acquisition in a decade.

In another 2011 acquisition that boosted its Latin American holdings Telecom Italia paid about $145 million to raise its ownership stake in Sofora Telecomunicaciones the holding company which owns Telecom Argentina from 58% to 68%. Closer to home Telecom Italia bought 71% of Italian mobile phone retailer 4G Holding from GIR Srl a company controlled by 4G's CEO 2011. The deal boosted the company's domestic retail presence by 200 shops as it works to get its brand out in front of more wireless customers in a saturated market. GIR retained 29% of 4G Holding.

Ownership

The former state-owned monopoly has one major institutional shareholder. An investment group made up primarily of Italian financial backers known as Telco SpA owns a 22% stake. Telco is made up of Telefonica (46%) Italian insurance giant Generali (31%) investment bank Mediobanca (12%) and commercial bank Intesa Sanpaolo (11%).

HISTORY

After gaining political power in Italy Benito Mussolini began a program of nationalization focusing first on three major banks and their equity portfolios. Included were three local phone companies that became the core of Societa Finanziaria Telefonica (STET) created in 1933 to handle Italy's phone services under the state's industrial holding company Istituto per La Ricostruzione Industriale (IRI).

Germany and Italy grew closer in the years leading up to WWII and Italian equipment makers entered a venture with Siemens to make phone equipment. STET came through the war with most of its infrastructure intact and a monopoly on phone service in Italy. Siemens' properties along with those of other equipment makers were taken over by another company TETI which was nationalized and put under STET's control in 1958. This expanded STET's monopoly to include equipment manufacturing.

Italy's industries were increasingly nationalized under IRI. Companies within the IRI family forged alliances with each other and with independent companies which frequently were absorbed into STET.

STET's scope expanded during the 1960s and 1970s to include satellite and data communications but its monopoly was undermined by new technologies such as faxes PCs and teleconferencing. In the technology race among equipment makers STET fell behind. And in a satellite communications era STET's status as a necessary long-distance carrier was threatened. Despite these pressures change did not come easily to STET. State monopolies maintained popular support not only on nationalistic grounds but also because of labor's strong anticompetitive stance.

Anticipating privatization however IRI reorganized STET in 1994 and poured new capital into the company. STET's five telecom companies —SIP (domestic phone operator) Italcable (intercontinental) Telespazio (satellite) SIRM (maritime) and Iritel (domestic long distance) —were merged into one Telecom Italia. Its mobile phone business was spun off as Telecom Italia Mobile (TIM) in 1995.

To end political feuding the government abruptly replaced the heads of STET and Telecom Italia in 1997. Telecom Italia was merged with STET which took the Telecom Italia name and was privatized that year. Berardino Libonati became chairman and Franco Bernabe formerly CEO of oil company ENI took the helm as CEO. The company began taking stakes in foreign telecom companies including mobilkom austria Spanish broadcaster Retevision and —as European Union competition began in 1998 —Telekom Austria.

Erstwhile rival Olivetti launched a hostile takeover bid for Telecom Italia in 1999. Though Telecom Italia tried to fend off the smaller firm with various maneuvers including a proposed merger with Deutsche Telekom Olivetti gained 55% of Telecom Italia. Olivetti CEO Roberto Colaninno took over as chairman and CEO.

That year Telecom Italia sold 50% of Stream its pay TV unit to an investor group led by News Corp. The company also announced plans to spin off and sell a stake in its ISP Tin.it. In 2000 however Telecom Italia instead combined Tin.it with SEAT Pagine Gialle a yellow pages directory publisher and Internet portal operator (spun off from the parent company and sold in 2003). Also that year the company sold off 81% of its telecom equipment unit Italtel and its 49% stake in installations firm Sirti.

In 2001 Colaninno and several other Telecom Italia officials were named as suspects in an investigation of whether the company had violated accounting conflict of interest and share manipulation laws. Colaninno was replaced when tire maker Pirelli and Edizione Holding the parent company of the Benetton Group acquired a 23% stake in Olivetti.

Telecom Italia teamed up with News Corp. to develop the Stream pay TV joint venture renamed Sky Italia. The venture gained a kick-start when the two companies teamed to buy Italian pay-TV business Telepiu from Vivendi Universal in a cash and debt assumption deal that was valued at $871 million. The deal included agreements to drop disputes between Telepiu and Stream. Telecom Italia then sold a 30% stake in the venture to News Corp. It retained a 20% share with News Corp. controlling 80%.

In 2003 the company abandoned plans to acquire phone directories group Pagine Utili from Fininvest in a deal that would have been worth more than $130 million because of protests by Italian regulators who claimed the deal would breach competition laws. It also spun off its international services division starting in 2003 into a separate company Telecom Italia Sparkle which concentrated on services to other fixed-line operators ISPs and international corporations and sold its nearly 62% stake in SEAT Pagine Gialle to an investor group for $3.55 billion.

Once the subsidiary Telecom Italia became the parent company after the 2003 merger with former parent Olivetti. The reorganization simplified a corporate structure that was at best confusing: Olivetti through its Tecnost unit had acquired a controlling 55% stake in Telecom Italia in 1999. Two years later tire maker Pirelli and the Benetton family teamed up to take control of Olivetti. Olivetti's largest shareholder was Olimpia a company owned by Pirelli and the Benetton Group among others.

Because Telecom Italia accounted for more than 95% of the revenues of Olivetti the reorganization also kept the focus on the core business. The merger was met with favor among market watchers and some shareholders although a group of international investors opposed the restructuring.

Reorganization continued at the company and it began selling some international fixed-line assets and putting some wireless operations outside Italy on the market. Disposals included Digitel the Venezuelan wireless carrier to Oswaldo Cisneros' Telvenco in a deal valued at about $425 million. It also sold its 81% stake in Greek wireless carrier Hellas Telecommunications to US-based private equity firms Texas Pacific Group and Apax Partners in a deal valued at $1.4 billion; stakes in Spanish joint venture Auna and satellite unit Telespazio (to Finmeccanica); and in 2005 it sold its holdings in IT services and consulting company Finsiel to Italian outsourcing firm Gruppo COS.

After spurning an offer from AT&T to buy the company Telecom Italia named Pasquale Pistorio chairman in 2007 replacing Guido Rossi who had held the position for only seven months. Telefonica subsequently won control of the company. Later that year Pistorio was replaced by Gabriele Galateri as chairman; Galateri was nominated by another top shareholder Mediobanca.

In 2010 the company began selling off interests not related to its businesses in Italy or Brazil. It sold its 70% stake in Elettra which specialized in laying submarine cables to France Telecom (later renamed Orange) for ?20 million ($27 million); its Netherlands fixed-line provider BBNed to Tele2 for ?50 million ($64 million); and its German broadband unit HanseNet to Telefonica for the tidy sum of ?900 million ($1.2 billion) in cash. The following year Telecom Italia sold its 27% stake in the state-run Cuban phone company ETECSA for $706 million to Rafin SA a financial services firm in that country. Also in 2011 the company sold subsidiary Loquendo to US-based Nuance Communications. The sales were part of Telecom Italia's ongoing effort to sell non-core businesses in order to reduce debt.

EXECUTIVES

Head Disposals; EVP of Telecom Italia Media and Head of the Media Business Unit, Giovanni Stella, age 65
Manager Consumer, Fabrizio Bona
Chairman, Gabriele Galateri di Genola, age 66
Head External Relations, Carlo Fornaro, age 53
Managing Director COO, Marco Patuano, age 49
Head Purchasing, Stefano Ciurli, age 51
Investor Relations Officer, Elisabetta Ripa, age 47
Manager Public Affairs Department, Paolo Annunziato, age 52
Head Audit and Compliance Services, Frederico M. D'Andrea
Head Human Resources Organization and Industrial Relations, Antonio Migliardi, age 54
Head Domestic Legal Affairs and Board Secretary, Antonino Cusimano, age 48
Head Quality of Service, Paolo D'Andrea
Head Administration Finance Control and International Business, Andrea Mangoni
CEO Assistant, Franco R. Brescia
Head Strategy and Innovation, Cesare Sironi
Chief Regulatory Officer, Alessandro Talotta
Head Security, Damiano Toselli, age 60
Head National Wholesale Services, Riccardo Delleani, age 53
CEO TIM Brasil, Luca Luciani, age 45
Manager Broadband Content, Luca Tomassini
Head International Operations, Francesco Armato
Manager Business, Pietro Labriola
Manager Top Clients Market and Networked IT Services, Gianfilippo D'Agostino, age 52
Investor Relations Contact Domestic Operations, Helen Mainardi-Rosenthal
Investor Relations Contact Internal Operations - Credit Analysts and Bondholders, Paolo Germiniani
Investor Relations Contact Sustainability Retail Investors and Benchmarking, Alessandra Cantu
Investor Relations Contact Sustainability Retail Investors and Benchmarking, Maria A. Ruggieri
Investor Relations Contact Sustainability Retail Investors and Benchmarking, Giorgio Tavolini
Press Office Assistant, Rita Carboni
Head Market Press Office, Marco Rosatella
Head Regulation Press Office, Marco Signoretti
IR Contact Officer, Alex Alex Bolis Bolis
Head of Domestic Media, Carlotta Carlotta Ventura Ventura
Head of TI Audit & Compliance Services, Federico Federico DAndrea DAndrea
Group Compliance Officer, Francesca Francesca Petralia Petralia
Chairman of the Board, Franco Franco Bernabe Bernabe
Chief Executive Officer of Telecom Argentina; Chairman of Telecom Personal, Franco Franco Bertone Bertone
Information Technology Director, Gianluca Gianluca Pancaccini Pancaccini
Head of Quality, Giuseppe Giuseppe Zaza Zaza
Head of Administration; Finance and Control; Financial Reporting Officer, Piergiorgio Piergiorgio Peluso Peluso
Head of IT & Security Compliance, Roberto Roberto Mazzilli Mazzilli
Head of Top Clients and Public Sector, Simone Simone Battiferri Battiferri
Director, Aldo Minucci, age 66
Director, Mauro Sentinelli, age 66
Director, Stefano Cao, age 62
Director, Elio Cosimo Catania, age 66
Director, Roland Berger, age 75
Chairman, Gabriele Galateri di Genola, age 66
Director, Renato Pagliaro, age 56
Director, Paolo Baratta, age 74
Director, Jean-Paul Fitoussi, age 71
Director, Tarak Ben Ammar, age 64
Director, Luigi Zingales, age 50
CEO and Director, Franco Bernabe, age 64
Director, Julio L. Lopez, age 68
Director, Gaetano Micciche, age 62
Director, Cesar Alierta
Non-Executive Director, Cesar Cesar Alierta Izuel Izuel
Non-Executive Director, Gabriele Gabriele Galateri di Genola Genola
Non-Executive Director, Gaetano Gaetano Micciche Micciche
Non-Executive Director, Julio Julio Linares Lopez Lopez
Non-Executive Independent Director, Lucia Lucia Calvosa Calvosa
Non-Executive Independent Director, Massimo Massimo Egidi Egidi
Non-Executive Director, Tarak Tarak Ben Ammar Ammar
Auditors: RecontaErnst&YoungS.p.A.

LOCATIONS

HQ: Telecom Italia SPA
Piazza degli Affari 2, Milan 20123
Phone: (39) 02 85 95 1
Web: www.telecomitalia.com

2011 Sales

	% of total
Italy	64
Other	36
Total	**100**

PRODUCTS/OPERATIONS

2011 Sales

	$ mil.	% of total
Services	93	
Equipment sales	7	
Total	**0**	**100**

COMPETITORS

America Movil
BT
Cable & Wireless
Canon
Deutsche Telekom
FastWeb
Hewlett-Packard
Hutchison Whampoa
IBM
KPN
Millicom
Orange
Ricoh Company
SFR
Swisscom
Tele2
Telefonica
Tiscali
Vivo Participac?es
Vodafone Omnitel
Wind Telecomunicazioni
Xerox

HISTORICAL FINANCIALS

Company Type: Public

Income Statement FYE: December 31

	REVENUE ($ mil.)	NET INCOME ($ mil.)	NET PROFIT MARGIN	EMPLOYEES
12/12	40,044	(2,144)	—	83,184
12/11	39,870	(6,112)	—	84,154
12/10	37,973	4,177	11.0%	84,200
12/09	40,278	2,277	5.7%	71,384
12/08	43,403	3,095	7.1%	77,825
Annual Growth	(2.0%)	—	—	1.7%

2012 Year-End Financials

Debt ratio: 68.3%
Return on equity: (-7.7%)
Cash ($ mil.): 9,801
Current ratio: 0.96
Long-term debt ($ mil.): 44,933
No. of shares (mil.): —
Dividends
Yield: 4.7%
Payout: —
Market value ($ mil.): —

	STOCK PRICE ($) FY Close	P/E High/Low	PER SHARE ($) Earnings	Dividends	Book Value
12/12	9.05	— —	(0.11)	0.43	1.93
12/11	10.65	— —	(0.31)	1.14	2.22
12/10	12.94	189105	0.21	0.45	2.91
12/09	15.43	489218	0.12	0.48	2.83
12/08	16.25	581163	0.15	0.91	2.76
Annual Growth	(13.6%)	— —	—	(17.1%)	(8.6%)

Telefonaktiebolaget LM Ericsson (Sweden)

LOCATIONS

HQ: Telefonaktiebolaget LM Ericsson (Sweden)
Torshamnsgatan 23, Stockholm SE-164 83
Phone: (46) 10 719 0000
Web: www.ericsson.com

HISTORICAL FINANCIALS

Company Type: Public

Income Statement FYE: December 31

	REVENUE ($ mil.)	NET INCOME ($ mil.)	NET PROFIT MARGIN	EMPLOYEES
12/12	34,964	886	2.5%	110,255
12/11	32,901	1,768	5.4%	0
12/10	30,325	1,662	5.5%	0
Annual Growth	7.4%	(27.0%)	—	—

2012 Year-End Financials

Debt ratio: 1.6%
Return on equity: 4.1%
Cash ($ mil.): 6,858
Current ratio: 1.98
Long-term debt ($ mil.): 3,668
No. of shares (mil.): —
Dividends
Yield: —
Payout: —
Market value ($ mil.): —

	STOCK PRICE ($) FY Close	P/E High/Low		PER SHARE ($) Earnings	Dividends	Book Value
12/12	0.00	—	—	0.27	0.00	6.52
12/11	0.00	—	—	0.55	0.00	6.46
Annual Growth	—	—	—	(29.3%)	—	0.5%

Telefonica, S.A.

Telefonica calls Spain home but customers in 25 countries call home with Telefonica. The company provides fixed and mobile phone service across Europe (55% of sales) and Latin America (45%). Its fixed-line portfolio includes voice Internet access cable and satellite television enterprise networking and hosting and wholesale services. Its mobile business encompasses voice messaging and corporate infrastructure services. Telefonica divides its business into three segments –Telefonica Espa?a Telefonica Europe and Telefonica Latinoamerica. Telefonica Espa?a has 24 million mobile customers and 13 million access lines and Telefonica Latinoamerica has almost 145 million mobile subscribers.

As the incumbent carrier in Spain Telefonica Espa?a is the leading fixed-line operator in Spain with more than 13 million access lines in service. Like other landline providers the company has seen its number of subscribers drop by about 1 million a year over the past couple of years as more people switch to cellular phones for their primary service. Mobile data and pay TV users continue to rise. The company counts almost 6 million Internet users and more than 775000 pay TV viewers. Telefonica Espa?a accounted for abouth 30% of the group's revenues in 2010.

Telefonica Europe oversees the group's operations in the Czech Republic Germany Ireland Slovakia and the UK; its services are marketed under the O2 brand. Altogether it has more than 3.5 million fixed-line customers 4.4 million Internet and data access users about 200000 pay TV viewers and almost 46 million mobile subscribers. Again while the number of fixed-line customers drop mobile data and pay TV users are on the rise. Telefonica Europe accounted for about 25% of the group's revenues in 2010.

Telefonica Latinoamerica is a top carrier in Argentina Brazil (with Portugal Telecom) Chile Colombia and Peru; the company also has substantial operations in Ecuador El Salvador Guatemala Mexico Nicaragua Panama Puerto Rico Uruguay and Venezuela. In these countries the company has 24 million fixed-line customers 8 million Internet and data access users 1.7 million pay TV viewers and almost 150 million mobile subscribers. Up against regional wireless leader America Movil the company is the dominant carrier in some markets. Telefonica Latinoamerica accounted for more than 40% of the group's revenues in 2010.

With the market cornered on traditional voice services Telefonica's acquisitions and divestures are centered around auxiliary services. In early 2010 it bought broadband service provider Hansenet from Telecom Italia for E900 million ($1.2 billion). The deal added about 2 million high-speed Internet customers to Telefonica's books and gave it a better foothold in Germany where its Telefonica O2 Germany struggles to gain ground on rivals Vodafone and United Internet not to mention incumbent provider Deutsche Telekom.

Later that year Telefonica got the green light from Spanish anti-trust regulators to acquire a 22% stake in Sogecable's Digital+ satellite TV service. Telefonica had originally wanted to make strategic decisions on Digital+'s business plan and govern its management; in the end regulators agreed to also give broadcaster Mediaset Espa?a (formerly Telecinco) a 22% stake and leave parent Prisa with the 56% majority control. Upon completion of the deal including financial terms Telefonica will likely strengthen its presence in the pay-TV market.

Telefonica has numerous stakes in companies outside of its core operating countries. It owns 100% of 3G Mobile AG Switzerland (inactive) call center Atento Brasil and media distributor Telefonica de Contenidos; 46% of Telco S.p.A. a holding company that controls more than 20% of Telecom Italia; 32% of Lycos Europe; and a 5% stake in China Unicom. The company is looking to reduce its debt load however by selling non-core operations. In late 2012 it agreed to sell Atento to private equity group Bain Capital for some E1 billion ($1.3 billion).

In 2013 it formed a mobile advertising network with US telecom giant Sprint Nextel that will offer advertisers access to more than 370 million customers in the Americas and Europe.

HISTORY

When a 1923 military coup brought General Miguel Primo de Rivera to power in Spain the government-run phone system was in shambles. More than half of the country's 90000 lines did not work. With little cash in the government coffers Primo de Rivera sought foreign assistance.

Supported by National City Bank (now Citigroup) US-based ITT bought three private Spanish phone companies later combining them to form Compa?ia Telefonica Nacional de Espa?a. The ITT unit gained the state phone concession in 1924 and the government agreed not to reclaim the system for 20 years. But when Franco came to power in 1939 he froze Telefonica's assets. ITT tried to sell the company to German buyers in 1941 but backed out when the US State Department objected. The Spanish government nationalized Telefonica in 1945 keeping 41% of its shares.

Long-distance service was introduced in 1960 satellite communications in 1967 and international service in 1971. Still when Spain entered the European Union (EU) in 1986 Telefonica was unprepared for the increase in demand for services and complaints rose.

The firm purchased a minority stake in Compa?ia de Telefonos de Chile in 1990 and a Telefonica-led consortium won a bid to manage the southern half of ENTEL Argentina's former state phone system. The company acquired a majority stake in Peru's telecom monopoly in 1994 and a year later joined Unisource a European telecom consortium.

The Spanish government at first defied the EU's directive to break up its telecom monopoly. But in 1994 the government announced it would meet the EU's 1998 deadline for opening telecom markets; in exchange Telefonica won permission to begin new businesses when competition arrived.

Flamboyant former investment banker Juan Villalonga took over as chairman in 1996. The boyhood friend of Spain's prime minister began expanding Telefonica's presence in Latin America with several acquisitions in 1997. They included 35% of Brazil's Companhia Riograndense de Telecomunicac?es (CRT); a large stake in Multicanal Argentina's #1 cable company (sold in 1998 to Grupo Clarin); and 35% of satellite TV service Via Digital.

That year Telefonica broke off with Unisource and allied with British Telecom (now BT Group) and MCI only to have the alliance break up when MCI agreed to be bought by WorldCom in 1998. Meanwhile the Spanish government had finished divesting its interest in the company in 1997 (retaining a golden share) and competition came to Spain the next year. The company revamped its corporate structure cut 10000 jobs and became Telefonica S.A. It also won fixed-line phone company Telesp and a cellular company in Brazil's auction of the former national phone company Telebras.

In 1999 Telefonica sold to the public a part of its Internet unit Terra Networks (formerly Telefonica Interactiva). The next year it took near-total ownership of four of its Latin American units: Telefonica de Argentina Telefonica del Peru Telesp and Tele Sudeste Celular (it later sold its stake in CRT to meet regulatory approval) and separated the mobile and data operations to reorganize by business units.

To expand its multimedia offerings Telefonica bought Netherlands-based independent TV producer Endemol for $5.3 billion in 2000 and formed Telefonica Media (it agreed to sell the stake back to a consortium including the company's founder John de Mol in 2007 for $3.65 billion). After dropping out of the UK wireless license auction the company teamed up with Finland's Sonera (later acquired by Telia) to win a license in the German auction. But when merger talks with Dutch telecom carrier KPN broke down Villalonga resigned over disagreements on the direction of the company.

In 2001 Telefonica combined its Brazilian mobile telephone holdings with those of Portugal Telecom to form market leader Brasilcel. It then spent $2.7 billion in Mexico in 2001 and 2002 to buy four wireless operators and a 65%-stake in a fifth (Pegaso PCS) to achieve #2 in that market.

Telefonica acquired the assets of BellSouth Latin America Group which had holdings in 10 South and Central American countries in a $5.8 billion deal in 2005.

The company sold its stake in phone directory business Telefonica Publicidad e Informacion (TPI) to Yell Group in 2006. Also that year Telefonica purchased the remaining 7% stake of its Telefonica Moviles wireless arm that it did not already own and integrated those operations. The company's 2006 acquisition of UK-based mobile phone operator O2 for more than $31 billion gave Telefonica a strong presence in the UK and Germany. The Spanish operator previously had no operations in those regions.

In partnership with a coalition of Italian financial backers the company bought a stake in Telecom Italia for about $5.58 billion in mid-2007. Telefonica also sold its 75% stake in Dutch TV producer Endemol for $3.65 billion in 2007.

Telefonica exited Morocco in 2009 when it sold its 32% stake in Medi Telecom for E400 million ($572 million). Later that year it bought California-based communications software developer JAJAH Inc. for E145 million ($207 million) in cash to enhance its ability to offer computer telephony services to customers regardless of their location. JAJAH specializes in applications that allow interoperability between wired and wireless IP-based communications systems.

EXECUTIVES

Vice-Chairman, Isidro Faine Casas, age 70
Director, Sir David G. Arculus, age 66
Director, Peter Erskine, age 61
Vice-Chairman, Vitalino M. Nafria Aznar, age 62
Director, Pablo Isla Alvarez de Tejera, age 48
Director, Gonzalo Hinojosa Fernandez de Angulo, age 67
Director, Alfonso Ferrari Herrero, age 70
Director, Carlos Colomer Casellas, age 68
Director, Jose M. Abril Perez, age 60
Director, Antonio Massanell Lavilla, age 58
Legal and Board Secretary and Director, Ramiro Sanchez de Lerin Garcia-Ovies
Director, Jose Fernando de Almansa Moreno-Barreda, age 64
COO and Director, Julio Linares Lopez
Director, Javier de Paz Mancho, age 54
Chairwoman and CEO Telefonica Europe and Director, Eva Castillo Sanz, age 50
Director, Luiz Fernando Furlan, age 66
Auditors: Ernst&YoungS.L.

LOCATIONS

HQ: Telefonica, S.A.
Distrito Telefonica, Ronda de la Comunicacion, s/n, Madrid 28050
Phone: (34) 91 482 8700 **Fax:** (34) 91 482 8600
Web: www.telefonica.com

2010 Sales

	% of total
Telefonica Latin	44
Telefonica	31
Telefonica	25
Total	**100**

PRODUCTS/OPERATIONS

Selected Subsidiaries

Atento Brasil S.A.
Brasilcel (Brazil)
Colombia Telecomunicaciones S.A. ESP.
Otecel S.A. (Ecuador)
Telcel S.A. (Venezuela)
Telecomunicac?es de S?o Paulo S.A (Brazil)
Telefonica Chile S.A.
Telefonica de Argentina S.A.
Telefonica del Peru S.A.A.
Telefonica Moviles Argentina S.A.
Telefonica Moviles Chile S.A.
Telefonica Moviles Colombia S.A.
Telefonica Moviles El Salvador S.A. de C.V.
Telefonica Moviles Guatemala S.A.
Telefonica Moviles Mexico S.A. de C.V.
Telefonica Moviles Nicaragua S.A.
Telefonica Moviles Panama S.A.
Telefonica Moviles Peru S.A.C.
Telefonica Moviles Uruguay S.A.
Telefonica O2 Czech Republic a. s.
Telefonica O2 Germany
Telefonica O2 Ireland Limited
Telefonica O2 Slovakia S R O
Telefonica O2 UK Limited

COMPETITORS

America Movil
BT
Brasil Telecom
COLT Group
Cableuropa
Carphone Warehouse
Hutchison Telecommunications
Jazztel
KPN
Orange
Orange Espa?a
Portugal Telecom
Telecom Italia
Telemar Norte Leste
TeliaSonera
Telmex
Virgin Mobile
Vodafone
Vodafone Espa?a

HISTORICAL FINANCIALS

Company Type: Public

Income Statement FYE: December 31

	REVENUE ($ mil.)	NET INCOME ($ mil.)	NET PROFIT MARGIN	EMPLOYEES
12/12	82,188	5,177	6.3%	133,186
12/11	81,276	6,988	8.6%	291,027
12/10	81,288	13,607	16.7%	285,106
12/09	81,724	11,201	13.7%	257,426
12/08	81,013	10,614	13.1%	257,035
Annual Growth	0.4%	(16.4%)	—	(15.2%)

2012 Year-End Financials

Debt ratio: 67.9%
Return on equity: 18.6%
Cash ($ mil.): 12,978
Current ratio: 0.81
Long-term debt ($ mil.): 74,612
No. of shares (mil.): —
Dividends
Yield: 15.4%
Payout: 151.2%
Market value ($ mil.): —

	STOCK PRICE ($) FY Close	P/E High/Low		PER SHARE ($) Earnings	Dividends	Book Value
12/12	13.49	36	19	1.15	2.08	5.99
12/11	17.19	108	24	1.53	3.93	6.25
12/10	68.42	75	39	2.96	1.72	7.26
12/09	83.52	113	55	2.46	1.42	6.86
12/08	67.39	128	51	2.28	1.00	5.12
Annual Growth	(33.1%)	—	—	(15.8%)	20.0%	4.0%

Telenor ASA

How do you say "can you hear me now" in Norwegian? Telenor knows. The company dominates the Norwegian telecommunications market with millions of accounts. It generates about 70% of sales from its mobile operations serving more than 150 million subscribers in about a dozen markets in the Nordic region Central and Eastern Europe and Asia. The company operates in 18 additional mobile markets thoughts its 36% stake in VimpelCom one of Russia's largest mobile operators with more than 200 million subscribers. Telenor also offers fixed-line communication services (telephone and Internet) and cable and satellite television (provided through Telenor Broadcast).

Operations

Telenor's fixed-line services account for just under 15% of sales and are declining year-over-year (down 6% in 2011). Telenor Broadcast is one of the leading providers of DTH television in the Nordic region through subsidiary Canal Digital. It also provides cable TV terrestrial transmission and encryption services and manages content rights through its Telenor Media and Content Services division.

Geographic Reach

Norway is Telenor's largest market representing nearly 30% of sales with the entire Nordic region accounting for nearly half. Malaysia Thailand and other Asian countries however are among the company's fastest-growing markets and currently account for about 40% of sales.

Financial Analysis

Telenor's revenue grew 4% in 2011 (on top of 5% growth in 2010) to 98.5 billion Norwegian kroner (about $16.4 billion). The results were powered by the addition of 29 million new mobile subscribers primarily due to strong organic growth from the company's Asian operations specifically in India and Bangladesh. Net income in 2011 however fell by more than 50% from 2010 when Telenor recorded a significant gain on disposal related to its ownership in VimpelCom. A 2011 impairment loss as a result of the cancellation of all existing 2G wireless network licenses by the Indian Supreme Court also negatively impacted net income.

Strategy

One of Telenor's strategic challenges as part of a fast-moving industry is making sure it is prepared for next-generation products and services. To address this the company established a new division in 2011 called Digital Services that is focused on innovation and working with partners to develop new services. It established a digital services company ComoYo that year and also partnered with Google to provide Telenor customers with more efficient access to mobile content and apps. In addition the company is working on mobile financial services (it has tested a mobile payment service with Norwegian banking giant DNB) as well as machine-to-machine (M2M) communications.

Telenor is also investing in network modernization initiatives to handle the anticipated growth in traffic as a result of smartphones and other mobile broadband devices. Network upgrades were completed in about half a dozen markets in 2011 (including Norway Sweden and Bangladesh) with more in the works for 2012 (including Thailand and Malaysia).

Mergers and Acquisitions

Telenor uses acquisitions to broaden and enhance its offerings. In 2010 it acquired an additional 18% of Indian carrier (and partner) Unitech Wireless. The deal put Telenor in control of more than two-thirds of the company which was rebranded Uninor and gave it significant access to the Indian wireless market (one the world's largest). Two years later it increased its stake in VimpelCom to about 36% (it had previously fallen to 32%).

Ownership

The Norwegian government through the Ministry of Trade and Industry owns about 54% of Telenor.

HISTORY

Telecommunications arrived in Norway in 1855 when the first telegraph line was opened and the Norwegian Telegraph Administration was created. By 1880 telephone systems were being installed followed by the first automatic phone exchange (1918) Telex services (1946) and a transmitter network for television which debuted in 1960. Mobile phone service was introduced in 1966 but it was not until 1969 that the agency's name was changed to Norwegian Telecommunications Administration.

Norway had progressed to its first computer-controlled phone exchange by the mid 1970s and in 1976 launched a national satellite system (NORSAT) that linked North Sea oil explorers with Norway's mainland. It opened the world's first fully automated coastal earth station in 1982 to carry maritime traffic as part of the INMARSAT system and a year later automated its last manually operated phone exchange. (Telenor held a stake in INMARSAT until it sold it in 2006.)

In the mid-1980s the national carrier became known as Norwegian Telecom (Televerket). In 1984 it introduced an upgraded mobile phone system and a numeric paging system (alphanumeric paging followed in 1991). The first digital phone exchanges arrived in 1986 and two years later Televerket was reorganized into three units: the national operator (Televerket) a sales subsidiary (TBK) and a state regulatory agency for equipment approval (STF).

The company in 1990 organized its mobile services under a single division (Tele-mobil) which a year later became a limited company. Two years later data transmission was opened to competition and the resale of surplus leased line capacity was allowed.

In 1993 Televerket reorganized under the name Norwegian Telecom Group and joined a consortium of Nordic and Hungarian companies to win a mobile operator license in Hungary. A year later it became a state-owned company and in 1995 was renamed Telenor. That year it teamed up with British Telecommunications (now BT Group) and Tele Danmark (now TDC) to create the Swedish telecom competitor Telenordia (Telenor and BT became 50-50 owners in 2000).

Telenor in 1997 took a 10% stake in VIAG Interkom a joint venture with BT and Germany's VIAG to operate both a mobile and fixed line network in Germany (BT bought Telenor's stake in 2000). That year the Norwegian telecom network was completely digitized and Telenor introduced its Internet unit Telenor Nextel (renamed Nextra in 2000).

Telenor expanded its Internet activities in Europe as deregulation of Norway's telecom market in 1998 increased competition there. The next year Telenor's plans to merge with Swedish telecom Telia fell through; Telia later merged with Sonera of Finland to form TeliaSonera. In 2000 Telenor changed the name of its installation and services unit to Bravida and spun it off. Telenor also acquired 54% of Danish mobile operator Sonofon. That year Norway's government sold about 20% of Telenor in a public offering.

The carrier beefed up its satellite operations in 2001 buying Lockheed Martin's COMSAT Mobile Communications. It also took full ownership of Telenordia the Swedish fixed-line venture it held with BT and it took full ownership of Hungarian mobile phone operator Pannon GSM. The company sold Telenor Media its directory-publishing unit to US-based private equity firm Texas Pacific Group for about $670 million. It also sold a 7.7% stake in Ukrainian mobile telecom operator Kyivstar to Storm in 2002 for $31 million.

Telenor sold Russian telecom subsidiaries Comincom and Combellga to Golden Telecom in 2003 in exchange for a nearly 21% stake in that firm. In 2004 Telenor acquired the Norwegian operation of Italian ISP Tiscali. The next year the company acquired Denmark's third-largest broadband provider Cybercity and Sweden's second-largest broadband provider Bredbandsbolaget (B2 Bredband).

Hoping to boost its market share in Denmark Telenor acquired Tele2 Denmark from Tele2 in 2007. Tele2 Denmark provided mobile broadband and fixed-line services. Meanwhile the company strengthened its position in the Nordic markets with the acquisitions of such smaller rivals as Sweden-based Spray Telecom and Norwegian competitor Talkmore.

Efforts to simplify the company's corporate structure included the 2007 sale of Telenor Satellite Services business and its minority stake in Austrian mobile carrier One. Telenor also reduced its controlling stake in Malaysian operator DiGi to 49% in 2008 and it sold its 18% stake in Russian carrier Golden Telecom to VimpleCom that year.

EXECUTIVES

EVP and CFO, Richard Olav Aa
President and CEO, Jon F. Baksaas, age 59, $793,350 total compensation
CEO Thailand, Jon Eddy Abdullah, age 47
EVP and Head Telenor Norway, Berit Svendsen, age 50
Manager Communication, Dag Melgaard
Chairman, Svein Aaser, age 67
CEO Serbia, Ove Fredheim, age 49
Manager Communication, Scott Engebrigtsen
Chairman, Harald Norvik, age 65
CEO DiGi Malaysia, Henrik Clausen
Deputy Chairman, Liselott Kilaas
Managing Director Uninor, Stein-Erik Vellan
EVP and Head European Operations, Kjell-Morten Johnsen, age 46
Manager Communication, Ingrid Schiefloe
EVP and Head Asia Operations, Sigve Brekke
EVP and Head Group People Development, Jon Erik Haug
EVP and Head Group Industrial Development, Hilde M. Tonne, $500,000 total compensation
Head Information Norway, Atle Lessum
Director Communications Asia, Glenn Mandelid
CEO Pannon, Anders Jensen
Head Investor Relations, Marianne Moe
CEO Telenor Connexion, Per Simonsen, age 49
CEO Sweden, Lars-?ke Norling
CEO Grameenphone, Oddvar Hesjedal
CEO Hungary, Christopher Laska
Head Telenor Russia; SVP Telenor Central and Eastern Europe, Ole Bj?rn Sjulstad
Interim EVP and Interim Head People and Organization, Ingvald Fergestad
EVP and Head Digital Services, Rolv-Erik Spilling
CEO Pakistan, Christian Albech
Director Communications Broadcast Holding, J?rgen Thaule
Executive Vice President, Kristin Lund
EVP and Head Strategy and RegulatoryAffairs, Morten K. Sorby
CEO Denmark, Marek Slacik
CEO Grameenphone Bangladesh, Vivek Sood
CEO Uninor India, Yogesh Malik
CEO Pakistan, Lars Christian Iuel
Executive Vice President Chief Financial Officer CFO, Richard Olav
Director, Burckhard Bergmann, age 69
Director, Sanjiv Ahuja, age 57
Deputy Chairman, Liselott Kilaas
Director, Barbara M. Thoralfsson, age 54
Director, Olav Volldal, age 63
Director, Kjersti Kleven, age 46
Employee Representative, Bj?rn Andre Anderssen
Employee Representative, Harald Stavn
Auditors: Ernst&YoungAS

LOCATIONS

HQ: Telenor ASA
Snaroyveien 30, Fornebu N-1331
Phone: (47) 810 77 000
Web: www.telenor.com

2011 Sales

	% of total
Norway	29
Sweden	12
Other	8
Other Western	1
Central	8
Thailand	14
Malaysia	11
Other	16
Other	1
Total	**100**

PRODUCTS/OPERATIONS

2011 Sales

	% of total
Mobile	69
Fixed-line	14
Satellite & TV	7
Customer	6
Other	4
Total	**100**

COMPETITORS

BT
Bharti Airtel
CELCOM
Computer Sciences Corp.
Deutsche Telekom
Hutchison Telecommunications
Mahanagar Telephone Nigam
Maxis
Modern Times Group AB
Orange
Pakistan Telecom
Reliance Communications
TDC
Tata Teleservices
Tele2
TeleComputing
TeliaSonera
Tieto
Vodafone India

HISTORICAL FINANCIALS

Company Type: Public

Income Statement

FYE: December 31

	REVENUE ($ mil.)	NET INCOME ($ mil.)	NET PROFIT MARGIN	EMPLOYEES
12/12	18,184	1,799	9.9%	32,900
12/11	16,385	1,191	7.3%	32,030
12/10	16,253	2,456	15.1%	33,220
12/09	16,949	1,501	8.9%	40,300
12/08	13,881	1,865	13.4%	38,800
Annual Growth	7.0%	(0.9%)	—	(4.0%)

2012 Year-End Financials

Debt ratio: 5.4%
Return on equity: 12.6%
Cash ($ mil.): 1,574
Current ratio: 0.68
Long-term debt ($ mil.): 7,347
No. of shares (mil.): 1,544
Dividends
Yield: 4.0%
Payout: 6.4%
Market value ($ mil.): 93,795

	STOCK PRICE ($) FY Close	P/E High	P/E Low	PER SHARE ($) Earnings	Dividends	Book Value
12/12	60.74	0	0	1.15	2.46	8.59
12/11	48.77	0	0	0.74	0.06	8.82
12/10	48.90	0	0	1.49	1.14	9.23
12/09	41.80	0	0	0.91	0.00	7.96
12/08	20.50	0	0	1.12	2.03	6.97
Annual Growth	31.2%	—	—	0.7%	4.8%	5.3%

TeliaSonera A B

An expert at cold calling TeliaSonera offers telecom services primarily in the chilly Nordic region as Europe's fifth-largest telco. Mobile and broadband services including TV to residential and business customers in Finland Norway and Sweden account for about 60% of sales. The company offers mobile services to Spain and countries across Eurasia such as Russia (nearly 65 million subscribers) and Turkey (nearly 35 million). With a leading position in most of its markets the company counts 175 million subscribers across its networks. The company's mobile business brings in about half of sales. Other activities include sales of telecom equipment and the provision of wholesale network capacity to other carriers.

The company has offered 4G data services using the Long Term Evolution (LTE) standard since 2009. TeliaSonera implemented LTE equipment from Ericsson for Stockholm and from Huawei Technologies for Oslo along with 4G data modems supplied by Samsung Electronics. TeliaSonera holds nationwide 4G licenses in seven countries — Denmark Estonia Finland Latvia Lithuania Norway and Sweden.

TeliaSonera offers both its mobile and broadband services only to its Baltic (Estonia Latvia and Lithuania) and Nordic customers. Outside of these regions the company offers wireless service to its only Western European holding Yoigo (Spain) which counts about 2.2 million subscribers. TeliaSonera's Eurasia division provides wireless service to Azerbaijan Georgia Kazakhstan Moldova Nepal Russia Tajikistan Turkey and Uzbekistan.

TeliaSonera saw 9% growth in volume largely in its mobile business but pricing pressure and foreign exchange effects drove overall revenue down 4% to about $15 billion. Mobility services were up nearly 1% and Eurasia revenues grew 5%. Sales in its largest market Sweden grew 7% while Spain increased by nearly one-third. The company also saw double digit growth in most of its Eurasian markets with Nepal nearly doubling.

Although TeliaSonera holds at least majority stakes in its companies in Eurasia its strategy includes increasing its ownership in its core business. In 2012 it agreed to pay $1.5 billion to incerase its ownership in its Kazakhstan subsidiary Kcell to nearly 62%. Kazakhstan is Central Asia's largest mobile market. Shedding a non-core business in 2011 TeliaSonera sold its subsidiary North Sea Comunication which provided communications services to the oil and gas industry operating in the North Sea between Norway and the UK. It was sold to HitecVision for about SEK170 million ($22 million).

The governments of Finland and Sweden together control 51% of TeliaSonera: The Kingdom of Sweden holds 37% while the Republic of Finland owns nearly 14%.

HISTORY

Telia's wires go back to 1853 when the Swedish government created Kongliga Elektriska Telegraf-Verket to operate a telegraph line linking Stockholm and Uppsala. The next year it opened a line that reached the main European continent; the company became Telegrafverket in 1860.

Just a year after the telephone was invented in 1876 the firm installed its first phone line. The 1880s saw private phone companies sprout up in Sweden's larger cities and by 1900 Telegrafverket had installed some 62000 telephones. Even though Sweden was open to telecom competition the company became a de facto monopoly in 1918 when it bought the country's largest exchange Stockholms Allmanna Telefon. In 1921 Telegrafverket began laying its first long-distance cable.

Telegrafverket began automating its phone systems in the 1930s. After WWII the company entered a major growth period: More than 110000 new telephone users were connected in 1947 alone. Also in the mid-1940s Telegrafverket launched one of the world's first mobile phone networks (closed radio).

Renamed Televerket the firm continued to grow rapidly in the 1960s and 1970s and introduced data communications services in 1965. It teamed up with equipment maker Ericsson in 1970 to form Ellemtel an R&D concern that developed the first all-digital public switching system. (Ellemtel ceased operations in 1999.) Televerket began moving into satellite services in 1970 when INTELSAT installed an earth station in the Nordic region. In the early 1980s it rolled out several new services including cable TV cellular and international packet switching.

Meanwhile the company began losing its monopoly status in the 1980s and lost its government funding in 1984. Fearing competition from giants such as AT&T and British Telecom (now BT Group) the company in 1991 joined the Netherlands' Royal KPN to form Unisource a global telecommunications provider; Swisscom joined the group two years later. Sweden's telecom deregulation was completed in 1993 and the firm became Telia. That year it ventured into the Baltic states.

AT&T teamed up with Unisource in 1994 to provide services to multinationals. In 1995 Telia began providing Internet access and announced it was installing an overlay Internet protocol (IP) backbone. Moving into the Americas in 1997 Telia led a consortium that secured rights to offer cellular service in Brazil.

Unisource never took off and after AT&T jumped ship in 1998 Telia and its partners began divesting the venture's assets. After Telia's proposed merger with Norway's Telenor fell through in 1999 the company began tweaking its strategy to become a strong global player. But conditions within the telecom industry forced the company to revamp its international carrier strategy cut 400 jobs within the unit and trim its operations.

The Swedish government floated 30% of Telia in 2000. A restructuring the next year created five new business areas. Telia acquired Norwegian mobile phone operator NetCom ASA and in 2002 it bought the UK operations of bankrupt Canadian network operator 360networks and acquired defunct KPNQwest's network in France.

Also in 2002 Telia acquired Nordic region competitor Sonera. That company's history as a telegraph company dates back almost as far as Telia's although the original connection between Helsinki and St. Petersburg was used primarily by the Russian government and the military. The Finnish government in 1877 created an entity that installed the country's first telephone lines and encouraged other companies to do the same; ultimately there were some 800 local telephone companies. The Finnish government established the Telegraph Office in 1917 (which included telephones) and combined it with the Post Office in 1927 forming the Finnish Post and Telegraph Office (PTT). The state-controlled PTT monopolized long-distance and international telephone service until 1992 (the individual companies which had become about 50 regional firms by the 1990s provided the local service). Two years later PTT became PT Finland which then was separated into Finland Post and Telecom Finland. The latter became Sonera in 1998 after Telecom Finland was partially privatized the year before. With the Telia acquisition the two companies were combined to form TeliaSonera; as a condition of the merger the group was required to sell Telia Mobile Finland.

The group acquired the Danish operations of Orange Communications the wireless unit of France Telecom (later renamed Orange) in 2004. The acquisition improved TeliaSonera's market position in Denmark moving it from fourth- to third-largest mobile operator. That year the company also paid $117 million to acquire a 35% stake in Omnitel from Motorola in a deal that increased TeliaSonera's stake in the Lithuanian mobile operator to 90%; it later acquired the remaining 10%. In 2004 it sold its Sonera Zed unit an aggregator and reseller of digital content to mobile phone users to Spanish interactive media group Wisdom Entertainment. It also unloaded its stake in satellite company Eutelsat.

TeliaSonera expanded its holdings in Norway in 2006 when it acquired an 82% stake in NextGenTel Holding the country's #2 broadband provider and 33% of retail holding company ComHouse. That year TeliaSonera also purchased the shares it did not already own of wireless services firm Paamies which operated via a network of retail shops throughout Finland. Acquisitions in 2007 included Cygate a Nordic provider of managed IP services and mobile carrier debitel Danmark. TeliaSonera bought the remaining two-thirds of ComHouse in 2008.

France Telecom offered to acquire TeliaSonera for nearly $42 billion in 2008; TeliaSonera ultimately rejected the bid.

In 2009 it acquired the remaining shares it did not already own of Estonian carrier AS Eesti Telekom and raised its stake in the Lithuanian firm TEO LT. Also that year the company acquired the Norwegian broadband and VoIP business of rival Tele2 through NextGenTel in a bid to build its assets in Norway.

EXECUTIVES

President and CEO, Lars Nyberg, age 61, $12,010,704 total compensation
Vice Chairman, Timo Peltola, age 67
President of Mobility Services, Tero E. Kivisaari, age 41
SVP General Counsel and Head Group Legal Affairs, Jan H. Ahrnell, age 54
Chairman, Anders Narvinger, age 65
SVP and Head Group Communications, Cecilia Edstrom, age 47
President and CEO Sonera Finland, Robert Andersson, age 53
President of Broadband Services, Malin Frenning, age 46
SVP and Head Group Human Resources, Karin Eliasson, age 62
EVP and CFO, Per-Arne Blomquist, age 51, $2,161,243 total compensation
SVP and Head of Sales Division Business Services, Sverker Hannervall, age 53
VP Investor Relations, Andreas Ekstrom, age 38
President and CEO, Johan Dennelind
SVP and CIO, Ake Sodermark, age 58
Senior Vice President; Chief Information Officer, Ake Ake Sodemark Sodemark
Senior Vice President; Head of Group Communications, Cecilia Cecilia Edstrom Edstrom
President and Chief Executive Officer of Sonera in Finland, Robert Robert Andersson Andersson
CEO Kcell; Head of Central Asia, Veysel Aral
Vice Chairman, Timo Peltola, age 67
Director, Per-Arne Sandstrom, age 67
Director, Maija-Liisa Friman, age 61
Director, Jon Risfelt, age 52
Director, Lars Renstrom, age 62
Director, Conny Karlsson, age 58
Director, Agneta Ahlstrom, age 53
Director, Magnus Brattstrom, age 60
Director, Srefan Carlsson, age 60
Director, Ingrid Jonasson Blank
Director; Employee Representative, Agneta Agneta Ahlstrom Ahlstrom
Independent Director, Lars Lars Renstrom Renstrom
Director; Employee Representative, Magnus Magnus Brattstrom Brattstrom
Independent Director, Per-Arne Per-Arne Sandstrom Sandstrom
Auditors: PricewaterhouseCoopersAB

LOCATIONS

HQ: TeliaSonera A B
Stureplan 8, Stockholm SE-106 63
Phone: (46) 8 504 550 00 **Fax:** (46) 8 504 550 01
Web: www.teliasonera.com

2011 Sales

	% of total
Sweden	35
Finland	14
Norway	9
Other	42
Total	**100**

PRODUCTS/OPERATIONS

2011 Sales

	% of total
Mobility	46
Broadband	34
Eurasia	16
Other	4
Total	**100**

2011 Sales

	% of total
Mobile	57
Fixed	32
Equipment sales & other	11
Total	**100**

Selected Brands

Amigo (Latvia)
Azercell (Azerbaijan)
Chess (Norway)
Diil (Estonia)
Elion (Estonia)
EMT (Estonia)
Ezys (Lithuania)
DLG Tele2 (Denmark)
Geocell (Georgia)
Halebop (Sweden)
Kcell (Kazakhstan)
Lattelecom (Latvia)
Life (Belarus Ukraine)
LMT (Latvia)
MegaFon (Russia)
Moldcell (Moldova)
Ncell (Nepal)
NetCom (Norway)
NextGenTel (Norway)
Okarte (Latvia)
Omnitel (Lithuania)
Sonera (Finland)
Tcell (Tajikistan)
TeleFinland (Finland)
Telia (Sweden Denmark)
TEO (Lithuania)
Turkcell (Turkey)
UCell (Uzbekistan)
Yoigo (Spain)

COMPETITORS

BT
COLT Group
Cable & Wireless
DNA Ltd.
Deutsche Telekom
Elisa Corporation
Hi3G Denmark
Invitel
KPN
Level 3 Communications
Liberty Global
Mobile TeleSystems
Orange
Orange Business Services
Rostelecom
TDC
Tele2
Telefonica
Telenor
VimpelCom
Vivo Participac?es
Vodafone

HISTORICAL FINANCIALS

Company Type: Public

Income Statement

FYE: December 31

	REVENUE ($ mil.)	NET INCOME ($ mil.)	NET PROFIT MARGIN	EMPLOYEES
12/12	16,102	3,052	19.0%	27,838
12/11	15,130	2,659	17.6%	28,412
12/10	15,894	3,170	19.9%	28,945
12/09	15,327	2,647	17.3%	29,734
12/08	13,263	2,434	18.4%	32,171
Annual Growth	5.0%	5.8%	—	(3.6%)

2012 Year-End Financials

Debt ratio: 5.5%
Return on equity: 17.5%
Cash ($ mil.): 4,575
Current ratio: 1.61
Long-term debt ($ mil.): 12,615
No. of shares (mil.): —
Dividends
Yield: 6.1%
Payout: 2.7%
Market value ($ mil.): —

	STOCK PRICE ($) FY Close	P/E High/Low		PER SHARE ($) Earnings	Dividends	Book Value
12/12	13.65	0	0	0.70	0.84	3.88
12/11	13.49	0	0	0.61	0.02	3.91
12/10	14.67	0	0	0.71	0.01	4.18
12/09	14.75	0	0	0.59	0.01	4.23
Annual Growth	(2.6%)	—	—	4.5%	224.4%	(2.2%)

Telstra Corp., Ltd.

As Australia's #1 telecommunications carrier Telstra provides fixed-line services to about 8 million access lines and it serves 12 million mobile phone customers. It is also the country's leading ISP through BigPond with more than 5 million broadband subscribers. Telstra's largest market is consumer and residential customers but its business and government segment comes in a close second. The company also provides wholesale network services to other communications companies while its Sensis telephone directory unit specializes in print online and wireless advertising. Telstra owns half of pay-television operator FOXTEL while News Corp. and Consolidated Media Holdings each own 25% of the joint venture.

Telstra was delivered a blow by the Australian government in 2008 when it was shut out of an auction (open to the company and rivals such as Singapore Telecommunications) to bid on the construction of an $11 billion nationwide broadband network. Telstra's proposal did not include plans for how the network would benefit small and midsized businesses as required by the government.

Subsequent negotiations between Telstra and the government during 2009 and 2010 became entangled in broader legislation related to changes to federal telecommunications regulations. The government has prodded Telstra to break up into two businesses in order to increase competition. In 2012 the company agreed to sell TelstraClear to Vodafone for NZ$840 million ($670 million).

The restructuring would divide the company into separate wholesale and retail businesses and make Telstra's landline telephone business part of the nationwide network operated under the government-owned National Broadband Network (NBN). Telstra would have to allow rivals access to its copper network through at least 2020 while NBN develops the fiber optic network. The company also have to sell its cable network and its stake in FOXTEL; it continues to negotiate with the government.

While revenues and profits rose overall in 2011 Telstra is trying to turn around underperforming units such as its fixed-line services and directories businesses which saw sales slip for the year. The company is hoping that new consumer products will appeal to broadband Internet and cable pay television customers and boost fixed-line subscriber numbers. It is marketing a new touchscreen communications device for the home known as T-Hub that combines wireless calling and Internet access. Another device T-Box is a set-top box that enables standard digital video recorder functions and adds Internet television capabilities. As part of its effort to address market demand for IP video services the company bought video conferencing and collaboration services provider iVision in 2011.

While Telstra derives the bulk of its sales from domestic operations it does some business overseas. Its Telstra International unit oversees the company's operations in Australasia from facilities in Hong Kong and Singapore. Hong Kong subsidiary CSL New World Limited counts almost 3 million wireless customers. Its 50-50 joint venture with PCCW known as REACH is Asia's largest international carrier of voice private line and Internet protocol data services. In China subsidiary LMobile provides mobile news and entertainment content. Telstra spun off Chinese real estate website SouFun in 2010.

HISTORY

When Australia gained independence in 1901 telecommunications were assigned to the new state-owned Postmaster-General's Department (PMG). Engineer H. P. Brown who had managed the UK's telegraph and telephone system became head of PMG in 1923. He set up research labs that year oversaw the first overseas call to London in 1930 and streamlined operations until his reign ended in 1939.

During WWII Australia quickly expanded its communications infrastructure to assist the Allied Front in the South Pacific. Following the war the government formed the Overseas Telecommunications Commission (OTC) in 1946 to handle international operations independent of PMG.

Even as new technology connected the continent and boosted the productivity of PMG its postal operations steadily recorded losses in the postwar era. In 1974 a Royal Commission recommended that postal and telecom services be split. Australian Telecommunications Commission (Telecom Australia) was launched in 1975 (OTC retained overseas services); it turned a profit in its first year.

Looking to connect residents in the outback the firm signed Japan's Nippon Electric (now NEC) in 1981 to set up a digital radio transmission system; by the next decade it connected some 50000 outback users. Also in 1981 Telecom Australia took a 25% stake in government-owned satellite operator AUSSAT and launched nationwide paging and mobile phone service in Melbourne and Sydney.

Renamed Australian Telecommunications in 1989 the carrier got its first whiff of competition as others were allowed to provide phone equipment. Two years later Optus Communications began competing with Telecom Australia; for the privilege it was forced to buy the unsuccessful AUSSAT. Long-distance competition began in 1991 and mobile phone competition began in 1992. In response Telecom Australia merged with OTC to become Australian and Overseas Telecommunications Corporation (AOTC).

AOTC became Telstra Corporation in 1993 and launched a digital wireless GSM-based network. It joined with Rupert Murdoch's News Corp. to form pay TV operator FOXTEL in 1995.

That year Telstra teamed with Microsoft to create ISP On Australia. Microsoft dropped out in 1996 but Telstra kept the service (Big Pond) and its portal (renamed Telstra.com in 1999). The government fully deregulated telecommunications and sold a third of Telstra to the public in 1997.

Kerry Packer's Publishing and Broadcasting bought a 25% stake in FOXTEL in 1998. The next year Telstra posted an Australian record-setting profit and the government floated an additional 17% stake.

Telstra combined its New Zealand operations with those of cable TV operator Austar United to form Telstra Saturn in 1999. Two years later it bought Clear Communications the New Zealand unit of BT Group (formerly British Telecommunications) in a deal worth about $182 million and merged it with Telstra Saturn to form TelstraClear.

In 2004 the company acquired Australia-based Trading Post Group for nearly $484 million that bolstered the company's advertising and publishing operations. Telstra also bought technology services provider Kaz Group that year for $252 million.

Former chairman Bob Mansfield resigned after conflicts with the board of directors over the proposed acquisition of publisher John Fairfax Holdings. Mansfield supported the acquisition. Late the same year CEO Ziggy Switkowski was sacked by the board after holding the position for six years during which time the company's share price dropped considerably. The company hired former Orange SA CEO Sol Trujillo to take his place in 2005. That year Trujillo outlined a plan to reduce the company's payroll by 12000 positions by 2010 in a long-term effort to cut costs.

In 2006 the company bought competitor New World Mobile Holdings and merged it with the operations of subsidiary Hong Kong CSL to create CSL New World. Also that year the company acquired a controlling stake in China-based real estate listings website SouFun in a move intended to boost revenues of its Sensis advertising business and to further build a presence in China. The Australian comonwealth reduced its majority stake in Telstra from 52% to 18% in 2007.

The company in 2008 completed phasing out its older network which was based on CDMA (code division multiple access) technology and migrated its customers onto the newer digital GSM (global system for mobile communications) system known as Next G. Telstra invested A$96 million in the upgrade in a bid to increase the capacity of its network to enable a wider range of mobile broadband services. The push for subscribers to upgrade contributed to increased sales of compatible wireless handsets that year.

Telstra expanded its operations in Asia particularly in the area of media communications during 2008. The company moved to boost ad revenue in China that year with the acquisition of controlling interests in Chinese Web content providers Norstar Media and Autohome/PCPop.

As part of its broader strategy of focusing on core telecom services business lines the company sold its IT services business KAZ Group to Fujitsu for A$200 million in 2009.

EXECUTIVES

Group Managing Director Media Services; CEO Sensis, Bruce J. Akhurst, age 53, $751,751 total compensation
Group Managing Director Business, Will Irving
CEO and Board Member, David Thodey, age 58, $962,783 total compensation
Group Managing Director Project New and Customer Experience, Robert A. Nason
Chief Operations Officer - Telstra Operations, Brendon Riley
Group Managing Director Finance and CFO, Andrew (Andy) Penn, age 50
Group Managing Director Applications and Ventures, Deena Shiff, $718,199 total compensation
Chairman, Catherine B. Livingstone, age 57
Group Managing Director Enterprise and Government, Paul Geason
Group Managing Director Innovation Products and Marketing, Kate McKenzie, $441,305 total compensation
Chief Executive Officer, Xiaowei Chen, age 45
Company Secretary, Carmel Mulhern
Director Investor Relations, Ben Spincer
Group Managing Director Telstra International, Tarek A. Robbiati
Executive Director Product Management, Ross Fielding
Acting Group Managing Director Wireless Data Applications and Services, Philip Jones
Group Managing Director and Chief Customer Officer, Gordon S. Ballantyne
Group Managing Director Country Wide, Brett Riley
Director Industry Analyst Relations, Catherine Payne
Executive Director Media Relations, Andrew Butcher
Acting Group Managing Director Wholesale, Glenn Osborne
Deputy CFO, Mark Hall
Company Secretary, Damien Coleman
Group Managing Director of Telstra Digital Media, Rick Ellis
Board Member, John D. Zeglis, age 65
CEO and Board Member, David Thodey, age 58
Board Member, John P. Mullen, age 61
Group Managing Director Finance and CFO, Andrew (Andy) Penn, age 50
Board Member, John M. Stewart, age 64
Director, Nora L. Scheinkestel, age 52
Board Member, John W. Stocker, age 66
Board Member, Geoffrey Cousins, age 70
Board Member, Russell A. Higgins
Board Member, Steven Vamos
Non-Executive Director, Margaret Seale
Auditors: Ernst&Young

LOCATIONS

HQ: Telstra Corp., Ltd.
Level 41, 242 Exhibition Street, Melbourne, Victoria 3000
Phone: (61) 8 8308 1721 **Fax:** (61) 3 9632 3215
Web: www.telstra.com.au

2011 Sales

	% of total
Australia	92
Other	8
Total	**100**

PRODUCTS/OPERATIONS

2011 Sales

	% of total
Consumer	40
Business	18
Enterprise &	17
Wholesale	8
Directories & advertising	7
Telstra	5
Other	5
Total	**100**

Selected Services

Advertising and directory services
Audio video and Internet conferencing
Broadband ISP
Cable TV
Data transmission
E-mail
Enhanced fax products and services
Freecall (toll-free 1-800 phone service)
Information technology (IT) services
Internet access
Mobile phone service
Prepaid telephony
Satellite transmission

COMPETITORS

Hutchison Telecommunications Australia
Optus
Pacnet
PowerTel
Telecom Corporation of New Zealand

HISTORICAL FINANCIALS

Company Type: Public

Income Statement FYE: June 30

	REVENUE ($ mil.)	NET INCOME ($ mil.)	NET PROFIT MARGIN	EMPLOYEES
06/13	23,684	3,517	14.8%	37,000
06/12	25,834	3,467	13.4%	39,972
06/11	26,897	3,463	12.9%	39,790
06/10	21,239	3,309	15.6%	45,220
06/09	20,781	3,318	16.0%	43,181
Annual Growth	3.3%	1.5%	—	(3.8%)

2013 Year-End Financials

Debt ratio: 36.0%
Return on equity: 31.6%
Cash ($ mil.): 2,286
Current ratio: 1.05
Long-term debt ($ mil.): 13,201
No. of shares (mil.): —
Dividends
Yield: 0.0%
Payout: 482.6%
Market value ($ mil.): —

	STOCK PRICE ($) FY Close	P/E High/Low	PER SHARE ($) Earnings	Dividends	Book Value
06/13	21.84	81 57	0.28	1.36	0.93
06/12	18.85	74 50	0.28	1.47	0.94
06/11	15.61	73 44	0.28	1.35	1.04
06/10	13.69	40 26	0.27	1.20	0.87
06/09	13.60	52 16	0.27	1.02	0.81
Annual Growth	12.6%	— —	1.3%	7.4%	3.5%

Tesco PLC (United Kingdom)

Tesco is the #1 retailer in the UK and one of the top retailers in the world by annual sales behind Wal-Mart and Carrefour. Tesco and its subsidiaries have more than 6200 stores in 14 countries in Europe Asia and North America with about half located in the UK. Although built on the "pile it high sell it cheap" creed of founder Sir Jack Cohen Tesco abandoned its discount format to become a multi-format retailer in stores and online. Among its banners are Tesco Extra superstores; Tesco Express Tesco Metro and One Stop convenience stores; Homeplus hypermarket small express and virtual stores in South Korea; and Dobbies gardening stores in the UK Scotland and northern Ireland.

Geographic Reach

Tesco's presence spans about a dozen countries worldwide. Outside of the UK which is its largest market the company's other European-based stores are located in the Czech Republic Hungary Ireland Poland Slovakia and Turkey. In

Asia it operates in China India Malaysia South Korea and Thailand. It is exiting the US market with the sale of its Fresh & Easy banner.

Operations

As a multi-format multi-channel retailer Tesco's various physical retail store operations are complemented by its online retailing operations including tesco.com (the world's largest online grocery retailer) and Tesco Direct. As a provider of financial services Tesco is the UK's largest supermarket bank through Tesco Personal Finance (which does business as Tesco Bank). Through wholly owned dunnhumby Tesco offers data analytics and customer insight to such clients as Coca-Cola Kroger and Procter & Gamble. The dunnhumby group includes marketing expert BzzAgent and price optimization company KSS Retail.

Tesco boasts an impressive presence in Asia. Homeplus in South Korea is the company's largest international business with some 475 stores consisting of large hypermarkets and small Tesco Express stores an online business and virtual stores in subway and bus stops where customers can buy products via their mobile devices and get them delivered to their homes. In Southeast Asia Tesco is a market leader in Thailand where it operates locally as Tesco Lotus. It operates in Malaysia with conglomerate partner Sime Darby while in India the company has an exclusive franchise agreement with the retail arm of Tata Group to develop Star Bazaar hypermarkets there.

In China Tesco is playing catch up to global rivals Wal-Mart and Carrefour which entered that market nearly a decade before Tesco. There it has more than 100 stores along the eastern seaboard provinces and it is developing shopping malls under the Lifespace brand that are anchored by Tesco hypermarkets. China is also a major sourcing market for Tesco; it has international sourcing headquarters in Hong Kong and a hub in Singapore.

Financial Performance

Tesco is under pressure to reverse a slide in its core UK business after 20 years of solid growth and profitability. In early 2012 the company issued its first earnings warning in two decades. While group sales rose about 5% in fiscal 2012 (ends February) compared to the previous year and group profit rose modestly Tesco lost money at home. The UK lagged Asia Europe and the US in sales growth and profitability.

Strategy

After being criticized for allowing its UK business to deteriorate while it focused on expansion abroad Tesco is refocusing its strategy on core UK growth which is still a key driver of sales and profit. In fiscal 2013 it is investing #1 billion (roughly $1.6 billion) to improve the shopping experience for its UK customers in stores and online. The retailer will overhaul its existing UK stores by adding more staff and improving in-store service accelerating its remodeling schedule and offering better prices and more personalized promotions. It will also add about 38% less retail space in Britain this year than last as it moves away from big stores in favor of smaller shops and the Internet. To that end Tesco will ramp up investment in its online operations and accelerate the roll out of its Click and Collect program which allows shoppers to pick up orders placed online.

Tesco has seen its market share decline in recent years as rival Wal-Mart-owned ASDA and deep discounters such as ALDI and Lidl increase their share of the fiercely competitive UK grocery market. To win the hearts of cash-strapped consumers and keep them in its stores Tesco has expanded its own Tesco Value line of discount products and its Tesco Finest brand —both of which exceed #1 billion in annual sales. Also Tesco is facing even stronger competition from its chief UK rival ASDA which recently acquired the Netto chain of discount stores in the UK. To bolster its One Stope Stores convenience chain Tesco acquired more than 75 stores from privately owned Mills Group (boosting its store count to more than 600 across England and Wales) in 2011.

Outside of the UK Tesco is strategically reviewing certain underperforming international operations including its US-based Fresh & Easy business a chain of 200 unprofitable stores launched in 2007. Indeed Tesco has struck a deal to exit the US with the sale of about 150 Fresh & Easy stores to The Yucaipa Cos. (It will close the remaining 50 stores). Across the Pacific in a two-stage process Tesco is selling its 50% stake in its loss-making Tesco Japan business to AEON for a nominal sum after after nine years of struggling in that market.

HISTORY

With WWI behind him in 1919 Jack Cohen invested his serviceman's gratuity in a grocery stall in London's East End. He introduced his first private-label product Tesco Tea in 1924 —the name was the combination of the initials of his tea supplier (T. E. Stockwell) and the first two letters of Cohen's last name. By the late 1920s Cohen had several stalls and in 1929 he opened his first store under the Tesco name in Edgeware London.

Cohen founded Tesco Stores Limited in 1932. During the rest of the decade the company added more than 100 stores mainly in London. Cohen visited the US in 1935 studying its self-service supermarkets and returned to England with a plan of using a similar "pile it high and sell it cheap" format. Delayed by WWII Tesco opened its first American-styled store in 1947 and went public that year as Tesco Stores Holdings. By 1950 the company ran 20 self-service stores.

Tesco grew primarily through acquisitions during the 1950s and 1960s adding about 600 stores. By the early 1970s however competition and a recession battered Tesco. Managing director Ian MacLaurin initiated radical changes including abandoning trading stamps and to shed its down-market image refurbishing stores with a more upscale decor. A price-slashing initiative in 1977 dramatically increased Tesco's market share within a year. Because cheap brands were best-sellers Tesco began creating its own private-label brands. The company also started closing unprofitable stores while opening superstores some with gas stations.

In 1979 the year Sir Jack Cohen died Tesco entered Ireland by buying Three Guys (abandoning the effort in 1986). In 1983 the company became Tesco and two years later it named MacLaurin as chairman. By 1991 Tesco was the UK's largest independent gasoline retailer.

Looking for new opportunities in 1992 Tesco introduced small urban stores called Tesco Metro and the next year began expanding outside England acquiring stores in France and Scotland. In 1994 it acquired an initial 51% stake in Global a 43-store grocery chain in Hungary. That year it also opened Tesco Express (combination convenience stores and gas stations).

Tesco acquired 31 Stavia stores in Poland in 1995; a year later it added 13 Kmart stores in the Czech Republic and Slovakia. Tesco returned to Ireland in 1997 by acquiring 109 Associated British Food stores. It also launched its financial services division —Tesco Personal Finance —that year and named John Gardiner as chairman (replacing the retiring MacLaurin) and Terry Leahy as CEO. In 1998 the retailer purchased 75% of food retailer Lotus with 13 stores in Thailand. The following year Tesco partnered with Samsung to develop Homeplus hypermarkets in South Korea.

By 2000 Tesco's profitable online shopping business was one of the world's most successful and the company made it a separate subsidiary Tesco.com. To build on that success Tesco bought a 35% stake in GroceryWorks a subsidiary of the US Safeway grocery chain in June 2001.

Tesco acquired the travel company First Class Leisure in March 2002 and renamed the business Tesco Freetime. The acquisition was yet another move by the supermarket chain to expand beyond groceries. Tesco became the market leader in the fragmented Polish food retailing arena by acquiring German hypermarket operator HIT in July 2002. In January 2003 Tesco completed the acquisition of the British convenience store chain T&S Stores for #519 million. In July it acquired a 95% stake in Japanese convenience store operator C Two-Network for about #139 million. In November Tesco acquired Kipa a small hypermarket operator in Turkey for #96 million.

To strengthen its presence in the convenience market Tesco bought T&S Stores (now One Stop Stores) in 2003 and has converted many of its 800-plus shops to its Express banner.

In April 2004 David Reid became non-executive chairman replacing Gardiner who retired from Tesco. In August Tesco sold the Dillons chain of newsstands to TM Retail for an undisclosed amount. Tesco had acquired Dillons when it purchased T&S Stores.

Tesco transferred some 770 back office jobs in January 2005 from the UK to Bangalore India where it opened a software development and accounting office. In mid-year Tesco opened its first Kipa store in Turkey since it acquired the Turkish chain in 2003. The 50000-sq.-ft. store brought Tesco's store count in Turkey to six.

In 2006 the company bought 27 small stores from Edeka in the Czech Republic. In the fall it launched a higher-end 30-piece apparel line for men and women called F&F Collection by Lee Rees-Oliviere (Tesco's head designer recruited in 2005 from Marks and Spencer). In October Tesco sold its 38% stake in Internet grocer GroceryWorks to Safeway its partner in the venture. In December Tesco increased its stake in China's Ting Hsin Holding Corp. to 90% from 50% in a deal valued at about $352 million. (Tesco entered China in 2004 paying approximately $275 million for 50% in Ting Hsin's subsidiary Ting Cao.)

Tesco increased its international selling space by 25% in the fiscal year ending in February 2007. In early November the British retailer opened its first US store: a Fresh & Easy Neighborhood Market in Hemet California (outside Los Angeles). Also in 2007 Tesco acquired nearly a two-thirds ownership stake in the Scottish garden center operator Dobbies Garden Centers PLC. (It increased its ownership to 100% in July 2008).

In August 2008 Tesco bought the UK operation of Handleman a leading UK-based distributor and store merchandiser of books music computer games and other products for about #9.4 million (about $16 million). Tesco retained a substantial portion of Handleman's UK workforce. Also that year Tesco made a major acquisition of a chain of hypermarkets in South Korea from E-Land Group for about $2 billion.

Tesco bought out its joint venture partner —Royal Bank of Scotland —in Tesco Personal Finance (TPF) for about $1.9 billion in 2008. TPF which was formed in 1997 has grown to serve more than 6 million customer accounts and offers insurance credit cards loans mortgages and savings products. The purchase is part of Tesco's strategy to expand into the service sector which is outpacing food in terms of growth. The timing of its push into retail banking —just ahead of the banking crisis in the UK —was auspicious. Tesco is enjoying increased demand for its banking services as distrust of traditional banks has grown in the aftermath of big bank bailouts in the UK during the financial crisis. TPF is also getting into the auto and home insurance markets via a partnership with the UK arm of Fortis Insurance.

In early 2011 international executive Philip Clarke replaced retiring longtime chief executive Terry Leahy.

Also that year Tesco acquired an 80% stake in the British video-on-demand (VoD) service Blinkbox which competes with Amazon.com's LoveFilm. Tesco entered the VoD market to position itself for the next phase of Internet-driven home entertainment even though the retailer is a huge seller of DVDs.

EXECUTIVES

Deputy Chairman, Patrick J. Cescau, age 64
CEO Tesco Personal Finance Limited (Tesco Bank), Benny Higgins, age 52
Board Member; CEO Retail Services, Andrew T. Higginson, age 55, $1,597,200 total compensation
Board Member; Deputy CEO and Chief Marketing Officer; President and CEO Fresh & Easy Neighborhood Market, Tim J. R. Mason, age 55, $1,995,322 total compensation
Marketing Director UK, Carolyn Bradley
Director Investor Relations, Steve Webb, age 52
Board Member; Corporate and Legal Affairs Director, Lucy Neville-Rolfe, age 60, $1,025,626 total compensation
Commercial Director Clothing Electronics and General Merchandise, Laura Wade-Gery, age 47
Head Retail Operations and Logistics UK, Noel W. Robbins
Chairman, Sir Richard Broadbent, age 59
Chief Clothing, Richard Jones
Board Member; Company Secretary, Jonathan Lloyd, age 47
CEO and Board Member, Philip (Phil) Clarke, age 52, $1,503,821 total compensation
CEO Tesco Mobile and Tesco Telecoms, Lance Batchelor
CFO and Board Member, Laurie McIlwee, age 50, $838,312 total compensation
Buyer Tea, Paul Grigg
Tesco Salad Food Buyer, Sam Wright
Senior Buying Manager, Dryell Simon
CEO Asia, Trevor Masters
Director Media Relations, Trevor Datson
Online Food and Internet Retailing Director, Ken Towle, age 48
COO UK, Bob Robbins
Director Finance UK, Mike Iddon
Group Director Digital and Marketing, Matt Atkinson
CIO, Mike McNamara, age 48
Group Chief Financial Officer; Executive Director, Laurie McIlwee
Senior Independent Director, Patrick J. Cescau, age 65
Board Member, Kenneth J. (Ken) Hydon, age 68
Board Member; CEO Retail Services, Andrew T. Higginson, age 55
Board Member; Deputy CEO and Chief Marketing Officer; President and CEO Fresh & Easy Neighborhood Market, Tim J. R. Mason, age 55
Board Member, Stuart Chambers, age 57
Board Member; Corporate and Legal Affairs Director, Lucy Neville-Rolfe, age 60
Board Member, Ken G. Hanna, age 60
Board Member, Karen Cook, age 59
Board Member, Gareth R. Bullock, age 60
Board Member; Company Secretary, Jonathan Lloyd, age 47
CEO and Board Member, Philip (Phil) Clarke, age 52
CFO and Board Member, Laurie McIlwee, age 50
Board Member, Jacqueline Tammenoms Bakker, age 59
Non-Executive Independent Director, Deanna Oppenheimer
Auditors: PricewaterhouseCoopersLLP

LOCATIONS

HQ: Tesco PLC (United Kingdom)
Tesco House, Delamare Road, Cheshunt, Hertfordshire EN8 9SL
Phone: (44) 1992 632222 **Fax:** (44) 1992 630794
Web: www.tescoplc.com

2012 Retail Sales

	% of total
Europe	
UK	67
Other	16
Asia	16
US	1
Total	**100**

2012 Stores

	No.
UK	2,979
Asia	1,719
Rest of	1,351
US	185
Total	**6,234**

PRODUCTS/OPERATIONS

2012 UK Stores

	No.
Tesco	1,427
One	613
Tesco	471
Tesco	230
Tesco	190
Dobbies	31
Tesco Home	13
Other	4
Total	**2,975**

Selected Subsidiaries and Joint Ventures

Dobbies Garden Centres PLC (100% Scotland)
dunnhumby Ltd. (100% data analysis England)
Ek-Chai Distribution System Co. Ltd. (86% Lotus stores Thailand)
One Stop Stores Ltd. (100% convenience stores England and Wales)
Tesco Ireland Ltd. (100% Republic of Ireland)
Tesco Japan Co. Ltd. (100% Japan)
Tesco Kipa (93% hypermarkets Turkey)
Tesco Mobile Ltd. (50% telecommunications)
Tesco Personal Finance Group Limited (50%; credit cards savings accounts loans online banking insurance)
Tesco Polska Sp. Z o.o. (100% Czestochowa stores Poland)
Tesco Stores CR a.s. (100% Czech Republic)
Tesco Stores SR a.s. (100% Slovakia)
Tesco Qinhuangdo Property Ltd. (50% PRC)

COMPETITORS

A.S. Watson
ALDI
ASDA
Alliance Boots
BP
Carphone Warehouse
Carrefour
Co-operative Group
Convenience Retail Asia
Dairy Farm International
Dunnes Stores
Exxon Mobil
Iceland Foods
J Sainsbury
John Lewis
LAWSON
LOVEFiLM
Lidl
METRO AG
Marks & Spencer
Matalan
Musgrave Retail Partners
NEXT plc
Primark
Royal Dutch Shell
SPAR Handels
Seven & i
Stater Bros.
T.K. Maxx
The Gap
Virgin Money
Vons
Waitrose
Wal-Mart
Wm Morrison Supermarkets
Wyevale Garden

HISTORICAL FINANCIALS

Company Type: Public

Income Statement

FYE: February 23

	REVENUE ($ mil.)	NET INCOME ($ mil.)	NET PROFIT MARGIN	EMPLOYEES
02/13	98,950	189	0.2%	954,225
02/12	101,973	4,433	4.3%	925,759
02/11	98,061	4,272	4.4%	877,103
02/10	86,770	3,547	4.1%	844,432
02/09	77,551	3,084	4.0%	832,523
Annual Growth	6.3%	(50.2%)	—	3.5%

2013 Year-End Financials

Debt ratio: 32.9%
Return on equity: 0.7%
Cash ($ mil.): 3,834
Current ratio: 0.70
Long-term debt ($ mil.): 15,367
No. of shares (mil.): —
Dividends
Yield: 0.0%
Payout: 6,911.3%
Market value ($ mil.): —

	STOCK PRICE ($) FY Close	P/E High/Low	PER SHARE ($) Earnings	Dividends	Book Value
02/13	17.14	27452127	0.02	1.62	3.15
02/12	15.24	155101	0.55	1.72	3.50
02/11	20.03	164118	0.53	1.44	3.31
02/10	19.21	190 90	0.45	1.29	2.79
02/09	14.23	266 96	0.39	1.58	2.34
Annual Growth	4.8%	— —	(50.4%)	0.7%	7.8%

Teva Pharmaceutical Industries Ltd

Teva Pharmaceutical Industries is the biggest name in the no-name world of generic pharmaceuticals. The company makes hundreds of generic versions of brand-name antibiotics heart drugs heartburn medications and more. Subsidiary Teva Pharmaceuticals USA generics product line include equivalents of such blockbusters as antidepressant Prozac and osteoporosis drug Fosamax. The company Israel's top drugmaker also develops and manufactures proprietary branded drugs including multiple sclerosis treatment Copaxone Parkinson's disease treatment Azilect and a portfolio of women's health treatments. Its active pharmaceutical ingredient (API) division makes drug components for Teva and other manufacturers.

Geographic Reach

While Teva has research and manufacturing operations in more than 60 countries in the Americas Europe Asia and the Middle East almost half of the company's sales come from its North American operations.

Operations

Although generics still account for half of the company's sales Teva is steadily building up its line of branded proprietary drugs which accounted for 35% of the company's sales in 2011. Its development pipeline includes drug candidates for neurological disorders autoimmune diseases and oncology targeting such ailments as Alzheimer's disease Crohn's disease and lupus. However joining in on the branded market has also made Teva more vulnerable to patent expirations of its own: its two bestsellers Provigil and Copaxone are facing generic competition soon.

Over-the-counter (OTC) drugs are still a small portion of its branded drug revenues but in 2011

Teva laid the groundwork to grow that business. It struck a joint-venture with Procter & Gamble to combine both companies' OTC drug businesses outside of the US. P&G brought big consumer health brand names to the deal (including Pepto Bismol and Vicks) while Teva brought international manufacturing and regulatory expertise.

While biotech drugs are more finicky to make they also have the potential for higher profit rewards that Teva does not want to miss out on. Generic biotech drugs are known as biosimilars or follow-on-biologics (FOBs) and Teva has built up its capacity to produce biosimilars through smaller acquisitions and a joint venture with Swiss API firm Lonza.

Marketing and Sales

Teva's finished product are sold directly to retailers and medical providers as well as through wholesale distribution firms.

Financial Performance

Teva's revenues have made a steady march upwards each year rising 11% to $20 billion in 2012. Likewise its net income bounced back from the 2008 recession until 2011 when it dropped 15% to $2.8 billion due to acquisition expenses. Net income fell another 29% in 2012 to some $2 billion.

Strategy

Following a strategic review of its operations in 2007 Teva set a goal of doubling its business by 2012 to achieve annual revenues of $20 billion. The company successfully achieved the goal by increasing its market share in key regions (including North America) expanding its R&D and production capacities and growing its generic and proprietary drug portfolios through acquisitions and organic growth programs.

Continuing growth strategies include expansion efforts in emerging markets and increasing its portfolio in over-the-counter medicines. Teva continues with its historical strategy of filing patent challenges on branded products thus attempting to gain a "first-to-market" advantage with its generic equivalents; however in recent years these patent challenges have grown more expensive and less exclusive which has eroded their usefulness.

Lingering impacts from acquisition expenses as well as the impending patent expiration of top-selling branded drug Copaxone prompted Teva to launch a cost control program in 2013 to cut $2 billion in annual expenses by 2017. The program includes a 10% workforce reduction; the first such downsizing program in the company's history.

After regulatory compliance expenses pinched the company's animal health business in 2011 Teva sold off those operations to Bayer HealthCare in early 2013 in a deal worth up to $145 million. The business included dermatology and food products for companion animals.

Mergers and Acquisitions

Several hefty acquisitions have helped it get closer to its goal and with its 2011 $6.8 billion buy of US drugmaker Cephalon Teva believes that it has indeed reached the $20 billion revenue mark. Cephalon's marketed specialty drugs promise to bolster Teva's brand name drug portfolio and fatten its pipeline of R&D candidates. Specifically the deal gave Teva more treatments for central nervous system disorders including narcolepsy drug Provigil as well as oncology and pain management drugs and 30 late-stage drugs in development.

Acquisitions around the globe have helped the company enter new markets and secure market dominance in others. In the emerging market of Japan the company paid some $150 million in 2011 to gain full control of Teva-Kowa Pharma a former joint venture with Kowa Company. An acquisition in Peru positioned the company to take advantage of better health care coverage in South America which is creating a new demand for pharmaceuticals.

HISTORY

Teva traces its origins to Salomon Levin and Elstein Ltd. a drug distribution firm based in Jerusalem which at the time was a Jewish section of British-controlled Palestine.

Ironically in the 1930s the company benefited from the emigration of Jewish people many of whom were scientists seeking to escape the Nazi regime in Germany which at the time was the global leader in drug development. The company went public in 1951.

In 1968 Eli Hurvitz was appointed to Teva's board of directors and scripted much of the company's growth. In 1970 Teva merged with Assia Chemical Laboratories (Hurvitz's old employer) and another company to form Teva Pharmaceutical Industries.

Ten years later Teva sold a 20% stake of itself to Koor Industries in exchange for Koor subsidiary Ikapharm Teva's closest competitor. (Koor later launched a takeover bid but the Founders Group Teva's controlling shareholders foiled the attempt.)

In 1985 Teva moved into the US. It formed a joint venture with W. R. Grace called TAG Pharmaceuticals (Teva bought out W. R. Grace's portion in 1991). In 1985 TAG bought Lemmon Co. famous — or infamous — for its tranquilizer Quaalude which had gained notoriety as the recreational drug of choice for many young people. Lemmon which ceased production of Quaalude prior to Teva's purchase became the acquirer's generic manufacturing division.

Teva bought Abic Israel's #2 drugmaker in a complex 1988 transaction that gave Canadian investor and Seagram's heir Charles Bronfman a stake in the company. British publisher Robert Maxwell also bought a substantial stake in Teva. (Following Maxwell's mysterious death in 1993 his estate sold his stake.)

In the 1990s Teva turned its attention to Europe buying companies in France Hungary Italy and the UK. In 1996 the company bought US firm Biocraft Laboratories merging it with Lemmon and forming Teva Pharmaceuticals USA.

In 1998 the company reorganized after officials realized that it had to evolve from being a collection of disparate operating entities to a more centralized operation. It also divested several operations –including its Russian joint venture its yeast and alcohol fermentation business and some of its German operations –in order to concentrate on pharmaceuticals.

Teva maintained a steady rate of acquisitions including generics firms Copley Pharmaceuticals and Novapharm in 1999 and 2000 respectively Bayer's French generic operations in 2002 and rival generics manufacturer IVAX Corporation in January 2006. To further its generics operations in Spain Teva acquired Bentley Pharmaceuticals in 2008.

The company's $7.5 billion purchase of Barr Pharmaceuticals expanded Teva's presence in both the US and European generic and branded drug markets in 2008. Coming at a time of rapid consolidation in the industry the deal set Teva even further ahead of the pack in the global generics arena. Within a year Barr Pharmaceuticals was fully integrated into Teva's operations though its European PLIVA subsidiary continued to operate independently. Teva also acquired Germany's Ratiopharm for some $5 billion in 2010.

EXECUTIVES

Chairman, Phillip Frost
EVP and CFO, Eyal Desheh, age 60
Corporate Vice President Chief Internal Auditor, Ron Grupel, age 62
Group Executive Vice President Institutional and Community Affairs, Aharon (Arik) Yaari, age 61
Vice Chairman, Prof Moshe Many, age 84
President and CEO Global Operations, Carlo de Notaristefani, age 55
Chairman Teva Japan and Teva South Korea, Prof Itzhak Krinsky, age 60
EVP Chief Legal Officer and Company Secretary, Richard S. Egosi, age 50
President and CEO Teva EMIA and Asia Pacific, Judith Vardi, age 54
EVP Human Resources and Chief Integration Officer, Isaac (Ika) Abravanel, age 58
President and CEO, Jeremy M. Levin
President and CEO Generics Europe, Dipankar Bhattacharjee
Group Executive Vice President and Global Head of Quality, Frances M. (Fran) Zipp
President and CEO Teva Americas Generics, Allan Oberman
President of Global R&D and Chief Scientific Officer, Michael Hayden
President and CEO Specialty Medicines, Robert Koremans
Group Executive Vice President & Chief Business Process Officer, Erez Israeli
Director, Abraham E. (Barry) Cohen, age 76
Director, Chaim Hurvitz, age 52
Director, Dan S. Suesskind, age 68
Director, Erez Vigodman, age 53
Director, Amir Elstein, age 57
Vice Chairman, Prof Moshe Many, age 84
Director, Ory Slonim, age 70
Director, Roger Abravanel, age 67
Director, Prof Roger D. Kornberg, age 65
Director, Joseph (Yosi) Nitzani, age 65
Director, Prof Elon Kohlberg, age 65
Auditors: Kesselman&Kesselman

LOCATIONS

HQ: Teva Pharmaceutical Industries Ltd
5 Basel Street, P.O. Box 3190, Petach Tikva 49131
Phone: (972) 3 926 7267
Web: www.tevapharm.com

2012 Sales

	$ mil.	% of total
US	10,438	51
Other regions	4,206	21

PRODUCTS/OPERATIONS

2012 Sales

	$ mil.	% of total
Generic products	9,589	47
Branded products		
Central nervous system	5,464	27
Respiratory	856	4
Women's health	448	2
Oncology	860	4
Other	522	3
Over the counter products	936	5
Active pharmaceutical ingredients	796	4
Other revenues	846	4
Total	**20,317**	**100**

Selected Products

Branded products
- Central nervous system
  - Azilect (Parkinson's)
  - Copaxone (multiple sclerosis)
  - Provigil (narcolepsy)
- Specialty respiratory
  - ProAir (bronchial spasms)
  - Qvar (chronic asthma)
- Women' s health
  - Enjuvia (menopausal hormone therapy)
  - Plan B (emergency oral contraceptive)
  - Seasonique

Biosimilar products
- Eporatio (erythopoietin treatment for chemotherapy-induced anemia)
- Granulocyte Colony Stimulating Factor (anti-infective for oncology patients)
- Tev-Tropin (human growth hormone)

Generic products
- Amoxicillin (Amoxil)
- Atorvastatin (Lipitor)
- Bromatapp (Dimetapp)
- Candesartan (Atacand)
- Cimetidine (Tagamet)
- Ciprofloxacin (Cipro)
- Clemastine fumarate (Tavist)
- Clotrimazole (Lotrimin)
- Diclofenac extended release (Voltaren XR)
- Diltiazem HCl (Cardizem)
- Donepezil (Aricept)
- Fluconazole Injection (Diflucan)
- Fluoxetine (Prozac)
- Galantamine (Reminyl)
- Ketoconazole cream (Nizoral Cream)
- Lamivudine (Epivir)
- Lovastatin (Mevacor)
- Metronidazole (Flagyl)
- Quetiapine (Seroquel)
- Sotalol hydrochloride (Betapace)
- Sulfamethoxazole and Trimethoprim (Bactrim)
- Tizanidine (Zanaflex)
- Tramadol hydrochloride (Ultram/Ultracet)

Selected Acquisitions

2011
- Cephalon ($6.8 billion US specialty drugs)
- Corporacion Infarmasa (Peru branded and generics)
- Taiyo Pharmaceutical Industry (Japan generics)
- Theramex (Europe women' s health)

2010
- ratiopharm ($4.95 billion Germany generics)

2008
- Barr Pharmaceuticals (US generics)
- CoGenesys ($400 million biosimilars)

COMPETITORS

Abbott Labs
Actavis Inc.
AstraZeneca
Bayer HealthCare Pharmaceuticals Inc.
Bio-Rad Labs
Biogen Idec
Boehringer Ingelheim
Bristol-Myers Squibb
Dr. Reddy' s
Forest Labs
GlaxoSmithKline
Johnson & Johnson
Merck
Mylan
Novartis
Perrigo
Pfizer
Ranbaxy Laboratories
Sandoz International GmbH
Sanofi
Taro
Wockhardt

HISTORICAL FINANCIALS

Company Type: Public

Income Statement FYE: December 31

	REVENUE ($ mil.)	NET INCOME ($ mil.)	NET PROFIT MARGIN	EMPLOYEES
12/13	20,314	1,269	6.2%	44,945
12/12	20,317	1,963	9.7%	45,948
12/11	18,312	2,759	15.1%	45,754
12/10	16,121	3,331	20.7%	39,660
12/09	13,899	2,000	14.4%	35,089
Annual Growth	10.0%	(10.8%)	—	6.4%

2013 Year-End Financials

Debt ratio: 25.6%
Return on equity: 5.6%
Cash ($ mil.): 1,038
Current ratio: 1.15
Long-term debt ($ mil.): 10,387
No. of shares (mil.): 848
Dividends
Yield: 2.7%
Payout: 72.9%
Market value ($ mil.): 33,988

	STOCK PRICE ($) FY Close	P/E High/Low		PER SHARE ($) Earnings	Dividends	Book Value
12/13	40.08	28	25	1.49	1.09	26.61
12/12	37.34	20	16	2.25	0.80	26.57
12/11	40.36	18	11	3.09	0.78	25.14
12/10	52.13	17	13	3.67	0.67	24.47
12/09	56.18	25	18	2.23	0.48	21.72
Annual Growth	(8.1%)	—	—	(9.6%)	22.5%	5.2%

THALES

Unlike the Greek philosopher for whom it is named Thales (Thay-leez) knows itself. It knows about C4I (command control communications computers & intelligence) worldwide. Thales' Defense & Security segment is primarily government-based providing systems for intelligence electronic warfare surveillance satellites radar navigation and communications for air land and naval applications; it also offers air traffic control. Its Aerospace & Transport segment which predominantly supports non-government markets designs and develops rail signaling ticketing systems avionics cabin systems and flight simulators. The French government owns about 27% of Thales while UK-based Dassault holds about 26%.

While some aerospace and defense companies fared better than other industries during the economic crisis their success remains contingent upon government spending. Thales is reliant upon its military orders representing about 75% of its revenues. With such a hefty percentage invested in that sector it's no wonder the company increased its sales during the national stimulus plan in France in 2009 but suffered when cuts in defense spending were announced a year later. Thales ended up posting a 6% loss in sales in 2010 over 2009; however its net income posting at a loss of more than $142 million is about 50% improved over 2009's bottom line loss of almost $300 million. The company attributes this to strong growth in the Aerospace & Transport segment especially in its space business. In 2011 the company landed a multi-year contract with Iridium in the US for more than E1 billion (more than $2 billion) to build 81 telecommunications satellites —launch date is scheduled for 2015.

Thales serves government and private-sector customers (OEMs and MROs) in the aeronautics space transport defense and security markets. Thales' mix of military and civil business is somewhat balanced which mitigates fluctuations in demand economy and federal spending. The company is capitalizing on the synergies between the two markets to develop technologies and products that address the needs of both. To utilize its resources most efficiently the company reorganized its operations in early 2010 to include two primary business segments (comprising seven divisions): Defense & Security and Aerospace & Transport.

The rationale for reorganization is based on the fact that cyber crime trafficking terrorism identity breaches satellite observation air and rail transport security et al constitute areas in need of threat detection technology –whether civil or military in nature. Thales further refined its new organization in 2010 by consolidating its divisions into three geographical areas; France holds its own division while the rest of the world is included in the other two divisions.

The company manufactures its products in one of 13 sites located throughout Europe in France the Netherlands Spain and the UK as well as in Australia. The company extends its global presence through acquisitions joint ventures and partnerships. In 2011 Thales agreed to form a joint venture with India-based Axis Aerospace & Technologies which will be majority shareholder. The two companies want to create a flight training center in Bangalore with Axis investing about $50 million in the project. Thales will supply the simulator equipment as well as its management expertise.

Thales is France's largest defense company by revenue but after its home country Great-Britain is where Thales is a significant player; the company is the UK's second largest military supplier. In 2009 the company won the competition to design the electronics as well as the missile seekers for the aircraft carrier Royal Navy Future Carrier (CVF). Thales is part of the Airtanker consortium the winning bid for the RAF's Future Strategic Tanker Aircraft and the British Army UAV program Watchkeeper. It also produces the SWARM remote weapon station.

Thales links to the US defense market by establishing a number of relationships with US companies on everything from missiles to radars to sonar. It makes components for Raytheon's missiles and the company's combat management system is at the core of Northrop Grumman's Integrated Combat Management system (which is a fixture on General Dynamics' Littoral Combat Ship).

On its home turf Thales in early 2011 took over France-based Societe Europeenne de Systemes Optiques (SESO) a maker of precision optical components such as mirrors and telescopes as well as solar simulators. SESO's acquisition enhances Thales' offerings to its space and defense and laser customers. In naval operations Thales supplies radars surveillance and communications systems and sonar products for use in the construction of the French-Italian Horizon frigates and FREMM multi-mission frigates programs.

Many of the company's defense systems apply to the aerospace market i.e. satellites. For example Thales Alenia Space the joint venture between Thales (67% stake) and Italy's aerospace group Finmeccanica (33%) seeks to snare a growing share of the global market for large commercial-communications satellites that are launched by commercial rockets. Catching the eye of the White House and Pentagon the venture develops a family of satellites built without US hardware –the US restricts the use of its hardware so that it can be used in Chinese satellites. Simultaneously the venture has set its sights on parlaying the scope of commercial satellite launch contracts into partnerships with interests like China whose price is less than launches on European Russian or US rockets. The French-Italian connection also marks a first for NASA. The venture creates Cupola a new surround-glass attachment for the International Space Station.

And while all this was going on Thales' ownership stakes were changing hands. Financially strapped Alcatel-Lucent was given the green light by the European Commission in 2009 to unload its 21% stake in Thales to Dassault. Dassault already owned over 5% giving the UK-based airplane maker about 26% of Thales. (On the heels of the sale Groupe Dassault's (GIMD) stake in Thales landed with Dassault Aviation.) The French government with its 27% stake preserves its dominant position in capital ownership and voting rights. However with the entry of the French government as a new key shareholder Chairman Denis Ranque was replaced with the state's candidate of choice Luc Vigneron. Careers ended also for 10 Thales directors.

HISTORY

Compagnie Francaise Thomson-Houston (CFTH) began as a subsidiary for US-based tramway-equipment maker Thomson-Houston Electric Corporation in 1893. French investors bought the subsidiary when Thomson-Houston and Edison General Electric merged to become General Electric (GE). The fledgling company kept its founder's name and maintained a licensing agreement with GE. Early interests included power stations and the electrification of tramways. Diversification in the 1920s included the acquisition of Societe des Usines du Pied-Selle (kitchen and heating equipment 1920) and the formation of a finance company Financiere Electricite (1925).

Alsthom was created in 1928 when Thomson and Societe Alsacienne de Constructions Mecaniques joined to make industrial electrical equipment. Radio and TV receivers were added in 1929 when Thomson acquired Etablissements Ducretet.

The 1930s brought the acquisition of Etablissement Kraemer (radio equipment 1936). During WWII however operations not used by the German military sat idle.

Postwar political conflict between France and the US plus Thomson's involvement in defense and nuclear technology caused it to end association with GE in 1953. A 1959 agreement with Pathe-Marconi began radio and TV production.

A 1966 merger with Hotchkiss-Brandt resulted in a new name Thomson-Brandt. In 1968 another merger and another name change Thomson-CSF occurred when Compagnie Generale de TSF joined Thomson. In 1981 the French nationalized Thomson-Brandt and in 1982 created holding company Thomson S.A. to manage it. Opposition to the government's nationalization in 1987 forced Thomson's return to the private sector and the company formed semiconductor unit SGS-Thomson Microelectronics. In 1989 the company acquired defense electronics businesses MBLE (Belgium) and Signaal (Denmark) from Philips.

Arms sales declined in 1991 and the company began to produce consumer goods such as satellite TV dishes. A 1992 agreement introduced IBM technology to Thomson defense and space products. UK-based GEC and Thomson began making sonar and antisubmarine systems after a 1995 agreement.

Thomson sold its interests in Credit Lyonnais Securities to the French government in 1996. The company sold its semiconductor unit in 1997. Thomson strengthened its defense business by taking a majority interest in Siemens Forvarssystemer (military communications Norway) in 1998 and striking a $500 million deal with Raytheon to make control systems for NATO in 1999. That year Thomson also purchased a 42% stake in Singapore-based optronics company Avimo Group.

Late in 1999 Shorts Missile Systems Ltd. (SMS) —Thomson's joint venture with Canada-based Bombardier —won a long-term $319 million contract to make short-range Starstreak anti-aircraft missiles for the UK. In 2000 Thomson-CSF acquired UK-based Racal Electronics a defense electronics firm for $2.17 billion and bought out Bombardier's share in the SMS venture. Also in 2000 the company announced plans to sell Crouzet-Automatismes (its electro-mechanical components division) to Schneider Electric. In December Thomson-CSF changed its name to Thales and agreed to form a joint air-defense venture (Thales-Raytheon Systems) with Raytheon.

In 2001 the company acquired majority control over optronics company Avimo. The same year Thales sold its 48.8% stake in Alcatel Space to joint venture partner Alcatel for about $700 million. (That deal and another sale of Thales' stock late in the year reduced Alcatel's stake to about 16%.) Thales also agreed to buy Orbital Science's GPS businesses Magellan Corporation and Navigation Solutions LLC (NavSol) a joint venture with Hertz for about $70 million. In November the company sold Thales Instruments (the former instruments business of Racal) to an investment firm consortium for about $120 million.

Thales agreed to sell its computer services arm Thales IS to French IT company GFI Informatique in 2002. However GFI abandoned the deal which would have been worth more than $300 million soon after it was announced.

In 2004 Thales gained ground when BAE lost prime contractor status in building the Royal Navy's new carriers; but the two companies would ultimately work together with US-based KBR coordinating things. The following year Thales inked a E236 million deal to supply 18 facilities with Tiger combat helicopter simulators.

In 2006 Thales and Germany's Diehl Stiftung & Co. merged their aerospace activities specifically cockpit avionics systems and flight and engine control to create a new joint venture company Diehl Aerospace GmbH. The two companies teamed up again to form Junghans Microtec GmbH a combination of the two companies' ammunition fuse and safety device operations.

In exchange for a near 21% stake in Thales plus cash Thales acquired the satellite-building and homeland security businesses of telecom-equipment maker Alcatel-Lucent in 2006. The deal included Alcatel-Lucent's transport systems division which makes signaling systems for railways and subway systems. As part of the acquisition the French government's stake in Thales decreased.

Thales acquired a 25% slice of shipyard concern Direction des Constructions Navales (DCN) in 2007 with an option to increase its stake to as much as 35%. In return Thales handed over its Naval France business to DCN and a stake in three of Thales's concerns. The tie-up pushes Thales's system capabilities to the front of the European naval market. Also that same year ITT Gilfillan and Thales inked a deal that would enable ITT radar systems to have the exclusive right to market and produce the Smart SMK II radar system for the US market. Thales also has a manufacturing facility in Maryland where it works on the Joint Tactical Radio System.

The company sold its Thales Computers unit to Kontron Modular Computers in 2008 for E11 million (over $14 million). It also divested its electronic payment business that same year; American Group Hypercom purchased it for over E93 million (almost $125 million).

To expand its information and communications systems security business the company pocketed nCipher in 2008 a supplier of encryption products for government financial institutions and enterprises that need to protect sensitive data. Also in 2008 Thales joined Emirates Advanced Investments subsidiary C4 Advanced Solutions (C4AS) to step up military communication systems and equipment in the Middle East and Northern Africa. Holding a 49% stake in the Abu Dhabi-based joint venture (Thales Advanced Solutions) Thales supplies tactical radio maintenance in-service support for products and systems and software for communications systems to UAE armed forces. The joint venture extended Thales's regional influence; the company already won a deal to integrate communications at Abu Dhabi International Airport's air traffic control center tower. India is a customer too and operates combat aircraft built by Dassault and Thales.

Thales purchased Israel-based medical imaging company CMT Medical Technologies in 2009 for about E20 million (more than $28 million). While its medical imaging business took a giant hit during the recession its joint venture with Philips and Siemens (Thales holds 51%) to make digital X-ray detectors offset the impact. The acquisition of CMT satisfies all the needs of OEM requirements.

EXECUTIVES

Chairman and CEO, Luc Vigneron, age 58
SVP Research and Technology, Marko Erman
EVP Area A; Chairman Thales UK, Alex Dorrian, age 67
SVP Avionics, Michel Mathieu, age 62
SVP Space Division, Reynald Seznec
Senior Vice President - Air Operations; Member of the Executive Committee, Guy Delevacque, age 55
SVP Defence and Security C41 Systems, Pascale Sourisse
Managing Director Thales Australia, Chris Jenkins
SVP; CEO Thales Germany, Markus Hellenthal
Chief Executive Officer, Victor Chavez
Senior Vice President - Defence and Security C4I Systems; Member of the Executive Committee, Marc Darmon, age 47
SVP Mission Defence Systems, Pierre-Eric Pommellet, age 48
SVP Land Defence, Alex Cresswell, age 48
SVP Area B, Blaise Jaeger, age 49
SVP Strategy, Herve Multon
SVP Air Operations, Jean-Loic Galle, age 53
SVP Transportation Systems, Jean-Pierre Forestier, age 65
Managing Director Simulation Business France, Pierre Segretain
Vice President General Manager Inflight Systems, Alan Pellegrini
Vice President Strategy and Business Development, Brad Foreman
Vice President General Manager Avionics Services World-Wide, Edward Senen
Vice President Legal & Contracts, Phyllis E. Andes
Vice President General Manager Naval Division, Robert G. Sprigg
IR Contact, Jean-Claude Climeau
Senior Vice President - Finance; Information Systems and Real Estate Services; Member of the Executive Committee, Pascal Bouchiat
Senior Vice President - Human Resources and Operations; Member of the Executive Committee, Patrick Fournie
Senior Vice President - Land Defence; Member of the Executive Committee, Serge Adrian
Vice President of Finance for the Land & Defense Division, Thomas Got
Vice President Operations, Adam Marks
Vice President Research & Technical, John Best
Vice President Director New Zealand, Peter Beggs
Vice President General Counsel Secretary, Howard Diamond
Vice President Naval, Chris Lloyd
Vice President Government Relations, Jim Fraser
Vice President Legal & Commercial, Michael Jackson
Vice President Protected Vehicles, Warwick Strachan
Senior Executive Vice-President Chief Operating Officer, Patrice Caine
Director, Charles Edelstenne, age 76
Director, Bernard Retat, age 73
Director, Yannick d'Escatha, age 65
Director, Loik Segalen
Director, Lord Roger Freeman, age 70
Director, Didier Lombard, age 72
Director, Amaury-Daniel de Seze, age 66
Director, Steve Gentili, age 63
Director, Eric Trappier
Director, Dominique Floch
Director, Philippe Lepinay
Director, Pierre Mutz, age 70
Director, Bruno Parent
Director, Oliver Bourges
Director, Martine Saunier
Independent Director, Ann Taylor
Independent Director, Anne-Claire Taittinger
Director - Representative of Employees Shareholders, Philippe Lepinay
Independent Director, Yannick dEscatha
Auditors: Ernst&YoungAudit

LOCATIONS

HQ: THALES
45, rue de Villiers, Neuilly-sur-Seine, Cedex 92200
Phone: (33) 1 57 77 80 00
Web: www.thalesgroup.com

2010 Sales

	% of total
Europe	
France	22
UK	11
Other	26
Asia/Pacific	14
North	10
Middle	10
Other	7
Total	**100**

PRODUCTS/OPERATIONS

2010 Sales

	% of total
Defense &	57
Aerospace &	42
Other	1
Total	**100**

Selected Divisions

Air operations
Avionics
Defense & security C4I systems
Defense mission systems
Land defense
Space
Transportation systems

Selected Subsidiaries

TDA Armements
Thales Air Systems
Thales Alenia Space
Thales Avionics
Thales Communications
Thales Electron Devices (TED)
Thales Optronique
Thales Raytheon Systems
Thales Security Solutions & Services SAS
Thales Services
Thales Systemes Aeroportes
Thales Underwater Systems

COMPETITORS

AT&T
Aero Simulation
Alliant Techsystems
Ansaldo STS
Argon ST
BAE SYSTEMS
Ball Aerospace
Boeing
CAE USA
Chemring
Cubic Corp.
Cubic Simulation Systems
Diebold
Ducommun LaBarge Technologies
EADS
FLIR Systems
GE
General Dynamics
Harris Corp.
Herley Industries
Honeywell International
IBM
ITT Corp.
Indra
Innovative Solutions
Invensys
Lockheed Martin
MBDA
Meggitt-USA
Motorola Solutions
Nokia
Nortel Networks
Northrop Grumman
RUAG Holding
Raytheon NCS
Saab AB
Siemens AG
Ultra Electronics

HISTORICAL FINANCIALS

Company Type: Public

Income Statement FYE: December 31

	REVENUE ($ mil.)	NET INCOME ($ mil.)	NET PROFIT MARGIN	EMPLOYEES
12/12	18,661	706	3.8%	65,992
12/11	16,851	661	3.9%	68,325
12/10	17,565	(144)	—	66,919
12/09	18,556	(290)	—	64,285
12/08	17,706	782	4.4%	63,248
Annual Growth	1.3%	(2.5%)	—	1.1%

2012 Year-End Financials

Debt ratio: 11.4%
Return on equity: 12.2%
Cash ($ mil.): 3,319
Current ratio: 0.93
Long-term debt ($ mil.): 1,121
No. of shares (mil.): 199
Dividends
Yield: —
Payout: —
Market value ($ mil.): 6,581

	STOCK PRICE ($) FY Close	P/E High/Low	PER SHARE ($) Earnings	Dividends	Book Value
12/12	32.98	25 19	3.55	0.00	30.23
12/11	30.20	33 18	3.36	0.00	26.81
12/10	35.25	— —	(0.74)	0.00	25.15
12/09	51.75	— —	(1.48)	0.00	27.59
12/08	42.10	51 23	3.98	0.00	28.32
Annual Growth	(5.9%)	— —	(2.9%)	—	1.6%

ThyssenKrupp AG

How do you say "giant engineering and steel company" in German? Try ThyssenKrupp and pronounce it "TISS-in kroop." The company is one of the world's largest steel producers and operates worldwide in two business areas: Materials and Technologies. The first comprises the company's steel (carbon and stainless steel) and materials services businesses. ThyssenKrupp's Technologies group consists of its elevators unit marine systems components technology (for the auto and engineering markets) and plant technology (construction and environmental services) segments. Although its combined interests range from elevators to shipbuilding the company has historically relied upon the steel market.

ThyssenKrupp's diversified industrial operations are split into seven operating business areas plus Inoxum (formerly Stainless Global) as a discontinued operation. The Materials division consists of the Steel Europe Steel Americas and Materials Services units. The Technologies division comprises the company's Elevator Technology Plant Technology Components Technology and Marine Systems units.

In 2011 ThyssenKrupp's revenues increased 15% from the previous year (for both continuing operations and before Stainless Global carve-out sales figures). Although growth continued to be weak in Europe and the US during 2011 the German economy was positive and the group's rise in orders and sales increased in most business areas. That year the company received strong demand for its flat carbon steel auto components and naval shipbuilding operations. Five business areas increased earnings from the previous year with Steel Europe being the largest contributor. The company's net loss of ?1.8 billion ($2.3 billion) in 2011 compared with a net income of ?927 million ($1.2 billion) in 2010 resulted from impairment charges for the discontinued operations of its Stainless Global business and its Steel Americas unit (from cost overruns in the build of its plant in Brazil and the weakness of markets in the US and Europe).

To pay down debt the company decided in 2011 to divest ?10 billion ($14.4 billion) worth of noncore assets. Stainless Global its stainless steel business was the largest asset on the chopping block. At 3 million tons a year Stainless Global was Europe's largest stainless steel producer. ThyssenKrupp followed in the footsteps of rival ArcelorMittal which spun off its stainless unit into a new company Aperam earlier in 2011.

ThyssenKrupp split off Stainless Global from its other operations and renamed it Inoxum. Inoxum's operations include the manufacture of stainless steel flat products and materials such as nickel alloys titanium and zirconium. Early in 2012 ThyssenKrupp agreed to sell Inoxum to Finnish company Outokumpu for ?2.7 billion ($3.54 billion). The deal awaits approval by the European Commission after Outokumpu divests some of its combined operations with Inoxum.

In 2012 the company also offloaded ThyssenKrupp Steel Europe's lightweight steel construction elements group to Irish company Kingspan.

In 2013 ArcelorMittal formed a joint venture with Nippon Steel & Sumitomo Metal to buy ThyssenKrupp Steel USA from ThyssenKrupp for $1.5 billion. The deal is expected to deliver $60 million in annual savings.

ThyssenKrupp sold its metal forming unit which supplies the automotive industry to Spain's Gestamp Automocion in 2011. The metals unit was no longer part of ThyssenKrupp's core business of Steel Europe. In another move to unload noncore businesses and pay down debt that year ThyssenKrupp sold Xervon a service provider for the processing construction and energy and power industries to German water and recycling services company Remondis.

In another exit that year ThyssenKrupp terminated its submarine sales joint venture with Ferrostaal which is owned by Germany's MAN group and Abu Dhabi's International Petroleum Investment Co. (IPIC). The company is reorganizing its Marine Systems business unit.

While continuing to divest noncore operations the group is making selective investments in key growth areas. It is making major investments in projects in Brazil and the US. Its Elevator Technology has made strategic acquisitions in the US and Canada as well as smaller buys in the Benelux countries France Italy and Spain. The Plant Technology unit has expanded its coke plant activities by acquiring Tokyo-based Otto Corporation. Through its Components Technology unit ThyssenKrupp has invested in crankshaft factories in Nanjing China.

ThyssenKrupp is a product of the 1999 merger of Thyssen AG and Fried. Krupp AG Hoesch-Krupp. The Alfried Krupp von Bohlen und Halbach Foundation owns 25% of the company.

HISTORY

Formed separately in the 1800s both Thyssen and Krupp flourished in their early years under family control. Friedrich Krupp opened his steel factory in 1811. He died in 1826 and left the nearly bankrupt factory in the hands of his 14-year-old son Alfred who turned the business around. At the first World's Fair in 1851 Alfred unveiled a steel cannon far superior to earlier bronze models.

Twenty years later August Thyssen founded a puddling and rolling mill near Mulheim. He bought small factories and mines and by WWI he ran Germany's largest iron and steel company. During the world wars the resources of both companies were turned toward military efforts.

Post-WWII years were tough for both companies. Thyssen was split up by the Allies and when it began production again in 1953 it consisted of one steel plant. In the Krupp camp Alfred's great-grandson Alfried was convicted in 1948 of using slave labor during WWII. Released from prison in 1951 Alfried rebuilt Krupp. After near ruin following WWII both companies emerged and enjoyed a resurgence along with the German economy in which they prospered and expanded during the 1950s.

By the 1980s Thyssen's businesses included ships locomotives offshore oil rigs specialty steel and metals trading and distribution. Krupp continued to grow and in 1992 it took over engineering and steelmaking concern Hoesch AG. (Eberhard Hoesch had begun making railroad tracks in the 1820s. The company grew and expanded into infrastructure and building products.)

The new Fried. Krupp AG Hoesch-Krupp bought Italian specialty steelmaker Acciai Speciali Terni chemical-plant builder Uhde and South African shipper J.H. Bachmann. Its automotive division formed a joint venture in Brazil and added production sites in China Mexico Romania and the US.

In 1997 Thyssen expanded in North America with its $675 million acquisition of Giddings & Lewis (machine tools US) and the purchase of Copper & Brass Sales (metals processing and distributing).

Krupp attempted a hostile takeover of Thyssen in 1997. The takeover failed but the companies soon agreed to merge their steel operations to form Thyssen Krupp Stahl. Bigger plans were in the works and in 1998 the two companies agreed to merge. That year Thyssen sold its Plusnet fixed-line phone business to Esprit Telecom Group.

In 1999 Krupp's automotive division (Krupp Hoesch Automotive) bought Cummins' Atlas Crankshaft subsidiary. Thyssen also bought US-based Dover's elevator business for $1.1 billion. Krupp and Thyssen completed their merger in 1999. The company planned to spin off its steel operations but held off due to its success in 2000. ThyssenKrupp did however sell its Krupp Kunststofftechnik unit (plastic molding machines) for about $183 million. To speed corporate decision-making the company made plans to scrap its dual-management structure in 2001.

Early in 2001 ThyssenKrupp agreed to buy 51% of Fiat unit Magneti Marelli's suspension-systems and shock-absorbers business. It also had the option of buying the remainder after 2004. In 2002 the company formed alliances with NKK and Kawasaki Steel to share its steel sheet making technologies while expanding its business with Japanese automotive makers in Europe. ThyssenKrupp's joint venture with Chinese steelmaker ANSC Angang New Steel known as TAGAL began producing galvanized coil of which about 80% will be used in China's burgeoning automotive industry.

In 2004 ThyssenKrupp sold its residential real estate unit for around $2.8 billion to a consortium of real estate funds operated by Morgan Stanley and Corpus-Immobiliengruppe. It divested the automotive segment of the capital goods unit in 2006 selling it off in pieces.

ThyssenKrupp opened three major new steel facilities in the Americas in 2010. A new integrated steel mill in Santa Cruz Brazil started production in mid-year. The $7 billion plant the company's biggest project ever is a partnership with South American giant Vale SA which owns a 25% stake in the venture. The company also began production at two plants in Calvert Alabama: a $3.6 billion carbon steel plant and a $1.4 billion stainless steel rolling plant. The company also constructed —and consolidated its corporate staff in —a new headquarters building in Essen Germany in 2010.

In 2010 ThyssenKrupp sold its Hamburg-based mega-yacht and shipbuilding operations to Abu Dhabi MAR Group. ThyssenKrupp is exiting the civil shipbuilding business to focus on constructing military vessels. The company also sold its interest in Hellenic Shipyards to Abu Dhabi MAR following difficulties related to the Greek government's financial problems.

Heinrich Hiesinger was named CEO of ThyssenKrupp in 2011. He replaced Ekkehard Schulz who retired. Hiesinger was previously an executive of German engineering company Siemens AG.

EXECUTIVES

Member Executive Board Technologies; CEO Elevator Technology, Olaf Berlien, age 51, $556,512 total compensation
Head Corporate Investor Relations, Claus Ehrenbeck
Chairman Executive Board, Heinrich Hiesinger, age 53
Vice Chairman, Bertin Eichler, age 61
Member Executive Board Materials; CEO Steel Europe and Steel Americas, Edwin Eichler, age 55, $700,320 total compensation
Member Executive Board Human Resources, Ralph Labonte, age 60, $653,280 total compensation
Member Executive Board Controlling and Risk, Guido Kerkhoff, age 46
Corporate Center Communications Strategy and Technology, Stefan Ettwig
Member Supervisory Board, M. Christian Streiff, age 57
Honorary Chairman, Gunter Vogelsang
Member Supervisory Board, Hans-Peter Keitel, age 66
Honorary Chairman, Berthold Beitz, age 70
Member Supervisory Board, Kersten von Schenck, age 63
Vice Chairman, Bertin Eichler, age 60
Member Supervisory Board, Prof Bernard Pellens, age 57
Member Supervisory Board, Wilhelm Segerath, age 61
Member Supervisory Board, Prof Ulrich Lehner, age 68
Member Supervisory Board, Peer Steinbruck, age 65
Member Supervisory Board, Jurgen R. Thumann, age 71
Member Supervisory Board, Prof Beatrice Weder di Mauro, age 49
Auditors: KPMGDeutscheTreuhand-GesellschaftAG

LOCATIONS

HQ: ThyssenKrupp AG
ThyssenKrupp Allee 1, Essen D-45143
Phone: (49) 201 844 0 **Fax:** (49) 201 844 53600
Web: www.thyssenkrupp.com

2011 Sales

	$ mil.	% of total
EU		
Other countries		29
Asia/Pacific		12
Total		**100**

PRODUCTS/OPERATIONS

2011 Sales (Continued Operations)

	$ mil.	% of total
Materials		
Materials Services		32
Steel		
Steel Europe		28
Steel America		2
Components Technology		15
Elevator Technology		11
Plant Technology		9
Marine Systems		3
Total		**100**

COMPETITORS

Acerinox
ArcelorMittal
Bechtel
Descours & Cabaud
GEA Group
ITOCHU
Ingersoll-Rand
JFE Holdings
Kobe Steel
MAN
Magna International
Marubeni
Nippon Steel & Sumitomo Metal Corporation
POSCO
Qingdao Iron and Steel
Schindler Holding
Sumitomo Metal Industries
Tata Europe
United States Steel
United Technologies

HISTORICAL FINANCIALS

Company Type: Public

Income Statement FYE: September 30

	REVENUE ($ mil.)	NET INCOME ($ mil.)	NET PROFIT MARGIN	EMPLOYEES
09/13	52,044	(1,884)	—	156,856
09/12	51,880	(6,035)	—	167,961
09/11	58,490	(1,741)	—	180,050
09/10	58,084	1,122	1.9%	177,346
09/09	59,373	(2,718)	—	187,495
Annual Growth	(3.2%)	—	—	(4.4%)

2013 Year-End Financials

Debt ratio: 33.9%
Return on equity: (-48.1%)
Cash ($ mil.): 5,146
Current ratio: 1.11
Long-term debt ($ mil.): 9,387
No. of shares (mil.): 514
Dividends
Yield: —
Payout: —
Market value ($ mil.): 12,317

	STOCK PRICE ($) FY Close	P/E High/Low	PER SHARE ($) Earnings	Dividends	Book Value
09/13	23.94	— —	(3.66)	0.00	5.88
09/12	21.50	— —	(11.73)	0.00	8.94
09/11	24.60	— —	(3.66)	0.00	23.63
09/10	31.95	45 23	2.41	0.00	27.96
09/09	34.47	— —	(5.87)	0.00	25.04
Annual Growth	(8.7%)	— —	—	—	(30.4%)

Tokio Marine Holdings Inc

Tokio Marine Holdings might have old roots but it still knows how to learn new tricks. Japan's oldest property/casualty insurance company the firm has one of the largest insurance sales networks in Japan and has expanded its insurance operations to about 40 additional countries in Asia Europe and North America. Through Tokio Marine & Nichido Fire (TMNF) Nisshin Fire Philadelphia Insurance Companies Kiln and other subsidiaries Tokio Marine Holdings provides marine property/casualty personal accident fire auto and life insurance as well as reinsurance. It also offers asset management pension plans and other services.

Geographic Reach

The firm has insurance operations in about 40 countries throughout Asia Europe and North America. The majority of Tokio Marine's revenue comes from Japan (about 85% in fiscal 2012).

Financial Performance

Tokio Marine's revenue has been trending upward during recent fiscal years. The firm claimed about $41.5 billion in revenue for fiscal 2012 up from the $39.7 billion it reported for fiscal 2011 and the $38.5 billion it brought in during fiscal 2010.

Mergers and Acquisitions

In mid-2012 Tokio Marine made another large US acquisition this time of property/casualty and specialty life insurer Delphi Financial Group. The $2.7 billion acquisition enhanced Tokio Marine's property/casualty offerings by adding Safety National Casualty's workers' compensation offerings and Matrix Absence Management's disability offerings; it will brought the company into the US life insurance market through the addition of Delphi's Reliance Standard Life unit which provides group employee benefits and individual annuities.

In 2011 TMNF bought up CNA Financial Corporation's 50% interest in First Insurance Company of Hawaii the state's largest property/casualty insurance firm. TMNF had held the other 50% of the company since 1999 and buying up the balance of First Insurance Company of Hawaii sped up its US expansion efforts.

Other potential countries targeted for growth efforts include China and India.

HISTORY

After the US forced Japan to open to trade in 1854 Western marine insurers began operating there. In 1878 Japan's government organized backers for a Japanese marine insurance firm. Tokio Marine and Fire Insurance was founded the next year.

Tokio grew quickly insuring trading companies like Mitsubishi and Mitsui; it soon had offices in London Paris and New York. Increased competition in the 1890s forced it to curtail its foreign operations and begin using brokers in most other countries.

Victory in the Russo-Japanese War of 1904-05 buoyed the country but the economy slowed as it demobilized. Businesses responded by forming cooperative groups known as "zaibatsu". Tokio Marine and Fire was allied with the Mitsubishi group.

Before WWI Tokio expanded by adding fire personal accident theft and auto insurance and it continued to buy foreign sales brokers. Japan's insurance industry consolidated in the 1920s and the company bought up smaller competitors. The 1923 Tokyo earthquake hit the industry hard but Tokio's new fire insurance operations had little exposure.

Most of Tokio's foreign operations were seized during WWII. In 1944 Tokio merged with Mitsubishi Marine Insurance and Meiji Fire Insurance. Business grew in WWII but wartime destruction left Tokio with nothing to insure and no money to pay claims.

After the war Tokio slowly recovered and resumed overseas operations. Although the US had dismantled the "zaibatsu" during occupation Tokio allied once again with Mitsubishi when Japan's government rebuilt most of the old groups as "keiretsu".

During the 1950s and 1960s the company grew its personal lines adding homeowners coverage. Domestic business slowed during the 1970s and 1980s and Tokio boosted operations overseas. It added commercial property/casualty insurer Houston General Insurance (a US company sold in 1997) Tokio Reinsurance and interests in insurance and investment management firms.

In the 1980s the firm invested heavily in real estate through "jusen" (mortgage companies). Japan's overheated real estate market collapsed in the early 1990s dumping masses of nonperforming assets on "jusen" and their investors (the country's major banks and insurers including Tokio).

Deregulation began in 1996 and economic recession soon followed. In 1998 Tokio joined other members of the Mitsubishi group including Bank of Tokyo-Mitsubishi and Meiji Life Insurance to form investment banking pension and trust joint ventures. The firm also formed its own investment trust and allied with such foreign financial companies as BANK ONE and United Asset Management to develop new investment products. Brokerage firm Charles Schwab Tokio Marine Securities a joint venture was launched in 1999. That year Tokio consolidated its foreign reinsurance operations into Tokio Marine Global Re in Dublin Ireland and kicked off a business push that included reorganizing its agent force and planning for online sales.

Millea Holdings was created in 2002 as the holding company for the merger between Tokio Marine and Fire and Nichido Fire and Marine. The two were combined and renamed Tokio Marine & Nichido Fire Insurance a subsidiary of Millea Holdings.

The company's 2005 acquisition of Real Seguros allowed the company to bring its life insurance products to Brazil (renamed Tokio Marine Seguradora). In 2006 Millea acquired Nisshin Fire and Marine Insurance Company as a separately operated subsidiary. In 2007 the firm purchased Asia General Holdings and its life insurance subsidiaries which operated in Singapore and Malaysia. It also purchased Japanese fire insurance provider Nihon Kousei Kyousaikai.

In 2008 Millea Holdings changed its name to Tokio Marine Holdings to reflect the positive brand recognition associated with the Tokio Marine name.

EXECUTIVES

Chairman, Kunio Ishihara, age 70
EVP, Takaaki Tamai, age 63
EVP, Hiroshi Amemiya, age 63
President Nisshin Fire, Hiroshi Miyajima, age 63
Chairman, Shuzo Sumi
Senior Managing Executive Officer International Business Development, Hiroshi Endo
President and CEO, Tsuyoshi Nagano
Managing Executive Officer, Masashi Oba
General Manager Personnel Planning Dept., Takefumi Horiuchi
General Manager of Domestic Business Development Dept, Mitsuhiko Uehira
Managing Director General Manager of Corporate Accounting Dept, Hirokazu Fujita
General Manager of International Business Development Dept, Ichiro Ishii
President Tokio Marine & Nichido Life, Toshifumi Kitazawa
EVP, Kazuo Kouduki
Auditors: ChuoAoyamaPricewaterhouseCoopers

LOCATIONS

HQ: Tokio Marine Holdings Inc
1-2-1 Marunouchi, Chiyoda-ku, Tokyo 100-0005
Phone: (81) 3 6212 3333
Web: www.tokiomarinehd.com/en/

2012 Sales

	% of total
Japan	85
Other	15
Total	**100**

PRODUCTS/OPERATIONS

2012 Sales

	% of total
Property/casualty	78
Life	13
Other	9
Total	**100**

Selected Mergers and Acquisitions

FY2012

Delphi Financial Group ($2.7 billion; Wilmington DE; specialty life insurer)

COMPETITORS

AIG
Allianz
Aviva
Brit Insurance
Chubb Corp
Dai-ichi Life
Daido Life
Equity Insurance
Fuji Fire and Marine
HCC Insurance
Hiscox
ING
MS&AD Holdings
Markel
NKSJ Holdings
Nippon Life Insurance
Prudential plc
Sumitomo Life
Travelers Companies
Zurich Insurance Group

HISTORICAL FINANCIALS

Company Type: Public

Income Statement

FYE: March 31

	ASSETS ($ mil.)	NET INCOME ($ mil.)	INCOME AS % OF ASSETS	EMPLOYEES
03/13	191,614	1,377	0.7%	33,006
03/12	199,176	73	0.0%	30,831
03/11	199,605	868	0.4%	29,758
03/10	184,844	1,374	0.7%	29,578
03/09	154,833	234	0.2%	28,063
Annual Growth	5.5%	55.6%	—	4.1%

2013 Year-End Financials

Return on assets: 0.7%
Return on equity: 6.2%
Long-term debt ($ mil.): —
No. of shares (mil.): 767
Sales ($ mil): 41,118
Dividends
Yield: —
Payout: —
Market value ($ mil.): 22,029

	STOCK PRICE ($) FY Close	P/E High/Low		PER SHARE ($) Earnings	Dividends	Book Value
03/13	28.72	—	—	1.79	0.00	32.74
03/12	27.66	—	—	0.10	0.00	29.53
03/11	26.78	—	—	1.12	0.59	29.99
03/10	28.20	—	—	1.74	0.52	29.70
03/09	24.57	—	—	0.30	0.54	21.14
Annual Growth	4.0%	—	—	56.9%	—	11.6%

Tokyo Electric Power Co. Inc. (The) (Japan)

Japan Inc. would grind to a halt without Tokyo Electric Power Company (TEPCO) which supplies power to 28.6 million customers in Tokyo Yokohama and the rest of the Kanto region. One of the world's largest electric utilities TEPCO's 190 power plants have the generating capacity of approximately 64500 MW primarily produced by thermal nuclear and hydroelectric power sources. In 2011 the company faced a major crisis when its Fukushima Dai-ichi nuclear plant complex experienced a partial meltdown at three reactors and radioactive material was released in the wake of a major earthquake and tsunami. The disaster confronted the company with the prospect of multi-billion dollar losses.

Public confidence had already been shaken by a rash of accidents within Japan's nuclear industry. The company had struggled to restore its credibility after the Japanese government shut down TEPCO's 17 nuclear reactors due to safety concerns prompted by the company's admittance of falsifying safety data to cover up faults at several of its nuclear facilities in 2002. In 2009 it reopened the Kashiwazaki-Kariwa Nuclear Power Station which was closed in 2007 due to a major earthquake in the region.

Through affiliates TEPCO also offers cable TV and Internet services international consulting and investing in non-Japan-based independent power producers. Other businesses include construction real estate and transportation companies.

The company is developing new green energy sources such as wind and solar in order to meet carbon emission reduction targets. In 2009 the company agreed to build a major solar project in Kawasaki Kanagawa to serve about 5900 households. In 2010 it teamed up with Toyota Tsusho to fund wind power company Eurus Energy Holdings which acquired solar power company Jindosun Park in 2011. Jindosun oversees the generation of 2974KW of electricity mostly in South Korea and will activate a 45000KW plant in the US in mid-2011.

Broadening its international power assets in 2011 the company agreed to buy 12% of Thailand-based independent power producer Electricity Generating PCL for about $274 million. However the daunting financial impact of the Fukushima disaster has cast a pall over the company's international expansion plans.

The company is selling assets to pay off its massive debt. In 2012 it agreed to sell its 67.5% stake in Australian power station Loy Yang A to the plant's minority owner AGL Resources for $1.6 billion.

HISTORY

The Tokyo Electric Power Company (TEPCO) descended from Tokyo Electric Light which was formed in 1883. In 1887 the company switched on Japan's first power plant a 25-KW fossil fuel generator. Fossil fuels were the main source of electricity in Japan until 1912 when long-distance transmission techniques became more efficient making hydroelectric power cheaper.

In 1938 Japan nationalized electric utilities despite strong objections from Yasuzaemon Matsunaga a leader in Japan's utility industry and former president of the Japan Electric Association. After WWII Matsunaga championed public ownership of Japan's power companies which helped in 1951 to establish the current system of 10 regional companies each with a service monopoly. Tokyo Electric Power was the largest. That year it was listed on the Tokyo Stock Exchange and was regulated by the Ministry of International Trade and Industry. (The ministry has regulated electric utilities since 1965.)

Fossil fuel plants made a comeback in Japan in the postwar era because they could be built more economically than hydroelectric plants. When the OPEC oil embargo of the 1970s demonstrated Japan's dependence on foreign oil TEPCO increased its use of liquefied natural gas (LNG) and nuclear energy sources. (It brought its first nuke online in 1971.) In 1977 it formed the Energy Conservation Center to promote conservation and related legislation.

To further reduce its oil dependence TEPCO joined other US and Japanese firms in building a coal gasification plant in California's Mojave Desert in 1982. Two years later TEPCO announced it would begin building its first coal-burning generator since the oil crisis. It established Tokyo Telecommunication Network (TTNet) a partnership to provide telecommunications services in 1986 and TEPCO Cable TV in 1989.

As part of its interest in alternative energy systems TEPCO established a global environment department in 1990 to conduct R&D on energy and the environment. Its environmental program has included reforestation and fuel cell research.

Liberalization in 1995 allowed Japan's electric utilities to buy power from independent power producers; TEPCO quickly lined up 10 suppliers. The company proceeded with energy experimentation in 1996 trying a 6000-KW sodium-sulfur battery at a Yokohama transformer station. The next year the company announced that it would become the first electric utility to sell liquefied natural gas as part of its energy mix and finished building the world's largest nuclear plant.

To gain experience in deregulating markets TEPCO invested in US power generating company Orion Power in 1999. (It agreed to sell its 5% stake to Reliant Energy in 2001.) At home the firm joined Microsoft and SOFTBANK to form SpeedNet which provides Internet access over TTNet's network. In 2000 TEPCO got its first taste of deregulation when large customers (accounting for about a third of the market) began choosing their electricity suppliers. Also in 2000 TEPCO joined a group of nine Japanese electric companies to create POWEREDCOM. (In 2005 TEPCO sold its stake in POWEREDCOM to KDDI in order to focus on its core power business).

In 2001 TEPCO joined up with Sumitomo and Electricite de France to build Vietnam's first independent power plant.

To raise cash in 2006 Mirant (now GenOn Energy) sold its power plants in the Philippines to TEPCO and Marubeni for $3.4 billion.

EXECUTIVES

Chairman, Tsunehisa Katsumata
EVP, Norio Tsuzumi
EVP, Hiroshi Yamaguchi
Managing Director and General Manager Business Development Division, Makio Fujiwara
Managing Director; Deputy General Manager Nuclear Power Plant Siting Division, Sakae Muto
Managing Director, Yoshihiro Naito
President, Toshio Nishizawa
EVP, Zengo Aizawa
Chairman, Kazuhiko Shimokobe
President, Naomi Hirose
EVP, Yoshiyuki Ishizaki
Director, Yoshihisa Morimoto
EVP and Director, Susumu Shirakawa
EVP General Manager Marketing and Sales and Director, Shigeru Kimura
EVP General Manager Engineering Research and Development and Director, Hiroyuki Ino
Director, Tomijirou Morita
Director, Yasushi Aoyama
Auditors: Ernst&YoungShinNihon

LOCATIONS

HQ: Tokyo Electric Power Co. Inc. (The) (Japan)
1-1-3 Uchisaiwai-cho, Chiyoda-Ku, Tokyo 100-8560
Phone: (81) 3 6373 1111
Web: www.tepco.co.jp

PRODUCTS/OPERATIONS

2010 Sales

	% of total
Electricity	89
Energy &	7
Living environment &	2
Information &	2
Total	**100**

Selected Subsidiaries

TEPCO CABLE TELEVISION Inc. (85% cable television)
TEPCO SYSTEMS CORPORATION (information software and services)
Toden Kogyo Co. Ltd. (facilities construction and maintenance)
Toden Real Estate Co. Inc. (property management)
Tokyo Densetsu Service Co. Ltd. (facilities construction and maintenance)
Tokyo Electric Power Environmental Engineering Company Incorporated (facilities construction and maintenance)
Tokyo Electric Power Services Company Limited (facilities construction and maintenance)

COMPETITORS

Chubu Electric Power
Chugoku Electric Power
Hokkaido Electric Power
Hokuriku Electric Power
Internet Initiative Japan
Jinpan International
KDDI
KEPCO
Korea Electric Power
Kyushu Electric Power
NTT
Osaka Gas
Shikoku Electric
Tohoku Electric Power
Tokyo Gas

HISTORICAL FINANCIALS

Company Type: Public

Income Statement FYE: March 31

	REVENUE ($ mil.)	NET INCOME ($ mil.)	NET PROFIT MARGIN	EMPLOYEES
03/13	63,514	(7,283)	—	0
03/12	65,213	(9,528)	—	52,046
03/11	64,832	(15,063)	—	52,970
03/10	53,702	1,432	2.7%	52,452
03/09	59,787	(858)	—	52,506
Annual Growth	1.5%	—	—	—

2013 Year-End Financials

Debt ratio: 0.5%
Return on equity: (-71.9%)
Cash ($ mil.): 18,651
Current ratio: 1.34
Long-term debt ($ mil.): 72,195
No. of shares (mil.): 1,600
Dividends
Yield: —
Payout: —
Market value ($ mil.): 3,913

	STOCK PRICE ($) FY Close	P/E High/Low	PER SHARE ($) Earnings	Dividends	Book Value
03/13	2.45	— —	(4.54)	0.00	7.56
03/12	2.58	— —	(5.95)	0.00	6.19
03/11	5.35	— —	(10.22)	0.68	12.09
03/10	26.25	— —	1.06	0.00	19.99
03/09	25.50	— —	(0.64)	0.00	18.23
Annual Growth	(44.4%)	— —	—	—	(19.8%)

TonenGeneral Sekiyu K.K.

TonenGeneral Sekiyu is a leading Japanese refiner that came into being in 2000 as the result of the merger of Japanese refiners Tonen and General Sekiyu both affiliates of global oil and gas behemoth Exxon Mobil. TonenGeneral Sekiyu (50.02%-owned by Exxon Mobil) combines Tonen's 505000 barrels a day of refining capacity in Kawasaki and Wakayama with General Sekiyu's 156000 barrels a day of capacity at Sakai. The oil producing company also operates a 100000 barrels-a-day refinery at Nishihara (in Okinawa) through its 87.5%-owned Nansei Sekiyu subsidiary. TonenGeneral Sekiyu operates a chain of gas stations across Japan under the Esso General and Mobil brands.

The company is trying to diversify its sources of crude oil supply (about 70% comes from the Middle East) and upgrade its refineries in order to reduce costs.

EXECUTIVES

Managing Director and Representative Director, Jun Mutoh
Auditor, Tetsuro Yamamoto
Auditor, Masaaki Ayukawa
President and Director, Kazuo Suzuki
Managing Director and Representative Director, W. J. Bogarty
Managing Director and Representative Director, Jun Mutoh
Director, Kyoji Yoshida
Director, S.K. Arnet
Director, D.R. Csapo
Director, P.P. Ducom
Auditors: PricewaterhouseCoopersLLP

LOCATIONS

HQ: TonenGeneral Sekiyu K.K.
1-8-15 Kohnan, Minato-ku, Tokyo 108-8005
Phone: (81) 3 6713 4400
Web: www.tonengeneral.co.jp

PRODUCTS/OPERATIONS

2007 Sales

	% of total
Oil	89
Chemical	11
Total	**100**

COMPETITORS

Idemitsu Kosan
JX Nippon Mining & Metals
JX Nippon Oil & Energy
Showa Shell Sekiyu

HISTORICAL FINANCIALS

Company Type: Public

Income Statement FYE: December 31

	REVENUE ($ mil.)	NET INCOME ($ mil.)	NET PROFIT MARGIN	EMPLOYEES
12/12	32,566	635	2.0%	2,805
12/11	34,594	1,715	5.0%	2,171
12/10	29,490	527	1.8%	2,178
12/09	22,856	(235)	—	2,354
12/08	36,185	876	2.4%	2,278
Annual Growth	(2.6%)	(7.7%)	—	5.3%

2012 Year-End Financials

Debt ratio: 0.2%
Return on equity: 16.8%
Cash ($ mil.): 155
Current ratio: 0.95
Long-term debt ($ mil.): 1,933
No. of shares (mil.): 364
Dividends
Yield: —
Payout: —
Market value ($ mil.): —

Toppan Printing Co., Ltd.

It would actually be a lot easier to list the items Toppan Printing "doesn't" print. The company prints commercial products (posters catalogs calendars) securities and cards (checks bank pass-books magnetic cards) publications (magazines books CD-ROMs) and packaging products (containers labels). In addition to traditional print products Toppan also specializes in electronics materials such as photomasks for semi-conductors and color filters for LCD TVs. The company has operations throughout the Asia/Pacific region as well as in Europe and North America. Toppan Printing was founded in 1900 by engineers from the printing bureau of Japan's Ministry of Finance.

Toppan Printing has grown to become one of the world's largest printing and publishing companies. The business operates through more than 190 subsidiaries and joint ventures. Just one of these is Toppan Photomasks which manufactures electronics-related materials and industrial materials (such as decorative sheeting and wallpaper). The company's printing businesses account for more than half of revenues. Efforts related to printing and publications include ramping up digital content distribution such as expanding its Shufoo! digital flyer business.

The company's printing operations provide a stable profit source that allows Toppan to invest in other growth industries such as clean energy-related packaging products and materials. In 2011 the company announced its intentions to be the world's only comprehensive supplier of packaging materials for lithium-ion batteries which have applications in personal computers mobile and smart phones and environmentally friendly vehicles. It is doing so through the formation of a joint venture partnership with Toyo Seikan Kaisha a provider of molding and sealant technologies. Previously Toppan focused on manufacturing for color filters and rear-projection TV screens. An example of such efforts was its 2010 formation of Ortus Technology a joint venture with CASIO COMPUTER CO. that manufactures organic light-emitting diode (OLED) displays and thin-film transistor (TFT) liquid crystals.

While the Japanese market accounts for about 90% of Toppan's sales the company is attempting to increase its international business and expand globally. Its International Division was created to grow foreign sales and bring information-related overseas business under central control. The company is particularly focused on emerging markets such as China Thailand and Indonesia.

HISTORY

Toppan Printing was established as Toppan Printing Limited Partnership in 1900 by engineers from Japan's Ministry of Finance who used the most advanced printing techniques of the day. It was renamed Toppan Printing Co. in 1908. In its early days the company focused primarily on securities (for the Ministry of Finance) books and business forms.

Toppan flourished during and immediately after WWI as book and magazine publishing increased. In 1926 it opened the Koishikawa Paper Container Plant. Printing declined in the 1930s however as the Japanese dictatorship banned books and stifled writers and publishers. WWII brought a paper shortage and recession which further depressed Japan's printing industry.

As the printing industry began to recover after the end of WWII Toppan expanded into specialty packaging materials (1952) and industrial materials (1958). It also acquired children's book publisher Froebel-Kan in 1961 and became the first Japanese printer to open a Hong Kong plant in 1963. The company grew at a steady pace throughout the 1960s eventually adding planning and designing to its stable of services. Toppan Moore Business Forms a joint venture between Toppan and Canada's Moore Corporation was established in 1965 (it would become Japan's largest business form printer by the 1980s).

Toppan formed a US subsidiary Toppan Printing (America) in New York City in 1971 and became the first Japanese printer to establish a production plant in the US with the 1979 opening of a separation plant in Mountainside New Jersey. During the late 1970s and early 1980s the company made several important breakthroughs in containers and packing products; it developed long-term liquid storage containers (1976) easy-to-uncap heat seals for packaging (1978) and long-term food storage containers (1980). In 1983 Toppan Moore developed a smart card with two embedded integrated circuits. Two years later the company purchased decorating products manufacturer Kyodo Kako. By the end of the decade Toppan had moved into the production of videotext batteries compact discs liquid crystal display filters lottery tickets postage stamps and portable smart card systems. It also began emphasizing distribution and direct marketing services and created an industrial materials division.

By 1990 Toppan had 21 printing plants and more than 50 sales offices throughout Japan as well as 21 international offices. That year the company formed a photomask joint venture company with Dallas-based Texas Instruments. Toppan executive Hiromichi Fujita was named president of the firm in 1991 (he later became chairman). The company established a multimedia unit in 1996 and acquired all of Toppan Moore –renamed Toppan Forms –the following year (it spun off Toppan Forms in a public offering in 1998).

In 1999 Toppan joined with Internet Initiative Japan Intel Sun Microsystems and IBM Japan to create Bitway which focuses on Internet marketing and distribution of digital content. The following year Toppan entered into a variety of partnerships and joint ventures with such firms as Chughwa Picture Tubes (photomasks) Gemplus (smart cards) and Baltimore Technologies Japan Co. (electronic authentication). Also in 2000 the company celebrated the 100th anniversary of its founding. In 2001 the company partnered with Taiwan's Powerchip Semiconductor Corp. to make chips for other companies.

That year the company invested in another Internet opportunity joining with NEC Corp. and SGI Japan Ltd. to support businesses using broadband Internet services.

EXECUTIVES

Chairman, Naoki Adachi
EVP, Jitsumei Takamiyagi
Senior Managing Director Electronics Division, Kiyoshi Otsuka
President, Shingo Kaneko
Senior Managing Director Information and Communication Division, Mitsuru Ominato
Senior Managing Director Living Environment Division, Yoshihiro Furuya
Senior Managing Director Material Solutions Division, Yuichi Kumamoto
Managing Director Higashinihon Division, Atsushi Ito
Managing Director Finance and Accounting Division, Hidetaka Kakiya
Board Member, Makoto Arai, age 61
Board Member, Kenichi Aoki
Board Member, Seiji Mitsui
Board Member, Kiyoshi Tsuji
Managing Director Purchasing, Hiroe Okazaki
Board Member, Toru Ito
Board Member, Syungo Hiromura
Board Member, Sawako Noma
Board Member, Hidetaka Kakiya
Board Member, Hideharu Maro
Auditors: KPMGAZSA&Co.

LOCATIONS

HQ: Toppan Printing Co., Ltd.
1 Kanda-Izumicho, Chiyoda-ku, Tokyo 101-0024
Phone: (81) 3 3835 5660
Web: www.toppan.co.jp

2011 Sales

	% of total
Japan	86
International	14
Total	**100**

PRODUCTS/OPERATIONS

2011 Sales

	% of total
Information and Networks (traditional print	57
Living Environment (packaging & decor	25
Electronics	18
Total	**100**

Selected Offerings

Information & Networks
- Publications Printing
  - Magazines
  - Books
  - Electronic publications
  - Publication planning & editing
  - Advertising
- Commercial Printing
  - Posters
  - Catalogs
  - Brochures
  - Flyers
  - Direct mail
  - Calendars
  - Corporate communications materials
- Business Forms
  - Cards
  - Envelopes
  - Continuous forms

Living Environment
- Packaging & industrial materials
- Interior decor materials

Electronics
- Displays
- Semiconductors

COMPETITORS

Corning Japan
Dai Nippon Printing
Hoya Corp.
Kodansha
Metro Packaging and Imaging
Nippon Carbide
Photronics
Quad/Graphics
R.R. Donnelley
Times Publishing Limited

HISTORICAL FINANCIALS

Company Type: Public

Income Statement FYE: March 31

	REVENUE ($ mil.)	NET INCOME ($ mil.)	NET PROFIT MARGIN	EMPLOYEES
03/13	15,966	197	1.2%	48,878
03/12	18,412	37	0.2%	47,872
03/11	18,796	146	0.8%	48,197
03/10	16,130	125	0.8%	47,650
03/09	16,423	(78)	—	47,522
Annual Growth	(0.7%)	—	—	0.7%

2013 Year-End Financials

Debt ratio: 0.1%
Return on equity: 2.5%
Cash ($ mil.): 1,770
Current ratio: 1.77
Long-term debt ($ mil.): 2,381
No. of shares (mil.): 644
Dividends
Yield: —
Payout: —
Market value ($ mil.): 4,661

	STOCK PRICE ($) FY Close	P/E High/Low		PER SHARE ($) Earnings	Dividends	Book Value
03/13	7.23	—	—	0.31	0.00	14.65
Annual Growth	—	—	—	—	—	—

Toronto Dominion Bank

The Toronto-Dominion Bank wants to score financial TDs at home and abroad. Also known as TD Bank or TD Financial the company ranks among the world's top online financial services firms and is one of the largest banks in Canada where it operates more than 1100 branches under the TD Trust banner. US subsidiary TD Bank N.A. has another 1300 branches in about 15 eastern states. TD also offers commercial financial and advisory services. Other units include TD Insurance TD Asset Management (mutual funds) and TD Securities (investment banking equities and foreign exchange). Its TD Waterhouse is the largest online brokerage in the UK and Canada; TD Bank also owns 45% of US discount brokerage TD Ameritrade.

TD had CDN$806 billion in assets as of July 31 2012. Over the years TD Bank has been building its US operations to increase its earnings beyond Canada –a mature market with limited growth potential and several large competitors. As US banks fell in record amounts as a result of the global financial crisis TD Bank and other Canadian firms took the opportunity to further boost their US holdings. To this end TD Bank and Target Corporation inked a deal in late 2012 for the purchase of the retailer's existing US Visa and private label credit card portfolio (with a gross outstanding balance of $5.9 billion). As part of an associated seven-year program agreement TD was granted exclusive rights as the issuer of the Target-branded Visa and private label credit cards to Target's US customers. TD benefits by taking over the established card program that enjoys one of the industry's leading rewards programs.

In 2010 TD Bank N.A. added more than 60 branches in Florida by acquiring three failed banks. It also bought The South Financial Group to further expand in the Sunshine State and establish a presence in the Carolinas; that deal added about 70 locations.

In 2011 TD Bank bought most of auto lender Chrysler Financial from Cerberus in a $6.3 billion deal. The acquisition provided a significant boost to the company's loan portfolio as well as some one million customers in the US and Canada. TD Bank rebranded the lender TD Auto Finance. It later expanded another segment of its consumer lending operations when it bought Bank of America's MBNA Canada credit card business adding some 1.8 million active accounts.

TD Bank sold the US operations of online discount brokerage TD Waterhouse to Ameritrade (now TD Ameritrade) in 2006. (TD Waterhouse continues to operate in Canada.) As part of the deal TD Bank acquired a 40% stake in TD Ameritrade. It upped its stake to 45% in 2009 and bought the operations of online broker thinkorswim Group in Canada. Also that year TD increased its stake in Luxembourg-based Internaxx to 75%; the move has helped it expand its online brokerage business in Europe. As of late 2012 TD boasted some 8.5 million online customers.

On the other side of the ledger TD Bank sold fund of funds manager TD Capital Private Equity Investors (now Northleaf Capital Partners) to the unit's management team in 2009. The move was designed to allow TD Bank to focus on its core operations.

HISTORY

The Bank of Toronto was established in 1855 by flour traders who wanted their own banking facilities. Its growth encouraged another group of businessmen to found the Dominion Bank in 1869. Dominion emphasized commercial banking and invested heavily in railways and construction.

As the new nation expanded westward both banks established branch networks. They helped fund Canada's primary industries –dairy mining oil pulp and textiles. True to its pioneering spirit a Bank of Toronto official claimed to be the first to have set up a branch office with the help of aviation (in Manitoba in the 1920s).

The demand for agricultural products and commodities dropped after WWI but production continued full throttle creating a world grain glut that helped trigger the stock market crash of 1929. Both the Bank of Toronto and Dominion Bank contracted during the 1930s. After growing during and subsequent to WWII The Bank of Toronto and Dominion Bank decided to increase their capital base merging into a 450-branch bank in 1955.

In the 1970s TD Bank opened offices in Bangkok Beirut and Frankfurt among other cities abroad. During the 1980s it was active in making loans to less-developed countries. After the deregulation of the Canadian securities industry in 1987 then-CEO Richard Thomson reduced international lending and began focusing on brokerage activities. The strategy paid off when several Latin American countries fell behind on their loans in the late 1980s.

As the North American economy slowed in the early 1990s TD Bank's nonperforming loans increased and with it its loan loss reserves. The bank still made acquisitions including Central Guaranty Trust (1993) and Lancaster Financial Holdings (1995 investment banking). It worked to build its financial services expanding its range of service offerings and geographic coverage and buying New York-based Waterhouse Investor Services (1996); 97% of Australia-based Pont Securities (1997); and California-based Kennedy Cabot & Co. (1997). In 1998 the bank sold its payroll services to Ceridian and its Waterhouse Securities unit bought US discount brokerage Jack White & Co.

That year the government nixed TD Bank's merger with Canadian Imperial on the same day it voided the Royal Bank of Canada/Bank of Montreal deal. The banks believed the consolidation was necessary to stave off foreign banks' encroachment into Canada but the government had domestic antitrust concerns: Though Canada has one-tenth the population of the US its five top banks all ranked in the top 15 in North America.

In 1999 TD Bank bought Trimark Financial's retail trust banking business and spun off part of Waterhouse Investor Services which would become part of TD Waterhouse Group. That year the bank ramped up its focus on Internet banking.

Not giving up on acquisition-fueled growth in 2000 the company bought CT Financial Services (now TD Canada Trust) from British American Tobacco. As a condition for government approval TD Bank had to sell its MasterCard credit portfolio (sold to Citibank Canada) and a dozen southern Ontario branches (to Bank of Montreal).

The company's plans to hitch a ride on the Wal-Mart gravy train derailed in 2001. Arrangements to open bank branches in some US-based Wal-Mart stores were squelched by regulators enforcing the banking and commerce barrier. TD Bank later closed all of its existing branches (more than 100 in all) inside Canadian Wal-Marts as part of a broader restructuring.

TD Bank suffered its first-ever annual loss during fiscal year 2002. Write-downs on loans to telecommunications technology and energy firms contributed mightily to the dismal results.

Frustrated by limited growth opportunities at home in 2005 TD Bank ventured south of the border with its purchase of a stake in Banknorth. TD Bank paid about $4.8 billion in cash and stock for its original 51% stake (it bought the rest in 2007). Additionally in 2006 the company assumed about a 40% ownership in TD AMERITRADE as part of the sale of TD Waterhouse.

In 2008 the company acquired New Jersey-based Commerce Bancorp. The $8.5 billion acquisition deal added some 450 branches along the eastern seaboard to TD Bank's US network and exemplified the company's plans to expand abroad. TD merged Commerce with its TD Banknorth unit to create TD Bank.

EXECUTIVES

Group Head Wealth Management Direct Channels and Corporate Shared Services, Mike Pedersen
Chairman, Brian M. Levitt, age 66
Group President and Chief Executive Officer, W. Edmund (Ed) Clark, age 66, $1,337,850 total compensation
Group Head Insurance Credit Cards and Enterprise Strategy, Riaz E. Ahmed
Deputy Chair, Frank J. McKenna, age 65
EVP; Head Regional Retail Banking and Direct Channels TD Bank, Brian J. Haier
Group Head Wholesale Banking; Chairman President and CEO TD Securities, Robert E. (Bob) Dorrance, age 57, $445,950 total compensation
EVP Senior Client Relationships and Shared Services Wealth Management, John G. See
Group Head Canadian Banking Auto Finance and Credit Cards; President and CEO TD Canada Trust, Timothy D. (Tim) Hockey, age 49, $490,250 total compensation
Chief Operating Officer, Bharat B. Masrani, age 56, $521,449 total compensation
EVP and Chief Risk Officer Risk Management, Mark R. Chauvin
Group Head Finance Sourcing and Corporate Communications and Chief Financial Officer, Colleen M. Johnston, $416,488 total compensation
Group Head Marketing Corporate and People Strategies TD Bank Group, Theresa L. (Teri) Currie
SVP Wealth Management, David P. (Dave) Pickett
EVP; Chief Operating Officer TD Securities, Paul M. Clark
Group Head Legal Compliance and Anti Money Laundering and General Counsel, Norie C. Campbell
SVP Wealth Management, Michael E. (Mike) Reilly
SVP Wealth Management, Kevin J. Whyte
SVP Wholesale Banking, Brian Smith
Vice President - Legal; Corporate Secretary, Kevin Thompson
Executive Vice President; Head - Retail Distribution and Products, Nandita Bakhshi
Group Head - Corporate Development; Enterprise Strategy and Treasury; Corporate Office, Raiz Ahmed
Group President and Chief Executive Officer, W. Edmund (Ed) Clark, age 66
Independent Director, Karen E. Maidment
Director, Nadir H. Mohamed, age 56
Director, Wilbur J. (Bill) Prezzano Jr., age 72
Director, Harold H. MacKay, age 72
Director, Irene R. Miller, age 60
Director, Carole S. Taylor, age 65
Deputy Chair, Frank J. McKenna, age 65
Director, John L. Bragg, age 72
Director, Colleen A. Goggins, age 58
Director, Wendy K. Dobson, age 70
Director, Henry H. Ketcham, age 63
Director, Pierre H. Lessard, age 69
Director, Helen K. Sinclair, age 61
Director, Hugh J. Bolton, age 74
Director, William E. Bennett, age 66
Director, John M. Thompson, age 69
Director, Amy W. Brinkley, age 57
Auditors: Ernst&YoungLLP

LOCATIONS

HQ: Toronto Dominion Bank
P.O. Box 1, Toronto Dominion Centre, Toronto, Ontario M5K 1A2
Phone: 416 307-6018 **Fax:** 416 308-1943
Web: www.td.com

PRODUCTS/OPERATIONS

2010 Sales

	% of total
Interest	
Deposits with	41
Loans	30
Securities	9
Noninterest	
Investments & securities	6
Service	4
Other	10
Total	**100**

Selected Canadian Subsidiaries

CT Financial Assurance Company (99.9%)
Meloche Monnex Inc.
Security National Insurance Company
Primmum Insurance Company
TD Direct Insurance Inc.
TD General Insurance Company
TD Home and Auto Insurance Company
TD Asset Finance Corp.
TD Asset Management Inc.
TD Waterhouse Private Investment Counsel Inc.
TD Investment Services Inc.
TD Life Insurance Company
TD Mortgage Corporation
The Canada Trust Company
TD Pacific Mortgage Corporation
TD Mortgage Investment Corporation
TD Nordique Investments Limited
TD Parellel Private Equity Investors Ltd.
TD Securities Inc.
TD Timberlane Investments Limited
TD McMurray Investments Limited
TD Redpath Investments Limited
TD Riverside Investments Limited
TD Vermillion Holdings ULC
TD Financial International Ltd. (Bermuda)
Canada Trustco International Limited (Barbados)
TD Reinsurance (Barbados) Inc.
Toronto Dominion International Inc. (Barbados)
TD Waterhouse Canada Inc.
thinkorswim Canada
Truscan Property Corporation

Selected US Subsidiaries

TDAM USA Inc.
Toronto Dominion Holdings (U.S.A.) Inc.
TD Holdings II Inc.
TD Securities (USA) LLC
Toronto Dominion (Texas) LLC
Toronto Dominion Capital (U.S.A.) Inc.
Toronto Dominion Investments Inc.

Selected Other International Subsidiaries

Internaxx Bank S.A. (Luxembourg)
NatWest Personal Financial Management Limited (50% UK)
NatWest Stockbrokers Limited
TD Ireland
TD Global Finance
TD Waterhouse Bank N.V. (The Netherlands)
TD Waterhouse Investor Services (UK) Limited
TD Waterhouse Investor Services (Europe) Limited (UK)
Toronto Dominion (South East Asia) Limited (Singapore)

COMPETITORS

BMO Financial Group
Bank of America
Berkshire Hills Bancorp
CI Financial
CIBC
Caisses centrale Desjardins
Charles Schwab
E*TRADE Financial
Edward Jones
FMR
KeyCorp
Laurentian Bank
Morgan Stanley
National Bank of Canada
RBC Financial Group
Scotiabank
Sovereign Bank

HISTORICAL FINANCIALS

Company Type: Public

Income Statement

FYE: October 31

	ASSETS ($ mil.)	NET INCOME ($ mil.)	INCOME AS % OF ASSETS	EMPLOYEES
10/13	824,651	6,092	0.7%	78,748
10/12	813,315	6,187	0.8%	78,397
10/11	738,424	5,783	0.8%	75,631
10/10	608,172	4,558	0.7%	68,725
10/09	513,755	2,876	0.6%	65,930
Annual Growth	12.6%	20.6%	—	4.5%

2013 Year-End Financials

Return on assets: 0.7%
Return on equity: 13.0%
Long-term debt ($ mil.): —
No. of shares (mil.): 1,835
Sales ($ mil): 32,575
Dividends
Yield: 7.0%
Payout: 98.0%
Market value ($ mil.): 168,306

	STOCK PRICE ($) FY Close	P/E High	P/E Low	PER SHARE ($) Earnings	Dividends	Book Value
10/13	91.72	24	20	3.30	3.17	26.29
10/12	81.34	26	18	3.39	2.89	26.01
10/11	75.28	29	20	3.23	2.63	23.69
10/10	72.20	29	21	2.50	2.40	23.63
10/09	57.24	33	11	1.60	2.25	20.78
Annual Growth	12.5%	—	—	19.9%	9.0%	6.1%

Toshiba Corp

Toshiba products play an active role be it in computing controlling powering or communicating —transporting playing or even just chillin'. The company's portfolio includes personal and professional computers (PCs point-of-sale systems) telecommunications and medical equipment (LCDs for mobile devices X-ray machines) industrial machinery (power plant reactors elevators) consumer appliances (air conditioners Blu-ray Disc recorders) electronic components (electron tubes batteries) and semiconductors. Its portfolio also includes air traffic control and railway transportation systems. Customers outside Japan account for 55% of Toshiba's revenues.

In 2009 the company announced its biggest ever annual loss. The global recession took its toll across all of Toshiba's primary product groups — digital products social infrastructure electronic devices and home appliances —with each experiencing a drop in revenues and only social infrastructure reporting positive operating income.

As the global recession eased in 2009 and 2010 Toshiba saw strengthening sales and better financial results in some segments such as digital products electronic devices and home appliances. Revenue rose 1% year-over-year in the fiscal year that ended in March 2011. The company also recorded net income in 2010 and 2011.

By segment sales of digital products (about 33% of sales) decreased by 3% in fiscal 2011. Social infrastructure (also 33%) was down 2%. Electronic devices (20%) rose 6%. Home appliances (9%) increased 3%.

By 2013 the company plans to increase sales of digital products by 10% electronic devices by 13% social infrastructure by 10% and home appliances by 4%. Geographically Toshiba wants to increase its proportion of international sales from 55% to more than 65% during the same time period. While increasing sales and improving profitability remain top strategic goals Toshiba also aspires to becoming a greener company reducing its CO2 emissions and promoting more environmentally friendly products and technologies.

Digital products includes personal computers visual products hard disk drives (HDDs) and multifunction peripherals. Social infrastructure consists of energy-related equipment medical equipment IT products and elevators. Under electronic devices are semiconductors and liquid crystal displays. The home appliance segment comprises refrigerators washing/drying machines light fixtures and air conditioners. Included in the other segment is logistics services.

In 2012 Toshiba made a move to increase the scope of its storage device portfolio specifically HDDs when it bought certain of Western Digital's 3.5 inch HDD assets. The deal gives Toshiba the ability to provide products covering all aspects of the HDD market and increase its capacity to supply nearline HDDs. Demand for nearline HDDs is growing along with continued expansion in the server market. As part of the sale Western Digital acquired Toshiba Storage Device (Thailand) a disk drive manufacturer that has not resumed operations since the Thailand flooding in 2011. The sale of the HDD assets were required for Western Digital to get regulatory approval for its purchase of Hitachi Global Storage Technologies.

In 2010 the company combined its wireless handset business with that of archrival Fujitsu to create Fujitsu Toshiba Mobile Communications Limited the largest cell phone maker in Japan. The companies hope to better compete with market leader Nokia and a number of key players from Asia and North America; Fujitsu owns an 80% stake in the new company while Toshiba owns around 20%. Fujitsu is now looking to acquire Toshiba's interest in the JV in an effort to boost its smartphone operations.

In 2011 the company announced a deal that would both increase its overseas sales and provide entry into the smart grid market. Toshiba bought Swiss smart meter hardware and communications module maker Landis+Gyr for $2.3 billion including debt. Founded in 1896 Landis+Gyr boasted more than 8000 utility customers worldwide and operations in more than 30 countries; it was selected to supply 10000 smart meters to the State Grid Corporation of China as that country constructs the world's largest smart grid. Toshiba is eager to enter the burgeoning smart grid market especially as concerns about the safety of nuclear power overshadow growth plans for its nuclear power division.

Toshiba which holds a 67% stake in Westinghouse Electric shares ownership with The Shaw Group (20%) and IHI (3%). The remaining 10% is held by Kazatomprom a state-owned uranium supplier based in Kazakhstan which acquired the stake from Toshiba for $540 million in 2007. In 2011 Toshiba announced that it would acquire Shaw's stake.

In 2011 Toshiba Medical Systems bought longtime partner Vital Images a developer of visualization and analysis software used in computed tomography (CT) scanners and magnetic resonance imaging (MRI) equipment. Toshiba Medical Systems paid about $273 million in cash for the company in an effort to further expand its global imaging business.

Toshiba has used partnerships (often with competitors) to fuel product development and reduce costs. The company has worked with rivals such as Fujitsu and NEC on semiconductor development. It has a strategic relationship with SanDisk for the production of NAND flash memories.

Toshiba bought out Panasonic's stake in another joint venture Toshiba Matsushita Display Technology in 2009. Toshiba took full ownership of the unit so it can more quickly implement restructuring measures. Renamed Toshiba Mobile Display the company is a leading provider of LCDs used in mobile phones in-vehicle displays and portable computers.

In 2012 Toshiba became part of a joint venture named Japan Display Inc. (JDI) that combined its small- and medium-sized LCD panel business with those of Hitachi and Sony along with investment by a Japanese government-backed fund. The government owns 70% of JDI while the three companies each hold 10%. Also that year subsidiary Toshiba TEC which offers point-of-sale systems for retailers bought IBM's retail store solutions business for about $850 million. The initial stage of the deal will be a joint venture Toshiba Global Commerce Solutions Holdings Corporation with IBM owning just shy of 20% and Toshiba TEC owning the rest and then buying out IBM three years later. The joint venture began operations in the US Canada Mexico and Australia. Late in 2011 Toshiba and OJSC Power Machines announced a joint venture for electrical power transformer manufacturing slated for a 2013 start. The plant is to be built in St. Petersburg with Toshiba holding a nearly 50/50 ownership with OJSC Power Machines.

HISTORY

Two Japanese electrical equipment manufacturers came together in 1939 to create Toshiba. Tanaka Seizo-sha Japan's first telegraph equipment manufacturer was founded in 1875 by Hisashige Tanaka the so-called Edison of Japan. In the 1890s the company started making heavier electrical equipment such as transformers and electric motors adopting the name Shibaura Seisakusho Works in 1893. Seisakusho went on to pioneer the production of hydroelectric generators (1894) and X-ray tubes (1915) in Japan.

The other half of Toshiba Hakunetsusha & Company was founded by Ichisuke Fujioka and Shoichi Miyoshi as Japan's first incandescent lamp maker (1890). Renamed Tokyo Electric Company (1899) the company developed the coiled filament lightbulb (1921) Japan's first radio receiver and cathode-ray tube (1924) and the internally frosted glass lightbulb (1925). In 1939 it merged with Shibaura Seisakusho to form Tokyo Shibaura Electric Company (Toshiba).

Toshiba was the first company in Japan to make fluorescent lamps (1940) radar systems (1942) broadcasting equipment (1952) and digital computers (1954). Production of black-and-white televisions began in 1949. Even so through the 1970s the company was considered an also-ran trailing other Japanese business groups known as keiretsu partly because of its bureaucratic management style.

Electrical engineer Shoichi Saba became president in 1980. Saba invested heavily in Toshiba's information and communications segments. The company became the first in the world to produce the powerful one-megabit DRAM chip (1985). That year it unveiled its first laptop PC. In the meantime Saba (named chairman 1986) pushed Toshiba into joint ventures to exchange technology with companies such as Siemens and Motorola.

But in 1987 Toshiba incurred the wrath of the US government. A subsidiary sold submarine sound-deadening equipment to the USSR resulting in threats of US sanctions and a precipitous decline in its stock price and in US sales. Chairman Saba and president Sugichiro Watari resigned in shame.

Toshiba in 1992 bought a $500 million stake in Time Warner (the stake was reduced in 1998). In 1996 the company appointed marketing and multimedia specialist Taizo Nishimuro as president breaking its tradition of filling the position with an engineer from its heavy electrical operations.

In 1997 Toshiba and IBM formed joint venture Dominion Semiconductor to develop memory chips. (IBM sold its stake to Toshiba in 1999.) The next year the company looked to boost earnings by cutting its workforce and allying with other manufacturers such as Fujitsu and General Electric in development deals. But continued semiconductor price declines and sluggish demand in Japan caused the company to record its first annual loss in more than two decades.

Nishimuro made plans to cut 5000 jobs and streamlined Toshiba's 15 divisions to eight in-house companies. Toshiba in 1999 agreed to take a $1 billion charge to settle a class-action lawsuit alleging some manufacturers supplied potentially corrupt disk drives in its portable computers –even though no Toshiba customer complaints were filed.

In 2000 Nishimuro stepped down as CEO. SVP and Information and Industrial Systems and Services subsidiary president Tadashi Okamura assumed the post. Nishimuro filled the vacant chairman's seat. Toshiba announced another restructuring effort in 2001 which included plans to reduce its workforce shift manufacturing to overseas plants and withdraw from unprofitable businesses. The following year it sold its DRAM manufacturing plant Dominion Semiconductor to Micron Technology.

In 2004 Toshiba partnered with Canon to develop surface conduction electron emitter display (SED) panels an alternative technology to LCD televisions. In 2005 Atsutoshi Nishida an executive that led the company's PC operations succeeded Okamura as CEO.

In 2006 Toshiba acquired nuclear power plant equipment and service provider Westinghouse Electric for $5.4 billion. Canon purchased Toshiba's stake in the SED joint venture in 2007.

The company acknowledged a setback for its consumer electronics business in 2008 when it announced the discontinuation of HD-DVD development. Toshiba was the primary backer of the HD-DVD format for high-definition DVD players and recorders –a market where it battled with Sony the primary backer of the competing Blu-ray format for support among manufacturers media companies and consumers.

In 2009 Norio Sasaki became CEO of Toshiba; Nishida was named chairman.

Toshiba acquired the hard-disk drive business of Fujitsu in 2009. In addition to augmenting Toshiba's consumer product-oriented disk drive line the purchase moved the company into the enterprise disk drive business. Toshiba formed three new subsidiaries with the purchase including Toshiba Storage Device Corp. The company also bought the Advanced Visual Imaging Systems division of imaging and graphics systems maker Barco that year. The purchase augmented its Toshiba Medical Systems unit which develops diagnostic medical imaging systems.

EXECUTIVES

Chairman, Atsutoshi Nishida, age 70
EVP, Hiroshi Saito
SEVP and Director, Fumio Muraoka, age 65
EVP, Shozo Saito
Vice Chairman, Norio Sasaki, age 64
President and CEO, Hisao Tanaka, age 63
SEVP, Hidejiro Shimomitsu, age 61

EVP, Toshiharu Watanabe
SEVP, Hideo Kitamura, age 61
VP, Shoji Yoshioka
EVP, Masahiko (Masa) Fukakushi, age 59
SEVP, Akira Sudo, age 62
SEVP, Makoto Kubo, age 62
EVP, Yasuharu Igarashi
EVP, Kiyoshi Kobayashi
VP, Masakazu Kakumu
VP, Hiroshi Igashira
VP, Munehiko Tsuchiya
VP, Takaaki Tanaka
VP, Hironobu Nishikori
VP, Yasuhiro Shimura
EVP, Toshio Masaki
General Manager Human Resources And Administration Division and Director, Hiroshi Horioka, age 60
Managing Executive Officer, Fumiaki Fumiaki Ushio Ushio
Managing Executive Officer; Director of Nuclear Power Business in Electric System Company, Kiyoshi Kiyoshi Okamura Okamura
Managing Executive Officer; Vice President of Semiconductor & Storage Company, Makoto Makoto Hideshima Hideshima
Managing Executive Officer; Senior Executive Officer; Chairman of Subsidiary, Masaaki Masaaki Ohsumi Ohsumi
Managing Executive Officer; Senior Executive Officer; President of Subsidiary, Masayasu Masayasu Toyohara Toyohara
Managing Executive Officer; President of Kansai Office, Naoki Naoki Takenaka Takenaka
Managing Executive Officer; Senior Executive Officer; Manager of Electric Power & Social System Technology Development Center, Osamu Osamu Maekawa Maekawa
Senior Managing Executive Officer; Vice President of Electric System Company; President of Subsidiary, Shigenori Shigenori Shiga Shiga
Managing Executive Officer; Senior Executive Officer; Vice President of Digital Products & Service Company, Shigenori Shigenori Tokumitsu Tokumitsu
Managing Executive Officer; Senior Director of Cloud & Solution Business, Shigeyoshi Shigeyoshi Shimotsuji Shimotsuji
Managing Executive Officer; Vice President of Social Infrastructure System Company, Takemi Takemi Adachi Adachi
Managing Executive Officer; Director of Electric Power Distribution System Business in Social Infrastructure System Company, Takeshi Takeshi Yokota Yokota
Managing Executive Officer; Chairman of the Board in Subsidiary, Teruo Teruo Kiriyama Kiriyama
Managing Executive Officer; Director of Memory Business in Semiconductor Company, Yasuo Yasuo Naruke Naruke
Managing Executive Officer; Director of Thermal Power and Water Power Business in Electricity System Company, Yoshihiro Yoshihiro Aburatani Aburatani
Director, Kiichiro Furusawa, age 73
Director, Shigeo Koguchi, age 67
SEVP and Director, Yoshihiro Maeda, age 64
SEVP and Director, Fumio Muraoka, age 65
SEVP and Director, Ichiro Tai, age 64
SEVP and Director, Masao Namiki, age 63
EVP and Director, Kazuo Tanigawa, age 63
SEVP and Director, Masashi Muromachi, age 62
Vice Chairman, Norio Sasaki, age 64
Director, Hiroshi Hirabayashi, age 72
Director, Takeshi Sasaki, age 70
General Manager Human Resources And Administration Division and Director, Hiroshi Horioka, age 60
Director, Takeo Kosugi, age 71
Independent Director, Hiroyuki Itami
Independent Director, Ken Shimanouchi
Auditors: Ernst&Young

LOCATIONS

HQ: Toshiba Corp
1-1-1 Shibaura, Minato-ku, Tokyo 105-8001
Phone: (81) 3 3457 4511 **Fax:** (81) 3 3456 1631
Web: www.toshiba.co.jp

2011 Sales

	% of total
Asia	
Japan	45
Other	20
North	18
Europe	13
Other	4
Total	**100**

PRODUCTS/OPERATIONS

2011 Sales

	% of total
Digital	33
Social	33
Electronic	20
Home	9
Other	5
Total	**100**

Selected Products

Digital products
- Digital Media Network Company
  - Digital cameras
  - Digital tuners
  - DVD players and recorders
  - Hard disk drives
  - Industrial and surveillance cameras
  - Optical disk drives
  - Projectors
  - Televisions
- Mobile Communications Company
  - Mobile phones
- Personal Computer & Network Company
  - Handheld computers
  - Notebook computers
  - Servers

Social infrastructure
- Industrial and Power Systems & Services Company
  - Boiling water reactor plants
  - Building energy management systems
  - Control and measurement system devices
  - Industrial computers
  - Nuclear fuel reprocessing plants
  - Power generating equipment (hydroelectric thermal geothermal)
  - Railway station service systems
  - Superconducting magnets
  - Transportation management systems
  - Water supply and sewage monitoring systems
- Social Network & Infrastructure Systems Company
  - Air traffic control and navigation aid systems
  - Automatic letter processing systems
  - Banknote processing machines
  - Broadcasting systems
  - Face recognition security systems

Electronic devices
- Semiconductor Company
  - LSI systems
  - Memory
  - Microprocessors

Home appliances
- Air conditioners
- Batteries
- Lighting
- Microwaves
- Refrigerators
- Washing machines

COMPETITORS

ABB
ALSTOM
AREVA
Mitsubishi Electric
NEC
NTT DATA
Acer
Alcatel-Lucent
Apple Inc.
CASIO COMPUTER
Canon
Dell
Electrolux
Emerson Electric
Ericsson
FUJIFILM
Fujitsu
GE
Hewlett-Packard
Hitachi
IBM
Ingersoll-Rand
Intel
KONE
Kyocera
Lenovo
Nokia
Oki Electric
Panasonic Corp
Philips Electronics
Pioneer Corporation
Ricoh Company
STMicroelectronics
Samsung Electronics
Schindler Holding
Seagate Technology
Seiko
Sharp Corp.
Siemens AG
Sony
Sony Mobile
Spansion
Texas Instruments
Unisys
Western Digital
Xerox

HISTORICAL FINANCIALS

Company Type: Public

Income Statement

FYE: March 31

	REVENUE ($ mil.)	NET INCOME ($ mil.)	NET PROFIT MARGIN	EMPLOYEES
03/13	63,079	824	1.3%	206,087
03/12	75,639	898	1.2%	209,784
03/11	78,417	1,664	2.1%	202,638
03/10	68,349	(211)	—	203,889
03/09	67,575	(3,488)	—	199,456
Annual Growth	(1.7%)	—	—	0.8%

2013 Year-End Financials

Debt ratio: 0.2%
Return on equity: 8.1%
Cash ($ mil.): 2,223
Current ratio: 1.15
Long-term debt ($ mil.): 11,036
No. of shares (mil.): —
Dividends
Yield: 0.0%
Payout: 0.0%
Market value ($ mil.): —

	STOCK PRICE ($) FY Close	P/E High/Low		PER SHARE ($) Earnings	Dividends	Book Value
03/13	30.40	0	0	0.19	0.00	2.60
03/12	26.57	0	0	0.21	0.00	2.50
03/11	29.60	0	0	0.38	0.02	2.48
03/10	30.80	—	—	(0.05)	0.00	2.02
Annual Growth	(0.4%)	—	—	—	—	6.5%

Total S.A.

TOTAL does it all. With operations in more than 130 countries TOTAL engages in all aspects of the petroleum industry including Upstream operations (oil and gas exploration development and production LNG) and Downstream operations (refining marketing and the trading and shipping of crude oil and petroleum products). TOTAL also produces base chemicals (petrochemicals and fertilizers) and specialty chemicals for the industrial and consumer markets (rubber processing adhesives resins and electroplating). In addition TOTAL has interests in the coal mining and power generation sectors.

Geographic Reach

TOTAL has operations in 130 countries. European countries excluding France generate the most revenues for TOTAL –44% in 2011.

Operations

The company's business is divided into three main segments: Upstream Downstream and Chemicals. Reshaping its organization to create greater efficiencies in 2012 TOTAL reorganized its Downstream operations into two divisions: Refining and Chemicals and Supply and Marketing (of petroleum products).

Upstream TOTAL explores for and produces oil and gas in 40 countries and has reserves of 11.4 billion barrels of oil equivalent. It is a major player in the global natural gas market with more than 60 years of experience in the field. Its expertise covers natural gas as well as liquid natural gas (LNG) and liquefied petroleum gas (LPG).

Downstream it has a refining capacity of 2.3 million barrels a day and some 16425 gas stations primarily under the TOTAL and Elf brands mostly in Europe and Africa.

TOTAL is also one of the world's largest integrated chemical producers and a leader in each of its markets —Petrochemicals and Fertilizers and Specialties.

Financial Analysis

Revenues increased by 19% thanks mainly to the 23% increase in upstream segment revenues due to higher oil prices an increase in liquids and natural gas price realization a 19% price-related jump in downstream segment revenues and a 12% increase in chemical segment revenues as a result of stronger global demand.

TOTAL's net income grew by 16.4% mainly due to the impact of the increase in oil and petroleum product prices and an after-tax inventory valuation effect and gains on asset sales.

The company saw an upward trend in revenue from 2007 to 2008 but slumped in 2009 during the global recession (which weakened demand) and regained momentum in 2010 and 2011 thanks to higher oil prices.

Strategy

Over the long term the company is committed to building its leading position in all three segments of its business through acquisitions divestitures and investments. It is investing heavily in refinery expansion in Jubail Saudi Arabia and in Port Arthur Texas. Other long-term growth initiatives include teaming up with Gazprom and Statoil to develop the vast Shtokman gas field in the Barents Sea.

TOTAL is also expanding its energy offerings and developing complementary next generation energy activities (solar biomass nuclear). It made a big move into renewable energy in 2011 buying 60% of solar company SunPower for $1.4 billion.

To raise $1 billion to pay down debt the company sold some mature assets in 2011 and 2012 including TEPMA BV (to Sinochem) a 5% stake in the Ocensa pipeline to Petrominerales and another 5% to Cepsa.

Furthering its investment in Canada's oil sands in late 2010 the company formed a strategic alliance with Suncor Energy in which it paid Suncor about $1.7 billion to acquire 19% of Suncor's holdings in the Fort Hills mining project and a 49% stake in the Voyageur Upgrader project near Fort McMurray. Suncor bought about 37 % of total's interest in the Joslyn project.

HISTORY

A French consortium formed the Compagnie Francaise des Petroles (CFP) in 1924 to develop an oil industry for the country. Lacking reserves within its borders France had a 24% stake in the Turkish Petroleum Company (TPC) acquired from Germany in 1920 as part of the spoils from WWI. When oil was discovered in Iraq in 1927 the TPC partners (CFP; Anglo-Persian Oil later BP; Royal Dutch Shell; and a consortium of five US oil companies) became major players in the oil game.

In 1929 France acquired a 25% stake in CFP (raised to 35% in 1931) but ensured the company's independence from government control. CFP began establishing refining and transporting capabilities and by the start of WWII it was a vertically integrated petroleum company.

With France's occupation by Germany during WWII CFP was effectively blocked from further expansion and its stake in Iraq Petroleum (formerly the TPC) was held by its partners until the end of the war. In 1948 over French protests the US partners ended the "Red Line" agreement a pact that limited members' competition in that Middle Eastern region.

After WWII CFP diversified its sources for crude opening a supply in 1947 from the Venezuelan company Pantepec and making several major discoveries in colonial Algeria in 1956. It also began supplying crude to Japan South Korea and Taiwan in the 1950s. To market its products in North Africa and France and other European areas it introduced the brand name TOTAL in 1954. It began making petrochemicals in 1956.

Algeria in 1971 became North Africa's first major oil-producing country to nationalize its petroleum industry. This was not as dire a blow to CFP as it could have been; by that time the company got only about 20% of its supplies from Algeria. Exploration had paid off with discoveries in Indonesia in the 1960s and the North Sea in the early 1970s.

CFP joined Elf Aquitaine in 1980 to buy Rhone-Poulenc's petrochemical segment. Ten years later it purchased state-owned Orkem's coating business (inks resins paints and adhesives).

In 1985 the company had adopted its brand name as part of its new name TOTAL Compagnie Francaise des Petroles shortened in 1991 to TOTAL. The firm was listed on the NYSE that year. The French government began reducing its stake in TOTAL in 1992 (ultimately to less than 1%). The company expanded reserves with stakes in fields in Argentina the Caspian Sea and Colombia.

In 1995 the year Thierry Desmarest became CEO TOTAL contracted to develop two large oil and gas fields in Iran despite US pressure not to do business there. The next year TOTAL led a consortium (including Russia's Gazprom and Malaysia's Petronas) in a $2 billion investment in Iran's gas sector just days after selling its 55% stake in its North American arm Total Petroleum to Ultramar Diamond Shamrock — insulating TOTAL from the threat of US sanctions.

TOTAL bought Belgium's Petrofina an integrated oil and gas company for $11 billion in 1999 and became TOTAL FINA. Within days the new TOTAL FINA launched a $43 billion hostile bid for rival Elf Aquitaine. Elf made a counterbid but TOTAL FINA wound up acquiring 95% of Elf in 2000 for $48.7 billion and became TOTAL FINA ELF. The new company gained control of the remainder of Elf later that year.

In 2001 the company in collaboration with Pertamina and Unocal Indonesia agreed to invest $500 million to boost its production of liquefied gas in Indonesia by 14%. That year the company also acquired generating assets in Argentina from AES for $370 million. Also that year an explosion in a TOTAL FINA ELF subsidiary's petrochemical and fertilizer plant in southern France killed 29 people and injured 2500. In 2003 a number of former Elf executives and state officials were named in a corruption scandal that implicated the former French oil giant in influence peddling and bribery in the early 1990s.

TOTAL FINA ELF was renamed TOTAL S.A. in 2003.

In 2006 the company spun off its Arkema unit which produces chlorochemicals intermediates and performance polymers.

With an eye to restructuring as a pure integrated oil business in 2007 TOTAL began to sell its then-18% stake in pharmaceutical manufacturer Sanofi. By mid-2009 the stake had fallen below 10%.

Oil sands has been a major source of growth. In 2008 it paid $470 million to buy Canada's Synenco Energy whose principal asset is a 60% stake in the Northern Lights oil sands project in the Athabasca region. Sinopec owns the remaining stake in the project. Again looking to expand its Canadian oil sands assets in 2009 TOTAL made a $617 million bid to acquire UTS Energy. That bid failed but TOTAL came back in 2010 with a $1.4 billion offer that led to an acquisition agreement for UTS. Following the acquisition it absorbed UTS's 20% stake in the Fort Hills oil sands project into its Canadian exploration and production unit and spun off the rump of UTS as a new oil sands explorer SilverBirch Energy.

To improve its cash flow in 2010 TOTAL merged its Italian retail operations with ERG's to create TotalERG the #3 gas station network in Italy with 3300 outlets and it sold two noncore oil fields in the Norwegian sector to BP for $991 million

In the US in early 2010 in a further expansion TOTAL also acquired 25% of Chesapeake Energy's Barnett Shale properties forming a $2.25 billion joint venture with that company.

The company made a couple of notable divestitures in 2011. To reduce its financial exposure in the refining sector the company agreed to sell its 49% stake in Spain's CEPSA to joint venture partner Abu Dhabi-based IPC. In a move to refocus its Chemicals segment TOTAL divested its coatings resins and photocure resins businesses to Arkema in a deal valued at $730 million.

EXECUTIVES

Chairman and CEO, Christophe de Margerie, age 62, $1,310,000 total compensation
Chief Administrative Officer, Jean-Jacques Guilbaud, age 60
President Chemicals, Francois Cornelis, age 64
President Exploration and Production, Yves-Louis Darricarrere, age 62
SVP Overseas Downstream, Alain Champeaux
SVP Marketing France Refining and Marketing, Andre Tricoire
SVP Marketing Europe Refining and Marketing, Eric de Menten
SVP Industrial Safety, Jean-Marc Jaubert
Chief Purchasing Officer, Sonia Sikorav
President Marketing and Services and New Energies, Philippe Boisseau, age 50
CFO, Patrick de La Chevardiere, age 56
President Refining and Chemicals, Patrick Pouyanne
SVP Scientific Development, Jean-Francois Minster
General Counsel, Peter Herbel
SVP Exploration and Production Africa, Jacques Marraud des Grottes, age 60
General Secretary Total Refining and Marketing, Bertrand Deroubaix, age 57
VP Strategy and Planning, Jean-Jacques Mosconi
EVP Sustainable Development and Environment, Manoelle Lepoutre
SVP Geosciences Exploration and Production, Marc Blaizot, age 59
VP Corporate Communications, Yves-Marie Dalibard
General Secretary Chemicals, Francoise Leroy
CEO and Director, Christophe de Margerie, age 62
Director, Serge Tchuruk, age 75
Director, Anne Lauvergeon, age 54
Director, Paul Desmarais Jr., age 58
Director, Michel Pebereau, age 70
Director, Daniel Bouton, age 62
Director, Bertrand P. Collomb, age 70
Director, Claude Mandil, age 72
Director, Bertrand Jacquillat, age 67

Director, Pierre Vaillaud, age 76
Director, Patricia Barbizet, age 58
Director, Antoine Jeancourt-Galignani, age 75
Director, Thierry de Rudder, age 64
Director, Lord Peter Levene, age 70
Director Training and Skills Management Specialties Sector and Director, Daniel Boeuf, age 63
Director, Maj. Patrick Artus, age 54
Auditors: KPMGAudit

LOCATIONS

HQ: Total S.A.
2, place Jean Millier, La Defense 6, Courbevoie 92400
Phone: (33) 1 47 44 45 46 **Fax:** (33) 1 47 44 49 44
Web: www.total.com

2011 Sales

	% of total
Europe	
France	23
Other	44
Africa	9
North	8
Other	16
Total	**100**

PRODUCTS/OPERATIONS

2011 Sales

Downstream	65
Chemicals	10

COMPETITORS

Akzo Nobel
Ashland Inc.
BASF SE
BHP Billiton
BP
Chevron
ConocoPhillips
DuPont
Eni
Exxon Mobil
Imperial Oil
MOL
Norsk Hydro ASA
Occidental Petroleum
PEMEX
PETROBRAS
Pakistan State Oil
Petroleos de Venezuela
Royal Dutch Shell
Statoil
ZaZa Energy

HISTORICAL FINANCIALS

Company Type: Public

Income Statement FYE: December 31

	REVENUE ($ mil.)	NET INCOME ($ mil.)	NET PROFIT MARGIN	EMPLOYEES
12/12	240,279	14,095	5.9%	97,126
12/11	215,424	15,878	7.4%	96,104
12/10	188,009	14,147	7.5%	92,855
12/09	161,564	12,168	7.5%	96,387
12/08	224,157	14,805	6.6%	96,959
Annual Growth	1.8%	(1.2%)	—	0.0%

2012 Year-End Financials

Debt ratio: 25.5%
Return on equity: 15.1%
Cash ($ mil.): 20,388
Current ratio: 1.38
Long-term debt ($ mil.): 29,358
No. of shares (mil.): —
Dividends
Yield: 5.4%
Payout: 47.2%
Market value ($ mil.): —

	STOCK PRICE ($) FY Close	P/E High/Low		PER SHARE ($) Earnings	Dividends	Book Value
12/12	52.01	21	14	6.22	2.86	42.57
12/11	51.11	23	13	7.04	0.00	39.04
12/10	53.48	28	15	6.30	2.93	36.14
12/09	64.04	37	21	5.45	3.28	33.90
12/08	55.30	42	16	6.59	3.10	30.73
Annual Growth	(1.5%)	—	—	(1.4%)	(2.1%)	8.5%

Toyota Motor Corp

Toyota Motor among the world's largest automotive manufacturers by auto sales (running a tight race with GM) designs and manufactures a diverse product line-up that ranges from subcompacts to luxury and sports vehicles to SUVs trucks minivans and buses. Its vehicles are produced either with combustion or hybrid engines as with the Prius. Toyota's subsidiaries also manufacture vehicles: Daihatsu Motor produces mini-vehicles while Hino Motors produces trucks and buses. Additionally Toyota makes automotive parts for its own use and for sale to others. Popular models include the Camry Corolla Land Cruiser and luxury Lexus line as well as the Tundra truck.

Major Toyota subsidiaries include Toyota Auto Body Co. Ltd. Toyota Motor Sales U.S.A. Toyota Motor North America Toyota Motor Engineering & Manufacturing North America Toyota Financial Services Corporation and Toyota Motor Credit Corporation.

Toyota divides its operations into the three segments of automotive (91 % of total sales) financial services (6%) and other (3%). Automotive is obviously Toyota's bread and butter; the segment makes passenger and commercial vehicles minivans trucks and related parts. Its less known financial services segment provides financing to dealers and their customers for the lease or purchase of Toyota vehicles.

Toyota maintains a vast geographical reach selling to 170 countries and regions through more than 500 consolidated subsidiaries and some 210 affiliated companies. Almost 60% of its sales come from Asia (Japan counts for 48%) while North America generates around 20 % of total sales. Countries in Europe Africa the Middle East Oceania and Latin America account for the remainder.

Toyota has been focused on regaining its financial footing after suffering through several economic disasters. From 2010 to 2011 its overall net revenue decreased by 2% due to the March 2011 Great East Japan Earthquake flood in Thailand and a shortage of parts supplies stemming from those disasters. Its geographical segments were also stung by volatile exchange rates. However despite these challenges the total number of overall vehicles sold in 2012 for Toyota was roughly 7.3 million vehicles up 0.6% compared to 2011.

Like its competitors Toyota is beefing up its Chinese operations by joining forces with local automotive players. With its partner China FAW Group Corporation Toyota builds nine models including Land Cruisers and Corollas in the country. The third factory operated by the JV began producing Corollas in May 2012.

Along with China India is generating a lot of interest in the automotive industry. Toyota in late 2010 opened a manufacturing plant near Bangalore through its Toyota Kirloskar Motor (TKM) joint venture with partner Kirloskar Group. The move established Toyota's presence in India's heartland by launching its compact Etios to the Indian market.

While Toyota shared the pain of its global competitors during the Great Recession it was spared the government-supervised bankruptcy reorganizations that Chrysler and GM endured. During the hard times Toyota focused on consolidating its North American operations shifting its resources and closing underperforming operations. In early 2010 it sold off Toyota Financial Services Securities Corp. (the brokerage unit of its financial arm Toyota Financial Services Corp.) to Tokai Tokyo Financial Holdings.

Toyota was met with massive recalls beginning in 2010 in regard to defective gas pedals faulty floor mats and problems with braking software. It recalled more than 8 million vehicles worldwide and halted production of the subject models including the top-selling Camry at US and Canadian plants. The recalls were the largest for Toyota in the US and the suspension of sales and production resulting from vehicle defects topped the industry's charts.

HISTORY

In 1926 Sakichi Toyoda founded Toyoda Automatic Loom Works. In 1930 he sold the rights to the loom he invented and gave the proceeds to his son Kiichiro Toyoda to begin an automotive business. Kiichiro opened an auto shop within the loom works in 1933. When protectionist legislation (1936) improved prospects for Japanese automakers Kiichiro split off the car department took it public (1937) and changed its name to Toyota.

During WWII the company made military trucks but financial problems after the war caused Toyota to reorganize in 1950. Its postwar commitment to R&D paid off with the launch of the four-wheel-drive Land Cruiser (1951); full-sized Crown (1955); and the small Corona (1957).

Toyota Motor Sales U.S.A. debuted the Toyopet Crown in the US in 1957 but it proved underpowered for the US market. Toyota had better luck with the Corona in 1965 and with the Corolla (which became the best-selling car of all time) in 1968. By 1970 Toyota was the world's fourth largest carmaker.

Toyota expanded rapidly in the US. During the 1970s the oil crisis caused demand for fuel-efficient cars and Toyota was there to grab market share from US makers. In 1975 Toyota displaced Volkswagen as the US's #1 auto importer. Toyota began auto production in the US in 1984 through NUMMI its joint venture with General Motors. The Lexus line was launched in the US in 1989.

Because of European restrictions on Japanese auto imports until 2000 Toyota's European expansion slowed. Toyota responded in 1992 by agreeing to distribute cars in Japan for Volkswagen and also by establishing an engine plant (later moved to full auto production) in the UK.

The SUV mania of the 1990s spurred Toyota's introduction of luxury minivans and light trucks. Hiroshi Okuda a 40-year veteran with Toyota and the first person from outside the Toyoda family to run the firm succeeded Tatsuro Toyoda as president in 1995. The next year Toyota consolidated its North American production units into Cincinnati-based Toyota Motor Manufacturing North America.

In 1997 Toyota introduced the Prius a hybrid electric- and gas-powered car. The next year Toyota boosted its stake in affiliate Daihatsu Motor (mini-vehicles) to about 51% and started Toyota Mapmaster (51% owned) to make map databases for car navigation systems. Okuda became chairman in 1999 replacing Shoichiro Toyoda and Fujio Cho became president (later chairman). Also that year Toyota agreed to form a joint venture with Isuzu Motors to manufacture buses.

In 2000 Toyota launched the WiLL Vi a sedan aimed at young people. It announced that it was building an online replacement parts marketplace with i2 Technologies and formed a financial services company (Toyota Financial Service) and a brokerage firm (Toyota Financial Services Securities Corp.). Toyota also bought a 5% stake in Yamaha Motor (the world's #2 motorcycle maker) and raised its stake in truck maker Hino Motors from about 20% to around 34%.

International developments included Toyota's agreement with the Chinese government to produce passenger cars for sale in China built by Tianjin Toyota Motor Corp. a joint venture between Chinese carmaker Tianjin Automobile Xiali and Toyota. In 2001 Toyota opened a plant in France. Later that year Toyota also increased its stake in Hino Motors to 50%. With partners Toyoda Gosei and Horie Metal Co. Ltd. Toyota formed a joint venture in 2002 to manufacture resin fuel tank systems. In 2004 Toyota forged a joint venture agreement with Guangzhou Automobile Group to build engines in China. The following year Toyota established 14 Lexus dealerships in China. The company began joint car production in Europe with Peugeot S.A. in 2005. Also in 2005 Toyota bought just under 9% of Fuji Heavy Industries –the Japanese maker of Subaru passenger vehicles. The two companies began production of Toyota Camrys at Fuji Heavy Industries' underutilized Subaru of Indiana plant in 2007.

After suffering through the Great Recession from 2008 to 2010 Toyota faced another unforeseen crisis. In March 2011 its business suffered unexpectedly from the Great East Japan Earthquake which triggered a deadly tsunami and subsequent nuclear crisis that forced Tokyo Electric Power (Tepco) to shut down reactors at two nuclear power plants and five other conventional power plants. The events forced manufacturers to reduce their output or move production to other regions. Toyota along with its rivals (Nissan Honda and Mazda) were forced to close their factories days after the devastation.

EXECUTIVES

Chairman, Fujio Cho, age 76
Vice Chairman, Katsuaki Watanabe, age 71
Vice Chairman, Kazuo Okamoto, age 69
Chairman, Takeshi Uchiyamada, age 67
Corporate Auditor, Masaki Nakatsugawa
VP Toyota Product Communications Toyota Motor Sales U.S.A., James H. (Jim) Colon
President and COO Toyota Motor North America; Chairman and CEO Toyota Motors Sales U.S.A., Yoshimi Inaba, age 67
President and Board Member, Akio Toyoda, age 57
EVP and Representative Director, Atsushi (Art) Niimi, age 65
EVP and Representative Director, Yukitoshi (Yuki) Funo, age 66
EVP and Representative Director, Shinichi Sasaki, age 66
Senior Managing Officer, Masanao Tomozoe
Managing Officer, Katsutada Masumoto
Managing Officer, James E. (Jim) Lentz III, age 57
Managing Officer; EVP Toyota Motor Engineering & Manufacturing North America; President Toyota Technical Center, Shigeki Terashi
Senior Managing Executive Officer, Takahiro Iwase, age 61
Senior Managing Officer, Yoshimasa Ishii, age 60
Senior Managing Officer, Takeshi Shirane
Chief Officer of the China Operations Group, Akira Sasaki, age 65
EVP and Board Member, Masamoto Maekawa
Senior Managing Executive Officer; Chief Director of Public Relations; Director, Mamoru Furuhashi, age 63
EVP and Representative Director, Satoshi Ozawa, age 64
EVP and Board Member, Seiichi Sudo
Senior Managing Officer, Tadashi Yamashina, age 62
EVP and Board Member, Yasumori Ihara, age 62
EVP and Board Member, Mitsuhisa Kato
President and COO Toyota Motor Engineering & Manufacturing North America, Tetsuo Agata, age 60
Managing Officer; EVP Toyota Motor Engineering & Manufacturing North America; Chief Quality Officer North American Quality Task Force; Chairman Toyota Motor Manufacturing Kentucky; Chairman Toyota Motor Manufactuing Mississippi, Steve St. Angelo, age 57
Managing Officer, Hiroyoshi Yoshiki
Managing Officer, Koichi Sugihara
Managing Officer, Osamu Nagata
Managing Officer, Shigeru Hayakawa
Senior Managing Officer, Hirofumi Muta
Managing Officer, Shigeki Suzuki
Managing Officer, Hisayuki Inoue
Managing Officer, Hiroji Onishi
Managing Officer, Keiji Masui
Managing Officer, Kenji Miura
Managing Officer Design Quality Innovation Sports Vehicle Management Product Development Management and LEXUS Development Center, Kiyotaka Ise
Managing Officer; Chief Quality Officer Europe, Didier Leroy
Managing Officer, Hiroyuki Yokoyama
Managing Officer, Koei Saga
Managing Officer, Takuo Matsui
Managing Officer, Hiroyuki Ochiai
Managing Officer, Yasuo Kawada
Managing Officer, Naoki Miyazaki
Managing Officer; VP Production Control Division and Corporate Strategy Division Toyota Motor Engineering & Manufacturing North America; Corporate Auditor Aisan Industry, Kazuhiro Miyauchi
VP Marketing, Bill Fay
VP Sales Administration, Randy Pflughaupt
Corporate Auditor, Kunihiro Matsuo
Corporate Auditor, Yoichi Morishita
Corporate Auditor, Akishige Okada
EVP and Board Member, Nobuyori Kodaira, age 64
Managing Officer, Shunichi Konishi
Managing Officer, Yoichi Inoue
Managing Officer, Yoshihiko Matsuda
Managing Officer, Satoru Mouri
Managing Officer, Moritaka Yoshida
Managing Officer, Johan van Zyl
Vice Chairman, Katsuaki Watanabe, age 71
Vice Chairman, Kazuo Okamoto, age 69
EVP and Representative Director, Takeshi Uchiyamada, age 66
President and Board Member, Akio Toyoda, age 57
EVP and Representative Director, Atsushi (Art) Niimi, age 65
EVP and Representative Director, Yukitoshi (Yuki) Funo, age 66
EVP and Representative Director, Shinichi Sasaki, age 66
EVP and Board Member, Masamoto Maekawa
Director; Chief Officer Government and Public Affairs Group, Mamoru Furuhashi, age 62
EVP and Representative Director, Satoshi Ozawa, age 64
EVP and Board Member, Seiichi Sudo
EVP and Board Member, Yasumori Ihara, age 62
EVP and Board Member, Mitsuhisa Kato
Director, Takahiko Ijichi, age 60
EVP and Board Member, Nobuyori Kodaira, age 64
Auditors: PricewaterhouseCoopersAarata

LOCATIONS

HQ: Toyota Motor Corp
1 Toyota-cho, Toyota, Aichi 471-8571
Phone: (81) 565 28 2121 **Fax:** (81) 565 23 5800
Web: www.toyota.co.jp

2012 Sales

	$ mil.	% of total
Asia		
Other countries	14	
Europe	9	
Total	**0**	**100**

2012 Unit Sales

Asia		
Other countries	1,326,829	18
Europe	797,993	11
Total	**7,351,929**	**100**

PRODUCTS/OPERATIONS

2012 Sales

	$ mil.	% of total
Automotive		91
Other		3

Selected Products

Vehicles
- 4Runner
- Allion (sold in Japan)
- Alphard (minivan sold in Japan)
- Aurus (hybrid)
- Avalon
- Camry (also hybrid)
- Corolla
- Corolla Rumion
- Crown
- FJ Cruiser
- Highlander (also hybrid)
- Land Cruiser
- Lexus
  - GX
  - LS600h (hybrid)
  - LX (SUV)
  - RX
  - SC
- Mark X (sold in Japan)
- Matrix
- Premio (sold in Japan)
- Prius (hybrid)
- RAV4
- Scion
- Sequoia
- Sienna (minivan)
- Tacoma (truck)
- Tundra (truck)
- Vanguard
- Vellfire (minivan)
- Venza
- Wish (minivan sold in Japan)
- Yaris (marketed in Japan as the Vitz)

Other products
- Factory automation equipment
- Forklifts and other industrial vehicles
- Housing products

Selected Investments

Daihatsu Motor (51% motor vehicles)
Hino Motors Ltd. (50% trucks)

COMPETITORS

BMW
Brilliance China
Caterpillar
Chery Automobile
Chrysler
Daimler
Deere
Fiat
Ford Motor
Fuji Heavy Industries
General Motors
Global Diversified Industries
Honda
Hyundai Motor
Isuzu
Kia Motors
Komatsu
Kubota
Land Rover
Mazda
Mitsubishi Motors
Nissan
Peugeot
Renault
Saab Automobile
Shanghai Automotive
Suzuki Motor
Tata Motors
Volkswagen
Volvo
Volvo Car Corp.

HISTORICAL FINANCIALS

Company Type: Public

Income Statement FYE: March 31

	REVENUE ($ mil.)	NET INCOME ($ mil.)	NET PROFIT MARGIN	EMPLOYEES
03/13	234,495	10,225	4.4%	333,498
03/12	226,546	3,456	1.5%	325,905
03/11	229,374	4,929	2.1%	317,716
03/10	202,885	2,242	1.1%	320,590
03/09	208,474	(4,437)	—	320,808
Annual Growth	3.0%	—	—	1.0%

2013 Year-End Financials

Debt ratio: 0.4%
Return on equity: 8.4%
Cash ($ mil.): 34,760
Current ratio: 1.07
Long-term debt ($ mil.): 77,985
No. of shares (mil.): —
Dividends
Yield: 0.0%
Payout: 0.0%
Market value ($ mil.): —

	STOCK PRICE ($) FY Close	P/E High	P/E Low	PER SHARE ($) Earnings	Dividends	Book Value
03/13	102.64	0	0	3.23	0.00	40.76
03/12	86.82	0	0	1.10	0.00	40.61
03/11	80.25	0	0	1.57	1.03	39.79
03/10	80.42	0	0	0.72	1.18	35.37
03/09	63.30	—	—	(1.41)	3.47	34.76
Annual Growth	12.8%	—	—	—	(91.3%)	4.1%

Toyota Tsusho Corp

Toyota Tsusho is the trading unit for the Toyota Group which includes Toyota Motor and auto parts maker DENSO. The company brokers a wide array of goods including metals such as steel and aluminum (comprising its largest division) machinery and electronics energy and chemicals and various consumer products. As its family relationship would imply Toyota Tsusho exports Toyota vehicles around the world but plenty of non-automotive consumer products also contribute to its business. Those other products include foodstuffs like produce and wine as well as personal nursing care equipment. Toyota Motor Corporation owns 22% of the company while Toyota Industries owns 11%.

With the global recession as a background Toyota Tusho's revenues fell almost 19% in 2010. The downturn was precipitated by an across-the-board drop in the company's sales led by a 28% dip in its Automotive division and 21% in its Metals unit. Correspondingly net income was off 32% over 2009.

In 2010 parent company Toyota Motor introduced a new low-carbon plastic material to be used in a number of its 2011 model vehicles. The "Ecological Plastic" developed by Toyota Tusho marks the world's first use of bio-polyethylene terephthalate derived from sugar cane. The new material is a second-generation bio-plastic that is more durable than earlier substances.

Also that year Eurus Energy Holdings a joint venture between Tokyo Electric Power and Toyota Tsusho acquired South Korean solar power company Jindosun Park Inc. Jindosun oversees the generation of 2974KW of electricity mostly in South Korea and will activate a 45000KW plant in the US in mid-2011.

In 2010 Toyota Tsusho acquired UK-based CalEnergy Gas's 5% stake in the Otway Gas Project and exploration rights in the Bass Straits in Australia. Toyota Tsusho considers Australia an important country for upstream investments in the gas value chain.

The company agreed in 2009 to separate its automotive fabrics business and join the unit with similar businesses of Toyota Boshoku and Kawashima Selkon. Toyota Tsusho own 30% of the resulting company. The move away from sole ownership of that business fits within Tsusho's general strategic plan to earn half of its revenue from the automotive sector by 2015.

The acquisition of TOMEN Corporation made Toyota Tsusho the sixth-largest trading company in Japan and it expanded the company's operations in the non-auto sector. Products under Tomen's purview include chemicals and plastics foodstuffs IT telecommunications and power supply equipment and textiles.

EXECUTIVES

Executive Officer; Deputy Chief Division Officer Automotive Division, Takashi Hattori
Executive Officer; Deputy Chief Division Officer Energy and Chemicals Division, Kuniaki Yamagiwa
Chairman, Junzo Shimizu, age 66
President Toyota Tsusho Asia Pacific, Jun Nakayama
Managing Executive Officer; President Toyota Tsusho America, Masanori Yamase
EVP, Mikio Asano
President and CEO, Jun Karube
Vice Chairman, Yoshio Shirai, age 62
Senior Managing Director, Hiroshi Takano
Managing Director, Takumi Shirai
Executive Officer; Deputy Chief Division Officer Machinery and Electronics Division, Soichiro Matsudaira
President of Toyota Tsusho Europe S.A, Seiichiro Adachi
President S.C. Toyota Tsusho do Brasil, Yoshifumi Araki
Executive Officer; President Toyota Tsusho Europe; President Toyota Tsusho (UK), Hiroki Sawayama
Executive Officer; Deputy Chief Division Officer Global Strategic Integration Division, Yuichi Oi
EVP, Akimasa Yokoi
President Toyota Tsusho America, Nobuyuki Minowa
Executive Officer; Deputy Chief Division Officer Metals Division, Minoru Murata
President Toyota Tsusho Europe, Kiyoshi Yamakawa
President Toyota Tsusho India, Shizuka Hayashi
President Toyota Tsusho (Thailand), Hirofumi Sato
Managing Director; Chief Division Officer Produce and Foodstuffs Division, Makoto Hyodo
Director, Hiroshi Kawakami, age 62
President and Representative Director, Junzo Shimizu, age 66
Senior Managing Director Chief Division Officer Energy and Chemicals Division and Representative Director, Yoshimasa Kondo
Vice Chairman, Yoji Toyohara, age 70
EVP Chief Representative of Tokyo Head Office and Representative Director, Kiyoshi Furubayashi, age 67
EVP and Representative Director, Katsunori Takahashi
Senior Managing Director Chief Division Officer Consumer Products Services and Materials Division and Representative Director, Koji Oshige, age 64
Managing Director; Chief Division Officer of Machinery & Electronics Division, Hisashi Yamamoto
Managing Director Chief Division Officer Administrative Division and Representative Director, Mikio Asano
Senior Managing Director; Chief Division Officer of Global Strategic Integration Division, Kenji Takanashi
Managing Director; Chief Division Officer Automotive Division, Seiichiro Adachi
Managing Director; Chief Division Officer Metals Division, Minoru Hayata
Auditors: PricewaterhouseCoopersAarata

LOCATIONS

HQ: Toyota Tsusho Corp
Century Toyota Bldg., 4-9-8 Meieki, Nakamura-ku, Nagoya, Aichi 450-8575
Phone: (81) 52 584 5482 **Fax:** (81) 52 584 5636
Web: www.toyota-tsusho.com

PRODUCTS/OPERATIONS

2010 Sales

Metals	30
Energy & chemicals	22
Produce & foodstuffs	6

COMPETITORS

Daewoo International
Mitsui
Nippon Steel Trading
Rieter Holding
Samsung C&T
Sojitz
Sumitomo
Yamato Kogyo

HISTORICAL FINANCIALS

Company Type: Public

Income Statement FYE: March 31

	REVENUE ($ mil.)	NET INCOME ($ mil.)	NET PROFIT MARGIN	EMPLOYEES
03/13	67,001	716	1.1%	48,336
03/12	72,129	807	1.1%	33,845
03/11	69,362	569	0.8%	31,081
03/10	54,623	292	0.5%	29,832
03/09	63,843	408	0.6%	27,909
Annual Growth	1.2%	15.1%	—	14.7%

2013 Year-End Financials

Debt ratio: 0.4%
Return on equity: 9.6%
Cash ($ mil.): 4,159
Current ratio: 1.30
Long-term debt ($ mil.): 8,509
No. of shares (mil.): 350
Dividends
Yield: —
Payout: —
Market value ($ mil.): 8,082

	STOCK PRICE ($) FY Close	P/E High	P/E Low	PER SHARE ($) Earnings	Dividends	Book Value
03/13	23.04	—	—	2.05	0.00	27.88
03/12	17.65	—	—	2.31	0.00	26.18
03/11	19.05	—	—	1.63	0.00	23.04
03/10	15.25	—	—	0.84	0.00	19.89
03/09	9.60	—	—	1.16	0.00	17.02
Annual Growth	24.5%	—	—	15.1%	—	13.1%

TUI AG

TUI has the European travel business cornered. Through its tourism umbrella of companies TUI holds a majority stake in TUI Travel which sells leisure travel packages and provides other travel services under some 200 brands in some 20 countries. TUI Travel & Resorts' hotel portfolio counts around 250 hotels in about 30 countries. (Hotel brands include Riu Grecotel and Dorfhotel.) The company's cruise segment includes subsidiary Hapag-Lloyd Cruises a leading provider of discovery and luxury cruises to the German market and TUI Cruises a joint venture with Royal Caribbean Cruises. The travel company also owns a majority stake in container ship operator Hapag-Lloyd AG.

The company's revenues (turnover) for fiscal year-end 2011 (ends September) increased by 7% compared to the prior year. Also operating earnings for that same year gained ground by 2% versus the prior year. TUI substantially reduced its debt load from ?2.3 billion ($3.1 billion) in 2010 to ?816.7 million ($1.1 billion) in 2011. This was accomplished by the improvement in working capital in the TUI Travel business and the lower cash flow impact from restructuring costs. Also payments from its investment in Hapag-Lloyd further reduced debt and the restructuring of loan payments to lower interest rates.

As for its segments the company's TUI Travel which accounted for around 95% of revenues in 2011 increased by 7% in 2011 compared to 2010. Its hotels & resorts segment gained by close to 3% in 2011 versus the prior year. The company's cruise ship operations gained good ground by some 12% in 2011.

Great Britain Germany and the other EU countries accounted for about 90% of revenues (turnover) in 2011. Great Britain and Germany represented 29% and 27% of revenues respectively.

TUI and Hapag-Lloyd's other owner are exploring taking the container ship operator public. A public offering would mark TUI's exit from the economically sensitive container shipping business something the travel company has been seeking since it sold it a majority stake in the business in 2009. TUI has said it may use the proceeds from the sale of Hapag-Lloyd to add to its 55% stake in TUI Travel. In addition to entertaining an IPO TUI is selling a roughly 17% stake in Hapag-Lloyd to majority owner Albert Ballin a consortium of investors that purchased a controlling stake in the container business in 2009. TUI is selling its stake for roughly ?475 million ($640 million) and will leave it with a remaining 22% stake in Hapag-Lloyd. The company had aimed to undertake the IPO during 2011 however the deals was postponed due to the weakened global equity markets.

S-Group Travel Holding GmbH owns about 25% of TUI AG. Activist TUI shareholder John Fredriksen owns about 15% of the company.

HISTORY

What became TUI was founded in Berlin in 1923 as Preussische Bergwerks-und Hutten-Aktiengesellschaft (Prussian Mine and Foundry Company) to operate former state-owned mining companies saltworks and smelters. Despite outmoded equipment and a war-shattered economy the company prospered. So in 1929 the Prussian parliament combined Preussag with Hibernia and Preussischen Elektrizitats to form the state-run VEBA group hoping to stimulate foreign investment.

Operating as part of VEBA didn't work out as well as Preussag had hoped and WWII left the company a shell of its former self. In 1952 as restrictions on steel production were lifted and industry rebounded Preussag relocated to Hanover. After taking steps to reestablish itself Preussag made a public offering in 1959; VEBA kept about 22%.

A worldwide steel glut that lasted through the 1960s forced Preussag to diversify. Acquisitions included railroad tank car and transport agent VTG and shipbuilding and chemical companies. The company also formed oil exploration unit Preussag Energie in 1968. In 1969 VEBA sold its remaining stake in Preussag to Westdeusche Landesbank (WestLB).

When the 1970s oil crisis drove up steel costs Preussag began international ventures to counter falling revenues at home. But the 1980s brought PR disasters. The European Commission fined Preussag and five other zinc producers for antitrust violations in 1984.

In 1989 Preussag reorganized into a holding company with four independent units: coal oil natural gas and plant construction. But it was about to take a sharp business turn. Michael Frenzel who had managed WestLB's industry holdings became CEO in 1994 in the midst of another steel recession. Frenzel was determined to shift Preussag away from its rusting past and toward services and technology. In 1997 it acquired container shipping and travel firm Hapag-Lloyd which had a 30% stake in Touristik Union International (TUI). By the end of 1998 the acquisitions of the rest of TUI First Reisebuero Management and a 25% stake in the UK's Thomas Cook (raised to 50.1% in 1999) had made Preussag Europe's top tourism group.

As part of its restructuring Preussag traded its plant engineering units and half of its shipbuilding unit (HDW) to Babcock Borsig for a 33% stake in that company in 1999. Preussag then made plans to transfer another 25% of HDW to Sweden's Celsius in a deal (along with Babcock Borsig) to merge Celsius' Kockums submarine shipyards with HDW. That year Hapag-Lloyd and TUI were merged into Hapag Touristik Union (renamed TUI Group in 2000); VTG merged with Lehnkering a 126-year-old freight forwarding group becoming VTG-Lehnkering.

Preussag also acquired a stake in French package tour leader Nouvelles Frontieres and sold a metals trading unit W. & O. Bergmann to Enron. By 2002 the company had sold off most of its nontourism operations changed its name to TUI and restructured its business to concentrate on travel-related businesses.

In 2004 TUI sold a division of its VTG-Lehnkering logistics operation to investors for an undisclosed amount. Also that year TUI Travel Solutions GmbH sold 50% of its stake in TQ3 Travel Solutions to Navigant International. (It sold the rest of TQ3 to Navigant two years later.)

WestLB surrendered its majority shareholding of TUI in 2004 freeing up 90% of the company's shares for free float.

In 2005 the company purchased Canada-based CP Ships for almost $2 billion making Hapag-Lloyd one of the world's largest container carriers.

Two years later TUI expanded its travel business by buying First Choice Holidays and combining the UK-based company with its existing tourism operations to form TUI Travel a publicly traded company in which TUI held a controlling stake. Around the same time the company decided to shed its container shipping operations and focus solely on its tourism and travel services businesses. To this end in March 2009 TUI sold Hapag-Lloyd to a German consortium but retained a 43% stake in the company. (TUI's stake in Hapag-Lloyd increased to about 50% as loans to the company were converted to equity.)

EXECUTIVES

Chairman, Michael Frenzel, age 66
Chief HR and Legal Affairs, Peter Engelen, age 57
Head Investor Relations, Bjorn Beroleit
Chief Tourism; CEO First Choice Holidays and TUI Travel, Peter Long, age 61
Deputy Chairman, Petra Gerstenkorn, age 59
CFO, Mikhail Noskov
Board Member, Manfred Schneider, age 75
Board Member, Roberto Lopez Abad, age 58
Board Member, Jurgen Krumnow, age 69
Board Member, Jella Susanne Benner-Heinacher, age 53
Board Member, Abel Matutes Juan, age 72
Board Member, Carmen Riu Guell, age 57
Board Member, Hans-Dieter Ruster, age 61
Board Member, Ingo Kronsfoth, age 56
Board Member, Andreas Barczewski, age 46
Board Member, Roland Schneider, age 64
Board Member, Henry Sieb, age 62
Board Member, Vladimir Yakushev, age 42
Board Member, Arnd Dunse, age 43
Board Member, Frank Jakobi, age 51
Deputy Chairman, Petra Gerstenkorn, age 59
Board Member, Anass H. Alami, age 45
Board Member, Peter F. Barrenstein, age 63
Board Member, Anette Strempel, age 47
Board Member, Ortwin Strubelt, age 49
Auditors:
PricewaterhouseCoopersAGWirtschaftsprufungsgesellschaft

LOCATIONS

HQ: TUI AG
Karl-Wiechert-Allee 4, Hanover D-30625
Phone: (49) 511 566 00 **Fax:** (49) 511 56 1901
Web: www.tui.com

2011 Sales

	$ mil.	% of total
Europe		
Great Britain		29
Germany		27
Spain		2
Other EU		32
Other Countries		4
North & South America		4
Other regions		2
Total	**0**	**100**

PRODUCTS/OPERATIONS

2011 Sales

	% of total
Tourism	
TUI	96
TUI Hotels &	2
Cruises	1
Central	1
Total	**100**

COMPETITORS

Accor
American Express
Carlson Wagonlit
Carnival Corporation
Club Med
Kuoni Travel
REWE
Royal Caribbean Cruises
Thomas Cook
Travelport

HISTORICAL FINANCIALS

Company Type: Public

Income Statement FYE: September 30

	REVENUE ($ mil.)	NET INCOME ($ mil.)	NET PROFIT MARGIN	EMPLOYEES
09/12	23,701	(19)	—	73,812
09/11	23,582	32	0.1%	73,707
09/10	22,282	138	0.6%	71,398
09/09*	19,180	487	2.5%	69,536
12/08	26,164	(169)	—	70,254
Annual Growth	(2.4%)	—	—	1.2%

*Fiscal year change

2012 Year-End Financials

Debt ratio: 24.0%	No. of shares (mil.): 252
Return on equity: (-0.6%)	Dividends
Cash ($ mil.): 2,945	Yield: —
Current ratio: 0.62	Payout: —
Long-term debt ($ mil.): 2,340	Market value ($ mil.): 2,187

	STOCK PRICE ($) FY Close	P/E High/Low		PER SHARE ($) Earnings	Dividends	Book Value
09/12	8.67	—	—	(0.21)	0.00	10.67
09/11	7.03	—	—	(0.01)	0.00	13.24
09/10	12.20	75	49	0.82	0.00	12.68
09/09*	10.30	28	6	1.83	0.00	11.97
12/08	10.30	—	—	(0.80)	0.00	10.77
Annual Growth	(4.2%)	—	—	—	—	(0.2%)

*Fiscal year change

TUI Travel Plc

The first step on a journey is likely to begin with TUI Travel. The group is the #1 or #2 source for leisure tour and travel services in many markets as well as Europe's largest provider of online package holidays. It also distributes accommodations through international online wholesalers and its online travel agent in the UK and increasingly Asia and Australia. TUI Travel runs some 3500 retail travel stores across Europe and operates with a fleet of 145 airplanes. In all the group does business under some 200 name brands serving millions of consumers worldwide. TUI Travel formed from the 2007 merger of TUI AG's travel business with Britain's First Choice Holidays. TUI AG controls about 55% of TUI Travel.

The group operates through four business segments. Mainstream holidays the largest segment comprise tours and airline flights based in three regions: "Northern" (the UK Ireland Nordic countries and Canada) Central Europe and Western Europe. TUI Travel's Specialist and Activity travel segment steers adventure education and marine activities along with a North American specialist sport and holiday group. An Accommodation and Destinations segment serves tour operators and travel agents corporate clients and individual travelers through four services: accommodation wholesale accommodation online travel agent destination services and cruise handling. Recently launched an Emerging Markets segment combines travel services with a presence in Russia and the Ukraine and increasingly Brazil India and China.

TUI Travel's operations are located in 31 national markets. It sells name brand services established across 180 countries. Europe generates about 95% of sales of which the UK accounts for nearly one-third.

Along with the rest of the tourism industry TUI Travel has faced a difficult few years as the geopolitical and economic landscape crumbled. The group managed in 2011 to regain profitability and approach its 2006 earnings record following three years of operating in the red. Underlying operating profit jumped 18% in 2011 over the prior year and cash generated from operations gained momentum. Results reflect a modest increase in sales led by the UK after a two-year slump. Several national markets the UK and Nordic region Belgium the Netherlands Austria and Canada reached record profits buoyed by cost cuts and streamlined operations. Growth was offset by weak to late consumer spending but most especially by a crisis in North Africa; TUI Travel was forced to move travel to Egypt and Tunisia –destinations that its French tour operators depend upon –to other locations such as Spain Greece and Turkey. The group also took a financial hit from such disasters as the earthquake and tsunami in Japan (2011) and volcanic ash clouds that closed much of European airspace for a period in 2010. The ensuing costs widened with merger related expenses attributable to the UK businesses and former TUI businesses based in Europe charged off as separately disclosed items in 2010 and less so in 2011.

TUI Travel's plans for growth focus on expanding its portfolio of diverse and exclusive travel offerings in multiple market segments. Its strategy includes tightening control of distribution with a concentration online a course intended to improve customer access and shave distribution costs. It is further developing its numerous existing brands: TUI (German tour operator) Moorings (yacht business) and Quark (cruises to the Polar Regions). Acquisitions are on its strategic map too. TUI Travel in mid-2011 acquired six operating companies that lease and manage more than a dozen Magic Life holiday clubs in Turkey Tunisia Egypt Greece and Spain from TUI AG for a nominal sum as the clubs are operating at a loss. The all-inclusive mid-priced Magic Life clubs cater to the Austrian and German markets which generate more than one-quarter of the group's sales.

HISTORY

The company that has evolved into TUI Travel began operating in the mid-1970s under the moniker Owners Abroad. It went public in 1982. In 1987 Owners Abroad opened its Air 2000 charter airline service and Howard Klein took over as chairman. In 1992 Klein began informal talks with David Crossland chairman of rival UK tour operator Airtours about a possible merger. The talks produced nothing. Later that year fearing a takeover attempt by Airtours (known for years as MyTravel Group) First Choice signed a deal with another rival UK travel agency Thomas Cook. The deal gave Thomas Cook a 10% stake in Owners Abroad in exchange for a distribution network in Europe.

Sure enough Airtours launched a takeover attempt in 1993 but Thomas Cook's stake helped block the maneuver. While the takeover attempt failed Owners Abroad's profits fell by half. (Klein blamed a fickle British public's change in taste regarding travel destinations. He and two other directors resigned.)

The company brought in Francis Baron who relaunched the company in 1994 under the name First Choice Holidays. It also bought Canada's International Travel Holdings (renamed Signature Vacations in 1995) making First Choice the market leader in that country. First Choice restructured consolidating its half-dozen brand names into three brands catering to luxury single and family traveling and sold off some non-essential businesses. In 1996 Baron was ousted in a boardroom coup by directors who complained of his management style. He was replaced as group managing director by Peter Long while Ian Clubb the company's deputy chairman moved into the role of chairman.

In late 1998 the rumor mill hinted that Thomas Cook was looking to buy out First Choice. Meanwhile First Choice scooped up smaller operators Unijet and Hayes & Jarvis. The following year First Choice shareholders rejected a $2.3 billion merger with Swiss travel group Kuoni Reisen. Shortly thereafter it was once again Airtours that launched a $1.3 billion bid for First Choice. The takeover bid came under scrutiny from the European Union Commission and ultimately was blocked.

In 2000 First Choice acquired the remaining 75% of retail travel shop chain Holiday Hypermarkets that it didn't already own (it bought a 25% stake in 1999). It also agreed to form a cruise line joint venture with Royal Caribbean Cruises which bought a 20% stake in the company. The company acquired Spain's Viejes Barcelo in exchange for a 21% stake in the company. Barcelo performs outbound tour operating and destination services businesses. In all First Choice bought seven tour operators in 2000 and another 10 in 2001 including I Viaggi Del Turchese (Italy) Sunrise BV (The Netherlands) Tourinter (France) and CIT Holidays in its own backyard. With the acquisitions First Choice gained a presence in every major market in Europe.

The company's 10-plus acquisitions in fiscal 2004 included that of StudentCity.com an online provider of travel packages targeting US high school and college students (think spring break and graduation trips). The StudentCity.com purchase bolstered First Choice's growth efforts in North America which previously had been focused on Canada.

In 2006 the company purchased California-based Your Man Tours which offers travel packages designed for older people under the YMT Vacations brand. In 2007 rival TUI bought First Choice and merged the company with its own tourism arm to form TUI Travel.

TUI Travel made almost 20 acquisitions in 2008 of companies in the UK US and Australia mainly for its activity holiday division. Also in 2008 the company agreed to take full ownership of Island Cruises its 50%-owned joint venture with Royal Caribbean Cruises.

Like other airline operators TUI Travel has been faced with higher-than-expected fuel prices and it has announced plans to scale back its flight capacity. To strengthen its airline operations the company discussed a combination of its TUIfly Germany business with Air Berlin. In 2009 TUI Travel bought a 10% stake in Air Berlin and Air Berlin took over TUIfly's scheduled flight business later that year. Using about a dozen of TUIfly's aircraft Air Berlin is operating its routes within Germany and to Italy and Austria. The deal reduced TUI Travel's exposure to TUIfly's losses in the past year.

EXECUTIVES

Deputy Chairman, Sir Michael S. (Mike) Hodgkinson, age 69, $347,939 total compensation

Chairman, Michael Frenzel, age 66

Managing Director UK and Ireland, Dermot Blastland, age 63, $744,999 total compensation

President Cunard Line, Peter Shanks

Managing Director Specialist and Emerging Markets, Richard Prosser, age 55

Group Legal Director and Company Secretary, Andrew John, age 60

Director Group Human Resources, Bill Logan, age 65

Managing Director Accommodation and Destinations, Joan Vila, age 50

Managing Director Specialist and Activity, John Wimbleton, age 54

Chief Financial Officer, William (Will) Waggott, age 49

CIO, Jim Mann

Director Corporate Communications, Lesley Allan

Managing Director Northern Region and Director, Johan Lundgren, age 46, $1,221,880 total compensation

Director Finance and Investor Relations, Andy Jones

Managing Director Western Europe, Bart Brackx, age 61

Managing Director Central Europe and Director, Volker Bottcher, age 54, $970,136 total compensation
Chief Marketing Officer, Michael Lambertz
Managing Director, Joan Vil+
Board Member, Jeremy Hicks, age 60
Deputy Chairman, Sir Michael S. (Mike) Hodgkinson, age 69
Director, Clare M. Chapman, age 53
Director, Rainer Feuerhake, age 69
Director, Erhard Schipporeit, age 64
Director, Albert Schunk, age 72
Board Member, Giles Thorley, age 46
Director, Tony A. Campbell, age 63
CFO and Director, William (Will) Waggott, age 49
Managing Director Northern Region and Director, Johan Lundgren, age 46
Director, William S. (Bill) Dalton, age 69
Managing Director Central Europe and Director, Volker Bottcher, age 54
Director, Harold Sher, age 66
Director, Horst Baier, age 56
Chief Executive and Director, Peter Long, age 60
Auditors: KPMGAuditPlc

LOCATIONS

HQ: TUI Travel Plc
TUI Travel House, Crawley Business Quarter, Fleming Way, Crawley, West Sussex RH10 9QL
Phone: (44) 1293 645 700 **Fax:** (44) 1293 645 704
Web: www.tuitravelplc.com

2011 Sales

	% of total
Europe	
UK	30
Germany	27
France	10
Other European	28
Other	5
Total	**100**

PRODUCTS/OPERATIONS

2011 Sales

Mainstream sector	73	
Accomodation & Destinations sector	14	
Specialist & Activity sector	13	
Total	**0**	**100**

Selected Brands

Accommodation and Destination sector (Spain UK and US)
- AsiaRooms
- Bedsonline
- Hotelbeds
- Intercruises
- LateRooms
- TUI Espa?a

Emerging Markets sector (Egypt Turkey and Spain)
- TUI Russia & CIS

Mainstream sector
- Central Europe (Germany Spain and US)
  - 1-2-FLY
  - I'tur
  - TUI
- Northern region (Spain Greece and Turkey)
  - First Choice
  - Fritidsresor
  - Thomson
- Western Europe (Spain Turkey and Morocco)
  - Arke
  - Holland International
  - Jetair
  - Marmara
  - Nouvelles Frontieres
  - Sunjets

Specialist and Activity sector (US France and Italy)
- Brightspark
- Crystal
- Educational Tours Inc.
- Hayes & Jarvis
- Le Boat
- The Moorings
- USA

COMPETITORS

Accor
American Express
BCD Travel
Carnival Corporation
Club Med
Holidaybreak
Kuoni Travel
REWE
Thomas Cook
Transat
Travelport

HISTORICAL FINANCIALS

Company Type: Public

Income Statement FYE: September 30

	REVENUE ($ mil.)	NET INCOME ($ mil.)	NET PROFIT MARGIN	EMPLOYEES
09/13	24,295	96	0.4%	55,406
09/12	23,418	223	1.0%	54,090
09/11	22,877	132	0.6%	53,247
09/10	21,289	(165)	—	48,724
09/09	22,337	(40)	—	49,463
Annual Growth	2.1%	—	—	2.9%

2013 Year-End Financials

Debt ratio: 27.2%
Return on equity: 3.9%
Cash ($ mil.): 2,829
Current ratio: 0.55
Long-term debt ($ mil.): 1,633
No. of shares (mil.): 1,118
Dividends
Yield: —
Payout: —
Market value ($ mil.): 6,272

	STOCK PRICE ($) FY Close	P/E High/Low	PER SHARE ($) Earnings	Dividends	Book Value
09/13	5.61	255188	0.09	0.00	2.09
09/12	3.53	74 48	0.20	0.00	2.27
09/11	2.20	139 71	0.12	0.00	2.63
09/10	3.42	— —	(0.15)	0.00	2.80
09/09	4.02	— —	(0.04)	0.00	3.29
Annual Growth	8.7%	— —	—	—	
(10.7%)					

Turkiye Garanti Bankasi A.S.

Turkiye Garanti Bankasi (Garanti Bank Turkey) provides banking services from about 966 domestic branches and more than 3700 ATMs. Subsidiaries and branches can also be found in China Cyprus Germany Luxembourg Malta Russia and the UK. In addition to traditional deposit products Garanti Bank provides brokerage factoring insurance leasing personal pension plans portfolio management and other services. The bank serves more than 12.2 million customers and has assets of more than $106 billion. Banco Bilbao Vizcaya Argentaria owns 25% of the bank once owned by the Dou Group which now holds 24%. Turkiye Garanti Bankasi was founded in 1946.

EXECUTIVES

President CEO and Director, Ergun Ozen
EVP Financial Institutions and Corporate Banking, Tolga Egemen
Executive Vice President Financial Institutions and Corporate Banking, Ali Fuat Erbil
Chairman, Ferit Faik Sahenk
Vice Chairman, Suleyman Sozen
Executive Vice President Technology Operational Services and Central Marketing, Husnu Erel
Executive Vice President Domestic & Overseas Subsidiaries Coordination, Turgay Gonensin
Executive Vice President Support Services, Adnan Memis
EVP Loans, Ali Temel
Executive Vice President Strategic and Financial Planning, Murat Mergin
EVP Treasury, Uruz Ersozoglu
EVP Human Resources Training Treasury & Investment Banking, Gokhan Erun
Executive Vice President SME Banking, Nafiz Karadere
Executive Vice President Technology Operations Management & Central Marketing, Husnu Erel
Executive Vice President CFO, Afzal M. Modak
Executive Vice President, Onur Genc
Executive Vice President - Loans, Erhan Adali
Executive Vice President Delivery Channels Social Platforms Management Customer Satisfaction, Didem Dincer Baser
Executive Vice President General Accounting & Financial Reporting, Ibrahim Aydinli
Executive Vice President Commercial Banking, Recep Bastug
Executive Vice President Legal Services and Retail Risk Monitoring, Aydin Duren
Executive Vice President Project and Acquisition Finance Sustainability, Ebru Dildar Edin
Executive Vice President Retail and Private Banking Call Center Garanti Payment Systems CEO, Onur Genc
Executive Vice President SME Banking Corporate Brand Management and Marketing Communication, Nafiz Karadere
Executive Vice President Purchasing & Tax Management, Aydin Senel
President CEO and Director, Ergun Ozen
Vice Chairman, Suleyman Sozen
Auditors: KPMG

LOCATIONS

HQ: Turkiye Garanti Bankasi A.S.
Levent, Nispetiye Mahallesi, Aytar Caddesi, No. 2, Besiktas, Istanbul, Istanbul Province 34340
Phone: (90) 212 318 23 50 **Fax:** (90) 212 216 59 02
Web: www.garantibank.com

COMPETITORS

Akbank
Finansbank
Isbank
Koc
Sabanci
Sekerbank
Turk Ekonomi Bankasi
Yapi Kredi

HISTORICAL FINANCIALS

Company Type: Public

Income Statement FYE: December 31

	ASSETS ($ mil.)	NET INCOME ($ mil.)	INCOME AS % OF ASSETS	EMPLOYEES
12/12	99,102	1,878	1.9%	20,287
12/11	85,900	1,789	2.1%	19,547
12/10	87,971	2,220	2.5%	19,497
12/09	77,183	2,056	2.7%	18,875
12/08	63,904	1,245	1.9%	18,391
Annual Growth	11.6%	10.8%	—	2.5%

2012 Year-End Financials

Return on assets: 1.9%
Return on equity: 16.8%
Long-term debt ($ mil.): —
No. of shares (mil.): —
Sales ($ mil): 9,804
Dividends
Yield: 1.1%
Payout: 3.8%
Market value ($ mil.): —

	STOCK PRICE ($) FY Close	P/E High/Low		PER SHARE ($) Earnings	Dividends	Book Value
12/12	5.20	2	1	0.45	0.06	0.03
12/11	3.11	2	1	0.43	0.02	0.02
12/10	5.15	4	2	0.53	0.07	0.03
12/09	3.95	3	1	0.49	0.01	0.02
12/08	1.35	8	1	0.42	0.98	1.53
Annual Growth	40.1%	—	—	1.7%	(50.9%)	(62.9%)

UBS AG (Switzerland)

If you be wealthy then UBS is for you. UBS is one of the world's largest private banks with operations in more than 50 countries. UBS also provides asset management and investment banking as well as traditional banking services in its home country of Switzerland. The group includes four primary segments: Wealth Management & Swiss Bank Wealth Management Americas Global Asset Management and UBS Investment Bank. Investment management clients include ultra-wealthy individuals corporations and institutional investors. Asset classes offered include internal and external mutual bonds money markets stocks and bonds. Investment banking options include securities underwriting advisory and foreign exchange.

After suffering billions in losses in the global recession UBS has been restructuring itself and cutting down its portfolio of businesses. It is also looking for ways to sharpen its focus on client-focused investment operations and move away from the proprietary trading business that contributed to its losses. The company plans to focus on its global wealth management and Swiss banking operations while utilizing its investment banking operations as a supporting partner to its core businesses. (Going forward it will report Wealth management and Retail & Corporate as separate divisions while its Wealth Management & Swiss Bank segment will go away.) Recent acquisitions that fall in line with that goal include Dutch wealth management firm VermogensGroep the French asset management operations of rival Commerzbank and ING Groep's investment management business in Australia. It also bought structured products boutique Luxembourg Financial Group boosting its global equities activities.

The group's corporate rejiggering and fiscal discipline along with the relative strength of the Swiss franc helped UBS return to profitability in 2010. Its investment bank operations provided the company with its greatest boost that year as it lessened its exposure to risky investments and turned around losses in fixed income currencies and commodities. However the lingering downturn and concerns over European sovereign debt have been a drain on the company. Investment banking activity slowed down in 2011 which was the primary reason profits slipped some 45% that year. On the other hand the company reported improved new client assets and wealth management revenues rose. UBS has a strong capital position with a core Tier 1 ratio ahead of many other European banks as they work to meet Basel III standards.

In 2011 the company reported a third-quarter loss after it discovered unauthorized trading in its London investment bank. The rogue trader was arrested under suspicion of fraud; losses from the speculative trading amounted to CHF 1.9 billion (more than $2 billion). Although UBS' risk system detected unauthorized trading the company did not investigate and controls were not put in place. The incident led to further declines in UBS' investment banking business.

HISTORY

Businessmen in Winterthur Switzerland formed the Bank of Winterthur in 1862 to serve trading interests finance railroads and operate a warehouse. In 1912 the bank merged with the Bank of Toggenburg (formed in 1863) to create Schweizerische Bankgesellschaft –Union Bank of Switzerland (UBS).

It expanded in Switzerland buying smaller banks and adding branches. After growing in the post-WWI era it was hit hard by the Depression. UBS benefited from Switzerland's neutrality in WWII gaining deposits from both Jews and Nazis. In 1946 the bank opened an office in New York. Expansion in Switzerland continued after the war with the purchase of Eidgenossische Bank of Zurich.

UBS continued its acquisitions in the 1950s; by 1962 it had 81 branches. Other purchases included Interhandel a cash-rich Swiss financial concern (1967) and four savings banks (1968). In 1967 it opened a full-service office in London and during the 1970s established several securities underwriting subsidiaries abroad.

International financial markets became supercharged in the 1980s and UBS resolved to catch up with its domestic peers in international operations. As London prepared for financial deregulation in 1986 UBS bought brokerage house Phillips & Drew.

The firm's UK brokerage business was hit hard by the 1987 US stock market crash; over the next two years losses continued prompting an overhaul of the London operations. Then its US operations were jarred by the collapse of the junk bond market in 1990. The next year UBS set up offices in Paris Singapore and Hong Kong and took over Chase Manhattan's (now JPMorgan Chase) New York money management unit.

Meanwhile the firm continued to expand within Switzerland buying five more banks to boost market share and fill in gaps in its branch network. These buys left UBS with overlapping operations and a bloated infrastructure when recession hit. Falling real estate values left the bank with a heavy load of nonperforming loans.

In 1994 profits plummeted. Stockholder Martin Ebner dissatisfied with the performance of president Robert Studer tried to gain control of UBS; failing that he sought to have Studer charged with criminal fraud. In 1996 he almost thwarted Studer's election to the chairmanship.

UBS launched a multiyear reorganization in 1994 by consolidating its consumer credit operations. The next year it joined with Swiss Life/Rentenanstalt to offer insurance products through its bank network.

In 1996 after rebuffing Credit Suisse Group's merger bid UBS began an even more draconian reorganization cutting domestic branches and writing down billions of francs in bad loans leading to UBS' first-ever loss (with another the next year). In 1998 the company merged with Swiss Bank Corp. then cut 23% of its staff. Later that year the bank lost $1.6 billion in the stumbling Long-Term Capital Management hedge fund prompting chairman Mathis Cabiallavetta to resign.

As UBS struggled to swallow Swiss Bank in 1999 it retreated somewhat from riskier markets began selling some $2 billion in real estate and sold its 25% stake in Swiss Life/Rentenanstalt. Looking to bulk up the firm that year bought Bank of America's European and Asian private banking operations and Allegis Realty Investors a US real estate investment management firm.

In 2000 UBS reorganized yet again and bought US broker Paine Webber (now UBS Paine Webber). UBS's integration of Paine Webber continued into the next year. Also in 2001 chairman Marcel Ospel was criticized for UBS's handling of Swissair's cash crisis which resulted in the air fleet's grounding.

The bank came under computer attack in 2002 when a disgruntled PaineWebber employee set off a "logic bomb" in UBS's computer system. Despite the deletion of 1000 files across the company network and $3 million in damages UBS and its stock price weathered the attack.

Continuing to target the mass affluent around the planet UBS acquired the South American wealth management operations of Dresdner Bank and the North American wealth management business of Julius Baer in 2004. It sold some of its private banking business in Switzerland to Julius Baer the following year.

In late 2004 UBS bought SoundView (renamed UBS Capital Markets) the capital markets and specialist business of US company Charles Schwab for $265 million in cash. UBS integrated the operations into the equities business of its investment bank making the unit one of the top market makers of Nasdaq stock.

UBS's 2006 acquisition of #2 Brazilian investment bank Banco Pactual for about $2.6 billion gave it a foothold in the volatile-yet-growing Brazilian private equity market (a market in which rival Credit Suisse was already active). Also that year with the commodities market at a fever pitch UBS bought ABN AMRO's futures and commodities trading business for an estimated $400 million. It bought the private client services business of Piper Jaffray Companies for $875 million and KeyCorp's McDonald Investments.

UBS suffered severe losses in 2007 and 2008 related to investments in the US subprime mortgage market. It was one of Europe's hardest-hit financial institutions and in late 2008 UBS received government bailout funds to the tune of CHF 68 billion ($60 billion). Ironically UBS' exposure to subprime mortgages had been undertaken as a way to play catch-up with competition in the bonds markets. UBS ended up writing down around $40 billion and closing its Dillon Read Capital Management operations (paying out some $300 million in the process).

In 2009 the company restructured to separate its struggling divisions into four autonomous units including splitting up the former Global Wealth Management & Business Bank segment to give each unit more accountability and flexibility. UBS cut costs as well including cutting some 12500 jobs (it cut 6000 jobs the previous year). In 2008 the company sold $15 billion in distressed mortgage assets to BlackRock shut down its municipal bond business and sold its 3.4 billion shares in Bank of China. It also sold UBS Fiduciary Trust to Wilmington Trust its mortgage servicing business to Impac Mortgage and its Canadian energy business to JPMorgan Chase.

The company ran into more trouble in 2009. To settle claims that it helped American clients avoid paying taxes to the US government the company paid a $780 million fine and turned over once-secret banking client records. It also exited the US cross-border banking business. Some UBS account-holders countered by suing the company in Swiss court. As the company cooperates with authorities to provide more transparency though UBS risks losing some of its uber-wealthy customers.

The turmoil was the final straw for CEO Marcel Rohrer who was replaced in 2009 by Oswald Grubel the former CEO of rival Credit Suisse.

Grubel retired from Credit Suisse in 2007 and was credited with turning that company around after a period of poor performance. UBS continued to clear out its top management that year and brought in former Swiss finance minister Kaspar Villiger as its chairman.

EXECUTIVES

Head Wealth Management International, Juerg Haller
Chief Group Internal Audit Swiss Bank, Stephan Zimmermann
Secretary, Luzius Cameron
Chairman and CEO Global Asset Management; Chairman UBS Saudi Arabia, John A. Fraser, age 62
Chairman Americas; President UBS Investment Bank, Robert Wolf, age 51
Group COO; CEO Corporate Center and UBS Group Europe Middle East and Africa, Ulrich Korner, age 51
Vice Chairman Wealth Management Americas; Vice Chairman UBS Bank USA, Rosemary T. Berkery, age 59
Head Wealth Management Origination UBS Financial Services, Robert E. (Bob) Mulholland, age 61
Co-Head Investment Banking EMEA, Hermann Prelle, age 48
Co-Head Wealth Management Advisor Group US Global Wealth Management Americas, James D. (Jamie) Price
Executive Chairman Fixed Income Currencies and Commodities (FICC); Head Complex Structured Products UBS Investment Bank, Jeffrey (Jeff) Mayer, age 54
Group CEO, Sergio P. Ermotti, age 53
CFO, Thomas C. (Tom) Naratil
Global Head Equity Capital Markets, Matthew Koder
Chief Executive UBS Jersey, Thomas R. (Tom) Hill, age 51
COO UBS Switzerland, Markus Ronner
Head Wealth Management Asia Pacific, Kathryn Shih
COO Wealth Management Advisor Group US, Anton Stadelmann
CEO Americas and Wealth Management Americas, Robert J. (Bob) McCann, age 55
Vice Chairman Wealth Management Americas, James M. Pierce
Chairman Investment Banking Division, J. Richard (Rick) Leaman III
Head Wealth Management Partnership Wealth Management Americas, Brian P. Hull
Global Chief Risk Officer, Philip J. Lofts
Head Group Compliance, Neil R. Stocks
Vice Chairman Wealth Management and Swiss Bank, Carlo Grigioni
Head Products and Services Wealth Management Americas, Michael A. Weisberg
Global Head Alternative and Quantitative Investments Global Asset Management, Joseph (Joe) Scoby, age 48
Head Human Resources, John F. Bradley, age 52
CFO Wealth Management and Swiss Bank, William F. Widdowson
Global Head Human Resources UBS Investment Bank, Maria Bentley
Head Banking Products and Wealth Services, Bernhard Buchs
Member of the Executive Board; Group General Counsel, Markus U. Diethelm, age 56
Chief Investment Officer Private Bank, Alexander S. Friedman
Co-Head Investment Banking Division, Simon Warshaw
CEO Russia and the Commonwealth of Independent States, Steven Meehan
Vice Chairman Saudi Arabia, Mohammed Al Dhoheyan
CEO UBS Saudi Arabia, Mohamed Sammakia
Head Human Resources and Education Wealth Management and Swiss Bank, Gabriela Maria Payer
Head Wealth Management Greater China and Deputy Head Wealth Management Asia Pacific, Allen C. L. Lo
General Counsel Wealth Management Americas, Mark Shelton
Special Counsel Wealth Management and Swiss Bank, Ursula Suter
Chairman Global Markets Asia, Peter W. Burnett
CFO Global Asset Management, Paresh Sodha
Deputy Global Head Alternative and Quantitative Investments Global Asset Management, William J. (Bill) Ferri
Global Head Equities, John C. Leonard
Chief Communication Officer, Michael Willi
CEO UBS Investment Bank, Carsten Kengeter, age 46, $711,178 total compensation
President UBS Global Asset Management (Japan) Ltd., Susumu Okamura
Co-Head Securities, Yassine Bouhara
Chief Economist Swiss Business and Private Bank, Andreas Hoefert, age 46
Head Asia Equity Syndicate, James Fleming
Managing Director and Head Corporate Communications Americas, Mark Arena
Co-Chairman and Co-CEO Asia Pacific, Chi-Won Yoon, age 54
Media Relations Europe Middle East and Africa, Oliver (Ollie) Gadney
Co-Head Global Debt Capital Markets, David Soanes
Co-Head Global Debt Capital Markets, Mike Davidson
Media Relations Investment Bank, Kelly Smith
Media Relations Investment Bank, Doug Morris
Media Relations Wealth Management US, Allison Chin-Leong
Media Relations Global Asset Management and Wealth Management US, Kris Kagel
Media Relations Canada, Graeme Harris
Global Head Securities UBS Investment Bank, Neal Shear
Co-Head Securities, Francois Gouws
Head Wealth Management Solutions Wealth Management Americas, John Brown
COO UBS Financial Services, Anita Sands
Head Wealth Management Germany, Axel Hoerger
Head Prime Broking Singapore, David Forsyth
COO UBS Investment Bank, Sam Molinaro
Co-Head Investment Banking Division, Matthew Grounds
Member of the Executive Board; Co-CEO of UBS Investment Bank, Andrea Orcel
Chairman of the Board of Directors, Axel Weber
Member of the Board of Directors, Beatrice Mauro
Member of the Board of Directors, Isabelle Romy
Member of the Executive Board; CEO of UBS Switzerland; CEO of UBS Retail & Corporate, Lukas Gaehwiler
Independent Vice Chairman of the Board, Michel Demare
Member of the Executive Board; Group Chief Operating Officer; CEO of Corporate Center; CEO of UBS Europe; Middle East and Africa, Ulrich Koerner
Account Vice President, Jeffrey C. Mull
Corporate Vice President, Timothy L. Andrews
Vice President Wealth Management, Dax P. McCracken
Director, Wolfgang Mayrhuber, age 66
Director, David H. Sidwell, age 59
Director, Helmut Panke, age 67
Director, Axel P. Lehmann, age 54
Director, Prof Bruno Gehrig, age 67
Director, Ann F. Godbehere, age 57
Director, William G. (Bill) Parrett, age 67
Vice Chairman, Michel Demare, age 56
Director, Rainer-Marc Frey, age 51
Director, Joseph Yam
Auditors: Ernst&YoungLtd.

LOCATIONS

HQ: UBS AG (Switzerland)
Bahnhofstrasse 45, Zurich CH-8001
Phone: (41) 44 234 11 11
Web: www.ubs.com

2011 Sales

	% of total
Europe	
Switzerland	41
UK	5
Other	6
US	34
Asia/Pacific	13
Other	1
Total	**100**

PRODUCTS/OPERATIONS

2011 Sales

	% of total
Interest	46
Net fees &	39
Net trading	11
Other	4
Total	**100**

2011 Sales by Segment

	% of total
Wealth Management & Bank	
Wealth	27
Retail &	15
Investment	32
Wealth Management	19
Global Asset	7
Total	**100**

COMPETITORS

Bank of America
Barclays
CIBC
Citigroup
Coutts Group
Credit Suisse
Goldman Sachs
HSBC
JPMorgan Chase
Julius Baer
Mitsubishi UFJ Financial Group
Mizuho Financial
Morgan Stanley
RBC Financial Group
UniCredit
Wells Fargo Advisors

HISTORICAL FINANCIALS

Company Type: Public

Income Statement

FYE: December 31

	ASSETS ($ mil.)	NET INCOME ($ mil.)	INCOME AS % OF ASSETS	EMPLOYEES
12/12	1,373,662	(2,739)	—	62,628
12/11	1,508,470	4,420	0.3%	64,820
12/10	1,407,629	8,050	0.6%	64,617
12/09	1,301,498	(2,656)	—	67,518
12/08	1,894,358	(19,635)	—	77,783
Annual Growth	(7.7%)	—	—	(5.3%)

2012 Year-End Financials

Return on assets: (-0.1%)
Return on equity: (-5.0%)
Long-term debt ($ mil.): —
No. of shares (mil.): —
Sales ($ mil): 38,764
Dividends
Yield: 0.6%
Payout: 14.0%
Market value ($ mil.): —

	STOCK PRICE ($) FY Close	P/E High/Low		PER SHARE ($) Earnings	Dividends	Book Value
12/12	15.74	—	—	(0.73)	0.11	13.36
12/11	11.83	22	11	1.15	0.00	15.16
12/10	16.47	10	6	2.09	0.00	13.19
12/09	15.51	—	—	(0.73)	0.00	11.31
12/08	14.30	—	—	(7.10)	0.00	10.74
Annual Growth	2.4%	—	—	—	—	5.6%

Umicore S.A.

Umicore aims to do more. Its diversified business includes four segments: Catalysis (automotive catalysts precious metals chemistry); Energy Metals (cobalt and specialty materials electro-optic materials thin film products fuel cells); Performance Materials (building products. electroplating platinum engineered materials zinc chemicals); and Recycling (precious metals refining battery recycling jewellery and industrial metals precious metals management). The company also owns 40% of Element Six Abrasives a joint venture with industrial diamond producer Element Six. Another joint venture with Zinifex combines the two companies' zinc businesses into the world's largest zinc producer called Nyrstar.

Umicore's revenues rebounded in 2010 gaining 16% over the previous year. The bounce was due to improving conditions in most of the company's end markets driving higher demand and an increase in prices. Sales in its Catalysis segment were up 19% based on the recovery of the automotive industry. The Recycling unit also grew by 19% while Energy Materials was up 14% and Performance Materials gained 10%. Net income almost tripled driven by solid sales growth and a reduction in operating expenses.

The company's growth strategy is to address key global challenges such as resource scarcity the electrification of automobiles the need to reduce carbon emissions and the need for renewable energy generation. The company plans to grow organically focusing its investments on expanding its capabilities in battery materials for hybrid and electrical vehicle and heavy-duty diesel production and technology. Umicore's goal is to average 10% growth through 2015.

Umicore is using investments to increase its precious metals refining and recycling activities. The company's recent growth has expanded Umicore into China and has increased its presence in North and South America. After selling off most of its copper and zinc businesses in the middle part of the 2000s Umicore has focused on producing higher-value-added products that can return profits even when metal prices are low.

It invested some $79 million in 2010 to increase its production of new generation cathodel materials for lithium-ion rechargeable batteries. The investment more than tripled Umicore's production capacity at its existing operations.

In 2007 Umicore and Zinifex took Nyrstar public gaining Umicore about $1 billion in the process.

HISTORY

Created in 1906 to exploit the rich mineral resources of the Belgian Congo (later called the Congo then Zaire now simply Congo) the company then known as Union Miniere du Haut Katanga (UM) mined cobalt copper precious metals tin and zinc in Belgium's African colony. UM smelted the mined ores in Africa and then transported them to Belgium for refining.

UM first cast copper in the Belgian Congo at Elisabethville (now Lubumbashi) in 1911; tin production began in 1918 gold and silver recovery in 1921 and radium production in 1922. In 1924 the company began smelting cobalt at its Jadotville-Panda plant. It added production of zinc in 1937 and uranium in 1943. (It exited the uranium business in 1960.) That year the Congo gained independence from Belgium and when widespread violence and unrest swept the country the United Nations sent in troops to restore order. UN forces withdrew from the country in 1964.

In 1965 Joseph Mobutu rose to power and began a reign of terror. He nationalized UM's mines and smelting operations in 1968. Mobutu's action forced the company to develop new mining operations in the 1970s and 1980s. During that period the company became a subsidiary of conglomerate Societe Generale de Belgique.

UM grew substantially in 1989 when it merged with Metallurgie Hoboken-Overplet (nonferrous and precious metals) Vielle-Montagne (zinc) and Mechim (engineering). Growth proved troublesome however and in 1995 saddled with high labor costs and too many noncore assets the company began to sell off operations. By 1999 UM had sold Asturienne Penamet Cananea its CSO trading companies Diamant Boart Overpelt-Plascobel Union Mines and Zinkgruvan. The divestitures lowered sales but returned the company to profitability.

With restructuring behind it UM acquired a controlling interest in four businesses in 2000: Padaeng Industry (zinc Thailand) Larvik Pigment (zinc for paint; Australia Malaysia Norway) and V&S Scientific and Tayside Optical Technology (both UK-based producers of finished optics products).

In 2001 UM acquired the 60% of optical materials maker Vertex (France) that it didn't own and sold its Sogemin metals trading unit to Belgian Natexis Banques Populaires (now called simply Natixis). That September UM changed its name to Umicore. The company continued its global growth in 2002 buying a zinc alloy processor in France and China's leading producer of zinc dust (used to make paint).

In 2003 the company acquired OM Group's precious metals group (PMG) for about $750 million diversifying its business and expanding its operations in North and South America. Also that year Franco-Belgian utility Suez divested its 15% stake in the company (Suez had acquired a controlling stake when it bought Societe Generale de Belgique).

In 2005 the company spun off its copper business as a separate company called Cumerio.

EXECUTIVES

EVP Recycling, Hugo Morel, age 63
Vice-President Umicore Japan, Luc Gellens
SVP Information Systems, Edwin D'Hondt
EVP Energy Materials, Marc van Sande, age 61
Chairman, Thomas Leysen, age 53
Vice-President Thin Film Products, Michel Cauwe
Chief Executive Officer, Marc Grynberg, age 48
Vice-President Environment, Guy Ethier
Vice-President Zinc Chemicals, Guy Beke
SVP Government Affairs, Stephan Csoma
SVP Human Resources, Ignace de Ruijter
SVP Colbalt and Specialty Materials, Dirk Uytdewilligen
EVP Performance Materials, Pascal Reymondet, age 54
SVP Umicore Battery Recycling, Jan Vliegen
Vice-President Technical Materials, Joerg Beuers
SVP Precious Metals Management, Ralf Drieselmann
SVP Automotive Catalysts Europe and Africa, Michael Neisel
SVP Umicore China, Klaus Ostgathe
EVP Catalysts, Bill Staron
Director Group Communications, Tim Weekes
External Communications, Bart Crols
Vice-President Jewellery & Industrial Metals, Dietmar Becker
CTO, Denis Goffaux, age 45
Honorary Chairman, Karel Vinck
Vice-President Government Affairs, Egbert Lox
SVP Legal Affairs, Geraldine Nolens
Head of Investor Relations, Geoffroy Raskin
Vice-President Precious Metals Refining, Koen Demesmaeker
Chief Financial Officer, Ludo Vandervelden
Vice-President Group Research & Development, Wilfried Muller
Vice-President Umicore Greater China, Bernhard Fuchs
Vice-President Automotive Catalysts Asia Pacific, Joerg Roden
Vice-President Human Resources, Ignace Ruijter
Vice-President Building Products, Pierre Bruaene
Vice-President Automotive Catalysts Research & Technology, Dieter Lindner
Vice-President Umicore South America, Marcos Lucchese
Director, Isabelle Bouillot, age 63
Director, Uwe-Ernst Bufe, age 69
Director, Jonathan M. E. Oppenheimer, age 44
Director, Jean-Luc Dehaene, age 70
Director, Guy Paquot, age 72
Director, Klaus Wendel, age 69
Director, Comte Arnoud de Pret, age 70
Honorary Chairman, Karel Vinck
Auditors: PricewaterhouseCoopersReviseursd'EntreprisesSCCRL

LOCATIONS

HQ: Umicore S.A.
Broekstraat 31 rue du Marais, Brussels B-1000
Phone: (32) 2 227 71 11 **Fax:** (32) 2 227 79 00
Web: www.umicore.com

PRODUCTS/OPERATIONS

2010 Sales

	$ mil.	% of total
Recycling		25

COMPETITORS

BASF Catalysts
Johnson Matthey
Mitsubishi Materials
Mitsui Mining and Smelting
OM Group
Recylex
Sumitomo Metal Mining
Teck

HISTORICAL FINANCIALS

Company Type: Public

Income Statement FYE: December 31

	REVENUE ($ mil.)	NET INCOME ($ mil.)	NET PROFIT MARGIN	EMPLOYEES
12/12	16,621	307	1.9%	14,438
12/11	18,804	420	2.2%	14,572
12/10	13,044	332	2.6%	14,386
12/09	10,099	106	1.1%	13,720
12/08	12,960	170	1.3%	15,447
Annual Growth	6.4%	16.0%	—	(1.7%)

2012 Year-End Financials

Debt ratio: 12.7%	No. of shares (mil.): 111
Return on equity: 13.6%	Dividends
Cash ($ mil.): 173	Yield: 1.9%
Current ratio: 1.52	Payout: 48.0%
Long-term debt ($ mil.): 3	Market value ($ mil.): 6,193

	STOCK PRICE ($) FY Close	P/E High/Low	PER SHARE ($) Earnings	Dividends	Book Value
12/12	55.35	48 32	2.74	1.42	20.64
12/11	39.75	38 21	3.69	1.29	19.47
12/10	52.00	43 21	2.93	1.07	17.88
12/09	33.80	116 42	0.94	0.94	16.83
12/08	18.25	477 25	1.47	0.91	16.08
Annual Growth	32.0%	— —	16.9%	11.8%	6.4%

Unicredito S.p.A. Roma

Let's give credit where credit is due: UniCredit (formerly UniCredito Italiano) is a giant among Europe's banking giants. The financial services group and its units operate in some 22 European countries with more than 9600 branches in about 50 markets. The company is also the largest foreign bank in Central and Eastern Europe (CEE) with roughly 4000 branches and units. UniCredit is organized into several divisions including retail banking (targeting families and small to midsized businesses) corporate and investment banking private banking and CEE. UniCredit's retail banking operations are led by its bank of the same name in Italy UniCredit Bank in Germany UniCredit Bank Austria and Bank Pekao in Poland.

UniCredit is the product of the merger of nine of Italy's largest banks and the subsequent combination with Germany's HVB Group and Italy's Capitalia. Former CEO Alessandro Profumo ushered in a series of mergers and acquisitions that helped push the company from being a purely domestic player into one of Europe's leading banking groups with a growing international presence. He oversaw the $18 billion acquisition of HVB and Bank Austria in 2005 (one of the largest cross-border banking deals ever seen in Europe) and the nearly $30 billion purchase of Italian bank Capitalia in 2007. The HVB acquisition made UniCredit a powerhouse in Germany and Austria and brought the company sizeable holdings in Central and Eastern Europe while the Capitalia acquisition strengthened its position at home.

After several years of expansion UniCredit was one of the harder-hit banks in the financial crisis as loan losses soared in its newer markets. The company coped with trying to recover from an 85% decline in share prices in 2009. It spent fiscal year 2010 restructuring its business: it expanded its leadership model by establishing a country chairman to oversee financial activities and operations in some of its markets; it merged seven subsidiaries including its former main Italian bank entity UniCredit Banca to simplify its corporate structure in Italy; it consolidated and rebranded its distribution networks; and it worked to divest certain noncore assets such as its Pioneer Global asset management unit and its MedioCredito Centrale public financing unit.

Also in 2010 Profumo resigned as CEO. Not only had he lost favor for his aggressive and risky expansion into Eastern Europe but he was also called to task for his role in Libya's acquisition of a 7.6% stake in UniCredit. (That development brought much-needed capital but made investors nervous about outside ownership and influence.) Deputy CEO Federico Ghizzoni a longtime veteran of the bank was named Profumo's successor.

HISTORY

UniCredito Italiano's ancestor Banca di Genova was formed in 1870 just after Italy unified. Within a year the bank was in a South American banking venture Banco de Italia y Rio de la Plata. A banking crisis beginning in the late 1880s threatened the company which was saved and reorganized with the aid of German banking interests. The changes gave the bank –which was renamed Credito Italiano –an advantage over home-grown rivals and pointed it in the direction of German-style universal banking including making direct investments in Italy's late-blooming industrial sector.

In the early 20th century Credito Italiano joined other banks in foreign ventures in Albania Brazil and China and opened offices in London and New York.

After the 1929 crash Credito Italiano acquired several failed banks. But Credito Italiano itself was none too healthy: Government attempts in the 1920s to peg the lira to the pound led to industrial stagnation leaving the bank holding highly illiquid industrial investments and by the early 1930s it was essentially an industrial holding company.

Credito Italiano's existence was threatened when the Depression hit in earnest. To save the bank and its peers Mussolini established the Istituto per la Ricostruzione Industriale (IRI) in 1933 as a "temporary" Resolution Trust-style holding company (IRI was finally liquidated in 2000) to take over the industrial assets of Credito Italiano and several other banks. IRI was instantly a major shareholder in Credito Italiano. IRI-held banks were designated "banks of national interest" three years later and were allowed to provide only short-term commercial banking services a limit that remained in effect for more than 50 years.

In 1946 to fill the need for long-term industrial credit to rebuild war-torn Italy Credito Italiano joined with Banca Commerciale Italiana (now part of IntesaBci) and Banco di Roma to form Mediobanca.

Credito Italiano went public in 1969 (IRI sold its interest in the bank in 1993). As a bank of national interest Credito Italiano was called upon to help bail out several of the country's industrial groups in 1979 (it did so reluctantly).

Changing laws allowed the company to expand its branch network in 1980 and in 1982 IRI allowed Credito Italiano to raise capital (although it was still obliged to prop up struggling state industries). But the 1987 US stock market crash caused Credito Italiano's earnings to plunge 33%. Two years later it bought a stake in Banca Nazionale dell'Agricoltura then Italy's largest private bank.

In 1995 the company joined forces with Rolo Banca 1473 (named for the year its progenitor was founded) to form Credito Italiano Group. Two years later Alessandro Profumo became CEO. He would usher in more than a decade of rapid and agressive expansion.

Credito Italiano merged in 1998 with UniCredito a collection of several northern Italian banks. One Cassa di Risparmio di Verona Vicenza Belluno e Ancona (Cariverona) began in 1501 as a pawnshop operated by monks.

Foreshadowing the bank's shift to an Internet growth strategy (announced after talks with Spain's Banco Bilbao Vizcaya Argentaria fell through) UniCredito in 1999 announced plans for an electronic stock market to include after-hours trading. It also continued to boost holdings in Eastern European banks. In 2000 the company entered into securities brokerage and mutual fund administration with its purchase of US-based Pioneer Investment Management.

In 2001 UniCredito bought 10% of the Pirelli/Benetton-owned holding company formed to control Italian telecommunications company Olivetti. The following year the company partnered with Koc Holding to take a majority stake in Yapi Kredi.

The bank acquired HVB and Bank Austria in 2005 in an $18 billion cross-border deal one of the largest such deals ever seen in Europe. The bank strengthened its hold at home in 2007 with the nearly $30 billion purchase of Italian bank Capitalia. Antitrust authorities ordered UniCredit to sell its stake in Assicurazioni Generali following the Capitalia transaction.

EXECUTIVES

Chairman, Dieter Rampl, age 66
Vice Chairman, Fabrizio Palenzona, age 60
Vice Chairman, Vincenzo C. Buonaura, age 67
Deputy General Manager and Head Corporate and Investment Banking, Jean-Pierre Mustier, age 52
Vice Chairman, Farhat O. Bengdara, age 48
COO, Paolo Fiorentino, age 58
General Manager, Roberto Nicastro, age 49
CEO, Federico Ghizzoni, age 58
Vice Chairman of the Board, Candido Fois
CFO, Marina Natale
Secretary, Lorenzo Lampiano
General Counsel and Group Compliance Officer, Nadine Faruque, age 53
Head Group Human Resources, Paolo Cornetta
Head Group Investor Relations, Simone Concetti
Chief Risk Officer, Alessandro Decio
Investor Relations Officer, Andrea Pavoncello
Chairman of the Board, Giuseppe Vita
Vice Chairman of the Board, Luca Montezemolo
Head of Internal Audit, Ranieri Marchis
Director, Manfred Bischoff, age 71
Director, Piero Gnudi, age 75
Director, Luigi Maramotti, age 56
Director, Hans-Jurgen Schinzler, age 73
Director, Anthony B. Wyand, age 70
Vice Chairman, Fabrizio Palenzona, age 60
Vice Chairman, Vincenzo C. Buonaura, age 67
Director, Carlo Pesenti, age 50
Director, Friedrich Kadrnoska, age 62
Director, Antonio M. Marocco, age 79
Director, Enrico T. Cucchiani, age 63
Vice Chairman, Farhat O. Bengdara, age 48
Director, Donato Fontanesi, age 71
Director, Francesco Giacomin, age 62
Director, Franz Zwickl, age 60
Vice Chairman of the Board, Candido Fois
Deputy Vice Chairman, Luigi Castelletti, age 57
Director, Giovanni Belluzzi, age 68
Director, Marinna Li Calzi, age 63
Director, Lucrezia Reichlin, age 59
Director, Theodore Waigel, age 73
Independent Director, Alessandro Caltagirone
Chairman of the Board, Giuseppe Vita
Non-Executive Director, Helga Jung
Independent Director, Henryka Bochniarz
Independent Director, Lorenzo Bianchi
Non-Executive Independent Director, Marianna Calzi
Independent Director, Mohamed Fahim
Auditors: KPMGS.p.A.

LOCATIONS

HQ: Unicredito S.p.A. Roma
Piazza Cordus, Milano 20123
Phone: (39) 2 88 621 **Fax:** (39) 2 8862 3463
Web: www.unicreditgroup.eu

2011 Sales

	% of total
Europe	

Italy	38
Germany	17
Austria	9
Other	34
Asia	1
Americas	1
Total	**100**

PRODUCTS/OPERATIONS

2011 Sales

	% of total
Retail	48
Corporate & investment	28
Central & Eastern	18
Private	3
Asset	3
Total	**100**

COMPETITORS

ABN AMRO Group
Antonveneta
BNL bc
BNP Paribas
Banca Popolare di Milano
Banco Popolare
Credit Suisse
Deutsche Bank
Intesa Sanpaolo
UBS

HISTORICAL FINANCIALS

Company Type: Public

Income Statement

FYE: December 31

	ASSETS ($ mil.)	NET INCOME ($ mil.)	INCOME AS % OF ASSETS	EMPLOYEES
12/12	1,221,604	1,139	0.1%	162,864
12/11	1,198,730	(11,908)	—	167,014
12/10	1,244,000	1,771	0.1%	167,914
12/09	1,337,942	2,452	0.2%	170,017
12/08	1,461,860	5,608	0.4%	174,519
Annual Growth	(4.4%)	(32.9%)	—	(1.7%)

2012 Year-End Financials

Return on assets: 0.0%
Return on equity: 1.4%
Long-term debt ($ mil.): —
No. of shares (mil.): —
Sales ($ mil): 55,028
Dividends
Yield: —
Payout: —
Market value ($ mil.): —

	STOCK PRICE ($) FY Close	P/E High/Low		PER SHARE ($) Earnings	Dividends	Book Value
12/12	4.89	71	30	0.20	0.00	15.10
Annual Growth	—	—	—	—	—	—

Unilever N.V.

Unilever N.V. is the numero uno Unilever. It has joint custody of food and personal care products giant Unilever. Along with Unilever PLC the Netherlands-based firm operates Unilever as a joint venture. The three companies operate as the Unilever Group which has a single board of directors and one set of financial statements. Unilever holds the No. 1 spot in manufacturing dressings savory and spreads with brand names Hellmann's Knorr Wish-Bone and Ragu. Its other top products include ice cream (Breyers Ben & Jerry's) tea (Lipton) soaps (Dove Lux) and Sunsilk (hair care). The company holds a leading position in laundry detergents. Unilever also operates tea and oil plantations.

The company boasts a vast products portfolio. In 2008 13 of its brands logged $1 billion or more in revenue. These were Knorr Hellmann's Lipton Becel/Flora (Healthy Heart) Rama/Blue Band (Family Goodness) Wall's/Algida (Heartbrand) Omo Surf Dove Lux Rexona (including Sure and Degree) Axe/Lynx and Sunsilk (including Seda and Sedal).

Unilever's primarily a food maker that participates in other niches to diversify. It generated 54% of its 2008 sales from food items while home and personal care products brought in the remaining 46%. The manufacturer's savory dressings and spreads segment (35%) logged the most revenue in 2008 followed by personal care (28%) ice cream and beverages (19%) and home care (18%).

Building upon its non-food offerings the company agreed to acquire Sara Lee's body care products and European detergents business for about ?1.3 billion (nearly $2 million) in cash. The deal which includes the Sanex Radox and Duschdas brands is subject to regulatory approval by the European Commission which is expected to rule on transaction by October 2010. The brands earned Sara Lee about ?750 million ($1 billion) in revenue in 2009. Unilever looks poised to expand the market of its new goods in developing countries where Sara Lee cultivated about 15% of personal care product sales.

During the past few years Unilever has felt intense heat on the competitor front despite its leader status in the consumer products arena for many years. When The Procter & Gamble Company (P&G) acquired The Gillette Company –overnight making P&G the largest consumer products maker in the world ahead of Unilever –Unilever launched a restructuring. The company also made sweeping changes to its leadership organization and abandoned its dual chairman/CEO structure that had been in place for decades. Antony Burgmans chairman stepped down and was replaced by Ericsson chairman Michael Treschow in 2007. Patrick Cescau the company's CEO retired at the end of 2008 and was replaced by Paul Polman an executive at Nestle USA who strategically had logged 26 years of experience at P&G.

To compete with rival P&G and climb back on top Unilever in mid-2007 implemented a four-year plan that involved slashing some 20000 jobs (or a tenth of its workforce) and selling off slow-growth businesses. Its job cuts were to be focused on Europe.

As part of its strategy to dispose of non-strategic brands Unilever is clearing its pantry. The company sold its Boursin cheese-making business in early 2008. In August 2008 Unilever sold its Lawry's and Adolph's seasoning brands to McCormick & Company for about $604 million in cash. It sold off of its North American laundry business which includes the All Wisk Sunlight Surf and Snuggle brands to private-equity firm Vestar Capital Partners in September 2008 in return for about $1.45 billion in cash and preferred stock in Sun Products (a new company formed by the integration of the Unilever laundry business and Vestar's Huish Detergents). Unilever made the move to focus on its laundry business in Europe Asia Africa and Latin America. The transaction includes the fabric-cleaning brands as well as Unilever's manufacturing plant in Baltimore. Unilever also sold its Bertolli olive oil and vinegar business to SOS Group for some $1 billion in December 2008. The deal is structured as a perpetual brand license by Unilever. The firm retained the Bertolli brand for other foods such as pasta and frozen meals until mid-2012 when it sold the brand (alongside its P.F. Chang's frozen food business) to ConAgra for $267 million.

Additionally in some cases Unilever has rewritten its expansion plans into certain countries. Despite efforts to expand its reach into the European chilled-products market in recent years Unilever announced in 2007 that due to stalled growth it planned to divest its European frozen foods unit while retaining its similar business in Italy. Its decision to keep a foothold in Italy is due in part a need to maintain a presence in the country to promote future trade relations there. Unilever also sold its Spanish frozen foods business to Bonduelle for several million euros in 2006 and sold the majority of its Western European frozen foods business to private-equity firm Permira for more than $2.2 billion. (The transaction included the Iglo and Birds Eye brands in Austria Belgium France Germany Greece Ireland the Netherlands Portugal and the UK.)

The company has earlier purged a handful of hair care brands signaling that it's not very interested in maintaining a portfolio rich in the hair care niche. Unilever sold its Finesse and Aqua Net brands in 2006 for some $130 million. (The two brands had generated more than $85 million in 2005 for Unilever which retained the Aqua Net brand in Mexico.) Lornamead picked up the two hair care products to breath new life into the "heritage" brands through rebranding and increased marketing. The company also sold its Unilever Cosmetics International business to Coty in 2005 for some $800 million.

Shares of Unilever N.V. trade in France Germany the Netherlands Switzerland the UK and the US. Unilever N.V. has an 85% stake in Unilever Indonesia.

EXECUTIVES

Chairman, Michael Treschow, age 70
Non-Executive Vice-Chairman of the Board and Senior Independent Director, Kornelis J. (Kees) Storm, age 71
Chief Operating Officer, Harish Manwani, age 61
Chief Human Resources Officer, Douglas A. (Doug) Baillie, age 58
CEO and Director, Paul Polman, age 56, $1,456,014 total compensation
Chief Marketing and Communication Officer, Keith Weed, age 51
Chief Human Resources Officer, Sandy Ogg, age 59
President Americas, David (Dave) Lewis, age 48
Chief Auditor, Alan Johnson, age 59
Chief Research and Development Officer, Prof Genevieve B. Berger, age 58
Group Controller, Charles Nichols, age 53
Chief Supply Chain Officer, Pier Luigi Sigismondi, age 47
EVP Global Skin, Antoine De-Saint-Affrique
VP IT Services Europe, Paulo de Sa
VP Nutrition and Health, Gert Meijer
Global Corporate Communications Manager, Lucila Zambrano
Chief Legal Officer and Group Secretary, Tonia Lovell, age 44
Corporate Media Relations Manager, Flip Dotsch
President; North Asia, Alan Jope
President - Foods, Antoine Saint-Affrique
President; Europe, Jan Zijderveld
Chief Financial Officer; Executive Director, Jean-Marc Huet
President; North America, Kees Kruythoff
President - Refreshment, Kevin Havelock
Director, Paul S. Walsh, age 58
Director, Charles E. Golden, age 66
Director, Ann M. Fudge, age 61
Director, Byron E. Grote, age 64
Vice Chairman, Kornelis J. (Kees) Storm, age 70
Non-Executive Independent Director, Sir Malcolm L. Rifkind, age 66
CEO and Director, Paul Polman, age 56
Director, T. Hixonia Nyasulu, age 59

CFO and Director, Jean-Marc Huet, age 43
Director, Louise O. Fresco, age 62
Director, Sunil Bharti Mittal, age 56
Non-Executive Independent Director, Sunil Mittal
Auditors: PricewaterhouseCoopersN.V.

LOCATIONS

HQ: Unilever N.V.
Weena 455, Rotterdam 3013 AL
Phone: (31) 10 217 4000 **Fax:** (31) 10 217 4798
Web: www.unilever.com

2010 Sales

	% of total
Asia Africa & Central & Eastern	40
The	33
Western	27
Total	**100**

PRODUCTS/OPERATIONS

2010 Sales

	% of total
Savory dressings &	32
Personal	31
Ice cream &	19
Home care &	18
Total	**100**

COMPETITORS

Alticor
Atkins Nutritionals
Avon
Beiersdorf
Boulder Brands
Campbell Soup
Church & Dwight
Clorox
Coca-Cola
Colgate-Palmolive
ConAgra
Dairy Farmers of America
Danone
Del Monte Foods
Estee Lauder
General Mills
Henkel
Johnson & Johnson
Kao
L' Oreal
LVMH
Mars Incorporated
McBride plc
Meda Pharmaceuticals
Mondelez International
Nestle
Procter & Gamble
R.C. Bigelow
Reckitt Benckiser
Republic of Tea
Revlon
S.C. Johnson
Shiseido
Tata Global Beverages
The Dial Corporation
Uniq

HISTORICAL FINANCIALS

Company Type: Public

Income Statement

FYE: December 31

	REVENUE ($ mil.)	NET INCOME ($ mil.)	NET PROFIT MARGIN	EMPLOYEES
12/12	67,647	5,904	8.7%	172,000
12/11	60,102	5,499	9.2%	169,000
12/10	59,239	5,680	9.6%	165,000
12/09	57,367	4,854	8.5%	168,000
12/08	56,654	7,028	12.4%	174,000
Annual Growth	4.5%	(4.3%)	—	(0.3%)

2012 Year-End Financials

Debt ratio: 29.1%
Return on equity: 30.3%
Cash ($ mil.): 3,248
Current ratio: 0.77
Long-term debt ($ mil.): 9,971
No. of shares (mil.): 1,706
Dividends
Yield: 3.2%
Payout: 60.4%
Market value ($ mil.): 65,366

	STOCK PRICE ($) FY Close	P/E High/Low		PER SHARE ($) Earnings	Dividends	Book Value
12/12	38.30	43	32	2.03	1.23	11.71
12/11	34.37	43	33	1.89	2.25	10.78
12/10	31.40	42	29	1.95	1.11	11.31
12/09	32.33	58	26	1.69	1.09	10.14
12/08	24.55	43	21	2.42	1.11	8.11
Annual Growth	11.8%	—	—	(4.3%)	2.6%	9.6%

Unilever Plc (United Kingdom)

It takes two parents –one Dutch and one British –to make one Unilever. Unilever N.V. and Unilever PLC together with their group companies constitute a global food personal care and household products powerhouse. The group's vast portfolio of consumer products includes a dozen global brands including Hellmann's (mayonnaise) Knorr (soups) Lipton (tea) and Dove and Lux (soaps) that each ring up more than ?1 billion ($1.4 billion) in sales. Unilever's consumer goods are sold in more than 190 countries. The company was the world's #1 consumer products maker until Procter & Gamble purchased Gillette in 2005. Based in England Unilever PLC trades on the London and New York stock exchanges.

Unilever acquired salon hair care products maker TIGI in 2009. The more than $410 million purchase which includes the firm's hair styling academies adds the Bed Head Catwalk and S-factor brands among others to Unilever's hair care products offering. TIGI remains headquartered in Dallas and operates as a stand-alone global business unit within Unilever.

The company has seen revenue gains in recent years despite rising commodity costs. Unilever points to several countries for its notable yet steady growth. These include Africa the Americas (including Brazil and Mexico) China Europe India and Russia. China Russia and Brazil are three of the company's biggest hair care markets in the world.

CEO Patrick Cescau retired at the end of 2008 and was replaced by Paul Polman an executive at Nestle USA who has some 25 years of experience at P&G.

EXECUTIVES

Chairman, Michael Treschow, age 70
President Asia Africa and Central & Eastern Europe, Harish Manwani, age 60
Group Controller and SVP Finance Categories, Howard Green
Innovation Project Leader Unilever Research Colworth UK, Shelagh Muir
Manager Product Design Global Research Center Vlaardingen Netherlands, Ingeborg van Heetvelde
Chief HR Officer, Douglas A. (Doug) Baillie, age 57
SVP Communications and Sustainability, Gavin Neath
Group VP; President Unilever U.S., Kevin Havelock, age 56
CEO and Director, Paul Polman, age 56
Chief Marketing and Communication Officer, Keith Weed, age 51
President Americas, David (Dave) Lewis, age 48
Managing Director and CEO Hindustan Unilever, Nitin Paranjpe, age 49
Group Secretary, Sven Dumoulin
VP Finance, Philip de Klerk
Chief Research and Development Officer, Prof Genevieve B. Berger, age 58
Brand Manager Domex Philippines, Patricia Niles
Director Customer Management Ghana, Cynthia Ifeagwu
Director Customer Development Argentina, Tomas Jans
Manager European Operations Kingston UK, Jane Mackie
Personal Assistant Jakarta Indonesia, Arif Hudaya
Manager Regional Management Development Home and Personal Care Categories Latin America Chile and South America, Katia Cuellar
Life sciences Colworth UK, Steve Colliver
Ice cream Colworth UK, Andrew Cox
Manager Research Unilever Research China Shanghai, David Liu
Beverages Colworth UK, Stella Peace
Director Customer and Channel Marketing Unilever Foodsolutions North America, Ted Skodol
Chief Supply Chain Officer, Pier Luigi Sigismondi, age 47
Chief Legal Officer and Secretary, Tonia Lovell, age 44
General Counsel, Steve Williams
Chief Auditor, Akhter Mateen
President; North Asia, Alan Alan Jope Jope
President - Foods, Antoine Antoine de Saint-Affrique Saint-Affrique
President; Europe, Jan Jan Zijderveld Zijderveld
Chief Financial Officer; Executive Director, Jean-Marc Jean-Marc Huet Huet
President; North America, Kees Kees Kruythoff Kruythoff
Chief Supply Chain Officer, Pier Sigismondi
Director, Paul S. Walsh, age 58
Director, Charles E. Golden, age 65
Director, Ann M. Fudge, age 61
Director, Byron E. Grote, age 64
Director, Kornelis J. (Kees) Storm, age 71
Non-Executive Independent Director, Sir Malcolm L. Rifkind, age 66
CEO and Director, Paul Polman, age 56
CFO and Director, Jean-Marc Huet, age 42
Director, Hixonia Nyalsulu, age 57
Director, Louise O. Fresco, age 61
Non-Executive Independent Director, Hixonia Hixonia Nyasulu Nyasulu
Non-Executive Independent Director, Sunil Sunil Mittal Mittal
Auditors: PricewaterhouseCoopersLLP

LOCATIONS

HQ: Unilever Plc (United Kingdom)
Unilever House, Blackfriars, London EC4Y 0DY
Phone: (44) 20 7822 5252 **Fax:** (44) 20 7822 6108
Web: www.unilever.com

PRODUCTS/OPERATIONS

Selected Global Brands

Axe/Lynx (male grooming)
Blue Band (margarine)
Dove (personal care)
Heartbrand ice creams
Hellmann's (mayonnaise)
Knorr (soup)
Lipton (tea)
Lux (soap)
Omo (detergent)
Rexona (deodorant)
Sunsilk (hair care)

COMPETITORS

Church & Dwight Canada
Premier Foods
Procter & Gamble

Henkel
Mondelez International
Nestle
R&R Ice Cream
Reckitt Benckiser

HISTORICAL FINANCIALS

Company Type: Public

Income Statement FYE: December 31

	REVENUE ($ mil.)	NET INCOME ($ mil.)	NET PROFIT MARGIN	EMPLOYEES
12/12	67,647	5,904	8.7%	172,000
12/11	60,102	5,499	9.2%	169,000
12/10	59,239	5,680	9.6%	165,000
12/09	57,367	4,854	8.5%	168,000
12/08	56,654	7,028	12.4%	174,000
Annual Growth	4.5%	(4.3%)	—	(0.3%)

2012 Year-End Financials

Debt ratio: 29.1%
Return on equity: 30.3%
Cash ($ mil.): 3,248
Current ratio: 0.77
Long-term debt ($ mil.): 9,971
No. of shares (mil.): 1,283
Dividends
Yield: 3.1%
Payout: 102.1%
Market value ($ mil.): 49,696

	STOCK PRICE ($) FY Close	P/E High	P/E Low	PER SHARE ($) Earnings	Dividends	Book Value
12/12	38.72	44	32	2.03	1.23	15.57
12/11	33.52	43	33	1.89	2.25	14.11
12/10	30.88	41	28	1.95	1.11	14.80
12/09	31.90	55	26	1.69	1.00	13.27
12/08	23.02	44	20	2.42	0.99	10.62
Annual Growth	13.9%	—	—	(4.3%)	5.5%	10.0%

Unione Di Banche Italiane S.c.p.a.

Unione di Banche Italiane combines several banks under one organization. Known as UBI Banca it serves individuals and businesses through nine subsidiary banks with some 2000 branches in Italy (concentrated in the Lombardy region) and offices in about a dozen other countries in Europe Asia and South America. The banks offer such standard deposit products as savings and checking accounts and CDs. They also provide asset management leasing operations private banking insurance corporate banking and mortgage and other types of lending. The group was formed in 2007 when Banche Popolari Unite acquired rival Banca Lombarda e Piemontese and changed its name to UBI Banca.

EXECUTIVES

Chairman Management Board, Emilio Zanetti, age 82
Deputy Chairman Supervisory Board, Alberto Folonari, age 76
General Manager, Riccardo Sora, age 63
Joint General Manager and Head Human Resources and Organization, Graziano Caldiani, age 63
Chief Executive Officer, Victor Massiah, age 55
General Manager UBI Banca Group, Francesco Iorio, age 45
Deputy General Manager and Operational Chairman UBI Sistemi and Servizi, Pierangelo Rigamonti
Head Investor Relations, Laura Ferraris
Senior Deputy Chairman Supervisory Board, Giuseppe Calvi, age 82
Deputy Chairman Supervisory Board, Mario Mazzoleni, age 70
Chairman Supervisory Board, Andrea Moltrasio, age 58
Deputy Chairman Management Board, Flavio Pizzini, age 58
Deputy General Manager Chief of Business, Rossella Leidi
Deputy General Manager and Head Credit and Credit Recovery, Giovanni Lupinacci
Deputy General Manager and Chief of General Affairs and Subsidiaries, Ettore Medda
Senior Deputy General Manager Chief Operating Officer, Elvio Sonnino
Senior Deputy Chairman, Mario Cera
Director, Carlo Garavaglia
Director, Pietro Gussalli Beretta, age 51
Director, Giovanni Bazoli, age 81
Deputy Chairman Supervisory Board, Alberto Folonari, age 75
Director, Mario G. Cattaneo, age 82
Director, Italo Lucchini
Director, Giuseppe Lucchini
Director, Alessandro (Att) Pedersoli, age 84
Senior Deputy Chairman Supervisory Board, Giuseppe Calvi, age 82
Director, Enio Fontana
Director, Giorgio Perolari
Director, Sergio Orlandi
Deputy Chairman Supervisory Board, Mario Mazzoleni, age 70
Director, Salvatore Toti Musumeci
Director, Roberto Sestini
Director, Sergio Pivato
Director, Federico Manzoni
Director, Virginio Fidanza
Director, Luigi Bellini
Director, Battista Albertani
Auditors: KPMGS.p.A.

LOCATIONS

HQ: Unione Di Banche Italiane S.c.p.a.
Piazza Vittorio Veneto 8, Bergamo 24122
Phone: (39) 035 392111
Web: www.ubibanca.it

PRODUCTS/OPERATIONS

Selected Subsidiaries

Aviva Assicurazioni Vita Spa (49.9%)
Banco di San Giorgio Spa (93%)
Banca Populare Commercio e Industria Spa (84%)
Banca Populare di Bergamo Spa
Banca Regionale Europea Spa (60%)
Capitalgest Alternative Investments SGR Spa
Centrobanca Spa (98%)
FinanzAttiva Servizi Srl
IW Bank Spa (80%)
Mercato Impresa Spa (99%)
Prestitalia Spa (23%)
S.B.I.M. Spa
UBI Assicurazioni Spa
UBI Banca Private Investment Spa
UBI Gestioni Fiduciarie Sim Spa
UBI Leasing Spa (99%)
UBI Pramerica SGR Spa (65%)

COMPETITORS

Antonveneta
BNL bc
BPER-Emilia Romagna
Banca Carige
Banca Popolare di Milano
Banco Popolare
HSBC
Intesa Sanpaolo
Monte dei Paschi di Siena
UniCredit

HISTORICAL FINANCIALS

Company Type: Public

Income Statement FYE: December 31

	ASSETS ($ mil.)	NET INCOME ($ mil.)	INCOME AS % OF ASSETS	EMPLOYEES
12/12	174,554	109	0.1%	19,114
12/11	167,894	(2,381)	—	19,405
12/10	174,735	230	0.1%	19,699
12/09	176,200	389	0.2%	20,285
12/08	170,505	96	0.1%	20,680
Annual Growth	0.6%	3.1%	—	(1.9%)

2012 Year-End Financials

Return on assets: 0.0%
Return on equity: 0.8%
Long-term debt ($ mil.): —
No. of shares (mil.): 900
Sales ($ mil): 7,415
Dividends
Yield: —
Payout: —
Market value ($ mil.): —

United Overseas Bank Ltd. (Singapore)

One of Singapore's top financial institutions United Overseas Bank (UOB) provides a range of commercial banking and personal financial services. Offerings include checking and savings accounts loans investment banking commodities trading and finance private banking and investments such as unit trusts which are similar to mutual funds; the bank also has issued more than 1.5 million credit cards making it one of the largest issuers in the Asia-Pacific region. UOB and its subsidiaries including Far Eastern Bank in Singapore and UOB Buana in Indonesia operate more than 500 offices including locations in more than a dozen additional nations in Asia Australia Western Europe and North America.

UOB is targeting Asia for growth. The company opened its first offices in China and India in 2008 and 2009 and acquired interests in China-based Evergrowing Bank and The Southern Commercial Joint Stock Bank. UOB also bought the physical assets of HSBC's Asian wholesale banknotes business which arranges the distribution of banknotes to central banking institutions and banks. The company has also been building its wealth management operations.

In 2010 UOB inked a deal to sell its life insurance unit to UK-based Prudential. As part of the deal UOB's branches in Singapore Indonesia and Thailand will sell Prudential's life and health insurance policies and products for 12 years. Gains from the sale helped boost UOB's results that year along with increases in earnings from investments lending and credit cards.

Entities associated with Citibank and DBS Group each own more than 15% of UOB.

EXECUTIVES

Chairman, Cho Yaw Wee, age 84
Head Group Retail, Francis Chin Yong Lee
Head Commercial Banking, Eng Cheong Yeo
Head Group Global Markets and Investment Management, Terence Sea Eng Ong
Head Corporate Banking, Joo Yeow Wee
Head Group Institutional Financial Services, Kie Cheong Chong

CFO and Head Group Corporate Services, Wai Fai Lee
Head Personal Financial Services, Eddie Boo Jin Khoo
Head Investment Banking, Tong Poh Tay
Head Risk Management, Ming Soong Tham
Head Group Compliance, Mei Lee Chew
Senior Vice President Group Audit, Victor Ngo
Executive Vice President Human Resources, Jenny Mei Leng Wong
Chief Executive Officer, Chan Seong
Executive Vice President Information Technology, Hwee Susan
Chief Financial Officer, Lee Fai
Executive Vice President Investment Banking, Tay Poh
Executive Vice President Risk Management, Tham Soong
Executive Vice President Corporate Banking, Wee Yeow
Deputy Chairman and CEO, Wee Ee Cheong, age 59
Director, Reggie Thein, age 72
Director, Tong Dow Ngiam, age 75
Director, Cham Tao Soon, age 73
Director, Philip Liat Kok Yeo, age 65
Director, Meng Meng Wong, age 64
Director, Pin Lim, age 76
Auditors: Ernst&YoungLLP

LOCATIONS

HQ: United Overseas Bank Ltd. (Singapore)
80 Raffles Place, UOB Plaza, 048624
Phone: (65) 6533 9898 **Fax:** (65) 6534 2334
Web: www.uobgroup.com

PRODUCTS/OPERATIONS

2010 Sales

	% of total
Interest	69
Noninterest	
Fees &	16
Rental	2
Dividends	1
Other	12
Total	**100**

COMPETITORS

Bangkok Bank
Bank of China
DBS Group Holdings
Edaran Otomobil
HSBC
Hang Seng Bank
Hong Leong Finance
Maybank
OCBC Bank
Standard Chartered

HISTORICAL FINANCIALS

Company Type: Public

Income Statement FYE: December 31

	ASSETS ($ mil.)	NET INCOME ($ mil.)	INCOME AS % OF ASSETS	EMPLOYEES
12/12	206,769	2,291	1.1%	0
12/11	182,320	1,790	1.0%	0
12/10	166,717	2,102	1.3%	0
12/09	132,402	1,356	1.0%	0
12/08	126,699	1,341	1.1%	0
Annual Growth	13.0%	14.3%	—	—

2012 Year-End Financials

Return on assets: 1.1%
Return on equity: 11.6%
Long-term debt ($ mil.): —
No. of shares (mil.): 1,574
Sales ($ mil): 7,249

Dividends
Yield: 2.9%
Payout: 44.7%
Market value ($ mil.): 51,731

	STOCK PRICE ($) FY Close	P/E High	P/E Low	PER SHARE ($) Earnings	Dividends	Book Value
12/12	32.85	13	9	1.40	0.95	13.02
12/11	23.56	16	9	1.09	0.71	11.23
12/10	28.36	10	8	1.32	0.84	10.86
12/09	27.94	13	4	0.85	0.83	8.99
12/08	18.00	13	5	0.86	0.94	7.16
Annual Growth	16.2%	—	—	13.0%	0.4%	16.1%

Vale S. A.

Vale has more than just one iron in the fire. Iron ore and pellets account for more than two-thirds of Vale's sales and the company accounts for a third of the world's ocean-shipped iron ore. Vale also mines for bauxite nickel kaolin and potash. Other products include steel copper and aluminum. It has holdings in hydroelectric power generation and in the rail and shipping businesses mainly to support its mining activities in Brazil. The company is the world's second-largest iron ore miner having grown dramatically with the 2006 acquisition of Vale Limited (formerly Vale Inco). To keep all of its materials coming out of the ground Vale maintains its exploration efforts in 24 countries around the world.

Vale's revenues almost doubled in 2010 growing more than 94% as a result of increased production and higher prices for its major products particularly metals including iron ore nickel and copper. Net income grew 223% for the year on the strength of higher sales volumes and profit on the sale of assets.

In early 2012 the company declared force majeure on a number of its iron ore sales contract after high rainfall in three Brazilian states curtailed Vale's operations. The company estimated a loss of 2 million metric tons in iron ore shipments.

In 2011 Vale agreed to buy out minority shareholders of its Vale Fertilizantes SA subsidiary in a $1.4 billion move to consolidate its fertilizer business. Vale sought to buy the 16% of Fertilizantes it did not already own. The subsidiary is a small part of Vale's overall fertilizer business which the company had planned to spin off in 2011 but canceled those plans when it proved to be more profitable than Vale had projected.

Vale spent much of 2010 acquiring fertilizer companies and forming ventures. Mitsui teamed up with US fertilizer company Mosaic in 2010 for a joint venture investing in a Vale phosphorus ore development project in Peru. Mitsui spent $275 million to acquire a 25% stake and voting rights in a Vale subsidiary while Mosaic holds a 24% stake. The project is located in northwestern Peru's Piura province. Vale also completed a $4.7 billion deal for Brazil's Fosfertil and US-based agribusiness Bunge Co. to create Vale Fertilizantes.

Also in 2011 Vale announced plans to acquire South Africa-based copper and cobalt miner Metorex Ltd. for about $1.1 billion. However prior to the deal's close China's Jinchuan Group countered Vale's bid for Metrorex with a $1.34 billion offer. Vale subsequently dropped its offer refusing to engage in a bidding war.

In 2010 Vale sold its Brazilian aluminum operations to Norwegian aluminum producer Norsk Hydro for $5.7 billion. Norsk Hydro paid Vale a combination of cash and a 22% stake in Norsk Hydro. Vale said it divested Paragominas one of the world's largest bauxite mines because it did not see enough growth potential in the operation.

Remaining active in the mining sector Vale is developing a copper mine in Zambia in a $400 million joint venture with African Rainbow Minerals. The Konkola North project is expected to begin production in 2013. In 2010 Vale acquired a 51% stake in Guinea iron-ore mining firm BSG Resources for $2.5 billion. The acquisition expands Vale's presence in Africa where it is also developing the Moatize coal deposit in Mozambique in a $6 billion joint venture with South Korean steelmaker POSCO.

In 2011 Vale resumed work on a $6.2 billion steelworks operation in Espirito Santo in southeast Brazil. The project part of a network of five mills planned around the country was dropped in 2009 after local authorities refused to issue an environmental permit. Now with permit in hand Vale is going forward with the redesigned project which is expected to produce about 5 million tons of slab steel a year beginning in 2014. Vale which had originally partnered with China's Baosteel Group is seeking another partner for the project.

To complement its rail port and shipping facilities Vale created a new logistics company for cargo transport in 2011. Vale Logistics Integrada will handle the company's general cargo assets including its operations for moving iron ore and other minerals from its mines to its customers. The company received $1.5 billion in sales from logistics services in 2010 primarily from the shipping of agricultural and steel products fuel and construction materials.

Murilo Pinto de Oliveira Ferreira was named president and CEO of Vale in 2011. He succeeds Roger Agnelli who completed his 10-year term in the position. Ferreira was previously the CEO of Vale Canada and Executive Director of Vale's Nickel and Base Metals Sales.

Investment group Valepar controls a third of Vale. The Brazilian government holds limited veto power on any permanent company changes.

HISTORY

During the 1890s as land reforms opened the way for foreign investments in Brazil the mineral-rich state of Minas Gerais caught the attention of mining companies from Europe and the US. British engineers founded the Itabira Iron Ore Company and took over the Doce River Valley's Vitoria-Minas Railroad. After Brazil's revolution (1930) Itabira was split up. One of the new companies Itabira Minerac?o began shipping iron ore in 1940.

A 1942 agreement prompted by the outbreak of WWII established iron export regulations from Brazil to the US and the UK. Later that year the Companhia Vale do Rio Doce (CVRD) was formed with the Brazilian government owning 80%. The new company received the assets of Itabira including Brazil's "iron mountain" Caue Peak. By the end of the 1940s 80% of Brazil's iron ore exports were mined by CVRD. During the 1950s CVRD invested in land holdings and shipping operations. The company set up a shipping and logistics subsidiary in 1962.

CVRD teamed up with US Steel in 1970 to mine iron ore at Carajas in Amazonian Brazil; two years later the site was found to hold the world's largest iron ore reserves (18 billion tons). By 1975 CVRD had become the world's largest iron ore exporter. A year later the company finished doubling the tracks of the Vitoria-Minas Railroad. It also set up a manganese mining company (Urucum Minerac?o) and an alumina production facility (Alumina do Norte do Brasil or Alunorte).

To support its Carajas mining operations CVRD added the Estrada de Ferro de Carajas railway (finished 1985) and a hydroelectric project. In all the giant Carajas project involved investments from the US Japan France the European Economic Community and the World Bank. (The Carajas area like many mining sites in Brazil has been the site of intense controversy because it attracts subsistence miners including children who work under dangerous circumstances.) By the late 1980s the company had become a major supplier of pelletized iron used as feed for steel mill blast furnaces.

In 1992 CVRD expanded into the production of chemicals (Rio Capim Quimica now Para Pigmentos SA). The company acquired stakes in two steel mills —Siderurgica de Tubar?o and Aco Minas Gerais SA —in 1993. In 1996 it invested in gold finds in Para state. CVRD was privatized in 1997 and the next year set the sales record for a private Brazilian company.

The company listed ADR shares on the NYSE in 2000. Acquisitions that year included Brazilian iron ore companies SOCOIMEX and SAMITRI (73%). CVRD sold its 50% stake in pulp and paper group Bahia Sul to Suzano for $320 million in 2001. It also sold its 51% share of pulp maker Cenibra and its share of steelmaker Companhia Siderurgica Nacional (CSN).

In 2002 the Brazilian Treasury and the National Social and Economic Bank (BNDES) sold 33% of CVRD's shares further privatizing the company. CVRD disposed of its last gold mine (Fazenda Brasileiro) in 2003. It also exited the dry bulk-shipping business that year.

Under pressure from increasing globalization Vale had been forced to trim some of its operations (including its stake in CSN) to focus on mining and bulk transport. Those asset sales helped fund Vale's win over Australian mining giant BHP Billiton the world's #2 iron ore producer in a battle for Brazil's iron miner Caemi Minerac?o e Metalurgia #4 worldwide. (From 2001 through 2006 the company picked up stakes in Caemi until it owned it fully.) The deal for Inco trumped offers from Canadian miner Teck and US copper producer Phelps Dodge.

Toward the end of 2007 the company —then called Companhia Vale do Rio Doce —decided that it wanted a new brand identity and so ditched its longtime nickname CVRD in favor of Vale. Two years later it changed its name legally dropping the more formal Companhia Vale do Rio Doce.

EXECUTIVES

Executive Officer Human Resources and Corporate Services, Carla Grasso, age 52
President and CEO, Roger Agnelli, age 54
Executive Officer Non-Ferrous Minerals and Basic Metals Operations; President and CEO Vale Inco, Tito Botelho Martins Jr., age 51
Vice Chairman, Mario da Silveira Teixeira Jr., age 68
Executive Officer Ferrous Minerals Marketing Sales and Strategy, Jose Carlos Martins, age 64
CFO, Guilherme Perboyre Cavalcanti
President Chief Executive Officer CEO, Murilo Pinto de Oliveira Ferreira
Executive Officer Integrated Operations Logistics Project Management and Sustainability, Eduardo de Salles Bartolomeo, age 50
Executive Officer Fertilizers, Mario Alves Barbosa Neto
Press Manager, Monica Ferreira
Media Contact National Press and Steel Mill, Marcos Henrique Almeida
Media Contact International, Fatima Cristina
Media Contact Research and Development Innovation and Technology, Murilo Fiuza
Media Contact Logistics Energy and Fertilizers, Renata Bellozi
Media Contact Financial Investor Relations and Human Resources, Patricia Malavez
Chairman of the Board, Dan Conrado
Member of the Board of Directors, Fuminobu Kawashima
Capital Projects Implementation Officer; Member of the Executive Board, Galib Chaim
Logistics and Mineral Research Officer; Member of the Executive Board, Humberto Freitas
Member of the Board of Directors, Jose Cunha
Chief Finan.; Investor Rel.; Supplies and Shared Services Officer; Member of the Exec. Board, Luciano Pires
Vice Chairman of the Board, Mario Teixeira
Member of the Board of Directors, Nelson Barbosa
Member of the Board of Directors, Paulo Souza
Member of the Board of Directors, Renato Gomes
Member of the Board of Directors, Robson Rocha
Human Resources; Health & Safety; Sustainability & Energy Officer; Member of the Executive Board, Vania Somavilla
Director, Renato da Cruz Gomes, age 61
Director, Oscar Augusto de Camargo Filho, age 76
Vice Chairman, Mario da Silveira Teixeira Jr., age 68
Director, Ken Abe, age 64
Director, Eduardo Fernando Jardim Pinto, age 49
Director, Jorge Luiz Pacheco, age 59
Director, Jose Ricardo Sasseron, age 57
Director, Sandro Kohler Marcondes, age 50
Director, Luciano Galv?o Coutinho, age 67
Auditors: PricewaterhouseCoopersAuditoresIndependentes

LOCATIONS

HQ: Vale S. A.
Av. Graca Aranha 26, 18 Andar, Centro, Rio de Janeiro, RJ 20030-900
Phone: (55) 21 3814 4477 **Fax:** (55) 21 3814 9935
Web: www.cvrd.com.br

2010 Sales

	$ mil.	% of total
Asia	24,791	53
South America	8,960	19
Europe	8,912	19
North America	2,028	5
Other	1,790	4
Adjustments	(1188)	-
Total	**45,293**	**100**

PRODUCTS/OPERATIONS

2010 Sales

Ores & minerals	39,422	85
Aluminum	2,554	5
Fertilizers	1,845	4
Other products	1,195	3
Adjustments	(1188)	-

COMPETITORS

AHMSA
Alcoa
Anglo American
BHP Billiton
BHP Billiton Plc
Cliffs Natural Resources
Exxaro
Freeport-McMoRan
Kumba Iron Ore
Norilsk Nickel
Rio Tinto Limited
Rio Tinto plc
Teck
Xstrata

HISTORICAL FINANCIALS

Company Type: Public

Income Statement

FYE: December 31

	REVENUE ($ mil.)	NET INCOME ($ mil.)	NET PROFIT MARGIN	EMPLOYEES
12/12	47,694	5,511	11.6%	70,785
12/11	58,990	22,885	38.8%	79,646
12/10	45,293	17,264	38.1%	70,785
12/09	23,311	5,349	22.9%	60,036
12/08	37,426	13,218	35.3%	39,525
Annual Growth	6.2%	(19.6%)	—	15.7%

2012 Year-End Financials

Debt ratio: 24.3%	No. of shares (mil.): —
Return on equity: 7.2%	Dividends
Cash ($ mil.): 5,832	Yield: 3.7%
Current ratio: 1.82	Payout: 92.9%
Long-term debt ($ mil.): 28,524	Market value ($ mil.): —

	STOCK PRICE ($) FY Close	P/E High/Low	PER SHARE ($) Earnings	Dividends	Book Value
12/12	20.96	25 15	1.07	0.99	14.41
12/11	21.45	9 5	4.33	1.56	15.25
12/10	34.57	11 7	3.23	0.45	13.24
12/09	29.03	30 12	0.97	0.45	10.92
12/08	12.11	17 3	2.58	0.47	8.16
Annual Growth	14.7%	— —	(19.8%)	20.4%	15.3%

Valeo S.A. (France)

Valeo hopes to live up to its name which in Latin means "I am doing well." The company is one of Europe's largest car parts suppliers making components for most global car makers. Valeo has reorganized from 10 component groups to four business groups: Comfort and Driving Assistance Systems (interior controls security systems); Powertrain Systems (engine and electrical systems transmissions); Thermal Systems (climate control compressors engine cooling); and Visibility Systems (lighting systems wiper systems). Valeo Service distributes products to the automotive aftermarket. Valeo has about 120 production sites in 27 countries; more than two-thirds of its sales come from Europe.

The worldwide economic recession hit auto parts makers particularly hard. As consumers cut spending on big-ticket items such as cars car makers with large unsold inventories slashed production and demand for parts plummeted. Unable to dodge the bullet for a second consecutive year Valeo posted a 13% drop in sales in 2009 from 2008 (its lowest level since 2005). The company managed to slightly narrow its losses in 2009 over 2008 however the negative results continued to reach beyond E153 million ($209 million). The decrease was driven in large part by the plunge in production of its core OEM customers primarily those located in Europe and North America. Its top five customers —Renault-Nissan Volkswagen Peugeot S.A. Ford and General Motors —account for close to two-thirds of sales.

Despite its lack luster performance Valeo has continued to spend on R&D. It is developing products identified as having strong growth potential particularly for CO2 emissions reduction that align with its business groups: driving assistance powertrain efficiency and comfort enhancement. Though not formally identified as an area of innovation the company also develops products for driver safety as part of its Visibility Systems business unit. All business groups are moving to introduce systems for hybrid and all-electric vehicles. A start-stop starter-alternator StARS touting reduced gas consumption and lower emissions went into volume production in 2010.

In the meantime Valeo is equally determined to refocus its business by shedding non-core activities. In mid-2010 the company sold its Telma speed controller business which makes electromagnetic retarders to the business' current management. Valeo sold its heavy-duty truck engine cooling division in 2008 to EQT a European private equity buyout firm. An electrical wiring unit Valeo Connecting Systems was also axed in 2007; the activity was sold to Germany's Leoni.

Geographically Valeo's footprint is widening in Asia (Japan China Thailand and India). The company in early 2011 inked a deal with Belgian investment group RHJ International and Nissan to buy up Japanese automotive supplier Niles. The acquisition valued at E320 million ($439 million) promises to strengthen both its geographic presence with regional car makers such as Nissan and its Comfort and Driving Assistance Systems business. Already Valeo has established plants in five major industry centers in China; Shanghai Wuhan Nanjing Guangzhou and Changchun support the company's local R&D facilities production plants and distribution center. In 2009 Valeo scooped up the remaining 40% stake in a compressor manufacturing joint venture based in Changchun. Renamed Valeo Compressor (Changchun) the operation produces compressors for markets across China and neighboring countries. Valeo also holds majority control in its FAW-Valeo Climate Control Systems joint venture that produces HVAC systems. In India the company deepened its footprint in 2010 by purchasing the stake held by its joint venture partner NK Minda Group in an electrical systems manufacturing business (established in 2008). The deal gives Valeo 100% ownership in the newly renamed Valeo Engine and Electrical Systems India. Valeo holds four other joint ventures in that country.

In early 2009 the French government invested E19 million (roughly $23 million) in Valeo taking an equity stake of about 8%. Chairman and CEO Thierry Morin then resigned citing strategic differences with the board. Board member Jacques Aschenbroich was named CEO to succeed him.

Morin's leave comes after 20 years with the company and eight years in the top posts. His proposed severance package of more than E3 million (about $3.7 million) stoked a political controversy in France over "golden parachute" benefits for executives of companies that received financial aid from the French government. Responding to the furor government officials opposed the severance payment which was voted down by shareholders at the 2009 annual meeting.

HISTORY

Englishman Herbert Frood drawing on a recollection of a carriage driver who jammed his shoe between the brake and wheel to hasten the carriage's arrest introduced an asbestos brake shoe for automobiles around 1910. The new product was an immediate hit and Frood sold the right to import (and later manufacture) his "Ferodo" linings to French businessman Eugene Buisson who founded Societe Anonyme Francaise du Ferodo in 1923. Over the years the company added clutches clutch linings and other parts to its product line.

In 1962 Ferodo acquired Sofica an automotive heating systems company. It then diversified into cooling systems and expanded into Italy Spain Asia and South America as the company followed its customers' international growth. Ferodo acquired several companies during the 1970s and its line of automotive parts soon included lighting systems electronics and transmissions. In 1980 the company changed its name to Valeo. Around the same time the company began diversifying into non-automotive businesses including construction steel and industrial equipment. Valeo lost money from 1984-86.

Carlo De Benedetti's Cerus gained a 19% stake (later increased to about 27%) in Valeo in 1986. The next year Benedetti tapped Noel Goutard (lured from Thomson) to replace CEO Andre Buisson. Goutard's first order of business was unloading Valeo's non-automotive interests. He also reduced costs by cutting the workforce by 25% and by slashing the number of its suppliers in half. Although Goutard cut the payroll he didn't do so at the expense of research and development; in a three-year span in the early 1990s he hired nearly 2000 engineers. The company routinely spent 6% of sales on R&D.

Meanwhile Goutard began a program of aggressive international growth. Undaunted by European recession in the early 1990s –when the European car market suffered its worst contraction in 50 years –Valeo had 80 plants and research centers in 17 countries by 1994. Its US operations figured heavily in the growth spurt; in five years Valeo's US sales grew from $50 million to $500 million. Other investments included the acquisition of German auto electronics company Borg Instruments (1994) and the formation of five joint ventures in China by the end of 1995. Cerus which had blocked any moves to raise capital that would dilute its interest in the company sold its stake in Valeo in 1996.

Valeo spent about $1.7 billion in 1998 for ITT Automotive's electrical systems unit. The next year Goutard announced that he would retire at the end of 2000 after showing his successor Andre Navarri the ropes. Navarri who previously headed ALSTOM's $5 billion-a-year transport division succeeded him in 2000. However Navarri was forced out in 2001 by major shareholder CGIP after disagreements concerning the company's strategy. CFO Thierry Morin replaced Navarri as chairman of the management board and Goutard was reinstated to head Valeo's newly formed supervisory board.

In 2000 Valeo announced plans to cut 6000 jobs –about 12% of its workforce –and to invest heavily in Latin America and Eastern Europe. The same year it bought a 20% stake in Japanese carlighting maker Ichikoh Industries from Nissan. The company also bought the automotive business of Labinal.

Early in 2001 the company announced that it would cut about 1000 jobs in the US in response to a slowdown in the North American auto market. Not long afterward it was reported that Valeo was in talks regarding the sale of its electric motors business to Hong Kong-based Johnson Electric. Also in 2001 Valeo sold Filtrauto S.A. (automotive oil fuel and air filters) to Italian filter company SOGEFI. Then in response to the depressed global automotive market Valeo announced 12 European plant closures including sites in France Germany and Spain. Later in 2001 Valeo sold Valeo Transmission Limited UK to three of the company's managers in an MBO. As 2001 neared its close US subsidiary Valeo Electrical Systems Inc. filed for Chapter 11 bankruptcy; it emerged from Chapter 11 in 2002.

In 2005 Valeo bought the engine electronics business of Johnson Controls for about $437 million. The division made engine management systems and components and operated two plants in France. Also that year Valeo formed a joint venture with Iranian auto parts maker Armco.

After deciding its motors and actuators business was not complementary to its focus on comfort enhancement driving assistance and powertrain efficiency Valeo sold the business to Nidec of Japan for E165 million in 2006. Two years later the company sold its Shanghai-based automotive motor manufacturing subsidiary to Nidec.

EXECUTIVES

Chief Executive Officer, Jacques Aschenbroich, age 60
Chairman, Pascal Colombani, age 67
SVP Technical, Andre Gold
VP Financial Affairs and Strategic Operations, Vincent Marcel
SVP Valeo Service Activity, Robert de la Serve
VP Transmissions Product Family, Michael Schwenzer
VP Climate Control Product Family, Alain Marmugi
Chief Financial Officer, Robert Charvier
VP Quality, Kazuo Kawashima
Director Communications, Kate Philipps
VP Human Resources, Michel Boulain
VP Engine Cooling Product Family, Maurizio Martinelli
SVP Sales and Business Development, Hans-Peter Kunze
President Comfort and Driving Assistance Systems Business Group, Marc Vrecko
Member Supervisory Board, Erich Spitz
Member Supervisory Board, Behdad Alizadeh, age 52
Auditors: SalustroReydel

LOCATIONS

HQ: Valeo S.A. (France)
43, rue Bayen, Paris, Cedex 17 75848
Phone: (33) 1 40 55 20 20 **Fax:** (33) 1 40 55 21 71
Web: www.valeo.com

2009 Sales

	% of total
Europe &	65
Asia &	17
North	10
South	8
Total	**100**

PRODUCTS/OPERATIONS

2009 Sales

	% of total
Thermal	31
Powertrain	27
Visibility	25
Comfort & driving assistance	17
Total	**100**

Selected Business & Product Groups

Comfort & driving assistance systems
- Access mechanisms
- Driving assistance
- Interior controls
- Interior electronics

Powertrain systems
- Air management systems
- Electrical systems
- Engine management systems
- Hybrid & electric vehicle systems
- Transmission systems

Thermal systems
- Climate control
- Compressors
- Front-end modules
- Powertrain thermal systems

Visibility systems
- Lighting systems
- Wiper motors
- Wiper systems

COMPETITORS

Axsys
BorgWarner
Continental AG
DENSO
Daimler
Dana Holding
Delphi Automotive Systems
Eaton
Faurecia
Federal-Mogul
Honeywell International
ITT Corp.
Johnson Controls
Key Safety Systems
LEONI
LKQ
Lear Corp
Magna International
Magna Mirrors
Meritor
Modine Manufacturing
Robert Bosch
SPX
TRW Automotive
TT electronics
Visteon

HISTORICAL FINANCIALS

Company Type: Public

Income Statement FYE: December 31

	REVENUE ($ mil.)	NET INCOME ($ mil.)	NET PROFIT MARGIN	EMPLOYEES
12/12	15,498	500	3.2%	72,600
12/11	14,057	552	3.9%	68,000
12/10	12,891	488	3.8%	57,930
12/09	10,802	(220)	—	52,110
12/08	12,324	(289)	—	51,200
Annual Growth	5.9%	—	—	9.1%

2012 Year-End Financials

Debt ratio: 30.6%	No. of shares (mil.): 76
Return on equity: 19.0%	Dividends
Cash ($ mil.): 1,758	Yield: 3.4%
Current ratio: 1.10	Payout: 21.9%
Long-term debt ($ mil.): 2,061	Market value ($ mil.): 1,956

	STOCK PRICE ($) FY Close	P/E High	P/E Low	PER SHARE ($) Earnings	Dividends	Book Value
12/12	25.70	10	6	6.63	0.88	35.54
12/11	19.78	12	5	7.33	1.60	33.38
12/10	28.45	11	4	6.50	0.00	30.44
12/09	17.55	—	—	(2.94)	0.00	23.51
12/08	7.50	—	—	(3.82)	0.94	24.42
Annual Growth	36.1%	—	—	—	(1.8%)	9.8%

Veolia Environnement

Voila! Veolia Environnement holds water —as well as wastewater waste management energy and passenger transportation —operations. The company provides more than 100 million people with drinking water. One of the world's leading wastewater companies it serves more than 70 million people a year. It also provides waste management services managing some 60 million metric tons of waste and provides energy at 120000 facilities. Majority-owned energy unit Dalkia (Veolia Energy Services) operates global cogeneration facilities and heating and cooling systems. Joint venture Veolia Transdev (now up for sale) is a top European provider of bus light-rail and rail transport and operates in about 30 countries.

Veolia Environnement offers a broad range of utility services: supplying water and recycling wastewater; collecting and treating waste; supplying heat and cooled air; and optimizing industrial processes. It provides technical services to its municipal and industrial customers in the water services market. It is exiting its transportation activities.

Its principal operating subsidiaries and divisions are now Veolia Eau —Compagnie Generale des Eaux (Veolia Water) Veolia Proprete (Veolia Environmental Services) and Dalkia (Veolia Energy Services) which is 34%-owned by French electricity group Electricite de France (EDF). Veolia's electricity production comes from its cogeneration facilities (generating both electricity and heat).

Veolia Environnement's expertise includes securing water and wastewater management contracts from large cities and industrial companies. In waste management it focuses on treating and recycling hazardous waste and on large concession contracts in the UK. Through its Dalkia unit it manages large public networks and local energy cycles. It plans to concentrate on high added-value services and technologies to attain more profitable growth.

Calling 2011 its year of transition Veolia Environnement faced several setbacks due to the declining economy and operational problems in markets such as Southern Europe North Africa and the US. However that year its revenue increase 3% from the previous year reaching $38.4 billion (E29.6 billion) in 2011. The increase resulted from higher prices in recycled raw materials for its Environmental Services unit growth in its Water unit (primarily from Germany and Central and Eastern Europe) and higher prices in its Energy Services division.

After binging on acquisitions from 2006 to 2008 Veolia started slimming down its operations in 2012 to combat worsening economic conditions. In late 2011 it presented a strategy to restructure its portfolio and cut debt streamline its organization and reduce costs. Its plan for 2012-2013 called for generating $6.6 billion (E5 billion) from asset sales. As part of that plan in 2012 the company sold its US solid waste operations part of its Veolia Environmental Services North America unit to US investment firm Highstar Capital for $1.9 billion (E1.5 billion).

The company also is selling a majority stake in its UK regulated water businesses —Veolia Water Central Veolia Water East and Veolia Water Southeast —for $1.9 billion (E1.5 billion) to Infracapital Partners an investment fund managed by the European investment arm of Prudential plc (M&G) and Morgan Stanley Infrastructure Partners.

In addition Veolia wants to sell its stake in Veolia Transdev its transportation joint venture with French state bank Caisse des Depots et Consignations (CDC). Although Veolia placed its 50% stake in the company up for sale in late 2011 CDC balked at Veolia's turnaround plan the following June. Veolia may have to delay the sale until 2013.

The divestitures will enable Veolia to focus on commercial outsourcing which combines its expertise in water waste and energy. Proceeds will be used to reduce its net debt to $15.7 billion (E12 billion) by the end of 2013.

Veolia has a strong presence in the European Union North America and northern Asia and its strategy includes continued development in those regions. It has been negotiating asset sales in 22 countries with the goal of reducing its presence to fewer than 40 countries in 2013 (down from 77 in 2011). The company's Water division was in 69 countries including Belgium the Czech Republic France Germany Italy Romania Slovakia and the US at the end of 2011.

Veolia Environnement was formed from the water waste energy and transport businesses of the former Vivendi group. (The name Veolia is derived from Aeolus the keeper of the winds in Greek mythology). The group spun off Veolia Environnement (then called Vivendi Environnement) sold a minority stake to the public and renamed itself Vivendi Universal in 2000 (and Vivendi in 2006).

HISTORY

What is now Veolia Environnement originated in 1853 as Compagnie Generale des Eaux in Paris. The company irrigated farmlands and subsequently supplied water. By 1860 Paris had granted the company a 50-year contract to provide the city's water. In 1880 it moved beyond France to provide water in Venice Italy. Operations in Turkey (Istanbul) and Portugal (Oporto) followed.

Compagnie Generale des Eaux extended its water network in 1924 and by WWII it supplied half of all urban households in France. After the war the company expanded into household waste collection (1953) and operation of household waste incineration and compost plants (1967). Wastewater treatment activities began in 1972.

In the next decade Compagnie Generale des Eaux dove into diversification. It increased its holding in energy-conversion systems operator Compagnie Generale de Chauffe to 100% (making it France's leading energy company) in 1980. That year it merged its wastewater treatment subsidiaries to create Omnium de Traitement et de Valorisation (OTV). Its waste operations were further augmented through the takeover of Compagnie Generale d'Entreprises Automobiles (CGEA) a transport and waste management firm. The company also ventured into telecommunications pay-TV and construction (it gained a controlling stake in builder SGE in 1988 but disposed of its interest in the firm later known as VINCI in 2000).

CGEA bid for and won control of several former British Rail lines in 1996 when the UK's railway system was privatized. Operating under the name Connex the company began to run trains throughout southeastern England the UK's largest commuting area.

In 1998 CGEA changed its name to Vivendi. The group (which came to include mobile phone provider Cegetel and a stake in the Havas media company) transferred the Compagnie Generale des Eaux name to its water business. Vivendi also organized its Compagnie Generale de Chauffe and Sithe Energies (now a part of Dynergy) subsidiaries into a single energy division named Dalkia. In 1999 Sithe Energies bought 23 thermal power plants from US utility GPU (later FirstEnergy) and became the leading independent power producer in the northeastern US.

Vivendi continued its charge into the US that year. The group acquired waste services company Superior Services (then the US's fourth-biggest solid waste company). Its purchase of USFilter transformed Vivendi into the world's largest water company and marked the biggest acquisition of a US firm by a French company.

The ever-evolving Vivendi transformed into a global media company and renamed itself Vivendi Universal in 2000. It bought Seagram and French pay-TV provider CANAL+ and spun off its water waste management transportation and energy operations (Vivendi Environnement) after turning down German utility RWE's $28 million offer to buy the business.

Vivendi Environnement's waste operations grew after snapping up operations in Brazil Hong Kong and Mexico from Waste Management. In 2001 the company merged its Dalkia energy operations with the energy services operations of Electricite de France (EDF).

In 2002 Vivendi Universal reduced its stake in Vivendi Environnement from 63% to about 20%; the following year Vivendi Environnement changed its name to Veolia Environnement. Vivendi finally divested all of its interest in Veolia in the middle of 2006.

In 2007 the company acquired Thermal North America Inc. the largest portfolio of district heating and cooling networks in the US.

Late in 2009 the company named Antoine Frerot as CEO. He had been in charge of Veolia's water division previously.

To generate cash in 2010 Veolia Environnement sold US waste-to-energy contractor Montenay International (which held its North American waste-to-energy assets) to Covanta Holding for $450 million. Marking a push for more green energy projects in Europe that year the company opened France's largest biomass-fueled boiler plant serving a district heating system in Val d'Oise.

In 2011 Veolia Transport merged with Transdev to create the world's largest private-sector transportation business jointly owned by Veolia Environnement and Caisse des Depots. Although the joint venture announced plans to seek a public listing when market conditions permitted by the end of 2011 Veolia Environnement had decided to sell its half of the venture.

EXECUTIVES

Vice Chairman, Louis Schweitzer, age 71
COO and SEVP, Denis Gasquet, age 59
CEO VeoliaTransdev, Jerome Gallot, age 53
EVP Human Resources, Jean-Marie Lambert
EVP Water, Jean-Michel Herrewyn, age 52
EVP Energy, Franck LaCroix
EVP and CFO, Pierre-Francois Riolacci, age 46
EVP and Secretary General, Olivier Orsini
EVP Public Entities and European Affairs, Jean-Pierre Fremont
Chairman of the Board; Chief Executive Officer; Member of the Executive Committee, Antoine Antoine Frerot Frerot
Senior Executive Vice President; Secretary General; Member of the Executive Committee, Helman Helman le Pas de Secheval Secheval
Senior Executive Vice President - Environmental Services Division; Member of the Executive Committee, Jerome Jerome Le Conte Conte
Independent Director - Representative of Groupe Industriel Marcel Dassault, Olivier Olivier Costa de Beauregard Beauregard
Secretary of the Executive Committee, Sylvain Sylvain Boucher Boucher
Chief Operating Officer; Member of the Executive Committee, Francois Bertreau
Senior Executive Vice President; Secretary General; Member of the Executive Committee, Helman le Pas de Secheval
Chairman and Chief Executive Officer of Veolia Transdev; Member of the Executive Committee, Jean-Marc Janaillac
Senior Executive Vice President - Environmental Services Division; Member of the Executive Committee, Jerome Le Conte
Vice Chairman, Louis Schweitzer, age 70
Director, Paolo Scaroni, age 67
Director, Jean-Francois Dehecq, age 73
Director, Baudouin Prot, age 61
Director, Daniel Bouton, age 62
Director, Pierre-Andre de Chalendar, age 54
Director, Henri Proglio, age 64
Director, Georges Ralli, age 64
Director, Serge Michel, age 86
Director, Paul-Louis Girardot, age 79
Director, Esther Koplowitz, age 60
Director, Philippe Kourilsky, age 70
Director, Olivier Costa de Beauregard
Director, Thierry Dassault, age 56
Director, Mohd Alhamadi, age 50
Director - Representative of Caisse des depots et consignations, Olivier Olivier Mareuse Mareuse
Independent Director, Pierre-Andre Pierre-Andre de Chalendar Chalendar
Auditors: KPMGAudit

LOCATIONS

HQ: Veolia Environnement
36/38, avenue Kleber, Paris 75116
Phone: (33) 1 71 75 00 00
Web: www.veolia.com

2011 Sales

	% of total
Europe	
France	39
Germany	9
UK	9
Other	19
North	8
Asia	6
Oceania	3
Other	7
Total	**100**

PRODUCTS/OPERATIONS

2011 Sales

	% of total
Water	42
Environmental	33
Energy	25
Transportation —	
Total	**100**

Selected Operations

Selected Operations

Water
Veolia Eau - Compagnie Generale des Eaux
Veolia Water S.A.
Environmental Services
Veolia Environmental Services North America Corp.
Energy
Dalkia (66%)
Transport
Veolia Transdev (50%)

COMPETITORS

Alpheus
American States Water
Anglian Water Group
Bouygues
COFELY
Electricite de France
Electricite de Strasbourg
Kelda
Northumbrian Water
Pennon
RWE
SABESP
SNCF
SUEZ Environnement
Severn Trent
Shanks
Stagecoach
Thames Water
ThermoEnergy
United Utilities
Vattenfall
Waste Management
Waste Recycling
Welsh Water

HISTORICAL FINANCIALS

Company Type: Public

Income Statement

FYE: December 31

	REVENUE ($ mil.)	NET INCOME ($ mil.)	NET PROFIT MARGIN	EMPLOYEES
12/12	38,801	519	1.3%	318,376
12/11	38,347	(633)	—	331,266
12/10	46,557	777	1.7%	317,034
12/09	49,773	841	1.7%	312,590
12/08	50,618	566	1.1%	336,013
Annual Growth	(6.4%)	(2.2%)	—	(1.3%)

2012 Year-End Financials

Debt ratio: 50.2%
Return on equity: 5.5%
Cash ($ mil.): 7,312
Current ratio: 1.18
Long-term debt ($ mil.): 17,244
No. of shares (mil.): 507
Dividends
Yield: 7.2%
Payout: 144.0%
Market value ($ mil.): 6,216

	STOCK PRICE ($) FY Close	P/E High/Low		PER SHARE ($) Earnings	Dividends	Book Value
12/12	12.24	38	20	1.03	0.89	18.56
12/11	11.05	—	—	(1.28)	3.20	18.09
12/10	29.36	60	32	1.62	1.45	21.99
12/09	32.88	68	29	1.79	1.69	22.44
12/08	31.71	217	42	1.23	3.12	21.39
Annual Growth	(21.2%)	—	—	(4.4%)	(27.0%)	(3.5%)

Vinci SA

Veni vidi vici ...VINCI. Through its VINCI Construction division this company conquers the world as one of the largest building civil engineering and maintenance contractors. VINCI operates in two divisions: concessions and contracting (85% of sales). Its concessions business which builds and operates motorways parking garages rail infrastructure stadiums and airports includes motorway operator VINCI Autoroutes and parking manager VINCI Park. Under the contracting umbrella VINCI provides electrical engineering maintenance and facilities management. Roadworks and transportation infrastructure is handled by Eurovia. VINCI is active in some 100 countries with France accounting for about 60% of sales.

VINCI has an aggressive growth strategy as it continues to increase revenues and grow organically and through acquisitions. Despite the depressed economy VINCI managed to show signs of growth and a revival in revenue in 2010. The success was due in part to increased vehicle traffic on the company's motorways coupled with a rebounding contracting business.

VINCI also is expanding internationally in regions with economic growth such as central and eastern Europe the Middle East and India. The company also sees opportunities in North America where ageing infrastructure needs to be replaced. VINCI has an on-going strategy to acquire specialty companies that have a global reach. Specific target areas include ground technologies oil and gas infrastructure and nuclear engineering. VINCI is aligning its growth areas with marketplace trends such as urban development mobility needs and growing demand for new energy infrastructure.

In 2010 VINCI boosted its cooperation with the Qatar-owned investment company Qatari Diar when it bought technology services firm Cegelec in exchange for a stake in VINCI. Qatari Diar now is one of VINCI's largest shareholders owning about 6% of the company. Cegelec joined VINCI's energy business to create VINCI Facilities which offers energy services and facilities management in Europe the Middle East and beyond.

VINCI and Quatri Diar continue to strengthen their partnership. Later in 2010 the two partners announced plans for a parking lot joint venture which will run lots in Qatar. The two already are working on a proposed E2.2 billion ($3 billion) bridge that would link Qatar and Bahrain.

VINCI's Eurovia subsidiary which builds roads motorways airports rail and light rail infrastructure has been investing heavily in the raw building materials. It has bought several European gravel quarry operations and road construction companies over the last several years. In 2010 it bought about 100 quarries from Tarmac. The deal helped expand operations in Central Europe where road construction is growing. Eurovia now operates a network of about 430 quarries.

Not to be left out of the growth spurt VINCI Park has been busy making acquisitions in the US Canada and Europe in efforts to make it one of the largest parking operators in the world. VINCI Park (and subsidiaries such as LAZ Parking in the US) manages more than a million on-street and off-street parking spaces in Europe North America and Asia.

VINCI merged the functions of its chairman and CEO in 2010. CEO Xavier Huillard took over as chairman and CEO while Chairman Yves-Thibault de Silguy became vice-chairman and senior director. The new structure is aimed at improving efficiency.

HISTORY

VINCI's origins lie with French conglomerate Vivendi (now Vivendi Universal) which was founded in 1853 as Compagnie Generale des Eaux. Its mission was to irrigate French farmland and supply water to towns. The company won contracts to serve Lyons (1853) Nantes (1854) Paris (1860) and Venice (1880). Generale des Eaux moved into construction in 1972 building an office tower (and later hotels and houses) in Paris. The company also entered communications in the 1980s.

In 1988 Generale des Eaux acquired control of construction and civil engineering giant Societe Generale d'Entreprises. SGE subsidiaries included Campenon Bernard SGE (part of Generale des Eaux since 1981) Sogea Freyssinet Cochery Bourdin Chausse Saunier Duval Tunzini Lefort Francheteau and Wanner. SGE traces its construction roots to 1910. It became a subsidiary of Generale d'Electricite in 1966. Glassmaker Saint-Gobain acquired control of SGE in 1984. Under Generale des Eaux SGE enhanced its European profile through acquisitions including British builder Norwest Holst (1989) German road builder VBU (1991) and German pipe and duct maker MLTU (1992).

Generale des Eaux acquired publisher Havas in 1998 and took the name Vivendi –representing vivacity and mobility. Its purchase of USFilter in 1999 made Vivendi the world's largest water company. Vivendi's SGE unit (renamed VINCI) agreed to acquire the construction arm of rival conglomerate Suez's GTM unit in 2000.

Groupe GTM traces its roots to Societe Lyonnaise des Eaux et de L'Eclairage a leading French water utility. Formed in 1880 Lyonnaise des Eaux built up its French and international operations to include water distribution as well as gas and electricity production and distribution. A century later the company had diversified into such businesses as heating (Cofreth) waste management (Sita) and communications acquiring a stake in Lyonnaise Communications (now Lyonnaise Cable) in 1986.

In 1990 Lyonnaise des Eaux acquired construction firm Dumez whose subsidiary GTM-Entrepose was France's largest car park manager. Four years later Dumez-GTM was formed to consolidate the construction and civil engineering businesses of Dumez and GTM-Entrepose. In 1997 Lyonnaise des Eaux and Compagnie de Suez merged to create a leading provider of private infrastructure services Suez Lyonnaise des Eaux (which shortened its name to SUEZ in 2001). Compagnie Universal du Canal Maritime de Suez the builder of the Suez Canal was founded in 1858 and became Financiere de Suez in 1958. In 1967 Financiere de Suez acquired control of Lyonnaise des Eaux.

SGE changed its name to VINCI in 2000. That year as part of their strategy to rationalize operations and focus on core businesses Vivendi and SUEZ agreed to a friendly takeover of GTM by VINCI. SUEZ emerged as the combined company's largest shareholder but by the following year both SUEZ and Vivendi Universal had exited most of VINCI's capital leaving no core stockholder.

To better control its car park management operations the company in 2001 created VINCI Park to operate as an umbrella of its VINCI Concessions unit. It expanded its concessions holdings even more in 2002 by hooking up with construction group Eiffage to grab a 17% stake in Europe's second-largest toll road operator ASF which was floated that year by the French government.

In 2003 the group won the contract to manage the restoration of the historic Hall of Mirrors. It also won the concession contract to operate along with joint venture partner Keolis the International Airport of Grenoble.

VINCI completed its acquisition of ASF in 2005. The deal was part of a government program to privatize motorway companies.

The company has had volatile internal struggles. There was unrest in the board room during 2006 as chairman Antoine Zacharias reportedly wanted to oust CEO Xavier Vuillard in favor of Nexity CEO Alain Dinin. Zacharias was the one who ended up resigning and at the end of 2006 Dinin resigned from VINCI's board.

In 2007 VINCI's top French construction businesses Sogea Construction and GTM Construction merged to create VINCI Construction France its domestic construction giant.

The company strengthened its position in the UK in 2008 when it bought British construction and facilities management firm Taylor Woodrow from Taylor Wimpey. The deal consolidated VINCI's position in UK facilities management and public-private partnership projects such as rail airports and energy infrastructure. In 2009 VINCI Construction acquired the troubled UK builder Haymills Group as that company teetered on the brink of collapse.

In 2008 Eurovia branched out from the road to the rails when it acquired rail infrastructure firm Vossloh Infrastructure Services (now ETF-Eurovia Travaux Ferroviaires) from Vossloh. The division specializes in rail track maintenance and installation.

EXECUTIVES

COO Energy Business Line, Yves Meignie, age 58
Chairman VINCI Autoroutes, Pierre Coppey, age 50
Executive Vice-President and Chief Financial Officer, Christian Labeyrie, age 57
Deputy Managing Director Eurovia, Dominique Collomp
VP Business Development, Jean-Luc Pommier, age 60
Chairman and Chief Executive Officer, Xavier Huillard, age 59
VP Human Resources and Sustainable Development, Franck Mougin, age 54
Chairman VINCI Construction, Jean Rossi, age 64
COO VINCI Construction, Bruno Dupety, age 57
Chairman VINCI PLC, John Stanion
Managing Director CFE, Renaud Bentegeat, age 59
Chairman Energy Business Line, Jean-Yves le Brouster, age 65
COO Eurovia, Guy Vacher
Executive Vice-President Contracting, Richard Francioli, age 54
Senior Vice-President International Development, Pascale Sourisse
Chairman Soletanche Freyssinet; Director, Jean-Pierre Lamoure
Chairman Chief Executive Officer, Dominique Bouvier
COO Eurovia, Pierre Anjolras
Chairman and Chief Executive Officer Eurovia, Jacques Tavernier, age 63
CEO VINCI Concessions, Louis-Roch Burgard, age 45
Director Corporate Communication, Pierre Duprat, age 50
General Counsel and Secretary, Patrick Richard, age 56
Deputy Managing Director Operations Autoroutes du Sud de la France, Sebastien Fraisse
Chairman and CEO Escota, Philippe E. Daussy
Deputy Managing Director Energy Business Line, Herve Adam
Chairman VINCI Construction France, Gerard Bienfait
Chairman VINCI Construction Grands Projets, Alain Bonnot
Deputy Managing Director Energy Business Line, Michel Cantet
Chairman and CEO Sogea-Satom, Philippe Chavent
President directeur general de VINCI Park, Serge Clemente
CEO Cofiroute, Arnaud Grison
Director Business Development VINCI Concessions, Fadi Selwan
Managing Director, Alain Bellanger
Director, Robert Castaigne, age 65
Director, Patrick Faure, age 67
Director, Michael P. Pragnell, age 66
Director, Francois David
Director, Dominique Ferrero, age 66
Director, Dominique Bazy, age 59
Director, Henri Saint Olive, age 66
Director, Jean-Bernard Levy, age 58
Director, Pascale Sourisse
Chairman Soletanche Freyssinet; Director, Jean-Pierre Lamoure
Director, Yousuf Ahmad Al Hammadi
Director, Elisabeth Boyer
Auditors: SalustroReydel

LOCATIONS

HQ: Vinci SA
1, cours Ferdinand-de-Lesseps, Rueil-Malmaison, Cedex 92500
Phone: (33) 1 47 16 35 00 **Fax:** (33) 1 47 51 91 02
Web: www.vinci.com

2010 Sales

	% of total
France	62
Central and Eastern	6
United	5
Germany	5
Africa	5
Benelux	4
Americas	3
Rest of	3
Asia Middle East and	2
Total	**100**

PRODUCTS/OPERATIONS

2010 Sales

	% of total
Contracting	85
Concessions	15
Total	**100**

Selected Subsidiaries

VINCI Construction
CFE (46.8%; Benelux)
DEME (50%; dredging)
VINCI Construction France
VINCI PLC (UK)
VINCI Construction Filiales Internationales (Germany Central Europe overseas France Africa)
VINCI Construction Grands Projets
Freyssinet (specialized civil engineering)
VINCI Concessions
VINCI Park
Eurovia
VINCI Energies
Actemium (industry solutions)
Axians (voice-data-image communication)
Citeos (urban lighting)
Graniou (telecommunications infrastructure)
Omexom (high-voltage power transmission)
Opteor (maintenance)

COMPETITORS

Atlantia
Bechtel
Bilfinger Berger
Bouygues
Bovis Lend Lease
EIFFAGE
FCC Barcelona
HOCHTIEF
Louis Berger
Parsons Corporation
Schneider Electric
Skanska
WS Atkins

HISTORICAL FINANCIALS

Company Type: Public

Income Statement FYE: December 31

	REVENUE ($ mil.)	NET INCOME ($ mil.)	NET PROFIT MARGIN	EMPLOYEES
12/12	52,062	2,526	4.9%	192,701
12/11	49,023	2,463	5.0%	183,320
12/10	45,821	2,376	5.2%	179,527
12/09	47,089	2,299	4.9%	161,746
12/08	47,773	2,224	4.7%	164,057
Annual Growth	2.2%	3.2%	—	4.1%

2012 Year-End Financials

Debt ratio: 43.2%
Return on equity: 14.5%
Cash ($ mil.): 8,352
Current ratio: 0.87
Long-term debt ($ mil.): 21,818

No. of shares (mil.): 536
Dividends
Yield: 6.1%
Payout: 20.0%
Market value ($ mil.): 6,435

	STOCK PRICE ($) FY Close	P/E High	P/E Low	PER SHARE ($) Earnings	Dividends	Book Value
12/12	12.00	6	4	4.67	0.73	32.77
12/11	10.86	9	5	4.50	1.08	30.86
12/10	13.65	9	5	4.42	0.51	30.42
12/09	14.35	10	4	4.62	0.57	28.27
12/08	10.45	13	4	4.61	0.41	24.88
Annual Growth	3.5%	—	—	0.3%	15.9%	7.1%

Vivendi

Vivendi wants to be the life of the party. More than half of the company's business is in telecom services and the rest is in movies TV games and music. Its telecom holdings include SFR (Europe's largest alternative telecom operator) (more than 40% of sales) a controlling stake in Maroc Telecom (the largest telecom company in Morocco) and GVT in Brazil (that country's leading alternative high-speed Internet company). Vivendi's media assets include Universal Music Group (UMG) and the world's #1 independent video game publisher Activision Blizzard. Vivendi also owns CANAL+ the top pay-television provider in France and Europe's largest distributor and producer of films.

Vivendi's telecom business provides mobile and fixed telecom services including broadband Internet. At less than half of its main telecom company SFR's size is Canal+ Group Vivendi's next largest business. Not much smaller than Canal+ is UMG which gets most of its revenues from recorded music by artists such as Justin Bieber Lady Gaga LMFAO and Rihanna. Activision Blizzard tops rival Electronic Arts and in fact every other video game publisher except Nintendo with game franchises such as Call of Duty (Activision) and World of Warcraft (Blizzard).

Vivendi has grown sales steadily (measured in its domestic currency) since 2005 but couldn't quite continue that for 2011 as revenues remained nearly flat at ?28.8 billion ($37.3 billion). Modest gains in many of its segments were counteracted by a 6% drop in UMG revenues and a 3% decline in SFR revenues. Like its competitors however SFR did see gains as revenue from mobile data services climbed 18% and broadband Internet & fixed services saw a marginal uptick. Vivendi kept costs at bay for the year and brought in other operating and non-operating income that ultimately boosted its profit by about 20%.

Although Vivendi's strategy concentrates on synergies among its business units and organic innovation acquisitions have also been important. In 2012 Canal+ agreed to acquire the free-to-air channels and advertising sales operations from Bollore. Vivendi announced in 2011 that it would expand UMG's music library by purchasing London-based music group EMI's recorded music division for #1.2 billion ($1.9 billion) from Citigroup. Already the global leader in recorded music with the largest catalog of musical works the deal would bring UMG more big names including Pink Floyd Miles Davis and arguably the biggest one in pop music ever The Beatles.

Also that year Vivendi funded an even more significant acquisition by selling its 20% stake in NBCUniversal to NBCUniversal's majority owner General Electric for $5.8 billion. General Electric pushed for the acquisition to facilitate the proposed sale of a controlling 51% interest in NBCUniversal to Philadelphia-based cable operator Comcast. The deal gave Vivendi the funds it needed to take full ownership and total control of its SFR telecom division and thereby bolster its position at home against industry leader France Telecom (later renamed Orange) and other rivals. The company bought out UK-based Vodafone's stake (44%) in SFR for nearly $11.5 billion. SFR and Vodafone are set to extend their commercial partnership for three more years as part of the deal. Maneuvering into an adjacent market Vivendi acquired ticketing companies See Tickets the #2 ticketing business in the UK (behind Live Nation's Ticketmaster) in 2011 and France's Digitick in 2010.

HISTORY

Authorized by an imperial decree Compagnie Generale des Eaux was founded in 1853 by investors such as the Rothschild family and Napoleon III's half-brother to irrigate French farmland and supply water to towns. It won contracts to serve Lyons (1853) Nantes (1854) Paris (1860) and Venice (1880).

After WWI Generale des Eaux created water engineering firm Societe Auxiliaire de Distribution d'Eau (Sade 1918) and extended its water distribution network to several areas of France. By 1953 the company had added trash collection to its services. In the 1960s it began managing district heating networks and waste incineration/composting plants. The company moved into construction in 1972. By the time Guy Dujouany became chairman in 1976 water distribution accounted for less than half of the company's sales.

Dujouany began an expansion drive. In 1980 Generale des Eaux became France's #1 private energy management firm when it bought Generale de Chauffe. Also that year it expanded its wastewater and waste management businesses and moved into transportation buying Compagnie Generale d'Entreprises Automobiles (CGEA). The company also entered communications in the 1980s: it took a 15% stake in pay-TV provider CANAL+ (1983) and it created mobile phone unit Societe Francaise de Radiotelephonie (SFR 1987).

Generale des Eaux took its water services global in the 1990s. Dujouany stepped down in 1996 and was succeeded by Jean-Marie Messier who immediately dumped some businesses. In 1997 the company launched telecom provider Cegetel and increased its stake in publisher Havas to 30%. In 1998 the firm bought the rest of Havas increased its ownership in CANAL+ and took the name Vivendi to represent "vivacity" and "mobility."

Its purchase of USFilter in 1999 made Vivendi the world's largest water company; it also bought US waste management company Superior Services.

Bulking up its media holdings it acquired US educational software and games firm Cendant Software and bought French film producer Pathe. Vivendi sold most of Pathe's assets but kept stakes in BSkyB and CANAL+'s CanalSatellite digital-TV unit. The company sold $985 million worth of real estate to Unibail and it sold its hotel and restaurant businesses to Accor the French hotels group.

In 2000 Vivendi and Vodafone launched an Internet portal Vizzavi. Vivendi brought its environmental services businesses together under the Vivendi Environnement umbrella and sold a minority stake in the company to the public.

Later that year in a $34 billion deal that set the stage for Vivendi's transformation into a global conglomerate the company bought Seagram and the portion of CANAL+ that it didn't already own. The combined company became Vivendi Universal (VU). To gain European Commission approval for the Seagram acquisition VU had to unload its stake in BSkyB. VU also sold Seagram's liquor business for $8.1 billion to Diageo and Pernod Ricard which split up the various Seagram's brands between them. VU also sold off its construction operations and real estate holdings.

In 2001 the company bought music download site MP3.com for its music group and textbook publisher Houghton Mifflin for its publishing unit. It also sold its 55% stake in AOL France. To reduce its reliance on magazine advertising revenue the company sold its trade and medical publishing businesses to British investment firm Cinven.

Also in 2001 the company struck the biggest deal in its history by agreeing to buy the entertainment assets of USA Networks (now named InterActiveCorp). The deal closed the following year and VU combined Universal Studios with the USA business –which included film and TV production and cable channels –into a company called Vivendi Universal Entertainment (VUE).

VU in 2002 struck a deal with Marvel Enterprises (now Marvel Entertainment) to license the comic book publisher's characters for online games. At the end of the year VU completely exited the publishing business by selling Vivendi Universal Publishing (now named Editis) to Lagardere for $1.2 billion and Houghton Mifflin to Thomas H. Lee and Bain Capital for $1.6 billion. The sales were part of VU's asset fire sale put in place by Fourtou.

In 2004 VU saw its Hollywood aspirations fade to black. A prominent part of Fourtou's debt reduction plan was the sale of 86%-owned VUE with the exception of Universal Music Group to General Electric the parent company to NBC TV network. In the deal that included Universal Studios cable TV channels and theme parks and created NBC Universal (which was later remane NBCUniversal) VU received $3.8 billion in cash and retained a 19% stake in the company.

In 2006 the company (through Universal Music Group) acquired BMG Music Publishing for $2.1 billion. The deal advanced Universal Music's lead in the music industry in which it already had a greater than 25% market share.

Vivendi also acquired the nearly 8% stake in Universal Studios Holding from Matsushita Electric Industrial (now Panasonic) for nearly $1.2 billion. The deal gave it 100% ownership in the holding company that owns Universal Music Group Universal Interactive and 20% of NBC Universal.

The company also combined its CANAL+ unit with rival French pay-TV provider Television Par Satellite (TPS) in a deal that gave Vivendi control over the group. Because French authorities wanted CANAL+ to remain independent Vivendi had earlier transferred the majority of its CANAL+ Group operations to Canal Plus SA a publicly traded entity; Vivendi retained a 49% stake.

Vivendi also held a 51% stake in Moroccan incumbent telecom carrier Maroc Telecom. Another telecom holding was Vivendi's 49% stake in Elektrim Telekomunikacja the Polish holding company that owned a 48% stake (as its only major asset) in Poland's leading wireless telecom carrier Polska Telefonia Cyfrowa (PTC). Polish industrial holding firm Elektrim which also owned 49% of Elektrim Telekomunikacja was battling Germany's Deutsche Telekom and the Polish courts over its stake. Deutsche Telekom seeking to control PTC claimed the transfer of a stake in PTC from Elektrim to Elektrim Telekomunikacja was invalid. In an attempt to settle the longstanding legal dispute Vivendi in 2006 made a $3.2 billion bid to buy Deutsche Telekom's stake. (In 2010 the companies were reportedly close to reaching an agreement that would give full control of PTC to Deutsche Telekom in exchange for a ?1 billion –about $1.3 billion –payment for Vivendi to drop its claims to PTC.)

To concentrate on its core businesses Vivendi sold the non-French assets of CANAL+ Group. It also sold its 55% stake in Monaco Telecom to Cable and Wireless in a cash deal valued at ?169 million and in 2006 it sold its remaining 5% stake in utilities unit Veolia Environnement.

Citing a desire to further reduce costs the company in 2006 ended its listing on the New York Stock Exchange. It dropped Universal from its name –and became simply Vivendi –also in 2006 as part of its agreements with GE that created NBCUniversal. (The Universal Music Group retained the right to use Universal as part of its name until 2029.)

Looking to better compete with global games leader Electronic Arts Vivendi acquired US-based video game developer Activision in 2008. It combined Activision with its Vivendi Games subsidiary to form Activision Blizzard. The move brought together a variety of leading game titles under a single brand including World of Warcraft Guitar Hero and Call of Duty.

Also that year Vivendi merged SFR and Neuf Cegetel into one company under the SFR brand; the combined entity is Europe's largest alternative telecommunications operator.

Vivendi is also looking to international markets for growth. The company acquired 51% of Brazilian telephone company GVT Holding for $4.1 billion in 2009 amid protests from GVT's other suitor Telefonica. Vivendi bought essentially all of the remaining shares the following year.

EXECUTIVES

Chairman Supervisory Board, Jean-Rene Fourtou, age 74
SEVP Telecoms Activity, Jean-Yves Charlier, age 49
Chairman Management Board, Jean-Francois Dubos, age 68
Chairman Executive Board CANAL+ Group, Bertrand Meheut, age 61
Senior Executive Vice President Communications and Public Affairs, Simon Gillham, age 56
Executive Vice President - Innovation; Deputy Financial Director, Sandrine Dufour, age 42
Senior Executive Vice President Mergers & Acquisitions, Regis Turrini, age 54
IR Contact Officer, Jean-Michel Bonamy, age 42
Senior Vice President Audit and Special Projects, Vincent Vallejo, age 48
Chairman and CEO Universal Music Group, Lucian Grainge, age 52
Chairman Management Board Maroc Telecom, Abdeslam Ahizoune, age 58
SEVP Human Resources, Stephane Roussel, age 51
CFO and Member Management Board, Philippe G. H. Capron, age 55
V.P. Investor Relations, Eileen McLAUGHLIN
Chief Executive Officer, Jean-Bernard Levy
Vice President Corporate Communications, Adam White
Senior Vice President Corporate Communications, Peter Lofrumento
Senior Vice President; Development in the Strategy and Development Department, Arnaud Arnaud Castille Castille
Independent Member of the Supervisory Board, Christophe Christophe de Margerie Margerie
Independent Member of the Supervisory Board, Claude Claude Bebear Bebear
Independent Member of the Supervisory Board, Dominique Dominique Heriard Dubreuil Dubreuil
Vice President; Management and Business Plan Control/Holding Company Accounts, Florent Florent de Cournuaud Cournuaud
Senior Vice President; Head of the Legal Department; Secretary of the Supervisory and Management Boards, Frederic Frederic Crepin Crepin
Independent Member of the Supervisory Board, Jacqueline Jacqueline Tammenoms Bakker Bakker
Member of the Management Board; Chairman and Chief Executive Officer of GVT, Amos Amos Genish Genish
Executive Vice President Human Resources, Mathieu Peycere
Member Supervisory Board, Christophe de Margerie, age 61
Member Supervisory Board, Henri Lachmann, age 74
Member Supervisory Board, Jean-Yves Charlier, age 48
Member Supervisory Board, Daniel Camus, age 61
Member Supervisory Board, Claude Bebear, age 77
Vice Chairman Supervisory Board, Dominique Heriard Dubreuil, age 66
Member Supervisory Board, Maureen Chiquet, age 50
Member Supervisory Board, Philippe Donnet, age 52
Member Supervisory Board, Pierre Rodocanachi, age 74
Member Supervisory Board, Aliza Jabes, age 50
Member Supervisory Board, Jacqualine Tammenoms Bakker, age 59
Auditors: KPMGAudit

LOCATIONS

HQ: Vivendi
42, avenue de Friedland, Paris, Cedex 08 75380
Phone: (33) 1 71 71 10 00 **Fax:** (33) 1 71 71 10 01
Web: www.vivendi.com

2011 Sales

	% of total
Europe	
France	58
Rest of	11
USA	11
Morocco	8
Brazil	5
Rest of the	7
Total	**100**

PRODUCTS/OPERATIONS

2011 Sales

	% of total
Telecommunication services	
SFR	42
Maroc Telecom	9
GVT	5
Canal+	17
Universal Music	15
Activision	12
Total	**100**

COMPETITORS

Al Jazeera
BMG Rights Management
Bouygues
Brasil Telecom
CKX
Capcom
Cherry Lane Music Publishing
Chrysalis
EMI Group
Eidos
Electronic Arts
ITV
Iliad S.A.
Konami
Lucasfilm Entertainment
Microsoft Game Studios
NCsoft
Net Servicos de Comunicac?o
Nintendo
Orange
Orange
Sony
Sony Music
THQ
Take-Two
Tele2
Telefonica Brasil
Telemar Norte Leste
Tiscali
Ubisoft
Virgin Group
Warner Music
Warner/Chappell
ZeniMax Media

HISTORICAL FINANCIALS

Company Type: Public

Income Statement

FYE: December 31

	REVENUE ($ mil.)	NET INCOME ($ mil.)	NET PROFIT MARGIN	EMPLOYEES
12/12	38,215	216	0.6%	58,050
12/11	37,268	3,467	9.3%	58,400
12/10	38,649	2,941	7.6%	51,272
12/09	39,085	1,195	3.1%	49,004
12/08	35,500	3,639	10.3%	43,208
Annual Growth	1.9%	(50.6%)	—	7.7%

2012 Year-End Financials

Debt ratio: 39.3%
Return on equity: 0.8%
Cash ($ mil.): 5,132
Current ratio: 0.69
Long-term debt ($ mil.): 16,695
No. of shares (mil.): 1,322
Dividends
Yield: 4.2%
Payout: 1,370.2%
Market value ($ mil.): 30,166

	STOCK PRICE ($) FY Close	P/E High/Low	PER SHARE ($) Earnings	Dividends	Book Value
12/12	22.81	309199	0.16	1.27	18.40
12/11	21.74	29 16	2.70	3.64	19.54
Annual Growth	4.9%	— —	(50.8%)	(23.1%)	(1.5%)

Vodafone Group Plc

Customers have voted with their phones to make Vodafone one of the world's top wireless phone carriers with more than 400 million customers in more than 30 countries. In terms of subscribers Vodafone trails only China Mobile. The company does around 70% of its business in Europe where it is a leader in the wireless markets of the UK and Germany. It also provides data broadband Internet and fixed-line phone services; in Germany its largest market those services are overseen by subsidiary Arcor. Vodafone increasingly serves callers in the Asia/Pacific Africa and Middle East regions through subsidiaries and joint ventures. It holds a 45% stake in US provider Verizon Wireless.

Revenue for 2012 inched up little more than 1%. Somewhat nominal growth in Germany the Netherlands and the UK and even 25% growth in Turkey was offset by continuing economic woes in Southern Europe. Regions farther east and south turned in an 8% increase headlined by India Egypt Ghana Qatar and Vodacom (southern Africa). Net income kept going the other way though falling more than 10% to #7 billion (about $11 billion).

One of the biggest hurdles Vodafone faces is customer acquisition and retention costs which are the largest single cost its business faces. The company also wants to improve growth in its average revenue per user which it will try to do through improvements to its network to customer service and by introducing new and differentiated handset services. Geographically emerging markets such as India and Africa continue to be a big area of focus for Vodafone.

In 2012 Vodafone acquired fellow country mate Cable & Wireless Worldwide (CWW) in a deal that valued the venerable telecom provider at approximately #1.04 billion (about $1.6 billion). The purchase has obvious benefits for Vodafone. Because CWW has more than 12000 miles of optical fiber –the largest fiber optic network in the UK –Vodafone will not need to rent as much landline from its competition primarily BT. CWW will also extend Vodafone's reach in managed voice and data and IP-based services and applications as well as bolster its stable of enterprise and government customers.

Supporting its strategy to grow in emerging markets the company paid $5 billion in 2011 to buy out partner Essar Group in wireless joint venture Vodafone Essar in a bid to bolster its position in India. The deal gave Vodafone a 75% stake in the business with the remaining shares controlled by the company's Indian partners in which Vodafone also holds minority interests. To comply with Indian foreign ownership rules Vodafone subsequently sold about 5% of Vodafone Essar (renamed Vodafone India) to Piramal Healthcare for $640 million.

Vodafone strengthened its Global Enterprise business which deals with its largest multinational clients with the 2011 acquisition of UK-based IT consultant and outsourcer Bluefish Communications. Bluefish became the centerpiece of a unified communications and collaboration unit within global enterprise.

Divestments have helped the company stay focused. The company sold back its stake in Tokyo-based technology investment firm SOFTBANK for $5 billion in 2010 and sold of its 3% stake in China Mobile for about $6.7 billion earlier that year. The following year closer to home Vodafone sold its stake in French wireless provider SFR to Vivendi for about $11.4 billion. SFR and Vodafone are set to extend their commercial partnership for three more years as part of the deal.

Vodafone also moved to strengthen its fixed communications portfolio in 2012 when it bought TelstraClear the New Zealand operations of Telstra Corporation for NZ$840 million ($670 million). As that country's #2 fixed infrastructure operator – behind Telecom New Zealand (TCNZ) –TelstraClear gives Vodafone a more level playing field against regional rival TCNZ in capitalizing on a government-backed infrastructure expansion planned for the next several years.

HISTORY

Vodafone was formed in 1983 as a joint venture between Racal Electronics (a UK electronics firm) and Millicom (a US telecom company) and was granted one of two mobile phone licenses in the UK. It launched service in 1985 as a Racal subsidiary. Vodafone and Cellnet the other licensee were swamped with demand. In 1988 Racal offered 20% of Vodafone to the public; three years later the rest of the firm was spun off to become Vodafone Group.

Vodafone moved beyond the UK in the 1990s. By 1993 it had interests in mobile phone networks in Australia Greece Hong Kong Malta and Scandinavia.

For a time Vodafone and Cellnet a joint venture of British Telecom (now BT Group) and Securicor enjoyed a duopoly in the UK. Regulators elected not to impose price controls and the pounds rolled in. But in 1993 a new wireless provider One 2 One (now T-Mobile UK) launched a digital network in London. Vodafone countered that year with its own GSM (global system for mobile communications) digital network.

With increasing competition at home Vodafone continued to expand in 1994. It launched or bought stakes in operations in Fiji Germany South Africa and Uganda.

Digital service took on a larger role in Vodafone's UK business and by 1997 some 85% of new subscribers were opting for digital GSM. In 1998 Vodafone sold its French service provider Vodafone SA and bought digital cellular carrier BellSouth New Zealand. It also expanded into Egypt by buying a minority stake in Misrfone marking the largest British investment in Egypt since the Suez Canal.

In 1999 Vodafone prevailed in a brief bidding war with Bell Atlantic (now Verizon) to buy AirTouch Communications for about $60 billion. Vodafone's Chris Gent took over as CEO of the new company Vodafone AirTouch. The prize for Vodafone: entry into the lucrative US market plus the opportunity to consolidate minority interests in European wireless carriers.

Vodafone AirTouch moved to significantly boost its European footprint in 1999 by launching a $131 billion hostile takeover bid for Germany's Mannesmann. The company acquired Mannesmann for about $180 billion in stock in 2000 and agreed to sell the conglomerate's engineering operations and its UK mobile phone unit Orange. (France Telecom –later itself renamed Orange – bought the Orange unit for $37.5 billion later that year.)

In 2000 Vodafone AirTouch expanded its presence in the US by combining its US wireless operations with those of Bell Atlantic and GTE to form Verizon Wireless. The company failed to strengthen its presence in that market two years previously when it lost a bidding war with Cingular Wireless (now AT&T Mobility) over the acquisition of AT&T Wireless.

That year the company dropped AirTouch from its name and became Vodafone Group once again. It also continued its expansion push investing in China Mobile and buying Irish mobile phone operator Eircell (now Vodafone Ireland) in a deal that was completed in 2001. That year Vodafone bought BT's remaining interest in Spain's Airtel (now Vodafone Espa?a). In 2003 Vodafone sold its stake in Mexico's Grupo Iusacell to Movil@ccess.

Vodafone sold its 98%-owned Vodafone Japan unit in 2006 to SOFTBANK in a deal valued at nearly $16 billion. The group's acquisitions in regions outside of Europe included the 2006 purchase of Telsim (formerly the number two mobile service operator in Turkey) for about $4.6 billion. The next year Vodafone outbid several rivals to win control of one of India's largest telecom companies Hutchison Essar in a deal valued at about $9 billion. Also in 2007 the group bought fixed-line broadband Internet businesses in Italy and Spain from Sweden-based Tele2 for more than $1 billion.

Arun Sarin resigned as Vodafone's CEO in 2008. He was replaced by deputy CEO Vittorio Colao. During his five year tenure Sarin spearheaded the company's push into emerging markets in Eastern Europe as well as India and Turkey. He came under fire from shareholders at times for his aggressive expansion strategy but Sarin succeeded in more than doubling Vodafone's subscriber base and boosted the company's share price by more than 30%.

Also in 2008 Vodafone bought the remaining one-quarter of German fixed-line operator Arcor's shares that it did not already own from Deutsche Post and Deutsche Bahn for about ?474 million. The transaction was part of the company's plan to focus on providing a more extensive range of bundled services to German subscribers.

Vittorio Colao stated that the company's plans included a continued expansion into Africa Asia and the Middle East through acquisitions and partnerships while exiting non-core markets. Its key areas for growth in terms of service segments were mobile data broadband and corporate accounts. To this end Vodafone in 2008 raised its stake in South Africa's largest wireless operator Vodacom from 50% to 65% and took a controlling stake in Ghana's third-largest mobile carrier. The company in 2009 combined its mobile operations in Australia with those of Hong Kong-based Hutchison Telecommunications. As part of the deal Hutchison Telecommunications Australia paid $500 million to acquire Vodafone Hutchison Australia.

EXECUTIVES

Regional President Americas, Terry D. Kramer, age 54

Deputy Chairman, Sir John G. S. Buchanan, age 69, $269,901 total compensation

Chief Executive; Executive Director, Vittorio A. Colao, age 51, $1,944,247 total compensation

Group General Counsel and Company Secretary, Rosemary Martin, age 53

Group Chief Commercial Officer, Morten Lundal, age 48

Managing Director and CEO Vodafone Essar Ltd India, Marten Pieters, age 60

CEO Czech Republic, Muriel Anton

CEO Asia Pacific and Middle East, Nicholas J. (Nick) Read, age 48

CEO Germany, Friedrich P. (Fritz) Joussen, age 50

CTO and Director, Stephen C. (Steve) Pusey, age 52, $491,000 total compensation

Chief Financial Officer; Executive Director, Andrew N. (Andy) Halford, age 55, $1,273,523 total compensation

Director; CEO Europe Region, Michel Combes, age 51

CEO Ireland, Charles Butterworth

Chief Executive; Southern Europe, Paolo Bertoluzzo, age 47

Group Financial Controlller, Margherita Della Valle

CFO Europe, John Townsend, age 50

CEO Qatar, Grahame Maher

CEO Australia, Nigel Dews

Chairman, Gerard J. Kleisterlee, age 68

CEO UK, Guy Laurence, age 51

CEO Albania, Haris Broumidis

Director Group External Affairs, Matthew Kirk, age 52

Director Mobile Payments, Cenk Serdar, age 44

Director Group Strategy and Business Development, Warren Finegold, age 57

Director Group Investor Relations, Richard C. Snow, age 46

CEO Partner Markets, Richard Daly

CEO Hungary, Gyorgy Beck, age 58

CEO Malta, I?aki Berroeta

CEO New Zealand, Russell Stanners

CEO Spain, Francisco (Paco) Roman

Group Chief Marketing Officer, Wendy Becker, age 46

Global Director Terminals, Patrick Chomet

CEO Egypt, Hatem Dowidar

Director Human Resources, Ronald Schellekens, age 49

CEO Netherlands, Jens Schulte-Bockum

CEO Turkey, Serpil Timuray

Chief Executive; Northern & Central Europe, Philipp Humm
President Americas, Chuck Pol
President Asia Pacific & Sub-Saharan Africa, Stevan Hoyle
Executive Vice President Managed Network & Services, Nick Lambert
Director, Alan W. Jebson, age 64
Director, Philip E. (Phil) Yea, age 59
Director, Samuel E. (Sam) Jonah, age 63
Director, Anne Lauvergeon, age 54
Deputy Chairman, Sir John G. S. Buchanan, age 69
Director, Luc Vandevelde, age 62
CTO and Director, Stephen C. (Steve) Pusey, age 52
CFO and Director, Andrew N. (Andy) Halford, age 54
Director; CEO Europe Region, Michel Combes, age 51
Director, Renee J. James, age 48
Director, Nick Land, age 66
Director, Anthony (Tony) Watson, age 69
Auditors: DeloitteLLP

LOCATIONS

HQ: Vodafone Group Plc
Vodafone House, The Connection, Newbury, Berkshire RG14 2FN
Phone: (44) 1635 33251 **Fax:** (44) 1635 238080
Web: www.vodafone.com

2012 Sales

	% of total
Europe	
Germany	18
Italy	12
UK	11
Spain	10
Other	18
Africa Middle East Asia/Pacif	
Vodacom (Southern	12
India	9
Other	9
Non-controlled interests & common	1
Total	**100**

PRODUCTS/OPERATIONS

2012 Sales

	% of total
Voice	60
Data	15
Messaging	12
Fixed	8
Other	5
Total	**100**

Countries of Operation interests)
Africa/the East/Asia-
Australia
Congo
Egypt
Fiji
Ghana
India
Lesotho
Mozambique
New Zealand
Qatar
South Africa
Tanzania
Europe
Albania
Czech Republic
Germany
Greece
Hungary
Ireland
Italy
Malta
The Netherland
Portugal
Romania
Spain
Turkey
UK

COMPETITORS

AT&T Mobility
BT
Belgacom
China Mobile
Deutsche Telekom
Hutchison Whampoa
KPN
M1
NTT DoCoMo
Orange
Orange
Swisscom
Telefonica Europe
Telekom Austria
Telstra
Virgin Mobile Telecoms

HISTORICAL FINANCIALS

Company Type: Public

Income Statement

FYE: March 31

	REVENUE ($ mil.)	NET INCOME ($ mil.)	NET PROFIT MARGIN	EMPLOYEES
03/13	67,539	651	1.0%	91,272
03/12	74,379	11,148	15.0%	86,373
03/11	73,826	12,820	17.4%	83,862
03/10	67,444	13,110	19.4%	84,990
03/09	58,677	4,403	7.5%	79,097
Annual Growth	3.6%	(38.0%)	—	3.6%

2013 Year-End Financials

Debt ratio: 44.0%
Return on equity: 0.5%
Cash ($ mil.): 11,584
Current ratio: 0.75
Long-term debt ($ mil.): 44,233
No. of shares (mil.): —
Dividends
Yield: 0.0%
Payout: 26,939.3%
Market value ($ mil.): —

	STOCK PRICE ($) FY Close	P/E High/Low	PER SHARE ($) Earnings	Dividends	Book Value
03/13	28.40	82396493	0.01	3.56	2.22
03/12	27.67	566442	0.22	5.31	2.48
03/11	28.75	509283	0.24	1.30	2.73
03/10	23.31	370230	0.25	1.27	2.60
03/09	17.42	1580526	0.08	1.35	2.35
Annual Growth	13.0%	— —	(36.8%)	27.4%	(1.4%)

Volkswagen A.G. (Germany, Fed. Rep.)

With cars named for climate patterns insects and small mammals Volkswagen (VW) leads the Continent as Europe's #1 carmaker. Along with Golf (Gulf Stream reference) and the New Beetle VW's annual production of more than 7 million cars trucks and vans includes such models as Passat (trade wind) Jetta (jet stream) Rabbit and Fox. VW also owns a garage full of luxury carmakers – AUDI Lamborghini Bentley and Bugatti. Other brands include SEAT (family cars Spain) and Skoda (family cars the Czech Republic). Late in 2009 VW acquired a 49.9% stake in Porsche for about E4 billion (almost $6 billion) as the first step in combining the two into an integrated car company.

Geographic Reach

VW sells its cars worldwide with operations in Europe North America South America Africa and Asia. The company holds a global market share of more than 11%.

Sales outside of Germany account for almost 65% of the company's revenue although the rest of Europe accounted for more than 40% of revenue in 2011.

Operations

VW's makes more than 7 million cars trucks and vans annually.

VW AG is the holding company for VW Group that comprises segments including Automotive and Financial Services which provides customer financing leasing banking insurance and fleet management.

VW manufactures its nine brands (10 including Porsche) and almost 200 models in its more than 60 production plants. In mid-2011 VW announced plans for two additional manufacturing plants in China with an expected annual production of 300000 automobiles by 2013.

For its commercial vehicles segment VW holds 68% of the voting rights in Swedish truck maker Scania. It holds more than 30% of MAN which is considered a majority stake.

Financial Performance

The company's revenue has been trending upward and steadily increasing over the course of recent fiscal years. Revenue increased about 17% in fiscal 2011 compared to fiscal 2010.

Strategy

VW has preserved Porsche's brand autonomy. VW sees the combined group –which includes 10 distinct and separate brands along with the Porsche Holding auto trading business currently held by the Porsche and Piech families –as a way to become an industry leader in terms of global market presence innovation purchasing and manufacturing.

Though sales are recovering in North America and Europe the company hopes to continue expanding in Brazil India and Russia –where sales continue to be strong –to offset difficult conditions in North America and Western Europe.

VW's environmentally-friendly orientation and focus on innovation is part of its plan to be the largest car company in the world by 2018. The goal is to increase unit sales to more than 10 million vehicles a year. As part of its quest the company will invest a reported E51.6 billion ($70.6 billion) between 2011 and 2015 to update its manufacturing plants and equipment.

Mergers and Acquisitions

VW has added companies that allow it to expand internationally as well as to develop its products. In early 2010 VW completed a $2.5 billion deal for a 20% stake in Suzuki Motor Corp.

The deal gave VW greater access to markets in India and Southeast Asia where Suzuki is established. Suzuki gained from VW's presence in China which is experiencing sustained growth. VW particularly likes Suzuki's savvy in manufacturing cars inexpensively and profitably and plans to learn from the process.

HISTORY

Since the early 1920s auto engineer Ferdinand Porsche (whose son later founded the Porsche car company) had wanted to make a small car for the masses. He found no backers until he met Adolf Hitler in 1934. Hitler formed the Gesellschaft zur Vorbereitung des deutschen Volkswagen (Company for the Development of the German People's Car) in 1937 and built a factory in Wolfsburg Germany. No cars were delivered during WWII as the company produced military vehicles using the slave labor of Jews and Russian prisoners of war.

Following WWII British occupation forces oversaw the rebuilding of the bomb-damaged plant and initial production of the odd-looking "people's car" (1945). The British appointed Heinz Nordhoff to manage Volkswagen (1948) and then turned the company over to the German government (1949).

In the 1950s VW launched the Microbus and built foreign plants. Although US sales began slowly by the end of the decade acceptance of the little car had increased. Advertising that coined the name "Beetle" helped carve VW's niche in the US.

VW sold stock to the German public in 1960. In 1966 it purchased Auto Union (AUDI) from Daimler-Benz. The Beetle became a counterculture symbol in the 1960s and US sales took off. By the time of Nordhoff's death in 1968 the Beetle had become the best-selling car in history.

In the 1970s the Beetle was discontinued in every country except Mexico. VW lost heavily during the model-changeover period.

VW agreed to several deals in the 1980s including a car venture in China (1984) the purchase of 75% of SEAT (1986; it bought the rest in 1990) and the merger of its suddenly faltering Brazilian unit with Ford's ailing Argentine operations to form Autolatina (1987). In 1990 the company began building China's largest auto plant and acquired a 70% stake in Czech auto company Skoda. After suffering a loss in excess of $1 billion the company put Ferdinand Piech in the driver's seat in 1993. Under his leadership the company cut costs and boosted sales by resuscitating the SEAT and Skoda brands and launching a bigger more luxurious Passat sedan in 1997.

VW acquired Rolls-Royce Motor Cars Vickers' Cosworth auto engines subsidiary Italian sportscar maker Bugatti and Italy's Automobili Lamborghini —all in 1998. Although less luxurious than VW's other pursuits the New Beetle helped boost US sales that year. Also in 1998 VW established a $12 million fund to compensate the surviving 2000 concentration-camp inmates forced to work as slave labor during WWII. However the company was hit with a class-action lawsuit filed on behalf of Holocaust survivors anyway.

In 1999 Piech announced an end to VW's acquisition binge saying that growth would be driven from within; the company announced it would pour more than $31 billion into modernizing its factories through 2004. VW hoped to tap the market in China after getting approval in 1999 to sell a newly developed minicar there. That year it announced plans to invest $1 billion in its Mexico plant over the next five years.

VW expanded into heavy commercial vehicles in 2000 by purchasing a 34% stake in Swedish truck maker Scania (from holding company Investor). That year it also bought the 30% of Skoda that it didn't already own. Anticipating China's entry into the World Trade Organization VW announced in 2001 that it would invest $1.7 billion in China and the Asia/Pacific region over the next five years. Later in the year —and half a world away —12500 workers at the company's Mexico plant went on strike for 19 days over a pay dispute.

In April 2002 former BMW head Bernd Pischetsrieder succeeded Piech as CEO. In July 2003 the final classic Beetle rolled off the VW assembly line in Mexico concluding a 70-year run of constant production. That year BMW took control of the Rolls-Royce brand from Volkswagen.

After a pretty terrible 2005 VW took steps to turn things around. The company sold its car rental company Europcar to European investment firm Eurazeo in early 2006 and it reorganized its Financial Services division of which Europcar had been a part.

As 2006 wound to a close then VW boss Bernd Pischetsrieder stepped down and was replaced by AUDI chief Martin Winterkorn. The management shake-up was attributed to an internal power struggle between Pischetsrieder and supervisory board chairman Ferdinand Piech a grandson of Porsche founder Ferdinand Porsche. Despite the internal struggle total sales for 2006 had increased by nearly 12% and operating profit jumped by a whopping 51%.

VW acquired a stake in Porsche just shy of 50% for about E3.9 billion (about $5.79 billion) in late 2009. It was the first step in combining the two car companies. That same year VW sold VW Truck & Bus to MAN for nearly E1.2 billion in cash.

In mid-2010 VW acquired a stake in excess of 90% in Italdesign-Giugiaro (IDG) an automobile design and engineering company based in Turin Italy. IDG was the design force behind the Golf I Passat Scirocco and the Audi 80.

Also in 2010 VW completed a $2.5 billion deal for a 20% stake in Suzuki Motor Corp. Domestically in 2010 VW acquired Raffay's 10-car dealer network with almost 80 offices and integrated it into its sales network.

EXECUTIVES

Chairman Supervisory Board, Ferdinand K. Piech, age 76
Member Management Board Group Production, Michael Macht, age 52
Member Management Board Procurement, Francisco Javier Garcia Sanz, age 56
Chairman Management Board; Manager R&D; Chairman Audi; Chairman Management Board Porsche Automobil Holdings, Martin Winterkorn, age 66
Member Management Board China, Jochem Heizmann, age 62
Member Management Board; Chairman Board of Management Audi AG, Rupert Stadler, age 50
Member Management Board Finance and Controlling; CFO Porsche Automobil, Hans D. Potsch, age 62
Member Management Board Human Resources and Organization, Horst G. Neumann, age 64
Member Management Board Sales and Marketing, Christian Klingler, age 45
Member Management Board Group Commercial Vehicles, Leif Ostling
Member Supervisory Board, Michael Frenzel, age 66
Deputy Chairman Supervisory Board, Berthold Huber, age 63
Member Supervisory Board, Hans Michel Piech, age 70
Member Supervisory Board, Wolfgang Porsche
Member Supervisory Board, Hartmut Meine
Member Supervisory Board, Peter Mosch, age 42
Member Supervisory Board, Bernd Osterloh, age 57
Member Supervisory Board, Jurgen Stumpf, age 59
Member Supervisory Board, Bernd Wehlauer, age 59
Member Supervisory Board, Babette Frohlich, age 48
Member Supervisory Board, Peter Jacobs, age 57
Member Supervisory Board, Wolfgang Ritmeier, age 66
Member Supervisory Board, Thomas Zwiebler
Member Supervisory Board, Jorg Bode
Member Supervisory Board, Hussain Ali Al-Abdulla
Member of the Supervisory Board, Annika Falkengren
Member of the Supervisory Board; Employee Representative, Babette Froehlich
Member of the Supervisory Board, David McAllister
Member of the Supervisory Board, Hans Piech
Member of the Supervisory Board, Jassim Kuwari
Member of the Supervisory Board, Ursula Piech
Auditors: PricewaterhouseCoopersAGWirtschaftsprufungsgesellschaft

LOCATIONS

HQ: Volkswagen A.G. (Germany, Fed. Rep.)
Brieffach 1848-2, Wolfsburg D-38436
Phone: (49) 5361 9 0 **Fax:** (49) 5361 928282
Web: www.volkswagen.com

2011 Sales

	$ mil.	% of total
Europe		80
Asia/Pacific		11
Africa		2
Total	**0**	**100**

PRODUCTS/OPERATIONS

Selected Brands

Audi
Bentley
Bugatti
Lamborghini
Scania
SEAT
Skoda
Volkswagen
Volkswagen Commercial Vehicles

Selected Makes and Models

AUDI
- A1
- A3
- A3 Cabriolet
- A3 Sportback
- A4
- A4 allroad quattro
- A4 Avant
- A5 Cabriolet
- A5 Coupe
- A5 Sportback
- A6
- A6 allroad quattro
- A6 Avant
- A7 Sportback
- A8
- A8L
- A8L W12
- Q5
- Q7
- Q7 V12 TDI
- R8
- R8 Spyder
- R8 Spyder FSI quattro
- RS5 Coupe
- RS6
- S3
- S3 Sportback
- S4
- S4 Avant
- S5 Cabriolet
- S5 Coupe
- S5 Sportback
- TT Coupe
- TT Roadster
- TT RS Coupe
- TT RS Roadster
- TTS Coupe
- TTS Roadster

Bentley
- Continental Flying Spur
- Continental Flying Spur Speed
- Continental GT
- Continental GTC
- Continental GTC Speed
- Continental SuperSports
- Continental SuperSports Convertible
- Mulsanne

Bugatti
- Veyron
- Veyron Grand Sport
- Veyron Super Sport

Lamborghini
- Gallardo LP
- Gallardo LP Spyder
- Gallardo LP Spyder Performante
- Gallardo LP Superleggera
- Murcielago LP Coupe
- Murcielago LP Roadster

Scania
- Buses
- Engines
- Trucks

SEAT
- Alhambra
- Alhambra ECOMOTIVE
- Altea
- Altea ECOMOTIVE

Altea Freetrack
Altea XL
Altea XL ECOMOTIVE
Cordoba
Exeo
Exeo ST
Ibiza
Ibiza Cupra
Ibiza ECOMOTIVE
Ibiza FR
Ibiza SC
Ibiza SC Bocanegra
Ibiza ST
Leon
Leon Cupra
Leon ECOMOTIVE
Leon FR

Skoda
Fabia
Fabia Combi
Fabia Combi GreenLine
Fabia Combi RS
Fabia Combi Scout
Fabia GreenLine
Fabia RS
Fabia Scout
Octavia
Octavia Combi
Octavia Combi GreenLine
Octavia Combi GreenLine
Octavia Combi LPG
Octavia GreenLine
Octavia LPG
Octavia RS
Octavia Scout
Octavia Tour
Octavia Tour Combi
Roomster
Roomster GreenLine
Roomster Scout
Praktik
Superb
Superb Combi
Superb Combi GreenLine
Superb GreenLine
Yeti
Yeti GreenLine

Volkswagen Commercial Vehicles
Caddy
California
Caravelle
Crafter
Multivan
Saveiro
Transporter shuttle

Volkswagen Passenger Vehicles
CrossPolo
CrossTouran
Eos
Fox
Golf
Golf Estate
New Beetle
New Beetle Cabriolet
Jetta
Passat
Phaeton
Polo
Routan
Scirocco
Sharan
Tiguan
Touareg
Touran
Voyage

COMPETITORS

BMW
Chrysler
Daimler
Ford Motor
Fuji Heavy Industries
General Motors
Honda
Isuzu
Mazda
Nissan
Peugeot
Renault
Saab Automobile
Suzuki Motor
Toyota

HISTORICAL FINANCIALS

Company Type: Public

Income Statement FYE: December 31

	REVENUE ($ mil.)	NET INCOME ($ mil.)	NET PROFIT MARGIN	EMPLOYEES
12/12	253,956	28,624	11.3%	549,763
12/11	206,094	19,930	9.7%	501,956
12/10	169,805	9,147	5.4%	399,381
12/09	151,529	1,382	0.9%	368,500
12/08	159,113	6,645	4.2%	369,928
Annual Growth	12.4%	44.1%	—	10.4%

2012 Year-End Financials

Debt ratio: 40.7%
Return on equity: 32.0%
Cash ($ mil.): —
Current ratio: 1.07
Long-term debt ($ mil.): 84,431
No. of shares (mil.): 295
Dividends
Yield: 1.3%
Payout: 1.6%
Market value ($ mil.): 12,828

	STOCK PRICE ($) FY Close	P/E High	P/E Low	PER SHARE ($) Earnings	Dividends	Book Value
12/12	43.47	2	1	61.18	0.58	346.23
12/11	26.69	2	1	42.81	0.93	252.20
12/10	28.55	4	2	20.30	0.53	208.56
12/09	22.35	67	19	3.43	0.38	172.28
12/08	71.55	32	7	16.61	0.44	165.97
Annual Growth	(11.7%)	—	—	38.5%	7.1%	20.2%

Volvo AB

Despite the fact that the name "Volvo" still conjures up visions of soccer moms Volvo should really only inspire images of burly truck drivers. The company is one of the world's largest makers of trucks buses and construction equipment. In North America the company makes big rigs through its Volvo Trucks North America unit; Volvo also owns controlling interests in the well-known Mack Trucks brand in North America and Renault Trucks in Europe. Other products include marine (Volvo Penta) and industrial engines. Volvo's most widely known business –auto making –belongs to Geely Automobile of China.

Geographic Reach

Volvo's main business segments (Trucks Construction Equipment Buses Financial Services [financing and insurance] and Penta) sell their products and services in 190 markets worldwide. Overall it has production facilities in nearly 20 countries.

Financial Analysis

As the global economy starts to recover then retreats again the company saw slight decreases in revenue across the board. Operating income dipped 34% but was helped by strong results in the consumer finance division. Volvo blamed decreased sales and restructuring charges for the drop.

Strategy

Part of the company's response to continued economic uncertainty is building smaller less expensive trucks particularly under its Renault label. It positions them for developing markets but lower price appeals to all. Volvo is also working to meet strict EU environmental requirements for trucks buses construction equipment and its Penta vehicles.

Speaking of developing markets Volvo positioned itself to take part in the world's largest economy when in 2013 it signed an agreement with China's Dongfeng Motor Group to produce heavy-duty trucks. The Swedish company will take a 45% stake in Dongfeng Commercial Vehicles a subsidiary of the Chinese firm that will make big trucks for China and other countries.

As it continues to strengthen its core truck construction equipment and other products in its target markets Volvo has been looking into divesting non-core businesses. In late 2012 it sold its Volvo Aero business to GKN for about SEK 6.9 billion (about $1 billion); Volvo already sold Aero's US subsidiary Volvo Aero Services in 2010. Aero accounted for about 3% of the company's total revenue in 2010.

Ownership

Nordic holding company owns about 6% of Volvo.

HISTORY

Swedish ball bearing maker SKF formed Volvo (Latin for "I roll") as a subsidiary in 1915. Volvo began building cars in 1926 trucks in 1928 and bus chassis in 1932 in Gothenburg. Sweden's winters and icy roads made the company keenly attentive to engineering and safety. Volvo bought an engine maker in 1931. In 1935 Volvo became an independent company led by Assar Gabrielsson and Gustaf Larson.

Sweden's neutrality during WWII allowed Volvo to grow and move into component manufacturing and tractor production. Output in 1949 exceeded 100000 units 80% of which were sold in Sweden. The purchase of Bolinder-Munktell (farm machinery diesel engines; Sweden; 1950) enhanced Volvo's position in the Swedish tractor market. Volvo introduced turbocharged diesel truck engines and windshield defrosters and washers in the 1950s. By 1956 car production had outstripped truck and bus output.

Aware that it was too small to compete in global markets Volvo diversified (energy industrial products food finance and trading). Volvo increased its market share by purchasing several trucking and construction equipment companies that included White Motors' truck unit (US 1981) and Leyland Bus (UK 1986). In the 1980s Volvo acquired drug and biotechnology concern Pharmacia (now Pfizer) and Custos (investments Sweden). The company consolidated its food and drug units with state-controlled holding company Procordia in 1990.

At that time however Volvo was facing stagnant sales. It embarked on the largest industrial undertaking in Swedish history spending more than $2 billion to modernize plants and develop a series of high-performance family sedans which it introduced in 1991. Still high costs and persistent recession in Europe kept the company in the red during the early 1990s.

Adding to its troubles there was public outcry against a planned merger with French automaker Renault. The plan was abandoned in 1993 and the company sold its drug and consumer product interests (which had landed back in Volvo's lap when the government divested Procordia in 1993). These sales brought Volvo back into the black.

In 1997 Volvo sold its 11% stake in Renault left over from the abandoned merger. The next year the company strengthened its line of excavators and its Far Eastern presence by buying Samsung Heavy Industries' construction equipment unit. Volvo also bought Mexico's bus maker Mexicana de Autobuses and GM's share in Volvo GM Heavy Truck (now Volvo Trucks North America).

Anticipating a lower demand for cars Volvo closed an assembly plant in Canada in 1998 and in 1999 Volvo acquired a 13% stake (later upped to 25%) in rival truck maker Scania. To pay for its new focus on making heavy trucks Volvo sold its auto brand and manufacturing operations in Sweden Belgium and the Netherlands to Ford Motor Company for $6.45 billion in 1999. Volvo then agreed to take a 20% stake in the truck and construction equipment operations of Japan's Mitsubishi Motors.

In 2000 Volvo boosted its stake in Scania to 46% but its hope of acquiring a majority interest died when the EU rejected the $7.53 billion deal. Volvo then turned to France's Renault and bought the company's Mack truck unit in exchange for a 15% stake in Volvo.

Volvo's Renault Trucks subsidiary inked a technology transfer deal in 2002 with Chinese truckmaker Dongfeng Motors. The agreement cleared the road for Dongfeng to equip its heavy- and medium-duty trucks with Renault engines. In 2003 Volvo became the first Western truck manufacturer to produce vehicles under its own name in Russia. The following year Volvo opened a new truck factory in China with its partner China National Heavy Truck Corporation. Also in 2004 Volvo Construction Equipment (Volvo CE) sold its line of compact motor graders to Champion LLC a company headed up by Gary Abernathy a former manager at Volvo CE. Volvo acquired the remaining 50% of bus manufacturer Prevost Car from Henlys Group in late 2004.

To boost its presence in Asia in early 2006 Volvo acquired a 13% stake in Nissan Diesel Motor (now named UD Trucks Corporation) for a reported $195 million. Later that year Volvo bought another 6% of Nissan Diesel Motor from Nissan Motor with the intention of acquiring the remaining outstanding shares (which it did in 2007). Also in 2006 the company negotiated with Nissan and the Chinese government to purchase Nissan's 50% stake in Dongfeng Motor Co. Ltd. –China's largest maker of commercial trucks.

In response to new emissions standards that went into effect in late 2006 in Europe and the beginning of 2007 in North America Volvo has been sprucing up the operations of its Mack and Renault brands. The move is in step with Volvo's other truck operations which also have been revamped to comply with the new standards.

Asia has also been the focus of group's development efforts. The 2007 acquisitions of Japanese truck manufacturer Nissan Diesel and Chinese wheel loader maker Lingong gave Volvo increased manufacturing capacity in the region. Part of its Asian expansion included buying for $1.3 billion. Though its manufacturing facilities are based in the US the target of the acquisition was the heavy compactors pavers and asphalt millers demanded by the growing number of infrastructure projects in China and India.

Scaling back on other operations the company sold its Volvo Material Handling Equipment business in mid-2008 to Linamar's Skyjack division. Volvo's Material Handling unit which had been part of Volvo's acquisition of Ingersoll Rand's road construction equipment business was considered to be peripheral to Volvo's operations.

Beginning in fall 2008 the company responded to the difficult business environment by scaling back production to reduce costs and match demand. Volvo also edged up new product pricing to offset lower sales volumes. Its simultaneous effort to slash inventories resulted in a robust rise cash flow in 2009 that has helped to sustain operations. A 20% reduction in headcount in 2008 through 2009 accompanied the resizing. Nonetheless Volvo suffered more than a SEK 14 million ($2 billion) loss in 2009.

EXECUTIVES

President Volvo Trucks, Staffan Jufors, age 61
Chairman, Louis Schweitzer, age 71
EVP Corporate Legal and Compliance and General Counsel, Eva Persson, age 60
SVP, Stefan Johnsson, age 54
Chairman, Carl-Henric Svanberg
EVP Corporate Strategy, Karin Falk
Chief Technology Officer; EVP Group Trucks Technology, Torbjorn Holmstrom
EVP Group Trucks Sales and Marketing EMEA, Peter Karlsten, age 56
EVP Trucks Sales & Marketing Americas, Dennis R. (Denny) Slagle, age 60
Head Investor Relations, Christer Johansson
Director Investor Relations, Patrik Stenberg
VP Investor Relations North America, John Hartwell
EVP Corporate Communications, M?rten Wikforss
EVP Business Areas, H?kan Karlsson, age 52
President Renault Trucks, Stefano Chmielewski, age 60
President CEO and Director, Olof Persson, age 48
President UD Trucks, Satoru Takeuchi, age 66
President Volvo Trucks Europe, Claes Nilsson
EVP Public and Environmental Affairs, Jan-Eric Sundgren, age 62
EVP Volvo Construction Equipment, Patrick (Pat) Olney
SVP Corporate Communications Volvo Trucks Global, Tommy Kohle
EVP Group Trucks Operations, Mikael Bratt, age 46
President Aero, Staffan Zackrisson, age 60
Director Investor Relations, Anders Christensson
CFO and EVP Finance and Control, Anders Osberg
President Volvo Business Services, Elisabeth Rocke, age 53
President Volvo Penta of the Americas, Clint Moore
EVP Corporate Human Resources, Kerstin Renard, age 53
CIO; EVP Corporate Process and IT, Magnus Carlander, age 59
EVP Group Truck Sales and Marketing and JVs APAC, Joachim Rosenberg
EVP Financial Services, Martin Weissburg
EVP Legal and Compliance; General Counsel, Sofia Frandberg
EVP Public and Environmental Affairs, Niklas Gustavsson
Director, Lars Westerberg, age 65
Director, Peter I. Bijur, age 71
Director, Jean-Baptiste Duzan, age 67
Director, Berth Thulin, age 62
Director, Ravi Venkatesan, age 51
Director, Anders Nyren, age 58
Director, Ying Yeh, age 65
President CEO and Director, Olof Persson, age 48
Director, Hanne de Mora, age 53
Director, Lars Ask, age 53
Director, Peteris Lauberts, age 66
Director, Mikael Sallstrom, age 53
Auditors: PricewaterhouseCoopersAB

LOCATIONS

HQ: Volvo AB
Volvo Bergegaards v., Goeteborg SE-405 08
Phone: (46) 31 66 00 00 **Fax:** (46) 31 53 72 96
Web: www.volvogroup.com

2012 Sales

	% of total
Western	30
Asia	23
North	23
South	10
Eastern	7
Other	7
Total	**100**

PRODUCTS/OPERATIONS

2012 Sales

	% of total
Trucks	64
Construction	21
Buses	7
Financial	3
Volvo	3
Volvo	2
Total	**100**

Selected Products & Brand Names

Buses
- Chassis
- City & intercity buses
- Coaches

Construction equipment
- Articulated haulers
- Asphalt milling machines
- Backhoe loaders
- Compaction equipment
- Crawler excavators
- Motor graders
- Pavers
- Skid steer loaders
- Wheel loaders
- Wheeled excavators

Financial services
- Customer & dealer financing

Trucks
- Mack
- Renault
- UD Trucks
- VE Commercial Vehicles (46% India)
- Volvo

Volvo Penta
- Industrial engines & drive systems (gensets & materials handling)
- Marine engines & drive systems (leisure & commercial boats)

COMPETITORS

Cummins Westport
Daimler
Daimler Trucks North America
Deere
Fiat
Fiat Industrial
Fuji Heavy Industries
General Motors
Hino Motors
Honda
Isuzu
MAN
Mitsubishi Motors
Navistar
Navistar International
Nissan
Oshkosh Truck
PACCAR
Penske
Rolls-Royce
Scania
Suzuki Motor
Terex
Toyota

HISTORICAL FINANCIALS

Company Type: Public

Income Statement

FYE: December 31

	REVENUE ($ mil.)	NET INCOME ($ mil.)	NET PROFIT MARGIN	EMPLOYEES
12/12	46,610	1,694	3.6%	98,717
12/11	45,000	2,573	5.7%	98,162
12/10	39,481	1,620	4.1%	90,409
12/09	30,659	(2,066)	—	90,208
12/08	38,883	1,273	3.3%	101,380
Annual Growth	4.6%	7.4%	—	(0.7%)

2012 Year-End Financials

Debt ratio: 5.9%
Return on equity: 12.9%
Cash ($ mil.): 3,954
Current ratio: 1.17
Long-term debt ($ mil.): 12,514
No. of shares (mil.): 2,027
Dividends
Yield: 3.2%
Payout: 1.2%
Market value ($ mil.): 27,718

	STOCK PRICE ($) FY Close	P/E High/Low	PER SHARE ($) Earnings	Dividends	Book Value
12/12	13.67	0 0	0.84	0.44	6.48
12/11	10.84	0 0	1.27	0.01	6.05
12/10	17.61	0 0	0.80	0.00	5.38
12/09	8.46	— —	(1.02)	0.24	4.60
12/08	5.66	0 0	0.63	0.93	5.31
Annual Growth	24.7%	— —	7.4%	(16.9%)	5.1%

Wesfarmers Ltd.

Wesfarmers got its start as a farmers' cooperative in Western Australia a century ago. Today it's one of the country's most diverse companies and largest retailers following its acquisition of food and liquor retailer Coles Group. Wesfarmers has interests in far-ranging businesses including general merchandise (Kmart and Target) home-improvement (Bunnings) and office products retailing; coal mining; gas processing and distribution; chemical and fertilizer production; building materials sales; distribution of maintenance repair and operating products and industrial and safety products; and insurance. True to its heritage Wesfarmers still provides agricultural merchandise and services.

Geographic Reach

Perth-based Wesfarmers rings up 98% of its sales in Australia. New Zealand accounts for the rest. The company also has operations in Bangladesh and the UK.

Operations

The Coles division (formed in 2007) is Wesfarmers' largest business (accounting for 60% of the group's sales and 41% of its EBIT). It is one of Australia's leading food liquor and convenience retailers with a national presence. Wesfarmers has more than 2200 outlets under the Coles and BiLO supermarkets banners First Choice Liquor Liquorland and Vintage Cellars names and Coles Express banner. Other retail operations include Kmart and Target stores home improvement and office supplies stores. Wesfarmers is also engaged in coal production and export insurance (commercial and consumer) chemicals energy and fertilizers as well as industrial and safety products.

Financial Performance

Since buying Australian supermarket and liquor store operator Coles (in 2007) Wesfarmers has seen its sales increase more than 500%. In fiscal 2013 (ended June) Wesfarmers' sales grew 3% (before the impact of currency translation) versus the prior year. Operating income rose 3% over the same period. Driving the annual sales increase was improved performance of Coles and Wesfarmers' other retail operations (with the exception of Target) as well as the insurance and chemicals energy and fertilizers divisions. The company's Resources and Industrial and Safety businesses posted declines.

Strategy

The $18-billion purchase of Cole Group was transformational for Wesfarmers. Indeed the acquisition —at the time ranked as the largest takeover in Australia's history —gave Wesfarmers the designation as the country's top retailer. A five-year turnaround focused on the Coles supermarket chain began soon after the acquisition. As part of the reorganization Coles Group sold its online pharmacy business —Pharmacy Direct —and also shed some supermarket and liquor stores in an effort to improve its overall store network. The grocer also improved its fresh food and produce offerings and remodeled stores. While Coles has made progress and is beginning to regain market share (after years of losses) the 740-store chain continues to trail archrival Woolworths. Together Woolworths and Coles account for almost 80% of supermarket sales in Australia.

Beyond the retail arena recent acquisitions include the purchase of the New Zealand-based packaging firm Expresspak. To strengthen its position in the food service industry Wesfarmers Industrial acquired Expresspak which specializes in paper and plastic food and beverage packaging to add to its Packaging House business. As part of the deal the firm operates independently under the Expresspak name but shares its resources with Wesfarmers' subsidiary Packaging House whose offerings are largely of the industrial sort (steel strapping tape film). The acquisition put Packaging House which provides hygiene food service cleaning and chemicals and industrial packaging in a market-leading position in the food service packaging sector.

In April 2010 the company merged its Wesfarmers Chemicals & Fertilizers and Wesfarmers Energy divisions to form Wesfarmers Chemicals Energy & Fertilisers and also made other organizational and management changes in the industrial divisions. More recently Westfarmers began mulling a bid for ammonia producer Burrup Fertilisers but is meeting resistance from Australia's competition regulator. As part of its reorganization the company in late 2011 sold its Premier Coal (exploration production and processing) businesses to China-based Yanzhou Coal Mining for roughly $296 million.

A series of recent catastrophic events including the 2010 Christchurch New Zealand earthquake brushfires in Western Australia and sereve weather events have led to higher reinsurance costs and claims activity for Wesfarmers' insurance division a tiny part of its overall business.

EXECUTIVES

Executive General Manager Corporate Affairs, Alan Carpenter
Managing Director Target, Dene L. Rogers, age 51
Managing Director Coles, Ian McLeod, age 55
Chief Human Resources Officer, Ben Lawrence
Managing Director, Richard J. Barr Goyder, age 51, $431,009 total compensation
Managing Director Home Improvement and Office Supplies, John Gillam
Managing Director Kmart, Guy Russo
Finance Director, Terry Bowen
Managing Director Wesfarmers Resources, Stewart Butel
Executive General Manager Business Development, Tim Bult
Managing Director Wesfarmers Insurance, Robert Scott
Chairman, Robert (Bob) Every, age 68
Chief Executive Chemicals, Ian Hansen
Managing Director Wesfarmers Industrial and Safety, Olivier Chretien
Managing Director Wesfarmers Chemicals Energy & Fertilizers, Tom O'Leary
Group General Counsel, Paul Meadows
Managing Director, Tom OLeary
Managing Director Wesfarmers Insurance, Anthony Gianotti
Non-Executive Director, Colin B. Carter, age 70
Non-Executive Director, Charles Macek, age 66
Non-Executive Director, James Graham
Auditors: Ernst&Young

LOCATIONS

HQ: Wesfarmers Ltd.
Level 11, Wesfarmers House, 40 The Esplanade, Perth, Western Australia 6000
Phone: (61) 8 9327 4211 **Fax:** (61) 8 9327 4216
Web: www.wesfarmers.com.au

2013 Sales

	% of total
Australia	98
New	2
Total	**100**

PRODUCTS/OPERATIONS

2013 Sales

	% of total
Coles	60
Home improvement & office	15
Kmart	7
Target	6
Chemicals energy &	3
Industrial &	3
Insurance	3
Resources	3
Total	**100**

Selected Retail Operations

Convenience
  Coles Express
General Merchandise
  Kmart
  Target
Home Improvement
  Bunnings
  Bunnings Trade
  Bunnings Warehouse
Liquor Stores
  First Choice Liquor
  Liquorland
  Vintage Cellars
Supermarkets
  BiLo
  Coles
  Coles Online
Office Supply
  Officeworks

COMPETITORS

ALDI
Australia and New Zealand Banking
Caltex Australia
Commonwealth Bank of Australia
Harvey Norman Holdings
Insurance Australia
Metcash
Woolworths Limited

HISTORICAL FINANCIALS

Company Type: Public

Income Statement

FYE: June 30

	REVENUE ($ mil.)	NET INCOME ($ mil.)	NET PROFIT MARGIN	EMPLOYEES
06/13	55,187	2,085	3.8%	200,000
06/12	59,148	2,165	3.7%	0
06/11	58,821	2,060	3.5%	200,000
06/10	44,176	1,333	3.0%	200,000
06/09	41,536	1,250	3.0%	201,202
Annual Growth	7.4%	13.6%	—	(0.1%)

2013 Year-End Financials

Debt ratio: 12.3%
Return on equity: 8.7%
Cash ($ mil.): 1,229
Current ratio: 1.11
Long-term debt ($ mil.): 5,265
No. of shares (mil.): 1,157
Dividends
  Yield: —
  Payout: —
Market value ($ mil.): 41,023

	STOCK PRICE ($) FY Close	P/E High/Low		PER SHARE ($) Earnings	Dividends	Book Value
06/13	35.45	22	15	1.80	0.00	20.74
06/12	29.15	19	15	1.87	0.00	22.56
06/11	33.20	25	12	1.78	0.00	23.46
06/10	24.15	17	8	1.15	1.07	18.19
06/09	17.90	16	3	1.30	0.90	17.08
Annual Growth	18.6%	—	—	8.5%	—	5.0%

Westdeutsche Genossenschafts-Zentralbank EG (Germany, Fed. Rep.)

WGZ BANK is one of Germany's largest banking institutions and the central bank for more than 220 Volksbanken and Raiffeisenbanken member banks in the state of North Rhine-Westphalia. Supported by branches in Dusseldorf Koblenz and Munster its banks primarily offer refinancing investment and payment transaction products and services in local markets. WGZ BANK's largest subsidiary WL BANK is a mortgage bank that engages in public-sector real estate lending. WGZ BANK also functions as a commercial bank that provides lending to small and midsized businesses. As a wholesale bank it acts as a trading partner in the currency foreign exchange and capital markets as well as in bond issuing and syndications.

Although WGZ BANK is dealing with a difficult market environment it is moving forward with plans to expand outsourcing services advisory services for overall bank management and cooperation models among member banks.

The company is owned by its member banks with about 92% of those shares pooled into WGZ Beteiligungs GmbH & Co. KG.

Auditors: Deloitte&ToucheGmbH

LOCATIONS

HQ: Westdeutsche Genossenschafts- Zentralbank EG (Germany, Fed. Rep.)
Ludwig-Erhard-Allee 20, Duesseldorf 40227
Phone: (49) 211 778 00 **Fax:** (49) 211 778 1277
Web: www.wgz-bank.de

2008 Sales

	% of total
Germany	92
Other European	8
Total	**100**

PRODUCTS/OPERATIONS

2008 Sales

	% of total
Other	48
Capital market	22
Member	15
Real	10
Corporate	5
Total	**100**

Selected Subsidiaries

Domestic
- WGZ Corporate Finance Beratung GmbH (investment banking advisory services)
- WGZ Immobilien + Treuhand GmbH (real estate services)
- WGZ Initiativkapital GmbH (equity business)
- WL BANK (mortgage bank)

Foreign
- WGZ BANK Ireland plc (international credit business)
- WGZ BANK Luxembourg S.A. (secondary services in foreign currency investment and financing)

COMPETITORS

BayernLB
Commerzbank
DZ BANK
Deutsche Bank
UniCredit Bank AG
WestLB

HISTORICAL FINANCIALS

Company Type: Public

Income Statement FYE: December 31

	ASSETS ($ mil.)	NET INCOME ($ mil.)	INCOME AS % OF ASSETS	EMPLOYEES
12/12	126,640	493	0.4%	1,243
12/11	121,513	(270)	—	1,239
12/10	125,915	199	0.2%	1,192
12/09	137,780	410	0.3%	1,159
12/08	129,536	(262)	—	1,171
Annual Growth	(0.6%)	—	—	1.5%

2012 Year-End Financials

Return on assets: 0.3%
Return on equity: 12.9%
Long-term debt ($ mil.): —
No. of shares (mil.): 6
Sales ($ mil): 4,183
Dividends
Yield: —
Payout: —
Market value ($ mil.): —

WestLB AG

WestLB acts as the central institution for the more than 100 "sparkassen" or savings banks in Germany's largest state North Rhine-Westphalia and Brandenburg. The bank also serves midsized companies public entities multinational corporations and individuals in Germany and abroad. A universal bank WestLB offers a range of financial services including loans trading asset management investment banking transaction processing private banking and real estate finance. It has about a dozen branches in Germany plus more than a dozen in financial capitals in Europe and around the world. WestLB's savings bank partners collectively operate more than 3000 branches.

WestLB has been working to get on financial stable footing after exposure to failing US mortgage-related investments caused it to nearly collapse. The bank has placed assets up for sale including noncore unit WestLB International which it sold to DekaBank Luxembourg in early 2011. The bank is weighing numerous bids for its Westdeutsche Immobilienbank real estate unit as well. The company has also sought to merge with another bank but talks to join forces with BayernLB ended in 2010 after BayernLB saw no value in the deal.

WestLB Mellon Asset Management a joint venture between WestLB and The Bank of New York Mellon has some E23.5 million in assets under management. Most of its assets are European fixed-income holdings.

The state of North Rhine-Westphalia and two local savings banks own WestLB.

HISTORY

WestLB traces its roots back to war reparations paid by Sweden to the province of Westphalia after the Napoleonic Wars. In 1832 the provincial government founded Westphalian Provinzialbank-Hulfskasse to distribute the funds to various government projects. Fifteen years later King Frederick William IV of Prussia bade the establishment of a similar bank in the Rhineland; Provinzial-Hulfskasse of the Rhineland opened in 1854. These two banks eventually became "Landesbanks" and funded the growth of the two productive regions through WWI.

The Westphalian and Rhineland banks survived the cyclic German economy of the early 20th century as two world wars raged through the region. During the post-WWII reconstruction the two began providing clearing services for the regional savings banks ("Sparkassen") adding "girozentrale" to their names. As the two regions grew closer in the 1950s so did the two banks but politics prevented an outright merger of Landesbank fur Westfalen Girozentrale and Rheinsche Girozentrale und Provinzialbank until 1969.

Enjoying certain credit advantages not shared by private banks WestLB grew at home by lending to both individuals and corporate clients and becoming one of Germany's largest banks by the mid-1970s. The company also focused on building its merchant banking services teaming with such firms as Chase Manhattan (now part of JPMorgan Chase).

When interest rates climbed in the 1980s WestLB found itself in a pinch. To stabilize the bank (and the region's economy) the North Rhine-Westphalia government infused capital and raised its ownership to more than 40%. Its risk reduced the company once again turned its attention to growth outside Germany in the mid- to late 1980s. It extended loans to the Soviet Union and set up banking ventures in the crumbling Soviet Bloc provided capital to the emerging economies of Latin America teamed with Japanese banks to sell securities on the Tokyo Exchange and wove a web of joint ventures and partnerships around the globe.

After German reunification WestLB began buying stakes in both banking and nonbanking entities to strengthen the economy. In the mid-1990s the company sought to raise its European investment banking through both internal growth and purchases; among them was Panmure Gordon a UK brokerage firm (1996).

In the late 1990s WestLB became embroiled in an ongoing controversy with the European Union (EU) over subsidies it received from the German government in 1992. The EU declared these subsidies illegal and demanded that the company repay the German government; WestLB in 2000 flatly refused to do so triggering a lawsuit from the EU. Later that year members of the bank's supervisory committee proposed a move that would partially privatize WestLB. In 2002 the WestLB commercial operations became a private business.

WestLB had provided state-guaranteed loans for economic growth and housing development in its home state; those duties are now carried out by NRW.BANK which was established in 2002. Competitors contended that state backing gave WestLB an unfair advantage and the European Union agreed. WestLB began operating as a stand-alone institution for the first time in 2005.

In 2008 the government of North Rhine-Westphalia injected E5 billion ($7 billion) into WestLB which neared bankruptcy as it buckled under the weight of investments in the crashing US subprime mortgage market. WestLB which had hoped to merge with a fellow German central bank Landesbank Baden-Wurttemberg began divesting some of its assets as a condition of the government rescue.

Heinz Hilgert also took over as CEO. He resigned the following year unable to come to an agreement with WestLB's owners over the best way to shrink the company's balance sheet. He was replaced by Dietrich Voigtlander.

EXECUTIVES

Chief Risk Officer, Thomas Gro?, age 48
Vice Chairman Managing Board, Hubert Beckmann, age 56
CFO, Hans-Jurgen Niehaus, age 56
Investor Relations, Holger Grawe
Member Managing Board, Werner Taiber, age 52
Chairman Supervisory Board, Michael Breuer
Member Managing Board, Klemens Breuer, age 46
Head of Corporate Communications London, Richard Bassett
Head of Communications and Press Spokesman, Walter Hillebrand-Droste
Press Spokesman, Eberhard Roll
Group Communications New York, Connie J. Kain
Managing Director Sub-Sahara Africa Financial Institutions, Charles Weller
Executive Director Ukraine Financial Institutions, Igor Potapov
Executive Director Czech Republic Slovakia Financial Institutions, Joachim von Massow
Member Supervisory Board, Rolf Gerlach
Deputy Chairman Supervisory Board, Doris Ludwig
Member Supervisory Board, Gerhard Langemeyer
Member Supervisory Board, Alexander Wueerst
Member Supervisory Board, Raimund Baer
Member Supervisory Board, Dietmar P. Binkowska
Member Supervisory Board, Rolf Finger
Member Supervisory Board, Dietmar Fischer
Member Supervisory Board, Cornelia Hintz
Member Supervisory Board, Sigrid Janetzko
Member Supervisory Board, Wolfgang Kirsch
Member Supervisory Board, Christiane Kutil-Bleibaum
Member Supervisory Board, Helmut Linssen
Member Supervisory Board, Annette Lipphaus
Member Supervisory Board, Siegfried Luther
Member Supervisory Board, Manfred Matthewes
Member Supervisory Board, Heinz-Guenter Sander
Member Supervisory Board, Hans-Georg Vogt
Member Supervisory Board, Harry Voigtsberger
Auditors: Ernst&YoungAG

LOCATIONS

HQ: WestLB AG
Herzogstrasse 15, Duesseldorf D-40217
Phone: (49) 211 826 01 **Fax:** (49) 211 826 6119
Web: www.portigon.com

PRODUCTS/OPERATIONS

Selected Subsidiaries

readybank ag
WestLB Hungaria ZRt.
WestLB Ireland plc
WestLB (Italia) Finanziaria S.p.A.
WestLB Mellon Asset Management Holdings Limited
West Pensions Consult GmbH

COMPETITORS

BayernLB
Citigroup
Commerzbank
Credit Suisse
Deutsche Bank
Goldman Sachs
ING
UBS
UniCredit Bank AG
WGZ BANK

HISTORICAL FINANCIALS

Company Type: Public

Income Statement

FYE: December 31

	ASSETS ($ mil.)	NET INCOME ($ mil.)	INCOME AS % OF ASSETS	EMPLOYEES
12/12	130,145	(1,779)	—	2,776
12/11	217,183	(62)	—	4,429
12/10	256,329	(321)	—	4,712
12/09	349,065	(764)	—	5,214
12/08	402,820	25	0.0%	5,957
Annual Growth	(24.6%)	—	—	(17.4%)

2012 Year-End Financials

Return on assets: (-1.0%)
Return on equity: (-50.6%)
Long-term debt ($ mil.): —
No. of shares (mil.): 22
Sales ($ mil): 4,507
Dividends
Yield: —
Payout: —
Market value ($ mil.): —

Weston (George) Limited

George Weston Limited fuels Canadians through those long winters. About 95% of the company's sales come from its 63%-owned Loblaw Companies Limited Canada's largest supermarket operator (with more than 1000 stores under some 20 banners including Loblaws Extra Foods T&T and Zehrs Markets) and the country's largest wholesale food distributor. The rest comes from Weston Foods with operations in Canada and the US that focus on freshly baked goods frozen dough biscuits and other bakery products. (Its Interbake Foods division is a major supplier of Girl Scout cookies in the US.) Chairman Galen Weston owns about 63% of the company which was founded by his grandfather in 1882.

Both Loblaw and Weston Foods are facing challenges resulting from changing consumer preferences concerning what to eat and where to shop. In response George Weston has been restructuring both businesses to better match changing tastes. The weak economy on both sides of the US and Canadian border have put a damper on sales. Total sales rose less than 1% in 2010 vs. 2009 and were slightly below 2008 levels. The Loblaw segment outperformed Weston Foods with sales up about 1% vs. a nearly 4% decline for Weston Foods. Loblaw's 2010 sales got a boost from the acquisition of T&T Supermarket in late 2009. (T&T is Canada's largest retailer of Asian foods.)

Looking to position itself on a more profitable path to growth George Weston purged a couple of its businesses. In early 2009 the company sold its US-based fresh baked and baked goods business Dunedin Holdings to Mexico's Grupo Bimbo for about $2.5 billion. The sale included the Arnold Brownberry Entemann's Freihofer Stroehmann and Thomas' brand names. (The company's Interbake Foods and Maplehurst Bakeries businesses in the US were not included in the transaction.) Previously George Weston had sold its Neilson Dairy business to Saputo.

Cash from the divestitures was used to introduce new higher-margin products that customers want to eat and to fund acquisitions. To this end George Weston acquired Keystone Bakery Holdings a US provider of frozen cupcakes doughnuts and cookies for in-store bakeries and foodservice firms. The $185-million deal expanded the frozen baked goods division of its Maplehurst Bakeries unit. Aside from sweet treats George Weston is looking to shift its product mix to include more whole grains as an increased focus on healthier breads has hurt sales of white-flour-based products. In late 2010 the company acquired artisan and European-style bread manufacturer ACE Bakery for C$110 million (US$108 million). Based in Toronto ACE was made a subsidiary of Weston Foods (Canada). Its breads are distributed in Canada and the US.

Loblaw which is in the last year of a five-year restructuring plan is facing increased competition from non-traditional rivals such as Wal-Mart Canada and Costco Wholesale Canada which are claiming a growing share of the retail grocery market. In response the company is cutting prices and sprucing up its retail stores. It's also aggressively expanding its low-price Real Canadian Superstore format which numbers more than 100 stores and its No Frill chain of discount supermarkets to better compete with foreign superstore operators. In recent years Loblaw has been shuttering struggling Provigo stores.

HISTORY

A baker's apprentice George Weston began delivering bread in Toronto with a single horse in 1882. He added the Model Bakery in 1896 and began making cookies and biscuits in 1908.

Upon George's death in 1924 his son Garfield gained control of the company and took it public as George Weston Limited in 1928. Having popularized the premium English biscuit in Canada Garfield acquired bakeries in the UK to make cheap biscuits (uncommon at the time). He grouped the bakeries as a separate public company called Allied Bakeries in 1935 (it later became Associated British Foods and is still controlled by the Weston family).

Expansion-minded Garfield led the company into the US with the purchase of Associated Biscuit in 1939. By the late 1930s George Weston was making cakes breads and almost 500 kinds of candy and biscuits.

During the 1940s the company made a number of acquisitions including papermaker E.B. Eddy (1943; sold 1998 to papermaker Domtar giving it a 20% stake in Domtar) Southern Biscuit (1944) Western Grocers (1944 its first distribution company) and William Neilson (1948 chocolate and dairy products).

In 1953 it acquired a controlling interest in Loblaw Groceterias Canada's largest grocery chain. George Weston continued its acquisitions during the 1950s and 1960s adding grocer National Tea and diversifying into packaging (Somerville Industries 1957) and fisheries (British Columbia Packers 1962; Conners Bros. 1967).

By 1970 when Garfield's son Galen became president the company's holdings were in disarray. Galen brought in new managers consolidated the food distribution and sales operations under Loblaw Companies Limited and cut back on National Tea (which shrank from over 900 stores in 1972 to 82 in 1993). When Garfield died in 1978 Galen became chairman.

Ever since Galen a polo-playing chum of Prince Charles was the target of a failed kidnapping attempt by the Irish Republican Army in 1983 the family has kept a low public profile.

George Weston became the #1 chocolate maker in Canada with its purchase of Cadbury Schweppes' Canadian assets in 1987. The 1980s concluded with a five-year price war in St. Louis among its National Tea stores Kroger and a local grocer. This ultimately proved fruitless and Loblaw sold its US supermarkets in 1995 ending its US retail presence. As part of its divestiture of underachieving subsidiaries the company sold its Neilson confectionery business back to Cadbury Schweppes in 1996 and sold its chocolate products company in 1998.

In early 1998 Loblaw set its sights on Quebec buying Montreal-based Provigo. Other George Weston acquisitions in the late 1990s included Oshawa Foods' 80-store Agora Foods franchise supermarket unit in eastern Canada and its Fieldfresh Farms dairy business the frozen-bagel business of Quaker Oats Pennsylvania-based Maier's Bakery and Bunge International's Australian meat processor Don Smallgoods. It also sold its British Columbia Packers fisheries unit.

Early in 2001 George Weston surprised analysts when it won Unilever's Bestfoods Baking Company (Entenmann's Oroweat) with a bid of $1.8 billion. The company reduced its stake in Loblaw by 2% and sold its Connors canned seafood business to fund the purchase which was completed in July 2001. To help pay down debt in early 2002 the company sold its Orowheat business in the western US to Mexican bread giant Grupo Bimbo for $610 million.

In 2003 Weston's food distribution business introduced about 1500 private label products. It sold its fisheries operations in Chile at a loss in 2004 for about $20 million. That September the company purchased Quebec-based Boulangerie Gadoua Ltee a family-owned baking business.

In 2005 the company sold its Heritage Salmon subsidiary thus exiting the unprofitable fisheries business entirely. The company also restructured its US biscuit operations and opened a new fresh bakery plant in Orlando Florida in 2005 as part of its push to increase its business in the southeastern US. A new bakery in the midwestern US began production of bread and English muffins in late 2006.

In early 2007 Weston's Loblaw subsidiary announced it was writing down its operations in Quebec to the tune of $768 million tied to its struggling Provigo grocery stores.

In December 2008 the company sold the Neilson dairy division of Weston Foods Canada to Saputo for some C$465 million in cash (about $373 million). It will use the money to pay down debt. In January 2009 it completed the sale of its fresh bread and baked goods business in the US. Later in the year Loblaw acquired T&T Supermarket Canada's largest retailer of Asian food.

In September 2010 George Weston through its Maplehurst Bakeries subsidiary acquired Keystone Bakery Holdings for approximately $185 million. Keystone is comprised of three operating companies: Freed's Bakery of Manchester New Hampshire a leading supplier of frozen thaw and sell iced cupcakes; Granny's Kitchens of Frankfort New York a leading supplier of both frozen pre-fried and frozen thaw and sell donuts; and Heartland Baking of DuQuoin Illinois a specialty supplier of frozen thaw and sell cookies. In November Weston Foods acquired artisan and European-style bread manufacturer ACE Bakery for C$110 million (US$108 million). Based in Toronto ACE was made a subsidiary of Weston Foods (Canada). Its breads are distributed in Canada and the US.

Chairman and president Galen Weston stepped down as the company's president in late 2011 but remained chairman.

EXECUTIVES

SVP Taxation, J. Bradley Holland, age 49
Executive Vice President Corporate Development, Robert G. (Bob) Vaux, age 65
SVP Financial Control and Investor Relations, Geoffrey H. (Geoff) Wilson, age 57
Chairman, W. Galen Weston, age 72, $1,018,300 total compensation
SVP General Counsel Canada and Secretary, Robert A. Balcom, age 51
SVP Finance; SVP Finance Loblaw Companies, Jeremy Roberts, age 49
President, Paviter S. (Pavi) Binning, age 53
Chairman, W. Galen G. Weston, age 40
EVP and CFO, Richard Dufresne
EVP and Chief Legal Officer, Gordon A. M. Currie, age 54
EVP and Chief Legal Officer, Gordon A.M. Currie
VP Commodities, David Farnfield, age 49
VP and Controller, Lina Taglieri, age 44
VP and Legal Counsel, Adam Walsh, age 39
Senior Vice President - Corporate Development, Khush Khush Dadyburjor Dadyburjor
Senior Vice President - Taxation, Bradley Holland
Director, Warren F. Bryant, age 67
Director, John S. Lacey, age 69
Director, A. Charles (Charlie) Baillie, age 73
Director, Isabelle Marcoux, age 43
Deputy Chairman, Allan L. Leighton, age 59
Director, J. Robert S. Prichard, age 64
Director, Robert J. Dart, age 73
Director, Anne L. Fraser, age 71
Director, Anthony R. Graham, age 56
Director, Peter B.M. Eby, age 74
Director, Thomas F. (Tom) Rahilly, age 69
Independent Director, Barbara Barbara Stymiest Stymiest
Independent Director, Darren Darren Entwistle Entwistle
Auditors: KPMGLLP

LOCATIONS

HQ: Weston (George) Limited
22 St. Clair Avenue East, Toronto, Ontario M4T 2S7
Phone: 416 922-2500 **Fax:** 416 922-4395
Web: www.weston.ca

2010 Sales

	% of total
Canada	98
US	2
Total	**100**

PRODUCTS/OPERATIONS

2010 Sales

	% of total
Loblaw	95
Weston	5
Total	**100**

Selected Operating Divisions

Food Distribution (selected Loblaw banners)
- Atlantic SaveEasy
- Dominion
- Extra Foods
- Fortinos
- Loblaws
- Maxi
- Maxi & Co.
- No frills
- The Real Canadian Superstore
- The Real Canadian Wholesale Club
- SuperValu
- T&T Supermarkets
- Your Independent Grocer
- Zehrs Markets

Food Processing (selected units)
- ACE Bakery (artisan breads)
- Interbake Foods Inc. (cookies and crackers US)
- Maplehurst Bakeries Inc. (frozen bakery products US)
- Weston Bakeries Limited (fresh baked goods)

COMPETITORS

7-Eleven
Bridgford Foods
Campbell Canada
Jean Coutu
Jim Pattison Group
Katz Group
Canada Safeway
Canadian Tire
Costco Wholesale Canada
Couche-Tard
Flowers Foods
Grupo Bimbo
H&M Company
Hostess Brands
IGA
Kellogg U.S. Snacks
METRO
Maple Leaf Foods
Otis Spunkmeyer
Shoppers Drug Mart
Sobeys
Urban Outfitters
Wal-Mart Canada
Zara

HISTORICAL FINANCIALS

Company Type: Public

Income Statement FYE: December 31

	REVENUE ($ mil.)	NET INCOME ($ mil.)	NET PROFIT MARGIN	EMPLOYEES
12/12	32,920	488	1.5%	140,000
12/11	31,738	622	2.0%	142,000
12/10	31,914	452	1.4%	142,000
12/09	30,351	987	3.3%	143,000
12/08	26,145	677	2.6%	145,000
Annual Growth	5.9%	(7.9%)	—	(0.9%)

2012 Year-End Financials

Debt ratio: 38.0%
Return on equity: 8.6%
Cash ($ mil.): 1,597
Current ratio: 1.47
Long-term debt ($ mil.): 6,295
No. of shares (mil.): 128
Dividends
Yield: 0.0%
Payout: 43.2%
Market value ($ mil.): 9,129

	STOCK PRICE ($) FY Close	P/E High/Low	PER SHARE ($) Earnings	Dividends	Book Value
12/12	71.20	21 15	3.40	1.47	44.63
12/11	65.49	19 13	4.46	9.01	41.75
12/10	83.08	27 19	2.93	1.44	40.56
12/09	62.70	7 5	7.32	1.37	51.30
12/08	46.94	7 5	4.95	1.17	37.41
Annual Growth	11.0%	— —	(9.0%)	5.8%	4.5%

Westpac Banking Corp

Westpac Banking keeps its pact to serve customers in Australia New Zealand and the neighboring Pacific Islands. The company serves some 12 million customers through about 1400 branches and is one of the largest banks in Australia. Retail banking division Australian Financial Services (AFS) group includes Westpac St. George Bank of Melbourne and BankSA branded banking locations. AFS also offers wealth management insurance and consulting through BT Financial Group. Meanwhile Westpac Institutional Bank offers corporate financial services and Westpac New Zealand provides retail wealth and institutional services.

Geographic Reach

Australia accounts for 90% of Westpac's annual revenues. In addition to branches and subsidiaries located across Australia New Zealand and neighboring islands Westpac's institutional division has offices in London New York City Hong Kong and Singapore.

Operations

Through its operating divisions Westpac has a total of some $675 billion in assets. The company's AFS division includes the Westpac Retail and Business Banking unit (consumer and small to midsized banking customers) the St. George Banking group and the BT Financial Group as well as the banking products and risk management segments. BT Financial operates under brands including

Ascalon Asgard Advance Asset Management Magnitude and Securitor.

Westpac Institutional Bank serves corporations institutions and government entities across Australia and New Zealand as well as overseas. New Zealand banking primarily serves small to mid-sized businesses and consumers in New Zealand.

Sales and Marketing

Westpac's retail services are promoted through its retail banking locations as well as through relationship managers wealth specialists business banking centers customer service channels and online. The institutional segment conducts sales through dedicated industry relationship and specialist product teams.

Financial Performance

Westpac reported a 2% decrease in revenues to some A$42 billion ($44 billion) in 2012 due to lower sales and services in the Australian retail banking market (offset by growth in the institutional banking segment). Net income also fell by 15% to A$6.0 billion ($6.2 billion) due to higher tax impairment and operating expenses.

Strategy

Westpac's primary operating vision is to become the largest financial services firm in Australia. The company also aims to build strong customer relationships and provide superior shareholder returns. Though it occasionally makes acquisitions Westpac is currently focused on organic growth measures to increase customer numbers. The firm is also working to increase products-per-customer numbers through deposit wealth and insurance cross-selling programs. In addition Westpac is expanding its operations in Asia.

In response to challenging financial service markets Westpac is also reducing costs through streamlining and simplification programs.

HISTORY

Westpac proudly calls itself Australia's "First Bank." But when predecessor Bank of New South Wales was founded in 1817 some 90% of the eponymous colony's inhabitants were convicts or their relatives. (The penal colony was established just 30 years before the bank.) The British challenged the bank's charter forcing it to become a joint-stock company.

New South Wales' parliament rechartered the company as a bank in 1850 amidst the country's first gold rushes. (Some bank branches consisted of tents in mining camps.) Heavy British investment and an influx of colonists kept the country growing. The bank's future partner Commercial Bank of Australia was founded in 1866 in Melbourne in the neighboring colony of Victoria. More than half of the country's banks disappeared in a panic at the end of the century when land speculation and a collapse in wool prices caused a depression.

Australia became a country with the onset of the 20th century and its government formed Commonwealth Bank a central bank. The Bank of New South Wales now known as "The Wales" helped finance Australia's WWI efforts. Along with the rest of the world the country and the bank rode up the Roaring '20s and down the Great Depression.

About 65% of the bank's male staff enlisted during WWII. Its New Guinea branches closed; others were hit by air raids. In 1947 the government moved to nationalize the prospering country's banks within the Commonwealth Bank but the courts helped the banks fend off the attack on their independence.

The Bank of New South Wales moved into the newly opened savings banking market in 1956. The next year it bought into Australian Guarantee Corporation (it bought the rest in 1988).

The bank expanded abroad and diversified operations in the 1970s. Battered by a lagging protectionist economy Australia moved to deregulate banking in the 1980s. As foreign banks hustled in Bank of New South Wales and Commercial Bank of Australia in 1982 made what was then the largest merger in Australia's history.

The new bank known as Westpac (for its Western Pacific market area) began building its non-teller-based banking networks in the early 1980s. The company developed an extensive ATM network and established telephone and computerized banking. Later that decade it bought a stake in London gold dealer Johnson Matthey (1986) and all of William E. Pollock Government Securities (1987).

In 1992 Australia's wealthiest man Kerry Packer took a 10% share in troubled Westpac gaining board seats for himself and friend "Chainsaw" Al Dunlap. Packer's power grab failed and he sold the stake in 1993.

After buying itself into the equities market in the mid-1980s Westpac sold its Ord Minnett brokerage division in 1993. The bank withdrew from Asia and expanded closer to home in the mid 1990s buying Western Australia's Challenge Bank in 1995 Trust Bank of New Zealand in 1996 and Victoria's Bank of Melbourne in 1997.

In 1998 the bank agreed to merge its back-office operations with those of ANZ Banking Group providing economies of scale while avoiding antitrust issues. The next year Westpac announced 3000 job cuts mainly through attrition to ready itself for increased competition from changes in Australian law. Pacific operations caused waves in 2000: Westpac said it would pull out of Kiribati in response to government action and a coup in Fiji prompted the bank to reduce employees' hours (a move that was criticized by the Fiji government). The next year however Westpac was strengthening ties to the Pacific market. It doubled its holdings in the Bank of Tonga (on the island of Tonga) and its share of Pacific Commercial Bank (on the island of Samoa).

In 2007 subsidiary Westpac Essential Services Trust formed a joint venture with another Australian firm to operate the Airport Link Company a rail-to-airport passenger service in Sydney. The trust was established so investors could invest in public-private partnership (PPP) assets.

Westpac's acquisition of St.George Bank in 2008 catapulted Westpac from fourth to second among Australia's leading banks. The combination set Westpac and its St.George subsidiary behind only the National Australia Bank in terms of assets.

EXECUTIVES

Group Executive People and Performance, Ilana Atlas, age 58, $428,502 total compensation
Managing Director and CEO, Gail P. Kelly, age 56
Chief Executive Australian Financial Services, Brian C. Hartzer, age 46
Chief Operating Officer; Senior Company Secretary, John Arthur
Chief Financial Officer, Philip (Phil) Coffey, age 55, $571,692 total compensation
CEO St.George Bank, Rob Chapman
COO Australian Financial Services, Peter Clare, age 50
Group Executive Human Resources and Corporate Affairs, Christine Parker
CEO Westpac New Zealand, George Frazis, age 48
Group Executive Westpac Institutional Bank, Rob Whitfield, age 46, $383,333 total compensation
Senior Media Relations Manager, Jane Counsel
Deputy Chairman, John S. Curtis, age 63
Chairman, Lindsay P. Maxsted
Chief Executive Officer of BT Financial Group, Brad Cooper, age 50, $331,252 total compensation
Group Executive Transformation and Productivity, Peter Hanlon, age 58, $444,805 total compensation
General Manager Consumer Banking New Zealand, Bruce McLachlan
Head Investor Relations, Andrew Bowden
CIO, Clive Whincup
Group Executive Westpac Retail and Business, Jason Yetton
Senior Manager Investor Relations, Hugh Devine
Finance Manager, Linda Schubert
Director, Gordon M. Cairns, age 59
Director, Peter Wilson, age 68
Managing Director and CEO, Gail P. Kelly, age 56
Director, Carolyn Hewson, age 57
Director, Graham J. Reaney, age 70
Director, Elizabeth B. Bryan, age 63
Director, Robert G. Elstone, age 58
Deputy Chairman, John S. Curtis, age 63
Director, Peter J. O. Hawkins, age 59
Auditors: PricewaterhouseCoopers

LOCATIONS

HQ: Westpac Banking Corp
275 Kent Street, Sydney, New South Wales 2000
Phone: (61) 2 9293 9270 **Fax:** (61) 2 8253 4128
Web: www.westpac.com.au

2012 Sales

Australia	90
Other countries	1

PRODUCTS/OPERATIONS

2012 Sales by Segment

	% of total
Westpac Retail and Business	36
St.George	19
Westpac Institutional	18
BT Financial Group	11
Westpac New	9
Other	7
Total	**100**

COMPETITORS

Australia and New Zealand Banking
Barclays
Commonwealth Bank of Australia
HBOS Australia
HSBC
Hang Seng Bank
Macquarie Group
National Australia Bank

HISTORICAL FINANCIALS

Company Type: Public

Income Statement

FYE: September 30

	ASSETS ($ mil.)	NET INCOME ($ mil.)	INCOME AS % OF ASSETS	EMPLOYEES
09/13	648,927	6,349	1.0%	35,597
09/12	704,404	6,230	0.9%	35,675
09/11	651,105	6,791	1.0%	37,806
09/10	598,553	6,143	1.0%	38,962
09/09	519,822	3,038	0.6%	37,032
Annual Growth	5.7%	20.2%	—	(1.0%)

2013 Year-End Financials

Return on assets: 0.9%
Return on equity: 15.0%
Long-term debt ($ mil.): —
No. of shares (mil.): —
Sales ($ mil): 36,128
Dividends
Yield: 28.5%
Payout: 82.6%
Market value ($ mil.): —

	STOCK PRICE ($) FY Close	P/E High/Low		PER SHARE ($) Earnings	Dividends	Book Value
09/13	30.67	77	11	2.01	8.75	14.03
09/12	128.33	73	47	1.99	1.72	15.06
09/11	96.06	63	37	2.17	7.73	13.47
09/10	112.30	56	33	2.00	5.38	12.37
09/09	115.44	70	20	1.09	4.68	10.38
Annual Growth	(28.2%)	—	—	16.6%	16.9%	7.8%

Wilmar International Ltd

Wilmar International Limited is among Asia's largest agribusiness groups. The company grows refines and sells palm soy and other edible oils and grains. It is divided into three units: plantations for growing palm and rubber trees; processing plants for refining the oil and grains; and a consumer division which sells the oils in China India and Indonesia. As part of its business Wilmar also makes and sells fertilizer and palm-based biodiesel sold in Europe and the US. Wilmar boasts operations in 20-plus countries on four continents and owns more than 300 processing plants across Southeast Asia. It sells its products in 50-plus countries worldwide. Beyond agribusiness it's acquiring property in China.

Since its inception Wilmar has continued to grow its operations with a focus on Indonesia Malaysia China India and Europe. In 2010 it teamed up with subsidiaries of two Hong Kong-listed property developers to bid for commercial and residential real estate in China. It also acquired Indonesian sugar refinery PT Jawamanis Rafinasi and a sugar trading company —Windsor and Brook Trading —in its home city of Singapore. Also in 2010 Wilmar bought Sucrogen an Australia-based producer of sugar and biofuel from CSR for nearly A$1.8 billion (about US$1.5 billion). Sucrogen generates some 40% of Australia's raw sugar and complements Wilmar's other businesses in the Asia/Pacific region. Soon after Sucrogen in 2011 inked a deal to buy a local sugar cooperative for A$115 million (more than US$122 million). In Africa the company entered into a joint venture with Britain's PZ Cussons to build a palm oil refinery in Nigeria to produce edible oils and nutritional spreads for the local market. The plant is expected to begin production in 2012.

In 2008 Wilmar teamed with Olam International to acquire a 20% stake in joint venture PureCircle for $106 million. PureCircle is a producer of natural sweeteners made from the stevia plant. In line with its long-term expansion strategy and to support the growing grain market in Queensland Australia the company in 2009 acquired a sugar terminal in the port of Brisbane. The company later refitted it to handle grain and other bulk and liquid commodities.

But all that growth comes with a price. Wilmar owns about 570000 hectares of plantation land in Indonesia and Malaysia. Since palm only grows in the tropical forests of Southeast Asia there has been high demand to use palm oil in the production of plant-based biofuels while the world looks for sustainable energy sources to replace coal. To help meet the growing demand for biofuels and related products Wilmar formed a joint venture with US-based Elevance Renewable Sciences to build a plant (with an initial capacity of about 400 million pounds) on the site of its new manufacturing complex in Surabaya Indonesia. The new facility came online in 2011 uses multiple renewable oil feedstocks such as palm mustard soybean jatropha or waste oils to make high-value performance chemicals advanced biofuels and oleochemicals.

Palm oil produces the most energy of any oil or seed crop and Wilmar claims it's an environmentally sensitive corporation. But a group based in the Netherlands (where its biodiesel is sold) filed a complaint with the Roundtable on Sustainable Palm Oil of which Wilmar is a member. The group claims Wilmar destroyed rainforests and didn't comply with the environmental permit process when developing new plantations in Indonesia. Wilmar maintains its land conservation policy is strict and falls within governmental regulations.

In 2007 Wilmar merged with the Malaysia-based Kuok Group in a $2.7 billion deal and restructured the businesses of Wilmar Holdings Pte Ltd for $1.6 billion. It's now one of the largest 15 companies listed on the Singapore Exchange.

EXECUTIVES

Executive Director Chief Operating Officer, Martua Sitorus, age 53
Executive Director Commercial and Board Member, Teo Kim Yong, age 59
Head Operations Indonesia, Hendri Saksti
Head Operations Malaysia, Yee Chek Toong
Head Technical, Matthew J. Morgenroth
Head Plantations Division, Goh Ing Sing
Financial Controller, Sng Ching
Vice Chairman, Mu Kui
Chief Executive Officer, Ian Glasson
Chief Scientific Advisor, Chua Nam-Hai
Executive Director Chief Operating Officer, Martua Sitorus, age 53
Executive Director Commercial and Board Member, Teo Kim Yong, age 59
Auditors: Ernst&YoungLLP

LOCATIONS

HQ: Wilmar International Ltd
56 Neil Road, 088830
Phone: (65) 6216 0244 **Fax:** (65) 6836 1709
Web: www.wilmar-international.com

2010 Sales

	% of total
China	52
Southeast	25
Europe	7
India	4
Others	12
Total	**100**

PRODUCTS/OPERATIONS

2010 Sales

	% of total
Palm &	53
Oilseeds &	28
Consumer	15
Plantation & palm oil	1
Others	3
Total	**100**

COMPETITORS

Amsteel
Anglo-Eastern Plantations
Asia Food & Properties
Bunge Limited
Genting Malaysia
Golden Agri-Resources
Hong Leong Malaysia
IOI Corporation
Inch Kenneth Kajang Rubber
Kuala Lumpur Kepong
Narborough Plantations
New Britain Palm
Sime Darby

HISTORICAL FINANCIALS

Company Type: Public

Income Statement FYE: December 31

	REVENUE ($ mil.)	NET INCOME ($ mil.)	NET PROFIT MARGIN	EMPLOYEES
12/12	45,463	1,255	2.8%	0
12/11	44,710	1,600	3.6%	0
12/10	30,377	1,323	4.4%	0
12/09	23,885	1,882	7.9%	0
12/08	29,145	1,530	5.3%	0
Annual Growth	11.8%	(4.8%)	—	—

2012 Year-End Financials

Debt ratio: 53.0%
Return on equity: 9.0%
Cash ($ mil.): 1,581
Current ratio: 1.11
Long-term debt ($ mil.): 4,505
No. of shares (mil.): —
Dividends
Yield: 1.3%
Payout: 186.7%
Market value ($ mil.): —

	STOCK PRICE ($) FY Close	P/E High/Low		PER SHARE ($) Earnings	Dividends	Book Value
12/12	27.35	240	126	0.20	0.37	2.24
12/11	38.48	197	138	0.25	0.38	2.09
12/10	43.94	257	188	0.21	0.55	1.85
12/09	45.60	168	59	0.27	0.48	1.71
Annual Growth	(15.7%)	—	—	(8.0%)	(6.7%)	7.0%

Wolseley Plc Jersey

In its 100-year history Wolseley's gone from shearing sheep in Australia to becoming the world's largest distributor of heating and plumbing supplies to professional contractors. The company distributes heating and cooling equipment plumbing supplies pipes valves safety equipment and fire protection products as well as building materials in about 23 countries throughout North America and Europe. Key customers include building contractors plumbing and heating engineers and industrial and mechanical contractors. Outside of the UK Wolseley subsidiaries include Ferguson Enterprises in the US Reseau Pro in France and Wasco in the Netherlands.

Wolseley offers a broad range of products. Its largest product segment plumbing heating and air conditioning equipment generated roughly 40% of revenues in fiscal 2011. Its building materials segment and its civil/waterworks commercial and industrial segment each accounted for about 30% of revenues while the remaining 2% came from the sale of electrical cables wiring and lighting as well as installation maintenance and customer inventory management services.

This product mix serves customers in the residential commercial and industrial sectors —both new construction and repair and maintenance. Customers range from individual plumbers and builders to national contractor chains and home builders. Professional contractors are Wolseley's main customer base; within that category building contractors and plumbing and heating engineers together generate about 50% of Wolseley's total revenues.

In fiscal 2011 as markets stabilized Wolseley reported revenues of #13.6 billion (about $22.3 billion) up a modest 3% from #13.2 billion (about $20.7 billion) in 2010. These results were driven mainly by improving new residential construction and the repair and maintenance market.

Wolseley's business is divided into six geographic regions. In the US and Canada –which together generate about half of the company's total sales –the group is bringing the business activities of Wolseley Canada under the management of Ferguson the US's largest wholesale distributor of plumbing supplies pipes valves and fittings and a major distributor of heating ventilation and air conditioning (HVAC) equipment. Ferguson operates in all 50 states and has 10 distribution centers across the US.

Its UK Nordic region and France units generated 18% 16% and 14% of revenue in 2011 respectively. The UK business is driven by its Plumb Center and Parts Center branches which are market leaders in the UK plumbing and heating distribution market. The Nordic region business comprises Finland Denmark Norway and Sweden and is represented by such brands as Beijer Neumann Silvan Stark and Starkki. Wolseley France's key brands include Reseau Pro (building materials) and Silverwood (timber).

In mid-2011 Wolseley sold Brossette its French plumbing and heating supplier and Build Center its building materials dealer in the UK to France's Compagnie de Saint-Gobain for a total of #310 million (about $487 million).

Wolseley's smallest geographic segment Central Europe accounts for about 6% of sales and covers Austria Luxembourg Netherlands and Switzerland. Its primary businesses are OAG an Austrian supplier of heating and plumbing supplies Tobler a Swiss distributor of heating and sanitation plumbing supplies and Wasco a Dutch distributor of central heating equipment.

HISTORY

In the late 1800s Irishman Frederick Wolseley immigrated to Australia where he developed the world's first mechanical sheep shearer. In 1889 he formed Wolseley Sheep Shearing Machine Company. Herbert Austin a young engineer who perfected Wolseley's machine moved back to England and became manager of the company's Birmingham factory when the company relocated there in 1893.

In 1895 Austin amazed by an automobile exhibition he attended in Paris obtained an advance from the company to develop an automobile; it went into production in 1901. The car manufacturing operations were separated from the company's other machinery operations and soon were bought by Vickers. (Austin went out on his own in 1905 and began producing cars under his own name –the venerable Austin line.)

By the middle of the century Wolseley Sheep Shearing had grown to include central heating and plumbing products distribution. In 1958 it joined with Geo. H. Hughes to form Wolseley-Hughes. At the time the company was a small manufacturer with 11 distribution depots.

The company's watershed transition began in 1976 when Jeremy Lancaster took over the chairmanship from his father. (In the 20 years that Lancaster was chairman profits rose from about $6 million in 1976 to more than $350 million in 1996.) In the late 1970s the company began expanding rapidly through acquisitions. In 1982 it went public and acquired Ferguson Enterprises a leading distributor of plumbing supplies on the US's East Coast. The acquisition marked the company's first substantial US purchase. Three years later the company formed Wolseley Centers which distributed building products under the names Plumb Center Controls Center and Pipeline Center. In 1986 the company changed its name to Wolseley plc. Acquisitions that year included Carolina Builders Corporation and M.P. Harris & Co. Late 1980s acquisitions included Familian (1987) the largest plumbing supplier on the US's West Coast and Familian Northwest (1988).

Wolseley then looked across the English Channel. In 1992 it bought Brossette France's largest specialist distributor of plumbing supplies. The company moved further eastward in 1994 acquiring OAG Group (now Wolseley Austria) Austria's largest wholesale plumbing supply business. In addition to 40 Austrian branches OAG also had five branches in both Hungary and Germany and four in the Czech Republic. The OAG deal solidified Wolseley's position as the world's #1 plumbing and heating merchant.

Wolseley turned its attention back to the US in the mid-1990s buying a half-dozen companies including Building Material Supply. John Young became CEO that year when Jeremy Lancaster retired from the company.

In 1998 the company began integrating California-based Familian and Virginia-based Ferguson Enterprises –together responsible for more than half of Wolseley's US distribution revenues –under Ferguson's management. The company continued making acquisitions that year and the next including its first Italian company (Manzardo plumbing and heating supplies); it also grew by opening new outlets. Wolseley sold some of its burner and boiler manufacturing operations in 1999.

Chairman Richard Ireland became acting chief executive in June 2000 with the retirement of Young for health reasons. That year the company sold most of its manufacturing businesses. It sold its remaining boiler and burner manufacturing businesses in early 2001. In May 2001 Ferguson Enterprises CEO Charles Banks was named group chief executive.

Also in 2001 Wolseley bought the heating and plumbing operations of Westburne Group (from France-based Rexel a distributor of electrical equipment) for $356 million to further expand in the US. In 2002 Wolseley bought Clayton Acquisition a Florida-based wholesale distributor of waterworks for $110 million. Additionally in 2002 the company bought Wasco a Dutch heating-equipment supplier for $58 million to expand in Europe. In December of that year Ireland was replaced as chairman by deputy chairman John Whybrow.

In July 2003 Wolseley bought Pinault Bois & Materiaux (now PB & M) which distributes lumber and building supplies in France from Pinault-Printemps-Redoute. Wolseley acquired three North American businesses JM Lumber Liberty Equipment & Supply and Nuroc Plumbing and Heating Supplies in September 2003.

The company acquired Tobler Management [now Wolseley (Schweiz)] a Swiss HVAC wholesaler from CapVis in December 2003. PB & M acquired Groupe Simoni a French building materials distributor in January 2004. Wolseley expanded its Irish business through the August 2004 acquisition of Brooks Group an Irish building supply company from UPM-Kymmene. Capping an acquisitive year Wolseley also acquired Parnell-Martin Management and Record Supply Company in the US and TAPS Wholesale Bath Centre in Canada in December 2004.

Overall in the fiscal year ended July 2005 the company spent #431 million on 26 acquisitions.

In April 2006 Wolseley acquired Brandon Hire for #72 million. The acquisition of DT Group in September brought Wolseley into new markets in Denmark Finland Norway and Sweden. In October the company purchased Woodcote - stavebni materialy a.s. a general builders merchant with operations in the Czech Republic the Slovak Republic Hungary Poland Romania and Croatia. Overall in fiscal 2006 the company added 279 new locations.

In August 2007 Wolseley purchased Davidson Pipe Company in the US thereby gaining access to the New York metropolitan market.

In 2008 the company acquired Gama Myjava in Slovakia.

In May 2009 Wolseley sold a 51% stake in Stock Building Supply to The Gores Group LLC a US private equity firm. In June Ian Meakins joined Wolseley as CEO. He succeeded Claude "Chip" Hornsby who resigned from the position after three years.

In July 2011 the company sold its Electric Center business to Edmundson Electrical. In November Wolseley sold its remaining 49% stake in Stock Building Supply to Gores Group.

EXECUTIVES

Chairman, Gareth Davis, age 63
Board Member; Chief Executive North America, Frank W. Roach, age 62, $953,727 total compensation
Group Chief Executive and Board Member, Ian K. Meakins, $74,229 total compensation
Group Treasurer and Tax, Mike Verrier
Secretary General Counsel and Board Member, Richard Shoylekov, age 47
Chief Financial Officer; Executive Director, John Martin, age 47
Director Corporate Communications, Mark Fearon
Board Member, Alain Le Goff, age 60
Board Member, Nigel M. Stein, age 58
Board Member; Chief Executive North America, Frank W. Roach, age 62
Board Member, Andrew J. (Andy) Duff, age 54
Group Chief Executive and Board Member, Ian K. Meakins
Secretary General Counsel and Board Member, Richard Shoylekov, age 47
Board Member, James I. K. Murray, age 66
Board Member, Michael P. (Mike) Wareing, age 59
CFO and Board Member, John Martin, age 46
Non-Executive Director, Michael Clarke
Auditors: PricewaterhouseCoopersLLP

LOCATIONS

HQ: Wolseley Plc Jersey
26 New Street, St Helier, Jersey JE2 3RA
Phone: (44) 118 929 8700 **Fax:** (44) 118 929 8701
Web: www.wolseley.com

2011 Sales

	% of total
North America	
US	40
Canada	6
UK	18
Nordic	16
France	14
Central	6
Total	**100**

PRODUCTS/OPERATIONS

2011 Sales by Market

	% of total
Residential repair maintenance &	36
Non-residential repair maintenance &	21
Residential new	20
Non-residential new	16
Civil	7
Total	**100**

2011 Sales by Product

	% of total
Plumbing heating & air	40
Building	30
Civil/waterworks commercial &	28
Other	2
Total	**100**

Selected Products

Building materials
- Beams and trusses
- Bricks blocks and aggregates
- Cement

- Doors and frames
- Glass
- Insulation
- Plaster and plasterboard
- Roofing materials
- Tiles and flooring
- Timber products

Civil/waterworks industrial and commercial
- Carbon and stainless steel pipes valves and fittings
- Drainage pipes
- Underground pressure pipes

Plumbing heating and air conditioning
- Air conditioning equipment
- Baths and showers
- Boilers and burners
- Brassware
- Control equipment
- Copper tubing
- Heat pumps
- Hot water cylinders
- Plastic pipes and fittings
- Radiators and valves
- Sanitaryware
- Solar equipment
- Ventilation equipment

Other
- Electrical cables
- Lighting
- Wiring
- Services
  - Customer inventory management
  - Installation
  - Maintenance

Selected Subsidiaries

CFM
- Heating appliances Luxembourg

DT Group
- Building materials Denmark

Ferguson Enterprises Inc.
- Wholesale distribution of plumbing heating and piping products US

Manzardo SpA
- Heating and plumbing equipment Italy

OAG AG
- Heating and plumbing products Austria

PB&M
- Building materials and wood distribution France

Tobler
- Heating and plumbing products Switzerland

Wasco Holding BV
- Heating equipment The Netherlands

Wolseley Canada
- Wholesale distribution of plumbing heating and ventilation products Canada

Wolseley France
- Building materials plumbing and heating products France

Wolseley UK Limited
- Construction products UK

Woodcote Group
- Construction materials Czech Republic

COMPETITORS

84 Lumber
B&Q
Castorama Dubois
Emco Corporation
Grafton Group
HD Supply
HSS Hire
Hewden Stuart
Interline Brands
Jewson
Kingfisher
Lowe' s
MPS Builders and Merchants
MSC Industrial Direct
Noland
SIG plc
Saint-Gobain Building Distribution
Speedy Hire
Thermador Groupe
Travis Perkins
Waxman

HISTORICAL FINANCIALS

Company Type: Public

Income Statement

FYE: July 31

	REVENUE ($ mil.)	NET INCOME ($ mil.)	NET PROFIT MARGIN	EMPLOYEES
07/13	20,003	463	2.3%	39,995
07/12	21,038	89	0.4%	43,170
07/11	22,095	441	2.0%	46,246
07/10	20,704	(533)	—	48,226
07/09	23,870	(1,938)	—	55,132
Annual Growth	(4.3%)	—	—	(7.7%)

2013 Year-End Financials

Debt ratio: 17.5%
Return on equity: 9.8%
Cash ($ mil.): 515
Current ratio: 1.51
Long-term debt ($ mil.): 1,139
No. of shares (mil.): 274
Dividends
Yield: —
Payout: —
Market value ($ mil.): 1,320

	STOCK PRICE ($) FY Close	P/E High	P/E Low	PER SHARE ($) Earnings	Dividends	Book Value
07/13	4.81	11	8	1.67	0.00	16.92
07/12	3.58	48	25	0.32	0.00	17.73
07/11	2.96	9	6	1.67	0.00	20.86
Annual Growth	27.5%	—	—	(0.1%)	—	(5.1%)

Woolworths Ltd.

Chow Down Under with Australia's #1 food retailer (ahead of Coles) — Woolworths (aka "Woolies"). The diversified retailer operates about 3200 stores in Australia and New Zealand including more than 1000 supermarkets under the Woolworths Foodtown Countdown and Thomas Dux banners. It also operates BWS and Dan Murphy's liquor stores. In addition Woolworths sells gasoline and leverages its distribution network to provide wholesale merchandise for third-party supermarkets. Woolworths' 165-odd general merchandise discount stores operate under the Big W name. It also runs about 395 consumer electronics shops under the Dick Smith and Tandy brand names. Woolworths also operates nearly 300 hotels.

Woolworths' total fiscal 2011 (ends June) sales rose nearly 5% vs. the previous year. The retailer's supermarket Australian supermarkets outperformed their counterparts in New Zealand. Indeed sales at the New Zealand markets declined slightly in 2011 vs. 2010 while the Australian markets rose more than 4%. Sales at the company's Big W general merchandise stores dipped while the consumer electronics category rose 4%. Online sales increased 63% with Woolworths onlne now available to 85% of Australia's population.

Woolworths along with other Australian retailers has been hit by weak consumer demand and competition from online retailers. Looking to streamline its operations the company in early 2012 announced plans to sell its Dick Smith consumer electronics business but will continue to participate in the category through its Big W stores and an expanded online offering. Stung by competition from Internet retailers the company is focused on expanding its online operations. (The company's pending exit from the Dick Smith business will not impact the its partnership with India's Tata Group for a chain of consumer electronics stores in India. Woolworths is supplying Tata's chain of 50 Croma stores there.)

The decision to sell Dick Smith followed the purchase by the firm's Australian Leisure and Hospitality Group (ALH) of about 30 hotels in New South Wales in late 2011. ALH operates sports bars and pubs restaurants retail liquor stores gaming outlets and nightclubs and hotels across Australia. To stock its liquor cabinet Woolworths in 2011 acquired The Cellarmasters Group from Archer Capital for A$340 million ($346 million). Cellarmasters is a leading direct-to-home wine retailer with operations in Australia and New Zealand. It also has a winemaking operation. The purchase complemented the company's existing liquor brands which include Dan Murphy's BWS Woolworth's Liquor and Langton's.

On the home front Woolworths is taking on the big-box home improvement market in partnership with the #2 home improvement chain in the US — Lowe's Companies. The Danks joint venture which is two-thirds owned by Woolworths has begun opening Lowe's-style home improvement stores in Australia under the Danks and Masters banners. Plans are for more than 150 such sites over the next five years. The stores will compete with market leader Bunnings owned by rival Wesfarmers which also owns Coles.

HISTORY

Harold Percival Christmas first tried a mail-order dress business before opening the popular Frock Salon retail store. Christmas and his partners opened a branch store in the Imperial Arcade in Sydney in 1924 renaming it "Woolworths Stupendous Bargain Basement" and luring customers with advertisements calling it "a handy place where good things are cheap ... you'll want to live at Woolworths." The company borrowed the name from Frank Woolworth's successful US chain after determining that chain had no plans to open stores in Australia. Woolworths was listed on the Australian stock exchange in 1924.

Food sales came more than 30 years later. Woolworths opened its first freestanding full-line supermarket in 1960 then diversified into specialty retail buying the Rockmans women's clothing store chain the next year (sold in 2000). It expanded into discounting with the Big W chain in 1976 and further diversified when it bought 60% of the Dick Smith Electronics store chain in 1981 (buying the remainder in 1983).

The purchase of the Safeway grocery chain (the Australian operations of the US-based chain) put Woolworths on the top of the supermarket heap in 1985. But the company was hurting (it lost $13 million in 1985-86) because of a restructuring in the early 1980s that had weakened management by bulking up the front offices and dividing responsibilities. Woolworths got a shot in the arm from Paul Simons who returned to the company in 1987 after running competitor Franklins. Simons cleaned house in the front offices closed unprofitable stores and began the successful "Fresh Food People" marketing strategy.

Industrial Equity Limited (IEL) bought the company in 1989; IEL then became part of the Adelaide Steamship group which spun off Woolworths as a public company in 1993. Career Woolworths manager Reg Clairs took over as CEO the following year following the untimely death (on a golf course) in 1993 of Harry Watts who was being groomed for the job. As a result the company has an unwritten rule of avoiding CEOs older than 60.

Clairs took the company in a variety of new directions. Woolworths began supplying fresh food to neighbor Asia in 1995. The company added Plus Petrol outlets adjacent to Woolworths Supermarkets in 1996. It also started a superstore concept for its Dick Smith Electronics chain (Power House) that year. In 1997 the company launched its Woolworths Metro store chain which targets commuters and other on-the-run shoppers in urban areas and it aggressively jumped into wholesaling to independent grocers.

Clairs (who was turning 60 in 1999) stepped down in late 1998 and Roger Corbett took over as CEO. Woolworths also began offering banking services to its customers and bought Dan Murphy a Victoria-based liquor chain in 1998. It divested its Chisholm Manufacturing meat plants in 2000.

In 2001 Woolworths acquired two liquor store chains (Liberty Liquor Booze Bros) more than 200 Tandy Electronics stores and 72 Franklins supermarkets from Hong Kong-based Dairy Farm International Holdings (most of which were later converted to the Woolworths and Food for Less banners). It sold its Crazy Prices general merchandise stores and began restructuring its liquor operations into four distinctive formats.

Woolworths exited the New Zealand market in 2002 when it sold its supermarkets group there to Foodland Associated for $690 million.

Supermarket division chief Bill Wavish resigned in May 2003 and was replaced by former chief general manager of supermarket operations Tom Flood. Wavish was considered one of the top candidates to replace CEO Corbett. Also in 2003 the company discontinued its Australian Independent Wholesalers (AIW) operations. Flood who like Wavish was considered a likely successor to Corbett resigned abruptly in August 2004.

The company acquired Australia's biggest pub owner Australian Leisure & Hospitality (ALH) in 2005. Woolworths operates ALH's retailing activities leaving the pubs and gaming operations to its partner in the purchase The Bruce Mathieson Group. (Previously the duo had acquired a 16% stake in ALH.) In mid-2005 the company acquired the New Zealand supermarkets of Foodland Associated and 22 Action stores in Western Australia Queensland and New South Wales for about $1.8 billion.

In September 2006 the company announced it had purchased a 10% stake in New Zealand's The Warehouse retail chain. Corbett retired as CEO in October. He was succeeded by Michael Luscombe the company's long-serving director of supermarkets.

Woolworths offered about $1.7 billion in 2008 to buy all of New Zealand's leading general merchandise retailer Warehouse Group. The purchase however which would have allowed Woolworths to expand from food into general merchandise in New Zealand was blocked by that country's competition regulator in mid-2008. An attempt to take over Australia's JB Hi-Fi an independent chain of home entertainment products also failed.

In February 2011 Woolworths acquired The Cellarmasters Group from Archer Capital for A$340 million ($346 million). In October Grant O'Brien was named CEO of the company.

EXECUTIVES

Group General Counsel and Company Secretary, Peter Horton
Finance Director, Thomas (Tom) Pockett, $773,894 total compensation
Director of BIG W, Julie Coates, $563,221 total compensation
Director Corporate and Public Affairs, Andrew Hall
General Manager Liquor, Steve Greentree
General Manager Logistics, Geoff Thomas
Director of Supermarkets, Tjeerd Jegen
Acting Director of Human Resources, Catherine Catherine Flynn Flynn
Chief Executive Officer; Managing Director; Executive Director, Grant Grant OBrien OBrien
Director - Multi Channel and Supply Chain, Penelope Penelope Winn Winn
Chairman of the Board, Ralph Ralph Waters Waters
Chief Operating Officer - Australian Supermarkets and Petrol, Steven Greentree
Director, Roderick S. Deane, age 71
Director, Ian J. Macfarlane, age 67
Director, Alison M. Watkins, age 49
Director, Diane J. Grady, age 64
Director, John Astbury, age 68
Managing Director and CEO, Grant O'Brien, age 50
Director, Leon M. L. Huillier, age 69
Non-Executive Director, Allan Allan Douglas Mackay Mackay
Non-Executive Independent Director, Carla Carla Hrdlicka Hrdlicka
Non-Executive Director, Christine Christine Cross Cross
Non-Executive Independent Director, Jillian Jillian Broadbent Broadbent
Non-Executive Director, Michael Michael Ullmer Ullmer
Auditors: DeloitteToucheTohmatsu

LOCATIONS

HQ: Woolworths Ltd.
1 Woolworths Way, Bella Vista, Sydney, New South Wales 2153
Phone: (61) 2 8885 0000 **Fax:** (61) 2 8888 1066
Web: www.woolworthslimited.com.au

2011 Supermarkets

	No.
Australia	840
New	156
Total	**996**

2011 Sales

	% of total
Australia	92
New	8
Total	**100**

PRODUCTS/OPERATIONS

2011 Sales

	% of total
Supermarkets	86
General	11
Hotels &	3
Total	**100**

COMPETITORS

ALDI
BP
Harvey Norman Holdings
Metcash
Royal Dutch Shell
Wesfarmers

HISTORICAL FINANCIALS

Company Type: Public

Income Statement FYE: June 30

	REVENUE ($ mil.)	NET INCOME ($ mil.)	NET PROFIT MARGIN	EMPLOYEES
06/13	54,119	2,084	3.9%	197,637
06/12	55,514	1,824	3.3%	0
06/11	57,313	2,242	3.9%	190,000
06/10	45,275	1,766	3.9%	188,000
06/09	40,075	1,480	3.7%	191,000
Annual Growth	7.8%	8.9%	—	0.9%

2013 Year-End Financials

Debt ratio: 18.4%
Return on equity: 25.8%
Cash ($ mil.): 783
Current ratio: 0.91
Long-term debt ($ mil.): 3,950
No. of shares (mil.): 1,250
Dividends
Yield: —
Payout: —
Market value ($ mil.): 38,318

	STOCK PRICE ($) FY Close	P/E High/Low		PER SHARE ($) Earnings	Dividends	Book Value
06/13	30.65	20	14	1.68	0.00	6.66
06/12	27.05	23	14	1.49	0.00	6.68
06/11	28.40	19	12	1.83	0.00	6.59
06/10	24.25	14	9	1.43	0.00	5.38
06/09	20.75	12	5	1.21	0.00	4.49
Annual Growth	10.2%	—	—	8.6%	—	10.4%

Woori Finance Holdings Co., Ltd

Woori Finance Holdings (aka Woori Financial Group) was formed in 2001 when the South Korean government consolidated its interests in Hanvit Bank (now Woori Bank) Kyongnam Bank Kwangju Bank Peace Bank and Hanaro Merchant Bank. Together the group has more than 1100 domestic and some 15 international locations. Most of these are Woori Bank branches; Woori Bank is the third-largest commercial bank in the nation by assets. It also owns regional banks Kyongnam Bank and Kwangju Bank. In addition to deposit and lending offerings the company provides securities brokerage asset management wealth management and insurance services. The South Korean government owns about 56% of Woori Financial Group.

The government intends to sell off blocks of its stake in Woori Financial and eventually privatize the company outright. It has had to put those plans on hold numerous times most recently due to the global credit crunch but it now hopes to have the sale completed in 2011. In early 2010 it sold about 10% to institutional investors.

Woori Financial Group has been focused on expansion abroad as well as on growing its non-banking businesses. Woori America Bank provides retail and corporate banking services in the US targeting Korean-American customers. The subsidiary has more than 40 offices in California Maryland New Jersey New York Pennsylvania and Virginia. Woori planned to expand its presence in Southern California with the acquisition of struggling bank Hanmi Financial which would have added about 30 branches but both parties called the deal off in mid-2011. Regulatory delays and the relatively weak capital levels of both Hanmi and Woori's US unit contributed to the companies' decision to cancel the acquisition. Woori will continue to seek opportunities in the West and has not ruled out buying Hanmi down the road.

Woori has also said it would acquire troubled banks in South Korea that have been laid low by real estate woes and it plans to spin off part of its credit card operations in efforts to strengthen that business.

Other units of the company include Woori Investment & Securities which provides investment banking and merchant banking services from about 130 offices. Credit Suisse Group bought a 30% stake of Woori Asset Management in 2006 but sold its stake back to Woori for an undisclosed amount in 2009.

LOCATIONS

HQ: Woori Finance Holdings Co., Ltd
20th Floor, 203 Hoehyon-dong, 1-ga, Jung-gu, Seoul 100-792
Phone: (82) 2 2125 2110 **Fax:** (82) 2 2125 2293
Web: www.woorifg.com

HISTORICAL FINANCIALS

Company Type: Public

Income Statement FYE: December 31

	ASSETS ($ mil.)	NET INCOME ($ mil.)	INCOME AS % OF ASSETS	EMPLOYEES
12/12	305,052	1,483	0.5%	136
12/11	269,951	1,844	0.7%	152
12/10	259,683	1,149	0.4%	142
12/09	246,234	886	0.4%	123
12/08	229,256	358	0.2%	23,000
Annual Growth	7.4%	42.7%	—	(72.3%)

2012 Year-End Financials

Return on assets: 0.4%
Return on equity: 8.7%
Long-term debt ($ mil.): —
No. of shares (mil.): 806
Sales ($ mil): 16,101
Dividends
Yield: 1.9%
Payout: 33.2%
Market value ($ mil.): 26,881

	STOCK PRICE ($) FY Close	P/E High/Low	PER SHARE ($) Earnings	Dividends	Book Value
12/12	33.35	— —	1.81	0.66	21.69
12/11	24.41	— —	2.29	0.00	18.76
12/10	41.55	— —	1.43	0.27	17.37
12/09	35.95	— —	1.10	0.00	14.71
12/08	14.27	— —	0.44	0.76	11.93
Annual Growth	23.6%	— —	42.0%	(3.5%)	16.1%

ZF Friedrichshafen AG (Germany)

ZF Friedrichshafen (ZF) shifts easily from land to air to sea. The company makes automatic and manual transmissions for commercial vehicles cars aircraft and marine vessels. ZF also makes rail transmissions and industrial drives such as servo gearboxes. Its off-road division makes transmissions for construction equipment and farm machinery. ZF's chassis unit makes automotive rear-axle systems and suspension modules. Through ZF Lenksysteme (a joint venture with Robert Bosch) the company makes steering systems. ZF was founded in 1915 by Ferdinand von Zeppelin (the Zeppelin inventor). The Zeppelin Stiftung Foundation which is largely controlled by the town of Friedrichshafen owns more than 90% of the company.

Geography continues to be an important subject for the company. As with most of its competitiors ZF has turned its attention toward the East. Automobile production in China is expected to increase by about 50% in 2010 compared to 2005. For continued growth the company is beefing up its sales activities in the emerging region. ZF is also keeping an eye out for partnerships and potential joint ventures that will help it strengthen its global footprint while complementing its product mix.

ZF has not forgotten about Western Europe the source of 60% of the company sales. In late 2010 ZF acquired Fonderie Lorraine a France-based supplier of light-alloy internal transmission parts and housings from fellow German manufacturer HONSEL. The deal strengthens the supply chain for ZF's automatic transmissions in the region and will allow the company to take advantage of the light-alloy foundry operations to facilitate the manufacture of the the company's new 8-speed automatic transmissions.

The company opened a new production plant for powertrain and suspension components at its Slovakian site in Levice and a production facility in Europe for the industrial manufacture of hybrid modules for passenger cars. It signed an agreement with Continental in May 2009 to develop and produce commercial vehicle hybrid drives; ZF will produce the drive system and Continental will supply the electronics. The company signed a supply agreement to produce 35000 dual-mass flywheels and clutches for Subaru's first diesel boxer engine and together with Porsche it developed the seven-speed dual clutch transmission which began volume production. ZF opened its new Development Center in Friedrichshafen for its Commercial Vehicle and Special Driveline Technology division.

Weakened by the ripple effects of Detroit's problems the beleaguered North American auto component industry is a target-rich environment for acquisitions. In North America ZF is restructuring its operations while keeping an eye out for potential acquisitions particularly for companies involved in gear technology as evidenced by its November 2008 acquisition of Cherry Corporation which it has renamed as ZF Electronics. The acquisition strengthened its technology position in the electronics sector. ZF is going forward with a joint venture with Chrysler to make axles for Chrysler and other customers beginning in 2010.

The company has expanded its after-sales business by merging key organizations to form the new Services business unit. This segment will be involved in logistics and infrastructure with an eye on building its range of products and services available to customers. ZF operates more than 100 production companies six main development locations over 40 after-market trading companies and sales and service centers over 10 marketing offices and has 650 service partners worldwide.

HISTORY

After the 1908 fiery demonstration of an early airship Count Ferdinand Graf von Zeppelin thought he was ruined. However despite its unfortunate fate the airship's brief flight managed to captivate the interest of the citizens of Friedrichshafen Germany. The townspeople donated funds to Count Zeppelin raising more than 6 million German marks. He used the money to found Luftschiffbau Zeppelin GmbH in 1908. The company was controlled by the Zeppelin Stiftung (founded by the count) for the town of Friedrichshafen.

In 1915 Zahnradfabrik Friedrichshafen GmbH (ZF) was created by Luftschiffbau Zeppelin for the development and manufacture of special gears for airships and other aircraft. Count Zeppelin died two years later.

ZF was converted from a private firm to a stock corporation in 1921. To reflect the change the company's name was changed to Zahnradfabrik Friedrichshafen AG. ZF AG developed the first helical-gear transmission in 1929. The company began producing automotive steering systems in 1932.

Like much of Germany's industrial production capacity Zahnradfabrik Friedrichshafen's operations were out of commission by the end of WWII. Reconstruction of the company's factories was completed in 1946 when production resumed with 1000 workers.

In accordance with the count's will complete ownership of the Zeppelin Stiftung foundation was transferred to the city of Friedrichshafen in 1947. Three years later most of ZF's ownership (90%) was assigned to the Zeppelin Stiftung.

ZF expanded into South America in 1959 with the establishment of ZF do Brasil SA. The company developed its first automatic transmission in 1961. A little over a decade later (1973) the company reached 1 billion German marks in sales and employed 18000 workers. ZF entered the US in 1979 with the founding of ZF of North America in Chicago. In 1986 the company expanded its US operations to include a factory for the production of pickup truck transmissions in Gainesville Georgia.

The company changed its name from Zahnradfabrik Friedrichshafen AG to the relatively less-cumbersome ZF Friedrichshafen AG in 1992. By 1997 ZF had established four joint ventures in China. The following year was busy for the company. It formed ZF Lenksysteme a joint venture with Robert Bosch for the manufacture of automotive steering systems. By mid-1998 ZF had also founded ZF Batavia LLC with Ford Motor Company in the US for the production of automatic transmissions for passenger cars and ZF Meritor with Meritor (now ArvinMeritor) for the production and distribution of commercial vehicle transmissions in North America.

In 2000 ZF and Sauer AG formed ZF Graziano Materials Handling Components GmbH a joint venture that combined their respective forklift transmission operations.

The following year ZF agreed to acquire Mannesmann Sachs AG (transmission and driveline components). The deal was completed in 2002 and the division was renamed ZF Sachs AG.

In 2008 to stay lean the company shed some noncore operations including its ZF Meritor joint venture with ArvinMeritor.

EXECUTIVES

Chairman of the Group Works Council of ZF Friedrichshafen AG, Johann Kirchgassner
Executive Vice President ZF Group, Michael Paul, age 61
VP Finance Commercial Vehicle and Special Driveline Technology Division and Member Supervisory Board, Rupert Baur
CEO, Stefan Sommer, age 54
EVP and Member Management Board, Reinhard Buhl, age 61
EVP and Member Management Board, Peter Ottenbruch, age 55
Chairman Supervisory Board, Prof Dr. Giorgio Behr, age 65
Member Management Board, Rolf Lutz, age 61
EVP and Member Management Board, Gerhard Wagner, age 59
EVP and Member Management Board, Jurgen Holeksa, age 47
EVP and Member Board of Management, Wilhelm Rehm
Communications Manager, Martin Meissner
Chief Financial Officer CFO, Thomas Henne
Member Supervisory Board, Franz-Josef Paefgen, age 66
Member Supervisory Board, Hans Dietmar Sauer
Vice Chairman, Johann Kirchgassner
VP Finance Commercial Vehicle and Special Driveline Technology Division and Member Supervisory Board, Rupert Baur
Member Supervisory Board, Uwe Christensen
Member Supervisory Board, Wolfgang Schuler
Member Supervisory Board, Barbara Kux, age 59
Member Supervisory Board, Josef Buchelmeier
Member Supervisory Board, Jurgen Bunge
Member Supervisory Board, Willy Dekant

Member Supervisory Board, Joachim Milberg
Member Supervisory Board, Martin Ocker
Member Supervisory Board, Helmut Petri
Member Supervisory Board, Lilo Rademacher
Member Supervisory Board, Hermann Sicklinger
Member Supervisory Board, Irmgard Ulderup
Member Supervisory Board, Henning Wallentowitz
Member Supervisory Board, Bernd Wiedmann
Auditors:
Ernst&YoungGmbHWirtschaftsprufungsgesellschaft

LOCATIONS

HQ: ZF Friedrichshafen AG (Germany)
Graf-von-Soden-Platz 1, Friedrichshafen D-88046
Phone: (49) 7541 77 0 **Fax:** (49) 7541 77 90 80 00
Web: www.zf.com

2009 Sales

	% of total
Europe	
Western	60
Eastern	5
Asia/Pacific	18
North	10
South	5
Africa	2
Total	**100**

PRODUCTS/OPERATIONS

2009 Sales

	% of total
Powertrain & suspension	21
Car driveline	19
Commercial vehicle & special driveline	19
Off-road driveline technology & axle	14
Car chassis	13
Steering	13
Services	11
Rubber-metal	5
Electronic	2
Marine propulsion	2
Aviation	1
Corporate R&D corporate headquarters & service	1
Total	**100**

2009 Sales by Market

	% of total
Cars & light commercial	65
Commercial	21
Construction & agricultural machinery marine craft aircraft special & rail	14
Total	**100**

Selected Divisions and Products

Aftermarket
- Spare parts

Aviation technology
- Aircraft transmissions

Car chassis technology
- Airbag housings
- Axle systems
- Gearshift systems
- Rubber-metal components
- Suspension joints
- Tie rods
- Wheel suspension modules

Car driveline technology
- Automatic transmissions
- Continuously variable transmissions
- Manual transmissions

Commercial vehicle and special driveline technology
- Automatic transmissions
- Electromagnetic clutches
- Hydrodynamic retarders
- Manual transmissions
- Torque converter units
- Transfer gearboxes

Marine propulsion systems
- Marine transmissions

Off-road driveline technology and axle systems
- Agricultural machinery axles
- Agricultural machinery transmissions
- Axles for fork-lift trucks
- Axle systems for commercial vehicles
- Construction machinery axles
- Construction machinery transmissions
- Transmissions for elevators
- Transmissions for fork-lift trucks
- Transmissions for mobile mixers

Powertrain and suspension components
- Axle modules
- Cab dampers
- Clutch systems
- Electric propulsion systems
- Powertrain automation
- Ride-height control systems
- Shock absorbers
- Torque converters

Rubber-metal technology
- Bumper impact dampers
- Chassis suspension
- Plastic components
- Powertrain suspension
- Vibration and noise control products

Steering technology
- Ball and nut power steerings for cars and commercial vehicles
- Electro-hydraulic steering systems
- Limited-slip differentials
- Rack and pinion power steerings
- Rear axle steering systems for commercial vehicles
- Steer by wire systems (electric steerings)
- Steering accessories
- Steering columns
- Steering pumps
- Steering shafts
- Steering valves

COMPETITORS

Aisin Seiki
American Axle & Manufacturing
Carraro
Continental AG
DENSO
Dana Holding
Delphi Automotive Systems
Eaton
GKN
Magna International
Meritor
Metaldyne
Robert Bosch LLC
TRW Automotive
Visteon

HISTORICAL FINANCIALS

Company Type: Public

Income Statement

FYE: December 31

	REVENUE ($ mil.)	NET INCOME ($ mil.)	NET PROFIT MARGIN	EMPLOYEES
12/12	22,889	402	1.8%	74,775
12/11	20,060	649	3.2%	71,488
12/10	17,274	546	3.2%	64,600
12/09	13,499	(629)	—	59,771
12/08	17,477	589	3.4%	63,288
Annual Growth	7.0%	(9.1%)	—	4.3%

2012 Year-End Financials

Debt ratio: 12.9%
Return on equity: 7.8%
Cash ($ mil.): 1,393
Current ratio: 1.61
Long-term debt ($ mil.): 1,294
No. of shares (mil.): 300
Dividends
Yield: —
Payout: —
Market value ($ mil.): —

Zurich Insurance Group Ltd

The operations of Zurich Insurance Group (formerly Zurich Financial Services) have crossed over the Alps and spread around the globe. Serving approximately 170 countries worldwide the company is a major global provider of property/casualty and life insurance. Focused on markets in Europe and North America the company's general insurance segment offers commercial and personal property/casualty and specialty coverage while its global life segment offers life insurance annuities and other investment policies. Zurich's Farmers Group division offers personal property/casualty insurance policies in the US. The company was founded in 1872.

Geographic Reach

With operations spread around the globe Zurich's general insurance division's core markets include Germany Italy Spain Switzerland the UK and the US in addition to the domestic Swiss market. Other international business units are focused in Latin America the Asia/Pacific region China South Africa and other emerging markets.

Operations

Zurich's general insurance segment which accounts for about half of the company's annual premiums and fees provides property/casualty and specialty insurance to a variety of clients. Its global corporate unit focuses on risk management for large international and domestic clients while the Europe general insurance division provides property/casualty and specialty lines for businesses and individuals. In the US Zurich provides commercial and specialty property/casualty policies for small to midsized business customers through its North America commercial unit which includes Zurich American Insurance Company and its subsidiaries.

Zurich's global life segment (40% of premiums and fees) offers life investment pension and savings plans for individuals and groups. Global life operates through regional subsidiaries to provide localized services to its clients. Its businesses include Farmers New World Life in the US Openwork in the UK and other subsidiaries and partnerships in Europe. The division is growing in emerging markets as well.

The company's third major division Farmers Group provides personal auto and homeowners' coverage in the US as well as small business life and specialty insurance policies. Its operating divisions include 21st Century Insurance and Bristol West Holdings.

Marketing and Sales

All of the Zurich operating segments use a mixture of distribution channels to promote their products. The company has affiliated agents and it also uses independent brokers financial advisors and bank representatives to promote its policies.

During 2012 Zurich strengthened its distribution network in emerging markets by expanding agreements to sell through bank representatives in Indonesia Italy Spain and the Middle East; the firm made similar banking arrangements in Latin America during 2011. In addition the Farmers network in the US expanded its network of exclusive agents during 2012.

Financial Performance

Zurich reported a 33% revenue increase to some $70 billion in 2012 as well as 5% profit growth to nearly $4 billion. The company attributed its success to portfolio management and pricing discipline measures especially during challenging market conditions including weather events in the US and disappointing results in the German general insurance market. Overall the US market showed solid returns and Zurich also highlighted successful integration of acquired businesses in Latin America and Malaysia.

The company which has undertaken extensive restructuring efforts in recent years has steadily increased profits over the last four years. However sales growth in 2012 followed a decrease in revenues in both 2010 and 2011.

Strategy

In 2012 the company changed its name from Zurich Financial Services to Zurich Insurance

Group to reflect its concentration on the insurance business. The company has undergone nearly ten years of strategic reorganization efforts to refocus its operations around its principal lines of business. The company's reorganization programs have aimed to help Zurich achieve its financial efficiency and expansion goals as well as to increase profitability.

Divestitures of noncore businesses continued into 2012 including the transfer of the UK general insurance portfolio of Eagle Star Insurance Group –a run-off business that does not actively market policies –through a reinsurance agreement with the RiverStone Insurance.

At the same time as it is focused on tightening its organization and improving returns in existing markets Zurich is also looking to expand in high-growth emerging markets such as Brazil China Russia Spain Turkey and Taiwan. Zurich has also benefited from its efforts to expand into markets deemed "under-represented." One strategy is to provide niche product offerings to reach targeted customer segments such as expatriates and minority groups. In the US market the Farmers division is working to expand its operations in the eastern states.

Mergers and Acquisitions

To further expansion efforts in the growing Latin American markets in 2011 Zurich acquired a 51% stake in general and life insurance divisions of Banco Santander in Argentina Brazil Chile Mexico and Uruguay; those divisions now operate as Zurich Santander. Also that year Zurich expanded in the Asia/Pacific region through the purchase of composite insurer Malaysian Assurance Alliance Berhad.

In 2010 it purchased Lebanese general insurance firm Compagnie Libanaise D'Assurances to accelerate its expansion measures in the Middle East.

HISTORY

The roots of Zurich Financial Services stretch back to the 1872 founding of a reinsurer for Switzerland Transport Insurance. The company soon branched out into accident travel and workers' compensation insurance and in 1875 it changed its name to Transport and Accident Insurance plc Zurich to reflect the changes. It then expanded into Berlin (the jumping-off point for its expansion into Scandinavia and Russia) and Stuttgart Germany. The company exited marine lines in 1880; it later left the reinsurance business and expanded into liability insurance; in 1894 it changed its name to Zurich General Accident and Liability Insurance.

In 1912 Zurich crossed the Atlantic expanding operations into the US. It agreed in 1925 to provide insurance for Ford cars at favorable terms. Zurich's business was hard hit during the war years of the late 1930s and 1940s. In 1955 the company changed its name to Zurich Insurance.

Starting in the 1960s Zurich began buying other insurers including Alpina (1965 Switzerland) Agrippina (1969 Germany) and Maryland Casualty Group (1989 US). It also bought the property liability operations of American General.

The company shifted its strategy in the early 1990s expanding into what it deemed underrepresented markets in the UK and the US. Being big wasn't enough; Zurich needed to find a focus. It also jettisoned such marginal or unprofitable business lines as commercial fire insurance in Germany.

In 1995 Zurich bought struggling Chicago-based asset manager Kemper and in 1997 bought lackluster mutual fund manager Scudder Stevens & Clark forming Scudder Kemper. That year it also bought failed Hong Kong investment bank Peregrine Investment Holdings.

Zurich merged in 1998 with the financial services businesses of B.A.T Industries formerly known as the British-American Tobacco Co. created in 1902 as a joint venture between UK-based Imperial Tobacco and American Tobacco. As public disapproval of smoking grew in the 1970s British-American Tobacco began diversifying; it changed its name to B.A.T Industries in 1976 and moved into insurance. In 1984 it rescued UK insurer Eagle Star from a hostile offer by German insurance giant Allianz. The next year it bought Hambro Life Assurance renaming it Allied Dunbar. Moving into the large US market in 1988 B.A.T bought Farmers Insurance Group.

While B.A.T battled the antismoking army of the 1990s the insurance industry struggled with stagnant growth. In 1997 Europe's largest insurance firms were named as defendants in class action lawsuits that sought recovery for unpaid claims on Holocaust-era insurance policies. In 1998 Zurich became a founding member of the International Commission on Holocaust Era Insurance Claims (ICHEIC).

Also in 1998 Zurich and B.A.T's insurance units merged to create Zurich Financial Services. The firm reshuffled some of its holdings and sold Eagle Star Reinsurance. In 1999 Zurich spun off its real estate holdings into PSP Swiss Property and at the turn of the century it focused on expansion buying the new business of insurer Abbey Life which it merged into Allied Dunbar. In 2000 the holding companies formed to own Zurich (Zurich Allied and Allied Zurich) were merged into the firm.

In 2002 Zurich completed the spinoff of reinsurance unit Zurich Re which became Converium. It also sold troubled asset manager Zurich Scudder to Deutsche Bank and acquired the bank's life insurance operations in Italy Spain and Portugal. It also acquired life insurance firm Deutsche Herold as well as German financial services provider Bonfinanz and mutual fund distributor DGV. Zurich also sold a large holding in its US-based Zurich Life to BANK ONE and sold its operations in Hungary Poland and Slovakia to Italian insurer Generali. Zurich paid out some $900 million in claims related to the September 11 2001 terrorist attacks in the US.

The write-off of assets and strengthening of non-life reserves resulted in Zurich posting a $3.4 billion loss for 2002. Rolf Huppi Zurich's legendary chairman and CEO stepped down while the company's asset management unit tumbled and investors pulled out. James Schiro previously with PricewaterhouseCoopers was named as the new chief executive and began guiding a turnaround at the company.

Schiro launched a restructuring initiative in 2004. The company began its "The Zurich Way" rebranding efforts the following year which began a financial turnaround for the company. The reorganization program sought to refocus the company's operations around its principal lines of business (including insurance underwriting and reserving risk management and investment management) and consolidate Zurich's General Insurance and Global Life businesses under the Zurich brand.

To enhance efficiencies the firm streamlined its distribution cross-selling customer service and claims management processes. The company estimated that achievements from The Zurich Way program would help save some $2.7 billion annually.

In 2009 after five years of successful restructuring efforts Schiro retired and chief investment officer Martin Senn took over the CEO role.

Continuing with its strategy to grow in emerging markets Zurich Financial entered the Turkish market through the acquisition of TEB Sigorta in 2008. It also acquired a majority stake in Russian insurance provider NASTA for $260 million. In 2009 the company purchased two Brazilian insurers.

To build up Farmers Group Zurich Financial spent $1.9 billion to acquire 21st Century Insurance the personal auto insurance arm of AIG in 2009. The addition of 21st Century's online products and geographic spread secured Farmers Group into the top tier of US auto insurers.

EXECUTIVES

Acting Chairman, Tom de Swaan, age 67
Head Mergers and Acquisition and Strategy, Christian Carl, age 41
Vice Chairman, Josef Ackermann, age 65
Regional Chairman Americas; Chairman Farmers Group, Paul N. Hopkins, age 57
CEO General Insurance, Mario Greco, age 54
Acting CFO, Vibhu R. Sharma, age 47
Chief Executive Officer Global Life, Kevin Hogan, age 51
CEO Global Corporate, Mario P. Vitale, age 58
Senior Advisor, John Amore, age 65
Chief Risk Officer and Regional Chairman Europe, Axel P. Lehmann, age 54
CEO Europe General Insurance, Annette Court, age 51
Regional Chairman Asia Pacific and Middle East, Geoffrey (Geoff) Riddell, age 57
CEO, Martin Senn, age 56
Chief Financial Officer CFO, Pierre Wauthier, age 52
CEO Farmer's Group, Jeffrey J. (Jeff) Dailey, age 55
Chief Underwriting Officer Europe General Insurance and Zurich Insurance plc, Alan Fairhead, age 49
Regional Chairman Europe, Dieter Wemmer, age 56
Group Chief Economist, Daniel M. Hofmann
Chairman, Manfred Gentz, age 71, $56,992 total compensation
CEO General Insurance, Michael G. (Mike) Kerner, age 47
CEO Western Europe, Markus Hongler, age 56
Global Chief Underwriting Officer and Head Organizational Transformation Management, Inga K. Beale, age 50
CEO North American Commercial; Regional Chairman Americas, Mike Foley, age 51
CEO Global Life, Kristof Terryn, age 46
CEO North America Shared Services Platform (ZFUS), Claudia Dill, age 47
CEO Support Office, Malcolm Gilbert
Director Media Relations Farmers, Jerry Davies
Global Head Corporate Communications, Angel Serna
Head Global Corporate Communications and Climate Office, Francis Bouchard, age 47
Head Investor Relations and Rating Agencies, Debra Broek, age 51
CEO Middle East and Africa, Saad Mered, age 46
CFO Australia, Iain C. Howie, age 49
Global Head Mergers and Acquisitions and Chief Underwriting Officer of Directors and Officers liability and Employment Practices Liability Insurance. Global Corporate, Paul Schiavone
Chief Integration Officer Personal Lines Auto US, Keitha Schofield
CEO General Insurance UK, Stephen Lewis
Chief Underwriting Officer, Lee Meyrick
Controller, Scott Egan, age 41
CEO Latin America, Peter Rebrin, age 50
Dipl. Event Manager (incl. Sponsoring) Investor Relations, Patricia Heina
Senior Investor Relations Officer, Andre Meier
Senior Investor Relations Officer, Roger Schluessel
Investor Relations Officer, Karin Winter
Information Specialist Research, Vassili Kirianoff

Senior Media Relations Officer, Tatjana Domke
Head Group Media Relations North America, Sean Keveligh an
Manager Media Relations Germany, Bernd O. Engelien
CFO Asia Pacific and Middle East, Pascal Perritaz, age 40
CFO Global Life, Joachim Masur, age 47
Chief Investment Officer, Cecilia Reyes, age 55
Head Investment Strategy Implementation, Urban Angehrn, age 49
Chief Information Technology Officer, Markus Nordlin, age 50
Head Alternative Investments; CEO Zurich Alternative Asset Management, Bernard Joei, age 56
Group General Counsel, Yannick Hausmann
Chief Administrative Officer, Christian Orator, age 50
Manager European Communications Italy, Riccardo Moretto
CEO Europe, Patrick Manley, age 52
CEO Asia/Pacific, Johnny Chen, age 52
Group Head Human Resources, Peter J. Wright, age 58
Chief Marketing Officer, Isabelle M. Conner
Regional Chairman of Asia-Pacific & Middle East, Geoffrey Geoff
Honorary Chairman of the Board, Fritz Fritz Gerber Gerber
President of Programs & Direct Markets, Kathleen Savio
Director, Tom de Swaan, age 67
Director, Susan S. Bies, age 65
Vice Chairman, Josef Ackermann, age 65
Director, Thomas K. Escher, age 64
Director, Armin Meyer, age 64
Director, Fred Kindle, age 54
Director, Rolf Urs Watter, age 55
Director, Vernon L. Sankey
Director, Donald T. (Don) Nicolaisen, age 67
Director, Victor L.L. Chu, age 56
Non-Executive Director, Tom Tom de Swaan Swaan
Auditors: PricewaterhouseCoopersAG

LOCATIONS

HQ: Zurich Insurance Group Ltd
Mythenquai 2, Zurich CH-8022
Phone: (41) 1 625 25 25 **Fax:** (41) 1 625 35 55
Web: www.zurich.com

PRODUCTS/OPERATIONS

2012 Premiums and Fees

	% of total
General	49
Global	41
Farmers	10
Total	**100**

Selected Subsidiaries

Farmers Group Inc. (property/casualty US)
21st Century Insurance Company (property/casualty US)
Farmers New World Life Insurance Company (life insurance US)
Foremost Insurance Company (specialty insurance US)
Bristol West Holdings Inc. (specialty insurance US)
Zurich American Insurance Company (general insurance US)
Zurich Insurance plc (general insurance UK)
Zurich International Life Limited (life insurance UK)

Selected Acquisitions

2011
Malaysian Assurance Alliance Berhad (Malaysia composite insurer)
Zurich Santander (51% Latin America general and life insurance divisions of Banco Santander)
2010
Compagnie Libanaise D'Assurances (Lebanon general insurance)

COMPETITORS

AEGON
AIG
AXA
Allianz
Aviva
CNA Financial
GEICO
Generali
ING
MetLife
Mitsui Sumitomo Insurance
Prudential
Prudential plc
State Farm
The Hartford
Travelers Companies

HISTORICAL FINANCIALS

Company Type: Public

Income Statement

FYE: December 31

	ASSETS ($ mil.)	NET INCOME ($ mil.)	INCOME AS % OF ASSETS	EMPLOYEES
12/12	409,267	3,878	0.9%	52,722
12/11	385,869	3,766	1.0%	52,648
12/10	375,661	3,434	0.9%	54,934
12/09	368,914	3,215	0.9%	56,668
12/08	327,944	3,039	0.9%	57,609
Annual Growth	5.7%	6.3%	—	(2.2%)

2012 Year-End Financials

Return on assets: 0.9%
Return on equity: 11.7%
Long-term debt ($ mil.): —
No. of shares (mil.): 146
Sales ($ mil): 70,414
Dividends
Yield: 6.8%
Payout: 6.9%
Market value ($ mil.): 3,938

	STOCK PRICE ($) FY Close	P/E High	P/E Low	PER SHARE ($) Earnings	Dividends	Book Value
12/12	26.80	1	1	26.31	1.82	234.73
12/11	22.68	1	1	25.61	1.83	216.67
12/10	25.89	1	1	23.44	1.47	220.29
12/09	21.74	1	0	22.35	0.96	205.81
12/08	21.85	2	1	21.63	1.46	161.45
Annual Growth	5.2%	—	—	5.0%	5.7%	9.8%

Hoover's Handbook of

World Business

Executive index

Index of Executives

A

A-nanthothai, Thongchai 61
Aa, Richard Olav 435
Aagaard-Svendsen, Birgit 147
Aaker, Tom 411
Aanestad, Ola M. 414
Aaser, Svein 435
Aasnaes, Hans 415
Abad, Alfredo Saenz 60
Abad, Roberto Lopez 457
Abadie, Laurent 338
Abadin, Antonio Abril 228
Abanumay, Mohammed S. 385
Abate, Rene 110
Abbasi, Osama 139
Abbott, John 370
Abdullah, Jon Eddy 435
Abe, Ken 295
Abe, Ken 296
Abe, Yasushi 307
Abe, Yasuyuki 417
Abe, Yasuyuki 418
Abe, Ken 468
Abella, Roland 156
Abello, Vincent 109
Abersoch, Lord E. Mervyn Davies of 156
Able, Michael 300
Aboud, Mark 384
Aboulafia, Itzhak 63
Aboumrad, Daniel Hajj 32
Abraham, Leopold 332
Abrahams, Samuel 235
Abrahamsson, Jonas 159
Abravanel, Isaac (Ika) 441
Abravanel, Roger 441
Abreu, Domingos 57
Abreu, Antonio 161
Abreu, Antonio M. Pita de 161
Abrial, Francois 261
Aburatani, Yoshihiro Yoshihiro Aburatani 452
Accum, Claude A. 422
Achatz, Reinhold 396
Achleitner, Paul 78
Achleitner, Paul 144
Achleitner, Paul 371
Achten, Dominik von 197
Achurra, Emiliano 185
Acker, Laurens G. van den 355
Ackermann, Josef 370
Ackermann, Josef 395
Ackermann, Josef 396
Ackermann, Josef 491
Ackermann, Josef 492
Acranis, Tina 278
Adachi, Yoroku (Joe) 105
Adachi, Yoroku (Joe) 106
Adachi, Michio 149
Adachi, Toshio 390
Adachi, Naoki 448
Adachi, Takemi Takemi Adachi 452
Adachi, Seiichiro 456
Adachi, Seiichiro 456
Adali, Erhan 459
Adam, Annette 335
Adam, Herve 472
Adamany, Linda 305
Adami, Norman J. 373
Adamo, Emma Emma Adamo 42
Addison, Niall 298
Adeson, Kevin 217
Adeva, Angel Durandez 356
Adler, Reuven 63
Adler, Lothar 396
Adrian, Horia 212
Adrian, Ken 321
Adrian, Serge 443
Advani, Deepak 266
Aegler, Mark 287
Afonso, Horacio Lisboa 168
Agar, James 87
Agarwal, Bhikam C. 39
Agata, Atsunobu 15
Agata, Atsunobu 16
Agata, Shintaro 334
Agata, Tetsuo 455
Ageborg, Katarina 44
Agius, Marcus 72
Agnelli, Roger 5
Agnelli, Andrea 172
Agnelli, Roger 468
Agnon, Udi 218
Agon, Jean Paul 261
Agoras, Michael 12
Agrawal, S. K. 86
Agreda, Ignacio 39
Agrusti, Raffaele 41
Aguignier, Philippe 391
Aguire, Jose M. Lucia 59
Agustin, Juan P. San 114
Ahizoune, Abdeslam 474
Ahlstrom, Agneta 436
Ahlstrom, Agneta Agneta Ahlstrom 436
Ahmad, Kamaludin 275
Ahmed, Riaz E. 450
Ahmed, Raiz 450
Ahn, Byung Mo 249
Ahn, Skott 267
Ahn, Charles 345
Ahn, Seung 398
Aho, Esko 318
Ahrnell, Jan H. 436
Ahtisaari, Marko 318
Ahuja, Sanjiv 435
Aiba, Koji 311
Aich, Andre 78
Aigrain, Jacques 151
Aiguo, Lin 339
Aihua, Pei 122
Aikawa, Tetsuro 293
Aikawa, Tetsuro 293
Aiken, Philip S. (Phil) 304
Aikyo, Katsunori 296
Aili, Liu 119
Aili, Liu 119
Aima, Abhay 196
Ainley, John 47
Aizawa, Shinichi 141
Aizawa, Naoki 424
Aizawa, Zengo 447
Akamatsu, Yoshio 238
Akerman, Christel Christel Akerman 401
Akermann, Markus 212
Akermann, Markus 212
Akhurst, Bruce J. 438
Akikawa, Tadashi 184
Akikawa, Tadashi 184
Akimoto, Nobuyuki 141
Akishige, Kunikazu 140
Akishige, Kunikazu 141
Akiyama, Tomofumi 184
Akiyoshi, Mitsuru 281
Akras, Juha 318
Akras, Juha 318
Aksyutin, Oleg E. 188
Al-Abdrabbuh, Samir A. 385
Al-Abdulla, Hussain Ali 477
Al-Amoudi, Omar A. 385
Al-Benyan, Yousef A. 385
Al-Humaid, Abdulaziz S. 385
Al-Issa, Abdullah M. 385
Al-Mady, Mohamed H. 385
Al-Mady, Mohamed H. 385
Al-Mahasher, Nasser 372
Al-Maker, Awadh 385
Al-Mana, Khaled 385
Al-Morished, Mutlaq 385
Al-Ohali, Mosaed 385
Al-Rabeeah, Abdullah S. 385
Al-Saud, Prince Saud bin Abdullah bin Thenayan 385
Al-Sheaibi, Fahad 385
Al-Subaie, Abdulla Abdulla Al-Subaie 210
Al-Tuwaijri, Homood A. 385
Al-Zamel, Yousef 385
Ala-Pietila, Pekka 384
Ala-Pietila, Pekka Pekka Ala-Pietila 384
Alacs, Lajos 297
Aladro, Manuel 55
Alami, Anass H. 457
Alary, Pierre 91
Albanel, Christine 333
Albanese, Tom 360
Albanese, Tom 360
Albanese, Tom 361
Albech, Christian 435
Albertani, Battista 466
Albrecht, Christoph 54
Albrecht, D. Michael 179
Albuquerque, Francisco Roberto de 340
Alcide, Peter 11
Alciturri, Jose Luis Gomez 60
Aldott, Zoltan 297
Alekperov, Vagit Y. 329
Alekperov, Vagit Y. 329
Alemany, Ellen 368
Alessandro, Dominic 423
Alexander, Deborah M. 69
Alexander, Dame Helen 365
Alexander, Gregor 410
Alexander, Gregor 410
Alexandre, Patrick 19
Alexandridis, Georgios P. 343
Alflatt, Mark 364
Alfonsi, Davide 234
Alford, George 235
Alhamadi, Mohd 471
Alias, Abdul Farid 275
Alierta, Cesar 432
Alimhamzah, Bapak Bapak Alimhamzah 275
Alizadeh, Behdad 469
Allan, John M. 305
Allan, Lesley 458
Allen, Barry Barry Allen 82
Allen, Nicholas C. 266
Allen, Stephen 273
Allert, Richard H. (Rick) 33
Alm, Thomas 400
Almanza, Ashley 85
Almeida, Augusto Augusto Espeschit de Almeida 39
Almeida, Manuel Antonio Ribeiro Serzedelo de 168
Almeida, Ann 218
Almeida, Marcos Henrique 468
Almestad, Anders 364
Alonso, Martin 12
Alonso, Juan 57
Alonso, Emilson 217
Alphandery, Edmond 189
Alsowaidi, Nasser A. 137
Altan, Par 381
Altenschmidt, Hans-Hermann 129
Althoff, Eric 323
Altman, Gideon 63
Alton, Steve 100
Altozano, Angel Manuel Garcia 10
Altozano, Angel Garcia 210
Alvarado, Cristobal Valderas 10
Alvarez, Joao Aguiar 57
Alvarez, Denise Aguiar 57
Alvarez, Fernando de Asua 60
Alvarez, Jose Antonio Alvarez 60
Alvarez, Fernando de Asua 60
Alvarez, Luis 100
Alvarez, Manuel 185
Alvera, Marco 163
Alvera, Marco 186
Alves, Nuno M. Pestana de Almeida 161
Alves, Nuno 161
Alvez, Leo S. 379
Alwan, Basil 25
Amado, Nuno 60
Amadori, Flavio 54
Amaral, Mario Mosqueira do 168
Amarelli, Giuseppina 54
Ambani, Mukesh D. 353
Ambani, Ramniklal H. 353
Ambe, Shintaro 296
Ambrose, Kathleen A. 396
Amemiya, Hiroshi 446
Ames, Richard D. 107
Amine, Ali Al 266
Amino, Yutaka 420
Ammar, Tarak Ben 284
Ammar, Tarak Ben 432
Ammar, Tarak Tarak Ben Ammar 432
Amore, John 491

INDEX OF EXECUTIVES

Amorim, Americo Ferreira de 59
Amoroso, Greg 169
Amos, Louise 130
Amstutz, Ernst 287
Amyot, Lise-Anne 302
Anand, V. 85
Ananenkov, Alexander G. 188
Ancelin, Bruno 355
Anderlini, Luca 376
Anders, Bettina 164
Anders, Steffi 364
Andersen, Tonny Thierry 146
Andersen, Ole Gjesso 147
Andersen, Thomas Thune 410
Anderson, Paul 51
Anderson, Paul M. 95
Anderson, John 100
Anderson, Sir John A. 130
Anderson, Sir Roy 192
Anderson, Roy 278
Anderson, William D. (Bill) 422
Anderssen, Bj?rn Andre 435
Andersson, Robert 318
Andersson, Johan Johan Andersson 399
Andersson, Magnus Magnus Andersson 401
Andersson, Robert 436
Andersson, Robert Robert Andersson 436
Andes, Phyllis E. 443
Ando, Ichiro 289
Ando, Goron 325
Ando, Goron 325
Andrade, Juan C. 9
Andrade, Miguel 161
Andrade, Miguel Stilwell de 161
Andreasen, Lars 147
Andreolli, Airton Celso Exel 56
Andres, Esteban Morras 162
Andres, Juan 323
Andresen, Johan Johan Andresen 399
Andreu, Joan 57
Andrew, Jim 258
Andrews, Nigel D. T. 330
Andrews, Timothy L. 461
Andrulewicz, Krzysztof 401
Ang, Eric T. L. 147
Ang, Ramon S. 379
Ang, Ramon S. 379
Angehrn, Urban 492
Angeli, Caroline 333
Angelo, Steve St. 455
Angelotti, Luiz C. 56
Angerbauer, Friedrich 136
Angulo, Gonzalo Hinojosa Fernandez de 434
Anjolras, Pierre 472
Annaka, Masahiro 307
Annovi, Emilio 54
Annunziato, Franco 97
Annunziato, Paolo 432
Annuscheit, Frank 128
Anthoine, Jean 109
Antinori, Thierry 151
Anto?anzas, Miguel 159
Anton, Muriel 475
Antoniadis, Christodoulos G. 343
Antoniadis, Christodoulos G. 344
Antonietti, Robert 54
Anuchitworawong, Shairit 61
Anwar, A. S. El 218
Anzai, Takashi 388
Anzai, Takashi 388
Anzai, Yuichiro 409
Aoki, Yoshihisa 238
Aoki, Yoshihisa 238
Aoki, Kenichi 448
Aoto, Shuichi 293
Aoto, Shuichi 293
Aoyama, Hajime 124
Aoyama, Shinji 215
Aoyama, Yasushi 447
Apalagaki, Chariklia A. 343
Aparicio, Francisco 59
Apenbrink, Rudolf 218
Apfalter, Guenther 274
Apitzsch, Wolfgang 158
Apitzsch, Hannes 396
Apotheker, Leo 387
Apotheker, Leo 387
Appel, Frank 153
Arai, Naoto 180
Arai, Jun 393
Arai, Jun 393
Arai, Shunichi 417
Arai, Makoto 448
Araki, Makoto 106
Araki, Makoto 106
Araki, Saburo 294
Araki, Ryuji 294
Araki, Yuji 326
Araki, Yoshifumi 456
Aral, Veysel 436
Aranha, Brian 39
Araujo, Julio de Siqueira Carvalho de 56
Araujo, Julio 57
Arbide, Juan Mata 10
Arboe, Susanne Susanne Arboe 147
Arculus, Sir David G. 434
Arena, Mark 461
Arenal, Pablo Garcia 10
Ariano, Lucia 234
Arias, Sebastian Battaner 223
Ariffin, Johan Johan bin Ariffin 275
Arikawa, Sadahiro 358
Arison, Micky 107
Aristizabal, Hector Castano 160
Armada, Jose Sainz 223
Armato, Francesco 432
Armbrust, Thomas 335
Armengol, Domingo 55
Armour, Mark H. 373
Armstrong, Graeme D. 24
Armstrong, Catherine 98
Armstrong, Danny 130
Armstrong, Anthony 139
Armstrong, Danny 301
Armstrong, Laurie 318
Armstrong, Philip 422
Arnault, Bernard 110
Arnault, Bernard 124
Arnault, Bernard 271
Arnault, Antoine 271
Arnault, Delphine 271
Arndt, Frank-Peter 81
Arnet, S.K. 448
Arnold, Michael (Mike) 330
Arnoldussen, Ludger 300
Arnone, John 91
Arnstad, Marit 414
Arnstad, Marit 414
Arora, Rajiv 224
Arora, Ankush 430
Arrago, Andre 195
Arribas, Fernando Garcia 10
Arseneault, Tom 51
Arthur, John 484
Arto, Philippe 212
Artoni, Anna Maria 376
Artus, Maj. Patrick 454
Arya, Karun 364
Asada, Teruo 281
Asada, Teruo 282
Asai, Shigeo 244
Asama, Yoshimasa 124
Asami, Takao 316
Asami, Hiroyasu 326
Asano, Tomoyasu 141
Asano, Tomoyasu 142
Asano, Mikio 456
Asano, Mikio 456
Asavanich, Bodin 394
Asavanich, Bodin 394
Aschenbroich, Jacques 469
Ashby, Ian R. 87
Asher-Topilsky, Lilach 62
Ashley, Steven 320
Asimopoulos, Spyros 303
Ask, Lars 479
Asmussen, Jorg 154
Aspar, Gerard 131
Assaf, Samir 217
Assaf, S. 218
Assakul, Kirati 141
Asshoff, Gregor 210
Assis, Franciso de 243
Astbury, John 488
Atack, Jonathan 24
Atan, Erin 364
Atarashi, Akira 390
Athanassopoulos, Antreas 303
Atieh, Michael G. (Mike) 9
Atkins, Chris 100
Atkinson, Kent 66
Atkinson, Kent 66
Atkinson, Stephen 411
Atkinson, Kent 413
Atkinson, Matt 440
Atlas, Ilana 484
Atsumi, Masanori 424
Attagrish, Grish 394
Attal, Alexandre 184
Attendu, Pierre 91
Attinger, Per-Olof 362
Au, Paul 130
Aubouin, Pierre 375
Audvard, Yves 355
Audvard, Yves 355
Auer, Werner 396
Auffret, Gilles 407
Aune, J. Brian 346
Auque, Francois 21
Auris, Jan-Dirk 202
Ausseil, Georges 127
Austin, Roxanne S. 166
Austin, Neal 298
Averbeck, Richard 144
Avila, Jose A. 136
Avner, David 63
Awori, Jeremy 412
Axford, Eric 423
Axmann, Michael 395
Aydinli, Ibrahim 459
Aynat, Julio de Miguel 223
Ayukawa, Masaaki 448
Ayuthaya, Ongorn Abhakorn Na 394
Ayuthaya, Chirayu Isarangkun Na 394
Ayyoubi, Silvia 362
Azema, Jean 284
Azema, Jean 402
Aziz, Zafrul Zafrul Abd Aziz 275
Aznar, Vitalino M. Nafria 434
Azuhata, Shigeru 208
Azuma, Kazunori 358
Azumi, Tooru 326

B

B.?ri, Robert 107
B?ving, Jesper 325
Ba, Shusong 229
Ba?ler, Engelbert 202
Baba, Kengo 236
Babani, Susie 46
Babe, Gregory S. (Greg) 78
Babeau, Emmanuel 387
Babeau, Emmauel 387
Babin, Jean-Christophe 271
Babrowski, Claire H. 169
Babu, Amar 266
Bach, Herbert 300
Bachant, Raymond 91
Bacher, Lars C. 414
Bachrach, Ernest G. 102
Back, Jan Erik 399
Backer, Christophe de 217
Backhouse, Peter 85
Backteman, Thomas 426
Bacon, Andrew 100
Baconnier, Robert 403
Baconnier, Robert 403
Bada, Hajime 244
Bader, Marcos 56
Badrinath, Vivek 333
Bae, Charlie 378
Baer, Jakob 12
Baer, Raimund 482
Baete, Oliver 28
Bagel, Friderike 202
Bagel-Trah, Simone 202
Bague, Hugo 361
Bahlmann, Tineke J.P. 231
Baier, Waltraud 164
Baier, Horst 459
Bailey, Irving W. 14
Bailey, George 409
Bailleres, Alberto 177
Baillie, Douglas A. (Doug) 464
Baillie, Douglas A. (Doug) 465
Baillie, A. Charles (Charlie) 483
Bailly, Jean-Paul 189
Bain, George S. 193
Bain, Peter 330
Bakey, Patrick (Pat) 384
Bakhshi, Sandeep 224
Bakhshi, Nandita 450
Bakker, Jacqueline Tammenoms 440
Bakker, Jacqueline Jacqueline Tammenoms Bakker 474
Bakker, Jacqualine Tammenoms 474
Bakkerud, Lill-Heidi 414
Baksaas, Jon F. 425
Baksaas, Jon F. 435
Baladron, Daniel Vega 10
Balaji, E. 352
Balakrishnan, Sudhakar 12
Balasubramanian, P. 86
Balbinot, Sergio 40
Balbinot, Sergio 41
Balbinot, Sergio 128
Balcom, Robert A. 483
Baldauf, Sari 24
Baldauf, Sari M. 144
Baldwin, Nick 410
Ball, Tony 101
Ball, Chris 384
Ballantyne, Gordon S. 438
Balmes, Christian 127
Balsells, Jaume 57
Balthazard, Michel 355
Balyan, A. K. 328
Balyan, A. K. 328
Balz, Manfred 154
Bamba, Ryoichi 106
Bamberger, Thomas 384
Bammann, Linda B. 278
Bancroft, Philip V. 9
Band, Sir Jonathon 107
Banerjee, Prith 5
Bang, Lars 321
Banga, Manvinder Manvinder Banga 280
Banham, Sir John 245
Bank, Ondra 88
Bank, Danske 147
Bansal, A.K. 85
Bansal, Arun 166
Bao-Lang, Chen 178
Baptista, Benjamin 39
Barahona, Pedro 55
Baraibar, Gonzalo Gomez-Zamalloa 10
Baratta, Paolo 432
Barbassa, Almir G. 340
Barbedo, Norberto Pinto 56
Barber, Ralph G. 217
Barber, Samantha 223
Barberis, Pierre 93
Barbier, Francois 176
Barbier, Denis 355
Barbieri, Pierlaurent 11
Barbizet, Patricia 93
Barbizet, Patricia 454
Barbosa, Rodrigo 364
Barbosa, Nelson 468
Barczewski, Andreas 457
Barge, Alan 44
Baril, Thierry Thierry Baril 21
Barker, Glyn 47
Barkla, Andrew 384

Barkov, Anatoly A. 329
Barnes, Peter 100
Barnett, Lee 33
Barollier, Pascal 383
Baron, Mali 62
Barr, G. 298
Barral, David 47
Barrenstein, Peter F. 457
Barrie, Chris Chris Barrie 42
Barrio, Miguel 356
Barros, Patrick Monteiro de 168
Barrow, Mark 100
Barrows, Charles 47
Bartels, Andreas 151
Barten, Heiko 263
Bartke, Rolf 21
Bartolomeo, Bill 27
Bartolomeo, Eduardo de Salles 468
Bartolotta, Peter 266
Bartoschek, Werner 159
Baschera, Pius 362
Basecqz, Bernard 168
Baser, Didem Dincer 459
Bashada, Stephen M. 396
Basham-Pyke, Sharanne 100
Bason, John G. 42
Bason, John G. 42
Bass, Jim 409
Bassermann, Rolf 144
Bassett, Richard 482
Bassil, Alain 19
Bastian, Ralf-Gerd 76
Bastug, Recep 459
Batchelor, Lance 440
Bates, M. 298
Batista, Joesley Mendonca 243
Batista, Wesley Mendonca 243
Batista, Wesley Mendonca 243
Batista, Jose 243
Batista, Luis Carlos Croissier 356
Batra, Sandeep 224
Battiferri, Simone Simone Battiferri 432
Bauer, Sabine 13
Bauer, Sabine 13
Bauer, Manuel 28
Bauer, Werner J. 309
Bauert, Ian 360
Baule, Rainer 179
Baumann, Werner 78
Baumann, Albert 287
Baumann, Wolfgang 332
Baumgartl, Wolf-Dieter 195
Baumgartl, Wolf-Dieter 429
Baumgartner, Fred 76
Baur, Rupert 489
Baur, Rupert 489
Bauwens, Alain 202
Bax, Jan Hein 352
Baxter, Peter 330
Baxter, Tim 412
Bayerle, Gunter 164
Bayle, Pierre 21
Bayswater, Lord Powell of 271
Bazid, Abdullah 385
Bazin, Sebastien 109
Bazin, Sebastien 110
Bazin, Benoit 131
Bazire, Nicolas 109
Bazire, Nicolas 271
Bazoli, Giovanni 234
Bazoli, Giovanni 466
Bazy, Dominique 472
Beale, Inga K. 491
Beamish, Brian 35
Beato, Manuel Perez 10
Beattie, W. Geoffrey (Geoff) 366
Beauchamp, Joan 302
Beaudoin, Laurent 91
Beaudoin, Pierre 91
Beaudoin, Pierre 91
Beaudoin, Pierre 345
Beaulieu, Martin E. (Marty) 422
Beauregard, Olivier Olivier Costa de Beauregard 47
Beauregard, Olivier Costa de 471
Beaven, Peter 88
BeavenBAcc, Peter 87
Bebear, Claude 90
Bebear, Claude 388
Bebear, Claude Claude Bebear 474
Bebear, Claude 474
Bech-Hansen, Henrik 147
Bechat, Jean-Paul 31
Becher, Jonathan D. 384
Beck, Richard S. 217
Beck, Gyorgy 475
Becke, Wolf 195
Becker, Michael 54
Becker, Hermann-Josef 154
Becker, Michael 395
Becker, Dietmar 462
Becker, Wendy 475
Beckers, Pierre-Olivier 169
Beckmann, Christoph 151
Beckmann, Hubert 482
Bedard, Normand 127
Bedford, M. 245
Beerli, Andreas 54
Beermann, Anita 335
Beeton, Jeremy 410
Beeuwsaert, Dirk 189
Beever, Doug 18
Beffa, Jean-Louis 131
Beffa, Jean-Louis 189
Beffa, Jean-Louis 396
Beggs, Peter 443
Beharel, Francois 352
Behr, Prof Dr. Giorgio 489
Behrendt, Michael 277
Beinecke, Candace K. 31
Beisheim, Michael 84
Beitz, Wolfgang 396
Beitz, Berthold 445
Beke, Guy 462
Belair, Douglas E. (Doug) 51
Belchior, Miriam Aparecida 340
Belda, Alain J. P. 355
Belier, Jean-Pierre 127
Belikov, Igor 329
Bell, Mike Mike Bell 250
Bell, Sir John Irving 362
Bell, Thomas A. 365
Bellanger, Alain 472
Bellinger, Patricia 403
Bellini, Luigi 466
Bellodi, Leonardo 163
Bellon, Pierre 403
Bellon, Astrid 403
Bellon, Bernard 403
Bellon, Francois-Xavier 403
Belloni, Aldo 268
Belloni, Antonio (Toni) 271
Belloni, Antonio (Toni) 271
Bellozi, Renata 468
Belluzzi, Giovanni 463
Belot, Stanislas 47
Belsham, David 348
Belzberg, Brent S. 104
Belzer, Joan Joan Belzer 139
Ben-Zeev, Itai 63
Bendavid, Laurent 109
Benenati, Benedikt Benedikt Benenati 250
Benetton, Gilberto 284
Beng, Na Wu 336
Bengdara, Farhat O. 463
Bengdara, Farhat O. 463
Bengoa, Angel Jado Becerro de 60
Benitez, Jorge L. 7
Benito, Javier de 212
Benjelloun, Othman 168
Benke, Richard 297
Benmosche, Robert H. (Bob) 139
Benner-Heinacher, Jella Susanne 457
Bennett, Brad 9
Bennett, Glenn 13
Bennett, D. Michael 51
Bennett, R. E. T. 217
Bennett, C J 245
Bennett, Jeremy 320
Bennett, William E. 450
Benoist, Gilles 126
Benquet, Alain 127
Bensaid, Mohamed Ali 212
Benson, David 320
Benson, Mel E. 423
Bentegeat, Renaud 472
Bentham, Jeremy B. 370
Bentler, Martin 395
Bentley, Phillip K. (Phil) 116
Bentley, Phillip K. (Phil) 116
Bentley, Maria 461
Benzecry, Oliver (Olly) 8
Ber, Hedva 63
Beracha, Solomon 343
Berard, Andre 82
Berard, Andre Andre Berard 82
Berard, Andre 91
Berchtold, Walter 139
Berdychowski, Marek 277
Berendji, Sacha 280
Beretta, Pietro Gussalli 466
Berg, Achim 84
Berg, H?kan 426
Bergelin, Sven 159
Bergendal, Evelyn 407
Berger, Genevieve 44
Berger, Roland 172
Berger, H. C. Roland 179
Berger, Roland 432
Berger, Prof Genevieve B. 464
Berger, Prof Genevieve B. 465
Bergh, Maarten A. van den 233
Bergh, Lodewijk Hijmans van den 255
Bergh, Rob F. van den 255
Berghausen, Rainer 113
Bergmann, Burckhard 128
Bergmann, Burckhard 188
Bergmann, Horst 335
Bergmann, Burckhard 435
Bergstrom, Henrik 3
Berkenhagen, Ulf 277
Berkenhagen, Ulf 277
Berkery, Rosemary T. 461
Berlien, Olaf 445
Bernabe, Franco 339
Bernabe, Franco Franco Bernabe 432
Bernabe, Franco 432
Bernal, Ignacio Sanin 160
Bernard, Daniel 25
Bernard, Michel 26
Bernard, Daniel 250
Berndt, Wolfgang C. G. 332
Berndt, Wolfgang C. G. 332
Bernhard, Wolfgang 143
Bernheim, Antoine 124
Bernheim, Antoine 271
Bernheim, Antoine 284
Bernicke, Jutta 202
Bernier, Jean 27
Berninghaus, Ernst Dieter 287
Bernini, Alessandro 163
Bernis, Valerie 189
Bernotat, Wulf H. 28
Bernotat, Wulf H. 84
Bernotat, Wulf H. 154
Bernotat, Wulf H. 286
Bernstein, David 107
Bernstein, Joel 384
Beroleit, Bjorn 457
Berroeta, I?aki 475
Berry, David 184
Berry, Craig J. 396
Berselli, Carlo 234
Bertamini, Stefano Paolo (Steve) 411
Bertamini, Stefano Paolo (Steve) 412
Bertazzoni, Roberto 284
Bertiere, Francois 93
Bertiere, Francois 127
Bertling, Lutz 21
Bertolini, Massimo 284
Bertolissi, Mario 234
Bertolissi, Mario 234
Bertoluzzo, Paolo 475
Bertone, Franco Franco Bertone 432
Bertrand, Luc 302
Bertrand, Luc 302
Bertreau, Francois 471
Bespalov, Alexander D. 188
Bessy, Patrick 31
Best, Ulrich 210
Best, John 443
Betteridge, David 98
Bettink, Jan 263
Betz, Ralph 66
Betz, Wolfgang 277
Beuers, Joerg 462
Beullier, Alain 189
Beuman, Willy 78
Beumer, Markus 128
Beyer, Uwe 352
Beynio, Wolfgang 202
Beynon, Ann 100
Beyrer, Markus 332
Bezaire, George E. 225
Bezard, Bruno 333
Bezieux, Geoffroy Roux de 342
Bhagat, Rahul N. 196
Bhakta, Mansingh L. 353
Bharami-uaychai, Krisorn 61
Bhargava, P. S. 85
Bhargava, Subodh 430
Bharucha, Kaizad 196
Bhatia, Vanisha Mittal 39
Bhatia, Vanisha Vanisha Mittal Bhatia 39
Bhatnagar, Vijay K. 39
Bhattacharjee, Dipankar 441
Bhattacharya, S. B. 86
Bhattacharya, Shyamal 328
Bhojwani, Gary C. 28
Biancarelli, Jean-Louis 170
Bianchi, Luigi A. 234
Bianchi, S. 376
Bianchi, Lorenzo 463
Biau, Patrick 355
Biau, Patrick 355
Bibeau, Marc A. 346
Bibert, Sascha 159
Bibic, Mirko 82
Bible, Geoffrey C. (Geoff) 373
Bicker, Uwe 383
Bickford, Natalie 403
Bickmeyer, Anette 159
Bicknell, Simon M. 191
Bienfait, Gerard 472
Bienz, Urs 54
Bies, Susan S. 492
Bignon, Jean-Yves 127
Bijur, Peter I. 479
Bilgi-Zapparoli, Elif 332
Billig, Jean-Michel 355
Bilodeau, Stephane 302
Bimson, Paul 100
Bindra, Jaspal Singh 411
Bindra, Jaspal Singh 412
Bing, Shang 122
Bing, Shang 122
Bingham, H. Raymond 176
Bingxun, Zhang 64
Biniek, Oliver 159
Binkowska, Dietmar P. 263
Binkowska, Dietmar P. 482
Binks, Ian 100
Binning, Paviter S. (Pavi) 483
Binswanger, Christine 212
Bird, Damien 85
Birken, Alexander 335
Birnbaum, Leonhard 371
Birnstiel, Constantin 395
Bironneau, Jean-Noel 109
Birrell, Andrew 330
Biscarolasaga, Isabel Tocino 60
Bischof, Jens 151
Bischoff, Werner 135
Bischoff, Werner 136
Bischoff, Manfred 143
Bischoff, Manfred 256
Bischoff, Sir Winfried F. W. (Win) 270

Bischoff, Werner 371
Bischoff, Manfred 463
Bishop, Tim 273
Bisnaire, Jean-Paul (J-P.) 278
Bissiritsas, Panagiotis 384
Bjorklund, Tomas 321
Bjorknert, Mikael 426
Bjorknert, Mikael Mikael Bjorknert 426
Bjorstedt, Marie Marie Bjorstedt 203
Blaafalk, Steen 147
Black, Jerry 16
Black, Jerry 16
Blackburn, Mike 100
Blackburn, Denis 302
Blackwell, Lord Norman 413
Blades, Tom 396
Blaffart, Henri 39
Blair, Simon 130
Blair, Carolyn 422
Blaizot, Marc 453
Blake, Kelvin 100
Blanc, Robert Le 71
Blanc, Robert Le 72
Blanc, Robert Le 74
Blanc, Jean-Louis 189
Blanco, Rafael Bermejo 56
Blanco, Alejandro Alvarez 352
Blanco, Paulina Beato 356
Blank, Ingrid Jonasson 436
Blasi, Simone 234
Blastland, Dermot 458
Blau, Peter 159
Blazheev, Victor 329
Blazquez, Nicholas B. (Nick) 155
Blazquez, Pedro Azagra 223
Bleasel, Len 350
Blessing, Martin 128
Blincow, Andrew 410
Blok, Eelco 256
Blomquist, Per-Arne 436
Blomqvist, Anders 401
Bloomberg, Lawrence S. 302
Blount, W. Frank 25
Blum, Clemens 387
Blunck, Thomas 300
Bly, Mark 95
Bo, Qiliang 339
Bo+?l, Nicolas 407
Boal, Greg 47
Boccard, Georges-Antoine 54
Boccassino, Piero 234
Boccolini, Giovanni 234
Bochniarz, Henryka 463
Bock, Kurt W. 76
Bode, Jorg 477
Body, Serge 127
Boeckmann, Alan L. 87
Boeckmann, Alan L. 88
Boehm-Bezing, Carl-Ludwig 371
Boehm-Bezing, Carl Ludwig von 371
Boehm-Bezing, Carl-Ludwig 371
Boekhoff, Hannes 135
Boel, Nicolas 407
Boer, A. Dick 255
Boersig, Clemens Clemens Boersig 144
Boesch, Dina Dina Boesch 300
Boethius, Ulrika 425
Boeuf, Daniel 454
Bogart, Thomas A. 421
Bogarty, W. J. 448
Bohmer, Gregor 263
Boilini, Enrique H. 102
Boireau, Christian 19
Bois, Michel 126
Boissard, Gael de 139
Boisseau, Philippe 453
Boldrini, Giosue 54
Bolis, Alex Alex Bolis 432
Bolland, Marc J. (M. J.) 280
Bolland, Marc J. (M. J.) 280
Bolliger, Herbert 287
Bollore, Vincent 40
Bollore, Vincent 41
Bollore, Vincent 284
Bollore, Thierry 355
Bolton, Hugh J. 450
Boman, Par 425
Bombardier, J.R. Andre 91
Bombardier, Janine 92
Bomhard, Nikolaus von 128
Bomhard, Nikolaus von 164
Bomhard, Nikolaus Nikolaus von Bomhard 300
Bommensath, Eric 72
Bommensath, Eric 74
Bona, Fabrizio 432
Bonamy, Jean-Michel 474
Bond, Sir John R. H. 2
Bondy, Rupert 95
Bonfield, Sir Peter L. 166
Bonfield, Andrew R. J. 250
Bonfield, Andrew R. J. 304
Bonfield, Andrew R. J. 304
Bonfield, Sir Peter L. 409
Bonfield, Sir Peter L. 429
Bonhomme, Thierry 333
Boni, Aurelio Conrado 56
Bonnafe, Jean-Laurent 89
Bonnafe, Jean-Laurent 90
Bonnafe, Jean-Laurent 90
Bonnafe, Jean-Laurent 110
Bonnell, Bruno 145
Bonnell, William 302
Bonnesen, Birgitte 426
Bonnot, Alain 472
Booker, Robert 85
Booker, Niall S. K. 217
Boone, Haynes 429
Booth, Clement B. 28
Booth, David 72
Booth, David 74
Booth, Richard 422
Bootsma, Pieter 19
Bordenave, Philippe 89
Bordet, A. 245
Borel, Daniel V. 309
Borgen, Thomas F. 146
Borghgraef, Paul 248
Borghi, Gilberto 54
Borgklint, Per G. 166
Borig, Klaus G. 157
Born, Jorge 102
Born, Ulrika 426
Bornia, Antonio 56
Bornia, Antonio 57
Boroughs, Timothy A. 9
Borowicz, Klaus 113
Borries, Daniel von 164
Borrini, Amerigo 41
Borsig, Clemens A. H. 78
Borsig, Clemens A. H. 144
Borsig, Clemens A. H. 268
Borwankar, Satish B. 430
Bosch, Jose 57
Bosch, Jose 57
Bosch, Dina 300
Boscia, Jon A. 422
Bose, U N 328
Bose, U N 328
Bossina, Bruno 234
Bosson, Oskar 24
Bostock, Kate 280
Bostock, Kate 280
Bostock, Nathan 368
Bostoen, Paul 248
Botes, Hermien 35
Botin, Ana P. 60
Botin, Javier 60
Bottcher, Volker 459
Bottcher, Volker 459
Botteghelz, Botteghelz Canga 10
Botteghelz, Alejandro Canga 10
Botti, Jean J. 21
Bottomley, Baroness Virginia 24
Bouc, Herve Le 93
Bouchard, Alain 26
Bouchard, Alain 27
Bouchard, Francis 491
Boucher, Richie 66
Boucher, Richie 66
Boucher, Sylvain Sylvain Boucher 471
Bouchiat, Pascal 443
Bouchut, Pierre B. 169
Bouckaert, Alfred 49
Bouckaert, Vincent 212
Boudreau, Danielle 91
Bougon, Philippe 387
Bouhara, Yassine 461
Bouillot, Isabelle 131
Bouillot, Isabelle 462
Boulain, Michel 469
Boulc'h, Laurent Le 127
Bourdon, Martine 127
Bourgeois, Michel 91
Bourges, Olivier 189
Bourges, Oliver 443
Bourgie, Pierre 302
Bourgon, Jacques 212
Bourke, Neville 66
Bousfield, Clare 14
Bousquet-Chavanne, Patrick 280
Boustridge, Michael 100
Bouton, Daniel 453
Bouton, Daniel 471
Bouts, Erik 24
Bouvier, A. 173
Bouvier, Dominique 472
Bouygues, Olivier 31
Bouygues, Olivier 93
Bouygues, Martin 93
Bouygues, Olivier 93
Bouygues, Olivier 127
Bowden, Andrew 484
Bowen, Terry 480
Bowes, Patrick 330
Bowles, Jack M. H. D. 98
Bowman, Adm. Frank L. (Skip) 95
Bowman, Mark J. 373
Boxmeer, Jean-Francois M. L. van 199
Boyer, Elisabeth 472
Boyle, Robert 233
Boyle, Duncan 350
Boyles, Peter W. 217
Bozzini, Giulio 376
Br?ndum, Helle 147
Brabec-Lagrange, Claire 189
Brabeck-Letmathe, Peter 139
Brabeck-Letmathe, Peter 139
Brabeck-Letmathe, Peter 309
Bracher, Candido Botelho 237
Brackx, Bart 458
Bradeen, Richard C. 91
Bradley, Carolyn 440
Bradley, John F. 461
Braekeleer, Marc de 352
Bragg, John L. 450
Brambilla, Giuseppe 109
Bramwell, Philip 51
Branco, Mario 407
Brandao, Lazaro 57
Brandenberger, Walter 287
Brandenstein, Gerd von 396
Brandenstein, Gerd 396
Brandgaard, Jesper 325
Brandjes, Michiel 370
Brandl, Monika 154
Brands, Andrew D. 193
Brandt, Werner 151
Brandt, Werner 384
Branham, Timothy L. 184
Bratt, Mikael 479
Brattstrom, Magnus 436
Brattstrom, Magnus Magnus Brattstrom 436
Bredimus, Andre 54
Breene, R. Timothy S. (Tim) 7
Breffort, Jean-Claude 131
Bregier, Fabrice Fabrice Bregier 21
Brekke, Sigve 435
Brendel, Olaf 335
Brenden, Jon 321
Brennan, David R. 44
Brennan, Vincent 66
Brenneman, Ronald A. (Ron) 69
Brenneman, Ronald A. (Ron) 82
Brenner, Catherine 33
Brentan, Andrea 162
Brescia, Franco R. 432
Breton, Thierry 109
Breton, Claude 302
Brettmann, Kai 84
Breuer, Michael 482
Breuer, Klemens 482
Breukink, Henk W. 231
Brien, Michael 423
Brillet, Rene 109
Brin, Jean-Francois 383
Brinded, Malcolm 370
Brink, Dolf van den 24
Brink, Dolf 24
Brink, Brian 35
Brinkley, Amy W. 450
Brinkmann, Hans-Georg 260
Briquet, Claude 387
Brisebois, Alain 27
Brissonneau, Phillippe 127
Brito, Carlos 37
Brittin, Matthew (Matt) 240
Broadbent, Sir Richard 440
Broadbent, Jillian Jillian Broadbent 488
Broadley, Philip 330
Broadman, Bart Joseph 147
Brochu, Sophie 82
Brockmann, Jan 3
Brodet, David 63
Brody, William 323
Broek, Lykele van der 78
Broek, Jacques van den 352
Broek, Debra 491
Broendum, Helle Helle Broendum 147
Broens, Daniel 407
Brogaard, Jakob 146
Brokatzky-Geiger, Juergen 323
Broman, Marianne 203
Bromley, Craig 278
Bronner, Goran 426
Brooks, Martha F. 92
Brooks, Simon 170
Broomhead, Malcolm W. 87
Broomhead, Malcolm W. 88
Brose, Dagmar 263
Brossard, Jean-Paul 127
Broughton, Sir Martin F. 233
Brouhns, Alexis 407
Broumidis, Haris 475
Broussard, Jason 26
Brouster, Jean-Yves le 472
Brown, Richard A. 5
Brown, Charles 82
Brown, Robert E. (Bob) 82
Brown, Malcolm 85
Brown, Alastair 218
Brown, Michael W. T. (Mike) 330
Brown, Robert E. (Bob) 360
Brown, John 461
Brownell, Nora 305
Brownett, Lesley 280
Bruaene, Pierre 462
Bruce, Chris 100
Brudermuller, Martin 76
Brugman, Robbin 352
Brummelen, Karin van 128
Bruns, Andreas 202
Bruseth, Stuart 370
Bruzelius, Peggy B. 3
Bruzelius, Peggy B. 3
Bruzelius, Peggy B. 24
Bruzelius, Peggy B. 156
Bryan, Elizabeth B. 484
Bryant, Warren F. 483
Bsirske, Frank 151
Bsirske, Frank 151
Bsirske, Frank 153
Bsirske, Frank 371
Bsirske, Frank 371
Buberl, Thomas 49
Buch, Rolf Eberhard 84
Buchan, Colin 413
Buchanan, Sir John G. S. 87
Buchanan, John G. S. 88

Buchanan, Alan K. 233
Buchanan, Sally 409
Buchanan, Sir John G. S. 475
Buchanan, Sir John G. S. 476
Buchel, Heinz 371
Buchelmeier, Josef 489
Buchholz, Bernd 84
Buchner, Stefan E. 144
Buchs, Bernhard 461
Buck, Helen 240
Buckelew, Alan B. 107
Bucker, Michael 79
Buckley, Warren 100
Budd, David C. 217
Buehler, Kevin J. 323
Bueno, Jose Luiz Rodrigues 56
Buey, Manuel Garcia 10
Bufe, Uwe-Ernst 24
Bufe, Uwe-Ernst 24
Bufe, Uwe-Ernst 462
Buhagiar, Mike 100
Buhl, Dieter 143
Buhl, Reinhard 489
Bula, Patrice 309
Bulcke, Paul 309
Bulkin, Michael H. 102
Bull, Mark 352
Bullock, Jonathan 157
Bullock, Gareth R. 412
Bullock, Gareth R. 440
Bult, Tim 480
Bundschuh, Russell G. 9
Bunge, Jurgen 489
Bunn, Jon 47
Bunyasaranan, Bunsong 61
Buonaura, Vincenzo C. 463
Buonaura, Vincenzo C. 463
Buono, Jean-Claude 261
Burbach, Willi 384
Burch, Simon 155
Burckhardt, Andreas 54
Burdis, Margie 100
Bures, Doris 332
Buresch, Bernd 151
Burg, Christophe 375
Burgard, Louis-Roch 472
Burger, Bas 100
Burger, Glynn R. 235
Burger, Glynn R. 235
Burgess, Mike 362
Burgmans, Antony 14
Burgmans, Antony 24
Burgmans, Antony 95
Burke, Catherine 29
Burke, Amy 66
Burke, Andrew J. (Drew) 102
Burke, Patrick J. (Pat) 217
Burkhart, Andreas 144
Burlington, Bruce 44
Burnett, Ken 227
Burnett, Peter W. 461
Burnley, Roger 240
Burns, Tom 25
Burns, Lord Terence (Terry) 60
Burns, Susan 102
Burns, Stephanie A. 192
Burns, Steven 350
Burr, Gwyn 240
Burreau, Britta 321
Burrows, Jessie 47
Burrows, Richard 98
Burrows, Richard 98
Burston, Claire 413
Burt, Tye Tye Burt 39
Burton, Paula 85
Bury, Hans Martin 154
Busch, Roland 395
Busetti, Alessandro 41
Bussche, Johan van den 91
Bussmann, Oliver 384
Bustamante, Ricardo Martin de 10
Bustin, Ian 364
Butcher, Andrew 438
Butel, Stewart 480
Butler, Pat 66
Butschek, Gunter Gunter Butschek 21
Butterworth, Charles 475
Buyse, Bart 151
Byanna, Vidya S. (Vid) 8
Bye, Gerry 95
Bylen, Hans Van 202
Bylund, Katarina 401
Bylund, Tommy 425
Byrne, Bernard 29
Byrne, Gerry 29
Byrom, Peter J. 365
Byun, Bo Kyung 247
Byun, Jun-Yeon 258
Byun, Jun-Yeon 258
Byung-Ki, Kim 345

C

Cabot, Cirus 57
Cabra, Luis 356
Caceres, Javier Nonzon de 10
Cagni, Pascal Pascal Cagni 250
Cahill, Gerald R. (Gerry) 107
Cai, Haoyi 64
Cailiao, Xu 122
Caille, Andre 302
Caille, Andre 302
Caine, Patrice 443
Caira, Marc 309
Cairns, Gordon M. 484
Caishi, Jiang 342
Calavia, Philippe 19
Calder, Rosemary 100
Calderon, Alberto 87
Caldiani, Graziano 466
Caltagirone, Francesco G. 40
Caltagirone, Francesco G. 41
Caltagirone, Alessandro 463
Calvi, Giuseppe 466
Calvi, Giuseppe 466
Calvo, Domingo Armengol 55
Calvosa, Lucia Lucia Calvosa 432
Calzi, Marinna Li 463
Calzi, Marianna 463
Camacho, Francisco 145
Camara, Braulio Medel 223
Cambier, Bernard 355
Cameron, Barry 413
Cameron, Luzius 461
Campany, Cate 74
Campau, Robert G. 26
Campbell, Kevin M. 7
Campbell, Chris 368
Campbell, Norie C. 450
Campbell, Tony A. 459
Campling, Andrew 100
Campos, Joselito D. 379
Camus, Philippe 25
Camus, Daniel 474
Candel, Filomeno Mira 279
Candel, Filomeno Mira 279
Canevari, Roberto 109
Cangeri, Antonio 41
Cano, Andre 57
Cantera, Jose Garcia 60
Cantet, Michel 472
Cantor-Grable, Marcia 348
Cantu, Alfredo Livas 177
Cantu, Alessandra 432
Cao, Xinghe 125
Cao, Shifan 343
Cao, Stefano 432
Caparroso, Ricardo A. Chavez 212
Caplan, Russell R. 370
Caple, Roy 218
Cappi, Luiz 57
Cappi, Luiz Carlos Trabuco 57
Capron, Philippe G. H. 474
Caraballo, Octavio 102
Carapiet, Michael 273
Carbajal, Jose A. Fernandez 114
Carbajal, Jose Antonio Fernandez 177
Carbajal, Francisco Javier Fernandez 177
Carbajal, Jose Antonio Fernandez 199
Carbajal, Jose Antonio Fernandez 199
Carboni, Rita 432
Cardell, Anna 47
Cardenas, Mauricio 160
Cardenuto, Rodolpho 384
Cardona, Maria 161
Cardoso, Aldo 189
Carey, Michael 370
Cargill, Jan 368
Carl, Christian 491
Carlander, Magnus 479
Carlberg, Inga-Lill 321
Carleton, Sean R. 225
Carlier, Didier 111
Carlo, Massimo Di 284
Carlsson, Magnus 399
Carlsson, Srefan 436
Carmichael, Brian 278
Carnwath, Alison J. 72
Carnwath, Alison J. 74
Caro, Alvaro Castaneda 160
Carolus, Cheryl 235
Caron, Joseph P. 278
Carpenter, Alan 480
Carpentier, Elisabeth 403
Carr, Keith 31
Carr, Sir Roger M. 116
Carr, Jeff 255
Carr, David 412
Carreiro, Maj. Paul 384
Carro, Fernando 84
Carroll, Cynthia B. 35
Carroll, Cynthia B. 95
Carron, Rene 172
Carron, Rene 189
Carruth, Richard A. 393
Carson, Neil A. P. 245
Carson, Neil A. P. 245
Carter, Stephen A. 25
Carter, Colin B. 480
Cartwright, Stacey 192
Carvalho, Michel de 199
Casar, Bernhard 54
Casas, Isidro Faine 65
Casas, Isidro 356
Casas, Isidro Faine 356
Casas, Isidro Faine 434
Casati, Gianfranco 7
Casellas, Ignacio 57
Casellas, Carlos Colomer 434
Caselli, Ettore 54
Caselli, G. 376
Casimir-Lambert, Charles 407
Casiraghi, Rosalba 234
Caso', Angelo 284
Cassaday, John M. 278
Cassidy, Rick 429
Casta?o, Martha Cecilia 160
Castagna, Giuseppe 234
Castaigne, Robert 383
Castaigne, Robert 402
Castaigne, Robert 472
Castell, Sir William M. (Bill) 95
Castella, Jose Carlos Cardoso 168
Castelletti, Luigi 463
Castille, Arnaud Arnaud Castille 474
Castillo, Federico 57
Castillo, Eva 330
Castries, Henri de 49
Castro, Manuel 55
Castro, Alberto 161
Catalano, Laura 364
Catania, Elio Cosimo 432
Cathomas, Robert 260
Catroga, Eduardo e Almeida 161
Catroga, Eduardo 161
Cattaneo, Mario G. 466
Catton, Mark 368
Caty, Linda 302
Catz, Safra A. 218
Caussemille, Thierry 127
Cauwe, Michel 462
Cavalcanti, Luiz C.B. 56
Cavalcanti, Guilherme Perboyre 468
Cavallaro, Richard (Rich) 400
Cazar, Jorge Luis 9
Cebulla, Jorg 151
Cederholm, Cenneth Cenneth Cederholm 203
Cedervall, Peter 91
Cefis, Alberta G. 69
Celeste, Lino J. 278
Cera, Mario 466
Cereda, Maurizio 284
Ceresa, Marco 352
Ceruti, Franco 234
Cerutti, Romeo 139
Cerutti, Giancarlo 284
Cesareo, Marco 234
Cescau, Patrick J. 440
Cescau, Patrick J. 440
Cette, Jean-Jacques 28
Cezar, Laercio 57
Cha, Laura M. L. 217
Cha, Laura M. L. 218
Chacko, Thomas 85
Chaevardiere, Partick de la 383
Chaigneau, Alain 189
Chaim, Galib 468
Chalendar, Pierre-Andre 131
Chalendar, Pierre-Andre de 131
Chalendar, Pierre-Andre de 471
Chalendar, Pierre-Andre Pierre-Andre de Chalendar
Chalitaporn, Kannikar 394
Chalitaporn, Kannikar 394
Challen, David 35
Chalmers, Sabine 37
Chalons-Browne, Roland W. 395
Chambers, Stuart 440
Chambon, Bruno 127
Champeaux, Alain 453
Champigneux, Alain 355
Champigneux, Alain 355
Chan, Cho Chak (John) 194
Chan, Caleb 216
Chan, Lily 278
Chan, Doris 278
Chancel, Pierre 382
Chandarasomboon, Amorn 61
Chandok, Vijay 224
Chandra, Vinit 74
Chandran, Ruban 95
Chandy, K. P. 86
Chaney, Michael A. 301
Chang, Fa-Te 112
Chang, Fa-Te 112
Chang, Jimmy 137
Chang, Ray-Chung 137
Chang, C. P. 178
Chang, Morris 428
Chang-Hee, Lee 345
Chanmugam, Anthony E. A. (Tony) 100
Chanmugam, Anthony E. A. (Tony) 101
Chantharawichai, Shuphorn 61
Chapa, Jaime 114
Chapman, Frank 85
Chapman, Clare Clare Chapman 100
Chapman, Barbara 130
Chapman, Clare M. 250
Chapman, Christopher (Chris) 330
Chapman, Clare M. 459
Chapman, Rob 484
Charalampidis, Damianos 303
Charbonnet, Michel 287
Charkova, Alisa 373
Charlier, Jean-Yves 474
Charlier, Jean-Yves 474
Charuwatthanachai, Chitwatthana 61
Charvier, Robert 469
Chateauvieux, Jacques de 49
Chaurasia, Bina 166
Chaussade, Jean-Louis 189
Chauvet, Jacques 355
Chauvin, Mark R. 450
Chavel, George 403
Chavent, Philippe 472
Chavez, Victor 443
Chawla, M. M. 86

Cheah, Teik Teik Seng Cheah 275
Chen, C. J. 69
Chen, Grace 112
Chen, Tsu-Pei 112
Chen, Tsu-Pei 112
Chen, Hongsheng 121
Chen, Wei 125
Chen, Bi 125
Chen, J. Y. 137
Chen, Ming-Huei 137
Chen, James 139
Chen, Thomas K. S. 139
Chen, James 139
Chen, Han-Ting 178
Chen, Han-Ting 178
Chen, Xudong 266
Chen, Kexiang 343
Chen, Su 343
Chen, Cheng-Kang 427
Chen, Jason C. S. 428
Chen, C.H. 429
Chen, Kok-Choo 429
Chen, Xiaowei 438
Chen, Johnny 492
Cheng, Moses M. C. 119
Cheng, Edgar W. K. 125
Cheng, Jack T. K. 139
Cheng, Christopher W. C. 147
Cheng, Cindy 278
Cheng, Neo Bock 336
Cheng, Christopher W. C. 342
Chengwen, Zhuo 90
Chengyu, Fu 120
Chenshuang, Zhang 122
Chenshuang, Zhang 122
Cheong, Yong Hwa 247
Cheong, Wee Ee 467
Cherepanov, Vsevolod 188
Cherner, Anatoly 186
Chertier, Dominique-Jean 375
Cheshire, Ian 250
Cheshire, Ian 250
Cheung, Kin 65
Cheung, Alex Y. S. 90
Cheung, LI Ka (Eric) 194
Cheung, Marvin K.T. 218
Cheung, Laura 219
Cheung, Louis C. Y. 343
Chevallon, Sophie 131
Chevardiere, Patrick de La 453
Chevet, Pierre-Franck 189
Chevre, Claude 195
Chevrier, Robert 131
Chew, Cynthia 11
Chew, Jeffrey S. T. 336
Chew, Paul 383
Chew, Mei Lee 467
Chey, Tae-Won 397
Chey, Jae-Won 398
Chi, Ting Pang 137
Chia-Wei, Prof Woo 266
Chiang, Shang-Yi 428
Chiaro, Preston 360
Chiaro, Preston 361
Chijiiwa, Ryoji 241
Child-Villiers, Roddy 309
Chillcott, John 51
Chin, Bobby 336
Chin, Elaine 411
Chin, Y. P. 429
Chin-Leong, Allison 461
Ching, Koh Ching 336
Ching, Man Kam 342
Ching, Sng 485
Chipchase, Graham 44
Chiquet, Maureen 474
Chirac, Bernadette 271
Chisholm, Bill Bill Chisholm 39
Chiu, Sung Hong 125
Chmielewski, Stefano 479
Cho, Dam 247
Cho, In-Kook 258
Cho, In-Kook 258
Cho, Shigeyoshi 328
Cho, Soon 397
Cho, Jae Ho 398
Cho, Ki Haeng 398
Cho, Fujio 409
Cho, Fujio 455
Choi, Young Han 247
Choi, In Gyu 247
Choi, Gee-Sung 378
Choi, Gee-Sung 378
Choi, Buhmsoo 391
Choi, Myung-Hae 397
Chokki, Morikazu 289
Chomet, Patrick 475
Chong, Kie Cheong 466
Choo, Michael 249
Choo, Kangsoo 259
Chou, Shu-Chang 427
Chou, Chun-Lung 427
Chou, Chen-Tsai 427
Choudhury, S. Roy 205
Chow, Sir Chung-Kong (C.K.) 35
Chow, Kareen 278
Chow, Gregory C. 429
Chowdhury, Ravneet 411
Chr, Lars 325
Chretien, Olivier 480
Christen, Hansruedi 287
Christensen, Claus 321
Christensen, Mariann Strid 325
Christensen, Uwe 489
Christensson, Anders 479
Christian, Ralf 396
Christiansen, Niels B. 146
Christley, S. M. 245
Christodoulou, Petros 303
Christodoulou, Nikos 303
Chrominska, Sylvia D. 69
Chronican, Philip (Phil) 46
Chu, Victor L.L. 492
Chuanzhi, Liu 266
Chubachi, Ryoji 408
Chubachi, Ryoji 409
Chuchottaworn, Pailin 349
Chugh, Davinder K. 39
Chulia, Francisco Vicent 177
Chung, Nuno 161
Chung, Dong-Rack 258
Chung, Hae-Joo 258
Chung, Joon-Yang 345
Chung, Joon-Yang 345
Chung, Jay Young 398
Chunguang, Li 120
Chutima, Sarunthorn 394
Chye, Spencer Lee Tien 275
Ch'ien, Raymond K. F. 194
Ciaccia, Mario 234
Cico, Carla 25
Cicognani, Giulio 54
Cicurel, Michel 402
Cid, Manuel 55
Cielo, Antonio C. Del 56
Cieslak, John B. 302
Cirelli, Jean-Francois 189
Cirelli, Jean-Francois 189
Cirillo-Goldberg, Mary A. 9
Ciurli, Stefano 432
Claesson, Pehr 166
Clairs, Reginald J. (Reg) 130
Clamadieu, Jean-Pierre 407
Clamens, Sophie 403
Clamon, Jean 89
Clappison, John H. 422
Clare, Peter 484
Clark, Richard P. 7
Clark, Brian 33
Clark, Gregory J. 46
Clark, Chris 90
Clark, Chris 100
Clark, Ian T. 362
Clark, Alan 373
Clark, Sue 373
Clark, Alan 373
Clark, W. Edmund (Ed) 450
Clark, Paul M. 450
Clark, W. Edmund (Ed) 450
Clarke, Timothy 42
Clarke, Charles 218
Clarke, Anthony 280
Clarke, Karin 352
Clarke, Tracy J. 411
Clarke, Philip (Phil) 440
Clarke, Philip (Phil) 440
Clarke, Michael 486
Clau?en, Hans-Peter 164
Clau?en, Hans-Peter 300
Clausen, Christian 321
Clausen, Henrik 435
Claussen, Hans Hans Claussen 300
Clavel, Pierre 189
Clayton, Bret 360
Clayton, Bret 361
Clayton, Annette K. 387
Cleave, Robert C. Van 53
Clemens, Jay 266
Clemente, Sergio 57
Clemente, Serge 472
Clements, Sean 325
Clemson, Nigel 47
Clifford, R. Leigh 74
Climeau, Jean-Claude 443
Clo, Alberto 163
Close, Katie 373
Clotte, Alain 127
Clouzard, Pascal 109
Clyne, Cameron A. 301
Clyne, Cameron A. 301
Coakwell, Todd 18
Coates, G. J. 245
Coates, Julie 488
Cobaleda, Manuel 185
Cobben, Mark M. 98
Cobee, Vincent 316
Cobo, Santiago 185
Coby, Paul 233
Cochet, Philippe 31
Cocker, Tony 159
Coelho, Alexandre da Paix?o 168
Coffey, Charlie 366
Coffey, Philip (Phil) 484
Cohen, Tzahi 62
Cohen, Dan 63
Cohen, Doron 63
Cohen, Florence Baranes 109
Cohen, David 129
Cohen, Abraham E. (Barry) 441
Coinaud, Ghislaine 333
Cojan, Jean-Pierre 375
Cojuangco, Eduardo M. (Danding) 379
Colafrancesco, Matteo 234
Colao, Vittorio A. 475
Colas, Gilles 131
Cole, Martin I. (Marty) 7
Cole, Michael 82
Cole, Robert 100
Coleman, Michael 273
Coleman, Damien 438
Colijn-Hooymans, C.M. 256
Collado, Alfredo 401
Coller, Stephen van 71
Colli, Salvatore 376
Collier, Declan 29
Collier, Christopher (Chris) 176
Collingwood, Carla F. 130
Collins, Donal 66
Collins, Deirdre 318
Collinson, Shawn 7
Colliver, Steve 465
Collomb, Bertrand P. 453
Collomp, Dominique 472
Colmenero, Antonio Perez 177
Colombani, Pascal 31
Colombani, Pascal 469
Colombara, Jean-Pierre 139
Colombo, Paolo Andrea 163
Colon, James H. (Jim) 455
Colonges, Guillaume de 109
Colotti, Salvatore 41
Colquitt, Julian 202
Colter, Gary F. 104
Colucci, Eugenio 41
Comadran, Sol 57
Combe, Emilie 93
Combes, Michel 25
Combes, Michel 475
Combes, Michel 476
Combret, Francois Polge de 375
Comyn, Matt 130
Concetti, Simone 463
Conick, Doug 278
Conn, Iain C. 95
Conn, Iain C. 95
Conn, Iain C. 365
Connelly, Deirdre P. 191
Conner, David P. 336
Conner, David P. 336
Conner, Steve 395
Conner, Isabelle M. 492
Connolly, Joe 66
Connor, Peter 100
Connor, Roger 192
Connor, Dean A. 422
Connor, Dean A. 422
Connors, Michael P. 9
Conrado, Dan 468
Consedine, Stephen 360
Considine, Tom 66
Constantine, Clem 280
Constantino, Ferdinand K. 379
Constantino, Ferdinand K. 379
Conte, Jerome Jerome Le Conte 471
Conte, Jerome Le 471
Conti, Fulvio 72
Conti, Fulvio 74
Convers, Enrique Velazquez 160
Conway, Mike 413
Conyers, Yolanda 266
Cook, Robert A. (Bob) 278
Cook, Karen 440
Cook-Bennett, Gail C. A. 278
Cooley, Paul 410
Coombe, John D. 218
Cooper, Kirstine 47
Cooper, Wendy 49
Cooper, Steve 74
Cooper, Alison J. 227
Cooper, Alison J. 227
Cooper, Brad 484
Coopmans, Baptiest 256
Cope, George A. 82
Cope, George A. 82
Cope, Nigel 250
Copeland, Garry 233
Copland, Carolyn 95
Coppey, Pierre 472
Coppinger, Francis 102
Corachan, Joaquin 57
Cordeiro, Carlos 87
Cordeiro, Carlos 88
Cordova, Harel 218
Corless, Kenneth (Ken) 8
Cornelis, Frans 352
Cornelis, Francois 453
Cornetta, Paolo 463
Cornier, Christophe 39
Cornu, Jo 248
Corominas, Blanca 57
Correa, Fabio Echeverri 160
Correa, Fabio Echeverri 160
Cortes, Antonio R. 276
Cosgrove, Tom 409
Cossiello, Ademir 56
Costa, Paulo C. 161
Costa, Antonio F. Melo Martins da 161
Costa, Carlos da Silva 170
Costa, Paulo R. 340
Costa, Mario 352
Cote, Nadia 9
Cote, Jacynthe 361
Cotte, Bruno 375
Cottet, Jean-Paul 333
Cottet, Jean 333
Coughlan, Anthony G. (Tony) 7
Coulombe, Gerard 302
Coulter, James G. (Jim) 266
Coulter, Douglas (Doug) 366
Counsel, Jane 484

Coupe, Mike 240
Coupe, Michael (Mike) 240
Courcel, Georges Chodron de 31
Courcel, Georges Chodron de 89
Courcel, Georges Chodron de 93
Coureil, Herve 387
Cournuaud, Florent Florent de Cournuaud 474
Court, Annette 491
Courtemanche, Robert 9
Courtemanche, Gilles 225
Courtier, Beth 100
Courtois, Jean-Philippe 44
Courtois, Jean-Philippe 44
Cousins, Richard J. 134
Cousins, Richard J. 134
Cousins, Geoffrey 438
Coutinho, Fernando Pedro Braga Pereira 168
Coutinho, Eric 257
Coutinho, Luciano Galv?o 340
Coutinho, Luciano Galv?o 468
Coutu, Marcel R. 193
Coutu, Marcel 345
Couture, Xavier 333
Cowan, Andrew 156
Cowdry, Miles A. 364
Cowen, Peter 100
Cox, Mitch 74
Cox, Chris 85
Cox, Pat 133
Cox, Philip G. 298
Cox, Vivienne 360
Cox, Vivienne 361
Cox, Andrew 465
Craig, Pamela J. (Pam) 7
Craig, David 129
Cramer, Ralf 135
Crampton, James 156
Crane, Lisa 156
Crawford, David A. 87
Crawford, David A. 88
Crawley, Andrew 233
Cremonini, Luigi 54
Crepin, Frederic Frederic Crepin 474
Cresswell, Alex 443
Creus, Jose 57
Cristina, Fatima 468
Crochon, Michel 387
Crockett, Bruce L. 9
Croisset, Charles F. W. de 271
Croisset, Charles F. W. de 355
Crols, Bart 462
Crombie, Sir Sandy 368
Cromme, Gerhard 28
Cromme, Gerhard 28
Cromme, Gerhard 131
Cromme, Gerhard 395
Croot, Giles 72
Crosby, Ralph D. 21
Crosby, Sir James R. 134
Cross, Patricia 301
Cross, Christine Christine Cross 488
Crossley, Andrew M. (Andy) 348
Crosthwaite, Peregrine 235
Crouch, Robert P. 11
Crowe, Sean 66
Crowe, John 131
Crowley, Kieran 29
Crowley, Des 66
Crowley, Jilinda 364
Cruickshank, Bert 91
Crull, Kevin W. 82
Crusemann, Michael E. 335
Cruz, Jennifer de la 107
Cruz, Joao 161
Csanyi, Sandor 297
Csanyi, Sandor 297
Csapo, D.R. 448
Cseh, Bela 297
Csoma, Stephan 462
Cuadrench, Alfonso Costa 10
Cuba, Yolanda Z. 71
Cucchiani, Enrico T. 28
Cucchiani, Enrico T. 234
Cucchiani, Enrico T. 463
Cuellar, Katia 465
Cullinan, Rory 368
Culmer, George 270
Culmer, George 270
Culp, H. Lawrence (Larry) 192
Cummins, John 368
Cunci, Delphine Delphine Ernotte Cunci 333
Cunha, Rui Ferin 161
Cunha, Sergio Quiroga da 166
Cunha, Pedro Guilherme Beauvillain de Brito e 168
Cunha, Jose 468
Cunningham, Ralph S. 18
Cunningham, Mark 66
Cunningham, Orla 66
Cunnington, Brian 74
Curadeau-Grou, Patricia 302
Curcuruto, Pier Luigi 234
Currie, Alistair 46
Currie, Theresa L. (Teri) 450
Currie, Gordon A. M. 483
Currie, Gordon A.M. 483
Currier, John D. 47
Curtaz, Philippe de Fontaine Vive 170
Curtis, John S. 28
Curtis, Miranda Miranda Curtis 280
Curtis, Christopher B. (Chris) 387
Curtis, John S. 484
Curtis, John S. 484
Curtius, Prof Julius Michael 113
Cusenier, Bernard 131
Cusenier, Bernard 131
Cusimano, Antonino 432
Cusumano, Robert F. (Bob) 9
Cutt, Tim 88
Cutting, David D. 411
Cuyper, Hans Hans De Cuyper 275
Cuyper, Vincent De 407
Cuyper, Vincent 407
Cypriano, Marcio Artur Laurelli 57
Cyr, Bernard 302

D

Daberkow, Mario 153
Dacey, John R. 49
Dachowski, Peter R. 131
Dadiseth, Keki B. 348
Dadyburjor, Khush Khush Dadyburjor 483
Dagenais, Jean 302
Dahan, Rene 255
Dahlvig, Anders Anders Dahlvig 203
Dahlvig, Anders 250
Dai, Guoliang 64
Daido, Issei 67
Daido, Issei 67
Dailey, Jeffrey J. (Jeff) 491
Dale, Thomas P. 364
Daleffe, P. 376
Daley, Jeffrey W. 289
Dalgaard, Lars 384
Dalibard, Barbara M. 133
Dalibard, Yves-Marie 453
Dalibor, Ulrich 286
Dalibot, Denis 124
Dalton, William S. (Bill) 459
dAlviella, Richard 145
Daly, Mike 95
Daly, John P. 98
Daly, John P. 98
Daly, Richard 475
Dam, Jan Van 255
Damesin, Marie-Francoise 355
DAmico, Michael 173
Damme, Alexandre Van 37
DAmours, Jacques 27
Dancausa, Maria Dolores 70
DAndrea, Federico Federico DAndrea 432
Danhan, Huang 64
Daniel, Dominik de 11
Daniel, Gary J. 18
Daniel, Wolfgang 76
Daniel, Patrick D. 104
Daniels, J. Eric 101
Danielsen, John 147
Danielsen, Mette Kruse 325
Danielsson, Anders 401
Dankner, Dan (Danny) 62
Danon, Laurence 156
Danon, Pierre Pierre Danon 413
Dantani, Shigeki 405
Daocheng, Wang 339
Daofu, Wang 339
Darchis, Francois 261
Darfoor, Andrew 330
Dargue, Robin 25
Darijtschuk, Niklas 84
Darmayan, Philippe 39
Darmon, Marc 443
Darner, Leif 24
Darricarrere, Yves-Louis 453
Darroch, Jeremy 280
Dart, Robert J. 483
Daruwala, Zarin 224
Das, Maarten M. 199
Das, Theo 352
Daschner, Georg 300
Dash, Sujogya 39
Dassault, Laurent 345
Dassault, Thierry 471
Dassler, Adi 13
Datar, Srikant M. 323
Datson, Trevor 440
Datta, B.K. 85
Datta, Partho 196
Dauger, Jean-Marie 189
Daum, Martin 143
Daussy, Philippe E. 472
David, George 95
David, Michael 164
David, Francois 472
David-Weill, Michel 145
Davidson, Janet G. 25
Davidson, Nicola 39
Davidson, James A. (Jim) 176
Davidson, John 373
Davidson, Mike 461
Davidsson, Kristina 166
Davies, Andrew 51
Davies, Pat 87
Davies, Mathew 100
Davies, Chris 155
Davies, Victoria 304
Davies, David C. 332
Davies, Sir Howard J. 348
Davies, Alan 361
Davies, Jerry 491
Davila, Carlos Alejandro Perez 373
Davila, Alejandro Santo Domingo 373
Davis, Darrell 26
Davis, Ian E. L. 95
Davis, Scott 97
Davis, Sally 100
Davis, Ian E. L. 364
Davis, Alison 368
Davis, Aaron L. 387
Davis, Scott T. 388
Davis, Scott M. 422
Davis, Gareth 486
Davoren, Peter J. 210
Davy, Francois 11
Dawe, Shirley A. 302
Dawson, Grant 116
Dawson, Douglas 318
Daxiong, Wang 119
De-Saint-Affrique, Antoine 464
Dean, Corey M. 104
Deane, Jonathan 33
Deane, Roderick S. 488
Debaillie, Luc 248
Deblaere, Johan G. (Jo) 7
Deborah, DiSanzo 258
Debrosse, Didier 199
DeBrusk, Ryan 91
Decarnin, Philippe 127
Decio, Alessandro 463
Dedi, Wang 342
dEeckenbrugge, Herve 407
Deek, Amnon 62
Deepak, Anurag 85
Deessen, Ulrich von 76
Defieuw, Luc 25
Defourny, Michel 407
Degen, Urs 54
Degenhart, Elmar 135
Degoumois, Christophe 91
Deguchi, Toshihisa 416
Dehaene, Jean-Luc 37
Dehaene, Jean-Luc 462
Dehaze, Alain 11
Dehecq, Jean-Francois 471
Dehen, Wolfgang 395
Deininger, Hermann 13
Deister, Michael 136
Dekang, Chen 229
Dekant, Willy 489
Dekkers, Marijn E. 78
Delamere, Sandra L. 422
Delbridge, Richard 412
Deleplace, Christian 355
Delevacque, Guy 443
Delfrate, Marco 234
Delgado, Luisa Deplazes 384
Delicourt, Patrick 402
Delleani, Riccardo 432
Delorme, Philippe 387
Delpit, Bernard 355
Delvecchio, Helena Irene Revoredo 59
Demare, Michel 5
Demare, Michel 461
Demare, Michel 461
Demel, Herbert 274
Demesmaeker, Koen 462
Demiddeleer, Leopold 407
Demoliere, Serge 263
Demosky, Bart W. 423
Denes, Ferenc 297
Denham, Robert E. 177
Denham, Gillian H. (Jill) 302
Denison, David 367
Dennelind, Johan 436
Denoke, Georg 268
Denozza, Francesco 284
Dentressangle, Norbert 49
Dentressangle, Norbert 49
Depail, Jean-Claude 189
Depickere, Franky 248
Deranleau, Richard 184
Deroubaix, Bertrand 453
Desautels, L. Denis 92
Descalzi, Claudio 163
Descalzi, Claudio 186
dEscatha, Yannick 443
Descheemaeker, Stefan 37
Desforges, Odile 355
Desheh, Eyal 441
Deshpande, Charudatta 224
Deshui, Li 120
Desjardins, Daniel 91
Desjardins, Luc 104
Deslarzes, Jean-Christophe 109
Desmarais, Paul 189
Desmarais, Andre R. 193
Desmarais, Paul 193
Desmarais, Paul 345
Desmarais, Andre R. 345
Desmarais, Paul 346
Desmarais, Andre R. 346
Desmarais, Paul 453
Desmarest, Thierry 91
Desmarest, Thierry 261
Desmarest, Thierry 355
Desmarest, Thierry 383
Desmartis, Charles 109
Desrosiers, Roger 27
Deus, Lutz 144
DeVard, Jerri L. 318
Devey, Robert A. (Rob) 348
Devey, Robert A. (Rob) 348
Devine, Hugh 484

Devisch, Noel 248
Devitre, Dinyar S. 373
Dewan, Shai 257
DeWolfe, Richard B. 278
DeWolfe, Richard B. 278
Dews, Nigel 475
Dhawan, Neelam 258
Dhoheyan, Mohammed Al 461
Diaconu, Lacramiorara 332
Diamond, Robert E. (Bob) 72
Diamond, Robert E. (Bob) 72
Diamond, Howard 443
Diamond-Gelinas, Nicole 302
Dianwu, Lei 120
Dias, Ricardo 57
Diaz, Alvaro 104
DiCiurcio, John A. 210
Dick, Brendan 100
Dickinson, Lawrence 74
Dickinson, Robert H. (Bob) 107
Diederich, Prof Francois 76
Diedrich, Christian 164
Diekmann, Michael 28
Diekmann, Michael 76
Diekmann, Michael 76
Diekmann, Michael 268
Diekmann, Michael 268
Diekmann, Michael 396
Diesbach, Patrice Lambert-de 109
Diess, Herbert 81
Diethelm, Markus U. 461
Dietrichs, Hans 202
Diezi, Reto 54
Diggelmann, Roland 362
Dijk, Robert J. van 57
Dikken, Tineke 24
Dill, Claudia 491
Dimopoulos, Dimitrios G. 303
Dimopoulos, Dimitrios G. 303
Dinaker, J. 86
Dineen, Robert E. 278
Dingemans, Simon 191
Dingemans, Simon 192
Dinges, Andreas 11
Dingle, David K. 107
Diniz, Abilio dos Santos 111
DiPietro, Kenneth A. (Ken) 266
dIribarne, Benoit 131
Dirks, Thorsten 256
Dirks, Detlef 277
DiSanzo, Deborah 257
Diskul, Mom Rajawongse Disnadda 394
Dixon, John 280
Dixon, John 280
Dixon, Mark 413
Dlamini, Kuseni 330
Dobashi, Akio 405
Dobson, Wendy K. 450
Dodge, David A. 69
Dodge, Tanith 280
Dodge, Colin 316
Dodge, Colin 316
Dodig, Victor 104
Dodson, Tim 414
Doets, Jan 205
Dohle, Markus 84
Doi, Nobuhiro 67
Doi, Nobuhiro 67
Doi, Masayuki 417
Doi, Masayuki 418
Doijer, Derk C. 255
Doimo, Daniel 387
Dolberg, Patrick 212
Domingues, Mario 91
Dominguez, Jaime 114
Domke, Tatjana 492
Donald, Arnold W. 107
Donald, Arnold W. 107
Donck, Frank 248
Dong-Sung, Cho 249
Dongping, Yang 65
Dongre, Sanjay 196
Donnelly, Nigel 273
Donnelly, Vincent 410
Donnet, Philippe 474
Donovan, M. J. (Mike) 53
Donovan, Denis 66
Donvil, Jos 256
Doo, William W. H. 65
Doo-Hee, Lee 249
Dore, John 218
Dorey, Gerard 109
Dorge, Philippe 342
Dorig, Rolf 11
Doris, Ennio 284
Dormann, Jurgen 85
Dorn, Jurgen 277
Dorner, I. M. 218
Dorrance, Robert E. (Bob) 450
Dorrepaal, Karin 164
Dorrian, Alex 443
Dotsch, Flip 464
Doucet, Michel 27
Dougan, Brady W. 139
Dougherty, Kevin P. 422
Doukeris, Michel Dimitrios 37
Douro, Lord 383
Douroux, Lucien 93
Douville, Jean 302
Dovey, John 100
Dovrat, Moshe 63
Dowd, Brian E. 9
Dowidar, Hatem 475
Dowling, Dame Ann 95
Downe, Andrew J. 273
Downey, Richard 18
Downey, A. 298
Downing, John 227
Downing, Wadham 265
Doye, Anthony P. (Tony) 183
Doyle, Jeff 11
Doyle, Noreen 139
Drabsch, Neil 350
Draeger, Klaus 81
Drake, Tomas Alfaro 56
Drake, Tomas 56
Dranse, Phil 225
Draxler, Helmut 332
Drees, Jeff 387
Drieselmann, Ralf 462
Driscoll, Sean O' 29
Dromer, Alain 47
Dror, Nira 62
Dror, Iris 62
Drori, Yehuda 63
Drouet, Dominique 212
Drozdovsky, Liliana 218
Drummond, Craig 301
Duan, Pang Cheng 278
Duarte, Helio 218
Duarte, Jose 384
Dubik, Nikolay N. 187
Dublon, Dina 8
Dubos, Jean-Francois 474
Dubourg, Saori 76
Dubreuil, Dominique Dominique Heriard Dubreuil 474
Dubreuil, Dominique Heriard 474
Duchesne, Marc 91
Ducom, P.P. 448
Ducra, Henri 189
Ducre, Henri 189
Ducroix, Daniel 127
Ducros, Pierre Y. 278
Dudley, Robert W. (Bob) 95
Dudley, Robert W. (Bob) 95
Dueholm, John Staunsbjerg 415
Dufau, Bernard 333
Duff, Andrew J. (Andy) 486
Duffaut, Eric 384
Duffy, David 29
Dufour, Pierre 261
Dufour, Sandrine 474
Dufresne, Pierre 24
Dufresne, Richard 483
Duggan, Frank 5
Duhnkrack, Thomas 157
Duijl, Milko Van 266
Dumas, Jacques 111
Dumoulin, Sven 24
Dumoulin, Sven 465
Duncan, Phillip 323
Dundas, Jamie F. T. 412
Dunhaupt, Aage 151
Dunkel, Gunter 136
Dunleavy, J.K. 245
Dunn, Craig 33
Dunn, Craig 33
Dunn, Michael 100
Dunne, Stephen 33
Dunoyer, Marc 44
Dunoyer, Marc 191
Dunse, Arnd 457
Dunselman, Ange 257
Dupety, Bruno 472
Duppre, Hans Jorg 263
Duppre, Hans 263
Duprat, Pierre 472
Duprieu, Jean-Pierre 261
Dupuy, Armand 375
Duque, Renato Renato de Souza Duque 340
Duquette, Pascal 302
Duran, Jose-Luis 333
Duran, Jose 333
Durana, Christina Aldamiz-Echevarria Gonzalez de 1
Durand, Philippe 127
Durand-Charlot, Veronique 189
Durante, Nicandro 98
Durante, Nicandro 98
Durbin, Annemarie 411
Dureau, Gaetan 91
Duren, Aydin 459
Durland, Michael (Mike) 69
Durrant, Mark 318
Durrant, Kath 365
Dusi, Sam 266
Dussard, Dominique 407
Dussault, Alain Alain Dussault 82
Dutil, Marcel 302
Dutra, Felipe 37
Dutschke, Michael 263
Duverne, Denis 49
Duverne, Denis 49
Duvoisin, Jean-Marc 309
Duzan, Jean-Baptiste 316
Duzan, Jean-Baptiste 479
Dvorin, Pnina 62
Dybal, Alexander 186
Dyer, Stephen G. (Steve) 18
Dyer, Melanie 404
Dyer, Robert 409
Dyrbus, Robert (Bob) 227
Dyrbus, Robert (Bob) 227
Dyukov, Alexander V. 186
Dyukov, Alexander V. 186
d'Adda, Tiberto Ruy Brandolini 172
D'Agostino, Gianfilippo 432
D'Alessandro, Dominic 104
D'Alessandro, Dominic 423
d'Alviella, Baron Richard Goblet 145
D'Amours, Jacques 26
D'Amours, Jacques 27
D'Andrea, Frederico M. 432
D'Andrea, Paolo 432
d'Aquino, Thomas P. 278
d'Eeckenbrugge, Baron Herve Coppens 407
d'Escatha, Yannick 443
d'Estaing, Antoine Giscard 111
d'Estaing, Henri M.E.V. Giscard 111
d'Estaing, Henri M.E.V. Giscard 353
d'Estais, Jacques 89
D'Hinnin, Dominique 21
D'Hondt, Edwin 462
d'Intignano, Beatrice Majnoni 261

E

Earl, Belinda Belinda Earl 280
Easthope, Dana J. 422
Eastwood, S. 298
Eastwood, Grant 298
Ebata, Makoto 208
Eberhardt, Wolfram 5
Ebi, Yutaka 358
Eby, Peter B.M. 483
Echavez, Luis 114
Echevarria, Jose I. Berroeta 223
Echeverri, Adriana M. 160
Eckes, Peter 76
Eddington, Sir Roderick I. (Rod) 360
Edelman, Keith 51
Edelstenne, Charles 109
Edelstenne, Charles 443
Ederer, Brigitte 396
Edey, Russell P. 330
Edin, Ebru Dildar 459
Edlund, Anders 321
Edmondson, Ralph 98
Edmonstone, Sandy 273
Edstrom, Cecilia 436
Edstrom, Cecilia Cecilia Edstrom 436
Edwards, David 100
Edwards, Steve 100
Edwards, Robert L. 176
Egan, Scott 491
Egawa, Keishi (Keith) 283
Egawa, Ryutaro Ryutaro Egawa 390
Egea, Ignacio 356
Egemen, Tolga 459
Eggberry, Charmaine 318
Egidi, Massimo Massimo Egidi 432
Egloff, German 54
Egloff, Sergio 212
Egmond, Marit van 255
Egosi, Richard S. 441
Eguchi, Masao 388
Eguren, Eduardo 74
Ehrat, Felix R. 323
Ehrenbeck, Claus 445
Ehrling, Marie 321
Ehrling, Marie 321
Ehrnrooth, Georg 318
Ehrnrooth, Georg 381
Eichel, Scott 368
Eichholz, Rainer 210
Eichiner, Friedrich 81
Eichler, Bertin 81
Eichler, Bertin 445
Eichler, Edwin 445
Eichler, Bertin 445
Eicholz, Rainer 210
Eickholt, Jochen 395
Eiken, Petter 400
Eilersen, Claus 325
Eilertsen, Carsten Carsten Eilertsen 147
Einarsson, Petra 381
Einersson, Petra 381
Eisenlohr, Thomas 268
Eizenstat, Stuart E. 25
Ejelov, Ulf 426
Ejima, Kikuo 253
Ekblom, Anders 44
Ekholm, E. Borje 166
Eklund, Petra 321
Ekstrom, Andreas 436
Ekvall, Niklas 321
Ekwall, Johan 321
Elfstrand, Bjorn 426
Elgibaly, Khalid 74
Eliasson, Tomas 3
Eliasson, Karin 436
Elie, Jean A. 27
Elix, Douglas T. (Doug) 366
Elizondo, Jaime G. 114
Elkann, Lapo 172
Elliot, David 47
Elliot, Guy R. 360
Elliot, Guy R. 360
Elliott, Shayne 46
Elliott, Ben 352
Elliott, Guy 361
Elliott, Guy 361
Elliott, Guy 370
Ellis, Glenn 206
Ellis, Rick 438
Ellwood, Peter 24

Elop, Stephen A. 318
Elstein, Amir 441
Elstone, Robert G. 484
Elverding, Peter A. F. W. 231
Elverding, Peter A. F. W. 231
Elzvik, Eric 5
Emmett, Dorian 35
Emura, Katsumi 307
Enami, Takatsugu 416
Enders, Thomas (Tom) 21
Endersby, Robert 147
Endo, Nobuhiro 306
Endo, Nobuhiro 307
Endo, Hidenobu 358
Endo, Hiroshi 446
Engebrigtsen, Scott 435
Engel, Hans-Ulrich 76
Engelen, Peter 457
Engelien, Bernd O. 492
Engels, William 102
Engels, Stephan 128
Engels, Stephan 143
Engibous, Thomas J. (Tom) 429
Engineer, Harish 196
Engineer, Harish 196
Engstrand, Mats 426
Enkawa, Takao 97
Ennerfelt, Goran 425
Enoki, Masahiro 281
Enomoto, Takashi 22
Enslin, Rob 384
Entenmann, Klaus 143
Entwistle, Darren Darren Entwistle 483
Eok-Jo, Kim 222
Eok-Jo, Kim 222
Epple, Alwin 143
Epple, Lukas 212
Epstein, David R. 323
Erbil, Ali Fuat 459
Erel, Husnu 459
Erel, Husnu 459
Eremina, Victoria 318
Eriksen, Jesper T. 256
Eriksen, Peter Bonne 325
Eriksen, Trond Finn 415
Erikson, Jonas 426
Erlen, Hubertus 113
Erman, Marko 443
Erming, Prof Xu 122
Ermotti, Sergio P. 461
Errard, Nathalie 21
Ersb.ll, Charlotte 325
Erskine, Peter 434
Ersozoglu, Uruz 459
Erun, Gokhan 459
Erwert, Jurgen 151
Escher, Thomas K. 492
Escobar, Ignacio Legorburu 10
Espenshade, Scott 87
Espinosa, Alicia del Carmen 381
Essoka, Ebenezer 411
Estevez, Xabier de Irala 223
Estlin, Peter 72
Estrada, Joaquin 114
Estrada, Genaro Borrego 177
Estrada, Genaro 177
Estrade-Bordry, Corinne 261
Etemesi, Richard 411
Ethier, Guy 462
Eto, Naomi 96
Eto, Akihiro 97
Ettwig, Stefan 445
Euh, Yoon-Dae 247
Eui-Sun, Chung 222
Eui-Sun, Chung 222
Euisun, Chung 249
Euisun, Chung 249
Eusman, Frans 199
Eustace, Kevin 396
Evans, William 46
Evans, Gay 47
Evans, Paul J. 49
Evans, Nicola 87
Evans, Paul 100
Everett, N. Ashleigh 69
Evers, Astrid 128
Evers, Johannes 263
Evers, John E. 395
Evertz, Andreas 381
Every, Robert (Bob) 480
Evin, Kerim 401
Ewaldsson, Ulf 166
Ewelme, Michael Michael Jay of Ewelme 42
Excell, Paul 100
Eyton, Trevor 274

F

Faber, Emmanuel 145
Faber, Joachim 218
Fabian, Heinz 205
Fabiani, Matteo 234
Fabritius, Hans Georg 149
Facchin, Claudio 5
Fady, Antoine 24
Fagen, Colin 350
Fagerlin, Karl Gunnar 203
Fagioli, Alessandro 54
Fagnoule, Dominique 302
Fahim, Mohamed 161
Fahim, Mohamed 463
Fahy, Nick 66
Fai, Chow (Edward) Kwong 119
Fai, Lee 467
Fainaro, Ron M. 63
Fainaro, Ron Ron Fainaro 63
Fairbairn, Mark 305
Fairbairn, Sally 410
Fairclough, Daniel 39
Fairey, Michael E. (Mike) 147
Fairey, Michael E. (Mike) 265
Fairhead, Rona A. 218
Fairhead, Alan 491
Faivre-Duboz, Michel 354
Fakie, Shauket A. 71
Falck, Alexandre 109
Falk, Per 325
Falk, Karin 479
Falkengren, Annika Annika Falkengren 300
Falkengren, Annika 399
Falkengren, Annika 399
Falkengren, Annika 477
Fallowfield, Tim 240
Fan, Yaosheng 64
Fan, Xulitai 121
Fan, Jiang 339
Fan, Yang-Jan 427
Fanelli, Angelo 163
Fanfei, Xin 119
Fang, Han 122
Fang, Zhi 125
Fangzheng, Jiao 120
Fante, Rich 44
Farnfield, David 483
Farnsworth, Richard 373
Farr, Jezz 218
Farrant, S. 245
Farrell, Garry 273
Farrington, Hugh G. 169
Faruque, Nadine 463
Farwerck, Joost 256
Fasimon, Sandor 297
Fassbind, Renato 260
Fassin, Frank 164
Fassin, Frank 300
Faure, Pascal 333
Faure, Patrick 472
Faust, Dieter 371
Fauter, Wolfgang 54
Faxander, Olof 380
Fay, Bill 455
Fayolle, Jean 202
Fazzio, Luiz 109
Fearon, Mark 486
Feder, Lenny 412
Fedorov, Igor 188
Fedun, Leonid A. 329
Fee, Tom 66
Fegan, Paul A. 33
Feger, Andres Ruiz 300
Feger, Andres Andres Ruiz Feger 300
Fehrenbach, Franz 76
Fei, Zhao Ke 141
Feick, Florian 276
Feiger, Robert 197
Feldhaus, Stephan 362
Feldman, Robert 334
Feldt, Erik 321
Felice, Gregorio de 234
Feliziani, Giuseppe 234
Fell, Anthony S. 82
Fell, David 98
Fell, Nick 373
Fenglan, Yin 119
Fenne, Rob 352
Fennell, Andy 156
Ferencz, Szabolcs I. 297
Fergestad, Ingvald 435
Ferguson, Iain 53
Ferguson, Alan 245
Ferguson, John T. 366
Ferguson, Karen 387
Ferguson, John T. 423
Fernandes, Ana Maria M. 161
Fernandez, Jose Maria Aguirre 10
Fernandez, Angel 55
Fernandez, Enrique Medina 56
Fernandez, Enrique 56
Fernandez, Daniel 109
Fernandez, Ignacio 114
Fernandez, Felipe 161
Fernandez, Carlos 185
Fernandez, Ramon 189
Feroni, Marco Cerrina 234
Ferran, Javier 42
Ferran, Javier Javier Ferran 42
Ferrari, Piero 54
Ferrari, Piero 54
Ferraris, Luigi 162
Ferraris, Laura 466
Ferreira, Paulo 57
Ferreira, Miguel Ribeiro 161
Ferreira, Murilo Pinto de Oliveira 468
Ferreira, Monica 468
Ferrer, Antonio Garcia 10
Ferrer, Antonio Garcia 10
Ferrero, Gianluca 234
Ferrero, Pietro 284
Ferrero, Dominique 472
Ferrero-Waldner, Benita 300
Ferri, Stefano 41
Ferri, William J. (Bill) 461
Ferro, Claudio Braz 37
Ferro, Claudio 37
Fessard, Jerome 131
Feuer, Zvi 396
Feuerhake, Rainer 459
Fiatte, Traci 352
Fibig, Andreas 78
Fidalgo, Julio Sacristan 10
Fidanza, Virginio 466
Field, Richard 47
Field, Bernard 131
Fielding, Ross 438
Filho, Armando Trivelato 56
Filho, Oscar Augusto de Camargo 468
Filippi, Charles-Henri 333
Finch, Yuki 412
Findlay, David 320
Finegold, Warren 475
Finger, Rolf 482
Fini, Vittorio 54
Fini, Vittorio 54
Fink, Johannes 13
Finlayson, Chris 85
Finlayson, Eric 360
Finne, Thomas 335
Fiorentino, Paolo 463
Firth, J. Roy 278
Fischer, Thomas 78
Fischer, Roland 396
Fischer, Dietmar 482
Fischl, Hans 136
Fisher, Ronald D. (Ron) 404
Fisher, Ronald D. (Ron) 404
Fishman, Mark C. 323
Fitoussi, Jean-Paul 234
Fitoussi, Martine 261
Fitoussi, Jean-Paul 432
Fitschen, Juergen 260
Fitting, Alwin 371
Fitzgerald, Bryan 129
Fitzpatrick, Ceri 100
Fitzpatrick, Michael 360
Fitzpatrick, Michael 361
Fiuza, Murilo 468
Fjell, Olav Olav Fjell 426
Flanagan, Brian 298
Flegel, Heinrich 144
Fleming, James 461
Flemming, William (Bill) 400
Fletcher, Rees 9
Fletcher, M. 298
Flett, Angus 100
Fleurant, Jacques 216
Flint, Douglas J. 217
Flint, John 218
Floch, Dominique 443
Flockhart, Alexander A. (Sandy) 194
Flockhart, Alexander A. (Sandy) 218
Floether, Karl-Heinz 7
Floriani, Lodovico 41
Floris, Jean-Pierre 131
Flowers, J. Christopher 392
Flynn, Patrick G. 231
Flynn, Catherine Catherine Flynn 488
Foerster, Christina 263
Fogarty, Des 350
Fogelberg, Anders 401
Fois, Candido 463
Fois, Candido 463
Fok, Canning K. N. 219
Foley, Donough 258
Foley, John 348
Foley, John 348
Foley, Dan 352
Foley, Mike 491
Folland, Nick 250
Folonari, Alberto 466
Folonari, Alberto 466
Folz, Jean-Martin 31
Folz, Jean-Martin 49
Folz, Jean-Martin 131
Folz, Jean-Martin 402
Folz, Jean-Martin 407
Font, Artur Carulla 356
Fontaine, Jean-Louis 91
Fontaine, Jean-Louis 91
Fontana, Bernard 39
Fontana, Enio 466
Fontanesi, Donato 463
Foong, Seong Seong Yew Foong 275
Forbes, Cindy 278
Ford, Anna 240
Ford, W. Douglas (Doug) 423
Foreman, Brad 443
Forestier, Jean-Pierre 443
Forgeard, Noel 387
Fornaro, Carlo 432
Forneck, Gunter 78
Forneri, Jean-Marc 375
Fornero, Elsa 234
Fornero, Elsa 234
Forrest, Mary 300
Forshaw, Robin 35
Forster, Christina 263
Forsyth, David 461
Fortier, Yves 360
Fortin, Richard 26
Fortin, Guy 345
Foschi, Pier Luigi 107
Foschi, Pier Luigi 107
Foster, Mike 183
Foster, Maria Maria das Gracas Silva Foster 340
Foster, Maria das Gracas Silva 340
Foster, David 423

Fotopoulos, Thane 82
Foullong, Uwe 128
Fourie, Jac 88
Fourlis, Vassilios S. 343
Fournie, Patrick 443
Fournier, Thierry 131
Fournier, Annie 261
Fourtou, Jean-Rene 309
Fourtou, Jean-Rene 383
Fourtou, Jean-Rene 474
Fourtounis, Petros 303
Fowler, J. B. 245
Fox, Martha Lane 280
Fox, Martha Martha Fox 280
Fragkiadakis, Leonidas 303
Fraisse, Sebastien 472
Framp, P. C. 245
Franchi, Thierry 333
Francioli, Richard 472
Francis, Mary 116
Francisco, Douglas T. 56
Francke, Ulrika 426
Franco, Andres 104
Franco, Vitor D. Seabra 161
Franco, G. 376
Frandberg, Sofia 479
Frangetis, Dimitris 303
Frangista, Maria (Marily) 303
Frank, Kenneth 25
Frank, Howard S. 107
Frank, Howard S. 107
Franke, Fritz 202
Franke, Ralf-Michael 396
Franklin, Roy 414
Fransson, Catrin 426
Franz, Christoph 151
Fraser, Simon J. 72
Fraser, Simon J. 74
Fraser, Rob 240
Fraser, Sheila 278
Fraser, Jim 443
Fraser, John A. 461
Fraser, Anne L. 483
Frasier, Curtis R. 370
Fraternali, Silvio 234
Frazis, George 484
Fredheim, Ove 435
Freedman, Larry 107
Freeman, Patrick J. (Pat) 18
Freeman, Lord Roger 443
Frei, Hansjorg 54
Frei, Hans 54
Freidel, Marc 342
Freitas, Carlos Augusto Machado de Almeida 168
Freitas, Humberto 468
Freixe, Laurent 309
Fremont, Jean-Pierre 471
French, Seamus 35
French, Robert 233
Frenning, Malin 436
Frenzel, Dirk 78
Frenzel, Michael 457
Frenzel, Michael 458
Frenzel, Michael 477
Frere, Baron Albert 189
Frere, Baron Albert 271
Frere, Gerald 346
Frere, Gerald 346
Frerichs, Robert N. (Bob) 7
Frerot, Antoine Antoine Frerot 471
Fresco, Louise O. 465
Fresco, Louise O. 465
Frese, Mark 286
Frew, Anita M. 270
Frey, Johann-Christoph 202
Frey, Rainer-Marc 461
Freyne, Colm J. 422
Frial, Pedro Fernandez 356
Frial, Pedro 356
Friberg, Lars 426
Frick, David P. 309
Fried, D. L. 218
Fried, Bradley 235
Friedberg, Daniel 345
Friedman, Alexander S. 461
Frieling, Hubert 286
Friese, Lard 231
Friis, Morten N 366
Friman, Maija-Liisa 436
Froehlich, Babette 477
Froger, Anne 91
Frohlich, Fritz W. 352
Frohlich, Babette 477
Frost, Phillip 441
Froud, Samantha 9
Fry, Dominic 280
Fryar, Bob 95
Frykhammar, Jan 166
Fu, Junyuan 117
Fu, Yuning 118
Fu, Chengyu 125
Fucheng, Wang 339
Fuchigami, Masao 253
Fuchita, Keizo 292
Fuchs, Bernhard 462
Fudge, Ann M. 323
Fudge, Ann M. 464
Fudge, Ann M. 465
Fueangfu, Charnsak 61
Fuerst, Tracy 274
Fuhrmann, Werner 24
Fuhrmann, Christian 300
Fuji, Yosaku 420
Fujie, Naofumi 22
Fujie, Naofumi 22
Fujiga, Takeshi 283
Fujii, Natsuki 96
Fujii, Takashi 141
Fujii, Tsunehiko 206
Fujii, Junsuke 420
Fujikake, Yasuo 236
Fujikawa, Kazuhisa 283
Fujiki, Satoru 34
Fujimori, Fumio 22
Fujimori, Fumio 22
Fujimoto, Shinji 206
Fujimoto, Muneaki 241
Fujimoto, Noboru 390
Fujimoto, Toshihiko 390
Fujimura, Kiyoshi 290
Fujino, Michimasa 215
Fujinuma, Tsuguoki 320
Fujinuma, Tsuguoki 420
Fujita, Masami 183
Fujita, Masami 184
Fujita, Masaaki 295
Fujita, Kunitaka 408
Fujita, Hirokazu 446
Fujitsuka, Mikio 253
Fujiwara, Kiyoshi 283
Fujiwara, Makio 447
Fujiyoshi, Yukihiro 307
Fujiyoshi, Yukihiro 307
Fukakusa, Janice R. 366
Fukakushi, Masahiko (Masa) 452
Fukaya, Sumio 206
Fukubayashi, Kenjiro 416
Fukuda, Haruko 235
Fukuda, Yuji 238
Fukuda, Takitaro 293
Fukuda, Takitaro 293
Fukui, Takeo 215
Fukui, Masaki 307
Fukunaga, Seiji 224
Fukunaga, Seiji 224
Fukunaga, Takashi 295
Fukuo, Koichi 214
Fukushima, Sakie Tachibana 97
Funabashi, Haruo 142
Funayama, Norio 392
Fung, Andrew H. C. 194
Fung, Anita Y. M. 218
Funo, Yukitoshi (Yuki) 455
Funo, Yukitoshi (Yuki) 455
Furihata, Toru 417
Furlan, Luiz Fernando 434
Furong, Zhang 229
Furong, Zhang 229
Furrer, Lilian 11
Furse, Dame Clara H. F. 265
Furubayashi, Kiyoshi 456
Furuhashi, Mamoru 455
Furuhashi, Mamoru 455
Furuichi, Takeshi 311
Furuichi, Takeshi 311
Furukawa, Toshimasa 295
Furumoto, Yoshiharu 252
Furumoto, Yoshiharu 252
Furusawa, Kiichiro 182
Furusawa, Kiichiro 452
Furuta, Takanobu 236
Furuta, Takanobu 236
Furuta, Takanobu 238
Furutama, Takashi 283
Furuya, Shigemi 140
Furuya, Kazuhiko 182
Furuya, Katsumasa 184
Furuya, Katsumasa 184
Furuya, Sadao 241
Furuya, Yoshihiro 448
Fushen, Li 122
Futaki, Shiro 293
Fuyao, Tong 266
Fyodorov, Igor Y. 188

G

Gabanna, Louis 127
Gabas, Antonio 185
Gabel, Yadl 49
Gabriel, Yves 93
Gabriel, Yves 93
Gabriel, Yves 127
Gachora, John 71
Gadney, Oliver (Ollie) 461
Gaehwiler, Lukas 461
Gaemperle, Chantal 271
Gaffney, M. 245
Gagnon, Pierre 293
Gajecka, Marta 170
Gal, Shimon 62
Galateri, Gabriele 41
Galateri, Gabriele 41
Galbraith, Colin R. 130
Galende, Marcos 57
Galhau, Francois Villeroy de 90
Galifi, Vincent J. 274
Galipeau, Linda 352
Galizzi, P. 376
Gallagher, Tim 107
Gallagher, Gerry 227
Gallagher, John 370
Galle, Jean-Loic 443
Gallia, Fabio 89
Gallia, Franco 234
Gallienne, Segolene 124
Gallinari, D. 376
Gallo, Juan 356
Gallo, Juan Abello 356
Gallois, Louis 21
Gallois, Louis 21
Gallois, Louis 133
Gallot, Jerome 387
Gallot, Jerome 471
Galloway, Jil 289
Galvin, Mike 100
Ganaye, Patrick 109
Gancedo, Eric 59
Gancia, Alessandro Vallarino 124
Gandil, Patrick 375
Gang, Xiao 90
Ganong, David A. 422
Gans, Prof Arieh 63
Gao, Yingxin 90
Gao, Renjie 139
Garanderie, Dominique de La 355
Garavaglia, Carlo 466
Garavini, Eugenio 54
Garavoglia, Luca 172
Garcia, Victor Revuelta 10
Garcia, Jose Alfonso Nebrera 10
Garcia, Jose Alvaro Cuervo 10
Garcia, Claudio 37
Garcia, Ricardo de Ramon 131
Garcia, Ricardo 131
Garcia, Felix Martin 145
Garcia, Felix 145
Garcia, Federico Reyes 177
Garcia, Bego?a Elices 356
Garcia, Begona 356
Garcia, Winston F. 379
Garcia-Ovies, Ramiro Sanchez de Lerin 434
Garcia-Suelto, Jose 56
Garcia-Tu?on, Antonio Basagoiti 60
Gardner, Sir Roy A. 134
Gardner, David 298
Gardner, Paul 423
Garfield, Gary 97
Garibaldi, Pietro 234
Garnadt, Karl U. 151
Garner, Joe D. 217
Garner, N. P. H. 245
Garnier, Thierry 109
Garnier, Jean-Pierre (JP) 355
Garrett, Sophie 47
Garrett, Michael W.O. 348
Garwood, Alan 51
Garza, Francisco 114
Garza, Luis 114
Garza, Rafael 114
Garza, Alfonso C. Romo 114
Garza, Alfonso Garza 177
Garza, Consuelo Garza de 177
Garzon, Sabine 263
Gaskin, Beverly J. 365
Gasquet, Denis 471
Gates, David 156
Gathoo, S. P. 85
Gatto, Carlo Carlo Gatto 163
Gatzke, Eckard 352
Gaul, Hans Michael 396
Gaulin, Jean R. 302
Gaulle, Yves de 189
Gaus, Norbert 395
Gauthey, Gabrielle 25
Gauthier, Sylvie 91
Gauthier, Daniel 197
Gauthier, Paule 366
Gautier, Bernard 131
Gavazzi, Alberto 155
Gavin, Mike 100
Gawaxab, Johannes 330
Gazizullin, Farit R. 188
Ge, Chen 120
Gearheard, Richard L. 18
Geary, Dave 25
Geason, Paul 438
Gebbia, A. 376
Geddes, Paul 368
Geeber, Magnus 426
Gehl, Walter N. 151
Gehrig, Prof Bruno 362
Gehrig, Prof Bruno 362
Gehrig, Prof Bruno 461
Gei?inger, Jurgen 136
Geissler, Nicole 136
Gellens, Luc 462
Gelmon, Mark 35
Gelsomino, Cosma 76
Gemkow, Stephan 151
Genc, Onur 459
Genc, Onur 459
Genestar, Thierry 127
Genestar, Thierry 127
Genish, Amos Amos Genish 474
Genma, Akira 252
Genola, Gabriele Galateri di 432
Genola, Gabriele Galateri di 432
Genola, Gabriele Gabriele Galateri di Genola 432
Genova, Juan Maria Nin 167
Genova, Juan Maria Nin 356
Gent, Sir Christopher Charles (Chris) 191
Gentili, Steve 443
Gentz, Manfred 491
Geoff, Geoffrey 492

Georganas, Iakovos G. 343
George, Jeffrey (Jeff) 323
George, Richard L. (Rick) 366
George, Richard L. (Rick) 423
George, Richard L. (Rick) 423
Gerber, Michel 5
Gerber, Charles 104
Gerber, Fritz Fritz Gerber 492
Gerhards, Tilmann 157
Gerhardsson, Peter 325
Gerlach, Rolf 482
Germiniani, Paolo 432
Gernandt, Karl 260
Gerner, Roland 205
Gerrand, Sarah 250
Gershon, Sir Peter 304
Gershon, Sir Peter 305
Gerstenkorn, Petra 457
Gerstenkorn, Petra 457
Gerth, Erich 47
Gervasoni, Carlo 212
Gerwert, Bernhard Bernhard Gerwert 21
Geschwind, Ben J. 8
Geurts, Ton 24
Geust, Jonas 318
Ghazali, Mohd Mohd Nazlan bin Mohd Ghazali 275
Ghizzoni, Federico 463
Ghosh, Pallav 86
Ghosh, Sujit 212
Ghosn, Carlos 316
Ghosn, Carlos 354
Ghostine, Gilbert 156
Giacomin, Francesco 463
Giancarlo, Charles H. 8
Giannidis, Ioannis C. 303
Gianno, Jean-Marie 90
Gianotti, Anthony 480
Giard, Diane 302
Gibara, Germaine 18
Gibor, Eyal 12
Gibson, Sir Ian 298
Gibson, Linda T. 330
Giesinger, Jim 422
Giffin, Gordon D. 104
Gilbert, Jackson B. 168
Gilbert, Daniel T. (Danny) 301
Gilbert, Steffen 330
Gilbert, Malcolm 491
Gilchrist, Sean 74
Gilead, Prof Israel 63
Giles, Colin 318
Gilibert, Pierluigi 170
Gillam, John 480
Gillard, Ian Guy 61
Gillespie, Alan R. 330
Gillham, Simon 474
Gilliam, Theron I. (Tig) 11
Gillies, Crawford 413
Gillingwater, Richard D. 410
Gilroy, Kevin J. 384
Gilstrap, Douglas L. 166
Gilvary, Brian 95
Gilvary, Brian 95
Gimbe, Peter 400
Gina, Jian 266
Giordano, Giovanni 98
Giordo, Giuseppe 173
Giovanni, Gianni Di 163
Girard, Elie 333
Girard, Elie 333
Girardot, Paul-Louis 471
Girgis, Gisele 287
Girling, Russell K. (Russ) 18
Giroday, Eric Boyer de la 231
Gittler, Juliana 278
Giusto, Mauro 41
Gj?stein, Ann-Mari 415
Gjostein, Ann-Mari 415
Gjurovski, Stojko 426
Gkolemis, Stylianos 344
Gladman, Ian 330
Gladstone, Mira 218
Glaser, William A. (Bill) 409
Glasier, Richard J. 107
Glass, Kevin 104
Glasson, Ian 485
Glazer, Rose 396
Gledhill, David 147
Gleeson, Evelyn Evelyn Gleeson 250
Glen, John 261
Glitza-Stamberger, Silke 276
Gluher, Alexandre 57
Glynn, Martin J. G. 422
Gnudi, Piero 463
Gobeil, Paul 302
Goda, Hirofumi Hirofumi Goda 184
Godal, Bjorn T. 414
Godbehere, Ann 98
Godbehere, Ann F. 348
Godbehere, Ann F. 360
Godbehere, Ann F. 461
Gode, Pierre 124
Gode, Pierre 271
Godwin, Ian D. 245
Goeltz, Richard K. 47
Goeschel, Burkhard 274
Goetz, Juergen 179
Goetzeler, Martin 395
Goff, Alain Le 486
Goffaux, Denis 462
Goggins, Colleen A. 450
Goh, Euleen Y. K. 47
Goh, Euleen Y. K. 147
Goh, Linus T. L. 336
Gold, Andre 469
Golden, Charles E. 464
Golden, Charles E. 465
Goldenstein, Ihno 113
Goldenstein, Ihno 113
Goldfarb, Shlomo 63
Goldman, Yaacov 63
Goldsworthy, Nigel 365
Golemis, Stilianos D. 343
Golko, Yaroslav Y. 188
Golubev, Valery 186
Golubev, Valery A. 187
Gomersall, Sir Stephen 208
Gomes, Sergio 5
Gomes, Antonio F. B. de Sousa 161
Gomes, Renato 468
Gomes, Renato da Cruz 468
Gomez, Eugenio Llorente 10
Gomez, Jose Ramon Arce 70
Gomez, Christa 84
Gomez, Hernando J. 160
Gomez-Lavin, Javier Polanco 10
Gomi, Kazuhiro 314
Gomwe, Godfrey G. 35
Goncalves, Vitor 161
Goncalves, Prof Vitor F. de Conceicao 161
Gonda, Toshihiro 22
Gonda, Barbara Garza Laguera 177
Gonda, Eva Garza Laguera 177
Gonda, Mariana Garza Laguera 177
Gonensin, Turgay 459
Gong, Huazhang 121
Gonzales, Miguel 169
Gonzales-Hurtado, Jose C. 109
Gonzalez, Juan Enrique Ruiz 10
Gonzalez, Jose Maria Aguirre 10
Gonzalez, Fernando A. 114
Gonzalez, Fernando A. 114
Gonzalez-Albo, Jose Romero de Avila 10
Gooding, Valerie F. (Val) 240
Gooding, Valerie F. (Val) 412
Goodmanson, Richard R. 360
Goodmanson, Richard R. 361
Goodson, Simon 364
Goodwin, Michael 350
Gordillo, Rodrigo Echenique 60
Gordo, Juan Ignacio Apoita 55
Gordo, Juan 55
Gordon, Helen 368
Gorman, Raymond (Ray) 266
Goschl, Peter 300
Gosnell, David 156
Goss, Andreas J. 395
Got, Thomas 443
Goto, Katsuhiro 388
Goto, Katsuhiro 388
Goto, Kazutoshi 390
Goto, Masahiro 393
Goto, Masahiro 393
Goto, Masao 405
Gottlob, Martin 146
Gottschalk, Helmut 158
Gottschalk, Helmut 158
Gotz, Gerd 257
Gou, Terry T.M. 213
Gough, V. E. 245
Gould, Andrew 85
Gould, Andrew 85
Gould, Andrew 360
Goulding, Richard F. 411
Gourbin, Jean-Louis 102
Gouws, Francois 461
Govindarajan, M. P. 86
Goyder, Richard J. Barr 480
Graafland, Rene Hooft 199
Graafland, Rene Hooft 199
Grabe, William O. 266
Grabicki, Michael 76
Grace, Adrian 14
Grace, I. 298
Gracian, Pablo Quiros 10
Grady, Diane 273
Grady, Diane J. 488
Graeber, Juergen 195
Graef, Roger 371
Graef, Roger 371
Graenicher, Walter 31
Graf, Anja 135
Graf, John 350
Grafemeyer, Andreas 84
Graff, Pierre 189
Graff, Michael J. (Mike) 261
Graham, John 95
Graham, Annie 240
Graham, Anthony R. 345
Graham, Anthony R. 346
Graham, John 384
Graham, Stuart E. (Stu) 400
Graham, Stuart E. (Stu) 401
Graham, James 480
Graham, Anthony R. 483
Grainge, Lucian 474
Grandin, Michael A. 216
Grandke, Gerhard 263
Granier, Jean-Laurent 49
Grant, Sir John 85
Grappotte, Francois 133
Grasso, Giancarlo 173
Grasso, Carla 468
Gratton, Robert 345
Gratton, Robert 345
Gratton, Robert 346
Gratz, Gabriele 159
Graves, H. David 193
Gravesen, Rachel Curtis 325
Grawe, Holger 482
Gray, Andrew 98
Gray, Eddie 191
Gray, Lisa 301
Graye, Mitchell T. G. 193
Grayfer, Valery 329
Greco, Mario 41
Greco, Mario 491
Green, William D. (Bill) 7
Green, Stephen K. 76
Green, Gary R. 134
Green, Gary R. 134
Green, Andrew 280
Green, Lars 325
Green, John 350
Green, Howard 465
Greenberg, Evan G. 9
Greenebaum, John de Zuleta 70
Greenhorn, Kevin 410
Greentree, Steve 488
Greentree, Steven 488
Gref, Herman 329
Grefstad, Odd Arild 415
Gregory, Mark 265
Gregory, Mark 265
Gregson, Prof Peter J. 365
Greisinger, Gunter 164
Gress, Felix 135
Grey, Curt 51
Grice, Greg 366
Grieg, Camilla Marianne 415
Griffin, Garth 71
Griffith, Chris 35
Griffiths, Guy 51
Griffiths, Gareth 159
Grigg, Paul 440
Grigioni, Carlo 461
Grigson, David David Grigson 413
Grimeh, Mohammed 411
Grimstone, Gerry E. 413
Grindel, Isabella 335
Grisard, Jean-Marie 111
Grison, Arnaud 472
Gritsch, Klaus 144
Grix, Alain Le 39
Gro?, Thomas 482
Groeneveld, Oscar Y. L. 360
Gronwall, Katarina 401
Gros, David-Alexandre 383
Gros-Pietro, Gian Maria 172
Gross, Marc 199
Grossett, James M. (Jim) 18
Grote, Byron E. 95
Grote, Byron E. 95
Grote, Byron E. 464
Grote, Byron E. 465
Grottes, Jacques Marraud des 453
Grounds, Matthew 461
Grover, James N.D. (Jim) 155
Grue, Kim 321
Grunberg, Hubertus von 5
Grunberg, Hubertus von 154
Grund, Frank 54
Grund, Birgit 179
Grundmann, Hans-Jorg 395
Grupel, Ron 441
Gruss, Peter 300
Gruss, Peter 396
Grynberg, Marc 462
Grzesiek, Artur 263
Gu, Jia-Yan 100
Gu, Liansong 139
Guajardo, Pablo Roberto Gonzalez 32
Guanghua, Zhang 119
Guarguaglini, Pier Francesco 173
Guay, Charles 413
Guelfand, Greg 300
Guell, Miquel 57
Guell, Carmen Riu 457
Guena, Yves 375
Guerlain, Eric 124
Guerlain, Eric 124
Guerrero, Pedro Guerrero 70
Guerrero, Jose-Luis 218
Guertin, Alexandre J. 193
Guetta, Bentzi 218
Guffey, Lawrence H. 154
Gugliermina, Pierre 39
Gui, Hao 121
Guilbaud, Jean-Jacques 453
Guilbert, Dan 47
Guilherme, Carlos Alberto Rodrigues 57
Guillaume, Gregory 249
Guillemet, Bruno 31
Guillemin, Jean-Francois 93
Guillemin, Jean-Francois 127
Guillemot, Philippe 25
Guillen, Federico 25
Guillot, Laurent 131
Guillot, Daniel 333
Guilmant, Phillipe 127
Guimaraes, Enderson 3
Guiotoko, Celso 316
Guiral, Philippe 168
Gulbrandsen, Per-Arne 11
Guldimann, Tobias 139
Guldstrand, Jonas 203
Gulliford, Simon 413

Gulliver, Stuart T. 217
Gulliver, Stuart T. 218
Guloien, Donald A. 278
Guloien, Donald A. 278
Gunawan, Hendra 147
Gunn, George 323
Gunning, Louis W. (Tex) 24
Guntermann, Ralf 395
Guo, Peizhang 121
Guohua, Xi 119
Guoliang, Wang 339
Guoliang, Wang 339
Guoxiong, Wei 229
Gupta, K.K. 85
Gupta, Piyush 147
Gupta, Piyush 147
Gupta, Sanjeev 392
Gupte, Lalita D. 318
Gurtler, Henrik 325
Gurunath, Prof Marti 224
Gustavsson, Jonas 380
Gustavsson, Niklas 479
Gut, Alexander 12
Gut, Rainer E. 139
Gutberlet, Kurt-Ludwig 395
Gutierrez, Carlos Bremer 32
Gutierrez, Fernando 55
Gutierrez, Mauricio Echeverry 160
Gutierrez-Barquin, Santos Marinze-Conde 10
Guttinger, Rene 54
Guttinger, Antoine 145
Guyette, James M. (Jim) 364
Guyette, James M. (Jim) 365
Guyton, Jeffrey H. 283
Guzman, Rami Avraham 63
Guzman, Avraham (Rami) 63
Guzman, Renato de 336
Gwon, Tae Tae Eun Gwon 392

H

H?dl, Hubert 274
H?gsted, Peter 250
H?jland, Peter 147
H?ltermand, Peter 399
Haank, D. J. 256
Haarmann, Wilhelm 384
Haas, Herbert K. 195
Haas, Herbert K. 429
Haasis, Heinrich 263
Haasteren, Jacobus van 385
Haba, Yasuhiro 224
Haber, Yaacov (Kobi) 63
Hachey, Guy C. 91
Hachigo, Takahiro 215
Hackenberger, Alfred 76
Hackett, James 102
Hadjisotiriou, Paula N. 303
Haeling, Karl 262
Haendler, Sascha 263
Haenggi, Rolf 309
Haenggi, Rolf 309
Hageman, Eric 256
Hageman, Jurn 257
Hager, Hans-Joerg 260
Hagger, Andrew 301
Hahm, Sang Moon 247
Hahn, Anatol von 69
Hahn, Harald 151
Hai, Zhu 387
Haibo, Huang 64
Haichao, Zhang 120
Haidinger, Michael 364
Haier, Brian J. 450
Haignere, Claudie 333
Haignere, Claudie 333
Haignere, Claudie 383
Hailwood, Janice 100
Haimao, Jia 342
Haimoto, Shuzo 180
Hainer, Herbert 13
Haines, David 227
Hajjar, Karim 35
Hakamata, Naoto 236
Hakii, Mitsuhiko 140
Hakii, Mitsuhiko 141
Hakim, Saad 364
Halary, Christian 375
Halbherr, Michael 318
Halford, Andrew N. (Andy) 475
Halford, Andrew N. (Andy) 476
Hall, David 218
Hall, G. 298
Hall, Mark 438
Hall, Andrew 488
Hallavo, Ilkka 146
Haller, Bettina 396
Haller, Juerg 461
Halling, Marie 426
Hallqvist, Louise Louise Hallqvist 401
Haltebourg, Patrice 127
Hamaba, Masaaki 183
Hamada, Tatsuro 97
Hamada, Akio 214
Hamada, Toyosaku 417
Hamada, Toyosaku 417
Hamakawa, Ichiro 294
Hamamoto, Yasuo 312
Hamamoto, Misao 393
Hamano, Toshishige 390
Hamasaki, Yuji 419
Hamatsuka, Junichi 405
Hambrecht, Jurgen 144
Hambrecht, Jurgen 151
Hamelmann, Stefan 202
Hamilton, Anthony J. 49
Hamli, Mohamed D. Al 137
Hamlin, Rick 26
Hammadi, Yousuf Ahmad Al 472
Hammer, Hans Jorg 335
Hampel, Daniel 128
Hampton, Sir Philip 35
Hampton, Sir Philip 305
Hampton, Sir Philip 368
Han, Jianguo 121
Han, Dae-Soo 258
Han, Dae-Soo 258
Han, Woosung 378
Han, Dong Woo 391
Han, Dong Woo 391
Han, Young-Suk 397
Han, In-Goo 397
Han, Seung-Soo 412
Hanada, Yoshihiko 183
Hanafin, Mark 116
Hanafin, Mark 116
Hanai, Masayuki 405
Hanashima, Kyoichi 117
Hanatani, Shinji 408
Hanazawa, Hiroyuki 124
Hand, Scott M. 278
Handelsbanken, Svenska 401
Handelsbanken, Svenska 401
Handrick, Gabriele 195
Hanggi, Rolf 309
Haniel, Franz M. 81
Haniel, Franz 286
Hanlon, Peter 484
Hanna, Ken G. 440
Hannah, Ashley 100
Hannam, Wendy G. 69
Hannasch, Brian P. 26
Hanneffy, Kay 66
Hannervall, Sverker 436
Hanratty, Paul 330
Hansen, Cecilie M. 2
Hansen, Stefan 151
Hansen, Jean-Pierre 189
Hansen, Elin K. 325
Hansen, Signhild Signhild Arnegard Hansen 399
Hansen, Erik Haug 415
Hansen, Ian 480
Hanss, Mary 384
Hanyu, Masaharu 208
Hao, Li 118
Hao, Gui 121
Haoyi, Cai 64
Hapke, Wolfgang 76
Happel, Otto 128
Hara, Hideo (Hank) 96
Hara, Yoshinari 307
Hara, Toshiki 357
Hara, Takashi 405
Harada, Masashi 236
Harada, Yuji 283
Harada, Yuji 283
Harada, Shozo 328
Harada, Shozo 328
Harada, Masatoshi 338
Haran, Paul M. 66
Harayama, Yuko 131
Harayama, Yasuhito 424
Harayama, Yasuhito 424
Harber, Bill 107
Hard, Karl 44
Harder, V. Peter 346
Hardie, Gordon 102
Harding, Mark 72
Harding, Mark 74
Harding, Ian 250
Harding, Robert J. (Bob) 278
Harding, Andrew 360
Harding, Andrew 361
Hardjapamekas, Erry Erry Riyana Hardjapamekas 275
Harings, Lothar A. 260
Harlow, Jo 318
Harper, Mike 330
Harris, Tim 47
Harris, Brendan 87
Harris, Richard 130
Harris, Mary E. 240
Harris, Sir Thomas 245
Harris, Michael D. (Mike) 274
Harris, John J. 309
Harris, Graeme 461
Harrison, Marianne 278
Harrison, Mark D. 298
Hart, Stephen P. 69
Harte, Michael R. 130
Hartert, Daniel 78
Hartman, Peter F. 19
Hartman, Natalie A. 151
Hartnall, Michael 51
Hartung, Matthias 371
Hartung, Hans-Jurgen 396
Hartwell, Terry 298
Hartwell, John 479
Hartwig, Roland 78
Hartz, Scott 278
Hartzer, Brian C. 484
Harun, Mohd Mohd Salleh bin Harun 275
Harunari, Hiroshi 293
Harunari, Hiroshi 293
Haruta, Junichi 241
Harvey, Kenneth G. (Ken) 305
Harvey, Harald 373
Harwerth, Noel Noel Harwerth 413
Harwig, Rick 257
Hasegawa, Nobuki 253
Hasegawa, Masao 294
Hasegawa, Toshiya 320
Hasegawa, Yoshisuke 390
Hasenfratz, Linda S. 104
Hasford, Heiner 164
Hasford, Heiner 277
Hashikawa, Masaki 405
Hashimoto, Yukiaki 105
Hashimoto, Noritomo 291
Hashimoto, Noritomo 291
Hashimoto, Masahiro 420
Hashimoto, Masahiro 420
Haskins, Jim 47
Hasold-Schilter, Marianne 69
Hassan, T. 245
Hassel, Gilbert Van 231
Hasunuma, Yoshio 180
Hatano, Shoichi 117
Hattersley, Gavin 373
Hatton, John D. 129
Hattori, Toshihiko 293
Hattori, Takashi 456
Hauenstein, Dieter 13
Haug, Knut Dyre 415
Haug, Jon Erik 435
Hauser, Gerard 31
Hausler, Gerd 79
Hausmann, Peter 78
Hausmann, Carl L. 102
Hausmann, Richard 396
Hausmann, Yannick 492
Hausser, Joachim 260
Havelock, Kevin 464
Havelock, Kevin 465
Havkin, Evgueni 329
Havu, Jussi 318
Hawker, Michael J. (Mike) 47
Hawker, Michael J. (Mike) 273
Hawkins, Peter J. O. 484
Hawksworth, Keith J. 53
Hawrysh, Fred J. 7
Haxel, Geoffrey C. (Geoff) 26
Hayakawa, Shigeru 455
Hayama, Nobuhiro 283
Hayama, Nobuhiro 283
Hayashi, Naoki 15
Hayashi, Naoki 16
Hayashi, Naoki 16
Hayashi, Naoki 16
Hayashi, Minoru 22
Hayashi, Toshihiro 184
Hayashi, Toshihiro 184
Hayashi, Motohiko 390
Hayashi, Kazuhiko 419
Hayashi, Shizuka 456
Hayashida, Eiji 244
Hayashida, Eiji 244
Hayata, Minoru 456
Hayden, Michael 441
Hayes, Tom 66
Hayes, William (Billy) 316
Haynes, Lawrie 364
Hayward, Godfrey R. (Geoff) 28
Hazarika, A. K. 328
Hazarika, A. K. 328
He, Wenbo 71
He, Guangbei 90
He, Guangbei 90
He, George Z. Q. 266
He, Wang 342
Head, Robert M. (Bob) 330
Headrick, Rick 422
Healey, Michaela J. 301
Healy, Andrew 146
Healy, Joseph 301
Heander, Carina Malmgren 3
Hearn, Timothy J. (Tim) 366
Heath, Jeffrey C. (Jeff) 69
Heath, Andrew 365
Heckmann, Fritz-Jurgen 197
Hedbeck, Ann-Marie 401
Hedberg, Jonny 91
Hedlund, Jan 166
Heere, Jan 280
Heetvelde, Ingeborg van 465
Heggen, Elmar 84
Heijden, R. L. P. J. van der 245
Heimbach, Stephan 395
Hein, Frank-Martin 364
Heina, Patricia 491
Heinricht, Frank 205
Heinz, Michael 76
Heiss, Franz 28
Heizmann, Jochem 477
Helash, Kevin R. 18
Heldt, Markus 76
Hellberg, Marita 166
Hellenthal, Markus 443
Heller, Michael 335
Helmersson, Helena Helena Helmersson 203
Helmont, Sue 47
Helmrich, Klaus 396
Helms, Luther S. 278
Helten-Kindlein, Birgit 202
Heltne, J?rn 364

Hemsley, Richard 368
Hemstritch, Jane S. 130
Henderson, Steve 100
Henderson, Jason 216
Henkel, Prof Hans-Olaf 78
Henkel, Prof Hans-Olaf 136
Hennah, James 100
Henne, Thomas 489
Henneberry, Robbie 29
Hennessy, Gilles 271
Henney, Jane E. 44
Henningsen, August-Wilhelm 151
Henrich, Andreas 371
Henriksen, Johnny 325
Henry, Susan A. 18
Henry, Mike 87
Henry, Mike 88
Henry, Simon 370
Henry, Simon 370
Henry, Pierre 403
Henschel, Gerhard 263
Hepher, Michael L. 193
Hepher, Michael L. 250
Heras, Javier Peralta de las 60
Herbel, Peter 453
Heremans, Dirk 248
Herlihy, Michael H. C. 227
Hermann, Wolfgang 396
Hermreck, Immanuel 84
Hern+indez, Luis 114
Hernadi, Zsolt 297
Hernandez, Judith 9
Hernandez, Robert M. 9
Hernandez, Adolfo 25
Hernandez, Javier 57
Hernandez, Luis 114
Hernandez, Luis 114
Hernandez, Roland A. 409
Hernandez-Blades, Catherine 176
Hernando, Jose Manuel Canal 177
Herr, David A. (Dave) 51
Herrando, Luis 59
Herrero, Fernando Masaveu 70
Herrero, Fernando 161
Herrero, Alfonso Ferrari 434
Herrewyn, Jean-Michel 471
Herring, Rick 255
Herring, Brooks 393
Herrmann, Gerald 263
Herrmann, Gerald 429
Herteman, Jean-Paul 375
Herwarth, Andreas 286
Hesjedal, Oddvar 435
Hesoun, Wolfgang 396
Hess, Marc 153
Hess, Beat W. 309
Hesse, Thomas 84
Hesselink, Arent Jan 257
Hessels, Jan-Michiel 199
Hester, Stephen A. M. 305
Hester, Stephen A. M. 368
Hester, Stephen A. M. 368
Hetzer, Rainer 136
Heuberger, Herta 335
Heumann, Josef 197
Heuser, Albert 76
Heutink, Chris 352
Hewett, Gareth 218
Hewins, Paul 401
Hewitt, Rt. Hon. Patricia 101
Hewson, Carolyn 87
Hewson, Carolyn 88
Hewson, Carolyn 484
Heydemann, Christel 25
Heynike, Petraea 144
Hiang, Cynthia 336
Hibberd, Robin S. 69
Hicks, Jeremy 459
Hidaka, Naoki 417
Hidema, Tomohiro 34
Hideshima, Makoto Makoto Hideshima 452
Hiekel, Dominique 151
Hiemstra, Siep 199
Hiesinger, Heinrich 445
Higaki, Seiji 356
Higaki, Seiji 357
Higashi, Kazuhiro 356
Higashi, Kazuhiro 357
Higashihara, Toshiaki 208
Higgins, Trevor 100
Higgins, Russell A. 438
Higgins, Benny 440
Higginson, Andrew T. 440
Higginson, Andrew T. 440
Highbury, Lord Simon of 189
Highcock, Andrew 373
Hightower, Dennis F. 8
Higuchi, Koukei 214
Higuchi, Shinya 312
Higuchi, Kazushige 314
Higuchi, Kazushige 314
Higuera, Roberto 59
Hikita, Sakae 141
Hikita, Sakae 141
Hildner, Rolf 157
Hill, David 266
Hill, Richard 412
Hill, Thomas R. (Tom) 461
Hillebrand, Rainer 335
Hillebrand, Rainer 335
Hillebrand-Droste, Walter 482
Hillel, Orit 12
Hillenius, Dorothy 231
Hilse, Jurgen 263
Hilton, Ralph 216
Himpe, Robrecht 39
Hin, Wong Chung 219
Hindle, Peter 131
Hinsch, Christian 429
Hintz, Cornelia 482
Hinz, Bernd 202
Hippe, Alan 362
Hirabayashi, Hiroshi 296
Hirabayashi, Hiroshi 452
Hirai, Kenji 184
Hirai, Kenji 184
Hirai, Toshifumi 316
Hirai, Kazuo (Kaz) 408
Hirakawa, Yoshio 180
Hirakawa, Yoji 391
Hirakawa, Haruki Haruki Hirakawa 392
Hirano, Hajime 289
Hirano, Nobuyuki 294
Hirano, Nobuyuki 294
Hirano, Atsuhiko 393
Hiranuma, Yoshiyuki 70
Hirao, Kohei 417
Hirayama, Kizo 312
Hirdman-Ryrberg, Viveka 399
Hirji, Rahim 278
Hirji, Zabeen 366
Hirobe, Toshihiko 390
Hiroki, Kazumasa 140
Hiroki, Kazumasa 141
Hiromoto, Yuichi 289
Hiromura, Syungo 448
Hironaka, Kazuo 149
Hironaka, Mamoru 253
Hirose, Takahisa 22
Hirose, Atsushi 316
Hirose, Hiroshi 416
Hirose, Naomi 447
Hirschheimer, Ruy 3
Hirshberg, Gary 145
Hiruma, Masato 96
Hiruma, Takahisa 224
Hisco, David 46
Hisham, Muzaffar 275
Hitomi, Mitsuo 283
Hitosugi, Itsuro 393
Ho, Vincent Y.S. 137
Ho, KwonPing 156
Ho, Edith 216
Ho, Edwina 278
Ho, Lora 429
Hoak, Jonathan S. (Jon) 176
Hoblyn, James 91
Hoch, Steven G. 309
Hochstrasser, Franz 167
Hocker, Ulrich 154
Hocker, Ulrich 159
Hockey, Timothy D. (Tim) 450
Hodges, Graham K. 46
Hodgkinson, Sir Michael S. (Mike) 458
Hodgkinson, Sir Michael S. (Mike) 459
Hodgson, Christopher J. (Chris) 69
Hodkinson, Phil 101
Hodnett, David W. P. 71
Hodnett, David W. P. 72
Hodson, Beverley C. 352
Hoefert, Andreas 461
Hoeg, Krystyna T. 225
Hoeg, Krystyna T. 422
Hoepfel, Uwe 286
Hoerger, Axel 461
Hoffman, Janet L. 7
Hoffman, Reiner 78
Hoffman, Andre 362
Hoffman, Andre 362
Hoffmann, Beate 129
Hoffmann, Charlotte 147
Hoffmann, Henrik 147
Hoffmann, Charlotte 147
Hoffmann, Per 157
Hofile?a, Hector L. 379
Hofmann, Jorg 144
Hofmann, Daniel M. 491
Hogan, Joseph M. (Joe) 5
Hogan, Kevin 491
Hogen, Kensaku 215
Hogg, Baroness Sarah 85
Hohler, Gertrud 54
Hohmann-Dennhardt, Christine 144
Hohmeister, Harry 151
Hojo, Yoichi 214
Hojo, Yoichi 215
Hoke, Dirk 396
Holden, Betsy D. 156
Holeksa, Jurgen 489
Holland, J. Bradley 483
Holland, Bradley 483
Hollander, Roberto S. 57
Hollanders, Nicolas 169
Hollick, Lord Clive R. 156
Holliday, Steven J. (Steve) 280
Holliday, Steven J. (Steve) 304
Holliday, Steven J. (Steve) 304
Holliday, Charles O. (Chad) 370
Hollifield, Matt 107
Holm, Sven 146
Holmes, Richard W. 412
Holmgren, Geir 415
Holmlund, Marianne 318
Holmstrom, Bengt 318
Holmstrom, Torbjorn 479
Holtmann, Claus Friedrich 263
Holz, Manfred 371
Holz, Manfred 371
Holzbacher, Enric 202
Holzherr, Christian 113
Holzwarth, Lothar 154
Homma, Toshio 106
Homma, Toshio 106
Hommen, Jan H. M. 231
Honda, Haruhisa 106
Honda, Haruhisa 106
Honda, Masahiro 314
Honda, Osamu 424
Honda, Osamu 424
Hong, Ching Wei 336
Hongbin, Liu 339
Hongler, Markus 491
Hongli, Zhang 229
Hongo, Shosuke 419
Hongru, Liu 339
Hongxia, Liu 119
Honjo, Masashi 328
Honjo, Masaya 420
Hood, John 85
Hood, Colin 410
Hood, Colin 410
Hoon, Linda 147
Hoong, Sim Sio 275
Hooper, Michele J. 44
Hooper, Marjorie 53
Hope, Donald I. (Don) 330
Hopkins, Paul N. 491
Hopwood, Andy 95
Hora, Hayao 34
Hora, Hayao 34
Horigome, Yoshio 194
Horigome, Yoshio 194
Horikawa, Masakazu 289
Horio, Norimitsu 141
Horioka, Hiroshi 452
Horioka, Hiroshi 452
Horiuchi, Takefumi 446
Horn, Michael 262
Horner, Russell J. 18
Horowitz, Beth 216
Horstedt, Richard 401
Horta-Osorio, Antonio 270
Horta-Osorio, Antonio 270
Hortensius, Peter D. 266
Horton, Greg J. 330
Horton, Peter 488
Horvath, Ferenc 297
Hosaka, Takemi 307
Hosek, Chaviva M. 193
Hoshi, Norikazu 390
Hoshino, Asako 316
Hoskins, Richard 47
Hosoda, Ryutaro (Ray) 182
Hosoi, Susumu 236
Hosoi, Susumu 236
Hosoya, Eiji 356
Hosoya, Eiji 358
Hotta, Takao 283
Hou, Cliff 429
Houel, Patrick 271
Houliang, Dai 120
Houliang, Dai 120
Hourican, John 368
Hours, Bernard 145
Hours, Bernard 145
House, Andrew 408
Houssaye, France 402
Houston, Martin 85
Houston, Martin 85
Houten, Frans van 257
Houze, Philippe 111
Hove, Mark ten 350
Hove, Kjetil 414
Hoving, Erik 256
Howard, Richard A. 143
Howe, Stephen 82
Howe, Stephen 156
Howeg, Stephan 12
Howie, Iain C. 491
Howlett, C. C. 245
Howorka, Johannes Johannes Howorka 210
Hoyle, Stevan 476
Hrdlicka, Carla Carla Hrdlicka 488
Hseih, Tsun-Yan 409
Hsieh, Tsun-yan 278
Hsieh, Chung-Dea 427
Hsiung, Ming-Ho 112
Hsiung, Ming-Ho 112
Hsu, J. H. 112
Hsu, J. H. 112
Hsu, Miao-Chiu 139
Hsu, Larry 139
Hsu, Michael 318
Hu, Shin-Tai 137
Hu, Hsiang 427
Hu, Fei-Ling 427
Hua, Yang 125
Hua, Yang 125
Hualin, Li 339
Huang, Danhan 64
Huang, Shizhong 64
Huang, Qing 121
Huang, Su Kuo 139
Huang, Ja-Tao 178
Huang, Arthur 213
Huart, Olivier 100
Huating, Hu 65
Hubber, Keith 85

Huber, Stefan 212
Huber, Walter 287
Huber, Berthold 395
Huber, Anton S. 396
Huber, Walter 396
Huber, Berthold 396
Huber, Berthold 477
Hubner, Thomas M. 109
Hudaya, Arif 465
Hude, Thomas 49
Hudon, Isabelle 422
Hudson, Paul 44
Hudson, Linda P. 51
Hudson, Linda P. 51
Hudson, Ian 84
Hudson, A. 298
Hudson, Isabel 350
Huet, Jean-Marc 464
Huet, Jean-Marc 465
Huet, Jean-Marc Jean-Marc Huet 465
Huet, Jean-Marc 465
Huettl, Reinhard Reinhard Huettl 81
Huff, John R. 423
Hugentobler, Paul 212
Hughes, Louis R. 5
Hughes, Louis R. 24
Hughes, Louis R. 25
Hughes, David 100
Hughes, Gary 240
Hughes, Penelope L. (Penny) 298
Hughes, Penelope L. (Penny) 368
Hughes, Gary 380
Hughes-Hallett, James W. J. 218
Hui, Chng Sok 147
Hui, Jenki 194
Hui, Jenkin 242
Huijskes, Jaap 332
Huillard, Xavier 472
Huillier, Leon M. L. 488
Huiman, Yi 229
Hull, Brian P. 461
Hulsbos, Peter J. 352
Hulst, Els van der 24
Hult, Bertil 330
Hultin, Richard 401
Humanes, Enrique 102
Humer, Franz B. 155
Humer, Franz B. 362
Humm, Philipp 476
Humphries, Paul 176
Hundsb?k-Pedersen, Susanne 325
Hungate, Alexander C. (Alex) 217
Hunt, Jonathan 44
Hunt, Stephen 100
Hunt, Cheney L. 278
Hunt, Jackie 413
Hunter, Don 330
Hunziker, Erich 212
Huon, Thierry 355
Hurst, A. C. 245
Hurvitz, Chaim 441
Hussain, Zulfi 100
Hussain, Abbas 191
Hussain, M. M. 218
Hutchins, Julie 330
Hutchinson, Howard 44
Hutchinson, Belinda J. 350
Hutchinson, Kevin 401
Hutmacher, Heiko 286
Huttl, Reinhard 81
Hwee, Jen Yap 156
Hydon, Kenneth J. (Ken) 440
Hyle, Kathleen 102
Hyman, Gary 364
Hyodo, Makoto 456
Hyun-Kook, Hong 249

I

Ibarra, I?igo V. de Oriol 223
Ibbotson, Terry 350
Ibuchi, Yoshiaki 390
Ichige, Masayuki 291
Ichihashi, Yasuhiko 206
Ichikawa, Masakazu 206
Ichikawa, Masakazu 206
Ichikawa, Hiizu 292
Ichikawa, Hiizu 293
Ichino, Naoshi 22
Icole, Jean-Yves 126
Idda, Lorenzo 76
Iddon, Mike 440
Ide, Akiko 326
Idei, Nobuyuki 8
Idermark, Lars 426
Idrac, Anne-Marie 131
Iersel, Erwin 11
Ifeagwu, Cynthia 465
Igarashi, Kazuhiro 183
Igarashi, Tsutomu 427
Igarashi, Tsutomu 427
Igarashi, Yasuharu 452
Igashira, Hiroshi 452
Igel, Anders Anders Igel 426
Iglhaut, Michael 136
Iguchi, Isao 291
Ihamuotila, Timo 318
Ihara, Yasumori 455
Ihara, Yasumori 455
Ihori, Eishin 211
Ihori, Kazutaka 390
Ihrie, Bob 107
Iida, Masami 180
Iijima, Kenji 241
Iijima, Masami 295
Iijima, Masami 296
Iio, Norinao 295
Iio, Norinao 296
Ijichi, Takahiko 455
Ike, Fumihiko 214
Ike, Fumihiko 215
Ikeda, Tomohiko 180
Ikeda, Morio 253
Ikeda, Homare 291
Ikeda, Kazuyoshi 356
Ikeda, Takashi 405
Ikegai, Kenji 183
Ikemura, Toshio 208
Ikoma, Toshiaki 106
Ikoma, Toshiaki 106
Ikuno, Hiroshi 282
Ikuta, Masaharu 16
Ikuta, Masaharu 16
Ikuta, Shoichi 281
Illera, Gregorio Panadero 55
Ilossi, Dario 179
Iltgen, Leslie 179
Ilyukhina, Elena A. 186
Imada, Kazuo Kazuo Imada 184
Imai, Masahiro 238
Imai, Kazuki 283
Imai, Michiro 293
Imai, Masamichi 307
Imai, Takashi 314
Imaki, Hisakazu 283
Imamura, Masashi 409
Imauven, Claude 131
Imazu, Hidetoshi 316
Imazu, Hidetoshi 316
Imrie, Alastair 51
Inaba, Takahiro 141
Inaba, Nobuo 358
Inaba, Yoshimi 455
Inamoto, Nobuhide 283
Inayama, Hideaki 419
Inbona, Yves 376
Inciarte, Matias Rodriguez 60
Inciarte, Juan Rodriguez 60
Inciarte, Matias Rodriguez 60
Inciarte, Juan Rodriguez 60
Ingold, Roger 7
Ingram, Duncan 100
Ingram, Louise 318
Inman, Lorna 130
Innis, Emmanuel van 189
Innocenzi, Fabio 234
Ino, Hiroyuki 447
Inoguchi, Junji 67
Inoguchi, Junji 67
Inohara, Hiroyuki 417
Inoue, Shinichi 34
Inoue, Yoshiharu 96
Inoue, Nobuaki 182
Inoue, Nobuaki 182
Inoue, Toshiki 206
Inoue, Hiroo 238
Inoue, Takeshi 290
Inoue, Mikoto 334
Inoue, Makoto 334
Inoue, Yuri 393
Inoue, Hisayuki 455
Inoue, Yoichi 455
Iorio, Anthony (Tony) Di 368
Iorio, Tony 368
Iorio, Francesco 466
Iperen, Rokus van 106
Iqbal, Shaheen 47
Irace, Gregory (Greg) 382
Irahara, Ryuichi 328
Irani, Jamshed J. (JJ) 430
Irby, Charles 350
Irie, Hiroyuki 314
Irie, Hiroyuki 314
Irujo, Carlos Loring Martinez de 56
Irujo, Carlos 56
Irvin, Kenneth B. 300
Irving, Will 438
Isaac, Bernardo Quintana 114
Isaka, Ryuichi 388
Isaka, Ryuchi 388
Isasi, Ricardo Alvarez 223
Isayama, Takeshi 355
Ise, Kiyotaka 455
Ishibashi, Shuichi 96
Ishibashi, Hidekazu 96
Ishida, Kazuo 184
Ishida, Yasuyuki 314
Ishida, Yasuyuki 314
Ishihara, Masayuki 358
Ishihara, Kunio 446
Ishii, Kazuma 141
Ishii, Kazuma 141
Ishii, Ichiro 446
Ishii, Yoshimasa 455
Ishikawa, Masanobu 22
Ishikawa, Toshiyuki 22
Ishikawa, Tsutomu 22
Ishikawa, Shigeaki 282
Ishikura, Yoko 184
Ishitobi, Osamu 416
Ishitobi, Osamu 416
Ishizaka, Masami 16
Ishizaka, Masami 16
Ishizaki, Yoshiyuki 447
Ishizuka, Yuichi 106
Ishizuka, Tatsuro 208
Iskander, Sami 85
Isola, Paulo Eduardo D'Avila 56
Isono, Kaoru 357
Isoyama, Seiji 314
Isoyama, Seiji 314
Isozaki, Yoshinori 252
Israel, Ronen 62
Israeli, Erez 441
Istephan, Sami 100
Itami, Hiroyuki 452
Itatani, Masanori 320
Ito, Shinichiro 34
Ito, Hiroyuki 34
Ito, Shinichiro 34
Ito, Hiroyuki 34
Ito, Haruo 184
Ito, Takanobu 214
Ito, Takanobu 215
Ito, Kazuhiko 236
Ito, Katsuhiro 289
Ito, Kunio 290
Ito, Kunio 390
Ito, Kunio 390
Ito, Seiya 393
Ito, Seiya 393
Ito, Jun 419
Ito, Yujiro 420
Ito, Atsushi 448
Ito, Toru 448
Itoh, Masaki 70
Itonaga, Takehide 141
Itou, Tomoaki 393
Iuel, Lars Christian 435
IV, August A. Busch 37
Ivanov, Igor 329
Iversen, Einar A. 414
Iwai, Mutsuo 241
Iwaki, Masakazu 312
Iwaki, Masakazu 312
Iwamura, Tetsuo 214
Iwamura, Tetsuo 215
Iwanami, Toshimitsu 307
Iwasa, Kaoru 282
Iwasaki, Fumio 326
Iwasaki, Fumio 327
Iwasaki, Nobuo 421
Iwasawa, Hideki 417
Iwase, Takahiro 455
Iwashita, Tomonori 106
Iwashita, Naoya 281
Iwata, Shinjiro 208
Iwata, Hidenobu 214
Iwata, Naoki 356
Iwatsuki, Takashi 424
Iyengar, Sridar A. 224
Iyobe, Tsuneo 290
Izakson, Irit 62
Izuel, Cesareo (Cesar) Alierta 122
Izuel, Cesar Cesar Alierta Izuel 432
Izumi, Fumihiro 124
Izumida, Ryugo 289

J

J?gtnes, Harald 157
J?rgensen, Niels B. 321
J?rgensen, Torsten Hagen 321
J?rgensen, Lars A. 325
J?rgensen, Lars F. 325
Jabes, Aliza 474
Jackman, Boris J. 423
Jackson, David J. 95
Jackson, Richard 343
Jackson, Tony 350
Jackson, Michael 443
Jacob, Mark 157
Jacobs, Andreas 11
Jacobs, Andreas 12
Jacobs, Brad 51
Jacobs, Peter 477
Jacobsen, Mads 146
Jacobsen, Lennart 321
Jacobsen, Svein S. 321
Jacobsen, Jon Arnt 415
Jacobson, Hans 321
Jacques, Jean-Sebastien 360
Jacquillat, Bertrand 453
Jaderberg, Tina 203
Jaderberg, Tina Tina Jaderberg 203
Jae-Rok, Lee 249
Jaeger, Blaise 443
Jaenichen, Michael 263
Jagdishan, Sashi 196
Jager, Wolfgang 13
Jager, Richard 352
Jaggia, Anil 196
Jain, Amit 24
Jain, Prof Dipak C. 353
Jairath, V. K. 430
Jakel, Julia 84
Jakobi, Frank 457
Jakobsen, Mads 321
Jakobsson, Sten 5
Jalil, Hadenan 275
Jallal, Bahija 44
Jamal, Arshil 193
Jamal, Zainal Zainal Abidin bin Jamal 275
James, Renee J. 476
Jamieson, P.L.A. 242
Janaillac, Jean-Marc 471
Janetzko, Sigrid 482

Jang-Hee, Yoo 345
Jannai, Alon 218
Jans, Tomas 465
Jansen, Peter 151
Janson, Kristina Kristina Janson 426
Jansson, Mats 147
Jansson, Mats 169
Jansson, Urban 399
Jansson, Urban 399
Japy, Nicholas 403
Jaquotot, Baldomero (Baldo) Falcones 177
Jaschinski, Siegfried 262
Jaubert, Jean-Marc 453
Jay, Lady Sylvia 25
Jay, Lord Michael 42
Jay, Lady Sylvia 131
Jeanbart, Paul 403
Jeancourt-Galignani, Antoine 454
Jeanniot, Lynn 302
Jeanson, Virginia 261
Jebson, Alan W. 476
Jeffery, Reuben 72
Jeffery, Reuben 74
Jegen, Tjeerd 488
Jenkins, Antony 71
Jenkins, Antony 72
Jenkins, Antony 74
Jenkins, Antony 74
Jenkins, Chris 443
Jennings, Austin 66
Jenny, Klaus 54
Jensen, Tommy 102
Jensen, Luke 240
Jensen, Anders 321
Jensen, Anders 435
Jenssen, Jens R. 414
Jentsch, Dieter W. 69
Jentzsch, Stefan 13
Jeremiah, Dai 100
Jerschke, Tobias 260
Jesudason, Rob 130
Jetzer-Chung, Alexandre F. 323
Jeunet, Philippe 189
Jewell, Tony 44
Jeworrek, Torsten 300
Jha, Prabir 430
Jiafu, Wei 118
Jiafu, Wei 119
Jian, Liu 125
Jian, Qiao 266
Jiang, Yansong 64
Jiang, Yongzhi 125
Jianguo, Han 121
Jianguo, Li 122
Jianguo, Li 122
Jianhua, Zhang 120
Jianhua, Zhang 120
Jianqing, Jiang 229
Jianzhou, Wang 119
Jichuan, Wu 122
Jidong, Zhao 122
Jie, Yang 122
Jie, Yang 122
Jiemin, Jiang 339
Jiemin, Jiang 339
Jikumaru, Yusuke 34
Jilian, Xue 121
Jilu, Tong 122
Jilu, Tong 122
Jimenez, Pedro Lopez 10
Jimenez, Frank 102
Jimenez, Pedro Pedro Jose Lopez Jimenez 210
Jimenez, Joseph (Joe) 323
Jimenez, Menardo R. 379
Jin, Shaoliang 343
Jinglian, Wu 122
Jinli, Wang 121
Jiping, Zhang 122
Jiping, Zhang 122
Jiping, Zhou 339
Jiping, Zhou 339
Joas, Irmgard 300
Joei, Bernard 492
Johannessen, Morten S. 414
Johannesson, Tuve 399
Johannpeter, Jorge Gerdau 340
Johansson, Hasse 3
Johansson, Leif 44
Johansson, Leif 166
Johansson, Ulf J. 166
Johansson, Ann-Sofie 203
Johansson, Martin 399
Johansson, Mats 400
Johansson, Inge 401
Johansson, Jan C. 425
Johansson, Christer 479
John, Andrew 458
Johnsen, Kjell-Morten 435
Johnson, Daniel 92
Johnson, K. L. 298
Johnson, Chris 309
Johnson, Edward 345
Johnson, Edward D. 346
Johnson, Mark 401
Johnson, Alan 464
Johnsson, Anders 399
Johnsson, Jimmy Jimmy Johnsson 426
Johnsson, Stefan 479
Johnston, J. Dave 193
Johnston, Camille 396
Johnston, Colleen M. 450
Joiner, Mark A. 301
Joiner, Mark A. 301
Joly, Alain 261
Jonah, Samuel E. (Sam) 476
Jonasson, Anders 203
Jones, Mark 44
Jones, Graham 47
Jones, Den 85
Jones, Den 85
Jones, Martyn 298
Jones, Martyn 298
Jones, Sheldon 323
Jones, Philip 438
Jones, Richard 440
Jones, Andy 458
Jong, Jan M. de 199
Jong, Peter 231
Jong, Ronald 258
Jong-Tae, Choi 345
Jono, Kazuya 420
Jonsson, Thomas 318
Jonsson, Jonas 330
Joo, In Ki 267
Joo, Jong Nam 267
Joon-Ho, Han 345
Jooss, Gerhard 164
Joosten, Ruud 24
Jope, Alan 464
Jope, Alan Alan Jope 465
Jorda, Daniel 185
Jordi, Markus 54
Jordi, Ignacio Ferrero 56
Jordis, Theresa 167
Jordis, Theresa 167
Joshi, S.K. 85
Josi, Jean-Louis Laurent 49
Joubert, Philippe 31
Jourquin, Christian 406
Jourquin, Christian 407
Joussen, Friedrich P. (Fritz) 475
Joyce, Tony 66
Joyce, Tony 218
Juan, Abel Matutes 60
Juan, Abel Matutes 457
Jucker, Bernhard 5
Judge, Lady Barbara T. 414
Juel, Steinar 321
Jufors, Staffan 479
Julius, DeAnne S. 362
Jun, Lei 65
Jung, Helga 28
Jung, David 267
Jung, David 267
Jung, Man Won 398
Jung, Man-Won 398
Jung, Helga 463
Jungels, Pierre H. 227
Junhui, Cui 339
Junyent, Miquel Roca i 10
Junyent, Miguel 57
Junyuan, Fu 119
Juranek, Herbert 167
Jurecka, Christoph 164

K

K?nig, Elke A. 195
Ka-cheung, Li (Eric) 65
Ka-shing, Li 219
Kaba, Franz 332
Kaden, Lewis B. (Lew) 39
Kadoorie, Sir Michael D. 219
Kadowaki, Katsutoshi 334
Kadrnoska, Friedrich 463
Kaemmerer, Peter A. 262
Kaeser, Joe 395
Kaeser, Christian 396
Kaga, Satoru 236
Kagawa, Shingo Shingo Kagawa 184
Kagawa, Akihiko 294
Kagel, Kris 461
Kagermann, Henning Henning Kagermann 81
Kagermann, Henning 300
Kagermann, Henning 318
Kageyama, Sachio 106
Kain, Connie J. 482
Kaiser, Regine 300
Kaisheng, Yang 229
Kaisheng, Yang 229
Kajiya, Tetsuro 253
Kakehi, Kazuo 96
Kakehi, Kazuo 97
Kakinoki, Masumi 282
Kakiuchi, Takehiko 289
Kakiya, Hidetaka 448
Kakiya, Hidetaka 448
Kakumu, Masakazu 452
Kalaris, Thomas L. (Tom) 72
Kalaris, Thomas L. (Tom) 74
Kalberer, Peter 54
Kalle, Volker 164
Kallmeier, Hans-Jurgen 154
Kamano, Hiroyuki 420
Kamata, Hiroshi 1
Kamata, Hiroshi 1
Kamath, Kundapur V. (K. V.) 224
Kambe, Mitsutaka 1
Kambe, Mitsutaka 1
Kameda, Shigeaki 393
Kamei, Katsunobu 334
Kamei, Atsushi 388
Kamei, Atsushi 388
Kamei, Yasuo 416
Kamijo, Masahito 357
Kamimae, Osamu 224
Kamimae, Osamu 225
Kamlani, Suneel 368
Kammerer, Thilo 268
Kamogawa, Tamaki 180
Kan, Tetsuya 357
Kanada, Yoshihiko 22
Kanai, Hiroshi 141
Kanai, Seita 283
Kanai, Seita 283
Kanai, Makoto 328
Kanai, Makoto 328
Kanazawa, Eiji 34
Kanazawa, Suguru 214
Kanazawa, Hirotaka 283
Kanazawa, Kaoru 314
Kanazawa, Kaoru 314
Kanda, Tokuji 141
Kanda, Yoshifumi 208
Kanda, Naoya 416
Kane, Archie 66
Kane, Julie 323
Kanegae, Michihiko 417
Kaneko, Shingo 448
Kanemaru, Kenichi 358
Kang, Il-Hyung 222
Kang, Chan Soo 247
Kang, Seog-Hoon 258
Kang, Yu-Sig 267
Kang, Yu-Sig 267
Kang, T.H. 372
Kangmin, Sun 122
Kangmin, Sun 122
Kani, Shigeru 392
Kann-Rasmussen, Lars E. 2
Kannan, N. S. 224
Kano, Noriaki 253
Kano, Noriaki 253
Kano, Takashi 417
Kant, Ravi 430
Kant, Ravi 430
Kantola, Birgitta Birgitta Kantola 399
Kantor, Bernard 235
Kantor, Bernard 235
Kantor, Ian 235
Kanwal, Ajay 412
Kao, Tsai-Shan 178
Kaperi, Ari 321
Kapil, Pawan K. 353
Kapil, Pawan K. 353
Kaplan, Larry 318
Kapur, Rajnish 212
Kapur, Dharam V. 353
Kara, Pal 297
Karadere, Nafiz 459
Karadere, Nafiz 459
Karatsu, Masanori 288
Karlsen, Lars Guldb?k 325
Karlsson, Per 318
Karlsson, Jessica 401
Karlsson, Anders 426
Karlsson, Conny 436
Karlsson, H?kan 479
Karlsten, Peter 479
Karlstrom, Johan 381
Karlstrom, Johan 400
Karlstrom, Johan Johan Karlstrom 401
Karlstrom, Johan 401
Karlstrom, Roger 401
Karlstrom, Roger Roger Karlstrom 401
Karnad, Renu S. 196
Karnchana, Manusiri 61
Karnebeek, Jan Derck van 199
Karnibad, Michal 218
Karnstrom, Tomas 381
Karnstrom, Tomas 381
Karpel, Yelena 188
Karpel, Elena E. 188
Karube, Hiroshi 316
Karube, Jun 456
Karytinos, Aristotelis 303
Kasai, Masahiro 180
Kasai, Manabu 206
Kasai, Kazuhiko 404
Kasai, Kazuhiko 404
Kaschke, Michael 202
Kasdorf, Helen 193
Kase, Yutaka 405
Kase, Yutaka 405
Kaseda, Tatsuya 211
Kashihara, Yasuo 67
Kashima, Ikusaburo 338
Kashiwagi, Yasuo 320
Kashiwagi, Shigesuke 320
Kasse, Philippe 31
Kasteel, Daniel 263
Kasui, Yoshitomo 419
Katagiri, Takao 316
Katanozaka, Shinya 34
Katayama, Ko 214
Katayama, Masanori 236
Katayama, Masanori 236
Katayama, Yasuyoshi 314
Katayama, Yasuyoshi 314
Katayama, Mikio 390
Katayama, Mikio 390
Katen, Karen L. 261
Kato, Yoshiaki 22
Kato, Mitsuharu 149
Kato, Kazuhiko 183

Kato, Kazuhiko 184
Kato, Kazuyasu 252
Kato, Seiji 289
Kato, Ryozo 290
Kato, Sadao 311
Kato, Sadao 311
Kato, Shigeaki 316
Kato, Kaoru 326
Kato, Kaoru 327
Kato, Makoto Makoto Kato 390
Kato, Shigeya 393
Kato, Hideaki 405
Kato, Masaru 408
Kato, Susumu 417
Kato, Susumu 417
Kato, Ikunori 420
Kato, Mitsuhisa 455
Kato, Mitsuhisa 455
Katoh, Nobuaki 149
Katsibas, Adam Adam Katsibas 240
Katsumata, Nobuo 281
Katsumata, Tsunehisa 447
Katsura, Yasuo 338
Katsura, Yasuo 338
Katsurayama, Naoki 22
Katsuyama, Norio 312
Katsuyama, Norio 312
Katte, Hans-Dieter 268
Katte, Hans-Dieter 268
Katz, Miryam (Miri) 63
Katzilieri-Zour, Ioanna 303
Kau, Melanie 27
Kauffmann, Herbert 13
Kaufman, Donna Soble 82
Kaul, Poonam 318
Kaushal, Sunil 412
Kaushik, A. K. 85
Kavitanon, Staporn 61
Kawabata, Yoshifumi 320
Kawada, Yasuo 455
Kawaguchi, Hitoshi 316
Kawahara, Makoto 236
Kawahara, Takuro 417
Kawahara, Takuro 418
Kawahata, Susumu 236
Kawai, Seiichiro 97
Kawai, Shinji 281
Kawai, Shinji 282
Kawai, Mitsuhiko 295
Kawai, Hideaki 338
Kawai, Fumiyoshi 419
Kawakami, Kozo 283
Kawakami, Hidenori 283
Kawakami, Hiroshi 456
Kawamata, Atsuhiro 241
Kawamoto, Yoshinori 224
Kawamoto, Soichi 314
Kawamoto, Soichi 314
Kawamura, Toshimitsu 182
Kawamura, Takashi 208
Kawamura, Yoshinori 420
Kawana, Kaoru 137
Kawanabe, Tomohiko 215
Kawanabe, Tomohiko 215
Kawano, Kaoru 208
Kawasaki, Yasumi 96
Kawasaki, Hironori 206
Kawasaki, Kazuhiko 405
Kawasaki, Yasuyuki 420
Kawashima, Takashi 141
Kawashima, Fuminobu 296
Kawashima, Isamu 307
Kawashima, Fuminobu 468
Kawashima, Kazuo 469
Kawata, Takeshi 22
Kawatsuma, Tsuneo 183
Kawazoe, Shinichiro 289
Kay, eng
Kay, S. Carolyn H. 130
Ke, Nigel 278
Kean, Sue 330
Keanly, Rose 330
Kearns, Roger 407
Keating, Andrew 66
Keck, Kirsten 13
Kehua, Zhang 120
Kehui, Zhang 121
Keijzer, Conrad 24
Keim, Marco 14
Keir, Alan M. 218
Keitel, Prof Hans-Peter 129
Keitel, Hans-Peter 445
Keller, Gottlieb A. 362
Kellner, Petr 41
Kellow, Glenn 88
Kelly, Tom 100
Kelly, Greg 316
Kelly, Gail P. 484
Kelly, Gail P. 484
Kelly-Ennis, Debra 107
Kelman, Naomi 323
Kelsall, Bruce 413
Kemball, Benjamin (Benj) 98
Kemmel, Gerard Van 383
Kemmochi, Masatoshi 334
Kemp, Adrian 44
Kemp, Jacques P.M. 247
Kemper, Nikola 300
Kengeter, Carsten 461
Kennedy, Patrick T. 66
Kennedy, Jerome J. 66
Kennedy, John 156
Kennedy, Keith N. 330
Kenyon-Slaney, Harry 361
Keogh, John W. 9
Keogh, John W. 9
Keon-Soo, Shin 249
Kerckhove, Ghislaine Van 248
Kerkhof, Paul P. M. van de 352
Kerkhoff, Guido 445
Kern, Andreas 197
Kern, Harald 396
Kerner, Jurgen 277
Kerner, Michael G. (Mike) 491
Kerr, John C. 69
Kerr, Graham 87
Kerr, Graham 88
Kerr, John 361
Kerr, David W. 422
Kerrmann, Dirk-Uwe 113
Keryer, Philippe 25
Kesner, Prof Idalene F. (Idie) 422
Kessel, Kevin 176
Kessler, Bruce L. 9
Kessler, Denis 90
Kesteren, Gerard van 260
Kesteren, Gerard 260
Keswick, Henry 242
Keswick, Simon L. 242
Ketcham, Henry H. 450
Keulen, Sjoerd 231
Keveligan, Sean 492
Khan, Afaq 411
Khandelwa, Sachin 224
Khavkin, Evgeny 329
Kheradpir, Shaygan 72
Kheradpir, Shaygan 74
Khoba, Lyubov 329
Khomyakov, Sergey F 187
Khoo, Edwin 147
Khoo, Eddie Boo Jin 467
Khoshoo, Raj 396
Khoza, Reuel 330
Khusrokhan, Homi R. 224
Kida, Yasushi 419
Kida, Tetsuhiro 427
Kida, Tetsuhiro 427
Kidowaki, Masaki 306
Kidwai, Naina L. 309
Kielholz, Walter B. 139
Kielholz, Walter B. 139
Kierans, Thomas E. (Tom) 278
Kiernan, Larry 66
Kiesel, Klaus-Armin 396
Kikuchi, Katsuyori 34
Kikuchi, Takashi 236
Kikuchi, Satoshi 238
Kilaas, Liselott 435
Kilaas, Liselott 435
Kildahl, J?rgen 159
Kim, Jeong H. 25
Kim, Henry 91
Kim, Kwang-Nyun 222
Kim, Ki Hong 247
Kim, Han 247
Kim, Chee Joong 247
Kim, Ssang-Su 258
Kim, Woo-Kyum 258
Kim, Jong-Ho 258
Kim, Chong-Young 258
Kim, Ssang-Su 258
Kim, Jung-Kook 258
Kim, Kyung-Min 258
Kim, Woo-Kyum 258
Kim, Jong-Ho 258
Kim, Chong-Young 258
Kim, Gan 336
Kim, Yangkyu Y.K. 378
Kim, Gi Gi Yeong Kim 391
Kim, Seok Seok Won Kim 392
Kim, Joon Ho 397
Kim, Joon Ho 397
Kim, Tai-Yoo 397
Kimsey, William L. (Bill) 8
Kimura, Misao 34
Kimura, Osamu 117
Kimura, Yaichi 137
Kimura, Yaichi 137
Kimura, Kazumasa 149
Kimura, Masakazu 180
Kimura, Hiroshi 241
Kimura, Hiroshi 241
Kimura, Shohei 316
Kimura, Keiji 408
Kimura, Toshihide 419
Kimura, Shigeru 447
Kin, Lam Kun 336
Kindle, Fred 492
King, Ian 51
King, Ian 51
King, Thomas (Tom) 72
King, Thomas (Tom) 74
King, Liz 100
King, Bill 184
King, M. J. W. 217
King, Justin 240
King, Justin 240
King, Annette 278
King, Thomas B. (Tom) 304
King, Thomas B. (Tom) 304
King, James 352
King, Mark 364
Kingo, Lise 325
Kingsmill, Baroness Denise 159
Kingsmill, Baroness Denise 233
Kingsmill, Stephani E. 278
Kinlochard, Lord John O. Kerr of 360
Kinlochard, Lord Kerr 361
Kinlochard, Lord John O. Kerr of 370
Kinlochard, Lord John O. Kerr of 370
Kinoshita, Masayuki 295
Kinoshita, Manabu 306
Kinoshita, Manabu 307
Kinukawa, Jun 289
Kirby, Michael J. L. 69
Kirby, Peter M. 273
Kirby, Pamela J. 325
Kirchgassner, Johann 489
Kirchgassner, Johann 489
Kirchhof, Ina 164
Kirchmann, Albert 143
Kirianoff, Vassili 491
Kiriyama, Teruo Teruo Kiriyama 452
Kirk, Matthew 475
Kirkby, Matthew 368
Kirsch, Wolfgang 157
Kirsch, Wolfgang 482
Kishi, Satoru 252
Kishida, Makoto 328
Kishida, Makoto 328
Kishimoto, Sumiyuki 244
Kishimoto, Sumiyuki 244
Kissling, Willy R. 387
Kist, Ewald 258
Kita, Hidetaka Hidetaka Kita 253
Kita, Toshihiko 405
Kitajima, Yoshitoshi 140
Kitajima, Yoshinari 140
Kitajima, Motoharu 140
Kitajima, Yoshitoshi 141
Kitajima, Yoshinari 141
Kitamatsu, Yoshihito 208
Kitamura, Tadashi 326
Kitamura, Kunitaro 421
Kitamura, Hideo 452
Kitayama, Yuji 67
Kitayama, Teisuke 182
Kitayama, Teisuke 182
Kitayama, Ryuichi 208
Kitayama, Teisuke 420
Kitayuguchi, Tatsuro 140
Kitazaki, Michiharu 314
Kitazaki, Michiharu 314
Kitazawa, Toshifumi 446
Kitsanayothin, Phornthep 61
Kivihuhta, Jari 321
Kivisaari, Tero E. 436
Kiyoshi, Tatsuya 289
Kjellgren, Jan 381
Klatten, Susanne 81
Klausner, Richard D. 382
Klaver, Piet C. 231
Klebe, Thomas 144
Klein, Philippe 355
Klein, Robert E. 422
Kleinfeld, Klaus 78
Kleinjohann, Norbert 396
Kleisterlee, Gerard J. 144
Kleisterlee, Gerard J. 370
Kleisterlee, Gerard J. 475
Klemm, Erich 143
Klemm, Erich 144
Klerk, Philip de 465
Kleven, Kjersti 435
Kley, Max D. 76
Kley, Karl-Ludwig 80
Kley, Karl-Ludwig 81
Kley, Karl-Ludwig 84
Kley, Max D. 197
Klingler, Christian 477
Klinpathum, Wanlapha 61
Klockhaus, Werner 286
Kloppers, Marius 87
Kloppers, Marius 87
Kloppers, Marius 88
Kluge, Holger 219
Kluhr, Thomas 151
Knauf, Jason 368
Knight, Christopher 411
Knight, John 414
Knobel, Carsten 202
Knox, Lesley 116
Knox, Lesley 373
Knutson, Lottie 203
Knutsson, Anne-Charlotte 44
Ko, May 219
Ko, Handy 429
Koba, Fumihiro 417
Kobayashi, Hisashi 137
Kobayashi, Ryo 22
Kobayashi, Katsumi 34
Kobayashi, Masayuki 67
Kobayashi, Masayuki 67
Kobayashi, Kenji 106
Kobayashi, Hisashi 137
Kobayashi, Koji 149
Kobayashi, Koji 149
Kobayashi, Hidetoshi 180
Kobayashi, Hiroshi 214
Kobayashi, Hiroshi 215
Kobayashi, Kiyonobu 224
Kobayashi, Yoichi 238
Kobayashi, Eizo 238
Kobayashi, Yoichi 238
Kobayashi, Hirotake 251
Kobayashi, Yoshimitsu 288
Kobayashi, Ken 289
Kobayashi, Ken 290
Kobayashi, Kazuo 311
Kobayashi, Kenichi 311

Kobayashi, Kazuo 311
Kobayashi, Kenichi 311
Kobayashi, Toshio 314
Kobayashi, Yotaro 314
Kobayashi, Toshio 314
Kobayashi, Toru 326
Kobayashi, Toshiaki 338
Kobayashi, Hiroshi 358
Kobayashi, Tsuyoshi 388
Kobayashi, Masayuki 393
Kobayashi, Kiyoshi 452
Kobei, Andrea 260
Kobi, Andrea 260
Koch, Brice 5
Koch, Urlich 83
Koch, Benoit-H. 212
Koch, Olaf 286
Kocher, Prof Renate 28
Kocher, Isabelle 49
Kocher, Prof Renate 81
Kocher, Isabelle 189
Kocher, Renate 277
Kochhar, Rakesh 316
Kochuparampil, Augustine 39
Kock, Gerard de 352
Kockmann, Siegfried 335
Kodaira, Nobuyori 455
Kodaira, Nobuyori 455
Koder, Matthew 461
Koecher, Renate 28
Koecher, Renate Renate Koecher 81
Koedijk, Dirk-Stephan 202
Koelbl, Konrad 179
Koerner, Ulrich 461
Koezuka, Masahiro 183
Koezuka, Masahiro 183
Koezuka, Masahiro 184
Koezuka, Masahiro 184
Koga, Akira 283
Kogai, Masamichi 283
Koguchi, Shigeo 452
Kogure, Makoto 408
Kohlberg, Prof Elon 441
Kohle, Tommy 479
Kohler, Roland 212
Kohler, Alexis 355
Kohlinger, Jorg 136
Kohnke, Gilbert 336
Koide, Sadayuki 194
Koide, Sadayuki 194
Koike, Tetsuya 117
Koike, Masato 140
Koike, Koh 327
Koizumi, Mitsuomi 241
Koizumi, Mitsuomi 241
Kojima, Keiji 208
Kojima, Yorihiko 289
Kojima, Nobuaki 289
Kojima, Kazuo 334
Kojima, Yorihiko 409
Kok, Wim 370
Kokubu, Fumiya 281
Kokubun, Ryosei 184
Kolakowska, Malgorzata 231
Kolbe, Martin 260
Kolbl, Konrad 179
Kolding, Eivind 147
Kolff, Han 352
Koll, Norbert 202
Kollatz-Ahnen, Matthias 170
Koller, Dan 62
Komai, Masayoshi 296
Komai, Masayoshi 296
Komaki, Tatsuo 141
Komamura, Yoshinori 253
Komatsu, Shunji 70
Komatsu, Hiroshi 180
Komatsu, Hiroshi 180
Komiya, Shinichirou 253
Komiyama, Masahiro 405
Komori, Shigetaka 182
Komori, Shigetaka 182
Komori, Mitsunobu 326
Komori, Mitsunobu 327
Komura, Yoshifumi 236
Konczaty, Michel 89
Kondo, Jun 180
Kondo, Jun 180
Kondo, Hiroaki Hiroaki Kondo 183
Kondo, Yoshiki Yoshiki Kondo 184
Kondo, Koichi 214
Kondo, Kunio 307
Kondo, Shiro 358
Kondo, Shiro 358
Kondo, Yoshimasa 456
Kong, Dong 121
Kong, Janis 250
Kong, Cheong Choong 336
Konijnenburg, Robin H. von 199
Konishi, Masahide 293
Konishi, Shunichi 455
Konno, Hidehiro 290
Konno, Masaru 320
Konoda, Tetsuya 405
Konstantakopoulos, Vassilios 303
Koo, Jeffrey L. S. 139
Koo, George C.G. 242
Koo, Bon Joon 267
Koo, Ja-Young 397
Koo, Ja-Young 397
Koop, Peter 384
Koopmann, Andreas N. 139
Koopmann, Andreas N. 309
Kopf, MaryKay 3
Koplowitz, Esther 471
Kopp, Cathy 387
Koremans, Robert 441
Koren, Moshe 62
Koren, Zvi 63
Koreyva, Ken 9
Kornberg, Prof Roger D. 441
Korner, Ulrich 461
Kornicker, Peter 323
Kornowski-Bonnet, Sophie 362
Korte, Daniel G. (Dan) 364
Kosakai, Yasuo 180
Koseki, Shuichi 238
Koshida, Susumu 70
Koskull, Casper von 321
Kossubek, Peter 28
Kostov, Todor 212
Kosugi, Takeo 452
Kotagiri, Seetarama 274
Kotake, Nobukazu 253
Kotler, Ofer 12
Kotz, Hans-Helmut 149
Kouduki, Kazuo 446
Kourilsky, Philippe 471
Kozano, Yoshiaki 392
Kozano, Yoshiaki 392
Kozlov, Alexander N. 187
Kozlov, Aleksandr 188
Kozuka, Syuichiro 312
Kraats, Robert-Jan van de 352
Kralingen, Bridget van 366
Kralingen, Bridget 367
Kralingen, Tony van 373
Kramer, Markus 76
Kramer, Marcus 79
Kramer, Terry D. 475
Kramp, Uwe 195
Krauel, Jose 185
Kraus, Peter S. 49
Kraut, Hans G. 197
Kravchenko, Kirill 186
Krayer, Georg F. 54
Krayer, Georg F. 54
Krebs, Prof Rolf 261
Krecke, Jeannot 39
Krecke, Jeannot Jeannot Krecke 39
Kreimeyer, Andreas 76
Kress, Robert E. (Bob) 8
Kretschmer, Eduardo 212
Kreutzer, Gerhard 277
Krieger, Alexandra 128
Krinsky, Prof Itzhak 441
Kristensen, Peter 325
Kritsanamara, Ayut 61
Kroener, Ulrike Ulrike Kroener 210
Kroese, Hayko 257
Krol, John A. (Jack) 9
Kron, Patrick 31
Kronau, Denice 396
Kronen, Petra 78
Kroner, Ulrike 210
Kronsfoth, Ingo 457
Kroon, Hans van der 352
Krossa, Hubertus 53
Krueger, Harald Harald Krueger 81
Kruger, Harald 81
Kruger, R. M. (Rich) 225
Kruglov, Andrey V. 186
Kruglov, Andrey V. 187
Krumnow, Jurgen 457
Kruse, Stein 107
Krusell, Tor 400
Kruyt, Peter 345
Kruythoff, Kees 464
Kruythoff, Kees Kees Kruythoff 465
Kubo, Takeshi 117
Kubo, Akito 419
Kubo, Tetsuya 420
Kubo, Ken 420
Kubo, Tetsuya 420
Kubo, Makoto 452
Kubori, Hideaki 320
Kubota, Isao 314
Kubota, Isao 314
Kubota, Akira 408
Kuchler, Gunter 151
Kucmin, Janusz 91
Kudelski, Andre 309
Kudo, Yoshikazu 184
Kudo, Hiroshi 281
Kudo, Hideyuki 392
Kuehn, Frithjof 371
Kuehn, Frithjof 371
Kuehne, Klaus-Michael 260
Kuepker, Horst 153
Kugler, Jean-Christophe 355
Kuhn, Frithjof 371
Kuhnast, Sylvia 154
Kuhnert, Marcus 202
Kui, Mu 485
Kuiper, Jaap 24
Kuiper, Joost 231
Kuisch, Eric 256
Kukielski, Peter G. J. 39
Kukura, Sergei P. 329
Kulartz, Hans Jurgen 263
Kulkarni, S.V. 86
Kulkarni, Girish 141
Kumagai, Bunya 326
Kumagai, Bunya 327
Kumagai, Osamu 408
Kumamoto, Yuichi 448
Kumar, P.V. 85
Kumar, Rupesh 224
Kumaraswamy, P. 86
Kume, Shinsuke 141
Kume, Shinsuke 141
Kummer, Werner 54
Kumura, Haruyoshi 316
Kun, Zsuzsanna 297
Kuneva, Meglena 90
Kung, Lin 61
Kung, Arthur H. 137
Kung, Patrick S. 257
Kunibe, Takeshi 420
Kunieda, Toshinari 326
Kunio, Takemitsu 307
Kunio, Takemitsu 307
Kuntz-Mayr, Christiane 384
Kunz, Thomas 145
Kunze, Hans-Peter 469
Kuok, Khoon ean 65
Kupfer, Peter 212
Kurahara, Fumiaki 420
Kurahashi, Masatsugu 289
Kuraishi, Seiji 214
Kuraishi, Seiji 215
Kuramochi, Junjiro 224
Kuramochi, Junjiro 224
Kurashige, Hideki 16
Kurashige, Hideki 16
Kurata, Yoshizumi 405
Kuri, Alejandro Soberon 32
Kurihara, Kazuhiro 208
Kurihara, Shinichi 293
Kurihara, Katsumi 358
Kuroda, Yujiro 140
Kuroda, Yujiro 141
Kuroda, Masami 311
Kuroda, Masami 311
Kuromoto, Kazunori 253
Kurosawa, Koji 283
Kurosawa, Tomohiro 327
Kuroyanagi, Nobuo 215
Kurtzhals, Peter 325
Kusakabe, Isao 137
Kusakabe, Isao 137
Kuschewski, Rainer 286
Kushan, Ravi 130
Kushihashi, Yasuo 224
Kusuhashi, Toshinori 283
Kutil-Bleibaum, Christiane 482
Kuwaiti, Alyazia 332
Kuwaiti, Alyazia Ali Saleh Al 332
Kuwari, Jassim 477
Kuwayama, Shoji 281
Kux, Barbara 395
Kux, Barbara 489
Kuzume, Kaoru 282
Kuzuoka, Toshiaki 208
Kvart, Sussi 203
Kverneland, Anne Marie 325
Kvilhaug, J?rn O. 157
Kwek, Alan 24
Kwist, Charlotte 199
Kwok, Thomas P. K. 65
Kwok, R. C. 242
Kwon, Havis 267
Kwon, Oh-Hyun 378
Kyriakopoulos, Ioannis 303
Kyriakos-Saad, Fawzi 139
Kysilka, Pavel 167

L

Laan, Sander van der 255
LaBarre, Ron 261
Laberge, Alice D. 366
Labeyrie, Christian 472
Labonte, Ralph 445
Labriffe, Christian De 124
Labriola, Pietro 432
Lacey, John S. 483
Lacharriere, Marc Ladreit de 111
Lacharriere, Marc Ladreit de 355
Lachman, Henri 387
Lachmann, Henri 474
LaCroix, Franck 471
Laflamme, Louise 302
Lafleur, Jean 173
Lafont, Bruno Bruno Lafont 39
Lafos, Hans-Peter 371
Lafuente, Francisco Fernandez 10
Lagard+?re, Arnaud 21
Lagardere, Arnaud Arnaud Lagardere 21
Lagardere, Arnaud 21
Lagayette, Philippe 355
Laguiche, Bernard 407
Laguiche, Bernard de 407
Lahoud, Marwan 21
Lai, Dominic K. M. 219
Laidlaw, W. Samuel H. (Sam) 116
Laidlaw, W. Samuel H. (Sam) 116
Laidlaw, W. Samuel H. (Sam) 218
Laidlaw, Roy 273
Laing, Melanie 130
Laing, Ian G. A. 318
Laisathit, Kirati 61
Laisathit, Niraman 61
Lajoux, Christian 382
Lajtha, Adrian J. 7
Lake, Spencer 217
Lam, Yim Nam 90
Lam, Cheung Wing (Linus) 122
Lam, Kam Hing 219

Lam, Kam Hing 219
Lamade, Lars Lars Lamade 384
Lamade, Lars 384
Lamarre, Jacques 366
Lamba, Sanjiv 268
Lambech, Arne 321
Lambert, Thierry 131
Lambert, Jean-Marie 471
Lambert, Nick 476
Lamberti, Hermann-Josef 21
Lamberton, Michelle 51
Lambertz, Michael 459
Lambkin, Charlotte 51
Lamlieng, Chumpol Na 394
Lamouche, Didier 12
Lamoure, Jean-Pierre 472
Lamoure, Jean-Pierre 472
Lampersbach, Andreas 277
Lampiano, Lorenzo 463
Lan, Yan 119
Lancaster, Geoff 42
Lanci, Gianfranco 266
Land, Nick 476
Landau, Igor 13
Landau, Igor 28
Landau, Igor 383
Landel, Michel 403
Landel, Michel 403
Landert, Karl 139
Landert, Karl 139
Landini, Bruce 27
Landiribar, Javier Echenique 10
Landiribar, Javier 57
Landiribar, Javier Echenique 356
Landiribar, Javier 356
Landis, Katrina 95
Landolt, Pierre 323
Lane, Robert W. (Bob) 81
Lane, Jon 100
Lane, Melanie 370
Lang, Teng Soon 336
Lange, Reinhard 260
Lange, Titia de 309
Langemeyer, Gerhard 371
Langemeyer, Gerhard 482
Langer, Jurgen 144
Langlois, Francois 423
Langner, Arne 39
Lanier, Jean 139
Laorakpong, Amrit 394
Lark, Andrew 129
Larkin, Joe 66
Larnaudie-Eiffel, Xavier 126
Larochelle, Pierre 345
Larson, Kirk 364
Larsson, Stefan 203
Larsson, Andreas 321
Larsson, Jan 321
Larsson, Carl 380
Larsson, Hans 399
Larsson, Claes 400
Larsson, Thomas 401
Larsson, Marie Hallander 426
Larsson, Marie Marie Hallander Larsson 426
Lasar, Jean 39
Laska, Christopher 435
Laskaris, George 304
Lassen, Lars Christian 325
Lastra, Juan March de la 10
Lategan, Willie T. 71
Latimer, Simon 51
Lau, Leng 87
Lau, Lawrence J. 125
Lau, M. 130
Lauberts, Peteris 479
Laubie, Christian 145
Lauble-Meffert, Inge 260
Lauder, Estee 280
Lauenroth-Mago, Jorg 113
Lauer, Stefan 151
Lauk, Kurt 274
Lauke, Harald 76
Lauraguais, Bernard de La Tour d'Auvergne 102
Lauraguais, Bernard 102
Laurence, Guy 475
Laurent, Jean Gaston Pierre Marie Victor 145
Laury-Deroubaix, Veronique 250
Lautenschlaeger-Peit, Sabine 150
Lauvergeon, Anne 189
Lauvergeon, Anne 453
Lauvergeon, Anne 476
Lavedrine, Christian 127
Lavilla, Antonio Massanell 434
Lavinay, Gerard 109
Lawrence, Paul J. 217
Lawrence, James A. (Jim) 233
Lawrence, Christian 300
Lawrence, Ken 370
Lawrence, Ben 480
Lawton, Keith 100
Lay, Patrick Le 127
Lazberger, Mark J. 130
Leach, Lord C. G. Rodney 242
Leaman, J. Richard (Rick) 461
Leary, Robert G. (Rob) 231
Lebel, Marie-Claude 302
Leclair, Nadine 355
Leclercq, Gerard 355
Lecorvaisier, Fabienne 261
Lede, Cees van 199
Lede, Cornelis J. A. (Cees) van 258
Lede, Cornelis 258
Lede, Cornelis van 261
Lederman, Baruch 63
Leduc, Eduardo 76
Lee, Suet-Fern 49
Lee, Shau-Kee 65
Lee, Chang-Ken 112
Lee, Alan 112
Lee, Chang-Ken 112
Lee, Ting Chang (Peter) 194
Lee, Jae-kye 220
Lee, Man-woo 220
Lee, Hyoung-Keun (Hank) 249
Lee, Hyoung-Keun (Hank) 249
Lee, Tae-Sik 258
Lee, Gi-Pyo 258
Lee, Kyu Min 267
Lee, Hin Hin Hock Lee 275
Lee, Helena 278
Lee, Suzanne 278
Lee, George L. W. 336
Lee, Irene 350
Lee, Yoon-Woo 378
Lee, Sang-Hoon 378
Lee, Gregory 378
Lee, In-Ho 378
Lee, Chae-Woong 378
Lee, Emile 384
Lee, Dong Hwan 391
Lee, Sin Gee 391
Lee, Sang Sang Gyeong Lee 392
Lee, Hoon-Kyu 397
Lee, Johnsee 429
Lee, Francis Chin Yong 466
Lee, Wai Fai 467
Leenaars, Eli P. 231
Leeuw, Sieto de 352
Lefakis, Demetrios 303
Lefebvre, Pierre-Emmanuel 47
Lefebvre, Vincent 212
Lefebvre, Jocelyn 346
Leger, Manfred 53
Leggett, Karen 302
Legros, Eric 109
Lehmann, Axel P. 461
Lehmann, Axel P. 491
Lehner, Ulrich 159
Lehner, Ulrich 323
Lehner, Ulrich 323
Lehner, Jean-Pierre 383
Lehner, Prof Ulrich 445
Lehtinen, Olli-Petteri 321
Leibig, Frank 335
Leibinger-Kammueller, Nicola 396
Leibinger-Kammuller, Nicola 151
Leibinger-Kammuller, Nicola 396
Leibowitz, Gary 373
Leidi, Rossella 466
Leighton, Allan L. 483
Leitner, Manfred 332
Lekatsas, Angela S. 18
Lekkakos, Stavros M. 343
Lekkakos, Stavros M. 343
Lels, Marike E. van Lier 256
Lemann, Jorge Paulo 37
Lemay, Stephane 345
Lemay, Stephane 345
Lemay, Stephane 346
Lembregts, Dirk 280
Lemesre, Rene 250
Lemoine, Mathilde 110
Lemoine, Frederic 131
Leng, James W. (Jim) 31
Leng, Leong Wai 336
Lentz, James E. (Jim) 455
Leonard, John C. 461
Leone, Raffaella Raffaella Leone 163
Leonelli, Candido 56
Leopold, Tess 311
Leopoulos, Agis 303
Lepasoon, Karin 401
Lepercq, Xavier 127
Lepetit, Prof Jean-Francois 90
Lepinay, Philippe 443
Lepinay, Philippe 443
Lepoutre, Manoelle 453
Lerberghe, Rose-Marie Van 111
Lerch, Hans 260
Lerer, Orit 62
Lereuth, Karsten 100
Lerman, Raz 218
Leroy, Jean Philippe 56
Leroy, Francoise 453
Leroy, Didier 455
Lerwill, Robert E. 98
Lesar, David 18
Leschly, Jan 2
Lessard, Pierre H. 450
Lessum, Atle 435
Letellier, Gerard 212
Leten, Ronnie 3
Leten, Ronnie 3
Letty, Laurence 49
Leu, Andreas 212
Leung, William Wing Cheung 194
Leung, Margaret K. M. Y. 194
Leung, Andrew 194
Leung, William Wing Cheung 194
Leung, Margaret K. M. Y. 194
Leung, Margaret K. M. Y. 218
Leung, Hans 219
Leung, Margaret K. M. Y. 219
Leupp, Peter 5
Levene, Lord Peter 454
Leveque, Didier 111
Leverton, Tim 430
Levesque, Rejean 302
Levey, Stuart 218
Levin, Edward 9
Levin, Anat (Moti) 62
Levin, Jeremy M. 441
Levitt, Brian M. 82
Levitt, Brian M. 450
Levy, Shemaya 14
Levy, Ofer 62
Levy, Jean-Marc 98
Levy, Shemaya 375
Levy, Jean-Bernard 402
Levy, Jean-Bernard 472
Levy, Jean-Bernard 474
Lewent, Judy C. 192
Lewis, Guy 218
Lewis, Martin 348
Lewis, Catherine (Cathy) 348
Lewis, M. George 366
Lewis, Stevan 422
Lewis, David (Dave) 464
Lewis, David (Dave) 465
Lewis, Stephen 491
Leye, Erik De 407
Leysen, Thomas 462
Lhernould, Gilles 382
Li, Gong 7
Li, Lihui 64
Li, David K. P. 65
Li, Richard T. K. 65
Li, Aubrey K. S. 65
Li, Fook-wo 65
Li, Prof Arthur K. C. 65
Li, Eric F. C. 65
Li, Stephen Charles K. S. 65
Li, Yinquan 119
Li, Dong 121
Li, Gang 122
Li, Gang 122
Li, Fanrong 125
Li, Fanrong 125
Li, Wenzhi 139
Li, Zhihong 139
Li, Victor T. K. 219
Li, Victor T. K. 219
Li, Renjie 229
Li, Ruoshan 229
Li, Xia 266
Li, William 266
Li, Lillian 278
Li, Michelle 422
Lianfeng, Xu 119
Liang, Linus G.T. 336
Liautaud, Bernard 384
Lichtenauer, Michael 335
Lieb, Eckhard 151
Liebelt, Uwe 76
Liebenberg, Andre 87
Liebman, Seymour E. 105
Ligresti, Jonella 284
Lihao, Zhu 122
Lihui, Li 64
Lihui, Li 64
Likierman, Sir Andrew 74
Lili, Wang 229
Lili, Wang 229
Lilja, Goran Goran Lilja 399
Lilja, Anders 400
Lim, Young-Rok 222
Lim, Suk Sig 247
Lim, Hyun Chin 398
Lim, Pin 467
Lima, Fabiano 258
Lin, Sheng-Chung 137
Lin, Shane S. I. 137
Lin, Jung-Lieh 137
Lin, Marc W.H. 137
Lin, Connie 139
Lin, Teresa 147
Lin, Keh-Yen 178
Lin, Bingkun 229
Lin, Lijun 343
Lin, Burn J. 429
Lin, J.K. 429
Linan, Zhu 266
Lindb?k, Jannik 414
Lindberg, Christina 3
Lindberg, Sanna 203
Lindberg, Nicklas 401
Lindblad, Anders 166
Lindelauf, Leo J.M.V. 352
Linden, Lars 166
Lindenberg, Frank 144
Lindgreen, Sarah 44
Lindner, Thomas 429
Lindner, Dieter 462
Lindsay, Ed 100
Lindsay, Donald R. (Don) 278
Lindskog, ?se 166
Linehan, Karen 382
Ling, Wen 121
Ling, Yinbao 139
Link, Matthias 179
Linssen, Helmut 482
Lintag, Mariquit 422
Lioi, Vittorio Corbo 60
Lion, Emmanuel 218
Lipp, Robert I. (Bob) 8
Lippert, Karl 373
Lipphaus, Annette 482

Lipps, Ben J. 179
Lipsky, John 218
Lischka, Horst 81
Liss?ker, Jan 380
Lissaker, Jan 381
Lissowski, Antoine 126
Lister, Paul 42
Lister, John 47
Lister, David W. 304
Littich, Wolfram 332
Little, Tom 82
Little, Mark 423
Littlefield, Christopher J. (Chris) 47
Littner, Leslie 62
Litzenberger, Waltraud 154
Liu, Yanfen 64
Liu, Lina 64
Liu, Peter Y. K. 90
Liu, Qitao 117
Liu, Benren 121
Liu, Cheng-Hsie 137
Liu, Jun 266
Liu, Yuhong 345
Liu, Sherry 368
Liu, Mark 429
Liu, David 465
Livfors, Mia Brunell 203
Livingston, Ian P. 100
Livingston, Ian P. 100
Livingston, Brian W. 225
Livingstone, Catherine B. 273
Livingstone, Catherine B. 438
Liwanag, Lils 278
Llopis, Ana Maria 98
Llorens, Juan Pi 56
Llorens, Juan 56
Lloveras, Maria 57
Lloyd, Chris 85
Lloyd, Mike 364
Lloyd, Jonathan 440
Lloyd, Jonathan 440
Lloyd, Chris 443
Lluansi, Olivier 131
Lo, Winston Yau-lai 65
Lo, Kenneth C. M. 65
Lo, Chi-Tong 178
Lo, Hong Sui (Vincent) 194
Lo, Sai Lai 343
Lo, Wei-Jen 429
Lo, Allen C. L. 461
Loader, Adrian 212
Locatelli, Piero 172
Lockstone, Paul 47
Loddesol, Lars 415
Loechelt, Dieter Dieter Loechelt 81
Loehr, Thomas O. 365
Loescher, Peter Peter Loescher 300
Loescher, Peter Peter Loescher 396
Loew, Willibald Willibald Loew 81
Loffler, Michael 154
Lofrumento, Peter 474
Lofts, Philip J. 461
Logan, Kevin 218
Logan, Bill 458
Lomax, Rachel 218
Lombard, Marie-Christine 286
Lombard, Didier 443
Lomelin, Carlos Salazar 177
Loney, D. Allen 193
Loney, D. Allen 193
Long, Annabelle Yu 84
Long, Xu 119
Long, Xu 119
Long, Brian 130
Long, Andrew P. 217
Long, Tom 373
Long, Peter 457
Long, Peter 459
Longde, Sun 339
Longpre, Roger 27
Lonsert, Michael 113
Looney, Bernard 95
Lopez, Belen 56
Lopez, Francisco Luzon 60
Lopez, Jose 185
Lopez, Francisco Luzon 228
Lopez, Carmelo de las Morenas 356
Lopez, Miguel-Angel 396
Lopez, Julio L. 432
Lopez, Julio Julio Linares Lopez 432
Lopez, Julio Linares 434
Lopez-Oca?a, Juan Manuel Urgoiti y 228
Lopez-Pi?ol, Jose Maria 10
Lopopolo, Nicola 277
Lord, Andy 233
Lorentz, Paul 278
Lorenzi, Alessandro Alessandro Lorenzi 163
Lorenzo, Domenic De 373
Loscher, Peter 300
Loscher, Peter 395
Lostao, Eduardo Arbizu 55
Louette, Pierre 333
Loughrey, Dan 66
Louie, Paul 320
Louie, Brandt C. 366
Louison, Mark 318
Louv, Bill 191
Louwhoff, Roel 100
Lovatt, William W. 193
Lovelace, Lori L. 7
Lovell, Tonia 464
Lovell, Tonia 465
Loveridge, Debbie 352
Low, Willibald 81
Lowe, John 18
Lowis, Stephan 371
Lowth, Simon 44
Lowth, Simon 44
Lowther, Julie 100
Lox, Egbert 462
Loyola, Gustavo Jorge Laboissiere 237
Lozano, Rafael 114
Lu, Guojun 161
Lubatti, Giulio 234
Lubov, Josh 404
Luby, Steve 396
Luca, S. De 173
Lucas, Christopher (Chris) 72
Lucas, Christopher (Chris) 72
Lucas, Christopher (Chris) 74
Lucas, Christopher (Chris) 74
Lucas, Steve 134
Lucchese, Marcos 462
Lucchini, Stefano 163
Lucchini, Italo 466
Lucchini, Giuseppe 466
Luchai, Kanung 61
Luciani, Luca 432
Ludkovsky, Gregory 39
Ludwig, Doris 482
Luengsuwan, Natthaphorn 61
Luff, Nick 116
Luff, Nick 116
Luge, Ingo 159
Luglini, Raffaella 173
Luk, Peter K. Y. 342
Lulin, Elisabeth 402
Lumb, Richard A. 7
Lumley, Edward C. 82
Lun, Shiaw-Yen 427
Lunardi, R. 173
Lunati, Elisabetta 234
Lund, Helge 414
Lund, Kristin 435
Lundal, Morten 475
Lundberg, Fredrik 381
Lundberg, Fredrik 401
Lundberg, Fredrik 425
Lundgren, Johan 458
Lundgren, Johan 459
Lundius, Annika 415
Lundquist, Bo 203
Lundy, Nicki 413
Lung, Cha (Laura) May 122
Luo, Lianfu 139
Luongo, Manfredi 54
Luongo, Piero 234
Lupica, John 9
Lupinacci, Giovanni 466
Lupo, John S. 3
Lupo, L. Patrick 102
Lupo, L. Patrick 102
Lupton, Laurie 278
Luscan, Philippe 382
Lusch, Andreas 31
Lusignani, Giuseppe 54
Luther, Siegfried 482
Lutkestratkotter, Herbert 197
Lutz, Frank H. 277
Lutz, Rolf 489
Luu, Hang 278
Luxembourg, Guillaume Guillaume de Luxembourg 39
Luxembourg, Prince Guillaume de 39
Lynam, Aidan 212
Lynas, Peter 51
Lynas, Peter 51
Lynch, Christopher 361
Lynton, Michael M. 408
Lyons, Gerard 411
Lyublinsky, Michael 368

M

M?rch, Lars Stensgaard 146
Ma, Yuzhu 122
Ma, Peter M. Z. 343
Ma, Yun 404
Maag-Spieler, Jacqueline 12
Mabuchi, Akira 180
Macaskill, Bridget A. 348
Macdonald, John Paul 91
Macedo, Jorge 161
Macek, Charles 480
MacFarlane, Stuart 37
Macfarlane, Ian J. 46
Macfarlane, Ian J. 488
Machado, Luiz Pasteur Vasconcellos 56
Machado, Diogo C. B. de Lacerda 161
MacHale, Joseph P. (Joe) 368
Machell, Simon 47
Macheras, Kostas 169
Machetti, Claudio 162
Machida, Yukio 405
Machida, Kiyomi 417
Macht, Michael 477
MacIntyre, Gregg 330
Mackay, Martin 44
Mackay, Iain J. 194
Mackay, Iain J. 217
Mackay, E.A. G. (Graham) 373
Mackay, E.A. G. (Graham) 373
MacKay, Harold H. 450
Mackay, Allan Allan Douglas Mackay 488
MacKenzie, John 35
Mackenzie, Amanda 47
Mackenzie, Andrew 87
Mackenzie, Andrew 88
Mackenzie, Andrew 116
Macker, Marielle de 352
Mackie, Jane 465
MacLaurin, Lord Ian C. 199
MacLeod, Robert 245
MacNicholas, Garry 193
Macpherson, Nina 166
MacSween, Mike 423
MacWillson, Alastair 7
Maddox, Paul 330
Madridejos, Ignacio 114
Maeda, Masaya 106
Maeda, Masaya 106
Maeda, Yasunori 224
Maeda, Yasunori 225
Maeda, Kiyoshi 314
Maeda, Yoshihiro 452
Maeji, Nobuyoshi 12
Maekawa, Osamu Osamu Maekawa 452
Maekawa, Masamoto 455
Maekawa, Masamoto 455
Maerki, Hans 5
Maesako, Shizumi 70
Maeseneire, Baron Patrick G. De 11
Maestri, Adriano 234
Maeyama, Tadashige 194
Maeyama, Tadashige 194
Maffe, France 302
Magano, Basetsana 330
Maganov, Ravil U. 329
Maganov, Ravil U. 329
Magner, Marjorie (Marge) 8
Magnus, George C. 219
Magnus, Birger 415
Magnusson, Bjorn 203
Magnusson, Bo 399
Magrath, Duncan 53
Magro, Charles V. (Chuck) 18
Magyer, Denise 29
Mahajan, Anand 131
Maher, Peter J. 273
Maher, Grahame 475
Maheshwari, Sudhir 39
Mahindra, Anand G. 387
Mahlan, Dierdre A. 156
Mahlan, Dierdre A. 156
Mahon, Paul A. 193
Mahoney, A. M. 218
Mahoney, Tony 218
Mahr, Wolfgang 113
Mahy, Helen M. 304
Mahy, Helen M. 305
Maia, Paulo 216
Maia, Paulo 218
Maidique, Modesto A. 107
Maidment, Karen E. 450
Maier, Gerhard 384
Mainardi-Rosenthal, Helen 432
Maitland, Alister Alister Maitland 275
Maizey, Silla 233
Majima, Nobuaki 358
Maki, Shinsuke 34
Makino, Fujiatsu 291
Makino, Masashi 338
Makridis, Alexandros 303
Malach, Itzhak 63
Malanga, J. D. 245
Malavez, Patricia 468
Malchuk, Daniel 87
Malchuk, Daniel 88
MalchukBE, Daniel 88
Maldonado, Bill 218
Malek, Philip G. (Phil) 422
Malik, Asif 24
Malik, Yogesh 435
Malkiel, Shahar 63
Mallac, David 373
Malliet, Dan 396
Mallinckrodt, Thomas von 429
Mallon, Mark 44
Mallon, Gerry 147
Maloney, Bill 414
Malungani, Mangalani 235
Mamillapalle, Venkatram 430
Manabe, Hiroshi 311
Manaf, Nora Nora Abd Manaf 275
Mancho, Javier de Paz 434
Manchot, Thomas 202
Mandelid, Glenn 435
Mandeng, Mathieu 412
Mandersson, Magnus 166
Mandil, Claude 453
Manduca, Paul 348
Mang, Thomas 263
Mangalaseril, Jasmine 278
Manger, Richard 157
Mangiagalli, Marco 234
Mangiagalli, Marco 376
Manglik, Harsh 7
Mangold, Klaus J. 31
Mangold, Klaus 136
Mangold, Klaus J. 286
Mangoni, Andrea 432
Manley, John P. 104
Manley, Patrick 492
Mann, Lindsay 130
Mann, Trevor 316
Mann, Peter 330
Mann, Jim 458

Mannekens, Henk 100
Manning, Sir David G. 85
Manning, Andre 257
Manning, Robert J. (Rob) 422
Manos, Alexandros S. 343
Manos, Alexandros S. 343
Manser, John 373
Manser, John 373
Manso, Joao 161
Mantakas, Georgios 343
Mantega, Guido 340
Manti?an, Jose Manuel Loureda 356
Mantilla, Luis Suarez de Lezo 356
Mantilla, Luis 356
Mantilla, Luis Suarez de Lezo 356
Mantovani, Massimo 163
Manwani, Harish 464
Manwani, Harish 465
Many, Prof Moshe 441
Many, Prof Moshe 441
Manzoni, John A. 373
Manzoni, Federico 466
Manzotti, Maurizio 234
Maouche, Marc 333
Maramotti, Luigi 463
Marbach, Alain 89
Marced, Maria 429
Marcel, Vincent 469
March, Bruce H. 225
March, Bruce H. 225
Marchal, Marie-Jeanne 407
Marchant, Ian 410
Marchesini, Gianni 234
Marchetti, Stefano 234
Marchioni, Paolo 163
Marchionne, Sergio 172
Marchis, Ranieri 463
Marcinowski, Stefan 76
Marco, Rafael 185
Marco, Rafael Villaseca 185
Marcondes, Sandro Kohler 468
Marcote, Flora Perez 228
Marcoux, Isabelle 345
Marcoux, Isabelle 483
Mardrus, Christian 355
Mareuse, Olivier Olivier Mareuse 471
Marey-Semper, Isabel 318
Margerie, Christophe de 453
Margerie, Christophe de 453
Margerie, Christophe Christophe de Margerie 474
Margerie, Christophe de 474
Margevich, Robert (Bob) 24
Margolian, Beverly S. 278
Mari?o, Jose Luis Vazquez 228
Maridet, Pascal 127
Marien, Philippe 31
Marien, Philippe 93
Marien, Philippe 127
Marin, Javier 60
Marino, Ricardo Villela 237
Markelov, Vitaly 188
Markham, Rudy H. P. 44
Markham, Rudy H. P. 265
Markham, Rudy H. P. 412
Marki, Hans Ulrich 5
Markland, Ruth 412
Markov, Vladimir 188
Marks, Alison 302
Marks, Adam 443
Marmugi, Alain 469
Maro, Hideharu 448
Marocco, Antonio M. 463
Marri, Alberto 54
Marrodan, Carlos 185
Marrone, Virgilio 172
Marroquin, Paulina Garza de 177
Marsden, Lorna R. 278
Marshall, Steven (Steve) 53
Marshall, Graham 329
Marshall, Roger 330
Martello, Wan Ling 309
Martensson, Cecilia Cecilia Martensson 399
Martin, Brad 84
Martin, Fiona 87
Martin, Andrew 134
Martin, Andrew 134
Martin, John 316
Martin, Miguel Martinez San 356
Martin, Miguel 356
Martin, Rosemary 475
Martin, John 486
Martin, John 486
Martin-Lof, Sverker 166
Martin-Lof, Sverker 166
Martin-Lof, Sverker 425
Martineau, Francois 49
Martinelli, Mark 218
Martinelli, Maurizio 469
Martinez, Maria del Carmen Becerril 162
Martinez, Jose 185
Martinez, Jose Luis Olivas 223
Martinez, Jose Manuel Martinez 279
Martinez-Lage, Santiago 223
Martiniere, Gerard de La 261
Martiniere, Gerard de La 387
Martins, Tito Botelho 468
Martins, Jose Carlos 468
Martirez, George 275
Martre, Henri 333
Martrenchar, Yves 90
Marulanda, Camilo 160
Marumoto, Akira 283
Marumoto, Akira 283
Maruta, Hideto 405
Maruyama, Kenji 34
Maruyama, Yoshinori 34
Maruyama, Haruya 149
Maruyama, Takao 307
Marwah, Sarabjit S. (Sabi) 69
Marwah, Sarabjit S. (Sabi) 69
Marzano, Stefano 3
Masachs, Enric 57
Masaki, Hideto 141
Masaki, Hideto 141
Masaki, Toshio 452
Mascher, Christof 28
Mascolo, Lisa M. 7
Maseda, Miguel 185
Masegi, Mitsuhiko 149
Mashaal, Jacob 63
Mashelkar, Raghunath Anant 353
Mashelkar, Ramesh A. 430
Maslyaev, Ivan 329
Maso, Philippe 47
Mason, Peter 33
Mason, Sir Peter J. 51
Mason, Stephen 66
Mason, Barbara F. (Barb) 69
Mason, Graham 348
Mason, Tim J. R. 440
Mason, Tim J. R. 440
Masperi, Valeriana 54
Masrani, Bharat B. 450
Masschelin, Paul J. 225
Massiah, Victor 466
Massow, Joachim von 482
Masters, Trevor 440
Masui, Keiji 455
Masuko, Osamu 292
Masuko, Osamu 293
Masumoto, Ryuhei 224
Masumoto, Katsutada 455
Masunaga, Mikio 96
Masunaga, Mikio 97
Masunaga, Shinichiro 141
Masur, Joachim 492
Masurel, Jean-Louis 342
Mateen, Akhter 465
Mather, Richard 373
Mathers, David 139
Matheu, Bruno 19
Mathews, Tomy 86
Mathews, Ben 360
Mathieu, Michel 443
Mathur, S. P. 85
Mathur, S. K. 86
Matic, Matthias 136
Matos, Jose Agostinho Martins de 103
Matsaira, Washington 411
Matschi, Helmut 135
Matsuba, Naoki 320
Matsubara, Nobuko 296
Matsubayashi, Kenichi 358
Matsuda, Yuji 215
Matsuda, Sakugoro 224
Matsuda, Yuzuru 252
Matsuda, Yoshihiko 455
Matsudaira, Soichiro 456
Matsui, Kenichi 224
Matsui, Kenichi 224
Matsui, Shunichi 289
Matsui, Nobusuke 311
Matsui, Hiroshi 326
Matsui, Hiroshi 327
Matsui, Takuo 455
Matsuki, Yukio 405
Matsumoto, Milton 56
Matsumoto, Shigeyuki 106
Matsumoto, Shigeyuki 106
Matsumoto, Tango Tango Matsumoto 184
Matsumoto, Yoshiyuki 214
Matsumoto, Yoshihisa 224
Matsumoto, Junichi 295
Matsumoto, Junichi 296
Matsumoto, Ryu 388
Matsumoto, Masafumi 390
Matsumoto, Oki 392
Matsumoto, Jun 405
Matsumoto, Masayoshi 419
Matsumoto, Masayoshi 419
Matsumoto, Tamiji 427
Matsumoto, Tamiji 427
Matsumura, Hideto 137
Matsumura, Hideto 137
Matsumura, Yukihiko 282
Matsuno, Junichi 358
Matsuo, Yasuhiro Yasuhiro Matsuo 253
Matsuo, Kenji 402
Matsuo, Kunihiro 455
Matsushige, Hiroshi 206
Matsushima, Tohru 238
Matsushita, Kazuya 293
Matsushita, Masayuki 338
Matsushita, Masayuki 338
Matsuura, Yoshimasa 358
Matsuura, Yohzoh 358
Matsuura, Yoshimasa 358
Matsuura, Yasuo 393
Matsuyama, Akihiro 291
Matsuyama, Yasuomi 311
Matsuyama, Yasuomi 311
Matthewes, Manfred 482
Matthews, Trevor J. 47
Matthews, Trevor J. 47
Matthews, Colin 245
Matthews, Paul 413
Matts, Mikael Mikael Matts 401
Matuschka, Nikolaus Nikolaus Graf von Matuschka 21
Matytsyn, Alexander K. 329
Maubach, Klaus-Dieter 159
Maughan, Sir Deryck 192
Maurange, Jean-Luc 39
Mauro, Prof Beatrice Weder di 164
Mauro, Prof Beatrice Weder di 362
Mauro, Prof Beatrice Weder di 445
Mauro, Beatrice 461
Maury, Pascal 90
Maxsted, Lindsay 87
Maxsted, Lindsay P. 484
May, Jonathan 47
May, Catherine 373
Mayberry, John T. 69
Mayer, Igal 47
Mayer, Jeffrey (Jeff) 461
Mayhew, George 304
Maynard, Roger P. 233
Mayrhuber, Wolfgang 81
Mayrhuber, Wolfgang 300
Mayrhuber, Wolfgang 461
Maystadt, Philippe 170
Mazankowski, Rt. Hon. Donald F. (Don) 193
Mazankowski, Rt. Hon. Donald F. (Don) 345
Mazankowski, Rt. Hon. Donald F. (Don) 346
Mazarakis, Babis 303
Mazuka, Michiyoshi 183
Mazur, Ilan 62
Mazzilli, Roberto Roberto Mazzilli 432
Mazzoleni, Mario 466
Mazzoleni, Mario 466
Mazzuchelli, Marco 368
Mbazima, Norman B. 35
McAdam, John D. G. 240
McAdam, John D. G. 365
McAllister, David 477
McAloon, Jane F. 87
McAloon, Jane F. 87
McAloon, Jane F. 88
McBride, Geraldine 384
McCain, Michael H. 366
McCann, James 255
McCann, H. Kevin 273
McCann, Robert J. (Bob) 461
McCarthy, Tony 233
McCaughey, Gerald T. (Gerry) 104
McCaughey, Gerald T. (Gerry) 104
McCaw, Maureen 423
McCormick, John 368
McCracken, Dax P. 461
McCrae, Neil 44
McCrone, Stewart 257
McCue, Thomas A. (Tom) 39
McCullough, A. J. 245
McCure, Matt 27
McDermott, William R. (Bill) 384
McDonagh, Baroness Margaret J. 413
McDonald, Andrew 25
McDonald, Stephen D. (Steve) 69
Mcdonald, Zsoka 156
McDonough, Peter 156
McDowell, Mary T. 318
McEwan, Ross 130
McEwan, Ross 368
McFarlane, John 47
McFarlane, John 47
McFarlane, John 368
McFeetors, Raymond L. 193
McFeetors, Raymond L. 345
McFeetors, Raymond L. 345
McFeetors, Raymond L. 346
McFeetors, Raymond L. 346
McGarvie, Blythe J. 8
McGee, Hugh E. (Skip) 72
McGee, Hugh E. (Skip) 74
McGivney, Tom 66
McGovern, Patrick F. 9
McGowan, David 66
McGowan, Nicola 413
McGrath, Mark G. 255
McGregor, G. L. 245
McGregor, A. Douglas (Doug) 366
McGuckin, Sean 69
McGuinness, Patrick 217
McIlwee, Laurie 440
McIlwee, Laurie 440
McInally, Jim 100
McInerney, Thomas J. (Tom) 231
McInnes, Ross 375
McInnis-Day, Brigette 384
McIntosh, Nayna 280
McIntyre, John 368
McKay, H. Lamar 95
McKay, David I. (Dave) 366
McKenna, Frank J. 450
McKenna, Frank J. 450
McKenzie, Kimberlee B. (Kim) 69
McKenzie, Kate 438
McKillip, Bob 368
McKinlay, Pamela (Pam) 323
McKinstry, Nancy 166
McLachlan, Bruce 484
McLaren, John 24
McLaren, George 364

McLaughlin, M. 273
McLaughlin, Joe 311
McLaughlin, Andrew 368
McLAUGHLIN, Eileen 474
McLellan, A. Anne 18
McLenaghan, Vince 350
McLeod, Ian 480
McLintock, Michael G.A. 348
McIlwee, Laurie 440
McLoughlin, Keith R. 3
McLoughlin, Keith R. 3
McLoughlin, Liam 66
McMahon, Greg 298
McMillan, David 47
McNally, Michael (Mike) 400
McNamara, Michael M. (Mike) 176
McNamara, Michael M. (Mike) 176
McNamara, Mike 440
McNaughton, Andrew 53
McPhedran, James 69
McPhee, Sarah 415
McPherson, Bill 24
McQuay, Michael 91
McRitchie, Alec 91
McStravick, Gregory (Greg) 384
Mead, Andy 304
Meadows, Rick 107
Meadows, Richard D. (Rick) 107
Meadows, Paul 480
Meakins, Ian K. 116
Meakins, Ian K. 486
Meakins, Ian K. 486
Medda, Ettore 466
Meddings, Richard H. 411
Meddings, Richard H. 412
Meder, Dietmar 144
Medina, Dionisio Garza 114
Medina, Dionisio 114
Medina, Amilkar Acosta 160
Medini, Paul B. 9
Medniuk, Tony 300
Medori, Rene 35
Medori, Rene 410
Medvedev, Alexander I. 187
Medvedev, Aleksandr 188
Meehan, Steven 461
Mehdorn, Hartmut 384
Meheut, Bertrand 474
Mehlman, Guillaume 31
Mehra, R. K. 85
Mehta, Tarak 5
Mehta, Aman 231
Meier, Hans-bernd Hans-bernd Meier 384
Meier, Andre 491
Meignie, Yves 472
Meijden, Erik van der 256
Meijer, Gert 464
Meiklejohn, David E. 46
Meine, Hartmut 136
Meine, Hartmut 477
Meinecke, Ulrich 335
Meirvenne, Dirk Van 78
Meissner, Martin 489
Meister, Edgar 128
Meister, Hans-Ulrich 139
Mekawi, Hesham 95
Melaniuk, Michal 401
Melgaard, Dag 435
Meli, Salvatore 163
Mellbye, Peter 414
Meller, Craig 33
Mello, Vasco M. G. Jose de 161
Mellor, Amanda 280
Mellor, Amanda 280
Meloni, Vittorio 234
Memis, Adnan 459
Menanteau, Jean-Pierre 47
Mendelson, Avner 63
Mendez, Fernando 9
Mendiola, Cristina Sanz 356
Mendiola, Cristina 356
Mendoza, Estelito P. 379
Menendez, Manuel Menendez 161
Menezes, Alfredo A. Lima de 56
Menezes, Alfredo 57
Menezes, Ivan M. 155
Menges, Kathrin 202
Menikoff, Peter 9
Menten, Eric de 453
Meo, Francesco De 179
Meo, Francesco 179
Merchan, Juan 9
Merck, Johannes 335
Merckle, Ludwig 197
Merckle, Tobias 197
Mered, Saad 491
Mergin, Murat 459
Merican, Mohamed 275
Merin, Mitchell M. (Mitch) 422
Merizzi, Robert 47
Merkamp, Christine 371
Merkamp, Christine 371
Meroi, Stefano 41
Merten, Alan 278
Mervis, Ari 373
Merz, Albrecht 157
Mesland, Jean-Michel 407
Messina, Carlo 234
Mestrallet, Gerard 131
Mestrallet, Gerard 189
Meswani, Hital R. 353
Meswani, Nikhil R. 353
Meswani, Hital R. 353
Meswani, Nikhil R. 353
Mettling, Bruno 333
Meulder, Jan 54
Meunier, Jean-Luc 26
Meux, Bruno Bernard Marie Joseph de Laage de 58
Meux, Bruno Bernard Marie Joseph de Laage de 58
Mexia, Antonio 161
Meyer, Frank 12
Meyer, Michael 153
Meyer, Lothar 164
Meyer, Armin 492
Meyers, Jean-Pierre 309
Meyrick, Lee 491
Meysel, Frank 263
Meziane, Mohamed 161
Mezquiriz, Juan Carlos Alvarez 56
Miao, Jianhua 122
Miao, Jianhua 122
Miau, Matthew F. C. 268
Micciche, Gaetano 432
Micciche, Gaetano Gaetano Micciche 432
Michael, Gavin 8
Michael, DeNoma 139
Michaelis, Alain 364
Michaud, Anik 35
Michel, Jacques 127
Michel, Gilles 333
Michel, Serge 471
Michelin, Pierre 133
Michels, Sir David M. C. 280
Michels, Sir David M. C. 280
Middelmann, Prof Ulrich 154
Middlemann, Prof Ulrich 128
Midunsky, Karl H. 195
Midura, Jennifer 24
Miele, Markus 164
Migliardi, Antonio 432
Mignonat, Eric 407
Miguel, Josu 356
Miguelsanz, Luis Nogueira 10
Mikhailov, Sergei 329
Mikhailova, Elena 188
Mikhaylova, Elena 188
Miki, Shigemitsu 291
Miki, Shohei 311
Mikkelsen, B?rd 159
Mikoshiba, Toshiaki 215
Milano, Enrico 234
Milberg, Joachim 80
Milberg, Joachim 84
Milberg, Joachim 384
Milberg, Joachim 490
Milde, Johannes 395
Milette, Nicolas 302
Milis, Ilias D. 343
Milis, Ilias D. 344
Miller, Eric 18
Miller, Serge 39
Miller, Alexey B. 186
Miller, Alexey B. 187
Miller, Aleksey 188
Miller, Alexey B. 188
Miller, Klaus 195
Miller, Irene R. 228
Miller, David 235
Miller, Thomas (Tom) 395
Miller, Timothy J. (Tim) 411
Miller, Irene R. 450
Millet, Jose M. Mas 59
Millett, Simon J. 411
Millian, John R. (Randy) 156
Milliken, Paul 370
Milliner, Mark 423
Millman, Chris 100
Milloy, Robert 100
Mills, Christina 360
Min, Jung Kee 391
Minakawa, Kunihito 358
Minami, Nobuya 141
Minami, Naohiro 241
Minardi, Eduardo 96
Minas, Mauricio 57
Minato, Yoshihiro 419
Mincato, Vittorio 172
Minekawa, Sho 214
Minekawa, Sho 215
Minemura, Ryuji 141
Mineno, Toshiyuki 306
Mineno, Toshiyuki 307
Ming, Wong Wai 122
Ming, Timpson Chung Shui 122
Mingchao, Gu 65
Mingchun, Zhou 339
Mingot, Antoni 185
Minnick, Mary E. 199
Minoru, Shimizu 96
Minowa, Nobuyuki 456
Minster, Jean-Francois 453
Minto, Jim 141
Mintz, Yoel 63
Mintz, J. M. (Jack) 225
Minucci, William R. 422
Minucci, Aldo 432
Minzberg, Samuel (Sam) 216
Miquel, Maria Isabel Gabarro 356
Miranda, Pedro 396
Mirtillo, Nunzio 166
Misailidis, Christos 12
Misra, Prof Ashok 353
Misra, Kabir 404
Missier, Jerry del 72
Missier, Jerry del 74
Mistry, Keki M. 196
Mistry, Cyrus P. 430
Mita, Daiju 289
Mitarai, Fujio 105
Mitarai, Naoki 208
Mitchell, Jessica 95
Mitchell, Dave 100
Mitchell-Keller, Lori 384
Mitchelmore, Lorraine 370
Mitchelson, Mark 403
Mitra, N. K. 328
Mitra, N. K. 328
Mitridati, Christophe 127
Mitsuda, Minoru 283
Mitsuhashi, Yasuo 105
Mitsuhashi, Yasuo 106
Mitsui, Seiji 448
Mitsuya, Makoto 22
Mitsuya, Makoto 22
Mitsuzaki, Chikao 236
Mitsuzaki, Chikao 236
Mitsuzuka, Tetsuji 211
Mittag, Andrew K. 18
Mittal, Lakshmi N. 21
Mittal, Lakshmi N. 39
Mittal, Aditya 39
Mittal, Lakshmi N. 224
Mittal, Sunil Bharti 465
Mittal, Sunil 465
Mittal, Sunil Sunil Mittal 465
Mittelholzer, Leo 212
Mittendorfer, Gernot 167
Miura, Satoru 295
Miura, Satoshi 314
Miura, Satoshi 314
Miura, Eiji 320
Miura, Zenji 358
Miura, Zenji 358
Miura, Kenji 455
Miwa, Akihisa 328
Miwa, Akihisa 328
Miyabe, Yoshiyuki 338
Miyahara, Ichiro 289
Miyahara, Kenji 307
Miyajima, Hiroshi 446
Miyakawa, Akira 388
Miyake, Senji 252
Miyake, Senji 252
Miyaki, Masahiko 149
Miyamoto, Yutaka 22
Miyamoto, Yutaka 22
Miyamoto, Satoshi 137
Miyamoto, Satoshi 137
Miyamoto, Michiko 142
Miyamoto, Ikuo 338
Miyanaga, Masato 124
Miyasaka, Akihiro 312
Miyashita, Hisato 320
Miyashita, Tsugie 408
Miyata, Koichi 420
Miyato, Naoteru 427
Miyauchi, Takahisa 289
Miyauchi, Yoshihiko 334
Miyauchi, Ken 404
Miyauchi, Ken 404
Miyauchi, Yoshihiko 405
Miyauchi, Kazuhiro 455
Miyawaki, Motohisa 180
Miyazaki, Hideki 241
Miyazaki, Naoki 455
Miyoshi, Takashi 208
Miyoshi, Takashi 208
Mizobuchi, Hiroaki 417
Mizui, Satoshi 405
Mizumoto, Yoshiaki 282
Mizusawa, Nobutoshi 106
Mizushima, Toshiyuki 22
Mizushima, Toshiyuki 22
Mizushima, Shigeaki 390
Mizutani, Haruki 236
Mizutani, Haruki 236
Mkhwanazi, Xolani 88
Mobius, Mark 329
Mocatta, William E. 219
Mochida, Nobuo 208
Mochizuki, Atsushi 70
Mochizuki, Atsushi 70
Mochizuki, Eiji 424
Modak, Afzal M. 459
Modi, Mahesh P. 353
Modruson, Frank B. 8
Moe, Marianne 435
Moenius, Werner 396
Moerch, Lars Lars Moerch 147
Mogami, Yoshihiko 208
Moghrabi, Jeff 9
Mogi, Yoshio 405
Mogren, H?kan 145
Mohamed, Datuk Syed Tamin Syed 275
Mohamed, Nadir H. 450
Mohan, S. 85
Mohl, Andrew M. 130
Mohn, Liz 83
Mohn, Christoph 84
Mohn, Liz 84
Mohn, Brigitte 84
Mohr, Peter 263
Molenaar, Rob 24
Molho, David 131
Molina, Federico Maya 160
Molinaro, Sam 461

Molinillo, Jose Luis Lopez 10
Molins, Casimiro 59
Moll, Magdalena 76
Moller, Arnold 2
Moller, Leise Maersk Mc-Kinney 2
Molleron, Henri 127
Molloy, Patrick J. 66
Molnar, Jozsef 297
Moltrasio, Andrea 466
Molyneux, Paul Paul Molyneux 390
Molyneux, Phil 409
Momoi, Katsushi 253
Monavon, Michele 375
Monceau, Evelyn du 407
Mond, Oliver van der 371
Mondal, Pralay 196
Mondazzi, Massimo 163
Mondlane, Eduardo C. 71
Mong, William M. W. 65
Mong-Koo, Chung 222
Mong-Koo, Chung 249
Mongin, Pierre 189
Monius, Werner 396
Monnas, Giovanna Kampouri 353
Montag, Bernd 395
Montague, Sir Adrian A. 401
Montalbano, John S. 366
Montanari, Fioravante 54
Monteiro, Manuel 161
Monteiro, Manuel F. de Macedo Alves 161
Monteith, Stuart 422
Montero, Rodolfo 212
Monteros, Carlos Espinosa de los 228
Montezemolo, Luca 463
Montouche, Thierry 127
Montoya, Pedro 21
Montuenga, Luis 59
Monty, Jean C. 25
Monty, Jean C. 91
Moody-Stuart, Sir Mark 8
Mookim, Rakesh 224
Moore, Nicholas W. 273
Moore, Nicholas W. 273
Moore, Lori 325
Moore, Martin R. 348
Moore, Niel Niel Moore 401
Moore, Clint 479
Moosmayer, Klaus 396
Mor, Nachiket 224
Mora, Ramon Bustamante y de la 55
Mora, Ramon 56
Mora, Hanne de 381
Mora, Hanne 381
Mora, Hanne de 479
Morad, Osman 411
Moraes, Pedro Luiz Bodin de 237
Moraes, Marcus Vinicius Pratini de 243
Morais, Jorge M. Pragana da Cruz 161
Morales, Ramiro 114
Morales, Petra Mateos-Aparicio 407
Morales, Petra 407
Morano, Hernan 401
Moranville, Guy de Selliers de 407
Moranville, Guy 407
Mordechay, Sasson 63
Moreau, Nicolas 49
Moreira, Prof Vital M. 161
Morel, Hugo 462
Morelli, Marco 234
Moreno, Vicente 8
Moreno, Pablo 57
Moreno, Hector 57
Moreno, Joaquin 160
Moreno, Sergio 185
Moreno-Barreda, Jose Fernando de Almansa 434
Moretto, Riccardo 492
Morgan, Flemming 145
Morgan, Andrew 155
Morgan, Gwyn 218
Morgan, Peter 364
Morgan, Jennifer 384
Morgenroth, Matthew J. 485
Mori, Yoshiki 15
Mori, Yoshiki 16
Mori, Yoshiki 16
Mori, Yoshiki 16
Mori, Shosuke 34
Mori, Shigeru 141
Mori, Ikuo 180
Mori, Takashi 183
Mori, Ryosuke 184
Mori, Kazuhiro 208
Mori, Kazuyuki 289
Mori, Takahiro 338
Mori, Yasutomo 358
Mori, Masayuki Masayuki Mori 390
Morikawa, Keizo 137
Morikawa, Keizo 137
Morikawa, Toshio 307
Morillo, Manuel 59
Morimoto, Mitsuo 34
Morimoto, Mitsuo 34
Morimoto, Yoshiyuki 96
Morimoto, Masao 117
Morimoto, Hiroshi 390
Morimoto, Yoshihisa 447
Morin, Isabelle 345
Morin, Isabelle 346
Morin-Postel, Christine 98
Morin-Postel, Christine 370
Morino, Tetsuji 140
Morino, Tetsuji 141
Morishita, Yoichi 455
Morita, Takashi 22
Morita, Takashi 22
Morita, Takayuki 306
Morita, Toshio 320
Morita, Ken 338
Morita, Masao 408
Morita, Tomijirou 447
Moritani, Mamoru 419
Moritz, Peter 396
Moriyama, Toru 289
Moriyama, Takahiro 417
Moriyasu, Masaharu 291
Moriyasu, Isao 327
Morland, Miles 373
Morlion, Lode 248
Mornhinweg, Volker 144
Moro, Masahiro 283
Morrin, Noel 401
Morris, Clive 44
Morris, Peter 66
Morris, Mark 364
Morris, Doug 409
Morris, Simon 411
Morris, Jonathan 412
Morris, Doug 461
Morrison, Briggs 44
Morschel, John P. 46
Morsiani, Gian Guido Sacchi 234
Morton, Paul 74
Morttinen, Leena 321
Morvan, Yves Alain Marie 168
Morzaria, Tushar 72
Morzaria, Tushar 74
Mosch, Peter 477
Mosconi, Jean-Jacques 453
Moser, Michael 352
Moses, Marc 217
Moses, Alan C. 325
Moskalenko, Anatoly 329
Mosonyi, Gyorgy 297
Mosonyi, Gyorgy 297
Moss, Andrew 47
Moss, Andrew 47
Mota, Antonio 161
Motobayashi, Tohru 208
Motohashi, Isaku 96
Motoki, Jun 236
Motta, Roberto Moses Thompson 37
Motton, Tania 46
Mougin, Franck 472
Mourer, Anne-Marie 189
Mouri, Takashige 307
Mouri, Satoru 455
Mousten, Niels-Ulrik 147
Moya, Valentin Montoya 162
Moynihan, James J. (Jim) 53
Moyo, Dambisa 72
Moyo, Dambisa 74
Moyo, Dambisa 373
Mperitsi, Ekaterini 343
Mu?oz, Manuel Alvarez 10
Mu?oz, David Ibarra 32
Muehlenfeld, Dagmar 371
Muehlenfeld, Dagmar 371
Mueller, Michael 54
Mueller, Klaus-Peter 179
Mueller, Otto 195
Mueller, Martin K. 263
Mueller, Silvia Silvia Mueller 300
Mueller, Stefan 355
Muguiro, Jaime 114
Muhlenfeld, Dagmar 371
Muina, Tomas 57
Muir, Ian 98
Muir, Shelagh 465
Mukai, Kazushi Kazushi Mukai 390
Mukawa, Tatsuhiko 180
Mukherjee, Bhaswar 205
Muko, Hiroaki 224
Mukohara, Kiyoshi 421
Mukrasch, Uwe 151
Mulhern, Carmel 438
Mulholland, Anna 35
Mulholland, Robert E. (Bob) 461
Mull, Jeffrey C. 461
Mullen, John P. 438
Muller, Alois 54
Muller, Klaus-Peter 128
Muller, Jochen 151
Muller, Frans W.H. 169
Muller, Klaus-Peter 179
Muller, Eberhard 195
Muller, Otto 195
Muller, Tina 202
Muller, Klaus-Peter 268
Muller, Frans W.H. 286
Muller, Silvia 300
Muller, Otto 430
Muller, Wilfried 462
Muller-Kirschbaum, Thomas 202
Muller-Mohl, Carolina 309
Mulliez, Christian 383
Mullin, Leo F. 9
Mullin, Mark W. 14
Multon, Herve 443
Mulvey, Vincent 66
Mulvihill, Patrick 66
Mulyak, Vladimir 329
Munday, Trevor S. 71
Mundul, Sujit 411
Muneoka, Shoji 312
Muneoka, Shoji 312
Muneyuki, Mitsuo 291
Munhoz, Jose Alcides 56
Munjee, Nasser M. 430
Munoz, Fernando 57
Munoz, Jose 316
Munro, Joanna 217
Munro, Bruce 301
Munro, Sean 366
Munroe-Blum, Heather E. L. 366
Mupita, Ralph 330
Murai, Shouhei 16
Murai, Shouhei 16
Murai, Takayuki 311
Murai, Jun 404
Murakami, Noriyuki 15
Murakami, Noriyuki 16
Murakami, Shinichi 241
Murakami, Motonori 295
Murakami, Hideto 316
Murali, K. 205
Muramatsu, Tetsuro Tetsuro Muramatsu 390
Muramoto, Morihiro 141
Muramoto, Shuzo 293
Muraoka, Shigeo 405
Muraoka, Fumio 451
Muraoka, Fumio 452
Murata, Noritoshi 388
Murata, Minoru 456
Murayama, Hiroyuki 149
Murayama, Hiroyoshi 291
Murayama, Hisao 358
Murdoch, James R. 192
Murdy, Wayne W. 87
Murdy, Wayne W. 88
Murofushi, Kimiko 97
Muromachi, Masashi 452
Murphy, John 66
Murphy, Senan 66
Murphy, Gerard 98
Murray, Duncan 53
Murray, Declan 66
Murray, Susan E. 134
Murray, Robert J. 169
Murray, Alan 197
Murray, Susan E. 227
Murray, Martin C. 330
Murray, James I. K. 486
Murrer, B. A. 245
Murthy, N. R. Narayana 218
Musin, Valery A. 188
Mussari, Giuseppe 49
Mustier, Jean-Pierre 463
Musumeci, Salvatore Toti 466
Muta, Hirofumi 455
Muto, Naoto 180
Muto, Toshiro 296
Muto, Sakae 447
Mutoh, Jun 448
Mutoh, Jun 448
Mutz, Pierre 443
Myklebust, Egil 381
Mylonas, Paul 303
Mylonas, Theordoros P. 344
Myochin, Toru 392
Myrmel-Johansen, Elin M. 415

N

Nabeshima, Hideyuki 289
Nabeshima, Hideyuki 290
Nabiullina, Elvira 188
Nachbar, Moacir 57
Nackstad, Caj 380
Nadeau, Bertin F. 422
Naert, Philippe 248
Nagae, Shusaku 338
Nagahama, Morinobu 141
Nagai, Takashi 215
Nagai, Katsumasa 236
Nagai, Katsumasa 236
Nagai, Yasuo 289
Nagai, Yasuo 290
Nagai, Noriaki 320
Nagai, Koji 320
Nagamatsu, Shoichi 320
Nagamatsu, Soichi 320
Nagamatsu, Shoichi 358
Nagano, Yoshiaki 141
Nagano, Hisashi 180
Nagano, Tsuyoshi 446
Nagao, Kimitsugu 1
Nagao, Kimitsugu 1
Nagarajan, Sridhar 412
Nagasawa, Kenichi 106
Nagase, Shin 34
Nagase, Shin 34
Nagata, Ryoko 241
Nagata, Kiyohito 326
Nagata, Osamu 455
Nagato, Masatsugu 180
Nagato, Masatsugu 180
Nagayama, Yoshiaki 1
Nagayama, Yoshiaki 1
Nagayama, Atsushi 141
Nagayama, Osamu 362
Nagayasu, Yojiro 67
Nagayasu, Katsunori 294
Nagayasu, Katsunori 294
Nagel, Alberto N. 41
Nagel, Alberto N. 41
Nagel, Thomas 151

Nagel, Wilfred F. 231
Nagel, Alberto N. 284
Nager, Lorenz 197
Naggan, Zvi 62
Nagle, Carl 9
Nagura, Toshikazu 22
Nagura, Toshikazu 22
Nahmias, Jacques-Alexandre 145
Naidoo, N. Alfie 71
Naito, Yoshihiro 447
Nakae, Gosuke 289
Nakae, Yasuyuki 307
Nakae, Kiyohiko 416
Nakagaki, Keiichi 289
Nakagawa, Hideki 289
Nakagawa, Junko 320
Nakagawa, Yutaka 408
Nakagome, Kenji 427
Nakagome, Kenji 427
Nakahara, Hideto 289
Nakahara, Hideto 290
Nakai, Tsuyoshi Tsuyoshi Nakai 180
Nakajima, Shigehiro 182
Nakajima, Junzo 208
Nakajima, Shigeki 224
Nakajima, Hajime 252
Nakajima, Kazuhiko 405
Nakamae, Koji 357
Nakamine, Yuji 283
Nakamura, Shunichi 22
Nakamura, Ryuji 22
Nakamura, Shunichi 22
Nakamura, Katsumi 34
Nakamura, Akihiko 34
Nakamura, Hisayoshi 67
Nakamura, Hisayoshi 67
Nakamura, Toyoaki 208
Nakamura, Ichiro 238
Nakamura, Tsuyoshi 291
Nakamura, Yoshikazu 293
Nakamura, Koji 295
Nakamura, Kimiyasu 316
Nakamura, Toshiyuki 316
Nakamura, Shiro 316
Nakamura, Katsuhiro 326
Nakamura, Katsuhiro 327
Nakamura, Yuji 328
Nakamura, Kunio 338
Nakamura, Kunio 338
Nakamura, Katsumi 354
Nakamura, Masahiro 358
Nakamura, Takashi 358
Nakamura, Yukio 392
Nakamura, Yukio 392
Nakamura, Akihiro 393
Nakamura, Moritaka 393
Nakamura, Akihiro 393
Nakamura, Makoto 417
Nakamura, Kuniharu 417
Nakamura, Masaru 417
Nakamura, Kuniharu 417
Nakanishi, Hiroaki 208
Nakanishi, Hiroaki 208
Nakanishi, Yasuyuki 291
Nakanishi, Akinori 292
Nakanishi, Katsunori 393
Nakanishi, Satoru 420
Nakanishi, Satoru 420
Nakanishi, Shinzo 424
Nakano, Takashi 211
Nakano, Kazuhisa 224
Nakano, Kazuhisa 224
Nakano, Masafumi 283
Nakano, Takahiro 419
Nakao, Ryugo 293
Nakao, Ryugo 293
Nakaoka, Masaki 106
Nakaoka, Masaki 106
Nakashima, Toshihiro 311
Nakata, Yuji 320
Nakatani, Yoshiaki 291
Nakatsugawa, Masaki 455
Nakayama, Hiroshi 208
Nakayama, Haruhide 326
Nakayama, Fujikazu 390
Nakayama, Jun 456
Nakhata, Yaowadee 61
Nakura, Shuji 295
Nam, Sung-Il 222
Nam, Dae-Woo 397
Nam-Hai, Chua 485
Namba, Hajime 141
Namgoong, Hun Hun Namgoong 392
Namiki, Masao 452
Nandakumar, E. 85
Nandkishore, Nandu 309
Nanterme, Pierre 7
Nanterme, Pierre 8
Nanthawithaya, Arthid 394
Naouri, Jean-Charles 111
Napier, Iain J. G. 227
Naratil, Thomas C. (Tom) 461
Narayanan, K. B. 86
Nardi, Yoav 63
Narev, Ian 130
Naruke, Yasuo Yasuo Naruke 452
Narvinger, Anders 436
Nasard, Alexis 199
Nascimento, Alvaro Jose Barrigas do 103
Nash, Glenn 409
Nason, Robert A. 438
Nasser, Jacques A. (Jac) 87
Natale, Marina 463
Natekar, R. P. 86
Nauffal, Rafael 57
Naughton, Des 98
Naumann, Susan 113
Navarre, Christophe 199
Navarri, Andre 91
Navarro, Pedro Alfonso Rosales 160
Navarro, Juan Villalonga 168
Navarro, Gustavo 212
Naveda, Marcelino Botin-Sanz de Sautola y 70
Nazmi, Nader 90
Neal, John 350
Neath, Gavin 465
Nebbia, Luciano 234
Nebuloni, Pierantonio 376
Neckmar, Thomas 321
Neeb, Marc J. 274
Neeteson, Paul 131
Neff, Thomas J. (Tom) 9
Nei, Yasushi 149
Neild, Ian 100
Neill, John M. 365
Neilson, John 51
Neira, Adriana Marcela 160
Neisel, Michael 462
Nekrasov, Vladimir I. 329
Nelles, Josef 159
Nelson, David J. 87
Nelson, Brendan 95
Nelson, John 250
Nelson, Brendan 368
Nelson, Shayne K. 411
Nemesch, Ferdinand 332
Nemoto, Takehiko 294
Nemoto, Shoji 408
Neoh, Anthony F. 64
Nergaard, Truls 415
Nesbitt, Richard W. 104
Neske, Rainer 153
Netland, Greg A. 352
Neto, Jo?o M. Manso 161
Neto, Mario Alves Barbosa 468
Neumann, Horst G. 477
Neumeister, Ulrich 113
Neville-Rolfe, Lucy 440
Neville-Rolfe, Lucy 440
Newbury, Karsten 396
Ng, Lynne 12
Ng, Andrew 147
Ng, Gary 266
Ng, Sing Yip 343
Ngamsopee, Kannika 394
Ngiam, Tong Dow 467
Ngo, Victor 467
Ngui, Karen 147
Ngwerume, Luke 330
Nhleko, Phuthuma F. 35
Nhleko, Phuthuma F. 95
Nho, Hwan Yong 267
Nicandrou, Nicolaos (Nic) 348
Nicastro, Roberto 463
Nicholas, David 95
Nicholls, Blair 350
Nichols, Keith 24
Nichols, Charles 464
Nickerson, Jerry E. A. 193
Nickerson, Jerry E. A. 345
Nickerson, Jerry E. A. 346
Nicolaisen, Donald T. (Don) 492
Nicolas, Eric 355
Nicolau, Neville F. 35
Nicolin, Tomas Tomas Nicolin 399
Nicolle, Gilles 127
Nicolson, John R. 199
Niehage, Udo 395
Niehaus, Hans-Jurgen 482
Nield, David A. 193
Nielsen, Niels 318
Nielsen, Kurt Anker 325
Nielsen, Peter 368
Nielsen, Kai 414
Nielsen, Birgitte 415
Nielsen, Helle Helle Kruse Nielsen 426
Niermann, Nils 79
Nightingale, Anthony J. L. 242
Nightingale, Anthony J. L. 242
Nigorra, Miguel 59
Niimi, Atsushi (Art) 455
Niimi, Atsushi (Art) 455
Niinami, Takeshi 334
Niino, Takashi 306
Nijns, Herman 352
Nikolaevich, Dubik Nikolai 186
Nikolin, Hans-Joachim 135
Niland, John R. 273
Niles, Patricia 465
Nilsson, Kjell-Olof 203
Nilsson, Bernth 380
Nilsson, Emil 381
Nilsson, Kenneth 401
Nilsson, Claes 479
Nimocks, Suzanne P. 39
Ningning, Ding 342
Nininger, James R. 345
Nish, David 413
Nish, David 413
Nishi, Yoshio 67
Nishi, Yoshio 67
Nishi, Hiroyuki 311
Nishida, Mitsuo 419
Nishida, Mitsuo 419
Nishida, Atsutoshi 451
Nishigai, Kazuhisa 96
Nishigai, Kazuhisa 97
Nishikawa, Seiji 326
Nishikori, Hironobu 452
Nishimae, Manabu 214
Nishimura, Ken 34
Nishimura, Tatsuya 140
Nishimura, Tomonori 306
Nishimura, Shuichi 316
Nishimura, Shozo 326
Nishimura, Akira 419
Nishina, Hiroaki 334
Nishina, Hiroaki 334
Nishino, Toshikazu 208
Nishinomiya, Kazuo 358
Nishio, Hiroki 420
Nishioka, Takashi 292
Nishioka, Hiroaki 326
Nishitani, Kiyoshi 408
Nishiyama, Asahiko (Duke) 96
Nishiyama, Raita 283
Nishiyori, Akiro 224
Nishiyori, Akiro 224
Nishizawa, Massaaki 316
Nishizawa, Toshio 447
Nitzani, Joseph (Yosi) 441
Niu, Ximing 65
Niubo, Antonio 185
Niubo, Antonio Brufau 185
Niubo, Antonio 356
Niwa, Uichiro 238
Nix, Kevin 384
Nixon, Gordon M. 366
Nixon, Gordon M. 366
Noack, Achim 78
Noakes, Baroness Sheila V. 368
Noakes, Baroness Sheila V. 368
Noda, Shigeru 419
Noerenberg, Marco Marco Noerenberg 300
Nogai, Yasunobu 180
Noguchi, Takashi 70
Noguchi, Akio 106
Noguchi, Kazuhiko 106
Noguchi, Tadahiko 328
Noguchi, Tadahiko 328
Nogueira, Nilton P. 57
Nohara, Sawako 307
Noji, Kunio 253
Noji, Kunio 253
Noji, Kunio 358
Nolan, Helen 66
Nolens, Geraldine 462
Nolker, Stefan 54
Noma, Eiji 328
Noma, Sawako 448
Nomakuchi, Tamotsu 290
Nomura, Kiyoshi 96
Nomura, Toru 117
Nomura, Motokiyo 180
Nomura, Yutaka 281
Nomura, Fumihide 320
Nomura, Junji 338
Nomura, Katsuaki 390
Nonaka, Hideyasu 291
Nonaka, Ikujiro 296
Nonaka, Terumoto 358
Nonaka, Ikujiro 388
Nooitgedagt, Jan 14
Noordaa, Hans van der 231
Noordende, Alexander (Sander) van 't 7
Noordende, Alexander M. (Sander) van't 8
Noordende, Alexander 8
Nopmuang, Ruchanee 61
Nor, Megat Zaharuddin Megat Mohd 275
Nordahl, Tomas 380
Nordberg, Bert 166
Nordberg, Bert 408
Nordfelt, Stig 203
Nordlin, Markus 492
Nordmann, Dick 136
Nordstrom, Gunilla 3
Nordstrom, Lars G. 321
Norenberg, Marco 164
Norenberg, Marco 300
Noriega, Carlos Rodado 160
Norin, Maria 3
Norling, Lars-?ke 435
Norman, Stephen 355
Norman, Andy 370
Normand, Gilles 316
Normann, Henrik 146
Normant, Emmanuel 131
Noro, Yukio 420
Noronha, Marcelo de Araujo 56
Norvik, Harald 435
Nosko, Roland 13
Noskov, Mikhail 457
Nota, Pieter 257
Notaristefani, Carlo de 441
Noteboom, Ben J. 255
Noteboom, Ben J. 352
Noth, Thomas 429
Nouchi, Yuzo 289
Novakovic, Christine 399
Nozaka, Yoshiki 141
Nozaka, Yoshiki 141
Nozaki, Kunio 416
Nqwababa, Bongani 330
Ntshingila, Happy 71
Nucci, Antonio 234

Nucleaires, Activites 189
Nugent, Helen M. 273
Nunn, Tom 278
Nursing, Nursing 130
Nusmeier, Nico 199
Nyalsulu, Hixonia 465
Nyasulu, T. Hixonia 464
Nyasulu, Hixonia Hixonia Nyasulu 465
Nyberg, Martti 321
Nyberg, Lars 436
Nyegaard, Peter 321
Nyembezi-Heita, Nonkululeko 330
Nymebezi-Heita, Nku 39
Nyquist, Peter 3
Nyren, Anders 166
Nyren, Anders 381
Nyren, Anders 425
Nyren, Anders 479
Nysschen, Johan de 316

O

O-sotsin, Chirana 61
O?Hare, Michael 199
O?Shea, Niall 66
Oba, Masashi 446
Obayashi, Takeo 328
Obayashi, Takeo 328
Oberlaender, Franz Franz Oberlaender 81
Oberlander, Franz 81
Oberman, Allan 441
Obermann, Rene 159
Obermeier, Georg 260
Oberson, Gilles 287
OBrien, David 366
OBrien, Grant Grant OBrien 488
OByrne, Kevin Kevin OByrne 250
Occhiello, Ernesto 385
Ochiai, Shinji 421
Ochiai, Shinji 421
Ochiai, Hiroyuki 455
Ocker, Martin 490
Oda, Shinya 307
Odegaard, Janice B. 423
Odelstam, Jan 401
Odone, Toby 95
ODonnell, Hugh 376
ODonoghue, Leslie 18
ODonovan, Anne 69
Odorici, Luigi 54
Odorici, Luigi 54
Odum, Marvin E. 370
Oechslin, Joachim 300
Oecking, Christian 395
Oeri, Andreas 362
Oers, Joris van 100
Oetker, Arend 54
Ogawa, Tadashi 69
Ogawa, Kazuto (Kevin) 106
Ogawa, Daisuke 182
Ogawa, Kazuhiko Kazuhiko Ogawa 184
Ogawa, Hiroshi 252
Ogawa, Katsumi 295
Ogawa, Kiyoshi 417
Ogg, Sandy 464
Ogura, Toshiyuki 282
Ogura, Satoru 419
Oh, Thomas 249
Oh, Se Se Yil Oh 391
Oh, Sei-Jong 397
Ohara, Wataru 420
Ohashi, Yoji 34
Ohashi, Mitsuo 208
Ohashi, Tetsuji 253
Ohashi, Tetsuji 253
Ohashi, Yutaka 291
Ohbatake, Masami 390
Ohira, Noriyoshi 288
Ohkawara, Masaki 180
Ohkubo, Hideyuki 291
Ohkubo, Tetsuo 421
Ohkubo, Tetsuo 421
Ohkuma, Nobuyuki 291
Ohmichi, Masao 293
Ohmori, Kazuo 417
Ohmori, Kazuo 417
Ohno, Koji 34
Ohno, Shigeru 405
Ohsumi, Masaaki Masaaki Ohsumi 452
Ohta, Seiichi 293
Ohta, Seiichi 293
Ohta, Kenji 390
Ohta, Jun 420
Ohtaka, Zenko 388
Ohtaka, Zenko 388
Ohtaki, Katsuhisa 137
Ohtani, Nobuo Nobuo Ohtani 184
Ohtani, Toshiaki 316
Ohtsubo, Fumio 338
Ohtsubo, Fumio 338
Ohya, Kenji 149
Ohyama, Yasuo 293
Oi, Atsushi 295
Oi, Yuichi 456
Oikawa, Hiroyuki 180
Oikawa, Hiroyuki 180
Oishi, Masakazu 393
Oiso, Kimio 142
Oistamo, Kai 318
Oistamo, Kai 318
Ojima, Koichi 206
Oka, Motoyuki 417
Okabe, Hitoshi 22
Okabe, Keiichiro 137
Okada, Motoya 15
Okada, Motoya 16
Okada, Motoya 16
Okada, Motoya 16
Okada, Keisuke 34
Okada, Akira 34
Okada, Keisuke 34
Okada, Masato 106
Okada, Hideki 214
Okada, Kenji 238
Okada, Shinichi 244
Okada, Tadashi 253
Okada, Daisuke 281
Okada, Joji 295
Okada, Takayuki 306
Okada, Kuniaki 307
Okada, Fujio 307
Okada, Moriyuki 390
Okada, Keiko Keiko Okada 390
Okada, Tomonori 393
Okada, Akishige 455
Okafuji, Masahiro 238
Okahashi, Terukazu 295
Okamoto, Hitoshi 238
Okamoto, Hitoshi 238
Okamoto, Kunie 311
Okamoto, Yoshihiko 416
Okamoto, Kazuo 455
Okamoto, Kazuo 455
Okamura, Sadamasa 314
Okamura, Sadamasa 314
Okamura, Kiyoshi Kiyoshi Okamura 452
Okamura, Susumu 461
Okano, Michiyuki 392
Okauchi, Kinya 294
Okauchi, Kinya 294
Okawa, Kazushi 289
Okawara, Eiji 214
Okawara, Makoto 289
Okazaki, Soichi 16
Okazaki, Soichi 16
Okazaki, Seiei 206
Okazaki, Seiei 206
Okazaki, Hiroe 448
OKeefe, Sean Sean OKeefe 21
Okihara, Takamune 294
Okimoto, Takashi 184
Oku, Norio 22
Oku, Masayuki 338
Oku, Masayuki 420
Okubo, Chiyuki 69
Okubo, Chiyuki 70
Okubo, Toshikazu 117
Okubo, Noriaki 241
Okubo, Noriaki 241
Okubo, Tsuneo 388
Okuda, Kentaro 320
Okuda, Takashi 390
Okuhara, Kazushige 180
Okuhara, Kazushige 180
Okuno, Hiroshi 67
Okuno, Jun 421
Olav, Richard 435
OLeary, Tom 480
Oletzky, Torsten 164
Olive, Henri Saint 472
Oliveira, Ramon de 49
Oliveira, Anibal da Costa Reis 168
Oliveira, Wagner Pinheiro de 243
Oliver, Dick 51
Olivieri, Fernando 114
Ollagnier, Jean-Marc 8
Ollila, Jorma 318
Ollila, Jorma 370
Olmos, Pascual 356
Olney, Patrick (Pat) 479
Olofsson, Pierre 401
Olsen, Robert C. 225
Olsson, Mats H. 166
Olvaso, Arpad 297
Omae, Takao 296
Omae, Takao 296
Omar, Abdul Abdul Wahid bin Omar 275
Omar, Abdul Wahid bin 275
Ominato, Mitsuru 448
Omiya, Shuichi 224
Omori, Shinichiro 208
Onda, Toru 214
ONeill, Thomas Thomas ONeill 82
Oneill, Michael 266
Onessimo, Laura 401
Ong, Alice N. L. 266
Ong, Susan 278
Ong, Terence Sea Eng 466
Ongpin, Roberto V. 379
Onillon, Julien 39
Onishi, Tetsuo 390
Onishi, Hiroji 455
Ono, Koichiro 34
Ono, Kazuto 106
Ono, Isao 208
Onodera, Makoto 429
Onoe, Seizo 326
Onorato, Gianni 107
Oosterman, Wade 82
Opelt, Marc 335
Ophamurathawong, Narin 61
Oppenheimer, Nicholas F. (Nicky) 35
Oppenheimer, Deanna 440
Oppenheimer, Jonathan M. E. 462
Oratis, Michael 303
Orator, Christian 492
Orcel, Andrea 461
Orchart, Paul 130
Orgler, Prof Yair E. 62
Orlandi, Sergio 466
Orlowski, Stefan 199
Ornelas, Jose Gonzalez 177
Ornelas, Jos 177
Orr, R. Jeffrey 193
Orr, R. Jeffrey 193
Orr, R. Jeffrey 345
Orr, R. Jeffrey 345
Orr, R. Jeffrey 346
Orr, R. Jeffrey 346
Orris, Mike 364
Orsi, Giuseppe 173
Orsini, Olivier 471
Ortoli, Antoine 382
Osawa, Masahiro 106
Osawa, Hidetoshi 338
Osawa, Toshiyuki Toshiyuki Osawa 390
Osawa, Yoshio 417
Osawa, Yoshio 418
Osberg, Anders 479
Osborne, Jeffrey (Jeff) 8
Osborne, Brian 53
Osborne, Glenn 438
Osculati, Gianemilio 402
Oshige, Koji 456
Oshima, Akio 326
Oshima, Akio 327
Oshima, Yuki 334
Osseforth, Ansgar 144
Ossenberg-Engels, Jorg 286
Ossip, Alon 274
Osterloh, Bernd 477
Ostermeier, Hans 205
Ostgathe, Klaus 462
Ostling, Leif 477
Ostrander, Paul 212
Ostrowski, Hartmut 83
OSullivan, Patrick 330
Osuna, Nicolas 59
Oswald, Robert 76
Oswald, Robert 76
Oswald, Andrin 323
Oswald, Gerhard 384
Ota, Mitsuhiko 34
Ota, Yasushi 97
Ota, Michihiko 281
Ota, Michihiko 282
Ota, Katsuhiko 312
Otani, Nobuo 183
Othman, Ahmad 218
Otomo, Nobuhiko 289
Otoshi, Takuma 294
Otsuka, Naoji 106
Otsuka, Kazuo 388
Otsuka, Hiromasa 408
Otsuka, Kiyoshi 448
Otsuki, Jiro 184
Otsuki, Hitoshi 338
Ott, Erhard 159
Ottenbruch, Peter 489
Otterbeck, Lars 330
Otterman, G. P. 245
Otto, Thomas 276
Otto, Thomas 277
Otto, Michael 335
Otto, Michael 335
Otto, Alexander 335
Oudeman, Marjan 24
Oura, Hiroshi 184
Ouziel, Sylvie 8
Ovesen, Jesper 399
Ovrum, Margareth 414
Owen-Jones, Lindsay 383
Oyama, Nagahisa 16
Oyama, Nagahisa 16
Oyama, Tatsuhiro 214
Oyama, Tatsuhiro 215
Oyamada, Takashi 294
Oz, Ran 62
Ozaki, Teruo 252
Ozaki, Kiyoshi 283
Ozaki, Kiyoshi 283
Ozawa, Hitoshi 61
Ozawa, Hideki 106
Ozawa, Hideki 106
Ozawa, Motoyuki Motoyuki Ozawa 184
Ozawa, Satoshi 455
Ozawa, Satoshi 455
Ozen, Ergun 459
Ozen, Ergun 459
O'Brien, Fiona 266
O'Brien, Patrick D. 338
O'Brien, David P. 366
O'Brien, Michael W. (Mike) 423
O'Brien, Grant 488
O'Byrne, Kevin 250
O'Byrne, Kevin 250
O'Callaghan, Jeremiah A. (Jerry) 243
O'Connell, B. M. 245
O'Connor, Richard 368
O'Connor, Michael J. 422
O'Day, Daniel 362
O'Donald, Lewis 320
O'Donnell, Hugh J. (James) 376
O'Donnell, Hugh J. (James) 376
O'Donoghue, Leslie A. 18
O'Donovan, Rose 29

O'Donovan, Anne Marie 69
O'Donovan, Kathleen A. 348
O'Dwyer, Barry 348
O'Halloran, Frank 350
O'Halloran, Frank 350
O'Hara, Jim 29
O'Keefe, Sean C. 21
O'Leary, Tom 480
O'Looney, Michael 74
O'Meara, John-Paul 13
O'Neill, Thomas 12
O'Neill, Tim 66
O'Neill, Thomas C. (Tom) 69
O'Neill, Brian D. 167
O'Neill, Sean 199
O'Neill, Michael J. 266
O'Rourke, Ray 35
O'Sullivan, Patrick H. 66
O'Sullivan, Patrick H. 66
O'Sullivan, Francis K. (Fran) 266
O'Sullivan, James J. (Jim) 283

P

Paasche, Sascha 143
Pachauri, Rajendra 332
Pacheco, Jorge Luiz 468
Pachler, Johan 212
Pachta-Reyhofen, Georg 276
Padilla, Raul 102
Padmanabhan, P. 86
Pae, Judy 267
Paefgen, Franz-Josef 489
Paesana, Bruno 234
Paesler, Klaus 195
Pagliaro, Renato 432
Pahne, Erika 426
Paiement, Luc 302
Paiva, Bernardo Pinto 37
Palacio, Vivian Kobeh de 318
Palande, Pandit 196
Palenzona, Fabrizio 284
Palenzona, Fabrizio 463
Palenzona, Fabrizio 463
Palia, S. M. (Sam) 430
Palladino, Camilla 163
Pallesen, Lars 2
Palmer, John 33
Palmer, Jeffrey O. 274
Palmer, John R. V. 278
Palmer, Andy 316
Palomo, Benjamin 356
Paltrinieri, Massimo 41
Pamer-Wieser, Charlotte 323
Pan, Nicholas D. Le 104
Pan, Richard 345
Pan, Richard 346
Panagiotopoulos, Theofanis 303
Panagopoulos, Ioannis P. 303
Pancaccini, Gianluca Gianluca Pancaccini 432
Pancini, Josue A. 56
Pande, Arvind 196
Pande, N. K. 328
Pande, N. K. 328
Pang, Joseph Y. W. 65
Pangalos, Menelas 44
Panicker, Prasad K. 86
Panizzo, Jose M. Carrera 356
Panizzo, Jose 356
Panke, Helmut 78
Panke, Helmut 461
Pannell, Derek G. 18
Panpiemras, Kosit 61
Panpiemrat, Kosit 61
Panpiemrat, Kosit 61
Pansa, Alessandro 173
Pansegrau, Wolfgang 263
Pantzar, Anna Tillberg 203
Pantzar, Anna Anna Pantzar 203
Panyarachun, Anand 394
Pao-In, Bussakorn 61
Paoli, Mary 422
Paolini, Nonce 93
Paolini, Nonce 93
Papagrigoris, Gregory 303
Papakonstantinou, Lambros 303
Papalexopoulou-Benop, Alexandra 303
Papaspyrou, Spyros A. 343
Papaspyrou, Spyros A. 344
Pape, Jacques 19
Papiasse, Alain 90
Paquot, Guy 462
Paranjpe, Nitin 465
Paras, Marios 352
Parayre, Jean-Paul 342
Pardo, Jaime Chico 32
Pare, Raymond 27
Pare, Raymond 27
Pare, Jean-Philippe 145
Pare, Jean-Philippe 145
Parent, Ghislain 302
Parent, Brigitte 422
Parent, Bruno 443
Parente, Pedro Pullen 102
Parikh, Bobby 196
Parisot, Laurence 133
Parizeau, Robert 345
Park, Jin-won 220
Park, Young-june 220
Park, Jong-Seok 267
Park, Oh-Soo 378
Parker, Sir John 21
Parker, Sir John 35
Parker, Sue Graham 69
Parker, Sue 69
Parker, Andrew 100
Parker, Sir John 107
Parker, Josh 368
Parker, Christine 484
Parkes, David 51
Parnaby, Nathan 413
Parr, Nick 195
Parrett, William G. (Bill) 461
Parsons, Alex 227
Parthasarthy, Ashish 196
Pascal, Amy 408
Pasch, Reinhard 164
Pasch, Reinhard 300
Paschalis, Konstantinos 343
Pascoe, Ricardo 302
Pasquali, L. 173
Pasquini, Fabio 234
Pastor, Jacques 127
Patel, Krishna 217
Paternot, Thierry 202
Paterson, David 278
Paterson, John 364
Patmore, Jeff 100
Pattanayak, Nilesh 91
Patten, Louise A.V.C. 280
Patterson, Gavin 100
Patterson, Gavin 101
Pattijn, Elbert 147
Patuano, Marco 432
Paul, George 86
Paul, Stuart 130
Paul, Sarah 156
Paul, Helmut 177
Paul, Michael 489
Paula, Jefferson 39
Paulsson, Magnus 401
Paus, William 399
Pavlova, Olga P. 186
Pavoncello, Andrea 463
Payer, Gabriela Maria 461
Payne, Catherine 438
Paynter, John 412
Paynter, John John Paynter 413
Peace, Sir John W. 411
Peace, Stella 465
Peacher, Stephen C. 422
Peacock, Lynne Lynne Peacock 413
Pearce, John 343
Pearcy, D. Benedict 102
Pearman, Rowan 156
Pearson, Mark 49
Peasland, Michael J. (Mike) 53
Pebereau, Michel 21
Pebereau, Michel Michel Pebereau 21
Pebereau, Michel 49
Pebereau, Michel 131
Pebereau, Michel 453
Peck, Eliott 106
Pecresse, Jerome 31
Pedersen, Klaus M. 147
Pedersen, Bent 157
Pedersen, Bent 157
Pedersen, Helge J. 321
Pedersen, Celena Lund 325
Pedersen, S?ren Thuesen 325
Pedersen, Mike 450
Pedersoli, Alessandro (Att) 41
Pedersoli, Alessandro (Att) 466
Pedini, Claire 131
Pedro, Jose Luis San 223
Pedrocchi, Luigi 287
Peeters, Paul 257
Peever, David 360
Peijs, Karla M.H. 14
Peiner, Wolfgang 260
Pelaz, Mario 356
Peled, Efrat 62
Pelisson, Gilles 8
Pellegrini, Alan 443
Pellens, Prof Bernard 445
Pellicioli, Lorenzo 41
Peltola, Timo 321
Peltola, Timo 321
Peltola, Timo 436
Peltola, Timo 436
Peluso, Piergiorgio Piergiorgio Peluso 432
Peman, Manuel Guerrero 168
Pemberthy, Javier G. Gutierrez 160
Pena, Rui 161
Penchas, Henri 237
Pene, Jean-Bernard 375
Peng, Darren T.S. 336
Penicaud, Muriel 145
Penicaud, Muriel 333
Penn, Andrew (Andy) 49
Penn, Andrew (Andy) 438
Penn, Andrew (Andy) 438
Pennings, Gerrit 210
Pennycook, Richard 298
Pennycook, Richard 298
Pentland, Louise 318
Pentz, Larry C. 245
Pentz, Larry C. 245
Percival, Matthew 33
Pereira, Luis 161
Pereira, Maria 161
Perera, Amal 47
Peres, Luiz F. 56
Perez, Jose Luis del Valle 10
Perez, Juan Perez Luis Garcia-Gelabert 10
Perez, Antonio 59
Perez, Arnaldo 107
Perez, Jorge 114
Perez, Jose Jose Luis del Valle Perez 210
Perez, Jose M. Abril 434
Perez-Guerra, Jaime 21
Perfetti, A. 173
Pergament, Shlomo 63
Perissinotto, Giovanni 41
Perlet, Helmut 128
Perolari, Giorgio 466
Perritaz, Pascal 492
Persson, Stefan 203
Persson, Karl-Johan 203
Persson, Madeleine 203
Persson, Anna Vikstrom 380
Persson, Eva 479
Persson, Olof 479
Persson, Olof 479
Pesenti, Carlo 284
Pesenti, Carlo 463
Pessi, Oliviero E. 41
Pester, Marion 158
Pestre, Jacques 131
Petalas, Constantin (Tino) 9
Peter, Joseph G. (Joe) 316
Peters, Pierre 27
Peters, Simon 51
Petersen, Grahame A. 129
Petersen, Sune Visti 147
Petersen, Heidi M. 321
Peterson, Sandra E. 78
Peterson, Ulf 399
Petit, Olivier 261
Petitjean, Patrick 189
Petracchini, Marco 163
Petracchini, Gerard Laffineur 168
Petralia, Francesca Francesca Petralia 432
Petram, Hans-Dieter 429
Petrelli, Paul O. 422
Petri, Roberto Roberto Petri 163
Petri, Helmut 490
Petter, John 100
Pettersson, Lars 401
Pettit, Stephen R. 304
Peugeot, Thierry 261
Peugeot, Jean-Philippe 342
Peugeot, Thierry 342
Peugeot, Robert 342
Peugeot, Jean-Philippe 342
Peura, Ingrid 318
Peverett, Jane L. 104
Peycere, Mathieu 474
Peyre, Philippe 382
Peyrelevade, Jean 93
Pfister, Michael 262
Pfitzner, Michael B. 39
Pflughaupt, Randy 455
Phashirat, Sutthirat 61
Phaswana, Tshmano Mohau Frederick (Fred) 35
Pheiffer, Natasha 51
Phelizon, Jean-Francois 131
Philipps, Kate 469
Philips, Dalton T. 298
Phillips, Joyce A. 46
Phillips, Ian 130
Phillips, Robin 218
Phillips, Roger 225
Phillips, Matthew 227
Phillips, Matthew 227
Phillips-Davies, Alistair 410
Phillips-Davies, Alistair 410
Phisitbuntoon, Sutharntip 394
Phokasub, Yol 394
Phornprapha, Phornthep 61
Phutrakun, Korbsak 61
Piacenza, Bruno 202
Picarelli, Sergio 11
Picca, Bruno 234
Pichottka, Andrea 202
Pickard, Ann 370
Pickavance, Norman 298
Pickel, Michael 195
Pickett, David P. (Dave) 450
Piech, Ferdinand K. 276
Piech, Ferdinand K. 477
Piech, Hans Michel 477
Piech, Hans 477
Piech, Ursula 477
Pierce, James M. 461
Pierson, George J. 53
Pieters, Marten 475
Pieterse, Robert (Rob) 373
Pigozzi, Lorenza 284
Pike, Gavin 156
Pilaud, Eric 387
Pilkington, Edward 156
Pillard, Larry G. 102
Pinault, Francois-Henri 93
Pingang, Wang 121
Pinger, Markus 113
Pinho, Ilidio 161
Pink, Charles 130
Pinkham, Gary 166
Pinoncely, Gilles 111
Pins, Christian de 127
Pinto, Alberto Alves de Oliveira 58
Pinto, Ari 62
Pinto, Paulo T. 161

Pinto, Francisco Eduardo de Almeida 237
Pinto, Eugenio 284
Pinto, Eduardo Fernando Jardim 468
Pinzer, Reinhard 395
Piou, Olivier 25
Piper, Martha 370
Piramal, Swati 224
Pires, Luciano 468
Piry, Laszlo 297
Pisano, Wayne F. 382
Pischetsrieder, Bernd 286
Pischetsrieder, Bernd 300
Pisharody, Ravindra 430
Pistorio, Pasquale 172
Pitfield, Robert H. (Rob) 69
Pivato, Sergio 466
Piyajitti, Supa 394
Pizzini, Flavio 466
Planta, Andreas von 212
Planta, Andreas von 212
Planta, Andreas von 323
Plantenga, Door 199
Plassat, Georges 109
Platsch, Matthias 396
Plattner, Prof Hasso 384
Playford, Ian 250
Pleasance, P. J. 298
Pleines, Thomas 54
Plessis, Jan Jan du Plessis 280
Plessis, Jan P. du 280
Plessis, Jan P. du 360
Plessis, Jan du 361
Plessis-Belair, Michel 193
Plessis-Belair, Michel 193
Plessis-Belair, Michel 345
Plessis-Belair, Michel 346
Plischke, Wolfgang 78
Ploix, Helene 90
Plougmann, Carsten 2
Plourde, Real 26
Plourde, Real 27
Plummer, Stephen B. 364
Poblador, Alexander J. 379
Pockett, Thomas (Tom) 488
Podolsky, Daniel K. 192
Podvin, Jean-Marc 382
Podyuk, Vasiliy 186
Poelvoorde, Geert Van 39
Poh, Lai Teck 336
Poh, Tay 467
Pohl, Reinfried 41
Pohle, Klaus 383
Pohlig, Rolf 371
Poian, Christophe Da 127
Poitou, Jean-Laurent 7
Pol, Ramon 57
Pol, Chuck 476
Polignac, Nicole 69
Polignac, Francois Melchior de 109
Politopoulou, Maria-Ioanna 303
Politopoulou, Marianna 303
Pollak, Andrea 195
Pollestad, Jan 321
Pollock, John 265
Pollock, John 265
Polman, Paul 464
Polman, Paul 464
Polman, Paul 465
Polman, Paul 465
Pommellet, Pierre-Eric 443
Pommier, Jean-Luc 472
Pons, Francisco Servando Verdu 10
Pontolillo, Vincenzo 76
Ponzellini, Gianluca 234
Poon, Stephen 130
Poon, Christine A. (Chris) 258
Poonen, Sanjay 384
Popham, Stuart 265
Popov, Alexander 13
Porro, Jose Manuel Gonzalez 279
Porro, Jose Manuel Gonzalez 279
Porsche, Wolfgang 477
Porter, Brian J. 69
Porth, Wilfried 21
Porth, Wilfried 143
Portman, Erin 91
Posayanon, Kowit 61
Posch, Guillaume de 84
Poshyananda, Kovit 61
Possne, Torbjorn 166
Postel, Christine 98
Posyagin, Boris S. 188
Potapov, Igor 482
Potier, Benoit 133
Potier, Benoit 145
Potsch, Hans D. 84
Potsch, Hans D. 477
Pott, Jeff 44
Pott, Richard 78
Potthoff, Christian 262
Poulopoulos, Georgios 343
Poulsen, John Axel 2
Poulsen, Kasper Roseeuw 325
Poupart-Lafarge, Henri 31
Poupart-Lafarge, Arnaud 39
Poux-Guillaume, Gregoire 31
Pouyanne, Patrick 453
Pouyat, Alain 93
Pouyat, Alain 93
Powell, Rod 25
Powell, David 87
Powell, David 88
Poynter, Kieran C. 98
Prabhu, Banesh 394
Pragnell, Michael P. 472
Prasad, P.M.S. 353
Prasad, P.M.S. 353
Preesman, Pim 257
Prelle, Hermann 461
Prentice, Rt. Hon. Jim 82
Prentice, Rt. Hon. Jim 104
Prentice, Rt. Hon. Jim 104
Prest, D. W. 245
Pret, Comte Arnoud de 37
Pret, Comte Arnoud de 462
Pretorius, Brand S.G. 71
Prettejohn, Nicholas E. T. (Nick) 265
Preuss, Michael 78
Prezzano, Wilbur J. (Bill) 450
Pri-Zan, Hanna 62
Price, Gary 47
Price, Jonathan 47
Price, Timothy R. (Tim) 216
Price, James D. (Jamie) 461
Prichard, J. Robert S. 483
Prideaux, Nigel 47
Prideaux, Michael 98
Priester, Barbara 128
Prince, David N. 12
Prior, Lawrence B. (Larry) 51
Prioux, Noel 109
Prock-Schauer, Wolfgang 151
Proctor, Christopher (Chris) 98
Proctor, Timothy D. (Tim) 155
Produkt, Vorstand 84
Proebstl, Siegmar 396
Profumo, Alessandro Alessandro Profumo 163
Proglio, Henri 471
Prondzynski, Heino von 258
Prondzynski, Heino 258
Prosser, David 235
Prosser, Richard 458
Prost, Jacques 355
Prot, Baudouin 89
Prot, Baudouin 471
Proto, Frank W. 18
Provera, Marco T. 284
Provera, Marco T. 284
Provident, Friends 401
Provoost, Rudy S. 257
Provost, Francois 355
Prufer, Hans 159
Pruksakit, Parnsak 61
Prune, Gabrielle 189
Pryor, Robert D. 184
Pucci, Roberto 382
Puente, Raul Llamazares de la 10
Puig, Jose 57
Pujari, Anup K. 224
Pulman, David 191
Punet, Andreu 356
Puno, Reynato S. 379
Punta, Stefano Del 234
Puri, Aditya 196
Puri, Navin 196
Puri, Aditya 196
Purinthawarakun, Amphorn 61
Puron, Jose M. Rincon Gallardo 114
Puron, Jose 114
Pusey, Stephen C. (Steve) 475
Pusey, Stephen C. (Steve) 476
Putkiranta, Juha 318
Putnam, Michael C. (Mike) 400
Putter, Bernd 210
Pye, Hugh 218
Pym, Richard A. 330

Q

Qi, Zhu 119
Qi, Lan 119
Qi, Gao 368
Qing, Huang 121
Qingshan, Wen 339
Qiu, Olivia 131
Qu, Zhang 229
Qu, Zhang 229
Quandt, Stefan 80
Quandt, Stefan 81
Quartermain, Mark 370
Qubaisi, Khadem 332
Qubaisi, Khadem A. Al 332
Querner, Immo 195
Querner, Immo 429
Quinn, Noel 218
Quintella, Antonio 139
Quintella, Sergio F. 340
Quirke, Kelly 87
Qureshi, Rima 166

R

R., Claudia L. Castellanos 160
R?d, St?le 401
R?ed, Anders 415
Raad, M. P. M. (Theo) de 286
Rabe, Thomas 83
Rabin, Anthony L. P. 53
Rabin, Anthony L. P. 53
Raby, Paul 53
Rachou, Nathalie 402
Rademacher, Tom 210
Rademacher, Lilo 490
Radke, Roger 396
Radley, Diane 330
Rae, John A. 345
Rae, John A. 345
Raffelhuschen, Prof Bernd 164
Raffin, Philippe 127
Rahilly, Thomas F. (Tom) 483
Rahl, Leslie 104
Raimondi, Christian 127
Rainer, Majda 280
Rajapakse, Suresh Suresh Rajapakse 39
Rake, Sir Michael D. V. (Mike) 72
Rake, Sir Michael D. V. (Mike) 74
Rake, Sir Michael D. V. (Mike) 74
Rake, Sir Michael D. V. (Mike) 100
Ralapanawa, Mahanama 212
Ralli, Georges 471
Ralph, Jay 28
Ramachandran, M. S. 224
Ramakrishnan, C. 430
Ramaphosa, M. Cyril 373
Ramberg, Agneta 203
Ramchander, Pranill 35
Ramesh, S. 85
Ramkumar, Krishnaswamy 224
Ramkumar, Krishnaswamy 224
Ramlau-Hansen, Henrik 147
Ramos, Jose Maldonado 55
Ramos, Maria 71
Ramos, Maria 72
Ramos, Maria 74
Ramos, Luis 91
Ramphele, Mamphela 35
Rampl, Dieter 284
Rampl, Dieter 463
Ramsay, Duncan 350
Ramsby, Ole 325
Rana, Basudev 85
Randle, Paul R. 283
Randolph, Marcus P. 87
Rannou, Jean 375
Ranong, Chok 61
Ranque, Denis 131
Rao, I. Srinivas 86
Rapaczynski, Wanda 12
Rapanos, Prof Vassilios T. 303
Rapiya, Marshall 330
Rappo, Bruno 54
Raps, Jurgen 151
Raschke, Klaus-Dieter 159
Rasinger, Wilhelm G. 167
Raskin, Geoffroy 462
Rasmussen, Michael P. 2
Rasmussen, Michael 321
Ratcliffe, Peter G. 107
Rath, Cornelia 371
Rathe, Bente 425
Rathmann, Thomas 396
Rattanacharoensiri, Chaiyong 61
Ravichandran, J. 85
Ravindran, K. N. 85
Ravn, Bo Sonne 147
Raybaud, Maria Helena Antolin 223
Raynaud, Eric 90
Rayner, Paul 116
Read, Giles 39
Read, Paul 176
Read, Rory 266
Read, Nicholas J. (Nick) 475
Reaney, Graham J. 484
Rebelato, Odair Afonso 56
Reboa, Marco 163
Rebrin, Peter 491
Rebuck, Dame Gail 83
Recchi, Giuseppe 163
Reckers, Hans 150
Recto, Eric O. 379
Recto, Eric O. 379
Reddy, D.M. 85
Redfearn, Dominic 156
Redfern, David 191
Redondo, Maximiliano Navascues 10
Ree, Mark Du 11
Reed, Alison 233
Rees, Alun M. G. (Mike) 411
Rees, Alun M. G. (Mike) 412
Reese, Thorsten 135
Reeves, Lee 107
Regan, Patrick C. (Pat) 47
Regendantz, Bernd 395
Regent, Tom 100
Rehder, W. M. Henning 113
Rehm, Wilhelm 489
Reibestein, Robert 231
Reich, Dirk 260
Reichlin, Lucrezia 463
Reichstul, Henri-Philippe 342
Reichstul, Henri-Philippe 356
Reid, Andrew 47
Reid, Thomas G. 422
Reilly, David 98
Reilly, Michael E. (Mike) 450
Reimann, Simon 151
Reina, Ramon 57
Reinbrecht, Jorg 28
Reiners, Hans W. 76
Reinhard, J. Pedro 366
Reinhardt, Alexander 21
Reinhardt, Jorg 78
Reiniche, Dominique 49
Reiniger, Wolfgang 371
Reinikkala, Veli-Matti 5

Reitan, Torgrim 414
Reiterman, Michael 396
Reithofer, Norbert 80
Reitinger, Philip R. 409
Reitler, Walter 159
Reitzle, Prof Wolfgang 135
Reitzle, Wolfgang H. 268
Rellier, Huguette 126
Rembde, Martin 84
Rembe, Ola 166
Remsperger, Prof Hermann 150
Ren, Alex H. C. 343
Renard, Kerstin 479
Rendon, Eduardo 114
Rengifo, Alvaro 91
Renjie, Li 229
Rennard, Marc 333
Rennemo, Svein 414
Renschler, Andreas 143
Renstrom, Lars 436
Renstrom, Lars Lars Renstrom 436
Reny, Luc 345
Reny, Luc 346
Renz, Gerhard 39
Renzi, Pierluigi Pierluigi Renzi 163
Reppien, Gunter 371
Represas, Carlos E. 91
Requardt, Hermann 395
Resca, Mario 163
Resnick, Donald 274
Retat, Bernard 443
Reu?, Dieter 179
Reuss, Dieter 179
Reutersberg, Bernhard 159
Reuther, Michael 128
Rey, Bernard 355
Reyes, Cecilia 492
Reymondet, Pascal 462
Reynish, Steve D. L. 423
Reynolds, Steve 25
Reynolds, Maj. Jon 100
Reynolds, Robert L. (Bob) 193
Riboud, Franck 145
Riboud, Franck 355
Ricci, Rich 72
Ricci, Rich 74
Ricciardi, Jose 161
Ricciardi, Jose M. E. Santo Silva 161
Ricciardi, Jose Maria Espirito Santo Silva 168
Rice, Susan 410
Richard, Pierre 19
Richard, Patrick 472
Richardson, Karen Karen Richardson 101
Richardson, Troy K. 384
Richter, Maria C. 305
Riddell, Geoffrey (Geoff) 491
Rider, Matthew J. 231
Ridolfi, Steven A. (Steve) 91
Rieck, Lars-Uwe 335
Riecken, Martin 151
Riedel, Jens 268
Rieger, Ralf 429
Rieger, Ralf 430
Riehl, Arnd 286
Riepe, Tobias 84
Rieth, Peter 136
Rifkind, Sir Malcolm L. 464
Rifkind, Sir Malcolm L. 465
Rigamonti, Pierangelo 466
Riis, Jakob 325
Rijckevorsel, Jacques van 407
Rijckevorsel, Jacques 407
Riley, Cathryn 47
Riley, James 242
Riley, Brendon 438
Riley, Brett 438
Ringsted, Sean 9
Riolacci, Pierre-Francois 471
Rios, Christian 104
Ripa, Elisabetta 432
Ripp, Robert 9
Rippert, Donald J. (Don) 7
Rippey, Michael G. (Mike) 39
Risfelt, Jon 436
Rishton, John F. 364
Rishton, John F. 365
Risseeuw, A. H. J. (Ton) 256
Ritchie, Doug 360
Ritmeier, Wolfgang 477
Ritter, Maria 356
Ritthaphirom, Thawilap 61
Riva, Ernesto 234
Riva, Renato Dalla 234
Riva, A. 376
Rivero, Jose Antonio Fernandez 56
Rivero, Jose 56
Rix, John 286
Rix, Kristian 356
Rizzo, Paul J. 301
Ro?, Heinz-Peter 429
Roach, Mark 129
Roach, Frank W. 486
Roach, Frank W. 486
Robbiati, Tarek A. 438
Robbins, Noel W. 440
Robbins, Bob 440
Robbroeckx, Lynn 39
Roberson, Simon 100
Robert, Don 134
Roberts, Steve 9
Roberts, Graham 53
Roberts, David L. 270
Roberts, David L. 270
Roberts, Julian V. F. 330
Roberts, Kenneth (Ken) 364
Roberts, Jeremy 483
Robertson, Ian 80
Robertson, Steve 100
Robertson, Brian 217
Robertson, Sir Simon 217
Robertson, Sir Simon 218
Robertson, Nigel 298
Robertson, Sir Simon 364
Robinson, David 9
Robinson, Sir Ian 134
Robinson, S. P. 245
Robinson, T. 298
Robinson, Thomas J. 422
Robredo, Rafael Miranda 162
Rocha, Robson 468
Rocke, Elisabeth 479
Roden, Neil 368
Roden, Joerg 462
Roder, Steve 278
Roder, Peter 300
Rodero, Vicente Rodero 55
Rodler, Friedrich 167
Rodocanachi, Pierre 474
Rodriguez, Florentino Perez 10
Rodriguez, Florentino Perez 10
Rodriguez, Paul 26
Rodriguez, Jose 57
Rodriguez, Jose R. 59
Rodriguez, Julio 387
Rodriguez, Julio 387
Roeder, Peter Peter Roeder 300
Roegner, Harry 268
Rogers, David 47
Rogers, Neil 100
Rogers, John 240
Rogers, John 240
Rogers, Dene L. 480
Roggemann, Gerhard 179
Rogowski, Michael 429
Rogstad, Gunnar 415
Rohatyn, Felix G. 271
Rohkamm, Prof Eckhard 429
Rohkamm, Prof Eckhard 429
Rohleder, Stephen J. (Steve) 7
Rohner, Urs 139
Rojas, Hector Manosalva 160
Rojas, Jose Fernando Calderon 177
Rojas, Julio 412
Roll, Eberhard 482
Rolland, Martial C. 309
Roller, Wolfgang 151
Rolli, Guy 131
Roma, Francesco 234
Roma, Eugenio 234
Roman, David A. 266
Roman, Francisco (Paco) 475
Romano, Massimo 40
Romano, Javier Marin 60
Romero, Guillermo de la Dehesa 60
Romero, Guillermo de la Dehesa 60
Romero, Juan 114
Rommer, Hans 325
Romojaro, Jaime 57
Romuld, Trine S?ther 157
Romy, Isabelle 461
Romyarup, Aphichat 61
Roncoroni, Marie-Helene 342
Rond, Theo de 199
Rondeau, Isabelle 91
Rondolat, Eric 258
Rondolat, Eric 387
Roney, Michael J. (Mike) 245
Ronner, Markus 461
Rooney, Paul L. 278
Rooney, Paul L. 278
Roos, Bill 157
Root, Jim 126
Rooy, Yvonne 231
Roquemaurel, Gerald de 111
Rorsg?rd, Veronica 401
Rorsgard, Veronica Veronica Rorsgard 401
Rorsted, Kasper B. 84
Rorsted, Kasper B. 202
Ros, Carl Wilhelm 399
Rosar, Alexander 78
Rosatella, Marco 432
Rose, Nicholas C. (Nick) 51
Rose, Andy 53
Rose, Nicholas Nicholas Rose 101
Rose, Marlies 151
Rose, George W. 304
Rosen, Michel de 5
Rosen, Andrea 278
Rosenberg, Philip 409
Rosenberg, Joachim 479
Rosenfeld, Klaus 136
Rosenstock, Josh 364
Rosenthal, Terese 300
Ross, Wilbur L. 39
Ross, Wayne 47
Ross, James H. 348
Rossetti, Eugenio 234
Rossi, Deanna 54
Rossi, Marco 57
Rossi, Orazio 234
Rossi, Jean 472
Rossmann, Martin 332
Rosso, Jean-Pierre 91
Rosson, Mark 100
Rossum, Anton Anton van Rossum 139
Rossum, Anton van 139
Rossum, Anton van 300
Rossum, Anton Anton van Rossum 300
Rossum, Anton van 407
Rossum, Anton 407
Rost, Uwe 335
Rosty, Nicolas von 396
Rosumek, Anke 300
Roth, Martin 158
Roth, Klaus 164
Roth, Jean-Pierre 309
Rothschild, David de 111
Rothwell, Dame Nancy 44
Roubin, Augustin de 261
Roubin, Augustin 261
Rouf, Shah 47
Roulet, Marcel 333
Roumeliotis, Panagiotis 343
Rouot, Mattieu 49
Roussat, Olivier 93
Rousseau, Henri-Paul 193
Rousseau, Henri-Paul 345
Rousseau, Henri-Paul 345
Rousseau, Henri-Paul 346
Rousseau, Henri-Paul 346
Rousseau, Luc 355
Roussel, Patrick 333
Roussel, Stephane 474
Roussinos, Don S. 365
Roussis, Theodoros 248
Routs, Rob J. 256
Rouvillois, Patrick 109
Roux, Didier 131
Rowe, Patrick B. F. 8
Rowe, Jeremy 24
Rowe, Steve 280
Rowland, David P. 7
Roy, Sumita Bose 85
Roy, Anami 196
Roy, Sylvie 302
Roy, Louise 346
Roychowdhury, Debasish 383
Royer, Raymond 193
Royer, Raymond 346
Royere, Jean-Marc 261
Rubio, Juan 114
Rudas, Andreas 84
Rudd, Henry 373
Rudder, Thierry de 189
Rudder, Thierry de 454
Rudengren, Pia Pia Rudengren 426
Ruding, H. Onno 212
Rudnicki, Yael 63
Ruechai, Khanueng 61
Ruf, Anton 81
Ruf, Anton 81
Ruggieri, Chiara 76
Ruggieri, Maria A. 432
Ruijter, Ignace de 462
Ruijter, Ignace 462
Ruiwen, Ke 122
Ruiz, Angel 166
Ruizendaal, Gerard 257
Rulis, Mike 325
Rumble, Keith C. 87
Rumble, Keith C. 88
Rumpler, John 350
Runau, Jan 13
Runevad, Anders 166
Runte, Roseann 302
Ruppik, Erich 84
Rupprecht, Gerhard 28
Rupprecht, Gerhard 179
Rupprecht, Gerhard 179
Rupprecht, Rudolf 277
Ruprecht, Hans 13
Ruprecht, Hans 13
Rusakova, Vlada V. 187
Rusckowski, Stephen H. (Steve) 257
Rusk, Jim 396
Ruslie, Kumala D. 278
Russak-Aminoach, Rakefet 63
Russo, Guy 480
Russwurm, Siegfried 395
Ruster, Hans-Dieter 457
Ruys, Anthony (Thony) 98
Ryan, Fergus D. 130
Ryan, Philip K. 193
Ryan, T. Timothy 270
Ryan, Arthur F. (Art) 368
Ryan, Jim 409
Rydberg-Dumont, Josephine 401
Ryopponen, Hannu 325
Rystedt, Fredrik 321
Ryu, Yul 372
Ryu, Seung Seung Heon Ryu 391
Ryuto, Yasuo 96

S

S.p.A, Generali 41
S?rensen, Lars R. 84
S?rensen, Lars Rebien 325
S?rensen, Lars 325
S?rensen, Lars Rebien 325
S?rensen, Lars Troen 414
Sa, Paulo de 464
Sabatacakis, Petros K. 303
Sabharwal, Rajiv 224
Sabino, Joao 57
Sabroe, Tania 325

Sach, Derek S. 368
Sachdev, Neil 240
Sachedina, Alaudin 35
Sada, Armando Garza 177
Sadeler, Sophie 127
Sadka, Prof Efraim 63
Sado, Masaaki 326
Saeki, Akira 241
Saetre, Eldar 414
Saez, Antonio Gomis 356
Saez, Antonio 356
Saga, Koei 455
Sagar, Madhu 86
Sagbakken, Per 157
Sage, Gordon H. 53
Sager, Oskar 287
Sahay, Anupam 47
Sahenk, Ferit Faik 459
Saiga, Daisuke 295
Saiga, Daisuke 296
Saikawa, Hiroto 316
Saikawa, Hiroto 316
Saikawa, Hiroto 355
Sailly, Michel 355
Saimpert, Philippe 189
Saines, Ian 129
Saint-Affrique, Antoine 464
Saint-Affrique, Antoine Antoine de Saint-Affrique
Saint-Geours, Frederic 111
Saito, Masayasu 22
Saito, Takashi 140
Saito, Katsutoshi 141
Saito, Katsutoshi 141
Saito, Yutaka 208
Saito, Fumihiko 214
Saito, Hiroki 393
Saito, Tadashi (Tan) 408
Saito, Shigeo 419
Saito, Hiroshi 451
Saito, Shozo 451
Saka, Yoshihiro 149
Sakai, Hitoshi 184
Sakai, Hitoshi 184
Sakai, Hiroyoshi 236
Sakai, Yoshikiyo 327
Sakamoto, Noriaki 296
Sakamoto, Hideyuki 316
Sakamoto, Toshihiro 338
Sakamoto, Yoshitsugu 416
Sakane, Masahiro 253
Sakane, Masahiro 320
Sakata, Ryo 236
Sakata, Shoichi 291
Sakata, Seiji 358
Sakellaris, Ploutarchos K. 170
Sakishima, Takafumi 281
Sakishima, Takafumi 282
Sako, Naohiro 320
Sako, Tatsunobu 405
Saksti, Hendri 485
Sakuma, Hidetoshi 117
Sakuma, Hidetoshi 117
Sakuma, Kaichiro 208
Sakunphram, Songkhram 61
Sakurai, Kenji 141
Sakurai, Akira 316
Sakurai, Masamitsu 358
Sakurai, Tohru 393
Sakurai, Tohru 393
Sakuyama, Masaki 291
Sala, Bernard 127
Salazar-Simpson, Luis Alberto 60
Salgado, Ricardo Espirito Santo Silva 57
Salgado, Ricardo Espirito Santo 58
Salgado, Ricardo Espirito Santo 58
Salguero, Carlos 177
Sallas, Michalis G. 343
Saller, Syl 155
Salles, Fernando Roberto Moreira 237
Sallstrom, Mikael 479
Salman, Samir 135
Salmons, Dan 74
Salomonsen, Henrik 325
Salt, Mark 95
Salter, Brian 33
Salvadore, Domenico 212
Salvino, Michael J. (Mike) 7
Salza, Enrico 234
Salzgeber, Guy 261
Samaddar, Sanjay Sanjay Samaddar 39
Samanta, Ashim 196
Samaram, Maris 394
Samarasekera, Indira V. 69
Samet, Haim 63
Samet, Zipora 63
Sammakia, Mohamed 461
Sampson, Chris 44
Sams, Steve 401
Samuel, Jonathan 35
Samuelson, Jonas 3
Samuelsson, H?kan 396
Sanches, Valter 144
Sanchez, Octavio del Real 10
Sanchez, Antonio Alfonzo 10
Sanchez, Enrique 12
Sanctis, S. de 376
Sande, Marc van 462
Sander, Heinz-Guenter 482
Sandford, W. F. (Bill) 245
Sandhaus, Nomi 63
Sands, Peter A. 411
Sands, Peter A. 412
Sands, Anita 461
Sandstrom, Per-Arne 436
Sandstrom, Per-Arne Per-Arne Sandstrom 436
Sang-Yong, Park 345
Sanjines, Javier Gerardo Astaburuaga 177
Sanjines, Javier Gerardo Astaburuaga 199
Sankey, Vernon L. 492
Sanson, Agathe 126
Santacana, Enrique 5
Santamans, Carlos 57
Santana, Vincente 59
Santesso, Adineu 56
Santiago, Ramon A. 379
Santiago, Carmelo L. 379
Santoni, Jean-Philippe 382
Santos, Luiz A. dos 56
Santos, Paulo A. dos 57
Santos, Tomas Milmo 114
Sants, Sir Hector 72
Sant'Albano, Carlo 172
Sanyal, Dev 95
Sanyalaksiri, Somchai 394
Sanz, Eva Castillo 434
Sanz, Francisco Javier Garcia 477
Sanzgiri, Dipti 85
Sapir, Amos 63
Saradhi, V. Vizia 205
Sardo, Salvatore 163
Sardo, Salvatore 376
Sarig, Oded 62
Sarnoff, Richard 83
Sarraf, D. K. 328
Sarraf, D. K. 328
Sarup, Deepak 394
Saruwatari, Satoshi 141
Sasakawa, Takashi 291
Sasaki, Tadashi 182
Sasaki, Toshio 236
Sasaki, Toshio 236
Sasaki, Junichi 238
Sasaki, Mikio 290
Sasaki, Mikio 291
Sasaki, Mikio 293
Sasaki, Takeshi 334
Sasaki, Shiro 358
Sasaki, Shinichi 417
Sasaki, Shinichi 417
Sasaki, Norio 451
Sasaki, Norio 452
Sasaki, Takeshi 452
Sasaki, Shinichi 455
Sasaki, Akira 455
Sasaki, Shinichi 455
Sasamoto, Hiroshi 214
Sasamoto, Sakio 244
Sasikala, I. 85
Saso, Hideyuki 183
Sassenfeld, Peter 210
Sasseron, Jose Ricardo 468
Sato, Reiichi 1
Sato, Reiichi 1
Sato, Toru 34
Sato, Yoichi 96
Sato, Kazuhiro 252
Sato, Masayuki 388
Sato, Hiroshi Hiroshi Sato 390
Sato, Hitomi 392
Sato, Yoji 405
Sato, Yoji 405
Sato, Yoshio 420
Sato, Yoshio 420
Sato, Hirofumi 456
Satomi, Kazuhiro 393
Satomi, Kazuhiro 393
Satou, Hironobu 392
Saucier, Guylaine 145
Sauer, Hans Dietmar 489
Saun, Bruce W. Van 368
Saun, Bruce 368
Saun, Bruce W. Van 368
Saunders, Mark S. 422
Saunier, Martine 443
Saupper, Eveline 54
Saura, Janet 107
Sauriol, Jean-Pierre 27
Savander, Niklas 318
Savart, Michel 111
Savio, Kathleen 492
Savorelli, Lorenzo 41
Sawamoto, Kazuo 291
Sawayama, Hiroki 456
Sawers, Rick 301
Saxon, Ulrika 3
Sayato, Junichi 421
Scalco, Jair D. 56
Scannapieco, Dario 170
Scarborough, Ranulf 100
Scardino, Dame Marjorie M. 318
Scardino, Dame Marjorie M. 318
Scaroni, Paolo 41
Scaroni, Paolo 163
Scaroni, Paolo 471
Scarratt, Mary 100
Schachler, Juergen Juergen Schachler 39
Schacht, Horst 260
Schad, Martin 144
Schade, Michael 78
Schaeffler, Georg F. W. 136
Schaeffler, Maria-Elisabeth 136
Schaekel, Julie 9
Schafer, Wolfgang 136
Schaferkordt, Anke 84
Schaffer, Thomas 396
Schaller, Andreas 197
Scharwath, Tim 260
Schatzman, Matt 85
Scheele, Sir Nicholas V. (Nick) 98
Scheen, Benoit 333
Scheen, Benoit 333
Scheffer, Henk 39
Scheibye, Sten 147
Scheibye, Sten 325
Scheifele, Bernd 197
Scheinkestel, Nora L. 33
Scheinkestel, Nora L. 438
Scheitor, Dieter 396
Schele, Staffan Staffan Schele 401
Schellekens, Ronald 475
Schellemans, Denise 76
Scheller, Richard H. 362
Schenck, Marcus 128
Schenck, Marcus 159
Schenck, Kersten von 445
Schenk, Dieter 179
Scheu, Greg 5
Scheuble, Bernhard 407
Scheuer, Albert 197
Schiavone, Paul 491
Schick, Elisabeth 76
Schick, Hartmut 143
Schiefloe, Ingrid 435
Schielke, Joachim E. 262
Schiendorfer, Michael 323
Schilfgaarde, Steven van 256
Schiller, Xaver 286
Schimmelmann, Wulf von 8
Schindera, Philipp 154
Schinzler, Hans-Jurgen 286
Schinzler, Hans-Jurgen 463
Schipporeit, Erhard 195
Schipporeit, Erhard 384
Schipporeit, Erhard 429
Schipporeit, Erhard 459
Schiro, James J. (Jim) 258
Schlatter, Theophil H. 212
Schlede, Klaus G. 151
Schleweis, Helmut 263
Schluessel, Roger 491
Schmedtmann, Markus 84
Schmeer, Dagmar 371
Schmid, Stefan 81
Schmid, Stefan 81
Schmid, Hans-Peter 153
Schmidheiny, Thomas 212
Schmidt, Thomas 5
Schmidt, Maria 81
Schmidt, Joachim 143
Schmidt, Becky 151
Schmidt, Matthias 202
Schmidt, Xaver 268
Schmidt, Kurt T. 309
Schmidt, Elin 325
Schmitt, Heinz 197
Schmitt, Heinz 197
Schmitt, Wolfram 429
Schmittmann, Stefan 128
Schmitz, Rolf Martin 371
Schmitz, Jochen 395
Schmoldt, Hubertus 78
Schmoldt, Hubertus 159
Schmoock, David 266
Schneider, Ralf 28
Schneider, Manfred 78
Schneider, Michael 79
Schneider, Ulf M. (Mark) 179
Schneider, Peter 263
Schneider, Manfred 268
Schneider, Jorg 300
Schneider, Don 330
Schneider, Manfred 371
Schneider, Manfred 371
Schneider, Manfred 457
Schneider, Roland 457
Schnepp, Maj. Gilles 131
Schoch, Manfred 80
Schoch, Manfred 81
Schofield, Keitha 491
Schonfelder, Jorg 136
Schorling, Melker 203
Schorling, Melker Melker Schorling 203
Schorsch, Louis (Lou) 39
Schraeder, Werner 197
Schram, Jacob 27
Schregle, Josef 268
Schreiber, Katja 13
Schreiber, Pierre 139
Schreyer, Peter 249
Schroder, Soren W. 102
Schroder, Lothar 154
Schroder, Ulrich 154
Schroeder, Lone F. 425
Schubert, John M. 87
Schubert, John M. 88
Schubert, Stefan 179
Schubert, Linda 484
Schubiger, Georg 146
Schubring-Giese, Friedrich 263
Schuessel, Wolfgang 371
Schuessel, Wolfgang 371
Schuler, Wolfgang 489
Schulman, Daniel H. (Dan) 176
Schulte-Bockum, Jens 475

Schulte-Laggenbeck, Jurgen 335
Schulte-Noelle, Henning 28
Schulte-Noelle, Henning 159
Schultz, Prof Majken 147
Schultz, Richard G. 193
Schulz, Ekkehard D. 78
Schulz, Ekkehard D. 276
Schulz, Ekkehard D. 277
Schulz, Ekkehard D. 371
Schulz, Thomas 380
Schulz, Stefan 384
Schulz-Drost, Michael 395
Schulze, Michael 384
Schulze-Delitzsch, Hermann 158
Schumm, Jochen 277
Schunk, Albert 459
Schurer, Wolfgang 212
Schussel, Wolfgang 371
Schuster, Helmut 95
Schutte, Tom 88
Schwaab, Stefan 144
Schwager, Harald 76
Schwan, Severin 362
Schwartz, Michael 12
Schwartz, Dafna 62
Schwartz, Menachem 63
Schwartz, Larry 155
Schwartz, Mark 404
Schwarz, Erich 277
Schweitzer, Roger 84
Schweitzer, Louis 90
Schweitzer, Louis 354
Schweitzer, John 384
Schweitzer, Louis 471
Schweitzer, Louis 471
Schweitzer, Louis 479
Schwenzer, Michael 469
Schwerdtle, Willi 13
Schwerdtle, Willi 13
Schwitalla, Jorg 276
Scibetta, Pierluigi 163
Scicluna, Martin A. 270
Sciolla, Corrado 100
Scoby, Joseph (Joe) 461
Scott, Gary R. 91
Scott, Philip G. 156
Scott, T. G. (Glenn) 225
Scott, Philip G. 368
Scott, Robert 480
Scotti, Giancarlo 41
Scotti, Gianni 131
Scotting, Bill 39
Seage, Ed 44
Seah, Peter L. H. 147
Seale, Margaret 438
Searle, Peter 11
Seber, Butch 26
Secheval, Helman le Pas de 93
Secheval, Helman Helman le Pas de Secheval 471
Secheval, Helman le Pas de 471
See, John G. 450
Sega, Franco Dalla 234
Segal, Nurit 63
Segal, Jillian S. 301
Segal, Hugh D. 422
Segalen, Loik 443
Segawa, Daisuke 358
Segerath, Wilhelm 445
Segovia, Armando J. Garcia 114
Segre, Paul 25
Segretain, Pierre 443
Segundo, Karen M. A. de 98
Segundo, Karen 98
Segundo, Karen de 159
Sehgal, Rajender 196
Seibert, Karl-Heinz 395
Seilliere, Ernest-Antoine 342
Seitz, Friedrich 76
Seki, Daisuke 224
Seki, Hiroshi 224
Seki, Tadayuki 238
Seki, Tadayuki 238
Seki, Fusao 253
Seki, Jun 316
Sekiguchi, Masakazu 97
Sekiguchi, Yoshiki (Steve) 149
Sekiguchi, Takashi 214
Sekihachi, Yoshihiro 211
Sekine, Yutaka 417
Sekiuchi, Masao 417
Sela, Dor 109
Seleznev, Kirill Gennadievich 186
Seleznev, Kirill Gennadievich 187
Selfors-Thomann, Karin 11
Seligman, Mark 85
Seligman, Mark Mark Seligman 250
Seligman, Nicole 408
Sell, Robert E. (Bob) 8
Selley, Clive 100
Selvas, Francesc 57
Selwan, Fadi 472
Semmel, Christina 151
Sen, Ting Lee 266
Sen, Michael 396
Sen, Ranendra 430
Senel, Aydin 459
Senen, Edward 443
Senequier, Dominique 388
Seng, Kwa Chong 147
Senn, Martin 491
Sentinelli, Mauro 432
Seong, Chan 467
Serdar, Cenk 475
Sereda, Mikhail L. 187
Sereda, Mikhail L. 188
Serfontein, Deward 330
Serna, Angel 491
Seroussi, Yair 62
Serrano, Manuel Soto 60
Serve, Robert de la 469
Servitje, Roberto 177
Seshadri, K. V. 86
Sestini, Roberto 466
Setbon, Philippe 41
Seth, Munish 25
Sethi, Ashmita 364
Seto, Shinichirou 392
Seton, John 100
Setrakian, Berge 227
Setubal, Roberto Egydio 237
Setubal, Alfredo Egydio 237
Setzer, Nikolai 135
Seung-Eun, Jeong 249
Sevaldsen, Erik 146
Sevang, Thomas 321
Severin, Bo 380
Severino, Jean 333
Seymour, Linda 216
Seze, Amaury-Daniel de 110
Seze, Amaury de 346
Seze, Amaury-Daniel de 443
Seznec, P. 173
Seznec, Reynald 443
Shafir, Robert S. (Rob) 139
Shah, Tushaar 224
Shahudin, Ismail 275
Shaked, Carol 218
Shakeel, Bassem A. 274
Shalev, Prof Gabriela 63
Shamsuarov, Azat 329
Shamsudin, Mohaiyani Mohaiyani binti Shamsudin 275
Shan, Tan Su 147
Shang, Oliver 139
Shankar, Viswanathan (Shankar) 411
Shankar, Viswanathan (Shankar) 412
Shanks, Eugene B. 9
Shanks, Peter 458
Shanley, Marlene 66
Shaopeng, Chen 266
Shapland, Darren 240
Shapland, Darren 240
Sharma, Sharad K. 85
Sharma, Pramod 86
Sharma, Mahendra Kumar 224
Sharma, R. S. 328
Sharma, Vibhu R. 491
Sharman, Lord Colin M. 47
Sharp, Julie 66
Sharp, Steven (Steve) 280
Sharp, Steven (Steve) 280
Shasta, Theodore E. (Ted) 9
Shaw, Allan C. 69
Shaw, Peter 412
Shaw, Candace G. 422
Shear, Neal 461
Shearan, Kevin 9
Sheard, Jim 364
Shearer, Craig 216
Shedden, Jill 116
Sheffy, F. K. 245
Shelton, Mark 461
Shengchen, Guo 342
Shenoy, K. V. 86
Sher, Harold 459
Shergold, Peter 33
Sheridan, Ronan 29
Sherman, Frank 24
Shern, Stephanie M. 255
Sherry, Ann C. 107
Shevlin, Bianca 373
Shevrin, Phil 404
Shibata, Tsukasa 34
Shibata, Takumi 320
Shibata, Masaharu 320
Shibata, Kenichi 328
Shiff, Deena 438
Shiga, Toshiyuki 316
Shiga, Toshiyuki 316
Shiga, Shigenori Shigenori Shiga 452
Shigeta, Osamu 291
Shih, Willy C. 176
Shih, Ming-Hsiung 178
Shih, Edith 219
Shih, Lee Tih 336
Shih, Stan 429
Shih, Kathryn 461
Shikama, Chihiro 281
Shikamura, Akio (Alex) 149
Shikata, Susumu 291
Shiki, Takashi 34
Shill, Walt 7
Shilo, Gabriella 63
Shilston, Andrew B. 95
Shilston, Andrew B. 365
Shim, Dal Sup 398
Shimada, Hideo 420
Shimada, Hideo 420
Shimanouchi, Ken 452
Shimanuki, Shizuo 22
Shimao, Matt 318
Shimizu, Minoru 97
Shimizu, Katsuichi 106
Shimizu, Takao 140
Shimizu, Takao 141
Shimizu, Masakazu 241
Shimizu, Minoru 278
Shimizu, Takaaki 307
Shimizu, Noritaka 388
Shimizu, Junzo 456
Shimizu, Junzo 456
Shimojima, Bunmei 183
Shimokawa, Ryoichi 180
Shimokobe, Kazuhiko 447
Shimomitsu, Hidejiro 451
Shimomura, Setsuhiro 291
Shimoni, Micha 62
Shimotsuji, Shigeyoshi Shigeyoshi Shimotsuji 452
Shimoyama, Yoichi 289
Shimura, Yasuhiro 452
Shin, Il-Soon 258
Shin, Moon-Bum 267
Shindo, Kosei 312
Shindo, Kosei 312
Shindou, Tsutomu 326
Shingai, Yasushi 241
Shingai, Yasushi 241
Shinobe, Osamu 34
Shinobe, Osamu 34
Shinohara, Hiromichi 314
Shinohara, Hiromichi 314
Shinohara, Minoru 316
Shinohara, Minoru 320
Shinohara, Masashi 405
Shinozuka, Hisashi 253
Shintaku, Masaaki 327
Shiokawa, Yorihisa 338
Shiomi, Takao 238
Shipway, Jane 100
Shirai, Yoshio 206
Shirai, Yoshio 456
Shirai, Takumi 456
Shiraishi, Toru 328
Shiraishi, Toru 328
Shiraji, Kozo 289
Shirakawa, Susumu 447
Shiraki, Seiji 289
Shirane, Takeshi 455
Shirasaki, Shinji 149
Shirota, Norihisa 408
Shiseki, Koji Koji Shiseki 184
Shiung, Albert 139
Shizhong, Huang 64
Shizuta, Atsushi 316
Shmatko, Sergey I. 188
Shobuda, Kiyotaka 283
Shokhin, Alexander 329
Shouji, Tetsuya 314
Shoylekov, Richard 486
Shoylekov, Richard 486
Shrikhande, Anil 364
Shui, Lo Ka 119
Shulin, Su 120
Shun, Wong (Peter) Tung 65
Shurniak, William 219
Shurui, Zhou 342
Shuxian, Zhao 342
Si, Khanit 61
Sicklinger, Hermann 490
Sicre, Alberto 223
Sicupira, Carlos A. 37
Sidorkina, Anna 186
Sidwell, David H. 461
Sieb, Henry 457
Sieber, Thomas 54
Sieber, Ulrich 128
Sieg, Rainer 396
Siegert, Theo 159
Siegert, Theo 164
Siegert, Theo 202
Sierau, Ullrich 371
Sierau, Ullrich 371
Sierra, Joan 57
Sievert, Christian Christian Sievert 203
Sigismondi, Pier Luigi 464
Sigismondi, Pier Luigi 465
Sigismondi, Pier 465
Signoretti, Marco 432
Siilasmaa, Risto 318
Sikka, Vishal 384
Sikorav, Sonia 453
Sikorski, Ralf 76
Silguy, Yves-Thibault de 271
Silguy, Yves-Thibault 407
Silva, Kleber Kleber Silva 39
Silva, Fernando d'Ornellas 162
Silva, Jose Manuel Pinheiro Espirito Santo 168
Silva, Jose Pedro Torres Garcia Caldeira da 168
Silva, Eduardo Padilla 177
Silva, Josue Christiano Gomes da 340
Silvant, Jean-Louis 342
Silvanus, Joseph 411
Sim, BoonKiat 5
Simmonds, Robert Robert Simmonds 82
Simola, Jozsef 297
Simon, Dryell 440
Simoni, Walter De 35
Simonin, Jean 333
Simonsen, Per 435
Simpfendorfer, Ben 368
Simpson, Richard 35
Simpson, Julia 233
Simpson, James 330
Simpson, James W. (Jim) 423
Sinclair, Charles J. F. 42

Sinclair, Helen K. 450
Sing, Goh Ing 485
Singelais, B. C. 245
Singh, R.K. 85
Singh, Brij Pal 86
Singh, Arun 86
Singh, James 309
Singh-Molares, Rajeev 25
Sintraphannathorn, Mali 61
Siong, Prof Neo Boon 336
Sirichot, Thanit 61
Siridej, Adm. Prachet 61
Siridet, Prachet 61
Siriphat, Saowani 61
Siriphokhi, Than 61
Sirois, Charles 104
Sironi, Cesare 432
Sirotkin, Mikhail 188
Sistino, Lorenzo 172
Sit, Dorothy K. Y. P. 194
Sit, Dorothy K. Y. P. 194
Sithi-Amnuai, Piti 61
Sitorus, Martua 485
Sitorus, Martua 485
Sitthiphong, Norkun 349
Sivignon, Pierre-Jean 109
Siwayathorn, Kunthida 61
Sixt, Frank J. 219
Sixt, Frank J. 219
Sj?blom, Tove Stuhr 414
Sjafril, Irwin 3
Sjulstad, Ole Bj?rn 435
Sk?r, ?smund 157
Skaaret, Heidi 415
Skalli, Jaafar 212
Skaugen, Grace Reksten 414
Skelt, Paul 100
Skene, Richard 212
Skeoch, Keith 413
Skeoch, Keith 413
Skinner, Paul D. 261
Skinner, Paul D. 412
Skodol, Ted 465
Skovhus, Per Damborg 146
Skudutis, Tom 274
Slacik, Marek 435
Slagle, Dennis R. (Denny) 479
Slaoui, Moncef 191
Slaoui, Moncef 192
Slater, Gavin R. 301
Sloan, Hugh W. 278
Slobodin, Mikhail 186
Slonim, Ory 441
Slonina, Kajetan 352
Sluitner, Zsolt 396
Slym, Karl 430
Smart, Jill B. 7
Smart, Ken 233
Smart, Katherine 373
Smeby-Udesen, Lena 426
Smedman, Johan 426
Smejc, Jiri 344
Smiles, P. 350
Smit, Willie 39
Smith, Peter 42
Smith, David 44
Smith, Michael R. P. 46
Smith, Michael R. P. 46
Smith, Wayne T. 76
Smith, Dorothy 100
Smith, Guy L. 156
Smith, David 156
Smith, Maura Abeln 169
Smith, Roland C. 169
Smith, Jeremy 212
Smith, Simon M. 225
Smith, Gerry P. 266
Smith, Malcolm 348
Smith, Jenni 350
Smith, David 360
Smith, Colin P. 364
Smith, Colin P. 365
Smith, James 370
Smith, Andrew 370
Smith, Kate 370
Smith, Keith J. 385
Smith, Lord Robert 410
Smith, Jim 410
Smith, Kris 423
Smith, Brian 450
Smith, Kelly 461
Smits, Peter 5
Smits, Ivar 24
Smits, Didier 169
Smoley, David E. 176
Snabe, Jim Hagemann 384
Snow, Richard C. 475
Snowball, Patrick 423
Snowball, Patrick 423
Soanes, David 461
Sobey, Paul D. 69
Sobrinho, Jose Batista 243
Sodeika, Lisa M. 217
Sodemark, Ake Ake Sodemark 436
Sodermark, Ake 436
Sodha, Paresh 461
Soete, Hendrik 248
Soeters, Martin H. 325
Soh, Vincent 336
Soh, Jae Gwang 391
Sohn, Dale 378
Soiron, Rolf 212
Sojo, Jose 350
Solis, Manuel Delgado 10
Solis, Miguel A. de 59
Solmssen, Peter Y. 395
Sologaistua, Pedro 57
Solvay, Denis 407
Solvay, Denis 407
Solvay, Jean-Marie 407
Somanath, T. 86
Somavilla, Vania 468
Somaya, M. M. 86
Sombutsiri, Sirichai 394
Somers, Michael 29
Somers, Michael 29
Somlyai, Dora 297
Sommer, Michael 154
Sommer, Richard 164
Sommer, Ron 300
Sommer, Richard 300
Sommer, Stefan 489
Sommerauer, Thomas 167
Son, Masayoshi 404
Soneda, Mitsuru 224
Sonet, Aurelien 403
Song, Qiao 266
Sonn, Crispin 330
Sonnino, Elvio 466
Sonshine, Edward 366
Sood, Vivek 435
Sookoo, Suresh 366
Soon, Cham Tao 467
Soong, Tham 467
Sophonpanich, Chartsiri 61
Sophonpanich, Chartsiri 61
Sophonpanich, Charn 61
Sophonpanit, Chatri 61
Sora, Riccardo 466
Soranno-Keating, Valerie (Val) 72
Soranno-Keating, Valerie (Val) 74
Sorbara, Nicole 273
Sorby, Morten K. 435
Sorensen, Torben B. 3
Sori, Takahisa 283
Soriot, Pascal 44
Sorrentino, Rob 83
Sostmann, Rafael Rangel 114
Sostmann, Rafael 114
Soto, Jose Zornoza 10
Sourisse, Pascale 355
Sourisse, Pascale 443
Sourisse, Pascale 472
Sourisse, Pascale 472
Southern, Martin 100
Souza, Altair A. de 56
Souza, Paulo 468
Sozen, Suleyman 459
Sozen, Suleyman 459
Spadacini, Marco 234
Spallanzani, Erminio 54
Spalt, Bernhard 167
Spalti, Dieter 212
Spangenberg, Jonas 401
Spannuth, Heiner 91
Spanswick, Paul 320
Speers, Laurie A. 193
Spek, Hanspeter 113
Spek, Hanspeter 382
Spelman, Mark 7
Spencer, Robin 47
Sperling, Katrine 325
Speth, Ralf 430
Speth, Ralf 430
Spiegel, Eric A. 396
Spies, Jorg 144
Spiesshofer, Ulrich 5
Spilling, Rolv-Erik 435
Spillmann, Antoine 39
Spina, Jessica 284
Spincer, Ben 438
Spinetta, Jean-Cyril 19
Spinetta, Jean-Cyril 25
Spinetta, Jean-Cyril 131
Spitz, Erich 469
Spoelberch, Gregoire de 37
Spoerry, Robert F. 212
Spohr, Carsten 151
Spoo, Sibylle 154
Sprieser, Judith A. (Judy) 255
Sprigg, Robert G. 443
Spring, Dick 29
Spring, Annabel F. 130
Spyriouni, Garyfallia 303
Sr., James J. (Jim) Tobin 274
Sr., Paul Desmarais 345
Sr., Paul Desmarais 346
Srejber, Eva 170
Srichukrin, Narong 394
Sridar, V. 224
Sriphaibun, Suthira 61
Srivastava, P. C. 86
Stachelhaus, Regine 159
Stack, John James 167
Stack, Robert J. (Bob) 240
Stadelmann, Anton 461
Stadler, Ines Macho 223
Stadler, Rupert 277
Stadler, Rupert 477
Staehelin, Thomas 260
Stagg, Nigel 100
Stahl, Jack J. 169
Stalker, Robin 13
Stamminger, Erich 13
Standish, Mark A. 366
Stang, Wolfgang 205
Stanion, John 472
Stanners, Russell 475
Stansfield, George 49
Stara, Friedrich 202
Starkov, Rinat 39
Staron, Bill 462
Stathopoulos, Miltiadis 303
Staudt, Daniel J. 396
Staunton, Henry E. 265
Staunton, Henry E. 265
Stausberg, Bertram 84
Stausholm, Jakob 414
Stavn, Harald 435
Stavrakis, Charilaos 170
Steacy, Robert J. (Bob) 104
Stecyk, Geoffrey Geoffrey Stecyk 275
Steed, Jacqueline 100
Steel, Gary 5
Steers, Bill 39
Stegemann, Klaus P. 396
Steimer, Olivier 9
Stein, Rainer 179
Stein, Darrell 280
Stein, Paul 364
Stein, Nigel M. 486
Steinberg, Scott A. 408
Steinborn, Birgit 396
Steinbruck, Peer 445
Steinebach, Lothar 202
Steininger, Frank-Dirk 197
Steinle, Karl 195
Steinmann, Katrin 335
Stella, Giovanni 432
Stemmer, Ralf 153
Stenberg, Patrik 479
Stenstadvold, Halvor 415
Stenvinkel, Kristina 203
Stephenson, I. F. 245
Stepic, Herbert 332
Sterling, Stephanie 370
Sterling, Eric 396
Stern, Prof Yedidia (Zvi) 63
Steur, Christine van der 100
Steven, Anna 100
Stevens, Ben 98
Stevens, Ben 98
Stevens, Franzo Grande 172
Stevens, Jason 289
Stevenson, Katharine B. (Kate) 104
Stevenson, Tim E. P. 245
Stewart, John D. 173
Stewart, John M. 265
Stewart, Alan 280
Stewart, John M. 438
Stickler, Peter A. 176
Stieger, Peter 286
Stimpson, Hayley 47
Stirrat, Ian 100
Stitzer, H. Todd 156
Stocken, Oliver 412
Stocker, John W. 438
Stocks, Neil R. 461
Stoker, Graeme 100
Stokes, Edmund 218
Stolberg, Doug 46
Stoll, Jerome 355
Stolyar, Nikolai F. 188
Stone, Rod 21
Stone, Jon 74
Storm, Kornelis J. (Kees) 14
Storm, Kornelis J. (Kees) 37
Storm, Kornelis J. (Kees) 37
Storm, Kornelis J. (Kees) 464
Storm, Kornelis J. (Kees) 464
Storm, Kornelis J. (Kees) 465
Storr, Hanns-Peter 153
Storrie, Colin 33
Story, John D. 423
Str?b?k, Stig 325
Straarup, Peter 146
Strachan, Ian C. 365
Strachan, Warwick 443
Strain, Kevin D. 422
Strassl, Wolfgang 300
Stratton, Kim 323
Strau?, Thorsten 84
Straub, Stefan 277
Straube, David 7
Strauss, Frank 153
Streiff, M. Christian 445
Strempel, Anette 457
Streppel, Joseph B.M. (Jos) 256
Stringer, Sir Howard 408
Strobel, Martin 54
Strohmaier, Walter 79
Stromberg, Charlotte 401
Stromberg, Charlotte Charlotte Stromberg 401
Stromberg, Charlotte Charlotte Stromberg 426
Stroomer, Kees 352
Strubelt, Ortwin 457
Struble, Mike 26
Strutz, Eric 284
Stuart, Mark 8
Stuart, Sandra 216
Stuckes, Richard 24
Studer, Robert 168
Stuger, Thomas 151
Stukalsky, Alan 352
Stumpf, Mark 225
Stumpf, Heribert 395
Stumpf, Jurgen 477
Stumpfoegger, Niko 179

Stumpfogger, Niko 179
Sturany, Klaus 78
Sturany, Klaus 195
Sturany, Klaus 195
Sturm, Stephan 179
Stymiest, Barbara G. 366
Stymiest, Barbara Barbara Stymiest 483
Su, C. Y. 178
Su?elbeck, Roswitha 78
Suarez, Joaquin 114
Subbotin, Valery 329
Suberville, Max Michel 177
Subotnick, Stuart 107
Subrahmanyam, Prof Marti G. 224
Subramanian, G. 196
Sucharitkun, Piyada 61
Suckale, Margret 76
Sud, Ashok 411
Suda, Zenichi 224
Sudhakar, S 353
Sudhoff, Stefan 202
Sudo, Fumio 244
Sudo, Fumio 244
Sudo, Noriyuki 253
Sudo, Akira 452
Sudo, Seiichi 455
Sudo, Seiichi 455
Sueki, Takayuki 291
Suematsu, Hiroyuki 106
Suematsu, Kouichi 182
Suess, Michael 396
Suesskind, Dan S. 441
Sueyoshi, Takejiro 16
Sueyoshi, Takejiro 16
Suffel, Holger 144
Sufrategui, Jose 57
Sugano, Nobuyuki 390
Sugano, Nobuyuki 390
Sugi, Hikaru 149
Sugi, Hikaru 149
Sugihara, Koichi 455
Sugiki, Akira Akira Sugiki 253
Sugimori, Masato 417
Sugimoto, Toyokazu 424
Sugiura, Masayasu 22
Sugiura, Yasuyuki 289
Sugiyama, Nao 328
Sugiyama, Toshiaki 393
Sugizaki, Tomoki 141
Suh, Jin Won 391
Suh, Jin Won 391
Suila, Keijo 318
Suita, Kiyotsugu 224
Sukkirdkijpiboon, Rungruang 394
Sukthankar, Paresh 196
Sukthankar, Paresh 196
Sullivan, Damien 9
Sullivan, Brian 95
Sullivan, Chris 368
Sumi, Shuzo 446
Sumihiro, Isao 206
Sumikawa, Masaaki 241
Summerer, Gerhard 157
Sun, Changji 90
Sun, Changji 90
Sun, David P. 112
Sun, David P. 112
Sun, Bo 339
Sun, Jianyi 343
Sun, Jianyi 343
Sun, Elizabeth 429
Sun, Jack 429
Sun, Irene 429
Sunaoshi, Hisashi 282
Sundberg, Matti 401
Sunderland, Sir John M. 72
Sunderland, Sir John M. 74
Sundgren, Jan-Eric 479
Sundstrom, Anders 426
Sundstrom, Anders Anders Sundstrom 426
Sundstrom, Karl-Henrik Karl-Henrik Sundstrom 426
Suning, Tian 266
Sunkunakorn, Manoon 394
Sunmonu, Mutiu 370
Suo, Masahiro 22
Suominen, Arja 318
Suraphongchai, Vichit 394
Suraphongchai, Vichit 394
Suri, Rajeev 318
Surinach, Ignacio Segura 10
Surjaudaja, Pramukti 336
Susan, Hwee 467
Sutanthawibun, Wirasak 61
Sutcliffe, Anthony Anthony Sutcliffe 250
Sutcliffe, James H. (Jim) 422
Suter, Ursula 461
Sutherland, Peter D. 28
Sutherland, Graham 100
Sutherland, David 225
Sutherland, Euan A. 250
Suttle, John 51
Sutton, Neil 100
Suzaki, Koichi 420
Suzaki, Koichi 420
Suzuki, Hideo 137
Suzuki, Toshiaki 182
Suzuki, Masahito 252
Suzuki, Toru 252
Suzuki, Yasuo 253
Suzuki, Makoto 296
Suzuki, Masatoshi 326
Suzuki, Tetsuya 326
Suzuki, Masatoshi 327
Suzuki, Toshifumi 388
Suzuki, Joji 405
Suzuki, Yoshihisa 405
Suzuki, Tomoyuki 408
Suzuki, Kunimasa 409
Suzuki, Osamu 424
Suzuki, Toshihiro 424
Suzuki, Toshihiro 424
Suzuki, Kazuo 448
Suzuki, Shigeki 455
Svaan, Morten 414
Svanberg, Carl-Henric 95
Svanberg, Carl-Henric 166
Svanberg, Carl-Henric 479
Svanholm, Poul J. 2
Svendsen, Berit 435
Svensson, Siv Siv Svensson 426
Swaan, Tom de 192
Swaan, Tom de 255
Swaan, Tom de 255
Swaan, Tom de 491
Swaan, Tom de 492
Swaan, Tom Tom de Swaan 492
Swannell, Robert 280
Swaroop, Neeraj 411
Sweeney, Mike 51
Sweeney, Mick 66
Sweet, Julie S. 8
Sweldens, Wim 25
Swift, Nick 233
Switzer, Frank T. 422
Symon, Carl G. 51
Symonds, Jonathan R. (Jon) 323
Symons, Baroness Elizabeth C. 233
Syriani, Aziz R.D. 139
Syz, David W. 139
Syzdek, Alan 202
Szabo, Nathalie 403
Szathmary, Emoke J. E. 193
Szathmary, Emoke 193
Szathmary, Emoke J. E. 345
Szathmary, Emoke 345
Szathmary, Emoke J. E. 346
Szathmary, Emoke 346

T

Tabacco, Marina 234
Tabernero, Jordi 185
Tachibana-Fukushima, Sakie 97
Tachikake, Satoshi 283
Tachimori, Takeshi 180
Tadaki, Keiichi 16
Tadaki, Keiichi 16
Tadaki, Yoshihiro 236
Tadeu, Ricardo 37
Taeuber, Annette 151
Tagami, Minoru 316
Tagawa, Joji 316
Taglieri, Lina 483
Tagomori, Satoshi 96
Taguchi, Yasuhiro 326
Tai, Jackson P. 258
Tai, Ichiro 452
Taiber, Werner 482
Tait, Duncan 183
Taittinger, Anne-Claire 109
Taittinger, Anne-Claire 443
Tajima, Akio 149
Takada, Mitsuru 180
Takada, Katsumi Katsumi Takada 184
Takada, Hisashi 419
Takagi, Shigeo 211
Takagi, Shigeru 214
Takagi, Shigeru 215
Takaha, Yasuo 388
Takahara, Hirokazu 307
Takahashi, Seiichi 22
Takahashi, Atsushi 141
Takahashi, Mitsuru 180
Takahashi, Toshio 182
Takahashi, Yoshisada 253
Takahashi, George 289
Takahashi, Hideaki 307
Takahashi, Yusuke 316
Takahashi, Kunio 388
Takahashi, Kunio 388
Takahashi, Kozo 390
Takahashi, Hiroyuki 392
Takahashi, Katsunori 456
Takahata, Koichi 417
Takamatsu, Norio 420
Takami, Kazunori 338
Takami, Kazunori 338
Takamiyagi, Jitsumei 448
Takamuku, Seizo 419
Takamura, Fujitoshi 253
Takanami, Koichi 140
Takanami, Koichi 141
Takanashi, Kenji 456
Takano, Kengo 70
Takano, Kengo 70
Takano, Hiroshi 456
Takao, Yoshimasa 416
Takao, Yoshimasa 416
Takasaki, Hideo 67
Takasaki, Hideo 67
Takase, Susumu 22
Takasugi, Tadashi 289
Takata, Kiyota 314
Takata, Kiyota 314
Takayanagi, Koji 238
Takayanagi, Koji 238
Takeda, Kunitoshi 96
Takeda, Yasuo 141
Takeda, Munetaka 241
Takeda, Yoshiyuki 326
Takedagawa, Masahiro 214
Takei, Masato 405
Takeishi, Hiroaki 106
Takemura, Shigeyuki 34
Takenaka, Hiroyuki 419
Takenaka, Naoki Naoki Takenaka 452
Takenami, Yuichiro 97
Taketomi, Masao 141
Takeuchi, Hirotaka 334
Takeuchi, Kazuhiro 417
Takeuchi, Akira 417
Takeuchi, Satoru 479
Takeyama, Yoshio 141
Takeyama, Yoshio 142
Takizawa, Soichiro 215
Talbot, Graham 370
Tali, Pietro Franco 376
Talotta, Alessandro 432
Tamagnini, Andrea 234
Tamai, Kouichi 182
Tamai, Hiroto 393
Tamai, Takaaki 446
Tamba, Toshihito 238
Tamura, Atsuto 137
Tamura, Atsuto 137
Tamura, Yoshihiro 405
Tamura, Minoru 424
Tamura, Minoru 424
Tamvakakis, Apostolos S. 303
Tamvakakis, Apostolos S. 303
Tan, Man-kou 65
Tan, Bernard 147
Tan, Lip-Bu 176
Tan, Tat Tat Wai Tan 275
Tan, Cynthia G. H. 336
Tanabe, Yasuo 208
Tanabe, Eiichi 289
Tanabe, Hiroyuki 405
Tanabe, Kazuo 421
Tanai, Tsuneo 214
Tanai, Tsuneo 215
Tanaka, Toshizo 105
Tanaka, Toshizo 106
Tanaka, Akio 141
Tanaka, Koji 208
Tanaka, Kazuaki 282
Tanaka, Masaaki (Masa) 294
Tanaka, Tatsuo 294
Tanaka, Tatsuo 294
Tanaka, Seiichi 295
Tanaka, Seiichi 296
Tanaka, Hiroshi 320
Tanaka, Takashi 326
Tanaka, Takashi 327
Tanaka, Yoshihiro 388
Tanaka, Tsutomu 405
Tanaka, Shigeru 419
Tanaka, Hisao 451
Tanaka, Takaaki 452
Tanbourgi, Gabriel 76
Tandon, Atul 364
Taneya, Mototaka Mototaka Taneya 390
Tang, Yat Sun (Richard) 194
Tang, Bin 229
Tang, Fred van der 352
Tangtatswas, Singh 61
Tani, Yasuhiro 106
Tani, Yasuhiro 106
Tani, Kenji 289
Tani, Makoto 419
Tanigaki, Masahide 208
Tanigawa, Yasuo 206
Tanigawa, Hiromichi 314
Tanigawa, Hiromichi 314
Tanigawa, Kazuo 452
Taniguchi, Norihiko 183
Taniguchi, Shinichi 312
Taniguchi, Shinichi 312
Taniguchi, Nobuyuki 390
Taniguchi, Nobuyuki 390
Taniguchi, Shinichi 405
Tanimoto, Michihisa 420
Tanizawa, Fumihiko 420
Tanna, Catherine 85
Tanner, Ernst 139
Tantazzi, Angelo 54
Tanthuwanit, Sumate 394
Tantisawetrat, Yokporn 394
Taohai, Xue 119
Taohai, Xue 119
Tapias, Alcides Lopes 237
Tapling, Mark 326
Taranto, Francesco 163
Tardif, Christian 24
Tardio, Vicente 59
Targetti, Ferdinando 234
Targova, Violeta 407
Tasaka, Hitoshi 149
Tassan, Franck 109
Tat, Lim Hong 275
Tat, Wai Tan 275
Tata, Ratan N. 172
Tata, Jimmy 196
Tateishi, Hisao 241
Tatsuta, Yasuto 283
Tauby, Anne 21

Tavares, Carlos 316
Tavares, Carlos 355
Tavernier, Jacques 472
Tavolini, Giorgio 432
Tay, Tong Poh 467
Tayanukorn, Kajornvut 61
Taylor, Roxanne 7
Taylor, Bob 24
Taylor, Kevin 51
Taylor, Carole S. 82
Taylor, C. 298
Taylor, Richard 298
Taylor, Joseph M. (Joe) 338
Taylor, Kathleen P. (Katie) 366
Taylor, Aileen 368
Taylor, Andy 381
Taylor, Alison 396
Taylor, Ann 443
Taylor, Carole S. 450
Tchuruk, Serge 453
Teare, David 399
Teck, Lim Cheng 411
Tedesi, Luca 234
Teerlink, Ron 368
Teirlynck, Yves 323
Teixeira, Vicente C. 102
Teixeira, Mario da Silveira 468
Teixeira, Mario 468
Teixeira, Mario da Silveira 468
Teixiera, Mario da Silveira 57
Tejada, Vicente Prados 10
Tejada, Jaime de Marichalar Y Saenz De 124
Tejera, Pablo Isla Alvarez de 228
Tejera, Pablo Isla Alvarez de 434
Tejima, Shunichiro 307
Telang, Prakash M. 430
Telles, Marcel H. 37
Tellier, Paul M. 82
Tellier, Marc P. 302
Tellier, Paul M. 360
Tembo, Akihiko 224
Temel, Ali 459
Temperley, Nick 156
Tena, Antonio 185
Tena, Nemesio Fernandez-Cuesta Luca de 356
Tena, Nemesio 356
Teo, Lay Lim 7
Teo, Melvin T. W. 147
Teragawa, Masatsugu 390
Terajima, Yoshinori 311
Terakado, Kazuyoshi 246
Teramoto, Hideo 141
Teranishi, Shinichi 405
Teraoka, Kazunori 405
Terashi, Shigeki 455
Terazawa, Tatsumaro 70
Terazawa, Tatsumaro 70
Terisse, Pierre-Andre 145
Terium, Peter 371
Terner, Franck 19
Terradas, Salvador 57
Terre, Jaon-David Grima i 10
Terrett, Mike J. 364
Terrett, Mike J. 365
Terry, Jane 364
Terry, James 422
Terryn, Kristof 491
Terver, Bernard 212
Tervonen, Jyrki 203
Tessmann, Patrick 263
Tessmar-Pfohl, Werner 167
Tetrault, Lynn 44
Teulie, Pierre Alexandre 109
Teuwsen, Bjorn 258
Tewell, Dennis 27
Teyssen, Johannes 159
Tezuka, Kazuo 252
Thabet, Pierre 302
Thackwray, Ian 212
Thaensathit, Suwan 61
Thaler-Veh, Heidi 13
Tham, Ming Soong 467
Thamm, Michael 107
Thananithi, Piyaphan 61
Thanatsrang, Thawisak 61
Thani, Jassim Jassim Al Thani 139
Thansathit, Suvarn 61
Thanyasiri, Tharisa 61
Thaule, J?rgen 435
Thein, Reggie 467
Thelin, Anders 380
Theoklitos, Leonidas 303
Theoklitos, H. E. the Metropolitan of Ioannina 303
Theoklitos, Leonidas 303
Thethi, Jo 85
Thiam, Tidjane C. 348
Thibaud, Laure 382
Thielen, Gunter 83
Thienemann, Sabina Flaxa 10
Thiessen, Gordon G. 278
Thirarotchanawong, Sa-ard 61
Thiratharathorn, Ratchada 61
Thodey, David 438
Thodey, David 438
Thoman, Gordon R. 387
Thomas, Barbara S. 69
Thomas, Patrick W. 78
Thomas, Patrick W. 85
Thomas, Claire 191
Thomas, Peter 235
Thomas, Ralf P. 395
Thomas, Eira M. 423
Thomas, Geoff 488
Thomas-Graham, Pamela A. 139
Thomlinson, David C. 7
Thomopoulos, Anthimos C. 303
Thomopoulos, Anthimos C. 303
Thompson, Jack E. 35
Thompson, Dorothy 245
Thompson, John M. 257
Thompson, John M. 258
Thompson, Simon 298
Thompson, Simon R. 381
Thompson, Peter M. 403
Thompson, Egil 415
Thompson, Westley V. (Wes) 421
Thompson, Kevin 450
Thompson, John M. 450
Thomsen, Mads K. 325
Thomsen-Bendixen, Carsten 159
Thomson, Alan M. 31
Thomson, Philip (Phil) 191
Thomson, Phil 192
Thomson, Alan M. 245
Thomson, Warren A. 278
Thoralfsson, Barbara M. 3
Thoralfsson, Barbara M. 435
Thorburn, Andrew 301
Thoresen, Roar 415
Thorley, Giles 459
Thormann, Dominique 355
Thorn, John G. 301
Thornburgh, Richard E. 139
Thorne, Grant 360
Thornton, John L. 122
Thornton, John L. 218
Thorpe, Annette 100
Thouin, Stephane 109
Thulin, Anders 166
Thulin, Berth 479
Thumann, Jurgen R. 445
Thun, Fredrick 18
Thurston, Paul A. 217
Thurston, Richard (Dick) 429
Thwaites, George 350
Tianpu, Wang 120
Tianpu, Wang 120
Tible, Phillippe 250
Tiel, Jeroen 352
Tieqi, Teng 65
Tierce, Stephane 333
Tigges, Uwe 371
Tiitinen, Pekka 5
Tilger, Carsten 202
Timmermans, J. V. (Koos) 231
Timuray, Serpil 475
Tin, Kng 336
Tin, Kng Hwee 336
Tiner, John 139
Tirri, Henry 318
Tissot, Nicolas 31
Titi, Fani 235
Tkach, Douglas 193
Toal, Anne 193
Toda, Yuzo 182
Toevs, Alden 130
Togashi, Kazuhisa 417
Togni, Fabrizio 54
Togni, Alberto 64
Toikkanen, Timo 318
Toit, Philippus Philippus du Toit 39
Toit, Hendrik 235
Tok, Dan 401
Tokubutsu, Fumio 420
Tokuda, Hiromi 149
Tokuda, Hiromi 149
Tokuhiro, Kiyoshi 326
Tokumitsu, Shigenori Shigenori Tokumitsu 452
Tokunaga, Takenori 253
Tokunari, Muneaki 294
Tokura, Masakazu 416
Tokura, Masakazu 416
Toledano, Sidney 124
Toledano, Sidney 124
Tolot, Jerome 189
Toma, Shigeki 392
Toma, Shigeki 392
Tomassini, Luca 432
Tomb, Greg 384
Tomita, Kimio 316
Tomlinson, D. J. 245
Tomlinson, Geoffrey A. (Geoff) 301
Tommiska, Kati 321
Tomono, Hiroshi 312
Tomozoe, Masanao 455
Tong, Hon shing 65
Tong, Lim Khiang 336
Tonne, Hilde M. 435
Tonomoto, Kiyoshi 34
Toong, Yee Chek 485
Toot, Joseph F. 342
Topholm, Jan 2
Torii, Keizo 282
Torii, Hiroyasu 419
Torio, Livio 234
Toriumi, Chie 320
Torpey, Michael 66
Torre, Alexis E. Rovzar de la 69
Torre, Alexis E. Rovzar de la 177
Torrego, Agustin Bateucas 10
Torres, Antonio Escamez 60
Torres, Juan 114
Torres, Alberto 318
Torstendahl, Mats 399
Toselli, Damiano 432
Tosti, Kim 325
Tostivin, Jean-Claude 93
Totsuka, Takehiko 328
Toubro, Per Alling 147
Toubro, Per Alling 147
Touche, Ricardo Guajardo 177
Tourek, Tim 26
Tourkolias, Alexandros G. 303
Tourkolias, Alexandros 303
Tournier, Philippe 127
Tourres, Christian 13
Toussan, Michel 375
Tov, Imri 62
Towle, Ken 440
Townsend, John 475
Toyama, Takashi 338
Toyobe, Katsuyuki 67
Toyobe, Katsuyuki 67
Toyoda, Kanshiro 22
Toyoda, Shoichiro 22
Toyoda, Shoichiro 149
Toyoda, Akio 455
Toyoda, Akio 455
Toyohara, Masayasu Masayasu Toyohara 452
Toyohara, Yoji 456
Toyoki, Noriyuki 183
Toyomasu, Shunichi 316
Toyoshima, Masaaki 16
Tracey, Jonathan 412
Traficant, Jim 8
Trapani, Francesco 271
Trappier, Eric 443
Treble, Nick 29
Treichl, Andreas 167
Trenholm, Steve 159
Treschow, Michael 5
Treschow, Michael 464
Treschow, Michael 465
Tretiak, Gregory D. 345
Tretiak, Gregory D. 346
Tretton, Jack 409
Trevisani, Valter 41
Trian, Pedro Ascorbe 10
Triana, Margarita Obregon 160
Triandafyllidis, Avraam 303
Tricoire, Jean-Pascal 387
Tricoire, Andre 453
Trivedi, Yogendra P. 353
Triwannakun, Thawat 61
Troger, Laurent 91
Troska, Hubertus 144
Trotter, Lloyd G. 144
Trowbridge, Kim J. 26
Troy, Dan 191
Troy, Daniel 192
Truong, Jack G. 3
Trutzschler, Klaus 113
Tsai, Hong-Tu 112
Tsai, Cheng-Ta 112
Tsai, Cheng-Chiu 112
Tsai, Cheng-Ta 112
Tsai, Cheng-Chiu 112
Tsai, Chiu-Jung 427
Tsai, Rick 429
Tsai, N. S. 429
Tsai, Rick 429
Tsang, Katherine 411
Tschage, Uwe 128
Tse, Aloysius H. Y. 122
Tse, Aloysius H. Y. 125
Tse, Edward 320
Tse, Edmund S.W. 342
Tseng, F. C. 428
Tseng, F. C. 429
Tsiddon, Prof Daniel 63
Tsien, Samuel N. (Sam) 336
Tso, Stephen T. (Steve) 429
Tsoumas, Athanasios 344
Tsuboi, Hiromichi 124
Tsubouchi, Kazuto 326
Tsubouchi, Kazuto 327
Tsuchida, Osamu 140
Tsuchida, Osamu 141
Tsuchiya, Jun-ichi 141
Tsuchiya, Sojiro 149
Tsuchiya, Sojiro 149
Tsuchiya, Munehiko 452
Tsuda, Toru 96
Tsuda, Toru 97
Tsuda, Shingo 282
Tsuda, Noboru 288
Tsue, Sik 125
Tsuga, Kazuhiro 338
Tsuji, Haruyoshi 16
Tsuji, Haruyoshi 16
Tsuji, Masahito 97
Tsuji, Haruo 320
Tsuji, Kiyoshi 448
Tsujigami, Hiroshi 327
Tsujimura, Kenji 22
Tsujimura, Kiyoyuki 326
Tsujimura, Kiyoyuki 327
Tsujiyama, Eiko 334
Tsukada, Masaki 141
Tsukada, Masaki 141
Tsukada, Tadao 141
Tsukamoto, Makoto 206
Tsukamoto, Shigeru 392
Tsukioka, Takashi 224
Tsukioka, Takashi 225

Tsukioka, Ryozo 236
Tsukioka, Ryozo 236
Tsukuda, Kazuo 290
Tsunekage, Hitoshi 421
Tsuritani, Naomasa 145
Tsuruta, Masaaki 408
Tsutsui, Yoshinobu 311
Tsutsui, Yoshinobu 311
Tsutsumi, Tomio 290
Tsutsumi, Kazuhiko 291
Tsuya, Masaaki 96
Tsuya, Masaaki 97
Tsuyuki, Shigeo 141
Tsuyuki, Shigeo 141
Tsuzumi, Norio 447
Tu, L.C. 429
Tucker, Greg 14
Tufano, Paul J. 25
Tuffy, William 51
Tulanan, Decha 61
Tulananda, Deja 61
Tulloch, Maurice 47
Tulloch, Angus 130
Tummel, Lord Iain D. T. Vallance of 396
Tummel, Iain 396
Tung, Chee-Chen 339
Tungesvik, Stale 414
Tunnacliffe, Paul D. 155
Tunwatthanachit, Panit 61
Tunwatthanachit, Phornnit 61
Turcke, Mary Ann 82
Turcotte, Martine 82
Turmel, Jean 27
Turmo, Rafael Sanchez-Lozano 233
Turnbull, Lord Andrew 348
Turner, Cathy 72
Turner, Cathy 74
Turner, David J. 129
Turner, Nigel 151
Turney, Sally 47
Turrini, Regis 474
Twardy, Achim 83
Twembeke, Willem van 189
Twigg, M. V. 245
Tyler, Ian P. 53
Tyler, David A. 240
Tyrwhitt, Hamish G. 210
Tysoe, Ronald W. (Ron) 104
Tytgadt, Alain 248
Tzakou-Lambropoulou, Nelly 303
Tzeng, M. C. 428

U

Ucelay, Juan Manuel Eguiagaray 21
Uchida, Nariaki 283
Uchida, Kozo 312
Uchimoto, Tsuneo 22
Uchinaga, Yukako 409
Uchino, Shuma 289
Uchino, Shuma 293
Uchioke, Fumikiyo 419
Uchiyamada, Takeshi 455
Uchiyamada, Takeshi 455
Uddenfeldt, Jan 166
Ueang-udomsin, Siridet 61
Uebber, Bodo 84
Uebber, Bodo 143
Ueda, Ryoichi 289
Ueda, Ryoichi 290
Uegaki, Masahiro 253
Uehara, Hirohisa 427
Uehira, Mitsuhiko 446
Uejima, Hirokazu 183
Ueno, Satoru 141
Ueno, Yasuo 180
Ueno, Mitsuru 253
Uenoyama, Makoto 338
Uesugi, Gayu 293
Uesugi, Gayu 293
Uggla, Ane Maersk Mc-Kinney 2
Uhm, Rak Yong 398
Ui-yamaphan, Pratsani 61
Uji, Noritaka 314
Uji, Noritaka 314
Ujihara, Kiyoshi 311
Ujiie, Teruhiko 1
Ulber, Peter 260
Ulderup, Irmgard 490
Ulissi, Roberto 163
Ullmer, Michael Michael Ullmer 488
Umaki, Tamio 334
Umeda, Mochio 358
Umemura, Hiroyuki 291
Umezawa, Toshinori 282
Umlauft, Rene 276
Unger, Konstantin von 202
Ungerer, Michael 107
Uno, Ikuo 338
Uno, Ikuo 420
Unoura, Hiroo 314
Unoura, Hiroo 314
Urabe, Toshimitsu 289
Urakawa, Chikafumi 183
Urano, Takashi 96
Urata, Haruyuki 334
Urata, Haruyuki 334
Urata, Haruo 420
Urata, Haruo 420
Urayama, Shigeru 314
Urayama, Shigeru 314
Urbain, Xavier 260
Ure?a-Raso, Domingo 21
Urena-Raso, Domingo Domingo Urena-Raso 21
Urlini, Franco 41
Urquijo, Gonzalo 39
Urushibata, Kenichi 419
Usami, Kazumi 22
Usbeck, Verner 147
Ushijima, Nozomi 419
Ushio, Fumiaki Fumiaki Ushio 452
Usui, Sadahiro 149
Usui, Sonosuke 427
Usui, Sonosuke 427
Utamura, Toru 283
Uthaisangchai, Prasong 61
Utsler, Mike 95
Utsuda, Shoei 295
Uyeda, Leslie 278
Uytdewilligen, Dirk 462
Uzawa, Shigeyuki 106

V

Vabres, Renaud Donnedieu de 124
Vacher, Guy 472
Vachon, Louis 302
Vachon, Louis 302
Vadell, Pablo Vallbona 10
Vadell, Pablo Vallbona 10
Vadera, Shriti 44
Vadera, Baroness Shriti 87
Vadera, Baroness Shriti 88
Vaghul, Narayanan 39
Vahlbrock, Martin 371
Vaillaud, Pierre 454
Vainboim, Israel 237
Valborgland, Kirsti 415
Valdemoro, Juan 356
Valdes, Lou 27
Valentine, Debra A. 360
Valentine, Debra A. 361
Valero, Karina 401
Vall, Luis 57
Vallance, Patrick 191
Vallance, Paul 364
Vallaude, Jean-Pierre 355
Valle, Diego Della 41
Valle, Dean Della 88
Valle, Margherita Della 116
Valle, Margherita Margherita Della Valle 116
Valle, Margherita Della 475
Vallejo, Victor de Urrutia 223
Vallejo, Vincent 474
Valls, Ramon 55
Vallverdu, Jaime 57
Valstorp, Per 325
Vamos, Steven 438
Vanaselja, Siim A. 82
Vandenhende, Christian 355
Vandervelden, Ludo 462
Vandevelde, Luc 402
Vandevelde, Luc 476
Vanhevel, Jan 248
Vanneste, Luc A. 69
Vanni, Enrico 323
Vanot, Jean-Philippe 333
Vanselow, Alex 88
Vansteenkiste, Baron Luc 169
Vantieghem, Germain 248
Vara, Fabiola Arredondo de 70
Varadarajan, S. 85
Varaldo, Riccardo 234
Vardi, Judith 441
Vardinogiannis, Ioannis 343
Varin, Philippe 85
Varley, John S. 44
Varley, John S. 360
Varone, P. 376
Varvel, Eric 139
Varwijk, Erik 19
Vasantasingh, Chulasingh 349
Vasella, Daniel L. 323
Vasilakis, Eftychios 344
Vasileva, Elena 188
Vasilyeva, Elena A. 187
Vasino, Christian 11
Vasseur, Denis Le 345
Vasseur, Denis 345
Vasseur, Denis Le 346
Vasseur, Denis 346
Vassiliadis, Michael 76
Vassiliadis, Michael 202
Vastrup, Prof Claus 147
Vasudev, C.M. 196
Vasudeva, Nishi 205
Vaswani, Ashok 72
Vaswani, Ashok 74
Vatier, Bernard 375
Vaucleroy, Jacques de 49
Vaucleroy, Jacques de 169
Vaughan, Chris 53
Vaux, Robert G. (Bob) 483
Vavalidis, Stefanos C. 303
Vawdrey, Rod 183
Vedrine, Hubert 271
Veer, Ben van der 14
Veer, Jeroen 231
Veer, Jeroen 258
Veer, Jeroen van der 370
Velasco, Ernesto Vega 32
Velasco, Pedro 223
Velasquez, Maria E. 160
Velayos, Rodrigo Martin 352
Vellan, Stein-Erik 435
Venkat, Sunder 91
Venkataramanan, PS (Venkat) 39
Venkatesan, Ravi 479
Venn, Richard E. 104
Ventre, Marc 375
Ventura, Carlotta Carlotta Ventura 432
Verbeek, Dirk P. M. 14
Verdes, Marcelino Fernandez 10
Verdes, Marcelino F. 210
Verdes, Marcelino F. 210
Verdier, Damien 403
Vereecke, Marc Marc Vereecke 39
Vereker, William 320
Verelst, Patrick 407
Vergine, Umberto 163
Verhaegen, Tom 373
Vermeulen, Raymond 231
Verneray, Laurent 387
Vernerey, Laurent 387
Vernieri, Marco 234
Verplancke, Jan 412
Verrier, Mike 486
Versteeg, C. H. (Cor) 352
Verwaayen, Ben 24
Verwaayen, Bernardus J. (Ben) 25
Verwilghen, Etienne 248
Vestberg, Hans 166
Vestberg, Hans 166
Vi?uela, Azucena 161
Vial, Arnaud 345
Vial, Arnaud 346
Viana, Miguel 161
Vianen, John van 256
Vicaire, Guillaume 109
Victor, Diane de Saint 5
Vidal, Jean 127
Vidarte, Susana Rodriguez 56
Vidarte, Susana 56
Vidman, Moshe 63
Viehbacher, Christopher A. (Chris) 382
Viehbacher, Christopher A. (Chris) 383
Vieira, Arnaldo Alves 56
Vieira, Vasco 161
Vietheer-Grupe, Monika 335
Vieweg, Cecilia 3
Vigneron, Luc 443
Vignial, Antoine 131
Vigodman, Erez 441
Viguri, Jose Maria Loizaga 10
Vijayakumar, S. 85
Vijayan, T. S. 224
Vil+, Joan 459
Vila, Carlos Torres 55
Vila, Joan 458
Vilagi, Oszkar 297
Vilagi, Oszkar 297
Villa, Gabriele 284
Villadiego, Oscar A. 160
Villarreal, Ramiro G. 114
Villarreal, Roberto Zambrano 114
Villela, Alfredo Egydio Arruda 237
Vincent, Jacques 145
Vincent, Jacques 145
Vinci, Francesco Saverio 284
Vinck, Karel 462
Vinck, Karel 462
Vinge, Nils 203
Vink, Lodewijk J.R. de 362
Vinter, Graham 85
Viola, Mike 32
Vione, Federico 11
Visconti, Diego 7
Visser, Marco 256
Vita, Giuseppe 463
Vita, Giuseppe 463
Vitale, Mario P. 491
Viteri, Xabier 223
Vlerick, Philippe 248
Vliegen, Jan 462
Vlissingen, Annemiek Fentener van 199
Vogel, Roland 195
Vogelsang, Harald 263
Vogelsang, Gunter 445
Vogg, Stefan 159
Vogt, Hans-Georg 482
Vohra, Pravir 224
Vohra, Pravir 224
Voigt, Hans Ole 325
Voigt, Thomas 335
Voigtsberger, Harry 482
Volldal, Olav 435
Vollmer, Alexander 144
Volpi, Michelangelo (Mike) 166
Volz, Werner 136
Voncina, Libor 256
Vonden, Stephanie 352
Vorobyev, Vadim 329
Voscherau, Eggert 76
Voscherau, Eggert Eggert Voscherau 210
Voser, Peter R. 370
Voser, Peter R. 370
Voss, Bernd W. 5
Voss, Bernd W. 136
Vrailas, Demetrios 303
Vranas, Andreas 303
Vranas, Andreas 303
Vranitzky, Rt. Hon. Franz 274
Vrcelj, Stevan 273
Vrecko, Marc 469
Vries, Maarten de 257

Vries, Ellen de 258
Vries, Roel De 316
Vriese, Hans de 24
Vrij, Robert 25
Vuursteen, Karel 24

W

W?rsted, Gunn 321
Waal, Lodewijk J. de 231
Waal, Lodewijk 231
Wachtler, Gert 195
Wada, Masahiko 140
Wada, Takashi 141
Wada, Masahiko 141
Wada, Masao 307
Wada, Norio 314
Wade, D. N. 298
Wade-Gery, Laura 280
Wade-Gery, Laura Laura Wade-Gery 280
Wade-Gery, Laura 440
Wadia, Nusli N. 430
Waechtler, Gert 195
Waelchli, Urs 12
Wageningen, Richard van 100
Waggott, William (Will) 458
Waggott, William (Will) 459
Wagner, Gerhard 489
Wagu, Kenji 206
Wagu, Kenji 206
Wah, George L.L. 336
Wahlberg, Klas 91
Wahlroos, Bjorn 321
Waigel, Theodore 463
Wainaina, Carole 258
Wainwright, Ross 384
Wakabayashi, Hiroyuki 149
Wakabayashi, Tatsuo 294
Wakabayashi, Tatsuo 294
Wakayama, Masazumi 283
Wakayama, Masazumi 283
Walbaum, Jean-Pierre 126
Waldenfels, Georg Freiherr von 159
Waldron, Patrick 66
Walker, Mervyn 35
Walker, Sir David A. 72
Walker, Sir David A. 74
Walker, Paul A. 156
Walker, Roland 212
Walker, J. F. 245
Walker, Donald J. 274
Walker, Donald J. 274
Walker, Bruce 311
Walkling, Adrian 412
Wallace, Sean 411
Wallenberg, Marcus 3
Wallenberg, Jacob 5
Wallenberg, Marcus 44
Wallenberg, Jacob 166
Wallenberg, Marcus 166
Wallenberg, Jacob 166
Wallenberg, Marcus 166
Wallenberg, Jacob 399
Wallenberg, Marcus 399
Wallenberg, Jacob 399
Wallentowitz, Henning 490
Waller, John 301
Wallette, Donald E. (Don) 329
Wallin, Ulrich 195
Wallin, Anders 380
Wallin, Peter 400
Wallin, Ulrich 429
Walls, Russell F. 47
Walls, Lindsay 51
Walmsley, Emma 191
Walprecht, Volker 395
Walsh, Joe 66
Walsh, Paul S. 155
Walsh, Paul S. 156
Walsh, Brian E. 193
Walsh, Imelda 240
Walsh, Paula 273
Walsh, Sam 360
Walsh, Sam 361
Walsh, Sam 361
Walsh, Pamela 410
Walsh, Paul S. 464
Walsh, Paul S. 465
Walsh, Adam 483
Walter, Bernhard 144
Walter, Bernhard 154
Walter, Bernhard 202
Walter, Bernhard 262
Walther, Klaus 151
Walton, Mia K. 364
Walvis, Robert J. W. (Rob) 53
Walvis, Robert J. W. (Rob) 245
Wanaptikun, Phakorn 61
Wanblad, Duncan 35
Wanders, Hans E. 352
Wandke, Simon 39
Wang, Gregory K.H. 112
Wang, Gregory K.H. 112
Wang, Ming Yang 118
Wang, Jinli 121
Wang, Pingang 121
Wang, Xiaolin 121
Wang, Tao 125
Wang, Jason 139
Wang, Wilfred 178
Wang, Xiaoyan 266
Wang, Liping 343
Wang, George 352
Wang, Sue-Chuan 427
Wang, J.K. 429
Wankel, Sibylle 396
Wankhede, G. S. 86
Warby, Sarah 240
Ward, Giles 9
Ward, Mary 25
Ward, Greg C. 273
Ward-Lilley, James 44
Wardlaw, Fiona 33
Wareby, Jan 166
Wareing, Michael P. (Mike) 486
Waring, Philip J. 283
Warne, Peter H. 273
Warner, Thomas E. (Tom) 18
Warren, Dipak 47
Warren, Joseph G. 106
Warshaw, Simon 461
Warsop, Simon 47
Wastler, Ernst 179
Watabe, Nobuhiko 283
Watanabe, Kunio 105
Watanabe, Kunio 106
Watanabe, Koichiro 141
Watanabe, Koichiro 141
Watanabe, Masaya 208
Watanabe, Katsushi 215
Watanabe, Ryuji 289
Watanabe, Hiroki 314
Watanabe, Hiroki 314
Watanabe, Akihito 320
Watanabe, Kunio 320
Watanabe, Kenichi 320
Watanabe, Toshiharu 452
Watanabe, Katsuaki 455
Watanabe, Katsuaki 455
Watanuki, Yusuke 283
Waterous, Johanna 298
Waters, Ralph Ralph Waters 488
Watkins, Alison M. 46
Watkins, William D. (Bill) 176
Watkins, Alison M. 488
Watson, John 82
Watson, Howard 100
Watson, Karl 114
Watson, Anthony (Tony) 270
Watson, Charles 370
Watson, Anthony (Tony) 476
Wattanasiritham, Khunying Jada 394
Watter, Rolf Urs 492
Watters, Stephanie 364
Waugh, Richard E. (Rick) 69
Waugh, Richard E. (Rick) 69
Wauthier, Pierre 491
Wayth, Nick 95
Weatherall, Percy 242
Weatherston, Anne 46
Webb, Robert 365
Webb, Steve 440
Weber, Stephan 35
Weber, Jurgen 78
Weber, Thomas 143
Weber, Jurgen 151
Weber, Jurgen 151
Weber, Christophe 192
Weber, Johanna 300
Weber, Chris 318
Weber, Manfred 371
Weber, Axel 461
Weber-Rey, Daniela 90
Webster, Sue 100
Webster, Jonathan 364
Wechsler, Juergen Juergen Wechsler 81
Wedborn, Erik 218
Wedel, J?rgen 325
Wee, Lee Seng 336
Wee, Cho Yaw 466
Wee, Joo Yeow 466
Weed, Keith 464
Weed, Keith 465
Weede, Marc A. van 14
Weekes, Tim 462
Wegmann, Jens M. 395
Wehlauer, Bernd 477
Wei, Ding 119
Weibel, Peter F. 139
Weiberg, Geor 144
Weidmann, Jens 150
Weidong, Hou 65
Weihe, Huang 339
Weihua, Ma 118
Weihua, Ma 119
Weihua, Ma 120
Weil, Laura A. 107
Weill, Veronique 49
Weinberg, Serge 382
Weinberg, Serge 387
Weir, Helen A. 373
Weir, Helen A. 373
Weisberg, Yoram 62
Weisberg, Michael A. 461
Weisenburger, Randall J. 107
Weiss, Paul R. 82
Weiss, Heinrich 91
Weiss, Heinrich 144
Weissburg, Martin 479
Weisser, Alberto 102
Weith, Joachim 179
Welinder, Margareta 203
Wellauer, Thomas 300
Weller, Charles 482
Wellink, Nout 64
Wells, David 82
Wells, Michael A. (Mike) 348
Wells, Michael A. (Mike) 348
Wemmer, Dieter 28
Wemmer, Dieter 491
Wendel, Klaus 462
Wendler, Olaf Olaf Wendler 210
Weng, Mok Kwong 261
Weng, Mok 261
Wenger, Kaspar 212
Wenk, Martin 54
Wenlin, Huang 119
Wenlin, Huang 119
Wenner, Christine 390
Wenning, Werner 159
Wenning, Joachim 300
Wente, Heinz-Gerhard 135
Wentzien, Ulf 202
Werner, Uwe 144
Werner, Herbert 332
Wessling, Holger 157
West, Darryl 74
Westbury-Haines, Denise 100
Westerberg, Lars 381
Westerberg, Lars 479
Westerstad, Stina 203
Westhoff, Frank 158
Westin, Bo 381
Westlake, W. James (Jim) 366
Weston, David 35
Weston, George G. 42
Weston, W. Galen 42
Weston, George G. 42
Weston, Chris 116
Weston, Chris 116
Weston, W. Galen 483
Weston, W. Galen G. 483
Westra, Marike 258
Westwell, Steve 95
Wettberg, Stefanie 76
Whaley, Jim 396
Wheway, Scott 47
Whincup, Clive 484
Whitaker, Anne C. 383
Whitbread, Jasmine Jasmine Whitbread 101
Whitchurch, Adrian 100
Whitcutt, Peter 35
White, Deanna 91
White, Christopher S. 102
White, Mark J. 134
White, Aleida 330
White, Adam 474
Whitehead, Nigel 51
Whitehouse, Janet V. 422
Whitfield, Rob 484
Whittaker, Sheelagh D. 225
Whittaker, Sheelagh D. 413
Whyte, Kevin J. 450
Wi, Sung Ho 391
Wibergh, Johan 166
Widdowson, William F. 461
Widhani, Monica 86
Widmann, Werner 176
Wieczorek, Roman 401
Wiedeking, Wendelin 323
Wiedmann, Bernd 490
Wiesehuegel, Klaus Klaus Wiesehuegel 210
Wiesehuegel, Klaus 210
Wiest, Christian 387
Wigger, Mechtild 335
Wiggers, Marcel 352
Wiggins, Andy 250
Wijers, Hans 199
Wijers, G. J. (Hans) 370
Wijk, Leo M. van 14
Wijk, Leo M. van 352
Wijk, Leo M. van 352
Wijk, Olle 381
Wijkstrom, Annika Annika Wijkstrom 426
Wijnen, Roland van 212
Wikforss, M?rten 479
Wikramanayake, Shemara 273
Wilhelm, Harald 21
Wilken, C. H. 242
Wilkins, Rayford (Ray) 32
Wilkinson, Ronald A. (Ron) 18
Wilkinson, Graham 100
Wilkinson, Brian 352
Wilks, Sharon 216
Will, Angelika 286
Willans, Andrew 411
Willard, Howard A. 373
Willemse, Johan B. 71
Willett, Steve 250
Willi, Michael 461
Williams, Nigel 46
Williams, Sheila 95
Williams, Sean M.G. 100
Williams, Suzi 100
Williams, Gareth 155
Williams, Keith 233
Williams, Keith 233
Williams, Damon 366
Williams, Mark 370
Williams, Steven W. (Steve) 423
Williams, Steven W. (Steve) 423
Williams, Steve 465
Williamson, J. David 104
Williamson, Sir Brian 218
Williamson, Mark 227
Williamson, Sir Malcolm 301

Williamson, Mats 400
Willis, Margaret 216
Wilmers, Robert G. (Bob) 29
Wilson, Stephen 9
Wilson, Michael M. (Mike) 18
Wilson, Michael M. (Mike) 18
Wilson, Thomas C. 28
Wilson, Jimmy 88
Wilson, Lynton R. 144
Wilson, Sir Robert P. 192
Wilson, Nigel 265
Wilson, Nigel 265
Wilson, Julia 265
Wilson, Charles 286
Wilson, Helen 330
Wilson, Andrew 368
Wilson, James (Jamie) 373
Wilson, James (Jamie) 373
Wilson, Geoffrey H. (Geoff) 483
Wilson, Peter 484
Wimbleton, John 458
Win, Thomas de 78
Win, Thomas de 78
Winckler, Georg 167
Winckler, Georg 167
Wine, Robert 95
Winkel, Michael (Mike) 159
Winkelman, Mark 37
Winkelmann, Ralf 262
Winkelmeier, Stephan 79
Winn, Penelope Penelope Winn 488
Winnacker, Ernst-Ludwig 78
Winqvist, Pontus 401
Winroth, Jorgen 44
Winser, Nick 304
Winser, Nick 305
Winsth, Annika 321
Winston, Sue 47
Winter, Jennifer 29
Winter, Jaap 353
Winter, Steven M. (Steve) 384
Winter, Josef 396
Winter, Karin 491
Winterkorn, Martin 477
Winyawong, Suraphong 61
Wirahadiraksa, Ron H. 257
Wirth, Ken 25
Wise, Barbara 100
Wissmann, Matthias 151
Withington, Neil 98
Withunchat, Kesini 61
Witoonchart, Gasinee 61
Witt, Peter 396
Witteck, Lars 202
Wittemans, Marc 248
Witten, Peer 335
Witts, Karen 250
Witty, Sir Andrew 191
Witty, Sir Andrew 192
Wixtead, James E. 9
Wodrich, Thomas 54
Woerkom, Floris van 199
Woicke, Peter 35
Wolf, Prof Siegfried 136
Wolf, David L. 257
Wolf, Frank 263
Wolf, Michael 426
Wolf, Robert 461
Wolfe, Kristin 373
Wolfinger, Uwe 268
Wolle, Joerg 260
Woller, Rolf 135
Wollitzer, Hans 159
Wollstadt, Michael 151
Wong, Allan C. Y. 65
Wong, Chung-hin 65
Wong, David S. H. 90
Wong, Frank K. S. 119
Wong, Jeanette 147
Wong, Tung Shun (Peter) 194
Wong, Kin Tung (Marvin) 194
Wong, Peter T. S. 217
Wong, Helen 218
Wong, Wai Ming 266
Wong, Ai Fong 318
Wong, Peter T. S. 343
Wong, Jenny Mei Leng 467
Wong, Meng Meng 467
Woo, Susan M. F. Chow 219
Woo, Mo 219
Woo, Susan M. F. Chow 219
Wood, Steven Steven Wood 39
Wood, Karen J. 87
Wood, Ian 100
Wood, Greg 116
Wood, Alan 130
Wood, John 240
Wood, Alison 304
Wood, Tony 364
Wood, Douglas 393
Wood, Malcolm 413
Woodman, Paul 100
Woodroffe, Sean N. 422
Woods, Catherine 29
Woods, Tom D. 104
Wook, Sun 345
Worle, Erwin 136
Worms, Nicholas C. 271
Worrall, Lawrence D. 274
Wrede, Bernd 260
Wrede, Bernd 260
Wrench, Mike 100
Wright, Troy 69
Wright, Ian 156
Wright, A. 245
Wright, Craig 366
Wright, Jeremy 368
Wright, Sam 440
Wright, Peter J. 492
Wroblowski, Peter 202
Wu, Andi 122
Wu, Andi 122
Wu, Guangqi 125
Wu, Guangqi 125
Wu, Zhenfang 125
Wu, Jong-Chang 137
Wu, Ching-Yang 137
Wu, Jung-Chung 137
Wu, Eric 139
Wu, Shengliang 161
Wu, Pe-Chu 427
Wubbenhorst, Klaus L. 164
Wucherer, Klaus 384
Wueerst, Alexander 482
Wulf, Alf H. 25
Wulff, Barbel 263
Wulff, Barbel 263
Wummer, Kathy Egan 166
Wurth, Michel 39
Wyand, Anthony B. 402
Wyand, Anthony B. 463
Wyatt-Tilby, James 35
Wybrew-Bond, Ian 376
Wyk, Steve Van 231
Wyman, Malcolm 227
Wymeersch, Charles Van 248
Wynaendts, Alexander R. (Alex) 14
Wyss, Andre (Andy) 323

X

Xia, Liping 343
Xianfeng, Sun 339
Xiangdong, Lu 119
Xiao, Gang 64
Xiao, Qin 122
Xiaobing, Chang 122
Xiaochu, Wang 122
Xiaojin, Chen 120
Xiaopeng, Li 229
Xiaopeng, Li 229
Xiaowei, Yang 122
Xiaowei, Yang 122
Xiaoyuan, Hong 119
Xie, Songlin 121
Xinhua, Wang 120
Xinhua, Li 339
Xiqun, Yi 119
Xiwu, Zhang 121
Xiyou, Cai 120
Xiyou, Cai 120
Xu, Bin 229
Xue, Jilian 121
Xuewu, Zhang 343
Xuezheng, Ma 266
Xuezheng, Ma 266
Xunsheng, Zuo 122
Xunsheng, Zuo 122

Y

Yaari, Aharon (Arik) 441
Yabe, Nobuhiro 282
Yabunaka, Mitoji 291
Yachi, Shotaro 184
Yadav, Ranjit 430
Yagi, Shinsuke 22
Yahagi, Mitsuaki 409
Yajima, Ryoji 141
Yajima, Ryoji 141
Yajima, Tsutomu 244
Yajima, Hidetoshi 293
Yakovlev, Vadim 186
Yakushev, Vladimir 457
Yali, Yu 65
Yam, Zipora Gal 63
Yam, Joseph 461
Yamabayashi, Naoyuki 419
Yamada, Masayuki 1
Yamada, Masanori 106
Yamada, Masayoshi 140
Yamada, Masayoshi 141
Yamada, Takuji 214
Yamada, Takuji 215
Yamada, Hiroyuki 215
Yamada, Tsutomu 236
Yamada, Tsutomu 236
Yamada, Noriaki 283
Yamada, Ryuji 314
Yamada, Ryuji 326
Yamada, Ryuji 327
Yamada, Yoshihiko (Yoshi) 338
Yamada, Yoshihiko (Yoshi) 338
Yamada, Kiyotaka 393
Yamagiwa, Kuniaki 456
Yamaguchi, Masato 141
Yamaguchi, Masanobu 307
Yamaguchi, Tsuyoshi 316
Yamaguchi, Yoji 420
Yamaguchi, Hiroshi 447
Yamakawa, Yoichiro 420
Yamakawa, Kiyoshi 456
Yamaki, Masaharu 283
Yamaki, Masaharu 283
Yamamoto, Yoshinori 124
Yamamoto, Tatsusaburo 141
Yamamoto, Tadahito 182
Yamamoto, Masami 183
Yamamoto, Mikio 184
Yamamoto, Takahiko 206
Yamamoto, Akimasa 206
Yamamoto, Takashi 214
Yamamoto, Yoshiharu 215
Yamamoto, Hiroshi 283
Yamamoto, Masato 307
Yamamoto, Toshihiko 393
Yamamoto, Toshihiko 393
Yamamoto, Tetsuro 448
Yamamoto, Hisashi 456
Yamamura, Shinichiro 22
Yamanaka, Yasushi 149
Yamanaka, Akira 183
Yamane, Yoshi 215
Yamane, Kosuke 253
Yamane, Kenji 338
Yamanishi, Kenichiro 291
Yamanouchi, Takashi 283
Yamanouchi, Takashi 283
Yamase, Masanori 456
Yamashina, Tadashi 455
Yamashita, Hideo 206
Yamashita, Masaya 214
Yamashita, Masaya 215
Yamashita, Mitsuhiko (Mike) 316
Yamashita, Mitsuhiko (Mike) 316
Yamashita, Yoshinori 358
Yamashita, Masashi 392
Yamauchi, Yasuhito 22
Yamauchi, Yasuhito 22
Yamauchi, Takashi 295
Yamauchi, Yasuhiro 316
Yamauchi, Yoshiaki 409
Yamauchi, Yoshiaki 420
Yamaura, Yoshiyuki 194
Yamaya, Yoshiyuki 334
Yamazaki, Kunio 34
Yamazaki, Fujio 140
Yamazaki, Toshikuni 244
Yamazaki, hajime 244
Yamazaki, Toshikuni 244
Yamazaki, hajime 244
Yamazaki, Hiromasa 320
Yamazawa, Noboru Noboru Yamazawa 390
Yamazoe, Shigeru 281
Yan, Lu 266
Yan, Wu 342
Yanaga, Fumihiro 96
Yanagihara, Tsunehiko 289
Yanaginuma, Nobuyuki 307
Yanai, Jun 289
Yanai, Shunji 291
Yanai, Tadashi 404
Yanakov, Konstantin 344
Yang, J. S. 137
Yang, Julie L. 139
Yang, Ya 161
Yang, Yuanqing 266
Yang, Marjorie M. T. 323
Yano, Masahide 290
Yano, Kaoru 306
Yano, Atsushi 419
Yano, Atsushi 419
Yao, Jun 343
Yaocang, Zhang 120
Yaocang, Zhang 120
Yaofeng, Cao 120
Yarom, Yosef 62
Yassur, Tamar 63
Yasuda, Shosuke 289
Yasuda, Ryuji 409
Yasue, Hideyuki 281
Yasui, Junji 306
Yasui, Junji 307
Yatagai, Atsuo Atsuo Yatagai 183
Yavetz, Efrat 62
Yea, Philip E. (Phil) 476
Yeager, J. Michael (Mike) 87
Yee, Ernest 216
Yeh, Ying 5
Yeh, Ying 479
Yen, Ta-Tsung 137
Yeo, Eng Cheong 466
Yeo, Philip Liat Kok 467
Yeoh, Susie 47
Yeoh, Peter B. A. 336
Yeoh, Patrick K. H. 336
Yeow, Wee 467
Yerushalmi, Dan 63
Yetton, Jason 484
Yeung, Jason C. W. 90
Yibing, Wu 266
Yim, Young-chul 222
Yimin, Lu 122
Yimin, Lu 122
Yincheng, Wang 342
Yincheng, Wang 342
Yip, Dicky Peter 65
Yip, Amy 147
Yogarajah, Ruban 87
Yokogawa, Masamichi 419
Yokoi, Akimasa 456
Yokoo, Hiroshi 16
Yokoo, Hiroshi 16
Yokota, Chitoshi 215
Yokota, Takeshi Takeshi Yokota 452
Yokoyama, Hideki 96
Yokoyama, Yoshinori 334

Yokoyama, Shinichi 420
Yokoyama, Yoshinori 420
Yokoyama, Terunori 427
Yokoyama, Terunori 427
Yokoyama, Hiroyuki 455
Yoneda, Seiichi 69
Yoneda, Seiichi 70
Yonekura, Eiichi 238
Yonekura, Hiromasa 416
Yoneyama, Yoshiteru 184
Yoneyama, Yoshiteru 184
Yong, Teo Kim 485
Yong, Teo Kim 485
Yong-Won, Yoon 345
Yongli, Wang 64
Yongwu, Li 339
Yongyuan, Liao 339
Yongyuan, Liao 339
Yoo, Jae Jae Geun Yoo 392
Yoon, Ju-Hwa 378
Yoon, Gye Gye Seop Yoon 392
Yoon, Chi-Won 461
Yoshida, Sam 106
Yoshida, Masahiro 214
Yoshida, Masahiro 215
Yoshida, Tomofumi 238
Yoshida, Mamoru 338
Yoshida, Kyoji 448
Yoshida, Moritaka 455
Yoshii, Toshio 117
Yoshikai, Masanori 419
Yoshikawa, Shigeaki 289
Yoshikawa, Atsushi 320
Yoshikawa, Masaki 326
Yoshiki, Hiroyoshi 455
Yoshimatsu, Hiroki 291
Yoshimatsu, Hiroki 291
Yoshimi, Mikio 215
Yoshimoto, Makoto 316
Yoshimura, Shotaro 288
Yoshimura, Hisanori 290
Yoshimura, Naoki 306
Yoshimura, Takeshi 405
Yoshimura, Toshiharu 405
Yoshinaga, Yasuyuki 180
Yoshinaga, Yasuyuki 180
Yoshinaga, Toru 291
Yoshino, Teruomi 140
Yoshino, Teruomi 141
Yoshioka, Tsutomu 393
Yoshioka, Hiroshi 408
Yoshioka, Takashi 419
Yoshioka, Shoji 452
Yoshizawa, Kazuhiro 326
Young, Victor L. 82
Young, Harrison H. 130
Young, Victor L. 225
Young, William L. 274
Young, Francine 311
Young, Victor L. 366
Young, Keith 413
Young-Jong, Seo 249
Young-Soo, Park 249
Yu, Raymond H. K. 65
Yuan, Guangyu 125
Yuan, Li 339
Yue, Li 119
Yue, Li 119
Yuejia, Sha 119
Yuejia, Sha 119
Yuen, Anthony K. T. 301
Yuen, Loretta 336
Yueshu, Wang 342
Yueying, Sun 119
Yugala, Prince Mongkolchaleam 61
Yuhara, Takao 358
Yukang, Zeng 339
Yukawa, Akihiro 149
Yukhon, Mongkhonchaloem 61
Yuki, Taihei 294
Yuki, Taihei 294
Yukun, Kang 229
Yun, Liu 120
Yun, Ke Sup 391
Yunming, Jiang 229
Yunoki, Tsukasa 358
Yusufov, Igor K. 188
Yuzhuo, Zhang 121

Z

Zachariah, Thomas 86
Zackrisson, Staffan 479
Zainal, Abidin Jamal 275
Zaiqun, Zhou 64
Zaitsu, Narumi (Nick) 96
Zaleschuk, Victor J. 18
Zaltsman, Yaron 12
Zambrano, Lorenzo H. 114
Zambrano, Lorenzo Milmo 114
Zambrano, Lorenzo H. 177
Zambrano, Lucila 464
Zanata, Alberto 3
Zanden, Tim van der 24
Zander, Andrea 260
Zanetti, Emilio 466
Zanias, George P. 303
Zanias, George P. 303
Zaohang, Li 64
Zaohang, Li 64
Zappa, Giorgio 173
Zaveri, Bhavesh 196
Zaza, Giuseppe Giuseppe Zaza 432
Zedelius, Werner 28
Zeebroeck, Jean van 407
Zeebroeck, Jean 407
Zeglis, John D. 438
Zeitler, Prof Franz-Christoph 149
Zelada, Jorge L. 340
Zengerly, Thomas G. 370
Zeqiao, Hua 121
Zerhouni, Elias A. 382
Zetsche, Dieter 143
Zetsche, Dieter 371
Zeuner, Louis L. von 71
Zeuner, Louis L. von 71
Zhai, Guiwu 121
Zhan, Weijian 64
Zhang, Qi 64
Zhang, Xiangdong 64
Zhang, Kehui 121
Zhang, Xiwu 121
Zhang, Yuzhuo 121
Zhang, Junan 122
Zhang, Junan 122
Zhang, Guohua 125
Zhang, Rutian 139
Zhang, Dingming 161
Zhang, Hongyi 343
Zhao, Liguo 125
Zheng, Taike 139
Zhengfei, Lu 342
Zhenghuan, Liu 342
Zhenghuan, Liu 342
Zhengxin, Jiang 122
Zhengzhang, Zhao 339
Zhigang, Wang 120
Zhigang, Wang 120
Zhigang, Song 229
Zhihong, Tang 119
Zhihua, Hong 64
Zhong, Hua 125
Zhongyu, Xie 120
Zhou, Wenyao 64
Zhou, Shouwei 125
Zhou, Qinye 229
Zhu, Weilin 125
Zibetti, Mario 172
Zichlinskey, Nir 62
Ziegler, Stefan 151
Zielke, Martin 128
Zierer, Werner 81
Zijderveld, Jan 464
Zijderveld, Jan Jan Zijderveld 465
Zimmerer, Maximilian 28
Zimmermann, Rolf 28
Zimmermann, Rolf 28
Zimmermann, Rolf 202
Zimmermann, Norbert 332
Zimmermann, Marcio Pereira 340
Zimmermann, Stephan 461
Zingales, Luigi 432
Zingoni, Maria 356
Zinkernagel, Rolf M. 323
Zinkin, Peter J. L. 53
Zinkula, Mark 265
Zipp, Frances M. (Fran) 441
Zobel, I?igo 379
Zohar, Shlomo 12
Zoller, Edgar 79
Zook, Tony P. 44
Zsuga, Janos 297
Zubkov, Victor A. 187
Zubkov, Viktor 188
Zubkov, Victor A. 188
Zubrickas, J. V. 245
Zucchelli, Mario 54
Zucker, Uzi 107
Zuhlke, Oliver 78
Zunino, Luigi 284
Zviedris, Andrea 422
Zwartendijk, Robert (Rob) 353
Zwickl, Franz 463
Zwiebler, Thomas 477
Zwirn, Randy H. 395
Zyl, Johan van 455